Y0-CGK-447

6th

SAN FRANCISCO

PUBLIC LIBRARY

REFERENCE BOOK

Not to be taken from the Library

THE UNIVERSAL REFERENCE SYSTEM

Public Policy
and the
Management of Science

Volume IX of the

POLITICAL SCIENCE, GOVERNMENT, AND

PUBLIC POLICY SERIES

Included in this series:

POLITICAL SCIENCE, GOVERNMENT, & PUBLIC POLICY SERIES

Volume IX

Public Policy
and the
Management of Science

An annotated and intensively indexed compilation of significant
books, pamphlets, and articles, selected and processed by
The UNIVERSAL REFERENCE SYSTEM—a computerized
information retrieval service in the social and behavioral sciences.

Prepared under the direction of

ALFRED DE GRAZIA, GENERAL EDITOR
Professor of Social Theory in Government, New York University,
and Founder, *The American Behavioral Scientist*

CARL E. MARTINSON, MANAGING EDITOR
and
JOHN B. SIMEONE, CONSULTANT

Published by
PRINCETON RESEARCH PUBLISHING COMPANY
Princeton, New Jersey

Copyright © 1967, 1968, 1969, Princeton Information Technology,
A Division of IFI/Plenum Data Corporation

All rights in this book are reserved. No part of this book,
including the index classification system, may be used
or reproduced in any manner whatsoever without
written permission except in the case of brief
quotations embodied in critical articles and reviews.

For information, address:

UNIVERSAL REFERENCE SYSTEM
32 Nassau Street, Princeton, N.J. 08540

. . . and see the subscription information contained
on the last page of this volume.

*16.3
Un34
v. 9

69 02

Standard Book No. 87635-009-0
Library of Congress Catalog Card No. 68-57825

Printed and Bound in the U.S.A. by
KINGSPORT PRESS, INC., KINGSPORT, TENN.

SAN FRANCISCO PUBLIC LIBRARY

Contents

Advisory Committee* for the UNIVERSAL REFERENCE SYSTEM

CHAIRMAN: Alfred de Grazia, *New York University*

Kenneth J. Arrow, *Stanford University*
Peter Bock, *Brooklyn College*
Kenneth E. Boulding, *University of Michigan*
Hadley Cantril, *The Institute for International Social Research, Princeton*
Bernard C. Cohen, *The University of Wisconsin*
Richard M. Cyert, *Carnegie Institute of Technology*
Karl W. Deutsch, *Harvard University*
Ward Edwards, *University of Michigan*
Luther H. Evans, *Director of International and Legal Collections, Columbia University Law Library*
Helen Fairbanks, *Woodrow Wilson School of Public and International Affairs*
Richard F. Fenno, Jr., *University of Rochester*
William J. Gore, *Indiana University*
E. de Grolier, *International Social Science Council, Paris*
Stanley Hoffmann, *Harvard University*
Thomas Hovet, *University of Oregon*
Morton A. Kaplan, *University of Chicago*
Harold D. Lasswell, *Yale University Law School*
Wayne Leys, *University of Southern Illinois*
Charles A. McClelland, *School of International Relations, University of Southern California*
Hans J. Morgenthau, *City University of New York*
Stuart S. Nagel, *University of Illinois*
Robert C. North, *Stanford University*
A. F. K. Organski, *University of Michigan*
Robert Pages, *Chef du Laboratoire de Psychologie Sociale a la Sorbonne*
E. Raymond Platig, *Director, External Research Division, U. S. Department of State*
James A. Robinson, *Ohio State University*
Stein Rokkan, *Bergen, Norway, and Chairman, International Committee on Documentation in the Social Sciences*
James N. Rosenau, *Douglass College, Rutgers University*
Giovanni Sartori, *University of Florence*
John R. Schmidhauser, *University of Iowa*
Glendon A. Schubert, Jr., *York University*
Martin Shubik, *Yale University*
David L. Sills, *The Population Council*
Herbert A. Simon, *Carnegie Institute of Technology*
J. David Singer, *Mental Health Research Institute, University of Michigan*
Richard C. Snyder, *University of California at Irvine*
Richard N. Swift, *New York University*
Joseph Tanenhaus, *University of Iowa*
S. Sidney Ulmer, *University of Kentucky*
Quincy Wright, *University of Virginia*

*Not all members advise in all areas.

Introduction to the CODEX of Public Policy and the Management of Science

The UNIVERSAL REFERENCE SYSTEM includes in its listings under *Public Policy and the Management of Science* selected books, articles, reports, and other documents concerning attempts of man to control the epitome of directed rational procedures, science itself. Public policy is here treated in the sense of an institutional and behavioral process framing decisions about questions affecting a whole people. The scientific enterprise, which is developing rapidly in this age, is directly enveloped in the process of government and management, and is peculiarly sensitive to and related to the central and perennial issues of freedom of thought and action in government. Under the management of science are included both internal organization and behavior of scientists in working groups and associations, and the external activities of scientific groups.

The number of documents annotated in the present CODEX is 1,258, and the number of Index entries is approximately 14,600. The term "science" itself is not indexed because in one way or another every document listed concerns science or proto-scientific processes in human relations. The field of Public Policy and the Management of Science is not presently recognized as a basic field of political science, although the problems it treats have always been part of the interest of every traditional field. The field applies to the internal governance of science the age-old concern of political writers to find the grounds on which public policy can be securely implanted, and therefore starts with the most ancient human documents of Egypt, Mesopotamia, India, and China that purport to give rulers advice on how to control science (e.g., astrology, navigation, and scholars in general).

In more recent times, the vocabulary of the field has greatly changed in conformity to the changing vocabulary of the sciences in general. Further, the stress has changed so as to emphasize now the validation by scientific method of the techniques for group management in the achievement of social ends. We begin to see the new development rather markedly in the positivist movement of the middle nineteenth Century in France under August Comte and Henri, Comte de St. Simon. The vocabulary of social action becomes scientific and the recommended technique of making public policy is the scientific method.

The present CODEX employs these observations in its focal concern with the politics of science. The politics of science is connected with the science of science (the total area of scientific behavior) and the sociology of science (the total social field in which scientific activity is generated), but is especially characterized by its preoccupation with the political behavior and political systems of science. Just as there is a political science that concerns itself with political parties and interest groups, there is a political science that concerns itself with *scientific* factions, ideologies, establishments, pressure groups, and politically relevant policies. It views scientists as constituting in part simply another politicized element in the political arena. This concept is specifically drawn by Alfred de Grazia in *The Velikovsky Affair* (1965); there the ways in which scientists in the large respond to the stimulus of outside threat, dissent, and novelty are systematized in the frame of a Reception System of Science.

In conclusion, the components of the field of Public Policy and the Management of Science are still scattered about and not as many works exist within it as are found in traditional fields. As the numbers of scientists multiply and as the influence of scientists grows in all aspects of life and throughout the world, this field of study is bound to grow also and to acquire increasing importance as a scientific discipline and source of aid to the makers of educational and public policy.

How To Use This CODEX
(Hypothetical Example is Used)

1. Frame your need as specifically as possible. (Example: "I want articles written in 1968 that deal with the activities of labor leaders and small business owners in city politics in America.")
2. Scan the Dictionary of Descriptors in this Volume, page xv and following, for URS terms that match your subject. (Example: for cities you find MUNIC and LOC/G; for labor, LABOR; for small companies, SML/CO.) Find the number of titles each Descriptor carries. For rapidity select terms having few entries; for comprehensiveness, select terms having many entries.
3. Having identified terms that match your subject, enter the Index at one of them, say SML/CO, which heads a list of works on small business. For rapid identification of highly relevant titles, search the narrow right-hand column, which contains the Critical Descriptors; these index the primary facets of a work. Even if you read every title under a Descriptor, the critical column will help you identify works of high probable value. Titles are arranged by year of publication and within each year by format: books (B), long articles (L), short articles (S), and chapters (C). The designation "N" covers serials and titles lacking dates or published over several years. The Index entry carries author, title, secondary Descriptors (which index secondary facets of the work), page of the Catalog containing full citation and annotation, and Catalog accession number. Secondary Descriptors are always arranged in the order of the Topical and Methodological Index.
4. Listings of the document would be found in fourteen

SAMPLE CATALOG LISTING

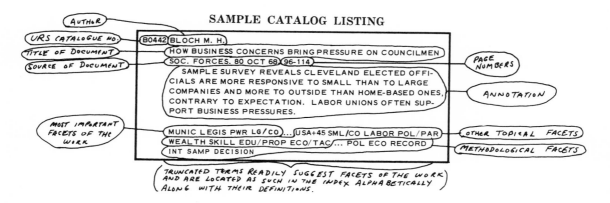

places in the Index, that is, under each of its numerous significant facets. One of them could be located in a search of "the small company in politics" as follows:

SAMPLE INDEX LISTING

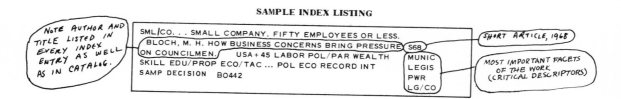

5. Jot down the page numbers and the accession numbers of items that interest you and look them up in the Catalog. There you will find the full citation and a brief annotation of each work.
6. You may locate information on methods authors employ, as well as topics they discuss. Survey the methodological Descriptors in the Grazian Index, pp. xiii-xiv, and locate the relevant Descriptors in the Index of Documents. (Example: if you wished to discover whether any studies of urban business politics had employed recorded interviews, you would look up the term INT [interviews]).
7. Read the Topical and Methodological classification of terms (Grazian Index System) once or twice to grasp the ways in which ideas and groups of related ideas are compressed. The truncated Descriptors, though obvious, are defined in the dictionary of the Index.
8. Although the Catalog is arranged alphabetically by author (except for Volumes II and III), accession numbers have been retained. The major exception to alphabetical arrangement is the group of journals and unsigned articles that begin the Catalog.
9. The Catalogs of Volumes I, IV, V, VI, VII, VIII, IX, and X do not carry Descriptors.
10. The Directory of Publishers pertains to all ten CODEXes.

Concerning the
UNIVERSAL REFERENCE SYSTEM
in General

The UNIVERSAL REFERENCE SYSTEM is a computerized documentation and information retrieval system employing citations of material above a modest level of quality, appearing in all social and behavioral sciences, annotated. It is indexed by author and employs a set of Standard Descriptors that are arranged according to a master system of topics and methodological techniques, plus various Unique Descriptors.

The flow chart on page x, entitled "The Universal Reference System," shows the numerous steps taken to process documents which come from the intellectual community until they cycle back into the same community as delivered instruments of improved scholarship.

Background of the Work

The many fields of social sciences have suffered for a long time from inadequate searching systems and information storage. The rate of development of periodical and book literature is well known to be far beyond the capacities of the existing book-form document retrieval services. Thousands of new books appear each year, dealing with society and man. Thousands of journals pour forth articles. Hundreds of periodicals are founded each year.

Countries outside of the United States have gone into the social sciences, so that the need for making available foreign publications in intelligible form is ever greater. If there is a light year's distance between present capabilities and the best available service in the social sciences, there is an even greater distance to be traversed in bringing into use the material being published in languages other than English.

A vicious economic cycle is at work in the matter of information retrieval, too: Scholars and students give up research because there are no tools to search with, and therefore their demand for searching tools decreases because they have learned to get along without the materials. Thus, the standards of all the social sciences are lowered because of an anticipated lack of success in handling the problem of information retrieval. The economic risk, therefore, of an information retrieval service has to be taken into account: Many professionals are like the Bengal peasant who cannot aid in his own economic development because he cannot conceive of the nature of the problem and has learned to live as a victim outside of it.

A study in the June, 1964, issue of *The American Behavioral Scientist* magazine showed what the need is today, even before the full capabilities of new systems are appreciated. One-half of a sample of social and behavioral scientists reported that, due to inadequate bibliographic aids, they had discovered significant information on some research too late to use it, and that this information would have significantly affected the scope and nature of their research. In a number of cases, the problem of the researcher was reported to be inadequate access to pre-existing materials, and in other cases was said to be insufficient means of addressing oneself to current material.

So the current ways of information retrieval, or lack thereof, are deficient with respect both to retrospective searching and to current material, not to mention the alarming problem of access to prospective material, in the form of current research project activities and current news of scientific development in relevant categories.

The international scholarly associations centered mainly in Paris have endeavored, with help of UNESCO and other sources of aid, to bring out bibliographies and abstracting services. These services are not fully used, because of their format, their incompleteness, their lack of selectivity, their formulation in traditional and conventional terms of the social sciences (slighting the so-called inter-disciplinary subject matters in methodology), and the simple indexing that they employ. Continuous efforts are being made to solve such problems. Lately, such solutions have been sought via computerized systems. The American Council of Learned Societies, for example, has funded projects at New York University to which the computer is integral.

The Universal Reference System is endeavoring to take an immediately practical view of the literature-access problem, while designing the system so that it will remain open to advances and permit a number of alterations. One must contemplate projects leading to automatic reading and indexing; retrieval of information in the form of propositions, historical dates, and other factual materials; encyclopedic information-providing services; movement into other scientific fields joining social and natural science materials; automatized printing and reproduction of a large variety of materials in quantities ranging from individual to thousands of copies, and provision for televised or other rapid-fire communication services from information retrieval centers.

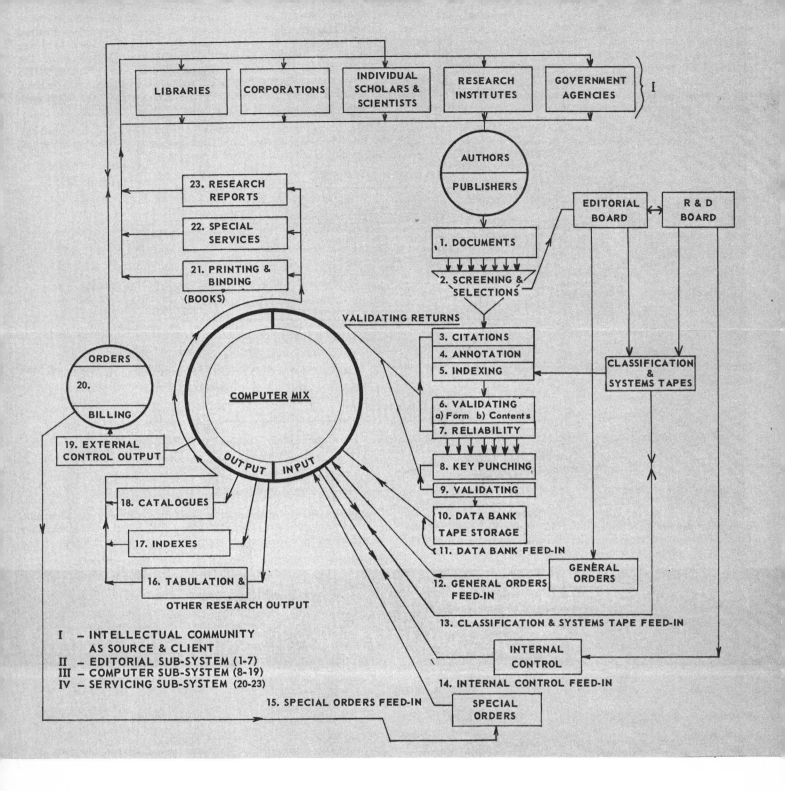

UNIVERSAL REFERENCE SYSTEM

A diagrammatic representation of the numerous steps taken to process documents which come from the intellectual community until they cycle back to the same community as pinpointed sources of information.

The Grazian Classification and Indexing System

The theory behind the URS Classification System is operational. It asks the question: *"Who says, 'Who does what with whom, where and when, by what means, why'* and *how does he know so?"* This question leads to the general categories and subcategories of the system, which is presented in its logical form on pages **xii-xiv**, along with the truncated terms used in the computerized Index of Documents. The advantage of reading the logical classification is that one will learn in a few minutes the general meaning of the truncated terms and can usually go directly and rapidly to the proper terms in the Index.

The Grazian classification cuts across various disciplines of social science to call attention to the methodological aspects of works which would appear to be important to scholars in the behavioral, instrumental, positivistic tradition of philosophy and science.

The constant recourse to method also serves as a screening device for eliminating numerous documents that are purely evaluative, journalistic, nonempirical, or of an intuitive type. The Grazian index contains some 351 Standard Descriptor categories at the present time. To them are added Unique Descriptors as they occur. Some additional categories logically subtending from the existing ones will be added as time goes on. These will be expanded as part of the original coding as the need is shown. (Several categories may be altered, too, on the same grounds.) From two to four of the Standard and Unique Descriptors are selected as most important facets of the work and are indicated as Critical Descriptors. These are printed apart in the Index of Documents.

The possibilities of utilizing cross-categories are immediate. Cross-categories can be used (both by the searcher and by the creator of the index) to provide a more specialized bibliography. This Cross-Faceting can permit adjusting to changes in the interests of scientists. An almost infinite number of cross-categories is possible, of course. The user of the system will find it set up beyond any existing system to facilitate this. In the future, and upon request, complicated cross-category or multi-faceted searches will be performed by the Universal Reference System's machinery. The ultimate instrumental goal is Controlled Faceting—contractible or expansible according to need and logic.

In practice, the Standard Descriptors, the Unique Descriptors, the Critical Descriptors, the Multiple Faceting, and the Cross-Faceting are interlaced in the operations of documentary analysis and control. Thus, to allow for gaps in the system, to go along with conventional practice, to employ more specialized terms, and to carry important proper nouns, the indexing rules permit the documentary analyst to add Unique Descriptors to the Standard Descriptors already taken from the master list. There are 63 of these in the *Codex of Legislative Process, Representation, and Decision-Making*. The total number of descriptors finally averaged 13 per item.

Some persons have inquired whether it might be useful to print out the whole descriptor rather than a truncated term. Several reasons arbitrate against this procedure, at least for the present. In most cases there is really no single term for which the printed-out truncated descriptor is the symbol. Most Standard Descriptors stand for several synonymous words and related ideas. Printing out the full descriptor *word* would be deluding in many cases, leading searchers to believe a word has only its face meaning.

Moreover, if all truncated descriptors were spelled out, the search time (after the first few searches) would be extended greatly since the eye would have to cover much more lettering and space. Furthermore, the size of the CODEX would be at least tripled, for the space provided for permuting would have to be open enough to carry the longest, not the average, words. There are other technical difficulties.

The repetition of numerous descriptors following each entry in the Index of Documents serves the purpose of targeting the search precisely. The richness of descriptors also postpones the moment of returning to the catalogue and thus enlarges the marginal utility of the first resort to the catalogue.

The intensive indexing of each document, which ranges from 10 to 20 entries, serves a purpose. Intensive indexing permits a document to exhibit all of its important facets to the searcher. The ratio of index carriage to title carriage is here termed the "carriage ratio." The carriage ratio of the URS is much higher than that of most bibliographies. The magnitude of the difference shows the meaning of high intensity indexing. Under other systems, unlike the URS CODEX, a topic is understated in the index. And, less obviously, topics other than the one carried as a flag in the title are sunk into oblivion; thus "Relations Between France and Indochina," which may be a valuable work on questions of economic development, would probably not be indexed on that question at all.

To sum up, the URS, when used as in this CODEX, thoroughly exposes the facets of a listed document. It makes the document thoroughly *retrievable*.

Also under consideration are suggestions to eliminate (or suppress) more of the descriptors. What is the optimal number? It is difficult to say, *a priori*. Experience and experiment will tell, over time. Meanwhile, the Critical Descriptors offer a researcher the "fast search," if he pleases. The more numerous group of descriptors in the final column offers a more complete faceting.

The search time of a researcher should be an important concern of a bibliographer. Search time begins to run, of course, with the knowledge of and access to a work that probably covers a searcher's need. It runs, too, with the ingenuity of the searcher's phrasing of his need. Then it runs with the presence of the works needed in the list searched; a missing document can be translated into lost time. An index saves time, too, when the term searched is the term under which a document is indexed; the need to compromise between detailed vocabularies and generalized ones is evident: it can reasonably be argued that more time is lost in research in social science in getting on the same semantic beam than in solving substantive problems of the "real world." Finally, the structure of an index should lessen search time while permitting a rich search.

Research and experimentation are in order, and it is hoped that a by-product of the initial publications of the Universal Reference System will be an increased stimulation of research into research procedures with respect to the URS' problems and to those of other reference systems.

Topical and Methodological Index (Grazian Index System)

The truncated descriptors (left of each column) and their expanded definitions (right of each column) that follow were employed in systematically computerizing the topics and methods of the Social and Behavioral Sciences. Truncated descriptors that are underscored in the listing that follows have not been carried in the left-hand index entry column of this CODEX; several others (denoted by a double underscore) have been entirely eliminated from this CODEX. Fuller definitions are included in the Index of Documents. So are proper names, place names, organization names, and incidents.

I. TOPICS

1. **TIME—SPACE—CULTURE INDEX:** Cultural-temporal location of subject.
   Centuries covered (e.g., -4; 14-19; 20)

PREHIST	Prehistoric.
MEDIT-7	Mediterranean and Near East, pre-Islamic.
PRE/AMER	Pre-European Americas.
CHRIST-17C	Christendom to 1700.
AFR	Sub-Sahara Africa.
ASIA	China, Japan, Korea.
S/ASIA	India, Southeast Asia, Oceania, except European settlements.
ISLAM	Islamic world.
MOD/EUR	Europe, 1700 to 1918, including European settlements.
USA-45	USA, 1700 to 1945.
WOR-45	Worldwide to 1945.
L/A+17C	Latin America since 1700.
EUR+WWI	Europe, 1918 to present, including colonies, but excluding Communist countries.
COM	Communist countries.
USA+45	USA since 1945.
WOR+45	Worldwide since 1945.
FUT	Future.
SPACE	Outer space.
UNIV	Free of historical position.
SEA	Locale of activity is aquatic.
AIR	Locale of activity is aerial.

   (Nations are readily identifiable.)

2. **INSTITUTIONAL INDEX:** (or subject treated).
   A. General

SOCIETY	Society as a whole.
CULTURE	Cultural patterns.
STRUCT	Social structure.
CONSTN	Constitution. Basic group structure.
LAW	Sanctioned practices, enforced ethics in a community.
ELITES	A power-holding group.
INTELL	Intelligentsia.
SOC/INTEG	Social integration.
STRATA	Social strata.
CLIENT	Clients.

   B. Economic type

ECO/UNDEV	Developing countries.
ECO/DEV	Developed countries.

   C. Economic function

AGRI	Agriculture, including hunting.
R+D	Research and development organization.
FINAN	Financial services.
INDUS	All or most industry.
COM/IND	Communications industry.
CONSTRUC	Construction and building.
DIST/IND	Distributive system: Includes transportation, warehousing.
EXTR/IND	Extractive industry.
MARKET	Marketing system.
PROC/MFG	Processing or manufacturing.
SERV/IND	Service industry.

   D. Organizations

SML/CO	Small company: 50 employees or less.
LG/CO	Company of more than 50 employees.
LABOR	Labor unions.
PROF/ORG	Professional organizations, including guilds.
PUB/INST	Habitational institutions: hospitals, prisons, sanitariums, etc.
POL/PAR	Political party.
SCHOOL	School (except University).
ACADEM	Higher learning.
PERF/ART	Performing arts groupings.

SECT	Church, sect, religious group.
FAM	Family.
KIN	Kinship groups.
NEIGH	Neighborhood.
LOC/G	Local governments.
MUNIC	Cities, villages, towns.
PROVS	State or province.
NAT/G	National governments.
FACE/GP	Acquaintance group: face-to-face association.
VOL/ASSN	Voluntary association.
INT/ORG	International organizations.

3. **ORGANIC OR INTERNAL STRUCTURE INDEX:** Sub-groupings or substructures treated.

CONSULT	Consultants.
FORCES	Armed forces and police.
DELIB/GP	Conferences, committees, boards, cabinets.
LEGIS	Legislatures.
CT/SYS	Court systems.
EX/STRUC	Formal executive establishment.
TOP/EX	Individuals holding executive positions.
CHIEF	Chief officer of a government.
WORKER	Workers and work conditions.

4. **PROCESSES AND PRACTICES:** Procedures or tactics used by subject or discussed as subject.
   A. Creating and Sciencing

CREATE	Creative and innovative processes.
ACT/RES	Combined research and social action.
COMPUTER	Computer techniques.
INSPECT	Inspecting quality, output, legality.
OP/RES	Operations research.
PLAN	Planning.
PROB/SOLV	Problem-solving and decision-making.
TEC/DEV	Development and change of technology.

   B. Economizing

ACCT	Accounting, bookkeeping.
BAL/PWR	Balance of power.
BARGAIN	Bargaining, trade.
BUDGET	Budgeting, fiscal planning.
CAP/ISM	Enterprise, entrepreneurship.
DIPLOM	Diplomacy.
ECO/TAC	Economic measures or tactics.
FOR/AID	Foreign aid.
INT/TRADE	International trade.
RATION	Rationing, official control of goods or costs.
RENT	Renting.
TARIFFS	Tariffs.
TAX	Taxation.

   C. Awarding

GIVE	Giving, philanthropy.
LICENSE	Legal permit.
PAY	Paying.
RECEIVE	Receiving of welfare.
REPAR	Reparations.
TRIBUTE	Payments to dominant by minor power, racketeering.
WORSHIP	Worship, ritual.

   D. Symbolizing

DOMIN	Domination.
EDU/PROP	Education or propaganda.
LEGIT	Legitimacy.
PRESS	Printed media.
RUMOR	Rumor, gossip.
TV	Television.
WRITING	Writing.

   E. Evaluating

CONFER	Group consultation.
DEBATE	Organized collective arguments.

ETIQUET	Etiquette, fashion, manners.
PRICE	Pricing.
SENIOR	Seniority.

F. Determining

ADJUD	Judicial behavior and personality.
ADMIN	Behavior of non-top executive personnel (except armed forces).
AGREE	Agreements, treaties, compacts.
AUTOMAT	Automation.
COLONIAL	Colonialism.
CONTROL	Specific ability of power to determine achievement.
EXEC	Executive, regularized management.
FEEDBACK	Feedback phenomena.
GAMBLE	Speculative activity.
LEAD	Leading.
LOBBY	Lobbying.
NEUTRAL	Neutralism, neutrality.
PARL/PROC	Parliamentary procedures (legislative).
PARTIC	Participation: civic apathy or activity.
REGION	Regionalism.
RISK	Risk, uncertainty, certainty.
ROUTINE	Procedural and work systems.
SANCTION	Sanctions of law and social law.
TASK	A specific operation within a work setting.
TIME	Timing, time-factor.

G. Forcing

ARMS/CONT	Arms control and disarmament.
COERCE	Force and violence.
CRIME	Criminal behavior.
CROWD	Mass behavior.
DEATH	Death-related behavior.
DETER	Military deterrence.
GUERRILLA	Guerrilla warfare.
MURDER	Murder, assassination.
NUC/PWR	All uses of nuclear energy.
REV	Revolution.
SUICIDE	Suicide.
WAR	War.
WEAPON	Conventional military weapons.

H. Choosing

APPORT	Apportionment of assemblies.
CHOOSE	Choice, election.
REPRESENT	Representation.
SUFF	Suffrage.

I. Consuming

DREAM	Dreaming.
LEISURE	Unobligated time expenditures.
SLEEP	Sleep-related behavior.
EATING	Eating, cuisine.

5. RELATIONS INDEX: Relationship of individuals and/or group under discussion.

CIVMIL/REL	Civil-military relation.
GOV/REL	Relations between local or state governments and governmental agencies.
GP/REL	Relations among groups, except nations.
INT/REL	Relations among sovereign states.
INGP/REL	Relations within groups.
PERS/REL	Relations between persons; interpersonal communication.
RACE/REL	Race relations.

6. CONDITIONS AND MEASURES (of activities being discussed).

ADJUST	Social adjustment, socialization.
BAL/PAY	Balance of payments.
CENTRAL	Centralization.
CONSEN	Consensus.
COST	Costs.
DEMAND	In economic sense, a demand.
DISCRIM	Social differentiation in support of inequalities.
EFFICIENCY	Effectiveness, measures.
EQUILIB	Equilibrium (technical).
FEDERAL	Federalism.
HAPPINESS	Satisfaction and unhappiness.
ILLEGIT	Bastardy.
INCOME	Income distribution, shares, earnings.
ISOLAT	Isolation and community.
LITERACY	Ability to read and write.
MAJORITY	Behavior of major parts of grouping.
MARRIAGE	Legal wedlock.

NAT/LISM	Nationalism.
OPTIMAL	Optimality in its economic usages.
OWN	Ownership.
PEACE	Freedom from conflict or termination of hostilities.
PRIVIL	Privilege, parliamentary.
PRODUC	Productivity.
PROFIT	Profit in economic sense.
RATIONAL	Instrumental rationality.
STRANGE	Estrangement or outsiders.
TOTALISM	Totalitarianism.
UTIL	Utility as in economics.
UTOPIA	Envisioned general social conditions.

7. PERSONALITY INDEX: Behavior of actors to their actions.

HABITAT	Ecology.
HEREDITY	Genetic influences on personality.
DRIVE	Drive, morale, or antithesis.
PERCEPT	Perception.
PERSON	Personality and human nature.
ROLE	Role, reference group feelings, cross-pressures.
AGE	Age factors in general.
AGE/C	Infants and children.
AGE/Y	Youth, adolescence.
AGE/A	Adults.
AGE/O	Old.
SEX	Sexual behavior.
SUPEGO	Conscience, superego, and responsibility.
RIGID/FLEX	Rigidity/flexibility; exclusive/inclusive.
ATTIT	Attitudes, opinions, ideology.
DISPL	Displacement and projection.
AUTHORIT	Authoritarianism, as personal behavior.
BIO/SOC	Bio-social processes: drugs, psychosomatic phenomena, etc.
ANOMIE	Alienation, anomie, generalized personal anxiety.

8. VALUES INDEX: Basically desired (or nondesired) conditions held or believed in by subjects.

HEALTH	Well-being, bodily and psychic integrity (sickness).
KNOWL	Enlightenment (ignorance).
LOVE	Affection, friendship (hatred).
MORAL	Rectitude, morality (immorality), goodness.
PWR	Power, participation in decision-making (impotence).
RESPECT	Respect, social class attitudes (contempt, disrespect).
SKILL	Skill, practical competence (incompetence).
WEALTH	Wealth, access to goods and services (poverty).
ALL/VALS	All, or six or more of above.
ORD/FREE	Security, order, restraint (change, experience, freedom).
SOVEREIGN	Sovereignty; home-rule.

9. IDEOLOGICAL TOPIC: Ideology discussed in work.

CATHISM	Roman Catholicism.
CONSERVE	Traditionalism.
FASCISM	Fascism.
LAISSEZ	Laissez-faire-ism (old liberal).
MARXISM	Marxism.
MYSTISM	Mysticism.
NEW/LIB	New Liberalism (welfare state).
OBJECTIVE	Value-free thought.
PACIFISM	Pacifism.
PLURISM	Socio-political order of autonomous groups.
POPULISM	Majoritarianism.
RELATISM	Relativism.
SOCISM	Socialism.
TECHRACY	Socio-political order dominated by technicians.
ALL/IDEOS	Three or more of above.

II. METHODOLOGY (What techniques are dealt with by the author and what techniques the document employs or describes).

10. ETHICAL STANDARDS APPLIED BY AUTHOR

| ETHIC | Personal ethics (private and professional). |
| LAW/ETHIC | Ethics of laws and court processes. |

POLICY   Treats ethics of public policies.

11. IDEOLOGY OF AUTHOR (where clear).

ANARCH	Anarchism.
CATH	Roman Catholic.
CONVNTL	Conventional: unsystematic acceptance of values in common currency.
FASCIST	Totalitarian with nonworker, upper class, or leader cult.
MAJORIT	Majoritarian, consensual.
MARXIST	Marxist Communist in viewpoint.
MYSTIC	Otherworldly, mystical.
OLD/LIB	Old liberal, laissez-faire.
PACIFIST	Pacifist
PLURIST	Pluralist.
REALPOL	Realpolitik, Machiavellism.
RELATIV	Relativist.
SOCIALIST	Socialist (except Communist).
TECHNIC	Technocratic.
TRADIT	Traditional or aristocratic.
WELF/ST	Welfare state advocate.

12. FIELD INDEX: Fields, discipline, or methodological approach of document.

ART/METH	Fine Arts, Graphics, Performing Arts, Aesthetics.
CRIMLGY	Criminology.
DECISION	Decision-making and gaming (game theory).
ECO	Economics and economic enterprise.
ECOMETRIC	Econometrics, mathematical economics.
EPIST	Epistemology, sociology of knowledge.
GEOG	Demography and geography.
HEAL	Health sciences.
HIST	History (including current events).
HUM	Methods of the "Humanities." Literary analysis.
INT/LAW	International law. Uses legal approach.
JURID	Uses legal approach. Concerns largely the laws.
MGT	Administrative management.
PHIL/SCI	Scientific method and Philosophy of Science.
POL	Deals with political and power process.
PSY	Psychology.
SOC	Sociology.
SOC/WK	Social services.

13. CONCEPTS: Document is noteworthy for systematic and/or basic treatment of:

CONCPT	Subject-matter abstract concepts.
METH/CNCPT	Methodological concepts.
MYTH	Treats assumptions unconsciously accepted, fictions.
NEW/IDEA	Word inventions, new concepts and ideas.

14. LOGIC, MATHEMATICS, AND LANGUAGE

LOG	Logic: syntax, semantics, pragmatics.
MATH	Mathematics.
STAT	Statistics.
AVERAGE	Mean, average behaviors.
PROBABIL	Probability, chance.
MODAL	Modal types, fashions.
CORREL	Correlations (statistical).
REGRESS	Regression analysis.
QUANT	Nature and limits of quantification.
CLASSIF	Classification, typology, set theory.
INDICATOR	Numerical indicator, index weights.
LING	Linguistics.
STYLE	The styles and terminology of scientific communications.

15. DIRECT OBSERVATION

OBS	Trained or participant observation.
SELF/OBS	Self-observation, psycho-drama.
OBS/ENVIR	Social milieu of and resistances to observation.
CONT/OBS	Controlled direct observation.
RECORD	Recording direct observations. (But not content analysis, q.v.)

16. INTERVIEWS

INT	Interviews, short or long, in general.
STAND/INT	Standardized interviews.
DEEP/INT	Depth interviews.
UNPLAN/INT	Impromptu interview.
RESIST/INT	Social resistance to interviewing.
REC/INT	Recording, systematizing, and analyzing of interviews.

17. QUESTIONNAIRES

QU	Questionnaires in general, short or long.
DEEP/QU	Depth questionnaires, including projective or probing.
QU/SEMANT	Semantic and social problems of questionnaires.
SYS/QU	Systematizing and analyzing questionnaires.

18. TESTS AND SCALES

TESTS	Theory and uses of tests and scales.
APT/TEST	Aptitude tests.
KNO/TEST	Tests for factual knowledge, beliefs, or abilities.
PERS/TEST	Personality tests.
PROJ/TEST	Projective tests.

19. UNIVERSES AND SAMPLING

CENSUS	Census.
SAMP	Sample survey in general.
SAMP/SIZ	Sizes and techniques of sampling.
NET/THEORY	Systematic group-member connections analysis.

20. ANALYSIS OF TEMPORAL SEQUENCES

BIOG	Biography, personality development, and psychoanalysis.
HIST/WRIT	Historiography.
TIME/SEQ	Chronology and genetic series of men, institutions, processes, etc.
TREND	Projection of trends, individual and social.
PREDICT	Prediction of future events.

21. COMMUNICATION CONTENT ANALYSIS

CON/ANAL	Quantitative content analysis.
DOC/ANAL	Conventional analysis of records or documents.

22. INFORMATION STORAGE AND RETRIEVAL

OLD/STOR	Conventional libraries, books, records, tape, film.
THING/STOR	Artifacts and material evidence.
COMPUT/IR	Mechanical and electronic information retrieval.

23. GRAPHICS AND AUDIO-VISUAL TECHNIQUES: Used in the research and/or in the presentation.

AUD/VIS	Film and sound, photographs.
CHARTS	Graphs, charts, diagrams, maps.
EXHIBIT	Exhibits.
PROG/TEAC	Programmed instruction.

24. COMPARATIVE ANALYSIS INDEX

METH/COMP	Of methods, approaches, styles.
IDEA/COMP	Of ideas, methods, ideologies.
PERS/COMP	Of persons.
GP/COMP	Of groups.
GOV/COMP	Of governments.
NAT/COMP	Of nations.

25. EXPERIMENTATION

LAB/EXP	Laboratory or strictly controlled groups.
SOC/EXP	"Social" experimentation.
HYPO/EXP	Hypothetical, intellectual constructs.

26. MODELS: Intellectual representations of objects or processes.

SIMUL	Scientific models.
ORG/CHARTS	Blueprints and organization charts.
STERTYP	Stereotypes, ideologies, utopias.
GAME	Game or Decision Theory models.

27. GENERAL THEORY

GEN/LAWS	Systems based on substantive relations, such as idealism, economic determinism.
GEN/METH	Systems based on methodology, such as cycles, pragmatism, sociometry.

28. SPECIAL FORMATS

ANTHOL	Anthology, symposium, collection.
BIBLIOG	Bibliography over fifty items, or of rare utility.
BIBLIOG/A	Contains bibliography over fifty items or of rare utility, annotated.
DICTIONARY	Dictionary.
INDEX	List of names or subjects.
METH	Document heavily emphasizes methodology (Part II) rather than topics (Part I).
T	Textbook.

Dictionary of Descriptors in this Volume
(*Incorporating List of Frequency of Descriptors in Index*)

This Dictionary contains all Descriptors employed in this volume, and thus enables you to identify in a few minutes every Descriptor that may pertain to your subject. The frequency list calls your attention to the number of works carried under each Descriptor and assists you in determining the term at which you may most advantageously begin your search in the Index. A modest system of cross-references may be found in the Dictionary that appears in the Index.

CATALOGUE OF DOCUMENTS

0001 CURRENT THOUGHT ON PEACE AND WAR.
DURHAM: CURRENT THOUGHT INC.
"WORLD AFFAIRS DIGEST" OF BOOKS AND ARTICLES, UNPUBLISHED MEMORANDA, AND REPORTS, UN AND GOVERNMENTAL DOCUMENTS, AND RESEARCH AND MANUSCRIPTS IN PROGRESS ON CURRENT INTERNATIONAL ISSUES. CONTENTS ARRANGED TOPICALLY: CRISES AREAS AND ISSUES, MILITARY, INTERNATIONAL ECONOMIC FACTORS IN INTERNATIONAL RELATIONS, ETC. EXTENSIVE ANNOTATION OF ABOUT 600 ITEMS. FIRST PUBLISHED 1959. APPEARS TWICE A YEAR.

0002 JOURNAL OF CONFLICT RESOLUTION.
ANN ARBOR: U MICH CONFL RESO.
QUARTERLY FOR RESEARCH ON WAR AND PEACE. FIRST PUBLISHED 1957. CONTAINS BOOK REVIEW SECTION WHICH TREATS INTERNATIONAL RELATIONS. EMPHASIZES RELATED ASPECTS OF THE SOCIAL AND BEHAVIORAL SCIENCES. COVERS PERIOD SINCE WWII AND REVIEWS BOOKS IN ENGLISH AND EUROPEAN LANGUAGES. LIST OF BOOKS IN ADDITION TO REVIEWS.

0003 ADVANCED MANAGEMENT.
NEW YORK: SOC ADVANCEMT MANAGEMT.
A MONTHLY PUBLICATION OF THE SOCIETY FOR THE ADVANCEMENT OF MANAGEMENT FIRST ISSUED IN 1934. ATTEMPTS TO PROMOTE DISCUSSION AND RESEARCH IN THE SCIENTIFIC STUDY OF THE PRINCIPLES GOVERNING ORGANIZED EFFORT IN INDUSTRIAL AND ECONOMIC LIFE. EARLIER ISSUES CONTAIN LENGTHY SECTION OF BIBLIOGRAPHIES AND SHORT BOOK REVIEWS.

0004 FOREIGN AFFAIRS.
NEW YORK: COUNCIL ON FOREIGN REL.
QUARTERLY, FIRST PUBLISHED 1922, CONTAINING BOOK REVIEW SECTION AND LISTS OF DOCUMENTS AND PAMPHLETS PUBLISHED BY US AND BRITISH GOVERNMENTS AND BY INTERNATIONAL ORGANIZATIONS. DEALS WITH INTERNATIONAL RELATIONS SINCE WWI. INCLUDES TITLES IN ENGLISH, GERMAN, AND FRENCH.

0005 INDIA: A REFERENCE ANNUAL.
NEW DELHI: INDIAN MIN OF INFO.
FIRST PUBLISHED IN 1953 BY PUBLICATIONS DIVISION OF THE MINISTRY OF INFORMATION AND BROADCASTING, WITH OBJECT OF PROVIDING AUTHENTIC INFORMATION ON VARIOUS ASPECTS ON NATIONAL LIFE WITHIN COUNTRY AND ABROAD. SELECT BIBLIOGRAPHY INCLUDES ADDITIONAL INFORMATION FROM GOVERNMENT REPORTS AND PUBLICATIONS, REFERENCE WORKS, AND OTHER BOOKS.

0006 JOURNAL OF PUBLIC ADMINISTRATION: JOURNAL OF THE ROYAL INSTITUTE OF PUBLIC ADMINISTRATION.
LONDON: ROYAL INST OF PUB ADMIN.
QUARTERLY JOURNAL FIRST PUBLISHED IN 1923. CONTAINS A FAIRLY EXTENSIVE CRITICAL BOOK REVIEW SECTION AND A QUARTERLY REVIEW OF RECENT PUBLICATIONS WITH DESCRIPTIVE ANNOTATIONS. THIS LATTER SECTION LISTS 30 RECENT WORKS. INCLUDES ALSO A LISTING OF NEW GOVERNMENT PUBLICATIONS IN THE FIELD. ALTHOUGH WORKS ARE IN ENGLISH THEY HAVE AN INTERNATIONAL SCOPE.

0007 THE MANAGEMENT REVIEW.
NEW YORK: AMER MANAGEMENT ASSN.
MONTHLY PUBLICATION, FIRST PUT OUT BY AMERICAN MANAGEMENT ASSOCIATION IN 1914. INCLUDES SURVEY OF BOOKS FOR EXECUTIVES, CRITICAL REVIEWS OF 10-22 RECENT WORKS, AND A LISTING OF RECENT PUBLICATIONS RECEIVED FROM PUBLISHERS. BOOKS COVER TOPICS ON LABOR RELATIONS AND HUMAN RELATIONS, ARBITRATION OF LABOR DISPUTES, UNION-MANAGEMENT RELATIONS, ETC.

0008 MARKETING INFORMATION GUIDE.
WASHINGTON: US BUS + DEF SERV.
MONTHLY PUBLICATION LISTING CURRENT US GOVERNMENT AND NONGOVERNMENTAL BOOKS, PAMPHLETS, REPORTS, AND ARTICLES ON MARKETING AND DISTRIBUTION. ENTRIES ARRANGED BY SUBJECT AND ANNOTATED. INCLUDES CUMULATIVE INDEX TWICE A YEAR. FIRST PUBLISHED 1954.

0009 PUBLIC ADMINISTRATION ABSTRACTS AND INDEX OF ARTICLES.
NEW DELHI: INDIAN INST PUB ADMIN.
MONTHLY PUBLICATION, FIRST ISSUED 1957, INDEXING ARTICLES FROM SELECTED ENGLISH-LANGUAGE JOURNALS PERTAINING TO PUBLIC ADMINISTRATION. PRIMARY EMPHASIS ON UNDERDEVELOPED AREAS.

0010 PERSONNEL.
NEW YORK: AMER MANAGEMENT ASSN.
BIMONTHLY PERIODICAL CONCERNED WITH MANAGEMENT OF PEOPLE AT WORK. INCLUDES BOOK REVIEW SECTION OF CURRENT PUBLICATIONS.

0011 FOREIGN AFFAIRS BIBLIOGRAPHY: A SELECTED AND ANNOTATED LIST OF BOOKS ON INTERNATIONAL RELATIONS 1919-1962 (4 VOLS.)
NEW YORK: FOREIGN AFFAIRS BIBL, 1933.
EACH VOLUME INCLUDES 19,000 ANNOTATED REFERENCES TO BOOKS ON INTERNATIONAL AFFAIRS. LISTS ITEMS IN ALL IMPORTANT LANGUAGES OF WORLD, INCLUDING PRINCIPAL ASIATIC LANGUAGES. CONTAINS REFERENCES TO WORKS ON POLITICAL, SOCIAL, CULTURAL AND RELIGIOUS FACTORS IN INTERNATIONAL RELATIONS; INTERNATIONAL LAW, ORGANIZATION AND GOVERNMENT; THE TWO WORLD WARS; AND PARTICULAR ISSUES OF GEOGRAPHIC REGIONS. 1ST VOL. 1933.

0012 "SELECTED CRITICAL BIBLIOGRAPHY ON THE METHODS AND TECHNIQUES OF POLITICAL BEHAVIOR RESEARCH."
AM. POL. SCI. REV., 46 (DEC. 52), 1033-1045.
ANNOTATED LISTING OF APPROXIMATELY 120 BOOKS AND ARTICLES PERTINENT TO POLITICAL BEHAVIOR RESEARCH. ORGANIZED INTO SECTIONS ON SCIENTIFIC METHOD IN POLITICAL RESEARCH, GENERAL SOCIAL SCIENCE RESEARCH, DOCUMENTARY ANALYSIS, PARTICIPANT OBSERVATION, INTERVIEWS, EXPERIMENTS, INSTITUTIONAL AND COMMUNITY RESEARCH, AND INTERPRETATION AND ANALYSIS. ENTRIES WRITTEN PRINCIPALLY IN PERIOD 1920-52.

0013 HISTORICAL ABSTRACTS.
SANTA BARBARA: CLIO, 1956, LC#56-56304.
AN ANNOTATED QUARTERLY REVIEWING WORLDWIDE PERIODICAL LITERATURE ON POLITICAL, DIPLOMATIC, ECONOMIC, SOCIAL, CULTURAL, AND INTELLECTUAL HISTORY ON THE PERIOD 1775-1945. INDEXED BY COMPUTER FROM A CODE OF MAIN CUES, AND ABSTRACTS ARRANGED IN SEVEN SUBJECT TOPICS. ANNUAL INDEX DIVIDED INTO A SUBJECT INDEX AND A GENERAL NAMES INDEX. FIRST PUBLICATION 1956.

0014 LIST OF PUBLICATIONS (PERIODICAL OR AD HOC) ISSUED BY VARIOUS MINISTRIES OF THE GOVERNMENT OF INDIA (3RD ED.)
NEW DELHI: LOK SABHA SECRETARIAT, 1958, 282 PP.
LISTING OF PUBLICATIONS OF ALL MINISTRIES UNDER MINISTRY ISSUING MATERIAL. EVERY EFFORT IS MADE TO KEEP VOLUME UP-TO-DATE BY ISSUING ADDENDA AND CORRIGENDA TO VOLUME FROM TIME TO TIME. MATERIAL IS LISTED IN TABLE FORM WITHOUT INDEXES.

0015 ARMS CONTROL.
DAEDALUS, 89 (FALL 60), 669-1075.
ESSAYS COVER PROBLEMS AND GOALS OF, AND PREREQUISITES FOR ARMS CONTROL. EXAMINE CHARACTER OF RECENT PROPOSALS AND AGREEMENTS. TREAT ARMS RACE, LIMITED WAR STRATEGY, ROLE OF SMALLER POWERS, INSPECTION TECHNIQUES, ARMS STABILIZATION, AND UNILATERAL DISARMAMENT.

0016 SOVIET STAND ON DISARMAMENT.
NEW YORK: CROSSCURRENTS, 1962, 150 PP.
DETAILED EXPOSITION OF SOVIET GOVERNMENT POSITION ON DISARMAMENT, NUCLEAR TEST-BAN, AND RELATED QUESTIONS. OUTLINES GRADUAL STEPS TO EASE TENSIONS AND LAY GROUNDWORK FOR COMPREHENSIVE MEASURES. ELABORATES FUTURE TEST-BAN TREATY.

0017 RECENT PUBLICATIONS ON GOVERNMENTAL PROBLEMS.
CHICAGO: JOINT REFERENCE LIBRARY, 1964.
A WEEKLY PERIODICAL CATALOGING THE MOST RECENT PUBLICATIONS ON GOVERNMENTAL PROBLEMS. PUBLISHED SINCE 1932.

0018 "FURTHER READING."
SEMINAR, (JUNE 64), 63-65.
BIBLIOGRAPHY ON KASHMIR AND "THE SUB-CONTINENTAL IMPLICATIONS OF A CRITICAL QUESTION."

0019 WHITE HOUSE CONFERENCE ON INTERNATIONAL COOPERATION(VOL.II)
WASHINGTON: NATL CITIZ COMN REP, 1965, 25 PP.
COMMITTEE REPORTS MADE AT 1965 WHITE HOUSE CONFERENCE. INCLUDED ARE REPORTS ON LABOR, MANPOWER, NATURAL RESOURCES, CONSERVATION AND DEVELOPMENT, ATOMIC ENERGY, PEACEKEEPING OPERATIONS, POPULATION, SCIENCE AND TECHNOLOGY, SOCIAL WELFARE, SPACE, TECHNICAL COOPERATION AND DEVELOPMENT, TRADE, TRANSPORATION, URBAN DEVELOPMENT, WOMEN, AND YOUTH ACTIVITIES.

0020 PEACE RESEARCH ABSTRACTS.
ONTARIO: CANADIAN PEACE RES INST, 1965.
MONTHLY PUBLICATION SINCE 1965, WHICH CONTAINS ABSTRACTS OF BOOKS AND ARTICLES. INCLUDES SUCH TOPICS AS DISARMAMENT, FALLOUT, AND ECONOMIC AID. APPROXIMATELY 12,000 ABSTRACTS PER YEAR.

0021 "FURTHER READING."
SEMINAR, (MAR. 66), 42-44.
BIBLIOGRAPHY ON URBAN DEVELOPMENT IN INDIA.

0022 "CHINESE STATEMENT ON NUCLEAR PROLIFERATION."
BUL. ATOMIC SCIENTISTS, 23 (MAY 67), 53-54.
COMMUNIST CHINESE STATEMENT CONDEMNING THE PROPOSED NONPROLIFERATION TREATY ON NUCLEAR WEAPONS. THE US AND USSR ARE SEEN AS ATTEMPTING TO KEEP A NUCLEAR MONOPOLY FOR THEIR OWN REASONS.

0023 "POLITICAL PARTIES ON FOREIGN POLICY IN THE INTER-ELECTION YEARS 1962-66."
INDIA Q., 23 (JAN.-MAR. 67), 47-75.
SUMMARIZES ATTITUDES OF VARIOUS POLITICAL PARTIES IN INDIA AS STATED IN THEIR DOCUMENTS, 1962-66, FROM TIME OF CHINESE ATTACK ON INDIA THROUGH CHINA'S DEVELOPMENT OF NUCLEAR WEAPONS.

0024 ABSHIRE D.M. ED., ALLEN R.V. ED.
NATIONAL SECURITY: POLITICAL, MILITARY, AND ECONOMIC STRATEGIES IN THE DECADE AHEAD.
NEW YORK: PRAEGER, 1963, 1039 PP., $10.00.
A NUMBER OF SPECIALISTS IN INTERNATIONAL POLITICS AND

SCIENCE ATTEMPT TO MAKE A SYSTEMATIC INQUIRY INTO CRITICAL
CHOICES WHICH CONFRONT U.S. AND THE FREE WORLD IN THE NEXT
TEN YEARS. COVERS SINO-SOVIET STRATEGY, POLITICAL REQUIRE-
MENTS FOR U.S. STRATEGY, MILITARY STRATEGIES, ECONOMIC
STRATEGIES, AND HOW STRATEGY REQUIREMENTS CAN BE MET WITHIN
FRAMEWORK OF FREE ECONOMY. OUTLINES IN DETAIL THE RANGE OF
ALTERNATIVES UPON WHICH OUR NATIONAL SECURITY MAY DEPEND.

0025 ABT C.C.
"THE PROBLEMS AND POSSIBILITIES OF SPACE ARMS CONTROL."
J. ARMS CONTR., 1 (JAN. 63), 18-43.
   DISCUSSES THE CONNECTION BETWEEN THE DEVELOPMENT OF SPACE
WEAPONS AND REQUIREMENTS FOR ARMS CONTROL AGREEMENT. RE-
COUNTS USEFULNESS OF SUCH WEAPONS IN VARYING STRATEGIES
AND PROBLEMS INVOLVED IN INTERNATIONALLY CONTROLLING THESE
WEAPONS BY LAW.

0026 ABT C.C.
"WAR GAMING."
INT. SCI. TECHNOL., (AUGUST 64), 29-37.
   WAR GAMES ARE EXPERIMENTS WITH ALTERNATIVES IN SIMUL-
ATED CONFLICT AND THEIR CONSEQUENCES. WITHOUT THE CERTAIN-
TY OF THE CORRECT TRUTHS OR COMPLETE TRUTHS, WAR GAMES CAN
ONLY EXERCISE, EXTEND, AND IMPROVE JUDGEMENT. THEY CANNOT
PREDICT THE FUTURE.

0027 ABT C.C.
"CONTROLLING FUTURE ARMS."
DISSERTATION ABSTRACTS, 3 (SPRING 65), 19-40.
   PROCEDURE OUTLINED FOR ANALYZING REQUIREMENTS OF CONTROL
SYSTEMS FOR FUTURE WEAPONS. POSSIBLE TECHNOLOGICAL ADVANCES
CONSIDERED FOR ARMS CONTROL FEASIBILITY. SECURITY RISKS AND
GAINS IN CONTROL ARE OUTLINED. SINCE A LONG LEAD IS NECES-
SARY TO DEVELOP ACCEPTABLE CONTROLS, THESE CONTROLS MUST BE
PREPARED PARALLEL WITH ARMS DEVELOPMENTS.

0028 ACKOFF R.L., RIVETT P.
A MANAGER'S GUIDE TO OPERATIONS RESEARCH.
NEW YORK: JOHN WILEY, 1963, 107 PP., LC#63-14115.
   ACQUAINTS INDUSTRIAL EXECUTIVE WITH TASK OF OPERATIONS
RESEARCH, ITS METHODS, AND PROCESS OF ESTABLISHING
OPERATIONS RESEARCH DEPARTMENT. EXPLAINS FORM AND CONTENT
OF PROBLEMS DISCUSSED UNDER OPERATIONS RESEARCH AND ITS
RELATION TO OTHER MANAGEMENT SERVICES.

0029 ADAMS E.W., FAGOT R.
"A MODEL OF RISKLESS CHOICE."
BEHAVIORAL SCIENCE, 4 (1959), 1-10.
   PRESENTS MODEL TO PREDICT AND EXPLAIN INDIVIDUAL DECISION
MAKING UNDER CONDITIONS OF RISKLESS CHOICE, AND EXPLAINS THE
FUNCTION AND APPLICATION OF MODEL. DISCUSSES CON-
CEPT OF "UTILITY" AS A MEASURING FUNCTION.

0030 AIR FORCE ACADEMY ASSEMBLY '59
INTERNATIONAL STABILITY AND PROGRESS (PAMPHLET)
COLORADO SPRINGS: USAF ACADEMY, 1959, 96 PP.
   REPORT OF 1959 CONFERENCE TO DISCUSS QUESTIONS OF FOREIGN
ASSISTANCE. CONCLUDES THAT MILITARY ASSISTANCE PROGRAMS
HAVE HELPED CREATE AND MAINTAIN A SUBSTANTIALLY LARGER AND
MORE EFFECTIVE DEFENSE POSTURE AROUND USSR THAN A SIMILAR
DOLLAR INVESTMENT IN US'S OWN DEFENSE ESTABLISHMENT COULD
HAVE PRODUCED. SUGGESTS EFFORTS BE MADE TO CREATE PUBLIC
UNDERSTANDING OF PROGRAM.

0031 AIR FORCE ACADEMY LIBRARY
INTERNATIONAL ORGANIZATIONS AND MILITARY SECURITY SYSTEMS
(PAMPHLET) (SPECIAL BIBLIOGRAPHY SERIES, NUMBER 25)
COLORADO SPRINGS: USAF ACADEMY, 1962, 28 PP.
   SELECTED LIST OF ABOUT 220 ITEMS ON THIS SUBJECT HELD BY
USAF ACADEMY LIBRARY. COVERS VARIOUS INTERNATIONAL ORGANIZA-
TIONS, WITH MOST EMPHASIS GIVEN TO UN. ARRANGED BY ORGANIZA-
TION TREATED; SUBDIVIDED INTO BOOKS, PERIODICALS, AND GOV-
ERNMENT DOCUMENTS. ALL IN ENGLISH. INDICATES SOURCES OF
ADDITIONAL INFORMATION.

0032 AIR UNIVERSITY LIBRARY
INDEX TO MILITARY PERIODICALS.
MONTGOMERY: MAXWELL AFB.
   QUARTERLY SINCE 1949, SUPERSEDED BY ANNUAL AND TRIENNIAL
CUMULATIVE ISSUES. INDEXES SIGNIFICANT ARTICLES, NEWS ITEMS,
AND EDITORIALS APPEARING IN 70 MILITARY AND AERONAUTICAL
PERIODICALS. ALL ENTRIES IN ENGLISH. ITEMS ARRANGED BY SUB-
JECT AND BY COUNTRY.

0033 ALBAUM G.
"INFORMATION FLOW AND DECENTRALIZED DECISION MAKING IN
MARKETING."
CALIF. MANAGEMENT REV., 9 (SUMMER 67), 59-70.
   DISCUSSES NECESSITY FOR INTERDEPARTMENTAL MARKETING IN-
FORMATION SYSTEMS IN BUSINESSES WHERE DECISION-MAKING POWER
IS NOT CENTRALIZED. NOTES IMPORTANT ASPECTS OF SYSTEM DESIGN
AND GIVES SAMPLE SYSTEM. DISCUSSES INTEGRATION OF MARKETING
INFORMATION SYSTEM WITH MASTER COMPANY FLOW SYSTEM HANDLING
VARIOUS KINDS OF DATA.

0034 ALBI F.
TRATADO DE LOS MODOS DE GESTION DE LAS CORPORACIONES LOCALES
MADRID: AGUILAR, 1960, 771 PP.
   EXAMINES MUNICIPAL PUBLIC ADMINISTRATION IN SPAIN IN ITS
LEGAL AND FUNCTIONAL ASPECTS. DISCUSSES RESPONSIBILITIES OF
MUNICIPAL GOVERNMENT AS OPPOSED TO NATIONAL GOVERNMENT,
EXPLAINING FINANCIAL AND POLITICAL OBLIGATION OF URBAN
GOVERNMENT TO MEET NEEDS OF LOCAL POPULATION. COVERS PROCESS
OF INCORPORATION AND MANAGEMENT.

0035 ALBONETTI A.
"IL SECONDO PROGRAMMA QUINQUENNALE 1963-67 ED IL BILANCIO
RICERCHE ED INVESTIMENTI PER IL 1963 DELL'ERATOM."
DR. ECON. NUCL., 4 (NO.2, 62), 163-78.
   HISTORICAL APPROACH TO QUESTION OF DEVELOPMENT OF RE-
SEARCH INSTITUTE. DEALS WITH NEW PROGRAM PLANS AND RELATES
THEM TO ITALIAN ECONOMY. POINTS OUT OTHER NATIONS' NUCLEAR
POWER POLITICS.

0036 ALEXANDER L.
"PROTECTION OF PRIVACY IN BEHAVIORAL RESEARCH."
LEX ET SCIENTIA, 4 (JAN.-MAR. 67), 34-38.
   STRESSES IMPORTANCE OF CREATING LEGAL PROTECTION OF RIGHT
TO PRIVACY IN VIEW OF DEVELOPING TECHNOLOGY AND BEHAVIORAL
RESEARCH. CITES WORK OF RUEBHAUSEN AND BRIM WHOSE FORMULA-
TION ACCORD WITH BOTH HIPPOCRATIC OATH AND NURENBERG CODE.

0037 ALEXANDER L.M.
THE LAW OF THE SEA: OFFSHORE BOUNDARIES AND ZONES.
COLUMBUS: OHIO STATE U PR, 1967, 321 PP., LC#67-16949.
   PAPER PRESENTED AT CONFERENCE OF LAW OF THE SEA INSTITUTE
DISCUSSING PROBLEMS INVOLVED IN REDEFINITION OF OFFSHORE
BOUNDARIES. EXAMINES STATE OF INTERNATIONAL LAWS OF SEA AND
ACCOMPLISHMENTS OF GENEVA CONFERENCE ON ISSUE. PRESENTS
QUESTION OF FISHING AND MINING RIGHTS AND FREEDOM OF
NAVIGATION. DISCUSSES USE OF FACTOR ANALYSIS IN SOLVING
PROBLEM.

0038 ALEXANDER Y.
INTERNATIONAL TECHNICAL ASSISTANCE EXPERTS* A CASE STUDY OF
THE U.N. EXPERIENCE.
NEW YORK: FREDERICK PRAEGER, 1966, 223 PP., LC#66-21767.
   STUDY OF THE FUNCTIONS AND CHARACTERISTICS OF TECHNICAL
ASSISTANCE AGENCIES, PROGRAMS AND PERSONNEL. FOCUS ON OBJEC-
TIVES, FINANCING, MACHINERY, AND PLANNING OF UN PROGRAMS FOR
TECHNICAL CO-OPERATION. FURTHER ANALYSIS OF PROBLEMS OF DE-
TERMINING QUALIFICATIONS FOR ASSISTANCE PERSONNEL AND THEIR
RECRUITMENT. INTERVIEWS WITHIN UN PERSONNEL, ND UN DOCUMENTS
USED; DATA REPORTED IN APPENDICES.

0039 ALEXANDER Y.
INTERNATIONAL TECHNICAL ASSISTANCE EXPERTS: A CASE STUDY OF
THE U.N. EXPERIENCE.
NEW YORK: FREDERICK PRAEGER, 1966, 223 PP., LC#66-21767.
   EXAMINATION OF SPECIAL CHARACTERISTICS OF TECHNICAL
ASSISTANCE EXPERTS, STANDARDS APPLIED, AND MACHINERY AND
PROCEDURES UTILIZED IN THEIR RECRUITMENT. CONCLUDES THAT
VAST MAJORITY OF PERSONNEL HAVE PERFORMED THEIR ASSIGN-
MENTS SATISFACTORILY.

0041 ALI S., JONES G.N.
PLANNING, DEVELOPMENT AND CHANGE: AN ANNOTATED BIBLIOGRAPHY
ON DEVELOPMENTAL ADMINISTRATION.
BALTIMORE: J HOPKINS SCHOOL HYG, 1966, 217 PP.
   ANNOTATED BIBLIOGRAPHY OF 655 BOOKS, JOURNAL ARTICLES,
AND GOVERNMENT PUBLICATIONS IN ENGLISH ON TOPICS OF PLANNING
AND DEVELOPMENT IN EMERGING NATIONS, AND PROCESS OF CHANGE
IN ALL SOCIETIES. ARRANGED ACCORDING TO TOPICS OF RESEARCH
METHODOLOGY AND TYPES OF PLANNING; ECONOMIC, SOCIAL,
POLITICAL, AND ADMINISTRATIVE DEVELOPMENT; AND
ORGANIZATIONAL THEORY AND BEHAVIOR.

0042 ALKER H.R. JR.
MATHEMATICS AND POLITICS.
NEW YORK: MACMILLAN, 1965, 152 PP., LC#65-15593.
   REVIEWS DEFINITIONS OF POLITICS, SCHEMES OF POLITICAL
ANALYSIS, IDEAS OF JUSTICE AND POLITICAL INEQUALITY, AND
WAYS OF FORMALLY STATING AND TESTING THEORIES. SHOWS THE
UTILITY OF A MATHEMATICAL APPROACH TO CONCEPT FORMATION
AND VERIFICATION OF HYPOTHESES. IDENTIFIES SEVERAL METHODS
FOR STUDYING THE DEGREE OF ASSOCIATION BETWEEN QUALITATIVE
ATTRIBUTES AND QUANTITATIVE VARIABLES.

0043 ALLEE D.
"AMERICAN AGRICULTURE - ITS RESOURCE ISSUES FOR THE COMING
YEARS."
DAEDALUS, 96 (FALL 67), 1071-1081.
   STATES THAT MORE EFFECTIVE WAYS SHOULD BE FOUND TO
DECREASE SOCIAL COSTS OF RAPID TECHNOLOGICAL CHANGE IN
AGRICULTURE WITHOUT UNDUE SACRIFICE IN EITHER DIRECT OUTPUT
OR ALTERNATIVE USES FOR RESOURCES INVOLVED. THIS
REQUIRES CONTROLLING "EXOTIC" AS WELL AS "COMMON" FORMS OF
POLLUTION, AND RECOGNIZING SOCIAL EFFECTS OF DISPLACED
RESOURCES.

0044 ALLEN S.
LETTER TO A CONSERVATIVE.

GARDEN CITY: DOUBLEDAY, 1965, 370 PP., LC#65-19904.
ATTITUDES OF "MODERATELY LIBERAL AMERICAN" ON THREAT OF
COMMUNISM, THE RADICAL RIGHT AND ITS REACTIONS, MORALITY
AND NUCLEAR WAR, EFFECTIVE ANTI-COMMUNISM, AND US
FOREIGN POLICY IN 20TH CENTURY.

0045 ALLISON D.
"THE GROWTH OF IDEAS."
INT. SCI. AND TECH., 67 (JULY 67), 24-32.
DISCUSSES TWO REPORTS RELATING TO ASPECTS OF THE PROCESS
OF INVENTION AND INNOVATION. ONE STUDY EXAMINED WEAPONS
SYSTEMS AND EVENTS WHICH CONTRIBUTED TO THEIR DEVELOPMENT.
SECOND STUDY EXAMINED TEN TECHNOLOGICAL ACCOMPLISHMENTS,
INCLUDING THE DEVELOPMENT OF SILICONES AND
PYROCERAM GLASS, AND THE "RESEARCH-ENGINEERING INTERACTIONS"
WHICH CONTRIBUTED TO THOSE DEVELOPMENTS.

0046 ALMOND G.A.
"COMPARATIVE POLITICAL SYSTEMS" (BMR)"
J. OF POLITICS, 18 (AUG. 56), 391-409.
SUGGESTS HOW APPLICATION OF CERTAIN SOCIOLOGICAL AND
ANTHROPOLOGICAL CONCEPTS MAY FACILITATE SYSTEMATIC
COMPARISON AMONG MAJOR TYPES OF POLITICAL SYSTEMS. DEALS
PARTICULARLY WITH PROBLEM OF CLASSIFYING POLITICAL SYSTEMS
OF TODAY.

0047 ALTSHULER A.
A LAND-USE PLAN FOR ST. PAUL (PAMPHLET)
INDIANAPOLIS: BOBBS-MERRILL, 1965.
DESCRIBES DRAFT OF NEW LAND USE PLAN BY CITY PLANNERS IN
ST. PAUL. CASTS OFF OLD MARKET-VALUE BIAS OF EARLIER CITY
PLANNERS. QUESTIONS OLD CRITERIA AND CAPABILITY OF NEWER
PLANNERS TO DETERMINE MERITS OF ALTERNATIVE SYSTEMS.

0048 AMERICAN COUNCIL LEARNED SOC
THE ACLS CONSTITUENT SOCIETY JOURNAL PROJECT.
NEW YORK: AMER COUN LEARNED SOC.
AMERICAN COUNCIL OF LEARNED SOCIETIES IS ESTABLISHING A
BIBLIOGRAPHICAL DATA PROCESSING CENTER IN CONJUNCTION WITH
NYU'S INSTITUTE FOR COMPUTER RESEARCH IN THE HUMANITIES.
ONE OF FIRST PROJECTS IS COMPILATION OF ABSTRACTS FROM LEAD-
ING JOURNALS IN THE SOCIAL SCIENCES AND HUMANITIES. DATA
WILL BE PROCESSED TO PRODUCE ANNUAL INDEX OF CONSTITUENT SO-
CIETY JOURNALS AND SPECIALIZED INDEXES.

0049 AMERICAN ASSEMBLY COLUMBIA U
A WORLD OF NUCLEAR POWERS?
NEW YORK: COLUMBIA U PRESS, 1966, 176 PP., LC#66-29073.
STUDY OF POSSIBLE PROLIFERATION OF NUCLEAR NATIONS IN
FUTURE. NON-NUCLEAR POWERS' REPRESENTATIVES ANALYZE PROB-
LEMS, COSTS, TECHNOLOGICAL POSSIBILITY OF NUCLEAR POWER'S
SPREADING, AND EFFECT ON INTERNATIONAL RELATIONS, SUGGESTING
METHOD TO PREVENT SPREAD EVEN WITHOUT ARMS CONTROL.

0050 AMERICAN DOCUMENTATION INST
AMERICAN DOCUMENTATION.
WASHINGTON: AMER DOCUMENT INST.
QUARTERLY PUBLICATION IN THE VARIOUS FIELDS OF DOCUMENTA-
TION. SERVES AS A FORUM FOR DISCUSSION AND EXPERIMENTATION.
EMPHASIZES ANALYSIS OF METHODOLOGY AND SYSTEM IN STORING
AND TRANSMITTING COMMUNICATIONS AND DOCUMENTATION.

0051 AMERICAN DOCUMENTATION INST
DOCUMENTATION ABSTRACTS.
WASHINGTON: AMER DOCUMENT INST.
QUARTERLY, FIRST PUBLISHED MARCH 1966, CONTAINS ABSTRACTS
FROM CURRENT BOOKS, PAPERS, GOVERNMENT DOCUMENTS, AND
RESEARCH PERTAINING TO INFORMATION RETRIEVAL. ENTRIES AR-
RANGED BY SUBJECT. INCLUDES REGIONAL, NATIONAL, AND INTER-
NATIONAL PROGRAMS, INFORMATION SYSTEMS AND TECHNIQUES, COM-
PUTERS, EQUIPMENT, ETC. MAJORITY ENGLISH-LANGUAGE SOURCES;
SOME EUROPEAN.

0052 AMERICAN DOCUMENTATION INST
CATALOGUE OF AUXILIARY PUBLICATIONS IN MICROFILMS AND PHOTO-
PRINTS.
WASHINGTON: AMER DOCUMENT INST, 1946, 51 PP.
AN UNANNOTATED LISTING OF DOCUMENTS DEPOSITED WITH THE
AMERICAN DOCUMENTATION INSTITUTE UNDER ITS AUXILIARY PUBLI-
CATION PROGRAM. COVERS PUBLICATIONS ISSUED OR TRANSLATED IN
ENGLISH ON A WIDE RANGE OF SUBJECTS. ARTICLES LISTED ARE
SCIENTIFIC OR SCHOLARLY PAPERS TOO LONG TO BE PUBLISHED IN
JOURNALS; CHARTS, DIAGRAMS, OR ILLUSTRATIONS INCLUDED WITH
THE ARTICLE ON MICROFILM. TOPICALLY CLASSIFIED LISTINGS.

0053 AMERICAN FRIENDS SERVICE COMM
IN PLACE OF WAR.
NEW YORK: GROSSMAN PUBL, 1967, 115 PP., LC#67-21234.
DEVOTED TO STRATEGY OF NONVIOLENT DEFENSE. BEGINS WITH
SHORT HISTORY OF THE POLICY AND OUTLINES EFFECTIVENESS AND
DIFFERENT KINDS OF NONVIOLENCE, ORGANIZATION OF THE
GOVERNMENT, PREPARATION OF THE NATION, AND FORMS PROTEST
SHOULD TAKE IN EVENT OF INVASION.

0054 AMERICAN LIBRARY ASSN
GUIDE TO JAPANESE REFERENCE BOOKS.
CHICAGO: AMER LIB ASSN, 1966, 303 PP., LC#66-23396.
RESTRICTED TO BOOKS AND PERIODICALS PUBLISHED UP TO
SEPTEMBER. DIVIDED INTO FOUR CATEGORIES: GENERAL WORKS,
HUMANITIES, SOCIAL SCIENCES, AND SCIENCE AND TECHNOLOGY.
ANNOTATED WITH CROSS REFERENCES AND INDEXES.

0055 AMRINE M.
THE GREAT DECISION: THE SECRET HISTORY OF THE ATOMIC BOMB.
NEW YORK: G P PUTNAM'S SONS, 1959, 251 PP.
REVIEWS PERIOD FROM ROOSEVELT'S DEATH TO THE ATOMIC BOMB-
ING OF HIROSHIMA, ANALYZING EVENTS LEADING UP TO THE MOMEN-
TOUS DECISION AND DISCUSSING ROLE OF POLITICIANS, MILITARY
MEN, SCIENTISTS, AND ESPIONAGE AGENTS IN DECISION-MAKING.
BELIEVES IMPORTANT POLICY DECISIONS ARE TAKEN WITHOUT SUF-
FICIENT DELIBERATION.

0056 ANDERSON C.A. ED., BOWMAN M.J. ED.
EDUCATION AND ECONOMIC DEVELOPMENT.
CHICAGO: ALDINE PUBLISHING CO, 1965, 436 PP., LC#65-12453.
HAS 22 ARTICLES ON INVESTMENT VIEW OF HUMAN RESOURCES:
FORMATION OF HUMAN COMPETENCIES; DIFFUSION OF SCHOOLING,
TECHNOLOGIES, AND EDUCATIONAL OPPORTUNITIES; AND HUMAN-
FACTOR PRECONDITIONS, THE TIMING OF EMERGENCE, AND THE PACE
OF CHANGE.

0057 ANDERSON N., NIJKERK K.F.
"INTERNATIONAL SEMINARS: AN ANALYSIS AND AN EVALUATION."
ADMIN SCI. QUART., 3 (SEPT. 58), 229-50.
SYSTEMATIC, SCIENTIFIC STUDY ON EFFECTIVENESS OF 24
INTERNATIONAL SEMINARS EVALUATED AND COMPARED BY SEMINAR
MEMBERS AND BY DELEGATES OF LARGER REGIONAL ORGANIZATIONS.

0058 ANDREWS R.B.
"URBAN ECONOMICS: AN APPRAISAL OF PROGRESS."
LAND ECONOMICS, 37 (AUG. 61), 219-227.
APPRAISAL OF GROWTH OF URBAN ECONOMICS AS A DISCIPLINE.
DISCUSSES DEFINITION OF THE DISCIPLINE, USE OF DATA, PROB-
LEMS IN PROCEDURE, AND PROPOSALS FOR THE IMPROVEMENT OF
URBAN ECONOMIC STUDY TECHNIQUES. PRIMARILY CONCERNED WITH
URBAN-ECONOMIC THEORY DEVELOPMENT.

0059 ANGELL N.
DEFENCE AND THE ENGLISH-SPEAKING ROLE.
LONDON: PALL MALL PRESS, 1958, 116 PP.
EXAMINES IMPLICATIONS OF MODERN THREAT TO PEACE BY RUSSO-
CHINESE TOTALITARIAN COMMUNISM. MAINTAINS THAT NEUTRALITY IS
INCOMPATIBLE WITH PEACE AND DEFENSE; THAT UN IS BEST-SUITED
VEHICLE FOR INTERNATIONAL UNDERSTANDING; THAT COMMUNIST
PROPAGANDA HAS USED LIBERAL SLOGANS TO UNDERMINE DEMOCRACY;
AND THAT BOTH BRITAIN AND US MUST TEMPER THEIR NATIONALISM
TO COOPERATE IN DEFENSE OF DEMOCRATIC IDEALS.

0060 ANGELL R.
"GOVERNMENTS AND PEOPLES AS FOCI FOR PEACE-ORIENTED
RESEARCH."
J. SOC. ISSUES, 11 (1955), 36-41.
APPRAISES EFFECTIVENESS OF SOCIOLOGY-ORIENTED STUDIES IN
INTERNATIONAL RELATIONS. CONSIDERS HISTORICAL ANALOGIES,
FUNCTIONING OF GOVERNMENT LEADERS AND INTERGOVERNMENTAL
BODIES AS VALID FOR STUDY. AS MEANS TO SOCIAL INTEGRATION,
CULTURAL LIKENESSES AND DIFFERENCES, SOCIAL TENSIONS AND
POSSIBLE INTER-CULTURAL BRIDGES SHOULD BE RECOGNIZED.

0061 ANTHONY R.N.
PLANNING AND CONTROL SYSTEMS.
CAMBRIDGE: HARVARD U, DIV OF RES, 1965, 180 PP., LC#65-18724
A BRIEF INQUIRY INTO THE NATURE AND FUNCTION OF CONTROL
SYSTEMS. EMPHASIZES SELECTION OF A FRAMEWORK UNDER WHICH
SUCH TOPICS AS STRATEGIC PLANNING, MANAGEMENT CONTROL,
AND OPERATIONAL CONTROL ARE DISCUSSED IN SYSTEMATIC DETAIL.
AN APPENDIX ON TERMINOLOGY IS INCLUDED.

0062 APPADORAI A.
THE SUBSTANCE OF POLITICS (6TH ED.)
MADRAS: OXFORD U PRESS, 1952, 524 PP.
TREATS ESSENTIAL PRINCIPLES OF POLITICAL THEORY AND
ORGANIZATION. PART ONE DISCUSSES THEORY; PART TWO TREATS
SPECIFIC POLITIES FROM THE GREEK CITY-STATES TO MAJOR MODERN
EUROPEAN STATES AND INDIA, AND CONSIDERS VARIOUS ASPECTS
OF POLITIES SUCH AS LEGISLATURES, JUDICIARY, AND EXECUTIVE.
INTENDED AS TEXTBOOK. BIBLIOGRAPHIES AT END OF EACH CHAPTER.

0063 APTHEKER H.
DISARMAMENT AND THE AMERICAN ECONOMY: A SYMPOSIUM.
NEW YORK: NEW CENTURY, 64 PP, 1960, $.75.
COLLECTION OF ARTICLES WITH MARXIST VIEWPOINT, ATTEMPTING
TO DEMONSTRATE THAT DISARMAMENT WILL NOT CREATE SEVERE ECO-
NOMIC CRISIS. ECONOMIC, POLITICAL AND IDEOLOGICAL FACTORS
ARE CONSIDERED.

0064 ARGYRIS C.
"SOME PROBLEMS IN CONCEPTUALIZING ORGANIZATIONAL CLIMATE:
A CASE STUDY OF A BANK" (BMR)"
ADMINISTRATIVE SCI. Q., 2 (MAR. 58), 501-520.
CONCERNED WITH WAY OF ORDERING COMPLEX OF VARIABLES
COMPRISING ORGANIZATIONS. USES MODEL OF A BANK TO STUDY

INTERPERSONAL RELATIONS. FINDS THREE SYSTEMS OF VARIABLES:
POLICIES, PROCEDURES, AND POSITIONS, PERSONALITY FACTORS
SUCH AS INDIVIDUAL'S NEEDS, VALUES, AND ABILITIES; AND
INDIVIDUAL'S EFFORTS TO ACCOMMODATE HIS OWN EFFORTS TO THE
ORGANIZATION'S.

0066 ARON R.
CENTURY OF TOTAL WAR.
NEW YORK: DOUBLEDAY, 1954, 379 PP.
     DISCUSSES HISTORY OF WAR IN THE TWENTIETH CENTURY THROUGH
ANALYSIS OF THE ORIGINS AND CONSEQUENCES OF WORLD WAR ONE,
AND HOW THEY LAY THE GROUNDWORK FOR WORLD WAR TWO AND THE
PRESENT COLD WAR SITUATION, AND THEIR IMPACT ON THE DEVELOP-
MENT OF POLITICAL IDEOLOGIES AND POLICIES IN TODAY'S WORLD.

0067 ARON R.
ON WAR: ATOMIC WEAPONS AND GLOBAL DIPLOMACY (TRANS. BY
TERENCE KILMARTIN)
LONDON: SECKER AND WARBURG, 1958, 126 PP.
     STATES THAT NO SINGLE WEAPON WILL SUFFICE TO CHANGE HUMAN
NATURE. CLAIMING A "REALIST" ATTITUDE, AUTHOR BELIEVES THAT
TREND OF INTERNATIONAL POLITICS DEPENDS AS MUCH ON MEN AND
SOCIETY AS UPON WEAPONS. CLAIMS ATOMIC WEAPONS HAVE PLAYED
ONLY A LATENT ROLE IN THE COURSE OF INTERNATIONAL EVENTS.

0068 ARON R.
THE GREAT DEBATE: THEORIES OF NUCLEAR STRATEGY.
GARDEN CITY: DOUBLEDAY, 1967, 265 PP., LC#65-10618.
     TRANSLATED FROM FRENCH AND ORIGINALLY WRITTEN TO EXPLAIN
AMERICAN NUCLEAR POSITIONS TO FRENCH. SETS FORTH THEORIES OF
DETERRENCE AND GRADUATED RETALIATION THAT GUIDE US.
CONSIDERS PROS AND CONS OF FRENCH NUCLEAR FORCE AND SMALL
FORCES GENERALLY, AND FUTURE OF THE ALLIANCE.

0069 ARONOWITZ D.S.
"CIVIL COMMITMENT OF NARCOTIC ADDICTS."
COLUMBIA LAW REV., 67 (MAR. 67), 405-429.
     ARGUES THAT INVOLUNTARY CIVIL COMMITMENT OF NONCRIMINAL
NARCOTIC ADDICTS NOT JUSTIFIED ON BASIS OF EXISTING KNOWL-
EDGE OF ADDICTION. EXAMINES CLAIMS BY PROPONENTS OF COMMIT-
MENT PROGRAMS TO SHOW THEIR INSUFFICIENCY IN SUPPORTING THIS
APPROACH TO PROBLEM. CONCLUDES THAT SUCH PROGRAMS REPRESENT
UNREASONABLE, IMPROPER DEPRIVATION OF LIBERTY FOR ADDICTS.

0070 ARROW K.J. ED., KARLIN S. ED., SUPPES P. ED.
MATHEMATICAL METHODS IN THE SOCIAL SCIENCES, 1959.
STANFORD: STANFORD U PRESS, 1960.
     23 PAPERS OF STANFORD SYMPOSIUM ON MATHEMATICAL METHODS
IN THE SOCIAL SCIENCES - JUNE 1959 - ON ECONOMICS (STABIL-
ITY, CAPITAL ACCUMULATION, CONSUMER BEHAVIOR AND TECHNOLOG-
ICAL CHANGE); MANAGEMENT SCIENCE (A PROBLEM IN QUEUING THEO-
RY AND INVENTORY PROBLEMS); AND ON PSYCHOLOGY (UTILITY, STO-
CHASTIC MODELS FOR INTELLIGENCE TEST SCORES, CHOICE BEHAV-
IOR, RESPONSE LATENCY, ETC).

0071 ARTHUR D LITTLE INC
SAN FRANCISCO COMMUNITY RENEWAL PROGRAM.
SAN FRANCISCO: COMM RENEWAL PROG, 1965, 173 PP.
     REPORT TO CITY PLANNING COMMISSION ON SAN FRANCISCO
PROGRAM. PRESENTS FIVE BASIC OBJECTIVES OF PROGRAM AND THE
ADMINISTRATIVE AND ORGANIZATIONAL PROCEDURES NECESSARY TO
ACHIEVE THEM. CONTENDS THAT MAINTAINING LIVABLE AND
PROSPERING COMMUNITY FOR PEOPLE OF ALL INCOME LEVELS IS
PUBLIC AND PRIVATE OBLIGATION.

0072 ASIAN STUDIES CENTER
FOUR ARTICLES ON POPULATION AND FAMILY LIFE IN TAIWAN (ASIAN
STUDIES PAPERS, REPRINT SERIES NO. 2)
E LANSING: ASIAN STUD CTR, MSU, 1967, 53 PP.
     FOUR ARTICLES ARE ENTITLED: 1) TAIWAN AS A LABORATORY FOR
STUDY OF CHINESE SOCIETY AND CULTURE, 2) MORE RURAL PEOPLE-
STRONG FAMILY LIFE, (3 URBANIZATION AND THE FAMILY, AND (4
MATRILATERAL AND AFFINAL RELATIONSHIPS OF A TAIWANESE VIL-
LAGE. DISCUSSION OF CHANGES AND PROBLEMS RESULTING FROM AG-
RICULTURAL AND INDUSTRIAL PROGRESS.

0073 ASTIA
HUMAN ENGINEERING: A REPORT BIBLIOGRAPHY.
WASHINGTON: US GOVERNMENT, 1962, 240 PP.
     CITATIONS OF UNCLASSIFIED DOCUMENTS CATALOGUED BY THE
ARMED SERVICES TECHNICAL INFORMATION AGENCY. ENTRIES DATE
1953-62. SUBJECTS INCLUDE COMMUNICATIONS SYSTEMS, CONTROL,
DATA PROCESSING SYSTEMS AND COMPUTERS, HUMAN FACTORS, ROCKET
SYSTEMS AND MISSILES, AND TRAINING; ALL ITEMS TREAT VARIOUS
ASPECTS OF AIRCRAFT.

0074 ASTIA
INFORMATION THEORY: A REPORT BIBLIOGRAPHY.
WASHINGTON: US GOVERNMENT, 1962, 58 PP.
     MATERIAL CATALOGUED BY ARMED SERVICES TECHNICAL INFORMA-
TION AGENCY 1953-62. DEFENSE CONTRACTOR REPORTS LISTED BY
SOURCE, CONTRACT, AND DATE; MILITARY RESEARCH DOCUMENTS
CATALOGUED BY SOURCE AND TITLE. SUBJECTS INCLUDE BEHAVIORAL
APPLICATIONS, COMMUNICATIONS SYSTEMS AND THEORY, DATA TRANS-
MISSION SYSTEMS, AND COMPUTER DESIGN.

0075 ATKIN J.M.
"THE FEDERAL GOVERNMENT, BIG BUSINESS, AND COLLEGES OF EDU-
CATION."
EDUCATIONAL FORUM, 31 (MAY 67), 391-402.
     A CRITIQUE OF THE ROLE OF THE FEDERAL GOVERNMENT AND OF
BIG BUSINESS IN EDUCATION. THE BACKGROUND OF THIS INVOLVE-
MENT, SOME OF ITS FEATURES, AND THE PROBLEMS IT HAS AND IS
CREATING ARE EXPLORED. MAJOR ISSUES ARE THAT PROFESSIONALLY
TRAINED EDUCATORS HAVE NOT BEEN SUFFICIENTLY INVOLVED IN THE
PROGRAMS, AND THAT TECHNIQUES AND APPROACHES OF BUSINESS AND
GOVERNMENT ARE SOMETIMES INAPPROPRIATELY USED IN EDUCATION.

0076 ATOMIC INDUSTRIAL FORUM
COMMENTARY ON LEGISLATION TO PERMIT PRIVATE OWNERSHIP OF
SPECIAL NUCLEAR MATERIAL (PAMPHLET)
NEW YORK: ATOMIC INDUS FORUM, 1963, 63 PP.
     DISCUSSES ATOMIC ENERGY COMMISSION'S BILL TO PERMIT
PRIVATE OWNERSHIP OF SPECIAL NUCLEAR MATERIAL AND TO REVISE
ATOMIC ENERGY ACT OF 1954 TO AUTHORIZE TRANSACTIONS BY AEC
WITH PRIVATE PERSONS. PRESENTS ATOMIC ENERGY ACT AND TEXT
OF BILL AND ANALYZES ADVISABILITY OF CHANGES. BASICALLY
SUPPORTS BILL.

0077 ATOMIC INDUSTRIAL FORUM
PUBLIC RELATIONS FOR THE ATOMIC INDUSTRY.
NEW YORK: ATOMIC INDUS FORUM, 1956, 160 PP.
     PAPERS ON USES OF ATOMIC ENERGY, ATOM AS NEWS, NEED TO
INFORM PUBLIC, SOURCES OF INFORMATION, PUBLIC OPINION OF
PEACEFUL USES OF ATOMIC ENERGY, SAFETY REQUIREMENTS NEEDED
TO RECEIVE PUBLIC SUPPORT, AND TOOLS AND TECHNIQUES OF
PUBLIC RELATIONS.

0078 ATOMIC INDUSTRIAL FORUM
MANAGEMENT AND ATOMIC ENERGY.
NEW YORK: ATOMIC INDUS FORUM, 1958, 460 PP.
     PROCEEDINGS OF ATOMIC ENERGY MANAGEMENT CONFERENCE ON
STATUS AND GROWTH OF ATOMIC INDUSTRY. CONSIDERS POLICY,
HEALTH AND SAFETY, ASSESSMENT OF US POWER REACTOR PROGRAM,
FEASIBILITY OF SMALL REACTORS, SALE OF NUCLEAR PRODUCTS
OUTSIDE US, AMENDMENTS TO ATOMIC ENERGY ACT, NUCLEAR SHIPS,
REDUCTION OF COST, INTERNATIONAL ACTIVITIES, PEACEFUL USES,
INDEMNIFICATION LAW, AND RESEARCH DEVELOPMENTS.

0079 ATOMIC INDUSTRIAL FORUM
THE IMPACT OF THE PEACEFUL USES OF ATOMIC ENERGY ON STATE
AND LOCAL GOVERNMENT.
NEW YORK: ATOMIC INDUS FORUM, 1959, 92 PP.
     SURVEYS EFFECTS OF ATOMIC ENERGY DEVELOPMENT AND PEACEFUL
USES ON STATE AND LOCAL GOVERNMENTAL AGENCIES. EMPHASIZES
DECISIONS THAT OFFICIALS MAY BE CALLED ON TO MAKE REGARDING
ATOMIC ENERGY. EXAMINES IMPACT ON REGULATORY AGENCIES AND ON
INDUSTRIAL DEVELOPMENT PROGRAMS. STUDIES ROLE OF STATE
LEGISLATURE, COORDINATION OF STATE PROGRAMS, FEDERAL
STANDARDIZATION, AND NATIONAL PROGRAMS.

0080 ATOMIC INDUSTRIAL FORUM
ATOMS FOR INDUSTRY: WORLD FORUM.
NEW YORK: ATOMIC INDUS FORUM, 1960, 160 PP.
     DESCRIBES GROWTH OF INDUSTRIAL USES OF ATOMIC ENERGY, AND
PROCEDURES. IDENTIFIES UNPRECEDENTED PROBLEMS OF
USING ATOMS FOR SOCIAL PURPOSES, SUCH AS COST, SAFETY,
FINANCES, LEGAL CONTROL, AND PUBLIC INTEREST.

0081 ATOMIC INDUSTRIAL FORUM
SAFEGUARDS AGAINST DIVERSION OF NUCLEAR MATERIALS FROM
PEACEFUL TO MILITARY PURPOSES.
NEW YORK: ATOMIC INDUS FORUM, 1965, 85 PP.
     PAPERS ON CONTROL OF NUCLEAR MATERIALS TO PREVENT
MILITARY USAGE AND ON DEVELOPMENT OF PEACEFUL USES.
DISCUSSES INTERNATIONAL ATOMIC ENERGY AGENCY'S INSPECTION
SYSTEM TO SAFEGUARD AGAINST MILITARY USE.

0082 AVTORKHANOV A.
"A NEW AGRARIAN REVOLUTION."
INST. FOR STUDY OF USSR, 14 (JULY 67), 3-19.
     COMPARES REFORMS IN SOVIET AGRICULTURE NOW CARRIED OUT
BY KHRUSHCHEV'S SUCCESSORS AND ESSENTIAL FEATURES OF KOLKHOZ
SYSTEM AS CREATED BY STALIN. BASES ARGUMENTS ON CONCEPT THAT
FREE MARKETS ARE THE ONLY SOLUTION TO ECONOMIC PROBLEMS.

0084 BAILEY S.K. ED.
AMERICAN POLITICS AND GOVERNMENT.
NEW YORK: BASIC BOOKS, 1965, 284 PP., LC#65-14968.
     ESSAYS ON VARIETY OF POLITICAL SCIENCE THEMES BY PROFES-
SORS AND POLITICAL LEADERS IN US. AMONG TOPICS ARE: AMERICAN
CONSTITUTIONAL SYSTEM, SUPREME COURT, PRESIDENCY, CONGRESS,
LEGISLATIVE POLICY-MAKING, AMERICAN PARTY SYSTEM, ELECTIONS,
PUBLIC OPINION, STATE GOVERNMENT, LOCAL GOVERNMENT, INTERNA-
TIONAL RELATIONS, FOREIGN POLICY, AND SCIENCE AND GOVERN-
MENT.

0085 BAKER G.W., COTTRELL L.S.
BEHAVIORAL SCIENCE AND CIVIL DEFENSE.
WASHINGTON: NATL ACAD OF SCI, 1962, 169 PP., LC#62-60093.
     DISCUSSES CIVIL DEFENSE AND ITS FACILITATION BY SOCIAL
SCIENCE METHODS. CONSIDERS ITS EFFECTIVENESS IN PUBLIC PLAN-

NING, DECISION-MAKING AND PUBLIC POLICY, APATHY CONTROL AND
ENCOURAGING COOPERATION. ALSO VIEWS ASPECTS OF TENSION AND
STRESS RELEASE, AND SYSTEMATIC APPLICATIONS OF BEHAVIORAL
SCIENCE TO DISASTER RECOVERY.

0086 BAKER H.
PROBLEMS OF REEMPLOYMENT AND RETRAINING OF MANPOWER DURING
THE TRANSITION FROM WAR TO PEACE.
PRINCETON: PRIN U INDUS REL CTR, 1945, 45 PP.
    APPROXIMATELY 275 ENTRIES INCLUDING BOOKS, GOVERNMENT
PUBLICATIONS, AND ARTICLES FROM TECHNICAL JOURNALS DEALING
WITH PROBLEMS OF RETRAINING VETERANS AND ENACTING MEASURES
TO ABSORB VETERANS INTO NORMAL, GAINFUL EMPLOYMENT. ALL EN-
TRIES ARE IN ENGLISH AND WERE PUBLISHED 1943-45. ARRANGED
BY SUBJECT AND ALPHABETICALLY BY AUTHOR.

0087 BALASSA B.
TRADE PROSPECTS FOR DEVELOPING COUNTRIES.
HOMEWOOD: RICHARD IRWIN, 1964, 450 PP., LC#64-17248.
    PROJECTION OF GENERAL TRADE PATTERNS AND THE PROSPECTS
FOR INDIVIDUAL COMMODITIES OF THE DEVELOPING WORLD TO 1975.
ASSUMES THAT FURTHER GROWTH IN THE DEVELOPED COUNTRIES WILL
AFFECT DEMAND SIDE OF PRICING WITH SUPPLY FLUCTUATIONS IN
POOR LANDS AFFECTING OTHER SIDE. DISCUSSES ROLE OF POLITICAL
TRADE POLICIES OF BOTH RICH AND POOR AND MAKES POLICY SUG-
GESTIONS. WEALTH OF EMPIRICAL MATERIAL.

0088 BALDWIN H.W.
"SLOW-DOWN IN THE PENTAGON."
FOREIGN AFFAIRS, 43 (JAN. 65), 262-280.
    A CRITIQUE OF THE BUREAUCRATIZATION AND OVER-CENTRALIZA-
TION OF THE DEPARTMENT OF DEFENSE, WHICH BALDWIN BELIEVES
HAS LED TO A DANGEROUS SLOW DOWN IN WEAPONS RESEARCH, AND
IMPLEMENTATION. CORROBORATIVE CASES AND SOURCES CITED.

0089 BALDWIN H.W.
THE PRICE OF POWER.
NEW YORK: HARPER & ROW, 1947, 361 PP.
    EXAMINES PROBLEM OF AMERICAN POWER AND ITS USE IN ATOMIC
AGE. DISCUSSES DILEMMA OF BUILDING MILITARY DEFENSE AND
STILL MAINTAINING DEMOCRACY. PRESENTS CHANGES IN US POWER'S
POLITICAL, MILITARY, ECONOMIC, AND PSYCHOLOGICAL POSITIONS.
STUDIES REVISION MADE IN POLICIES AND COSTS OF SWITCHES.
EXPLORES ALTERNATIVES OPEN IN FUTURE AND PRICE OF US POWER.
STATES THAT COMMON IDEAL IS ONLY SOLUTION.

0090 BARAGWANATH L.E., FENDER B.E.F., SMITH E.B.
"SCIENTIFIC CO-OPERATION BETWEEN THE UNIVERSITIES AND
INDUSTRY - A RESEARCH NOTE."
J. MANAGEMENT STUDIES, 5 (FEB. 68), 83-90.
    REPORTS ON SURVEY DESIGNED TO DETERMINE FREQUENCY OF
TECHNICAL CONTACT BETWEEN UNIVERSITY SCIENTISTS AND INDUS-
TRY AND EXTENT TO WHICH INDUSTRY IS SATISFIED WITH THE
PRESENT DEGREE OF COLLABORATION. ALSO SEEKS TO FIND IF IN-
DUSTRY HAS TROUBLE FINDING UNIVERSITY SCIENTISTS IN AREAS
OF INTEREST, WHAT SUBJECTS NEED CLOSER CONTACT, AND IF IN-
DUSTRY FEELS GRADUATE RESEARCHERS COULD MAKE CLOSER LINK.

0091 BARAN P.
"THE FUTURE COMPUTER UTILITY."
PUBLIC INTEREST, 8 (SUMMER 67), 75-87.
    DISCUSSES POSSIBILITY OF "NATIONAL COMPUTER PUBLIC UTILI-
TY SYSTEM" IN FUTURE. FEELS IT WILL OPERATE ON PRINCIPLE OF
"TIME-SHARING," ONLY WITH MANY MORE PEOPLE OWNING COMPUTERS
THAN DO NOW. COVERS DEVELOPMENT OF COMPUTER OVER YEARS,
ITS BENEFITS, ETC. CONCENTRATES ON PROBLEM OF REGULATING
SUCH SYSTEM.

0092 BARANSON J.
TECHNOLOGY FOR UNDERDEVELOPED AREAS: AN ANNOTATED BIBLIOG-
RAPHY.
NEW YORK: PERGAMON PRESS, 1967, 81 PP., LC#67-14273.
    INTERDISCIPLINARY BIBLIOGRAPHY OF 319 ITEMS FROM JOURNALS
AND BOOKS SELECTED FROM 2,000 EUROPEAN AND AMERICAN SOURCES.
ENTRIES, ARRANGED BY SUBJECT, TREAT SOCIO-CULTURAL INFLU-
ENCES ON TECHNOLOGY, PRODUCTS AND SYSTEMS, INSTITUTIONAL
ARRANGEMENTS, AND MAJOR ASPECTS OF ECONOMIC THEORY. ITEMS
ARE ANNOTATED.

0093 BARISH N.N. ED., VERHULST M. ED.
MANAGEMENT SCIENCES IN THE EMERGING COUNTRIES.
NEW YORK: PERGAMON PRESS, 1965, 261 PP., LC#63-18929.
    EXPLORES WAYS IN WHICH MANAGEMENT TOOLS DEVELOPED FOR USE
IN MORE ADVANCED ECONOMIES MAY BE APPLIED TO NEWLY EMERGING
COUNTRIES. SURVEYS SIGNIFICANT ENVIRONMENTAL DIFFERENCES
BETWEEN THESE ECONOMIES TO AVOID ILL-ADVISED APPLICATIONS
OF OPERATIONS RESEARCH AND MANAGEMENT SCIENCE TECHNIQUES.
SOME PAPERS PRESENTED IN FRENCH.

0094 BARKER E.
POLITICAL THOUGHT IN ENGLAND: FROM HERBERT SPENCER TO THE
PRESENT DAY.
NEW YORK: HOLT RINEHART WINSTON, 1928, 256 PP.
    PRESENTS HISTORY OF ENGLISH POLITICAL THOUGHT. DISCUSSES
T.H. GREEN, BRADLEY, AND BOSANQUET IN IDEALIST SCHOOL,
ALSO HERBERT SPENCER AND SCIENTIFIC SCHOOL. ANALYZES THE

"LAWYERS" OF MID- AND LATE-19TH CENTURY, AND ECONOMICS AND
POLITICS OF BENTHAM, PEARSON, AND MAITLAND.

0095 BARKER E.
THE DEVELOPMENT OF PUBLIC SERVICES IN WESTERN EUROPE:
1660-1930.
LONDON: OXFORD U PR, 1944, 93 PP.
    HISTORY OF THE DEVELOPMENT OF PUBLIC ADMINISTRATION IN
ENGLAND, FRANCE, AND PRUSSIA, WITH COMPARISONS OF STRUCTURES
AND FUNCTIONS. CONCENTRATES ON MILITARY CONSCRIPTION,
TAXATION, SOCIAL WELFARE, AND EDUCATION.

0096 BARNET R.
WHO WANTS DISARMAMENT.
BOSTON: BEACON, 1960, 141 PP.
    RELATIONSHIP OF DISARMAMENT TO AMERICAN SECURITY AND TO
SOVIET GOALS IS OBSERVED. A CRITICAL EXAMINATION OF VARIOUS
PROPOSALS THAT HAVE SOUGHT TO ACHIEVE 'ARMS CONTROL' IS ALSO
PRESENTED.

0097 BARNETT H.J.
"RESEARCH AND DEVELOPMENT, ECONOMIC GROWTH, AND
NATIONAL SECURITY."
ANN. AMER. ACAD. POLIT. SOC. SCI., 327 (JAN. 60), 36-49.
    QUESTIONS THE PREVALENT BELIEF THAT GOVERNMENT-SPONSORED
RESEARCH AND DEVELOPMENT CAN BE EQUATED WITH ECONOMIC
GROWTH. CORRELATION BETWEEN THE TWO DOES EXIST BUT IT IS
NECESSARY TO EXAMINE PATHS 'OPEN TO GOVERNMENT' IN SELECTING
POLICY. ENDS BEST ACHIEVED IF GOVERNMENT INDICATES ONLY
OBJECTIVES ALLOWING RESEARCH-DECISIONS TO BE MADE AT-LARGE.

0098 BARRO S.
"ECONOMIC IMPACT OF SPACE EXPENDITURES: SOME BROAD ISSUES
DEALING WITH COSTS AND BENEFITS."
BUSINESS HORIZONS, 10 (SUMMER 67), 71-80.
    PROVIDES BACKGROUND ON HOW SPACE PROGRAM FUNDING DECI-
SIONS MAY IMPINGE ON OVER-ALL ECONOMIC ACTIVITY AND ECONOMIC
POLICY; SUGGESTS POSSIBILITY THAT SPACE OPERATIONS MAY MAKE
MAJOR CONTRIBUTIONS TO ECONOMIC WELFARE.

0099 BARRON J.A.
"ACCESS TO THE PRESS."
HARVARD LAW REV., 80 (JUNE 67), 1641-1678.
    STATES THAT 18TH-CENTURY VIEW OF FIRST AMENDMENT AS
ENCOURAGEMENT TO "FULL AND FREE DISCUSSION" IN PRESS IS NO
LONGER WORKING. EXAMINES NEW TECHNOLOGY OF COMMUNICATIONS
INDUSTRY, WHICH LIMITS ACCESS TO MEDIA AND TYPES OF NEWS
COVERED. EXAMINES SEVERAL COURT CASES AND URGES PASSAGE OF
LAW THAT WOULD GUARANTEE FREE ACCESS TO ALL MEDIA FOR ALL
POINTS OF VIEW.

0100 BASS M.E., MARTIN E.D.
SELECTIVE BIBLIOGRAPHY ON MUNICIPAL GOVERNMENT FROM THE
FILES OF THE MUNICIPAL TECHNICAL ADVISORY SERVICE.
KNOXVILLE: U TENN MUNIC TECH ADV, 1963, 40 PP.
    BIBLIOGRAPHIC LISTING OF PUBLICATIONS PERTAINING TO EVERY
AREA OF MUNICIPAL ADMINISTRATION. MATERIAL LISTED COVERS
SPECIFIC TOPICS WITHIN BROADER FIELDS OF FINANCE, PUBLIC
SERVICES, ADMINISTRATION, AND PLANNING.

0101 BATES J.
"A MODEL FOR THE SCIENCE OF DECISION."
PHILOSOPHY OF SCIENCE, 21 (OCT. 54), 326-339.
    FORMULATES A MODEL FOR DECISION MAKING IN POLITICAL,
ETHICAL, ECONOMIC, POLICY SCIENCE FIELDS. STRESSES NEED FOR
METHODS OTHER THAN INTUITIVE AND SEMI-INTUITIVE PROCEDURES
CURRENTLY EMPLOYED. CONDITIONS FOR DECISION PROCEDURE MODEL
ARE BASED ON GENERAL PRINCIPLES PREVIOUSLY FORMULATED BY
MATHEMATICIANS IN THIS FIELD.

0102 BAUCHET P.
ECONOMIC PLANNING.
LONDON: HEINEMANN, 1964, 299 PP., LC#64-16665.
    DESCRIBES THE FRENCH EXPERIENCE IN ECONOMIC PLANNING AS A
MAJOR TRANSFORMATION OF CAPITALIST STRUCTURE. CONSIDERS
PLANNING AND DEMOCRACY, BUSINESS FIRMS, AND SOCIAL CLASSES,
AS WELL AS THE STRATEGY OF PLANNING FOR AN OPTIMUM.

0103 BAUER P.T.
ECONOMIC ANALYSIS AND POLICY IN UNDERDEVELOPED COUNTRIES.
DURHAM: DUKE U PR, 1957, 145 PP., LC#57-8814.
    DESCRIBES SCOPE, METHOD, AND POSSIBILITIES OF ECONOMICS
IN STUDY OF UNDERDEVELOPED NATIONS; AND REPERCUSSIONS OF
INCREASED INTEREST IN FIELD. STUDIES CHARACTERISTIC
FEATURES OF ECONOMIC LANDSCAPE AND ISSUES OF POLICY.

0104 BAUMGARTEL H.
"LEADERSHIP STYLE AS A VARIABLE IN RESEARCH ADMINISTRATION."
ADMINISTRATIVE SCI. Q., 2 (DEC. 57), 344-360.
    REPORT ON THE RELATIONSHIP BETWEEN LEADERSHIP STYLES OF
LABORATORY DIRECTORS IN A GOVERNMENT RESEARCH ORGANIZATION
AND CERTAIN ATTITUDES AND MOTIVATIONS OF THE SCIENTISTS
WITHIN THOSE LABORATORIES. SAYS THAT SCIENTISTS WORK BEST
WHEN THEY FEEL REPRESENTED IN MANAGEMENT'S DECISION-MAKING.

0105 BAUMOL W.J.

BUSINESS BEHAVIOR, VALUE AND GROWTH (REV. ED.)
NEW YORK: HARCOURT BRACE, 1967, 159 PP., LC#67-14320.
DISCUSSION OF STATIC OLIGOPOLY THEORY AND THE THEORY OF
ECONOMIC DEVELOPMENT. ANALYZES OLIGOPOLISTIC INTERDEPEN-
DENCE, FUNDS LIMITATION AND PROFIT, AND REVENUE MAXIMIZA-
TION PROCESS. OUTLINES DETAILED STATIC OLIGOPOLY MODEL AND
SUGGESTS SOME IMPLICATIONS OF MODEL. EXTENDS SCHUMPETERIAN
ANALYSIS OF GROWTH MECHANISM IN MODERN CAPITALISTIC ECON-
OMIES AND MAINTAINS EXISTENCE OF INSTITUTIONAL FORCES.

0106 BAVELAS A.
"COMMUNICATION PATTERNS IN TASK-ORIENTED GROUPS" (BMR)".
J. OF ACOUSTICAL SOCIETY OF AMERICA, 22 (NOV. 50), 725-730.
DESCRIBES TREND OF RESEARCH AND EXPERIMENTAL ACTIVITY IN
AREA OF COMMUNICATION PATTERNS. RESEARCH CONCENTRATES
UPON EFFECTS THAT PATTERN, AS SUCH, CAN HAVE UPON EMERGENCE
OF LEADERSHIP, DEVELOPMENT OF ORGANIZATION, DEGREE OF
RESISTANCE TO GROUP DISRUPTION, AND ABILITY TO ADAPT
SUCCESSFULLY TO SUDDEN CHANGES IN THE WORKING ENVIRONMENT.

0107 BAXTER J.P.
SCIENTISTS AGAINST TIME.
BOSTON: LITTLE BROWN, 1946, 473 PP.
OFFICIAL HISTORY OF THE OFFICE OF SCIENTIFIC RESEARCH
AND DEVELOPMENT. DESCRIBES RAPID TRANSITION FROM
SEVENTEENTH CENTURY-STYLE WARFARE TO NUCLEAR-AGE WARFARE.
ASSAYS STRENGTH OF DEMOCRATIC SOCIETIES TO PREPARE FOR
WAR.

0108 BEARD C.A.
PUBLIC POLICY AND THE GENERAL WELFARE.
NEW YORK: FARRAR + RINEHART, 1941, 176 PP.
ILLUMINATES CONFLICTS OVER INTERPRETATION AND APPLICATION
OF CONCEPT OF GENERAL WELFARE. STATES THAT CONCEPT IS ROOTED
IN DEMOCRATIC VIEW OF NATURE OF MAN AND STATE. MAINTAINS
THAT ESSENCE OF GOVERNMENT IS POWER. THIS MUST BE RECONCILED
WITH BELIEF THAT LIBERTY AND GENERAL WELFARE ARE HIGHEST
UNDER LAISSEZ-FAIRE SYSTEM. SOLUTION IS TO REINTERPRET
"LIBERTY" TO ACCORD WITH POWERFUL, BUT FREE SOCIETY.

0109 BEATON L.
MUST THE BOMB SPREAD?
BALTIMORE: PENGUIN BOOKS, 1966, 147 PP.
STUDIES PROBLEM OF CONTROLLING PROLIFERATION OF NUCLEAR
POWER. DISCUSSES TECHNICAL REQUIREMENTS, PRESTIGE AND
MILITARY SECURITY AS INCENTIVES FOR DEVELOPMENT OF NUCLEAR
WEAPONS, AND PROBABLE RATE OF PROLIFERATION WITHOUT
CONTROLS. EXAMINES POSSIBILITY OF SPREAD OF PLUTONIUM, NOT
ACTUAL WEAPONS; PRESENTS ANTI-PROLIFERATION PLAN; AND STATES
THAT DECISION IS POLITICAL, NOT TECHNICAL.

0110 BEAUFRE A.
"THE SHARING OF NUCLEAR RESPONSIBILITIES* A PROBLEM IN NEED
OF SOLUTION."
INTL AFFAIRS (UK), 41 (JULY 65), 411-419
ON THE ASSUMPTIONS THAT STRATEGIC SITUATIONS ARE ALWAYS
IN FLUX AND THAT PRESENT SITUATION-- LOW THREAT, LOW CREDI-
BILITY, HIGH NUCLEAR THRESHOLD-- HAS "EXCESS OF STABILITY"
COORDINATED THROUGH PEACETIME "FOREWARD PLANNING" OF "CRISIS
MANAGEMENT" AND A MULTINATIONAL STRATEGIC STUDIES GROUP.

0111 BEAUFRE A.
AN INTRODUCTION TO STRATEGY, WITH PARTICULAR REFERENCE TO
PROBLEMS OF DEFENSE, POLITICS, ECONOMICS IN THE NUCLEAR AGE.
NEW YORK: FREDERICK PRAEGER, 1965, 138 PP.
SPEAKS OF STRATEGY AS A METHOD OF THOUGHT WHOSE OBJECT
IS TO CODIFY EVENTS, SET THEM IN ORDER OF PRIORITY, THEN
CHOOSE MOST EFFECTIVE COURSE OF ACTION. STRATEGY MUST BE
EFFECTIVE AT ALL LEVELS FROM INTERNATIONAL PLANNING TO
MILITARY TACTICS, AND MUST BE ORGANIZED ALONG LINES
APPROPRIATE TO WORLD SITUATION TODAY.

0112 BECK H.P.
MEN WHO CONTROL OUR UNIVERSITIES.
NEW YORK: OXFORD U PR, 1947, 229 PP., LC#47-30526.
A STUDY OF THE ECONOMIC AND SOCIAL COMPOSITION OF
GOVERNING BOARDS OF THIRTY LEADING AMERICAN UNIVERSITIES,
AS AN INVESTIGATION INTO SOCIAL FORCES. GIVES POWERS AND
FUNCTIONS OF BOARDS, USUAL QUALIFICATIONS OF MEMBERS,
THEIR BUSINESS CONNECTIONS, THE METHODS OF APPOINTMENT
(DISCUSSING REPRESENTATIVE ASPECTS), AND LENGTH OF SERVICE.
DISCUSSES BIAS AND ADDS RECOMMENDATIONS.

0113 BECKER A.S.
"COMPARISIONS OF UNITED STATES AND USSR NATIONAL OUTPUT:
SOME RULES OF THE GAME."
WORLD POLIT., 13 (OCT. 60), 99-111.
CONTENDS THAT SIGNIFICANT DIFFERENCES IN THE ECONOMIC
STRUCTURES OF THE USA AND USSR MAKE COMPARISONS OF NATIONAL
OUTPUTS ERRONEOUS AND MISLEADING. BELIEVES THAT AVERAGING
INDEX-NUMBERS IS WRONG AND PROPOSES SOME 'RULES' WHICH
SHOULD BE APPLIED IN PUBLIC DISCUSSION OF THIS VITAL MATTER.

0114 BEGUIN H.
"ASPECTS GEOGRAPHIQUE DE LA POLARISATION."
TIERS-MONDE, 4 (NO. 16, 63), 559-608.

DEALS WITH FIRST STAGES OF DEVELOPMENT OF THIRD WORLD
COUNTRIES. RELATES PATTERN OF THEIR DEVELOPMENT TO
GEOGRAPHIC ENVIRONMENT. CALLS FOR INCREASED KNOWLEDGE OF
GEOGRAPHIC FACTORS INFLUENCING POLARIZATION PROCESS.

0115 BELL J.R., STEEDMAN L.B.
PERSONNEL PROBLEMS IN CONVERTING TO AUTOMATION (PAMPHLET)
INDIANAPOLIS: BOBBS-MERRILL, 1959, 14 PP.
ACCOUNT OF CALIFORNIA STATE DEPARTMENT OF EMPLOYMENT'S
CONVERSION FROM CONVENTIONAL TO AUTOMATED COMPUTERS. FOCUSES
ON PLAN DEVELOPED TO AVOID LAYOFFS AS RESULT OF CHANGE IN
PROCEDURE.

0116 BELLMAN R., DREYFUS S.E.
APPLIED DYNAMIC PROGRAMMING.
PRINCETON: PRINCETON U PRESS, 1962.
USING THE RAND JOHNNIAC COMPUTER, ATTEMPTS TO PRESENT
A DETAILED ACCOUNT OF THE APPLICATION OF THE THEORY OF DY-
NAMIC PROGRAMMING TO THE NUMERICAL SOLUTION OF OPTIMIZATION
PROBLEMS. APPLIES DATA TO MARKOV DECISION PROCESSES AND TO
ECONOMIC MODELS.

0117 BENDIX R.
"INDUSTRIALIZATION, IDEOLOGIES, AND SOCIAL STRUCTURE" (BMR)"
AMER. SOCIOLOGICAL REV., 24 (OCT. 59), 613-623.
ILLUSTRATES BASIC DIFFERENCE BETWEEN MANAGERIAL IDEOLOGY
IN ENGLAND AND RUSSIA, AND RELATES IT TO STRUCTURAL
DIFFERENCES IN BUREAUCRACY. STUDIES EFFECTIVENESS OF
IDEOLOGY PRESUPPOSING SELF-RELIANCE AND GOOD FAITH.

0118 BENJAMIN A.C.
SCIENCE, TECHNOLOGY, AND HUMAN VALUES.
COLUMBIA: U OF MO PR, 1965, 296 PP., LC#65-10698.
DISCUSSES LANGUAGE AND THOUGHT PATTERNS OF MODERN SCIENCE
AND ANALYZES PLACE OF EDUCATION, RELIGION, AND PHILOSOPHY
IN TECHNOLOGICAL SOCIETY. EMPHASIZES IMPORTANT SOCIAL ROLE
OF SCIENCE. FEELS SCIENCE IS ESSENTIAL PART OF MODERN
DESIGN FOR LIVING, BUT WORLD "WILL BE SAVED" NOT BY SCIENCE
ALONE, BUT BY MEN OF KNOWLEDGE AND VISION WHO USE SCIENCE
TO PROMOTE TRUTH AND "THE GOOD LIFE."

0119 BENN W.
"TECHNOLOGY HAS AN INEXORABLE EFFECT."
SCIENCE AND TECHNOLOGY, 69 (SEPT. 67), 8-52.
DISCUSSES BRITISH ATTEMPT TO MERGE COMPETING COMPANIES
SO THAT FOREIGN COMPETITION CAN BE MET. FEELS ONLY LARGE
INDUSTRIES CAN EMPLOY TECHNOLOGY NEEDED TO MAKE BRITAIN
TECHNOLOGICAL LEADER OF EUROPE. ANALYZES CHANGES NEEDED IN
ADMINISTRATION, PRODUCTION, AND EDUCATIONAL SYSTEM. AUTHOR
IS BRITAIN'S MINISTER OF TECHNOLOGY.

0120 BENNETT J.C. ED.
NUCLEAR WEAPONS AND THE CONFLICT OF CONSCIENCE.
NEW YORK: CHAS SCRIBNER'S SONS, 1962, 191 PP., LC#62-9653.
EXAMINES MORAL AND ETHICAL ISSUES INVOLVED IN USE OF
NUCLEAR WEAPONS. STATES PROBLEM IN LIGHT OF HISTORY OF
WARFARE, CURRENT INTERNATIONAL SITUATION, AND SCIENTIFIC
ESTIMATES OF EFFECT OF NUCLEAR WAR. DISCUSSES IMPACT OF
DESTRUCTIVE POWER ON MEANING OF HISTORY AND ON "FAITH IN
PROVIDENCE AND HUMAN DESTINY.

0121 BENNETT J.W.
HUTTERIAN BRETHREN; THE AGRICULTURAL ECONOMY AND SOCIAL
ORGANIZATION OF A COMMUNAL PEOPLE.
STANFORD: STANFORD U PRESS, 1967, 228 PP.
EXAMINES SIX COLONIES OF HUTTERIAN SECT TO SHOW HOW
COMMUNAL FARMS WERE ESTABLISHED AND RELATIONS WERE FORMED
WITH OTHER LOCAL PEOPLE. DISCUSSES FAMILY AND KINSHIP,
AGRICULTURAL MANAGEMENT AND DECISION-MAKING, METHODS OF
PRODUCTION, AND CHANGES IN HUTTERIAN SOCIETY AND TECHNOLOGY
TO DETERMINE CAUSES OF COMMUNES' SUCCESS. COMPARES COLONY
WITH ISRAELI KIBBUTZ.

0122 BENNION E.G.
"ECONOMETRICS FOR MANAGEMENT."
HARVARD BUSINESS REV., 39 (MAR. 61), 100-112.
INTRODUCES ECONOMETRIC AND PROGRAMMING MODELS AND SHOWS
HOW THEY MAY BE USED TO THE COMPANY'S ADVANTAGE IN DECISION-
MAKING. ASSESSES RELUCTANCE OF BUSINESS TO ADOPT THESE
MODELS. ASSERTS VALUE OF SUCH MODELS IN AIDING CHOICE-MAKING
ON COMPLEX ISSUES BY ENHANCING COMPREHENSION OF VARIABLES
AND BY FACILITATING COMPREHENSIBLE, PRECISE ANALYSIS OF AL-
TERNATIVE ASSUMPTIONS.

0123 BENNIS W.G., BENNE K.D., CHIN R.
THE PLANNING OF CHANGE: READINGS IN THE APPLIED BEHAVIORAL
SCIENCES.
NEW YORK: HOLT RINEHART WINSTON, 1962, 780 PP., LC#61-14602.
A COLLECTION OF READINGS ON THE APPLICATION AND ADAPTA-
TION OF THEORIES OF SOCIAL AND PERSONAL CHANGE TO PLANNED
CHANGE. THE BOOK IS DIVIDED INTO FOUR PARTS: THE ROOTS OF
PLANNED CHANGES, CONCEPTUAL TOOL FOR THE CHANGE AGENT: SOC-
SYSTEMS AND CHANGE MODELS, DYNAMICS OF THE INFLUENCE PROCESS
PROCESS AND PROGRAMS AND TECHNOLOGIES OF PLANNED CHANGE.

0124 BENTHAM J.

DEFENCE OF USURY (1787)
ORIGINAL PUBLISHER NOT AVAILABLE, 1788, 232 PP.
DENOUNCES PROHIBITORY USURY LAWS CONTROLLING RATE OF INTEREST ON LENDING MONEY; FEELS THAT IT BENEFITS PUBLIC TO HAVE UNLIMITED RATES. DISCIPLE OF ADAM SMITH INSISTS ON EXTREME LOGICAL APPLICATION OF PRINCIPLES AND ARGUES AGAINST SMITH'S APPROVAL OF FIVE-PER-CENT LIMITATION. ARGUES THAT LOANS ON SECURITY WOULD HELP TECHNOLOGICAL PROGRESS EVEN IF PROJECTS FAILED.

0125 BENTWICH J.S.
EDUCATION IN ISRAEL.
PHILA: JEWISH PUBL SOC AMER, 1965, 204 PP.
ACCOUNT OF FORMS OF EDUCATION IN ISRAEL AND THEIR PRESENT ORGANIZATION AND CURRICULA. DISCUSSES ISRAELI ATTEMPTS TO SOLVE PROBLEMS OF CREATING MEANINGFUL VALUES IN A HEDONISTIC WORLD, BREAKING DOWN CLASS BARRIERS, BUILDING A SYNTHESIS OF RELIGION AND SCIENCE, AND CREATING A BETTER WAY OF LIFE IN A TECHNOLOGICAL SOCIETY.

0126 BERGMANN G.
"IDEOLOGY" (BMR)"
ETHICS, 61 (APR. 51), 205-218.
SEEKS TO DEMONSTRATE NATURE OF LOGICAL ANALYSIS BY APPLYING ITS METHODOLOGY TO STUDY OF IDEOLOGY. DISCUSSES DICHOTOMY OF FACT AND VALUE; INCLUDES CAUSAL FACTORS THAT MUST BE REPRESENTED IN ALL LAWS OF BEHAVIOR. DEFINES TERMS CAREFULLY THROUGHOUT, IN MANNER OF LOGICAL POSITIVISTS, BEFORE DISCUSSING SYSTEMS OF IDEAS. FEELS GOAL TO STRIVE FOR IS AN IDEOLOGY-FREE SOCIETY.

0127 BERGSON H.
CREATIVE EVOLUTION.
NEW YORK: HOLT, 1911, 407 PP.
DISCUSSES THE HUMAN INTELLECT IN ITS ATTEMPT TO ADJUST TO ITS ENVIRONMENT. PHILOSOPHICALLY ORIENTED DISCUSSION OF THE PROCESS OF EVOLUTION AND A POSSIBLE COMPARISON OF A THEORY OF KNOWLEDGE AND A THEORY OF LIFE.

0128 BERKELEY E.C.
THE COMPUTER REVOLUTION.
GARDEN CITY: DOUBLEDAY, 1962, 268 PP.
DISCUSSION OF COMPUTERS; THEIR HISTORY, OPERATION, CAPA-BILITIES, AND FUTURE APPLICATIONS. NOTES DANGERS AND SOCIAL IMPLICATIONS OF "COMPUTER REVOLUTION." GLOSSARY.

0129 BERKS R.N.
"THE US AND WEAPONS CONTROL."
CURRENT HIST., 47 (AUG. 64), 65-116.
EIGHT ARTICLES EXPLORING UNITED STATES VIEWS ON WEAPONS CONTROL, DISARMAMENT, AND ALTERNATE PATHS TOWARD PEACE AND MILITARY SECURITY.

0130 BERNAL J.D.
THE SOCIAL FUNCTION OF SCIENCE.
CAMBRIDGE: M I T PRESS, 1967, 482 PP., LC#67-14526.
ANALYZES RELATION OF SCIENCE TO SOCIAL AND ECONOMIC DE-VELOPMENTS. INVESTIGATES EXTENT TO WHICH SCIENTISTS ARE RE-SPONSIBLE FOR ADVERSE EFFECTS OF TECHNOLOGICAL PROGRESS. SUGGESTS STEPS TO FRUITFUL UTILIZATION OF SCIENCE. DISCUSSES GOVERNMENTAL INFLUENCE ON SCIENTIFIC DEVELOPMENTS.

0131 BERND J.L. ED.
MATHEMATICAL APPLICATIONS IN POLITICAL SCIENCE, II.
DALLAS: SOUTHERN METHODIST U PR, 1966, 208 PP.
SEVEN ESSAYS ON APPLICATION OF MATHEMATICAL AS WELL AS VERBAL EXPRESSION IN POLITICAL SCIENCE. TREATS USES OF MATH-EMATICS IN METHODOLOGICAL PROBLEMS, STATISTICAL TECHNIQUES APPLICABLE IN POLITICAL SCIENCE, AND APPLICATIONS OF MATH-EMATICS TO PRACTICAL POLITICS. CLOSES WITH MODELS OF THE POLITICAL SYSTEM.

0132 BERNSTEIN I.
THE NEW DEAL COLLECTIVE BARGAINING PROCESS.
BERKELEY: U OF CALIF PR, 1950, 178 PP.
HISTORICAL INTRODUCTION TO LEGISLATIVE POLICY CONCERNED WITH COLLECTIVE BARGAINING. TRACES EMERGENCE OF NEW CONCEPT OF ROLE OF GOVERNMENT IN INDUSTRIAL RELATIONS. DEALS SPECIF-ICALLY WITH YEARS 1933-35. AUTHOR ARGUES THAT COLLECTIVE BARGAINING CAN BE CONSTRUCTIVE INSTITUTION IN A DEMOCRATIC SOCIETY. CONTAINS EXTENSIVE BIBLIOGRAPHY.

0133 BETHE H.
"DISARMAMENT AND STRATEGY."
BULL. AT. SCI., 18 (SEPT. 62), 14-22.
USSR'S NEED FOR SECRECY, AND USA'S NEED FOR INSPECTION IN ARMS CONTROL NEGOTIATIONS ARE DISCUSSED IN TERMS OF TECHNOLOGICAL DEVELOPMENT AND STRATEGY. SOLUTION IS FOUND IN SOHN PLAN ACCOMODATING BOTH NEEDS. BALANCE OF TERROR, STABLE DETERRENT, COUNTERFORCE AND ARMS REDUCTION DISCUSSED.

0134 BETTEN J.K.
"ARMS CONTROL AND THE PROBLEM OF EVASION."
PRINCETON: U. PR., 1962, 28 PP., $1.00.
SEEKS TO DEFINE THE MOTIVATIONS AND STRATEGIES BEHIND ALTERNATIVE METHODS OF EVADING AN ARMS-CONTROL AGREEMENT.

FACTORS WHICH MIGHT MAXIMIZE OR MINIMIZE THE SUCCESS OF THE EVASION ARE INVESTIGATED.

0135 BIDWELL P.W.
RAW MATERIALS: A STUDY OF AMERICAN POLICY.
NEW YORK: HARPER, 1958, 403 PP., $5.95.
EXAMINES U.S. POLICY AS IT AFFECTS SUPPLY OF RAW MATERI-ALS FOR AMERICAN INDUSTRIES. SUCCESSES AND FAILURES OF THIS POLICY ARE DISCUSSED AS WELL AS PROPOSED MEASURES FOR REFORM WHICH INCLUDE CHANGES IN NATIONAL POLICIES TO MAKE THEM MORE ADAPTABLE TO CHANGES IN TECHNOLOGY AND INTERNATIONAL RELATIONS.

0136 BINGHAM A.M.
THE TECHNIQUES OF DEMOCRACY.
NEW YORK: DUELL, SLOAN & PEARCE, 1942, 314 PP.
ANALYZES VARIOUS INSTITUTIONAL DEVICES AND METHODS OF GROUP ACTION, EMPHASIZING DEMOCRATIC PUBLIC ADMINISTRATION. DESCRIBES TRADITIONAL TECHNIQUES OF VOTING, FEDERALISM, AND CONSTITUTIONS. DISCUSSES FAILURE OF THESE AND RISE OF TOTALITARIAN TECHNIQUES OF DISCIPLINE AND CENTRALISM. STUDIES MODERN DEMOCRATIC TECHNIQUES OF PUBLIC MANAGEMENT AND FREEDOM.

0137 BIRNBAUM K.
"SWEDEN'S NUCLEAR POLICY."
INTERNATIONAL JOURNAL, 20 (SUMMER 65) 297-311.
FEARS OF NUCLEAR PROLIFERATION, AND THE COMPLEX CONTIN-GENT STRATEGIES OF TECHNOLOGICALLY SOPHISTICATED, NEUTRAL SWEDEN INTERACT TO CAUSE INERTIA AND DISAGREEMENT AMONG HER POLITCAL AND MILITARY GROUPS PERTAINING TO ACQUISITION OF NUCLEAR CAPABILITY. POLICY IS TO BUY TIME AND OPTIONS.

0138 BLACKETT P.M.S.
ATOMIC WEAPONS AND EAST-WEST RELATIONS.
NEW YORK: CAMBRIDGE U. PR., 1956, 107 PP.
DISCUSSES THE EFFECT OF THE NUCLEAR WEAPONS ON CURRENT WORLD SITUATION ANALYZES THOUGHTS AND OPINIONS ABOUT NUCLEAR WEAPONS AND ABOUT CONTROVERSY ON THEIR USE. CON-CLUDES WITH SOME GENERAL OUTLINES FOR FUTURE MILITARY POLICIES.

0139 BLOOMFIELD L., CLEMENS W.C., GRIFFITHS F.
SOVIET INTERESTS IN ARMS CONTROL AND DISARMAMENT* THE DECADE UNDER KHRUSHCHEV 1954-1964.
CAMBRIDGE: MIT CTR INTL STUDIES, 1965, 249 PP.
RESEARCH MEMORANDUM PREPARED FOR THE US ARMS CONTROL AND DISARMAMENT AGENCY. ATTEMPTS TO IDENTIFY CHIEF FACTORS, INTERNAL AND EXTERNAL, WORKING ON SOVIET ARMS CONTROL POLICY FROM 1954-1964, AND TO CORRELATE CHANGES IN FACTORS WITH UPS AND DOWNS OF SOVIET INTERESTS IN ARMS CONTROL. GOOD DISCUS-SION OF PROBLEMS OF SCIENTIFIC ANALYSIS OF SOVIET BEHAVIOR.

0140 BLOOMFIELD L.P., PADELFORD N.J.
"THREE EXPERIMENTS IN POLITICAL GAMING."
AMER. POLIT. SCI. REV., 53 (DEC. 59), 105-115.
DESCRIBES METHODS OF CONSTRUCTING GAMES AND ANALYZES DIFFUCULTIES ENCOUNTERED. EVALUATES POLITICAL GAMING AS APPLIED TO INTERNATIONAL RELATIONS STRATAGEMS.

0141 BLOOMFIELD L.P.
OUTER SPACE: A PATTERN OF WAR IN A NEW DIMENSION.
ENGLEWOOD CLIFFS: PRENTICE HALL, 1962, 203 PP.
FOCUSES ATTENTION ON ANTICIPATED IMPACT OF TECHNOLOGICAL INNOVATIONS ON ECONOMIC, SOCIAL, AND POLITICAL ENVIRONMENT, QUESTIONING THE MILITARY AND LEGAL IMPLICATIONS OF THE WORLD'S ENTRY INTO THE 'SPACE AGE'.

0142 BLOOMFIELD L.P., LEIS A.C.
"ARMS CONTROL AND THE DEVELOPING COUNTRIES."
WORLD POLITICS, 18 (OCT. 65), 1-19.
STUDIES BY REGION LATIN AMERICA, MIDDLE EAST, ASIA, AND AFRICA, THE PROBLEMS OF NUCLEAR PROLIFERATION IN RELATION TO LOCAL ARMS COMPETITION, AND THE POSSIBILITIES OF PREVENT-IVE STATESMANSHIP TO DEAL WITH THESE DANGERS IN A BROADER SECURITY CONTEXT. PROPOSES SET OF UNIVERSALLY APPLICABLE PRINCIPLES AS BASIS FOR US POLICY ON A BROAD-SPECTRUM, NOT A PARTICULAR-REGION, APPROACH TO ARMS CONTROL.

0143 BLOOMFIELD L.P., CLEMENS W.C. JR., GRIFFITHS F.
KHRUSHCHEV AND THE ARMS RACE.
CAMBRIDGE: M I T PRESS, 1966, 338 PP., LC#66-19361.
SOVIET ATTITUDES AND POLICIES TOWARD ARMS IN KHRUSHCHEV DECADE LISTED BY THREE PERIODS, TO SPUTNIK, TO CUBA, TO OUSTER OF KHRUSHCHEV. INCLUDES CONSIDERATION OF FACTORS IN-FLUENCING ARMS CONTROL POLICY.

0144 BLOUSTEIN E.J. ED.
NUCLEAR ENERGY, PUBLIC POLICY, AND THE LAW.
NEW YORK: OCEANA PUBLISHING, 1964, 113 PP., LC#64-22787.
CONSIDERS PROBLEMS OF NUCLEAR POWER FOR PEACEFUL USAGE: HOW TO CAUSE LEAST RESENTMENT IN ESTABLISHING IT, ROLE OF GOVERNMENT IN PROMOTING IT, SAFETY MEASURES, AND ECONOMIC AND MORAL RESPONSIBILITY FOR ITS USE.

0145 BOBROW D.B. ED.

COMPONENTS OF DEFENSE POLICY.
NEW YORK: RAND MCNALLY & CO, 1965, 445 PP., LC#65-11368.
A SERIES OF ARTICLES WHICH SET BOUNDARIES AND CATALOGUE
PROBLEMS OF SOCIAL SCIENCE SECTOR OF DEFENSE POLICY
ANALYSIS. DEALS WITH THE STRATEGIC CONTEXT, DEFENSE POLICY-
MAKING, STRATEGIC ALTERNATIVES, AND QUALITY CONTROL.
ARTICLES BY HILSMAN, KAHN, SCHELLING, KISSINGER,
HUNTINGTON, VERBA, ET AL.

0146 BOCK E.A. ED., CAMPBELL A.K. ED.
CASE STUDIES IN AMERICAN GOVERNMENT.
ENGLEWOOD CLIFFS: PRENTICE HALL, 1962, 368 PP., LC#62-12624.
COLLECTION OF CASE STUDIES TO BE USED AS TEXTBOOK SUPPLE-
MENT IN UNDERGRADUATE CLASSES IN POLITICAL SCIENCE. MAIN
TOPIC HEADINGS INCLUDE: CONSTITUTION, COURTS AND CIVIL
RIGHTS, POLITICS, LEGISLATIVE PROCESS, PRESIDENCY, GOVERN-
MENT, SCIENCE, AND THE ECONOMY. BOOK IS PART OF INTER-UNI-
VERSITY CASE PROGRAM.

0148 BOHN L.C.
"WHOSE NUCLEAR TEST: NON-PHYSICAL INSPECTION AND TEST BAN."
J. CONFL. RESOLUT., 7 (SEPT. 63), 379-393.
SPECULATES ON ADVANTAGES OFFERED BY CONCEALED NUCLEAR-
TESTING WITH REGARD TO WEAPONS DEVELOPMENT AND THE
N-TH NATION PROBLEM. INABILITY OF PHYSICAL METHODS TO DETECT
MID-OCEAN OR SPACE EXPLOSIONS HAS NECESSITATED EMPLOYMENT
OF NON-PHYSICAL TECHNIQUES ANALOGOUS TO CRIMINAL INVESTIGAT-
ION AND COURT SYSTEMS.

0149 BOHN L.C.
"ATOMS FOR PEACE AND ATOMS FOR WAR."
DISSERTATION ABSTRACTS, 3 (SPRING 65), 1-18.
AUTHOR SUGGESTS THAT "ATOMS FOR PEACE" TYPE PROGRAMS MAY
CONTRIBUTE TO NUCLEAR ARMAMENT, AS THE NUCLEAR FUELS USED,
AND HUMAN RESOURCES INVOLVED IN PEACEFUL PROLIFERATION ARE
EASILY TRANSFERRABLE TO WARTIME ARMAMENT NEEDS. THIS DILEMMA
CAN BEST BE MET BY DEVELOPING NON-NUCLEAR ENERGY RESOURCES
AND BY MEETING NATIONAL SECURITY NEEDS IN NON-NUCLEAR WAYS.

0150 BOLTON R.E. ED.
DEFENSE AND DISARMAMENT: THE ECONOMICS OF TRANSITION.
ENGLEWOOD CLIFFS: PRENTICE HALL, 1966, 180 PP., LC#66-22609.
STUDIES ON ECONOMIC ASPECTS OF DEFENSE AND DISARMAMENT.
DISCUSSES SCOPE OF DISARMAMENT; ECONOMIC IMPLICATIONS OF
LARGE DEFENSE REDUCTIONS; PROBLEMS OF ECONOMIC TRANSITION
FROM SWORD TO PLOWSHARE. ALSO STUDIES PUBLIC AND
PRIVATE ARMS EXPENDITURES AND DANGERS OF POLITICAL
PRESSURES.

0151 BONER H.A.
"HUNGRY GENERATIONS."
LONDON: OXFORD U PR, 1955.
HISTORY OF THE ACCEPTANCE AND EVENTUAL REJECTION OF MAL-
THUSIAN THEORY IN 19TH-CENTURY ENGLAND. ARGUES THAT THE
ENTIRE MALTHUSIAN THEORY, INCLUDING "ITS FALLACIOUS AND
SOCIALLY DISASTROUS" CONCLUSION THAT THE MAJOR CAUSE OF
POVERTY WAS THE RECKLESS OVERBREEDING OF THE POOR, WAS AN
INVIDIOUS INSTRUMENT FOR CONCEALING EXPLOITATION AND ECONOM-
IC INJUSTICE. BIBLIOGRAPHY OF WORKS PUBLISHED SINCE 1840.

0152 BONINI C.P.
SIMULATION OF INFORMATION AND DECISION SYSTEMS IN THE FIRM.
ENGLEWOOD CLIFFS: PRENTICE HALL, 1963, 152 PP., LC#63-16585.
DESCRIBES SIMULATION MODEL OF HYPOTHETICAL BUSINESS FIRM.
SYNTHESIS OF RELEVANT THEORY FROM DISCIPLINES OF ECONOMICS,
ACCOUNTING, ORGANIZATION THEORY, AND BEHAVIORAL SCIENCE
WITHIN SETTING OF TRADITIONAL CONCEPTS OF BUSINESS PRACTICE.
STUDIES EFFECTS OF INFORMATIONAL, ORGANIZATIONAL, AND ENVI-
RONMENTAL FACTORS UPON DECISIONS OF BUSINESS FIRM.

0153 BONNEFOUS M.
EUROPE ET TIERS MONDE.
LEYDEN: SYTHOFF, 1961, 116 PP.
CONSIDERS EUROPE'S AID TO THE UNDERDEVELOPED COUNTRIES
OF AFRICA AND QUESTIONS WHETHER THESE TECHNICAL CONNECTIONS
WILL MORE FAVORABLY BIND THE COUNTRIES THAN THE FORMER
HISTORICAL ONES.

0154 BORKOF H. ED.
COMPUTER APPLICATIONS IN THE BEHAVIORAL SCIENCES.
ENGLEWOOD CLIFFS: PRENTICE HALL, 1962, 605 PP., LC#62-8229.
GENERAL INTRODUCTION TO COMPUTERS WHICH PROVIDES SPECIFIC
INFORMATION ON THEIR USE AS RESEARCH TOOLS. EMPHASIS PLACED
ON NON-COMPUTATIONAL USE OF COMPUTER. DISCUSSION OF COMPUTER
SYSTEMS, NATURE OF MECHANICAL THOUGHT, HISTORY OF DATA PRO-
CESSING, COMPUTER PRINCIPLES AND APPLICATIONS, ETC.

0155 BOSANQUET B.
"SCIENCE AND PHILOSOPHY" IN J. MUIRHEAD AND R.B.
BOSANQUET, EDS., SCIENCE AND PHILOSOPHY AND OTHER ESSAYS."
LONDON: ALLEN & UNWIN, 1927.
CONCERNED WITH WHETHER PHILOSOPHY DEALS WITH CONCRETE
FACT. BELIEVES THAT IT IS NOT POSSIBLE TO SET UP SPECIFIC
DOMAINS WITH WHICH SCIENCE AND PHILOSOPHY WILL BE CONCERNED.
BELIEVES PHILOSOPHY HAS THE "RIGHT OF DIRECT INQUIRY INTO
REALITY AT FIRST HAND." PHILOSOPHY IS A CONSIDERATION OF

TOTALITIES, OR THE WHOLE OF AN IMPRESSION. PHILOSOPHY CAN
NOT BE REVOLUTIONIZED BY DISCOVERY, BUT IT IS PROGRESSIVE.

0156 BOULDING K.E., SPIVEY W.A.
LINEAR PROGRAMMING AND THE THEORY OF THE FIRM.
NEW YORK: MACMILLAN, 1960.
REVIEW OF RECENT DEVELOPMENTS IN FIELD RELEVANT TO THE
THEORY OF THE FIRM. DISCUSSES PRESENT CONCEPT OF THEORY AND
ADAPTABILITY OF DATA TO LINEAR PROGRAMMING. PRESENTS STUDY
OF RELATION OF OPERATIONS RESEARCH TO ECONOMIC APPLICATION,
ESPECIALLY IN RELATION TO CYCLICAL CHANGES.

0157 BOULDING K.E.
CONFLICT AND DEFENSE: A GENERAL THEORY.
NEW YORK: HARPER/ROW, 1962, 491 PP.
INTERNATIONAL RELATIONS ARE SUBJECTED TO MATHEMATICS BY
AN ECONOMIST TO DETERMINE IF CONFLICTS AMONG NATIONS CAN BE
PREDICTED TO A USEFUL DEGREE. AN ABSTRACT SOCIAL THEORY WITH
A RATIONAL METHODOLOGY. PART 1 EVOLVES A GENERAL THEORY OF
WAR AND PART 2 APPLIES IT TO SPECIAL CASES, EMPHASIZING THE
DIFFERENCES. EXPLORES GAME THEORY AND VIEWS OF BEHAVIORISTS.

0158 BOULDING K.E.
"THE PREVENTION OF WORLD WAR THREE."
VIRGINIA QUART. REV., 38 (WINTER 62), 1-12.
ASSERTS THAT CLOSE INTER-RELATIONS AMONG ALL GOVERNMENTS
OF THE WORLD IS A DANGER THAT MUST BE ADAPTED TO AND MADE
VIABLE THROUGH MUTUAL AGREEMENTS LEADING TO DISARMAMENT AND
WORLD FEDERATION.

0159 BOULDING K.E.
"UNIVERSITY, SOCIETY, AND ARMS CONTROL."
J. CONFL. RESOLUT., 7 (SEPT. 63), 458-63.
CONSIDERS ARMS CONTROL COMPARABLE TO INFLATION, AS
PROBLEM OF SOCIAL SYSTEMS. VAST EXPENDITURES ON ARMS HAVE
NOT SWUNG BALANCE TO EITHER SIDE, BUT HAVE CONSTITUTED AN
ECONOMIC DRAIN AND INCREASED INSECURITY. UNIVERSITIES HAVE
CRITICAL ROLES AS BARGAINING POWERS FOR DISARMAMENT.

0160 BOWEN H.R. ED., MANGUM G.L. ED.
AUTOMATION AND ECONOMIC PROGRESS.
ENGLEWOOD CLIFFS: PRENTICE HALL, 1966, 170 PP., LC#66-28109.
STUDIES REPORT OF THE NATIONAL COMMISSION ON TECHNOLOGY,
AUTOMATION, AND ECONOMIC PROGRESS. CONTAINS A SELECTION
OF EIGHT EXPERT STUDIES AND PAPERS COMPRISING COMMISSION'S
REPORT. THESE STUDIES COVER GENERAL OUTLOOK FOR
TECHNOLOGICAL CHANGE, ITS PACE, AND EMPLOYMENT ASPECTS
OF TECHNOLOGICAL CHANGE. INCLUDES ONE STUDY ON CHANGE
IN WESTERN EUROPE; REMAINING ESSAYS CONCERN PROBLEM IN US.

0161 BOWMAN I.
GEOGRAPHY IN RELATION TO THE SOCIAL SCIENCES.
NEW YORK: CHAS SCRIBNER'S SONS, 1934, 382 PP.
EXPLORES GEOGRAPHY'S PLACE IN, AND CONTRIBUTION TO, SO-
CIAL SCIENCES. DESCRIBES DATA USED BY GEOGRAPHERS, PRECISION
AND QUALITY OF THEIR CONTRIBUTION, AND TECHNIQUES OF
GEOGRAPHICAL ANALYSIS. STUDIES ECONOMIC, POLITICAL, AND
CULTURAL PHASES OF FIELD.

0162 BRADLEY D.
NO PLACE TO HIDE.
BOSTON: LITTLE BROWN, 1948, 179 PP.
THE LOG OF A DOCTOR WHO WAS ASSIGNED TO DUTY WITH OPER-
ATIONS CROSSROADS - BETTER KNOWN AS THE ATOMIC BOMB TESTS AT
BIKINI. SEEKS TO MAKE KNOWN THE 'MENACING ASPECTS OF ATOMIC
ENERGY' IN ORDER THAT LIFE AS WE KNOW IT MAY CONTINUE.

0163 BRADY R.A.
ORGANIZATION, AUTOMATION, AND SOCIETY.
BERKELEY: U OF CALIF PR, 1961, 481 PP., LC#61-7535.
STUDY CONCENTRATES ON INDUSTRIAL TECHNOLOGY, WITH SPE-
CIAL ATTENTION TO THAT LEVEL OF DEVELOPMENT WHEREIN THE
CLEANING-UP OPERATIONS NECESSARY TO BRING PRACTICE FULLY
IN LINE WITH SCIENTIFIC THEORY ARE ALREADY WELL ADVANCED.
TRIES TO DECIDE BEST WAY TO ORGANIZE PRODUCTIVE RESOURCES
OF ECONOMY WHEN DECISION-MAKERS ARE PREPARED TO USE POTEN-
TIALITIES OF ADVANCED SCIENCE AND ENGINEERING.

0164 BRENNAN D.G.
"SETTING AND GOALS OF ARMS CONTROL."
DAEDALUS, 89 (WINTER 1960), 681-707.
ANALYZES THE STRATEGY ON WHICH ARMS CONTROL IS BASED,
INCLUDING A REVIEW OF THE CONTEMPORARY MILITARY GOALS OF
DETERRENCE, LIMITED WAR AND GENERAL WAR. ELABORATES ON
EFFECTS OF THERMONUCLEAR ACTIONS IN CONFINED AREAS AND
CONTENDS THEIR OCCURRENCE CAN BE AVOIDED BY ACHIEVING A
WORKABLE ARMAMENT AGREEMENT WITH THE SOVIET UNION BASED ON
COMMON OBJECTIVES AND ENFORCED BY INTERNATIONAL SANCTIONS.

0165 BRENNAN D.G. ED.
"ARMS CONTROL AND CIVIL DEFENSE."
HARMON-ON-HUDSON: HUDSON INST. 1963, 47 PP.
STUDIES POSSIBLE IMPACT OF CD PROGRAMS ON ARMS CONTROL
AND IVCE VERSA. EVALUATES CURRENT SITUATION AND CURRENT
STRATEGY. NOTES SOCIAL, POLITICAL AND PSYCHOLOGICAL EFFECTS
OF CD. FAVORS INTERNATIONAL COOPERATION ON CD PROGRAMS.

0166 BRETNOR R.
"DESTRUCTIVE FORCE AND THE MILITARY EQUATIONS."
MILITARY REV., 47 (MAY 67), 28-35.
    ANALYZES VARIOUS ASPECTS OF DESTRUCTIVE FORCE AND VULNER-
ABILITY FACTORS. TREATS PREPARATION, APPROACH, MANEUVER, AND
WEAPONS IN PRIMARY AND SECONDARY "RADIUS OF EXPRESSION." DE-
FINES TERMS AND CONCEPTS PERTINENT TO ASSESSING DESTRUCTIVE
POTENTIALS OF A WEAPON OR NATION IN GIVEN SITUATION. JUDGES
HOW NEW TECHNIQUES, SUCH AS AUTOMATION AND COMPUTERS, MIGHT
AFFECT DESTRUCTIVE FORCE.

0167 BRETTON H.L.
STRESEMANN AND THE REVISION OF VERSAILLES: A FIGHT FOR
REASON.
STANFORD: STANFORD U PRESS, 1953, 199 PP., LC#53-6446.
    STUDIES POLITICAL AND DIPLOMATIC PHASES OF PROCESS OF
REVISIONISM THROUGH WHICH TREATY OF VERSAILLES PASSED.
CONCENTRATES ON PERIOD 1918-30. EXAMINES ROLE OF GUSTAV
STRESEMANN IN MAKING AND CONDUCTING A REVISIONIST FOREIGN
POLICY. ATTEMPTS TO DISCOVER SEQUENCE OF ATTACKS ON TREATY,
AND INTERNATIONAL AND GERMAN BACKGROUND OF STRESEMANN'S
STRATEGY.

0168 BRIGHT J.R.
RESEARCH, DEVELOPMENT AND TECHNOLOGICAL INNOVATION.
HOMEWOOD: RICHARD IRWIN, 1964, 764 PP., LC#64-11711.
    DISCUSSION OF TECHNOLOGICAL INNOVATION AND ITS PROBLEMS.
TYPICAL BUSINESS PROBLEMS ANALYZED IN ATTEMPT TO ILLUMINATE
METHODS OF HANDLING ISSUES CONCERNING IDENTIFICATION OF,
SUPPORT FOR, AND DEFENSE AGAINST RADICAL TECHNOLOGICAL CON-
CEPTS. CHANGE AND INNOVATION IN POPULATION, SOCIAL TRENDS,
NATURAL RESOURCE POSITIONS, ETC. ARE CONSIDERED.

0169 BRILLOUIN L.
SCIENTIFIC UNCERTAINTY AND INFORMATION.
NY & LONDON: ACADEMIC PRESS, 1964, 152 PP., LC#64-19689.
    REAPPRAISAL OF PHILOSOPHICAL FOUNDATIONS OF SCIENCE. CON-
SIDERS VALIDITY OF THEORIES DEVELOPED IN EXPERIMENTAL SCI-
ENCES. GENERAL PROBLEMS OF SCIENTIFIC RESEARCH FOCUSING ON
ROLES OF OBSERVATION, INFORMATION, AND IMAGINATION. SCRUTINY
OF POINCARE THEORY.

0170 BRITISH COMMONWEALTH BUR AGRI
WORLD AGRICULTURAL ECONOMICS AND RURAL SOCIOLOGY ABSTRACTS.
LONDON: COMMONWEALTH AGRI BUR.
    AN INTERNATIONAL ABSTRACT JOURNAL COVERING THE LITERATURE
ON ECONOMIC AND SOCIAL ASPECTS OF AGRICULTURE. ENCOMPASSES
ONLY NEWLY PUBLISHED MATERIAL OF INTEREST TO RESEARCH WORK-
ERS, GOVERNMENT OFFICIALS, AND EXTENSION WORKERS. MATERIAL
IS SYSTEMATICALLY ARRANGED BY SUBJECTS: GOVERNMENTAL POLI-
CIES, LAND REFORM, FARM MANAGEMENT, MARKETING, ETC. SELEC-
TIONS ARE INTERNATIONAL IN SCOPE.

0171 BRODIE B.
THE OBSOLETE WEAPON: ATOMIC POWER AND WORLD ORDER.
NEW YORK: HARCOURT, 1946, 214 PP.
    EXPLORES PROBLEM OF WAR IN ATOMIC AGE. POINTS OUT MILI-
TARY AND POLITICAL CONSEQUENCES OF POLICIES RELATED TO NU-
CLEAR WEAPONS. FOCUSES ON EFFECT OF WEAPONS ON INTERNATIONAL
ORGANIZATION AND ON SOVIET-AMERICAN. CONCLUDES WITH STUDY OF
INTERNATIONAL CONTROL OF NUCLEAR WEAPONS.

0172 BRODIE B.
ESCALATION AND THE NUCLEAR OPTION.
PRINCETON: PRINCETON U PRESS, 1966, 151 PP., LC#66-23765.
    AUTHOR PRESENTS CASE FOR DEVELOPING A STRATEGY FOR THE
TACTICAL USE OF NUCLEAR WEAPONRY. CLAIMS THAT SUCH A STRATE-
GY WILL SERVE TO DETER THE LIMITED CONFLICTS WHICH THROUGH
ESCALATION ARE THE GREATEST THREAT TO NUCLEAR WAR. FAILING
DETERRENCE HE CLAIMS TACTICAL NUCS CAN BE USED TO DE-ESCA-
LATE CONFLICTS. PRESENTS AND COUNTERS CRITICISMS TO THIS AP-
PROACH.

0173 BRODY R.A.
"DETERRENCE STRATEGIES: AN ANNOTATED BIBLIOGRAPHY."
J. OF CONFLICT RESOLUTION, 4 (DEC. 60), 443-457.
    AN ANNOTATED BIBLIOGRAPHY ON DETERRENCE STRATEGIES.
MATERIAL PUBLISHED IN ENGLISH, RANGING FROM 1955 TO 1959.
CONTAINS 38 ENTRIES.

0174 BROOKINGS INSTITUTION
UNITED STATES FOREIGN POLICY: STUDY NO 9: THE FORMULATION
AND ADMINISTRATION OF UNITED STATES FOREIGN POLICY.
WASHINGTON: BROOKINGS INST, 1960, 191 PP.
    STUDY DONE FOR US SENATE COMMITTEE ON FOREIGN RELATIONS.
APPRAISES ENDS AND MEANS OF US FOREIGN POLICY IN RELATION TO
CHANGING WORLD CONDITIONS. COVERS CONGRESSIONAL AND EXECU-
TIVE PROCEDURE, ROLE OF MULTILATERAL ORGANIZATIONS, RELATION
WITH MILITARY ESTABLISHMENT, OUR AMBASSADORIAL SETUP, PER-
SONNEL MANAGEMENT, AND INTELLIGENCE AND INFORMATIONAL OPERA-
TIONS. MAKES MANY RECOMMENDATIONS.

0175 BROOKINGS INSTITUTION
DEVELOPMENT OF THE EMERGING COUNTRIES; AN AGENDA FOR
RESEARCH.
WASHINGTON: BROOKINGS INST, 1962, 239 PP., LC#62-12716.

SUGGESTS RESEARCH THAT MAY CONTRIBUTE TO REMEDYING
PRESENT DEFICIENCY IN KNOWLEDGE OF ECONOMICS, POLITICS,
SOCIOLOGY, AND PSYCHOLOGY OF DEVELOPMENT. EXAMINES COUNTRY
PROGRAMMING, RURAL PROBLEMS, ECONOMIC AND POLITICAL CHANGE,
TECHNOLOGICAL CHANGE, ROLE OF EDUCATION, AND FOREIGN AID.

0176 BROUDE H.W.
STEEL DECISIONS AND THE NATIONAL ECONOMY.
NEW HAVEN: YALE U PR, 1963, 332 PP., LC#63-13958.
    DISCUSSES PROBLEM OF US ECONOMIC DEPENDENCE ON STEEL AND
THE INDUSTRY'S UNWILLINGNESS TO EXPAND AS GOVERNMENT POLICY
DICTATES. ATTEMPTS TO DEFINE LIMITS OF DEPENDENCE, AND
SUGGESTS THEORETICAL AND PRATICAL POLICIES WHICH MIGHT ALTER
PRACTICES OF STEEL INDUSTRY.

0177 BROWN N.
NUCLEAR WAR* THE IMPENDING STRATEGIC DEADLOCK.
NEW YORK: FREDERICK PRAEGER, 1964, 238 PP., LC#64-25586.
    DETAILED ANALYSIS OF MILITARY TECHNOLOGY CIRCA 1963. BAL-
ANCES EAST AND WEST, OFFENSIVE AND DEFENSIVE WEAPONS AND
TACTICS. SEES IMPORTANT DIPLO-STRATEGIC DEADLOCK CAUSED BY
RELATIVE BALANCE OF THERMO-NUCLEAR MISSILES. REGARDS NATO
AND UN AS KEYS TO STABILIZING THE ARMS RACE.

0178 BROWN N.
"BRITISH ARMS AND THE SWITCH TOWARD EUROPE."
INTER-AM. ECO. AFFAIRS, 43 (JULY 67), 468-482.
    EXAMINES CHANGES IN BRITAIN'S DEFENSE SYSTEM. SEES SHIFT
TOWARD INCREASING COOPERATION WITH EUROPE AND RECOGNITION OF
BRITAIN AS EUROPEAN, NOT WORLD, POWER. PREDICTS FORMATION
OF ATLANTIC ALLIANCE BASED ON WESTERN EUROPEAN UNION AND US
AS PEACEKEEPING FORCE IN WORLD.

0179 BROWN W.B.
"MODEL-BUILDING AND ORGANIZATIONS."
ACADEMY OF MANAGEMENT JOURNAL, 10 (JUNE 67), 169-178.
    EXAMINES SEVERAL TECHNIQUES FOR DEVELOPING ORGANIZATIONAL
THEORY, BOTH VERBAL AND NON-VERBAL, WITH PARTICULAR ATTEN-
TION PAID TO NEW DEVELOPMENTS IN MODEL-BUILDING. DISCUSSES
VARIOUS ATTEMPTS, FOR EXAMPLE, THROUGH USE OF COMPUTERS, TO
PROVIDE MORE PRECISE AND PREDICTIVE MODELS THAN VERBAL
THEORIES HAVE PREVIOUSLY AFFORDED.

0180 BROWN W.M.
THE DESIGN AND PERFORMANCE OF "OPTIMUM" BLAST SHELTER
PROGRAMS (PAMPHLET)
HARMON-ON-HUDSON: HUDSON INST, 1964, 38 PP.
    RESEARCH REPORT ON BLAST SHELTERS, INCLUDING DESCRIPTION
OF MODEL AND SUGGESTIONS FOR ITS IMPROVEMENT, ITS COST, AND
ITS EFFECTIVENESS.

0181 BROWNLIE I.
"NUCLEAR PROLIFERATION* SOME PROBLEMS OF CONTROL."
INTL AFFAIRS (UK), 42 (OCT. 66), 600-608
    COMPARES SOVIET AND AMERICAN DRAFT TREATIES. POSSIBILITY
OF REGIONAL TREATIES, DISTRUST OF NON-NUCLEAR STATES IN MON-
OPOLY OF OTHERS, PROBLEMS OF "PEACEFUL USE" CONVERSIONS, EX-
PERIENCE WITH TEST BAN TREATY, AND FEARS OF ALLIANCE SHAR-
ING. CONCLUDES WITH 5 CONDITIONS FOR MAKING NON-PROLIFERA-
TION A PRACTICAL PROPOSAL.

0182 BRUNHILD G., BURTON R.H.
"THEORY OF 'TECHNICAL UNEMPLOYMENT'."
AMER. J. OF ECO. AND SOC., 26 (JULY 67), 265-277.
    THEORY PRESENTED INCORPORATES ONE TYPE OF "STRUCTURAL
NEMPLOYMENT" CALLED "TECHNICAL UNEMPLOYMENT," INTO A KEYNES-
IAN MODEL TO DEMONSTRATE THE COMPLEMENTARY RELATIONSHIP
BETWEEN THE TWO THEORIES. BELIEVES THAT SOLUTION TO
UNEMPLOYMENT LIES BOTH IN INCREASED DEMAND AND EASIER
STRUCTURAL TRANSFORMATION.

0183 BRYSON L.
SCIENCE AND FREEDOM.
NEW YORK: COLUMBIA U PRESS, 1947, 191 PP.
    A CRITICAL INQUIRY INTO THE NATURE OF FREEDOM AS A SOCIAL
CONDITION. THE AUTHOR DISCUSSES THE RELEVANCE OF SCIENCE IN
ACHIEVING A "GOOD SOCIETY." EMPHASIZES SOCIAL CHANGE THROUGH
"CULTURAL AND SOCIAL ENGINEERING."

0184 BUDER S.
PULLMAN: AN EXPERIMENT IN INDUSTRIAL ORDER AND COMMUNITY
PLANNING, 1880-1930.
NEW YORK: OXFORD U PR, 1967, 263 PP., LC#67-25456.
    CONCERNS MODEL TOWN PULLMAN CONSTRUCTED OUTSIDE CHICAGO
FOR PRODUCTION OF HIS RAILROAD CARS AND HOUSING OF WORKERS.
BEGINS WITH DEVELOPMENT OF PULLMAN'S INDUSTRY; EXAMINES
SOCIAL AND INDUSTRIAL PROBLEMS. COVERS PHYSICAL PLANNING
OF TOWN AND FACTORY, RELATIONS OF COMMUNITY AND COMPANY,
EMPLOYEE DISSATISFACTION, AND LABOR STRIFE AND STRIKE.
ENDS WITH SEPARATION OF FACTORY AND TOWN.

0185 BULMER-THOMAS I.
"SO, ON TO THE GREAT SOCIETY."
TWENTIETH CENTURY, 175 (JUL-SEP 67), 12-13
    GENERAL ESSAY ON SOCIAL AND SCIENTIFIC ADVANCES IN THE
20TH CENTURY. DISCUSSES ADVANCES IN PHYSICS, TECHNICAL

DEVELOPMENTS, FUTURE SCIENTIFIC ACCOMPLISHMENTS, WARS, THE BALANCE OF POWER, RELIGION, AND ARTISTIC DEVELOPMENTS. EXTREMELY OPTIMISTIC PICTURE OF THE WORLD YESTERDAY, TODAY, AND TOMORROW.

0186 BUNDY M.
"THE SCIENTIST AND NATIONAL POLICY."
SCIENCE, 139 (MAR. 63), 805-809.
SCIENTISTS SHOULD PARTICIPATE IN GOVERNMENT BUT MUST BE GIVEN SHARED RESPONSIBILITY FOR INTERPRETING SCIENCE AND MUST NOT OVERSTATE THEIR AREA OF AUTHORITATIVE KNOWLEDGE. THE EXPLOITATION OF NUCLEAR ENERGY FOR MILITARY PURPOSES CONCERNS POLITICS AND THE SCIENTIST SHOULD PROVIDE A FULL SPECTRUM OF POSSIBILITIES TO THE POLITICAL AUTHORITIES TO ALLOW FREEDOM OF ACTION TO THE LATTER.

0187 BUNGE M. ED.
THE SEARCH FOR SYSTEM. VOL. 3, PART 1 OF STUDIES IN THE FOUNDATIONS METHODOLOGY, AND PHILOSOPHY OF SCIENCE.
NEW YORK: SPRINGER-VERLAG, 1967, 536 PP.
PRESENTS LOGICAL, SEMANTICAL, AND METHODOLOGICAL TOOLS OF SCIENTIFIC INQUIRY. BEGINS WITH EXAMINATION OF PROBLEMS RATHER THAN WITH DATA OR FINISHED THEORIES. STUDIES HYPOTHESES, PARTICULARLY SCIENTIFIC LAWS. DISCUSSES STRUCTURE AND MEANING OF SCIENTIFIC THEORIES.

0188 BUNGE M. ED.
THE SEARCH FOR TRUTH, VOL. 3, PART 2 OF STUDIES IN THE FOUNDATIONS, METHODOLOGY, AND PHILOSOPHY OF SCIENCE.
NEW YORK: SPRINGER-VERLAG, 1967, 374 PP.
COVERS THE APPLICATION OF THEORIES OF EXPLANATION, PREDICTION, AND RATIONAL ACTION. ANALYZES THE TEST OF THEORIES THROUGH OBSERVATION, MEASUREMENT, EXPERIMENT-PLANNING AND INTERPRETATION BY FURTHER THEORIES. DISCUSSES CORRELATION OF IDEAS WITH DATA AND EVALUATES BOTH.

0189 BURKE A.E.
ENOUGH GOOD MEN.
CLEVELAND: WORLD, 1962, 254 PP., LC#62-17152.
DISCUSSES NATURE OF COMMUNIST CHALLENGE TO AMERICA. PROBLEMS OF UNDERDEVELOPED COUNTRIES, AND NECESSARY RESPONSE OF FREE WORLD AND US.

0190 BURNS A.L.
"THE NEW WEAPONS AND INTERNATIONAL RELATIONS."
AUSTRAL OUTLOOK, 12 (JUNE 58), 32-42.
SURVEYS DEVELOPMENT OF INTERNATIONAL RELATIONS AND DEALS WITH PROBLEMS INVOLVED. STUDIES EFFECTS OF H-BOMBS, BALLISTIC MISSILES, AND 'OUTER-SPACE OBJECTS' ON DIPLOMACY. FAVORS UNIVERSAL INSPECTION.

0191 BURNS A.L.
"THE RATIONALE OF CATALYTIC WAR."
PRINCETON: CENT. INT. STUD., 1959, 20 PP.
EXAMINES ALTERNATIVES POSSIBLE IF A THIRD COUNTRY WERE TO TRY TO DECEIVE NUCLEAR POWERS INTO ATTACKING EACH OTHER. ALSO EXAMINES, THROUGH HYPOTHETICAL SITUATIONS, HOW DEVELOPMENT OF TECHNOLOGY OR SPREAD OF WEAPONS WOULD AFFECT PROBABILITY OF ATTACK. FAVORS COMMON WARNING SYSTEM.

0192 BURNS A.L.
"POWER POLITICS AND THE GROWING NUCLEAR CLUB."
PRINCETON: CENT. INT. STUD., 1959, 20 PP.
EVALUATES EFFECT OF 'NTH COUNTRY' NUCLEAR CAPABILITY ON POWER BALANCE, ON PROBABILITY OF ACCIDENTAL NUCLEAR WAR, ON DETERRENT STRATEGIES, ETC. URGES NUCLEAR POWERS TO SPEED UP QUALITATIVE ARMS RACE.

0193 BURNS E.L.M.
MEGAMURDER.
NEW YORK: PANTHEON BOOKS, 1967, 297 PP., LC#67-13323.
UNSPARING EXAMINATION OF AMERICAN MILITARY STRATEGY. POINTS OUT THAT MILITARY MEN HAVE FORGOTTEN "RAISON D'ETRE" OF MILITARY STRATEGY: PROTECTION OF CIVILIAN POPULATION, NOT FURTHER DEVELOPMENT OF WEAPONS AND STRATEGIES "PER SE."

0194 BURSK E.C., CHAPMAN J.F.
NEW DECISION-MAKING TOOLS FOR MANAGERS.
CAMBRIDGE: HARVARD U PR, 1963.
PRESENTS MATHEMATICAL DECISION-MAKING AS A USEFUL AND ESSENTIAL AID TO THE BUSINESS MANAGER. ATTEMPTS TO SHOW THE SPECIFIC APPLICATIONS OF THE MATHEMATICAL APPROACH IN COLLECTION AND INTERPRETATION OF DATA. WARNS OF POSSIBILITY OF SACRIFICING UTILITY IN PRESERVING TECHNIQUE.

0195 BUSH V.
SCIENCE, THE ENDLESS FRONTIER.
WASHINGTON: G.P.O., 1945, 184 PP.
REPORT TO PRESIDENT BY DIRECTOR OF THE OFFICE OF SCIENTIFIC RESEARCH AND DEVELOPMENT, AND SALVAGES WARTIME ENGENDERED THINKING AND EXPERIENCES, IN GOVERNMENT SPONSORED RESEARCH, FOR PEACETIME APPLICATION. PROPOSES ESTABLISHMENT OF NATIONAL RESEARCH FOUNDATION AND POLICY FOR IMPROVING SCIENTIFIC DEVELOPMENT AND THE TRAINING OF SCIENTISTS.

0196 BUSH V.

ENDLESS HORIZONS.
WASHINGTON: PUBL. AFF. PR., 1946, 182 PP.
COLLECTION OF AUTHOR'S SPEECHES, WRITINGS AND REPORTS, ASSERTING NEED FOR UNIMPEDED INTERNATIONAL FLOW OF SCIENTIFIC DATA TO FOSTER PEACE AND FREEDOM, CITING BENEFITS OF COORDINATED BASIC RESEARCH, AND CALLING ATTENTION TO UNSOLVED PROBLEMS.

0197 BUTLER J. ED., CASTAGNO A.A. ED.
BOSTON UNIVERSITY PAPERS ON AFRICA* TRANSITION IN AFRICAN POLITICS.
NEW YORK: FREDERICK PRAEGER, 1967, 342 PP., LC#67-16665.
COLLECTION OF PAPERS ON RECENT CHANGES IN AFRICAN AFFAIRS GENERALLY OF POLITICAL NATURE. STRESS IS ON EAST AFRICA, AND CONSTITUTIONAL DEVELOPMENT ALSO COMES UP. LABOR QUESTIONS, LAW, IDEOLOGY ARE ALSO CONSIDERED.

0198 BUTOW R.J.C.
JAPAN'S DECISION TO SURRENDER.
STANFORD: STANFORD U PRESS, 1954, 259 PP., LC#54-8145.
NARRATES EVENTS OF EARLY MONTHS OF JAPAN'S WWII MILITARY CONQUEST. DESCRIBES SUCCESSIVE CRISES GROWING OUT OF JAPAN'S MOUNTING DEFEATS LATER IN THE WAR. TELLS OF DEVELOPMENTS OF LAST DAYS OF JAPAN'S TRAGEDY. SHOWS HOW SMALL GROUP WITHIN RULING ELITE COMMITTED JAPANESE GOVERNMENT TO SALVAGING, THROUGH NEGOTIATION, A PART OF WHAT THE MILITARY COULD NO LONGER MAINTAIN.

0199 BYRNES F.C.
"ASSIGNMENT TO AMBIGUITY: WORK PERFORMANCE IN CROSS-CULTURAL TECHNICAL ASSISTANCE."
HUM. ORGAN., 23 (1964), 196-209.
STUDY OF 34 FORMER TECHNICAL ADVISORS OF THE ICA WITH REFERENCE TO PERCEPTIONS AND REACTIONS TO THEIR OVERSEAS EXPERIENCE. EXPLORES BEHAVIOR IN TERMS OF POSITION, ROLES PERFORMED, RESPONSIBILITY TO WORK ORGANIZATIONS, FORMAL AND INFORMAL NETWORKS OF COMMUNICATION.

0200 CALDER R.
LIVING WITH THE ATOM.
CHICAGO: U. CHI. PR., 1962, 275 PP.
EDUCATES THE LAYMAN IN THE PEACEFUL USES OF NUCLEAR ENERGY ON THE PUBLIC HEALTH. IT DESCRIBES THE SAFE METHODS USED TO DESTROY RADIOACTIVE WASTE THROUGH A WASTE TRENCH SYSTEM. RAISES THE NEEDS FOR NEW PUBLIC HEALTH LAWS AND REGULATION DUE TO USES OF ATOMIC ENERGY.

0201 CALDWELL L.K.
RESEARCH METHODS IN PUBLIC ADMINISTRATION; AN OUTLINE OF TOPICS AND READINGS (PAMPHLET)
ALBANY: STATE U OF NY AT ALBANY, 1953, 35 PP.
A DESCRIPTIVELY ANNOTATED BIBLIOGRAPHY DESIGNED TO ASSIST THE EFFECTIVE APPLICATION OF TOOLS AND TECHNIQUES OF SOCIAL RESEARCH TO ADMINISTRATIVE PROBLEMS OF THE PUBLIC SERVICE. ATTENTION GIVEN TO INTERPRETATION OF STATISTICS, PUNCH-CARD METHODS OF PROCESSING DATA, BIBLIOGRAPHICAL RESEARCH, AND THE DOCUMENTATION OF RESEARCH PAPERS. ENTRIES LISTED ALPHABETICALLY BY AUTHOR WITHIN EACH TOPICAL DIVISION.

0202 CALDWELL L.K.
"THE GOVERNMENT AND ADMINISTRATION OF NEW YORK."
NEW YORK: THOMAS Y CROWELL, 1954.
DESCRIPTIVE STUDY OF GOVERNMENT AND PUBLIC ADMINISTRATION IN NEW YORK STATE. SELECTED, PARTIALLY-ANNOTATED BIBLIOGRAPHY OF PUBLIC RECORDS AND DOCUMENTARY MATERIALS RELATING TO NY STATE GOVERNMENT; LIMITED TO ESSENTIAL OFFICIAL AND SEMI-OFFICIAL SOURCES AND TO THE MORE COMPREHENSIVE GENERAL WORKS. MOST ENTRIES CONSIST OF ANNUAL PUBLICATIONS OR POST-1949 WORKS.

0203 CALDWELL L.K.
"BIOPOLITICS: SCIENCE, ETHICS, AND PUBLIC POLICY."
YALE REV., 54(64), 1-16.
RE-EXAMINES RELATIONSHIP BETWEEN SCIENCE AND POLITICS. QUESTIONS WHETHER THE POLITICAL CAPACITIES OF MAN ARE CAPABLE OF CONFRONTING CONTEMPORARY SCIENTIFIC KNOWLEDGE. 'WITHOUT THE INTERRELATION AND DISTILLATION OF SCIENTIFIC FINDINGS INTO ISSUES AMENABLE TO POLITICAL ACTION, THE GAP BETWEEN SCIENCE AND POLITICS CANNOT BE SUCCESSFULLY BRIDGED.'

0204 CALKINS R.D.
"THE DECISION PROCESS IN ADMINISTRATION."
BUSINESS HORIZONS, 2 (FALL 59).
ANALYZES DECISION-MAKING PROCESS IN ORGANIZATIONS. STUDIES PROBLEM IDENTIFICATION, GOAL DEFINITION, ALTERNATIVE CHOICE SOLUTION AND CONSEQUENCE ANALYSIS AS PART OF THE APPRAISAL-CHOICE SYNDROME. PROPOSES MORE SYSTEMATIC APPROACHES TO PROMOTE INCREASED EFFICIENCY.

0205 CALLOT E.
LA SOCIETE ET SON ENVIRONNEMENT: ESSAI SUR LES PRINCIPES DES SCIENCES SOCIALES.
PARIS: LIBRAIRIE MARCEL RIVIERE, 1952, 580 PP.
THEORETICAL AND GENERAL WORK ON PRINCIPLES OF SOCIOLOGY. AUTHOR BELIEVES SCIENTIFIC AND PHILOSOPHIC METHODS SHOULD

BE INCORPORATED IN SOCIOLOGICAL STUDIES. DESCRIBES SOCIAL
REALITY AS A PARTICULAR AREA AND OBJECT OF SCIENCE.
DISCUSSES PHILOSOPHY OF AREA. DELINEATES LIMITS OF SOCIOLOGY
AND DISTINGUISHES IT FROM OTHER SCIENCES.

0206 CANTRIL H. ED.
TENSIONS THAT CAUSE WAR.
URBANA: U. ILLINOIS PR., 1950, 303 PP.
COLLECTION OF ESSAYS, BY LEADING SOCIAL SCIENTISTS,
HOLDING THAT THE STUDY OF THE SCIENCES OF MAN 'TASK OF AC-
QUIRING SELF-KNOWLEDGE AND SOCIAL INSIGHT) IS AS VITAL AS
STUDY OF PHYSICAL AND BIOLOGICAL SCIENCES. ATTEMPTS TO STUDY
SCIENTIFICALLY THE CAUSES OF MAN'S TENSIONS WHICH LEAD TO
WAR.

0207 CARMICHAEL D.M.
"FORTY YEARS OF WATER POLLUTION CONTROL IN WISCONSIN: A CASE
STUDY."
WISC. LAW REV., 67 (SPRING 67), 350-419.
HISTORY OF POLLUTION CONTROL EMPHASIZING PRESENT POLICY
AND ENFORCEMENT AND OF DEPARTMENT OF RESOURCE DEVELOPMENT
AND DRAINAGE BASIN HEARINGS.

0208 CARNEGIE ENDOWMENT INT. PEACE
"POLITICAL QUESTIONS (ISSUES BEFORE THE NINETEENTH GENERAL
ASSEMBLY)."
INT. CONCIL., 550 (NOV. 64), 5-62.
DISCUSSES FOLLOWING PROBLEMS WHICH WERE RAISED DURING
NINETEENTH SESSION: FINANCES, PEACE KEEPING FORCES, DISARM-
AMENT, ARMS CONTROL, CHARTER REVISION, RED CHINA, RADIATION,
PALESTINE REFUGEES, CYPRUS, AND THE PEACEFUL USES OF ATOMIC
ENERGY.

0209 CARNEGIE ENDOWMENT INT. PEACE
"ECONOMIC AND SOCIAL QUESTION (ISSUES BEFORE THE NINETEENTH
GENERAL ASSEMBLY)."
INT. CONCIL., 550 (NOV. 64), 117-87.
DISCUSSES PROBLEMS CONCERNING THE FOLLOWING WHICH WERE
RAISED DURING NINETEENTH SESSION: GATT, COMMODITY TRADE,
TECHNICAL COOPERATION, PATENTS, UN SPECIAL FUND, AND UN
TRAINING AND RESEARCH INSTITUTE.

0210 CARNELL F. ED.
THE POLITICS OF THE NEW STATES: A SELECT ANNOTATED BIBLIOG-
RAPHY WITH SPECIAL REFERENCE TO THE COMMONWEALTH.
LONDON: OXFORD U PR, 1961, 171 PP.
PARTIALLY ANNOTATED BIBLIOGRAPHY OF 1599 TITLES ON THE
NEW STATES OF AFRICA AND ASIA IN FRENCH AND ENGLISH. ITEMS
ARE ARRANGED BY TOPIC, CROSS-REFERENCED AND INDEXED BY
AUTHOR AND GEOGRAPHICAL LOCATION. SECTION ON APPROACHES TO
THE STUDY OF POLITICS INCLUDES WORKS ON WESTERN STATES.
COVERS GENERAL HISTORICAL BACKGROUND ON COLONIALISM AND
STUDIES OF PROBLEMS IN COLONIALISM.

0211 CARPENTER E. ED., MCLUHAN M. ED.
EXPLORATIONS IN COMMUNICATION.
BOSTON: BEACON PRESS, 1960, 210 PP., LC#60-7938.
ESSAYS THAT HAVE APPEARED IN "EXPLORATIONS." PURPOSE IS
TO DEVELOP AN AWARENESS ABOUT PRINT AND NEWER TECHNOLOGIES
OF COMMUNICATION TO MINIMIZE THEIR MUTUAL FRUSTRATIONS AND
CLASHES, ORCHESTRATE THEM, AND GET BEST OF EACH IN
EDUCATIONAL PROCESS.

0212 CARPER E.T.
THE DEFENSE APPROPRIATIONS RIDER (PAMPHLET)
UNIVERSITY: U ALABAMA PR, 1960, 28 PP.
CASE STUDY OF 1955 RIDER TO DEFENSE BUDGET BILL, WHICH
GAVE CONGRESSIONAL COMMITTEES RIGHT TO DISAPPROVE SHUTDOWN
BY DEFENSE DEPARTMENT OF CERTAIN LOCAL INSTALLATIONS.
CONGRESS FELT IT ILLEGAL, YET PRESIDENT COULD NOT VETO BILL.
STUDY SHOWS FIGHT BETWEEN LEGISLATURE AND EXECUTIVE.
ANALYZES LOCAL PRESSURE IN NATIONAL POLICY-MAKING, USING
BOSTON NAVAL INSTALLATION AS EXAMPLE.

0213 CARPER E.T.
REORGANIZATION OF THE U.S. PUBLIC HEALTH SERVICE.
INDIANAPOLIS: BOBBS-MERRILL, 1965.
ANALYZES PROBLEMS FACED BY PUBLIC HEALTH SERVICE IN
REORGANIZING ITS PLANS FOR IMMEDIATE AND FUTURE PROCEDURES.
FACTORS NECESSITATING REORGANIZATION ARE CHANGES IN AMERICAN
ENVIRONMENT, CONGRESSIONAL DEMANDS, AND PUBLIC EXPECTATIONS.
FORCES AT PLAY INCLUDE CONFLICT OF INTEREST WITH NATIONAL
INSTITUTE OF MENTAL HEALTH, RESISTANCE TO CHANGE, AND
INTERNAL RELATIONSHIPS.

0214 CARR E.H.
"REVOLUTION FROM ABOVE."
NEW LEFT REV., 46 (NOV. 67), 17-29.
DISCUSSES WHAT AUTHOR CONSIDERS TRAGEDY OF SOVIET COLLEC-
TIVIZATION. BELIEVES THAT STALIN'S DECISION (IN 1929) TO
COLLECTIVIZE WAS HAPHAZARD AND IMPULSIVE. LENIN HAD PRO-
POSED GRADUAL COLLECTIVIZATION; BUT AS A RESULT OF LOW AGRI-
CULTURAL PRODUCTION, ESPECIALLY IN GRAIN, STALIN DECIDED TO
PROCEED IMMEDIATELY. MECHANIZATION HAD NOT PROGRESSED FAR
ENOUGH, AND PEASANTS OFFERED MINIMAL ASSISTANCE.

0215 CARROLL K.J.
"SECOND STEP TOWARD ARMS CONTROL."
MILITARY REV., 47 (MAY 67), 77-84.
AFTER SURVEYING DIFFICULTIES IN THE HISTORY OF ARMS CON-
TROL DURING PAST TWO DECADES, THE AUTHOR PRESENTS THE
CRITERIA FOR SURE AND ACCEPTABLE INSPECTION. SHOWS HOW
SUBMARINES COULD BE RESTRICTED WITH SHORELINE INSPECTION
AND ON-BOARD OBSERVERS. SUGGESTS THAT USA- USSR ACCORD IN
THIS AREA COULD SERVE AS PILOT EXPERIMENT FOR FUTURE DIS-
ARMAMENT.

0216 CARSON R.
SILENT SPRING.
BOSTON: HOUGHTON MIFFLIN, 1962, 368 PP., LC#60-5148.
DESCRIBES IN DETAIL THE NATURE, VARIETY, EXTENT, AND
EFFECTS OF POLLUTION, RAISING QUESTIONS OF HUMAN BEHAVIOR
AND RESPONSIBILITY IN ECOLOGICAL SYSTEM OF PLANET.

0217 CARY G.D.
"THE QUIET REVOLUTION IN COPYRIGHT* THE END OF THE 'PUBLICA-
TION' CONCEPT."
G. WASH. LAW REV., 35 (MAY 67), 652-674.
EXAMINES BACKGROUND OF COPYRIGHT LAW REVISION BILL, SOME
CASES WHICH ILLUSTRATE NEED FOR CHANGE, AND THE INNOVATION
BROUGHT ABOUT BY NEW BILL. IN PARTICULAR DISCUSSES CONCEPT
OF PUBLICATION WHICH DEVELOPMENT OF 20TH CENTURY COMMUNICA-
TIONS REVOLUTION HAS MADE OBSCURE AND ARTIFICIAL. ANALYZES
IMPLICATION OF APPLICATION OF PUBLICATION CONCEPT TO EXHI-
BITION OF PAINTINGS AND SALE OF PHONOGRAPH RECORDS.

0218 CAVERS D.F.
"ADMINISTRATIVE DECISION-MAKING IN NUCLEAR FACILITIES
LICENSING."
U. PENN. LAW REV., 110 (JAN. 62), 330-370.
AEC IS CHARGED WITH UPHOLDING PUBLIC INTEREST IN AREAS
OF SAFETY, EFFICIENCY, ETC., BUT HAS NOT DONE SO, SINCE MOST
OF ITS LICENSING ACTIONS ARE UNCONTESTED. IT OFTEN SERVES
MERELY AS A RUBBER STAMP FOR THE PLANS OF PRIVATE POWER
CORPORATIONS.

0219 CETRON M.J.
"FORECASTING TECHNOLOGY."
SCIENCE AND TECHNOLOGY, 69 (SEPT. 67), 3-92.
DEFINES TECHNOLOGICAL FORECAST AS A "PREDICTION, WITH A
LEVEL OF CONFIDENCE, OF A TECHNICAL ACHIEVEMENT IN A GIVEN
TIME FRAME WITH A SPECIFIED LEVEL OF SUPPORT." REVIEWS CUR-
RENT PHILOSOPHY AND FORECASTING TECHNIQUES USED. APPRAISES
UTILITY OF FORECASTING AND ITS ROLE IN MILITARY AND INDUS-
TRIAL PLANNING.

0220 CHANDLER A.D.
STRATEGY AND STRUCTURE: CHAPTERS IN THE HISTORY OF THE
INDUSTRIAL ENTERPRISE.
CAMBRIDGE: M I T PRESS, 1962, 463 PP., LC#62-11990.
STUDY OF AMERICAN BIG BUSINESS: FINDS THAT DIFFERENT
ORGANIZATIONAL FORMS RESULT FROM DIFFERENT TYPES OF
GROWTH. MAINLY STUDIES DUPONT, GENERAL MOTORS, STANDARD OIL,
AND SEARS, THEIR CHANGING STRUCTURE AND THE STRATEGY WHICH
CREATES CHANGE.

0221 CHAPPLE E.D., SAYLES L.R.
THE MEASURE OF MANAGEMENT.
NEW YORK: MACMILLAN, 1961, 218 PP., LC#60-6654.
CONSIDERATION OF METHODS BY WHICH MANAGEMENT CAN EFFI-
CIENTLY UTILIZE HUMAN ORGANIZATIONAL RESOURCES, ADVOCATING
A CONSISTENT SCIENTIFIC SYSTEM OF MEASUREMENT. ARGUES THAT
MEASUREMENTS, PROVIDING CRITERIA FOR MANAGEMENT ACTION, ARE
BASIC TO ORGANIZATIONAL AND ADMINISTRATIVE DECISIONS, AND
THAT HUMAN BEHAVIOR IN THE ORGANIZATION IS QUANTIFIABLE. DE-
VELOPS AN ORGANIZATION OF WORK - TECHNOLOGY, METHOD, ETC.

0222 CHARLESWORTH J.C. ED.
CONTEMPORARY POLITICAL ANALYSIS.
NEW YORK: MACMILLAN, 1967, 480 PP.
TWENTY AUTHORITIES DISCUSS MAJOR CONTEMPORARY
METHODOLOGIES IN POLITICAL SCIENCE RESEARCH. EACH APPROACH
IS DESCRIBED, ANALYZED, AND EVALUATED; 8 METHODOLOGIES DIS-
CUSSED ARE BEHAVIORALISM, FUNCTIONAL ANALYSIS, QUANTITATIVE
APPROACH, SYSTEMS THEORY, DECISION-MAKING THEORY, GAME
THEORY, COMMUNICATIONS THEORY, AND POLITICAL DEVELOPMENT
THEORY.

0223 CHASE S.
LIVE AND LET LIVE.
NEW YORK: HARPER & ROW, 1960, 146 PP., LC#60-07522.
PRESENTS A PROGRAM FOR AMERICANS IN SIXTIES, INCLUDING
CHANGES OF RECENT TIMES, CURRENT SOCIAL AND POLITICAL
PROBLEMS, AND SUGGESTED SOLUTIONS OF AUTHOR AND OTHER
OBSERVERS.

0224 CHASE S.
THE PROPER STUDY OF MANKIND (2ND REV. ED.)
NEW YORK: HARPER & ROW, 1962, 320 PP.
ATTEMPTS TO SHOW THAT WHILE HUMAN BEHAVIOR MAY BE
DIFFICULT TO STUDY, SCIENTIFIC METHOD IS APPLICABLE TO BOTH
MAN AND HIS WORLD. DISCUSSES HISTORY OF SOCIAL SCIENCE.

PRINCIPLES UPON WHICH IT IS BASED, AND METHODS IT EMPLOYS.
ENUMERATES VARIOUS PROBLEMS SOCIAL SCIENTISTS HAVE EXAMINED
OR SHOULD EXAMINE. DESCRIBES GROWTH OF FIELD DURING WWII
AND PROPOSES A WIDENED "SCIENCE OF MAN."

0225 CHEEK G.
ECONOMIC AND SOCIAL IMPLICATIONS OF AUTOMATION: A BIBLIO-
GRAPHIC REVIEW (PAMPHLET)
E LANSING: MSU LABOR & IND REL, 1958, 125 PP.
SOME 600 WELL-ANNOTATED BIBLIOGRAPHIES, BOOKS, ARTICLES,
CONFERENCE REPORTS, CASE STUDIES, AND SPEECHES ARRANGED TOP-
ICALLY AND PUBLISHED FROM 1948-57. SUBJECTS INCLUDE
MANPOWER, SOCIETY AND GOVERNMENT, HUMAN RELATIONS, COLLEC-
TIVE BARGAINING, AND MANAGEMENT ORGANIZATION. SUBJECT AND
AUTHOR INDEX.

0226 CHENG C.-.Y.
SCIENTIFIC AND ENGINEERING MANPOWER IN COMMUNIST CHINA,
1949-1963.
WASHINGTON: NATL SCIENCE FDN, 1965, 588 PP.
PROVIDES BACKGROUND INFORMATION ON TRAINING, UTILIZATION,
AND EMPLOYMENT OF SCIENTIFIC AND ENGINEERING MANPOWER IN
COMMUNIST CHINA FROM 1949-63. DISCUSSES GOVERNMENTAL
POLICIES AND CONTROLS AND ROLE OF USSR IN DEVELOPING CHINA'S
SPECIALIZED MANPOWER. GIVES BIOGRAPHICAL DATA ON 1,200
PROMINENT SCIENTISTS AND ENGINEERS IN MAINLAND CHINA.

0227 CHILDS J.R.
AMERICAN FOREIGN SERVICE.
NEW YORK: HOLT RINEHART WINSTON, 1948, 261 PP.
STUDIES EVOLUTION OF US FOREIGN SERVICE AND DISCUSSES
ITS NATURE AS A CAREER. SHOWS RELATIONS BETWEEN SERVICE AND
DEPARTMENT OF STATE AND OTHER GOVERNMENT AGENCIES. ANALYZES
PROFESSION AND PRACTICE OF DIPLOMACY, AND PORTRAYS AN
EMBASSY AND AMBASSADOR IN ACTION. DESCRIBES EMBASSY'S
POLITICAL, CONSULAR, ECONOMIC, INFORMATION, AND CULTURAL
RELATIONS SECTIONS.

0228 CHIU S.M.
"CHINA'S MILITARY POSTURE."
CURRENT HISTORY, 53 (SEPT. 67), 155-160.
ATTEMPTS TO EVALUATE CHINA'S MILITARY POWER, CONCENTRA-
TING ON STRENGTH OF PEOPLE'S LIBERATION ARMY (PLA) AND NU-
CLEAR DEVELOPMENT. DISCUSSES ROLE OF PLA IN SUPPORTING CUL-
TURAL REVOLUTION AND POLITICAL CONTROL SYSTEM WHICH MANAGES
ARMY. MAINTAINS THAT UNTIL NUCLEAR WEAPONS SYSTEM IS OPERA-
TIONAL, PEKING'S MILITARY POSTURE WILL BE DEFENSIVE.

0229 CHRIST R.F.
"REORGANIZATION OF FRENCH ARMED FORCES."
MILITARY REV., 47 (MAY 67), 66-70.
SURVEYS STRUCTURE OF FRENCH MILITARY MIGHT, ITS REORGAN-
IZATION UNDER SINGLE AUTHORITY, THE MISSION OF ITS DOT, ITS
INTRODUCTION OF HIGH-PERFORMANCE AIRCRAFT LIKE THE MIRAGE,
THE BUILD-UP OF EQUIPMENT, AND OTHER FACETS. CONCLUDES THAT
NUCLEAR WEAPONS HAVE BEEN GIVEN PRIORITY AND THAT THE ARMY'S
ROLE IS SECONDARY. NEITHER CRITICIZES NOR FAVORS THIS
STRATEGY.

0230 CHU K., NAYLOR T.H.
"A DYNAMIC MODEL OF THE FIRM."
MANAGEMENT SCIENCE, 2 (MAY 65), 736-50.
UTILIZES TRADITIONAL MICRO-ECONOMIC THEORY AND ELEMENTARY
QUEUING THEORY TO DEVELOP A COMPUTER SIMULATION MODEL OF A
SINGLE-PRODUCT, MULTI-PROCESS FIRM. DEMONSTRATES "THEORY OF
THE FIRM" MAY BE USED TO PROVIDE CONVENIENT FRAME OF REFER-
ENCE IN APPLYING RECENTLY DEVELOPED ANALYTICAL TOOLS OF
OPERATIONS RESEARCH AND COMPUTER TECHNOLOGY TO THE ANALYSIS
OF THE BEHAVIOR OF THE FIRM.

0231 CLARK G., SOHN L.B.
WORLD PEACE THROUGH WORLD LAW; TWO ALTERNATIVE PLANS.
CAMBRIDGE: HARVARD U PR, 1966, 535 PP., LC#66-21198.
PRESENTS PLAN FOR MAINTENANCE OF WORLD PEACE IN FORM OF
REVISED UN CHARTER. MAINTAINS THAT WORLD PEACE CANNOT EXIST
WITHOUT ENFORCEABLE WORLD LAW FOR PREVENTION OF WAR.
REVISES MEMBERSHIP, GENERAL ASSEMBLY, EXECUTIVE COUNCIL,
ECONOMIC AND SOCIAL AND TRUSTEESHIP COUNCILS, DISARMAMENT
PROCESS, WORLD POLICY FORCE, JUDICIAL AND REVENUE SYSTEMS,
PENALTIES, PRIVILEGES, AND RATIFICATION AND AMENDMENT PLANS.

0232 CLARKE A.C.
PROFILES OF THE FUTURE; AN INQUIRY INTO THE LIMITS OF THE
POSSIBLE.
NEW YORK: HARPER & ROW, 1962, 234 PP., LC#62-14563.
DEFINES BOUNDARIES OF TECHNOLOGY WITHIN WHICH POSSIBLE
FUTURES ARE CONFINED. TREATS TRANSPORTATION, COMMUNICATION,
TIME, PRODUCTIVITY, INVISIBLE MEN, SIZE REDUCTION, MEMORY,
AND LIFE SPAN.

0233 CLEAVELAND F.N.
SCIENCE AND STATE GOVERNMENT.
CHAPEL HILL: U OF N CAR PR, 1959, 161 PP.
EXPLORATION OF ROLE OF STATE GOVERNMENTS IN SCIENTIFIC
EFFORTS OF NATION. MEASURES EFFORTS BY DOLLAR EXPENDITURES
AND MANPOWER INVESTMENTS. DISCOVERS PLACE OF SCIENTIFIC

ACTIVITY IN STATE OPERATIONS. IDENTIFIES POLICIES FORMULATED
BY STATE TO GUIDE SCIENTIFIC ACTIVITIES, AND DISCOVERS
ACTIVITIES' PLACE IN STRUCTURE OF STATE ADMINISTRATION.

0234 CLEMENS W.C.
"CHINESE NUCLEAR TESTS: TRENDS AND PORTENTS."
CHINA Q., 32 (OCT.-DEC. 67), 111-131.
EXPLORES EFFECTS OF CHINESE DEVELOPMENT OF A NUCLEAR
WEAPON UPON INTERNATIONAL RELATIONS, PARTICULARLY STRATEGIC
AND DIPLOMATIC CONSIDERATIONS OF US AND RUSSIA. ALSO EVAL-
UATES POSSIBLE CHANGES IN CHINESE POLICY TOWARD BOTH THE
SUPERPOWERS AND THE THIRD WORLD. FORESEES NECESSITY FOR
FULL RE-EXAMINATION OF POLICY IN MAJOR POWERS TO COPE WITH
CHINA'S GROWING MILITARY MIGHT.

0235 CLEVELAND H.
"CRISIS DIPLOMACY."
FOREIGN AFFAIRS, 41 (JULY 63), 638-649.
DISCUSSES MANAGEMENT OF A FOREIGN POLICY CRISIS. SUGGESTS
FIVE "LESSONS" FOR SUCH DECISION-MAKING: KEEPING OBJECTIVES
LIMITED, DECIDING LIMITS OF ACTION, SELECTING THE GENTLEST
FORM OF FORCE NECESSARY, WIDENING THE COMMUNITY OF THE
CONCERNED, RECOGNIZING THAT DECISION-MAKERS MUST ABIDE BY
THE LAWS, AND TAKING NOTICE OF PRECEDENTS MADE.

0236 COCH L., FRENCH J.R.P. JR.
"OVERCOMING RESISTANCE TO CHANGE" (BMR)"
HUMAN RELATIONS, 1 (1948), 512-532.
REPORTS A RESEARCH PROGRAM CONDUCTED FOR THE BENEFIT OF
FACTORY MANAGEMENT IN ORDER TO DETERMINE: (1) WHY WORKERS
RESIST CHANGE SO STRONGLY AND (2) WHAT CAN BE DONE TO OVER-
COME THIS RESISTANCE. ON THE BASIS OF A PRELIMINARY THEORY
DEVISED BY THE RESEARCHERS TO ACCOUNT FOR THIS RESISTANCE,
A REAL LIFE ACTION EXPERIMENT WAS CONDUCTED WITHIN THE CON-
TEXT OF THE FACTORY SITUATION. THE RESULTS ARE INTERPRETED.

0237 COENEN E.
LA "KONJUNKTURFORSCHUNG" EN ALLEMAGNE ET EN AUTRICHE,
1925-1935.
LOUVAIN: EDITIONS NAUWELAERTS, 1964, 352 PP.
"KONJUNKTURFORSCHUNG" WAS RESEARCH SERIES ON ECONOMIC
MOVEMENTS UNDERTAKEN BETWEEN WWI AND II. ADHERENTS DEVISED A
THEORY OF POLITICAL ECONOMY THAT SYNTHESIZED DEDUCTIVE AND
INDUCTIVE METHODS. BOOK STUDIES LEADING IDEAS AND
METHODOLOGICAL PRINCIPLES IN ATTEMPT TO SHOW RELEVANCE TO
CURRENT ECONOMIC STUDIES. INCLUDES BIBLIOGRAPHY OF ABOUT 180
ITEMS.

0238 COFFEY J.I.
"THE ANTI-BALLISTIC MISSILE DEBATE."
FOREIGN AFFAIRS, 45 (APR. 67), 403-413.
DISCUSSES CONTROVERSY SURROUNDING BUILD-UP OF ANTI-BAL-
ISTIC MISSILE PROGRAM. MAINTAINS THAT THIS INCREASE IN STRA-
TEGIC ARMAMENTS WOULD INCREASE TENSION AMONG NUCLEAR POWERS
AND ALIENATE POWERS SEEKING NUCLEAR DISARMAMENT. THUS, THE
PRODUCTION OF ABMS MIGHT LEAD TO INHIBITION OF FURTHER ARMS
CONTROL NEGOTIATIONS. HE PROPOSES EITHER A MORATORIUM ON
ABMS OR RESTRICTIONS GOVERNING THEIR NUMBERS AND TYPES.

0239 COHEN A.
"THE TECHNOLOGY/ELITE APPROACH TO THE DEVELOPMENTAL PROCESS*
PERUVIAN CASE STUDY."
ECO. DEV. AND CULTURAL CHANGE, 14 (APR. 66), 323-333.
TECHNOLOGY/ELITE THEORY OF ECONOMIC GROWTH USING ONLY
TWO VARIABLES PERMITS GENERALIZATIONS ABOUT NATURE AND
DIRECTION OF DEVELOPMENTAL PROCESS. THE LESS VERTICAL MOBIL-
ITY AND THE SLOWER THE RATE OF GROWTH IN A PARTICULAR BACK-
WARD SOCIETY, THE MORE RELEVANT BECOMES TECHNOLOGY/ELITE
EXPLANATION .IT IS FREQUENTLY APPLIED TO LATIN AMERICA.

0240 COHEN K.J., RHENMAN E.
"THE ROLE OF MANAGEMENT GAMES IN EDUCATION AND RESEARCH."
MANAGEMENT SCIENCE, 7 (JAN. 61), 131-66.
STRESSES THAT, FOR TRAINING PURPOSES, MORE ATTENTION
SHOULD BE GIVEN IN GAMES TO FINANCIAL, LABOR, PUBLIC RELA-
TIONS ASPECTS. THEY MIGHT ALSO BE USED TO DISCOVER OPTIMAL
PATTERNS OF BUSINESS BEHAVIOR.

0241 COHEN M. ED.
LAW AND POLITICS IN SPACE: SPECIFIC AND URGENT PROBLEMS IN
THE LAW OF OUTER SPACE.
MONTREAL: MCGILL U. PR., 1964, 221 PP.
CONFERENCE PAPERS PERTAIN TO INTERNATIONAL ARRANGEMENTS
FOR SATELLITE COMMUNICATIONS, POLLUTION AND CONTAMINATION IN
SPACE, ARMS CONTROL, DISARMAMENT AND OBSERVATION IN SPACE,
PROSPECTS FOR AN OUTER SPACE REGIME. FIND THAT MAJOR POWERS
USE LAW TO SERVE NATIONAL INTERESTS.

0242 COHEN M.R., NAGEL E.
AN INTRODUCTION TO LOGIC AND SCIENTIFIC METHOD.
NEW YORK: HARCOURT BRACE, 1934, 467 PP.
ELEMENTARY TEXT ON HISTORY OF LOGIC. ILLUSTRATES LOGICAL
DOCTRINE WITH EXAMPLES FROM MANY DIFFERENT AREAS OF THOUGHT.
STUDIES FORMAL LOGIC, ANALYSIS OF PROPOSITIONS, THEIR
INTERRELATIONS, CATEGORICAL SYLLOGISMS, MATHEMATICAL LOGIC,
AND PROBABLE INFERENCE. EXPLAINS APPLIED LOGIC AND

SCIENTIFIC METHOD, HYPOTHESES, DEFINITION, INDUCTION, MEASUREMENT, AND FALLACIES.

0243 COLEMAN J.R.
THE CHANGING AMERICAN ECONOMY.
NEW YORK: BASIC BOOKS, 1967, 275 PP., LC#67-15951.
ESSAYS DEAL WITH CHANGE IN WAYS AMERICANS ARE DOING BUSINESS WITH EACH OTHER. STUDY THE "ECONOMY IN FLUX," LARGE AND SMALL CORPORATIONS, COMPETITION, THE AFFLUENT CONSUMER, PROBLEMS OF AGRICULTURE, POVERTY, AND LABOR. DISCUSS FISCAL POLICIES WHICH SEEK TO AVOID INFLATION AND DEPRESSION, FINANCING OF FOREIGN AID, AND THE INDIVIDUAL IN A CHANGING ECONOMY.

0244 COLM G., GEIGER T.
THE ECONOMY OF THE AMERICAN PEOPLE.
WASHINGTON: NATL PLANNING ASSN, 1967, 220 PP., LC#66-30437.
WIDELY USED IN HIGH SCHOOL AND COLLEGE ECONOMICS COURSES. PRESENTS SIMPLE BUT ACCURATE ACCOUNT OF HOW AMERICAN ECONOMY OPERATES AND ACHIEVES HIGH PRODUCTIVITY AND LIVING STAN-DARDS AND WHAT PROBLEMS IT FACES FOR THE FUTURE.

0245 COMBS C.H. ED., THRALL R.M. ED., DAVIS R.L. ED.
DECISION PROCESSES.
NEW YORK: WILEY, 1954, 332 PP.
INDIVIDUAL PAPERS RANGING FROM PURE MATHEMATICS TO EXPER-IMENTS IN GROUP DYNAMICS - ALL DIRECTED AT APPLYING MATHEMA-TICS TO BEHAVIORAL SCIENCES IN GENERAL AND TO DECISION PRO-CESSES IN PARTICULAR.

0246 COMMITTEE ECONOMIC DEVELOPMENT
TAXES AND TRADE: 20 YEARS OF CED POLICY (PAMPHLET)
NEW YORK: COMM FOR ECO DEV, 1963, 53 PP.
DEALS WITH ROLE OF COMMITTEE FOR ECONOMIC DEVELOPMENT IN BUSINESS LEADERSHIP. DISCUSSES COMMITTEE'S FUNCTION IN MAINTAINING REALISM IN FISCAL AND MONETARY POLICY. ANALYZES IMPORTANCE OF TRADE POLICY AS A KEY TO ECONOMIC STRENGTH.

0247 COMMONER B.
SCIENCE AND SURVIVAL.
NEW YORK: VIKING PRESS, 1967, 150 PP.
ARGUMENTATIVE ANALYSIS OF INVERSE EFFECTS OF SCIENTIFIC ACHIEVEMENT ON HEALTH OF SOCIETY. QUESTIONS CONTROL OF NEW POWERS SCIENCE HAS GIVEN MAN. ATTRIBUTES CAUSE OF EROSION OF SCIENTIFIC INTEGRITY TO SECRECY RESTRICTIONS AND POLITICAL PRESSURE. POLITICAL CRISIS HAS BEEN GENERATED BY AWARENESS OF THESE INVERSE EFFECTS.

0248 CONANT J.B.
SCIENCE AND COMMON SENSE.
NEW HAVEN: YALE U. PR., 1951 371 PP.
DISCUSSES METHODS AND HISTORY OF EXPERIMENTAL SCIENCE IN ORDER TO GIVE INFORMATION TO LAYMEN ENGAGED IN WORK OUTSIDE NATURAL SCIENCE. POINTS OUT THAT THERE IS NO SINGLE SCIEN-TIFIC METHOD BUT MANY WHICH ARE BASED ON HYPOTHESES DEVELOP-ED FROM EXPERIMENTATION. FINDS SCIENTIFIC ACTIVITIES CLOSELY RELATED TO CONTEMPORARY SOCIAL LIFE.

0249 CONANT J.B.
TWO MODES OF THOUGHT: MY ENCOUNTERS WITH SCIENCE AND EDUCATION.
NEW YORK: TRIDENT PR, 1964, 96 PP., LC#64-18874.
ARGUES THAT A FREE SOCIETY REQUIRES BOTH THE EMPIRICAL-INDUCTIVE METHOD OF INQUIRY AND THE THEORETICAL-DEDUCTIVE OUTLOOK, THOUGH BOTH HAVE THEIR DANGERS. PLOTS RELATIONS BETWEEN THE TWO, HOW THEY OPERATE IN THE NATURAL SCIENCES, THE PRACTICAL ARTS, AND SOCIAL SCIENCES. SHOWS HOW THE PREPONDERANCE OF ONE OR THE OTHER IN THE STUDY OF LAW CRE-ATED RADICALLY DIFFERENT BUSINESS AND EDUCATION PRACTICES.

0250 CONNOLLY W.E.
POLITICAL SCIENCE AND IDEOLOGY.
NEW YORK: ATHERTON PRESS, 1967, 179 PP., LC#67-18273.
ANALYZES TWO REPRESENTATIVE THEORIES OF POWER IN AMERI-CAN SOCIETY: THOSE OF THE PLURALISTS WHO AFFIRM, AND THE ELITISTS WHO DISPUTE, THE CASE FOR DEMOCRACY. DEMONSTRATES HOW PERSONAL PREFERENCES AND GROUP INTERESTS ENTER INTO THE DEVELOPMENT OF THESE CONCEPTS. DETAILS METHODS BY WHICH INVESTIGATOR CAN UNCOVER AND EFFECTIVELY CONTROL THE IDEOLOGICAL ASPECTS OF HIS OWN WORK AND THAT OF OTHERS.

0251 CONOVER H.L. ED.
CIVILIAN DEFENSE: A SELECTED LIST OF RECENT REFERENCES (PAMPHLET)
WASHINGTON: LIBRARY OF CONGRESS, 1941, 43 PP.
BIBLIOGRAPHY OF 429 LISTINGS IN ENGLISH COMPILED FOR LIBRARY OF CONGRESS, DIVISION OF BIBLIOGRAPHIES ON PROBLEMS OF CIVILIAN DEFENSE ORGANIZATION. INCLUDES BIBLIOGRAPHIES, BULLETINS AND ARTICLES ON STATE, REGIONAL, MUNICIPAL AND LOCAL PLANNING. HOUSING, BUILDING, PUBLIC UTILITIES AND TRANSPORT, CONSUMER-MARKETING, AIR RAID PRO-TECTION AND ITS ACCOMPANYING PROBLEMS ARE INCLUDED.

0252 CONWAY J.E.
"MAKING RESEARCH EFFECTIVE IN LEGISLATION."
WISC. LAW REV., 67 (WINTER 67), 252-266.
ASKS QUESTION IS THERE WAY OF ORGANIZING AND ADMINISTER-ING RESEARCH PROJECT SO THAT LAWMAKERS MORE LIKELY TO ADOPT LEGISLATION BASED ON RESEARCH. ARGUES THAT CERTAIN FUNCTIONS MUST BE ORGANIZATIONALLY LOCATED IF RESEARCH IS TO BE BEST POSSIBLE AND CHANCES OF ADOPTION MAXIMIZED. ADVOCATES ADVI-SORY AND EXECUTIVE COMMITTEES TO CARRY OUT RESEARCH AND SEP-ARATION OF EXECUTIVE DIRECTION FROM SPONSORING GROUP.

0253 COOKE E.F.
"RESEARCH: AN INSTRUMENT OF POWER."
POLIT. SCI. QUART., 76 (MAR. 61), 69-87.
A CASE STUDY OF A TAXPAYER'S ASSOCIATION, THE PENNSYLVANIA ECONOMY LEAGUE, WHICH "HAS COME TO WIELD GREAT INFLUENCE OVER THE MAKING OF PUBLIC POLICY INSTEAD OF BEING ONLY A RESEARCH AGENCY." NOTES THAT GOVERNMENT, BY RESEARCH, IS GAINING CONSTANT ADHERENTS IN AN ERA WHERE SCIENCE AND RESEARCH HAVE PUBLIC SUPPORT WHICH EXCEEDS THE PUBLIC UNDERSTANDING OF ISSUES.

0254 COOMBS C.H.
A THEORY OF DATA.
NEW YORK: JOHN WILEY, 1964, 585 PP., LC#63-20629.
CONSTRUCTS A COMPREHENSIVE SYSTEM FOR DISTINGUISHING AND RELATING FOUR TYPES OF DATA WITH WHICH MEASUREMENT AND SCALING THEORIES DEAL: PREFERENTIAL CHOICE DATA, SINGLE STIMULUS DATA, STIMULI COMPARISON DATA, AND SIMILARITIES DATA. CONCLUDES WITH ANALYSIS OF THE INTERRELATIONS AMONG VARIOUS KINDS OF DATA AND FACTORS COMMON TO ALL. ANALYZ-ES FOUNDATIONS OF PSYCHOLOGICAL MEASUREMENT AND SCALING.

0255 COOPER A.C.
"R&D IS MORE EFFICIENT IN SMALL COMPANIES."
HARVARD BUSINESS REV., 42 (MAY 64), 75-83.
IN WIDE AND IMPORTANT SEGMENTS OF AMERICAN INDUSTRIAL RESEARCH, LARGE FIRMS TEND TO SPEND SUBSTANTIALLY MORE THAN SMALL ONES TO DEVELOP PRODUCTS. PIONEERING INQUIRY BY MEANS OF INTERVIEWS WITH EXPERIENCED PERSONNEL IN BOTH LARGE AND SMALL COMPANIES IN ELECTRONICS AND CHEMICALS. INCLUDES STUDY OF LARGE AND SMALL COMPANIES INDEPENDENTLY DEVELOPING SAME PRODUCT. ASSESSES ADVANTAGES OF BOTH SIZES OF COMPANY.

0256 CORDIER A.W. ED., FOOTE W. ED.
THE QUEST FOR PEACE.
NEW YORK: COLUMBIA U PRESS, 1965, 390 PP., LC#65-10357.
ARTICLES DISCUSSING MECHANICS OF PEACE-MAKING, INCLUDING APPRAISAL OF UN, KEEPING THE PEACE, DISARMAMENT, NEW ATTITUDES IN ECONOMIC RELATIONS, AND HUMAN RIGHTS IN WORLD AFFAIRS.

0257 CORY R.H. JR.
"FORGING A PUBLIC INFORMATION POLICY FOR THE UNITED NATIONS."
INT. ORG., 7 (MAY 53), 229-42.
ATTEMPTS TO CLARIFY WHAT ARE PROBLEMS FACING UN DELEGATES DECIDING WAY IN WHICH INTERNATIONAL SECRETARIAT SHOULD ATTEMPT TO INFLUENCE PUBLIC OPINION.

0258 CORY R.H. JR.
"INTERNATIONAL INSPECTION FROM PROPOSALS TO REALIZATION."
INT. ORG., 13 (AUTUMN 59), 495-504.
SURVEYS ADMINISTRATIVE, BUDGETARY, ORGANIZATIONAL, LEGAL, AND POLITICAL PROBLEMS BARRING ESTABLISHMENT OF EFFECTIVE INSPECTORATE CHECKING DEVELOPMENT AND SPREAD OF WEAPONS. DISCUSSES RELATIONSHIPS OF INSPECTORATE WITH OTHER PARALLEL INTERNATIONAL ORGANIZATIONS.

0259 CRAIG J.
ELEMENTS OF POLITICAL SCIENCE (3 VOLS.)
EDINBURGH: WILLIAM BLACKWOOD, 1814, 1186 PP.
EARLY ATTEMPT AT A GENERAL OVERVIEW OF SCIENCE OF GOVERNMENT. BOOK ONE DEALS WITH THE NATURE OF GOVERNMENT: ITS RIGHTS, RIGHTS OF THE INDIVIDUAL AND OF SOCIETY, AND THE DISTRIBUTION OF POLITICAL POWER. BOOK TWO CONCERNS DUTIES OF GOVERNMENT: ADMINISTRATION OF LAW, NATIONAL DEFENSE, ECONOMIC REGULATION, PROPER DISTRIBUTION OR WEALTH. BOOK THREE DISCUSSES REVENUE AND TAXATION.

0260 CRANBERG L.
"SCIENCE, ETHICS, AND LAW."
SOUTHERN HUMANITIES REV., 1 (SPRING 67), 30-40.
ARGUES AGAINST THE VIEW THAT A FUNDAMENTAL DICHOTOMY SEP-ARATES SCIENCE AND ETHICS, AND SUGGESTS INSTEAD THAT THE MO-TIVATING FORCE OF SCIENTIFIC INVESTIGATION, A SEARCH FOR NATURAL TRUTH, IS AN ETHICAL STANDARD. VALID SOCIAL LAW CAN INCORPORATE BOTH SCIENTIFIC KNOWLEDGE AND ETHICAL JUDGMENT.

0261 CRANE R.D.
"LAW AND STRATEGY IN SPACE."
ORBIS, 6 (SUMMER 62), 281-300.
USA MUST TAKE INITIATIVE IN FORMULATING SPACE LAWS WHICH WOULD SERVE TO PROMOTE SCIENTIFIC RESEARCH AND ECONOMIC PROGRESS. IN ORDER TO FACILITATE GROWTH OF A FREE AND PEACEFUL WORLD ORDER, IT'S NECESSARY TO IMPLEMENT ON A HIGHER MORAL LEVEL USA MILITARY AND POLITICAL STRATEGIES.

0262 CRAUMER L.V. ED.

BUSINESS PERIODICALS INDEX (8VOLS.)
NEW YORK: H W WILSON, 1960, 6240 PP.
   CUMULATIVE SUBJECT INDEX TO PERIODICALS IN FIELD OF
BUSINESS AND RELATED AREAS. COVERS ACCOUNTING, ADVERTISING,
FINANCE, BANKING, LABOR, INSURANCE, TAXATION, ETC. ARRANGED
ALPHABETICALLY BY TOPIC. COVERS 1958-66.

0263 CROSSON F.J. ED.
SCIENCE AND CONTEMPORARY SOCIETY.
SOUTH BEND: U OF NOTRE DAME, 1967, 251 PP., LC#67-22148.
   ESSAYS SURVEY CONTEMPORARY RELATION BETWEEN PHILOSOPHY
AND SCIENCE, TRACE CURRENT CENTRAL PROBLEMS, AND CHART
DEMISE OF POSITIVIST THEORY OF SCIENCE. ANALYZES ISSUES
INVOLVED IN SCIENCE-RELIGION DICHOTOMY, AND EXAMINES SOURCE
OF CONFLICT. PREDICTS CHANGES SOCIETY WILL UNDERGO IN NEXT
100 YEARS AS RESULT OF SCIENTIFIC AND TECHNICAL INNOVATIONS.

0264 CROWE S.
THE LANDSCAPE OF POWER.
LONDON: THE ARCHITECTURAL PRESS, 1958, 115 PP.
   EXAMINES THE LANDSCAPE OF THE BRITISH ISLES AND THE
CHALLENGE OF GIGANTIC CONSTRUCTIONS AND POWER LINES. STUDIES
NATURAL, PRACTICAL METHODS FOR THE NEW INDUSTRIAL AGE. IN-
CLUDES POWER, NATIONAL PARKS, NUCLEAR POWER STATIONS, HYDRO-
ELECTRIC POWER, ELECTRIC AND OIL TRANSMISSION, AIRFIELDS,
AND NEW INDUSTRIES IN OLD AREAS. CONCLUDES THAT MAN MUST RE-
GAIN HIS SENSE OF VALUE AND BEAUTY, THEN ACT FOR THE FUTURE.

0265 CROWTHER J.G., WHIDDINGTON R.
SCIENCE AT WAR.
NEW YORK: PHILO/LIBRARY, 1950, 185 PP.
   ACCOUNT BASED ON OFFICIAL BRITISH ARCHIVES OF THE
SCIENTIFIC CONTRIBUTIONS TO BRITAIN'S WAR EFFORT DURING
WORLD WAR II. RESEARCH IN RADAR, ATOMIC ENERGY AND MARINE
OPERATIONS BROUGHT SCIENCE INTO NEW ROLE OF FORMATIVE
INFLUENCE ON THE STRATEGY AND TACTICS OF MODERN WARFARE.

0266 CURRENT TRENDS IN PSYCHOLOGY
PSYCHOLOGY IN THE WORLD EMERGENCY.
PITTSBURGH: U. PR., 1952, 199 PP.
   SERIES OF LECTURES DEFINING THE CONTEMPORARY ROLE OF
SERVICE AND RESEARCH PSYCHOLOGY IN THE US DEFENSE DEPARTMENT
IN PROBLEMS OF PERSONNEL TRAINING METHODS, MEASURES OF
PERSONNEL TASK PROFICIENCY AND MORALE STIMULATION. QUESTION
REMAINS WHETHER ROLE SHOULD EMPHASIZE RESEARCH OR SERVICE.

0267 CYERT R.M., FEIGENBAUM E.A., MARCH J.G.
"MODELS IN A BEHAVIORAL THEORY OF THE FIRM."
BEHAVIORAL SCIENCE, 4 (APR. 59), 81-96.
   PROPOSES A COMPLEX MODEL OF THE FIRM AS A DECISION-MAKING
ORGANIZATION WHICH CAN YIELD ECONOMICALLY RELEVANT AND TEST-
ABLE PREDICTIONS OF BUSINESS BEHAVIOR. EMPLOYS COMPUTER
SIMULATION TECHNIQUES.

0268 D'AMATO D.
"LEGAL ASPECTS OF THE FRENCH NUCLEAR TESTS."
AMER. J. OF INT. LAW, 61 (JAN. 67).
   DISCUSSES FRANCE'S RESPONSIBILITY UNDER INTERNATIONAL LAW
FOR ITS 1966 NUCLEAR TESTING IN TAHITI. DISCUSSES THE COM-
PLEX PROBLEMS IN PROVING THE ILLEGALITY OF THE TESTS, BUT
IMPLIES THAT PREVIOUS EVIDENCE OF RADIOACTIVE CONTAMINATION
IN OTHER TESTS CAN BE THE BASIS FOR A STRONG CLAIM.

0269 DADDARIO E.Q.
"CONGRESS FACES SPACE POLICIES."
BUL. ATOMIC SCIENTISTS, 23 (MAY 67), 10-16.
   DISCUSSION OF SPACE POLICIES, WITH SPECIAL REFERENCE TO
THE ROLE OF CONGRESS, BY A CONGRESSMAN. DISCUSSES THE
PROBLEMS OF PRIORITIES, OF MILITARY VS. CIVILIAN SPACE VEN-
TURES, OF FUNDING, AND OF THE RELATIONSHIP BETWEEN SPACE
RESEARCH AND SCIENTIFIC RESEARCH, WHICH ARE NOT ALWAYS THE
SAME. SPACE PROGRAMS WILL CONTINUE, BUT COST MUST BE A FAC-
TOR. CONGRESS TODAY UNDERSTANDS PROBLEMS OF PROGRAM BETTER.

0270 DAENIKER G.
STRATEGIE DES KLEIN STAATS.
STUTTGART: VERL HUBER FRAUENFELD, 1966, 230 PP.
   DISCUSSES THE STRATEGY OF A SMALL STATE, SWITZERLAND, IN
MAINTAINING ITSELF IN THE ATOMIC AGE. ARGUES FOR NUCLEAR
ARMAMENT OF SWITZERLAND, MILITARY DEFENSE, AND CONTINUED
POLITICAL EXISTENCE. DESCRIBES NEW DIMENSIONS OF THREAT
DERIVING FROM NUCLEAR WEAPONS. QUESTIONS EXPHASIS ON
CONVENTIONAL WEAPONS IN SWITZERLAND.

0271 DAHRENDORF R.
CLASS AND CLASS CONFLICT IN INDUSTRIAL SOCIETY.
STANFORD: STANFORD U PRESS, 1959, 336 PP., LC#59-7425.
   PART TWO OF THIS BOOK, "TOWARD A SOCIOLOGICAL THEORY
OF CONFLICT IN INDUSTRIAL SOCIETY," DEALS WITH GROUP
THEORY RELEVANT TO REPRESENTATION, THE ROLE OF LATENT AND
MANIFEST INTERESTS OF GROUPSAND QUASI-GROUPS, AND THE
FUNCTIONS AND MEDIATION OF SOCIAL AND GROUP CONFT ARE

0272 DALAND R.T. ED.
PERSPECTIVES OF BRAZILIAN PUBLIC ADMINISTRATION (VOL. I)
LOS ANGELES: U OF S CAL, PUB ADM, 1963, 171 PP.

PAPERS WRITTEN FOR BRAZILIAN SCHOOL OF PUBLIC ADMINIS-
TRATION. CONCERNED PRIMARILY WITH OVER-ALL VIEW OF BRAZILIAN
ADMINISTRATION IN NATIONAL GOVERNMENT, FOCUSING ON THE
ADMINISTRATION DEPARTMENT OF PUBLIC SERVICE, PERSONNEL SYS-
TEM, AND PLANNING.

0273 DALKEY N.C.
"SOLVABLE NUCLEAR WAR MODELS."
MANAGEMENT SCIENCE, 11 (JULY 65), 783-791.
   DEALS WITH AN AGGREGATED TWO-SIDED WAR GAME, ONE OF SEV-
ERAL DESIGNED TO STUDY THE USE OF ABSTRACT MODELS FOR STRA-
TEGIC PLANNING. A PAY-OFF FUNCTION FOR WAR GAME IS DEFINED,
USING AN ASSUMPTION OF INCREASING CONCERN AS A CRITICAL LEV-
EL OF DAMAGE IS APPROACHED. A SIMPLE, ONE-WEAPON VERSION
OF THE CENTRAL NUCLEAR WAR GAME HAS AN ANALYTIC SOLUTION
AND, IF NO SIDE HAS COUNTERFORCE, AN EQUILIBRIUM POINT.

0274 DALTON G.
"ECONOMIC THEORY AND PRIMITIVE SOCIETY" (BMR)"
AMERICAN ANTHROPOLOGIST, 63 (FEB. 61), 1-21.
   PRESENTS REASONS WHY ECONOMIC THEORY CANNOT BE
SUCCESSFULLY APPLIED TO STUDY OF PRIMITIVE COMMUNITIES.
EXAMINES TECHNOLOGICAL PROCESSES, LEVEL OF MATERIAL
SUBSISTANCE, ECOLOGICAL CONDITIONS, ETC. SUGGESTS
ALTERNATIVE APPROACH TO ANALYTICAL TREATMENT OF PRIMITIVE
ECONOMY.

0276 DAVENPORT J.
"ARMS AND THE WELFARE STATE."
YALE REV., 47 (SPR. 58), 335-346.
   BELIEVES THAT US NEEDS A STRONG AND EFFECTIVE GOVERNMENT
FOR NATIONAL DEFENSE, DIPLOMACY, SOUND MONEY, AND TO RESIST
MONOPOLY IN BUSINESS AND LABOR, BUT THIS DOES NOT HAVE TO
MEAN 'WELFARE STATE'. ARGUES FOR A NEW 'INTELLECTUAL COM-
MUNITY SYNTHESIS', WHICH WILL TAKE THE THREAT OF RUSSIAN
DANGER SERIOUSLY, WHILE KEEPING FREE SOCIETY AT HOME. ANSWER
TO TOBIN'S 'DEFENSE, DOLLARS AND DOCTINES' OF SAME ISSUE.

0277 DAVIS E.
TWO MINUTES TO MIDNIGHT.
INDIANAPOLIS: BOBBS-MERRILL, 1955, 207 PP., LC#55-6823.
   TREATS POLITICAL AND PSYCHOLOGICAL CONDITIONS THAT MAY
BRING ABOUT OR DISCOURAGE THERMONUCLEAR WAR. ALSO DISCUSSES
MEANS OF ALIGNING NEUTRAL NATIONS WITH US ON INTERNATIONAL
QUESTIONS.

0278 DAVIS K.C.
ADMINISTRATIVE LAW TREATISE (VOLS. I AND IV)
MINNEAPOLIS: WEST PUBL CO, 1958, 1310 PP.
   VOL. I DISCUSSES NATURE AND PROCESS OF ADMINISTRATIVE
LAW. EXAMINES CONCEPT OF DELEGATION OF POWER, RULE-MAKING
FUNCTION OF ADMINISTRATIVE AGENCIES, ADJUDICATIVE PROCEDURE,
AND SUBDELEGATION OF POWER. VOL. IV DISCUSSES NATURE OF UN-
REVIEWABLE ADMINISTRATIVE ACTION, SCOPE OF REVIEWABLE EVI-
DENCE, AND SCOPE OF REVIEW OF LEGAL CONCEPTS AS APPLIED TO
FACTS.

0279 DAVIS P.C.
"THE COMING CHINESE COMMUNIST NUCLEAR THREAT AND U.S. SEA
BASED ABM OPTIONS."
ORBIS, 11 (SPRING 67), 45-66.
   DISCUSSES BACKGROUND OF US DEVELOPMENT OF ANTIBALLISTIC
MISSILES, AND WAYS IN WHICH DEVELOPMENT MAY BE AFFECTED BY
CHINESE NUCLEAR POWER. BELIEVES ABM'S WOULD BE EFFECTIVE
AGAINST CHINESE WARHEADS DIRECTED AT US, BUT THINKS THAT
EVENT UNLIKELY IN NEXT DECADE. CONSIDERS CHINESE ATTACK ON
OR BLACKMAIL OF ASIAN COUNTRIES MORE LIKELY, AND RECOMMENDS
US ABM'S, ESPECIALLY A SEA-BASED SYSTEM, FOR SUCH COUNTRIES.

0280 DAVIS V.
THE POLITICS OF INNOVATION: PATTERNS IN NAVY CASES
(PAMPHLET)
DENVER: U OF DENVER, 1967, 69 PP.
   STUDY OF NATIONAL SECURITY POLICY FOCUSING ON BEHAVIOR OF
INDIVIDUALS IN US NAVY. CONSIDERS PROPOSALS THAT NAVY SHOULD
DEVELOP TECHNOLOGICAL INNOVATION AS PART OR ALL OF A WEAPONS
SYSTEM. INCLUDES BIBLIOGRAPHICAL CITATIONS OF BOOKS, ARTI-
CLES, AND PAPERS; MAJORITY PUBLISHED 1960'S IN US.

0281 DAWSON R.H.
"CONGRESSIONAL INNOVATION AND INTERVENTION IN DEFENSE
POLICY: LEGISLATIVE AUTHORIZATION OF WEAPONS SYSTEMS."
AM. POL. SCI. REV., 56 (MAR. 62), 42-57.
   PROVIDES INSIGHTS INTO LEGISLATIVE FUNCTIONS AND ROLE OF
CONGRESS IN POLITICAL PROCESSES OF DEFENSE. EXAMINES
CONDITIONS OF ACTIVE AND EFFECTIVE LEGISLATIVE INTERVENTION
IN STRATEGIC DECISIONS. URGES EXPANSION OF ROLE OF CON-
GRESSIONAL LEADERS IN DEFENSE POLICY-MAKING.

0282 DAY E.E.
EDUCATION FOR FREEDOM AND RESPONSIBILITY.
ITHACA: CORNELL U. PR., 1952.
   DISCUSSES IMPACT OF PROFESSIONALISM AND TREND TOWARDS
SPECIALIZATION IN RESEARCH. ADVOCATES RE-ORIENTATION OF
LIBERAL EDUCATION REJECTING THE CONANT PLAN AS INFLEXIBLE.
IN WAKE OF COLD WAR SUGGESTS TRAINING OF LOYAL LEADERSHIP

AND EXPANSION OF EDUCATION IN GENERAL.

0283 DE BLIJ H.J.
SYSTEMATIC POLITICAL GEOGRAPHY.
NEW YORK: JOHN WILEY, 1967, 618 PP., LC#66-28752.
PRESENTS INTRODUCTION TO FIELD OF POLITICAL GEOGRAPHY,
WITH PROFESSIONAL PAPERS AND CASE STUDIES. DISCUSSES RISE
OF NATION-STATE, ITS ELEMENTS, RESTRICTIONS, FUNCTIONS,
AND ROLE IN GEOPOLITICAL ACTIVITY, AND ITS INTERNAL
STRUCTURE. APPLIES STUDY TO COLONIALISM, SUPRA-NATIONALISM,
AND EMERGENT WORLD FORCES.

0284 DE FOREST J.D.
"LOW LEVELS OF TECHNOLOGY AND ECONOMIC DEVELOPMENT
PROSPECTS."
SOC. SCI., 38 (JUNE 63), 131-139.
DISCUSSES ROLE OF TECHNIQUE AND LEVEL OF PRODUCTIVE ARTS
AS OBSTACLES TO ECONOMIC PROGRESS IN THE 'POOR' WORLD. CITES
PROBLEMS OF TECHNOLOGICAL INNOVATION AS THEY RELATE TO
GENERAL FACTORS. STRESSES THE VALUE OF LOCAL APPLIED
RESEARCH ACTIVITY AS MEANS OF RAISING PRODUCTIVITY.

0285 DE JOUVENEL B.
THE ART OF CONJECTURE.
NEW YORK: BASIC BOOKS, 1967, 307 PP., LC#67-12649.
CONCERNS METHODS OF PREDICTING FUTURE SOCIAL, POLITICAL,
AND ECONOMIC DEVELOPMENTS WITH ACCURACY. INCLUDES HISTORICAL
AND SCIENTIFIC FORECASTING. OUTLINES WAYS OF CONCEIVING
FUTURE, RELATION OF FUTURE TO PAST AND PRESENT, AND TER-
MINOLOGY. CONSIDERS RELATION OF CONJECTURE TO MAKING DECI-
SIONS, PRINCIPLE OF UNCERTAINTY, FORECASTING OF IDEAS, AND
PRAGMATISM OF CONJECTURE AND CONSEQUENCES.

0286 DE NEUFVILLE R.
"EDUCATION AT THE ACADEMIES."
MILITARY REV., 47 (MAY 67), 3-9.
ASSESSES, DESCRIBES, AND DEFENDS GOALS, TECHNIQUES, AND
CURRICULA OF MILITARY ACADEMIES. SHOWS HOW ACADEMIES HAVE
ADOPTED NEW TEACHING METHODS WITH EMPHASIS ON ANALYSIS,
NEW SUBJECT MATTER SUCH AS COMPUTER TRAINING, AND NEW GOALS
AS DEFINED BY MILITARY OFFICERS. BROACHES QUESTION OF
OBSOLESCENT LEARNING, INTERDISCIPLINARY TRAINING, ETC.

0287 DEAN A.L. ED.
FEDERAL AGENCY APPROACHES TO FIELD MANAGEMENT (PAMPHLET)
CHICAGO: AMER SOC FOR PUB ADMIN, 1963, 28 PP., LC#63-21421.
SYMPOSIUM DRAWN FROM PAPERS PRESENTED AT 1963 NATIONAL
CONFERENCE ON PUBLIC ADMINISTRATION. INCLUDES BRIEF NOTES
ON GENERAL AREA OF FEDERAL FIELD MANAGEMENT AND STUDIES OF
FIELD MANAGEMENT IN THE INTERNAL REVENUE SERVICE; POST
OFFICE DEPARTMENT; A MULTI-PURPOSE AGENCY (HEW); A RESEARCH
AND DEVELOPMENT AGENCY (NASA); AND AN INTEGRATED AGENCY
(FAA).

0288 DEAN B.V.
"APPLICATION OF OPERATIONS RESEARCH TO MANAGERIAL DECISION
MAKING"
ADMINISTRATIVE SCI. Q., 3 (1958), 412-428.
OUTLINES DECISION-MAKING PROCESS AND ROLE OF DECISION
MAKER IN THIS PROCESS. INDICATES UTILITY OF OPERATIONS
RESEARCH IN SOLVING DECISION-MAKING PROBLEMS. SHOWS HOW
ANALYTIC MODELS ARE CONSTRUCTED AND SOLVED, NOTES SOME
TOOLS AND TECHNIQUES FOR SOLVING SUCH MODELS, AND FORECASTS
POSSIBLE FUTURE DEVELOPMENTS OF OPERATIONS RESEARCH TECH-
NIQUES AND THEIR POSSIBLE EFFECTS ON DECISION-MAKING.

0289 DEAN B.V., CULHAN R.H.
"CONTRACT RESEARCH PROPOSAL PREPARATION STRATEGIES."
MANAGEMENT SCIENCE, 11 (JUNE 65), 187-199.
A BIDDING MODEL IS DEVELOPED AND USED TO EXAMINE CONTRACT
RESEARCH PROPOSAL PREPARATION STRATEGIES. EXPECTED PROFITS
DUE TO SALES FROM INITIAL AND FOLLOW-ON PRODUCTION ORDERS
ARE RELATED TO PROPOSAL PREPARATION COST, CONTRACT VALUE,
AND THE PROBABILITY OF CONTRACT AWARD. THE MODEL IS TESTED
AND APPLIED IN THE PROPOSAL PREPARATION ACTIVITY OF AN
AEROSPACE COMPANY.

0290 DECHERT C.R.
"THE DEVELOPMENT OF CYBERNETICS."
AMER. BEHAVIORAL SCIENTIST, 8 (JUNE 65), 15-20.
PRESENTS THE THEORETICAL INNOVATIONS IN THE DEVELOPMENT
OF CYBERNETIC OR SELF-REGULATING SYSTEMS AND APPLICATIONS
IN POLITICAL ECONOMY AND SOCIAL RELATIONS. THE SCOPE OF
CYBERNETICS IS OUTLINED. THE ROLE OF COMPUTERS IS DISCUSSED
IN RELATION TO COMMUNICATION OF INFORMATION IN CYBERNETIC
SYSTEMS. A CYBERNETIC MODEL REQUIRES DISTINCTIONS AMONG
PERCEPTION, DECISION-MAKING, AND ACTION.

0291 DEES J.W. JR.
URBAN SOCIOLOGY AND THE EMERGING ATOMIC MEGALOPOLIS,
PART I.
ANN ARBOR: ANN ARBOR PUBL, 1950, 267 PP.
INTRODUCTORY TEXT AND CASEBOOK IN FIELD OF URBAN SOCIETY
AND SOCIAL PATHOLOGY. ATTEMPTS TO ENLARGE SCOPE OF URBANISM
INTO DEVELOPMENT OF EMERGING ATOMIC MEGALOPOLIS. FOCUSES ON
PROBLEMS OF FRINGE DEVELOPMENT, SOCIOLOGY OF WATER AND

SEWAGE, SCIENTIFIC MEASUREMENT OF CITIES, THEORIES OF URBAN
ECOLOGICAL EXPANSION, PLANS FOR PUBLIC HOUSING, AND
NEIGHBORHOODS.

0292 DEGLER C.N.
THE AGE OF THE ECONOMIC REVOLUTION 1876-1900.
CHICAGO: SCOTT, FORESMAN & CO, 1967, 213 PP., LC#67-14492.
STUDIES FACTORS LEADING TO INDUSTRIALIZATION IN US,
RESULTING TRANSFORMATION IN AMERICAN SOCIETY, ADVENT OF
FACTORIES, AND GROWTH OF LARGE CITIES. DISCUSSES CONCOMITANT
POLITICAL REFORMATION AND AGRICULTURAL REVOLUTION,
SECULARIZATION OF RELIGION, ANTITRUST MOVEMENT, INFLUENCE
OF DARWINISM, AND POLITICAL PARTY CAMPAIGNS AND ISSUES.
COMPARES US TO EUROPEAN COUNTRIES.

0293 DELLIN L.A.D.
"BULGARIA UNDER SOVIET LEADERSHIP."
CURR. HIST., 44 (MAY 63), 281-287.
REVEALS EXCESSIVE SUBSERVIENCE TO USSR. DE-STALINIZATION
MORE NOMINAL THAN REAL. USA REMAINS PUBLIC ENEMY NO.1 OF
REGIME YET SOURCE OF HOPE TO PEOPLE. COUNTRY'S TENSIONS
FOUND IN ECONOMIC FIELD: CRISIS IN AGRICULTURE ACUTE.

0294 DESAI M.J.
"INDIA AND NUCLEAR WEAPONS."
DISSERTATION ABSTRACTS, 3 (FALL 65), 135-142.
THOUGH INDIA'S REFUSAL TO HAVE NUCLEAR WEAPONS IS DEEPLY
INGRAINED, GROWING FEAR OF CHINA MAY MAKE THIS REFUSAL
IMPOSSIBLE TO UPHOLD. AUTHOR INSISTS THAT INDIA CAN ONLY
GUARANTEE TO REMAIN NON-NUCLEAR IF THE NUCLEAR POWERS
ELIMINATE UNDERGROUND TESTING, PROGRESSIVELY REDUCE ALL ARM-
AMENTS, AND EVENTUALLY ELIMINATE NUCLEAR ARMS.

0295 DEUTSCH K.W.
"GAME THEORY AND POLITICS: SOME PROBLEMS OF APPLICATION."
CANAD. ECO. POLIT. SCI., 20 (FEB. 54), 76-83.
CONSIDERS THE SIMILARITY OF CERTAIN SOCIAL SITUATIONS AND
CERTAIN GAMES. APPLICATION OF GAME THEORIES TO POLITICAL
BEHAVIOR REQUIRES EXACT, MEASURABLE DATA FROM POLITICAL
SCIENTISTS. STATES GAME THEORIES DRAWBACK IS THAT THEY PLACE
HUMAN AFFAIRS IN STATIC CATEGORIES.

0297 DEUTSCH K.W.
"THE IMPACT OF SCIENCE AND TECHNOLOGY ON INTERNATIONAL
POLITICS."
DAEDALUS, 88 (FALL 59), 669-685.
PRESENTS AS MYTHS THE OVERESTIMATION OF SCIENTIFIC
PROWESS OF ONE'S OWN CULTURE, OF PARTIAL MILITARY INNOVA-
TION, OF SMALL MILITARY ELITES, OF HIGHLY CENTRALIZED
POLITICAL POWER AND REANALYZES SOME BASIC CONCEPTS OF NA-
TIONAL INTERESTS AND FOREIGN POLICY. BELIEVES THAT WITH
SCIENCE'S IMPACT, THERE MAY BE PREMIUM ON LEADERSHIP.

0298 DEUTSCH K.W.
"TOWARD AN INVENTORY OF BASIC TRENDS AND PATTERNS IN COM-
PARATIVE AND INTERNATIONAL POLITICS."
AMER. POLIT. SCI. REV., 54 (MARCH 60), 34-58.
ANALYZES TYPES AND MODELS OF POLITICAL BEHAVIOR IN ORDER
FIND BEHAVIOR PATTERN OF PARTICULAR STATE UNDER PARTICULAR
CIRCUMSTANCES. DISCUSSES METHODS OF EVALUATING QUANTATIVE
DATE WITH HELP OF NUMEROUS DATA CHARTS AND STATISTICS.

0299 DEUTSCH K.W., MADOW W.G.
"A NOTE ON THE APPEARANCE OF WISDOM IN LARGE BUREAUCRATIC
ORGANIZATIONS."
BEHAVIORAL SCIENCE, 6 (JAN. 61), 72-85.
STATISTICAL MODEL TO DETERMINE PROBABILITY FOR OFFICIALS
TO MAKE CORRECT DECISIONS WHEN DECISION-MAKERS OF COMPAR-
ABLE COMPETENCE HAVE FAILED. DISCUSSES APPLICABILITY OF RE-
SULTS TO POLITICAL AND ORGANIZATIONAL BEHAVIOR.

0300 DEUTSCH K.W.
"ARMS CONTROL AND EUROPEAN UNITY* THE NEXT TEN YEARS."
BUL. ATOMIC SCIENTISTS, 23 (MAY 67), 21-24.
A DISCUSSION, BASED ON EXTENSIVE RESEARCH FOR A FORTH-
COMING BOOK, OF EUROPEAN ATTITUDES TOWARD ARMS CONTROL,
EUROPEAN UNITY AND THE ATLANTIC ALLIANCE, AND INDEPENDENT
NUCLEAR FORCES. WHILE EUROPEAN INTEGRATION IS EXPECTED TO
PROCEED SLOWLY, THERE IS GENERAL AGREEMENT AS TO THE DESIR-
ABILITY OF DECREASED INTERNATIONAL TENSION AND OF ARMS CON-
TROL, AND THE UNDESIRABILITY OF EXPANDED NUCLEAR FORCES.

0301 DEWEY J.
THE QUEST FOR CERTAINTY.
NEW YORK: MINTON, BALCH & CO, 1929, 313 PP.
OUTLINES METHODS OF INVESTIGATION FOR MODERN AGE. SHOWS
CHANGES IN MODELS OF CONSECUTIVE INVESTIGATION IN SCIENCE
AND PHILOSOPHY FROM PRE-SCIENTIFIC ANALYSIS OF CLASSIC AND
MIDDLE AGES TO WAYS OF THOUGHT CHARACTERISTIC OF MODERN
SCIENCE AND PHILOSOPHY.

0302 DICKSON P.G.M.
THE FINANCIAL REVOLUTION IN ENGLAND.
NEW YORK: ST MARTIN'S PRESS, 1967, 580 PP., LC#67-12509.
CITES AND EXPLORES IMPORTANCE OF DEVELOPMENT OF PUBLIC
CREDIT SYSTEMS TO POLITICAL, SOCIAL, AND ECONOMIC HISTORY

OF 18TH CENTURY ENGLAND. NATIONAL DEBT, ADMINISTRATIVE PROBLEMS, PUBLIC CREDITORS, GOVERNMENT BORROWING, SECURITY MARKETS, ARE ALL ANALYZED IN DEPTH. COMPREHENSIVE WORK INCLUDING WIDE RANGE OF DISCIPLINES.

0303 DIEBOLD J.
BEYOND AUTOMATION: MANAGERIAL PROBLEMS OF AN EXPLODING TECHNOLOGY.
NEW YORK: MCGRAW HILL, 1964, 220 PP., LC#64-25598.
STRESSES THE IMPERATIVES OF ADJUSTING TO THE NEW TECHNOLOGY, ONLY ONE OF WHOSE CHALLENGES IS INCREASE IN EMPLOYMENT PROBLEMS, WHICH MUST BE UNDERSTOOD AGAINST THE PROSPECT OF A RADICALLY TRANSFORMED SOCIETY. VOLUME IS BASED ON PUBLIC ADDRESSES OF THE AUTHOR, WHO HAS ADVISED THE SECRETARY OF LABOR.

0304 DODDS H.W.
THE ACADEMIC PRESIDENT "EDUCATOR OR CARETAKER?
NEW YORK: MCGRAW HILL, 1962, 294 PP., LC#61-18625.
DEALS WITH MANY REPRESENTATIONAL ISSUES, SUCH AS THE ADMINISTRATIVE COUNCIL, FACULTY PARTICIPATION IN ADMINISTRATION, BOARD OF TRUSTEES, FORMAL AND INFORMAL POWER CENTERS, AND THE NATURE OF ACADEMIC LEADERSHIP. A COMPANION VOLUME IS AN ANNOTATED BIBLIOGRAPHY (1961) PREPARED BY W.C. EELLS AND E.V. HOLLIS.

0305 DONAHO J.A.
"PLANNING-PROGRAMMING-BUDGETING SYSTEMS."
MUNICIPAL FINANCE, 40 (AUG. 67), 17-25.
DESCRIBES AND EVALUATES ADMINISTRATIVE TECHNIQUES OF PLANNED BUDGET SYSTEMS FOR GOVERNMENTAL SPENDING. DISCUSSES ROLE IN PUBLIC ADMINISTRATION AND RELATES METHODOLOGY OF ECONOMETRICS.

0306 DONALD A.G.
MANAGEMENT, INFORMATION, AND SYSTEMS.
NEW YORK: PERGAMON PRESS, 1967, 178 PP.
PROVIDES FRAMEWORK FOR NEW MANAGEMENT TECHNIQUES. OUTLINES CONCEPT OF SYSTEMS, FEEDBACK CONTROL, AND PROBLEMS IN CONTROLLING SYSTEMS. APPLIES CONCEPTS TO BUSINESS ENTERPRISES AND NON-PROFIT MAKING CONCERNS.

0307 DONNELLY D.
"THE POLITICS AND ADMINISTRATION OF PLANNING."
POLIT. QUART., 33 (OCT.-DEC. 62), 404-413.
HISTORY OF ECONOMIC AND SOCIAL WELFARE PLANNING IN UK, AND HOW POOR LOCAL GOVERNMENT ORGANIZATION AND RESOURCES HAVE HINDERED OPERATION OF PLANS.

0308 DORFMAN R. ED.
MEASURING BENEFITS OF GOVERNMENT INVESTMENTS.
WASHINGTON: BROOKINGS INST, 1965, 429 PP., LC#65-18313.
PAPERS FROM 1963 CONFERENCE, AND COMMENTS OF PARTICIPANTS ON SEVEN TYPES OF GOVERNMENT PROJECTS. EXPLORES THE FEASIBILITY OF APPLYING BENEFIT-COST ANALYSIS AND OTHER MEANS OF MEASURING GOVERNMENT INVESTMENTS. PROJECTS INCLUDE R&D, OUTDOOR RECREATION, PREVENTING HIGH SCHOOL DROP-OUTS, CIVIL AVIATION EXPENDITURES, URBAN HIGHWAYS, URBAN RENEWAL, AND SYPHILIS CONTROL.

0309 DOTSON A.
PRODUCTION PLANNING IN THE PATENT OFFICE (PAMPHLET)
INDIANAPOLIS: BOBBS-MERRILL, 1952, 13 PP.
DESCRIBES 1945 TROUBLES OF US PATENT OFFICE REGARDING DISTRIBUTION OF PATENT COPIES TO PUBLIC. ILLUSTRATES USE OF SCIENTIFIC MANAGEMENT TO EXPEDITE GOVERNMENT CLERICAL OPERATION.

0310 DOTY P.M.
"THE ROLE OF THE SMALLER POWERS."
DAEDULUS, 89 (FALL 60), 818-30.
QUESTIONS THE DESIRABILITY OF SMALLER POWERS POSSESSING NUCLEAR ARMS. PRESENTS ALTERNATIVES FOR COUNTRIES DENIED ARMS. CONCLUDES THAT ALTHOUGH A NUMBER OF SMALLER POWERS POSSESS TECHNICAL ABILITY, REJECTION OF SUCH WEAPONS IS MORE BENEFICIAL TO THEM.

0311 DOUGHERTY J.E.
"KEY TO SECURITY: DISARMAMENT OR ARMS STABILITY."
ORBIS, 4 (FALL 60), 261-83.
SEES PROPOSALS FOR ARMS CONTROL AS FAILING DUE TO LACK OF APPROPRIATE LEGAL BASIS AND ABUNDANCE OF TECHNICAL COMPLEXITIES. CRITICIZES NUCLEAR MORATORIUM EXPERIENCE AS LACKING IN INSPECTION SAFEGUARDS AND LIMITING NEEDED RESEARCH. ADVOCATES OPEN EXPRESSION OF STRENGTH ON BOTH SIDES AND CONCRETE REDUCTIONS, AS ONLY WAY TO EFFECTIVE PROGRAM.

0312 DOUGHERTY J.E.
"THE CATHOLIC CHURCH, WAR AND NUCLEAR WEAPONS."
ORBIS, 9 (WINTER 66), 845-897.
IN THE LIGHT OF THE SECOND VATICAN COUNCIL'S STAND ON THE POSSESSION AND USE OF NUCLEAR WEAPONS IN DETERRENCE AND MODERN WAR, THE AUTHOR TRACES THE CHURCH'S HISTORICAL THINKING ON THE MORALITY AND USES OF WAR. THE CONFLICTS WITHIN VATICAN TWO ARE PRESENTED, WITH SPEECHES OF MAJOR PARTICIPANTS.

0313 DOYLE S.E.
"COMMUNICATION SATELLITES* INTERNAL ORGANIZATION FOR DEVELOPMENT AND CONTROL."
CALIF. LAW REV., 55 (MAY 67), 431-448.
ARGUES THAT PROBLEM POSED BY COMMUNICATION SATELLITES IS ORGANIZATION OF INTERNATIONAL COOPERATIVE TO DEVELOP AND EXPLOIT SYSTEM. EXAMINES COMMUNICATIONS SATELLITE COOPERATION AND INTELSAT AND EXPLORES POLICY PROBLEMS THAT BECOME DIFFICULT AS SATELLITE TECHNOLOGY ADVANCES INCLUDING QUESTIONS OF PRIVATE OWNERSHIP AND DIRECT BROADCASTING.

0314 DRAPER J.W.
HISTORY OF THE CONFLICT BETWEEN RELIGION AND SCIENCE.
NEW YORK: APPLETON, 1923, 367 PP.
HOLDS THAT RELIGION AND SCIENCE ARE QUALITATIVELY DIFFERENT. RELIGIOUS FAITH IS UNCHANGEABLE AND STATIONARY, WHILE SCIENCE IS PROGRESSIVE. CHRISTIANITY (NOTABLY ROMAN CATHOLICISM) HAS USED ITS ACQUIRED POLITICAL POWER TO HINDER THE SCIENTIFIC PURSUIT OF TRUTH.

0315 DRUCKER P.F.
"'MANAGEMENT SCIENCE' AND THE MANAGER."
MANAGEMENT SCIENCE, 1 (JAN. 55), 115-118.
LOOKS AT 'MANAGEMENT SCIENCE' FROM POINT OF VIEW OF MANAGER. FOCUSES ON DETERMINING METHODOLOGY, TOOLS, AND TECHNIQUES NECESSARY TO AN ORDERLY AND SYSTEMATIC JOB OF MANAGING. CONCENTRATES ON DECISION-MAKING AND BUSINESS ENTERPRISE AND ITS STRUCTURE.

0316 DRUCKER P.F.
AMERICA'S NEXT TWENTY YEARS.
NEW YORK: HARPER & ROW, 1957, 114 PP., LC#57-7974.
EXAMINES LABOR SHORTAGES AND ENROLLMENT PRESSURES ON COLLEGES AND UNIVERSITIES IN US IN LIGHT OF POPULATION EXPLOSION. DISCUSSES ROLE OF AUTOMATION IN ECONOMY AND CONCLUDES WITH ANALYSIS OF FOREIGN AID ISSUES AND SOME PRESSING ISSUES IN DOMESTIC POLITICS (TRANSPORTATION, HOUSING, URBAN RENEWAL, MEDICAL CARE, ETC.).

0317 DUBIN R.
THE WORLD OF WORK: INDUSTRIAL SOCIETY AND HUMAN RELATIONS.
ENGLEWOOD CLIFFS: PRENTICE HALL, 1958, 448 PP., LC#58-9615.
BOOK CONCERNS AMERICAN INDUSTRY AND COMMERCE. ANALYZES WHAT PEOPLE DO WHILE WORKING AND REASONS FOR THEIR BEHAVIOR. MANY FACETS OF ORGANIZATION OF WORK: WORKING POPULATION, PRODUCTION, AND MANAGEMENT OF WORK ORGANIZATIONS ARE EXPLORED, WITH EMPHASIS UPON HUMAN FACTOR. BIBLIOGRAPHY INCLUDES SUPPLEMENTARY READINGS ON EVERY CHAPTER IN BOOK: THEORY, THE JOB, THE WORKER, AND HIS ROLE, MANAGEMENT, ETC.

0318 DUBRIDGE L.A.
"POLICY AND THE SCIENTISTS."
FOREIGN AFFAIRS, 41 (APR. 63), 571-588.
A SURVEY OF THE ROLE OF SCIENTISTS IN GOVERNMENT WITH SPECIAL ATTENTION GIVEN TO THE OFFICE OF SCIENTIFIC RESEARCH AND DEVELOPMENT, THE AEC, THE PRESIDENT'S SCIENCE ADVISORY COMMITTEE, NSF, NASA, AND VARIOUS OTHER AGENCIES.

0319 DUCKWORTH W.E.
A GUIDE TO OPERATIONAL RESEARCH.
LONDON: METHUEN, 1962, 145 PP.
DEFINES AND EXPLAINS OPERATIONAL RESEARCH AS IT APPLIES TO THE STUDY OF ADMINISTRATIVE SYSTEMS. SUMMARIZES TECHNIQUES OF APPLYING SCIENTIFIC METHODOLOGY TO STUDY OF COMPLEX ORGANIZATIONS, THEIR FUNCTIONS AND PROCESSES. INCLUDES: STATISTICS, LINEAR PROGRAMMING, QUEUEING, MONTE CARLO AND SIMULATION, GAME THEORY, CYBERNETICS, AND DECISION THEORY.

0320 DUNBAR L.W.
A REPUBLIC OF EQUALS.
ANN ARBOR: U OF MICH PR, 1966, 132 PP., LC#66-17027.
ESTIMATES COMBINED IMPACT OF CIVIL RIGHTS MOVEMENT ON US AND ITS POLITICAL IDEAS AND INSTITUTIONS. DISCUSSES SOUTH'S KEY IMPORTANCE WITHIN REPUBLIC'S CONSTITUTIONAL ORDER AND SIGNIFICANCE OF FEDERALISM TO US.

0321 DUNCAN O.D.
"THE MEASUREMENT OF POPULATION DISTRIBUTION" (BMR)"
POPULATION STUDIES, 11 (JULY 57), 27-45.
SUMMARIZES MAJOR TECHNIQUES OF DESCRIBING AND MEASURING POPULATION DISTRIBUTION. INCLUDES SPATIAL AND CATEGORICAL MEASURES OF DENSITY, CONCENTRATION, SPACING, POPULATION POTENTIAL, CENTROGRAPHY, COMMUNITY SIZE, PROXIMITY TO CENTERS, AND RURAL-URBAN CLASSIFICATION. INDICATES PROBLEMS OF EACH METHOD THAT NEED FURTHER RESEARCH.

0322 DUPRE J.S., SANFORD S.A.
SCIENCE AND THE NATION: POLICY AND POLITICS.
ENGLEWOOD CLIFFS: PRENTICE HALL, 1962, 181 PP., LC#62-9307.
APPRAISAL OF HOW GOVERNMENT CONTRACTS FOR RESEARCH HAVE ALTERED SEPARATION OF PUBLIC AND PRIVATE SPHERES; HOW INDUSTRY, GOVERNMENT, AND UNIVERSITIES HAVE FORMED A NEW PARTNERSHIP; THE ROLE PLAYED BY SCIENTISTS IN SHAPING US MILITARY AND FOREIGN POLICY; AND SCIENCE ADVISORY COMMISSION.

0323 DUPRE S., LAKOF S.A.
SCIENCE AND THE NATION.
ENGLEWOOD CLIFFS: PRENTICE HALL, 1962, 181 PP., LC#62-9307.
AN ATTEMPT TO PROVIDE A CONCISE SURVEY OF DEVELOPMENTS
DEALING WITH SCIENCE, TECHNOLOGY, AND POLITICS, WHICH ARE
DESCRIBED ONLY IN LARGE NUMBERS OF GOVERNMENT DOCUMENTS AND
SECONDARY SOURCES. SUBJECTS SUCH AS THE RELATIONSHIP BETWEEN
INDUSTRY AND RESEARCH OR BETWEEN UNIVERSITIES AND GOVERNMENT
ARE TREATED; SCIENCE AS WELL AS SCIENTISTS ARE EXAMINED
IN RELATION TO ARMS, POLITICS, AND SECURITY.

0324 DUPREE A.H.
SCIENCE IN THE FEDERAL GOVERNMENT; A HISTORY OF POLICIES AND
ACTIVITIES TO 1940.
CAMBRIDGE: HARVARD U PR, 1957, 460 PP., LC#57-5484.
TRACES POLICIES AND ACTIVITIES OF US GOVERNMENT IN
SCIENCE FROM 1789 TO 1940. BEGINS WITH ENCOURAGEMENT OF
EDUCATION BY CONSTITUTION FOUNDERS. DISCUSSES JEFFERSONIAN
ERA, EXPLORATIONS AND SURVEYS, BEGINNINGS OF CENTRAL
SCIENTIFIC ORGANIZATION, AGRICULTURAL RESEARCH, ALLISON
COMMISSION, FEDERAL SCIENCE ESTABLISHMENT, AND IMPACT OF
WWI, DEPRESSION, AND NEW DEAL.

0325 DUPUY R.E., DUPUY T.N.
"MILITARY HERITAGE OF AMERICA."
NEW YORK: MCGRAW HILL, 1956.
COMPREHENSIVE TEXT ON AMERICAN MILITARY HISTORY WHICH
TOUCHES ON IMPORTANT FOREIGN MILITARY EVENTS BEFORE AND
AFTER 1775. SPECIAL EMPHASIS PLACED ON MODERN WAR TACTICS
AND HISTORY. STRESSES TWO THEMES OF IMMUTABILITY OF PRINCI-
PLES OF WAR AND CONSTANTLY CHANGING NATURE OF ACTUAL WAGING
OF WAR. EXTENSIVE BIBLIOGRAPHY CONTAINS ITEMS ON THEORY,
POLICY, HISTORY, AND MILITARY ANALYSIS.

0326 DUSCHA J.
ARMS, MONEY, AND POLITICS.
NEW YORK: IVES WASHBURN, INC, 1964, 210 PP., LC#65-20066.
EXAMINES POLITICS OF DEFENSE SPENDING, INCLUDING ATTI-
TUDES OF CONGRESS, DEFENSE DEPARTMENT'S RELATION TO INDUS-
TRY. CONSIDERS SPENDING TOO GREAT. PROPOSES PLAN FOR PEACE
AND FOR REDUCTION IN SPENDING.

0327 DYKMAN J.W.
"REVIEW ARTICLE* PLANNING AND DECISION THEORY."
J. OF AM. INST. OF PLANNERS, 27 (NOV. 61), 335-345.
"PLANNING IS ITSELF A KIND OF DECISION-MAKING," REQUIRING
GOALS OF EQUITY AND LEGALITY, SOCIAL ACCEPTABILITY AND EFFI-
CIENCY. ANALYZES HISTORICAL FOUNDATIONS OF DECISION THEORY
FROM UTILITARIAN RATIONALITY TO NORMATIVE. QUALITATIVE THE-
ORIES. PLANNERS MUST COMBINE THEORY EXTREMES, NORMATIVE
TASKS, AND RATIONAL ACTION.

0328 DYSON F.J.
"THE FUTURE DEVELOPMENT OF NUCLEAR WEAPONS."
FOR. AFF, 38 (APRIL 60), 457-64.
RADICALLY NEW KINDS OF NUCLEAR WEAPONS ARE TECHNICALLY
POSSIBLE. MILITARY AND POLITICAL EFFECTS OF SUCH WEAPONS
WOULD BE IMPORTANT. DEVELOPMENT OF WEAPONS CAN BE ARRESTED
ONLY BY INTERNATIONAL CONTROL OF ALL NUCLEAR OPERATIONS.
AN INTERNATIONAL DETECTIVE FORCE WITH UNRESTRICTED RIGHTS
OF TRAVEL AND INSPECTION IS IMPERATIVE.

0329 EASTON D.
THE POLITICAL SYSTEM, AN INQUIRY INTO THE STATE POLITICAL
SCIENCE.
NEW YORK: KNOPF, 1953, 320 PP.
DEALS WITH CONDITION OF THE SCIENCE OF POLITICS AS IT IS
KNOWN IN THE UNITED STATES, AND WITH THE RELATIONSHIP TO IT
OF POLITICAL THEORY. DISCUSSES ROLE SCIENTIFIC REASONING HAS
PLAYED IN WESTERN WORLD AND RECENT DISILLUSIONMENT WITH IT.
DISCUSSES METHODS AND OUTLOOK FOR POLITICAL RESEARCH AND IN-
QUIRY. CRITICIZES GENERAL POLITICAL THEORY.

0330 EASTON D.
"LIMITS OF THE EQUILIBRIUM MODEL IN SOCIAL RESEARCH."
BEHAVIORAL SCIENCE, 1 (1956), 96-104.
DEALS WITH EQUILIBRIUM AS A CENTRAL THEORETICAL CONCEPT.
A MAJOR SHORTCOMING OF THIS MODEL AT PRESENT IS THE LACK OF
QUANTIFIABLE DATA IN SOCIAL RESEARCH, ESPECIALLY FOR AN
INDEX OF THE AMOUNT OF POWER HELD BY GROUPS OR INDIVIDUALS.

0331 EASTON D.
"AN APPROACH TO THE ANALYSIS OF POLITICAL SYSTEMS."
WORLD POLIT, 9 (1957), 383-401.
BELIEVES THAT SYSTEM THEORY 'WITH ITS SENSITIVITY TO THE
INPUT-OUTPUT EXCHANGE BETWEEN A SYSTEM AND ITS SETTING' IS
THE BEST METHOD OF ORGANIZING PRESENTLY DISCONNECTED POLITI-
CAL DATA INTO A GENERAL STUDY OF POLITICAL LIFE. MENTIONS
MAJOR ATTRIBUTES OF POLITICAL SYSTEMS WHICH REQUIRE SPECIAL
ATTENTION IN ORDER TO DEVELOPE A GENERALIZED APPROACH.

0332 ECKSTEIN A.
COMMUNIST CHINA'S ECONOMIC GROWTH AND FOREIGN TRADE* IMPLI-
CATIONS FOR US POLICY.
NEW YORK: MCGRAW HILL, 1966, 359 PP., LC#65-28588.
CAREFUL BREAKDOWN AND ANALYSIS OF THE FACTORS AFFECTING

THE ECONOMIC DEVELOPMENT OF COMMUNIST CHINA, ESPECIALLY
IN TERMS OF HER INFRASTRUCTURE AND TRADING PATTERNS. WEALTH
OF DATA (ALL INCLUDE 1963, SOME 1964) IS ANALYZED IN TERMS
OF CHINA'S INTERNATIONAL CAPABILITIES AND VULNERABILITIES
TO ECONOMIC PRESSURE WITH REFERENCE TO US POLICY.

0333 EDELMAN M.
THE SYMBOLIC USES OF POWER.
URBANA: U OF ILLINOIS PR, 1964, 201 PP., LC#64-20654.
GENERAL THEORETICAL TEXT. DISCUSSES REPRESENTATION IN
ADMINISTRATIVE AGENCIES WITH REFERENCE TO THE MAINTENANCE
AND DEVELOPMENT OF POWER OF AGENCY AND ITS PERSONNEL. HOLDS
THAT AN AGENCY WILL HEED ONLY THE WISHES OF THOSE PERSONS OR
ORGANIZATIONS WHICH CAN HARM THE AGENCY. IN GENERAL,
AGENCIES REPRESENT THE GROUPS THEY ARE INTENDED TO REGULATE
RATHER THAN THE PUBLIC INTEREST.

0334 EDMONDS M.
"INTERNATIONAL COLLABORATION IN WEAPONS PROCUREMENT* THE IM-
PLICATIONS OF THE ANGLO-FRENCH CASE."
INTER-AMERICAN ECON. AFF, 43 (1967), 252-264.
CONTENDS COLLABORATION BETWEEN BRITISH & FRENCH AERO-
SPACE INDUSTRIES HAS NOT OCCURRED UNIFORMLY AT ALL LEVELS.
COOPERATION AT PRODUCTION, DEVELOPMENT, ADMINISTRATIVE
LEVELS FAR OUTRANKS PROGRESS MADE AT DECISION-MAKING LEVELS.
ARGUES COLLABORATION NOT BENEFICIAL UNLESS FREE FLOW OF IN-
FORMATION ABOUT INTELLIGENCE AND RESEARCH TAKES PLACE.
DISCUSSES DIFFICULTIES, REWARDS OF EFFICIENT COLLABORATION.

0335 EHRHARD J.
LE DESTIN DU COLONIALISME.
PARIS: EDITIONS EYROLLES, 1958, 242 PP.
DISCUSSES PROBLEMS OF UNDERDEVELOPMENT IN AFRICAN NA-
TIONS, FRENCH AID AND COMMERCE, LEVELS OF INDUSTRIALIZATION
AND TECHNOLOGICAL PROGRESS, INTERNAL PRODUCTION AND EXPORTS,
AGRICULTURE, AND NECESSITY OF LONG-TERM PLANNING AND PRICE
STABILIZATION.

0336 EINAUDI L., GOLDHAMER H.
"ANNOTATED BIBLIOGRAPHY OF LATIN AMERICAN MILITARY JOURNALS"
J. OF LATIN AM. RES. REV, 2 (SPRING 67), 95-122.
ARRANGED BY COUNTRY, THIS SELECTION CONTAINS A DESCRIP-
TION OF SIZE, SCOPE, AND FORMAT OF EACH MAGAZINE AS WELL AS
ANY OTHER INFORMATION THAT SEEMS PERTINENT OR IMPORTANT.
PREPARED UNDER RAND CORPORATION AUSPICES. ALSO INCLUDES
UNANNOTATED REVIEWS AND AN APPENDIX OF REVIEWS NO LONGER
AVAILABLE.

0337 EINSTEIN A.
THE WORLD AS I SEE IT.
NEW YORK: COVICI/FRIEDE, 1939, 290 PP.
A COLLECTION OF ESSAYS AND CORRESPONDENCE PRESENTING
VIEWS ON SUCH SUBJECTS AS HISTORY, SCIENCE, PACIFISM,
NATIONALISM, DISARMAMENT, ETHICS, AND THE MEANING OF LIFE
AND RELIGION.

0338 EINSTEIN A., NATHAN O. ED., MORDAN H. ED.
EINSTEIN ON PEACE.
NEW YORK: SIMON SCHUSTER, 1960, 704 PP.
COMPILATION OF EINSTEIN'S LETTERS AND THOUGHTS ON INTER-
NATIONAL RELATIONS, ATOMIC POWER, TOTALITARIANISM, CIVIL
LIBERTIES AND RELATED MATTERS. ALSO INCLUDES SYMPATHETIC
COMMENTARY ON HIS POSITIONS BY THE EDITORS.

0339 EISENDRATH C.
"THE OUTER SPACE TREATY."
FOREIGN SERVICE J, 44 (MAY 67), 27-44.
DISCUSSES EVOLUTION OF TREATY ON OUTER SPACE EXPLORATION
COMPLETED THROUGH UN IN 1966. WORK ON TREATY BEGAN IN 1957,
WAS FOSTERED BY NASA, UN COMMITTEE ON THE PEACEFUL USES OF
OUTER SPACE, AND HAD PRECEDENT IN THE ANTARCTIC TREATY OF
1959. TREATY'S MAIN SUCCESS WAS IN CREATING DEMILITARIZED
ZONE IN OUTER SPACE.

0340 EISENMENGER R.W.
THE DYNAMICS OF GROWTH IN NEW ENGLAND'S ECONOMY, 1870-1964.
MIDDLETON: WESLEYAN U PR, 1967, 201 PP., LC#66-23926.
DESPITE ITS FEW NATURAL RESOURCES, NEW ENGLAND ENJOYS A
UNIQUE AND PRIVILEGED POSITION IN THE AMERICAN ECONOMY. THE
AUTHOR OF THIS STUDY ATTEMPTS TO ACCOUNT FOR ITS PROSPERITY
BY THE USE OF AGGREGATE ECONOMIC, SOCIAL, AND HISTORICAL
FACTORS. HE ANALYZES THE ROLE OF INHERITED WEALTH, LABOR,
EDUCATION, AND FEDERAL FISCAL POLICIES IN THE REGION'S
DEVELOPMENT.

0341 ELDERSVELD S.J., HEARD A. ET AL.
"RESEARCH IN POLITICAL BEHAVIOR" (BMR)"
AM. POL. SCI. REV, 46 (DEC. 52), 1003-1045.
FIVE PAPERS DEFINE AND ILLUSTRATE SIGNIFICANT
CONTEMPORARY DEVELOPMENTS IN POLITICAL RESEARCH. OUTLINE
REQUIREMENTS, CHARACTERISTICS, AND IMPLICATIONS OF POLITICAL
BEHAVIOR RESEARCH. SKETCH PLANS FOR SEVERAL RESEARCH
PROJECTS. INCLUDE SELECTED BIBLIOGRAPHY ON METHODS AND
TECHNIQUES OF POLITICAL BEHAVIOR RESEARCH.

0342 ELDREDGE H.W. ED.

TAMING MEGALOPOLIS: HOW TO MANAGE AN URBANIZED WORLD.
GARDEN CITY: DOUBLEDAY, 1967, 586 PP., LC#67-12878.
ESSAYS CONCERNED WITH METHODS AND WAYS TO MANAGE CITIES.
BEGIN WITH PLANNING AS A PROFESSION, AND THEN DISCUSS DATA
RESEARCH AND COMPUTER MODELS. TREAT GOVERNMENT STRUCTURE FOR
PLANNING AND NEW TOOLS FOR ANALYSIS AND CONTROL. INCLUDE
SOCIAL PLANNING, URBAN POVERTY, CITIZEN PARTICIPATION, AND
URBANIZATION OF DEVELOPING NATIONS. CONCLUDE WITH FUNCTIONAL
AND SPATIAL MACRO-PLANNING.

0343 ELDRIDGE H.T.
THE MATERIALS OF DEMOGRAPHY: A SELECTED AND ANNOTATED
BIBLIOGRAPHY.
NY: INTL UNION SCI STUDY POPULAT, 1959, 222 PP.
IDENTIFIES AND DESCRIBES SIGNIFICANT PUBLISHED WORKS IN
THE FIELD OF POPULATION ANALYSIS. CITATIONS LIMITED TO POST-
1940 PUBLICATIONS IN ENGLISH; COMPILATIONS IN OTHER LANU
GAGES ISSUED SEPARATELY. BIBLIOGRAPHY IS TOPICALLY CLAS-
SIFIED ACCORDING TO THE COMPONENTS OF POPULATION CHANGE:
BIRTH, DEATH, AND MIGRATION. CONTAINS AN AUTHOR INDEX.

0344 ELLUL J.
THE TECHNOLOGICAL SOCIETY.
NEW YORK: ALFRED KNOPF, 1964, 447 PP., LC#62-15562.
FORMULATES A COMPREHENSIVE SOCIAL PHILOSOPHY OF TECHNICAL
CIVILIZATION. EMPHASIZES THE EROSION OF MORAL VALUES BROUGHT
ON BY TECHNICISM. DISCUSSES THE HISTORICAL DEVELOPMENT OF
TECHNICAL CIVILIZATION, CHARACTERISTICS OF TECHNICAL SOCIE-
TIES, AND IMPLICATIONS FOR THE FUTURE.

0345 ELSNER H.
THE TECHNOCRATS, PROPHETS OF AUTOMATION.
SYRACUSE: SYRACUSE U PRESS, 1967, 252 PP., LC#67-14522.
STUDY OF THE TECHNOCRACY MOVEMENT FROM BEGINNING IN 1919,
TO MOVEMENT AS IT EXISTS IN THE 1960'S. THE CONCLUDING CHAP-
TER IS A SOCIOLOGICAL-POLITICAL INTERPRETATION OF TECH-
NOCRACY.

0346 EMME E.M. ED.
THE IMPACT OF AIR POWER - NATIONAL SECURITY AND WORLD
POLITICS.
PRINCETON: VAN NOSTRAND, 1959, 914 PP., LC#59-8554.
COLLECTION OF ESSAYS ON NATURE AND THEORIES OF AIR
WARFARE. DISCUSSES AIR WARFARE IN WWII AND LESSONS DRAWN.
COMPARES SOVIET AND US AIR POLICY AND EXAMINES AIR POWER IN
EUROPE AND ASIA.

0347 ENKE S.
"GOVERNMENT-INDUSTRY DEVELOPMENT OF A COMMERCIAL SUPERSONIC
TRANSPORT."
AMER. ECO. REVIEW, 57 (MAY 67), 71-79.
DISCUSSES THE PROBLEMS OF DEVELOPING AND EFFECTIVELY
USING THE SST AS A COMMERCIAL VENTURE. EXPENSE OF SUCH PRO-
GRAMS REQUIRES HEAVY FEDERAL FINANCING. CONCLUDES THAT UN-
LESS THE GOVERNMENT CAN BE GUARANTEED AT LEAST 10 PER CENT
RETURN ON INVESTMENT, COMMITMENT TO AN SST PROGRAM IS IMMA-
TURE. SUGGESTS A SEVEN-POINT GUIDELINE FOR DEVELOPING SUCH A
PROGRAM THROUGH PRIVATE ENTERPRISE BUT WITH FEDERAL AID.

0348 ENKE S. ED.
DEFENSE MANAGEMENT.
ENGLEWOOD CLIFFS: PRENTICE HALL, 1967, 404 PP., LC#67-10540.
ESSAYS EXAMINING CHANGES IN DECISION-MAKING AT THE PENTA-
GON, APPLICATION OF COST-BENEFIT ANALYSIS TO SPECIFIC DE-
FENSE PROGRAMS, PROBLEMS IN RESEARCH AND DEVELOPMENT, AND
ECONOMIC IMPACT OF DEFENSE SPENDING. ALSO DISCUSS PROBLEMS
OTHER FEDERAL AGENCIES WILL FACE IN SHIFTING TO COST-EFFEC-
TIVENESS TECHNIQUES.

0349 ENTHOVEN A.C.
"ECONOMIC ANALYSIS IN THE DEPARTMENT OF DEFENSE."
AMER. ECO. REVIEW, 53 (MAY 63), 413-423.
PROGRESS REPORT ON ECONOMISTS' WORK IN DEFENSE DEPARTMENT
ON PROBLEMS OF DETERMINING REQUIREMENTS FOR WEAPON SYSTEMS
AND FORCES. REDESIGNS PROGRAMMING SYSTEM TO HAVE COST
AND BENEFITS PLANNED TOGETHER TO REDUCE BUDGET GAP. DEVISES
PLAN FOR ALLOCATION OF RESOURCES FOR NUCLEAR AND
CONVENTIONAL FORCE REQUIREMENTS. SUGGESTS WAYS OF DEALING
WITH UNCERTAINTIES IN DEFENSE PLANNING.

0350 ERSKINE H.G.
"THE POLLS: ATOMIC WEAPONS AND NUCLEAR ENERGY."
PUB. OPIN. QUART., 27 (SUMMER 63), 155-90.
COLLECTION OF POLL RESULTS OF AMERICAN REACTIONS TO THE
EFFECT AND MEANING OF ATOMIC AND NUCLEAR ENERGY FROM 1945
TO THE PRESENT. FINDINGS OF AIPO, NORC, ROPER, AND IRA.

0351 ESTEP R.
AN AIR POWER BIBLIOGRAPHY.
MONTGOMERY: AIR U, 1956, 199 PP.
COVERS PUBLICATIONS 1950-56 ON AIR POWER, EQUIPMENT,
PERFORMANCE, LAW, PUBLIC RELATIONS, BUDGETING AND
AREAS RELATED TO USAF; 3,250 ENTRIES.

0352 ETZIONI A.
THE MOON-DOGGLE: DOMESTIC AND INTERNATIONAL IMPLICATIONS
OF THE SPACE RACE.
GARDEN CITY: DOUBLEDAY, 1964, 195 PP., $4.50.
ANALYZES AMERICAN SPACE POLICY IN TERMS OF EXCELLENT
SHORT TERM PLANNING MIRED BY A LACK OF LONG-RANGE PERSPEC-
TIVES. EXAMINES THE PATTERNS OF POLICY-MAKING, POWER
COALITIONS, INTEREST GROUPS, AND THE COLLABORATIONS OF
AGENCIES AND SERVICES INVOLVED IN THE RACE TO THE MOON
WHICH MUST BE CHANGED IF AMERICA IS TO FACE ITS DOMESTIC
AND INTERNATIONAL PROBLEMS WITHOUT LOOKING TO THE SKY FOR
SOLUTIONS.

0353 ETZIONI A.
"ON THE NATIONAL GUIDANCE OF SCIENCE."
ADMINISTRATIVE SCI. Q., 10 (JUNE-AUG. 65), 466-487.
EXAMINES MANNER IN WHICH DECISIONS ARE MADE TO SUPPORT
SCIENTIFIC ACTIVITIES. SHOWS THAT PRESENT "PLURALISTIC"
APPROACH IGNORES SCARCITY OF SCIENTIFIC MANPOWER AND URGES
ADOPTION OF MORE "SYSTEMATIC" APPROACHES, ESPECIALLY CEN-
TRALIZATION OF POLICY.

0354 EWALD R.F.
"ONE OF MANY POSSIBLE GAMES."
BACKGROUND, 9 (FEB. 66), 275-282.
AUTHOR EXPLAINS HOW CLARK AND SOHN'S MODEL OF THE DIS-
ARMED FUTURE WORLD LENDS ITSELF THROUGH GAMING AS A SOUND
TEACHING DEVICE IN INTERNATIONAL LAW AND ORGANIZATION.

0355 EYRAUD M.
"LA FRANCE FACE A UN EVENTUEL TRAITE DE NON DISSEMINATION
DES ARMES NUCLEAIRES."
POLITIQUE ETRANGERE, 32 (1967), 441-452, 4-5.
ANALYZES ECONOMIC CONSEQUENCES FOR FRANCE OF REJECTION
OF NUCLEAR DISARMAMENT TREATY, ESPECIALLY IF A LARGE NUMBER
OF NATIONS SIGN IT. ANALYZES AMERICAN INDUSTRIAL PRODUCTION
DEPENDENT UPON NUCLEAR ENERGY, AND NOTES THAT THE US HAS
THE GREATEST STOCKPILE OF NUCLEAR MATERIAL. BELIEVES THAT
IF AFRICAN COUNTRIES GRANTING FRANCE MINING CONCESSIONS
SIGN TREATY, FRENCH INDUSTRY WILL BE SERIOUSLY ENDANGERED.

0356 FADDEYEV N.
"CMEA CO-OPERATION OF EQUAL NATIONS."
INTER-AM. ECO. AFFAIRS, 4 (APR. 67).
DISCUSSION OF FIRST INTERNATIONAL ORGANIZATION OF SO
CIALIST COUNTRIES WHICH EMBODIES PRINCIPLES OF SOCIALIST
INTERNATIONALISM. PROVIDES SYSTEM OF MUTUAL ECONOMIC TIES TO
PROMOTE SOCIAL PRODUCTION AND ECONOMIC DEVELOPMENT. TRACES
HISTORY, FORMS OF ECONOMIC COOPERATION, AND PROCESSES OF
SPECIALIZATION AND COMBINATION.

0357 FAIR M.L.
"PORT AUTHORITIES IN THE UNITED STATES."
LAW AND CONTEMPORARY PROB., 26 (FALL 61), 703-714.
DISCUSSES HISTORICAL EVOLUTION OF THE PORT CONCEPT, ITS
DEVELOPMENT IN THE UNITED STATES, THE TYPES OF PORT
AUTHORITIES AND TRENDS IN TYPES OF PORT AUTHORITIES.

0358 FALK L.A., MUSHRUSH G.J., SKRIVANEK M.S.
ADMINISTRATIVE ASPECTS OF GROUP PRACTICE.
PITTSBURGH: UNIVERSITY PR, 1964, 100 PP., LC#64-16014.
LISTS 222 REFERENCES RELATED TO ADMINISTRATIVE
ASPECTS OF GROUP HEALTH PLANS PAID FOR BY INSTALLMENTS
THAT WERE PUBLISHED 1950-64. ENTRIES ARRANGED BY SUB-
JECT AND AUTHOR.

0359 FALK R.A., TUCKER R.C., YOUNG O.R.
ON MINIMIZING THE USE OF NUCLEAR WEAPONS; THREE ESSAYS;
RESEARCH MONOGRAPH NO. 23.
PRINCETON: CTR OF INTL STUDIES, 1966, 145 PP.
THREE EXTENDED ESSAYS ON THE DANGERS TO THE EXISTENCE,
STABILITY, AND REFORM OF THE INTERNATIONAL SYSTEM WHICH CAN
BE ATTRIBUTED TO THE USE OF NUCLEAR WEAPONS IN THE SYSTEM,
USE BEING GIVEN A VARIETY OF MEANINGS. FALK SEES PARADOXICAL
PROBLEMS IN THE NEED FOR BOTH REVOLUTION AND REFORMATION IN
THE SYSTEM. YOUNG FINDS INTERNATIONAL SYSTEM FAIRLY STABLE,
WHILE TUCKER'S ESSAY ON US-USSR RELATIONS IS MIDDLE-GROUND.

0360 FALK S.L.
"DISARMAMENT IN HISTORICAL PERSPECTIVE."
MILITARY REVIEW, 44 (DEC. 64), 36-48.
IN A REVIEW OF HISTORY OF PROPOSALS AND ATTEMPTS TO A-
CHIEVE ARMS CONTROL, AUTHOR DESCRIBES FOUR GENERAL CATEGOR-
IES, DISARMAMENT BY EXTERMINATION, DISARMAMENT BY IMPOSI-
TION, DISARMAMENT BY NEGOTIATION, AND UNILATERAL DISARMA-
MENT. AUTHOR SUGGESTS CAREFUL STUDY OF EARLIER PROPOSALS TO
DETERMINE APPLICABILITY OF PREVIOUS CONCEPTS IN NUCLEAR AGE.

0361 FEI J.C.H., RANIS G.
DEVELOPMENT OF THE LABOR SURPLUS ECONOMY: THEORY AND
POLICY.
HOMEWOOD: RICHARD IRWIN, 1964, 324 PP., LC#64-21024.
PRESENTS A THEORY OF DEVELOPMENT RELEVANT TO ORDINARY
LABOR SURPLUS TYPE OF UNDERDEVELOPED ECONOMY, AND ATTEMPTS
TO EXTRACT SOME POLICY CONCLUSIONS. APPROACHES PROBLEM FROM
VIEWPOINTS OF ANALYTICAL ECONOMICS, INSTITUTIONAL ECONOMICS,
AND STATISTICS. PRESENTS ANALYTICAL FRAMEWORK AT AGGREGATE
LEVEL TO EXPLAIN GROWTH IN PARTICULAR TYPE OF UNDERDEVELOPED

COUNTRY.

0362 FEIS H.
THE ATOMIC BOMB AND THE END OF WORLD WAR II.
PRINCETON: PRINCETON U PRESS, 1966, 213 PP., LC#66-13312.
TRACING OF AMERICAN AND JAPANESE POLICIES LEADING TO THE
DEFEAT OF JAPAN; RANGE OF ALTERNATIVES DISCUSSED. CONCENTRA-
TION ON ATOMIC DEVELOPMENT AND DECISIONS. POTSDAM AND SUR-
RENDER CHRONOLOGIES PRESENTED. SPECULATIONS ON FUTURE OF
THE BOMB, JAPAN AND SURVIVAL OF HUMANITY.

0363 FELD B.T.
"A PLEDGE* NO FIRST USE."
BUL. ATOMIC SCIENTISTS, 23 (MAY 67), 46-48.
AN ARGUMENT FOR THE ADOPTION OF A TREATY PLEDGING NO
FIRST USE OF NUCLEAR WEAPONS AGAINST NON-NUCLEAR NATIONS.
SUCH A TREATY MIGHT PROVIDE IMPETUS TO FURTHER STEPS FOR
ARMS CONTROL, AS WELL AS INHIBITING NUCLEAR PROLIFERATION.
SUCH A TREATY WOULD ALSO BE AN ACKNOWLEDGMENT OF THE LIMIT-
ED UTILITY OF NUCLEAR WEAPONS IN THE SOLUTION OF CONFLICT.

0364 FERBER R., VERDOORN P.J.
RESEARCH METHODS IN ECONOMICS AND BUSINESS.
NEW YORK: MACMILLAN, 1962, 573 PP., LC#62-7080.
RECOGNIZING SIMILARITIES BETWEEN PROBLEM-SOLVING
TECHNIQUES USED FOR BUSINESS AND ECONOMIC ANALYSIS OF
AGGREGATES, THIS STUDY PROVIDES GENERAL OUTLINE OF
ORGANIZATION OF RESEARCH OPERATIONS, EXPOSITION OF MAIN
APPROACHES TO RESEARCH PROBLEMS, AND DESCRIPTIONS OF
SPECIFIC RESEARCH TECHNIQUES, WITH RELATIVE MERITS OF EACH.

0365 FERRETTI B.
"IMPORTANZA E PROSPETTIVE DELL ENERGIA DI ORIGINE NUCLEARE."
MULINO, 12 (NO.131, 63), 837-46.
ANSWERS SOME GENERAL QUESTIONS ABOUT NUCLEAR ENERGY.
GIVES DIRECTIONS FOR ITS IMPROVED USE IN ITALY, AND FOR
ITS UTILIZATION AS ECONOMIC RESOURCE. DISCUSSES IMPACT OF
NUCLEAR ENERGY ON MANKIND.

0366 FIELD M.G.
SOVIET SOCIALIZED MEDICINE.
NEW YORK: FREE PRESS OF GLENCOE, 1967, 253 PP.
THIS VOLUME ILLUMINATES THE HISTORY, PROBLEMS, AND PRES-
ENT CIRCUMSTANCES OF THE SOVIET MEDICAL ESTABLISHMENT. EM-
PLOYS A SYSTEMATIC SOCIOLOGICAL APPROACH IN EXAMINING SO-
CIALIZED MEDICINE IN RELATION TO SOVIET IDEOLOGY AND POLITI-
CAL AND ECONOMIC SYSTEMS. DESCRIBES BACKGROUND, PRINCIPLES,
ORGANIZATION, ADMINISTRATION, AND FINANCES.

0367 FINK C.F.
"MORE CALCULATIONS ABOUT DETERRENCE."
J. OF CONFLICT RESOLUTION, 9 (MAR. 65), 54-65.
WEAKNESSES DEMONSTRATED IN RUSSETT'S "CALCULUS OF DETER-
RENCE" INTERPRETATIONS BECAUSE OF ASSUMPTIONS CONCERNING
NECESSARY AND SUFFICIENT QUALITIES OF HIS "CREDIBILITY AND
EFFECTIVENESS" VARIABLES AND DATA. REINTERPRETS DATA USING
2 X 2 CONTINGENCY TABLES AND FISHER'S EXACT TEST. THUS DE-
VELOPING ALTERNATE "ATTACK-NO ATTACK" HYPOTHESES.

0368 FINKELSTEIN L.S.
"THE UNITED NATIONS AND ORGANIZATIONS FOR CONTROL OF ARMA-
MENT."
INT. ORGAN., 16 (WINTER 62', 1-19.
DISCUSSES INDEPENDENT ROLE OF DISARMAMENT NEGOTIATIONS
UNDER UN GUIDANCE. SUGGESTS THAT SUBORDINATING ARMS CONTROL
TO UN MAKES TASK HARDER BECAUSE INTERESTED POWERS FAVOR
AUTONOMOUS HANDLING OF PROBLEM. SUGGESTS ARMS CONTROL
MIGHT BENEFIT IF THERE WERE A LIASON BETWEEN UN AND AGENCIES
AND IF THE AGENCIES COULD REFER FOR SETTLEMENT BY UN
CERTAIN POLITICAL QUESTIONS.

0369 FINKELSTEIN L.S.
"ARMS INSPECTION."
INT. CONCIL., 540 (JAN. 62), 5-89.
DISCUSSES FUNCTIONS OF AND NECESSARY ENVIRONMENT FOR IN-
SPECTION. POINTS OUT PROBLEMS OF INSPECTION: DETECTION AND
IDENTIFICATION, INSPECTION OF DISARMAMENT OR ARMAMENT,
THREAT TO SECURITY, SAMPLING, TACTICAL-STRATEGIC MEASURES,
PREPARATIONS TO VIOLATE, COMPLETE VS. PARTIAL PROHIBITIONS,
INTERACTION EFFECTS. DISCUSSES ORGANIZATION. MAKES RECOM-
MENDATIONS FOR MINIMAL INSPECTION AND COMPROMISE.

0370 FISHMAN B.G., FISHMAN L.
"PUBLIC POLICY AND POLITICAL CONSIDERATIONS."
REV. ECON. STAT., 39 (NOV. 57), 457-462.
PROBES VALIDITY OF VIEW-POINT URGING ECONOMISTS TO
CONCENTRATE ATTENTION ON ECONOMIC CONSIDERATIONS AND NOT
TAKE INTO ACCOUNT POLITICAL FACTORS. POINTS OUT THAT THE TWO
ARE OFTEN SO CLOSELY ALLIED AND INTERMIXED THAT THEY CANNOT
ALWAYS BE SEPARATELY CONSIDERED.

0371 FLEMING W.G.
"AUTHORITY, EFFICIENCY, AND ROLE STRESS: PROBLEMS IN THE
DEVELOPMENT OF EAST AFRICAN BUREAUCRACIES."
ADMINISTRATIVE SCI. Q., 2 (DEC. 66), 386-404.
AN ANALYSIS BY COUNTRY OF BRITISH EXPERIENCES IN EAST
AFRICA IN ATTEMPTING TO IMPOSE BUREAUCRATIC STRUCTURES UPON
EXISTING POLITICAL SYSTEMS. STRESSES IMPOSSIBILITY OF MAXI-
MIZING BOTH EFFICIENCY AND AUTHORITY, AND EXPLORES CURRENT
ATTEMPTS BY THESE NATIONS TO MODERNIZE THE NATIONAL POLITI-
CAL STRUCTURE. INCLUDES BACKGROUND FOR RESEARCH INTO VARIOUS
ASPECTS OF COLONIALISM, SOCIOLOGY, AND POLITICAL SYSTEMS.

0372 FLOOD M.M.
"STOCHASTIC LEARNING THEORY APPLIED TO CHOICE EXPERIMENTS
WITH RATS, DOGS, AND MEN."
BEHAVIORAL SCIENCE, 3 (JULY 62), 289-314.
DISCUSSES DEVELOPMENT OF NEW TECHNIQUE TO STUDY STOCHAS-
TIC BEHAVIOR USING MODERN COMPUTERS.

0373 FLORES E.
LAND REFORM AND THE ALLIANCE FOR PROGRESS (PAMPHLET)
PRINCETON: CTR FOR INTL STUDIES, 1963, 14 PP.
DISCUSSES PROSPECTS OF ALLIANCE FOR PROGRESS, ARGUING
THAT IT CAN SUCCEED ONLY IF IT ACCEPTS DRASTIC REVOLUTIONARY
CHANGE IN LATIN AMERICA, EMPHASIZING IMPORTANCE OF LAND
REFORM AS INTEGRAL PART OF CHANGE.

0374 FLORINSKY M.T.
"TRENDS IN THE SOVIET ECONOMY."
CURR. HIST., 47 (NOV. 64), 266-271.
WHEN DEALING WITH USSR DIFFICULT TO RESIST TEMPTATION TO
COMPARE WITH USA. POPULAR GROUND FOR COMPARISON IS RATE OF
ECONOMIC GROWTH WHICH AUTHOR (AND OTHERS FAMILIAR WITH
STATISTICAL METHODS) ASSERTS IS AN UNSOUND METHOD.

0375 FOGELMAN E.
HIROSHIMA: THE DECISION TO USE THE A-BOMB.
NEW YORK: CHAS SCRIBNER'S SONS, 1964, 116 PP., LC#64-21291.
COLLECTION OF WRITTEN SOURCES ON DECISION TO USE THE
ATOMIC BOMB. IN ADDITION TO SOURCES INCLUDES A GUIDE TO
RESEARCH, AN ACCOUNT OF THE RATIONALE AND METHODS OF RE-
SEARCH; INTRODUCTION TO TOPIC OF ANTHOLOGY; SUGGESTED
TOPICS FOR CONTROLLED RESEARCH; AND SUGGESTED SOURCES AND
TOPICS FOR LIBRARY RESEARCH.

0376 FOLDES L.
"UNCERTAINTY, PROBABILITY AND POTENTIAL SURPRISE."
ECONOMICA, 99 (AUG. 58), 246-254.
PRESENTS A REFUTATION OF KNIGHT'S DISTINCTION BETWEEN
RISK AND UNCERTAINTY. ARGUES THAT THE CONCEPT OF "PROBABIL-
ITY" IS SUFFICIENT TO ANALYSE BUSINESS BEHAVIOR.

0377 FOLSOM M.B., PRICE D.K., ROLL E.
BETTER MANAGEMENT OF THE PUBLIC'S BUSINESS (PAMPHLET)
NEW YORK: COMM FOR ECO DEV, 1964, 39 PP.
EXAMINES ADMINISTRATION OF GOVERNMENTAL AGENCIES, AREAS
IN GREATEST NEED OF CHANGE, AND METHODS BY WHICH BUSINESSMEN
MAY ACCOMPLISH THESE CHANGES. INCLUDES DISCUSSION OF COMMIT-
TEE FOR ECONOMIC DEVELOPMENT AND ITS ROLE IN ACCOMPLISHING
REFORMS IN GOVERNMENTAL ADMINISTRATION.

0378 FORBES H.W.
THE STRATEGY OF DISARMAMENT.
WASHINGTON: PUBL. AFF. PR., 1962, 158 PP.
DISCUSSES STEPS TAKEN TOWARDS GENERAL DISARMAMENT AND
CONCLUDES 'SUBSTANTIAL AGREEMENT AMONG THE GREAT POWERS ON
DISARMAMENT IS IMPOSSIBLE SO LONG AS EACH OF THEM SUSPECTS
OTHERS OF AGGRESSIVE INTENTIONS.'

0379 FOREIGN POLICY ASSOCIATION
"US CONCERN FOR WORLD LAW."
INTERCOM, 9 (MAY-JUNE 67), 40-47.
DISCUSSES THE CONTROVERSY OVER US ADOPTION OF THE UNI-
VERSAL DECLARATION OF HUMAN RIGHTS AND OVER THE CONNALLY
AMMENDMENT TO THE JURISDICTION OF THE INTERNATIONAL COURT
OF JUSTICE. DEMONSTRATES THE NECESSITY OF WORLD LAW FOR THE
SUPERVISION OF DISARMAMENT AND THE MAINTENANCE OF PEACE.

0380 FOREIGN POLICY ASSOCIATION
"HOW WORLD LAW DEVELOPS* A CASE STUDY OF THE OUTER SPACE
TREATY."
INTERCOM, 9 (MAY-JUNE 67), 30-32.
RELATES GOLDBERG'S SPEECH ON THE OUTER SPACE TREATY, "IN-
TERNATIONAL LAW IN THE UNITED NATIONS." GOLDBERG TREATS
THREE SUBJECTS IN SPEECH: HOW INTERNATIONAL LAW DEVELOPS,
THE RELATION OF LAW TO DIPLOMACY, AND THE RELEVANCE OF LAW
IN UN DEALING WITH PROBLEMS OF MANKIND. THE OUTER SPACE
TREATY PROMOTES COOPERATION IN SPACE EFFORTS BY THE PROHIBI-
TION OF NUCLEAR WEAPONS & BY UNIVERSAL EXPLORATION RIGHTS.

0381 FORM W.H.
"THE PLACE OF SOCIAL STRUCTURE IN THE DETERMINATION OF LAND
USE: SOME IMPLICATIONS FOR A THEORY OF URBAN ECOLOGY" (BMR)"
SOCIAL FORCES, 32 (MAY 54), 317-323.
IN STUDYING LAND CHANGE USE, AUTHOR PROPOSES THAT ECOLOGY
ABANDON ITS SUB-SOCIAL NON-ORGANIZATION ORIENTATIONS AND USE
THE FRAME OF REFERENCE OF GENERAL SOCIOLOGY. FIRST STEP IS
TO ANALYZE SOCIAL FORCES OPERATING ON LAND MARKET. FROM
A STUDY OF THIS STRUCTURE ONE OBTAINS PICTURE OF PARAMETERS
OF ECOLOGICAL BEHAVIOR, PATTERNS OF LAND CHANGE USE, AND
INSTITUTIONAL PRESSURES ON ECOLOGICAL ORDER.

0382 FORRESTER J.W.
"INDUSTRIAL DYNAMICS* A MAJOR BREAKTHROUGH FOR DECISION
MAKERS."
HARVARD BUSINESS REV., 4 (JULY-AUG. 58), 37-66.
PROPOSES NEW STUDY METHODS AND TECHNIQUES, INCLUDING COM-
PUTER TECHNOLOGY, AS WELL AS NEW CONCEPTS IN ATTEMPT TO
MAKE THE "ART OF MANAGEMENT" A PROFESSION.

0383 FORTUNE EDITORS
THE SPACE INDUSTRY: AMERICA'S NEWEST GIANT.
ENGLEWOOD CLIFFS: PRENTICE HALL, 1962, 192 PP., LC#62-18428.
DESCRIBES WHY AND HOW OF US COMMITMENT TO PROBE SPACE,
SPACE AS TODAY'S BIGGEST MANAGEMENT JOB, AND CHALLENGE TO
FREE ENTERPRISE'S TALENTS; MYSTERIES AND HAZARDS TO BE FACED
BY SPACE EXPLORERS.

0384 FOSKETT D.J.
CLASSIFICATION AND INDEXING IN THE SOCIAL SCIENCES.
LONDON: BUTTERWORTHS, 1963, 190 PP.
DEALS WITH PROBLEM OF INFORMATION DISSEMINATION AND RE-
TRIEVAL IN THE SOCIAL SCIENCES. AUTHOR DISCUSSES NATURE
OF SOCIAL SCIENCE DATA, ORGANIZATION OF SUBJECT INDEXES, AND
CLASSIFICATION SCHEMES. BIBLIOGRAPHIES AT CHAPTER ENDS WHICH
ENCOMPASS GOVERNMENT DOCUMENTS, JOURNAL ARTICLES, AND BOOKS
OF ENGLISH-LANGUAGE PUBLICATIONS AND A FEW GERMAN AND
FRENCH PUBLICATIONS FROM 1929 THROUGH 1962.

0385 FOSTER P.
EDUCATION AND SOCIAL CHANGE IN GHANA.
CHICAGO: U OF CHICAGO PRESS, 1965, 322 PP.
A CASE STUDY OF EDUCATIONAL DEVELOPMENT IN GHANA AS THE
FIRST AND MOST COMPLEX AFRICAN NATION TO ACHIEVE RECENT
INDEPENDENCE. STUDIES DOCUMENTS RELATING TO HISTORICAL
BACKGROUND OF GOLD COAST, TRADITIONS OF WESTERN EDUCATION,
AND CONTEMPORARY PRACTICES, ESPECIALLY IN SECONDARY SCHOOLS.
EXAMINES ROLE OF SCHOOL SYSTEMS AND EDUCATIONAL DEMANDS
OF ECONOMIC AND SOCIAL GROWTH.

0386 FOSTER R.B.
"UNILATERAL ARMS CONTROL MEASURES AND DISARMAMENT
NEGOTIATION."
ORBIS, 6 (SUMMER 62), 258-280.
ASSERTS THAT THE DEVELOPING ECONOMIC STRENGTH AND TECHNO-
LOGICAL CAPACITY OF THE WEST COULD INCREASE ITS MILITARY
POWER VIS-A-VIS RUSSIA. RECOMMENDS THAT USA ASSUME THE
INITIATIVE IN FUTURE DIPLOMATIC NEGOTIATIONS BY UNILATERALLY
ADOPTING LIMITED, STRATEGIC ARMS CONTROL MEASURES TO REDUCE
LIKELIHOOD OF WARS RESULTING FROM ACCIDENTS AND ESCALATION.

0387 FOSTER W.C.
"ARMS CONTROL AND DISARMAMENT IN A DIVIDED WORLD."
ANN. AMER. ACAD. POLIT. SOC. SCI., 342 (JULY 62), 80-8.
DISCUSSES REVOLUTION IN NUCLEAR WEAPONS AND THE NEED FOR
ARMS CONTROL DESPITE THE CLASH IN IDEOLOGIES. SUGGESTS EX-
PLORING POSSIBILITIES OF PEACEFUL SOLUTION ON BASIS OF
NUCLEAR STRATEGIC STANDOFF, EVOLUTION OF SOVIET UNION,
ATLANTIC COMMUNITY AND THE UN, AND COMMON INTERESTS OF THE
WESTERN AND COMMUNIST WORLDS. PRESENTS THE USA POSITION AND
HOPE FOR THE FUTURE.

0388 FOX A.B.
"NATO AND CONGRESS."
POLIT. SCI. QUART., 80 (SEPT. 65), 395-414.
ANALYSIS OF RELATIONS BETWEEN THE EXECUTIVE BRANCH AND
PERTINENT CONGRESSIONAL COMMITTEES VIS-A-VIS NATO POLICY.
THE DISPERSION OF CONGRESSIONAL CONTROL BECAUSE OF A PLETH-
ORA OF COMPETING COMMITTEES IS CONTRASTED TO POWER OF THE
JOINT COMMITTEE ON ATOMIC ENERGY.

0389 FOX W.T.R.
UNITED STATES POLICY IN A TWO POWER WORLD.
NEW HAVEN: YALE U PR, 1947, 17 PP.
DISCUSSES US-SOVIET RELATIONS, DECLARING NEED FOR US TO
SUPPORT NATIONS OF WESTERN EUROPE SO THAT THEY MAY FUNCTION
AS BUFFER STATES. ENCOURAGES FOREIGN AID TO NEUTRALS AS
SOUND ACTION, SINCE US DOES NOT NEED TO DOMINATE EUROPE TO
PREVENT SOVIETS FROM DOMINATING IT. MAJOR UNCERTAINTY
REVEALED IS EFFECT OF NUCLEAR WEAPONS IN INTERNATIONAL
AFFAIRS.

0390 FRANCIS R.G.
THE PREDICTIVE PROCESS.
RIO PIEDRAS: SOCIAL SCI RES CTR, 1960, 142 PP.
EXAMINES ROLE OF PREDICTION IN SCIENCE AND TRACES IDEA OF
PROGRESS AS ADVANCED BY STATESMEN AND PHILOSOPHERS IN
WESTERN SOCIETY, WITH PARTICULAR EMPHASIS ON ITS DEVELOP-
MENT IN US. DISCUSSES BRIEFLY PREDICTIVE PROCESS IN ECONOMIC
SPHERE.

0391 FREIDEL F. ED., POLLACK N. ED.
AMERICAN ISSUES IN THE TWENTIETH CENTURY.
SKOKIE: RAND MCNALLY & CO, 1966, 526 PP., LC#66-10803.
CONSIDER BASIC NATIONAL POLICY PROBLEMS OF EVERY DECADE
OF 20TH CENTURY. SPECIALISTS IN VARIOUS FIELDS DISCUSS
CRUCIAL DOMESTIC AND INTERNATIONAL ISSUES THAT THREATENED
US SECURITY IN EACH PERIOD. RELEVANT PHILOSOPHIES OR

PROGRAMS OF PRESIDENTS TREATED.

0392 FREYMOND J.
WESTERN EUROPE SINCE THE WAR.
NEW YORK: FREDERICK PRAEGER, 1964, 236 PP., LC#64-13495.
HISTORICAL ESSAY ON ATLANTIC EUROPE SINCE WWII, INCLUDING
APPRAISAL OF POST-WAR OUTLOOK AND STRATEGY, ECONOMIC RE-
DEVELOPMENT, CRISES OF 1950'S, AND DEBATE OF GRAND DESIGN,
USUALLY FROM FRENCH POINT OF VIEW.

0393 FRIED M.
"FUNCTIONS OF THE WORKING CLASS COMMUNITY IN MODERN URBAN
SOCIETY* IMPLICATIONS FOR FORCED RELOCATION."
J. OF AM. INST. OF PLANNERS, 33 (MAR. 67), 90-102.
AUTHOR STUDIES PROBLEMS OF RELOCATION IN URBAN CENTERS
AND FINDS THAT ADAPTATION TO RESIDENTIAL DISPLACEMENT DE-
PENDS ON VARIETY OF PSYCHOLOGICAL AND SOCIAL FACTORS. CHAR-
ACTERISTICS OF PRE-RELOCATION ENVIRONMENT INFLUENCE ADAPTA-
BILITY TO NEW ENVIRONMENT. EXAMINES WORKING-CLASS LIFE,
COMMUNITY RELATIONSHIPS, ABILITY TO ADJUST, ETC.

0394 FRIEDRICH-EBERT-STIFTUNG
THE SOVIET BLOC AND DEVELOPING COUNTRIES.
HANNOVER: VERLAG FUR LITERATUR, 1962, 39 PP.
DESCRIBES FOREIGN AID POLICIES OF SOVIET BLOC NATIONS AS
BEING PART OF POLITICAL PROGRAM TO GAIN ALLIES AMONG UNDER-
DEVELOPED NATIONS IN ECONOMIC COMPETITION WITH WEST. TAKES
NOTE OF ORGANIZATIONS FOR THIS PURPOSE AND FOR CULTURAL AND
SCIENTIFIC COOPERATION. FOCUSES PARTICULARLY ON USSR,
COMMUNIST CHINA, AND EAST GERMANY.

0395 FRISCH D.
ARMS REDUCTION: PROGRAM AND ISSUES.
NEW YORK: TWENTIETH CENTURY FUND, 1961, 162 PP.
DISCUSSES SPECIFIC PLANS FOR, AND IMPORTANT COMPONENTS
OF ARMS CONTROL. AIMS TO ADVANCE INTELLECTUAL ASPECT OF
POLICY FORMULATION.

0396 FRUTKIN A.W.
SPACE AND THE INTERNATIONAL COOPERATION YEAR: A NATIONAL
CHALLENGE (PAMPHLET)
WASHINGTON: GOVT PR OFFICE, 1965, 19 PP.
SHORT STUDY OF PRESENT SPACE PROJECTS, ROLE OF INTERNA-
TIONAL SCIENTIFIC COMMUNITY, EUROPEAN REGIONAL ORGANIZA-
TIONS, AND GLOBAL COMMERCIAL COMMUNICATIONS SATELLITE
SYSTEM.

0397 FRYKLUND R.
100 MILLION LIVES: MAXIMUM SURVIVAL IN A NUCLEAR WAR.
NEW YORK: MACMILLAN, 1962, 175 PP., LC#62-12896.
A REPORTER'S ATTEMPT TO EXPLAIN CONFLICTING PROPOSALS FOR
NUCLEAR-WAR STRATEGY. DESCRIBES IN DETAIL PROPOSED STRATEGY
WHICH COULD BROADEN US DETERRENT AND DEFENSE ABILITY, AND
HELP US TO ENDURE AN ACCIDENTAL WAR WITHOUT SENSELESS
SLAUGHTER.

0398 FULLER G.A. ED.
DEMOBILIZATION: A SELECTED LIST OF REFERENCES.
WASHINGTON: LIBRARY OF CONGRESS, 1945, 193 PP.
COMPILES A LIST OF SELECTED REFERENCES ON DEMOBILIZATION
FROM BOOKS, PAMPHLETS, AND ARTICLES WRITTEN 1943-45.
MATERIAL IS ARRANGED IN FIVE AREAS: GENERAL TREATISES, DE-
MOBILIZATION OF ARMED FORCES, INDUSTRIAL DEMOBILIZATION, DE-
MOBILIZATION OF ECONOMIC CONTROLS, AND AGRICULTURE IN THE
TRANSITIONAL PERIOD. 1,222 ENTRIES.

0399 FULLER G.H. ED.
A SELECTED LIST OF REFERENCES ON THE EXPANSION OF THE US
NAVY, 1933-1939 (PAMPHLET)
WASHINGTON: LIBRARY OF CONGRESS, 1939, 34 PP.
CONTAINS 410 LISTINGS OF CONGRESSIONAL COMMITTEE REPORTS
AND GENERAL PUBLICATION ARTICLES DISCUSSING DEVELOPMENT OF
US NAVAL FORCES PRIOR TO WWII.

0400 FULLER G.H. ED., BADEN A.L. ED.
SELECTED LIST OF RECENT REFERENCES ON AMERICAN NATIONAL
DEFENSE (PAMPHLET)
WASHINGTON: LIBRARY OF CONGRESS, 1940, 79 PP.
1,134 ARTICLES ALL PUBLISHED 1937-40 ON MANY ASPECTS OF
AMERICAN DEFENSE POLICIES, SYSTEMS, AND STRATEGIES. MANY
ARTICLES DEAL WITH DEVELOPMENT OF A LARGE US NAVY AND THE
FINANCIAL BURDEN OF AN EXPANDING ARMED SERVICE.

0401 FULLER G.H. ED.
DEFENSE FINANCING: A SELECTED LIST OF REFERENCES (PAMPHLET)
WASHINGTON: LIBRARY OF CONGRESS, 1941, 40 PP.
CONTAINS 354 LISTINGS OF CONGRESSIONAL REPORTS AND PUB-
LICATIONS OF GENERAL INTEREST ON ISSUES OF NATIONAL DEFENSE
FINANCING IN US AND FOREIGN COUNTRIES 1939-41. ALSO CONTAINS
LISTING OF ARTICLES ON WWI DEFENSE SPENDING.

0402 FULLER G.H. ED.
A LIST OF BIBLIOGRAPHIES ON QUESTIONS RELATING TO NATIONAL
DEFENSE (PAMPHLET)
WASHINGTON: LIBRARY OF CONGRESS, 1941, 21 PP.
LISTS BIBLIOGRAPHICAL RECORDS (MOST PUBLISHED BY GOVERN-

MENT AGENCIES) ON TOPICS RELATING TO US NATIONAL DEFENSE UP
TO 1940. MOST OF THE 188 ENTRIES RELATE TO THE LATE 1930'S.

0403 FULLER G.H. ED.
DEFENSE FINANCING: A SUPPLEMENTARY LIST OF REFERENCES
(PAMPHLET)
WASHINGTON: LIBRARY OF CONGRESS, 1942, 45 PP.
CONTAINS 451 LISTINGS OF BOOKS AND ARTICLES SUPPLEMENTING
1941 BIBLIOGRAPHY "DEFENSE FINANCING." HAS SEPARATE CLASSI-
FICATIONS FOR US, UK, CANADA, AUSTRALIA, AND MISCELLANEOUS.
MANY LISTINGS ARE CONGRESSIONAL DISCUSSIONS AND REPORTS.

0404 FULLER G.H. ED.
MILITARY GOVERNMENT: A LIST OF REFERENCES (A PAMPHLET)
WASHINGTON: LIBRARY OF CONGRESS, 1944, 14 PP.
CONTAINS 122 ENTRIES OF ARTICLES IN FRENCH, GERMAN, AND
ENGLISH CONCERNING LEGAL, ADMINISTRATIVE, AND SOCIOLOGICAL
PROBLEMS INVOLVED IN MILITARY JURISDICTION IN OCCUPIED
COUNTRIES. COMPILED FOR LIBRARY OF CONGRESS.

0405 GALLAHER A. JR. ED.
PERSPECTIVES IN DEVELOPMENTAL CHANGE.
LEXINGTON: U OF KY PR, 1968, 263 PP., LC#67-17844.
ANTHOLOGY OF SOCIAL SCIENTISTS' EXPLORATIONS OF ESSENTIAL
PROBLEMS OF DEVELOPMENTAL CHANGE AGAINST THE THEORETICAL
BACKGROUND AND EMPIRICAL DATA OF THE SOCIAL SCIENCES. CON-
SIDERATIONS INCLUDE PROBLEMS THAT ARISE WHEN HUMAN BEINGS
ARE CONFRONTED BY CHANGE; INVESTMENT PLANNING AND DECISION-
MAKING IN A SPECIAL CASE; AND THE PROBLEM OF WHAT CONSTI-
TUTES DEVELOPMENT.

0406 GANDILHON J.
"LA SCIENCE ET LA TECHNIQUE A L'AIDE DES REGIONS PEU DE-
VELOPPEES."
POLIT. ETRANG., (NO.3, 63), 221-40.
RECOMMENDS CLOSER ECONOMIC RELATIONS WITH UNDERDEVELOPED
REGIONS. SCIENTIFIC AID PROGRAMS SHOULD AIM TO APPLY
RESEARCH TO TECHNOLOGY. GIVES INSIGHTS INTO FRENCH SCIEN-
TIFIC SITUATION AND UN SCIENTIFIC AID PROGRAM.

0407 GANGE J.
UNIVERSITY RESEARCH ON INTERNATIONAL AFFAIRS.
WASHINGTON: AMER. COUNC. EDUC., 1958, 145 PP., $3.00.
REPORTS SURVEY OF 60 UNIVERSITIES ON STATUS, SUPPORT,
ADMINISTRATION AND PROBLEMS, OF INTERNATIONAL RESEARCH
AGENCIES. CONCLUDES THERE IS NEED FOR MORE OBJECTIVE MEA-
SURES IN ORDER TO GIVE FIELD A MORE SCIENTIFIC STATUS.

0408 GANZ G.
"THE CONTROL OF INDUSTRY BY ADMINISTRATIVE PROCESS."
PUBLIC LAW, (SUMMER 67), 93-106.
ASSESSES SUITABILITY OF INDUSTRIAL DEVELOPMENT ACT OF
1966 AND LOCAL EMPLOYMENT ACT OF 1960 AND ADMINISTRATIVE
MACHINERY THEY PROVIDE FOR IMPLEMENTING GOVERNMENT POLICY IN
RELATION TO INDUSTRY. EXAMINES EXTENT OF PROTECTION OF
INDIVIDUALS UNDER TWO LAWS. SHOWS MOVEMENT AWAY FROM LEGAL
CONTROL OVER INDUSTRY TO ADMINISTRATIVE CONTROL.

0409 GARCIA ROBLES A.
THE DENUCLEARIZATION OF LATIN AMERICA (TRANS. BY MARJORIE
URQUIDI)
NEW YORK: TAPLINGER PUBL CO, 1967, 167 PP.
COLLECTION OF SPEECHES BY AUTHOR AND OF INTERNATIONAL
DOCUMENTS TREATING ORIGINS, SCOPE, AND OBJECTIVES OF
DENUCLEARIZATION PLANS IN LATIN AMERICA. MOST IMPORTANT
EVENTS LEADING TO WORLD-WIDE TREATY ARE JOINT DECLARATION OF
1963, UN RESOLUTION 1911, FORMATION OF PREPARATORY
COMMISSION OF DENUCLEARIZATION IN LATIN AMERICA AND ITS
FIRST THREE SESSIONS.

0410 GARDNER R.N.
"COOPERATION IN OUTER SPACE."
FOR. AFF., 41 (JAN. 63), 344-59.
DEALS WITH COOPERATION IN OUTER SPACE AFFAIRS ON A BI-
LATERAL AND WORLD-WIDE BASIS FOR ULTIMATE ATTAINMENT OF
WORLD PEACE. PRESENT UN ACTIVITIES REVEAL MULTITUDE OF CO-
OPERATIVE PROJECTS DESPITE WHAT IS FELT TO BE OBSTRUCTIVE
EFFORTS BY USSR.

0411 GARDNER R.N.
"GATT AND THE UNITED NATIONS CONFERENCE ON TRADE AND DEVEL-
OPMENT."
INT. ORGAN., 18 (AUTUMN 64), 685-704.
NOTES UN'S ROLE IN HELPING TO DEFINE AND SOLVE PROBLEMS
OF INTERNATIONAL TRADE BARRIERS AND SPECIFIC PROBLEMS FACING
TRADE OF SMALL UNDER-DEVELOPED NATIONS. CITES AMBITIOUS
GOALS OF KENNEDY ROUND ON TARIFFS, AND SHOWS GATT'S COMPLEX
ROLE IN DEALING WITH THIS NEW POLICY OF ACROSS-THE-BOARD
TRADE. POINTS TO NEED FOR POLICY OF SELF-DEVELOPMENT.

0412 GARFINKEL H.
"THE RATIONAL PROPERTIES OF SCIENTIFIC AND COMMON SENSE
ACTIVITIES."
BEHAV. SCI., 5 (60), 72-83.
ARGUES THAT SCIENTIFIC RATIONALITY IS A STABLE AND
SANCTIONABLE IDEAL ONLY IN SCIENTIFIC THEORIZING ACTIONS.

WITHIN THIS METHODOLOGY, RATIONAL NORMS SHOULD BE REGARDED
AS DATA.

0413 GAUSSENS J., BONNET R.
"THE APPLICATIONS OF NUCLEAR ENERGY - TECHNICAL, ECONOMIC
AND SOCIAL ASPECTS."
IMPACT OF SCIENCE ON SOCIETY, 17 (1967), 75-99.
DISCUSSES THE NECESSARY DEVELOPMENT OF A NUCLEAR ECONOMY
AND ITS TECHNICAL PROBLEMS, EXPLORING DIFFERENT NUCLEAR
SYSTEMS AND TRAINING DEMANDS. CONCLUDES THAT THE SOCIAL
CHANGES WILL BE POSITIVE, RAISING LIVING STANDARDS AND IN-
DUSTRIAL CAPABILITY.

0414 GAVIN J.M.
WAR AND PEACE IN THE SPACE AGE.
NEW YORK: HARPER & ROW, 1958, 304 PP., LC#58-11396.
US MISSILE, SPACE, ATOMIC POWER DEVELOPMENT FOUND BEHIND
USSR. SUGGESTS VITAL ALTERATIONS OF MILITARY, SCIENTIFIC,
TECHNOLOGICAL GOALS, TRAINING IMPROVEMENTS, PSYCHOLOGICAL
INVENTIVENESS, MOBILE WEAPONS SYSTEM, HIGH PRIORITY FOR
SATELLITE PROGRAM, AND STRATEGY FOR PEACE TO MAKE WAR
UNLIKELY.

0415 GEERTZ C. ED.
OLD SOCIETIES AND NEW STATES: THE QUEST FOR MODERNITY IN
ASIA AND AFRICA.
NEW YORK: FREE PRESS OF GLENCOE, 1963, 310 PP., LC#63-8416.
STUDIES POLITICAL DEVELOPMENT IN STATES WHICH HAVE
ACHIEVED INDEPENDENCE SINCE 1945. INCLUDES COMPARATIVE
STUDIES OF NEW STATES; CULTURAL POLICY; POLITICAL RELIGION;
THE INTEGRATIVE REVOLUTION; EQUALITY, MODERNITY
AND CIVIL POLITICS; PROBLEMS OF LAW IN AFRICA; ROLE OF
EDUCATION DEVELOPMENT; AND POLITICAL SOCIALIZATION AND
CULTURE CHANGE.

0416 GERMANY FOREIGN MINISTRY
DOCUMENTS ON GERMAN FOREIGN POLICY 1918-1945, SERIES C
(1933-1937) VOLS. I-V.
WASHINGTON: US GOVERNMENT, 1954, 3562 PP.
CHRONICLES RISE OF THIRD REICH IN GERMANY, CONSISTING
ENTIRELY OF DOCUMENTS DESCRIBING IMMENSE RANGE OF GERMAN
DIPLOMATIC ACTIVITY, INCLUDING LETTERS, TELEGRAMS, AND
MEMORANDA, SENT AND RECEIVED BY GERMAN FOREIGN MINISTRY.
PUBLISHED DURING 1954-66.

0417 GILPIN R.
AMERICAN SCIENTISTS AND NUCLEAR WEAPONS POLICY.
PRINCETON: U. PR., 1962, 352 PP.
TRACES AMERICAN SCIENTIFIC THOUGHT FROM EARLY POST-HIRO-
SHIMA POLICY (OR LACK OF SIGNIFICANT POLICY) THROUGH DEVEL-
OPMENT OF VARIOUS IDEALISTIC THEORIES TO THE EVENTUAL EMERG-
ENCE OF PRESENT SOCIAL MATURITY. DEPICTS SCIENTISTS AS BE-
ING FACED WITH THE CHOICE OF WORKING FOR DISARMAMENT OR DE-
TERRENCE IN SEEKING WORLD STABILITY, BUT AS BECOMING RESOLV-
ED TO THE INEVITABILITY OF THE LATTER.

0418 GINZBERG E.
MANPOWER FOR GOVERNMENT (PAMPHLET)
CHICAGO: PUBLIC PERSONNEL ASSN, 1958, 31 PP.
ATTEMPTS 10-YEAR FORECAST OF MAJOR MANPOWER ISSUES FACING
GOVERNMENT. DIVIDED INTO THREE PARTS, IT DISCUSSES: BASIC
TRENDS, SUGGESTED ACTION TO SECURE RESOURCES, AND
CONSIDERATION OF HOW BEST TO USE RESOURCES AVAILABLE. LISTS
WAYS OF INDUCING YOUTHS TO JOIN GOVERNMENT SERVICE AND MEANS
OF IMPROVING PUBLIC RELATIONS.

0419 GLADDEN E.N.
BRITISH PUBLIC SERVICE ADMINISTRATION.
NEW YORK: STAPLES PRESS, 1961, 328 PP.
DETAILED HISTORICAL AND ANALYTICAL STUDY OF THE FUNC-
TIONS, STRUCTURE, AND ORGANIZATION OF ALL BRANCHES OF
BRITISH PUBLIC ADMINISTRATION: EMPHASIS IS ON EFFICIENCY
RATHER THAN RESPONSIBILITY.

0420 GLADSTONE A.E.
"THE POSSIBILITY OF PREDICTING REACTIONS TO INTERNATIONAL
EVENTS."
J. SOC. ISSUES, 11 (1955), 21-28.
SEES GREAT UNCERTAINTY AS TO WHICH VARIABLES ARE RELEVANT
FOR PREDICTION OF WAR, AS RETARDING PROBLEM IN ANY SCIENTIF-
IC INVESTIGATION OF WAR. SUGGESTS DEVISING CONCEPTUAL SCHEME
AS FRAMEWORK FOR INVESTIGATION AND PROCEEDS TO OFFER PRE-
LIMINARY OUTLINE OF SCHEME OF FACTORS IN INTERNATIONAL SITU-
ATION WHICH MAY BE RELEVANT TO OCCURANCE OF WAR.

0421 GLAZER M.
THE FEDERAL GOVERNMENT AND THE UNIVERSITY.
PRINCETON: PRIN U INDUS REL CTR, 1966, 4 PP.
CONTAINS MAGAZINE AND JOURNAL ARTICLES DEALING WITH
FEDERAL GOVERNMENT SUPPORT OF SOCIAL SCIENCE RESEARCH AND
IMPACT OF PROJECT CAMELOT. ALL ENTRIES ARE IN ENGLISH AND
WERE PUBLISHED 1960-66. ARRANGED ACCORDING TO FOLLOWING
TOPICS: GOVERNMENT-UNIVERSITY RELATIONS, GOVERNMENT SUPPORT
FOR SOCIAL SCIENCE RESEARCH, AND PROJECT CAMELOT.

0422 GOBER J.L.

"FEDERALISM AT WORK."
NATIONAL CIVIC REV., 56 (MAY 67), 260-264.
DISCUSSION OF PROBLEMS OF INTERAGENCY COOPERATION AS IL-
LUSTRATED IN JELLICO, TENNESSEE. CITES SUDDEN GROWTH OF PRO-
GRAMS AND FACILITIES AND REACTION OF MUNICIPAL GOVERNMENT IN
SEEKING STATE AID IN COORDINATING STATE AND FEDERAL AGEN-
CIES. DISCUSSES CONSTRICTIVE EFFORTS OF TVA AND STATE PLAN-
NING COMMISSION.

0423 GODDARD V.
THE ENIGMA OF MENACE.
LONDON: STEVENS, 1959, 110 PP.
PHILOSOPHICAL DISCUSSION OF PEACE THROUGH STRENGTH. DIS-
CUSSES PEACE AND DEFENSE AS STATES OF MIND THAT MUST BE
ACHIEVED THROUGH REALIZATION THAT WEAPONS AND WARFARE ARE
NOT VALID MEANS OF SETTLING DIFFERENCES AMONG MEN.

0424 GOLD N.L.
REGIONAL ECONOMIC DEVELOPMENT AND NUCLEAR POWER IN INDIA.
WASHINGTON: NATL PLANNING ASSN, 1957, 110 PP., LC#57-14761.
EXAMINES CASE STUDY IN INDIA OF USE OF ATOMIC ENERGY TO
AID ECONOMIC DEVELOPMENT THROUGH INDUSTRIAL DEVELOP-
MENT. DISCUSSES POWER NEEDS, INDUSTRY EXPANSION EFFECTS ON
TRADE, FINANCING, AND FUTURE USE OF IT.

0425 GOLDBERG A.
"ATOMIC ORIGINS OF THE BRITISH NUCLEAR DETERRENT."
INT. AFF., 40 (JULY 64), 409-429.
'BRITISH ATOMIC ENERGY PROGRAMME IN BOTH ITS MILITARY AND
CIVIL ASPECTS WAS A LOGICAL AND INEVITABLE HISTORIC
EVOLUTION.'

0426 GOLDHAMMER H., SPEIER H.
"SOME OBSERVATIONS ON POLITICAL GAMING."
WORLD POLIT., 12 (59), 71-83.
REVIEWS RECENT ADVANCES BY SOCIAL SCIENCE DIVISION OF
RAND CORPORATION IN PROCEDURE FOR STUDYING FOREIGN AFFAIRS
BY POLITICAL GAMING. POINTS OUT VALUE OF SUCH METHODS IN
DEVELOPING A LEVEL OF PREDICTABILITY OF POLITICAL BEHAVIOR.

0427 GOLDSEN J.M. ED.
INTERNATIONAL POLITICAL IMPLICATIONS OF ACTIVITIES IN OUT-
ER SPACE.
SANTA MONICA: RAND, 1960.
TRANSCRIPT OF OCT. 59 CONFERENCE. INCLUDES PAPERS ON
'PUBLIC OPINION AND THE DEVELOPMENT OF SPACE TECHNOLOGY' BY
G. A. ALMOND, ON 'INTERNATIONAL IMPLICATIONS OF OUTER SPACE
ACTIVITIES' BY K. KNORR, AND ON 'OUTER SPACE AND INTERNA-
TIONAL POLITICS' BY K. W. DEUTSCH.

0428 GOLDSEN J.M. ED.
OUTER SPACE IN WORLD POLITICS.
NEW YORK: PRAEGER, 1963, 180 PP., $5.00.
ESSAYS EXPLORING THE CONSEQUENCES OF SPACE TECHNOLOGY
FOR DIPLOMATIC AND MILITARY POLICY-MAKERS.

0429 GOLDSTEIN W.
"KEEPING THE GENIE IN THE BOTTLE* THE FEASIBILITY OF A
NUCLEAR NON-PROLIFERATION AGREEMENT."
BACKGROUND, 9 (AUG. 65), 137-146.
BELIEVES THAT THE NON-NUCLEAR NATIONS WILL BE COMPELLED
TO GO NUCLEAR IN THE 'SEVENTIES IF THE 5 NUCLEAR POWERS DO
NOT REACH A NON-PROLIFERATION AGREEMENT SOON. ANALYZES ROAD-
BLOCKS TO SUCH AGREEMENT AND PROPOSES SPECIFIC STEPS FOR
AVOIDING THEM NOW WHILE THERE IS TIME.

0430 GOLDSTEIN W.
"THE SCIENCE ESTABLISHMENT AND ITS POLITICAL CONTROL."
VIRGINIA QUART. REV., 43 (SUMMER 67), 353-371.
EXAMINES DIFFERENTIAL RATE OF CHANGE BETWEEN SCIENTIFIC
INNOVATION AND POLITICAL ADJUSTMENT. CONSIDERS RESULTING
NEED FOR NEW INSTITUTIONS OF POLITICAL CONTROL. DISCUSSES
CONSEQUENCES OF SCIENTIFIC DEVELOPMENT AND MEASUREMENT OF
SIZE OF SCIENTIFIC ESTABLISHMENT. ADVOCATES RATIONAL
ORDERING OF SCIENTIFIC ACTIVITY TO ENCOURAGE ENLARGEMENT OF
INDIVIDUAL FREEDOM AND OF SOCIAL WELFARE.

0431 GOLEMBIEWSKI R.T.
ORGANIZING MEN AND POWER: PATTERNS OF BEHAVIOR AND LINE-
STAFF MODELS.
NEW YORK: RAND MCNALLY & CO, 1967, 277 PP., LC#66-19446.
CHALLENGES NOTION THAT "STAFF" IN COOPERATIVE ENTERPRISES
SHOULD BE OUTSIDE CHAIN OF COMMAND, AND THAT IT SHOULD AND
DOES PROVIDE SERVICE RATHER THAN EXERT CONTROL. DEVELOPS NEW
MODEL OF LINE-STAFF RELATIONS THAT WILL PERMIT EFFECTIVE
MANAGERIAL ACTION.

0432 GOLOVINE M.N.
CONFLICT IN SPACE: A PATTERN OF WAR IN A NEW DIMENSION.
NEW YORK: ST. MARTIN'S, 1962, 146 PP.
TRACES DEVELOPMENT OF ORBITAL SYSTEMS, GROWTH OF AERO-
SPACE TECHNOLOGY. STUDIES POTENTIAL UTILIZATION OF AEROSPACE
WEAPONRY AND ITS EFFECT ON STRATEGY. SUPPORTS PANAMA HYPO-
THESIS AFFIRMING USA NEED TO OCCUPY STRATEGIC AREAS OF
SPACE. SUGGESTS EVENTUAL FULL-SCALE ORBITAL WAR AS ONLY
HUMANE SOLUTION TO EAST-WEST CONFLICTS.

0433 GORDON B.K.
"NUCLEAR WEAPONS: RUSSIAN AND AMERICAN."
CURR. HIST., 42 (MAY 62), 281-286.
DISCLOSES NO 'GLARING MISSILE-GAP' AND ASSESSES USA
STRATEGIC FORCES ('VARIETY OF NUMBERS AND POTENTIAL
INVULNERABILITY'). USA, STILL PROFITING PARTLY FROM ITS
GEOGRAPHY, SEEMS TO BE FAVORED. BECAUSE OF TARGET-PLACEMENTS
(ONES THE COMMUNISTS WOULD HAVE TO NEUTRALIZE ALL AT ONCE
IN ORDER TO MAKE AGGRESSION PROFITABLE), USA ARSENAL MORE
POWERFUL WITHOUT POSSESSING MILITARY INSTRUMENTS OF VICTORY.

0434 GORDON G.
THE LEGISLATIVE PROCESS AND DIVIDED GOVERNMENT; A CASE STUDY
OF THE 86TH CONGRESS.
AMHERST: U MASS, BUR OF GOVT RES, 1966, 112 PP.
CASE STUDY OF HOUSING ACT OF 1959 SEEKS TO DETERMINE
EFFICACY OF RESPONSIBLE DEMOCRATIC GOVERNMENT IN NON-
PARLIAMENTARY SYSTEM; DISCUSSES PROBLEMS OF LEGISLATION WHEN
PRESIDENT IS OF DIFFERENT PARTY THAN CONGRESSIONAL
MAJORITY. REVIEWS CONCEPT OF DIVIDED GOVERNMENT, PRESIDENCY
OF EISENHOWER, AND VARIABLES AFFECTING LEGISLATIVE PROCESS.
HOUSING ACT EXAMINED AT EACH STAGE FROM PROPOSAL TO BILL.

0435 GORDON L.
"THE ORGANIZATION FOR EUROPEAN ECONOMIC COOPERATION."
INT. ORGAN., 10 (FEB. 56), 1-11.
CONTENDS OEEC HAS HAD INFLUENCE ON ATTITUDES AND ACTIONS
OF MEMBER STATES. EXAMINES SUCCESSES IN ALLOCATION OF AID,
TRADE AND PAYMENTS LIBERALIZATION, PRODUCTIVITY INCREASE,
AND CURRENCY STABILIZATION. OEEC FAILED IN RECOVERY PRO-
GRAMS, ECONOMIC INTEGRATION.

0436 GORDON W.J.J.
SYNECTICS; THE DEVELOPMENT OF CREATIVE CAPACITY.
NEW YORK: HARPER & ROW, 1961, 177 PP., LC#61-10237.
DATED ACCOUNT OF GORDON'S FIRM, ITS DEVELOPMENT, AND HIS
METHOD OF INSPIRING CREATIVITY. TRACES HISTORY OF RESEARCH
INTO DEVELOPMENT OF CREATIVITY, DESCRIBES HOW IT OPERATES,
AND DISCUSSES SOME OF ITS APPLICATIONS IN INDUSTRY. AIMED
AT TOP EXECUTIVES AND RESEARCHERS, THE PROGRAM ORIGINATED
AND UTILIZED MANY TECHNIQUES NOW CURRENT.

0437 GOULD J.M.
THE TECHNICAL ELITE.
NEW YORK: AUGUSTUS M KELLEY, 1966, 178 PP., LC#66-15566.
ANALYZES EMERGENCE AND SCOPE OF TECHNICIANS WHO
INFLUENCE DECISION-MAKING IN GOVERNMENT AND BUSINESS TODAY.
STUDIES THEIR CHARACTERISTICS AND THREAT THAT "PUBLIC POLICY
CAN BE CAPTIVATED BY THEM IN FUTURE." CONCENTRATES ON MEN IN
INDUSTRIAL FIELD WHO DETERMINE AMOUNT OF US PRODUCTIVITY.

0438 GOULDNER A.W.
"PATTERNS OF INDUSTRIAL BUREAUCRACY."
NEW YORK: FREE PRESS OF GLENCOE, 1954.
STUDY OF BUREAUCRATIC ORGANIZATION DERIVED FROM DIRECT
SYSTEMATIC OBSERVATION OF MODERN FACTORY ADMINISTRATION. IN-
QUIRES INTO TENSIONS AND PROBLEMS EVOKED BY BUREAUCRATIZA-
TION UNDERMINING THE CONSENT OF THOSE GOVERNED. BIBLIOGRAPHY
OF BOOKS AND ARTICLES PUBLISHED IN FRENCH AND ENGLISH
BETWEEN 1921-51. ARRANGED IN ONE ALPHABETICAL LISTING.

0439 GOWING M.
BRITAIN AND ATOMIC ENERGY 1939-1945.
NEW YORK: ST MARTIN'S PRESS, 1964, 464 PP.
FIRST AUTHORITATIVE ACCOUNT OF ROLE PLAYED BY BRITAIN IN
DEVELOPMENT OF THE FIRST ATOMIC BOMBS. AUTHOR IS HISTORIAN
AND ARCHIVIST FOR UK ATOMIC ENERGY AUTHORITY. ILLUSTRATES
RELATIONSHIP BETWEEN SCIENCE AND GOVERNMENT.

0440 GRANICK D.
THE RED EXECUTIVE.
NEW YORK: DOUBLEDAY, 1960, 334 PP.
SOVIET INDUSTRIAL SYSTEM RUN BY MANAGERIAL CLASS SIMILAR
TO AMERICAN COUNTERPART. AMERICAN AND RED EXECUTIVES POSSESS
SIMILAR EDUCATION AND EXPERIENTIAL BACKGROUNDS. RED EXECU-
TIVES ENJOYS GREATER STATUS AND WEALTH, BUT LACK DECISION
MAKING POWER AND PERSONAL SECURITY.

0441 GRANICK D.
THE EUROPEAN EXECUTIVE.
GARDEN CITY: DOUBLEDAY, 1962, 384 PP., LC#62-07635.
ANALYZES EUROPEAN ECONOMIC MANAGEMENT, ESPECIALLY IN
GREAT BRITAIN, BELGIUM, GERMANY, AND FRANCE. DISCUSSES THE
TECHNOCRAT, ENTREPRENEURSHIP, LABOR PRACTICES, MANAGEMENT
CONCEPTS, AND OWNER-MANAGER RELATIONS.

0442 GRAVIER J.F.
AMENAGEMENT DU TERRITOIRE ET L'AVENIR DES REGIONS FRANCAISES
PARIS: FLAMMARION, 1964, 336 PP.
CONCERNS TOWN AND COUNTRY PLANNING, ESPECIALLY IN FRANCE.
DISCUSSES GEOGRAPHIC CONDITIONS AND HOW THEY AFFECT THE
ECONOMY, INDUSTRIALIZATION, REFORM IN CITY AND COUNTRY
PLANNING, REFORMS IN PARIS, ETC. AUTHOR BELIEVES REFORM
TO BE IMPEDED BY BUREAUCRACY.

0443 GREEN H.P., ROSENTHAL A.

GOVERNMENT OF THE ATOM.
NEW YORK: ATHERTON PRESS, 1963, 281 PP., LC#63-8916.
STUDY OF JOINT COMMITTEE ON ATOMIC ENERGY, FOCUSING ON
COMMITTEE'S POWER RELATIONS WITH EXECUTIVE BRANCH AND
CONGRESS. ANALYZES COMMITTEE'S SOURCES OF AUTHORITY AND
ITS TECHNIQUES AS LEGISLATOR AND POLICY-MAKER. STUDY IS
BASED ON THEORY THAT COMMITTEE'S BEHAVIOR RESEMBLES THAT OF
HIGHER ECHELONS IN EXECUTIVE BRANCH.

0444 GREEN P.
DEADLY LOGIC* THE THEORY OF NUCLEAR DETERRENCE.
COLUMBUS: OHIO STATE U PR, 1966, 361 PP., LC#66-23258.
ANALYSIS OF THE INTELLECTUAL ARGUMENTS, GENERAL THEORIES,
AND "SCIENTIFIC METHODS" ADVOCATED AND EMPLOYED BY THE "REP-
UTABLE" SOCIAL SCIENTISTS WHO CONCERN THEMSELVES WITH SPEC-
ULATING ON, AND AFFECTING AMERICAN DETERRENCE POLICY. FINDS
THEIR SCIENTISM "SPURIOUS" AND METHODS INAPPROPRIATE. IS A
SERIOUS, THOROUGH STUDY.

0445 GREENBERG D.S.
"THE SCIENTIFIC PORK BARREL."
HARPER'S, 232 (JAN. 66), 90-92.
NOTES TREMENDOUS INCREASE IN GOVERNMENT SUPPORT OF SCI-
ENTIFIC RESEARCH SINCE WWII, EMPHASIZING GROWING TENSION
BETWEEN GOVERNMENT AND SCIENTISTS OVER HOW MONEY IS TO BE
SPENT, AND DEFINING MECHANICS OF GRANT DISTRIBUTION AS
INFLUENCED BY POLITICS.

0446 GREENFIELD K.R.
COMMAND DECISIONS.
NEW YORK: HARCOURT., 1959, 575 PP.
CHRONOLOGICAL TREATMENT OF THE TWENTY MOST IMPORTANT
MILITARY DECISIONS OF WW 2. MORAL AND POLITICAL PRINCIPLES
HASTENED USA ENTRY INTO FULL-SCALE WAR. LATER IN WAR, AXIS
AND ALLIED MILITARY STRATEGY (ASIA AND EUROPE) PREVAILED
FOCUSES ATTENTION ON ARDENNES COUNTER-OFFENSIVE AND
EVALUATES DECISION TO USE THE ATOMIC BOMB.

0447 GREGG P.M., BANKS A.S.
"DIMENSIONS OF POLITICAL SYSTEMS: FACTOR ANALYSIS OF A CROSS
POLITY SURVEY."
AM. POL. SCI. REV., 59 (1965), 602-614.
DATA OF SURVEY PROVIDES EVIDENCE FOR INFERRING 7 BASIC
POLITICAL DIMENSIONS: ACCESS, DIFFERENTIATION, CONSENSUS,
SECTIONALISM, LEGITIMATION, INTEREST, AND LEADERSHIP. STUDY
PROVIDES CONCEPTS AROUND WHICH THEORY CONSTRUCTION AND
RESEARCH SHOULD PROCEED.

0448 GRENIEWSKI H.
"INTENTION AND PERFORMANCE: A PRIMER OF CYBERNETICS OF PLAN-
NING."
MANAGEMENT SCIENCE, 11 (JULY 65), 263-282.
THE OBJECT OF A GOAL IS ALWAYS A RELATIVELY ISOLATED PRO-
SPECTIVE SYSTEM; THE GOAL IS A CERTAIN STATE OF THE OUTPUT;
THE MEANS ARE THE STATES OF THE CONTROLLED INPUTS. RELATIONS
AMONG GOALS, MEANS, AND CIRCUMSTANCES ARE ANALYZED; PLANNING
IS GIVEN A GAME THEORETICAL INTERPRETATION; THE IMPLEMENTA-
TION OF A PLAN IS A 2 PERSON GAME, THE PLANNER AND THE CIR-
CUMSTANCES BEING THE TWO PLAYERS.

0449 GRETTON P.
MARITIME STRATEGY - A STUDY OF DEFENSE PROBLEMS.
NEW YORK: FREDERICK PRAEGER, 1965, LC#65-25485.
DISCUSSES HISTORY AND PRINCIPLES OF MARITIME STRATEGY,
FACTORS AFFECTING IT (NUCLEAR WEAPONS), AND INSTRUMENTS
OF MARITIME STRATEGY (SUBMARINES, AIR-CRAFT CARRIERS,ETC.).
EXAMINES SIZE OF BRITISH FORCES AND THAT OF POTENTIAL
ENEMIES.

0450 GRIFFITH E.S.
"THE CHANGING PATTERN OF PUBLIC POLICY FORMATION."
AM. POL. SCI. REV., 38 (JUNE 44), 445-459.
CONSIDERS CHANGES IN OVER-ALL CULTURE OF WHICH PUBLIC
POLICY FORMATION IS A PART AND MORE PRECISE CHANGES IN
POLICY FORMATION.

0451 GRIFFITH E.S. ED.
RESEARCH IN POLITICAL SCIENCE: THE WORK OF PANELS OF RE-
SEARCH COMMITTEE, APSA.
PRINCETON* UNIV. REF. SYSTEM, 1948, 238 PP., LC#49-63042.
ARTICLES, MANY BY LEADING MEN IN THE FIELD, DISCUSSING
PROBLEMS OF POLITICAL SCIENCE RESEARCH. IN ADDITION TO
STANDARD DIVISIONS, STUDY OF WAR, MILITARY OCCUPATION,
AND POLITICAL COMMUNICATIONS ARE INCLUDED. EDITOR
CLOSES WITH CHAPTERS ON METHOD AND PROSPECTS. INCLUDES
LIST OF SOURCES.

0452 GRIFFITH S.B.
"COMMUNIST CHINA'S CAPACITY TO MAKE WAR."
FOR. AFF., 43 (JAN. 62), 217-236.
ASSESSES COMMUNIST CHINA'S MILITARY CAPABILITIES IN TERMS
OF: ATOMIC-NUCLEAR SYSTEMS, PRESENT LEADERSHIP AND REGIME,
EXISTANT AND POTENTIAL POPULATION, TECHNICAL PERSONNEL, GEO-
GRAPHICAL POSITION, AND LEVEL OF IDEOLOGICAL COMMITMENT TO
THE PARTY. ALSO EXAMINES STRUCTURE AND RESOURCES OF PEOPLE'S
LIBERATION ARMY.

0453 GRIFFITHS F.
"THE POLITICAL SIDE OF 'DISARMAMENT'."
INT. J., 22 (SPRING 67), 293-305.
CONTENDS THAT APPROACH TO DISARMAMENT AND ARMS CONTROL
IGNORED RECENT METHODS OF POLITICAL ANALYSIS. EXPRESSES NEED
FOR THEORETICAL PERSPECTIVE ON ARMS PROBLEM. POLITICAL AC-
TION NECESSARY FOR INTERNATIONAL CHANGE CAN COME ABOUT ONLY
THROUGH DEVELOPMENT OF THEORY OF INTERNATIONAL RELATIONS.
PREDICTS A POSSIBLE TRANSNATIONALIZATION OF INTERESTS IN
WHICH NATIONAL SELF-DETERMINATION BECOMES OBSOLETE.

0454 GRODZINS M. ED., RABINOWITCH E. ED.
THE ATOMIC AGE: FORTY-FIVE SCIENTISTS AND SCHOLARS SPEAK
ON NATIONAL AND WORLD AFFAIRS.
NEW YORK: BASIC, 1963, 616 PP.
DOCUMENTS EVOLUTION OF INTERRELATIONSHIP OF WORLD OF SCI-
ENCE AND POLITICS. TRACES FAILURE TO ACHIEVE INTERNATIONAL
CONTROL OF ATOMIC ENERGY, ATTEMPTS TO PREVENT WAR, END OF
USA NUCLEAR MONOPOLY, DEVELOPMENT OF ATOMIC WEAPONS AND
POLICY, PROSPECTS FOR DISARMAMENT AND ARMS CONTROL.

0455 GROSSER G.H. ED. ET AL.
THE THREAT OF IMPENDING DISASTER: CONTRIBUTIONS TO THE
PSYCHOLOGY OF STRESS.
CAMBRIDGE: M.I.T. PR., 1964, 335 PP.
THEORETICAL AND CLINICAL STUDY OF REACTIONS TO PERSONAL
AND IMPERSONAL THREATS: NUCLEAR DISASTER, SOMATIC DISEASES,
TORTURE, DEATH FROM NATURAL CAUSES. STUDIES PERSONALITIES OF
MERCURY ASTRONAUTS. ATTEMPS TO ESTABLISH PATTERN OF REACTION
AND TO RELATE REACTIONS TO ETHNIC VALUE-SYSTEMS.

0456 GROSSMAN G.
ECONOMIC SYSTEMS.
ENGLEWOOD CLIFFS: PRENTICE HALL, 1967, 120 PP., LC#67-10741.
COMPARES AND ANALYZES SYSTEMATIC APPROACHES TO BALANCING
NATIONAL ECONOMY UNDER CAPITALIST, SOCIALIST, AND MIXED
ECONOMIES. DISCUSSES THEORIES AND PRACTICE TODAY IN US,
USSR, AND YUGOSLAVIA AND IMPORTANCE OF WORKER, MANAGER, AND
CONSUMER IN EACH SYSTEM.

0457 GRUBER R. ED.
SCIENCE AND THE NEW NATIONS.
NEW YORK: BASIC, 1961, 314 PP., $6.50.
DISCUSS SCIENTIFIC AID TO SOCIAL AND ECONOMIC PROBLEMS
OF NEWLY DEVELOPING COUNTRIES.

0458 GRUNEWALD D., BASS H.L.
PUBLIC POLICY AND THE MODERN COOPERATION: SELECTED
READINGS.
NEW YORK: APPLETON, 1966, 380 PP., LC#66-10939.
STUDIES IN PUBLIC POLICY AND MODES OF COOPERATION. VIEWS
ISSUE OF LARGENESS IN BUSINESS COOPERATIONS AS
ECONOMICALLY, SOCIALLY, AND POLITICALLY SIGNIFICANT.
DISCUSSES ANTITRUST LAW AND POLICY; PUBLIC POLICY
TOWARD REGULATED SECTOR; TARIFFS, CARTELS, AND BUSINESS
ABROAD; AND SOCIAL SIGNIFICANCE OF THE MODERN COOPERATION.

0459 GUETZKOW H. ED.
SIMULATION IN SOCIAL SCIENCE: READINGS.
ENGLEWOOD CLIFFS: PRENTICE HALL, 1962, 188 PP., LC#62-16887.
CONSIDERS SUCH TOPICS AS SIMULATED BUREAUCRACIES, USE OF
SIMULATION IN INTER-NATION RELATIONS, CARNEGIE TECH MANAGE-
MENT GAME, AND COMPUTER SIMULATION OF PEAK-HOUR OPERATIONS
IN BUS TERMINALS. DEALS WITH NATURE AND PURPOSE OF SIMULA-
TION AND FURNISHES SOURCE MATERIAL ON ITS USE IN MILITARY
AND INDUSTRIAL OPERATIONS. CLASSIFIED BIBLIOGRAPHY
INCLUDED.

0460 GUILBAUD G.T.
WHAT IS CYBERNETICS?
NEW YORK: CRITERION, 1959, 126 PP.
DISCUSSES CYBERNETICS IN THE BROADEST SENSE - THE THEORY
OF NETWORKS, COMMUNICATION, AND CONTROL. DISCUSSION IS NOT
LIMITED TO ELECTRONICS AND AUTOMATION, BUT INCLUDES BIOLOG-
ICAL AND PSYCHOLOGICAL ASPECTS OF COMMUNICATION THEORY.

0461 GULICK L. ED., URWICK L. ED.
PAPERS ON THE SCIENCE OF ADMINISTRATION.
NY: COLUMBIA U, INST PUB ADMIN, 1937, 195 PP., LC#37-25327.
DISCUSSES ADMINISTRATION FROM SCIENTIFIC ORIENTATION,
ATTEMPTING TO FORMULATE WHAT HAS COME TO BE KNOWN AS
OPERATIONAL RESEARCH. TREATS ADMINISTRATION AS A
TECHNICAL PROBLEM, CONTROL PROCESSES, STANDARDIZATION OF
NOMENCLATURE, ENVIRONMENTAL ASPECTS, AND BASIC
FUNCTIONALISM. GULICK ATTEMPTS INTEGRATION OF SCIENCE,
VALUES, AND ADMINISTRATION.

0462 GULICK M.C.
NONCONVENTIONAL INFORMATION SYSTEMS SERVING THE SOCIAL
SCIENCES AND THE HUMANITIES; A BIBLIOGRAPHIC ESSAY (PAPER)
AVAILABLE THRU URS: UNPUBLISHED, 1967, 24 PP.
GUIDE TO LITERATURE ON UNCONVENTIONAL INFORMATION SYSTEMS
AND CENTERS. INCLUDES ABSTRACTING JOURNALS, SPECIFIC ARTI-
CLES, INDEXES, ANNUALS, GOVERNMENT REPORTS, UNPUBLISHED RE-
PORTS, AND BIBLIOGRAPHIES. MAJORITY OF ENTRIES PUBLISHED IN
1960'S. OVER 200 ITEMS COVERED. AUTHOR DEFINES PROBLEM AND

SCOPE.

0463 GUTMANN P.M. ED.
ECONOMIC GROWTH: AN AMERICAN PROBLEM.
ENGLEWOOD CLIFFS: PRENTICE HALL, 1964, 181 PP., LC#64-16246.
AMERICA'S ECONOMIC GROWTH IS COMPARED TO THAT OF
OTHER COUNTRIES. INCLUDES ANALYSIS OF ANATOMY OF US
ECONOMIC GROWTH. SPECIFIC ASPECTS OF ECONOMIC GROWTH
COVERED INCLUDE: GOALS IN THIS DECADE; COMPARATIVE
GROWTH RATES; CAUSES OF ECONOMIC GROWTH; IMPEDIMENTS
TO IT; POLICIES FOR GROWTH.

0464 HAAS E.B., SCHMITTER P.C.
"ECONOMICS AND DIFFERENTIAL PATTERNS OF POLITICAL INTEGRA-
TION: PROJECTIONS ABOUT UNITY IN LATIN AMERICA."
INT. ORGAN., 18 (AUTUMN 64), 705-37.
PRESENTS THESIS THAT 'UNDER MODERN CONDITIONS THE RELA-
TIONSHIP BETWEEN ECONOMIC AND POLITICAL UNION HAD BEST BE
TREATED AS A CONTINUUM.... POLITICAL IMPLICATIONS CAN BE
ASSOCIATED WITH MOST MOVEMENTS TOWARD ECONOMIC INTEGRATION
EVEN WHEN THE CHIEF ACTORS THEMSELVES DO NOT ENTERTAIN SUCH
NOTIONS AT THE TIME OF ADOPTING THEIR NEW CONSTUITIVE CHAR-
TER.' CITES LAFTA AS EXAMPLE.

0465 HABERER J.
"POLITICS AND THE COMMUNITY OF SCIENCE."
AMER. BEHAVIORAL SCIENTIST, 10 (MAY 67), 0-22.
BERATES SCIENTIFIC COMMUNITY IN GENERAL FOR LACK OF SO-
CIAL CONSCIENCE AND COWARDICE IN FACE OF POLITICAL PRES-
SURES.

0466 HADLEY A.T.
THE NATIONS SAFETY AND ARMS CONTROL.
NEW YORK: VIKING, 1961, 150 PP.
COMPREHENSIVE EXPLORATION OF SOME PRACTICAL MEASURES
THAT CAN BE USED TO SOLVE PROBLEM OF NUCLEAR TESTING.
PROVIDES CERTAIN CRITERIA BY WHICH ARMS CONTROL SCHEMES CAN
BE JUDGED.

0467 HAINES G., HEIDER F., REMINGTON D.
"THE COMPUTER AS A SMALL-GROUP MEMBER."
ADMINISTRATIVE SCI. Q., 6 (DEC. 61), 360-374.
A STUDY OF A COMPUTER AS A MEMBER IN A TASK ORIENTED
GROUP; SHOWING ORGANIZATION CHANGES, EMOTIONAL REACTIONS,
HOW TO FACILITATE SUCH A CHANGE, DISCUSSION OF MECHANISMS
TENDING TO RETARD SUCH AN INNOVATION, AND QUESTIONS FOR
FURTHER STUDY OF THE RELATIONS BETWEEN MAN AND THINKING
MACHINES.

0468 HALEY A.G. ED., HEINRICH W. ED.
FIRST COLLOQUIUM ON THE LAW OF OUTER SPACE.
VIENNA: SPRINGER VERLAG, 1959.
RECORD OF PROCEEDINGS OF SPACE LAW CONFERENCE, DISCUSSING
LEGAL BOUNDARIES, SCIENTIFIC SPACE STRATEGY, PROBLEMS OF
SOVEREIGNTY, AND INTERNATIONALIZATION OF OUTER SPACE.

0469 HALEY A.G.
SPACE LAW AND GOVERNMENT.
NEW YORK: APPLETON, 1963, 584 PP., $15.00.
RANGES FROM THE TRADITIONAL BASES OF INTERNATIONAL LAW
AND PROBLEMS OF NATIONAL SOVEREIGNTY, ACROSS TECHNOLOGICAL
CAPABILITIES AND QUESTIONS OF LIABILITY AND REGULATION, TO
THE ROLE OF INTERGOVERNMENTAL AND NONGOVERNMENTAL AGENCIES
IN FOCUSING ATTENTION ON SCIENTIFIC AND LEGAL ASPECTS OF
SPACE EXPLORATION. A COMPREHENSIVE, DEFINITIVE STUDY OF
LEGAL AND SOCIOLOGICAL ISSUES OF SPACE FLIGHT.

0470 HALLE L.J.
THE COLD WAR AS HISTORY.
NEW YORK: HARPER & ROW, 1967, 434 PP.
INTERPRETATION OF COLD WAR AS CYCLICAL PHENOMENON IN
HISTORY OF ALL INTERNATIONAL CONFLICTS. ANALYZES HISTORICAL
CIRCUMSTANCES AND DIPLOMATIC RELATIONS OF EAST AND WEST FROM
WWII THROUGH KENNEDY ADMINISTRATION AND CUBAN CRISIS.

0471 HALPERIN M.H.
LIMITED WAR: AN ESSAY ON THE DEVELOPMENT OF THE THEORY AND
AN ANNOTATED BIBLIOGRAPHY (OCCASIONAL PAPER NO. 3)
CAMBRIDGE: HARV CTR INTL AFFAIRS, 1962.
ANNOTATED LISTING OF OVER 300 BOOKS AND ARTICLES ON LIM-
ITED WARFARE. ARRANGED BY AUTHOR.

0472 HALPERIN M.H.
CHINA AND THE BOMB.
NEW YORK: FREDERICK PRAEGER, 1965, 166 PP., LC#65-15646.
AN ANALYSIS OF CHINESE FOREIGN POLICY OBJECTIVES, AND THE
ROLE OF NUCLEAR WEAPONS IN CHINESE DOCTRINE. THE EFFECTS OF
AMERICAN CONFRONTATIONS WITH CHINA IN ASIA AS A MOTIVE FOR
OBTAINING AND USING NUCLEAR WEAPONS. DISCUSSES THE COST
OF THE PROGRAM TO CHINA AND OUTLINES DIFFERENT CAPABILITY
LEVELS AND STRATEGIES SHE MAY ATTAIN. SINO-SOVIET DISPUTE
AND AMERICAN RESPONSES TO A NUCLEAR CHINA ARE DISCUSSED.

0473 HALPERIN M.H., PERKINS D.H.
COMMUNIST CHINA AND ARMS CONTROL.
CAMBRIDGE: HARV CTR ASIAN STUD, 1965, 191 PP.

ATTEMPTS TO IDENTIFY AND CLARIFY FACTORS AFFECTING
FORMULATION OF COMMUNIST CHINA'S POLICIES TOWARD ARMS
CONTROL AND DISARMAMENT ISSUES. ASSESSES IMPLICATIONS OF
SUCH POLICIES, PARTICULARLY FOR US SECURITY AND ARMS CONTROL
OBJECTIVES. CONSIDERS RELEVANT POLITICAL, IDEOLOGICAL,
ECONOMIC, TECHNOLOGICAL, MILITARY, AND CULTURAL FACTORS, AS
WELL AS HISTORICAL AND TRADITIONAL ATTITUDES OF THE CHINESE.

0474 HALPERIN M.H.
CHINA AND NUCLEAR PROLIFERATION (PAMPHLET)
CHICAGO: U CHI, CTR POLICY STUDY, 1966, 48 PP.
EXAMINES CHINESE ATTITUDES TOWARD NUCLEAR PROLIFERATION.
FINDS THAT CHINESE POLICY HAS BEEN MARKED BY GREAT CAUTION
IN DESIRE TO AVOID NUCLEAR ATTACK. FEELS THAT CHINESE
DEVELOPMENT OF NUCLEAR CAPACITY MIGHT LEAD THEM TO TAKE
GREATER RISKS IN CARRYING OUT COMMUNIST REVOLUTION. ALSO
DISCUSSES CHINA'S LIKELY EVALUATION OF DANGERS AND
OPPORTUNITIES OF FURTHER NUCLEAR EXPANSION TO INDIA, JAPAN.

0475 HALPIN A.W.
THEORY AND RESEARCH IN ADMINISTRATION.
NEW YORK: MACMILLAN, 1966, 352 PP., LC#66-11578.
TREATS THEORIES BEHIND RESEARCH ON EDUCATIONAL
ADMINISTRATION AND PRESENTS SUBSTANTIVE RESEARCH RESULTS.
STUDIES RELATIONSHIP BETWEEN VERBAL AND NONVERBAL BEHAVIOR
AND RESULTS OF DISCREPANCIES; REFLECTS ON NATURE OF
SCIENTIFIC INQUIRY AND ITS PERTINENCE FOR RESEARCH IN
EDUCATION.

0476 HALSEY A.H.
"THE CHANGING FUNCTIONS OF UNIVERSITIES IN ADVANCED
INDUSTRIAL SOCIETIES."
HARVARD EDUCATIONAL REV., 30 (SPRING 60), 118-127.
WESTERN CULTURE'S COLLEGES AND UNIVERSITIES, IN
ASSUMING ADDED FUNCTIONS OF RESEARCH AND PROFESSIONAL
TRAINING, HAVE BECOME MORE CLOSELY INTEGRATED WITH SOCIETY
IN GENERAL AND HAVE INCREASED THEIR POTENTIAL AS SOURCES
OF ECONOMIC AND SOCIAL CHANGE.

0477 HAMBERG D.
"SIZE OF ENTERPRISE AND TECHNICAL CHANGE."
ANTI-TRUST LAW AND ECO. REVIEW, 1 (JULY-AUG. 67), 43-52.
STUDIES IMPACT, PAST AND PRESENT, OF TECHNICAL CHANGE
ON OPTIMAL SIZE OF ENTERPRISES, AND RELATIONSHIP OF SIZE
TO TECHNICAL INNOVATION. DISPUTES EQUATING LARGENESS WITH
INCREASED EFFICIENCY, STATING THAT MANY LARGE FIRMS WERE
MERELY AMALGAMATIONS OF PREVIOUSLY EXISTING COMPANIES.
CONCEDES THAT PRODUCTION OF NEW TECHNOLOGY IS LINKED TO
SIZE OF ENTERPRISE.

0478 HAMMOND P.E. ED.
SOCIOLOGISTS AT WORK.
NEW YORK: BASIC BOOKS, 1964, 391 PP., LC#64-21090.
ACCOUNT OF HISTORIES OF MAJOR RESEARCH PROJECTS BY
13 SOCIOLOGISTS. ANSWERS SUCH QUESTIONS AS WHY
INVESTIGATORS UNDERTAKE RESEARCH, HOW TO ADAPT THEORY TO
REALITY, HOW TO CAPITALIZE ON UNLUCKY ACCIDENTS.

0479 HANSON A.H.
"PLANNING AND THE POLITICIANS* SOME REFLECTIONS ON ECONOMIC
PLANNING IN WESTERN EUROPE."
INT. REV. OF ADMIN. SCI., 32 (1966), 277-286.
AUTHOR CONTENDS THAT ECONOMIC PLANNING SHOULD BE A COMBI-
NATION OF ECONOMISTS, POLITICIANS, AND ADMINISTRATORS WORK-
ING TOGETHER JOINTLY. ADMINISTRATORS AND POLITICIANS ARE
NEEDED TO DEVISE THE MACHINERY AND FORMULATE RULES AND REGU-
LATIONS WHEREBY BROAD OBJECTIVES MAY BE TRANSLATED INTO DE-
TAILED AND CONSISTENT DECISIONS. COMPARES AND CONTRASTS WHAT
INDIVIDUAL COUNTRIES IN EUROPE ARE NOW DOING.

0480 HARDIN L.M.
"REFLECTIONS ON AGRICULTURAL POLICY FORMATION IN THE
UNITED STATES."
AM. POL. SCI. REV., 42 (OCT. 48), 881-905.
CRITICISM OF AGRICULTURAL ADMINISTRATION AND CONTENT OF
AGRICULTURAL POLICY.

0481 HARDT J.P., HOFFENBERG M. ET AL.
MATHEMATICS AND COMPUTERS IN SOVIET ECONOMIC PLANNING.
NEW HAVEN: YALE U PR, 1967, 320 PP., LC#67-13435.
AMERICAN ECONOMISTS DESCRIBE PROGRESS SOVIETS HAVE MADE
IN DEVELOPING AND APPLYING MATHEMATICAL METHODS AND COMPUTER
TECHNIQUES IN ACTUAL SOVIET PLANNING. DISCUSS PROBLEMS THAT
WILL FACE THEM IN FUTURE. ANALYZE ASPECTS OF INFORMATION,
CONTROL, LINEAR PROGRAMMING, AND USE OF OPTIMIZING MODELS
IN PLANNING.

0482 HARMAN H.H.
MODERN FACTOR ANALYSIS (2ND REV. ED.)
CHICAGO: U OF CHICAGO PRESS, 1967, 474 PP., LC#67-20572.
COVERS BASIC FOUNDATIONS OF FACTOR ANALYSIS, DIRECT AND
DERIVED SOLUTIONS, FACTOR MEASUREMENTS, AND PROBLEM
MATERIAL. INCLUDES DISCUSSION OF IMPACT OF COMPUTERS.

0483 HARPER S.N.
THE GOVERNMENT OF THE SOVIET UNION.

PRINCETON: VAN NOSTRAND, 1938, 204 PP.
DISCUSSES SOVIET INSTITUTIONS, GOVERNMENTAL STRUCTURES,
AND METHODS OF GOVERNING IMMEDIATELY PRECEDING AND AFTER
BOLSHEVIK RISE TO POWER. INCLUDES ECONOMIC STRUCTURES AND
PLANS, PARTY POLICY, LAW-MAKING, PUBLIC ADMINISTRATION, AND
PUBLIC SERVICES. ALSO TREATS ROLE OF INDIVIDUAL IN A
COLLECTIVIZED STATE, INTERNATIONAL RELATIONSHIPS, GOAL OF
WORLD REVOLUTION, AND 1937-38 TREASON TRIALS.

0484 HARRIS F.R.
"POLITICAL SCIENCE AND THE PROPOSAL FOR A NATIONAL SOCIAL
SCIENCE FOUNDATION."
AM. POL. SCI. REV. 61 (FALL 67), 1088-1095.
US SENATOR DISCUSSES NEED FOR A NATIONAL SOCIAL SCIENCE
FOUNDATION TO PROMOTE INNOVATIVE AND ORIGINAL RESEARCH INTO
US SOCIAL AND POLITICAL PROBLEMS. FEELS SUCH A FOUNDATION
WOULD GIVE NEW AUTHORITY, PRESTIGE, AND FUNDS TO SOCIAL
SCIENCES, PRESENTLY "SECOND CLASS CITIZENS" OF NSF AND
RECEIVING AT BEST ONLY TEN PER CENT OF NSF BUDGET.

0485 HARRISON S.L.
"NTH NATION CHALLENGES* THE PRESENT PERSPECTIVE."
ORBIS, 9 (SPRING 65), 155-170.
THE SPREAD OF NUCLEAR WEAPONS TO MANY COUNTRIES IS ALMOST
CERTAIN IN THE NEXT THREE DECADES. THE SPREAD OF NUCLEAR
TECHNOLOGY AND FACILITIES FOR PEACEFUL USE SEEN AS PRIME
FACTOR. AUTHOR URGES USA TO GIVE NUCLEAR WEAPONS TO NATO, AS
IT WILL AID SOLIDARITY WHILE ONLY HURRYING THE INEVITABLE.

0486 HART B.H.L.
STRATEGY (REV. ED.)
NEW YORK: FREDERICK PRAEGER, 1954, 420 PP., LC#54-09111.
HISTORY OF MILITARY STRATEGY FROM FIFTH CENTURY B.C. TO
PRESENT, EMPHASIZING WORLD WARS, FUNDAMENTALS OF STRATEGY,
AND GRAND STRATEGY.

0487 HARTIGAN R.S.
"NONCOMBAT IMMUNITY* REFLECTIONS ON ITS ORIGINS AND PRESENT
STATUS."
REV. OF POLITICS, 29 (APR. 67), 204-220.
CONTENDS THAT STATEMENT OF NONCOMBATANT CIVILIAN IMMUNITY
IN INTERNATIONAL LAW DOES NOT REPRESENT ETHICAL & MORAL
OBLIGATIONS. FEELS LAW ACHIEVED PRESENT FORM THROUGH CUSTOM
RATHER THAN DEDUCTIVE MORAL REASONING. SUMMARIZES PHILOSOPH-
ICAL/HISTORICAL EVOLUTION OF CIVILIAN IMMUNITY DURING MIL-
ITARY ATTACK. EXAMINES DEBATE ON RELEVANCY OF NONCOMBATANT
IMMUNITY DURING NUCLEAR ATTACK. PROPOSES SOLUTION OF DEBATE.

0488 HARVARD UNIVERSITY LAW SCHOOL
INTERNATIONAL PROBLEMS OF FINANCIAL PROTECTION AGAINST
NUCLEAR RISK.
NEW YORK: ATOMIC INDUS FORUM, 1959, 96 PP.
STUDIES PROBLEMS DERIVING FROM POSSIBILITY OF SERIOUS
NUCLEAR INDUSTRIAL ACCIDENT AS TO LIABILITY LIMITATIONS,
INSURANCE, PROCESSING OF CLAIMS, COMPUTING PREMIUMS, AND
ROLE OF GOVERNMENT. ALSO CONCERNED WITH PROBLEMS OF
INTERNATIONAL COOPERATION IN THESE LAWSUITS.

0489 HASKINS C.P.
THE SCIENTIFIC REVOLUTION AND WORLD POLITICS.
NEW YORK: HARPER & ROW, 1964, 115 PP., LC#63-8132.
SCANS NATURE AND DIRECTION OF CURRENTS IN SCIENCE AND
TECHNOLOGY AS THEY AFFECT PRESENT AND FUTURE ASPECTS OF US
FOREIGN POLICY. SHOWS HOW GROWTH OF TECHNOLOGY HAS
INFLUENCED NEW AND SEMI-DEVELOPED NATIONS, COMMUNIST
COUNTRIES, AND US ATTITUDES TOWARD THESE NATIONS.

0490 HASSON J.A.
THE ECONOMICS OF NUCLEAR POWER.
LONDON: LONGMANS, GREEN & CO, 1965, 160 PP.
DEVELOPMENT OF METHODOLOGICAL FRAMEWORK TO STUDY NEW IN-
DUSTRY OF NUCLEAR POWER AND ITS EFFECT ON SOCIAL WELFARE IN-
CLUDING NUCLEAR PROGRAMS IN US, UNITED KINGDOM, AND INDIA,
AND ECONOMIC DECISIONS OF NUCLEAR DEVELOPMENT.

0491 HATHAWAY D.A.
GOVERNMENT AND AGRICULTURE: PUBLIC POLICY IN A DEMOCRATIC
SOCIETY.
NEW YORK: MACMILLAN, 1963, 412 PP., LC#61-11797.
DISCUSSION OF THE ROLE OF GOVERNMENT IN DETERMINING FARM
POLICY. SEES AGRICULTURAL POLICY AS PART OF A NATIONAL
ATTEMPT AT DEVELOPING A UNIFORMLY PROSPEROUS, STABLE,
CAPITALIST ECONOMY.

0492 HAUSMAN W.H. ED.
MANAGING ECONOMIC DEVELOPMENT IN AFRICA.
CAMBRIDGE: M I T PRESS, 1963, 253 PP., LC#63-16233.
ANTHOLOGY OF PAPERS ON MANAGEMENT OF AFRICAN ECONOMIC DE-
VELOPMENT COVERING PLANNING, MANPOWER, TECHNICAL ASSISTANCE,
CAPITAL, FOREIGN AID, LEGAL ASPECTS, AND US ROLE.

0493 HAWLEY A.H.
"ECOLOGY AND HUMAN ECOLOGY"
SOCIAL FORCES, 22 (MAY 44), 398-405.
INDICATES DEFICIENCIES IN STUDY OF HUMAN ECOLOGY AND PRO-
POSES METHODS FOR REORGANIZATION OF THE SUBJECT. CRITICIZES

FAILURE TO MAINTAIN WORKING RELATIONSHIP BETWEEN HUMAN
ECOLOGY AND BIOECOLOGY, PREOCCUPATION WITH CONCEPT OF
COMPETITION, AND PERSISTENT EMPHASIS ON "SPATIAL
RELATIONS." CALLS FOR ECOLOGISTS TO RECOGNIZE THEIR SUBJECT
AS A SOCIAL SCIENCE.

0494 HAYEK F.A.
THE COUNTER-REVOLUTION OF SCIENCE.
GLENCOE: FREE PR., 1952, 225 PP.
EXAMINATION OF HISTORICAL ROLES ASSUMED BY NATURAL AND
SOCIAL SCIENCES. THEORETICAL DISCUSSION OF MAJOR ISSUES IN
LATTER INCLUDES CONCEPTS OF SAINT-SIMON AND COMTE. SEVERAL
DIFFERENT METHODS AS WELL AS CERTAIN SIGNIFICANT ASPECTS OF
THE SOCIAL SCIENCES ARE REVIEWED.

0495 HAYTON R.D.
"THE ANTARCTIC SETTLEMENT OF 1959."
AMER. J. INT. LAW, 54 (APR. 60), 349-71.
BRIEF HISTORY OF ANTARCTIC EXPLORATION. ACCOUNTS OF IGY
AND WASHINGTON CONFERENCE ON ANTARCTICA. PRINCIPLES OF
CONFERENCE EMBODIED IN TREATY ENSURING USE OF ANTARCTICA
FOR EXCLUSIVELY PEACEFUL PURPOSES. INCLUDES CRITICAL ANALY-
SIS OF TREATY PROVISIONS AND SPECULATIONS CONCERNING FUTURE
INTERNATIONAL ROLE OF AREA.

0496 HAZARD J.N.
"POST-DISARMAMENT INTERNATIONAL LAW."
AMER. J. OF INT. LAW, 61 (JAN. 67), 78-83.
DISCUSSES THE LIMITATIONS OF A PROPOSAL BY O.V. BOGDANOV
(USSR) AT 1966 CONFERENCE OF INTERNATIONAL LAW ASSOCIATION,
THAT COMPLETE WORLD DISARMAMENT WILL NOT ONLY ELIMINATE THE
NEED FOR LARGE STANDING ARMIES, BUT ALSO CREATE A PACIFISTIC
INTERNATIONAL SPIRIT WHICH WILL MAKE EVEN A UN ARMY UNNECES-
SARY. AUTHOR SUGGESTS THAT BOGDANOV'S REPORT GIVES VAL-
ID GOAL, BUT UNDERESTIMATES THE STEPS TO REACH IT.

0497 HAZLEWOOD A.
THE ECONOMICS OF DEVELOPMENT: AN ANNOTATED LIST OF BOOKS
AND ARTICLES PUBLISHED 1958-1962.
LONDON: OXFORD U PR, 1964, 104 PP.
CONFINED TO ENGLISH-LANGUAGE PUBLICATIONS OF PERIOD 1958-
1962. ORGANIZED BY CONTENT AND TYPE OF STUDY: THEORIES AND
PROBLEMS; HISTORICAL STUDIES; AREA STUDIES; NATIONAL IN-
COME AND COMPONENTS; POPULATION, LABOR, AND MANAGEMENT;
AGRICULTURE AND LAND; INDUSTRY; COMMERCE AND TRANSPORT;
MONEY AND BANKING; GOVERNMENT; INTERNATIONAL ECONOMICS.

0498 HEADLEY J.C., LEWIS J.N.
PESTICIDE PROBLEM: AN ECONOMIC APPROACH TO PUBLIC POLICY.
BALTIMORE: JOHNS HOPKINS PRESS, 1967, 141 PP., LC#66-28503.
DEALS WITH STUDY OF ENVIRONMENTAL PROBLEMS TO DEVELOP
ANALYSES AND INFORMATION AS BASIS FOR POLICY ON USE OF
PESTICIDES. PROPOSES THAT USE MUST BE CONCERNED WITH COSTS
AND RETURNS AND URGES "DEVELOPMENT OF REASONABLE POLICIES
GOVERNING USE." GIVES BACKGROUND, ALTERNATIVES, PROBLEMS OF
EFFECT AND DETERMINATION OF EFFECT, AND RESEARCH NEEDS.

0499 HECKSCHER G.
"GROUP ORGANIZATION IN SWEDEN."
PUBLIC OPINION QUART., 3 (JAN. 39), 130-135.
DISCUSSES END OF LAISSEZ-FAIRE AND DEVELOPMENT OF CO-
OPERATIVE ASSOCIATIONS AND INDUSTRIAL UNIONS IN SWEDEN SINCE
THE 1880'S. EMPHASIZES TREND TOWARD CENTRALIZED AUTHORITY.
NOTES RAPID EXPANSION OF AGRICULTURAL ASSOCIATIONS FROM
1929-1939.

0500 HEER D.M.
AFTER NUCLEAR ATTACK: A DEMOGRAPHIC INQUIRY.
NEW YORK: FREDERICK PRAEGER, 1965, 405 PP., LC#65-12928.
FOCUSES ON THE DEMOGRAPHIC IMPACT ON THE US OF TWO TYPES
OF NUCLEAR ATTACKS: ATTACKS ON MILITARY AND INDUSTRIAL TAR-
GETS, AND ATTACKS ON ONLY MILITARY TARGETS. DISCUSSES THE
PROBABLE COMPOSITION OF US POPULATION AFTER NUCLEAR ATTACK,
PRESSURES FOR MIGRATION FOLLOWING ATTACK AND THE CONGRUENCE
OF MIGRATION WITH NATIONAL NEEDS, PREDICTION OF POPULATION
COMPOSITION 20 YEARS AFTER ATTACK, AND POST-ATTACK ECONOMY.

0501 HEILBRONER R.L.
THE FUTURE AS HISTORY.
NEW YORK: HARPER, 1960, 211 PP.
DEMONSTRATES EFFECTS OF MILITARY TECHNOLOGY AND UNDER-
DEVELOPED COUNTRIES ON AMERICA. THE ABILITY TO UNDERSTAND
AND COPE WITH A FUTURE ANTAGONISTIC TO THE WEST IS STRESSED.
COMMUNISM, SOCIALISM, TECHNOLOGY AND PLANNING APPRAISED.

0502 HEILBRONER R.L.
THE LIMITS OF AMERICAN CAPITALISM.
NEW YORK: HARPER & ROW, 1967, 134 PP., LC#66-21708.
DISCUSSION OF IMPACT OF CORPORATE SYSTEM ON TOTAL ENVIRON-
MENT. CHANGES IN POWER, INFLUENCE, AND TECHNOLOGY AS THEY
AFFECT CORPORATE SECTOR OF ECONOMY. HIGH MILITARY PRODUCTION
HAS SLOWED DECLINE, BUT IN FUTURE CORPORATE STRUCTURE WILL
BE MUCH LESS INFLUENTIAL.

0503 HEKHUIS D.J. ED., MCCLINTOCK C.G. ED., BURNS A.L. ED.
INTERNATIONAL STABILITY: MILITARY, ECONOMIC AND POLITICAL

DIMENSIONS.
NEW YORK: WILEY, 1964, 296 PP., $6.00.
    ESSAYS DEFINE STABILITY, ANALYZE THREATS TO STABILITY,
AND STUDY MEANS FOR ALLEVIATING INSTABILITY. STUDY MUTUAL
DETERRENCE, REGIONAL DEFENSE, DISARMAMENT, ARMS CONTROL.

0504 HELLER D.
THE KENNEDY CABINET--AMERICA'S MEN OF DESTINY.
DERBY: MONARCH BOOKS, INC, 1961, 159 PP.
    DISCUSSES INTERNAL FUNCTION OF JUSTICE DEPARTMENT,
DEPARTMENT OF DEFENSE, STATE DEPARTMENT, TREASURY,
COMMERCE, DEPARTMENT OF INTERIOR, LABOR, AFRICULTURE,
HEALTH, EDUCATION, AND WELFARE, AND POST OFFICE DEPARTMENT
UNDER KENNEDY ADMINISTRATION.

0505 HELLMAN F.S.
THE NEW DEAL: SELECTED LIST OF REFERENCES.
WASHINGTON: LIBRARY OF CONGRESS, 1940, 71 PP.
    INDEXED, ANNOTATED, AND CLASSIFIED BIBLIOGRAPHY INCLUDES
586 ITEMS RELATING TO 36 SEPARATE AGENCIES, AS WELL AS
SPECIFIC POLICIES AND ISSUES OF THE NEW DEAL. CONCERNED WITH
HOUSING, FINANCIAL, AND FOREIGN POLICY; COURT-PACKING;
LABOR RELATIONS; REORGANIZATION OF EXECUTIVE DEPARTMENTS;
THE TVA, WPA, SEC, SOCIAL SECURITY BOARD, NRA, CCC, AAA,
ETC.

0506 HENKIN L.
ARMS CONTROL: ISSUES FOR THE PUBLIC.
ENGLEWOOD CLIFFS: PRENTICE HALL, 1961, 207 PP.
    REPORT ON THE NINETEENTH AMERICAN ASSEMBLY ON ARMS
CONTROL. ESSAYS ON VARIOUS ASPECTS OF DISARMAMENT PROBLEMS
OF INSPECTION AND US FOREIGN POLICY. PARTICULAR EMPHASIS
FOCUSED ON QUESTION OF SOVIET NATIONAL INTEREST AND EUROPEAN
VIEWS OF USA ARMS CONTROL PROJECTS.

0507 HERNDON J. ED., PRESS C. ED., WILLIAMS D.P. ED.
A SELECTED BIBLIOGRAPHY OF MATERIALS IN STATE GOVERNMENT AND
POLITICS (PAMPHLET)
LEXINGTON: U KY BUR GOVT RES, 1963, 143 PP.
    AN UNANNOTATED BIBLIOGRAPHY OF RECENT MATERIAL IN POLITI-
CAL SCIENCE, EMPHASIZING THE BEHAVIORAL APPROACH. STRESS IS
ANALYTICAL AND EMPIRICAL AND FOCUSES ON MATERIAL IN DECI-
SION-MAKING BY PUBLIC OFFICIALS. CLASSIFICATIONS DIVIDED IN-
TO BACKGROUND MATERIALS, POLITICAL ANALYSES, AND BIBLIOGRA-
PHIC STUDIES. ARRANGED ALPHABETICALLY BY STATE.

0508 HERRING P., MOSLEY P.E., HITCH C.J.
"RESEARCH FOR PUBLIC POLICY: BROOKINGS DEDICATION LECTURES."
WASHINGTON: BROOKINGS INST., 1961, 126 PP.
    APPRAISE GOVERNMENTAL, FOREIGN POLICY, AND ECONOMIC
STUDIES. ANALYZE PROBLEMS OF RESEARCH. MAKE RECOMMENDATIONS
FOR MORE EFFECTIVE RESEARCH TECHNIQUES.

0509 HEYEL C. ED.
THE ENCYCLOPEDIA OF MANAGEMENT.
LONDON: REINHOLD PUBLISHING CO, 1963, 1084 PP.
    EXTENSIVE ALPHABETIZED DESCRIPTIONS OF AREAS PERTAINING
TO MANAGEMENT. SEEKS TO SHOW CONCERNS OF TOP MANAGEMENT,
MARKETING, AND FINANCE; DEFINES PROBLEMS OF PRODUCTION AND
PLANT ENGINEERING AND ADVANCES IN NEW MANAGEMENT SCIENCES,
SUCH AS GAME THEORY, HUMAN ENGINEERING, AND APPLIED
PROBABILITY THEORY. CONTAINS 300 DEFINITIONS, EACH ENTRY
FOLLOWED BY SUGGESTED READINGS.

0510 HIBBS A.R.
"SPACE TECHNOLOGY* THE THREAT AND THE PROMISE."
DISSERTATION ABSTRACTS, 3 (SPRING 65), 63-74.
    AT PRESENT, SPACE WEAPONS SYSTEMS CANNOT COMPETE ON A
COST EFFECTIVENESS BASIS WITH EARTH-BASED MILITARY SYSTEMS.
THUS, IT IS A PROPITIOUS TIME FOR COMBINING A BAN ON WEAPONS
DEVELOPMENT WITH ARRANGEMENTS FOR COOPERATION IN SCIENTIFIC
SPACE RESEARCH

0511 HICKMAN B.G. ED.
QUANTITATIVE PLANNING OF ECONOMIC POLICY.
WASHINGTON: BROOKINGS INST, 1965, 266 PP., LC#65-18314.
    SURVEY OF THEORETICAL AND EMPIRICAL DEVELOPMENTS IN
QUANTITATIVE PLANNING OF ECONOMIC POLICY. APPRAISAL OF TECH-
NIQUES OF QUANTITATIVE POLICY ANALYSIS AND OF SPECIFIC AP-
PLICATION IN NETHERLANDS, FRANCE, AND JAPAN. PROPOSALS FOR
FUTURE RESEARCH INCLUDE METHODS OF DETERMINING POLICY AL-
TERNATIVES, AND PRACTICAL EXAMINATION OF POLITICAL DECISION-
MAKING PROCESS. ECONOMETRIC MODELS INCLUDED.

0512 HILL R.
"SOCIAL ASPECTS OF FAMILY PLANNING."
WOLRD JUSTICE, 9 (DEC. 67), 167-173.
    DISCUSSES SOCIAL AND PSYCHOLOGICAL ASPECTS OF FAMILY
PLANNING, SUCH AS SOCIAL CONDITIONS REQUIRED FOR FERTILITY
CONTROL. BELIEVES THAT KOREA, TAIWAN, INDIA, PAKISTAN,
MEXICO, AND CHILE ARE READY FOR FERTILITY DECLINE, AND
THAT MOTIVATION FOR BIRTH CONTROL SHOULD NOW BE SPURRED
THROUGH PROGRAMS OF MASS COMMUNICATION AND EDUCATION.

0513 HIRSCHMAN A.O.
DEVELOPMENT PROJECTS OBSERVED.

WASHINGTON: BROOKINGS INST, 1967, 197 PP., LC#67-27683.
    POLITICAL ECONOMIST STUDIES COMPARATIVE BEHAVIOR AND
STRUCTURAL CHARACTERISTICS OF DEVELOPMENT PROJECTS. USES 11
WORLD BANK PROJECTS IN 11 COUNTRIES AS BASIS. BELIEVES
EVEN BEST-RESEARCHED PROJECTS ARE SUBJECT TO UNFORESEEN
PROBLEMS AND WINDFALLS. DISCUSSES UNCERTAINTIES IN SUPPLY
OF TECHNOLOGY, ADMINISTRATION, FINANCE; AND IN DEMAND. EX-
AMINES PROJECT IMPLEMENTATION, DESIGN, AND APPRAISAL.

0514 HITCH C.J., MCKEAN R.
THE ECONOMICS OF DEFENSE IN THE NUCLEAR AGE.
CAMBRIDGE: HARVARD U. PR., 1960, 442 PP., $9.50.
    ESTABLISHES MUTUAL RELATIONS OF MILITARY AND ECONOMIC
PROBLEMS, DEMONSTRATING CAUSAL CONNECTION BETWEEN AVAILABLE
RESOURCES AND DEFENSE STRATEGY. DISCUSSES THE ECONOMICS OF
MILITARY ALLIANCES, DISARMAMENT, AND MOBILIZATION. STRESS
PLACED ON PROBLEMS ARISING FROM REVOLUTION IN TECHNOLOGY.

0515 HITCH C.J.
DECISION-MAKING FOR DEFENSE.
BERKELEY: U OF CALIF PR, 1965, 83 PP., LC#65-27885.
    TRACES EVOLUTION OF "DEFENSE PROBLEM" IN US HISTORY.
DESCRIBES PURPOSE AND FUNCTION OF "PROGRAMMING" SYSTEM
INSTALLED BY DEFENSE DEPARTMENT IN 1961 AND HOW IT FITS IN
WITH OVER-ALL MANAGEMENT OF DEFENSE ESTABLISHMENT. DESCRIBES
APPLICATION OF TECHNIQUES OF OPERATIONS RESEARCH OR SYSTEMS
ANALYSIS TO DEFENSE DECISION-MAKING, EMPHASIZING CHOICE OF
WEAPONS SYSTEMS. EVALUATES LATER INNOVATIONS.

0516 HODGE G.
"THE RISE AND DEMISE OF THE UN TECHNICAL ASSISTANCE ADMIN-
ISTRATION."
CAN. PUBLIC ADMIN., 10 (MAR. 67), 1-24.
    AN EXPLORATION OF THE FACTORS CONTRIBUTING TO THE DECLINE
OF THE TAA OF THE UN. FACTORS STUDIED INCLUDE INTERNAL AND
EXTERNAL PRESSURES, LEADERSHIP AND PERSONALITIES, MAINTE-
NANCE OF GOALS, INTERGROUP RIVALRIES, COALITIONS, AND ITS
EXPENDABILITY. CHIEF FAULT OF AN ORGANIZATION IS THAT IT IS
A TOOL CREATED TO DO A SPECIFIC JOB RATHER THAN A NATURAL
PRODUCT OF SOCIAL NEEDS AND PRESSURES.

0517 HODGETTS J.E.
ADMINISTERING THE ATOM FOR PEACE.
NEW YORK: ATHERTON PRESS, 1964, 193 PP., LC#64-11506.
    STUDY OF ADMINISTRATIVE PROBLEMS ASSOCIATED WITH PEACEFUL
APPLICATIONS OF NUCLEAR ENERGY. COMPARATIVE ANALYSIS OF IM-
PACT OF INSTITUTIONAL, ECONOMIC, AND TECHNOLOGICAL FEATURES
OF EACH COUNTRY ON ITS RESPECTIVE SOLUTIONS TO PROBLEMS
POSED BY EMERGENT USES OF ATOMIC ENERGY.

0518 HODGKINS J.A.
SOVIET POWER: ENERGY RESOURCES, PRODUCTION AND POTENTIALS.
ENGLEWOOD CLIFFS: PRENTICE HALL, 1961, 189 PP., LC#61-12382.
    RESEARCH INTO SOVIET ECONOMIC RESOURCES, ESPECIALLY
MINERAL FUELS. DISCUSSES GEOGRAPHIC DISTRIBUTION; ENERGY
POTENTIAL; PRODUCTION AND CONSUMPTION OF COAL, OIL
SHALE, AND NATURAL GAS. EXTENSIVE STATISTICAL TABLES.

0519 HODGKINSON R.G.
THE ORIGINS OF THE NATIONAL HEALTH SERVICE: THE MEDICAL
SERVICES OF THE NEW POOR LAW, 1834-1871.
BERKELEY: U OF CALIF PR, 1967, 725 PP.
    STUDIES GROWTH OF BRITISH STATE MEDICAL SERVICES FROM
POOR LAW OF 1834 TO 20TH-CENTURY WELFARE STATE.
EXAMINES INADEQUACIES OF THIS LAW WHICH DETHRONED WEALTHY
RISTOCRATS BUT OFFERED LITTLE MEDICAL RELIEF FOR POOR IN NEW
RBAN SLUMS. REVIEWS LATER NATIONAL HEALTH SERVICE WHICH GREW
OUT OF OMISSIONS OF POOR LAW AND GAVE RISE TO A NEW POLITICS
OF POVERTY. DISCUSSES PRESENT FAILURES AND WEAKNESSES.

0520 HODGSON J.G.
THE OFFICIAL PUBLICATIONS OF AMERICAN COUNTIES: A UNION LIST
NEW YORK: COL U, INST WAR-PEACE, 1956.
    UNANNOTATED BIBLIOGRAPHY OF 5,243 OFFICIAL DOCUMENTS OF
AMERICAN COUNTIES, ARRANGED BY STATE AND COUNTY, THROUGH
1936. LISTS LOCATIONS OF ALL INDEXED DOCUMENTS. INDEX OF
SUBJECTS.

0521 HOFFER J.R.
"RELATIONSHIP OF NATURAL AND SOCIAL SCIENCES TO SOCIAL
PROBLEMS AND CONTRIBUTION OF... SCIENTISTS TO SOLUTIONS."
AMER. DOCUMENTATION, 18 (OCT. 67), 228-234.
    EXPLORES PREMISE THAT INFORMATION SCIENCE AND INFORMATION
SPECIALISTS CAN MAKE A MAJOR CONTRIBUTION TO SOLUTION OF
BASIC SOCIAL PROBLEMS BY COLLECTING AND INTEGRATING
PERTINENT KNOWLEDGE FROM PHYSICAL, BIOLOGICAL, AND SOCIAL
SCIENCES AND BY RELATING IT DIRECTLY TO SELECTED CRITICAL
AREAS. SUGGESTS THAT PERIODICAL INDEXES BE DEVELOPED FOR
FIELD OF SOCIAL WELFARE.

0522 HOFSTADTER R.
ANTI-INTELLECTUALISM IN AMERICAN LIFE.
NEW YORK: ALFRED KNOPF, 1963, 434 PP., LC#63-14086.
    DISCUSSES THE INFLUENCE OF ANTI-INTELLECTUALISM ON RE-
LIGION, POLITICS, TECHNOLOGY, AND EDUCATION. DEFINES ANTI-
INTELLECTUALISM AND DISCUSSES THE REASONS FOR THE UNPOPULAR-

ITY OF THE INTELLECTUAL. AUTHOR BELIEVES THAT ANTI-INTELLEC-
TUALISM IS A PERVASIVE FORCE IN AMERICAN SOCIETY.

0523 HOLSTI O.R.
"EAST-WEST CONFLICT AND SINO-SOVIET RELATIONS"
J OF APPLIED BEHAVIORAL SCIENCE, 1 (APR.-JUNE 65), 115-130.
EXAMINES THE HYPOTHESIS THAT A HIGH LEVEL OF INTERCOALI-
TION CONFLICT TENDS TO INCREASE INTRACOALITION UNITY,
WHEREAS MORE RELAXED RELATIONS BETWEEN BLOCS TEND TO
MAGNIFY DIFFERENCES WITHIN THE ALLIANCE. SEVENTY-EIGHT
DOCUMENTS WRITTEN BY LEADING CHINESE AND SOVIET DECISION-
MAKERS BETWEEN 1959 AND 1963 WERE CONTENT-ANALYZED ON IBM
7090. HYPOTHESIS CONFIRMED FOR SINO-SOVIET RELATIONS.

0524 HOLTON G. ED.
"ARMS CONTROL."
DAEDALUS, 89 (FALL 60), 674-1075.
COORDINATED GROUP OF PAPERS ON ART AND SCIENCE OF CON-
TROLLING WAR. COMPRISES HANDBOOK ON PROBLEMS OF ARMS CONTROL
AND NATIONAL POLICY. ALSO INCLUDES SELECTED CRITICAL
BIBLIOGRAPHY.

0525 HOLZMAN B.G.
"BASIC RESEARCH FOR NATIONAL SURVIVAL."
AIR UNIV. QUART. REV., 12 (SPRING 1960), 28-52.
OUTLINES BASIC RESEARCH FUNCTIONS OF INDIVIDUAL DIVISIONS
AND DIRECTORATES AFFILIATED WITH AIR FORCE OFFICE OF
SCIENTIFIC RESEARCH. DESCRIBES THEIR ACCOMPLISHMENTS IN
NUCLEAR PHYSICS, MATHEMATICS, SOLID-STATE SCIENCE, BIOLOGY,
PROPULSION, MECHANICS AND THE BEHAVORIAL SCIENCES. EXAMINES
AIR FORCE INFORMATION RETRIEVAL STUDIES DESIGNED TO REDUCE
HUMAN LABOR IN HANDLING SCIENTIFIC AND TECHNICAL DATA.

0526 HOMANS G.C.
"THE WESTERN ELECTRIC RESEARCHES" IN S. HOSLETT, ED., HUMAN
FACTORS IN MANAGEMENT (BMR)"
NEW YORK: HARPER & ROW, 1951.
A DISCUSSION OF THE PROGRAM OF MANAGEMENT RESEARCH AND
OF THE WORKER, CONDUCTED AT THE CHICAGO WORKS OF THE WESTERN
ELECTRIC COMPANY. EXAMINES A NUMBER OF EXPERIMENTS TESTING
THE HAPPINESS AND RESULTING PRODUCTIVITY OF THE WORKERS IN
THIS PLANT. ANALYZES THE FAILURE AND SUCCESS OF THESE
EXPERIMENTS.

0527 HOOPES T.
"CIVILIAN-MILITARY BALANCE."
YALE REV., 43 (WINTER 54), 218-234.
DISCUSSES NEED FOR BALANCE BETWEEN CIVILIAN AND MILITARY
AUTHORITIES IN FEDERAL GOVERNMENT: NEED TO KEEP MILITARY
OFFICIALS OUT OF PARTISAN POLITICS, TO LIMIT INFLUENCE OF
MILITARY ON FOREIGN POLICY, AND TO GIVE FULLER AUTHORITY TO
SECRETARY OF DEFENSE.

0528 HOPKINS J.F.K. ED.
ARABIC PERIODICAL LITERATURE, 1961.
CAMBRIDGE: HEFFER & SONS, LTD, 1966, 104 PP.
ANNOTATED BIBLIOGRAPHICAL GUIDE TO 23 ARABIC PERIOD-
ICALS PUBLISHED IN 1961, BOTH WITHIN AND OUTSIDE ARABIC-
SPEAKING AREAS. LIST WAS COMPILED UNDER AUSPICES OF THE
MIDDLE EAST CENTRE OF CAMBRIDGE UNIVERSITY. ARTICLES ARE
CLASSIFIED IN 18 TOPICAL CATEGORIES COVERING CURRENT AF-
FAIRS, SOCIAL SCIENCES, SCIENCE AND TECHNOLOGY, AND POLITI-
CAL QUESTIONS. ALL ARABIC NAMES AND TITLES TRANSLITERATED.

0529 HOROWITZ I.L. ED.
THE RISE AND FALL OF PROJECT CAMELOT: STUDIES IN THE
RELATIONSHIP BETWEEN SOCIAL SCIENCE AND PRACTICAL POLITICS.
CAMBRIDGE: M I T PRESS, 1967, 385 PP., LC#67-14204.
EXAMINES EXTENT TO WHICH SOCIAL SCIENCE COMMUNITY SHOULD
ASSIST IN GOVERNMENTAL STUDIES AND COMMENT UPON MATTERS
RELEVANT TO MILITARY SCIENCE AND TECHNOLOGY. OUTLINES AIMS,
FEASIBILITY, ETHICS, METHODS, AND OPERATIONS OF PROJECT
CAMELOT, A STUDY IN POLITICAL ASPECTS OF SOCIAL CHANGE IN
ALL NATIONS. GIVES REPRESENTATIVE RESEARCH FINDINGS. NOTES
REASONS OF CONFLICT AND POLITICS LEADING TO END OF PROJECT.

0530 HOSKINS H.L.
"ARAB SOCIALISM IN THE UAR."
CURR. HIST., 44 (JAN. 63), 8-12.
NASSER'S PROGRAM FOR THE IMPROVEMENT OF EGYPTIAN LIVING
STANDARDS IS FOREDOOMED TO FAILURE WHATEVER THE SUCCESS OF
INDUSTRIALIZATION AND RECOVERY OF WASTE LANDS IF POPULATION
CONTINUES TO INCREASE AT PRESENT RATE. THE THREE PERCENT
INCREASE MIGHT OVERRUN IMPROVEMENTS IN ECONOMY WITHIN A
FEW YEARS.

0531 HOVLAND C.I., JANIS I.L., KELLEY H.H.
COMMUNICATION AND PERSUASION: PSYCHOLOGICAL STUDIES OF
OPINION CHANGE.
NEW HAVEN: YALE U. PR., 1953, 315 PP.
STUDIES CREDIBILITY OF COMMUNICATION AND ORGANIZATION OF
PERSUASIVE ARGUMENTS. DISCUSSES GROUP MEMBERSHIP, RESISTANCE
TO INFLUENCE AND SUSCEPTIBILITY TO PERSUASION. OBSERVES THAT
CONVICTION ACQUIRED THROUGH ACTIVE PARTICIPATION. CONCLUDES
WITH STUDY ON RETENTION OF OPINION CHANGE.

0532 HOWER R.M., ORTH C.D.
MANAGERS AND SCIENTISTS.
CAMBRIDGE: HARVARD U, DIV OF RES, 1963, 310 PP., LC#63-10191
STUDY INTO PERSONAL RELATIONS BETWEEN SCIENTISTS AND
MANAGEMENT, INTERNAL TO RESEARCH ORGANIZATIONS. FOCUSES
ON HUMAN RELATIONS, STATUS, COMMUNICATION, MOTIVATION,
MORALE, MANAGER DEVELOPMENT, ETC. DESCRIPTION AND ANALYSIS
OF CASE SITUATIONS IN TWO COMPANIES.

0533 HSIEH A.L.
"THE SINO-SOVIET NUCLEAR DIALOGUE* 1963."
BUL. ATOMIC SCIENTISTS, 21 (JAN. 65), 16-21.
HSIEH ANALYZES CRUCIAL CHINESE AND SOVIET FOREIGN AND
MILITARY POLICY DOCUMENTS, SEEKING TO ISOLATE FACTORS WHICH
DEEPEN SINO-SOVIET DISPUTE. CITES FEAR OF ESCALATION OF
LOCAL WARS, CHINEESE AMBITIONS IN ASIA, AND SOVIET DESIRES
FOR UNIFIED COMMAND OVER COMMUNIST STRATEGIC FORCES.

0534 HUGHES E.M.
AMERICA THE VINCIBLE.
GARDEN CITY: DOUBLEDAY, 1959, 306 PP., LC#59-9783.
EXAMINES US FOREIGN POLICY AND ATTEMPTS TO EXPLAIN
TODAY'S PREDICAMENTS. SUGGESTS THAT IMPROVEMENT OF
INTERNATIONAL RELATIONS ON PERSONAL LEVEL MIGHT HELP
SOLVE COLD WAR PROBLEMS. FEELS US "POWER" POLICIES
INCREASE TENSION.

0535 HUGHES T.L.
"SCHOLARS AND FOREIGN POLICY* VARIETIES OF RESEARCH EXPER-
IENCE."
BACKGROUND, 9 (NOV. 65), 199-214.
IN THIS ARTICLE THE DIRECTOR, BUREAU OF INTELLIGENCE
AND RESEARCH, DEPARTMENT OF STATE, OUTLINES THE GOVERNMENT'S
PLAN FOR LICENSING SOCIAL SCIENCE RESEARCH IN THE WAKE OF
THE "CAMELOT AFFAIR." HOW ALL INVOLVED, FROM THE SCHOLAR,
THE HOST SUBJECT, UP TO THE PRESIDENT, WILL BE TREATED AND
BENEFIT IS PRESENTED.

0536 HULL E.W.S.
"THE POLITICAL OCEAN."
FOREIGN AFFAIRS, 45 (APR. 67), 492-502.
PREDICTS THAT THE OCEANS WILL ASSUME NEW DIMENSIONS AMONG
INTERNATIONAL PROBLEMS. NEW USES OF SEA RESOURCES WILL PRO-
DUCE VAST ECONOMIC, POLITICAL, TECHNOLOGICAL, AND INDUSTRIAL
CHANGES. ADVOCATES INTERNATIONAL ADMINISTRATION OF LAWS TO
PROTECT THE OCEANS SO THAT ALL NATIONS WILL BENEFIT FROM
RESOURCES. OCEANOGRAPHY CAN SERVE AS BRIDGE FOR CONTACT AND
COOPERATION IN THE FUTURE TO TRANSCEND NATIONAL INTERESTS.

0537 HUNTINGTON S.P.
"ARMS RACES: PREREQUISITES AND RESULTS."
PUB. POLICY, 8 (MAR. 58), 41-86.
ARMS RACES ARE EITHER PRELUDES TO, OR SUBSTITUTES FOR,
WAR. QUANTITATIVE AND QUALITATIVE RACES ARE CONTRASTED AND
INFLUENCE ON POWER-BALANCES, DOMESTIC ECONOMIES AND
POSSIBILITIES OF WAR IS ASSESSED. CONCLUDES THAT IT'S
IMPOSSIBLE TO SEPARATE TECHNICAL FROM POLITICAL ASPECTS
IN ARMS CONTROL.

0538 HUNTINGTON S.P.
"STRATEGIC PLANNING AND THE POLITICAL PROCESS."
FOR. AFF., 38 (JAN. 60), 285-89.
CRITICIZES LEGISLATIVE LEADERSHIP AND SCOPE OF THE
STRATEGIC CONSENSUS IN THE EXECUTIVE BRANCH AS WEAK AND
LIMITED AND SUGGESTS BOTH BE CLARIFIED TO IMPROVE THE
CONTENT OF MILITARY DECISIONS. URGES THE ADMINISTRATION
ABANDON ITS DEFENSIVE ROLE REGARDING STRATEGIC PROGRAMS AND
PERMIT THEIR BROADER AND EARLIER PUBLIC DISCUSSION TO
ASCERTAIN ACCURATELY WHAT THE PEOPLE WILL SUPPORT.

0539 HUTCHINSON C.E.
"AN INSTITUTE FOR NATIONAL SECURITY AFFAIRS."
AMER. BEHAV. SCI., 4 (SEPT. 60), 31-35.
NATIONAL SECURITY POLICY DEPENDENT UPON QUESTIONS OF
TIMING PROCESS AND AVAILABLE RESOURCES PREDICTION. COMMUN-
ICATION AND TECHNICAL UTILIZATION REQUIRE RESEARCH AND DE-
VELOPMENT, AND PROFESSIONAL ADVISORS FOR NATIONAL LEADERS.

0540 HUXLEY J.
FREEDOM AND CULTURE.
NEW YORK: COLUMBIA U PRESS, 1951, 270 PP.
SIX ARTICLES ON FREEDOM IN MODERN WORLD, INCLUDING
FREEDOMS OF EDUCATION, INFORMATION, SCIENCE, AND RIGHTS OF
CREATIVE ARTIST.

0541 HUZAR E.
THE PURSE AND THE SWORD: CONTROL OF THE ARMY BY CONGRESS
THROUGH MILITARY APPROPRIATIONS 1933-1950.
ITHACA: CORNELL U PRESS, 1950, 417 PP.
STUDIES LEGISLATIVE-ADMINISTRATIVE AND CIVIL-MILITARY RE-
LATIONS WITH REGARD TO CONGRESSIONAL MILITARY APPROPRIATIONS
FROM DEPRESSION TO COLD WAR FOR THE ARMY. STUDIES CONGRES-
SIONAL COMMITTEE, SUBCOMMITTEE, AND HEARINGS ON MILITARY AP-
PROPRIATION; RELATION TO MILITARY POLICY; ARMY ADMINISTRA-
TION; LEGISLATIVE CONTROL; AND ADMINISTRATIVE DISCRETION.
RECOMMENDS OVERHAULING CONGRESSIONAL PROCEDURES AND GOALS.

0542 IANNI O.
ESTADO E CAPITALISMO.
RIO DE JANEIRO: ED CIVIL BRASIL, 1965, 270 PP.
ANALYZES ECONOMIC AND SOCIAL STRUCTURE OF BRAZIL SINCE INDUSTRIALIZATION IN 20TH CENTURY. EXAMINES ACTIONS OF PRIVATE SECTOR IN DEVELOPMENT AND TREATS ROLE OF NATIONAL GOVERNMENT IN PARTICIPATING IN AND ENCOURAGING DEVELOPMENT OF INDUSTRY.

0543 IKLE F.C.
"NTH COUNTRIES AND DISARMAMENT."
BULL. AT. SCI., 16 (DEC. 60), 391-94.
PRESENTS COUNTERARGUMENTS TO GENERAL PROPOSALS FOR CONTROLLING SPREAD OF NUCLEAR WEAPONS. CITES RELUCTANCE OF SMALLER POWERS TO STARTING NUCLEAR WAR FOR FEAR OF MAJOR POWERS. NOTES LIMITATIONS OF ATTEMPTS TO ENFORCE UNIVERSAL TEST BAN AND CONTENDS ENFORCEMENT MAY BE EASIER FOR INTERNATIONAL BODIES TO ACCOMPLISH AS EVEN MORE COUNTRIES ACQUIRE NUCLEAR CAPABILITIES.

0544 INGLIS D.R.
"MISSILE DEFENSE, NUCLEAR SPREAD, AND VIETNAM."
BUL. ATOMIC SCIENTISTS, 23 (MAY 67), 49-52.
DISCUSSES THE INTERRELATION OF ANTI-BALLISTIC MISSILE SYSTEMS, NUCLEAR PROLIFERATION, AND THE VIETNAM WAR. AN ABM SYSTEM MIGHT HAVE SERIOUS EFFECTS ON THE ARMS RACE, AS WELL AS ON THE ECONOMY AND RELATIONS WITH RUSSIA. NUCLEAR PROLIFERATION MUST BE STOPPED AND DIPLOMACY ENCOURAGED. THE VIETNAM WAR IS A POSSIBLE FACTOR IN CHINESE NUCLEAR DEVELOPMENT. SO FAR HAWKS HAVE HAD TOO MUCH THEIR OWN WAY.

0545 INGLIS D.R., SANDLER C.R.
"PROSPECTS AND PROBLEMS: THE NONMILITARY USES OF NUCLEAR EXPLOSIVES."
BUL. ATOMIC SCIENTISTS, 23 (DEC. 67), 46-53.
ASSESS PROSPECTIVE PEACEFUL USES OF NUCLEAR EXPLOSIVES. CONCERNED WITH TECHNICAL AND ECONOMIC ASPECTS, ALSO RELATIONSHIP WITH ARMS CONTROL. DISCUSS USE OF NUCLEAR EXPLOSIVES FOR CANAL EXCAVATION, UNEARTHING OF NATURAL RESOURCES, AND EXPERIMENTS IN PURE SCIENCE. EMPHASIZE RELEVANCE OF PROPOSED NONPROLIFERATION TREATY TO SCIENTIFIC USE OF NUCLEAR WEAPONS.

0546 INST D'ETUDE POL L'U GRENOBLE
ADMINISTRATION TRADITIONELLE ET PLANIFICATION REGIONALE.
PARIS: COLIN (LIB ARMAND), 1964, 306 PP.
STUDY OF TRADITIONAL FRENCH ADMINISTRATION, WHICH CANNOT MEET MODERN PROBLEMS OF CITY PLANNING. ANALYZES NEW PLANNING EFFORTS, THEIR FUNCTIONAL CHARACTERISTICS, AND THEIR POLITICAL DIMENSIONS. ANALYZES IN DETAIL STEPS OF NEW PLANNING. BIBLIOGRAPHY OF 394 ITEMS.

0547 INSTITUTE PSYCHOLOGICAL RES
HUMAN ENGINEERING BIBLIOGRAPHY, 1959-1960.
WASHINGTON: US GOVERNMENT, 1961, 349 PP.
REFERENCES ON METHODOLOGY, FACILITIES, AND EQUIPMENT FOR PSYCHOLOGICAL RESEARCH; SYSTEMS OF MACHINES AND MEN; WORK CONDITIONS AND INDIVIDUAL FACTORS; AND TRAINING AIDS AND DEVICES.

0548 INT. BANK RECONSTR. DEVELOP.
ECONOMIC DEVELOPMENT OF KUWAIT.
BALTIMORE: JOHNS HOPKINS PR., 1965, 194 PP.
KUWAIT IS FOURTH LARGEST OIL PRODUCER IN WORLD AND SECOND ONLY TO VENEZUELA AS AN OIL EXPORTER. SUMMARIZES RESULTS OF FINDINGS AND RECOMMENDATIONS OF TWO 'ECONOMIC MISSIONS' TO COUNTRY. DOMESTIC NEEDS AND INVESTMENT OPPORTUNITIES ARE EMPHASIZED WITH REVALUATION OF TARIFFS AND IMPORT RESTRICTIONS.

0549 INTERNATIONAL CITY MGRS ASSN
COUNCIL-MANAGER GOVERNMENT, 1940-64: AN ANNOTATED BIBLIOGRAPHY.
CHICAGO: INT CITY MANAGER'S ASSN, 1965, 38 PP.
ANNOTATED BIBLIOGRAPHY OF 340 REFERENCES TO BOOKS, ARTICLES, AND GOVERNMENT PUBLICATIONS IN ENGLISH OR ENGLISH TRANSLATIONS; ARRANGED UNDER TOPICS OF HISTORY OF COUNCIL-MANAGER GOVERNMENT, INITIATION OF PLAN, CITY MANAGER, BASIC COUNCIL-MANAGER PLAN AND INTERGOVERNMENTAL RELATIONS.

0550 JACKSON W.G.F.
"NUCLEAR PROLIFERATION AND THE GREAT POWERS."
MILITARY REV., 47 (JUNE 67), 72-81.
BRITISH MAJOR GENERAL ANALYZES WHAT FACTORS HAVE CAUSED NUCLEAR PROLIFERATION AND HOW IT CAN BE CONTROLLED. CITES NATIONALISM AND FEAR AS CHIEF MOTIVES OF ARMS RACE. DISCUSSES VARIOUS WAYS IN WHICH NATIONS MIGHT SUBMIT TO SUPRANATIONAL AUTHORITY TO MAINTAIN PEACE. CONCLUDES THAT BRITAIN MUST BOTH SUPPORT SUCH EFFORTS AT COOPERATION AND MAINTAIN HER OWN INTERESTS.

0551 JACOB H.
GERMAN ADMINISTRATION SINCE BISMARCK: CENTRAL AUTHORITY VERSUS LOCAL AUTONOMY.
NEW HAVEN: YALE U PR, 1963, 324 PP., LC#63-7937.
ANALYZES AND COMPARES SECOND REICH, WEIMAR REPUBLIC, THIRD REICH, AND GERMAN FEDERAL REPUBLIC IN HISTORICAL PERSPECTIVE. STUDIES INSTITUTIONS AND ADMINISTRATIVE POLICIES. EXAMINES DEVELOPMENT OF CONTROLS, LEGALISTIC PERSPECTIVES, PARTY INFILTRATION, AND LARGE-SCALE PERSONNEL CHANGES. INCLUDES GERMAN CIVIL SERVICE, QUEST FOR RESPONSIVENESS, AND ADAPTIVE CHARACTERISTICS.

0552 JACOB P.E.
"THE DISARMAMENT CONSENSUS."
INT. ORGAN., 14 (SPRING 60), 235-60.
DISCUSSES AREAS OF EAST-WEST AGREEMENT. LIST AREAS OF DISAGREEMENT SUCH AS: EXTENT OF ACCESS BY CONTROL TEAMS AND SCOPE OF THE VETO. SUSPECTS RUSSIA MORE WILLING TO COMPROMISE THAN HAS BEEN GENERALLY BELIEVED. RECOMMENDS DIVORCING POLITICAL CONDITIONS FROM DISARMAMENT PROPOSALS.

0553 JACOBS N. ED.
CULTURE FOR THE MILLIONS?
PRINCETON: VAN NOSTRAND, 1959, 200 PP.
DISCUSSIONS OF MASS CULTURE AS RELATED TO ARTS AND MASS MEDIA BY SEVERAL ARTISTS, CRITICS, AND SOCIAL SCIENTISTS. ALSO CONSIDERS SOCIO-POLITICAL CHANGES WHICH HAVE CONTRIBUTED TO DEVELOPMENT OF MASS CULTURE.

0554 JACOBSON H.K., STEIN E.
DIPLOMATS, SCIENTISTS, AND POLITICIANS* THE UNITED STATES AND THE NUCLEAR TEST BAN NEGOTIATIONS.
ANN ARBOR: U OF MICH PR, 1966, 538 PP., LC#66-11622.
DETAILED ANALYSIS OF THE NEGOTIATIONS, AND RELATED POLITICAL AND SCIENTIFIC EVENTS, CULMINATING IN THE MOSCOW TREATY BANNING NUCLEAR TESTING--FIRST FORMAL ARMS CONTROL AGREEMENT OF THE COLD WAR. RESULT OF ATTEMPT TO ASSESS THE IMPACT OF SCIENCE AND MODERN TECHNOLOGY ON THE PROCESS OF NEGOTIATION AND ON STRUCTURE AND FUNCTIONS OF INTERNATIONAL ORGANIZATION.

0555 JAFFEE A.J.
"POPULATION TRENDS AND CONTROLS IN UNDERDEVELOPED COUNTRIES."
LAW CONTEMP. PROBL., 25 (SUMMER 60), 508-535.
OFFERS HISTORY OF POPULATION GROWTH, AND ANALYSIS OF POPULATION DISTRIBUTION AND BIRTH-DEATH RATES. COMPARES SOCIO-ECONOMIC FACTORS RELATED TO POPULATION GROWTH AND FERTILITY IN UNDERDEVELOPED COUNTRIES WITH THOSE IN DEVELOPED ONES. SPECULATES ON POSSIBLE FUTURE GROWTH OF POPULATION AND ITS EFFECT ON ECONOMIC DEVELOPMENT, EMPLOYMENT, AND STANDARD OF LIVING.

0556 JAIN G.
"INDIA REJECTS THE POWER RACE* REALISM ABOUT NUCLEAR WEAPONS."
ROUND TABLE, (APR. 67), 135-140.
POINTS OUT RECENT INDIAN NON-INTEREST IN CHINESE NUCLEAR TESTING AS LOGICAL DEVELOPMENT. DISCUSSES INDIAN FOREIGN POLICY AS IT RELATES TO NUCLEAR WEAPONS. ALSO CONSIDERS NEHRU'S ACTIONS DURING 1950'S.

0557 JANDA K.
DATA PROCESSING: APPLICATIONS TO POLITICAL RESEARCH.
EVANSTON: NORTHWESTERN U PRESS, 1965, 288 PP., LC#65-15476.
INTRODUCTION TO SOME ADVANTAGES AND APPLICATIONS OF DATA PROCESSING BY PUNCH-CARD. SHOWS WAYS IN WHICH DIFFERENTS TYPES OF POLITICAL INFORMATION CAN BE RECORDED, MANIPULATED, COMPILED, AND ANALYZED.

0558 JANOWITZ M.
"MILITARY ELITES AND THE STUDY OF WAR."
J. CONFL. RESOLUT., 1 (MAR. 57), 9-18.
IDENTIFIES DIFFERENT MODELS OF POLITICAL-MILITARY ELITE ORGANIZATION REFLECTIVE OF DIFFERENT SOCIAL STRUCTURES. CONSIDERS CONSEQUENCES OF VAST TECHNOLOGICAL DEVELOPMENTS IN WAR-MAKING ON THE ORGANIZATION OF THESE ELITES. STUDIES RECENT TRENDS IN INDOCTRINATION AND CONCLUDES MILITARY ESTABLISHMENT CANNOT BE CONTROLLED AND STILL REMAIN EFFECTIVE BY CIVILIANIZING IT.

0559 JANOWITZ M.
"CHANGING PATTERNS OF ORGANIZATIONAL AUTHORITY: THE MILITARY ESTABLISHMENT" (BMR)"
ADMINISTRATIVE SCI. Q., 3 (MAR. 59), 473-493.
ANALYZES BASES AND MANIFESTATIONS OF TREND IN MILITARY ESTABLISHMENT TOWARD LESS DIRECT, ARBITRARY, AND AUTHORITARIAN BUREAUCRACY. SHOWS CHANGE IS FROM AN AUTHORITY SYSTEM BASED UPON DOMINATION TO ONE BASED UPON TECHNIQUES OF MANIPULATION BROUGHT ABOUT BY NEW WEAPONS, AUTOMATION OF WARFARE, DEMANDS OF TECHNICAL EXPERTISE, AND EMPHASIS UPON INDIVIDUAL INITIATIVE.

0560 JANOWITZ M.
THE PROFESSIONAL SOLDIER.
NEW YORK: FREE PRESS OF GLENCOE, 1960, 454 PP., LC#60-7090.
ATTEMPTS TO DESCRIBE PROFESSIONAL LIFE, ORGANIZATIONAL SETTING, AND LEADERSHIP OF AMERICAN MILITARY. ASSESSMENT OF MODERN MILITARY'S POWER POSITION IN US SOCIETY AND ITS BEHAVIOR IN INTERNATIONAL RELATIONS.

0561 JANOWITZ M. ED.
COMMUNITY POLITICAL SYSTEMS.
NEW YORK: FREE PRESS OF GLENCOE, 1961, 259 PP., LC#59-13864.
A STUDY OF COMMUNITY ORGANIZATION APPROACHED FROM THE BE-
HAVIORAL POINT OF VIEW. ANALYZES LEADERSHIP AND POWER
STRUCTURES, THE EFFECT OF INDUSTRIALIZATION, METHODOLOGICAL
PROBLEMS IN SOCIOLOGICAL RESEARCH, AND STUDIES OF SAMPLE
CITIES.

0562 JASNY H.
KHRUSHCHEV'S CROP POLICY.
GLASGOW: GEORGE OUTRAM CO. LTD, 1965, 243 PP.
ANALYZES KHRUSHCHEV'S AGRICULTURAL PROGRAMS THAT BROUGHT
ABOUT FAILURES IN ECONOMY. CONCLUDES THAT EXCESSIVE CONCERN
WITH MAIZE, PULSE, AND SUGARBEET CAUSED FAILURE. COMPARES
SOVIET CROP PRACTICES WITH THOSE OF OTHER NATIONS. FEELS
KHRUSHCHEV MAY HAVE BEEN JUSTIFIED, OWING TO UNIQUENESS OF
NATURAL RESOURCES.

0563 JENKS C.W.
SPACE LAW.
NEW YORK: FREDERICK PRAEGER, 1965, 476 PP., LC#65-17859.
ANALYSIS OF DEVELOPMENT AND STATUS OF SPACE LAW. EXAMINES
LAW AND CONCEPTS OF JURISDICTION EXISTING TODAY, UN ACTION
ON ISSUE OF OUTER SPACE ACTIVITIES AND RIGHTS, AND LEGAL
LITERATURE AVAILABLE.

0564 JOHNSTON D.M.
"LAW, TECHNOLOGY AND THE SEA."
CALIF. LAW REV., 55 (MAY 67), 449-472.
EXPLORES CONFLICT BETWEEN INTERNATIONAL LAW AND VALUE OF
EFFICIENCY INHERENT IN MODERN TECHNOLOGY AS EXPRESSED IN
CHANGES TAKING PLACE IN LAW OF THE SEA. CATEGORIZES USES
OF SEA SUGGESTED BY TECHNOLOGY AND FIELDS IMPLIED FOR INTER-
NATIONAL LEGISLATION. DISCUSSES SPECIFIC ASPECTS OF CURRENT
TREATIES AND LEGISLATION. DISPUTES NOTION OF TERRITORIALITY
AT SEA. RECOMMENDS NEW APPROACHES TO PROPER LEGAL FRAMEWORK.

0565 JOINT ECONOMIC COMMITTEE
"DIMENSIONS OF SOVIET ECONOMIC POWER."
WASHINGTON: US GOVERNMENT, 1962.
COMPILATION OF STUDY PAPERS PREPARED BY A GROUP OF EX-
PERTS ON THE SOVIET ECONOMY FOR 87TH CONGRESS. ANALYZES
SOVIET POLICY FRAMEWORK IN TERMS OF RESOURCE ALLOCATION,
MILITARY ESTABLISHMENT, AND RECENT DEVELOPMENTS IN PLANNING.
EXAMINES THE MEASURE AND STRATEGY OF PRODUCTION AND PRODUC-
TIVITY, DEVELOPMENT OF HUMAN RESOURCES, AND DEMOGRAPHY.
SELECTED BIBLIOGRAPHY OF RECENT SOVIET ECONOMIC MONOGRAPHS.

0566 JONES G.S.
"STRATEGIC PLANNING."
MILITARY REV., 47 (SEPT. 67), 14-19.
ANALYZES ROLE OF JOINT CHIEFS OF STAFF IN POLICY FORMA-
TION IN AREA OF SECURITY. DISCUSSES RELATIONSHIP OF JCS
TO PRESIDENT AND DEVELOPMENT OF THE JOINT STRATEGIC OBJEC-
TIVES PLAN, STARTING POINT IN PREPARING MILITARY BUDGET.

0567 JONES J.M.
THE FIFTEEN WEEKS (FEBRUARY 21-JUNE 5, 1947)
NEW YORK: VIKING PRESS, 1955, 296 PP., LC#55-8923.
HISTORY OF MARSHALL PLAN AND TRUMAN DOCTRINE. DETAILS
SITUATION THAT LED UP TO THEIR CONCEPTION. ATTEMPTS AN
INTIMATE STORY OF POLITICAL BACKGROUND IN WASHINGTON
DURING FIFTEEN CRUCIAL WEEKS.

0568 JUNGK R.
BRIGHTER THAN A THOUSAND SUNS: THE MORAL AND POLITICAL
HISTORY OF THE ATOMIC SCIENTISTS.
LONDON: VICTOR GOLLANCZ, 1958, 350 PP.
ANALYSIS OF NUCLEAR DEVELOPMENTS, ACHIEVEMENTS, AND
FAILURES OF WESTERN POWERS THROUGH OPINIONS OF SCIENTISTS
IN EACH COUNTRY THAT CONTRIBUTED TO OR INVENTED NUCLEAR
PROJECTS. QUOTES THEIR WORKS AND ANALYZES THEIR VIEWS ON
MORALITY AND WORLD CONSEQUENCES OF THEIR WORK. COVERS
POST-WWI TO ABOUT 1955.

0569 KAHN H.
ON THERMONUCLEAR WAR.
PRINCETON: U. PR., 1961, 625 PP.
EXAMINES THE MILITARY SIDE OF WHAT MAY BE THE MAJOR PROB-
LEM THAT FACES CIVILIZATION, COMPARING SOME OF THE ALTERNA-
TIVES THAT SEEM AVAILABLE AND SOME OF THE IMPLICATIONS IN
THESE CHOICES.

0570 KAHN H.
THINKING ABOUT THE UNTHINKABLE.
NEW YORK: HORIZON, 1962, 254 PP.
DISCUSSES PROBLEMS CREATED BY MODERN TECHNOLOGY AND BY
CONTEMPORARY INTERNATIONAL RELATIONS. CALLS FOR A WORLD
GOVERNMENT TO HANDLE THE PROBLEMS PRESENTED BY THE THERMO-
NUCLEAR AGE.

0571 KAHN H., DIBBLE C.
"CRITERIA FOR LONG-RANGE NUCLEAR CONTROL POLICIES."
CALIF. LAW REV., 55 (MAY 67), 473-492.
ARGUES THAT TECHNICAL AND FINANCIAL OBSTACLES TO NUCLEAR

PROLIFERATION WILL NO LONGER BE IMPORTANT IN THE FUTURE,
THAT PROLIFERATION WILL BE RADICALLY DIFFERENT PROBLEM FROM
TODAY. SUGGESTS CRITERIA BY WHICH NUCLEAR POLICY SHOULD BE
JUDGED. INCLUDES SUGGESTIONS ON MERITS OF "LEX TALIONIS" AND
REGIONAL DEFENSE SYSTEMS. ADVOCATES UNIVERSE OF SEMI-EQUAL
NATIONAL POWERS.

0572 KANTOROVICH L.V.
THE BEST USE OF ECONOMIC RESOURCES.
CAMBRIDGE: HARVARD U PR, 1965, 349 PP., LC#64-21300.
DEMONSTRATES THE TECHNIQUES OF LINEAR PROGRAMMING. PRE-
SENTS EVIDENCE THAT THIS TECHNIQUE, WITH ITS IMPLICATIONS
FOR THE SETTING OF PRICES IN THE PRODUCER-GOODS MARKET,
SHOULD BE MORE WIDELY ADOPTED IN THE PLANNING OF THE RUSSIAN
ECONOMY. ILLUMINATES ASPECTS OF RUSSIAN ECONOMIC PLANNING
AND SHOWS THAT MANAGERIAL PROBLEMS ARE ESSENTIALLY SIMILAR
WHATEVER THE GENERAL ECONOMIC STRUCTURE OF THE COUNTRY.

0573 KAPLAN A.
"CONTENT ANALYSIS AND THE THEORY OF SIGNS" (BMR)"
PHILOSOPHY OF SCIENCE, 10 (1943), 230-247.
PROPOSES TO ELUCIDATE CONTENT ANALYSIS FROM POINT OF VIEW
OF GENERAL THEORY OF SIGNS, ESPECIALLY IN THE FORM IN WHICH
THE LATTER HAS BEEN ESTABLISHED BY C. W. MORRIS AND THE
SCIENTIFIC EMPIRICISTS. DEVELOPS VIEWPOINT THAT CONTENT
ANALYSIS IS STATISTICAL SEMANTICS OF POLITICAL DISCOURSE,
SEMANTICS BEING DEFINED AS A SPECIAL BRANCH OF SEMIOLOGY.
INCLUDES LIST OF 21 RELATED READINGS.

0574 KAPLAN A., SKOGSTAD A.L., GIRSHICK M.A.
"THE PREDICTION OF SOCIAL AND TECHNOLOGICAL EVENTS."
PUB. OPIN. QUART., 14 (SPRING 50), 93-110.
POLICY-MAKING IS A RESULT OF: ANTICIPATION OF THE FUTURE,
PREDICTIONS OF CONDITIONS WHICH POLICY MUST FACE, AND
EXPECTATION OF CONSEQUENCES OF RESPONSES AND ALTERNATE
COURSES OF ACTION. REPORT ON A PILOT-STUDY CONCERNING THE
THREE BASIC PROBLEMS IN PREDICTION, EVALUATION, IMPROVEMENT,
AND APPRAISAL.

0575 KAPLAN B.
AN UNHURRIED VIEW OF COPYRIGHT.
NEW YORK: COLUMBIA U PRESS, 1967, 142 PP., LC#67-13539.
ANALYSIS OF LAW OF COPYRIGHT IN LIGHT OF TECHNOLOGICAL
AND SOCIAL DEVELOPMENTS AS CONTAINED IN THREE SPEECHES MADE
BY AUTHOR IN MARCH, 1966. FIRST LECTURE ON HISTORY OF
COPYRIGHT, SECOND ON PLAGIARISM, AND THIRD ON FUTURE OF
COPYRIGHT. TABLE OF CASES CITED.

0576 KAPLAN M.A., BURNS A.L., QUANDT R.E.
"THEORETICAL ANALYSIS OF THE BALANCE OF POWER."
BEHAV. SCI., 5 (JULY 60), 240-52.
PROPOSES THEORY OF COMPETITIVE GAME OF INTERNATIONAL
POLITICS. DEPICTS FORMATION OF ALLIANCES AND COUNTER ALLIAN-
CES. OUTLINES PROBLEMS OF SUPRANATIONAL NATIONS. DISCUSSES
THE STABILITY OF A BALANCE OF POWER SYSTEM.

0577 KAPLAN M.A.
"THE NEW GREAT DEBATE* TRADITIONALISM VS SCIENCE IN INTER-
NATIONAL RELATIONS."
WORLD POLITICS, 19 (OCT. 66), 1-20.
SCATHING REBUTTAL TO "TRADITIONALISTS" LIKE HEDLEY BULL
WHO CRITICIZE THE USERS OF THE SCIENTIFIC METHOD IN IR FOR
SLIGHTING THE ROLE OF HUMAN PURPOSE AND DEIFYING SIMPLISTIC
MODELS. ILLUSTRATIONS PROVIDED FROM AUTHOR'S USE OF INTER-
NATIONAL SYSTEMS THEORY AND FROM THE WORKS OF DEUTSCH, RUS-
SETT, BURNS, SCHELLING AND OTHERS.

0578 KARNJAHAPRAKORN C.
MUNICIPAL GOVERNMENT IN THAILAND AS AN INSTITUTION AND PRO-
CESS OF SELF-GOVERNMENT.
BRUSSELS: THAMMASAT U PUB ADMIN, 1962, 249 PP.
ANALYZES DEVELOPMENT OF PHILOSOPHY AND PRACTICE OF
MUNICIPAL SELF-GOVERNMENT. FINDS THAT THAILAND CAN
ACCEPT FORM OF SELF-GOVERNMENT USED IN WESTERN DEMOCRACIES
BUT NOT ITS PHILOSOPHY. DISCUSSES PROBLEM OF KEEPING
MUNICIPAL GOVERNMENT IN THAILAND AND SUGGESTS WAYS TO GAIN
ACCEPTANCE FOR IT.

0579 KASER M.
COMECON* INTEGRATION PROBLEMS OF THE PLANNED ECONOMIES.
LONDON: OXFORD U PR, 1965, 215 PP.
THE LACK OF AUTOMATIC REGULATION THROUGH THE PRICE MECH-
ANISM HAS MADE TRADE A DIFFICULT PROBLEM WITHIN THE REGIONAL
ECONOMIC ORGANIZATION OF THE EUROPEAN COMMUNIST STATES. IN-
STITUTIONAL HISTORY OF COMECON SHOWS INTERPLAY BETWEEN PO-
LITICAL FACTORS LIKE NATIONALISM AND ECONOMIC PLANNING PARA-
DOXES SUCH AS PROFITS. INTEGRATION PROBLEMS COMPARED TO
THOSE FACING EEC.

0580 KASSOF A.
"THE ADMINISTERED SOCIETY: TOTALITARIANISM WITHOUT TERROR."
WORLD POLIT., 16 (JULY 64), 558-75.
PROPOSES THE CONCEPT OF THE ADMINISTERED SOCIETY AS A
TOOL TO SUMMARIZE AND EVALUATE RECENT CHANGES IN THE
SOVIET SYSTEM AND TO IDENTIFY CURRENT TRENDS. ASSERTS
THAT SOVIET SOCIETY IS BEING SUBJECTED TO NEW AND MORE

SUBTLE FORMS OF TOTALISM -TOTALISM WITHOUT TERROR. THE
STALINIST PAST IS BEING ADAPTED RATHER THAN REJECTED.

0581 KAST F.E. ED., ROSENWEIG J.E. ED.
SCIENCE, TECHNOLOGY, AND MANAGEMENT.
NEW YORK: MCGRAW HILL, 1963, 368 PP., LC#63-11852.
PROCEEDINGS OF 1962 NATIONAL ADVANCED-TECHNOLOGY
MANAGEMENT CONFERENCE ON PROBLEMS OF MANAGING VERY LARGE
PROGRAMS USING LATEST TECHNOLOGICAL DEVELOPMENTS. SHOWS
PROGRESS IN SOLVING PROBLEMS AND AREAS THAT NEED FURTHER
IMPOVEMENT. SEEKS TO DEVELOP MANAGERIAL SCIENCE TO DEAL
WITH TECHNICAL PROGRAMS, SUCH AS DEFENSE, NASA, AND NUCLEAR
POWER PROGRAMS.

0582 KATZ S.M., MCGOWEN F.
A SELECTED LIST OF US READINGS ON DEVELOPMENT.
WASHINGTON: AGENCY FOR INTL DEV, 1963, 362 PP.
LIST OF SELECTED READINGS ON APPLICATION OF SCIENCE AND
TECHNOLOGY TO PROBLEMS OF LESS-DEVELOPED NATIONS. REPRESEN-
TATIVE SAMPLE OF CURRENT AMERICAN RESEARCH PAPERS, ACADEMIC
STUDIES, AND OPERATIONAL REPORTS ON MAJOR AREAS OF SCIENCE
AND TECHNOLOGY. CONTAINS FAIRLY EXTENSIVE ANNOTATIONS OF
1,195 ITEMS PUBLISHED AFTER 1950. MATERIAL ORGANIZED BY
SUBJECT; INCLUDES AUTHOR INDEX.

0584 KAUFMAN J.L.
COMMUNITY RENEWAL PROGRAMS (PAMPHLET)
EUGENE, ORE: EXCHANGE BIBLIOGS, 1965, 23 PP.
CONTAINS 200 REFERENCES ARRANGED BY STATE AND CITY.
DOES NOT DIFFERENTIATE ACCORDING TO QUALITY OR
SIGNIFICANCE, SO AS TO PROVIDE A STARTING POINT IN THE
ACCUMULATION OF MATERIAL ON RENEWAL PROGRAMS.

0585 KAUFMANN F.
METHODOLOGY OF THE SOCIAL SCIENCES.
LONDON: OXFORD U PR, 1944, 271 PP.
GENERAL CONSIDERATION OF PHILOSOPHY OF SCIENCE. ALSO
DEALS WITH RELATION OF PRAGMATISM, RATIONALISM, AND RELA-
TIVITY TO FORMULATION OF RESEARCH PARADIGMS. DISCUSSES AP-
PLICATIONS IN SOCIAL SCIENCES AND DIFFICULTIES IN APPLICA-
TION, ESPECIALLY IN ECONOMICS. ATTEMPTS TO GIVE BASIC
FOUNDATION FOR CONSIDERATION OF BEHAVIOR.

0586 KAUFMANN W.W.
THE MC NAMARA STRATEGY.
NEW YORK: HARPER & ROW, 1964, 339 PP., LC#64-12672.
DISCUSSES MC NAMARA'S POLICY AND INNOVATIONS IN DEFENSE
DEPARTMENT. EXPLAINS CHANGES IN DECISION-MAKING PROCESS AND
PROCEDURAL REFORMS, SUCH AS COST-EFFECTIVENESS APPROACH TO
PROJECTS AND SYSTEMS. DETAILED DESCRIPTION OF SHIFT FROM
CONCEPT OF MASSIVE RETALIATION TO STRATEGY OF FLEXIBLE
RESPONSE AND LIMITED WARFARE. DRAWN LARGELY FROM DIRECT
TESTIMONY OF THE SECRETARY AND PENTAGON OFFICIALS.

0587 KAWALKOWSKI A.
"POUR UNE EUROPE INDEPENDENTE ET REUNIFIEE."
POLIT. ETRANG., 28 (NO.3, 63), 195-221.
POINTS UP NECESSITY OF NUCLEAR AUTONOMY. FOCUSES ATTEN-
TION ON DE GAULLE'S POLITICAL PLANS AND ECONOMIC OBJECTIVES.
ANALYZES AMERICAN AND RUSSIAN ATTITUDES WITH RESPECT TO
THESE AIMS.

0588 KAYSEN C.
"DATA BANKS AND DOSSIERS."
PUBLIC INTEREST, 7 (SPRING 67), 52-60.
GIVES BACKGROUND ON CONCEPTION OF NATIONAL DATA CENTER.
SUGGESTS PROBLEMS RAISED BY INTENSIVE CENTRALIZATION OF
INFORMATION BUT ARGUES THAT CENTRALIZATION NECESSARY TO
COUNTER INEFFICIENCIES OF OVER DECENTRALIZED STATISTICAL
SYSTEM. PROPOSES CHECKS TO DANGERS TO PRIVACY IN DISTIN-
GUISHING BETWEEN "DOSSIER" & "STATISTICAL DATA FILE."

0589 KECSKEMETI P.
"THE 'POLICY SCIENCES': ASPIRATION AND OUTLOOK."
WORLD POLIT., 4 (JULY 52), 520-35.
SUGGESTS THAT SOCIETY NEEDS TO CONSTRUCT A COMPREHENSIVE
THEORY OF BEHAVIOR BECAUSE FACTUAL AND SPECIALIZED KNOWLEDGE
OF SOCIAL PHENOMENA. IF APPLIED BY POLICY MAKERS, WOULD
BRING AS GREAT TRANSFORMATION TO SOCIAL AND POLITICAL FIELDS
AS THE TECHNOLOGICAL APPLICATION OF NATURAL SCIENCES DID IN
FIELD OF MASTERY OVER NATURAL FORCES. PRESENTS IDEAS OF
LEADING AUTHORITIES IN THE FIELD OF METHODOLOGY.

0590 KEISER N.F.
"PUBLIC RESPONSIBILITY AND FEDERAL ADVISORY GROUPS: A CASE
STUDY."
WESTERN POLIT. QUART., 11 (JUNE 58), 251-264.
STUDY OF THE BUSINESS ADVISORY COUNCIL OF DEPARTMENT OF
COMMERCE. BAC IS TYPICAL OF MANY PRIVATE GROUPS WHICH ARE
OFFICIAL DUTIES AND PRIVILEGES OFTEN MASK A SPECIFIC
INTEREST AT THE EXPENSE OF THE PUBLIC INTEREST.

0591 KELLEY G.A.
"THE POLITICAL BACKGROUND OF THE FRENCH A-BOMB."
ORBIS, 4 (FALL 60), 251-67.
TRACES FRENCH ATOMIC POLICY RE NATIONAL INTEREST AND

FOLLOWS POLICIES OF PRE-DE GAULLE GOVERNMENTS. ADVOCATES
CLAIM VALUE FOR PRESTIGE BARGAINING FOR EUROPEAN AND UNIVER-
SAL LEADERSHIP. OPPONENTS EMPHASIZE USELESSNESS, ECONOMIC
COST AND DIFFICULTY OF NEGOTIATIONS WITH USSR, HOLDING
REALISM REQUIRES ACCEPTANCE OF THIS FACT.

0592 KENNEDY J.F.
TO TURN THE TIDE.
NEW YORK: HARPER & ROW, 1962, 235 PP., LC#61-12221.
SELECTION OF PRESIDENT KENNEDY'S SPEECHES AND WRITINGS
FROM HIS ELECTION THROUGH 1961 ADJOURNMENT OF CONGRESS.
GREATEST EMPHASIS IS ON IMPORTANT INTERNATIONAL ISSUES BUT
ALSO INCLUDES DISCUSSION OF DOMESTIC ECONOMIC SITUATION,
SPACE PROGRAM, CIVIL RIGHTS, AND OTHER INTERNAL AFFAIRS.

0593 KENT A.
SPECIALIZED INFORMATION CENTERS.
WASHINGTON: SPARTAN BOOKS, 1965, 290 PP., LC#65-16172.
ANALYSIS OF PROBLEM OF "MEMORY" AS RELATED TO LIBRARY,
INSTITUTION, STUDENT, AND COMMUNICATION. DISCUSSES PURPOSE
AND METHOD OF INFORMATION RETRIEVAL. INCLUDES ACQUISITION OF
MATERIALS, ANALYSIS, TERMINOLOGY, INDEXING ON SEARCHABLE
MEDIUM, STORAGE OF SOURCE MATERIALS, SEARCH, AND DELIVERY
OF RESULTS. ADVANCES IN MECHANIZATION AND AUTOMATION WILL
ENABLE EFFICIENT STORAGE AND RETRIEVAL OF NEEDED DATA.

0594 KENWORTHY L.S.
FREE AND INEXPENSIVE MATERIALS ON WORLD AFFAIRS (PAMPHLET)
WASHINGTON: PUBLIC AFFAIRS PRESS, 1954, 94 PP., LC#54-10983.
TOPICAL AND NATIONAL LISTING OF MAPS, PAMPHLETS, AND FILM
STRIPS WITH MINIMAL ANNOTATION. MATERIALS ARE INTENDED TO BE
TEACHING AIDS FOR SUBUNIVERSITY PUPILS. ADDRESSES OF
PUBLISHERS FOLLOW 1300 LISTINGS. ALL IN ENGLISH-LANGUAGE
SOURCES.

0595 KIETH-LUCAS A.
DECISIONS ABOUT PEOPLE IN NEED, A STUDY OF ADMINISTRATIVE
RESPONSIVENESS IN PUBLIC ASSISTANCE.
CHAPEL HILL: U OF N CAR PR, 1957, 318 PP.
ANALYZES DECISION-MAKING SETTINGS AND PROCESSES IN PUB-
LIC WELFARE ADMINISTRATION INCLUDING SOCIAL, MORAL, AND POL-
ITICAL FACTORS. DISCUSSES IMPORTANT IMPLICATIONS OF AGENCY-
RECIPIENT RELATIONSHIP AND PROPOSES FORCES AND IDEAS TO
WHICH AGENCY ADMINISTRATION SHOULD BE RESPONSIVE. OUTLINES
STUDY OF AID TO DEPENDENT CHILDREN PROGRAM IN TWO STATES,
USED TO ANALYZES DECISION-MAKING PROCEDURES AND EFFECTS.

0596 KILE O.M.
THE FARM BUREAU MOVEMENT: THE FARM BUREAU THROUGH THREE
DECADES.
BALTIMORE: WAVERLY, 1948, 416 PP.
DESCRIBES THE RISE OF ORGANIZED AGRICULTURE, THE
FOUNDING CONVENTION OF THE AFBF AND ITS ORGANIZATION,
VARIOUS AFBF "ADMINISTRATIONS" MEMBERSHIP DRIVES. THE
"FARM BLOC" AND LOBBYING, BUREAU FINANCING, PUBLICITY,
PRESS, INTERGROUP CONFERENCES AND RELATIONSHIPS, AS WELL AS
SERVICES FOR MEMBERS AND STRUCTURAL ANALYSIS.

0597 KINGSTON-MCCLOUG E.
DEFENSE; POLICY AND STRATEGY.
NEW YORK: FREDERICK PRAEGER, 1960, 272 PP., LC#60-7612.
KINGSTON-MCCLOUGHTY EXPLAINS PROBLEMS INVOLVED IN
EVOLUTION OF DEFENSE POLICY AND IN DEVELOPMENT OF
INTERNATIONAL FRAMEWORK OF PLANNING. EMPHASIZES INCREASED
IMPORTANCE OF POLITICAL LEADER IN MAKING DEFENSE POLICY
AND STRATEGIC DECISIONS. DISCUSSES VARIOUS TYPES OF
DEFENSE SYSTEMS AND THEIR ORGANIZATION.

0598 KINTNER W.R., PFALTZGRAFF RL J.R.
"THE PROSPECTS FOR WESTERN SCIENCE AND TECHNOLOGY."
ORBIS, 9 (FALL 65), 565-586.
A PRIORITY ITEM AMONG THE NATIONS OF WESTERN EUROPE AND
THE US SHOULD BE IN THE AREA OF FINDING WAYS TO SURMOUNT
THE OBSTACLES TO TECHNICAL COLLABORATION. AUTHORS PREDICT
THAT USSR HAS DEVELOPED THE EDUCATIONAL AND SCIENTIFIC BASE
TO CHALLENGE US SUPERIORITY IN NEXT GENERATION AND THUS
GREATER WESTERN UNITY IS ESSENTIAL.

0599 KINTNER W.R.
PEACE AND THE STRATEGY CONFLICT.
NEW YORK: FREDERICK PRAEGER, 1967.
CONCERNED WITH THE PROPER ROLE OF US STRATEGIC POWER IN
PRESERVING WORLD PEACE AND AMERICAN SECURITY. CENTRAL THEME
IS THAT US STRATEGIC SUPERIORITY IS AN ESSENTIAL AND STRATE-
GIC INGREDIENT IN KEEPING PEACE. AUTHOR BELIEVES PEACE BEING
THREATENED BY US POLICY-PLANNERS SEEKING TO COPE WITH TWO
CONFLICTING GOALS--MAINTENANCE OF STRATEGIC SUPERIORITY AND
THE SLOWDOWN OF THE ARMS RACE.

0601 KISER M.
"ORGANIZATION OF AMERICAN STATES."
WASHINGTON: PAN AMER. UNION, 1955, 74 PP.
A HANDBOOK ABOUT ORGANIZATION DESCRIBING WHAT IT IS, HOW
IT IS ORGANIZED, WHAT IT DOES, AND THE INTER-AMERICAN
AGENCIES.

0602 KISSINGER H.A.
NUCLEAR WEAPONS AND FOREIGN POLICY.
NEW YORK: HARPER, 1957, 455 PP.
ATTEMPTS TO MODIFY ASSUMPTIONS ABOUT NUCLEAR WAR, DIPLOM-
ACY, NATURE OF PEACE. PROPOSES PLAN OF STRATEGY, COUNSELS
GUIDED DOCTRINE INCLUDING FULLER COMMUNICATION OF INTENTIONS
TO POWERS. REVIEWS FACTS ON SURVIVAL AFTER NUCLEAR ATTACK.

0603 KISSINGER H.A.
"ARMS CONTROL, INSPECTION AND SURPRISE ATTACK."
FOR. AFF., 38 (JULY 60), 557-75.
OUTLINES A PLAN DESIGNED TO MEET SOME OF THE OBJECTIONS
TO INSPECTION AND YET MAXIMIZE STABILITY. STATES THAT
SECURITY MUST BE RECOGNIZED AS THE PRIME OBJECTIVE OF ANY
ARMS CONTROL PROGRAM.

0604 KISSINGER H.A.
THE NECESSITY FOR CHOICE.
NEW YORK: HARPER, 1961, 370 PP.
APPRAISAL OF MAJOR ISSUES CONFRONTING USA FOREIGN POLICY.
FEELS UNITED STATES' POSITION IN WORLD HAS DETERIORATED IN
PAST DECADE AND CHALLENGES POLICY MAKERS TO RESOLVE THE MANY
ISSUES WHICH HAVE BEEN IGNORED SINCE 1945, PRIMARILY,
DETERRENCE, LIMITED WAR PLANS, ARMS CONTROL AND THE ATLANTIC
COMMUNITY.

0605 KLAPPER J.T.
"WHAT WE KNOW ABOUT THE EFFECTS OF MASS COMMUNICATION: THE
BRINK OF HOPE" (BMR)
PUBLIC OPINION QUART., 21 (WINTER 58), 453-474.
AUTHOR FEELS NEW ORIENTATION TOWARD RESEARCH IN MASS
COMMUNICATIONS AND NEW GENERALIZATIONS TO ORDER ITS
SEEMINGLY DIVERSE AND UNRELATED FINDINGS ARE NECESSARY FOR
SUCCESSFUL FUTURE RESEARCH. ARTICLE DESCRIBES NEW ORIENTA-
TION, EMERGING GENERALIZATIONS, AND FINDINGS WHICH THEORY
WILL MOLD INTO A BODY OF ORGANIZED KNOWLEDGE. AUTHOR
INCLUDES A SELECTIVE BIBLIOGRAPHY OF 53 WORKS.

0606 KLOTSCHE J.M.
THE URBAN UNIVERSITY AND THE FUTURE OF OUR CITIES.
NEW YORK: HARPER & ROW, 1966, 149 PP.
SKETCHES HISTORY OF THE URBAN UNIVERSITY AND POSES
SALIENT QUESTIONS ABOUT RELATION OF UNIVERSITY TO THE CITY
AND ITS PROBLEMS. POINTS UP OPPORTUNITY FACING UNIVERSITY.
DESCRIBES NEW TECHNIQUES AND MECHANISMS REQUIRED BY
MAGNITUDE AND COMPLEXITY OF CITY'S AFFAIRS.

0607 KNAPP D.C.
"CONGRESSIONAL CONTROL OF AGRICULTURAL CONSERVATION POLICY:
A CASE STUDY OF THE APPROPRIATIONS PROCESS."
POLIT. SCI. QUART., 71 (JUNE 56), 257-281.
EXAMINATION OF THE CONTROL WHICH CONGRESS EXERCISED OVER
AGRICULTURAL CONSERVATION POLICY IN THE APPROPRIATIONS PROC-
ESS 1940-50. ANALYSIS OF BOTH THE ADMINISTRATIVE ISSUES
RAISED AND THE INFLUENCE IN THE SETTLEMENT. AIM IS TO PRE-
SENT A COMPLETE PICTURE OF THE ROLE OF POLICY-MAKING IN THE
APPROPRIATIONS PROCESS. GIVES DETAILED ANALYSIS OF THE
AGRICULTURAL CONSERVATION PROGRAM.

0608 KNORR K., MORGENSTERN O.
SCIENCE AND DEFENSE: SOME CRITICAL THOUGHTS ON MILITARY
RESEARCH AND DEVELOPMENT.
PRINCETON: CTR OF INTL STUDIES, 1965, 58 PP.
CLAIMS MANAGEMENT OF MILITARY R&D IN US IS NOT CONDUCIVE
TO THE ASSERTION AND SURVIVAL OF NEW IDEAS, THAT WE FAIL TO
NURTURE THE NATION'S ASSETS FOR R&D, THAT THE MILITARY FAIL
TO GIVE PROPER DIRECTION AND INSPIRATION TO THE SCIENTISTS
AND ENGINEERS, THAT THE CONCEPT OF R&D IS TOO NARROWLY
CONFINED TO MILITARY WEAPONS, THAT INNOVATION IN MILI-
TARY-POLITICAL STRATEGY IS NEGLECTED.

0609 KOENIG L.W.
THE SALE OF THE TANKERS.
WASHINGTON: COMM ON PUBLIC ADMIN, 1950, 184 PP.
STUDY RELATES 1947-48 US GOVERNMENT SALE OF 83 TANKERS TO
13 FOREIGN NATIONS. EXAMINES ENSUING DIFFICULTIES AMONG
PUBLIC AND PRIVATE GROUPS IN AMERICAN POLITICAL AND ADMINIS-
TRATIVE LIFE. REVIEWS ATTITUDES AND ACTIONS OF ALL INVOLVED
PARTIES.

0610 KOENIG L.W.
THE TRUMAN ADMINISTRATION: ITS PRINCIPLES AND PRACTICE.
NEW YORK: NEW YORK U PR, 1956, 394 PP., LC#56-7425.
ANALYZES COMPLEX PROBLEMS TRUMAN FACED ASSUMING POWER IN
MIDDLE OF WORLD WAR AND IN FOUR MONTHS COPING WITH PROBLEM
OF DEMOBILIZING NATION GEARED FOR WAR FOR THREE YEARS.
INCLUDES PROBLEM OF USING BOMB AND POLITICAL SCENE AT
POTSDAM, WHICH INITIATED COLD WAR. FOLLOWS HIM THROUGH IKE'S
ELECTION.

0611 KOHL W.L.
"NUCLEAR SHARING IN NATO AND THE MULTILATERAL FORCE."
POLIT. SCI. QUART., 80 (MAR. 65), 88-109.
AUTHOR HOPES FOR ACKNOWLEDGMENT THAT THERE IS A NUCLEAR
SHARING PROBLEM IN NATO THAT MUST BE SOLVED. HE BELIEVES THE
MLF OR A VARIATION OF IT, OFFERS BEST MEANS OF MEETING

SHARING PROBLEM. HE DISCUSSES US POLICIES ON SHARING, FEA-
SIBILITY, PURPOSES, MILITARY VALUE, PROBLEM OF CONTROL, PO-
CITICAL EFFECTS AND VALUE, AND EFFECTS ON EAST-WEST RELA-
TIONS OF MLF.

0612 KOLDZIEF E.A.
"CONGRESSIONAL RESPONSIBILITY FOR THE COMMON DEFENSE: THE
MONEY PROBLEM."
WESTERN POLIT. QUART., 16 (MAR. 63), 149-160.
DISCUSSES THE PROPER ROLE FOR CONGRESS IN POLICY-MAKING,
FOCUSING PRIMARILY ON ONE AREA--CONGRESS' ANNUAL AUTHORIZA-
TION AND APPROPRIATION OF FUNDS FOR THE MILITARY ESTABLISH-
MENT. BRIEFLY DESCRIBES THE PRINCIPAL DISADVANTAGES HAMPER-
ING CONGRESS AND DELINEATES A NUMBER OF CRITICALLY IMPORTANT
FUNCTIONS WHICH IT SHOULD DISCHARGE IN DEFENSE POLICY DE-
VELOPMENT.

0613 KOMESAR N.K. ED., MARSON C.C. ED.
"SECURITY INTERESTS IN GOVERNMENT CONTRACTS* WHEREIN THE
TORTOISE WINS THE RES."
UNIV. CHICAGO LAW REV., 34 (SPRING 67), 661-685.
REVIEWS POLICY OF FEDERAL COURTS IN ALLOWING DEFENSE
DEP'T TO ENFORCE ITS SECURITY INTERESTS WITHOUT NOTIFYING
THIRD PARTIES. SUGGESTS GOVERNMENT SHOULD FILE SECURITY IN-
TERESTS SO THAT PROSPECTIVE CREDITORS HAVE WAY TO DETERMINE
WHETHER CONTRACTOR'S PROPERTY ENCUMBERED BY GOVERNMENT AGEN-
CY. PROPOSES SEVERAL METHODS BY WHICH SUCH REQUIREMENTS MAY
BE EFFECTED.

0614 KORNHAUSER W.
SCIENTISTS IN INDUSTRY: CONFLICT AND ACCOMMODATION.
BERKELEY: U OF CALIF PR, 1963, 230 PP., LC#62-8491.
STUDIES SCIENTISTS AND ENGINEERS WHO CONDUCT RESEARCH FOR
INDUSTRY. PRIMARY SOURCE OF DATA IS SERIES OF INTERVIEWS
WITH RESEARCH SCIENTISTS, ENGINEERS, AND MANAGERS.
IDENTIFIES MAJOR PROBLEMS AND VARIABLES OF PROFESSIONAL
RELATIONS IN ORGANIZATIONS. DISCUSSES PROFESSIONAL GOALS,
STRAINS BETWEEN PROFESSIONS AND ORGANIZATIONS, CONTROLS,
ADAPTATIONS, AND PROFESSIONAL INFLUENCE IN INDUSTRY.

0615 KOROL A.G.
SOVIET RESEARCH AND DEVELOPMENT.
CAMBRIDGE: M I T PRESS, 1965, 375 PP., LC#64-8312.
ORGANIZATION, PERSONNEL, AND FUNDS USED FOR SOVIET
RESEARCH AND DEVELOPMENT. STUDY TO EXAMINE MAGNITUDE AND
DISTRIBUTION OF NATURAL RESOURCES ALLOCATED TO SCIENTIFIC
RESEARCH.

0616 KRAFT J.
THE GRAND DESIGN.
NEW YORK: HARPER, 1962, 122 PP.
DESCRIBES GENESIS OF ATLANTIC PARTNERSHIP, AND ITS INTER-
NATIONAL IMPLICATIONS AS WELL AS THOSE FOR THE US.

0617 KRANZBERG M. ED., PURSELL G.W.E. ED.
TECHNOLOGY IN WESTERN CIVILIZATION VOLUME ONE.
NEW YORK: OXFORD U PR, 1967, 802 PP., LC#67-15129.
CONTAINS 45 ARTICLES WRITTEN IN DIRECTION OF EMPHASIZING
IMPORTANCE OF TECHNOLOGY IN HUMAN AFFAIRS. COMMENCING WITH
HISTORICAL PERSPECTIVES, CONTINUES ON TO INDUSTRIAL REVOLU-
TION, STEAM AGE, MECHANICAL AND ELECTRICAL ADVANCES, MASS
PRODUCTION, AND PUBLIC POLICY.

0618 KRAUS J.
"A MARXIST IN GHANA."
PROBLEMS OF COMMUNISM, 16 (MAY-JUNE 67), 42-49.
PORTRAYS THE RISE AND FALL OF NKRUMAH, HIS EFFORTS TO
ESTABLISH SOCIALIST STATE IN GHANA, HIS ATTEMPTS TO DISSEM-
INATE MARXIST VIEWPOINT THROUGHOUT AFRICA, AND THE POLI-
TICAL AND IDEOLOGICAL FORCES BEHIND HIS IDEAS AND PROGRAMS.
DESCRIBES EXTENT OF SOCIALIZATION, ITS ECONOMIC AND SOCIAL
EFFECTS, ITS INTERNATIONAL REPERCUSSIONS. CONCLUDES THAT
SOCIALISM HAS BEEN A "MANIPULATIVE MYTH" TO ADVANCE NKRUMAH.

0619 KREITH K.
"PEACE RESEARCH AND GOVERNMENT POLICY."
BACKGROUND, 8 (FEB. 65), 269-277.
NOTES THAT GOVERNMENT RECOGNIZES NEED FOR SERIOUS EFFORTS
IN PEACE RESEARCH FIELD, BUT BELIEVES THAT MORE IMPORTANT
AND VALID WORK CAN AND SHOULD BE MADE OUTSIDE OF THE GOVERN-
MENT. THE EXCEPTION TO THIS IS IN THE AREA OF ARMS CONTROL
AND OTHER MECHANICAL METHODS FOR SUPPRESSING WAR.

0620 KREPS J., LAWS R.
AUTOMATION AND THE OLDER WORKER: AN ANNOTATED BIBLIOGRAPHY
(PAMPHLET)
NEW YORK: NAT COUNCIL ON AGING, 1963, 43 PP.
ANNOTATED LISTING ARRANGED ALPHABETICALLY BY AUTHOR AND
INCLUDING BOOKS, PAMPHLETS, PERIODICALS, AND OFFICIAL DOCU-
MENTS. APPROXIMATELY 130 ITEMS ALL IN ENGLISH.

0621 KRICKUS R.J.
"ON THE MORALITY OF CHEMICAL/BIOLOGICAL WAR."
J. OF CONFLICT RESOLUTION, 9 (JUNE 65), 200-210.
BASED ON A SUMMARY OF BELIEFS CONCERNING THE RELEVANCE OF
JUST WAR DOCTRINES IN AN AGE OF NUCLEAR WEAPONS OF MASS DES-

TRUCTION, KRICKUS DISCUSSES MORALITY OF CHEMICAL/BIOLOGICAL WEAPONS, TABOO ON RATIONAL DISCUSSION, DISTINCTION BETWEEN THE TWO TYPES OF AGENTS, RANGE OF POSSIBLE MILITARY USES AND POSITIVE MORALITY OF NONLETHAL WEAPONS. ON BALANCE, ADVOCATES CB ARMS CONTROL WORLDWIDE.

0622 KRUPP S.
PATTERN IN ORGANIZATIONAL ANALYSIS: A CRITICAL EXAMINATION.
NEW YORK: CHILTON BOOKS, 1961, 185 PP., LC#61-11614.
CONCERNED WITH METHODOLOGICAL AND PHILOSOPHICAL ISSUES OF ORGANIZATION THEORY. THE LATTER HAS EXCLUDED, UNDULY, PHENOMENA OF POWER, CONFLICT, RESOURCE ALLOCATION, INCOME DISTRIBUTION AND FOLLETT'S "LAW OF THE SITUATION," AND HAS OBSCURED THE FACT THAT STRUCTURE OF AUTHORITY CAN BE AN OBJECT OF CONCERTED PARTICIPANT CONTEST.

0623 KRUSCHE H.
"THE STRIVING OF THE KIESINGER-STRAUS GOVERNMENT FOR NUCLEAR WEAPONS IS A THREAT TO EUROPEAN SECURITY."
GERMAN FOREIGN POLICY, 6 (FEB. 67), 152-160.
ARGUES THAT BONN POLICIES POTENTIALLY THREATEN EUROPEAN AND WORLD PEACE. NECESSARY TO LIMIT ARMS RACE AND DANGERS OF NUCLEAR CONFLICT. WESTBGERMANY OPPOSED TO ARMS CONTROL AND THUS EVENTUAL GERMAN REUNIFICATION. ARGUES THAT WEST GERMANY CONSTITUTES MAIN SOURCE OF TENSION BETWEEN EUROPEAN STATES. SOME DOCUMENTATION.

0624 KRUTILLA J.V.
CONSERVATION RECONSIDERED.
AMER. ECO. REVIEW, 57 (SEPT. 67), 77-786.
EXAMINES BASIS ON WHICH DECISIONS CAN BE MADE IN CHOICE ENTAILING ACTION WHICH WILL HAVE IRREVERSIBLE ADVERSE CONSEQUENCE FOR "RARE PHENOMENA OF NATURE." URGES DEVELOPMENT OF POLICY THAT CONSIDERS USE OF AREA FOR SPECIALIZED RECREATION AND MAINTENANCE OF BIOLOGICAL DIVERSITY FOR SCIENTIFIC RESEARCH AND EDUCATION.

0625 KUENNE R.E.
THE POLARIS MISSILE STRIKE* A GENERAL ECONOMIC SYSTEMS ANALYSIS.
COLUMBUS: OHIO STATE U PR, 1966, 434 PP., LC#66-10715.
STUDY OF THE POLARIS DETERRENCE SYSTEM DEALING WITH ITS EFFECTIVENESS IN PREVENTING SOVIET UNION FROM LAUNCHING A THERMONUCLEAR ATTACK. OFFERS ECONOMIC SOLUTIONS AND PRESENTS A PROBABILISTIC MODEL SUSCEPTIBLE TO USE BY COMPUTER. HYPOTHESIZES ABOUT NATIONAL SECURITY AND ARMS CONTROL.

0626 KURAKOV I.G.
SCIENCE, TECHNOLOGY AND COMMUNISM; SOME QUESTIONS OF DEVELOPMENT (TRANS. BY CARIN DEDIJER)
NEW YORK: PERGAMON PRESS, 1966, 126 PP., LC#66-12657.
IN LIGHT OF MARXIST SOCIAL THEORY AND METHODS OF MARXIST ECONOMICS, TREATS PROBLEMS OF ECONOMICS, RESEARCH POLICY, AND INDUSTRIAL MANAGEMENT. EMPHASIZES ACCOUNTING FOR RESEARCH WORK INPUTS IN COST BENEFIT ANALYSES. CRITICIZES SOVIET RESEARCH PLANNING AND USE OF MATERIAL INCENTIVES. SHOWS ROLE OF SCIENCE AND TECHNOLOGY IN SOVIET PRODUCTION AND EXPLAINS DIRECTION OF THEIR DEVELOPMENT.

0627 KUZMACK A.M.
"TECHNOLOGICAL CHANGE AND STABLE DETERRENCE."
J. OF CONFLICT RESOLUTION, 9 (SEPT. 65), 309-317.
COUNTERS ARGUMENT THAT TECHNOLOGICAL CHANGE, HENCE, CONTINUED MILITARY R AND D, MUST HAVE DESTABILIZING EFFECT ON STABLE DETERRENCE. CITES HISTORY, LONG LEAD TIMES FOR INNOVATION, AND SHORTER TIME FOR COUNTERMEASURES AS KEY REASONS.

0628 LA PORTE T.
"DIFFUSION AND DISCONTINUITY IN SCIENCE, TECHNOLOGY AND PUBLIC AFFAIRS: RESULTS OF A SEARCH IN THE FIELD."
AMER. BEHAVIORAL SCIENTIST, 10 (MAY 67), 23-29.
IN AN EXTENSIVE SERIES OF INTERVIEWS WITH INDIVIDUAL SCHOLARS AND FEDERAL ADMINISTRATORS, AUTHOR FOUND A "DISTRESSING" DISCONTINUITY BETWEEN SCHOLAR AND RESEARCHER. SUGGESTS THE TWO BEGIN ACCOMMODATION PROCESS.

0629 LAHAYE R.
LES ENTREPRISES PUBLIQUES AU MAROC.
PARIS: LIBRAIRIE DE MEDICIS, 1961, 340 PP.
ANALYSIS OF STATE OWNERSHIP AND PARTICIPATION IN PUBLIC SERVICES AND INDUSTRY IN MOROCCO. DESCRIBES ENTERPRISES, ANALYZES THEIR STRUCTURE, AND DISCUSSES THEIR ECONOMIC AND ADMINISTRATIVE EVOLUTION. STATE PARTNERSHIP IN PRIVATE INDUSTRY IS IMPORTANT TO ECONOMIC DEVELOPMENT, AS WELL AS STATE OWNERSHIP WHERE INDUSTRY HAS NOT DEVELOPED SUCCESSFULLY. DISCUSSES GROWTH OF ADMINISTRATIVE JURISPRUDENCE.

0630 LALL B.G.
"GAPS IN THE ABM DEBATE."
BUL. ATOMIC SCIENTISTS, 23 (APR. 67), 45-46.
POINTS OUT THAT US OFFICIALS IN DISCUSSING HOPES FOR AN AGREEMENT WITH THE USSR AGAINST BUILDING AN ANTI-BALLISTIC MISSILE SYSTEM FAIL TO POINT OUT ESTABLISHED SOVIET DISINTEREST IN SUCH A MOVE WHEN UNACCOMPANIED BY REDUCTIONS IN OFFENSIVE STRENGTH. ALSO NOTES LACK OF COUNTER-PRESSURE IN US EXECUTIVE ESTABLISHMENT TO MILITARY DESIRES.

0631 LAMBERT J.
LATIN AMERICA: SOCIAL STRUCTURES AND POLITICAL INSTITUTIONS.
BERKELEY: U OF CALIF PR, 1967, 330 PP.
EXAMINES LATIN AMERICAN POLITICS AND SOCIETIES IN TERMS OF DISTINCT, INDIVIDUAL CATEGORIES RATHER THAN TREATING LATIN AMERICA AS ONE LARGE ENTITY. STUDIES THREE TYPES OF DIVISIONS: THOSE OF WESTERN EUROPE WITH FULLY DEVELOPED ECONOMIC AND SOCIAL STRUCTURES, UNDERDEVELOPED COUNTRIES WITH ARCHAIC SOCIAL STRUCTURES, AND COUNTRIES OF UNEQUAL DEVELOPMENT AND DUAL SOCIAL STRUCTURES.

0632 LANG A.S., SOBERMAN R.M.
URBAN RAIL TRANSIT.
CAMBRIDGE: M I T PRESS, 1964, 139 PP., LC#63-23379.
DISCUSSES ECONOMICS AND TECHNOLOGY OF MASS RAIL-TRANSPORTATION SYSTEMS. DESCRIBES THE PHYSICAL COMPONENTS OF THESE SYSTEMS, THEIR OPERATIONAL REQUIREMENTS, AND THEIR COSTS. EMPHASIZES CHARACTERISTICS OF CAPACITY AND QUALITY OF SERVICE AND RELATES THESE FACTORS TO COST. ATTEMPTS TO RELATE RAIL TRANSIT TO THE ENTIRE URBAN TRANSPORTATION SCENE.

0633 LANG D.
FROM HIROSHIMA TO THE MOON: CHRONICLES OF LIFE IN THE ATOMIC AGE.
NEW YORK: SIMON AND SCHUSTER, 1959, 496 PP., LC#59-13877.
STUDY OF DEVELOPMENT AND MAJOR USES OR PROJECTS OF NUCLEAR POWER SINCE BOMB IN 1945. OPINIONATED ANALYSIS BY NEWSPAPER REPORTER OF MEN AND MACHINES THAT TOOK US TO MOON. CONCENTRATES ON FEELINGS AND OPINIONS OF PUBLIC BYSTANDER KEPT IN DARK UNTIL BOMB.

0634 LANGER W.L., GLEASON S.E.
THE UNDECLARED WAR, 1940-1941.
NEW YORK: HARPER & ROW, 1953, 963 PP., LC#53-7738.
EXTENSIVELY AND IN GREAT DETAIL DESCRIBES WORLD CRISIS AT INCEPTION OF EUROPEAN PHASE OF WWII AND DEVELOPMENT OF US POLICY IN ITS GLOBAL SETTING, ANALYZING "THE TORTURED EMERGENCE" OF US AS WORLD LEADER.

0635 LAPP R.E.
THE NEW PRIESTHOOD; THE SCIENTIFIC ELITE AND THE USES OF POWER.
NEW YORK: HARPER & ROW, 1965, 244 PP., LC#65-14686.
STATES THAT SCIENTIFIC REVOLUTION IS DANGEROUS TO DEMOCRATIC TRADITIONS IN THAT SCIENTIFIC ADVISERS WIELD ENORMOUS POWER OVER DECISIONS BUT ARE OUTSIDE SYSTEM OF CHECKS AND BALANCES. SOCIETY MUST DESIGN AND APPLY PROPER CONTROLS OVER SCIENTISTS AND THEIR DEVELOPMENTS. DISCUSSES RELATION OF SCIENTISTS TO MILITARY. PUBLIC, CONGRESS, AND PRESIDENT.

0636 LARSEN K.
NATIONAL BIBLIOGRAPHIC SERVICES: THEIR CREATION AND OPERATION.
PARIS: UNESCO, 1953, 146 PP.
DEFINES PURPOSE, SCOPE, AND TECHNIQUES FOR ESTABLISHING A BIBLIOGRAPHIC CENTER UNDER THE AUSPICES OF UNESCO; OUTLINES ITS FUNCTIONS. STRESSES ITS IMPORTANCE, AND SPECIFIES TECHNIQUES. DESCRIBES THE MEANS FOR PROCURING, PRODUCING, AND PROMOTING MATERIALS; DEALS WITH THE UNION CATALOGUE, DIRECTORIES, INFORMATION SERVICE, ADMINISTRATION OF THE CENTER, ETC.

0637 LASKI H.J.
REFLECTIONS ON THE REVOLUTIONS OF OUR TIME.
NEW YORK: VIKING PRESS, 1943, 417 PP.
ATTACKS CAPITALISM AS DYSFUNCTIONAL FOR THE WELFARE OF THE MASSES AND CLAIMS EARLY CRITICISMS OF SOVIET UNION ARE UNWARRANTED AND PREMATURE. LAUDS USSR AS PORTENTOUS OF NEW CIVILIZATION. PROPOSES A PLANNED DEMOCRACY AS IDEAL STATE SINCE IT WOULD BE IMMUNE TO FLUCTUATIONS OF "FREE" MARKET SYSTEM, CLAIMING GOVERNMENT INTERVENTION HAS BEEN PROVED NECESSARY BY FAILURE OF CAPITALISM TO SOLVE SOCIAL PROBLEMS.

0638 LASSWELL H.D.
"THE RELATION OF IDEOLOGICAL INTELLIGENCE TO PUBLIC POLICY."
ETHICS, 53 (OCT. 42), 25-34.
STUDY OF FACTS ABOUT THOUGHT AND FEELINGS IN THE MAKING OF IMPORTANT PUBLIC DECISIONS WITH THE EMPHASIS ON THE CONTRIBUTION OF SUCH FACTS TO THE CLARIFICATION OF GOALS AND ALTERNATIVES. DEPLORES TIMIDITY IN DEMOCRATIC SOCIETY INHIBITING THE REALIZATION OF DEMOCRATIC ASPIRATIONS.

0639 LASSWELL H.D.
THE ANALYSIS OF POLITICAL BEHAVIOUR: AN EMPIRICAL APPROACH.
NEW YORK: OXFORD U. PR., 1947, 314 PP.
ARTICLES AND ESSAYS DIVIDED INTO THREE MAJOR FIELDS OF INQUIRY: HOW TO INTEGRATE SCIENCE, MORALS AND POLITICS, HOW TO ANALYZE POLITICS AND HOW TO OBSERVE AND RECORD POLITICS. INCLUDES CRITIQUE OF LEGAL EDUCATION, MILITARY STATE, THE FASCIST STATE AND DESCRIBES VARIOUS SCIENTIFIC TECHNIQUES FOR POLITICAL SCIENCE RESEARCH.

0641 LASSWELL H.D. ED.
"RESEARCH IN POLITICAL BEHAVIOR."

AM. POL. SCI. REV., 46 (DEC. 52), 1003-1045.
DEFINES AND ILLUSTRATES SIGNIFICANT CONTEMPORARY
DEVELOPMENTS IN POLITICAL RESEARCH. OUTLINES REQUIREMENTS,
CHARACTERISTICS, AND IMPLICATIONS OF RESEARCH AND PRESENTS
THREE RESEARCH PROJECTS THAT MEET THESE SPECIFICATIONS.
INCLUDES BIBLIOGRAPHY ON METHODS AND TECHNIQUES OF RESEARCH.

0642 LASSWELL H.D.
"THE SCIENTIFIC STUDY OF INTERNATIONAL RELATIONS."
YRB. WORLD AFF., 12 (58), 1-28.
SURVEY OF SCIENTIFIC CONTRIBUTIONS TO INTERNATIONAL
STUDIES IN RECENT YEARS. FOCUSES ON THEORIES OF WORLD POLI-
TICAL EQUILIBRIUM, THEORIES OF MILITARY, DIPLOMATIC, IDEO-
LOGICAL AND ECONOMIC STRATEGY AND METHODS OF OBTAINING AND
PROCESSING DATA.

0643 LASSWELL H.D.
THE FUTURE OF POLITICAL SCIENCE.
ENGLEWOOD CLIFFS: PRENTICE HALL, 1963, 256 PP., LC#63-16401.
DISCUSSES GROWTH AND RELEVANCE OF POLITICAL SCIENCE
IN INCREASINGLY INDUSTRIALIZED AND URBANIZED SOCIETY.
EMPHASIZES CULTIVATION OF CREATIVITY AND APPLAUDS CREATION
OF CENTERS OF POLITICAL SCIENCE AS INSTITUTIONAL MEANS OF
FACING CHALLENGE.

0644 LASSWELL H.D.
"THE POLICY SCIENCES OF DEVELOPMENT."
WORLD POLIT., 17 (JAN. 65), 286-309.
'SELF-SUSTAINING LEVEL OF CREATIVE CONCERN WITH THE POWER
VALUE AND ITS DIVERSE MODES OF INSTITUTIONAL EXPRESSION...
CAN PROVIDE AN INCLUSIVE FRAME OF REFERENCE FOR THE
DECISION-MAKERS AND CHOOSERS INVOLVED IN GIVING OR
RECEIVING ASSISTANCE OR IN DIRECTING SELF-SUSTAINING
AND INTEGRATED GROWTH.'

0645 LAWRENCE S.A.
THE BATTERY ADDITIVE CONTROVERSY (PAMPHLET)
UNIVERSITY: U ALABAMA PR, 1962, 34 PP.
RELATES EPISODE OF JESS M. RITCHIE, WHO SOUGHT TO MARKET
A PREPARATION CLAIMING TO PROLONG BATTERY LIFE. CHARGED WITH
MISLEADING ADVERTISING, HE ATTACKED FTC AND CHALLENGED
SCIENTIFIC ACCURACY OF NATIONAL BUREAU OF STANDARD'S TEST
FINDINGS. DESCRIBES TACTICS OF DIFFERENT GROUPS OF
SCIENTISTS IN CASE.

0646 LAY S.H., POOLE R.E.
"EXCLUSIVE GOVERNMENTAL LIABILITY FOR SPACE ACCIDENTS."
AMER BAR ASSN., 53 (SEPT. 67), 831-836.
GAP BETWEEN SPACE TECHNOLOGY AND SPACE LAW INCLUDES
THIRD-PARTY LIABILITY PROBLEMS ARISING FROM SPACE ACCIDENTS.
ANALYZES CONFLICTING OBJECTIVES OF ANY SOLUTION: QUICK AND
FULL COMPENSATION, POPULAR SUPPORT, PRIVATE INDUSTRIAL
PARTICIPATION, PREVENTION OF ACCIDENTS, AND FAIRNESS IN
DISTRIBUTION OF LOSSES. ADVOCATES GOVERNMENT LIABILITY
PROGRAM AS BEST SOLUTION.

0647 LE GHAIT E.
NO CARTE BLANCHE TO CAPRICORN; THE FOLLY OF NUCLEAR WAR.
NEW YORK: BOOKFIELD HOUSE, 1960, 114 PP.
ANALYSIS OF NATO NUCLEAR STRATEGY. EXAMINES DANGERS OF
INCREASED BUILD-UP OF NUCLEAR WEAPONS IN EUROPE RELATIVE TO
POPULATION AND CREATION OF HOSTILITIES IN WESTERN EUROPEAN
NATIONS BACAUSE OF RISKS FROM DEPLOYMENT OF SUCH WEAPONS.

0648 LEAR J.
"PEACE: SCIENCE'S NEXT GREAT EXPLORATION."
SAT. REV., (DEC. 60), 51-52.
DISCUSSES JEROME WEISNER'S VIEWS ON ARMS CONTROL AND DIS-
ARMAMENT. MAINTAINS ARMS CONTROL SYSTEM FEASIBLE NOW. AD-
VOCATES PRESIDENTIAL ENDORSEMENT OF PLAN, REORGANIZATION OF
SCIENCE STRUCTURE IN FEDERAL GOVERNMENT, AND FORMATION OF
PEACE ORGANIZATION.

0649 LECHT L.
GOAL, PRIORITIES, AND DOLLARS: THE NEXT DECADE.
NEW YORK: FREE PRESS OF GLENCOE, 1966, 365 PP., LC#66-19798.
ATTEMPTS SYNTHESIS OF REQUIRED, DESIRED, AND FEASIBLE
GOALS OF PUBLIC EXPENDITURE. SURVEYS THESE GOALS IN TERMS
OF SOCIAL, ECONOMIC, AND POLITICAL OBJECTIVES: WELFARE,
URBAN DEVELOPMENT, HEALTH, EDUCATION, TRANSPORTATION,
DEFENSE, HOUSING, INTERNATIONAL AID, SPACE, AND AGRICULTURE.

0650 LECLERCQ H., WEST R.L.
"ECONOMIC RESEARCH AND DEVELOPMENT IN TROPICAL AFRICA."
SOCIAL RESEARCH, 32 (FALL 65), 299-320.
WHILE THE PRESENT CAPABILITY FOR RESEARCH IS DEFINITELY
LOW BY STANDARDS OF INTERNATIONAL COMPARISON, A SHARP IN-
CREASE OF RESEARCH ACTIVITY HAS OCCURRED SINCE 1960. ARTICLE
COVERS THE STRUCTURE OF ECONOMIC RESEARCH FACILITIES THAT
EXISTED IN COLONIAL AFRICA, AND THE GROWTH OF THE TEN MAJOR
ACADEMIC RESEARCH CENTERS SINCE INDEPENDENCE.

0651 LEE R.R., FLEISCHER G.A., ROGGEVEEN V.J.
ENGINEERING-ECONOMIC PLANNING MISCELLANEOUS SUBJECTS: A
SELECTED BIBLIOGRAPHY (MIMEOGRAPHED)
STANFORD: STAN U PROJ ENG & ECO, 1961, 53 PP.

SELECTION OF REFERENCES TO CITY AND REGIONAL PLANNING.
SPECIAL EMPHASIS ON ADMINISTRATIVE, ECONOMIC, LEGISLATIVE,
AND POLITICAL ASPECTS. INCLUDES SECTIONS ON ENGINEERING
ECONOMY THEORY, INVESTMENT DECISION-MAKING, LAND AND NATURAL
RESOURCES, PUBLIC FINANCE, AND URBAN RENEWAL. INCLUDES BRIEF
DESCRIPTIONS OF MANY BOOKS AND ARTICLES LISTED. STUDIES ARE
BOTH GENERAL AND OF SPECIFIC TOPICS.

0652 LEFEVER E.W.
ARMS AND ARMS CONTROL.
NEW YORK: PRAEGER, 1962, 337 PP.
FOCUSES ATTENTION ON THE PRICE OF MILITARY STABILITY,
TECHNOLOGY, CO-EXISTENCE OF WAR AND DISARMAMENT AND THE
SOVIET ATTITUDE TOWARDS DISARMAMENT.

0653 LEFTON M.
"DECISION MAKING IN A MENTAL HOSPITAL: REAL, PERCEIVED,
AND IDEAL."
AMER. SOCIOLOGICAL REV., 24 (DEC. 59), 822-829.
A STUDY OF 5I MENTAL HEALTH SPECIALISTS AS TO
THEIR DECISION-MAKING PROCESSES IN A SMALL PSYCHIATRIC
HOSPITAL, USING THE CRITERIA OF ORGANIZATION AND THE
EQUALITARIAN APPROACH REGARDING CARE AND TREATMENT OF
PATIENTS.

0654 LEISERSON A.
"SCIENTISTS AND THE POLICY PROCESS."
AM. POL. SCI. REV., 52 (JUNE 65), 408-416.
REPORT ON INFLUENCE OF SCIENTISTS AND SCIENTIFIC METHODS
ON FEDERAL GOVERNMENT, WITH CONCENTRATION OF ROLES OF
SCIENTISTS IN THE EXECUTIVE OFFICE OF THE PRESIDENT.

0655 LENTZ T.F.
"REPORT ON A SURVEY OF SOCIAL SCIENTISTS CONDUCTED BY THE
ATTITUDE RESEARCH LABORATORY."
INT. J. OPIN. ATT. RES., 14 (SPRING 50), 97-102.
SUMMARY OF OPINIONS OF SOCIAL SCIENTISTS IN THE USA ABOUT
THE VALUE AND FEASIBILITY OF, AND POSSIBLE TECHNIQUES FOR
RELATING SOCIAL SCIENCE TO WAR AND PEACE.

0656 LEPAWSKY A.
ADMINISTRATION.
NEW YORK: ALFRED KNOPF, 1949, 675 PP.
DISCUSSES ADMINISTRATION AS ART, SCIENCE, AND VOCATION,
EMPHASIZING ROLE OF ADMINISTRATIVE MACHINERY IN SOCIAL,
ECONOMIC, AND POLITICAL AFFAIRS. ATTEMPTS TO DEVELOP
APPRECIATION OF SOUND AND TESTED ADMINISTRATIVE METHODS,
MANAGERIAL TECHNIQUES, AND ORGANIZATIONAL DEVICES, AND TO
AID RECOGNITION OF UNSOUND ADMINISTRATIVE PRACTICES.

0657 LERNER A.P.
"NUCLEAR SYMMETRY AS A FRAMEWORK FOR COEXISTENCE."
SOC. RES., 31 (SUMMER 64), 141-54.
ARGUES THAT IMPOSSIBILITY OF WINNING A NUCLEAR WAR IN ANY
REAL SENSE SHOULD LEAD TO POLICY IN WHICH WINNING IS RULED
OUT AND IDEAL BECOMES SYMMETRY. OFFERS AGGRESSION-RESPONSE
RATIOS BASED ON THIS PRINCIPLE. SUGGESTS PRINCIPLE OF
SYMMETRY BE ADOPTED AS EXPRESSION OF JOINT DESIRE FOR
SURVIVAL AND FEELS THIS WOULD BE FIRST MOVE TOWARD
ACCEPTANCE OF EQUALITY UNDER WORLD LAW.

0658 LERNER D. ED., LASSWELL H.D. ED.
"THE POLICY SCIENCES: RECENT DEVELOPMENTS IN SCOPE AND
METHODS."
STANFORD: U. PR., 1951, 344 PP., $7.50.
SUGGESTS HOW SCIENTIFIC METHODS OF INVESTIGATION AND
MEASUREMENT CAN BE APPLIED TO PROBLEMS IN FIELD OF HUMAN
RELATIONS. DEMONSTRATES HOW COMBINED EFFORTS OF POLICY SCI-
ENTISTS WOULD BENEFIT BOTH NATIONAL AND INTERNATIONAL
POLICY-MAKERS.

0659 LERNER D. ED., SCHRAMM W. ED.
COMMUNICATION AND CHANGE IN DEVELOPING COUNTRIES.
HONOLULU: EAST WEST CENTER PRESS, 1967, 333 PP., LC#66-13022
ANTHOLOGY OF PAPERS EXAMINING GENERAL PROBLEMS OF COM-
MUNICATION AND CHANGE AND SOME CASE STUDIES OF COMMUNICA-
TION AND CHANGE IN INDIA, COMMUNIST CHINA, AND PHILIP-
PINES. OCCASION FOR PAPERS WAS CONFERENCE SPONSORED BY
INSTITUTE OF ADVANCED PROJECTS OF THE EAST-WEST CENTER IN
HONOLULU, 1964.

0660 LEVENSTEIN A.
"TECHNOLOGICAL CHANGE, WORK, AND HUMAN VALUES."
SOCIAL SCIENCE, 42 (APR. 67), 80-85.
DISCUSSES THE IMPACT OF TECHNOLOGY UPON UTILIZATION
OF TIME AS WORK AND LEISURE. CONCLUDES THAT AUTOMATION, BY
CREATING "FREE" TIME FOR LARGER POPULATIONS, FORCES US TO
RE-EXAMINE OUR VALUES. SUGGESTS THAT THIS FREEDOM CAN LEAD
TO A HIGHER LEVEL OF CIVILIZATION IN WHICH INDIVIDUALS
RECOGNIZE THEIR SOCIAL OBLIGATIONS AS A REWARDING DIMENSION
OF TIME-STRUCTURING.

0661 LEWIN K.
FIELD THEORY IN SOCIAL SCIENCE: SELECTED THEORETICAL PA-
PERS.
NEW YORK: HARPER, 1951, 346 PP.

A SYSTEMATIC EXPOSITION SHOWING FIELD THEORY TO BE A METHOD OF ANALYZING CAUSAL RELATIONS, OF BUILDING SCIENTIFIC CONSTRUCTS. DISCUSSES BASIC PROBLEMS OF SCIENTIFIC METHOD.

0662 LEWIS R.L.
"GOAL AND NO GOAL* A NEW POLICY IN SPACE."
BUL. ATOMIC SCIENTISTS, 23 (MAY 67), 17-20.
WITH RECOMMENDED FUNDING IN 1968 OF APOLLO APPLICATIONS PROGRAM, THERE APPEARS TO HAVE BEEN DECIDED THAT THE GOAL OF SPACE RESEARCH IS NOW BASICALLY MANNED LUNAR AND EXTRA-PLANETARY SCIENTIFIC EXPLORATION. OTHER FORMS OF RESEARCH HERETOFORE CONNECTED WITH THE PROGRAM ARE SUFFERING. REDUCED SUPPORT TO UNIVERSITY LABORATORIES IS THREATENING A BREAKDOWN IN VALUABLE RESEARCH. PRIORITIES MAY BE WRONG.

0663 LEWIS W.A.
DEVELOPMENT PLANNING; THE ESSENTIALS OF ECONOMIC POLICY.
NEW YORK: HARPER & ROW, 1966, 278 PP., LC#66-10655.
CONCERNED WITH TECHNIQUES AND ECONOMICS OF DEVELOPMENT PLANNING; EMPHASIZES POLICY. BEGINS WITH PATTERNS OF PLANNING, THEN EXAMINES STRATEGY. ARITHMETIC AND STATISTICAL FRAMEWORK OF A PLAN EXPLAINED IN DETAIL. CLOSES WITH PROCESS OF PLANNING. AREAS COVERED INCLUDE ADMINISTRATIVE STRUCTURE OF FEDERAL AND PRIVATE PLANNING AGENCIES AND COMMITTEES, FOREIGN TRADE AND AID, LINEAR PROGRAMMING, CAPITAL.

0664 LEYDER J.
BIBLIOGRAPHIE DE L'ENSEIGNEMENT SUPERIEUR ET DE LA RECHERCHE SCIENTIFIQUE EN AFRIQUE INTERTROPICALE (2 VOLS.)
BRUSSELS: CEN DOC ECO ET SOC AFR, 1960, 287 PP.
ANNOTATED BIBLIOGRAPHY OF 1,025 WORKS IN WESTERN LANGUAGES COVERING PERIOD 1940-59. MATERIAL IS CHRONOLOGICALLY ARRANGED AND PROVIDES ANALYTICAL ANNOTATIONS IN FRENCH TOGETHER WITH COMPLETE BIBLIOGRAPHICAL INFORMATION. MANY SOURCES GATHERED FROM DOCUMENTS OF OFFICIAL ORGANS AND SCIENTIFIC INSTITUTIONS. CONTAINS A COMPREHENSIVE ALPHABETICAL INDEX.

0665 LI C.M. ED.
INDUSTRIAL DEVELOPMENT IN COMMUNIST CHINA.
NEW YORK: PRAEGER, 1964, 205 PP., $5.00.
PRESENTS UP TO DATE INFORMATION AND CRITICAL ANALYSES ON CAPITAL FORMATION, WORK-INCENTIVE POLICY, ECONOMIC PLANNING, CHANGES IN THE STEEL INDUSTRY, HANDICRAFTS AND AGRICULTURE, SINO-SOVIET TRADE AND EXCHANGE RATES, AND THE DIFFICULTIES IN MEASURING CHINESE INDUSTRIAL OUTPUT.

0666 LILIENTHAL D.E.
CHANGE, HOPE, AND THE BOMB.
PRINCETON: U. PR., 1963, 168 PP.
'THINKS THAT THE PRESENT DISARMAMENT NEGOTIATIONS ARE DECEPTIVELY DANGEROUS, THAT OUR VIEW OF THE PLACE OF THE ATOM IN THE MODERN WORLD HAS BEEN MAINLY WRONG AND THAT WE HAVE ALLOWED OUR SCIENTIFIC LEADERS TOO MUCH INFLUENCE IN NON-SCIENTIFIC AREAS OF PUBLIC POLICY.'

0667 LILLEY S.
MEN, MACHINES AND HISTORY: THE STORY OF TOOLS AND MACHINES IN RELATION TO SOCIAL PROGRESS.
NEW YORK: INTERNATIONAL PUBLRS, 1966, 352 PP., LC#66-21951.
SURVEYS HISTORY OF TECHNOLOGY AND SOCIAL EFFECTS OF SCIENTIFIC DISCOVERY AND INVENTION FROM BEGINNINGS OF AGRICULTURE IN 8,000 BC TO SPACE AGE. DETAILS EFFORTS OF INNOVATIONS - FROM PRIMITIVE TOOLS TO THE MOTOR - AND DESCRIBES DEVELOPMENTS IN NEW FIELDS OF NUCLEAR POWER, COMPUTERS, AUTOMATION, AND CONQUEST OF SPACE. EXPLORES POLICY PROBLEMS ARISING FROM NEW FIELDS.

0668 LINDFORS G.V.
INTERCOLLEGIATE BIBLIOGRAPHY; CASES IN BUSINESS ADMINISTRATION (VOL. X)
BOSTON: INTERCOL CASE CLEAR HSE, 1966, 197 PP.
TEN-VOLUME BIBLIOGRAPHY CONTAINING 5,000 CASES IN BUSINESS ADMINISTRATION SUBMITTED BY 1,200 CONTRIBUTORS (AUTHORS AND SUPERVISORS) FROM 190 INSTITUTIONS. BOTH FOREIGN AND DOMESTIC. SPECIAL BIBLIOGRAPHIES FREQUENTLY ISSUED DOCUMENTING POPULAR CASES OR SPECIAL LISTINGS. ENTRIES ARE TOPICALLY ORGANIZED AND ARRANGED IN ONE COMPREHENSIVE TABLE WHICH PROVIDES A SUMMARY AND COMPLETE BIBLIOGRAPHICAL DATA.

0669 LINDSAY F.A.
"PLANNING IN FOREIGN AFFAIRS: THE MISSING ELEMENT."
FOR. AFF. 39 (JAN. 61), 271-78.
PRESSURE OF OPERATING NEEDS FORCES USA DIPLOMACY TO FACE PROBLEMS OF CONFLICTING GROUPS WITHIN POWER STRUCTURE. RECOMMENDS REORGANIZATION OF PROGRAMS AND OF MUTUALLY DEPENDENT PLANS.

0670 LINDVEIT E.N.
SCIENTISTS IN GOVERNMENT.
WASHINGTON: PUBLIC AFFAIRS PRESS, 1960, 84 PP., LC#59-15849.
STUDY OF PROBLEMS OF RETAINING SCIENTIFIC PERSONNEL IN US GOVERNMENT AND DEVELOPMENT OF GREATER NEED FOR THEM IN GOVERNMENT SINCE WWII. COVERS ALL FIELDS OF SCIENCE EXCEPT MEDICAL AND STRESSES RESPONSIBILITY OF GOVERNMENT TO KEEP QUALITY SCIENTISTS IN TECHNICAL AGE. BIBLIOGRAPHY OF WORKS CITED IN TEXT AND GOVERNMENT PUBLICATIONS ON SUBJECT SINCE 1945.

0671 LINS L.J. ED.
"BASIS FOR DECISION: A COMPOSITE OF CURRENT INSTITUTIONAL RESEARCH METHODS OF COLLEGES AND UNIVERSITIES"
J. EXPERIMENTAL EDUCATION, 31 (DEC. 62), 88-229.
MANY FACETS OF INSTITUTIONAL RESEARCH PROBLEMS FACING AMERICAN UNIVERSITIES ARE BROUGHT TO EXAMINATION IN THIS SYMPOSIUM BY EXPERTS. PROVIDES AN AVENUE FOR EXCHANGE OF METHODS AND RESULTS OF RESEARCH. INCLUDES DISCUSSION ON RESEARCH PLANNING, INSTITUTIONAL COST ANALYSIS, SELF-STUDY PROGRAMS, TEACHING LOADS, SCHOLASTIC PROGRESS, FORECASTING.

0672 LIPPITT R., WATSON J., WESTLEY B.
DYNAMICS OF PLANNED CHANGE.
NEW YORK: HARCOURT BRACE, 1958, 312 PP., LC#58-898.
FOCUSING ON PLANNED CHANGE, THE BOOK ANALYZES PURPOSEFUL DECISIONS TO IMPROVE CLIENT SYSTEMS BY PROFESSIONAL CHANGE AGENTS. EXPLORES AREAS OF CHANGE POTENTIAL, CHANGE FORCES, RESISTANCE FORCES, AND PHASES AND METHODS OF CHANGE. ADMITS IMSPIRATION OF KURT LEWIN. CONTAINS USEFUL BIBLIOGRAPHY ON ORGANIZATIONSAND COMMUNITIES AS CLIENT SYSTEMS. PRESENTS METHODS WHICH ARE THE OPPOSITES TO REPRESENTATIONAL MEANS.

0673 LIPPMAN W.
THE PUBLIC PHILOSOPHY.
BOSTON: LITTLE BROWN, 1955, 189 PP., LC#55-6533.
TALKS ABOUT PROBLEMS IN DEMOCRACIES. ANALYZES STRUCTURE OF EXISTING DEMOCRACIES WITH THE IDEA THAT WHERE MASS OPINION DOMINATES GOVERNMENT, THERE IS A MORBID DERANGEMENT OF THE TRUE FUNCTIONS OF POWER. EXAMINES MALADY OF DEMOCRACIES DERANGEMENT OF POWER, PUBLIC INTEREST, THE ADVERSARIES OF LIBERAL DEMOCRACY, AND THE DEFENSE OF CIVILITY. CONCLUDES THAT PUBLIC PHILOSOPHY CAN BE REVIVED AND CAN SURVIVE.

0674 LITTERER J.A.
ORGANIZATIONS: STRUCTURE AND BEHAVIOR.
NEW YORK: JOHN WILEY, 1963, 418 PP., LC#63-12285.
A COLLECTION OF PAPERS ON FORMAL AND INFORMAL ORGANIZATIONS, WITH BASIC CONCEPTS, PROBLEMS AND ANATOMY, AND THEIR INTERRELATIONS. INFORMAL LEADERSHIP, "STRATEGIC LENIENCY," INTERNALIZED STANDARDS OF BUREAUCRACY AS SUBSTITUTES FOR REPRESENTATION, COMPETITION OF STAFF AND LINE FOR POWER, FORMAL-INFORMAL ORGANIZATION NEXUS, AND ORGANIZATIONAL ADAPTATION ARE TREATED IN DETAIL.

0675 LOCKLIN D.P.
ECONOMICS OF TRANSPORTATION (4TH ED.)
HOMEWOOD: RICHARD IRWIN, 1954, 916 PP.
EXTENSIVE ANALYSIS OF ORGANIZATION OF TRANSPORTATION SYSTEM IN US. BEGINS WITH OVER-ALL LOOK AT VARIOUS MODES OF TRANSPORTATION; NOTES SIGNIFICANT DIFFERENCES IN THEIR ORGANIZATION AND DEVELOPMENT. COVERS GOVERNMENTAL CONTROLS, MAJOR PROBLEMS, FINANCING, AND SERVICES. MAJOR PORTION DEVOTED TO RAILROADS; INCLUDES HIGHWAY, WATER, AND AIR TRANSPORTATION. ENDS WITH TRANSPORT COMPETITION.

0676 LONG N.E.
"PUBLIC POLICY AND ADMINISTRATION: THE GOALS OF RATIONALITY AND RESPONSIBILITY."
PUBLIC ADMIN. REV., 14 (WINTER 54), 22-31.
POLICY AND FACT-GATHERING ARE PART OF SAME PROCESS. SUBORDINATES SHOULD PRESENT AS WIDE A RANGE OF CHOICES AS POSSIBLE TO THE POLITICAL DECISION-MAKERS: THIS WILL INCREASE CHANCES OF PUBLIC WILL BEING SERVED BY AN ADMINISTRATIVE DECISION.

0677 LOWENSTEIN L. ED.
GOVERNMENT RESOURCES AVAILABLE FOR FOREIGN AFFAIRS RESEARCH.
WASHINGTON: DEPT OF STATE, 1965, 56 PP.
A DIRECTORY OF GOVERNMENT FACILITIES, FINANCIAL SUPPORT, AND A BIBLIOGRAPHY OF GOVERNMENT RESOURCES AVAILABLE TO THE PRIVATE SCHOLAR FOR RESEARCH ON FOREIGN AFFAIRS.

0678 LUNDBERG G.A.
"THE CONCEPT OF LAW IN THE SOCIAL SCIENCES"(BMR)"
PHILOSOPHY OF SCIENCE, 5 (APR. 38), 189-203.
DEMONSTRATES THAT THE APPARENT DIFFICULTY OF APPLYING THE METHODS OF NATURAL SCIENCE OF SOCIOLOGICAL PHENOMENA RESULTS NOT FROM ANY INTRINSIC CHARACTERISTICS OF SOCIOLOGICAL DATA, BUT FROM THE RETENTION IN SOCIOLOGY OF POSTULATES LONG SINCE REPUDIATED IN SCIENCE. CONTENDS THAT THE TERM SCIENTIFIC LAW CAN AND SHOULD MEAN EXACTLY WHAT IT MEANS IN THE OTHER SCIENCES.

0679 LUNDBERG G.A.
CAN SCIENCE SAVE US.
NEW YORK: LONGMANS, 1961, 150 PP.
EXPLORES PRE-SCIENTIFIC THOUGHTWAYS IN TECHNOLOGICAL AGE. DEPICTS THE TRANSITION TO SCIENCE IN HUMAN RELATIONS. STUDIES PROBLEM OF EDUCATION, ARTS, LITERATURE AND THE SPIRITUAL LIFE IN A SCIENTIFIC CONTEXT. GIVES INSIGHT INTO ATTITUDES OF TOTALITARIAN REGIMES.

0680 LUTZ V.

FRENCH PLANNING.
WASHINGTON: AMER ENTERPRISE INST, 1965, 105 PP., LC#65-22084
FINDS IMPOSSIBLE TO ASCERTAIN EFFECT OF FRENCH ECONOMIC
PLANNING ON POSTWAR ECONOMIC GROWTH OR TO DISCOVER WHETHER
PLAN WILL BECOME AN INSTRUMENT OF REGIMENTATION. DESCRIBES
PLAN AS IN AN UNSTABLE POSITION. DETAILS ITS ADMINISTRATIVE
MACHINERY, PREPARATION, OBJECTIVES, OPTIONS, INSTRUMENTS,
AND RECORD OF PAREDICTIVE SUCCESSES.

0681 LYONS G.M.
"THE NEW CIVIL-MILITARY RELATIONS."
AM. POL. SCI. REV., 55 (MAR. 61), 53-63.
DEFENSE ESTABLISHMENT HAS BECOME POLITICIZED AND MILITARY
TAKES ACTIVE INTEREST IN POLICY FORMULATION.

0682 MAASS A.
MUDDY WATERS: THE ARMY ENGINEERS AND THE NATIONS RIVERS.
CAMBRIDGE: HARVARD U PR, 1951, 306 PP.
CASE STUDY OF POWERFUL GROUP, ITS WORKINGS AND RELATIONS
TO EXECUTIVE, LEGISLATIVE ESTABLISHMENTS. ATTEMPTS TO ESTAB-
LISH CRITERIA WHICH WILL BE USEFUL IN DETERMINING EXTENT TO
WHICH ANY ADMINISTRATIVE AGENCY CONDUCTS ITSELF AS A RESPON-
SIBLE INSTRUMENT OF GOVERNMENT.

0683 MAASS A.A.
"CONGRESS AND WATER RESOURCES."
AM. POL. SCI. REV., 44 (SEPT. 50), 576-593.
APPRAISAL OF CONGRESS'S DUTIES AND LOCAL CONSERVATION
INTERESTS. DISCUSSES PAST AND FUTURE LEGISLATION IN THIS
AREA, PRESENT ARRANGEMENTS, WATER RESOURCE-PLANNING.

0684 MACAVOY P.W., SLOSS J.
REGULATION OF TRANSPORT INNOVATION.
NEW YORK: RANDOM HOUSE, INC, 1967, 143 PP., LC#67-10910.
INVESTIGATES PROBLEM OF LONG DELAY IN ADOPTION OF UNIT
TRAIN SERVICE TO EASTERN SEABOARD. DESCRIBES UNIT TRAIN AS
AN INNOVATION AND EXAMINES LEGAL CONSTRAINTS WHICH AFFECTED
ITS ADOPTION. INDICATES EXTENT TO WHICH LEGAL DECISIONS
RESULTED IN NEGATIVE ECONOMIC ATTITUDE TOWARD ADOPTION OF
NEW TRANSPORT SYSTEM.

0685 MACBRIDE R.
THE AUTOMATED STATE; COMPUTER SYSTEMS AS A NEW FORCE IN
SOCIETY.
NEW YORK: CHILTON BOOKS, 1967, 407 PP., LC#67-22758.
EXAMINES WAYS IN WHICH DIGITAL COMPUTERS AFFECT PEOPLE,
THEIR JOBS, AND PERSONAL DECISIONS. STATES THAT FUTURE OF
COMPUTERS WILL BE DETERMINED BY THEIR APPLICABILITY FOR
SOLVING SOCIAL AND ECONOMIC PROBLEMS. DISCUSSES ROLE OF
COMPUTER SYSTEM IN EMPLOYMENT AND IN SOCIAL PLANNING.
EXPLORES INVASION-OF-PRIVACY ISSUE, IMPACT OF COMPUTERS ON
FEDERAL GOVERNMENT, AND EVOLUTION OF NATIONWIDE SYSTEMS.

0686 MACCORQUODALE K., MEEHL P.E.
"ON A DISTINCTION BETWEEN HYPOTHETICAL CONSTRUCTS AND
INTERVENING VARIABLES."
PSYCHOLOGICAL REVIEW, 55 (MAR. 48), 95-107.
SUGGESTS THAT A FAILURE TO DISTINGUISH BETWEEN THE
PHRASES "INTERVENING VARIABLE" AND "HYPOTHETICAL CONSTRUCT"
LEADS TO FUNDAMENTAL CONFUSIONS. PROPOSES A LINGUISTIC
CONVENTION THAT THE FIRST PHRASE BE RESTRICTED TO CONSTRUCTS
WHICH MERELY ABSTRACT THE EMPIRICAL RELATIONSHIPS AND THAT
THE SECOND PHRASE BE USED FOR CONSTRUCTS WHICH INVOLVE
THE SUPPOSITION OF ENTITIES NOT AMONG THE OBSERVED.

0687 MACDONALD G.J.F.
"SCIENCE AND SPACE POLICY* HOW DOES IT GET PLANNED?"
BUL. ATOMIC SCIENTISTS, 67 (MAY 67), 2-9.
A DISCUSSION OF THE STRUCTURE OF NASA, THE PROCEDURES
AND PRIORITIES IN PLANNING SPACE PROGRAMS AND FLIGHTS, AND
THE ROLE OF SCIENTISTS IN PLANNING. THE NECESSITY OF LONG-
RANGE PLANNING IS STRESSED, AS IS THE IMPORTANCE OF GREATER
SCIENTIFIC INFLUENCE IN THE SPACE AGENCY.

0688 MACHLUP F.
THE PRODUCTION AND DISTRIBUTION OF KNOWLEDGE IN THE UNITED
STATES.
PRINCETON: PRINCETON U PRESS, 1962, 416 PP., LC#63-07072.
INTERDISCIPLINARY WORK ON KNOWLEDGE AS AN ECONOMIC FAC-
TOR, ITS PRODUCTION, DISTRIBUTION, AND VALUE. EFFECT OF
KNOWLEDGE ON ECONOMIC GROWTH, AND TECHNOLOGICAL INFLUENCE ON
NATIONS' WEALTH DISCUSSED. ECONOMIC ANALYSIS OF VALUE OF
LEARNING, RESEARCH, EDUCATION, AND TECHNOLOGY.

0689 MACHOWSKI K.
"SELECTED PROBLEMS OF NATIONAL SOVEREIGNTY WITH REFERENCE
TO THE LAW OF OUTER SPACE."
PROC. AMER. SOC. INT. LAW, 55 (APR. 61), 169-74.
WARNS AGAINST POSSIBILITY OF USING OUTER SPACE FOR MILIT-
ARY PURPOSES. ASSERTS THAT ANY LEGAL SETTLEMENT ON MAN'S
ACTIVITY MUST BE BASED ON THE SAME PREMISES, NAMELY THE PRE-
SERVATION OF SECURITY OF STATES.

0690 MACK R.T.
RAISING THE WORLDS STANDARD OF LIVING.
NEW YORK: CITADEL, 1953, 285 PP.
DEALS WITH FOREIGN AID PROGRAMS OF POST-WAR PERIOD. DE-
TAILS SEVERAL AID PROGRAMS SUCH AS POINT FOUR AND TECHNICAL
ASSISTANCE CONFERENCE OF THE UN. CITES IRAN AS EXAMPLE.

0691 MACKINTOSH J.M.
JUGGERNAUT.
NEW YORK: MACMILLAN, 1967, 352 PP.
HISTORY OF THE SOVIET ARMY FROM ITS FOUNDATION IN CIVIL
WAR TO ITS PRESENT STATUS AS ONE OF THE MOST DOMINANT MILI-
TARY FORCES IN THE WORLD. DESCRIBES HOW ITS RECONSTRUCTION
FROM A WEAK ORGANIZATION OCCURRED AND AT WHAT COST. RECOUNTS
ITS BATTLES AND CAMPAIGNS OF WWII, AND DESCRIBES THE ARMY
UNDER THE REGIMES OF STALIN AND KHRUSHCHEV.

0692 MACPHERSON C.
"TECHNICAL CHANGE AND POLITICAL DECISION."
INT. SOC. SCI. J., 12 (1960), 357-405.
OUTLINES THE RATIONALIZATION OF METHODS AND MEANS OF
ACTION IN PUBLIC ADMINISTRATION, SHOWING EFFECTS OF TECH-
NICAL INNOVATIONS ON THE RELATIONSHIP BETWEEN CENTRAL AND
LOCAL AUTHORITIES. EVALUATES RECRUITMENT AND TRAINING OF
CIVIL SERVANTS.

0693 MACRAE D.G.
"THE BOLSHEVIK IDEOLOGY; THE INTELLECTUAL AND EMOTIONAL FAC-
TORS IN COMMUNIST AFFILIATION" (BMR)"
CAMBRIDGE JOURNAL, 5 (DEC. 51), 164-177.
ATTEMPTS TO EXAMINE MARXISM IN ITS BOLSHEVIK FORM NOT AS
A SYSTEM OR METHOD, BUT AS THE SOCIAL OPERATION OF AN
IDEOLOGY. CONSIDERS THE APPEAL OF BOLSHEVISM AS A POLITICO-
SOCIAL CREED: ITS INTELLECTUAL CLAIM TO SCIENTIFIC STATUS,
ITS EMOTIONAL CLAIM AS A SALVATIONIST RELIGION, AND ITS
IDEALISTIC CLAIM TO EQUALITY. VIEWS THESE LEVELS OF APPEAL
AGAINST THE SUCCESSION OF MARXIST PROPHETS AND LEADERS.

0694 MAGGS P.B.
"SOVIET VIEWPOINT ON NUCLEAR WEAPONS IN INTERNATIONAL LAW."
LAW CONTEMP. PROBL., 29 (AUTUMN 64), 956-70.
EXPLAINS SOVIET APPROACH TO LEGAL PROBLEMS CONNECTED WITH
THE MILITARY USE OF NUCLEAR WEAPONS AS WELL AS THE TESTING,
CONSTRUCTION, POSSESSION, STATIONING AND TRANSFER OF SUCH
WEAPONS.

0695 MAHALANOBIS P.C.
"PERSPECTIVE PLANNING IN INDIA: STATISTICAL TOOLS."
CO-EXISTENCE, 1 (MAY 64), 60-73.
EXPLAINS WHY LONG-RANGE (20-30 YEARS) PLANNING IS
NECESSARY IN DEVELOPING NATIONS AND GIVES EXAMPLES OF THE
STATISTICAL INFORMATION AND METHODS USED IN INDIA.

0696 MAINZER L.C.
"SCIENTIFIC FREEDOM IN GOVERNMENT-SPONSORED RESEARCH."
J. OF POLITICS, 23 (MAY 61), 212-230.
INVESTIGATES DEGREE OF SCIENTIFIC DISCRETION RETAINED BY
SCIENTIFIC RESEARCHERS WITHIN FEDERAL AGENCIES OR OTHERWISE
FEDERALLY FUNDED. EXAMINES ASPECTS OF PROGRAM PLANNING, FUND
ALLOTMENT, AND PROJECT SELECTION. DISCUSSES POLITICAL AND
ADMINISTRATIVE PRESSURES ON RESEARCHERS. ARGUES AGAINST
COMPLETE SCIENTIFIC FREEDOM. CLAIMS MANY SCIENTISTS HAVE
"LIMITED INTELLECTUAL RANGE AND LIMITED NEED FOR FREEDOM."

0697 MALENBAUM W.
"GOVERNMENT, ENTREPRENEURSHIP, AND ECONOMIC GROWTH IN POOR
LANDS."
WORLD POLITICS, 19 (OCT. 66), 52-68.
DEVELOPMENT PROJECTS IN THE LAST DECADE HAVE SPURRED SOME
GROWTH, BUT TOO LITTLE TO REDUCE THE DIFFERENTIAL BETWEEN
RICH AND POOR NATIONS, AND BETWEEN THE MODERN AND TRADITION-
AL ELEMENTS IN THE STRUCTURE OF THE DEVELOPING NATIONS.
DEVELOPMENT PLANS MUST RELATE GROWTH IN MODERN SECTORS TO
CHANGE IN THE TRADITIONAL. THIS REQUIRES ENTERPRENEURSHIP
WHICH ONLY GOVERNMENT CAN PROVIDE IN THE POOR NATIONS

0698 MALONE D.K.
"THE COMMANDER AND THE COMPUTER."
MILITARY REV., 47 (JUNE 67), 51-58.
EXAMINES ROLE OF COMPUTER IN ARMED FORCES AND SUGGESTS
HOW IT CAN BE USED TO COMPLEMENT COMMAND DECISIONS. STRESSES
THAT EVEN THE MOST ADVANCED SYSTEM EMPLOYS ONLY "MODERN,
PROVED TECHNIQUES" AND THAT IT IS BASICALLY A TOOL DEPENDENT
UPON HUMAN JUDGMENT. GIVES EXAMPLES OF HOW COMPUTERS CAN
BE USED TO ADJUST STRATEGY, DETERMINE LOGISTICS, ETC.

0699 MANGELSDORF J.E.
"HUMAN DECISIONS IN MISSILE YSTEMS."
ANN. N.Y. ACAD. SCI. 89 (JAN. 61), 717-725.
A STUDY OF THE CRITICAL PROBLEMS IN COMMUNICATION BETWEEN
PERSONNEL AND TO SUGGEST A FORM THAT THE SOLUTION MIGHT
TAKE.

0700 MANNHEIM K.
FREEDOM, POWER, AND DEMOCRATIC PLANNING.
NEW YORK: OXFORD U. PR., 1950, 313 PP.
OUTLINES PRINCIPLES OF A SOCIETY THAT IS PLANNED YET
DEMOCRATIC. END OF LAISSEZ-FAIRE ERA HAS SIGNALLED NEED FOR
REAL PLANNING CONSISTING OF THE CO-ORDINATION OF

INSTITUTIONS, EDUCATION, VALUATIONS AND PSYCHOLOGY.

0701 MANSFIELD E. ED.
MONOPOLY POWER AND ECONOMIC PERFORMANCE: AN INTRODUCTION TO
A CURRENT ISSUE OF PUBLIC POLICY.
NEW YORK: W W NORTON, 1964, 174 PP., LC#63-21710.
COLLECTION OF ARTICLES DEALS WITH THE EFFICIENCY OF MO-
NOPOLIES IN THE US. SUBJECTS CONSIDERED ARE: MARKET STRUC-
TURE, RESOURCE ALLOCATION, AND ECONOMIC PROGRESS; INDUSTRIAL
CONCENTRATION, COLLUSION, AND THE SOCIAL RESPONSIBILITY OF
BIG BUSINESS; AND THE ANTITRUST LAWS - THEIR PROVISIONS,
EFFECTIVENESS, AND STANDARDS.

0702 MARCHANT A. ED., SHELBY C. ED.
INVESTIGATIONS IN PROGRESS IN THE UNITED STATES IN THE FIELD
OF LATIN AMERICAN HUMANISTIC AND SOCIAL SCIENCE STUDIES.
WASHINGTON: LIBRARY OF CONGRESS, 1942, 236 PP.
COMPILATION OF RECORD OF INVESTIGATIONS IN PROGRESS IN US
IN FIELD OF LATIN AMERICAN SOCIAL SCIENCES. VARIOUS SOURCES
UTILIZED TO COMPILE NAMES. EFFORT MADE TO INCLUDE PERSONS
ASSISTING ALL RESEARCH. INFORMATION CONTAINED IN RECORD IS
AS OF NOV. 1, 1941.

0703 MARCUSE H.
SOVIET MARXISM, A CRITICAL ANALYSIS.
NEW YORK: COLUMBIA U PRESS, 1958, 271 PP., LC#57-10943.
DISCUSSES THEORY OF SOVIET MARXISM, DEVELOPS IDEOLOGICAL
AND SOCIOLOGICAL CONSEQUENCES OF PREMISES, AND THEN
REVALUATES THEORY IN LIGHT OF CONSEQUENCES. DIVIDED INTO
PARTS ON POLITICAL AND ETHICAL TENETS.

0704 MARCY C.
"THE RESEARCH PROGRAM OF THE SENATE COMMITTEE ON FOREIGN
RELATIONS."
PROD, 2 (NOV. 58), 28-30.
DISCUSSES NATURE OF COMMITTEE ON FOREIGN RELATIONS, AND
SKETCHES ITS PROGRAMS AND R AIMS. COMMITTEE CONCENTRATES
ON FUNDAMENTAL FORCES AT WORK IN WORLD POLITICS WHICH MUST
BE UNDERSTOOD TO IMPROVE US FOREIGN POLICY.

0705 MARES V.E.
"EAST EUROPE'S SECOND CHANCE."
CURR. HIST., 47 (NOV. 64), 272-9.
DISCUSSES TRENDS AT WORK IN EAST EUROPE. DE-STALINIZATION
HAS ASSUMED DE-SATELLIZATION. AUTHOR LABELS INDEPENDENT
ACTIONS (YUGOSLAVIA IN 1948, HUNGARY IN 1956 AND RUMANIA IN
1964) AS AMAZING. ASSERTS THAT POLICIES BE CO-ORDINATED IN
ORDER TO BUILD A STRONG EAST EUROPE COMMONWEALTH.

0706 MARK M.
"BEYOND SOVEREIGNTY."
WASHINGTON: PUBLIC AFFAIRS PRESS, 1965.
AN ESSAY ON THE "POST-NATION-STATE ERA" AND THE TRANSI-
TION TO TRANSNATIONALISM. WARNING AGAINST A US NEO-ISOLA-
TIONISM. BIBLIOGRAPHY OF ABOUT 150 ITEMS IN ENGLISH TO 1964,
LIMITED TO WORKS ON VARIOUS ASPECTS OF CONTEMPORARY INTERNA-
TIONAL POLITICS SUCH AS NATIONALISM, INTERNATIONAL ECONOMY,
UNDERDEVELOPED NATIONS, POWER BLOCS, AND MILITARY MATTERS.
ARRANGED BY SUBJECT AND AUTHOR.

0707 MARKHAM J.W.
AN ECONOMIC-MEDIA STUDY OF BOOK PUBLISHING.
NY: AMER TEXTBOOK PUBLRS COUNCIL, 1966, 267 PP.
SURVEYS POLICIES AND PRACTICES OF FEDERAL GOVERNMENT AS
THEY BEAR UPON BOOK PUBLISHING; DESCRIBES PRESENT AND FUTURE
TECHNOLOGY USED IN TRANSFER OF INFORMATION; AND ANALYZES
COPYING PRACTICES IN SCHOOLS AND COLLEGES. PROVIDES
INFORMATION REQUIRED FOR LONG-RANGE BUSINESS DECISIONS AND
DISCUSSES CURRENT COPYRIGHT LEGISLATION. SUPPLEMENTED WITH
DETAILED AND EXTENSIVE STATISTICAL DATA.

0708 MARQUIS D.G.
"RESEARCH PLANNING AT THE FRONTIERS OF SCIENCE" (BMR)"
AMER. PSYCHOLOGIST, 3 (OCT. 48), 30-438.
THE AUTHOR MAINTAINS THAT MORE ATTENTION TO PLANNING CAN
GREATLY ACCELERATE THE RATE OF RESEARCH DEVELOPMENT.
DISTINGUISHES THREE LEVELS OF RESEARCH PLANNING:
EXPERIMENTAL DESIGN, PROGRAM DESIGN, AND POLICY DESIGN.
THESE ARE DEFINED AS THE PLANNING OF A SINGLE SPECIFIC
PROJECT, AN INTEGRATED SET OF PROJECTS, AND AN OVER-ALL EF-
FORT AMONG AREAS. MAPS OBJECTIVES AND PROCEDURES.

0709 MARRIS R.
THE ECONOMIC THEORY OF "MANAGERIAL" CAPITALISM.
NEW YORK: FREE PRESS OF GLENCOE, 1964, 346 PP., LC#64-10371.
STUDIES SEPARATION OF MANAGEMENT CONTROL FROM OWNERSHIP
IN FIRMS, INCLUDING INSTITUTIONAL FRAMEWORK, SUPPLY AND
DEMAND, AND BEHAVIOR AND EVIDENCE. BIBLIOGRAPHY OF ENGLISH
BOOKS AND ARTICLES, LISTED ALPHABETICALLY BY AUTHOR, 1932-
1962; 125 ENTRIES.

0710 MARS D.
SUGGESTED LIBRARY IN PUBLIC ADMINISTRATION.
LOS ANGELES: U OF S CAL, PUB ADM, 1962, 133 PP.
INDEXED BIBLIOGRAPHY ON PUBLIC ADMINISTRATION AIMS AT
SELECTING MOST IMPORTANT WORKS IN THIS FIELD. ALSO INCLUDES

PERIODICALS DEALING WITH PUBLIC ADMINISTRATION AND MANAGE-
MENT. AN OUTGROWTH OF THE BERKELY BRAZIL PROJECT DESIGNED
PRIMARILY FOR OVERSEAS LIBRARIES.

0711 MARSCH P.E., GORTNER R.A.
FEDERAL AID TO SCIENCE EDUCATION: TWO PROGRAMS.
SYRACUSE: SYRACUSE U PRESS, 1963, 97 PP., LC#63-11007.
COMPARES TWO FEDERALLY SUPPORTED PROGRAMS TO IMPROVE
SCIENCE EDUCATION IN PUBLIC SCHOOLS, THEIR METHODS AND
EFFICIENCY.

0712 MARTIN A., YOUNG W.
"PROLIFERATION."
DISSERTATION ABSTRACTS, 3 (FALL 65), 107-134.
REJECTS FORCIBLE MEANS TO HALT PROLIFERATION AND FAVORS
UNDERGROUND TEST BAN, NON-NUCLEAR ZONES, PLUS NON-DISSEMIN-
ATION AND NON-ACQUISITION TREATIES. PROLIFERATION CAN BE
HALTED ONLY BY MASSIVE ARMS REDUCTIONS OF EXISTING NUCLEAR
POWERS.

0713 MARTIN L.
"THE AMERICAN ABM DECISION."
SURVIVAL, 9 (DEC. 67), 384-387.
EXAMINES EFFECTS OF US DECISION TO BEGIN DEPLOYMENT OF
A LIMITED BALLISTIC MISSILE DEFENSE SYSTEM UPON INTERNA-
TIONAL RELATIONS, ARMS RACE, AND POLICY DECISIONS OF OTHER
NATIONS ON WEAPONRY. CLAIMS IT DOES NOT NEGATE USEFULNESS
OF EUROPEAN NUCLEAR FORCE.

0714 MARTIN L.W.
"THE MARKET FOR STRATEGIC IDEAS IN BRITAIN: THE 'SANDYS
ERA'"
AM. POL. SCI. REV., 56 (MAR. 62), 23-40.
ANALYSIS OF BRITISH DEFENSE MEASURES AND COMMITMENTS. IN-
CLUDES STUDY OF MILITARY, DIPLOMATIC,AND ECONOMIC RESOURCES
AND VARIOUS DEFENSE STRATEGIES. CONSIDERS PROBLEMS FACED BY
MINISTER OF DEFENCE IN SEARCH FOR ADVANCED MODES OF
DEFENSE.

0715 MARTIN L.W.
"BALLISTIC MISSILE DEFENSE AND EUROPE."
BUL. ATOMIC SCIENTISTS, 23 (MAY 67), 42-46.
DISCUSSION OF EUROPEAN ATTITUDES TOWARD POSSIBLE US DE-
PLOYMENT OF ABM DEFENSE SYSTEMS OR OTHER US RESPONSE TO
SUCH DEPLOYMENT BY THE USSR. EUROPEAN CONCERNS INCLUDE
MAINTENANCE OF THE EAST-WEST DETENTE, RELIABILITY OF US
GUARANTEES TO EUROPE, AND THE PRESENT INDEFENSIBILITY OF
EUROPE AGAINST IRBM OR ICBM ATTACK.

0716 MARTINO R.L.
PROJECT MANAGEMENT AND CONTROL: VOL. 2 APPLIED OPERATIONAL
PLANNING.
NEW YORK: AMER MANAGEMENT ASSN, 1964, 184 PP., LC#64-18544.
SECOND BOOK IN SERIES DESCRIBING HOW THE PERT/CPM TECH-
NIQUES MAY BE USED TO ARRIVE AT BEST METHOD OF CARRYING OUT
A PROJECT, TO ESTIMATE TIME AND COST OF PROJECT, TO MEET
SCHEDULED COMPLETION DATES, AND TO BEST ALLOCATE RESOURCES.

0717 MARTINS A.F.
REVOLUCAO BRANCA NO CAMPO.
SAO PAULO: EDITORA BRASILIENSE, 1962, 202 PP.
EXAMINES RURAL AGRICULTURAL ECONOMY OF BRAZIL, EXPLAINING
IMPORTANCE OF MODERNIZATION OF PRODUCTION BY MORE EXTENSIVE
ELECTRICAL FACILITIES AND USE OF MODERN MACHINERY. COMPARES
DEVELOPMENT OF US AGRICULTURE THROUGH APPLICATION OF MODERN
ELECTRICAL POWER TO THE SLOW DEVELOPMENT OF BRAZILIAN RURAL
AREAS.

0718 MASSART L.
"L'ORGANISATION DE LA RECHERCHE SCIENTIFIQUE EN EUROPE."
TABLE RONDE, 181 (FEB. 63), 23-30.
ANALYZES STAGES OF EVOLUTION OF ORGANIZATION OF
SCIENTIFIC RESEARCH IN EUROPEAN COUNTRIES. DEFINES IDEA
OF SCIENTIFIC POLITICS, ITS PURPOSES AND ACTIVITIES.
EXAMINES PROBLEMS POSED BY THIS SCIENCE. DISCUSSES EUROPEAN
SCIENTIFIC RESEARCH UNDERTAKEN BY INTERNATIONAL ORGANIZA-
TIONS.

0719 MASTERS D. ED.
"ONE WORLD OR NONE."
NEW YORK: MCGRAW HILL, 1946, 79 PP., $1.00.
REPORT TO PUBLIC ON FULL MEANING OF ATOMIC BOMB. ANALYSIS
OF BASIC PROBLEMS INVOLVED VIA ARTICLES BY LEADERS IN
ATOMIC ENGINEERING. STRESSES APPROACHES TO AVERTING
INEVITABLE HORROR IMPLIED IN ATOMIC DISASTER.

0720 MASTERS N.A., SALISBURY R.H., ELIOT T.H.
STATE POLITICS AND THE PUBLIC SCHOOLS.
NEW YORK: ALFRED KNOPF, 1964, 319 PP., LC#63-20402.
A DESCRIPTION OF THE POSITION OF EDUCATORS IN THREE STATE
POLITICAL SYSTEMS, WITH AN ASSESSMENT OF THEIR POWER, AND
A DETERMINATION OF WHERE THEY FIND SUPPORT FOR THEIR
DEMANDS. DESCRIBES ROLES OF STATE TEACHER ASSOCIATIONS,
EDUCATIONAL LOBBIES, GROUP REPRESENTATION ON, AND OPERATION
OF, THE ILLINOIS SCHOOL PROBLEMS COMMISSION, AND LACK OF
A STATE-WIDE SCHOOL DISTRICT PLAN IN MICHIGAN.

0721 MATHEWS J.M.
AMERICAN STATE GOVERNMENT.
NEW YORK: APPLETON, 1925, 660 PP.
SURVEYS AMERICAN SYSTEM OF STATE GOVERNMENT. DISCUSSES
POSITION OF STATES IN FEDERAL SYSTEM, STATE CONSTITUTIONS,
LEGISLATURES, COURTS, AND EXECUTIVES. EXAMINES STATE POWERS,
ADMINISTRATIVE ORGANIZATION, ELECTIONS AND POLITICS, AND
CONTROL OVER TAXES, FINANCE, BUSINESS, AND UNIONS. DESCRIBES
RELATIONSHIP BETWEEN STATE AND LOCAL GOVERNMENTS.

0722 MATTHEWS M.A.
INTERNATIONAL POLICE (PAMPHLET)
WASHINGTON: CARNEGIE ENDOWMENT, 1944, 18 PP.
UNANNOTATED BIBLIOGRAPHY OF PROPOSALS FOR COOPERATIVE
DEFENSE THROUGH THE USE OF INTERNATIONAL ARMIES, NAVIES, AND
AIR FORCES. SOURCES ARE INTERNATIONAL IN SCOPE AND DATE FROM
1930.

0723 MAYDA J. ED.
ATOMIC ENERGY AND LAW.
SAN JUAN: U OF PUERTO RICO, 1959, 254 PP.
CONSIDERS PROBLEMS OF BOTH TECHNICAL AND LEGAL ASPECTS
IN USE OF ATOMIC POWER IN UNDERDEVELOPED COUNTRIES. DIS-
CUSSES PRODUCTION, STORAGE, SALE, APPLICATION, AND DISPOSAL
IN ATTEMPTING TO SET NEW POLICY FOR SOUTH AMERICAN
GOVERNMENTS TO FOLLOW.

0724 MAYNE R.
THE COMMUNITY OF EUROPE.
LONDON: GOLLANCZ, 1963, 192 PP.
BRIEF HISTORY OF EVOLVING ENTITY OF THE EUROPEAN COMMUN-
ITY, INCLUDING POLITICAL AND ECONOMIC BACKGROUND, POST-WAR
DEBATES, BRITISH 'DILEMMA,' AND EUROPE'S RELATION TO REST OF
WORLD. ALSO DISCUSSES VARIOUS EUROPEAN REGIONAL ORGANIZA-
TIONS.

0725 MAYO E.
THE SOCIAL PROBLEMS OF AN INDUSTRIAL CIVILIZATION.
CAMBRIDGE: HARVARD U PR, 1945, 150 PP.
DISCUSSES PROBLEMS OF EFFECTIVE COOPERATION IN 20TH CEN-
TURY INDUSTRIAL SOCIETY. DEALS WITH DEFECTS OF POLITICAL AS
WELL AS ECONOMIC THINKING IN OUR SOCIETY. CALLS ATTENTION
TO IMBALANCE IN SYSTEMATIC STUDIES; CONFLICT BETWEEN
TECHNICAL AND SCIENTIFIC; AND HUMAN AND SOCIAL. COMMENTS
ON THE HAWTHORNE EXPERIMENT.

0726 MAZOUR A.G.
SOVIET ECONOMIC DEVELOPMENT: OPERATION OUTSTRIP: 1921-1965.
PRINCETON: VAN NOSTRAND, 1967, 191 PP.
SIMPLE HISTORICAL ANALYSIS OF SOVIET ECONOMIC PROGRESS
FROM 1921 TO 1965 INITIATION OF KHRUSHCHEV-KOSYGIN CO-EXIS-
TENCE POLICY. EMPHASIS ON NEP AND FIVE-YEAR PLANS WITH
ABOUT HALF OF BOOK DEVOTED TO EXCERPTED READINGS FROM RUS-
SIAN GOVERNMENT DOCUMENTS AND COMMENTARY SOURCES.

0727 MCBRIDE J.H.
THE TEST BAN TREATY: MILITARY, TECHNOLOGICAL, AND POLITICAL
IMPLICATIONS.
WASHINGTON: US GOVERNMENT, 1967, 197 PP., LC#67-14660.
TRACES BACKGROUND OF TREATY, INCLUDING RELATIVE LEVELS OF
NUCLEAR DEVELOPMENT IN US AND USSR. NOTES OPPOSITE CONCLU-
SIONS REACHED BY TWO SENATE COMMITTEES INVESTIGATING TREATY
INDEPENDENTLY. ANALYZES MILITARY AND TECHNOLOGICAL ADVAN-
TAGES AND DISADVANTAGES FOR US. DISCUSSES TESTING AND SAFE-
GUARDS DEMANDED BY JOINT CHIEFS. ANALYZES POLITICAL ADVAN-
TAGES CLAIMED, NOTING ONLY ONE AS PERSUASIVE.

0728 MCCLELLAND C.A.
"THE FUNCTION OF THEORY IN INTERNATIONAL RELATIONS."
J. CONFL. RESOLUT., 4 (JULY 60), 303-36.
ASSERTS THEORY SHOULD BE A MEANS TOWARDS DEMONSTRABLE
KNOWLEDGE OF THE REGULARITIES IN INTERNATIONAL RELATIONS.
SHOULD HAVE WITHIN IT, A MEANS OF DECIPHERING THE SPECIAL
FIELD OF INTERNATIONAL RELATIONS FROM THE MILIEU OF THE
TOTAL SOCIAL REALITY.

0729 MCCLELLAND C.A. ED.
NUCLEAR WEAPONS, MISSILES, AND FUTURE WAR: PROBLEM FOR
THE SIXTIES.
SAN FRANCISCO: CHANDLER, 1960, 235 PP., LC#60-8430.
EXAMINES PROBLEMS RELATING TO NUCLEAR WEAPONS AND THE
THREAT OF WAR. STUDIES ARE ORGANIZED AROUND THEMES OF
DEFINING THE INTERNATIONAL SITUATION; IMPLICATIONS, HOPES,
AND FEARS; PROPOSALS AND DESCRIPTIONS.

0730 MCCLINTOCK R.
THE MEANING OF LIMITED WAR.
BOSTON: HOUGHTON MIFFLIN, 1967, 239 PP., LC#67-10558.
EMPHASIS OF STUDY IS ON OBJECTIVES OF 20TH-CENTURY LIMIT-
ED WARFARE. STUDIES MANNER IN WHICH CONFLICTS OF THE PAST 2
DECADES HAVE BEEN SETTLED. SPECIFIC WARS STUDIED INCLUDE
GREEK CIVIL WAR, KOREAN WAR, ARAB-ISERAELI WARS OF 1946-49
AND 1956, "WARS OF NATIONAL LIBERATION" IN VIETNAM, AND CHI-
NESE ATTACK ON HIMALAYAN FRONTIERS OF INDIA. INCLUDES EXAMI-
NATION OF US DEFENSE POLICY.

0731 MCCLOSKEY J.F. ED., TREFETHEN F.N. ED.
OPERATIONS RESEARCH FOR MANAGEMENT.
BALTIMORE: JOHNS HOPKINS PRESS, 1954, 972 PP., LC#54-13114.
PAPERS COVER HISTORY, METHODOLOGY, EXPERIMENTAL ANALYSIS,
INFORMATION HANDLING, AND CASE HISTORIES IN OPERATIONS
RESEARCH FOR MANAGEMENT AND ARE PRODUCTS OF SEMINAR HELD AT
JOHN HOPKINS UNIVERSITY IN 1952.

0732 MCCRACKEN H.L.
KEYNESIAN ECONOMICS IN THE STREAM OF ECONOMIC THOUGHT.
BATON ROUGE: LOUISIANA ST U PR, 1961, 205 PP., LC#61-13012.
ANALYZES AND EVALUATES KEYNES'S SYSTEM OF ECONOMICS, WITH
SPECIAL EMPHASIS ON PLACING IT INTO CONTEXT OF EVOLVING ECO-
NOMIC THOUGHT, RELATING IT TO, AND SHOWING CONTRIBUTIONS
FROM, PREVIOUS ECONOMIC THEORIES.

0733 MCDIARMID J.
"THE MOBILIZATION OF SOCIAL SCIENTISTS," IN L. WHITE'S CIVIL
CIVIL SERVICE IN WARTIME."
CHICAGO: U OF CHICAGO PRESS, 1945.
DISCUSSES PROCESS BY WHICH AMERICAN SOCIAL SCIENTISTS
WERE MOBILIZED FOR THEIR PART IN WWII. DESCRIBES CIVIL
SERVICE COMMISSION'S WAR-RECRUITING AND REPLACEMENT
PROGRAM, SHOWING METHODS OF DECENTRALIZATION AND DELEGATION
OF AUTHORITY.

0734 MCDONALD L.C.
"VOEGELIN AND THE POSITIVISTS: A NEW SCIENCE OF POLITICS."
MIDWEST. J. POLIT. SCI., 1 (NOV. 57), 233-51.
DESCRIBES POSITIVISM AND VOEGELIN'S REJECTION OF IT VIA
HIS NEW SCIENCE, WHICH ATTACKS VALUE-FREE METHOD AS BEING
IMPROPER AND A DESTROYER OF MEN'S SOULS. OBJECTS TO
VOEGELIN'S VIEWS AND INDICATES A COURSE BETWEEN DEPERSONAL-
IZATION AND IMMEASURABILITY SHOULD BE TAKEN RATHER THAN A
DOGMATIC APPROACH FROM EITHER THE POSITIVISTIC OR ANTI-
POSITIVISTIC SIDE.

0735 MCDONOUGH A.M.
INFORMATION ECONOMICS AND MANAGEMENT SYSTEMS.
NEW YORK: MCGRAW HILL, 1963, 321 PP., LC#63-15459.
EXAMINES STUDIES IN INFORMATION FIELD, ESTABLISHES
THEORETICAL FRAMEWORK UNDER WHICH VALUES PLACED ON
KNOWLEDGE AND INFORMATION ARE DISCUSSED, AND PROBES INTO
INFORMATION-RETRIEVAL SYSTEMS IN CONTEXT OF MANAGEMENT
SYSTEMS.

0736 MCDOUGAL M.S., LIPSON L.
"PERSPECTIVES FOR A LAW OF OUTER SPACE."
AMER. J. INT. LAW, 2 (JULY, 58), 407-31.
DUE TO INTERDEPENDENCE OF SCIENTIFIC, MILITARY, AND COM-
MERCIAL OBJECTIVES, AND ACTIVITIES IN OUTER SPACE AN INTER-
NATIONAL CONVENTION FOR OUTER SPACE LAW IS NOT NOW POSSIBLE.
FORECAST LAUNCHING OF SATELLITES FOR AND REGISTRATION BY
U.N. AND UNILATERAL DISARMAMENT AS FIRST STEPS IN FUTURE
CODE OF LAWS.

0737 MCDOUGAL M.S., LASSWELL H.D.
"THE IDENTIFICATION AND APPRAISAL OF DIVERSE SYSTEMS OF PUB-
LIC ORDER (BMR)"
AMER. J. OF INT. LAW, 53 (1959), 1-29.
DISCUSSES ROLE OF SCHOLAR IN RESEARCHING SYSTEMS OF GOV-
ERNMENT AND MODERNIZING INTERNATIONAL LAW TO MAKE IT EFFEC-
TIVE IN TODAY'S POLITICAL SITUATION. EXAMINES PROBLEMS OF
RECONCILING DIFFERENT IDEOLOGIES TO PEACEFUL COEXISTENCE.

0738 MCDOUGAL M.S., LASSWELL H.D.
"THE ENJOYMENT AND ACQUISITION OF RESOURCES IN OUTER
SPACE."
U. PENN. LAW REV., 3 (MAR. 63), 521-636.
A COMPREHENSIVE REVIEW OF THE MORE PROMINENT FEATURES
OF THE PROBABLE PROCESS OF INTERACTION FOR THEIR POTENTIAL
SIGNFICANCE TO CLAIM, POLICY, AND DECISION.' THE ARTICLE
COMPRISES A CHAPTER FROM THE FORTHCOMING BOOK, LAW AND
PUBLIC ORDER IN SPACE. THE DESCRIPTION OF POTENTIAL SPACE
RESOURCES, ESPECIALLY THE CELESTIAL BODIES AND THEIR RANGE
OF POSSIBLE USES, IS UNIQUE.

0739 MCDOUGAL M.S., LASSWELL H.D., VLASIC I.A.
LAW AND PUBLIC ORDER IN SPACE.
NEW HAVEN: YALE U PR, 1963, 11½7 PP., LC#63-13968.
ANALYSIS OF PRESENT STATUS AND LAW, AND NATIONAL POLICY
RELATED TO OUTER SPACE. EXAMINES MAJOR PROBLEMS IN DECI-
SION-MAKING REGARDING EARTH-SPACE ACTIVITY AND INTERNATIONAL
RELATIONS AS MAN MORE DEEPLY EXPLORES SPACE.

0740 MCDOUGAL M.S., LASSWELL H.D., MILLER J.C.
THE INTERPRETATION OF AGREEMENTS AND WORLD PUBLIC ORDER:
PRINCIPLES OF CONTENT AND PROCEDURE.
NEW HAVEN: YALE U PR, 1967, 448 PP., LC#67-13442.
RELATES INTERNATIONAL AGREEMENTS TO PROCESS OF
COMMUNICATION, AND DISCUSSES NEW APPROACHES TO THEORY OF
COMMUNICATION AND PARTICIPATION OF NEW NATIONS. APPRAISES
ADEQUACY OF TRADITIONAL PRINCIPLES OF INTERPRETATION AND
SUGGESTS A SYSTEMIZATION AND MODERIZATION OF THESE
PRINCIPLES.

0741 MCGREGOR D.
THE HUMAN SIDE OF ENTERPRISE.
NEW YORK: MCGRAW HILL, 1960, 246 PP., LC#60-10608.
DISCUSSES WHETHER SUCCESSFUL MANAGERS ARE BORN OR MADE.
FINDS THAT MAKING OF MANAGERS IS ONLY SLIGHTLY THE RESULT
OF MANAGEMENT'S FORMAL EFFORTS IN MANAGEMENT DEVELOPMENT.
IT IS MORE THE RESULT OF MANAGEMENT'S CONCEPTION OF
NATURE OF ITS TASK AND OF ALL POLICIES AND PRACTICES
CONSTRUCTED TO IMPLEMENT THIS CONCEPTION. SUGGESTS MORE
ADEQUATE ASSUMPTIONS UPON WHICH TO BASE TRAINING.

0742 MCGUIRE M.C.
SECRECY AND THE ARMS RACE* A THEORY OF THE ACCUMULATION OF
STRATEGIC WEAPONS AND HOW SECRECY AFFECTS IT.
CAMBRIDGE: HARVARD U PR, 1965, 249 PP., LC#65-22062.
THEORETICAL STRUCTURE FOR EXPLAINING ARMS RACES DEVELOPED
USING GAME THEORETIC FORMULATIONS. ASSUMES THAT SELECTION
OF LEVEL AND QUALITY OF ARMAMENTS ARE RATIONAL CHOICES BAL-
ANCING CONTRIBUTIONS TO NATIONAL OBJECTIVES AGAINST COSTS.
INTERACTION MODEL BUILT IN WHICH SECRECY IS A KEY VARIABLE.

0743 MCKINNEY E.R.
A BIBLIOGRAPHY OF CYBERNETICS AND INFORMATION THEORY.
NEW YORK: FORD FOUNDATION, 1957, 194 PP.
AN ANNOTATED BIBLIOGRAPHY OF 2,900 WORKS, MOSTLY ON THE
INTERMEDIATE AND ADVANCED LEVELS, OF CYBERNETICS AND INFOR-
MATION THEORY. MATERIAL LISTED ALPHABETICALLY WITHIN 15 TOP-
ICAL CLASSIFICATIONS. FOREIGN WORKS IN WESTERN LANGUAGES
INCLUDED. MOST SOURCES DATE FROM THE 1950'S.

0744 MCKINNEY R.
REVIEW OF THE INTERNATIONAL ATOMIC POLICIES AND PROGRAMS OF
THE UNITED STATES (5 VOLS.)
WASHINGTON: US GOVERNMENT, 1960, 2079 PP.
STUDIES INTERNATIONAL PROGRAMS AND POLICIES OF THE US
CONCERNING PEACEFUL USES OF ATOMIC ENERGY. APPRAISES AND
EVALUATES THESE POLICIES IN RELATION TO ORIGINAL PREMISES
AND PURPOSES. EXPLORES ALTERNATIVE COURSES OF ACTION.
COVERS US RELATIONSHIPS WITH DEVELOPED AND LESS-DEVELOPED
COUNTRIES, ALLIES, AND COMMUNIST NATIONS.

0745 MCLAUGHLIN M.R.
RELIGIOUS EDUCATION AND THE STATE: DEMOCRACY FINDS A WAY.
CAMBRIDGE: HARVARD LAW SCHOOL, 1967, 439 PP., LC#67-21368.
DESCRIBES HOW WESTERN DEMOCRACIES, OTHER THAN US, HAVE
SOLVED PROBLEMS OF RELIGION'S ROLE IN PUBLIC EDUCATION AND
RELATION OF STATE TO CHURCH-AFFILIATED SCHOOLS. FINDS THAT
RELIGION IS GIVEN IMPORTANT ROLE IN EDUCATION AND THAT
CHURCHRELATED SCHOOLS ARE SUPPORTED BY STATE. BELIEVES
THAT CONTROVERSY CAN BE SOLVED BY DEMOCRATIC METHODS.
AUTHOR IS CATHOLIC NUN.

0746 MCLEAN J.M.
THE PUBLIC SERVICE AND UNIVERSITY EDUCATION.
PRINCETON: PRINCETON U PRESS, 1949, 241 PP.
CONSIDERS BASIC ISSUES OF SOCIAL AND GOVERNMENTAL ORGAN-
IZATION, SOCIAL AND ADMINISTRATIVE VALUES, AND BASIC TRENDS
IN PUBLIC ADMINISTRATION. IS PRIMARILY CONCERNED WITH ROLE
OF UNIVERSITY IN TRAINING ABLE AND RESPONSIBLE ADMINISTRA-
TORS TO MEET GROWING NEED FOR QUALIFIED GOVERNMENT PERSON-
NEL. COMPARES AMERICAN AND BRITISH ATTEMPTS.

0747 MCNAMARA R.L.
"THE NEED FOR INNOVATIVENESS IN DEVELOPING SOCIETIES."
RURAL SOCIOLOGY, 32 (DEC. 67), 395-399.
EXAMINES COLOMBIA AS CASE OF DEVELOPING SOCIETY'S ATTEMPT
TO ASCERTAIN GENERAL SITUATIONAL FEATURES THAT REQUIRE
INNOVATION BY LEADERS, ADMINISTRATORS, AND OFFICIALS IN
DEALING WITH PROBLEMS. POINTS TO FAILURE OF CONVENTIONAL
SCHEMES TO HANDLE PROBLEMS SUCCESSFULLY, ILLUSTRATING
IDEAS WITH SELECT PROBLEMS.

0748 MCRAE R.
THE PROBLEM OF THE UNITY OF THE SCIENCES: BACON TO KANT.
TORONTO: TORONTO UNIV PRESS, 1961, 193 PP.
A PHILOSOPHICAL ACCOUNT OF THE IDEAS BY WHICH BACON,
DESCARTES, LEIBNIZ, CONDILLAC, DIDEROT, AND KANT TRIED
TO IMPOSE UNITY ON SCIENCE. THESE MEN WERE SYSTEMATIZERS
OF CURRENT KNOWLEDGE, RATHER THAN PIONEERS AT THE FRONTIERS
OF KNOWLEDGE. HENCE, THEY WERE MORE LIKE SOCIAL REFORMERS
THAN SOCIAL INNOVATORS.

0749 MEANS G.C.
ADMINISTRATIVE INFLATION AND PUBLIC POLICY (PAMPHLET)
WASHINGTN: ANDERSON KRAMER ASSOC, 1959, 47 PP., LC#59-13956.
STATEMENTS MADE TO SENATE ANTITRUST AND MONOPOLY SUBCOM-
MITTEE BY US ECONOMISTS IN 1957 TO PROVE THAT "ADMINISTERED
PRICES" CAN CAUSE INFLATION. THEORY SUPPORTED IN 1959 WHEN
1957 INFLATION DID NOT RESPOND TO TRADITIONAL CURBING
METHODS, DUE TO UNEMPLOYMENT AND LACK OF CONSUMER DEMAND.
PRESENTS PROGRAM TO CONTROL ADMINISTERED INFLATION AND
HAVE FULL EMPLOYMENT.

0750 MECRENSKY E.
SCIENTIFIC MANPOWER IN EUROPE.
NEW YORK: PERGAMON PRESS, 1958, 188 PP., LC#58-14062.
COMPARATIVE STUDY OF SKILLED SCIENTIFIC MANPOWER IN PUB-
LIC SERVICE OF ENGLAND, US, AND EUROPEAN NATIONS. COVERS
TRAINING, SALARIES, AND AIMS TO FIND WAYS OF HOLDING THEM
IN GOVERNMENT JOBS. BIBLIOGRAPHY OF SPECIFIC STUDIES BY
COUNTRIES. CHARTS OF PEOPLE INTERVIEWED, SCHOOLS FOR
SCIENTISTS, ETC.

0751 MEHTA A.
"INDIA* POVERTY AND CHANGE."
DISSENT, (MAR.-APR. 67), 191-199.
INDIAN SOCIETY AS IT FACES MODERNIZATION. BREAKUP OF TRA-
DITIONAL SOCIETY BECAUSE OF SCIENCE, INDUSTRY, AGRICULTURAL
TECHNOLOGY. SOCIAL SCIENCES READY TO CHANGE MOTIVATION AND
ATTITUDES. GOAL FOR INDIA IS NOW ECONOMIC FREEDOM. COVERS
CASTE, NATIONAL INCOME, INDUSTRY, TECHNOLOGY, RESEARCH, AND
FOREIGN AID. CONSIDERS SOCIAL CHANGE AND ECONOMIC
DEVELOPMENT AS INTERDEPENDENT.

0752 MELMAN S. ED.
DISARMAMENT: ITS POLITICS AND ECONOMICS.
BOSTON: AMER. ACAD. ARTS SCI., 1962, 398 PP.
A COLLECTION OF PAPERS BY VARIOUS AUTHORS ON THE GENEVA
NEGOTIATIONS AND OTHER CONFERENCES, THE EFFECTIVENESS OF
DISARMAMENT AS A PEACE MEASURE, PROBLEMS OF ENFORCEMENT,
INTERNAL ECONOMIC REPERCUSSIONS, OPPOSITION WITHIN THE US
AND USSR AND SPREAD OF NUCLEAR WEAPONS TECHNOLOGY.

0753 MELMANS S.
OUR DEPLETED SOCIETY.
NEW YORK: HOLT RINEHART WINSTON, 1965, 366 PP., LC#65-14453.
EFFECT OF COLD WAR MILITARY EXPENDITURES ON ECONOMIC
CONDITIONS OF US. DEFENSE RESEARCH AND DEVELOPMENT CON-
TRACTS; SPACE PROGRAM PRIORITIES AND ARMS SALE BUSINESS SEEN
AS DESTRUCTIVE TO THE SOCIAL WELFARE OF THE AMERICAN PEOPLE.

0754 MENEZES A.J.
SUBDESENVOLVIMENTO E POLITICA INTERNACIONAL.
RIO DE JANEIRO: EDICIONES GRD, 1963, 223 PP.
STUDY OF UNDERDEVELOPED WORLD IN FIELD OF INTERNATIONAL
POLITICS. DISCUSSES NATIONALISM AND WORLD WIDE POLITICAL AND
ECONOMIC COMPETITION AMONG NATIONS. DEALS WITH POSITION OF
BRAZIL AND ITS PLANS FOR INDEPENDENT GROWTH IN POWER AND
INFLUENCE.

0755 MERRIAM C.E.
PUBLIC AND PRIVATE GOVERNMENT.
NEW HAVEN: YALE U PR, 1944, 78 PP.
LECTURES DEALING WITH PRIVATE GOVERNMENT, NOTING THE
CONTRIBUTIONS OF GIERKE, DUGNIT, AND GUILD SOCIALISTS,
AS WELL AS INDUSTRIAL SELF-GOVERNMENT. THE PROBLEMS OF
PUBLIC AND PRIVATE INTERDEPENDENCE, PLURALISM, POLITICAL
ORGANIZATION, AND DEMOCRACY.

0756 MERTON R.
"THE ROLE OF APPLIED SOCIAL SCIENCE IN THE FORMATION OF
POLICY: A RESEARCH MEMORANDUM."
PHIL. SCI., 16 (JULY 49), 161-181.
FOCUSES ON THE RECIPROCAL RELATIONS BETWEEN THEORY AND
METHODOLOGY, AND APPLIED SOCIAL SCIENCE IN POLICY FORMULA-
TION. URGES THE USE OF BASIC SCIENTIFIC METHODS IN THE CREA-
TION OF POLICIES.

0757 MERTON R.K.
"THE BEARING OF EMPIRICAL RESEARCH UPON THE DEVELOPMENT OF
SOCIAL THEORY" (BMR)"
AMER. SOCIOLOGICAL REV., 13 (OCT. 48), 505-515.
DISCUSSION OF FOUR IMPACTS OF RESEARCH UPON DEVELOPMENT
OF SOCIAL THEORY: INITIATION, REFORMULATION, REFOCUSING,
AND CLARIFICATION OF THEORY. SUGGESTS THAT AN EXPLICITLY
FORMULATED THEORY DOES NOT INVARIABLY PRECEDE EMPIRICAL
INQUIRY, AND THAT THE SEQUENCE IS OFTEN REVERSED. DEFINES
THE RECIPROCITY OF ROLES BETWEEN EMPIRICISM AND PRINCIPLE.

0758 , LAZARSFELD P.F. ED.
CONTINUITIES IN SOCIAL RESEARCH; STUDIES IN SCOPE AND METHOD
OF "THE AMERICAN SOLDIER"
NEW YORK: FREE PRESS OF GLENCOE, 1950, 255 PP.
EXAMINES NEW TECHNIQUES OF DATA ANALYSIS INTRODUCED IN
"THE AMERICAN SOLDIER." DISCUSSES WAYS IN WHICH SYSTEMATIC
DATA OF STUDY CLARIFIES AND EXTENDS SOCIAL THEORY MORE THAN
DOES ANECDOTAL DATA. EXPLORES STUDY'S IMPLICATIONS FOR
THEORY OF REFERENCE GROUP BEHAVIOR, SURVEY ANALYSIS,
SOCIOLOGY OF MILITARY, OPINION RESEARCH, AND SOCIAL
PSYCHOLOGY.

0759 MERTON R.K.
SOCIAL THEORY AND SOCIAL STRUCTURE (REV. ED.)
NEW YORK: FREE PRESS OF GLENCOE, 1957, 645 PP.
DISCUSSES FUNCTIONAL ANALYSIS AND INTERRELATIONSHIP OF
SOCIOLOGICAL THEORY AND RESEARCH. USING FUNCTIONAL ANALYSIS,
STUDIES SOCIAL STRUCTURE AND ANOMIE, BUREAUCRACY AND
PERSONALITY, THEORY OF REFERENCE GROUPS, AND PATTERNS OF
INFLUENCE. EXAMINES THEORIES OF SOCIOLOGY OF KNOWLEDGE AND
MASS COMMUNICATION AND STUDIES IN SOCIOLOGY OF SCIENCE.

0760 METZLER L.A., ET A.L.

INCOME, EMPLOYMENT, AND PUBLIC POLICY.
NEW YORK: W W NORTON, 1948, 381 PP.
   DISCUSSES RELATIONSHIP OF DETERMINANTS OF INCOME: INVEST-
MENT, REDISTRIBUTION, PRODUCTIVITY, EMPLOYMENT. CONSIDERS
SOCIAL SETTING AND EFFECTS OF PUBLIC POLICY ON INCOME.
EXAMINES CREDIT CONTROLS, INTEREST RATES, PUBLIC EXPENDI-
TURES, AND EXPANSIONISTIC FISCAL POLICIES. RELATION OF PRO-
DUCTIVITY TO WAGES IS ALSO STUDIED.

0761 MEZERIK A.G. ED.
ATOM TESTS AND RADIATION HAZARDS (PAMPHLET)
NEW YORK: INTL REVIEW SERVICE, 1961, 59 PP.
   EXAMINES POSTWAR PROBLEMS OF NUCLEAR ARMS CONTROL IN
REGARD TO HEALTH DANGERS, AND UN ACTIVITIES TO LIMIT USE AND
SPREAD OF NUCLEAR WEAPONS. DISCUSSES TEST BAN TREATY AND
CONFERENCES ON TOPIC.

0762 MEZERIK A.G. ED.
INTERNATIONAL POLICY 1965 (PAMPHLET)
NEW YORK: INTL REVIEW SERVICE, 1965, 95 PP.
   REVIEWS VARIOUS INTERNATIONAL PROBLEMS OF 1965 AND VIEWS
OF NATIONS AND LEADERS ON THEM AS VOICED BEFORE UN,
INCLUDING VIETNAM, KASHMIR, APARTHEID, AND DISARMAMENT.

0763 MEZERIK AG
OUTER SPACE: UN, US, USSR (PAMPHLET)
NEW YORK: INTL REVIEW SERVICE, 1960, 52 PP.
   SHORT OUTLINE OF RECENT ACTIVITIES OF US AND USSR IN AND
CONCERNING SPACE EXPLORATION. SURVEYS ROLE OF UN IN ATTEMPTS
AT TREATY-MAKING AND REVIEWS VARIOUS THEORIES OF SOVEREIGNTY
IN SPACE, COMMITTEES AND ORGANIZATIONS CONCERNED, AND
PRACTICAL AND LEGAL PROBLEMS INVOLVED.

0764 MICHAEL D.N.
PROPOSED STUDIES ON THE IMPLICATIONS OF PEACEFUL SPACE AC-
TIVITIES FOR HUMAN AFFAIRS.
WASHINGTON: GOVT PR OFFICE, 1961, 272 PP.
   DESIGNATES SEVERAL AREAS OF STUDY AND SUGGESTS RESEARCH
PROGRAMS FOR FUTURE EXAMINATION OF PROBLEMS AND CONSEQUENCES
OF SPACE ACTIVITY AS RELATED TO SOCIAL INSTITUTIONS AND VAR-
IOUS AREAS OF SOCIAL ENDEAVOR. PROVIDES DETAILED ANALYSES OF
PROSPECTIVE PLANS FOR STUDYING IMPLICATIONS FOR INDUSTRY,
COMMUNICATIONS, NATIONAL GOALS, AND OTHER IMPORTANT TOPICS
AND ISSUES IN DEVELOPMENT OF US SPACE PROGRAM.

0765 MIKSCHE F.O.
ATOMIC WEAPONS AND ARMIES.
LONDON: FABER, 1955, 222 PP.
   ANALYZES DEVELOPMENT OF WAR TECHNIQUES FROM 1914 TO
PRESENT. DISCUSSES POSSIBLE EFFECTS ON ARMY TACTICS AND
ORGANIZATION OF USE OF NUCLEAR WEAPONS.

0766 MIKSCHE F.O.
THE FAILURE OF ATOMIC STRATEGY.
NEW YORK: PRAEGER, 1959, 224 PP.
   CONTENDS WESTERN STRATEGY RELIES CHIEFLY ON PROGRESSIVE
ARMS TECHNIQUE INCOMMENSURABLE WITH POLITICAL REALITIES.
OVERWHELMING CONCENTRATION OF NUCLEAR POWER LEAVES ALLIES
WITH NO CHOICE EXCEPT SUICIDE OR RETREAT AGAINST SOVIET
AGGRESSION. PROPOSES INCREASED STRENGTH IN CONVENTIONAL
WEAPONS AND FORCES ALONG WITH COMPLETE SOLIDARITY OF ALL
ALLIES. ADVOCATES REVISION OF WESTERN MILITARY POLICY.

0767 MILBRATH L.W.
THE WASHINGTON LOBBYISTS.
NEW YORK: RAND MCNALLY & CO, 1963, 358 PP.
   STUDY OF LOBBYISTS AS SPECIAL POLITICAL SKILL GROUP, AS
PERSONS, AS POLITICAL ACTORS. EXAMINATION OF COMMUNICATION
PROCESS BY WHICH POLICY DESIRES OF SPECIAL-INTEREST GROUPS
ARE FED INTO GOVERNMENTAL DECISION PROCESS. DISCUSSES ROLE
OF LOBBYING IN AMERICAN DEMOCRACY. EXTENSIVE TABLES
INCLUDED.

0768 MILBURN T.W.
"WHAT CONSTITUTES EFFECTIVE DETERRENCE."
J. CONFL. RESOLUT., 3 (JUNE 59), 138-45.
   WEIGHS FACTORS ACTING AS DETERRENTS AND EVALUATES THEIR
CONTRIBUTING EFFECT ON PREVENTION OF WAR. FINDS BEHAVIOR OF
BOTH USA AND USSR INFLUENCED BY THREAT OF RETALIATORY PUN-
ISHMENT. INFERS THAT EFFECTIVENESS OF DETERRENCE COULD BE
DETERMINED BY KNOWLEDGE OF ENEMY'S EXPECTATIONS OF GAINS AND
WILLINGNESS TO SACRIFICE. STUDY OF ATTITUDES IS ALSO OF
GREAT IMPORTANCE IN DETERMINING DETERRENCE.

0769 MILIBAND R. ED., SAVILLE J. ED.
THE SOCIALIST REGISTER: 1964.
NEW YORK: MONTHLY REVIEW PR, 1964, 308 PP.
   SOME 18 ESSAYS ON CURRENT SOCIALIST AND COMMUNIST THEORY,
POLITICS, ECONOMICS, AND BEHAVIOR. EMPHASIS IS ON EVENTS AND
PROGRESS IN ENGLAND, BUT 1964 EDITION INCLUDES COMMENTARY ON
NASSER, MAOISM, WEST GERMANY, ALLIANCE FOR PROGRESS, AND
OTHER ITEMS OF INTERNATIONAL SIGNIFICANCE. ALSO INCLUDES
REVIEWS OF PERTINENT BOOKS AND ARTICLES.

0770 MILLAR R.
THE NEW CLASSES.

LONDON: LONGMANS, GREEN & CO, 1966, 296 PP.
   BELIEVES THAT CLASS GROUPINGS WHICH GREW OUT OF FIRST
INDUSTRIAL REVOLUTION ARE BEING DESTROYED BY TECHNOLOGICAL
AND MECHANIZED REVOLUTION. EXAMINES REASONS FOR
DISINTEGRATION OF OLD SOCIAL AND ECONOMIC STRUCTURE, SYSTEM
THAT IS TAKING ITS PLACE, AND EFFECTS ON BRITISH PEOPLE.
STUDIES STATUS SYMBOLS AND MOBILITY. MAINTAINS THAT NEW
SYSTEM WILL ELIMINATE TRADITIONAL CLASS ANTAGONISMS.

0771 MILLER G.A.
"WHAT IS INFORMATION MEASUREMENT?"
AMER. PSYCHOLOGIST, 8 (JAN. 53), 3-11.
   AN INTRODUCTORY ANALYSIS TO BASIC CONCEPTS OF INFORMATION
THEORY. DEFINES AND MATHEMATICALLY ILLUSTRATES CONCEPTS OF
"AMOUNT OF INFORMATION," "BIT," "SOURCE," "AVERAGE AMOUNT
OF INFORMATION," AND "RELATED SOURCES." EXAMINES BOTH THE
TRANSMISSION AND THE SEQUENTIAL SITUATION AND IDENTIFIES THE
VARIABLES IN EACH SITUATION WITH DIFFERENT QUANTITIES OF
INFORMATION.

0772 MILLER G.A.
"THE MAGICAL NUMBER SEVEN, PLUS OR MINUS TWO: SOME LIMITS ON
OUR CAPACITY FOR PROCESSING INFORMATION."
PSYCHOLOGICAL REVIEW, 63 (MAR. 56), 81-97.
   EXAMINATION OF EXPERIMENTS ON HUMAN CAPACITY TO TRANSMIT
INFORMATION. EXPERIMENTS MEASURED THE DEGREE OF ACCURACY
WITH WHICH PEOPLE CAN ASSIGN NUMBERS TO THE MAGNITUDES OF
VARIOUS ASPECTS OF A STIMULUS. EXPERIMENTAL RESULTS ARE
ANALYZED IN TERMS OF THE CONCEPTS OF INFORMATION THEORY.
INCLUDES AN UNANNOTATED BIBLIOGRAPHY OF 20 REFERENCES.

0773 MILLER J.G.
"TOWARD A GENERAL THEORY FOR THE BEHAVIORAL SCIENCES" (BMR)"
AMER. PSYCHOLOGIST, 10 (SEPT. 55), 513-531.
   A CONSIDERATION OF MODELS, PROPOSITIONS, AND OTHER AS-
PECTS OF A GENERAL THEORY FOR THE BEHAVIORAL SCIENCES.
DISCUSSES SPECIFIC ASPECTS OF THE THEORY SUCH AS SYSTEMS,
BOUNDARIES, SUBSYSTEMS, CODING, AND EQUIFINALITY.
EXAMINES THE NECESSITY FOR RECOGNIZING ANALOGIES OR FORMAL
IDENTITIES FOR GENERALIZATION TO BE EFFECTIVE. OUTLINES 19
PROPOSITIONS EMPIRICALLY TESTABLE AT ALL SYSTEM LEVELS.

0774 MILLER W.E.
"PRESIDENTIAL COATTAILS: A STUDY IN POLITICAL MYTH AND
METHODOLOGY" (BMR)"
PUBLIC OPINION QUART., 19 (WINTER 56), 353-368.
   EXAMINES DISCREPANCIES IN TRADITIONAL ANALYSES OF
INFLUENCE OF PRESIDENTIAL CANDIDATE WHICH EQUATE ABILITY
TO GET VOTES WITH DEMONSTRATION OF STRENGTH. DESCRIBES A
MODEL FOR IDENTIFYING AND ANALYZING VOTE-PULLING POWER OF
PRESIDENTIAL CANDIDATES. INCLUDES MOTIVATION OF
PRESIDENTIAL VOTING, SEQUENCE OF VOTE DECISIONS, AND
CANDIDATE PARTISANSHIP.

0775 GT BRIT MIN OVERSEAS DEV, LIB
TECHNICAL CO-OPERATION -- A BIBLIOGRAPHY.
LONDON: MIN OF OVERSEAS DEVEL.
   MONTHLY LISTING, FIRST PUBLISHED 1964, OF CURRENT
OFFICIAL PUBLICATIONS OF THE COMMONWEALTH, DOCUMENTS, PRO-
CESSED AND UNPUBLISHED MATERIALS, AND OTHER REPORTS AND
BULLETINS FROM FOREIGN INSTITUTIONS. ENTRIES PERTAIN TO ECO-
NOMIC, SOCIAL, LEGAL, AND STATISTICAL ASPECTS OF TECHNICAL
DEVELOPMENT.

0776 MOCH J.
HUMAN FOLLY: DISARM OR PERISH.
LONDON: GOLLANCZ, 1955, 220 PP.
   DEVELOPS THE DISARMAMENT QUESTION THROUGH FIRST STUDYING
THE MILITARY-TECHNICAL SITUATION AS IT DEVELOPED SINCE CRE-
ATION OF ATOMIC BOMB, AND THEN REVIEWING USA'S ATTEMPTS TO
REACH A PEACEFUL SOLUTION. FORSEES INEVIBILITY OF CONFLICT
UNLESS PROGRESS MADE IN FIELD OF DISARMAMENT.

0777 MODELSKI G
ATOMIC ENERGY IN THE COMMUNIST BLOC.
NEW YORK: CAMBRIDGE, 1959, 221 PP.
   THE COMMUNIST BLOC'S INCREASED KNOWLEDGE IN THE ATOMIC
ENERGY FIELD DURING THE PAST DECADE IS SPECTACULAR NOT ONLY
IN ITS GROWTH, BUT ALSO IN ITS DIVERSIFICATION AND DISSEMIN-
ATION OF ACQUIRED KNOWLEDGE. THIS SPREAD OF KNOWLEDGE AMONG
THE NATIONS WILL HAVE DEFINITE REPERCUSSIONS IN THE QUEST
FOR INTERNATIONAL CONTROL OF ATOMIC ENERGY.

0778 MOON P.T.
"SYLLABUS ON INTERNATIONAL RELATIONS."
LONDON: MACMILLAN, 1925.
   COMPREHENSIVE SURVEY OF ECONOMIC, GEOGRAPHIC, SOCIOLOGI-
CAL ASPECTS OF INTERNATIONAL RELATIONS FOR UNDERGRADUATE
USE. CITATION OF SOURCE MATERIAL GENERALLY CONFINED TO THAT
LEVEL. GENERAL BIBLIOGRAPHY AT END AND BIBLIOGRAPHICAL
REFERENCES FOR EACH CHAPTER INCLUDED. TRACES HISTORY OF
INTERNATIONAL RELATIONS UP TO 1920'S.

0779 MOOR E.J.
"THE INTERNATIONAL IMPACT OF AUTOMATION."
LEX ET SCIENTIA, 4 (JAN.-MAR. 67), 10-14.

GIVES REPRESENTATIVE OPERATIONAL, ADMINISTRATIVE, AND
PLANNING EXAMPLES TO FORECAST AUTOMATION'S FUTURE IMPACT.
ADVOCATES RESPONSIVE RELATIONSHIP WITH DEVICES ADOPTED TO
AID OUR CONGNITIVE POWERS.

0780 MOORE J.R.
THE ECONOMIC IMPACT OF THE TVA.
KNOXVILLE: U OF TENN PR, 1967, 160 PP., LC#67-12217.
COLLECTION OF ESSAYS FROM SYMPOSIUM CELEBRATING TVA'S
30TH ANNIVERSARY. CONSIDERS ROLE OF ELECTRIC POWER IN ECO-
NOMIC DEVELOPMENT. PROBLEMS OF TVA MODELED PROJECTS IN IRAN
AND COLUMBIA. RELATION OF REGIONAL DEVELOPMENT TO NATIONAL
PROSPERITY. CONTROVERSIES OVER SOCIALISM AND ANTI-TRUST EX-
POSURES REVIEWED. WANTS CONGRESSIONAL SANCTION FOR INCREASED
SCOPE OF ACTIVITY TO MEET GENERAL ECONOMIC MATURITY.

0781 MORGENSTERN O.
"THE N-COUNTRY PROBLEM."
FORTUNE, MARCH 61.
EFFORT TO FORESEE MAIN OUTLINES OF NUCLEAR PROBLEM.
EXAMINES THE ABILITY TO PRODUCE AND DELIVER AND PROBES PROB-
LEMS OF STABILITY AND DETERRENCE. CONCLUDES THAT THE SPREAD
OF NUCLEAR WEAPONS AFFECTS THE EXISTING BALANCE OF POWER.

0782 MORGENTHAU H.J.
SCIENTIFIC MAN VS POWER POLITICS.
CHICAGO: U. CHI. PR., 1946, 245 PP.
ASSERTS THAT THE 'REDEEMING POWER' OF SCIENCE HAS BEEN
MISPLACED. CITES CONTENTS INHERENT IN PHILOSOPHICAL AND
POLITICAL THOUGHT FROM WHICH THIS 'BELIEF' HAS EMANATED.
EXPOSTULATION THAT PROBLEMS OF THE SOCIAL WORLD MUST YIELD
TO THE MORAL AND INTELLECTUAL FACULTIES OF MAN.

0783 MORGENTHAU H.J.
"A POLITICAL THEORY OF FOREIGN AID."
AMER. POLIT. SCI. REV., 56 (JUNE 62) 301-309.
SEES NEED TO DEVELOPE INTELLIGIBLE THEORY OF FOREIGN AID,
SO TO PROVIDE STANDARDS FOR DISCUSSION. CLASSIFIES AID INTO
6 TYPES AND PARTICULARY DISCUSSES THE ASPECTS AND SUCCESSES
OF AID 'FOR ECONOMIC DEVELOPMENT.' CONCLUDES THAT US MUST
LEARN TO CHOOSE QUANTITY AND QUALITY OF AID APPROPRIATE TO
SITUATION, TO ATTUNE DIFFERENT TYPES OF AID TO EACH OTHER,
AND TREAT FOREIGN AID AS INTEGRAL PART OF POLITICAL POLICY.

0784 MORRIS M.D.
THE EMERGENCE OF AN INDUSTRIAL LABOR FORCE IN INDIA: A
STUDY OF THE BOMBAY COTTON MILLS, 1854-1947.
BERKELEY: U OF CALIF PR, 1965, 263 PP., LC#65-13143.
DISCUSSES PROBLEM OF HOW A LABOR FORCE IS MOBILIZED AND
ORGANIZED FOR FACTORY EMPLOYMENT DURING EARLY STAGES OF
INDUSTRIALIZATION. ARGUES THAT IN PARTICULAR STUDY SUPPLY OF
LABOR FOR INDUSTRIAL REQUIREMENTS WAS NOT HARD TO GET AND
THAT THE LEVEL OF LABOR FORCE'S PERFORMANCE WAS ALMOST
ENTIRELY SET BY NATURE OF INDUSTRIAL ORGANIZATION AND
DEVELOPMENT.

0785 MORRIS W.T.
ENGINEERING ECONOMY.
HOMEWOOD: RICHARD IRWIN, 1960, 506 PP., LC#60-12922.
A PRESENTATION OF ENGINEERING ECONOMY WITHIN THE LARGER
CONTEXT OF MANAGEMENT DECISION ANALYSIS. DISCUSSES FUNDAMEN-
TALS OF ENGINEERING DECISIONS IN TERMS OF APPROACHES, GOALS,
MODELS, AND CASES UNDER CERTAINTY, UNCERTAINTY, AND RISK.
EXAMINES SOURCES OF INFORMATION, PREDICTION AND JUDGMENT,
EVALUATION OF INTANGIBLES, REPLACEMENT POLICY, AND PROBABIL-
ITY THEORY. ANALYZES ECONOMICS OF AUTOMATION IN MANAGEMENT.

0786 MORSTEIN-MARX F. ED.
PUBLIC MANAGEMENT IN THE NEW DEMOCRACY.
NEW YORK: HARPER & ROW, 1940, 266 PP.
COLLECTION OF PAPERS DISCUSSING HISTORICAL BASIS OF NEW,
BIG BUREAUCRACY, TENETS OF PUBLIC MANAGEMENT, POWERS IN AND
OF CIVIL SERVICE.

0787 MORTON J.A.
"A SYSTEMS APPROACH TO THE INNOVATION PROCESS: ITS USE IN
THE BELL SYSTEM."
BUSINESS HORIZONS, 10 (SUMMER 67), 7-36.
AS A PROCESS, INNOVATION CAN BE STUDIED AND MANAGED FROM
SYSTEMS VIEWPOINT; IN LAB STAGE, SPECIALIZED FUNCTIONS
OF BASIC RESEARCH, APPLIED RESEARCH, AND DEVELOPMENT DESIGN
CAN BE PROVIDED WITH OVER-ALL GUIDANCE, JUDGMENTS, AND CA-
TALYSIS BY SYSTEMS ENGINEERING.

0788 MORTON L.
"THE DECISION TO USE THE BOMB."
FOREIGN AFFAIRS, 35 (JAN. 57), 334-353.
A LOOK AT THE DEVELOPMENT OF THE ATOMIC BOMB AND ITS USE
FROM A PERSPECTIVE OF TEN YEARS. DOES NOT RESOLVE ANY OF THE
CONFUSION OR MORAL QUESTIONS SURROUNDING THE EVENT; PURELY
THE RECORDING OF HISTORICAL FACT.

0789 MOSK S.A.
INDUSTRIAL REVOLUTION IN MEXICO.
BERKELEY: U OF CALIF PR, 1954, 331 PP.
ANALYZES REVOLUTION IN MEXICAN ECONOMY SINCE 1940, BASIC

ATTITUDES OF INDUSTRIAL DRIVE, AND PERSPECTIVES OF
BUSINESS, GOVERNMENT, AND LABOR. DISCUSSES GOVERNMENTAL
POLICIES ENCOURAGING INDUSTRIAL DEVELOPMENT. SURVEYS
DEVELOPMENTS IN PRINCIPAL INDUSTRIAL FIELDS.

0790 MOSKOWITZ H., ROBERTS J.
US SECURITY, ARMS CONTROL, AND DISARMAMENT 1961-1965.
WASHINGTON: DEPT OF THE ARMY, 1965, 140 PP.
CONTAINS 1400 LISTINGS IN ENGLISH FROM BOOKS, ARTICLES,
AND DOCUMENTS. ARRANGED BY SUBJECT; PUBLICATION DATES OF
ENTRIES OCTOBER, 1961-JANUARY, 1965. EXCERPTS FROM LISTINGS
IN ANNOTATIONS.

0791 MOSS F.M.
THE WATER CRISIS.
NEW YORK: FREDERICK PRAEGER, 1967.
EXAMINES WATER PROBLEMS THE US FACES TODAY - POLLUTION,
SHORTAGE, VARIABILITY, DEPLETION, AND WASTE. PROPOSES
SOLUTIONS - STEPS TO REORGANIZE OUR WATER MANAGEMENT ACTIVI-
TIES AND ACHIEVE A FUNDAMENTAL NATIONAL WATER POLICY. SUG-
GESTS THE CREATION OF A DEPT. OF NATURAL RESOURCES.

0792 MULLENBACH P.
CIVILIAN NUCLEAR POWER: ECONOMIC ISSUES AND POLICY FOR-
MATION.
NEW YORK: TWENTIETH CENT. FUND, 1963, 406 PP., $8.50.
CONCERNED WITH THE EXTENT TO WHICH THE U.S. CAN MAINTAIN
WORLD LEADERSHIP IN PEACETIME DEVELOPMENT OF NUCLEAR ENERGY.
EVALUATES POLICY FORMATION, BASED ON ECONOMIC ANALYSIS OF
THE ISSUES UNDERLYING POWER REACTOR DEVELOPMENT DURING THE
PERIOD 1953-1961.

0793 MULLER H.J.
FREEDOM IN THE WESTERN WORLD.
NEW YORK: HARPER & ROW, 1963, 428 PP., LC#63-8427.
SYNTHESIS OF VARIOUS MAJOR DEVELOPMENTS THAT AFFECTED
WESTERN CIVILIZATION THROUGH DARK AGES TO MODERN DEMOCRACY.
RELIGIOUS AND POLITICAL STRUGGLES, ADVANCES OF COLLECTIVE
WEALTH AND POWER THROUGH COMMERCE AND TECHNOLOGY, CREATIVITY
IN ART AND SCIENTIFIC THOUGHT, AND EVOLVEMENT OF IDEAS THAT
PROMOTED BELIEF IN MAN'S DIGNITY AND FITNESS FOR FREEDOM ARE
DEVELOPMENTS THAT ARE DISCUSSED.

0794 MUMFORD L.
"AUTHORITARIAN AND DEMOCRATIC TECHNIQUES."
SCI. TECH., 5 (WINTER 1964), 1-8.
THIS STUDY CONTENDS THAT THE PRESENT AGE HAS SURRENDERED
TO A SYSTEM-CENTERED AUTHORITARIAN TECHNOLOGY WHICH IS SLOW-
LY DESTROYING HUMAN AUTONOMY AND CREATIVITY. IT URGES A RE-
SURGENCE OF DEMOCRATIC TECHNIQUES DEVELOPED AND DIRECTED BY
INDIVIDUALS AND BASED ON SMALL-SCALE PRODUCTION.

0795 MUMFORD L.
THE MYTH OF THE MACHINE: TECHNICS AND HUMAN DEVELOPMENT.
NEW YORK: HARCOURT BRACE, 1966, 342 PP., LC#67-16088.
QUESTIONS BOTH THE ASSUMPTIONS AND THE PREDICTIONS UPON
WHICH OUR COMMITMENT TO THE PRESENT FORMS OF TECHNICAL AND
SCIENTIFIC PROGRESS, TREATED AS ENDS IN THEMSELVES, HAVE
BEEN BASED. AUTHOR BELIEVES THAT THE ROLE OF MACHINES HAS
BEEN OVERRATED. PRESENTS A PHILOSOPHICAL HISTORY OF TECHNI-
CAL DEVELOPMENT SINCE THE STONE AGE.

0796 MURDOCK J.C. ED., GRAVES J. ED.
RESEARCH AND REGIONS.
COLUMBIA: U OF MO, BUS & PUB ADM, 1966, 211 PP., LC#66-65231
A KWIC (KEYWORD-IN-CONTEXT) INDEXED BIBLIOGRAPHY OF MA-
TERIAL IN ECONOMIC AND ADMINISTRATIVE RESEARCH AND REGIONAL
DEVELOPMENT. APPLIES COMPUTER TECHNIQUES TO INFORMATION RE-
TRIEVAL. PART I LISTS ENTRIES BY SEVEN KEYWORDS; PART II IS
AUTHOR-ALPHABETIZED BIBLIOGRAPHY; PART III, AN AUTHOR CROSS
REFERENCE. INCLUDES LISTING OF RESEARCH FACILITIES.

0797 MURPHY E.F.
WATER PURITY: A STUDY IN LEGAL CONTROL OF NATURAL RESOURCES.
MADISON: U OF WISCONSIN PR, 1961, 212 PP., LC#61-5902.
STUDIES LOCAL REGULATION AND STATE ADMINISTRATION OF
WATER PURIFICATION PROGRAMS IN WISCONSIN. PRESENTS LEGAL
RESOLUTION OF ECONOMIC PROBLEMS IN NATURAL RESOURCE
CONSERVATION AND INTERPLAY OF LAW AND INTEREST GROUPS.
ANALYZES TRANSLATION OF BIOLOGICAL KNOWLEDGE INTO PUBLIC
WORKS PROGRAMS. DISCUSSES PUBLIC AND OFFICIAL ATTITUDES
TOWARD VARIOUS ASPECTS OF STATE ADMINISTRATIVE CONTROL.

0798 MYERS S.
"TECHNOLOGY AND URBAN TRANSIT: THE ENORMOUS POTENTIAL OF BUS
AND RAIL SYSTEMS."
BUSINESS HORIZONS, 10 (SUMMER 67), 3-70.
SUGGESTS THAT EXISTING RAIL AND BUS SYSTEMS CAN BE GREAT-
LY IMPROVED USING TODAY'S TECHNOLOGY, WHILE RESEARCH GOES ON
SEEKING NEW FORMS. TRANSPORTATION IMPROVEMENT SHOULD BE MADE
IN QUALITY RATHER THAN QUANTITY OF TRANSPORT SYSTEMS; USE OF
ELECTRONIC HIGHWAY CONTROL AND OFF-PEAK PRICING IS SUGGEST-
ED.

0799 NADER R., PAGE J.A.
"AUTOMOBILE DESIGN AND THE JUDICIAL PROCESS."

CALIF. LAW REV., 55 (AUG. 67), 645-677.
DISCUSSES PAST AND POTENTIAL INTERACTION BETWEEN JUDICIAL
PROCESS AND CONTRIBUTION OF AUTOMOBILE DESIGN TO TRAFFIC
ACCIDENTS. CONSIDERS LEGAL FRAMEWORK INVOLVED, REASONS FOR
REFUSING DAMAGES IN SEVERAL COURT CASES, AND PRACTICAL
PROBLEMS OF SUCH SUITS. DISCUSSES TRAFFIC AND MOTER VEHICLE
SAFETY ACT AND ITS IMPLICATIONS FOR COURT PROCEDURES AND
DECISIONS.

0800 NADLER E.B.
"SOME ECONOMIC DISADVANTAGES OF THE ARMS RACE."
J. CONFL. RESOLUT., 7 (SEPT. 63), 503-09.
STUDIES WAYS IN WHICH GROWTH OF MILITARY-INDUSTRIAL COM-
PLEX PREVENTS EFFECTIVE CONTROL OF AMERICAN ECONOMY. PROBLEM
CONTRIBUTES TO BUSINESS STAGNATION AND UNEMPLOYMENT. OFFERS
SOLUTIONS.

0801 NAFZIGER R.O. ED., WHITE D.M.
INTRODUCTION TO MASS COMMUNICATIONS RESEARCH (REV. ED.)
BATON ROUGE: LOUISIANA ST U PR, 1963, 281 PP., LC#63-8223.
ESSAYS ON RESEARCH METHODS IN MASS COMMUNICATION FROM
BEHAVIORAL POINT OF VIEW. INCLUDE DISCUSSION OF CONTENT
ANALYSIS, STATISTICS, SCIENTIFIC METHOD, FIELD METHODS,
AND RESEARCH PLANNING.

0802 NAKICENOVIC S.
NUCLEAR ENERGY IN YUGOSLAVIA.
BELGRADE, YUGO: EXPORT PRESS, 1961, 537 PP.
SURVEY OF BASIC AND APPLIED NUCLEAR RESEARCH. PROGRAMS
ARE CONFINED TO PEACEFUL PURPOSES AND INCLUDE APPLICATION OF
RADIOACTIVE ISOTOPES TO INDUSTRY, AGRICULTURE, AND MEDICINE.
DESCRIBES IN DETAIL WORK OF VARIOUS INSTITUTES AND PROGRESS
IN GENERAL FIELDS AND SPECIFIC PROGRAMS. CONTAINS EXTENSIVE
BIBLIOGRAPHY OF ATOMIC RESEARCH SINCE YUGOSLAVIA'S ENTRANCE
INTO THE FIELD IN 1947.

0803 NANES A.
"DISARMAMENT: THE LAST SEVEN YEARS."
CURR. HIST., 42 (MAY 62), 267-274.
SUMMARIZING NEGOTIATIONS SINCE 1955, AUTHOR CALLS
ATTENTION TO 'CRUCIAL POINT THAT HAS NEVER BEEN RESOLVED...
USA INSISTENCE ON EFFECTIVE INTERNATIONAL INSPECTION AND
SOVIET SUSPICION OF SAME AS COVER FOR ESPIONAGE.' ESSENTIAL-
LY, DISARMAMENT TALKS HAVE FAILED: PROSPECTS FOR A TEST-BAN
ARE CURRENTLY DIM. ONE REASON FOR HOPE IS GROWING PUBLIC
CONSCIOUSNESS OF DESTRUCTIVE NATURE OF MODERN WEAPONS.

0804 NASA
CONFERENCE ON SPACE, SCIENCE, AND URBAN LIFE.
WASHINGTON: US GOVERNMENT, 1963, 254 PP.
EXAMINES POSSIBILITIES OF APPLYING SPACE EXPLORATION
PROGRAM TO PROBLEMS OF DAILY LIFE IN URBAN AREAS. SEEKS
WAYS TO USE NEW KNOWLEDGE DEVELOPING IN SCIENTIFIC AND
TECHNOLOGICAL REVOLUTION TO HELP FIND ANSWERS TO CRITICAL
ISSUES FACING URBAN POPULATIONS.

0805 NASA
PROCEEDINGS OF CONFERENCE ON THE LAW OF SPACE AND OF
SATELLITE COMMUNICATIONS: CHICAGO 1963.
WASHINGTON: US GOVERNMENT, 1964, 205 PP.
SURVEYS LEGAL PROBLEMS OF SPACE AGE AND FORMULATES TENTA-
TIVE LEGAL VIEWS ON SPACE. TREATS PROBLEMS OF LAW AND FOR-
EIGN DIPLOMACY THAT ARE EXPECTED IN HANDLING COMMUNICATIONS
SATELLITE, BECAUSE IT IS A "YANKEE INVENTION COMMITTED
TO FREE ENTERPRISE." INCLUDES TEXT OF SATELLITE ACT OF 1962.

0806 NASH M.
MACHINE AGE MAYA.
CHICAGO: U OF CHICAGO PRESS, 1967, 155 PP.
DISCUSSES THE INDUSTRIALIZATION OF A GUATEMALAN COMMUNI-
TY. DESCRIBES AN INDIAN MOUNTAIN COMMUNITY, WHICH HAS SUC-
CESSFULLY ADAPTED TO THE OPERATION OF LATIN AMERICA'S LARG-
EST TEXTILE MILL. DISCUSSES IMPACT OF THE FACTORY ON THE
COMMUNITY, E.G., RAISING THE STANDARD OF LIVING AND CREAT-
ING NEW WORK HABITS. COMPARES THE RELIGIOUS PRACTICES AND
BELIEFS OF FACTORY AND FARM WORKER.

0807 NATHAN O. ED. ET AL.
EINSTEIN ON PEACE.
NEW YORK: SIMON SCHUSTER, 1961, 704 PP., $8.50.
DEPICTS EINSTEIN'S LIFE-TIME CONCERN FOR INDIVIDUAL
LIBERTY. REVIEWS DECLARATIONS REGARDING DISARMAMENT AND
SURVIVAL OF MANKIND.

0808 NATIONAL ACADEMY OF SCIENCES
CIVIL DEFENSE: PROJECT HARBOR SUMMARY REPORT (PAMPHLET)
WASHINGTON: NATL ACADEMY OF SCI, 1964, 39 PP., LC#64-62988.
CONDENSED VERSION OF REPORT OF SUMMER STUDY GROUP AT
WOOD'S HOLE, MASSACHUSETTS. CONCLUDES THAT EXISTING FALLOUT
SHELTER PROGRAM IS EFFECTIVE BUT THAT INCREASED EDUCATION
OF PUBLIC, FURTHER STOCKPILING OF NEEDED COMMODITIES, AND
GREATER FEDERAL INVOLVEMENT IN COORDINATION OF OPERATIONS
WOULD SUBSTANTIALLY BETTER US CHANCES FOR SURVIVAL OF
NUCLEAR ATTACK.

0809 NATIONAL ACADEMY OF SCIENCES

BASIC RESEARCH AND NATIONAL GOALS.
WASHINGTON: NATL ACAD OF SCI, 1965, 336 PP.
A REPORT TO THE COMMITTEE ON SCIENCE AND ASTRONAUTICS OF
THE HOUSE OF REPRESENTATIVES BY THE NATIONAL ACADEMY OF SCI-
ENCES. INVESTIGATES THE LEVEL OF FEDERAL SUPPORT NEEDED TO
MAINTAIN US LEADERSHIP IN BASIC RESEARCH. COMPENDIUM OF AR-
TICLES ON VARIOUS SCIENCES' NEEDS FOR FEDERAL AID. SCIENCES
DISCUSSED INCLUDE BASIC RESEARCH, GEOLOGY, AND BIOMEDICAL,
PHYSICAL, AND BEHAVIORAL SCIENCES.

0810 NATIONAL PLANNING ASSOCIATION
1970 WITHOUT ARMS CONTROL (PAMPHLET)
WASHINGTON: NATL PLANNING ASSN, 1958, 72 PP., LC#58-11014.
STUDIES EXTENT TO WHICH TECHNOLOGY OF MODERN WEAPONS
SYSTEMS CAN ASSURE NATIONAL SECURITY, FACTORS OF SECURITY
PROGRAM THAT WILL MOTIVATE STABLE WORLD SECURITY BALANCE,
FEASIBILITY OF INTERNATIONAL REGULATION OF ARMAMENTS, AND
METHODS OF LIMITING INTERNATIONAL VIOLENCE THROUGH ARMS
CONTROL. EXAMINES PRESENT AND FUTURE WEAPONS SYSTEMS.

0811 NATIONAL REFERRAL CENTER SCI
A DIRECTORY OF INFORMATION RESOURCES IN THE UNITED STATES;
SOCIAL SCIENCES.
WASHINGTON: LIBRARY OF CONGRESS, 1965, 218 PP., LC#65-62583.
ANNOTATED GUIDE TO INFORMATION ACTIVITY CENTERS IN THE
US. ENTRIES LISTED ALPHABETICALLY BY ORGANIZATIONAL NAME.
SUBJECT INDEX IS PROVIDED IN WHICH FULL NAMES OF THE IN-
FORMATION RESOURCES ARE LISTED UNDER SUBJECT HEADINGS. CON-
TAINS DATA ON LOCATION, INTERESTS, SERVICE RESTRICTIONS, AND
PUBLICATIONS OF EACH AGENCY.

0812 NATIONAL SCIENCE FOUNDATION
CURRENT RESEARCH AND DEVELOPMENT IN SCIENTIFIC
DOCUMENTATION - NO. 12.
WASHINGTON: NATL SCIENCE FON, 1965, 401 PP.
BIBLIOGRAPHY OF REFERENCES CITED IN VOLUMES 1-11 OF NA-
TIONAL SCIENCE FOUNDATION'S SERIES DESCRIBING RESEARCH PROJ-
ECTS IN SCIENTIFIC DOCUMENTATION AND RELATED FIELDS. LISTS
ARTICLES, BOOKS, REPORTS, AND GOVERNMENT PUBLICATIONS. MOST
ENTRIES DATED 1955 THROUGH 1962. ENGLISH-LANGUAGE SOURCES
PRIMARILY; SOME FOREIGN, INCLUDING RUSSIAN. ABOUT 2500
ITEMS, LISTED BY TOPIC AND ORGANIZATION.

0813 NATIONAL SCIENCE FOUNDATION
SIXTEENTH ANNUAL REPORT FOR THE FISCAL YEAR ENDED JUNE 30,
1966.
WASHINGTON: US GOVERNMENT, 1966, 175 PP.
DESCRIBES PROGRAM ACTIVITIES OF NATIONAL SCIENCE FOUNDA-
TION IN RESEARCH, GRADUATE AND UNDERGRADUATE EDUCATION IN
SCIENCE, INSTITUTIONAL PROGRAMS, INTERNATIONAL SCIENCE
ACTIVITIES, AND SCIENCE POLICY PLANNING. INCLUDES APPENDIXES
ON COMMITTEES, FISCAL NEEDS, ADVANCED SEMINARS, AND PUBLICA-
TIONS OF NATIONAL SCIENCE FOUNDATION.

0814 NATIONAL SCIENCE FOUNDATION
DIRECTORY OF SELECTED RESEARCH INSTITUTES IN EASTERN EUROPE.
NEW YORK: COLUMBIA U PRESS, 1967, 445 PP., LC#66-20496.
DESCRIPTIVE GUIDE TO LOCATION AND CHARACTER OF
SCIENTIFIC RESEARCH INSTITUTES IN SIX COUNTRIES: BULGARIA,
CZECHOSLOVAKIA, HUNGARY, POLAND, RUMANIA AND YUGOSLAVIA.
PRIME PURPOSE IS TO DESCRIBE SCOPE OF CURRENT SCIENTIFIC
ACTIVITIES IN EASTERN EUROPE AND TO LIST NAMES OF
PERSONNEL IN CHARGE OF THESE ACTIVITIES AND THEIR CORRESPON-
DENCE ADDRESSES.

0815 NEEDHAM T.
"SCIENCE AND SOCIETY IN EAST AND WEST."
SCI. SOC., 28 (64), 385-408.
DISCUSSES THE PROBLEM OF HUMANIZING BUREAUCRACY THROUGH-
OUT CHINESE HISTORY. 'CHINA WAS HOMEOSTATIC, CYBERNETIC IF
YOU LIKE, BUT NEVER STAGNANT.' CHINESE INVENTIONS THAT
SHOCKED EUROPEAN CULTURE TIME AFTER TIME WERE TAKEN IN
STRIDE BY CHINA. NOTES THOSE FEATURES OF CHINESE SOCIETY
WHICH ALLOW THE INTEGRATION AND ASSIMILATION OF IDEAS OF
SOCIAL CHANGE.

0816 NIEBURG H.L.
"THE EISENHOWER AEC AND CONGRESS: A STUDY IN EXECUTIVE-LEG-
ISLATIVE RELATIONS."
MIDWEST J. OF POLI. SCI., 6 (MAY 62), 115-148.
SHOWS HOW POLICY-MAKING INITIATIVE DURING 1956-60 RESTED
WITH CONGRESSIONAL JOINT COMMITTEE ON ATOMIC ENERGY RATHER
THAN WITH EXECUTIVE BRANCH. USES MICROCOSM OF EISENHOWER
ADMINISTRATION. COVERS AEC AND PRE-1953 RELATIONS WITH
CONGRESS, ALSO, EFFECT OF DEMOCRATIC VICTORIES, AND ROLE OF
LEWIS STRAUSS. CONCLUDES THAT STRONGER PRESIDENTIAL LEADER-
SHIP ISNECESSARY.

0817 NELSON R.R., PECK M.J., KALACHEK E.D.
TECHNOLOGY, ECONOMIC GROWTH, AND PUBLIC POLICY.
WASHINGTON: BROOKINGS INST, 1967, 238 PP., LC#67-14973.
RELATES ECONOMY TO TECHNOLOGICAL ADVANCE, UNEMPLOYMENT,
INTEGRATION OF DEVELOPMENT INTO ECONOMY. RESEARCH AND
INNOVATION ARE TIED TO GROWTH. ANALYZES IMPACT UPON ECONOMY,
GOVERNMENT POLICY, AND PUBLIC. PROPOSES CHANGES IN PUBLIC
POLICY. CREATES UNDERSTANDING BASIC TO COMPREHENSION OF

PUBLIC POLICY.

0818 NEW ZEALAND COMM OF ST SERVICE
THE STATE SERVICES IN NEW ZEALAND.
WELLINGTON, N.Z.: RE OWEN, 1962, 470 PP.
REPORT OF ROYAL COMMISSION OF INQUIRY INTO ORGANIZATION,
STAFFING, AND METHODS OF CONTROL AND OPERATION OF DEPART-
MENTS OF STATE. RECOMMENDS SEVERAL CHANGES TOWARD INCREASED
EFFICIENCY, ECONOMY, AND IMPROVED SERVICE IN DISCHARGE OF
PUBLIC BUSINESS.

0819 NEWELL A.C., SHAW J.C., SIMON H.A.
"ELEMENTS OF A THEORY OF HUMAN PROBLEM SOLVING" (BMR)"
PSYCHOLOGICAL REVIEW, 65 (1958), 151-166.
PROVIDES ELEMENTS OF A THEORY OF HUMAN PROBLEM-SOLVING,
TOGETHER WITH SOME EVIDENCE FOR ITS VALIDITY DRAWN FROM
CURRENTLY ACCEPTED FACTS ABOUT NATURE OF PROBLEM-SOLVING.
STATED REQUIREMENTS FOR SUCH A THEORY INVOLVE: PREDICTING
THE PERFORMANCE OF A PERSON HANDLING SPECIFIED TASKS;
EXPLAINING THE OPERATION OF PROCESSES AND MECHANISMS IN
PERFORMING THE TASK; AND PREDICTING INCIDENTAL PHENOMENA.

0820 NIEBURG H.
"EURATOM: A STUDY IN COALITION POLITICS."
WORLD POLIT., 15 (JULY 63), 597-622.
CONCLUDES THAT ANGLO-AMERICAN COALITION OF POLITICAL
POWER TO MAINTAIN EXCLUSIVE CONTROL OVER THE PRODUCTION OF
NUCLEAR WEAPONS AND STRATEGIC PREDOMINANCE IN NATO ALLIANCE
HAS LED TO EUROPEAN DISUNITY WHILE PERILLING STABILITY OF
NATO. ANALYZES ORIGINS AND DEVELOPMENT OF EURATOM AND ENEA.
RE-APPRAISAL OF U.S. AND BRITISH ROLE IN EUROPE IS
BECOMING INCREASINGLY NECESSARY.

0821 NIEBURG H.L.
"THE EISENHOWER ATOMIC ENERGY COMMISSION AND CONGRESS"
MIDWEST J. OF POLI. SCI., 6 (MAY 62), 115-148.
CASE STUDY IN EXECUTIVE-LEGISLATIVE RELATIONS. AEC SAID
TO BE DOMINATED BY CONGRESSIONAL JOINT COMMITTEE ON
ATOMIC ENERGY. SINCE CONGRESS IS PRONE TO INTERPRET NATIONAL
INTEREST IN TERMS OF DOMESTIC CONSTITUENCIES, US WORLD
LEADERSHIP IS SAID TO SUFFER.

0822 NIEBURG H.L.
IN THE NAME OF SCIENCE.
CHICAGO: QUADRANGLE BOOKS, INC, 1966, 431 PP., LC#66-11868.
ANALYSIS OF US FEDERAL SCIENCE POLICIES AND GOVERNMENT
CONTRACTS IN TECHNOLOGICAL AND SCIENTIFIC FIELDS. EXAMINES
SOCIOLOGICAL IMPLICATIONS OF NATIONALIZATION OF SCIENCE AND
NUMEROUS LARGE-SCALE TRANSACTIONS BETWEEN GOVERNMENT AND
INDUSTRIAL PROFIT ORGANIZATIONS. ANALYZES FEDERAL CONTRACT
AS POWERFUL SOCIAL MANAGEMENT TOOL IN STIMULATION OF ECONOM-
IC AND POLITICAL ACTIVITY AND IN DISTRIBUTION OF POWER.

0823 NOEL-BAKER D.
THE ARMS RACE.
NEW YORK: OCEANA, 1958, 603 PP.
ASSESSMENT OF DANGER OF THE ARMS RACE AND IMPORTANCE OF
DISARMAMENT IN NATIONAL AND INTERNATIONAL POLICY. LISTS
TECHNICAL AND POLITICAL PROBLEMS THAT ARISE WHEN GOVERNMENTS
CONSIDER DISARMAMENT. OUTLINES HISTORY OF 'NUCLEAR
NEGOTIATIONS' AND ADVOCATES TOTAL AND COMPLETE DISARMAMENT.

0824 NOGEE J.L.
SOVIET POLICY TOWARD INTERNATIONAL CONTROL OF ATOMIC
ENERGY.
SOUTH BEND: NOTRE DAME PR., 1961, 306 PP., $6.50.
ANALYZES SOVIET ATTITUDES TOWARD INTERNATIONALIZATION OF
THE ATOM. OBSERVES THAT IMMODERATE SELF-INTEREST IS BASIS OF
USSR POLICY. CLAIMS THAT USSR IS ABLE TO DEDICATE ITSELF TO
ANY GIVEN TASK BUT IS WEAK IN ITS ABILITY TO WITHSTAND
EXPOSURE TO AN ATMOSPHERE OF FREEDOM. CONCLUDES THAT SOVIET
UNION CAN ONLY VIEW THE OUTSIDE WORLD WITH SUSPICION.

0825 NORTH R.C. ET AL.
CONTENT ANALYSIS: A HANDBOOK WITH APPLICATIONS FOR THE
STUDY OF INTERNATIONAL CRISIS.
EVANSTON: NORTHWESTERN U. PR., 1963, 182 PP., $2.95.
A VALUABLE INTRODUCTION TO A USEFUL RESEARCH TECHNIQUE.
INCLUDES CONCRETE ILLUSTRATIONS PLUS GUIDES 'FOR DECIDING
WHETHER, WHEN, AND WHAT FORM OF CONTENT ANALYSIS SHOULD BE
USED.' THE EXAMPLES COME FROM RESEARCH ON THE ORIGINS OF
WORLD WAR I AND ON CONTEMPORARY SINO-SOVIET RELATIONS.
SPECIAL FORMS DISCUSSED INCLUDE: THE CONVENTIONAL FREQUENCY
COUNT AND QUALITATIVE IDENTIFICATIONS, Q-SORTS, PAIR COM-
PARISONS, AND EVALUATIVE ASSERTION ANALYSIS.

0826 NORTHROP F.S.C.
THE MEETING OF EAST AND WEST.
NEW YORK: MACMILLAN, 1946, 531 PP.
ANALYZES GERMAN IDEALISM, RUSSIAN COMMUNISM, THE UNIQUE
ELEMENTS OF BRITISH DEMOCRACY AND SIGNIFICANCE OF EASTERN
CIVILIZATION. STATES THAT TIME HAS COME WHEN IDEOLOGICAL
CONFLICTS MUST BE FACED AND, WHEN POSSIBLE, RESOLVED.
FURNISHES INSTRUCTIONS FOR SOLUTION OF BASIC PROBLEMS.

0827 NORTHRUP H.R.
RESTRICTIVE LABOR PRACTICES IN THE SUPERMARKET INDUSTRY.
PHILA: U OF PENN PR, 1967, 202 PP., LC#67-26220.
STUDIES LABOR-MANAGEMENT RELATIONS AND PROBLEMS IN SUPER-
MARKET INDUSTRY. SEEKS TO DETERMINE WHETHER LABOR PRACTICES
WORK AGAINST CONSUMER INTERESTS AND EFFICIENT MARKETING
OPERATIONS. DISCUSSES POTENTIALS FOR CHANGE, PRESENTS DE-
TAILS OF TECHNOLOGICAL PROGRESS, AND SUGGESTS NEW APPROACH
TO LABOR RELATIONS. INCLUDES HISTORY OF DEVELOPMENT OF
SUPERMARKETS AND UNIONIZATION MOVEMENT.

0828 NOVE A.
THE SOVIET ECONOMY.
NEW YORK: FREDERICK PRAEGER, 1961, 328 PP., LC#61-16579.
INTRODUCTION SURVEY OF SOVIET ECONOMY, INCLUDING ITS PRO-
DUCTIVE ENTERPRISES, ADMINISTRATION, CHANGING NATURE OF ITS
PROBLEMS, AND BASIC CONCEPTS OF SOVIET ECONOMICS.

0829 ODEGARD P.H.
POLITICAL POWER AND SOCIAL CHANGE.
NEW BRUNSWICK: RUTGERS U PR, 1966, 111 PP., LC#62-28215.
ETHICS OF GOVERNMENT, PAST, PRESENT, AND FUTURE, COMPARED
AND RELATED TO ECONOMIC, HISTORICAL, AND SOCIAL EVOLUTION.
SKETCHES EFFECT OF TECHNOLOGY AND POPULATION ON POWER AND
GIVES BRIEF HISTORY OF ITS ABUSE.

0830 OECD
SCIENCE AND THE POLICIES OF GOVERNMENTS: THE IMPLICATIONS
OF SCIENCE AND TECHNOLOGY FOR NATL AND INTL AFFAIRS.
PARIS: ORG FOR ECO COOP AND DEV, 1963, 55 PP.
EXPLORES NEED FOR NATIONAL AND INTERNATIONAL POLICIES TO
STRENGTHEN SCIENCE AND TECHNOLOGY. EXAMINES MUTUAL EFFECTS
AND IMPLICATIONS OF SCIENCE AND OF POLICIES GOVERNING
NATIONAL AND INTERNATIONAL AFFAIRS GENERALLY. SUGGESTS WAYS
TO MEET PARTICULAR NEEDS WITHIN AND AMONG NATIONS. FOCUSES
ON POLICY IMPLICATIONS OF NATURAL SCIENCES. STRESSES CLOSE
RELATION BETWEEN SCIENCE POLICY AND EDUCATIONAL POLICY.

0831 OECD
MEDITERRANEAN REGIONAL PROJECT: TURKEY; EDUCATION AND
DEVELOPMENT.
PARIS: ORG FOR ECO COOP AND DEV, 1965, 189 PP.
REVIEWS PRESENT EDUCATIONAL STRUCTURE AND POLICY IN
TURKEY; TREATS ROLE OF EDUCATION IN SOCIAL AND ECONOMIC
DEVELOPMENT. DISCUSSES FACILITIES, TEACHER TRAINING AND
SUPPLY, AND ADMINISTRATION. EXAMINES COST OF EDUCATIONAL
DEVELOPMENT, PRESENT EXPENDITURES, AND FUTURE NEEDS. COVERS
ECONOMIC TARGETS AND MANPOWER, OCCUPATIONAL CLASSIFICATIONS,
DEMAND AND SUPPLY, AND PARTICIPATION.

0832 OECD
THE MEDITERRANEAN REGIONAL PROJECT: PORTUGAL; EDUCATION AND
DEVELOPMENT.
PARIS: ORG FOR ECO COOP AND DEV, 1965, 225 PP.
ECONOMIC ANALYSIS OF EDUCATIONAL DEVELOPMENT. BEGINS WITH
METHODOLOGY AND FUTURE REQUIREMENTS FOR SKILLED PERSONNEL;
INCLUDES BREAKDOWN OF EMPLOYMENT BY EDUCATIONAL LEVEL.
ANALYZES PRESENT STRUCTURE AND ESTIMATES GROWTH OF SCHOOL
ENROLLMENT; DISCUSSES FACILITIES AND TEACHERS, PRESENT AND
FUTURE, ACCORDING TO TYPE OF EDUCATIONAL INSTITUTION. CLOSES
WITH EXPENDITURES ON EDUCATION.

0833 OECD
THE MEDITERRANEAN REGIONAL PROJECT: ITALY; EDUCATION AND
DEVELOPMENT.
PARIS: ORG FOR ECO COOP AND DEV, 1965, 216 PP.
CONCERNED WITH RELATION OF EDUCATIONAL PLANNING TO
ECONOMIC DEVELOPMENT AND SOCIAL ADVANCEMENT. OPENS WITH
SURVEY OF TRENDS IN PAST AND TARGETS FOR 1975; EXAMINES
OCCUPATIONAL STRUCTURE OF EMPLOYMENT AND TRAINING FACILITIES
IN PAST DECADE. DISCUSSES WAYS OF ACHIEVING PROPOSED GOALS,
STRUCTURE OF SYSTEM, FINANCING. ENDS WITH METHODOLOGY FOR
ESTIMATING OCCUPATIONAL STRUCTURE IN 1951, 1961, AND 1975.

0834 OECD
THE MEDITERRANEAN REGIONAL PROJECT: GREECE; EDUCATION AND
DEVELOPMENT.
PARIS: ORG FOR ECO COOP AND DEV, 1965, 195 PP.
BEGINS WITH ECONOMIC FRAMEWORK AND ROLE OF EDUCATION.
RELATES EDUCATIONAL PLANNING TO ECONOMIC GROWTH AND SOCIAL
ADVANCEMENT; DISCUSSES EXISTING SYSTEM AND GOAL FOR 1974.
EXAMINES ADJUSTMENTS THAT WILL HAVE TO BE MADE, RESOURCES
FOR EXPANSION, AND OUTLINE OF PLAN; INCLUDES STRUCTURE OF
SYSTEM, MANPOWER NEEDS, AND EDUCATIONAL NEEDS IN
AGRICULTURE. CLOSES WITH EXPENDITURES FOR EDUCATION TO 1974.

0835 OECD
THE MEDITERRANEAN REGIONAL PROJECT: SPAIN; EDUCATION AND
DEVELOPMENT.
PARIS: ORG FOR ECO COOP AND DEV, 1965, 135 PP.
SURVEYS PRESENT EDUCATIONAL SYSTEM, ASSESSES LONG-TERM
EDUCATIONAL NEEDS, AND FORMULATES PLANS AND FINANCIAL
ESTIMATES TO MEET NEEDS. BEGINS WITH SUMMARY OF PRESENT
EDUCATIONAL POLICY; DISCUSSES ORGANIZATION AND
ADMINISTRATION OF EDUCATION, COST, QUALITY, OCCUPATIONAL
STRUCTURE OF LABOR FORCE, AND EDUCATIONAL LEVELS. CLOSES
WITH EXPENDITURES ON EDUCATION.

0836 OECD DEVELOPMENT CENTRE
CATALOGUE OF SOCIAL AND ECONOMIC DEVELOPMENT INSTITUTES AND
PROGRAMMES* RESEARCH.
PARIS: ORG FOR ECO COOP AND DEV, 1966, 452 PP.
LISTING OF RESEARCH INSTITUTES AND THEIR ACTIVITIES IN
FIELD OF SOCIAL AND ECONOMIC DEVELOPMENT. THIRTY NON-IRON-
CURTAIN NATIONS SURVEYED. ALL DATA IN ENGLISH.

0837 OGBURN W.
TECHNOLOGY AND INTERNATIONAL RELATIONS.
CHICAGO: U. CHI. PR., 1949, 201 PP., $4.00.
EXAMINES POSTWAR LEGACY OF INVENTIONS AND SCIENTIFIC DIS-
COVERIES AND RELATES THEM TO THEIR AFFECTS UPON INTERNATION-
AL RELATIONS. FOCUSES UPON INFLUENCES OF STEAM, STEEL, ATOM
BOMB, AVIATION AND MASS COMMUNICATIONS UPON THE RANKING OF
POWERS, SPHERES OF INFLUENCE, FEDERATION OF NATIONS, AND
SOCIAL INSTITUTIONS.

0838 OGDEN F.D.
THE POLL TAX IN THE SOUTH.
UNIVERSITY: U ALABAMA PR, 1958, 301 PP., LC#58-08773.
STUDIES WHAT POLL TAX IS, HOW IT OPERATES, AND ITS VALUE
AS VOTING PREREQUISITE. PRESENTS HISTORICAL SUMMARY, MEANS
OF ADMINISTERING IT, ITS EFFECTS ON VOTER PARTICIPATION AND
RELATION BETWEEN TAX AND CORRUPTION.

0839 ONYEMELUKWE C.C.
PROBLEMS OF INDUSTRIAL PLANNING AND MANAGEMENT IN NIGERIA.
LONDON: LONGMANS, GREEN & CO, 1966, 330 PP.
STUDY OF BACKGROUND AND NATURE OF PROBLEMS OF INDUSTRI-
ALIZATION IN NIGERIA, A REPRESENTATIVE AFRICAN NATION; SHOWS
THAT SOCIAL CHANGES MUST TAKE PLACE ALONGSIDE TECHNOLOGICAL
OR PROGRESS WILL NOT TAKE PLACE. AUTHOR HOPES OTHER UNDER-
DEVELOPED NATIONS CAN LEARN FROM NIGERIA'S ATTEMPT TO SOLVE
MODERN PROBLEMS.

0840 OPERATIONS RESEARCH SOCIETY
A COMPREHENSIVE BIBLIOGRAPHY ON OPERATIONS RESEARCH; THROUGH
1956 WITH SUPPLEMENT FOR 1957.
CLEVELAND: CASE INST OF TECH, 1958, 188 PP., LC#58-9681.
CODED BIBLIOGRAPHY CONTAINING 300,0 TITLES OF BOOKS, AR-
TICLES, REPORTS, PROCEEDINGS, ETC., PUBLISHED THROUGH 1956.
INTENDED FOR AN OPERATIONS RESEARCH AUDIENCE. EACH AU-
THOR GIVEN A SERIAL WHICH REPRESENTS SHORTHAND VERSION OF
COMPLETE ENTRY; SERIALS USED FOR COMPUTERIZED CODING OF
CROSS REFERENCES. TEN-DIGIT CLASSIFICATION TO LEFT OF EACH
ENTRY INFORMS READER ON CONTENT OF WORK CITED.

0841 OPLER M.E.
"SOCIAL ASPECTS OF TECHNICAL ASSISTANCE IN OPERATION."
PARIS: UNESCO, 1954, 79 PP.
REPORT OF JOINT CONFERENCE OF U.N. AGENCIES ON PROBLEMS
OF ADMINISTRATION OF TECHNICAL ASSISTANCE. DEALS WITH
SOCIAL, CULTURAL, ECONOMIC, AND POLITICAL IMPEDIMENTS TO
EXECUTION OF TECHNICAL ASSISTANCE MISSIONS AND POSSIBLE
SOLUTIONS.

0842 OPPENHEIMER R.
THE OPEN MIND.
NEW YORK: SIMON SCHUSTER, 1955, 146 PP.
DISCUSSES ATOMIC WEAPONS AND POLICY ISSUES AND RELATION-
SHIP BETWEEN SCIENCE AND CONTEMPORARY CULTURE. ARGUES THAT
ATOMIC WEAPONS CAN HELP PREVENT WAR BECAUSE THEY CREATE
SENSE OF URGENCY TO END ARMS RACE AND ENCOURAGE PEACEFUL USE
OF ATOMIC ENERGY. URGES REGULATION AND EVENTUAL ABOLITION OF
ATOMIC WEAPONS WHEN IDEOLOGICAL BATTLE SUBSIDES.

0843 ORG FOR ECO COOP AND DEVEL
THE MEDITERRANEAN REGIONAL PROJECT: YUGOSLAVIA; EDUCATION
AND DEVELOPMENT.
PARIS: ORG FOR ECO COOP AND DEV, 1965, 143 PP.
REVIEWS ECONOMIC AND SOCIAL DEVELOPMENTS, PAST AND PRES-
ENT, AND SURVEYS YUGOSLAV EDUCATIONAL SYSTEM. DISCUSSES
ECONOMIC AND MANPOWER PROJECTIONS, 1961-75, AND SKILL
STRUCTURE; INCLUDES PROSPECTIVE VERSUS REQUIRED OUTPUTS OF
EDUCATIONAL SYSTEM FOR 1961-75 AND PRESENTS METHODOLOGICAL
APPROACH. CLOSING SECTION DEALS WITH TEACHING STAFF AND
FINANCIAL EXPENDITURE.

0844 ORGANIZATION AMERICAN STATES
ECONOMIC SURVEY OF LATIN AMERICA, 1962.
BALTIMORE: JOHNS HOPKINS PR., 1964, 444 PP.
DEMONSTRATES IMPACT OF ALLIANCE OR PROGRESS ON LATIN-
AMERICAN ECONOMY, ASSESSING CAPACITY TO IMPORT AND
DEVELOPMENT OF PRODUCTIVE STRUCTURE. EVALUATES EXECUTION OF
ECONOMIC PROGRAMS UNDER ALLIANCE FOR PROGRESS.

0845 ORLANS H.
CONTRACTING FOR ATOMS.
WASHINGTON: BROOKINGS INST, 1967, 242 PP., LC#67-17131.
DISCUSSES CURRENT ATOMIC ENERGY COMMISSION CONTRACT POLI-
CIES AND PROBLEMS, MEN INVOLVED, AND COMMISSION'S FUTURE
ROLE. RECOMMENDS DEFINITION OF AIMS, COMPETITION FOR GROWTH,
AND CLARIFICATION OF MISSION OF AEC.

0846 ORTEGA Y GASSET J.

MAN AND CRISIS.
NEW YORK: W W NORTON, 1958, 217 PP., LC#58-9282.
PRESENT DAY VIEWED, IN TERMS OF THEORY OF CYCLES OF
CRISIS IN HISTORY, AS PERIOD OF CRISIS IN WHICH AGE WHICH
BEGAN WITH GALILEO WILL END. IN SUCH PERIODS OF CRISIS, MEN
CHARACTERISTICALLY TURN INWARD AND LOOK BACKWARD IN HISTORY
TOWARD PURER AND SIMPLER MODES OF THOUGHT AND BEING.
RENAISSANCE AS WELL AS PRESENT A PERIOD OF CRISIS. MODERN
CRISIS IS RESULT OF COMPLEXITY.

0847 ORTH C.D., BAILEY J.C., WOLEK F.W.
ADMINISTERING RESEARCH AND DEVELOPMENT.
HOMEWOOD: DORSEY, 1964, 585 PP., LC#64-24699.
DETAILED CASE STUDIES OF PROBLEMS IN MANAGEMENT OF RE-
SEARCH AND DEVELOPMENT GROUPS FOCUSING ON ADMINISTRATIVE AC-
TIVITIES OF SEVERAL LARGE CORPORATIONS. ALSO CONTAINS COL-
LECTIONS OF GENERAL DISCUSSIONS OF RESEARCH STUDIES PROBLEMS
AND CONCEPTUAL PROBLEMS.

0848 OSGOOD C.E.
"A CASE FOR GRADUATED UNILATERAL DISENGAGEMENT."
BULL. AT. SCI., 16 (APR.60), 127-31.
ANALYZES CAUSES OF COLD WAR AND OFFERS SUGGESTIONS FOR
CHANGES IN PRESENT POLICIES. PROPOSES RE-EXAMINATION OF
POLICY GOALS ASSERTING UNILATERAL DISENGAGEMENT IS A
'PRIMER' STAGE TO A REVERSAL OF PRESENT TENSIONS AND THE
ARMS RACE DILEMMA.

0849 OSGOOD C.E.
AN ALTERNATIVE TO WAR OR SURRENDER.
URBANA: U. ILL. PR., 1962, 183 PP., $1.45.
PRESENTS MODEL OF SOCIAL-PSYCHOLOGICAL LOGIC AND KNOWL-
EDGE APPLIED TO WORLD PEACE. DESCRIBES A PROGRAM FOR ORGANI-
ZATION CALLED GRADUATED RECIPROCATION IN TENSION-REDUCTION.
ARGUES THAT UNDERLYING SOCIAL DYNAMICS OF INTERNATIONAL RE-
LATIONS WILL BRING INEVITABLE MUTUAL DISASTER AND FOIL PRO-
CESS OF TENSION-REDUCTION.

0850 OSSENBECK F.J. ED., KROECK P.C. ED.
OPEN SPACE AND PEACE.
STANFORD: HOOVER INSTITUTE, 1964, 227 PP., LC#64-18827.
COLLECTION OF PAPERS GIVEN AT OPEN SPACE AND PEACE SYM-
POSIUM ON SATELLITE OBSERVATION. COVERS BACKGROUND, TECH-
NOLOGY, SOCIOLOGICAL AND POLITICAL IMPLICATIONS, IMPLEMENTA-
TION OF FURTHER RESEARCH, AND FUTURE PROGRAMS IN US.

0851 OTTOSON H.W. ED.
LAND USE POLICY AND PROBLEMS IN THE UNITED STATES.
LINCOLN: U OF NEB PR, 1963, 469 PP., LC#63-9096.
COMPREHENSIVE STUDY OF LAND POLICY IN US FROM HOMESTEAD
ACT OF 1862 TO PRESENT. PRESENTS SOCIAL FACTORS INVOLVED IN
LAND POLICY, DEMANDS FOR AND CONFLICTS OVER LAND, AND
CHANGES IN OUR POLICY, AND APPLICATION IN DEVELOPING
COUNTRIES.

0852 OVERSEAS DEVELOPMENT INST.
EFFECTIVE AID.
LONDON: MIN OF OVERSEAS DEVEL, 1967, 129 PP.
EXAMINES AID ADMINISTRATION, TERMS AND CONDITIONS OF
FOREIGN AID, AND TECHNICAL ASSISTANCE TO UNDERDEVELOPED NA-
TIONS. DISCUSSES PRACTICES IN GERMANY, FRANCE, UK, AND US.

0853 VON BORCH H.
FRIEDETROTZ KRIEG.
MUNICH: R PIPER AND CO VERLAG, 1966, 375 PP.
DISCUSSES INTERNATIONAL TENSIONS SINCE 1950. EXAMINES
ESCALATION IN ARMAMENT, GERMAN UNIFICATION PROBLEM, DEVELOP-
MENT OF NEW COLD WAR POLITICS, AND "WORLD ANXIETY" PRODUCED
BY THREAT OF NUCLEAR WAR.

0854 PACHTER H.M.
COLLISION COURSE; THE CUBAN MISSILE CRISIS AND COEXISTENCE.
NEW YORK: FREDERICK PRAEGER, 1963, 261 PP., LC#63-18528.
CURRENT HISTORY OF EVENTS INVOLVED IN THE CUBAN
MISSILE CRISIS OF OCTOBER, 1962. DISCUSSES PRINCIPAL
PERSONS INVOLVED - KHRUSHCHEV, CASTRO, KENNEDY, U THANT.
POINTS OUT FORCES WHICH MOTIVATED THEIR ACTIONS. ANALYZES
AND FORMULATES GENERAL CONCLUSIONS ABOUT POWER CONFLICTS IN
NUCLEAR AGE; PRESENTS PRINCIPLES OF COEXISTENCE WHICH
MAY PREVENT COLD WAR FROM BEING ACTIVATED.

0855 PACKENHAM R.A.
"POLITICAL-DEVELOPMENT DOCTRINES IN THE AMERICAN FOREIGN
AID PROGRAM."
WORLD POLITICS, 18 (JAN. 66), 194-235.
AUTHOR GIVES BRIEF, BUT SUBSTANTIAL COVERAGE OF IMPORTANT
THEORISTS VIEWS ON FIVE CONDITIONS OF POLITICAL DEVELOPMEMT
AND DISCUSSES LACK OF ATTENTION SPENT ON THE DEPENDENT VAR-
IABLE, POLITICAL DEVELOPMENT ITSELF. HE THEN SHOWS THAT U.S.
A.I.D. ADMINISTRATORS AND DOCTRINES PAY LITTLE ATTENTION TO
POLITICAL DEVELOPMENT BECAUSE IT IS BELIEVED LITTLE POLITI-
CAL CHANGE CAN BE EFFECTED BY AID.

0856 PADELFORD N.J., LINCOLN G.A.
THE DYNAMICS OF INTERNATIONAL POLITICS (2ND ED.)
NEW YORK: MACMILLAN, 1967, 640 PP.

DESCRIBES BACKGROUND OF INTERNATIONAL POLITICS AND DIS-
CUSSES MAJOR FACTORS. EMPHASIS IS PLACED ON DECISION-MAKING
PROCESS. INCLUDES INSTRUMENTS AND PATTERNS OF FOREIGN POL-
ICY, ORGANIZATION OF INTERNATIONAL COMMUNITY, ECONOMIC AND
POLITICAL PRINCIPLES, IMPACT OF TECHNOLOGICAL CHANGE, GROW-
ING POPULATION, AND SHIFTING RELATIONSHIPS WITHIN POWER
BLOCS. TEXTS TO IMPORTANT TREATIES INCLUDED.

0857 PANAMERICAN UNION
DOCUMENTOS OFICIALES DE LA ORGANIZACION DE LOS ESTADOS
AMERICANOS, INDICE Y LISTA (VOL. III, 1962)
WASHINGTON: PAN AMERICAN UNION, 1963, 501 PP.
     OFFICIAL OAS DOCUMENTS FOR 1962, ARRANGED BY SERIES, WITH
FULL ALPHABETICAL INDEX INDICATING PROPER SERIES AND DOCU-
MENT NUMBER. VOLUMES I AND II APPEARED AS "INDICE Y LISTA
GENERAL DE LOS DOCUMENTOS OFICIALES."

0858 PARANJAPE H.K.
THE FLIGHT OF TECHNICAL PERSONNEL IN PUBLIC UNDERTAKINGS.
NEW DELHI: INDIAN INST PUB ADMIN, 1964, 191 PP.
     INVESTIGATES "FLIGHT OF TECHNICAL PERSONNEL" FROM ONE
PUBLIC ENTERPRISE TO ANOTHER OR TO PRIVATE ENTERPRISE IN
INDIA, ITS EXTENT, ACUTENESS OF PROBLEM, WHICH INDUSTRIES
AND TYPES OF PERSONNEL ARE AFFECTED, PROBLEMS IT CAUSES SUCH
AS NONAVAILABILITY OF PERSONNEL, CAUSES OF MIGRATION, AND
SOLUTIONS TO MAINTAIN STEADY AVAILABILITY OF TECHNICAL
PERSONNEL.

0859 PARRY A.
RUSSIA'S ROCKETS AND MISSILES.
NEW YORK: DOUBLEDAY, 1960, 382 PP.
     SUMS UP MYTHS AND REALITIES OF RUSSIAN TECHNICAL DEVELOP-
MENTS. BRINGS INFORMATION ABOUT THE GERMAN ROLE IN RUSSIAN
ROCKETS. ANALYZES PSYCHO-POLITICAL FACTORS OF SPACE-RACE.
USES LATEST SCIENTIFIC DOCUMENTS.

0860 PASLEY R.S.
"ORGANIZATIONAL CONFLICTS OF INTEREST IN GOVERNMENT CON-
TRACTS."
WISC. LAW REV., 67 (WINTER 67), 1-42.
     THE GROWTH OF DEFENSE AND SPACE EFFORTS BY THE FEDERAL
GOVT. AND THE DEVELOPMENT OF AN IMMENSE MILITARY-INDUSTRIAL
OMPLEX HAVE BROUGHT WITH THEM THE ORGANIZATIONAL CONFLICT OF
INTEREST, WHICH ARISES WHEN AN INDUSTRY ENGAGES IN RESEARCH
AND DVLPMT. OF PRODUCTS AND THEN SUPPLIES THOSE PRODUCTS TO
THE GOVT. PASLEY DESCRIBES 2 MAJOR AREAS OF CONFLICT - PRO-
CUREMENT AND EMPLOYMENT.

0861 PAULING L.
"GENETIC EFFECTS OF WEAPONS TESTS."
BULL. AT. SCI., 18 (DECEMBER 1962), 15-18.
     EXAMINES GENETIC EFFECTS OF NUCLEAR EXPLOSIONS UPON
CHILDREN. ESTIMATES TOTAL NUMBER OF CHILDREN WITH GROSS
PHYSICAL OR MENTAL DEFECTS AND NUMBER OF EMBRYONIC OR CHILD-
HOOD DEATH COMBINED TO BE 1.2 MILLION FROM RADIOACTIVE FALL-
OUT AND 16 MILLION FROM IRRADIATION BY CARBON-14. USES THESE
ESTIMATES TO SUPPORT PLEA FOR CESSATION OF NUCLEAR TESTING.

0862 PEABODY R.L. ED., POLSBY N.W. ED.
NEW PERSPECTIVES ON THE HOUSE OF REPRESENTATIVES.
NEW YORK: RAND MCNALLY & CO, 1963, 381 PP., LC#63-17450.
     REAPPRAISAL OF POLITICS, PROCEDURES, AND TRADITIONS OF
HOUSE. INCLUDES ESSAYS ON ENLARGED RULES COMMITTEE, COM-
MITTEE ASSIGNMENTS, FEDERAL AID TO EDUCATION , AND MAKING
OF MILITARY POLICY.

0863 PEARSELL M.
MEDICAL BEHAVIORAL SCIENCE: A SELECTED BIBLIOGRAPHY OF CUL-
TURAL ANTHROPOLOGY, SOCIAL PSYCHOLOGY, AND SOCIOLOGY...
LEXINGTON: U OF KY PR, 1963, 134 PP., LC#62-19381.
     FIRST IN SERIES OF MONOGRAPHS PUBLISHED BY DEPARTMENT
OF BEHAVIORAL SCIENCE IN UNIVERSITY OF KENTUCKY MEDICAL CEN-
TER. CONTAINS ITEMS ON CULTURAL ANTHROPOLOGY, SOCIAL PSY-
CHOLOGY, MEDICAL SOCIOLOGY, AND MEDICAL STATISTICS.
INCLUDES 3,000 ITEMS COVERING PERIOD FROM 1930 THROUGH
1962. ORGANIZED BY SUBJECT CONTENT. INCLUDES AUTHOR
INDEX. ONLY ENGLISH TITLES INCLUDED.

0864 PEDERSEN E.S.
NUCLEAR ENERGY IN SPACE.
ENGLEWOOD CLIFFS: PRENTICE HALL, 1964, 516 PP.
     ANALYSIS OF NUCLEAR ENERGY AS ESSENTIAL AND INEVITABLE IN
SPACE. INCLUDES HISTORICAL BACKGROUND, THEORY OF NUCLEAR
PROPULSION, HEAT TRANSFER, AND FLUID FLOW. EXAMINES MATER-
IALS FOR SPACE, NUCLEAR ENGINE DESIGN, ADVANCED PROPULSION
SYSTEMS, DIRECT SPACE POWER CONVERSION, NUCLEAR WEAPONS IN
SPACE, AND ENVIRONMENT AND RADIATION HAZARDS IN SPACE.

0865 PEIRCE W.S.
SELECTIVE MANPOWER POLICIES AND THE TRADE-OFF BETWEEN RISING
PRICES AND UNEMPLOYMENT (DISSERTATION)
PRINCETON: PRIN U, DEPT OF ECO, 1966, 207 PP.
     CONCEPTUAL CONSIDERATIONS ON DILEMMA OF APPARENT
INCOMPATIBILITY OF FULL EMPLOYMENT WITH STABLE PRICES,
ESTABLISHING CONDITIONS UNDER WHICH SELECTIVE MANPOWER
POLICIES CAN DEAL WITH PROBLEM IN PARTICULAR MODELS OF

LABOR MARKETS.

0866 PENNEY N.
"BANK STATEMENTS, CANCELLED CHECKS, AND ARTICLE FOUR IN THE
ELECTRONIC AGE."
MICH. LAW REV., 65 (MAY 67), 1341-1360.
     EXAMINES EFFECT OF ACCELERATING OPERATIONAL AND
TECHNOLOGICAL CHANGES IN BANKING INDUSTRY ON ARTICLE FOUR
OF UNIFORM COMMERCIAL CODE. MEASURES WORKABILITY OF CODE FOR
PRESENT AND CONTEMPLATED OPERATIONAL INNOVATIONS. FOCUSES
ON BANKS' PROCEDURE OF ISSUING CHECKING-ACCOUNT STATEMENTS.

0867 PENTONY D.E. ED.
THE UNDERDEVELOPED LANDS.
SAN FRANCISCO: CHANDLER, 1960, 196 PP, $1.50.
     STUDIES PROBLEMS OF UNDERDEVELOPMENT IN ASIA, AFRICA AND
LATIN AMERICA, 'STRIPPED OF SOME OF ITS COLD-WAR OVERTONES'.
INCLUDES DISCUSSION OF: RUBLE DIPLOMACY, TRADE AND AID,
OBSTACLES TO ECONOMIC DEVELOPMENT, GANDHI'S VIEWS ON
MACHINES AND TECHNOLOGY, AND ECONOMIC COOPERATION UNDER UN
AUSPICES.

0868 PERKINS J.A.
"ADMINISTRATION OF THE NATIONAL SECURITY PROGRAM."
PUBLIC ADMIN. REV., 13 (SPRING 53), 80-86.
     SECURITY POLICY DETERMINATION REQUIRES CHANGES IN FORM
AND FUNCTION: DISCUSSES ROLES OF DEFENSE DEPARTMENT, STATE
DEPARTMENT, NATIONAL SECURITY COUNCIL, AND CONGRESS IN
SECURITY PLANNING.

0869 PERLO V.
MILITARISM AND INDUSTRY.
NEW YORK: INTERNATIONAL PUBLRS, 1963, 63-8584 PP.
     SUGGESTS THAT MUNITIONS AND AIRCRAFT INDUSTRIES ARE
LARGELY RESPONSIBLE FOR CONTINUATION OF ARMS RACE. SHOWS HOW
COMPANIES HOLDING FOREIGN INVESTMENTS STAND TO LOSE MONEY IF
DISARMAMENT OCCURS. SUPPORTING DOCUMENTATION SHOWS HOW BUSI-
NESS INFLUENCES GOVERNMENT POLICY.

0870 PERRE J.
LES MUTATIONS DE LA GUERRE MODERNE: DE LA REVOLUTION
FRANCAISE A LA REVOLUTION NUCLEAIRE.
PARIS: PAYOT, 1962, 419 PP.
     HISTORY OF NATIONAL WARS, WORLD WARS, AND POST WAR
CONDITIONS FROM 1792 TO 1962. TRACES CAUSES, GOALS, EXTENTS,
MURDEROUS EFFECTS, FORMS, AND CONSEQUENCES. AUTHOR
OFFERS HISTORICAL PROJECTIONS. BELIEVES ANOTHER WORLD WAR IS
NOT INEVITABLE, BUT ROAD TO PEACE IS NARROW, UPHILL,
UNEVEN, ARDUOUS, EXHAUSTING.

0871 PETERSON W.
THE POLITICS OF POPULATION.
GARDEN CITY: DOUBLEDAY, 1964, 350 PP., $4.95.
     ESSAYS RELATING POPULATION TRENDS TO SOCIAL POLICY. THE
TWO MAIN TOPICS ARE POPULATION GROWTH AND FAMILY PLANNING
AND MIGRATION AND THE ACCULTURATION OF ETHNIC MINORITIES.
SIX OF THE ESSAYS DEAL WITH FAMILY PLANNING IN THE U.S. OR
WITH IMMIGRATION TO OR MIGRATION WITHIN THE U.S. OTHERS
ANALYZE THE PRO-NATALIST LAWS OF THE NETHERLANDS AND THE
SOVIET UNION AND THE IMMIGRATION POLICIES OF AUSTRALIA,
CANADA, AND ISRAEL.

0872 PFIFFNER J.M.
RESEARCH METHODS IN PUBLIC ADMINISTRATION.
NEW YORK: RONALD PRESS, 1940, 447 PP.
     TEXTBOOK FOR TRAINING IN PRACTICAL OPERATING METHODS AND
TECHNIQUES OF FACT-FINDING IN PUBLIC ADMINISTRATION.
FOCUSES ON PROBLEMS OF MANAGEMENT. DESCRIBES CAREER
OPPORTUNITIES IN RESEARCH, AND STAFF RELATIONSHIPS WITHIN
ORGANIZATIONS. ANALYZES RESEARCH PLANNING, HANDLING OF DATA,
INTERVIEWS, QUESTIONNAIRES, AND METHODS OF PREPARING THE
RESEARCH REPORT.

0873 PHELPS E.S. ED.
PRIVATE WANTS AND PUBLIC NEEDS - AN INTRODUCTION TO A
CURRENT ISSUE OF PUBLIC POLICY (REV. ED.)
NEW YORK: W W NORTON, 1965, 178 PP., LC#65-12517.
     PRESENTS 14 ESSAYS DEALING WITH QUESTION OF GOVERNMENT
EXPENDITURE (EXCLUDING "TRANSFER PAYMENTS" AND PURCHASES
FOR ANTI-CYCLICAL PURPOSES), WHICH HAS BEEN MADE CENTRAL
ISSUE CONCERNING ROLE OF GOVERNMENT AND PUBLIC POLICY DUE TO
INCREASING EXPANSION OF PUBLIC SECTOR AND POPULAR PRESSURES
SURROUNDING IT. CONTRASTS ECONOMIC AND POLITICAL VIEWPOINTS,
TRACING THE THEORETICAL DEVELOPMENTS.

0874 PHELPS J.
"STUDIES IN DETERRENCE VIII: MILITARY STABILITY AND ARMS
CONTROL: A CRITICAL SURVEY."
CHINA LAKE: U.S.N.O.T.S., 1963, 22 PP., (NOTS TP 3173).
     EXAMINES THE TRENDS TOWARD MILITARY STABILITY IN ORDER
TO DRAW FORTH IMPLICATIONS FOR SEABORNE DETERRENCE FORCES
AND NAVY PLANNING. ANALYZES THE DEPENDENCE OF STRATEGIC
STABILITY ON WEAPONS. PROPOUNDS SOME RESEARCH PROBLEMS
ASSOCIATED WITH EXTENDING THE TIME PERIOD FOR A STABLE
MILITARY ENVIRONMENT. QUESTIONS THE USEFULNESS OF STABIL-
ITY AS AN ANALYTIC TOOL IN CONSIDERING AND EVALUATING

MEASURES TO INCREASE MILITARY SECURITY.

0875 PHELPS J.
"INFORMATION AND ARMS CONTROL."
J. ARMS CONTR., 1 (APR. 63), 44-55.
FUNDAMENTAL DIFFICULTY IN NEGOTIATING DISARMAMENT HAS
BEEN GREAT DIFFERENCE IN VIEWS ON DISSEMINATION OF ARMS
INFORMATION, AND ON INSPECTION.

0876 PHIPPS T.E.
"THE CASE FOR DETERRENCE."
CURR. HIST., 42 (MAY 62) 275-280.
'ONCE WEST HAS SATISFIED REQUIREMENTS (POLITICAL UNITY OF
WEST AND DETERMINATION TO HALT SOVIET BLOC'S WINNING OF COLD
WAR) IT IS ENTIRELY WITHIN CAPABILITY UNILATERALLY TO END
OUR PART OF ARMS RACE AND TO ACCOMPLISH MOST EFFECTIVE FORM
OF ARMS CONTROL, NAMELY, SELF-CONTROL.' ASSERTS THAT USA
MUST RECOGNIZE 'RETALIATORY SUFFICIENCY' AND ELIMINATE
CONCEPT OF COUNTER-FORCE AND RELATED OBJECTIVES.

0877 PILISUK M., RAPOPORT A.
"STEPWISE DISARMAMENT & SUDDEN DESTRUCTION IN A TWO-
PERSON GAME: A RESEARCH TOOL."
J. CONFL. RESOLUT., 8 (MAR. 64), 36-49.
DESCRIBES AN EXPERIMENTAL GAME WHICH IS INTERMEDIATE IN
COMPLEXITY BETWEEN INTRICATE SMALL GROUP SIMULATIONS OF
INTERNATIONAL CONFLICT AND SIMPLE TWO-PERSON TWO-CHOICE
GAMES PROMINENT IN GAME-THEORY-INSPIRED STUDIES OF COOPERA-
TIVE AND COMPETITIVE BEHAVIOR. INCLUDES A SECTION ON THE
SELECTION OF VARIABLES TO BE STUDIED WITH THIS METHOD.

0878 PILISUK M., HAYDEN T.
"IS THERE A MILITARY INDUSTRIAL COMPLEX WHICH PREVENTS PEACE
CONSENSUS; COUNTERVAILING POWER IN PLURALIST SYSTEMS."
J. SOCIAL ISSUES, 21 (JULY 65), 67-117.
STUDY OF LITERATURE ON QUESTION OF EXISTENCE OF MILITA-
RISTIC POWER ELITE IN AMERICAN SOCIETY. ISOLATES VARIABLES
NECESSARY FOR ITS EXISTENCE IN LIGHT OF PLURALIST-DEMOCRACY
THEORIES. DETERMINE THAT RIGIDITY TO PEACE PLANS WILL OCCUR
WHEN PROPOSALS CALL FOR "REDISTRIBUTING INCONTROVERTIBLE"
INVESTMENTS. AUTHORS PROPOSE THAT PERMANENT PEACE CAN ONLY
COME WHEN INCONTROVERTIBILITY IS UNDERSTOOD AND ELIMINATED.

0879 PIPER D.C.
THE INTERNATIONAL LAW OF THE GREAT LAKES.
DURHAM: DUKE U PR, 1967, 165 PP., LC#67-29860.
EXTRACTS FROM CONVENTIONAL RULES AND CUSTOMARY PRACTICES
OF INTERNATIONAL LAW GOVERNING CANADIAN-AMERICAN RELATIONS
WITH REGARD TO GREAT LAKES. TOPICS ARE INTERNATIONAL
BOUNDARY, CRIMINAL AND ADMIRALITY JURISDICTION FOR WHICH
LAKES ARE CONSIDERED HIGH SEAS, USE OF WATER RESOURCES,
FISHING INDUSTRY, NAVIGATION RIGHTS, NAVAL ARMAMENTS, MUNI-
CIPAL PROBLEMS. APPENDIX OF TREATIES.

0880 PLATT J.R.
"RESEARCH AND DEVELOPMENT FOR SOCIAL PROBLEMS."
BUL. ATOMIC SCIENTISTS, (JUNE 64), 27-29.
BRIEF RESTATEMENT OF THE NATURE OF THE NEED FOR SO-
CIAL INVENTION AS AN ORGANIZED ACTIVITY. CITES PAST EXAMPLES
AND FUTURE POSSIBILITIES AND CALLS FOR SOCIAL R&D ORGANIZA-
TIONS CORRESPONDING TO THOSE ENGAGED IN TECHNOLOGICAL AND
SCIENTIFIC PROBLEMS.

0881 POKROVSKY G.I.
SCIENCE AND TECHNOLOGY IN CONTEMPORARY WAR.
NEW YORK: PRAEGER, 1959, 180 PP.
CONCERNED WITH THE EFFECTS OF NUCLEAR, BACTERIOLOGICAL
AND CHEMICAL TECHNOLOGY UPON MODERN WARFARE.

0882 POLANYI M.
"ON THE INTRODUCTION OF SCIENCE INTO MORAL SUBJECTS."
CAMBRIDGE J., 7 (JAN. 54), 195-207.
MAINTAINS THAT STUDENT OF MAN AND SOCIETY SHOULD UTILIZE
PERSONAL EXPERIENCE. NEW CONCEPTION OF SCIENTIFIC STUDY.

0883 POLLARD W.G.
ATOMIC ENERGY AND SOUTHERN SCIENCE.
OAK RIDGE: OAK R ASSOCIATED U, 1966, 147 PP., LC#66-29119.
REPORTS ON IMPACT OF ATOMIC ENERGY ON DEVELOPMENT OF
SCIENCE IN SOUTH. AREAS OF CONTRIBUTIONS INCLUDE NUCLEAR
AND NON-NUCLEAR PHYSICS, CHEMISTRY, IOLOGY, AND MEDICINE.

0884 POMEROY W.J.
HALF A CENTURY OF SOCIALISM.
NEW YORK: INTERNATIONAL PUBLRS, 1967, 126 PP., LC#67-28137.
DISCUSSES STATE OF SOVIET SOCIETY AFTER ITS FIRST 50
YEARS, DECIDING THAT GREAT STRIDES HAVE BEEN MADE IN ALL
FIELDS TOWARD INTEGRATING CULTURE, TECHNOLOGY, AND PERSON-
ALITY IN USSR. CLAIMS TREND IS TOWARD PRODUCING COLLEC-
TIVIST MENTALITY COUPLED WITH AN EXCELLENT GRASP OF TECH-
NOLOGY. FROM THIS, PREDICTS REALIZATION OF COMMUNIST
SOCIETY WITHIN 50 YEARS.

0885 PONTECORVO G.
"THE LAW OF THE SEA."
BUL. ATOMIC SCIENTISTS, 23 (APR. 67), 46-48.

REPORT ON 1966 CONFERENCE ON LAW OF THE SEA, POINTING
UP MAJOR ISSUES FACING DEVELOPMENT OF SUCH LAW. MAJOR ISSUE
WAS WHETHER OCEAN RESOURCES SHOULD BE INTERNATIONALIZED AND,
IF SO, WHAT THE FRAMEWORK FOR INTERNATIONALIZATION SHOULD
BE. TECHNICAL PROBLEMS AND A BRIEF MENTION OF THE US POSI-
TION ARE ALSO INCLUDED.

0886 PORWIT K.
CENTRAL PLANNING: EVALUATION OF VARIANTS.
NEW YORK: PERGAMON PRESS, 1967, 200 PP., LC#66-17808.
ANALYSIS OF CIRCUMSTANCES UNDER WHICH PLANNING CALCULA-
TIONS CAN BECOME A REAL BASIS FOR IMPLEMENTATION OF THE
PRINCIPLE OF RATIONAL MANAGEMENT. DEALS WITH THE TYPE OF
CALCULATIONS IN WHICH MAIN ATTENTION IS FOCUSED ON MATERIAL,
REAL-TERMSRELATIONSHIPS IN THE ECONOMY. CONSIDERS THEM
PRIMARILY FROM THE POINT OF VIEW OF THE CENTRAL PLAN COV-
ERING THE WHOLE ECONOMY.

0887 POWELSON J.P.
LATIN AMERICA: TODAY'S ECONOMIC AND SOCIAL REVOLUTION.
NEW YORK: MCGRAW HILL, 1964, 303 PP., LC#63-20719.
DISCUSSION OF LATIN AMERICAN ECONOMICS BY LATIN AND NORTH
AMERICANS. STUDIES THE ECONOMIC REVOLUTION; INDIVIDUAL AND
COLLECTIVE APPROACHES TO DEVELOPMENT; AGRARIAN REFORM; MON-
OPOLY; PRIMARY PRODUCTS; EXPERIENCES WITH COPPER, SUGAR,
OIL, AND COFFEE; INFLATION; ECONOMIC INTEGRATION; FOREIGN
AID; NATIONAL ECONOMIC PLANNING; AND REVOLUTION - OLD AND
NEW.

0888 PO414COLUMBIA BUR OF APP SOC R
ATTITUDES OF PROMINENT AMERICANS TOWARD "WORLD PEACE THROUGH
WORLD LAW" (SUPRA-NATL ORGANIZATION FOR WAR PREVENTION)
NEW YORK: COLUMBIA U APP SOC RES, 1959.
ANALYZES OPINION OF PERSONS LISTED IN "WHO'S WHO
IN AMERICA" CONCERNING TWO PLANS FOR AN INTERNATIONAL AGENCY
TO SETTLE NATIONAL DISPUTES IN WORLD LAW COURTS. OPINION
ANALYSIS IS BASED ON ATTITUDINAL CHARACTERISTICS AND SOCIAL
VARIABLES; EXTENSIVE USE OF TABLES AND STATISTICS.

0889 PRINCETON U INDUSTRIAL REL SEC
THE FEDERAL GOVERNMENT AND THE UNIVERSITY: SUPPORT FOR SO-
CIAL SCIENCE RESEARCH AND THE IMPACT OF PROJECT CAMELOT.
PRINCETON: PRIN U INDUS REL CTR, 1966, 4 PP.
ANNOTATED BIBLIOGRAPHY OF BOOKS AND ARTICLES PUBLISHED IN
ENGLISH, 1960-66. ITEMS ARRANGED BY TOPIC. PAMPHLET NO. 132.

0890 PRINCETON U INDUSTRIAL REL SEC
RECENT MATERIAL ON COLLECTIVE BARGAINING IN GOVERNMENT
(PAMPHLET NO. 130)
PRINCETON: PRIN U INDUS REL CTR, 1966, 4 PP.
ANNOTATED BIBLIOGRAPHY OF BOOKS, ARTICLES, AND DOCUMENTS
PUBLISHED IN ENGLISH, 1962-66; LISTED TOPICALLY.

0891 PRINCETON U INDUSTRIAL REL SEC
COLLECTIVE BARGAINING IN THE PUBLIC SCHOOLS
(PAMPHLET NO. 33)
PRINCETON: PRIN U INDUS REL CTR, 1967, 4 PP.
ANNOTATED BIBLIOGRAPHY OF BOOKS, ARTICLES, AND DOCUMENTS
IN ENGLISH, 1961-66; LISTED ALPHABETICALLY BY AUTHOR.

0892 PRINCETON UNIVERSITY
SELECTED REFERENCES: INDUSTRIAL RELATIONS SECTION.
PRINCETON: PRIN U INDUS REL CTR.
SELECTED ANNOTATED REFERENCES TO RECENT WORKS IN INDUS-
TRIAL RELATIONS: EMPLOYMENT AND INCOME; COLLECTIVE BARGAIN-
ING; WAGE POLICIES; ARBITRATION OF LABOR DISPUTES; ADMINIS-
TRATION OF UNION CONTRACTS; ETC.. FIRST PUBLISHED IN 1945
BY DEPARTMENT OF SOCIOLOGY AND ECONOMICS.

0893 PUBLIC ADMIN CLEARING HOUSE
PUBLIC ADMINISTRATIONS ORGANIZATIONS: A DIRECTORY, 1954.
CHICAGO: PUBLIC ADMIN CLEAR HSE, 1954, 150 PP.
SEVENTH EDITION OF DIRECTORY OF VOLUNTARY ORGANIZATIONS
WORKING IN PUBLIC ADMINISTRATION. EMPHASIZES NATIONAL
ORGANIZATIONS. PREVIOUS EDITIONS INCLUDE CANADA AS WELL
AS US. INCLUDES DESCRIPTIONS OF ACTIVITIES. DESCRIBES 513
NATIONAL ORGANIZATIONS; ARRANGEMENT IS ALPHABETICAL.

0894 PUBLIC ADMINISTRATION SERVICE
YOUR BUSINESS OF GOVERNMENT: A CATALOG OF PUBLICATIONS IN
THE FIELD OF PUBLIC ADMINISTRATION (PAMPHLET)
CHICAGO: PUBLIC ADMIN SERVICE, 1944, 30 PP.
UNANNOTATED BIBLIOGRAPHY OF PUBLICATIONS ISSUED BY 15
PRIVATE AND GOVERNMENTAL ASSOCIATIONS ON THE SUBJECT OF
GOVERNMENT ADMINISTRATION. INCLUDES PUBLICATIONS WHICH MAKE
AVAILABLE FOR GENERAL USE THE PRINCIPLES, FINDINGS, AND
RECOMMENDATIONS DEVELOPED AS A RESULT OF SURVEY, REORGANIZA-
TION, AND INSTALLATION PROJECTS. MOST WORKS POSTDATE 1934.
ARRANGED ALPHABETICALLY BY ISSUING ORGANIZATION.

0895 PUBLIC ADMINISTRATION SERVICE
SOURCE MATERIALS IN PUBLIC ADMINISTRATION: A SELECTED
BIBLIOGRAPHY (PAS PUBLICATION NO. 102)
CHICAGO: PUBLIC ADMIN SERVICE, 1948, 30 PP.
GUIDE TO CURRENT AND RECENT LITERATURE IN FIELD OF PUBLIC
ADMINISTRATION. SELECTIVE LISTS OF BASIC SOURCES AND REFER-

ENCE BOOKS. WITH BRIEF ANNOTATIONS AND COMPREHENSIVE LIST-
ING OF MORE RECENT TEXTS, TREATISES, AND SPECIAL STUDIES IN
FIELD; CLASSIFIED BY SUBJECT, AND SUBJECT BIBLIOGRAPHIES.
INCLUDES LIST OF PUBLISHERS AND PERIODICALS CITED.

0896 PYE L.W.
"EASTERN NATIONALISM AND WESTERN POLICY."
WORLD POLIT., 6 (JAN. 54), 248-265.
ADVANCES VIEW THAT GENERAL BACKGROUND STUDIES OF HISTOR-
ICAL, SOCIOLOGICAL, ECONOMIC AND TECHNOLOGICAL DEVELOPMENTS
ARE INADEQUATE FOR PURPOSES OF POLICY-FORMULATION. SUGGESTS
MORE CASE-STUDIES ON THE INTERACTION BETWEEN POLITICAL
BEHAVIOR AND THE GENERAL FRAMEWORK OF ASIAN SOCIETIES.

0897 PYE L.W. ED., VERBA S. ED.
POLITICAL CULTURE AND DEVELOPMENT.
PRINCETON: PRINCETON U PRESS, 1965, 574 PP., LC#65-10840.
DEFINES POLITICAL CULTURE AS SYSTEM OF EMPIRICAL BELIEFS,
EXPRESSIVE SYMBOLS, AND VALUES DEFINING LOCUS OF POLITICAL
ACTION, AND APPLIES IT TO POLITICAL DEVELOPMENT OF TEN
NATIONS, STUDYING PATTERNS OF CHANGE AND PROBLEM OF
TRADITION FOR MODERNIZATION.

0898 RAMO S. ED.
PEACETIME USES OF OUTER SPACE.
NEW YORK: MCGRAW HILL, 1961, 279 PP.
ANALYZES DEVELOPMENTS IN SCIENCE AND TECHNOLOGY IN RELA-
TION TO FUTURE SPACE VENTURES. SEVERAL AUTHORITIES STUDY
SPACE RESEARCH, IMPACT OF WORLD SITUATION, COMMUNICATIONS
IN SPACE, NAVIGATIONAL AIDS, EARTH STUDY, ROLE OF GOVERNMENT
AND PRIVATE ENTERPRISE, THE CHALLENGE OF SPACE TO MAN,
AND POSSIBILITIES FOR SPACE TRAVEL. DISCUSS POTENTIAL OF
AND POSSIBLE LIMITS TO MAN'S CONQUEST OF SPACE.

0899 RAMSEY J.A.
"THE STATUS OF INTERNATIONAL COPYRIGHTS."
LEX ET SCIENTIA, 4 (JAN.-MAR. 67), 1-9.
DISCUSSION OF INTERNATIONAL COPYRIGHT AGREEMENTS FROM
BERNE UNION TO UNIVERSAL COPYRIGHT CONVENTION, THE SUPPLE-
MENTARY NETWORK OF BILATERAL ARRANGEMENTS BETWEEN VARIOUS
STATES, AND INTERNATIONAL AGREEMENTS ON NEW MEDIA. TREATS
RELATIONS OF COMMUNIST COUNTRIES TO TRADITIONAL TREATIES AND
NON-COMMUNIST COUNTRIES RE COMMUNICATIONS COPYRIGHTS.

0900 RAND SCHOOL OF SOCIAL SCIENCE
INDEX TO LABOR ARTICLES.
LONDON: MEYER LONDON MEM LIB.
MONTHLY UNANNOTATED GUIDE TO ARTICLES CURRENTLY APPEAR-
ING IN SELECTED PERIODICALS. COVERS BUSINESS AND LABOR CON-
DITIONS, TRADE UNIONISM, LABOR LEGISLATION, DISPUTES AND AR-
BITRATION, AND INTERNATIONAL ORGANIZATIONS. FIRST ISSUED IN
1926.

0901 RANSOM H.H.
CAN AMERICAN DEMOCRACY SURVIVE COLD WAR.
GARDEN CITY: DOUBLEDAY, 1964, 262 PP., $1.25.
HISTORY OF DEFENSE ORGANIZATION IN AMERICA WITH EMPHASIS
ON THE POST-WAR PERIOD. ANALYSIS OF THE STRUCTURE AND PER-
FORMANCE OF THE DEFENSE DEPARTMENT, THE NATIONAL SECURITY
COUNCIL, THE DEFENSE BUDGET PROCESS, AND THE CIA AND OTHER
INTELLIGENCE AGENCIES. PRIMARY QUESTION DEALT WITH IS THE
RELATIONSHIP BETWEEN COMPLEX, PARTIALLY SECRET BUREAUCRACIES
AND THE IDEALS OF DEMOCRATIC GOVERNMENT.

0902 RAPOPORT A.
FIGHTS, GAMES AND DEBATES.
ANN ARBOR: U. MICH. PR., 1960, 400 PP., $6.95.
STUDY BASED ON MATHEMATICAL ANALYSIS METHOD. OUTLINES
STRUCTURE OF TYPES OF CONFLICTS. REVIEWS POSSIBILITY OF
INDIVIDUAL DECISIONS WIELDING INFLUENCE.

0903 RAPP W.F.
"MANAGEMENT ANALYSIS AT THE HEADQUARTERS OF FEDERAL
AGENCIES."
INT. REV. OF ADMIN. SCI., 26 (1960), 235-248.
A SURVEY OF MANAGEMENT ANALYSIS STAFFS AND FUNCTIONS:
"COLLABORATIVE WORKING ARRANGEMENTS ARE TYPICAL, STAFFS ARE
SMALL, THERE ARE MANY CONCEPTS AND PRACTICES."

0904 RASER J.R.
"WEAPONS DESIGN AND ARMS CONTROL* THE POLARIS EXAMPLE."
J. OF CONFLICT RESOLUTION, 9 (DEC. 65), 450-462.
ONE CRITERION FOR WEAPONS SYSTEM SELECTION ACCORDING TO
RASER SHOULD BE THE ADAPTABILITY OF THE SYSTEM TO FUTURE
ARMS CONTROL AGREEMENTS. HE DEMONSTRATES THAT THE IMPROVED
3000-MILE RANGE POLARIS VIOLATES THIS TENET. HE THEN ILLUS-
TRATES MYRIAD OF ARMS-CONTROL AND STRATEGIC ADVANTAGES AC-
CRUING TO A SHORTER RANGED "DEPLOYED OFF STATION" POLARIS.

0905 RASER J.R.
"DETERRENCE RESEARCH* PAST PROGRESS AND FUTURE NEEDS."
JOURNAL OF PEACE RESEARCH, (1966), 297-327.
INCREASED UNDERSTANDING OF CONFLICT PROCESSES SUCH AS
DETERRENCE IS ESSENTIAL. THE DEVELOPMENT OF THINKING ABOUT
NUCLEAR DETERRENCE IS EXAMINED AND AN ANALYTICAL FRAMEWORK
FOR STUDYING DETERRENCE (INCLUDING SOCIOLOGICAL AND PSYCHO-

LOGICAL VARIABLES) IS PROPOSED. FUTURE DIRECTIONS FOR STUDY
ARE SUGGESTED.

0906 RAUDSEPP E.
MANAGING CREATIVE SCIENTISTS AND ENGINEERS.
NEW YORK: MACMILLAN, 1963, 249 PP., LC#63-07448.
EXPLORES RELATIONSHIP BETWEEN RESEARCH AND MANAGEMENT IN
CONTEMPORARY US ECONOMY. DISCUSSES CREATIVE PROCESS AND
CHARACTERISTICS OF CREATIVE PROFESSIONAL; CREATIVITY IN CUL-
TURE AND INDUSTRY; AND MANAGING CREATIVE RESEARCH.

0907 RAWLINSON J.L.
CHINA'S STRUGGLE FOR NAVAL DEVELOPMENT 1839-1895.
CAMBRIDGE: HARVARD U PR, 1967, 318 PP., LC#66-10127.
DESCRIBES CHINA'S EFFORT TO BUILD POWERFUL NAVAL FORCE
IN LATE 19TH CENTURY. DISCUSSES INABILITY TO CONTRAVENE
TRADITIONAL ORGANIZATION AS IT CONTRIBUTED TO FAILURE OF
EFFORT. DISCUSSES DAMAGING DEFEATS BY JAPAN IN 1894-5 THAT
ALTERED HISTORY OF PACIFIC AREA IN 20TH CENTURY.

0908 REDFORD E.S. ED.
PUBLIC ADMINISTRATION AND POLICY FORMATION: STUDIES IN OIL,
GAS, BANKING, RIVER DEVELOPMENT AND CORPORATE INVESTIGATIONS
AUSTIN: U OF TEXAS PR, 1956, 319 PP., LC#56-7507.
FIVE CASE STUDIES OF ADMINISTRATIVE REGULATION EMPHASIZE
RELATIONSHIP BETWEEN CONTROL, EFFICIENCY, AND PUBLIC
INTEREST. DISCUSSES INTERRELATIONSHIPS BETWEEN AGENCIES,
CLIENTELE, AND SPECIFIC INDIVIDUALS.

0909 REED E. ED.
CHALLENGES TO DEMOCRACY: THE NEXT TEN YEARS.
NEW YORK: FREDERICK PRAEGER, 1963, 245 PP., LC#64-12516.
GOVERNMENT LEADERS AIM TO BRING US POLITICAL GOALS,
VALUES, AND POLICIES TO 20TH-CENTURY TERMS. EMPHASIS IS ON
ADVANCING CIVILIZATION AND FUTURE KNOWLEDGE BY CRITICAL
DISCUSSIONS AND ANALYSIS OF OUTDATED 18TH-CENTURY BELIEFS.
PART OF PROGRAM IS BY CENTER FOR DEMOCRATIC INSTITUTIONS.

0910 REICH C.A.
BUREAUCRACY AND THE FORESTS (PAMPHLET)
SANTA BARBARA: CTR DEMO INST, 1962, 13 PP.
ARGUES THAT MORE PUBLIC PARTICIPATION IS DESIRABLE IN
MANAGEMENT AND PLANNING FOR OUR FORESTS.

0911 REINTANZ G.
"THE SPACE TREATY."
GERMAN FOREIGN POLICY, 6 (FEB. 67), 147-152.
ANALYSIS OF 1966 UN SPACE TREATY. SOME DISCUSSION OF ITS
EVOLUTION. EMPHASIZES EFFECTS OF "ALL-STATES" PROVISIONS
CLAUSE, I.E. THE PRINCIPLE OF UNIVERSALITY APPLIED FOR THE
FIRST TIME TO INTERNATIONAL TREATY. ANALYZES WEST GERMAN
REACTION TO TREATY RE HER RELATIONS TO EAST GERMANY. AUTHOR
IS EAST GERMAN AND ANTI-AMERICAN.

0912 REISS A.J. JR. ED.
SCHOOLS IN A CHANGING SOCIETY.
NEW YORK: FREE PRESS OF GLENCOE, 1965, 224 PP., LC#65-25255.
ESSAYS CONTRIBUTED TO A CONFERENCE ON RESEARCH IN THE
ADMINISTRATIVE ORGANIZATION OF SCHOOL SYSTEMS AND ON ITS
EFFECT ON THE SOCIALIZATION OF YOUTH IN THE SCHOOL AND THE
COMMUNITY. THEMES INCLUDE ORGANIZATIONAL DISPARITY, YOUTH
CULTURE, COMMUNITY LINKAGES OF PUBLIC SCHOOLS, SCHOOLS IN
A CHANGING SOCIETY, USES OF AUTHORITY, POLICE AND PROBATION,
INTEGRATION PLANS, CONTEMPORARY PROBLEMS, AND PUBLIC POLICY.

0913 RENAN E.
THE FUTURE OF SCIENCE.
ORIGINAL PUBLISHER NOT AVAILABLE, 1891, 497 PP.
ADVOCATES RETURN TO SIMPLER LIFE. SCIENCE IS SAID TO BE
OF USE, BUT INSUFFICIENT TO RESOLVE MYSTERIES OF LIFE.
ALTHOUGH FEELING THAT FAITH AND CHRISTIANITY ARE MOST IMPOR-
TANT THINGS IN LIFE, CLAIMS THAT KNOWLEDGE GIVES ONE FOUNDA-
TIONS FOR LIVING AND INSIGHTS INTO WAYS TO ATTAIN FAITH.
ADVOCATES FREEDOM BUT FEELS THAT PEACE LEADS TO WEAKNESS.
RELATES HISTORY TO PHILOSOPHY.

0914 REVES E.
THE ANATOMY OF PEACE.
NEW YORK: HARPER, 1945, 293 PP.
ANAYLZES HISTORICAL SIGNIFICANCE OF SOVEREIGNTY. EXAMINES
RELATIONSHIP BETWEEN INDIVIDUAL BEHAVIOR AND STATE POLICIES.
POINTS OUT 'FALLACY' OF INTERNATIONALISM AND OF SELF-
DETERMINISM OF NATIONS. ANALYZES PROBLEM OF NUCLEAR POWER.

0915 REYNOLDS P.A.
BRITISH FOREIGN POLICY IN THE INTER-WAR YEARS.
LONDON: LONGMANS, GREEN & CO, 1954, 182 PP.
TRACES COURSE OF POLICY DEVELOPMENT, 1919-39, DISCUSSING
CHANGES BY RELATING THEM TO POLITICAL PRESSURES, ECONOMIC
INFLUENCES, PUBLIC OPINION, AND NEGOTIATIONS. ALSO DISCUSSES
RELATIONS WITH US AND EFFECT ON BRITISH POLICY.

0916 RICH G.S.
"THE PROPOSED PATENT LEGISLATION* SOME COMMENTS."
G. WASH. LAW REV., 35 (MAY 67), 641-651.
CRITICISM OF RECOMMENDATIONS OF REPORT OF THE PRESIDENT'S

COMMISSION TO STUDY THE PATENT SYSTEM, ARGUING THAT PRESUMPTION OF VALIDITY ARGUMENT IS MEANINGLESS, THAT THERE IS TOO MUCH EMPHASIS ON HARMONIZATION OF US AND WESTERN EUROPE SYSTEMS. ATTACKS FOUR SPECIFIC RECOMMENDATIONS WHICH WORK UNNECESSARY HARDSHIP ON INVENTOR.

0917 RICHMAN B.M.
"SOVIET MANAGEMENT IN TRANSITION."
BUSINESS TOPICS, 15 (SPRING 67), 27-41.
CONCERNED WITH PROBLEMS FACING MANAGEMENT AS SOVIET INDUSTRIAL ECONOMY EXPANDS AND GROWS MORE COMPLEX. DISCUSSES LIBERMAN PLAN, DECENTRALIZATION OF AUTHORITY, NEED FOR OVERHAUL OF PRICING SYSTEM, MARKETING PRACTICES, USE OF SCIENTIFIC TOOLS AND TECHNIQUES FOR PLANNING AND CONTROL FINANCING, REFORMS UNDER KOSYGIN, INCENTIVE PLANS, SKILLS, AND ESTABLISHMENT OF NEW MINISTRIES.

0918 RICHSTEIN A.R.
"LEGAL RULES IN NUCLEAR WEAPONS EMPLOYMENTS."
MIL. REV., 41(JULY 61), 91-98.
DESTRUCTIVE SCALE OF NUCLEAR WEAPONS AND GUIDANCE ERRORS OF MISSILE SYSTEMS CREATE PROBLEMS AS TO EFFECTS ON CIVILIAN NON-COMBATANS IN TARGET AREAS.

0919 RIDKER R.G.
ECONOMIC COSTS OF AIR POLLUTION* STUDIES IN MEASUREMENT.
NEW YORK: FREDERICK PRAEGER, 1967, 214 PP., LC#66-26571.
SETS UP MEASUREMENT SYSTEM FOR ECONOMIC COST OF AIR POLLUTION. INCLUDES AS RELEVANT MEDICAL COSTS, DAMAGE TO MATERIALS, EFFECT ON MARKETS. PROVIDES CASE STUDY GIVING TECHNIQUES, DATA ANALYSIS. CONSIDERS PROPERTY VALUES, BOTH IN CROSSSECTION AND TIME-SERIES STUDIES. ADVISES FOR FUTURE RESEARCH.

0920 RIES J.C.
THE MANAGEMENT OF DEFENSE: ORGANIZATION AND CONTROL OF THE US ARMED SERVICES.
BALTIMORE: JOHNS HOPKINS PRESS, 1964, 212 PP., LC#64-18122.
REAPPRAISAL OF DEFENSE ORGANIZATION. FAVORS COMMITTEE METHOD OF ORGANIZATION--CONCLUDING THAT AMERICAN POLITICAL ENVIRONMENT DEMANDS PLURALISTIC DEFENSE STRUCTURE WHICH ALLOCATES RESPONSIBILITY IN KEEPING WITH AUTHORITY. URGES RATIONALIZATION OF DECISION-MAKING AND RESTORATION OF ORGANIZATIONAL EQUILIBRIUM.

0921 RIKER W.H.
THE THEORY OF POLITICAL COALITIONS.
NEW HAVEN: YALE U. PR., 1962, 300 PP.
MATHEMATICAL FORMULAE OF GAME-THEORY USED TO DERIVE THEORIES OF POLITICAL BEHAVIOR WHICH WILL SERVE AS FOUNDATION FOR FUTURE STUDY OF POLITICS. EVENTUALLY WILL JOIN WITH ECONOMICS AND PSYCHOLOGY IN NEW SCIENCE OF HUMAN BEHAVIOR. CONSTRUCTION OF MODEL TO INTERPRET COALITIONS AND APPENDIX WITH DERIVATION OF MODELS. APPLICATION TO USA AS LEADER IN POTENTIAL WORLD-DOMINATING ALLIANCE.

0922 RILEY V., ALLEN R.L.
INTERINDUSTRY ECONOMIC STUDIES.
BALTIMORE: JOHNS HOPKINS PRESS, 1955, 280 PP.
ANNOTATED AND INDEXED BIBLIOGRAPHY ALSO PRESENTS AND DISCUSSES ASPECTS OF INTERINDUSTRY ECONOMICS. DEALS WITH THEORETICAL ECONOMY STRUCTURE, MATHEMATICAL AND COMPUTATIONAL TECHNIQUES OF ANALYSIS, PROBLEMS AND MEANS OF CLASSIFICATION, AS WELL AS SPECIFIC FACETS OF THE US ECONOMIC SYSTEM. CONTAINS A SEPARATE SECTION OF GENERAL DISCUSSION AND INCLUDES A LIST OF GENERAL REFERENCES.

0923 RIVKIN A.
"AFRICAN ECONOMIC DEVELOPMENT: ADVANCED TECHNOLOGY AND THE STAGES OF GROWTH."
J. HUM. REL., 8 (SUMMER 60), 617-645.
CONCERNED WITH BASIC PROBLEM AREAS OF AFRICAN ECONOMIC DEVELOPMENT (INCLUDING AGRICULTURE, MINING, TRANSPORTATION, AND LABOR), AND ROLE ADVANCED FREE WORLD TECHNOLOGY CAN PLAY IN ENSURING FREEDOM AND INDEPENDENCE OF AFRICAN STATES. POINTS OUT DANGERS OF EXCESSIVE RAPIDITY IN GROWTH, AND INCORPORATING TECHNOLOGY INTO CULTURAL PROCESSES OF AFRICA.

0924 RIZOS E.J.
"SCIENCE AND TECHNOLOGY IN COUNTRY DEVELOPMENT* TOWARDS AN UNDERSTANDING OF THE ROLE OF PUBLIC ADMINISTRATION."
INT. REV. OF ADMIN. SCI., 32 (1966), 335-345.
EXAMINES ROLE THAT PUBLIC ADMINISTRATION PLAYS IN BRINGING ABOUT GOAL OF ECONOMIC, TECHNOLOGICAL, AND SCIENTIFIC DEVELOPMENT IN UNDERDEVELOPED COUNTRIES. TREATS FUNCTIONS, GOALS, AND METHODS IN ADMINISTRATION, INTERPLAY OF SCIENCE AND TECHNOLOGY, DEFICIENCIES OF PUBLIC ADMINISTRATION, ORGANIZATIONAL STRUCTURE, PROCESS OF ADMINISTRATIVE DECISIONS, AND PROBLEMS OF EFFICIENT MANPOWER.

0925 ROACH J.R. ED.
THE UNITED STATES AND THE ATLANTIC COMMUNITY; ISSUES AND PROSPECTS.
AUSTIN: U OF TEXAS PR, 1967, 87 PP., LC#67-27782.
STUDIES PRESENT PLACE OF NATO AS PEACE-KEEPING FORCE. ADVOCATES REVISION OF POLICIES AND FUNCTIONS OF NATO TO MEET CHANGES IN WORLD SITUATION PARTIALLY CAUSED BY NATO ITSELF. CONSIDERS IMPLICATIONS OF ECONOMIC RECOVERY OF EUROPE, END OF COLONIALISM, LESSENING OF SOVIET THREAT, ADVANTAGES IN MODERN TECHNOLOGY, AND UNIFICATION OF EUROPE FOR US POSITION IN NATO AND FOREIGN POLICY.

0926 ROBERTS E.B.
"THE PROBLEM OF AGING ORGANIZATIONS."
BUSINESS HORIZONS, 10 (WINTER 67), 51-60.
DESCRIBES RISE AND FALL IN EFFICIENCY AND OUTPUT OF R&D FIRMS. BASED ON INDUSTRIAL DYNAMICS, PROPOSES THAT PROBLEMS ARE NATURAL OUTGROWTH OF FIRMS' DEVELOPMENT. DISCUSSES APPLICATION OF FEEDBACK LOOPS AND EFFECT OF VARIOUS DIVISIONS WITHIN THE ORGANIZATION UPON ONE ANOTHER, PROPOSING SOLUTIONS AND CORRECTIVE MEASURES.

0927 ROBERTS W.
"DIVERSITY, CONSENSUS, AND ECLECTICISM IN POLITICAL SCIENCE"
S.W. SOCIAL SCI. QUART., 48 (SEPT. 67), 133-141.
DISCUSSES DISCIPLINE OF POLITICAL SCIENCE. ARGUES THAT DIVERSITY OF APPROACHES TO DISCIPLINE FORMS HEALTHY DEBATE. MAINTAINS THAT AMONG DIVERSE OPINIONS CONSENSUS STILL EXISTS ON NECESSITY OF POLITICAL SCIENCE AND ON USE OF SCIENTIFIC METHOD. SUGGESTS THAT BEST HOPE FOR FUTURE IS ECLECTIC APPROACH.

0928 ROBERTS HL
FOREIGN AFFAIRS BIBLIOGRAPHY, 1952-1962.
NEW YORK: RR BOWKER, 1964, 752 PP., LC#33-7094.
A SELECTED AND ANNOTATED CUMULATIVE BIBLIOGRAPHY OF BOOKS ON INTERNATIONAL RELATIONS BASED LARGELY UPON NOTES APPEARING QUARTERLY IN "FOREIGN AFFAIRS". RETAINS SCHEMATIC CLASSIFICATION OF EARLIER VOLUMES: GENERAL INTERNATIONAL RELATIONS, THE WORLD SINCE 1914, AND THE WORLD BY REGIONS. EMPHASIZING ANALYTICAL, CHRONOLOGICAL, AND REGIONAL TREATMENTS RESPECTIVELY. LIMITED TO WORKS PUBLISHED FROM 1953-62.

0929 ROBINSON E.A.G.
THE STRUCTURE OF COMPETITIVE INDUSTRY.
NEW YORK: CAMBRIDGE U PRESS, 1953, 179 PP.
DISCUSSES MEANS AVAILABLE TO GREAT BRITAIN FOR INCREASING ITS NATIONAL PRODUCT, THROUGH CONSIDERATION OF INDUSTRIAL EFFICIENCY. DEFENDS FREE MARKET SYSTEM AS MOST EFFICIENT BECAUSE IT ADJUSTS TO DEMANDS OF CONSUMER. ATTEMPTS TO DEFINE AND DESCRIBE WORKINGS OF FREE MARKET SYSTEM.

0930 ROBINSON J.A.T.
"ABORTION* THE CASE FOR A FREE DECISION."
TWENTIETH CENTURY, 174 (1967), 5-8.
DISCUSSES APPROACHES TO LEGISLATING ABOUT ABORTION. ADVOCATES REPEAL OF LAWS MAKING ABORTION A CRIME. ARGUES SUCH DECISIONS ARE MORAL RATHER THAN LEGAL AND CANNOT BE LEGISLATIVELY REGULATED. ADVOCATES TOTAL AVAILIBILITY OF BIRTH CONTROL INFORMATION AND DEVICES TO REMOVE NECESSITY OF ABORTION AS MUCH AS POSSIBLE.

0931 ROBINSON T.W.
"A NATIONAL INTEREST ANALYSIS OF SINO-SOVIET RELATIONS."
INTERNATIONAL STUDIES Q., 11 (JUNE 67), 135-175.
APPLIES HANS MORGENTHAU'S NATIONAL-INTEREST FORMULATION TO SINO-SOVIET RELATIONS TO STUDY APPLICATION OF TRADITIONAL THEORY TO COMMUNIST WORLD. DISCUSSES NATIONAL INTEREST THEORY IN DETAIL; INQUIRES INTO NATIONAL INTERESTS OF CHINA AND USSR, RELATION OF POWER AND INTEREST, AND INFLUENCE OF NUCLEAR WEAPONS ON INTERESTS. ANALYZES SINO-SOVIET ALLIANCE IN TERMS OF COUNTRIES' NATIONAL INTERESTS.

0932 ROCKEFELLER BROS. FUND INC.
INTERNATIONAL SECURITY - THE MILITARY ASPECT.
GARDEN CITY: DOUBLEDAY, 1958, 63 PP.
REPORT ON STRATEGIC PROBLEMS, DEFENSE ORGANIZATION, NUCLEAR WEAPON SYSTEMS, ALLIANCES, CIVIL DEFENSE, DISARMAMENT, AND BUDGETS FOR NATIONAL SECURITY. MAINTAINS THAT RETALIATORY FORCE OF US IS INADEQUATELY DISPERSED AND PROTECTED.

0933 ROMANIECKI L.
"THE ATOM AND INTERNATIONAL COOPERATION."
POLISH PERSPECTIVES, (FEB. 67), 3-9.
BELIEVES THAT THE INTERNATIONAL ATOMIC ENERGY AGENCY SHOULD HAVE A GREATER ROLE IN THE CONTROL OF NUCLEAR WEAPONS. DISCUSSES A POLISH PROPOSAL AT THE TENTH GENERAL CONFERENCE OF THE IAEA, HELD IN SEPT., 1966, THAT POLAND WOULD SUBMIT HER ATOMIC INSTALLATIONS TO THE CONTROL OF THE IAEA IF WEST GERMANY WOULD DO THE SAME.

0934 ROSE A.M.
THEORY AND METHOD IN THE SOCIAL SCIENCES.
MINNEAPOLIS: U OF MINN PR, 1954, 351 PP., LC#54-6369.
THE FIRST SECTION, DEALING WITH SOCIAL THEORY, DISCUSSES SOCIAL ORGANIZATION AND DISORGANIZATION AND A THEORY OF THE FUNCTION OF VOLUNTARY ASSOCIATIONS IN CONTEMPORARY SOCIAL STRUCTURE. THE SECOND SECTION DEALS WITH THE SOCIAL RESPONSIBILITIES OF THE SOCIAL SCIENTIST. OTHER SECTIONS DEAL WITH INTERDISCIPLINARY PROBLEMS, METHODOLOGY, AND RESEARCH TECHNIQUES.

0935 ROSECRANCE R.N. ED.
THE DISPERSION OF NUCLEAR WEAPONS: STRATEGY AND POLITICS.
NEW YORK: COLUMB. U. PR., 1964, 343 PP., $7.50.
DISCUSSES THE EXPERIENCE OF BRITAIN AND FRANCE IN
THEIR ATTEMPT TO ACQUIRE DETERRENT CAPABILITIES COMPARABLE
TO THAT OF THE U.S. AND THE SOVIET UNION. EVALUATES THE
EFFECT ON RED CHINA'S POSITIONS IN SOUTHEAST ASIA WHEN SHE
ACHIEVES NUCLEAR STATUS. AND CONSIDERS THE QUESTION OF
WHETHER THE SPREAD OF NUCLEAR WEAPONS WILL JEOPARDIZE
INTERNATIONAL PEACE.

0936 ROSENAU J.N. ED.
INTERNATIONAL POLITICS AND FOREIGN POLICY: A READER IN
RESEARCH AND THEORY.
NEW YORK: FREE PRESS OF GLENCOE, 1961, 511 PP., LC#61-14106.
ANTHOLOGY OF 55 ARTICLES ON THEORETICAL MODELS OF INTER-
NATIONAL POLITICS OR POLICY; INQUIRES INTO MEANING OF BASIC
CONCEPTS IN FIELD; CASE STUDIES ILLUSTRATING OPERATION OF
KEY PROCESSES IN DECISION-MAKING IN WESTERN AND NON-WESTERN
SOCIETIES. EACH STUDY IS FOLLOWED BY SERIES OF NOTES WITH
BIBLIOGRAPHICAL REFERENCES.

0937 ROSENHAUPT H.W.
HOW TO WAGE PEACE.
NEW YORK: DAY, 1949, 249 PP.
ASSESSES THE NECESSITY OF CREATIVE COMMON ACTION IN ORDER
TO ACHIEVE POSITIVE RESULTS. ANALYZES INTRANATIONAL GROUPS
INTERESTED IN PROBLEM OF MAINTAINING PEACE. DISCUSSES RELE-
VANT POLITICAL MOVEMENTS WITHIN THE CONGRESS. EXPLORES CER-
TAIN RESEARCH INSTITUTES.

0938 ROSHOLT R.L.
AN ADMINISTRATIVE HISTORY OF NASA, 1958-1963.
WASHINGTON: GOVT PR OFFICE, 1966, 381 PP., LC#66-60083.
HISTORICAL STUDY OF ADMINISTRATION OF NASA, ITS
ANTECEDENTS AND BEGINNING, AND CHANGES AS SPACE PROGRAM
ACCELERATED AND POLITICAL ADMINISTRATIONS CHANGED.

0939 ROSS R.
SYMBOLS AND CIVILIZATION.
NEW YORK: HARCOURT BRACE, 1962, 243 PP., LC#62-21848.
AN ATTEMPT TO EXPLORE THE BASIS OF CIVILIZATION UNDER-
LYING ISSUES OF ECONOMICS AND POLITICS. ESSENTIALLY A
TREATMENT OF EPISTEMOLOGICAL QUESTIONS, WITH PARTICULAR
EMPHASIS ON SCIENCE. FOCUSES ON THE QUESTION OF HOW
MAN USES HIS KNOWLEDGE TO UNDERSTAND THE WORLD.

0940 ROTHENBERG J.
ECONOMIC EVALUATION OF URBAN RENEWAL: CONCEPTUAL FOUNDATION
OF BENEFIT-COST ANALYSIS.
WASHINGTON: BROOKINGS INST, 1967, 277 PP., LC#67-19190.
CONCENTRATES ON REDEVELOPMENT ASPECTS OF URBAN RENEWAL
PROGRAM IN US. FORMULATES A PROCEDURE BY WHICH A BENEFIT-
COST ANALYSIS OF URBAN RENEWAL CAN BE CARRIED OUT.
ILLUSTRATES PROCEDURE BY ANALYSIS OF FIVE SELECTED RENEWAL
PROJECTS.

0941 ROTHSCHILD J.H.
TOMORROW'S WEAPONS: CHEMICAL AND BIOLOGICAL.
NEW YORK: MCGRAW HILL, 1964, 271 PP., LC#63-22553.
DISCUSSES MORAL AND POLITICAL ASPECTS OF CHEMICAL AND
BIOLOGICAL WARFARE. STUDIES USE OF CHEMICAL WEAPONS FOR
OFFENSE. ADVOCATES USE OF SUCH WEAPONS AS DETERRENCE IN
TOTALLY DISARMED WORLD TO INSURE PEACE.

0942 ROTHSTEIN R.L.
"NUCLEAR PROLIFERATION AND AMERICAN POLICY."
POLIT. SCI. QUART., 82 (MAR. 67), 14-34.
EXAMINES BRITISH AND FRENCH DECISIONS TO DEVELOP NUCLEAR
EAPONS, THE NUCLEAR DEBATES IN INDIA, AND THE CREDIBILITY OF
NUCLEAR GUARANTEES. CONCLUDES THAT AMERICAN POLICY SHOULD BE
TO PREVENT NUCLEAR PROLIFERATION BY A COMBINATION OF GUARAN-
TEES AND CONTROLS ON PRODUCTION, AND IN LIMITED INSTANCES, A
POLICY OF TRANSFERRING CONTROL, WHEN ALTERNATIVE IS AN
IMMEDIATE LOCAL WAR OR UNCONTROLLED ARMS PARE.

0943 ROYAL INST. INT. AFF.
"ANNUAL REPORT OF THE COUNCIL: 1951-1952."
LONDON: CHATHAM, 1952, 71 PP.
SCIENTIFIC STUDY OF INTERNATIONAL QUESTIONS AS DETERMINED
BY ECLECTICISM WITH RESPECT TO THE SIGNIFICANCE OF SPECIFIC
CONTEMPORARY INTERNATIONAL PROBLEMS. ABBREVIATED ACCOUNT OF
ACTIVITIES OF SIX COMMONWEALTH INSTITUTES.

0944 RUBINSTEIN A.Z.
"POLITICAL BARRIERS TO DISARMAMENT."
ORBIS, 9 (SPRING 65), 140-154.
THE OVERCOMING OF DEEPLY INGRAINED NATIONAL ANXIETIES
WILL NOT SOON OR READILY BE MANAGED. MOST NATIONAL LEADERS
ARE RECONCILED TO A CONTINUATION OF THE BALANCE OF TERROR.
YET NEGOTIATION OUT OF FEAR MAY BRING RESULTS AS EFFECTIVE
AND ENDURING AS THOSE BASED ON TRUST. CONCLUDES THAT A COM-
PLETE AND GENERAL DISARMAMENT AGREEMENT BETWEEN THE US AND
THE USSR IS UNLIKELY BECAUSE OF ATTITUDES AND DANGERS.

0945 RUITENBEER H.M.
THE DILEMMA OF ORGANIZATIONAL SOCIETY.
NEW YORK: EP DUTTON, 1963, 220 PP., LC#63-24814.
EXPLORES EFFECTS OF MASS SOCIETY UPON INDIVIDUALS.
FRIEDMAN CONSIDERS LOYALTY AND AUTHORITY. REISMAN, WHYTE,
MERTON, AND MEAD COVER TECHNICAL ADVANCES, EDUCATION, AND
LEISURE, AND KARL JASPERS DISCUSSES BUREAUCRACY AS FORM OF
TOTALITARIANISM. ALSO CONSIDERS EFFECTS ON URBANISM AND
RELIGION.

0946 RUPPENTHAL K.M. ED., MCKINNELL H.A. JR. ED.
TRANSPORTATION AND TOMORROW.
STANFORD: STANFORD U. BUS ADMIN, 1966, 180 PP., LC#66-23037.
DISCUSSES SEVERAL TYPES OF TRANSPORTATION: RAILROADS,
TRUCKING, PIPELINES, SHIPPPING, AIR, AND SPACE. STUDIES
CHANGES NECESSARY TO MEET INDUSTRIAL AND MILITARY NEEDS,
SUCH AS MORE EFFICIENT ORGANIZATION AND CLOSER COOPERATION
AMONG TYPES. PREDICTS TYPES OF TRANSPORTATION IN 2000.

0947 RUSHING W.A.
THE PSYCHIATRIC PROFESSIONS.
CHAPEL HILL: U OF N CAR PR, 1964, 267 PP., LC#64-13559.
DEALS WITH POWER, CONFLICT, AND ADAPTATION IN A
PSYCHIATRIC HOSPITAL STAFF, FROM A SOCIOLOGICAL VIEWPOINT.
SOCIAL SYSTEMS OF PSYCHIATRIC NURSES, THEIR INFLUENCE ON
DOCTORS, STUDY OF SOCIAL WORKERS, ND RECREATION SERVICES ALL
SHED LIGHT ON "ANCILLARY" PROFESSIONS AIDING PSYCHIATRY.

0948 RUSSELL B.
COMMON SENSE AND NUCLEAR WARFARE.
LONDON: ALLEN UNWIN, 1959, 93 PP.
SURVIVAL OF MAN IN NUCLEAR AGE IS PRIMARILY CONCERN OF
POLICY MAKERS. ALL EFFORTS SHOULD BE MADE TO SETTLE DISPUTES
PEACEFULLY AND TO OUTLAW WAR AS AN INSTRUMENT OF POLICY.
CHANGES IN EDUCATION CAN HELP BRING SECURITY. EAST AND WEST
MUST UNITE TO ELIMINATE THREAT OF NUCLEAR WARFARE.

0949 RUSSELL B.
WAR CRIMES IN VIETNAM.
LONDON: ALLEN & UNWIN, 1967, 178 PP., LC#67-23969.
BERTRAND RUSSELL APPEALS TO AMERICAN CONSCIENCE TO STOP
WAR CRIMES IN VIETNAM. TELLS OF NAPALM, "LAZY BOMBS,"
CHEMICALS THAT NOT ONLY DEFOLIATE BUT POISON AND KILL, AND
OF CONCENTRATION CAMPS POLITELY CALLED "RELOCATION CENTERS."
FEELS RACISM IN US HAS CREATED CLIMATE IN WHICH IT IS
DIFFICULT FOR AMERICANS TO UNDERSTAND WAR.

0950 RUSSETT B.M., COOPER C.C.
ARMS CONTROL IN EUROPE: PROPOSALS AND POLITICAL CONSTRAINTS.
DENVER: U OF DENVER, 1967, 85 PP.
DESCRIBES VARIOUS POLICIES ON GERMAN REUNIFICATION AND
ARMS CONTROL TO ASSESS RELATIVE IMPORTANCE OF POLICIES TO
NATIONS AND THEIR POLITICAL PARTIES. POINTS OUT CONFLICTS
IN POLICIES AND SHIFTS OVER TIME. INFERS FROM PATTERNS OF
CONFLICTS AND SHIFTS THE CONSTRAINTS ON INTERNATIONAL BAR-
GAINING. BELIEVES THAT BETTER UNDERSTANDING OF THESE LIMITA-
TIONS WILL OPEN UP NEW AVENUES OF AGREEMENT.

0951 RUTGERS U GRADUATE SCH LIB SCI
BIBLIOGRAPHY OF RESEARCH RELATING TO THE COMMUNICATION OF
SCIENTIFIC AND TECHNICAL INFORMATION.
NEW BRUNSWICK: RUTGERS U PR, 1967, 764 PP., LC#67-63792.
INCLUDES WORKS ON ALL ASPECTS OF GENERATION, ACQUISITION,
PROCESSING, STORAGE, RETRIEVAL, AND USE OF INFORMATION 1955-
1965. CONCERNED WITH RESEARCH AND DEVELOPMENT RELATING TO
COMMUNICATION WITH UNKNOWN PERSONS IN THE INDEFINITE FUTURE.

0952 RUTH J.M.
"THE ADMINISTRATION OF WATER RESOURCES IN GUATEMALA."
PUBLIC & INTL. AFF., 5 (SPRING 67), 249-278.
STUDIES CONTROL OF WATER IN GUATEMALA AS A MODEL OF PROB-
LEMS IN HANDLING NATURAL RESOURCES. CONSIDERS THE ROLE OF
GOVERNMENT IN COORDINATING DEMANDS OF HYDRO-ELECTRIC PROJ-
ECTS, IRRIGATION, COMMUNITY WATER SUPPLY, RECREATION, AND
FLOOD CONTROL. SUGGESTS MORE DETAILED, COORDINATED, AND COM-
PREHENSIVE PLANNING, EITHER ON THE CABINET LEVEL OR ON AN
AUTONOMOUS PROJECT LEVEL, LIKE TVA.

0953 SALISBURY H.E.
"THE WAR IN VIETNAM."
CURRENT, (FEB. 67), 15-20.
REPORTS ON US BOMBING DAMAGE TO CIVILIAN AREAS IN NORTH.
ALSO SAW DIKES BOMBED, EVIDENCE OF EXTENSIVE CIVILIAN CASU-
ALTIES. SOME EVIDENCE SHOWS PILOTS DUMP EXTRA LOADS ON OTHER
THAN SPECIFIED TARGETS, CAUSING CIVILIAN DEATHS, AND ALSO
SHOWS PILOT ERRORS. EFFECTIVENESS OF BOMBING ON SUPPLY ROUTE
HAS BEEN MINIMAL DUE TO ABILITY TO REBUILD VERY QUICKLY AND
EASILY. REPRINTED FROM SEVERAL ISSUES OF NY TIMES.

0954 SALMOND J.A.
THE CIVILIAN CONSERVATION CORPS, 1933-1942.
DURHAM: DUKE U PR, 1967, 240 PP., LC#66-30206.
STUDY OF CENTRAL ORGANIZATION OF CIVILIAN CONSERVATION
CORPS. FOCUSES ON ADMINISTRATIVE OPERATIONS AND FIELD WORK.
NOTES NEED FOR, AND CREATION OF, CCC; SHOWS HOW IT WAS MO-
BILIZED. DESCRIBES ADMINISTRATORS AND DETAILS POLICIES OF
EXPANSION AND PROBLEMS ENCOUNTERED.

0955 SANDERS R.
"NUCLEAR DYNAMITE: A NEW DIMENSION IN FOREIGN POLICY."
ORBIS, 4 (FALL 60), 307-322.
CONTENDS THAT UNDERGROUND TESTS HAVE PROVED UNLIMITED USE
OF ATOMIC ENERGY COULD BE ULTIMATELY UTILIZED FOR PEACEFUL
PURPOSES. CONTROLLED NUCLEAR UNDERGROUND EXPLOSIONS COULD BE
MADE SAFE ENOUGH FOR THEIR APPLICATION TO VARIOUS SCIENTIFIC
PROJECTS. HOPES THAT FURTHER DEVELOPMENT OF NUCLEAR DYNAMITE
WILL DEPEND ON UNIVERSAL AGREEMENT ON TEST BAN TREATY.

0956 SANFORD T.
BUT WHAT ABOUT THE PEOPLE?
NEW YORK: HARPER & ROW, 1966, 172 PP., LC#66-10638.
GOVERNOR OF NORTH CAROLINA DISCUSSES EVENTS IN HIS STATE
IN FIELD OF EDUCATION FROM 1961 TO 1964. PROVIDES REASONS
FOR PREVIOUS FAILURES IN EDUCATION, METHOD OF SETTING GOALS
FOR IMPROVED EDUCATION, STRATEGY FOR GAINING PUBLIC SUPPORT,
AND MEASURES OF INPROVEMENT OR INNOVATION ATTEMPTED. SHOWS
COOPERATION OF POLITICAL AND EDUCATIONAL LEADERS. SUPPORTS
INCREASED STATE RESPONSIBILITY FOR EDUCATION.

0957 SAPARINA Y.
CYBERNETICS WITHIN US.
HOLLYWOOD: WILSHIRE BOOK CO, 1967, 315 PP., LC#66-30621.
EXAMINES CYBERNETICS, SCIENCE OF CONTROL AND
COMMUNICATION. LOOKS AT BIOLOGICAL SELF-REGULATORY SYSTEMS
IN HUMAN BODY AND COMPARES THESE TO ELECTRONIC REGULATORY
SYSTEMS DEVELOPED BY MAN. INVESTIGATES SYSTEM OF HUMAN
THINKING AND DISCUSSES SIMILAR SYSTEMS OF THOUGHT,
LEARNING, AND PERCEPTION IN MACHINES.

0958 SAYLES L.R., STRAUSS G.
THE LOCAL UNION.
NEW YORK: HARPER & ROW, 1953, 269 PP., LC#53-5477.
BOOK STUDIES LOCAL INDUSTRIAL UNIONS, GRIEVANCE PROCED-
URES AND GROUP PRESSURES, THE ROLES OF OFFICERS AND STEW-
ARDS, MEMBERSHIP AND UNION DEMOCRACY AND THUS PRESENTS A
VALUABLE SOURCE FOR STUDENTS OF REPRESENTATION. GRIEVANCE
PROCEDURES, THE DECLINE OF THE STEWARDS' COMMUNICATION
FUNCTION, CROSS-PRESSURES, UNION ELECTIONS, AND UPWARD
COMMUNICATIONS FROM MEMBERS AT UNION MEETINGS ARE DISCUSSED.

0959 SCARROW H.A.
THE HIGHER PUBLIC SERVICE OF THE COMMONWEALTH OF AUSTRALIA.
DURHAM: DUKE U PR, 1957, 180 PP., LC#57-13024.
CASE STUDY OF PUBLIC SERVICE BUREAUCRACY IN AUSTRALIA,
FROM ITS BEGINNINGS AS MACHINERY WAS SET UP THROUGH ITS
GROWTH AND DEVELOPMENT TO PRESENT ORGANIZATION. DISCUSSES
COMPOSITION OF SERVICE AND ITS ROLE IN GOVERNMENTAL
STRUCTURE.

0960 SCHAAF R.W.
DOCUMENTS OF INTERNATIONAL MEETINGS.
WASHINGTON: LIBRARY OF CONGRESS, 1953, 210 PP., LC#59-60030.
ANNOTATED BIBLIOGRAPHY OF DOCUMENTS EMANATING FROM MEET-
INGS OF INTERNATIONAL NONGOVERNMENTAL ORGANIZATIONS DURING
1953. DOCUMENTS INCLUDE OFFICIAL REORDS AND OTHER PUBLICA-
TIONS ISSUED BY THE ORGANIZATIONS IN VARIOUS FIELDS: ECON-
OMIC DEVELOPMENT, INTERNATIONAL RELATIONS, SOCIAL SCIENCE,
HEALTH AND MEDICAL SCIENCE, TRANSPORTATION, AGRICULTURE,
EDUCATION, LABOR, AND OTHERS.

0961 SCHACTER O.
"SCIENTIFIC ADVANCES AND INTERNATIONAL LAWMAKING."
CALIF. LAW REV., 55 (MAY 67), 423-430.
ARGUES THAT GROWTH OF INTERNATIONAL INSTITUTIONS HAS BEEN
CHARACTERISTIC RESPONSE OF GOVERNMENTS AND SCIENTIFIC BOD-
IES TO SCIENTIFIC AND TECHNOLOGICAL ADVANCES. DISCUSSES
TYPES OF INTERNATIONAL ORGANIZATIONS AND POLICY ALTERNATIVES
WHICH ARE ARTICULATED IN LAW. ASSUMES THAT CONSCIOUS LAW-
MAKING MUST BE SOUGHT THROUGH MULTILATERAL TREATIES, AND
STATISTIC RETRIEVAL HAS BECOME CRUCIAL TO POLICY-MAKING.

0962 SCHEINMAN L.
ATOMIC ENERGY POLICY IN FRANCE UNDER THE FOURTH REPUBLIC.
PRINCETON: PRINCETON U PRESS, 1965, 259 PP., LC#65-10839.
ATTEMPTS TO DESCRIBE NATURE AND DEVELOPMENT OF FRENCH
ATOMIC POLICY DURING FOURTH REPUBLIC AND TO DISCOVER PROCESS
BY WHICH THIS POLICY WAS MADE. REVIEWS NATURE OF POLITICS
DURING PERIOD, AND ALSO BACKGROUND, ORGANIZATION, AND
COMPOSITION OF COMMISSARIAT A L'ENERGIE ATOMIQUE.

0963 SCHEINMAN L.
EURATOM* NUCLEAR INTEGRATION IN EUROPE.
NEW YORK: CARNEGIE ENDOWMENT, 1967, 66 PP.
AN ANALYSIS OF EURATOM REVOLVING AROUND FIVE FACTORS* THE
ENERGY CONTEXT, NATIONAL DISPARITIES, NUCLEAR NATIONALISM,
EXECUTIVE LEADERSHIP, AND THE NATURE OF THE BARGAIN IN CON-
TEXT. WHILE EURATOM IS UNLIKELY TO SURVIVE IN ITS PRESENT
FORM, AUTHOR SUGGESTS THAT EUROPEAN CONCERN ABOUT THE TECHNO-
LOGICAL GAP BETWEEN EUROPE AND THE US MIGHT PROVIDE THE IMPE
TUS FOR THE REBIRTH OF A RESTYLED SCIENTIFIC COMMUNITY.

0964 SCHELLING T.C.
"SIGNALS AND FEEDBACK IN THE ARMS DIALOGUE."
BUL. ATOMIC SCIENTISTS, 21 (JAN. 65), 5-10.
SPECULATES THAT INDIRECT MEANS OF COMMUNICATION MAY HAVE
MORE SALIENCY FOR US AND USSR IN ARMS CONTROL AND STRATEGIC
DIALOGUE THAN DIRECT MEANS SYMBOLIZED BY "HOT-LINE" AND GEN-
EVA DEBATES. DEMONSTRATES THAT SERIOUS SPEECHES AND STRATE-
GIC WORKS FOR INTERNAL CONSUMPTION WILL BE "OVERHEARD" AND
LISTENING TO ADVERSARY'S THOUGHTS GAINS "HIS EAR."

0965 SCHERER F.M.
THE WEAPONS ACQUISITION PROCESS: ECONOMIC INCENTIVES.
BOSTON: DIVISION OF RESEARCH, GRADUATE SCHOOL OF BUSINESS.
ADMIN., HARVARD U., 1964, 447 PP., $7.50.
DEALS WITH PROBLEMS OF INTEREST TO THOSE RESPONSIBLE
FOR FORMULATING AND EXECUTING PROCUREMENT POLICIES WITHIN
CONTRACTOR ORGANIZATIONS. EXPLORES QUESTION OF MOTIVATION,
RISK, UNCERTAINTY, AND BUSINESS BEHAVIOR WHICH CONCERN
SOCIAL SCIENTISTS.

0966 SCHILLING W.R.
"THE H-BOMB: HOW TO DECIDE WITHOUT ACTUALLY CHOOSING."
POLIT. SCI. QUART., 76 (MAR. 61) 26-46.
CONTRASTS CONTENT AND FORM OF TRUMAN'S DECISION ON JAN.3,
1945 WITH POLICY DISCUSSION THAT HAD PRECEDED IT. ADVANCES
EXPLANATION FOR CHARACTER OF DECISION AND INDICATES POLIT-
ICAL CONSEQUENCES.

0967 SCHILLING W.R.
"SCIENTISTS, FOREIGN POLICY AND POLITICS."
AMER. POLIT. SCI. REV., 56 (JUNE 62), 287-300.
ASSERTS THE TECHNOLOGICAL ADVANCES OF THE TWENTIETH
CENTURY NECESSITATE A CLOSE RELATIONSHIP BETWEEN SCIENCE AND
GOVERNMENT. CONCLUDES STATESMEN WILL DETERMINE TO WHAT EX-
TENT SCIENCE WILL BE PUT TO FUTURE USE.

0968 SCHILLING W.R., HAMMOND P.Y., SNYDER O.H.
STRATEGY, POLITICS, AND DEFENSE BUDGETS.
NEW YORK: COLUMB. U. PR., 1962.
THREE STUDIES OF THE POLITICAL PROCESS AS IT OPERATED TO
DEFINE NATIONAL SECURITY IN THE CRITICAL PERIOD OF TRANSI-
TION FROM AMERICAN ATOMIC MONOPOLY TO THERMONUCLEAR WEAPONS
BEING ON BOTH SIDES. DEAL IN TURN WITH THE WARNING PHASE OF
1948-49, THE REACTION TO DRAMATIC EVENTS BEGINNING IN 1950,
AND THE RESETTING OF MILITARY POLICY IN THE FIRST YEARS OF
THE EISENHOWER ADMINISTRATION.

0970 SCHMIDT H.
VERTEIDIGUNG ODER VERGELTUNG.
MUNICH: SEEWALD VERLAG, 1961, 290 PP.
A GERMAN CONTRIBUTION TO THE STRATEGIC PROBLEM OF NATO.
BOOK LARGELY LIMITED TO ASPECTS OF MILITARY STRATEGY.
REVIEWS VARIOUS PROBLEMS: KOREA, CUBA, DETERRENCE, SOVIET
STRATEGY, US POLICY AND THE STRATEGIC VACUUM, THE ABILITY OF
NATO TO DEFEND GERMANY, AND THE QUESTION OF STABILITY.

0971 SCHMITT H.A.
THE PATH TO EUROPEAN UNITY.
BATON ROUGE: LOUISIANA ST U PR, 1962, 272 PP., LC#62-18669.
ANALYSIS OF EUROPEAN PLAN FOR UNION FROM POSTWAR DRIVE
OF MARSHALL PLAN TO FORMATION OF COMMON MARKET. STUDIES US
AID AND POLICY REGARDING EUROPEAN UNION AND STRUCTURE AND
OPERATION OF EUROPEAN COAL AND STEEL COMMUNITY'S ECONOMIC
AND POLITICAL EFFECTS TOWARD UNITY.

0972 SCHMITT H.A.
"THE EUROPEAN COMMUNITIES."
CURR. HIST., 45 (NOV. 63), 257-263.
WITHIN COMMON MARKET MEMBERSHIP IS STAGNANT. TOO MANY
OBSTACLES TO POLITICAL UNION. BRIEF SURVEY OF MARSHALL PLAN,
SCHUMAN PLAN, EUROPEAN DEFENSE COMMUNITY, COMMON MARKET AND
ECSC. PRESSURES AND FEARS HAVE RECEDED AND PROSPERITY IS
ORDER OF DAY. IT APPEARS TO AUTHOR THAT EUROPE WILL PROGRESS
TOWARD UNION ONLY UNDER LASH OF DISASTER.

0973 SCHOECK H. ED., WIGGINS J.W. ED.
THE NEW ARGUMENT IN ECONOMICS.
PRINCETON: VAN NOSTRAND, 1963, 264 PP.
ESSAYS PRESENTING VARIOUS VIEWS ON ECONOMIC ISSUES SUCH
AS NEOMERCANTILISM, ECONOMIC ROLE OF STATE, PRIVATE AND
PUBLIC EXPENDITURES, AND TRADE UNIONISM. ALSO DISCUSSES
NATURAL RESOURCES, FOREIGN AID PROGRAM IN BOLIVIA, GROWTH
OF BUREAUCRATIC POWER, AND PUBLIC VS. PRIVATE SECTOR IN
BRITAIN.

0974 SCHOECK H. ED., WIGGINS J.W. ED.
CENTRAL PLANNING AND NEOMERCANTILISM.
PRINCETON: VAN NOSTRAND, 1964, 227 PP.
CRITICAL ANALYSES OF SEVERAL ASPECTS OF PHILOSOPHY,
LIMITS, AND DEVELOPMENT OF CENTRAL OR GOVERNMENT PLANNING.
CONSIDERS CENTRALIZED ALLOCATION OF RESOURCES TO PAY FOR
PLANNED PROGRAMS, AS MEANS TO TOTAL, PERFECT STATE. COVERS
LATIN AMERICA AND ENGLAND AS EXAMPLES OF EXISTING PLANNED
ECONOMIES.

0975 SCHON D.A.
TECHNOLOGY AND CHANGE* THE NEW HERACLITUS.
NEW YORK: DELACORTE PRESS, 1967, 248 PP.
THESIS: TODAY'S LARGE BUSINESS CORPORATIONS, ENTIRE

INDUSTRIES, AND GOVERNMENT AGENCIES, CANNOT LIVE WITHOUT A STREAM OF NEW INVENTIONS AND INNOVATIONS - BUT THEY CANNOT LIVE WITH THEM OR READILY RESPOND TO THEM. BOOK DISCUSSES MATTERS THAT HELP OR HINDER CHANGE, AND OFFERS REMEDIES TO INDUSTRY'S CURRENT RESPONSE TO INNOVATION.

0976 SCHRADER R.
SCIENCE AND POLICY.
NEW YORK: PERGAMON PRESS, 1963, 81 PP., LC#63-11117.
DISCUSSES INTERACTION OF SCIENTIFIC AND POLITICAL AFFAIRS. TREATS IMPACT OF SCIENCE AND TECHNOLOGY ON POLICY PROBLEMS, MILITARY AFFAIRS, ADMINISTRATION, INTERNATIONAL RELATIONS, AND UNDERDEVELOPED WORLD, PROPOSING NEW GOVERN- MENTAL POLICIES.

0977 SCHRAMM W. ED.
"MASS COMMUNICATIONS: A BOOK OF READINGS (2ND ED.)"
URBANA: U OF ILLINOIS PR, 1960.
INTERPRETATION OF MASS COMMUNICATIONS AS BRANCH OF SOCIAL SCIENCES. EMPHASIS ON MASS MEDIA AS ORGANIZATIONS, ON STRUC- TURE AND FUNCTION OF MASS COMMUNICATIONS. NEW RE-EVALUATION OF CONCEPTION OF "THE TWO-STEP" FLOW OF COMMUNICATION. ADDITIONAL STUDIES OF RESPONSIBILITY AND ETHIC OF COMMUN- ICATIONS. ANTHOLOGY CONCLUDED WITH NOTE ON SUGGESTIONS FOR FURTHER READING.

0978 SCHRAMM W.
"MASS MEDIA AND NATIONAL DEVELOPMENT: THE ROLE OF INFORMATION IN DEVELOPING COUNTRIES."
STANFORD: STANFORD U PRESS, 1964.
STUDY CONDUCTED UNDER AUSPICES OF UNESCO DESIGNED TO EXAMINE CONTRIBUTION OF EFFECTIVE COMMUNICATION TO SOCIAL AND EXONOMIC DEVELOPMENT. ANALYZES COMMUNICATIONS RESEARCH AS FACET OF ECONOMIC AND SOCIAL DEVELOPMENT; HOW IT MAY EFFECT SOCIAL CHANGE; DISTRIBUTION OF MASS MEDIA THROUGHOUT WORLD; DEVELOPMENT OF MASS MEDIA. INCLUDES EXTENSIVE NOTES AND LARGE SELECT BIBLIOGRAPHY.

0979 SCHULTZ T.H.
FOOD FOR THE WORLD.
CHICAGO: U. CHI. PR., 1945, 352 PP.
INVESTIGATES THE EFFECT OF POPULATION GROWTH ON FOOD AND THE CONSIDERATION OF NUTRITION WITHIN A FOOD POLICY. DEPICTS POSTWAR TRADE POLICY, ANALYZES MAJOR OBSTACLES IN THE PATH OF INTERNATIONAL COLLABORATION IN FOOD AND AGRICULTURE.

0980 SCHUMACHER B.G.
COMPUTER DYNAMICS IN PUBLIC ADMINISTRATION.
WASHINGTON: SPARTAN BOOKS, 1967, 195 PP., LC#67-17365.
TRACT URGING AUTOMATION OF PUBLIC AGENCIES ON ALL ADMINISTRATIVE LEVELS, DETAILING IMPLEMENTATION OF COMPUTER HARDWARE. EVALUATES COMPUTERS AND DISCUSSES EVOLUTIONARY STAGES OF USE IN PUBLIC SERVICE. ATTEMPTS TO PRESENT AS NEARLY COMPLETE TAXONOMIC STRUCTURE OF SYSTEMS AND THEORIES AS POSSIBLE. GLOSSARY.

0981 SCHURMANN F.
IDEOLOGY AND ORGANIZATION IN COMMUNIST CHINA.
BERKELEY: U OF CALIF PR, 1966, 540 PP., LC#66-15324.
THEORIZES THAT IDEOLOGY AND ORGANIZATION AROSE IN RED CHINA BECAUSE A TRADITIONAL SOCIAL SYSTEM NO LONGER EXISTED TO GIVE UNITY TO SOCIETY. TRACES STRUGGLE IN MAINLAND COUNTRYSIDE AND CITIES TO CREATE AND IMPOSE STRUCTURES OF ORGANIZATION ON THE NATION. STUDIES THE PARTY, GOVERNMENT BUREAUCRACY AND MANAGEMENT, CONCEPTS OF CONTROL, AND ORGANIZATION OF CITIES AND VILLAGES.

0982 SCHWARTZ L.E.
INTERNATIONAL ORGANIZATIONS AND SPACE COOPERATION.
DURHAM: DUKE U PR, 1962, 108 PP.
COLLECTS BASIC DATA ON PUBLIC AND PRIVATE INTERNATIONAL ORGANIZATIONS INVOLVED IN SPACE PROGRAMS. STUDIES ORIGINS, HISTORY, AIMS, STRUCTURE, PAST ACHIEVEMENTS, AND PLANS OF ALL BODIES WITH ROLES IN SPACE COORDINATION, INCLUDING INTERNATIONAL COUNCIL OF SCIENTIFIC UNIONS, INTERNATIONAL GEOPHYSICAL YEAR, COMMITTEE ON SPACE RESEARCH, UN AND ITS COMMITTEES, AND INTERNATIONAL CIVIL AVIATION ORGANIZATION.

0983 SCHWARTZ M.D. ED.
CONFERENCE ON SPACE SCIENCE AND SPACE LAW.
S HACKENSACK: FRED B ROTHMAN CO, 1964, 176 PP.
ARTICLES IN LAW AND SCIENCE ON FUTURE OF MAN IN SPACE, INCLUDING PEACEFUL USES, MILITARY STRATEGY, INTERNATIONAL COOPERATION, SPACE AND NATIONAL ECONOMY, AND LEGAL PROBLEMS.

0984 SCHWEBEL M. ED.
"BEHAVIORAL SCIENCE AND HUMAN SURVIVAL."
NEW YORK: TRIDENT PR, 1965.
ANTHOLOGY OF PAPERS PRESENTED AT AMERICAN ORTHOPSYCHIAT- RIC ASSOCIATION MEETING IN 1963. SAMPLING OF GENERAL PAPERS ON OVER-ALL TOPIC OF SURVIVAL, THOSE SPECIFICALLY THEO- RETICAL, THOSE DRAWING ON EMPIRICAL DATA, AND SELECTION OF PAPERS ON CURRENT REPORTS ON PEACE RESEARCH ACTIVITIES. CONTAINS INDIVIDUAL REFERENCES AND CONCLUDING ANNOTATED BIBLIOGRAPHY OF PUBLISHED LITERATURE ON PEACE.

0985 SCOVILLE W.J.
"GOVERNMENT REGULATION AND GROWTH IN THE FRENCH PAPER INDUS- TRY DURING THE EIGHTEENTH CENTURY."
AMER. ECO. REVIEW, 57 (MAY 67), 283-293.
EXAMINATION OF ECONOMIC HISTORY OF PAPER INDUSTRY. AUTHOR FINDS DIRECT CORRELATION BETWEEN THE INDUSTRY'S EXPANSION AND RELAXATION OF DIRECT GOVERNMENTAL CONTROLS. IN THIS PER- IOD LARGE-SCALE CAPITALISTIC ENTERPRISE BECAME MORE COMMON. EXPLORES CHANGING ROLE OF GOVERNMENT, METHODS IT USED TO RE- LAX CONTROL AND ENCOURAGE INDIVIDUALS, AND AREAS WHERE GOV- ERNMENT CONTROL SHOULD HAVE BEEN RELAXED BUT WASN'T.

0986 SEABERG G.P.
"THE DRUG ABUSE PROBLEMS AND SOME PROPOSALS."
J. CRIM. LAW CRIM. POLICE SCI., 58 (SEPT. 67), 349-375.
DISCUSSES COMMON DRUGS INVOLVED IN DRUG ABUSE AND ASPECTS OF DEPENDENCE, TOLERATION, AND HABITUATION. PRESENTS LAWS RELATING TO DRUG USE AND PROBLEMS OF INTERPRETATION AND ENFORCEMENT. URGES LAWS PROVIDING HUMANE TREATMENT FOR ADDICTS AND PUNISHMENT FOR PROFITEERS. ADVOCATES BETTER AFTER-CARE PROGRAMS, RETRIAL OF DISPENSARY TECHNIQUE, AND REVISION OF LAWS IN ACCORD WITH DIFFERENCES IN DRUGS.

0987 SEARA M.V.
"COSMIC INTERNATIONAL LAW."
DETROIT: WAYNE STATE U PR, 1965.
A GENERAL STUDY OF PROBLEMS IN INTERNATIONAL LAW AND SPACE, MODIFIED FROM SPANISH EDITION. BIBLIOGRAPHY OF ABOUT 400 BOOKS AND PERIODICALS IN ALL MAJOR LANGUAGES, UP TO 1963. ARRANGED BY AREA, INCLUDING GENERAL AND SPECIAL PROBLEMS OF INTERNATIONAL LAW, AIR LAW, OUTER SPACE, AND TECHNICAL WORKS.

0988 SEIDMAN H.
"THE GOVERNMENT CORPORATION IN THE UNITED STATES."
PUBLIC ADMINISTRATION, 37 (SUMMER 59), 103-109.
GOVERNMENT CORPORATIONS IN THE US ARE SET UP TO HELP PRIVATE ENTERPRISE. CONTROL OVER THESE CORPORATIONS IS LESS SPECIFIC THAN IN BRITAIN, BUT CONGRESS AND THE PRESIDENT DO HAVE SUFFICIENT CONTROL.

0989 SHARP G.
"THE NEED OF A FUNCTIONAL SUBSTITUTE FOR WAR."
INTL. RELATIONS, 3 (APR. 67), 187-207.
ATTEMPT TO RE-EXAMINE PROBLEM OF WAR IN CONTEXT OF GEN- ERAL VIOLENT SOCIAL AND POLITICAL CONFLICT. ADVOCATES RESEARCH ON THREE TASKS AS POSSIBLE CONTRIBUTIONS TO ABOLI- ON OF WAR: ESTABLISH VALIDITY OF FUNCTIONAL ANALYSIS OF WAR, EXAMINE NATURE OF SUBSTITUTE TECHNIQUES TO REPLACE VIOLENT CONFLICT, DEVELOP DETAILED SUBSTITUTE FOR WAR TO REPLACE SPECIFIC CONFLICT SITUATIONS.

0990 SHEEHAN D.
"PUBLIC CORPORATIONS AND PUBLIC ACTION."
POLIT. QUART., 35 (JAN.-MAR. 64), 58-68.
PUBLIC CORPORATIONS IN GREAT BRITAIN, DESPITE SOME FAILINGS, HAVE SERVED THE NATIONAL ECONOMY AND THE PUBLIC WELL AS SHOWN BY ECONOMIC GROWTH RATE AND HIGH EMPLOYMENT.

0991 SHUBIK M.
READINGS IN GAME THEORY AND POLITICAL BEHAVIOR.
GARDEN CITY: DOUBLEDAY, 1955, 74 PP., $0.95.
ESSAYS ATTEMPT APPLICATION OF THE MATHEMATICAL TOOL OF GAME THEORY TO SELECTED POLITICAL SITUATIONS AND PROBLEMS. AN ANALYSIS OF SOCIAL BEHAVIOR IN DIFFERENT STRATEGIC SITUA- TIONS IN WHICH COMPETITION AND CONFLICT IMPEL DECISION- MAKING.

0992 SHUBIK M.
"BIBLIOGRAPHY ON SIMULATION, GAMING, ARTIFICIAL INTELLIGENCE AND ALLIED TOPICS."
J. OF THE AMERICAN STAT ASSN., 55 (DEC. 60), 736-751.
UNANNOTATED BIBLIOGRAPHY OF 350 REFERENCES ON THE SUB- JECTS OF SIMULATION, GAMING, MONTE CARLO METHODS, ARTIFICIAL INTELLIGENCE, AND SYSTEMS. LISTS BOOKS, BIBLIOG- RAPHIES, PAPERS, AND ARTICLES SELECTED FROM ENGLISH-LANGUAGE PUBLICATIONS COVERING PERIOD 1943-60; MOST SELECTIONS POSTDATE 1957.

0994 SHUBIK M. ED.
GAME THEORY AND RELATED APPROACHES TO SOCIAL BEHAVIOR: SELECTIONS.
NEW YORK: JOHN WILEY, 1964, 390 PP.
READINGS FOR THE NONMATHEMATICIAN DEALING WITH GAME THEORY IN GENERAL, THE CONCEPT OF POWER, ASPECT OF INTERNA- TIONAL RELATIONS, AND GAMING AND SIMULATIONS.

0995 SHULMAN M.D.
"'EUROPE' VERSUS 'DETENTE'."
FOREIGN AFFAIRS, 45 (APR. 67), 389-402.
HOLDS THAT THERE IS NO CONTRADICTION IN AMERICAN EFFORTS TO STRENGTHEN US-EUROPEAN ALLIANCE WHILE IMPROVING US-USSR RELATIONS. MAINTAINS SOVIET THREAT MORE POLITICAL-ECONOMIC THAN MILITARY, THEREFORE US-EUROPEAN ALLIANCE IS NOW UNITED BY SHARED VALUES AND GOALS RATHER THAN BY MILITARY THREAT FROM SOVIETS. ADVOCATES A LIMITED DETENTE BETWEEN US-USSR

TO SOLVE EUROPEAN PROBLEMS AND AVOID NUCLEAR WAR.

0996 SILBERMAN C.E.
THE MYTHS OF AUTOMATION.
NEW YORK: HARPER & ROW, 1967, 148 PP., LC#66-13927.
ATTEMPTS TO SEPARATE FACTS OF AUTOMATION FROM MYTHS. AR-
GUES THAT AUTOMATION IS NOT A SIGNIFICANT CAUSE OF UNEMPLOY-
MENT; NEW TECHNOLOGY IS EXERTING LESS IMPACT THAN ASSUMED
ON KIND OF WORK MEN DO AND AMOUNT OF EDUCATION AND SKILL
THEY NEED TO DO IT; TECHNOLOGY IS NOT TAKING OVER, NOR IS IT
EFFACING HUMAN WILL.

0997 SILK L.S.
THE RESEARCH REVOLUTION.
NEW YORK: MCGRAW HILL, 1960, 244 PP., LC#60-15866.
SEES HOW TO ACHIEVE SATISFACTORY RATE OF GROWTH AS MAIN
US ECONOMIC PROBLEM TODAY. DESCRIBES INCESSANT TECHNOLOGICAL
INNOVATION THROUGH SCIENTIFIC ADVANCE AS NEW FORCE WHICH
ENABLES OUR ECONOMIC ENGINE TO INCREASE ITS SPEED. MAINTAINS
THAT DEPENDENCE ON PERPETUAL FLOW OF INNOVATION CREATES NEW
PROBLEMS FOR BUSINESS AND GOVERNMENT.

0998 SILVERT K.H.
"AMERICAN ACADEMIC ETHICS AND SOCIAL RESEARCH ABROAD* THE
LESSON OF PROJECT CAMELOT."
BACKGROUND, 9 (NOV. 65), 215-236.
SCATHING CRITICISM OF THE MANAGEMENT OF PROJECT CAMELOT,
ESPECIALLY OF THE QUESTIONABLE ACADEMIC DIPLOMACY AND POOR
COMMUNICATIONS WITH CHILE. SILVERT ARTICULATES GENERAL RULES
AND FUNCTIONS FOR THE SCHOLAR DOING INTERNATIONAL RESEARCH
WHILE UNDER GOVERNMENT EMPLOY. LASTLY, HE COMMENTS ON THE
REASONS BEHIND THE GENERAL INEPTNESS OF THE LATIN AMERICAN
AREA PROGRAMS IN AMERICAN POLITICAL RESEARCH.

0999 SIMMONS L.W., WOLFE H.G.
SOCIAL SCIENCE IN MEDICINE.
NEW YORK: RUSSELL SAGE FDN., 1954, 254 PP., LC#54-9401.
EXAMINATION OF THE INTEGRATION OF MEDICAL ARTS WITH BIO-
LOGICAL AND PHYSICAL SCIENCES. STUDIES THE HISTORICAL BACK-
GROUNDS AND PERSPECTIVES FOR NEW FIELD. ANALYZES THE THOUGHT
THAT LINKS SOCIETY, CULTURE, AND THE INDIVIDUAL. DISCUSSES
THE EFFECTS OF SOCIOCULTURAL SYSTEM AND LINKS BETWEEN STRESS
AND DISEASE. REVIEWS HOSPITAL PRACTICE FROM THIS VIEWPOINT,
AND CONCLUDES THAT A CLOSE, RELATED STUDY IS NEEDED.

1000 SIMON R.
"THE STATE OF PUBLIC RELATIONS SCHOLARLY RESEARCH."
PUBLIC RELATIONS J., 22 (JULY 66), 27-28.
STATISTICS SHOW THAT FOUR TIMES AS MANY DOCTORAL DISSER-
TATIONS ON SUBJECTS RELATING TO PUBLIC RELATIONS HAVE BEEN
WRITTEN IN 1960-64 THAN IN 1950-59 AND ONE-AND-ONE-HALF
TIMES AS MANY MASTERS' THESES. ALTHOUGH GAPS EXIST IN SOME
AREAS, THE LISTS BY SUBJECT MATTER PROVIDE EVIDENCE THAT
PUBLIC RELATIONS AS A SEPARATE FIELD IS GAINING STATURE.

1001 SIMONS H.
"WORLD-WIDE CAPABILITIES FOR PRODUCTION AND CONTROL OF
NUCLEAR WEAPONS."
DAEDALUS, 88 (SUMMER 59), 385-409.
REPORT DEALS WITH SIGNIFICANT PROBLEMS OF NUCLEAR DISSEM-
INATION. DISCUSSES COUNTRY'S REQUIREMENTS, CAPABILITY,
ACCESS TO FISSIONABLE MATERIALS, AND TECHNICAL PROB-
LEMS ARISING FROM THE NUCLEAR REACTOR INSTALLATIONS. OFFERS
SOLUTIONS TO LIMIT ATOMIC ENERGY TO PEACEFUL USES.

1002 SINGER J.D.
"THREAT PERCEPTION AND THE ARMAMENT TENSION DILEMMA."
J. CONFL. RESOLUT., 2 (MAR. 58), 90-105.
EXPOSES RISKS IMPLICIT IN PERPETUATION OF ARMS RACE. DIS-
CRIBES VARIOUS APPROACHES TO DISARMAMENT. CRITICIZES THREE
MAIN APPROACHES FOR AVOIDING ISSUE OF THREAT TO NATIONAL
SECURITY PERCEIVED BY DECISION MAKERS. OFFERS SUGGESTIONS ON
INTERNATIONAL ARMS CONTROL.

1003 SINGER J.D.
DETERRENCE, ARMS CONTROL AND DISARMAMENT: TOWARD A
SYNTHESIS IN NATIONAL SECURITY POLICY.
COLUMBUS: OHIO STATE U. PR., 1962, 279 PP.
THOUGH DETERRENCE, ARMS CONTROL AND DISARMAMENT ARE
VIEWED AS REPRESENTING THREE DIFFERENT SETS OF PROBLEMS,
AUTHOR MAINTAINS THAT THEY MUST BE DEALT WITH IN TERMS OF
A SINGLE CONTEXT. ALL FACETS OF A SINGLE PROBLEM: NATIONAL
SECURITY IN THE NUCLEAR-MISSILE ERA.

1004 SINGER J.D.
"STABLE DETERRENCE AND ITS LIMITS."
WEST. POLIT. QUART., 44 (SEPT. 62), 449-64.
DISCUSSES WAYS FOR STABILIZING BALANCE OF TERROR. ANA-
LYZES LIMITS TO STABILITY. CONSIDERS IT ONLY A WAY-STATION-
TOWARD COMPREHENSIVE DISARMAMENT UNDER SUPERNATURAL CONTROL.

1005 SINGER J.D. ED.
"WEAPONS MANAGEMENT IN WORLD POLITICS: PROCEEDINGS OF
THE INTERNATIONAL ARMS CONTROL SYMPOSIUM, DECEMBER, 1962."
J. CONFL. RESOLUT., 7 (MAR. 63), 185-652/J. ARMS CONTR., 1
(NO.4, 63), 279-746.

SOME 43 ESSAYS AND RESEARCH REPORTS BY MEN SUCH AS
KARL DEUTSCH, QUINCY WRIGHT, HUBERT HUMPHREY. DISCUSSES IN
DETAIL, AMONG OTHER THINGS, HOW TO MANAGE WEAPONS, DISARM
NATIONS, AND NEGOTIATE DISARMAMENT. SEEKS 'PRIMARILY A MIX
OF INNOCENCE AND REALISM, FRESHNESS AND SOPHISTICATION, SO
THAT THE HARD-SOFT DICHOTOMY WOULD BE BLURRED IN A PROBLEM-
ORIENTED--AS OPPOSED TO A POLICY-ORIENTED--CONTEXT.'

1006 SINGER J.D. ED.
HUMAN BEHAVIOR AND INTERNATIONAL POLITICS* CONTRIBUTIONS
FROM THE SOCIAL-PSYCHOLOGICAL SCIENCES.
NEW YORK: RAND MCNALLY & CO, 1965, 466 PP., LC#65-14105.
COLLECTION OF ESSAYS FROM THE BEHAVIORAL SCIENCES CONSID-
ERED RELEVANT TO INTERNATIONAL POLITICS THROUGH ANALOGY.
AUTHOR PROPOSES BERTALANFFY'S GENERAL SYSTEMS THEORY AS AN
INTEGRATING FRAMEWORK FOR THE VARIOUS DISCIPLINES: CONTRIBU-
TIONS ORGANIZED AROUND, THE INTERNATIONAL SYSTEM AS ENVIRON-
MENT, THE NATION-STATE AS PRIMARY ACTOR, POLITICS AS INTER-
ACTION, AND SYSTEM TRANSFORMATION. GOOD BIBLIOGRAPHY.

1007 SINGH B.
"ITALIAN EXPERIENCE IN REGIONAL ECONOMIC DEVELOPMENT AND
LESSONS FOR OTHER COUNTRIES."
ECO. DEV. AND CULTURAL CHANGE, 15 (APR. 67).
AFTER ANALYZING ITALY'S ATTEMPT TO DEVELOP ITS SOUTH TO
BALANCE THE RAPID ECONOMIC EXPANSION OF ITS NORTH, AUTHOR
CONCLUDES THAT EFFICIENCY IN REGIONAL ECONOMIC DEVELOPMENT
WOULD BE MORE EFFECTIVE IF IT IS MORE DISCRIMINATORY, FAVOR-
ING HIGHER YIELDING ZONES IN WHICH COMPLETELY INTERRELATED
PROGRAMS CAN BE DEVELOPED ON ALL LEVELS INSTEAD OF BROAD BUT
LESS DIRECTED PLANNING.

1008 SKINNER B.F.
"FREEDOM AND THE CONTROL OF MEN" (BMR)"
AMER. SCHOLAR, 25 (WINTER 55), 47-65.
STATES THAT "DEMOCRATIC PHILOSOPHY" OF HUMAN BEHAVIOR
WHICH SCIENCE HAS CREATED IS INCREASINGLY IN CONFLICT WITH
APPLICATION OF SCIENCE TO HUMAN AFFAIRS. FEELS THAT UNLESS
WESTERN DEMOCRACY WELCOMES THE SUPPORT OF SCIENCE, THE
STRENGTH OF SCIENCE MAY FALL INTO DESPOTS' HANDS AND
DEMOCRACY MAY BE DEFEATED.

1009 SKOLNIKOFF E.B.
"MAKING FOREIGN POLICY"
CURRENT, (JAN. 67), 27-32.
STRESSES IMPORTANCE OF SCIENCE AND TECHNOLOGY TO FOREIGN
POLICY CONCERNS, ESPECIALLY IN NATIONAL DEFENSE. ADVOCATES
REACTIVATION OF SCIENCE OFFICE AT STATE DEPT TO BE SOURCE OF
CONSTANT RELEVANT INFORMATION. SCIENCE OFFICE FUNCTION IS TO
CORRELATE ACTIVITIES OF VARIOUS AGENCIES AS WELL AS RESEARCH
WORK AND DATA-GATHERING AROUND THE WORLD ABOUT TECHNOLOGICAL
CHANGE.

1010 SKOLNIKOFF E.B.
SCIENCE, TECHNOLOGY, AND AMERICAN FOREIGN POLICY.
CAMBRIDGE: M I T PRESS, 1967, 330 PP., LC#67-15239.
DESCRIBES ROLE OF SCIENCE IN US FOREIGN POL-
ICY. SHOWS HOW UNCERTAINTIES INHERENT IN JUDGMENTS ABOUT
SCIENCE AND TECHNOLOGY ARE AFFECTED BY POLITICAL FACTORS.
QUESTIONS EFFICIENCY OF US DEPARTMENT OF STATE. DISCUSSES
AREAS OF POLICY SUCH AS ARMS CONTROL, SPACE, ATOMIC ENERGY,
BILATERAL RELATIONS, AND INTERNATIONAL ORGANIZATIONS.

1011 SLOAN P.
"FIFTY YEARS OF SOVIET RULE."
QUARTERLY REV., 305 (OCT. 67), 367-378.
DISCUSSES SOVIET PROGRESS SINCE 1917 REVOLUTION. NOTES
BACKWARDNESS AND OPPRESSIVENESS OF TSARIST RULE. BELIEVES
THAT PRESS DOES NOT GIVE ADEQUATE COVERAGE TO GREAT PROGRESS
MADE IN RUSSIA. USSR HAS INDEED INTRODUCED A NEW SOCIAL SYS-
TEM AND CULTURE THAT ARE FIRMLY ESTABLISHED. DESCRIBES
ADVANCES IN LAND AND ECONOMIC REFORM, EDUCATIONAL SYSTEM,
HEALTH, HOUSING, AND PRODUCTION OF CONSUMER GOODS.

1012 SLUCKIN W.
MINDS AND MACHINES (REV. ED.)
BALTIMORE: PENGUIN BOOKS, 1960, 239 PP.
COMPARES FUNCTION AND MECHANICS OF ELECTRONIC COMPUTERS
WITH THOSE OF THE HUMAN BRAIN. DESCRIBES THE NERVOUS SYSTEM
IN DETAIL. THEN DISCUSSES CONTROL AND COMMUNICATION IN
MACHINES AND IN LIVING CREATURES - CYBERNETICS. CONCERNED
WITH THE INFLUENCE THAT THE STUDY OF COMPUTERS HAS HAD
ON MODERN PSYCHOLOGY.

1013 SMITH D.O.
"WHAT IS A WAR DETERRENT."
ORBIS, 7 (SPRING 63), 96-104.
NO 'STABLE DETERRENT' BASED EITHER ON MILITARY PARITY OR
MILITARY SUPERIORITY CAN BE DEVISED. WHEN GERMAN FLEET
BECAME COMPARABLE TO BRITISH 'FIRST LINE OF DEFENSE', THE
INTERNATIONAL SITUATION LAPSED INTO INSTABILITY. HUNGARY
ROSE AGAINST SOVIETS WHO WERE GREATLY SUPERIOR IN MILITARY
STRENGTH. SUGGESTS THAT BEST PROTECTION FOR USA IS TO
RETAIN PREPONDERANCE IN MILITARY WEAPONS.

1014 SMITH E.A.

SOCIAL WELFARE: PRINCIPLES AND CONCEPTS.
NEW YORK: ASSOCIATION PRESS, 1965, 478 PP., LC#65-11095.
WINNER OF THE ASSOCIATION PRESS AWARD, PRESENTS A SYSTEM
OF PRINCIPLES AND CONCEPTS AS TOOLS OF THOUGHT ABOUT THE
ENTIRE FIELD OF SOCIAL WELFARE. PROVIDES A SCHEME TO ANALYZE
SOCIAL WELFARE NEEDS, RESOURCES, AND PROGRAMS, AND TO
UNDERSTAND THE DYNAMICS OF CHANGE IN THE SOCIAL WELFARE
FIELD AS WELL AS IN ASSOCIATED PROFESSIONS, FROM NURSING AND
SOCIAL SCIENCE TO LAW AND THE MINISTRY.

1015 SMITH H.H.
THE CITIZEN'S GUIDE TO PLANNING.
TRENTON: CHANDLER-DAVIS PUBLG, 1961, 104 PP., LC#61-13706.
DISCUSSES NEED FOR URBAN PLANNING AND FUNCTIONS OF PLAN-
NING BOARD. DESCRIBES RELATION OF BOARD TO SCHOOL BOARDS,
ZONING BOARDS, AND URBAN RENEWAL PROGRAMS. INCLUDES
PROBLEMS MET BY PLANNING BOARD SUCH AS LAND SUBDIVISION,
CAPITAL IMPROVEMENTS, AND COMMUNITY RELATIONS.

1016 SMITHIES A.
THE BUDGETARY PROCESS IN THE UNITED STATES.
NEW YORK: MCGRAW HILL, 1955, 486 PP., LC#54-11767.
HOW FEDERAL GOVERNMENT MAKES EXPENDITURE DECISIONS, IN-
CLUDING PARTS PLAYED BY PRESIDENT, CONGRESS, AND DEPARTMENT-
AL BUREAUS. MAKES RECOMMENDATIONS, STARTING WITH IDEA THAT
DECISION-MAKING CAN BE IMPROVED BY CLEAR FORMULATION OF AL-
TERNATIVES. COVERS DEFENSE AND NON-DEFENSE BUDGETS, ECONOMIC
IMPACT OF BUDGET, HISTORY OF BUDGETARY PROCESS, RELATION TO
NATIONAL POLICY, FORMULATION, EXECUTION, REVIEW OF BUDGET.

1017 SMYTH H.D.
ATOMIC ENERGY FOR MILITARY PURPOSES.
PRINCETON: U. PR., 1945, 254 PP.
TECHNICAL AND ADMINISTRATIVE HISTORY OF THE DEVELOPMENT
OF THE ATOMIC BOMB. BASIC PROBLEMS WHICH CONFRONTED THE
SCIENTISTS ARE PRESENTED FOR ENGINEERS AND INFORMED LAYMEN.
PROJECTIONS OF MILITARY AND CIVILIAN POSSIBILITIES OF
NUCLEAR ENERGY ARE SUBMITTED.

1018 SNYDER R.C. ED., BRUCK H. ED., SAPIN B. ED.
FOREIGN POLICY DECISION-MAKING.
NEW YORK: FREE PRESS, 1962, 274 PP.
CONSTRUCT SCHEMA FOR ANALYSIS OF SUBJECT. EMPHASIZE
VARIABLES OF DECISION-MAKING. DEVELOP TESTABLE HYPOTHESIS
BY CONSIDERING CASE STUDIES AND ORGANIZATIONAL STUDIES.

1019 SOCIAL SCIENCE RESEARCH COUN
PUBLIC REACTION TO THE ATOMIC BOMB AND WORLD AFFAIRS.
ITHACA: CORNELL U PRESS, 1947, 310 PP.
RESULTS OF SURVEYS TAKEN BEFORE AND AFTER NAVAL ATOMIC
BOMB PROJECT AT BIKINI, USING BOTH EXTENSIVE SURVEY
TECHNIQUES AND INTENSIVE INTERVIEWS. PRESENTS RELATIONSHIP
BETWEEN OPINIONS AND SOCIAL BACKGROUND AND INTERRELATIONS
OF SELECTED ATTITUDES. FINDS THAT PUBLIC FELT US SHOULD
CONTINUE TO DEVELOP BOMBS AND THAT US COULD CONTROL THEM.

1020 SOHN L.B.
ZONAL DISARMAMENT: VARIATIONS ON A THEME.
BULL. AT. SCI., 18 (SEPT. 62), 4-10.
PROPOSES METHOD OF PROGRESSIVE ZONAL INSPECTION AND
DISARMAMENT THROUGH THREE CATEGORIES: SYSTEMATIC, SELECTIVE,
AND AT RANDOM. CITES POSSIBILITIES OF THEIR APPLICATION.
COMPLEX PROBLEM OF THE LINK BETWEEN DISARMAMENT AND
INSPECTION SHOULD BE DEVELOPED ALONG ZONAL LINKS WHEREIN
FUTURE TOTAL DISARMAMENT MAY BE ACHIEVED.

1021 SOROKIN P.
CONTEMPORARY SOCIOLOGICAL THEORIES.
NEW YORK: HARPER, 1928, 785 PP.
SURVEYS PRINCIPLE SOCIOLOGICAL THEORIES IN ORDER TO
ESTABLISH TO WHAT EXTENT THEY ARE SCIENTIFICALLY VALID.
DESCRIBES VARIOUS INTERPRETATIONS OF THE STRUGGLE FOR EXIST-
ENCE AND THE SOCIOLOGY OF WAR. CONCLUDES WITH ANALYSIS AND
DEFINITION OF SOCIOLOGY.

1022 SOUERS S.W.
"POLICY FORMULATION FOR NATIONAL SECURITY."
AM. POL. SCI. REV., 43 (JUNE 49), 534-543.
OUTLINE OF THE GENESIS OF THE NATIONAL SECURITY COUNCIL
TO SHOW ITS ROLE IN GOVERNMENT ACTIONS. ANALYZES COUNCIL'S
DESIGN, MEMBERSHIP OF COUNCIL, AND WORKINGS OF COUNCIL AS
WELL AS THE COUNCIL'S RELATION TO THE PRESIDENT AND HIS CAB-
INET. CONCLUDES THAT NATIONAL SECURITY COUNCIL IS PROVING
TO BE A VALUABLE MEANS FOR PROTECTING OUR NATIONAL SECURITY
AND SAFEGUARDING INTERNATIONAL PEACE.

1023 SPANIER J.W.
THE TRUMAN-MACARTHUR CONTROVERSY AND THE KOREAN WAR.
CAMBRIDGE: HARVARD U PR, 1959, 311 PP., LC#59-12976.
EXAMINES TRUMAN-MACARTHUR BY ANALYZING BASIC
DECISIONS WHICH AMERICAN POLICY-MAKERS HAD TO MAKE DURING
KOREAN WAR: HOW DIFFERENCES AROSE AND ESCALATED SO THAT TRU-
MAN HAD TO DISMISS MACARTHUR. SECONDLY, ANALYZES PROBLEMS OF
CIVIL-MILITARY RELATIONS DURING A LIMITED WAR. ALSO REVIEWS
THE MACARTHUR HEARINGS.

1024 SPEIER H.
GERMAN REARMAMENT AND ATOMIC WAR: THE VIEWS OF GERMAN
MILITARY AND POLITICAL LEADERS.
EVANSTON: ROW PETERSON, 1957, 272 PP.
DISCLOSES THAT GERMAN MILITARY EXPERTS DO NOT EXPECT ANY
FUTURE USE OF NUCLEAR WEAPONS AND WILL RELY MAINLY ON LARGE
HOME FORCES TO MEET THREAT OF WAR.

1025 SPENCER R.F. ED.
METHOD AND PERSPECTIVE IN ANTHROPOLOGY.
MINNEAPOLIS: U OF MINN PR, 1954, 323 PP., LC#54-8210.
COLLECTION OF 12 ARTICLES IN ETHNOGRAPHY, CULTURAL
ANTHROPOLOGY, LINGUISTICS, ETHNOGEOGRAPHY, AND SOCIOLOGY,
CENTERING AROUND PHILOSOPHY AND METHOD OF ORGANIZING A FIELD
OF STUDY IN THESE AREAS. INCLUDES SAMPLE STUDY EVALUATION,
COMPARATIVE METHODS, VALUE SYSTEMS, AND QUANTITATIVE
TECHNIQUE, ESPECIALLY IN LINGUISTICS. SUMMARY AND CRITICAL
ANALYSIS OF EACH ARTICLE IS INCLUDED.

1026 SPONSLER G.C.
"THE MILITARY ROLE IN SPACE."
BULL. AT. SCI., (JUNE 64), 31-34.
WHILE SKEPTICAL OF THE AGGRESSIVE USES OF SPACE SUCH
AS AN ORBITING BOMB, EMPHASIZES THE IMPORTANCE OF SURVEIL-
LANCE FROM SPACE OF MILITARY DEVELOPMENTS ON LAND, IN THE
SEA, AND IN SPACE ITSELF. PRIORITY IS GIVEN TO DEVELOP-
MENT OF A MANNED ORBITAL LABORATORY.

1027 SPROTT W.J.H.
SCIENCE AND SOCIAL ACTION.
NEW YORK: FREE PRESS OF GLENCOE, 1954, 164 PP.
EXAMINES SOCIOLOGY AS MEANS OF IMPROVING LIFE SITUATION.
GENERALLY DISCUSSES BASIC THEORIES OF SOCIOLOGY DEALING WITH
ASSIMILATION, GROUPS, KNOWLEDGE, AND PERSONALITY.

1028 SPULBER N.
THE STATE AND ECONOMIC DEVELOPMENT IN EASTERN EUROPE.
NEW YORK: RANDOM HOUSE, INC, 1966, 179 PP., LC#66-14883.
EXAMINES ROLE OF STATE IN ECONOMIC DEVELOPMENT OF SOVIET
TYPE OF COUNTRY. STUDIES HISTORY OF STATE WITH RESPECT TO
INDUSTRIALIZATION, CITING THE BALKAN COUNTRIES 1860-1960
IN THEIR CHANGE OF ECONOMIC STRUCTURE - CHANGE ACCOMPANIED
BY EXPANSION OF STATE OWNERSHIP AND ECONOMIC ACTIVITY.
COMPARES CAPITALISM TO STRUCTURED DEVELOPMENT WITH ITS
CONCOMITANT DISCRIMINATION AND SELF-STYLED SUCCESS.

1029 STAAR R.F.
"RETROGRESSION IN POLAND."
CURR. HIST., 48 (MAR. 65), 154-160.
TIGHTENING OF POLICY IN AGRICULTURE, EDUCATION, MILITARY
SECURITY AND ECONOMIC PLANNING INDICATES GOMULKA PUSHING
TOWARDS GREATER CONFORMITY EVEN THOUGH LIBERALIZATION
BEING PERMITTED IN OTHER COMMUNIST REGIMES.

1030 STAHL O.G.
PUBLIC PERSONNEL ADMINISTRATION.
LONDON: HARPER & ROW, 1962, 531 PP., LC#62-19728.
TRACES TREND OF INCREASING PROFESSIONALISM IN GOVERNMENT
AND THE EXPANSION OF THE CIVIL SERVICE. EXAMINES CURRENT
METHODS OF RECRUITMENT AND TRAINING, AND DISCUSSES RECENT
INNOVATIONS IN MANAGEMENT. ALSO DESCRIBES SUCH OCCUPATIONAL
ASPECTS OF PUBLIC WORK AS WAGES, BENEFITS, AND TURNOVER.

1031 STAMP S.
THE SCIENCE OF SOCIAL ADJUSTMENT.
LONDON: MACMILLAN, 1937, 174 PP.
EXAMINES RELATION OF SCIENTIFIC METHOD TO SOCIETY, AND
PROBLEMS ARISING FROM ADVANCES IN TECHNOLOGY. DISCUSSES PO-
TENTIALITIES OF PROPER APPLICATION OF SCIENCE TO HUMAN
PROBLEMS, BUT EMPHASIZES THAT QUALITIES OF FREEDOM AND INDI-
VIDUALISM MUST BE PRESERVED.

1032 STANFORD RESEARCH INSTITUTE
POSSIBLE NONMILITARY SCIENTIFIC DEVELOPMENTS AND THEIR PO-
TENTIAL IMPACT ON FOREIGN POLICY PROBLEMS OF THE UNITED.
STATES.
WASHINGTON: G.P.O., 1959, 100 PP.
THEORIZING THAT INCREASED SCIENTIFIC KNOWLEDGE PRODUCES
INCREASED WORLD TENSION, THE INITIATION OF A DEFINITE NON-
MILITARY SCIENTIFIC RESEARCH PROGRAM IS DESIRABLE. THIS
WOULD COVER USE OF RESEARCH AND DEVELOPMENT IN FIELDS OF FOR
EIGN POLICY, WEATHER CONTROL OR WHEREVER NECESSARY.

1033 STEIN W., ANSCOMBE G.E.M. ET AL.
NUCLEAR WEAPONS: A CATHOLIC RESPONSE.
NEW YORK: SHEED AND WARD, 1961, 151 PP., LC#62-15284.
PRESENTS ROMAN CATHOLIC IDEAS ON NUCLEAR WEAPONS,
EXAMINING MORAL AND SPIRITUAL ISSUES INVOLVED. DISCUSSES
MORAL DISTINCTION BETWEEN KILLING AND MURDER IN WAR, AND
APPLIES THIS ANALYSIS TO PROBLEMS OF NUCLEAR WAR AND
DETERRENCE. REVIEWS TRADITIONAL FORMULATIONS OF THE "JUST
WAR" CONCEPT AND THE CHURCH'S PRESENT APPROACH TO THESE
MATTERS.

1034 STEINER G.A. ED.
THE CREATIVE ORGANIZATION.

CHICAGO: U OF CHICAGO PRESS, 1965, 267 PP., LC#65-17301.
COLLECTION OF ARTICLES ADDRESSES ITSELF TO PROBLEMS ARIS-
ING FROM THE INCREASING NEED FOR, AND EMPHASIS ON, CREATIV-
ITY IN BUSINESS OPERATIONS. DEALS WITH DEFINING, MEASURING,
AND FOSTERING CREATIVITY, AS WELL AS METHODS OF DISCOVERING
CREATIVE INDIVIDUALS IN MANAGEMENT SPHERES.

1035 STERN A.C. ED.
AIR POLLUTION (2 VOLS.)
NY & LONDON: ACADEMIC PRESS, 1962, 1242 PP., LC#61-18293.
A DETAILED ANALYSIS OF THE CAUSE, EFFECT, TRANSPORT,
MEASUREMENT, AND CONTROL OF AIR POLLUTION BY 45 AUTHORS.
INCLUDES CHAPTERS ON THE NATURE OF POLLUTANTS; THEIR
DISPERSAL AND EFFECTS UPON PLANTS, ANIMALS, HUMANS, MATTER,
AND VISIBILITY; AND SAMPLING, ANALYSIS, MEASURING, AND
MONITORING. DISCUSSES PRINCIPAL SOURCES, CONTROL TECHNIQUES,
AND LEGAL REGULATIONS AND THEIR ADMINISTRATION.

1036 STEWART I.
ORGANIZING SCIENTIFIC RESEARCH FOR WAR: ADMINISTRATIVE
HISTORY OF OFFICE OF SCIENTIFIC RESEARCH AND DEVELOPMENT.
BOSTON: LITTLE BROWN, 1948, 360 PP.
DESCRIBES ADMINISTRATIVE FRAMEWORK OF THE ORGANIZATION
THAT DEVELOPED, IMPROVED, AND BROUGHT INTO USE CERTAIN NEW
WEAPONS IN WWII. STUDIES BEGINNINGS AND NATURE OF OFFICE OF
SCIENTIFIC RESEARCH AND DEVELOPMENT. ANALYZES ITS FUNCTION
AS A LIAISON WITH ARMED SERVICES AND ALLIED GOVERNMENTS.
DISCUSSES FISCAL POLICY, SECURITY, LABOR, AND PUBLIC
RELATIONS OF OSRD.

1037 STOESSINGER J.G.
"THE INTERNATIONAL ATOMIC ENERGY AGENCY: THE FIRST PHASE."
INT. ORG., 13 (SUMMER 59), 394-411.
DESCRIBES AGENCY'S POLICY MAKING PROCESS, ADMINISTRATION,
RESEARCH PROBLEMS, COORDINATION WITH OTHER INTERNATIONAL
AGENCIES, AND ITS STRUGGLE TO MAINTAIN PEACE. EXAMINES
RELATIONSHIPS BETWEEN ATOMIC AND NON-ATOMIC NATIONS.
POINTS OUT WEAKNESS OF BILATERAL AGREEMENTS ON MATTERS OF
ATOMIC AID AND FAVORS AGREEMENTS ARRANGED THROUGH THE
AGENCY.

1038 STONE J.J.
CONTAINING THE ARMS RACE* SOME SPECIFIC PROPOSALS.
CAMBRIDGE: M I T PRESS, 1966, 252 PP., LC#66-17757.
BASED ON THE ASSUMPTIONS THAT PUBLIC SOURCES AND THE PRES-
ENT TECHNICAL AND POLITICAL STATE OF MILITARY AFFAIRS ARE
SUFFICIENTLY CANDID AND UNDERSTANDABLE FOR INTELLIGENT PUB-
LIC SPECULATIONS, HUDSON INSTITUTE ANALYST JEREMY STONE
OFFERS SOME SPECIFIC PROPOSALS FOR FUTURE US PLANS FOR ARMS
CONTROL. THESE INCLUDE A FREEZE IN PROCUREMENT OF NEW STRA-
TEGIC WEAPONS, AND RESTRAINT IN MISSILE DEFENSE PROGRAMS.

1039 STONE P.A.
"DECISION TECHNIQUES FOR TOWN DEVELOPMENT."
OPERATIONAL RESEARCH Q., 15 (SEPT. 64), 185-205.
QUANTITATIVE ANALYSIS OF CONSEQUENCES OF TOWN DEVELOPMENT
WITH PURPOSE OF REDUCING MASS OF PROBLEMS TO COMPREHENSIBLE
STATISTICS. DRAWS DISTINCTION BETWEEN COST-BENEFIT ANALYSIS,
COST-BENEFIT CRITERIA AND COSTS-IN-USE CRITERIA. CONTENDS
CONSEQUENCES CAN ONLY BE MEASURED BY TRACING THEIR INCIDENCE
BEYOND EFFECTS ON MARKET AND LOOKING AT THEIR TOTAL SOCIO-
ECONOMIC IMPACT BY EVALUATING THEIR COSTS AND BENEFITS.

1040 STORER N.W.
"SOME SOCIOLOGICAL ASPECTS OF FEDERAL SCIENCE POLICY."
AMER. BEHAVIORAL SCIENTIST, 6 (DEC. 62), 27-30.
ADVOCATES A GOVERNMENT POLICY TO PROTECT INCENTIVE SYSTEM
AND, THEREBY, THE VALUES OF SCIENCE. SUGGESTS DEVELOPMENT OF
SCIENTIFIC ENCLAVES IN WHICH PROFESSIONAL RECOGNITION RE-
TAINS CENTRAL IMPORTANCE, AND CHOICE OF RESEARCH IS GROUNDED
IN SCIENTIFIC INTEREST. ENCOURAGES IDENTIFICATION OF NEW
FIELDS AND NEW MEDIA FOR INTERCOMMUNICATION, AND OTHER
PSYCHOLOGICALLY REWARDING METHODS.

1041 STOVER C.F.
THE GOVERNMENT OF SCIENCE (PAMPHLET)
SANTA BARBARA: CTR DEMO INST, 1962.
FOCUSES ON GOVERNMENTAL INSTITUTIONS LINKING SCIENCE AND
TECHNOLOGY TO POLITICS AND LAW. INQUIRES INTO ADEQUACY OF
EXISTING FORMS AND SUGGESTS ESSENTIAL CHANGES. DISCUSSES
EXPLOITATION OF SCIENCE AND TECHNOLOGY, POLITICS AND
SCIENTIFIC FREEDOM, PROFESSIONAL RESPONSIBILITY, AND
GOVERNMENT CONTRACT SYSTEM. INCLUDES CREATION OF DEPARTMENT
FOR SCIENCE AND TECHNOLOGY IN US GOVERNMENT.

1042 STRAUSS L.L.
MEN AND DECISIONS.
GARDEN CITY: DOUBLEDAY, 1962, 468 PP., LC#62-11304.
RECOLLECTIONS OF FORMER PRIVATE SECRETARY TO PRESIDENT
HOOVER ABOUT IMPORTANT DECISIONS AND THEIR HISTORICAL CIR-
CUMSTANCES. BEGINS WITH HOOVER'S DECISION TO AID HUNGRY AND
HOMELESS IN BELGIUM AND FRANCE, DISCUSSES EVENTS LEADING TO
DROPPING OF ATOM BOMB IN 1945, AND CONCLUDES WITH RUSSIAN-
AMERICAN EFFORTS TO AGREE ON SUPERVISION OF NUCLEAR TESTS.

1043 STREAT R.

"GOVERNMENT CONSULTATION WITH INDUSTRY."
PUBLIC ADMINISTRATION, 37 (SPRING 59), 1-8.
AS A RESULT OF WORLD WAR II, RELATIONS BETWEEN INDUSTRY
AND GOVERNMENT HAVE BECOME CLOSE: THERE IS CONSTANT
CONSULTATION ON ALL TOPICS BETWEEN BUREAUCRATS AND
INDUSTRIALISTS.

1044 STREET D., VINTER R.D., PERROW C.
ORGANIZATION FOR TREATMENT.
NEW YORK: FREE PRESS OF GLENCOE, 1966, 330 PP., LC#66-17696.
COMPARATIVE STUDY OF SIX INSTITUTIONS FOR MALE
DELINQUENTS, DEALING WITH ADMINISTRATIVE STRATEGY, GOALS
AND THEIR EFFECTS ON INMATE SOCIAL SYSTEMS AND REHABILITA-
TION POLICIES. POWER DISTRIBUTION, ORGANIZATION STRUCTURE,
ROLES, CONFLICT, AND PERSPECTIVES AS WELL AS SOCIAL CONTROLS
ARE EXAMINED FROM BOTH INMATE AND STAFF POINT OF VIEW.
CONTAINS VALUABLE BIBLIOGRAPHY AND REFERENCES.

1045 STYCOS J.M.
"POLITICS AND POPULATION CONTROL IN LATIN AMERICA."
WORLD POLITICS, 20 (OCT. 67), 66-82.
STUDIES LATIN AMERICAN ATTITUDES TOWARD POPULATION
CONTROL. SHOWS INFLUENTIAL POLICIES OF CATHOLIC CHURCH,
NATIONAL GOVERNMENTS, AND MARXIST MINORITIES. FORESEES
THAT US SPONSORSHIP TOGETHER WITH HELP FROM UN AND A CHANGE
IN CATHOLIC ATTITUDES WILL EVENTUALLY CREATE A FAVORABLE
ENVIRONMENT FOR INTRODUCTION OF NATIONAL FAMILY-PLANNING
PROGRAMS IN LATIN AMERICA.

1046 SUINN R.M.
"THE DISARMAMENT FANTASY* PSYCHOLOGICAL FACTORS THAT MAY
PRODUCE WARFARE."
J. HUMAN RELATIONS, 15 (1967), 36-42.
REPORTS ON A WAR-GAME EXPERIMENT IN WHICH PSYCHOLOGICAL
FACTORS OF FEAR, MISTRUST, AND COMPETITIVENESS LED THE
PARTICIPANTS TO STOCKPILE COUNTERS (WEAPONS) AND TO "PUSH
THE BUTTON" (START NUCLEAR WAR) DESPITE INTENTIONS OF GOOD
WILL. CONCLUDES THAT SUCH FACTORS MAY MAKE DISARMAMENT SOLU-
TIONS MORE FANTASY THAN PROBABILITY.

1047 SURANYI-UNGER T.
PRIVATE ENTERPRISE AND GOVERNMENTAL PLANNING.
NEW YORK: MCGRAW HILL, 1950, 389 PP.
STARTING WITH A DISCUSSION OF INDIVIDUAL AND GROUP
"WANTS" AND A HIERARCHY OF "WANTS," THEIR SATISFACTION
THROUGH PRIVATE OR SEMI-PUBLIC GROUP, AND PARTIAL COLLECTIVE
PLANNING, AUTHOR ASKS QUESTIONS ABOUT OPTIMAL EXTENT OF
COLLECTIVE PLANNING, STRUCTURAL TRANSFORMATIONS, COORDINA-
TION OF PRIVATE AND PUBLIC PLANNING REPRIVATIZATION OF WEL-
FARE WITH STATISTICAL, ECONOMIC, AND MATHEMATICAL ANALYSIS.

1048 SWIFT R.
"THE UNITED NATIONS AND ITS PUBLIC."
INT. ORGAN., 14 (WINTER 60), 60-91.
CRITICIZES UN TECHNICAL ADVISORY COMMITTEE ON INFORMATION
AND OFFICE OF PUBLIC INFORMATION. PRESENTS A COMMITTEE AP-
PRAISAL OF OPI EFFICIENCY, ITS IMPACT ON WORLD OPINION, ITS
FINANCIAL ARRANGEMENTS.

1049 TAGIL S.
"WEGENER, RAEDER, AND THE GERMAN NAVAL STRATEGY: VIEWPOINTS
ON THE CONDITIONS FOR THE INFLUENCE OF IDEAS."
COOPERATION AND CONFLICT, 2 (1967), 102-111.
REVIEWS THEORIES OF GERMAN HISTORIANS WEGENER AND RAEDER
ON NAVAL STRATEGY BETWEEN TWO WARS. AIMS TO USE THIS AS
EXAMPLE OF TYPES OF CONDITIONS NECESSARY FOR HISTORIAN TO
DEAL WITH PROBLEMS OF INFLUENCE OF IDEAS. POINTS OUT THAT
BOTH HISTORIANS HAVE SIMILAR IDEAS, AND WROTE AT SAME TIME.
TO MEASURE THEIR INFLUENCE, STUDIED PEOPLE THEY CONTACTED.
FOUND THEY HAD MANY SIMILAR EXPERIENCES.

1051 TANNENBAUM P.H.
"COMMUNICATION OF SCIENCE INFORMATION."
SCIENCE, 140 (MAY 63), 579-583.
SURVEYS RESEARCH ON INADEQUACIES OF PRESS REPORTAGE OF
SCIENCE IN RELATION TO EDITORIAL AND ENTERTAINING FUNCTIONS
CONCLUDES THAT MASS-MEDIA CAN NEVER BECOME RELIABLE
DISSEMINATORS OF SCIENCE INFORMATION.

1052 TARKOWSKI Z.M., TURNBULL A.V.
"SCIENTISTS VERSUS ADMINISTRATORS: AN APPROACH TOWARD
ACHIEVING GREATER UNDERSTANDING."
PUBLIC ADMINISTRATION, 37 (SUMMER 59), 213-259.
IN BRITISH GOVERNMENT, SCIENTISTS TEND TO PURSUE OWN
GOALS WHILE ADMINISTRATORS ARE MORE LOYAL TO THEIR
ORGANIZATION AND MORE RESPONSIVE TO PARLIAMENT: THERE IS
MUCH FRICTION BETWEEN THE TWO GROUPS. ARTICLE SUGGESTS
WAYS OF IMPROVING COMMUNICATIONS BETWEEN THE TWO GROUPS.

1053 TASHJEAN J.E.
"RESEARCH ON ARMS CONTROL."
AMER. BEHAV. SCI., 6 (JAN. 63) 15-17.
AN ANALYSIS OF SOME OF THE TERMS OF WAR AND PEACE LEADS
TO THE SUGGESTION THAT BOTH THE USA AND USSR ARE TOO TECH-
NOCRATIC TO KNOW HOW TO SUBJECT ARMS PROBLEMS TO POLICY
SCIENCE AND POLITICAL WISDOM.

1054 TAUBENFELD H.J.
"OUTER SPACE--PAST POLITICS AND FUTURE POLICY."
PROC. AMER. SOC. INT. LAW., 55 (APR. 61), 176-89.
OUTLINES THE INHERENT DANGER OF NUCLEAR POWERS USING
SPACE AS A HIGHWAY FOR DESTRUCTIVE MECHANISMS. SPECULATES
THAT LIMITED CONFLICTS ARISING IN THE FUTURE IN OUTER
SPACE MAY BE EXTENDED. ADVOCATES ATTAINMENT OF SPECIFIC REG-
ULATIONS WITHIN LEGISLATIVE AND ENFORCEMENT FRAMEWORK OF
AN INTERNATIONAL COSMIC SURVEILLANCE AUTHORITY.

1055 TAUBENFELD H.J.
"A TREATY FOR ANTARCTICA."
INT. COUNCIL., 531 (JAN. 61), 243-322.
APPRAISES SPECIAL FACTORS WHICH MADE POSSIBLE THE 1957
TWELVE-NATION AGREEMENT ON SCIENTIFIC RESEARCH. CONSIDERS
ITS POTENTIAL RELEVANCE TO POLITICAL ISSUES.

1056 TAUBENFELD H.J.
"A REGIME FOR OUTER SPACE."
NORTHWEST. U. LAW REV., 56 (MAR.-APR. 61), 129-67.
EXPLORES LEGAL CONCEPTS WHICH COULD GOVERN OUTER SPACE
TO PREVENT IT FROM BECOMING A SOURCE OF OR THEATER FOR CON-
FLICT. DISCUSSES INADEQUACY OF SEA AIR ANALOGIES, SCIENTIFIC
DELINEATION, AND GEOCENTRIC POLITICS. PROPOSES A NEW AP-
PROACH, RECOGNIZING THAT PROBLEM CANNOT BE COMPLETELY SOLVED
AS IT IS A PROJECTION OF COLD WAR.

1057 TAUBENFELD H.J. ED.
SPACE AND SOCIETY.
NEW YORK: OCEANA PUBLISHING, 1964, 172 PP., LC#64-21185.
PAPERS FROM SEMINAR ON PROBLEMS OF OUTER SPACE SPONSORED
BY CARNEGIE ENDOWMENT FOR INTERNATIONAL PEACE, CONCERNING
IMPACT OF MAN IN SPACE ON MAN'S SOCIETY ON EARTH. COVERS
TOPICS OF LAW, POLITICS, SPACE SCIENCE, VALUES AND GOALS
OF SPACE EXPLORATION, SPACE COMMUNICATION, CLAIMS TO USE
OF SPACE, MILITARY USE, AND FUTURE PROSPECTS OF SPACE
EXPLORATION.

1058 TAYLOR M.G.
"THE ROLE OF THE MEDICAL PROFESSION IN THE FORMULATION AND
EXECUTION OF PUBLIC POLICY" (BMR)"
CAN. J. OF ECO. AND POL. SCI., 26 (FEB. 60), 108-127.
EXAMINES RELATION OF MEDICAL PROFESSION TO CANADIAN
GOVERNMENT. DISCUSSES ROLE OF PROFESSION AS SELF-GOVERNING
GROUP AND ITS RESISTANCE TO OUTSIDE CONTROL. TREATS CANADIAN
MEDICAL ASSOCIATION'S FUNCTION AS INTEREST OR PRESSURE
GROUP IN AREAS OF MEDICAL PRACTICES AND STANDARDS AND
ORGANIZING AND FINANCING OF MEDICAL SERVICES. REVEALS GROUP
INVOLVEMENT IN PUBLIC ADMINISTRATION IN SEVERAL AREAS.

1059 TAYLOR P.S.
"THE RELATION OF RESEARCH TO LEGISLATIVE AND ADMINISTRATIVE
DECISIONS."
J. SOCIAL ISSUES, 3 (FALL 57).
SOCIAL SCIENTISTS CONTRIBUTE TO INTELLIGENT POLITICAL
DECISIONS, BUT MUCH MUST STILL BE DONE TO UNDERSTAND DECI-
SION PROCESS, TO CLARIFY ISSUES, AND TO DEVELOP POLICY
ALTERNATIVES.

1060 TEKINER S.
"SINKIAN AND THE SINO-SOVIET CONFLICT."
INST. FOR STUDY OF USSR, 14 (AUG. 67), 9-16.
ANALYZES BORDER DISPUTE BETWEEN USSR AND CHINA OVER
PROVINCE OF SINKIANG FROM STRATEGIC VIEWPOINT. THIS PROV-
INCE, ONCE OF LITTLE VALUE, NOW HAS IMPORTANCE AS TESTING
GROUND FOR NUCLEAR WEAPONS, ACCESS TO INDIA, AND ROUTE OF
CHINESE REFUGEES INTO USSR.

1061 TELLER E.
"PLANNING FOR PEACE."
ORBIS, 10 (SUMMER 66), 341-359
PRESENTS VIEWS ON WIDE RANGE OF TOPICS RELATING TO PEACE.
ARGUES THAT SOLUTION TO DANGERS OF NUCLEAR PROLIFERATION
LIES IN DEVELOPING ADEQUATE RETALIATORY FORCE AND CIVIL DE-
FENSE. PUTS DOWN FRENCH CLAIM THAT MILITARY ALLIANCES ARE
ANACHRONISTIC IN NUCLEAR AGE. CONCLUDES THAT "BEST GUARANTEE
OF PEACE IS APPROPRIATE FORCE IN THE HANDS OF THOSE WHO WANT
PEACE."

1062 TELLER E.
OUR NUCLEAR FUTURE.
NEW YORK: CRITERION, 1958, 184 PP.
SIMPLIFIED EXPLANATION OF ASPECTS OF NUCLEAR PHYSICS:
RADIOACTIVITY, NUCLEAR REACTIONS AND EFFECTS. DISCUSSES
ALL-OUT WAR AND LIMITED WAR. CONCLUDES PEACE DEPENDENT ON
EXTENT OF COOPERATION.

1063 TENDLER J.D.
"TECHNOLOGY AND ECONOMIC DEVELOPMENT* THE CASE OF HYDRO VS
THERMAL POWER."
POLIT. SCI. QUART., 80 (JUNE 65), 236-253.
A COMPARISON OF ARGENTINE AND BRAZILIAN EXPERIENCES IN
THE DEVELOPMENT OF PUBLIC POWER FACILITIES OVER THE LAST TWO
DECADES. ADVISES THAT THE DEVELOPMENT OF ELECTRIC CAPACITY
THROUGH HYDRO POWER, WHILE ORIGINALLY MORE EXPENSIVE, IS IN
LONG RUN BETTER FOR THE DEVELOPING COUNTRY BECAUSE IT PRO-

MOTES LOCAL INDUSTRY, SKILLS AND INTEGRATION RATHER THAN
HIGH TECHNOLOGY IMPORTS NECESSITATED BY THERMAL SYSTEMS.

1064 THANT U.
THE UNITED NATIONS' DEVELOPMENT DECADE: PROPOSALS FOR
ACTION.
NEW YORK: UNITED NATIONS, 1962, 125 PP., $1.25.
PROPOSES UN SPONSORED WORLD WIDE PROMOTION OF SOCIAL AND
ECONOMIC GROWTH AMONG MEMBER NATIONS. THE ROLE OF FINANCIAL
AND TECHNOLOGICAL ASSISTANCE ARE DISCUSSED AS KEY FACTORS IN
THE PROGRAM.

1065 THANT U.
TOWARD WORLD PEACE.
NEW YORK: THOMAS YOSELOFF, 1964, 404 PP., LC#64-21343.
COLLECTION OF MAJOR PUBLIC ADDRESSES OF U THANT SINCE
1961. SPEECHES ON PURPOSE OF UN, MIDDLE EAST CRISIS, EDUCA-
TION, SMALL NATIONS AND UN, SCIENCE, ETC.

1066 THAYER F.C. JR.
AIR TRANSPORT POLICY AND NATIONAL SECURITY: A POLITICAL,
ECONOMIC, AND MILITARY ANALYSIS.
CHAPEL HILL: U OF N CAR PR, 1965, 352 PP., LC#65-25600.
HISTORICAL ACCOUNT OF NATURE AND DEVELOPMENT OF
MILITARY AND COMMERCIAL LONG-HAUL AIRLIFT SYSTEMS. DISCUSSES
NATIONAL AND INTERNATIONAL POLICY BEFORE WORLD WAR II TO
PRESENT, AND RELATIONS BETWEEN MILITARY AND PRIVATE USE FROM
ECONOMIC AND DEFENSE VIEWPOINTS. SUGGESTS VARIOUS REVISIONS
TO AIRLINE REGULATORY PROCESS AND REFINEMENTS OF ECONOMIC
THEORY. COMMENTS ON SPECIFIC MILITARY STRATEGIES FOR 1960'S.

1067 THOMAS M.
ATOMIC ENERGY AND CONGRESS.
ANN ARBOR: U. MICH. PR., 1956, 301 PP.
EXAMINES THE ROLE OF CONGRESS IN THE DEVELOPMENT OF
ATOMIC ENERGY SINCE WW 2. DEALS WITH THE GROWTH OF U.S.
ATOMIC PROGRAM WITH EMPHASIS ON THE ROLE OF THE ATOMIC
ENERGY COMMISSION.

1068 THOMPSON K.W.
"NATIONAL SECURITY IN A NUCLEAR AGE."
SOC. RES., 25 (WINTER 58), 439-448.
EXAMINATION OF FALLACIES OF A THERMONUCLEAR BALANCE OF
POWER SYSTEM TO MAINTAIN PEACE. PROPOSES THAT DIPLOMATS TAKE
THE INITIATIVE IN ARRIVING AT NEW AND SANER POLICIES.

1069 THOMPSON V.A.
"HIERARACHY, SPECIALIZATION, AND ORGANIZATIONAL CONFLICT"
(BMR)"
ADMINISTRATIVE SCI. Q., 5 (MAR. 61), 485-521.
STATES THAT COMBINATION IN MODERN BUREAUCRACY OF
TECHNOLOGICAL SPECIALIZATION AND HIERARCHY HAS PRODUCED AN
ORGANIZATIONALLY DETERMINED PATTERN OF CONFLICT, WHICH
ULTIMATELY REFLECTS GROWING GAP BETWEEN AUTHORITY AND
PERCEPTIONS OF TECHNICAL NEEDS. DISCUSSES SPECIFIC CAUSES OF
INTRAORGANIZATIONAL CONFLICT.

1070 THOMPSON V.A.
"ADMINISTRATIVE OBJECTIVES FOR DEVELOPMENT ADMINISTRA-
TION."
ADMIN. SCI. QUART., 9 (JUNE 64), 91-108.
ADMINISTRATIVE PRACTICES AND PRINCIPLES OF THE WEST
HAVE DERIVED FROM PREOCCUPATION WITH CONTROL AND THEREFORE
HAVE LITTLE VALUE FOR DEVELOPMENT ADMINISTRATION IN UNDER-
DEVELOPED COUNTRIES WHERE THE NEED IS FOR AN ADOPTIVE
ADMINISTRATION, ONE THAT CAN INCORPORATE CONSTANT CHANGE.

1071 THOMSON G.P.
NUCLEAR ENERGY IN BRITAIN DURING THE LAST WAR: THE CHERWELL
SIMON LECTURE (MONOGRAPH)
LONDON: CLARENDON PRESS, 1962, 16 PP.
DISCUSSES INTERNATIONAL SCIENTIFIC RESEARCH IN ATOMIC
THEORY IN US AND EUROPE THAT LED TO THE UK'S PROJECT MAUD
(MILITARY APPLICATIONS OF URANIUM DETONATION) IN 1940.
EXPLAINS PROBLEM OF ISOTOPE SEPARATION WHICH FINALLY LED TO
CREATION OF INSTRUMENT CAPABLE OF RELEASING LARGE AMOUNTS
OF RADIOACTIVE SUBSTANCE. TELLS OF COLLABORATION WITH US AND
CONTRIBUTIONS OF PARTICIPATING SCIENTISTS.

1072 THORELLI H.B., GRAVES R.L., HOWELLS L.T.
"THE INTERNATIONAL OPERATIONS SIMULATION AT THE UNIVER-
SITY OF CHICAGO."
J. BUS., 35 (JULY 62), 287-97.
A GENERAL DESCRIPTION OF INTERNATIONAL OPERATIONS SIMU-
LATION (INTOP), THE FIRST MAJOR BUSINESS SIMULATION EXER-
CISE ORIENTED TOWARD SPECIFIC PROBLEMS OF INTERNATIONAL
TRADE AND OVERSEAS OPERATIONS.

1073 THORELLI H.B., GRAVES R.L., HOWELLS L.T.
INTOP: INTERNATIONAL OPERATIONS SIMULATION: PLAYER'S MANUAL.
NEW YORK: FREE PRESS OF GLENCOE, 1963, 58 PP., LC#63-13249.
PLAYER'S MANUAL FOR ONE OF THE FIRST MAJOR BUSINESS
SIMULATION EXERCISES ORIENTED TOWARD SPECIFIC PROBLEM OF
INTERNATIONAL AND OVERSEAS OPERATIONS; DESIGNED TO INCREASE
UNDERSTANDING OF PROBLEMS OF MULTINATIONAL CORPORATIONS AND
TO YIELD SUBSTANTIAL PAYOFF IN GENERAL MANAGEMENT TRAINING.

1074 TIVEY L.
"THE POLITICAL CONSEQUENCES OF ECONOMIC PLANNING."
PARLIAMENTARY AFFAIRS, 20 (FALL 67), 297-314.
    BELIEVES THAT POLITICAL VALUES IN ECONOMIC PLANNING HAVE
BEEN NEGLECTED. MAIN PROBLEM LIES WITH FACT THAT GOVERNMENT
HAS NEITHER CONTROL NOR PREROGATIVE OVER THE PRIME AGENTS OF
PRODUCTION. INTEREST GROUPS PLAY TOO GREAT A ROLE IN PLAN-
NING. BELIEVES THAT PRIMACY OF TRADITIONAL POLITICAL PROCESS
MUST BE MAINTAINED, AND THAT FINAL AUTHORITY ON ECONOMIC
PLANNING MATTERS MUST REST WITH GOVERNMENT.

1075 TOMKINS S.S. ED., MESSICK S. ED.
COMPUTER SIMULATION OF PERSONALITY.
NEW YORK: JOHN WILEY, 1963, 317 PP., LC#62-22072.
    SELECTION OF ESSAYS ON COMPUTER SIMULATION AND PERSONALI-
TY DESIGNED TO SERVE AS INTRODUCTION TO FIELD. PROVIDES
A SURVEY OF WHAT HAS BEEN ACCOMPLISHED IN COMPUTER SIMULA-
TION. DISCUSSION OF GENERAL PROBLEMS, COMPUTER SIMULATION,
PSYCHOANALYTIC THEORY, AND APPLICATIONS IN STUDY OF
COGNITION AND EFFECT.

1076 TOMPKINS D.C.
CIVIL DEFENSE IN THE STATES: A BIBLIOGRAPHY (DEFENSE
BIBLIOGRAPHIES NO. 3: PAMPHLET)
BERKELEY: U CALIF, BUR PUB ADMIN, 1953, 56 PP., LC#53-62488.
    LISTING OF CURRENT LITERATURE AND BACKGROUND OF DOMESTIC
ASPECTS OF NATIONAL DEFENSE AND WAR ADMINISTRATION. CONTAINS
MATERIAL ON FEDERAL CIVIL DEFENSE ADMINISTRATION: STATE
CIVIL DEFENSE PROGRAMS AND LEGISLATION: MUTUAL AID: WORK-
MAN'S COMPENSATION FOR VOLUNTEERS. INCLUDES SELECTED
BIBLIOGRAPHY ON STATE CIVIL DEFENSE.

1077 TOMPKINS D.C.
STATE GOVERNMENT AND ADMINISTRATION: A BIBLIOGRAPHY.
BERKELEY: U CALIF, BUR PUB ADMIN, 1954, 269 PP.
    GUIDE TO PRIMARY SOURCES OF IMFORMATION WHICH ARE BASIC
TO A STUDY OF STATE GOVERNMENT AND ADMINISTRATION. DRAWS
ON MATERIALS ISSUED SINCE 1930. ANNOTATIONS CLARIFY
OBSCURE TITLES OR INDICATE CONTENT. CONTAINS AUTHOR AND
SUBJECT INDEX. SECOND PART OF VOLUME IS DEVOTED TO LEGIS-
LATIVE PROCESS, WITH PARTICULAR REFERENCE TO ORGANIZATION
AND PROCEDURE OF LEGISLATIVE AND JUDICIAL ADMINISTRATION.

1078 TRAVERS H. JR.
"AN EXAMINATION OF THE CAB'S MERGER POLICY."
U. KANSAS LAW J., 15 (MAR. 67), 227-263.
    EXAMINES 3 RECENT CASES TO DETERMINE CAB'S POLICY AND
STANDARDS FOR DECISION REGARDING AIRLINE MERGERS. DISCUSSES
POLICY PRIOR TO 1938, CIVIL AERONAUTICS ACT, ECONOMIC DETER-
MINANTS OF POLICY, STRUCTURE OF AIRLINES INDUSTRY, COMPETI-
TION, IMPACT OF MERGERS, AND ANTI-MONOPOLY PROVISO. AUTHOR
PRESENTS IDEAS FOR REFORM.

1079 TRUMAN D.B.
"SELECTED CRITICAL BIBLIOGRAPHY ON THE METHODS AND TECH-
NIQUES OF POLITICAL BEHAVIOR RESEARCH."
AM. POL. SCI. REV., 46 (DEC. 52), 1033-1045.
    ANNOTATED BIBLIOGRAPHY ON METHODS AND TECHNIQUES OF PO-
LITICAL BEHAVIOR RESEARCH. ITEMS GROUPED UNDER EIGHT HEAD-
INGS: SCIENTIFIC METHOD IN POLITICAL RESEARCH, DOCUMENTARY
ANALYSIS, PARTICIPANT OBSERVATION, INTERVIEW TECHNIQUES,
EXPERIMENTS, INSTITUTIONAL AND COMMUNITY RESEARCH, INTER-
PRETATION AND ANALYSIS, HANDBOOKS ON SOCIAL SCIENCE RE-
SEARCH. 147 ENTRIES. 20TH CENTURY, ENGLISH-LANGUAGE SOURCES.

1080 TRYTTEN M.H.
"THE MOBILIZATION OF SCIENTISTS," IN L. WHITE, CIVIL SERVICE
IN WARTIME."
CHICAGO: U OF CHICAGO PRESS, 1945.
    STUDIES PROCESS BY WHICH AMERICAN SCIENTISTS ARE
MOBILIZED FOR THEIR PART IN WAR. DESCRIBES EMERGENCE IN
WWII OF A NEW CIVILIAN SCIENTIFIC ORGANIZATION TO
SUPPLEMENT ACTIVITIES OF SERVICE LABORATORIES. ANALYZES
PERSONALITIES AND ROLE OF OFFICE OF SCIENTIFIC RESEARCH AND
DEVELOPMENT.

1081 TURKEVICH J.
"SOVIET SCIENCE APPRAISED."
FOREIGN AFFAIRS, 44 (APR. 66), 489-500.
    COMPARISON OF STRENGTHS AND WEAKNESSES, ACHIEVEMENTS AND
FAILURES OF AMERICAN AND SOVIET SCIENTIFIC ESTABLISHMENTS.
DISCUSSES GENERAL MILITARY, PROPAGANDA, AND PEACEFUL EFFECTS
OF SCIENTIFIC DISCOVERIES, THEN GIVES SCIENCE-BY-SCIENCE
BREAKDOWN.

1082 TURNER A.N., LAWRENCE P.R.
INDUSTRIAL JOBS AND THE WORKER.
CAMBRIDGE: HARVARD U. DIV OF RES, 1965, 177 PP., LC#64-07523
    STUDIES RESPONSE OF WORKERS TO TECHNOLOGICAL DEVELOPMENTS
IN INDUSTRY. CONSIDERS TASK ATTRIBUTES AND JOB SATISFACTION,
EFFECT OF TOWN AND CITY SUBCULTURES, AND TASK ATTRIBUTES AND
ATTENDANCE.

1083 TURNER R.H.
"THE NAVY DISBURSING OFFICER AS A BUREAUCRAT" (BMR)"
AMER. SOCIOLOGICAL REV., 12 (JUNE 47), 342-348.

DESCRIBES SOCIOLOGICALLY RELEVANT INFLUENCES THAT BEAR
ON ONE BUREAUCRAT: THE NAVY DISBURSING OFFICER.
STATES THAT DURING WWII, CERTAIN INFLUENCES DIVERTED HIM
FROM FUNCTIONING AS AN IDEAL, TYPICAL BUREAUCRAT. HE
BEGAN TO FUNCTION IN A PERSONAL WAY, RELEGATING SYSTEMATIC,
BUREAUCRATIC RULES TO A SECONDARY ROLE.

1084 TYBOUT R.A.
ECONOMICS OF RESEARCH AND DEVELOPMENT.
COLUMBUS: OHIO STATE U PR, 1965, 458 PP., LC#65-18734.
    TOPICS INCLUDE6 HISTORY OF SCIENCE, INDUSTRIAL R&D,
INTERNATIONAL ORGANIZATION, PUBLIC POLICY, MILITARY R&D,
INTERNATIONAL COLLABORATION, AND THE EMERGENT NATIONS.
RESULTS OF A CONFERENCE. INCLUDES COMMENTS ON PAPERS.

1085 U OF MICHIGAN LAW SCHOOL
ATOMS AND THE LAW.
ANN ARBOR: U OF MICH LAW SCHOOL, 1959, 1512 PP.
    CONCERNS LEGAL PROBLEMS INVOLVED IN PEACEFUL USES OF
ATOMIC ENERGY. CONCENTRATES ON TORT LIABILITY FOR RADIATION
INJURIES, WORKMEN'S COMPENSATION, FEDERAL STATUTORY AND
ADMINISTRATIVE PROVISIONS REGULATING ATOMIC ACTIVITIES, AND
STATE REGULATION OF ATOMIC ENERGY. INCLUDES ESSAYS ON
INTERNATIONAL ASPECTS OF THE SUBJECT.

1086 UN
SPACE ACTIVITIES AND RESOURCES: REVIEW OF UNITED NATION'S
NATIONAL AND INTERNATIONAL PROGRAMS.
NEW YORK: UNITED NATIONS, 1965, 172 PP.
    OVER-ALL VIEW OF DEVELOPMENTS IN USE OF SPACE FOR PEACE
AND BENEFIT OF MAN. COVERS ACTIVITIES OF SPECIAL AGENCIES
AND INTERNATIONAL GROUPS AIDING UN. GIVES BREAKDOWN OF SPACE
ACTIVITIES IN 37 SEPARATE NATIONS. EXPLANATIONS AND EVALUA-
TIONS BY SECRETARY-GENERAL.

1087 UN HEADQUARTERS LIBRARY
BIBLIOGRAPHY OF INDUSTRIALIZATION IN UNDERDEVELOPED
COUNTRIES (BIBLIOGRAPHICAL SERIES NO. 6)
NEW YORK: UNITED NATIONS, 1956, 216 PP.
    LISTS PUBLICATIONS OF UN AND SPECIALIZED AGENCIES ON
SUBJECT OF INDUSTRIALIZATION AND INFORMATION ON PERTINENT
RESEARCH PROJECTS BEING CARRIED OUT BY GOVERNMENTS, UNIVER-
SITIES, AND SCIENTIFIC INSTITUTIONS. RECORDS ALSO RELEVANT
PUBLICATIONS AND UNPUBLISHED RESEARCH. ITEMS ARRANGED BY
GEOGRAPHY. WRITTEN IN SPANISH, ENGLISH, AND FRENCH. ITEMS
IN ALL RELEVANT LANGUAGES, INCLUDING ORIENTAL.

1088 UN INTL CONF ON PEACEFUL USE
PROGRESS IN ATOMIC ENERGY (VOL. I)
GENEVA: UN INTL CONF PEACEFUL ATOM, 1958, 525 PP.
    PAPERS PRESENTED AT SECOND UN INTERNATIONAL CONFERENCE ON
PEACEFUL USES OF ATOMIC ENERGY. TREATS FUTURE OF NUCLEAR
POWER DEVELOPMENTS AND PROGRAMS ALL OVER WORLD. DISCUSSES
SUPPLY AND TRAINING OF TECHNICAL PERSONNEL. EXAMINES
DEVELOPMENT OF INTERNATIONAL COLLABORATION IN RESEARCH,
FOUNDATION OF NUCLEAR CENTER IN BAGHDAD, AND INTERNATIONAL
ASPECTS OF CONTAMINATION.

1089 UN SECRETARY GENERAL
PLANNING FOR ECONOMIC DEVELOPMENT.
NEW YORK: UNITED NATIONS, 1963, 156 PP.
    REPORTS ON ECONOMIC PLANNING AND TECHNIQUES USED IN
SEVERAL COUNTRIES. EXAMINES ORGANIZATION AND MANAGEMENT OF
PLANS, AS WELL AS NATIONAL AND INTERNATIONAL POLICIES.

1090 UNESCO
HANDBOOK OF INTERNATIONAL EXCHANGES.
PARIS: UNESCO, 1965.
    REFERENCE SUPPLIES INFORMATION ON AIMS, PROGRAMS, AND
ACTIVITIES OF NATIONAL AND INTERNATIONAL ORGANIZATIONS:
AND ON INTERNATIONAL AGREEMENTS CONCERNING INTERNATIONAL
RELATIONS AND EXCHANGES IN THE FIELDS OF EDUCATION,
SCIENCE, CULTURE, AND MASS COMMUNICATION. CONTAINS DATA ON
THE ACTIVITIES OF 272 INTERNATIONAL AND 5,000 GOVERNMENTAL
AGENCIES: LISTS 4,200 AGREEMENTS.

1091 UNESCO
PRINCIPLES AND PROBLEMS OF NATIONAL SCIENCE POLICIES.
NEW YORK: UNITED NATIONS, 1967, 99 PP.
    REPORT OF MEETING OF COORDINATORS OF SCIENCE POLICY
STUDIES OF UN. TWELVE NATIONS STATED THEIR GOVERNMENTS'
POLICIES, PLANS FOR SCIENTIFIC RESEARCH, AND PROBLEMS. AIM
IS TO DEFINE COMMON FEATURES OF SCIENTIFIC POLICY AND
DETERMINE DATA NEEDED TO PREPARE SCIENTIFIC POLICIES FOR
NATIONS AT DIFFERENT DEVELOPING STAGES.

1092 UNITED NATIONS
OFFICIAL RECORDS OF THE UNITED NATIONS' ATOMIC ENERGY
COMMISSION - DISARMAMENT COMMISSION.
NEW YORK: UNITED NATIONS.
    OFFICIAL RECORDS OF THE UN ATOMIC ENERGY COMMISSION
DISARMAMENT COMMISSION. CONSIST OF VERBATIM RECORDS OF ALL
PLENARY MEETINGS, ANNEXED ESSENTIAL DOCUMENTS, AND SPECIAL
SUPPLEMENTS COMPRISING THE REPORT TO THE SECURITY COUNCIL.
PUBLISHED ANNUALLY.

1093 UNITED NATIONS
INTERNATIONAL SPACE BIBLIOGRAPHY.
NEW YORK: UNITED NATIONS, 1966, 166 PP.
LISTS ABOUT 3,000 BOOKS, REPORTS, BULLETINS, GOVERNMENT
DOCUMENTS, AND PERIODICALS PUBLISHED IN 1960'S IN 34 MAJOR
COUNTRIES OF THE WORLD. PREPARED TO ASSIST COMMITTEE ON
PEACEFUL PURPOSES OF OUTER SPACE. ENTRIES ARRANGED BY TYPE
OF MATERIAL UNDER COUNTRY; SUBDIVIDED BY SUBJECT.

1094 UNIVERSAL REFERENCE SYSTEM
LEGISLATIVE PROCESS, REPRESENTATION, AND DECISION-MAKING
(VOLUME II)
PRINCETON* UNIV. REF. SYSTEM, 1967, 1200 PP.
COMPUTERIZED INFORMATION RETRIEVAL SYSTEM FOR THE SOCIAL
AND BEHAVIORAL SCIENCES. ANNOTATED AND EXTENSIVELY INDEXED,
UTILIZING "TOPICAL-METHODOLOGICAL INDEX" DEVELOPED BY PRO-
FESSOR ALFRED DE GRAZIA. APPROXIMATELY 3,000 CITATIONS FROM
SCHOLARLY JOURNALS, BOOKS, GOVERNMENT DOCUMENTS IN ENGLISH
AND EUROPEAN LANGUAGES. INCLUDES CLASSICAL SOURCES THROUGH
1967. PUBLISHED JAN., 1968, WITH QUARTERLY GAZETTES.

1095 UNIVERSAL REFERENCE SYSTEM
BIBLIOGRAPHY OF BIBLIOGRAPHIES IN POLITICAL SCIENCE, GOVERN-
MENT, AND PUBLIC POLICY (VOLUME III)
PRINCETON* UNIV. REF. SYSTEM, 1967, 1200 PP.
COMPUTERIZED INFORMATION RETRIEVAL SYSTEM FOR THE SOCIAL
AND BEHAVIORAL SCIENCES. ANNOTATED AND EXTENSIVELY INDEXED,
UTILIZING "TOPICAL-METHODOLOGICAL INDEX" DEVELOPED BY PRO-
FESSOR ALFRED DE GRAZIA. APPROXIMATELY 3,000 CITATIONS FROM
SCHOLARLY JOURNALS, BOOKS, GOVERNMENT DOCUMENTS IN ENGLISH
AND EUROPEAN LANGUAGES. INCLUDES CLASSICAL SOURCES THROUGH
1967. TO BE PUBLISHED EARLY 1968 WITH QUARTERLY GAZETTES.

1096 UNIVERSAL REFERENCE SYSTEM
ADMINISTRATIVE MANAGEMENT: PUBLIC AND PRIVATE BUREAUCRACY
(VOLUME IV)
PRINCETON* UNIV. REF. SYSTEM, 1967, 1200 PP.
COMPUTERIZED INFORMATION RETRIEVAL SYSTEM. ANNOTATED AND
EXTENSIVELY INDEXED, UTILIZING "TOPICAL-METHODOLOGICAL IN-
DEX" DEVELOPED BY PROFESSOR ALFRED DE GRAZIA. APPROXIMATELY
3,000 CITATIONS FROM BOOKS, GOVERNMENT PUBLICATIONS, AND
JOURNALS. ENGLISH AND EUROPEAN LANGUAGES. MATERIALS SELECT-
ED FROM CLASSICAL SOURCES THROUGH 1967. TO BE PUBLISHED
EARLY 1968, WITH SUBSEQUENT QUARTERLY GAZETTES.

1097 UNIVERSAL REFERENCE SYSTEM
CURRENT EVENTS AND PROBLEMS OF MODERN SOCIETY (VOLUME V)
PRINCETON* UNIV. REF. SYSTEM, 1967, 1200 PP.
TREATS BOOKS, ARTICLES, REPORTS, AND GOVERNMENT DOCUMENTS
CONCERNED WITH SOCIAL, POLITICAL, EDUCATIONAL, AND ECONOMIC
CONTROVERSIES OF THE PRESENT PERIOD. MAJORITY OF ITEMS ARE
PUBLICATIONS OF THE 1960'S, AND ARE IN ENGLISH AND EUROPEAN
LANGUAGES. ABOUT 3000 ITEMS CITED. TO BE PUBLISHED EARLY
1968. QUARTERLY GAZETTES BEGAN AUG., 1967. COMPUTERIZED
INFORMATION RETRIEVAL SYSTEM.

1098 UNIVERSAL REFERENCE SYSTEM
PUBLIC OPINION, MASS BEHAVIOR, AND POLITICAL PSYCHOLOGY
(VOLUME VI)
PRINCETON* UNIV. REF. SYSTEM, 1967, 1200 PP.
COMPUTERIZED INFORMATION RETRIEVAL SYSTEM. ANNOTATED AND
EXTENSIVELY INDEXED, UTILIZING "TOPICAL-METHODOLOGICAL IN-
DEX" DEVELOPED BY PROFESSOR ALFRED DE GRAZIA. APPROXIMATELY
3,000 CITATIONS FROM BOOKS, JOURNALS, AND GOVERNMENT DOCU-
MENTS IN ENGLISH AND EUROPEAN LANGUAGES. TO BE PUBLISHED
EARLY 1968. QUARTERLY GAZETTES BEGAN JUNE, 1967.
CLASSIC SOURCES UP THROUGH 1967 MATERIALS.

1099 UNIVERSAL REFERENCE SYSTEM
ECONOMIC REGULATION, BUSINESS, AND GOVERNMENT (VOLUME VIII)
PRINCETON* UNIV. REF. SYSTEM, 1967, 1200 PP.
COMPUTERIZED INFORMATION RETRIEVAL SYSTEM DEALING WITH
VARIOUS FACETS OF INTERNAL GOVERNANCE OF BUSINESS ACTIVITIES
AND THEIR RELATION TO POLITICS. ABOUT 3000 ANNOTATIONS
FROM ALL TYPES OF PUBLICATIONS IN ENGLISH AND EUROPEAN LAN-
GUAGES. SOURCES RANGE FROM CLASSICS WITH EMPHASIS ON MATE-
RIALS OF 1960'S. TO BE PUBLISHED EARLY 1968. QUARTERLY
GAZETTES BEGAN AUG., 1967.

1100 UNIVERSAL REFERENCE SYSTEM
PUBLIC POLICY AND THE MANAGEMENT OF SCIENCE (VOLUME IX)
PRINCETON* UNIV. REF. SYSTEM, 1967, 1200 PP.
ABOUT 3000 SELECTED BOOKS, ARTICLES, AND DOCUMENTS CON-
CERNED WITH INSTITUTIONAL AND BEHAVIORAL PROCESS OF SCIEN-
TIFIC DECISION-MAKING. MAJORITY OF ITEMS FROM 1960'S; IN-
CLUDES ENGLISH-LANGUAGE AND EUROPEAN SOURCES. USES PROFESSOR
ALFRED DE GRAZIA'S "TOPICAL-METHODOLOGICAL INDEX." TO BE
PUBLISHED EARLY 1968. QUARTERLY GAZETTES BEGAN AUG., 1967.

1101 UNIVERSAL REFERENCE SYSTEM
LAW, JURISPRUDENCE, AND JUDICIAL PROCESS (VOLUME VII)
PRINCETON: UNIVERSAL REF SYSTEM, 1967, 1200 PP.
COMPUTERIZED INFORMATION RETRIEVAL SYSTEM. TREATS SCIENCE
OF STUDY OF LAW AND ITS METHODOLOGY. ANNOTATED AND EXTEN-
SIVELY INDEXED USING PROFESSOR ALFRED DE GRAZIA'S "TOPICAL-
METHODOLOGICAL INDEX." APPROXIMATELY 3,000 CITATIONS FROM

ENGLISH AND EUROPEAN-LANGUAGE BOOKS, JOURNALS, DOCUMENTS
RANGING FROM CLASSICS TO PRESENT. TO BE PUBLISHED EARLY
1968. QUARTERLY GAZETTES BEGAN JUNE, 1967.

1102 UNRUH J.M.
"SCIENTIFIC INPUTS TO LEGISLATIVE DECISION-MAKING
(SUPPLEMENT)"
WESTERN POLIT. QUART., 17 (SEPT. 64), 53-60.
AUTHOR, A CALIFORNIA STATE LEGISLATOR, CRITIS THE FACT
THAT MOST SCIENTISTS AND SCHOLARS DEVOTE THEIR TECHNICAL
QUALITIES AND CREATIVE CAPABILITIES TO THE FEDERAL GOVERN-
MENT AND DO NOT PAY HEED TO THE NEEDS OF STATE GOVERNMENT.
OUTLINES THE UNFORTUNATE CONSEQUENCES, PARTICULARLY IN STATE
LEGISLATURES, AND REPORTS ON STEPS CURRENTLY BEING TAKEN
IN CALIFORNIA TO FOSTER MORE PRODUCTIVE COOPERATION.

1103 US AIR FORCE ACADEMY
"AMERICAN DEFENSE POLICY."
BALTIMORE: JOHNS HOPKINS PRESS, 1965.
ANTHOLOGY OF STUDIES ON PROVISIONS FOR US MILITARY SECUR-
ITY. DEALS WITH PRINCIPAL ISSUES OF STRATEGY AND INSTITU-
TIONS AND PROCESSES THROUGH WHICH STRATEGY IS FORMULATED.
BIBLIOGRAPHICAL ESSAY IS SELECTIVE AND CONSISTS OF PRELIMI-
NARY SURVEYS OF EACH TOPIC, IDENTIFIED BY CHAPTER. STUDIES
NOT CONFINED TO ANALYSIS OF US POLICY BUT INCLUDE EXAMINA-
TIONS OF COMMUNIST AND CHINESE STRATEGIC DOCTRINES.

1104 US AIR FORCE ACADEMY ASSEMBLY
OUTER SPACE: FINAL REPORT APRIL 1-4, 1964.
NEW YORK: AMERICAN ASSEMBLY, 1964, 94 PP.
SPEECHES GIVEN AT ACADEMY BY EXPERTS ON PROBLEMS OF
CONTROLLING OUTER SPACE. COVERS BOTH PEACEFUL AND HARMFUL
POSSIBILITIES FOR WORLD. EVALUATES US PROGRESS, REASONS FOR
PROJECTS, AND FUTURE PLANS.

1105 US ARMY LIBRARY
THESES AND DISSERTATIONS IN THE HOLDINGS OF THE ARMY LIBRARY
(PAMPHLET)
WASHINGTON: DEPT OF THE ARMY, 1957, 55 PP.
APPROXIMATELY 400 TITLES, MANY UNPUBLISHED, IN ALL AREAS
WITH EMPHASIS ON MILITARY ARTS AND SCIENCES AND THE PHYSICAL
SCIENCES. ARRANGED BY SUBJECT, THESE ITEMS ARE NOT ANNOTATED
AND MOST ARE POST-1950 THESIS. THIS EDITION FOLLOWED BY 1961
AND 1966 EDITIONS ON THE SAME FORMAT.

1106 US ATOMIC ENERGY COMMISSION
ATOMIC ENERGY IN USE (PAMPHLET)
WASHINGTON: US GOVERNMENT, 1965, 77 PP.
SERIES OF ILLUSTRATED ARTICLES EXPLAIN IN LAY TERMS THE
NATURE AND USES OF ATOMIC ENERGY. SEPARATE ESSAYS DESCRIBE
THE PURPOSES AND EMPLOYMENT OF URANIUM, NUCLEAR RADIATION,
REACTORS, RADIOISOTOPES, AND ATOM SMASHERS. THE FUSION POWER
OF THE ATOM IS EXPLAINED. SAFETY IN PREPARATION AND USE OF
REACTORS AND OTHER NUCLEAR DEVICES IS STRESSED.

1107 US ATOMIC ENERGY COMMISSION
ATOMIC ENERGY IN THE SOVIET UNION: TRIP REPORT OF THE US
ATOMIC ENERGY DELEGATION, MAY 1933.
WASHINGTON: US GOVERNMENT, 1963, 83 PP.
DETAILED DESCRIPTION OF ELEVEN-DAY TOUR OF 14 SITES,
INCLUDING TEN LARGEST SCIENTIFIC INSTALLATIONS. US DELEGA-
TION WAS TREATED MOST CORDIALLY, WITH ALL QUESTIONS ANSWERED
FREELY. USSR PROGRAM WAS FOUND ESPECIALLY AMBITIOUS IN HIGH
ENERGY ACCELERATORS, CONTROLLED THERMONUCLEAR REACTIONS, AND
TRANSURANIUM RESEARCH, BUT HAD LITTLE BIOLOGICAL WORK. US-
USSR TECHNIQUES COMPARED. GIVES TEXT OF EXCHANGE AGREEMENT.

1108 US BUREAU OF THE BUDGET
THE ADMINISTRATION OF GOVERNMENT SUPPORTED RESEARCH AT
UNIVERSITIES (PAMPHLET)
WASHINGTON: GOVT PR OFFICE, 1966, 141 PP.
REPORT UNDERTAKEN IN RESPONSE TO EXECUTIVE BRANCH'S CON-
TINUING CONCERN THAT ITS RESEARCH BE WELL MANAGED.
IDENTIFIES ADMINISTRATIVE PROCEDURES WHICH FOSTER GOOD RE-
SEARCH, HELP INSTITUTION, AND GUARANTEE PRUDENT STEWARDSHIP
OF PUBLIC FUNDS. PARTICULARLY CONCERNED WITH MANAGEMENT
OF FEDERALLY-FUNDED RESEARCH PROGRAMS IN PHYSICAL, LIFE,
AND BEHAVIORAL SCIENCES.

1109 US CHAMBER OF COMMERCE
THE SIGNIFICANCE OF CONCENTRATION RATIOS (PAMPHLET)
WASHINGTON: US CHAMBER OF COMM, 1957, 8 PP.
CLOSE LOOK AT GAUGE BEING USED TO MEASURE ECONOMIC CON-
CENTRATION. IN ORDER TO DETERMINE WHETHER CONCENTRATION RA-
TIOS ARE CONCEPTUALLY VALID MEASURES, AND WHETHER THEY ARE
STATISTICALLY ACCURATE. MAINTAINS THAT CONCENTRATION RATIOS
ARE CONCEPTUALLY INVALID AS MEASURES OF INDUSTRIAL CONCEN-
TRATION OR MARKET POWER.

1110 US CONGRESS
COMMUNICATIONS SATELLITE LEGISLATION: HEARINGS BEFORE COMM
ON AERON AND SPACE SCIENCES ON BILLS S2550 AND 2814.
WASHINGTON: US GOVERNMENT, 1962, 485 PP.
TESTIMONIES BY GOVERNMENT OFFICIALS CONCERNING CREATION
OF WORLDWIDE COMMUNICATIONS SYSTEM, AS AMENDMENT TO NSA ACT
OF 1958. INCLUDES EVIDENCE BY REPRESENTATIVES OF PRIVATE

INDUSTRY, DISCUSSION OF PARTICIPANTS ON NEED FOR
INTERNATIONAL COOPERATION, AND SPECIFIC TESTIMONY ON
OWNERSHIP, OPERATION, AND CONTROL OF SUCH SYSTEM.

1111 US CONGRESS JT ATOM ENRGY COMM
SELECTED MATERIALS ON FEDERAL-STATE COOPERATION IN THE
ATOMIC ENERGY FIELD.
WASHINGTON: GOVT PR OFFICE, 1959, 517 PP.
OUTLINES POLICY QUESTIONS AND ALTERNATIVES FOR JOINT
COMMITTEE ON ATOMIC ENERGY. COLLECTS REPORTS AND MATERIALS
SUMMARIZING ACTIVITIES OF FEDERAL, STATE, AND LOCAL AGENCIES
AND CERTAIN NONGOVERNMENTAL ORGANIZATIONS IN ATOMIC ENERGY
FIELD. INCLUDES ARTICLES, LEGAL ANALYSES, AND A BIBLIOGRAPHY
ON FEDERAL-STATE COOPERATION IN ATOMIC ENERGY.

1112 US CONGRESS JT ATOM ENRGY COMM
PEACEFUL USES OF ATOMIC ENERGY, HEARING.
WASHINGTON: US GOVERNMENT, 1962, 148 PP.
WITNESSES' STATEMENTS DESCRIBE SPECIFIC PEACEFUL USES OF
ATOMIC POWER. PRINCIPAL EMPHASIS ON ANALYSIS OF EDUCATIONAL
SYSTEM IN USSR INCLUDING STANDARDS, POLICIES, AND PUBLIC
ATTITUDES. COMPARES US EDUCATION TO USSR AND GIVES RECOMMEN-
DATIONS FOR IMPROVEMENTS. COMMENTS ON LACK OF QUALIFIED
SCIENTISTS, ENGINEERS, AND TEACHERS; NOTES POSSIBLE
SOLUTIONS TO PROBLEM . NOTES SOVIET SCHOOL EXAMINATIONS.

1113 US CONGRESS JT ATOM ENRGY COMM
PEACEFUL APPLICATIONS OF NUCLEAR EXPLOSIVES: PLOWSHARE,
HEARING.
WASHINGTON: GOVT PR OFFICE, 1965, 620 PP.
CONCENTRATES ON EXPERTS' FORMAL RESEARCH ON DANGERS AND
ADVANTAGES OF USING UNDERGROUND NUCLEAR BLASTS FOR CONSTRUC-
TIVE PURPOSES. DISCUSSES FEASIBILITY OF BLASTING NEW PANAMA
CANAL AND USE OF NUCLEAR EXPLOSIVES FOR INCREASING PETROLEUM
RECOVERY. INCLUDES GENERAL SURVEY OF NUCLEAR EXCAVATION
TECHNOLOGY; AND DISCUSSES INTERNATIONAL POLITICAL ASPECTS
OF NUCLEAR BLASTING. TESTIMONY IS MINIMAL.

1114 US CONGRESS JT ATOM ENRGY COMM
ATOMIC ENERGY LEGISLATION THROUGH 89TH CONGRESS, 1ST SESSION
WASHINGTON: GOVT PR OFFICE, 1965, 328 PP.
COLLECTION OF STATUTES AND MATERIAL PERTAINING TO ATOMIC
ENERGY. INCLUDES ATOMIC ENERGY ACT OF 1954 AS AMENDED, AEC
AUTHORIZATION ACTS, EURATOM COOPERATION ACT, AND
INTERNATIONAL ATOMIC ENERGY PARTICIPATION ACT OF 1957.
LISTS APPROPRIATIONS FOR ATOMIC ENERGY PROGRAM, 1947-66.

1115 US CONGRESS JT ATOM ENRGY COMM
PROPOSED AMENDMENT TO SECTION 271 OF THE ATOMIC ENERGY ACT
OF 1954.
WASHINGTON: US GOVERNMENT, 1965, 199 PP.
HEARINGS BEFORE JOINT COMMITTEE ON ATOMIC ENERGY HELD IN
MAY AND JUNE, 1965. TESTIMONY SHOWED THAT ATOMIC ENERGY
COMMISSION HAD BEEN PREVENTED FROM BUILDING AN ELECTRIC
POWERLINE TO STANFORD LINEAR ACCELERATOR. PROPOSED
AMENDMENT WOULD CLARIFY LAW TO SHOW CONGRESS DID NOT INTEND
TO PREVENT AEC FROM TAKING ACTIONS SUCH AS THIS.

1116 US CONGRESS JT COMM ECO GOVT
BACKGROUND MATERIAL ON ECONOMY IN GOVERNMENT 1967 (PAMPHLET)
WASHINGTON: US GOVERNMENT, 1967, 229 PP.
ANALYSIS OF FEDERAL PROPERTY HOLDINGS AND PROPERTY MAN-
AGEMENT ACTIVITIES IN ORDER TO IMPROVE OPERATIONS AND LOWER
COSTS. LISTS AMOUNT AND COST OF REAL PROPERTY HOLDINGS AND
EXTENT OF DEFENSE DEPARTMENT PROPERTY ACTIVITIES AND YEARLY
EXPENDITURES.

1117 US DEPARTMENT OF ARMY
MILITARY PROTECTIVE CONSTRUCTION: NUCLEAR WARFARE AND
CHEMICAL AND BIOLOGICAL OPERATIONS (MANUAL)
CHICAGO: HENRY REGNERY CO, 1965, 225 PP.
TECHNICAL MANUAL ILLUSTRATES METHODS OF CONSTRUCTING
TEMPORARY SHELTERS FOR PERSONNEL, EQUIPMENT, AND SUPPLIES.
DISCUSSES EFFECTS OF CONVENTIONAL AND CHEMICAL-BIOLOGICAL
WEAPONS AND NUCLEAR BLAST AND RADIATION ON STRUCTURES. USE
OF EXISTING FACILITIES AND ADAPTATION TO TERRAIN ARE
STRESSED. EXAMPLE DESIGNS INCLUDE PROVISION FOR AIR AND DUCT
SYSTEMS, FILTER UNITS, SANITATION, POWER, AND STORAGE.

1118 US DEPARTMENT OF DEFENSE
US SECURITY ARMS CONTROL, AND DISARMAMENT 1961-1965
(PAMPHLET)
WASHINGTON: US GOVERNMENT, 1965, 140 PP.
CONTAINS 750 PAPERS DEALING WITH THE PROBLEMS OF ARMS
CONTROL AND DISARMAMENT AND PUBLISHED FROM OCTOBER, 1961, TO
JANUARY, 1965. MATERIALS ON POLICIES, STRATEGIES, CONCEPTS,
NEGOTIATIONS, NUCLEAR WEAPONRY, AND SPACE AS THE NEW DIMEN-
SION OF POLITICO-MILITARY CONFLICT ARE INCLUDED.

1119 US DEPARTMENT OF LABOR
PRODUCTIVITY: A BIBLIOGRAPHY.
WASHINGTON: US GOVERNMENT, 1966, 129 PP.
ANNOTATED BIBLIOGRAPHY OF 454 PUBLICATIONS ISSUED BETWEEN
1957-64. COVERS MATERIAL ON PRODUCTIVITY RATIOS, WITH EMPHA-
SIS ON LABOR INPUT; EXCLUDES MATERIAL RELATED TO TIME AND
MOTION STUDIES AT THE JOB LEVEL AND MATERIAL IN FIELD OF

PSYCHOLOGY. ITEMS DIVIDED INTO SIX SUBJECT CLASSIFICATIONS,
INCLUDING CONCEPTS, FACTORS, PRODUCTIVITY LEVELS, INTERNA-
TIONAL WORKS, AND BIBLIOGRAPHIES.

1120 US DEPARTMENT OF LABOR
TECHNOLOGICAL TRENDS IN MAJOR AMERICAN INDUSTRIES.
WASHINGTON: US GOVERNMENT, 1966, 269 PP.
APPRAISES SOME OF MAJOR TECHNOLOGICAL CHANGES EMERG-
ING AMONG AMERICAN INDUSTRIES AND PROJECTS THE IMPACT OF
THESE CHANGES OVER NEXT 5-10 YEARS. EVALUATES GENERAL
EFFECTS OF TECHNOLOGICAL PROGRESS ON FUTURE PATTERNS OF EM-
PLOYMENT, OCCUPATION, AND ISSUE OF LABOR-MANAGEMENT ADJUST-
MENT. INCLUDES LENGTHY UNANNOTATED BIBLIOGRAPHY PRIMARILY
CONSISTING OF POST-1962 PUBLICATIONS ON THE SUBJECT.

1121 US DEPARTMENT OF STATE
POINT FOUR: COOPERATIVE PROGRAM FOR AID IN THE DEVELOPMENT
OF ECONOMICALLY UNDERDEVELOPED AREAS.
WASHINGTON: GOVT PR OFFICE, 1950, 167 PP.
EXPLAINS NATURE, PURPOSE, SCOPE, AND OPERATING ARRANGE-
MENTS OF POINT FOUR PROGRAM AND ITS RELATION TO UN PROGRAM
OF ECONOMIC ASSISTANCE. DISCUSSES PROMOTION OF PEACE AND
ECONOMIC PROGRESS, US INTEREST. AGRICULTURE, EDUCATION,
AND HOUSING. STUDIES DEVELOPMENT OF INDUSTRY, NEED FOR
ASSISTANCE, FINANCING OF PROGRAM THROUGH CAPITAL INVESTMENT
AND TECHNICAL COOPERATION, AND LIVING STANDARDS.

1122 US DEPARTMENT OF STATE
PUBLICATIONS OF THE DEPARTMENT OF STATE, OCTOBER 1,1929 TO
JANUARY 1, 1953.
WASHINGTON: DEPT OF STATE, 1954, 207 PP.
COMPLETE LIST OF NUMBERED DEPARTMENT OF STATE PUBLICA-
TIONS, ARRANGED ALPHABETICALLY AND WITH CROSS REFERENCES.
SEPARATE INDEX FOR SERIES PUBLICATIONS.

1123 US DEPARTMENT OF STATE
PUBLICATIONS OF THE DEPARTMENT OF STATE, JANUARY 1,1953 TO
DECEMBER 31, 1957.
WASHINGTON: DEPT OF STATE, 1958, 230 PP.
COMPLETE LIST OF NUMBERED STATE DEPARTMENT PUBLICATIONS,
ARRANGED ALPHABETICALLY AND WITH CROSS REFERENCES. SEPARATE
INDEX BY SERIES FOR SERIES PUBLICATIONS.

1124 US DEPARTMENT OF STATE
FOREIGN AFFAIRS RESEARCH (PAMPHLET)
WASHINGTON: DEPT OF STATE, 1967, 83 PP., LC#67-61715.
DESCRIPTIVE LISTINGS OF US GOVERNMENT RESOURCES
AVAILABLE FOR SOCIAL AND BEHAVIORAL SCIENCE RESEARCH ON
FOREIGN AREAS AND INTERNATIONAL AFFAIRS. SOURCES LISTED
ALPHABETICALLY BY AGENCY AND DEFINE TYPE OF RESEARCH IN
WHICH EACH IS ENGAGED. INCLUDES BIBLIOGRAPHY.

1125 US DEPARTMENT OF THE ARMY
AMERICAN MILITARY HISTORY.
WASHINGTON: DEPT OF THE ARMY, 1956, 494 PP.
UNANNOTATED BIBLIOGRAPHIES AT CHAPTER ENDS TRACE US ARMY
ACTIONS FROM FRENCH AND INDIAN WAR THROUGH KOREAN CONFLICT.
CONCENTRATES ON HISTORICAL SETTINGS FOR CONFLICT AND STRA-
TEGIC AND TACTICAL CONCEPTS AS THEY HAVE DEVELOPED IN THE
ARMY. ALSO CHANGES IN MILITARY TECHNOLOGY AND THEIR EFFECTS
ON MILITARY AND POLITICAL THINKING. TRACES CHANGES IN ORGA-
NIZATION OF US MILITARY. APPROXIMATELY 200 TITLES.

1126 US DEPARTMENT OF THE ARMY
RESEARCH AND DEVELOPMENT (AND RELATED ASPECTS) IN FOREIGN
COUNTRIES.
WASHINGTON: DEPT OF THE ARMY, 1956, 316 PP.
LISTS AND ANNOTATES ITEMS DEALING WITH RESEARCH AND
DEVELOPMENT THROUGHOUT THE WORLD. CAREFULLY CLASSIFIED BY
SUBJECT AND COUNTRY. ITEMS WERE SCREENED FROM 15,000 TITLES,
OF WHICH 1,600 APPEAR IN TWO SEPARATE SECTIONS. THE FIRST
DEALS WITH COMMUNIST AND THE SECOND WITH NON-COMMUNIST
COUNTRIES. INCLUDES A LIST OF INDEXES AND BIBLIOGRAPHIES.

1127 US DEPARTMENT OF THE ARMY
BIBLIOGRAPHY ON LIMITED WAR (PAMPHLET)
WASHINGTON: DEPT OF THE ARMY, 1958, 53 PP.
ANNOTATED BIBLIOGRAPHY OF UNCLASSIFIED MATERIAL DEALING
WITH LIMITED WAR AND THE VITAL IMPORTANCE OF IT IN RELATION
TO THE POLITICAL AND MILITARY OBJECTIVES OF THE US. DIVIDED
INTO SUBJECT CATEGORIES SUCH AS NUCLEAR WEAPONS, SOCIOLOG-
ICAL ASPECTS, ETC. APPROXIMATELY 300 ITEMS INCLUDED.

1128 US DEPARTMENT OF THE ARMY
DISARMAMENT: A BIBLIOGRAPHIC RECORD: 1916-1960.
WASHINGTON: US GOVERNMENT, 1960, 122 PP.
CONTAINS 1,000 ENTRIES IN ENGLISH, FRENCH, AND RUSSIAN
ARRANGED BY SUBJECT. PUBLICATION DATES OF LISTINGS RANGE
FROM 1900-1961. ENTRIES ARE FROM BOOKS, ARTICLES, DOCUMENTS,
AND DISSERTATIONS. EXCERPTS FROM LISTINGS IN ANNOTATION; IN-
CLUDES CHRONOLOGY ON DISARMAMENT.

1129 US DEPARTMENT OF THE ARMY
SOVIET RUSSIA: STRATEGIC SURVEY (PAMPHLET)
WASHINGTON: DEPT OF THE ARMY, 1963, 223 PP.
MORE THAN 1,000 SHORT ABSTRACTS OF SCHOLARLY AND POPULAR

ARTICLES AND BOOKS MOSTLY IN ENGLISH. TONE OF BIBLIOGRAPHY IS ADMITTEDLY HOSTILE TO RUSSIA AND PORTRAYS "SOVIET UNION AS A WORLD POWER INTENT ON EXTENDING ITS INFLUENCE BEYOND ITS NATIONAL BORDERS AND DOMINATING THE WORLD. " WORKS FROM 1960-63. TOPICALLY ARRANGED WITH CONCLUDING SECTION OF CONGRESSIONAL DOCUMENTS.

1130 US DEPARTMENT OF THE ARMY
US OVERSEAS BASES: PRESENT STATUS AND FUTURE PROSPECTS (PAMPHLET)
WASHINGTON: DEPT OF THE ARMY, 1963, 133 PP.
ABOUT 400 ARTICLES, BOOKS, GOVERNMENT DOCUMENTS, AND SPEECHES HAVING OVER-ALL FAVORABLE OPINION OF EFFICACY OF US BASES ALTHOUGH SOME SOVIET OPINIONS ARE INCLUDED. MANY OF THE HEAVILY ANNOTATED SOURCES DO NOT DEVOTE ENTIRE CONTENT TO BASES. ITEMS TOPICALLY ARRANGED; PUBLISHED FROM 1955-63.

1131 US DEPARTMENT OF THE ARMY
NUCLEAR WEAPONS AND THE ATLANTIC ALLIANCE: A BIBLIOGRAPHIC SURVEY.
WASHINGTON: DEPT OF THE ARMY, 1965, 179 PP.
WIDE RANGING ANNOTATED BIBLIOGRAPHY ABSTRACTING OVER 750 UNCLASSIFIED ITEMS ON THE ATLANTIC ALLIANCE IN GENERAL AND THE IMPACT OF NUCLEAR WEAPONS POLICIES ON IT IN PARTICULAR. SUPPLEMENT ON "RED CHINA'S A-BOMB."

1132 US DEPARTMENT OF THE ARMY
MILITARY MANPOWER POLICY.
WASHINGTON: DEPT OF THE ARMY, 1965, 142 PP.
ANNOTATED BIBLIOGRAPHY ON MILITARY MANPOWER POLICY, CITING 700 BOOKS, DOCUMENTS, AND ARTICLES IN ENGLISH; ARRANGED TOPICALLY, 1948-64.

1133 US DEPARTMENT OF THE ARMY
COMMUNIST CHINA: A STRATEGIC SURVEY: A BIBLIOGRAPHY (PAMPHLET NO. 20-67)
WASHINGTON: DEPT OF THE ARMY, 1966, 143 PP.
BIBLIOGRAPHICAL PROBE INTO THE ECONOMIC, SOCIOLOGICAL, MIL-ITARY, AND POLITICAL MAKE-UP OF COMMUNIST CHINA. FOCUSES ON EMERGENCE AS STRATEGIC THREAT. ABSTRACTS FROM OVER 650 PER-IODICAL ARTICLES, BOOKS, AND STUDIES IN ENGLISH. INCLUDES CHINA'S POLICY TO SOUTH ASIA AS A WHOLE AND TO INDIVIDUAL COUNTRIES. MAPS, CHARTS, AND DATA APPENDED.

1134 US DEPARTMENT OF THE ARMY
CIVILIAN IN PEACE, SOLDIER IN WAR: A BIBLIOGRAPHIC SURVEY OF THE ARMY AND AIR NATIONAL GUARD (PAMPHLET, NOS. 130-2)
WASHINGTON: DEPT OF THE ARMY, 1967, 192 PP.
ANNOTATED BIBLIOGRAPHY OF PERIODICAL ARTICLES, BOOKS, UN-PUBLISHED MATERIALS, AND GOVERNMENT PUBLICATIONS PERTAINING TO THE ROLE AND FUNCTIONS OF THE MILITARY IN THE US. SOURCES CITED PUBLISHED 1938 THROUGH 1966. OVER 800 ITEMS ARRANGED BY SUBJECT. INCLUDES SECTION ON MILITIAS OF FOREIGN COUN-TRIES AND ONE ON STATE MILITIAS. MAJORITY OF ENTRIES ARE GOVERNMENT PUBLICATIONS.

1135 US DEPT COMMERCE OFF TECH SERV
TECHNICAL TRANSLATIONS.
WASHINGTON: GOVT PR OFFICE.
SEMI-MONTHLY ABSTRACTING JOURNAL OF OTS WHICH LISTS NEW TRANSLATIONS AVAILABLE FROM OTS, LIBRARY OF CONGRESS, AND OTHER SOURCES.

1136 US FOOD AND DRUG ADMIN
CIVIL DEFENSE INFORMATION FOR FOOD AND DRUG OFFICIALS (2ND ED.) (PAMPHLET)
WASHINGTON: US GOVERNMENT, 1956, 221 PP.
HANDBOOK TO SUPPLEMENT COURSE IN CIVIL DEFENSE CONTAINING METHODS TO DEAL WITH RADIOACTIVE CONTAMINATION, DESCRIPTIONS OF BIOLOGICAL EFFECTS OF RADIOACTIVITY AND CHEMICAL AND BIOLOGICAL WARFARE, AND REVIEW OF PRINCIPLES OF MATHEMATICS, PHYSICS, CHEMISTRY, AND ATOMIC THEORY.

1137 US HOUSE COMM APPROPRIATIONS
PUBLIC WORKS AND ATOMIC ENERGY COMMISSION APPROPRIATION BILL, 1968 (PAMPHLET)
WASHINGTON: US GOVERNMENT, 1967, 103 PP.
REPORT EXPLAINS APPROPRIATIONS MADE FOR PUBLIC WORKS ENGINEERING, DESIGN, AND CONSTRUCTION. GIVES BREAKDOWN FOR VARIOUS PROJECTS THROUGHOUT THE US AND PANAMA CANAL, AND RESPECTIVE ALLOCATION OF FUNDS.

1138 US HOUSE COMM FOREIGN AFFAIRS
REPORT OF SPECIAL STUDY MISSION TO THE NEAR EAST (PAMPHLET)
WASHINGTON: US GOVERNMENT, 1967, 70 PP.
REPORT TO COMMITTEE ON FOREIGN AFFAIRS GIVES FINDINGS OF SPECIAL STUDY MISSION TO NEAR EAST, NOVEMBER-DECEMBER, 1966. MEMBERS EXAMINED UN PEACEKEEPING AND OTHER ACTIVITIES; MILI-TARY AND POLITICAL SIGNIFICANCE OF DIPLOMATIC ACTIVITIES; YEMEN WAR; ASSISTANCE PROGRAMS; WATER DEVELOPMENT IN ISRAEL; EXPROPRIATION AND NATIONALIZATION OF AMERICAN FIRMS AND PROPERTY; AND THE ARMS RACE.

1139 US HOUSE COMM GOVT OPERATIONS
CIVIL DEFENSE.
WASHINGTON: US GOVERNMENT, 1958, 519 PP.

HEARINGS BEFORE SUBCOMMITTEE OF COMMITTEE ON GOVERNMENT OPERATIONS HEADED BY CHET HOLIFIELD ON TESTS MADE ON TYPES OF ATOMIC SHELTERS AND OTHER RADIATION PROTECTION DEVICES, AND ON REORGANIZATION OF CIVIL DEFENSE PROGRAM TO FIT PRESENT NEEDS.

1140 US HOUSE COMM GOVT OPERATIONS
THE COMPUTER AND INVASION OF PRIVACY.
WASHINGTON: US GOVERNMENT, 1966, 318 PP.
HEARINGS BEFORE SUBCOMMITTEE OF COMMITTEE ON GOVERNMENT OPERATIONS, ON INVASION OF PRIVACY. DEALS WITH COMPUTER AND ESTABLISHMENT OF NATIONAL DATA CENTERS WITHIN FEDERAL GOVERNMENT.

1141 US HOUSE COMM ON JUDICIARY
CIVIL COMMITMENT AND TREATMENT OF NARCOTIC ADDICTS.
WASHINGTON: GOVT PR OFFICE, 1966, 465 PP.
US CONGRESSIONAL HEARINGS STUDY CONCEPT OF CIVIL COMMITMENT OF CERTAIN ADDICTION CASES INSTEAD OF CRIMINAL PROSECUTION. DISCUSSION INCLUDES REVIEW OF SENTENCING PROCEDURES AND MEDICAL TESTIMONY ON TREATMENT AND REHABILITATION.

1142 US HOUSE COMM SCI ASTRONAUT
THE ORGANIZATION OF THE US NATIONAL SPACE EFFORT.
WASHINGTON: G.P.O., 1960, 13 PP.
STATES THAT RACE FOR SPACE IS MATTER OF NATIONAL CONCERN AND PRESTIGE. ADVISES MAINTAINING LEADERSHIP IN PEACEFUL EXPLOITATION OF SPACE AND ASTRONAUTICAL SCIENCES. WARNS THAT MILITARY APPLICATIONS IN SPACE MUST BE ENERGETICALLY PROSECUTED IN THE INTEREST OF NATIONAL SECURITY.

1143 US HOUSE COMM SCI ASTRONAUT
GOVERNMENT, SCIENCE, AND PUBLIC POLICY (PAMPHLET)
WASHINGTON: US GOVERNMENT, 1966, 58 PP.
SEVEN PAPERS BY LEADING AUTHORITIES, WITH SUBJECTS RANG-ING FROM THE APPLICATION OF SCIENCE TO GOVERNMENTAC ADMINIS-TRATION, TO THE FURURE POSSIBILITIES OF PLASTICS. FIRST PRESENTED IN CONFERENCE OF PANEL ON SCIENCE AND TECHNOLOGY, COMMITTEE ON SCIENCE AND ASTRONAUTICS.

1144 US HOUSE COMM SCI ASTRONAUT
INQUIRIES, LEGISLATION, POLICY STUDIES RE: SCIENCE AND TECH-NOLOGY: REVIEW AND FORECAST (PAMPHLET)
WASHINGTON: GOVT PR OFFICE, 1966, 28 PP.
SUMMARY OF ACTIVITY AND RESULTS TO DATE OF SUB-COMMITTEE ON SCIENCE, RESEARCH, AND DEVELOPMENT, COMMITTEE ON SCIENCE AND ASTRONAUTICS. ALSO SETS OUT PROBLEMS OF SCIENCE AND TECHNOLOGY THAT WILL NEED FUTURE STUDY.

1145 US HOUSE COMM SCI ASTRONAUT
THE ADEQUACY OF TECHNOLOGY FOR POLLUTION ABATEMENT (PAMPHLET)
WASHINGTON: GOVT PR OFFICE, 1966, 17 PP.
REPORT OF COMMITTEE ON SCIENCE AND ASTRONAUTICS. SECTION VI RAISES ISSUES OF PUBLIC POLICY AS IT RELATES BOTH TO ACTUAL TECHNOLOGY AND TO ADMINISTRATION AND SOCIAL ASPECTS OF POLLUTION CONTROL.

1146 US HOUSE COMM SCI ASTRONAUT
GOVERNMENT, SCIENCE, AND INTERNATIONAL POLICY.
WASHINGTON: US GOVERNMENT, 1967, 220 PP.
PROCEEDINGS BEFORE CONGRESSIONAL COMMITTEE ON SCIENCE AND ASTRONAUTICS. PURPOSE WAS TO IDENTIFY SPHERES OF RESEARCH WHICH OFFER EXCEPTIONAL PROMISE; DISCUSS CURRENT METHODS OF RESEARCH; PROVIDE INFORMATION ON AVAILABILITY OF SCIENTIFIC MANPOWER AND EDUCATIONAL NEEDS; PROVIDE INFORMATION ON MAT-TERS OF INTERNATIONAL COOPERATION AND ORGANIZATION.

1147 US HOUSE COMM SCI ASTRONAUT
AMENDING NATIONAL SCIENCE FOUNDATION ACT OF 1950 TO MAKE IM-PROVEMENTS IN ORGANIZATION AND OPERATION OF FOUNDAT'N(PAMPH)
WASHINGTON: US GOVERNMENT, 1967, 55 PP.
REPORT RECOMMENDS PASSAGE TO AMEND NATIONAL SCIENCE FOUNDATION ACT OF 1950 TO MAKE CHANGES AND IMPROVEMENTS IN ITS ORGANIZATION AND OPERATION. ELUCIDATES MAJOR GOALS OF NEW BILL. INCLUDES BACKGROUND INFORMATION AND EVALUATION.

1148 US HOUSE COMM SCI ASTRONAUT
THE JUNIOR COLLEGE AND EDUCATION IN THE SCIENCES (PAMPHLET)
WASHINGTON: US GOVERNMENT, 1967, 103 PP.
REPORT OF NATIONAL SCIENCE FOUNDATION FOR SUBCOMMITTEE ON SCIENCE, RESEARCH, AND DEVELOPMENT. DEALS WITH SCIENCE EDU-CATION ON JUNIOR COLLEGE LEVEL. DISCUSSES UNIVERSAL COLLEGE EDUCATION; MODEL LAW FOR JUNIOR COLLEGES, THEIR GROWTH, RESOURCES, PROGRAMS, AND FACULTY.

1149 US HOUSE COMM SCI ASTRONAUT
AUTHORIZING APPROPRIATIONS TO THE NATIONAL AERONAUTICS AND SPACE ADMINISTRATION (PAMPHLET)
WASHINGTON: US GOVERNMENT, 1967, 194 PP.
AUTHORIZES 1968 NASA APPROPRIATIONS. FUNDS ALLOCATED FOR RESEARCH AND DEVELOPMENT, CONSTRUCTION OF FACILITIES, ADMIN-ISTRATIVE OPERATIONS, AND OTHER USES. EXPLAINS AUTHORIZA-TIONS OF FUNDS FOR SEPARATE NASA PROGRAMS.

1150 US HOUSE COMM SCI ASTRONAUT
AUTHORIZING SECY OF COMMERCE TO PROVIDE FOR COLLECTION, COM-
PILATION, CRIT EVALUATION, PUBLICATION, SALE OF STD REF DATA
WASHINGTON: US GOVERNMENT, 1967, 18 PP.
AUTHORIZES SECRETARY OF COMMERCE TO PROVIDE FOR THE
COLLECTION, COMPILATION, CRITICAL EVALUATION, PUBLICATION,
AND SALE OF STANDARD REFERENCE DATA. PURPOSE IS TO MAKE
SUCH DATA ACCESSIBLE TO SCIENTISTS, ENGINEERS, AND GENERAL
PUBLIC, FACILITATED BY MODERN COMPUTER TECHNIQUES.

1151 US HOUSE COMM SCI ASTRONAUT
SCIENCE, TECHNOLOGY, AND PUBLIC POLICY DURING THE 89TH
CONGRESS, JANUARY, 1965 THROUGH DECEMBER, 1966.
WASHINGTON: US GOVERNMENT, 1967, 212 PP.
REPORT OF SUBCOMMITTEE ON SCIENCE, RESEARCH, AND
DEVELOPMENT OF HOUSE COMMITTEE ON SCIENCE AND ASTRONAUTICS
IDENTIFYING CHANGES IN NATIONAL POLICY FOR SCIENCE AND
TECHNOLOGY FROM 1965-66. SUGGESTS HOW STRONGLY SCIENCE AND
TECHNOLOGY ARE INVOLVED IN STRUCTURE OF GOVERNMENT. INCLUDES
SELECTED REFERENCES FROM BOOKS, ARTICLES AND GOVERNMENT
PUBLICATIONS FROM 1965-66.

1152 US HOUSE COMM SCI ASTRONAUT
GOVERNMENT, SCIENCE, AND INTERNATIONAL POLICY (PAMPHLET)
WASHINGTON: US GOVERNMENT, 1967, 81 PP.
SIX PAPERS, BY SCIENTISTS FROM VARIOUS NATIONS, PRESENTED
TO PANEL ON SCIENCE AND TECHNOLOGY OF SCIENCE AND
ASTRONAUTICS COMMITTEE. MOST DEAL PRIMARILY WITH BACKGROUND
OF SCIENTIFIC RESEARCH, GOVERNMENT SCIENCE POLICIES, AND
SCIENCE-INDUSTRY RELATION IN SPECIFIC COUNTRIES. SI LESS
CONCERNED WITH SCIENCE AND FOREIGN AFFAIRS THAN TITLE
INDICATES, BUT SOME ATTENTION IS GIVEN TO THIS SUBJECT.

1153 US HOUSE COMM. SCI. ASTRONAUT.
OCEAN SCIENCES AND NATIONAL SECURITY.
WASHINGTON: G.P.O., 1960, 180 PP.
AN INVESTIGATION INTO THE EXTENT TO WHICH RESEARCH IS
DESIRABLE AND EXAMINES OCEONOGRAPHIC CAPABILITIES,
PROPOSED PROGRAMS AND IMMEDIATE AND EMERGING ISSUES BEFORE
CONGRESS. MAIN GOALS ARE ECONOMIC AND MILITARY. RESEARCH
RATHER THAN DEVELOPMENT IS THE MOST CRUCIAL NEED. THE
POSSIBILITY OF GAINING FOOD FROM THE OCEAN FOR POPULATION
EXPLOSIAN AND ANTISUBMARINE WARFARE ARE SPECIAL CONCERNS.

1154 US LIBRARY OF CONGRESS
CLASSIFIED GUIDE TO MATERIAL IN THE LIBRARY OF CONGRESS
COVERING URBAN COMMUNITY DEVELOPMENT.
WASHINGTON: US NATL RESOURC COMM, 1936, 102 PP.
LISTS NO BOOKS, BUT CONSISTS OF 850 SUBJECT HEADINGS AND
SUBHEADINGS RELATED TO URBAN MATTERS, CHOSEN FROM LIST OF
SUBJECT HEADINGS USED IN DICTIONARY CATALOGUES OF LIBRARY OF
CONGRESS. ARRANGED BY ANALOGICAL LIST OF CLASSES OF RELATED
SUBJECTS; BY CALL NUMBERS CORRESPONDING TO SUBJECT HEADINGS,
ARRANGED ACCORDING TO ALPHABETICAL AND NUMERICAL SEQUENCE OF
LIBRARY-CONGRESS CLASSIFICATIONS; ALPHABETICAL BY SUBJECT.

1155 US LIBRARY OF CONGRESS
CONDUCT OF THE WAR (APRIL 1941-MARCH 1942)
WASHINGTON: LIBRARY OF CONGRESS, 1942, 95 PP.
SELECTED AND ANNOTATED BIBLIOGRAPHY ON THE OPERATIONS OF
THE ARMED FORCES IN WORLD WAR II; 685 ITEMS ARRANGED
TOPICALLY AND INDEXED BY AUTHOR. LISTS REFERENCES AND
BIBLIOGRAPHIES. DEALS WITH BACKGROUND, PROSECUTION OF THE
WAR, PRISONS; EACH BRANCH OF THE SERVICES SEPARATELY AND
IN GENERAL; ACTIVITIES ON ALL FRONTS. ALSO CONTAINS A SUB-
JECT INDEX.

1156 US LIBRARY OF CONGRESS
A DIRECTORY OF INFORMATION RESOURCES IN THE UNITED STATES:
SOCIAL SCIENCES.
WASHINGTON: LIBRARY OF CONGRESS, 1965, 218 PP., LC#65-62583.
PROVIDES A DIRECTORY OF ORGANIZATIONS, BOTH PRIVATE AND
GOVERNMENTAL, WHICH CAN PROVIDE INFORMATION FOR RESEARCH-
ERS IN THE SOCIAL SCIENCES. PERTINENT INFORMATION ABOUT
EACH ORGANIZATION INCLUDES LOCATION, DESCRIPTION OF
COLLECTIONS, AND PUBLICATIONS. ARRANGES ORGANIZATIONS BY
NAME AND BY SUBJECTS WITH WHICH THEY WORK.
APPROXIMATELY 1,000 ORGANIZATIONS ARE LISTED.

1157 US OFFICE OF THE PRESIDENT
REPORT TO CONGRESS ON THE MUTUAL SECURITY PROGRAM FOR THE
SIX MONTHS ENDED JUNE 30, 1955.
WASHINGTON: US GOVERNMENT, 1955, 60 PP.
PROGRESS REPORT ON OPERATIONS AND EXPENDITURES DURING
FIRST HALF OF 1955. MAJOR PORTION OF MILITARY AID SHIPMENTS
WENT TO EUROPE. LARGEST INVESTMENT IN NONMILITARY FUNDS WAS
IN ASIA. DETAILED ANALYSES OF PROGRAMS IN FREE ASIA, NEAR
EAST, AFRICA, LATIN AMERICA, AND EUROPE COVER 70 COUNTRIES.
INTERNATIONAL COOPERATION ADMINISTRATION WAS ESTABLISHED IN
STATE DEPARTMENT TO DIRECT MUTUAL SECURITY PROGRAMS.

1158 US OFFICE OF THE PRESIDENT
REPORT TO CONGRESS ON THE MUTUAL SECURITY PROGRAM FOR THE
SIX MONTHS ENDED DECEMBER 31, 1955.
WASHINGTON: US GOVERNMENT, 1956, 37 PP.
PROGRESS REPORT ON OPERATIONS AND EXPENDITURES DURING

SECOND HALF OF 1955 AND ANTICIPATED NEEDS FOR 1956. USSR'S
AID TO COUNTRIES OUTSIDE COMMUNIST BLOC SEEN AS MAJOR
THREAT. BUDGET OF $2.9 BILLION NEEDED PRIMARILY FOR
MILITARY AID AND DEFENSE SUPPORT WITH 52% OF FUNDS EARMARKED
FOR ASIA. USE OF ECONOMIC RESOURCES ABROAD AND SHARING
TECHNICAL SKILLS EMPHASIZED.

1159 US PRES COMM ECO IMPACT DEFENS
REPORT* JULY 1965.
WASHINGTON: GOVT PR OFFICE, 1966, 92 PP., LC#66-60269.
BASIC CONCENTRATION ON INTERNAL IMPACT OF CHANGING DE-
FENSE EXPENDITURES. ALSO A CONCERN FOR EFFECTS ON BALANCE OF
PAYMENTS. MOST VALUABLE FOR INCLUSIVECOLLECTION OF ALL DE-
FENSE-RELATED EXPENDITURE DATA.

1160 US PRES COMN LAW ENFORCE-JUS
THE CHALLENGE OF CRIME IN A FREE SOCIETY.
WASHINGTON: US GOVERNMENT, 1967, 340 PP.
THE REPORT OF THE PRESIDENT'S COMMISSION ON LAW ENFORCE-
MENT AND ADMINISTRATION OF JUSTICE DISCUSSES THE PROBLEMS OF
CRIME IN AMERICA TODAY AND RECOMMENDS WAYS TO REDUCE CRIME
AND IMPROVE FAIRNESS AND EFFECTIVENESS OF POLICE, COURTS,
AND CORRECTIONAL AGENCIES. PROPOSALS ARE PRESENTED FOR RADI-
CALLY RESTRUCTURING POLICE PERSONNEL PRACTICES, MODERNIZING
LOWER COURTS, AND REORIENTING OFFENDERS INTO THE COMMUNITY.

1161 US SEN SPEC COMM SPACE ASTRO
SPACE LAW; A SYMPOSIUM (PAMPHLET)
CHICAGO: HENRY REGNERY CO, 1959, 573 PP.
COLLECTION OF ESSAYS AND REPORTS ON SPACE LAW PREPARED
FOR SENATE SPECIAL COMMITTEE ON SPACE AND ASTRONAUTICS. COV-
ERS LEGAL CONCEPTS OF EXPERTS ON INTERNATIONAL LAW AND SPACE
DEVELOPMENTS. INCLUDES VIEWPOINTS FROM SEVERAL COUNTRIES IN-
CLUDING USSR.

1162 US SENATE
DOCUMENTS ON INTERNATIONAL ASPECTS OF EXPLORATION AND USE OF
OUTER SPACE, 1954-62: STAFF REPORT FOR COMM AERON SPACE SCI.
WASHINGTON: US GOVERNMENT, 1963, 407 PP.
EXERPTS OF OFFICIAL DOCUMENTS CONCERNING POLICY VIEWS OF
US AND RUSSIA ON SPACE MATTERS. CONTAINS ANALYSIS BY US
OFFICIALS. COVERS HISTORICAL EVENTS OF BOTH NATIONS, STATE-
MENTS BY THEIR LEADERS, AND ALL LEGISLATION CONCERNING OUTER
SPACE LAWS AND PROJECTS.

1163 US SENATE
US INTERNATIONAL SPACE PROGRAMS, 1959-65: STAFF REPORT FOR
COMM ON AERONAUTICAL AND SPACE SCIENCES.
WASHINGTON: US GOVERNMENT, 1965, 575 PP.
COMPILATION OF EXECUIVEE AGREEMENTS, LETTERS, MEMORANDA
OF UNDERSTANDING, AND ALL INTERNATIONAL ARRANGEMENTS
CONCERNING OUTER SPACE, FROM 1959-65. AIMS TO REVEAL SCOPE
OF US SPACE EFFORTS AND METHODS OF ACHIEVING INTERNATIONAL
COOPERATION DOCUMENTS ARE ARRANGED ALPHABETICALLY BY
COUNTRY OF ORIGIN.

1164 US SENATE
POLICY PLANNING FOR AERONAUTICAL RESEARCH AND DEVELOPMENT:
STAFF REPORT FOR COMM ON AERONAUTICAL AND SPACE SCIENCES.
WASHINGTON: US GOVERNMENT, 1966, 279 PP.
SURVEY REPORT OF POSSIBILITIES OF AVIATION IN TERMS OF
NATIONAL GOALS FOR TRANSPORTATION, MILITARY SECURITY, AND
ECONOMIC STRENGTH. CONCENTRATES ON OPERATIONS NOW IN PROG-
RESS AND METHODS OF FINANCING THEM. AIM IS TO EVALUATE
NEEDS OF FUTURE AND MAKE APPROPRIATE POLICY CHANGES IN
RESEARCH AND DEVELOPMENT.

1165 US SENATE
STATUS OF THE DEVELOPMENT OF THE ANTI-BALLISTIC MISSILE
SYSTEMS IN THE UNITED STATES (PAMPHLET)
WASHINGTON: US GOVERNMENT, 1967, 4 PP.
STATEMENT OF J.S. FOSTER (DEFENSE DEPARTMENT DIRECTOR OF
DEFENSE RESEARCH AND ENGINEERING) ON TECHNICAL STATUS OF
ANTI-BALLISTIC MISSILE SYSTEMS. DISCUSSES CAPABILITIES OF
NIKE-ZEUS SYSTEM, NIKE X, SPRINT, AND SPARTAN MISSILES.
EVALUATES THEIR EFFECTIVENESS IN LIMITED OR ALL-OUT NUCLEAR
ATTACK.

1166 US SENATE COMM AERO SPACE SCI
NATIONAL SPACE GOALS FOR THE POST-APOLLO PERIOD.
WASHINGTON: US GOVERNMENT, 1965, 383 PP.
AUGUST, 1967. HEARINGS BEFORE SENATE COMMITTEE ON AERO-
NAUTICAL AND SPACE SCIENCES. NASA OFFICIALS AND CONGRESSMEN
DISCUSSED ALTERNATIVE GOALS OF SPACE PROGRAM FOR 1975, 1985,
AND BEYOND. CONSIDERED COMPARATIVE MERITS OF MANNED AND UN-
MANNED MISSIONS. ALSO DISCUSSED MONEY, TIME, AND TECHNOLOGY
NEEDED FOR APOLLO EXTENSION SYSTEMS, AND ROLE OF DEFENSE
DEPARTMENT.

1167 US SENATE COMM AERO SPACE SCI
INTERNATIONAL COOPERATION AND ORGANIZATION FOR OUTER SPACE.
WASHINGTON: US GOVERNMENT, 1965, 580 PP.
STAFF REPORT PREPARED FOR SENATE COMMITTEE ON AERONAUTI-
CAL AND SPACE SCIENCES. SURVEYS ORGANIZATIONS WITH SPACE AND
SPACE-RELATED PRGRAMS AND THEIR INTERRELATIONSHIPS. ANALY-
ZES IMPACT OF FRONTIER OF OUTER SPACE UPON US FOREIGN RELA-

TIONS, RELATIONS AMONG OTHER NATIONS, QUESTION OF ARMS CON-
TROL. DISCUSSES INTERNATIONAL ECONOMIC AND TECHNICAL DEVEL-
OPMENTS, PROGRAMS, AND POLICIES OF UN AND ITS AGENCIES.

1168 US SENATE COMM AERO SPACE SCI
SOVIET SPACE PROGRAMS, 1962-65; GOALS AND PURPOSES, ACHIEVE-
MENTS, PLANS, AND INTERNATIONAL IMPLICATIONS.
WASHINGTON: US GOVERNMENT, 1966, 920 PP.
    STAFF REPORT PREPARED FOR SENATE COMMITTEE ON AERONAUTI-
CAL AND SPACE SCIENCES. SUMMARIZES SOVIET SPACE PROGRAMS,
AND ANALYZES INTERNATIONAL, POLITICAL, AND LEGAL IMPLI-
CATIONS. DISCUSSES SOVIET GOALS, WESTERN PROJECTIONS OF FU-
TURE SOVIET SPACE PLANS AND CAPABILITIES, AND SOVIET ATTI-
TUDE TOWARD INTERNATIONAL SPACE COOPERATION.

1169 US SENATE COMM AERO SPACE SCI
AERONAUTICAL RESEARCH AND DEVELOPMENT POLICY (PAMPHLET)
WASHINGTON: US GOVERNMENT, 1967, 189 PP.
    HEARINGS BEFORE COMMITTEE ON AERONAUTICAL AND SPACE
SCIENCES, US SENATE. REVIEWS ADEQUACY OF POLICY PLANNING
FOR RESEARCH IN THIS AREA. ASSESSES WHAT CONGRESS, THE EXEC-
UTIVE, AND PRIVATE INDUSTRY CAN DO TO IMPLEMENT NEEDED
PROGRAMS.

1170 US SENATE COMM AERO SPACE SCI
TREATY ON PRINCIPLES GOVERNING ACTIVITIES OF STATES IN EX-
PLORATION AND USE OF OUTER SPACE, INCLUDING...BODIES.
WASHINGTON: US GOVERNMENT, 1967, 84 PP.
    REPORT ON "TREATY ON OUTER SPACE," INCLUDING NEGOTIATION
OF TREATY PROVISIONS, TEXT AND ANALYSIS OF TREATY, AND BACK-
GROUND DOCUMENTS (UN AND US RESOLUTIONS, ANTARCTIC TREATY,
NUCLEAR TEST BAN TREATY). ALSO INCLUDES US AND USSR MOON
EXPLORATION RECORDS. PREPARED FOR USE OF COMMITTEE ON
AERONAUTICAL AND SPACE SCIENCES.

1171 US SENATE COMM AERO SPACE SCI
POLICY PLANNING FOR TECHNOLOGY TRANSFER (PAMPHLET)
WASHINGTON: US GOVERNMENT, 1967, 183 PP.
    EXAMINATION OF APPLICATION OF SCIENCE AND TECHNOLOGY TO
PROBLEMS IN COMMERCIAL OR PUBLIC PROGRAMS. DISCUSSES DEVEL-
OPMENT OF US AND FOREIGN TECHNOLOGY AND ITS IMPORTANCE FOR
NATIONAL ECONOMY. ANALYZES NEW TECHNOLOGICAL NEEDS IN CREA-
TION.

1172 US SENATE COMM AERO SPACE SCI
HEARINGS BEFORE THE COMMITTEE ON AERONAUTICAL AND SPACE
SCIENCES UNITED STATES SENATE NINETIETH CONGRESS (PAMPHLET)
WASHINGTON: US GOVERNMENT, 1967, 189 PP.
    STATEMENTS AND TESTIMONIES ON ADEQUACY OF POLICY PLANNING
FOR AERONAUTICAL RESEARCH AND DEVELOPMENT. CONCLUDES THAT
MAJOR REORGANIZATION IS REQUIRED AND RECOMMENDS THAT AN
AERONAUTICAL RESEARCH AND DEVELOPMENT ADVISORY COUNCIL BE
CREATED.

1173 US SENATE COMM AERO SPACE SCI
APOLLO ACCIDENT (PARTS 1-7)
WASHINGTON: US GOVERNMENT, 1967, 785 PP.
    HEARINGS PREPARED BEFORE THE COMMITTEE ON AERONAUTICAL
AND SPACE SCIENCES REGARDING APOLLO ACCIDENT OF JAN. 27,
1967. CONTAINS FULL INVESTIGATIVE REPORT; PLANS FOR HARDWARE
MODIFICATION; PLANS FOR CHANGES IN PROGRAM COSTS AND
SCHEDULES; NORTH AMERICAN AVIATION HEARING; APOLLO
PROGRAM REVISED SCHEDULES; ACTIONS TAKEN ON BOARD'S
DETERMINATIONS, AND AS RESULT OF ACCIDENT.

1174 US SENATE COMM AERO SPACE SCI
AERONAUTICAL RESEARCH AND DEVELOPMENT POLICY; HEARINGS,
COMM ON AERONAUTICAL AND SPACE SCIENCES...1967 (PAMPHLET)
WASHINGTON: GOVT PR OFFICE, 1967, 189 PP.
    HEARINGS DEALT WITH ADEQUACY OF POLICY PLANNING IN AERO-
NAUTICAL RESEARCH AND DEVELOPMENT, AND WITH PROPER ROLES OF
CONGRESS, EXECUTIVE BRANCH, AND PRIVATE INDUSTRY. BOTH
SPACE AND NONSPACE ACTIVITIES TREATED.

1175 US SENATE COMM APPROPRIATIONS
PERSONNEL ADMINISTRATION AND OPERATIONS OF AGENCY FOR INTER-
NATIONAL DEVELOPMENT: SPECIAL HEARING.
WASHINGTON: GOVT PR OFFICE, 1963, 404 PP.
    ANALYSIS OF PEOPLE WHO ARE APPOINTED TO AID AGENCY TO
ADMINISTER FOREIGN AID FUNDS AND PROGRAMS. FEELS PEOPLE ARE
INEFFICIENT AND UNDESERVING, AND WASTE US MONEY. SUGGESTS
AGENCY PEOPLE HAVE CIVIL SERVICE STATUS AND BE OF TOP
QUALITY. INVESTIGATES CERTAIN NATIONS, THEIR PROGRAMS, AND
LEADERS.

1176 US SENATE COMM GOVT OPERATIONS
ORGANIZING FOR NATIONAL SECURITY.
WASHINGTON: US GOVERNMENT, 1961, 1338 PP.
    VOLUME TWO OF THREE- VOLUME PUBLICATION OF SUBCOMMITTEE
ON NATIONAL POLICY MACHINERY. CONTAINS STUDIES AND BACK-
GROUND MATERIALS ON THE DEVELOPMENT, COORDINATION AND EXECU-
TION OF FOREIGN AND DEFENSE POLICY. VOLUMES ONE AND THREE
CONTAIN HEARINGS AND FINDINGS AND RECOMMENDATIONS.

1177 US SENATE COMM GOVT OPERATIONS
ADMINISTRATION OF NATIONAL SECURITY.

WASHINGTON: GOVT PR OFFICE, 1962, 201 PP.
    DESCRIBES ADMINISTRATION OF SECURITY PROGRAMS UNDER
KENNEDY AND EFFECT OF THIS ON FOREIGN POLICY DEVELOPMENT
IN THAT PERIOD. INCLUDES TEXTS OF RELEVANT OFFICIAL
STATEMENTS BY JFK, RUSK, MCNAMARA, AND BUNDY. ALSO GIVES
RECENT COMMENTS BY ACHESON, NEUSTADT, AND HERTER.

1178 US SENATE COMM GOVT OPERATIONS
ADMINISTRATION OF NATIONAL SECURITY (9 PARTS)
WASHINGTON: US GOVERNMENT, 1963, 600 PP.
    COLLECTION OF US GOVERNMENT DOCUMENTS OF THE HEARINGS
BEFORE SUBCOMMITTEE ON NATIONAL SECURITY STAFFING AND
OPERATIONS DURING THE 88TH CONGRESS, FIRST AND SECOND SES-
SIONS. CONTAINS OPENING STATEMENTS, TESTIMONY, MEMORANDA,
EXHIBITS, AND COMMENTARY OF PARTICIPANTS IN THE INVESTIGA-
TION. COMMITTEE CHAIRED BY JOHN L. MCCLELLAN OF ARKANSAS.

1179 US SENATE COMM GOVT OPERATIONS
ORGANIZATION OF FEDERAL EXECUTIVE DEPARTMENTS AND AGENCIES:
REPORT OF MARCH 23, 1965.
WASHINGTON: GOVT PR OFFICE, 1965, 67 PP.
    REVIEWS ORGANIZATIONAL CHANGES IN EXECUTIVE BRANCH DURING
1964. IS 25TH OF SERIES. DETAILED ORGANIZATION CHART. COVERS
BUREAUS OF DEPARTMENTS OF AGRICULTURE, COMMERCE, DEFENSE,
THREE MILITARY DEPARTMENTS, HEALTH, EDUCATION, AND WELFARE,
INTERIOR, LABOR, POST OFFICE, STATE, TREASURY, ALSO
INDEPENDENT AGENCIES; ALSO EMPLOYEE STATISTICS AND SUMMARY
CHARTS.

1180 US SENATE COMM ON COMMERCE
URBAN MASS TRANSPORTATION.
WASHINGTON: GOVT PR OFFICE, 1960, 308 PP.
    HEARING BEFORE SUBCOMMITTEE ON SURFACE TRANSPORTATION OF
US SENATE COMMITTEE ON COMMERCE. DISCUSSES THREE PROPOSED
BILLS ON URBAN MASS TRANSPORTATION. FIRST BILL PROVIDES
FINANCIAL ASSISTANCE FOR PUBLIC AND PRIVATE SYSTEMS; SECOND
ENCOURAGES STATE AND LOCAL INITIATIVE IN URBAN TRANSIT
DEVELOPMENT; THIRD ALSO PROVIDES FUNDS. ALL PROVIDE FOR
LONG-RANGE PROGRAMS AND FOR RESEARCH PROJECTS.

1181 US SENATE COMM ON FOREIGN REL
ARMS SALES AND FOREIGN POLICY (PAMPHLET)
WASHINGTON: US GOVERNMENT, 1967, 13 PP.
    STAFF STUDY OF COMMITTEE ON FOREIGN POLICY. CONCLUDES
THAT SALE OF ARMS HAS REPLACED GIVING ARMS AS PREDOMINANT
FORM OF US MILITARY ASSISTANCE. BELIEVES THAT US
MUST REAPPRAISE ADEQUACY OF PRESENT MACHINERY OF POLICY
CONTROL AND LEGISLATIVE OVERSIGHT GOVERNING SALE OF
ARMS. MAKES SPECIFIC RECOMMENDATIONS FOR IMPROVEMENT.

1182 US SENATE COMM ON FOREIGN REL
TREATY ON OUTER SPACE.
WASHINGTON: US GOVERNMENT, 1967, 162 PP.
    HEARINGS BEFORE SENATE COMMITTEE ON FOREIGN RELATIONS,
HEADED BY J. W. FULBRIGHT, TO CONSIDER TREATY ON OUTER SPACE
SIGNED BY US AND 59 OTHER COUNTRIES INCLUDING USSR ON
JANUARY 27, 1967. SECRETARY OF STATE RUSK, CYRUS R. VANCE,
GENERAL EARLE WHEELER, AND AMBASSADOR TO UN ARTHUR GOLDBERG
TESTIFIED.

1183 US SENATE COMM ON FOREIGN REL
ARMS SALES TO NEAR EAST AND SOUTH ASIAN COUNTRIES.
WASHINGTON: US GOVERNMENT, 1967, 102 PP.
    HEARINGS BEFORE SUBCOMMITTEE ON NEAR EASTERN AND SOUTH
ASIAN AFFAIRS OF SENATE COMMITTEE ON FOREIGN RELATIONS
HEADED BY STUART SYMINGTON ON US ARMS SALES TO IRAN. INVES-
TIGATES COORDINATION OF GOVERNMENT MACHINERY IN SALES; ASKS
WHETHER OR NOT CONGRESS IS PROPERLY CONSULTED AND INFORMED
ABOUT SALE DECISIONS. ALSO DEALS WITH SALES TO INDIA AND
PAKISTAN AND ROLE OF COMMERCIAL ARMS SUPPLIERS.

1184 US SENATE COMM ON FOREIGN REL
UNITED STATES ARMAMENT AND DISARMAMENT PROBLEMS.
WASHINGTON: US GOVERNMENT, 1967, 181 PP.
    HEARINGS BEFORE SUBCOMMITTEE ON DISARMAMENT OF COMMITTEE
ON FOREIGN RELATIONS HEADED BY ALBERT GORE. INCLUDES DIS-
CUSSION OF STATUS OF DEVELOPMENT OF BALLISTIC AND ANTI-
BALLISTIC SYSTEMS IN US AND BRIEFING ON NONPROLIFERATION
TREATY, DEPLOYMENT OF NIKE X ANTI-BALLISTIC MISSILE SYSTEM,
ARMS SALES, AND OTHER DISARMAMENT AND ARMANENT PROBLEMS.

1185 US SENATE COMM ON FOREIGN REL
FOREIGN ASSISTANCE ACT OF 1967.
WASHINGTON: US GOVERNMENT, 1967, 393 PP.
    HEARINGS BEFORE SENATE COMMITTEE ON FOREIGN RELATIONS ON
FOREIGN ASSISTANCE BILL OF 1967. WITNESSES INCLUDE SECRETARY
OF DEFENSE ROBERT MC NAMARA, SECRETARY OF STATE DEAN RUSK,
AND WILLIAM E. MORAN OF INTERNATIONAL ECONOMIC POLICY ASSO-
CIATION. COVERS ALL AREAS OF FOREIGN AID IN SEVERAL PARTS OF
WORLD.

1186 US SENATE COMM ON FOREIGN REL
SURVEY OF THE ALLIANCE FOR PROGRESS; THE POLITICAL ASPECTS
(PAMPHLET)
WASHINGTON: US GOVERNMENT, 1967, 24 PP.
    STUDY FOR SUBCOMMITTEE ON AMERICAN REPUBLICS AFFAIRS OF

COMMITTEE ON FOREIGN RELATIONS TREATING LONG-TERM POLITICAL
ASPECTS OF CURRENT LATIN AMERICAN SITUATION. SEES PROBLEM AS
ONE OF TECHNOLOGICAL REVOLUTION AND GREAT POPULATION GROWTH
IN SOCIETIES WITH TRADITIONAL POLITICAL AND SOCIAL
INSTITUTIONS. DISCUSSES US POLICY IN LIGHT OF SITUATION.

1187 US SENATE COMM ON PUBLIC WORKS
AIR QUALITY ACT OF 1967 (PAMPHLET)
WASHINGTON: US GOVERNMENT, 1967, 86 PP.
REPORT OF COMMITTEE ON PUBLIC WORKS RECOMMENDS PASSAGE
OF AMENDMENT TO CLEAN AIR ACT. EXPANDS AUTHORITY TO CONDUCT
RESEARCH RELATING TO AIR POLLUTANTS; ESTABLISH REGIONAL
AIR QUALITY COMMISSIONS; CONTROL INDUSTRIAL EMISSIONS;
ESTABLISH AND INSPECT AUTOMOBILE EMISSION CONTROL DEVICES.

1188 US SUPERINTENDENT OF DOCUMENTS
TRANSPORTATION: HIGHWAYS, ROADS, AND POSTAL SERVICE (PRICE
LIST 25)
WASHINGTON: GOVT PR OFFICE.
SERIES PUBLICATION OF US GOVERNMENT LISTING MATERIALS
CURRENTLY AVAILABLE FOR SALE. ENTRIES GROUPED BY SUBJECT:
INCLUDE TOPICS SUCH AS FEDERAL MARITIME COMMISSION, MARITIME
ADMINISTRATION, PORTS, POSTAL SERVICE, NAVIGATION, MERCHANT
MARINE, PUBLIC ROADS BUREAU, RAILROADS, FIRST AID AT SEA,
AND INTRACOASTAL WATERWAY. 50 EDITIONS TO DATE. MATERIALS
PUBLISHED 1952 THROUGH 1967.

1189 US SUPERINTENDENT OF DOCUMENTS
LIBRARY OF CONGRESS (PRICE LIST 83)
WASHINGTON: GOVT PR OFFICE.
SERIAL PUBLICATION LISTING US GOVERNMENT PUBLICATIONS
CURRENTLY AVAILABLE FOR SALE. MAJORITY OF ITEMS ANNOTATED.
INCLUDES BIBLIOGRAPHICAL PUBLICATIONS, 13 EDITIONS TO DATE,
CONTAINING PUBLICATIONS FROM 1957 THROUGH 1966. ITEMS AR-
RANGED BY SUBJECT, INCLUDE MATERIALS ON AFRICA, COPYRIGHTS,
CIVIL WAR, EUROPE, SOVIET UNION, INTERNATIONAL MEETINGS AND
SCIENTIFIC ORGANIZATIONS, KENNEDY, AND PRESIDENTS OF US.

1190 US SUPERINTENDENT OF DOCUMENTS
SPACE: MISSILES, THE MOON, NASA, AND SATELLITES (PRICE
LIST 79A)
WASHINGTON: GOVT PR OFFICE, 1967, 21 PP.
FIRST EDITION OF US GOVERNMENT SERIES LISTING GOVERNMENT
MATERIALS CURRENTLY AVAILABLE FOR SALE. MAJORITY OF SOURCES
ANNOTATED; ENTRIES PUBLISHED 1959 THROUGH 1966. TOPICS IN-
CLUDE SPACE EDUCATION, EXPLORATION, RESEARCH TECHNOLOGY,
NASA CONGRESSIONAL REPORTS, PROJECT APOLLO AND GEMINI, COM-
MUNICATIONS SATELLITES, INSPECTION, INTERNATIONAL COOPERA-
TION, ETC.

1191 VAN DYKE V.
PRIDE AND POWER: THE RATIONALE OF THE SPACE PROGRAM.
URBANA: U. ILL. PR., 1964, 285 PP., $6.50.
CONSIDERS HOW SPACE DECISIONS ARE MADE AND THE HISTORY OF
THE U.S. PROGRAM. EXAMINES THE VARIOUS REASONS GIVEN TO
SUPPORT AND JUSTIFY THE SPACE PROGRAM. DESCRIBES THE ORGAN-
IZATION OF THE FEDERAL GOVERNMENT FOR THE IMPLEMENTATION OF
THE PROGRAM. DEMONSTRATES THAT WHAT STARTED AS A SCIENTIFIC
PROGRAM HAS COME TO BE DOMINATED BY A CONCERN FOR PRIDE AND
POWER, EVEN BY THE SCIENTISTS WORKING ON THE LUNAR PROGRAM.

1192 VAN WAGENEN R.W.
SOME VIEWS OF AMERICAN DEFENSE OFFICIALS ABOUT THE UNITED
NATIONS (PAPER)
CAMBRIDGE: MIT CTR INTL STUDIES, 1959, 47 PP.
ANALYZES OPINIONS TOWARD UN AND ITS ROLE IN PROMOTING US
NATIONAL OBJECTIVES; BASED ON INTERVIEWS WITH 25 DEPARTMENT
OF DEFENSE OFFICIALS. PRIMARILY CONCERNED WITH THREE ISSUES:
ABILITY OF US TO SURVIVE NUCLEAR WAR IN NEAR FUTURE,
POSSIBILITY THAT WORLD PEACE CAN EVER BE ACHIEVED AND UN AS
VEHICLE TO CARRY OUT US POLICY OR AS MECHANISM TO NARROW
GAP BETWEEN EAST AND WEST.

1193 VEINOTT A.F. JR. ED.
MATHEMATICAL STUDIES IN MANAGEMENT SCIENCE.
NEW YORK: MACMILLAN, 1965, 481 PP., LC#55-17819.
SURVEY OF CURRENT TOPICS OF DISCUSSION IN MANAGEMENT
SCIENCES. PAPERS DEAL WITH DETERMINISTIC DECISION MODELS
AND STOCHASTIC DECISION MODELS; TREAT TRANSPORTATION AND
NETWORK PROBLEMS, TOPICS IN LINEAR AND QUADRATIC
PROGRAMMING, AND PRODUCTION AND INVENTORY CONTROL; ANALYZE
PROGRAMMING UNDER UNCERTAINTY, AND INVENTORY MODELS.

1194 VERGIN R.C.
"COMPUTER INDUCED ORGANIZATION CHANGES."
BUSINESS TOPICS, 15 (SUMMER 67), 60-68.
EXAMINES EFFECT OF COMPUTER ON DECISION-MAKING,
CONCOMITANT CHANGES IN STRUCTURE OF ORGANIZATION, AND
POSITION OF DATA PROCESSING. DISCUSSES MIDDLE MANAGEMENT,
DECENTRALIZATION, AND RESISTANCE TO ORGANIZATIONAL CHANGE.
COMMENTS ON IMPACT OF COMPUTER IN FUTURE.

1195 VERMOT-GAUCHY M.
L'EDUCATION NATIONALE DANS LA FRANCE DE 1975.
MONACO: ED DU ROCHER, 1965, 335 PP.
ANALYZES CURRENT THOUGHT CONCERNING EDUCATIONAL POLICY

IN FRANCE. DISCUSSES RESULTS THAT APPLICATION OF THIS POLICY
WILL HAVE FROM 1960-75. DISCUSSES PAST TRADITIONS AND EXIST-
ING POLICIES, FORECASTS FUTURE POLICIES, AND OUTLINES PROS-
PECTS FROM 1970-75. BELIEVES THAT GROWTH IN EDUCATIONAL
INSTITUTIONS HAS BEGUN TO BRING ABOUT DESIRABLE CURRICULUM
AND OTHER EDUCATIONAL REFORMS.

1196 VERNEY D.V.
PUBLIC ENTERPRISE IN SWEDEN.
LIVERPOOL: LIVERPOOL U PRESS, 1959, 132 PP.
EXPLAINS SWEDISH ECONOMIC SYSTEM, PAYING PARTICULAR
ATTENTION TO PUBLIC ACCOUNTABILITY. BEGINS WITH PUBLIC
ENTERPRISE WITHOUT NATIONALIZATION AND COMPARES WITH UK.
DISCUSSES GROWTH OF TRADING AGENCIES AND STATE COMPANIES,
FORM OF SWEDISH PUBLIC ENTERPRISE, AND PROBLEM OF
ACCOUNTABILITY. INCLUDES CIVIL SERVICE FORMALISM, SOCIAL
DEMOCRATIC PARTY, ALTERNATIVES, AND FUTURE REFORMS.

1197 VERNON R.
THE MYTH AND REALITY OF OUR URBAN PROBLEMS (PAMPHLET)
CAMBRIDGE: JOINT CTR URBAN STUD, 1962, 84 PP.
STAFFORD LITTLE LECTURES PRESENTED AT PRINCETON
UNIVERSITY, 1961. OFFER PRESCRIPTION FOR, RATHER THAN PROG-
NOSIS OF, METROPOLITAN ILLS. PROPOSE SEVERAL PROGRAMS, IN-
CLUDING LAND-USE PLANNING, REBUILDING CITIES, GOVERNMENT
INTERVENTION, AND THE LIKE.

1198 VIETORISZ T.
"PRELIMINARY BIBLIOGRAPHY FOR INDUSTRIAL DEVELOPMENT
PROGRAMMING."
UN INDUSTRIALIZ & PRODUC BULL., 5 (1962), 68-82.
AN ANNOTATED BIBLIOGRAPHY FOR INDUSTRIAL DEVELOPMENT PRO-
GRAMMING. MATERIAL PUBLISHED IN ENGLISH, FRENCH, SPANISH,
RUSSIAN, AND GERMAN LANGUAGES RANGING FROM 1929 TO 1960.
CONTAINS 374 ENTRIES.

1199 VIETORISZ T.
"PRELIMINARY BIBLIOGRAPHY FOR INDUSTRIAL DEVELOPMENT
PROGRAMMING."
UN INDUSTRIALIZ & PRODUC BULL., 6 (1963), 67-77.
AN ANNOTATED BIBLIOGRAPHY FOR INDUSTRIAL DEVELOPMENT PRO-
GRAMMING. MATERIAL PUBLISHED IN ENGLISH, FRENCH, SPANISH,
RUSSIAN, AND GERMAN LANGUAGES RANGING FROM 1939 TO 1962.
CONTAINS 332 ENTRIES.

1200 VINER J. ET AL.
SYMPOSIUM ON ATOMIC ENERGY AND ITS IMPLICATIONS.
NEW YORK: PHILO/LIBRARY, VOL. 90, 1946, 79 PP.
REVIEWS FIFTY YEARS OF ATOMIC PHYSICS. DESCRIBES SOCIAL
ADJUSTMENTS TO ATOMIC ENERGY. EXPLORES QUESTION OF INTER-
NATIONAL CONTROL OF ATOMIC ENERGY. CONCLUDES WITH STUDY
OF POSSIBLE BENEFITS OF ATOMIC ENERGY.

1201 VLASIC I.A.
"THE SPACE TREATY* A PRELIMINARY EVALUATION."
CALIF. LAW REV., 55 (MAY 67), 507-519.
GIVES BACKGROUND OF SPACE TREATY AND DISCUSSES CONDITIONS
WHICH INFLUENCED ITS FORMULATION. ANALYSIS OF PRINCIPAL
FEATURES AND DEFICIENCIES OF TREATY. DISCUSSES EMERGENCE
OF GENERAL ASSEMBLY AS PRINCIPAL WORLD COMMUNITY ORGAN FOR
SETTING STANDARDS OF CONDUCT IN SPACE AGE AND THE DAMAGE
DONE TO PRESTIGE BY CONCLUSION OF SPACE TREATY.

1202 VON NEUMANN J.
"CAN WE SURVIVE TECHNOLOGY?"
FORTUNE, 51 (JUNE 55), 106-108, 151-152.
STATES THAT INCREASED TECHNOLOGY IS CAUSING SERIOUS
SHORTAGE OF SPACE AND "MAN IS RUNNING OUT OF ROOM." FEELS
THIS CRISIS IS INHERENT IN TECHNOLOGY'S RELATION TO
GEOGRAPHY AND TO POLITICAL ORGANIZATION. CONSIDERS PROBLEMS
OF AIR POLLUTION, POSSIBILITIES OF WEATHER CONTROL, AND
DANGERS OF NUCLEAR MISUSE. HOPES MAN'S FLEXIBILITY WILL
ENABLE HIM TO PRODUCE ADJUSTMENTS NECESSARY FOR SURVIVAL.

1203 VUCINICH A.
THE SOVIET ACADEMY OF SCIENCES.
STANFORD: STANFORD U PRESS, 1956, 157 PP., LC#55-11552.
EXAMINES TWO INTERRELATED PROBLEMS: THE ORGANIZATION OF
SCIENTIFIC INQUIRY IN SOVIET UNION, AND THE SOCIAL ROLE OF
SOVIET SCIENCE AND SCIENTISTS. TREATS THESE PROBLEMS IN
TERMS OF THEIR BEARING UPON THE ACADEMY OF SCIENCES OF
THE USSR.

1204 WAGER P.W. ED.
"COUNTY GOVERNMENT ACROSS THE NATION."
PRINCETON* UNIV. REF. SYSTEM, 1950.
DESCRIPTION OF ORGANIZATION AND OPERATIONS OF PARTICULAR
COUNTY GOVERNMENTS IN 48 STATES WITH THE EXCLUSION OF METRO-
POLITAN COUNTIES. INTRODUCTION SURVEYS GENERAL FEATURES OF
COUNTY GOVERNMENT: SCHOOL DISTRICTS, TOWNSHIP GOVERNMENTS,
TOWN GOVERNMENT, STATE ADMINISTRATIVE SUPERVISION, REVENUES
AND EXPENDITURES, COURTS AND COURT OFFICIALS, ETC. SHORT
GENERAL BIBLIOGRAPHY INCLUDED.

1205 WALDO D. ED.
THE RESEARCH FUNCTION OF UNIVERSITY BUREAUS AND INSTITUTES

FOR GOVERNMENTAL-RELATED RESEARCH.
BERKELEY: U CALIF, BUR PUB ADMIN, 1960.
ISSUED BY BUREAU OF PUBLIC ADMINISTRATION, BOOK IS
RESULT OF A 1959 CONFERENCE AT UNIVERSITY OF CALIFORNIA.
DEALS WITH RESEARCH IN PUBLIC ADMINISTRATION, POLITICS,
COMPARATIVE GOVERNMENTS, METROPOLISES, AND PUBLIC POLICY.
ALSO DEALS WITH METHODS OF RESEARCH. THE RELATION BETWEEN
THEIR OUTPUT AND THE HOW AND WHY OF THEIR ORGANIZATION IS
NOT ADEQUATELY EXPLAINED.

1206 WALES H.G., FERBER R.
A BASIC BIBLIOGRAPHY ON MARKETING RESEARCH (REV. ED.)
CHICAGO: AMER MARKETING ASSN, 1963, 182 PP.
PROVIDES ANNOTATED SET OF REFERENCES IN AREA OF
MARKETING RESEARCH THROUGH 1962. INCLUDES NOT ONLY REFER-
ENCES DEALING DIRECTLY WITH MARKETING RESEARCH BUT ALSO
REFERENCES PERTAINING TO CONCEPTS AND METHODS IN RELATED
AREAS. CRITERIA OF SELECTION ARE RELIABILITY, BROADNESS OF
INTEREST, AND AVAILABILITY. ANNOTATIONS INDICATE THE VALUE
OF EACH PUBLICATION FOR VARIOUS TYPES OF RESEARCH.

1207 WALSTON H.
AGRICULTURE UNDER COMMUNISM.
CHESTER SPRINGS: DUFOUR, 1962, 108 PP., LC#62-10661.
DESCRIBES AGRARIAN HISTORY OF COMMUNIST COUNTRIES AND
METHODS USED TO SOLVE PROBLEM OF AGRICULTURAL WORKERS'
RESISTANCE TO GOVERNMENT INTERFERENCE. EVALUATES SUCCESS
OF COMMUNIST CHANGES. MAINTAINS INNOVATOR MUST SEE THAT
CHANGE BRINGS "BETTER AND HAPPIER LIFE" TO CULTIVATORS.

1208 WALTER E.
"VERS UNE CLASSIFICATION SCIENTIFIQUE DE LA SOCIOLOGIA."
DIALECTICA, 16 (NO., 62), 354-60.
DEALS WITH EPISTEMOLOGIC PROBLEM IN EMPIRICAL SCIENCES.
SUGGESTS BETTER CLASSIFICATION OF METHODS IN ORDER TO ADAPT
THEM TO MODERN TECHNOLOGY AND POLICY PLANNING DEVICES.

1209 WALTERS R.E.
"THE ROLE OF NUCLEAR WEAPONS FOR THE WEST."
ROYAL UNITED SERVICE INST. J., 62 (AUG. 67), 249-256.
EXAMINES DEVELOPMENT OF NUCLEAR WEAPONS BY WESTERN POWERS
AND POLICY EFFECTS OF IT. CRITICIZES LACK OF PLANNING AND
DECISION-MAKING AFTER WEAPONS ARE DEVELOPED. ADVOCATES USE
OF CHEMICAL AND BIOLOGICAL WARFARE AS MORE EFFECTIVE AND
MERCIFUL, AND LAUDS PREDEVELOPMENTAL PLANNING.

1210 WARD B.
5 IDEAS THAT CHANGE THE WORLD.
NEW YORK: NORTON, 1959, 188 PP.
TRACES HISTORY OF THEORY AND PRACTICE OF NATIONALISM AND
SHOWS HOW IT CHANGES AND IS CHANGED BY FOUR OTHER BASIC
IDEAS: INDUSTRIALISM, COLONIALISM, COMMUNISM AND INTER-
NATIONALISM.

1211 WARD B.
NATIONALISM AND IDEOLOGY.
NEW YORK: W W NORTON, 1966, 125 PP., LC#66-15318.
NATIONALISM AND IDEOLOGY ARE PRESENTED AS TWO DEAD-END
PATHS IN MAN'S QUEST FOR MEANINGFUL KINSHIP. AMERICAN CAP-
ITALISM AND RUSSIAN COMMUNISM ARE SIGNIFICANT FAILURES AS
ATTEMPTS TO USE TECHNOLOGICAL ADVANCES TO UNITE MAN. THESE
IDEOLOGIES PREVENT THE NECESSARY HUMANITARIAN ASSISTANCE TO
BE GIVEN THE POOR LANDS, THEREBY AVOIDING CATASTROPHE.

1212 WARD C.
"THE 'NEW MYTHS' AND 'OLD REALITIES' OF NUCLEAR WAR."
ORBIS, 7 (SUMMER 64), 255-91.
SEES THE 'NUCLEAR STALEMATE' THEORY AS A NEW MYTH WHICH
IS ACCEPTED BY PERSONS IN THE SCIENTIFIC COMMUNITY COG-
NIZANT OF DEFENSE MATTERS. ASSERTS THAT THE REALITIES ARE
SUCH THAT THE USA MUST CONTINUE TO EMPLOY TRADITIONAL
SAFEGUARDS BEFORE ACCEPTING BELIEF IN A SOVIET DETENTE.

1213 WARE R.S.
"FORECAST A.D. 2000."
MILITARY REV., 47 (JUNE 67), 30-39.
PROJECTS FUTURE CONDITIONS BASED ON EXIGENCIES OF POPULA-
TION EXPLOSION AND SCIENTIFIC REVOLUTION. FORESEES SHARPEN-
ING OF CONFLICT BETWEEN "HAVES" AND "HAVE NOTS" DUE TO IN-
CREASED COMMUNICATION AND WORSENING OVERALL ECONOMIC CONDI-
TIONS IN SMALL COUNTRIES. DESCRIBES FUTURE POSSIBILITIES OF
LIMITED WAR. CONCLUSIONS ARE BASED ON AVAILABLE SCIENTIFIC
HYPOTHESES AND PRESUME NO INTERNATIONAL ACCORD.

1214 WARNER A.W. ED., MORSE D. ED., EICHNER A.S. ED.
THE IMPACT OF SCIENCE ON TECHNOLOGY.
NEW YORK: COLUMBIA U PRESS, 1965, 218 PP., LC#65-19945.
ARTICLES BY LEADING SCIENTISTS AND PUBLIC OFFICIALS.
C. WRIGHT NOTES THAT INTERACTION OF SCIENCE AND TECHNOLOGY
IS INCREASING, SUBJECT TO POLICY CHOICES. PROBES FACTORS
MOST PRODUCTIVE OF SCIENTIFIC ADVANCE. ASKS: CAN TECHNOLOGY
ACCELERATE GROWTH IN THE CIVILIAN SECTOR OF ECONOMY.

1215 WARNER W.L. ED.
THE EMERGENT AMERICAN SOCIETY VOL I, LARGE-SCALE ORGANIZA-
TIONS.

NEW HAVEN: YALE U PR, 1967, 667 PP., LC#67-13450.
A COLLECTION OF ESSAYS BY RESEARCH EXPERTS ON THE SEVERAL
VARIETIES OF LARGE STRUCTURES IN US: FEDERAL GOVERNMENT,
LARGE CORPORATIONS, UNIONS, TRADE AND PROFESSIONAL GROUPS.
THE CHANGING ROLE OF THE SCHOOLS AND CHURCHES IS ALSO DIS-
CUSSED. THE EVOLUTION OF THESE VARIOUS ORGANIZATIONS IS ANA-
LYZED IN DEPTH AND THE EFFECT OF TECHNOLOGY IS EXAMINED.

1216 WASHBURN A.M.
"NUCLEAR PROLIFERATION IN A REVOLUTIONARY INTERNATIONAL
SYSTEM."
PUBLIC & INTL AFF., 5 (SPRING 67), 111-133.
DANGER OF NOT RECOGNIZING NUCLEAR PROLIFERATION AS A CON-
TINUING PROBLEM AND REASONS FOR THIS DECREASING CONCERN.
NUCLEAR PROLIFERATION IS SUBJECT TO ANALYSIS ON TWO LEVELS,
THAT OF THE INTERNATIONAL SYSTEM AND THAT OF THE NATION-
STATE. IMPLICATIONS OF THESE APPROACHES AND THEIR RELEVANCE
TO SPRING, 1967, EIGHTEEN NATION DISARMAMENT CONFERENCES ARE
DISCUSSED.

1217 WASHBURNE N.F.
INTERPRETING SOCIAL CHANGE IN AMERICA.
NEW YORK: RANDOM HOUSE, INC, 1954, 50 PP., LC#54-10158.
TREATS EFFECT OF SOCIAL STRUCTURE ON CHANGE. INTERCONNEC-
TIONS AMONG INSTITUTIONAL FUNCTIONS, SOCIAL PROCESSES, AND
SOCIAL MOVEMENTS. EMPHASIZES TRENDS IN URBANIZATION, BUREAU-
CRATIZATION, AND TECHNOLOGICAL DEVELOPMENTS.

1218 WASKOW A.I.
KEEPING THE WORLD DISARMED.
SANTA BARBARA: CTR DEMO INST, 1965, 88 PP.
EXAMINES POSSIBILITIES FOR DEMILITARIZED WORLD ORDER
SUCH AS GRADUATED DETERRENTS, NON-LETHAL EQUIVALENTS OF
WAR, AND HYPOTHETICAL POLICE MISSIONS.

1219 WASSERMAN P.
INFORMATION FOR ADMINISTRATORS: A GUIDE TO PUBLICATIONS AND
SERVICES FOR MANAGEMENT IN BUSINESS AND GOVERNMENT.
ITHACA, NY: CORNELL SCH BUS ADM, 1956, 375 PP.
OUTLINES SOURCES OF INFORMATION USEFUL IN BUSINESS AND
GOVERNMENTAL MANAGEMENT. DISCUSSES PARTICULAR UTILITY OF
EACH KIND OF PUBLICATION LISTED. INCLUDES LIBRARIES, GOVERN-
MENT PUBLICATIONS, PERIODICALS AND NEWSPAPERS, SOURCES OF
STATISTICAL DATA, AND PUBLICATIONS ASSOCIATED WITH CHAMBERS
OF COMMERCE, PROFESSIONAL ORGANIZATIONS, VARIOUS RESEARCH
INSTITUTIONS, AND BUSINESS AND PUBLIC ADMINISTRATION GROUPS.

1220 WASSERMAN P. ED.
MEASUREMENT AND ANALYSIS OF ORGANIZATIONAL PERFORMANCE.
ITHACA, NY: CORNELL SCH BUS ADM, 1959, 109 PP.
COVERS TOTAL, UNIT, AND INDIVIDUAL EFFICIENCY IN ORGAN-
IZATIONS OF ALL TYPES. GENERAL AND THEORETICAL MATERIAL ON
IMPROVEMENT OF EFFICIENCY.

1221 WEBSTER J.A.
A GENERAL STUDY OF THE DEPARTMENT OF DEFENSE INTERNAL
SECURITY PROGRAM.
LOS ANGELES: U OF S CALIF PR, 1960, 78 PP.
EXAMINES ADMINISTRATIVE SUCCESS, PROBLEMS, AND FAILINGS
OF INDUSTRIAL SECURITY PROGRAM. CONSIDERS COST OF ADMIN-
ISTRATION, NEED FOR SECURITY, LEGAL ASPECTS OF SECURITY,
AND RELATION OF JUDICIAL TO EXECUTIVE BRANCHES IN THESE
PROBLEMS.

1222 WEIGLEY R.F.
HISTORY OF THE UNITED STATES ARMY.
NEW YORK: MACMILLAN, 1967, 688 PP.
EMPHASIZES INTERNAL, INSTITUTIONAL DEVELOPMENT OF THE AR-
MY RATHER THAN STRESSING BATTLES AND CAMPAIGNS. CONSIDERS
PLACE OF ARMY WITHIN AMERICAN GOVERNMENT AND SOCIETY AT
LARGE AND INCLUDES METHODS OF WARMAKING.

1223 WEIL G.L.
"THE MERGER OF THE INSTITUTIONS OF THE EUROPEAN COMMUNITIES"
AMER. J. OF INT. LAW, 61 (JAN. 67), 57-65.
REPORTS ON NATURE AND SIGNIFICANCE OF MERGER TREATY OF
1965 WHICH REPLACED EEC, EURATOM, AND ECSC WITH A SINGLE
COUNCIL AND COMMISSION. THIS SINGLE COMMISSION DEALING WITH
EUROPEAN NATURAL POWER CONTROL IS CONSIDERED AS A MAJOR
CONSTITUTIONAL DEVELOPMENT IN PROGRESS TOWARD EUROPEAN UNI-
TY.

1224 WEINBERG A.M.
"CAN TECHNOLOGY REPLACE SOCIAL ENGINEERING?"
AMER. BEHAVIORAL SCIENTIST, 10 (MAY 67), 7-10.
DISCUSSES COMPARATIVE UTILITY OF SOCIAL SCIENTIST AND
TECHNOLOGIST IN SOLVING SOCIAL PROBLEMS. FINDS THAT NEED IS
GREAT FOR BETTER UNDERSTANDING BETWEEN THE TWO. FEELS THAT
THE MORE PRESSING SOCIAL PROBLEMS CAN BEST BE SOLVED VIA
TECHNOLOGICAL ADVANCES. SUGGESTS THAT EARTH, NOT SPACE, BE
THE FOCUS OF SCIENTIFIC ENDEAVOR.

1225 WEINBERG A.M.
REFLECTIONS ON BIG SCIENCE.
CAMBRIDGE: M I T PRESS, 1967, 181 PP., LC#67-14205.
DISCUSSES SEVERAL AREAS OF RECENT SCIENTIFIC PROGRESS AND

OUTLINES SCOPE AND RATE OF PRESENT ACHIEVEMENTS. NOTES
PROBLEMS OF COMMUNICATION WITHIN SCIENTIFIC COMMUNITY AND
POSSIBLE BOUNDS FOR PRESENT TECHNOLOGIES. DISCUSSES CRITERIA
FOR CHOOSING FIELDS FOR CONCENTRATION OF RESEARCH. NOTES
ROLE OF NATIONAL LABORATORIES. COMMENTS ON FUTURE OF
BIOMEDICAL SCIENCE AND NOTES ROLE OF UNIVERSITIES.

1226 WEINER N.
CYBERNETICS.
NEW YORK: JOHN WILEY, 1948, 203 PP., LC#61-13034.
STUDY OF HUMAN CONTROL FUNCTIONS AND MECHANICO-ELECTRICAL
SYSTEMS DESIGNED TO REPLACE THEM. DESCRIBES APPLICATION
OF STATISTICAL MECHANICS METHODS TO COMMUNICATIONS ENGINEER-
ING. COVERS MATHEMATICAL CALCULATORS AS WELL AS NERVES AND
BRAIN OF HUMAN BODY.

1227 WEISBROD B.A.
ECONOMICS OF PUBLIC HEALTH.
PHILA: U OF PENN PR, 1961, 127 PP., LC#61-5545.
ANALYSIS OF PUBLIC HEALTH AS FACTOR IN ECONOMY AND ITS
IMPORTANCE TO OVER-ALL SOCIETY. EXAMINES LOSS TO US DUE TO
MAJOR DISEASES AND BENEFITS OBTAINABLE BY IMPROVED HEALTH.

1228 WEISNER J.B.
WHERE SCIENCE AND POLITICS MEET.
NEW YORK: MCGRAW HILL, 1965, 302 PP., LC#65-16157.
MIRRORS BROAD RANGE OF SCIENTIFIC AND TECHNICAL ISSUES
THAT CONFRONT MODERN PRESIDENT. INCLUDES DOMESTIC ISSUES OF
BASIC RESEARCH AND SCIENCE, AS STIMULANTS TO ECONOMIC
GROWTH, INTERNATIONAL ISSUES OF NATIONAL DEFENSE, MILITARY
RESEARCH PROJECTS, TECHNOLOGY IN FOREIGN AID, AND THE
LIKE. AUTHOR SERVED AS SCIENTIFIC ADVISER TO PRESIDENTS
KENNEDY AND JOHNSON.

1229 WELTON H.
THE THIRD WORLD WAR; TRADE AND INDUSTRY, THE NEW
BATTLEGROUND.
NEW YORK: PHILOSOPHICAL LIB, 1959, 330 PP.
CLAIMS NO MILITARY CONFLICT WILL DEVELOP BETWEEN COM-
MUNIST AND WESTERN NATIONS, SINCE WAR, ALREADY IN PROGRESS
IN TRADE AND INDUSTRY, WILL ITSELF DETERMINE FUTURE OF
WORLD. DEFEAT IS BASED ON ECONOMIC DESTRUCTION BY DISPLACE-
MENT OF EXPORTS IN WORLD MARKETS.

1230 WENDT P.F.
HOUSING POLICY - THE SEARCH FOR SOLUTIONS.
BERKELEY: U CAL BUR BUS ECON RES, 1962, 283 PP., LC#62-11497.
EVALUATES NATIONAL HOUSING PROGRAMS AND POLICIES IN UK,
SWEDEN, WEST GERMANY, AND US SINCE WWII. COMPARES POSTWAR
POLICIES, PRODUCTION, AND RELATIVE IMPROVEMENT IN HOUSING
STANDARDS AMONG ALTERNATIVE POLICIES. EXAMINES RELATION
BETWEEN HOUSING AND GENERAL ECONOMIC POLICIES.

1231 WHEELER-BENNETT J.W.
THE NEMESIS OF POWER (2ND ED.)
NEW YORK: ST MARTIN'S PRESS, 1964, 831 PP.
HISTORY OF GERMAN ARMY, FROM DEFEAT IN WWI TO ITS
REESTABLISHMENT IN WEST GERMANY. EMPHASIZES ROLE OF OFFICER
CORPS AS RESPONSIBLE FOR NATURE AND CONTINUITY OF ARMY'S
EMBROILMENT IN POLITICS. PRIMARILY COVERS WWII PERIOD. THE
PECULIAR RELATIONSHIP BETWEEN HITLER AND THE GENERAL STAFF.

1232 WHITE L.D.
"CONGRESSIONAL CONTROL OF THE PUBLIC SERVICE."
AM. POL. SCI. REV., 39 (FEB. 45), 1-11.
SEES CONGRESS DECLINING IN PUBLIC ESTEEM AND IN ITS CON-
TROL OF THE ADMINISTRATION. SUGGESTS REFORMS FOR CONGRESS SO
IT MAY REGAIN THE CONTROL WHICH IS DEMOCRATICALLY ESSENTIAL
TO ENSURE THAT ITS MANDATES ON PUBLIC POLICY PREVAIL AND TO
ENSURE THAT THE EXECUTION OF PUBLIC POLICY AVOIDS WASTE, IN-
COMPETENCE, AND UNNECESSARY PUBLIC INCONVENIENCE.

1233 WHITE L.D. ED.
CIVIL SERVICE IN WARTIME.
CHICAGO: U OF CHICAGO PRESS, 1945, 253 PP.
DISCUSSES THE DISCOVERY AND USE OF CIVILIAN PERSONNEL
IN THE EXPANDED GOVERNMENTAL ACTIVITIES, AND THE ROLE OF
VARIOUS COMMISSIONS, EMPLOYMENT SERVICES, AND CIVILIAN
AGENCIES IN MEETING THE NEEDS OF WARTIME. DISCUSSES THE USE
OF NATIONAL ROSTER OF SCIENTIFIC AND SPECIALIZED
PERSONNEL AND ITS USEFUL FUNCTION IN RECRUITING SOCIAL
SCIENTISTS AS EXPERTS.

1234 WHITEHEAD T.N.
LEADERSHIP IN A FREE SOCIETY; A STUDY IN HUMAN RELATIONS
BASED ON AN ANALYSIS OF PRESENT-DAY INDUSTRIAL CIVILIZATION.
CAMBRIDGE: HARVARD U PR, 1947, 266 PP.
CONCERNED WITH IMPACT OF BUSINESS AND INDUSTRIAL
INSTITUTIONS ON SOCIETY AND WITH TYPE OF SOCIAL STRUCTURE
WHICH CAN MAINTAIN ITSELF BEST IN TECHNOLOGICALLY DEVELOPING
WORLD. STUDIES FUNCTIONING OF WORKING GROUPS AND ROLE OF
LEADERSHIP IN COLLECTIVE ACTION; INVESTIGATES INTERACTION
BETWEEN HUMAN MOTIVES AND SHAPE AND DEVELOPMENT OF ORGANIZED
INSTITUTIONS. REVIEWS TYPES OF SOCIAL SYSTEMS.

1235 WHITNAH D.R.

SAFER SKYWAYS.
AMES: IOWA STATE U PR, 1966, 417 PP., LC#66-24402.
EXAMINES FEDERAL CONTROL OF AVIATION IN US 1926-66.
TRACING TECHNOLOGICAL ADVANCES SINCE THEN, UNDERSCORES
PRIMARY PURPOSE OF GOVERNMENTAL REGULATION - MAKING
AIRWAYS SAFER. ALSO CONSIDERS PROBLEMS OF PERSONNEL AND
ADMINISTRATION IN RAPIDLY GROWING CONCERNS. NOTES
INTERACTION OF FAA-CAB AND MILITARY.

1236 WHITTIER J.M.
"COMPULSORY POOLING AND UNITIZATION* DIE-HARD KANSAS."
U. KANSAS LAW J., 15 (MAR. 67), 307-323.
AUTHOR DEFINES THE PROBLEM, ANALYZES AND EVALUATES LEGAL-
ECONOMIC CONTROVERSY, DISCUSSES NEED FOR LEGISLATION IN KAN-
SAS, COMPARES KANSAS TO OTHER STATES, AND PROPOSES POSSIBLE
SOLUTIONS. KANSAS HAS REFUSED TO ENACT COMPULSORY POOLING &
UNITIZATION LEGISLATION APPLICABLE TO GAS AND OIL INDUS-
TRIES, AND AUTHOR FINDS THIS DUE TO FACT THAT LANDOWNERS DO
NOT REALIZE THEY WOULD RECEIVE AS MUCH OIL ON WIDER SPACING.

1237 WIGHTMAN D.
TOWARD ECONOMIC CO-OPERATION IN ASIA.
NEW HAVEN: YALE U. PR., 1963, 400 PP.
INDEPENDENT HISTORY AS WELL AS AN APPRAISAL OF THE WORK
OF THE U.N. ECONOMIC COMMISSION FOR ASIA AND THE FAR EAST
'ECAFE). INCLUDES APPROACHES TO ECONOMIC DEVELOPMENT
COMMONLY PROPOUNDED AND ACCEPTED IN THE REGION. CITES
ABILITY OF ECAFE TO INFLUENCE AND SHAPE THE POLICIES AND
ACTIONS OF THE INDIVIDUAL GOVERNMENTS.

1238 WILCOX J.K.
OFFICIAL DEFENSE PUBLICATIONS, 1941-1945 (NINE VOLS.)
BERKELEY: U OF CALIF PR, 1946.
AN ANNOTATED GUIDE TO OFFICIAL DEFENSE AND WAR PUBLICA-
TIONS OF FEDERAL, STATE, AND CANADIAN AGENCIES, COVERING THE
PERIOD FROM JUNE 1940 TO JANUARY 1945. THE NINE-VOLUME SET
LISTS 19,000 ITEMS, OF WHICH 655 ARE CANADIAN, 4,887 STATE,
AND 13,392 FEDERAL. MATERIAL LISTED ALPHABETICALLY BY NAME
OF ISSUING AGENCY; BOTH AUTHOR AND SUBJECT INDEX APPENDED TO
GUIDE.

1239 WILENSKY H.L.
SYLLABUS OF INDUSTRIAL RELATIONS: A GUIDE TO READING
AND RESEARCH.
CHICAGO: U OF CHICAGO PRESS, 1954, 305 PP.
GUIDE TO READING AND RESEARCH IN INDUSTRIAL RELATIONS.
REFERENCES TO MATERIAL ON STUDY OF INDUSTRIAL RELATIONS;
URBAN INDUSTRIAL SETTING; ORGANIZATION OF WORK; TRADE
UNION HISTORY, ORGANIZATION, ADMINISTRATION AND IMPACT;
COLLECTIVE BARGAINING SYSTEMS, PROCESSES AND ISSUES;
PUBLIC POLICY AND INDUSTRIAL RELATIONS.

1240 WILES P.J.D.
"WILL CAPITALISM AND COMMUNISM SPONTANEOUSLY CONVERGE."
ENCOUNTER, 20 (JUNE 63), 86-90.
DISCOUNTS BELIEF THAT CAPITALISM AND COMMUNISM WILL
CONVERGE. POINTS OUT THAT NEW MATHEMATICAL TECHNIQUES AND
USE OF COMPUTERS WILL MAKE POSSIBLE MORE EFFICIENT CONTROL
OF RUSSIA'S COMMAND-ECONOMY.

1241 WILLIAMS B.H.
"SCIENTIFIC METHOD IN FOREIGN POLICY."
BULL. ATOM. SCI., 15 (DEC. 59) 419-21.
URGES POLICY MAKERS TO USE BASIC CONCEPTS OF SCIENTIFIC
METHOD IN POLICY FORMULATION TO AVOID ANOTHER WAR. POLICY
SHOULD BE BASED ON FACTS, DISREGARDING EMOTIONAL PRESSURES.

1242 WILLIAMS C.
"REGIONAL MANAGEMENT OVERSEAS."
HARVARD BUSINESS REV., 45 (JAN. 67), 87-91.
CONSIDERS THE ADVANTAGES OF REGIONAL MANAGEMENT AND THE
COMPANIES IN WHICH IT WORKS BEST. ADVISES BRUSSELS, LONDON,
GENEVA, ZURICH, AND PARIS AS HQ SITES FOR EXPANDING EURO-
PEAN MARKETS. CONCLUDES THAT INCREASE IN OVERHEAD AND COM-
PLEXITY OF COMMUNICATION IS OFFSET BY ADVANTAGES OF
ON-THE-SPOT DECISION-MAKING.

1243 WILLIAMS S.P. ED.
TOWARD A GENUINE WORLD SECURITY SYSTEM (PAMPHLET)
BOSTON: UNITED WORLD FEDERALISTS, 1964, 65 PP., LC#64-20453.
ANNOTATED BIBLIOGRAPHY OF SOURCES FOR AREAS OF WORLD
LAW, ORDER, AND PEACE. INCLUDES INTRODUCTORY BOOKS AND SYM-
POSIA FOR THE BEGINNER, TOPICAL FOCUS ON DETAILED AREAS,
INDEX OF AUTHORS, EDITORS, PERIODICALS. CONTAINS 355
ENTRIES, MAJORITY DATED 1962-1963.

1244 WILLIAUS T.H.
AMERICANS AT WAR: THE DEVELOPMENT OF THE AMERICAN MILITARY
SYSTEM.
BATON ROUGE: LOUISIANA ST U PR, 1960, 139 PP., LC#60-8287.
ILLUSTRATED ESSAYS PRIMARILY CONCERNED WITH THE ARMY
DISCUSS MILITARY ORGANIZATION, ADMINISTRATION, AND TACTICS,
INCLUDING COMPARISON OF NORTH AND SOUTH DURING THE CIVIL
WAR. BIBLIOGRAPHY OF 100 WORKS PUBLISHED 1901-55 IN ENGLISH;
SOURCES DISCUSSED TOPICALLY.

1246 WILTZ J.E.
IN SEARCH OF PEACE: THE SENATE MUNITIONS INQUIRY, 1934-36.
BATON ROUGE: LOUISIANA ST U PR, 1963, 277 PP., LC#63-16656.
ILLUSTRATED STUDY OF SENATE INVESTIGATION ATTEMPTING TO
PROVE THAT INDUSTRIES WHICH PROFITED FROM THE WAR WERE RE-
SPONSIBLE FOR WAR. INCLUDES MUNITIONS MANUFACTURE, ARMS EM-
BARGO, AND CONSCRIPTION.

1247 WINSTON O.
"AN URBANIZATION PATTERN FOR THE US* SOME CONSIDERATIONS
FOR THE DECENTRALIZATION OF EXCELLENCE."
LAND ECONOMICS, 43 (FEB. 67), 1-9.
EXAMINES PROBLEMS INHERENT IN TRYING TO CREATE
PHYSICAL, SOCIAL, AND AESTHETIC ENVIRONMENT IN LARGE URBAN
CENTERS WHICH WILL STIMULATE RISE IN CULTURAL LEVEL OF
INDIVIDUALS. AUTHOR STRESSES NEED FOR QUALITY RATHER THAN
QUANTITY.

1248 WINTHROP H.
"THE MEANING OF DECENTRALIZATION FOR TWENTIETH-CENTURY MAN."
AMER. J. OF ECO. AND SOC., 26 (OCT. 67), 351-366.
EXAMINES ASPECTS OF MODERN DECENTRALIST THOUGHT.
CONSIDERS NEW DECENTRALISM AS ONE OF MANY PHILOSOPHIES
PRESENTLY COMPETING FOR THE RIGHT TO STRUCTURE
THE COMING SOCIAL ORDER. STATES THAT DECENTRALIZATION, WITH
THE HELP OF SCIENCE AND TECHNOLOGY, CAN FURNISH SOLUTIONS TO
MANY MODERN PROBLEMS, ADMINISTRATIVE, EDUCATIONAL, AND
POLITICAL.

1249 WIRTH L.
ON CITIES AND SOCIAL LIFE: SELECTED PAPERS.
CHICAGO: U OF CHICAGO PRESS, 1964, 350 PP., LC#64-24970.
SELECTED PAPERS OF LOUIS WIRTH, SOCIOLOGICAL THEORIST.
EXCERPTS HIS THOUGHTS ON SOCIAL ORGANIZATION, SOCIOLOGY OF
KNOWLEDGE, THE COMMUNITY, AND SOCIAL PROBLEMS AND PLANNING.
PAPERS DEAL WITH CONCEPTS OF PERSONALITY, VALUE, HUMAN
ECOLOGY, RACE AND PUBLIC POLICY, AND CONSENSUS.

1250 WISH J.R.
ECONOMIC DEVELOPMENT IN LATIN AMERICA: AN ANNOTATED BIBLIOG-
RAPHY.
NEW YORK: FREDERICK PRAEGER, 1965, 144 PP., LC#65-21105.
ANNOTATED BIBLIOGRAPHY EMPHASIZING ITEMS PUBLISHED SINCE
1955 AND RELEVANT TO OBJECTIVE OF MAKING OPERATIVE ROSTOW'S
"NATIONAL MARKET" CONCEPT. FOCUSES ON MARKETING AND COMMUNI-
CATION IN AGRICULTURAL RESEARCH. INCLUDES SECTIONS DEALING
WITH WRITINGS AND ISSUES OF SOCIAL SCIENCE RESEARCH, AND
ECONOMIC DEVELOPMENT. APPENDEXES CONTAIN SHORT LISTING OF
INFORMATION SOURCES AND SHORT BIBLIOGRAPHY OF KEY SOURCES.

1251 WOETZEL R.K.
THE INTERNATIONAL CONTROL OF AIRSPACE AND OUTERSPACE.
BAD-GOPESBERG: ASGARD, 1960, 97 PP.
ANALYZES LEGAL ASPECTS OF SPACE PENETRATION. PROBES INTO
THE MANY UNSOLVED PROBLEMS OF SOVEREIGNTY AND SOVEREIGN
RIGHTS. CONSIDERS LEGAL CHARACTER OF SPACE IN TERMS OF
INTERNATIONAL LAW. CONCLUDES THAT AIR SPACE BE LIMITED TO
SIXTY MILES BASED ON THE LIMITING FACTOR OF CONVENTIONAL
AIRCRAFTS IMPOSED BY CONDITIONS OF NATURE. SUGGESTS SPACE
ABOVE SIXTY MILES BE CONSIDERED AS RES COMMUNIS UNDER SOME
INTERNATIONAL CONTROL.

1252 WOHLSTETTER A.
"NUCLEAR SHARING: NATO AND THE NTH COUNTRY."
FOR AFF., 39 (APR. 61), 355-87.
DISCUSSES VALUE OF SPREAD OF NUCLEAR STRIKE FORCES.
FAVORS CENTRALIZED CONTROL OVER NUCLEAR POWER. OPPOSES
SPREAD OF NUCLEAR WEAPONS.

1253 WOHLSTETTER A.
"SCIENTISTS, SEERS AND STRATEGY."
FOR. AFF., 41 (APRIL 63), 466-478.
ASSERTS THAT SCIENTISTS ARE NOT NECESSARILY QUALIFIED TO
MAKE STRATEGY AND OTHER ARMS-POLICY DECISIONS. NON-SCIENTIST
DECISION-MAKERS ARE COMPETENT, GIVEN THE TIME, IN PRESCRIB-
INT COURSES OF ACTION.

1254 WOLFE T.W.
"SOVIET MILITARY POLICY AT THE FIFTY YEAR MARK."
CURRENT HISTORY, 53 (OCT. 67), 208-216.
STUDIES BACKGROUND OF SOVIET MILITARY POLICY INHERITED
BY BREZHNEV AND KOSYGIN. BELIEVES THAT PRESENT POLICY IS
ATTEMPT AT BROADENING MILITARY CAPACITIES IN NEGLECTED
AREAS, WITH BASIC POLICY REMAINING. EXAMINES RESOURCE
ALLOCATION ISSUE, QUESTION OF PREPARATION FOR LIMITED WAR,
AND POLITICAL-MILITARY RELATIONS. DESCRIBES EFFECTS OF
WARSAW PACT AND VIETNAM WAR.

1255 WOLFERS A., OSGOOD R.E. ET AL.
THE UNITED STATES IN A DISARMED WORLD: A STUDY OF THE US
OUTLINE FOR GENERAL AND COMPLETE DISARMAMENT.
BALTIMORE: JOHNS HOPKINS PRESS, 1966, 236 PP., LC#66-16036.
EXPLORES INTERESTS OF US THAT REQUIRE PROTECTION.
INQUIRES INTO RESOURCES FOR DETERRENCE AND DEFENSE THAT US
COULD COMMAND. EVALUATES PROPOSED PEACE-KEEPING MEASURES IN
TERMS OF THEIR PRACTICABILITY AND EFFECTIVENESS AS SUPPLE-

MENTS TO OR SUBSTITUTES FOR ARMAMENTS WHICH WOULD BE
ELIMINATED IN THE PROCESS OF DISARMAMENT.

1256 WOODRUFF W.
IMPACT OF WESTERN MAN.
NEW YORK: ST MARTIN'S PRESS, 1967, 375 PP., LC#66-17299.
EXAMINES CAREFULLY AND EXTENSIVELY THE EFFECT UPON THE
MODERN WORLD OF EUROPEAN IDEAS AND DEVELOPMENTS, CONCENTRA-
TING ON THE ECONOMIC SPHERE. COMMENCES WITH COLONIAL EMPIRES
OF 1750, GOES THROUGH WORLD-WIDE DISPERSAL, EUROPEAN BANKING
CENTERS, TECHNOLOGICAL PROGRESS, CHANGING TRADE PATTERNS.
COVERS ECONOMIC DEVELOPMENTS THROUGH 2 CENTURIES.

1257 WRIGHT Q.
PROBLEMS OF STABILITY AND PROGRESS IN INTERNATIONAL
RELATIONSHIPS.
BERKELEY: U. CALIF. PR., 1954, 378 PP.
DISCUSSES POSSIBILITY OF USING SCIENCE, EDUCATION, ORGAN-
IZATION, LAW AND POLITICS TO CREATE GREATER HARMONY IN FIELD
OF INTERNATIONAL RELATIONS. FAVORS CENTRALIZATION OF INSTI-
TUTIONS THROUGH UN FRAMEWORK. STUDIES GROUP BEHAVIOR.

1258 WRIGHT Q.
"THE PEACEFUL ADJUSTMENT OF INTERNATIONAL RELATIONS:
PROBLEMS AND RESEARCH APPROACHES."
J. SOC. ISSUES, 11 (1955), 3-12.
SEES PROBLEM SOLUTION FOR PEACEFUL WORLD AS VARIED, AND
THEREFORE TYPES OF RESEARCH RELEVANT TO EACH CLASS OF PROB-
LEMS AS VARIED ALSO. DEVISES SCHEME OF CLASSIFICATION OF
PROBLEMS IN INTERNATIONAL RELATIONS INTO 4 TYPES, AS WELL AS
CLASSIFICATION OF 4 TYPES OF RESEARCH.

1259 WRIGHT Q. ED.
PREVENTING WORLD WAR THREE.
NEW YORK: SIMON SCHUSTER, 1962, 450 PP.
ESSAYS ON PROBLEMS OF WAR AND PEACE WHICH HAVE BEEN
DIVIDED INTO THREE PARTS: PROBLEMS CAUSED BY THE ARMS RACE,
PROPOSALS REDUCING INTERNATIONAL TENSIONS CREATING A CLIMATE
IN WHICH FRUITFUL NEGOTIATIONS MIGHT BE POSSIBLE AND STEPS
THAT MUST BE TAKEN IF PROBLEMS DISCUSSED IN PARTS ONE AND
TWO ARE NOT TO RECUR. ADVOCATES CHANGES IN THINKING AND
SOCIAL ORGANIZATION OF HUMAN BEINGS.

1260 WYLIE J.C.
MILITARY STRATEGY: GENERAL THEORY OF POWER CONTROL.
NEW BRUNSWICK: RUTGERS U PR, 1967, 111 PP., LC#67-13076.
STUDY OF STRATEGIC THEORY IN US INCLUDES EXISTING
THEORIES AND THEIR LIMITATIONS, CUMULATIVE AND SEQUENTIAL
STRATEGY, AND METHODS OF STUDYING STRATEGY.

1261 YALEN R.
REGIONALISM AND WORLD ORDER.
INT. AFF., 38 (OCT. 62), 460-471.
EXAMINES THE REASONS FOR THE GROWTH OF CONTEMPORARY
REGIONALISM, TRACING THE LINES OF COMPATABILITY AND CONFLICT
BETWEEN REGIONAL AND UNIVERSAL FORMS OF INTERNATIONAL
ORGANIZATION. DISTINGUISHES BETWEEN REGIONALISM AND THE
CONCEPT OF WORLD ORDER.

1262 YAMAMURA K.
ECONOMIC POLICY IN POSTWAR JAPAN.
BERKELEY: U OF CALIF PR, 1967, 320 PP.
EXAMINES TWO POSTWAR ECONOMIC POLICIES - DEMOCRATIZATION
IMPOSED BY "ALLIED POWERS" AND SUBSEQUENT REACTION OF
DE-DEMOCRATIZATION PURSUED AND FORMULATED BY THE INDEPENDENT
GOVERNMENT. CONSIDERS BOTH POLICIES IN TERMS OF WHAT, WHY,
AND HOW. INCLUDES EXAMINATION OF JAPANESE ECONOMIC
INSTITUTIONS AND POSTWAR GROWTH.

1263 YAVITZ B.
AUTOMATION IN COMMERCIAL BANKING.
NEW YORK: FREE PRESS OF GLENCOE, 1967, 224 PP.
EXAMINATION OF RECENT INTRODUCTION OF ELECTRONIC COMPUTER
INTO BANKING. DESCRIBES AND ANALYZES PROCESSES OF AUTOMATION
REVELANT TO COMPUTER INSTALLATIONS. FOUR CASE STUDIES USED.
ALSO INCLUDES TOPICS AS DECISION TO AUTOMATE, DIVERSI-
FICATION OF COMPUTER APPLICATIONS, IMPACT OF AUTOMATION ON
EMPLOYMENT, ORGANIZATIONAL STRUCTURE, MANAGERIAL FUNCTIONS,
AND BANKING SERVICES.

1264 YEMELYANOV V.S.
"ATOMIC ENERGY FOR PEACE: THE USSR AND INTERNATIONAL
CO-OPERATION."
FOR. AFF., 38 (APRIL 60), 465-475.
SOVIET AUTHOR DISCUSSES THE MANY USES OF ATOMIC ENERGY
FOR PEACEFUL PURPOSES SUCH AS: ELECTRIC POWER, CHEMICAL
PROCESSES AND OXIDATION OF ORGANIC COMPOUNDS. ASSERTS THAT
IF USSR IS TO CONTINUE SHARING ITS RESEARCH RESULTS WITH
OTHER NATIONS COMPLETE DISARMAMENT IS IMPERATIVE. ONLY UNDER
SUCH CONDITIONS CAN SCIENTISTS ATTAIN CO-OPERATION.

1265 YOUNG O.R.
"ACTIVE DEFENSE AND INTERNATIONAL ORDER."
BUL. ATOMIC SCIENTISTS, 23 (MAY 67), 35-42.
AN ATTEMPT TO DELINEATE THE POLITICAL AND OTHER CONSE-
QUENCES OF NUMBER OF ALTERNATIVE PATTERNS OF ANTI-BALLISTIC-

MISSILES DEVELOPMENT, INCLUDING MUTUAL DEVELOPMENT OF
DEFENSIVE SYSTEMS, COUNTERING ABM DEPLOYMENT BY INCREASED
DEVELOPMENT OF OFFENSIVE WEAPONS, AND UNILATERAL ABM DE-
PLOYMENT WITHOUT ANY COUNTER-RESPONSE. THE OFFENSIVE-
DEFENSIVE PATTERN IS MOST DANGEROUS.

1266 YOUNG W. ED.
EXISTING MECHANISMS OF ARMS CONTROL.
NEW YORK: PERGAMON PRESS, 1966, 150 PP., LC#65-25010.
FOR NEW ARMS CONTROL MEASURES TO WORK THEY NEED TO BE
BASED ON EXPERIENCE AS WELL AS ANALOGY AND IMAGINATION. EDI-
TOR YOUNG HAS COLLECTED ESSAYS ON EXPERIENCES OF 5 INSTITU-
TIONS IN CONTROLLING THE WARLIKE USES OF FISSIONABLE MATTER.
CONTRIBUTORS: MEN SUCH AS SEABORG EXPERIENCED IN THE OPERA-
TIONS OF THE ATOMIC ENERGY COMMISSION, EURATON, ETC.

1267 ZELLER B. ED.
"AMERICAN STATE LEGISLATURES: REPORT ON THE COMMITTEE ON
AMERICAN LEGISLATURES."
NEW YORK: THOMAS Y CROWELL, 1954.
PRESENTS RESULTS OF FOUR-YEAR STUDY OF STATE LEGISLA-
TURES. CONCLUDES THAT STATE LEGISLATURES ARE POORLY EQUIPPED
TO SERVE AS POLICY-MAKING AGENCIES. EXTENSIVE BIBLIOGRAPHY
COVERS FIELDS OF REPRESENTATION, ORGANIZATION, PROCEDURE,
LEGISLATIVE AIDS, EXECUTIVE-LEGISLATIVE RELATIONS. APPEN-
DIXES DEVOTED TO RESULTS OF CASE STUDIES IN NEBRASKA,
MAINE, CONNECTICUT, AND MASSACHUSETTS.

1268 ZLOTNICK M.
WEAPONS IN SPACE (PAMPHLET)
HARMON-ON-HUDSON: HUDSON INST, 1963, 67 PP.
ANALYSIS OF OPERATIONAL POSSIBILITIES OF WAGING WAR IN
SPACE TO SAVE EARTH. INCLUDES STUDY OF PRACTICAL TACTICAL
PROBLEMS OF WAR AND PSYCHOLOGICAL EFFECTS ON PEOPLE.
CONSIDERS TECHNIQUES OF INSPECTION AND NEGOTIATIONS WITH
SPACE WEAPONS.

1269 ZNANIECKI F.
THE SOCIAL ROLE OF THE MAN OF KNOWLEDGE.
NEW YORK: COLUMBIA U PRESS, 1940, 212 PP.
ATTEMPTS TO ASCERTAIN PLACE OF "SCIENTIST" IN SOCIETY.
APPROACHES PROBLEM FROM STANDPOINT OF SOCIOLOGY OF
KNOWLEDGE. SURVEYS GROWTH OF SCIENCE IN 20TH CENTURY, AND
FUNCTION OF LEARNED SCHOOLS AND SCHOLARS. BELIEVES THAT ALL
NEW DEVELOPMENTS IN HISTORY OF KNOWLEDGE ARE OWING TO
THOSE SCIENTISTS WHO DID MORE IN THEIR SOCIAL ROLES THAN
THEIR CIRCLES WANTED OF THEM.

1270 ZOPPO C.E.
"NUCLEAR TECHNOLOGY, MULTIPOLARITY, AND INTERNATIONAL
STABILITY."
WORLD POLITICS, 18 (JULY 66), 579-606.
ZOPPO DESCRIBES UNBALANCING EFFECT OF NUCLEAR WEAPONS ON
THE INTERNATIONAL SYSTEM: ARMS-CONTROL CONCEPTS ARE CONTRA-
DICTORY TO TRADITIONAL BALANCE OF POWER THEORY, WAR HAS LOST
MUCH OF ITS PAST LEGITIMACY, AND TECHNOLOGICAL FACTORS OF
WAR MAKE POLITICAL AND MILITARY MISCALCULATIONS IRREVERSIBLE
AND INTOLERABLE. ABILITY OF LEADERS TO ADJUST TO TECHNICAL
CHANGE IS PROPOSED FOR GREATER SYSTEM STABILITY.

1271 ZUCKERMAN S.
SCIENTISTS AND WAR.
NEW YORK: HARPER & ROW, 1967, 177 PP., LC#67-11333.
RELATION OF SCIENCE TO MILITARY AND POLITICAL DECISIONS
IS DISCUSSED. ADVOCATES INTERNATIONAL COOPERATION IN RE-
SEARCH AND DEVELOPMENT, IN INDUSTRY AND SCIENCE. DISMISSES
CONCEPT OF NUCLEAR POWER AS TACTICAL FORCE, AND PREDICTS
GREATER SEPARATION OF DEVELOPED AND UNDEVELOPED NATIONS.
ASKS FOR SCIENTISTS' ROLE IN DECISION-MAKING. STRESSES
SOCIAL FUNCTION OF SCIENCE.

ABA....AMERICAN BAR ASSOCIATION

ABILITY TESTS....SEE KNO/TEST

ABM/DEFSYS....ANTI-BALLISTIC MISSILE DEFENSE SYSTEMS

L67
DAVIS P.C.,"THE COMING CHINESE COMMUNIST NUCLEAR   NUC/PWR
THREAT AND U.S. SEA BASED ABM OPTIONS." ASIA   DETER
CHINA/COM FUT USA+45 SEA NAT/G FORCES PLAN TEC/DEV   WEAPON
LEAD ARMS/CONT...GEOG METH/COMP 20 ABM/DEFSYS.   DIPLOM
PAGE 14 G0279

S67
MARTIN L.,"THE AMERICAN ABM DECISION." ASIA COM   WEAPON
EUR+WWI UK USA+45 USSR FORCES DIPLOM PEACE...POLICY   DETER
20 ABM/DEFSYS. PAGE 36 G0713   NUC/PWR
  WAR

ABORIGINES....ABORIGINES (AUSTRALIA)

ABORTION....ABORTION

S67
ROBINSON J.A.T.,"ABORTION* THE CASE FOR A FREE   PLAN
DECISION." LAW PROB/SOLV SANCTION ATTIT MORAL...PSY   ILLEGIT
IDEA/COMP 20 ABORTION. PAGE 47 G0930   SEX
  HEALTH

ABRIKOSSOV, DIMITRI....SEE ABRIKSSV/D

ABRIKSSV/D....DIMITRI ABRIKOSSOV

ABSHIRE D.M. G0024

ABT C.C. G0025,G0026,G0027

ACAD/ASST....ACADEMIC ASSISTANCE COUNCIL (U.K.)

ACADEM....UNIVERSITY, COLLEGE, GRADUATE SCHOOL, HIGHER
  EDUCATION

B42
MARCHANT A.,INVESTIGATIONS IN PROGRESS IN THE   ACT/RES
UNITED STATES IN THE FIELD OF LATIN AMERICAN   SOC
HUMANISTIC AND SOCIAL SCIENCE STUDIES. USA+45   R+D
ACADEM...QU ANTHOL. PAGE 36 G0702   L/A+17C

S44
HAWLEY A.H.,"ECOLOGY AND HUMAN ECOLOGY" WOR+45   HABITAT
INTELL ACADEM PLAN GP/REL ADJUST PERSON...PHIL/SCI   GEOG
SOC METH/CNCPT METH 20. PAGE 25 G0493   GEN/LAWS
  METH/COMP

B47
BECK H.P.,MEN WHO CONTROL OUR UNIVERSITIES.   EDU/PROP
EX/STRUC CHOOSE INGP/REL DISCRIM PERSON WEALTH   ACADEM
...POLICY TREND CON/ANAL CHARTS BIBLIOG. PAGE 6   CONTROL
G0112   LEAD

S48
MARQUIS D.G.,"RESEARCH PLANNING AT THE FRONTIERS OF   PLAN
SCIENCE" (BMR)" INTELL ACADEM CREATE UTIL...PSY 20.   ACT/RES
PAGE 36 G0708   EFFICIENCY
  GEN/METH

B49
MCLEAN J.M.,THE PUBLIC SERVICE AND UNIVERSITY   ACADEM
EDUCATION. UK USA-45 DELIB/GP EX/STRUC TOP/EX ADMIN   NAT/G
...GOV/COMP METH/COMP NAT/COMP ANTHOL 20. PAGE 38   EXEC
G0746   EDU/PROP

B51
HUXLEY J.,FREEDOM AND CULTURE. UNIV LAW SOCIETY R+D   CULTURE
ACADEM SCHOOL CREATE SANCTION ATTIT KNOWL...HUM   ORD/FREE
ANTHOL 20. PAGE 27 G0540   PHIL/SCI
  IDEA/COMP

B53
SCHAAF R.W.,DOCUMENTS OF INTERNATIONAL MEETINGS.   BIBLIOG/A
AGRI INDUS ACADEM DIPLOM NUC/PWR RACE/REL AGE/Y   DELIB/GP
HEALTH...SOC 20. PAGE 49 G0960   INT/ORG
  POLICY

B56
UN HEADQUARTERS LIBRARY,BIBLIOGRAPHY OF   BIBLIOG
INDUSTRIALIZATION IN UNDERDEVELOPED COUNTRIES   ECO/UNDEV
(BIBLIOGRAPHICAL SERIES NO. 6). WOR+45 R+D ACADEM   TEC/DEV
INT/ORG NAT/G. PAGE 55 G1087

B56
VUCINICH A.,THE SOVIET ACADEMY OF SCIENCES. USSR   PHIL/SCI
STRUCT ACADEM NAT/G EDU/PROP ADMIN LEAD ROLE   CREATE
...BIBLIOG 20 ACADEM/SCI. PAGE 61 G1203   INTELL

B57
DRUCKER P.F.,AMERICA'S NEXT TWENTY YEARS. USA+45   WORKER
DIST/IND ACADEM MUNIC SCHOOL DIPLOM ECO/TAC AUTOMAT   FOR/AID
HABITAT HEALTH...SOC/WK TREND 20 URBAN/RNWL   CENSUS
PUB/TRANS. PAGE 16 G0316   GEOG

B58
GANGE J.,UNIVERSITY RESEARCH ON INTERNATIONAL   R+D
AFFAIRS. USA+45 ACADEM INT/ORG CONSULT CREATE EXEC   MGT
ROUTINE...QUANT STAT INT STERTYP GEN/METH TOT/POP   DIPLOM
VAL/FREE 20. PAGE 21 G0407

B60
LEYDER J.,BIBLIOGRAPHIE DE L'ENSEIGNEMENT SUPERIEUR   BIBLIOG/A
ET DE LA RECHERCHE SCIENTIFIQUE EN AFRIQUE   ACT/RES
INTERTROPICALE (2 VOLS.). AFR CULTURE ECO/UNDEV   ACADEM
AGRI PLAN EDU/PROP ADMIN COLONIAL...GEOG SOC/INTEG   R+D
20 NEGRO. PAGE 34 G0664

B60
WALDO D.,THE RESEARCH FUNCTION OF UNIVERSITY   ADMIN
BUREAUS AND INSTITUTES FOR GOVERNMENTAL-RELATED   R+D
RESEARCH. FINAN ACADEM NAT/G INGP/REL ROLE...POLICY   MUNIC
CLASSIF GOV/COMP. PAGE 61 G1205

S60
HALSEY A.H.,"THE CHANGING FUNCTIONS OF UNIVERSITIES   ACADEM
IN ADVANCED INDUSTRIAL SOCIETIES." R+D EDU/PROP   CREATE
REPRESENT ROLE ORD/FREE PWR TREND. PAGE 24 G0476   CULTURE
  ADJUST

B62
DODDS H.W.,THE ACADEMIC PRESIDENT "EDUCATOR OR   ACADEM
CARETAKER? FINAN DELIB/GP EDU/PROP PARTIC ATTIT   ADMIN
ROLE PWR...POLICY RECORD INT. PAGE 16 G0304   LEAD
  CONTROL

B62
DUPRE J.S.,SCIENCE AND THE NATION: POLICY AND   R+D
POLITICS. USA+45 LAW ACADEM FORCES ADMIN CIVMIL/REL   INDUS
GOV/REL EFFICIENCY PEACE...TREND 20 SCI/ADVSRY.   TEC/DEV
PAGE 16 G0322   NUC/PWR

B62
DUPRE S.,SCIENCE AND THE NATION. USA+45 ECO/DEV   ARMS/CONT
ACADEM ORD/FREE TECHNIC. PAGE 17 G0323   DECISION
  TEC/DEV
  INDUS

B62
MACHLUP F.,THE PRODUCTION AND DISTRIBUTION OF   ACADEM
KNOWLEDGE IN THE UNITED STATES. USA+45 COM/IND   TEC/DEV
INDUS SCHOOL SECT WORKER COMPUTER CREATE CIVMIL/REL   EDU/PROP
COST EFFICIENCY WEALTH 20. PAGE 35 G0688   R+D

L62
LINS L.J.,"BASIS FOR DECISION: A COMPOSITE OF   DECISION
CURRENT INSTITUTIONAL RESEARCH METHODS OF COLLEGES   ACADEM
AND UNIVERSITIES" ADMIN MGT. PAGE 34 G0671   R+D
  ACT/RES

N62
US CONGRESS JT ATOM ENRGY COMM,PEACEFUL USES OF   NUC/PWR
ATOMIC ENERGY, HEARING. USA+45 USSR TEC/DEV ATTIT   ACADEM
RIGID/FLEX...TESTS CHARTS EXHIBIT METH/COMP 20   SCHOOL
CONGRESS. PAGE 57 G1112   NAT/COMP

B63
HOFSTADTER R.,ANTI-INTELLECTUALISM IN AMERICAN   INTELL
LIFE. USA+45 AGRI INDUS ACADEM TEC/DEV EDU/PROP   EPIST
INGP/REL ATTIT...SOC WORSHIP 20 MCCARTHY/J   CULTURE
STEVENSN/A. PAGE 26 G0522   SOCIETY

B63
LASSWELL H.D.,THE FUTURE OF POLITICAL SCIENCE.   CREATE
SOCIETY ECO/DEV ACADEM NAT/G PROB/SOLV...OBS   ACT/RES
SOC/INTEG. PAGE 33 G0643   FUT

B63
NASA,CONFERENCE ON SPACE, SCIENCE, AND URBAN LIFE.   MUNIC
USA+45 SOCIETY INDUS ACADEM ACT/RES ECO/TAC ADMIN   SPACE
20. PAGE 41 G0804   TEC/DEV
  PROB/SOLV

S63
BOULDING K.E.,"UNIVERSITY, SOCIETY, AND ARMS   SOCIETY
CONTROL." WOR+45 WOR-45 ACADEM NAT/G CONSULT FORCES   ARMS/CONT
ACT/RES PLAN TEC/DEV BAL/PWR ECO/TAC COERCE DETER
WAR ATTIT RIGID/FLEX KNOWL ORD/FREE PWR WEALTH
...CONCPT COLD/WAR TOT/POP 20. PAGE 8 G0159

S63
DUBRIDGE L.A.,"POLICY AND THE SCIENTISTS." ELITES   POLICY
PROB/SOLV ROLE KNOWL PWR. PAGE 16 G0318   PHIL/SCI

RECENT PUBLICATIONS ON GOVERNMENTAL PROBLEMS. FINAN
INDUS ACADEM PLAN PROB/SOLV EDU/PROP ADJUD ADMIN
BIO/SOC...MGT SOC. PAGE 1 G0017

ACADEM
DECISION

B64
BIBLIOG
AUTOMAT
LEGIS
JURID

UNRUH J.M.,"SCIENTIFIC INPUTS TO LEGISLATIVE
DECISION-MAKING (SUPPLEMENT)" USA+45 ACADEM NAT/G
PROVS GOV/REL GOV/COMP. PAGE 56 G1102

S64
CREATE
DECISION
LEGIS
PARTIC

BENTWICH J.S.,EDUCATION IN ISRAEL. ISRAEL CULTURE
STRATA PROB/SOLV TEC/DEV ADJUST ALL/VALS 20 JEWS.
PAGE 7 G0125

B65
SECT
EDU/PROP
ACADEM
SCHOOL

CHENG C.-.Y.,SCIENTIFIC AND ENGINEERING MANPOWER IN
COMMUNIST CHINA, 1949-1963. CHINA/COM USSR ELITES
ECO/DEV R+D ACADEM LABOR NAT/G EDU/PROP CONTROL
UTIL...POLICY BIBLIOG 20. PAGE 12 G0226

B65
WORKER
CONSULT
MARXISM
BIOG

KOROL A.G.,SOVIET RESEARCH AND DEVELOPMENT. USSR
ACADEM SCHOOL WORKER ROUTINE COST...STAT T 20.
PAGE 31 G0615

B65
COM
R+D
FINAN
DIST/IND

LOWENSTEIN L.,GOVERNMENT RESOURCES AVAILABLE FOR
FOREIGN AFFAIRS RESEARCH. NAT/G DIPLOM GOV/REL.
PAGE 34 G0677

B65
R+D
ACADEM
ACT/RES
BIBLIOG/A

NATIONAL ACADEMY OF SCIENCES,BASIC RESEARCH AND
NATIONAL GOALS. R+D ACADEM DELIB/GP PLAN EDU/PROP
...POLICY HEAL PHIL/SCI PSY SOC ANTHOL 20 CONGRESS
HOUSE/REP HS/SCIASTR. PAGE 41 G0809

B65
LEGIS
BUDGET
NAT/G
CREATE

NATIONAL REFERRAL CENTER SCI,A DIRECTORY OF
INFORMATION RESOURCES IN THE UNITED STATES; SOCIAL
SCIENCES. USA+45 PROF/ORG...PSY SOC 20. PAGE 41
G0811

B65
INDEX
R+D
ACADEM
ACT/RES

OECD,MEDITERRANEAN REGIONAL PROJECT: TURKEY;
EDUCATION AND DEVELOPMENT. FUT TURKEY SOCIETY
STRATA FINAN NAT/G PROF/ORG PLAN PROB/SOLV ADMIN
COST...STAT CHARTS 20 OECD. PAGE 42 G0831

B65
EDU/PROP
ACADEM
SCHOOL
ECO/UNDEV

OECD,THE MEDITERRANEAN REGIONAL PROJECT: PORTUGAL;
EDUCATION AND DEVELOPMENT. PORTUGAL SOCIETY STRATA
FINAN PROF/ORG WORKER PLAN PROB/SOLV ADMIN...POLICY
STAT CHARTS METH 20 OECD. PAGE 42 G0832

B65
EDU/PROP
SCHOOL
ACADEM
ECO/UNDEV

OECD,THE MEDITERRANEAN REGIONAL PROJECT: ITALY;
EDUCATION AND DEVELOPMENT. ITALY SOCIETY STRATA
FINAN NAT/G PROF/ORG WORKER PLAN PROB/SOLV ADMIN
...STAT CHARTS METH 20 OECD. PAGE 42 G0833

B65
SCHOOL
EDU/PROP
ECO/UNDEV
ACADEM

OECD,THE MEDITERRANEAN REGIONAL PROJECT: GREECE;
EDUCATION AND DEVELOPMENT. FUT GREECE SOCIETY AGRI
FINAN NAT/G PROF/ORG WORKER PLAN PROB/SOLV ADMIN
DEMAND ATTIT 20 OECD. PAGE 42 G0834

B65
EDU/PROP
SCHOOL
ACADEM
ECO/UNDEV

OECD,THE MEDITERRANEAN REGIONAL PROJECT: SPAIN;
EDUCATION AND DEVELOPMENT. FUT SPAIN STRATA FINAN
NAT/G WORKER PLAN PROB/SOLV ADMIN COST...POLICY
STAT CHARTS 20 OECD. PAGE 42 G0835

B65
ECO/UNDEV
EDU/PROP
ACADEM
SCHOOL

ORG FOR ECO COOP AND DEVEL,THE MEDITERRANEAN
REGIONAL PROJECT: YUGOSLAVIA; EDUCATION AND
DEVELOPMENT. YUGOSLAVIA SOCIETY FINAN PROF/ORG PLAN
ADMIN COST DEMAND MARXISM...STAT TREND CHARTS METH
20 OECD. PAGE 43 G0843

B65
EDU/PROP
ACADEM
SCHOOL
ECO/UNDEV

UNESCO,HANDBOOK OF INTERNATIONAL EXCHANGES. COM/IND
R+D ACADEM PROF/ORG VOL/ASSN CREATE TEC/DEV
EDU/PROP AGREE 20 TREATY. PAGE 55 G1090

B65
INDEX
INT/ORG
DIPLOM
PRESS

US LIBRARY OF CONGRESS,A DIRECTORY OF INFORMATION

B65
BIBLIOG

RESOURCES IN THE UNITED STATES: SOCIAL SCIENCES.
USA+45 ACADEM INT/ORG LABOR PROF/ORG PUB/INST
SCHOOL SECT 20. PAGE 59 G1156

R+D
COMPUT/IR

VERMOT-GAUCHY M.,L'EDUCATION NATIONALE DANS LA
FRANCE DE 1975. FRANCE FUT CULTURE ELITES R+D
SCHOOL PLAN EDU/PROP EFFICIENCY...POLICY PREDICT
CHARTS INDEX 20. PAGE 61 G1195

B65
ACADEM
CREATE
TREND
INTELL

PILISUK M.,"IS THERE A MILITARY INDUSTRIAL COMPLEX
WHICH PREVENTS PEACE CONSENSUS; COUNTERVAILING
POWER IN PLURALIST SYSTEMS." INDUS R+D ACADEM
FEEDBACK CIVMIL/REL ADJUST CONSEN ATTIT RIGID/FLEX
...CENSUS IDEA/COMP BIBLIOG. PAGE 45 G0878

L65
ELITES
WEAPON
PEACE
ARMS/CONT

HUGHES T.L.,"SCHOLARS AND FOREIGN POLICY* VARIETIES
OF RESEARCH EXPERIENCE." COM/IND DIPLOM ADMIN EXEC
ROUTINE...MGT OBS CONGRESS PRESIDENT CAMELOT.
PAGE 27 G0535

S65
ACT/RES
ACADEM
CONTROL
NAT/G

LECLERCQ H.,"ECONOMIC RESEARCH AND DEVELOPMENT IN
TROPICAL AFRICA." ECO/UNDEV INT/ORG CREATE PLAN UN.
PAGE 33 G0650

S65
AFR
R+D
ACADEM
ECO/TAC

SCHELLING T.C.,"SIGNALS AND FEEDBACK IN THE ARMS
DIALOGUE." USA+45 USSR R+D ACADEM FORCES ACT/RES
ADJUST COST GEN/LAWS. PAGE 49 G0964

S65
FEEDBACK
DETER
EDU/PROP
ARMS/CONT

SILVERT K.H.,"AMERICAN ACADEMIC ETHICS AND SOCIAL
RESEARCH ABROAD* THE LESSON OF PROJECT CAMELOT."
CHILE L/A+17C USA+45 FINAN ADMIN...PHIL/SCI SOC
GEN/LAWS CAMELOT. PAGE 51 G0998

S65
ACADEM
NAT/G
ACT/RES
POLICY

SEARA M.V.,"COSMIC INTERNATIONAL LAW." LAW ACADEM
ACT/RES DIPLOM COLONIAL CONTROL NUC/PWR SOVEREIGN
...GEN/LAWS BIBLIOG UN. PAGE 50 G0987

C65
SPACE
INT/LAW
IDEA/COMP
INT/ORG

GLAZER M.,THE FEDERAL GOVERNMENT AND THE
UNIVERSITY. CHILE PROB/SOLV DIPLOM GIVE ADMIN WAR
...POLICY SOC 20. PAGE 21 G0421

B66
BIBLIOG/A
NAT/G
PLAN
ACADEM

GREEN P.,DEADLY LOGIC* THE THEORY OF NUCLEAR
DETERRENCE. USA+45 ACT/RES OP/RES NUC/PWR RATIONAL
ALL/VALS PWR...DECISION MGT PHIL/SCI QUANT
IDEA/COMP GAME. PAGE 23 G0444

B66
DETER
ACADEM
GEN/LAWS
RECORD

KLOTSCHE J.M.,THE URBAN UNIVERSITY AND THE FUTURE
OF OUR CITIES. FUT USA+45 USA-45 LOC/G NEIGH GIVE
19/20. PAGE 31 G0606

B66
ACADEM
MUNIC
PROB/SOLV
TEC/DEV

MARKHAM J.W.,AN ECONOMIC-MEDIA STUDY OF BOOK
PUBLISHING. USA+45 LAW COM/IND ACADEM SCHOOL
EDU/PROP AUTOMAT CONTROL...DECISION STAT CHARTS 20
CONGRESS. PAGE 36 G0707

B66
PRESS
ECO/TAC
TEC/DEV
NAT/G

NATIONAL SCIENCE FOUNDATION,SIXTEENTH ANNUAL REPORT
FOR THE FISCAL YEAR ENDED JUNE 30, 1966. USA+45
CREATE BUDGET SKILL 20 NSF. PAGE 41 G0813

B66
NAT/G
EDU/PROP
ACADEM
KNOWL

OECD DEVELOPMENT CENTRE,CATALOGUE OF SOCIAL AND
ECONOMIC DEVELOPMENT INSTITUTES AND PROGRAMMES*
RESEARCH. ACT/RES PLAN TEC/DEV EDU/PROP...SOC
GP/COMP NAT/COMP. PAGE 43 G0836

B66
ECO/UNDEV
ECO/DEV
R+D
ACADEM

PRINCETON U INDUSTRIAL REL SEC,THE FEDERAL
GOVERNMENT AND THE UNIVERSITY: SUPPORT FOR SOCIAL
SCIENCE RESEARCH AND THE IMPACT OF PROJECT CAMELOT.
USA+45 ACT/RES CONTROL GP/REL PWR...POLICY 20.
PAGE 45 G0889

B66
BIBLIOG/A
NAT/G
ACADEM
PLAN

SANFORD T.,BUT WHAT ABOUT THE PEOPLE? ACADEM SCHOOL
BUDGET TAX CONTROL SKILL WEALTH 20 NORTH/CAR.
PAGE 49 G0956

B66
EDU/PROP
PROB/SOLV
POLICY
PROVS

US BUREAU OF THE BUDGET,THE ADMINISTRATION OF
GOVERNMENT SUPPORTED RESEARCH AT UNIVERSITIES
(PAMPHLET). USA+45 CONSULT TOP/EX ADMIN INCOME
WEALTH...MGT PHIL/SCI INT. PAGE 56 G1108
ACT/RES
NAT/G
ACADEM
GP/REL
B66

EWALD R.F.,"ONE OF MANY POSSIBLE GAMES." ACADEM
INT/ORG ARMS/CONT...INT/LAW GAME. PAGE 18 G0354
SIMUL
HYPO/EXP
PROG/TEAC
RECORD
S66

GREENBERG D.S.,"THE SCIENTIFIC PORK BARREL." USA+45
ECO/DEV PUB/INST CHIEF LEGIS BUDGET GIVE GP/REL PWR
WEALTH 20. PAGE 23 G0445
R+D
NAT/G
ACADEM
ATTIT
S66

SIMON R.,"THE STATE OF PUBLIC RELATIONS SCHOLARLY
RESEARCH." TEC/DEV TASK MAJORITY PRODUC...TREND
CHARTS BIBLIOG 20. PAGE 51 G1000
ACADEM
CREATE
STAT
GP/REL
S66

TURKEVICH J.,"SOVIET SCIENCE APPRAISED." USA+45 R+D
ACADEM FORCES DIPLOM EDU/PROP WAR EFFICIENCY PEACE
SKILL OBS. PAGE 55 G1081
USSR
TEC/DEV
NAT/COMP
ATTIT
S66

US HOUSE COMM SCI ASTRONAUT,GOVERNMENT, SCIENCE,
AND PUBLIC POLICY (PAMPHLET). R+D ACADEM DELIB/GP
COMPUTER BUDGET CONFER ADMIN...PHIL/SCI PREDICT
TREND 20 CONGRESS HS/SCIASTR. PAGE 58 G1143
NAT/G
POLICY
TEC/DEV
CREATE
N66

HOROWITZ I.L.,THE RISE AND FALL OF PROJECT CAMELOT:
STUDIES IN THE RELATIONSHIP BETWEEN SOCIAL SCIENCE
AND PRACTICAL POLITICS. USA+45 WOR+45 CULTURE
FORCES LEGIS EXEC CIVMIL/REL KNOWL...POLICY SOC
METH/CNCPT 20. PAGE 27 G0529
NAT/G
ACADEM
ACT/RES
GP/REL
B67

NATIONAL SCIENCE FOUNDATION,DIRECTORY OF SELECTED
RESEARCH INSTITUTES IN EASTERN EUROPE. BULGARIA
CZECHOSLVK HUNGARY POLAND ROMANIA INTELL ACADEM
NAT/G ACT/RES 20. PAGE 41 G0814
INDEX
R+D
COM
PHIL/SCI
B67

ORLANS H.,CONTRACTING FOR ATOMS. USA+45 LAW INTELL
ACADEM LG/CO NAT/G PLAN TEC/DEV CONTROL DETER
...TREND 20 AEC. PAGE 43 G0845
NUC/PWR
R+D
PRODUC
PEACE
B67

US DEPARTMENT OF STATE,FOREIGN AFFAIRS RESEARCH
(PAMPHLET). USA+45 WOR+45 ACADEM NAT/G...PSY SOC
CHARTS 20. PAGE 57 G1124
BIBLIOG
INDEX
R+D
DIPLOM
B67

US HOUSE COMM SCI ASTRONAUT,THE JUNIOR COLLEGE AND
EDUCATION IN THE SCIENCES (PAMPHLET). USA+45 AGE/Y
...CHARTS SIMUL HOUSE/REP. PAGE 58 G1148
ACADEM
EDU/PROP
PHIL/SCI
R+D
B67

WARNER W.L.,THE EMERGENT AMERICAN SOCIETY VOL I,
LARGE-SCALE ORGANIZATIONS. USA+45 USA-45 ACADEM
PROF/ORG SCHOOL SECT EX/STRUC TEC/DEV GP/REL
...TREND CHARTS. PAGE 62 G1215
ANTHOL
NAT/G
LABOR
LG/CO
B67

WEINBERG A.M.,REFLECTIONS ON BIG SCIENCE. FUT
USA+45 NAT/G EDU/PROP CHOOSE PERS/REL COST OPTIMAL
...PHIL/SCI TREND. PAGE 62 G1225
ACADEM
KNOWL
R+D
PLAN
B67

ATKIN J.M.,"THE FEDERAL GOVERNMENT, BIG BUSINESS,
AND COLLEGES OF EDUCATION." PROF/ORG CONSULT CREATE
PLAN PROB/SOLV ADMIN EFFICIENCY. PAGE 4 G0075
SCHOOL
ACADEM
NAT/G
INDUS
S67

DE NEUFVILLE R.,"EDUCATION AT THE ACADEMIES."
USA+45 ELITES CONSULT EX/STRUC COMPUTER PLAN
PROB/SOLV TASK CIVMIL/REL ORD/FREE 20. PAGE 15
G0286
FORCES
ACADEM
TEC/DEV
SKILL
S67

LA PORTE T.,"DIFFUSION AND DISCONTINUITY IN
SCIENCE, TECHNOLOGY AND PUBLIC AFFAIRS: RESULTS OF
A SEARCH IN THE FIELD." USA+45 ACT/RES TEC/DEV
PERS/REL ATTIT PHIL/SCI. PAGE 32 G0628
INTELL
ADMIN
ACADEM
GP/REL
S67

WEINBERG A.M.,"CAN TECHNOLOGY REPLACE SOCIAL
ENGINEERING?" SPACE USA+45 SOCIETY ACADEM GP/REL.
PAGE 62 G1224
TEC/DEV
ACT/RES
PROB/SOLV
INTELL
S67

US HOUSE COMM SCI ASTRONAUT,GOVERNMENT, SCIENCE,
AND INTERNATIONAL POLICY (PAMPHLET). INDIA
NETHERLAND ECO/DEV ECO/UNDEV R+D ACADEM PLAN DIPLOM
FOR/AID CONFER...PREDICT 20 CHINJAP. PAGE 59 G1152
NAT/G
POLICY
CREATE
TEC/DEV
N67

BARAGWANATH L.E.,"SCIENTIFIC CO-OPERATION BETWEEN
THE UNIVERSITIES AND INDUSTRY - A RESEARCH NOTE."
UK LG/CO CREATE TEC/DEV EDU/PROP ATTIT...PHIL/SCI
STAT QU 20. PAGE 5 G0090
R+D
ACADEM
INDUS
GP/REL
S68

ACADEM/SCI....ACADEMY OF SCIENCES (U.S.S.R.)

VUCINICH A.,THE SOVIET ACADEMY OF SCIENCES. USSR
STRUCT ACADEM NAT/G EDU/PROP ADMIN LEAD ROLE
...BIBLIOG 20 ACADEM/SCI. PAGE 61 G1203
PHIL/SCI
CREATE
INTELL
PROF/ORG
B56

ACADEMIC ASSISTANCE COUNCIL (U.K.)....SEE ACAD/ASST

ACADEMY OF SCIENCES (U.S.S.R.)....SEE ACADEM/SCI

ACBC....ACTION COUNCIL FOR BETTER CITIES

ACCOUNTING....SEE ACCT

ACCT....ACCOUNTING, BOOKKEEPING

ACCULTURATION....SEE CULTURE

ACD....UNITED STATES ARMS CONTROL AND DISARMAMENT AGENCY

ACHESON/D....DEAN ACHESON

ACKOFF R.L. G0028

ACLU....AMERICAN CIVIL LIBERTIES UNION

ACQUAINTANCE GROUP....SEE FACE/GP

ACT/RES....RESEARCH FACILITATING SOCIAL ACTION

ACTION COUNCIL FOR BETTER CITIES....SEE ACBC

ACTION....ALLEGHENY COUNCIL TO IMPROVE OUR NEIGHBORHOODS

ACTON/LORD....LORD ACTON

ADA....AMERICANS FOR DEMOCRATIC ACTION

ADAMS E.W. G0029

ADAMS/J....PRESIDENT JOHN ADAMS

ADAMS/JQ....PRESIDENT JOHN QUINCY ADAMS

ADAMS/SAM....SAMUEL ADAMS

ADDICTION....ADDICTION

ADENAUER/K....KONRAD ADENAUER

ADJUD....JUDICIAL AND ADJUDICATIVE PROCESSES

RAND SCHOOL OF SOCIAL SCIENCE,INDEX TO LABOR
ARTICLES. ECO/DEV INT/ORG LEGIS DIPLOM GP/REL
...NAT/COMP 20. PAGE 46 G0900
BIBLIOG
LABOR
MGT
ADJUD
N

US SEN SPEC COMM SPACE ASTRO,SPACE LAW: A SYMPOSIUM
(PAMPHLET). USA+45 TEC/DEV CONFER CONTROL SOVEREIGN
...INT/LAW 20 SEN/SPACE. PAGE 59 G1161
SPACE
ADJUD
DIPLOM
INT/ORG
N19

MATHEWS J.M.,AMERICAN STATE GOVERNMENT. USA-45
LOC/G CHIEF EX/STRUC LEGIS ADJUD CONTROL CT/SYS
ROUTINE GOV/REL PWR 20 GOVERNOR. PAGE 37 G0721
PROVS
ADMIN
FEDERAL
CONSTN
B25

FULLER G.H.,DEFENSE FINANCING: A SUPPLEMENTARY LIST
OF REFERENCES (PAMPHLET). CANADA UK USA-45 ECO/DEV
NAT/G DELIB/GP BUDGET ADJUD ARMS/CONT WEAPON COST
PEACE PWR 20 AUSTRAL CHINJAP CONGRESS. PAGE 21
BIBLIOG/A
FINAN
FORCES
DIPLOM
B42

G0403

B53
SAYLES L.R.,THE LOCAL UNION. CONSTN CULTURE   LABOR
DELIB/GP PARTIC CHOOSE GP/REL INGP/REL ATTIT ROLE   LEAD
...MAJORIT DECISION MGT. PAGE 49 G0958   ADJUD
                                                     ROUTINE

B54
WRIGHT Q.,PROBLEMS OF STABILITY AND PROGRESS IN   INT/ORG
INTERNATIONAL RELATIONSHIPS. FUT WOR+45 WOR-45   CONCPT
SOCIETY LEGIS CREATE TEC/DEV ECO/TAC EDU/PROP ADJUD DIPLOM
WAR PEACE ORD/FREE PWR...KNO/TEST TREND GEN/LAWS
20. PAGE 64 G1257

S55
WRIGHT Q.,"THE PEACEFUL ADJUSTMENT OF INTERNATIONAL R+D
RELATIONS: PROBLEMS AND RESEARCH APPROACHES." UNIV   METH/CNCPT
INTELL EDU/PROP ADJUD ROUTINE KNOWL SKILL...INT/LAW PEACE
JURID PHIL/SCI CLASSIF 20. PAGE 64 G1258

B58
DAVIS K.C.,ADMINISTRATIVE LAW TREATISE (VOLS. I AND ADMIN
IV). NAT/G JUDGE PROB/SOLV ADJUD GP/REL 20   JURID
SUPREME/CT. PAGE 14 G0278   CT/SYS
                                                     EX/STRUC

B58
OGDEN F.D.,THE POLL TAX IN THE SOUTH. USA+45 USA-45 TAX
CONSTN ADJUD ADMIN PARTIC CRIME...TIME/SEQ GOV/COMP CHOOSE
METH/COMP 18/20 SOUTH/US. PAGE 43 G0838   RACE/REL
                                                     DISCRIM

B59
HARVARD UNIVERSITY LAW SCHOOL,INTERNATIONAL   NUC/PWR
PROBLEMS OF FINANCIAL PROTECTION AGAINST NUCLEAR   ADJUD
RISK. WOR+45 NAT/G DELIB/GP PROB/SOLV DIPLOM   INDUS
CONTROL ATTIT...POLICY INT/LAW MATH 20. PAGE 25   FINAN
G0488

B59
US CONGRESS JT ATOM ENRGY COMM,SELECTED MATERIALS   NAT/G
ON FEDERAL-STATE COOPERATION IN THE ATOMIC ENERGY   NUC/PWR
FIELD. USA+45 LAW LOC/G PROVS CONSULT LEGIS ADJUD   GOV/REL
...POLICY BIBLIOG 20 AEC. PAGE 57 G1111   DELIB/GP

S59
CORY R.H. JR.,"INTERNATIONAL INSPECTION FROM   STRUCT
PROPOSALS TO REALIZATION." WOR+45 TEC/DEV ECO/TAC   PSY
ADJUD ORD/FREE PWR WEALTH...RECORD VAL/FREE 20.   ARMS/CONT
PAGE 13 G0258   NUC/PWR

B60
CARPER E.T.,THE DEFENSE APPROPRIATIONS RIDER   GOV/REL
(PAMPHLET). USA+45 CONSTN CHIEF DELIB/GP LEGIS   ADJUD
BUDGET LOBBY CIVMIL/REL...POLICY 20 CONGRESS   LAW
EISNHWR/DD DEPT/DEFEN PRESIDENT BOSTON. PAGE 11   CONTROL
G0212

B60
WEBSTER J.A.,A GENERAL STUDY OF THE DEPARTMENT OF   ORD/FREE
DEFENSE INTERNAL SECURITY PROGRAM. USA+45 WORKER   PLAN
TEC/DEV ADJUD CONTROL CT/SYS EXEC GOV/REL COST   ADMIN
...POLICY DECISION MGT 20 DEPT/DEFEN SUPREME/CT.   NAT/G
PAGE 62 G1221

B60
WOETZEL R.K.,THE INTERNATIONAL CONTROL OF AIRSPACE   INT/ORG
AND OUTERSPACE. FUT WOR+45 AIR CONSTN STRUCT   JURID
CONSULT PLAN TEC/DEV ADJUD RIGID/FLEX KNOWL   SPACE
ORD/FREE PWR...TECHNIC GEOG MGT NEW/IDEA TREND   INT/LAW
COMPUT/IR VAL/FREE 20 TREATY. PAGE 64 G1251

B61
CARNELL F.,THE POLITICS OF THE NEW STATES: A SELECT BIBLIOG/A
ANNOTATED BIBLIOGRAPHY WITH SPECIAL REFERENCE TO   AFR
THE COMMONWEALTH. CONSTN ELITES LABOR NAT/G POL/PAR ASIA
EX/STRUC DIPLOM ADJUD ADMIN...GOV/COMP 20   COLONIAL
COMMONWLTH. PAGE 11 G0210

L61
TAUBENFELD H.J.,"A REGIME FOR OUTER SPACE." FUT   INT/ORG
UNIV R+D ACT/RES PLAN BAL/PWR LEGIT ARMS/CONT   ADJUD
ORD/FREE...POLICY JURID TREND UN TOT/POP 20   SPACE
COLD/WAR. PAGE 54 G1056

B62
MARS D.,SUGGESTED LIBRARY IN PUBLIC ADMINISTRATION. BIBLIOG
FINAN DELIB/GP EX/STRUC WORKER COMPUTER ADJUD   ADMIN
...DECISION PSY SOC METH/COMP 20. PAGE 36 G0710   METH
                                                     MGT

B62
US CONGRESS,COMMUNICATIONS SATELLITE LEGISLATION: SPACE
HEARINGS BEFORE COMM ON AERON AND SPACE SCIENCES ON COM/IND
BILLS S2550 AND 2814. WOR+45 LAW VOL/ASSN PLAN   ADJUD

DIPLOM CONTROL OWN PEACE...NEW/IDEA CONGRESS NASA.   GOV/REL
PAGE 56 G1110

S62
FINKELSTEIN L.S.,"THE UNITED NATIONS AND   INT/ORG
ORGANIZATIONS FOR CONTROL OF ARMAMENT." FUT   PWR
VOL/ASSN DELIB/GP TOP/EX CREATE EDU/PROP LEGIT   ARMS/CONT
ADJUD NUC/PWR ATTIT RIGID/FLEX ORD/FREE...POLICY
DECISION CONCPT OBS TREND GEN/LAWS TOT/POP
COLD/WAR. PAGE 19 G0368

B63
MCDOUGAL M.S.,LAW AND PUBLIC ORDER IN SPACE. FUT   SPACE
USA+45 ACT/RES TEC/DEV ADJUD...POLICY INT/LAW JURID ORD/FREE
20. PAGE 37 G0739   DIPLOM
                                                     DECISION

S63
BOHN L.,"WHOSE NUCLEAR TEST: NON-PHYSICAL   ADJUD
INSPECTION AND TEST BAN." WOR+45 R+D INT/ORG   ARMS/CONT
VOL/ASSN ORD/FREE...GEN/LAWS GEN/METH COLD/WAR 20.   TEC/DEV
PAGE 8 G0148   NUC/PWR

B64
RECENT PUBLICATIONS ON GOVERNMENTAL PROBLEMS. FINAN BIBLIOG
INDUS ACADEM PLAN PROB/SOLV EDU/PROP ADJUD ADMIN   AUTOMAT
BIO/SOC...MGT SOC. PAGE 1 G0017   LEGIS
                                                     JURID

B64
BLOUSTEIN E.J.,NUCLEAR ENERGY, PUBLIC POLICY, AND   TEC/DEV
THE LAW. USA+45 NAT/G ADJUD ADMIN GP/REL OWN PEACE   LAW
ATTIT HEALTH...ANTHOL 20. PAGE 7 G0144   POLICY
                                                     NUC/PWR

B64
NASA,PROCEEDINGS OF CONFERENCE ON THE LAW OF SPACE   SPACE
AND OF SATELLITE COMMUNICATIONS: CHICAGO 1963. FUT   COM/IND
WOR+45 DELIB/GP PROB/SOLV TEC/DEV CONFER ADJUD   LAW
NUC/PWR...POLICY IDEA/COMP 20 NASA. PAGE 41 G0805   DIPLOM

B64
TAUBENFELD H.J.,SPACE AND SOCIETY. USA+45 LAW   SPACE
FORCES CREATE TEC/DEV ADJUD CONTROL COST PEACE   SOCIETY
...PREDICT ANTHOL 20. PAGE 54 G1057   ADJUST
                                                     DIPLOM

B66
CLARK G.,WORLD PEACE THROUGH WORLD LAW: TWO   INT/LAW
ALTERNATIVE PLANS. WOR+45 DELIB/GP FORCES TAX   PEACE
CONFER ADJUD SANCTION ARMS/CONT WAR CHOOSE PRIVIL   PLAN
20 UN COLD/WAR. PAGE 12 G0231   INT/ORG

B66
DUNBAR L.W.,A REPUBLIC OF EQUALS. USA+45 CREATE   LAW
ADJUD PEACE NEW/LIB...POLICY 20 SOUTH/US   CONSTN
CIV/RIGHTS. PAGE 16 G0320   FEDERAL
                                                     RACE/REL

B66
US SENATE COMM AERO SPACE SCI,SOVIET SPACE   CONSULT
PROGRAMS, 1962-65: GOALS AND PURPOSES,   SPACE
ACHIEVEMENTS, PLANS, AND INTERNATIONAL   FUT
IMPLICATIONS. USA+45 USSR R+D FORCES PLAN EDU/PROP   DIPLOM
PRESS ADJUD ARMS/CONT ATTIT MARXISM. PAGE 60 G1168

B67
MACAVOY P.W.,REGULATION OF TRANSPORT INNOVATION.   DIST/IND
ACT/RES ADJUD COST DEMAND...POLICY CHARTS 20.   CONTROL
PAGE 35 G0684   PRICE
                                                     PROFIT

B67
UNIVERSAL REFERENCE SYSTEM,LAW, JURISPRUDENCE, AND   BIBLIOG/A
JUDICIAL PROCESS (VOLUME VII). WOR+45 WOR-45 CONSTN LAW
NAT/G LEGIS JUDGE CT/SYS...INT/LAW COMPUT/IR   JURID
GEN/METH METH. PAGE 56 G1101   ADJUD

L67
BARRON J.A.,"ACCESS TO THE PRESS." USA+45 TEC/DEV   ORD/FREE
PRESS TV ADJUD AUD/VIS. PAGE 5 G0099   COM/IND
                                                     EDU/PROP
                                                     LAW

L67
CARMICHAEL D.M.,"FORTY YEARS OF WATER POLLUTION   HEALTH
CONTROL IN WISCONSIN: A CASE STUDY." LAW EXTR/IND   CONTROL
INDUS MUNIC DELIB/GP PLAN PROB/SOLV SANCTION   ADMIN
...CENSUS CHARTS 20 WISCONSIN. PAGE 11 G0207   ADJUD

L67
NADER R.,"AUTOMOBILE DESIGN AND THE JUDICIAL   LAW
PROCESS." USA+45 CT/SYS SUPEGO JURID. PAGE 40 G0799 ADJUD
                                                     TEC/DEV
                                                     PROC/MFG

SEABERG G.P.,"THE DRUG ABUSE PROBLEMS AND SOME
PROPOSALS." UK USA+45 MARKET SANCTION CRIME
...POLICY NEW/IDEA. PAGE 50 G0986

L67
BIO/SOC
LAW
ADJUD
PROB/SOLV

TRAVERS H. JR.,"AN EXAMINATION OF THE CAB'S MERGER
POLICY." USA+45 USA-45 LAW NAT/G LEGIS PLAN ADMIN
...DECISION 20 CONGRESS. PAGE 55 G1078

L67
ADJUD
LG/CO
POLICY
DIST/IND

ALEXANDER L.,"PROTECTION OF PRIVACY IN BEHAVIORAL
RESEARCH." WOR+45 ADJUD SANCTION ORD/FREE...JURID
INT. PAGE 2 G0036

S67
ACT/RES
POLICY
OBS/ENVIR

D'AMATO D.,"LEGAL ASPECTS OF THE FRENCH NUCLEAR
TESTS." FRANCE WOR+45 ACT/RES COLONIAL RISK GOV/REL
EQUILIB ORD/FREE PWR DECISION. PAGE 14 G0268

S67
INT/LAW
DIPLOM
NUC/PWR
ADJUD

JOHNSTON D.M.,"LAW, TECHNOLOGY AND THE SEA." WOR+45
PLAN PROB/SOLV TEC/DEV CONFER ADJUD ORD/FREE
...POLICY JURID. PAGE 29 G0564

S67
INT/LAW
INT/ORG
DIPLOM
NEUTRAL

LAY S.H.,"EXCLUSIVE GOVERNMENTAL LIABILITY FOR
SPACE ACCIDENTS." USA+45 LAW FINAN SERV/IND TEC/DEV
ADJUD. PAGE 33 G0646

S67
NAT/G
SUPEGO
SPACE
PROB/SOLV

PENNEY N.,"BANK STATEMENTS, CANCELLED CHECKS, AND
ARTICLE FOUR IN THE ELECTRONIC AGE." USA+45 TEC/DEV LAW
COST EFFICIENCY WEALTH. PAGE 44 G0866

S67
CREATE
LAW
ADJUD
FINAN

ADJUST....SOCIAL ADJUSTMENT, SOCIALIZATION. SEE ALSO INGP/REL

STAMP S.,THE SCIENCE OF SOCIAL ADJUSTMENT. WOR-45
ACT/RES CREATE PLAN PROB/SOLV TEC/DEV ECO/TAC
EFFICIENCY SOC/INTEG 20. PAGE 52 G1031

B37
ADJUST
ORD/FREE
PHIL/SCI

HAWLEY A.H.,"ECOLOGY AND HUMAN ECOLOGY" WOR+45
INTELL ACADEM PLAN GP/REL ADJUST PERSON...PHIL/SCI
SOC METH/CNCPT METH 20. PAGE 25 G0493

S44
HABITAT
GEOG
GEN/LAWS
METH/COMP

BAKER H.,PROBLEMS OF REEMPLOYMENT AND RETRAINING OF
MANPOWER DURING THE TRANSITION FROM WAR TO PEACE.
USA+45 INDUS LABOR LG/CO NAT/G PLAN ADMIN PEACE
...POLICY MGT 20. PAGE 5 G0086

B45
BIBLIOG/A
ADJUST
WAR
PROB/SOLV

BALDWIN H.W.,THE PRICE OF POWER. USA+45 FORCES PLAN
NUC/PWR ADJUST COST ORD/FREE...POLICY PSY BIBLIOG
20. PAGE 5 G0089

B47
PROB/SOLV
PWR
POPULISM
PRICE

WEINER N.,CYBERNETICS. SOCIETY COMPUTER ADJUST
EFFICIENCY UTIL PERCEPT...PSY MATH REGRESS TIME.
PAGE 63 G1226

B48
FEEDBACK
AUTOMAT
CONTROL
TEC/DEV

CALLOT E.,LA SOCIETE ET SON ENVIRONNEMENT: ESSAI
SUR LES PRINCIPES DES SCIENCES SOCIALES. GP/REL
ADJUST CONSEN ISOLAT HABITAT PERCEPT PERSON
...BIBLIOG SOC/INTEG 20. PAGE 10 G0205

B52
SOCIETY
PHIL/SCI
CULTURE

VON NEUMANN J.,"CAN WE SURVIVE TECHNOLOGY?" WOR+45
AIR INDUS ADMIN ADJUST RIGID/FLEX...GEOG PHIL/SCI
NEW/IDEA 20. PAGE 61 G1202

S55
TEC/DEV
NUC/PWR
FUT
HABITAT

US DEPARTMENT OF THE ARMY,BIBLIOGRAPHY ON LIMITED
WAR (PAMPHLET). USA+45 TEC/DEV CONTROL RISK COERCE
DETER NUC/PWR WEAPON ADJUST PEACE ALL/VALS ORD/FREE
20. PAGE 57 G1127

B58
BIBLIOG/A
WAR
FORCES
CIVMIL/REL

US HOUSE COMM GOVT OPERATIONS,CIVIL DEFENSE. USA+45
FORCES...CHARTS 20 CONGRESS CIV/DEFENS HOLIFLD/C.
PAGE 58 G1139

B58
NUC/PWR
WAR
PLAN
ADJUST

ARGYRIS C.,"SOME PROBLEMS IN CONCEPTUALIZING
ORGANIZATIONAL CLIMATE: A CASE STUDY OF A BANK"
(BMR)" USA+45 EX/STRUC ADMIN PERS/REL ADJUST PERSON
...POLICY HYPO/EXP SIMUL 20. PAGE 3 G0064

S58
FINAN
CONCPT
LG/CO
INGP/REL

HALSEY A.H.,"THE CHANGING FUNCTIONS OF UNIVERSITIES
IN ADVANCED INDUSTRIAL SOCIETIES." R+D EDU/PROP
REPRESENT ROLE ORD/FREE PWR TREND. PAGE 24 G0476

S60
ACADEM
CREATE
CULTURE
ADJUST

BROOKINGS INSTITUTION,DEVELOPMENT OF THE EMERGING
COUNTRIES; AN AGENDA FOR RESEARCH. WOR+45 AGRI
TEC/DEV FOR/AID EDU/PROP ADJUST HABITAT KNOWL...PSY
SOC ANTHOL 20 THIRD/WRLD. PAGE 9 G0175

B62
ECO/UNDEV
R+D
SOCIETY
PROB/SOLV

HEYEL C.,THE ENCYCLOPEDIA OF MANAGEMENT. WOR+45
MARKET TOP/EX TEC/DEV AUTOMAT LEAD ADJUST...STAT
CHARTS GAME ANTHOL BIBLIOG. PAGE 26 G0509

B63
MGT
INDUS
ADMIN
FINAN

KORNHAUSER W.,SCIENTISTS IN INDUSTRY: CONFLICT AND
ACCOMMODATION. USA+45 R+D LG/CO NAT/G TEC/DEV
CONTROL ADJUST ATTIT...MGT STAT INT BIBLIOG 20.
PAGE 31 G0614

B63
CREATE
INDUS
PROF/ORG
GP/REL

LITTERER J.A.,ORGANIZATIONS: STRUCTURE AND
BEHAVIOR. PLAN DOMIN CONTROL LEAD ROUTINE SANCTION
INGP/REL EFFICIENCY PRODUC DRIVE RIGID/FLEX PWR.
PAGE 34 G0674

B63
ADMIN
CREATE
MGT
ADJUST

INST D'ETUDE POL L'U GRENOBLE,ADMINISTRATION
TRADITIONELLE ET PLANIFICATION REGIONALE. FRANCE
LAW POL/PAR PROB/SOLV ADJUST RIGID/FLEX...CHARTS
ANTHOL BIBLIOG T 20 REFORMERS. PAGE 28 G0546

B64
ADMIN
MUNIC
PLAN
CREATE

POWELSON J.P.,LATIN AMERICA: TODAY'S ECONOMIC AND
SOCIAL REVOLUTION. L/A+17C INTELL SOCIETY STRUCT
AGRI INDUS NAT/G DIPLOM ECO/TAC REV...POLICY 20.
PAGE 45 G0887

B64
ECO/UNDEV
WEALTH
ADJUST
PLAN

TAUBENFELD H.J.,SPACE AND SOCIETY. USA+45 LAW
FORCES CREATE TEC/DEV ADJUD CONTROL COST PEACE
...PREDICT ANTHOL 20. PAGE 54 G1057

B64
SPACE
SOCIETY
ADJUST
DIPLOM

BENTWICH J.S.,EDUCATION IN ISRAEL. ISRAEL CULTURE
STRATA PROB/SOLV TEC/DEV ADJUST ALL/VALS 20 JEWS.
PAGE 7 G0125

B65
SECT
EDU/PROP
ACADEM
SCHOOL

KASER M.,COMECON* INTEGRATION PROBLEMS OF THE
PLANNED ECONOMIES. INT/ORG TEC/DEV INT/TRADE PRICE
ADMIN ADJUST CENTRAL...STAT TIME/SEQ ORG/CHARTS
COMECON. PAGE 29 G0579

B65
PLAN
ECO/DEV
COM
REGION

REISS A.J. JR.,SCHOOLS IN A CHANGING SOCIETY.
CULTURE PROB/SOLV INSPECT DOMIN CONFER INGP/REL
RACE/REL AGE/C AGE/Y ALL/VALS...ANTHOL SOC/INTEG 20
NEWYORK/C. PAGE 46 G0912

B65
SCHOOL
EX/STRUC
ADJUST
ADMIN

PILISUK M.,"IS THERE A MILITARY INDUSTRIAL COMPLEX
WHICH PREVENTS PEACE CONSENSUS; COUNTERVAILING
POWER IN PLURALIST SYSTEMS." INDUS R+D ACADEM
FEEDBACK CIVMIL/REL ADJUST CONSEN ATTIT RIGID/FLEX
...CENSUS IDEA/COMP BIBLIOG. PAGE 45 G0878

L65
ELITES
WEAPON
PEACE
ARMS/CONT

MARTIN A.,"PROLIFERATION." FUT WOR+45 PROB/SOLV
REGION ADJUST...PREDICT NAT/COMP UN TREATY. PAGE 36
G0712

S65
RECORD
NUC/PWR
ARMS/CONT
VOL/ASSN

SCHELLING T.C.,"SIGNALS AND FEEDBACK IN THE ARMS
DIALOGUE." USA+45 USSR R+D ACADEM FORCES ACT/RES
ADJUST COST GEN/LAWS. PAGE 49 G0964

S65
FEEDBACK
DETER
EDU/PROP
ARMS/CONT

ONYEMELUKWE C.C.,PROBLEMS OF INDUSTRIAL PLANNING
AND MANAGEMENT IN NIGERIA. AFR FINAN LABOR DELIB/GP
TEC/DEV ADJUST...MGT TREND BIBLIOG. PAGE 43 G0839

B66
ECO/UNDEV
ECO/TAC
INDUS
PLAN

B66
ROSHOLT R.L.,AN ADMINISTRATIVE HISTORY OF NASA, ADMIN
1958-1963. SPACE USA+45 FINAN LEAD...MGT CHARTS EX/STRUC
BIBLIOG 20 NASA. PAGE 48 G0938 ADJUST
DELIB/GP

B67
BENNETT J.W.,HUTTERIAN BRETHREN; THE AGRICULTURAL SECT
ECONOMY AND SOCIAL ORGANIZATION OF A COMMUNAL AGRI
PEOPLE. USA+45 SOCIETY FAM KIN TEC/DEV ADJUST...MGT STRUCT
AUD/VIS GP/COMP 20. PAGE 6 G0121 GP/REL

B67
BERNAL J.D.,THE SOCIAL FUNCTION OF SCIENCE. WOR+45 ROLE
WOR-45 R+D NAT/G PROB/SOLV DOMIN WAR...PHIL/SCI 20. TEC/DEV
PAGE 7 G0130 SOCIETY
ADJUST

B67
EISENMENGER R.W.,THE DYNAMICS OF GROWTH IN NEW ECO/DEV
ENGLAND'S ECONOMY, 1870-1964. USA+45 USA-45 ECO/TAC AGRI
TAX PAY AUTOMAT GOV/REL ADJUST HABITAT...STAT INDUS
19/20. PAGE 17 G0340 CAP/ISM

B67
MACBRIDE R.,THE AUTOMATED STATE; COMPUTER SYSTEMS COMPUTER
AS A NEW FORCE IN SOCIETY. FUT WOR+45 FINAN MUNIC AUTOMAT
NAT/G WORKER PLAN TEC/DEV CONTROL PERS/REL RACE/REL PROB/SOLV
ADJUST. PAGE 35 G0685 SOCIETY

B67
ROACH J.R.,THE UNITED STATES AND THE ATLANTIC INT/ORG
COMMUNITY; ISSUES AND PROSPECTS. WOR+45 TEC/DEV POLICY
ECO/TAC COLONIAL REGION PEACE ROLE...ANTHOL NATO ADJUST
COLD/WAR EEC. PAGE 47 G0925 DIPLOM

S67
CRANBERG L.,"SCIENCE, ETHICS, AND LAW." UNIV CREATE LAW
PLAN EDU/PROP INGP/REL PERS/REL ADJUST RATIONAL PHIL/SCI
KNOWL MORAL...CONCPT IDEA/COMP 20. PAGE 13 G0260 INTELL

S67
FRIED M.,"FUNCTIONS OF THE WORKING CLASS COMMUNITY CLASSIF
IN MODERN URBAN SOCIETY* IMPLICATIONS FOR FORCED WORKER
RELOCATION." USA+45 INDUS R+D NEIGH PLAN TEC/DEV MUNIC
PARTIC GP/REL ATTIT...SOC STAT CHARTS. PAGE 20 ADJUST
G0393

S67
GAUSSENS J.,"THE APPLICATIONS OF NUCLEAR ENERGY - NUC/PWR
TECHNICAL, ECONOMIC AND SOCIAL ASPECTS." WOR+45 TEC/DEV
INDUS R+D ACT/RES EFFICIENCY PRODUC SKILL PREDICT. ECO/DEV
PAGE 21 G0413 ADJUST

S67
GOLDSTEIN W.,"THE SCIENCE ESTABLISHMENT AND ITS CREATE
POLITICAL CONTROL." WOR+45 SOCIETY GP/REL RATIONAL ADJUST
ORD/FREE. PAGE 22 G0430 CONTROL

S67
LEVENSTEIN A.,"TECHNOLOGICAL CHANGE, WORK, AND TEC/DEV
HUMAN VALUES." WOR+45 SOCIETY AUTOMAT ROUTINE CULTURE
LEISURE INGP/REL ADJUST TECHRACY...MGT CONCPT. ALL/VALS
PAGE 33 G0660 TIME/SEQ

S67
MEHTA A.,"INDIA* POVERTY AND CHANGE." STRATA INDUS INDIA
CREATE ECO/TAC FOR/AID NEUTRAL GP/REL ADJUST INCOME SOCIETY
...NEW/IDEA 20. PAGE 38 G0751 ECO/UNDEV
TEC/DEV

S67
VERGIN R.C.,"COMPUTER INDUCED ORGANIZATION COMPUTER
CHANGES." FUT USA+45 R+D CREATE OP/RES TEC/DEV DECISION
ADJUST CENTRAL...MGT INT CON/ANAL COMPUT/IR. AUTOMAT
PAGE 61 G1194 EX/STRUC

ADJUSTMENT, SOCIAL.....SEE ADJUST

ADLER/A....ALFRED ADLER

ADMIN....ORGANIZATIONAL BEHAVIOR, NONEXECUTIVE

N
CONOVER H.L.,CIVILIAN DEFENSE: A SELECTED LIST OF BIBLIOG
RECENT REFERENCES (PAMPHLET). USA+45 LOC/G MUNIC PLAN
PROB/SOLV ADMIN LEAD TASK WEAPON GOV/REL...POLICY WAR
CON/ANAL 20 CIV/DEFENS. PAGE 13 G0251 CIVMIL/REL

N
WEIGLEY R.F.,HISTORY OF THE UNITED STATES ARMY. FORCES
USA+45 USA-45 SOCIETY NAT/G LEAD WAR GP/REL PWR ADMIN
...SOC METH/COMP COLD/WAR. PAGE 62 G1222 ROLE
CIVMIL/REL

N
ADVANCED MANAGEMENT. INDUS EX/STRUC WORKER OP/RES MGT
...DECISION BIBLIOG/A 20. PAGE 1 G0003 ADMIN
LABOR
GP/REL

N
JOURNAL OF PUBLIC ADMINISTRATION: JOURNAL OF THE BIBLIOG/A
ROYAL INSTITUTE OF PUBLIC ADMINISTRATION. UK PLAN ADMIN
GP/REL INGP/REL 20. PAGE 1 G0006 NAT/G
MGT

N
THE MANAGEMENT REVIEW. FINAN EX/STRUC PROFIT LABOR
BIBLIOG/A. PAGE 1 G0007 MGT
ADMIN
MARKET

N
MARKETING INFORMATION GUIDE. USA+45 ECO/DEV FINAN BIBLIOG/A
ADMIN GP/REL. PAGE 1 G0008 DIST/IND
MARKET
ECO/TAC

N
PUBLIC ADMINISTRATION ABSTRACTS AND INDEX OF BIBLIOG/A
ARTICLES. WOR+45 PLAN PROB/SOLV...POLICY 20. PAGE 1 ADMIN
G0009 ECO/UNDEV
NAT/G

N
PERSONNEL. USA+45 LAW LABOR LG/CO WORKER CREATE BIBLIOG/A
GOV/REL PERS/REL ATTIT WEALTH. PAGE 1 G0010 ADMIN
MGT
GP/REL

N
US SUPERINTENDENT OF DOCUMENTS,TRANSPORTATION: BIBLIOG/A
HIGHWAYS, ROADS, AND POSTAL SERVICE (PRICE LIST DIST/IND
25). PANAMA USA+45 LAW FORCES DIPLOM ADMIN GOV/REL SERV/IND
HEALTH MGT. PAGE 61 G1188 NAT/G

N19
DOTSON A.,PRODUCTION PLANNING IN THE PATENT OFFICE EFFICIENCY
(PAMPHLET). USA+45 DIST/IND PROB/SOLV PRODUC...MGT PLAN
PHIL/SCI 20 BUR/BUDGET PATENT/OFF. PAGE 16 G0309 NAT/G
ADMIN

N19
FOLSOM M.B.,BETTER MANAGEMENT OF THE PUBLIC'S ADMIN
BUSINESS (PAMPHLET). USA+45 DELIB/GP PAY CONFER NAT/G
CONTROL REGION GP/REL...METH/COMP ANTHOL 20. MGT
PAGE 19 G0377 PROB/SOLV

N19
GINZBERG E.,MANPOWER FOR GOVERNMENT (PAMPHLET). WORKER
USA+45 FORCES PLAN PROB/SOLV PAY EDU/PROP ADMIN CONSULT
GP/REL COST...MGT PREDICT TREND 20 CIVIL/SERV. NAT/G
PAGE 21 G0418 LOC/G

N19
US CHAMBER OF COMMERCE,THE SIGNIFICANCE OF MARKET
CONCENTRATION RATIOS (PAMPHLET). USA+45 FINAN INDUS PREDICT
ADMIN...METH/CNCPT SAMP CHARTS 20. PAGE 56 G1109 LG/CO
CONTROL

N19
VERNON R.,THE MYTH AND REALITY OF OUR URBAN PLAN
PROBLEMS (PAMPHLET). USA+45 SOCIETY LOC/G ADMIN MUNIC
COST 20 PRINCETN/U INTERVENT URBAN/RNWL. PAGE 61 HABITAT
G1197 PROB/SOLV

B25
MATHEWS J.M.,AMERICAN STATE GOVERNMENT. USA-45 PROVS
LOC/G CHIEF EX/STRUC LEGIS ADJUD CONTROL CT/SYS ADMIN
ROUTINE GOV/REL PWR 20 GOVERNOR. PAGE 37 G0721 FEDERAL
CONSTN

B36
US LIBRARY OF CONGRESS,CLASSIFIED GUIDE TO MATERIAL BIBLIOG
IN THE LIBRARY OF CONGRESS COVERING URBAN COMMUNITY CLASSIF
DEVELOPMENT. USA+45 CREATE PROB/SOLV ADMIN 20. MUNIC
PAGE 59 G1154 PLAN

B37
GULICK L.,PAPERS ON THE SCIENCE OF ADMINISTRATION. OP/RES
INDUS PROB/SOLV TEC/DEV COST EFFICIENCY PRODUC CONTROL
HABITAT...PHIL/SCI METH/COMP 20. PAGE 23 G0461 ADMIN
MGT

B38
HARPER S.N.,THE GOVERNMENT OF THE SOVIET UNION. COM MARXISM
USSR LAW CONSTN ECO/DEV PLAN TEC/DEV DIPLOM NAT/G
INT/TRADE ADMIN REV NAT/LISM...POLICY 20. PAGE 24 LEAD
G0483 POL/PAR

HELLMAN F.S.,THE NEW DEAL: SELECTED LIST OF
REFERENCES. USA-45 FINAN LABOR EX/STRUC CREATE
INT/TRADE ADMIN CT/SYS 20 SUPREME/CT. PAGE 26 G0505

B40
BIBLIOG/A
ECO/TAC
PLAN
POLICY

MORSTEIN-MARX F.,PUBLIC MANAGEMENT IN THE NEW
DEMOCRACY. REPRESENT...MGT 20. PAGE 40 G0786

B40
EX/STRUC
ADMIN
EXEC
PWR

PFIFFNER J.M.,RESEARCH METHODS IN PUBLIC
ADMINISTRATION. USA-45 R+D...MGT STAT INT QU T 20.
PAGE 44 G0872

B40
ADMIN
OP/RES
METH
TEC/DEV

BINGHAM A.M.,THE TECHNIQUES OF DEMOCRACY. USA-45
CONSTN STRUCT POL/PAR LEGIS PLAN PARTIC CHOOSE
REPRESENT NAT/LISM TOTALISM...MGT 20. PAGE 7 G0136

B42
POPULISM
ORD/FREE
ADMIN
NAT/G

BARKER E.,THE DEVELOPMENT OF PUBLIC SERVICES IN
WESTERN WUROPE: 1660-1930. FRANCE GERMANY UK SCHOOL
CONTROL REPRESENT ROLE...WELF/ST 17/20. PAGE 5
G0095

B44
GOV/COMP
ADMIN
EX/STRUC

FULLER G.H.,MILITARY GOVERNMENT: A LIST OF
REFERENCES (A PAMPHLET). ITALY UK USA-45 WOR-45 LAW
FORCES DOMIN ADMIN ARMS/CONT ORD/FREE PWR
...DECISION 20 CHINJAP. PAGE 21 G0404

B44
BIBLIOG
DIPLOM
CIVMIL/REL
SOVEREIGN

MERRIAM C.E.,PUBLIC AND PRIVATE GOVERNMENT.
VOL/ASSN EDU/PROP ADMIN REPRESENT EFFICIENCY PWR
PLURISM...MAJORIT CONCPT. PAGE 38 G0755

B44
NAT/G
NEIGH
MGT
POLICY

PUBLIC ADMINISTRATION SERVICE,YOUR BUSINESS OF
GOVERNMENT: A CATALOG OF PUBLICATIONS IN THE FIELD
OF PUBLIC ADMINISTRATION (PAMPHLET). FINAN R+D
LOC/G ACT/RES OP/RES PLAN 20. PAGE 45 G0894

B44
BIBLIOG
ADMIN
NAT/G
MUNIC

GRIFFITH E.S.,"THE CHANGING PATTERN OF PUBLIC
POLICY FORMATION." MOD/EUR WOR+45 FINAN CHIEF
CONFER ADMIN LEAD CONSERVE SOCISM TECHRACY...SOC
CHARTS CONGRESS. PAGE 23 G0450

S44
LAW
POLICY
TEC/DEV

BAKER H.,PROBLEMS OF REEMPLOYMENT AND RETRAINING OF
MANPOWER DURING THE TRANSITION FROM WAR TO PEACE.
USA+45 INDUS LABOR LG/CO NAT/G PLAN ADMIN PEACE
...POLICY MGT 20. PAGE 5 G0086

B45
BIBLIOG/A
ADJUST
WAR
PROB/SOLV

BUSH V.,SCIENCE, THE ENDLESS FRONTIER. FUT USA-45
INTELL STRATA ACT/RES CREATE PLAN EDU/PROP ADMIN
NUC/PWR PEACE ATTIT HEALTH KNOWL...MAJORIT HEAL MGT
PHIL/SCI CONCPT OBS TREND 20. PAGE 10 G0195

B45
R+D
NAT/G

WHITE L.D.,CIVIL SERVICE IN WARTIME. CONSULT
DELIB/GP PARTIC WAR CHOOSE. PAGE 63 G1233

B45
REPRESENT
ADMIN
INTELL
NAT/G

MCDIARMID J.,"THE MOBILIZATION OF SOCIAL
SCIENTISTS," IN L. WHITE'S CIVIL CIVIL SERVICE IN
WARTIME." USA-45 TEC/DEV CENTRAL...SOC 20
CIVIL/SERV. PAGE 37 G0733

C45
INTELL
WAR
DELIB/GP
ADMIN

AMERICAN DOCUMENTATION INST,CATALOGUE OF AUXILIARY
PUBLICATIONS IN MICROFILMS AND PHOTOPRINTS. USA-45
LAW AGRI CREATE TEC/DEV ADMIN...GEOG LING MATH 20.
PAGE 3 G0052

B46
BIBLIOG
EDU/PROP
PSY

WILCOX J.K.,OFFICIAL DEFENSE PUBLICATIONS,
1941-1945 (NINE VOLS.). USA-45 AGRI INDUS R+D LABOR
FORCES TEC/DEV EFFICIENCY PRODUC SKILL WEALTH 20.
PAGE 63 G1238

B46
BIBLIOG/A
WAR
CIVMIL/REL
ADMIN

LASSWELL H.D.,THE ANALYSIS OF POLITICAL BEHAVIOUR:
AN EMPIRICAL APPROACH. WOR+45 CULTURE NAT/G FORCES
EDU/PROP ADMIN ATTIT PERCEPT KNOWL...PHIL/SCI PSY
SOC NEW/IDEA OBS INT GEN/METH NAZI 20. PAGE 32
G0639

B47
R+D
ACT/RES
ELITES

TURNER R.H.,"THE NAVY DISBURSING OFFICER AS A
BUREAUCRAT" (BMR)" USA-45 LAW STRATA DIST/IND WAR
PWR...SOC 20 BUREAUCRCY. PAGE 55 G1083

S47
FORCES
ADMIN
PERSON
ROLE

CHILDS J.R.,AMERICAN FOREIGN SERVICE. USA+45
SOCIETY NAT/G ROUTINE GOV/REL 20 DEPT/STATE
CIVIL/SERV. PAGE 12 G0227

B48
DIPLOM
ADMIN
GP/REL

PUBLIC ADMINISTRATION SERVICE,SOURCE MATERIALS IN
PUBLIC ADMINISTRATION: A SELECTED BIBLIOGRAPHY (PAS
PUBLICATION NO. 102). USA+45 LAW FINAN LOC/G MUNIC
NAT/G PLAN RECEIVE EDU/PROP CT/SYS CHOOSE HEALTH
20. PAGE 45 G0895

B48
BIBLIOG/A
GOV/REL
MGT
ADMIN

STEWART I.,ORGANIZING SCIENTIFIC RESEARCH FOR WAR:
ADMINISTRATIVE HISTORY OF OFFICE OF SCIENTIFIC
RESEARCH AND DEVELOPMENT. USA-45 INTELL R+D LABOR
WORKER CREATE BUDGET WEAPON CIVMIL/REL GP/REL
EFFICIENCY...POLICY 20. PAGE 53 G1036

B48
DELIB/GP
ADMIN
WAR
TEC/DEV

COCH L.,"OVERCOMING RESISTANCE TO CHANGE" (BMR)"
USA+45 CONSULT ADMIN ROUTINE GP/REL EFFICIENCY
PRODUC PERCEPT SKILL...CHARTS SOC/EXP 20. PAGE 12
G0236

S48
WORKER
OP/RES
PROC/MFG
RIGID/FLEX

HARDIN L.M.,"REFLECTIONS ON AGRICULTURAL POLICY
FORMATION IN THE UNITED STATES." LEGIS PLAN BUDGET
ECO/TAC LEAD CENTRAL...MGT SOC NEW/IDEA STAT FAO.
PAGE 24 G0480

S48
AGRI
POLICY
ADMIN
NEW/LIB

LEPAWSKY A.,ADMINISTRATION. FINAN INDUS LG/CO
SML/CO INGP/REL PERS/REL COST EFFICIENCY OPTIMAL
SKILL 20. PAGE 33 G0656

B49
ADMIN
MGT
WORKER
EX/STRUC

MCLEAN J.M.,THE PUBLIC SERVICE AND UNIVERSITY
EDUCATION. UK USA-45 DELIB/GP EX/STRUC TOP/EX ADMIN
...GOV/COMP METH/COMP NAT/COMP ANTHOL 20. PAGE 38
G0746

B49
ACADEM
NAT/G
EXEC
EDU/PROP

ROSENHAUPT H.W.,HOW TO WAGE PEACE. USA+45 SOCIETY
STRATA STRUCT R+D INT/ORG POL/PAR LEGIS ACT/RES
CREATE PLAN EDU/PROP ADMIN EXEC ATTIT ALL/VALS
...TIME/SEQ TREND COLD/WAR 20. PAGE 48 G0937

B49
INTELL
CONCPT
DIPLOM

DEES J.W. JR.,URBAN SOCIOLOGY AND THE EMERGING
ATOMIC MEGALOPOLIS, PART I. USA+45 TEC/DEV ADMIN
NUC/PWR HABITAT...SOC AUD/VIS CHARTS GEN/LAWS 20
WATER. PAGE 15 G0291

B50
PLAN
NEIGH
MUNIC
PROB/SOLV

HUZAR E.,THE PURSE AND THE SWORD: CONTROL OF THE
ARMY BY CONGRESS THROUGH MILITARY APPROPRIATIONS
1933-1950. NAT/G DELIB/GP EX/STRUC FORCES PROB/SOLV
BARGAIN CONFER ADMIN ROUTINE GOV/REL EFFICIENCY
...POLICY COLD/WAR. PAGE 27 G0541

B50
CIVMIL/REL
BUDGET
CONTROL
LEGIS

KOENIG L.W.,THE SALE OF THE TANKERS. USA+45 SEA
DIST/IND POL/PAR DIPLOM ADMIN CIVMIL/REL ATTIT
...DECISION 20 PRESIDENT DEPT/STATE. PAGE 31 G0609

B50
NAT/G
POLICY
PLAN
GOV/REL

US DEPARTMENT OF STATE,POINT FOUR: COOPERATIVE
PROGRAM FOR AID IN THE DEVELOPMENT OF ECONOMICALLY
UNDERDEVELOPED AREAS. WOR+45 AGRI INDUS INT/ORG
PLAN TEC/DEV DIPLOM EDU/PROP ADMIN PEACE PRODUC
WEALTH 20 CONGRESS UN. PAGE 57 G1121

B50
ECO/UNDEV
FOR/AID
FINAN
INT/TRADE

WAGER P.W.,"COUNTY GOVERNMENT ACROSS THE NATION."
USA+45 CONSTN COM/IND FINAN SCHOOL DOMIN CT/SYS
LEAD GOV/REL...STAT BIBLIOG 20. PAGE 61 G1204

C50
LOC/G
PROVS
ADMIN
ROUTINE

MAASS A.,MUDDY WATERS: THE ARMY ENGINEERS AND THE
NATIONS RIVERS. USA-45 PROF/ORG CONSULT LEGIS ADMIN
EXEC ROLE PWR...SOC PRESIDENT 20. PAGE 35 G0682

B51
FORCES
GP/REL
LOBBY
CONSTRUC

LASSWELL H.D.,"RESEARCH IN POLITICAL BEHAVIOR."

L52
PHIL/SCI

LOC/G MUNIC POL/PAR CONSULT ADMIN PARTIC...CHARTS ANTHOL BIBLIOG/A 20. PAGE 32 G0641 — METH R+D

B53
CALDWELL L.K.,RESEARCH METHODS IN PUBLIC ADMINISTRATION; AN OUTLINE OF TOPICS AND READINGS (PAMPHLET). LAW ACT/RES COMPUTER KNOWL...SOC STAT GEN/METH 20. PAGE 10 G0201 — BIBLIOG/A METH/COMP ADMIN OP/RES

B53
LARSEN K.,NATIONAL BIBLIOGRAPHIC SERVICES: THEIR CREATION AND OPERATION. WOR+45 COM/IND CREATE PLAN DIPLOM PRESS ADMIN ROUTINE...MGT UNESCO. PAGE 32 G0636 — BIBLIOG/A INT/ORG WRITING

B53
ROBINSON E.A.G.,THE STRUCTURE OF COMPETITIVE INDUSTRY. UK ECO/DEV DIST/IND MARKET TEC/DEV DIPLOM EDU/PROP ADMIN EFFICIENCY WEALTH...MGT 19/20. PAGE 47 G0929 — INDUS PRODUC WORKER OPTIMAL

B53
TOMPKINS D.C.,CIVIL DEFENSE IN THE STATES: A BIBLIOGRAPHY (DEFENSE BIBLIOGRAPHIES NO. 3; PAMPHLET). USA+45 LABOR LOC/G NAT/G PROVS LEGIS. PAGE 55 G1076 — BIBLIOG WAR ORD/FREE ADMIN

S53
CORY R.H. JR.,"FORGING A PUBLIC INFORMATION POLICY FOR THE UNITED NATIONS." FUT WOR+45 SOCIETY ADMIN PEACE ATTIT PERSON SKILL...CONCPT 20 UN. PAGE 13 G0257 — INT/ORG EDU/PROP BAL/PWR

S53
PERKINS J.A.,"ADMINISTRATION OF THE NATIONAL SECURITY PROGRAM." USA+45 EX/STRUC FORCES ADMIN CIVMIL/REL ORD/FREE 20. PAGE 44 G0868 — CONTROL GP/REL REPRESENT PROB/SOLV

B54
LOCKLIN D.P.,ECONOMICS OF TRANSPORTATION (4TH ED.). USA+45 USA-45 SEA AIR LAW FINAN LG/CO EX/STRUC ADMIN CONTROL...STAT CHARTS 19/20 RAILROAD PUB/TRANS. PAGE 34 G0675 — ECO/DEV DIST/IND ECO/TAC TEC/DEV

B54
MCCLOSKEY J.F.,OPERATIONS RESEARCH FOR MANAGEMENT. STRUCT COMPUTER ADMIN ROUTINE...PHIL/SCI CONCPT METH/CNCPT TREND ANTHOL BIBLIOG 20. PAGE 37 G0731 — OP/RES MGT METH/COMP TEC/DEV

B54
MOSK S.A.,INDUSTRIAL REVOLUTION IN MEXICO. MARKET LABOR CREATE CAP/ISM ADMIN ATTIT SOCISM...POLICY 20 MEXIC/AMER. PAGE 40 G0789 — INDUS TEC/DEV ECO/UNDEV NAT/G

B54
PUBLIC ADMIN CLEARING HOUSE,PUBLIC ADMINISTRATIONS ORGANIZATIONS: A DIRECTORY, 1954. USA+45 R+D PROVS ACT/RES...MGT 20. PAGE 45 G0893 — INDEX VOL/ASSN NAT/G ADMIN

B54
TOMPKINS D.C.,STATE GOVERNMENT AND ADMINISTRATION: A BIBLIOGRAPHY. USA+45 USA-45 CONSTN LEGIS JUDGE BUDGET CT/SYS LOBBY...CHARTS 20. PAGE 55 G1077 — BIBLIOG/A LOC/G PROVS ADMIN

B54
WILENSKY H.L.,SYLLABUS OF INDUSTRIAL RELATIONS: A GUIDE TO READING AND RESEARCH. USA+45 MUNIC ADMIN INGP/REL...POLICY MGT PHIL/SCI 20. PAGE 63 G1239 — BIBLIOG INDUS LABOR WORKER

S54
LONG N.E.,"PUBLIC POLICY AND ADMINISTRATION: THE GOALS OF RATIONALITY AND RESPONSIBILITY." EX/STRUC ADMIN LEAD 20. PAGE 34 G0676 — PROB/SOLV EXEC REPRESENT

C54
CALDWELL L.K.,"THE GOVERNMENT AND ADMINISTRATION OF NEW YORK." LOC/G MUNIC POL/PAR SCHOOL CHIEF LEGIS PLAN TAX CT/SYS...MGT SOC/WK BIBLIOG 20 NEWYORK/C. PAGE 10 G0202 — PROVS ADMIN CONSTN EX/STRUC

C54
GOULDNER A.W.,"PATTERNS OF INDUSTRIAL BUREAUCRACY." GP/REL CONSEN ATTIT DRIVE...BIBLIOG 20. PAGE 22 G0438 — ADMIN INDUS OP/RES WORKER

C54
ZELLER B.,"AMERICAN STATE LEGISLATURES: REPORT ON THE COMMITTEE ON AMERICAN LEGISLATURES." CONSTN POL/PAR EX/STRUC CONFER ADMIN CONTROL EXEC LOBBY — REPRESENT LEGIS PROVS

ROUTINE GOV/REL...POLICY BIBLIOG 20. PAGE 65 G1267 — APPORT

B55
RILEY V.,INTERINDUSTRY ECONOMIC STUDIES. USA+45 COMPUTER ADMIN OPTIMAL PRODUC...MGT CLASSIF STAT. PAGE 47 G0922 — BIBLIOG ECO/DEV PLAN STRUCT

B55
SMITHIES A.,THE BUDGETARY PROCESS IN THE UNITED STATES. ECO/DEV AGRI EX/STRUC FORCES LEGIS PROB/SOLV TAX ROUTINE EFFICIENCY...MGT CONGRESS PRESIDENT. PAGE 52 G1016 — NAT/G ADMIN BUDGET GOV/REL

L55
KISER M.,"ORGANIZATION OF AMERICAN STATES." L/A+17C USA+45 ECO/UNDEV INT/ORG NAT/G PLAN TEC/DEV DIPLOM ECO/TAC INT/TRADE EDU/PROP ADMIN ALL/VALS...POLICY MGT RECORD ORG/CHARTS OAS 20. PAGE 30 G0601 — VOL/ASSN ECO/DEV REGION

S55
VON NEUMANN J.,"CAN WE SURVIVE TECHNOLOGY?" WOR+45 AIR INDUS ADMIN ADJUST RIGID/FLEX...GEOG PHIL/SCI NEW/IDEA 20. PAGE 61 G1202 — TEC/DEV NUC/PWR FUT HABITAT

B56
KOENIG L.W.,THE TRUMAN ADMINISTRATION: ITS PRINCIPLES AND PRACTICE. USA+45 POL/PAR CHIEF LEGIS DIPLOM DEATH NUC/PWR WAR CIVMIL/REL PEACE ...DECISION 20 TRUMAN/HS PRESIDENT TREATY. PAGE 31 G0610 — ADMIN POLICY EX/STRUC GOV/REL

B56
REDFORD E.S.,PUBLIC ADMINISTRATION AND POLICY FORMATION: STUDIES IN OIL, GAS, BANKING, RIVER DEVELOPMENT AND CORPORATE INVESTIGATIONS. USA+45 CLIENT NAT/G ADMIN LOBBY REPRESENT GOV/REL INGP/REL 20. PAGE 46 G0908 — EX/STRUC PROB/SOLV CONTROL EXEC

B56
THOMAS M.,ATOMIC ENERGY AND CONGRESS. USA+45 NAT/G ACT/RES PLAN TEC/DEV EDU/PROP ROUTINE KNOWL PWR SKILL...PHIL/SCI NEW/IDEA TIME/SEQ CHARTS METH CONGRESS VAL/FREE 20 AEC. PAGE 54 G1067 — LEGIS ADMIN NUC/PWR

B56
VUCINICH A.,THE SOVIET ACADEMY OF SCIENCES. USSR STRUCT ACADEM NAT/G EDU/PROP ADMIN LEAD ROLE ...BIBLIOG 20 ACADEM/SCI. PAGE 61 G1203 — PHIL/SCI CREATE INTELL PROF/ORG

B57
KIETH-LUCAS A.,DECISIONS ABOUT PEOPLE IN NEED, A STUDY OF ADMINISTRATIVE RESPONSIVENESS IN PUBLIC ASSISTANCE. USA+45 GIVE RECEIVE INGP/REL PERS/REL MORAL RESPECT WEALTH...SOC OBS BIBLIOG 20. PAGE 30 G0595 — ADMIN RIGID/FLEX SOC/WK DECISION

B57
MERTON R.K.,SOCIAL THEORY AND SOCIAL STRUCTURE (REV. ED.). INTELL SECT WORKER OP/RES EDU/PROP ADMIN INGP/REL ANOMIE PERSON...AUD/VIS T 20 BUREAUCRCY. PAGE 38 G0759 — SOC GEN/LAWS SOCIETY STRUCT

B57
SCARROW H.A.,THE HIGHER PUBLIC SERVICE OF THE COMMONWEALTH OF AUSTRALIA. LAW SENIOR LOBBY ROLE 20 AUSTRAL CIVIL/SERV COMMONWLTH. PAGE 49 G0959 — ADMIN NAT/G EX/STRUC GOV/COMP

S57
BAUMGARTEL H.,"LEADERSHIP STYLE AS A VARIABLE IN RESEARCH ADMINISTRATION." USA+45 ADMIN REPRESENT PERS/REL 20. PAGE 5 G0104 — LEAD EXEC MGT INGP/REL

B58
LIST OF PUBLICATIONS (PERIODICAL OR AD HOC) ISSUED BY VARIOUS MINISTRIES OF THE GOVERNMENT OF INDIA (3RD ED.). INDIA ECO/UNDEV PLAN...POLICY MGT 20. PAGE 1 G0014 — BIBLIOG NAT/G ADMIN

B58
DAVIS K.C.,ADMINISTRATIVE LAW TREATISE (VOLS. I AND IV). NAT/G JUDGE PROB/SOLV ADJUD GP/REL 20 SUPREME/CT. PAGE 14 G0278 — ADMIN JURID CT/SYS EX/STRUC

B58
OGDEN F.D.,THE POLL TAX IN THE SOUTH. USA+45 USA-45 CONSTN ADJUD ADMIN PARTIC CRIME...TIME/SEQ GOV/COMP METH/COMP 18/20 SOUTH/US. PAGE 43 G0838 — TAX CHOOSE RACE/REL DISCRIM

OPERATIONS RESEARCH SOCIETY,A COMPREHENSIVE
BIBLIOGRAPHY ON OPERATIONS RESEARCH; THROUGH 1956
WITH SUPPLEMENT FOR 1957. COM/IND DIST/IND INDUS
ADMIN...DECISION MATH STAT METH 20. PAGE 43 G0840
BIBLIOG/A
COMPUT/IR
OP/RES
MGT
B58

ARGYRIS C.,"SOME PROBLEMS IN CONCEPTUALIZING
ORGANIZATIONAL CLIMATE: A CASE STUDY OF A BANK"
(BMR)" USA+45 EX/STRUC ADMIN PERS/REL ADJUST PERSON
...POLICY HYPO/EXP SIMUL 20. PAGE 3 G0064
FINAN
CONCPT
LG/CO
INGP/REL
S58

DAVENPORT J.,"ARMS AND THE WELFARE STATE." INTELL
STRUCT FORCES CREATE ECO/TAC FOR/AID DOMIN LEGIT
ADMIN WAR ORD/FREE PWR...POLICY SOC CONCPT MYTH OBS
TREND COLD/WAR TOT/POP 20. PAGE 14 G0276
USA+45
NAT/G
USSR
S58

FOLDES L.,"UNCERTAINTY, PROBABILITY AND POTENTIAL
SURPRISE." MARKET PROB/SOLV RISK PERSON...DECISION
MGT HYPO/EXP GAME. PAGE 19 G0376
PROBABIL
ADMIN
ROUTINE
S58

KEISER N.F.,"PUBLIC RESPONSIBILITY AND FEDERAL
ADVISORY GROUPS: A CASE STUDY." NAT/G ADMIN CONTROL
LOBBY...POLICY 20. PAGE 30 G0590
REPRESENT
ELITES
GP/REL
EX/STRUC
S58

AIR FORCE ACADEMY ASSEMBLY '59,INTERNATIONAL
STABILITY AND PROGRESS (PAMPHLET). USA+45 USSR
ECO/UNDEV PROB/SOLV BUDGET DIPLOM ADMIN DETER COST
ATTIT...TREND 20. PAGE 2 G0030
FOR/AID
FORCES
WAR
PLAN
B59

MAYDA J.,ATOMIC ENERGY AND LAW. ECO/UNDEV FINAN
TEC/DEV FOR/AID EFFICIENCY PRODUC WEALTH...POLICY
TECHNIC 20. PAGE 37 G0723
NUC/PWR
L/A+17C
LAW
ADMIN
B59

U OF MICHIGAN LAW SCHOOL,ATOMS AND THE LAW. USA+45
PROVS WORKER PROB/SOLV DIPLOM ADMIN GOV/REL ANTHOL.
PAGE 55 G1085
NUC/PWR
NAT/G
CONTROL
LAW
B59

TARKOWSKI Z.M.,"SCIENTISTS VERSUS ADMINISTRATORS:
AN APPROACH TOWARD ACHIEVING GREATER
UNDERSTANDING." UK EXEC EFFICIENCY 20. PAGE 53
G1052
INGP/REL
GP/REL
ADMIN
EX/STRUC
L59

BENDIX R.,"INDUSTRIALIZATION, IDEOLOGIES, AND
SOCIAL STRUCTURE" (BMR)" UK USA-45 USSR STRUCT
WORKER GP/REL EFFICIENCY...IDEA/COMP 20. PAGE 6
G0117
INDUS
ATTIT
MGT
ADMIN
S59

CALKINS R.D.,"THE DECISION PROCESS IN
ADMINISTRATION." EX/STRUC PROB/SOLV ROUTINE MGT.
PAGE 10 G0204
ADMIN
OP/RES
DECISION
CON/ANAL
S59

JANOWITZ M.,"CHANGING PATTERNS OF ORGANIZATIONAL
AUTHORITY: THE MILITARY ESTABLISHMENT" (BMR)"
USA+45 ELITES STRUCT EX/STRUC PLAN DOMIN AUTOMAT
NUC/PWR WEAPON 20. PAGE 28 G0559
FORCES
AUTHORIT
ADMIN
TEC/DEV
S59

SEIDMAN H.,"THE GOVERNMENT CORPORATION IN THE
UNITED STATES." USA+45 LEGIS ADMIN PLURISM 20.
PAGE 50 G0988
CONTROL
GOV/REL
EX/STRUC
EXEC
S59

SHEENAN D.,"PUBLIC CORPORATIONS AND PUBLIC ACTION."
UK ADMIN CONTROL REPRESENT SOCISM 20. PAGE 50 G0990
ECO/DEV
EFFICIENCY
EX/STRUC
EXEC
S59

STOESSINGER J.G.,"THE INTERNATIONAL ATOMIC ENERGY
AGENCY: THE FIRST PHASE." FUT WOR+45 NAT/G VOL/ASSN
DELIB/GP BAL/PWR LEGIT ADMIN ROUTINE PWR...OBS
CON/ANAL GEN/LAWS VAL/FREE 20 IAEA. PAGE 53 G1037
INT/ORG
ECO/DEV
FOR/AID
NUC/PWR
S59

STREAT R.,"GOVERNMENT CONSULTATION WITH INDUSTRY."
UK 20. PAGE 53 G1043
REPRESENT
ADMIN
EX/STRUC
INDUS
S59

ALBI F.,TRATADO DE LOS MODOS DE GESTION DE LAS
CORPORACIONES LOCALES. SPAIN FINAN NAT/G BUDGET
CONTROL EXEC ROUTINE GOV/REL ORD/FREE SOVEREIGN
...MGT 20. PAGE 2 G0034
LOC/G
LAW
ADMIN
MUNIC
B60

GRANICK D.,THE RED EXECUTIVE. COM USA+45 SOCIETY
ECO/DEV INDUS NAT/G POL/PAR EX/STRUC PLAN ECO/TAC
EDU/PROP ADMIN EXEC ATTIT DRIVE...GP/COMP 20.
PAGE 22 G0440
PWR
STRATA
USSR
ELITES
B60

KINGSTON-MCCLOUG E.,DEFENSE; POLICY AND STRATEGY.
UK SEA AIR TEC/DEV DIPLOM ADMIN LEAD WAR ORD/FREE
...CHARTS 20. PAGE 30 G0597
FORCES
PLAN
POLICY
DECISION
B60

LEYDER J.,BIBLIOGRAPHIE DE L'ENSEIGNEMENT SUPERIEUR
ET DE LA RECHERCHE SCIENTIFIQUE EN AFRIQUE
INTERTROPICALE (2 VOLS.). AFR CULTURE ECO/UNDEV
AGRI PLAN EDU/PROP ADMIN COLONIAL...GEOG SOC/INTEG
20 NEGRO. PAGE 34 G0664
BIBLIOG/A
ACT/RES
ACADEM
R+D
B60

LINDVEIT E.N.,SCIENTISTS IN GOVERNMENT. USA+45 PAY
EDU/PROP ADMIN DRIVE HABITAT ROLE...TECHNIC BIBLIOG
20. PAGE 34 G0670
TEC/DEV
ECO/TAC
PHIL/SCI
GOV/REL
B60

MCKINNEY R.,REVIEW OF THE INTERNATIONAL ATOMIC
POLICIES AND PROGRAMS OF THE UNITED STATES (5
VOLS.). COM FUT USA+45 ECO/DEV ECO/UNDEV INT/ORG
DELIB/GP PLAN ADMIN 20 THIRD/WRLD. PAGE 38 G0744
NUC/PWR
PEACE
DIPLOM
POLICY
B60

WALDO D.,THE RESEARCH FUNCTION OF UNIVERSITY
BUREAUS AND INSTITUTES FOR GOVERNMENTAL-RELATED
RESEARCH. FINAN ACADEM NAT/G INGP/REL ROLE...POLICY
CLASSIF GOV/COMP. PAGE 61 G1205
ADMIN
R+D
MUNIC
B60

WEBSTER J.A.,A GENERAL STUDY OF THE DEPARTMENT OF
DEFENSE INTERNAL SECURITY PROGRAM. USA+45 WORKER
TEC/DEV ADJUD CONTROL CT/SYS EXEC GOV/REL COST
...POLICY DECISION MGT 20 DEPT/DEFEN SUPREME/CT.
PAGE 62 G1221
ORD/FREE
PLAN
ADMIN
NAT/G
B60

BRENNAN D.G.,"SETTING AND GOALS OF ARMS CONTROL."
FUT USA+45 USSR WOR+45 INTELL INT/ORG NAT/G
VOL/ASSN CONSULT PLAN DIPLOM ECO/TAC ADMIN KNOWL
PWR...POLICY CONCPT TREND COLD/WAR 20. PAGE 8 G0164
FORCES
COERCE
ARMS/CONT
DETER
L60

JACOB P.E.,"THE DISARMAMENT CONSENSUS." USA+45 USSR
WOR+45 INT/ORG NAT/G ACT/RES TEC/DEV BAL/PWR
EDU/PROP ADMIN COERCE DETER NUC/PWR CONSEN
RIGID/FLEX PWR...CONCPT RECORD CHARTS COLD/WAR 20.
PAGE 28 G0552
DELIB/GP
ATTIT
ARMS/CONT
L60

MACPHERSON C.,"TECHNICAL CHANGE AND POLITICAL
DECISION." WOR+45 NAT/G CREATE CAP/ISM DIPLOM
ROUTINE RIGID/FLEX...CONCPT OBS GEN/METH 20.
PAGE 35 G0692
TEC/DEV
ADMIN
L60

RAPP W.F.,"MANAGEMENT ANALYSIS AT THE HEADQUARTERS
OF FEDERAL AGENCIES." USA+45 NAT/G 20. PAGE 46
G0903
INGP/REL
ADMIN
EX/STRUC
MGT
S60

SWIFT R.,"THE UNITED NATIONS AND ITS PUBLIC."
WOR+45 CONSTN FINAN CONSULT DELIB/GP ACT/RES ADMIN
ROUTINE RIGID/FLEX SKILL UN 20. PAGE 53 G1048
INT/ORG
EDU/PROP
S60

TAYLOR M.G.,"THE ROLE OF THE MEDICAL PROFESSION IN
THE FORMULATION AND EXECUTION OF PUBLIC POLICY"
(BMR)" CANADA NAT/G CONSULT ADMIN REPRESENT GP/REL
ROLE SOVEREIGN...DECISION 20 CMA. PAGE 54 G1058
PROF/ORG
HEALTH
LOBBY
POLICY
S60

SCHRAMM W.,"MASS COMMUNICATIONS: A BOOK OF READINGS
(2ND ED.)" LG/CO PRESS ADMIN CONTROL ROUTINE ATTIT
ROLE SUPEGO...CHARTS ANTHOL BIBLIOG 20. PAGE 50
G0977
COM/IND
EDU/PROP
CROWD
MAJORIT
C60

BRADY R.A.,ORGANIZATION, AUTOMATION, AND SOCIETY.
USA+45 AGRI COM/IND DIST/IND MARKET CREATE
...DECISION MGT 20. PAGE 8 G0163
TEC/DEV
INDUS
AUTOMAT
B61

ADMIN

B61
CARNELL F.,THE POLITICS OF THE NEW STATES: A SELECT BIBLIOG/A
ANNOTATED BIBLIOGRAPHY WITH SPECIAL REFERENCE TO AFR
THE COMMONWEALTH. CONSTN ELITES LABOR NAT/G POL/PAR ASIA
EX/STRUC DIPLOM ADJUD ADMIN...GOV/COMP 20 COLONIAL
COMMONWLTH. PAGE 11 G0210

B61
CHAPPLE E.D.,THE MEASURE OF MANAGEMENT. USA+45 MGT
WORKER ADMIN GP/REL EFFICIENCY...DECISION OP/RES
ORG/CHARTS SIMUL 20. PAGE 11 G0221 PLAN
METH/CNCPT

B61
GLADDEN E.N.,BRITISH PUBLIC SERVICE ADMINISTRATION. EFFICIENCY
UK...CHARTS 20. PAGE 21 G0419 ADMIN
EX/STRUC
EXEC

B61
HELLER D.,THE KENNEDY CABINET--AMERICA'S MEN OF EX/STRUC
DESTINY. NAT/G CHIEF CONSULT ADMIN CONTROL GOV/REL CONFER
...MGT 20 DEPT/LABOR DEPT/STATE DEPT/JUST DELIB/GP
DEPT/DEFEN KENNEDY/J. PAGE 26 G0504 TOP/EX

B61
JANOWITZ M.,COMMUNITY POLITICAL SYSTEMS. USA+45 MUNIC
SOCIETY INDUS VOL/ASSN TEC/DEV ADMIN LEAD CHOOSE STRUCT
...SOC SOC/WK 20. PAGE 29 G0561 POL/PAR

B61
LAHAYE R.,LES ENTREPRISES PUBLIQUES AU MAROC. NAT/G
FRANCE MOROCCO LAW DIST/IND EXTR/IND FINAN CONSULT INDUS
PLAN TEC/DEV ADMIN AGREE CONTROL OWN...POLICY 20. ECO/UNDEV
PAGE 32 G0629 ECO/TAC

B61
LEE R.R.,ENGINEERING-ECONOMIC PLANNING BIBLIOG/A
MISCELLANEOUS SUBJECTS: A SELECTED BIBLIOGRAPHY PLAN
(MIMEOGRAPHED). FINAN LOC/G MUNIC NEIGH ADMIN REGION
CONTROL INGP/REL HABITAT...GEOG MGT SOC/WK 20
RESOURCE/N. PAGE 33 G0651

B61
NOVE A.,THE SOVIET ECONOMY. USSR ECO/DEV FINAN PLAN
NAT/G ECO/TAC PRICE ADMIN EFFICIENCY MARXISM PRODUC
...TREND BIBLIOG 20. PAGE 42 G0828 POLICY

L61
THOMPSON V.A.,"HIERARACHY, SPECIALIZATION, AND PERS/REL
ORGANIZATIONAL CONFLICT" (BMR)" WOR+45 STRATA PROB/SOLV
STRUCT WORKER TEC/DEV GP/REL INGP/REL ATTIT ADMIN
AUTHORIT 20 BUREAUCRCY. PAGE 54 G1069 EX/STRUC

S61
DEUTSCH K.W.,"A NOTE ON THE APPEARANCE OF WISDOM IN ADMIN
LARGE BUREAUCRATIC ORGANIZATIONS." ROUTINE PERSON PROBABIL
KNOWL SKILL...DECISION STAT. PAGE 15 G0299 PROB/SOLV
SIMUL

S61
DYKMAN J.W.,"REVIEW ARTICLE* PLANNING AND DECISION DECISION
THEORY." ELITES LOC/G MUNIC CONSULT ADMIN...POLICY PLAN
MGT. PAGE 17 G0327 RATIONAL

S61
FAIR M.L.,"PORT AUTHORITIES IN THE UNITED STATES." MUNIC
PROB/SOLV ADMIN LEAD REPRESENT PWR...DECISION GEOG. REGION
PAGE 18 G0357 LOC/G
GOV/REL

S61
LYONS G.M.,"THE NEW CIVIL-MILITARY RELATIONS." CIVMIL/REL
USA+45 NAT/G EX/STRUC TOP/EX PROB/SOLV ADMIN EXEC PWR
PARTIC 20. PAGE 35 G0681 REPRESENT

S61
SCHILLING W.R.,"THE H-BOMB: HOW TO DECIDE WITHOUT PERSON
ACTUALLY CHOOSING." FUT USA+45 INTELL CONSULT ADMIN LEGIT
CT/SYS MORAL...JURID OBS 20 TRUMAN/HS. PAGE 49 NUC/PWR
G0966

S61
TAUBENFELD H.J.,"OUTER SPACE--PAST POLITICS AND PLAN
FUTURE POLICY." FUT USA+45 USA-45 WOR+45 AIR INTELL SPACE
STRUCT ECO/DEV NAT/G TOP/EX ACT/RES ADMIN ROUTINE INT/ORG
NUC/PWR ATTIT DRIVE...CONCPT TIME/SEQ TREND TOT/POP
20. PAGE 54 G1054

B62
BAKER G.W.,BEHAVIORAL SCIENCE AND CIVIL DEFENSE. NUC/PWR
USA+45 PROB/SOLV ADMIN GP/REL INGP/REL PERS/REL WAR
ANOMIE DRIVE PERSON...DECISION MGT SOC 20 POLICY
CIV/DEFENS. PAGE 4 G0085 ACT/RES

B62
CARSON R.,SILENT SPRING. USA+45 AIR CULTURE AGRI HABITAT
INDUS ADMIN ATTIT RIGID/FLEX ORD/FREE PWR...POLICY TREND
20. PAGE 11 G0216 SOCIETY
CONTROL

B62
CHANDLER A.D.,STRATEGY AND STRUCTURE: CHAPTERS IN LG/CO
THE HISTORY OF THE INDUSTRIAL ENTERPRISE. USA+45 PLAN
USA-45 ECO/DEV EX/STRUC ECO/TAC EXEC...DECISION 20. ADMIN
PAGE 11 G0220 FINAN

B62
DODDS H.W.,THE ACADEMIC PRESIDENT "EDUCATOR OR ACADEM
CARETAKER? FINAN DELIB/GP EDU/PROP PARTIC ATTIT ADMIN
ROLE PWR...POLICY RECORD INT. PAGE 16 G0304 LEAD
CONTROL

B62
DUCKWORTH W.E.,A GUIDE TO OPERATIONAL RESEARCH. OP/RES
INDUS PLAN PROB/SOLV EXEC EFFICIENCY PRODUC KNOWL GAME
...MGT MATH STAT SIMUL METH 20 MONTECARLO. PAGE 16 DECISION
G0319 ADMIN

B62
DUPRE J.S.,SCIENCE AND THE NATION: POLICY AND R+D
POLITICS. USA+45 LAW ACADEM FORCES ADMIN CIVMIL/REL INDUS
GOV/REL EFFICIENCY PEACE...TREND 20 SCI/ADVSRY. TEC/DEV
PAGE 16 G0322 NUC/PWR

B62
GUETZKOW H.,SIMULATION IN SOCIAL SCIENCE: READINGS. SIMUL
STRUCT OP/RES ADMIN AUTOMAT FEEDBACK...MGT PSY SOC TEC/DEV
STYLE BIBLIOG. PAGE 23 G0459 COMPUTER
GAME

B62
KARNJAHAPRAKORN C.,MUNICIPAL GOVERNMENT IN THAILAND LOC/G
AS AN INSTITUTION AND PROCESS OF SELF-GOVERNMENT. MUNIC
THAILAND CULTURE FINAN EX/STRUC LEGIS PLAN CONTROL ORD/FREE
GOV/REL EFFICIENCY ATTIT...POLICY 20. PAGE 29 G0578 ADMIN

B62
KENNEDY J.F.,TO TURN THE TIDE. SPACE AGRI INT/ORG DIPLOM
FORCES TEC/DEV ADMIN NUC/PWR PEACE WEALTH...ANTHOL CHIEF
20 KENNEDY/JF CIV/RIGHTS. PAGE 30 G0592 POLICY
NAT/G

B62
MARS D.,SUGGESTED LIBRARY IN PUBLIC ADMINISTRATION. BIBLIOG
FINAN DELIB/GP EX/STRUC WORKER COMPUTER ADJUD ADMIN
...DECISION PSY SOC METH/COMP 20. PAGE 36 G0710 METH
MGT

B62
NEW ZEALAND COMM OF ST SERVICE.THE STATE SERVICES ADMIN
IN NEW ZEALAND. NEW/ZEALND CONSULT EX/STRUC ACT/RES WORKER
...BIBLIOG 20. PAGE 42 G0818 TEC/DEV
NAT/G

B62
REICH C.A.,BUREAUCRACY AND THE FORESTS (PAMPHLET). ADMIN
USA+45 LOBBY...POLICY MGT 20. PAGE 46 G0910 CONTROL
EX/STRUC
REPRESENT

B62
SNYDER R.C.,FOREIGN POLICY DECISION-MAKING. FUT TEC/DEV
KOREA WOR+45 R+D CREATE ADMIN ROUTINE PWR HYPO/EXP
...DECISION PSY SOC CONCPT METH/CNCPT CON/ANAL DIPLOM
CHARTS GEN/METH METH 20. PAGE 52 G1018

B62
STAHL O.G.,PUBLIC PERSONNEL ADMINISTRATION. LOC/G ADMIN
TOP/EX CREATE PLAN ROUTINE...TECHNIC MGT T. PAGE 52 WORKER
G1030 EX/STRUC
NAT/G

B62
THANT U.,THE UNITED NATIONS' DEVELOPMENT DECADE: INT/ORG
PROPOSALS FOR ACTION. WOR+45 SOCIETY ECO/UNDEV AGRI ALL/VALS
COM/IND FINAN R+D MUNIC SCHOOL VOL/ASSN CONSULT
PLAN TEC/DEV ECO/TAC EDU/PROP ADMIN ROUTINE
RIGID/FLEX...MGT SOC CONCPT UNESCO UN TOT/POP
VAL/FREE. PAGE 54 G1064

B62
US SENATE COMM GOVT OPERATIONS.ADMINISTRATION OF ORD/FREE
NATIONAL SECURITY. USA+45 CHIEF PLAN PROB/SOLV ADMIN
TEC/DEV DIPLOM ATTIT...POLICY DECISION 20 NAT/G
KENNEDY/JF RUSK/D MCNAMARA/R BUNDY/M HERTER/C. CONTROL
PAGE 60 G1177

B62
WENDT P.F.,HOUSING POLICY - THE SEARCH FOR PLAN

SOLUTIONS. GERMANY/W SWEDEN UK USA+45 OP/RES   ADMIN
HABITAT WEALTH...SOC/WK CHARTS 20. PAGE 63 G1230   METH/COMP
                                                    NAT/G

                                                    B62
WRIGHT Q.,PREVENTING WORLD WAR THREE. FUT WOR+45   CREATE
CULTURE INT/ORG NAT/G CONSULT FORCES ADMIN   ATTIT
ARMS/CONT DRIVE RIGID/FLEX ORD/FREE SOVEREIGN
...POLICY CONCPT TREND STERTYP COLD/WAR 20. PAGE 64
G1259

                                                    L62
CAVERS D.F.,"ADMINISTRATIVE DECISION-MAKING IN   REPRESENT
NUCLEAR FACILITIES LICENSING." USA+45 CLIENT ADMIN   LOBBY
EXEC 20 AEC. PAGE 11 G0218   PWR
                                                    CONTROL

                                                    L62
LINS L.J.,"BASIS FOR DECISION: A COMPOSITE OF   DECISION
CURRENT INSTITUTIONAL RESEARCH METHODS OF COLLEGES   ACADEM
AND UNIVERSITIES" ADMIN MGT. PAGE 34 G0671   R+D
                                                    ACT/RES

                                                    L62
NEIBURG H.L.,"THE EISENHOWER AEC AND CONGRESS: A   CHIEF
STUDY IN EXECUTIVE-LEGISLATIVE RELATIONS." USA+45   LEGIS
NAT/G POL/PAR DELIB/GP EX/STRUC TOP/EX ADMIN EXEC   GOV/REL
LEAD ROUTINE PWR...POLICY COLD/WAR CONGRESS   NUC/PWR
PRESIDENT AEC. PAGE 41 G0816

                                                    L62
NIEBURG H.L.,"THE EISENHOWER ATOMIC ENERGY   NUC/PWR
COMMISSION AND CONGRESS" R+D INT/ORG OP/RES DIPLOM   TOP/EX
ADMIN CONTROL 20 PRESIDENT CONGRESS AEC. PAGE 42   LOBBY
G0821   DELIB/GP

                                                    S62
DONNELLY D.,"THE POLITICS AND ADMINISTRATION OF   GOV/REL
PLANNING." UK ROUTINE FEDERAL 20. PAGE 16 G0307   EFFICIENCY
                                                    ADMIN
                                                    EX/STRUC

                                                    S62
SCHILLING W.R.,"SCIENTISTS, FOREIGN POLICY AND   NAT/G
POLITICS." WOR+45 WOR-45 INTELL INT/ORG CONSULT   TEC/DEV
TOP/EX ACT/RES PLAN ADMIN KNOWL...CONCPT OBS TREND   DIPLOM
LEAGUE/NAT 20. PAGE 49 G0967   NUC/PWR

ACKOFF R.L.,A MANAGER'S GUIDE TO OPERATIONS   OP/RES
RESEARCH. STRUCT INDUS PROB/SOLV ROUTINE 20. PAGE 2   MGT
G0028   GP/REL
                                                    ADMIN

                                                    B63
BASS M.E.,SELECTIVE BIBLIOGRAPHY ON MUNICIPAL   BIBLIOG
GOVERNMENT FROM THE FILES OF THE MUNICIPAL   LOC/G
TECHNICAL ADVISORY SERVICE. USA+45 FINAN SERV/IND   ADMIN
PLAN 20. PAGE 5 G0100   MUNIC

                                                    B63
BONINI C.P.,SIMULATION OF INFORMATION AND DECISION   INDUS
SYSTEMS IN THE FIRM. MARKET BUDGET DOMIN EDU/PROP   SIMUL
ADMIN COST ATTIT HABITAT PERCEPT PWR...CONCPT   DECISION
PROBABIL QUANT PREDICT HYPO/EXP BIBLIOG. PAGE 8   MGT
G0152

                                                    B63
BROUDE H.W.,STEEL DECISIONS AND THE NATIONAL   PROC/MFG
ECONOMY. USA+45 LG/CO PLAN ADMIN COST DECISION.   NAT/G
PAGE 9 G0176   CONTROL
                                                    ECO/TAC

                                                    B63
DALAND R.T.,PERSPECTIVES OF BRAZILIAN PUBLIC   ADMIN
ADMINISTRATION (VOL. I). BRAZIL LAW ECO/UNDEV   NAT/G
SCHOOL CHIEF TEC/DEV CONFER CONTROL GP/REL ATTIT   PLAN
ROLE PWR...ANTHOL 20. PAGE 14 G0272   GOV/REL

                                                    B63
DEAN A.L.,FEDERAL AGENCY APPROACHES TO FIELD   ADMIN
MANAGEMENT (PAMPHLET). R+D DELIB/GP EX/STRUC   MGT
PROB/SOLV GOV/REL...CLASSIF BIBLIOG 20 FAA NASA   NAT/G
DEPT/HEW POSTAL/SYS IRS. PAGE 15 G0287   OP/RES

                                                    B63
GREEN H.P.,GOVERNMENT OF THE ATOM. USA+45 LEGIS   GOV/REL
PROB/SOLV ADMIN CONTROL PWR...POLICY DECISION 20   EX/STRUC
PRESIDENT CONGRESS. PAGE 22 G0443   NUC/PWR
                                                    DELIB/GP

                                                    B63
HATHAWAY D.A.,GOVERNMENT AND AGRICULTURE: PUBLIC   AGRI
POLICY IN A DEMOCRATIC SOCIETY. USA+45 LEGIS ADMIN   GOV/REL
EXEC LOBBY REPRESENT PWR 20. PAGE 25 G0491   PROB/SOLV
                                                    EX/STRUC

                                                    B63
HERNDON J.,A SELECTED BIBLIOGRAPHY OF MATERIALS IN   BIBLIOG
STATE GOVERNMENT AND POLITICS (PAMPHLET). USA+45   GOV/COMP
POL/PAR LEGIS ADMIN CHOOSE MGT. PAGE 26 G0507   PROVS
                                                    DECISION

                                                    B63
HEYEL C.,THE ENCYCLOPEDIA OF MANAGEMENT. WOR+45   MGT
MARKET TOP/EX TEC/DEV AUTOMAT LEAD ADJUST...STAT   INDUS
CHARTS GAME ANTHOL BIBLIOG. PAGE 26 G0509   ADMIN
                                                    FINAN

                                                    B63
HOWER R.M.,MANAGERS AND SCIENTISTS. EX/STRUC CREATE   R+D
ADMIN REPRESENT ATTIT DRIVE ROLE PWR SKILL...SOC   MGT
INT. PAGE 27 G0532   PERS/REL
                                                    INGP/REL

                                                    B63
JACOB H.,GERMAN ADMINISTRATION SINCE BISMARCK: ADMIN
CENTRAL AUTHORITY VERSUS LOCAL AUTONOMY. GERMANY   NAT/G
GERMANY/W LAW POL/PAR CONTROL CENTRAL TOTALISM   LOC/G
FASCISM...MAJORIT DECISION STAT CHARTS GOV/COMP   POLICY
19/20 BISMARCK/O HITLER/A WEIMAR/REP. PAGE 28 G0551

                                                    B63
LITTERER J.A.,ORGANIZATIONS: STRUCTURE AND   ADMIN
BEHAVIOR. PLAN DOMIN CONTROL LEAD ROUTINE SANCTION   CREATE
INGP/REL EFFICIENCY PRODUC DRIVE RIGID/FLEX PWR.   MGT
PAGE 34 G0674   ADJUST

                                                    B63
MAYNE R.,THE COMMUNITY OF EUROPE. UK CONSTN NAT/G   EUR+WWI
CONSULT DELIB/GP CREATE PLAN ECO/TAC LEGIT ADMIN   INT/ORG
ROUTINE ORD/FREE PWR WEALTH...CONCPT TIME/SEQ EEC   REGION
EURATOM 20. PAGE 37 G0724

                                                    B63
NASA,CONFERENCE ON SPACE, SCIENCE, AND URBAN LIFE.   MUNIC
USA+45 SOCIETY INDUS ACADEM ACT/RES ECO/TAC ADMIN   SPACE
20. PAGE 41 G0804   TEC/DEV
                                                    PROB/SOLV

                                                    B63
PEABODY R.L.,NEW PERSPECTIVES ON THE HOUSE OF   NEW/IDEA
REPRESENTATIVES. AGRI FINAN SCHOOL FORCES CONFER   LEGIS
LEAD CHOOSE REPRESENT FEDERAL...POLICY DECISION   PWR
HOUSE/REP. PAGE 44 G0862   ADMIN

                                                    B63
RUITENBEER H.M.,THE DILEMMA OF ORGANIZATIONAL   PERSON
SOCIETY. CULTURE ECO/DEV MUNIC SECT TEC/DEV   ROLE
EDU/PROP NAT/LISM ORD/FREE...NAT/COMP 20 RIESMAN/D   ADMIN
WHYTE/WF MERTON/R MEAD/MARG JASPERS/K. PAGE 48   WORKER
G0945

                                                    B63
SCHOECK H.,THE NEW ARGUMENT IN ECONOMICS. UK USA+45   WELF/ST
INDUS MARKET LABOR NAT/G ECO/TAC ADMIN ROUTINE   FOR/AID
BAL/PAY PWR...POLICY BOLIV. PAGE 49 G0973   ECO/DEV
                                                    ALL/IDEOS

                                                    B63
SCHRADER R.,SCIENCE AND POLICY. WOR+45 ECO/DEV   TEC/DEV
ECO/UNDEV R+D FORCES PLAN DIPLOM GOV/REL TECHRACY   NAT/G
BIBLIOG. PAGE 50 G0976   POLICY
                                                    ADMIN

                                                    B63
THORELLI H.B.,INTOP: INTERNATIONAL OPERATIONS   GAME
SIMULATION: PLAYER'S MANUAL. BRAZIL FINAN OP/RES   INT/TRADE
ADMIN GP/REL INGP/REL PRODUC PERCEPT...DECISION MGT   EDU/PROP
EEC. PAGE 54 G1073   LG/CO

                                                    B63
UN SECRETARY GENERAL,PLANNING FOR ECONOMIC   PLAN
DEVELOPMENT. ECO/UNDEV FINAN BUDGET INT/TRADE   ECO/TAC
TARIFFS TAX ADMIN 20 UN. PAGE 55 G1089   MGT
                                                    NAT/COMP

                                                    B63
US ATOMIC ENERGY COMMISSION,ATOMIC ENERGY IN THE   METH/COMP
SOVIET UNION: TRIP REPORT OF THE US ATOMIC ENERGY   OP/RES
DELEGATION, MAY 1933. USSR R+D NAT/G CONSULT CREATE   TEC/DEV
DIPLOM ADMIN ROUTINE EFFICIENCY PRODUC KNOWL SKILL   NUC/PWR
...NAT/COMP 20 AEC TRAVEL TREATY. PAGE 56 G1107

                                                    B63
US SENATE COMM APPROPRIATIONS,PERSONNEL   ADMIN
ADMINISTRATION AND OPERATIONS OF AGENCY FOR   FOR/AID
INTERNATIONAL DEVELOPMENT: SPECIAL HEARING. FINAN   EFFICIENCY
LEAD COST UTIL SKILL...CHARTS 20 CONGRESS AID   DIPLOM
CIVIL/SERV. PAGE 60 G1175

B63

US SENATE COMM GOVT OPERATIONS,ADMINISTRATION OF
NATIONAL SECURITY (9 PARTS). ADMIN...INT REC/INT
CHARTS 20 SENATE CONGRESS. PAGE 60 G1178

DELIB/GP
NAT/G
OP/RES
ORD/FREE

L63

BEGUIN H.,"ASPECTS GEOGRAPHIQUE DE LA
POLARISATION." FUT WOR+45 SOCIETY STRUCT ECO/DEV
R+D BAL/PWR ADMIN ATTIT RIGID/FLEX HEALTH WEALTH
...CHARTS 20. PAGE 6 G0114

ECO/UNDEV
GEOG
DIPLOM

B64

RECENT PUBLICATIONS ON GOVERNMENTAL PROBLEMS. FINAN
INDUS ACADEM PLAN PROB/SOLV EDU/PROP ADJUD ADMIN
BIO/SOC...MGT SOC. PAGE 1 G0017

BIBLIOG
AUTOMAT
LEGIS
JURID

B64

BAUCHET P.,ECONOMIC PLANNING. FRANCE STRATA LG/CO
CAP/ISM ADMIN PARL/PROC DEMAND OPTIMAL ATTIT PWR
SOCISM...POLICY CHARTS 20. PAGE 5 G0102

ECO/DEV
NAT/G
PLAN
ECO/TAC

B64

BLOUSTEIN E.J.,NUCLEAR ENERGY, PUBLIC POLICY, AND
THE LAW. USA+45 NAT/G ADJUD ADMIN GP/REL OWN PEACE
ATTIT HEALTH...ANTHOL 20. PAGE 7 G0144

TEC/DEV
LAW
POLICY
NUC/PWR

B64

FALK L.A.,ADMINISTRATIVE ASPECTS OF GROUP PRACTICE.
USA+45 FINAN PROF/ORG PLAN MGT. PAGE 18 G0358

BIBLIOG/A
HEAL
ADMIN
SERV/IND

B64

GRAVIER J.F.,AMENAGEMENT DU TERRITOIRE ET L'AVENIR
DES REGIONS FRANCAISES. FRANCE ECO/DEV AGRI INDUS
CREATE...GEOG CHARTS 20. PAGE 22 G0442

PLAN
MUNIC
NEIGH
ADMIN

B64

HODGETTS J.E.,ADMINISTERING THE ATOM FOR PEACE.
OP/RES TEC/DEV ADMIN...IDEA/COMP METH/COMP 20.
PAGE 26 G0517

PROB/SOLV
NUC/PWR
PEACE
MGT

B64

INST D'ETUDE POL L'U GRENOBLE,ADMINISTRATION
TRADITIONELLE ET PLANIFICATION REGIONALE. FRANCE
LAW POL/PAR PROB/SOLV ADJUST RIGID/FLEX...CHARTS
ANTHOL BIBLIOG T 20 REFORMERS. PAGE 28 G0546

ADMIN
MUNIC
PLAN
CREATE

B64

MASTERS N.A.,STATE POLITICS AND THE PUBLIC SCHOOLS.
STRUCT FINAN ADMIN LOBBY GP/REL PWR BIBLIOG.
PAGE 36 G0720

EDU/PROP
PROVS
DOMIN

B64

ORTH C.D.,ADMINISTERING RESEARCH AND DEVELOPMENT.
FINAN PLAN PROB/SOLV ADMIN ROUTINE...METH/CNCPT
STAT CHARTS METH 20. PAGE 43 G0847

MGT
R+D
LG/CO
INDUS

B64

PARANJAPE H.K.,THE FLIGHT OF TECHNICAL PERSONNEL IN
PUBLIC UNDERTAKINGS. INDIA PAY DEMAND HAPPINESS
ORD/FREE...MGT QU 20 MIGRATION. PAGE 44 G0858

ADMIN
NAT/G
WORKER
PLAN

B64

WHEELER-BENNETT J.W.,THE NEMESIS OF POWER (2ND
ED.). EUR+WWI GERMANY TOP/EX TEC/DEV ADMIN WAR
PERS/REL RIGID/FLEX ROLE ORD/FREE PWR FASCISM 20
HITLER/A. PAGE 63 G1231

FORCES
NAT/G
GP/REL
STRUCT

S64

KASSOF A.,"THE ADMINISTERED SOCIETY:
TOTALITARIANISM WITHOUT TERROR." COM USSR STRATA
AGRI INDUS NAT/G PERF/ART SCHOOL TOP/EX EDU/PROP
ADMIN ORD/FREE PWR...POLICY SOC TIME/SEQ GEN/LAWS
VAL/FREE 20. PAGE 29 G0580

SOCIETY
DOMIN
TOTALISM

S64

NEEDHAM T.,"SCIENCE AND SOCIETY IN EAST AND WEST."
INTELL STRATA R+D LOC/G NAT/G PROVS CONSULT ACT/RES
CREATE PLAN TEC/DEV EDU/PROP ADMIN ATTIT ALL/VALS
...POLICY RELATIV MGT CONCPT NEW/IDEA TIME/SEQ WORK
WORK. PAGE 41 G0815

ASIA
STRUCT

S64

STONE P.A.,"DECISION TECHNIQUES FOR TOWN
DEVELOPMENT." PLAN COST PROFIT...DECISION MGT
CON/ANAL CHARTS METH/COMP BIBLIOG 20. PAGE 53 G1039

OP/RES
MUNIC
ADMIN
PROB/SOLV

B65

ARTHUR D LITTLE INC,SAN FRANCISCO COMMUNITY RENEWAL
PROGRAM. USA+45 FINAN PROVS ADMIN INCOME...CHARTS
20 CALIFORNIA SAN/FRAN URBAN/RNWL. PAGE 4 G0071

HABITAT
MUNIC
PLAN
PROB/SOLV

B65

BAILEY S.K.,AMERICAN POLITICS AND GOVERNMENT.
USA+45 CONSTN FINAN LABOR POL/PAR DIPLOM ADMIN WAR
INGP/REL RACE/REL NEW/LIB 20 SUPREME/CT PRESIDENT
CONGRESS. PAGE 4 G0084

ANTHOL
LEGIS
PWR

B65

INT. BANK RECONSTR. DEVELOP.,ECONOMIC DEVELOPMENT
OF KUWAIT. ISLAM KUWAIT AGRI FINAN MARKET EX/STRUC
TEC/DEV ECO/TAC ADMIN WEALTH...OBS CON/ANAL CHARTS
20. PAGE 28 G0548

INDUS
NAT/G

B65

INTERNATIONAL CITY MGRS ASSN,COUNCIL-MANAGER
GOVERNMENT, 1940-64: AN ANNOTATED BIBLIOGRAPHY.
USA+45 ADMIN GOV/REL ROLE...MGT 20. PAGE 28 G0549

BIBLIOG/A
MUNIC
CONSULT
PLAN

B65

KASER M.,COMECON* INTEGRATION PROBLEMS OF THE
PLANNED ECONOMIES. INT/ORG TEC/DEV INT/TRADE PRICE
ADMIN ADJUST CENTRAL...STAT TIME/SEQ ORG/CHARTS
COMECON. PAGE 29 G0579

PLAN
ECO/DEV
COM
REGION

B65

LUTZ V.,FRENCH PLANNING. FRANCE TEC/DEV RIGID/FLEX
ORD/FREE 20. PAGE 34 G0680

PLAN
ADMIN
FUT

B65

MELMANS S.,OUR DEPLETED SOCIETY. SPACE USA+45
ECO/DEV FORCES BUDGET ECO/TAC ADMIN WEAPON
EFFICIENCY 20 COLD/WAR. PAGE 38 G0753

CIVMIL/REL
INDUS
EDU/PROP
CONTROL

B65

MORRIS M.D.,THE EMERGENCE OF AN INDUSTRIAL LABOR
FORCE IN INDIA: A STUDY OF THE BOMBAY COTTON MILLS,
1854-1947. INDIA WORKER OP/RES ADMIN 19/20. PAGE 40
G0784

INDUS
LABOR
ECO/UNDEV
CAP/ISM

B65

OECD,MEDITERRANEAN REGIONAL PROJECT: TURKEY;
EDUCATION AND DEVELOPMENT. FUT TURKEY SOCIETY
STRATA FINAN NAT/G PROF/ORG PLAN PROB/SOLV ADMIN
COST...STAT CHARTS 20 OECD. PAGE 42 G0831

EDU/PROP
ACADEM
SCHOOL
ECO/UNDEV

B65

OECD,THE MEDITERRANEAN REGIONAL PROJECT: PORTUGAL;
EDUCATION AND DEVELOPMENT. PORTUGAL SOCIETY STRATA
FINAN PROF/ORG WORKER PLAN PROB/SOLV ADMIN...POLICY
STAT CHARTS METH 20 OECD. PAGE 42 G0832

EDU/PROP
SCHOOL
ACADEM
ECO/UNDEV

B65

OECD,THE MEDITERRANEAN REGIONAL PROJECT: ITALY;
EDUCATION AND DEVELOPMENT. ITALY SOCIETY STRATA
FINAN NAT/G PROF/ORG WORKER PLAN PROB/SOLV ADMIN
...STAT CHARTS METH 20 OECD. PAGE 42 G0833

SCHOOL
EDU/PROP
ECO/UNDEV
ACADEM

B65

OECD,THE MEDITERRANEAN REGIONAL PROJECT: GREECE;
EDUCATION AND DEVELOPMENT. FUT GREECE SOCIETY AGRI
FINAN NAT/G PROF/ORG WORKER PLAN PROB/SOLV ADMIN
DEMAND ATTIT 20 OECD. PAGE 42 G0834

EDU/PROP
SCHOOL
ACADEM
ECO/UNDEV

B65

OECD,THE MEDITERRANEAN REGIONAL PROJECT: SPAIN;
EDUCATION AND DEVELOPMENT. FUT SPAIN STRATA FINAN
NAT/G WORKER PLAN PROB/SOLV ADMIN COST...POLICY
STAT CHARTS 20 OECD. PAGE 42 G0835

ECO/UNDEV
EDU/PROP
ACADEM
SCHOOL

B65

ORG FOR ECO COOP AND DEVEL,THE MEDITERRANEAN
REGIONAL PROJECT: YUGOSLAVIA; EDUCATION AND
DEVELOPMENT. YUGOSLAVIA SOCIETY FINAN PROF/ORG PLAN
ADMIN COST DEMAND MARXISM...STAT TREND CHARTS METH
20 OECD. PAGE 43 G0843

EDU/PROP
ACADEM
SCHOOL
ECO/UNDEV

B65

REISS A.J. JR.,SCHOOLS IN A CHANGING SOCIETY.
CULTURE PROB/SOLV INSPECT DOMIN CONFER INGP/REL
RACE/REL AGE/C AGE/Y ALL/VALS...ANTHOL SOC/INTEG 20
NEWYORK/C. PAGE 46 G0912

SCHOOL
EX/STRUC
ADJUST
ADMIN

B65

SINGER J.D.,HUMAN BEHAVIOR AND INTERNATINAL
POLITICS* CONTRIBUTIONS FROM THE SOCIAL-
PSYCHOLOGICAL SCIENCES. ACT/RES PLAN EDU/PROP ADMIN
KNOWL...DECISION PSY SOC NET/THEORY HYPO/EXP

DIPLOM
PHIL/SCI
QUANT
SIMUL

LAB/EXP SOC/EXP GEN/METH ANTHOL BIBLIOG. PAGE 51
G1006

B65
STEINER G.A.,THE CREATIVE ORGANIZATION. ELITES   CREATE
LG/CO PLAN PROB/SOLV TEC/DEV INSPECT CAP/ISM   MGT
CONTROL EXEC PERSON...METH/COMP HYPO/EXP 20.   ADMIN
PAGE 52 G1034   SOC

B65
TYBOUT R.A.,ECONOMICS OF RESEARCH AND DEVELOPMENT.   R+D
ECO/DEV ECO/UNDEV INDUS PROFIT DECISION. PAGE 55   FORCES
G1084   ADMIN
   DIPLOM

B65
US SENATE COMM GOVT OPERATIONS,ORGANIZATION OF   ADMIN
FEDERAL EXECUTIVE DEPARTMENTS AND AGENCIES: REPORT   EX/STRUC
OF MARCH 23, 1965. USA+45 FORCES LEGIS DIPLOM   GOV/REL
ROUTINE CIVMIL/REL EFFICIENCY FEDERAL...MGT STAT.   ORG/CHARTS
PAGE 60 G1179

B65
VEINOTT A.F. JR.,MATHEMATICAL STUDIES IN MANAGEMENT   MATH
SCIENCE. UNIV INDUS COMPUTER ADMIN...DECISION   MGT
NET/THEORY SIMUL 20. PAGE 61 G1193   PLAN
   PRODUC

L65
LASSWELL H.D.,"THE POLICY SCIENCES OF DEVELOPMENT."   PWR
CULTURE SOCIETY EX/STRUC CREATE ADMIN ATTIT KNOWL   METH/CNCPT
...SOC CONCPT SIMUL GEN/METH. PAGE 33 G0644   DIPLOM

S65
BALDWIN H.,"SLOW-DOWN IN THE PENTAGON." USA+45   RECORD
CREATE PLAN GOV/REL CENTRAL COST EFFICIENCY PWR   R+D
...MGT MCNAMARA/R. PAGE 5 G0088   WEAPON
   ADMIN

S65
HUGHES T.L.,"SCHOLARS AND FOREIGN POLICY* VARIETIES   ACT/RES
OF RESEARCH EXPERIENCE." COM/IND DIPLOM ADMIN EXEC   ACADEM
ROUTINE...MGT OBS CONGRESS PRESIDENT CAMELOT.   CONTROL
PAGE 27 G0535   NAT/G

S65
LEISERSON A.,"SCIENTISTS AND THE POLICY PROCESS."   PHIL/SCI
USA+45 NAT/G LEAD PARTIC REPRESENT. PAGE 33 G0654   ADMIN
   EX/STRUC
   EXEC

S65
SILVERT K.H.,"AMERICAN ACADEMIC ETHICS AND SOCIAL   ACADEM
RESEARCH ABROAD* THE LESSON OF PROJECT CAMELOT."   NAT/G
CHILE L/A+17C USA+45 FINAN ADMIN...PHIL/SCI SOC   ACT/RES
GEN/LAWS CAMELOT. PAGE 51 G0998   POLICY

B66
ALEXANDER Y.,INTERNATIONAL TECHNICAL ASSISTANCE   ECO/TAC
EXPERTS* A CASE STUDY OF THE U.N. EXPERIENCE.   INT/ORG
ECO/UNDEV CONSULT EX/STRUC CREATE PLAN DIPLOM   ADMIN
FOR/AID TASK EFFICIENCY...ORG/CHARTS UN. PAGE 2   MGT
G0038

B66
ALI S.,PLANNING, DEVELOPMENT AND CHANGE: AN   BIBLIOG/A
ANNOTATED BIBLIOGRAPHY ON DEVELOPMENTAL   ADMIN
ADMINISTRATION. PAKISTAN SOCIETY ORD/FREE 20.   ECO/UNDEV
PAGE 2 G0041   PLAN

B66
GLAZER M.,THE FEDERAL GOVERNMENT AND THE   BIBLIOG/A
UNIVERSITY. CHILE PROB/SOLV DIPLOM GIVE ADMIN WAR   NAT/G
...POLICY SOC 20. PAGE 21 G0421   PLAN
   ACADEM

B66
HALPIN A.W.,THEORY AND RESEARCH IN ADMINISTRATION.   GEN/LAWS
ACT/RES LEAD...MGT IDEA/COMP METH/COMP. PAGE 24   EDU/PROP
G0475   ADMIN
   PHIL/SCI

B66
LEWIS W.A.,DEVELOPMENT PLANNING; THE ESSENTIALS OF   PLAN
ECONOMIC POLICY. USA+45 FINAN INDUS NAT/G WORKER   ECO/DEV
FOR/AID INT/TRADE ADMIN ROUTINE WEALTH...CONCPT   POLICY
STAT. PAGE 34 G0663   CREATE

B66
LINDFORS G.V.,INTERCOLLEGIATE BIBLIOGRAPHY; CASES   BIBLIOG/A
IN BUSINESS ADMINISTRATION (VOL. X). FINAN MARKET   ADMIN
LABOR CONSULT PLAN GP/REL PRODUC 20. PAGE 34 G0668   MGT
   OP/RES

B66
MURDOCK J.C.,RESEARCH AND REGIONS. AGRI FINAN INDUS   BIBLIOG

LOC/G MUNIC NAT/G PROB/SOLV TEC/DEV ADMIN REGION   ECO/DEV
20. PAGE 40 G0796   COMPUT/IR
   R+D

B66
ROSHOLT R.L.,AN ADMINISTRATIVE HISTORY OF NASA,   ADMIN
1958-1963. SPACE USA+45 FINAN LEAD...MGT CHARTS   EX/STRUC
BIBLIOG 20 NASA. PAGE 48 G0938   ADJUST
   DELIB/GP

B66
SCHURMANN F.,IDEOLOGY AND ORGANIZATION IN COMMUNIST   MARXISM
CHINA. CHINA/COM LOC/G MUNIC POL/PAR ECO/TAC   STRUCT
CONTROL ATTIT...MGT STERTYP 20 COM/PARTY. PAGE 50   ADMIN
G0981   NAT/G

B66
STREET D.,ORGANIZATION FOR TREATMENT. CLIENT PROVS   GP/COMP
PUB/INST PLAN CONTROL PARTIC REPRESENT ATTIT PWR   AGE/Y
...POLICY BIBLIOG. PAGE 53 G1044   ADMIN
   VOL/ASSN

B66
US BUREAU OF THE BUDGET,THE ADMINISTRATION OF   ACT/RES
GOVERNMENT SUPPORTED RESEARCH AT UNIVERSITIES   NAT/G
(PAMPHLET). USA+45 CONSULT TOP/EX ADMIN INCOME   ACADEM
WEALTH...MGT PHIL/SCI INT. PAGE 56 G1108   GP/REL

B66
WHITNAH D.R.,SAFER SKYWAYS. DIST/IND DELIB/GP   ADMIN
FORCES TOP/EX WORKER TEC/DEV ROUTINE WAR CIVMIL/REL   NAT/G
COST...TIME/SEQ 20 FAA CAB. PAGE 63 G1235   AIR
   GOV/REL

B66
YOUNG W.,EXISTING MECHANISMS OF ARMS CONTROL.   ARMS/CONT
PROC/MFG OP/RES DIPLOM TASK CENTRAL...MGT TREATY.   ADMIN
PAGE 65 G1266   NUC/PWR
   ROUTINE

S66
"FURTHER READING." INDIA LOC/G NAT/G PLAN ADMIN   BIBLIOG
WEALTH...GEOG SOC CONCPT CENSUS 20. PAGE 1 G0021   ECO/UNDEV
   TEC/DEV
   PROVS

S66
FLEMING W.G.,"AUTHORITY, EFFICIENCY, AND ROLE   DOMIN
STRESS: PROBLEMS IN THE DEVELOPMENT OF EAST AFRICAN   EFFICIENCY
BUREAUCRACIES." AFR UGANDA STRUCT PROB/SOLV ROUTINE   COLONIAL
INGP/REL ROLE...MGT SOC GP/COMP GOV/COMP 20   ADMIN
TANGANYIKA AFRICA/20. PAGE 19 G0371

S66
HANSON A.H.,"PLANNING AND THE POLITICIANS* SOME   PLAN
REFLECTIONS ON ECONOMIC PLANNING IN WESTERN   ECO/DEV
EUROPE." MARKET NAT/G TEC/DEV CONSEN ROLE   EUR+WWI
...METH/COMP NAT/COMP. PAGE 24 G0479   ADMIN

S66
RIZOS E.J.,"SCIENCE AND TECHNOLOGY IN COUNTRY   ADMIN
DEVELOPMENT* TOWARDS AN UNDERSTANDING OF THE ROLE   TEC/DEV
OF PUBLIC ADMINISTRATION." WOR+45 STRUCT INT/ORG   ECO/UNDEV
EX/STRUC CREATE PLAN PROB/SOLV EFFICIENCY ROLE   PHIL/SCI
DECISION. PAGE 47 G0924

N66
US HOUSE COMM SCI ASTRONAUT,GOVERNMENT, SCIENCE,   NAT/G
AND PUBLIC POLICY (PAMPHLET). R+D ACADEM DELIB/GP   POLICY
COMPUTER BUDGET CONFER ADMIN...PHIL/SCI PREDICT   TEC/DEV
TREND 20 CONGRESS HS/SCIASTR. PAGE 58 G1143   CREATE

N66
US HOUSE COMM SCI ASTRONAUT,THE ADEQUACY OF   HEALTH
TECHNOLOGY FOR POLLUTION ABATEMENT (PAMPHLET).   POLICY
WOR+45 PLAN PROB/SOLV CONFER ADMIN...JURID 20   TEC/DEV
POLLUTION. PAGE 58 G1145   LEGIS

B67
AMERICAN FRIENDS SERVICE COMM,IN PLACE OF WAR.   PEACE
NAT/G ACT/RES DIPLOM ADMIN NUC/PWR EFFICIENCY   PACIFISM
...POLICY 20. PAGE 3 G0053   WAR
   DETER

B67
DE BLIJ H.J.,SYSTEMATIC POLITICAL GEOGRAPHY. WOR+45   GEOG
STRUCT INT/ORG NAT/G EDU/PROP ADMIN COLONIAL   CONCPT
ROUTINE ORD/FREE PWR...IDEA/COMP T 20. PAGE 15   METH
G0283

B67
DICKSON P.G.M.,THE FINANCIAL REVOLUTION IN ENGLAND.   ECO/DEV
UK NAT/G TEC/DEV ADMIN GOV/REL...SOC METH/CNCPT   FINAN
CHARTS GP/COMP BIBLIOG 17/18. PAGE 15 G0302   CAP/ISM
   MGT

DONALD A.G.,MANAGEMENT, INFORMATION, AND SYSTEMS. WOR+45 LG/CO PROB/SOLV CONTROL FEEDBACK KNOWL MGT. PAGE 16 G0306
B67
ROUTINE
TEC/DEV
CONCPT
ADMIN

ENKE S.,DEFENSE MANAGEMENT. USA+45 R+D FORCES WORKER PLAN ECO/TAC ADMIN NUC/PWR BAL/PAY UTIL WEALTH...MGT DEPT/DEFEN. PAGE 18 G0348
B67
DECISION
DELIB/GP
EFFICIENCY
BUDGET

FIELD M.G.,SOVIET SOCIALIZED MEDICINE. USSR FINAN R+D PROB/SOLV ADMIN SOCISM...MGT SOC CONCPT 20. PAGE 19 G0366
B67
PUB/INST
HEALTH
NAT/G
MARXISM

GOLEMBIEWSKI R.T.,ORGANIZING MEN AND POWER: PATTERNS OF BEHAVIOR AND LINESTAFF MODELS. WOR+45 EX/STRUC ACT/RES DOMIN PERS/REL...NEW/IDEA 20. PAGE 22 G0431
B67
ADMIN
CONTROL
SIMUL
MGT

LAMBERT J.,LATIN AMERICA: SOCIAL STRUCTURES AND POLITICAL INSTITUTIONS. STRUCT TEC/DEV DIPLOM ADMIN COLONIAL LEAD ATTIT...SOC CLASSIF NAT/COMP 17/20. PAGE 32 G0631
B67
L/A+17C
NAT/G
ECO/UNDEV
SOCIETY

MACKINTOSH J.M.,JUGGERNAUT. USSR NAT/G POL/PAR ADMIN LEAD CIVMIL/REL COST TOTALISM PWR MARXISM ...GOV/COMP 20. PAGE 35 G0691
B67
WAR
FORCES
COM
PROF/ORG

OVERSEAS DEVELOPMENT INSTIT,EFFECTIVE AID. WOR+45 INT/ORG TEC/DEV DIPLOM INT/TRADE ADMIN. PAGE 43 G0852
B67
FOR/AID
ECO/UNDEV
ECO/TAC
NAT/COMP

RAWLINSON J.L.,CHINA'S STRUGGLE FOR NAVAL DEVELOPMENT 1839-1895. ASIA DIPLOM ADMIN WAR ...BIBLIOG DICTIONARY 19 CHINJAP. PAGE 46 G0907
B67
SEA
FORCES
PWR

ROTHENBERG J.,ECONOMIC EVALUATION OF URBAN RENEWAL: CONCEPTUAL FOUNDATION OF BENEFIT-COST ANALYSIS. USA+45 ECO/DEV NEIGH TEC/DEV ADMIN GEN/LAWS. PAGE 48 G0940
B67
PLAN
MUNIC
PROB/SOLV
COST

SALMOND J.A.,THE CIVILIAN CONSERVATION CORPS, 1933-1942. USA-45 NAT/G CREATE EXEC EFFICIENCY WEALTH...BIBLIOG 20 ROOSEVLT/F. PAGE 48 G0954
B67
ADMIN
ECO/TAC
TASK
AGRI

SCHUMACHER B.G.,COMPUTER DYNAMICS IN PUBLIC ADMINISTRATION. USA+45 CREATE PLAN TEC/DEV...MGT LING CON/ANAL BIBLIOG/A 20. PAGE 50 G0980
B67
COMPUTER
COMPUT/IR
ADMIN
AUTOMAT

UNIVERSAL REFERENCE SYSTEM,BIBLIOGRAPHY OF BIBLIOGRAPHIES IN POLITICAL SCIENCE, GOVERNMENT, AND PUBLIC POLICY (VOLUME III). WOR+45 WOR-45 LAW ADMIN...SOC CON/ANAL COMPUT/IR GEN/METH. PAGE 56 G1095
B67
BIBLIOG/A
NAT/G
DIPLOM
POLICY

UNIVERSAL REFERENCE SYSTEM,ADMINISTRATIVE MANAGEMENT: PUBLIC AND PRIVATE BUREAUCRACY (VOLUME IV). WOR+45 WOR-45 ECO/DEV LG/CO LOC/G PUB/INST VOL/ASSN GOV/REL...COMPUT/IR GEN/METH. PAGE 56 G1096
B67
BIBLIOG/A
MGT
ADMIN
NAT/G

US DEPARTMENT OF THE ARMY,CIVILIAN IN PEACE, SOLDIER IN WAR: A BIBLIOGRAPHIC SURVEY OF THE ARMY AND AIR NATIONAL GUARD (PAMPHLET, NOS. 130-2). USA+45 USA-45 LOC/G NAT/G PROVS LEGIS PLAN ADMIN ATTIT ORD/FREE...POLICY 19/20. PAGE 58 G1134
B67
BIBLIOG/A
FORCES
ROLE
DIPLOM

US HOUSE COMM SCI ASTRONAUT,GOVERNMENT, SCIENCE, AND INTERNATIONAL POLICY. R+D OP/RES PLAN 20. PAGE 58 G1146
B67
ADMIN
PHIL/SCI
ACT/RES
DIPLOM

CARMICHAEL D.M.,"FORTY YEARS OF WATER POLLUTION CONTROL IN WISCONSIN: A CASE STUDY." LAW EXTR/IND INDUS MUNIC DELIB/GP PLAN PROB/SOLV SANCTION
L67
HEALTH
CONTROL
ADMIN

...CENSUS CHARTS 20 WISCONSIN. PAGE 11 G0207
ADJUD

RUTH J.M.,"THE ADMINISTRATION OF WATER RESOURCES IN GUATEMALA." GUATEMALA L/A+17C DIST/IND LOC/G NAT/G EX/STRUC ADMIN GOV/REL DEMAND EQUILIB WEALTH...GEOG MGT 20. PAGE 48 G0952
L67
EFFICIENCY
ECO/UNDEV
PLAN
ACT/RES

TRAVERS H. JR.,"AN EXAMINATION OF THE CAB'S MERGER POLICY." USA+45 USA-45 LAW NAT/G LEGIS PLAN ADMIN ...DECISION 20 CONGRESS. PAGE 55 G1078
L67
ADJUD
LG/CO
POLICY
DIST/IND

ALLISON D.,"THE GROWTH OF IDEAS." USA+45 LG/CO ADMIN. PAGE 3 G0045
S67
R+D
OP/RES
INDUS
TEC/DEV

ATKIN J.M.,"THE FEDERAL GOVERNMENT, BIG BUSINESS, AND COLLEGES OF EDUCATION." PROF/ORG CONSULT CREATE PLAN PROB/SOLV ADMIN EFFICIENCY. PAGE 4 G0075
S67
SCHOOL
ACADEM
NAT/G
INDUS

AVTORKHANOV A.,"A NEW AGRARIAN REVOLUTION." COM USSR ECO/DEV PLAN TEC/DEV ADMIN CONTROL OPTIMAL WEALTH SOCISM 20 KHRUSH/N STALIN/J. PAGE 4 G0082
S67
AGRI
METH/COMP
MARXISM
OWN

BENN W.,"TECHNOLOGY HAS AN INEXORABLE EFFECT." FUT UK ECO/DEV INT/ORG CONSULT PLAN EDU/PROP ADMIN LEAD GP/REL PRODUC...INT 20 EEC. PAGE 6 G0119
S67
R+D
LG/CO
TEC/DEV
INDUS

BROWN W.B.,"MODEL-BUILDING AND ORGANIZATIONS." CONTROL FEEDBACK...PROBABIL CHARTS METH/COMP. PAGE 9 G0179
S67
MGT
ADMIN
GAME
COMPUTER

CONWAY J.E.,"MAKING RESEARCH EFFECTIVE IN LEGISLATION." LAW R+D CONSULT EX/STRUC PLAN CONFER ADMIN LEAD ROUTINE TASK INGP/REL DECISION. PAGE 13 G0252
S67
ACT/RES
POLICY
LEGIS
PROB/SOLV

DONAHO J.A.,"PLANNING-PROGRAMMING-BUDGETING SYSTEMS." USA+45 LOC/G NAT/G ROUTINE. PAGE 16 G0305
S67
PLAN
BUDGET
ADMIN
ECOMETRIC

GANZ G.,"THE CONTROL OF INDUSTRY BY ADMINISTRATIVE PROCESS." UK DELIB/GP WORKER 20. PAGE 21 G0408
S67
INDUS
LAW
ADMIN
CONTROL

GOBER J.L.,"FEDERALISM AT WORK." USA+45 NAT/G CONSULT ACT/RES PLAN CONFER ADMIN LEAD PARTIC FEDERAL ATTIT. PAGE 21 G0422
S67
MUNIC
TEC/DEV
R+D
GOV/REL

HODGE G.,"THE RISE AND DEMISE OF THE UN TECHNICAL ASSISTANCE ADMINISTRATION." RISK TASK INGP/REL CONSEN EFFICIENCY 20 UN. PAGE 26 G0516
S67
ADMIN
TEC/DEV
EX/STRUC
INT/ORG

KAYSEN C.,"DATA BANKS AND DOSSIERS." FUT USA+45 COM/IND NAT/G PLAN PROB/SOLV TEC/DEV BUDGET ADMIN ROUTINE. PAGE 30 G0588
S67
CENTRAL
EFFICIENCY
CENSUS
ACT/RES

LA PORTE T.,"DIFFUSION AND DISCONTINUITY IN SCIENCE, TECHNOLOGY AND PUBLIC AFFAIRS: RESULTS OF A SEARCH IN THE FIELD." USA+45 ACT/RES TEC/DEV PERS/REL ATTIT PHIL/SCI. PAGE 32 G0628
S67
INTELL
ADMIN
ACADEM
GP/REL

MACDONALD G.J.F.,"SCIENCE AND SPACE POLICY* HOW DOES IT GET PLANNED?" R+D CREATE TEC/DEV BUDGET ADMIN ROUTINE...DECISION NASA. PAGE 35 G0687
S67
SPACE
PLAN
MGT
EX/STRUC

MCNAMARA R.L.,"THE NEED FOR INNOVATIVENESS IN DEVELOPING SOCIETIES." L/A+17C EDU/PROP ADMIN LEAD WEALTH...POLICY PSY SOC METH 20 COLOMB. PAGE 38
S67
PROB/SOLV
PLAN
ECO/UNDEV

G0747   NEW/IDEA

S67

ROBERTS E.B.,"THE PROBLEM OF AGING ORGANIZATIONS." INDUS
INTELL PROB/SOLV ADMIN EXEC FEEDBACK EFFICIENCY   R+D
PRODUC...GEN/LAWS 20. PAGE 47 G0926   MGT
                                               PLAN

S67

SCOVILLE W.J.,"GOVERNMENT REGULATION AND GROWTH IN NAT/G
THE FRENCH PAPER INDUSTRY DURING THE EIGHTEENTH   PROC/MFG
CENTURY." FRANCE MOD/EUR FINAN CAP/ISM TAX ADMIN   ECO/DEV
CONTROL PRIVIL LAISSEZ...POLICY 18. PAGE 50 G0985 INGP/REL

S67

TIVEY L.,"THE POLITICAL CONSEQUENCES OF ECONOMIC   PLAN
PLANNING." UK CONSTN INDUS ACT/RES ADMIN CONTROL   POLICY
LOBBY REPRESENT EFFICIENCY SUPEGO SOVEREIGN   NAT/G
...DECISION 20. PAGE 55 G1074

S67

WILLIAMS C.,"REGIONAL MANAGEMENT OVERSEAS." USA+45 MGT
WOR+45 DIST/IND LG/CO EX/STRUC INT/TRADE TARIFFS   EUR+WWI
ADMIN TASK CENTRAL. PAGE 63 G1242   ECO/DEV
                                               PLAN

S67

WINTHROP H.,"THE MEANING OF DECENTRALIZATION FOR   ADMIN
TWENTIETH-CENTURY MAN." FUT WOR+45 SOCIETY TEC/DEV. STRUCT
PAGE 64 G1248   CENTRAL
                                               PROB/SOLV

N67

US SUPERINTENDENT OF DOCUMENTS,SPACE: MISSILES, THE BIBLIOG/A
MOON, NASA, AND SATELLITES (PRICE LIST 79A). USA+45 SPACE
COM/IND R+D NAT/G DIPLOM EDU/PROP ADMIN CONTROL   TEC/DEV
HEALTH...POLICY SIMUL NASA CONGRESS. PAGE 61 G1190 PEACE

N67

US HOUSE COMM SCI ASTRONAUT,AMENDING NATIONAL   PHIL/SCI
SCIENCE FOUNDATION ACT OF 1950 TO MAKE IMPROVEMENTS DELIB/GP
IN ORGANIZATION AND OPERATION OF FOUNDAT'N(PAMPH). TEC/DEV
USA+45 GIVE ADMIN...POLICY HOUSE/REP NSF. PAGE 58 R+D
G1147

N67

US SENATE COMM ON FOREIGN REL,ARMS SALES AND   ARMS/CONT
FOREIGN POLICY (PAMPHLET). FINAN FOR/AID CONTROL ADMIN
20. PAGE 60 G1181   OP/RES
                                             DIPLOM

ADMINISTRATIVE MANAGEMENT....SEE MGT

ADOLESCENCE....SEE AGE/Y

ADVERT/ADV....ADVERTISING ADVISORY COMMISSION

ADVERTISING....SEE SERV/IND+EDU/PROP; SEE ALSO TV, PRESS

AEA....ATOMIC ENERGY AUTHORITY OF UN; SEE ALSO NUC/PWR

B64

GOWING M.,BRITAIN AND ATOMIC ENERGY 1939-1945.   NUC/PWR
FRANCE UK USA+45 USA-45 NAT/G CREATE...PHIL/SCI 20 DIPLOM
AEA. PAGE 22 G0439   TEC/DEV

AEC....ATOMIC ENERGY COMMISSION; SEE ALSO NUC/PWR

N19

ATOMIC INDUSTRIAL FORUM,COMMENTARY ON LEGISLATION NUC/PWR
TO PERMIT PRIVATE OWNERSHIP OF SPECIAL NUCLEAR   MARKET
MATERIAL (PAMPHLET). USA+45 DELIB/GP LEGIS PLAN OWN INDUS
...POLICY 20 AEC CONGRESS. PAGE 4 G0076   LAW

N19

US ATOMIC ENERGY COMMISSION,ATOMIC ENERGY IN USE OP/RES
(PAMPHLET). R+D RISK EFFICIENCY HEALTH KNOWL   TEC/DEV
ORD/FREE...PHIL/SCI CONCPT METH/CNCPT CHARTS   NUC/PWR
LAB/EXP 20 AEC. PAGE 56 G1106   CREATE

B56

THOMAS M.,ATOMIC ENERGY AND CONGRESS. USA+45 NAT/G LEGIS
ACT/RES PLAN TEC/DEV EDU/PROP ROUTINE KNOWL PWR   ADMIN
SKILL...PHIL/SCI NEW/IDEA TIME/SEQ CHARTS METH   NUC/PWR
CONGRESS VAL/FREE 20 AEC. PAGE 54 G1067

B59

LANG D.,FROM HIROSHIMA TO THE MOON: CHRONICLES OF NUC/PWR
LIFE IN THE ATOMIC AGE. USA+45 OP/RES CONTROL   SPACE
ARMS/CONT WAR CIVMIL/REL PEACE HABITAT MORAL PWR   HEALTH
...OBS INT 20 AEC. PAGE 32 G0633   TEC/DEV

B59

US CONGRESS JT ATOM ENRGY COMM,SELECTED MATERIALS NAT/G
ON FEDERAL-STATE COOPERATION IN THE ATOMIC ENERGY NUC/PWR
FIELD. USA+45 LAW LOC/G PROVS CONSULT LEGIS ADJUD GOV/REL
...POLICY BIBLIOG 20 AEC. PAGE 57 G1111   DELIB/GP

L62

CAVERS D.F.,"ADMINISTRATIVE DECISION-MAKING IN   REPRESENT
NUCLEAR FACILITIES LICENSING." USA+45 CLIENT ADMIN LOBBY
EXEC 20 AEC. PAGE 11 G0218   PWR
                                             CONTROL

L62

NEIBURG H.L.,"THE EISENHOWER AEC AND CONGRESS: A   CHIEF
STUDY IN EXECUTIVE-LEGISLATIVE RELATIONS." USA+45 LEGIS
NAT/G POL/PAR DELIB/GP EX/STRUC TOP/EX ADMIN EXEC GOV/REL
LEAD ROUTINE PWR...POLICY COLD/WAR CONGRESS   NUC/PWR
PRESIDENT AEC. PAGE 41 G0816

L62

NIEBURG H.L.,"THE EISENHOWER ATOMIC ENERGY   NUC/PWR
COMMISSION AND CONGRESS" R+D INT/ORG OP/RES DIPLOM TOP/EX
ADMIN CONTROL 20 PRESIDENT CONGRESS AEC. PAGE 42 LOBBY
G0821   DELIB/GP

B63

LILIENTHAL D.E.,CHANGE, HOPE, AND THE BOMB. USA+45 ATTIT
WOR+45 R+D INT/ORG NAT/G DELIB/GP FORCES ACT/RES   MYTH
DETER RIGID/FLEX ORD/FREE...POLICY CONCPT OBS AEC ARMS/CONT
20. PAGE 34 G0666   NUC/PWR

B63

US ATOMIC ENERGY COMMISSION,ATOMIC ENERGY IN THE   METH/COMP
SOVIET UNION: TRIP REPORT OF THE US ATOMIC ENERGY OP/RES
DELEGATION, MAY 1933. USSR R+D NAT/G CONSULT CREATE TEC/DEV
DIPLOM ADMIN ROUTINE EFFICIENCY PRODUC KNOWL SKILL NUC/PWR
...NAT/COMP 20 AEC TRAVEL TREATY. PAGE 56 G1107

B65

US CONGRESS JT ATOM ENRGY COMM,ATOMIC ENERGY   NUC/PWR
LEGISLATION THROUGH 89TH CONGRESS, 1ST SESSION.   FORCES
USA+45 LAW INT/ORG DELIB/GP BUDGET DIPLOM 20 AEC   PEACE
CONGRESS CASEBOOK EURATOM IAEA. PAGE 57 G1114   LEGIS

B65

US CONGRESS JT ATOM ENRGY COMM,PROPOSED AMENDMENT LAW
TO SECTION 271 OF THE ATOMIC ENERGY ACT OF 1954. LEGIS
USA+45 CONSTRUC PLAN INSPECT CONTROL CT/SYS 20   DELIB/GP
CONGRESS AEC. PAGE 57 G1115   NUC/PWR

B67

COMMONER B.,SCIENCE AND SURVIVAL. SOCIETY INDUS   PHIL/SCI
PLAN NUC/PWR KNOWL PWR...SOC 20 AEC. PAGE 13 G0247 CONTROL
                                             PROB/SOLV
                                           EQUILIB

B67

ORLANS H.,CONTRACTING FOR ATOMS. USA+45 LAW INTELL NUC/PWR
ACADEM LG/CO NAT/G PLAN TEC/DEV CONTROL DETER   R+D
...TREND 20 AEC. PAGE 43 G0845   PRODUC
                                             PEACE

S67

EYRAUD M.,"LA FRANCE FACE A UN EVENTUEL TRAITE DE NUC/PWR
NON DISSEMINATION DES ARMES NUCLEAIRES." FRANCE   ARMS/CONT
USA+45 EXTR/IND INDUS R+D INT/ORG ACT/RES TEC/DEV POLICY
AGREE PRODUC ATTIT 20 TREATY AEC EURATOM. PAGE 18
G0355

N67

US HOUSE COMM APPROPRIATIONS,PUBLIC WORKS AND   BUDGET
ATOMIC ENERGY COMMISSION APPROPRIATION BILL, 1968 NUC/PWR
(PAMPHLET). USA+45 ECO/DEV NAT/G...GEOG DEEP/INT   PROVS
CHARTS HOUSE/REP AEC DEPT/DEFEN TVA. PAGE 58 G1137 PLAN

AFGHANISTN....SEE ALSO ISLAM, ASIA

AFL/CIO....AMERICAN FEDERATION OF LABOR, CONGRESS OF
    INDUSTRIAL ORGANIZATIONS

AFLAK/M....MICHEL AFLAK

AFR....AFRICA

B58

EHRHARD J.,LE DESTIN DU COLONIALISME. AFR FRANCE   COLONIAL
ECO/UNDEV AGRI FINAN MARKET CREATE PLAN TEC/DEV   FOR/AID
BUDGET DIPLOM PRICE 20. PAGE 17 G0335   INT/TRADE
                                             INDUS

B60

LEYDER J.,BIBLIOGRAPHIE DE L'ENSEIGNEMENT SUPERIEUR BIBLIOG/A
ET DE LA RECHERCHE SCIENTIFIQUE EN AFRIQUE   ACT/RES
INTERTROPICALE (2 VOLS.). AFR CULTURE ECO/UNDEV   ACADEM
AGRI PLAN EDU/PROP ADMIN COLONIAL...GEOG SOC/INTEG R+D
20 NEGRO. PAGE 34 G0664

S60
JAFFEE A.J.,"POPULATION TRENDS AND CONTROLS IN   ECO/UNDEV
UNDERDEVELOPED COUNTRIES." AFR FUT ISLAM L/A+17C   GEOG
S/ASIA CULTURE R+D FAM PLAN EDU/PROP
BIO/SOC RIGID/FLEX HEALTH...SOC STAT OBS CHARTS 20.
PAGE 28 G0555

S60
RIVKIN A.,"AFRICAN ECONOMIC DEVELOPMENT: ADVANCED   AFR
TECHNOLOGY AND THE STAGES OF GROWTH." CULTURE   TEC/DEV
ECO/UNDEV AGRI COM/IND EXTR/IND PLAN ECO/TAC ATTIT   FOR/AID
DRIVE RIGID/FLEX SKILL WEALTH...MGT SOC GEN/LAWS
WORK TOT/POP 20. PAGE 47 G0923

B61
BONNEFOUS M.,EUROPE ET TIERS MONDE. EUR+WWI SOCIETY   AFR
INT/ORG NAT/G VOL/ASSN ACT/RES TEC/DEV CAP/ISM   ECO/UNDEV
ECO/TAC ATTIT ORD/FREE SOVEREIGN...POLICY CONCPT   FOR/AID
TREND 20. PAGE 8 G0153   INT/TRADE

B61
CARNELL F.,THE POLITICS OF THE NEW STATES: A SELECT   BIBLIOG/A
ANNOTATED BIBLIOGRAPHY WITH SPECIAL REFERENCE TO   AFR
THE COMMONWEALTH. CONSTN ELITES LABOR NAT/G POL/PAR   ASIA
EX/STRUC DIPLOM ADJUD ADMIN...GOV/COMP 20   COLONIAL
COMMONWLTH. PAGE 11 G0210

B63
GEERTZ C.,OLD SOCIETIES AND NEW STATES: THE QUEST   ECO/UNDEV
FOR MODERNITY IN ASIA AND AFRICA. AFR ASIA LAW   TEC/DEV
CULTURE SECT EDU/PROP REV...GOV/COMP NAT/COMP 20.   NAT/LISM
PAGE 21 G0415   SOVEREIGN

B63
HAUSMAN W.H.,MANAGING ECONOMIC DEVELOPMENT IN   ECO/UNDEV
AFRICA. AFR USA+45 LAW FINAN WORKER TEC/DEV WEALTH   PLAN
...ANTHOL 20. PAGE 25 G0492   FOR/AID
                                                        MGT

B65
BARISH N.N.,MANAGEMENT SCIENCES IN THE EMERGING   ECO/UNDEV
COUNTRIES. AFR CHINA/COM WOR+45 FINAN INDUS PLAN   OP/RES
PRODUC HABITAT...ANTHOL 20. PAGE 5 G0093   MGT
                                                        TEC/DEV

B65
WASKOW A.I.,KEEPING THE WORLD DISARMED. AFR   ARMS/CONT
GERMANY/E DIPLOM CONTROL WAR 20 UN. PAGE 62 G1218   PEACE
                                                        FORCES
                                                        PROB/SOLV

S65
BLOOMFIELD L.P.,"ARMS CONTROL AND THE DEVELOPING   ARMS/CONT
COUNTRIES." AFR ISLAM S/ASIA USA+45 VOL/ASSN   ECO/UNDEV
TEC/DEV DIPLOM REGION NUC/PWR...PREDICT TREND.   HYPO/EXP
PAGE 7 G0142   OBS

S65
LECLERCQ H.,"ECONOMIC RESEARCH AND DEVELOPMENT IN   AFR
TROPICAL AFRICA." ECO/UNDEV INT/ORG CREATE PLAN UN.   R+D
PAGE 33 G0650   ACADEM
                                                        ECO/TAC

B66
ONYEMELUKWE C.C.,PROBLEMS OF INDUSTRIAL PLANNING   ECO/UNDEV
AND MANAGEMENT IN NIGERIA. AFR FINAN LABOR DELIB/GP   ECO/TAC
TEC/DEV ADJUST...MGT TREND BIBLIOG. PAGE 43 G0839   INDUS
                                                        PLAN

S66
FLEMING W.G.,"AUTHORITY, EFFICIENCY, AND ROLE   DOMIN
STRESS: PROBLEMS IN THE DEVELOPMENT OF EAST AFRICAN   EFFICIENCY
BUREAUCRACIES." AFR UGANDA STRUCT PROB/SOLV ROUTINE   COLONIAL
INGP/REL ROLE...MGT SOC GP/COMP GOV/COMP 20   ADMIN
TANGANYIKA AFRICA/E. PAGE 19 G0371

B67
BUTLER J.,BOSTON UNIVERSITY PAPERS ON AFRICA*   IDEA/COMP
TRANSITION IN AFRICAN POLITICS. AFR LAW CONSTN   NAT/G
LABOR POL/PAR TEC/DEV 20. PAGE 10 G0197   PWR

B67
US SUPERINTENDENT OF DOCUMENTS,LIBRARY OF CONGRESS   BIBLIOG/A
(PRICE LIST 83). AFR ASIA EUR+WWI USA-45 USSR NAT/G   USA+45
DIPLOM CONFER CT/SYS WAR...DECISION PHIL/SCI   AUTOMAT
CLASSIF 19/20 CONGRESS PRESIDENT. PAGE 61 G1189   LAW

AFR/STATES....ORGANIZATION OF AFRICAN STATES

AFRICA/CEN....CENTRAL AFRICA

AFRICA/E....EAST AFRICA

S66
FLEMING W.G.,"AUTHORITY, EFFICIENCY, AND ROLE   DOMIN

STRESS: PROBLEMS IN THE DEVELOPMENT OF EAST AFRICAN   EFFICIENCY
BUREAUCRACIES." AFR UGANDA STRUCT PROB/SOLV ROUTINE   COLONIAL
INGP/REL ROLE...MGT SOC GP/COMP GOV/COMP 20   ADMIN
TANGANYIKA AFRICA/E. PAGE 19 G0371

AFRICA/N....NORTH AFRICA

AFRICA/SW....SOUTH WEST AFRICA

AFRICA/W....WEST AFRICA

AFTA....ATLANTIC FREE TRADE AREA

AGE....AGE FACTORS

B60
JANOWITZ M.,THE PROFESSIONAL SOLDIER. CULTURE   FORCES
STRATA STRUCT FAM PROB/SOLV TEC/DEV COERCE WAR   MYTH
CIVMIL/REL NAT/LISM AGE HEREDITY ALL/VALS CONSERVE   LEAD
...MGT WORSHIP. PAGE 28 G0560   ELITES

B62
CLARKE A.C.,PROFILES OF THE FUTURE; AN INQUIRY INTO   FUT
THE LIMITS OF THE POSSIBLE. COM/IND DIST/IND PRODUC   TEC/DEV
AGE PERCEPT...TECHNIC NEW/IDEA TIME. PAGE 12 G0232   PREDICT
                                                        SPACE

B65
ANDERSON C.A.,EDUCATION AND ECONOMIC DEVELOPMENT.   ANTHOL
INDUS R+D SCHOOL TEC/DEV ECO/TAC EDU/PROP AGE   ECO/DEV
HEREDITY PERCEPT SKILL 20. PAGE 3 G0056   ECO/UNDEV
                                                        WORKER

B67
SILBERMAN C.E.,THE MYTHS OF AUTOMATION. INDUS   MYTH
WORKER COST PRODUC AGE WEALTH 20. PAGE 51 G0996   AUTOMAT
                                                        CHARTS
                                                        TEC/DEV

AGE/A....ADULTS

AGE/C....INFANTS AND CHILDREN

S62
PAULING L.,"GENETIC EFFECTS OF WEAPONS TESTS."   HEAL
WOR+45 SOCIETY FAM ACT/RES EDU/PROP AGE/C HEALTH   ARMS/CONT
ORD/FREE...GEOG STAT CONT/OBS PROJ/TEST CHARTS   NUC/PWR
TOT/POP 20. PAGE 44 G0861

B65
REISS A.J. JR.,SCHOOLS IN A CHANGING SOCIETY.   SCHOOL
CULTURE PROB/SOLV INSPECT DOMIN CONFER INGP/REL   EX/STRUC
RACE/REL AGE/C AGE/Y ALL/VALS...ANTHOL SOC/INTEG 20   ADJUST
NEWYORK/C. PAGE 46 G0912   ADMIN

S67
STYCOS J.M.,"POLITICS AND POPULATION CONTROL IN   PLAN
LATIN AMERICA." USA+45 FAM NAT/G GP/REL AGE/C ATTIT   CENSUS
CATHISM MARXISM...POLICY UN WHO. PAGE 53 G1045   CONTROL
                                                        L/A+17C

AGE/O....OLD PEOPLE

B63
KREPS J.,AUTOMATION AND THE OLDER WORKER: AN   BIBLIOG/A
ANNOTATED BIBLIOGRAPHY (PAMPHLET). USA+45 STRUCT   WORKER
ECO/DEV INDUS TEC/DEV. PAGE 31 G0620   AGE/O
                                                        AUTOMAT

AGE/Y....YOUTH AND ADOLESCENCE

B53
SCHAAF R.W.,DOCUMENTS OF INTERNATIONAL MEETINGS.   BIBLIOG/A
AGRI INDUS ACADEM DIPLOM NUC/PWR RACE/REL AGE/Y   DELIB/GP
HEALTH...SOC 20. PAGE 49 G0960   INT/ORG
                                                        POLICY

B65
WHITE HOUSE CONFERENCE ON INTERNATIONAL   R+D
COOPERATION(VOL.II). SPACE WOR+45 EXTR/IND INT/ORG   CONFER
LABOR WORKER NUC/PWR PEACE AGE/Y...CENSUS ANTHOL 20   TEC/DEV
RESOURCE/N URBAN/RNWL PUB/TRANS. PAGE 1 G0019   DIPLOM

B65
REISS A.J. JR.,SCHOOLS IN A CHANGING SOCIETY.   SCHOOL
CULTURE PROB/SOLV INSPECT DOMIN CONFER INGP/REL   EX/STRUC
RACE/REL AGE/C AGE/Y ALL/VALS...ANTHOL SOC/INTEG 20   ADJUST
NEWYORK/C. PAGE 46 G0912   ADMIN

B66
STREET D.,ORGANIZATION FOR TREATMENT. CLIENT PROVS   GP/COMP
PUB/INST PLAN CONTROL PARTIC REPRESENT ATTIT PWR   AGE/Y
...POLICY BIBLIOG. PAGE 53 G1044   ADMIN
                                                        VOL/ASSN

B67
US HOUSE COMM SCI ASTRONAUT,THE JUNIOR COLLEGE AND   ACADEM
EDUCATION IN THE SCIENCES (PAMPHLET). USA+45 AGE/Y   EDU/PROP
...CHARTS SIMUL HOUSE/REP. PAGE 58 G1148   PHIL/SCI
                                                     R+D

AGGRESSION....SEE WAR, COERCE+ DIPLOM

AGGRESSION, PHYSICAL....SEE COERCE, DRIVE

AGREE....AGREEMENTS, CONTRACTS, TREATIES, CONCORDATS,
    INTERSTATE COMPACTS

N47
FOX W.T.R.,UNITED STATES POLICY IN A TWO POWER   DIPLOM
WORLD. COM USA+45 USSR FORCES DOMIN AGREE NEUTRAL   FOR/AID
NUC/PWR ORD/FREE SOVEREIGN 20 COLD/WAR TREATY   POLICY
EUROPE/W INTERVENT. PAGE 20 G0389

B55
US OFFICE OF THE PRESIDENT,REPORT TO CONGRESS ON   DIPLOM
THE MUTUAL SECURITY PROGRAM FOR THE SIX MONTHS   FORCES
ENDED JUNE 30, 1955. ECO/DEV INT/ORG NAT/G CREATE   PLAN
TEC/DEV BAL/PWR ECO/TAC AGREE DETER COST ORD/FREE   FOR/AID
20 DEPT/STATE DEPT/DEFEN. PAGE 59 G1157

B56
US OFFICE OF THE PRESIDENT,REPORT TO CONGRESS ON   DIPLOM
THE MUTUAL SECURITY PROGRAM FOR THE SIX MONTHS   FORCES
ENDED DECEMBER 31, 1955. ASIA USSR ECO/DEV   PLAN
ECO/UNDEV INT/ORG CREATE TEC/DEV BAL/PWR ECO/TAC   FOR/AID
AGREE DETER COST ORD/FREE 20 DEPT/STATE DEPT/DEFEN
EISNHWR/DD. PAGE 59 G1158

B61
LAHAYE R.,LES ENTREPRISES PUBLIQUES AU MAROC.   NAT/G
FRANCE MOROCCO LAW DIST/IND EXTR/IND FINAN CONSULT   INDUS
PLAN TEC/DEV ADMIN AGREE CONTROL OWN...POLICY 20.   ECO/UNDEV
PAGE 32 G0629   ECO/TAC

B65
UNESCO,HANDBOOK OF INTERNATIONAL EXCHANGES. COM/IND   INDEX
R+D ACADEM PROF/ORG VOL/ASSN CREATE TEC/DEV   INT/ORG
EDU/PROP AGREE 20 TREATY. PAGE 55 G1090   DIPLOM
                                                     PRESS

S67
EYRAUD M.,"LA FRANCE FACE A UN EVENTUEL TRAITE DE   NUC/PWR
NON DISSEMINATION DES ARMES NUCLEAIRES." FRANCE   ARMS/CONT
USA+45 EXTR/IND INDUS R+D INT/ORG ACT/RES TEC/DEV   POLICY
AGREE PRODUC ATTIT 20 TREATY AEC EURATOM. PAGE 18
G0355

S67
INGLIS D.R.,"PROSPECTS AND PROBLEMS: THE   NUC/PWR
NONMILITARY USES OF NUCLEAR EXPLOSIVES." CREATE   INDUS
PROB/SOLV TEC/DEV AGREE PEACE...INT/LAW PHIL/SCI   ARMS/CONT
NEW/IDEA 20 TREATY. PAGE 28 G0545   EXTR/IND

S67
WOLFE T.W.,"SOVIET MILITARY POLICY AT THE FIFTY   FORCES
YEAR MARK." USSR VIETNAM WOR+45 RATION AGREE WAR   POLICY
WEAPON CIVMIL/REL TREATY. PAGE 64 G1254   TIME/SEQ
                                                     PLAN

AGRI....AGRICULTURE (INCLUDING HUNTING AND GATHERING)

N
FULLER G.A.,DEMOBILIZATION: A SELECTED LIST OF   BIBLIOG/A
REFERENCES. USA+45 LAW AGRI LABOR WORKER ECO/TAC   INDUS
RATION RECEIVE EDU/PROP ROUTINE ARMS/CONT ALL/VALS   FORCES
20. PAGE 20 G0398   NAT/G

B
BRITISH COMMONWEALTH BUR AGRI,WORLD AGRICULTURAL   BIBLIOG/A
ECONOMICS AND RURAL SOCIOLOGY ABSTRACTS. NAT/G   AGRI
OP/RES PLAN TEC/DEV LEAD PRODUC...GEOG MGT NAT/COMP   SOC
20. PAGE 9 G0170   WORKER

B11
BERGSON H.,CREATIVE EVOLUTION. FUT WOR+45 WOR-45   BIO/SOC
INTELL AGRI R+D ATTIT PERCEPT PERSON RIGID/FLEX   KNOWL
...RELATIV PHIL/SCI PSY METH/CNCPT MATH HIST/WRIT
TREND HYPO/EXP TOT/POP. PAGE 7 G0127

B14
CRAIG J.,ELEMENTS OF POLITICAL SCIENCE (3 VOLS.).   PHIL/SCI
CONSTN AGRI INDUS SCHOOL FORCES TAX CT/SYS SUFF   NAT/G
MORAL WEALTH...CONCPT 19 CIVIL/LIB. PAGE 13 G0259   ORD/FREE

S39
HECKSCHER G.,"GROUP ORGANIZATION IN SWEDEN." SWEDEN   LAISSEZ
STRATA ECO/DEV AGRI INDUS LABOR NAT/G PROF/ORG   SOC
ECO/TAC CENTRAL SOCISM...MGT 19/20. PAGE 25 G0499

B45
SCHULTZ T.H.,FOOD FOR THE WORLD. UNIV SOCIETY INDUS   AGRI
R+D ECO/TAC...GEOG TREND GEN/LAWS 20. PAGE 50 G0979   TEC/DEV

B46
AMERICAN DOCUMENTATION INST,CATALOGUE OF AUXILIARY   BIBLIOG
PUBLICATIONS IN MICROFILMS AND PHOTOPRINTS. USA-45   EDU/PROP
LAW AGRI CREATE TEC/DEV ADMIN...GEOG LING MATH 20.   PSY
PAGE 3 G0052

B46
WILCOX J.K.,OFFICIAL DEFENSE PUBLICATIONS,   BIBLIOG/A
1941-1945 (NINE VOLS.). USA-45 AGRI INDUS R+D LABOR   WAR
FORCES TEC/DEV EFFICIENCY PRODUC SKILL WEALTH 20.   CIVMIL/REL
PAGE 63 G1238   ADMIN

B48
KILE O.M.,THE FARM BUREAU MOVEMENT: THE FARM BUREAU   AGRI
THROUGH THREE DECADES. NAT/G LEGIS LEAD LOBBY   STRUCT
GP/REL INCOME POLICY. PAGE 30 G0596   VOL/ASSN
                                                     DOMIN

S48
HARDIN L.M.,"REFLECTIONS ON AGRICULTURAL POLICY   AGRI
FORMATION IN THE UNITED STATES." LEGIS PLAN BUDGET   POLICY
ECO/TAC LEAD CENTRAL...MGT SOC NEW/IDEA STAT FAO.   ADMIN
PAGE 24 G0480   NEW/LIB

B50
US DEPARTMENT OF STATE,POINT FOUR: COOPERATIVE   ECO/UNDEV
PROGRAM FOR AID IN THE DEVELOPMENT OF ECONOMICALLY   FOR/AID
UNDERDEVELOPED AREAS. WOR+45 AGRI INDUS INT/ORG   FINAN
PLAN TEC/DEV DIPLOM EDU/PROP ADMIN PEACE PRODUC   INT/TRADE
WEALTH 20 CONGRESS UN. PAGE 57 G1121

L50
MAASS A.A.,"CONGRESS AND WATER RESOURCES." LOC/G   REGION
TEC/DEV CONTROL SANCTION...WELF/ST GEOG CONGRESS.   AGRI
PAGE 35 G0683   PLAN

B53
SCHAAF R.W.,DOCUMENTS OF INTERNATIONAL MEETINGS.   BIBLIOG/A
AGRI INDUS ACADEM DIPLOM NUC/PWR RACE/REL AGE/Y   DELIB/GP
HEALTH...SOC 20. PAGE 49 G0960   INT/ORG
                                                     POLICY

B54
US DEPARTMENT OF STATE,PUBLICATIONS OF THE   BIBLIOG
DEPARTMENT OF STATE, OCTOBER 1,1929 TO JANUARY 1,   DIPLOM
1953. AGRI INT/ORG FORCES FOR/AID EDU/PROP
ARMS/CONT NUC/PWR ATTIT 20 DEPT/STATE OAS UN NATO.
PAGE 57 G1122

B55
SMITHIES A.,THE BUDGETARY PROCESS IN THE UNITED   NAT/G
STATES. ECO/DEV AGRI EX/STRUC FORCES LEGIS   ADMIN
PROB/SOLV TAX ROUTINE EFFICIENCY...MGT CONGRESS   BUDGET
PRESIDENT. PAGE 52 G1016   GOV/REL

S56
KNAPP D.C.,"CONGRESSIONAL CONTROL OF AGRICULTURAL   LEGIS
CONSERVATION POLICY: A CASE STUDY OF THE   AGRI
APPROPRIATIONS PROCESS." DELIB/GP PLAN PROB/SOLV   BUDGET
CONFER PARL/PROC...POLICY INT CONGRESS. PAGE 31   CONTROL
G0607

B57
BAUER P.T.,ECONOMIC ANALYSIS AND POLICY IN   ECO/UNDEV
UNDERDEVELOPED COUNTRIES. WOR+45 AGRI INT/TRADE TAX   METH/COMP
PRICE...GEN/METH BIBLIOG/A 20 COMMONWLTH. PAGE 5   POLICY
G0103

B57
DUPREE A.H.,SCIENCE IN THE FEDERAL GOVERNMENT; A   NAT/G
HISTORY OF POLICIES AND ACTIVITIES TO 1940. USA-45   R+D
AGRI SCHOOL DELIB/GP WAR GOV/REL...PHIL/SCI BIBLIOG   CREATE
18/20 DEPRESSION NEW/DEAL WWI JEFFERSN/T. PAGE 17   TEC/DEV
G0324

B58
BIDWELL P.W.,RAW MATERIALS: A STUDY OF AMERICAN   EXTR/IND
POLICY. USA+45 USA-45 ECO/UNDEV AGRI INDUS KIN   ECO/DEV
CREATE PLAN ECO/TAC WAR PEACE ATTIT DRIVE WEALTH
...STAT CHARTS CONGRESS VAL/FREE. PAGE 7 G0135

B58
EHRHARD J.,LE DESTIN DU COLONIALISME. AFR FRANCE   COLONIAL
ECO/UNDEV AGRI FINAN MARKET CREATE PLAN TEC/DEV   FOR/AID
BUDGET DIPLOM PRICE 20. PAGE 17 G0335   INT/TRADE
                                                     INDUS

B58
US DEPARTMENT OF STATE,PUBLICATIONS OF THE   BIBLIOG
DEPARTMENT OF STATE, JANUARY 1,1953 TO DECEMBER 31,   DIPLOM
1957. AGRI INT/ORG FORCES FOR/AID EDU/PROP
ARMS/CONT NUC/PWR ATTIT 20 DEPT/STATE OAS UN NATO.

PAGE 57 G1123   VAL/FREE. PAGE 54 G1064

                                                     B59
CLEAVELAND F.N.,SCIENCE AND STATE GOVERNMENT. AGRI   TEC/DEV
EXTR/IND FINAN INDUS PROVS...METH/CNCPT STAT CHARTS   PHIL/SCI
20 NEW/YORK CONNECTICT WISCONSIN CALIFORNIA   GOV/REL
NEW/MEXICO. PAGE 12 G0233   METH/COMP

                                                     B59
WARD B.,5 IDEAS THAT CHANGE THE WORLD. WOR+45   ECO/UNDEV
WOR-45 SOCIETY STRUCT AGRI INDUS INT/ORG NAT/G   ALL/VALS
FORCES ACT/RES ARMS/CONT TOTALSM ATTIT DRIVE   NAT/LISM
GEN/LAWS. PAGE 62 G1210   COLONIAL

                                                     B60
LEYDER J.,BIBLIOGRAPHIE DE L'ENSEIGNEMENT SUPERIEUR   BIBLIOG/A
ET DE LA RECHERCHE SCIENTIFIQUE EN AFRIQUE   ACT/RES
INTERTROPICALE (2 VOLS). AFR CULTURE ECO/UNDEV   ACADEM
AGRI PLAN EDU/PROP ADMIN COLONIAL...GEOG SOC/INTEG   R+D
20 NEGRO. PAGE 34 G0664

                                                     B60
PENTONY D.E.,THE UNDERDEVELOPED LANDS. FUT WOR+45   ECO/UNDEV
CULTURE AGRI FINAN INDUS MARKET INT/ORG LABOR NAT/G   POLICY
VOL/ASSN CONSULT TEC/DEV ECO/TAC EDU/PROP COLONIAL   FOR/AID
ATTIT WEALTH...OBS RECORD SAMP TREND GEN/METH WORK   INT/TRADE
UN 20. PAGE 44 G0867

                                                     S60
BECKER A.S.,"COMPARISIONS OF UNITED STATES AND USSR   STAT
NATIONAL OUTPUT: SOME RULES OF THE GAME." COM   USSR
USA+45 ECO/DEV AGRI DIST/IND INDUS R+D CONSULT PLAN
ECO/TAC RIGID/FLEX KNOWL...METH/CNCPT CHARTS 20.
PAGE 6 G0113

                                                     S60
RIVKIN A.,"AFRICAN ECONOMIC DEVELOPMENT: ADVANCED   AFR
TECHNOLOGY AND THE STAGES OF GROWTH." CULTURE   TEC/DEV
ECO/UNDEV AGRI COM/IND EXTR/IND PLAN ECO/TAC ATTIT   FOR/AID
DRIVE RIGID/FLEX SKILL WEALTH...MGT SOC GEN/LAWS
WORK TOT/POP 20. PAGE 47 G0923

                                                     B61
BRADY R.A.,ORGANIZATION, AUTOMATION, AND SOCIETY.   TEC/DEV
USA+45 AGRI COM/IND DIST/IND MARKET CREATE   INDUS
...DECISION MGT 20. PAGE 8 G0163   AUTOMAT
                                                     ADMIN

                                                     B61
NAKICENOVIC S.,NUCLEAR ENERGY IN YUGOSLAVIA.   R+D
YUGOSLAVIA AGRI INDUS CREATE OP/RES ROUTINE   ECO/DEV
EFFICIENCY KNOWL...HEAL STAT CHARTS LAB/EXP BIBLIOG   TEC/DEV
20. PAGE 41 G0802   NUC/PWR

                                                     S61
DALTON G.,"ECONOMIC THEORY AND PRIMITIVE SOCIETY"   ECO/UNDEV
(BMR)" UNIV AGRI KIN TEC/DEV ECO/TAC REGION HABITAT   METH
SKILL...METH/COMP BIBLIOG. PAGE 14 G0274   PHIL/SCI
                                                     SOC

                                                     B62
BROOKINGS INSTITUTION.DEVELOPMENT OF THE EMERGING   ECO/UNDEV
COUNTRIES; AN AGENDA FOR RESEARCH. WOR+45 AGRI   R+D
TEC/DEV FOR/AID EDU/PROP ADJUST HABITAT KNOWL...PSY   SOCIETY
SOC ANTHOL 20 THIRD/WRLD. PAGE 9 G0175   PROB/SOLV

                                                     B62
CARSON R.,SILENT SPRING. USA+45 AIR CULTURE AGRI   HABITAT
INDUS ADMIN ATTIT RIGID/FLEX ORD/FREE PWR...POLICY   TREND
20. PAGE 11 G0216   SOCIETY
                                                     CONTROL

                                                     B62
KENNEDY J.F.,TO TURN THE TIDE. SPACE AGRI INT/ORG   DIPLOM
FORCES TEC/DEV ADMIN NUC/PWR PEACE WEALTH...ANTHOL   CHIEF
20 KENNEDY/JF CIV/RIGHTS. PAGE 30 G0592   POLICY
                                                     NAT/G

                                                     B62
KRAFT J.,THE GRAND DESIGN. EUR+WWI USA+45 AGRI   VOL/ASSN
FINAN INDUS MARKET INT/ORG NAT/G PLAN ECO/TAC   ECO/DEV
TARIFFS REGION DRIVE ORD/FREE WEALTH...POLICY OBS   INT/TRADE
TREND EEC 20. PAGE 31 G0616

                                                     B62
MARTINS A.F.,REVOLUCAO BRANCA NO CAMPO. L/A+17C   AGRI
SERV/IND DEMAND EFFICIENCY PRODUC...POLICY   ECO/UNDEV
METH/COMP. PAGE 36 G0717   TEC/DEV
                                                     NAT/COMP

                                                     B62
THANT U.,THE UNITED NATIONS' DEVELOPMENT DECADE: INT/ORG
PROPOSALS FOR ACTION. WOR+45 SOCIETY ECO/UNDEV AGRI   ALL/VALS
COM/IND FINAN R+D MUNIC SCHOOL VOL/ASSN CONSULT
PLAN TEC/DEV ECO/TAC EDU/PROP ADMIN ROUTINE
RIGID/FLEX...MGT SOC CONCPT UNESCO UN TOT/POP

                                                     B62
WALSTON H.,AGRICULTURE UNDER COMMUNISM. CHINA/COM   AGRI
COM PROB/SOLV HAPPINESS RIGID/FLEX...POLICY   MARXISM
METH/COMP 20. PAGE 62 G1207   PLAN
                                                     CREATE

                                                     B63
FLORES E.,LAND REFORM AND THE ALLIANCE FOR PROGRESS   AGRI
(PAMPHLET). L/A+17C USA+45 STRUCT ECO/UNDEV NAT/G   INT/ORG
WORKER CREATE PLAN ECO/TAC COERCE REV 20. PAGE 19   DIPLOM
G0373   POLICY

                                                     B63
HATHAWAY D.A.,GOVERNMENT AND AGRICULTURE: PUBLIC   AGRI
POLICY IN A DEMOCRATIC SOCIETY. USA+45 LEGIS ADMIN   GOV/REL
EXEC LOBBY REPRESENT PWR 20. PAGE 25 G0491   PROB/SOLV
                                                     EX/STRUC

                                                     B63
HOFSTADTER R.,ANTI-INTELLECTUALISM IN AMERICAN   INTELL
LIFE. USA+45 AGRI INDUS ACADEM TEC/DEV EDU/PROP   EPIST
INGP/REL ATTIT...SOC WORSHIP 20 MCCARTHY/J   CULTURE
STEVENSN/A. PAGE 26 G0522   SOCIETY

                                                     B63
KATZ S.M.,A SELECTED LIST OF US READINGS ON   BIBLIOG/A
DEVELOPMENT. AGRI COM/IND DIST/IND INDUS LABOR PLAN   ECO/UNDEV
FOR/AID EDU/PROP HEALTH...POLICY SOC/WK 20. PAGE 30   TEC/DEV
G0582   ACT/RES

                                                     B63
OTTOSON H.W.,LAND USE POLICY AND PROBLEMS IN THE   PROB/SOLV
UNITED STATES. USA+45 USA-45 LAW AGRI INDUS NAT/G   UTIL
GP/REL...CHARTS ANTHOL 19/20 HOMEST/ACT. PAGE 43   HABITAT
G0851   POLICY

                                                     B63
PEABODY R.L.,NEW PERSPECTIVES ON THE HOUSE OF   NEW/IDEA
REPRESENTATIVES. AGRI FINAN SCHOOL FORCES CONFER   LEGIS
LEAD CHOOSE REPRESENT FEDERAL...POLICY DECISION   PWR
HOUSE/REP. PAGE 44 G0862   ADMIN

                                                     S63
DELLIN L.A.D.,"BULGARIA UNDER SOVIET LEADERSHIP."   AGRI
BULGARIA COM USA+45 USSR ECO/DEV INDUS POL/PAR   NAT/G
EX/STRUC TOP/EX COERCE ATTIT RIGID/FLEX...POLICY   TOTALISM
TIME/SEQ 20. PAGE 15 G0293

                                                     S63
HOSKINS H.L.,"ARAB SOCIALISM IN THE UAR." ISLAM   ECO/DEV
USSR AGRI INDUS NAT/G TOP/EX CREATE DIPLOM EDU/PROP   PLAN
DRIVE KNOWL PWR SOCISM...POLICY CONCPT TREND SUEZ   UAR
20. PAGE 27 G0530

                                                     B64
BALASSA B.,TRADE PROSPECTS FOR DEVELOPING   INT/TRADE
COUNTRIES. WOR+45 ECO/DEV AGRI EXTR/IND INDUS   ECO/UNDEV
CREATE PLAN PRICE...ECOMETRIC CLASSIF TIME/SEQ   TREND
GEN/METH. PAGE 5 G0087   STAT

                                                     B64
FEI J.C.H.,DEVELOPMENT OF THE LABOR SURPLUS   ECO/TAC
ECONOMY: THEORY AND POLICY. WOR+45 AGRI INDUS   POLICY
MARKET PROB/SOLV TEC/DEV...STAT CHARTS GEN/LAWS   WORKER
METH 20 THIRD/WRLD. PAGE 18 G0361   ECO/UNDEV

                                                     B64
GRAVIER J.F.,AMENAGEMENT DU TERRITOIRE ET L'AVENIR   PLAN
DES REGIONS FRANCAISES. FRANCE ECO/DEV AGRI INDUS   MUNIC
CREATE...GEOG CHARTS 20. PAGE 22 G0442   NEIGH
                                                     ADMIN

                                                     B64
HAZLEWOOD A.,THE ECONOMICS OF DEVELOPMENT: AN   BIBLIOG/A
ANNOTATED LIST OF BOOKS AND ARTICLES PUBLISHED   ECO/UNDEV
1958-1962. AGRI FINAN INDUS LABOR NAT/G DIPLOM   TEC/DEV
INT/TRADE INCOME...MGT 20. PAGE 25 G0497

                                                     B64
LI C.M.,INDUSTRIAL DEVELOPMENT IN COMMUNIST CHINA.   ASIA
CHINA/COM ECO/DEV ECO/UNDEV AGRI FINAN INDUS MARKET   TEC/DEV
LABOR NAT/G ECO/TAC INT/TRADE EXEC ALL/VALS
...POLICY RELATIV TREND WORK TOT/POP VAL/FREE 20.
PAGE 34 G0665

                                                     B64
ORGANIZATION AMERICAN STATES,ECONOMIC SURVEY OF   ECO/UNDEV
LATIN AMERICA, 1962. L/A+17C AGRI DIST/IND INDUS   CHARTS
MARKET PROC/MFG R+D PLAN TEC/DEV ECO/TAC REGION
BAL/PAY ALL/VALS...CON/ANAL ORG/CHARTS GEN/METH OAS
20. PAGE 43 G0844

                                                     B64
POWELSON J.P.,LATIN AMERICA: TODAY'S ECONOMIC AND   ECO/UNDEV

SOCIAL REVOLUTION. L/A+17C INTELL SOCIETY STRUCT   WEALTH
AGRI INDUS NAT/G DIPLOM ECO/TAC REV...POLICY 20.   ADJUST
PAGE 45 G0887   PLAN

S64
FLORINSKY M.T.,"TRENDS IN THE SOVIET ECONOMY." COM   ECO/DEV
USA+45 USSR INDUS LABOR NAT/G PLAN TEC/DEV ECO/TAC   AGRI
ALL/VALS SOCISM...MGT METH/CNCPT STYLE CON/ANAL
GEN/METH WORK 20. PAGE 19 G0374

S64
KASSOF A.,"THE ADMINISTERED SOCIETY: SOCIETY
TOTALITARIANISM WITHOUT TERROR." COM USSR STRATA   DOMIN
AGRI INDUS NAT/G PERF/ART SCHOOL TOP/EX EDU/PROP   TOTALSM
ADMIN ORD/FREE PWR...POLICY SOC TIME/SEQ GEN/LAWS
VAL/FREE 20. PAGE 29 G0580

S64
MAHALANOBIS P.C.,"PERSPECTIVE PLANNING IN INDIA: PLAN
STATISTICAL TOOLS." INDIA S/ASIA STRATA AGRI   STAT
DIST/IND FINAN INDUS SERV/IND NAT/G ECO/TAC
ORD/FREE WEALTH...POLICY TREND SIMUL VAL/FREE 20.
PAGE 35 G0695

B65
INT. BANK RECONSTR. DEVELOP.,ECONOMIC DEVELOPMENT   INDUS
OF KUWAIT. ISLAM KUWAIT AGRI FINAN MARKET EX/STRUC   NAT/G
TEC/DEV ECO/TAC ADMIN WEALTH...OBS CON/ANAL CHARTS
20. PAGE 28 G0548

B65
JASNY H.,KHRUSHCHEV'S CROP POLICY. USSR ECO/DEV   AGRI
PLAN MARXISM...STAT 20 KHRUSH/N RESOURCE/N. PAGE 29   NAT/G
G0562   POLICY
                                                         ECO/TAC

B65
OECD,THE MEDITERRANEAN REGIONAL PROJECT: GREECE;   EDU/PROP
EDUCATION AND DEVELOPMENT. FUT GREECE SOCIETY AGRI   SCHOOL
FINAN NAT/G PROF/ORG WORKER PLAN PROB/SOLV ADMIN   ACADEM
DEMAND ATTIT 20 OECD. PAGE 42 G0834   ECO/UNDEV

B65
WISH J.R.,ECONOMIC DEVELOPMENT IN LATIN AMERICA: AN   BIBLIOG/A
ANNOTATED BIBLIOGRAPHY. L/A+17C COM/IND MARKET R+D   ECO/UNDEV
CREATE CAP/ISM ATTIT...STAT METH 20. PAGE 64 G1250   TEC/DEV
                                                         AGRI

S65
STAAR R.F.,"RETROGRESSION IN POLAND." COM USSR AGRI   TOP/EX
INDUS NAT/G CREATE EDU/PROP TOTALSM RIGID/FLEX   ECO/TAC
ORD/FREE PWR SOCISM...RECORD CHARTS 20. PAGE 52   POLAND
G1029

B66
LECHT L.,GOAL, PRIORITIES, AND DOLLARS: THE NEXT   IDEA/COMP
DECADE. SPACE USA+45 SOCIETY AGRI BUDGET FOR/AID   POLICY
...HEAL SOC/WK STAT CHARTS 20 URBAN/RNWL PUB/TRANS.   CONSEN
PAGE 33 G0649   PLAN

B66
LILLEY S.,MEN, MACHINES AND HISTORY: THE STORY OF   AGRI
TOOLS AND MACHINES IN RELATION TO SOCIAL PROGRESS.   TEC/DEV
PREHIST SPACE STRUCT COMPUTER AUTOMAT NUC/PWR   SOCIETY
...POLICY SOC. PAGE 34 G0667

B66
MURDOCK J.C.,RESEARCH AND REGIONS. AGRI FINAN INDUS   BIBLIOG
LOC/G MUNIC NAT/G PROB/SOLV TEC/DEV ADMIN REGION   ECO/DEV
20. PAGE 40 G0796   COMPUT/IR
                                                         R+D

B67
BENNETT J.W.,HUTTERIAN BRETHREN; THE AGRICULTURAL   SECT
ECONOMY AND SOCIAL ORGANIZATION OF A COMMUNAL   AGRI
PEOPLE. USA+45 SOCIETY FAM KIN TEC/DEV ADJUST...MGT   STRUCT
AUD/VIS GP/COMP 20. PAGE 6 G0121   GP/REL

B67
COLEMAN J.R.,THE CHANGING AMERICAN ECONOMY. USA+45   BUDGET
AGRI FINAN LABOR FOR/AID INT/TRADE AUTOMAT GP/REL   ECO/TAC
INGP/REL ANTHOL. PAGE 13 G0243   ECO/DEV
                                                         WEALTH

B67
DEGLER C.N.,THE AGE OF THE ECONOMIC REVOLUTION   INDUS
1876-1900. USA+45 AGRI MUNIC POL/PAR SECT ECO/TAC   SOCIETY
CHOOSE...PHIL/SCI CHARTS NAT/COMP 19 NEGRO. PAGE 15   ECO/DEV
G0292   TEC/DEV

B67
EISENMENGER R.W.,THE DYNAMICS OF GROWTH IN NEW   ECO/DEV
ENGLAND'S ECONOMY, 1870-1964. USA+45 USA-45 ECO/TAC   AGRI
TAX PAY AUTOMAT GOV/REL ADJUST HABITAT...STAT   INDUS
19/20. PAGE 17 G0340   CAP/ISM

B67
HEADLEY J.C.,PESTICIDE PROBLEM: AN ECONOMIC   HABITAT
APPROACH TO PUBLIC POLICY. AGRI TEC/DEV GOV/REL   POLICY
COST ATTIT CHARTS. PAGE 25 G0498   BIO/SOC
                                                         CONTROL

B67
MAZOUR A.G.,SOVIET ECONOMIC DEVELOPMENT: OPERATION   ECO/TAC
OUTSTRIP: 1921-1965. USSR ECO/UNDEV FINAN CHIEF   AGRI
WORKER PROB/SOLV CONTROL PRODUC MARXISM...CHARTS   INDUS
ORG/CHARTS 20 STALIN/J. PAGE 37 G0726   PLAN

B67
MOORE J.R.,THE ECONOMIC IMPACT OF THE TVA. AGRI   ECO/UNDEV
INDUS PLAN BARGAIN CONTROL REGION GOV/REL DEMAND   ECO/DEV
EFFICIENCY SOCISM 20 TVA. PAGE 40 G0780   NAT/G
                                                         CREATE

B67
NASH M.,MACHINE AGE MAYA. GUATEMALA L/A+17C STRUCT   INDUS
AGRI WORKER CREATE INCOME ATTIT RIGID/FLEX ROLE   CULTURE
...IDEA/COMP SOC/EXP WORSHIP 20 INDIAN/AM. PAGE 41   SOC
G0806   MUNIC

B67
POMEROY W.J.,HALF A CENTURY OF SOCIALISM. USSR LAW   SOCISM
AGRI INDUS NAT/G CREATE DIPLOM EDU/PROP PERSON   MARXISM
ORD/FREE WEALTH...POLICY TREND 20. PAGE 45 G0884   COM
                                                         SOCIETY

B67
SALMOND J.A.,THE CIVILIAN CONSERVATION CORPS,   ADMIN
1933-1942. USA-45 NAT/G CREATE EXEC EFFICIENCY   ECO/TAC
WEALTH...BIBLIOG 20 ROOSEVLT/F. PAGE 48 G0954   TASK
                                                         AGRI

S67
ALLEE D.,"AMERICAN AGRICULTURE - ITS RESOURCE   AGRI
ISSUES FOR THE COMING YEARS." FUT USA+45 PLAN   SOCIETY
PROB/SOLV 20. PAGE 2 G0043   EFFICIENCY
                                                         AUTOMAT

S67
AVTORKHANOV A.,"A NEW AGRARIAN REVOLUTION." COM   AGRI
USSR ECO/DEV PLAN TEC/DEV ADMIN CONTROL OPTIMAL   METH/COMP
WEALTH SOCISM 20 KHRUSH/N STALIN/J. PAGE 4 G0082   MARXISM
                                                         OWN

S67
CARR E.H.,"REVOLUTION FROM ABOVE." USSR STRATA   AGRI
FINAN INDUS NAT/G DOMIN LEAD GP/REL INGP/REL OWN   POLICY
PRODUC PWR 20 STALIN/J. PAGE 11 G0214   COM
                                                         EFFICIENCY

N67
ASIAN STUDIES CENTER,FOUR ARTICLES ON POPULATION   ASIA
AND FAMILY LIFE IN TAIWAN (ASIAN STUDIES PAPERS,   FAM
REPRINT SERIES NO. 2). CULTURE STRATA ECO/UNDEV   CENSUS
AGRI INDUS R+D KIN MUNIC...GEOG SOC CHARTS 20.   ANTHOL
PAGE 4 G0072

AGRICULTURE....SEE AGRI

AHRCO....ALLEGHENY HOUSING REHABILITATION CORPORATION

AID ....US AGENCY FOR INTERNATIONAL DEVELOPMENT

B63
US SENATE COMM APPROPRIATIONS,PERSONNEL   ADMIN
ADMINISTRATION AND OPERATIONS OF AGENCY FOR   FOR/AID
INTERNATIONAL DEVELOPMENT: SPECIAL HEARING. FINAN   EFFICIENCY
LEAD COST UTIL SKILL...CHARTS 20 CONGRESS AID   DIPLOM
CIVIL/SERV. PAGE 60 G1175

L66
PACKENHAM R.A.,"POLITICAL-DEVELOPMENT DOCTRINES IN   FOR/AID
THE AMERICAN FOREIGN AID PROGRAM." STRUCT R+D   ECO/UNDEV
CREATE DIPLOM AID. PAGE 43 G0855   GEN/LAWS

AIR POLLUTION....SEE POLLUTION

AIR....LOCALE OF SUBJECT ACTIVITY IS AERIAL

B53
LANGER W.L.,THE UNDECLARED WAR, 1940-1941. EUR+WWI   WAR
GERMANY USA-45 USSR AIR FORCES TEC/DEV CONFER   POLICY
CONTROL COERCE PERCEPT ORD/FREE PWR 20 CHINJAP   DIPLOM
EUROPE. PAGE 32 G0634

B54
LOCKLIN D.P.,ECONOMICS OF TRANSPORTATION (4TH ED.).   ECO/DEV
USA+45 USA-45 SEA AIR LAW FINAN LG/CO EX/STRUC   DIST/IND
ADMIN CONTROL...STAT CHARTS 19/20 RAILROAD   ECO/TAC
PUB/TRANS. PAGE 34 G0675   TEC/DEV

                                                          S55
VON NEUMANN J.,"CAN WE SURVIVE TECHNOLOGY?" WOR+45   TEC/DEV
AIR INDUS ADMIN ADJUST RIGID/FLEX...GEOG PHIL/SCI   NUC/PWR
NEW/IDEA 20. PAGE 61 G1202   FUT
                                                     HABITAT

                                                          S58
MCDOUGAL M.S.,"PERSPECTIVES FOR A LAW OF OUTER   INT/ORG
SPACE." FUT WOR+45 AIR CONSULT DELIB/GP TEC/DEV   SPACE
CT/SYS ORD/FREE...POLICY JURID 20 UN. PAGE 37 G0736   INT/LAW

                                                          B59
EMME E.M.,THE IMPACT OF AIR POWER - NATIONAL   DETER
SECURITY AND WORLD POLITICS. USA+45 USSR FORCES   AIR
DIPLOM WEAPON PEACE TOTALISM...POLICY NAT/COMP 20   WAR
EUROPE. PAGE 18 G0346   ORD/FREE

                                                          B60
GOLDSEN J.M.,INTERNATIONAL POLITICAL IMPLICATIONS   R+D
OF ACTIVITIES IN OUTER SPACE. FUT USA+45 WOR+45 AIR   SPACE
LAW ACT/RES LEGIT ATTIT KNOWL ORD/FREE PWR...CONCPT
20. PAGE 22 G0427

                                                          B60
KINGSTON-MCCLOUG E.,DEFENSE; POLICY AND STRATEGY.   FORCES
UK SEA AIR TEC/DEV DIPLOM ADMIN LEAD WAR ORD/FREE   PLAN
...CHARTS 20. PAGE 30 G0597   POLICY
                                                     DECISION

                                                          B60
US SENATE COMM ON COMMERCE,URBAN MASS   DIST/IND
TRANSPORTATION. FUT USA+45 AIR ECO/DEV FINAN LOC/G   PLAN
MUNIC LEGIS CREATE PROB/SOLV TEC/DEV 20 PUB/TRANS.   NAT/G
PAGE 60 G1180   LAW

                                                          B60
WOETZEL R.K.,THE INTERNATIONAL CONTROL OF AIRSPACE   INT/ORG
AND OUTERSPACE. FUT WOR+45 AIR CONSTN STRUCT   JURID
CONSULT PLAN TEC/DEV ADJUD RIGID/FLEX KNOWL   SPACE
ORD/FREE PWR...TECHNIC GEOG MGT NEW/IDEA TREND   INT/LAW
COMPUT/IR VAL/FREE 20 TREATY. PAGE 64 G1251

                                                          N60
US HOUSE COMM SCI ASTRONAUT,THE ORGANIZATION OF THE   ACT/RES
US NATIONAL SPACE EFFORT. USA+45 WOR+45 AIR ECO/DEV   SKILL
NAT/G PLAN TEC/DEV DIPLOM EDU/PROP ATTIT DRIVE PWR   SPACE
...OBS TIME/SEQ TREND TOT/POP 20. PAGE 58 G1142

                                                          S61
MACHOWSKI K.,"SELECTED PROBLEMS OF NATIONAL   UNIV
SOVEREIGNTY WITH REFERENCE TO THE LAW OF OUTER   ACT/RES
SPACE." FUT WOR+45 AIR LAW INTELL SOCIETY ECO/DEV   NUC/PWR
PLAN EDU/PROP DETER DRIVE PERCEPT SOVEREIGN   SPACE
...POLICY INT/LAW OBS TREND TOT/POP 20. PAGE 35
G0689

                                                          S61
TAUBENFELD H.J.,"OUTER SPACE--PAST POLITICS AND   PLAN
FUTURE POLICY." FUT USA+45 USA-45 WOR+45 AIR INTELL   SPACE
STRUCT ECO/DEV NAT/G TOP/EX ACT/RES ADMIN ROUTINE   INT/ORG
NUC/PWR ATTIT DRIVE...CONCPT TIME/SEQ TREND TOT/POP
20. PAGE 54 G1054

                                                          B62
BLOOMFIELD L.P.,OUTER SPACE: A PATTERN OF WAR IN A   CREATE
NEW DIMENSION. FUT USA+45 AIR TEC/DEV PWR   ACT/RES
...DECISION CONCPT GEN/LAWS 20. PAGE 7 G0141   ARMS/CONT
                                                     SPACE

                                                          B62
CARSON R.,SILENT SPRING. USA+45 AIR CULTURE AGRI   HABITAT
INDUS ADMIN ATTIT RIGID/FLEX ORD/FREE PWR...POLICY   TREND
20. PAGE 11 G0216   SOCIETY
                                                     CONTROL

                                                          B62
GOLOVINE M.N.,CONFLICT IN SPACE: A PATTERN OF WAR   CREATE
IN A NEW DIMENSION. FUT USA+45 WOR+45 AIR FORCES   TEC/DEV
PLAN DIPLOM DOMIN ATTIT...STAT AUD/VIS CHARTS   NUC/PWR
COLD/WAR 20. PAGE 22 G0432   SPACE

                                                          B62
STERN A.C.,AIR POLLUTION (2 VOLS.). LAW INDUS   AIR
PROB/SOLV TEC/DEV INSPECT RISK BIO/SOC HABITAT   OP/RES
...OBS/ENVIR TESTS SAMP 20 POLLUTION. PAGE 53 G1035   CONTROL
                                                     HEALTH

                                                          S62
CRANE R.D.,"LAW AND STRATEGY IN SPACE." FUT USA+45   CONCPT
WOR+45 AIR LAW INT/ORG NAT/G FORCES ACT/RES PLAN   SPACE
BAL/PWR LEGIT ARMS/CONT COERCE ORD/FREE...POLICY
INT/LAW JURID SOC/EXP 20 TREATY. PAGE 13 G0261

                                                          S63
ABT C.C.,"THE PROBLEMS AND POSSIBILITIES OF SPACE   ACT/RES
ARMS CONTROL." FUT USA+45 WOR+45 AIR SOCIETY NAT/G   ORD/FREE

                                                          ARMS/CONT
BAL/PWR EDU/PROP ATTIT PWR WEALTH...HYPO/EXP   SPACE
TOT/POP 20. PAGE 2 G0025

                                                          S63
GARDNER R.N.,"COOPERATION IN OUTER SPACE." FUT USSR   INT/ORG
WOR+45 AIR LAW COM/IND CONSULT DELIB/GP CREATE   ACT/RES
KNOWL 20 TREATY. PAGE 21 G0410   PEACE
                                                     SPACE

                                                          S64
SPONSLER G.C.,"THE MILITARY ROLE IN SPACE." FUT   TEC/DEV
USA+45 SEA AIR NAT/G ACT/RES PLAN COERCE NUC/PWR   FORCES
WEAPON KNOWL ORD/FREE PWR RESPECT...TREND 20.   SPACE
PAGE 52 G1026

                                                          B65
THAYER F.C. JR.,AIR TRANSPORT POLICY AND NATIONAL   AIR
SECURITY: A POLITICAL, ECONOMIC, AND MILITARY   FORCES
ANALYSIS. DIST/IND OP/RES PLAN TEC/DEV DIPLOM DETER   CIVMIL/REL
WAR COST EFFICIENCY...POLICY BIBLIOG 20 DEPT/DEFEN   ORD/FREE
FAA CAB. PAGE 54 G1066

                                                          B66
RUPPENTHAL K.M.,TRANSPORTATION AND TOMORROW. FUT   DIST/IND
SPACE USA+45 SEA AIR FORCES TEC/DEV INT/TRADE   PLAN
...ANTHOL 20 RAILROAD. PAGE 48 G0946   CIVMIL/REL
                                                     PREDICT

                                                          B66
US SENATE,POLICY PLANNING FOR AERONAUTICAL RESEARCH   SPACE
AND DEVELOPMENT: STAFF REPORT FOR COMM ON   CIVMIL/REL
AERONAUTICAL AND SPACE SCIENCES. USA+45 AIR   GOV/REL
DIST/IND PLAN...POLICY CHARTS 20 CONGRESS NASA.   R+D
PAGE 59 G1164

                                                          B66
WHITNAH D.R.,SAFER SKYWAYS. DIST/IND DELIB/GP   ADMIN
FORCES TOP/EX WORKER TEC/DEV ROUTINE WAR CIVMIL/REL   NAT/G
COST...TIME/SEQ 20 FAA CAB. PAGE 63 G1235   AIR
                                                     GOV/REL

                                                          B67
US SENATE COMM ON FOREIGN REL,TREATY ON OUTER   SPACE
SPACE. WOR+45 AIR FORCES PROB/SOLV NUC/PWR SENATE   DIPLOM
TREATY UN. PAGE 60 G1182   ARMS/CONT
                                                     LAW

                                                          B67
US SENATE COMM ON FOREIGN REL,UNITED STATES   ARMS/CONT
ARMAMENT AND DISARMAMENT PROBLEMS. USA+45 AIR   WEAPON
BAL/PWR DIPLOM FOR/AID NUC/PWR ORD/FREE SENATE   FORCES
TREATY. PAGE 60 G1184   PROB/SOLV

                                                          N67
US SENATE COMM AERO SPACE SCI,AERONAUTICAL RESEARCH   AIR
AND DEVELOPMENT POLICY (PAMPHLET). SPACE USA+45   R+D
INDUS CIVMIL/REL CONGRESS PRESIDENT NASA SENATE.   POLICY
PAGE 60 G1169   PLAN

                                                          N67
US SENATE COMM ON PUBLIC WORKS,AIR QUALITY ACT OF   HEALTH
1967 (PAMPHLET). USA+45 INDUS R+D LEGIS SENATE.   AIR
PAGE 61 G1187   HABITAT
                                                     CONTROL

ALGERIA....SEE ALSO ISLAM

ALGIER/CHR....CHARTER OF ALGIERS

ALI S. G0041

ALIENATION....SEE STRANGE

ALKER H.R. G0042

ALL/IDEOS....CONCERNS THREE OR MORE OF THE TERMS LISTED IN
THE IDEOLOGICAL TOPIC INDEX, P. XIII

B28
BARKER E.,POLITICAL THOUGHT IN ENGLAND: FROM   INTELL
HERBERT SPENCER TO THE PRESENT DAY. UK ALL/IDEOS   GEN/LAWS
...PHIL/SCI 19/20 SPENCER/H GREEN/TH BENTHAM/J   IDEA/COMP
MAITLAND/F. PAGE 5 G0094

S51
BERGMANN G.,"IDEOLOGY" (BMR)" UNIV PERCEPT KNOWL   PHIL/SCI
...IDEA/COMP METH. PAGE 7 G0126   CONCPT
                                                      LOG
                                                      ALL/IDEOS

S56
ALMOND G.A.,"COMPARATIVE POLITICAL SYSTEMS" (BMR)"   GOV/COMP
WOR+45 WOR-45 PROB/SOLV DIPLOM EFFICIENCY   CONCPT
...PHIL/SCI SOC METH 17/20. PAGE 3 G0046   ALL/IDEOS
                                                      NAT/COMP

L59
MCDOUGAL M.S.,"THE IDENTIFICATION AND APPRAISAL OF   INT/LAW
DIVERSE SYSTEMS OF PUBLIC ORDER (BMR)" WOR+45 NAT/G   DIPLOM
CONSULT EDU/PROP POLICY. PAGE 37 G0737   ALL/IDEOS

B63
SCHOECK H.,THE NEW ARGUMENT IN ECONOMICS. UK USA+45   WELF/ST
INDUS MARKET LABOR NAT/G ECO/TAC ADMIN ROUTINE   FOR/AID
BAL/PAY PWR...POLICY BOLIV. PAGE 49 G0973   ECO/DEV
                                                      ALL/IDEOS

B65
PYE L.W.,POLITICAL CULTURE AND DEVELOPMENT. WOR+45   PHIL/SCI
WOR-45 CULTURE ECO/UNDEV NAT/G ALL/VALS ORD/FREE   TEC/DEV
PWR WEALTH ALL/IDEOS...TRADIT TREND 20. PAGE 46   SOCIETY
G0897

B66
ODEGARD P.H.,POLITICAL POWER AND SOCIAL CHANGE.   PWR
UNIV NAT/G CREATE ALL/IDEOS...POLICY GEOG SOC   TEC/DEV
CENSUS TREND. PAGE 42 G0829   IDEA/COMP

B67
BAUMOL W.J.,BUSINESS BEHAVIOR, VALUE AND GROWTH   ALL/IDEOS
(REV. ED.). WOR+45 FINAN LG/CO TEC/DEV CAP/ISM   PHIL/SCI
DEMAND EQUILIB...METH/COMP SIMUL 20. PAGE 5 G0105   PLAN
                                                      ECO/DEV

B67
PADELFORD N.J.,THE DYNAMICS OF INTERNATIONAL   DIPLOM
POLITICS (2ND ED.). WOR+45 LAW INT/ORG FORCES   NAT/G
TEC/DEV REGION NAT/LISM PEACE ATTIT PWR ALL/IDEOS   POLICY
UN COLD/WAR NATO TREATY. PAGE 43 G0856   DECISION

ALL/PROG....ALLIANCE FOR PROGRESS

ALL/VALS....CONCERNS SIX OR MORE OF THE TERMS LISTED IN
THE VALUES INDEX, P. XIII

N
FULLER G.A.,DEMOBILIZATION: A SELECTED LIST OF   BIBLIOG/A
REFERENCES. USA+45 LAW AGRI LABOR WORKER ECO/TAC   INDUS
RATION RECEIVE EDU/PROP ROUTINE ARMS/CONT ALL/VALS   FORCES
20. PAGE 20 G0398   NAT/G

B34
EINSTEIN A.,THE WORLD AS I SEE IT. WOR-45 INTELL   SOCIETY
R+D INT/ORG NAT/G SECT VOL/ASSN FORCES CREATE   PHIL/SCI
EDU/PROP LEGIT ARMS/CONT WAR WEAPON NAT/LISM   DIPLOM
ALL/VALS...POLICY CONCPT 20. PAGE 17 G0337   PACIFISM

B45
REVES E.,THE ANATOMY OF PEACE. WOR-45 LAW CULTURE   ACT/RES
NAT/G PLAN TEC/DEV EDU/PROP WAR NAT/LISM ATTIT   CONCPT
ALL/VALS SOVEREIGN...POLICY HUM TIME/SEQ 20.   NUC/PWR
PAGE 46 G0914   PEACE

B46
NORTHROP F.S.C.,THE MEETING OF EAST AND WEST.   DRIVE
EUR+WWI FUT MOD/EUR UNIV WOR+45 WOR-45 INTELL   TREND
SOCIETY EX/STRUC TOP/EX ACT/RES LEGIT CHOOSE ATTIT   PEACE
PERCEPT RIGID/FLEX ALL/VALS...POLICY JURID OBS
TOT/POP. PAGE 42 G0826

B48
BRADLEY D.,NO PLACE TO HIDE. USA+45 SOCIETY NAT/G   R+D
FORCES TEC/DEV EDU/PROP DETER PEACE BIO/SOC   LAB/EXP
ALL/VALS...POLICY PHIL/SCI OBS RECORD SAMP BIOG   ARMS/CONT
GEN/METH COLD/WAR 20. PAGE 8 G0162   NUC/PWR

B49
ROSENHAUPT H.W.,HOW TO WAGE PEACE. USA+45 SOCIETY   INTELL
STRATA STRUCT R+D INT/ORG POL/PAR LEGIS ACT/RES   CONCPT
CREATE PLAN EDU/PROP ADMIN EXEC ATTIT ALL/VALS   DIPLOM
...TIME/SEQ TREND COLD/WAR 20. PAGE 48 G0937

L54
OPLER M.E.,"SOCIAL ASPECTS OF TECHNICAL ASSISTANCE   INT/ORG
IN OPERATION." WOR+45 VOL/ASSN CREATE PLAN TEC/DEV   CONSULT
EDU/PROP ALL/VALS...METH/CNCPT OBS RECORD TREND UN   FOR/AID
20. PAGE 43 G0841

L55
KISER M.,"ORGANIZATION OF AMERICAN STATES." L/A+17C   VOL/ASSN
USA+45 ECO/UNDEV INT/ORG NAT/G PLAN TEC/DEV DIPLOM   ECO/DEV
ECO/TAC INT/TRADE EDU/PROP ADMIN ALL/VALS...POLICY   REGION
MGT RECORD ORG/CHARTS OAS 20. PAGE 30 G0601

S55
MILLER J.G.,"TOWARD A GENERAL THEORY FOR THE   CONCPT
BEHAVIORAL SCIENCES" (BMR)" CREATE ALL/VALS KNOWL   OP/RES
...CON/ANAL CHARTS HYPO/EXP SIMUL BIBLIOG 20.   METH/CNCPT
PAGE 39 G0773   COMPUTER

B58
US DEPARTMENT OF THE ARMY,BIBLIOGRAPHY ON LIMITED   BIBLIOG/A
WAR (PAMPHLET). USA+45 TEC/DEV CONTROL RISK COERCE   WAR
DETER NUC/PWR WEAPON ADJUST PEACE ALL/VALS ORD/FREE   FORCES
20. PAGE 57 G1127   CIVMIL/REL

B59
HUGHES E.M.,AMERICA THE VINCIBLE. USA+45 FOR/AID   ORD/FREE
ARMS/CONT NUC/PWR PERS/REL RATIONAL ATTIT ALL/VALS   DIPLOM
20 COLD/WAR. PAGE 27 G0534   WAR

B59
WARD B.,5 IDEAS THAT CHANGE THE WORLD. WOR+45   ECO/UNDEV
WOR-45 SOCIETY STRUCT AGRI INDUS INT/ORG NAT/G   ALL/VALS
FORCES ACT/RES ARMS/CONT TOTALISM ATTIT DRIVE   NAT/LISM
GEN/LAWS. PAGE 62 G1210   COLONIAL

B60
JANOWITZ M.,THE PROFESSIONAL SOLDIER. CULTURE   FORCES
STRATA STRUCT FAM PROB/SOLV TEC/DEV COERCE WAR   MYTH
CIVMIL/REL NAT/LISM AGE HEREDITY ALL/VALS CONSERVE   LEAD
...MGT WORSHIP. PAGE 28 G0560   ELITES

B60
PARRY A.,RUSSIA'S ROCKETS AND MISSILES. COM FUT   PLAN
GERMANY USA+45 WOR+45 INTELL ECO/DEV ACT/RES   TEC/DEV
NUC/PWR WEAPON ATTIT ALL/VALS...OBS TIME/SEQ   SPACE
COLD/WAR 20. PAGE 44 G0859   USSR

S60
KAPLAN M.A.,"THEORETICAL ANALYSIS OF THE BALANCE OF   CREATE
POWER." FUT USA+45 WOR+45 INTELL ECO/DEV INT/ORG   NEW/IDEA
NAT/G CONSULT TOP/EX ACT/RES PLAN TEC/DEV ATTIT   DIPLOM
ALL/VALS...METH/CNCPT TOT/POP 20. PAGE 29 G0576   NUC/PWR

S60
OSGOOD C.E.,"A CASE FOR GRADUATED UNILATERAL   ATTIT
DISENGAGEMENT." FUT WOR+45 CULTURE SOCIETY NAT/G   EDU/PROP
NUC/PWR WAR PERSON SUPEGO ALL/VALS...POLICY PSY   ARMS/CONT
CONCPT COLD/WAR TOT/POP VAL/FREE 20. PAGE 43 G0848

B61
KAHN H.,ON THERMONUCLEAR WAR. FUT UNIV WOR+45   DETER
ECO/DEV CONSULT EX/STRUC TOP/EX ACT/RES CREATE PLAN   NUC/PWR
COERCE WAR PERSON ALL/VALS...POLICY GEOG CONCPT   SOCIETY
METH/CNCPT OBS TREND 20. PAGE 29 G0569

B61
LUNDBERG G.A.,CAN SCIENCE SAVE US. UNIV CULTURE   ACT/RES
INTELL SOCIETY ECO/DEV R+D PLAN EDU/PROP ROUTINE   CONCPT
CHOOSE ATTIT PERCEPT ALL/VALS...TREND 20. PAGE 34   TOTALISM
G0679

B62
BOULDING K.E.,CONFLICT AND DEFENSE: A GENERAL   MATH
THEORY. FUT SOCIETY INT/ORG NAT/G CREATE BAL/PWR   SIMUL
COERCE NAT/LISM DRIVE ALL/VALS...PLURIST DECISION   PEACE
CONCPT METH/CNCPT TREND HYPO/EXP TOT/POP 20. PAGE 8   WAR
G0157

B62
ROSS R.,SYMBOLS AND CIVILIZATION. UNIV CULTURE SECT   PHIL/SCI
CREATE ALL/VALS MORAL ART/METH. PAGE 48 G0939   KNOWL
                                                      EPIST
                                                      SOCIETY

B62

THANT U.,THE UNITED NATIONS' DEVELOPMENT DECADE: INT/ORG
PROPOSALS FOR ACTION. WOR+45 SOCIETY ECO/UNDEV AGRI ALL/VALS
COM/IND FINAN R+D MUNIC SCHOOL VOL/ASSN CONSULT
PLAN TEC/DEV ECO/TAC EDU/PROP ADMIN ROUTINE
RIGID/FLEX...MGT SOC CONCPT UNESCO UN TOT/POP
VAL/FREE. PAGE 54 G1064

S62

STORER N.W.,"SOME SOCIOLOGICAL ASPECTS OF FEDERAL   POLICY
SCIENCE POLICY." USA+45 INTELL PUB/INST PLAN GP/REL CREATE
PERS/REL DRIVE PERSON ROLE...PSY SOC SIMUL 20 NIH   NAT/G
NSF. PAGE 53 G1040   ALL/VALS

B63

NORTH R.C.,CONTENT ANALYSIS: A HANDBOOK WITH   METH/CNCPT
APPLICATIONS FOR THE STUDY OF INTERNATIONAL CRISIS. COMPUT/IR
ASIA COM EUR+WWI MOD/EUR INT/ORG TEC/DEV DOMIN   USSR
EDU/PROP ROUTINE COERCE PERCEPT RIGID/FLEX ALL/VALS
...QUANT TESTS CON/ANAL SIMUL GEN/LAWS VAL/FREE.
PAGE 42 G0825

S63

SCHMITT H.A.,"THE EUROPEAN COMMUNITIES." EUR+WWI   VOL/ASSN
FRANCE DELIB/GP EX/STRUC TOP/EX CREATE TEC/DEV   ECO/DEV
ECO/TAC LEGIT REGION COERCE DRIVE ALL/VALS
...METH/CNCPT EEC 20. PAGE 49 G0972

B64

LI C.M.,INDUSTRIAL DEVELOPMENT IN COMMUNIST CHINA.   ASIA
CHINA/COM ECO/DEV ECO/UNDEV AGRI FINAN INDUS MARKET TEC/DEV
LABOR NAT/G ECO/TAC INT/TRADE EXEC ALL/VALS
...POLICY RELATIV TREND WORK TOT/POP VAL/FREE 20.
PAGE 34 G0665

B64

ORGANIZATION AMERICAN STATES,ECONOMIC SURVEY OF   ECO/UNDEV
LATIN AMERICA, 1962. L/A+17C AGRI DIST/IND INDUS   CHARTS
MARKET PROC/MFG R+D PLAN TEC/DEV ECO/TAC REGION
BAL/PAY ALL/VALS...CON/ANAL ORG/CHARTS GEN/METH OAS
20. PAGE 43 G0844

L64

BERKS R.N.,"THE US AND WEAPONS CONTROL." WOR+45 LAW USA+45
INT/ORG NAT/G LEGIS EXEC COERCE PEACE ATTIT   PLAN
RIGID/FLEX ALL/VALS PWR...POLICY TOT/POP 20. PAGE 7 ARMS/CONT
G0129

L64

CARNEGIE ENDOWMENT INT. PEACE,"POLITICAL QUESTIONS   INT/ORG
(ISSUES BEFORE THE NINETEENTH GENERAL ASSEMBLY)."   PEACE
SPACE WOR+45 CONSTN FINAN NAT/G CONSULT DELIB/GP
FORCES LEGIS TEC/DEV EDU/PROP LEGIT ARMS/CONT
COERCE NUC/PWR ATTIT ALL/VALS...CONCPT OBS UN
COLD/WAR 20. PAGE 11 G0208

L64

WARD C.,"THE 'NEW MYTHS' AND 'OLD REALITIES' OF   FORCES
NUCLEAR WAR." COM FUT USA+45 USSR WOR+45 INT/ORG   COERCE
NAT/G DOMIN LEGIT EXEC ATTIT PERCEPT ALL/VALS   ARMS/CONT
...POLICY RELATIV PSY MYTH TREND 20. PAGE 62 G1212   NUC/PWR

S64

BYRNES F.C.,"ASSIGNMENT TO AMBIGUITY: WORK   INTELL
PERFORMANCE IN CROSSCULTURAL TECHNICAL ASSISTANCE." QU
USA+45 WOR+45 PROF/ORG CONSULT PLAN EDU/PROP ATTIT
DISPL PERCEPT PERSON ALL/VALS...POLICY INT CHARTS
NATO 20. PAGE 10 G0199

S64

CALDWELL L.K.,"BIOPOLITICS: SCIENCE, ETHICS, AND   TEC/DEV
PUBLIC POLICY." FUT USA+45 WOR+45 INTELL STRATA R+D POLICY
NAT/G CONSULT PLAN EDU/PROP ALL/VALS...RELATIV
PHIL/SCI 20. PAGE 10 G0203

S64

FLORINSKY M.T.,"TRENDS IN THE SOVIET ECONOMY." COM   ECO/DEV
USA+45 USSR INDUS LABOR NAT/G PLAN TEC/DEV ECO/TAC   AGRI
ALL/VALS SOCISM...MGT METH/CNCPT STYLE CON/ANAL
GEN/METH WORK 20. PAGE 19 G0374

S64

NEEDHAM T.,"SCIENCE AND SOCIETY IN EAST AND WEST."   ASIA
INTELL STRATA R+D LOC/G NAT/G PROVS CONSULT ACT/RES STRUCT
CREATE PLAN TEC/DEV EDU/PROP ADMIN ATTIT ALL/VALS
...POLICY RELATIV MGT CONCPT NEW/IDEA TIME/SEQ WORK
WORK. PAGE 41 G0815

S64

PLATT J.R.,"RESEARCH AND DEVELOPMENT FOR SOCIAL   R+D
PROBLEMS." INTELL SOCIETY PROB/SOLV GP/REL ATTIT   ACT/RES
ALL/VALS CONT/OBS. PAGE 45 G0880   PLAN
                                                     SOC

B65

BENTWICH J.S.,EDUCATION IN ISRAEL. ISRAEL CULTURE   SECT
STRATA PROB/SOLV TEC/DEV ADJUST ALL/VALS 20 JEWS.   EDU/PROP
PAGE 7 G0125   ACADEM
                                                     SCHOOL

B65

FOSTER P.,EDUCATION AND SOCIAL CHANGE IN GHANA.   SCHOOL
GHANA CULTURE STRUCT ECO/UNDEV TEC/DEV REGION   CREATE
EFFICIENCY LITERACY ALL/VALS SOVEREIGN...STAT   SOCIETY
METH/COMP 19/20 GOLD/COAST. PAGE 20 G0385

B65

PYE L.W.,POLITICAL CULTURE AND DEVELOPMENT. WOR+45   PHIL/SCI
WOR-45 CULTURE ECO/UNDEV NAT/G ALL/VALS ORD/FREE   TEC/DEV
PWR WEALTH ALL/IDEOS...TRADIT TREND 20. PAGE 46   SOCIETY
G0897

B65

REISS A.J. JR.,SCHOOLS IN A CHANGING SOCIETY.   SCHOOL
CULTURE PROB/SOLV INSPECT DOMIN CONFER INGP/REL   EX/STRUC
RACE/REL AGE/C AGE/Y ALL/VALS...ANTHOL SOC/INTEG 20 ADJUST
NEWYORK/C. PAGE 46 G0912   ADMIN

B65

US DEPARTMENT OF DEFENSE,US SECURITY ARMS CONTROL,   BIBLIOG/A
AND DISARMAMENT 1961-1965 (PAMPHLET). CHINA/COM COM ARMS/CONT
GERMANY/W ISRAEL SPACE USA+45 USSR WOR+45 FORCES   NUC/PWR
EDU/PROP DETER EQUILIB PEACE ALL/VALS...GOV/COMP 20 DIPLOM
NATO. PAGE 57 G1118

B66

GREEN P.,DEADLY LOGIC* THE THEORY OF NUCLEAR   DETER
DETERRENCE. USA+45 ACT/RES OP/RES NUC/PWR RATIONAL   ACADEM
ALL/VALS PWR...DECISION MGT PHIL/SCI QUANT   GEN/LAWS
IDEA/COMP GAME. PAGE 23 G0444   RECORD

B66

US HOUSE COMM GOVT OPERATIONS,THE COMPUTER AND   ORD/FREE
INVASION OF PRIVACY. USA+45 SOCIETY ALL/VALS...PSY   COMPUTER
SOC CHARTS HOUSE/REP PRIVACY. PAGE 58 G1140   TEC/DEV
                                                     NAT/G

B66

WARD B.,NATIONALISM AND IDEOLOGY. ECO/UNDEV KIN   IDEA/COMP
CREATE CAP/ISM FOR/AID ALL/VALS MARXISM...POLICY   NAT/LISM
SOC. PAGE 62 G1211   ATTIT

L66

DOUGHERTY J.E.,"THE CATHOLIC CHURCH, WAR AND   CATHISM
NUCLEAR WEAPONS." COM EUR+WWI SECT TOP/EX LEAD   MORAL
DETER ALL/VALS. PAGE 16 G0312   WAR
                                                     NUC/PWR

S67

LEVENSTEIN A.,"TECHNOLOGICAL CHANGE, WORK, AND   TEC/DEV
HUMAN VALUES." WOR+45 SOCIETY AUTOMAT ROUTINE   CULTURE
LEISURE INGP/REL ADJUST TECHRACY...MGT CONCPT.   ALL/VALS
PAGE 33 G0660   TIME/SEQ

ALLEE D. G0043

ALLEGHENY COUNCIL TO IMPROVE OUR NEIGHBORHOODS....SEE
    ACTION

ALLEGHENY HOUSING REHABILITATION CORPORATION....SEE AHRCO

ALLEN R.L. G0922

ALLEN R.V. G0024

ALLEN S. G0044

ALLIANCE FOR PROGRESS....SEE ALL/PROG

ALLIANCES, MILITARY....SEE FORCES+INT/REL

ALLISON D. G0045

ALMOND G.A. G0046

ALTO/ADIGE....ALTO-ADIGE REGION OF ITALY

ALTSHULER A. G0047

AM/LEGION....AMERICAN LEGION

AMA....AMERICAN MEDICAL ASSOCIATION

AMBITION....SEE DRIVE

AMEND/I....CONCERNED WITH FREEDOMS GRANTED IN THE
    FIRST AMENDMENT

AMEND/IV....CONCERNED WITH FREEDOMS GRANTED IN THE
    FOURTH AMENDMENT

AMEND/V....CONCERNED WITH FREEDOMS GRANTED IN THE
FIFTH AMENDMENT

AMEND/VI....CONCERNED WITH FREEDOMS GRANTED IN THE
SIXTH AMENDMENT

AMEND/XIV....CONCERNED WITH FREEDOMS GRANTED IN THE
FOURTEENTH AMENDMENT

AMERICAN COUNCIL OF LEARNED SOC. G0048

AMERICAN BAR ASSOCIATION....SEE ABA

AMERICAN CIVIL LIBERTIES UNION....SEE ACLU

AMERICAN FARM BUREAU FEDERATION....SEE FARM/BUR

AMERICAN FEDERATION OF LABOR, CONGRESS OF INDUSTRIAL
ORGANIZATIONS....SEE AFL/CIO, LABOR

AMERICAN INDIANS....SEE INDIAN/AM

AMERICAN LEGION....SEE AM/LEGION

AMERICAN POLITICAL SCIENCE ASSOCIATION....SEE APSA

AMERICAN TELEPHONE AND TELEGRAPH....SEE AT+T

AMERICAN ASSEMBLY COLUMBIA U G0049

AMERICAN DOCUMENTATION INST G0050,G0051,G0052

AMERICAN FRIENDS SERVICE COMM G0053

AMERICAN LIBRARY ASSN G0054

AMERICAS, PRE/EUROPEAN....SEE PRE/AMER

AMMAN/MAX....MAX AMMAN

AMRINE M. G0055

ANARCH....ANARCHISM; SEE ALSO ATTIT, VALUES INDEX

ANARCHISM....SEE ANARCH

ANCIENT EGYPT....SEE EGYPT/ANC

ANCIENT GREECE....SEE GREECE/ANC

ANDALUSIA....SEE ALSO SPAIN

ANDERSON C.A. G0056

ANDERSON N. G0057

ANDORRA....SEE ALSO APPROPRIATE TIME/SPACE/CULTURE INDEX

ANDREWS R.B. G0058

ANGELL N. G0059

ANGELL R. G0060

ANGLO/SAX....ANGLO-SAXON

ANGOLA....ANGOLA

ANNEXATION....ANNEXATION

ANOMIE....GENERALIZED PERSONAL ANXIETY; SEE DISPL

| | | B54 |
| SPROTT W.J.H.,SCIENCE AND SOCIAL ACTION. STRUCT ACT/RES CRIME GP/REL INGP/REL ANOMIE...PSY SOC/INTEG 19/20. PAGE 52 G1027 | SOC CULTURE PHIL/SCI | |

| | | B57 |
| MERTON R.K.,SOCIAL THEORY AND SOCIAL STRUCTURE (REV. ED.). INTELL SECT WORKER OP/RES EDU/PROP ADMIN INGP/REL ANOMIE PERSON...AUD/VIS T 20 BUREAUCRCY. PAGE 38 G0759 | SOC GEN/LAWS SOCIETY STRUCT | |

| | | B62 |
| BAKER G.W.,BEHAVIORAL SCIENCE AND CIVIL DEFENSE. USA+45 PROB/SOLV ADMIN GP/REL INGP/REL PERS/REL ANOMIE DRIVE PERSON...DECISION MGT SOC 20 CIV/DEFENS. PAGE 4 G0085 | NUC/PWR WAR POLICY ACT/RES | |

| | | B63 |
| TOMKINS S.S.,COMPUTER SIMULATION OF PERSONALITY. R+D TEC/DEV AUTOMAT FEEDBACK ANOMIE PERCEPT...STYLE PERS/TEST PREDICT COMPUT/IR GP/COMP. PAGE 55 G1075 | COMPUTER PERSON SIMUL PROG/TEAC | |

| | | B64 |
| ELLUL J.,THE TECHNOLOGICAL SOCIETY. FUT STRUCT CREATE AUTOMAT ROUTINE STRANGE ANOMIE MORAL PHIL/SCI. PAGE 18 G0344 | SOC SOCIETY TECHNIC TEC/DEV | |

| | | B66 |
| VON BORCH H,FRIEDE TROTZ KRIEG. GERMANY USSR WOR+45 PEACE ANOMIE ATTIT 20. PAGE 43 G0853 | DIPLOM NUC/PWR WAR COERCE | |

| | | S67 |
| SUINN R.M.,"THE DISARMAMENT FANTASY* PSYCHOLOGICAL FACTORS THAT MAY PRODUCE WARFARE." DIPLOM RISK ARMS/CONT DETER ANOMIE PERSON GAME. PAGE 53 G1046 | DECISION NUC/PWR WAR PSY | |

ANSCOMBE G.E.M. G1033

ANTARCTICA

| | | L61 |
| TAUBENFELD H.J.,"A TREATY FOR ANTARCTICA." FUT USA+45 INTELL INT/ORG LABOR 20 TREATY ANTARCTICA. PAGE 54 G1055 | R+D ACT/RES DIPLOM | |

ANTHOL....ANTHOLOGY, SYMPOSIUM, PANEL OF WRITERS

| | | N19 |
| FOLSOM M.B.,BETTER MANAGEMENT OF THE PUBLIC'S BUSINESS (PAMPHLET). USA+45 DELIB/GP PAY CONFER CONTROL REGION GP/REL...METH/COMP ANTHOL 20. PAGE 19 G0377 | ADMIN NAT/G MGT PROB/SOLV | |

| | | B42 |
| MARCHANT A.,INVESTIGATIONS IN PROGRESS IN THE UNITED STATES IN THE FIELD OF LATIN AMERICAN HUMANISTIC AND SOCIAL SCIENCE STUDIES. USA+45 ACADEM...QU ANTHOL. PAGE 36 G0702 | ACT/RES SOC R+D L/A+17C | |

| | | B48 |
| GRIFFITH E.S.,RESEARCH IN POLITICAL SCIENCE: THE WORK OF PANELS OF RESEARCH COMMITTEE, APSA. WOR+45 WOR-45 COM/IND R+D FORCES ACT/RES WAR...GOV/COMP ANTHOL 20. PAGE 23 G0451 | BIBLIOG PHIL/SCI DIPLOM JURID | |

| | | B49 |
| MCLEAN J.M.,THE PUBLIC SERVICE AND UNIVERSITY EDUCATION. UK USA-45 DELIB/GP EX/STRUC TOP/EX ADMIN ...GOV/COMP METH/COMP NAT/COMP ANTHOL 20. PAGE 38 G0746 | ACADEM NAT/G EXEC EDU/PROP | |

| | | B50 |
| CANTRIL H.,TENSIONS THAT CAUSE WAR. UNIV CULTURE R+D CREATE EDU/PROP DRIVE PERSON KNOWL ORD/FREE ...HUM PSY SOC OBS CENSUS TREND CON/ANAL SOC/EXP SIMUL GEN/METH ANTHOL COLD/WAR TOT/POP. PAGE 11 G0206 | SOCIETY PHIL/SCI PEACE | |

| | | B50 |
| CONTINUITIES IN SOCIAL RESEARCH; STUDIES IN SCOPE AND METHOD OF "THE AMERICAN SOLDIER" USA+45 FORCES INGP/REL ATTIT...PSY SAMP CON/ANAL CHARTS GEN/LAWS ANTHOL 20. PAGE 38 G0758 | SOC PHIL/SCI METH | |

| | | B51 |
| HUXLEY J.,FREEDOM AND CULTURE. UNIV LAW SOCIETY R+D ACADEM SCHOOL CREATE SANCTION ATTIT KNOWL...HUM ANTHOL 20. PAGE 27 G0540 | CULTURE ORD/FREE PHIL/SCI IDEA/COMP | |

| | | L52 |
| LASSWELL H.D.,"RESEARCH IN POLITICAL BEHAVIOR." LOC/G MUNIC POL/PAR CONSULT ADMIN PARTIC...CHARTS ANTHOL BIBLIOG/A 20. PAGE 32 G0641 | PHIL/SCI METH R+D | |

| | | B54 |
| GERMANY FOREIGN MINISTRY,DOCUMENTS ON GERMAN FOREIGN POLICY 1918-1945, SERIES C (1933-1937) VOLS. I-V. GERMANY MOD/EUR FORCES PLAN ECO/TAC ...FASCIST CHARTS ANTHOL 20. PAGE 21 G0416 | NAT/G DIPLOM POLICY | |

| | | B54 |
| MCCLOSKEY J.F.,OPERATIONS RESEARCH FOR MANAGEMENT. STRUCT COMPUTER ADMIN ROUTINE...PHIL/SCI CONCPT METH/CNCPT TREND ANTHOL BIBLIOG 20. PAGE 37 G0731 | OP/RES MGT METH/COMP TEC/DEV | |

| | | B54 |
| SPENCER R.F.,METHOD AND PERSPECTIVE IN ANTHROPOLOGY ....GEOG LING QUANT STAT TESTS SAMP/SIZ CON/ANAL IDEA/COMP METH/COMP ANTHOL BIBLIOG 20. PAGE 52 G1025 | PHIL/SCI SOC PSY METH | |

ATOMIC INDUSTRIAL FORUM,PUBLIC RELATIONS FOR THE
ATOMIC INDUSTRY. WOR+45 PLAN PROB/SOLV EDU/PROP
PRESS CONFER...AUD/VIS ANTHOL 20. PAGE 4 G0077
B56
NUC/PWR
INDUS
GP/REL
ATTIT

ATOMIC INDUSTRIAL FORUM,MANAGEMENT AND ATOMIC
ENERGY. WOR+45 SEA LAW MARKET NAT/G TEC/DEV INSPECT
INT/TRADE CONFER PEACE HEALTH...ANTHOL 20. PAGE 4
G0078
B58
NUC/PWR
INDUS
MGT
ECO/TAC

UN INTL CONF ON PEACEFUL USE,PROGRESS IN ATOMIC
ENERGY (VOL. I). WOR+45 R+D PLAN TEC/DEV CONFER
CONTROL PEACE SKILL...CHARTS ANTHOL 20 UN BAGHDAD.
PAGE 55 G1088
B58
NUC/PWR
DIPLOM
WORKER
EDU/PROP

HALEY A.G.,FIRST COLLOQUIUM ON THE LAW OF OUTER
SPACE. WOR+45 INT/ORG ACT/RES PLAN BAL/PWR CONFER
ATTIT PWR...POLICY JURID CHARTS ANTHOL 20. PAGE 24
G0468
B59
SPACE
LAW
SOVEREIGN
CONTROL

JACOBS N.,CULTURE FOR THE MILLIONS? INTELL SOCIETY
NAT/G...POLICY SOC OBS ANTHOL 20. PAGE 28 G0553
B59
CULTURE
COM/IND
PERF/ART
CONCPT

U OF MICHIGAN LAW SCHOOL,ATOMS AND THE LAW. USA+45
PROVS WORKER PROB/SOLV DIPLOM ADMIN GOV/REL ANTHOL.
PAGE 55 G1085
B59
NUC/PWR
NAT/G
CONTROL
LAW

ARROW K.J.,MATHEMATICAL METHODS IN THE SOCIAL
SCIENCES, 1959. TEC/DEV CHOOSE UTIL PERCEPT
...KNO/TEST GAME SIMUL ANTHOL. PAGE 4 G0070
B60
MATH
PSY
MGT

ATOMIC INDUSTRIAL FORUM,ATOMS FOR INDUSTRY: WORLD
FORUM. WOR+45 FINAN COST UTIL...JURID ANTHOL 20.
PAGE 4 G0080
B60
NUC/PWR
INDUS
PLAN
PROB/SOLV

CARPENTER E.,EXPLORATIONS IN COMMUNICATION. USSR
CULTURE SCHOOL SECT EDU/PROP PRESS TV AUTOMAT
FEEDBACK ATTIT PERSON...ART/METH PSY 20. PAGE 11
G0211
B60
ANTHOL
COM/IND
TEC/DEV
WRITING

MCCLELLAND C.A.,NUCLEAR WEAPONS, MISSILES, AND
FUTURE WAR: PROBLEM FOR THE SIXTIES. WOR+45 FORCES
ARMS/CONT DETER MARXISM...POLICY ANTHOL COLD/WAR.
PAGE 37 G0729
B60
DIPLOM
NUC/PWR
WAR
WEAPON

SCHRAMM W.,"MASS COMMUNICATIONS: A BOOK OF READINGS
(2ND ED.)" LG/CO PRESS ADMIN CONTROL ROUTINE ATTIT
ROLE SUPEGO...CHARTS ANTHOL BIBLIOG 20. PAGE 50
G0977
C60
COM/IND
EDU/PROP
CROWD
MAJORIT

RAMO S.,PEACETIME USES OF OUTER SPACE. FUT DIST/IND
INT/ORG CONSULT NUC/PWR...AUD/VIS ANTHOL 20.
PAGE 46 G0898
B61
PEACE
TEC/DEV
SPACE
CREATE

ROSENAU J.N.,INTERNATIONAL POLITICS AND FOREIGN
POLICY: A READER IN RESEARCH AND THEORY. ELITES
ATTIT SOVEREIGN...DECISION CHARTS HYPO/EXP GAME
SIMUL ANTHOL BIBLIOG METH 20. PAGE 48 G0936
B61
ACT/RES
DIPLOM
CONCPT
POLICY

STEIN W.,NUCLEAR WEAPONS: A CATHOLIC RESPONSE.
WOR+45 FORCES ARMS/CONT DETER MURDER MORAL...POLICY
CATH IDEA/COMP ANTHOL 20. PAGE 52 G1033
B61
NUC/PWR
WAR
CATHISM
ATTIT

BENNETT J.C.,NUCLEAR WEAPONS AND THE CONFLICT OF
CONSCIENCE. WOR+45 PROB/SOLV DIPLOM WEAPON SUPEGO
MORAL...ANTHOL WORSHIP 20. PAGE 6 G0120
B62
POLICY
NUC/PWR
WAR

BROOKINGS INSTITUTION,DEVELOPMENT OF THE EMERGING
COUNTRIES: AN AGENDA FOR RESEARCH. WOR+45 AGRI
TEC/DEV FOR/AID EDU/PROP ADJUST HABITAT KNOWL...PSY
SOC ANTHOL 20 THIRD/WRLD. PAGE 9 G0175
B62
ECO/UNDEV
R+D
SOCIETY
PROB/SOLV

KENNEDY J.F.,TO TURN THE TIDE. SPACE AGRI INT/ORG
B62
DIPLOM

FORCES TEC/DEV ADMIN NUC/PWR PEACE WEALTH...ANTHOL
20 KENNEDY/JF CIV/RIGHTS. PAGE 30 G0592
CHIEF
POLICY
NAT/G

ABSHIRE D.M.,NATIONAL SECURITY: POLITICAL,
MILITARY, AND ECONOMIC STRATEGIES IN THE DECADE
AHEAD. ASIA COM USA+45 WOR+45 ECO/DEV ECO/UNDEV
INT/ORG DELIB/GP FORCES ECO/TAC COERCE ATTIT
RIGID/FLEX HEALTH ORD/FREE PWR WEALTH...POLICY STAT
CHARTS ANTHOL COLD/WAR VAL/FREE. PAGE 1 G0024
B63
FUT
ACT/RES
BAL/PWR

DALAND R.T.,PERSPECTIVES OF BRAZILIAN PUBLIC
ADMINISTRATION (VOL. I). BRAZIL LAW ECO/UNDEV
SCHOOL CHIEF TEC/DEV CONFER CONTROL GP/REL ATTIT
ROLE PWR...ANTHOL 20. PAGE 14 G0272
B63
ADMIN
NAT/G
PLAN
GOV/REL

GOLDSEN J.M.,OUTER SPACE IN WORLD POLITICS. COM
USA+45 NAT/G FORCES ACT/RES PLAN EDU/PROP
COERCE ORD/FREE PWR...TECHNIC STAT INT SAMP TREND
ANTHOL VAL/FREE 20. PAGE 22 G0428
B63
TEC/DEV
DIPLOM
SPACE

HAUSMAN W.H.,MANAGING ECONOMIC DEVELOPMENT IN
AFRICA. AFR USA+45 LAW FINAN WORKER TEC/DEV WEALTH
...ANTHOL 20. PAGE 25 G0492
B63
ECO/UNDEV
PLAN
FOR/AID
MGT

HEYEL C.,THE ENCYCLOPEDIA OF MANAGEMENT. WOR+45
MARKET TOP/EX TEC/DEV AUTOMAT LEAD ADJUST...STAT
CHARTS GAME ANTHOL BIBLIOG. PAGE 26 G0509
B63
MGT
INDUS
ADMIN
FINAN

KAST F.E.,SCIENCE, TECHNOLOGY, AND MANAGEMENT.
SPACE USA+45 FORCES CONFER DETER NUC/PWR...PHIL/SCI
CHARTS ANTHOL BIBLIOG 20 NASA. PAGE 30 G0581
B63
MGT
PLAN
TEC/DEV
PROB/SOLV

OTTOSON H.W.,LAND USE POLICY AND PROBLEMS IN THE
UNITED STATES. USA+45 USA-45 LAW AGRI INDUS NAT/G
GP/REL...CHARTS ANTHOL 19/20 HOMEST/ACT. PAGE 43
G0851
B63
PROB/SOLV
UTIL
HABITAT
POLICY

REED E.,CHALLENGES TO DEMOCRACY: THE NEXT TEN
YEARS. FUT USA+45 ECO/DEV DELIB/GP TEC/DEV CONFER
GOV/REL KNOWL ORD/FREE...MAJORIT IDEA/COMP ANTHOL
20. PAGE 46 G0909
B63
POLICY
EDU/PROP
ECO/TAC
NAT/G

US SENATE,DOCUMENTS ON INTERNATIONAL AS"ECTS OF
EXPLORATION AND USE OF OUTER SPACE, 1954-62: STAFF
REPORT FOR COMM AERON SPACE SCI. USA+45 USSR LEGIS
LEAD CIVMIL/REL PEACE...POLICY INT/LAW ANTHOL 20
CONGRESS NASA KHRUSH/N. PAGE 59 G1162
B63
SPACE
UTIL
GOV/REL
DIPLOM

BLOUSTEIN E.J.,NUCLEAR ENERGY, PUBLIC POLICY, AND
THE LAW. USA+45 NAT/G ADJUD ADMIN GP/REL OWN PEACE
ATTIT HEALTH...ANTHOL 20. PAGE 7 G0144
B64
TEC/DEV
LAW
POLICY
NUC/PWR

FOGELMAN E.,HIROSHIMA: THE DECISION TO USE THE A-
BOMB. USA-45 DIPLOM EFFICIENCY PEACE...ANTHOL
BIBLIOG T 20 CHINJAP. PAGE 19 G0375
B64
INTELL
DECISION
NUC/PWR
WAR

GUTMANN P.M.,ECONOMIC GROWTH: AN AMERICAN PROBLEM.
USA+45 FINAN R+D...POLICY NAT/COMP ANTHOL BIBLIOG
20. PAGE 24 G0463
B64
WEALTH
ECO/DEV
CAP/ISM
ORD/FREE

INST D'ETUDE POL L'U GRENOBLE,ADMINISTRATION
TRADITIONELLE ET PLANIFICATION REGIONALE. FRANCE
LAW POL/PAR PROB/SOLV ADJUST RIGID/FLEX...CHARTS
ANTHOL BIBLIOG T 20 REFORMERS. PAGE 28 G0546
B64
ADMIN
MUNIC
PLAN
CREATE

OSSENBECK F.J.,OPEN SPACE AND PEACE. CHINA/COM FUT
USA+45 USSR LAW PROB/SOLV TEC/DEV EDU/PROP NEUTRAL
PEACE...AUD/VIS ANTHOL 20. PAGE 43 G0850
B64
SPACE
ORD/FREE
DIPLOM
CREATE

SCHWARTZ M.D.,CONFERENCE ON SPACE SCIENCE AND SPACE
LAW. FUT COM/IND NAT/G FORCES ACT/RES PLAN BUDGET
DIPLOM NUC/PWR WEAPON...POLICY ANTHOL 20. PAGE 50
G0983
B64
SPACE
LAW
PEACE
TEC/DEV

TAUBENFELD H.J.,SPACE AND SOCIETY. USA+45 LAW
FORCES CREATE TEC/DEV ADJUD CONTROL COST PEACE
...PREDICT ANTHOL 20. PAGE 54 G1057
B64
SPACE
SOCIETY
ADJUST
DIPLOM

US AIR FORCE ACADEMY ASSEMBLY,OUTER SPACE: FINAL
REPORT APRIL 1-4, 1964. FUT USA+45 WOR+45 LAW
DELIB/GP CONFER ARMS/CONT WAR PEACE ATTIT MORAL
...ANTHOL 20 NASA. PAGE 56 G1104
B64
SPACE
CIVMIL/REL
NUC/PWR
DIPLOM

WIRTH L.,ON CITIES AND SOCIAL LIFE: SELECTED
PAPERS. PLAN PROB/SOLV RACE/REL CONSEN ATTIT
HABITAT PERSON...POLICY SOC CONCPT ANTHOL BIBLIOG
20. PAGE 64 G1249
B64
GEN/LAWS
SOCIETY
NEIGH
STRUCT

WHITE HOUSE CONFERENCE ON INTERNATIONAL
COOPERATION(VOL.II). SPACE WOR+45 EXTR/IND INT/ORG
LABOR WORKER NUC/PWR PEACE AGE/Y...CENSUS ANTHOL 20
RESOURCE/N URBAN/RNWL PUB/TRANS. PAGE 1 G0019
B65
R+D
CONFER
TEC/DEV
DIPLOM

ANDERSON C.A.,EDUCATION AND ECONOMIC DEVELOPMENT.
INDUS R+D SCHOOL TEC/DEV ECO/TAC EDU/PROP AGE
HEREDITY PERCEPT SKILL 20. PAGE 3 G0056
B65
ANTHOL
ECO/DEV
ECO/UNDEV
WORKER

ATOMIC INDUSTRIAL FORUM,SAFEGUARDS AGAINST
DIVERSION OF NUCLEAR MATERIALS FROM PEACEFUL TO
MILITARY PURPOSES. WOR+45 DELIB/GP FORCES PLAN
DIPLOM CONFER PEACE...ANTHOL 20 IAEA. PAGE 4 G0081
B65
NUC/PWR
CIVMIL/REL
INSPECT
CONTROL

BAILEY S.K.,AMERICAN POLITICS AND GOVERNMENT.
USA+45 CONSTN FINAN LABOR POL/PAR DIPLOM ADMIN WAR
INGP/REL RACE/REL NEW/LIB 20 SUPREME/CT PRESIDENT
CONGRESS. PAGE 4 G0084
B65
ANTHOL
LEGIS
PWR

BARISH N.N.,MANAGEMENT SCIENCES IN THE EMERGING
COUNTRIES. AFR CHINA/COM WOR+45 FINAN INDUS PLAN
PRODUC HABITAT...ANTHOL 20. PAGE 5 G0093
B65
ECO/UNDEV
OP/RES
MGT
TEC/DEV

CORDIER A.W.,THE QUEST FOR PEACE. WOR+45 NAT/G PLAN
BAL/PWR ECO/TAC ARMS/CONT NUC/PWR PWR...ANTHOL UN
COLD/WAR. PAGE 13 G0256
B65
PEACE
DIPLOM
POLICY
INT/ORG

NATIONAL ACADEMY OF SCIENCES,BASIC RESEARCH AND
NATIONAL GOALS. R+D ACADEM DELIB/GP PLAN EDU/PROP
...POLICY HEAL PHIL/SCI PSY SOC ANTHOL 20 CONGRESS
HOUSE/REP HS/SCIASTR. PAGE 41 G0809
B65
LEGIS
BUDGET
NAT/G
CREATE

REISS A.J. JR.,SCHOOLS IN A CHANGING SOCIETY.
CULTURE PROB/SOLV INSPECT DOMIN CONFER INGP/REL
RACE/REL AGE/C AGE/Y ALL/VALS...ANTHOL SOC/INTEG 20
NEWYORK/C. PAGE 46 G0912
B65
SCHOOL
EX/STRUC
ADJUST
ADMIN

SINGER J.D.,HUMAN BEHAVIOR AND INTERNATIONAL
POLITICS* CONTRIBUTIONS FROM THE SOCIAL-
PSYCHOLOGICAL SCIENCES. ACT/RES PLAN EDU/PROP ADMIN
KNOWL...DECISION PSY SOC NET/THEORY HYPO/EXP
LAB/EXP SOC/EXP GEN/METH ANTHOL BIBLIOG. PAGE 51
G1006
B65
DIPLOM
PHIL/SCI
QUANT
SIMUL

SCHWEBEL M.,"BEHAVIORAL SCIENCE AND HUMAN
SURVIVAL." FORCES ARMS/CONT COERCE NUC/PWR WAR
GP/REL NAT/LISM PERCEPT...POLICY PSY ANTHOL
BIBLIOG/A 20 COLD/WAR. PAGE 50 G0984
C65
PEACE
ACT/RES
DIPLOM
HEAL

US AIR FORCE ACADEMY,"AMERICAN DEFENSE POLICY." COM
INT/ORG TEC/DEV FOR/AID ARMS/CONT DETER NUC/PWR
...POLICY DECISION CONCPT ANTHOL BIBLIOG/A 20
COLD/WAR NATO. PAGE 56 G1103
C65
PLAN
FORCES
WAR
COERCE

AMERICAN ASSEMBLY COLUMBIA U,A WORLD OF NUCLEAR
POWERS? FUT WOR+45 ECO/DEV BAL/PWR ECO/TAC CONTROL
RISK EFFICIENCY ATTIT PWR...METH/COMP ANTHOL 20.
PAGE 3 G0049
B66
NUC/PWR
DIPLOM
TEC/DEV
ARMS/CONT

BOLTON R.E.,DEFENSE AND DISARMAMENT: THE ECONOMICS
OF TRANSITION. USA+45 R+D FORCES PLAN LOBBY DETER
B66
ARMS/CONT
POLICY

WAR COST PEACE...ANTHOL BIBLIOG 20. PAGE 8 G0150
INDUS

BOWEN H.R.,AUTOMATION AND ECONOMIC PROGRESS.
EUR+WWI USA+45 ECO/DEV INCOME ORD/FREE WEALTH
...POLICY ANTHOL 20. PAGE 8 G0160
B66
AUTOMAT
TEC/DEV
WORKER
LEISURE

FREIDEL F.,AMERICAN ISSUES IN THE TWENTIETH
CENTURY. SOCIETY FINAN ECO/TAC FOR/AID CONTROL
NUC/PWR WAR RACE/REL PEACE ATTIT...ANTHOL T 20
WILSON/W ROOSEVLT/F KENNEDY/JF TRUMAN/HS. PAGE 20
G0391
B66
DIPLOM
POLICY
NAT/G
ORD/FREE

GRUNEWALD D.,PUBLIC POLICY AND THE MODERN
COOPERATION: SELECTED READINGS. USA+45 LAW MARKET
VOL/ASSN CAP/ISM INT/TRADE CENTRAL OWN...SOC ANTHOL
20. PAGE 23 G0458
B66
LG/CO
POLICY
NAT/G
CONTROL

RUPPENTHAL K.M.,TRANSPORTATION AND TOMORROW. FUT
SPACE USA+45 SEA AIR FORCES TEC/DEV INT/TRADE
...ANTHOL 20 RAILROAD. PAGE 48 G0946
B66
DIST/IND
PLAN
CIVMIL/REL
PREDICT

WOLFERS A.,THE UNITED STATES IN A DISARMED WORLD: A
STUDY OF THE US OUTLINE FOR GENERAL AND COMPLETE
DISARMAMENT. USA+45 NAT/G CONTROL DETER NUC/PWR
EFFICIENCY...ANTHOL 20. PAGE 64 G1255
B66
ARMS/CONT
POLICY
FORCES
PEACE

ALEXANDER L.M.,THE LAW OF THE SEA: OFFSHORE
BOUNDARIES AND ZONES. WOR+45 INT/ORG TEC/DEV
CONTROL PRIVIL HABITAT SOVEREIGN...CON/ANAL CHARTS
ANTHOL. PAGE 2 G0037
B67
SEA
INT/LAW
EXTR/IND

CHARLESWORTH J.C.,CONTEMPORARY POLITICAL ANALYSIS.
INTELL...DECISION METH/CNCPT MATH STYLE CON/ANAL
GAME ANTHOL 20. PAGE 11 G0222
B67
R+D
IDEA/COMP
CONCPT
METH/COMP

COLEMAN J.R.,THE CHANGING AMERICAN ECONOMY. USA+45
AGRI FINAN LABOR FOR/AID INT/TRADE AUTOMAT GP/REL
INGP/REL ANTHOL. PAGE 13 G0243
B67
BUDGET
ECO/TAC
ECO/DEV
WEALTH

CROSSON F.J.,SCIENCE AND CONTEMPORARY SOCIETY. FUT
WOR+45 SECT CREATE PROB/SOLV...HUM PREDICT TREND
IDEA/COMP ANTHOL. PAGE 14 G0263
B67
PHIL/SCI
SOCIETY
TEC/DEV
CONCPT

ELDREDGE H.W.,TAMING MEGALOPOLIS: HOW TO MANAGE AN
URBANIZED WORLD. WOR+45 SOCIETY ECO/DEV ECO/UNDEV
NAT/G COMPUTER CREATE PARTIC EFFICIENCY WEALTH
...MGT ANTHOL. PAGE 17 G0342
B67
MUNIC
TEC/DEV
PLAN
PROB/SOLV

GARCIA ROBLES A.,THE DENUCLEARIZATION OF LATIN
AMERICA (TRANS. BY MARJORIE URQUIDI). LAW PLAN
DIPLOM...ANTHOL 20 TREATY UN. PAGE 21 G0409
B67
NUC/PWR
ARMS/CONT
L/A+17C
INT/ORG

LERNER D.,COMMUNICATION AND CHANGE IN DEVELOPING
COUNTRIES. CHINA/COM INDIA PHILIPPINE COM/IND
CREATE TEC/DEV...ANTHOL 20. PAGE 33 G0659
B67
EDU/PROP
ORD/FREE
PERCEPT
ECO/UNDEV

ROACH J.R.,THE UNITED STATES AND THE ATLANTIC
COMMUNITY: ISSUES AND PROSPECTS. WOR+45 TEC/DEV
ECO/TAC COLONIAL REGION PEACE ROLE...ANTHOL NATO
COLD/WAR EEC. PAGE 47 G0925
B67
INT/ORG
POLICY
ADJUST
DIPLOM

WARNER W.L.,THE EMERGENT AMERICAN SOCIETY VOL I,
LARGE-SCALE ORGANIZATIONS. USA+45 USA-45 ACADEM
PROF/ORG SCHOOL SECT EX/STRUC TEC/DEV GP/REL
...TREND CHARTS. PAGE 62 G1215
B67
ANTHOL
NAT/G
LABOR
LG/CO

ASIAN STUDIES CENTER,FOUR ARTICLES ON POPULATION
AND FAMILY LIFE IN TAIWAN (ASIAN STUDIES PAPERS,
REPRINT SERIES NO. 2). CULTURE STRATA ECO/UNDEV
AGRI INDUS R+D KIN MUNIC...GEOG SOC CHARTS 20.
PAGE 4 G0072
N67
ASIA
FAM
CENSUS
ANTHOL

GALLAHER A. JR.,PERSPECTIVES IN DEVELOPMENTAL
B68
TECHNIC

CHANGE. MUNIC PLAN INSPECT EDU/PROP...POLICY   TEC/DEV
DECISION GEOG PSY SOC IDEA/COMP ANTHOL 20   PROB/SOLV
MODERNIZE. PAGE 21 G0405   CREATE

ANTHONY R.N. G0061

ANTHROPOLOGY, CULTURAL....SEE SOC

ANTHROPOLOGY, PSYCHOLOGICAL....SEE PSY

ANTI/SEMIT....ANTI-SEMITISM; SEE ALSO JEWS, GP/REL

ANTIBALLISTIC MISSILE DEFENSE SYSTEMS....SEE ABM/DEFSYS

ANTI-SEMITISM....SEE JEWS, GP/REL, ANTI/SEMIT

ANTI-TRUST ACTIONS....SEE MONOPOLY, INDUS, CONTROL

ANXIETY....SEE ANOMIE

APACHE....APACHE INDIANS

APARTHEID....APARTHEID

APPADORAI A. G0062

APPALACHIA

APPELLATE COURT SYSTEM....SEE CT/APPEALS, CT/SYS

APPORT....DELINEATION OF LEGISLATIVE DISTRICTS

                                                              C54
ZELLER B.."AMERICAN STATE LEGISLATURES: REPORT ON   REPRESENT
THE COMMITTEE ON AMERICAN LEGISLATURES." CONSTN   LEGIS
POL/PAR EX/STRUC CONFER ADMIN CONTROL EXEC LOBBY   PROVS
ROUTINE GOV/REL...POLICY BIBLIOG 20. PAGE 65 G1267   APPORT

APRA....ALIANZA POPULAR REVOLUCIONARIA AMERICANA, A PERUVIAN
    POLITICAL PARTY

APSA....AMERICAN POLITICAL SCIENCE ASSOCIATION

APT/TEST....APTITUDE TESTS

                                                              B52
CURRENT TRENDS IN PSYCHOLOGY.PSYCHOLOGY IN THE   NAT/G
WORLD EMERGENCY. USA+45 CONSULT FORCES ACT/RES PLAN PSY
SKILL...DECISION OBS APT/TEST KNO/TEST PERS/TEST
TREND CHARTS 20. PAGE 14 G0266

APTHEKER H. G0063

APTITUDE TESTS....SEE APT/TEST

AQUINAS/T....SAINT THOMAS AQUINAS

ARA....AREA REDEVELOPMENT ACT

ARABIA/SOU....SOUTH ARABIA

ARABS....ARAB WORLD, INCLUDING ITS CULTURE

ARBITRATION....SEE DELIB/GP, CONSULT, AND FUNCTIONAL GROUP
    CONCERNED (E.G., LABOR)

AREA STUDIES....SEE NAT/COMP

ARGENTINA....SEE ALSO L/A&17C

                                                              S65
TENDLER J.D.."TECHNOLOGY AND ECONOMIC DEVELOPMENT*   BRAZIL
THE CASE OF HYDRO VS THERMAL POWER." CONSTRUC   INDUS
DIST/IND CREATE TEC/DEV INT/TRADE CENTRAL PWR SKILL ECO/UNDEV
WEALTH...MGT NAT/COMP ARGEN. PAGE 54 G1063

ARGYRIS C. G0064

ARISTOCRATIC....SEE TRADIT, STRATA, ELITES

ARISTOTLE....ARISTOTLE

ARIZONA....ARIZONA

ARKANSAS....ARKANSAS

ARMED FORCES....SEE FORCES

ARMS CONTROL....SEE ARMS/CONT, ACD

ARMS CONTROL AND DISARMAMENT AGENCY (U.S.)....SEE ACD

ARMS/CONT....ARMS CONTROL, DISARMAMENT

                                                              N
FULLER G.A..DEMOBILIZATION: A SELECTED LIST OF   BIBLIOG/A
REFERENCES. USA+45 LAW AGRI LABOR WORKER ECO/TAC   INDUS
RATION RECEIVE EDU/PROP ROUTINE ARMS/CONT ALL/VALS   FORCES
20. PAGE 20 G0398   NAT/G

                                                              N
JOURNAL OF CONFLICT RESOLUTION. FUT WOR+45 INT/ORG   BIBLIOG/A
NAT/G FORCES CREATE PROB/SOLV ARMS/CONT NUC/PWR   DIPLOM
WEAPON SOC. PAGE 1 G0002   WAR

                                                              N
FOREIGN AFFAIRS. SPACE WOR+45 WOR-45 CULTURE   BIBLIOG
ECO/UNDEV FINAN NAT/G TEC/DEV INT/TRADE ARMS/CONT   DIPLOM
NUC/PWR...POLICY 20 UN EURATOM ECSC EEC. PAGE 1   INT/ORG
G0004   INT/LAW

                                                              N
AIR UNIVERSITY LIBRARY.INDEX TO MILITARY   BIBLIOG/A
PERIODICALS. FUT SPACE WOR+45 REGION ARMS/CONT   FORCES
NUC/PWR WAR PEACE INT/LAW. PAGE 2 G0032   NAT/G
                                                     DIPLOM

                                                              N
UNITED NATIONS.OFFICIAL RECORDS OF THE UNITED   ARMS/CONT
NATIONS' ATOMIC ENERGY COMMISSION - DISARMAMENT   INT/ORG
COMMISSION. WOR+45 TEC/DEV DIPLOM WRITING NUC/PWR   DELIB/GP
20 UN. PAGE 55 G1092   CONFER

                                                              N19
MEZERIK A.G..ATOM TESTS AND RADIATION HAZARDS   NUC/PWR
(PAMPHLET). WOR+45 INT/ORG DIPLOM DETER 20 UN   ARMS/CONT
TREATY. PAGE 39 G0761   CONFER
                                                     HEALTH

                                                              N19
MEZERIK A.G..INTERNATIONAL POLICY 1965 (PAMPHLET).   DIPLOM
KASHMIR S/ASIA SPACE USA+45 VIETNAM WOR+45   INT/ORG
ARMS/CONT RACE/REL DISCRIM PEACE PWR 20 UN. PAGE 39 POLICY
G0762   WAR

                                                              N19
ZLOTNICK M..WEAPONS IN SPACE (PAMPHLET). FUT WOR+45 SPACE
TEC/DEV DIPLOM ARMS/CONT CIVMIL/REL PEACE HABITAT   WEAPON
...CONCPT NEW/IDEA CHARTS. PAGE 65 G1268   NUC/PWR
                                                     WAR

                                                              B34
EINSTEIN A..THE WORLD AS I SEE IT. WOR-45 INTELL   SOCIETY
R+D INT/ORG NAT/G SECT VOL/ASSN FORCES CREATE   PHIL/SCI
EDU/PROP LEGIT ARMS/CONT WAR WEAPON NAT/LISM   DIPLOM
ALL/VALS...POLICY CONCPT 20. PAGE 17 G0337   PACIFISM

                                                              B35
FOREIGN AFFAIRS BIBLIOGRAPHY: A SELECTED AND   BIBLIOG/A
ANNOTATED LIST OF BOOKS ON INTERNATIONAL RELATIONS   DIPLOM
1919-1962 (4 VOLS.). CONSTN FORCES COLONIAL   INT/ORG
ARMS/CONT WAR NAT/LISM PEACE ATTIT DRIVE...POLICY
INT/LAW 20. PAGE 1 G0011

                                                              B39
FULLER G.H..A SELECTED LIST OF REFERENCES ON THE   BIBLIOG
EXPANSION OF THE US NAVY, 1933-1939 (PAMPHLET).   FORCES
MOD/EUR USA-45 NAT/G PLAN DIPLOM DOMIN RISK   WEAPON
ARMS/CONT EQUILIB PWR 20 NAVY. PAGE 20 G0399   WAR

                                                              B40
FULLER G.H..SELECTED LIST OF RECENT REFERENCES ON   BIBLIOG
AMERICAN NATIONAL DEFENSE (PAMPHLET). USA-45 FINAN   CIVMIL/REL
NAT/G ARMS/CONT WAR GOV/REL CENTRAL COST PEACE PWR   FORCES
20. PAGE 20 G0400   WEAPON

                                                              B41
FULLER G.H..DEFENSE FINANCING: A SELECTED LIST OF   BIBLIOG/A
REFERENCES (PAMPHLET). MOD/EUR USA-45 ECO/DEV NAT/G FINAN
DELIB/GP RATION ARMS/CONT WEAPON COST PEACE PWR 20   FORCES
CONGRESS. PAGE 20 G0401   BUDGET

                                                              B41
FULLER G.H..A LIST OF BIBLIOGRAPHIES ON QUESTIONS   BIBLIOG/A
RELATING TO NATIONAL DEFENSE (PAMPHLET). USA-45   FORCES
NAT/G ARMS/CONT WAR GOV/REL COST PEACE 20. PAGE 20   CIVMIL/REL
G0402   WEAPON

                                                              B42
FULLER G.H..DEFENSE FINANCING: A SUPPLEMENTARY LIST BIBLIOG/A
OF REFERENCES (PAMPHLET). CANADA UK USA-45 ECO/DEV   FINAN
NAT/G DELIB/GP BUDGET ADJUD ARMS/CONT WEAPON COST   FORCES
PEACE PWR 20 AUSTRAL CHINJAP CONGRESS. PAGE 21   DIPLOM
G0403

                                                              B44
FULLER G.H..MILITARY GOVERNMENT: A LIST OF   BIBLIOG
REFERENCES (A PAMPHLET). ITALY UK USA-45 WOR-45 LAW DIPLOM
FORCES DOMIN ADMIN ARMS/CONT ORD/FREE PWR   CIVMIL/REL
...DECISION 20 CHINJAP. PAGE 21 G0404   SOVEREIGN

G0067   DIPLOM

B44
MATTHEWS M.A.,INTERNATIONAL POLICE (PAMPHLET).   BIBLIOG
WOR-45 DIPLOM ARMS/CONT WAR 20. PAGE 37 G0722   INT/ORG
                                                     FORCES
                                                     PEACE

B46
BRODIE B.,THE OBSOLETE WEAPON: ATOMIC POWER AND   INT/ORG
WORLD ORDER. COM USA+45 USSR WOR-45 DELIB/GP PLAN   TEC/DEV
ORD/FREE PWR...CONCPT TIME/SEQ TREND UN 20. PAGE 9   ARMS/CONT
G0171   NUC/PWR

L46
MASTERS D.,"ONE WORLD OR NONE." FUT WOR-45 INTELL   POLICY
INT/ORG ACT/RES EDU/PROP DETER ATTIT RIGID/FLEX   PHIL/SCI
SUPEGO KNOWL...STAT TREND ORG/CHARTS 20. PAGE 36   ARMS/CONT
G0719   NUC/PWR

B47
SOCIAL SCIENCE RESEARCH COUN,PUBLIC REACTION TO THE ATTIT
ATOMIC BOMB AND WORLD AFFAIRS. SOCIETY CONFER   NUC/PWR
ARMS/CONT...STAT QU SAMP CHARTS 20. PAGE 52 G1019   DIPLOM
                                                     WAR

B48
BRADLEY D.,NO PLACE TO HIDE. USA+45 SOCIETY NAT/G   R+D
FORCES TEC/DEV EDU/PROP DETER PEACE BIO/SOC   LAB/EXP
ALL/VALS...POLICY PHIL/SCI OBS RECORD SAMP BIOG   ARMS/CONT
GEN/METH COLD/WAR 20. PAGE 8 G0162   NUC/PWR

S49
SOUERS S.W.,"POLICY FORMULATION FOR NATIONAL   DELIB/GP
SECURITY." EX/STRUC FORCES PROB/SOLV DIPLOM CONFER   CHIEF
EXEC ARMS/CONT DETER NUC/PWR GOV/REL PEACE   DECISION
COLD/WAR. PAGE 52 G1022   POLICY

B53
BRETTON H.L.,STRESEMANN AND THE REVISION OF   POLICY
VERSAILLES: A FIGHT FOR REASON. EUR+WWI GERMANY   DIPLOM
FORCES BUDGET ARMS/CONT WAR SUPEGO...BIBLIOG 20   BIOG
TREATY VERSAILLES STRESEMN/G. PAGE 9 G0167

B54
KENWORTHY L.S.,FREE AND INEXPENSIVE MATERIALS ON   BIBLIOG/A
WORLD AFFAIRS (PAMPHLET). WOR+45 CULTURE ECO/UNDEV   NAT/G
INT/TRADE ARMS/CONT NUC/PWR UN. PAGE 30 G0594   INT/ORG
                                                     DIPLOM

B54
REYNOLDS P.A.,BRITISH FOREIGN POLICY IN THE INTER-   DIPLOM
WAR YEARS. CZECHOSLVK GERMANY POLAND UK USA-45   POLICY
POL/PAR FORCES ECO/TAC ARMS/CONT WAR ATTIT 20.   NAT/G
PAGE 46 G0915

B54
US DEPARTMENT OF STATE,PUBLICATIONS OF THE   BIBLIOG
DEPARTMENT OF STATE, OCTOBER 1,1929 TO JANUARY 1,   DIPLOM
1953. AGRI INT/ORG FORCES FOR/AID EDU/PROP
ARMS/CONT NUC/PWR ATTIT 20 DEPT/STATE OAS UN NATO.
PAGE 57 G1122

B55
DAVIS E.,TWO MINUTES TO MIDNIGHT. WOR+45 PLAN   NUC/PWR
CONTROL NEUTRAL ARMS/CONT ATTIT ORD/FREE...PSY 20   WAR
COLD/WAR. PAGE 14 G0277   DETER
                                                     DIPLOM

B55
MOCH J.,HUMAN FOLLY: DISARM OR PERISH. USA+45   FUT
WOR+45 SOCIETY INT/ORG NAT/G ACT/RES EDU/PROP ATTIT DELIB/GP
PERSON KNOWL ORD/FREE PWR...MAJORIT TOT/POP   ARMS/CONT
COLD/WAR 20. PAGE 39 G0776   NUC/PWR

B55
OPPENHEIMER R.,THE OPEN MIND. USA+45 WOR+45 NAT/G   CREATE
DELIB/GP DETER MORAL ORD/FREE...MYTH GEN/LAWS 20.   PWR
PAGE 43 G0842   ARMS/CONT
                                                     NUC/PWR

B56
BLACKETT P.M.S.,ATOMIC WEAPONS AND EAST-WEST   FORCES
RELATIONS. FUT WOR+45 INT/ORG DELIB/GP COERCE ATTIT PWR
RIGID/FLEX KNOWL...RELATIV HIST/WRIT TREND GEN/METH ARMS/CONT
COLD/WAR 20. PAGE 7 G0138   NUC/PWR

B57
KISSINGER H.A.,NUCLEAR WEAPONS AND FOREIGN POLICY.   PLAN
FUT USA+45 WOR+45 INT/ORG FORCES ACT/RES TEC/DEV   DETER
DIPLOM ARMS/CONT COERCE ATTIT KNOWL PWR...DECISION   NUC/PWR
GEOG CHARTS 20. PAGE 31 G0602

B58
ARON R.,ON WAR: ATOMIC WEAPONS AND GLOBAL DIPLOMACY ARMS/CONT
(TRANS. BY TERENCE KILMARTIN). WOR+45 SOCIETY   NUC/PWR
FORCES BAL/PWR WAR WEAPON PERSON...SOC 20. PAGE 4   COERCE

B58
GAVIN J.M.,WAR AND PEACE IN THE SPACE AGE. SPACE   WAR
USA+45 USSR FORCES PLAN TEC/DEV BAL/PWR DIPLOM   DETER
ARMS/CONT WEAPON CIVMIL/REL...CHARTS GP/COMP 20   NUC/PWR
NATO COLD/WAR. PAGE 21 G0414   PEACE

B58
NATIONAL PLANNING ASSOCIATION,1970 WITHOUT ARMS   ARMS/CONT
CONTROL (PAMPHLET). WOR+45 PROB/SOLV TEC/DEV DIPLOM ORD/FREE
CONFER DETER NUC/PWR WAR...CHARTS 20 COLD/WAR.   WEAPON
PAGE 41 G0810   PREDICT

B58
NOEL-BAKER D.,THE ARMS RACE. WOR+45 NAT/G DELIB/GP   FUT
ACT/RES TEC/DEV EDU/PROP NUC/PWR ATTIT KNOWL PWR   INT/ORG
...CONCPT OBS LEAGUE/NAT 20 COLD/WAR. PAGE 42 G0823 ARMS/CONT
                                                     PEACE

B58
ROCKEFELLER BROTH FUND INC,INTERNATIONAL SECURITY - NUC/PWR
THE MILITARY ASPECT. USA+45 INT/ORG NAT/G BUDGET   DETER
ARMS/CONT WAR WEAPON PEACE ORD/FREE 20 NATO.   FORCES
PAGE 47 G0932   DIPLOM

B58
US DEPARTMENT OF STATE,PUBLICATIONS OF THE   BIBLIOG
DEPARTMENT OF STATE, JANUARY 1,1953 TO DECEMBER 31, DIPLOM
1957. AGRI INT/ORG FORCES FOR/AID EDU/PROP
ARMS/CONT NUC/PWR ATTIT 20 DEPT/STATE OAS UN NATO.
PAGE 57 G1123

S58
BURNS A.L.,"THE NEW WEAPONS AND INTERNATIONAL   TEC/DEV
RELATIONS." SPACE WOR+45 NAT/G VOL/ASSN FORCES   ARMS/CONT
NUC/PWR 20. PAGE 10 G0190   DIPLOM

S58
HUNTINGTON S.P.,"ARMS RACES: PREREQUISITES AND   FORCES
RESULTS." EUR+WWI MOD/EUR USA+45 WOR+45 WOR-45   PWR
NAT/G TEC/DEV BAL/PWR COERCE DETER ATTIT...POLICY   ARMS/CONT
TREND 20. PAGE 27 G0537

S58
SINGER J.D.,"THREAT PERCEPTION AND THE ARMAMENT   PERCEPT
TENSION DILEMMA." WOR+45 WOR-45 ELITES INT/ORG   ARMS/CONT
NAT/G DELIB/GP PLAN LEGIT COERCE DETER ATTIT   BAL/PWR
RIGID/FLEX PWR...DECISION PSY 20. PAGE 51 G1002

S58
THOMPSON K.W.,"NATIONAL SECURITY IN A NUCLEAR AGE." FORCES
USA+45 WOR+45 SOCIETY INT/ORG NAT/G TOP/EX DIPLOM   PWR
DOMIN EDU/PROP LEGIT ARMS/CONT COERCE ORD/FREE   BAL/PWR
...TREND STERTYP TOT/POP VAL/FREE COLD/WAR 20.
PAGE 54 G1068

B59
GODDARD V.,THE ENIGMA OF MENACE. WOR+45 SECT LEAD   PEACE
NUC/PWR WAR WEAPON CHOOSE PERSON PWR...POLICY   ARMS/CONT
PHIL/SCI PACIFIST 20 COLD/WAR. PAGE 22 G0423   DIPLOM
                                                     ATTIT

B59
HUGHES E.M.,AMERICA THE VINCIBLE. USA+45 FOR/AID   ORD/FREE
ARMS/CONT NUC/PWR PERS/REL RATIONAL ATTIT ALL/VALS   DIPLOM
20 COLD/WAR. PAGE 27 G0534   WAR

B59
LANG D.,FROM HIROSHIMA TO THE MOON: CHRONICLES OF   NUC/PWR
LIFE IN THE ATOMIC AGE. USA+45 OP/RES CONTROL   SPACE
ARMS/CONT WAR CIVMIL/REL PEACE HABITAT MORAL PWR   HEALTH
...OBS INT 20 AEC. PAGE 32 G0633   TEC/DEV

B59
MIKSCHE F.O.,THE FAILURE OF ATOMIC STRATEGY. COM   ACT/RES
EUR+WWI INTELL POL/PAR FORCES PLAN ECO/TAC NUC/PWR   ORD/FREE
ATTIT DRIVE RIGID/FLEX PWR...DECISION GEOG PSY   DIPLOM
CONCPT RECORD TREND CHARTS VAL/FREE 20. PAGE 39   ARMS/CONT
G0766

B59
RUSSELL B.,COMMON SENSE AND NUCLEAR WARFARE. WOR+45 ORD/FREE
INTELL SOCIETY STRATA NAT/G TOP/EX EDU/PROP ATTIT   ARMS/CONT
PERSON KNOWL MORAL PWR...POLICY CONCPT MYTH   NUC/PWR
CON/ANAL COLD/WAR 20. PAGE 48 G0948

B59
WARD B.,5 IDEAS THAT CHANGE THE WORLD. WOR+45   ECO/UNDEV
WOR-45 SOCIETY STRUCT AGRI INDUS INT/ORG NAT/G   ALL/VALS
FORCES ACT/RES ARMS/CONT TOTALISM ATTIT DRIVE   NAT/LISM
GEN/LAWS. PAGE 62 G1210   COLONIAL

L59
BURNS A.L.,"POWER POLITICS AND THE GROWING NUCLEAR   FORCES
CLUB." FUT WOR+45 TEC/DEV EXEC ARMS/CONT COERCE   BAL/PWR

DETER...DECISION HYPO/EXP 20. PAGE 10 G0192   NUC/PWR

S59
CORY R.H. JR.,"INTERNATIONAL INSPECTION FROM   STRUCT
PROPOSALS TO REALIZATION." WOR+45 TEC/DEV ECO/TAC   PSY
ADJUD ORD/FREE PWR WEALTH...RECORD VAL/FREE 20.   ARMS/CONT
PAGE 13 G0258   NUC/PWR

S59
SIMONS H.,"WORLD-WIDE CAPABILITIES FOR PRODUCTION   TEC/DEV
AND CONTROL OF NUCLEAR WEAPONS." FUT WOR+45 INDUS   ARMS/CONT
INT/ORG NAT/G ECO/TAC ATTIT PWR SKILL...TREND   NUC/PWR
CHARTS VAL/FREE 20. PAGE 51 G1001

B60
ARMS CONTROL. FUT UNIV WOR+45 INTELL R+D INT/ORG   DELIB/GP
NAT/G VOL/ASSN CONSULT CREATE EDU/PROP PEACE...HUM   ORD/FREE
GEN/LAWS TOT/POP 20. PAGE 1 G0015   ARMS/CONT
                                                        NUC/PWR

B60
APTHEKER H.,DISARMAMENT AND THE AMERICAN ECONOMY: A   MARXIST
SYMPOSIUM. FUT USA+45 ECO/DEV DIST/IND FINAN INDUS   ARMS/CONT
PROC/MFG LABOR NAT/G POL/PAR CONSULT PLAN CAP/ISM
INT/TRADE PEACE ATTIT MORAL WEALTH...TREND GEN/LAWS
TOT/POP 20. PAGE 3 G0063

B60
BARNET R.,WHO WANTS DISARMAMENT. COM EUR+WWI USA+45   PLAN
USSR INT/ORG NAT/G BAL/PWR DIPLOM EDU/PROP COERCE   FORCES
DETER NUC/PWR WAR WEAPON ATTIT PWR...TIME/SEQ   ARMS/CONT
COLD/WAR CONGRESS 20. PAGE 5 G0096

B60
CHASE S.,LIVE AND LET LIVE. USA+45 ECO/DEV   NAT/G
PROB/SOLV TEC/DEV ECO/TAC ARMS/CONT NUC/PWR WAR   DIPLOM
NAT/LISM PEACE...GEOG TREND 20 COLD/WAR. PAGE 11   SOCIETY
G0223   TASK

B60
EINSTEIN A.,EINSTEIN ON PEACE. FUT WOR+45 WOR-45   INT/ORG
SOCIETY PLAN BAL/PWR CAP/ISM DIPLOM ARMS/CONT   ATTIT
DETER NAT/LISM...POLICY RELATIV HUM PHIL/SCI CONCPT   NUC/PWR
BIOG COLD/WAR LEAGUE/NAT NAZI. PAGE 17 G0338   PEACE

B60
MCCLELLAND C.A.,NUCLEAR WEAPONS, MISSILES, AND   DIPLOM
FUTURE WAR: PROBLEM FOR THE SIXTIES. WOR+45 FORCES   NUC/PWR
ARMS/CONT DETER MARXISM...POLICY ANTHOL COLD/WAR.   WAR
PAGE 37 G0729   WEAPON

B60
US DEPARTMENT OF THE ARMY,DISARMAMENT: A   BIBLIOG/A
BIBLIOGRAPHIC RECORD: 1916-1960. DETER WAR WEAPON   ARMS/CONT
PEACE 20 UN LEAGUE/NAT COLD/WAR NATO. PAGE 57 G1128   NUC/PWR
                                                        DIPLOM

L60
BRENNAN D.G.,"SETTING AND GOALS OF ARMS CONTROL."   FORCES
FUT USA+45 USSR WOR+45 INTELL INT/ORG NAT/G   COERCE
VOL/ASSN CONSULT PLAN DIPLOM ECO/TAC ADMIN KNOWL   ARMS/CONT
PWR...POLICY CONCPT TREND COLD/WAR 20. PAGE 8 G0164   DETER

L60
HOLTON G.,"ARMS CONTROL." FUT WOR+45 CULTURE   ACT/RES
INT/ORG NAT/G FORCES TOP/EX PLAN EDU/PROP COERCE   CONSULT
ATTIT RIGID/FLEX ORD/FREE...POLICY PHIL/SCI SOC   ARMS/CONT
TREND COLD/WAR. PAGE 27 G0524   NUC/PWR

L60
JACOB P.E.,"THE DISARMAMENT CONSENSUS." USA+45 USSR   DELIB/GP
WOR+45 INT/ORG NAT/G ACT/RES TEC/DEV BAL/PWR   ATTIT
EDU/PROP ADMIN COERCE DETER NUC/PWR CONSEN   ARMS/CONT
RIGID/FLEX PWR...CONCPT RECORD CHARTS COLD/WAR 20.
PAGE 28 G0552

S60
BRODY R.A.,"DETERRENCE STRATEGIES: AN ANNOTATED   BIBLIOG/A
BIBLIOGRAPHY." WOR+45 PLAN ARMS/CONT NUC/PWR WAR   FORCES
WEAPON DECISION. PAGE 9 G0173   DETER
                                                        DIPLOM

S60
DOTY P.M.,"THE ROLE OF THE SMALLER POWERS." FUT   PWR
WOR+45 NAT/G TEC/DEV BAL/PWR DOMIN LEGIT CHOOSE   POLICY
DISPL DRIVE RESPECT...DECISION 20. PAGE 16 G0310   ARMS/CONT
                                                        NUC/PWR

S60
DOUGHERTY J.E.,"KEY TO SECURITY: DISARMAMENT OR   FORCES
ARMS STABILITY." COM USA+45 USSR INT/ORG NAT/G   ORD/FREE
CREATE EDU/PROP COERCE DETER ATTIT PWR...DECISION   ARMS/CONT
CONCPT MYTH NEW/IDEA TREND 20 COLD/WAR. PAGE 16   NUC/PWR
G0311

S60
DYSON F.J.,"THE FUTURE DEVELOPMENT OF NUCLEAR   INT/ORG
WEAPONS." FUT WOR+45 DELIB/GP ACT/RES PLAN DETER   ARMS/CONT
WEAPON ATTIT PWR...POLICY 20. PAGE 17 G0328   NUC/PWR

S60
IKLE F.C.,"NTH COUNTRIES AND DISARMAMENT." WOR+45   FUT
DELIB/GP ECO/TAC DOMIN EDU/PROP LEGIT ROUTINE   INT/ORG
COERCE RIGID/FLEX ORD/FREE...MARXIST TREND 20.   ARMS/CONT
PAGE 28 G0543   NUC/PWR

S60
KISSINGER H.A.,"ARMS CONTROL, INSPECTION AND   FORCES
SURPRISE ATTACK." COM USA+45 NAT/G ACT/RES PLAN   ORD/FREE
TEC/DEV DIPLOM EDU/PROP DETER WAR RIGID/FLEX   ARMS/CONT
...CONCPT GEN/METH TOT/POP 20. PAGE 31 G0603   NUC/PWR

S60
LEAR J.,"PEACE: SCIENCE'S NEXT GREAT EXPLORATION."   EX/STRUC
USA+45 INT/ORG TOP/EX TEC/DEV EDU/PROP ROUTINE   ARMS/CONT
PEACE KNOWL SKILL 20. PAGE 33 G0648   NUC/PWR

S60
OSGOOD C.E.,"A CASE FOR GRADUATED UNILATERAL   ATTIT
DISENGAGEMENT." FUT WOR+45 CULTURE SOCIETY NAT/G   EDU/PROP
NUC/PWR WAR PERSON SUPEGO ALL/VALS...POLICY PSY   ARMS/CONT
CONCPT COLD/WAR TOT/POP VAL/FREE 20. PAGE 43 G0848

S60
YEMELYANOV V.S.,"ATOMIC ENERGY FOR PEACE: THE USSR   VOL/ASSN
AND INTERNATIONAL CO-OPERATION." FUT USSR WOR+45   TEC/DEV
R+D CREATE EDU/PROP...CONCPT GEN/LAWS 20. PAGE 64   ARMS/CONT
G1264   NUC/PWR

B61
FRISCH D.,ARMS REDUCTION: PROGRAM AND ISSUES.   PLAN
USA+45 INT/ORG NAT/G ACT/RES REGION NUC/PWR ATTIT   FORCES
PWR...POLICY 20. PAGE 20 G0395   ARMS/CONT
                                                        DIPLOM

B61
HENKIN L.,ARMS CONTROL: ISSUES FOR THE PUBLIC.   WOR+45
EUR+WWI FUT USA+45 USSR INT/ORG NAT/G DIPLOM   DELIB/GP
EDU/PROP DETER NUC/PWR ATTIT PWR...CONCPT RECORD   ARMS/CONT
HIST/WRIT TIME/SEQ TOT/POP COLD/WAR 20. PAGE 26
G0506

B61
KISSINGER H.A.,THE NECESSITY FOR CHOICE. FUT USA+45   TOP/EX
ECO/UNDEV NAT/G PLAN BAL/PWR ECO/TAC ARMS/CONT   TREND
DETER NUC/PWR ATTIT...POLICY CONCPT RECORD GEN/LAWS   DIPLOM
COLD/WAR 20. PAGE 31 G0604

B61
NOGEE J.L.,SOVIET POLICY TOWARD INTERNATIONAL   INT/ORG
CONTROL OF ATOMIC ENERGY. COM USA+45 WOR+45 INTELL   ATTIT
NAT/G ACT/RES DIPLOM EDU/PROP NUC/PWR TOTALISM   ARMS/CONT
PERCEPT KNOWL PWR...TIME/SEQ COLD/WAR 20. PAGE 42   USSR
G0824

B61
SCHMIDT H.,VERTEIDIGUNG ODER VERGELTUNG. COM CUBA   PLAN
GERMANY/W USSR FORCES DIPLOM ARMS/CONT DETER   WAR
NUC/PWR...POLICY CHARTS HYPO/EXP SIMUL BIBLIOG 20   BAL/PWR
NATO COLD/WAR. PAGE 49 G0970   ORD/FREE

B61
STEIN W.,NUCLEAR WEAPONS: A CATHOLIC RESPONSE.   NUC/PWR
WOR+45 FORCES ARMS/CONT DETER MURDER MORAL...POLICY   WAR
CATH IDEA/COMP ANTHOL 20. PAGE 52 G1033   CATHISM
                                                        ATTIT

L61
TAUBENFELD H.J.,"A REGIME FOR OUTER SPACE." FUT   INT/ORG
UNIV R+D ACT/RES PLAN BAL/PWR LEGIT ARMS/CONT   ADJUD
ORD/FREE...POLICY JURID TREND UN TOT/POP 20   SPACE
COLD/WAR. PAGE 54 G1056

S61
RICHSTEIN A.R.,"LEGAL RULES IN NUCLEAR WEAPONS   NUC/PWR
EMPLOYMENTS." FUT WOR+45 LAW SOCIETY FORCES PLAN   TEC/DEV
WEAPON RIGID/FLEX...HEAL CONCPT TREND VAL/FREE 20.   MORAL
PAGE 47 G0918   ARMS/CONT

S61
WOHLSTETTER A.,"NUCLEAR SHARING: NATO AND THE NTH   TREND
COUNTRY." EUR+WWI FUT SOCIETY DIPLOM EXEC DETER PWR   TEC/DEV
SKILL...POLICY TECHNIC CONCPT 20 NATO. PAGE 64   NUC/PWR
G1252   ARMS/CONT

B62
SOVIET STAND ON DISARMAMENT. COM EUR+WWI FUT USA+45   ACT/RES
NAT/G TOP/EX NUC/PWR PEACE ATTIT...POLICY CONCPT   ORD/FREE
TOT/POP 20. PAGE 1 G0016   ARMS/CONT
                                                        USSR

BLOOMFIELD L.P.,OUTER SPACE: A PATTERN OF WAR IN A NEW DIMENSION. FUT USA+45 AIR TEC/DEV PWR ...DECISION CONCPT GEN/LAWS 20. PAGE 7 G0141

B62 CREATE ACT/RES ARMS/CONT SPACE

CALDER R.,LIVING WITH THE ATOM. FUT USA+45 WOR+45 R+D INT/ORG VOL/ASSN DELIB/GP ARMS/CONT...STYLE 20. PAGE 10 G0200

B62 TEC/DEV HEALTH NUC/PWR

DUPRE S.,SCIENCE AND THE NATION. USA+45 ECO/DEV ACADEM ORD/FREE TECHNIC. PAGE 17 G0323

B62 ARMS/CONT DECISION TEC/DEV INDUS

FORBES H.W.,THE STRATEGY OF DISARMAMENT. FUT WOR+45 INT/ORG VOL/ASSN CONSULT ARMS/CONT COERCE NUC/PWR WAR DRIVE RIGID/FLEX ORD/FREE PWR...POLICY CONCPT OBS TREND STERTYP 20. PAGE 19 G0378

B62 PLAN FORCES DIPLOM

GILPIN R.,AMERICAN SCIENTISTS AND NUCLEAR WEAPONS POLICY. COM FUT USA+45 WOR+45 INT/ORG NAT/G PROF/ORG CONSULT FORCES CREATE TEC/DEV BAL/PWR EDU/PROP ARMS/CONT WAR PERCEPT KNOWL MORAL PWR ...PHIL/SCI SOC CONCPT GEN/LAWS 20. PAGE 21 G0417

B62 INTELL ATTIT DETER NUC/PWR

HALPERIN M.H.,LIMITED WAR; AN ESSAY ON THE DEVELOPMENT OF THE THEORY AND AN ANNOTATED BIBLIOGRAPHY (OCCASIONAL PAPER NO. 3). WOR+45 WOR-45 NUC/PWR...CONCPT IDEA/COMP METH/COMP 19/20. PAGE 24 G0471

B62 BIBLIOG/A WAR ARMS/CONT FORCES

KAHN H.,THINKING ABOUT THE UNTHINKABLE. FUT USA+45 LAW NAT/G CONSULT FORCES ACT/RES CREATE TEC/DEV BAL/PWR DIPLOM EDU/PROP ARMS/CONT DETER ATTIT...CONCPT OBS TREND COLD/WAR 20. PAGE 29 G0570

B62 INT/ORG ORD/FREE NUC/PWR PEACE

LEFEVER E.W.,ARMS AND ARMS CONTROL. COM USA+45 INT/ORG TEC/DEV DIPLOM ORD/FREE 20. PAGE 33 G0652

B62 ATTIT PWR ARMS/CONT BAL/PWR

MELMAN S.,DISARMAMENT: ITS POLITICS AND ECONOMICS. WOR+45 DELIB/GP FORCES ECO/TAC DOMIN EDU/PROP LEGIT COERCE PWR...POLICY CONCPT 20. PAGE 38 G0752

B62 NAT/G ORD/FREE ARMS/CONT NUC/PWR

PERRE J.,LES MUTATIONS DE LA GUERRE MODERNE: DE LA REVOLUTION FRANCAISE A LA REVOLUTION NUCLEAIRE. DIPLOM ARMS/CONT DEATH REV WEAPON GP/REL PEACE ATTIT...STAT PREDICT BIBLIOG 18/20 WWI. PAGE 44 G0870

B62 WAR FORCES NUC/PWR

SINGER J.D.,DETERRENCE, ARMS CONTROL AND DISARMAMENT: TOWARD A SYNTHESIS IN NATIONAL SECURITY POLICY. COM USA+45 INT/ORG BAL/PWR DETER ORD/FREE...POLICY COLD/WAR 20. PAGE 51 G1003

B62 FUT ACT/RES ARMS/CONT

SOHN L.B.,ZONAL DISARMAMENT: VARIATIONS ON A THEME. FUT WOR+45 SOCIETY ACT/RES PLAN NUC/PWR PEACE ATTIT ...POLICY GEOG CONT/OBS HYPO/EXP 20. PAGE 52 G1020

B62 ORD/FREE NEW/IDEA ARMS/CONT

WRIGHT Q.,PREVENTING WORLD WAR THREE. FUT WOR+45 CULTURE INT/ORG NAT/G CONSULT FORCES ADMIN ARMS/CONT DRIVE RIGID/FLEX ORD/FREE SOVEREIGN ...POLICY CONCPT TREND STERTYP COLD/WAR 20. PAGE 64 G1259

B62 CREATE ATTIT

YALEN R.,REGIONALISM AND WORLD ORDER. EUR+WWI WOR+45 WOR-45 INT/ORG VOL/ASSN DELIB/GP TOP/EX BAL/PWR DIPLOM DOMIN REGION ARMS/CONT PWR ...JURID HYPO/EXP COLD/WAR 20. PAGE 64 G1261

B62 ORD/FREE POLICY

BETTEN J.K.,"ARMS CONTROL AND THE PROBLEM OF EVASION." WOR+45 FORCES CREATE DIPLOM DETER PWR ...PSY TREND GEN/LAWS COLD/WAR 20. PAGE 7 G0134

L62 NAT/G PLAN ARMS/CONT

FINKELSTEIN L.S.,"ARMS INSPECTION." FUT WOR+45 NAT/G DIPLOM ATTIT PERCEPT RIGID/FLEX ORD/FREE COLD/WAR 20. PAGE 19 G0369

L62 FORCES PWR ARMS/CONT

BETHE H.,"DISARMAMENT AND STRATEGY." COM USA+45 USSR WOR+45 VOL/ASSN TEC/DEV EDU/PROP NUC/PWR CHOOSE PEACE...POLICY DECISION NEW/IDEA OBS GEN/LAWS COLD/WAR 420. PAGE 7 G0133

S62 PLAN ORD/FREE ARMS/CONT DIPLOM

BOULDING K.E.,"THE PREVENTION OF WORLD WAR THREE." FUT WOR+45 INT/ORG PLAN BAL/PWR PEACE ORD/FREE PWR ...NEW/IDEA TREND TOT/POP COLD/WAR 20. PAGE 8 G0158

S62 VOL/ASSN NAT/G ARMS/CONT DIPLOM

CRANE R.D.,"LAW AND STRATEGY IN SPACE." FUT USA+45 WOR+45 AIR LAW INT/ORG NAT/G FORCES ACT/RES PLAN BAL/PWR LEGIT ARMS/CONT COERCE ORD/FREE...POLICY INT/LAW JURID SOC/EXP 20 TREATY. PAGE 13 G0261

S62 CONCPT SPACE

DAWSON R.H.,"CONGRESSIONAL INNOVATION AND INTERVENTION IN DEFENSE POLICY: LEGISLATIVE AUTHORIZATION OF WEAPONS SYSTEMS." CONSTN PLAN ARMS/CONT GOV/REL EFFICIENCY PEACE NEW/LIB OLD/LIB. PAGE 14 G0281

S62 LEGIS PWR CONTROL WEAPON

FINKELSTEIN L.S.,"THE UNITED NATIONS AND ORGANIZATIONS FOR CONTROL OF ARMAMENT." FUT WOR+45 VOL/ASSN DELIB/GP TOP/EX CREATE EDU/PROP LEGIT ADJUD NUC/PWR ATTIT RIGID/FLEX ORD/FREE...POLICY DECISION CONCPT OBS TREND GEN/LAWS TOT/POP COLD/WAR. PAGE 19 G0368

S62 INT/ORG PWR ARMS/CONT

FOSTER R.B.,"UNILATERAL ARMS CONTROL MEASURES AND DISARMAMENT NEGOTIATION." WOR+45 VOL/ASSN DELIB/GP ACT/RES ECO/TAC EDU/PROP ATTIT RIGID/FLEX...CONCPT MYTH TIME/SEQ COLD/WAR 20. PAGE 20 G0386

S62 PLAN ORD/FREE ARMS/CONT DETER

FOSTER W.C.,"ARMS CONTROL AND DISARMAMENT IN A DIVIDED WORLD." COM FUT USA+45 USSR WOR+45 INTELL INT/ORG NAT/G VOL/ASSN CONSULT CREATE PLAN TEC/DEV EDU/PROP LEGIT NUC/PWR ATTIT RIGID/FLEX...CONCPT TREND TOT/POP 20 UN. PAGE 20 G0387

S62 DELIB/GP POLICY ARMS/CONT DIPLOM

MARTIN L.W.,"THE MARKET FOR STRATEGIC IDEAS IN BRITAIN: THE 'SANDYS ERA'." UK ARMS/CONT WAR GOV/REL OPTIMAL...POLICY DECISION GOV/COMP COLD/WAR CMN/WLTH. PAGE 36 G0714

S62 DIPLOM COERCE FORCES PWR

NANES A.,"DISARMAMENT: THE LAST SEVEN YEARS." COM EUR+WWI USA+45 USSR INT/ORG FORCES TOP/EX CREATE LEGIT NUC/PWR DISPL ORD/FREE...CONCPT TIME/SEQ CON/ANAL 20. PAGE 41 G0803

S62 DELIB/GP RIGID/FLEX ARMS/CONT

PAULING L.,"GENETIC EFFECTS OF WEAPONS TESTS." WOR+45 SOCIETY FAM ACT/RES EDU/PROP AGE/C HEALTH ORD/FREE...GEOG STAT CONT/OBS PROJ/TEST CHARTS TOT/POP 20. PAGE 44 G0861

S62 HEAL ARMS/CONT NUC/PWR

PHIPPS T.E.,"THE CASE FOR DETERRENCE." FUT WOR+45 SOCIETY EX/STRUC FORCES ACT/RES CREATE PLAN TEC/DEV ROUTINE RIGID/FLEX ORD/FREE...POLICY MYTH NEW/IDEA STERTYP COLD/WAR 20. PAGE 45 G0876

S62 ATTIT COERCE DETER ARMS/CONT

SINGER J.D.,"STABLE DETERRENCE AND ITS LIMITS." FUT WOR+45 R+D INT/ORG CONSULT ACT/RES TEC/DEV ARMS/CONT COERCE DRIVE PERCEPT RIGID/FLEX ORD/FREE PWR...MYTH SIMUL TOT/POP 20. PAGE 51 G1004

S62 NAT/G FORCES DETER NUC/PWR

LILIENTHAL D.E.,CHANGE, HOPE, AND THE BOMB. USA+45 WOR+45 R+D INT/ORG NAT/G DELIB/GP FORCES ACT/RES DETER RIGID/FLEX ORD/FREE...POLICY CONCPT OBS AEC 20. PAGE 34 G0666

B63 ATTIT MYTH ARMS/CONT NUC/PWR

PACHTER H.M.,COLLISION COURSE; THE CUBAN MISSILE CRISIS AND COEXISTENCE. CUBA USA+45 DIPLOM ARMS/CONT PEACE MARXISM...DECISION INT/LAW 20 COLD/WAR KHRUSH/N KENNEDY/JF CASTRO/F. PAGE 43 G0854

B63 WAR BAL/PWR NUC/PWR DETER

PERLO V.,MILITARISM AND INDUSTRY. USA+45 INT/TRADE EDU/PROP DETER KNOWL...CHARTS MAPS 20. PAGE 44 G0869

B63 CIVMIL/REL INDUS LOBBY ARMS/CONT

US DEPARTMENT OF THE ARMY,SOVIET RUSSIA: STRATEGIC
SURVEY (PAMPHLET). USSR POL/PAR PLAN DOMIN EDU/PROP
ARMS/CONT GUERRILLA WAR WEAPON...TREND CHARTS
ORG/CHARTS 20. PAGE 57 G1129

B63
BIBLIOG/A
MARXISM
DIPLOM
COERCE

WILTZ J.E.,IN SEARCH OF PEACE: THE SENATE MUNITIONS
INQUIRY, 1934-36. EUR+WWI USA+45 ELITES INDUS LG/CO
LEGIS INT/TRADE LOBBY NEUTRAL ARMS/CONT...POLICY
CONGRESS 20 LEAGUE/NAT PRESIDENT SENATE CONSCRIPTN.
PAGE 64 G1246

B63
DELIB/GP
PROFIT
WAR
WEAPON

BRENNAN D.G.,"ARMS CONTROL AND CIVIL DEFENSE."
USA+45 WOR+45 NAT/G BAL/PWR ROUTINE ATTIT
RIGID/FLEX ORD/FREE...SOC TOT/POP 20. PAGE 8 G0165

L63
PLAN
HEALTH
ARMS/CONT
DETER

PHELPS J.,"STUDIES IN DETERRENCE VIII: MILITARY
STABILITY AND ARMS CONTROL: A CRITICAL SURVEY."
FUT WOR+45 INT/ORG ACT/RES EDU/PROP COERCE NUC/PWR
WAR HEALTH PWR...POLICY TECHNIC TREND SIMUL TOT/POP
20. PAGE 44 G0874

L63
FORCES
ORD/FREE
ARMS/CONT
DETER

ABT C.C.,"THE PROBLEMS AND POSSIBILITIES OF SPACE
ARMS CONTROL." FUT USA+45 WOR+45 AIR SOCIETY NAT/G
BAL/PWR EDU/PROP ATTIT PWR WEALTH...HYPO/EXP
TOT/POP 20. PAGE 2 G0025

S63
ACT/RES
ORD/FREE
ARMS/CONT
SPACE

BOHN L.,"WHOSE NUCLEAR TEST: NON-PHYSICAL
INSPECTION AND TEST BAN." WOR+45 R+D INT/ORG
VOL/ASSN ORD/FREE...GEN/LAWS GEN/METH COLD/WAR 20.
PAGE 8 G0148

S63
ADJUD
ARMS/CONT
TEC/DEV
NUC/PWR

BOULDING K.E.,"UNIVERSITY, SOCIETY, AND ARMS
CONTROL." WOR+45 WOR-45 ACADEM NAT/G CONSULT FORCES
ACT/RES PLAN TEC/DEV BAL/PWR ECO/TAC COERCE DETER
WAR ATTIT RIGID/FLEX KNOWL ORD/FREE PWR WEALTH
...CONCPT COLD/WAR TOT/POP 20. PAGE 8 G0159

S63
SOCIETY
ARMS/CONT

PHELPS J.,"INFORMATION AND ARMS CONTROL." COM SPACE
USA+45 USSR WOR+45 R+D INT/ORG NAT/G DELIB/GP
DIPLOM ORD/FREE...CONCPT 20. PAGE 45 G0875

S63
KNOWL
ARMS/CONT
NUC/PWR

SMITH D.O.,"WHAT IS A WAR DETERRENT." FUT GERMANY
HUNGARY UK USA+45 WOR+45 WOR-45 NAT/G TEC/DEV
BAL/PWR PWR...CONCPT GEN/LAWS COLD/WAR 20. PAGE 51
G1013

S63
ACT/RES
FORCES
ARMS/CONT
DETER

TASHJEAN J.E.,"RESEARCH ON ARMS CONTROL." COM
USA+45 USSR FORCES ACT/RES PLAN DOMIN COERCE
ORD/FREE PWR...TIME/SEQ GEN/LAWS 20 COLD/WAR.
PAGE 53 G1053

S63
NAT/G
POLICY
ARMS/CONT

WOHLSTETTER A.,"SCIENTISTS, SEERS AND STRATEGY."
USA+45 ELITES R+D NAT/G CONSULT FORCES TOP/EX
EDU/PROP ARMS/CONT KNOWL ORD/FREE...DECISION MYTH
20. PAGE 64 G1253

S63
INTELL
ACT/RES

BROWN N.,NUCLEAR WAR* THE IMPENDING STRATEGIC
DEADLOCK. USA+45 USSR TEC/DEV BUDGET RISK ARMS/CONT
NUC/PWR WEAPON COST BIO/SOC...GEOG IDEA/COMP
NAT/COMP GAME NATO WARSAW/P. PAGE 9 G0177

B64
FORCES
OP/RES
WAR
GEN/LAWS

GRODZINS M.,THE ATOMIC AGE: FORTY-FIVE SCIENTISTS
AND SCHOLARS SPEAK ON NATIONAL AND WORLD AFFAIRS.
FUT USA+45 WOR+45 R+D INT/ORG NAT/G CONSULT TEC/DEV
EDU/PROP ATTIT PERSON ORD/FREE...HUM CONCPT
TIME/SEQ CON/ANAL. PAGE 23 G0454

B64
INTELL
ARMS/CONT
NUC/PWR

ROBERTS HL,FOREIGN AFFAIRS BIBLIOGRAPHY, 1952-1962.
ECO/DEV SECT PLAN FOR/AID INT/TRADE ARMS/CONT
NAT/LISM ATTIT...INT/LAW GOV/COMP IDEA/COMP 20.
PAGE 47 G0928

B64
BIBLIOG/A
DIPLOM
INT/ORG
WAR

ROTHSCHILD J.H.,TOMORROW'S WEAPONS: CHEMICAL AND
BIOLOGICAL. FUT PROB/SOLV ARMS/CONT PEACE MORAL
...CHARTS BIBLIOG 20. PAGE 48 G0941

B64
WAR
WEAPON
BIO/SOC
DETER

US AIR FORCE ACADEMY ASSEMBLY,OUTER SPACE: FINAL
REPORT APRIL 1-4, 1964. FUT USA+45 WOR+45 LAW

B64
SPACE
CIVMIL/REL

DELIB/GP CONFER ARMS/CONT WAR PEACE ATTIT MORAL
...ANTHOL 20 NASA. PAGE 56 G1104

NUC/PWR
DIPLOM

WILLIAMS S.P.,TOWARD A GENUINE WORLD SECURITY
SYSTEM (PAMPHLET). WOR+45 INT/ORG FORCES PLAN
NUC/PWR ORD/FREE...INT/LAW CONCPT UN PRESIDENT.
PAGE 63 G1243

B64
BIBLIOG/A
ARMS/CONT
DIPLOM
PEACE

BERKS R.N.,"THE US AND WEAPONS CONTROL." WOR+45 LAW
INT/ORG NAT/G LEGIS EXEC COERCE PEACE ATTIT
RIGID/FLEX ALL/VALS PWR...POLICY TOT/POP 20. PAGE 7
G0129

L64
USA+45
PLAN
ARMS/CONT

CARNEGIE ENDOWMENT INT. PEACE,"POLITICAL QUESTIONS
(ISSUES BEFORE THE NINETEENTH GENERAL ASSEMBLY)."
SPACE WOR+45 CONSTN FINAN NAT/G CONSULT DELIB/GP
FORCES LEGIS TEC/DEV EDU/PROP LEGIT ARMS/CONT
COERCE NUC/PWR ATTIT ALL/VALS...CONCPT OBS UN
COLD/WAR 20. PAGE 11 G0208

L64
INT/ORG
PEACE

WARD C.,"THE 'NEW MYTHS' AND 'OLD REALITIES' OF
NUCLEAR WAR." COM FUT USA+45 USSR WOR+45 INT/ORG
NAT/G DOMIN LEGIT EXEC ATTIT PERCEPT ALL/VALS
...POLICY RELATIV PSY MYTH TREND 20. PAGE 62 G1212

L64
FORCES
COERCE
ARMS/CONT
NUC/PWR

FALK S.L.,"DISARMAMENT IN HISTORICAL PERSPECTIVE."
WOR-45 NAT/G PLAN NUC/PWR PEACE ORD/FREE PWR
...TIME/SEQ AUD/VIS VAL/FREE LEAGUE/NAT 20. PAGE 18
G0360

S64
INT/ORG
COERCE
ARMS/CONT

MAGGS P.B.,"SOVIET VIEWPOINT ON NUCLEAR WEAPONS IN
INTERNATIONAL LAW." USSR WOR+45 INT/ORG FORCES
DIPLOM ARMS/CONT ATTIT ORD/FREE PWR...POLICY JURID
CONCPT OBS TREND CON/ANAL GEN/LAWS VAL/FREE 20.
PAGE 35 G0694

S64
COM
LAW
INT/LAW
NUC/PWR

PILISUK M.,"STEPWISE DISARMAMENT & SUDDEN
DESTRUCTION IN A TWOPERSON GAME: A RESEARCH TOOL."
NAT/G FORCES ACT/RES ECO/TAC EDU/PROP EXEC ROUTINE
COERCE ORD/FREE...SIMUL GEN/LAWS VAL/FREE. PAGE 45
G0877

S64
PWR
DECISION
ARMS/CONT

PEACE RESEARCH ABSTRACTS. FUT WOR+45 R+D INT/ORG
NAT/G PLAN TEC/DEV BAL/PWR DIPLOM FOR/AID NUC/PWR
HEALTH. PAGE 1 G0020

B65
BIBLIOG/A
PEACE
ARMS/CONT
WAR

BLOOMFIELD L.,SOVIET INTERESTS IN ARMS CONTROL AND
DISARMAMENT* THE DECADE UNDER KHRUSHCHEV 1954-1964.
ASIA FORCES ACT/RES EDU/PROP DETER NUC/PWR WEAPON
COST ATTIT...PHIL/SCI CLASSIF STAT NET/THEORY GAME
BIBLIOG. PAGE 7 G0139

B65
USSR
ARMS/CONT
DIPLOM
TREND

BOBROW D.B.,COMPONENTS OF DEFENSE POLICY. ASIA
EUR+WWI USA+45 WOR+45 INTELL INT/ORG NAT/G PROF/ORG
CONSULT LEGIS ACT/RES CREATE ARMS/CONT COERCE
ORD/FREE...DECISION SIMUL. PAGE 7 G0145

B65
DETER
NUC/PWR
PLAN
FORCES

CORDIER A.W.,THE QUEST FOR PEACE. WOR+45 NAT/G PLAN
BAL/PWR ECO/TAC ARMS/CONT NUC/PWR PWR...ANTHOL UN
COLD/WAR. PAGE 13 G0256

B65
PEACE
DIPLOM
POLICY
INT/ORG

HALPERIN M.H.,CHINA AND THE BOMB. USA+45 USSR
INT/ORG FORCES ARMS/CONT DETER PRODUC ORD/FREE PWR
TREND. PAGE 24 G0472

B65
ASIA
NUC/PWR
WAR
DIPLOM

HALPERIN M.H.,COMMUNIST CHINA AND ARMS CONTROL.
CHINA/COM FUT USA+45 CULTURE FORCES TEC/DEV ECO/TAC
WAR PEACE ORD/FREE MARXISM 20 COLD/WAR. PAGE 24
G0473

B65
ATTIT
POLICY
ARMS/CONT
NUC/PWR

MCGUIRE M.C.,SECRECY AND THE ARMS RACE* A THEORY OF
THE ACCUMULATION OF STRATEGIC WEAPONS AND HOW
SECRECY AFFECTS IT. DIPLOM NUC/PWR WEAPON ISOLAT
RATIONAL ORD/FREE WEALTH...ECOMETRIC MATH GEN/LAWS.
PAGE 38 G0742

B65
DETER
ARMS/CONT
SIMUL
GAME

MOSKOWITZ H.,US SECURITY, ARMS CONTROL, AND
DISARMAMENT 1961-1965. FORCES DIPLOM DETER WAR

B65
BIBLIOG/A
ARMS/CONT

WEAPON...CHARTS 20 UN COLD/WAR NATO. PAGE 40 G0790   NUC/PWR
PEACE

B65
US DEPARTMENT OF DEFENSE,US SECURITY ARMS CONTROL,   BIBLIOG/A
AND DISARMAMENT 1961-1965 (PAMPHLET). CHINA/COM COM   ARMS/CONT
GERMANY/W ISRAEL SPACE USA+45 USSR WOR+45 FORCES   NUC/PWR
EDU/PROP DETER EQUILIB PEACE ALL/VALS...GOV/COMP 20   DIPLOM
NATO. PAGE 57 G1118

B65
US DEPARTMENT OF THE ARMY,NUCLEAR WEAPONS AND THE   BIBLIOG/A
ATLANTIC ALLIANCE: A BIBLIOGRAPHIC SURVEY. ASIA COM   ARMS/CONT
EUR+WWI USA+45 FORCES DIPLOM WEAPON...STAT 20 NATO.   NUC/PWR
PAGE 58 G1131   BAL/PWR

B65
US SENATE COMM AERO SPACE SCI,INTERNATIONAL   DIPLOM
COOPERATION AND ORGANIZATION FOR OUTER SPACE. FUT   SPACE
USA+45 WOR+45 PROF/ORG VOL/ASSN CONSULT DELIB/GP   R+D
PLAN TEC/DEV ARMS/CONT GP/REL PEACE 20 UN NASA.   NAT/G
PAGE 59 G1167

B65
WASKOW A.I.,KEEPING THE WORLD DISARMED. AFR   ARMS/CONT
GERMANY/E DIPLOM CONTROL WAR 20 UN. PAGE 62 G1218   PEACE
FORCES
PROB/SOLV

L65
PILISUK M.,"IS THERE A MILITARY INDUSTRIAL COMPLEX   ELITES
WHICH PREVENTS PEACE CONSENSUS; COUNTERVAILING   WEAPON
POWER IN PLURALIST SYSTEMS." INDUS R+D ACADEM   PEACE
FEEDBACK CIVMIL/REL ADJUST CONSEN ATTIT RIGID/FLEX   ARMS/CONT
...CENSUS IDEA/COMP BIBLIOG. PAGE 45 G0878

S65
ABT C.C.,"CONTROLLING FUTURE ARMS." USSR PLAN   PREDICT
BAL/PWR DIPLOM NUC/PWR COST...CLASSIF STAT CHARTS.   FUT
PAGE 2 G0027   ARMS/CONT
TEC/DEV

S65
BIRNBAUM K.,"SWEDEN'S NUCLEAR POLICY." WOR+45   SWEDEN
POL/PAR CREATE TEC/DEV NEUTRAL RISK WAR ORD/FREE   NUC/PWR
...DECISION IDEA/COMP NAT/COMP TIME. PAGE 7 G0137   DIPLOM
ARMS/CONT

S65
BLOOMFIELD L.P.,"ARMS CONTROL AND THE DEVELOPING   ARMS/CONT
COUNTRIES." AFR ISLAM S/ASIA USA+45 VOL/ASSN   ECO/UNDEV
TEC/DEV DIPLOM REGION NUC/PWR...PREDICT TREND.   HYPO/EXP
PAGE 7 G0142   OBS

S65
BOHN L.C.,"ATOMS FOR PEACE AND ATOMS FOR WAR."   NUC/PWR
WOR+45 INT/ORG TEC/DEV DIPLOM IDEA/COMP. PAGE 8   ARMS/CONT
G0149   RECORD

S65
DESAI M.J.,"INDIA AND NUCLEAR WEAPONS." ASIA   INDIA
BAL/PWR DIPLOM NUC/PWR WEAPON PEACE RECORD. PAGE 15   ARMS/CONT
G0294

S65
GOLDSTEIN W.,"KEEPING THE GENIE IN THE BOTTLE* THE   NUC/PWR
FEASIBILITY OF A NUCLEAR NON-PROLIFERATION   CREATE
AGREEMENT." ASIA FRANCE UK USA+45 WOR+45   COST
ECO/UNDEV VOL/ASSN ACT/RES PLAN RISK ARMS/CONT WAR
PEACE ATTIT PERCEPT...RECORD TREND TIME. PAGE 22
G0429

S65
HARRISON S.L.,"NTH NATION CHALLENGES* THE PRESENT   ARMS/CONT
PERSPECTIVE." EUR+WWI FUT USA+45 BAL/PWR CONTROL   NUC/PWR
RISK COERCE WAR...PREDICT COLD/WAR. PAGE 25 G0485   NAT/G
DIPLOM

S65
HIBBS A.R.,"SPACE TECHNOLOGY* THE THREAT AND THE   SPACE
PROMISE." FUT VOL/ASSN TEC/DEV NUC/PWR COST   ARMS/CONT
EFFICIENCY UTIL UN TREATY. PAGE 26 G0510   PREDICT

S65
KOHL W.L.,"NUCLEAR SHARING IN NATO AND THE   ARMS/CONT
MULTILATERAL FORCE." FUT USSR VOL/ASSN TEC/DEV   OBS
DIPLOM NUC/PWR WAR WEAPON NATO. PAGE 31 G0611   IDEA/COMP

S65
KREITH K.,"PEACE RESEARCH AND GOVERNMENT POLICY."   PEACE
INTELL NAT/G DIPLOM ECO/TAC CONTROL ARMS/CONT WAR   STYLE
PERCEPT...DECISION IDEA/COMP. PAGE 31 G0619   OBS

S65
KRICKUS R.J.,"ON THE MORALITY OF   MORAL
CHEMICAL/BIOLOGICAL WAR." ECO/UNDEV ARMS/CONT DETER   BIO/SOC

NUC/PWR RIGID/FLEX HEALTH INT/LAW. PAGE 31 G0621   WEAPON
WAR

S65
KUZMACK A.M.,"TECHNOLOGICAL CHANGE AND STABLE   R+D
DETERRENCE." CREATE EDU/PROP ARMS/CONT WEAPON   DETER
CHOOSE COST DRIVE PERCEPT...RECORD STERTYP TIME.   EQUILIB
PAGE 32 G0627

S65
MARTIN A.,"PROLIFERATION." FUT WOR+45 PROB/SOLV   RECORD
REGION ADJUST...PREDICT NAT/COMP UN TREATY. PAGE 36   NUC/PWR
G0712   ARMS/CONT
VOL/ASSN

S65
RASER J.R.,"WEAPONS DESIGN AND ARMS CONTROL* THE   ARMS/CONT
POLARIS EXAMPLE." DETER NUC/PWR WEAPON CHOOSE   R+D
PERCEPT...STERTYP TIME. PAGE 46 G0904   GEOG
ACT/RES

S65
RUBINSTEIN A.Z.,"POLITICAL BARRIERS TO   COM
DISARMAMENT." FUT DIPLOM COERCE NUC/PWR WAR   USA+45
NAT/LISM ORD/FREE PREDICT. PAGE 48 G0944   ARMS/CONT
ATTIT

S65
SCHELLING T.C.,"SIGNALS AND FEEDBACK IN THE ARMS   FEEDBACK
DIALOGUE." USA+45 USSR R+D ACADEM FORCES ACT/RES   DETER
ADJUST COST GEN/LAWS. PAGE 49 G0964   EDU/PROP
ARMS/CONT

C65
SCHWEBEL M.,"BEHAVIORAL SCIENCE AND HUMAN   PEACE
SURVIVAL." FORCES ARMS/CONT COERCE NUC/PWR WAR   ACT/RES
GP/REL NAT/LISM PERCEPT...POLICY PSY ANTHOL   DIPLOM
BIBLIOG/A 20 COLD/WAR. PAGE 50 G0984   HEAL

C65
US AIR FORCE ACADEMY,"AMERICAN DEFENSE POLICY." COM   PLAN
INT/ORG TEC/DEV FOR/AID ARMS/CONT DETER NUC/PWR   FORCES
...POLICY DECISION CONCPT ANTHOL BIBLIOG/A 20   WAR
COLD/WAR NATO. PAGE 56 G1103   COERCE

B66
AMERICAN ASSEMBLY COLUMBIA U,A WORLD OF NUCLEAR   NUC/PWR
POWERS? FUT WOR+45 ECO/DEV BAL/PWR ECO/TAC CONTROL   DIPLOM
RISK EFFICIENCY ATTIT PWR...METH/COMP ANTHOL 20.   TEC/DEV
PAGE 3 G0049   ARMS/CONT

B66
BEATON L.,MUST THE BOMB SPREAD? WOR+45 TEC/DEV   NUC/PWR
DIPLOM DRIVE ORD/FREE PWR...CHARTS 20. PAGE 6 G0109   ARMS/CONT
PLAN
PROB/SOLV

B66
BLOOMFIELD L.P.,KHRUSHCHEV AND THE ARMS RACE.   ARMS/CONT
USA+45 USSR ECO/DEV BAL/PWR EDU/PROP CONFER NUC/PWR   COM
ATTIT...CHARTS 20 KHRUSH/N. PAGE 7 G0143   POLICY
DIPLOM

B66
BOLTON R.E.,DEFENSE AND DISARMAMENT: THE ECONOMICS   ARMS/CONT
OF TRANSITION. USA+45 R+D FORCES PLAN LOBBY DETER   POLICY
WAR COST PEACE...ANTHOL BIBLIOG 20. PAGE 8 G0150   INDUS

B66
CLARK G.,WORLD PEACE THROUGH WORLD LAW; TWO   INT/LAW
ALTERNATIVE PLANS. WOR+45 DELIB/GP FORCES TAX   PEACE
CONFER ADJUD SANCTION ARMS/CONT WAR CHOOSE PRIVIL   PLAN
20 UN COLD/WAR. PAGE 12 G0231   INT/ORG

B66
HALPERIN M.H.,CHINA AND NUCLEAR PROLIFERATION   NUC/PWR
(PAMPHLET). CHINA/COM FUT INDIA USA+45 USSR   FORCES
ARMS/CONT WAR 20 CHINJAP. PAGE 24 G0474   POLICY
DIPLOM

B66
JACOBSON H.K.,DIPLOMATS, SCIENTISTS, AND   DIPLOM
POLITICIANS* THE UNITED STATES AND THE NUCLEAR TEST   ARMS/CONT
BAN NEGOTIATIONS. USA+45 USSR ACT/RES PLAN CONFER   TECHRACY
DETER NUC/PWR CONSEN ORD/FREE...INT TREATY. PAGE 28   INT/ORG
G0554

B66
KUENNE R.E.,THE POLARIS MISSILE STRIKE* A GENERAL   NUC/PWR
ECONOMIC SYSTEMS ANALYSIS. USA+45 USSR NAT/G   FORCES
BAL/PWR ARMS/CONT WAR...MATH PROBABIL COMPUT/IR   DETER
CHARTS HYPO/EXP SIMUL. PAGE 32 G0625   DIPLOM

B66
STONE J.J.,CONTAINING THE ARMS RACE* SOME SPECIFIC   ARMS/CONT
PROPOSALS. ASIA USA+45 USSR PROB/SOLV BARGAIN   FEEDBACK

DIPLOM DETER NUC/PWR RATIONAL...GAME 20 DEPT/DEFEN COST
TREATY. PAGE 53 G1038   ATTIT

                                                        B66
UNITED NATIONS,INTERNATIONAL SPACE BIBLIOGRAPHY.   BIBLIOG
FUT INT/ORG TEC/DEV DIPLOM ARMS/CONT NUC/PWR   SPACE
...JURID SOC UN. PAGE 56 G1093   PEACE
                                                     R+D

                                                        B66
US PRES COMM ECO IMPACT DEFENS,REPORT* JULY 1965.   ACT/RES
USA+45 ECO/DEV INDUS DELIB/GP FORCES OP/RES   STAT
ARMS/CONT NUC/PWR WEAPON BAL/PAY...PREDICT SIMUL.   WAR
PAGE 59 G1159   BUDGET

                                                        B66
US SENATE COMM AERO SPACE SCI,SOVIET SPACE   CONSULT
PROGRAMS, 1962-65: GOALS AND PURPOSES,   SPACE
ACHIEVEMENTS, PLANS, AND INTERNATIONAL   FUT
IMPLICATIONS. USA+45 USSR R+D FORCES PLAN EDU/PROP   DIPLOM
PRESS ADJUD ARMS/CONT ATTIT MARXISM. PAGE 60 G1168

                                                        B66
WOLFERS A.,THE UNITED STATES IN A DISARMED WORLD: A ARMS/CONT
STUDY OF THE US OUTLINE FOR GENERAL AND COMPLETE   POLICY
DISARMAMENT. USA+45 NAT/G CONTROL DETER NUC/PWR   FORCES
EFFICIENCY...ANTHOL 20. PAGE 64 G1255   PEACE

                                                        B66
YOUNG W.,EXISTING MECHANISMS OF ARMS CONTROL.   ARMS/CONT
PROC/MFG OP/RES DIPLOM TASK CENTRAL...MGT TREATY.   ADMIN
PAGE 65 G1266   NUC/PWR
                                                     ROUTINE

                                                        S66
BROWNLIE I.,"NUCLEAR PROLIFERATION* SOME PROBLEMS   NUC/PWR
OF CONTROL." USA+45 USSR ECO/UNDEV INT/ORG FORCES   ARMS/CONT
TEC/DEV REGION CONSEN...RECORD TREATY. PAGE 9 G0181 VOL/ASSN
                                                     ORD/FREE

                                                        S66
EWALD R.F.,"ONE OF MANY POSSIBLE GAMES." ACADEM   SIMUL
INT/ORG ARMS/CONT...INT/LAW GAME. PAGE 18 G0354   HYPO/EXP
                                                     PROG/TEAC
                                                     RECORD

                                                        B67
GARCIA ROBLES A.,THE DENUCLEARIZATION OF LATIN   NUC/PWR
AMERICA (TRANS. BY MARJORIE URQUIDI). LAW PLAN   ARMS/CONT
DIPLOM...ANTHOL 20 TREATY UN. PAGE 21 G0409   L/A+17C
                                                     INT/ORG

                                                        B67
KINTNER W.R.,PEACE AND THE STRATEGY CONFLICT. PLAN   ROLE
BAL/PWR DIPLOM CONTROL ARMS/CONT DETER WEAPON 20.   PEACE
PAGE 30 G0599   NUC/PWR
                                                     ORD/FREE

                                                        B67
MCBRIDE J.H.,THE TEST BAN TREATY: MILITARY,   ARMS/CONT
TECHNOLOGICAL, AND POLITICAL IMPLICATIONS. USA+45   DIPLOM
USSR DELIB/GP FORCES LEGIS TEC/DEV BAL/PWR TREATY.   NUC/PWR
PAGE 37 G0727

                                                        B67
PIPER D.C.,THE INTERNATIONAL LAW OF THE GREAT   CONCPT
LAKES. CANADA EXTR/IND MUNIC LICENSE ARMS/CONT   DIPLOM
CRIME...GEOG 19/20. PAGE 45 G0879   INT/LAW

                                                        B67
RUSSETT B.M.,ARMS CONTROL IN EUROPE: PROPOSALS AND   ARMS/CONT
POLITICAL CONSTRAINTS. GERMANY WOR+45 POL/PAR   REGION
BARGAIN DIPLOM...TREND CHARTS 20 COLD/WAR. PAGE 48   METH/COMP
G0950

                                                        B67
SKOLNIKOFF E.B.,SCIENCE, TECHNOLOGY, AND AMERICAN   PHIL/SCI
FOREIGN POLICY. SPACE USA+45 INT/ORG TEC/DEV   DIPLOM
ARMS/CONT NUC/PWR 29 DEPT/STATE. PAGE 51 G1010   NAT/G
                                                     EFFICIENCY

                                                        B67
US SENATE COMM ON FOREIGN REL,TREATY ON OUTER   SPACE
SPACE. WOR+45 AIR FORCES PROB/SOLV NUC/PWR SENATE   DIPLOM
TREATY UN. PAGE 60 G1182   ARMS/CONT
                                                     LAW

                                                        B67
US SENATE COMM ON FOREIGN REL,UNITED STATES   ARMS/CONT
ARMAMENT AND DISARMAMENT PROBLEMS. USA+45 AIR   WEAPON
BAL/PWR DIPLOM FOR/AID NUC/PWR ORD/FREE SENATE   FORCES
TREATY. PAGE 60 G1184   PROB/SOLV

                                                        L67
DAVIS P.C.,"THE COMING CHINESE COMMUNIST NUCLEAR   NUC/PWR
THREAT AND U.S. SEA BASED ABM OPTIONS." ASIA   DETER

CHINA/COM FUT USA+45 SEA NAT/G FORCES PLAN TEC/DEV   WEAPON
LEAD ARMS/CONT...GEOG METH/COMP 20 ABM/DEFSYS.   DIPLOM
PAGE 14 G0279

                                                        S67
"CHINESE STATEMENT ON NUCLEAR PROLIFERATION."   NUC/PWR
CHINA/COM USA+45 USSR DOMIN COLONIAL PWR. PAGE 1   BAL/PWR
G0022   ARMS/CONT
                                                     DIPLOM

                                                        S67
BROWN N.,"BRITISH ARMS AND THE SWITCH TOWARD   FORCES
EUROPE." EUR+WWI UK ARMS/CONT. PAGE 9 G0178   PLAN
                                                     DIPLOM
                                                     INT/ORG

                                                        S67
CARROLL K.J.,"SECOND STEP TOWARD ARMS CONTROL."   ARMS/CONT
WOR+45 INT/ORG VOL/ASSN FORCES PROB/SOLV RISK   DIPLOM
WEAPON 20 COLD/WAR. PAGE 11 G0215   PLAN
                                                     NUC/PWR

                                                        S67
CLEMENS W.C.,"CHINESE NUCLEAR TESTS: TRENDS AND   NUC/PWR
PORTENTS." CHINA/COM USA+45 USSR FORCES PLAN   WEAPON
TEC/DEV ARMS/CONT WAR PWR...DECISION 20 MAO   POLICY
KHRUSH/N. PAGE 12 G0234   DIPLOM

                                                        S67
COFFEY J.I.,"THE ANTI-BALLISTIC MISSILE DEBATE."   ARMS/CONT
USA+45 USSR TEC/DEV BAL/PWR 20. PAGE 12 G0238   NUC/PWR
                                                     DETER
                                                     DIPLOM

                                                        S67
DEUTSCH K.W.,"ARMS CONTROL AND EUROPEAN UNITY* THE   ARMS/CONT
NEXT TEN YEARS." USA+45 ELITES NAT/G BAL/PWR DIPLOM PEACE
NUC/PWR...INT KNO/TEST NATO EEC. PAGE 15 G0300   REGION
                                                     PLAN

                                                        S67
EDMONDS M.,"INTERNATIONAL COLLABORATION IN WEAPONS   DIPLOM
PROCUREMENT* THE IMPLICATIONS OF THE ANGLO-FRENCH   VOL/ASSN
CASE." FRANCE UK CONSULT OP/RES PROB/SOLV TEC/DEV   BAL/PWR
CONFER CONTROL EFFICIENCY 20. PAGE 17 G0334   ARMS/CONT

                                                        S67
EISENDRATH C.,"THE OUTER SPACE TREATY." CHINA/COM   SPACE
COM USA+45 DIPLOM CONTROL NUC/PWR...INT/LAW 20 UN   INT/ORG
COLD/WAR TREATY. PAGE 17 G0339   PEACE
                                                     ARMS/CONT

                                                        S67
EYRAUD M.,"LA FRANCE FACE A UN EVENTUEL TRAITE DE   NUC/PWR
NON DISSEMINATION DES ARMES NUCLEAIRES." FRANCE   ARMS/CONT
USA+45 EXTR/IND INDUS R+D INT/ORG ACT/RES TEC/DEV   POLICY
AGREE PRODUC ATTIT 20 TREATY AEC EURATOM. PAGE 18
G0355

                                                        S67
FELD B.T.,"A PLEDGE* NO FIRST USE." DELIB/GP   ARMS/CONT
BAL/PWR DOMIN DETER. PAGE 19 G0363   NUC/PWR
                                                     DIPLOM
                                                     PEACE

                                                        S67
FOREIGN POLICY ASSOCIATION,"US CONCERN FOR WORLD   INT/LAW
LAW." USA+45 WOR+45 DELIB/GP JUDGE BAL/PWR CONFER   INT/ORG
PEACE ORD/FREE 20 UN. PAGE 19 G0379   DIPLOM
                                                     ARMS/CONT

                                                        S67
FOREIGN POLICY ASSOCIATION,"HOW WORLD LAW DEVELOPS* INT/LAW
A CASE STUDY OF THE OUTER SPACE TREATY." SPACE   DIPLOM
WOR+45 BAL/PWR NEUTRAL NUC/PWR PEACE KNOWL 20 UN   ARMS/CONT
TREATY. PAGE 19 G0380   INT/ORG

                                                        S67
GRIFFITHS F.,"THE POLITICAL SIDE OF 'DISARMAMENT'." ARMS/CONT
FUT WOR+45 NUC/PWR NAT/LISM PEACE...NEW/IDEA   DIPLOM
PREDICT METH/COMP GEN/LAWS 20. PAGE 23 G0453

                                                        S67
HARTIGAN R.S.,"NONCOMBAT IMMUNITY* REFLECTIONS ON   INT/LAW
ITS ORIGINS AND PRESENT STATUS." WOR+45 PROB/SOLV   NUC/PWR
WAR PRIVIL MORAL...POLICY 20. PAGE 25 G0487   ARMS/CONT
                                                     DIPLOM

                                                        S67
HAZARD J.N.,"POST-DISARMAMENT INTERNATIONAL LAW."   INT/LAW
FUT USSR WOR+45 INT/ORG DELIB/GP FORCES DETER   ARMS/CONT
EQUILIB SOVEREIGN MARXISM 20 UN. PAGE 25 G0496   PWR
                                                     PLAN

                                                        S67
INGLIS D.R.,"MISSILE DEFENSE, NUCLEAR SPREAD, AND   NUC/PWR

VIETNAM." CHINA/COM USA+45 USSR VIETNAM INDUS
BAL/PWR DETER WAR COST NAT/LISM PEACE. PAGE 28
G0544

ARMS/CONT
DIPLOM
FORCES

S67

INGLIS D.R.,"PROSPECTS AND PROBLEMS: THE
NONMILITARY USES OF NUCLEAR EXPLOSIVES." CREATE
PROB/SOLV TEC/DEV AGREE PEACE...INT/LAW PHIL/SCI
NEW/IDEA 20 TREATY. PAGE 28 G0545

NUC/PWR
INDUS
ARMS/CONT
EXTR/IND

S67

JACKSON W.G.F.,"NUCLEAR PROLIFERATION AND THE GREAT
POWERS." FUT UK WOR+45 INT/ORG DOMIN ARMS/CONT
DETER ORD/FREE PACIFIST. PAGE 28 G0550

NUC/PWR
ATTIT
BAL/PWR
NAT/LISM

S67

JAIN G.,"INDIA REJECTS THE POWER RACE* REALISM
ABOUT NUCLEAR WEAPONS." FORCES PROB/SOLV FOR/AID
ARMS/CONT COST PWR...GOV/COMP 20. PAGE 28 G0556

INDIA
CHINA/COM
NUC/PWR
DIPLOM

S67

KAHN H.,"CRITERIA FOR LONG-RANGE NUCLEAR CONTROL
POLICIES." WOR+45 INT/ORG TEC/DEV DOMIN DETER WAR
WEAPON ISOLAT ORD/FREE POLICY. PAGE 29 G0571

NUC/PWR
ARMS/CONT
BAL/PWR
DIPLOM

S67

KRUSCHE H.,"THE STRIVING OF THE KIESINGER-STRAUS
GOVERNMENT FOR NUCLEAR WEAPONS IS A THREAT TO
EUROPEAN SECURITY." EUR+WWI GERMANY BAL/PWR
SANCTION WEAPON PEACE ORD/FREE...MARXIST 20 NATO
COLD/WAR. PAGE 32 G0623

ARMS/CONT
INT/ORG
NUC/PWR
DIPLOM

S67

LALL B.G.,"GAPS IN THE ABM DEBATE." NAT/G DIPLOM
DETER CIVMIL/REL 20. PAGE 32 G0630

NUC/PWR
ARMS/CONT
EX/STRUC
FORCES

S67

MARTIN L.W.,"BALLISTIC MISSILE DEFENSE AND EUROPE."
EUR+WWI USA+45 FORCES PLAN BAL/PWR DEBATE PEACE
...POLICY COLD/WAR NATO. PAGE 36 G0715

ATTIT
ARMS/CONT
NUC/PWR
DETER

S67

REINTANZ G.,"THE SPACE TREATY." WOR+45 DIPLOM
CONTROL ARMS/CONT NUC/PWR WAR...MARXIST 20 COLD/WAR
UN TREATY. PAGE 46 G0911

SPACE
INT/LAW
INT/ORG
PEACE

S67

ROMANIECKI L.,"THE ATOM AND INTERNATIONAL
COOPERATION." PROB/SOLV DIPLOM PEACE ORD/FREE 20.
PAGE 47 G0933

INT/ORG
NUC/PWR
ARMS/CONT
CONTROL

S67

ROTHSTEIN R.L.,"NUCLEAR PROLIFERATION AND AMERICAN
POLICY." PROB/SOLV BAL/PWR DIPLOM ARMS/CONT
EFFICIENCY 20. PAGE 48 G0942

NUC/PWR
CONTROL
DETER
WOR+45

S67

SHARP G.,"THE NEED OF A FUNCTIONAL SUBSTITUTE FOR
WAR." FUT UNIV WOR+45 CULTURE SOCIETY INT/ORG
CONSULT DELIB/GP ACT/RES CREATE BAL/PWR CONFER
ARMS/CONT NUC/PWR 20. PAGE 50 G0989

PEACE
WAR
DIPLOM
PROB/SOLV

S67

SHULMAN M.D.,"'EUROPE' VERSUS 'DETENTE'." USA+45
USSR INT/ORG CONTROL ARMS/CONT DETER 20. PAGE 50
G0995

DIPLOM
BAL/PWR
NUC/PWR

S67

SUINN R.M.,"THE DISARMAMENT FANTASY* PSYCHOLOGICAL
FACTORS THAT MAY PRODUCE WARFARE." DIPLOM RISK
ARMS/CONT DETER ANOMIE PERSON GAME. PAGE 53 G1046

DECISION
NUC/PWR
WAR
PSY

S67

TELLER E.,"PLANNING FOR PEACE." CHINA/COM WOR+45
DELIB/GP TEC/DEV RISK COERCE DETER WAR ATTIT
ORD/FREE 20 NATO. PAGE 54 G1061

ARMS/CONT
NUC/PWR
PEACE
DOMIN

S67

VLASCIC I.A.,"THE SPACE TREATY* A PRELIMINARY
EVALUATION." FUT USSR WOR+45 R+D ACT/RES TEC/DEV
DIPLOM CONFER ARMS/CONT PEACE...PREDICT UN TREATY.
PAGE 61 G1201

SPACE
INT/LAW
INT/ORG
NEUTRAL

S67

WASHBURN A.M.,"NUCLEAR PROLIFERATION IN A

ARMS/CONT

REVOLUTIONARY INTERNATIONAL SYSTEM." WOR+45 NAT/G
DELIB/GP PLAN TEC/DEV...POLICY 20. PAGE 62 G1216

NUC/PWR
DIPLOM
CONFER

S67

YOUNG O.R.,"ACTIVE DEFENSE AND INTERNATIONAL
ORDER." FORCES BAL/PWR DEBATE GAMBLE COST PEACE.
PAGE 64 G1265

ARMS/CONT
DETER
PLAN
DECISION

N67

US HOUSE COMM FOREIGN AFFAIRS,REPORT OF SPECIAL
STUDY MISSION TO THE NEAR EAST (PAMPHLET). ISRAEL
USA+45 YEMEN ECO/UNDEV INT/ORG FOR/AID ARMS/CONT
WAR WEAPON NAT/LISM PEACE...GEOG 20 UN HOUSE/REP.
PAGE 58 G1138

ISLAM
DIPLOM
FORCES

N67

US SENATE COMM ON FOREIGN REL,ARMS SALES AND
FOREIGN POLICY (PAMPHLET). FINAN FOR/AID CONTROL
20. PAGE 60 G1181

ARMS/CONT
ADMIN
OP/RES
DIPLOM

ARMY....ARMY (ALL NATIONS)

ARNOLD/M....MATTHEW ARNOLD

ARON R. G0066,G0067,G0068

ARONOWITZ D.S. G0069

ARROW K.J. G0070

ART/METH....FINE AND PERFORMING ARTS

B60

CARPENTER E.,EXPLORATIONS IN COMMUNICATION. USSR
CULTURE SCHOOL SECT EDU/PROP PRESS TV AUTOMAT
FEEDBACK ATTIT PERSON...ART/METH PSY 20. PAGE 11
G0211

ANTHOL
COM/IND
TEC/DEV
WRITING

B62

ROSS R.,SYMBOLS AND CIVILIZATION. UNIV CULTURE SECT
CREATE ALL/VALS MORAL ART/METH. PAGE 48 G0939

PHIL/SCI
KNOWL
EPIST
SOCIETY

B64

CONANT J.B.,TWO MODES OF THOUGHT: MY ENCOUNTERS
WITH SCIENCE AND EDUCATION....ART/METH JURID SOC
TREND. PAGE 13 G0249

PHIL/SCI
SKILL
MYTH
STYLE

S67

BULMER-THOMAS I.,"SO, ON TO THE GREAT SOCIETY." FUT
UNIV TEC/DEV BAL/PWR WAR BIO/SOC KNOWL...ART/METH
SOC PREDICT TREND WORSHIP 20 GREAT/SOC. PAGE 9
G0185

PHIL/SCI
SOCIETY
CREATE

ARTHUR D LITTLE INC G0071

ARTHUR/CA....PRESIDENT CHESTER ALAN ARTHUR

ARTISTIC ACHIEVEMENT....SEE CREATE

ASIA....SEE ALSO APPROPRIATE TIME/SPACE/CULTURE INDEX

S54

PYE L.W.,"EASTERN NATIONALISM AND WESTERN POLICY."
ASIA S/ASIA USA+45 USA-45 SOCIETY PLAN DIPLOM KNOWL
TOT/POP 20. PAGE 46 G0896

CREATE
ACT/RES
NAT/LISM

B56

US OFFICE OF THE PRESIDENT,REPORT TO CONGRESS ON
THE MUTUAL SECURITY PROGRAM FOR THE SIX MONTHS
ENDED DECEMBER 31, 1955. ASIA USSR ECO/DEV
ECO/UNDEV INT/ORG CREATE TEC/DEV BAL/PWR ECO/TAC
AGREE DETER COST ORD/FREE 20 DEPT/STATE DEPT/DEFEN
EISNHWR/DD. PAGE 59 G1158

DIPLOM
FORCES
PLAN
FOR/AID

B59

GREENFIELD K.R.,COMMAND DECISIONS. ASIA EUR+WWI
S/ASIA USA-45 WOR-45 NAT/G CONSULT DELIB/GP COERCE
NUC/PWR PWR...OBS 20 CHINJAP. PAGE 23 G0446

PLAN
FORCES
WAR
WEAPON

B61

CARNELL F.,THE POLITICS OF THE NEW STATES: A SELECT
ANNOTATED BIBLIOGRAPHY WITH SPECIAL REFERENCE TO
THE COMMONWEALTH. CONSTN ELITES LABOR NAT/G POL/PAR
EX/STRUC DIPLOM ADJUD ADMIN...GOV/COMP 20
COMMONWLTH. PAGE 11 G0210

BIBLIOG/A
AFR
ASIA
COLONIAL

ABSHIRE D.M.,NATIONAL SECURITY: POLITICAL,   FUT
MILITARY, AND ECONOMIC STRATEGIES IN THE DECADE   ACT/RES
AHEAD. ASIA COM USA+45 WOR+45 ECO/DEV ECO/UNDEV   BAL/PWR
INT/ORG DELIB/GP FORCES ECO/TAC COERCE ATTIT
RIGID/FLEX HEALTH ORD/FREE PWR WEALTH...POLICY STAT
CHARTS ANTHOL COLD/WAR VAL/FREE. PAGE 1 G0024
                                                    B63

GEERTZ C.,OLD SOCIETIES AND NEW STATES: THE QUEST   ECO/UNDEV
FOR MODERNITY IN ASIA AND AFRICA. AFR ASIA LAW   TEC/DEV
CULTURE SECT EDU/PROP REV...GOV/COMP NAT/COMP 20.   NAT/LISM
PAGE 21 G0415   SOVEREIGN
                                                    B63

NORTH R.C.,CONTENT ANALYSIS: A HANDBOOK WITH   METH/CNCPT
APPLICATIONS FOR THE STUDY OF INTERNATIONAL CRISIS. COMPUT/IR
ASIA COM EUR+WWI MOD/EUR INT/ORG TEC/DEV DOMIN   USSR
EDU/PROP ROUTINE COERCE PERCEPT RIGID/FLEX ALL/VALS
...QUANT TESTS CON/ANAL SIMUL GEN/LAWS VAL/FREE.
PAGE 42 G0825

WIGHTMAN D.,TOWARD ECONOMIC CO-OPERATION IN ASIA.   ECO/UNDEV
ASIA S/ASIA VOL/ASSN ACT/RES PLAN TEC/DEV ECO/TAC   CREATE
EDU/PROP RIGID/FLEX SKILL...POLICY METH/CNCPT OBS
INT GEN/LAWS UN 20 ECAFE. PAGE 63 G1237
                                                    B64

LI C.M.,INDUSTRIAL DEVELOPMENT IN COMMUNIST CHINA. ASIA
CHINA/COM ECO/DEV ECO/UNDEV AGRI FINAN INDUS MARKET TEC/DEV
LABOR NAT/G ECO/TAC INT/TRADE EXEC ALL/VALS
...POLICY RELATIV TREND WORK TOT/POP VAL/FREE 20.
PAGE 34 G0665
                                                    B64

ROSECRANCE R.N.,THE DISPERSION OF NUCLEAR WEAPONS: EUR+WWI
STRATEGY AND POLITICS. ASIA COM FUT S/ASIA USA+45   PWR
INT/ORG NAT/G DELIB/GP FORCES ACT/RES TEC/DEV   PEACE
BAL/PWR COERCE DETER ATTIT RIGID/FLEX ORD/FREE
...POLICY CHARTS VAL/FREE. PAGE 48 G0935
                                                    S64

NEEDHAM T.,"SCIENCE AND SOCIETY IN EAST AND WEST." ASIA
INTELL STRATA R+D LOC/G NAT/G PROVS CONSULT ACT/RES STRUCT
CREATE PLAN TEC/DEV EDU/PROP ADMIN ATTIT ALL/VALS
...POLICY RELATIV MGT CONCPT NEW/IDEA TIME/SEQ WORK
WORK. PAGE 41 G0815
                                                    B65

BLOOMFIELD L.,SOVIET INTERESTS IN ARMS CONTROL AND USSR
DISARMAMENT* THE DECADE UNDER KHRUSHCHEV 1954-1964. ARMS/CONT
ASIA FORCES ACT/RES EDU/PROP DETER NUC/PWR WEAPON   DIPLOM
COST ATTIT...PHIL/SCI CLASSIF STAT NET/THEORY GAME TREND
BIBLIOG. PAGE 7 G0139
                                                    B65

BOBROW D.B.,COMPONENTS OF DEFENSE POLICY. ASIA   DETER
EUR+WWI USA+45 WOR+45 INTELL INT/ORG NAT/G PROF/ORG NUC/PWR
CONSULT LEGIS ACT/RES CREATE ARMS/CONT COERCE   PLAN
ORD/FREE...DECISION SIMUL. PAGE 7 G0145   FORCES
                                                    B65

GRETTON P.,MARITIME STRATEGY - A STUDY OF DEFENSE   FORCES
PROBLEMS. ASIA UK USSR DIPLOM COERCE DETER NUC/PWR PLAN
WEAPON...CONCPT NAT/COMP 20. PAGE 23 G0449   WAR
                                                    SEA
                                                    B65

HALPERIN M.H.,CHINA AND THE BOMB. USA+45 USSR   ASIA
INT/ORG FORCES ARMS/CONT DETER PRODUC ORD/FREE PWR NUC/PWR
TREND. PAGE 24 G0472   WAR
                                                    DIPLOM
                                                    B65

US DEPARTMENT OF THE ARMY,NUCLEAR WEAPONS AND THE   BIBLIOG/A
ATLANTIC ALLIANCE: A BIBLIOGRAPHIC SURVEY. ASIA COM ARMS/CONT
EUR+WWI USA+45 FORCES DIPLOM WEAPON...STAT 20 NATO. NUC/PWR
PAGE 58 G1131   BAL/PWR
                                                    S65

DESAI M.J.,"INDIA AND NUCLEAR WEAPONS." ASIA   INDIA
BAL/PWR DIPLOM NUC/PWR WEAPON PEACE RECORD. PAGE 15 ARMS/CONT
G0294
                                                    S65

GOLDSTEIN W.,"KEEPING THE GENIE IN THE BOTTLE* THE NUC/PWR
FEASIBILITY OF A NUCLEAR NON-PROLIFERATION   CREATE
AGREEMENT." ASIA FRANCE UK USA+45 USSR WOR+45   COST
ECO/UNDEV VOL/ASSN ACT/RES PLAN RISK ARMS/CONT WAR
PEACE ATTIT PERCEPT...RECORD TREND TIME. PAGE 22
G0429
                                                    S65

GRIFFITH S.B.,"COMMUNIST CHINA'S CAPACITY TO MAKE   FORCES
WAR." CHINA/COM COM NAT/G TOP/EX PLAN DOMIN COERCE PWR

NUC/PWR ATTIT RESPECT SKILL...CONCPT MYTH TIME/SEQ WEAPON
TREND COLD/WAR 20. PAGE 23 G0452   ASIA
                                                    S65

HSIEH A.L.,"THE SINO-SOVIET NUCLEAR DIALOGUE*   ASIA
1963." S/ASIA USA+45 RISK DETER REV WAR SOVEREIGN   USSR
IDEA/COMP. PAGE 27 G0533   NUC/PWR
                                                    B66

BRODIE B.,ESCALATION AND THE NUCLEAR OPTION. ASIA   NUC/PWR
CUBA EUR+WWI KOREA USA+45 USSR VIETNAM RISK ATTIT   GUERRILLA
DRIVE PERCEPT PROBABIL. PAGE 9 G0172   WAR
                                                    DETER
                                                    B66

ECKSTEIN A.,COMMUNIST CHINA'S ECONOMIC GROWTH AND   ASIA
FOREIGN TRADE* IMPLICATIONS FOR US POLICY. COM   ECO/UNDEV
USA+45 USSR STRUCT INDUS MARKET DIPLOM ECO/TAC   CREATE
FOR/AID INT/TRADE...STAT CHARTS. PAGE 17 G0332   PWR
                                                    B66

STONE J.J.,CONTAINING THE ARMS RACE* SOME SPECIFIC ARMS/CONT
PROPOSALS. ASIA USA+45 USSR PROB/SOLV BARGAIN   FEEDBACK
DIPLOM DETER NUC/PWR RATIONAL...GAME 20 DEPT/DEFEN COST
TREATY. PAGE 53 G1038   ATTIT
                                                    L66

ZOPPO C.E.,"NUCLEAR TECHNOLOGY, MULTIPOLARITY, AND NET/THEORY
INTERNATIONAL STABILITY." ASIA RUSSIA USA+45 STRUCT ORD/FREE
TOP/EX BAL/PWR DIPLOM DETER CIVMIL/REL NAT/COMP.   DECISION
PAGE 65 G1270   NUC/PWR
                                                    B67

RAWLINSON J.L.,CHINA'S STRUGGLE FOR NAVAL   SEA
DEVELOPMENT 1839-1895. ASIA DIPLOM ADMIN WAR   FORCES
...BIBLIOG DICTIONARY 19 CHINJAP. PAGE 46 G0907   PWR
                                                    B67

US SUPERINTENDENT OF DOCUMENTS,LIBRARY OF CONGRESS BIBLIOG/A
(PRICE LIST 83). AFR ASIA EUR+WWI USA+45 USSR NAT/G USA+45
DIPLOM CONFER CT/SYS WAR...DECISION PHIL/SCI   AUTOMAT
CLASSIF 19/20 CONGRESS PRESIDENT. PAGE 61 G1189   LAW
                                                    B67

YAMAMURA K.,ECONOMIC POLICY IN POSTWAR JAPAN. ASIA ECO/DEV
FINAN POL/PAR DIPLOM LEAD NAT/LISM ATTIT NEW/LIB   POLICY
POPULISM 20 CHINJAP. PAGE 64 G1262   NAT/G
                                                    TEC/DEV
                                                    L67

"POLITICAL PARTIES ON FOREIGN POLICY IN THE INTER- POL/PAR
ELECTION YEARS 1962-66." ASIA COM INDIA USA+45 PLAN DIPLOM
ATTIT...DECISION 20. PAGE 1 G0023   POLICY
                                                    L67

DAVIS P.C.,"THE COMING CHINESE COMMUNIST NUCLEAR   NUC/PWR
THREAT AND U.S. SEA BASED ABM OPTIONS." ASIA   DETER
CHINA/COM FUT USA+45 SEA NAT/G FORCES PLAN TEC/DEV WEAPON
LEAD ARMS/CONT...GEOG METH/COMP 20 ABM/DEFSYS.   DIPLOM
PAGE 14 G0279
                                                    S67

MARTIN L.,"THE AMERICAN ABM DECISION." ASIA COM   WEAPON
EUR+WWI UK USA+45 USSR FORCES DIPLOM PEACE...POLICY DETER
20 ABM/DEFSYS. PAGE 36 G0713   NUC/PWR
                                                    WAR
                                                    S67

TEKINER S.,"SINKIAN AND THE SINO-SOVIET CONFLICT." DIPLOM
ASIA COM USSR FORCES PLAN BAL/PWR CONTROL NUC/PWR   PWR
WAR WEAPON...DECISION 20. PAGE 54 G1060   MARXISM
                                                    S67

WALTERS R.E.,"THE ROLE OF NUCLEAR WEAPONS FOR THE   PLAN
WEST." ASIA UK USA+45 USSR DIPLOM COERCE WAR PEACE NUC/PWR
...POLICY DECISION 20. PAGE 62 G1209   WEAPON
                                                    FORCES
                                                    N67

ASIAN STUDIES CENTER,FOUR ARTICLES ON POPULATION   ASIA
AND FAMILY LIFE IN TAIWAN (ASIAN STUDIES PAPERS,   FAM
REPRINT SERIES NO. 2). CULTURE STRATA ECO/UNDEV   CENSUS
AGRI INDUS R+D KIN MUNIC...GEOG SOC CHARTS 20.   ANTHOL
PAGE 4 G0072

ASIAN STUDIES CENTER G0072

ASIANS....ASIANS, ASIAN MINORITIES

ASQUITH/HH....HERBERT HENRY ASQUITH

ASSASSINATION....SEE MURDER

ASSIMILATION....SEE GP/REL+INGP/REL

ASSOCIATIONS....SEE VOL/ASSN

ASTIA G0073,G0074

AT+T....AMERICAN TELEPHONE AND TELEGRAPH

ATATURK/MK....MUSTAFA KEMAL ATATURK

ATHENS....ATHENS, GREECE

ATKIN J.M. G0075

ATLAN/ALL....ATLANTIC ALLIANCE

ATLANTA....ATLANTA, GEORGIA

ATLANTIC ALLIANCE....SEE ATLAN/ALL

ATLANTIC FREE TRADE AREA....SEE AFTA

ATLASES....SEE MAPS

ATOM BOMB....SEE NUC/PWR

ATOMIC ENERGY AUTHORITY OF UN....SEE AEA

ATOMIC ENERGY COMMISSION....SEE AEC + COUNTRY'S NAME

ATOMIC INDUSTRIAL FORUM G0076,G0077,G0078,G0079,G0080,G0081

ATTENTION....SEE PERCEPT

ATTIT....ATTITUDES, OPINIONS, IDEOLOGY

CURRENT THOUGHT ON PEACE AND WAR. WOR+45 INT/ORG
FORCES PROB/SOLV DIPLOM NUC/PWR PERCEPT...POLICY
SOC 20 UN NATO. PAGE 1 G0001
— B / BIBLIOG/A / PEACE / ATTIT / WAR

PERSONNEL. USA+45 LAW LABOR LG/CO WORKER CREATE
GOV/REL PERS/REL ATTIT WEALTH. PAGE 1 G0010
— N / BIBLIOG/A / ADMIN / MGT / GP/REL

BERGSON H.,CREATIVE EVOLUTION. FUT WOR+45 WOR-45
INTELL AGRI R+D ATTIT PERCEPT PERSON RIGID/FLEX
...RELATIV PHIL/SCI PSY METH/CNCPT MATH HIST/WRIT
TREND HYPO/EXP TOT/POP. PAGE 7 G0127
— B11 / BIO/SOC / KNOWL

DRAPER J.W.,HISTORY OF THE CONFLICT BETWEEN
RELIGION AND SCIENCE. WOR-45 INTELL SOCIETY R+D
CREATE PLAN TEC/DEV EDU/PROP ATTIT PWR...PHIL/SCI
CONCPT OBS TIME/SEQ TREND GEN/LAWS TOT/POP. PAGE 16
G0314
— B23 / SECT / KNOWL

SOROKIN P.,CONTEMPORARY SOCIOLOGICAL THEORIES.
MOD/EUR UNIV SOCIETY R+D SCHOOL ECO/TAC EDU/PROP
ROUTINE ATTIT DRIVE...PSY CONCPT TIME/SEQ TREND
GEN/LAWS 20. PAGE 52 G1021
— B28 / CULTURE / SOC / WAR

DEWEY J.,THE QUEST FOR CERTAINTY. GP/REL RATIONAL
UTOPIA ATTIT MORAL ORD/FREE PWR...MYTH HIST/WRIT.
PAGE 15 G0301
— B29 / PHIL/SCI / PERSON / PERCEPT / KNOWL

FOREIGN AFFAIRS BIBLIOGRAPHY: A SELECTED AND
ANNOTATED LIST OF BOOKS ON INTERNATIONAL RELATIONS
1919-1962 (4 VOLS.). CONSTN FORCES COLONIAL
ARMS/CONT WAR NAT/LISM PEACE ATTIT DRIVE...POLICY
INT/LAW 20. PAGE 1 G0011
— B35 / BIBLIOG/A / DIPLOM / INT/ORG

LASSWELL H.D.,"THE RELATION OF IDEOLOGICAL
INTELLIGENCE TO PUBLIC POLICY." WOR+45 WOR-45
SOCIETY DELIB/GP ACT/RES CREATE PLAN DIPLOM
EDU/PROP CHOOSE KNOWL PWR...POLICY SOC TREND
GEN/LAWS 20. PAGE 32 G0638
— S42 / ATTIT / DECISION

BUSH V.,SCIENCE, THE ENDLESS FRONTIER. FUT USA-45
INTELL STRATA ACT/RES CREATE PLAN EDU/PROP ADMIN
NUC/PWR PEACE ATTIT HEALTH KNOWL...MAJORIT HEAL MGT
PHIL/SCI CONCPT OBS TREND 20. PAGE 10 G0195
— B45 / R+D / NAT/G

REVES E.,THE ANATOMY OF PEACE. WOR-45 LAW CULTURE
NAT/G PLAN TEC/DEV EDU/PROP WAR NAT/LISM ATTIT
ALL/VALS SOVEREIGN...POLICY HUM TIME/SEQ 20.
PAGE 46 G0914
— B45 / ACT/RES / CONCPT / NUC/PWR / PEACE

BAXTER J.P.,SCIENTISTS AGAINST TIME. EUR+WWI
MOD/EUR USA+45 USA-45 WOR+45 WOR-45 R+D NAT/G PLAN
ATTIT PWR...PHIL/SCI RECORD CON/ANAL 17/20. PAGE 6
G0107
— B46 / FORCES / WAR / NUC/PWR

NORTHROP F.S.C.,THE MEETING OF EAST AND WEST.
EUR+WWI FUT MOD/EUR UNIV WOR+45 WOR-45 INTELL
SOCIETY EX/STRUC TOP/EX ACT/RES LEGIT CHOOSE ATTIT
PERCEPT RIGID/FLEX ALL/VALS...POLICY JURID OBS
TOT/POP. PAGE 42 G0826
— B46 / DRIVE / TREND / PEACE

MASTERS D.,"ONE WORLD OR NONE." FUT WOR+45 INTELL
INT/ORG ACT/RES EDU/PROP DETER ATTIT RIGID/FLEX
SUPEGO KNOWL...STAT TREND ORG/CHARTS 20. PAGE 36
G0719
— L46 / POLICY / PHIL/SCI / ARMS/CONT / NUC/PWR

LASSWELL H.D.,THE ANALYSIS OF POLITICAL BEHAVIOUR:
AN EMPIRICAL APPROACH. WOR+45 CULTURE NAT/G FORCES
EDU/PROP ADMIN ATTIT PERCEPT KNOWL...PHIL/SCI PSY
SOC NEW/IDEA OBS INT GEN/METH NAZI 20. PAGE 32
G0639
— B47 / R+D / ACT/RES / ELITES

SOCIAL SCIENCE RESEARCH COUN.PUBLIC REACTION TO THE
ATOMIC BOMB AND WORLD AFFAIRS. SOCIETY CONFER
ARMS/CONT...STAT QU SAMP CHARTS 20. PAGE 52 G1019
— B47 / ATTIT / NUC/PWR / DIPLOM / WAR

ROSENHAUPT H.W.,HOW TO WAGE PEACE. USA+45 SOCIETY
STRATA STRUCT R+D INT/ORG POL/PAR LEGIS ACT/RES
CREATE PLAN EDU/PROP ADMIN EXEC ATTIT ALL/VALS
...TIME/SEQ TREND COLD/WAR 20. PAGE 48 G0937
— B49 / INTELL / CONCPT / DIPLOM

BERNSTEIN I.,THE NEW DEAL COLLECTIVE BARGAINING
PROCESS. USA-45 GOV/REL ATTIT...BIBLIOG 20
ROOSEVLT/F. PAGE 7 G0132
— B50 / LABOR / LEGIS / POLICY / NEW/LIB

KOENIG L.W.,THE SALE OF THE TANKERS. USA+45 SEA
DIST/IND POL/PAR DIPLOM ADMIN CIVMIL/REL ATTIT
...DECISION 20 PRESIDENT DEPT/STATE. PAGE 31 G0609
— B50 / NAT/G / POLICY / PLAN / GOV/REL

MANNHEIM K.,FREEDOM, POWER, AND DEMOCRATIC
PLANNING. FUT USSR WOR+45 ELITES INTELL SOCIETY
NAT/G EDU/PROP ROUTINE ATTIT DRIVE SUPEGO SKILL
...POLICY PSY CONCPT TREND GEN/LAWS 20. PAGE 35
G0700
— B50 / TEC/DEV / PLAN / CAP/ISM / UK

CONTINUITIES IN SOCIAL RESEARCH; STUDIES IN SCOPE
AND METHOD OF "THE AMERICAN SOLDIER" USA+45 FORCES
INGP/REL ATTIT...PSY SAMP CON/ANAL CHARTS GEN/LAWS
ANTHOL 20. PAGE 38 G0758
— B50 / SOC / PHIL/SCI / METH

LENTZ T.F.,"REPORT ON A SURVEY OF SOCIAL SCIENTISTS
CONDUCTED BY THE ATTITUDE RESEARCH LABORATORY." FUT
WOR+45 CREATE EDU/PROP...PSY STAT RECORD SYS/QU
SAMP/SIZ CON/ANAL VAL/FREE 20. PAGE 33 G0655
— S50 / ACT/RES / ATTIT / DIPLOM

HUXLEY J.,FREEDOM AND CULTURE. UNIV LAW SOCIETY R+D
ACADEM SCHOOL CREATE SANCTION ATTIT KNOWL...HUM
ANTHOL 20. PAGE 27 G0540
— B51 / CULTURE / ORD/FREE / PHIL/SCI / IDEA/COMP

MACRAE D.G.,"THE BOLSHEVIK IDEOLOGY: THE
INTELLECTUAL AND EMOTIONAL FACTORS IN COMMUNIST
AFFILIATION" (BMR)" COM LEAD REV ATTIT ORD/FREE
...SOC CON/ANAL 20 BOLSHEVISM. PAGE 35 G0693
— S51 / MARXISM / INTELL / PHIL/SCI / SECT

DAY E.E.,EDUCATION FOR FREEDOM AND RESPONSIBILITY.
FUT USA+45 CULTURE CONSULT EDU/PROP ATTIT SKILL
...MGT CONCPT OBS GEN/LAWS COLD/WAR 20. PAGE 14
G0282
— B52 / SCHOOL / KNOWL

ELDERSVELD S.J.,"RESEARCH IN POLITICAL BEHAVIOR"
(BMR)" USA+45 PLAN TEC/DEV ATTIT...BIBLIOG/A METH
20. PAGE 17 G0341
— L52 / ACT/RES / GEN/LAWS / CREATE

KECSKEMETI P.,"THE 'POLICY SCIENCES': ASPIRATION
AND OUTLOOK." UNIV CULTURE INTELL SOCIETY STRUCT
EDU/PROP ATTIT PERCEPT RIGID/FLEX KNOWL...PHIL/SCI
— S52 / CREATE / NEW/IDEA

METH/CNCPT OBS 20. PAGE 30 G0589

B53
HOVLAND C.I.,COMMUNICATION AND PERSUASION: PSY
PSYCHOLOGICAL STUDIES OF OPINION CHANGE. INTELL   EDU/PROP
SOCIETY ECO/DEV COM/IND R+D SERV/IND CREATE TEC/DEV
ATTIT RIGID/FLEX KNOWL NEW/IDEA. PAGE 27 G0531

B53
SAYLES L.R.,THE LOCAL UNION. CONSTN CULTURE   LABOR
DELIB/GP PARTIC CHOOSE GP/REL INGP/REL ATTIT ROLE   LEAD
...MAJORIT DECISION MGT. PAGE 49 G0958   ADJUD
  ROUTINE

S53
CORY R.H. JR.,"FORGING A PUBLIC INFORMATION POLICY   INT/ORG
FOR THE UNITED NATIONS." FUT WOR+45 SOCIETY ADMIN   EDU/PROP
PEACE ATTIT PERSON SKILL...CONCPT 20 UN. PAGE 13   BAL/PWR
G0257

B54
ARON R.,CENTURY OF TOTAL WAR. FUT WOR+45 WOR-45   ATTIT
SOCIETY INT/ORG NAT/G FORCES TOP/EX CREATE BAL/PWR   WAR
DOMIN EDU/PROP COERCE DETER PEACE TOTALISM PWR
...TIME/SEQ TREND COLD/WAR TOT/POP VAL/FREE
LEAGUE/NAT 20. PAGE 4 G0066

B54
MOSK S.A.,INDUSTRIAL REVOLUTION IN MEXICO. MARKET   INDUS
LABOR CREATE CAP/ISM ADMIN ATTIT SOCISM...POLICY 20   TEC/DEV
MEXIC/AMER. PAGE 40 G0789   ECO/UNDEV
  NAT/G

B54
REYNOLDS P.A.,BRITISH FOREIGN POLICY IN THE INTER-   DIPLOM
WAR YEARS. CZECHOSLVK GERMANY POLAND UK USA-45   POLICY
POL/PAR FORCES ECO/TAC ARMS/CONT WAR ATTIT 20.   NAT/G
PAGE 46 G0915

B54
US DEPARTMENT OF STATE,PUBLICATIONS OF THE   BIBLIOG
DEPARTMENT OF STATE, OCTOBER 1,1929 TO JANUARY 1,   DIPLOM
1953. AGRI INT/ORG FORCES FOR/AID EDU/PROP
ARMS/CONT NUC/PWR ATTIT 20 DEPT/STATE OAS UN NATO.
PAGE 57 G1122

S54
POLANYI M.,"ON THE INTRODUCTION OF SCIENCE INTO   INTELL
MORAL SUBJECTS." FUT WOR+45 ACT/RES ATTIT KNOWL   PHIL/SCI
...CONCPT NEW/IDEA 20. PAGE 45 G0882

C54
GOULDNER A.W.,"PATTERNS OF INDUSTRIAL BUREAUCRACY."   ADMIN
GP/REL CONSEN ATTIT DRIVE...BIBLIOG 20. PAGE 22   INDUS
G0438   OP/RES
  WORKER

B55
DAVIS E.,TWO MINUTES TO MIDNIGHT. WOR+45 PLAN   NUC/PWR
CONTROL NEUTRAL ARMS/CONT ATTIT ORD/FREE...PSY 20   WAR
COLD/WAR. PAGE 14 G0277   DETER
  DIPLOM

B55
MOCH J.,HUMAN FOLLY: DISARM OR PERISH. USA+45   FUT
WOR+45 SOCIETY INT/ORG NAT/G ACT/RES EDU/PROP ATTIT   DELIB/GP
PERSON KNOWL ORD/FREE PWR...MAJORIT TOT/POP   ARMS/CONT
COLD/WAR 20. PAGE 39 G0776   NUC/PWR

S55
ANGELL R.,"GOVERNMENTS AND PEOPLES AS FOCI FOR   FUT
PEACE-ORIENTED RESEARCH." WOR+45 CULTURE SOCIETY   SOC
FACE/GP ACT/RES CREATE PLAN DIPLOM EDU/PROP ROUTINE   PEACE
ATTIT PERCEPT SKILL...POLICY CONCPT OBS TREND
GEN/METH 20. PAGE 3 G0060

S55
GLADSTONE A.E.,"THE POSSIBILITY OF PREDICTING   PHIL/SCI
REACTIONS TO INTERNATIONAL EVENTS." UNIV SOCIETY   CONCPT
NAT/G FORCES CREATE EDU/PROP COERCE WAR ATTIT
PERSON KNOWL PWR SKILL...METH/CNCPT NEW/IDEA
ORG/CHARTS. PAGE 21 G0420

S55
SKINNER B.F.,"FREEDOM AND THE CONTROL OF MEN"   ORD/FREE
(BMR)" FUT WOR+45 CONTROL CHOOSE GP/REL ATTIT MORAL   TEC/DEV
PWR POPULISM...POLICY 20. PAGE 51 G1008   PHIL/SCI
  INTELL

B56
HISTORICAL ABSTRACTS. NAT/G CREATE DIPLOM ATTIT   WOR-45
...SOC DICTIONARY INDEX 18/20. PAGE 1 G0013   COMPUT/IR
  BIBLIOG/A

B56
ATOMIC INDUSTRIAL FORUM,PUBLIC RELATIONS FOR THE   NUC/PWR

ATOMIC INDUSTRY. WOR+45 PLAN PROB/SOLV EDU/PROP   INDUS
PRESS CONFER...AUD/VIS ANTHOL 20. PAGE 4 G0077   GP/REL
  ATTIT

B56
BLACKETT P.M.S.,ATOMIC WEAPONS AND EAST-WEST   FORCES
RELATIONS. FUT WOR+45 INT/ORG DELIB/GP COERCE ATTIT   PWR
RIGID/FLEX KNOWL...RELATIV HIST/WRIT TREND GEN/METH   ARMS/CONT
COLD/WAR 20. PAGE 7 G0138   NUC/PWR

S56
MILLER W.E.,"PRESIDENTIAL COATTAILS: A STUDY IN   CHIEF
POLITICAL MYTH AND METHODOLOGY" (BMR)" USA+45   CHOOSE
CREATE PARTIC ATTIT DRIVE PWR...DECISION CONCPT   POL/PAR
CHARTS SIMUL 20 PRESIDENT CONGRESS. PAGE 39 G0774   MYTH

B57
KISSINGER H.A.,NUCLEAR WEAPONS AND FOREIGN POLICY.   PLAN
FUT USA+45 WOR+45 INT/ORG FORCES ACT/RES TEC/DEV   DETER
DIPLOM ARMS/CONT COERCE ATTIT KNOWL PWR...DECISION   NUC/PWR
GEOG CHARTS 20. PAGE 31 G0602

B57
SPEIER H.,GERMAN REARMAMENT AND ATOMIC WAR: THE   TOP/EX
VIEWS OF GERMAN MILITARY AND POLITICAL LEADERS. FUT   FORCES
WOR+45 INT/ORG NAT/G WEAPON ATTIT PWR...INT QU   NUC/PWR
TOT/POP VAL/FREE COLD/WAR 20. PAGE 52 G1024   GERMANY

S57
JANOWITZ M.,"MILITARY ELITES AND THE STUDY OF WAR."   FORCES
USA+45 WOR-45 STRATA NAT/G PROF/ORG TEC/DEV DOMIN   ELITES
EDU/PROP COERCE WAR ATTIT RIGID/FLEX PWR RESPECT
...MGT TREND STERTYP GEN/METH 20. PAGE 28 G0558

S57
MCDONALD L.C.,"VOEGELIN AND THE POSITIVISTS: A NEW   PHIL/SCI
SCIENCE OF POLITICS." WOR+45 WOR-45 INTELL CREATE   CONCPT
PLAN ATTIT...METH/CNCPT NEW/IDEA OBS VAL/FREE 20.   GEN/METH
PAGE 37 G0734

B58
BIDWELL P.W.,RAW MATERIALS: A STUDY OF AMERICAN   EXTR/IND
POLICY. USA+45 USA-45 ECO/UNDEV AGRI INDUS KIN   ECO/DEV
CREATE PLAN ECO/TAC WAR PEACE ATTIT DRIVE WEALTH
...STAT CHARTS CONGRESS VAL/FREE. PAGE 7 G0135

B58
MARCUSE H.,SOVIET MARXISM, A CRITICAL ANALYSIS.   MARXISM
USSR CONSTN PLAN PRODUC RATIONAL SOCISM...IDEA/COMP   ATTIT
20 COM/PARTY. PAGE 36 G0703   POLICY

B58
NOEL-BAKER D.,THE ARMS RACE. WOR+45 NAT/G DELIB/GP   FUT
ACT/RES TEC/DEV EDU/PROP NUC/PWR ATTIT KNOWL PWR   INT/ORG
...CONCPT OBS LEAGUE/NAT 20 COLD/WAR. PAGE 42 G0823   ARMS/CONT
  PEACE

B58
US DEPARTMENT OF STATE,PUBLICATIONS OF THE   BIBLIOG
DEPARTMENT OF STATE, JANUARY 1,1953 TO DECEMBER 31,   DIPLOM
1957. AGRI INT/ORG FORCES FOR/AID EDU/PROP
ARMS/CONT NUC/PWR ATTIT 20 DEPT/STATE OAS UN NATO.
PAGE 57 G1123

S58
ANDERSON N.,"INTERNATIONAL SEMINARS: AN ANALYSIS   INT/ORG
AND AN EVALUATION." WOR+45 R+D ACT/RES CREATE PLAN   DELIB/GP
REGION ATTIT KNOWL SKILL...SOC REC/INT PERS/TEST
CHARTS 20. PAGE 3 G0057

S58
HUNTINGTON S.P.,"ARMS RACES: PREREQUISITES AND   FORCES
RESULTS." EUR+WWI MOD/EUR USA+45 WOR+45 WOR-45   PWR
NAT/G TEC/DEV BAL/PWR COERCE DETER ATTIT...POLICY   ARMS/CONT
TREND 20. PAGE 27 G0537

S58
LASSWELL H.D.,"THE SCIENTIFIC STUDY OF   PHIL/SCI
INTERNATIONAL RELATIONS." USA+45 INT/ORG CREATE   GEN/METH
EDU/PROP DETER ATTIT PERCEPT PWR...DECISION CONCPT   DIPLOM
METH/CNCPT STYLE CON/ANAL 20. PAGE 33 G0642

S58
SINGER J.D.,"THREAT PERCEPTION AND THE ARMAMENT   PERCEPT
TENSION DILEMMA." WOR+45 WOR-45 ELITES INT/ORG   ARMS/CONT
NAT/G DELIB/GP PLAN LEGIT COERCE DETER ATTIT   BAL/PWR
RIGID/FLEX PWR...DECISION PSY 20. PAGE 51 G1002

B59
AIR FORCE ACADEMY ASSEMBLY '59,INTERNATIONAL   FOR/AID
STABILITY AND PROGRESS (PAMPHLET). USA+45 USSR   FORCES
ECO/UNDEV PROB/SOLV BUDGET DIPLOM ADMIN DETER COST   WAR
ATTIT...TREND 20. PAGE 2 G0030   PLAN

B59
GODDARD V.,THE ENIGMA OF MENACE. WOR+45 SECT LEAD   PEACE

NUC/PWR WAR WEAPON CHOOSE PERSON PWR...POLICY
PHIL/SCI PACIFIST 20 COLD/WAR. PAGE 22 G0423

ARMS/CONT
DIPLOM
ATTIT

B59

HALEY A.G..FIRST COLLOQUIUM ON THE LAW OF OUTER
SPACE. WOR+45 INT/ORG ACT/RES PLAN BAL/PWR CONFER
ATTIT PWR...POLICY JURID CHARTS ANTHOL 20. PAGE 24
G0468

SPACE
LAW
SOVEREIGN
CONTROL

B59

HARVARD UNIVERSITY LAW SCHOOL,INTERNATIONAL
PROBLEMS OF FINANCIAL PROTECTION AGAINST NUCLEAR
RISK. WOR+45 NAT/G DELIB/GP PROB/SOLV DIPLOM
CONTROL ATTIT...POLICY INT/LAW MATH 20. PAGE 25
G0488

NUC/PWR
ADJUD
INDUS
FINAN

B59

HUGHES E.M..AMERICA THE VINCIBLE. USA+45 FOR/AID
ARMS/CONT NUC/PWR PERS/REL RATIONAL ATTIT ALL/VALS
20 COLD/WAR. PAGE 27 G0534

ORD/FREE
DIPLOM
WAR

B59

MIKSCHE F.O..THE FAILURE OF ATOMIC STRATEGY. COM
EUR+WWI INTELL POL/PAR FORCES PLAN ECO/TAC NUC/PWR
ATTIT DRIVE RIGID/FLEX PWR...DECISION GEOG PSY
CONCPT RECORD TREND CHARTS VAL/FREE 20. PAGE 39
G0766

ACT/RES
ORD/FREE
DIPLOM
ARMS/CONT

B59

COLUMBIA U BUREAU APPL SOC R, ATTITUDES OF
PROMINENT AMERICANS TOWARD "WORLD PEACE THROUGH
WORLD LAW" (SUPRA-NATL ORGANIZATION FOR WAR
PREVENTION). USA+45 USSR ELITES FORCES PLAN
PROB/SOLV CONTROL WAR PWR...POLICY SOC QU IDEA/COMP
20 UN. PAGE 45 G0888

ATTIT
ACT/RES
INT/LAW
STAT

B59

RUSSELL B..COMMON SENSE AND NUCLEAR WARFARE. WOR+45
INTELL SOCIETY STRATA NAT/G TOP/EX EDU/PROP ATTIT
PERSON KNOWL MORAL PWR...POLICY CONCPT MYTH
CON/ANAL COLD/WAR 20. PAGE 48 G0948

ORD/FREE
ARMS/CONT
NUC/PWR

B59

SPANIER J.W..THE TRUMAN-MACARTHUR CONTROVERSY AND
THE KOREAN WAR. USA+45 TOP/EX PROB/SOLV LEAD ATTIT
PWR...POLICY BIBLIOG/A UN. PAGE 52 G1023

CIVMIL/REL
FORCES
CHIEF
WAR

B59

VAN WAGENEN R.W..SOME VIEWS OF AMERICAN DEFENSE
OFFICIALS ABOUT THE UNITED NATIONS (PAPER). FUT
USA+45 NAT/G DIPLOM WAR EFFICIENCY PEACE...POLICY
INT 20 UN DEPT/DEFEN. PAGE 61 G1192

INT/ORG
LEAD
ATTIT
FORCES

B59

WARD B..5 IDEAS THAT CHANGE THE WORLD. WOR+45
WOR-45 SOCIETY STRUCT AGRI INDUS INT/ORG NAT/G
FORCES ACT/RES ARMS/CONT TOTALISM ATTIT DRIVE
GEN/LAWS. PAGE 62 G1210

ECO/UNDEV
ALL/VALS
NAT/LISM
COLONIAL

S59

BENDIX R.."INDUSTRIALIZATION, IDEOLOGIES, AND
SOCIAL STRUCTURE" (BMR) UK USA-45 USSR STRUCT
WORKER GP/REL EFFICIENCY...IDEA/COMP 20. PAGE 6
G0117

INDUS
ATTIT
MGT
ADMIN

S59

GOLDHAMMER H.."SOME OBSERVATIONS ON POLITICAL
GAMING." FUT WOR+45 R+D NAT/G ACT/RES CREATE CHOOSE
ATTIT PWR...POLICY CONCPT METH/CNCPT STYLE KNO/TEST
TREND HYPO/EXP GAME GEN/METH METH 20. PAGE 22 G0426

COMPUT/IR
DECISION
DIPLOM

S59

MILBURN T.W.."WHAT CONSTITUTES EFFECTIVE
DETERRENCE." USA+45 USSR WOR+45 STRUCT FORCES
ACT/RES PLAN SUPEGO KNOWL ORD/FREE PWR...RELATIV
PSY CONCPT VAL/FREE 20 COLD/WAR. PAGE 39 G0768

INTELL
ATTIT
DETER
NUC/PWR

S59

SIMONS H.."WORLD-WIDE CAPABILITIES FOR PRODUCTION
AND CONTROL OF NUCLEAR WEAPONS." FUT WOR+45 INDUS
INT/ORG NAT/G ECO/TAC ATTIT PWR SKILL...TREND
CHARTS VAL/FREE 20. PAGE 51 G1001

TEC/DEV
ARMS/CONT
NUC/PWR

S59

WILLIAMS B.H.."SCIENTIFIC METHOD IN FOREIGN
POLICY." WOR+45 NAT/G FORCES TOP/EX DOMIN LEGIT
COERCE PEACE ATTIT KNOWL ORD/FREE PWR...GEN/LAWS
GEN/METH TOT/POP COLD/WAR NAZI. PAGE 63 G1241

PLAN
PHIL/SCI
DIPLOM

B60

APTHEKER H..DISARMAMENT AND THE AMERICAN ECONOMY: A
SYMPOSIUM. FUT USA+45 ECO/DEV DIST/IND FINAN INDUS
PROC/MFG LABOR NAT/G POL/PAR CONSULT PLAN CAP/ISM
INT/TRADE PEACE ATTIT MORAL WEALTH...TREND GEN/LAWS

MARXIST
ARMS/CONT

TOT/POP 20. PAGE 3 G0063

B60

BARNET R..WHO WANTS DISARMAMENT. COM EUR+WWI USA+45
USSR INT/ORG NAT/G BAL/PWR DIPLOM EDU/PROP COERCE
DETER NUC/PWR WAR WEAPON ATTIT PWR...TIME/SEQ
COLD/WAR CONGRESS 20. PAGE 5 G0096

PLAN
FORCES
ARMS/CONT

B60

CARPENTER E..EXPLORATIONS IN COMMUNICATION. USSR
CULTURE SCHOOL SECT EDU/PROP PRESS TV AUTOMAT
FEEDBACK ATTIT PERSON...ART/METH PSY 20. PAGE 11
G0211

ANTHOL
COM/IND
TEC/DEV
WRITING

B60

EINSTEIN A..EINSTEIN ON PEACE. FUT WOR+45 WOR-45
SOCIETY NAT/G PLAN BAL/PWR CAP/ISM DIPLOM ARMS/CONT
DETER NAT/LISM...POLICY RELATIV HUM PHIL/SCI CONCPT
BIOG COLD/WAR LEAGUE/NAT NAZI. PAGE 17 G0338

INT/ORG
ATTIT
NUC/PWR
PEACE

B60

GOLDSEN J.M..INTERNATIONAL POLITICAL IMPLICATIONS
OF ACTIVITIES IN OUTER SPACE. FUT USA+45 WOR+45 AIR
LAW ACT/RES LEGIT ATTIT KNOWL ORD/FREE PWR...CONCPT
20. PAGE 22 G0427

R+D
SPACE

B60

GRANICK D..THE RED EXECUTIVE. COM USA+45 SOCIETY
ECO/DEV INDUS NAT/G POL/PAR EX/STRUC PLAN ECO/TAC
EDU/PROP ADMIN EXEC ATTIT DRIVE...GP/COMP 20.
PAGE 22 G0440

PWR
STRATA
USSR
ELITES

B60

HEILBRONER R.L..THE FUTURE AS HISTORY. USA+45
WOR+45 WOR-45 SOCIETY ECO/DEV ECO/UNDEV VOL/ASSN
PLAN CAP/ISM NUC/PWR CHOOSE NAT/LISM ATTIT ORD/FREE
RESPECT WEALTH SOCISM 20. PAGE 25 G0501

TEC/DEV
TREND

B60

HITCH C.J..THE ECONOMICS OF DEFENSE IN THE NUCLEAR
AGE. USA+45 WOR+45 CREATE PLAN NUC/PWR ATTIT
...CON/ANAL CHARTS HYPO/EXP NATO 20. PAGE 26 G0514

R+D
FORCES

B60

MCGREGOR D..THE HUMAN SIDE OF ENTERPRISE. USA+45
LEAD ROUTINE GP/REL INGP/REL...CONCPT GEN/LAWS 20.
PAGE 38 G0741

MGT
ATTIT
SKILL
EDU/PROP

B60

PARRY A..RUSSIA'S ROCKETS AND MISSILES. COM FUT
GERMANY USA+45 INTELL ECO/DEV ACT/RES
NUC/PWR WEAPON ATTIT ALL/VALS...OBS TIME/SEQ
COLD/WAR 20. PAGE 44 G0859

PLAN
TEC/DEV
SPACE
USSR

B60

PENTONY D.E..THE UNDERDEVELOPED LANDS. FUT WOR+45
CULTURE AGRI FINAN INDUS MARKET INT/ORG LABOR NAT/G
VOL/ASSN CONSULT TEC/DEV ECO/TAC EDU/PROP COLONIAL
ATTIT WEALTH...OBS RECORD SAMP TREND GEN/METH WORK
UN 20. PAGE 44 G0867

ECO/UNDEV
POLICY
FOR/AID
INT/TRADE

L60

HOLTON G.."ARMS CONTROL." FUT WOR+45 CULTURE
INT/ORG NAT/G FORCES TOP/EX PLAN EDU/PROP COERCE
ATTIT RIGID/FLEX ORD/FREE...POLICY PHIL/SCI SOC
TREND COLD/WAR. PAGE 27 G0524

ACT/RES
CONSULT
ARMS/CONT
NUC/PWR

L60

JACOB P.E.."THE DISARMAMENT CONSENSUS." USA+45 USSR
WOR+45 INT/ORG NAT/G ACT/RES TEC/DEV BAL/PWR
EDU/PROP ADMIN COERCE DETER NUC/PWR CONSEN
RIGID/FLEX PWR...CONCPT RECORD CHARTS COLD/WAR 20.
PAGE 28 G0552

DELIB/GP
ATTIT
ARMS/CONT

S60

BARNETT H.J.."RESEARCH AND DEVELOPMENT, ECONOMIC
GROWTH, AND NATIONAL SECURITY." USA+45 R+D CREATE
ECO/TAC ATTIT DRIVE PWR...POLICY SOC METH/CNCPT
QUANT STAT TIME/SEQ ORG/CHARTS COLD/WAR 20. PAGE 5
G0097

ACT/RES
PLAN

S60

DOUGHERTY J.E.."KEY TO SECURITY: DISARMAMENT OR
ARMS STABILITY." COM USA+45 USSR INT/ORG NAT/G
CREATE EDU/PROP COERCE DETER ATTIT PWR...DECISION
CONCPT MYTH NEW/IDEA TREND 20 COLD/WAR. PAGE 16
G0311

FORCES
ORD/FREE
ARMS/CONT
NUC/PWR

S60

DYSON F.J.."THE FUTURE DEVELOPMENT OF NUCLEAR
WEAPONS." FUT WOR+45 DELIB/GP ACT/RES PLAN DETER
WEAPON ATTIT PWR...POLICY 20. PAGE 17 G0328

INT/ORG
ARMS/CONT
NUC/PWR

S60

HAYTON R.D.."THE ANTARCTIC SETTLEMENT OF 1959." FUT

DELIB/GP

USA+45 WOR+45 WOR-45 STRUCT R+D INT/ORG EX/STRUC JURID
CREATE TEC/DEV LEGIT PEACE ATTIT SOVEREIGN DIPLOM
...TIME/SEQ 20 TREATY IGY. PAGE 25 G0495 REGION

S60
HUTCHINSON C.E.,"AN INSTITUTE FOR NATIONAL SECURITY POLICY
AFFAIRS." USA+45 R+D NAT/G CONSULT TOP/EX ACT/RES METH/CNCPT
CREATE PLAN TEC/DEV EDU/PROP ROUTINE NUC/PWR ATTIT ELITES
ORD/FREE PWR...DECISION MGT PHIL/SCI CONCPT RECORD DIPLOM
GEN/LAWS GEN/METH 20. PAGE 27 G0539

S60
KAPLAN M.A.,"THEORETICAL ANALYSIS OF THE BALANCE OF CREATE
POWER." FUT USA+45 WOR+45 INTELL ECO/DEV INT/ORG NEW/IDEA
NAT/G CONSULT TOP/EX ACT/RES PLAN TEC/DEV ATTIT DIPLOM
ALL/VALS...METH/CNCPT TOT/POP 20. PAGE 29 G0576 NUC/PWR

S60
KELLEY G.A.,"THE POLITICAL BACKGROUND OF THE FRENCH NAT/G
A-BOMB." EUR+WWI USSR FORCES TOP/EX TEC/DEV NUC/PWR RESPECT
ATTIT PWR...CONCPT OBS/ENVIR TREND 20. PAGE 30 NAT/LISM
G0591 FRANCE

S60
OSGOOD C.E.,"A CASE FOR GRADUATED UNILATERAL ATTIT
DISENGAGEMENT." FUT WOR+45 CULTURE SOCIETY NAT/G EDU/PROP
NUC/PWR WAR PERSON SUPEGO ALL/VALS...POLICY PSY ARMS/CONT
CONCPT COLD/WAR TOT/POP VAL/FREE 20. PAGE 43 G0848

S60
RIVKIN A.,"AFRICAN ECONOMIC DEVELOPMENT: ADVANCED AFR
TECHNOLOGY AND THE STAGES OF GROWTH." CULTURE TEC/DEV
ECO/UNDEV AGRI COM/IND EXTR/IND PLAN ECO/TAC ATTIT FOR/AID
DRIVE RIGID/FLEX SKILL WEALTH...MGT SOC GEN/LAWS
WORK TOT/POP 20. PAGE 47 G0923

C60
SCHRAMM W.,"MASS COMMUNICATIONS: A BOOK OF READINGS COM/IND
(2ND ED.)" LG/CO PRESS ADMIN CONTROL ROUTINE ATTIT EDU/PROP
ROLE SUPEGO...CHARTS ANTHOL BIBLIOG 20. PAGE 50 CROWD
G0977 MAJORIT

N60
US HOUSE COMM SCI ASTRONAUT,THE ORGANIZATION OF THE ACT/RES
US NATIONAL SPACE EFFORT. USA+45 WOR+45 AIR ECO/DEV SKILL
NAT/G PLAN TEC/DEV DIPLOM EDU/PROP ATTIT DRIVE PWR SPACE
...OBS TIME/SEQ TREND TOT/POP 20. PAGE 58 G1142

B61
BONNEFOUS M.,EUROPE ET TIERS MONDE. EUR+WWI SOCIETY AFR
INT/ORG NAT/G VOL/ASSN ACT/RES TEC/DEV CAP/ISM ECO/UNDEV
ECO/TAC ATTIT ORD/FREE SOVEREIGN...POLICY CONCPT FOR/AID
TREND 20. PAGE 8 G0153 INT/TRADE

B61
FRISCH D.,ARMS REDUCTION: PROGRAM AND ISSUES. PLAN
USA+45 INT/ORG NAT/G ACT/RES REGION NUC/PWR ATTIT FORCES
PWR...POLICY 20. PAGE 20 G0395 ARMS/CONT
DIPLOM

B61
HADLEY A.T.,THE NATIONS SAFETY AND ARMS CONTROL. ACT/RES
FUT USA+45 WOR+45 TOP/EX PLAN TEC/DEV ATTIT DRIVE ROUTINE
...CONCPT OBS TIME/SEQ TREND 20. PAGE 24 G0466 DETER
NUC/PWR

B61
HENKIN L.,ARMS CONTROL: ISSUES FOR THE PUBLIC. WOR+45
EUR+WWI FUT USA+45 USSR INT/ORG NAT/G DIPLOM DELIB/GP
EDU/PROP DETER NUC/PWR ATTIT PWR...CONCPT RECORD ARMS/CONT
HIST/WRIT TIME/SEQ TOT/POP COLD/WAR 20. PAGE 26
G0506

B61
KISSINGER H.A.,THE NECESSITY FOR CHOICE. FUT USA+45 TOP/EX
ECO/UNDEV NAT/G PLAN ECO/TAC ARMS/CONT TREND
DETER NUC/PWR ATTIT...POLICY CONCPT RECORD GEN/LAWS DIPLOM
COLD/WAR 20. PAGE 31 G0604

B61
KRUPP S.,PATTERN IN ORGANIZATIONAL ANALYSIS: A MGT
CRITICAL EXAMINATION. INGP/REL PERS/REL RATIONAL CONTROL
ATTIT AUTHORIT DRIVE PWR...DECISION PHIL/SCI SOC CONCPT
IDEA/COMP. PAGE 32 G0622 METH/CNCPT

B61
LUNDBERG G.A.,CAN SCIENCE SAVE US. UNIV CULTURE ACT/RES
INTELL SOCIETY ECO/DEV R+D PLAN EDU/PROP ROUTINE CONCPT
CHOOSE ATTIT PERCEPT ALL/VALS...TREND 20. PAGE 34 TOTALISM
G0679

B61
MURPHY E.F.,WATER PURITY: A STUDY IN LEGAL CONTROL SEA
OF NATURAL RESOURCES. LOC/G ACT/RES PLAN TEC/DEV LAW
LOBBY GP/REL COST ATTIT HEALTH ORD/FREE...HEAL PROVS
JURID 20 WISCONSIN WATER. PAGE 40 G0797 CONTROL

B61
NOGEE J.L.,SOVIET POLICY TOWARD INTERNATIONAL INT/ORG
CONTROL OF ATOMIC ENERGY. COM USA+45 WOR+45 INTELL ATTIT
NAT/G ACT/RES DIPLOM EDU/PROP NUC/PWR TOTALISM ARMS/CONT
PERCEPT KNOWL PWR...TIME/SEQ COLD/WAR 20. PAGE 42 USSR
G0824

B61
ROSENAU J.N.,INTERNATIONAL POLITICS AND FOREIGN ACT/RES
POLICY: A READER IN RESEARCH AND THEORY. ELITES DIPLOM
ATTIT SOVEREIGN...DECISION CHARTS HYPO/EXP GAME CONCPT
SIMUL ANTHOL BIBLIOG METH 20. PAGE 48 G0936 POLICY

B61
STEIN W.,NUCLEAR WEAPONS: A CATHOLIC RESPONSE. NUC/PWR
WOR+45 FORCES ARMS/CONT DETER MURDER MORAL...POLICY WAR
CATH IDEA/COMP ANTHOL 20. PAGE 52 G1033 CATHISM
ATTIT

L61
THOMPSON V.A.,"HIERARARCHY, SPECIALIZATION, AND PERS/REL
ORGANIZATIONAL CONFLICT" (BMR)" WOR+45 STRATA PROB/SOLV
STRUCT WORKER TEC/DEV GP/REL INGP/REL ATTIT ADMIN
AUTHORIT 20 BUREAUCRCY. PAGE 54 G1069 EX/STRUC

S61
MORGENSTERN O.,"THE N-COUNTRY PROBLEM." EUR+WWI FUT
UNIV USA+45 WOR+45 SOCIETY CONSULT TOP/EX ACT/RES BAL/PWR
PLAN EDU/PROP ATTIT DRIVE...POLICY OBS TREND NUC/PWR
TOT/POP 20. PAGE 40 G0781 TEC/DEV

S61
TAUBENFELD H.J.,"OUTER SPACE--PAST POLITICS AND PLAN
FUTURE POLICY." FUT USA+45 USA-45 WOR+45 AIR INTELL SPACE
STRUCT ECO/DEV NAT/G TOP/EX ACT/RES ADMIN ROUTINE INT/ORG
NUC/PWR ATTIT DRIVE...CONCPT TIME/SEQ TREND TOT/POP
20. PAGE 54 G1054

B62
SOVIET STAND ON DISARMAMENT. COM EUR+WWI FUT USA+45 ACT/RES
NAT/G TOP/EX NUC/PWR PEACE ATTIT...POLICY CONCPT ORD/FREE
TOT/POP 20. PAGE 1 G0016 ARMS/CONT
USSR

B62
CARSON R.,SILENT SPRING. USA+45 AIR CULTURE AGRI HABITAT
INDUS ADMIN ATTIT RIGID/FLEX ORD/FREE PWR...POLICY TREND
20. PAGE 11 G0216 SOCIETY
CONTROL

B62
DODDS H.W.,THE ACADEMIC PRESIDENT "EDUCATOR OR ACADEM
CARETAKER? FINAN DELIB/GP EDU/PROP PARTIC ATTIT ADMIN
ROLE PWR...POLICY RECORD INT. PAGE 16 G0304 LEAD
CONTROL

B62
GILPIN R.,AMERICAN SCIENTISTS AND NUCLEAR WEAPONS INTELL
POLICY. COM FUT USA+45 WOR+45 INT/ORG NAT/G ATTIT
PROF/ORG CONSULT FORCES CREATE TEC/DEV BAL/PWR DETER
EDU/PROP ARMS/CONT WAR PERCEPT KNOWL MORAL PWR NUC/PWR
...PHIL/SCI SOC CONCPT GEN/LAWS 20. PAGE 21 G0417

B62
GOLOVINE M.N.,CONFLICT IN SPACE: A PATTERN OF WAR CREATE
IN A NEW DIMENSION. FUT USA+45 WOR+45 AIR FORCES TEC/DEV
PLAN DIPLOM DOMIN ATTIT...STAT AUD/VIS CHARTS NUC/PWR
COLD/WAR 20. PAGE 22 G0432 SPACE

B62
KAHN H.,THINKING ABOUT THE UNTHINKABLE. FUT USA+45 INT/ORG
LAW NAT/G CONSULT FORCES ACT/RES CREATE PLAN ORD/FREE
TEC/DEV BAL/PWR DIPLOM EDU/PROP ARMS/CONT DETER NUC/PWR
ATTIT...CONCPT OBS TREND COLD/WAR 20. PAGE 29 G0570 PEACE

B62
KARNJAHAPRAKORN C.,MUNICIPAL GOVERNMENT IN THAILAND LOC/G
AS AN INSTITUTION AND PROCESS OF SELF-GOVERNMENT. MUNIC
THAILAND CULTURE FINAN EX/STRUC LEGIS PLAN CONTROL ORD/FREE
GOV/REL EFFICIENCY ATTIT...POLICY 20. PAGE 29 G0578 ADMIN

B62
LEFEVER E.W.,ARMS AND ARMS CONTROL. COM USA+45 ATTIT
INT/ORG TEC/DEV DIPLOM ORD/FREE 20. PAGE 33 G0652 PWR
ARMS/CONT
BAL/PWR

B62
OSGOOD C.E.,AN ALTERNATIVE TO WAR OR SURRENDER. FUT ORD/FREE
UNIV CULTURE INTELL SOCIETY R+D INT/ORG CONSULT EDU/PROP
DELIB/GP ACT/RES PLAN CHOOSE ATTIT PERCEPT KNOWL PEACE
...PHIL/SCI PSY SOC TREND GEN/LAWS 20. PAGE 43 WAR
G0849

PERRE J.,LES MUTATIONS DE LA GUERRE MODERNE: DE LA | WAR
REVOLUTION FRANCAISE A LA REVOLUTION NUCLEAIRE. | FORCES
DIPLOM ARMS/CONT DEATH REV WEAPON GP/REL PEACE | NUC/PWR
ATTIT...STAT PREDICT BIBLIOG 18/20 WWI. PAGE 44
G0870
B62

RIKER W.H.,THE THEORY OF POLITICAL COALITIONS. | FUT
WOR+45 INTELL NAT/G CREATE PLAN ATTIT DRIVE PERCEPT | SIMUL
...DECISION PSY SOC METH/CNCPT NEW/IDEA MATH CHARTS
GAME TOT/POP 20. PAGE 47 G0921
B62

SOHN L.B.,ZONAL DISARMAMENT: VARIATIONS ON A THEME. | ORD/FREE
FUT WOR+45 SOCIETY ACT/RES PLAN NUC/PWR PEACE ATTIT | NEW/IDEA
...POLICY GEOG CONT/OBS HYPO/EXP 20. PAGE 52 G1020 | ARMS/CONT
B62

US SENATE COMM GOVT OPERATIONS,ADMINISTRATION OF | ORD/FREE
NATIONAL SECURITY. USA+45 CHIEF PLAN PROB/SOLV | ADMIN
TEC/DEV DIPLOM ATTIT...POLICY DECISION 20 | NAT/G
KENNEDY/JF RUSK/D MCNAMARA/R BUNDY/M HERTER/C. | CONTROL
PAGE 60 G1177
B62

WRIGHT Q.,PREVENTING WORLD WAR THREE. FUT WOR+45 | CREATE
CULTURE INT/ORG NAT/G CONSULT FORCES ADMIN | ATTIT
ARMS/CONT DRIVE RIGID/FLEX ORD/FREE SOVEREIGN
...POLICY CONCPT TREND STERTYP COLD/WAR 20. PAGE 64
G1259
B62

FINKELSTEIN L.S.,"ARMS INSPECTION." FUT WOR+45 | FORCES
NAT/G DIPLOM ATTIT PERCEPT RIGID/FLEX ORD/FREE | PWR
COLD/WAR 20. PAGE 19 G0369 | ARMS/CONT
L62

ALBONETTI A.,"IL SECONDO PROGRAMMA QUINQUENNALE | R+D
1963-67 ED IL BILANCIO RICERCHE ED INVESTIMENTI PER | PLAN
IL 1963 DELL'ERATOM." EUR+WWI FUT ITALY WOR+45 | NUC/PWR
ECO/DEV SERV/IND INT/ORG TEC/DEV ECO/TAC ATTIT
SKILL WEALTH...MGT TIME/SEQ OEEC 20. PAGE 2 G0035
S62

FINKELSTEIN L.S.,"THE UNITED NATIONS AND | INT/ORG
ORGANIZATIONS FOR CONTROL OF ARMAMENT." FUT WOR+45 | PWR
VOL/ASSN DELIB/GP TOP/EX CREATE EDU/PROP LEGIT | ARMS/CONT
ADJUD NUC/PWR ATTIT RIGID/FLEX ORD/FREE...POLICY
DECISION CONCPT OBS TREND GEN/LAWS TOT/POP
COLD/WAR. PAGE 19 G0368
S62

FOSTER R.B.,"UNILATERAL ARMS CONTROL MEASURES AND | PLAN
DISARMAMENT NEGOTIATION." WOR+45 VOL/ASSN DELIB/GP | ORD/FREE
ACT/RES ECO/TAC EDU/PROP ATTIT RIGID/FLEX...CONCPT | ARMS/CONT
MYTH TIME/SEQ COLD/WAR 20. PAGE 20 G0386 | DETER
S62

FOSTER W.C.,"ARMS CONTROL AND DISARMAMENT IN A | DELIB/GP
DIVIDED WORLD." COM FUT USA+45 USSR WOR+45 INTELL | POLICY
INT/ORG NAT/G VOL/ASSN CONSULT CREATE PLAN TEC/DEV | ARMS/CONT
EDU/PROP LEGIT NUC/PWR ATTIT RIGID/FLEX...CONCPT | DIPLOM
TREND TOT/POP 20 UN. PAGE 20 G0387
S62

PHIPPS T.E.,"THE CASE FOR DETERRENCE." FUT WOR+45 | ATTIT
SOCIETY EX/STRUC FORCES ACT/RES CREATE PLAN TEC/DEV | COERCE
ROUTINE RIGID/FLEX ORD/FREE...POLICY MYTH NEW/IDEA | DETER
STERTYP COLD/WAR 20. PAGE 45 G0876 | ARMS/CONT
S62

WALTER E.,"VERS UNE CLASSIFICATION SCIENTIFIQUE DE | PLAN
LA SOCIOLOGIE." UNIV CULTURE INTELL SOCIETY R+D | CONCPT
ACT/RES LEGIT ROUTINE ATTIT KNOWL...JURID MGT TREND
GEN/LAWS 20. PAGE 62 G1208
S62

US CONGRESS JT ATOM ENRGY COMM,PEACEFUL USES OF | NUC/PWR
ATOMIC ENERGY, HEARING. USA+45 USSR TEC/DEV ATTIT | ACADEM
RIGID/FLEX...TESTS CHARTS EXHIBIT METH/COMP 20 | SCHOOL
CONGRESS. PAGE 57 G1112 | NAT/COMP
N62

ABSHIRE D.M.,NATIONAL SECURITY: POLITICAL, | FUT
MILITARY, AND ECONOMIC STRATEGIES IN THE DECADE | ACT/RES
AHEAD. ASIA COM USA+45 WOR+45 ECO/DEV ECO/UNDEV | BAL/PWR
INT/ORG DELIB/GP FORCES ECO/TAC COERCE ATTIT
RIGID/FLEX HEALTH ORD/FREE PWR WEALTH...POLICY STAT
CHARTS ANTHOL COLD/WAR VAL/FREE. PAGE 1 G0024
B63

BONINI C.P.,SIMULATION OF INFORMATION AND DECISION | INDUS
SYSTEMS IN THE FIRM. MARKET BUDGET DOMIN EDU/PROP | SIMUL
ADMIN COST ATTIT HABITAT PERCEPT PWR...CONCPT | DECISION
PROBABIL QUANT PREDICT HYPO/EXP BIBLIOG. PAGE 8 | MGT
B63

G0152

DALAND R.T.,PERSPECTIVES OF BRAZILIAN PUBLIC | ADMIN
ADMINISTRATION (VOL. I). BRAZIL LAW ECO/UNDEV | NAT/G
SCHOOL CHIEF TEC/DEV CONFER CONTROL GP/REL ATTIT | PLAN
ROLE PWR...ANTHOL 20. PAGE 14 G0272 | GOV/REL
B63

HALEY A.G.,SPACE LAW AND GOVERNMENT. FUT USA+45 | INT/ORG
WOR+45 LEGIS ACT/RES CREATE ATTIT RIGID/FLEX | LAW
ORD/FREE PWR SOVEREIGN...POLICY JURID CONCPT CHARTS | SPACE
VAL/FREE 20. PAGE 24 G0469
B63

HOFSTADTER R.,ANTI-INTELLECTUALISM IN AMERICAN | INTELL
LIFE. USA+45 AGRI INDUS ACADEM TEC/DEV EDU/PROP | EPIST
INGP/REL ATTIT...SOC WORSHIP 20 MCCARTHY/J | CULTURE
STEVENSN/A. PAGE 26 G0522 | SOCIETY
B63

HOWER R.M.,MANAGERS AND SCIENTISTS. EX/STRUC CREATE | R+D
ADMIN REPRESENT ATTIT DRIVE ROLE PWR SKILL...SOC | MGT
INT. PAGE 27 G0532 | PERS/REL
| INGP/REL
B63

KORNHAUSER W.,SCIENTISTS IN INDUSTRY: CONFLICT AND | CREATE
ACCOMMODATION. USA+45 R+D LG/CO NAT/G TEC/DEV | INDUS
CONTROL ADJUST ATTIT...MGT STAT INT BIBLIOG 20. | PROF/ORG
PAGE 31 G0614 | GP/REL
B63

LILIENTHAL D.E.,CHANGE, HOPE, AND THE BOMB. USA+45 | ATTIT
WOR+45 R+D INT/ORG NAT/G DELIB/GP FORCES ACT/RES | MYTH
DETER RIGID/FLEX ORD/FREE...POLICY CONCPT OBS AEC | ARMS/CONT
20. PAGE 34 G0666 | NUC/PWR
B63

MULLENBACH P.,CIVILIAN NUCLEAR POWER: ECONOMIC | USA+45
ISSUES AND POLICY FORMATION. FINAN INT/ORG DELIB/GP | ECO/DEV
ACT/RES ECO/TAC ATTIT SUPEGO HEALTH ORD/FREE PWR | NUC/PWR
...POLICY CONCPT MATH STAT CHARTS VAL/FREE 20
COLD/WAR. PAGE 40 G0792
B63

PEARSELL M.,MEDICAL BEHAVIORAL SCIENCE: A SELECTED | BIBLIOG
BIBLIOGRAPHY OF CULTURAL ANTHROPOLOGY, SOCIAL | SOC
PSYCHOLOGY, AND SOCIOLOGY... USA+45 USA-45 R+D | PSY
ATTIT ROLE 20. PAGE 44 G0863 | HEALTH
B63

US DEPARTMENT OF THE ARMY,US OVERSEAS BASES: | BIBLIOG/A
PRESENT STATUS AND FUTURE PROSPECTS (PAMPHLET). | WAR
USA+45 DIPLOM NUC/PWR ATTIT ORD/FREE...POLICY | BAL/PWR
CHARTS 20. PAGE 58 G1130 | DETER
B63

WALES H.G.,A BASIC BIBLIOGRAPHY ON MARKETING | BIBLIOG/A
RESEARCH (REV. ED.). ATTIT...MGT STAT INT QU SAMP | MARKET
TREND 20. PAGE 62 G1206 | OP/RES
| METH/COMP
B63

BEGUIN H.,"ASPECTS GEOGRAPHIQUE DE LA | ECO/UNDEV
POLARISATION." FUT WOR+45 SOCIETY STRUCT ECO/DEV | GEOG
R+D BAL/PWR ADMIN ATTIT RIGID/FLEX HEALTH WEALTH | DIPLOM
...CHARTS 20. PAGE 6 G0114
L63

BRENNAN D.G.,"ARMS CONTROL AND CIVIL DEFENSE." | PLAN
USA+45 WOR+45 NAT/G BAL/PWR ROUTINE ATTIT | HEALTH
RIGID/FLEX ORD/FREE...SOC TOT/POP 20. PAGE 8 G0165 | ARMS/CONT
| DETER
L63

NIEBURG H.,"EURATOM: A STUDY IN COALITION | VOL/ASSN
POLITICS." EUR+WWI UK USA+45 ELITES NAT/G DELIB/GP | ACT/RES
LEGIS TOP/EX ECO/TAC NUC/PWR ATTIT ORD/FREE PWR
TOT/POP EEC OEEC 20 NATO EURATOM. PAGE 42 G0820
L63

ABT C.,"THE PROBLEMS AND POSSIBILITIES OF SPACE | ACT/RES
ARMS CONTROL." FUT USA+45 WOR+45 AIR SOCIETY NAT/G | ORD/FREE
BAL/PWR EDU/PROP ATTIT PWR WEALTH...HYPO/EXP | ARMS/CONT
TOT/POP 20. PAGE 2 G0025 | SPACE
S63

BOULDING K.E.,"UNIVERSITY, SOCIETY, AND ARMS | SOCIETY
CONTROL." WOR+45 ACADEM NAT/G CONSULT FORCES | ARMS/CONT
ACT/RES PLAN TEC/DEV BAL/PWR ECO/TAC COERCE DETER
WAR ATTIT RIGID/FLEX KNOWL ORD/FREE PWR WEALTH
...CONCPT COLD/WAR TOT/POP 20. PAGE 8 G0159
S63

DELLIN L.A.D.,"BULGARIA UNDER SOVIET LEADERSHIP." | AGRI
S63

BULGARIA COM USA+45 USSR ECO/DEV INDUS POL/PAR   NAT/G
EX/STRUC TOP/EX COERCE ATTIT RIGID/FLEX...POLICY   TOTALISM
TIME/SEQ 20. PAGE 15 G0293

S63
ERSKINE H.G.,"THE POLLS: ATOMIC WEAPONS AND NUCLEAR ATTIT
ENERGY." USA+45 COERCE ORD/FREE...POLICY SOC STAT   INT
CENSUS SAMP VAL/FREE 20. PAGE 18 G0350   NUC/PWR

S63
KOLDZIEF E.A.,"CONGRESSIONAL RESPONSIBILITY FOR THE LEGIS
COMMON DEFENSE: THE MONEY PROBLEM." PLAN DEBATE   NAT/G
EFFICIENCY ATTIT PWR DECISION. PAGE 31 G0612   FORCES
POLICY

B64
BAUCHET P.,ECONOMIC PLANNING. FRANCE STRATA LG/CO   ECO/DEV
CAP/ISM ADMIN PARL/PROC DEMAND OPTIMAL ATTIT PWR   NAT/G
SOCISM...POLICY CHARTS 20. PAGE 5 G0102   PLAN
ECO/TAC

B64
BLOUSTEIN E.J.,NUCLEAR ENERGY, PUBLIC POLICY, AND   TEC/DEV
THE LAW. USA+45 NAT/G ADJUD ADMIN GP/REL OWN PEACE   LAW
ATTIT HEALTH...ANTHOL 20. PAGE 7 G0144   POLICY
NUC/PWR

B64
COHEN M.,LAW AND POLITICS IN SPACE: SPECIFIC AND   DELIB/GP
URGENT PROBLEMS IN THE LAW OF OUTER SPACE.   LAW
CHINA/COM COM USA+45 USSR COM/IND INT/ORG   INT/LAW
NAT/G LEGIT NUC/PWR ATTIT BIO/SOC...JURID CONCPT   SPACE
CONGRESS 20 STALIN/J. PAGE 12 G0241

B64
DUSCHA J.,ARMS, MONEY, AND POLITICS. USA+45 INDUS   NAT/G
POL/PAR ECO/TAC TAX DETER NUC/PWR WAR WEAPON   FORCES
GOV/REL ATTIT...BIBLIOG/A 20 CONGRESS MONEY   POLICY
DEPT/DEFEN. PAGE 17 G0326   BUDGET

B64
GRODZINS M.,THE ATOMIC AGE: FORTY-FIVE SCIENTISTS   INTELL
AND SCHOLARS SPEAK ON NATIONAL AND WORLD AFFAIRS.   ARMS/CONT
FUT USA+45 WOR+45 R+D INT/ORG NAT/G CONSULT TEC/DEV NUC/PWR
EDU/PROP ATTIT PERSON ORD/FREE...HUM CONCPT
TIME/SEQ CON/ANAL. PAGE 23 G0454

B64
GROSSER G.H.,THE THREAT OF IMPENDING DISASTER: HEALTH
CONTRIBUTIONS TO THE PSYCHOLOGY OF STRESS. SPACE   PSY
UNIV SOCIETY R+D TEC/DEV EDU/PROP COERCE WAR ATTIT   NUC/PWR
BIO/SOC DISPL PERCEPT PERSON...SOC MYTH SELF/OBS
CONT/OBS BIOG CON/ANAL TOT/POP 20. PAGE 23 G0455

B64
HASKINS C.P.,THE SCIENTIFIC REVOLUTION AND WORLD   TEC/DEV
POLITICS. COM FUT USA+45 ECO/DEV ECO/UNDEV ATTIT   POLICY
...PHIL/SCI BIBLIOG 20 THIRD/WRLD. PAGE 25 G0489   DIPLOM
TREND

B64
RANSOM H.H.,CAN AMERICAN DEMOCRACY SURVIVE COLD   USA+45
WAR. USA-45 CONSTN NAT/G CONSULT DELIB/GP LEGIS   ROUTINE
ACT/RES LEGIT EXEC ATTIT KNOWL ORD/FREE PWR SKILL
...POLICY TIME/SEQ TREND GEN/LAWS 20 COLD/WAR.
PAGE 46 G0901

B64
ROBERTS H.L.,FOREIGN AFFAIRS BIBLIOGRAPHY,1952-2962. BIBLIOG/A
ECO/DEV SECT PLAN FOR/AID INT/TRADE ARMS/CONT   DIPLOM
NAT/LISM ATTIT...INT/LAW GOV/COMP IDEA/COMP 20.   INT/ORG
PAGE 47 G0928   WAR

B64
ROSECRANCE R.N.,THE DISPERSION OF NUCLEAR WEAPONS: EUR+WWI
STRATEGY AND POLITICS. ASIA COM FUT S/ASIA USA+45   PWR
INT/ORG NAT/G DELIB/GP FORCES ACT/RES TEC/DEV   PEACE
BAL/PWR COERCE DETER ATTIT RIGID/FLEX ORD/FREE
...POLICY CHARTS VAL/FREE. PAGE 48 G0935

B64
RUSHING W.A.,THE PSYCHIATRIC PROFESSIONS. DOMIN   ATTIT
INGP/REL DRIVE RIGID/FLEX ROLE HEALTH PWR...POLICY   PUB/INST
GP/COMP. PAGE 48 G0947   PROF/ORG
BAL/PWR

B64
US AIR FORCE ACADEMY ASSEMBLY,OUTER SPACE: FINAL   SPACE
REPORT APRIL 1-4, 1964. FUT USA+45 WOR+45 LAW   CIVMIL/REL
DELIB/GP CONFER ARMS/CONT WAR PEACE ATTIT MORAL   NUC/PWR
...ANTHOL 20 NASA. PAGE 56 G1104   DIPLOM

B64
VAN DYKE V.,PRIDE AND POWER: THE RATIONALE OF THE   TEC/DEV
SPACE PROGRAM. FUT USA+45 INTELL R+D NAT/G POL/PAR   ATTIT
DELIB/GP EX/STRUC LEGIS TOP/EX ACT/RES PLAN ECO/TAC POLICY

EDU/PROP ORD/FREE PWR RESPECT SKILL...TIME/SEQ
VAL/FREE. PAGE 61 G1191

B64
WIRTH L.,ON CITIES AND SOCIAL LIFE: SELECTED   GEN/LAWS
PAPERS. PLAN PROB/SOLV RACE/REL CONSEN ATTIT   SOCIETY
HABITAT PERSON...POLICY SOC CONCPT ANTHOL BIBLIOG   NEIGH
20. PAGE 64 G1249   STRUCT

L64
BERKS R.N.,"THE US AND WEAPONS CONTROL." WOR+45 LAW USA+45
INT/ORG NAT/G LEGIS EXEC COERCE PEACE ATTIT   PLAN
RIGID/FLEX ALL/VALS PWR...POLICY TOT/POP 20. PAGE 7 ARMS/CONT
G0129

L64
CARNEGIE ENDOWMENT INT. PEACE,"POLITICAL QUESTIONS   INT/ORG
(ISSUES BEFORE THE NINETEENTH GENERAL ASSEMBLY)."   PEACE
SPACE WOR+45 CONSTN FINAN NAT/G CONSULT DELIB/GP
FORCES LEGIS TEC/DEV EDU/PROP LEGIT ARMS/CONT
COERCE NUC/PWR ATTIT ALL/VALS...CONCPT OBS UN
COLD/WAR 20. PAGE 11 G0208

L64
GOLDBERG A.,"ATOMIC ORIGINS OF THE BRITISH NUCLEAR   CREATE
DETERRENT." EUR+WWI UK NAT/G TOP/EX PLAN BAL/PWR   FORCES
DOMIN DETER CHOOSE ATTIT DRIVE HEALTH ORD/FREE PWR   NUC/PWR
RESPECT...CONCPT VAL/FREE COLD/WAR 20 CMN/WLTH.
PAGE 22 G0425

L64
HAAS E.B.,"ECONOMICS AND DIFFERENTIAL PATTERNS OF   L/A+17C
POLITICAL INTEGRATION: PROJECTIONS ABOUT UNITY IN   INT/ORG
LATIN AMERICA." SOCIETY NAT/G DELIB/GP ACT/RES   MARKET
CREATE PLAN ECO/TAC REGION ROUTINE ATTIT DRIVE PWR
WEALTH...CONCPT TREND CHARTS LAFTA 20. PAGE 24
G0464

L64
WARD C.,"THE 'NEW MYTHS' AND 'OLD REALITIES' OF   FORCES
NUCLEAR WAR." COM FUT USA+45 USSR WOR+45 INT/ORG   COERCE
NAT/G DOMIN LEGIT EXEC ATTIT PERCEPT ALL/VALS   ARMS/CONT
...POLICY RELATIV PSY MYTH TREND 20. PAGE 62 G1212   NUC/PWR

S64
"FURTHER READING." INDIA PAKISTAN SECT WAR PEACE   BIBLIOG
ATTIT...POLICY 20. PAGE 1 G0018   GP/REL
DIPLOM
NAT/G

S64
BYRNES F.C.,"ASSIGNMENT TO AMBIGUITY: WORK   INTELL
PERFORMANCE IN CROSSCULTURAL TECHNICAL ASSISTANCE." QU
USA+45 WOR+45 PROF/ORG CONSULT PLAN EDU/PROP ATTIT
DISPL PERCEPT PERSON ALL/VALS...POLICY INT CHARTS
NATO 20. PAGE 10 G0199

S64
MAGGS P.B.,"SOVIET VIEWPOINT ON NUCLEAR WEAPONS IN   COM
INTERNATIONAL LAW." USSR WOR+45 INT/ORG FORCES   LAW
DIPLOM ARMS/CONT ATTIT ORD/FREE PWR...POLICY JURID   INT/LAW
CONCPT OBS TREND CON/ANAL GEN/LAWS VAL/FREE 20.   NUC/PWR
PAGE 35 G0694

S64
NEEDHAM T.,"SCIENCE AND SOCIETY IN EAST AND WEST."   ASIA
INTELL STRATA R+D LOC/G NAT/G PROVS CONSULT ACT/RES   STRUCT
CREATE PLAN TEC/DEV EDU/PROP ADMIN ATTIT ALL/VALS
...POLICY RELATIV MGT CONCPT NEW/IDEA TIME/SEQ WORK
WORK. PAGE 41 G0815

S64
PLATT J.R.,"RESEARCH AND DEVELOPMENT FOR SOCIAL   R+D
PROBLEMS." INTELL SOCIETY PROB/SOLV GP/REL ATTIT   ACT/RES
ALL/VALS CONT/OBS. PAGE 45 G0880   PLAN
SOC

S64
THOMPSON V.A.,"ADMINISTRATIVE OBJECTIVES FOR   ECO/UNDEV
DEVELOPMENT ADMINISTRATION." WOR+45 CREATE PLAN   MGT
DOMIN EDU/PROP EXEC ROUTINE ATTIT ORD/FREE PWR
...POLICY GEN/LAWS VAL/FREE. PAGE 54 G1070

B65
ALLEN S.,LETTER TO A CONSERVATIVE. SOCIETY NAT/G   ORD/FREE
DIPLOM EDU/PROP NUC/PWR GP/REL ATTIT MORAL   MARXISM
...MAJORIT CONCPT 20. PAGE 2 G0044   POLICY
LAISSEZ

B65
BENJAMIN A.C.,SCIENCE, TECHNOLOGY, AND HUMAN   PHIL/SCI
VALUES. WOR+45 SECT EDU/PROP GP/REL ATTIT...TECHNIC CREATE
LING IDEA/COMP WORSHIP 20. PAGE 6 G0118   ROLE
SOCIETY

B65

BLOOMFIELD L.,SOVIET INTERESTS IN ARMS CONTROL AND
DISARMAMENT* THE DECADE UNDER KHRUSHCHEV 1954-1964.
ASIA FORCES ACT/RES EDU/PROP DETER NUC/PWR WEAPON
COST ATTIT...PHIL/SCI CLASSIF STAT NET/THEORY GAME
BIBLIOG. PAGE 7 G0139
 USSR
 ARMS/CONT
 DIPLOM
 TREND

B65

HALPERIN M.H.,COMMUNIST CHINA AND ARMS CONTROL.
CHINA/COM FUT USA+45 CULTURE FORCES TEC/DEV ECO/TAC
WAR PEACE ORD/FREE MARXISM 20 COLD/WAR. PAGE 24
G0473
 ATTIT
 POLICY
 ARMS/CONT
 NUC/PWR

B65

OECD,THE MEDITERRANEAN REGIONAL PROJECT: GREECE;
EDUCATION AND DEVELOPMENT. FUT GREECE SOCIETY AGRI
FINAN NAT/G PROF/ORG WORKER PLAN PROB/SOLV ADMIN
DEMAND ATTIT 20 OECD. PAGE 42 G0834
 EDU/PROP
 SCHOOL
 ACADEM
 ECO/UNDEV

B65

TURNER A.N.,INDUSTRIAL JOBS AND THE WORKER. USA+45
CULTURE ECO/DEV LABOR MUNIC ACT/RES AUTOMAT TASK
...CHARTS BIBLIOG 20. PAGE 55 G1082
 WORKER
 INDUS
 ATTIT
 TEC/DEV

B65

US SENATE COMM AERO SPACE SCI,NATIONAL SPACE GOALS
FOR THE POST-APOLLO PERIOD. USA+45 CONSULT DELIB/GP
TEC/DEV BUDGET GP/REL ATTIT...CHARTS IDEA/COMP TIME
20 DEPT/DEFEN NASA CONGRESS. PAGE 59 G1166
 SPACE
 FUT
 R+D
 LEGIS

B65

WISH J.R.,ECONOMIC DEVELOPMENT IN LATIN AMERICA: AN
ANNOTATED BIBLIOGRAPHY. L/A+17C COM/IND MARKET R+D
CREATE CAP/ISM ATTIT...STAT METH 20. PAGE 64 G1250
 BIBLIOG/A
 ECO/UNDEV
 TEC/DEV
 AGRI

L65

LASSWELL H.D.,"THE POLICY SCIENCES OF DEVELOPMENT."
CULTURE SOCIETY EX/STRUC CREATE ADMIN ATTIT KNOWL
...SOC CONCPT SIMUL GEN/METH. PAGE 33 G0644
 PWR
 METH/CNCPT
 DIPLOM

L65

PILISUK M.,"IS THERE A MILITARY INDUSTRIAL COMPLEX
WHICH PREVENTS PEACE CONSENSUS; COUNTERVAILING
POWER IN PLURALIST SYSTEMS." INDUS R+D ACADEM
FEEDBACK CIVMIL/REL ADJUST CONSEN ATTIT RIGID/FLEX
...CENSUS IDEA/COMP BIBLIOG. PAGE 45 G0878
 ELITES
 WEAPON
 PEACE
 ARMS/CONT

S65

GOLDSTEIN W.,"KEEPING THE GENIE IN THE BOTTLE* THE
FEASIBILITY OF A NUCLEAR NON-PROLIFERATION
AGREEMENT." ASIA FRANCE UK USA+45 USSR WOR+45
ECO/UNDEV VOL/ASSN ACT/RES PLAN RISK ARMS/CONT WAR
PEACE ATTIT PERCEPT...RECORD TREND TIME. PAGE 22
G0429
 NUC/PWR
 CREATE
 COST

S65

GRIFFITH S.B.,"COMMUNIST CHINA'S CAPACITY TO MAKE
WAR." CHINA/COM COM NAT/G TOP/EX PLAN DOMIN COERCE
NUC/PWR ATTIT RESPECT SKILL...CONCPT MYTH TIME/SEQ
TREND COLD/WAR 20. PAGE 23 G0452
 FORCES
 PWR
 WEAPON
 ASIA

S65

RUBINSTEIN A.Z.,"POLITICAL BARRIERS TO
DISARMAMENT." FUT DIPLOM COERCE NUC/PWR WAR
NAT/LISM ORD/FREE PREDICT. PAGE 48 G0944
 COM
 USA+45
 ARMS/CONT
 ATTIT

B66

AMERICAN ASSEMBLY COLUMBIA U,A WORLD OF NUCLEAR
POWERS? FUT WOR+45 ECO/DEV BAL/PWR ECO/TAC CONTROL
RISK EFFICIENCY ATTIT PWR...METH/COMP ANTHOL 20.
PAGE 3 G0049
 NUC/PWR
 DIPLOM
 TEC/DEV
 ARMS/CONT

B66

BLOOMFIELD L.P.,KHRUSHCHEV AND THE ARMS RACE.
USA+45 USSR ECO/DEV BAL/PWR EDU/PROP CONFER NUC/PWR
ATTIT...CHARTS 20 KHRUSH/N. PAGE 7 G0143
 ARMS/CONT
 COM
 POLICY
 DIPLOM

B66

BRODIE B.,ESCALATION AND THE NUCLEAR OPTION. ASIA
CUBA EUR+WWI KOREA USA+45 USSR VIETNAM RISK ATTIT
DRIVE PERCEPT PROBABIL. PAGE 9 G0172
 NUC/PWR
 GUERRILLA
 WAR
 DETER

B66

FREIDEL F.,AMERICAN ISSUES IN THE TWENTIETH
CENTURY. SOCIETY FINAN ECO/TAC FOR/AID CONTROL
NUC/PWR WAR RACE/REL PEACE ATTIT...ANTHOL T 20
WILSON/W ROOSEVLT/F KENNEDY/JF TRUMAN/HS. PAGE 20
G0391
 DIPLOM
 POLICY
 NAT/G
 ORD/FREE

B66

GORDON G.,THE LEGISLATIVE PROCESS AND DIVIDED
 LEGIS

GOVERNMENT; A CASE STUDY OF THE 86TH CONGRESS.
USA+45 POL/PAR PROVS PROB/SOLV BAL/PWR CHOOSE
REPRESENT EFFICIENCY ATTIT...POLICY DECISION STAT
20 CONGRESS EISNHWR/DD. PAGE 22 G0434
 HABITAT
 CHIEF
 NAT/G

B66

VON BORCH H.,FRIEDE TROTZ KRIEG. GERMANY USSR
WOR+45 PEACE ANOMIE ATTIT 20. PAGE 43 G0853
 DIPLOM
 NUC/PWR
 WAR
 COERCE

B66

SCHURMANN F.,IDEOLOGY AND ORGANIZATION IN COMMUNIST
CHINA. CHINA/COM LOC/G MUNIC POL/PAR ECO/TAC
CONTROL ATTIT...MGT STERTYP 20 COM/PARTY. PAGE 50
G0981
 MARXISM
 STRUCT
 ADMIN
 NAT/G

B66

STONE J.J.,CONTAINING THE ARMS RACE* SOME SPECIFIC
PROPOSALS. ASIA USA+45 USSR PROB/SOLV BARGAIN
DIPLOM DETER NUC/PWR RATIONAL...GAME 20 DEPT/DEFEN
TREATY. PAGE 53 G1038
 ARMS/CONT
 FEEDBACK
 COST
 ATTIT

B66

STREET D.,ORGANIZATION FOR TREATMENT. CLIENT PROVS
PUB/INST PLAN CONTROL PARTIC REPRESENT ATTIT PWR
...POLICY BIBLIOG. PAGE 53 G1044
 GP/COMP
 AGE/Y
 ADMIN
 VOL/ASSN

B66

US DEPARTMENT OF THE ARMY,COMMUNIST CHINA: A
STRATEGIC SURVEY: A BIBLIOGRAPHY (PAMPHLET NO.
20-67). CHINA/COM COM INDIA USSR NAT/G POL/PAR
EX/STRUC FORCES NUC/PWR REV ATTIT...POLICY GEOG
CHARTS. PAGE 58 G1133
 BIBLIOG/A
 MARXISM
 S/ASIA
 DIPLOM

B66

US SENATE COMM AERO SPACE SCI,SOVIET SPACE
PROGRAMS, 1962-65; GOALS AND PURPOSES,
ACHIEVEMENTS, PLANS, AND INTERNATIONAL
IMPLICATIONS. USA+45 USSR R+D FORCES PLAN EDU/PROP
PRESS ADJUD ARMS/CONT ATTIT MARXISM. PAGE 60 G1168
 CONSULT
 SPACE
 FUT
 DIPLOM

B66

WARD B.,NATIONALISM AND IDEOLOGY. ECO/UNDEV KIN
CREATE CAP/ISM FOR/AID ALL/VALS MARXISM...POLICY
SOC. PAGE 62 G1211
 IDEA/COMP
 NAT/LISM
 ATTIT

S66

GREENBERG D.S.,"THE SCIENTIFIC PORK BARREL." USA+45
ECO/DEV PUB/INST CHIEF LEGIS BUDGET GIVE GP/REL PWR
WEALTH 20. PAGE 23 G0445
 R+D
 NAT/G
 ACADEM
 ATTIT

S66

TURKEVICH J.,"SOVIET SCIENCE APPRAISED." USA+45 R+D
ACADEM FORCES DIPLOM EDU/PROP WAR EFFICIENCY PEACE
SKILL OBS. PAGE 55 G1081
 USSR
 TEC/DEV
 NAT/COMP
 ATTIT

B67

BUDER S.,PULLMAN: AN EXPERIMENT IN INDUSTRIAL ORDER
AND COMMUNITY PLANNING, 1880-1930. USA-45 SOCIETY
LABOR LG/CO CREATE PROB/SOLV CONTROL GP/REL
EFFICIENCY ATTIT...MGT BIBLIOG 19/20 PULLMAN.
PAGE 9 G0184
 DIST/IND
 INDUS
 MUNIC
 PLAN

B67

CONNOLLY W.E.,POLITICAL SCIENCE AND IDEOLOGY.
UTOPIA ATTIT KNOWL...MAJORIT EPIST PHIL/SCI SOC
IDEA/COMP HYPO/EXP GEN/LAWS METH HUME/D MARX/KARL.
PAGE 13 G0250
 PWR
 PLURISM
 ELITES
 CONCPT

B67

DAVIS V.,THE POLITICS OF INNOVATION: PATTERNS IN
NAVY CASES (PAMPHLET). WOR+45 NAT/G CREATE WEAPON
INGP/REL ATTIT...POLICY SOC METH/COMP METH. PAGE 14
G0280
 BIBLIOG
 FORCES
 NUC/PWR
 TEC/DEV

B67

ELSNER H.,THE TECHNOCRATS, PROPHETS OF AUTOMATION.
SOCIETY INDUS VOL/ASSN COST INCOME ATTIT 20.
PAGE 18 G0345
 AUTOMAT
 TECHRACY
 PRODUC
 HIST/WRIT

B67

HEADLEY J.C.,PESTICIDE PROBLEM: AN ECONOMIC
APPROACH TO PUBLIC POLICY. AGRI TEC/DEV GOV/REL
COST ATTIT CHARTS. PAGE 25 G0498
 HABITAT
 POLICY
 BIO/SOC
 CONTROL

B67

HODGKINSON R.G.,THE ORIGINS OF THE NATIONAL HEALTH
SERVICE: THE MEDICAL SERVICES OF THE NEW POOR LAW,
1834-1871. UK INDUS MUNIC WORKER PROB/SOLV
EFFICIENCY ATTIT HEALTH WEALTH SOCISM...JURID
 HEAL
 NAT/G
 POLICY
 LAW

SOC/WK 19/20. PAGE 26 G0519

LAMBERT J.,LATIN AMERICA: SOCIAL STRUCTURES AND   L/A+17C
POLITICAL INSTITUTIONS. STRUCT TEC/DEV DIPLOM ADMIN   NAT/G
COLONIAL LEAD ATTIT...SOC CLASSIF NAT/COMP 17/20.   ECO/UNDEV
PAGE 32 G0631   SOCIETY
   B67

NASH M.,MACHINE AGE MAYA. GUATEMALA L/A+17C STRUCT   INDUS
AGRI WORKER CREATE INCOME ATTIT RIGID/FLEX ROLE   CULTURE
...IDEA/COMP SOC/EXP WORSHIP 20 INDIAN/AM. PAGE 41   SOC
G0806   MUNIC
   B67

PADELFORD N.J.,THE DYNAMICS OF INTERNATIONAL   DIPLOM
POLITICS (2ND ED.). WOR+45 LAW INT/ORG FORCES   NAT/G
TEC/DEV REGION NAT/LISM PEACE ATTIT PWR ALL/IDEOS   POLICY
UN COLD/WAR NATO TREATY. PAGE 43 G0856   DECISION
   B67

RUSSELL B.,WAR CRIMES IN VIETNAM. USA+45 VIETNAM   WAR
FORCES DIPLOM WEAPON RACE/REL DISCRIM ISOLAT   CRIME
BIO/SOC 20 COLD/WAR RUSSELL/B. PAGE 48 G0949   ATTIT
   POLICY
   B67

UNIVERSAL REFERENCE SYSTEM,CURRENT EVENTS AND   BIBLIOG/A
PROBLEMS OF MODERN SOCIETY (VOLUME V). WOR+45 LOC/G   SOCIETY
MUNIC NAT/G PLAN EDU/PROP CRIME RACE/REL WEALTH   PROB/SOLV
...COMPUT/IR GEN/METH. PAGE 56 G1097   ATTIT
   B67

UNIVERSAL REFERENCE SYSTEM,PUBLIC OPINION, MASS   BIBLIOG/A
BEHAVIOR, AND POLITICAL PSYCHOLOGY (VOLUME VI).   ATTIT
WOR+45 WOR-45 SOCIETY EDU/PROP PRESS PARTIC CHOOSE   CROWD
PERSON...TREND COMPUT/IR GEN/METH. PAGE 56 G1098   PSY
   B67

US DEPARTMENT OF THE ARMY,CIVILIAN IN PEACE,   BIBLIOG/A
SOLDIER IN WAR: A BIBLIOGRAPHIC SURVEY OF THE ARMY   FORCES
AND AIR NATIONAL GUARD (PAMPHLET, NOS. 130-2).   ROLE
USA+45 USA-45 LOC/G NAT/G PROVS LEGIS PLAN ADMIN   DIPLOM
ATTIT ORD/FREE...POLICY 19/20. PAGE 58 G1134
   B67

YAMAMURA K.,ECONOMIC POLICY IN POSTWAR JAPAN. ASIA   ECO/DEV
FINAN POL/PAR DIPLOM LEAD NAT/LISM ATTIT NEW/LIB   POLICY
POPULISM 20 CHINJAP. PAGE 64 G1262   NAT/G
   TEC/DEV
   L67

"POLITICAL PARTIES ON FOREIGN POLICY IN THE INTER-   POL/PAR
ELECTION YEARS 1962-66." ASIA COM INDIA USA+45 PLAN   DIPLOM
ATTIT...DECISION 20. PAGE 1 G0023   POLICY
   L67

ROBINSON T.W.,"A NATIONAL INTEREST ANALYSIS OF   MARXISM
SINO-SOVIET RELATIONS." CHINA/COM USSR NAT/G   DIPLOM
NUC/PWR ATTIT PWR...CONCPT CHARTS 20. PAGE 47 G0931   SOVEREIGN
   GEN/LAWS
   S67

EYRAUD M.,"LA FRANCE FACE A UN EVENTUEL TRAITE DE   NUC/PWR
NON DISSEMINATION DES ARMES NUCLEAIRES." FRANCE   ARMS/CONT
USA+45 EXTR/IND INDUS R+D INT/ORG ACT/RES TEC/DEV   POLICY
AGREE PRODUC ATTIT 20 TREATY AEC EURATOM. PAGE 18
G0355
   S67

FRIED M.,"FUNCTIONS OF THE WORKING CLASS COMMUNITY   CLASSIF
IN MODERN URBAN SOCIETY* IMPLICATIONS FOR FORCED   WORKER
RELOCATION." USA+45 INDUS R+D NEIGH PLAN TEC/DEV   MUNIC
PARTIC GP/REL ATTIT...SOC STAT CHARTS. PAGE 20   ADJUST
G0393
   S67

GOBER J.L.,"FEDERALISM AT WORK." USA+45 NAT/G   MUNIC
CONSULT ACT/RES PLAN CONFER ADMIN LEAD PARTIC   TEC/DEV
FEDERAL ATTIT. PAGE 21 G0422   R+D
   GOV/REL
   S67

HABERER J.,"POLITICS AND THE COMMUNITY OF SCIENCE."   LEAD
USA+45 SOCIETY ACT/RES PARTIC ATTIT PHIL/SCI.   SUPEGO
PAGE 24 G0465   INTELL
   LOBBY
   S67

HILL R.,"SOCIAL ASPECTS OF FAMILY PLANNING." INDIA   FAM
KOREA TAIWAN ECO/UNDEV PLAN PROB/SOLV TEC/DEV   BIO/SOC
EDU/PROP CONTROL ATTIT DRIVE...HEAL PSY SOC 20   GEOG
BIRTH/CON UN. PAGE 26 G0512   MARRIAGE
   S67

JACKSON W.G.F.,"NUCLEAR PROLIFERATION AND THE GREAT   NUC/PWR

POWERS." FUT UK WOR+45 INT/ORG DOMIN ARMS/CONT   ATTIT
DETER ORD/FREE PACIFIST. PAGE 28 G0550   BAL/PWR
   NAT/LISM
   S67

KRAUS J.,"A MARXIST IN GHANA." GHANA ELITES CHIEF   MARXISM
PROB/SOLV TEC/DEV DIPLOM ECO/TAC COLONIAL PARTIC   PLAN
PWR 20 NKRUMAH/K. PAGE 31 G0618   ATTIT
   CREATE
   S67

LA PORTE T.,"DIFFUSION AND DISCONTINUITY IN   INTELL
SCIENCE, TECHNOLOGY AND PUBLIC AFFAIRS: RESULTS OF   ADMIN
A SEARCH IN THE FIELD." USA+45 ACT/RES TEC/DEV   ACADEM
PERS/REL ATTIT PHIL/SCI. PAGE 32 G0628   GP/REL
   S67

MARTIN L.W.,"BALLISTIC MISSILE DEFENSE AND EUROPE."   ATTIT
EUR+WWI USA+45 FORCES PLAN BAL/PWR DEBATE PEACE   ARMS/CONT
...POLICY COLD/WAR NATO. PAGE 36 G0715   NUC/PWR
   DETER
   S67

ROBINSON J.A.T.,"ABORTION* THE CASE FOR A FREE   PLAN
DECISION." LAW PROB/SOLV SANCTION ATTIT MORAL...PSY   ILLEGIT
IDEA/COMP 20 ABORTION. PAGE 47 G0930   SEX
   HEALTH
   S67

STYCOS J.M.,"POLITICS AND POPULATION CONTROL IN   PLAN
LATIN AMERICA." USA+45 FAM NAT/G GP/REL AGE/C ATTIT   CENSUS
CATHISM MARXISM...POLICY UN WHO. PAGE 53 G1045   CONTROL
   L/A+17C
   S67

TELLER E.,"PLANNING FOR PEACE." CHINA/COM WOR+45   ARMS/CONT
DELIB/GP TEC/DEV RISK COERCE DETER WAR ATTIT   NUC/PWR
ORD/FREE 20 NATO. PAGE 54 G1061   PEACE
   DOMIN
   S67

WARE R.S.,"FORECAST A.D. 2000." SOCIETY STRATA   NUC/PWR
ECO/UNDEV INDUS FORCES EDU/PROP AUTOMAT COERCE REV   GEOG
WEAPON ATTIT PREDICT. PAGE 62 G1213   TEC/DEV
   WAR
   S67

WHITTIER J.M.,"COMPULSORY POOLING AND UNITIZATION*   LEGIS
DIE-HARD KANSAS." LAW PLAN EDU/PROP ATTIT...POLICY   MUNIC
JURID PREDICT TREND METH/COMP 20. PAGE 63 G1236   INDUS
   ECO/TAC
   N67

US SENATE COMM AERO SPACE SCI,POLICY PLANNING FOR   TEC/DEV
TECHNOLOGY TRANSFER (PAMPHLET). WOR+45 INDUS CREATE   POLICY
PLAN EFFICIENCY ATTIT. PAGE 60 G1171   NAT/G
   ECO/DEV
   S68

BARAGWANATH L.E.,"SCIENTIFIC CO-OPERATION BETWEEN   R+D
THE UNIVERSITIES AND INDUSTRY - A RESEARCH NOTE."   ACADEM
UK LG/CO CREATE TEC/DEV EDU/PROP ATTIT...PHIL/SCI   INDUS
STAT QU 20. PAGE 5 G0090   GP/REL
   B88

BENTHAM J.,DEFENCE OF USURY (1787). UK LAW NAT/G   TAX
TEC/DEV ECO/TAC CONTROL ATTIT...CONCPT IDEA/COMP 18   FINAN
SMITH/ADAM. PAGE 6 G0124   ECO/DEV
   POLICY

ATTLEE/C....CLEMENT ATLEE

ATTORNEY GENERAL....SEE ATTRNY/GEN

ATTRNY/GEN....ATTORNEY GENERAL

AUD/VIS....FILM AND SOUND (INCLUDING PHOTOGRAPHY)

AMERICAN DOCUMENTATION INST,AMERICAN DOCUMENTATION.   BIBLIOG
PROF/ORG CONSULT PLAN PERCEPT...MATH STAT AUD/VIS   TEC/DEV
CHARTS METH/COMP INDEX METH 20. PAGE 3 G0050   COM/IND
   COMPUT/IR
   N
   B50

DEES J.W. JR.,URBAN SOCIOLOGY AND THE EMERGING   PLAN
ATOMIC MEGALOPOLIS. PART I. USA+45 TEC/DEV ADMIN   NEIGH
NUC/PWR HABITAT...SOC AUD/VIS CHARTS GEN/LAWS 20   MUNIC
WATER. PAGE 15 G0291   PROB/SOLV
   B56

ATOMIC INDUSTRIAL FORUM,PUBLIC RELATIONS FOR THE   NUC/PWR
ATOMIC INDUSTRY. WOR+45 PLAN PROB/SOLV EDU/PROP   INDUS
PRESS CONFER...AUD/VIS ANTHOL 20. PAGE 4 G0077   GP/REL
   ATTIT

MERTON R.K.,SOCIAL THEORY AND SOCIAL STRUCTURE (REV. ED.). INTELL SECT WORKER OP/RES EDU/PROP ADMIN INGP/REL ANOMIE PERSON...AUD/VIS T 20 BUREAUCRCY. PAGE 38 G0759 — B57 — SOC GEN/LAWS SOCIETY STRUCT

TELLER E.A.,OUR NUCLEAR FUTURE. SOCIETY FORCES TEC/DEV EDU/PROP KNOWL ORD/FREE...STAND/INT SYS/QU KNO/TEST AUD/VIS CHARTS SIMUL 20. PAGE 54 G1062 — B58 — FUT PHIL/SCI NUC/PWR WAR

RAMO S.,PEACETIME USES OF OUTER SPACE. FUT DIST/IND INT/ORG CONSULT NUC/PWR...AUD/VIS ANTHOL 20. PAGE 46 G0898 — B61 — PEACE TEC/DEV SPACE CREATE

GOLOVINE M.N.,CONFLICT IN SPACE: A PATTERN OF WAR IN A NEW DIMENSION. FUT USA+45 WOR+45 AIR FORCES PLAN DIPLOM DOMIN ATTIT...STAT AUD/VIS CHARTS COLD/WAR 20. PAGE 22 G0432 — B62 — CREATE TEC/DEV NUC/PWR SPACE

OSSENBECK F.J.,OPEN SPACE AND PEACE. CHINA/COM FUT USA+45 USSR LAW PROB/SOLV TEC/DEV EDU/PROP NEUTRAL PEACE...AUD/VIS ANTHOL 20. PAGE 43 G0850 — B64 — SPACE ORD/FREE DIPLOM CREATE

FALK S.L.,"DISARMAMENT IN HISTORICAL PERSPECTIVE." WOR-45 NAT/G PLAN NUC/PWR PEACE ORD/FREE PWR ...TIME/SEQ AUD/VIS VAL/FREE LEAGUE/NAT 20. PAGE 18 G0360 — S64 — INT/ORG COERCE ARMS/CONT

BENNETT J.W.,HUTTERIAN BRETHREN: THE AGRICULTURAL ECONOMY AND SOCIAL ORGANIZATION OF A COMMUNAL PEOPLE. USA+45 SOCIETY FAM KIN TEC/DEV ADJUST...MGT AUD/VIS GP/COMP 20. PAGE 6 G0121 — B67 — SECT AGRI STRUCT GP/REL

BARRON J.A.,"ACCESS TO THE PRESS." USA+45 TEC/DEV PRESS TV ADJUD AUD/VIS. PAGE 5 G0099 — L67 — ORD/FREE COM/IND EDU/PROP LAW

AUGUSTINE....SAINT AUGUSTINE

AUST/HUNG....AUSTRIA-HUNGARY

AUSTRALIA....SEE ALSO S/ASIA, COMMONWLTH

FULLER G.H.,DEFENSE FINANCING: A SUPPLEMENTARY LIST OF REFERENCES (PAMPHLET). CANADA UK USA-45 ECO/DEV NAT/G DELIB/GP BUDGET ADJUD ARMS/CONT WEAPON COST PEACE PWR 20 AUSTRAL CHINJAP CONGRESS. PAGE 21 G0403 — B42 — BIBLIOG/A FINAN FORCES DIPLOM

SCARROW H.A.,THE HIGHER PUBLIC SERVICE OF THE COMMONWEALTH OF AUSTRALIA. LAW SENIOR LOBBY ROLE 20 AUSTRAL CIVIL/SERV COMMONWLTH. PAGE 49 G0959 — B57 — ADMIN NAT/G EX/STRUC GOV/COMP

MCLAUGHLIN M.R.,RELIGIOUS EDUCATION AND THE STATE: DEMOCRACY FINDS A WAY. CANADA EUR+WWI GP/REL POPULISM...CATH NAT/COMP 20 AUSTRAL. PAGE 38 G0745 — B67 — SECT NAT/G EDU/PROP POLICY

AUSTRIA....SEE ALSO APPROPRIATE TIME/SPACE/CULTURE INDEX

COENEN E.,LA "KONJUNKTURFORSCHUNG" EN ALLEMAGNE ET EN AUTRICHE, 1925-1935. AUSTRIA GERMANY OP/RES PLAN COST PERCEPT...METH/CNCPT BIBLIOG 20. PAGE 12 G0237 — B64 — METH/COMP R+D ECO/TAC

AUSTRIA-HUNGARY....SEE AUST/HUNG

AUTHORIT....AUTHORITARIANISM, PERSONAL; SEE ALSO DOMIN

JANOWITZ M.,"CHANGING PATTERNS OF ORGANIZATIONAL AUTHORITY: THE MILITARY ESTABLISHMENT" (BMR)" USA+45 ELITES STRUCT EX/STRUC PLAN DOMIN AUTOMAT NUC/PWR WEAPON 20. PAGE 28 G0559 — S59 — FORCES AUTHORIT ADMIN TEC/DEV

KRUPP S.,PATTERN IN ORGANIZATIONAL ANALYSIS: A CRITICAL EXAMINATION. INGP/REL PERS/REL RATIONAL ATTIT AUTHORIT DRIVE PWR...DECISION PHIL/SCI SOC — B61 — MGT CONTROL CONCPT

IDEA/COMP. PAGE 32 G0622 — METH/CNCPT

THOMPSON V.A.,"HIERARACHY, SPECIALIZATION, AND ORGANIZATIONAL CONFLICT" (BMR)" WOR+45 STRATA STRUCT WORKER TEC/DEV GP/REL INGP/REL ATTIT AUTHORIT 20 BUREAUCRCY. PAGE 54 G1069 — L61 — PERS/REL PROB/SOLV ADMIN EX/STRUC

MAINZER L.C.,"SCIENTIFIC FREEDOM IN GOVERNMENT-SPONSORED RESEARCH." USA+45 INTELL PUB/INST BUDGET LOBBY AUTHORIT PWR...POLICY PHIL/SCI 20 NIH NSF. PAGE 35 G0696 — S61 — CREATE ORD/FREE NAT/G R+D

RICHMAN B.M.,"SOVIET MANAGEMENT IN TRANSITION." USSR FINAN MARKET EX/STRUC PLAN PROB/SOLV TEC/DEV CONTROL LEAD CENTRAL EFFICIENCY...METH/COMP 20 REFORMERS. PAGE 47 G0917 — S67 — MGT MARXISM POLICY AUTHORIT

AUTHORITY....SEE DOMIN

AUTOMAT....AUTOMATION; SEE ALSO COMPUTER, PLAN

AMERICAN DOCUMENTATION INST,DOCUMENTATION ABSTRACTS. WOR+45 NAT/G COMPUTER CREATE TEC/DEV DIPLOM EDU/PROP REGION KNOWL...PHIL/SCI CLASSIF LING. PAGE 3 G0051 — N — BIBLIOG/A AUTOMAT COMPUT/IR R+D

US DEPT COMMERCE OFF TECH SERV,TECHNICAL TRANSLATIONS. WOR+45 INDUS COMPUTER CREATE NUC/PWR ...PHIL/SCI COMPUT/IR METH/COMP METH. PAGE 58 G1135 — B — BIBLIOG R+D TEC/DEV AUTOMAT

BELL J.R.,PERSONNEL PROBLEMS IN CONVERTING TO AUTOMATION (PAMPHLET). USA+45 COMPUTER PLAN ...METH/CNCPT 20 CALIFORNIA. PAGE 6 G0115 — N19 — WORKER AUTOMAT PROB/SOLV PROVS

WEINER N.,CYBERNETICS. SOCIETY COMPUTER ADJUST EFFICIENCY UTIL PERCEPT...PSY MATH REGRESS TIME. PAGE 63 G1226 — B48 — FEEDBACK AUTOMAT CONTROL TEC/DEV

US DEPARTMENT OF THE ARMY,RESEARCH AND DEVELOPMENT (AND RELATED ASPECTS) IN FOREIGN COUNTRIES. WOR+45 DIST/IND INDUS CONSULT FORCES CREATE EDU/PROP AUTOMAT DETER WEAPON. PAGE 57 G1126 — B56 — BIBLIOG/A R+D TEC/DEV NUC/PWR

DRUCKER P.F.,AMERICA'S NEXT TWENTY YEARS. USA+45 DIST/IND ACADEM MUNIC SCHOOL DIPLOM ECO/TAC AUTOMAT HABITAT HEALTH...SOC/WK TREND 20 URBAN/RNWL PUB/TRANS. PAGE 16 G0316 — B57 — WORKER FOR/AID CENSUS GEOG

CHEEK G.,ECONOMIC AND SOCIAL IMPLICATIONS OF AUTOMATION: A BIBLIOGRAPHIC REVIEW (PAMPHLET). USA+45 LG/CO WORKER CREATE PLAN CONTROL ROUTINE PERS/REL EFFICIENCY PRODUC...METH/COMP 20. PAGE 12 G0225 — B58 — BIBLIOG/A SOCIETY INDUS AUTOMAT

DUBIN R.,THE WORLD OF WORK: INDUSTRIAL SOCIETY AND HUMAN RELATIONS. MARKET PROC/MFG LABOR TEC/DEV CAP/ISM AUTOMAT TASK GP/REL EFFICIENCY...CONCPT CHARTS BIBLIOG 20. PAGE 16 G0317 — B58 — WORKER ECO/TAC PRODUC DRIVE

GUILBAUD G.T.,WHAT IS CYBERNETICS? COMPUTER OP/RES TEC/DEV AUTOMAT ROUTINE PERS/REL PERCEPT...PSY MATH COMPUT/IR SIMUL GEN/METH. PAGE 23 G0460 — B59 — CONTROL COM/IND FEEDBACK NET/THEORY

JANOWITZ M.,"CHANGING PATTERNS OF ORGANIZATIONAL AUTHORITY: THE MILITARY ESTABLISHMENT" (BMR)" USA+45 ELITES STRUCT EX/STRUC PLAN DOMIN AUTOMAT NUC/PWR WEAPON 20. PAGE 28 G0559 — S59 — FORCES AUTHORIT ADMIN TEC/DEV

CARPENTER E.,EXPLORATIONS IN COMMUNICATION. USSR CULTURE SCHOOL SECT EDU/PROP PRESS TV AUTOMAT FEEDBACK ATTIT PERSON...ART/METH PSY 20. PAGE 11 G0211 — B60 — ANTHOL COM/IND TEC/DEV WRITING

MORRIS W.T.,ENGINEERING ECONOMY. AUTOMAT RISK RATIONAL...PROBABIL STAT CHARTS GAME SIMUL BIBLIOG T 20. PAGE 40 G0785 — B60 — OP/RES DECISION MGT PROB/SOLV

B60

SLUCKIN W.,MINDS AND MACHINES (REV. ED.). PROB/SOLV PSY
TEC/DEV AUTOMAT TASK PERCEPT HEALTH KNOWL COMPUTER
...DECISION MATH PROBABIL COMPUT/IR GAME 20. PERSON
PAGE 51 G1012 SIMUL

B61

BRADY R.A.,ORGANIZATION, AUTOMATION, AND SOCIETY. TEC/DEV
USA+45 AGRI COM/IND DIST/IND MARKET CREATE INDUS
...DECISION MGT 20. PAGE 8 G0163 AUTOMAT
ADMIN

S61

MANGELSDORF J.E.,"HUMAN DECISIONS IN MISSILE DECISION
YSTEMS." OP/RES CHARTS. PAGE 35 G0699 PROB/SOLV
AUTOMAT
CONTROL

B62

BERKELEY E.C.,THE COMPUTER REVOLUTION. WOR+45 COMPUTER
CREATE TEC/DEV EFFICIENCY TECHRACY...SOC TREND 20. CONTROL
PAGE 7 G0128 AUTOMAT
SOCIETY

B62

BORKOF H.,COMPUTER APPLICATIONS IN THE BEHAVIORAL R+D
SCIENCES. AUTOMAT UTIL...DECISION PHIL/SCI PSY COMPUTER
METH/CNCPT LING LOG MATH STYLE NET/THEORY COMPUT/IR PROB/SOLV
PROG/TEAC SIMUL. PAGE 8 G0154 FEEDBACK

B62

GUETZKOW H.,SIMULATION IN SOCIAL SCIENCE: READINGS. SIMUL
STRUCT OP/RES ADMIN AUTOMAT FEEDBACK...MGT PSY SOC TEC/DEV
STYLE BIBLIOG. PAGE 23 G0459 COMPUTER
GAME

S62

VIETORISZ T.,"PRELIMINARY BIBLIOGRAPHY FOR BIBLIOG/A
INDUSTRIAL DEVELOPMENT PROGRAMMING." ECO/DEV TEC/DEV
ECO/UNDEV R+D LABOR PROB/SOLV AUTOMAT PRODUC. ACT/RES
PAGE 61 G1198 PLAN

B63

FOSKETT D.J.,CLASSIFICATION AND INDEXING IN THE PROB/SOLV
SOCIAL SCIENCES. WOR+45 R+D ACT/RES CREATE OP/RES CON/ANAL
TEC/DEV AUTOMAT ROLE...SOC COMPUT/IR BIBLIOG. CLASSIF
PAGE 20 G0384

B63

HEYEL C.,THE ENCYCLOPEDIA OF MANAGEMENT. WOR+45 MGT
MARKET TOP/EX TEC/DEV AUTOMAT LEAD ADJUST...STAT INDUS
CHARTS GAME ANTHOL BIBLIOG. PAGE 26 G0509 ADMIN
FINAN

B63

KREPS J.,AUTOMATION AND THE OLDER WORKER: AN BIBLIOG/A
ANNOTATED BIBLIOGRAPHY (PAMPHLET). USA+45 STRUCT WORKER
ECO/DEV INDUS TEC/DEV. PAGE 31 G0620 AGE/O
AUTOMAT

B63

MCDONOUGH A.M.,INFORMATION ECONOMICS AND MANAGEMENT COMPUT/IR
SYSTEMS. ECO/DEV OP/RES AUTOMAT EFFICIENCY 20. MGT
PAGE 37 G0735 CONCPT
COMPUTER

B63

OECD,SCIENCE AND THE POLICIES OF GOVERNMENTS: THE CREATE
IMPLICATIONS OF SCIENCE AND TECHNOLOGY FOR NATL AND TEC/DEV
INTL AFFAIRS. WOR+45 INT/ORG EDU/PROP AUTOMAT DIPLOM
...POLICY PHIL/SCI 20. PAGE 42 G0830 NAT/G

B63

TOMKINS S.S.,COMPUTER SIMULATION OF PERSONALITY. COMPUTER
R+D TEC/DEV AUTOMAT FEEDBACK ANOMIE PERCEPT...STYLE PERSON
PERS/TEST PREDICT COMPUT/IR GP/COMP. PAGE 55 G1075 SIMUL
PROG/TEAC

S63

VIETORISZ T.,"PRELIMINARY BIBLIOGRAPHY FOR BIBLIOG/A
INDUSTRIAL DEVELOPMENT PROGRAMMING." ECO/DEV TEC/DEV
ECO/UNDEV R+D LABOR PROB/SOLV AUTOMAT PRODUC. ACT/RES
PAGE 61 G1199 PLAN

B64

RECENT PUBLICATIONS ON GOVERNMENTAL PROBLEMS. FINAN BIBLIOG
INDUS ACADEM PLAN PROB/SOLV EDU/PROP ADJUD ADMIN AUTOMAT
BIO/SOC...MGT SOC. PAGE 1 G0017 LEGIS
JURID

B64

BRIGHT J.R.,RESEARCH, DEVELOPMENT AND TECHNOLOGICAL TEC/DEV
INNOVATION. CULTURE R+D CREATE PLAN PROB/SOLV NEW/IDEA
AUTOMAT RISK PERSON...DECISION CONCPT PREDICT INDUS
BIBLIOG. PAGE 9 G0168 MGT

B64

BRILLOUIN L.,SCIENTIFIC UNCERTAINTY AND PHIL/SCI
INFORMATION. PROB/SOLV AUTOMAT PERCEPT ORD/FREE NEW/IDEA
...MATH REGRESS STAT STYLE OBS IDEA/COMP SIMUL METH/CNCPT
TIME. PAGE 9 G0169 CREATE

B64

DIEBOLD J.,BEYOND AUTOMATION: MANAGERIAL PROBLEMS FUT
OF AN EXPLODING TECHNOLOGY. SOCIETY ECO/DEV CREATE INDUS
ECO/TAC AUTOMAT SKILL...TECHNIC MGT WORK. PAGE 16 PROVS
G0303 NAT/G

B64

ELLUL J.,THE TECHNOLOGICAL SOCIETY. FUT STRUCT SOC
CREATE AUTOMAT ROUTINE STRANGE ANOMIE MORAL SOCIETY
PHIL/SCI. PAGE 18 G0344 TECHNIC
TEC/DEV

B64

LANG A.S.,URBAN RAIL TRANSIT. OP/RES PLAN PROB/SOLV MUNIC
TEC/DEV AUTOMAT COST...TECHNIC MATH CON/ANAL CHARTS DIST/IND
METH/COMP SIMUL 20 RAILROAD PUB/TRANS. PAGE 32 ECOMETRIC
G0632

B65

NATIONAL SCIENCE FOUNDATION,CURRENT RESEARCH AND BIBLIOG
DEVELOPMENT IN SCIENTIFIC DOCUMENTATION - NO. 12. COMPUT/IR
WOR+45 INTELL COM/IND NAT/G COMPUTER TEC/DEV R+D
AUTOMAT KNOWL...PSY LING 20. PAGE 41 G0812 PHIL/SCI

B65

TURNER A.N.,INDUSTRIAL JOBS AND THE WORKER. USA+45 WORKER
CULTURE ECO/DEV LABOR MUNIC ACT/RES AUTOMAT TASK INDUS
...CHARTS BIBLIOG 20. PAGE 55 G1082 ATTIT
TEC/DEV

B66

BOWEN H.R.,AUTOMATION AND ECONOMIC PROGRESS. AUTOMAT
EUR+WWI USA+45 ECO/DEV INCOME ORD/FREE WEALTH TEC/DEV
...POLICY ANTHOL 20. PAGE 8 G0160 WORKER
LEISURE

B66

LILLEY S.,MEN, MACHINES AND HISTORY: THE STORY OF AGRI
TOOLS AND MACHINES IN RELATION TO SOCIAL PROGRESS. TEC/DEV
PREHIST SPACE STRUCT COMPUTER AUTOMAT NUC/PWR SOCIETY
...POLICY SOC. PAGE 34 G0667

B66

MARKHAM J.W.,AN ECONOMIC-MEDIA STUDY OF BOOK PRESS
PUBLISHING. USA+45 LAW COM/IND ACADEM SCHOOL ECO/TAC
EDU/PROP AUTOMAT CONTROL...DECISION STAT CHARTS 20 TEC/DEV
CONGRESS. PAGE 36 G0707 NAT/G

B66

MILLAR R.,THE NEW CLASSES. UK ELITES SOCIETY INDUS STRUCT
AUTOMAT GP/REL SOC/INTEG 20 INDUS/REV. PAGE 39 STRATA
G0770 TEC/DEV
CREATE

B66

MUMFORD L.,THE MYTH OF THE MACHINE: TECHNICS AND WORKER
HUMAN DEVELOPMENT. UNIV WOR-45 CREATE KNOWL TEC/DEV
PERCEPT KNOWL...EPIST PHIL/SCI SOC LING TREND SOCIETY
SOC/INTEG 20 MARX/KARL. PAGE 40 G0795

B66

NIEBURG H.L.,IN THE NAME OF SCIENCE. USA+45 NAT/G
EX/STRUC LEGIS TEC/DEV BUDGET PAY AUTOMAT LOBBY PWR INDUS
...OBS 20. PAGE 42 G0822 TECHRACY

B66

US DEPARTMENT OF LABOR,PRODUCTIVITY: A BIBLIOG/A
BIBLIOGRAPHY. ECO/DEV INDUS MARKET OP/RES AUTOMAT PRODUC
COST...STAT 20. PAGE 57 G1119 LABOR
PLAN

B66

US DEPARTMENT OF LABOR,TECHNOLOGICAL TRENDS IN TEC/DEV
MAJOR AMERICAN INDUSTRIES. USA+45 R+D LABOR GP/REL INDUS
PRODUC...MGT BIBLIOG 20. PAGE 57 G1120 TREND
AUTOMAT

B67

BARANSON J.,TECHNOLOGY FOR UNDERDEVELOPED AREAS: AN BIBLIOG/A
ANNOTATED BIBLIOGRAPHY. FUT WOR+45 CULTURE INDUS ECO/UNDEV
INT/ORG CREATE PROB/SOLV INT/TRADE EDU/PROP AUTOMAT TEC/DEV
...CONCPT METH. PAGE 5 G0092 R+D

B67

COLEMAN J.R.,THE CHANGING AMERICAN ECONOMY. USA+45 BUDGET
AGRI FINAN LABOR FOR/AID INT/TRADE AUTOMAT GP/REL ECO/TAC
INGP/REL ANTHOL. PAGE 13 G0243 ECO/DEV
WEALTH

COLM G.,THE ECONOMY OF THE AMERICAN PEOPLE. USA+45
ECO/DEV FINAN WORKER INT/TRADE AUTOMAT GP/REL.
PAGE 13 G0244
B67
ECO/TAC
PRODUC
TREND
TEC/DEV

EISENMENGER R.W.,THE DYNAMICS OF GROWTH IN NEW
ENGLAND'S ECONOMY, 1870-1964. USA+45 USA-45 ECO/TAC
TAX PAY AUTOMAT GOV/REL ADJUST HABITAT...STAT
19/20. PAGE 17 G0340
B67
ECO/DEV
AGRI
INDUS
CAP/ISM

ELSNER H.,THE TECHNOCRATS, PROPHETS OF AUTOMATION.
SOCIETY INDUS VOL/ASSN COST INCOME ATTIT 20.
PAGE 18 G0345
B67
AUTOMAT
TECHRACY
PRODUC
HIST/WRIT

KRANZBERG M.,TECHNOLOGY IN WESTERN CIVILIZATION
VOLUME ONE. UNIV INDUS SKILL. PAGE 31 G0617
B67
TEC/DEV
ACT/RES
AUTOMAT
POLICY

MACBRIDE R.,THE AUTOMATED STATE: COMPUTER SYSTEMS
AS A NEW FORCE IN SOCIETY. FUT WOR+45 FINAN MUNIC
NAT/G WORKER PLAN TEC/DEV CONTROL PERS/REL RACE/REL
ADJUST. PAGE 35 G0685
B67
COMPUTER
AUTOMAT
PROB/SOLV
SOCIETY

SCHUMACHER B.G.,COMPUTER DYNAMICS IN PUBLIC
ADMINISTRATION. USA+45 CREATE PLAN TEC/DEV...MGT
LING CON/ANAL BIBLIOG/A 20. PAGE 50 G0980
B67
COMPUTER
COMPUT/IR
ADMIN
AUTOMAT

SILBERMAN C.E.,THE MYTHS OF AUTOMATION. INDUS
WORKER COST PRODUC AGE WEALTH 20. PAGE 51 G0996
B67
MYTH
AUTOMAT
CHARTS
TEC/DEV

US SUPERINTENDENT OF DOCUMENTS,LIBRARY OF CONGRESS
(PRICE LIST 83). AFR ASIA EUR+WWI USA-45 USSR NAT/G
DIPLOM CONFER CT/SYS WAR...DECISION PHIL/SCI
CLASSIF 19/20 CONGRESS PRESIDENT. PAGE 61 G1189
B67
BIBLIOG/A
USA+45
AUTOMAT
LAW

ALLEE D.,"AMERICAN AGRICULTURE - ITS RESOURCE
ISSUES FOR THE COMING YEARS." FUT USA+45 PLAN
PROB/SOLV 20. PAGE 2 G0043
S67
AGRI
SOCIETY
EFFICIENCY
AUTOMAT

BRETNOR R.,"DESTRUCTIVE FORCE AND THE MILITARY
EQUATIONS." UNIV COMPUTER PLAN PROB/SOLV AUTOMAT
CONTROL COERCE DETER NUC/PWR WEAPON DRIVE PWR.
PAGE 9 G0166
S67
FORCES
TEC/DEV
DOMIN
WAR

LEVENSTEIN A.,"TECHNOLOGICAL CHANGE, WORK, AND
HUMAN VALUES." WOR+45 SOCIETY AUTOMAT ROUTINE
LEISURE INGP/REL ADJUST TECHRACY...MGT CONCPT.
PAGE 33 G0660
S67
TEC/DEV
CULTURE
ALL/VALS
TIME/SEQ

MALONE D.K.,"THE COMMANDER AND THE COMPUTER."
USA+45 OP/RES PROB/SOLV TEC/DEV AUTOMAT CENTRAL 20.
PAGE 35 G0698
S67
COMPUTER
FORCES
ELITES
PLAN

MOOR E.J.,"THE INTERNATIONAL IMPACT OF AUTOMATION."
WOR+45 ACT/RES COMPUTER CREATE PLAN CAP/ISM ROUTINE
EFFICIENCY PREDICT. PAGE 39 G0779
S67
TEC/DEV
OP/RES
AUTOMAT
INDUS

MORTON J.A.,"A SYSTEMS APPROACH TO THE INNOVATION
PROCESS: ITS USE IN THE BELL SYSTEM." USA+45 INTELL
INDUS LG/CO CONSULT WORKER COMPUTER AUTOMAT DEMAND
...MGT CHARTS 20. PAGE 40 G0787
S67
TEC/DEV
GEN/METH
R+D
COM/IND

MYERS S.,"TECHNOLOGY AND URBAN TRANSIT: THE
ENORMOUS POTENTIAL OF BUS AND RAIL SYSTEMS." USA+45
FINAN LOC/G MUNIC WORKER PLAN PROB/SOLV PRICE
AUTOMAT 20. PAGE 40 G0798
S67
R+D
TEC/DEV
DIST/IND
ACT/RES

VERGIN R.C.,"COMPUTER INDUCED ORGANIZATION
CHANGES." FUT USA+45 R+D CREATE OP/RES TEC/DEV
ADJUST CENTRAL...MGT INT CON/ANAL COMPUT/IR.
PAGE 61 G1194
S67
COMPUTER
DECISION
AUTOMAT
EX/STRUC

WARE R.S.,"FORECAST A.D. 2000." SOCIETY STRATA
ECO/UNDEV INDUS FORCES EDU/PROP AUTOMAT COERCE REV
WEAPON ATTIT PREDICT. PAGE 62 G1213
S67
NUC/PWR
GEOG
TEC/DEV
WAR

AUTOMOBILE....AUTOMOBILE

AVERAGE....MEAN, AVERAGE BEHAVIORS

AVTORKHANOV A. G0082

AZERBAIJAN....AZERBAIJAN, IRAN

B

BA/MBUTI....BA MBUTI - THE FOREST PEOPLE (CONGO)

BABIES....SEE AGE/C

BACKUS/I....ISAAC BACKUS

BACON/F....FRANCIS BACON

MCRAE R.,THE PROBLEM OF THE UNITY OF THE SCIENCES:
BACON TO KANT. CREATE TASK KNOWL...PERS/COMP 16/18
BACON/F DESCARTE/R LEIBNITZ/G KANT/I DIDEROT/D.
PAGE 38 G0748
B61
PHIL/SCI
IDEA/COMP
PERSON

BADEN A.L. G0400

BADEN....BADEN

BAGHDAD....BAGHDAD, IRAQ

UN INTL CONF ON PEACEFUL USE,PROGRESS IN ATOMIC
ENERGY (VOL. I). WOR+45 R+D PLAN TEC/DEV CONFER
CONTROL PEACE SKILL...CHARTS ANTHOL 20 UN BAGHDAD.
PAGE 55 G1088
B58
NUC/PWR
DIPLOM
WORKER
EDU/PROP

BAHAWALPUR....BAHAWALPUR, PAKISTAN

BAHIA....BAHIA

BAIL....BAIL

BAILEY J.C. G0847

BAILEY S.K. G0084

BAILEY/JM....JOHN MORAN BAILEY

BAILEY/S....S. BAILEY

BAILEY/T....THOMAS BAILEY

BAKER G.W. G0085

BAKER H. G0086

BAKUBA....BAKUBA TRIBE

BAL/PAY....BALANCE OF PAYMENTS

GOLD N.L.,REGIONAL ECONOMIC DEVELOPMENT AND NUCLEAR
POWER IN INDIA. FUT INDIA FINAN FOR/AID INT/TRADE
BAL/PAY EFFICIENCY OPTIMAL PRODUC WEALTH...PREDICT
20. PAGE 22 G0424
B57
ECO/UNDEV
TEC/DEV
NUC/PWR
INDUS

SCHOECK H.,THE NEW ARGUMENT IN ECONOMICS. UK USA+45
INDUS MARKET LABOR NAT/G ECO/TAC ADMIN ROUTINE
BAL/PAY PWR...POLICY BOLIV. PAGE 49 G0973
B63
WELF/ST
FOR/AID
ECO/DEV
ALL/IDEOS

NADLER E.B.,"SOME ECONOMIC DISADVANTAGES OF THE
ARMS RACE." USA+45 INDUS R+D FORCES PLAN TEC/DEV
ECO/TAC FOR/AID EDU/PROP PWR WEALTH...TREND
COLD/WAR 20. PAGE 41 G0800
S63
ECO/DEV
MGT
BAL/PAY

ORGANIZATION AMERICAN STATES,ECONOMIC SURVEY OF
LATIN AMERICA, 1962. L/A+17C AGRI DIST/IND INDUS
MARKET PROC/MFG R+D PLAN TEC/DEV ECO/TAC REGION
BAL/PAY ALL/VALS...CON/ANAL ORG/CHARTS GEN/METH OAS
20. PAGE 43 G0844
B64
ECO/UNDEV
CHARTS

CARNEGIE ENDOWMENT INT. PEACE,"ECONOMIC AND SOCIAL
QUESTION (ISSUES BEFORE THE NINETEENTH GENERAL
ASSEMBLY)." WOR+45 ECO/DEV ECO/UNDEV INDUS R+D
DELIB/GP CREATE PLAN TEC/DEV ECO/TAC FOR/AID
BAL/PAY...RECORD UN 20. PAGE 11 G0209
L64
INT/ORG
INT/TRADE

US PRES COMM ECO IMPACT DEFENS,REPORT* JULY 1965.
USA+45 ECO/DEV INDUS DELIB/GP FORCES OP/RES
ARMS/CONT NUC/PWR WEAPON BAL/PAY...PREDICT SIMUL.
PAGE 59 G1159
B66 ACT/RES STAT WAR BUDGET

ENKE S.,DEFENSE MANAGEMENT. USA+45 R+D FORCES
WORKER PLAN ECO/TAC ADMIN NUC/PWR BAL/PAY UTIL
WEALTH...MGT DEPT/DEFEN. PAGE 18 G0348
B67 DECISION DELIB/GP EFFICIENCY BUDGET

US SENATE COMM ON FOREIGN REL,FOREIGN ASSISTANCE
ACT OF 1967. VIETNAM WOR+45 DELIB/GP CONFER CONTROL
WAR WEAPON BAL/PAY...CENSUS CHARTS SENATE. PAGE 60
G1185
B67 FOR/AID LAW DIPLOM POLICY

BAL/PWR....BALANCE OF POWER

SURANYI-UNGER T.,PRIVATE ENTERPRISE AND
GOVERNMENTAL PLANNING. STRUCT FINAN BAL/PWR
HAPPINESS DRIVE NEW/LIB PLURISM...MATH QUANT STAT
TREND BIBLIOG. PAGE 53 G1047
B50 PLAN NAT/G LAISSEZ POLICY

CORY R.H. JR.,"FORGING A PUBLIC INFORMATION POLICY
FOR THE UNITED NATIONS." FUT WOR+45 SOCIETY ADMIN
PEACE ATTIT PERSON SKILL...CONCPT 20 UN. PAGE 13
G0257
S53 INT/ORG EDU/PROP BAL/PWR

ARON R.,CENTURY OF TOTAL WAR. FUT WOR+45 WOR-45
SOCIETY INT/ORG NAT/G FORCES TOP/EX CREATE BAL/PWR
DOMIN EDU/PROP COERCE DETER PEACE TOTALISM PWR
...TIME/SEQ TREND COLD/WAR TOT/POP VAL/FREE
LEAGUE/NAT 20. PAGE 4 G0066
B54 ATTIT WAR

JONES J.M.,THE FIFTEEN WEEKS (FEBRUARY 21-JUNE 5,
1947). EUR+WWI USA+45 PROB/SOLV BAL/PWR...POLICY
TIME/SEQ 20 COLD/WAR MARSHL/PLN TRUMAN/HS
WASHING/DC. PAGE 29 G0567
B55 DIPLOM ECO/TAC FOR/AID

US OFFICE OF THE PRESIDENT,REPORT TO CONGRESS ON
THE MUTUAL SECURITY PROGRAM FOR THE SIX MONTHS
ENDED JUNE 30, 1955. ECO/DEV INT/ORG NAT/G CREATE
TEC/DEV BAL/PWR ECO/TAC AGREE DETER COST ORD/FREE
20 DEPT/STATE DEPT/DEFEN. PAGE 59 G1157
B55 DIPLOM FORCES PLAN FOR/AID

US OFFICE OF THE PRESIDENT,REPORT TO CONGRESS ON
THE MUTUAL SECURITY PROGRAM FOR THE SIX MONTHS
ENDED DECEMBER 31, 1955. ASIA USSR ECO/DEV
ECO/UNDEV INT/ORG CREATE TEC/DEV BAL/PWR ECO/TAC
AGREE DETER COST ORD/FREE 20 DEPT/STATE DEPT/DEFEN
EISNHWR/DD. PAGE 59 G1158
B56 DIPLOM FORCES PLAN FOR/AID

ARON R.,ON WAR: ATOMIC WEAPONS AND GLOBAL DIPLOMACY
(TRANS. BY TERENCE KILMARTIN). WOR+45 SOCIETY
FORCES BAL/PWR WAR WEAPON PERSON...SOC 20. PAGE 4
G0067
B58 ARMS/CONT NUC/PWR COERCE DIPLOM

GAVIN J.M.,WAR AND PEACE IN THE SPACE AGE. SPACE
USA+45 USSR FORCES PLAN TEC/DEV BAL/PWR DIPLOM
ARMS/CONT WEAPON CIVMIL/REL...CHARTS GP/COMP 20
NATO COLD/WAR. PAGE 21 G0414
B58 WAR DETER NUC/PWR PEACE

HUNTINGTON S.P.,"ARMS RACES: PREREQUISITES AND
RESULTS." EUR+WWI MOD/EUR USA+45 WOR+45 WOR-45
NAT/G TEC/DEV BAL/PWR COERCE DETER ATTIT...POLICY
TREND 20. PAGE 27 G0537
S58 FORCES PWR ARMS/CONT

SINGER J.D.,"THREAT PERCEPTION AND THE ARMAMENT
TENSION DILEMMA." WOR+45 WOR-45 ELITES INT/ORG
NAT/G DELIB/GP PLAN LEGIT COERCE DETER ATTIT
RIGID/FLEX PWR...DECISION PSY 20. PAGE 51 G1002
S58 PERCEPT ARMS/CONT BAL/PWR

THOMPSON K.W.,"NATIONAL SECURITY IN A NUCLEAR AGE."
USA+45 WOR+45 SOCIETY INT/ORG NAT/G TOP/EX DIPLOM
DOMIN EDU/PROP LEGIT ARMS/CONT COERCE ORD/FREE
...TREND STERTYP TOT/POP VAL/FREE COLD/WAR 20.
PAGE 54 G1068
S58 FORCES PWR BAL/PWR

HALEY A.G.,FIRST COLLOQUIUM ON THE LAW OF OUTER
SPACE. WOR+45 INT/ORG ACT/RES PLAN BAL/PWR CONFER
ATTIT PWR...POLICY JURID CHARTS ANTHOL 20. PAGE 24
G0468
B59 SPACE LAW SOVEREIGN CONTROL

BURNS A.L.,"POWER POLITICS AND THE GROWING NUCLEAR
CLUB." FUT WOR+45 TEC/DEV EXEC ARMS/CONT COERCE
DETER...DECISION HYPO/EXP 20. PAGE 10 G0192
L59 FORCES BAL/PWR NUC/PWR

STOESSINGER J.G.,"THE INTERNATIONAL ATOMIC ENERGY
AGENCY: THE FIRST PHASE." FUT WOR+45 NAT/G VOL/ASSN
DELIB/GP BAL/PWR LEGIT ADMIN ROUTINE PWR...OBS
CON/ANAL GEN/LAWS VAL/FREE 20 IAEA. PAGE 53 G1037
S59 INT/ORG ECO/DEV FOR/AID NUC/PWR

BARNET R.,WHO WANTS DISARMAMENT. COM EUR+WWI USA+45
USSR INT/ORG NAT/G BAL/PWR DIPLOM EDU/PROP COERCE
DETER NUC/PWR WAR WEAPON ATTIT PWR...TIME/SEQ
COLD/WAR CONGRESS 20. PAGE 5 G0096
B60 PLAN FORCES ARMS/CONT

BROOKINGS INSTITUTION,UNITED STATES FOREIGN POLICY:
STUDY NO 9: THE FORMULATION AND ADMINISTRATION OF
UNITED STATES FOREIGN POLICY. USA+45 WOR+45
EX/STRUC LEGIS BAL/PWR FOR/AID EDU/PROP CIVMIL/REL
GOV/REL...INT COLD/WAR. PAGE 9 G0174
B60 DIPLOM INT/ORG CREATE

EINSTEIN A.,EINSTEIN ON PEACE. FUT WOR+45 WOR-45
SOCIETY NAT/G PLAN BAL/PWR CAP/ISM DIPLOM ARMS/CONT
DETER NAT/LISM...POLICY RELATIV HUM PHIL/SCI CONCPT
BIOG COLD/WAR LEAGUE/NAT NAZI. PAGE 17 G0338
B60 INT/ORG ATTIT NUC/PWR PEACE

LE GHAIT E.,NO CARTE BLANCHE TO CAPRICORN; THE
FOLLY OF NUCLEAR WAR. WOR+45 INT/ORG BAL/PWR DIPLOM
RISK COERCE...CENSUS 20 NATO. PAGE 33 G0647
B60 DETER NUC/PWR PLAN DECISION

JACOB P.E.,"THE DISARMAMENT CONSENSUS." USA+45 USSR
WOR+45 INT/ORG NAT/G ACT/RES TEC/DEV BAL/PWR
EDU/PROP ADMIN COERCE DETER NUC/PWR CONSEN
RIGID/FLEX PWR...CONCPT RECORD CHARTS COLD/WAR 20.
PAGE 28 G0552
L60 DELIB/GP ATTIT ARMS/CONT

DOTY P.M.,"THE ROLE OF THE SMALLER POWERS." FUT
WOR+45 NAT/G TEC/DEV BAL/PWR DOMIN LEGIT CHOOSE
DISPL DRIVE RESPECT...DECISION 20. PAGE 16 G0310
S60 PWR POLICY ARMS/CONT NUC/PWR

KISSINGER H.A.,THE NECESSITY FOR CHOICE. FUT USA+45
ECO/UNDEV NAT/G PLAN BAL/PWR ECO/TAC ARMS/CONT
DETER NUC/PWR ATTIT...POLICY CONCPT RECORD GEN/LAWS
COLD/WAR 20. PAGE 31 G0604
B61 TOP/EX TREND DIPLOM

SCHMIDT H.,VERTEIDIGUNG ODER VERGELTUNG. COM CUBA
GERMANY/W USSR FORCES DIPLOM ARMS/CONT DETER
NUC/PWR...POLICY CHARTS HYPO/EXP SIMUL BIBLIOG 20
NATO COLD/WAR. PAGE 49 G0970
B61 PLAN WAR BAL/PWR ORD/FREE

TAUBENFELD H.J.,"A REGIME FOR OUTER SPACE." FUT
UNIV R+D ACT/RES PLAN BAL/PWR LEGIT ARMS/CONT
ORD/FREE...POLICY JURID TREND UN TOT/POP 20
COLD/WAR. PAGE 54 G1056
L61 INT/ORG ADJUD SPACE

HAINES G.,"THE COMPUTER AS A SMALL-GROUP MEMBER."
DELIB/GP BAL/PWR TASK 20. PAGE 24 G0467
S61 INGP/REL COMPUTER PROB/SOLV EFFICIENCY

MORGENSTERN O.,"THE N-COUNTRY PROBLEM." EUR+WWI
UNIV USA+45 WOR+45 SOCIETY CONSULT TOP/EX ACT/RES
PLAN EDU/PROP ATTIT DRIVE...POLICY OBS TREND
TOT/POP 20. PAGE 40 G0781
S61 FUT BAL/PWR NUC/PWR TEC/DEV

BOULDING K.E.,CONFLICT AND DEFENSE: A GENERAL
THEORY. FUT SOCIETY INT/ORG NAT/G CREATE BAL/PWR
COERCE NAT/LISM DRIVE ALL/VALS...PLURIST DECISION
CONCPT METH/CNCPT TREND HYPO/EXP TOT/POP 20. PAGE 8
G0157
B62 MATH SIMUL PEACE WAR

GILPIN R.,AMERICAN SCIENTISTS AND NUCLEAR WEAPONS
POLICY. COM FUT USA+45 WOR+45 INT/ORG NAT/G
PROF/ORG CONSULT FORCES CREATE TEC/DEV BAL/PWR
EDU/PROP ARMS/CONT WAR PERCEPT KNOWL MORAL PWR
...PHIL/SCI SOC CONCPT GEN/LAWS 20. PAGE 21 G0417
B62 INTELL ATTIT DETER NUC/PWR

KAHN H.,THINKING ABOUT THE UNTHINKABLE. FUT USA+45
B62 INT/ORG

LAW NAT/G CONSULT FORCES ACT/RES CREATE PLAN
TEC/DEV BAL/PWR DIPLOM EDU/PROP ARMS/CONT DETER
ATTIT...CONCPT OBS TREND COLD/WAR 20. PAGE 29 G0570

ORD/FREE
NUC/PWR
PEACE

B62

LEFEVER E.W.,ARMS AND ARMS CONTROL. COM USA+45
INT/ORG TEC/DEV DIPLOM ORD/FREE 20. PAGE 33 G0652

ATTIT
PWR
ARMS/CONT
BAL/PWR

B62

SCHILLING W.R.,STRATEGY, POLITICS, AND DEFENSE
BUDGETS. USA+45 R+D NAT/G CONSULT DELIB/GP FORCES
LEGIS ACT/RES PLAN BAL/PWR LEGIT EXEC NUC/PWR
RIGID/FLEX PWR...TREND COLD/WAR CONGRESS 20
EISNHWR/DD. PAGE 49 G0968

ROUTINE
POLICY

B62

SINGER J.D.,DETERRENCE, ARMS CONTROL AND
DISARMAMENT: TOWARD A SYNTHESIS IN NATIONAL
SECURITY POLICY. COM USA+45 INT/ORG BAL/PWR DETER
ORD/FREE...POLICY COLD/WAR 20. PAGE 51 G1003

FUT
ACT/RES
ARMS/CONT

B62

YALEN R.,REGIONALISM AND WORLD ORDER. EUR+WWI
WOR+45 WOR-45 INT/ORG VOL/ASSN DELIB/GP FORCES
TOP/EX BAL/PWR DIPLOM DOMIN REGION ARMS/CONT PWR
...JURID HYPO/EXP COLD/WAR 20. PAGE 64 G1261

ORD/FREE
POLICY

S62

BOULDING K.E.,"THE PREVENTION OF WORLD WAR THREE."
FUT WOR+45 INT/ORG PLAN BAL/PWR PEACE ORD/FREE PWR
...NEW/IDEA TREND TOT/POP COLD/WAR 20. PAGE 8 G0158

VOL/ASSN
NAT/G
ARMS/CONT
DIPLOM

S62

CRANE R.D.,"LAW AND STRATEGY IN SPACE." FUT USA+45
WOR+45 AIR LAW INT/ORG NAT/G FORCES ACT/RES PLAN
BAL/PWR LEGIT ARMS/CONT COERCE ORD/FREE...POLICY
INT/LAW JURID SOC/EXP 20 TREATY. PAGE 13 G0261

CONCPT
SPACE

B63

ABSHIRE D.M.,NATIONAL SECURITY: POLITICAL,
MILITARY, AND ECONOMIC STRATEGIES IN THE DECADE
AHEAD. ASIA COM USA+45 WOR+45 ECO/DEV ECO/UNDEV
INT/ORG DELIB/GP FORCES ECO/TAC COERCE ATTIT
RIGID/FLEX HEALTH ORD/FREE PWR WEALTH...POLICY STAT
CHARTS ANTHOL COLD/WAR VAL/FREE. PAGE 1 G0024

FUT
ACT/RES
BAL/PWR

B63

MENEZES A.J.,SUBDESENVOLVIMENTO E POLITICA
INTERNACIONAL. BRAZIL WOR+45 PLAN CONTROL LEAD
NAT/LISM ORD/FREE 20 THIRD/WRLD. PAGE 38 G0754

ECO/UNDEV
DIPLOM
POLICY
BAL/PWR

B63

MILBRATH L.W.,THE WASHINGTON LOBBYISTS. CONSTN
BAL/PWR CONTROL LEAD TASK CHOOSE SUPEGO...DECISION
STAT CHARTS BIBLIOG. PAGE 39 G0767

LOBBY
POLICY
PERS/REL

B63

PACHTER H.M.,COLLISION COURSE; THE CUBAN MISSILE
CRISIS AND COEXISTENCE. CUBA USA+45 DIPLOM
ARMS/CONT PEACE MARXISM...DECISION INT/LAW 20
COLD/WAR KHRUSH/N KENNEDY/JF CASTRO/F. PAGE 43
G0854

WAR
BAL/PWR
NUC/PWR
DETER

B63

US DEPARTMENT OF THE ARMY,US OVERSEAS BASES:
PRESENT STATUS AND FUTURE PROSPECTS (PAMPHLET).
USA+45 DIPLOM NUC/PWR ATTIT ORD/FREE...POLICY
CHARTS 20. PAGE 58 G1130

BIBLIOG/A
WAR
BAL/PWR
DETER

L63

BEGUIN H.,"ASPECTS GEOGRAPHIQUE DE LA
POLARISATION." FUT WOR+45 SOCIETY STRUCT ECO/DEV
R+D BAL/PWR ADMIN ATTIT RIGID/FLEX HEALTH WEALTH
...CHARTS 20. PAGE 6 G0114

ECO/UNDEV
GEOG
DIPLOM

L63

BRENNAN D.G.,"ARMS CONTROL AND CIVIL DEFENSE."
USA+45 WOR+45 NAT/G BAL/PWR ROUTINE ATTIT
RIGID/FLEX ORD/FREE...SOC TOT/POP 20. PAGE 8 G0165

PLAN
HEALTH
ARMS/CONT
DETER

S63

ABT C.,"THE PROBLEMS AND POSSIBILITIES OF SPACE
ARMS CONTROL." FUT USA+45 WOR+45 AIR SOCIETY NAT/G
BAL/PWR EDU/PROP ATTIT PWR WEALTH...HYPO/EXP
TOT/POP 20. PAGE 2 G0025

ACT/RES
ORD/FREE
ARMS/CONT
SPACE

S63

BOULDING K.E.,"UNIVERSITY, SOCIETY, AND ARMS
CONTROL." WOR+45 WOR-45 ACADEM NAT/G CONSULT FORCES
ACT/RES PLAN TEC/DEV BAL/PWR ECO/TAC COERCE DETER
WAR ATTIT RIGID/FLEX KNOWL ORD/FREE PWR WEALTH

SOCIETY
ARMS/CONT

...CONCPT COLD/WAR TOT/POP 20. PAGE 8 G0159

S63

SMITH D.O.,"WHAT IS A WAR DETERRENT." FUT GERMANY
HUNGARY UK USA+45 WOR+45 WOR-45 NAT/G TEC/DEV
BAL/PWR PWR...CONCPT GEN/LAWS COLD/WAR 20. PAGE 51
G1013

ACT/RES
FORCES
ARMS/CONT
DETER

B64

HEKHUIS D.J.,INTERNATIONAL STABILITY: MILITARY,
ECONOMIC AND POLITICAL DIMENSIONS. FUT WOR+45 LAW
ECO/UNDEV INT/ORG NAT/G VOL/ASSN FORCES ACT/RES
BAL/PWR PWR WEALTH...STAT UN 20. PAGE 25 G0503

TEC/DEV
DETER
REGION

B64

KAUFMANN W.W.,THE MC NAMARA STRATEGY. TOP/EX
INSPECT BAL/PWR DIPLOM CONTROL DETER GUERRILLA
NUC/PWR WEAPON COST PWR...METH/COMP 20 MCNAMARA/R
KENNEDY/JF JOHNSON/LB NATO DEPT/DEFEN. PAGE 30
G0586

FORCES
WAR
PLAN
PROB/SOLV

B64

ROSECRANCE R.N.,THE DISPERSION OF NUCLEAR WEAPONS:
STRATEGY AND POLITICS. ASIA COM FUT S/ASIA USA+45
INT/ORG NAT/G DELIB/GP FORCES ACT/RES TEC/DEV
BAL/PWR COERCE DETER ATTIT RIGID/FLEX ORD/FREE
...POLICY CHARTS VAL/FREE. PAGE 48 G0935

EUR+WWI
PWR
PEACE

B64

RUSHING W.A.,THE PSYCHIATRIC PROFESSIONS. DOMIN
INGP/REL DRIVE RIGID/FLEX ROLE HEALTH PWR...POLICY
GP/COMP. PAGE 48 G0947

ATTIT
PUB/INST
PROF/ORG
BAL/PWR

L64

GOLDBERG A.,"ATOMIC ORIGINS OF THE BRITISH NUCLEAR
DETERRENT." EUR+WWI UK NAT/G TOP/EX PLAN BAL/PWR
DOMIN DETER CHOOSE ATTIT DRIVE HEALTH ORD/FREE PWR
RESPECT...CONCPT VAL/FREE COLD/WAR 20 CMN/WLTH.
PAGE 22 G0425

CREATE
FORCES
NUC/PWR

B65

PEACE RESEARCH ABSTRACTS. FUT WOR+45 R+D INT/ORG
NAT/G PLAN TEC/DEV BAL/PWR DIPLOM FOR/AID NUC/PWR
HEALTH. PAGE 1 G0020

BIBLIOG/A
PEACE
ARMS/CONT
WAR

B65

CORDIER A.W.,THE QUEST FOR PEACE. WOR+45 NAT/G PLAN
BAL/PWR ECO/TAC ARMS/CONT NUC/PWR PWR...ANTHOL UN
COLD/WAR. PAGE 13 G0256

PEACE
DIPLOM
POLICY
INT/ORG

B65

US DEPARTMENT OF THE ARMY,NUCLEAR WEAPONS AND THE
ATLANTIC ALLIANCE: A BIBLIOGRAPHIC SURVEY. ASIA COM
EUR+WWI USA+45 FORCES DIPLOM WEAPON...STAT 20 NATO.
PAGE 58 G1131

BIBLIOG/A
ARMS/CONT
NUC/PWR
BAL/PWR

S65

ABT C.C.,"CONTROLLING FUTURE ARMS." USSR PLAN
BAL/PWR DIPLOM NUC/PWR COST...CLASSIF STAT CHARTS.
PAGE 2 G0027

PREDICT
FUT
ARMS/CONT
TEC/DEV

S65

DALKEY N.C.,"SOLVABLE NUCLEAR WAR MODELS." FORCES
BAL/PWR DIPLOM COERCE PEACE DECISION. PAGE 14 G0273

GAME
SIMUL
WAR
NUC/PWR

S65

DESAI M.J.,"INDIA AND NUCLEAR WEAPONS." ASIA
BAL/PWR DIPLOM NUC/PWR WEAPON PEACE RECORD. PAGE 15
G0294

INDIA
ARMS/CONT

S65

HARRISON S.L.,"NTH NATION CHALLENGES* THE PRESENT
PERSPECTIVE." EUR+WWI FUT USA+45 BAL/PWR CONTROL
RISK COERCE WAR...PREDICT COLD/WAR. PAGE 25 G0485

ARMS/CONT
NUC/PWR
NAT/G
DIPLOM

C65

MARK M.,"BEYOND SOVEREIGNTY." WOR+45 WOR-45
ECO/UNDEV BAL/PWR INT/TRADE NUC/PWR REV WAR MARXISM
NEW/LIB BIBLIOG. PAGE 36 G0706

NAT/LISM
NAT/G
DIPLOM
INTELL

B66

AMERICAN ASSEMBLY COLUMBIA U,A WORLD OF NUCLEAR
POWERS? FUT WOR+45 ECO/DEV BAL/PWR ECO/TAC CONTROL
RISK EFFICIENCY ATTIT PWR...METH/COMP ANTHOL 20.
PAGE 3 G0049

NUC/PWR
DIPLOM
TEC/DEV
ARMS/CONT

B66

BLOOMFIELD L.P.,KHRUSHCHEV AND THE ARMS RACE.

ARMS/CONT

USA+45 USSR ECO/DEV BAL/PWR EDU/PROP CONFER NUC/PWR COM
ATTIT...CHARTS 20 KHRUSH/N. PAGE 7 G0143   POLICY
                                                           DIPLOM

                                                           B66
GORDON G.,THE LEGISLATIVE PROCESS AND DIVIDED   LEGIS
GOVERNMENT; A CASE STUDY OF THE 86TH CONGRESS.   HABITAT
USA+45 POL/PAR PROVS PROB/SOLV BAL/PWR CHOOSE   CHIEF
REPRESENT EFFICIENCY ATTIT...POLICY DECISION STAT   NAT/G
20 CONGRESS EISNHWR/DD. PAGE 22 G0434

                                                           B66
KUENNE R.E.,THE POLARIS MISSILE STRIKE* A GENERAL   NUC/PWR
ECONOMIC SYSTEMS ANALYSIS. USA+45 USSR NAT/G   FORCES
BAL/PWR ARMS/CONT WAR...MATH PROBABIL COMPUT/IR   DETER
CHARTS HYPO/EXP SIMUL. PAGE 32 G0625   DIPLOM

                                                           L66
ZOPPO C.E.,"NUCLEAR TECHNOLOGY, MULTIPOLARITY, AND   NET/THEORY
INTERNATIONAL STABILITY." ASIA RUSSIA USA+45 STRUCT   ORD/FREE
TOP/EX BAL/PWR DIPLOM DETER CIVMIL/REL NAT/COMP.   DECISION
PAGE 65 G1270   NUC/PWR

                                                           B67
ARON R.,THE GREAT DEBATE: THEORIES OF NUCLEAR   NUC/PWR
STRATEGY. FRANCE USA+45 INT/ORG PLAN TREND. PAGE 4   DETER
G0068   BAL/PWR
                                                           DIPLOM

                                                           B67
BURNS E.L.M.,MEGAMURDER. WOR+45 LAW INT/ORG NAT/G   FORCES
BAL/PWR DIPLOM DETER MURDER WEAPON CIVMIL/REL PEACE   PLAN
...INT/LAW TREND 20. PAGE 10 G0193   WAR
                                                           NUC/PWR

                                                           B67
HALLE L.J.,THE COLD WAR AS HISTORY. USSR WOR+45   DIPLOM
ECO/TAC FOR/AID NUC/PWR WAR PEACE ORD/FREE   BAL/PWR
...MAJORIT TREND 20 COLD/WAR KENNEDY/JF KHRUSH/N
BERLIN/BLO. PAGE 24 G0470

                                                           B67
KINTNER W.R.,PEACE AND THE STRATEGY CONFLICT. PLAN   ROLE
BAL/PWR DIPLOM CONTROL ARMS/CONT DETER WEAPON 20.   PEACE
PAGE 30 G0599   NUC/PWR
                                                           ORD/FREE

                                                           B67
MCBRIDE J.H.,THE TEST BAN TREATY: MILITARY,   ARMS/CONT
TECHNOLOGICAL, AND POLITICAL IMPLICATIONS. USA+45   DIPLOM
USSR DELIB/GP FORCES LEGIS TEC/DEV BAL/PWR TREATY.   NUC/PWR
PAGE 37 G0727

                                                           B67
MCCLINTOCK R.,THE MEANING OF LIMITED WAR. FUT   WAR
WOR+45 NAT/G FORCES GUERRILLA REV...POLICY SAMP/SIZ   NUC/PWR
TREND NAT/COMP 45 COLD/WAR. PAGE 37 G0730   BAL/PWR
                                                           DIPLOM

                                                           B67
US SENATE COMM ON FOREIGN REL,ARMS SALES TO NEAR   WEAPON
EAST AND SOUTH ASIAN COUNTRIES. INDIA IRAN PAKISTAN   FOR/AID
WOR+45 PROC/MFG BAL/PWR DIPLOM...DECISION SENATE.   FORCES
PAGE 60 G1183   POLICY

                                                           B67
US SENATE COMM ON FOREIGN REL,UNITED STATES   ARMS/CONT
ARMAMENT AND DISARMAMENT PROBLEMS. USA+45 AIR   WEAPON
BAL/PWR DIPLOM FOR/AID NUC/PWR ORD/FREE SENATE   FORCES
TREATY. PAGE 60 G1184   PROB/SOLV

                                                           S67
"CHINESE STATEMENT ON NUCLEAR PROLIFERATION."   NUC/PWR
CHINA/COM USA+45 USSR DOMIN COLONIAL PWR. PAGE 1   BAL/PWR
G0022   ARMS/CONT
                                                           DIPLOM

                                                           S67
BULMER-THOMAS I.,"SO, ON TO THE GREAT SOCIETY." FUT   PHIL/SCI
UNIV TEC/DEV BAL/PWR WAR BIO/SOC KNOWL...ART/METH   SOCIETY
SOC PREDICT TREND WORSHIP 20 GREAT/SOC. PAGE 9   CREATE
G0185

                                                           S67
CHRIST R.F.,"REORGANIZATION OF FRENCH ARMED   CHIEF
FORCES." FRANCE CREATE PLAN TEC/DEV BAL/PWR DOMIN   DETER
COERCE CENTRAL EFFICIENCY 20. PAGE 12 G0229   NUC/PWR
                                                           FORCES

                                                           S67
COFFEY J.I.,"THE ANTI-BALLISTIC MISSILE DEBATE."   ARMS/CONT
USA+45 USSR TEC/DEV BAL/PWR 20. PAGE 12 G0238   NUC/PWR
                                                           DETER
                                                           DIPLOM

                                                           S67
DEUTSCH K.W.,"ARMS CONTROL AND EUROPEAN UNITY* THE   ARMS/CONT
NEXT TEN YEARS." USA+45 ELITES NAT/G BAL/PWR DIPLOM   PEACE
NUC/PWR...INT KNO/TEST NATO EEC. PAGE 15 G0300   REGION
                                                           PLAN

                                                           S67
EDMONDS M.,"INTERNATIONAL COLLABORATION IN WEAPONS   DIPLOM
PROCUREMENT* THE IMPLICATIONS OF THE ANGLO-FRENCH   VOL/ASSN
CASE." FRANCE UK CONSULT OP/RES PROB/SOLV TEC/DEV   BAL/PWR
CONFER CONTROL EFFICIENCY 20. PAGE 17 G0334   ARMS/CONT

                                                           S67
FELD B.T.,"A PLEDGE* NO FIRST USE." DELIB/GP   ARMS/CONT
BAL/PWR DOMIN DETER. PAGE 19 G0363   NUC/PWR
                                                           DIPLOM
                                                           PEACE

                                                           S67
FOREIGN POLICY ASSOCIATION,"US CONCERN FOR WORLD   INT/LAW
LAW." USA+45 WOR+45 DELIB/GP JUDGE BAL/PWR CONFER   INT/ORG
PEACE ORD/FREE 20 UN. PAGE 19 G0379   DIPLOM
                                                           ARMS/CONT

                                                           S67
FOREIGN POLICY ASSOCIATION,"HOW WORLD LAW DEVELOPS*   INT/LAW
A CASE STUDY OF THE OUTER SPACE TREATY." SPACE   DIPLOM
WOR+45 BAL/PWR NEUTRAL NUC/PWR PEACE KNOWL 20 UN   ARMS/CONT
TREATY. PAGE 19 G0380   INT/ORG

                                                           S67
HULL E.W.S.,"THE POLITICAL OCEAN." FUT UNIV WOR+45   DIPLOM
EXTR/IND R+D VOL/ASSN PLAN BAL/PWR ECO/TAC PEACE   ECO/UNDEV
WEALTH 20 UN. PAGE 27 G0536   INT/ORG
                                                           INT/LAW

                                                           S67
INGLIS D.R.,"MISSILE DEFENSE, NUCLEAR SPREAD, AND   NUC/PWR
VIETNAM." CHINA/COM USA+45 USSR VIETNAM INDUS   ARMS/CONT
BAL/PWR DETER WAR COST NAT/LISM PEACE. PAGE 28   DIPLOM
G0544   FORCES

                                                           S67
JACKSON W.G.F.,"NUCLEAR PROLIFERATION AND THE GREAT   NUC/PWR
POWERS." FUT UK WOR+45 INT/ORG DOMIN ARMS/CONT   ATTIT
DETER ORD/FREE PACIFIST. PAGE 28 G0550   BAL/PWR
                                                           NAT/LISM

                                                           S67
KAHN H.,"CRITERIA FOR LONG-RANGE NUCLEAR CONTROL   NUC/PWR
POLICIES." WOR+45 INT/ORG TEC/DEV DOMIN DETER WAR   ARMS/CONT
WEAPON ISOLAT ORD/FREE POLICY. PAGE 29 G0571   BAL/PWR
                                                           DIPLOM

                                                           S67
KRUSCHE H.,"THE STRIVING OF THE KIESINGER-STRAUS   ARMS/CONT
GOVERNMENT FOR NUCLEAR WEAPONS IS A THREAT TO   INT/ORG
EUROPEAN SECURITY." EUR+WWI GERMANY BAL/PWR   NUC/PWR
SANCTION WEAPON PEACE ORD/FREE...MARXIST 20 NATO   DIPLOM
COLD/WAR. PAGE 32 G0623

                                                           S67
MARTIN L.W.,"BALLISTIC MISSILE DEFENSE AND EUROPE."   ATTIT
EUR+WWI USA+45 FORCES PLAN BAL/PWR DEBATE PEACE   ARMS/CONT
...POLICY COLD/WAR NATO. PAGE 36 G0715   NUC/PWR
                                                           DETER

                                                           S67
ROTHSTEIN R.L.,"NUCLEAR PROLIFERATION AND AMERICAN   NUC/PWR
POLICY." PROB/SOLV BAL/PWR DIPLOM ARMS/CONT   CONTROL
EFFICIENCY 20. PAGE 48 G0942   DETER
                                                           WOR+45

                                                           S67
SHARP G.,"THE NEED OF A FUNCTIONAL SUBSTITUTE FOR   PEACE
WAR." FUT UNIV WOR+45 CULTURE SOCIETY INT/ORG   WAR
CONSULT DELIB/GP ACT/RES CREATE BAL/PWR CONFER   DIPLOM
ARMS/CONT NUC/PWR 20. PAGE 50 G0989   PROB/SOLV

                                                           S67
SHULMAN M.D.,"'EUROPE' VERSUS 'DETENTE'." USA+45   DIPLOM
USSR INT/ORG CONTROL ARMS/CONT DETER 20. PAGE 50   BAL/PWR
G0995   NUC/PWR

                                                           S67
TEKINER S.,"SINKIAN AND THE SINO-SOVIET CONFLICT."   DIPLOM
ASIA COM USSR FORCES PLAN BAL/PWR CONTROL NUC/PWR   PWR
WAR WEAPON...DECISION 20. PAGE 54 G1060   MARXISM

                                                           S67
YOUNG O.R.,"ACTIVE DEFENSE AND INTERNATIONAL   ARMS/CONT
ORDER." FORCES BAL/PWR DEBATE GAMBLE COST PEACE.   DETER
PAGE 64 G1265   PLAN
                                                           DECISION

BALANCE OF PAYMENTS....SEE BAL/PAY

BALANCE OF POWER....SEE BAL/PWR

BALASSA B. G0087

BALDWIN H.W. G0088,G0089

BALDWIN/J....JAMES BALDWIN

BALKANS....BALKANS

BALTIMORE....BALTIMORE, MD.

BANDA/HK....H.K. BANDA, PRIME MINISTER OF MALAWI

BANK/ENGL....THE BANK OF ENGLAND

BANKING....SEE FINAN

BANKRUPTCY....BANKRUPTCY

BANKS A.S. G0447

BANTU....BANTU NATION AND CULTURE

BANTUSTANS....BANTUSTANS, REPUBLIC OF SOUTH AFRICA

BAO/DAI....BAO DAI

BARAGWANATH L.E. G0090

BARAN P. G0091

BARANSON J. G0092

BARBARIAN....BARBARIAN

BARGAIN....BARGAINING; SEE ALSO ECO/TAC, MARKET, DIPLOM

HUZAR E.,THE PURSE AND THE SWORD: CONTROL OF THE   CIVMIL/REL
ARMY BY CONGRESS THROUGH MILITARY APPROPRIATIONS   BUDGET
1933-1950. NAT/G DELIB/GP EX/STRUC FORCES PROB/SOLV   CONTROL
BARGAIN CONFER ADMIN ROUTINE GOV/REL EFFICIENCY   LEGIS
...POLICY COLD/WAR. PAGE 27 G0541   B50

MCCRACKEN H.L.,KEYNESIAN ECONOMICS IN THE STREAM OF   ECO/TAC
ECONOMIC THOUGHT. FINAN MARKET BARGAIN EFFICIENCY   DEMAND
OPTIMAL...PHIL/SCI CONCPT IDEA/COMP BIBLIOG 18/20   ECOMETRIC
KEYNES/JM. PAGE 37 G0732   B61

STONE J.J.,CONTAINING THE ARMS RACE* SOME SPECIFIC   ARMS/CONT
PROPOSALS. ASIA USA+45 USSR PROB/SOLV BARGAIN   FEEDBACK
DIPLOM DETER NUC/PWR RATIONAL...GAME 20 DEPT/DEFEN   COST
TREATY. PAGE 53 G1038   ATTIT   B66

PRINCETON U INDUSTRIAL REL SEC,RECENT MATERIAL ON   BIBLIOG/A
COLLECTIVE BARGAINING IN GOVERNMENT (PAMPHLET NO.   BARGAIN
130). USA+45 ECO/DEV LABOR WORKER ECO/TAC GOV/REL   NAT/G
...MGT 20. PAGE 45 G0890   GP/REL   N66

MOORE J.R.,THE ECONOMIC IMPACT OF THE TVA. AGRI   ECO/UNDEV
INDUS PLAN BARGAIN CONTROL REGION GOV/REL DEMAND   ECO/DEV
EFFICIENCY SOCISM 20 TVA. PAGE 40 G0780   NAT/G
                                                          CREATE   B67

NORTHRUP H.R.,RESTRICTIVE LABOR PRACTICES IN THE   DIST/IND
SUPERMARKET INDUSTRY. USA+45 INDUS WORKER TEC/DEV   MARKET
BARGAIN PAY CONTROL GP/REL COST...STAT CHARTS NLRB.   LABOR
PAGE 42 G0827   MGT   B67

RUSSETT B.M.,ARMS CONTROL IN EUROPE: PROPOSALS AND   ARMS/CONT
POLITICAL CONSTRAINTS. GERMANY WOR+45 POL/PAR   REGION
BARGAIN DIPLOM...TREND CHARTS 20 COLD/WAR. PAGE 48   METH/COMP
G0950   B67

PRINCETON U INDUSTRIAL REL SEC,COLLECTIVE   BIBLIOG/A
BARGAINING IN THE PUBLIC SCHOOLS (PAMPHLET NO. 33).   SCHOOL
USA+45 LABOR PROB/SOLV PWR MGT. PAGE 45 G0891   BARGAIN
                                                          GP/REL   N67

US CONGRESS JT COMM ECO GOVT,BACKGROUND MATERIAL ON   BUDGET
ECONOMY IN GOVERNMENT 1967 (PAMPHLET). WOR+45   COST
ECO/DEV BARGAIN PRICE DEMAND OPTIMAL...STAT   MGT
DEPT/DEFEN. PAGE 57 G1116   NAT/G   N67

BARISH N.N. G0093

BARKER E. G0094,G0095

BARNET R. G0096

BARNETT H.J. G0097

BARNETT/R....ROSS BARNETT

BAROTSE....BAROTSE TRIBE OF RHODESIA

BARRO S. G0098

BARRON J.A. G0099

BASHILELE....BASHILELE TRIBE

BASS H.L. G0458

BASS M.E. G0100

BATAK....BATAK TRIBE, PHILIPPINES

BATES J. G0101

BATISTA/J....JUAN BATISTA

BAUCHET P. G0102

BAUER P.T. G0103

BAUMGARTEL H. G0104

BAUMOL W.J. G0105

BAVARIA....BAVARIA

BAVELAS A. G0106

BAWONGO....BAWONGO TRIBE

BAXTER J.P. G0107

BAYESIAN INFLUENCE....SEE SIMUL

BEARD C.A. G0108

BEARD/CA....CHARLES A. BEARD

BEATON L. G0109

BEAUFRE A. G0110,G0111

BECCARIA/C....CAESARE BONESARA BECCARIA

BECK H.P. G0112

BECKER A.S. G0113

BECKER/E....ERNEST BECKER

BEGUIN H. G0114

BEHAV/SCI....BEHAVIORAL SCIENCES

BEHAVIOR TESTS....SEE PERS/TEST

BEHAVIORAL SCIENCES....SEE BEHAV/SCI

BEHAVIORSM....BEHAVIORISM

BELGIUM....BELGIUM

GRANICK D.,THE EUROPEAN EXECUTIVE. BELGIUM FRANCE   MGT
GERMANY/W UK INDUS LABOR LG/CO SML/CO EX/STRUC PLAN   ECO/DEV
TEC/DEV CAP/ISM COST DEMAND...POLICY CHARTS 20.   ECO/TAC
PAGE 22 G0441   EXEC   B62

BELIEF....SEE SECT, ATTIT

BELL J.R. G0115

BELLAS/HES....NATIONAL BELLAS HESS

BELLMAN R. G0116

BEN/BELLA....AHMED BEN BELLA

BENDIX R. G0117

BENESE....BENES

BENGAL....BENGAL + BENGALIS

BENIN....BENIN   DISTRICT IN NIGERIA

BENJAMIN A.C. G0118

BENN W. G0119

BENNE K.D. G0123

BENNETT J.C. G0120

BENNETT J.W. G0121

BENNION E.G. G0122

BENNIS W.G. G0123

BENTHAM J. G0124

BENTHAM/J....JEREMY BENTHAM

                                                    B28

    BARKER E.,POLITICAL THOUGHT IN ENGLAND: FROM   INTELL
HERBERT SPENCER TO THE PRESENT DAY. UK ALL/IDEOS   GEN/LAWS
...PHIL/SCI 19/20 SPENCER/H GREEN/TH BENTHAM/J   IDEA/COMP
MAITLAND/F. PAGE 5 G0094

BENTLEY/AF....ARTHUR F. BENTLEY

BENTWICH J.S. G0125

BERGMANN G. G0126

BERGSON H. G0127

BERGSON/H....HENRI BERGSON

BERGSON/WJ....W. JAMES BERGSON

BERKELEY E.C. G0128

BERKELEY....BERKELEY, CALIFORNIA

BERKS R.N. G0129

BERLIN....BERLIN

BERLIN/BLO....BERLIN BLOCKADE

                                                      B67

    HALLE L.J.,THE COLD WAR AS HISTORY. USSR WOR+45   DIPLOM
ECO/TAC FOR/AID NUC/PWR WAR PEACE ORD/FREE   BAL/PWR
...MAJORIT TREND 20 COLD/WAR KENNEDY/JF KHRUSH/N
BERLIN/BLO. PAGE 24 G0470

BERNAL J.D. G0130

BERNAYS/EL....EDWARD L. BERNAYS

BERND J.L. G0131

BERNSTEIN I. G0132

BESSARABIA....BESSARABIA; SEE ALSO USSR

BETHE H. G0133

BETTEN J.K. G0134

BHUMIBOL/A....BHUMIBOL ADULYADEJ

BHUTAN....SEE ALSO ASIA

BIAFRA....BIAFRA

BIBLE....BIBLE: OLD AND NEW TESTAMENTS

BIBLIOG....BIBLIOGRAPHY OVER 50 ITEMS

                                                      N

    AMERICAN DOCUMENTATION INST,AMERICAN DOCUMENTATION. BIBLIOG
PROF/ORG CONSULT PLAN PERCEPT...MATH STAT AUD/VIS   TEC/DEV
CHARTS METH/COMP INDEX METH 20. PAGE 3 G0050   COM/IND
                                                      COMPUT/IR

                                                      N

    CONOVER H.L.,CIVILIAN DEFENSE: A SELECTED LIST OF   BIBLIOG
RECENT REFERENCES (PAMPHLET). USA+45 LOC/G MUNIC   PLAN
PROB/SOLV ADMIN LEAD TASK WEAPON GOV/REL...POLICY WAR
CON/ANAL 20 CIV/DEFENS. PAGE 13 G0251   CIVMIL/REL

                                                      B

    US DEPT COMMERCE OFF TECH SERV,TECHNICAL   BIBLIOG
TRANSLATIONS. WOR+45 INDUS COMPUTER CREATE NUC/PWR R+D
...PHIL/SCI COMPUT/IR METH/COMP METH. PAGE 58 G1135 TEC/DEV
                                                      AUTOMAT

                                                      N

    FOREIGN AFFAIRS. SPACE WOR+45 WOR-45 CULTURE
                                                  BIBLIOG

ECO/UNDEV FINAN NAT/G TEC/DEV INT/TRADE ARMS/CONT DIPLOM
NUC/PWR...POLICY 20 UN EURATOM ECSC EEC. PAGE 1   INT/ORG
G0004   INT/LAW

                                                    N

INDIA: A REFERENCE ANNUAL. INDIA CULTURE COM/IND   CONSTN
R+D FORCES PLAN RECEIVE EDU/PROP HEALTH...STAT   LABOR
CHARTS BIBLIOG 20. PAGE 1 G0005   INT/ORG

                                                    N

GT BRIT MIN OVERSEAS DEV, LIB, TECHNICAL CO-   BIBLIOG
OPERATION -- A BIBLIOGRAPHY. UK LAW SOCIETY DIPLOM TEC/DEV
ECO/TAC FOR/AID...STAT 20 CMN/WLTH. PAGE 39 G0775 ECO/DEV
                                                      NAT/G

                                                    N

RAND SCHOOL OF SOCIAL SCIENCE,INDEX TO LABOR   BIBLIOG
ARTICLES. ECO/DEV INT/ORG LEGIS DIPLOM GP/REL   LABOR
...NAT/COMP 20. PAGE 46 G0900   MGT
                                                    ADJUD

                                                N19

KAUFMAN J.L.,COMMUNITY RENEWAL PROGRAMS (PAMPHLET). LOC/G
USA+45 CONSTRUC PROVS CREATE PLAN CONTROL WEALTH 20 MUNIC
URBAN/RNWL. PAGE 30 G0584   ACT/RES
                                                    BIBLIOG

                                                C25

MOON P.T.,"SYLLABUS ON INTERNATIONAL RELATIONS."   INT/ORG
EUR+WWI MOD/EUR USA-45 FORCES COLONIAL WAR WEAPON DIPLOM
NAT/LISM...POLICY BIBLIOG T 19/20. PAGE 39 G0778   NAT/G

                                                B36

US LIBRARY OF CONGRESS,CLASSIFIED GUIDE TO MATERIAL BIBLIOG
IN THE LIBRARY OF CONGRESS COVERING URBAN COMMUNITY CLASSIF
DEVELOPMENT. USA+45 CREATE PROB/SOLV ADMIN 20.   MUNIC
PAGE 59 G1154   PLAN

                                              B37

HODGSON J.G.,THE OFFICIAL PUBLICATIONS OF AMERICAN BIBLIOG
COUNTIES: A UNION LIST. SCHOOL BUDGET...HEAL MGT   LOC/G
SOC/WK 19/20. PAGE 26 G0520   PUB/INST

                                              B39

FULLER G.H.,A SELECTED LIST OF REFERENCES ON THE   BIBLIOG
EXPANSION OF THE US NAVY, 1933-1939 (PAMPHLET).   FORCES
MOD/EUR USA-45 NAT/G PLAN DIPLOM DOMIN RISK   WEAPON
ARMS/CONT EQUILIB PWR 20 NAVY. PAGE 20 G0399   WAR

                                              B40

FULLER G.H.,SELECTED LIST OF RECENT REFERENCES ON BIBLIOG
AMERICAN NATIONAL DEFENSE (PAMPHLET). USA-45 FINAN CIVMIL/REL
NAT/G ARMS/CONT WAR GOV/REL CENTRAL COST PEACE PWR FORCES
20. PAGE 20 G0400   WEAPON

                                              S43

KAPLAN A.,"CONTENT ANALYSIS AND THE THEORY OF   LOG
SIGNS" (BMR)" PERS/REL...PSY CONCPT LING IDEA/COMP CON/ANAL
SIMUL BIBLIOG 20 MORRIS/CW. PAGE 29 G0573   STAT
                                                      PHIL/SCI

                                              B44

FULLER G.H.,MILITARY GOVERNMENT: A LIST OF   BIBLIOG
REFERENCES (A PAMPHLET). ITALY UK USA-45 WOR-45 LAW DIPLOM
FORCES DOMIN ADMIN ARMS/CONT ORD/FREE PWR   CIVMIL/REL
...DECISION 20 CHINJAP. PAGE 21 G0404   SOVEREIGN

                                              B44

MATTHEWS M.A.,INTERNATIONAL POLICE (PAMPHLET).   BIBLIOG
WOR-45 DIPLOM ARMS/CONT WAR 20. PAGE 37 G0722   INT/ORG
                                                    FORCES
                                                    PEACE

                                              B44

PUBLIC ADMINISTRATION SERVICE,YOUR BUSINESS OF   BIBLIOG
GOVERNMENT: A CATALOG OF PUBLICATIONS IN THE FIELD ADMIN
OF PUBLIC ADMINISTRATION (PAMPHLET). FINAN R+D   NAT/G
LOC/G ACT/RES OP/RES PLAN 20. PAGE 45 G0894   MUNIC

                                              B46

AMERICAN DOCUMENTATION INST,CATALOGUE OF AUXILIARY BIBLIOG
PUBLICATIONS IN MICROFILMS AND PHOTOPRINTS. USA+45 EDU/PROP
LAW AGRI CREATE TEC/DEV ADMIN...GEOG LING MATH 20. PSY
PAGE 3 G0052

                                              B47

BALDWIN H.W.,THE PRICE OF POWER. USA+45 FORCES PLAN PROB/SOLV
NUC/PWR ADJUST COST ORD/FREE...POLICY PSY BIBLIOG PWR
20. PAGE 5 G0089   POPULISM
                                                    PRICE

                                              B47

BECK H.P.,MEN WHO CONTROL OUR UNIVERSITIES.   EDU/PROP
EX/STRUC CHOOSE INGP/REL DISCRIM PERSON WEALTH   ACADEM
...POLICY TREND CON/ANAL CHARTS BIBLIOG. PAGE 6   CONTROL
G0112   LEAD

B48

GRIFFITH E.S.,RESEARCH IN POLITICAL SCIENCE: THE WORK OF PANELS OF RESEARCH COMMITTEE. APSA. WOR-45 WOR-45 COM/IND R+D FORCES ACT/RES WAR...GOV/COMP ANTHOL 20. PAGE 23 G0451
BIBLIOG PHIL/SCI DIPLOM JURID

S48

MACCORQUODALE K.,"ON A DISTINCTION BETWEEN HYPOTHETICAL CONSTRUCTS AND INTERVENING VARIABLES." ...METH/CNCPT LING IDEA/COMP HYPO/EXP SOC/EXP BIBLIOG 20. PAGE 35 G0686
PSY PHIL/SCI CONCPT GEN/METH

B50

BERNSTEIN I.,THE NEW DEAL COLLECTIVE BARGAINING PROCESS. USA-45 GOV/REL ATTIT...BIBLIOG 20 ROOSEVLT/F. PAGE 7 G0132
LABOR LEGIS POLICY NEW/LIB

B50

SURANYI-UNGER T.,PRIVATE ENTERPRISE AND GOVERNMENTAL PLANNING. STRUCT FINAN BAL/PWR HAPPINESS DRIVE NEW/LIB PLURISM...MATH QUANT STAT TREND BIBLIOG. PAGE 53 G1047
PLAN NAT/G LAISSEZ POLICY

C50

WAGER P.W.,"COUNTY GOVERNMENT ACROSS THE NATION." USA+45 CONSTN COM/IND FINAN SCHOOL DOMIN CT/SYS LEAD GOV/REL...STAT BIBLIOG 20. PAGE 61 G1204
LOC/G PROVS ADMIN ROUTINE

B52

APPADORAI A.,THE SUBSTANCE OF POLITICS (6TH ED.). EX/STRUC LEGIS DIPLOM CT/SYS CHOOSE FASCISM MARXISM SOCISM...BIBLIOG T. PAGE 3 G0062
PHIL/SCI NAT/G

B52

CALLOT E.,LA SOCIETE ET SON ENVIRONNEMENT: ESSAI SUR LES PRINCIPES DES SCIENCES SOCIALES. GP/REL ADJUST CONSEN ISOLAT HABITAT PERCEPT PERSON ...BIBLIOG SOC/INTEG 20. PAGE 10 G0205
SOCIETY PHIL/SCI CULTURE

B53

BRETTON H.L.,STRESEMANN AND THE REVISION OF VERSAILLES: A FIGHT FOR REASON. EUR+WWI GERMANY FORCES BUDGET ARMS/CONT WAR SUPEGO...BIBLIOG 20 TREATY VERSAILLES STRESEMN/G. PAGE 9 G0167
POLICY DIPLOM BIOG

B53

TOMPKINS D.C.,CIVIL DEFENSE IN THE STATES: A BIBLIOGRAPHY (DEFENSE BIBLIOGRAPHIES NO. 3; PAMPHLET). USA+45 LABOR LOC/G NAT/G PROVS LEGIS. PAGE 55 G1076
BIBLIOG WAR ORD/FREE ADMIN

B54

BUTOW R.J.C.,JAPAN'S DECISION TO SURRENDER. USA-45 USSR CHIEF FORCES DOMIN NUC/PWR...BIBLIOG 20 TREATY CHINJAP. PAGE 10 G0198
ELITES DIPLOM WAR PEACE

B54

MCCLOSKEY J.F.,OPERATIONS RESEARCH FOR MANAGEMENT. STRUCT COMPUTER ADMIN ROUTINE...PHIL/SCI CONCPT METH/CNCPT TREND ANTHOL BIBLIOG 20. PAGE 37 G0731
OP/RES MGT METH/COMP TEC/DEV

B54

SIMMONS L.W.,SOCIAL SCIENCE IN MEDICINE. USA+45 USA-45 SOCIETY CONSULT PLAN PROB/SOLV CONTROL PERS/REL...POLICY HEAL TREND BIBLIOG 20. PAGE 51 G0999
PUB/INST HABITAT HEALTH BIO/SOC

B54

SPENCER R.F.,METHOD AND PERSPECTIVE IN ANTHROPOLOGY ....GEOG LING QUANT STAT TESTS SAMP/SIZ CON/ANAL IDEA/COMP METH/COMP ANTHOL BIBLIOG 20. PAGE 52 G1025
PHIL/SCI SOC PSY METH

B54

US DEPARTMENT OF STATE,PUBLICATIONS OF THE DEPARTMENT OF STATE, OCTOBER 1,1929 TO JANUARY 1, 1953. AGRI INT/ORG FORCES FOR/AID EDU/PROP ARMS/CONT NUC/PWR ATTIT 20 DEPT/STATE OAS UN NATO. PAGE 57 G1122
BIBLIOG DIPLOM

B54

WILENSKY H.L.,SYLLABUS OF INDUSTRIAL RELATIONS: A GUIDE TO READING AND RESEARCH. USA+45 MUNIC ADMIN INGP/REL...POLICY MGT PHIL/SCI 20. PAGE 63 G1239
BIBLIOG INDUS LABOR WORKER

C54

CALDWELL L.K.,"THE GOVERNMENT AND ADMINISTRATION OF NEW YORK." LOC/G MUNIC POL/PAR SCHOOL CHIEF LEGIS PLAN TAX CT/SYS...MGT SOC/WK BIBLIOG 20 NEWYORK/C. PAGE 10 G0202
PROVS ADMIN CONSTN EX/STRUC

C54

GOULDNER A.W.,"PATTERNS OF INDUSTRIAL BUREAUCRACY." GP/REL CONSEN ATTIT DRIVE...BIBLIOG 20. PAGE 22 G0438
ADMIN INDUS OP/RES WORKER

C54

ZELLER B.,"AMERICAN STATE LEGISLATURES: REPORT ON THE COMMITTEE ON AMERICAN LEGISLATURES." CONSTN POL/PAR EX/STRUC CONFER ADMIN CONTROL EXEC LOBBY ROUTINE GOV/REL...POLICY BIBLIOG 20. PAGE 65 G1267
REPRESENT LEGIS PROVS APPORT

B55

RILEY V.,INTERINDUSTRY ECONOMIC STUDIES. USA+45 COMPUTER ADMIN OPTIMAL PRODUC...MGT CLASSIF STAT. PAGE 47 G0922
BIBLIOG ECO/DEV PLAN STRUCT

S55

MILLER J.G.,"TOWARD A GENERAL THEORY FOR THE BEHAVIORAL SCIENCES" (BMR)" CREATE ALL/VALS KNOWL ...CON/ANAL CHARTS HYPO/EXP SIMUL BIBLIOG 20. PAGE 39 G0773
CONCPT OP/RES METH/CNCPT COMPUTER

C55

BONER H.A.,"HUNGRY GENERATIONS." UK WOR+45 WOR-45 STRATA INDUS FAM LABOR CAP/ISM...MGT BIBLIOG 19/20. PAGE 8 G0151
ECO/DEV PHIL/SCI CONCPT WEALTH

B56

UN HEADQUARTERS LIBRARY,BIBLIOGRAPHY OF INDUSTRIALIZATION IN UNDERDEVELOPED COUNTRIES (BIBLIOGRAPHICAL SERIES NO. 6). WOR+45 R+D ACADEM INT/ORG NAT/G. PAGE 55 G1087
BIBLIOG ECO/UNDEV TEC/DEV

B56

US DEPARTMENT OF THE ARMY,AMERICAN MILITARY HISTORY. USA+45 USA-45 EX/STRUC PROB/SOLV TEC/DEV DIPLOM NUC/PWR REV WAR WEAPON...PSY 18/20. PAGE 57 G1125
BIBLIOG FORCES NAT/G

B56

VUCINICH A.,THE SOVIET ACADEMY OF SCIENCES. USSR STRUCT ACADEM NAT/G EDU/PROP ADMIN LEAD, ROLE ...BIBLIOG 20 ACADEM/SCI. PAGE 61 G1203
PHIL/SCI CREATE INTELL PROF/ORG

B56

WASSERMAN P.,INFORMATION FOR ADMINISTRATORS: A GUIDE TO PUBLICATIONS AND SERVICES FOR MANAGEMENT IN BUSINESS AND GOVERNMENT. R+D LOC/G NAT/G PROF/ORG VOL/ASSN PRESS...PSY SOC STAT 20. PAGE 62 G1219
BIBLIOG MGT KNOWL EDU/PROP

S56

MILLER G.A.,"THE MAGICAL NUMBER SEVEN, PLUS OR MINUS TWO: SOME LIMITS ON OUR CAPACITY FOR PROCESSING INFORMATION." PERS/REL...PSY METH/CNCPT LING CHARTS BIBLIOG 20. PAGE 39 G0772
LAB/EXP KNOWL PERCEPT COMPUT/IR

C56

DUPUY R.E.,"MILITARY HERITAGE OF AMERICA." USA+45 USA-45 TEC/DEV DIPLOM ROUTINE...POLICY TREND CHARTS IDEA/COMP BIBLIOG COLD/WAR. PAGE 17 G0325
FORCES WAR CONCPT

B57

DUPREE A.H.,SCIENCE IN THE FEDERAL GOVERNMENT; A HISTORY OF POLICIES AND ACTIVITIES TO 1940. USA-45 AGRI SCHOOL DELIB/GP WAR GOV/REL...PHIL/SCI BIBLIOG 18/20 DEPRESSION NEW/DEAL WWI JEFFERSN/T. PAGE 17 G0324
NAT/G R+D CREATE TEC/DEV

B57

KIETH-LUCAS A.,DECISIONS ABOUT PEOPLE IN NEED, A STUDY OF ADMINISTRATIVE RESPONSIVENESS IN PUBLIC ASSISTANCE. USA+45 GIVE RECEIVE INGP/REL PERS/REL MORAL RESPECT WEALTH...SOC OBS BIBLIOG 20. PAGE 30 G0595
ADMIN RIGID/FLEX SOC/WK DECISION

N57

US ARMY LIBRARY,THESES AND DISSERTATIONS IN THE HOLDINGS OF THE ARMY LIBRARY (PAMPHLET). USA+45 ...INT/LAW PSY SOC 20. PAGE 56 G1105
BIBLIOG FORCES MGT CONTROL

B58

LIST OF PUBLICATIONS (PERIODICAL OR AD HOC) ISSUED BY VARIOUS MINISTRIES OF THE GOVERNMENT OF INDIA (3RD ED.). INDIA ECO/UNDEV PLAN...POLICY MGT 20. PAGE 1 G0014
BIBLIOG NAT/G ADMIN

B58

DUBIN R.,THE WORLD OF WORK: INDUSTRIAL SOCIETY AND HUMAN RELATIONS. MARKET PROC/MFG LABOR TEC/DEV
WORKER ECO/TAC

CAP/ISM AUTOMAT TASK GP/REL EFFICIENCY...CONCPT
CHARTS BIBLIOG 20. PAGE 16 G0317
    PRODUC
    DRIVE

B58
LIPPITT R.,DYNAMICS OF PLANNED CHANGE. STRUCT
ACT/RES ROUTINE INGP/REL PWR...POLICY METH/CNCPT
BIBLIOG. PAGE 34 G0672
    VOL/ASSN
    ORD/FREE
    PLAN
    CREATE

B58
MECRENSKY E.,SCIENTIFIC MANPOWER IN EUROPE. WOR+45
EDU/PROP GOV/REL SKILL...TECHNIC PHIL/SCI INT
CHARTS BIBLIOG 20. PAGE 38 G0750
    ECO/TAC
    TEC/DEV
    METH/COMP
    NAT/COMP

B58
US DEPARTMENT OF STATE,PUBLICATIONS OF THE
DEPARTMENT OF STATE, JANUARY 1,1953 TO DECEMBER 31,
1957. AGRI INT/ORG FORCES FOR/AID EDU/PROP
ARMS/CONT NUC/PWR ATTIT 20 DEPT/STATE OAS UN NATO.
PAGE 57 G1123
    BIBLIOG
    DIPLOM

S58
KLAPPER J.T.,"WHAT WE KNOW ABOUT THE EFFECTS OF
MASS COMMUNICATION: THE BRINK OF HOPE" (BMR)"
COM/IND KNOWL...METH/CNCPT GEN/LAWS BIBLIOG METH
20. PAGE 31 G0605
    ACT/RES
    PERCEPT
    CROWD
    PHIL/SCI

S58
NEWELL A.C.,"ELEMENTS OF A THEORY OF HUMAN PROBLEM
SOLVING" (BMR)" TASK PERCEPT...CONCPT LOG METH/COMP
LAB/EXP BIBLIOG 20. PAGE 42 G0819
    PROB/SOLV
    COMPUTER
    COMPUT/IR
    OP/RES

B59
US CONGRESS JT ATOM ENRGY COMM,SELECTED MATERIALS
ON FEDERAL-STATE COOPERATION IN THE ATOMIC ENERGY
FIELD. USA+45 LAW LOC/G PROVS CONSULT LEGIS ADJUD
...POLICY BIBLIOG 20 AEC. PAGE 57 G1111
    NAT/G
    NUC/PWR
    GOV/REL
    DELIB/GP

B60
LINDVEIT E.N.,SCIENTISTS IN GOVERNMENT. USA+45 PAY
EDU/PROP ADMIN DRIVE HABITAT ROLE...TECHNIC BIBLIOG
20. PAGE 34 G0670
    TEC/DEV
    ECO/TAC
    PHIL/SCI
    GOV/REL

B60
MORRIS W.T.,ENGINEERING ECONOMY. AUTOMAT RISK
RATIONAL...PROBABIL STAT CHARTS GAME SIMUL BIBLIOG
T 20. PAGE 40 G0785
    OP/RES
    DECISION
    MGT
    PROB/SOLV

S60
SHUBIK M.,"BIBLIOGRAPHY ON SIMULATION, GAMING,
ARTIFICIAL INTELLIGENCE AND ALLIED TOPICS."
COMPUTER ROUTINE...DECISION MGT STAT 20. PAGE 50
G0992
    BIBLIOG
    SIMUL
    GAME
    OP/RES

C60
SCHRAMM W.,"MASS COMMUNICATIONS: A BOOK OF READINGS
(2ND ED.)" LG/CO PRESS ADMIN CONTROL ROUTINE ATTIT
ROLE SUPEGO...CHARTS ANTHOL BIBLIOG 20. PAGE 50
G0977
    COM/IND
    EDU/PROP
    CROWD
    MAJORIT

B61
MCCRACKEN H.L.,KEYNESIAN ECONOMICS IN THE STREAM OF
ECONOMIC THOUGHT. FINAN MARKET BARGAIN EFFICIENCY
OPTIMAL...PHIL/SCI CONCPT IDEA/COMP BIBLIOG 18/20
KEYNES/JM. PAGE 37 G0732
    ECO/TAC
    DEMAND
    ECOMETRIC

B61
NAKICENOVIC S.,NUCLEAR ENERGY IN YUGOSLAVIA.
YUGOSLAVIA AGRI INDUS CREATE OP/RES ROUTINE
EFFICIENCY KNOWL...HEAL STAT CHARTS LAB/EXP BIBLIOG
20. PAGE 41 G0802
    R+D
    ECO/DEV
    TEC/DEV
    NUC/PWR

B61
NOVE A.,THE SOVIET ECONOMY. USSR ECO/DEV FINAN
NAT/G ECO/TAC PRICE ADMIN EFFICIENCY MARXISM
...TREND BIBLIOG 20. PAGE 42 G0828
    PLAN
    PRODUC
    POLICY

B61
ROSENAU J.N.,INTERNATIONAL POLITICS AND FOREIGN
POLICY: A READER IN RESEARCH AND THEORY. ELITES
ATTIT SOVEREIGN...DECISION CHARTS HYPO/EXP GAME
SIMUL ANTHOL BIBLIOG METH 20. PAGE 48 G0936
    ACT/RES
    DIPLOM
    CONCPT
    POLICY

B61
SCHMIDT H.,VERTEIDIGUNG ODER VERGELTUNG. COM CUBA
GERMANY/W USSR FORCES DIPLOM ARMS/CONT DETER
NUC/PWR...POLICY CHARTS HYPO/EXP SIMUL BIBLIOG 20
NATO COLD/WAR. PAGE 49 G0970
    PLAN
    WAR
    BAL/PWR
    ORD/FREE

B61
US SENATE COMM GOVT OPERATIONS,ORGANIZING FOR
NATIONAL SECURITY. COM USA+45 BUDGET DIPLOM DETER
    POLICY
    PLAN

NUC/PWR WAR WEAPON ORD/FREE...BIBLIOG 20 COLD/WAR.
PAGE 60 G1176
    FORCES
    COERCE

S61
DALTON G.,"ECONOMIC THEORY AND PRIMITIVE SOCIETY"
(BMR)" UNIV AGRI KIN TEC/DEV ECO/TAC REGION HABITAT
SKILL...METH/COMP BIBLIOG. PAGE 14 G0274
    ECO/UNDEV
    METH
    PHIL/SCI
    SOC

B62
AIR FORCE ACADEMY LIBRARY,INTERNATIONAL
ORGANIZATIONS AND MILITARY SECURITY SYSTEMS
(PAMPHLET) (SPECIAL BIBLIOGRAPHY SERIES, NUMBER
25). DIPLOM FOR/AID INT/TRADE NUC/PWR PEACE 20 UN
NATO OAS SEATO LEAGUE/NAT. PAGE 2 G0031
    BIBLIOG
    INT/ORG
    FORCES
    DETER

B62
CHASE S.,THE PROPER STUDY OF MANKIND (2ND REV.
ED.). WOR+45 WOR-45 INTELL WAR...METH/CNCPT
SAMP/SIZ GEN/LAWS BIBLIOG METH 16/20. PAGE 11 G0224
    PHIL/SCI
    SOC
    PROB/SOLV
    PERSON

B62
GUETZKOW H.,SIMULATION IN SOCIAL SCIENCE: READINGS.
STRUCT OP/RES ADMIN AUTOMAT FEEDBACK...MGT PSY SOC
STYLE BIBLIOG. PAGE 23 G0459
    SIMUL
    TEC/DEV
    COMPUTER
    GAME

B62
MARS D.,SUGGESTED LIBRARY IN PUBLIC ADMINISTRATION.
FINAN DELIB/GP EX/STRUC WORKER COMPUTER ADJUD
...DECISION PSY SOC METH/COMP 20. PAGE 36 G0710
    BIBLIOG
    ADMIN
    METH
    MGT

B62
NEW ZEALAND COMM OF ST SERVICE,THE STATE SERVICES
IN NEW ZEALAND. NEW/ZEALND CONSULT EX/STRUC ACT/RES
...BIBLIOG 20. PAGE 42 G0818
    ADMIN
    WORKER
    TEC/DEV
    NAT/G

B62
PERRE J.,LES MUTATIONS DE LA GUERRE MODERNE: DE LA
REVOLUTION FRANCAISE A LA REVOLUTION NUCLEAIRE.
DIPLOM ARMS/CONT DEATH REV WEAPON GP/REL PEACE
ATTIT...STAT PREDICT BIBLIOG 18/20 WWI. PAGE 44
G0870
    WAR
    FORCES
    NUC/PWR

C62
JOINT ECONOMIC COMMITTEE,"DIMENSIONS OF SOVIET
ECONOMIC POWER." USSR R+D FORCES ACT/RES OP/RES
TEC/DEV...GEOG STAT BIBLIOG 20. PAGE 29 G0565
    ECO/DEV
    PLAN
    PRODUC
    LABOR

B63
BASS M.E.,SELECTIVE BIBLIOGRAPHY ON MUNICIPAL
GOVERNMENT FROM THE FILES OF THE MUNICIPAL
TECHNICAL ADVISORY SERVICE. USA+45 FINAN SERV/IND
PLAN 20. PAGE 5 G0100
    BIBLIOG
    LOC/G
    ADMIN
    MUNIC

B63
BONINI C.P.,SIMULATION OF INFORMATION AND DECISION
SYSTEMS IN THE FIRM. MARKET BUDGET DOMIN EDU/PROP
ADMIN COST ATTIT HABITAT PERCEPT PWR...CONCPT
PROBABIL QUANT PREDICT HYPO/EXP BIBLIOG. PAGE 8
G0152
    INDUS
    SIMUL
    DECISION
    MGT

B63
DEAN A.L.,FEDERAL AGENCY APPROACHES TO FIELD
MANAGEMENT (PAMPHLET). R+D DELIB/GP EX/STRUC
PROB/SOLV GOV/REL...CLASSIF BIBLIOG 20 FAA NASA
DEPT/HEW POSTAL/SYS IRS. PAGE 15 G0287
    ADMIN
    MGT
    NAT/G
    OP/RES

B63
FOSKETT D.J.,CLASSIFICATION AND INDEXING IN THE
SOCIAL SCIENCES. WOR+45 R+D ACT/RES CREATE OP/RES
TEC/DEV AUTOMAT ROLE...SOC COMPUT/IR BIBLIOG.
PAGE 20 G0384
    PROB/SOLV
    CON/ANAL
    CLASSIF

B63
HERNDON J.,A SELECTED BIBLIOGRAPHY OF MATERIALS IN
STATE GOVERNMENT AND POLITICS (PAMPHLET). USA+45
POL/PAR LEGIS ADMIN CHOOSE MGT. PAGE 26 G0507
    BIBLIOG
    GOV/COMP
    PROVS
    DECISION

B63
HEYEL C.,THE ENCYCLOPEDIA OF MANAGEMENT. WOR+45
MARKET TOP/EX TEC/DEV AUTOMAT LEAD ADJUST...STAT
CHARTS GAME ANTHOL BIBLIOG. PAGE 26 G0509
    MGT
    INDUS
    ADMIN
    FINAN

B63
KAST F.E.,SCIENCE, TECHNOLOGY, AND MANAGEMENT.
SPACE USA+45 FORCES CONFER DETER NUC/PWR...PHIL/SCI
CHARTS ANTHOL BIBLIOG 20 NASA. PAGE 30 G0581
    MGT
    PLAN
    TEC/DEV
    PROB/SOLV

KORNHAUSER W.,SCIENTISTS IN INDUSTRY: CONFLICT AND
ACCOMMODATION. USA+45 R+D LG/CO NAT/G TEC/DEV
CONTROL ADJUST ATTIT...MGT STAT INT BIBLIOG 20.
PAGE 31 G0614
CREATE INDUS PROF/ORG GP/REL
B63

MILBRATH L.W.,THE WASHINGTON LOBBYISTS. CONSTN
BAL/PWR CONTROL LEAD TASK CHOOSE SUPEGO...DECISION
STAT CHARTS BIBLIOG. PAGE 39 G0767
LOBBY POLICY PERS/REL
B63

PANAMERICAN UNION,DOCUMENTOS OFICIALES DE LA
ORGANIZACION DE LOS ESTADOS AMERICANOS, INDICE Y
LISTA (VOL. III, 1962). L/A+17C DELIB/GP INT/TRADE
EDU/PROP REGION NUC/PWR...HEAL INT/LAW SOC/WK 20
OAS. PAGE 44 G0857
BIBLIOG INT/ORG DIPLOM
B63

PEARSELL M.,MEDICAL BEHAVIORAL SCIENCE: A SELECTED
BIBLIOGRAPHY OF CULTURAL ANTHROPOLOGY, SOCIAL
PSYCHOLOGY, AND SOCIOLOGY... USA+45 USA-45 R+D
ATTIT ROLE 20. PAGE 44 G0863
BIBLIOG SOC PSY HEALTH
B63

SCHRADER R.,SCIENCE AND POLICY. WOR+45 ECO/DEV
ECO/UNDEV R+D FORCES PLAN DIPLOM GOV/REL TECHRACY
BIBLIOG. PAGE 50 G0976
TEC/DEV NAT/G POLICY ADMIN
B63

RECENT PUBLICATIONS ON GOVERNMENTAL PROBLEMS. FINAN
INDUS ACADEM PLAN PROB/SOLV EDU/PROP ADJUD ADMIN
BIO/SOC...MGT SOC. PAGE 1 G0017
BIBLIOG AUTOMAT LEGIS JURID
B64

BRIGHT J.R.,RESEARCH, DEVELOPMENT AND TECHNOLOGICAL
INNOVATION. CULTURE R+D CREATE PLAN PROB/SOLV
AUTOMAT RISK PERSON...DECISION CONCPT PREDICT
BIBLIOG. PAGE 9 G0168
TEC/DEV NEW/IDEA INDUS MGT
B64

COENEN E.,LA "KONJUNKTURFORSCHUNG" EN ALLEMAGNE ET
EN AUTRICHE, 1925-1935. AUSTRIA GERMANY OP/RES PLAN
COST PERCEPT...METH/CNCPT BIBLIOG 20. PAGE 12 G0237
METH/COMP R+D ECO/TAC
B64

FOGELMAN E.,HIROSHIMA: THE DECISION TO USE THE A-
BOMB. USA-45 DIPLOM EFFICIENCY PEACE...ANTHOL
BIBLIOG T 20 CHINJAP. PAGE 19 G0375
INTELL DECISION NUC/PWR WAR
B64

FREYMOND J.,WESTERN EUROPE SINCE THE WAR. COM
EUR+WWI USA+45 DIPLOM...BIBLIOG 20 NATO UN EEC.
PAGE 20 G0392
INT/ORG POLICY ECO/DEV ECO/TAC
B64

GUTMANN P.M.,ECONOMIC GROWTH: AN AMERICAN PROBLEM.
USA+45 FINAN R+D...POLICY NAT/COMP ANTHOL BIBLIOG
20. PAGE 24 G0463
WEALTH ECO/DEV CAP/ISM ORD/FREE
B64

HASKINS C.P.,THE SCIENTIFIC REVOLUTION AND WORLD
POLITICS. COM FUT USA+45 ECO/DEV ECO/UNDEV ATTIT
...PHIL/SCI BIBLIOG 20 THIRD/WRLD. PAGE 25 G0489
TEC/DEV POLICY DIPLOM TREND
B64

INST D'ETUDE POL L'U GRENOBLE,ADMINISTRATION
TRADITIONELLE ET PLANIFICATION REGIONALE. FRANCE
LAW POL/PAR PROB/SOLV ADJUST RIGID/FLEX...CHARTS
ANTHOL BIBLIOG T 20 REFORMERS. PAGE 28 G0546
ADMIN MUNIC PLAN CREATE
B64

MARRIS R.,THE ECONOMIC THEORY OF "MANAGERIAL"
CAPITALISM. USA+45 ECO/DEV LG/CO ECO/TAC DEMAND
...CHARTS BIBLIOG 20. PAGE 36 G0709
CAP/ISM MGT CONTROL OP/RES
B64

MASTERS N.A.,STATE POLITICS AND THE PUBLIC SCHOOLS.
STRUCT FINAN ADMIN LOBBY GP/REL PWR BIBLIOG.
PAGE 36 G0720
EDU/PROP PROVS DOMIN
B64

RIES J.C.,THE MANAGEMENT OF DEFENSE: ORGANIZATION
AND CONTROL OF THE US ARMED SERVICES. PROF/ORG
DELIB/GP EX/STRUC LEGIS GOV/REL PERS/REL CENTRAL
RATIONAL PWR...POLICY TREND GOV/COMP BIBLIOG.
PAGE 47 G0920
FORCES ACT/RES DECISION CONTROL
B64

ROTHSCHILD J.H.,TOMORROW'S WEAPONS: CHEMICAL AND
BIOLOGICAL. FUT PROB/SOLV ARMS/CONT PEACE MORAL
...CHARTS BIBLIOG 20. PAGE 48 G0941
WAR WEAPON BIO/SOC DETER
B64

WIRTH L.,ON CITIES AND SOCIAL LIFE: SELECTED
PAPERS. PLAN PROB/SOLV RACE/REL CONSEN ATTIT
HABITAT PERSON...POLICY SOC CONCPT ANTHOL BIBLIOG
20. PAGE 64 G1249
GEN/LAWS SOCIETY NEIGH STRUCT
B64

"FURTHER READING." INDIA PAKISTAN SECT WAR PEACE
ATTIT...POLICY 20. PAGE 1 G0018
BIBLIOG GP/REL DIPLOM NAT/G
S64

STONE P.A.,"DECISION TECHNIQUES FOR TOWN
DEVELOPMENT." PLAN COST PROFIT...DECISION MGT
CON/ANAL CHARTS METH/COMP BIBLIOG 20. PAGE 53 G1039
OP/RES MUNIC ADMIN PROB/SOLV
S64

SCHRAMM W.,"MASS MEDIA AND NATIONAL DEVELOPMENT:
THE ROLE OF INFORMATION IN DEVELOPING COUNTRIES."
FINAN R+D ACT/RES PLAN TEC/DEV DIPLOM CHOOSE SUPEGO
ORD/FREE...BIBLIOG 20. PAGE 50 G0978
ECO/UNDEV COM/IND EDU/PROP MAJORIT
C64

BLOOMFIELD L.,SOVIET INTERESTS IN ARMS CONTROL AND
DISARMAMENT* THE DECADE UNDER KHRUSHCHEV 1954-1964.
ASIA FORCES ACT/RES EDU/PROP DETER NUC/PWR WEAPON
COST ATTIT...PHIL/SCI CLASSIF STAT NET/THEORY GAME
BIBLIOG. PAGE 7 G0139
USSR ARMS/CONT DIPLOM TREND
B65

CHENG C.-,Y.,SCIENTIFIC AND ENGINEERING MANPOWER IN
COMMUNIST CHINA, 1949-1963. CHINA/COM USSR ELITES
ECO/DEV R+D ACADEM LABOR NAT/G EDU/PROP CONTROL
UTIL...POLICY BIBLIOG 20. PAGE 12 G0226
WORKER CONSULT MARXISM BIOG
B65

NATIONAL SCIENCE FOUNDATION,CURRENT RESEARCH AND
DEVELOPMENT IN SCIENTIFIC DOCUMENTATION - NO. 12.
WOR+45 INTELL COM/IND NAT/G COMPUTER TEC/DEV
AUTOMAT KNOWL...PSY LING 20. PAGE 41 G0812
BIBLIOG COMPUT/IR R+D PHIL/SCI
B65

SCHEINMAN L.,ATOMIC ENERGY POLICY IN FRANCE UNDER
THE FOURTH REPUBLIC. FRANCE UK USA+45 ELITES
POL/PAR PLAN PROB/SOLV DIPLOM LEAD GOV/REL
...BIBLIOG 20 DEGAULLE/C. PAGE 49 G0962
NUC/PWR NAT/G DELIB/GP POLICY
B65

SINGER J.D.,HUMAN BEHAVIOR AND INTERNATINAL
POLITICS* CONTRIBUTIONS FROM THE SOCIAL-
PSYCHOLOGICAL SCIENCES. ACT/RES PLAN EDU/PROP ADMIN
KNOWL...DECISION PSY SOC NET/THEORY HYPO/EXP
LAB/EXP SOC/EXP GEN/METH ANTHOL BIBLIOG. PAGE 51
G1006
DIPLOM PHIL/SCI QUANT SIMUL
B65

THAYER F.C. JR.,AIR TRANSPORT POLICY AND NATIONAL
SECURITY: A POLITICAL, ECONOMIC, AND MILITARY
ANALYSIS. DIST/IND OP/RES PLAN TEC/DEV DIPLOM DETER
WAR COST EFFICIENCY...POLICY BIBLIOG 20 DEPT/DEFEN
FAA CAB. PAGE 54 G1066
AIR FORCES CIVMIL/REL ORD/FREE
B65

TURNER A.N.,INDUSTRIAL JOBS AND THE WORKER. USA+45
CULTURE ECO/DEV LABOR MUNIC ACT/RES AUTOMAT TASK
...CHARTS BIBLIOG 20. PAGE 55 G1082
WORKER INDUS ATTIT TEC/DEV
B65

US CONGRESS JT ATOM ENRGY COMM,PEACEFUL
APPLICATIONS OF NUCLEAR EXPLOSIVES: PLOWSHARE,
HEARING. USA+45 LEGIS CREATE PLAN PEACE...CHARTS
EXHIBIT BIBLIOG CONGRESS PANAMA/CNL. PAGE 57 G1113
NUC/PWR DELIB/GP TEC/DEV NAT/G
B65

US LIBRARY OF CONGRESS,A DIRECTORY OF INFORMATION
RESOURCES IN THE UNITED STATES: SOCIAL SCIENCES.
USA+45 ACADEM INT/ORG LABOR PROF/ORG PUB/INST
SCHOOL SECT 20. PAGE 59 G1156
BIBLIOG R+D COMPUT/IR
B65

PILISUK M.,"IS THERE A MILITARY INDUSTRIAL COMPLEX
WHICH PREVENTS PEACE CONSENSUS; COUNTERVAILING
POWER IN PLURALIST SYSTEMS." INDUS R+D ACADEM
FEEDBACK CIVMIL/REL ADJUST CONSEN ATTIT RIGID/FLEX
...CENSUS IDEA/COMP BIBLIOG. PAGE 45 G0878
ELITES WEAPON PEACE ARMS/CONT
L65

MARK M.,"BEYOND SOVEREIGNTY." WOR+45 WOR-45   NAT/LISM
ECO/UNDEV BAL/PWR INT/TRADE NUC/PWR REV WAR MARXISM   NAT/G
NEW/LIB BIBLIOG. PAGE 36 G0706   DIPLOM
                                                     INTELL
                                     C65

SEARA M.V.,"COSMIC INTERNATIONAL LAW." LAW ACADEM   SPACE
ACT/RES DIPLOM COLONIAL CONTROL NUC/PWR SOVEREIGN   INT/LAW
...GEN/LAWS BIBLIOG UN. PAGE 50 G0987   IDEA/COMP
                                                     INT/ORG
                                     B66

ALEXANDER Y.,INTERNATIONAL TECHNICAL ASSISTANCE   SKILL
EXPERTS: A CASE STUDY OF THE U.N. EXPERIENCE.   INT/ORG
USA+45 WOR+45 WORKER CREATE PLAN PROB/SOLV ECO/TAC   TEC/DEV
FOR/AID GIVE EDU/PROP...CHARTS BIBLIOG 20 UN.   CONSULT
PAGE 2 G0039

ALEXANDER — B66

BOLTON R.E.,DEFENSE AND DISARMAMENT: THE ECONOMICS   ARMS/CONT
OF TRANSITION. USA+45 R+D FORCES PLAN LOBBY DETER   POLICY
WAR COST PEACE...ANTHOL BIBLIOG 20. PAGE 8 G0150   INDUS

                                     B66

MURDOCK J.C.,RESEARCH AND REGIONS. AGRI FINAN INDUS   BIBLIOG
LOC/G MUNIC NAT/G PROB/SOLV TEC/DEV ADMIN REGION   ECO/DEV
20. PAGE 40 G0796   COMPUT/IR
                                                     R+D
                                     B66

ONYEMELUKWE C.C.,PROBLEMS OF INDUSTRIAL PLANNING   ECO/UNDEV
AND MANAGEMENT IN NIGERIA. AFR FINAN LABOR DELIB/GP   ECO/TAC
TEC/DEV ADJUST...MGT TREND BIBLIOG. PAGE 43 G0839   INDUS
                                                     PLAN
                                     B66

ROSHOLT R.L.,AN ADMINISTRATIVE HISTORY OF NASA,   ADMIN
1958-1963. SPACE USA+45 FINAN LEAD...MGT CHARTS   EX/STRUC
BIBLIOG 20 NASA. PAGE 48 G0938   ADJUST
                                                     DELIB/GP
                                     B66

STREET D.,ORGANIZATION FOR TREATMENT. CLIENT PROVS   GP/COMP
PUB/INST PLAN CONTROL PARTIC REPRESENT ATTIT PWR   AGE/Y
...POLICY BIBLIOG. PAGE 53 G1044   ADMIN
                                                     VOL/ASSN
                                     B66

UNITED NATIONS,INTERNATIONAL SPACE BIBLIOGRAPHY.   BIBLIOG
FUT INT/ORG TEC/DEV DIPLOM ARMS/CONT NUC/PWR   SPACE
...JURID SOC UN. PAGE 56 G1093   PEACE
                                                     R+D
                                     B66

US DEPARTMENT OF LABOR,TECHNOLOGICAL TRENDS IN   TEC/DEV
MAJOR AMERICAN INDUSTRIES. USA+45 R+D LABOR GP/REL   INDUS
PRODUC...MGT BIBLIOG 20. PAGE 57 G1120   TREND
                                                     AUTOMAT
                                     S66

"FURTHER READING." INDIA LOC/G NAT/G PLAN ADMIN   BIBLIOG
WEALTH...GEOG SOC CONCPT CENSUS 20. PAGE 1 G0021   ECO/UNDEV
                                                     TEC/DEV
                                                     PROVS
                                     S66

SIMON R.,"THE STATE OF PUBLIC RELATIONS SCHOLARLY   ACADEM
RESEARCH." TEC/DEV TASK MAJORITY PRODUC...TREND   CREATE
CHARTS BIBLIOG 20. PAGE 51 G1000   STAT
                                                     GP/REL
                                     B67

BUDER S.,PULLMAN: AN EXPERIMENT IN INDUSTRIAL ORDER   DIST/IND
AND COMMUNITY PLANNING, 1880-1930. USA-45 SOCIETY   INDUS
LABOR LG/CO CREATE PROB/SOLV CONTROL GP/REL   MUNIC
EFFICIENCY ATTIT...MGT BIBLIOG 19/20 PULLMAN.   PLAN
PAGE 9 G0184

                                     B67

DAVIS V.,THE POLITICS OF INNOVATION: PATTERNS IN   BIBLIOG
NAVY CASES (PAMPHLET). WOR+45 NAT/G CREATE WEAPON   FORCES
INGP/REL ATTIT...POLICY SOC METH/COMP METH. PAGE 14   NUC/PWR
G0280   TEC/DEV

                                     B67

DE JOUVENEL B.,THE ART OF CONJECTURE. WOR+45   FUT
EFFICIENCY PERCEPT KNOWL...DECISION PHIL/SCI CONCPT   PREDICT
METH/COMP BIBLIOG 20. PAGE 15 G0285   SIMUL
                                                     METH
                                     B67

DICKSON P.G.M.,THE FINANCIAL REVOLUTION IN ENGLAND.   ECO/DEV
UK NAT/G TEC/DEV ADMIN GOV/REL...SOC METH/CNCPT   FINAN
CHARTS GP/COMP BIBLIOG 17/18. PAGE 15 G0302   CAP/ISM
                                                     MGT

HARMAN H.H.,MODERN FACTOR ANALYSIS (2ND REV. ED.).   CON/ANAL
COMPUTER...DECISION CHARTS BIBLIOG T. PAGE 24 G0482   METH/CNCPT
                                                     SIMUL
                                                     MATH
                                     B67

NELSON R.R.,TECHNOLOGY, ECONOMIC GROWTH, AND PUBLIC   R+D
POLICY. USA+45 PLAN GP/REL UTIL KNOWL...POLICY   CONSULT
PHIL/SCI CHARTS BIBLIOG 20. PAGE 41 G0817   CREATE
                                                     ACT/RES
                                     B67

PORWIT K.,CENTRAL PLANNING: EVALUATION OF VARIANTS.   PLAN
PRICE OPTIMAL PRODUC...DECISION MATH CHARTS SIMUL   MGT
BIBLIOG 20. PAGE 45 G0886   ECOMETRIC

                                     B67

RAWLINSON J.L.,CHINA'S STRUGGLE FOR NAVAL   SEA
DEVELOPMENT 1839-1895. ASIA DIPLOM ADMIN WAR   FORCES
...BIBLIOG DICTIONARY 19 CHINJAP. PAGE 46 G0907   PWR

                                     B67

SALMOND J.A.,THE CIVILIAN CONSERVATION CORPS,   ADMIN
1933-1942. USA-45 NAT/G CREATE EXEC EFFICIENCY   ECO/TAC
WEALTH...BIBLIOG 20 ROOSEVLT/F. PAGE 48 G0954   TASK
                                                     AGRI
                                     B67

US DEPARTMENT OF STATE,FOREIGN AFFAIRS RESEARCH   BIBLIOG
(PAMPHLET). USA+45 WOR+45 ACADEM NAT/G...PSY SOC   INDEX
CHARTS 20. PAGE 57 G1124   R+D
                                                     DIPLOM
                                     B67

US HOUSE COMM SCI ASTRONAUT,SCIENCE, TECHNOLOGY,   POLICY
AND PUBLIC POLICY DURING THE 89TH CONGRESS,   TEC/DEV
JANUARY, 1965 THROUGH DECEMBER, 1966. USA+45   CREATE
...CHARTS BIBLIOG. PAGE 59 G1151   NAT/G

                                     B67

WOODRUFF W.,IMPACT OF WESTERN MAN. ECO/DEV INDUS   EUR+WWI
CREATE PLAN PROB/SOLV COLONIAL GOV/REL...CHARTS   MOD/EUR
GOV/COMP BIBLIOG 18/20. PAGE 64 G1256   CAP/ISM

BIBLIOG/A....BIBLIOGRAPHY OVER 50 ITEMS ANNOTATED

AMERICAN DOCUMENTATION INST,DOCUMENTATION   BIBLIOG/A
ABSTRACTS. WOR+45 NAT/G COMPUTER CREATE TEC/DEV   AUTOMAT
DIPLOM EDU/PROP REGION KNOWL...PHIL/SCI CLASSIF   COMPUT/IR
LING. PAGE 3 G0051   R+D
                                     N

FULLER G.A.,DEMOBILIZATION: A SELECTED LIST OF   BIBLIOG/A
REFERENCES. USA+45 LAW AGRI LABOR WORKER ECO/TAC   INDUS
RATION RECEIVE EDU/PROP ROUTINE ARMS/CONT ALL/VALS   FORCES
20. PAGE 20 G0398   NAT/G
                                     N

CURRENT THOUGHT ON PEACE AND WAR. WOR+45 INT/ORG   BIBLIOG/A
FORCES PROB/SOLV DIPLOM NUC/PWR PERCEPT...POLICY   PEACE
SOC 20 UN NATO. PAGE 1 G0001   ATTIT
                                                     WAR
                                     B

BRITISH COMMONWEALTH BUR AGRI,WORLD AGRICULTURAL   BIBLIOG/A
ECONOMICS AND RURAL SOCIOLOGY ABSTRACTS. NAT/G   AGRI
OP/RES PLAN TEC/DEV LEAD PRODUC...GEOG MGT NAT/COMP   SOC
20. PAGE 9 G0170   WORKER
                                     N

JOURNAL OF CONFLICT RESOLUTION. FUT WOR+45 INT/ORG   BIBLIOG/A
NAT/G FORCES CREATE PROB/SOLV ARMS/CONT NUC/PWR   DIPLOM
WEAPON SOC. PAGE 1 G0002   WAR

                                     N

ADVANCED MANAGEMENT. INDUS EX/STRUC WORKER OP/RES   MGT
...DECISION BIBLIOG/A 20. PAGE 1 G0003   ADMIN
                                                     LABOR
                                                     GP/REL
                                     N

JOURNAL OF PUBLIC ADMINISTRATION: JOURNAL OF THE   BIBLIOG/A
ROYAL INSTITUTE OF PUBLIC ADMINISTRATION. UK PLAN   ADMIN
GP/REL INGP/REL 20. PAGE 1 G0006   NAT/G
                                                     MGT
                                     N

THE MANAGEMENT REVIEW. FINAN EX/STRUC PROFIT   LABOR
BIBLIOG/A. PAGE 1 G0007   MGT
                                                     ADMIN
                                                     MARKET

MARKETING INFORMATION GUIDE. USA+45 ECO/DEV FINAN ADMIN GP/REL. PAGE 1 G0008

N
BIBLIOG/A
DIST/IND
MARKET
ECO/TAC

PUBLIC ADMINISTRATION ABSTRACTS AND INDEX OF ARTICLES. WOR+45 PLAN PROB/SOLV...POLICY 20. PAGE 1 G0009

N
BIBLIOG/A
ADMIN
ECO/UNDEV
NAT/G

PERSONNEL. USA+45 LAW LABOR LG/CO WORKER CREATE GOV/REL PERS/REL ATTIT WEALTH. PAGE 1 G0010

N
BIBLIOG/A
ADMIN
MGT
GP/REL

AIR UNIVERSITY LIBRARY,INDEX TO MILITARY PERIODICALS. FUT SPACE WOR+45 REGION ARMS/CONT NUC/PWR WAR PEACE INT/LAW. PAGE 2 G0032

N
BIBLIOG/A
FORCES
NAT/G
DIPLOM

AMER COUNCIL OF LEARNED SOCIET,THE ACLS CONSTITUENT SOCIETY JOURNAL PROJECT. FUT USA+45 LAW NAT/G PLAN DIPLOM PHIL/SCI. PAGE 3 G0048

N
BIBLIOG/A
HUM
COMPUT/IR
COMPUTER

PRINCETON UNIVERSITY,SELECTED REFERENCES: INDUSTRIAL RELATIONS SECTION. USA+45 EX/STRUC WORKER TEC/DEV...MGT 20. PAGE 45 G0892

N
BIBLIOG/A
LABOR
INDUS
GP/REL

US SUPERINTENDENT OF DOCUMENTS,TRANSPORTATION: HIGHWAYS, ROADS, AND POSTAL SERVICE (PRICE LIST 25). PANAMA USA+45 LAW FORCES DIPLOM ADMIN GOV/REL HEALTH MGT. PAGE 61 G1188

N
BIBLIOG/A
DIST/IND
SERV/IND
NAT/G

FOREIGN AFFAIRS BIBLIOGRAPHY: A SELECTED AND ANNOTATED LIST OF BOOKS ON INTERNATIONAL RELATIONS 1919-1962 (4 VOLS.). CONSTN FORCES COLONIAL ARMS/CONT WAR NAT/LISM PEACE ATTIT DRIVE...POLICY INT/LAW 20. PAGE 1 G0011

B35
BIBLIOG/A
DIPLOM
INT/ORG

HELLMAN F.S.,THE NEW DEAL: SELECTED LIST OF REFERENCES. USA-45 FINAN LABOR EX/STRUC CREATE INT/TRADE ADMIN CT/SYS 20 SUPREME/CT. PAGE 26 G0505

B40
BIBLIOG/A
ECO/TAC
PLAN
POLICY

FULLER G.H.,DEFENSE FINANCING: A SELECTED LIST OF REFERENCES (PAMPHLET). MOD/EUR USA-45 ECO/DEV NAT/G DELIB/GP RATION ARMS/CONT WEAPON COST PEACE PWR 20 CONGRESS. PAGE 20 G0401

B41
BIBLIOG/A
FINAN
FORCES
BUDGET

FULLER G.H.,A LIST OF BIBLIOGRAPHIES ON QUESTIONS RELATING TO NATIONAL DEFENSE (PAMPHLET). USA-45 NAT/G ARMS/CONT WAR GOV/REL COST PEACE 20. PAGE 20 G0402

B41
BIBLIOG/A
FORCES
CIVMIL/REL
WEAPON

FULLER G.H.,DEFENSE FINANCING: A SUPPLEMENTARY LIST OF REFERENCES (PAMPHLET). CANADA UK USA-45 ECO/DEV NAT/G DELIB/GP BUDGET ADJUD ARMS/CONT WEAPON COST PEACE PWR 20 AUSTRAL CHINJAP CONGRESS. PAGE 21 G0403

B42
BIBLIOG/A
FINAN
FORCES
DIPLOM

US LIBRARY OF CONGRESS,CONDUCT OF THE WAR (APRIL 1941-MARCH 1942). USA-45 WOR-45 LAW INDUS PUB/INST TEC/DEV EDU/PROP CIVMIL/REL 20. PAGE 59 G1155

B42
BIBLIOG/A
WAR
FORCES
PLAN

BAKER H.,PROBLEMS OF REEMPLOYMENT AND RETRAINING OF MANPOWER DURING THE TRANSITION FROM WAR TO PEACE. USA+45 INDUS LABOR LG/CO NAT/G PLAN ADMIN PEACE ...POLICY MGT 20. PAGE 5 G0086

B45
BIBLIOG/A
ADJUST
WAR
PROB/SOLV

WILCOX J.K.,OFFICIAL DEFENSE PUBLICATIONS, 1941-1945 (NINE VOLS.). USA-45 AGRI INDUS R+D LABOR FORCES TEC/DEV EFFICIENCY PRODUC SKILL WEALTH 20. PAGE 63 G1238

B46
BIBLIOG/A
WAR
CIVMIL/REL
ADMIN

PUBLIC ADMINISTRATION SERVICE,SOURCE MATERIALS IN PUBLIC ADMINISTRATION: A SELECTED BIBLIOGRAPHY (PAS PUBLICATION NO. 102). USA+45 LAW FINAN LOC/G MUNIC

B48
BIBLIOG/A
GOV/REL
MGT

NAT/G PLAN RECEIVE EDU/PROP CT/SYS CHOOSE HEALTH 20. PAGE 45 G0895

ADMIN

ELDERSVELD S.J.,"RESEARCH IN POLITICAL BEHAVIOR" (BMR)" USA+45 PLAN TEC/DEV ATTIT...BIBLIOG/A METH 20. PAGE 17 G0341

L52
ACT/RES
GEN/LAWS
CREATE

LASSWELL H.D.,"RESEARCH IN POLITICAL BEHAVIOR." LOC/G MUNIC POL/PAR CONSULT ADMIN PARTIC...CHARTS ANTHOL BIBLIOG/A 20. PAGE 32 G0641

L52
PHIL/SCI
METH
R+D

"SELECTED CRITICAL BIBLIOGRAPHY ON THE METHODS AND TECHNIQUES OF POLITICAL BEHAVIOR RESEARCH." ...PHIL/SCI OBS QU SYS/QU TESTS CON/ANAL. PAGE 1 G0012

S52
BIBLIOG/A
METH
SOC
EDU/PROP

TRUMAN D.B.,"SELECTED CRITICAL BIBLIOGRAPHY ON THE METHODS AND TECHNIQUES OF POLITICAL BEHAVIOR RESEARCH." R+D PARTIC...SOC OBS RECORD INT. PAGE 55 G1079

S52
BIBLIOG/A
ACT/RES
METH/CNCPT

CALDWELL L.K.,RESEARCH METHODS IN PUBLIC ADMINISTRATION: AN OUTLINE OF TOPICS AND READINGS (PAMPHLET). LAW ACT/RES COMPUTER KNOWL...SOC STAT GEN/METH 20. PAGE 10 G0201

B53
BIBLIOG/A
METH/COMP
ADMIN
OP/RES

LARSEN K.,NATIONAL BIBLIOGRAPHIC SERVICES: THEIR CREATION AND OPERATION. WOR+45 COM/IND CREATE PLAN DIPLOM PRESS ADMIN ROUTINE...MGT UNESCO. PAGE 32 G0636

B53
BIBLIOG/A
INT/ORG
WRITING

SCHAAF R.W.,DOCUMENTS OF INTERNATIONAL MEETINGS. AGRI INDUS ACADEM DIPLOM NUC/PWR RACE/REL AGE/Y HEALTH...SOC 20. PAGE 49 G0960

B53
BIBLIOG/A
DELIB/GP
INT/ORG
POLICY

MILLER G.A.,"WHAT IS INFORMATION MEASUREMENT?" CREATE...CONCPT METH/CNCPT QUANT STAT CHARTS BIBLIOG/A 20. PAGE 39 G0771

S53
COMPUTER
TEC/DEV
PSY
MATH

KENWORTHY L.S.,FREE AND INEXPENSIVE MATERIALS ON WORLD AFFAIRS (PAMPHLET). WOR+45 CULTURE ECO/UNDEV INT/TRADE ARMS/CONT NUC/PWR UN. PAGE 30 G0594

B54
BIBLIOG/A
NAT/G
INT/ORG
DIPLOM

TOMPKINS D.C.,STATE GOVERNMENT AND ADMINISTRATION: A BIBLIOGRAPHY. USA+45 USA-45 CONSTN LEGIS JUDGE BUDGET CT/SYS LOBBY...CHARTS 20. PAGE 55 G1077

B54
BIBLIOG/A
LOC/G
PROVS
ADMIN

HISTORICAL ABSTRACTS. NAT/G CREATE DIPLOM ATTIT ...SOC DICTIONARY INDEX 18/20. PAGE 1 G0013

B56
WOR-45
COMPUT/IR
BIBLIOG/A

ESTEP R.,AN AIR POWER BIBLIOGRAPHY. USA+45 TEC/DEV BUDGET DIPLOM EDU/PROP DETER CIVMIL/REL...DECISION INT/LAW 20. PAGE 18 G0351

B56
BIBLIOG/A
FORCES
WEAPON
PLAN

US DEPARTMENT OF THE ARMY,RESEARCH AND DEVELOPMENT (AND RELATED ASPECTS) IN FOREIGN COUNTRIES. WOR+45 DIST/IND INDUS CONSULT FORCES CREATE EDU/PROP AUTOMAT DETER WEAPON. PAGE 57 G1126

B56
BIBLIOG/A
R+D
TEC/DEV
NUC/PWR

BAUER P.T.,ECONOMIC ANALYSIS AND POLICY IN UNDERDEVELOPED COUNTRIES. WOR+45 AGRI INT/TRADE TAX PRICE...GEN/METH BIBLIOG/A 20 COMMONWLTH. PAGE 5 G0103

B57
ECO/UNDEV
METH/COMP
POLICY

MCKINNEY E.R.,A BIBLIOGRAPHY OF CYBERNETICS AND INFORMATION THEORY. COMPUTER OP/RES...DECISION PHIL/SCI PSY LING LOG MATH PROBABIL GAME 20. PAGE 38 G0743

B57
BIBLIOG/A
FEEDBACK
SIMUL
CONTROL

CHEEK G.,ECONOMIC AND SOCIAL IMPLICATIONS OF AUTOMATION: A BIBLIOGRAPHIC REVIEW (PAMPHLET). USA+45 LG/CO WORKER CREATE PLAN CONTROL ROUTINE PERS/REL EFFICIENCY PRODUC...METH/COMP 20. PAGE 12 G0225

B58
BIBLIOG/A
SOCIETY
INDUS
AUTOMAT

B58
OPERATIONS RESEARCH SOCIETY,A COMPREHENSIVE
BIBLIOGRAPHY ON OPERATIONS RESEARCH: THROUGH 1956
WITH SUPPLEMENT FOR 1957. COM/IND DIST/IND INDUS
ADMIN...DECISION MATH STAT METH 20. PAGE 43 G0840
BIBLIOG/A
COMPUT/IR
OP/RES
MGT

B58
US DEPARTMENT OF THE ARMY,BIBLIOGRAPHY ON LIMITED
WAR (PAMPHLET). USA+45 TEC/DEV CONTROL RISK COERCE
DETER NUC/PWR WEAPON ADJUST PEACE ALL/VALS ORD/FREE
20. PAGE 57 G1127
BIBLIOG/A
WAR
FORCES
CIVMIL/REL

B59
ELDRIDGE H.T.,THE MATERIALS OF DEMOGRAPHY: A
SELECTED AND ANNOTATED BIBLIOGRAPHY. R+D DEATH
...SAMP METH/COMP NAT/COMP 20. PAGE 18 G0343
BIBLIOG/A
GEOG
STAT
TREND

B59
SPANIER J.W.,THE TRUMAN-MACARTHUR CONTROVERSY AND
THE KOREAN WAR. USA+45 TOP/EX PROB/SOLV LEAD ATTIT
PWR...POLICY BIBLIOG/A UN. PAGE 52 G1023
CIVMIL/REL
FORCES
CHIEF
WAR

B59
WASSERMAN P.,MEASUREMENT AND ANALYSIS OF
ORGANIZATIONAL PERFORMANCE. FINAN MARKET EX/STRUC
TEC/DEV EDU/PROP CONTROL ROUTINE TASK...MGT 20.
PAGE 62 G1220
BIBLIOG/A
ECO/TAC
OP/RES
EFFICIENCY

B60
CRAUMER L.V.,BUSINESS PERIODICALS INDEX (8VOLS.).
USA+45 LABOR TAX 20. PAGE 13 G0262
BIBLIOG/A
FINAN
ECO/DEV
MGT

B60
LEYDER J.,BIBLIOGRAPHIE DE L'ENSEIGNEMENT SUPERIEUR
ET DE LA RECHERCHE SCIENTIFIQUE EN AFRIQUE
INTERTROPICALE (2 VOLS.). AFR CULTURE ECO/UNDEV
AGRI PLAN EDU/PROP ADMIN COLONIAL...GEOG SOC/INTEG
20 NEGRO. PAGE 34 G0664
BIBLIOG/A
ACT/RES
ACADEM
R+D

B60
US DEPARTMENT OF THE ARMY,DISARMAMENT: A
BIBLIOGRAPHIC RECORD: 1916-1960. DETER WAR WEAPON
PEACE 20 UN LEAGUE/NAT COLD/WAR NATO. PAGE 57 G1128
BIBLIOG/A
ARMS/CONT
NUC/PWR
DIPLOM

B60
WILLIAUS T.H.,AMERICANS AT WAR: THE DEVELOPMENT OF
THE AMERICAN MILITARY SYSTEM. USA+45 USA-45
EDU/PROP LEAD REV...GP/COMP BIBLIOG/A 18/20
PRESIDENT. PAGE 63 G1244
FORCES
WAR
NAT/G
POLICY

S60
BRODY R.A.,"DETERRENCE STRATEGIES: AN ANNOTATED
BIBLIOGRAPHY." WOR+45 PLAN ARMS/CONT NUC/PWR WAR
WEAPON DECISION. PAGE 9 G0173
BIBLIOG/A
FORCES
DETER
DIPLOM

B61
CARNELL F.,THE POLITICS OF THE NEW STATES: A SELECT
ANNOTATED BIBLIOGRAPHY WITH SPECIAL REFERENCE TO
THE COMMONWEALTH. CONSTN ELITES LABOR NAT/G POL/PAR
EX/STRUC DIPLOM ADJUD ADMIN...GOV/COMP 20
COMMONWLTH. PAGE 11 G0210
BIBLIOG/A
AFR
ASIA
COLONIAL

B61
INSTITUTE PSYCHOLOGICAL RES,HUMAN ENGINEERING
BIBLIOGRAPHY, 1959-1960. USA+45 WORKER EDU/PROP
PERSON METH/COMP. PAGE 28 G0547
BIBLIOG/A
METH
PSY
R+D

B61
LEE R.R.,ENGINEERING-ECONOMIC PLANNING
MISCELLANEOUS SUBJECTS: A SELECTED BIBLIOGRAPHY
(MIMEOGRAPHED). FINAN LOC/G MUNIC NEIGH ADMIN
CONTROL INGP/REL HABITAT...GEOG MGT SOC/WK 20
RESOURCE/N. PAGE 33 G0651
BIBLIOG/A
PLAN
REGION

B62
ASTIA,HUMAN ENGINEERING: A REPORT BIBLIOGRAPHY.
USA+45 R+D FORCES ACT/RES COMPUTER CREATE OP/RES
EDU/PROP CONTROL WEAPON...SOC NEW/IDEA. PAGE 4
G0073
BIBLIOG/A
COM/IND
COMPUT/IR
METH

B62
ASTIA,INFORMATION THEORY: A REPORT BIBLIOGRAPHY.
USA+45 COMPUTER CREATE OP/RES PLAN TEC/DEV CONTROL
...CONCPT METH/COMP. PAGE 4 G0074
BIBLIOG/A
COM/IND
FORCES
METH

B62
HALPERIN M.H.,LIMITED WAR; AN ESSAY ON THE
BIBLIOG/A

DEVELOPMENT OF THE THEORY AND AN ANNOTATED
BIBLIOGRAPHY (OCCASIONAL PAPER NO. 3). WOR+45
WOR-45 NUC/PWR...CONCPT IDEA/COMP METH/COMP 19/20.
PAGE 24 G0471
WAR
ARMS/CONT
FORCES

S62
VIETORISZ T.,"PRELIMINARY BIBLIOGRAPHY FOR
INDUSTRIAL DEVELOPMENT PROGRAMMING." ECO/DEV
ECO/UNDEV R+D LABOR PROB/SOLV AUTOMAT PRODUC.
PAGE 61 G1198
BIBLIOG/A
TEC/DEV
ACT/RES
PLAN

B63
KATZ S.M.,A SELECTED LIST OF US READINGS ON
DEVELOPMENT. AGRI COM/IND DIST/IND INDUS LABOR PLAN
FOR/AID EDU/PROP HEALTH...POLICY SOC/WK 20. PAGE 30
G0582
BIBLIOG/A
ECO/UNDEV
TEC/DEV
ACT/RES

B63
KREPS J.,AUTOMATION AND THE OLDER WORKER: AN
ANNOTATED BIBLIOGRAPHY (PAMPHLET). USA+45 STRUCT
ECO/DEV INDUS TEC/DEV. PAGE 31 G0620
BIBLIOG/A
WORKER
AGE/O
AUTOMAT

B63
US DEPARTMENT OF THE ARMY,SOVIET RUSSIA: STRATEGIC
SURVEY (PAMPHLET). USSR POL/PAR PLAN DOMIN EDU/PROP
ARMS/CONT GUERRILLA WAR WEAPON...TREND CHARTS
ORG/CHARTS 20. PAGE 57 G1129
BIBLIOG/A
MARXISM
DIPLOM
COERCE

B63
US DEPARTMENT OF THE ARMY,US OVERSEAS BASES:
PRESENT STATUS AND FUTURE PROSPECTS (PAMPHLET).
USA+45 DIPLOM NUC/PWR ATTIT ORD/FREE...POLICY
CHARTS 20. PAGE 58 G1130
BIBLIOG/A
WAR
BAL/PWR
DETER

B63
WALES H.G.,A BASIC BIBLIOGRAPHY ON MARKETING
RESEARCH (REV. ED.). ATTIT...MGT STAT INT QU SAMP
TREND 20. PAGE 62 G1206
BIBLIOG/A
MARKET
OP/RES
METH/COMP

S63
VIETORISZ T.,"PRELIMINARY BIBLIOGRAPHY FOR
INDUSTRIAL DEVELOPMENT PROGRAMMING." ECO/DEV
ECO/UNDEV R+D LABOR PROB/SOLV AUTOMAT PRODUC.
PAGE 61 G1199
BIBLIOG/A
TEC/DEV
ACT/RES
PLAN

B64
DUSCHA J.,ARMS, MONEY, AND POLITICS. USA+45 INDUS
POL/PAR ECO/TAC TAX DETER NUC/PWR WAR WEAPON
GOV/REL ATTIT...BIBLIOG/A 20 CONGRESS MONEY
DEPT/DEFEN. PAGE 17 G0326
NAT/G
FORCES
POLICY
BUDGET

B64
FALK L.A.,ADMINISTRATIVE ASPECTS OF GROUP PRACTICE.
USA+45 FINAN PROF/ORG PLAN MGT. PAGE 18 G0358
BIBLIOG/A
HEAL
ADMIN
SERV/IND

B64
HAZLEWOOD A.,THE ECONOMICS OF DEVELOPMENT: AN
ANNOTATED LIST OF BOOKS AND ARTICLES PUBLISHED
1958-1962. AGRI FINAN INDUS LABOR NAT/G DIPLOM
INT/TRADE INCOME...MGT 20. PAGE 25 G0497
BIBLIOG/A
ECO/UNDEV
TEC/DEV

B64
ROBERTS HL,FOREIGN AFFAIRS BIBLIOGRAPHY, 1952-1962.
ECO/DEV SECT PLAN FOR/AID INT/TRADE ARMS/CONT
NAT/LISM ATTIT...INT/LAW GOV/COMP IDEA/COMP 20.
PAGE 47 G0928
BIBLIOG/A
DIPLOM
INT/ORG
WAR

B64
WILLIAMS S.P.,TOWARD A GENUINE WORLD SECURITY
SYSTEM (PAMPHLET). WOR+45 INT/ORG FORCES PLAN
NUC/PWR ORD/FREE...INT/LAW CONCPT UN PRESIDENT.
PAGE 63 G1243
BIBLIOG/A
ARMS/CONT
DIPLOM
PEACE

B65
PEACE RESEARCH ABSTRACTS. FUT WOR+45 R+D INT/ORG
NAT/G PLAN TEC/DEV BAL/PWR DIPLOM FOR/AID NUC/PWR
HEALTH. PAGE 1 G0020
BIBLIOG/A
PEACE
ARMS/CONT
WAR

B65
INTERNATIONAL CITY MGRS ASSN,COUNCIL-MANAGER
GOVERNMENT, 1940-64: AN ANNOTATED BIBLIOGRAPHY.
USA+45 ADMIN GOV/REL ROLE...MGT 20. PAGE 28 G0549
BIBLIOG/A
MUNIC
CONSULT
PLAN

B65
LOWENSTEIN L.,GOVERNMENT RESOURCES AVAILABLE FOR
FOREIGN AFFAIRS RESEARCH. NAT/G DIPLOM GOV/REL.
PAGE 34 G0677
R+D
ACADEM
ACT/RES
BIBLIOG/A

MOSKOWITZ H.,US SECURITY, ARMS CONTROL, AND
DISARMAMENT 1961-1965. FORCES DIPLOM DETER WAR
WEAPON...CHARTS 20 UN COLD/WAR NATO. PAGE 40 G0790
B65
BIBLIOG/A
ARMS/CONT
NUC/PWR
PEACE

US DEPARTMENT OF DEFENSE,US SECURITY ARMS CONTROL,
AND DISARMAMENT 1961-1965 (PAMPHLET). CHINA/COM COM
GERMANY/W ISRAEL SPACE USA+45 USSR WOR+45 FORCES
EDU/PROP DETER EQUILIB PEACE ALL/VALS...GOV/COMP 20
NATO. PAGE 57 G1118
B65
BIBLIOG/A
ARMS/CONT
NUC/PWR
DIPLOM

US DEPARTMENT OF THE ARMY,NUCLEAR WEAPONS AND THE
ATLANTIC ALLIANCE: A BIBLIOGRAPHIC SURVEY. ASIA COM
EUR+WWI USA+45 FORCES DIPLOM WEAPON...STAT 20 NATO.
PAGE 58 G1131
B65
BIBLIOG/A
ARMS/CONT
NUC/PWR
BAL/PWR

US DEPARTMENT OF THE ARMY,MILITARY MANPOWER POLICY.
USA+45 LEGIS EXEC WAR 20 CONGRESS. PAGE 58 G1132
B65
BIBLIOG/A
POLICY
FORCES
TREND

WISH J.R.,ECONOMIC DEVELOPMENT IN LATIN AMERICA: AN
ANNOTATED BIBLIOGRAPHY. L/A+17C COM/IND MARKET R+D
CREATE CAP/ISM ATTIT...STAT METH 20. PAGE 64 G1250
B65
BIBLIOG/A
ECO/UNDEV
TEC/DEV
AGRI

SCHWEBEL M.,"BEHAVIORAL SCIENCE AND HUMAN
SURVIVAL." FORCES ARMS/CONT COERCE NUC/PWR WAR
GP/REL NAT/LISM PERCEPT...POLICY PSY ANTHOL
BIBLIOG/A 20 COLD/WAR. PAGE 50 G0984
C65
PEACE
ACT/RES
DIPLOM
HEAL

US AIR FORCE ACADEMY,"AMERICAN DEFENSE POLICY." COM
INT/ORG TEC/DEV FOR/AID ARMS/CONT DETER NUC/PWR
...POLICY DECISION CONCPT ANTHOL BIBLIOG/A 20
COLD/WAR NATO. PAGE 56 G1103
C65
PLAN
FORCES
WAR
COERCE

ALI S.,PLANNING, DEVELOPMENT AND CHANGE: AN
ANNOTATED BIBLIOGRAPHY ON DEVELOPMENTAL
ADMINISTRATION. PAKISTAN SOCIETY ORD/FREE 20.
PAGE 2 G0041
B66
BIBLIOG/A
ADMIN
ECO/UNDEV
PLAN

AMERICAN LIBRARY ASSN,GUIDE TO JAPANESE REFERENCE
BOOKS....HUM 20 CHINJAP. PAGE 3 G0054
B66
BIBLIOG/A
SOC
TEC/DEV
PHIL/SCI

GLAZER M.,THE FEDERAL GOVERNMENT AND THE
UNIVERSITY. CHILE PROB/SOLV DIPLOM GIVE ADMIN WAR
...POLICY SOC 20. PAGE 21 G0421
B66
BIBLIOG/A
NAT/G
PLAN
ACADEM

HOPKINS J.F.K.,ARABIC PERIODICAL LITERATURE, 1961.
ISLAM LAW CULTURE SECT...GEOG HEAL PHIL/SCI PSY SOC
20. PAGE 27 G0528
B66
BIBLIOG/A
NAT/LISM
TEC/DEV
INDUS

LINDFORS G.V.,INTERCOLLEGIATE BIBLIOGRAPHY; CASES
IN BUSINESS ADMINISTRATION (VOL. X). FINAN MARKET
LABOR CONSULT PLAN GP/REL PRODUC 20. PAGE 34 G0668
B66
BIBLIOG/A
ADMIN
MGT
OP/RES

PRINCETON U INDUSTRIAL REL SEC,THE FEDERAL
GOVERNMENT AND THE UNIVERSITY: SUPPORT FOR SOCIAL
SCIENCE RESEARCH AND THE IMPACT OF PROJECT CAMELOT.
USA+45 ACT/RES CONTROL GP/REL PWR...POLICY 20.
PAGE 45 G0889
B66
BIBLIOG/A
NAT/G
ACADEM
PLAN

SPULBER N.,THE STATE AND ECONOMIC DEVELOPMENT IN
EASTERN EUROPE. BULGARIA COM CZECHOSLVK HUNGARY
POLAND YUGOSLAVIA CULTURE PLAN CAP/ISM INT/TRADE
CONTROL...POLICY CHARTS METH/COMP BIBLIOG/A 19/20.
PAGE 52 G1028
B66
ECO/DEV
ECO/UNDEV
NAT/G
TOTALISM

US DEPARTMENT OF LABOR,PRODUCTIVITY: A
BIBLIOGRAPHY. ECO/DEV INDUS MARKET OP/RES AUTOMAT
COST...STAT 20. PAGE 57 G1119
B66
BIBLIOG/A
PRODUC
LABOR
PLAN

US DEPARTMENT OF THE ARMY,COMMUNIST CHINA: A
STRATEGIC SURVEY: A BIBLIOGRAPHY (PAMPHLET NO.
B66
BIBLIOG/A
MARXISM

20-67). CHINA/COM COM INDIA USSR NAT/G POL/PAR
EX/STRUC FORCES NUC/PWR REV ATTIT...POLICY GEOG
CHARTS. PAGE 58 G1133
S/ASIA
DIPLOM

RASER J.R.,"DETERRENCE RESEARCH* PAST PROGRESS AND
FUTURE NEEDS." INTELL PLAN TEC/DEV NUC/PWR PERCEPT
...DECISION PSY SOC NET/THEORY. PAGE 46 G0905
L66
DETER
BIBLIOG/A
FUT

PRINCETON U INDUSTRIAL REL SEC,RECENT MATERIAL ON
COLLECTIVE BARGAINING IN GOVERNMENT (PAMPHLET NO.
130). USA+45 ECO/DEV LABOR WORKER ECO/TAC GOV/REL
...MGT 20. PAGE 45 G0890
N66
BIBLIOG/A
BARGAIN
NAT/G
GP/REL

BARANSON J.,TECHNOLOGY FOR UNDERDEVELOPED AREAS: AN
ANNOTATED BIBLIOGRAPHY. FUT WOR+45 CULTURE INDUS
INT/ORG CREATE PROB/SOLV INT/TRADE EDU/PROP AUTOMAT
...CONCPT METH. PAGE 5 G0092
B67
BIBLIOG/A
ECO/UNDEV
TEC/DEV
R+D

GULICK M.C.,NONCONVENTIONAL INFORMATION SYSTEMS
SERVING THE SOCIAL SCIENCES AND THE HUMANITIES: A
BIBLIOGRAPHIC ESSAY (PAPER). USA+45 COMPUTER CREATE
EDU/PROP KNOWL...SOC METH 20. PAGE 23 G0462
B67
BIBLIOG/A
R+D
COMPUT/IR
HUM

RUTGERS U GRADUATE SCH LIB SCI,BIBLIOGRAPHY OF
RESEARCH RELATING TO THE COMMUNICATION OF
SCIENTIFIC AND TECHNICAL INFORMATION. FUT CREATE
FEEDBACK...PHIL/SCI NEW/IDEA COMPUT/IR HYPO/EXP.
PAGE 48 G0951
B67
BIBLIOG/A
COM/IND
R+D
TEC/DEV

SCHUMACHER B.G.,COMPUTER DYNAMICS IN PUBLIC
ADMINISTRATION. USA+45 CREATE PLAN TEC/DEV...MGT
LING CON/ANAL BIBLIOG/A 20. PAGE 50 G0980
B67
COMPUTER
COMPUT/IR
ADMIN
AUTOMAT

UNIVERSAL REFERENCE SYSTEM,LEGISLATIVE PROCESS,
REPRESENTATION, AND DECISION-MAKING (VOLUME II).
WOR+45 WOR-45 CONSTN LOC/G NAT/G...POLICY CON/ANAL
COMPUT/IR GEN/METH. PAGE 56 G1094
B67
BIBLIOG/A
LEGIS
REPRESENT
DECISION

UNIVERSAL REFERENCE SYSTEM,BIBLIOGRAPHY OF
BIBLIOGRAPHIES IN POLITICAL SCIENCE, GOVERNMENT,
AND PUBLIC POLICY (VOLUME III). WOR+45 WOR-45 LAW
ADMIN...SOC CON/ANAL COMPUT/IR GEN/METH. PAGE 56
G1095
B67
BIBLIOG/A
NAT/G
DIPLOM
POLICY

UNIVERSAL REFERENCE SYSTEM,ADMINISTRATIVE
MANAGEMENT: PUBLIC AND PRIVATE BUREAUCRACY (VOLUME
IV). WOR+45 WOR-45 ECO/DEV LG/CO LOC/G PUB/INST
VOL/ASSN GOV/REL...COMPUT/IR GEN/METH. PAGE 56
G1096
B67
BIBLIOG/A
MGT
ADMIN
NAT/G

UNIVERSAL REFERENCE SYSTEM,CURRENT EVENTS AND
PROBLEMS OF MODERN SOCIETY (VOLUME V). WOR+45 LOC/G
MUNIC NAT/G PLAN EDU/PROP CRIME RACE/REL WEALTH
...COMPUT/IR GEN/METH. PAGE 56 G1097
B67
BIBLIOG/A
SOCIETY
PROB/SOLV
ATTIT

UNIVERSAL REFERENCE SYSTEM,PUBLIC OPINION, MASS
BEHAVIOR, AND POLITICAL PSYCHOLOGY (VOLUME VI).
WOR+45 WOR-45 SOCIETY EDU/PROP PRESS PARTIC CHOOSE
PERSON...TREND COMPUT/IR GEN/METH. PAGE 56 G1098
B67
BIBLIOG/A
ATTIT
CROWD
PSY

UNIVERSAL REFERENCE SYSTEM,ECONOMIC REGULATION,
BUSINESS, AND GOVERNMENT (VOLUME VIII). WOR+45
WOR-45 ECO/DEV ECO/UNDEV FINAN LABOR TEC/DEV
ECO/TAC INT/TRADE GOV/REL...POLICY COMPUT/IR.
PAGE 56 G1099
B67
BIBLIOG/A
CONTROL
NAT/G

UNIVERSAL REFERENCE SYSTEM,PUBLIC POLICY AND THE
MANAGEMENT OF SCIENCE (VOLUME IX). FUT SPACE WOR+45
LAW NAT/G TEC/DEV CONTROL NUC/PWR GOV/REL
...COMPUT/IR GEN/METH. PAGE 56 G1100
B67
BIBLIOG/A
POLICY
MGT
PHIL/SCI

UNIVERSAL REFERENCE SYSTEM,LAW, JURISPRUDENCE, AND
JUDICIAL PROCESS (VOLUME VII). WOR+45 WOR-45 CONSTN
NAT/G LEGIS JUDGE CT/SYS...INT/LAW COMPUT/IR
GEN/METH METH. PAGE 56 G1101
B67
BIBLIOG/A
LAW
JURID
ADJUD

US DEPARTMENT OF THE ARMY,CIVILIAN IN PEACE,
SOLDIER IN WAR: A BIBLIOGRAPHIC SURVEY OF THE ARMY
AND AIR NATIONAL GUARD (PAMPHLET, NOS. 130-2).
USA+45 USA-45 LOC/G NAT/G PROVS LEGIS PLAN ADMIN
B67
BIBLIOG/A
FORCES
ROLE
DIPLOM

ATTIT ORD/FREE...POLICY 19/20. PAGE 58 G1134

B67
US SUPERINTENDENT OF DOCUMENTS.LIBRARY OF CONGRESS   BIBLIOG/A
(PRICE LIST 83). AFR ASIA EUR+WWI USA-45 USSR NAT/G   USA+45
DIPLOM CONFER CT/SYS WAR...DECISION PHIL/SCI   AUTOMAT
CLASSIF 19/20 CONGRESS PRESIDENT. PAGE 61 G1189   LAW

L67
EINAUDI L.,"ANNOTATED BIBLIOGRAPHY OF LATIN   BIBLIOG/A
AMERICAN MILITARY JOURNALS" LAW TEC/DEV DOMIN   NAT/G
EDU/PROP COERCE WAR CIVMIL/REL 20. PAGE 17 G0336   FORCES
                                                        L/A+17C

N67
US SUPERINTENDENT OF DOCUMENTS.SPACE: MISSILES, THE   BIBLIOG/A
MOON, NASA, AND SATELLITES (PRICE LIST 79A). USA+45   SPACE
COM/IND R+D NAT/G DIPLOM EDU/PROP ADMIN CONTROL   TEC/DEV
HEALTH...POLICY SIMUL NASA CONGRESS. PAGE 61 G1190   PEACE

N67
PRINCETON U INDUSTRIAL REL SEC.COLLECTIVE   BIBLIOG/A
BARGAINING IN THE PUBLIC SCHOOLS (PAMPHLET NO. 33).   SCHOOL
USA+45 LABOR PROB/SOLV PWR MGT. PAGE 45 G0891   BARGAIN
                                                        GP/REL

BICAMERALISM....SEE LEGIS, CONGRESS, HOUSE/REP, SENATE

BIDWELL P.W. G0135

BIGLER/W....WILLIAM BIGLER

BILL/RIGHT....BILL OF RIGHTS

BINGHAM A.M. G0136

BINNS/JJ....JOSEPH J. BINNS

BIO/SOC....BIO-SOCIAL PROCESSES, DRUGS, SEXUALITY

B11
BERGSON H.,CREATIVE EVOLUTION. FUT WOR+45 WOR-45   BIO/SOC
INTELL AGRI R+D ATTIT PERCEPT PERSON RIGID/FLEX   KNOWL
...RELATIV PHIL/SCI PSY METH/CNCPT MATH HIST/WRIT
TREND HYPO/EXP TOT/POP. PAGE 7 G0127

B48
BRADLEY D.,NO PLACE TO HIDE. USA+45 SOCIETY NAT/G   R+D
FORCES TEC/DEV EDU/PROP DETER PEACE BIO/SOC   LAB/EXP
ALL/VALS...POLICY PHIL/SCI OBS RECORD SAMP BIOG   ARMS/CONT
GEN/METH COLD/WAR 20. PAGE 8 G0162   NUC/PWR

B54
SIMMONS L.W.,SOCIAL SCIENCE IN MEDICINE. USA+45   PUB/INST
USA-45 SOCIETY CONSULT PLAN PROB/SOLV CONTROL   HABITAT
PERS/REL...POLICY HEAL TREND BIBLIOG 20. PAGE 51   HEALTH
G0999   BIO/SOC

B60
US HOUSE COMM. SCI. ASTRONAUT.,OCEAN SCIENCES AND   R+D
NATIONAL SECURITY. FUT SEA ECO/DEV EXTR/IND INT/ORG   ORD/FREE
NAT/G FORCES ACT/RES TEC/DEV ECO/TAC COERCE WAR
BIO/SOC KNOWL PWR...CONCPT RECORD LAB/EXP 20.
PAGE 59 G1153

S60
JAFFEE A.J.,"POPULATION TRENDS AND CONTROLS IN   ECO/UNDEV
UNDERDEVELOPED COUNTRIES." AFR FUT ISLAM L/A+17C   GEOG
S/ASIA CULTURE R+D FAM ACT/RES PLAN EDU/PROP
BIO/SOC RIGID/FLEX HEALTH...SOC STAT OBS CHARTS 20.
PAGE 28 G0555

B62
STERN A.C.,AIR POLLUTION (2 VOLS.). LAW INDUS   AIR
PROB/SOLV TEC/DEV INSPECT RISK BIO/SOC HABITAT   OP/RES
...OBS/ENVIR TESTS SAMP 20 POLLUTION. PAGE 53 G1035   CONTROL
                                                        HEALTH

B64
RECENT PUBLICATIONS ON GOVERNMENTAL PROBLEMS. FINAN   BIBLIOG
INDUS ACADEM PLAN PROB/SOLV EDU/PROP ADJUD ADMIN   AUTOMAT
BIO/SOC...MGT SOC. PAGE 1 G0017   LEGIS
                                                        JURID

B64
BROWN N.,NUCLEAR WAR* THE IMPENDING STRATEGIC   FORCES
DEADLOCK. USA+45 USSR TEC/DEV BUDGET RISK ARMS/CONT   OP/RES
NUC/PWR WEAPON COST BIO/SOC...GEOG IDEA/COMP   WAR
NAT/COMP GAME NATO WARSAW/P. PAGE 9 G0177   GEN/LAWS

B64
COHEN M.,LAW AND POLITICS IN SPACE: SPECIFIC AND   DELIB/GP
URGENT PROBLEMS IN THE LAW OF OUTER SPACE.   LAW
CHINA/COM COM USA+45 USSR WOR+45 COM/IND INT/ORG   INT/LAW
NAT/G LEGIT NUC/PWR ATTIT BIO/SOC...JURID CONCPT   SPACE
CONGRESS 20 STALIN/J. PAGE 12 G0241

B64
GROSSER G.H.,THE THREAT OF IMPENDING DISASTER: HEALTH
CONTRIBUTIONS TO THE PSYCHOLOGY OF STRESS. SPACE   PSY
UNIV SOCIETY R+D TEC/DEV EDU/PROP COERCE WAR ATTIT   NUC/PWR
BIO/SOC DISPL PERCEPT PERSON...SOC MYTH SELF/OBS
CONT/OBS BIOG CON/ANAL TOT/POP 20. PAGE 23 G0455

B64
PETERSON W.,THE POLITICS OF POPULATION. COM EUR+WWI   PLAN
FUT MOD/EUR S/ASIA USA+45 USA-45 WOR+45 LAW CULTURE   CENSUS
FAM SECT DOMIN EDU/PROP BIO/SOC HEALTH ORD/FREE   POLICY
...GEOG STAT TIME/SEQ TREND VAL/FREE. PAGE 44 G0871

B64
ROTHSCHILD J.H.,TOMORROW'S WEAPONS: CHEMICAL AND   WAR
BIOLOGICAL. FUT PROB/SOLV ARMS/CONT PEACE MORAL   WEAPON
...CHARTS BIBLIOG 20. PAGE 48 G0941   BIO/SOC
                                                        DETER

B65
US DEPARTMENT OF ARMY.MILITARY PROTECTIVE   FORCES
CONSTRUCTION: NUCLEAR WARFARE AND CHEMICAL AND   CONSTRUC
BIOLOGICAL OPERATIONS (MANUAL). OP/RES TEC/DEV RISK   TASK
COERCE NUC/PWR WAR WEAPON EFFICIENCY UTIL BIO/SOC   HEALTH
HABITAT ORD/FREE 20. PAGE 57 G1117

S65
KRICKUS R.J.,"ON THE MORALITY OF   MORAL
CHEMICAL/BIOLOGICAL WAR." ECO/UNDEV ARMS/CONT DETER   BIO/SOC
NUC/PWR RIGID/FLEX HEALTH INT/LAW. PAGE 31 G0621   WEAPON
                                                        WAR

B66
US HOUSE COMM ON JUDICIARY.CIVIL COMMITMENT AND   BIO/SOC
TREATMENT OF NARCOTIC ADDICTS. USA+45 SOCIETY FINAN   CRIME
LEGIS PROB/SOLV GIVE CT/SYS SANCTION HEALTH   IDEA/COMP
...POLICY HEAL 20. PAGE 58 G1141   CONTROL

B67
HEADLEY J.C.,PESTICIDE PROBLEM: AN ECONOMIC   HABITAT
APPROACH TO PUBLIC POLICY. AGRI TEC/DEV GOV/REL   POLICY
COST ATTIT CHARTS. PAGE 25 G0498   BIO/SOC
                                                        CONTROL

B67
RUSSELL B.,WAR CRIMES IN VIETNAM. USA+45 VIETNAM   WAR
FORCES DIPLOM WEAPON RACE/REL DISCRIM ISOLAT   CRIME
BIO/SOC 20 COLD/WAR RUSSELL/B. PAGE 48 G0949   ATTIT
                                                        POLICY

L67
SEABERG G.P.,"THE DRUG ABUSE PROBLEMS AND SOME   BIO/SOC
PROPOSALS." UK USA+45 MARKET SANCTION CRIME   LAW
...POLICY NEW/IDEA. PAGE 50 G0986   ADJUD
                                                        PROB/SOLV

S67
BULMER-THOMAS I.,"SO, ON TO THE GREAT SOCIETY." FUT   PHIL/SCI
UNIV TEC/DEV BAL/PWR WAR BIO/SOC KNOWL...ART/METH   SOCIETY
SOC PREDICT TREND WORSHIP 20 GREAT/SOC. PAGE 9   CREATE
G0185

S67
HILL R.,"SOCIAL ASPECTS OF FAMILY PLANNING." INDIA   FAM
KOREA TAIWAN ECO/UNDEV PLAN PROB/SOLV TEC/DEV   BIO/SOC
EDU/PROP CONTROL ATTIT DRIVE...HEAL PSY SOC 20   GEOG
BIRTH/CON UN. PAGE 26 G0512   MARRIAGE

BIOG....BIOGRAPHY (INCLUDES PSYCHOANALYSIS)

B48
BRADLEY D.,NO PLACE TO HIDE. USA+45 SOCIETY NAT/G   R+D
FORCES TEC/DEV EDU/PROP DETER PEACE BIO/SOC   LAB/EXP
ALL/VALS...POLICY PHIL/SCI OBS RECORD SAMP BIOG   ARMS/CONT
GEN/METH COLD/WAR 20. PAGE 8 G0162   NUC/PWR

B53
BRETTON H.L.,STRESEMANN AND THE REVISION OF   POLICY
VERSAILLES: A FIGHT FOR REASON. EUR+WWI GERMANY   DIPLOM
FORCES BUDGET ARMS/CONT WAR SUPEGO...BIBLIOG 20   BIOG
TREATY VERSAILLES STRESEMN/G. PAGE 9 G0167

B54
COMBS C.H.,DECISION PROCESSES. INTELL SOCIETY   MATH
DELIB/GP CREATE TEC/DEV DOMIN LEGIT EXEC CHOOSE   DECISION
DRIVE RIGID/FLEX KNOWL PWR...PHIL/SCI SOC
METH/CNCPT CONT/OBS REC/INT PERS/TEST SAMP/SIZ BIOG
SOC/EXP WORK. PAGE 13 G0245

B60
EINSTEIN A.,EINSTEIN ON PEACE. FUT WOR+45 WOR-45   INT/ORG
SOCIETY NAT/G PLAN BAL/PWR CAP/ISM DIPLOM ARMS/CONT   ATTIT
DETER NAT/LISM...POLICY RELATIV HUM PHIL/SCI CONCPT   NUC/PWR
BIOG COLD/WAR LEAGUE/NAT NAZI. PAGE 17 G0338   PEACE

B61
NATHAN O.,EINSTEIN ON PEACE. WOR+45 WOR-45 INTELL   CONCPT
NUC/PWR WAR PERSON MORAL...BIOG VAL/FREE NAZI 20   PEACE
EINSTEIN/A. PAGE 41 G0807

B64
GROSSER G.H.,THE THREAT OF IMPENDING DISASTER: HEALTH
CONTRIBUTIONS TO THE PSYCHOLOGY OF STRESS. SPACE   PSY
UNIV SOCIETY R+D TEC/DEV EDU/PROP COERCE WAR ATTIT   NUC/PWR
BIO/SOC DISPL PERCEPT PERSON...SOC MYTH SELF/OBS
CONT/OBS BIOG CON/ANAL TOT/POP 20. PAGE 23 G0455

B64
HAMMOND P.E.,SOCIOLOGISTS AT WORK. VOL/ASSN OP/RES   R+D
TEC/DEV CONFER ROUTINE TASK EFFICIENCY...MGT   BIOG
NEW/IDEA STYLE SAMP. PAGE 24 G0478   SOC

B64
THANT U.,TOWARD WORLD PEACE. DELIB/GP TEC/DEV   DIPLOM
EDU/PROP WAR SOVEREIGN...INT/LAW 20 UN MID/EAST.   BIOG
PAGE 54 G1065   PEACE
                                                         COERCE

B65
CHENG C.-Y.,SCIENTIFIC AND ENGINEERING MANPOWER IN   WORKER
COMMUNIST CHINA. 1949-1963. CHINA/COM USSR ELITES   CONSULT
ECO/DEV R+D ACADEM LABOR NAT/G EDU/PROP CONTROL   MARXISM
UTIL...POLICY BIBLIOG 20. PAGE 12 G0226   BIOG

BIRCH/SOC....JOHN BIRCH SOCIETY

BIRNBAUM K. G0137

BIRTH/CON....BIRTH CONTROL POLICIES AND TECHNIQUES

S67
HILL R.,"SOCIAL ASPECTS OF FAMILY PLANNING." INDIA   FAM
KOREA TAIWAN ECO/UNDEV PLAN PROB/SOLV TEC/DEV   BIO/SOC
EDU/PROP CONTROL ATTIT DRIVE...HEAL PSY SOC 20   GEOG
BIRTH/CON UN. PAGE 26 G0512   MARRIAGE

BISMARCK/O....OTTO VON BISMARCK

B63
JACOB H.,GERMAN ADMINISTRATION SINCE BISMARCK: ADMIN
CENTRAL AUTHORITY VERSUS LOCAL AUTONOMY. GERMANY   NAT/G
GERMANY/W LAW POL/PAR CONTROL CENTRAL TOTALISM   LOC/G
FASCISM...MAJORIT DECISION STAT CHARTS GOV/COMP   POLICY
19/20 BISMARCK/O HITLER/A WEIMAR/REP. PAGE 28 G0551

BLACK/EUG....EUGENE BLACK

BLACK/HL....HUGO L. BLACK

BLACK/MUS....BLACK MUSLIMS

BLACK/PWR....BLACK POWER; SEE ALSO NEGRO

BLACK/ZION....BLACK ZIONISM

BLACKETT P.M.S. G0138

BLACKSTN/W....SIR WILLIAM BLACKSTONE

BLACKSTONE, SIR WILLIAM....SEE BLACKSTN/W

BLOCH/E....ERNEST BLOCH

BLOOMFIELD L.P. G0139,G0140,G0141,G0142,G0143

BLOUSTEIN E.J. G0144

BLUEPRINTS....SEE ORG/CHARTS

BMA....BRITISH MEDICAL ASSOCIATION

BOARD....SEE DELIB/GP

BOARD/MDCN....BOARD ON MEDICINE

BOAS/FRANZ....FRANZ BOAS

BOBROW D.B. G0145

BOCK E.A. G0146

BODIN/JEAN....JEAN BODIN

BOER/WAR....BOER WAR

BOGARDUS....BOGARDUS SCALE

BOHME/H....HELMUT BOHME

BOHN L.C. G0148,G0149

BOLIVIA....SEE ALSO L/A+17C

B63
SCHOECK H.,THE NEW ARGUMENT IN ECONOMICS. UK USA+45   WELF/ST
INDUS MARKET LABOR NAT/G ECO/TAC ADMIN ROUTINE   FOR/AID
BAL/PAY PWR...POLICY BOLIV. PAGE 49 G0973   ECO/DEV
                                                         ALL/IDEOS

BOLSHEVISM....BOLSHEVISM AND BOLSHEVISTS

S51
MACRAE D.G.,"THE BOLSHEVIK IDEOLOGY: THE   MARXISM
INTELLECTUAL AND EMOTIONAL FACTORS IN COMMUNIST   INTELL
AFFILIATION" (BMR)" COM LEAD REV ATTIT ORD/FREE   PHIL/SCI
...SOC CON/ANAL 20 BOLSHEVISM. PAGE 35 G0693   SECT

BOLTON R.E. G0150

BONAPART/L....LOUIS BONAPARTE (KING OF HOLLAND)

BONER H.A. G0151

BONINI C.P. G0152

BONNEFOUS M. G0153

BONNET R. G0413

BONTOC....BONTOC, A MOUNTAIN TRIBE OF LUZON, PHILIPPINES

BOONE/DANL....DANIEL BOONE

BORDEN/R....SIR ROBERT BORDEN

BORKOF H. G0154

BORNEO....SEE ALSO S/ASIA

BOSANQUET B. G0155

BOSCH/JUAN....JUAN BOSCH

BOSSISM....BOSSISM; MONOPOLY OF POLITICAL POWER (U.S.)

BOSTON....BOSTON, MASSACHUSETTS

B60
CARPER E.T.,THE DEFENSE APPROPRIATIONS RIDER   GOV/REL
(PAMPHLET). USA+45 CONSTN CHIEF DELIB/GP LEGIS   ADJUD
BUDGET LOBBY CIVMIL/REL...POLICY 20 CONGRESS   LAW
EISNHWR/DD DEPT/DEFEN PRESIDENT BOSTON. PAGE 11   CONTROL
G0212

BOTSWANA....BOTSWANA

BOULDER....BOULDER, COLORADO

BOULDING K.E. G0156,G0157,G0158,G0159

BOURASSA/H....HENRI BOURASSA

BOWEN H.R. G0160

BOWMAN I. G0161

BOWMAN M.J. G0056

BOXER/REBL....BOXER REBELLION

BRADLEY D. G0162

BRADLEY/FH....FRANCIS HERBERT BRADLEY

BRADY R.A. G0163

BRAHMIN....BRAHMIN CASTE

BRAINWASHING....SEE EDU/PROP

BRANDEIS/L....LOUIS BRANDEIS

BRANNAN/C....CHARLES BRANNAN (SECRETARY OF AGRICULTURE)

BRAZIL....SEE ALSO L/A+17C

B63
DALAND R.T.,PERSPECTIVES OF BRAZILIAN PUBLIC   ADMIN
ADMINISTRATION (VOL. I). BRAZIL LAW ECO/UNDEV   NAT/G

SCHOOL CHIEF TEC/DEV CONFER CONTROL GP/REL ATTIT   PLAN
ROLE PWR...ANTHOL 20. PAGE 14 G0272   GOV/REL

B63
MENEZES A.J.,SUBDESENVOLVIMENTO E POLITICA   ECO/UNDEV
INTERNACIONAL. BRAZIL WOR+45 PLAN CONTROL LEAD   DIPLOM
NAT/LISM ORD/FREE 20 THIRD/WRLD. PAGE 38 G0754   POLICY
                                                   BAL/PWR

B63
THORELLI H.B.,INTOP: INTERNATIONAL OPERATIONS   GAME
SIMULATION: PLAYER'S MANUAL. BRAZIL FINAN OP/RES   INT/TRADE
ADMIN GP/REL INGP/REL PRODUC PERCEPT...DECISION MGT EDU/PROP
EEC. PAGE 54 G1073   LG/CO

S65
TENDLER J.D.,"TECHNOLOGY AND ECONOMIC DEVELOPMENT* BRAZIL
THE CASE OF HYDRO VS THERMAL POWER." CONSTRUC   INDUS
DIST/IND CREATE TEC/DEV INT/TRADE CENTRAL PWR SKILL ECO/UNDEV
WEALTH...MGT NAT/COMP ARGEN. PAGE 54 G1063

BREHON....BREHON LAW (ANCIENT CELTIC)

BRENNAN D.G. G0164,G0165

BRETNOR R. G0166

BRETTON H.L. G0167

BRIAND/A....ARISTIDE BRIAND

BRIDGEPORT....BRIDGEPORT, CONNECTICUT

BRIGHT J.R. G0168

BRILLOUIN L. G0169

BRIT/COLUM....BRITISH COLUMBIA, CANADA

BRITISH COLUMBIA, CANADA....SEE BRIT/COLUM

BRITISH COMMONWEALTH OF NATIONS....SEE COMMONWLTH

BRITISH GUIANA....SEE GUIANA/BR + GUYANA

BRITISH MEDICAL ASSOCIATION....SEE BMA

BRITISH COMMONWEALTH BUR AGRI G0170

BRODIE B. G0171,G0172

BRODY R.A. G0173

BROOK/EDGR....EDGAR H. BROOKES

BROOKINGS INSTITUTION G0174,G0175

BROOKINGS....BROOKINGS INSTITUTION, THE

BROUDE H.W. G0176

BROWN N. G0177,G0178

BROWN W.B. G0179

BROWN W.M. G0180

BROWN/JOHN....JOHN BROWN

BROWNELL/H....HERBERT BROWNELL

BROWNLIE I. G0181

BRUCK H. G1018

BRUNHILD G. G0182

BRYAN/WJ....WILLIAM JENNINGS BRYAN

BRYCE/J....JAMES BRYCE

BRYSON L. G0183

BRZEZNSK/Z....ZBIGNIEW K. BRZEZINSKI

BUCHANAN/J....PRESIDENT JAMES BUCHANAN

BUCKLEY/WF....WILLIAM F. BUCKLEY

BUDDHISM....BUDDHISM

BUDER S. G0184

BUDGET....BUDGETING, BUDGETS, FISCAL PLANNING

B37
HODGSON J.G.,THE OFFICIAL PUBLICATIONS OF AMERICAN BIBLIOG
COUNTIES: A UNION LIST. SCHOOL BUDGET...HEAL MGT   LOC/G
SOC/WK 19/20. PAGE 26 G0520   PUB/INST

B41
FULLER G.H.,DEFENSE FINANCING: A SELECTED LIST OF   BIBLIOG/A
REFERENCES (PAMPHLET). MOD/EUR USA-45 ECO/DEV NAT/G FINAN
DELIB/GP RATION ARMS/CONT WEAPON COST PEACE PWR 20 FORCES
CONGRESS. PAGE 20 G0401   BUDGET

B42
FULLER G.H.,DEFENSE FINANCING: A SUPPLEMENTARY LIST BIBLIOG/A
OF REFERENCES (PAMPHLET). CANADA UK USA-45 ECO/DEV FINAN
NAT/G DELIB/GP BUDGET ADJUD ARMS/CONT WEAPON COST   FORCES
PEACE PWR 20 AUSTRAL CHINJAP CONGRESS. PAGE 21   DIPLOM
G0403

B48
STEWART I.,ORGANIZING SCIENTIFIC RESEARCH FOR WAR: DELIB/GP
ADMINISTRATIVE HISTORY OF OFFICE OF SCIENTIFIC   ADMIN
RESEARCH AND DEVELOPMENT. USA-45 INTELL R+D LABOR   WAR
WORKER CREATE BUDGET WEAPON CIVMIL/REL GP/REL   TEC/DEV
EFFICIENCY...POLICY 20. PAGE 53 G1036

S48
HARDIN L.M.,"REFLECTIONS ON AGRICULTURAL POLICY   AGRI
FORMATION IN THE UNITED STATES." LEGIS PLAN BUDGET POLICY
ECO/TAC LEAD CENTRAL...MGT SOC NEW/IDEA STAT FAO.   ADMIN
PAGE 24 G0480   NEW/LIB

B50
HUZAR E.,THE PURSE AND THE SWORD: CONTROL OF THE   CIVMIL/REL
ARMY BY CONGRESS THROUGH MILITARY APPROPRIATIONS   BUDGET
1933-1950. NAT/G DELIB/GP EX/STRUC FORCES PROB/SOLV CONTROL
BARGAIN CONFER ADMIN ROUTINE GOV/REL EFFICIENCY   LEGIS
...POLICY COLD/WAR. PAGE 27 G0541

B53
BRETTON H.L.,STRESEMANN AND THE REVISION OF   POLICY
VERSAILLES: A FIGHT FOR REASON. EUR+WWI GERMANY   DIPLOM
FORCES BUDGET ARMS/CONT WAR SUPEGO...BIBLIOG 20   BIOG
TREATY VERSAILLES STRESEMN/G. PAGE 9 G0167

B54
TOMPKINS D.C.,STATE GOVERNMENT AND ADMINISTRATION: BIBLIOG/A
A BIBLIOGRAPHY. USA+45 USA-45 CONSTN LEGIS JUDGE   LOC/G
BUDGET CT/SYS LOBBY...CHARTS 20. PAGE 55 G1077   PROVS
                                                   ADMIN

B55
SMITHIES A.,THE BUDGETARY PROCESS IN THE UNITED   NAT/G
STATES. ECO/DEV AGRI EX/STRUC FORCES LEGIS   ADMIN
PROB/SOLV TAX ROUTINE EFFICIENCY...MGT CONGRESS   BUDGET
PRESIDENT. PAGE 52 G1016   GOV/REL

B56
ESTEP R.,AN AIR POWER BIBLIOGRAPHY. USA+45 TEC/DEV BIBLIOG/A
BUDGET DIPLOM EDU/PROP DETER CIVMIL/REL...DECISION FORCES
INT/LAW 20. PAGE 18 G0351   WEAPON
                                                   PLAN

S56
KNAPP D.C.,"CONGRESSIONAL CONTROL OF AGRICULTURAL   LEGIS
CONSERVATION POLICY: A CASE STUDY OF THE   AGRI
APPROPRIATIONS PROCESS." DELIB/GP PLAN PROB/SOLV   BUDGET
CONFER PARL/PROC...POLICY INT CONGRESS. PAGE 31   CONTROL
G0607

B58
EHRHARD J.,LE DESTIN DU COLONIALISME. AFR FRANCE   COLONIAL
ECO/UNDEV AGRI FINAN MARKET CREATE PLAN TEC/DEV   FOR/AID
BUDGET DIPLOM PRICE 20. PAGE 17 G0335   INT/TRADE
                                                   INDUS

B58
ROCKEFELLER BROTH FUND INC,INTERNATIONAL SECURITY - NUC/PWR
THE MILITARY ASPECT. USA+45 INT/ORG NAT/G BUDGET   DETER
ARMS/CONT WAR WEAPON PEACE ORD/FREE 20 NATO.   FORCES
PAGE 47 G0932   DIPLOM

B59
AIR FORCE ACADEMY ASSEMBLY '59,INTERNATIONAL   FOR/AID
STABILITY AND PROGRESS (PAMPHLET). USA+45 USSR   FORCES
ECO/UNDEV PROB/SOLV BUDGET DIPLOM ADMIN DETER COST WAR
ATTIT...TREND 20. PAGE 2 G0030   PLAN

B59
MEANS G.C.,ADMINISTRATIVE INFLATION AND PUBLIC   ECO/TAC
POLICY (PAMPHLET). USA+45 ECO/DEV FINAN INDUS   POLICY
WORKER PLAN BUDGET GOV/REL COST DEMAND WEALTH 20   RATION
CONGRESS MONOPOLY GOLD/STAND. PAGE 38 G0749   CONTROL

B60
ALBI F.,TRATADO DE LOS MODOS DE GESTION DE LAS   LOC/G
CORPORACIONES LOCALES. SPAIN FINAN NAT/G BUDGET   LAW

CONTROL EXEC ROUTINE GOV/REL ORD/FREE SOVEREIGN
...MGT 20. PAGE 2 G0034
ADMIN
MUNIC

B60
CARPER E.T.,THE DEFENSE APPROPRIATIONS RIDER
(PAMPHLET). USA+45 CONSTN CHIEF DELIB/GP LEGIS
BUDGET LOBBY CIVMIL/REL...POLICY 20 CONGRESS
EISNHWR/DD DEPT/DEFEN PRESIDENT BOSTON. PAGE 11
G0212
GOV/REL
ADJUD
LAW
CONTROL

B61
US SENATE COMM GOVT OPERATIONS,ORGANIZING FOR
NATIONAL SECURITY. COM USA+45 BUDGET DIPLOM DETER
NUC/PWR WAR WEAPON ORD/FREE...BIBLIOG 20 COLD/WAR.
PAGE 60 G1176
POLICY
PLAN
FORCES
COERCE

S61
MAINZER L.C.,"SCIENTIFIC FREEDOM IN GOVERNMENT-
SPONSORED RESEARCH." USA+45 INTELL PUB/INST BUDGET
LOBBY AUTHORIT PWR...POLICY PHIL/SCI 20 NIH NSF.
PAGE 35 G0696
CREATE
ORD/FREE
NAT/G
R+D

B62
FORTUNE EDITORS,THE SPACE INDUSTRY: AMERICA'S
NEWEST GIANT. USA+45 FINAN NAT/G BUDGET 20. PAGE 20
G0383
SPACE
INDUS
TEC/DEV
MGT

B63
BONINI C.P.,SIMULATION OF INFORMATION AND DECISION
SYSTEMS IN THE FIRM. MARKET BUDGET DOMIN EDU/PROP
ADMIN COST ATTIT HABITAT PERCEPT PWR...CONCPT
PROBABIL QUANT PREDICT HYPO/EXP BIBLIOG. PAGE 8
G0152
INDUS
SIMUL
DECISION
MGT

B63
UN SECRETARY GENERAL,PLANNING FOR ECONOMIC
DEVELOPMENT. ECO/UNDEV FINAN BUDGET INT/TRADE
TARIFFS TAX ADMIN 20 UN. PAGE 55 G1089
PLAN
ECO/TAC
MGT
NAT/COMP

S63
ENTHOVEN A.C.,"ECONOMIC ANALYSIS IN THE DEPARTMENT
OF DEFENSE." USA+45 NAT/G DELIB/GP PROB/SOLV RATION
NUC/PWR WEAPON COST...DECISION 20 DEPT/DEFEN
RESOURCE/N. PAGE 18 G0349
PLAN
BUDGET
ECO/TAC
FORCES

N63
COMMITTEE ECONOMIC DEVELOPMENT,TAXES AND TRADE: 20
YEARS OF CED POLICY (PAMPHLET). USA+45 ECO/DEV PLAN
BUDGET LEAD...POLICY KENNEDY/JF PRESIDENT. PAGE 13
G0246
FINAN
ECO/TAC
NAT/G
DELIB/GP

B64
BROWN N.,NUCLEAR WAR* THE IMPENDING STRATEGIC
DEADLOCK. USA+45 USSR TEC/DEV BUDGET RISK ARMS/CONT
NUC/PWR WEAPON COST BIO/SOC...GEOG IDEA/COMP
NAT/COMP GAME NATO WARSAW/P. PAGE 9 G0177
FORCES
OP/RES
WAR
GEN/LAWS

B64
DUSCHA J.,ARMS, MONEY, AND POLITICS. USA+45 INDUS
POL/PAR ECO/TAC TAX DETER NUC/PWR WAR WEAPON
GOV/REL ATTIT...BIBLIOG/A 20 CONGRESS MONEY
DEPT/DEFEN. PAGE 17 G0326
NAT/G
FORCES
POLICY
BUDGET

B64
SCHOECK H.,CENTRAL PLANNING AND NEOMERCANTILISM.
L/A+17C UK WOR+45 BUDGET ECO/TAC PRICE CONTROL
GOV/REL UTOPIA 20. PAGE 49 G0974
PLAN
CENTRAL
NAT/G
POLICY

B64
SCHWARTZ M.D.,CONFERENCE ON SPACE SCIENCE AND SPACE
LAW. FUT COM/IND NAT/G FORCES ACT/RES PLAN BUDGET
DIPLOM NUC/PWR WEAPON...POLICY ANTHOL 20. PAGE 50
G0983
SPACE
LAW
PEACE
TEC/DEV

N64
NATIONAL ACADEMY OF SCIENCES,CIVIL DEFENSE: PROJECT
HARBOR SUMMARY REPORT (PAMPHLET). USA+45 MUNIC
NAT/G ACT/RES BUDGET EDU/PROP DETER WEAPON EATING
...GEOG 20. PAGE 41 G0808
NUC/PWR
FORCES
WAR
PLAN

B65
FRUTKIN A.W.,SPACE AND THE INTERNATIONAL
COOPERATION YEAR: A NATIONAL CHALLENGE (PAMPHLET).
EUR+WWI USA+45 FINAN TEC/DEV BUDGET...MGT 20 NASA.
PAGE 20 G0396
SPACE
INDUS
NAT/G
DIPLOM

B65
HITCH C.J.,DECISION-MAKING FOR DEFENSE. USA+45
CREATE BUDGET COERCE WAR WEAPON EFFICIENCY...SIMUL
20. PAGE 26 G0515
DECISION
OP/RES
PLAN
FORCES

B65
KNORR K.,SCIENCE AND DEFENSE: SOME CRITICAL
THOUGHTS ON MILITARY RESEARCH AND DEVELOPMENT.
USA+45 ACT/RES CREATE BUDGET ECO/TAC DEMAND
DECISION. PAGE 31 G0608
CIVMIL/REL
R+D
FORCES
PLAN

B65
MELMANS S.,OUR DEPLETED SOCIETY. SPACE USA+45
ECO/DEV FORCES BUDGET ECO/TAC ADMIN WEAPON
EFFICIENCY 20 COLD/WAR. PAGE 38 G0753
CIVMIL/REL
INDUS
EDU/PROP
CONTROL

B65
NATIONAL ACADEMY OF SCIENCES,BASIC RESEARCH AND
NATIONAL GOALS. R+D ACADEM DELIB/GP PLAN EDU/PROP
...POLICY HEAL PHIL/SCI PSY SOC ANTHOL 20 CONGRESS
HOUSE/REP HS/SCIASTR. PAGE 41 G0809
LEGIS
BUDGET
NAT/G
CREATE

B65
US CONGRESS JT ATOM ENRGY COMM,ATOMIC ENERGY
LEGISLATION THROUGH 89TH CONGRESS, 1ST SESSION.
USA+45 LAW INT/ORG DELIB/GP BUDGET DIPLOM 20 AEC
CONGRESS CASEBOOK EURATOM IAEA. PAGE 57 G1114
NUC/PWR
FORCES
PEACE
LEGIS

B65
US SENATE COMM AERO SPACE SCI,NATIONAL SPACE GOALS
FOR THE POST-APOLLO PERIOD. USA+45 CONSULT DELIB/GP
TEC/DEV BUDGET GP/REL ATTIT...CHARTS IDEA/COMP TIME
20 DEPT/DEFEN NASA CONGRESS. PAGE 59 G1166
SPACE
FUT
R+D
LEGIS

B65
WARNER A.W.,THE IMPACT OF SCIENCE ON TECHNOLOGY.
UNIV INTELL SOCIETY NAT/G ACT/RES PLAN PROB/SOLV
BUDGET OPTIMAL GEN/METH. PAGE 62 G1214
DECISION
TEC/DEV
CREATE
POLICY

S65
FOX A.B.,"NATO AND CONGRESS." CONSTN DELIB/GP
EX/STRUC FORCES TOP/EX BUDGET NUC/PWR GOV/REL
...GP/COMP CONGRESS NATO TREATY. PAGE 20 G0388
CONTROL
DIPLOM

B66
LECHT L.,GOAL, PRIORITIES, AND DOLLARS: THE NEXT
DECADE. SPACE USA+45 SOCIETY AGRI BUDGET FOR/AID
...HEAL SOC/WK STAT CHARTS 20 URBAN/RNWL PUB/TRANS.
PAGE 33 G0649
IDEA/COMP
POLICY
CONSEN
PLAN

B66
NATIONAL SCIENCE FOUNDATION,SIXTEENTH ANNUAL REPORT
FOR THE FISCAL YEAR ENDED JUNE 30, 1966. USA+45
CREATE BUDGET SKILL 20 NSF. PAGE 41 G0813
NAT/G
EDU/PROP
ACADEM
KNOWL

B66
NIEBURG H.L.,IN THE NAME OF SCIENCE. USA+45
EX/STRUC LEGIS TEC/DEV BUDGET PAY AUTOMAT LOBBY PWR
...OBS 20. PAGE 42 G0822
NAT/G
INDUS
TECHRACY

B66
SANFORD T.,BUT WHAT ABOUT THE PEOPLE? ACADEM SCHOOL
BUDGET TAX CONTROL SKILL WEALTH 20 NORTH/CAR.
PAGE 49 G0956
EDU/PROP
PROB/SOLV
POLICY
PROVS

B66
US PRES COMM ECO IMPACT DEFENS,REPORT* JULY 1965.
USA+45 ECO/DEV INDUS DELIB/GP FORCES OP/RES
ARMS/CONT NUC/PWR WEAPON BAL/PAY...PREDICT SIMUL.
PAGE 59 G1159
ACT/RES
STAT
WAR
BUDGET

S66
GREENBERG D.S.,"THE SCIENTIFIC PORK BARREL." USA+45
ECO/DEV PUB/INST CHIEF LEGIS BUDGET GIVE GP/REL PWR
WEALTH 20. PAGE 23 G0445
R+D
NAT/G
ACADEM
ATTIT

N66
US HOUSE COMM SCI ASTRONAUT,GOVERNMENT, SCIENCE,
AND PUBLIC POLICY (PAMPHLET). R+D ACADEM DELIB/GP
COMPUTER BUDGET CONFER ADMIN...PHIL/SCI PREDICT
TREND 20 CONGRESS HS/SCIASTR. PAGE 58 G1143
NAT/G
POLICY
TEC/DEV
CREATE

B67
COLEMAN J.R.,THE CHANGING AMERICAN ECONOMY. USA+45
AGRI FINAN LABOR FOR/AID INT/TRADE AUTOMAT GP/REL
INGP/REL ANTHOL. PAGE 13 G0243
BUDGET
ECO/TAC
ECO/DEV
WEALTH

B67
ENKE S.,DEFENSE MANAGEMENT. USA+45 R+D FORCES
WORKER PLAN ECO/TAC ADMIN NUC/PWR BAL/PAY UTIL
WEALTH...MGT DEPT/DEFEN. PAGE 18 G0348
DECISION
DELIB/GP
EFFICIENCY
BUDGET

B67
US SENATE COMM AERO SPACE SCI,APOLLO ACCIDENT
PROB/SOLV

(PARTS 1-7). USA+45 DELIB/GP LEGIS...INT CHARTS SPACE
NASA. PAGE 60 G1173 BUDGET
GOV/REL

S67
DADDARIO E.Q.,"CONGRESS FACES SPACE POLICIES." R+D SPACE
NAT/G FORCES CREATE LEAD...DECISION CONGRESS NASA. PLAN
PAGE 14 G0269 BUDGET
POLICY

S67
DONAHO J.A.,"PLANNING-PROGRAMMING-BUDGETING PLAN
SYSTEMS." USA+45 LOC/G NAT/G ROUTINE. PAGE 16 G0305 BUDGET
ADMIN
ECOMETRIC

S67
HARRIS F.R.,"POLITICAL SCIENCE AND THE PROPOSAL FOR PROF/ORG
A NATIONAL SOCIAL SCIENCE FOUNDATION." FUT CONSULT R+D
DELIB/GP PLAN PROB/SOLV BUDGET CONFER SANCTION CREATE
CRIME...POLICY SOC/WK 20 NSF NSSF. PAGE 25 G0484 NAT/G

S67
KAYSEN C.,"DATA BANKS AND DOSSIERS." FUT USA+45 CENTRAL
COM/IND NAT/G PLAN PROB/SOLV TEC/DEV BUDGET ADMIN EFFICIENCY
ROUTINE. PAGE 30 G0588 CENSUS
ACT/RES

S67
LEWIS R.L.,"GOAL AND NO GOAL* A NEW POLICY IN SPACE
SPACE." R+D BUDGET COST...POLICY DECISION PHIL/SCI. PLAN
PAGE 34 G0662 EFFICIENCY
CREATE

S67
MACDONALD G.J.F.,"SCIENCE AND SPACE POLICY* HOW SPACE
DOES IT GET PLANNED?" R+D CREATE TEC/DEV BUDGET PLAN
ADMIN ROUTINE...DECISION NASA. PAGE 35 G0687 MGT
EX/STRUC

N67
US CONGRESS JT COMM ECO GOVT,BACKGROUND MATERIAL ON BUDGET
ECONOMY IN GOVERNMENT 1967 (PAMPHLET). WOR+45 COST
ECO/DEV BARGAIN PRICE DEMAND OPTIMAL...STAT MGT
DEPT/DEFEN. PAGE 57 G1116 NAT/G

N67
US HOUSE COMM APPROPRIATIONS,PUBLIC WORKS AND BUDGET
ATOMIC ENERGY COMMISSION APPROPRIATION BILL, 1968 NUC/PWR
(PAMPHLET). USA+45 ECO/DEV NAT/G...GEOG DEEP/INT PROVS
CHARTS HOUSE/REP AEC DEPT/DEFEN TVA. PAGE 58 G1137 PLAN

N67
US HOUSE COMM SCI ASTRONAUT,AUTHORIZING SPACE
APPROPRIATIONS TO THE NATIONAL AERONAUTICS AND R+D
SPACE ADMINISTRATION (PAMPHLET). USA+45 NAT/G PHIL/SCI
OP/RES TEC/DEV BUDGET NASA HOUSE/REP. PAGE 58 G1149 NUC/PWR

BUENOS/AIR....BUENOS AIRES, ARGENTINA

BUGANDA....BUGANDA, UGANDA

BUKHARIN/N....NIKOLAI BUKHARIN

BULGARIA....BULGARIA; SEE ALSO COM

S63
DELLIN L.A.D.,"BULGARIA UNDER SOVIET LEADERSHIP." AGRI
BULGARIA COM USA+45 USSR ECO/DEV INDUS POL/PAR NAT/G
EX/STRUC TOP/EX COERCE ATTIT RIGID/FLEX...POLICY TOTALISM
TIME/SEQ 20. PAGE 15 G0293

B66
SPULBER N.,THE STATE AND ECONOMIC DEVELOPMENT IN ECO/DEV
EASTERN EUROPE. BULGARIA COM CZECHOSLVK HUNGARY ECO/UNDEV
POLAND YUGOSLAVIA CULTURE PLAN CAP/ISM INT/TRADE NAT/G
CONTROL...POLICY CHARTS METH/COMP BIBLIOG/A 19/20. TOTALISM
PAGE 52 G1028

B67
NATIONAL SCIENCE FOUNDATION,DIRECTORY OF SELECTED INDEX
RESEARCH INSTITUTES IN EASTERN EUROPE. BULGARIA R+D
CZECHOSLVK HUNGARY POLAND ROMANIA INTELL ACADEM COM
NAT/G ACT/RES 20. PAGE 41 G0814 PHIL/SCI

BULLITT/WC....WILLIAM C. BULLITT

BULMER-THOMAS I. G0185

BUNCHE/R....RALPH BUNCHE

BUNDY M. G0186

BUNDY/M....MCGEORGE BUNDY

B62
US SENATE COMM GOVT OPERATIONS,ADMINISTRATION OF ORD/FREE
NATIONAL SECURITY. USA+45 CHIEF PLAN PROB/SOLV ADMIN
TEC/DEV DIPLOM ATTIT...POLICY DECISION 20 NAT/G
KENNEDY/JF RUSK/D MCNAMARA/R BUNDY/M HERTER/C. CONTROL
PAGE 60 G1177

BUNGE M. G0187,G0188

BUR/BUDGET....BUREAU OF THE BUDGET

N19
DOTSON A.,PRODUCTION PLANNING IN THE PATENT OFFICE EFFICIENCY
(PAMPHLET). USA+45 DIST/IND PROB/SOLV PRODUC...MGT PLAN
PHIL/SCI 20 BUR/BUDGET PATENT/OFF. PAGE 16 G0309 NAT/G
ADMIN

BUR/STNDRD....BUREAU OF STANDARDS

N19
LAWRENCE S.A.,THE BATTERY ADDITIVE CONTROVERSY PHIL/SCI
(PAMPHLET). USA+45 LAW MARKET PROC/MFG R+D CAP/ISM LOBBY
CT/SYS GOV/REL OWN FTC CONGRESS BUR/STNDRD INSPECT
RITCHIE/JM. PAGE 33 G0645

BURAGR/ECO....BUREAU OF AGRICULTURAL ECONOMICS

BUREAU OF AGRICULTURAL ECONOMICS....SEE BURAGR/ECO

BUREAU OF STANDARDS....SEE BUR/STNDRD

BUREAU OF THE BUDGET....SEE BUR/BUDGET

BUREAUCRCY....BUREAUCRACY; SEE ALSO ADMIN

S47
TURNER R.H.,"THE NAVY DISBURSING OFFICER AS A FORCES
BUREAUCRAT" (BMR)" USA-45 LAW STRATA DIST/IND WAR ADMIN
PWR...SOC 20 BUREAUCRCY. PAGE 55 G1083 PERSON
ROLE

B54
WASHBURNE N.F.,INTERPRETING SOCIAL CHANGE IN CULTURE
AMERICA. USA+45 STRATA FAM NAT/G SECT OP/RES STRUCT
ECO/TAC EDU/PROP HABITAT...SOC TIME/SEQ TREND 20 CREATE
BUREAUCRCY. PAGE 62 G1217 TEC/DEV

B57
MERTON R.K.,SOCIAL THEORY AND SOCIAL STRUCTURE SOC
(REV. ED.). INTELL SECT WORKER OP/RES EDU/PROP GEN/LAWS
ADMIN INGP/REL ANOMIE PERSON...AUD/VIS T 20 SOCIETY
BUREAUCRCY. PAGE 38 G0759 STRUCT

L61
THOMPSON V.A.,"HIERARACHY, SPECIALIZATION, AND PERS/REL
ORGANIZATIONAL CONFLICT" (BMR)" WOR+45 STRATA PROB/SOLV
STRUCT WORKER TEC/DEV GP/REL INGP/REL ATTIT ADMIN
AUTHORIT 20 BUREAUCRCY. PAGE 54 G1069 EX/STRUC

BURKE A.E. G0189

BURKE/EDM....EDMUND BURKE

BURMA....BURMA

BURNS A.L. G0190,G0191,G0192,G0503,G0576

BURNS E.L.M. G0193

BURR/AARON....AARON BURR

BURSK E.C. G0194

BURTON R.H. G0182

BURUNDI....SEE ALSO AFR

BUSH V. G0195,G0196

BUSINESS CYCLE....SEE FINAN

BUSINESS MANAGEMENT....SEE MGT

BUTLER J. G0197

BUTOW R.J.C. G0198

BYRNES F.C. G0199

BYZANTINE....BYZANTINE EMPIRE

─────────────────── C ───────────────────
CAB....CIVIL AERONAUTICS BOARD

B65
THAYER F.C. JR.,AIR TRANSPORT POLICY AND NATIONAL AIR
SECURITY: A POLITICAL, ECONOMIC, AND MILITARY FORCES

ANALYSIS. DIST/IND OP/RES PLAN TEC/DEV DIPLOM DETER CIVMIL/REL
WAR COST EFFICIENCY...POLICY BIBLIOG 20 DEPT/DEFEN ORD/FREE
FAA CAB. PAGE 54 G1066

B66
WHITNAH D.R.,SAFER SKYWAYS. DIST/IND DELIB/GP ADMIN
FORCES TOP/EX WORKER TEC/DEV ROUTINE WAR CIVMIL/REL NAT/G
COST...TIME/SEQ 20 FAA CAB. PAGE 63 G1235 AIR
GOV/REL

CABINET....SEE ALSO EX/STRUC, DELIB/GP, CONSULT

CAESAR/JUL....JULIUS CAESAR

CAIRO....CAIRO, EGYPT

CALCUTTA....CALCUTTA, INDIA

CALDER R. G0200

CALDWELL L.K. G0201,G0202,G0203

CALHOUN/JC....JOHN C. CALHOUN

CALIFORNIA....CALIFORNIA

N19
BELL J.R.,PERSONNEL PROBLEMS IN CONVERTING TO WORKER
AUTOMATION (PAMPHLET). USA+45 COMPUTER PLAN AUTOMAT
...METH/CNCPT 20 CALIFORNIA. PAGE 6 G0115 PROB/SOLV
PROVS

B59
CLEAVELAND F.N.,SCIENCE AND STATE GOVERNMENT. AGRI TEC/DEV
EXTR/IND FINAN INDUS PROVS...METH/CNCPT STAT CHARTS PHIL/SCI
20 NEW/YORK CONNECTICT WISCONSIN CALIFORNIA GOV/REL
NEW/MEXICO. PAGE 12 G0233 METH/COMP

B65
ARTHUR D LITTLE INC,SAN FRANCISCO COMMUNITY RENEWAL HABITAT
PROGRAM. USA+45 FINAN PROVS ADMIN INCOME...CHARTS MUNIC
20 CALIFORNIA SAN/FRAN URBAN/RNWL. PAGE 4 G0071 PLAN
PROB/SOLV

CALKINS R.D. G0204

CALLOT E. G0205

CALVIN/J....JOHN CALVIN

CAMB/SOMER....CAMBRIDGE-SOMERVILLE YOUTH STUDY

CAMBODIA....SEE ALSO S/ASIA

CAMBRIDGE-SOMERVILLE YOUTH STUDY....SEE CAMB/SOMER

CAMELOT....PROJECT CAMELOT (CHILE)

S65
HUGHES T.L.,"SCHOLARS AND FOREIGN POLICY* VARIETIES ACT/RES
OF RESEARCH EXPERIENCE." COM/IND DIPLOM ADMIN EXEC ACADEM
ROUTINE...MGT OBS CONGRESS PRESIDENT CAMELOT. CONTROL
PAGE 27 G0535 NAT/G

S65
SILVERT K.H.,"AMERICAN ACADEMIC ETHICS AND SOCIAL ACADEM
RESEARCH ABROAD* THE LESSON OF PROJECT CAMELOT." NAT/G
CHILE L/A+17C USA+45 FINAN ADMIN...PHIL/SCI SOC ACT/RES
GEN/LAWS CAMELOT. PAGE 51 G0998 POLICY

CAMEROON....SEE ALSO AFR

CAMPBELL A.K. G0146

CANAD/CRWN....CANADIAN CROWN CORPORATIONS

CANADA....SEE ALSO COMMONWLTH

B42
FULLER G.H.,DEFENSE FINANCING: A SUPPLEMENTARY LIST BIBLIOG/A
OF REFERENCES (PAMPHLET). CANADA UK USA-45 ECO/DEV FINAN
NAT/G DELIB/GP BUDGET ADJUD ARMS/CONT WEAPON COST FORCES
PEACE PWR 20 AUSTRAL CHINJAP CONGRESS. PAGE 21 DIPLOM
G0403

S60
TAYLOR M.G.,"THE ROLE OF THE MEDICAL PROFESSION IN PROF/ORG
THE FORMULATION AND EXECUTION OF PUBLIC POLICY" HEALTH
(BMR)" CANADA NAT/G CONSULT ADMIN REPRESENT GP/REL LOBBY
ROLE SOVEREIGN...DECISION 20 CMA. PAGE 54 G1058 POLICY

B67
MCLAUGHLIN M.R.,RELIGIOUS EDUCATION AND THE STATE: SECT
DEMOCRACY FINDS A WAY. CANADA EUR+WWI GP/REL NAT/G
POPULISM...CATH NAT/COMP 20 AUSTRAL. PAGE 38 G0745 EDU/PROP
POLICY

B67
PIPER D.C.,THE INTERNATIONAL LAW OF THE GREAT CONCPT
LAKES. CANADA EXTR/IND MUNIC LICENSE ARMS/CONT DIPLOM
CRIME...GEOG 19/20. PAGE 45 G0879 INT/LAW

CANADIAN CROWN CORPORATIONS....SEE CANAD/CRWN

CANADIAN MEDICAL ASSOCIATION....SEE CMA

CANAL/ZONE....CANAL ZONE

CANNON/JG....JOSEPH G. CANNON

CANON/LAW....CANON LAW

CANTRIL H. G0206

CANTRIL/H....HADLEY CANTRIL

CAP/ISM....CAPITALISM

N19
LAWRENCE S.A.,THE BATTERY ADDITIVE CONTROVERSY PHIL/SCI
(PAMPHLET). USA+45 LAW MARKET PROC/MFG R+D CAP/ISM LOBBY
CT/SYS GOV/REL OWN FTC CONGRESS BUR/STNDRD INSPECT
RITCHIE/JM. PAGE 33 G0645

B43
LASKI H.J.,REFLECTIONS ON THE REVOLUTIONS OF OUR CAP/ISM
TIME. COM USSR NAT/G WORKER UTOPIA ORD/FREE WEALTH WELF/ST
MARXISM SOCISM 19/20. PAGE 32 G0637 ECO/TAC
POLICY

B50
MANNHEIM K.,FREEDOM, POWER, AND DEMOCRATIC TEC/DEV
PLANNING. FUT USSR WOR+45 ELITES INTELL SOCIETY PLAN
NAT/G EDU/PROP ROUTINE ATTIT DRIVE SUPEGO SKILL CAP/ISM
...POLICY PSY CONCPT TREND GEN/LAWS 20. PAGE 35 UK
G0700

B54
MOSK S.A.,INDUSTRIAL REVOLUTION IN MEXICO. MARKET INDUS
LABOR CREATE CAP/ISM ADMIN ATTIT SOCISM...POLICY 20 TEC/DEV
MEXIC/AMER. PAGE 40 G0789 ECO/UNDEV
NAT/G

C55
BONER H.A.,"HUNGRY GENERATIONS." UK WOR+45 WOR-45 ECO/DEV
STRATA INDUS FAM LABOR CAP/ISM...MGT BIBLIOG 19/20. PHIL/SCI
PAGE 8 G0151 CONCPT
WEALTH

B58
DUBIN R.,THE WORLD OF WORK: INDUSTRIAL SOCIETY AND WORKER
HUMAN RELATIONS. MARKET PROC/MFG LABOR TEC/DEV ECO/TAC
CAP/ISM AUTOMAT TASK GP/REL EFFICIENCY...CONCPT PRODUC
CHARTS BIBLIOG 20. PAGE 16 G0317 DRIVE

B59
VERNEY D.V.,PUBLIC ENTERPRISE IN SWEDEN. FUT SWEDEN ECO/DEV
UK INDUS POL/PAR LEGIS PROB/SOLV CAP/ISM INT/TRADE POLICY
CONTROL SOCISM...MGT CONCPT NAT/COMP 20 SOCDEM/PAR LG/CO
CIVIL/SERV. PAGE 61 G1196 NAT/G

B60
APTHEKER H.,DISARMAMENT AND THE AMERICAN ECONOMY: A MARXIST
SYMPOSIUM. FUT USA+45 ECO/DEV DIST/IND FINAN INDUS ARMS/CONT
PROC/MFG LABOR NAT/G POL/PAR CONSULT PLAN CAP/ISM
INT/TRADE PEACE ATTIT MORAL WEALTH...TREND GEN/LAWS
TOT/POP 20. PAGE 3 G0063

B60
EINSTEIN A.,EINSTEIN ON PEACE. FUT WOR+45 WOR-45 INT/ORG
SOCIETY NAT/G PLAN BAL/PWR CAP/ISM DIPLOM ARMS/CONT ATTIT
DETER NAT/LISM...POLICY RELATIV HUM PHIL/SCI CONCPT NUC/PWR
BIOG COLD/WAR LEAGUE/NAT NAZI. PAGE 17 G0338 PEACE

B60
HEILBRONER R.L.,THE FUTURE AS HISTORY. USA+45 TEC/DEV
WOR+45 WOR-45 SOCIETY ECO/DEV ECO/UNDEV VOL/ASSN TREND
PLAN CAP/ISM NUC/PWR CHOOSE NAT/LISM ATTIT ORD/FREE
RESPECT WEALTH SOCISM 20. PAGE 25 G0501

B60
SILK L.S.,THE RESEARCH REVOLUTION. USA+45 FINAN ECO/DEV
CAP/ISM ECO/TAC PRICE EQUILIB PRODUC...STAT TREND R+D
CHARTS. PAGE 51 G0997 TEC/DEV
PROB/SOLV

L60
MACPHERSON C.,"TECHNICAL CHANGE AND POLITICAL TEC/DEV
DECISION." WOR+45 NAT/G CREATE CAP/ISM DIPLOM ADMIN
ROUTINE RIGID/FLEX...CONCPT OBS GEN/METH 20.
PAGE 35 G0692

B61
BONNEFOUS M.,EUROPE ET TIERS MONDE. EUR+WWI SOCIETY AFR
INT/ORG NAT/G VOL/ASSN ACT/RES TEC/DEV CAP/ISM   ECO/UNDEV
ECO/TAC ATTIT ORD/FREE SOVEREIGN...POLICY CONCPT   FOR/AID
TREND 20. PAGE 8 G0153   INT/TRADE

B62
GRANICK D.,THE EUROPEAN EXECUTIVE. BELGIUM FRANCE   MGT
GERMANY/W UK INDUS LABOR LG/CO SML/CO EX/STRUC PLAN   ECO/DEV
TEC/DEV CAP/ISM COST DEMAND...POLICY CHARTS 20.   ECO/TAC
PAGE 22 G0441   EXEC

S63
WILES P.J.D.,"WILL CAPITALISM AND COMMUNISM   PLAN
SPONTANEOUSLY CONVERGE." COM FUT USA+45 ECO/DEV   TEC/DEV
DIST/IND MARKET CAP/ISM ECO/TAC RIGID/FLEX WEALTH   USSR
MARXISM SOCISM...MATH STAT TREND COMPUT/IR 20.
PAGE 63 G1240

B64
BAUCHET P.,ECONOMIC PLANNING. FRANCE STRATA LG/CO   ECO/DEV
CAP/ISM ADMIN PARL/PROC DEMAND OPTIMAL ATTIT PWR   NAT/G
SOCISM...POLICY CHARTS 20. PAGE 5 G0102   PLAN
                                                      ECO/TAC

B64
GUTMANN P.M.,ECONOMIC GROWTH: AN AMERICAN PROBLEM.   WEALTH
USA+45 FINAN R+D...POLICY NAT/COMP ANTHOL BIBLIOG   ECO/DEV
20. PAGE 24 G0463   CAP/ISM
                                                      ORD/FREE

B64
MANSFIELD E.,MONOPOLY POWER AND ECONOMIC   LG/CO
PERFORMANCE: AN INTRODUCTION TO A CURRENT ISSUE OF   PWR
PUBLIC POLICY. ECO/DEV INDUS NAT/G PLAN CAP/ISM   ECO/TAC
PRICE CONTROL LOBBY EFFICIENCY PRODUC...POLICY 20   MARKET
CONGRESS KENNEDY/JF MONOPOLY. PAGE 36 G0701

B64
MARRIS R.,THE ECONOMIC THEORY OF "MANAGERIAL"   CAP/ISM
CAPITALISM. USA+45 ECO/DEV LG/CO ECO/TAC DEMAND   MGT
...CHARTS BIBLIOG 20. PAGE 36 G0709   CONTROL
                                                      OP/RES

B64
MILIBAND R.,THE SOCIALIST REGISTER: 1964. GERMANY/W   MARXISM
ITALY UK LABOR POL/PAR ECO/TAC FOR/AID NUC/PWR   SOCISM
...POLICY SOCIALIST IDEA/COMP 20 MAO NASSER/G.   CAP/ISM
PAGE 39 G0769   PROB/SOLV

B65
ALTSHULER A.,A LAND-USE PLAN FOR ST. PAUL   MUNIC
(PAMPHLET). USA+45 CREATE CAP/ISM RIGID/FLEX ROLE   PLAN
...NEW/IDEA 20 ST/PAUL. PAGE 3 G0047   ECO/DEV
                                                      GEOG

B65
MORRIS M.D.,THE EMERGENCE OF AN INDUSTRIAL LABOR   INDUS
FORCE IN INDIA: A STUDY OF THE BOMBAY COTTON MILLS,   LABOR
1854-1947. INDIA WORKER OP/RES ADMIN 19/20. PAGE 40   ECO/UNDEV
G0784   CAP/ISM

B65
PHELPS E.S.,PRIVATE WANTS AND PUBLIC NEEDS - AN   NAT/G
INTRODUCTION TO A CURRENT ISSUE OF PUBLIC POLICY   POLICY
(REV. ED.). USA+45 PLAN CAP/ISM INGP/REL ROLE   DEMAND
...DECISION TIME/SEQ 20. PAGE 44 G0873

B65
STEINER G.A.,THE CREATIVE ORGANIZATION. ELITES   CREATE
LG/CO PLAN PROB/SOLV TEC/DEV INSPECT CAP/ISM   MGT
CONTROL EXEC PERSON...METH/COMP HYPO/EXP 20.   ADMIN
PAGE 52 G1034   SOC

B65
WISH J.R.,ECONOMIC DEVELOPMENT IN LATIN AMERICA: AN   BIBLIOG/A
ANNOTATED BIBLIOGRAPHY. L/A+17C COM/IND MARKET R+D   ECO/UNDEV
CREATE CAP/ISM ATTIT...STAT METH 20. PAGE 64 G1250   TEC/DEV
                                                      AGRI

B66
GRUNEWALD D.,PUBLIC POLICY AND THE MODERN   LG/CO
COOPERATION: SELECTED READINGS. USA+45 LAW MARKET   POLICY
VOL/ASSN CAP/ISM INT/TRADE CENTRAL OWN...SOC ANTHOL   NAT/G
20. PAGE 23 G0458   CONTROL

B66
SPULBER N.,THE STATE AND ECONOMIC DEVELOPMENT IN   ECO/DEV
EASTERN EUROPE. BULGARIA COM CZECHOSLVK HUNGARY   ECO/UNDEV
POLAND YUGOSLAVIA CULTURE PLAN CAP/ISM INT/TRADE   NAT/G
CONTROL...POLICY CHARTS METH/COMP BIBLIOG/A 19/20.   TOTALISM
PAGE 52 G1028

B66
WARD B.,NATIONALISM AND IDEOLOGY. ECO/UNDEV KIN   IDEA/COMP
CREATE CAP/ISM FOR/AID ALL/VALS MARXISM...POLICY   NAT/LISM

SOC. PAGE 62 G1211   ATTIT

B67
BAUMOL W.J.,BUSINESS BEHAVIOR, VALUE AND GROWTH   ALL/IDEOS
(REV. ED.). WOR+45 FINAN LG/CO TEC/DEV CAP/ISM   PHIL/SCI
DEMAND EQUILIB...METH/COMP SIMUL 20. PAGE 5 G0105   PLAN
                                                      ECO/DEV

B67
DICKSON P.G.M.,THE FINANCIAL REVOLUTION IN ENGLAND.   ECO/DEV
UK NAT/G TEC/DEV ADMIN GOV/REL...SOC METH/CNCPT   FINAN
CHARTS GP/COMP BIBLIOG 17/18. PAGE 15 G0302   CAP/ISM
                                                      MGT

B67
EISENMENGER R.W.,THE DYNAMICS OF GROWTH IN NEW   ECO/DEV
ENGLAND'S ECONOMY, 1870-1964. USA+45 USA-45 ECO/TAC AGRI
TAX PAY AUTOMAT GOV/REL ADJUST HABITAT...STAT   INDUS
19/20. PAGE 17 G0340   CAP/ISM

B67
GROSSMAN G.,ECONOMIC SYSTEMS. USA+45 USA-45 USSR   ECO/DEV
YUGOSLAVIA WORKER CAP/ISM PRICE GP/REL EQUILIB   PLAN
WEALTH MARXISM SOCISM...MGT METH/COMP 19/20.   TEC/DEV
PAGE 23 G0456   DEMAND

B67
HEILBRONER R.L.,THE LIMITS OF AMERICAN CAPITALISM.   ELITES
FUT ECO/DEV INDUS LG/CO EX/STRUC LEAD PWR TECHRACY   CREATE
20. PAGE 25 G0502   TEC/DEV
                                                      CAP/ISM

B67
WOODRUFF W.,IMPACT OF WESTERN MAN. ECO/DEV INDUS   EUR+WWI
CREATE PLAN PROB/SOLV COLONIAL GOV/REL...CHARTS   MOD/EUR
GOV/COMP BIBLIOG 18/20. PAGE 64 G1256   CAP/ISM

S67
ENKE S.,"GOVERNMENT-INDUSTRY DEVELOPMENT OF A   INDUS
COMMERCIAL SUPERSONIC TRANSPORT." USA+45 ECO/DEV   FINAN
R+D LG/CO NAT/G TEC/DEV PRICE RISK COST PROFIT.   SERV/IND
PAGE 18 G0347   CAP/ISM

S67
FADDEYEV N.,"CMEA CO-OPERATION OF EQUAL NATIONS."   MARXISM
COM R+D PLAN CAP/ISM DIPLOM FOR/AID WEALTH...POLICY   ECO/TAC
MARXIST. PAGE 18 G0356   INT/ORG
                                                      ECO/UNDEV

S67
MOOR E.J.,"THE INTERNATIONAL IMPACT OF AUTOMATION."   TEC/DEV
WOR+45 ACT/RES COMPUTER CREATE PLAN CAP/ISM ROUTINE   OP/RES
EFFICIENCY PREDICT. PAGE 39 G0779   AUTOMAT
                                                      INDUS

S67
RICH G.S.,"THE PROPOSED PATENT LEGISLATION* SOME   LICENSE
COMMENTS." USA+45 LAW R+D ACT/RES TEC/DEV CONFER   POLICY
EFFICIENCY OWN JURID. PAGE 46 G0916   CREATE
                                                      CAP/ISM

S67
SCOVILLE W.J.,"GOVERNMENT REGULATION AND GROWTH IN   NAT/G
THE FRENCH PAPER INDUSTRY DURING THE EIGHTEENTH   PROC/MFG
CENTURY." FRANCE MOD/EUR FINAN CAP/ISM TAX ADMIN   ECO/DEV
CONTROL PRIVIL LAISSEZ...POLICY 18. PAGE 50 G0985   INGP/REL

CARRANZA/V....VENUSTIANZO CARRANZA

CARROLL K.J. G0215

CARSON R. G0216

CARY G.D. G0217

CASE STUDIES....CARRIED UNDER THE SPECIAL TECHNIQUES USED,
   OR TOPICS COVERED

CASEBOOK....CASEBOOK, SUCH AS LEGAL OR SOCIOLOGICAL CASEBOOK

	B62
BOCK E.A.,CASE STUDIES IN AMERICAN GOVERNMENT.	POLICY
USA+45 ECO/DEV CHIEF EDU/PROP CT/SYS RACE/REL	LEGIS
ORD/FREE...JURID MGT PHIL/SCI PRESIDENT CASEBOOK.	IDEA/COMP
PAGE 8 G0146	NAT/G

	B65
US CONGRESS JT ATOM ENRGY COMM,ATOMIC ENERGY	NUC/PWR
LEGISLATION THROUGH 89TH CONGRESS, 1ST SESSION.	FORCES
USA+45 LAW INT/ORG DELIB/GP BUDGET DIPLOM 20 AEC	PEACE
CONGRESS CASEBOOK EURATOM IAEA. PAGE 57 G1114	LEGIS

CASTAGNO A.A. G0197

CASTE....SEE INDIA + STRATA, HINDU

CASTRO/F....FIDEL CASTRO

	B63
PACHTER H.M.,COLLISION COURSE; THE CUBAN MISSILE	WAR
CRISIS AND COEXISTENCE. CUBA USA+45 DIPLOM	BAL/PWR
ARMS/CONT PEACE MARXISM...DECISION INT/LAW 20	NUC/PWR
COLD/WAR KHRUSH/N KENNEDY/JF CASTRO/F. PAGE 43	DETER
G0854	

CATH....ROMAN CATHOLIC

	B61
STEIN W.,NUCLEAR WEAPONS: A CATHOLIC RESPONSE.	NUC/PWR
WOR+45 FORCES ARMS/CONT DETER MURDER MORAL...POLICY	WAR
CATH IDEA/COMP ANTHOL 20. PAGE 52 G1033	CATHISM
	ATTIT

	B67
MCLAUGHLIN M.R.,RELIGIOUS EDUCATION AND THE STATE:	SECT
DEMOCRACY FINDS A WAY. CANADA EUR+WWI GP/REL	NAT/G
POPULISM...CATH NAT/COMP 20 AUSTRAL. PAGE 38 G0745	EDU/PROP
	POLICY

CATHISM....ROMAN CATHOLICISM

	B61
STEIN W.,NUCLEAR WEAPONS: A CATHOLIC RESPONSE.	NUC/PWR
WOR+45 FORCES ARMS/CONT DETER MURDER MORAL...POLICY	WAR
CATH IDEA/COMP ANTHOL 20. PAGE 52 G1033	CATHISM
	ATTIT

	L66
DOUGHERTY J.E.,"THE CATHOLIC CHURCH, WAR AND	CATHISM
NUCLEAR WEAPONS." COM EUR+WWI SECT TOP/EX LEAD	MORAL
DETER ALL/VALS. PAGE 16 G0312	WAR
	NUC/PWR

	S67
STYCOS J.M.,"POLITICS AND POPULATION CONTROL IN	PLAN
LATIN AMERICA." USA+45 FAM NAT/G GP/REL AGE/C ATTIT	CENSUS
CATHISM MARXISM...POLICY UN WHO. PAGE 53 G1045	CONTROL
	L/A+17C

'CATHOLICISM....SEE CATH, CATHISM

CAUCUS....SEE PARL/PROC

CAVERS D.F. G0218

CED....COMMITTEE FOR ECONOMIC DEVELOPMENT

CENSORSHIP....SEE EDU/PROP

CENSUS....POPULATION ENUMERATION

	B50
CANTRIL H.,TENSIONS THAT CAUSE WAR. UNIV CULTURE	SOCIETY
R+D CREATE EDU/PROP DRIVE PERSON KNOWL ORD/FREE	PHIL/SCI
...HUM PSY SOC OBS CENSUS TREND CON/ANAL SOC/EXP	PEACE
SIMUL GEN/METH ANTHOL COLD/WAR TOT/POP. PAGE 11	
G0206	

	S50
KAPLAN A.,"THE PREDICTION OF SOCIAL AND	PWR
TECHNOLOGICAL EVENTS." VOL/ASSN CONSULT ACT/RES	KNO/TEST

CREATE OP/RES PLAN ROUTINE PERSON...POLICY
METH/CNCPT STAT QU/SEMANT SYS/QU TESTS CENSUS TREND
20. PAGE 29 G0574

	B57
DRUCKER P.F.,AMERICA'S NEXT TWENTY YEARS. USA+45	WORKER
DIST/IND ACADEM MUNIC SCHOOL DIPLOM ECO/TAC AUTOMAT	FOR/AID
HABITAT HEALTH...SOC/WK TREND 20 URBAN/RNWL	CENSUS
PUB/TRANS. PAGE 16 G0316	GEOG

	S57
DUNCAN O.D.,"THE MEASUREMENT OF POPULATION	GEOG
DISTRIBUTION" (BMR)" WOR+45...QUANT STAT CENSUS	PHIL/SCI
CHARTS 20. PAGE 16 G0321	PROB/SOLV
	CLASSIF

	B60
LE GHAIT E.,NO CARTE BLANCHE TO CAPRICORN; THE	DETER
FOLLY OF NUCLEAR WAR. WOR+45 INT/ORG BAL/PWR DIPLOM	NUC/PWR
RISK COERCE...CENSUS 20 NATO. PAGE 33 G0647	PLAN
	DECISION

	S63
ERSKINE H.G.,"THE POLLS: ATOMIC WEAPONS AND NUCLEAR	ATTIT
ENERGY." USA+45 COERCE ORD/FREE...POLICY SOC STAT	INT
CENSUS SAMP VAL/FREE 20. PAGE 18 G0350	NUC/PWR

	B64
PETERSON W.,THE POLITICS OF POPULATION. COM EUR+WWI	PLAN
FUT MOD/EUR S/ASIA USA+45 USA-45 WOR+45 LAW CULTURE	CENSUS
FAM SECT DOMIN EDU/PROP BIO/SOC HEALTH ORD/FREE	POLICY
...GEOG STAT TIME/SEQ TREND VAL/FREE. PAGE 44 G0871	

	B65
WHITE HOUSE CONFERENCE ON INTERNATIONAL	R+D
COOPERATION(VOL.II). SPACE WOR+45 EXTR/IND INT/ORG	CONFER
LABOR WORKER NUC/PWR PEACE AGE/Y...CENSUS ANTHOL 20	TEC/DEV
RESOURCE/N URBAN/RNWL PUB/TRANS. PAGE 1 G0019	DIPLOM

	B65
HEER D.M.,AFTER NUCLEAR ATTACK: A DEMOGRAPHIC	GEOG
INQUIRY. USA+45 ECO/DEV SECT WORKER SEX...HEAL SOC	NUC/PWR
STAT PREDICT CHARTS 20 NEGRO. PAGE 25 G0500	CENSUS
	WAR

	L65
PILISUK M.,"IS THERE A MILITARY INDUSTRIAL COMPLEX	ELITES
WHICH PREVENTS PEACE CONSENSUS; COUNTERVAILING	WEAPON
POWER IN PLURALIST SYSTEMS." INDUS R+D ACADEM	PEACE
FEEDBACK CIVMIL/REL ADJUST CONSEN ATTIT RIGID/FLEX	ARMS/CONT
...CENSUS IDEA/COMP BIBLIOG. PAGE 45 G0878	

	B66
ODEGARD P.H.,POLITICAL POWER AND SOCIAL CHANGE.	PWR
UNIV NAT/G CREATE ALL/IDEOS...POLICY GEOG SOC	TEC/DEV
CENSUS TREND. PAGE 42 G0829	IDEA/COMP

	S66
"FURTHER READING." INDIA LOC/G NAT/G PLAN ADMIN	BIBLIOG
WEALTH...GEOG SOC CONCPT CENSUS 20. PAGE 1 G0021	ECO/UNDEV
	TEC/DEV
	PROVS

	B67
US SENATE COMM ON FOREIGN REL,FOREIGN ASSISTANCE	FOR/AID
ACT OF 1967. VIETNAM WOR+45 DELIB/GP CONFER CONTROL	LAW
WAR WEAPON BAL/PAY...CENSUS CHARTS SENATE. PAGE 60	DIPLOM
G1185	POLICY

	L67
CARMICHAEL D.M.,"FORTY YEARS OF WATER POLLUTION	HEALTH
CONTROL IN WISCONSIN: A CASE STUDY." LAW EXTR/IND	CONTROL
INDUS MUNIC DELIB/GP PLAN PROB/SOLV SANCTION	ADMIN
...CENSUS CHARTS 20 WISCONSIN. PAGE 11 G0207	ADJUD

	S67
KAYSEN C.,"DATA BANKS AND DOSSIERS." FUT USA+45	CENTRAL
COM/IND NAT/G PLAN PROB/SOLV TEC/DEV BUDGET ADMIN	EFFICIENCY
ROUTINE. PAGE 30 G0588	CENSUS
	ACT/RES

	S67
STYCOS J.M.,"POLITICS AND POPULATION CONTROL IN	PLAN
LATIN AMERICA." USA+45 FAM NAT/G GP/REL AGE/C ATTIT	CENSUS
CATHISM MARXISM...POLICY UN WHO. PAGE 53 G1045	CONTROL
	L/A+17C

	N67
ASIAN STUDIES CENTER,FOUR ARTICLES ON POPULATION	ASIA
AND FAMILY LIFE IN TAIWAN (ASIAN STUDIES PAPERS,	FAM
REPRINT SERIES NO. 2). CULTURE STRATA ECO/UNDEV	CENSUS
AGRI INDUS R+D KIN MUNIC...GEOG SOC CHARTS 20.	ANTHOL
PAGE 4 G0072	

	N67
US SENATE COMM ON FOREIGN REL,SURVEY OF THE	L/A+17C

ALLIANCE FOR PROGRESS; THE POLITICAL ASPECTS   POLICY
(PAMPHLET). CONSTN SOCIETY ECO/UNDEV INT/ORG   PROB/SOLV
TEC/DEV DIPLOM...CENSUS 20. PAGE 60 G1186

CENTER/PAR....CENTER PARTY (ALL NATIONS)

CENTO....CENTRAL TREATY ORGANIZATION

CENTRAL AFRICA....SEE AFRICA/CEN

CENTRAL AFRICAN REPUBLIC....SEE CENTRL/AFR

CENTRAL TREATY ORGANIZATION....SEE CENTO

CENTRAL....CENTRALIZATION

                                                      S39
HECKSCHER G.,"GROUP ORGANIZATION IN SWEDEN." SWEDEN LAISSEZ
STRATA ECO/DEV AGRI INDUS LABOR NAT/G PROF/ORG   SOC
ECO/TAC CENTRAL SOCISM...MGT 19/20. PAGE 25 G0499

                                                      B40
FULLER G.H.,SELECTED LIST OF RECENT REFERENCES ON   BIBLIOG
AMERICAN NATIONAL DEFENSE (PAMPHLET). USA-45 FINAN   CIVMIL/REL
NAT/G ARMS/CONT WAR GOV/REL CENTRAL COST PEACE PWR   FORCES
20. PAGE 20 G0400   WEAPON

                                                      C45
MCDIARMID J.,"THE MOBILIZATION OF SOCIAL   INTELL
SCIENTISTS," IN L. WHITE'S CIVIL CIVIL SERVICE IN   WAR
WARTIME." USA-45 TEC/DEV CENTRAL...SOC 20   DELIB/GP
CIVIL/SERV. PAGE 37 G0733   ADMIN

                                                      S48
HARDIN L.M.,"REFLECTIONS ON AGRICULTURAL POLICY   AGRI
FORMATION IN THE UNITED STATES." LEGIS PLAN BUDGET   POLICY
ECO/TAC LEAD CENTRAL...MGT SOC NEW/IDEA STAT FAO.   ADMIN
PAGE 24 G0480   NEW/LIB

                                                      S50
BAVELAS A.,"COMMUNICATION PATTERNS IN TASK-ORIENTED ACT/RES
GROUPS" (BMR)" R+D OP/RES INSPECT LEAD CENTRAL   PERS/REL
EFFICIENCY HAPPINESS RIGID/FLEX...PROBABIL 20.   TASK
PAGE 6 G0106   INGP/REL

                                                      B63
JACOB H.,GERMAN ADMINISTRATION SINCE BISMARCK: ADMIN
CENTRAL AUTHORITY VERSUS LOCAL AUTONOMY. GERMANY   NAT/G
GERMANY/W LAW POL/PAR CONTROL CENTRAL TOTALISM   LOC/G
FASCISM...MAJORIT DECISION STAT CHARTS GOV/COMP   POLICY
19/20 BISMARCK/O HITLER/A WEIMAR/REP. PAGE 28 G0551

                                                      B64
RIES J.C.,THE MANAGEMENT OF DEFENSE: ORGANIZATION   FORCES
AND CONTROL OF THE US ARMED SERVICES. PROF/ORG   ACT/RES
DELIB/GP EX/STRUC LEGIS GOV/REL PERS/REL CENTRAL   DECISION
RATIONAL PWR...POLICY TREND GOV/COMP BIBLIOG.   CONTROL
PAGE 47 G0920

                                                      B64
SCHOECK H.,CENTRAL PLANNING AND NEOMERCANTILISM.   PLAN
L/A+17C UK WOR+45 BUDGET ECO/TAC PRICE CONTROL   CENTRAL
GOV/REL UTOPIA 20. PAGE 49 G0974   NAT/G
                                                     POLICY

                                                      B65
KASER M.,COMECON* INTEGRATION PROBLEMS OF THE   PLAN
PLANNED ECONOMIES. INT/ORG TEC/DEV INT/TRADE PRICE   ECO/DEV
ADMIN ADJUST CENTRAL...STAT TIME/SEQ ORG/CHARTS   COM
COMECON. PAGE 29 G0579   REGION

                                                      S65
BALDWIN H.,"SLOW-DOWN IN THE PENTAGON." USA+45   RECORD
CREATE PLAN GOV/REL CENTRAL COST EFFICIENCY PWR   R+D
...MGT MCNAMARA/R. PAGE 5 G0088   WEAPON
                                                     ADMIN

                                                      S65
TENDLER J.D.,"TECHNOLOGY AND ECONOMIC DEVELOPMENT*   BRAZIL
THE CASE OF HYDRO VS THERMAL POWER." CONSTRUC   INDUS
DIST/IND CREATE TEC/DEV INT/TRADE CENTRAL PWR SKILL ECO/UNDEV
WEALTH...MGT NAT/COMP ARGEN. PAGE 54 G1063

                                                      B66
GRUNEWALD D.,PUBLIC POLICY AND THE MODERN   LG/CO
COOPERATION: SELECTED READINGS. USA+45 LAW MARKET   POLICY
VOL/ASSN CAP/ISM INT/TRADE CENTRAL OWN...SOC ANTHOL NAT/G
20. PAGE 23 G0458   CONTROL

                                                      B66
YOUNG W.,EXISTING MECHANISMS OF ARMS CONTROL.   ARMS/CONT
PROC/MFG OP/RES DIPLOM TASK CENTRAL...MGT TREATY.   ADMIN
PAGE 65 G1266   NUC/PWR
                                                     ROUTINE

                                                      B67
ZUCKERMAN S.,SCIENTISTS AND WAR. ELITES INDUS   R+D
DIPLOM CENTRAL EFFICIENCY KNOWL 20. PAGE 65 G1271   CONSULT
                                                     ACT/RES
                                                     GP/REL

                                                      S67
CHRIST R.F.,"REORGANIZATION OF FRENCH ARMED   CHIEF
FORCES." FRANCE CREATE PLAN TEC/DEV BAL/PWR DOMIN   DETER
COERCE CENTRAL EFFICIENCY 20. PAGE 12 G0229   NUC/PWR
                                                     FORCES

                                                      S67
KAYSEN C.,"DATA BANKS AND DOSSIERS." FUT USA+45   CENTRAL
COM/IND NAT/G PLAN PROB/SOLV TEC/DEV BUDGET ADMIN   EFFICIENCY
ROUTINE. PAGE 30 G0588   CENSUS
                                                     ACT/RES

                                                      S67
MALONE D.K.,"THE COMMANDER AND THE COMPUTER."   COMPUTER
USA+45 OP/RES PROB/SOLV TEC/DEV AUTOMAT CENTRAL 20. FORCES
PAGE 35 G0698   ELITES
                                                     PLAN

                                                      S67
RICHMAN B.M.,"SOVIET MANAGEMENT IN TRANSITION."   MGT
USSR FINAN MARKET EX/STRUC PLAN PROB/SOLV TEC/DEV   MARXISM
CONTROL LEAD CENTRAL EFFICIENCY...METH/COMP 20   POLICY
REFORMERS. PAGE 47 G0917   AUTHORIT

                                                      S67
VERGIN R.C.,"COMPUTER INDUCED ORGANIZATION   COMPUTER
CHANGES." FUT USA+45 R+D CREATE OP/RES TEC/DEV   DECISION
ADJUST CENTRAL...MGT INT CON/ANAL COMPUT/IR.   AUTOMAT
PAGE 61 G1194   EX/STRUC

                                                      S67
WEIL G.L.,"THE MERGER OF THE INSTITUTIONS OF THE   ECO/TAC
EUROPEAN COMMUNITIES" EUR+WWI ECO/DEV INT/TRADE   INT/ORG
CONSEN PLURISM...DECISION MGT 20 EEC EURATOM ECSC   CENTRAL
TREATY. PAGE 62 G1223   INT/LAW

                                                      S67
WILLIAMS C.,"REGIONAL MANAGEMENT OVERSEAS." USA+45   MGT
WOR+45 DIST/IND LG/CO EX/STRUC INT/TRADE TARIFFS   EUR+WWI
ADMIN TASK CENTRAL. PAGE 63 G1242   ECO/DEV
                                                     PLAN

                                                      S67
WINTHROP H.,"THE MEANING OF DECENTRALIZATION FOR   ADMIN
TWENTIETH-CENTURY MAN." FUT WOR+45 SOCIETY TEC/DEV. STRUCT
PAGE 64 G1248   CENTRAL
                                                     PROB/SOLV

CENTRAL/AM....CENTRAL AMERICA

CENTRL/AFR....CENTRAL AFRICAN REPUBLIC

CERMAK/AJ....ANTON J. CERMAK

CETRON M.J. G0219

CEWA....CEWA (AFRICAN TRIBE)

CEYLON....CEYLON

CHACO/WAR....CHACO WAR

CHAD....SEE ALSO AFR

CHAMBERS/J....JORDAN CHAMBERS

CHAMBR/DEP....CHAMBER OF DEPUTIES (FRANCE)

CHAMBRLN/J....JOSEPH CHAMBERLAIN

CHAMBRLN/N....NEVILLE CHAMBERLAIN

CHANDLER A.D. G0220

CHANGE (AS GOAL)....SEE ORD/FREE

CHANGE (AS INNOVATION)....SEE CREATE

CHANGE (SOCIAL MOBILITY)....SEE GEOG, STRATA

CHAPMAN J.F. G0194

CHAPPLE E.D. G0221

CHARACTER....SEE PERSON

CHARISMA....CHARISMA

CHARLES/I....CHARLES I OF ENGLAND

CHARLESWORTH J.C. G0222

CHARTISM....CHARTISM

CHARTS....GRAPHS, CHARTS, DIAGRAMS, MAPS

CHASE S. G0223,G0224

CHASE/S....STUART CHASE

CHATEAUB/F....VICOMTE FRANCOIS RENE DE CHATEAUBRIAND

CHATTANOOG....CHATTANOOGA, TENNESSEE

CHECKS AND BALANCES SYSTEM....SEE BAL/PWR

CHEEK G. G0225

CHEN/YUN....CH'EN YUN

CHENG C-Y. G0226

CHIANG....CHIANG KAI-SHEK

CHICAGO....CHICAGO, ILLINOIS

CHIEF....PRESIDENT, MONARCH, PRESIDENCY, PREMIER, CHIEF
   OFFICER OF ANY GOVERNMENT

MATHEWS J.M.,AMERICAN STATE GOVERNMENT. USA-45   PROVS   B25
LOC/G CHIEF EX/STRUC LEGIS ADJUD CONTROL CT/SYS   ADMIN
ROUTINE GOV/REL PWR 20 GOVERNOR. PAGE 37 G0721   FEDERAL
                                                   CONSTN

GRIFFITH E.S.,"THE CHANGING PATTERN OF PUBLIC   LAW   S44
POLICY FORMATION." MOD/EUR WOR+45 FINAN CHIEF   POLICY
CONFER ADMIN LEAD CONSERVE SOCISM TECHRACY...SOC   TEC/DEV
CHARTS CONGRESS. PAGE 23 G0450

SOUERS S.W.,"POLICY FORMULATION FOR NATIONAL   DELIB/GP S49
SECURITY." EX/STRUC FORCES PROB/SOLV DIPLOM CONFER CHIEF
EXEC ARMS/CONT DETER NUC/PWR GOV/REL PEACE   DECISION
COLD/WAR. PAGE 52 G1022   POLICY

BUTOW R.J.C.,JAPAN'S DECISION TO SURRENDER. USA-45 ELITES   B54
USSR CHIEF FORCES DOMIN NUC/PWR...BIBLIOG 20 TREATY DIPLOM
CHINJAP. PAGE 10 G0198   WAR
                                                   PEACE

HOOPES T.,"CIVILIAN-MILITARY BALANCE." USA+45 CHIEF CIVMIL/REL S54
FORCES PLAN CONTROL WAR GOV/REL GP/REL INGP/REL   LEAD
...POLICY 19/20. PAGE 27 G0527   PWR
                                                   NAT/G

CALDWELL L.K.,"THE GOVERNMENT AND ADMINISTRATION OF PROVS   C54
NEW YORK." LOC/G MUNIC POL/PAR SCHOOL CHIEF LEGIS ADMIN
PLAN TAX CT/SYS...MGT SOC/WK BIBLIOG 20 NEWYORK/C. CONSTN
PAGE 10 G0202   EX/STRUC

KOENIG L.W.,THE TRUMAN ADMINISTRATION: ITS   ADMIN   B56
PRINCIPLES AND PRACTICE. USA+45 POL/PAR CHIEF LEGIS POLICY
DIPLOM DEATH NUC/PWR WAR CIVMIL/REL PEACE   EX/STRUC
...DECISION 20 TRUMAN/HS PRESIDENT TREATY. PAGE 31 GOV/REL
G0610

MILLER W.E.,"PRESIDENTIAL COATTAILS: A STUDY IN   CHIEF   S56
POLITICAL MYTH AND METHODOLOGY" (BMR)" USA+45   CHOOSE
CREATE PARTIC ATTIT DRIVE PWR...DECISION CONCPT   POL/PAR
CHARTS SIMUL 20 PRESIDENT CONGRESS. PAGE 39 G0774 MYTH

SPANIER J.W.,THE TRUMAN-MACARTHUR CONTROVERSY AND CIVMIL/REL B59
THE KOREAN WAR. USA+45 TOP/EX PROB/SOLV LEAD ATTIT FORCES
PWR...POLICY BIBLIOG/A UN. PAGE 52 G1023   CHIEF
                                                   WAR

CARPER E.T.,THE DEFENSE APPROPRIATIONS RIDER   GOV/REL B60
(PAMPHLET). USA+45 CONSTN CHIEF DELIB/GP LEGIS   ADJUD
BUDGET LOBBY CIVMIL/REL...POLICY 20 CONGRESS   LAW
EISNHWR/DD DEPT/DEFEN PRESIDENT BOSTON. PAGE 11   CONTROL
G0212

HELLER D.,THE KENNEDY CABINET--AMERICA'S MEN OF   EX/STRUC B61
DESTINY. NAT/G CHIEF CONSULT ADMIN CONTROL GOV/REL CONFER
...MGT 20 DEPT/LABOR DEPT/STATE DEPT/JUST   DELIB/GP
DEPT/DEFEN KENNEDY/J. PAGE 26 G0504   TOP/EX

BOCK E.A.,CASE STUDIES IN AMERICAN GOVERNMENT.   POLICY   B62
USA+45 ECO/DEV CHIEF EDU/PROP CT/SYS RACE/REL   LEGIS
ORD/FREE...JURID MGT PHIL/SCI PRESIDENT CASEBOOK. IDEA/CCMP
PAGE 8 G0146   NAT/G

KENNEDY J.F.,TO TURN THE TIDE. SPACE AGRI INT/ORG DIPLOM   B62
FORCES TEC/DEV ADMIN NUC/PWR PEACE WEALTH...ANTHOL CHIEF
20 KENNEDY/JF CIV/RIGHTS. PAGE 30 G0592   POLICY
                                                   NAT/G

US SENATE COMM GOVT OPERATIONS,ADMINISTRATION OF   ORD/FREE B62
NATIONAL SECURITY. USA+45 CHIEF PLAN PROB/SOLV   ADMIN
TEC/DEV DIPLOM ATTIT...POLICY DECISION 20   NAT/G
KENNEDY/JF RUSK/D MCNAMARA/R BUNDY/M HERTER/C.   CONTROL
PAGE 60 G1177

NEIBURG H.L.,"THE EISENHOWER AEC AND CONGRESS: A   CHIEF   L62
STUDY IN EXECUTIVE-LEGISLATIVE RELATIONS." USA+45 LEGIS
NAT/G POL/PAR DELIB/GP EX/STRUC TOP/EX ADMIN EXEC GOV/REL
LEAD ROUTINE PWR...POLICY COLD/WAR CONGRESS   NUC/PWR
PRESIDENT AEC. PAGE 41 G0816

DALAND R.T.,PERSPECTIVES OF BRAZILIAN PUBLIC   ADMIN   B63
ADMINISTRATION (VOL. I). BRAZIL LAW ECO/UNDEV   NAT/G
SCHOOL CHIEF TEC/DEV CONFER CONTROL GP/REL ATTIT   PLAN
ROLE PWR...ANTHOL 20. PAGE 14 G0272   GOV/REL

LAPP R.E.,THE NEW PRIESTHOOD; THE SCIENTIFIC ELITE TEC/DEV B65
AND THE USES OF POWER. USA+45 ELITES INTELL SOCIETY TECHRACY
R+D NAT/G CHIEF LEGIS CIVMIL/REL GP/REL PWR 20   CONTROL
PRESIDENT CONGRESS. PAGE 32 G0635   POPULISM

WEISNER J.B.,WHERE SCIENCE AND POLITICS MEET.   CHIEF   B65
USA+45 ECO/DEV R+D FORCES PROB/SOLV DIPLOM FOR/AID NAT/G
CONTROL...PHIL/SCI PRESIDENT KENNEDY/JF JOHNSON/LB. POLICY
PAGE 63 G1228   TEC/DEV

GORDON G.,THE LEGISLATIVE PROCESS AND DIVIDED   LEGIS   B66
GOVERNMENT; A CASE STUDY OF THE 86TH CONGRESS.   HABITAT
USA+45 POL/PAR PROVS PROB/SOLV BAL/PWR CHOOSE   CHIEF
REPRESENT EFFICIENCY ATTIT...POLICY DECISION STAT NAT/G
20 CONGRESS EISNHWR/DD. PAGE 22 G0434

GREENBERG D.S.,"THE SCIENTIFIC PORK BARREL." USA+45 R+D   S66
ECO/DEV PUB/INST CHIEF LEGIS BUDGET GIVE GP/REL PWR NAT/G
WEALTH 20. PAGE 23 G0445   ACADEM
                                                   ATTIT

MAZOUR A.G.,SOVIET ECONOMIC DEVELOPMENT: OPERATION ECO/TAC B67
OUTSTRIP: 1921-1965. USSR ECO/UNDEV FINAN CHIEF   AGRI
WORKER PROB/SOLV CONTROL PRODUC MARXISM...CHARTS   INDUS
ORG/CHARTS 20 STALIN/J. PAGE 37 G0726   PLAN

CHRIST R.F.,"REORGANIZATION OF FRENCH ARMED   CHIEF   S67
FORCES." FRANCE CREATE PLAN TEC/DEV BAL/PWR DOMIN DETER
COERCE CENTRAL EFFICIENCY 20. PAGE 12 G0229   NUC/PWR
                                                   FORCES

KRAUS J.,"A MARXIST IN GHANA." GHANA ELITES CHIEF MARXISM S67
PROB/SOLV TEC/DEV DIPLOM ECO/TAC COLONIAL PARTIC   PLAN
PWR 20 NKRUMAH/K. PAGE 31 G0618   ATTIT
                                                   CREATE

CHILDREN....SEE AGE/C

CHILDS J.R. G0227

CHILDS/RS....RICHARD SPENCER CHILDS

CHILE....SEE ALSO L/A+17C

SILVERT K.H.,"AMERICAN ACADEMIC ETHICS AND SOCIAL ACADEM   S65
RESEARCH ABROAD* THE LESSON OF PROJECT CAMELOT."   NAT/G
CHILE L/A+17C USA+45 FINAN ADMIN...PHIL/SCI SOC   ACT/RES
GEN/LAWS CAMELOT. PAGE 51 G0998   POLICY

GLAZER M.,THE FEDERAL GOVERNMENT AND THE   BIBLIOG/A B66
UNIVERSITY. CHILE PROB/SOLV DIPLOM GIVE ADMIN WAR NAT/G
...POLICY SOC 20. PAGE 21 G0421   PLAN
                                                   ACADEM

CHIN R. G0123

CHINA....PEOPLE'S REPUBLIC OF CHINA: SEE CHINA/COM
    REPUBLIC OF CHINA: SEE TAIWAN

CHINA/COM....COMMUNIST CHINA

ANGELL N.,DEFENCE AND THE ENGLISH-SPEAKING ROLE. | DIPLOM
CHINA/COM UK USSR INT/ORG FORCES EDU/PROP NEUTRAL | WAR
NUC/PWR NAT/LISM PEACE TOTALISM 20 COLD/WAR | MARXISM
COEXIST. PAGE 3 G0059 | ORD/FREE
B58

FRIEDRICH-EBERT-STIFTUNG,THE SOVIET BLOC AND | MARXISM
DEVELOPING COUNTRIES. CHINA/COM COM GERMANY/E USSR | DIPLOM
WOR+45 ECO/UNDEV INT/ORG NAT/G TEC/DEV NEUTRAL PWR | ECO/TAC
...POLICY 20. PAGE 20 G0394 | FOR/AID
B62

WALSTON H.,AGRICULTURE UNDER COMMUNISM. CHINA/COM | AGRI
COM PROB/SOLV HAPPINESS RIGID/FLEX...POLICY | MARXISM
METH/COMP 20. PAGE 62 G1207 | PLAN
| CREATE
B62

COHEN M.,LAW AND POLITICS IN SPACE: SPECIFIC AND | DELIB/GP
URGENT PROBLEMS IN THE LAW OF OUTER SPACE. | LAW
CHINA/COM COM USA+45 USSR WOR+45 COM/IND INT/ORG | INT/LAW
NAT/G LEGIT NUC/PWR ATTIT BIO/SOC...JURID CONCPT | SPACE
CONGRESS 20 STALIN/J. PAGE 12 G0241
B64

LI C.M.,INDUSTRIAL DEVELOPMENT IN COMMUNIST CHINA. | ASIA
CHINA/COM ECO/DEV ECO/UNDEV AGRI FINAN INDUS MARKET | TEC/DEV
LABOR NAT/G ECO/TAC INT/TRADE EXEC ALL/VALS
...POLICY RELATIV TREND WORK TOT/POP VAL/FREE 20.
PAGE 34 G0665
B64

OSSENBECK F.J.,OPEN SPACE AND PEACE. CHINA/COM FUT | SPACE
USA+45 USSR LAW PROB/SOLV TEC/DEV EDU/PROP NEUTRAL | ORD/FREE
PEACE...AUD/VIS ANTHOL 20. PAGE 43 G0850 | DIPLOM
| CREATE
B64

BARISH N.N.,MANAGEMENT SCIENCES IN THE EMERGING | ECO/UNDEV
COUNTRIES. AFR CHINA/COM WOR+45 FINAN INDUS PLAN | OP/RES
PRODUC HABITAT...ANTHOL 20. PAGE 5 G0093 | MGT
| TEC/DEV
B65

CHENG C.--Y.,SCIENTIFIC AND ENGINEERING MANPOWER IN | WORKER
COMMUNIST CHINA, 1949-1963. CHINA/COM USSR ELITES | CONSULT
ECO/DEV R+D ACADEM LABOR NAT/G EDU/PROP CONTROL | MARXISM
UTIL...POLICY BIBLIOG 20. PAGE 12 G0226 | BIOG
B65

HALPERIN M.H.,COMMUNIST CHINA AND ARMS CONTROL. | ATTIT
CHINA/COM FUT USA+45 CULTURE FORCES TEC/DEV ECO/TAC | POLICY
WAR PEACE ORD/FREE MARXISM 20 COLD/WAR. PAGE 24 | ARMS/CONT
G0473 | NUC/PWR
B65

US DEPARTMENT OF DEFENSE,US SECURITY ARMS CONTROL, | BIBLIOG/A
AND DISARMAMENT 1961-1965 (PAMPHLET). CHINA/COM COM | ARMS/CONT
GERMANY/W ISRAEL SPACE USA+45 USSR WOR+45 FORCES | NUC/PWR
EDU/PROP DETER EQUILIB PEACE ALL/VALS...GOV/COMP 20 | DIPLOM
NATO. PAGE 57 G1118
B65

GRIFFITH S.B.,"COMMUNIST CHINA'S CAPACITY TO MAKE | FORCES
WAR." CHINA/COM COM NAT/G TOP/EX PLAN DOMIN COERCE | PWR
NUC/PWR ATTIT RESPECT SKILL...CONCPT MYTH TIME/SEQ | WEAPON
TREND COLD/WAR 20. PAGE 23 G0452 | ASIA
S65

HOLSTI O.R.,"EAST-WEST CONFLICT AND SINO-SOVIET | VOL/ASSN
RELATIONS" CHINA/COM USSR COMPUTER REGION DECISION. | DIPLOM
PAGE 27 G0523 | CON/ANAL
| COM
S65

HALPERIN M.H.,CHINA AND NUCLEAR PROLIFERATION | NUC/PWR
(PAMPHLET). CHINA/COM FUT INDIA USA+45 USSR | FORCES
ARMS/CONT WAR 20 CHINJAP. PAGE 24 G0474 | POLICY
| DIPLOM
B66

SCHURMANN F.,IDEOLOGY AND ORGANIZATION IN COMMUNIST | MARXISM
CHINA. CHINA/COM LOC/G MUNIC POL/PAR ECO/TAC | STRUCT
CONTROL ATTIT...MGT STERTYP 20 COM/PARTY. PAGE 50 | ADMIN
G0981 | NAT/G
B66

US DEPARTMENT OF THE ARMY,COMMUNIST CHINA: A | BIBLIOG/A
STRATEGIC SURVEY: A BIBLIOGRAPHY (PAMPHLET NO. | MARXISM
B66

20-67). CHINA/COM COM INDIA USSR NAT/G POL/PAR | S/ASIA
EX/STRUC FORCES NUC/PWR REV ATTIT...POLICY GEOG | DIPLOM
CHARTS. PAGE 58 G1133

LERNER D.,COMMUNICATION AND CHANGE IN DEVELOPING | EDU/PROP
COUNTRIES. CHINA/COM INDIA PHILIPPINE COM/IND | ORD/FREE
CREATE TEC/DEV...ANTHOL 20. PAGE 33 G0659 | PERCEPT
| ECO/UNDEV
B67

DAVIS P.C.,"THE COMING CHINESE COMMUNIST NUCLEAR | NUC/PWR
THREAT AND U.S. SEA BASED ABM OPTIONS." ASIA | DETER
CHINA/COM FUT USA+45 SEA NAT/G FORCES PLAN TEC/DEV | WEAPON
LEAD ARMS/CONT...GEOG METH/COMP 20 ABM/DEFSYS. | DIPLOM
PAGE 14 G0279
L67

ROBINSON T.W.,"A NATIONAL INTEREST ANALYSIS OF | MARXISM
SINO-SOVIET RELATIONS." CHINA/COM USSR NAT/G | DIPLOM
NUC/PWR ATTIT PWR...CONCPT CHARTS 20. PAGE 47 G0931 | SOVEREIGN
| GEN/LAWS
L67

"CHINESE STATEMENT ON NUCLEAR PROLIFERATION." | NUC/PWR
CHINA/COM USA+45 USSR DOMIN COLONIAL PWR. PAGE 1 | BAL/PWR
G0022 | ARMS/CONT
| DIPLOM
S67

CHIU S.M.,"CHINA'S MILITARY POSTURE." CHINA/COM | FORCES
ELITES NAT/G POL/PAR TEC/DEV ECO/TAC DOMIN CONTROL | CIVMIL/REL
LEAD REV MARXISM 20 MAO. PAGE 12 G0228 | NUC/PWR
| DIPLOM
S67

CLEMENS W.C.,"CHINESE NUCLEAR TESTS: TRENDS AND | NUC/PWR
PORTENTS." CHINA/COM USA+45 USSR FORCES PLAN | WEAPON
TEC/DEV ARMS/CONT WAR PWR...DECISION 20 MAO | POLICY
KHRUSH/N. PAGE 12 G0234 | DIPLOM
S67

EISENDRATH C.,"THE OUTER SPACE TREATY." CHINA/COM | SPACE
COM USA+45 DIPLOM CONTROL NUC/PWR...INT/LAW 20 UN | INT/ORG
COLD/WAR TREATY. PAGE 17 G0339 | PEACE
| ARMS/CONT
S67

INGLIS D.R.,"MISSILE DEFENSE, NUCLEAR SPREAD, AND | NUC/PWR
VIETNAM." CHINA/COM USA+45 USSR VIETNAM INDUS | ARMS/CONT
BAL/PWR DETER WAR COST NAT/LISM PEACE. PAGE 28 | DIPLOM
G0544 | FORCES
S67

JAIN G.,"INDIA REJECTS THE POWER RACE* REALISM | INDIA
ABOUT NUCLEAR WEAPONS." FORCES PROB/SOLV FOR/AID | CHINA/COM
ARMS/CONT COST PWR...GOV/COMP 20. PAGE 28 G0556 | NUC/PWR
| DIPLOM
S67

TELLER E.,"PLANNING FOR PEACE." CHINA/COM WOR+45 | ARMS/CONT
DELIB/GP TEC/DEV RISK COERCE DETER WAR ATTIT | NUC/PWR
ORD/FREE 20 NATO. PAGE 54 G1061 | PEACE
| DOMIN
S67

CHINESE/AM....CHINESE IMMIGRANTS TO US AND THEIR DESCENDANTS

CHITTAGONG....CHITTAGONG HILL TRIBES

CHIU S.M. G0228

CHOICE (IN DECISION-MAKING)....SEE PROB/SOLV

CHOOSE....CHOICE, ELECTION

BINGHAM A.M.,THE TECHNIQUES OF DEMOCRACY. USA-45 | POPULISM
CONSTN STRUCT POL/PAR LEGIS PLAN PARTIC CHOOSE | ORD/FREE
REPRESENT NAT/LISM TOTALISM...MGT 20. PAGE 7 G0136 | ADMIN
| NAT/G
B42

LASSWELL H.D.,"THE RELATION OF IDEOLOGICAL | ATTIT
INTELLIGENCE TO PUBLIC POLICY." WOR+45 WOR-45 | DECISION
SOCIETY DELIB/GP ACT/RES CREATE PLAN DIPLOM
EDU/PROP CHOOSE KNOWL PWR...POLICY SOC TREND
GEN/LAWS 20. PAGE 32 G0638
S42

WHITE L.D.,CIVIL SERVICE IN WARTIME. CONSULT | REPRESENT
DELIB/GP PARTIC WAR CHOOSE. PAGE 63 G1233 | ADMIN
| INTELL
| NAT/G
B45

NORTHROP F.S.C.,THE MEETING OF EAST AND WEST. | DRIVE
B46

EUR+WWI FUT MOD/EUR UNIV WOR+45 WOR-45 INTELL   TREND
SOCIETY EX/STRUC TOP/EX ACT/RES LEGIT CHOOSE ATTIT   PEACE
PERCEPT RIGID/FLEX ALL/VALS...POLICY JURID OBS
TOT/POP. PAGE 42 G0826

                                                        B47
BECK H.P.,MEN WHO CONTROL OUR UNIVERSITIES.   EDU/PROP
EX/STRUC CHOOSE INGP/REL DISCRIM PERSON WEALTH   ACADEM
...POLICY TREND CON/ANAL CHARTS BIBLIOG. PAGE 6   CONTROL
G0112   LEAD

                                                        B48
PUBLIC ADMINISTRATION SERVICE,SOURCE MATERIALS IN   BIBLIOG/A
PUBLIC ADMINISTRATION: A SELECTED BIBLIOGRAPHY (PAS   GOV/REL
PUBLICATION NO. 102). USA+45 LAW FINAN LOC/G MUNIC   MGT
NAT/G PLAN RECEIVE EDU/PROP CT/SYS CHOOSE HEALTH   ADMIN
20. PAGE 45 G0895

                                                        S49
MERTON R.,"THE ROLE OF APPLIED SOCIAL SCIENCE IN   PLAN
THE FORMATION OF POLICY: A RESEARCH MEMORANDUM."   SOC
WOR+45 INDUS NAT/G EXEC ROUTINE CHOOSE ORD/FREE PWR   DIPLOM
SKILL...POLICY MGT PSY METH/CNCPT TESTS CHARTS METH
VAL/FREE 20. PAGE 38 G0756

                                                        B52
APPADORAI A.,THE SUBSTANCE OF POLITICS (6TH ED.).   PHIL/SCI
EX/STRUC LEGIS DIPLOM CT/SYS CHOOSE FASCISM MARXISM   NAT/G
SOCISM...BIBLIOG T. PAGE 3 G0062

                                                        B53
SAYLES L.R.,THE LOCAL UNION. CONSTN CULTURE   LABOR
DELIB/GP PARTIC CHOOSE GP/REL INGP/REL ATTIT ROLE   LEAD
...MAJORIT DECISION MGT. PAGE 49 G0958   ADJUD
                                                        ROUTINE

                                                        B54
COMBS C.H.,DECISION PROCESSES. INTELL SOCIETY   MATH
DELIB/GP CREATE TEC/DEV DOMIN LEGIT EXEC CHOOSE   DECISION
DRIVE RIGID/FLEX KNOWL PWR...PHIL/SCI SOC
METH/CNCPT CONT/OBS REC/INT PERS/TEST SAMP/SIZ BIOG
SOC/EXP WORK. PAGE 13 G0245

                                                        S55
SKINNER B.F.,"FREEDOM AND THE CONTROL OF MEN"   ORD/FREE
(BMR)" FUT WOR+45 CONTROL CHOOSE GP/REL ATTIT MORAL   TEC/DEV
PWR POPULISM...POLICY 20. PAGE 51 G1008   PHIL/SCI
                                                        INTELL

                                                        S56
MILLER W.E.,"PRESIDENTIAL COATTAILS: A STUDY IN   CHIEF
POLITICAL MYTH AND METHODOLOGY" (BMR)" USA+45   CHOOSE
CREATE PARTIC ATTIT DRIVE PWR...DECISION CONCPT   POL/PAR
CHARTS SIMUL 20 PRESIDENT CONGRESS. PAGE 39 G0774   MYTH

                                                        S57
TAYLOR P.S.,"THE RELATION OF RESEARCH TO   DECISION
LEGISLATIVE AND ADMINISTRATIVE DECISIONS." ELITES   LEGIS
ACT/RES PLAN PROB/SOLV CONFER CHOOSE POLICY.   MGT
PAGE 54 G1059   PWR

                                                        B58
OGDEN F.D.,THE POLL TAX IN THE SOUTH. USA+45 USA-45   TAX
CONSTN ADJUD ADMIN PARTIC CRIME...TIME/SEQ GOV/COMP   CHOOSE
METH/COMP 18/20 SOUTH/US. PAGE 43 G0838   RACE/REL
                                                        DISCRIM

                                                        B59
GODDARD V.,THE ENIGMA OF MENACE. WOR+45 SECT LEAD   PEACE
NUC/PWR WAR WEAPON CHOOSE PERSON PWR...POLICY   ARMS/CONT
PHIL/SCI PACIFIST 20 COLD/WAR. PAGE 22 G0423   DIPLOM
                                                        ATTIT

                                                        S59
GOLDHAMMER H.,"SOME OBSERVATIONS ON POLITICAL   COMPUT/IR
GAMING." FUT WOR+45 R+D NAT/G ACT/RES CREATE CHOOSE   DECISION
ATTIT PWR...POLICY CONCPT METH/CNCPT STYLE KNO/TEST   DIPLOM
TREND HYPO/EXP GAME GEN/METH METH 20. PAGE 22 G0426

                                                        B60
ARROW K.J.,MATHEMATICAL METHODS IN THE SOCIAL   MATH
SCIENCES, 1959. TEC/DEV CHOOSE UTIL PERCEPT   PSY
...KNO/TEST GAME SIMUL ANTHOL. PAGE 4 G0070   MGT

                                                        B60
HEILBRONER R.L.,THE FUTURE AS HISTORY. USA+45   TEC/DEV
WOR+45 WOR-45 SOCIETY ECO/DEV ECO/UNDEV VOL/ASSN   TREND
PLAN CAP/ISM NUC/PWR CHOOSE NAT/LISM ATTIT ORD/FREE
RESPECT WEALTH SOCISM 20. PAGE 25 G0501

                                                        S60
DOTY P.M.,"THE ROLE OF THE SMALLER POWERS." FUT   PWR
WOR+45 NAT/G TEC/DEV BAL/PWR DOMIN LEGIT CHOOSE   POLICY
DISPL DRIVE RESPECT...DECISION 20. PAGE 16 G0310   ARMS/CONT
                                                        NUC/PWR

                                                        S60
GARFINKEL H.,"THE RATIONAL PROPERTIES OF SCIENTIFIC   CREATE
AND COMMON SENSE ACTIVITIES." SOCIETY STRATA   PHIL/SCI
ACT/RES CHOOSE...SOC METH/CNCPT NEW/IDEA CONT/OBS
SIMUL TOT/POP VAL/FREE. PAGE 21 G0412

                                                        S60
HUNTINGTON S.P.,"STRATEGIC PLANNING AND THE   EXEC
POLITICAL PROCESS." USA+45 NAT/G DELIB/GP LEGIS   FORCES
ACT/RES ECO/TAC LEGIT ROUTINE CHOOSE RIGID/FLEX PWR   NUC/PWR
...POLICY MAJORIT MGT 20. PAGE 27 G0538   WAR

                                                        B61
JANOWITZ M.,COMMUNITY POLITICAL SYSTEMS. USA+45   MUNIC
SOCIETY INDUS VOL/ASSN TEC/DEV ADMIN LEAD CHOOSE   STRUCT
...SOC SOC/WK 20. PAGE 29 G0561   POL/PAR

                                                        B61
LUNDBERG G.A.,CAN SCIENCE SAVE US. UNIV CULTURE   ACT/RES
INTELL SOCIETY ECO/DEV R+D PLAN EDU/PROP ROUTINE   CONCPT
CHOOSE ATTIT PERCEPT ALL/VALS...TREND 20. PAGE 34   TOTALISM
G0679

                                                        B62
OSGOOD C.E.,AN ALTERNATIVE TO WAR OR SURRENDER. FUT   ORD/FREE
UNIV CULTURE INTELL SOCIETY R+D INT/ORG CONSULT   EDU/PROP
DELIB/GP ACT/RES PLAN CHOOSE ATTIT PERCEPT KNOWL   PEACE
...PHIL/SCI PSY SOC TREND GEN/LAWS 20. PAGE 43   WAR
G0849

                                                        S62
BETHE H.,"DISARMAMENT AND STRATEGY." COM USA+45   PLAN
USSR WOR+45 VOL/ASSN TEC/DEV EDU/PROP NUC/PWR   ORD/FREE
CHOOSE PEACE...POLICY DECISION NEW/IDEA OBS   ARMS/CONT
GEN/LAWS COLD/WAR 420. PAGE 7 G0133   DIPLOM

                                                        B63
HERNDON J.,A SELECTED BIBLIOGRAPHY OF MATERIALS IN   BIBLIOG
STATE GOVERNMENT AND POLITICS (PAMPHLET). USA+45   GOV/COMP
POL/PAR LEGIS ADMIN CHOOSE MGT. PAGE 26 G0507   PROVS
                                                        DECISION

                                                        B63
MILBRATH L.W.,THE WASHINGTON LOBBYISTS. CONSTN   LOBBY
BAL/PWR CONTROL LEAD TASK CHOOSE SUPEGO...DECISION   POLICY
STAT CHARTS BIBLIOG. PAGE 39 G0767   PERS/REL

                                                        B63
PEABODY R.L.,NEW PERSPECTIVES ON THE HOUSE OF   NEW/IDEA
REPRESENTATIVES. AGRI FINAN SCHOOL FORCES CONFER   LEGIS
LEAD CHOOSE REPRESENT FEDERAL...POLICY DECISION   PWR
HOUSE/REP. PAGE 44 G0862   ADMIN

                                                        L64
GOLDBERG A.,"ATOMIC ORIGINS OF THE BRITISH NUCLEAR   CREATE
DETERRENT." EUR+WWI UK NAT/G TOP/EX PLAN BAL/PWR   FORCES
DOMIN DETER CHOOSE ATTIT DRIVE HEALTH ORD/FREE PWR   NUC/PWR
RESPECT...CONCPT VAL/FREE COLD/WAR 20 CMN/WLTH.
PAGE 22 G0425

                                                        C64
SCHRAMM W.,"MASS MEDIA AND NATIONAL DEVELOPMENT: ECO/UNDEV
THE ROLE OF INFORMATION IN DEVELOPING COUNTRIES."   COM/IND
FINAN R+D ACT/RES PLAN TEC/DEV DIPLOM CHOOSE SUPEGO   EDU/PROP
ORD/FREE...BIBLIOG 20. PAGE 50 G0978   MAJORIT

                                                        S65
KUZMACK A.M.,"TECHNOLOGICAL CHANGE AND STABLE   R+D
DETERRENCE." CREATE EDU/PROP ARMS/CONT WEAPON   DETER
CHOOSE COST DRIVE PERCEPT...RECORD STERTYP TIME.   EQUILIB
PAGE 32 G0627

                                                        S65
RASER J.R.,"WEAPONS DESIGN AND ARMS CONTROL* THE   ARMS/CONT
POLARIS EXAMPLE." DETER NUC/PWR WEAPON CHOOSE   R+D
PERCEPT...STERTYP TIME. PAGE 46 G0904   GEOG
                                                        ACT/RES

                                                        B66
CLARK G.,WORLD PEACE THROUGH WORLD LAW; TWO   INT/LAW
ALTERNATIVE PLANS. WOR+45 DELIB/GP FORCES TAX   PEACE
CONFER ADJUD SANCTION ARMS/CONT WAR CHOOSE PRIVIL   PLAN
20 UN COLD/WAR. PAGE 12 G0231   INT/ORG

                                                        B66
GORDON G.,THE LEGISLATIVE PROCESS AND DIVIDED   LEGIS
GOVERNMENT; A CASE STUDY OF THE 86TH CONGRESS.   HABITAT
USA+45 POL/PAR PROVS PROB/SOLV BAL/PWR CHOOSE   CHIEF
REPRESENT EFFICIENCY ATTIT...POLICY DECISION STAT   NAT/G
20 CONGRESS EISNHWR/DD. PAGE 22 G0434

                                                        B67
DEGLER C.N.,THE AGE OF THE ECONOMIC REVOLUTION   INDUS
1876-1900. USA-45 AGRI MUNIC POL/PAR SECT ECO/TAC   SOCIETY
CHOOSE...PHIL/SCI CHARTS NAT/COMP 19 NEGRO. PAGE 15   ECO/DEV
G0292   TEC/DEV

UNIVERSAL REFERENCE SYSTEM.PUBLIC OPINION, MASS
BEHAVIOR, AND POLITICAL PSYCHOLOGY (VOLUME VI).
WOR+45 WOR-45 SOCIETY EDU/PROP PRESS PARTIC CHOOSE
PERSON...TREND COMPUT/IR GEN/METH. PAGE 56 G1098
B67 BIBLIOG/A ATTIT CROWD PSY

WEINBERG A.M.,REFLECTIONS ON BIG SCIENCE. FUT
USA+45 NAT/G EDU/PROP CHOOSE PERS/REL COST OPTIMAL
...PHIL/SCI TREND. PAGE 62 G1225
B67 ACADEM KNOWL R+D PLAN

CHOU/ENLAI....CHOU EN-LAI

CHRIS/DEM....CHRISTIAN DEMOCRATIC PARTY (ALL NATIONS)

CHRIST R.F. G0229

CHRISTIAN DEMOCRATIC PARTY....SEE CHRIS/DEM

CHRISTIAN....CHRISTIAN BELIEFS OR CHURCHES

CHRIST-17C.... CHRISTENDOM TO 1700

HART B.H.L.,STRATEGY (REV. ED.). CHRIST-17C EUR+WWI
MEDIT-7 MOD/EUR TEC/DEV LEAD REV WEAPON...POLICY
CHARTS. PAGE 25 G0486
B54 WAR PLAN FORCES PHIL/SCI

MCDOUGAL M.S.,"THE ENJOYMENT AND ACQUISITION OF
RESOURCES IN OUTER SPACE." CHRIST-17C FUT WOR+45
WOR-45 LAW EXTR/IND INT/ORG ACT/RES CREATE TEC/DEV
ECO/TAC LEGIT COERCE HEALTH KNOWL ORD/FREE PWR
WEALTH...JURID HIST/WRIT VAL/FREE. PAGE 37 G0738
L63 PLAN TREND

CHRONOLOGY....SEE TIME/SEQ

CHU K. G0230

CHURCH....SEE SECT

CHURCH/STA....CHURCH-STATE RELATIONS (ALL NATIONS)

CHURCHLL/W....SIR WINSTON CHURCHILL

CIA....CENTRAL INTELLIGENCE AGENCY

CICERO....CICERO

CINCINNATI....CINCINNATI, OHIO

CINEMA....SEE FILM

CITIES....SEE MUNIC

CITIZENSHIP....SEE CITIZENSHP

CITIZENSHP....CITIZENSHIP

CITY/MGT....CITY MANAGEMENT, CITY MANAGERS; SEE ALSO MUNIC,
ADMIN, MGT, LOC/G

CIV/DEFENS....CIVIL DEFENSE

CONOVER H.L.,CIVILIAN DEFENSE: A SELECTED LIST OF
RECENT REFERENCES (PAMPHLET). USA+45 LOC/G MUNIC
PROB/SOLV ADMIN LEAD TASK WEAPON GOV/REL...POLICY
CON/ANAL 20 CIV/DEFENS. PAGE 13 G0251
N BIBLIOG PLAN WAR CIVMIL/REL

US FOOD AND DRUG ADMIN,CIVIL DEFENSE INFORMATION
FOR FOOD AND DRUG OFFICIALS (2ND ED.) (PAMPHLET).
USA+45 PROB/SOLV RISK HABITAT...MATH CHARTS
DICTIONARY 20 CIV/DEFENS. PAGE 58 G1136
N19 NUC/PWR WAR EATING HEALTH

US HOUSE COMM GOVT OPERATIONS,CIVIL DEFENSE. USA+45
FORCES...CHARTS 20 CONGRESS CIV/DEFENS HOLIFLD/C.
PAGE 58 G1139
B58 NUC/PWR WAR PLAN ADJUST

BAKER G.W.,BEHAVIORAL SCIENCE AND CIVIL DEFENSE.
USA+45 PROB/SOLV ADMIN GP/REL INGP/REL PERS/REL
ANOMIE DRIVE PERSON...DECISION MGT SOC 20
CIV/DEFENS. PAGE 4 G0085
B62 NUC/PWR WAR POLICY ACT/RES

CIV/DISOBD....CIVIL DISOBEDIENCE

CIV/RIGHTS....CIVIL RIGHTS: CONTEMPORARY CIVIL RIGHTS
MOVEMENTS; SEE ALSO RACE/REL, CONSTN + LAW

KENNEDY J.F.,TO TURN THE TIDE. SPACE AGRI INT/ORG
FORCES TEC/DEV ADMIN NUC/PWR PEACE WEALTH...ANTHOL
20 KENNEDY/JF CIV/RIGHTS. PAGE 30 G0592
B62 DIPLOM CHIEF POLICY NAT/G

DUNBAR L.W.,A REPUBLIC OF EQUALS. USA+45 CREATE
ADJUD PEACE NEW/LIB...POLICY 20 SOUTH/US
CIV/RIGHTS. PAGE 16 G0320
B66 LAW CONSTN FEDERAL RACE/REL

CIVIL AERONAUTICS BOARD....SEE CAB

CIVIL DEFENSE....SEE CIV/DEFENS

CIVIL DISOBEDIENCE....SEE CIV/DISOBD

CIVIL RIGHTS....SEE CIV/RIGHTS

CIVIL SERVICE....SEE ADMIN

CIVIL/CODE....CIVIL CODE (FRANCE)

CIVIL/LAW....CIVIL LAW

CIVIL/LIB....CIVIL LIBERTIES; SEE ALSO CONSTN + LAW

CRAIG J.,ELEMENTS OF POLITICAL SCIENCE (3 VOLS.).
CONSTN AGRI INDUS SCHOOL FORCES TAX CT/SYS SUFF
MORAL WEALTH...CONCPT 19 CIVIL/LIB. PAGE 13 G0259
B14 PHIL/SCI NAT/G ORD/FREE

CIVIL/SERV....CIVIL SERVICE; SEE ALSO ADMIN

GINZBERG E.,MANPOWER FOR GOVERNMENT (PAMPHLET).
USA+45 FORCES PLAN PROB/SOLV PAY EDU/PROP ADMIN
GP/REL COST...MGT PREDICT TREND 20 CIVIL/SERV.
PAGE 21 G0418
N19 WORKER CONSULT NAT/G LOC/G

MCDIARMID J.,"THE MOBILIZATION OF SOCIAL
SCIENTISTS," IN L. WHITE'S CIVIL CIVIL SERVICE IN
WARTIME." USA-45 TEC/DEV CENTRAL...SOC 20
CIVIL/SERV. PAGE 37 G0733
C45 INTELL WAR DELIB/GP ADMIN

CHILDS J.R.,AMERICAN FOREIGN SERVICE. USA+45
SOCIETY NAT/G ROUTINE GOV/REL 20 DEPT/STATE
CIVIL/SERV. PAGE 12 G0227
B48 DIPLOM ADMIN GP/REL

SCARROW H.A.,THE HIGHER PUBLIC SERVICE OF THE
COMMONWEALTH OF AUSTRALIA. LAW SENIOR LOBBY ROLE 20
AUSTRAL CIVIL/SERV COMMONWLTH. PAGE 49 G0959
B57 ADMIN NAT/G EX/STRUC GOV/COMP

VERNEY D.V.,PUBLIC ENTERPRISE IN SWEDEN. FUT SWEDEN
UK INDUS POL/PAR LEGIS PROB/SOLV CAP/ISM INT/TRADE
CONTROL SOCISM...MGT CONCPT NAT/COMP 20 SOCDEM/PAR
CIVIL/SERV. PAGE 61 G1196
B59 ECO/DEV POLICY LG/CO NAT/G

US SENATE COMM APPROPRIATIONS,PERSONNEL
ADMINISTRATION AND OPERATIONS OF AGENCY FOR
INTERNATIONAL DEVELOPMENT: SPECIAL HEARING. FINAN
LEAD COST UTIL SKILL...CHARTS 20 CONGRESS AID
CIVIL/SERV. PAGE 60 G1175
B63 ADMIN FOR/AID EFFICIENCY DIPLOM

CIVIL/WAR....CIVIL WAR

CIVIL-MILITARY RELATIONS....SEE CIVMIL/REL

CIVMIL/REL....CIVIL-MILITARY RELATIONS

CONOVER H.L.,CIVILIAN DEFENSE: A SELECTED LIST OF
RECENT REFERENCES (PAMPHLET). USA+45 LOC/G MUNIC
PROB/SOLV ADMIN LEAD TASK WEAPON GOV/REL...POLICY
CON/ANAL 20 CIV/DEFENS. PAGE 13 G0251
N BIBLIOG PLAN WAR CIVMIL/REL

WEIGLEY R.F.,HISTORY OF THE UNITED STATES ARMY.
USA+45 USA-45 SOCIETY NAT/G LEAD WAR GP/REL PWR
...SOC METH/COMP COLD/WAR. PAGE 62 G1222
N FORCES ADMIN ROLE CIVMIL/REL

ZLOTNICK M.,WEAPONS IN SPACE (PAMPHLET). FUT WOR+45
TEC/DEV DIPLOM ARMS/CONT CIVMIL/REL PEACE HABITAT
...CONCPT NEW/IDEA CHARTS. PAGE 65 G1268
N19 SPACE WEAPON NUC/PWR WAR

FULLER G.H.,SELECTED LIST OF RECENT REFERENCES ON AMERICAN NATIONAL DEFENSE (PAMPHLET). USA-45 FINAN NAT/G ARMS/CONT WAR GOV/REL CENTRAL COST PEACE PWR 20. PAGE 20 G0400
B40
BIBLIOG
CIVMIL/REL
FORCES
WEAPON

FULLER G.H.,A LIST OF BIBLIOGRAPHIES ON QUESTIONS RELATING TO NATIONAL DEFENSE (PAMPHLET). USA-45 NAT/G ARMS/CONT WAR GOV/REL COST PEACE 20. PAGE 20 G0402
B41
BIBLIOG/A
FORCES
CIVMIL/REL
WEAPON

US LIBRARY OF CONGRESS,CONDUCT OF THE WAR (APRIL 1941-MARCH 1942). USA-45 WOR-45 LAW INDUS PUB/INST TEC/DEV EDU/PROP CIVMIL/REL 20. PAGE 59 G1155
B42
BIBLIOG/A
WAR
FORCES
PLAN

FULLER G.H.,MILITARY GOVERNMENT: A LIST OF REFERENCES (A PAMPHLET). ITALY UK USA-45 WOR-45 LAW FORCES DOMIN ADMIN ARMS/CONT ORD/FREE PWR ...DECISION 20 CHINJAP. PAGE 21 G0404
B44
BIBLIOG
DIPLOM
CIVMIL/REL
SOVEREIGN

WILCOX J.K.,OFFICIAL DEFENSE PUBLICATIONS, 1941-1945 (NINE VOLS.). USA-45 AGRI INDUS R+D LABOR FORCES TEC/DEV EFFICIENCY PRODUC SKILL WEALTH 20. PAGE 63 G1238
B46
BIBLIOG/A
WAR
CIVMIL/REL
ADMIN

STEWART I.,ORGANIZING SCIENTIFIC RESEARCH FOR WAR: ADMINISTRATIVE HISTORY OF OFFICE OF SCIENTIFIC RESEARCH AND DEVELOPMENT. USA-45 INTELL R+D LABOR WORKER CREATE BUDGET WEAPON CIVMIL/REL GP/REL EFFICIENCY...POLICY 20. PAGE 53 G1036
B48
DELIB/GP
ADMIN
WAR
TEC/DEV

HUZAR E.,THE PURSE AND THE SWORD: CONTROL OF THE ARMY BY CONGRESS THROUGH MILITARY APPROPRIATIONS 1933-1950. NAT/G DELIB/GP EX/STRUC FORCES PROB/SOLV BARGAIN CONFER ADMIN ROUTINE GOV/REL EFFICIENCY ...POLICY COLD/WAR. PAGE 27 G0541
B50
CIVMIL/REL
BUDGET
CONTROL
LEGIS

KOENIG L.W.,THE SALE OF THE TANKERS. USA+45 SEA DIST/IND POL/PAR DIPLOM ADMIN CIVMIL/REL ATTIT ...DECISION 20 PRESIDENT DEPT/STATE. PAGE 31 G0609
B50
NAT/G
POLICY
PLAN
GOV/REL

PERKINS J.A.,"ADMINISTRATION OF THE NATIONAL SECURITY PROGRAM." USA+45 EX/STRUC FORCES ADMIN CIVMIL/REL ORD/FREE 20. PAGE 44 G0868
S53
CONTROL
GP/REL
REPRESENT
PROB/SOLV

HOOPES T.,"CIVILIAN-MILITARY BALANCE." USA+45 CHIEF FORCES PLAN CONTROL WAR GOV/REL GP/REL INGP/REL ...POLICY 19/20. PAGE 27 G0527
S54
CIVMIL/REL
LEAD
PWR
NAT/G

ESTEP R.,AN AIR POWER BIBLIOGRAPHY. USA+45 TEC/DEV BUDGET DIPLOM EDU/PROP DETER CIVMIL/REL...DECISION INT/LAW 20. PAGE 18 G0351
B56
BIBLIOG/A
FORCES
WEAPON
PLAN

KOENIG L.W.,THE TRUMAN ADMINISTRATION: ITS PRINCIPLES AND PRACTICE. USA+45 POL/PAR CHIEF LEGIS DIPLOM DEATH NUC/PWR WAR CIVMIL/REL PEACE ...DECISION 20 TRUMAN/HS PRESIDENT TREATY. PAGE 31 G0610
B56
ADMIN
POLICY
EX/STRUC
GOV/REL

GAVIN J.M.,WAR AND PEACE IN THE SPACE AGE. SPACE USA+45 USSR FORCES PLAN TEC/DEV BAL/PWR DIPLOM ARMS/CONT WEAPON CIVMIL/REL...CHARTS GP/COMP 20 NATO COLD/WAR. PAGE 21 G0414
B58
WAR
DETER
NUC/PWR
PEACE

US DEPARTMENT OF THE ARMY,BIBLIOGRAPHY ON LIMITED WAR (PAMPHLET). USA+45 TEC/DEV CONTROL RISK COERCE DETER NUC/PWR WEAPON ADJUST PEACE ALL/VALS ORD/FREE 20. PAGE 57 G1127
B58
BIBLIOG/A
WAR
FORCES
CIVMIL/REL

LANG D.,FROM HIROSHIMA TO THE MOON: CHRONICLES OF LIFE IN THE ATOMIC AGE. USA+45 OP/RES CONTROL ARMS/CONT WAR CIVMIL/REL PEACE HABITAT MORAL PWR ...OBS INT 20 AEC. PAGE 32 G0633
B59
NUC/PWR
SPACE
HEALTH
TEC/DEV

SPANIER J.W.,THE TRUMAN-MACARTHUR CONTROVERSY AND THE KOREAN WAR. USA+45 TOP/EX PROB/SOLV LEAD ATTIT
B59
CIVMIL/REL
FORCES

PWR...POLICY BIBLIOG/A UN. PAGE 52 G1023
CHIEF
WAR

BROOKINGS INSTITUTION,UNITED STATES FOREIGN POLICY: STUDY NO 9: THE FORMULATION AND ADMINISTRATION OF UNITED STATES FOREIGN POLICY. USA+45 WOR+45 EX/STRUC LEGIS BAL/PWR FOR/AID EDU/PROP CIVMIL/REL GOV/REL...INT COLD/WAR. PAGE 9 G0174
B60
DIPLOM
INT/ORG
CREATE

CARPER E.T.,THE DEFENSE APPROPRIATIONS RIDER (PAMPHLET). USA+45 CONSTN CHIEF DELIB/GP LEGIS BUDGET LOBBY CIVMIL/REL...POLICY 20 CONGRESS EISNHWR/DD DEPT/DEFEN PRESIDENT BOSTON. PAGE 11 G0212
B60
GOV/REL
ADJUD
LAW
CONTROL

JANOWITZ M.,THE PROFESSIONAL SOLDIER. CULTURE STRATA STRUCT FAM PROB/SOLV TEC/DEV COERCE WAR CIVMIL/REL NAT/LISM AGE HEREDITY ALL/VALS CONSERVE ...MGT WORSHIP. PAGE 28 G0560
B60
FORCES
MYTH
LEAD
ELITES

LYONS G.M.,"THE NEW CIVIL-MILITARY RELATIONS." USA+45 NAT/G EX/STRUC TOP/EX PROB/SOLV ADMIN EXEC PARTIC 20. PAGE 35 G0681
S61
CIVMIL/REL
PWR
REPRESENT

DUPRE J.S.,SCIENCE AND THE NATION: POLICY AND POLITICS. USA+45 LAW ACADEM FORCES ADMIN CIVMIL/REL GOV/REL EFFICIENCY PEACE...TREND 20 SCI/ADVSRY. PAGE 16 G0322
B62
R+D
INDUS
TEC/DEV
NUC/PWR

MACHLUP F.,THE PRODUCTION AND DISTRIBUTION OF KNOWLEDGE IN THE UNITED STATES. USA+45 COM/IND INDUS SCHOOL SECT WORKER COMPUTER CREATE CIVMIL/REL COST EFFICIENCY WEALTH 20. PAGE 35 G0688
B62
ACADEM
TEC/DEV
EDU/PROP
R+D

THOMSON G.P.,NUCLEAR ENERGY IN BRITAIN DURING THE LAST WAR: THE CHERWELL SIMON LECTURE (MONOGRAPH). UK R+D CONSULT FORCES PLAN DIPLOM TASK CIVMIL/REL ROLE...PHIL/SCI NEW/IDEA LAB/EXP 20 MAUD. PAGE 54 G1071
B62
CREATE
TEC/DEV
WAR
NUC/PWR

PERLO V.,MILITARISM AND INDUSTRY. USA+45 INT/TRADE EDU/PROP DETER KNOWL...CHARTS MAPS 20. PAGE 44 G0869
B63
CIVMIL/REL
INDUS
LOBBY
ARMS/CONT

US SENATE,DOCUMENTS ON INTERNATIONAL AS"ECTS OF EXPLORATION AND USE OF OUTER SPACE, 1954-62: STAFF REPORT FOR COMM AERON SPACE SCI. USA+45 USSR LEGIS LEAD CIVMIL/REL PEACE...POLICY INT/LAW ANTHOL 20 CONGRESS NASA KHRUSH/N. PAGE 59 G1162
B63
SPACE
UTIL
GOV/REL
DIPLOM

US AIR FORCE ACADEMY ASSEMBLY,OUTER SPACE: FINAL REPORT APRIL 1-4, 1964. FUT USA+45 WOR+45 LAW DELIB/GP CONFER ARMS/CONT WAR PEACE ATTIT MORAL ...ANTHOL 20 NASA. PAGE 56 G1104
B64
SPACE
CIVMIL/REL
NUC/PWR
DIPLOM

ATOMIC INDUSTRIAL FORUM,SAFEGUARDS AGAINST DIVERSION OF NUCLEAR MATERIALS FROM PEACEFUL TO MILITARY PURPOSES. WOR+45 DELIB/GP FORCES PLAN DIPLOM CONFER PEACE...ANTHOL 20 IAEA. PAGE 4 G0081
B65
NUC/PWR
CIVMIL/REL
INSPECT
CONTROL

BEAUFRE A.,AN INTRODUCTION TO STRATEGY, WITH PARTICULAR REFERENCE TO PROBLEMS OF DEFENSE, POLITICS, ECONOMICS IN THE NUCLEAR AGE. WOR+45 FORCES DIPLOM DETER CIVMIL/REL GP/REL...NEW/IDEA IDEA/COMP 20. PAGE 6 G0111
B65
PLAN
NUC/PWR
WEAPON
DECISION

KNORR K.,SCIENCE AND DEFENSE: SOME CRITICAL THOUGHTS ON MILITARY RESEARCH AND DEVELOPMENT. USA+45 ACT/RES CREATE BUDGET ECO/TAC DEMAND DECISION. PAGE 31 G0608
B65
CIVMIL/REL
R+D
FORCES
PLAN

LAPP R.E.,THE NEW PRIESTHOOD; THE SCIENTIFIC ELITE AND THE USES OF POWER. USA+45 ELITES INTELL SOCIETY R+D NAT/G CHIEF LEGIS CIVMIL/REL GP/REL PWR 20 PRESIDENT CONGRESS. PAGE 32 G0635
B65
TEC/DEV
TECHRACY
CONTROL
POPULISM

MELMANS S.,OUR DEPLETED SOCIETY. SPACE USA+45 ECO/DEV FORCES BUDGET ECO/TAC ADMIN WEAPON EFFICIENCY 20 COLD/WAR. PAGE 38 G0753
B65
CIVMIL/REL
INDUS
EDU/PROP
CONTROL

B65
THAYER F.C. JR.,AIR TRANSPORT POLICY AND NATIONAL AIR
SECURITY: A POLITICAL, ECONOMIC, AND MILITARY FORCES
ANALYSIS. DIST/IND OP/RES PLAN TEC/DEV DIPLOM DETER CIVMIL/REL
WAR COST EFFICIENCY...POLICY BIBLIOG 20 DEPT/DEFEN ORD/FREE
FAA CAB. PAGE 54 G1066

B65
US SENATE,US INTERNATIONAL SPACE PROGRAMS, 1959-65: SPACE
STAFF REPORT FOR COMM ON AERONAUTICAL AND SPACE DIPLOM
SCIENCES. WOR+45 VOL/ASSN CIVMIL/REL 20 CONGRESS PLAN
NASA TREATY. PAGE 59 G1163 GOV/REL

B65
US SENATE COMM GOVT OPERATIONS,ORGANIZATION OF ADMIN
FEDERAL EXECUTIVE DEPARTMENTS AND AGENCIES: REPORT EX/STRUC
OF MARCH 23, 1965. USA+45 FORCES LEGIS DIPLOM GOV/REL
ROUTINE CIVMIL/REL EFFICIENCY FEDERAL...MGT STAT. ORG/CHARTS
PAGE 60 G1179

L65
PILISUK M.,"IS THERE A MILITARY INDUSTRIAL COMPLEX ELITES
WHICH PREVENTS PEACE CONSENSUS: COUNTERVAILING WEAPON
POWER IN PLURALIST SYSTEMS." INDUS R+D ACADEM PEACE
FEEDBACK CIVMIL/REL ADJUST CONSEN ATTIT RIGID/FLEX ARMS/CONT
...CENSUS IDEA/COMP BIBLIOG. PAGE 45 G0878

B66
RUPPENTHAL K.M.,TRANSPORTATION AND TOMORROW. FUT DIST/IND
SPACE USA+45 SEA AIR FORCES TEC/DEV INT/TRADE PLAN
...ANTHOL 20 RAILROAD. PAGE 48 G0946 CIVMIL/REL
PREDICT

B66
US SENATE,POLICY PLANNING FOR AERONAUTICAL RESEARCH SPACE
AND DEVELOPMENT: STAFF REPORT FOR COMM ON CIVMIL/REL
AERONAUTICAL AND SPACE SCIENCES. USA+45 AIR GOV/REL
DIST/IND PLAN...POLICY CHARTS 20 CONGRESS NASA. R+D
PAGE 59 G1164

B66
WHITNAH D.R.,SAFER SKYWAYS. DIST/IND DELIB/GP ADMIN
FORCES TOP/EX WORKER TEC/DEV ROUTINE WAR CIVMIL/REL NAT/G
COST...TIME/SEQ 20 FAA CAB. PAGE 63 G1235 AIR
GOV/REL

L66
ZOPPO C.E.,"NUCLEAR TECHNOLOGY, MULTIPOLARITY, AND NET/THEORY
INTERNATIONAL STABILITY." ASIA RUSSIA USA+45 STRUCT ORD/FREE
TOP/EX BAL/PWR DIPLOM DETER CIVMIL/REL NAT/COMP. DECISION
PAGE 65 G1270 NUC/PWR

S66
COHEN A.,"THE TECHNOLOGY/ELITE APPROACH TO THE ECO/UNDEV
DEVELOPMENTAL PROCESS* PERUVIAN CASE STUDY." ELITES
L/A+17C STRUCT CREATE ECO/TAC FOR/AID CIVMIL/REL PERU
MARXISM TECHRACY HYPO/EXP. PAGE 12 G0239

B67
BURNS E.L.M.,MEGAMURDER. WOR+45 LAW INT/ORG NAT/G FORCES
BAL/PWR DIPLOM DETER MURDER WEAPON CIVMIL/REL PEACE PLAN
...INT/LAW TREND 20. PAGE 10 G0193 WAR
NUC/PWR

B67
HOROWITZ I.L.,THE RISE AND FALL OF PROJECT CAMELOT: NAT/G
STUDIES IN THE RELATIONSHIP BETWEEN SOCIAL SCIENCE ACADEM
AND PRACTICAL POLITICS. USA+45 WOR+45 CULTURE ACT/RES
FORCES LEGIS EXEC CIVMIL/REL KNOWL...POLICY SOC GP/REL
METH/CNCPT 20. PAGE 27 G0529

B67
MACKINTOSH J.M.,JUGGERNAUT. USSR NAT/G POL/PAR WAR
ADMIN LEAD CIVMIL/REL COST TOTALSM PWR MARXISM FORCES
...GOV/COMP 20. PAGE 35 G0691 COM
PROF/ORG

L67
EINAUDI L.,"ANNOTATED BIBLIOGRAPHY OF LATIN BIBLIOG/A
AMERICAN MILITARY JOURNALS" LAW TEC/DEV DOMIN NAT/G
EDU/PROP COERCE WAR CIVMIL/REL 20. PAGE 17 G0336 FORCES
L/A+17C

S67
CHIU S.M.,"CHINA'S MILITARY POSTURE." CHINA/COM FORCES
ELITES NAT/G POL/PAR TEC/DEV ECO/TAC DOMIN CONTROL CIVMIL/REL
LEAD REV MARXISM 20 MAO. PAGE 12 G0228 NUC/PWR
DIPLOM

S67
DE NEUFVILLE R.,"EDUCATION AT THE ACADEMIES." FORCES
USA+45 ELITES CONSULT EX/STRUC COMPUTER PLAN ACADEM
PROB/SOLV TASK CIVMIL/REL ORD/FREE 20. PAGE 15 TEC/DEV
G0286 SKILL

S67
LALL B.G.,"GAPS IN THE ABM DEBATE." NAT/G DIPLOM NUC/PWR
DETER CIVMIL/REL 20. PAGE 32 G0630 ARMS/CONT
EX/STRUC
FORCES

S67
TAGIL S.,"WEGENER, RAEDER, AND THE GERMAN NAVAL SEA
STRATEGY: VIEWPOINTS ON THE CONDITIONS FOR THE POLICY
INFLUENCE OF IDEAS." GERMANY WOR-45...IDEA/COMP HIST/WRIT
METH 20. PAGE 53 G1049 CIVMIL/REL

S67
WOLFE T.W.,"SOVIET MILITARY POLICY AT THE FIFTY FORCES
YEAR MARK." USSR VIETNAM WOR+45 RATION AGREE WAR POLICY
WEAPON CIVMIL/REL TREATY. PAGE 64 G1254 TIME/SEQ
PLAN

N67
US SENATE COMM AERO SPACE SCI,AERONAUTICAL RESEARCH AIR
AND DEVELOPMENT POLICY (PAMPHLET). SPACE USA+45 R+D
INDUS CIVMIL/REL CONGRESS PRESIDENT NASA SENATE. POLICY
PAGE 60 G1169 PLAN

CLAN....SEE KIN

CLARK G. G0231

CLARK/JB....JOHN BATES CLARK

CLARKE A.C. G0232

CLASS DIVISION....SEE STRATA

CLASS, SOCIAL....SEE STRATA

CLASSIF....CLASSIFICATION, TYPOLOGY, SET THEORY

N
AMERICAN DOCUMENTATION INST,DOCUMENTATION BIBLIOG/A
ABSTRACTS. WOR+45 NAT/G COMPUTER CREATE TEC/DEV AUTOMAT
DIPLOM EDU/PROP REGION KNOWL...PHIL/SCI CLASSIF COMPUT/IR
LING. PAGE 3 G0051 R+D

B36
US LIBRARY OF CONGRESS,CLASSIFIED GUIDE TO MATERIAL BIBLIOG
IN THE LIBRARY OF CONGRESS COVERING URBAN COMMUNITY CLASSIF
DEVELOPMENT. USA+45 CREATE PROB/SOLV ADMIN 20. MUNIC
PAGE 59 G1154 PLAN

B55
RILEY V.,INTERINDUSTRY ECONOMIC STUDIES. USA+45 BIBLIOG
COMPUTER ADMIN OPTIMAL PRODUC...MGT CLASSIF STAT. ECO/DEV
PAGE 47 G0922 PLAN
STRUCT

S55
WRIGHT Q.,"THE PEACEFUL ADJUSTMENT OF INTERNATIONAL R+D
RELATIONS: PROBLEMS AND RESEARCH APPROACHES." UNIV METH/CNCPT
INTELL EDU/PROP ADJUD ROUTINE KNOWL SKILL...INT/LAW PEACE
JURID PHIL/SCI CLASSIF 20. PAGE 64 G1258

S56
EASTON D.,"LIMITS OF THE EQUILIBRIUM MODEL IN METH/CNCPT
SOCIAL RESEARCH." STRUCT GP/REL PWR...PHIL/SCI GEN/METH
CLASSIF. PAGE 17 G0330 R+D
QUANT

S57
DUNCAN O.D.,"THE MEASUREMENT OF POPULATION GEOG
DISTRIBUTION" (BMR)" WOR+45...QUANT STAT CENSUS PHIL/SCI
CHARTS 20. PAGE 16 G0321 PROB/SOLV
CLASSIF

B59
DAHRENDORF R.,CLASS AND CLASS CONFLICT IN VOL/ASSN
INDUSTRIAL SOCIETY. LABOR NAT/G COERCE ROLE PLURISM STRUCT
...POLICY MGT CONCPT CLASSIF. PAGE 14 G0271 SOC
GP/REL

B60
WALDO D.,THE RESEARCH FUNCTION OF UNIVERSITY ADMIN
BUREAUS AND INSTITUTES FOR GOVERNMENTAL-RELATED R+D
RESEARCH. FINAN ACADEM NAT/G INGP/REL ROLE...POLICY MUNIC
CLASSIF GOV/COMP. PAGE 61 G1205

B63
DEAN A.L.,FEDERAL AGENCY APPROACHES TO FIELD ADMIN
MANAGEMENT (PAMPHLET). R+D DELIB/GP EX/STRUC MGT
PROB/SOLV GOV/REL...CLASSIF BIBLIOG 20 FAA NASA NAT/G
DEPT/HEW POSTAL/SYS IRS. PAGE 15 G0287 OP/RES

B63
FOSKETT D.J.,CLASSIFICATION AND INDEXING IN THE PROB/SOLV
SOCIAL SCIENCES. WOR+45 R+D ACT/RES CREATE OP/RES CON/ANAL
TEC/DEV AUTOMAT ROLE...SOC COMPUT/IR BIBLIOG. CLASSIF

PAGE 20 G0384

BALASSA B..TRADE PROSPECTS FOR DEVELOPING
COUNTRIES. WOR+45 ECO/DEV AGRI EXTR/IND INDUS
CREATE PLAN PRICE...ECOMETRIC CLASSIF TIME/SEQ
GEN/METH. PAGE 5 G0087
B64
INT/TRADE
ECO/UNDEV
TREND
STAT

COOMBS C.H..A THEORY OF DATA....MGT PHIL/SCI SOC
CLASSIF MATH PROBABIL STAT QU. PAGE 13 G0254
B64
CON/ANAL
GEN/METH
TESTS
PSY

ALKER H.R. JR..MATHEMATICS AND POLITICS. PROB/SOLV
...DECISION PHIL/SCI CLASSIF QUANT STAT GAME
GEN/LAWS INDEX. PAGE 2 G0042
B65
GEN/METH
CONCPT
MATH

BLOOMFIELD L..SOVIET INTERESTS IN ARMS CONTROL AND
DISARMAMENT* THE DECADE UNDER KHRUSHCHEV 1954-1964.
ASIA FORCES ACT/RES EDU/PROP DETER NUC/PWR WEAPON
COST ATTIT...PHIL/SCI CLASSIF STAT NET/THEORY GAME
BIBLIOG. PAGE 7 G0139
B65
USSR
ARMS/CONT
DIPLOM
TREND

ABT C.C.."CONTROLLING FUTURE ARMS." USSR PLAN
BAL/PWR DIPLOM NUC/PWR COST...CLASSIF STAT CHARTS.
PAGE 2 G0027
S65
PREDICT
FUT
ARMS/CONT
TEC/DEV

GREGG P.M.."DIMENSIONS OF POLITICAL SYSTEMS: FACTOR
ANALYSIS OF A CROSS POLITY SURVEY." TEC/DEV
...DECISION PHIL/SCI CONCPT STAT IDEA/COMP
GEN/LAWS. PAGE 23 G0447
S65
SIMUL
GEN/METH
CLASSIF

LAMBERT J..LATIN AMERICA: SOCIAL STRUCTURES AND
POLITICAL INSTITUTIONS. STRUCT TEC/DEV DIPLOM ADMIN
COLONIAL LEAD ATTIT...SOC CLASSIF NAT/COMP 17/20.
PAGE 32 G0631
B67
L/A+17C
NAT/G
ECO/UNDEV
SOCIETY

US SUPERINTENDENT OF DOCUMENTS.LIBRARY OF CONGRESS
(PRICE LIST 83). AFR ASIA EUR+WWI USA-45 USSR NAT/G
DIPLOM CONFER CT/SYS WAR...DECISION PHIL/SCI
CLASSIF 19/20 CONGRESS PRESIDENT. PAGE 61 G1189
B67
BIBLIOG/A
USA+45
AUTOMAT
LAW

FRIED M.."FUNCTIONS OF THE WORKING CLASS COMMUNITY
IN MODERN URBAN SOCIETY* IMPLICATIONS FOR FORCED
RELOCATION." USA+45 INDUS R+D NEIGH PLAN TEC/DEV
PARTIC GP/REL ATTIT...SOC STAT CHARTS. PAGE 20
G0393
S67
CLASSIF
WORKER
MUNIC
ADJUST

SKOLNIKOFF E.B.."MAKING FOREIGN POLICY" PROB/SOLV
EFFICIENCY PERCEPT PWR...MGT METH/CNCPT CLASSIF 20.
PAGE 51 G1009
S67
TEC/DEV
CONTROL
USA+45
NAT/G

CLAUSWTZ/K....KARL VON CLAUSEWITZ

CLEAVELAND F.N. G0233

CLEMENCE/G....GEORGES CLEMENCEAU

CLEMENCEAU, GEORGES....SEE CLEMENCE/G

CLEMENS W.C. G0139,G0143,G0234

CLEMSON....CLEMSON UNIVERSITY

CLEVELAND H. G0235

CLEVELAND....CLEVELAND, OHIO

CLEVELND/G....PRESIDENT GROVER CLEVELAND

CLIENT....CLIENTS, CLIENTELE (BUT NOT CUSTOMERS)

REDFORD E.S..PUBLIC ADMINISTRATION AND POLICY
FORMATION: STUDIES IN OIL, GAS, BANKING, RIVER
DEVELOPMENT AND CORPORATE INVESTIGATIONS. USA+45
CLIENT NAT/G ADMIN LOBBY REPRESENT GOV/REL INGP/REL
20. PAGE 46 G0908
B56
EX/STRUC
PROB/SOLV
CONTROL
EXEC

CAVERS D.F.."ADMINISTRATIVE DECISION-MAKING IN
NUCLEAR FACILITIES LICENSING." USA+45 CLIENT ADMIN
EXEC 20 AEC. PAGE 11 G0218
L62
REPRESENT
LOBBY
PWR
CONTROL

EDELMAN M..THE SYMBOLIC USES OF POWER. USA+45
EX/STRUC CONTROL GP/REL INGP/REL...MGT T. PAGE 17
G0333
B64
CLIENT
PWR
EXEC
ELITES

STREET D..ORGANIZATION FOR TREATMENT. CLIENT PROVS
PUB/INST PLAN CONTROL PARTIC REPRESENT ATTIT PWR
...POLICY BIBLIOG. PAGE 53 G1044
B66
GP/COMP
AGE/Y
ADMIN
VOL/ASSN

CLIFFORD/C....CLARK CLIFFORD

CLIQUES....SEE FACE/GP

CLUBS....SEE VOL/ASSN, FACE/GP

CMA....CANADIAN MEDICAL ASSOCIATION

TAYLOR M.G.."THE ROLE OF THE MEDICAL PROFESSION IN
THE FORMULATION AND EXECUTION OF PUBLIC POLICY"
(BMR)" CANADA NAT/G CONSULT ADMIN REPRESENT GP/REL
ROLE SOVEREIGN...DECISION 20 CMA. PAGE 54 G1058
S60
PROF/ORG
HEALTH
LOBBY
POLICY

CMN/WLTH

GT BRIT MIN OVERSEAS DEV, LIB, TECHNICAL CO-
OPERATION -- A BIBLIOGRAPHY. UK LAW SOCIETY DIPLOM
ECO/TAC FOR/AID...STAT 20 CMN/WLTH. PAGE 39 G0775
N
BIBLIOG
TEC/DEV
ECO/DEV
NAT/G

ROYAL INST. INT. AFF.."ANNUAL REPORT OF THE
COUNCIL: 1951-1952." WOR+45 CREATE KNOWL...MGT
COLD/WAR CMN/WLTH TOT/POP VAL/FREE 20. PAGE 48
G0943
L52
R+D
EDU/PROP

MARTIN L.W.."THE MARKET FOR STRATEGIC IDEAS IN
BRITAIN: THE 'SANDYS ERA'" UK ARMS/CONT WAR GOV/REL
OPTIMAL...POLICY DECISION GOV/COMP COLD/WAR
CMN/WLTH. PAGE 36 G0714
S62
DIPLOM
COERCE
FORCES
PWR

GOLDBERG A.."ATOMIC ORIGINS OF THE BRITISH NUCLEAR
DETERRENT." EUR+WWI UK NAT/G TOP/EX PLAN BAL/PWR
DOMIN DETER CHOOSE ATTIT DRIVE HEALTH ORD/FREE PWR
RESPECT...CONCPT VAL/FREE COLD/WAR 20 CMN/WLTH.
PAGE 22 G0425
L64
CREATE
FORCES
NUC/PWR

COALITIONS....SEE VOL/ASSN

COASTGUARD....COAST GUARD

COBB/HOWLL....HOWELL COBB

COCH L. G0236

COENEN E. G0237

COERCE....COERCION, VIOLENCE; SEE ALSO FORCES,
     PROCESSES AND PRACTICES INDEX, PART G, P. XIII

OGBURN W..TECHNOLOGY AND INTERNATIONAL RELATIONS.
WOR+45 WOR-45 ECO/DEV CREATE PLAN ECO/TAC EDU/PROP
COERCE PWR SKILL WEALTH...TECHNIC PSY SOC NEW/IDEA
CHARTS TOT/POP 20. PAGE 43 G0837
B49
TEC/DEV
DIPLOM
INT/ORG

CROWTHER J.G..SCIENCE AT WAR. EUR+WWI PLAN TEC/DEV
DOMIN COERCE NUC/PWR WEAPON KNOWL PWR...CONCPT OBS
TREND VAL/FREE 20. PAGE 14 G0265
B50
R+D
FORCES
WAR
UK

LANGER W.L..THE UNDECLARED WAR, 1940-1941. EUR+WWI
GERMANY USA-45 USSR AIR FORCES TEC/DEV CONFER
CONTROL COERCE PERCEPT ORD/FREE PWR 20 CHINJAP
EUROPE. PAGE 32 G0634
B53
WAR
POLICY
DIPLOM

ARON R..CENTURY OF TOTAL WAR. FUT WOR+45 WOR-45
SOCIETY INT/ORG NAT/G FORCES TOP/EX CREATE BAL/PWR
DOMIN EDU/PROP COERCE DETER PEACE TOTALISM PWR
...TIME/SEQ TREND COLD/WAR TOT/POP VAL/FREE
LEAGUE/NAT 20. PAGE 4 G0066
B54
ATTIT
WAR

MIKSCHE F.O..ATOMIC WEAPONS AND ARMIES. FUT WOR+45
WOR-45 SOCIETY COERCE DETER WEAPON PWR...POLICY
B55
TEC/DEV
FORCES

WELF/ST PSY CONCPT INT SYS/QU KNO/TEST TOT/POP 20. NUC/PWR
PAGE 39 G0765

S55
GLADSTONE A.E.,"THE POSSIBILITY OF PREDICTING PHIL/SCI
REACTIONS TO INTERNATIONAL EVENTS." UNIV SOCIETY CONCPT
NAT/G FORCES CREATE EDU/PROP COERCE WAR ATTIT
PERSON KNOWL PWR SKILL...METH/CNCPT NEW/IDEA
ORG/CHARTS. PAGE 21 G0420

B56
BLACKETT P.M.S.,ATOMIC WEAPONS AND EAST-WEST FORCES
RELATIONS. FUT WOR+45 INT/ORG DELIB/GP COERCE ATTIT PWR
RIGID/FLEX KNOWL...RELATIV HIST/WRIT TREND GEN/METH ARMS/CONT
COLD/WAR 20. PAGE 7 G0138 NUC/PWR

B57
KISSINGER H.A.,NUCLEAR WEAPONS AND FOREIGN POLICY. PLAN
FUT WOR+45 INT/ORG ACT/RES TEC/DEV ECO/TAC DETER
DIPLOM ARMS/CONT COERCE ATTIT KNOWL PWR...DECISION NUC/PWR
GEOG CHARTS 20. PAGE 31 G0602

S57
JANOWITZ M.,"MILITARY ELITES AND THE STUDY OF WAR." FORCES
USA+45 WOR-45 STRATA NAT/G PROF/ORG TEC/DEV DOMIN ELITES
EDU/PROP COERCE WAR ATTIT RIGID/FLEX PWR RESPECT
...MGT TREND STERTYP GEN/METH 20. PAGE 28 G0558

S57
MORTON L.,"THE DECISION TO USE THE BOMB." FORCES NUC/PWR
TOP/EX DOMIN COERCE PEACE. PAGE 40 G0788 DIPLOM
WAR

B58
ARON R.,ON WAR: ATOMIC WEAPONS AND GLOBAL DIPLOMACY ARMS/CONT
(TRANS. BY TERENCE KILMARTIN). WOR+45 SOCIETY NUC/PWR
FORCES BAL/PWR WAR WEAPON PERSON...SOC 20. PAGE 4 COERCE
G0067 DIPLOM

B58
US DEPARTMENT OF THE ARMY,BIBLIOGRAPHY ON LIMITED BIBLIOG/A
WAR (PAMPHLET). USA+45 TEC/DEV CONTROL RISK COERCE WAR
DETER NUC/PWR WEAPON ADJUST PEACE ALL/VALS ORD/FREE FORCES
20. PAGE 57 G1127 CIVMIL/REL

S58
HUNTINGTON S.P.,"ARMS RACES: PREREQUISITES AND FORCES
RESULTS." EUR+WWI MOD/EUR USA+45 WOR+45 WOR-45 PWR
NAT/G TEC/DEV BAL/PWR COERCE DETER ATTIT...POLICY ARMS/CONT
TREND 20. PAGE 27 G0537

S58
SINGER J.D.,"THREAT PERCEPTION AND THE ARMAMENT PERCEPT
TENSION DILEMMA." WOR+45 WOR-45 ELITES INT/ORG ARMS/CONT
NAT/G DELIB/GP PLAN LEGIT COERCE DETER ATTIT BAL/PWR
RIGID/FLEX PWR...DECISION PSY 20. PAGE 51 G1002

S58
THOMPSON K.W.,"NATIONAL SECURITY IN A NUCLEAR AGE." FORCES
USA+45 WOR+45 SOCIETY INT/ORG NAT/G TOP/EX DIPLOM PWR
DOMIN EDU/PROP LEGIT ARMS/CONT COERCE ORD/FREE BAL/PWR
...TREND STERTYP TOT/POP VAL/FREE COLD/WAR 20.
PAGE 54 G1068

B59
DAHRENDORF R.,CLASS AND CLASS CONFLICT IN VOL/ASSN
INDUSTRIAL SOCIETY. LABOR NAT/G COERCE ROLE PLURISM STRUCT
...POLICY MGT CONCPT CLASSIF. PAGE 14 G0271 SOC
GP/REL

B59
GREENFIELD K.R.,COMMAND DECISIONS. ASIA EUR+WWI PLAN
S/ASIA EUR+45 WOR-45 NAT/G CONSULT DELIB/GP COERCE FORCES
NUC/PWR PWR...OBS 20 CHINJAP. PAGE 23 G0446 WAR
WEAPON

L59
BURNS A.L.,"THE RATIONALE OF CATALYTIC WAR." COM COERCE
USA+45 WOR+45 R+D NAT/G FORCES ACT/RES TEC/DEV PWR NUC/PWR
...DECISION HYPO/EXP TOT/POP 20. PAGE 10 G0191 WAR

L59
BURNS A.L.,"POWER POLITICS AND THE GROWING NUCLEAR FORCES
CLUB." FUT WOR+45 TEC/DEV EXEC ARMS/CONT COERCE BAL/PWR
DETER...DECISION HYPO/EXP 20. PAGE 10 G0192 NUC/PWR

S59
WILLIAMS B.H.,"SCIENTIFIC METHOD IN FOREIGN PLAN
POLICY." WOR+45 NAT/G FORCES TOP/EX DOMIN LEGIT PHIL/SCI
COERCE PEACE ATTIT KNOWL ORD/FREE PWR...GEN/LAWS DIPLOM
GEN/METH TOT/POP COLD/WAR NAZI. PAGE 63 G1241

B60
BARNET R.,WHO WANTS DISARMAMENT. COM EUR+WWI USA+45 PLAN
USSR INT/ORG NAT/G BAL/PWR DIPLOM EDU/PROP COERCE FORCES
DETER NUC/PWR WAR WEAPON ATTIT PWR...TIME/SEQ ARMS/CONT

COLD/WAR CONGRESS 20. PAGE 5 G0096

B60
JANOWITZ M.,THE PROFESSIONAL SOLDIER. CULTURE FORCES
STRATA STRUCT FAM PROB/SOLV TEC/DEV COERCE WAR MYTH
CIVMIL/REL NAT/LISM AGE HEREDITY ALL/VALS CONSERVE LEAD
...MGT WORSHIP. PAGE 28 G0560 ELITES

B60
LE GHAIT E.,NO CARTE BLANCHE TO CAPRICORN; THE DETER
FOLLY OF NUCLEAR WAR. WOR+45 INT/ORG BAL/PWR DIPLOM NUC/PWR
RISK COERCE...CENSUS 20 NATO. PAGE 33 G0647 PLAN
DECISION

B60
US HOUSE COMM. SCI. ASTRONAUT.,OCEAN SCIENCES AND R+D
NATIONAL SECURITY. FUT SEA ECO/DEV EXTR/IND INT/ORG ORD/FREE
NAT/G FORCES ACT/RES TEC/DEV ECO/TAC COERCE WAR
BIO/SOC KNOWL PWR...CONCPT RECORD LAB/EXP 20.
PAGE 59 G1153

L60
BRENNAN D.G.,"SETTING AND GOALS OF ARMS CONTROL." FORCES
FUT USA+45 WOR+45 INTELL INT/ORG NAT/G COERCE
VOL/ASSN CONSULT PLAN DIPLOM ECO/TAC ADMIN KNOWL ARMS/CONT
PWR...POLICY CONCPT TREND COLD/WAR 20. PAGE 8 G0164 DETER

L60
HOLTON G.,"ARMS CONTROL." FUT WOR+45 CULTURE ACT/RES
INT/ORG NAT/G FORCES TOP/EX PLAN EDU/PROP COERCE CONSULT
ATTIT RIGID/FLEX ORD/FREE...POLICY PHIL/SCI SOC ARMS/CONT
TREND COLD/WAR. PAGE 27 G0524 NUC/PWR

L60
JACOB P.E.,"THE DISARMAMENT CONSENSUS." USA+45 USSR DELIB/GP
WOR+45 INT/ORG NAT/G ACT/RES TEC/DEV BAL/PWR ATTIT
EDU/PROP ADMIN COERCE DETER NUC/PWR CONSEN ARMS/CONT
RIGID/FLEX PWR...CONCPT RECORD CHARTS COLD/WAR 20.
PAGE 28 G0552

S60
DOUGHERTY J.E.,"KEY TO SECURITY: DISARMAMENT OR FORCES
ARMS STABILITY." COM USA+45 USSR INT/ORG NAT/G ORD/FREE
CREATE EDU/PROP COERCE DETER ATTIT PWR...DECISION ARMS/CONT
CONCPT MYTH NEW/IDEA TREND 20 COLD/WAR. PAGE 16 NUC/PWR
G0311

S60
IKLE F.C.,"NTH COUNTRIES AND DISARMAMENT." WOR+45 FUT
DELIB/GP ECO/TAC DOMIN EDU/PROP LEGIT ROUTINE INT/ORG
COERCE RIGID/FLEX ORD/FREE...MARXIST TREND 20. ARMS/CONT
PAGE 28 G0543 NUC/PWR

B61
KAHN H.,ON THERMONUCLEAR WAR. FUT UNIV WOR+45 DETER
ECO/DEV CONSULT EX/STRUC TOP/EX ACT/RES CREATE PLAN NUC/PWR
COERCE WAR PERSON ALL/VALS...POLICY GEOG CONCPT SOCIETY
METH/CNCPT OBS TREND 20. PAGE 29 G0569

B61
US SENATE COMM GOVT OPERATIONS,ORGANIZING FOR POLICY
NATIONAL SECURITY. COM USA+45 BUDGET DIPLOM DETER PLAN
NUC/PWR WAR WEAPON ORD/FREE...BIBLIOG 20 COLD/WAR. FORCES
PAGE 60 G1176 COERCE

B62
BOULDING K.E.,CONFLICT AND DEFENSE: A GENERAL MATH
THEORY. FUT SOCIETY INT/ORG NAT/G CREATE BAL/PWR SIMUL
COERCE NAT/LISM DRIVE ALL/VALS...PLURIST DECISION PEACE
CONCPT METH/CNCPT TREND HYPO/EXP TOT/POP 20. PAGE 8 WAR
G0157

B62
FORBES H.W.,THE STRATEGY OF DISARMAMENT. FUT WOR+45 PLAN
INT/ORG VOL/ASSN CONSULT ARMS/CONT COERCE NUC/PWR FORCES
WAR DRIVE RIGID/FLEX ORD/FREE PWR...POLICY CONCPT DIPLOM
OBS TREND STERTYP 20. PAGE 19 G0378

B62
MELMAN S.,DISARMAMENT: ITS POLITICS AND ECONOMICS. NAT/G
WOR+45 DELIB/GP FORCES ECO/TAC DOMIN EDU/PROP LEGIT ORD/FREE
COERCE PWR...POLICY CONCPT 20. PAGE 38 G0752 ARMS/CONT
NUC/PWR

S62
CRANE R.D.,"LAW AND STRATEGY IN SPACE." FUT USA+45 CONCPT
WOR+45 AIR LAW INT/ORG NAT/G FORCES ACT/RES PLAN SPACE
BAL/PWR LEGIT ARMS/CONT COERCE ORD/FREE...POLICY
INT/LAW JURID SOC/EXP 20 TREATY. PAGE 13 G0261

S62
GORDON B.K.,"NUCLEAR WEAPONS: RUSSIAN AND ORD/FREE
AMERICAN." COM USA+45 USSR NAT/G FORCES ACT/RES COERCE
TEC/DEV PERCEPT RIGID/FLEX PWR SKILL...MGT NUC/PWR
METH/CNCPT QUANT OBS TIME/SEQ CON/ANAL GEN/METH
TOT/POP VAL/FREE 20. PAGE 22 G0433

MARTIN L.W.,"THE MARKET FOR STRATEGIC IDEAS IN BRITAIN: THE 'SANDYS ERA'" UK ARMS/CONT WAR GOV/REL OPTIMAL...POLICY DECISION GOV/COMP COLD/WAR CMN/WLTH. PAGE 36 G0714
S62 DIPLOM COERCE FORCES PWR

PHIPPS T.E.,"THE CASE FOR DETERRENCE." FUT WOR+45 SOCIETY EX/STRUC FORCES ACT/RES CREATE PLAN TEC/DEV ROUTINE RIGID/FLEX ORD/FREE...POLICY MYTH NEW/IDEA STERTYP COLD/WAR 20. PAGE 45 G0876
S62 ATTIT COERCE DETER ARMS/CONT

SINGER J.D.,"STABLE DETERRENCE AND ITS LIMITS." FUT WOR+45 R+D INT/ORG CONSULT ACT/RES TEC/DEV ARMS/CONT COERCE DRIVE PERCEPT RIGID/FLEX ORD/FREE PWR...MYTH SIMUL TOT/POP 20. PAGE 51 G1004
S62 NAT/G FORCES DETER NUC/PWR

ABSHIRE D.M.,NATIONAL SECURITY: POLITICAL, MILITARY, AND ECONOMIC STRATEGIES IN THE DECADE AHEAD. ASIA COM USA+45 WOR+45 ECO/DEV ECO/UNDEV INT/ORG DELIB/GP FORCES ECO/TAC COERCE ATTIT RIGID/FLEX HEALTH ORD/FREE PWR WEALTH...POLICY STAT CHARTS ANTHOL COLD/WAR VAL/FREE. PAGE 1 G0024
B63 FUT ACT/RES BAL/PWR

FLORES E.,LAND REFORM AND THE ALLIANCE FOR PROGRESS (PAMPHLET). L/A+17C USA+45 STRUCT ECO/UNDEV NAT/G WORKER CREATE PLAN ECO/TAC COERCE REV 20. PAGE 19 G0373
B63 AGRI INT/ORG DIPLOM POLICY

GOLDSEN J.M.,OUTER SPACE IN WORLD POLITICS. COM USA+45 NAT/G FORCES ACT/RES PLAN DOMIN EDU/PROP COERCE ORD/FREE PWR...TECHNIC STAT INT SAMP TREND ANTHOL VAL/FREE 20. PAGE 22 G0428
B63 TEC/DEV DIPLOM SPACE

NORTH R.C.,CONTENT ANALYSIS: A HANDBOOK WITH APPLICATIONS FOR THE STUDY OF INTERNATIONAL CRISIS. ASIA COM EUR+WWI MOD/EUR INT/ORG TEC/DEV DOMIN EDU/PROP ROUTINE COERCE PERCEPT RIGID/FLEX ALL/VALS ...QUANT TESTS CON/ANAL SIMUL GEN/LAWS VAL/FREE. PAGE 42 G0825
B63 METH/CNCPT COMPUT/IR USSR

US DEPARTMENT OF THE ARMY,SOVIET RUSSIA: STRATEGIC SURVEY (PAMPHLET). USSR POL/PAR PLAN DOMIN EDU/PROP ARMS/CONT GUERRILLA WAR WEAPON...TREND CHARTS ORG/CHARTS 20. PAGE 57 G1129
B63 BIBLIOG/A MARXISM DIPLOM COERCE

MCDOUGAL M.S.,"THE ENJOYMENT AND ACQUISITION OF RESOURCES IN OUTER SPACE." CHRIST-17C FUT WOR+45 WOR-45 LAW EXTR/IND INT/ORG ACT/RES CREATE TEC/DEV ECO/TAC LEGIT COERCE HEALTH KNOWL ORD/FREE PWR WEALTH...JURID HIST/WRIT VAL/FREE. PAGE 37 G0738
L63 PLAN TREND

PHELPS J.,"STUDIES IN DETERRENCE VIII: MILITARY STABILITY AND ARMS CONTROL: A CRITICAL SURVEY." FUT WOR+45 INT/ORG ACT/RES EDU/PROP COERCE NUC/PWR WAR HEALTH PWR...POLICY TECHNIC TREND SIMUL TOT/POP 20. PAGE 44 G0874
L63 FORCES ORD/FREE ARMS/CONT DETER

BOULDING K.E.,"UNIVERSITY, SOCIETY, AND ARMS CONTROL." WOR-45 WOR+45 ACADEM NAT/G CONSULT FORCES ACT/RES PLAN TEC/DEV BAL/PWR ECO/TAC COERCE DETER WAR ATTIT RIGID/FLEX KNOWL ORD/FREE PWR WEALTH ...CONCPT COLD/WAR TOT/POP 20. PAGE 8 G0159
S63 SOCIETY ARMS/CONT

DELLIN L.A.D.,"BULGARIA UNDER SOVIET LEADERSHIP." BULGARIA COM USA+45 USSR ECO/DEV INDUS POL/PAR EX/STRUC TOP/EX COERCE ATTIT RIGID/FLEX...POLICY TIME/SEQ 20. PAGE 15 G0293
S63 AGRI NAT/G TOTALISM

ERSKINE H.G.,"THE POLLS: ATOMIC WEAPONS AND NUCLEAR ENERGY." USA+45 COERCE ORD/FREE...POLICY SOC STAT CENSUS SAMP VAL/FREE 20. PAGE 18 G0350
S63 ATTIT INT NUC/PWR

SCHMITT H.A.,"THE EUROPEAN COMMUNITIES." EUR+WWI FRANCE DELIB/GP EX/STRUC TOP/EX CREATE TEC/DEV ECO/TAC LEGIT REGION COERCE DRIVE ALL/VALS ...METH/CNCPT EEC 20. PAGE 49 G0972
S63 VOL/ASSN ECO/DEV

TASHJEAN J.E.,"RESEARCH ON ARMS CONTROL." COM USA+45 USSR FORCES ACT/RES PLAN DOMIN COERCE ORD/FREE PWR...TIME/SEQ GEN/LAWS 20 COLD/WAR. PAGE 53 G1053
S63 NAT/G POLICY ARMS/CONT

GROSSER G.H.,THE THREAT OF IMPENDING DISASTER: CONTRIBUTIONS TO THE PSYCHOLOGY OF STRESS. SPACE UNIV SOCIETY R+D TEC/DEV EDU/PROP COERCE WAR ATTIT BIO/SOC DISPL PERCEPT PERSON...SOC MYTH SELF/OBS CONT/OBS BIOG CON/ANAL TOT/POP 20. PAGE 23 G0455
B64 HEALTH PSY NUC/PWR

ROSECRANCE R.N.,THE DISPERSION OF NUCLEAR WEAPONS: STRATEGY AND POLITICS. ASIA COM FUT S/ASIA USA+45 INT/ORG NAT/G DELIB/GP FORCES ACT/RES TEC/DEV BAL/PWR COERCE DETER ATTIT RIGID/FLEX ORD/FREE ...POLICY CHARTS VAL/FREE. PAGE 48 G0935
B64 EUR+WWI PWR PEACE

THANT U.,TOWARD WORLD PEACE. DELIB/GP TEC/DEV EDU/PROP WAR SOVEREIGN...INT/LAW 20 UN MID/EAST. PAGE 54 G1065
B64 DIPLOM BIOG PEACE COERCE

BERKS R.N.,"THE US AND WEAPONS CONTROL." WOR+45 LAW INT/ORG NAT/G LEGIS EXEC COERCE PEACE ATTIT RIGID/FLEX ALL/VALS PWR...POLICY TOT/POP 20. PAGE 7 G0129
L64 USA+45 PLAN ARMS/CONT

CARNEGIE ENDOWMENT INT. PEACE,"POLITICAL QUESTIONS (ISSUES BEFORE THE NINETEENTH GENERAL ASSEMBLY)." SPACE WOR+45 CONSTN FINAN NAT/G CONSULT DELIB/GP FORCES LEGIS TEC/DEV EDU/PROP LEGIT ARMS/CONT COERCE NUC/PWR ATTIT ALL/VALS...CONCPT OBS UN COLD/WAR 20. PAGE 11 G0208
L64 INT/ORG PEACE

WARD C.,"THE 'NEW MYTHS' AND 'OLD REALITIES' OF NUCLEAR WAR." COM FUT USA+45 WOR+45 INT/ORG NAT/G DOMIN LEGIT EXEC ATTIT PERCEPT ALL/VALS ...POLICY RELATIV PSY MYTH TREND 20. PAGE 62 G1212
L64 FORCES COERCE ARMS/CONT NUC/PWR

ABT C.,"WAR GAMING." USA+45 NAT/G TOP/EX ACT/RES TEC/DEV COERCE KNOWL ORD/FREE PWR...DECISION MATH TIME/SEQ COMPUT/IR CHARTS LAB/EXP VAL/FREE. PAGE 2 G0026
S64 FORCES SIMUL WAR

FALK S.L.,"DISARMAMENT IN HISTORICAL PERSPECTIVE." WOR-45 NAT/G PLAN NUC/PWR PEACE ORD/FREE PWR ...TIME/SEQ AUD/VIS VAL/FREE LEAGUE/NAT 20. PAGE 18 G0360
S64 INT/ORG COERCE ARMS/CONT

LERNER A.P.,"NUCLEAR SYMMETRY AS A FRAMEWORK FOR COEXISTENCE." COM FUT USA+45 NAT/G ACT/RES CREATE PLAN DIPLOM EDU/PROP COERCE WAR RIGID/FLEX PWR SKILL...CONCPT METH/CNCPT GEN/LAWS TOT/POP VAL/FREE COLD/WAR 20. PAGE 33 G0657
S64 FORCES ORD/FREE DETER NUC/PWR

PILISUK M.,"STEPWISE DISARMAMENT & SUDDEN DESTRUCTION IN A TWOPERSON GAME: A RESEARCH TOOL." NAT/G FORCES ACT/RES ECO/TAC EDU/PROP EXEC ROUTINE COERCE ORD/FREE...SIMUL GEN/LAWS VAL/FREE. PAGE 45 G0877
S64 PWR DECISION ARMS/CONT

SPONSLER G.C.,"THE MILITARY ROLE IN SPACE." FUT USA+45 SEA AIR NAT/G ACT/RES PLAN COERCE NUC/PWR WEAPON KNOWL ORD/FREE PWR RESPECT...TREND 20. PAGE 52 G1026
S64 TEC/DEV FORCES SPACE

BOBROW D.B.,COMPONENTS OF DEFENSE POLICY. ASIA EUR+WWI USA+45 WOR+45 INTELL INT/ORG NAT/G PROF/ORG CONSULT LEGIS ACT/RES CREATE ARMS/CONT COERCE ORD/FREE...DECISION SIMUL. PAGE 7 G0145
B65 DETER NUC/PWR PLAN FORCES

GRETTON P.,MARITIME STRATEGY - A STUDY OF DEFENSE PROBLEMS. ASIA UK USSR DIPLOM COERCE DETER NUC/PWR WEAPON...CONCPT NAT/COMP 20. PAGE 23 G0449
B65 FORCES PLAN WAR SEA

HITCH C.J.,DECISION-MAKING FOR DEFENSE. USA+45 CREATE BUDGET COERCE WAR WEAPON EFFICIENCY...SIMUL 20. PAGE 26 G0515
B65 DECISION OP/RES PLAN FORCES

US DEPARTMENT OF ARMY,MILITARY PROTECTIVE CONSTRUCTION: NUCLEAR WARFARE AND CHEMICAL AND BIOLOGICAL OPERATIONS (MANUAL). OP/RES TEC/DEV RISK COERCE NUC/PWR WAR WEAPON EFFICIENCY UTIL BIO/SOC
B65 FORCES CONSTRUC TASK HEALTH

HABITAT ORD/FREE 20. PAGE 57 G1117

S65
DALKEY N.C.,"SOLVABLE NUCLEAR WAR MODELS." FORCES   GAME
BAL/PWR DIPLOM COERCE PEACE DECISION. PAGE 14 G0273   SIMUL
                                                     WAR
                                                     NUC/PWR

S65
GRIFFITH S.B.,"COMMUNIST CHINA'S CAPACITY TO MAKE   FORCES
WAR." CHINA/COM COM NAT/G TOP/EX PLAN DOMIN COERCE   PWR
NUC/PWR ATTIT RESPECT SKILL...CONCPT MYTH TIME/SEQ   WEAPON
TREND COLD/WAR 20. PAGE 23 G0452   ASIA

S65
HARRISON S.L.,"NTH NATION CHALLENGES* THE PRESENT   ARMS/CONT
PERSPECTIVE." EUR+WWI FUT USA+45 BAL/PWR CONTROL   NUC/PWR
RISK COERCE WAR...PREDICT COLD/WAR. PAGE 25 G0485   NAT/G
                                                     DIPLOM

S65
RUBINSTEIN A.Z.,"POLITICAL BARRIERS TO   COM
DISARMAMENT." FUT DIPLOM COERCE NUC/PWR WAR   USA+45
NAT/LISM ORD/FREE PREDICT. PAGE 48 G0944   ARMS/CONT
                                                     ATTIT

C65
SCHWEBEL M.,"BEHAVIORAL SCIENCE AND HUMAN   PEACE
SURVIVAL." FORCES ARMS/CONT COERCE NUC/PWR WAR   ACT/RES
GP/REL NAT/LISM PERCEPT...POLICY PSY ANTHOL   DIPLOM
BIBLIOG/A 20 COLD/WAR. PAGE 50 G0984   HEAL

C65
US AIR FORCE ACADEMY,"AMERICAN DEFENSE POLICY." COM PLAN
INT/ORG TEC/DEV FOR/AID ARMS/CONT DETER NUC/PWR   FORCES
...POLICY DECISION CONCPT ANTHOL BIBLIOG/A 20   WAR
COLD/WAR NATO. PAGE 56 G1103   COERCE

B66
VON BORCH H,FRIEDE TROTZ KRIEG. GERMANY USSR   DIPLOM
WOR+45 PEACE ANOMIE ATTIT 20. PAGE 43 G0853   NUC/PWR
                                                     WAR
                                                     COERCE

L67
EINAUDI L.,"ANNOTATED BIBLIOGRAPHY OF LATIN   BIBLIOG/A
AMERICAN MILITARY JOURNALS" LAW TEC/DEV DOMIN   NAT/G
EDU/PROP COERCE WAR CIVMIL/REL 20. PAGE 17 G0336   FORCES
                                                     L/A+17C

S67
BRETNOR R.,"DESTRUCTIVE FORCE AND THE MILITARY   FORCES
EQUATIONS." UNIV COMPUTER PLAN PROB/SOLV AUTOMAT   TEC/DEV
CONTROL COERCE DETER NUC/PWR WEAPON DRIVE PWR.   DOMIN
PAGE 9 G0166   WAR

S67
CHRIST R.F.,"REORGANIZATION OF FRENCH ARMED   CHIEF
FORCES." FRANCE CREATE PLAN TEC/DEV BAL/PWR DOMIN   DETER
COERCE CENTRAL EFFICIENCY 20. PAGE 12 G0229   NUC/PWR
                                                     FORCES

S67
TELLER E.,"PLANNING FOR PEACE." CHINA/COM WOR+45   ARMS/CONT
DELIB/GP TEC/DEV RISK COERCE DETER WAR ATTIT   NUC/PWR
ORD/FREE 20 NATO. PAGE 54 G1061   PEACE
                                                     DOMIN

S67
WALTERS R.E.,"THE ROLE OF NUCLEAR WEAPONS FOR THE   PLAN
WEST." ASIA UK USA+45 USSR DIPLOM COERCE WAR PEACE   NUC/PWR
...POLICY DECISION 20. PAGE 62 G1209   WEAPON
                                                     FORCES

S67
WARE R.S.,"FORECAST A.D. 2000." SOCIETY STRATA   NUC/PWR
ECO/UNDEV INDUS FORCES EDU/PROP AUTOMAT COERCE REV   GEOG
WEAPON ATTIT PREDICT. PAGE 62 G1213   TEC/DEV
                                                     WAR

COERCION....SEE COERCE

COEXIST....COEXISTENCE; SEE ALSO COLD/WAR, PEACE

B58
ANGELL N.,DEFENCE AND THE ENGLISH-SPEAKING ROLE.   DIPLOM
CHINA/COM UK USSR INT/ORG FORCES EDU/PROP NEUTRAL   WAR
NUC/PWR NAT/LISM PEACE TOTALISM 20 COLD/WAR   MARXISM
COEXIST. PAGE 3 G0059   ORD/FREE

COEXISTENCE....SEE COLD/WAR, PEACE, COEXIST

COFFEY J.I. G0238

COFFIN/WS....WILLIAM SLOANE COFFIN, JR.

COGNITION....SEE PERCEPT

COGNITIVE DISSONANCE....SEE PERCEPT, ROLE

COHEN A. G0239

COHEN K.J. G0240

COHEN M. G0241

COHEN M.R. G0242

COHESION....SEE CONSEN

COLD/WAR....COLD WAR

N
WEIGLEY R.F.,HISTORY OF THE UNITED STATES ARMY.   FORCES
USA+45 USA-45 SOCIETY NAT/G LEAD WAR GP/REL PWR   ADMIN
...SOC METH/COMP COLD/WAR. PAGE 62 G1222   ROLE
                                                     CIVMIL/REL

N47
FOX W.T.R.,UNITED STATES POLICY IN A TWO POWER   DIPLOM
WORLD. COM USA+45 USSR FORCES DOMIN AGREE NEUTRAL   FOR/AID
NUC/PWR ORD/FREE SOVEREIGN 20 COLD/WAR TREATY   POLICY
EUROPE/W INTERVENT. PAGE 20 G0389

B48
BRADLEY D.,NO PLACE TO HIDE. USA+45 SOCIETY NAT/G   R+D
FORCES TEC/DEV EDU/PROP DETER PEACE BIO/SOC   LAB/EXP
ALL/VALS...POLICY PHIL/SCI OBS RECORD SAMP BIOG   ARMS/CONT
GEN/METH COLD/WAR 20. PAGE 8 G0162   NUC/PWR

B49
ROSENHAUPT H.W.,HOW TO WAGE PEACE. USA+45 SOCIETY   INTELL
STRATA STRUCT R+D INT/ORG POL/PAR LEGIS ACT/RES   CONCPT
CREATE PLAN EDU/PROP ADMIN EXEC ATTIT ALL/VALS   DIPLOM
...TIME/SEQ TREND COLD/WAR 20. PAGE 48 G0937

S49
SOUERS S.W.,"POLICY FORMULATION FOR NATIONAL   DELIB/GP
SECURITY." EX/STRUC FORCES PROB/SOLV DIPLOM CONFER   CHIEF
EXEC ARMS/CONT DETER NUC/PWR GOV/REL PEACE   DECISION
COLD/WAR. PAGE 52 G1022   POLICY

B50
CANTRIL H.,TENSIONS THAT CAUSE WAR. UNIV CULTURE   SOCIETY
R+D CREATE EDU/PROP DRIVE PERSON KNOWL ORD/FREE   PHIL/SCI
...HUM PSY SOC OBS CENSUS TREND CON/ANAL SOC/EXP   PEACE
SIMUL GEN/METH ANTHOL COLD/WAR TOT/POP. PAGE 11
G0206

B50
HUZAR E.,THE PURSE AND THE SWORD: CONTROL OF THE   CIVMIL/REL
ARMY BY CONGRESS THROUGH MILITARY APPROPRIATIONS   BUDGET
1933-1950. NAT/G DELIB/GP EX/STRUC FORCES PROB/SOLV CONTROL
BARGAIN CONFER ADMIN ROUTINE GOV/REL EFFICIENCY   LEGIS
...POLICY COLD/WAR. PAGE 27 G0541

B52
DAY E.E.,EDUCATION FOR FREEDOM AND RESPONSIBILITY.   SCHOOL
FUT USA+45 CULTURE CONSULT EDU/PROP ATTIT SKILL   KNOWL
...MGT CONCPT OBS GEN/LAWS COLD/WAR 20. PAGE 14
G0282

L52
ROYAL INST. INT. AFF.,"ANNUAL REPORT OF THE   R+D
COUNCIL: 1951-1952." WOR+45 CREATE KNOWL...MGT   EDU/PROP
COLD/WAR CMN/WLTH TOT/POP VAL/FREE 20. PAGE 48
G0943

B54
ARON R.,CENTURY OF TOTAL WAR. FUT WOR+45 WOR-45   ATTIT
SOCIETY INT/ORG NAT/G FORCES TOP/EX CREATE BAL/PWR   WAR
DOMIN EDU/PROP COERCE DETER PEACE TOTALISM PWR
...TIME/SEQ TREND COLD/WAR TOT/POP VAL/FREE
LEAGUE/NAT 20. PAGE 4 G0066

B55
DAVIS E.,TWO MINUTES TO MIDNIGHT. WOR+45 PLAN   NUC/PWR
CONTROL NEUTRAL ARMS/CONT ATTIT ORD/FREE...PSY 20   WAR
COLD/WAR. PAGE 14 G0277   DETER
                                                     DIPLOM

B55
JONES J.M.,THE FIFTEEN WEEKS (FEBRUARY 21-JUNE 5,   DIPLOM
1947). EUR+WWI USA+45 PROB/SOLV BAL/PWR...POLICY   ECO/TAC
TIME/SEQ 20 COLD/WAR MARSHL/PLN TRUMAN/HS   FOR/AID
WASHING/DC. PAGE 29 G0567

B55
MOCH J.,HUMAN FOLLY: DISARM OR PERISH. USA+45   FUT
WOR+45 SOCIETY INT/ORG NAT/G ACT/RES EDU/PROP ATTIT DELIB/GP
PERSON KNOWL ORD/FREE PWR...MAJORIT TOT/POP   ARMS/CONT
COLD/WAR 20. PAGE 39 G0776   NUC/PWR

B56
BLACKETT P.M.S.,ATOMIC WEAPONS AND EAST-WEST FORCES
RELATIONS. FUT WOR+45 INT/ORG DELIB/GP COERCE ATTIT PWR
RIGID/FLEX KNOWL...RELATIV HIST/WRIT TREND GEN/METH ARMS/CONT
COLD/WAR 20. PAGE 7 G0138 NUC/PWR

C56
DUPUY R.E.,"MILITARY HERITAGE OF AMERICA." USA+45 FORCES
USA-45 TEC/DEV DIPLOM ROUTINE...POLICY TREND CHARTS WAR
IDEA/COMP BIBLIOG COLD/WAR. PAGE 17 G0325 CONCPT

B57
SPEIER H.,GERMAN REARMAMENT AND ATOMIC WAR: THE TOP/EX
VIEWS OF GERMAN MILITARY AND POLITICAL LEADERS. FUT FORCES
WOR+45 INT/ORG NAT/G WEAPON ATTIT PWR...INT QU NUC/PWR
TOT/POP VAL/FREE COLD/WAR 20. PAGE 52 G1024 GERMANY

B58
ANGELL N.,DEFENCE AND THE ENGLISH-SPEAKING ROLE. DIPLOM
CHINA/COM UK USSR INT/ORG FORCES NEUTRAL WAR
NUC/PWR NAT/LISM PEACE TOTALISM 20 COLD/WAR MARXISM
COEXIST. PAGE 3 G0059 ORD/FREE

B58
GAVIN J.M.,WAR AND PEACE IN THE SPACE AGE. SPACE WAR
USA+45 USSR FORCES PLAN TEC/DEV BAL/PWR DIPLOM DETER
ARMS/CONT WEAPON CIVMIL/REL...CHARTS GP/COMP 20 NUC/PWR
NATO COLD/WAR. PAGE 21 G0414 PEACE

B58
NATIONAL PLANNING ASSOCIATION,1970 WITHOUT ARMS ARMS/CONT
CONTROL (PAMPHLET). WOR+45 PROB/SOLV TEC/DEV DIPLOM ORD/FREE
CONFER DETER NUC/PWR WAR...CHARTS 20 COLD/WAR. WEAPON
PAGE 41 G0810 PREDICT

B58
NOEL-BAKER D.,THE ARMS RACE. WOR+45 NAT/G DELIB/GP FUT
ACT/RES TEC/DEV EDU/PROP NUC/PWR ATTIT KNOWL PWR INT/ORG
...CONCPT OBS LEAGUE/NAT 20 COLD/WAR. PAGE 42 G0823 ARMS/CONT
PEACE

S58
DAVENPORT J.,"ARMS AND THE WELFARE STATE." INTELL USA+45
STRUCT FORCES CREATE ECO/TAC FOR/AID DOMIN LEGIT NAT/G
ADMIN WAR ORD/FREE PWR...POLICY SOC CONCPT MYTH OBS USSR
TREND COLD/WAR TOT/POP 20. PAGE 14 G0276

S58
THOMPSON K.W.,"NATIONAL SECURITY IN A NUCLEAR AGE." FORCES
USA+45 WOR+45 SOCIETY INT/ORG NAT/G TOP/EX DIPLOM PWR
DOMIN EDU/PROP LEGIT ARMS/CONT COERCE ORD/FREE BAL/PWR
...TREND STERTYP TOT/POP VAL/FREE COLD/WAR 20.
PAGE 54 G1068

B59
GODDARD V.,THE ENIGMA OF MENACE. WOR+45 SECT LEAD PEACE
NUC/PWR WAR WEAPON CHOOSE PERSON PWR...POLICY ARMS/CONT
PHIL/SCI PACIFIST 20 COLD/WAR. PAGE 22 G0423 DIPLOM
ATTIT

B59
HUGHES E.M.,AMERICA THE VINCIBLE. USA+45 FOR/AID ORD/FREE
ARMS/CONT NUC/PWR PERS/REL RATIONAL ATTIT ALL/VALS DIPLOM
20 COLD/WAR. PAGE 27 G0534 WAR

B59
POKROVSKY G.I.,SCIENCE AND TECHNOLOGY IN TEC/DEV
CONTEMPORARY WAR. SPACE USSR WOR+45 NAT/G CONSULT FORCES
ACT/RES PLAN DETER WEAPON...MARXIST METH/CNCPT NUC/PWR
CHARTS STERTYP COLD/WAR 20. PAGE 45 G0881 WAR

B59
RUSSELL B.,COMMON SENSE AND NUCLEAR WARFARE. WOR+45 ORD/FREE
INTELL SOCIETY STRATA NAT/G TOP/EX EDU/PROP ATTIT ARMS/CONT
PERSON KNOWL MORAL PWR...POLICY CONCPT MYTH NUC/PWR
CON/ANAL COLD/WAR 20. PAGE 48 G0948

B59
WELTON H.,THE THIRD WORLD WAR: TRADE AND INDUSTRY, INT/TRADE
THE NEW BATTLEGROUND. WOR+45 ECO/DEV INDUS MARKET PLAN
TASK...MGT IDEA/COMP COLD/WAR. PAGE 63 G1229 DIPLOM

S59
MILBURN T.W.,"WHAT CONSTITUTES EFFECTIVE INTELL
DETERRENCE." USA+45 USSR WOR+45 STRUCT FORCES ATTIT
ACT/RES PLAN SUPEGO KNOWL ORD/FREE PWR...RELATIV DETER
PSY CONCPT VAL/FREE 20 COLD/WAR. PAGE 39 G0768 NUC/PWR

S59
WILLIAMS B.H.,"SCIENTIFIC METHOD IN FOREIGN PLAN
POLICY." WOR+45 NAT/G FORCES TOP/EX DOMIN LEGIT PHIL/SCI
COERCE PEACE ATTIT KNOWL ORD/FREE PWR...GEN/LAWS DIPLOM
GEN/METH TOT/POP COLD/WAR NAZI. PAGE 63 G1241

B60
BARNET R.,WHO WANTS DISARMAMENT. COM EUR+WWI USA+45 PLAN
USSR INT/ORG NAT/G BAL/PWR DIPLOM EDU/PROP COERCE FORCES
DETER NUC/PWR WAR WEAPON ATTIT PWR...TIME/SEQ ARMS/CONT
COLD/WAR CONGRESS 20. PAGE 5 G0096

B60
BROOKINGS INSTITUTION,UNITED STATES FOREIGN POLICY: DIPLOM
STUDY NO 9: THE FORMULATION AND ADMINISTRATION OF INT/ORG
UNITED STATES FOREIGN POLICY. USA+45 WOR+45 CREATE
EX/STRUC LEGIS BAL/PWR FOR/AID EDU/PROP CIVMIL/REL
GOV/REL...INT COLD/WAR. PAGE 9 G0174

B60
CHASE S.,LIVE AND LET LIVE. USA+45 ECO/DEV NAT/G
PROB/SOLV TEC/DEV ECO/TAC ARMS/CONT NUC/PWR WAR DIPLOM
NAT/LISM PEACE...GEOG TREND 20 COLD/WAR. PAGE 11 SOCIETY
G0223 TASK

B60
EINSTEIN A.,EINSTEIN ON PEACE. FUT WOR+45 WOR-45 INT/ORG
SOCIETY NAT/G PLAN BAL/PWR CAP/ISM DIPLOM ARMS/CONT ATTIT
DETER NAT/LISM...POLICY RELATIV HUM PHIL/SCI CONCPT NUC/PWR
BIOG COLD/WAR LEAGUE/NAT NAZI. PAGE 17 G0338 PEACE

B60
MCCLELLAND C.A.,NUCLEAR WEAPONS, MISSILES, AND DIPLOM
FUTURE WAR: PROBLEM FOR THE SIXTIES. WOR+45 FORCES NUC/PWR
ARMS/CONT DETER MARXISM...POLICY ANTHOL COLD/WAR. WAR
PAGE 37 G0729 WEAPON

B60
PARRY A.,RUSSIA'S ROCKETS AND MISSILES. COM FUT PLAN
GERMANY USA+45 WOR+45 INTELL ECO/DEV ACT/RES TEC/DEV
NUC/PWR WEAPON ATTIT ALL/VALS...OBS TIME/SEQ SPACE
COLD/WAR 20. PAGE 44 G0859 USSR

B60
US DEPARTMENT OF THE ARMY,DISARMAMENT: A BIBLIOG/A
BIBLIOGRAPHIC RECORD: 1916-1960. DETER WAR WEAPON ARMS/CONT
PEACE 20 UN LEAGUE/NAT COLD/WAR NATO. PAGE 57 G1128 NUC/PWR
DIPLOM

L60
BRENNAN D.G.,"SETTING AND GOALS OF ARMS CONTROL." FORCES
FUT USA+45 USSR WOR+45 INTELL INT/ORG NAT/G COERCE
VOL/ASSN CONSULT PLAN DIPLOM ECO/TAC ADMIN KNOWL ARMS/CONT
PWR...POLICY CONCPT TREND COLD/WAR 20. PAGE 8 G0164 DETER

L60
HOLTON G.,"ARMS CONTROL." FUT WOR+45 CULTURE ACT/RES
INT/ORG NAT/G FORCES TOP/EX PLAN EDU/PROP COERCE CONSULT
ATTIT RIGID/FLEX ORD/FREE...POLICY PHIL/SCI SOC ARMS/CONT
TREND COLD/WAR. PAGE 27 G0524 NUC/PWR

L60
JACOB P.E.,"THE DISARMAMENT CONSENSUS." USA+45 USSR DELIB/GP
WOR+45 INT/ORG NAT/G ACT/RES TEC/DEV BAL/PWR ATTIT
EDU/PROP ADMIN COERCE DETER NUC/PWR CONSEN ARMS/CONT
RIGID/FLEX PWR...CONCPT RECORD CHARTS COLD/WAR 20.
PAGE 28 G0552

S60
BARNETT H.J.,"RESEARCH AND DEVELOPMENT, ECONOMIC ACT/RES
GROWTH, AND NATIONAL SECURITY." USA+45 R+D CREATE PLAN
ECO/TAC ATTIT DRIVE PWR...POLICY SOC METH/CNCPT
QUANT STAT TIME/SEQ ORG/CHARTS COLD/WAR 20. PAGE 5
G0097

S60
DOUGHERTY J.E.,"KEY TO SECURITY: DISARMAMENT OR FORCES
ARMS STABILITY." COM USA+45 USSR INT/ORG NAT/G ORD/FREE
CREATE EDU/PROP COERCE DETER ATTIT PWR...DECISION ARMS/CONT
CONCPT MYTH NEW/IDEA TREND 20 COLD/WAR. PAGE 16 NUC/PWR
G0311

S60
OSGOOD C.E.,"A CASE FOR GRADUATED UNILATERAL ATTIT
DISENGAGEMENT." FUT WOR+45 CULTURE SOCIETY NAT/G EDU/PROP
NUC/PWR WAR PERSON SUPEGO ALL/VALS...POLICY PSY ARMS/CONT
CONCPT COLD/WAR TOT/POP VAL/FREE 20. PAGE 43 G0848

B61
HENKIN L.,ARMS CONTROL: ISSUES FOR THE PUBLIC. WOR+45
EUR+WWI FUT USA+45 USSR INT/ORG NAT/G DIPLOM DELIB/GP
EDU/PROP DETER NUC/PWR ATTIT PWR...CONCPT RECORD ARMS/CONT
HIST/WRIT TIME/SEQ TOT/POP COLD/WAR 20. PAGE 26
G0506

B61
KISSINGER H.A.,THE NECESSITY FOR CHOICE. FUT USA+45 TOP/EX
ECO/UNDEV NAT/G PLAN BAL/PWR ECO/TAC ARMS/CONT TREND
DETER NUC/PWR ATTIT...POLICY CONCPT RECORD GEN/LAWS DIPLOM
COLD/WAR 20. PAGE 31 G0604

NOGEE J.L.,SOVIET POLICY TOWARD INTERNATIONAL
CONTROL OF ATOMIC ENERGY. COM USA+45 WOR+45 INTELL
NAT/G ACT/RES DIPLOM EDU/PROP NUC/PWR TOTALISM
PERCEPT KNOWL PWR...TIME/SEQ COLD/WAR 20. PAGE 42
G0824
B61
INT/ORG
ATTIT
ARMS/CONT
USSR

SCHMIDT H.,VERTEIDIGUNG ODER VERGELTUNG. COM CUBA
GERMANY/W USSR FORCES DIPLOM ARMS/CONT DETER
NUC/PWR...POLICY CHARTS HYPO/EXP SIMUL BIBLIOG 20
NATO COLD/WAR. PAGE 49 G0970
B61
PLAN
WAR
BAL/PWR
ORD/FREE

US SENATE COMM GOVT OPERATIONS.ORGANIZING FOR
NATIONAL SECURITY. COM USA+45 BUDGET DIPLOM DETER
NUC/PWR WAR WEAPON ORD/FREE...BIBLIOG 20 COLD/WAR.
PAGE 60 G1176
B61
POLICY
PLAN
FORCES
COERCE

TAUBENFELD H.J.,"A REGIME FOR OUTER SPACE." FUT
UNIV R+D ACT/RES PLAN BAL/PWR LEGIT ARMS/CONT
ORD/FREE...POLICY JURID TREND UN TOT/POP 20
COLD/WAR. PAGE 54 G1056
L61
INT/ORG
ADJUD
SPACE

BURKE A.E.,ENOUGH GOOD MEN. USA+45 WOR+45 ECO/UNDEV
FORCES TEC/DEV GUERRILLA NUC/PWR REV WAR ORD/FREE
MARXISM...GEOG 20 COLD/WAR. PAGE 10 G0189
B62
DIPLOM
POLICY
NAT/G
TASK

GOLOVINE M.N.,CONFLICT IN SPACE: A PATTERN OF WAR
IN A NEW DIMENSION. FUT USA+45 WOR+45 AIR FORCES
PLAN DIPLOM DOMIN ATTIT...STAT AUD/VIS CHARTS
COLD/WAR 20. PAGE 22 G0432
B62
CREATE
TEC/DEV
NUC/PWR
SPACE

KAHN H.,THINKING ABOUT THE UNTHINKABLE. FUT USA+45
LAW NAT/G CONSULT FORCES ACT/RES CREATE PLAN
TEC/DEV BAL/PWR DIPLOM EDU/PROP ARMS/CONT DETER
ATTIT...CONCPT OBS TREND COLD/WAR 20. PAGE 29 G0570
B62
INT/ORG
ORD/FREE
NUC/PWR
PEACE

SCHILLING W.R.,STRATEGY, POLITICS, AND DEFENSE
BUDGETS. USA+45 R+D NAT/G CONSULT DELIB/GP FORCES
LEGIS ACT/RES PLAN BAL/PWR LEGIT EXEC NUC/PWR
RIGID/FLEX PWR...TREND COLD/WAR CONGRESS 20
EISNHWR/DD. PAGE 49 G0968
B62
ROUTINE
POLICY

SINGER J.D.,DETERRENCE, ARMS CONTROL AND
DISARMAMENT: TOWARD A SYNTHESIS IN NATIONAL
SECURITY POLICY. COM USA+45 INT/ORG BAL/PWR DETER
ORD/FREE...POLICY COLD/WAR 20. PAGE 51 G1003
B62
FUT
ACT/RES
ARMS/CONT

WRIGHT Q.,PREVENTING WORLD WAR THREE. FUT WOR+45
CULTURE INT/ORG NAT/G CONSULT FORCES ADMIN
ARMS/CONT DRIVE RIGID/FLEX ORD/FREE SOVEREIGN
...POLICY CONCPT TREND STERTYP COLD/WAR 20. PAGE 64
G1259
B62
CREATE
ATTIT

YALEN R.,REGIONALISM AND WORLD ORDER. EUR+WWI
WOR+45 WOR-45 INT/ORG VOL/ASSN DELIB/GP FORCES
TOP/EX BAL/PWR DIPLOM DOMIN REGION ARMS/CONT PWR
...JURID HYPO/EXP COLD/WAR 20. PAGE 64 G1261
B62
ORD/FREE
POLICY

BETTEN J.K.,"ARMS CONTROL AND THE PROBLEM OF
EVASION." WOR+45 FORCES CREATE DIPLOM DETER PWR
...PSY TREND GEN/LAWS COLD/WAR 20. PAGE 7 G0134
L62
NAT/G
PLAN
ARMS/CONT

FINKELSTEIN L.S.,"ARMS INSPECTION." FUT WOR+45
NAT/G DIPLOM ATTIT PERCEPT RIGID/FLEX ORD/FREE
COLD/WAR 20. PAGE 19 G0369
L62
FORCES
PWR
ARMS/CONT

NEIBURG H.L.,"THE EISENHOWER AEC AND CONGRESS: A
STUDY IN EXECUTIVE-LEGISLATIVE RELATIONS." USA+45
NAT/G POL/PAR DELIB/GP EX/STRUC TOP/EX ADMIN EXEC
LEAD ROUTINE PWR...POLICY COLD/WAR CONGRESS
PRESIDENT AEC. PAGE 41 G0816
L62
CHIEF
LEGIS
GOV/REL
NUC/PWR

BETHE H.,"DISARMAMENT AND STRATEGY." COM USA+45
USSR WOR+45 VOL/ASSN TEC/DEV EDU/PROP NUC/PWR
CHOOSE PEACE...POLICY DECISION NEW/IDEA OBS
GEN/LAWS COLD/WAR 420. PAGE 7 G0133
S62
PLAN
ORD/FREE
ARMS/CONT
DIPLOM

BOULDING K.E.,"THE PREVENTION OF WORLD WAR THREE."
FUT WOR+45 INT/ORG PLAN BAL/PWR PEACE ORD/FREE PWR
...NEW/IDEA TREND TOT/POP COLD/WAR 20. PAGE 8 G0158
S62
VOL/ASSN
NAT/G
ARMS/CONT

FINKELSTEIN L.S.,"THE UNITED NATIONS AND
ORGANIZATIONS FOR CONTROL OF ARMAMENT." FUT WOR+45
VOL/ASSN DELIB/GP TOP/EX CREATE EDU/PROP LEGIT
ADJUD NUC/PWR ATTIT RIGID/FLEX ORD/FREE...POLICY
DECISION CONCPT OBS TREND GEN/LAWS TOT/POP
COLD/WAR. PAGE 19 G0368
S62
INT/ORG
PWR
ARMS/CONT

FOSTER R.B.,"UNILATERAL ARMS CONTROL MEASURES AND
DISARMAMENT NEGOTIATION." WOR+45 VOL/ASSN DELIB/GP
ACT/RES ECO/TAC EDU/PROP ATTIT RIGID/FLEX...CONCPT
MYTH TIME/SEQ COLD/WAR 20. PAGE 20 G0386
S62
PLAN
ORD/FREE
ARMS/CONT
DETER

MARTIN L.W.,"THE MARKET FOR STRATEGIC IDEAS IN
BRITAIN: THE 'SANDYS ERA'" UK ARMS/CONT WAR GOV/REL
OPTIMAL...POLICY DECISION GOV/COMP COLD/WAR
CMN/WLTH. PAGE 36 G0714
S62
DIPLOM
COERCE
FORCES
PWR

PHIPPS T.E.,"THE CASE FOR DETERRENCE." FUT WOR+45
SOCIETY EX/STRUC FORCES ACT/RES CREATE PLAN TEC/DEV
ROUTINE RIGID/FLEX ORD/FREE...POLICY MYTH NEW/IDEA
STERTYP COLD/WAR 20. PAGE 45 G0876
S62
ATTIT
COERCE
DETER
ARMS/CONT

ABSHIRE D.M.,NATIONAL SECURITY: POLITICAL,
MILITARY, AND ECONOMIC STRATEGIES IN THE DECADE
AHEAD. ASIA COM USA+45 WOR+45 ECO/DEV ECO/UNDEV
INT/ORG DELIB/GP FORCES ECO/TAC COERCE ATTIT
RIGID/FLEX HEALTH ORD/FREE PWR WEALTH...POLICY STAT
CHARTS ANTHOL COLD/WAR VAL/FREE. PAGE 1 G0024
B63
FUT
ACT/RES
BAL/PWR

MULLENBACH P.,CIVILIAN NUCLEAR POWER: ECONOMIC
ISSUES AND POLICY FORMATION. FINAN INT/ORG DELIB/GP
ACT/RES ECO/TAC ATTIT SUPEGO HEALTH ORD/FREE PWR
...POLICY CONCPT MATH STAT CHARTS VAL/FREE 20
COLD/WAR. PAGE 40 G0792
B63
USA+45
ECO/DEV
NUC/PWR

PACHTER H.M.,COLLISION COURSE; THE CUBAN MISSILE
CRISIS AND COEXISTENCE. CUBA USA+45 DIPLOM
ARMS/CONT PEACE MARXISM...DECISION INT/LAW 20
COLD/WAR KHRUSH/N KENNEDY/JF CASTRO/F. PAGE 43
G0854
B63
WAR
BAL/PWR
NUC/PWR
DETER

BOHN L.C.,"WHOSE NUCLEAR TEST: NON-PHYSICAL
INSPECTION AND TEST BAN." WOR+45 R+D INT/ORG
VOL/ASSN ORD/FREE...GEN/LAWS GEN/METH COLD/WAR 20.
PAGE 8 G0148
S63
ADJUD
ARMS/CONT
TEC/DEV
NUC/PWR

BOULDING K.E.,"UNIVERSITY, SOCIETY, AND ARMS
CONTROL." WOR+45 WOR-45 ACADEM NAT/G CONSULT FORCES
ACT/RES PLAN TEC/DEV BAL/PWR ECO/TAC COERCE DETER
WAR RIGID/FLEX KNOWL ORD/FREE PWR WEALTH
...CONCPT COLD/WAR TOT/POP 20. PAGE 8 G0159
S63
SOCIETY
ARMS/CONT

NADLER E.B.,"SOME ECONOMIC DISADVANTAGES OF THE
ARMS RACE." USA+45 INDUS R+D FORCES PLAN TEC/DEV
ECO/TAC FOR/AID EDU/PROP PWR WEALTH...TREND
COLD/WAR 20. PAGE 41 G0800
S63
ECO/DEV
MGT
BAL/PAY

SMITH D.O.,"WHAT IS A WAR DETERRENT." FUT GERMANY
HUNGARY UK USA+45 WOR+45 WOR-45 NAT/G TEC/DEV
BAL/PWR PWR...CONCPT GEN/LAWS COLD/WAR 20. PAGE 51
G1013
S63
ACT/RES
FORCES
ARMS/CONT
DETER

TASHJEAN J.E.,"RESEARCH ON ARMS CONTROL." COM
USA+45 USSR FORCES ACT/RES PLAN DOMIN COERCE
ORD/FREE PWR...TIME/SEQ GEN/LAWS 20 COLD/WAR.
PAGE 53 G1053
S63
NAT/G
POLICY
ARMS/CONT

RANSOM H.H.,CAN AMERICAN DEMOCRACY SURVIVE COLD
WAR. USA-45 CONSTN NAT/G CONSULT DELIB/GP LEGIS
ACT/RES LEGIT EXEC ATTIT KNOWL ORD/FREE PWR SKILL
...POLICY TIME/SEQ TREND GEN/LAWS 20 COLD/WAR.
PAGE 46 G0901
B64
USA+45
ROUTINE

CARNEGIE ENDOWMENT INT. PEACE,"POLITICAL QUESTIONS
(ISSUES BEFORE THE NINETEENTH GENERAL ASSEMBLY)."
SPACE WOR+45 CONSTN FINAN NAT/G CONSULT DELIB/GP
FORCES LEGIS TEC/DEV LEGIT ARMS/CONT
COERCE NUC/PWR ATTIT ALL/VALS...CONCPT OBS UN
COLD/WAR 20. PAGE 11 G0208
L64
INT/ORG
PEACE

L64
GOLDBERG A.,"ATOMIC ORIGINS OF THE BRITISH NUCLEAR   CREATE
DETERRENT." EUR+WWI UK NAT/G TOP/EX PLAN BAL/PWR   FORCES
DOMIN DETER CHOOSE ATTIT DRIVE HEALTH ORD/FREE PWR   NUC/PWR
RESPECT...CONCPT VAL/FREE COLD/WAR 20 CMN/WLTH.
PAGE 22 G0425

S64
LERNER A.P.,"NUCLEAR SYMMETRY AS A FRAMEWORK FOR   FORCES
COEXISTENCE." COM FUT USA+45 NAT/G ACT/RES CREATE   ORD/FREE
PLAN DIPLOM EDU/PROP COERCE WAR RIGID/FLEX PWR   DETER
SKILL...CONCPT METH/CNCPT GEN/LAWS TOT/POP VAL/FREE   NUC/PWR
COLD/WAR 20. PAGE 33 G0657

B65
CORDIER A.W.,THE QUEST FOR PEACE. WOR+45 NAT/G PLAN   PEACE
BAL/PWR ECO/TAC ARMS/CONT NUC/PWR PWR...ANTHOL UN   DIPLOM
COLD/WAR. PAGE 13 G0256   POLICY
                                                         INT/ORG

B65
HALPERIN M.H.,COMMUNIST CHINA AND ARMS CONTROL.   ATTIT
CHINA/COM FUT USA+45 CULTURE FORCES TEC/DEV ECO/TAC   POLICY
WAR PEACE ORD/FREE MARXISM 20 COLD/WAR. PAGE 24   ARMS/CONT
G0473   NUC/PWR

B65
MELMANS S.,OUR DEPLETED SOCIETY. SPACE USA+45   CIVMIL/REL
ECO/DEV FORCES BUDGET ECO/TAC ADMIN WEAPON   INDUS
EFFICIENCY 20 COLD/WAR. PAGE 38 G0753   EDU/PROP
                                                        CONTROL

B65
MOSKOWITZ H.,US SECURITY, ARMS CONTROL, AND   BIBLIOG/A
DISARMAMENT 1961-1965. FORCES DIPLOM DETER WAR   ARMS/CONT
WEAPON...CHARTS 20 UN COLD/WAR NATO. PAGE 40 G0790   NUC/PWR
                                                        PEACE

S65
GRIFFITH S.B.,"COMMUNIST CHINA'S CAPACITY TO MAKE   FORCES
WAR." CHINA/COM COM NAT/G TOP/EX PLAN DOMIN COERCE   PWR
NUC/PWR ATTIT RESPECT SKILL...CONCPT MYTH TIME/SEQ   WEAPON
TREND COLD/WAR 20. PAGE 23 G0452   ASIA

S65
HARRISON S.L.,"NTH NATION CHALLENGES* THE PRESENT   ARMS/CONT
PERSPECTIVE." EUR+WWI FUT USA+45 BAL/PWR CONTROL   NUC/PWR
RISK COERCE WAR...PREDICT COLD/WAR. PAGE 25 G0485   NAT/G
                                                        DIPLOM

C65
SCHWEBEL M.,"BEHAVIORAL SCIENCE AND HUMAN   PEACE
SURVIVAL." FORCES ARMS/CONT COERCE NUC/PWR WAR   ACT/RES
GP/REL NAT/LISM PERCEPT...POLICY PSY ANTHOL   DIPLOM
BIBLIOG/A 20 COLD/WAR. PAGE 50 G0984   HEAL

C65
US AIR FORCE ACADEMY,"AMERICAN DEFENSE POLICY." COM   PLAN
INT/ORG TEC/DEV FOR/AID ARMS/CONT DETER NUC/PWR   FORCES
...POLICY DECISION CONCPT ANTHOL BIBLIOG/A 20   WAR
COLD/WAR NATO. PAGE 56 G1103   COERCE

B66
CLARK G.,WORLD PEACE THROUGH WORLD LAW: TWO   INT/LAW
ALTERNATIVE PLANS. WOR+45 DELIB/GP FORCES TAX   PEACE
CONFER ADJUD SANCTION ARMS/CONT WAR CHOOSE PRIVIL   PLAN
20 UN COLD/WAR. PAGE 12 G0231   INT/ORG

B66
DAENIKER G.,STRATEGIE DES KLEIN STAATS. SWITZERLND   NUC/PWR
ACT/RES CREATE DIPLOM NEUTRAL DETER WAR WEAPON PWR   PLAN
SOVEREIGN...IDEA/COMP 20 COLD/WAR. PAGE 14 G0270   FORCES
                                                        NAT/G

B67
HALLE L.J.,THE COLD WAR AS HISTORY. USSR WOR+45   DIPLOM
ECO/TAC FOR/AID NUC/PWR WAR PEACE ORD/FREE   BAL/PWR
...MAJORIT TREND 20 COLD/WAR KENNEDY/JF KHRUSH/N
BERLIN/BLO. PAGE 24 G0470

B67
MCCLINTOCK R.,THE MEANING OF LIMITED WAR. FUT   WAR
WOR+45 NAT/G FORCES GUERRILLA REV...POLICY SAMP/SIZ   NUC/PWR
TREND NAT/COMP 45 COLD/WAR. PAGE 37 G0730   BAL/PWR
                                                        DIPLOM

B67
PADELFORD N.J.,THE DYNAMICS OF INTERNATIONAL   DIPLOM
POLITICS (2ND ED.). WOR+45 LAW INT/ORG FORCES   NAT/G
TEC/DEV REGION NAT/LISM PEACE ATTIT PWR ALL/IDEOS   POLICY
UN COLD/WAR NATO TREATY. PAGE 43 G0856   DECISION

B67
ROACH J.R.,THE UNITED STATES AND THE ATLANTIC   INT/ORG
COMMUNITY: ISSUES AND PROSPECTS. WOR+45 TEC/DEV   POLICY
ECO/TAC COLONIAL REGION PEACE ROLE...ANTHOL NATO   ADJUST

COLD/WAR EEC. PAGE 47 G0925   DIPLOM

B67
RUSSELL B.,WAR CRIMES IN VIETNAM. USA+45 VIETNAM   WAR
FORCES DIPLOM WEAPON RACE/REL DISCRIM ISOLAT   CRIME
BIO/SOC 20 COLD/WAR RUSSELL/B. PAGE 48 G0949   ATTIT
                                                        POLICY

B67
RUSSETT B.M.,ARMS CONTROL IN EUROPE: PROPOSALS AND   ARMS/CONT
POLITICAL CONSTRAINTS. GERMANY WOR+45 POL/PAR   REGION
BARGAIN DIPLOM...TREND CHARTS 20 COLD/WAR. PAGE 48   METH/COMP
G0950

S67
CARROLL K.J.,"SECOND STEP TOWARD ARMS CONTROL."   ARMS/CONT
WOR+45 INT/ORG VOL/ASSN FORCES PROB/SOLV RISK   DIPLOM
WEAPON 20 COLD/WAR. PAGE 11 G0215   PLAN
                                                        NUC/PWR

S67
EISENDRATH C.,"THE OUTER SPACE TREATY." CHINA/COM   SPACE
COM USA+45 DIPLOM CONTROL NUC/PWR...INT/LAW 20 UN   INT/ORG
COLD/WAR TREATY. PAGE 17 G0339   PEACE
                                                        ARMS/CONT

S67
KRUSCHE H.,"THE STRIVING OF THE KIESINGER-STRAUS   ARMS/CONT
GOVERNMENT FOR NUCLEAR WEAPONS IS A THREAT TO   INT/ORG
EUROPEAN SECURITY." EUR+WWI GERMANY BAL/PWR   NUC/PWR
SANCTION WEAPON PEACE ORD/FREE...MARXIST 20 NATO   DIPLOM
COLD/WAR. PAGE 32 G0623

S67
MARTIN L.W.,"BALLISTIC MISSILE DEFENSE AND EUROPE."   ATTIT
EUR+WWI USA+45 FORCES PLAN BAL/PWR DEBATE PEACE   ARMS/CONT
...POLICY COLD/WAR NATO. PAGE 36 G0715   NUC/PWR
                                                        DETER

S67
REINTANZ G.,"THE SPACE TREATY." WOR+45 DIPLOM   SPACE
CONTROL ARMS/CONT NUC/PWR WAR...MARXIST 20 COLD/WAR   INT/LAW
UN TREATY. PAGE 46 G0911   INT/ORG
                                                        PEACE

COLE/GEO....GEORGE COLE

COLEMAN J.R. G0243

COLLECTIVE BARGAINING....SEE BARGAIN+LABOR+GP/REL

COLLECTIVE SECURITY....SEE INT/ORG+FORCES

COLLEGES....SEE ACADEM

COLM G. G0244

COLOMBIA....SEE ALSO L/A&17C

S67
MCNAMARA R.L.,"THE NEED FOR INNOVATIVENESS IN   PROB/SOLV
DEVELOPING SOCIETIES." L/A+17C EDU/PROP ADMIN LEAD   PLAN
WEALTH...POLICY PSY SOC METH 20 COLOMB. PAGE 38   ECO/UNDEV
G0747   NEW/IDEA

COLONIAL....COLONIALISM; SEE ALSO DOMIN

C25
MOON P.T.,"SYLLABUS ON INTERNATIONAL RELATIONS."   INT/ORG
EUR+WWI MOD/EUR USA-45 FORCES COLONIAL WAR WEAPON   DIPLOM
NAT/LISM...POLICY BIBLIOG T 19/20. PAGE 39 G0778   NAT/G

B35
FOREIGN AFFAIRS BIBLIOGRAPHY: A SELECTED AND   BIBLIOG/A
ANNOTATED LIST OF BOOKS ON INTERNATIONAL RELATIONS   DIPLOM
1919-1962 (4 VOLS.). CONSTN FORCES COLONIAL   INT/ORG
ARMS/CONT WAR NAT/LISM PEACE ATTIT DRIVE...POLICY
INT/LAW 20. PAGE 1 G0011

B58
EHRHARD J.,LE DESTIN DU COLONIALISME. AFR FRANCE   COLONIAL
ECO/UNDEV AGRI FINAN MARKET CREATE PLAN TEC/DEV   FOR/AID
BUDGET DIPLOM PRICE 20. PAGE 17 G0335   INT/TRADE
                                                        INDUS

B59
WARD B.,5 IDEAS THAT CHANGE THE WORLD. WOR+45   ECO/UNDEV
WOR-45 SOCIETY STRUCT AGRI INDUS INT/ORG NAT/G   ALL/VALS
FORCES ACT/RES ARMS/CONT TOTALISM ATTIT DRIVE   NAT/LISM
GEN/LAWS. PAGE 62 G1210   COLONIAL

B60
LEYDER J.,BIBLIOGRAPHIE DE L'ENSEIGNEMENT SUPERIEUR BIBLIOG/A
ET DE LA RECHERCHE SCIENTIFIQUE EN AFRIQUE   ACT/RES
INTERTROPICALE (2 VOLS.). AFR CULTURE ECO/UNDEV   ACADEM
AGRI PLAN EDU/PROP ADMIN COLONIAL...GEOG SOC/INTEG   R+D
20 NEGRO. PAGE 34 G0664

B60
PENTONY D.E.,THE UNDERDEVELOPED LANDS. FUT WOR+45   ECO/UNDEV
CULTURE AGRI FINAN INDUS MARKET INT/ORG LABOR NAT/G   POLICY
VOL/ASSN CONSULT TEC/DEV ECO/TAC EDU/PROP COLONIAL   FOR/AID
ATTIT WEALTH...OBS RECORD SAMP TREND GEN/METH WORK   INT/TRADE
UN 20. PAGE 44 G0867

B61
CARNELL F.,THE POLITICS OF THE NEW STATES: A SELECT   BIBLIOG/A
ANNOTATED BIBLIOGRAPHY WITH SPECIAL REFERENCE TO   AFR
THE COMMONWEALTH. CONSTN ELITES LABOR NAT/G POL/PAR   ASIA
EX/STRUC DIPLOM ADJUD ADMIN...GOV/COMP 20   COLONIAL
COMMONWLTH. PAGE 11 G0210

C65
SEARA M.V.,"COSMIC INTERNATIONAL LAW." LAW ACADEM   SPACE
ACT/RES DIPLOM COLONIAL CONTROL NUC/PWR SOVEREIGN   INT/LAW
...GEN/LAWS BIBLIOG UN. PAGE 50 G0987   IDEA/COMP
                                                       INT/ORG

S66
FLEMING W.G.,"AUTHORITY, EFFICIENCY, AND ROLE   DOMIN
STRESS: PROBLEMS IN THE DEVELOPMENT OF EAST AFRICAN   EFFICIENCY
BUREAUCRACIES." AFR UGANDA STRUCT PROB/SOLV ROUTINE   COLONIAL
INGP/REL ROLE...MGT SOC GP/COMP GOV/COMP 20   ADMIN
TANGANYIKA AFRICA/E. PAGE 19 G0371

B67
DE BLIJ H.J.,SYSTEMATIC POLITICAL GEOGRAPHY. WOR+45   GEOG
STRUCT INT/ORG NAT/G EDU/PROP ADMIN COLONIAL   CONCPT
ROUTINE ORD/FREE PWR...IDEA/COMP T 20. PAGE 15   METH
G0283

B67
LAMBERT J.,LATIN AMERICA: SOCIAL STRUCTURES AND   L/A+17C
POLITICAL INSTITUTIONS. STRUCT TEC/DEV DIPLOM ADMIN   NAT/G
COLONIAL LEAD ATTIT...SOC CLASSIF NAT/COMP 17/20.   ECO/UNDEV
PAGE 32 G0631   SOCIETY

B67
ROACH J.R.,THE UNITED STATES AND THE ATLANTIC   INT/ORG
COMMUNITY; ISSUES AND PROSPECTS. WOR+45 TEC/DEV   POLICY
ECO/TAC COLONIAL REGION PEACE ROLE...ANTHOL NATO   ADJUST
COLD/WAR EEC. PAGE 47 G0925   DIPLOM

B67
WOODRUFF W.,IMPACT OF WESTERN MAN. ECO/DEV INDUS   EUR+WWI
CREATE PLAN PROB/SOLV COLONIAL GOV/REL...CHARTS   MOD/EUR
GOV/COMP BIBLIOG 18/20. PAGE 64 G1256   CAP/ISM

S67
"CHINESE STATEMENT ON NUCLEAR PROLIFERATION."   NUC/PWR
CHINA/COM USA+45 USSR DOMIN COLONIAL PWR. PAGE 1   BAL/PWR
G0022   ARMS/CONT
                                                       DIPLOM

S67
D'AMATO D.,"LEGAL ASPECTS OF THE FRENCH NUCLEAR   INT/LAW
TESTS." FRANCE WOR+45 ACT/RES COLONIAL RISK GOV/REL   DIPLOM
EQUILIB ORD/FREE PWR DECISION. PAGE 14 G0268   NUC/PWR
                                                       ADJUD

S67
KRAUS J.,"A MARXIST IN GHANA." GHANA ELITES CHIEF   MARXISM
PROB/SOLV TEC/DEV DIPLOM ECO/TAC COLONIAL PARTIC   PLAN
PWR 20 NKRUMAH/K. PAGE 31 G0618   ATTIT
                                                       CREATE

COLORADO....COLORADO
COLUMBIA U BUREAU APPL SOC RES G0888
COLUMBIA/U....COLUMBIA UNIVERSITY

COM....COMMUNIST COUNTRIES, EXCEPT CHINA; SEE ALSO
    APPROPRIATE NATIONS, MARXISM

B38
HARPER S.N.,THE GOVERNMENT OF THE SOVIET UNION. COM   MARXISM
USSR LAW CONSTN ECO/DEV PLAN TEC/DEV DIPLOM   NAT/G
INT/TRADE ADMIN REV NAT/LISM...POLICY 20. PAGE 24   LEAD
G0483   POL/PAR

B43
LASKI H.J.,REFLECTIONS ON THE REVOLUTIONS OF OUR   CAP/ISM
TIME. COM USSR NAT/G WORKER UTOPIA ORD/FREE WEALTH   WELF/ST
MARXISM SOCISM 19/20. PAGE 32 G0637   ECO/TAC
                                                       POLICY

B46
BRODIE B.,THE OBSOLETE WEAPON: ATOMIC POWER AND   INT/ORG

WORLD ORDER. COM USA+45 USSR WOR+45 DELIB/GP PLAN   TEC/DEV
ORD/FREE PWR...CONCPT TIME/SEQ TREND UN 20. PAGE 9   ARMS/CONT
G0171   NUC/PWR

N47
FOX W.T.R.,UNITED STATES POLICY IN A TWO POWER   DIPLOM
WORLD. COM USA+45 USSR FORCES DOMIN AGREE NEUTRAL   FOR/AID
NUC/PWR ORD/FREE SOVEREIGN 20 COLD/WAR TREATY   POLICY
EUROPE/W INTERVENT. PAGE 20 G0389

S51
MACRAE D.G.,"THE BOLSHEVIK IDEOLOGY: THE   MARXISM
INTELLECTUAL AND EMOTIONAL FACTORS IN COMMUNIST   INTELL
AFFILIATION" (BMR)" COM LEAD REV ATTIT ORD/FREE   PHIL/SCI
...SOC CON/ANAL 20 BOLSHEVISM. PAGE 35 G0693   SECT

B59
MIKSCHE F.O.,THE FAILURE OF ATOMIC STRATEGY. COM   ACT/RES
EUR+WWI INTELL POL/PAR FORCES PLAN ECO/TAC NUC/PWR   ORD/FREE
ATTIT DRIVE RIGID/FLEX PWR...DECISION GEOG PSY   DIPLOM
CONCPT RECORD TREND CHARTS VAL/FREE 20. PAGE 39   ARMS/CONT
G0766

B59
MODELSKI G.,ATOMIC ENERGY IN THE COMMUNIST BLOC.   TEC/DEV
FUT INT/ORG CONSULT FORCES ACT/RES PLAN KNOWL SKILL   NUC/PWR
...PHIL/SCI STAT CHARTS 20. PAGE 39 G0777   USSR
                                                       COM

L59
BURNS A.L.,"THE RATIONALE OF CATALYTIC WAR." COM   COERCE
USA+45 WOR+45 R+D NAT/G FORCES ACT/RES TEC/DEV PWR   NUC/PWR
...DECISION HYPO/EXP TOT/POP 20. PAGE 10 G0191   WAR

B60
BARNET R.,WHO WANTS DISARMAMENT. COM EUR+WWI USA+45   PLAN
USSR INT/ORG NAT/G BAL/PWR DIPLOM EDU/PROP COERCE   FORCES
DETER NUC/PWR WAR WEAPON ATTIT PWR...TIME/SEQ   ARMS/CONT
COLD/WAR CONGRESS 20. PAGE 5 G0096

B60
GRANICK D.,THE RED EXECUTIVE. COM USA+45 SOCIETY   PWR
ECO/DEV INDUS NAT/G POL/PAR EX/STRUC PLAN ECO/TAC   STRATA
EDU/PROP ADMIN EXEC ATTIT DRIVE...GP/COMP 20.   USSR
PAGE 22 G0440   ELITES

B60
MCKINNEY R.,REVIEW OF THE INTERNATIONAL ATOMIC   NUC/PWR
POLICIES AND PROGRAMS OF THE UNITED STATES (5   PEACE
VOLS.). COM FUT USA+45 ECO/DEV ECO/UNDEV INT/ORG   DIPLOM
DELIB/GP PLAN ADMIN 20 THIRD/WRLD. PAGE 38 G0744   POLICY

B60
PARRY A.,RUSSIA'S ROCKETS AND MISSILES. COM FUT   PLAN
GERMANY USA+45 WOR+45 INTELL ECO/DEV ACT/RES   TEC/DEV
NUC/PWR WEAPON ATTIT ALL/VALS...OBS TIME/SEQ   SPACE
COLD/WAR 20. PAGE 44 G0859   USSR

S60
BECKER A.S.,"COMPARISIONS OF UNITED STATES AND USSR   STAT
NATIONAL OUTPUT: SOME RULES OF THE GAME." COM   USSR
USA+45 ECO/DEV AGRI DIST/IND INDUS R+D CONSULT PLAN
ECO/TAC RIGID/FLEX KNOWL...METH/CNCPT CHARTS 20.
PAGE 6 G0113

S60
DOUGHERTY J.E.,"KEY TO SECURITY: DISARMAMENT OR   FORCES
ARMS STABILITY." COM USA+45 USSR INT/ORG NAT/G   ORD/FREE
CREATE EDU/PROP COERCE DETER ATTIT PWR...DECISION   ARMS/CONT
CONCPT MYTH NEW/IDEA TREND 20 COLD/WAR. PAGE 16   NUC/PWR
G0311

S60
KISSINGER H.A.,"ARMS CONTROL, INSPECTION AND   FORCES
SURPRISE ATTACK." COM USA+45 NAT/G ACT/RES PLAN   ORD/FREE
TEC/DEV DIPLOM EDU/PROP DETER WAR RIGID/FLEX   ARMS/CONT
...CONCPT GEN/METH TOT/POP 20. PAGE 31 G0603   NUC/PWR

B61
NOGEE J.L.,SOVIET POLICY TOWARD INTERNATIONAL   INT/ORG
CONTROL OF ATOMIC ENERGY. COM USA+45 WOR+45 INTELL   ATTIT
NAT/G ACT/RES DIPLOM EDU/PROP NUC/PWR TOTALISM   ARMS/CONT
PERCEPT KNOWL PWR...TIME/SEQ COLD/WAR 20. PAGE 42   USSR
G0824

B61
SCHMIDT H.,VERTEIDIGUNG ODER VERGELTUNG. COM CUBA   PLAN
GERMANY/W USSR FORCES DIPLOM ARMS/CONT DETER   WAR
NUC/PWR...POLICY CHARTS HYPO/EXP SIMUL BIBLIOG 20   BAL/PWR
NATO COLD/WAR. PAGE 49 G0970   ORD/FREE

B61
US SENATE COMM GOVT OPERATIONS,ORGANIZING FOR   POLICY
NATIONAL SECURITY. COM USA+45 BUDGET DIPLOM DETER   PLAN
NUC/PWR WAR WEAPON ORD/FREE...BIBLIOG 20 COLD/WAR.   FORCES
PAGE 60 G1176   COERCE

SOVIET STAND ON DISARMAMENT. COM EUR+WWI FUT USA+45 ACT/RES NAT/G TOP/EX NUC/PWR PEACE ATTIT...POLICY CONCPT TOT/POP 20. PAGE 1 G0016
B62
ACT/RES
ORD/FREE
ARMS/CONT
USSR

FRIEDRICH-EBERT-STIFTUNG,THE SOVIET BLOC AND DEVELOPING COUNTRIES. CHINA/COM COM GERMANY/E USSR WOR+45 ECO/UNDEV INT/ORG NAT/G TEC/DEV NEUTRAL PWR ...POLICY 20. PAGE 20 G0394
B62
MARXISM
DIPLOM
ECO/TAC
FOR/AID

GILPIN R.,AMERICAN SCIENTISTS AND NUCLEAR WEAPONS POLICY. COM FUT USA+45 WOR+45 INT/ORG NAT/G PROF/ORG CONSULT FORCES CREATE TEC/DEV BAL/PWR EDU/PROP ARMS/CONT WAR PERCEPT KNOWL MORAL PWR ...PHIL/SCI SOC CONCPT GEN/LAWS 20. PAGE 21 G0417
B62
INTELL
ATTIT
DETER
NUC/PWR

LEFEVER E.W.,ARMS AND ARMS CONTROL. COM USA+45 INT/ORG TEC/DEV DIPLOM ORD/FREE 20. PAGE 33 G0652
B62
ATTIT
PWR
ARMS/CONT
BAL/PWR

SINGER J.D.,DETERRENCE, ARMS CONTROL AND DISARMAMENT: TOWARD A SYNTHESIS IN NATIONAL SECURITY POLICY. COM USA+45 INT/ORG BAL/PWR DETER ORD/FREE...POLICY COLD/WAR 20. PAGE 51 G1003
B62
FUT
ACT/RES
ARMS/CONT

WALSTON H.,AGRICULTURE UNDER COMMUNISM. CHINA/COM COM PROB/SOLV HAPPINESS RIGID/FLEX...POLICY METH/COMP 20. PAGE 62 G1207
B62
AGRI
MARXISM
PLAN
CREATE

BETHE H.,"DISARMAMENT AND STRATEGY." COM USA+45 USSR WOR+45 VOL/ASSN TEC/DEV EDU/PROP NUC/PWR CHOOSE PEACE...POLICY DECISION NEW/IDEA OBS GEN/LAWS COLD/WAR 420. PAGE 7 G0133
S62
PLAN
ORD/FREE
ARMS/CONT
DIPLOM

FOSTER W.C.,"ARMS CONTROL AND DISARMAMENT IN A DIVIDED WORLD." COM FUT USA+45 USSR WOR+45 INTELL INT/ORG NAT/G VOL/ASSN CONSULT CREATE PLAN TEC/DEV EDU/PROP LEGIT NUC/PWR ATTIT RIGID/FLEX...CONCPT TREND TOT/POP 20 UN. PAGE 20 G0387
S62
DELIB/GP
POLICY
ARMS/CONT
DIPLOM

GORDON B.K.,"NUCLEAR WEAPONS: RUSSIAN AND AMERICAN." COM USA+45 USSR NAT/G FORCES ACT/RES TEC/DEV PERCEPT RIGID/FLEX PWR SKILL...MGT METH/CNCPT QUANT OBS TIME/SEQ CON/ANAL GEN/METH TOT/POP VAL/FREE 20. PAGE 22 G0433
S62
ORD/FREE
COERCE
NUC/PWR

NANES A.,"DISARMAMENT: THE LAST SEVEN YEARS." COM EUR+WWI USA+45 USSR INT/ORG FORCES TOP/EX CREATE LEGIT NUC/PWR DISPL ORD/FREE...CONCPT TIME/SEQ CON/ANAL 20. PAGE 41 G0803
S62
DELIB/GP
RIGID/FLEX
ARMS/CONT

ABSHIRE D.M.,NATIONAL SECURITY: POLITICAL, MILITARY, AND ECONOMIC STRATEGIES IN THE DECADE AHEAD. ASIA COM EUR+WWI MOD/EUR INT/ORG DELIB/GP FORCES ECO/TAC COERCE ATTIT RIGID/FLEX HEALTH ORD/FREE PWR WEALTH...POLICY STAT CHARTS ANTHOL COLD/WAR VAL/FREE. PAGE 1 G0024
B63
FUT
ACT/RES
BAL/PWR

GOLDSEN J.M.,OUTER SPACE IN WORLD POLITICS. COM USA+45 NAT/G FORCES ACT/RES PLAN DOMIN EDU/PROP COERCE ORD/FREE PWR...TECHNIC STAT INT SAMP TREND ANTHOL VAL/FREE 20. PAGE 22 G0428
B63
TEC/DEV
DIPLOM
SPACE

NORTH R.C.,CONTENT ANALYSIS: A HANDBOOK WITH APPLICATIONS FOR THE STUDY OF INTERNATIONAL CRISIS. ASIA COM EUR+WWI MOD/EUR INT/ORG TEC/DEV DOMIN EDU/PROP ROUTINE COERCE PERCEPT RIGID/FLEX ALL/VALS ...QUANT TESTS CON/ANAL SIMUL GEN/LAWS VAL/FREE. PAGE 42 G0825
B63
METH/CNCPT
COMPUT/IR
USSR

DELLIN L.A.D.,"BULGARIA UNDER SOVIET LEADERSHIP." BULGARIA COM USA+45 USSR ECO/DEV INDUS POL/PAR EX/STRUC TOP/EX COERCE ATTIT RIGID/FLEX...POLICY TIME/SEQ 20. PAGE 15 G0293
S63
AGRI
NAT/G
TOTALISM

PHELPS J.,"INFORMATION AND ARMS CONTROL." COM SPACE USA+45 USSR WOR+45 R+D INT/ORG NAT/G DELIB/GP DIPLOM ORD/FREE...CONCPT 20. PAGE 45 G0875
S63
KNOWL
ARMS/CONT
NUC/PWR

TASHJEAN J.E.,"RESEARCH ON ARMS CONTROL." COM USA+45 USSR FORCES ACT/RES PLAN DOMIN COERCE ORD/FREE PWR...TIME/SEQ GEN/LAWS 20 COLD/WAR. PAGE 53 G1053
S63
NAT/G
POLICY
ARMS/CONT

WILES P.J.D.,"WILL CAPITALISM AND COMMUNISM SPONTANEOUSLY CONVERGE." COM FUT USA+45 ECO/DEV DIST/IND MARKET CAP/ISM ECO/TAC RIGID/FLEX WEALTH MARXISM SOCISM...MATH STAT TREND COMPUT/IR 20. PAGE 63 G1240
S63
PLAN
TEC/DEV
USSR

COHEN M.,LAW AND POLITICS IN SPACE: SPECIFIC AND URGENT PROBLEMS IN THE LAW OF OUTER SPACE. CHINA/COM COM USA+45 USSR WOR+45 COM/IND INT/ORG NAT/G LEGIT NUC/PWR ATTIT BIO/SOC...JURID CONCPT CONGRESS 20 STALIN/J. PAGE 12 G0241
B64
DELIB/GP
LAW
INT/LAW
SPACE

FREYMOND J.,WESTERN EUROPE SINCE THE WAR. COM EUR+WWI USA+45 DIPLOM...BIBLIOG 20 NATO UN EEC. PAGE 20 G0392
B64
INT/ORG
POLICY
ECO/DEV
ECO/TAC

HASKINS C.P.,THE SCIENTIFIC REVOLUTION AND WORLD POLITICS. COM FUT USA+45 ECO/DEV ECO/UNDEV ATTIT ...PHIL/SCI BIBLIOG 20 THIRD/WRLD. PAGE 25 G0489
B64
TEC/DEV
POLICY
DIPLOM
TREND

PETERSON W.,THE POLITICS OF POPULATION. COM EUR+WWI FUT MOD/EUR S/ASIA USA+45 USA-45 WOR+45 LAW CULTURE FAM SECT DOMIN EDU/PROP BIO/SOC HEALTH ORD/FREE ...GEOG STAT TIME/SEQ TREND VAL/FREE. PAGE 44 G0871
B64
PLAN
CENSUS
POLICY

ROSECRANCE R.N.,THE DISPERSION OF NUCLEAR WEAPONS: STRATEGY AND POLITICS. ASIA COM FUT S/ASIA USA+45 INT/ORG NAT/G DELIB/GP FORCES ACT/RES TEC/DEV BAL/PWR COERCE DETER ATTIT RIGID/FLEX ORD/FREE ...POLICY CHARTS VAL/FREE. PAGE 48 G0935
B64
EUR+WWI
PWR
PEACE

WARD C.,"THE 'NEW MYTHS' AND 'OLD REALITIES' OF NUCLEAR WAR." COM FUT USA+45 USSR WOR+45 INT/ORG NAT/G DOMIN LEGIT EXEC ATTIT PERCEPT ALL/VALS ...POLICY RELATIV PSY MYTH TREND 20. PAGE 62 G1212
L64
FORCES
COERCE
ARMS/CONT
NUC/PWR

FLORINSKY M.T.,"TRENDS IN THE SOVIET ECONOMY." COM USA+45 USSR INDUS LABOR N/G PLAN TEC/DEV ECO/TAC ALL/VALS SOCISM...MGT METH/CNCPT STYLE CON/ANAL GEN/METH WORK 20. PAGE 19 G0374
S64
ECO/DEV
AGRI

KASSOF A.,"THE ADMINISTERED SOCIETY: TOTALITARIANISM WITHOUT TERROR." COM USSR STRATA AGRI INDUS NAT/G PERF/ART SCHOOL TOP/EX EDU/PROP ADMIN ORD/FREE PWR...POLICY SOC TIME/SEQ GEN/LAWS VAL/FREE 20. PAGE 29 G0580
S64
SOCIETY
DOMIN
TOTALISM

LERNER A.P.,"NUCLEAR SYMMETRY AS A FRAMEWORK FOR COEXISTENCE." COM FUT USA+45 USSR ACT/RES CREATE PLAN DIPLOM EDU/PROP COERCE WAR RIGID/FLEX PWR SKILL...CONCPT METH/CNCPT GEN/LAWS TOT/POP VAL/FREE COLD/WAR 20. PAGE 33 G0657
S64
FORCES
ORD/FREE
DETER
NUC/PWR

MAGGS P.B.,"SOVIET VIEWPOINT ON NUCLEAR WEAPONS IN INTERNATIONAL LAW." USSR WOR+45 INT/ORG FORCES DIPLOM ARMS/CONT ATTIT ORD/FREE PWR...POLICY JURID CONCPT OBS TREND CON/ANAL GEN/LAWS VAL/FREE 20. PAGE 35 G0694
S64
COM
LAW
INT/LAW
NUC/PWR

MARES V.E.,"EAST EUROPE'S SECOND CHANCE." COM EUR+WWI HUNGARY ROMANIA USSR YUGOSLAVIA ECO/UNDEV NAT/G TOP/EX CREATE PLAN TEC/DEV REGION NAT/LISM RIGID/FLEX PWR...CONCPT STAT COMECON 20. PAGE 36 G0705
S64
VOL/ASSN
ECO/TAC

KASER M.,COMECON* INTEGRATION PROBLEMS OF THE PLANNED ECONOMIES. INT/ORG TEC/DEV INT/TRADE PRICE ADMIN ADJUST CENTRAL...STAT TIME/SEQ ORG/CHARTS COMECON. PAGE 29 G0579
B65
PLAN
ECO/DEV
COM
REGION

KOROL A.G.,SOVIET RESEARCH AND DEVELOPMENT. USSR ACADEM SCHOOL WORKER ROUTINE COST...STAT T 20. PAGE 31 G0615
B65
COM
R+D
FINAN

DIST/IND

US DEPARTMENT OF DEFENSE,US SECURITY ARMS CONTROL, BIBLIOG/A
AND DISARMAMENT 1961-1965 (PAMPHLET). CHINA/COM COM ARMS/CONT
GERMANY/W ISRAEL SPACE USA+45 USSR WOR+45 FORCES NUC/PWR
EDU/PROP DETER EQUILIB PEACE ALL/VALS...GOV/COMP 20 DIPLOM
NATO. PAGE 57 G1118

B65

US DEPARTMENT OF THE ARMY,NUCLEAR WEAPONS AND THE BIBLIOG/A
ATLANTIC ALLIANCE: A BIBLIOGRAPHIC SURVEY. ASIA ARMS/CONT
EUR+WWI USA+45 FORCES DIPLOM WEAPON...STAT 20 NATO. NUC/PWR
PAGE 58 G1131 BAL/PWR

S65

GRIFFITH S.B.,"COMMUNIST CHINA'S CAPACITY TO MAKE FORCES
WAR." CHINA/COM COM NAT/G TOP/EX PLAN DOMIN COERCE PWR
NUC/PWR ATTIT RESPECT SKILL...CONCPT MYTH TIME/SEQ WEAPON
TREND COLD/WAR 20. PAGE 23 G0452 ASIA

S65

HOLSTI O.R.,"EAST-WEST CONFLICT AND SINO-SOVIET VOL/ASSN
RELATIONS" CHINA/COM USSR COMPUTER REGION DECISION. DIPLOM
PAGE 27 G0523 CON/ANAL
COM

S65

RUBINSTEIN A.Z.,"POLITICAL BARRIERS TO COM
DISARMAMENT." FUT DIPLOM COERCE NUC/PWR WAR USA+45
NAT/LISM ORD/FREE PREDICT. PAGE 48 G0944 ARMS/CONT
ATTIT

S65

STAAR R.F.,"RETROGRESSION IN POLAND." COM USSR AGRI TOP/EX
INDUS NAT/G CREATE EDU/PROP TOTALISM RIGID/FLEX ECO/TAC
ORD/FREE PWR SOCISM...RECORD CHARTS 20. PAGE 52 POLAND
G1029

C65

US AIR FORCE ACADEMY,"AMERICAN DEFENSE POLICY." COM PLAN
INT/DEV TEC/DEV FOR/AID ARMS/CONT DETER NUC/PWR FORCES
...POLICY DECISION CONCPT ANTHOL BIBLIOG/A 20 WAR
COLD/WAR NATO. PAGE 56 G1103 COERCE

B66

BLOOMFIELD L.P.,KHRUSHCHEV AND THE ARMS RACE. ARMS/CONT
USA+45 USSR ECO/DEV BAL/PWR EDU/PROP CONFER NUC/PWR COM
ATTIT...CHARTS 20 KHRUSH/N. PAGE 7 G0143 POLICY
DIPLOM

B66

ECKSTEIN A.,COMMUNIST CHINA'S ECONOMIC GROWTH AND ASIA
FOREIGN TRADE* IMPLICATIONS FOR US POLICY. COM ECO/UNDEV
USA+45 USSR STRUCT INDUS MARKET DIPLOM ECO/TAC CREATE
FOR/AID INT/TRADE...STAT CHARTS. PAGE 17 G0332 PWR

B66

SPULBER N.,THE STATE AND ECONOMIC DEVELOPMENT IN ECO/DEV
EASTERN EUROPE. BULGARIA COM CZECHOSLVK HUNGARY ECO/UNDEV
POLAND YUGOSLAVIA CULTURE PLAN CAP/ISM INT/TRADE NAT/G
CONTROL...POLICY CHARTS METH/COMP BIBLIOG/A 19/20. TOTALISM
PAGE 52 G1028

B66

US DEPARTMENT OF THE ARMY,COMMUNIST CHINA: A BIBLIOG/A
STRATEGIC SURVEY: A BIBLIOGRAPHY (PAMPHLET NO. MARXISM
20-67). CHINA/COM COM INDIA USSR NAT/G POL/PAR S/ASIA
EX/STRUC FORCES NUC/PWR REV ATTIT...POLICY GEOG DIPLOM
CHARTS. PAGE 58 G1133

L66

DOUGHERTY J.E.,"THE CATHOLIC CHURCH, WAR AND CATHISM
NUCLEAR WEAPONS." COM EUR+WWI SECT TOP/EX LEAD MORAL
DETER ALL/VALS. PAGE 16 G0312 WAR
NUC/PWR

B67

HARDT J.P.,MATHEMATICS AND COMPUTERS IN SOVIET PLAN
ECONOMIC PLANNING. COM USSR OP/RES PROB/SOLV TEC/DEV
OPTIMAL...MODAL SIMUL 20. PAGE 24 G0481 MATH
COMPUT/IR

B67

MACKINTOSH J.M.,JUGGERNAUT. USSR NAT/G POL/PAR WAR
ADMIN LEAD CIVMIL/REL COST TOTALISM PWR MARXISM FORCES
...GOV/COMP 20. PAGE 35 G0691 COM
PROF/ORG

B67

NATIONAL SCIENCE FOUNDATION,DIRECTORY OF SELECTED INDEX
RESEARCH INSTITUTES IN EASTERN EUROPE. BULGARIA R+D
CZECHOSLVK HUNGARY POLAND ROMANIA INTELL ACADEM COM
NAT/G ACT/RES 20. PAGE 41 G0814 PHIL/SCI

B67

POMEROY W.J.,HALF A CENTURY OF SOCIALISM. USSR LAW SOCISM
AGRI INDUS NAT/G CREATE DIPLOM EDU/PROP PERSON MARXISM
ORD/FREE WEALTH...POLICY TREND 20. PAGE 45 G0884 COM
SOCIETY

L67

"POLITICAL PARTIES ON FOREIGN POLICY IN THE INTER- POL/PAR
ELECTION YEARS 1962-66." ASIA COM INDIA USA+45 PLAN DIPLOM
ATTIT...DECISION 20. PAGE 1 G0023 POLICY

S67

AVTORKHANOV A.,"A NEW AGRARIAN REVOLUTION." COM AGRI
USSR ECO/DEV PLAN TEC/DEV ADMIN CONTROL OPTIMAL METH/COMP
WEALTH SOCISM 20 KHRUSH/N STALIN/J. PAGE 4 G0082 MARXISM
OWN

S67

CARR E.H.,"REVOLUTION FROM ABOVE." USSR STRATA AGRI
FINAN INDUS NAT/G DOMIN LEAD GP/REL INGP/REL OWN POLICY
PRODUC PWR 20 STALIN/J. PAGE 11 G0214 COM
EFFICIENCY

S67

EISENDRATH C.,"THE OUTER SPACE TREATY." CHINA/COM SPACE
COM USA+45 DIPLOM CONTROL NUC/PWR...INT/LAW 20 UN INT/ORG
COLD/WAR TREATY. PAGE 17 G0339 PEACE
ARMS/CONT

S67

FADDEYEV N.,"CMEA CO-OPERATION OF EQUAL NATIONS." MARXISM
COM R+D PLAN CAP/ISM DIPLOM FOR/AID WEALTH...POLICY ECO/TAC
MARXIST. PAGE 18 G0356 INT/ORG
ECO/UNDEV

S67

MARTIN L.,"THE AMERICAN ABM DECISION." ASIA COM WEAPON
EUR+WWI UK USA+45 USSR FORCES DIPLOM PEACE...POLICY DETER
20 ABM/DEFSYS. PAGE 36 G0713 NUC/PWR
WAR

S67

TEKINER S.,"SINKIAN AND THE SINO-SOVIET CONFLICT." DIPLOM
ASIA COM USSR FORCES PLAN BAL/PWR CONTROL NUC/PWR PWR
WAR WEAPON...DECISION 20. PAGE 54 G1060 MARXISM

COM/IND....COMMUNICATIONS INDUSTRY

N

AMERICAN DOCUMENTATION INST,AMERICAN DOCUMENTATION. BIBLIOG
PROF/ORG CONSULT PLAN PERCEPT...MATH STAT AUD/VIS TEC/DEV
CHARTS METH/COMP INDEX METH 20. PAGE 3 G0050 COM/IND
COMPUT/IR

N

INDIA: A REFERENCE ANNUAL. INDIA CULTURE COM/IND CONSTN
R+D FORCES PLAN RECEIVE EDU/PROP HEALTH...STAT LABOR
CHARTS BIBLIOG 20. PAGE 1 G0005 INT/ORG

B48

GRIFFITH E.S.,RESEARCH IN POLITICAL SCIENCE: THE BIBLIOG
WORK OF PANELS OF RESEARCH COMMITTEE. APSA. WOR+45 PHIL/SCI
WOR-45 COM/IND R+D FORCES ACT/RES WAR...GOV/COMP DIPLOM
ANTHOL 20. PAGE 23 G0451 JURID

C50

WAGER P.W.,"COUNTY GOVERNMENT ACROSS THE NATION." LOC/G
USA+45 CONSTN COM/IND FINAN SCHOOL DOMIN CT/SYS PROVS
LEAD GOV/REL...STAT BIBLIOG 20. PAGE 61 G1204 ADMIN
ROUTINE

B53

HOVLAND C.I.,COMMUNICATION AND PERSUASION: PSY
PSYCHOLOGICAL STUDIES OF OPINION CHANGE. INTELL EDU/PROP
SOCIETY ECO/DEV COM/IND R+D SERV/IND CREATE TEC/DEV
ATTIT RIGID/FLEX KNOWL NEW/IDEA. PAGE 27 G0531

B53

LARSEN K.,NATIONAL BIBLIOGRAPHIC SERVICES: THEIR BIBLIOG/A
CREATION AND OPERATION. WOR+45 COM/IND CREATE PLAN INT/ORG
DIPLOM PRESS ADMIN ROUTINE...MGT UNESCO. PAGE 32 WRITING
G0636

B58

OPERATIONS RESEARCH SOCIETY,A COMPREHENSIVE BIBLIOG/A
BIBLIOGRAPHY ON OPERATIONS RESEARCH: THROUGH 1956 COMPUT/IR
WITH SUPPLEMENT FOR 1957. COM/IND DIST/IND INDUS OP/RES
ADMIN...DECISION MATH STAT METH 20. PAGE 43 G0840 MGT

S58

KLAPPER J.T.,"WHAT WE KNOW ABOUT THE EFFECTS OF ACT/RES
MASS COMMUNICATION: THE BRINK OF HOPE" (BMR)" PERCEPT
COM/IND KNOWL...METH/CNCPT GEN/LAWS BIBLIOG METH CROWD
20. PAGE 31 G0605 PHIL/SCI

GUILBAUD G.T.,WHAT IS CYBERNETICS? COMPUTER OP/RES
TEC/DEV AUTOMAT ROUTINE PERS/REL PERCEPT...PSY MATH
COMPUT/IR SIMUL GEN/METH. PAGE 23 G0460
B59
CONTROL
COM/IND
FEEDBACK
NET/THEORY

JACOBS N.,CULTURE FOR THE MILLIONS? INTELL SOCIETY
NAT/G...POLICY SOC OBS ANTHOL 20. PAGE 28 G0553
B59
CULTURE
COM/IND
PERF/ART
CONCPT

CARPENTER E.,EXPLORATIONS IN COMMUNICATION. USSR
CULTURE SCHOOL SECT EDU/PROP PRESS TV AUTOMAT
FEEDBACK ATTIT PERSON...ART/METH PSY 20. PAGE 11
G0211
B60
ANTHOL
COM/IND
TEC/DEV
WRITING

RIVKIN A.,"AFRICAN ECONOMIC DEVELOPMENT: ADVANCED
TECHNOLOGY AND THE STAGES OF GROWTH." CULTURE
ECO/UNDEV AGRI COM/IND EXTR/IND PLAN ECO/TAC ATTIT
DRIVE RIGID/FLEX SKILL WEALTH...MGT SOC GEN/LAWS
WORK TOT/POP 20. PAGE 47 G0923
S60
AFR
TEC/DEV
FOR/AID

SCHRAMM W.,"MASS COMMUNICATIONS: A BOOK OF READINGS
(2ND ED.)" LG/CO PRESS ADMIN CONTROL ROUTINE ATTIT
ROLE SUPEGO...CHARTS ANTHOL BIBLIOG 20. PAGE 50
G0977
C60
COM/IND
EDU/PROP
CROWD
MAJORIT

BRADY R.A.,ORGANIZATION, AUTOMATION, AND SOCIETY.
USA+45 AGRI COM/IND DIST/IND MARKET CREATE
...DECISION MGT 20. PAGE 8 G0163
B61
TEC/DEV
INDUS
AUTOMAT
ADMIN

MICHAEL D.N.,PROPOSED STUDIES ON THE IMPLICATIONS
OF PEACEFUL SPACE ACTIVITIES FOR HUMAN AFFAIRS.
COM/IND INDUS FORCES DIPLOM PEACE PERSON...PSY SOC
20. PAGE 39 G0764
B61
FUT
SPACE
ACT/RES
PROB/SOLV

ASTIA,HUMAN ENGINEERING: A REPORT BIBLIOGRAPHY.
USA+45 R+D FORCES ACT/RES COMPUTER CREATE OP/RES
EDU/PROP CONTROL WEAPON...SOC NEW/IDEA. PAGE 4
G0073
B62
BIBLIOG/A
COM/IND
COMPUT/IR
METH

ASTIA,INFORMATION THEORY: A REPORT BIBLIOGRAPHY.
USA+45 COMPUTER CREATE OP/RES PLAN TEC/DEV CONTROL
...CONCPT METH/COMP. PAGE 4 G0074
B62
BIBLIOG/A
COM/IND
FORCES
METH

CLARKE A.C.,PROFILES OF THE FUTURE: AN INQUIRY INTO
THE LIMITS OF THE POSSIBLE. COM/IND DIST/IND PRODUC
AGE PERCEPT...TECHNIC NEW/IDEA TIME. PAGE 12 G0232
B62
FUT
TEC/DEV
PREDICT
SPACE

MACHLUP F.,THE PRODUCTION AND DISTRIBUTION OF
KNOWLEDGE IN THE UNITED STATES. USA+45 COM/IND
INDUS SCHOOL SECT WORKER COMPUTER CREATE CIVMIL/REL
COST EFFICIENCY WEALTH 20. PAGE 35 G0688
B62
ACADEM
TEC/DEV
EDU/PROP
R+D

THANT U.,THE UNITED NATIONS' DEVELOPMENT DECADE:
PROPOSALS FOR ACTION. WOR+45 SOCIETY ECO/UNDEV AGRI
COM/IND FINAN R+D MUNIC SCHOOL VOL/ASSN CONSULT
PLAN TEC/DEV ECO/TAC EDU/PROP ADMIN ROUTINE
RIGID/FLEX...MGT SOC CONCPT UNESCO UN TOT/POP
VAL/FREE. PAGE 54 G1064
B62
INT/ORG
ALL/VALS

US CONGRESS,COMMUNICATIONS SATELLITE LEGISLATION:
HEARINGS BEFORE COMM ON AERON AND SPACE SCIENCES ON
BILLS S2550 AND 2814. WOR+45 LAW VOL/ASSN PLAN
DIPLOM CONTROL OWN PEACE...NEW/IDEA CONGRESS NASA.
PAGE 56 G1110
B62
SPACE
COM/IND
ADJUD
GOV/REL

KATZ S.M.,A SELECTED LIST OF US READINGS ON
DEVELOPMENT. AGRI COM/IND DIST/IND INDUS LABOR PLAN
FOR/AID EDU/PROP HEALTH...POLICY SOC/WK 20. PAGE 30
G0582
B63
BIBLIOG/A
ECO/UNDEV
TEC/DEV
ACT/RES

NAFZIGER R.O.,INTRODUCTION TO MASS COMMUNICATIONS
RESEARCH (REV. ED.). ACT/RES...STAT CON/ANAL METH
20. PAGE 41 G0801
B63
COM/IND
CONCPT
PHIL/SCI
CREATE

GARDNER R.N.,"COOPERATION IN OUTER SPACE." FUT USSR
S63
INT/ORG

WOR+45 AIR LAW COM/IND CONSULT DELIB/GP CREATE
KNOWL 20 TREATY. PAGE 21 G0410
ACT/RES
PEACE
SPACE

TANNENBAUM P.H.,"COMMUNICATION OF SCIENCE
INFORMATION." USA+45 TEC/DEV ROUTINE...PHIL/SCI
STYLE 20. PAGE 53 G1051
S63
COM/IND
PRESS
OP/RES
METH/CNCPT

COHEN M.,LAW AND POLITICS IN SPACE: SPECIFIC AND
URGENT PROBLEMS IN THE LAW OF OUTER SPACE.
CHINA/COM COM USA+45 USSR WOR+45 COM/IND INT/ORG
NAT/G LEGIT NUC/PWR ATTIT BIO/SOC...JURID CONCPT
CONGRESS 20 STALIN/J. PAGE 12 G0241
B64
DELIB/GP
LAW
INT/LAW
SPACE

NASA,PROCEEDINGS OF CONFERENCE ON THE LAW OF SPACE
AND OF SATELLITE COMMUNICATIONS: CHICAGO 1963. FUT
WOR+45 DELIB/GP PROB/SOLV TEC/DEV CONFER ADJUD
NUC/PWR...POLICY IDEA/COMP 20 NASA. PAGE 41 G0805
B64
SPACE
COM/IND
LAW
DIPLOM

SCHWARTZ M.D.,CONFERENCE ON SPACE SCIENCE AND SPACE
LAW. FUT COM/IND NAT/G FORCES ACT/RES PLAN BUDGET
DIPLOM NUC/PWR WEAPON...POLICY ANTHOL 20. PAGE 50
G0983
B64
SPACE
LAW
PEACE
TEC/DEV

SCHRAMM W.,"MASS MEDIA AND NATIONAL DEVELOPMENT:
THE ROLE OF INFORMATION IN DEVELOPING COUNTRIES."
FINAN R+D ACT/RES PLAN TEC/DEV DIPLOM CHOOSE SUPEGO
ORD/FREE...BIBLIOG 20. PAGE 50 G0978
C64
ECO/UNDEV
COM/IND
EDU/PROP
MAJORIT

NATIONAL SCIENCE FOUNDATION,CURRENT RESEARCH AND
DEVELOPMENT IN SCIENTIFIC DOCUMENTATION - NO. 12.
WOR+45 INTELL COM/IND NAT/G COMPUTER TEC/DEV
AUTOMAT KNOWL...PSY LING 20. PAGE 41 G0812
B65
BIBLIOG
COMPUT/IR
R+D
PHIL/SCI

UNESCO,HANDBOOK OF INTERNATIONAL EXCHANGES. COM/IND
R+D ACADEM PROF/ORG VOL/ASSN CREATE TEC/DEV
EDU/PROP AGREE 20 TREATY. PAGE 55 G1090
B65
INDEX
INT/ORG
DIPLOM
PRESS

WISH J.R.,ECONOMIC DEVELOPMENT IN LATIN AMERICA: AN
ANNOTATED BIBLIOGRAPHY. L/A+17C COM/IND MARKET R+D
CREATE CAP/ISM ATTIT...STAT METH 20. PAGE 64 G1250
B65
BIBLIOG/A
ECO/UNDEV
TEC/DEV
AGRI

HUGHES T.L.,"SCHOLARS AND FOREIGN POLICY* VARIETIES
OF RESEARCH EXPERIENCE." COM/IND DIPLOM ADMIN EXEC
ROUTINE...MGT OBS CONGRESS PRESIDENT CAMELOT.
PAGE 27 G0535
S65
ACT/RES
ACADEM
CONTROL
NAT/G

MARKHAM J.W.,AN ECONOMIC-MEDIA STUDY OF BOOK
PUBLISHING. USA+45 LAW COM/IND ACADEM SCHOOL
EDU/PROP AUTOMAT CONTROL...DECISION STAT CHARTS 20
CONGRESS. PAGE 36 G0707
B66
PRESS
ECO/TAC
TEC/DEV
NAT/G

LERNER D.,COMMUNICATION AND CHANGE IN DEVELOPING
COUNTRIES. CHINA/COM INDIA PHILIPPINE COM/IND
CREATE TEC/DEV...ANTHOL 20. PAGE 33 G0659
B67
EDU/PROP
ORD/FREE
PERCEPT
ECO/UNDEV

RUTGERS U GRADUATE SCH LIB SCI,BIBLIOGRAPHY OF
RESEARCH RELATING TO THE COMMUNICATION OF
SCIENTIFIC AND TECHNICAL INFORMATION. FUT CREATE
FEEDBACK...PHIL/SCI NEW/IDEA COMPUT/IR HYPO/EXP.
PAGE 48 G0951
B67
BIBLIOG/A
COM/IND
R+D
TEC/DEV

BARRON J.A.,"ACCESS TO THE PRESS." USA+45 TEC/DEV
PRESS TV ADJUD AUD/VIS. PAGE 5 G0099
L67
ORD/FREE
COM/IND
EDU/PROP
LAW

CARY G.D.,"THE QUIET REVOLUTION IN COPYRIGHT* THE
END OF THE 'PUBLICATION' CONCEPT." USA+45 LAW
OP/RES TEC/DEV CONFER DEBATE EFFICIENCY...JURID
CONGRESS. PAGE 11 G0217
S67
COM/IND
POLICY
LICENSE
PRESS

DOYLE S.E.,"COMMUNICATION SATELLITES* INTERNAL
ORGANIZATION FOR DEVELOPMENT AND CONTROL." USA+45
R+D ACT/RES DIPLOM NAT/LISM...POLICY INT/LAW
PREDICT UN. PAGE 16 G0313
S67
TEC/DEV
SPACE
COM/IND
INT/ORG

S67
KAYSEN C.,"DATA BANKS AND DOSSIERS." FUT USA+45   CENTRAL
COM/IND NAT/G PLAN PROB/SOLV TEC/DEV BUDGET ADMIN   EFFICIENCY
ROUTINE. PAGE 30 G0588   CENSUS
                                                     ACT/RES

S67
MORTON J.A.,"A SYSTEMS APPROACH TO THE INNOVATION   TEC/DEV
PROCESS: ITS USE IN THE BELL SYSTEM." USA+45 INTELL   GEN/METH
INDUS LG/CO CONSULT WORKER COMPUTER AUTOMAT DEMAND   R+D
...MGT CHARTS 20. PAGE 40 G0787   COM/IND

S67
RAMSEY J.A.,"THE STATUS OF INTERNATIONAL   INT/LAW
COPYRIGHTS." WOR+45 CREATE TEC/DEV DIPLOM CONFER   INT/ORG
CONTROL SANCTION OWN...POLICY JURID. PAGE 46 G0899   COM/IND
                                                     PRESS

N67
US SUPERINTENDENT OF DOCUMENTS,SPACE: MISSILES, THE   BIBLIOG/A
MOON, NASA, AND SATELLITES (PRICE LIST 79A). USA+45   SPACE
COM/IND R+D NAT/G DIPLOM EDU/PROP ADMIN CONTROL   TEC/DEV
HEALTH...POLICY SIMUL NASA CONGRESS. PAGE 61 G1190   PEACE

COM/PARTY....COMMUNIST PARTY (ALL NATIONS)

B58
MARCUSE H.,SOVIET MARXISM, A CRITICAL ANALYSIS.   MARXISM
USSR CONSTN PLAN PRODUC RATIONAL SOCISM...IDEA/COMP   ATTIT
20 COM/PARTY. PAGE 36 G0703   POLICY

B66
SCHURMANN F.,IDEOLOGY AND ORGANIZATION IN COMMUNIST   MARXISM
CHINA. CHINA/COM LOC/G MUNIC POL/PAR ECO/TAC   STRUCT
CONTROL ATTIT...MGT STERTYP 20 COM/PARTY. PAGE 50   ADMIN
G0981   NAT/G

COMBS C.H. G0245

COMECON....COMMUNIST ECONOMIC ORGANIZATION EAST EUROPE

S64
MARES V.E.,"EAST EUROPE'S SECOND CHANCE." COM   VOL/ASSN
EUR+WWI HUNGARY ROMANIA USSR YUGOSLAVIA ECO/UNDEV   ECO/TAC
NAT/G TOP/EX CREATE PLAN TEC/DEV REGION NAT/LISM
RIGID/FLEX PWR...CONCPT STAT COMECON 20. PAGE 36
G0705

B65
KASER M.,COMECON* INTEGRATION PROBLEMS OF THE   PLAN
PLANNED ECONOMIES. INT/ORG TEC/DEV INT/TRADE PRICE   ECO/DEV
ADMIN ADJUST CENTRAL...STAT TIME/SEQ ORG/CHARTS   COM
COMECON. PAGE 29 G0579   REGION

COMINFORM....COMMUNIST INFORMATION BUREAU

COMINTERN....COMMUNIST THIRD INTERNATIONAL

COMM/SPACE....COMMITTEE ON SPACE RESEARCH

COMMANDS....SEE LEAD, DOMIN

COMMISSIONS....SEE CONFER, DELIB/GP

COMMITTEE ECONOMIC DEVELOPMENT G0246

COMMITTEE FOR ECONOMIC DEVELOPMENT....SEE CED

COMMITTEE ON SCIENCE AND TECHNOLOGY (OF THE BRITISH
     PARLIAMENT)....SEE COM/SCITEC

COMMITTEES....SEE CONFER, DELIB/GP

COMMON/LAW....COMMON LAW

COMMONER B. G0247

COMMONWEALTH....SEE COMMONWLTH

COMMONWLTH....BRITISH COMMONWEALTH OF NATIONS; SEE ALSO
     VOL/ASSN, APPROPRIATE NATIONS, CMN/WLTH

B57
BAUER P.T.,ECONOMIC ANALYSIS AND POLICY IN   ECO/UNDEV
UNDERDEVELOPED COUNTRIES. WOR+45 AGRI INT/TRADE TAX   METH/COMP
PRICE...GEN/METH BIBLIOG/A 20 COMMONWLTH. PAGE 5   POLICY
G0103

B57
SCARROW H.A.,THE HIGHER PUBLIC SERVICE OF THE   ADMIN
COMMONWEALTH OF AUSTRALIA. LAW SENIOR LOBBY ROLE 20   NAT/G
AUSTRAL CIVIL/SERV COMMONWLTH. PAGE 49 G0959   EX/STRUC
                                                     GOV/COMP

B61
CARNELL F.,THE POLITICS OF THE NEW STATES: A SELECT   BIBLIOG/A
ANNOTATED BIBLIOGRAPHY WITH SPECIAL REFERENCE TO   AFR
THE COMMONWEALTH. CONSTN ELITES LABOR NAT/G POL/PAR   ASIA
EX/STRUC DIPLOM ADJUD ADMIN...GOV/COMP 20   COLONIAL
COMMONWLTH. PAGE 11 G0210

COMMUN/DEV....COMMUNITY DEVELOPMENT MOVEMENT IN INDIA

COMMUNES....COMMUNES

COMMUNICATION, MASS....SEE EDU/PROP

COMMUNICATION, PERSONAL....SEE PERS/REL

COMMUNICATION, POLITICAL....SEE EDU/PROP

COMMUNICATIONS INDUSTRY....SEE COM/IND

COMMUNISM....SEE MARXISM

COMMUNIST CHINA....SEE CHINA/COM

COMMUNIST COUNTRIES (EXCEPT CHINA)....SEE COM

COMMUNIST ECONOMIC ORGANIZATION....SEE COMECON

COMMUNIST INFORMATION BUREAU....SEE COMINFORM

COMMUNIST THIRD INTERNATIONAL....SEE COMINTERN

COMMUNITY....SEE NEIGH

COMPANY, LARGE....SEE LG/CO

COMPANY, SMALL....SEE SML/CO

COMPARATIVE....SEE APPROPRIATE COMPARATIVE ANALYSIS INDEX

COMPETITION....SEE APPROPRIATE RELATIONS AND VALUES INDEXES

COMPNY/ACT....COMPANIES ACT (U.K., 1882)

COMPULSORY NATIONAL SERVICE....SEE NAT/SERV

COMPUT/IR....INFORMATION RETRIEVAL

N
AMERICAN DOCUMENTATION INST,AMERICAN DOCUMENTATION.   BIBLIOG
PROF/ORG CONSULT PLAN PERCEPT...MATH STAT AUD/VIS   TEC/DEV
CHARTS METH/COMP INDEX METH 20. PAGE 3 G0050   COM/IND
                                                     COMPUT/IR

N
AMERICAN DOCUMENTATION INST,DOCUMENTATION   BIBLIOG/A
ABSTRACTS. WOR+45 NAT/G COMPUTER CREATE TEC/DEV   AUTOMAT
DIPLOM EDU/PROP REGION KNOWL...PHIL/SCI CLASSIF   COMPUT/IR
LING. PAGE 3 G0051   R+D

B
US DEPT COMMERCE OFF TECH SERV,TECHNICAL   BIBLIOG
TRANSLATIONS. WOR+45 INDUS COMPUTER CREATE NUC/PWR   R+D
...PHIL/SCI COMPUT/IR METH/COMP METH. PAGE 58 G1135   TEC/DEV
                                                     AUTOMAT

N
AMER COUNCIL OF LEARNED SOCIET,THE ACLS CONSTITUENT   BIBLIOG/A
SOCIETY JOURNAL PROJECT. FUT USA+45 LAW NAT/G PLAN   HUM
DIPLOM PHIL/SCI. PAGE 3 G0048   COMPUT/IR
                                                     COMPUTER

B56
HISTORICAL ABSTRACTS. NAT/G CREATE DIPLOM ATTIT   WOR-45
...SOC DICTIONARY INDEX 18/20. PAGE 1 G0013   COMPUT/IR
                                                     BIBLIOG/A

S56
MILLER G.A.,"THE MAGICAL NUMBER SEVEN, PLUS OR   LAB/EXP
MINUS TWO: SOME LIMITS ON OUR CAPACITY FOR   KNOWL
PROCESSING INFORMATION." PERS/REL...PSY METH/CNCPT   PERCEPT
LING CHARTS BIBLIOG 20. PAGE 39 G0772   COMPUT/IR

B58
OPERATIONS RESEARCH SOCIETY,A COMPREHENSIVE   BIBLIOG/A
BIBLIOGRAPHY ON OPERATIONS RESEARCH; THROUGH 1956   COMPUT/IR
WITH SUPPLEMENT FOR 1957. COM/IND DIST/IND INDUS   OP/RES
ADMIN...DECISION MATH STAT METH 20. PAGE 43 G0840   MGT

S58
NEWELL A.C.,"ELEMENTS OF A THEORY OF HUMAN PROBLEM   PROB/SOLV
SOLVING" (BMR)" TASK PERCEPT...CONCPT LOG METH/COMP   COMPUTER
LAB/EXP BIBLIOG 20. PAGE 42 G0819   COMPUT/IR
                                                     OP/RES

B59
GUILBAUD G.T.,WHAT IS CYBERNETICS? COMPUTER OP/RES   CONTROL

TEC/DEV AUTOMAT ROUTINE PERS/REL PERCEPT...PSY MATH COM/IND
COMPUT/IR SIMUL GEN/METH. PAGE 23 G0460   FEEDBACK
                                                          NET/THEORY

                                                          S59
GOLDHAMMER H.,"SOME OBSERVATIONS ON POLITICAL   COMPUT/IR
GAMING." FUT WOR+45 R+D NAT/G ACT/RES CREATE CHOOSE   DECISION
ATTIT PWR...POLICY CONCPT METH/CNCPT STYLE KNO/TEST   DIPLOM
TREND HYPO/EXP GAME GEN/METH METH 20. PAGE 22 G0426

                                                          B60
SLUCKIN W.,MINDS AND MACHINES (REV. ED.). PROB/SOLV   PSY
TEC/DEV AUTOMAT TASK PERCEPT HEALTH KNOWL   COMPUTER
...DECISION MATH PROBABIL COMPUT/IR GAME 20.   PERSON
PAGE 51 G1012   SIMUL

                                                          B60
WOETZEL R.K.,THE INTERNATIONAL CONTROL OF AIRSPACE   INT/ORG
AND OUTERSPACE. FUT WOR+45 AIR CONSTN STRUCT   JURID
CONSULT PLAN TEC/DEV ADJUD RIGID/FLEX KNOWL   SPACE
ORD/FREE PWR...TECHNIC GEOG MGT NEW/IDEA TREND   INT/LAW
COMPUT/IR VAL/FREE 20 TREATY. PAGE 64 G1251

                                                          B62
ASTIA,HUMAN ENGINEERING: A REPORT BIBLIOGRAPHY.   BIBLIOG/A
USA+45 R+D FORCES ACT/RES COMPUTER CREATE OP/RES   COM/IND
EDU/PROP CONTROL WEAPON...SOC NEW/IDEA. PAGE 4   COMPUT/IR
G0073   METH

                                                          B62
BORKOF H.,COMPUTER APPLICATIONS IN THE BEHAVIORAL   R+D
SCIENCES. AUTOMAT UTIL...DECISION PHIL/SCI PSY   COMPUTER
METH/CNCPT LING LOG MATH STYLE NET/THEORY COMPUT/IR   PROB/SOLV
PROG/TEAC SIMUL. PAGE 8 G0154   FEEDBACK

                                                          B63
FOSKETT D.J.,CLASSIFICATION AND INDEXING IN THE   PROB/SOLV
SOCIAL SCIENCES. WOR+45 R+D ACT/RES CREATE OP/RES   CON/ANAL
TEC/DEV AUTOMAT ROLE...SOC COMPUT/IR BIBLIOG.   CLASSIF
PAGE 20 G0384

                                                          B63
MCDONOUGH A.M.,INFORMATION ECONOMICS AND MANAGEMENT   COMPUT/IR
SYSTEMS. ECO/DEV OP/RES AUTOMAT EFFICIENCY 20.   MGT
PAGE 37 G0735   CONCPT
                                                          COMPUTER

                                                          B63
NORTH R.C.,CONTENT ANALYSIS: A HANDBOOK WITH   METH/CNCPT
APPLICATIONS FOR THE STUDY OF INTERNATIONAL CRISIS.   COMPUT/IR
ASIA COM EUR+WWI MOD/EUR INT/ORG TEC/DEV DOMIN   USSR
EDU/PROP ROUTINE COERCE PERCEPT RIGID/FLEX ALL/VALS
...QUANT TESTS CON/ANAL SIMUL GEN/LAWS VAL/FREE.
PAGE 42 G0825

                                                          B63
TOMKINS S.S.,COMPUTER SIMULATION OF PERSONALITY.   COMPUTER
R+D TEC/DEV AUTOMAT FEEDBACK ANOMIE PERCEPT...STYLE   PERSON
PERS/TEST PREDICT COMPUT/IR GP/COMP. PAGE 55 G1075   SIMUL
                                                          PROG/TEAC

                                                          S63
WILES P.J.D.,"WILL CAPITALISM AND COMMUNISM   PLAN
SPONTANEOUSLY CONVERGE." COM FUT USA+45 ECO/DEV   TEC/DEV
DIST/IND MARKET CAP/ISM ECO/TAC RIGID/FLEX WEALTH   USSR
MARXISM SOCISM...MATH STAT TREND COMPUT/IR 20.
PAGE 63 G1240

                                                          S64
ABT C.,"WAR GAMING." USA+45 NAT/G TOP/EX ACT/RES   FORCES
TEC/DEV COERCE KNOWL ORD/FREE PWR...DECISION MATH   SIMUL
TIME/SEQ COMPUT/IR CHARTS LAB/EXP VAL/FREE. PAGE 2   WAR
G0026

                                                          B65
KENT A.,SPECIALIZED INFORMATION CENTERS. INTELL R+D   COMPUT/IR
VOL/ASSN CONSULT COMPUTER KNOWL...DECISION HUM   CREATE
PHIL/SCI METH/CNCPT TREND CHARTS 20. PAGE 30 G0593   TEC/DEV
                                                          METH/COMP

                                                          B65
NATIONAL SCIENCE FOUNDATION,CURRENT RESEARCH AND   BIBLIOG
DEVELOPMENT IN SCIENTIFIC DOCUMENTATION - NO. 12.   COMPUT/IR
WOR+45 INTELL COM/IND NAT/G COMPUTER TEC/DEV   R+D
AUTOMAT KNOWL...PSY LING 20. PAGE 41 G0812   PHIL/SCI

                                                          B65
US LIBRARY OF CONGRESS,A DIRECTORY OF INFORMATION   BIBLIOG
RESOURCES IN THE UNITED STATES: SOCIAL SCIENCES.   R+D
USA+45 ACADEM INT/ORG LABOR PROF/ORG PUB/INST   COMPUT/IR
SCHOOL SECT 20. PAGE 59 G1156

                                                          S65
DECHERT C.R.,"THE DEVELOPMENT OF CYBERNETICS."   SIMUL
ACT/RES CREATE SKILL...STERTYP METH. PAGE 15 G0290   COMPUT/IR
                                                          PLAN

                                                          B66
KUENNE R.E.,THE POLARIS MISSILE STRIKE* A GENERAL   NUC/PWR
ECONOMIC SYSTEMS ANALYSIS. USA+45 USSR NAT/G   FORCES
BAL/PWR ARMS/CONT WAR...MATH PROBABIL COMPUT/IR   DETER
CHARTS HYPO/EXP SIMUL. PAGE 32 G0625   DIPLOM

                                                          B66
MURDOCK J.C.,RESEARCH AND REGIONS. AGRI FINAN INDUS   BIBLIOG
LOC/G MUNIC NAT/G PROB/SOLV TEC/DEV ADMIN REGION   ECO/DEV
20. PAGE 40 G0796   COMPUT/IR
                                                          R+D

                                                          B67
GULICK M.C.,NONCONVENTIONAL INFORMATION SYSTEMS   BIBLIOG/A
SERVING THE SOCIAL SCIENCES AND THE HUMANITIES; A   R+D
BIBLIOGRAPHIC ESSAY (PAPER). USA+45 COMPUTER CREATE   COMPUT/IR
EDU/PROP KNOWL...SOC METH 20. PAGE 23 G0462   HUM

                                                          B67
HARDT J.P.,MATHEMATICS AND COMPUTERS IN SOVIET   PLAN
ECONOMIC PLANNING. COM USSR OP/RES PROB/SOLV   TEC/DEV
OPTIMAL...MODAL SIMUL 20. PAGE 24 G0481   MATH
                                                          COMPUT/IR

                                                          B67
RUTGERS U GRADUATE SCH LIB SCI,BIBLIOGRAPHY OF   BIBLIOG/A
RESEARCH RELATING TO THE COMMUNICATION OF   COM/IND
SCIENTIFIC AND TECHNICAL INFORMATION. FUT CREATE   R+D
FEEDBACK...PHIL/SCI NEW/IDEA COMPUT/IR HYPO/EXP.   TEC/DEV
PAGE 48 G0951

                                                          B67
SCHUMACHER B.G.,COMPUTER DYNAMICS IN PUBLIC   COMPUTER
ADMINISTRATION. USA+45 CREATE PLAN TEC/DEV...MGT   COMPUT/IR
LING CON/ANAL BIBLIOG/A 20. PAGE 50 G0980   ADMIN
                                                          AUTOMAT

                                                          B67
UNIVERSAL REFERENCE SYSTEM,LEGISLATIVE PROCESS,   BIBLIOG/A
REPRESENTATION, AND DECISION-MAKING (VOLUME II).   LEGIS
WOR+45 WOR-45 CONSTN LOC/G NAT/G...POLICY CON/ANAL   REPRESENT
COMPUT/IR GEN/METH. PAGE 56 G1094   DECISION

                                                          B67
UNIVERSAL REFERENCE SYSTEM,BIBLIOGRAPHY OF   BIBLIOG/A
BIBLIOGRAPHIES IN POLITICAL SCIENCE, GOVERNMENT,   NAT/G
AND PUBLIC POLICY (VOLUME III). WOR+45 WOR-45 LAW   DIPLOM
ADMIN...SOC CON/ANAL COMPUT/IR GEN/METH. PAGE 56   POLICY
G1095

                                                          B67
UNIVERSAL REFERENCE SYSTEM,ADMINISTRATIVE   BIBLIOG/A
MANAGEMENT: PUBLIC AND PRIVATE BUREAUCRACY (VOLUME   MGT
IV). WOR+45 WOR-45 ECO/DEV LG/CO LOC/G PUB/INST   ADMIN
VOL/ASSN GOV/REL...COMPUT/IR GEN/METH. PAGE 56   NAT/G
G1096

                                                          B67
UNIVERSAL REFERENCE SYSTEM,CURRENT EVENTS AND   BIBLIOG/A
PROBLEMS OF MODERN SOCIETY (VOLUME V). WOR+45 LOC/G   SOCIETY
MUNIC NAT/G PLAN EDU/PROP CRIME RACE/REL WEALTH   PROB/SOLV
...COMPUT/IR GEN/METH. PAGE 56 G1097   ATTIT

                                                          B67
UNIVERSAL REFERENCE SYSTEM,PUBLIC OPINION, MASS   BIBLIOG/A
BEHAVIOR, AND POLITICAL PSYCHOLOGY (VOLUME VI).   ATTIT
WOR+45 WOR-45 SOCIETY EDU/PROP PRESS PARTIC CHOOSE   CROWD
PERSON...TREND COMPUT/IR GEN/METH. PAGE 56 G1098   PSY

                                                          B67
UNIVERSAL REFERENCE SYSTEM,ECONOMIC REGULATION,   BIBLIOG/A
BUSINESS, AND GOVERNMENT (VOLUME VIII). WOR+45   CONTROL
WOR-45 ECO/DEV ECO/UNDEV FINAN LABOR TEC/DEV   NAT/G
ECO/TAC INT/TRADE GOV/REL...POLICY COMPUT/IR.
PAGE 56 G1099

                                                          B67
UNIVERSAL REFERENCE SYSTEM,PUBLIC POLICY AND THE   BIBLIOG/A
MANAGEMENT OF SCIENCE (VOLUME IX). FUT SPACE WOR+45   POLICY
LAW NAT/G TEC/DEV CONTROL NUC/PWR GOV/REL   MGT
...COMPUT/IR GEN/METH. PAGE 56 G1100   PHIL/SCI

                                                          B67
UNIVERSAL REFERENCE SYSTEM,LAW, JURISPRUDENCE, AND   BIBLIOG/A
JUDICIAL PROCESS (VOLUME VII). WOR+45 WOR-45 CONSTN   LAW
NAT/G LEGIS JUDGE CT/SYS...INT/LAW COMPUT/IR   JURID
GEN/METH METH. PAGE 56 G1101   ADJUD

                                                          B67
US HOUSE COMM SCI ASTRONAUT,AUTHORIZING SECY OF   PHIL/SCI
COMMERCE TO PROVIDE FOR COLLECTION, COMPILATION,   CON/ANAL
CRIT EVALUATION, PUBLICATION, SALE OF STD REF DATA.   STAT
USA+45 TEC/DEV...COMPUT/IR HOUSE/REP. PAGE 59 G1150   R+D

YAVITZ B.,AUTOMATION IN COMMERCIAL BANKING. USA+45
STRUCT WORKER CREATE OP/RES PLAN ROLE...DECISION
SAMP/SIZ. PAGE 64 G1263

B67
TEC/DEV
FINAN
COMPUT/IR
MGT

VERGIN R.C.,"COMPUTER INDUCED ORGANIZATION
CHANGES." FUT USA+45 R+D CREATE OP/RES TEC/DEV
ADJUST CENTRAL...MGT INT CON/ANAL COMPUT/IR.
PAGE 61 G1194

S67
COMPUTER
DECISION
AUTOMAT
EX/STRUC

COMPUTER....COMPUTER TECHNIQUES AND TECHNOLOGY

AMERICAN DOCUMENTATION INST,DOCUMENTATION
ABSTRACTS. WOR+45 NAT/G COMPUTER CREATE TEC/DEV
DIPLOM EDU/PROP REGION KNOWL...PHIL/SCI CLASSIF
LING. PAGE 3 G0051

N
BIBLIOG/A
AUTOMAT
COMPUT/IR
R+D

US DEPT COMMERCE OFF TECH SERV,TECHNICAL
TRANSLATIONS. WOR+45 INDUS COMPUTER CREATE NUC/PWR
...PHIL/SCI COMPUT/IR METH/COMP METH. PAGE 58 G1135

B
BIBLIOG
R+D
TEC/DEV
AUTOMAT

AMER COUNCIL OF LEARNED SOCIET,THE ACLS CONSTITUENT
SOCIETY JOURNAL PROJECT. FUT USA+45 LAW NAT/G PLAN
DIPLOM PHIL/SCI. PAGE 3 G0048

N
BIBLIOG/A
HUM
COMPUT/IR
COMPUTER

BELL J.R.,PERSONNEL PROBLEMS IN CONVERTING TO
AUTOMATION (PAMPHLET). USA+45 COMPUTER PLAN
...METH/CNCPT 20 CALIFORNIA. PAGE 6 G0115

N19
WORKER
AUTOMAT
PROB/SOLV
PROVS

WEINER N.,CYBERNETICS. SOCIETY COMPUTER ADJUST
EFFICIENCY UTIL PERCEPT...PSY MATH REGRESS TIME.
PAGE 63 G1226

B48
FEEDBACK
AUTOMAT
CONTROL
TEC/DEV

CALDWELL L.K.,RESEARCH METHODS IN PUBLIC
ADMINISTRATION: AN OUTLINE OF TOPICS AND READINGS
(PAMPHLET). LAW ACT/RES COMPUTER KNOWL...SOC STAT
GEN/METH 20. PAGE 10 G0201

B53
BIBLIOG/A
METH/COMP
ADMIN
OP/RES

MILLER G.A.,"WHAT IS INFORMATION MEASUREMENT?"
CREATE...CONCPT METH/CNCPT QUANT STAT CHARTS
BIBLIOG/A 20. PAGE 39 G0771

S53
COMPUTER
TEC/DEV
PSY
MATH

MCCLOSKEY J.F.,OPERATIONS RESEARCH FOR MANAGEMENT.
STRUCT COMPUTER ADMIN ROUTINE...PHIL/SCI CONCPT
METH/CNCPT TREND ANTHOL BIBLIOG 20. PAGE 37 G0731

B54
OP/RES
MGT
METH/COMP
TEC/DEV

RILEY V.,INTERINDUSTRY ECONOMIC STUDIES. USA+45
COMPUTER ADMIN OPTIMAL PRODUC...MGT CLASSIF STAT.
PAGE 47 G0922

B55
BIBLIOG
ECO/DEV
PLAN
STRUCT

MILLER J.G.,"TOWARD A GENERAL THEORY FOR THE
BEHAVIORAL SCIENCES" (BMR)" CREATE ALL/VALS KNOWL
...CON/ANAL CHARTS HYPO/EXP SIMUL BIBLIOG 20.
PAGE 39 G0773

S55
CONCPT
OP/RES
METH/CNCPT
COMPUTER

MCKINNEY E.R.,A BIBLIOGRAPHY OF CYBERNETICS AND
INFORMATION THEORY. COMPUTER OP/RES...DECISION
PHIL/SCI PSY LING LOG MATH PROBABIL GAME 20.
PAGE 38 G0743

B57
BIBLIOG/A
FEEDBACK
SIMUL
CONTROL

FORRESTER J.W.,"INDUSTRIAL DYNAMICS* A MAJOR
BREAKTHROUGH FOR DECISION MAKERS." COMPUTER OP/RES
...DECISION CONCPT NEW/IDEA. PAGE 20 G0382

L58
INDUS
ACT/RES
MGT
PROB/SOLV

NEWELL A.C.,"ELEMENTS OF A THEORY OF HUMAN PROBLEM
SOLVING" (BMR)" TASK PERCEPT...CONCPT LOG METH/COMP
LAB/EXP BIBLIOG 20. PAGE 42 G0819

S58
PROB/SOLV
COMPUTER
COMPUT/IR
OP/RES

GUILBAUD G.T.,WHAT IS CYBERNETICS? COMPUTER OP/RES
TEC/DEV AUTOMAT ROUTINE PERS/REL PERCEPT...PSY MATH
COMPUT/IR SIMUL GEN/METH. PAGE 23 G0460

B59
CONTROL
COM/IND
FEEDBACK

BOULDING K.E.,LINEAR PROGRAMMING AND THE THEORY OF
THE FIRM. ACT/RES PLAN...MGT MATH. PAGE 8 G0156

B60
LG/CO
NEW/IDEA
COMPUTER

SLUCKIN W.,MINDS AND MACHINES (REV. ED.). PROB/SOLV
TEC/DEV AUTOMAT TASK PERCEPT HEALTH KNOWL
...DECISION MATH PROBABIL COMPUT/IR GAME 20.
PAGE 51 G1012

B60
PSY
COMPUTER
PERSON
SIMUL

SHUBIK M.,"BIBLIOGRAPHY ON SIMULATION, GAMING,
ARTIFICIAL INTELLIGENCE AND ALLIED TOPICS."
COMPUTER ROUTINE...DECISION MGT STAT 20. PAGE 50
G0992

S60
BIBLIOG
SIMUL
GAME
OP/RES

BENNION E.G.,"ECONOMETRICS FOR MANAGEMENT." USA+45
INDUS EX/STRUC ACT/RES COMPUTER UTIL...MATH STAT
PREDICT METH/COMP HYPO/EXP. PAGE 6 G0122

S61
ECOMETRIC
MGT
SIMUL
DECISION

HAINES G.,"THE COMPUTER AS A SMALL-GROUP MEMBER."
DELIB/GP BAL/PWR TASK 20. PAGE 24 G0467

S61
INGP/REL
COMPUTER
PROB/SOLV
EFFICIENCY

ASTIA,HUMAN ENGINEERING: A REPORT BIBLIOGRAPHY.
USA+45 R+D FORCES ACT/RES COMPUTER CREATE OP/RES
EDU/PROP CONTROL WEAPON...SOC NEW/IDEA. PAGE 4
G0073

B62
BIBLIOG/A
COM/IND
COMPUT/IR
METH

ASTIA,INFORMATION THEORY: A REPORT BIBLIOGRAPHY.
USA+45 COMPUTER CREATE OP/RES PLAN TEC/DEV CONTROL
...CONCPT METH/COMP. PAGE 4 G0074

B62
BIBLIOG/A
COM/IND
FORCES
METH

BELLMAN R.,APPLIED DYNAMIC PROGRAMMING. OPTIMAL
...DECISION STAT SIMUL. PAGE 6 G0116

B62
COMPUTER
ECOMETRIC
GAME
MATH

BERKELEY E.C.,THE COMPUTER REVOLUTION. WOR+45
CREATE TEC/DEV EFFICIENCY TECHRACY...SOC TREND 20.
PAGE 7 G0128

B62
COMPUTER
CONTROL
AUTOMAT
SOCIETY

BORKOF H.,COMPUTER APPLICATIONS IN THE BEHAVIORAL
SCIENCES. AUTOMAT UTIL...DECISION PHIL/SCI PSY
METH/CNCPT LING LOG MATH STYLE NET/THEORY COMPUT/IR
PROG/TEAC SIMUL. PAGE 8 G0154

B62
R+D
COMPUTER
PROB/SOLV
FEEDBACK

GUETZKOW H.,SIMULATION IN SOCIAL SCIENCE: READINGS.
STRUCT OP/RES ADMIN AUTOMAT FEEDBACK...MGT PSY SOC
STYLE BIBLIOG. PAGE 23 G0459

B62
SIMUL
TEC/DEV
COMPUTER
GAME

MACHLUP F.,THE PRODUCTION AND DISTRIBUTION OF
KNOWLEDGE IN THE UNITED STATES. USA+45 COM/IND
INDUS SCHOOL SECT WORKER COMPUTER CREATE CIVMIL/REL
COST EFFICIENCY WEALTH 20. PAGE 35 G0688

B62
ACADEM
TEC/DEV
EDU/PROP
R+D

MARS D.,SUGGESTED LIBRARY IN PUBLIC ADMINISTRATION.
FINAN DELIB/GP EX/STRUC WORKER COMPUTER ADJUD
...DECISION PSY SOC METH/COMP 20. PAGE 36 G0710

B62
BIBLIOG
ADMIN
METH
MGT

FLOOD M.M.,"STOCHASTIC LEARNING THEORY APPLIED TO
CHOICE EXPERIMENTS WITH RATS, DOGS, AND MEN."...PSY
LAB/EXP METH. PAGE 19 G0372

S62
DECISION
COMPUTER
HYPO/EXP
TEC/DEV

BURSK E.C.,NEW DECISION-MAKING TOOLS FOR MANAGERS.
COMPUTER PLAN PROB/SOLV ROUTINE COST. PAGE 10 G0194

B63
DECISION
MGT
MATH
RIGID/FLEX

MCDONOUGH A.M.,INFORMATION ECONOMICS AND MANAGEMENT
SYSTEMS. ECO/DEV OP/RES AUTOMAT EFFICIENCY 20.
PAGE 37 G0735

B63
COMPUT/IR
MGT
CONCPT
COMPUTER

TOMKINS S.S.,COMPUTER SIMULATION OF PERSONALITY. COMPUTER B63
R+D TEC/DEV AUTOMAT FEEDBACK ANOMIE PERCEPT...STYLE PERSON
PERS/TEST PREDICT COMPUT/IR GP/COMP. PAGE 55 G1075 SIMUL
PROG/TEAC

MARTINO R.L.,PROJECT MANAGEMENT AND CONTROL: VOL. 2 DECISION B64
APPLIED OPERATIONAL PLANNING. COMPUTER...MATH PLAN
CHARTS SIMUL METH TIME. PAGE 36 G0716 TEC/DEV
OP/RES

JANDA K.,DATA PROCESSING: APPLICATIONS TO POLITICAL DECISION B65
RESEARCH....STAT CON/ANAL. PAGE 28 G0557 COMPUTER
TEC/DEV
METH

KENT A.,SPECIALIZED INFORMATION CENTERS. INTELL R+D COMPUT/IR B65
VOL/ASSN CONSULT COMPUTER KNOWL...DECISION HUM CREATE
PHIL/SCI METH/CNCPT TREND CHARTS 20. PAGE 30 G0593 TEC/DEV
METH/COMP

NATIONAL SCIENCE FOUNDATION,CURRENT RESEARCH AND BIBLIOG B65
DEVELOPMENT IN SCIENTIFIC DOCUMENTATION - NO. 12. COMPUT/IR
WOR+45 INTELL COM/IND NAT/G COMPUTER TEC/DEV R+D
AUTOMAT KNOWL...PSY LING 20. PAGE 41 G0812 PHIL/SCI

VEINOTT A.F. JR.,MATHEMATICAL STUDIES IN MANAGEMENT MATH B65
SCIENCE. UNIV INDUS COMPUTER ADMIN...DECISION MGT
NET/THEORY SIMUL 20. PAGE 61 G1193 PLAN
PRODUC

CHU K.,"A DYNAMIC MODEL OF THE FIRM." OP/RES INDUS S65
PROB/SOLV...DECISION ECOMETRIC NEW/IDEA STAT GAME COMPUTER
ORG/CHARTS SIMUL. PAGE 12 G0230 TEC/DEV

HOLSTI O.R.,"EAST-WEST CONFLICT AND SINO-SOVIET VOL/ASSN S65
RELATIONS" CHINA/COM USSR COMPUTER REGION DECISION. DIPLOM
PAGE 27 G0523 CON/ANAL
COM

BERND J.L.,MATHEMATICAL APPLICATIONS IN POLITICAL METH B66
SCIENCE, II. COMPUTER...PROBABIL STAT CHARTS. MATH
PAGE 7 G0131 METH/CNCPT

LILLEY S.,MEN, MACHINES AND HISTORY: THE STORY OF AGRI B66
TOOLS AND MACHINES IN RELATION TO SOCIAL PROGRESS. TEC/DEV
PREHIST SPACE STRUCT COMPUTER AUTOMAT NUC/PWR SOCIETY
...POLICY SOC. PAGE 34 G0667

US HOUSE COMM GOVT OPERATIONS,THE COMPUTER AND ORD/FREE B66
INVASION OF PRIVACY. USA+45 SOCIETY ALL/VALS...PSY COMPUTER
SOC CHARTS HOUSE/REP PRIVACY. PAGE 58 G1140 TEC/DEV
NAT/G

US HOUSE COMM SCI ASTRONAUT,GOVERNMENT, SCIENCE, NAT/G N66
AND PUBLIC POLICY (PAMPHLET). R+D ACADEM DELIB/GP POLICY
COMPUTER BUDGET CONFER ADMIN...PHIL/SCI PREDICT TEC/DEV
TREND 20 CONGRESS HS/SCIASTR. PAGE 58 G1143 CREATE

ELDREDGE H.W.,TAMING MEGALOPOLIS; HOW TO MANAGE AN MUNIC B67
URBANIZED WORLD. WOR+45 SOCIETY ECO/DEV ECO/UNDEV TEC/DEV
NAT/G COMPUTER CREATE PARTIC EFFICIENCY WEALTH PLAN
...MGT ANTHOL. PAGE 17 G0342 PROB/SOLV

GULICK M.C.,NONCONVENTIONAL INFORMATION SYSTEMS BIBLIOG/A B67
SERVING THE SOCIAL SCIENCES AND THE HUMANITIES; A R+D
BIBLIOGRAPHIC ESSAY (PAPER). USA+45 COMPUTER CREATE COMPUT/IR
EDU/PROP KNOWL...SOC METH 20. PAGE 23 G0462 HUM

HARMAN H.H.,MODERN FACTOR ANALYSIS (2ND REV. ED.). CON/ANAL B67
COMPUTER...DECISION CHARTS BIBLIOG T. PAGE 24 G0482 METH/CNCPT
SIMUL
MATH

MACBRIDE R.,THE AUTOMATED STATE; COMPUTER SYSTEMS COMPUTER B67
AS A NEW FORCE IN SOCIETY. FUT WOR+45 FINAN MUNIC AUTOMAT
NAT/G WORKER PLAN TEC/DEV CONTROL PERS/REL RACE/REL PROB/SOLV
ADJUST. PAGE 35 G0685 SOCIETY

SAPARINA Y.,CYBERNETICS WITHIN US. WOR+45 EDU/PROP COMPUTER B67
FEEDBACK PERCEPT HEALTH...DECISION METH/CNCPT METH/COMP
NEW/IDEA 20. PAGE 49 G0957 CONTROL
SIMUL

SCHUMACHER B.G.,COMPUTER DYNAMICS IN PUBLIC COMPUTER B67
ADMINISTRATION. USA+45 CREATE PLAN TEC/DEV...MGT COMPUT/IR
LING CON/ANAL BIBLIOG/A 20. PAGE 50 G0980 ADMIN
AUTOMAT

ALBAUM G.,"INFORMATION FLOW AND DECENTRALIZED LG/CO S67
DECISION MAKING IN MARKETING." EX/STRUC COMPUTER ROUTINE
OP/RES PROB/SOLV EFFICIENCY OPTIMAL...METH/COMP KNOWL
ORG/CHARTS 20. PAGE 2 G0033 MARKET

BARAN P.,"THE FUTURE COMPUTER UTILITY." USA+45 COMPUTER S67
NAT/G PLAN CONTROL COST...POLICY 20. PAGE 5 G0091 UTIL
FUT
TEC/DEV

BRETNOR R.,"DESTRUCTIVE FORCE AND THE MILITARY FORCES S67
EQUATIONS." UNIV COMPUTER PLAN PROB/SOLV AUTOMAT TEC/DEV
CONTROL COERCE DETER NUC/PWR WEAPON DRIVE PWR. DOMIN
PAGE 9 G0166 WAR

BROWN W.B.,"MODEL-BUILDING AND ORGANIZATIONS." MGT S67
CONTROL FEEDBACK...PROBABIL CHARTS METH/COMP. ADMIN
PAGE 9 G0179 GAME
COMPUTER

DE NEUFVILLE R.,"EDUCATION AT THE ACADEMIES." FORCES S67
USA+45 ELITES CONSULT EX/STRUC COMPUTER PLAN ACADEM
PROB/SOLV TASK CIVMIL/REL ORD/FREE 20. PAGE 15 TEC/DEV
G0286 SKILL

HOFFER J.R.,"RELATIONSHIP OF NATURAL AND SOCIAL PROB/SOLV S67
SCIENCES TO SOCIAL PROBLEMS AND CONTRIBUTION OF... SOCIETY
SCIENTISTS TO SOLUTIONS." USA+45 COMPUTER TEC/DEV INTELL
GP/REL KNOWL...SOC TREND. PAGE 26 G0521 ACT/RES

MALONE D.K.,"THE COMMANDER AND THE COMPUTER." COMPUTER S67
USA+45 OP/RES PROB/SOLV TEC/DEV AUTOMAT CENTRAL 20. FORCES
PAGE 35 G0698 ELITES
PLAN

MOOR E.J.,"THE INTERNATIONAL IMPACT OF AUTOMATION." TEC/DEV S67
WOR+45 ACT/RES COMPUTER CREATE PLAN CAP/ISM ROUTINE OP/RES
EFFICIENCY PREDICT. PAGE 39 G0779 AUTOMAT
INDUS

MORTON J.A.,"A SYSTEMS APPROACH TO THE INNOVATION TEC/DEV S67
PROCESS: ITS USE IN THE BELL SYSTEM." USA+45 INTELL GEN/METH
INDUS LG/CO CONSULT WORKER COMPUTER AUTOMAT DEMAND R+D
...MGT CHARTS 20. PAGE 40 G0787 COM/IND

VERGIN R.C.,"COMPUTER INDUCED ORGANIZATION COMPUTER S67
CHANGES." FUT USA+45 R+D CREATE OP/RES TEC/DEV DECISION
ADJUST CENTRAL...MGT INT CON/ANAL COMPUT/IR. AUTOMAT
PAGE 61 G1194 EX/STRUC

COMTE/A....AUGUST COMTE

CON/ANAL....QUANTITATIVE CONTENT ANALYSIS

CONOVER H.L.,CIVILIAN DEFENSE: A SELECTED LIST OF BIBLIOG N
RECENT REFERENCES (PAMPHLET). USA+45 LOC/G MUNIC PLAN
PROB/SOLV ADMIN LEAD TASK WEAPON GOV/REL...POLICY WAR
CON/ANAL 20 CIV/DEFENS. PAGE 13 G0251 CIVMIL/REL

KAPLAN A.,"CONTENT ANALYSIS AND THE THEORY OF LOG S43
SIGNS" (BMR)" PERS/REL...PSY CONCPT LING IDEA/COMP CON/ANAL
SIMUL BIBLIOG 20 MORRIS/CW. PAGE 29 G0573 STAT
PHIL/SCI

SMYTH H.D.,ATOMIC ENERGY FOR MILITARY PURPOSES. R+D B45
USA-45 NAT/G PLAN TEC/DEV KNOWL...MATH CON/ANAL TIME/SEQ
CHARTS LAB/EXP SIMUL 20. PAGE 52 G1017 NUC/PWR

BAXTER J.P.,SCIENTISTS AGAINST TIME. EUR+WWI FORCES B46
MOD/EUR USA+45 USA-45 WOR+45 WOR-45 R+D NAT/G PLAN WAR

ATTIT PWR...PHIL/SCI RECORD CON/ANAL 17/20. PAGE 6   NUC/PWR
G0107

B47
BECK H.P.,MEN WHO CONTROL OUR UNIVERSITIES.   EDU/PROP
EX/STRUC CHOOSE INGP/REL DISCRIM PERSON WEALTH   ACADEM
...POLICY TREND CON/ANAL CHARTS BIBLIOG. PAGE 6   CONTROL
G0112   LEAD

B50
CANTRIL H.,TENSIONS THAT CAUSE WAR. UNIV CULTURE   SOCIETY
R+D CREATE EDU/PROP DRIVE PERSON KNOWL ORD/FREE   PHIL/SCI
...HUM PSY SOC OBS CENSUS TREND CON/ANAL SOC/EXP   PEACE
SIMUL GEN/METH ANTHOL COLD/WAR TOT/POP. PAGE 11
G0206

B50
CONTINUITIES IN SOCIAL RESEARCH; STUDIES IN SCOPE   SOC
AND METHOD OF "THE AMERICAN SOLDIER" USA+45 FORCES   PHIL/SCI
INGP/REL ATTIT...PSY SAMP CON/ANAL CHARTS GEN/LAWS   METH
ANTHOL 20. PAGE 38 G0758

S50
LENTZ T.F.,"REPORT ON A SURVEY OF SOCIAL SCIENTISTS ACT/RES
CONDUCTED BY THE ATTITUDE RESEARCH LABORATORY." FUT ATTIT
WOR+45 CREATE EDU/PROP...PSY STAT RECORD SYS/QU   DIPLOM
SAMP/SIZ CON/ANAL VAL/FREE 20. PAGE 33 G0655

S51
MACRAE D.G.,"THE BOLSHEVIK IDEOLOGY; THE   MARXISM
INTELLECTUAL AND EMOTIONAL FACTORS IN COMMUNIST   INTELL
AFFILIATION" (BMR) COM LEAD REV ATTIT ORD/FREE   PHIL/SCI
...SOC CON/ANAL 20 BOLSHEVISM. PAGE 35 G0693   SECT

S52
"SELECTED CRITICAL BIBLIOGRAPHY ON THE METHODS AND   BIBLIOG/A
TECHNIQUES OF POLITICAL BEHAVIOR RESEARCH."   METH
...PHIL/SCI OBS QU SYS/QU TESTS CON/ANAL. PAGE 1   SOC
G0012   EDU/PROP

B54
SPENCER R.F.,METHOD AND PERSPECTIVE IN ANTHROPOLOGY PHIL/SCI
...GEOG LING QUANT STAT TESTS SAMP/SIZ CON/ANAL   SOC
IDEA/COMP METH/COMP ANTHOL BIBLIOG 20. PAGE 52   PSY
G1025   METH

S54
BATES J.,"A MODEL FOR THE SCIENCE OF DECISION."   QUANT
UNIV ROUTINE...CONT/OBS CON/ANAL HYPO/EXP GAME.   DECISION
PAGE 5 G0101   PHIL/SCI
                                                     METH/CNCPT

S55
MILLER J.G.,"TOWARD A GENERAL THEORY FOR THE   CONCPT
BEHAVIORAL SCIENCES" (BMR)" CREATE ALL/VALS KNOWL   OP/RES
...CON/ANAL CHARTS HYPO/EXP SIMUL BIBLIOG 20.   METH/CNCPT
PAGE 39 G0773   COMPUTER

S58
LASSWELL H.D.,"THE SCIENTIFIC STUDY OF   PHIL/SCI
INTERNATIONAL RELATIONS." USA+45 INT/ORG CREATE   GEN/METH
EDU/PROP DETER ATTIT PERCEPT PWR...DECISION CONCPT   DIPLOM
METH/CNCPT STYLE CON/ANAL 20. PAGE 33 G0642

B59
RUSSELL B.,COMMON SENSE AND NUCLEAR WARFARE. WOR+45 ORD/FREE
INTELL SOCIETY STRATA NAT/G TOP/EX EDU/PROP ATTIT   ARMS/CONT
PERSON KNOWL MORAL PWR...POLICY CONCPT MYTH   NUC/PWR
CON/ANAL COLD/WAR 20. PAGE 48 G0948

S59
CALKINS R.D.,"THE DECISION PROCESS IN   ADMIN
ADMINISTRATION." EX/STRUC PROB/SOLV ROUTINE MGT.   OP/RES
PAGE 10 G0204   DECISION
                                                     CON/ANAL

S59
STOESSINGER J.G.,"THE INTERNATIONAL ATOMIC ENERGY   INT/ORG
AGENCY: THE FIRST PHASE." FUT WOR+45 NAT/G VOL/ASSN ECO/DEV
DELIB/GP BAL/PWR LEGIT ADMIN ROUTINE PWR...OBS   FOR/AID
CON/ANAL GEN/LAWS VAL/FREE 20 IAEA. PAGE 53 G1037   NUC/PWR

B60
HITCH C.J.,THE ECONOMICS OF DEFENSE IN THE NUCLEAR   R+D
AGE. USA+45 WOR+45 CREATE PLAN NUC/PWR ATTIT   FORCES
...CON/ANAL CHARTS HYPO/EXP NATO 20. PAGE 26 G0514

B60
RAPOPORT A.,FIGHTS, GAMES AND DEBATES. INTELL   METH/CNCPT
SOCIETY R+D EX/STRUC PERCEPT PERSON SKILL...PSY SOC MATH
GAME. PAGE 46 G0902   DECISION
                                                     CON/ANAL

L60
DEUTSCH K.W.,"TOWARD AN INVENTORY OF BASIC TRENDS   R+D
AND PATTERNS IN COMPARATIVE AND INTERNATIONAL   PERCEPT

POLITICS." UNIV WOR+45 SOCIETY STRUCT INT/ORG NAT/G
CREATE PLAN EDU/PROP KNOWL...PHIL/SCI METH/CNCPT
STAT SELF/OBS OBS/ENVIR SAMP TREND CON/ANAL CHARTS
SOC/EXP GEN/METH 20. PAGE 15 G0298

B62
SNYDER R.C.,FOREIGN POLICY DECISION-MAKING. FUT   TEC/DEV
KOREA WOR+45 R+D CREATE ADMIN ROUTINE PWR   HYPO/EXP
...DECISION PSY SOC CONCPT METH/CNCPT CON/ANAL   DIPLOM
CHARTS GEN/METH METH 20. PAGE 52 G1018

S62
GORDON B.K.,"NUCLEAR WEAPONS: RUSSIAN AND   ORD/FREE
AMERICAN." COM USA+45 USSR NAT/G FORCES ACT/RES   COERCE
TEC/DEV PERCEPT RIGID/FLEX PWR SKILL...MGT   NUC/PWR
METH/CNCPT QUANT OBS TIME/SEQ CON/ANAL GEN/METH
TOT/POP VAL/FREE 20. PAGE 22 G0433

S62
NANES A.,"DISARMAMENT: THE LAST SEVEN YEARS." COM   DELIB/GP
EUR+WWI USA+45 USSR INT/ORG FORCES TOP/EX CREATE   RIGID/FLEX
LEGIT NUC/PWR DISPL ORD/FREE...CONCPT TIME/SEQ   ARMS/CONT
CON/ANAL 20. PAGE 41 G0803

B63
FOSKETT D.J.,CLASSIFICATION AND INDEXING IN THE   PROB/SOLV
SOCIAL SCIENCES. WOR+45 R+D ACT/RES CREATE OP/RES   CON/ANAL
TEC/DEV AUTOMAT ROLE...SOC COMPUT/IR BIBLIOG.   CLASSIF
PAGE 20 G0384

B63
NAFZIGER R.O.,INTRODUCTION TO MASS COMMUNICATIONS   COM/IND
RESEARCH (REV. ED.). ACT/RES...STAT CON/ANAL METH   CONCPT
20. PAGE 41 G0801   PHIL/SCI
                                                     CREATE

B63
NORTH R.C.,CONTENT ANALYSIS: A HANDBOOK WITH   METH/CNCPT
APPLICATIONS FOR THE STUDY OF INTERNATIONAL CRISIS. COMPUT/IR
ASIA COM EUR+WWI MOD/EUR INT/ORG TEC/DEV DOMIN   USSR
EDU/PROP ROUTINE COERCE PERCEPT RIGID/FLEX ALL/VALS
...QUANT TESTS CON/ANAL SIMUL GEN/LAWS VAL/FREE.
PAGE 42 G0825

B64
COOMBS C.H.,A THEORY OF DATA....MGT PHIL/SCI SOC   CON/ANAL
CLASSIF MATH PROBABIL STAT QU. PAGE 13 G0254   GEN/METH
                                                     TESTS
                                                     PSY

B64
GRODZINS M.,THE ATOMIC AGE: FORTY-FIVE SCIENTISTS   INTELL
AND SCHOLARS SPEAK ON NATIONAL AND WORLD AFFAIRS.   ARMS/CONT
FUT USA+45 WOR+45 R+D INT/ORG NAT/G CONSULT TEC/DEV NUC/PWR
EDU/PROP ATTIT PERSON ORD/FREE...HUM CONCPT
TIME/SEQ CON/ANAL. PAGE 23 G0454

B64
GROSSER G.H.,THE THREAT OF IMPENDING DISASTER: HEALTH
CONTRIBUTIONS TO THE PSYCHOLOGY OF STRESS. SPACE   PSY
UNIV SOCIETY R+D TEC/DEV EDU/PROP COERCE WAR ATTIT   NUC/PWR
BIO/SOC DISPL PERCEPT PERSON...SOC MYTH SELF/OBS
CONT/OBS BIOG CON/ANAL TOT/POP 20. PAGE 23 G0455

B64
LANG A.S.,URBAN RAIL TRANSIT. OP/RES PLAN PROB/SOLV MUNIC
TEC/DEV AUTOMAT COST...TECHNIC MATH CON/ANAL CHARTS DIST/IND
METH/COMP SIMUL 20 RAILROAD PUB/TRANS. PAGE 32   ECOMETRIC
G0632

B64
ORGANIZATION AMERICAN STATES,ECONOMIC SURVEY OF   ECO/UNDEV
LATIN AMERICA, 1962. L/A+17C AGRI DIST/IND INDUS   CHARTS
MARKET PROC/MFG R+D PLAN TEC/DEV ECO/TAC REGION
BAL/PAY ALL/VALS...CON/ANAL ORG/CHARTS GEN/METH OAS
20. PAGE 43 G0844

S64
FLORINSKY M.T.,"TRENDS IN THE SOVIET ECONOMY." COM   ECO/DEV
USA+45 USSR INDUS LABOR NAT/G PLAN TEC/DEV ECO/TAC   AGRI
ALL/VALS SOCISM...MGT METH/CNCPT STYLE CON/ANAL
GEN/METH WORK 20. PAGE 19 G0374

S64
MAGGS P.B.,"SOVIET VIEWPOINT ON NUCLEAR WEAPONS IN   COM
INTERNATIONAL LAW." USSR WOR+45 INT/ORG FORCES   LAW
DIPLOM ARMS/CONT ATTIT ORD/FREE PWR...POLICY JURID   INT/LAW
CONCPT OBS TREND CON/ANAL GEN/LAWS VAL/FREE 20.   NUC/PWR
PAGE 35 G0694

S64
STONE P.A.,"DECISION TECHNIQUES FOR TOWN   OP/RES
DEVELOPMENT." PLAN COST PROFIT...DECISION MGT   MUNIC
CON/ANAL CHARTS METH/COMP BIBLIOG 20. PAGE 53 G1039 ADMIN
                                                     PROB/SOLV

B65

INT. BANK RECONSTR. DEVELOP.,ECONOMIC DEVELOPMENT
OF KUWAIT. ISLAM KUWAIT AGRI FINAN MARKET EX/STRUC
TEC/DEV ECO/TAC ADMIN WEALTH...OBS CON/ANAL CHARTS
20. PAGE 28 G0548

INDUS
NAT/G

B65

JANDA K.,DATA PROCESSING: APPLICATIONS TO POLITICAL
RESEARCH....STAT CON/ANAL. PAGE 28 G0557

DECISION
COMPUTER
TEC/DEV
METH

S65

HOLSTI O.R.,"EAST-WEST CONFLICT AND SINO-SOVIET
RELATIONS" CHINA/COM USSR COMPUTER REGION DECISION.
PAGE 27 G0523

VOL/ASSN
DIPLOM
CON/ANAL
COM

S66

KAPLAN M.A.,"THE NEW GREAT DEBATE* TRADITIONALISM
VS SCIENCE IN INTERNATIONAL RELATIONS."...DECISION
HUM QUANT STYLE NET/THEORY CON/ANAL STERTYP
GEN/LAWS. PAGE 29 G0577

PHIL/SCI
CONSERVE
DIPLOM
SIMUL

B67

ALEXANDER L.M.,THE LAW OF THE SEA: OFFSHORE
BOUNDARIES AND ZONES. WOR+45 INT/ORG TEC/DEV
CONTROL PRIVIL HABITAT SOVEREIGN...CON/ANAL CHARTS
ANTHOL. PAGE 2 G0037

SEA
INT/LAW
EXTR/IND

B67

CHARLESWORTH J.C.,CONTEMPORARY POLITICAL ANALYSIS.
INTELL...DECISION METH/CNCPT MATH STYLE CON/ANAL
GAME ANTHOL 20. PAGE 11 G0222

R+D
IDEA/COMP
CONCPT
METH/COMP

B67

HARMAN H.H.,MODERN FACTOR ANALYSIS (2ND REV. ED.).
COMPUTER...DECISION CHARTS BIBLIOG T. PAGE 24 G0482

CON/ANAL
METH/CNCPT
SIMUL
MATH

B67

MCDOUGAL M.S.,THE INTERPRETATION OF AGREEMENTS AND
WORLD PUBLIC ORDER: PRINCIPLES OF CONTENT AND
PROCEDURE. WOR+45 CONSTN PROB/SOLV TEC/DEV
...CON/ANAL TREATY. PAGE 37 G0740

INT/LAW
STRUCT
ECO/UNDEV
DIPLOM

B67

SCHUMACHER B.G.,COMPUTER DYNAMICS IN PUBLIC
ADMINISTRATION. USA+45 CREATE PLAN TEC/DEV...MGT
LING CON/ANAL BIBLIOG/A 20. PAGE 50 G0980

COMPUTER
COMPUT/IR
ADMIN
AUTOMAT

B67

UNIVERSAL REFERENCE SYSTEM,LEGISLATIVE PROCESS,
REPRESENTATION, AND DECISION-MAKING (VOLUME II).
WOR+45 WOR-45 CONSTN LOC/G NAT/G...POLICY CON/ANAL
COMPUT/IR GEN/METH. PAGE 56 G1094

BIBLIOG/A
LEGIS
REPRESENT
DECISION

B67

UNIVERSAL REFERENCE SYSTEM,BIBLIOGRAPHY OF
BIBLIOGRAPHIES IN POLITICAL SCIENCE, GOVERNMENT,
AND PUBLIC POLICY (VOLUME III). WOR+45 WOR-45 LAW
ADMIN...SOC CON/ANAL COMPUT/IR GEN/METH. PAGE 56
G1095

BIBLIOG/A
NAT/G
DIPLOM
POLICY

B67

US HOUSE COMM SCI ASTRONAUT,AUTHORIZING SECY OF
COMMERCE TO PROVIDE FOR COLLECTION, COMPILATION,
CRIT EVALUATION, PUBLICATION, SALE OF STD REF DATA.
USA+45 TEC/DEV...COMPUT/IR HOUSE/REP. PAGE 59 G1150

PHIL/SCI
CON/ANAL
STAT
R+D

S67

VERGIN R.C.,"COMPUTER INDUCED ORGANIZATION
CHANGES." FUT USA+45 R+D CREATE OP/RES TEC/DEV
ADJUST CENTRAL...MGT INT CON/ANAL COMPUT/IR.
PAGE 61 G1194

COMPUTER
DECISION
AUTOMAT
EX/STRUC

CON/INTERP....CONSTITUTIONAL INTERPRETATION

CONANT J.B. G0248,G0249

CONCEN/CMP....CONCENTRATION CAMPS

CONCEPT....SEE CONCPT

CONCPT....SUBJECT-MATTER CONCEPTS

CONDEMNATION OF LAND OR PROPERTY....SEE CONDEMNATN

CONDEMNATN....CONDEMNATION OF LAND OR PROPERTY

CONDOTTIER....CONDOTTIERI - HIRED MILITIA

CONFER....CONFERENCES; SEE ALSO DELIB/GP

S58

MARCY C.,"THE RESEARCH PROGRAM OF THE SENATE
COMMITTEE ON FOREIGN RELATIONS." EUR+WWI ECO/UNDEV
ACT/RES PLAN PARL/PROC GOV/REL...GEOG CONFE
CONGRESS. PAGE 36 G0704

DELIB/GP
LEGIS
FOR/AID
POLICY

N

UNITED NATIONS,OFFICIAL RECORDS OF THE UNITED
NATIONS' ATOMIC ENERGY COMMISSION - DISARMAMENT
COMMISSION. WOR+45 TEC/DEV DIPLOM WRITING NUC/PWR
20 UN. PAGE 55 G1092

ARMS/CONT
INT/ORG
DELIB/GP
CONFER

N19

FOLSOM M.B.,BETTER MANAGEMENT OF THE PUBLIC'S
BUSINESS (PAMPHLET). USA+45 DELIB/GP PAY CONFER
CONTROL REGION GP/REL...METH/COMP ANTHOL 20.
PAGE 19 G0377

ADMIN
NAT/G
MGT
PROB/SOLV

N19

MEZERIK A.G.,ATOM TESTS AND RADIATION HAZARDS
(PAMPHLET). WOR+45 INT/ORG DIPLOM DETER 20 UN
TREATY. PAGE 39 G0761

NUC/PWR
ARMS/CONT
CONFER
HEALTH

N19

US SEN SPEC COMM SPACE ASTRO,SPACE LAW; A SYMPOSIUM
(PAMPHLET). USA+45 TEC/DEV CONFER CONTROL SOVEREIGN
...INT/LAW 20 SEN/SPACE. PAGE 59 G1161

SPACE
ADJUD
DIPLOM
INT/ORG

S44

GRIFFITH E.S.,"THE CHANGING PATTERN OF PUBLIC
POLICY FORMATION." MOD/EUR WOR+45 FINAN CHIEF
CONFER ADMIN LEAD CONSERVE SOCISM TECHRACY...SOC
CHARTS CONGRESS. PAGE 23 G0450

LAW
POLICY
TEC/DEV

B47

SOCIAL SCIENCE RESEARCH COUN,PUBLIC REACTION TO THE
ATOMIC BOMB AND WORLD AFFAIRS. SOCIETY CONFER
ARMS/CONT...STAT QU SAMP CHARTS 20. PAGE 52 G1019

ATTIT
NUC/PWR
DIPLOM
WAR

S49

SOUERS S.W.,"POLICY FORMULATION FOR NATIONAL
SECURITY." EX/STRUC FORCES PROB/SOLV DIPLOM CONFER
EXEC ARMS/CONT DETER NUC/PWR GOV/REL PEACE
COLD/WAR. PAGE 52 G1022

DELIB/GP
CHIEF
DECISION
POLICY

B50

HUZAR E.,THE PURSE AND THE SWORD: CONTROL OF THE
ARMY BY CONGRESS THROUGH MILITARY APPROPRIATIONS
1933-1950. NAT/G DELIB/GP EX/STRUC FORCES PROB/SOLV
BARGAIN CONFER ADMIN ROUTINE GOV/REL EFFICIENCY
...POLICY COLD/WAR. PAGE 27 G0541

CIVMIL/REL
BUDGET
CONTROL
LEGIS

B53

LANGER W.L.,THE UNDECLARED WAR, 1940-1941. EUR+WWI
GERMANY USA-45 USSR AIR FORCES TEC/DEV CONFER
CONTROL COERCE PERCEPT ORD/FREE PWR 20 CHINJAP
EUROPE. PAGE 32 G0634

WAR
POLICY
DIPLOM

C54

ZELLER B.,"AMERICAN STATE LEGISLATURES: REPORT ON
THE COMMITTEE ON AMERICAN LEGISLATURES." CONSTN
POL/PAR EX/STRUC CONFER ADMIN CONTROL EXEC LOBBY
ROUTINE GOV/REL...POLICY BIBLIOG 20. PAGE 65 G1267

REPRESENT
LEGIS
PROVS
APPORT

B56

ATOMIC INDUSTRIAL FORUM,PUBLIC RELATIONS FOR THE
ATOMIC INDUSTRY. WOR+45 PLAN PROB/SOLV EDU/PROP
PRESS CONFER...AUD/VIS ANTHOL 20. PAGE 4 G0077

NUC/PWR
INDUS
GP/REL
ATTIT

S56

KNAPP D.C.,"CONGRESSIONAL CONTROL OF AGRICULTURAL
CONSERVATION POLICY: A CASE STUDY OF THE
APPROPRIATIONS PROCESS." DELIB/GP PLAN PROB/SOLV
CONFER PARL/PROC...POLICY INT CONGRESS. PAGE 31
G0607

LEGIS
AGRI
BUDGET
CONTROL

S57

TAYLOR P.S.,"THE RELATION OF RESEARCH TO
LEGISLATIVE AND ADMINISTRATIVE DECISIONS." ELITES
ACT/RES PLAN PROB/SOLV CONFER CHOOSE POLICY.
PAGE 54 G1059

DECISION
LEGIS
MGT
PWR

B58

ATOMIC INDUSTRIAL FORUM,MANAGEMENT AND ATOMIC
ENERGY. WOR+45 SEA LAW MARKET NAT/G TEC/DEV INSPECT
INT/TRADE CONFER PEACE HEALTH...ANTHOL 20. PAGE 4
G0078

NUC/PWR
INDUS
MGT
ECO/TAC

B58

NATIONAL PLANNING ASSOCIATION,1970 WITHOUT ARMS

ARMS/CONT

CONTROL (PAMPHLET). WOR+45 PROB/SOLV TEC/DEV DIPLOM ORD/FREE
CONFER DETER NUC/PWR WAR...CHARTS 20 COLD/WAR. WEAPON
PAGE 41 G0810 PREDICT

B58
UN INTL CONF ON PEACEFUL USE,PROGRESS IN ATOMIC NUC/PWR
ENERGY (VOL. I). WOR+45 R+D PLAN TEC/DEV CONFER DIPLOM
CONTROL PEACE SKILL...CHARTS ANTHOL 20 UN BAGHDAD. WORKER
PAGE 55 G1088 EDU/PROP

B59
HALEY A.G.,FIRST COLLOQUIUM ON THE LAW OF OUTER SPACE
SPACE. WOR+45 INT/ORG ACT/RES PLAN BAL/PWR CONFER LAW
ATTIT PWR...POLICY JURID CHARTS ANTHOL 20. PAGE 24 SOVEREIGN
G0468 CONTROL

S59
LEFTON M.,"DECISION MAKING IN A MENTAL HOSPITAL: ACT/RES
REAL, PERCEIVED, AND IDEAL." R+D PUB/INST CONSULT PROB/SOLV
CONFER INGP/REL PERCEPT...MODAL 20. PAGE 33 G0653 DECISION
PSY

B61
HELLER D.,THE KENNEDY CABINET--AMERICA'S MEN OF EX/STRUC
DESTINY. NAT/G CHIEF CONSULT ADMIN CONTROL GOV/REL CONFER
...MGT 20 DEPT/LABOR DEPT/STATE DEPT/JUST DELIB/GP
DEPT/DEFEN KENNEDY/J. PAGE 26 G0504 TOP/EX

B62
SCHMITT H.A.,THE PATH TO EUROPEAN UNITY. EUR+WWI INT/ORG
USA+45 PLAN TEC/DEV DIPLOM FOR/AID CONFER...INT/LAW INT/TRADE
20 EEC EURCOALSTL MARSHL/PLN UNIFICA. PAGE 49 G0971 REGION
ECO/DEV

B63
DALAND R.T.,PERSPECTIVES OF BRAZILIAN PUBLIC ADMIN
ADMINISTRATION (VOL. I). BRAZIL LAW ECO/UNDEV NAT/G
SCHOOL CHIEF TEC/DEV CONFER CONTROL GP/REL ATTIT PLAN
ROLE PWR...ANTHOL 20. PAGE 14 G0272 GOV/REL

B63
KAST F.E.,SCIENCE, TECHNOLOGY, AND MANAGEMENT. MGT
SPACE USA+45 FORCES CONFER DETER NUC/PWR...PHIL/SCI PLAN
CHARTS ANTHOL BIBLIOG 20 NASA. PAGE 30 G0581 TEC/DEV
PROB/SOLV

B63
PEABODY R.L.,NEW PERSPECTIVES ON THE HOUSE OF NEW/IDEA
REPRESENTATIVES. AGRI FINAN SCHOOL FORCES CONFER LEGIS
LEAD CHOOSE REPRESENT FEDERAL...POLICY DECISION PWR
HOUSE/REP. PAGE 44 G0862 ADMIN

B63
REED E.,CHALLENGES TO DEMOCRACY: THE NEXT TEN POLICY
YEARS. FUT USA+45 ECO/DEV DELIB/GP TEC/DEV CONFER EDU/PROP
GOV/REL KNOWL ORD/FREE...MAJORIT IDEA/COMP ANTHOL ECO/TAC
20. PAGE 46 G0909 NAT/G

B64
HAMMOND P.E.,SOCIOLOGISTS AT WORK. VOL/ASSN OP/RES R+D
TEC/DEV CONFER ROUTINE TASK EFFICIENCY...MGT BIOG
NEW/IDEA STYLE SAMP. PAGE 24 G0478 SOC

B64
NASA,PROCEEDINGS OF CONFERENCE ON THE LAW OF SPACE SPACE
AND OF SATELLITE COMMUNICATIONS: CHICAGO 1963. FUT COM/IND
WOR+45 DELIB/GP PROB/SOLV TEC/DEV CONFER ADJUD LAW
NUC/PWR...POLICY IDEA/COMP 20 NASA. PAGE 41 G0805 DIPLOM

B64
US AIR FORCE ACADEMY ASSEMBLY,OUTER SPACE: FINAL SPACE
REPORT APRIL 1-4, 1964. FUT USA+45 WOR+45 LAW CIVMIL/REL
DELIB/GP CONFER ARMS/CONT WAR PEACE ATTIT MORAL NUC/PWR
...ANTHOL 20 NASA. PAGE 56 G1104 DIPLOM

B65
WHITE HOUSE CONFERENCE ON INTERNATIONAL R+D
COOPERATION(VOL.II). SPACE WOR+45 EXTR/IND INT/ORG CONFER
LABOR WORKER NUC/PWR PEACE AGE/Y...CENSUS ANTHOL 20 TEC/DEV
RESOURCE/N URBAN/RNWL PUB/TRANS. PAGE 1 G0019 DIPLOM

B65
ATOMIC INDUSTRIAL FORUM,SAFEGUARDS AGAINST NUC/PWR
DIVERSION OF NUCLEAR MATERIALS FROM PEACEFUL TO CIVMIL/REL
MILITARY PURPOSES. WOR+45 DELIB/GP FORCES PLAN INSPECT
DIPLOM CONFER PEACE...ANTHOL 20 IAEA. PAGE 4 G0081 CONTROL

B65
REISS A.J. JR.,SCHOOLS IN A CHANGING SOCIETY. SCHOOL
CULTURE PROB/SOLV INSPECT DOMIN CONFER INGP/REL EX/STRUC
RACE/REL AGE/C AGE/Y ALL/VALS...ANTHOL SOC/INTEG 20 ADJUST
NEWYORK/C. PAGE 46 G0912 ADMIN

B66
BLOOMFIELD L.P.,KHRUSHCHEV AND THE ARMS RACE. ARMS/CONT
USA+45 USSR ECO/DEV BAL/PWR EDU/PROP CONFER NUC/PWR COM

ATTIT...CHARTS 20 KHRUSH/N. PAGE 7 G0143 POLICY
DIPLOM

B66
CLARK G.,WORLD PEACE THROUGH WORLD LAW: TWO INT/LAW
ALTERNATIVE PLANS. WOR+45 DELIB/GP FORCES TAX PEACE
CONFER ADJUD SANCTION ARMS/CONT WAR CHOOSE PRIVIL PLAN
20 UN COLD/WAR. PAGE 12 G0231 INT/ORG

B66
FEIS H.,THE ATOMIC BOMB AND THE END OF WORLD WAR USA+45
II. FORCES PLAN PROB/SOLV DIPLOM CONFER WAR PEACE
...TIME/SEQ TREND CHINJAP PRESIDENT TIME. PAGE 19 NUC/PWR
G0362

B66
JACOBSON H.K.,DIPLOMATS, SCIENTISTS, AND DIPLOM
POLITICIANS* THE UNITED STATES AND THE NUCLEAR TEST ARMS/CONT
BAN NEGOTIATIONS. USA+45 USSR ACT/RES PLAN CONFER TECHRACY
DETER NUC/PWR CONSEN ORD/FREE...INT TREATY. PAGE 28 INT/ORG
G0554

N66
US HOUSE COMM SCI ASTRONAUT,GOVERNMENT, SCIENCE, NAT/G
AND PUBLIC POLICY (PAMPHLET). R+D ACADEM DELIB/GP POLICY
COMPUTER BUDGET CONFER ADMIN...PHIL/SCI PREDICT TEC/DEV
TREND 20 CONGRESS HS/SCIASTR. PAGE 58 G1143 CREATE

N66
US HOUSE COMM SCI ASTRONAUT,THE ADEQUACY OF HEALTH
TECHNOLOGY FOR POLLUTION ABATEMENT (PAMPHLET). POLICY
WOR+45 PLAN PROB/SOLV CONFER ADMIN...JURID 20 TEC/DEV
POLLUTION. PAGE 58 G1145 LEGIS

B67
UNESCO,PRINCIPLES AND PROBLEMS OF NATIONAL SCIENCE NAT/COMP
POLICIES. WOR+45 ECO/DEV ECO/UNDEV R+D INT/ORG POLICY
PROB/SOLV CONFER...PHIL/SCI CHARTS 20 UNESCO UN. TEC/DEV
PAGE 55 G1091 CREATE

B67
US SENATE COMM ON FOREIGN REL,FOREIGN ASSISTANCE FOR/AID
ACT OF 1967. VIETNAM WOR+45 DELIB/GP CONFER CONTROL LAW
WAR WEAPON BAL/PAY...CENSUS CHARTS SENATE. PAGE 60 DIPLOM
G1185 POLICY

B67
US SUPERINTENDENT OF DOCUMENTS,LIBRARY OF CONGRESS BIBLIOG/A
(PRICE LIST 83). AFR ASIA EUR+WWI USA-45 USSR NAT/G USA+45
DIPLOM CONFER CT/SYS WAR...DECISION PHIL/SCI AUTOMAT
CLASSIF 19/20 CONGRESS PRESIDENT. PAGE 61 G1189 LAW

S67
CARY G.D.,"THE QUIET REVOLUTION IN COPYRIGHT* THE COM/IND
END OF THE 'PUBLICATION' CONCEPT." USA+45 LAW POLICY
OP/RES TEC/DEV CONFER DEBATE EFFICIENCY...JURID LICENSE
CONGRESS. PAGE 11 G0217 PRESS

S67
CONWAY J.E.,"MAKING RESEARCH EFFECTIVE IN ACT/RES
LEGISLATION." LAW R+D CONSULT EX/STRUC PLAN CONFER POLICY
ADMIN LEAD ROUTINE TASK INGP/REL DECISION. PAGE 13 LEGIS
G0252 PROB/SOLV

S67
EDMONDS M.,"INTERNATIONAL COLLABORATION IN WEAPONS DIPLOM
PROCUREMENT* THE IMPLICATIONS OF THE ANGLO-FRENCH VOL/ASSN
CASE." FRANCE UK CONSULT OP/RES PROB/SOLV TEC/DEV BAL/PWR
CONFER CONTROL EFFICIENCY 20. PAGE 17 G0334 ARMS/CONT

S67
FOREIGN POLICY ASSOCIATION,"US CONCERN FOR WORLD INT/LAW
LAW." USA+45 WOR+45 DELIB/GP JUDGE BAL/PWR CONFER INT/ORG
PEACE ORD/FREE 20 UN. PAGE 19 G0379 DIPLOM
ARMS/CONT

S67
GOBER J.L.,"FEDERALISM AT WORK." USA+45 NAT/G MUNIC
CONSULT ACT/RES PLAN CONFER ADMIN LEAD PARTIC TEC/DEV
FEDERAL ATTIT. PAGE 21 G0422 R+D
GOV/REL

S67
HARRIS F.R.,"POLITICAL SCIENCE AND THE PROPOSAL FOR PROF/ORG
A NATIONAL SOCIAL SCIENCE FOUNDATION." FUT CONSULT R+D
DELIB/GP PLAN PROB/SOLV BUDGET CONFER SANCTION CREATE
CRIME...POLICY SOC/WK 20 NSF NSSF. PAGE 25 G0484 NAT/G

S67
JOHNSTON D.M.,"LAW, TECHNOLOGY AND THE SEA." WOR+45 INT/LAW
PLAN PROB/SOLV TEC/DEV CONFER ADJUD ORD/FREE INT/ORG
...POLICY JURID. PAGE 29 G0564 DIPLOM
NEUTRAL

S67
PONTECORVO G.,"THE LAW OF THE SEA." ECO/DEV CONFER

ECO/UNDEV TEC/DEV GEOG. PAGE 45 G0885 — INT/LAW EXTR/IND SEA

S67
RAMSEY J.A.,"THE STATUS OF INTERNATIONAL COPYRIGHTS." WOR+45 CREATE TEC/DEV DIPLOM CONFER CONTROL SANCTION OWN...POLICY JURID. PAGE 46 G0899 — INT/LAW INT/ORG COM/IND PRESS

S67
RICH G.S.,"THE PROPOSED PATENT LEGISLATION* SOME COMMENTS." USA+45 LAW R+D ACT/RES TEC/DEV CONFER EFFICIENCY OWN JURID. PAGE 46 G0916 — LICENSE POLICY CREATE CAP/ISM

S67
SCHACTER O.,"SCIENTIFIC ADVANCES AND INTERNATIONAL LAWMAKING." FUT R+D PLAN PROB/SOLV CONFER CONTROL ...POLICY PREDICT 20 UN. PAGE 49 G0961 — TEC/DEV INT/LAW INT/ORG ACT/RES

S67
SHARP G.,"THE NEED OF A FUNCTIONAL SUBSTITUTE FOR WAR." FUT UNIV WOR+45 CULTURE SOCIETY ACT/RES CREATE BAL/PWR CONFER ARMS/CONT NUC/PWR 20. PAGE 50 G0989 — PEACE WAR DIPLOM PROB/SOLV

S67
VLASCIC I.A.,"THE SPACE TREATY* A PRELIMINARY EVALUATION." FUT USSR WOR+45 R+D ACT/RES TEC/DEV DIPLOM CONFER ARMS/CONT PEACE...PREDICT UN TREATY. PAGE 61 G1201 — SPACE INT/LAW INT/ORG NEUTRAL

S67
WASHBURN A.M.,"NUCLEAR PROLIFERATION IN A REVOLUTIONARY INTERNATIONAL SYSTEM." WOR+45 NAT/G DELIB/GP PLAN TEC/DEV...POLICY 20. PAGE 62 G1216 — ARMS/CONT NUC/PWR DIPLOM CONFER

N67
US HOUSE COMM SCI ASTRONAUT,GOVERNMENT, SCIENCE, AND INTERNATIONAL POLICY (PAMPHLET). INDIA NETHERLAND ECO/DEV ECO/UNDEV R+D ACADEM PLAN DIPLOM FOR/AID CONFER...PREDICT 20 CHINJAP. PAGE 59 G1152 — NAT/G POLICY CREATE TEC/DEV

N67
US SENATE COMM AERO SPACE SCI,HEARINGS BEFORE THE COMMITTEE ON AERONAUTICAL AND SPACE SCIENCES UNITED STATES SENATE NINETIETH CONGRESS (PAMPHLET). USA+45 CONSULT PLAN CONFER EFFICIENCY SENATE. PAGE 60 G1172 — NAT/G DELIB/GP SPACE CREATE

CONFERENCES....SEE CONFER, DELIB/GP

CONFIDENCE, PERSONAL....SEE SUPEGO

CONFLICT, MILITARY....SEE WAR, FORCES+COERCE

CONFLICT, PERSONAL....SEE PERS/REL, ROLE

CONFLICT....CONFLICT THEORY

CONFORMITY....SEE CONSEN, DOMIN

CONFRONTATION....SEE CONFRONTN

CONFRONTN....CONFRONTATION

CONFUCIUS....CONFUCIUS

CONGO....CONGO, PRE-INDEPENDENCE OR GENERAL

CONGO/BRAZ....CONGO, BRAZZAVILLE; SEE ALSO AFR

CONGO/KINS....CONGO, KINSHASA; SEE ALSO AFR

CONGRESS OF RACIAL EQUALITY....SEE CORE

CONGRESS....CONGRESS (ALL NATIONS); SEE ALSO LEGIS, HOUSE/REP, SENATE, DELIB/GP

N19
ATOMIC INDUSTRIAL FORUM,COMMENTARY ON LEGISLATION TO PERMIT PRIVATE OWNERSHIP OF SPECIAL NUCLEAR MATERIAL (PAMPHLET). USA+45 DELIB/GP LEGIS PLAN OWN ...POLICY 20 AEC CONGRESS. PAGE 4 G0076 — NUC/PWR MARKET INDUS LAW

N19
LAWRENCE S.A.,THE BATTERY ADDITIVE CONTROVERSY (PAMPHLET). USA+45 LAW MARKET PROC/MFG R+D CAP/ISM CT/SYS GOV/REL OWN FTC CONGRESS BUR/STNDRD RITCHIE/JM. PAGE 33 G0645 — PHIL/SCI LOBBY INSPECT

B41
FULLER G.H.,DEFENSE FINANCING: A SELECTED LIST OF — BIBLIOG/A

REFERENCES (PAMPHLET). MOD/EUR USA-45 ECO/DEV NAT/G DELIB/GP RATION ARMS/CONT WEAPON COST PEACE PWR 20 CONGRESS. PAGE 20 G0401 — FINAN FORCES BUDGET

B42
FULLER G.H.,DEFENSE FINANCING: A SUPPLEMENTARY LIST OF REFERENCES (PAMPHLET). CANADA UK USA-45 ECO/DEV NAT/G DELIB/GP BUDGET ADJUD ARMS/CONT WEAPON COST PEACE PWR 20 AUSTRAL CHINJAP CONGRESS. PAGE 21 G0403 — BIBLIOG/A FINAN FORCES DIPLOM

S44
GRIFFITH E.S.,"THE CHANGING PATTERN OF PUBLIC POLICY FORMATION." MOD/EUR WOR+45 FINAN CHIEF CONFER ADMIN LEAD CONSERVE SOCISM TECHRACY...SOC CHARTS CONGRESS. PAGE 23 G0450 — LAW POLICY TEC/DEV

S45
WHITE L.D.,"CONGRESSIONAL CONTROL OF THE PUBLIC SERVICE." USA-45 NAT/G CONSULT DELIB/GP PLAN SENIOR CONGRESS. PAGE 63 G1232 — LEGIS EXEC POLICY CONTROL

B50
US DEPARTMENT OF STATE,POINT FOUR: COOPERATIVE PROGRAM FOR AID IN THE DEVELOPMENT OF ECONOMICALLY UNDERDEVELOPED AREAS. WOR+45 AGRI INDUS INT/ORG PLAN TEC/DEV DIPLOM EDU/PROP ADMIN PEACE PRODUC WEALTH 20 CONGRESS UN. PAGE 57 G1121 — ECO/UNDEV FOR/AID FINAN INT/TRADE

L50
MAASS A.A.,"CONGRESS AND WATER RESOURCES." LOC/G TEC/DEV CONTROL SANCTION...WELF/ST GEOG CONGRESS. PAGE 35 G0683 — REGION AGRI PLAN

B55
SMITHIES A.,THE BUDGETARY PROCESS IN THE UNITED STATES. ECO/DEV AGRI EX/STRUC FORCES LEGIS PROB/SOLV TAX ROUTINE EFFICIENCY...MGT CONGRESS PRESIDENT. PAGE 52 G1016 — NAT/G ADMIN BUDGET GOV/REL

B56
THOMAS M.,ATOMIC ENERGY AND CONGRESS. USA+45 NAT/G ACT/RES PLAN TEC/DEV EDU/PROP ROUTINE KNOWL PWR SKILL...PHIL/SCI NEW/IDEA TIME/SEQ CHARTS METH CONGRESS VAL/FREE 20 AEC. PAGE 54 G1067 — LEGIS ADMIN NUC/PWR

S56
KNAPP D.C.,"CONGRESSIONAL CONTROL OF AGRICULTURAL CONSERVATION POLICY: A CASE STUDY OF THE APPROPRIATIONS PROCESS." DELIB/GP PLAN PROB/SOLV CONFER PARL/PROC...POLICY INT CONGRESS. PAGE 31 G0607 — LEGIS AGRI BUDGET CONTROL

S56
MILLER W.E.,"PRESIDENTIAL COATTAILS: A STUDY IN POLITICAL MYTH AND METHODOLOGY" (BMR)" USA+45 CREATE PARTIC ATTIT DRIVE PWR...DECISION CONCPT CHARTS SIMUL 20 PRESIDENT CONGRESS. PAGE 39 G0774 — CHIEF CHOOSE POL/PAR MYTH

B58
BIDWELL P.W.,RAW MATERIALS: A STUDY OF AMERICAN POLICY. USA+45 USA-45 ECO/UNDEV AGRI INDUS KIN CREATE PLAN ECO/TAC WAR PEACE ATTIT DRIVE WEALTH ...STAT CHARTS CONGRESS VAL/FREE. PAGE 7 G0135 — EXTR/IND ECO/DEV

B58
US HOUSE COMM GOVT OPERATIONS,CIVIL DEFENSE. USA+45 FORCES...CHARTS 20 CONGRESS CIV/DEFENS HOLIFLD/C. PAGE 58 G1139 — NUC/PWR WAR PLAN ADJUST

S58
MARCY C.,"THE RESEARCH PROGRAM OF THE SENATE COMMITTEE ON FOREIGN RELATIONS." EUR+WWI ECO/UNDEV ACT/RES PLAN PARL/PROC GOV/REL...GEOG CONFE CONGRESS. PAGE 36 G0704 — DELIB/GP LEGIS FOR/AID POLICY

B59
MEANS G.C.,ADMINISTRATIVE INFLATION AND PUBLIC POLICY (PAMPHLET). USA+45 ECO/DEV FINAN INDUS WORKER PLAN BUDGET GOV/REL COST DEMAND WEALTH 20 CONGRESS MONOPOLY GOLD/STAND. PAGE 38 G0749 — ECO/TAC POLICY RATION CONTROL

B60
BARNET R.,WHO WANTS DISARMAMENT. COM EUR+WWI USA+45 USSR INT/ORG NAT/G BAL/PWR DIPLOM EDU/PROP COERCE DETER NUC/PWR WAR WEAPON ATTIT PWR...TIME/SEQ COLD/WAR CONGRESS 20. PAGE 5 G0096 — PLAN FORCES ARMS/CONT

B60
CARPER E.T.,THE DEFENSE APPROPRIATIONS RIDER (PAMPHLET). USA+45 CONSTN CHIEF DELIB/GP LEGIS BUDGET LOBBY CIVMIL/REL...POLICY 20 CONGRESS EISNHWR/DD DEPT/DEFEN PRESIDENT BOSTON. PAGE 11 G0212 — GOV/REL ADJUD LAW CONTROL

SCHILLING W.R.,STRATEGY, POLITICS, AND DEFENSE BUDGETS. USA+45 R+D NAT/G CONSULT DELIB/GP FORCES LEGIS ACT/RES PLAN BAL/PWR LEGIT EXEC NUC/PWR RIGID/FLEX PWR...TREND COLD/WAR CONGRESS 20 EISNHWR/DD. PAGE 49 G0968
B62
ROUTINE
POLICY

US CONGRESS,COMMUNICATIONS SATELLITE LEGISLATION: HEARINGS BEFORE COMM ON AERON AND SPACE SCIENCES ON BILLS S2550 AND 2814. WOR+45 LAW VOL/ASSN PLAN DIPLOM CONTROL OWN PEACE...NEW/IDEA CONGRESS NASA. PAGE 56 G1110
B62
SPACE
COM/IND
ADJUD
GOV/REL

NEIBURG H.L.,"THE EISENHOWER AEC AND CONGRESS: A STUDY IN EXECUTIVE-LEGISLATIVE RELATIONS." USA+45 NAT/G POL/PAR DELIB/GP EX/STRUC TOP/EX ADMIN EXEC LEAD ROUTINE PWR...POLICY COLD/WAR CONGRESS PRESIDENT AEC. PAGE 41 G0816
L62
CHIEF
LEGIS
GOV/REL
NUC/PWR

NIEBURG H.L.,"THE EISENHOWER ATOMIC ENERGY COMMISSION AND CONGRESS" R+D INT/ORG OP/RES DIPLOM ADMIN CONTROL 20 PRESIDENT CONGRESS AEC. PAGE 42 G0821
L62
NUC/PWR
TOP/EX
LOBBY
DELIB/GP

US CONGRESS JT ATOM ENRGY COMM,PEACEFUL USES OF ATOMIC ENERGY, HEARING. USA+45 USSR TEC/DEV ATTIT RIGID/FLEX...TESTS CHARTS EXHIBIT METH/COMP 20 CONGRESS. PAGE 57 G1112
N62
NUC/PWR
ACADEM
SCHOOL
NAT/COMP

GREEN H.P.,GOVERNMENT OF THE ATOM. USA+45 LEGIS PROB/SOLV ADMIN CONTROL PWR...POLICY DECISION 20 PRESIDENT CONGRESS. PAGE 22 G0443
B63
GOV/REL
EX/STRUC
NUC/PWR
DELIB/GP

US SENATE,DOCUMENTS ON INTERNATIONAL AS"ECTS OF EXPLORATION AND USE OF OUTER SPACE, 1954-62: STAFF REPORT FOR COMM AERON SPACE SCI. USA+45 USSR LEGIS LEAD CIVMIL/REL PEACE...POLICY INT/LAW ANTHOL 20 CONGRESS NASA KHRUSH/N. PAGE 59 G1162
B63
SPACE
UTIL
GOV/REL
DIPLOM

US SENATE COMM APPROPRIATIONS,PERSONNEL ADMINISTRATION AND OPERATIONS OF AGENCY FOR INTERNATIONAL DEVELOPMENT: SPECIAL HEARING. FINAN LEAD COST UTIL SKILL...CHARTS 20 CONGRESS AID CIVIL/SERV. PAGE 60 G1175
B63
ADMIN
FOR/AID
EFFICIENCY
DIPLOM

US SENATE COMM GOVT OPERATIONS,ADMINISTRATION OF NATIONAL SECURITY (9 PARTS). ADMIN...INT REC/INT CHARTS 20 SENATE CONGRESS. PAGE 60 G1178
B63
DELIB/GP
NAT/G
OP/RES
ORD/FREE

WILTZ J.E.,IN SEARCH OF PEACE: THE SENATE MUNITIONS INQUIRY, 1934-36. EUR+WWI USA-45 ELITES INDUS LG/CO LEGIS INT/TRADE LOBBY NEUTRAL ARMS/CONT...POLICY CONGRESS 20 LEAGUE/NAT PRESIDENT SENATE CONSCRIPTN. PAGE 64 G1246
B63
DELIB/GP
PROFIT
WAR
WEAPON

COHEN M.,LAW AND POLITICS IN SPACE: SPECIFIC AND URGENT PROBLEMS IN THE LAW OF OUTER SPACE. CHINA/COM COM USA+45 USSR WOR+45 COM/IND INT/ORG NAT/G LEGIT NUC/PWR ATTIT BIO/SOC...JURID CONCPT CONGRESS 20 STALIN/J. PAGE 12 G0241
B64
DELIB/GP
LAW
INT/LAW
SPACE

DUSCHA J.,ARMS, MONEY, AND POLITICS. USA+45 INDUS POL/PAR ECO/TAC TAX DETER NUC/PWR WAR WEAPON GOV/REL ATTIT...BIBLIOG/A 20 CONGRESS MONEY DEPT/DEFEN. PAGE 17 G0326
B64
NAT/G
FORCES
POLICY
BUDGET

MANSFIELD E.,MONOPOLY POWER AND ECONOMIC PERFORMANCE: AN INTRODUCTION TO A CURRENT ISSUE OF PUBLIC POLICY. ECO/DEV INDUS NAT/G PLAN CAP/ISM PRICE CONTROL LOBBY EFFICIENCY PRODUC...POLICY 20 CONGRESS KENNEDY/JF MONOPOLY. PAGE 36 G0701
B64
LG/CO
PWR
ECO/TAC
MARKET

BAILEY S.K.,AMERICAN POLITICS AND GOVERNMENT. USA+45 CONSTN FINAN LABOR POL/PAR DIPLOM ADMIN WAR INGP/REL RACE/REL NEW/LIB 20 SUPREME/CT PRESIDENT CONGRESS. PAGE 4 G0084
B65
ANTHOL
LEGIS
PWR

CARPER E.T.,REORGANIZATION OF THE U.S. PUBLIC HEALTH SERVICE. FUT USA+45 INTELL R+D LOBBY GP/REL
B65
HEAL
PLAN

INGP/REL PERS/REL RIGID/FLEX ROLE HEALTH...PHIL/SCI 20 CONGRESS PHS. PAGE 11 G0213
NAT/G
OP/RES

LAPP R.E.,THE NEW PRIESTHOOD; THE SCIENTIFIC ELITE AND THE USES OF POWER. USA+45 ELITES INTELL SOCIETY R+D NAT/G CHIEF LEGIS CIVMIL/REL GP/REL PWR 20 PRESIDENT CONGRESS. PAGE 32 G0635
B65
TEC/DEV
TECHRACY
CONTROL
POPULISM

NATIONAL ACADEMY OF SCIENCES,BASIC RESEARCH AND NATIONAL GOALS. R+D ACADEM DELIB/GP PLAN EDU/PROP ...POLICY HEAL PHIL/SCI PSY SOC ANTHOL 20 CONGRESS HOUSE/REP HS/SCIASTR. PAGE 41 G0809
B65
LEGIS
BUDGET
NAT/G
CREATE

US CONGRESS JT ATOM ENRGY COMM,PEACEFUL APPLICATIONS OF NUCLEAR EXPLOSIVES: PLOWSHARE, HEARING. USA+45 LEGIS CREATE PLAN PEACE...CHARTS EXHIBIT BIBLIOG CONGRESS PANAMA/CNL. PAGE 57 G1113
B65
NUC/PWR
DELIB/GP
TEC/DEV
NAT/G

US CONGRESS JT ATOM ENRGY COMM,ATOMIC ENERGY LEGISLATION THROUGH 89TH CONGRESS, 1ST SESSION. USA+45 LAW INT/ORG DELIB/GP BUDGET DIPLOM 20 AEC CONGRESS CASEBOOK EURATOM IAEA. PAGE 57 G1114
B65
NUC/PWR
FORCES
PEACE
LEGIS

US CONGRESS JT ATOM ENRGY COMM,PROPOSED AMENDMENT TO SECTION 271 OF THE ATOMIC ENERGY ACT OF 1954. USA+45 CONSTRUC PLAN INSPECT CONTROL CT/SYS 20 CONGRESS AEC. PAGE 57 G1115
B65
LAW
LEGIS
DELIB/GP
NUC/PWR

US DEPARTMENT OF THE ARMY,MILITARY MANPOWER POLICY. USA+45 LEGIS EXEC WAR 20 CONGRESS. PAGE 58 G1132
B65
BIBLIOG/A
POLICY
FORCES
TREND

US SENATE,US INTERNATIONAL SPACE PROGRAMS, 1959-65: STAFF REPORT FOR COMM ON AERONAUTICAL AND SPACE SCIENCES. WOR+45 VOL/ASSN CIVMIL/REL 20 CONGRESS NASA TREATY. PAGE 59 G1163
B65
SPACE
DIPLOM
PLAN
GOV/REL

US SENATE COMM AERO SPACE SCI,NATIONAL SPACE GOALS FOR THE POST-APOLLO PERIOD. USA+45 CONSULT DELIB/GP TEC/DEV BUDGET GP/REL ATTIT...CHARTS IDEA/COMP TIME 20 DEPT/DEFEN NASA CONGRESS. PAGE 59 G1166
B65
SPACE
FUT
R+D
LEGIS

FOX A.B.,"NATO AND CONGRESS." CONSTN DELIB/GP EX/STRUC FORCES TOP/EX BUDGET NUC/PWR GOV/REL ...GP/COMP CONGRESS NATO TREATY. PAGE 20 G0388
S65
CONTROL
DIPLOM

HUGHES T.L.,"SCHOLARS AND FOREIGN POLICY* VARIETIES OF RESEARCH EXPERIENCE." COM/IND DIPLOM ADMIN EXEC ROUTINE...MGT OBS CONGRESS PRESIDENT CAMELOT. PAGE 27 G0535
S65
ACT/RES
ACADEM
CONTROL
NAT/G

GORDON G.,THE LEGISLATIVE PROCESS AND DIVIDED GOVERNMENT; A CASE STUDY OF THE 86TH CONGRESS. USA+45 POL/PAR PROVS PROB/SOLV BAL/PWR CHOOSE REPRESENT EFFICIENCY ATTIT...POLICY DECISION STAT 20 CONGRESS EISNHWR/DD. PAGE 22 G0434
B66
LEGIS
HABITAT
CHIEF
NAT/G

MARKHAM J.W.,AN ECONOMIC-MEDIA STUDY OF BOOK PUBLISHING. USA+45 LAW COM/IND ACADEM SCHOOL EDU/PROP AUTOMAT CONTROL...DECISION STAT CHARTS 20 CONGRESS. PAGE 36 G0707
B66
PRESS
ECO/TAC
TEC/DEV
NAT/G

US SENATE,POLICY PLANNING FOR AERONAUTICAL RESEARCH AND DEVELOPMENT: STAFF REPORT FOR COMM ON AERONAUTICAL AND SPACE SCIENCES. USA+45 AIR DIST/IND PLAN...POLICY CHARTS 20 CONGRESS NASA. PAGE 59 G1164
B66
SPACE
CIVMIL/REL
GOV/REL
R+D

US HOUSE COMM SCI ASTRONAUT,GOVERNMENT, SCIENCE, AND PUBLIC POLICY (PAMPHLET). R+D ACADEM DELIB/GP COMPUTER BUDGET CONFER ADMIN...PHIL/SCI PREDICT TREND 20 CONGRESS HS/SCIASTR. PAGE 58 G1143
N66
NAT/G
POLICY
TEC/DEV
CREATE

US HOUSE COMM SCI ASTRONAUT,INQUIRIES, LEGISLATION, POLICY STUDIES RE: SCIENCE AND TECHNOLOGY: REVIEW AND FORECAST (PAMPHLET). FUT WOR+45 DELIB/GP PROB/SOLV...POLICY JURID TREND 20 CONGRESS. PAGE 58 G1144
N66
TEC/DEV
R+D
PLAN
LEGIS

US SUPERINTENDENT OF DOCUMENTS,LIBRARY OF CONGRESS
(PRICE LIST 83). AFR ASIA EUR+WWI USA-45 USSR NAT/G
DIPLOM CONFER CT/SYS WAR...DECISION PHIL/SCI
CLASSIF 19/20 CONGRESS PRESIDENT. PAGE 61 G1189
    B67 BIBLIOG/A USA+45 AUTOMAT LAW

TRAVERS H. JR.,"AN EXAMINATION OF THE CAB'S MERGER
POLICY." USA+45 USA-45 LAW NAT/G LEGIS PLAN ADMIN
...DECISION 20 CONGRESS. PAGE 55 G1078
    L67 ADJUD LG/CO POLICY DIST/IND

CARY G.D.,"THE QUIET REVOLUTION IN COPYRIGHT* THE
END OF THE 'PUBLICATION' CONCEPT." USA+45 LAW
OP/RES TEC/DEV CONFER DEBATE EFFICIENCY...JURID
CONGRESS. PAGE 11 G0217
    S67 COM/IND POLICY LICENSE PRESS

DADDARIO E.Q.,"CONGRESS FACES SPACE POLICIES." R+D
NAT/G FORCES CREATE LEAD...DECISION CONGRESS NASA.
PAGE 14 G0269
    S67 SPACE PLAN BUDGET POLICY

US SUPERINTENDENT OF DOCUMENTS,SPACE: MISSILES, THE
MOON, NASA, AND SATELLITES (PRICE LIST 79A). USA+45
COM/IND R+D NAT/G DIPLOM EDU/PROP ADMIN CONTROL
HEALTH...POLICY SIMUL NASA CONGRESS. PAGE 61 G1190
    N67 BIBLIOG/A SPACE TEC/DEV PEACE

US SENATE COMM AERO SPACE SCI,AERONAUTICAL RESEARCH
AND DEVELOPMENT POLICY (PAMPHLET). SPACE USA+45
INDUS CIVMIL/REL CONGRESS PRESIDENT NASA SENATE.
PAGE 60 G1169
    N67 AIR R+D POLICY PLAN

US SENATE COMM AERO SPACE SCI,AERONAUTICAL RESEARCH
AND DEVELOPMENT POLICY; HEARINGS, COMM ON
AERONAUTICAL AND SPACE SCIENCES...1967 (PAMPHLET).
R+D PROB/SOLV EXEC GOV/REL 20 DEPT/DEFEN FAA NASA
CONGRESS. PAGE 60 G1174
    N67 DIST/IND SPACE NAT/G PLAN

CONGRESS/P....CONGRESS PARTY (ALL NATIONS)

CONNECTICT....CONNECTICUT

CLEAVELAND F.N.,SCIENCE AND STATE GOVERNMENT. AGRI
EXTR/IND FINAN INDUS PROVS...METH/CNCPT STAT CHARTS
20 NEW/YORK CONNECTICT WISCONSIN CALIFORNIA
NEW/MEXICO. PAGE 12 G0233
    B59 TEC/DEV PHIL/SCI GOV/REL METH/COMP

CONNOLLY W.E. G0250

CONOVER H.L. G0251

CONRAD/JOS....JOSEPH CONRAD

CONSCIENCE....SEE SUPEGO

CONSCN/OBJ....CONSCIENTIOUS OBJECTION TO WAR AND KILLING

CONSCRIPTN....CONSCRIPTION

WILTZ J.E.,IN SEARCH OF PEACE: THE SENATE MUNITIONS
INQUIRY, 1934-36. EUR+WWI USA-45 ELITES INDUS LG/CO
LEGIS INT/TRADE LOBBY NEUTRAL ARMS/CONT...POLICY
CONGRESS 20 LEAGUE/NAT PRESIDENT SENATE CONSCRIPTN.
PAGE 64 G1246
    B63 DELIB/GP PROFIT WAR WEAPON

CONSEN....CONSENSUS

CALLOT E.,LA SOCIETE ET SON ENVIRONNEMENT: ESSAI
SUR LES PRINCIPES DES SCIENCES SOCIALES. GP/REL
ADJUST CONSEN ISOLAT HABITAT PERCEPT PERSON
...BIBLIOG SOC/INTEG 20. PAGE 10 G0205
    B52 SOCIETY PHIL/SCI CULTURE

GOULDNER A.W.,"PATTERNS OF INDUSTRIAL BUREAUCRACY."
GP/REL CONSEN ATTIT DRIVE...BIBLIOG 20. PAGE 22
G0438
    C54 ADMIN INDUS OP/RES WORKER

JACOB P.E.,"THE DISARMAMENT CONSENSUS." USA+45 USSR
WOR+45 INT/ORG NAT/G ACT/RES TEC/DEV BAL/PWR
EDU/PROP ADMIN COERCE DETER NUC/PWR CONSEN
RIGID/FLEX PWR...CONCPT RECORD CHARTS COLD/WAR 20.
PAGE 28 G0552
    L60 DELIB/GP ATTIT ARMS/CONT

WIRTH L.,ON CITIES AND SOCIAL LIFE: SELECTED
PAPERS. PLAN PROB/SOLV RACE/REL CONSEN ATTIT
    B64 GEN/LAWS SOCIETY

HABITAT PERSON...POLICY SOC CONCPT ANTHOL BIBLIOG
20. PAGE 64 G1249
    NEIGH STRUCT

PILISUK M.,"IS THERE A MILITARY INDUSTRIAL COMPLEX
WHICH PREVENTS PEACE CONSENSUS; COUNTERVAILING
POWER IN PLURALIST SYSTEMS." INDUS R+D ACADEM
FEEDBACK CIVMIL/REL ADJUST CONSEN ATTIT RIGID/FLEX
...CENSUS IDEA/COMP BIBLIOG. PAGE 45 G0878
    L65 ELITES WEAPON PEACE ARMS/CONT

JACOBSON H.K.,DIPLOMATS, SCIENTISTS, AND
POLITICIANS* THE UNITED STATES AND THE NUCLEAR TEST
BAN NEGOTIATIONS. USA+45 USSR ACT/RES PLAN CONFER
DETER NUC/PWR CONSEN ORD/FREE...INT TREATY. PAGE 28
G0554
    B66 DIPLOM ARMS/CONT TECHRACY INT/ORG

LECHT L.,GOAL, PRIORITIES, AND DOLLARS: THE NEXT
DECADE. SPACE USA+45 SOCIETY AGRI BUDGET FOR/AID
...HEAL SOC/WK STAT CHARTS 20 URBAN/RNWL PUB/TRANS.
PAGE 33 G0649
    B66 IDEA/COMP POLICY CONSEN PLAN

BROWNLIE I.,"NUCLEAR PROLIFERATION* SOME PROBLEMS
OF CONTROL." USA+45 USSR ECO/UNDEV INT/ORG FORCES
TEC/DEV REGION CONSEN...RECORD TREATY. PAGE 9 G0181
    S66 NUC/PWR ARMS/CONT VOL/ASSN ORD/FREE

HANSON A.H.,"PLANNING AND THE POLITICIANS* SOME
REFLECTIONS ON ECONOMIC PLANNING IN WESTERN
EUROPE." MARKET NAT/G TEC/DEV CONSEN ROLE
...METH/COMP NAT/COMP. PAGE 24 G0479
    S66 PLAN ECO/DEV EUR+WWI ADMIN

HODGE G.,"THE RISE AND DEMISE OF THE UN TECHNICAL
ASSISTANCE ADMINISTRATION." RISK TASK INGP/REL
CONSEN EFFICIENCY 20 UN. PAGE 26 G0516
    S67 ADMIN TEC/DEV EX/STRUC INT/ORG

ROBERTS W.,"DIVERSITY, CONSENSUS, AND ECLECTICISM
IN POLITICAL SCIENCE"...PHIL/SCI 20. PAGE 47 G0927
    S67 CONSEN DEBATE GEN/METH

WEIL G.L.,"THE MERGER OF THE INSTITUTIONS OF THE
EUROPEAN COMMUNITIES" EUR+WWI ECO/DEV INT/TRADE
CONSEN PLURALISM...DECISION MGT 20 EEC EURATOM ECSC
TREATY. PAGE 62 G1223
    S67 ECO/TAC INT/ORG CENTRAL INT/LAW

CONSENSUS....SEE CONSEN

CONSERVATISM....SEE CONSERVE

CONSERVE....TRADITIONALISM

GRIFFITH E.S.,"THE CHANGING PATTERN OF PUBLIC
POLICY FORMATION." MOD/EUR WOR+45 FINAN CHIEF
CONFER ADMIN LEAD CONSERVE SOCISM TECHRACY...SOC
CHARTS CONGRESS. PAGE 23 G0450
    S44 LAW POLICY TEC/DEV

ORTEGA Y GASSET J.,MAN AND CRISIS. SECT CREATE
PERSON CONSERVE...GEN/LAWS RENAISSAN. PAGE 43 G0846
    B58 PHIL/SCI CULTURE CONCPT

JANOWITZ M.,THE PROFESSIONAL SOLDIER. CULTURE
STRATA STRUCT FAM PROB/SOLV TEC/DEV COERCE WAR
CIVMIL/REL NAT/LISM AGE HEREDITY ALL/VALS CONSERVE
...MGT WORSHIP. PAGE 28 G0560
    B60 FORCES MYTH LEAD ELITES

FALK R.A.,ON MINIMIZING THE USE OF NUCLEAR WEAPONS;
THREE ESSAYS; RESEARCH MONOGRAPH NO. 23. WOR+45
STRUCT CREATE NUC/PWR REV CONSERVE...POLICY
NET/THEORY IDEA/COMP GEN/LAWS GEN/METH. PAGE 18
G0359
    B66 DIPLOM EQUILIB PHIL/SCI PROB/SOLV

KAPLAN M.A.,"THE NEW GREAT DEBATE* TRADITIONALISM
VS SCIENCE IN INTERNATIONAL RELATIONS."...DECISION
HUM QUANT STYLE NET/THEORY CON/ANAL STERTYP
GEN/LAWS. PAGE 29 G0577
    S66 PHIL/SCI CONSERVE DIPLOM SIMUL

MALENBAUM W.,"GOVERNMENT, ENTREPRENEURSHIP, AND
ECONOMIC GROWTH IN POOR LANDS." ELITES ECO/UNDEV
INDUS CREATE DRIVE. PAGE 35 G0697
    S66 ECO/TAC PLAN CONSERVE NAT/G

CONSRV/PAR....CONSERVATIVE PARTY (ALL NATIONS)

CONSTITUTION....SEE CONSTN

CONSTN....CONSTITUTIONS

INDIA: A REFERENCE ANNUAL. INDIA CULTURE COM/IND R+D FORCES PLAN RECEIVE EDU/PROP HEALTH...STAT CHARTS BIBLIOG 20. PAGE 1 G0005
CONSTN LABOR INT/ORG
N

CRAIG J.,ELEMENTS OF POLITICAL SCIENCE (3 VOLS.). CONSTN AGRI INDUS SCHOOL FORCES TAX CT/SYS SUFF MORAL WEALTH...CONCPT 19 CIVIL/LIB. PAGE 13 G0259
PHIL/SCI NAT/G ORD/FREE
B14

MATHEWS J.M.,AMERICAN STATE GOVERNMENT. USA-45 LOC/G CHIEF EX/STRUC LEGIS ADJUD CONTROL CT/SYS ROUTINE GOV/REL PWR 20 GOVERNOR. PAGE 37 G0721
PROVS ADMIN FEDERAL CONSTN
B25

FOREIGN AFFAIRS BIBLIOGRAPHY: A SELECTED AND ANNOTATED LIST OF BOOKS ON INTERNATIONAL RELATIONS 1919-1962 (4 VOLS.). CONSTN FORCES COLONIAL ARMS/CONT WAR NAT/LISM PEACE ATTIT DRIVE...POLICY INT/LAW 20. PAGE 1 G0011
BIBLIOG/A DIPLOM INT/ORG
B35

HARPER S.N.,THE GOVERNMENT OF THE SOVIET UNION. COM USSR LAW CONSTN ECO/DEV PLAN TEC/DEV DIPLOM INT/TRADE ADMIN REV NAT/LISM...POLICY 20. PAGE 24 G0483
MARXISM NAT/G LEAD POL/PAR
B38

BEARD C.A.,PUBLIC POLICY AND THE GENERAL WELFARE. USA-45 CONSTN LAISSEZ POPULISM...POLICY MAJORIT 20. PAGE 6 G0108
CONCPT ORD/FREE PWR NAT/G
B41

BINGHAM A.M.,THE TECHNIQUES OF DEMOCRACY. USA-45 CONSTN STRUCT POL/PAR LEGIS PLAN PARTIC CHOOSE REPRESENT NAT/LISM TOTALISM...MGT 20. PAGE 7 G0136
POPULISM ORD/FREE ADMIN NAT/G
B42

WAGER P.W.,"COUNTY GOVERNMENT ACROSS THE NATION." USA+45 CONSTN COM/IND FINAN SCHOOL DOMIN CT/SYS LEAD GOV/REL...STAT BIBLIOG 20. PAGE 61 G1204
LOC/G PROVS ADMIN ROUTINE
C50

SAYLES L.R.,THE LOCAL UNION. CONSTN CULTURE DELIB/GP PARTIC CHOOSE GP/REL INGP/REL ATTIT ROLE ...MAJORIT DECISION MGT. PAGE 49 G0958
LABOR LEAD ADJUD ROUTINE
B53

TOMPKINS D.C.,STATE GOVERNMENT AND ADMINISTRATION: A BIBLIOGRAPHY. USA+45 USA-45 CONSTN LEGIS JUDGE BUDGET CT/SYS LOBBY...CHARTS 20. PAGE 55 G1077
BIBLIOG/A LOC/G PROVS ADMIN
B54

CALDWELL L.K.,"THE GOVERNMENT AND ADMINISTRATION OF NEW YORK." LOC/G MUNIC POL/PAR SCHOOL CHIEF LEGIS PLAN TAX CT/SYS...MGT SOC/WK BIBLIOG 20 NEWYORK/C. PAGE 10 G0202
PROVS ADMIN CONSTN EX/STRUC
C54

ZELLER B.,"AMERICAN STATE LEGISLATURES: REPORT ON THE COMMITTEE ON AMERICAN LEGISLATURES." CONSTN POL/PAR EX/STRUC CONFER ADMIN CONTROL EXEC LOBBY ROUTINE GOV/REL...POLICY BIBLIOG 20. PAGE 65 G1267
REPRESENT LEGIS PROVS APPORT
C54

MARCUSE H.,SOVIET MARXISM, A CRITICAL ANALYSIS. USSR CONSTN PLAN PRODUC RATIONAL SOCISM...IDEA/COMP 20 COM/PARTY. PAGE 36 G0703
MARXISM ATTIT POLICY
B58

OGDEN F.D.,THE POLL TAX IN THE SOUTH. USA+45 USA-45 CONSTN ADJUD ADMIN PARTIC CRIME...TIME/SEQ GOV/COMP METH/COMP 18/20 SOUTH/US. PAGE 43 G0838
TAX CHOOSE RACE/REL DISCRIM
B58

CARPER E.T.,THE DEFENSE APPROPRIATIONS RIDER (PAMPHLET). USA+45 CONSTN CHIEF DELIB/GP LEGIS BUDGET LOBBY CIVMIL/REL...POLICY 20 CONGRESS EISNHWR/DD DEPT/DEFEN PRESIDENT BOSTON. PAGE 11 G0212
GOV/REL ADJUD LAW CONTROL
B60

WOETZEL R.K.,THE INTERNATIONAL CONTROL OF AIRSPACE AND OUTERSPACE. FUT WOR+45 AIR CONSTN STRUCT
INT/ORG JURID
B60

CONSULT PLAN TEC/DEV ADJUD RIGID/FLEX KNOWL ORD/FREE PWR...TECHNIC GEOG MGT NEW/IDEA TREND COMPUT/IR VAL/FREE 20 TREATY. PAGE 64 G1251
SPACE INT/LAW

SWIFT R.,"THE UNITED NATIONS AND ITS PUBLIC." WOR+45 CONSTN FINAN CONSULT DELIB/GP ACT/RES ADMIN ROUTINE RIGID/FLEX SKILL UN 20. PAGE 53 G1048
INT/ORG EDU/PROP
S60

CARNELL F.,THE POLITICS OF THE NEW STATES: A SELECT ANNOTATED BIBLIOGRAPHY WITH SPECIAL REFERENCE TO THE COMMONWEALTH. CONSTN ELITES LABOR NAT/G POL/PAR EX/STRUC DIPLOM ADJUD ADMIN...GOV/COMP 20 COMMONWLTH. PAGE 11 G0210
BIBLIOG/A AFR ASIA COLONIAL
B61

DAWSON R.H.,"CONGRESSIONAL INNOVATION AND INTERVENTION IN DEFENSE POLICY: LEGISLATIVE AUTHORIZATION OF WEAPONS SYSTEMS." CONSTN PLAN ARMS/CONT GOV/REL EFFICIENCY PEACE NEW/LIB OLD/LIB. PAGE 14 G0281
LEGIS PWR CONTROL WEAPON
S62

MAYNE R.,THE COMMUNITY OF EUROPE. UK CONSTN NAT/G CONSULT DELIB/GP CREATE PLAN ECO/TAC LEGIT ADMIN ROUTINE ORD/FREE PWR WEALTH...CONCPT TIME/SEQ EEC EURATOM 20. PAGE 37 G0724
EUR+WWI INT/ORG REGION
B63

MILBRATH L.W.,THE WASHINGTON LOBBYISTS. CONSTN BAL/PWR CONTROL LEAD TASK CHOOSE SUPEGO...DECISION STAT CHARTS BIBLIOG. PAGE 39 G0767
LOBBY POLICY PERS/REL
B63

RANSOM H.H.,CAN AMERICAN DEMOCRACY SURVIVE COLD WAR. USA+45 CONSTN NAT/G CONSULT DELIB/GP LEGIS ACT/RES LEGIT EXEC ATTIT KNOWL ORD/FREE PWR SKILL ...POLICY TIME/SEQ TREND GEN/LAWS 20 COLD/WAR. PAGE 46 G0901
USA+45 ROUTINE
B64

CARNEGIE ENDOWMENT INT. PEACE.,"POLITICAL QUESTIONS (ISSUES BEFORE THE NINETEENTH GENERAL ASSEMBLY)." SPACE WOR+45 CONSTN FINAN NAT/G CONSULT DELIB/GP FORCES LEGIS TEC/DEV EDU/PROP LEGIT ARMS/CONT COERCE NUC/PWR ATTIT ALL/VALS...CONCPT OBS UN COLD/WAR 20. PAGE 11 G0208
INT/ORG PEACE
L64

BAILEY S.K.,AMERICAN POLITICS AND GOVERNMENT. USA+45 CONSTN FINAN LABOR POL/PAR DIPLOM ADMIN WAR INGP/REL RACE/REL NEW/LIB 20 SUPREME/CT PRESIDENT CONGRESS. PAGE 4 G0084
ANTHOL LEGIS PWR
B65

FOX A.B.,"NATO AND CONGRESS." CONSTN DELIB/GP EX/STRUC FORCES TOP/EX BUDGET NUC/PWR GOV/REL ...GP/COMP CONGRESS NATO TREATY. PAGE 20 G0388
CONTROL DIPLOM
S65

DUNBAR L.W.,A REPUBLIC OF EQUALS. USA+45 CREATE ADJUD PEACE NEW/LIB...POLICY 20 SOUTH/US CIV/RIGHTS. PAGE 16 G0320
LAW CONSTN FEDERAL RACE/REL
B66

BUTLER J.,BOSTON UNIVERSITY PAPERS ON AFRICA* TRANSITION IN AFRICAN POLITICS. AFR LAW CONSTN LABOR POL/PAR TEC/DEV 20. PAGE 10 G0197
IDEA/COMP NAT/G PWR
B67

MCDOUGAL M.S.,THE INTERPRETATION OF AGREEMENTS AND WORLD PUBLIC ORDER: PRINCIPLES OF CONTENT AND PROCEDURE. WOR+45 CONSTN PROB/SOLV TEC/DEV ...CON/ANAL TREATY. PAGE 37 G0740
INT/LAW STRUCT ECO/UNDEV DIPLOM
B67

UNIVERSAL REFERENCE SYSTEM,LEGISLATIVE PROCESS, REPRESENTATION, AND DECISION-MAKING (VOLUME II). WOR+45 WOR-45 CONSTN LOC/G NAT/G...POLICY CON/ANAL COMPUT/IR GEN/METH. PAGE 56 G1094
BIBLIOG/A LEGIS REPRESENT DECISION
B67

UNIVERSAL REFERENCE SYSTEM,LAW, JURISPRUDENCE, AND JUDICIAL PROCESS (VOLUME VII). WOR+45 WOR-45 CONSTN NAT/G LEGIS JUDGE CT/SYS...INT/LAW COMPUT/IR GEN/METH METH. PAGE 56 G1101
BIBLIOG/A LAW JURID ADJUD
B67

TIVEY L.,"THE POLITICAL CONSEQUENCES OF ECONOMIC PLANNING." UK CONSTN INDUS ACT/RES ADMIN CONTROL LOBBY REPRESENT EFFICIENCY SUPEGO SOVEREIGN ...DECISION 20. PAGE 55 G1074
PLAN POLICY NAT/G
S67

US SENATE COMM ON FOREIGN REL,SURVEY OF THE
ALLIANCE FOR PROGRESS; THE POLITICAL ASPECTS
(PAMPHLET). CONSTN SOCIETY ECO/UNDEV INT/ORG
TEC/DEV DIPLOM...CENSUS 20. PAGE 60 G1186
N67 L/A+17C POLICY PROB/SOLV

CONSTN/CNV....CONSTITUTIONAL CONVENTION

CONSTRUC....CONSTRUCTION INDUSTRY

KAUFMAN J.L.,COMMUNITY RENEWAL PROGRAMS (PAMPHLET).
USA+45 CONSTRUC PROVS CREATE PLAN CONTROL WEALTH 20
URBAN/RNWL. PAGE 30 G0584
N19 LOC/G MUNIC ACT/RES BIBLIOG

MAASS A.,MUDDY WATERS: THE ARMY ENGINEERS AND THE
NATIONS RIVERS. USA-45 PROF/ORG CONSULT LEGIS ADMIN
EXEC ROLE PWR...SOC PRESIDENT 20. PAGE 35 G0682
B51 FORCES GP/REL LOBBY CONSTRUC

US CONGRESS JT ATOM ENRGY COMM,PROPOSED AMENDMENT
TO SECTION 271 OF THE ATOMIC ENERGY ACT OF 1954.
USA+45 CONSTRUC PLAN INSPECT CONTROL CT/SYS 20
CONGRESS AEC. PAGE 57 G1115
B65 LAW LEGIS DELIB/GP NUC/PWR

US DEPARTMENT OF ARMY,MILITARY PROTECTIVE
CONSTRUCTION: NUCLEAR WARFARE AND CHEMICAL AND
BIOLOGICAL OPERATIONS (MANUAL). OP/RES TEC/DEV RISK
COERCE NUC/PWR WAR WEAPON EFFICIENCY UTIL BIO/SOC
HABITAT ORD/FREE 20. PAGE 57 G1117
B65 FORCES CONSTRUC TASK HEALTH

TENDLER J.D.,"TECHNOLOGY AND ECONOMIC DEVELOPMENT*
THE CASE OF HYDRO VS THERMAL POWER." CONSTRUC
DIST/IND CREATE TEC/DEV INT/TRADE CENTRAL PWR SKILL
WEALTH...MGT NAT/COMP ARGEN. PAGE 54 G1063
S65 BRAZIL INDUS ECO/UNDEV

CONSTRUCTION INDUSTRY....SEE CONSTRUC

CONSULT....CONSULTANTS

AMERICAN DOCUMENTATION INST,AMERICAN DOCUMENTATION.
PROF/ORG CONSULT PLAN PERCEPT...MATH STAT AUD/VIS
CHARTS METH/COMP INDEX METH 20. PAGE 3 G0050
N BIBLIOG TEC/DEV COM/IND COMPUT/IR

GINZBERG E.,MANPOWER FOR GOVERNMENT (PAMPHLET).
USA+45 FORCES PLAN PROB/SOLV PAY EDU/PROP ADMIN
GP/REL COST...MGT PREDICT TREND 20 CIVIL/SERV.
PAGE 21 G0418
N19 WORKER CONSULT NAT/G LOC/G

WHITE L.D.,CIVIL SERVICE IN WARTIME. CONSULT
DELIB/GP PARTIC WAR CHOOSE. PAGE 63 G1233
B45 REPRESENT ADMIN INTELL NAT/G

WHITE L.D.,"CONGRESSIONAL CONTROL OF THE PUBLIC
SERVICE." USA-45 NAT/G CONSULT DELIB/GP PLAN SENIOR
CONGRESS. PAGE 63 G1232
S45 LEGIS EXEC POLICY CONTROL

BUSH V.,ENDLESS HORIZONS. FUT USA+45 INTELL NAT/G
CONSULT ACT/RES CREATE PLAN EDU/PROP DRIVE
...MAJORIT HEAL MGT PHIL/SCI CONCPT OBS TREND
GEN/METH TOT/POP 20. PAGE 10 G0196
B46 R+D KNOWL PEACE

COCH L.,"OVERCOMING RESISTANCE TO CHANGE" (BMR)"
USA+45 CONSULT ADMIN ROUTINE GP/REL EFFICIENCY
PRODUC PERCEPT SKILL...CHARTS SOC/EXP 20. PAGE 12
G0236
S48 WORKER OP/RES PROC/MFG RIGID/FLEX

KAPLAN A.,"THE PREDICTION OF SOCIAL AND
TECHNOLOGICAL EVENTS." VOL/ASSN CONSULT ACT/RES
CREATE OP/RES PLAN ROUTINE PERSON...POLICY
METH/CNCPT STAT QU/SEMANT SYS/QU TESTS CENSUS TREND
20. PAGE 29 G0574
S50 PWR KNO/TEST

CONANT J.B.,SCIENCE AND COMMON SENSE. WOR+45 WOR-45 CREATE
R+D SCHOOL CONSULT TEC/DEV EDU/PROP SKILL...PLURIST PHIL/SCI
METH/CNCPT RECORD TIME/SEQ SIMUL GEN/METH METH.
PAGE 13 G0248
B51

MAASS A.,MUDDY WATERS: THE ARMY ENGINEERS AND THE
B51 FORCES

NATIONS RIVERS. USA-45 PROF/ORG CONSULT LEGIS ADMIN
EXEC ROLE PWR...SOC PRESIDENT 20. PAGE 35 G0682
GP/REL LOBBY CONSTRUC

LERNER D.,"THE POLICY SCIENCES: RECENT DEVELOPMENTS
IN SCOPE AND METHODS." R+D SERV/IND CREATE DIPLOM
ROUTINE PWR...METH/CNCPT TREND GEN/LAWS METH 20.
PAGE 33 G0658
S51 CONSULT SOC

CURRENT TRENDS IN PSYCHOLOGY,PSYCHOLOGY IN THE
WORLD EMERGENCY. USA+45 CONSULT FORCES ACT/RES PLAN
SKILL...DECISION OBS APT/TEST KNO/TEST PERS/TEST
TREND CHARTS 20. PAGE 14 G0266
B52 NAT/G PSY

DAY E.E.,EDUCATION FOR FREEDOM AND RESPONSIBILITY.
FUT USA+45 CULTURE CONSULT EDU/PROP ATTIT SKILL
...MGT CONCPT OBS GEN/LAWS COLD/WAR 20. PAGE 14
G0282
B52 SCHOOL KNOWL

LASSWELL H.D.,"RESEARCH IN POLITICAL BEHAVIOR."
LOC/G MUNIC POL/PAR CONSULT ADMIN PARTIC...CHARTS
ANTHOL BIBLIOG/A 20. PAGE 32 G0641
L52 PHIL/SCI METH R+D

SIMMONS L.W.,SOCIAL SCIENCE IN MEDICINE. USA+45
USA-45 SOCIETY CONSULT PLAN PROB/SOLV CONTROL
PERS/REL...POLICY HEAL TREND BIBLIOG 20. PAGE 51
G0999
B54 PUB/INST HABITAT HEALTH BIO/SOC

OPLER M.E.,"SOCIAL ASPECTS OF TECHNICAL ASSISTANCE
IN OPERATION." WOR+45 VOL/ASSN CREATE PLAN TEC/DEV
EDU/PROP ALL/VALS...METH/CNCPT OBS RECORD TREND UN
20. PAGE 43 G0841
L54 INT/ORG CONSULT FOR/AID

US DEPARTMENT OF THE ARMY,RESEARCH AND DEVELOPMENT
(AND RELATED ASPECTS) IN FOREIGN COUNTRIES. WOR+45
DIST/IND INDUS CONSULT FORCES CREATE EDU/PROP
AUTOMAT DETER WEAPON. PAGE 57 G1126
B56 BIBLIOG/A R+D TEC/DEV NUC/PWR

GORDON L.,"THE ORGANIZATION FOR EUROPEAN ECONOMIC
COOPERATION." EUR+WWI INDUS INT/ORG NAT/G CONSULT
DELIB/GP ACT/RES CREATE PLAN TEC/DEV EDU/PROP LEGIT
WEALTH OEEC 20. PAGE 22 G0435
S56 VOL/ASSN ECO/DEV

FISHMAN B.G.,"PUBLIC POLICY AND POLITICAL
CONSIDERATIONS." USA+45 SOCIETY NAT/G ACT/RES
CREATE PLAN DIPLOM KNOWL ORD/FREE...CONCPT GEN/METH
20. PAGE 19 G0370
S57 ECO/DEV CONSULT

CROWE S.,THE LANDSCAPE OF POWER. UK CULTURE
SERV/IND NAT/G CONSULT PARTIC NUC/PWR LEISURE...SOC
EXHIBIT 20. PAGE 14 G0264
B58 HABITAT TEC/DEV PLAN CONTROL

GANGE J.,UNIVERSITY RESEARCH ON INTERNATIONAL
AFFAIRS. USA+45 ACADEM INT/ORG CONSULT CREATE EXEC
ROUTINE...QUANT STAT INT STERTYP GEN/METH TOT/POP
VAL/FREE 20. PAGE 21 G0407
B58 R+D MGT DIPLOM

JUNGK R.,BRIGHTER THAN A THOUSAND SUNS: THE MORAL
AND POLITICAL HISTORY OF THE ATOMIC SCIENTISTS.
WOR+45 WOR-45 CONSULT CREATE RISK UTIL DRIVE
PERCEPT PWR...INT 20. PAGE 29 G0568
B58 NUC/PWR MORAL GOV/REL PERSON

MCDOUGAL M.S.,"PERSPECTIVES FOR A LAW OF OUTER
SPACE." FUT WOR+45 AIR CONSULT DELIB/GP TEC/DEV
CT/SYS ORD/FREE...POLICY JURID 20 UN. PAGE 37 G0736
S58 INT/ORG SPACE INT/LAW

GREENFIELD K.R.,COMMAND DECISIONS. ASIA EUR+WWI
S/ASIA USA+45 WOR-45 NAT/G CONSULT DELIB/GP COERCE
NUC/PWR PWR...OBS 20 CHINJAP. PAGE 23 G0446
B59 PLAN FORCES WAR WEAPON

MODELSKI G.,ATOMIC ENERGY IN THE COMMUNIST BLOC.
FUT INT/ORG CONSULT FORCES ACT/RES PLAN KNOWL SKILL
...PHIL/SCI STAT CHARTS 20. PAGE 39 G0777
B59 TEC/DEV NUC/PWR USSR COM

POKROVSKY G.I.,SCIENCE AND TECHNOLOGY IN
CONTEMPORARY WAR. SPACE USSR WOR+45 NAT/G CONSULT
ACT/RES PLAN DETER WEAPON...MARXIST METH/CNCPT
B59 TEC/DEV FORCES NUC/PWR

CHARTS STERTYP COLD/WAR 20. PAGE 45 G0881   WAR

B59
STANFORD RESEARCH INSTITUTE,POSSIBLE NONMILITARY   R+D
SCIENTIFIC DEVELOPMENTS AND THEIR POTENTIAL IMPACT   TEC/DEV
ON FOREIGN POLICY PROBLEMS OF THE UNITED. FUT
USA+45 INT/ORG PROF/ORG CONSULT ACT/RES CREATE PLAN
PEACE KNOWL SKILL...TECHNIC PHIL/SCI NEW/IDEA
UNESCO 20. PAGE 52 G1032

B59
US CONGRESS JT ATOM ENRGY COMM,SELECTED MATERIALS   NAT/G
ON FEDERAL-STATE COOPERATION IN THE ATOMIC ENERGY   NUC/PWR
FIELD. USA+45 LAW LOC/G PROVS CONSULT LEGIS ADJUD   GOV/REL
...POLICY BIBLIOG 20 AEC. PAGE 57 G1111   DELIB/GP

L59
MCDOUGAL M.S.,"THE IDENTIFICATION AND APPRAISAL OF   INT/LAW
DIVERSE SYSTEMS OF PUBLIC ORDER (BMR)" WOR+45 NAT/G   DIPLOM
CONSULT EDU/PROP POLICY. PAGE 37 G0737   ALL/IDEOS

S59
LEFTON M.,"DECISION MAKING IN A MENTAL HOSPITAL: ACT/RES
REAL, PERCEIVED, AND IDEAL." R+D PUB/INST CONSULT   PROB/SOLV
CONFER INGP/REL PERCEPT...MODAL 20. PAGE 33 G0653   DECISION
                                                          PSY

B60
ARMS CONTROL. FUT UNIV WOR+45 INTELL R+D INT/ORG   DELIB/GP
NAT/G VOL/ASSN CONSULT CREATE EDU/PROP PEACE...HUM   ORD/FREE
GEN/LAWS TOT/POP 20. PAGE 1 G0015   ARMS/CONT
                                                          NUC/PWR

B60
APTHEKER H.,DISARMAMENT AND THE AMERICAN ECONOMY: A   MARXIST
SYMPOSIUM. FUT USA+45 ECO/DEV DIST/IND INDUS   ARMS/CONT
PROC/MFG LABOR NAT/G POL/PAR CONSULT PLAN CAP/ISM
INT/TRADE PEACE ATTIT MORAL WEALTH...TREND GEN/LAWS
TOT/POP 20. PAGE 3 G0063

B60
PENTONY D.E.,THE UNDERDEVELOPED LANDS. FUT WOR+45   ECO/UNDEV
CULTURE AGRI FINAN INDUS MARKET INT/ORG LABOR NAT/G   POLICY
VOL/ASSN CONSULT PLAN TEC/DEV ECO/TAC EDU/PROP COLONIAL   FOR/AID
ATTIT WEALTH...OBS RECORD SAMP TREND GEN/METH WORK   INT/TRADE
UN 20. PAGE 44 G0867

B60
WOETZEL R.K.,THE INTERNATIONAL CONTROL OF AIRSPACE   INT/ORG
AND OUTERSPACE. FUT WOR+45 AIR CONSTN STRUC   JURID
CONSULT PLAN TEC/DEV ADJUD RIGID/FLEX KNOWL   SPACE
ORD/FREE PWR...TECHNIC GEOG MGT NEW/IDEA TREND   INT/LAW
COMPUT/IR VAL/FREE 20 TREATY. PAGE 64 G1251

L60
BRENNAN D.G.,"SETTING AND GOALS OF ARMS CONTROL."   FORCES
FUT USA+45 USSR WOR+45 INTELL INT/ORG NAT/G   COERCE
VOL/ASSN CONSULT PLAN DIPLOM ECO/TAC ADMIN KNOWL   ARMS/CONT
PWR...POLICY CONCPT TREND COLD/WAR 20. PAGE 8 G0164   DETER

L60
HOLTON G.,"ARMS CONTROL." FUT WOR+45 CULTURE   ACT/RES
INT/ORG NAT/G FORCES TOP/EX PLAN EDU/PROP COERCE   CONSULT
ATTIT RIGID/FLEX ORD/FREE...POLICY PHIL/SCI SOC   ARMS/CONT
TREND COLD/WAR. PAGE 27 G0524   NUC/PWR

S60
BECKER A.S.,"COMPARISIONS OF UNITED STATES AND USSR   STAT
NATIONAL OUTPUT: SOME RULES OF THE GAME." COM   USSR
USA+45 ECO/DEV AGRI DIST/IND INDUS R+D CONSULT PLAN
ECO/TAC RIGID/FLEX KNOWL...METH/CNCPT CHARTS 20.
PAGE 6 G0113

S60
HUTCHINSON C.E.,"AN INSTITUTE FOR NATIONAL SECURITY   POLICY
AFFAIRS." USA+45 R+D NAT/G CONSULT TOP/EX ACT/RES   METH/CNCPT
CREATE PLAN TEC/DEV EDU/PROP ROUTINE NUC/PWR ATTIT   ELITES
ORD/FREE PWR...DECISION MGT PHIL/SCI CONCPT RECORD   DIPLOM
GEN/LAWS GEN/METH 20. PAGE 27 G0539

S60
KAPLAN M.A.,"THEORETICAL ANALYSIS OF THE BALANCE OF   CREATE
POWER." FUT USA+45 WOR+45 INTELL ECO/DEV INT/ORG   NEW/IDEA
NAT/G CONSULT TOP/EX ACT/RES PLAN TEC/DEV ATTIT   DIPLOM
ALL/VALS...METH/CNCPT TOT/POP 20. PAGE 29 G0576   NUC/PWR

S60
SANDERS R.,"NUCLEAR DYNAMITE: A NEW DIMENSION IN   INDUS
FOREIGN POLICY." FUT WOR+45 ECO/DEV CONSULT TEC/DEV   PWR
PERCEPT...CONT/OBS TIME/SEQ TREND GEN/LAWS TOT/POP   DIPLOM
20 TREATY. PAGE 49 G0955   NUC/PWR

S60
SWIFT R.,"THE UNITED NATIONS AND ITS PUBLIC."   INT/ORG
WOR+45 CONSTN FINAN CONSULT DELIB/GP ACT/RES ADMIN   EDU/PROP
ROUTINE RIGID/FLEX SKILL UN 20. PAGE 53 G1048

S60
TAYLOR M.G.,"THE ROLE OF THE MEDICAL PROFESSION IN   PROF/ORG
THE FORMULATION AND EXECUTION OF PUBLIC POLICY"   HEALTH
(BMR)" CANADA NAT/G CONSULT ADMIN REPRESENT GP/REL   LOBBY
ROLE SOVEREIGN...DECISION 20 CMA. PAGE 54 G1058   POLICY

B61
HELLER D.,THE KENNEDY CABINET--AMERICA'S MEN OF   EX/STRUC
DESTINY. NAT/G CHIEF CONSULT ADMIN CONTROL GOV/REL   CONFER
...MGT 20 DEPT/LABOR DEPT/STATE DEPT/JUST   DELIB/GP
DEPT/DEFEN KENNEDY/J. PAGE 26 G0504   TOP/EX

B61
KAHN H.,ON THERMONUCLEAR WAR. FUT UNIV WOR+45   DETER
ECO/DEV CONSULT EX/STRUC TOP/EX ACT/RES CREATE PLAN   NUC/PWR
COERCE WAR PERSON ALL/VALS...POLICY GEOG CONCPT   SOCIETY
METH/CNCPT OBS TREND 20. PAGE 29 G0569

B61
LAHAYE R.,LES ENTREPRISES PUBLIQUES AU MAROC.   NAT/G
FRANCE MOROCCO LAW DIST/IND EXTR/IND FINAN CONSULT   INDUS
PLAN TEC/DEV ADMIN AGREE CONTROL OWN...POLICY 20.   ECO/UNDEV
PAGE 32 G0629   ECO/TAC

B61
RAMO S.,PEACETIME USES OF OUTER SPACE. FUT DIST/IND   PEACE
INT/ORG CONSULT NUC/PWR...AUD/VIS ANTHOL 20.   TEC/DEV
PAGE 46 G0898   SPACE
                                                          CREATE

B61
SMITH H.H.,THE CITIZEN'S GUIDE TO PLANNING. USA+45   MUNIC
LAW SCHOOL CREATE PROB/SOLV EDU/PROP GP/REL ROLE 20   PLAN
URBAN/RNWL OPEN/SPACE. PAGE 52 G1015   DELIB/GP
                                                          CONSULT

L61
HERRING P.,"RESEARCH FOR PUBLIC POLICY: BROOKINGS   R+D
DEDICATION LECTURES." USA+45 CONSULT DELIB/GP   ACT/RES
ROUTINE PERCEPT SKILL...MGT 20. PAGE 26 G0508   DIPLOM

S61
DYKMAN J.W.,"REVIEW ARTICLE* PLANNING AND DECISION   DECISION
THEORY." ELITES LOC/G MUNIC CONSULT ADMIN...POLICY   PLAN
MGT. PAGE 17 G0327   RATIONAL

S61
MORGENSTERN O.,"THE N-COUNTRY PROBLEM." EUR+WWI   FUT
UNIV USA+45 WOR+45 SOCIETY CONSULT TOP/EX ACT/RES   BAL/PWR
PLAN EDU/PROP ATTIT DRIVE...POLICY OBS TREND   NUC/PWR
TOT/POP 20. PAGE 40 G0781   TEC/DEV

S61
SCHILLING W.R.,"THE H-BOMB: HOW TO DECIDE WITHOUT   PERSON
ACTUALLY CHOOSING." FUT USA+45 INTELL CONSULT ADMIN   LEGIT
CT/SYS MORAL...JURID OBS 20 TRUMAN/HS. PAGE 49   NUC/PWR
G0966

B62
FERBER R.,RESEARCH METHODS IN ECONOMICS AND   ACT/RES
BUSINESS. ECO/DEV FINAN MARKET LG/CO SML/CO CONSULT   PROB/SOLV
CONTROL COST...STAT METH/COMP 20. PAGE 19 G0364   ECO/TAC
                                                          MGT

B62
FORBES H.W.,THE STRATEGY OF DISARMAMENT. FUT WOR+45   PLAN
INT/ORG VOL/ASSN CONSULT ARMS/CONT COERCE NUC/PWR   FORCES
WAR DRIVE RIGID/FLEX ORD/FREE PWR...POLICY CONCPT   DIPLOM
OBS TREND STERTYP 20. PAGE 19 G0378

B62
GILPIN R.,AMERICAN SCIENTISTS AND NUCLEAR WEAPONS   INTELL
POLICY. COM FUT USA+45 WOR+45 INT/ORG NAT/G   ATTIT
PROF/ORG CONSULT FORCES CREATE TEC/DEV BAL/PWR   DETER
EDU/PROP ARMS/CONT WAR PERCEPT KNOWL MORAL PWR   NUC/PWR
...PHIL/SCI SOC CONCPT GEN/LAWS 20. PAGE 21 G0417

B62
KAHN H.,THINKING ABOUT THE UNTHINKABLE. FUT USA+45   INT/ORG
LAW NAT/G CONSULT FORCES ACT/RES CREATE PLAN   ORD/FREE
TEC/DEV BAL/PWR DIPLOM EDU/PROP ARMS/CONT DETER   NUC/PWR
ATTIT...CONCPT OBS TREND COLD/WAR 20. PAGE 29 G0570   PEACE

B62
NEW ZEALAND COMM OF ST SERVICE,THE STATE SERVICES   ADMIN
IN NEW ZEALAND. NEW/ZEALND CONSULT EX/STRUC ACT/RES   WORKER
...BIBLIOG 20. PAGE 42 G0818   TEC/DEV
                                                          NAT/G

B62
OSGOOD C.E.,AN ALTERNATIVE TO WAR OR SURRENDER. FUT   ORD/FREE
UNIV CULTURE INTELL SOCIETY R+D INT/ORG CONSULT   EDU/PROP
DELIB/GP ACT/RES PLAN CHOOSE ATTIT PERCEPT KNOWL   PEACE
...PHIL/SCI PSY SOC TREND GEN/LAWS 20. PAGE 43   WAR
G0849

SCHILLING W.R.,STRATEGY, POLITICS, AND DEFENSE **B62** ROUTINE
BUDGETS. USA+45 R+D NAT/G CONSULT DELIB/GP FORCES POLICY
LEGIS ACT/RES PLAN BAL/PWR LEGIT EXEC NUC/PWR
RIGID/FLEX PWR...TREND COLD/WAR CONGRESS 20
EISNHWR/DD. PAGE 49 G0968

SCHWARTZ L.E.,INTERNATIONAL ORGANIZATIONS AND SPACE **B62** INT/ORG
COOPERATION. VOL/ASSN CONSULT CREATE TEC/DEV DIPLOM
SANCTION...POLICY INT/LAW PHIL/SCI 20 UN. PAGE 50 R+D
G0982 SPACE

STRAUSS L.L.,MEN AND DECISIONS. USA+45 USA-45 USSR **B62** DECISION
CONSULT FORCES TOP/EX WAR PEACE 20. PAGE 53 G1042 PWR
NUC/PWR
DIPLOM

THANT U.,THE UNITED NATIONS' DEVELOPMENT DECADE: **B62** INT/ORG
PROPOSALS FOR ACTION. WOR+45 SOCIETY ECO/UNDEV AGRI ALL/VALS
COM/IND FINAN R+D MUNIC SCHOOL VOL/ASSN CONSULT
PLAN TEC/DEV ECO/TAC EDU/PROP ADMIN ROUTINE
RIGID/FLEX...MGT SOC CONCPT UNESCO UN TOT/POP
VAL/FREE. PAGE 54 G1064

THOMSON G.P.,NUCLEAR ENERGY IN BRITAIN DURING THE **B62** CREATE
LAST WAR: THE CHERWELL SIMON LECTURE (MONOGRAPH). TEC/DEV
UK R+D CONSULT FORCES PLAN DIPLOM TASK CIVMIL/REL WAR
ROLE...PHIL/SCI NEW/IDEA LAB/EXP 20 MAUD. PAGE 54 NUC/PWR
G1071

WRIGHT Q.,PREVENTING WORLD WAR THREE. FUT WOR+45 **B62** CREATE
CULTURE INT/ORG NAT/G CONSULT FORCES ADMIN ATTIT
ARMS/CONT DRIVE RIGID/FLEX ORD/FREE SOVEREIGN
...POLICY CONCPT TREND STERTYP COLD/WAR 20. PAGE 64
G1259

FOSTER W.C.,"ARMS CONTROL AND DISARMAMENT IN A **S62** DELIB/GP
DIVIDED WORLD." COM FUT USA+45 USSR WOR+45 INTELL POLICY
INT/ORG NAT/G VOL/ASSN CONSULT CREATE PLAN TEC/DEV ARMS/CONT
EDU/PROP LEGIT NUC/PWR ATTIT RIGID/FLEX...CONCPT DIPLOM
TREND TOT/POP 20 UN. PAGE 20 G0387

SCHILLING W.R.,"SCIENTISTS, FOREIGN POLICY AND **S62** NAT/G
POLITICS." WOR+45 WOR-45 INTELL INT/ORG CONSULT TEC/DEV
TOP/EX ACT/RES PLAN ADMIN KNOWL...CONCPT OBS TREND DIPLOM
LEAGUE/NAT 20. PAGE 49 G0967 NUC/PWR

SINGER J.D.,"STABLE DETERRENCE AND ITS LIMITS." FUT **S62** NAT/G
WOR+45 R+D INT/ORG CONSULT ACT/RES TEC/DEV FORCES
ARMS/CONT COERCE DRIVE PERCEPT RIGID/FLEX ORD/FREE DETER
PWR...MYTH SIMUL TOT/POP 20. PAGE 51 G1004 NUC/PWR

MAYNE R.,THE COMMUNITY OF EUROPE. UK CONSTN NAT/G **B63** EUR+WWI
CONSULT DELIB/GP CREATE PLAN ECO/TAC LEGIT ADMIN INT/ORG
ROUTINE ORD/FREE PWR WEALTH...CONCPT TIME/SEQ EEC REGION
EURATOM 20. PAGE 37 G0724

US ATOMIC ENERGY COMMISSION,ATOMIC ENERGY IN THE **B63** METH/COMP
SOVIET UNION: TRIP REPORT OF THE US ATOMIC ENERGY OP/RES
DELEGATION, MAY 1933. USSR R+D NAT/G CONSULT CREATE TEC/DEV
DIPLOM ADMIN ROUTINE EFFICIENCY PRODUC KNOWL SKILL NUC/PWR
...NAT/COMP 20 AEC TRAVEL TREATY. PAGE 56 G1107

BOULDING K.E.,"UNIVERSITY, SOCIETY, AND ARMS **S63** SOCIETY
CONTROL." WOR+45 WOR-45 ACADEM VOL/ASSN CONSULT FORCES ARMS/CONT
ACT/RES PLAN TEC/DEV BAL/PWR ECO/TAC COERCE DETER
WAR ATTIT RIGID/FLEX KNOWL ORD/FREE PWR WEALTH
...CONCPT COLD/WAR TOT/POP 20. PAGE 8 G0159

GARDNER R.N.,"COOPERATION IN OUTER SPACE." FUT USSR **S63** INT/ORG
WOR+45 AIR LAW COM/IND CONSULT DELIB/GP CREATE ACT/RES
KNOWL 20 TREATY. PAGE 21 G0410 PEACE
SPACE

WOHLSTETTER A.,"SCIENTISTS, SEERS AND STRATEGY." **S63** INTELL
USA+45 ELITES R+D NAT/G CONSULT FORCES TOP/EX ACT/RES
EDU/PROP ARMS/CONT KNOWL ORD/FREE...DECISION MYTH
20. PAGE 64 G1253

GRODZINS M.,THE ATOMIC AGE: FORTY-FIVE SCIENTISTS **B64** INTELL
AND SCHOLARS SPEAK ON NATIONAL AND WORLD AFFAIRS. ARMS/CONT

FUT USA+45 WOR+45 R+D INT/ORG NAT/G CONSULT TEC/DEV NUC/PWR
EDU/PROP ATTIT PERSON ORD/FREE...HUM CONCPT
TIME/SEQ CON/ANAL. PAGE 23 G0454

PEDERSEN E.S.,NUCLEAR ENERGY IN SPACE. FUT INTELL **B64** SPACE
R+D CONSULT...NEW/IDEA CHARTS METH T 20. PAGE 44 TEC/DEV
G0864 NUC/PWR
LAB/EXP

RANSOM H.H.,CAN AMERICAN DEMOCRACY SURVIVE COLD **B64** USA+45
WAR. USA-45 CONSTN NAT/G CONSULT DELIB/GP LEGIS ROUTINE
ACT/RES LEGIT EXEC ATTIT KNOWL ORD/FREE PWR SKILL
...POLICY TIME/SEQ TREND GEN/LAWS 20 COLD/WAR.
PAGE 46 G0901

CARNEGIE ENDOWMENT INT. PEACE,"POLITICAL QUESTIONS **L64** INT/ORG
(ISSUES BEFORE THE NINETEENTH GENERAL ASSEMBLY)." PEACE
SPACE WOR+45 CONSTN FINAN NAT/G CONSULT DELIB/GP
FORCES LEGIS TEC/DEV EDU/PROP LEGIT ARMS/CONT
COERCE NUC/PWR ATTIT ALL/VALS...CONCPT OBS UN
COLD/WAR 20. PAGE 11 G0208

BYRNES F.C.,"ASSIGNMENT TO AMBIGUITY: WORK **S64** INTELL
PERFORMANCE IN CROSSCULTURAL TECHNICAL ASSISTANCE." QU
USA+45 WOR+45 PROF/ORG CONSULT PLAN EDU/PROP ATTIT
DISPL PERCEPT PERSON ALL/VALS...POLICY INT CHARTS
NATO 20. PAGE 10 G0199

CALDWELL L.K.,"BIOPOLITICS: SCIENCE, ETHICS, AND **S64** TEC/DEV
PUBLIC POLICY." FUT USA+45 WOR+45 INTELL STRATA R+D POLICY
NAT/G CONSULT PLAN EDU/PROP ALL/VALS...RELATIV
PHIL/SCI 20. PAGE 10 G0203

NEEDHAM T.,"SCIENCE AND SOCIETY IN EAST AND WEST." **S64** ASIA
INTELL STRATA R+D LOC/G NAT/G PROVS CONSULT ACT/RES STRUCT
CREATE PLAN TEC/DEV EDU/PROP ADMIN ATTIT ALL/VALS
...POLICY RELATIV MGT CONCPT NEW/IDEA TIME/SEQ WORK
WORK. PAGE 41 G0815

BOBROW D.B.,COMPONENTS OF DEFENSE POLICY. ASIA **B65** DETER
EUR+WWI USA+45 WOR+45 INTELL INT/ORG NAT/G PROF/ORG NUC/PWR
CONSULT LEGIS ACT/RES CREATE ARMS/CONT COERCE PLAN
ORD/FREE...DECISION SIMUL. PAGE 7 G0145 FORCES

CHENG C.-Y.,SCIENTIFIC AND ENGINEERING MANPOWER IN **B65** WORKER
COMMUNIST CHINA, 1949-1963. CHINA/COM USSR ELITES CONSULT
ECO/DEV R+D ACADEM LABOR NAT/G EDU/PROP CONTROL MARXISM
UTIL...POLICY BIBLIOG 20. PAGE 12 G0226 BIOG

INTERNATIONAL CITY MGRS ASSN,COUNCIL-MANAGER **B65** BIBLIOG/A
GOVERNMENT, 1940-64: AN ANNOTATED BIBLIOGRAPHY. MUNIC
USA+45 ADMIN GOV/REL ROLE...MGT 20. PAGE 28 G0549 CONSULT
PLAN

KENT A.,SPECIALIZED INFORMATION CENTERS. INTELL R+D **B65** COMPUT/IR
VOL/ASSN CONSULT COMPUTER KNOWL...DECISION HUM CREATE
PHIL/SCI METH/CNCPT TREND CHARTS 20. PAGE 30 G0593 TEC/DEV
METH/COMP

SMITH E.A.,SOCIAL WELFARE: PRINCIPLES AND CONCEPTS. **B65** CONCPT
STRATA STRUCT CONSULT WORKER ACT/RES CREATE PLAN SOC/WK
TEC/DEV ROUTINE GP/REL UTOPIA...SOC 20. PAGE 51 RECEIVE
G1014 ORD/FREE

US SENATE COMM AERO SPACE SCI,NATIONAL SPACE GOALS **B65** SPACE
FOR THE POST-APOLLO PERIOD. USA+45 CONSULT DELIB/GP FUT
TEC/DEV BUDGET GP/REL ATTIT...CHARTS IDEA/COMP TIME R+D
20 DEPT/DEFEN NASA CONGRESS. PAGE 59 G1166 LEGIS

US SENATE COMM AERO SPACE SCI,INTERNATIONAL **B65** DIPLOM
COOPERATION AND ORGANIZATION FOR OUTER SPACE. FUT SPACE
USA+45 WOR+45 PROF/ORG VOL/ASSN CONSULT DELIB/GP R+D
PLAN TEC/DEV ARMS/CONT GP/REL PEACE 20 UN NASA. NAT/G
PAGE 59 G1167

ALEXANDER Y.,INTERNATIONAL TECHNICAL ASSISTANCE **B66** ECO/TAC
EXPERTS* A CASE STUDY OF THE U.N. EXPERIENCE. INT/ORG
ECO/UNDEV CONSULT EX/STRUC CREATE PLAN DIPLOM ADMIN
FOR/AID TASK EFFICIENCY...ORG/CHARTS UN. PAGE 2 MGT
G0038

ALEXANDER Y.,INTERNATIONAL TECHNICAL ASSISTANCE   SKILL
EXPERTS: A CASE STUDY OF THE U.N. EXPERIENCE.   INT/ORG
USA+45 WOR+45 WORKER CREATE PLAN PROB/SOLV ECO/TAC   TEC/DEV
FOR/AID GIVE EDU/PROP...CHARTS BIBLIOG 20 UN.   CONSULT
PAGE 2 G0039
                                                          B66

LINDFORS G.V.,INTERCOLLEGIATE BIBLIOGRAPHY; CASES   BIBLIOG/A
IN BUSINESS ADMINISTRATION (VOL. X). FINAN MARKET   ADMIN
LABOR CONSULT PLAN GP/REL PRODUC 20. PAGE 34 G0668   MGT
                                                          OP/RES
                                                          B66

US BUREAU OF THE BUDGET,THE ADMINISTRATION OF   ACT/RES
GOVERNMENT SUPPORTED RESEARCH AT UNIVERSITIES   NAT/G
(PAMPHLET). USA+45 CONSULT TOP/EX ADMIN INCOME   ACADEM
WEALTH...MGT PHIL/SCI INT. PAGE 56 G1108   GP/REL
                                                          B66

US SENATE COMM AERO SPACE SCI,SOVIET SPACE   CONSULT
PROGRAMS, 1962-65; GOALS AND PURPOSES,   SPACE
ACHIEVEMENTS, PLANS, AND INTERNATIONAL   FUT
IMPLICATIONS. USA+45 USSR R+D FORCES PLAN EDU/PROP   DIPLOM
PRESS ADJUD ARMS/CONT ATTIT MARXISM. PAGE 60 G1168
                                                          B67

HIRSCHMAN A.O.,DEVELOPMENT PROJECTS OBSERVED. INDUS   ECO/UNDEV
INT/ORG CONSULT EX/STRUC CREATE OP/RES ECO/TAC   R+D
DEMAND...POLICY MGT METH/COMP 20 WORLD/BANK.   FINAN
PAGE 26 G0513   PLAN
                                                          B67

NELSON R.R.,TECHNOLOGY, ECONOMIC GROWTH, AND PUBLIC   R+D
POLICY. USA+45 PLAN GP/REL UTIL KNOWL...POLICY   CONSULT
PHIL/SCI CHARTS BIBLIOG 20. PAGE 41 G0817   CREATE
                                                          ACT/RES
                                                          B67

US PRES COMN LAW ENFORCE-JUS,THE CHALLENGE OF CRIME   CT/SYS
IN A FREE SOCIETY. LAW STRUCT CONSULT ACT/RES   PUB/INST
TEC/DEV INGP/REL...SOC/WK 20. PAGE 59 G1160   CRIMLGY
                                                          CRIME
                                                          B67

ZUCKERMAN S.,SCIENTISTS AND WAR. ELITES INDUS   R+D
DIPLOM CENTRAL EFFICIENCY KNOWL 20. PAGE 65 G1271   CONSULT
                                                          ACT/RES
                                                          GP/REL
                                                          S67

ATKIN J.M.,"THE FEDERAL GOVERNMENT, BIG BUSINESS,   SCHOOL
AND COLLEGES OF EDUCATION." PROF/ORG CONSULT CREATE   ACADEM
PLAN PROB/SOLV ADMIN EFFICIENCY. PAGE 4 G0075   NAT/G
                                                          INDUS
                                                          S67

BARRO S.,"ECONOMIC IMPACT OF SPACE EXPENDITURES: SPACE
SOME BROAD ISSUES DEALING WITH COSTS AND BENEFITS."   FINAN
USA+45 PROC/MFG R+D LG/CO CONSULT COST PRODUC 20.   ECO/TAC
PAGE 5 G0098   NAT/G
                                                          S67

BENN W.,"TECHNOLOGY HAS AN INEXORABLE EFFECT." FUT   R+D
UK ECO/DEV INT/ORG CONSULT PLAN EDU/PROP ADMIN LEAD   LG/CO
GP/REL PRODUC...INT 20 EEC. PAGE 6 G0119   TEC/DEV
                                                          INDUS
                                                          S67

CONWAY J.E.,"MAKING RESEARCH EFFECTIVE IN   ACT/RES
LEGISLATION." LAW R+D CONSULT EX/STRUC PLAN CONFER   POLICY
ADMIN LEAD ROUTINE TASK INGP/REL DECISION. PAGE 13   LEGIS
G0252   PROB/SOLV
                                                          S67

DE NEUFVILLE R.,"EDUCATION AT THE ACADEMIES."   FORCES
USA+45 ELITES CONSULT EX/STRUC COMPUTER PLAN   ACADEM
PROB/SOLV TASK CIVMIL/REL ORD/FREE 20. PAGE 15   TEC/DEV
G0286   SKILL
                                                          S67

EDMONDS M.,"INTERNATIONAL COLLABORATION IN WEAPONS   DIPLOM
PROCUREMENT: THE IMPLICATIONS OF THE ANGLO-FRENCH   VOL/ASSN
CASE." FRANCE UK CONSULT OP/RES PROB/SOLV TEC/DEV   BAL/PWR
CONFER CONTROL EFFICIENCY 20. PAGE 17 G0334   ARMS/CONT
                                                          S67

GOBER J.L.,"FEDERALISM AT WORK." USA+45 NAT/G   MUNIC
CONSULT ACT/RES PLAN CONFER ADMIN LEAD PARTIC   TEC/DEV
FEDERAL ATTIT. PAGE 21 G0422   R+D
                                                          GOV/REL
                                                          S67

HARRIS F.R.,"POLITICAL SCIENCE AND THE PROPOSAL FOR   PROF/ORG
A NATIONAL SOCIAL SCIENCE FOUNDATION." FUT CONSULT   R+D
DELIB/GP PLAN PROB/SOLV BUDGET CONFER SANCTION   CREATE

CRIME...POLICY SOC/WK 20 NSF NSSF. PAGE 25 G0484   NAT/G
                                                          S67

MORTON J.A.,"A SYSTEMS APPROACH TO THE INNOVATION   TEC/DEV
PROCESS: ITS USE IN THE BELL SYSTEM." USA+45 INTELL   GEN/METH
INDUS LG/CO CONSULT WORKER COMPUTER AUTOMAT DEMAND   R+D
...MGT CHARTS 20. PAGE 40 G0787   COM/IND
                                                          S67

SHARP G.,"THE NEED OF A FUNCTIONAL SUBSTITUTE FOR   PEACE
WAR." FUT UNIV WOR+45 CULTURE SOCIETY INT/ORG   WAR
CONSULT DELIB/GP ACT/RES CREATE BAL/PWR CONFER   DIPLOM
ARMS/CONT NUC/PWR 20. PAGE 50 G0989   PROB/SOLV
                                                          N67

US SENATE COMM AERO SPACE SCI,HEARINGS BEFORE THE   NAT/G
COMMITTEE ON AERONAUTICAL AND SPACE SCIENCES UNITED   DELIB/GP
STATES SENATE NINETIETH CONGRESS (PAMPHLET). USA+45   SPACE
CONSULT PLAN CONFER EFFICIENCY SENATE. PAGE 60   CREATE
G1172

CONSULTANTS....SEE CONSULT

CONSUMER....SEE MARKET

CONT/OBS....CONTROLLED DIRECT OBSERVATION
                                                          B51

LEWIN K.,FIELD THEORY IN SOCIAL SCIENCE: SELECTED   PHIL/SCI
THEORETICAL PAPERS. UNIV CREATE DRIVE PERCEPT KNOWL   HYPO/EXP
...METH/CNCPT CONT/OBS CHARTS GEN/METH METH
VAL/FREE 20. PAGE 33 G0661
                                                          B53

MACK R.T.,RAISING THE WORLDS STANDARD OF LIVING.   WOR+45
IRAN INT/ORG VOL/ASSN EX/STRUC ECO/TAC WEALTH...MGT   FOR/AID
METH/CNCPT STAT CONT/OBS INT TOT/POP VAL/FREE 20   INT/TRADE
UN. PAGE 35 G0690
                                                          B54

COMBS C.H.,DECISION PROCESSES. INTELL SOCIETY   MATH
DELIB/GP CREATE TEC/DEV DOMIN LEGIT EXEC CHOOSE   DECISION
DRIVE RIGID/FLEX KNOWL PWR...PHIL/SCI SOC
METH/CNCPT CONT/OBS REC/INT PERS/TEST SAMP/SIZ BIOG
SOC/EXP WORK. PAGE 13 G0245
                                                          S54

BATES J.,"A MODEL FOR THE SCIENCE OF DECISION."   QUANT
UNIV ROUTINE...CONT/OBS CON/ANAL HYPO/EXP GAME.   DECISION
PAGE 5 G0101   PHIL/SCI
                                                          METH/CNCPT
                                                          S60

GARFINKEL H.,"THE RATIONAL PROPERTIES OF SCIENTIFIC   CREATE
AND COMMON SENSE ACTIVITIES." SOCIETY STRATA   PHIL/SCI
ACT/RES CHOOSE...SOC METH/CNCPT NEW/IDEA CONT/OBS
SIMUL TOT/POP VAL/FREE. PAGE 21 G0412
                                                          S60

SANDERS R.,"NUCLEAR DYNAMITE: A NEW DIMENSION IN   INDUS
FOREIGN POLICY." FUT WOR+45 ECO/DEV CONSULT TEC/DEV   PWR
PERCEPT...CONT/OBS TIME/SEQ TREND GEN/LAWS TOT/POP   DIPLOM
20 TREATY. PAGE 49 G0955   NUC/PWR
                                                          B62

SOHN L.B.,ZONAL DISARMAMENT: VARIATIONS ON A THEME.   ORD/FREE
FUT WOR+45 SOCIETY ACT/RES PLAN NUC/PWR PEACE ATTIT   NEW/IDEA
...POLICY GEOG CONT/OBS HYPO/EXP 20. PAGE 52 G1020   ARMS/CONT
                                                          S62

PAULING L.,"GENETIC EFFECTS OF WEAPONS TESTS."   HEAL
WOR+45 SOCIETY FAM ACT/RES EDU/PROP AGE/C HEALTH   ARMS/CONT
ORD/FREE...GEOG STAT CONT/OBS PROJ/TEST CHARTS   NUC/PWR
TOT/POP 20. PAGE 44 G0861
                                                          B64

GROSSER G.H.,THE THREAT OF IMPENDING DISASTER: HEALTH
CONTRIBUTIONS TO THE PSYCHOLOGY OF STRESS. SPACE   PSY
UNIV SOCIETY R+D TEC/DEV EDU/PROP COERCE WAR ATTIT   NUC/PWR
BIO/SOC DISPL PERCEPT PERSON...SOC MYTH SELF/OBS
CONT/OBS BIOG CON/ANAL TOT/POP 20. PAGE 23 G0455
                                                          S64

PLATT J.R.,"RESEARCH AND DEVELOPMENT FOR SOCIAL   R+D
PROBLEMS." INTELL SOCIETY PROB/SOLV GP/REL ATTIT   ACT/RES
ALL/VALS CONT/OBS. PAGE 45 G0880   PLAN
                                                          SOC

CONTEMPT....SEE RESPECT

CONTENT ANALYSIS....SEE CON/ANAL

CONTROL....CONTROL OF HUMAN GROUP OPERATIONS
                                                          N19

FOLSOM M.B.,BETTER MANAGEMENT OF THE PUBLIC'S   ADMIN

BUSINESS (PAMPHLET). USA+45 DELIB/GP PAY CONFER
CONTROL REGION GP/REL...METH/COMP ANTHOL 20.
PAGE 19 G0377
NAT/G
MGT
PROB/SOLV

N19
KAUFMAN J.L.,COMMUNITY RENEWAL PROGRAMS (PAMPHLET).
USA+45 CONSTRUC PROVS CREATE PLAN CONTROL WEALTH 20
URBAN/RNWL. PAGE 30 G0584
LOC/G
MUNIC
ACT/RES
BIBLIOG

N19
MEZERIK AG,OUTER SPACE: UN, US, USSR (PAMPHLET).
USSR DELIB/GP FORCES DETER NUC/PWR SOVEREIGN
...POLICY 20 UN TREATY. PAGE 39 G0763
SPACE
CONTROL
DIPLOM
INT/ORG

N19
US CHAMBER OF COMMERCE,THE SIGNIFICANCE OF
CONCENTRATION RATIOS (PAMPHLET). USA+45 FINAN INDUS
ADMIN...METH/CNCPT SAMP CHARTS 20. PAGE 56 G1109
MARKET
PREDICT
LG/CO
CONTROL

N19
US SEN SPEC COMM SPACE ASTRO,SPACE LAW: A SYMPOSIUM
(PAMPHLET). USA+45 TEC/DEV CONFER CONTROL SOVEREIGN
...INT/LAW 20 SEN/SPACE. PAGE 59 G1161
SPACE
ADJUD
DIPLOM
INT/ORG

B25
MATHEWS J.M.,AMERICAN STATE GOVERNMENT. USA-45
LOC/G CHIEF EX/STRUC LEGIS ADJUD CONTROL CT/SYS
ROUTINE GOV/REL PWR 20 GOVERNOR. PAGE 37 G0721
PROVS
ADMIN
FEDERAL
CONSTN

B37
GULICK L.,PAPERS ON THE SCIENCE OF ADMINISTRATION.
INDUS PROB/SOLV TEC/DEV COST EFFICIENCY PRODUC
HABITAT...PHIL/SCI METH/COMP 20. PAGE 23 G0461
OP/RES
CONTROL
ADMIN
MGT

B44
BARKER E.,THE DEVELOPMENT OF PUBLIC SERVICES IN
WESTERN WUROPE: 1660-1930. FRANCE GERMANY UK SCHOOL
CONTROL REPRESENT ROLE...WELF/ST 17/20. PAGE 5
G0095
GOV/COMP
ADMIN
EX/STRUC

S45
WHITE L.D.,"CONGRESSIONAL CONTROL OF THE PUBLIC
SERVICE." USA-45 NAT/G CONSULT DELIB/GP PLAN SENIOR
CONGRESS. PAGE 63 G1232
LEGIS
EXEC
POLICY
CONTROL

B47
BECK H.P.,MEN WHO CONTROL OUR UNIVERSITIES.
EX/STRUC CHOOSE INGP/REL DISCRIM PERSON WEALTH
...POLICY TREND CON/ANAL CHARTS BIBLIOG. PAGE 6
G0112
EDU/PROP
ACADEM
CONTROL
LEAD

B48
WEINER N.,CYBERNETICS. SOCIETY COMPUTER ADJUST
EFFICIENCY UTIL PERCEPT...PSY MATH REGRESS TIME.
PAGE 63 G1226
FEEDBACK
AUTOMAT
CONTROL
TEC/DEV

B50
HUZAR E.,THE PURSE AND THE SWORD: CONTROL OF THE
ARMY BY CONGRESS THROUGH MILITARY APPROPRIATIONS
1933-1950. NAT/G DELIB/GP EX/STRUC FORCES PROB/SOLV
BARGAIN CONFER ADMIN ROUTINE GOV/REL EFFICIENCY
...POLICY COLD/WAR. PAGE 27 G0541
CIVMIL/REL
BUDGET
CONTROL
LEGIS

L50
MAASS A.A.,"CONGRESS AND WATER RESOURCES." LOC/G
TEC/DEV CONTROL SANCTION...WELF/ST GEOG CONGRESS.
PAGE 35 G0683
REGION
AGRI
PLAN

B53
LANGER W.L.,THE UNDECLARED WAR, 1940-1941. EUR+WWI
GERMANY USA-45 USSR AIR FORCES TEC/DEV CONFER
CONTROL COERCE PERCEPT ORD/FREE PWR 20 CHINJAP
EUROPE. PAGE 32 G0634
WAR
POLICY
DIPLOM

S53
PERKINS J.A.,"ADMINISTRATION OF THE NATIONAL
SECURITY PROGRAM." USA+45 EX/STRUC FORCES ADMIN
CIVMIL/REL ORD/FREE 20. PAGE 44 G0868
CONTROL
GP/REL
REPRESENT
PROB/SOLV

B54
LOCKLIN D.P.,ECONOMICS OF TRANSPORTATION (4TH ED.).
USA+45 USA-45 SEA AIR LAW FINAN LG/CO EX/STRUC
ADMIN CONTROL...STAT CHARTS 19/20 RAILROAD
PUB/TRANS. PAGE 34 G0675
ECO/DEV
DIST/IND
ECO/TAC
TEC/DEV

B54
SIMMONS L.W.,SOCIAL SCIENCE IN MEDICINE. USA+45
PUB/INST

USA-45 SOCIETY CONSULT PLAN PROB/SOLV CONTROL
PERS/REL...POLICY HEAL TREND BIBLIOG 20. PAGE 51
G0999
HABITAT
HEALTH
BIO/SOC

S54
HOOPES T.,"CIVILIAN-MILITARY BALANCE." USA+45 CHIEF
FORCES PLAN CONTROL WAR GOV/REL GP/REL INGP/REL
...POLICY 19/20. PAGE 27 G0527
CIVMIL/REL
LEAD
PWR
NAT/G

C54
ZELLER B.,"AMERICAN STATE LEGISLATURES: REPORT ON
THE COMMITTEE ON AMERICAN LEGISLATURES." CONSTN
POL/PAR EX/STRUC CONFER ADMIN CONTROL EXEC LOBBY
ROUTINE GOV/REL...POLICY BIBLIOG 20. PAGE 65 G1267
REPRESENT
LEGIS
PROVS
APPORT

B55
DAVIS E.,TWO MINUTES TO MIDNIGHT. WOR+45 PLAN
CONTROL NEUTRAL ARMS/CONT ATTIT ORD/FREE...PSY 20
COLD/WAR. PAGE 14 G0277
NUC/PWR
WAR
DETER
DIPLOM

S55
SKINNER B.F.,"FREEDOM AND THE CONTROL OF MEN"
(BMR)" FUT WOR+45 CONTROL CHOOSE GP/REL ATTIT MORAL
PWR POPULISM...POLICY 20. PAGE 51 G1008
ORD/FREE
TEC/DEV
PHIL/SCI
INTELL

B56
REDFORD E.S.,PUBLIC ADMINISTRATION AND POLICY
FORMATION: STUDIES IN OIL, GAS, BANKING, RIVER
DEVELOPMENT AND CORPORATE INVESTIGATIONS. USA+45
CLIENT NAT/G ADMIN LOBBY REPRESENT GOV/REL INGP/REL
20. PAGE 46 G0908
EX/STRUC
PROB/SOLV
CONTROL
EXEC

S56
KNAPP D.C.,"CONGRESSIONAL CONTROL OF AGRICULTURAL
CONSERVATION POLICY: A CASE STUDY OF THE
APPROPRIATIONS PROCESS." DELIB/GP PLAN PROB/SOLV
CONFER PARL/PROC...POLICY INT CONGRESS. PAGE 31
G0607
LEGIS
AGRI
BUDGET
CONTROL

B57
MCKINNEY E.R.,A BIBLIOGRAPHY OF CYBERNETICS AND
INFORMATION THEORY. COMPUTER OP/RES...DECISION
PHIL/SCI PSY LING LOG MATH PROBABIL GAME 20.
PAGE 38 G0743
BIBLIOG/A
FEEDBACK
SIMUL
CONTROL

N57
US ARMY LIBRARY,THESES AND DISSERTATIONS IN THE
HOLDINGS OF THE ARMY LIBRARY (PAMPHLET). USA+45
...INT/LAW PSY SOC 20. PAGE 56 G1105
BIBLIOG
FORCES
MGT
CONTROL

B58
CHEEK G.,ECONOMIC AND SOCIAL IMPLICATIONS OF
AUTOMATION: A BIBLIOGRAPHIC REVIEW (PAMPHLET).
USA+45 LG/CO WORKER CREATE PLAN CONTROL ROUTINE
PERS/REL EFFICIENCY PRODUC...METH/COMP 20. PAGE 12
G0225
BIBLIOG/A
SOCIETY
INDUS
AUTOMAT

B58
CROWE S.,THE LANDSCAPE OF POWER. UK CULTURE
SERV/IND NAT/G CONSULT PARTIC NUC/PWR LEISURE...SOC
EXHIBIT 20. PAGE 14 G0264
HABITAT
TEC/DEV
PLAN
CONTROL

B58
UN INTL CONF ON PEACEFUL USE,PROGRESS IN ATOMIC
ENERGY (VOL. I). WOR+45 R+D PLAN TEC/DEV CONFER
CONTROL PEACE SKILL...CHARTS ANTHOL 20 UN BAGHDAD.
PAGE 55 G1088
NUC/PWR
DIPLOM
WORKER
EDU/PROP

B58
US DEPARTMENT OF THE ARMY,BIBLIOGRAPHY ON LIMITED
WAR (PAMPHLET). USA+45 TEC/DEV CONTROL RISK COERCE
DETER NUC/PWR WEAPON ADJUST PEACE ALL/VALS ORD/FREE
20. PAGE 57 G1127
BIBLIOG/A
WAR
FORCES
CIVMIL/REL

S58
KEISER N.F.,"PUBLIC RESPONSIBILITY AND FEDERAL
ADVISORY GROUPS: A CASE STUDY." NAT/G ADMIN CONTROL
LOBBY...POLICY 20. PAGE 30 G0590
REPRESENT
ELITES
GP/REL
EX/STRUC

B59
ATOMIC INDUSTRIAL FORUM,THE IMPACT OF THE PEACEFUL
USES OF ATOMIC ENERGY ON STATE AND LOCAL
GOVERNMENT. USA+45 INDUS NAT/G LEGIS PLAN CONTROL
GOV/REL. PAGE 4 G0079
PROVS
LOC/G
NUC/PWR
PEACE

B59
GUILBAUD G.T.,WHAT IS CYBERNETICS? COMPUTER OP/RES
TEC/DEV AUTOMAT ROUTINE PERS/REL PERCEPT...PSY MATH
COMPUT/IR SIMUL GEN/METH. PAGE 23 G0460
CONTROL
COM/IND
FEEDBACK
NET/THEORY

HALEY A.G.,FIRST COLLOQUIUM ON THE LAW OF OUTER SPACE. WOR+45 INT/ORG ACT/RES PLAN BAL/PWR CONFER ATTIT PWR...POLICY JURID CHARTS ANTHOL 20. PAGE 24 G0468
SPACE
LAW
SOVEREIGN
CONTROL
B59

HARVARD UNIVERSITY LAW SCHOOL,INTERNATIONAL PROBLEMS OF FINANCIAL PROTECTION AGAINST NUCLEAR RISK. WOR+45 NAT/G DELIB/GP PROB/SOLV DIPLOM CONTROL ATTIT...POLICY INT/LAW MATH 20. PAGE 25 G0488
NUC/PWR
ADJUD
INDUS
FINAN
B59

LANG D.,FROM HIROSHIMA TO THE MOON: CHRONICLES OF LIFE IN THE ATOMIC AGE. USA+45 OP/RES CONTROL ARMS/CONT WAR CIVMIL/REL PEACE HABITAT MORAL PWR ...OBS INT 20 AEC. PAGE 32 G0633
NUC/PWR
SPACE
HEALTH
TEC/DEV
B59

MEANS G.C.,ADMINISTRATIVE INFLATION AND PUBLIC POLICY (PAMPHLET). USA+45 ECO/DEV FINAN INDUS WORKER PLAN BUDGET GOV/REL COST DEMAND WEALTH 20 CONGRESS MONOPOLY GOLD/STAND. PAGE 38 G0749
ECO/TAC
POLICY
RATION
CONTROL
B59

COLUMBIA U BUREAU APPL SOC R, ATTITUDES OF PROMINENT AMERICANS TOWARD "WORLD PEACE THROUGH WORLD LAW" (SUPRA-NATL ORGANIZATION.FOR WAR PREVENTION). USA+45 USSR ELITES FORCES PLAN PROB/SOLV CONTROL WAR PWR...POLICY SOC QU IDEA/COMP 20 UN. PAGE 45 G0888
ATTIT
ACT/RES
INT/LAW
STAT
B59

U OF MICHIGAN LAW SCHOOL,ATOMS AND THE LAW. USA+45 PROVS WORKER PROB/SOLV DIPLOM ADMIN GOV/REL ANTHOL. PAGE 55 G1085
NUC/PWR
NAT/G
CONTROL
LAW
B59

VERNEY D.V.,PUBLIC ENTERPRISE IN SWEDEN. FUT SWEDEN UK INDUS POL/PAR LEGIS PROB/SOLV CAP/ISM INT/TRADE CONTROL SOCISM...MGT CONCPT NAT/COMP 20 SOCDEM/PAR CIVIL/SERV. PAGE 61 G1196
ECO/DEV
POLICY
LG/CO
NAT/G
B59

WASSERMAN P.,MEASUREMENT AND ANALYSIS OF ORGANIZATIONAL PERFORMANCE. FINAN MARKET EX/STRUC TEC/DEV EDU/PROP CONTROL ROUTINE TASK...MGT 20. PAGE 62 G1220
BIBLIOG/A
ECO/TAC
OP/RES
EFFICIENCY
B59

SEIDMAN H.,"THE GOVERNMENT CORPORATION IN THE UNITED STATES." USA+45 LEGIS ADMIN PLURISM 20. PAGE 50 G0988
CONTROL
GOV/REL
EX/STRUC
EXEC
S59

SHEENAN D.,"PUBLIC CORPORATIONS AND PUBLIC ACTION." UK ADMIN CONTROL REPRESENT SOCISM 20. PAGE 50 G0990
ECO/DEV
EFFICIENCY
EX/STRUC
EXEC
S59

ALBI F.,TRATADO DE LOS MODOS DE GESTION DE LAS CORPORACIONES LOCALES. SPAIN FINAN NAT/G BUDGET CONTROL EXEC ROUTINE GOV/REL ORD/FREE SOVEREIGN ...MGT 20. PAGE 2 G0034
LOC/G
LAW
ADMIN
MUNIC
B60

CARPER E.T.,THE DEFENSE APPROPRIATIONS RIDER (PAMPHLET). USA+45 CONSTN CHIEF DELIB/GP LEGIS BUDGET LOBBY CIVMIL/REL...POLICY 20 CONGRESS EISNHWR/DD DEPT/DEFEN PRESIDENT BOSTON. PAGE 11 G0212
GOV/REL
ADJUD
LAW
CONTROL
B60

WEBSTER J.A.,A GENERAL STUDY OF THE DEPARTMENT OF DEFENSE INTERNAL SECURITY PROGRAM. USA+45 WORKER TEC/DEV ADJUD CONTROL CT/SYS EXEC GOV/REL COST ...POLICY DECISION MGT 20 DEPT/DEFEN SUPREME/CT. PAGE 62 G1221
ORD/FREE
PLAN
ADMIN
NAT/G
B60

SCHRAMM W.,"MASS COMMUNICATIONS: A BOOK OF READINGS (2ND ED.)" LG/CO PRESS ADMIN CONTROL ROUTINE ATTIT ROLE SUPEGO...CHARTS ANTHOL BIBLIOG 20. PAGE 50 G0977
COM/IND
EDU/PROP
CROWD
MAJORIT
C60

HELLER D.,THE KENNEDY CABINET--AMERICA'S MEN OF DESTINY. NAT/G CHIEF CONSULT ADMIN CONTROL GOV/REL ...MGT 20 DEPT/LABOR DEPT/STATE DEPT/JUST DEPT/DEFEN KENNEDY/J. PAGE 26 G0504
EX/STRUC
CONFER
DELIB/GP
TOP/EX
B61

KRUPP S.,PATTERN IN ORGANIZATIONAL ANALYSIS: A CRITICAL EXAMINATION. INGP/REL PERS/REL RATIONAL ATTIT AUTHORIT DRIVE PWR...DECISION PHIL/SCI SOC IDEA/COMP. PAGE 32 G0622
MGT
CONTROL
CONCPT
METH/CNCPT
B61

LAHAYE R.,LES ENTREPRISES PUBLIQUES AU MAROC. FRANCE MOROCCO LAW DIST/IND EXTR/IND FINAN CONSULT PLAN TEC/DEV ADMIN AGREE CONTROL OWN...POLICY 20. PAGE 32 G0629
NAT/G
INDUS
ECO/UNDEV
ECO/TAC
B61

LEE R.R.,ENGINEERING-ECONOMIC PLANNING MISCELLANEOUS SUBJECTS: A SELECTED BIBLIOGRAPHY (MIMEOGRAPHED). FINAN LOC/G MUNIC NEIGH ADMIN CONTROL INGP/REL HABITAT...GEOG MGT SOC/WK 20 RESOURCE/N. PAGE 33 G0651
BIBLIOG/A
PLAN
REGION
B61

MURPHY E.F.,WATER PURITY: A STUDY IN LEGAL CONTROL OF NATURAL RESOURCES. LOC/G ACT/RES PLAN TEC/DEV LOBBY GP/REL COST ATTIT HEALTH ORD/FREE...HEAL JURID 20 WISCONSIN WATER. PAGE 40 G0797
SEA
LAW
PROVS
CONTROL
B61

MANGELSDORF J.E.,"HUMAN DECISIONS IN MISSILE YSTEMS." OP/RES CHARTS. PAGE 35 G0699
DECISION
PROB/SOLV
AUTOMAT
CONTROL
S61

ASTIA,HUMAN ENGINEERING: A REPORT BIBLIOGRAPHY. USA+45 R+D FORCES ACT/RES COMPUTER CREATE OP/RES EDU/PROP CONTROL WEAPON...SOC NEW/IDEA. PAGE 4 G0073
BIBLIOG/A
COM/IND
COMPUT/IR
METH
B62

ASTIA,INFORMATION THEORY: A REPORT BIBLIOGRAPHY. USA+45 COMPUTER CREATE OP/RES PLAN TEC/DEV CONTROL ...CONCPT METH/COMP. PAGE 4 G0074
BIBLIOG/A
COM/IND
FORCES
METH
B62

BERKELEY E.C.,THE COMPUTER REVOLUTION. WOR+45 CREATE TEC/DEV EFFICIENCY TECHRACY...SOC TREND 20. PAGE 7 G0128
COMPUTER
CONTROL
AUTOMAT
SOCIETY
B62

CARSON R.,SILENT SPRING. USA+45 AIR CULTURE AGRI INDUS ADMIN ATTIT RIGID/FLEX ORD/FREE PWR...POLICY 20. PAGE 11 G0216
HABITAT
TREND
SOCIETY
CONTROL
B62

DODDS H.W.,THE ACADEMIC PRESIDENT "EDUCATOR OR CARETAKER? FINAN DELIB/GP EDU/PROP PARTIC ATTIT ROLE PWR...POLICY RECORD INT. PAGE 16 G0304
ACADEM
ADMIN
LEAD
CONTROL
B62

FERBER R.,RESEARCH METHODS IN ECONOMICS AND BUSINESS. ECO/DEV FINAN MARKET LG/CO SML/CO CONSULT CONTROL COST...STAT METH/COMP 20. PAGE 19 G0364
ACT/RES
PROB/SOLV
ECO/TAC
MGT
B62

FRYKLUND R.,100 MILLION LIVES: MAXIMUM SURVIVAL IN A NUCLEAR WAR. USA+45 USSR CONTROL WEAPON ...IDEA/COMP NAT/COMP 20. PAGE 20 G0397
NUC/PWR
WAR
PLAN
DETER
B62

KARNJAHAPRAKORN C.,MUNICIPAL GOVERNMENT IN THAILAND AS AN INSTITUTION AND PROCESS OF SELF-GOVERNMENT. THAILAND CULTURE FINAN EX/STRUC LEGIS PLAN CONTROL GOV/REL EFFICIENCY ATTIT...POLICY 20. PAGE 29 G0578
LOC/G
MUNIC
ORD/FREE
ADMIN
B62

REICH C.A.,BUREAUCRACY AND THE FORESTS (PAMPHLET). USA+45 LOBBY...POLICY MGT 20. PAGE 46 G0910
ADMIN
CONTROL
EX/STRUC
REPRESENT
B62

STERN A.C.,AIR POLLUTION (2 VOLS.). LAW INDUS PROB/SOLV TEC/DEV INSPECT RISK BIO/SOC HABITAT ...OBS/ENVIR TESTS SAMP 20 POLLUTION. PAGE 53 G1035
AIR
OP/RES
CONTROL
HEALTH
B62

STOVER C.F.,THE GOVERNMENT OF SCIENCE (PAMPHLET). USA+45 SOCIETY PROF/ORG EX/STRUC CREATE CONTROL NUC/PWR WAR GOV/REL PEACE ORD/FREE 20. PAGE 53 G1041
PHIL/SCI
TEC/DEV
LAW
NAT/G
B62

US CONGRESS,COMMUNICATIONS SATELLITE LEGISLATION: SPACE
HEARINGS BEFORE COMM ON AERON AND SPACE SCIENCES ON COM/IND
BILLS S2550 AND 2814. WOR+45 LAW VOL/ASSN PLAN ADJUD
DIPLOM CONTROL OWN PEACE...NEW/IDEA CONGRESS NASA. GOV/REL
PAGE 56 G1110
B62

US SENATE COMM GOVT OPERATIONS,ADMINISTRATION OF ORD/FREE
NATIONAL SECURITY. USA+45 CHIEF PLAN PROB/SOLV ADMIN
TEC/DEV DIPLOM ATTIT...POLICY DECISION 20 NAT/G
KENNEDY/JF RUSK/D MCNAMARA/R BUNDY/M HERTER/C. CONTROL
PAGE 60 G1177
B62

CAVERS D.F.,"ADMINISTRATIVE DECISION-MAKING IN REPRESENT
NUCLEAR FACILITIES LICENSING." USA+45 CLIENT ADMIN LOBBY
EXEC 20 AEC. PAGE 11 G0218 PWR
CONTROL
L62

NIEBURG H.L.,"THE EISENHOWER ATOMIC ENERGY NUC/PWR
COMMISSION AND CONGRESS" R+D INT/ORG OP/RES DIPLOM TOP/EX
ADMIN CONTROL 20 PRESIDENT CONGRESS AEC. PAGE 42 LOBBY
G0821 DELIB/GP
L62

DAWSON R.H.,"CONGRESSIONAL INNOVATION AND LEGIS
INTERVENTION IN DEFENSE POLICY: LEGISLATIVE PWR
AUTHORIZATION OF WEAPONS SYSTEMS." CONSTN PLAN CONTROL
ARMS/CONT GOV/REL EFFICIENCY PEACE NEW/LIB OLD/LIB. WEAPON
PAGE 14 G0281
S62

BROUDE H.W.,STEEL DECISIONS AND THE NATIONAL PROC/MFG
ECONOMY. USA+45 LG/CO PLAN ADMIN COST DECISION. NAT/G
PAGE 9 G0176 CONTROL
ECO/TAC
B63

DALAND R.T.,PERSPECTIVES OF BRAZILIAN PUBLIC ADMIN
ADMINISTRATION (VOL. I). BRAZIL LAW ECO/UNDEV NAT/G
SCHOOL CHIEF TEC/DEV CONFER CONTROL GP/REL ATTIT PLAN
ROLE PWR...ANTHOL 20. PAGE 14 G0272 GOV/REL
B63

GREEN H.P.,GOVERNMENT OF THE ATOM. USA+45 LEGIS GOV/REL
PROB/SOLV ADMIN CONTROL PWR...POLICY DECISION 20 EX/STRUC
PRESIDENT CONGRESS. PAGE 22 G0443 NUC/PWR
DELIB/GP
B63

JACOB H.,GERMAN ADMINISTRATION SINCE BISMARCK: ADMIN
CENTRAL AUTHORITY VERSUS LOCAL AUTONOMY. GERMANY NAT/G
GERMANY/W LAW POL/PAR CONTROL CENTRAL TOTALISM LOC/G
FASCISM...MAJORIT DECISION STAT CHARTS GOV/COMP POLICY
19/20 BISMARCK/O HITLER/A WEIMAR/REP. PAGE 28 G0551
B63

KORNHAUSER W.,SCIENTISTS IN INDUSTRY: CONFLICT AND CREATE
ACCOMMODATION. USA+45 R+D LG/CO NAT/G TEC/DEV INDUS
CONTROL ADJUST ATTIT...MGT STAT INT BIBLIOG 20. PROF/ORG
PAGE 31 G0614 GP/REL
B63

LITTERER J.A.,ORGANIZATIONS: STRUCTURE AND ADMIN
BEHAVIOR. PLAN DOMIN CONTROL LEAD ROUTINE SANCTION CREATE
INGP/REL EFFICIENCY PRODUC DRIVE RIGID/FLEX PWR. MGT
PAGE 34 G0674 ADJUST
B63

MENEZES A.J.,SUBDESENVOLVIMENTO E POLITICA ECO/UNDEV
INTERNACIONAL. BRAZIL WOR+45 PLAN CONTROL LEAD DIPLOM
NAT/LISM ORD/FREE 20 THIRD/WRLD. PAGE 38 G0754 POLICY
BAL/PWR
B63

MILBRATH L.W.,THE WASHINGTON LOBBYISTS. CONSTN LOBBY
BAL/PWR CONTROL LEAD TASK CHOOSE SUPEGO...DECISION POLICY
STAT CHARTS BIBLIOG. PAGE 39 G0767 PERS/REL
B63

EDELMAN M.,THE SYMBOLIC USES OF POWER. USA+45 CLIENT
EX/STRUC CONTROL GP/REL INGP/REL...MGT T. PAGE 17 PWR
G0333 EXEC
ELITES
B64

KAUFMANN W.W.,THE MC NAMARA STRATEGY. TOP/EX FORCES
INSPECT BAL/PWR DIPLOM CONTROL DETER GUERRILLA WAR
NUC/PWR WEAPON COST PWR...METH/COMP 20 MCNAMARA/R PLAN
KENNEDY/JF JOHNSON/LB NATO DEPT/DEFEN. PAGE 30 PROB/SOLV
G0586
B64

MANSFIELD E.,MONOPOLY POWER AND ECONOMIC LG/CO
PERFORMANCE: AN INTRODUCTION TO A CURRENT ISSUE OF PWR
PUBLIC POLICY. ECO/DEV INDUS NAT/G PLAN CAP/ISM ECO/TAC
PRICE CONTROL LOBBY EFFICIENCY PRODUC...POLICY 20 MARKET
CONGRESS KENNEDY/JF MONOPOLY. PAGE 36 G0701
B64

MARRIS R.,THE ECONOMIC THEORY OF "MANAGERIAL" CAP/ISM
CAPITALISM. USA+45 ECO/DEV LG/CO ECO/TAC DEMAND MGT
...CHARTS BIBLIOG 20. PAGE 36 G0709 CONTROL
OP/RES
B64

RIES J.C.,THE MANAGEMENT OF DEFENSE: ORGANIZATION FORCES
AND CONTROL OF THE US ARMED SERVICES. PROF/ORG ACT/RES
DELIB/GP EX/STRUC LEGIS GOV/REL PERS/REL CENTRAL DECISION
RATIONAL PWR...POLICY TREND GOV/COMP BIBLIOG. CONTROL
PAGE 47 G0920
B64

SCHOECK H.,CENTRAL PLANNING AND NEOMERCANTILISM. PLAN
L/A+17C UK WOR+45 BUDGET ECO/TAC PRICE CONTROL CENTRAL
GOV/REL UTOPIA 20. PAGE 49 G0974 NAT/G
POLICY
B64

TAUBENFELD H.J.,SPACE AND SOCIETY. USA+45 LAW SPACE
FORCES CREATE TEC/DEV ADJUD CONTROL COST PEACE SOCIETY
...PREDICT ANTHOL 20. PAGE 54 G1057 ADJUST
DIPLOM
B64

ANTHONY R.N.,PLANNING AND CONTROL SYSTEMS. UNIV CONTROL
OP/RES...DECISION MGT LING. PAGE 3 G0061 PLAN
METH
HYPO/EXP
B65

ATOMIC INDUSTRIAL FORUM,SAFEGUARDS AGAINST NUC/PWR
DIVERSION OF NUCLEAR MATERIALS FROM PEACEFUL TO CIVMIL/REL
MILITARY PURPOSES. WOR+45 DELIB/GP FORCES PLAN INSPECT
DIPLOM CONFER PEACE...ANTHOL 20 IAEA. PAGE 4 G0081 CONTROL
B65

CHENG C.-,Y.,SCIENTIFIC AND ENGINEERING MANPOWER IN WORKER
COMMUNIST CHINA: 1949-1963. CHINA/COM USSR ELITES CONSULT
ECO/DEV R+D ACADEM LABOR NAT/G EDU/PROP CONTROL MARXISM
UTIL...POLICY BIBLIOG 20. PAGE 12 G0226 BIOG
B65

JENKS C.W.,SPACE LAW. DIPLOM DEBATE CONTROL SPACE
ORD/FREE TREATY 20 UN. PAGE 29 G0563 INT/LAW
JURID
INT/ORG
B65

KANTOROVICH L.V.,THE BEST USE OF ECONOMIC PLAN
RESOURCES. USSR SOCIETY FINAN ACT/RES TEC/DEV MATH
ECO/TAC PRICE CONTROL COST DEMAND EFFICIENCY DECISION
OPTIMAL...MGT STAT. PAGE 29 G0572
B65

LAPP R.E.,THE NEW PRIESTHOOD; THE SCIENTIFIC ELITE TEC/DEV
AND THE USES OF POWER. USA+45 ELITES INTELL SOCIETY TECHRACY
R+D NAT/G CHIEF LEGIS CIVMIL/REL GP/REL PWR 20 CONTROL
PRESIDENT CONGRESS. PAGE 32 G0635 POPULISM
B65

MELMANS S.,OUR DEPLETED SOCIETY. SPACE USA+45 CIVMIL/REL
ECO/DEV FORCES BUDGET ECO/TAC ADMIN WEAPON INDUS
EFFICIENCY 20 COLD/WAR. PAGE 38 G0753 EDU/PROP
CONTROL
B65

STEINER G.A.,THE CREATIVE ORGANIZATION. ELITES CREATE
LG/CO PLAN PROB/SOLV TEC/DEV INSPECT CAP/ISM MGT
CONTROL EXEC PERSON...METH/COMP HYPO/EXP 20. ADMIN
PAGE 52 G1034 SOC
B65

US CONGRESS JT ATOM ENRGY COMM,PROPOSED AMENDMENT LAW
TO SECTION 271 OF THE ATOMIC ENERGY ACT OF 1954. LEGIS
USA+45 CONSTRUC PLAN INSPECT CONTROL CT/SYS 20 DELIB/GP
CONGRESS AEC. PAGE 57 G1115 NUC/PWR
B65

WASKOW A.I.,KEEPING THE WORLD DISARMED. AFR ARMS/CONT
GERMANY/E DIPLOM CONTROL WAR 20 UN. PAGE 62 G1218 PEACE
FORCES
PROB/SOLV
B65

WEISNER J.B.,WHERE SCIENCE AND POLITICS MEET. CHIEF
USA+45 ECO/DEV R+D FORCES PROB/SOLV DIPLOM FOR/AID NAT/G
CONTROL...PHIL/SCI PRESIDENT KENNEDY/JF JOHNSON/LB. POLICY
B65

PAGE 63 G1228   TEC/DEV

                                                  S65
BEAUFRE A.,"THE SHARING OF NUCLEAR   DETER
RESPONSIBILITIES* A PROBLEM IN NEED OF SOLUTION." RISK
FRANCE USA+45 INT/ORG NAT/G DELIB/GP FORCES CONTROL ACT/RES
NUC/PWR RIGID/FLEX...CONCPT IDEA/COMP NATO. PAGE 6 WAR
G0110

                                                  S65
FOX A.B.,"NATO AND CONGRESS." CONSTN DELIB/GP   CONTROL
EX/STRUC FORCES TOP/EX BUDGET NUC/PWR GOV/REL   DIPLOM
...GP/COMP CONGRESS NATO TREATY. PAGE 20 G0388

                                                  S65
HARRISON S.L.,"NTH NATION CHALLENGES* THE PRESENT ARMS/CONT
PERSPECTIVE." EUR+WWI FUT USA+45 BAL/PWR CONTROL NUC/PWR
RISK COERCE WAR...PREDICT COLD/WAR. PAGE 25 G0485 NAT/G
                                                  DIPLOM

                                                  S65
HUGHES T.L.,"SCHOLARS AND FOREIGN POLICY* VARIETIES ACT/RES
OF RESEARCH EXPERIENCE." COM/IND DIPLOM ADMIN EXEC ACADEM
ROUTINE...MGT OBS CONGRESS PRESIDENT CAMELOT   CONTROL
PAGE 27 G0535   NAT/G

                                                  S65
KREITH K.,"PEACE RESEARCH AND GOVERNMENT POLICY." PEACE
INTELL NAT/G DIPLOM ECO/TAC CONTROL ARMS/CONT WAR STYLE
PERCEPT...DECISION IDEA/COMP. PAGE 31 G0619   OBS

                                                  C65
SEARA M.V.,"COSMIC INTERNATIONAL LAW." LAW ACADEM SPACE
ACT/RES DIPLOM COLONIAL CONTROL NUC/PWR SOVEREIGN INT/LAW
...GEN/LAWS BIBLIOG UN. PAGE 50 G0987   IDEA/COMP
                                                  INT/ORG

                                                  B66
AMERICAN ASSEMBLY COLUMBIA U,A WORLD OF NUCLEAR NUC/PWR
POWERS? FUT WOR+45 ECO/DEV BAL/PWR ECO/TAC CONTROL DIPLOM
RISK EFFICIENCY ATTIT PWR...METH/COMP ANTHOL 20. TEC/DEV
PAGE 3 G0049   ARMS/CONT

                                                  B66
FREIDEL F.,AMERICAN ISSUES IN THE TWENTIETH   DIPLOM
CENTURY. SOCIETY FINAN ECO/TAC FOR/AID CONTROL   POLICY
NUC/PWR WAR RACE/REL PEACE ATTIT...ANTHOL T 20   NAT/G
WILSON/W ROOSEVLT/F KENNEDY/JF TRUMAN/HS. PAGE 20 ORD/FREE
G0391

                                                  B66
GRUNEWALD D.,PUBLIC POLICY AND THE MODERN   LG/CO
COOPERATION: SELECTED READINGS. USA+45 LAW MARKET POLICY
VOL/ASSN CAP/ISM INT/TRADE CENTRAL OWN...SOC ANTHOL NAT/G
20. PAGE 23 G0458   CONTROL

                                                  B66
MARKHAM J.W.,AN ECONOMIC-MEDIA STUDY OF BOOK   PRESS
PUBLISHING. USA+45 LAW COM/IND ACADEM SCHOOL   ECO/TAC
EDU/PROP AUTOMAT CONTROL...DECISION STAT CHARTS 20 TEC/DEV
CONGRESS. PAGE 36 G0707   NAT/G

                                                  B66
PRINCETON U INDUSTRIAL REL SEC,THE FEDERAL   BIBLIOG/A
GOVERNMENT AND THE UNIVERSITY: SUPPORT FOR SOCIAL NAT/G
SCIENCE RESEARCH AND THE IMPACT OF PROJECT CAMELOT. ACADEM
USA+45 ACT/RES CONTROL GP/REL PWR...POLICY 20.   PLAN
PAGE 45 G0889

                                                  B66
SANFORD T.,BUT WHAT ABOUT THE PEOPLE? ACADEM SCHOOL EDU/PROP
BUDGET TAX CONTROL SKILL WEALTH 20 NORTH/CAR.   PROB/SOLV
PAGE 49 G0956   POLICY
                                                  PROVS

                                                  B66
SCHURMANN F.,IDEOLOGY AND ORGANIZATION IN COMMUNIST MARXISM
CHINA. CHINA/COM LOC/G MUNIC POL/PAR ECO/TAC   STRUCT
CONTROL ATTIT...MGT STERTYP 20 COM/PARTY. PAGE 50 ADMIN
G0981   NAT/G

                                                  B66
SPULBER N.,THE STATE AND ECONOMIC DEVELOPMENT IN ECO/DEV
EASTERN EUROPE. BULGARIA COM CZECHOSLVK HUNGARY ECO/UNDEV
POLAND YUGOSLAVIA CULTURE PLAN CAP/ISM INT/TRADE NAT/G
CONTROL...POLICY CHARTS METH/COMP BIBLIOG/A 19/20. TOTALISM
PAGE 52 G1028

                                                  B66
STREET D.,ORGANIZATION FOR TREATMENT. CLIENT PROVS GP/COMP
PUB/INST PLAN CONTROL PARTIC REPRESENT ATTIT PWR AGE/Y
...POLICY BIBLIOG. PAGE 53 G1044   ADMIN
                                                  VOL/ASSN

                                                  B66
US HOUSE COMM ON JUDICIARY,CIVIL COMMITMENT AND BIO/SOC

TREATMENT OF NARCOTIC ADDICTS. USA+45 SOCIETY FINAN CRIME
LEGIS PROB/SOLV GIVE CT/SYS SANCTION HEALTH   IDEA/COMP
...POLICY HEAL 20. PAGE 58 G1141   CONTROL

                                                  B66
WOLFERS A.,THE UNITED STATES IN A DISARMED WORLD: A ARMS/CONT
STUDY OF THE US OUTLINE FOR GENERAL AND COMPLETE POLICY
DISARMAMENT. USA+45 NAT/G CONTROL DETER NUC/PWR FORCES
EFFICIENCY...ANTHOL 20. PAGE 64 G1255   PEACE

                                                  B67
ALEXANDER L.M.,THE LAW OF THE SEA: OFFSHORE   SEA
BOUNDARIES AND ZONES. WOR+45 INT/ORG TEC/DEV   INT/LAW
CONTROL PRIVIL HABITAT SOVEREIGN...CON/ANAL CHARTS EXTR/IND
ANTHOL. PAGE 2 G0037

                                                  B67
BUDER S.,PULLMAN: AN EXPERIMENT IN INDUSTRIAL ORDER DIST/IND
AND COMMUNITY PLANNING, 1880-1930. USA-45 SOCIETY INDUS
LABOR LG/CO CREATE PROB/SOLV CONTROL GP/REL   MUNIC
EFFICIENCY ATTIT...MGT BIBLIOG 19/20 PULLMAN.   PLAN
PAGE 9 G0184

                                                  B67
COMMONER B.,SCIENCE AND SURVIVAL. SOCIETY INDUS PHIL/SCI
PLAN NUC/PWR KNOWL PWR...SOC 20 AEC. PAGE 13 G0247 CONTROL
                                                  PROB/SOLV
                                                  EQUILIB

                                                  B67
DONALD A.G.,MANAGEMENT, INFORMATION, AND SYSTEMS. ROUTINE
WOR+45 LG/CO PROB/SOLV CONTROL FEEDBACK KNOWL MGT. TEC/DEV
PAGE 16 G0306   CONCPT
                                                  ADMIN

                                                  B67
GOLEMBIEWSKI R.T.,ORGANIZING MEN AND POWER: ADMIN
PATTERNS OF BEHAVIOR AND LINESTAFF MODELS. WOR+45 CONTROL
EX/STRUC ACT/RES DOMIN PERS/REL...NEW/IDEA 20.   SIMUL
PAGE 22 G0431   MGT

                                                  B67
HEADLEY J.C.,PESTICIDE PROBLEM: AN ECONOMIC   HABITAT
APPROACH TO PUBLIC POLICY. AGRI TEC/DEV GOV/REL POLICY
COST ATTIT CHARTS. PAGE 25 G0498   BIO/SOC
                                                  CONTROL

                                                  B67
KINTNER W.R.,PEACE AND THE STRATEGY CONFLICT. PLAN ROLE
BAL/PWR DIPLOM CONTROL ARMS/CONT DETER WEAPON 20. PEACE
PAGE 30 G0599   NUC/PWR
                                                  ORD/FREE

                                                  B67
MACAVOY P.W.,REGULATION OF TRANSPORT INNOVATION. DIST/IND
ACT/RES ADJUD COST DEMAND...POLICY CHARTS 20.   CONTROL
PAGE 35 G0684   PRICE
                                                  PROFIT

                                                  B67
MACBRIDE R.,THE AUTOMATED STATE: COMPUTER SYSTEMS COMPUTER
AS A NEW FORCE IN SOCIETY. FUT WOR+45 FINAN MUNIC AUTOMAT
NAT/G WORKER PLAN TEC/DEV CONTROL PERS/REL RACE/REL PROB/SOLV
ADJUST. PAGE 35 G0685   SOCIETY

                                                  B67
MAZOUR A.G.,SOVIET ECONOMIC DEVELOPMENT: OPERATION ECO/TAC
OUTSTRIP: 1921-1965. USSR ECO/UNDEV FINAN CHIEF AGRI
WORKER PROB/SOLV CONTROL PRODUC MARXISM...CHARTS INDUS
ORG/CHARTS 20 STALIN/J. PAGE 37 G0726   PLAN

                                                  B67
MOORE J.R.,THE ECONOMIC IMPACT OF THE TVA. AGRI ECO/UNDEV
INDUS PLAN BARGAIN CONTROL REGION GOV/REL DEMAND ECO/DEV
EFFICIENCY SOCISM 20 TVA. PAGE 40 G0780   NAT/G
                                                  CREATE

                                                  B67
MOSS F.M.,THE WATER CRISIS. PROB/SOLV CONTROL   GEOG
...POLICY NEW/IDEA. PAGE 40 G0791   ACT/RES
                                                  PRODUC
                                                  WEALTH

                                                  B67
NORTHRUP H.R.,RESTRICTIVE LABOR PRACTICES IN THE DIST/IND
SUPERMARKET INDUSTRY. USA+45 INDUS WORKER TEC/DEV MARKET
BARGAIN PAY CONTROL GP/REL COST...STAT CHARTS NLRB. LABOR
PAGE 42 G0827   MGT

                                                  B67
ORLANS H.,CONTRACTING FOR ATOMS. USA+45 LAW INTELL NUC/PWR
ACADEM LG/CO NAT/G PLAN TEC/DEV CONTROL DETER   R+D
...TREND 20 AEC. PAGE 43 G0845   PRODUC
                                                  PEACE

SAPARINA Y.,CYBERNETICS WITHIN US. WOR+45 EDU/PROP FEEDBACK PERCEPT HEALTH...DECISION METH/CNCPT NEW/IDEA 20. PAGE 49 G0957
B67
COMPUTER
METH/COMP
CONTROL
SIMUL

SCHON D.A.,TECHNOLOGY AND CHANGE* THE NEW HERACLITUS. TEC/DEV CONTROL COST DEMAND EFFICIENCY RIGID/FLEX...MYTH 20. PAGE 49 G0975
B67
INDUS
PROB/SOLV
R+D
CREATE

UNIVERSAL REFERENCE SYSTEM,ECONOMIC REGULATION, BUSINESS, AND GOVERNMENT (VOLUME VIII). WOR+45 WOR-45 ECO/DEV ECO/UNDEV FINAN LABOR TEC/DEV ECO/TAC INT/TRADE GOV/REL...POLICY COMPUT/IR. PAGE 56 G1099
B67
BIBLIOG/A
CONTROL
NAT/G

UNIVERSAL REFERENCE SYSTEM,PUBLIC POLICY AND THE MANAGEMENT OF SCIENCE (VOLUME IX). FUT SPACE WOR+45 LAW NAT/G TEC/DEV CONTROL NUC/PWR GOV/REL ...COMPUT/IR GEN/METH. PAGE 56 G1100
B67
BIBLIOG/A
POLICY
MGT
PHIL/SCI

US SENATE COMM ON FOREIGN REL,FOREIGN ASSISTANCE ACT OF 1967. VIETNAM WOR+45 DELIB/GP CONFER CONTROL WAR WEAPON BAL/PAY...CENSUS CHARTS SENATE. PAGE 60 G1185
B67
FOR/AID
LAW
DIPLOM
POLICY

WYLIE J.C.,MILITARY STRATEGY: GENERAL THEORY OF POWER CONTROL. CUBA USA+45 VIETNAM/N WOR+45 ELITES CONTROL WAR PWR...POLICY METH/COMP 20 MAO. PAGE 64 G1260
B67
FORCES
PLAN
DECISION
IDEA/COMP

CARMICHAEL D.M.,"FORTY YEARS OF WATER POLLUTION CONTROL IN WISCONSIN: A CASE STUDY." LAW EXTR/IND INDUS MUNIC DELIB/GP PLAN PROB/SOLV SANCTION ...CENSUS CHARTS 20 WISCONSIN. PAGE 11 G0207
L67
HEALTH
CONTROL
ADMIN
ADJUD

PASLEY R.S.,"ORGANIZATIONAL CONFLICTS OF INTEREST IN GOVERNMENT CONTRACTS." ELITES R+D ROUTINE NUC/PWR DEMAND EFFICIENCY 20. PAGE 44 G0860
L67
NAT/G
ECO/TAC
RATION
CONTROL

AVTORKHANOV A.,"A NEW AGRARIAN REVOLUTION." COM USSR ECO/DEV PLAN TEC/DEV ADMIN CONTROL OPTIMAL WEALTH SOCISM 20 KHRUSH/N STALIN/J. PAGE 4 G0082
S67
AGRI
METH/COMP
MARXISM
OWN

BARAN P.,"THE FUTURE COMPUTER UTILITY." USA+45 NAT/G PLAN CONTROL COST...POLICY 20. PAGE 5 G0091
S67
COMPUTER
UTIL
FUT
TEC/DEV

BRETNOR R.,"DESTRUCTIVE FORCE AND THE MILITARY EQUATIONS." UNIV COMPUTER PLAN PROB/SOLV AUTOMAT CONTROL COERCE DETER NUC/PWR WEAPON DRIVE PWR. PAGE 9 G0166
S67
FORCES
TEC/DEV
DOMIN
WAR

BROWN W.B.,"MODEL-BUILDING AND ORGANIZATIONS." CONTROL FEEDBACK...PROBABIL CHARTS METH/COMP. PAGE 9 G0179
S67
MGT
ADMIN
GAME
COMPUTER

CHIU S.M.,"CHINA'S MILITARY POSTURE." CHINA/COM ELITES NAT/G POL/PAR TEC/DEV ECO/TAC DOMIN CONTROL LEAD REV MARXISM 20 MAO. PAGE 12 G0228
S67
FORCES
CIVMIL/REL
NUC/PWR
DIPLOM

EDMONDS M.,"INTERNATIONAL COLLABORATION IN WEAPONS PROCUREMENT* THE IMPLICATIONS OF THE ANGLO-FRENCH CASE." FRANCE UK CONSULT OP/RES PROB/SOLV TEC/DEV CONFER CONTROL EFFICIENCY 20. PAGE 17 G0334
S67
DIPLOM
VOL/ASSN
BAL/PWR
ARMS/CONT

EISENDRATH C.,"THE OUTER SPACE TREATY." CHINA/COM COM USA+45 DIPLOM CONTROL NUC/PWR...INT/LAW 20 UN COLD/WAR TREATY. PAGE 17 G0339
S67
SPACE
INT/ORG
PEACE
ARMS/CONT

GANZ G.,"THE CONTROL OF INDUSTRY BY ADMINISTRATIVE PROCESS." UK DELIB/GP WORKER 20. PAGE 21 G0408
S67
INDUS
LAW
ADMIN
CONTROL

GOLDSTEIN W.,"THE SCIENCE ESTABLISHMENT AND ITS POLITICAL CONTROL." WOR+45 SOCIETY GP/REL RATIONAL ORD/FREE. PAGE 22 G0430
S67
CREATE
ADJUST
CONTROL

HILL R.,"SOCIAL ASPECTS OF FAMILY PLANNING." INDIA KOREA TAIWAN ECO/UNDEV PLAN PROB/SOLV TEC/DEV EDU/PROP CONTROL ATTIT DRIVE...HEAL PSY SOC 20 BIRTH/CON UN. PAGE 26 G0512
S67
FAM
BIO/SOC
GEOG
MARRIAGE

RAMSEY J.A.,"THE STATUS OF INTERNATIONAL COPYRIGHTS." WOR+45 CREATE TEC/DEV DIPLOM CONFER CONTROL SANCTION OWN...POLICY JURID. PAGE 46 G0899
S67
INT/LAW
INT/ORG
COM/IND
PRESS

REINTANZ G.,"THE SPACE TREATY." WOR+45 DIPLOM CONTROL ARMS/CONT NUC/PWR WAR...MARXIST 20 COLD/WAR UN TREATY. PAGE 46 G0911
S67
SPACE
INT/LAW
INT/ORG
PEACE

RICHMAN B.M.,"SOVIET MANAGEMENT IN TRANSITION." USSR FINAN MARKET EX/STRUC PLAN PROB/SOLV TEC/DEV CONTROL LEAD CENTRAL EFFICIENCY...METH/COMP 20 REFORMERS. PAGE 47 G0917
S67
MGT
MARXISM
POLICY
AUTHORIT

ROMANIECKI L.,"THE ATOM AND INTERNATIONAL COOPERATION." PROB/SOLV DIPLOM PEACE ORD/FREE 20. PAGE 47 G0933
S67
INT/ORG
NUC/PWR
ARMS/CONT
CONTROL

ROTHSTEIN R.L.,"NUCLEAR PROLIFERATION AND AMERICAN POLICY." PROB/SOLV BAL/PWR DIPLOM ARMS/CONT EFFICIENCY 20. PAGE 48 G0942
S67
NUC/PWR
CONTROL
DETER
WOR+45

SCHACTER O.,"SCIENTIFIC ADVANCES AND INTERNATIONAL LAWMAKING." FUT R+D PLAN PROB/SOLV CONFER CONTROL ...POLICY PREDICT 20 UN. PAGE 49 G0961
S67
TEC/DEV
INT/LAW
INT/ORG
ACT/RES

SCOVILLE W.J.,"GOVERNMENT REGULATION AND GROWTH IN THE FRENCH PAPER INDUSTRY DURING THE EIGHTEENTH CENTURY." FRANCE MOD/EUR FINAN CAP/ISM TAX ADMIN CONTROL PRIVIL LAISSEZ...POLICY 18. PAGE 50 G0985
S67
NAT/G
PROC/MFG
ECO/DEV
INGP/REL

SHULMAN M.D.,"'EUROPE' VERSUS 'DETENTE'." USA+45 USSR INT/ORG CONTROL ARMS/CONT DETER 20. PAGE 50 G0995
S67
DIPLOM
BAL/PWR
NUC/PWR

SINGH B.,"ITALIAN EXPERIENCE IN REGIONAL ECONOMIC DEVELOPMENT AND LESSONS FOR OTHER COUNTRIES." EUR+WWI ITALY INDUS NAT/G ACT/RES REGION GP/REL EFFICIENCY EQUILIB PRODUC WEALTH. PAGE 51 G1007
S67
ECO/UNDEV
PLAN
ECO/TAC
CONTROL

SKOLNIKOFF E.B.,"MAKING FOREIGN POLICY" PROB/SOLV EFFICIENCY PERCEPT PWR...MGT METH/CNCPT CLASSIF 20. PAGE 51 G1009
S67
TEC/DEV
CONTROL
USA+45
NAT/G

STYCOS J.M.,"POLITICS AND POPULATION CONTROL IN LATIN AMERICA." USA+45 FAM NAT/G GP/REL AGE/C ATTIT CATHISM MARXISM...POLICY UN WHO. PAGE 53 G1045
S67
PLAN
CENSUS
CONTROL
L/A+17C

TEKINER S.,"SINKIAN AND THE SINO-SOVIET CONFLICT." ASIA COM USSR FORCES PLAN BAL/PWR CONTROL NUC/PWR WAR WEAPON...DECISION 20. PAGE 54 G1060
S67
DIPLOM
PWR
MARXISM

TIVEY L.,"THE POLITICAL CONSEQUENCES OF ECONOMIC PLANNING." UK CONSTN INDUS ACT/RES ADMIN CONTROL LOBBY REPRESENT EFFICIENCY SUPEGO SOVEREIGN ...DECISION 20. PAGE 55 G1074
S67
PLAN
POLICY
NAT/G

US SUPERINTENDENT OF DOCUMENTS,SPACE: MISSILES, THE MOON, NASA, AND SATELLITES (PRICE LIST 79A). USA+45 COM/IND R+D NAT/G DIPLOM EDU/PROP ADMIN CONTROL HEALTH...POLICY SIMUL NASA CONGRESS. PAGE 61 G1190
N67
BIBLIOG/A
SPACE
TEC/DEV
PEACE

US SENATE COMM ON FOREIGN REL,ARMS SALES AND
N67
ARMS/CONT

FOREIGN POLICY (PAMPHLET). FINAN FOR/AID CONTROL   ADMIN
20. PAGE 60 G1181   OP/RES
                                                         DIPLOM

                                                         N67
US SENATE COMM ON PUBLIC WORKS,AIR QUALITY ACT OF   HEALTH
1967 (PAMPHLET). USA+45 INDUS R+D LEGIS SENATE.   AIR
PAGE 61 G1187   HABITAT
                                                        CONTROL

                                                         B88
BENTHAM J.,DEFENCE OF USURY (1787). UK LAW NAT/G   TAX
TEC/DEV ECO/TAC CONTROL ATTIT...CONCPT IDEA/COMP 18   FINAN
SMITH/ADAM. PAGE 6 G0124   ECO/DEV
                                                        POLICY

CONTROLLED DIRECT OBSERVATION....SEE CONT/OBS

CONV/LEASE....CONVICT LEASE SYSTEM IN SOUTH

CONVENTIONAL....SEE CONVNTL

CONVNTL....CONVENTIONAL

CONWAY J.E. G0252

COOKE E.F. G0253

COOLIDGE/C....CALVIN COOLIDGE

COOMBS C.H. G0254

COOPER A.C. G0255

COOPER C.C. G0950

COOPERATION....SEE AGREE

COOPERATIVE....SEE VOL/ASSN

COORDINATION....SEE CENTRAL

COPYRIGHT....COPYRIGHT

CORDIER A.W. G0256

CORE....CONGRESS OF RACIAL EQUALITY

CORN/LAWS....CORN LAWS (U.K.)

CORNELL/U....CORNELL UNIVERSITY

CORPORATION....SEE CORPORATN

CORPORATN....CORPORATION

CORRECTIONAL INSTITUTION....SEE PUB/INST

CORREL....STATISTICAL CORRELATIONS

CORY R.H. G0257,G0258

COST....ECONOMIC VALUE; SEE ALSO PROFIT

                                                         N19
BROWN W.M.,THE DESIGN AND PERFORMANCE OF "OPTIMUM"   HABITAT
BLAST SHELTER PROGRAMS (PAMPHLET). USA+45 ACT/RES   NUC/PWR
PLAN DEATH COST EFFICIENCY OPTIMAL...POLICY CHARTS   WAR
20. PAGE 9 G0180   HEALTH

                                                         N19
GINZBERG E.,MANPOWER FOR GOVERNMENT (PAMPHLET).   WORKER
USA+45 FORCES PLAN PROB/SOLV PAY EDU/PROP ADMIN   CONSULT
GP/REL COST...MGT PREDICT TREND 20 CIVIL/SERV.   NAT/G
PAGE 21 G0418   LOC/G

                                                         N19
VERNON R.,THE MYTH AND REALITY OF OUR URBAN   PLAN
PROBLEMS (PAMPHLET). USA+45 SOCIETY LOC/G ADMIN   MUNIC
COST 20 PRINCETN/U INTERVENT URBAN/RNWL. PAGE 61   HABITAT
G1197   PROB/SOLV

                                                         B37
GULICK L.,PAPERS ON THE SCIENCE OF ADMINISTRATION.   OP/RES
INDUS PROB/SOLV TEC/DEV COST EFFICIENCY PRODUC   CONTROL
HABITAT...PHIL/SCI METH/COMP 20. PAGE 23 G0461   ADMIN
                                                        MGT

                                                         B40
FULLER G.H.,SELECTED LIST OF RECENT REFERENCES ON   BIBLIOG
AMERICAN NATIONAL DEFENSE (PAMPHLET). USA-45 FINAN   CIVMIL/REL
NAT/G ARMS/CONT WAR GOV/REL CENTRAL COST PEACE PWR   FORCES
20. PAGE 20 G0400   WEAPON

                                                         B41
FULLER G.H.,DEFENSE FINANCING: A SELECTED LIST OF   BIBLIOG/A
REFERENCES (PAMPHLET). MOD/EUR USA-45 ECO/DEV NAT/G   FINAN
DELIB/GP RATION ARMS/CONT WEAPON COST PEACE PWR 20   FORCES
CONGRESS. PAGE 20 G0401   BUDGET

                                                         B41
FULLER G.H.,A LIST OF BIBLIOGRAPHIES ON QUESTIONS   BIBLIOG/A
RELATING TO NATIONAL DEFENSE (PAMPHLET). USA-45   FORCES
NAT/G ARMS/CONT WAR GOV/REL COST PEACE 20. PAGE 20   CIVMIL/REL
G0402   WEAPON

                                                         B42
FULLER G.H.,DEFENSE FINANCING: A SUPPLEMENTARY LIST   BIBLIOG/A
OF REFERENCES (PAMPHLET). CANADA UK USA-45 ECO/DEV   FINAN
NAT/G DELIB/GP BUDGET ADJUD ARMS/CONT WEAPON COST   FORCES
PEACE PWR 20 AUSTRAL CHINJAP CONGRESS. PAGE 21   DIPLOM
G0403

                                                         B47
BALDWIN H.W.,THE PRICE OF POWER. USA+45 FORCES PLAN   PROB/SOLV
NUC/PWR ADJUST COST ORD/FREE...POLICY PSY BIBLIOG   PWR
20. PAGE 5 G0089   POPULISM
                                                        PRICE

                                                         B48
METZLER L.A.,INCOME, EMPLOYMENT, AND PUBLIC POLICY.   INCOME
FINAN INDUS LOC/G NAT/G TAX GIVE PAY COST PRODUC   WEALTH
...MGT TIME/SEQ 20. PAGE 38 G0760   POLICY
                                                        ECO/TAC

                                                         B49
LEPAWSKY A.,ADMINISTRATION. FINAN INDUS LG/CO   ADMIN
SML/CO INGP/REL PERS/REL COST EFFICIENCY OPTIMAL   MGT
SKILL 20. PAGE 33 G0656   WORKER
                                                        EX/STRUC

                                                         B55
US OFFICE OF THE PRESIDENT,REPORT TO CONGRESS ON   DIPLOM
THE MUTUAL SECURITY PROGRAM FOR THE SIX MONTHS   FORCES
ENDED JUNE 30, 1955. ECO/DEV INT/ORG NAT/G CREATE   PLAN
TEC/DEV BAL/PWR ECO/TAC AGREE DETER COST ORD/FREE   FOR/AID
20 DEPT/STATE DEPT/DEFEN. PAGE 59 G1157

                                                         B56
US OFFICE OF THE PRESIDENT,REPORT TO CONGRESS ON   DIPLOM
THE MUTUAL SECURITY PROGRAM FOR THE SIX MONTHS   FORCES
ENDED DECEMBER 31, 1955. ASIA USSR ECO/DEV   PLAN
ECO/UNDEV INT/ORG CREATE TEC/DEV BAL/PWR ECO/TAC   FOR/AID
AGREE DETER COST ORD/FREE 20 DEPT/STATE DEPT/DEFEN
EISNHWR/DD. PAGE 59 G1158

                                                         B59
AIR FORCE ACADEMY ASSEMBLY '59,INTERNATIONAL   FOR/AID
STABILITY AND PROGRESS (PAMPHLET). USA+45 USSR   FORCES
ECO/UNDEV PROB/SOLV BUDGET DIPLOM ADMIN DETER COST   WAR
ATTIT...TREND 20. PAGE 2 G0030   PLAN

                                                         B59
MEANS G.C.,ADMINISTRATIVE INFLATION AND PUBLIC   ECO/TAC
POLICY (PAMPHLET). USA+45 ECO/DEV FINAN INDUS   POLICY
WORKER PLAN BUDGET GOV/REL COST DEMAND WEALTH 20   RATION
CONGRESS MONOPOLY GOLD/STAND. PAGE 38 G0749   CONTROL

                                                         B60
ATOMIC INDUSTRIAL FORUM,ATOMS FOR INDUSTRY: WORLD   NUC/PWR
FORUM. WOR+45 FINAN COST UTIL...JURID ANTHOL 20.   INDUS
PAGE 4 G0080   PLAN
                                                        PROB/SOLV

                                                         B60
WEBSTER J.A.,A GENERAL STUDY OF THE DEPARTMENT OF   ORD/FREE
DEFENSE INTERNAL SECURITY PROGRAM. USA+45 WORKER   PLAN
TEC/DEV ADJUD CONTROL CT/SYS EXEC GOV/REL COST   ADMIN
...POLICY DECISION MGT 20 DEPT/DEFEN SUPREME/CT.   NAT/G
PAGE 62 G1221

                                                         B61
MURPHY E.F.,WATER PURITY: A STUDY IN LEGAL CONTROL   SEA
OF NATURAL RESOURCES. LOC/G ACT/RES PLAN TEC/DEV   LAW
LOBBY GP/REL COST ATTIT HEALTH ORD/FREE...HEAL   PROVS
JURID 20 WISCONSIN WATER. PAGE 40 G0797   CONTROL

                                                         B62
FERBER R.,RESEARCH METHODS IN ECONOMICS AND   ACT/RES
BUSINESS. ECO/DEV FINAN MARKET LG/CO SML/CO CONSULT   PROB/SOLV
CONTROL COST...STAT METH/COMP 20. PAGE 19 G0364   ECO/TAC
                                                        MGT

                                                         B62
GRANICK D.,THE EUROPEAN EXECUTIVE. BELGIUM FRANCE   MGT
GERMANY/W UK INDUS LABOR LG/CO SML/CO EX/STRUC PLAN   ECO/DEV
TEC/DEV CAP/ISM COST DEMAND...POLICY CHARTS 20.   ECO/TAC
PAGE 22 G0441   EXEC

B62

MACHLUP F.,THE PRODUCTION AND DISTRIBUTION OF   ACADEM
KNOWLEDGE IN THE UNITED STATES. USA+45 COM/IND   TEC/DEV
INDUS SCHOOL SECT WORKER COMPUTER CREATE CIVMIL/REL EDU/PROP
COST EFFICIENCY WEALTH 20. PAGE 35 G0688   R+D

B63

BONINI C.P.,SIMULATION OF INFORMATION AND DECISION INDUS
SYSTEMS IN THE FIRM. MARKET BUDGET DOMIN EDU/PROP   SIMUL
ADMIN COST ATTIT HABITAT PERCEPT PWR...CONCPT   DECISION
PROBABIL QUANT PREDICT HYPO/EXP BIBLIOG. PAGE 8   MGT
G0152

B63

BROUDE H.W.,STEEL DECISIONS AND THE NATIONAL   PROC/MFG
ECONOMY. USA+45 LG/CO PLAN ADMIN COST DECISION.   NAT/G
PAGE 9 G0176   CONTROL
                                                   ECO/TAC

B63

BURSK E.C.,NEW DECISION-MAKING TOOLS FOR MANAGERS. DECISION
COMPUTER PLAN PROB/SOLV ROUTINE COST. PAGE 10 G0194 MGT
                                                   MATH
                                                   RIGID/FLEX

B63

US SENATE COMM APPROPRIATIONS,PERSONNEL   ADMIN
ADMINISTRATION AND OPERATIONS OF AGENCY FOR   FOR/AID
INTERNATIONAL DEVELOPMENT: SPECIAL HEARING. FINAN EFFICIENCY
LEAD COST UTIL SKILL...CHARTS 20 CONGRESS AID   DIPLOM
CIVIL/SERV. PAGE 60 G1175

S63

ENTHOVEN A.C.,"ECONOMIC ANALYSIS IN THE DEPARTMENT PLAN
OF DEFENSE." USA+45 NAT/G DELIB/GP PROB/SOLV RATION BUDGET
NUC/PWR WEAPON COST...DECISION 20 DEPT/DEFEN   ECO/TAC
RESOURCE/N. PAGE 18 G0349   FORCES

B64

BROWN N.,NUCLEAR WAR* THE IMPENDING STRATEGIC   FORCES
DEADLOCK. USA+45 USSR TEC/DEV BUDGET RISK ARMS/CONT OP/RES
NUC/PWR WEAPON COST BIO/SOC...GEOG IDEA/COMP   WAR
NAT/COMP GAME NATO WARSAW/P. PAGE 9 G0177   GEN/LAWS

B64

COENEN E.,LA "KONJUNKTURFORSCHUNG" EN ALLEMAGNE ET METH/COMP
EN AUTRICHE, 1925-1935. AUSTRIA GERMANY OP/RES PLAN R+D
COST PERCEPT...METH/CNCPT BIBLIOG 20. PAGE 12 G0237 ECO/TAC

B64

KAUFMANN W.W.,THE MC NAMARA STRATEGY. TOP/EX   FORCES
INSPECT BAL/PWR DIPLOM CONTROL DETER GUERRILLA   WAR
NUC/PWR WEAPON COST PWR...METH/COMP 20 MCNAMARA/R PLAN
KENNEDY/JF JOHNSON/LB NATO DEPT/DEFEN. PAGE 30   PROB/SOLV
G0586

B64

LANG A.S.,URBAN RAIL TRANSIT. OP/RES PLAN PROB/SOLV MUNIC
TEC/DEV AUTOMAT COST...TECHNIC MATH CON/ANAL CHARTS DIST/IND
METH/COMP SIMUL 20 RAILROAD PUB/TRANS. PAGE 32   ECOMETRIC
G0632

B64

TAUBENFELD H.J.,SPACE AND SOCIETY. USA+45 LAW   SPACE
FORCES CREATE TEC/DEV ADJUD CONTROL COST PEACE   SOCIETY
...PREDICT ANTHOL 20. PAGE 54 G1057   ADJUST
                                                   DIPLOM

S64

STONE P.A.,"DECISION TECHNIQUES FOR TOWN   OP/RES
DEVELOPMENT." PLAN COST PROFIT...DECISION MGT   MUNIC
CON/ANAL CHARTS METH/COMP BIBLIOG 20. PAGE 53 G1039 ADMIN
                                                   PROB/SOLV

B65

BLOOMFIELD L.,SOVIET INTERESTS IN ARMS CONTROL AND USSR
DISARMAMENT* THE DECADE UNDER KHRUSHCHEV 1954-1964. ARMS/CONT
ASIA FORCES ACT/RES EDU/PROP DETER NUC/PWR WEAPON DIPLOM
COST ATTIT...PHIL/SCI CLASSIF STAT NET/THEORY GAME TREND
BIBLIOG. PAGE 7 G0139

B65

HASSON J.A.,THE ECONOMICS OF NUCLEAR POWER. INDIA NUC/PWR
UK USA+45 WOR+45 INT/ORG TEC/DEV COST...SOC STAT   INDUS
CHARTS 20 EURATOM. PAGE 25 G0490   ECO/DEV
                                                   METH

B65

KANTOROVICH L.V.,THE BEST USE OF ECONOMIC   PLAN
RESOURCES. USSR SOCIETY FINAN ACT/RES TEC/DEV   MATH
ECO/TAC PRICE CONTROL COST DEMAND EFFICIENCY   DECISION
OPTIMAL...MGT STAT. PAGE 29 G0572

B65

KOROL A.G.,SOVIET RESEARCH AND DEVELOPMENT. USSR   COM
ACADEM SCHOOL WORKER ROUTINE COST...STAT T 20.   R+D

PAGE 31 G0615   FINAN
                                                   DIST/IND

B65

OECD,MEDITERRANEAN REGIONAL PROJECT: TURKEY;   EDU/PROP
EDUCATION AND DEVELOPMENT. FUT TURKEY SOCIETY   ACADEM
STRATA FINAN NAT/G PROF/ORG PLAN PROB/SOLV ADMIN   SCHOOL
COST...STAT CHARTS 20 OECD. PAGE 42 G0831   ECO/UNDEV

B65

OECD,THE MEDITERRANEAN REGIONAL PROJECT: SPAIN;   ECO/UNDEV
EDUCATION AND DEVELOPMENT. FUT SPAIN STRATA FINAN EDU/PROP
NAT/G WORKER PLAN PROB/SOLV ADMIN COST...POLICY   ACADEM
STAT CHARTS 20 OECD. PAGE 42 G0835   SCHOOL

B65

ORG FOR ECO COOP AND DEVEL,THE MEDITERRANEAN   EDU/PROP
REGIONAL PROJECT: YUGOSLAVIA; EDUCATION AND   ACADEM
DEVELOPMENT. YUGOSLAVIA SOCIETY FINAN PROF/ORG PLAN SCHOOL
ADMIN COST DEMAND MARXISM...STAT TREND CHARTS METH ECO/UNDEV
20 OECD. PAGE 43 G0843

B65

THAYER F.C. JR.,AIR TRANSPORT POLICY AND NATIONAL AIR
SECURITY: A POLITICAL, ECONOMIC, AND MILITARY   FORCES
ANALYSIS. DIST/IND OP/RES PLAN TEC/DEV DIPLOM DETER CIVMIL/REL
WAR COST EFFICIENCY...POLICY BIBLIOG 20 DEPT/DEFEN ORD/FREE
FAA CAB. PAGE 54 G1066

S65

ABT C.C.,"CONTROLLING FUTURE ARMS." USSR PLAN   PREDICT
BAL/PWR DIPLOM NUC/PWR COST...CLASSIF STAT CHARTS. FUT
PAGE 2 G0027   ARMS/CONT
                                                   TEC/DEV

S65

BALDWIN H.,"SLOW-DOWN IN THE PENTAGON." USA+45   RECORD
CREATE PLAN GOV/REL CENTRAL COST EFFICIENCY PWR   R+D
...MGT MCNAMARA/R. PAGE 5 G0088   WEAPON
                                                   ADMIN

S65

GOLDSTEIN W.,"KEEPING THE GENIE IN THE BOTTLE* THE NUC/PWR
FEASIBILITY OF A NUCLEAR NON-PROLIFERATION   CREATE
AGREEMENT." ASIA FRANCE UK USA+45 USSR WOR+45   COST
ECO/UNDEV VOL/ASSN ACT/RES PLAN RISK ARMS/CONT WAR
PEACE ATTIT PERCEPT...RECORD TREND TIME. PAGE 22
G0429

S65

HIBBS A.R.,"SPACE TECHNOLOGY* THE THREAT AND THE   SPACE
PROMISE." FUT VOL/ASSN TEC/DEV NUC/PWR COST   ARMS/CONT
EFFICIENCY UTIL UN TREATY. PAGE 26 G0510   PREDICT

S65

KUZMACK A.M.,"TECHNOLOGICAL CHANGE AND STABLE   R+D
DETERRENCE." CREATE EDU/PROP ARMS/CONT WEAPON   DETER
CHOOSE COST DRIVE PERCEPT...RECORD STERTYP TIME.   EQUILIB
PAGE 32 G0627

S65

SCHELLING T.C.,"SIGNALS AND FEEDBACK IN THE ARMS   FEEDBACK
DIALOGUE." USA+45 USSR R+D ACADEM FORCES ACT/RES   DETER
ADJUST COST GEN/LAWS. PAGE 49 G0964   EDU/PROP
                                                   ARMS/CONT

B66

BOLTON R.E.,DEFENSE AND DISARMAMENT: THE ECONOMICS ARMS/CONT
OF TRANSITION. USA+45 R+D FORCES PLAN LOBBY DETER POLICY
WAR COST PEACE...ANTHOL BIBLIOG 20. PAGE 8 G0150   INDUS

B66

KURAKOV I.G.,SCIENCE, TECHNOLOGY AND COMMUNISM;   CREATE
SOME QUESTIONS OF DEVELOPMENT (TRANS. BY CARIN   TEC/DEV
DEDIJER). USSR INDUS PLAN PROB/SOLV COST PRODUC   MARXISM
...MGT MATH CHARTS METH 20. PAGE 32 G0626   ECO/TAC

B66

STONE J.J.,CONTAINING THE ARMS RACE* SOME SPECIFIC ARMS/CONT
PROPOSALS. ASIA USA+45 USSR PROB/SOLV BARGAIN   FEEDBACK
DIPLOM DETER NUC/PWR RATIONAL...GAME 20 DEPT/DEFEN COST
TREATY. PAGE 53 G1038   ATTIT

B66

US DEPARTMENT OF LABOR,PRODUCTIVITY: A   BIBLIOG/A
BIBLIOGRAPHY. ECO/DEV INDUS MARKET OP/RES AUTOMAT PRODUC
COST...STAT 20. PAGE 57 G1119   LABOR
                                                   PLAN

B66

WHITNAH D.R.,SAFER SKYWAYS. DIST/IND DELIB/GP   ADMIN
FORCES TOP/EX WORKER TEC/DEV ROUTINE WAR CIVMIL/REL NAT/G
COST...TIME/SEQ 20 FAA CAB. PAGE 63 G1235   AIR
                                                   GOV/REL

ELSNER H.,THE TECHNOCRATS, PROPHETS OF AUTOMATION. AUTOMAT
SOCIETY INDUS VOL/ASSN COST INCOME ATTIT 20. TECHRACY
PAGE 18 G0345 PRODUC
HIST/WRIT
B67

HEADLEY J.C.,PESTICIDE PROBLEM: AN ECONOMIC HABITAT
APPROACH TO PUBLIC POLICY. AGRI TEC/DEV GOV/REL POLICY
COST ATTIT CHARTS. PAGE 25 G0498 BIO/SOC
CONTROL
B67

MACAVOY P.W.,REGULATION OF TRANSPORT INNOVATION. DIST/IND
ACT/RES ADJUD COST DEMAND...POLICY CHARTS 20. CONTROL
PAGE 35 G0684 PRICE
PROFIT
B67

MACKINTOSH J.M.,JUGGERNAUT. USSR NAT/G POL/PAR WAR
ADMIN LEAD CIVMIL/REL COST TOTALISM PWR MARXISM FORCES
...GOV/COMP 20. PAGE 35 G0691 COM
PROF/ORG
B67

NORTHRUP H.R.,RESTRICTIVE LABOR PRACTICES IN THE DIST/IND
SUPERMARKET INDUSTRY. USA+45 INDUS WORKER TEC/DEV MARKET
BARGAIN PAY CONTROL GP/REL COST...STAT CHARTS NLRB. LABOR
PAGE 42 G0827 MGT
B67

ROTHENBERG J.,ECONOMIC EVALUATION OF URBAN RENEWAL: PLAN
CONCEPTUAL FOUNDATION OF BENEFIT-COST ANALYSIS. MUNIC
USA+45 ECO/DEV NEIGH TEC/DEV ADMIN GEN/LAWS. PROB/SOLV
PAGE 48 G0940 COST
B67

SCHON D.A.,TECHNOLOGY AND CHANGE* THE NEW INDUS
HERACLITUS. TEC/DEV CONTROL COST DEMAND EFFICIENCY PROB/SOLV
RIGID/FLEX...MYTH 20. PAGE 49 G0975 R+D
CREATE
B67

SILBERMAN C.E.,THE MYTHS OF AUTOMATION. INDUS MYTH
WORKER COST PRODUC AGE WEALTH 20. PAGE 51 G0996 AUTOMAT
CHARTS
TEC/DEV
B67

WEINBERG A.M.,REFLECTIONS ON BIG SCIENCE. FUT ACADEM
USA+45 NAT/G EDU/PROP CHOOSE PERS/REL COST OPTIMAL KNOWL
...PHIL/SCI TREND. PAGE 62 G1225 R+D
PLAN
S67

BARAN P.,"THE FUTURE COMPUTER UTILITY." USA+45 COMPUTER
NAT/G PLAN CONTROL COST...POLICY 20. PAGE 5 G0091 UTIL
FUT
TEC/DEV
S67

BARRO S.,"ECONOMIC IMPACT OF SPACE EXPENDITURES: SPACE
SOME BROAD ISSUES DEALING WITH COSTS AND BENEFITS." FINAN
USA+45 PROC/MFG R+D LG/CO CONSULT COST PRODUC 20. ECO/TAC
PAGE 5 G0098 NAT/G
S67

ENKE S.,"GOVERNMENT-INDUSTRY DEVELOPMENT OF A INDUS
COMMERCIAL SUPERSONIC TRANSPORT." USA+45 ECO/DEV FINAN
R+D LG/CO NAT/G TEC/DEV PRICE RISK COST PROFIT. SERV/IND
PAGE 18 G0347 CAP/ISM
S67

INGLIS D.R.,"MISSILE DEFENSE, NUCLEAR SPREAD, AND NUC/PWR
VIETNAM." CHINA/COM USA+45 USSR VIETNAM INDUS ARMS/CONT
BAL/PWR DETER WAR COST NAT/LISM PEACE. PAGE 28 DIPLOM
G0544 FORCES
S67

JAIN G.,"INDIA REJECTS THE POWER RACE* REALISM INDIA
ABOUT NUCLEAR WEAPONS." FORCES PROB/SOLV FOR/AID CHINA/COM
ARMS/CONT COST PWR...GOV/COMP 20. PAGE 28 G0556 NUC/PWR
DIPLOM
S67

LEWIS R.L.,"GOAL AND NO GOAL* A NEW POLICY IN SPACE
SPACE." R+D BUDGET COST...POLICY DECISION PHIL/SCI. PLAN
PAGE 34 G0662 EFFICIENCY
CREATE
S67

PENNEY N.,"BANK STATEMENTS, CANCELLED CHECKS, AND CREATE
ARTICLE FOUR IN THE ELECTRONIC AGE." USA+45 TEC/DEV LAW
COST EFFICIENCY WEALTH. PAGE 44 G0866 ADJUD
FINAN

YOUNG O.R.,"ACTIVE DEFENSE AND INTERNATIONAL ARMS/CONT
ORDER." FORCES BAL/PWR DEBATE GAMBLE COST PEACE. DETER
PAGE 64 G1265 PLAN
DECISION
S67

US CONGRESS JT COMM ECO GOVT,BACKGROUND MATERIAL ON BUDGET
ECONOMY IN GOVERNMENT 1967 (PAMPHLET). WOR+45 COST
ECO/DEV BARGAIN PRICE DEMAND OPTIMAL...STAT MGT
DEPT/DEFEN. PAGE 57 G1116 NAT/G
N67

COSTA/RICA....SEE ALSO L/A+17C

COTTRELL L.S. G0085

COUGHLIN/C....CHARLES EDWARD COUGHLIN

COUNCIL-MANAGER SYSTEM OF LOCAL GOVERNMENT....SEE
COUNCL/MGR

COUNCL/EUR....COUNCIL OF EUROPE

COUNCL/MGR....COUNCIL-MANAGER SYSTEM OF LOCAL GOVERNMENT

COUNTIES....SEE LOC/G

COUNTY AGRICULTURAL AGENT....SEE COUNTY/AGT

COUNTY/AGT....COUNTY AGRICULTURAL AGENT

COURAGE....SEE DRIVE

COURT OF APPEALS....SEE CT/APPEALS

COURT SYSTEMS....SEE CT/SYS

COURT/DIST....DISTRICT COURTS

COWPER/W....WILLIAM COWPER

CRAIG J. G0259

CRANBERG L. G0260

CRANE R.D. G0261

CRAUMER L.V. G0262

CREATE....CREATIVE PROCESSES

AMERICAN DOCUMENTATION INST,DOCUMENTATION BIBLIOG/A
ABSTRACTS. WOR+45 NAT/G COMPUTER CREATE TEC/DEV AUTOMAT
DIPLOM EDU/PROP REGION KNOWL...PHIL/SCI CLASSIF COMPUT/IR
LING. PAGE 3 G0051 R+D
N

KRUTILLA J.V.,CONSERVATION RECONSIDERED. USA+45 PROB/SOLV
CREATE EDU/PROP. PAGE 32 G0624 POLICY
HABITAT
GEOG
N

US DEPT COMMERCE OFF TECH SERV,TECHNICAL BIBLIOG
TRANSLATIONS. WOR+45 INDUS COMPUTER CREATE NUC/PWR R+D
...PHIL/SCI COMPUT/IR METH/COMP METH. PAGE 58 G1135 TEC/DEV
AUTOMAT
B

JOURNAL OF CONFLICT RESOLUTION. FUT WOR+45 INT/ORG BIBLIOG/A
NAT/G FORCES CREATE PROB/SOLV ARMS/CONT NUC/PWR DIPLOM
WEAPON SOC. PAGE 1 G0002 WAR
N

PERSONNEL. USA+45 LAW LABOR LG/CO WORKER CREATE BIBLIOG/A
GOV/REL PERS/REL ATTIT WEALTH. PAGE 1 G0010 ADMIN
MGT
GP/REL
N

KAUFMAN J.L.,COMMUNITY RENEWAL PROGRAMS (PAMPHLET). LOC/G
USA+45 CONSTRUC PROVS CREATE PLAN CONTROL WEALTH 20 MUNIC
URBAN/RNWL. PAGE 30 G0584 ACT/RES
BIBLIOG
N19

US ATOMIC ENERGY COMMISSION,ATOMIC ENERGY IN USE OP/RES
(PAMPHLET). R+D RISK EFFICIENCY HEALTH KNOWL TEC/DEV
ORD/FREE...PHIL/SCI CONCPT METH/CNCPT CHARTS NUC/PWR
LAB/EXP 20 AEC. PAGE 56 G1106 CREATE
N19

DRAPER J.W.,HISTORY OF THE CONFLICT BETWEEN SECT
B23

RELIGION AND SCIENCE. WOR-45 INTELL SOCIETY R+D KNOWL CREATE PLAN EDU/PROP ATTIT PWR...PHIL/SCI CONCPT OBS TIME/SEQ TREND GEN/LAWS TOT/POP. PAGE 16 G0314

B49
ROSENHAUPT H.W.,HOW TO WAGE PEACE. USA+45 SOCIETY INTELL STRATA STRUCT R+D INT/ORG POL/PAR LEGIS ACT/RES CONCPT CREATE PLAN EDU/PROP ADMIN EXEC ATTIT ALL/VALS DIPLOM ...TIME/SEQ TREND COLD/WAR 20. PAGE 48 G0937

C27
BOSANQUET B.,"SCIENCE AND PHILOSOPHY" IN J. PHIL/SCI MUIRHEAD AND R.B. BOSANQUET, EDS., SCIENCE AND CREATE PHILOSOPHY AND OTHER ESSAYS."...CONCPT METH/COMP METH/CNCPT GEN/METH. PAGE 8 G0155 NEW/IDEA

B50
CANTRIL H.,TENSIONS THAT CAUSE WAR. UNIV CULTURE SOCIETY R+D CREATE EDU/PROP DRIVE PERSON KNOWL ORD/FREE PHIL/SCI ...HUM PSY SOC OBS CENSUS TREND CON/ANAL SOC/EXP PEACE SIMUL GEN/METH ANTHOL COLD/WAR TOT/POP. PAGE 11 G0206

B34
EINSTEIN A.,THE WORLD AS I SEE IT. WOR-45 INTELL SOCIETY R+D INT/ORG NAT/G SECT VOL/ASSN FORCES CREATE PHIL/SCI EDU/PROP LEGIT ARMS/CONT WAR WEAPON NAT/LISM DIPLOM ALL/VALS...POLICY CONCPT 20. PAGE 17 G0337 PACIFISM

S50
KAPLAN A.,"THE PREDICTION OF SOCIAL AND PWR TECHNOLOGICAL EVENTS." VOL/ASSN CONSULT ACT/RES KNO/TEST CREATE OP/RES PLAN ROUTINE PERSON...POLICY METH/CNCPT STAT QU/SEMANT SYS/QU TESTS CENSUS TREND 20. PAGE 29 G0574

B36
US LIBRARY OF CONGRESS,CLASSIFIED GUIDE TO MATERIAL BIBLIOG IN THE LIBRARY OF CONGRESS COVERING URBAN COMMUNITY CLASSIF DEVELOPMENT. USA+45 CREATE PROB/SOLV ADMIN 20. MUNIC PAGE 59 G1154 PLAN

S50
LENTZ T.F.,"REPORT ON A SURVEY OF SOCIAL SCIENTISTS ACT/RES CONDUCTED BY THE ATTITUDE RESEARCH LABORATORY." FUT ATTIT WOR+45 CREATE EDU/PROP...PSY STAT RECORD SYS/QU DIPLOM SAMP/SIZ CON/ANAL VAL/FREE 20. PAGE 33 G0655

B37
STAMP S.,THE SCIENCE OF SOCIAL ADJUSTMENT. WOR-45 ADJUST ACT/RES CREATE PLAN PROB/SOLV TEC/DEV ECO/TAC ORD/FREE EFFICIENCY SOC/INTEG 20. PAGE 52 G1031 PHIL/SCI

B51
CONANT J.B.,SCIENCE AND COMMON SENSE. WOR+45 WOR-45 CREATE R+D SCHOOL CONSULT TEC/DEV EDU/PROP SKILL...PLURIST PHIL/SCI METH/CNCPT RECORD TIME/SEQ SIMUL GEN/METH METH. PAGE 13 G0248

S38
LUNDBERG G.A.,"THE CONCEPT OF LAW IN THE SOCIAL EPIST SCIENCES"(BMR)" CULTURE INTELL SOCIETY STRUCT GEN/LAWS CREATE...NEW/IDEA 20. PAGE 34 G0678 CONCPT PHIL/SCI

B51
HUXLEY J.,FREEDOM AND CULTURE. UNIV LAW SOCIETY R+D CULTURE ACADEM SCHOOL CREATE SANCTION ATTIT KNOWL...HUM ORD/FREE ANTHOL 20. PAGE 27 G0540 PHIL/SCI IDEA/COMP

B40
HELLMAN F.S.,THE NEW DEAL: SELECTED LIST OF BIBLIOG/A REFERENCES. USA-45 FINAN LABOR EX/STRUC CREATE ECO/TAC INT/TRADE ADMIN CT/SYS 20 SUPREME/CT. PAGE 26 G0505 PLAN POLICY

B51
LEWIN K.,FIELD THEORY IN SOCIAL SCIENCE: SELECTED PHIL/SCI THEORETICAL PAPERS. UNIV CREATE DRIVE PERCEPT KNOWL HYPO/EXP ...METH/CNCPT CONT/OBS CHARTS GEN/METH METH VAL/FREE 20. PAGE 33 G0661

S42
LASSWELL H.D.,"THE RELATION OF IDEOLOGICAL ATTIT INTELLIGENCE TO PUBLIC POLICY." WOR+45 WOR-45 DECISION SOCIETY DELIB/GP ACT/RES CREATE PLAN DIPLOM EDU/PROP CHOOSE KNOWL PWR...POLICY SOC TREND GEN/LAWS 20. PAGE 32 G0638

S51
LERNER D.,"THE POLICY SCIENCES: RECENT DEVELOPMENTS CONSULT IN SCOPE AND METHODS." R+D SERV/IND CREATE DIPLOM SOC ROUTINE PWR...METH/CNCPT TREND GEN/LAWS METH 20. PAGE 33 G0658

B45
BUSH V.,SCIENCE, THE ENDLESS FRONTIER. FUT USA-45 R+D INTELL STRATA ACT/RES CREATE PLAN EDU/PROP ADMIN NAT/G NUC/PWR PEACE ATTIT HEALTH KNOWL...MAJORIT HEAL MGT PHIL/SCI CONCPT OBS TREND 20. PAGE 10 G0195

B52
HAYEK F.A.,THE COUNTER-REVOLUTION OF SCIENCE. UNIV PERCEPT INTELL R+D VOL/ASSN CREATE EDU/PROP...PHIL/SCI SOC KNOWL OBS TIME/SEQ TREND GEN/METH. PAGE 25 G0494

B46
AMERICAN DOCUMENTATION INST,CATALOGUE OF AUXILIARY BIBLIOG PUBLICATIONS IN MICROFILMS AND PHOTOPRINTS. USA-45 EDU/PROP LAW AGRI CREATE TEC/DEV ADMIN...GEOG LING MATH 20. PSY PAGE 3 G0052

L52
ELDERSVELD S.J.,"RESEARCH IN POLITICAL BEHAVIOR" ACT/RES (BMR)" USA+45 PLAN TEC/DEV ATTIT...BIBLIOG/A GEN/LAWS 20. PAGE 17 G0341 CREATE METH

B46
BUSH V.,ENDLESS HORIZONS. FUT USA-45 INTELL NAT/G R+D CONSULT ACT/RES CREATE PLAN EDU/PROP DRIVE KNOWL ...MAJORIT HEAL MGT PHIL/SCI CONCPT OBS TREND PEACE GEN/METH TOT/POP 20. PAGE 10 G0196

L52
ROYAL INST. INT. AFF.,"ANNUAL REPORT OF THE R+D COUNCIL: 1951-1952." WOR+45 CREATE KNOWL...MGT EDU/PROP COLD/WAR CMN/WLTH TOT/POP VAL/FREE 20. PAGE 48 G0943

B46
MORGENTHAU H.J.,SCIENTIFIC MAN VS POWER POLITICS. UNIV USA+45 WOR+45 INTELL SOCIETY ACT/RES CREATE PLAN MORAL EDU/PROP...CONCPT TREND TOT/POP 20. PAGE 40 G0782 PEACE

S52
KECSKEMETI P.,"THE 'POLICY SCIENCES': ASPIRATION CREATE AND OUTLOOK." UNIV CULTURE INTELL SOCIETY STRUCT NEW/IDEA EDU/PROP ATTIT PERCEPT RIGID/FLEX KNOWL...PHIL/SCI METH/CNCPT OBS 20. PAGE 30 G0589

B47
BRYSON L.,SCIENCE AND FREEDOM. WOR+45 ACT/RES CONCPT CREATE TECHRACY...TECHNIC SOC/INTEG. PAGE 9 G0183 ORD/FREE CULTURE SOC

B53
EASTON D.,THE POLITICAL SYSTEM, AN INQUIRY INTO THE R+D STATE POLITICAL SCIENCE. USA+45 INTELL CREATE PERCEPT EDU/PROP RIGID/FLEX KNOWL SKILL...PHIL/SCI NEW/IDEA STERTYP TOT/POP 20. PAGE 17 G0329

B48
STEWART I.,ORGANIZING SCIENTIFIC RESEARCH FOR WAR: DELIB/GP ADMINISTRATIVE HISTORY OF OFFICE OF SCIENTIFIC ADMIN RESEARCH AND DEVELOPMENT. USA-45 INTELL R+D LABOR WAR WORKER CREATE BUDGET WEAPON CIVMIL/REL GP/REL TEC/DEV EFFICIENCY...POLICY 20. PAGE 53 G1036

B53
HOVLAND C.I.,COMMUNICATION AND PERSUASION: PSY PSYCHOLOGICAL STUDIES OF OPINION CHANGE. INTELL EDU/PROP SOCIETY ECO/DEV COM/IND R+D SERV/IND CREATE TEC/DEV ATTIT RIGID/FLEX KNOWL NEW/IDEA. PAGE 27 G0531

S48
MARQUIS D.G.,"RESEARCH PLANNING AT THE FRONTIERS OF PLAN SCIENCE" (BMR)" INTELL ACADEM CREATE UTIL...PSY 20. ACT/RES PAGE 36 G0708 EFFICIENCY GEN/METH

B53
LARSEN K.,NATIONAL BIBLIOGRAPHIC SERVICES: THEIR BIBLIOG/A CREATION AND OPERATION. WOR+45 COM/IND CREATE PLAN INT/ORG DIPLOM PRESS ADMIN ROUTINE...MGT UNESCO. PAGE 32 WRITING G0636

B49
OGBURN W.,TECHNOLOGY AND INTERNATIONAL RELATIONS. TEC/DEV WOR+45 WOR-45 ECO/DEV CREATE PLAN ECO/TAC EDU/PROP DIPLOM COERCE PWR SKILL WEALTH...TECHNIC PSY SOC NEW/IDEA INT/ORG CHARTS TOT/POP 20. PAGE 43 G0837

S53
MILLER G.A.,"WHAT IS INFORMATION MEASUREMENT?" COMPUTER CREATE...CONCPT METH/CNCPT QUANT STAT CHARTS TEC/DEV BIBLIOG/A 20. PAGE 39 G0771 PSY MATH

B54
ARON R.,CENTURY OF TOTAL WAR. FUT WOR+45 WOR-45   ATTIT
SOCIETY INT/ORG NAT/G FORCES TOP/EX CREATE BAL/PWR   WAR
DOMIN EDU/PROP COERCE DETER PEACE TOTALSM PWR
...TIME/SEQ TREND COLD/WAR TOT/POP VAL/FREE
LEAGUE/NAT 20. PAGE 4 G0066

B54
COMBS C.H.,DECISION PROCESSES. INTELL SOCIETY   MATH
DELIB/GP CREATE TEC/DEV DOMIN LEGIT EXEC CHOOSE   DECISION
DRIVE RIGID/FLEX KNOWL PWR...PHIL/SCI SOC
METH/CNCPT CONT/OBS REC/INT PERS/TEST SAMP/SIZ BIOG
SOC/EXP WORK. PAGE 13 G0245

B54
MOSK S.A.,INDUSTRIAL REVOLUTION IN MEXICO. MARKET   INDUS
LABOR CREATE CAP/ISM ADMIN ATTIT SOCISM...POLICY 20   TEC/DEV
MEXIC/AMER. PAGE 40 G0789   ECO/UNDEV
                                                         NAT/G

B54
WASHBURNE N.F.,INTERPRETING SOCIAL CHANGE IN   CULTURE
AMERICA. USA+45 STRATA FAM NAT/G SECT OP/RES   STRUCT
ECO/TAC EDU/PROP HABITAT...SOC TIME/SEQ TREND 20   CREATE
BUREAUCRCY. PAGE 62 G1217   TEC/DEV

B54
WRIGHT Q.,PROBLEMS OF STABILITY AND PROGRESS IN   INT/ORG
INTERNATIONAL RELATIONSHIPS. FUT WOR+45 WOR-45   CONCPT
SOCIETY LEGIS CREATE TEC/DEV ECO/TAC EDU/PROP ADJUD   DIPLOM
WAR PEACE ORD/FREE PWR...KNO/TEST TREND GEN/LAWS
20. PAGE 64 G1257

L54
OPLER M.E.,"SOCIAL ASPECTS OF TECHNICAL ASSISTANCE   INT/ORG
IN OPERATION." WOR+45 VOL/ASSN CREATE PLAN TEC/DEV   CONSULT
EDU/PROP ALL/VALS...METH/CNCPT OBS RECORD TREND UN   FOR/AID
20. PAGE 43 G0841

S54
PYE L.W.,"EASTERN NATIONALISM AND WESTERN POLICY."   CREATE
ASIA S/ASIA USA+45 USA-45 SOCIETY PLAN DIPLOM KNOWL   ACT/RES
TOT/POP 20. PAGE 46 G0896   NAT/LISM

B55
OPPENHEIMER R.,THE OPEN MIND. USA+45 WOR+45 NAT/G   CREATE
DELIB/GP DETER MORAL ORD/FREE...MYTH GEN/LAWS 20.   PWR
PAGE 43 G0842   ARMS/CONT
                                                         NUC/PWR

B55
SHUBIK M.,READINGS IN GAME THEORY AND POLITICAL   MATH
BEHAVIOR. WOR+45 FORCES CREATE ROUTINE WAR PEACE   DECISION
PERCEPT KNOWL PWR...PSY SOC CONCPT METH/CNCPT STAT   DIPLOM
CHARTS HYPO/EXP GAME METH VAL/FREE 20. PAGE 50
G0991

B55
US OFFICE OF THE PRESIDENT,REPORT TO CONGRESS ON   DIPLOM
THE MUTUAL SECURITY PROGRAM FOR THE SIX MONTHS   FORCES
ENDED JUNE 30, 1955. ECO/DEV INT/ORG NAT/G CREATE   PLAN
TEC/DEV BAL/PWR ECO/TAC AGREE DETER COST ORD/FREE   FOR/AID
20 DEPT/STATE DEPT/DEFEN. PAGE 59 G1157

S55
ANGELL R.,"GOVERNMENTS AND PEOPLES AS A FOCI FOR   FUT
PEACE-ORIENTED RESEARCH." WOR+45 CULTURE SOCIETY   SOC
FACE/GP ACT/RES CREATE PLAN DIPLOM EDU/PROP ROUTINE   PEACE
ATTIT PERCEPT SKILL...POLICY CONCPT OBS TREND
GEN/METH 20. PAGE 3 G0060

S55
GLADSTONE A.E.,"THE POSSIBILITY OF PREDICTING   PHIL/SCI
REACTIONS TO INTERNATIONAL EVENTS." UNIV SOCIETY   CONCPT
NAT/G FORCES CREATE EDU/PROP COERCE WAR ATTIT
PERSON KNOWL PWR SKILL...METH/CNCPT NEW/IDEA
ORG/CHARTS. PAGE 21 G0420

S55
MILLER J.G.,"TOWARD A GENERAL THEORY FOR THE   CONCPT
BEHAVIORAL SCIENCES" (BMR)" CREATE ALL/VALS KNOWL   OP/RES
...CON/ANAL CHARTS HYPO/EXP SIMUL BIBLIOG 20.   METH/CNCPT
PAGE 39 G0773   COMPUTER

B56
HISTORICAL ABSTRACTS. NAT/G CREATE DIPLOM ATTIT   WOR-45
...SOC DICTIONARY INDEX 18/20. PAGE 1 G0013   COMPUT/IR
                                                        BIBLIOG/A

B56
US DEPARTMENT OF THE ARMY,RESEARCH AND DEVELOPMENT   BIBLIOG/A
(AND RELATED ASPECTS) IN FOREIGN COUNTRIES. WOR+45   R+D
DIST/IND INDUS CONSULT FORCES CREATE EDU/PROP   TEC/DEV
AUTOMAT DETER WEAPON. PAGE 57 G1126   NUC/PWR

B56
US OFFICE OF THE PRESIDENT,REPORT TO CONGRESS ON   DIPLOM
THE MUTUAL SECURITY PROGRAM FOR THE SIX MONTHS   FORCES
ENDED DECEMBER 31, 1955. ASIA USSR ECO/DEV   PLAN
ECO/UNDEV INT/ORG CREATE TEC/DEV BAL/PWR ECO/TAC   FOR/AID
AGREE DETER COST ORD/FREE 20 DEPT/STATE DEPT/DEFEN.
EISNHWR/DD. PAGE 59 G1158

B56
VUCINICH A.,THE SOVIET ACADEMY OF SCIENCES. USSR   PHIL/SCI
STRUCT ACADEM NAT/G EDU/PROP ADMIN LEAD ROLE   CREATE
...BIBLIOG 20 ACADEM/SCI. PAGE 61 G1203   INTELL
                                                        PROF/ORG

S56
GORDON L.,"THE ORGANIZATION FOR EUROPEAN ECONOMIC   VOL/ASSN
COOPERATION." EUR+WWI INDUS INT/ORG NAT/G CONSULT   ECO/DEV
DELIB/GP ACT/RES CREATE PLAN TEC/DEV EDU/PROP LEGIT
WEALTH OEEC 20. PAGE 22 G0435

S56
MILLER W.E.,"PRESIDENTIAL COATTAILS: A STUDY IN   CHIEF
POLITICAL MYTH AND METHODOLOGY" (BMR)" USA+45   CHOOSE
CREATE PARTIC ATTIT DRIVE PWR...DECISION CONCPT   POL/PAR
CHARTS SIMUL 20 PRESIDENT CONGRESS. PAGE 39 G0774   MYTH

B57
DUPREE A.H.,SCIENCE IN THE FEDERAL GOVERNMENT: A   NAT/G
HISTORY OF POLICIES AND ACTIVITIES TO 1940. USA-45   R+D
AGRI SCHOOL DELIB/GP WAR GOV/REL...PHIL/SCI BIBLIOG   CREATE
18/20 DEPRESSION NEW/DEAL WWI JEFFERSN/T. PAGE 17   TEC/DEV
G0324

S57
FISHMAN B.G.,"PUBLIC POLICY AND POLITICAL   ECO/DEV
CONSIDERATIONS." USA+45 SOCIETY NAT/G ACT/RES   CONSULT
CREATE PLAN DIPLOM KNOWL ORD/FREE...CONCPT GEN/METH
20. PAGE 19 G0370

S57
MCDONALD L.C.,"VOEGELIN AND THE POSITIVISTS: A NEW   PHIL/SCI
SCIENCE OF POLITICS." WOR+45 WOR-45 INTELL CREATE   CONCPT
PLAN ATTIT...METH/CNCPT NEW/IDEA OBS VAL/FREE 20.   GEN/METH
PAGE 37 G0734

B58
BIDWELL P.W.,RAW MATERIALS: A STUDY OF AMERICAN   EXTR/IND
POLICY. USA+45 USA-45 ECO/UNDEV AGRI INDUS KIN   ECO/DEV
CREATE PLAN ECO/TAC WAR PEACE ATTIT DRIVE WEALTH
...STAT CHARTS CONGRESS VAL/FREE. PAGE 7 G0135

B58
CHEEK G.,ECONOMIC AND SOCIAL IMPLICATIONS OF   BIBLIOG/A
AUTOMATION: A BIBLIOGRAPHIC REVIEW (PAMPHLET).   SOCIETY
USA+45 LG/CO WORKER CREATE PLAN CONTROL ROUTINE   INDUS
PERS/REL EFFICIENCY PRODUC...METH/COMP 20. PAGE 12   AUTOMAT
G0225

B58
EHRHARD J.,LE DESTIN DU COLONIALISME. AFR FRANCE   COLONIAL
ECO/UNDEV AGRI FINAN MARKET CREATE PLAN TEC/DEV   FOR/AID
BUDGET DIPLOM PRICE 20. PAGE 17 G0335   INT/TRADE
                                                        INDUS

B58
GANGE J.,UNIVERSITY RESEARCH ON INTERNATIONAL   R+D
AFFAIRS. USA+45 ACADEM INT/ORG CONSULT CREATE EXEC   MGT
ROUTINE...QUANT STAT INT STERTYP GEN/METH TOT/POP   DIPLOM
VAL/FREE 20. PAGE 21 G0407

B58
JUNGK R.,BRIGHTER THAN A THOUSAND SUNS: THE MORAL   NUC/PWR
AND POLITICAL HISTORY OF THE ATOMIC SCIENTISTS.   MORAL
WOR+45 WOR-45 CONSULT CREATE RISK UTIL DRIVE   GOV/REL
PERCEPT PWR...INT 20. PAGE 29 G0568   PERSON

B58
LIPPITT R.,DYNAMICS OF PLANNED CHANGE. STRUCT   VOL/ASSN
ACT/RES ROUTINE INGP/REL PWR...POLICY METH/CNCPT   ORD/FREE
BIBLIOG. PAGE 34 G0672   PLAN
                                                        CREATE

B58
ORTEGA Y GASSET J.,MAN AND CRISIS. SECT CREATE   PHIL/SCI
PERSON CONSERVE...GEN/LAWS RENAISSAN. PAGE 43 G0846   CULTURE
                                                        CONCPT

S58
ANDERSON N.,"INTERNATIONAL SEMINARS: AN ANALYSIS   INT/ORG
AND AN EVALUATION." WOR+45 R+D ACT/RES CREATE PLAN   DELIB/GP
REGION ATTIT KNOWL SKILL...SOC REC/INT PERS/TEST
CHARTS 20. PAGE 3 G0057

S58
DAVENPORT J.,"ARMS AND THE WELFARE STATE." INTELL   USA+45
STRUCT FORCES CREATE ECO/TAC FOR/AID DOMIN LEGIT   NAT/G

ADMIN WAR ORD/FREE PWR...POLICY SOC CONCPT MYTH OBS USSR
TREND COLD/WAR TOT/POP 20. PAGE 14 G0276

                                                                    S58
LASSWELL H.D.,"THE SCIENTIFIC STUDY OF   PHIL/SCI
INTERNATIONAL RELATIONS." USA+45 INT/ORG CREATE   GEN/METH
EDU/PROP DETER ATTIT PERCEPT PWR...DECISION CONCPT   DIPLOM
METH/CNCPT STYLE CON/ANAL 20. PAGE 33 G0642

                                                                    B59
STANFORD RESEARCH INSTITUTE,POSSIBLE NONMILITARY   R+D
SCIENTIFIC DEVELOPMENTS AND THEIR POTENTIAL IMPACT   TEC/DEV
ON FOREIGN POLICY PROBLEMS OF THE UNITED. FUT
USA+45 INT/ORG PROF/ORG CONSULT ACT/RES CREATE PLAN
PEACE KNOWL SKILL...TECHNIC PHIL/SCI NEW/IDEA
UNESCO 20. PAGE 52 G1032

                                                                    S59
ADAMS E.W.,"A MODEL OF RISKLESS CHOICE." CREATE   GAME
PROB/SOLV UTIL...PROBABIL PREDICT HYPO/EXP. PAGE 2   SIMUL
G0029   RISK
                                                          DECISION

                                                                    S59
BLOOMFIELD L.P.,"THREE EXPERIMENTS IN POLITICAL   TEC/DEV
GAMING." ACT/RES CREATE PWR...GAME GEN/METH METH.   METH/CNCPT
PAGE 7 G0140   DECISION

                                                                    S59
DEUTSCH K.W.,"THE IMPACT OF SCIENCE AND TECHNOLOGY   PHIL/SCI
ON INTERNATIONAL POLITICS." UNIV INTELL NAT/G   MYTH
ACT/RES CREATE TEC/DEV EDU/PROP EXEC KNOWL...CONCPT   DIPLOM
TREND TOT/POP 20. PAGE 15 G0297   NAT/LISM

                                                                    S59
GOLDHAMMER H.,"SOME OBSERVATIONS ON POLITICAL   COMPUT/IR
GAMING." FUT WOR+45 R+D NAT/G ACT/RES CREATE CHOOSE   DECISION
ATTIT PWR...POLICY CONCPT METH/CNCPT STYLE KNO/TEST   DIPLOM
TREND HYPO/EXP GAME GEN/METH METH 20. PAGE 22 G0426

                                                                    B60
ARMS CONTROL. FUT UNIV WOR+45 INTELL R+D INT/ORG   DELIB/GP
NAT/G VOL/ASSN CONSULT CREATE EDU/PROP PEACE...HUM   ORD/FREE
GEN/LAWS TOT/POP 20. PAGE 1 G0015   ARMS/CONT
                                                          NUC/PWR

                                                                    B60
BROOKINGS INSTITUTION,UNITED STATES FOREIGN POLICY: DIPLOM
STUDY NO 9: THE FORMULATION AND ADMINISTRATION OF   INT/ORG
UNITED STATES FOREIGN POLICY. USA+45 WOR+45   CREATE
EX/STRUC LEGIS BAL/PWR FOR/AID EDU/PROP CIVMIL/REL
GOV/REL...INT COLD/WAR. PAGE 9 G0174

                                                                    B60
HITCH C.J.,THE ECONOMICS OF DEFENSE IN THE NUCLEAR   R+D
AGE. USA+45 WOR+45 CREATE PLAN NUC/PWR ATTIT   FORCES
...CON/ANAL CHARTS HYPO/EXP NATO 20. PAGE 26 G0514

                                                                    B60
US SENATE COMM ON COMMERCE,URBAN MASS   DIST/IND
TRANSPORTATION. FUT USA+45 AIR ECO/DEV FINAN LOC/G   PLAN
MUNIC LEGIS CREATE PROB/SOLV TEC/DEV 20 PUB/TRANS.   NAT/G
PAGE 60 G1180   LAW

                                                                    L60
DEUTSCH K.W.,"TOWARD AN INVENTORY OF BASIC TRENDS   R+D
AND PATTERNS IN COMPARATIVE AND INTERNATIONAL   PERCEPT
POLITICS." UNIV WOR+45 SOCIETY STRUCT INT/ORG NAT/G
CREATE EDU/PROP KNOWL...PHIL/SCI METH/CNCPT
STAT SELF/OBS OBS/ENVIR SAMP TREND CON/ANAL CHARTS
SOC/EXP GEN/METH 20. PAGE 15 G0298

                                                                    L60
MACPHERSON C.,"TECHNICAL CHANGE AND POLITICAL   TEC/DEV
DECISION." WOR+45 NAT/G CREATE CAP/ISM DIPLOM   ADMIN
ROUTINE RIGID/FLEX...CONCPT OBS GEN/METH 20.
PAGE 35 G0692

                                                                    S60
BARNETT H.J.,"RESEARCH AND DEVELOPMENT, ECONOMIC   ACT/RES
GROWTH, AND NATIONAL SECURITY." USA+45 R+D CREATE   PLAN
ECO/TAC ATTIT DRIVE PWR...POLICY SOC METH/CNCPT
QUANT STAT TIME/SEQ ORG/CHARTS COLD/WAR 20. PAGE 5
G0097

                                                                    S60
DOUGHERTY J.E.,"KEY TO SECURITY: DISARMAMENT OR   FORCES
ARMS STABILITY." COM USA+45 USSR INT/ORG NAT/G   ORD/FREE
CREATE EDU/PROP COERCE DETER ATTIT PWR...DECISION   ARMS/CONT
CONCPT MYTH NEW/IDEA TREND 20 COLD/WAR. PAGE 16   NUC/PWR
G0311

                                                                    S60
GARFINKEL H.,"THE RATIONAL PROPERTIES OF SCIENTIFIC   CREATE
AND COMMON SENSE ACTIVITIES." SOCIETY STRATA   PHIL/SCI
ACT/RES CHOOSE...SOC METH/CNCPT NEW/IDEA CONT/OBS

SIMUL TOT/POP VAL/FREE. PAGE 21 G0412

                                                                    S60
HALSEY A.H.,"THE CHANGING FUNCTIONS OF UNIVERSITIES   ACADEM
IN ADVANCED INDUSTRIAL SOCIETIES." R+D EDU/PROP   CREATE
REPRESENT ROLE ORD/FREE PWR TREND. PAGE 24 G0476   CULTURE
                                                        ADJUST

                                                                    S60
HAYTON R.D.,"THE ANTARCTIC SETTLEMENT OF 1959." FUT   DELIB/GP
USA+45 WOR+45 WOR-45 STRUCT R+D INT/ORG EX/STRUC   JURID
CREATE TEC/DEV LEGIT PEACE ATTIT SOVEREIGN   DIPLOM
...TIME/SEQ 20 TREATY IGY. PAGE 25 G0495   REGION

                                                                    S60
HUTCHINSON C.E.,"AN INSTITUTE FOR NATIONAL SECURITY   POLICY
AFFAIRS." USA+45 R+D NAT/G CONSULT TOP/EX ACT/RES   METH/CNCPT
CREATE PLAN TEC/DEV EDU/PROP ROUTINE NUC/PWR ATTIT   ELITES
ORD/FREE PWR...DECISION MGT PHIL/SCI CONCPT RECORD   DIPLOM
GEN/LAWS GEN/METH 20. PAGE 27 G0539

                                                                    S60
KAPLAN M.A.,"THEORETICAL ANALYSIS OF THE BALANCE OF   CREATE
POWER." FUT USA+45 WOR+45 INTELL ECO/DEV INT/ORG   NEW/IDEA
NAT/G CONSULT TOP/EX ACT/RES PLAN TEC/DEV ATTIT   DIPLOM
ALL/VALS...METH/CNCPT TOT/POP 20. PAGE 29 G0576   NUC/PWR

                                                                    S60
YEMELYANOV V.S.,"ATOMIC ENERGY FOR PEACE: THE USSR   VOL/ASSN
AND INTERNATIONAL CO-OPERATION." FUT USSR WOR+45   TEC/DEV
R+D CREATE EDU/PROP...CONCPT GEN/LAWS 20. PAGE 64   ARMS/CONT
G1264   NUC/PWR

                                                                    B61
BRADY R.A.,ORGANIZATION, AUTOMATION, AND SOCIETY.   TEC/DEV
USA+45 AGRI COM/IND DIST/IND MARKET CREATE   INDUS
...DECISION MGT 20. PAGE 8 G0163   AUTOMAT
                                                        ADMIN

                                                                    B61
GORDON W.J.J.,SYNECTICS; THE DEVELOPMENT OF   CREATE
CREATIVE CAPACITY. USA+45 PLAN TEC/DEV KNOWL WEALTH   PROB/SOLV
...DECISION MGT 20. PAGE 22 G0436   ACT/RES
                                                        TOP/EX

                                                                    B61
GRUBER R.,SCIENCE AND THE NEW NATIONS. WOR+45 NAT/G   ECO/UNDEV
CREATE SKILL...CONCPT GEN/LAWS 20. PAGE 23 G0457   KNOWL

                                                                    B61
KAHN H.,ON THERMONUCLEAR WAR. FUT UNIV WOR+45   DETER
ECO/DEV CONSULT EX/STRUC TOP/EX ACT/RES CREATE PLAN   NUC/PWR
COERCE WAR PERSON ALL/VALS...POLICY GEOG CONCPT   SOCIETY
METH/CNCPT OBS TREND 20. PAGE 29 G0569

                                                                    B61
MCRAE R.,THE PROBLEM OF THE UNITY OF THE SCIENCES: PHIL/SCI
BACON TO KANT. CREATE TASK KNOWL...PERS/COMP 16/18   IDEA/COMP
BACON/F DESCARTE/R LEIBNITZ/G KANT/I DIDEROT/D.   PERSON
PAGE 38 G0748

                                                                    B61
NAKICENOVIC S.,NUCLEAR ENERGY IN YUGOSLAVIA.   R+D
YUGOSLAVIA AGRI INDUS CREATE OP/RES ROUTINE   ECO/DEV
EFFICIENCY KNOWL...HEAL STAT CHARTS LAB/EXP BIBLIOG   TEC/DEV
20. PAGE 41 G0802   NUC/PWR

                                                                    B61
RAMO S.,PEACETIME USES OF OUTER SPACE. FUT DIST/IND   PEACE
INT/ORG CONSULT NUC/PWR...AUD/VIS ANTHOL 20.   TEC/DEV
PAGE 46 G0898   SPACE
                                                        CREATE

                                                                    B61
SMITH H.H.,THE CITIZEN'S GUIDE TO PLANNING. USA+45   MUNIC
LAW SCHOOL CREATE PROB/SOLV EDU/PROP GP/REL ROLE 20   PLAN
URBAN/RNWL OPEN/SPACE. PAGE 52 G1015   DELIB/GP
                                                        CONSULT

                                                                    S61
MAINZER L.C.,"SCIENTIFIC FREEDOM IN GOVERNMENT-   CREATE
SPONSORED RESEARCH." USA+45 INTELL PUB/INST BUDGET   ORD/FREE
LOBBY AUTHORIT PWR...POLICY PHIL/SCI 20 NIH NSF.   NAT/G
PAGE 35 G0696   R+D

                                                                    B62
ASTIA,HUMAN ENGINEERING: A REPORT BIBLIOGRAPHY.   BIBLIOG/A
USA+45 R+D FORCES ACT/RES COMPUTER CREATE OP/RES   COM/IND
EDU/PROP CONTROL WEAPON...SOC NEW/IDEA. PAGE 4   COMPUT/IR
G0073   METH

                                                                    B62
ASTIA,INFORMATION THEORY: A REPORT BIBLIOGRAPHY.   BIBLIOG/A
USA+45 COMPUTER CREATE OP/RES PLAN TEC/DEV CONTROL   COM/IND
...CONCPT METH/COMP. PAGE 4 G0074   FORCES
                                                        METH

B62
BENNIS W.G.,THE PLANNING OF CHANGE: READINGS IN THE PROB/SOLV
APPLIED BEHAVIORAL SCIENCES. CULTURE STRATA STRUCT   CREATE
PLAN GP/REL...SOC T. PAGE 6 G0123   ACT/RES
                                                     OP/RES

B62
BERKELEY E.C.,THE COMPUTER REVOLUTION. WOR+45   COMPUTER
CREATE TEC/DEV EFFICIENCY TECHRACY...SOC TREND 20.   CONTROL
PAGE 7 G0128   AUTOMAT
                                                     SOCIETY

B62
BLOOMFIELD L.P.,OUTER SPACE: A PATTERN OF WAR IN A   CREATE
NEW DIMENSION. FUT USA+45 AIR TEC/DEV PWR   ACT/RES
...DECISION CONCPT GEN/LAWS 20. PAGE 7 G0141   ARMS/CONT
                                                     SPACE

B62
BOULDING K.E.,CONFLICT AND DEFENSE: A GENERAL   MATH
THEORY. FUT SOCIETY INT/ORG NAT/G CREATE BAL/PWR   SIMUL
COERCE NAT/LISM DRIVE ALL/VALS...PLURIST DECISION   PEACE
CONCPT METH/CNCPT TREND HYPO/EXP TOT/POP 20. PAGE 8 WAR
G0157

B62
GILPIN R.,AMERICAN SCIENTISTS AND NUCLEAR WEAPONS   INTELL
POLICY. COM FUT USA+45 WOR+45 INT/ORG NAT/G   ATTIT
PROF/ORG CONSULT FORCES CREATE TEC/DEV BAL/PWR   DETER
EDU/PROP ARMS/CONT WAR PERCEPT KNOWL MORAL PWR   NUC/PWR
...PHIL/SCI SOC CONCPT GEN/LAWS 20. PAGE 21 G0417

B62
GOLOVINE M.N.,CONFLICT IN SPACE: A PATTERN OF WAR   CREATE
IN A NEW DIMENSION. FUT USA+45 WOR+45 AIR FORCES   TEC/DEV
PLAN DIPLOM DOMIN ATTIT...STAT AUD/VIS CHARTS   NUC/PWR
COLD/WAR 20. PAGE 22 G0432   SPACE

B62
KAHN H.,THINKING ABOUT THE UNTHINKABLE. FUT USA+45   INT/ORG
LAW NAT/G CONSULT FORCES ACT/RES CREATE PLAN   ORD/FREE
TEC/DEV BAL/PWR DIPLOM EDU/PROP ARMS/CONT DETER   NUC/PWR
ATTIT...CONCPT OBS TREND COLD/WAR 20. PAGE 29 G0570 PEACE

B62
MACHLUP F.,THE PRODUCTION AND DISTRIBUTION OF   ACADEM
KNOWLEDGE IN THE UNITED STATES. USA+45 COM/IND   TEC/DEV
INDUS SCHOOL SECT WORKER COMPUTER CREATE CIVMIL/REL EDU/PROP
COST EFFICIENCY WEALTH 20. PAGE 35 G0688   R+D

B62
RIKER W.H.,THE THEORY OF POLITICAL COALITIONS.   FUT
WOR+45 INTELL NAT/G CREATE PLAN ATTIT DRIVE PERCEPT SIMUL
...DECISION PSY SOC METH/CNCPT NEW/IDEA MATH CHARTS
GAME TOT/POP 20. PAGE 47 G0921

B62
ROSS R.,SYMBOLS AND CIVILIZATION. UNIV CULTURE SECT PHIL/SCI
CREATE ALL/VALS MORAL ART/METH. PAGE 48 G0939   KNOWL
                                                     EPIST
                                                     SOCIETY

B62
SCHWARTZ L.E.,INTERNATIONAL ORGANIZATIONS AND SPACE INT/ORG
COOPERATION. VOL/ASSN CONSULT CREATE TEC/DEV   DIPLOM
SANCTION...POLICY INT/LAW PHIL/SCI 20 UN. PAGE 50   R+D
G0982   SPACE

B62
SNYDER R.C.,FOREIGN POLICY DECISION-MAKING. FUT   TEC/DEV
KOREA WOR+45 R+D CREATE ADMIN ROUTINE PWR   HYPO/EXP
...DECISION PSY SOC CONCPT METH/CNCPT CON/ANAL   DIPLOM
CHARTS GEN/METH METH 20. PAGE 52 G1018

B62
STAHL O.G.,PUBLIC PERSONNEL ADMINISTRATION. LOC/G   ADMIN
TOP/EX CREATE PLAN ROUTINE...TECHNIC MGT T. PAGE 52 WORKER
G1030   EX/STRUC
                                                     NAT/G

B62
STOVER C.F.,THE GOVERNMENT OF SCIENCE (PAMPHLET).   PHIL/SCI
USA+45 SOCIETY PROF/ORG EX/STRUC CREATE CONTROL   TEC/DEV
NUC/PWR WAR GOV/REL PEACE ORD/FREE 20. PAGE 53   LAW
G1041   NAT/G

B62
THOMSON G.P.,NUCLEAR ENERGY IN BRITAIN DURING THE   CREATE
LAST WAR: THE CHERWELL SIMON LECTURE (MONOGRAPH).   TEC/DEV
UK R+D CONSULT FORCES PLAN DIPLOM TASK CIVMIL/REL   WAR
ROLE...PHIL/SCI NEW/IDEA LAB/EXP 20 MAUD. PAGE 54   NUC/PWR
G1071

B62
WALSTON H.,AGRICULTURE UNDER COMMUNISM. CHINA/COM   AGRI

B62
COM PROB/SOLV HAPPINESS RIGID/FLEX...POLICY   MARXISM
METH/COMP 20. PAGE 62 G1207   PLAN
                                                     CREATE

B62
WRIGHT Q.,PREVENTING WORLD WAR THREE. FUT WOR+45   CREATE
CULTURE INT/ORG NAT/G CONSULT FORCES ADMIN   ATTIT
ARMS/CONT DRIVE RIGID/FLEX ORD/FREE SOVEREIGN
...POLICY CONCPT TREND STERTYP COLD/WAR 20. PAGE 64
G1259

L62
BETTEN J.K.,"ARMS CONTROL AND THE PROBLEM OF   NAT/G
EVASION." WOR+45 FORCES CREATE DIPLOM DETER PWR   PLAN
...PSY TREND GEN/LAWS COLD/WAR 20. PAGE 7 G0134   ARMS/CONT

S62
FINKELSTEIN L.S.,"THE UNITED NATIONS AND   INT/ORG
ORGANIZATIONS FOR CONTROL OF ARMAMENT." FUT WOR+45   PWR
VOL/ASSN DELIB/GP TOP/EX CREATE EDU/PROP LEGIT   ARMS/CONT
ADJUD NUC/PWR ATTIT RIGID/FLEX ORD/FREE...POLICY
DECISION CONCPT OBS TREND GEN/LAWS TOT/POP
COLD/WAR. PAGE 19 G0368

S62
FOSTER W.C.,"ARMS CONTROL AND DISARMAMENT IN A   DELIB/GP
DIVIDED WORLD." COM FUT USA+45 USSR WOR+45 INTELL   POLICY
INT/ORG NAT/G VOL/ASSN CONSULT CREATE PLAN TEC/DEV   ARMS/CONT
EDU/PROP LEGIT NUC/PWR ATTIT RIGID/FLEX...CONCPT   DIPLOM
TREND TOT/POP 20 UN. PAGE 20 G0387

S62
NANES A.,"DISARMAMENT: THE LAST SEVEN YEARS." COM   DELIB/GP
EUR+WWI USA+45 WOR+45 INT/ORG FORCES TOP/EX CREATE   RIGID/FLEX
LEGIT NUC/PWR DISPL ORD/FREE...CONCPT TIME/SEQ   ARMS/CONT
CON/ANAL 20. PAGE 41 G0803

S62
PHIPPS T.E.,"THE CASE FOR DETERRENCE." FUT WOR+45   ATTIT
SOCIETY EX/STRUC FORCES ACT/RES CREATE TEC/DEV   COERCE
ROUTINE RIGID/FLEX ORD/FREE...POLICY MYTH NEW/IDEA   DETER
STERTYP COLD/WAR 20. PAGE 45 G0876   ARMS/CONT

S62
STORER N.W.,"SOME SOCIOLOGICAL ASPECTS OF FEDERAL   POLICY
SCIENCE POLICY." USA+45 INTELL PUB/INST PLAN GP/REL CREATE
PERS/REL DRIVE PERSON ROLE...PSY SOC SIMUL 20 NIH   NAT/G
NSF. PAGE 53 G1040   ALL/VALS

S62
THORELLI H.B.,"THE INTERNATIONAL OPERATIONS   ECO/TAC
SIMULATION AT THE UNIVERSITY OF CHICAGO." FUT   SIMUL
USA+45 WOR+45 ECO/DEV DIST/IND FINAN INDUS INT/ORG   INT/TRADE
DELIB/GP ACT/RES CREATE TEC/DEV WEALTH...STAT
VAL/FREE 20. PAGE 54 G1072

B63
FLORES E.,LAND REFORM AND THE ALLIANCE FOR PROGRESS AGRI
(PAMPHLET). L/A+17C USA+45 STRUCT ECO/UNDEV NAT/G   INT/ORG
WORKER CREATE PLAN ECO/TAC COERCE REV 20. PAGE 19   DIPLOM
G0373   POLICY

B63
FOSKETT D.J.,CLASSIFICATION AND INDEXING IN THE   PROB/SOLV
SOCIAL SCIENCES. WOR+45 R+D ACT/RES CREATE OP/RES   CON/ANAL
TEC/DEV AUTOMAT ROLE...SOC COMPUT/IR BIBLIOG.   CLASSIF
PAGE 20 G0384

B63
HALEY A.G.,SPACE LAW AND GOVERNMENT. FUT USA+45   INT/ORG
WOR+45 LEGIS ACT/RES CREATE ATTIT RIGID/FLEX   LAW
ORD/FREE PWR SOVEREIGN...POLICY JURID CONCPT CHARTS SPACE
VAL/FREE 20. PAGE 24 G0469

B63
HOWER R.M.,MANAGERS AND SCIENTISTS. EX/STRUC CREATE R+D
ADMIN REPRESENT ATTIT DRIVE ROLE PWR SKILL...SOC   MGT
INT. PAGE 27 G0532   PERS/REL
                                                     INGP/REL

B63
KORNHAUSER W.,SCIENTISTS IN INDUSTRY: CONFLICT AND   CREATE
ACCOMMODATION. USA+45 R+D LG/CO NAT/G TEC/DEV   INDUS
CONTROL ADJUST ATTIT...MGT STAT INT BIBLIOG 20.   PROF/ORG
PAGE 31 G0614   GP/REL

B63
LASSWELL H.D.,THE FUTURE OF POLITICAL SCIENCE.   CREATE
SOCIETY ECO/DEV ACADEM NAT/G PROB/SOLV...OBS   ACT/RES
SOC/INTEG. PAGE 33 G0643   FUT

B63
LITTERER J.A.,ORGANIZATIONS: STRUCTURE AND   ADMIN
BEHAVIOR. PLAN DOMIN CONTROL LEAD ROUTINE SANCTION   CREATE
INGP/REL EFFICIENCY PRODUC DRIVE RIGID/FLEX PWR.   MGT
PAGE 34 G0674   ADJUST

MAYNE R.,THE COMMUNITY OF EUROPE. UK CONSTN NAT/G
CONSULT DELIB/GP CREATE PLAN ECO/TAC LEGIT ADMIN
ROUTINE ORD/FREE PWR WEALTH...CONCPT TIME/SEQ EEC
EURATOM 20. PAGE 37 G0724
B63
EUR+WWI
INT/ORG
REGION

MULLER H.J.,FREEDOM IN THE WESTERN WORLD. PREHIST
CULTURE SECT CREATE TEC/DEV DOMIN PWR WEALTH
...MAJORIT SOC CONCPT. PAGE 40 G0793
B63
ORD/FREE
TIME/SEQ
SOCIETY

NAFZIGER R.O.,INTRODUCTION TO MASS COMMUNICATIONS
RESEARCH (REV. ED.). ACT/RES...STAT CON/ANAL METH
20. PAGE 41 G0801
B63
COM/IND
CONCPT
PHIL/SCI
CREATE

OECD,SCIENCE AND THE POLICIES OF GOVERNMENTS: THE
IMPLICATIONS OF SCIENCE AND TECHNOLOGY FOR NATL AND
INTL AFFAIRS. WOR+45 INT/ORG EDU/PROP AUTOMAT
...POLICY PHIL/SCI 20. PAGE 42 G0830
B63
CREATE
TEC/DEV
DIPLOM
NAT/G

RAUDSEPP E.,MANAGING CREATIVE SCIENTISTS AND
ENGINEERS. USA+45 ECO/DEV LG/CO GP/REL PERS/REL
PRODUC. PAGE 46 G0906
B63
MGT
CREATE
R+D
ECO/TAC

US ATOMIC ENERGY COMMISSION,ATOMIC ENERGY IN THE
SOVIET UNION: TRIP REPORT OF THE US ATOMIC ENERGY
DELEGATION, MAY 1933. USSR R+D NAT/G CONSULT CREATE
DIPLOM ADMIN ROUTINE EFFICIENCY PRODUC KNOWL SKILL
...NAT/COMP 20 AEC TRAVEL TREATY. PAGE 56 G1107
B63
METH/COMP
OP/RES
TEC/DEV
NUC/PWR

WIGHTMAN D.,TOWARD ECONOMIC CO-OPERATION IN ASIA.
ASIA S/ASIA VOL/ASSN ACT/RES PLAN TEC/DEV ECO/TAC
EDU/PROP RIGID/FLEX SKILL...POLICY METH/CNCPT OBS
INT GEN/LAWS UN 20 ECAFE. PAGE 63 G1237
B63
ECO/UNDEV
CREATE

MCDOUGAL M.S.,"THE ENJOYMENT AND ACQUISITION OF
RESOURCES IN OUTER SPACE." CHRIST-17C FUT WOR+45
WOR-45 LAW EXTR/IND INT/ORG ACT/RES CREATE TEC/DEV
ECO/TAC LEGIT COERCE HEALTH KNOWL ORD/FREE PWR
WEALTH...JURID HIST/WRIT VAL/FREE. PAGE 37 G0738
L63
PLAN
TREND

DE FOREST J.D.,"LOW LEVELS OF TECHNOLOGY AND
ECONOMIC DEVELOPMENT PROSPECTS." WOR+45 WOR-45
CULTURE ACT/RES CREATE PLAN ECO/TAC ROUTINE PERCEPT
WEALTH...METH/CNCPT GEN/LAWS 20. PAGE 15 G0284
S63
ECO/UNDEV
TEC/DEV

FERRETTI B.,"IMPORTANZA E PROSPETTIVE DELL ENERGIA
DI ORIGINE NUCLEARE." FUT ITALY WOR+45 INTELL R+D
ACT/RES CREATE HEALTH WEALTH...METH/CNCPT TIME/SEQ
20. PAGE 19 G0365
S63
TEC/DEV
EXEC
NUC/PWR

GARDNER R.N.,"COOPERATION IN OUTER SPACE." FUT USSR
WOR+45 AIR LAW COM/IND CONSULT DELIB/GP CREATE
KNOWL 20 TREATY. PAGE 21 G0410
S63
INT/ORG
ACT/RES
PEACE
SPACE

HOSKINS H.L.,"ARAB SOCIALISM IN THE UAR." ISLAM
USSR AGRI INDUS NAT/G TOP/EX CREATE DIPLOM EDU/PROP
DRIVE KNOWL PWR SOCISM...POLICY CONCPT TREND SUEZ
20. PAGE 27 G0530
S63
ECO/DEV
PLAN
UAR

MASSART L.,"L'ORGANISATION DE LA RECHERCHE
SCIENTIFIQUE EN EUROPE." EUR+WWI WOR+45 ACT/RES
PLAN TEC/DEV EDU/PROP EXEC KNOWL...METH/CNCPT EEC
20. PAGE 36 G0718
S63
R+D
CREATE

SCHMITT H.A.,"THE EUROPEAN COMMUNITIES." EUR+WWI
FRANCE DELIB/GP EX/STRUC TOP/EX CREATE TEC/DEV
ECO/TAC LEGIT REGION COERCE DRIVE ALL/VALS
...METH/CNCPT EEC 20. PAGE 49 G0972
S63
VOL/ASSN
ECO/DEV

BALASSA B.,TRADE PROSPECTS FOR DEVELOPING
COUNTRIES. WOR+45 ECO/DEV AGRI EXTR/IND INDUS
CREATE PLAN PRICE...ECOMETRIC CLASSIF TIME/SEQ
GEN/METH. PAGE 5 G0087
B64
INT/TRADE
ECO/UNDEV
TREND
STAT

BRIGHT J.R.,RESEARCH, DEVELOPMENT AND TECHNOLOGICAL
INNOVATION. CULTURE R+D CREATE PLAN PROB/SOLV
AUTOMAT RISK PERSON...DECISION CONCPT PREDICT
B64
TEC/DEV
NEW/IDEA
INDUS

BIBLIOG. PAGE 9 G0168
MGT

BRILLOUIN L.,SCIENTIFIC UNCERTAINTY AND
INFORMATION. PROB/SOLV AUTOMAT PERCEPT ORD/FREE
...MATH REGRESS STAT STYLE OBS IDEA/COMP SIMUL
TIME. PAGE 9 G0169
B64
PHIL/SCI
NEW/IDEA
METH/CNCPT
CREATE

DIEBOLD J.,BEYOND AUTOMATION: MANAGERIAL PROBLEMS
OF AN EXPLODING TECHNOLOGY. SOCIETY ECO/DEV CREATE
ECO/TAC AUTOMAT SKILL...TECHNIC MGT WORK. PAGE 16
G0303
B64
FUT
INDUS
PROVS
NAT/G

ELLUL J.,THE TECHNOLOGICAL SOCIETY. FUT STRUCT
CREATE AUTOMAT ROUTINE STRANGE ANOMIE MORAL
PHIL/SCI. PAGE 18 G0344
B64
SOC
SOCIETY
TECHNIC
TEC/DEV

GOWING M.,BRITAIN AND ATOMIC ENERGY 1939-1945.
FRANCE UK USA+45 USA-45 NAT/G CREATE...PHIL/SCI 20
AEA. PAGE 22 G0439
B64
NUC/PWR
DIPLOM
TEC/DEV

GRAVIER J.F.,AMENAGEMENT DU TERRITOIRE ET L'AVENIR
DES REGIONS FRANCAISES. FRANCE ECO/DEV AGRI INDUS
CREATE...GEOG CHARTS 20. PAGE 22 G0442
B64
PLAN
MUNIC
NEIGH
ADMIN

INST D'ETUDE POL L'U GRENOBLE,ADMINISTRATION
TRADITIONELLE ET PLANIFICATION REGIONALE. FRANCE
LAW POL/PAR PROB/SOLV ADJUST RIGID/FLEX...CHARTS
ANTHOL BIBLIOG T 20 REFORMERS. PAGE 28 G0546
B64
ADMIN
MUNIC
PLAN
CREATE

OSSENBECK F.J.,OPEN SPACE AND PEACE. CHINA/COM FUT
USA+45 USSR LAW PROB/SOLV TEC/DEV EDU/PROP NEUTRAL
PEACE...AUD/VIS ANTHOL 20. PAGE 43 G0850
B64
SPACE
ORD/FREE
DIPLOM
CREATE

SHUBIK M.,GAME THEORY AND RELATED APPROACHES TO
SOCIAL BEHAVIOR: SELECTIONS. INTELL SOCIETY ACT/RES
CREATE PLAN PROB/SOLV...DECISION MATH. PAGE 50
G0994
B64
SOC
SIMUL
GAME
PWR

TAUBENFELD H.J.,SPACE AND SOCIETY. USA+45 LAW
FORCES CREATE TEC/DEV ADJUD CONTROL COST PEACE
...PREDICT ANTHOL 20. PAGE 54 G1057
B64
SPACE
SOCIETY
ADJUST
DIPLOM

CARNEGIE ENDOWMENT INT. PEACE,"ECONOMIC AND SOCIAL
QUESTION (ISSUES BEFORE THE NINETEENTH GENERAL
ASSEMBLY)." WOR+45 ECO/DEV ECO/UNDEV INDUS R+D
DELIB/GP CREATE PLAN TEC/DEV ECO/TAC FOR/AID
BAL/PAY...RECORD UN 20. PAGE 11 G0209
L64
INT/ORG
INT/TRADE

GOLDBERG A.,"ATOMIC ORIGINS OF THE BRITISH NUCLEAR
DETERRENT." EUR+WWI UK TOP/EX PLAN BAL/PWR
DOMIN DETER CHOOSE ATTIT DRIVE HEALTH ORD/FREE PWR
RESPECT...CONCPT VAL/FREE COLD/WAR 20 CMN/WLTH.
PAGE 22 G0425
L64
CREATE
FORCES
NUC/PWR

HAAS E.B.,"ECONOMICS AND DIFFERENTIAL PATTERNS OF
POLITICAL INTEGRATION: PROJECTIONS ABOUT UNITY IN
LATIN AMERICA." SOCIETY NAT/G DELIB/GP ACT/RES
CREATE PLAN ECO/TAC REGION ROUTINE ATTIT DRIVE PWR
WEALTH...CONCPT TREND CHARTS LAFTA 20. PAGE 24
G0464
L/A-17C
INT/ORG
MARKET

COOPER A.C.,"R&D IS MORE EFFICIENT IN SMALL
COMPANIES." USA+45 LG/CO SML/CO WEALTH...RECORD INT
LAB/EXP 20. PAGE 13 G0255
S64
R+D
INDUS
CREATE
GP/COMP

LERNER A.P.,"NUCLEAR SYMMETRY AS A FRAMEWORK FOR
COEXISTENCE." COM FUT USA+45 NAT/G ACT/RES CREATE
PLAN DIPLOM EDU/PROP COERCE WAR RIGID/FLEX PWR
SKILL...CONCPT METH/CNCPT GEN/LAWS TOT/POP VAL/FREE
COLD/WAR 20. PAGE 33 G0657
S64
FORCES
ORD/FREE
DETER
NUC/PWR

MARES V.E.,"EAST EUROPE'S SECOND CHANCE." COM
EUR+WWI HUNGARY ROMANIA USSR YUGOSLAVIA ECO/UNDEV
NAT/G TOP/EX CREATE PLAN TEC/DEV REGION NAT/LISM
RIGID/FLEX PWR...CONCPT STAT COMECON 20. PAGE 36
G0705
S64
VOL/ASSN
ECO/TAC

MUMFORD L.,"AUTHORITARIAN AND DEMOCRATIC
TECHNIQUES." INDUS PROC/MFG LG/CO SML/CO CREATE
PLAN KNOWL...POLICY TREND WORK 20. PAGE 40 G0794
S64 ECO/DEV TEC/DEV

NEEDHAM T.,"SCIENCE AND SOCIETY IN EAST AND WEST." INTELL STRATA R+D LOC/G NAT/G PROVS CONSULT ACT/RES
CREATE PLAN TEC/DEV EDU/PROP ADMIN ATTIT ALL/VALS
...POLICY RELATIV MGT CONCPT NEW/IDEA TIME/SEQ WORK
WORK. PAGE 41 G0815
S64 ASIA STRUCT

THOMPSON V.A.,"ADMINISTRATIVE OBJECTIVES FOR
DEVELOPMENT ADMINISTRATION." WOR+45 CREATE PLAN
DOMIN EDU/PROP EXEC ROUTINE ATTIT ORD/FREE PWR
...POLICY GEN/LAWS VAL/FREE. PAGE 54 G1070
S64 ECO/UNDEV MGT

UNRUH J.M.,"SCIENTIFIC INPUTS TO LEGISLATIVE
DECISION-MAKING (SUPPLEMENT)" USA+45 ACADEM NAT/G
PROVS GOV/REL GOV/COMP. PAGE 56 G1102
S64 CREATE DECISION LEGIS PARTIC

ALTSHULER A.,A LAND-USE PLAN FOR ST. PAUL
(PAMPHLET). USA+45 CREATE CAP/ISM RIGID/FLEX ROLE
...NEW/IDEA 20 ST/PAUL. PAGE 3 G0047
B65 MUNIC PLAN ECO/DEV GEOG

BENJAMIN A.C.,SCIENCE, TECHNOLOGY, AND HUMAN
VALUES. WOR+45 SECT EDU/PROP GP/REL ATTIT...TECHNIC
LING IDEA/COMP WORSHIP 20. PAGE 6 G0118
B65 PHIL/SCI CREATE ROLE SOCIETY

BOBROW D.B.,COMPONENTS OF DEFENSE POLICY. ASIA
EUR+WWI USA+45 WOR+45 INTELL INT/ORG NAT/G PROF/ORG
CONSULT LEGIS ACT/RES CREATE ARMS/CONT COERCE
ORD/FREE...DECISION SIMUL. PAGE 7 G0145
B65 DETER NUC/PWR PLAN FORCES

FOSTER P.,EDUCATION AND SOCIAL CHANGE IN GHANA.
GHANA CULTURE STRUCT ECO/UNDEV TEC/DEV REGION
EFFICIENCY LITERACY ALL/VALS SOVEREIGN...STAT
METH/COMP 19/20 GOLD/COAST. PAGE 20 G0385
B65 SCHOOL CREATE SOCIETY

HITCH C.J.,DECISION-MAKING FOR DEFENSE. USA+45
CREATE BUDGET COERCE WAR WEAPON EFFICIENCY...SIMUL
20. PAGE 26 G0515
B65 DECISION OP/RES PLAN FORCES

KENT A.,SPECIALIZED INFORMATION CENTERS. INTELL R+D
VOL/ASSN CONSULT COMPUTER KNOWL...DECISION HUM
PHIL/SCI METH/CNCPT TREND CHARTS 20. PAGE 30 G0593
B65 COMPUT/IR CREATE TEC/DEV METH/COMP

KNORR K.,SCIENCE AND DEFENSE: SOME CRITICAL
THOUGHTS ON MILITARY RESEARCH AND DEVELOPMENT.
USA+45 ACT/RES CREATE BUDGET ECO/TAC DEMAND
DECISION. PAGE 31 G0608
B65 CIVMIL/REL R+D FORCES PLAN

NATIONAL ACADEMY OF SCIENCES,BASIC RESEARCH AND
NATIONAL GOALS. R+D ACADEM DELIB/GP PLAN EDU/PROP
...POLICY HEAL PHIL/SCI PSY SOC ANTHOL 20 CONGRESS
HOUSE/REP HS/SCIASTR. PAGE 41 G0809
B65 LEGIS BUDGET NAT/G CREATE

SMITH E.A.,SOCIAL WELFARE: PRINCIPLES AND CONCEPTS.
STRATA STRUCT CONSULT WORKER ACT/RES CREATE PLAN
TEC/DEV ROUTINE GP/REL UTOPIA...SOC 20. PAGE 51
G1014
B65 CONCPT SOC/WK RECEIVE ORD/FREE

STEINER G.A.,THE CREATIVE ORGANIZATION. ELITES
LG/CO PLAN PROB/SOLV TEC/DEV INSPECT CAP/ISM
CONTROL EXEC PERSON...METH/COMP HYPO/EXP 20.
PAGE 52 G1034
B65 CREATE MGT ADMIN SOC

UNESCO,HANDBOOK OF INTERNATIONAL EXCHANGES. COM/IND
R+D ACADEM PROF/ORG VOL/ASSN CREATE TEC/DEV
EDU/PROP AGREE 20 TREATY. PAGE 55 G1090
B65 INDEX INT/ORG DIPLOM PRESS

US CONGRESS JT ATOM ENRGY COMM,PEACEFUL
APPLICATIONS OF NUCLEAR EXPLOSIVES: PLOWSHARE.
HEARING. USA+45 LEGIS CREATE PLAN PEACE...CHARTS
EXHIBIT BIBLIOG CONGRESS PANAMA/CNL. PAGE 57 G1113
B65 NUC/PWR DELIB/GP TEC/DEV NAT/G

VERMOT-GAUCHY M.,L'EDUCATION NATIONALE DANS LA
FRANCE DE 1975. FRANCE FUT CULTURE ELITES R+D
SCHOOL PLAN EDU/PROP EFFICIENCY...POLICY PREDICT
CHARTS INDEX 20. PAGE 61 G1195
B6 ACADEM CREATE TREND INTELL

WARNER A.W.,THE IMPACT OF SCIENCE ON TECHNOLOGY.
UNIV INTELL SOCIETY NAT/G ACT/RES PLAN PROB/SOLV
BUDGET OPTIMAL GEN/METH. PAGE 62 G1214
B6 DECISION TEC/DEV CREATE POLICY

WISH J.R.,ECONOMIC DEVELOPMENT IN LATIN AMERICA: AN
ANNOTATED BIBLIOGRAPHY. L/A+17C COM/IND MARKET R+D
CREATE CAP/ISM ATTIT...STAT METH 20. PAGE 64 G1250
B6 BIBLIOG/A ECO/UNDEV TEC/DEV AGRI

LASSWELL H.D.,"THE POLICY SCIENCES OF DEVELOPMENT."
CULTURE SOCIETY EX/STRUC CREATE ADMIN ATTIT KNOWL
...SOC CONCPT SIMUL GEN/METH. PAGE 33 G0644
L6 PWR METH/CNCP DIPLOM

BALDWIN H.,"SLOW-DOWN IN THE PENTAGON." USA+45
CREATE PLAN GOV/REL CENTRAL COST EFFICIENCY PWR
...MGT MCNAMARA/R. PAGE 5 G0088
S6 RECORD R+D WEAPON ADMIN

BIRNBAUM K.,"SWEDEN'S NUCLEAR POLICY." WOR+45
POL/PAR CREATE TEC/DEV NEUTRAL RISK WAR ORD/FREE
...DECISION IDEA/COMP NAT/COMP TIME. PAGE 7 G0137
S6 SWEDEN NUC/PWR DIPLOM ARMS/CONT

DECHERT C.R.,"THE DEVELOPMENT OF CYBERNETICS."
ACT/RES CREATE SKILL...STERTYP METH. PAGE 15 G0290
S6 SIMUL COMPUT/IR PLAN DECISION

ETZIONI A.,"ON THE NATIONAL GUIDANCE OF SCIENCE."
USA+45 FINAN NAT/G LEGIS GIVE 20. PAGE 18 G0353
S6 PHIL/SCI CREATE POLICY EFFICIENCY

GOLDSTEIN W.,"KEEPING THE GENIE IN THE BOTTLE* THE
FEASIBILITY OF A NUCLEAR NON-PROLIFERATION
AGREEMENT." ASIA FRANCE UK USA+45 USSR WOR+45
ECO/UNDEV VOL/ASSN ACT/RES PLAN RISK ARMS/CONT WAR
PEACE ATTIT PERCEPT...RECORD TREND TIME. PAGE 22
G0429
S6 NUC/PWR CREATE COST

KUZMACK A.M.,"TECHNOLOGICAL CHANGE AND STABLE
DETERRENCE." CREATE EDU/PROP ARMS/CONT WEAPON
CHOOSE COST DRIVE PERCEPT...RECORD STERTYP TIME.
PAGE 32 G0627
S65 R+D DETER EQUILIB

LECLERCQ H.,"ECONOMIC RESEARCH AND DEVELOPMENT IN
TROPICAL AFRICA." ECO/UNDEV INT/ORG CREATE PLAN UN.
PAGE 33 G0650
S65 AFR R+D ACADEM ECO/TAC

STAAR R.F.,"RETROGRESSION IN POLAND." COM USSR AGRI
INDUS NAT/G CREATE EDU/PROP TOTALISM RIGID/FLEX
ORD/FREE PWR SOCISM...RECORD CHARTS 20. PAGE 52
G1029
S65 TOP/EX ECO/TAC POLAND

TENDLER J.D.,"TECHNOLOGY AND ECONOMIC DEVELOPMENT*
THE CASE OF HYDRO VS THERMAL POWER." CONSTRUC
DIST/IND CREATE TEC/DEV INT/TRADE CENTRAL PWR SKILL
WEALTH...MGT NAT/COMP ARGEN. PAGE 54 G1063
S65 BRAZIL INDUS ECO/UNDEV

ALEXANDER Y.,INTERNATIONAL TECHNICAL ASSISTANCE
EXPERTS* A CASE STUDY OF THE U.N. EXPERIENCE.
ECO/UNDEV CONSULT EX/STRUC CREATE PLAN DIPLOM
FOR/AID TASK EFFICIENCY...ORG/CHARTS UN. PAGE 2
G0038
B66 ECO/TAC INT/ORG ADMIN MGT

ALEXANDER Y.,INTERNATIONAL TECHNICAL ASSISTANCE
EXPERTS: A CASE STUDY OF THE U.N. EXPERIENCE.
USA+45 WOR+45 WORKER CREATE PLAN PROB/SOLV ECO/TAC
FOR/AID GIVE EDU/PROP...CHARTS BIBLIOG 20 UN.
PAGE 2 G0039
B66 SKILL INT/ORG TEC/DEV CONSULT

DAENIKER G.,STRATEGIE DES KLEIN STAATS. SWITZERLND
B66 NUC/PWR

ACT/RES CREATE DIPLOM NEUTRAL DETER WAR WEAPON PWR   PLAN
SOVEREIGN...IDEA/COMP 20 COLD/WAR. PAGE 14 G0270   FORCES
   NAT/G

                                    B66
DUNBAR L.W.,A REPUBLIC OF EQUALS. USA+45 CREATE   LAW
ADJUD PEACE NEW/LIB...POLICY 20 SOUTH/US   CONSTN
CIV/RIGHTS. PAGE 16 G0320   FEDERAL
   RACE/REL

                                    B66
ECKSTEIN A.,COMMUNIST CHINA'S ECONOMIC GROWTH AND   ASIA
FOREIGN TRADE* IMPLICATIONS FOR US POLICY. COM   ECO/UNDEV
USA+45 USSR STRUCT INDUS MARKET DIPLOM ECO/TAC   CREATE
FOR/AID INT/TRADE...STAT CHARTS. PAGE 17 G0332   PWR

                                    B66
FALK R.A.,ON MINIMIZING THE USE OF NUCLEAR WEAPONS;   DIPLOM
THREE ESSAYS; RESEARCH MONOGRAPH NO. 23. WOR+45   EQUILIB
STRUCT CREATE NUC/PWR REV CONSERVE...POLICY   PHIL/SCI
NET/THEORY IDEA/COMP GEN/LAWS GEN/METH. PAGE 18   PROB/SOLV
G0359

                                    B66
KURAKOV I.G.,SCIENCE, TECHNOLOGY AND COMMUNISM;   CREATE
SOME QUESTIONS OF DEVELOPMENT (TRANS. BY CARIN   TEC/DEV
DEDIJER). USSR INDUS PLAN PROB/SOLV COST PRODUC   MARXISM
...MGT MATH CHARTS METH 20. PAGE 32 G0626   ECO/TAC

                                    B66
LEWIS W.A.,DEVELOPMENT PLANNING; THE ESSENTIALS OF   PLAN
ECONOMIC POLICY. USA+45 FINAN INDUS NAT/G WORKER   ECO/DEV
FOR/AID INT/TRADE ADMIN ROUTINE WEALTH...CONCPT   POLICY
STAT. PAGE 34 G0663   CREATE

                                    B66
MILLAR R.,THE NEW CLASSES. UK ELITES SOCIETY INDUS   STRUCT
AUTOMAT GP/REL SOC/INTEG 20 INDUS/REV. PAGE 39   STRATA
G0770   TEC/DEV
   CREATE

                                    B66
MUMFORD L.,THE MYTH OF THE MACHINE: TECHNICS AND   WORKER
HUMAN DEVELOPMENT. UNIV WOR-45 CREATE AUTOMAT   TEC/DEV
PERCEPT KNOWL...EPIST PHIL/SCI SOC LING TREND   SOCIETY
SOC/INTEG 20 MARX/KARL. PAGE 40 G0795

                                    B66
NATIONAL SCIENCE FOUNDATION,SIXTEENTH ANNUAL REPORT   NAT/G
FOR THE FISCAL YEAR ENDED JUNE 30, 1966. USA+45   EDU/PROP
CREATE BUDGET SKILL 20 NSF. PAGE 41 G0813   ACADEM
   KNOWL

                                    B66
ODEGARD P.H.,POLITICAL POWER AND SOCIAL CHANGE.   PWR
UNIV NAT/G CREATE ALL/IDEOS...POLICY GEOG SOC   TEC/DEV
CENSUS TREND. PAGE 42 G0829   IDEA/COMP

                                    B66
POLLARD W.G.,ATOMIC ENERGY AND SOUTHERN SCIENCE.   NUC/PWR
USA+45 HEALTH. PAGE 45 G0883   GP/REL
   PHIL/SCI
   CREATE

                                    B66
WARD B.,NATIONALISM AND IDEOLOGY. ECO/UNDEV KIN   IDEA/COMP
CREATE CAP/ISM FOR/AID ALL/VALS MARXISM...POLICY   NAT/LISM
SOC. PAGE 62 G1211   ATTIT

                                    L66
PACKENHAM R.A.,"POLITICAL-DEVELOPMENT DOCTRINES IN   FOR/AID
THE AMERICAN FOREIGN AID PROGRAM." STRUCT R+D   ECO/UNDEV
CREATE DIPLOM AID. PAGE 43 G0855   GEN/LAWS

                                    S66
COHEN A.,"THE TECHNOLOGY/ELITE APPROACH TO THE   ECO/UNDEV
DEVELOPMENTAL PROCESS* PERUVIAN CASE STUDY."   ELITES
L/A+17C STRUCT CREATE ECO/TAC FOR/AID CIVMIL/REL   PERU
MARXISM TECHRACY HYPO/EXP. PAGE 12 G0239

                                    S66
MALENBAUM W.,"GOVERNMENT, ENTREPRENEURSHIP, AND   ECO/TAC
ECONOMIC GROWTH IN POOR LANDS." ELITES ECO/UNDEV   PLAN
INDUS CREATE DRIVE. PAGE 35 G0697   CONSERVE
   NAT/G

                                    S66
RIZOS E.J.,"SCIENCE AND TECHNOLOGY IN COUNTRY   ADMIN
DEVELOPMENT* TOWARDS AN UNDERSTANDING OF THE ROLE   TEC/DEV
OF PUBLIC ADMINISTRATION." WOR+45 STRUCT INT/ORG   ECO/UNDEV
EX/STRUC CREATE PLAN PROB/SOLV EFFICIENCY ROLE   PHIL/SCI
DECISION. PAGE 47 G0924

                                    S66
SIMON R.,"THE STATE OF PUBLIC RELATIONS SCHOLARLY   ACADEM
RESEARCH." TEC/DEV TASK MAJORITY PRODUC...TREND   CREATE

CHARTS BIBLIOG 20. PAGE 51 G1000   STAT
   GP/REL

                                    N66
US HOUSE COMM SCI ASTRONAUT,GOVERNMENT, SCIENCE,   NAT/G
AND PUBLIC POLICY (PAMPHLET). R+D ACADEM DELIB/GP   POLICY
COMPUTER BUDGET CONFER ADMIN...PHIL/SCI PREDICT   TEC/DEV
TREND 20 CONGRESS HS/SCIASTR. PAGE 58 G1143   CREATE

                                    B67
BARANSON J.,TECHNOLOGY FOR UNDERDEVELOPED AREAS: AN   BIBLIOG/A
ANNOTATED BIBLIOGRAPHY. FUT WOR+45 CULTURE INDUS   ECO/UNDEV
INT/ORG CREATE PROB/SOLV INT/TRADE EDU/PROP AUTOMAT   TEC/DEV
...CONCPT METH. PAGE 5 G0092   R+D

                                    B67
BUDER S.,PULLMAN: AN EXPERIMENT IN INDUSTRIAL ORDER   DIST/IND
AND COMMUNITY PLANNING, 1880-1930. USA-45 SOCIETY   INDUS
LABOR LG/CO CREATE PROB/SOLV CONTROL GP/REL   MUNIC
EFFICIENCY ATTIT...MGT BIBLIOG 19/20 PULLMAN.   PLAN
PAGE 9 G0184

                                    B67
CROSSON F.J.,SCIENCE AND CONTEMPORARY SOCIETY. FUT   PHIL/SCI
WOR+45 SECT CREATE PROB/SOLV...HUM PREDICT TREND   SOCIETY
IDEA/COMP ANTHOL. PAGE 14 G0263   TEC/DEV
   CONCPT

                                    B67
DAVIS V.,THE POLITICS OF INNOVATION: PATTERNS IN   BIBLIOG
NAVY CASES (PAMPHLET). WOR+45 NAT/G CREATE WEAPON   FORCES
INGP/REL ATTIT...POLICY SOC METH/COMP METH. PAGE 14   NUC/PWR
G0280   TEC/DEV

                                    B67
ELDREDGE H.W.,TAMING MEGALOPOLIS; HOW TO MANAGE AN   MUNIC
URBANIZED WORLD. WOR+45 SOCIETY ECO/DEV ECO/UNDEV   TEC/DEV
NAT/G COMPUTER CREATE PARTIC EFFICIENCY WEALTH   PLAN
...MGT ANTHOL. PAGE 17 G0342   PROB/SOLV

                                    B67
GULICK M.C.,NONCONVENTIONAL INFORMATION SYSTEMS   BIBLIOG/A
SERVING THE SOCIAL SCIENCES AND THE HUMANITIES; A   R+D
BIBLIOGRAPHIC ESSAY (PAPER). USA+45 COMPUTER CREATE   COMPUT/IR
EDU/PROP KNOWL...SOC METH 20. PAGE 23 G0462   HUM

                                    B67
HEILBRONER R.L.,THE LIMITS OF AMERICAN CAPITALISM.   ELITES
FUT ECO/DEV INDUS LG/CO EX/STRUC LEAD PWR TECHRACY   CREATE
20. PAGE 25 G0502   TEC/DEV
   CAP/ISM

                                    B67
HIRSCHMAN A.O.,DEVELOPMENT PROJECTS OBSERVED. INDUS   ECO/UNDEV
INT/ORG CONSULT EX/STRUC CREATE OP/RES ECO/TAC   R+D
DEMAND...POLICY MGT METH/COMP 20 WORLD/BANK.   FINAN
PAGE 26 G0513   PLAN

                                    B67
LERNER D.,COMMUNICATION AND CHANGE IN DEVELOPING   EDU/PROP
COUNTRIES. CHINA/COM INDIA PHILIPPINE COM/IND   ORD/FREE
CREATE TEC/DEV...ANTHOL 20. PAGE 33 G0659   PERCEPT
   ECO/UNDEV

                                    B67
MOORE J.R.,THE ECONOMIC IMPACT OF THE TVA. AGRI   ECO/UNDEV
INDUS PLAN BARGAIN CONTROL REGION GOV/REL DEMAND   ECO/DEV
EFFICIENCY SOCISM 20 TVA. PAGE 40 G0780   NAT/G
   CREATE

                                    B67
NASH M.,MACHINE AGE MAYA. GUATEMALA L/A+17C STRUCT   INDUS
AGRI WORKER CREATE INCOME ATTIT RIGID/FLEX ROLE   CULTURE
...IDEA/COMP SOC/EXP WORSHIP 20 INDIAN/AM. PAGE 41   SOC
G0806   MUNIC

                                    B67
NELSON R.R.,TECHNOLOGY, ECONOMIC GROWTH, AND PUBLIC   R+D
POLICY. USA+45 PLAN GP/REL UTIL KNOWL...POLICY   CONSULT
PHIL/SCI CHARTS BIBLIOG 20. PAGE 41 G0817   CREATE
   ACT/RES

                                    B67
POMEROY W.J.,HALF A CENTURY OF SOCIALISM. USSR LAW   SOCISM
AGRI INDUS NAT/G CREATE DIPLOM EDU/PROP PERSON   MARXISM
ORD/FREE WEALTH...POLICY TREND 20. PAGE 45 G0884   COM
   SOCIETY

                                    B67
RUTGERS U GRADUATE SCH LIB SCI,BIBLIOGRAPHY OF   BIBLIOG/A
RESEARCH RELATING TO THE COMMUNICATION OF   COM/IND
SCIENTIFIC AND TECHNICAL INFORMATION. FUT CREATE   R+D
FEEDBACK...PHIL/SCI NEW/IDEA COMPUT/IR HYPO/EXP.   TEC/DEV
PAGE 48 G0951

SALMOND J.A.,THE CIVILIAN CONSERVATION CORPS,
1933-1942. USA-45 NAT/G CREATE EXEC EFFICIENCY
WEALTH...BIBLIOG 20 ROOSEVLT/F. PAGE 48 G0954

ADMIN
ECO/TAC
TASK
AGRI

B67

SCHON D.A.,TECHNOLOGY AND CHANGE* THE NEW
HERACLITUS. TEC/DEV CONTROL COST DEMAND EFFICIENCY
RIGID/FLEX...MYTH 20. PAGE 49 G0975

INDUS
PROB/SOLV
R+D
CREATE

B67

SCHUMACHER B.G.,COMPUTER DYNAMICS IN PUBLIC
ADMINISTRATION. USA+45 CREATE PLAN TEC/DEV...MGT
LING CON/ANAL BIBLIOG/A 20. PAGE 50 G0980

COMPUTER
COMPUT/IR
ADMIN
AUTOMAT

B67

UNESCO,PRINCIPLES AND PROBLEMS OF NATIONAL SCIENCE
POLICIES. WOR+45 ECO/DEV ECO/UNDEV R+D INT/ORG
PROB/SOLV CONFER...PHIL/SCI CHARTS 20 UNESCO UN.
PAGE 55 G1091

NAT/COMP
POLICY
TEC/DEV
CREATE

B67

US HOUSE COMM SCI ASTRONAUT,SCIENCE, TECHNOLOGY,
AND PUBLIC POLICY DURING THE 89TH CONGRESS,
JANUARY, 1965 THROUGH DECEMBER, 1966. USA+45
...CHARTS BIBLIOG. PAGE 59 G1151

POLICY
TEC/DEV
CREATE
NAT/G

B67

WOODRUFF W.,IMPACT OF WESTERN MAN. ECO/DEV INDUS
CREATE PLAN PROB/SOLV COLONIAL GOV/REL...CHARTS
GOV/COMP BIBLIOG 18/20. PAGE 64 G1256

EUR+WWI
MOD/EUR
CAP/ISM

B67

YAVITZ B.,AUTOMATION IN COMMERCIAL BANKING. USA+45
STRUCT WORKER CREATE OP/RES PLAN ROLE...DECISION
SAMP/SIZ. PAGE 64 G1263

TEC/DEV
FINAN
COMPUT/IR
MGT

B67

ATKIN J.M.,"THE FEDERAL GOVERNMENT, BIG BUSINESS,
AND COLLEGES OF EDUCATION." PROF/ORG CONSULT CREATE
PLAN PROB/SOLV ADMIN EFFICIENCY. PAGE 4 G0075

SCHOOL
ACADEM
NAT/G
INDUS

S67

BULMER-THOMAS I.,"SO, ON TO THE GREAT SOCIETY." FUT
UNIV TEC/DEV BAL/PWR WAR BIO/SOC KNOWL...ART/METH
SOC PREDICT TREND WORSHIP 20 GREAT/SOC. PAGE 9
G0185

PHIL/SCI
SOCIETY
CREATE

S67

CHRIST R.F.,"REORGANIZATION OF FRENCH ARMED
FORCES." FRANCE CREATE PLAN TEC/DEV BAL/PWR DOMIN
COERCE CENTRAL EFFICIENCY 20. PAGE 12 G0229

CHIEF
DETER
NUC/PWR
FORCES

S67

CRANBERG L.,"SCIENCE, ETHICS, AND LAW." UNIV CREATE
PLAN EDU/PROP INGP/REL PERS/REL ADJUST RATIONAL
KNOWL MORAL...CONCPT IDEA/COMP 20. PAGE 13 G0260

LAW
PHIL/SCI
INTELL

S67

DADDARIO E.Q.,"CONGRESS FACES SPACE POLICIES." R+D
NAT/G FORCES CREATE LEAD...DECISION CONGRESS NASA.
PAGE 14 G0269

SPACE
PLAN
BUDGET
POLICY

S67

GOLDSTEIN W.,"THE SCIENCE ESTABLISHMENT AND ITS
POLITICAL CONTROL." WOR+45 SOCIETY GP/REL RATIONAL
ORD/FREE. PAGE 22 G0430

CREATE
ADJUST
CONTROL

S67

HAMBERG D.,"SIZE OF ENTERPRISE AND TECHNICAL
CHANGE." USA+45 LG/CO SML/CO CREATE OP/RES PROFIT
...TREND 20. PAGE 24 G0477

TEC/DEV
INDUS
R+D
WEALTH

S67

HARRIS F.R.,"POLITICAL SCIENCE AND THE PROPOSAL FOR
A NATIONAL SOCIAL SCIENCE FOUNDATION." FUT CONSULT
DELIB/GP PLAN PROB/SOLV BUDGET CONFER SANCTION
CRIME...POLICY SOC/WK 20 NSF NSSF. PAGE 25 G0484

PROF/ORG
R+D
CREATE
NAT/G

S67

INGLIS D.R.,"PROSPECTS AND PROBLEMS: THE
NONMILITARY USES OF NUCLEAR EXPLOSIVES." CREATE
PROB/SOLV TEC/DEV AGREE PEACE...INT/LAW PHIL/SCI
NEW/IDEA 20 TREATY. PAGE 28 G0545

NUC/PWR
INDUS
ARMS/CONT
EXTR/IND

S67

KRAUS J.,"A MARXIST IN GHANA." GHANA ELITES CHIEF
PROB/SOLV TEC/DEV DIPLOM ECO/TAC COLONIAL PARTIC

MARXISM
PLAN

S67

PWR 20 NKRUMAH/K. PAGE 31 G0618

ATTIT
CREATE

LEWIS R.L.,"GOAL AND NO GOAL* A NEW POLICY IN
SPACE." R+D BUDGET COST...POLICY DECISION PHIL/SCI.
PAGE 34 G0662

SPACE
PLAN
EFFICIENCY
CREATE

S67

MACDONALD G.J.F.,"SCIENCE AND SPACE POLICY* HOW
DOES IT GET PLANNED?" R+D CREATE TEC/DEV BUDGET
ADMIN ROUTINE...DECISION NASA. PAGE 35 G0687

SPACE
PLAN
MGT
EX/STRUC

S67

MEHTA A.,"INDIA* POVERTY AND CHANGE." STRATA INDUS
CREATE ECO/TAC FOR/AID NEUTRAL GP/REL ADJUST INCOME
...NEW/IDEA 20. PAGE 38 G0751

INDIA
SOCIETY
ECO/UNDEV
TEC/DEV

S67

MOOR E.J.,"THE INTERNATIONAL IMPACT OF AUTOMATION."
WOR+45 ACT/RES COMPUTER CREATE PLAN CAP/ISM ROUTINE
EFFICIENCY PREDICT. PAGE 39 G0779

TEC/DEV
OP/RES
AUTOMAT
INDUS

S67

PENNEY N.,"BANK STATEMENTS, CANCELLED CHECKS, AND
ARTICLE FOUR IN THE ELECTRONIC AGE." USA+45 TEC/DEV
COST EFFICIENCY WEALTH. PAGE 44 G0866

CREATE
LAW
ADJUD
FINAN

S67

RAMSEY J.A.,"THE STATUS OF INTERNATIONAL
COPYRIGHTS." WOR+45 CREATE TEC/DEV DIPLOM CONFER
CONTROL SANCTION OWN...POLICY JURID. PAGE 46 G0899

INT/LAW
INT/ORG
COM/IND
PRESS

S67

RICH G.S.,"THE PROPOSED PATENT LEGISLATION* SOME
COMMENTS." USA+45 LAW R+D ACT/RES TEC/DEV CONFER
EFFICIENCY OWN JURID. PAGE 46 G0916

LICENSE
POLICY
CREATE
CAP/ISM

S67

SHARP G.,"THE NEED OF A FUNCTIONAL SUBSTITUTE FOR
WAR." FUT UNIV WOR+45 CULTURE SOCIETY INT/ORG
CONSULT DELIB/GP ACT/RES CREATE BAL/PWR CONFER
ARMS/CONT NUC/PWR 20. PAGE 50 G0989

PEACE
WAR
DIPLOM
PROB/SOLV

S67

SLOAN P.,"FIFTY YEARS OF SOVIET RULE." USSR INDUS
EDU/PROP EFFICIENCY PRODUC HEALTH KNOWL MORAL
WEALTH MARXISM...POLICY 20. PAGE 51 G1011

CREATE
NAT/G
PLAN
INSPECT

S67

VERGIN R.C.,"COMPUTER INDUCED ORGANIZATION
CHANGES." FUT USA+45 R+D CREATE OP/RES TEC/DEV
ADJUST CENTRAL...MGT INT CON/ANAL COMPUT/IR.
PAGE 61 G1194

COMPUTER
DECISION
AUTOMAT
EX/STRUC

S67

US HOUSE COMM SCI ASTRONAUT,GOVERNMENT, SCIENCE,
AND INTERNATIONAL POLICY (PAMPHLET). INDIA
NETHERLAND ECO/DEV ECO/UNDEV R+D ACADEM PLAN DIPLOM
FOR/AID CONFER...PREDICT 20 CHINJAP. PAGE 59 G1152

NAT/G
POLICY
CREATE
TEC/DEV

N67

US SENATE COMM AERO SPACE SCI,POLICY PLANNING FOR
TECHNOLOGY TRANSFER (PAMPHLET). WOR+45 INDUS CREATE
PLAN EFFICIENCY ATTIT. PAGE 60 G1171

TEC/DEV
POLICY
NAT/G
ECO/DEV

N67

US SENATE COMM AERO SPACE SCI,HEARINGS BEFORE THE
COMMITTEE ON AERONAUTICAL AND SPACE SCIENCES UNITED
STATES SENATE NINETIETH CONGRESS (PAMPHLET). USA+45
CONSULT PLAN CONFER EFFICIENCY SENATE. PAGE 60
G1172

NAT/G
DELIB/GP
SPACE
CREATE

N67

GALLAHER A. JR.,PERSPECTIVES IN DEVELOPMENTAL
CHANGE. MUNIC PLAN INSPECT EDU/PROP...POLICY
DECISION GEOG PSY SOC IDEA/COMP ANTHOL 20
MODERNIZE. PAGE 21 G0405

TECHNIC
TEC/DEV
PROB/SOLV
CREATE

B68

BARAGWANATH L.E.,"SCIENTIFIC CO-OPERATION BETWEEN
THE UNIVERSITIES AND INDUSTRY - A RESEARCH NOTE."
UK LG/CO CREATE TEC/DEV EDU/PROP ATTIT...PHIL/SCI
STAT QU 20. PAGE 5 G0090

R+D
ACADEM
INDUS
GP/REL

S68

CREDIT....CREDIT

CRIME....SEE ALSO ANOMIE

B54
SPROTT W.J.H.,SCIENCE AND SOCIAL ACTION. STRUCT SOC
ACT/RES CRIME GP/REL INGP/REL ANOMIE...PSY CULTURE
SOC/INTEG 19/20. PAGE 52 G1027 PHIL/SCI

B58
OGDEN F.D.,THE POLL TAX IN THE SOUTH. USA+45 USA-45 TAX
CONSTN ADJUD ADMIN PARTIC CRIME...TIME/SEQ GOV/COMP CHOOSE
METH/COMP 18/20 SOUTH/US. PAGE 43 G0838 RACE/REL
DISCRIM

B66
US HOUSE COMM ON JUDICIARY,CIVIL COMMITMENT AND BIO/SOC
TREATMENT OF NARCOTIC ADDICTS. USA+45 SOCIETY FINAN CRIME
LEGIS PROB/SOLV GIVE CT/SYS SANCTION HEALTH IDEA/COMP
...POLICY HEAL 20. PAGE 58 G1141 CONTROL

B67
PIPER D.C.,THE INTERNATIONAL LAW OF THE GREAT CONCPT
LAKES. CANADA EXTR/IND MUNIC LICENSE ARMS/CONT DIPLOM
CRIME...GEOG 19/20. PAGE 45 G0879 INT/LAW

B67
RUSSELL B.,WAR CRIMES IN VIETNAM. USA+45 VIETNAM WAR
FORCES DIPLOM WEAPON RACE/REL DISCRIM ISOLAT CRIME
BIO/SOC 20 COLD/WAR RUSSELL/B. PAGE 48 G0949 ATTIT
POLICY

B67
UNIVERSAL REFERENCE SYSTEM,CURRENT EVENTS AND BIBLIOG/A
PROBLEMS OF MODERN SOCIETY (VOLUME V). WOR+45 LOC/G SOCIETY
MUNIC NAT/G PLAN EDU/PROP CRIME RACE/REL WEALTH PROB/SOLV
...COMPUT/IR GEN/METH. PAGE 56 G1097 ATTIT

B67
US PRES COMN LAW ENFORCE-JUS,THE CHALLENGE OF CRIME CT/SYS
IN A FREE SOCIETY. LAW STRUCT CONSULT ACT/RES PUB/INST
TEC/DEV INGP/REL...SOC/WK 20. PAGE 59 G1160 CRIMLGY
CRIME

L67
SEABERG G.P.,"THE DRUG ABUSE PROBLEMS AND SOME BIO/SOC
PROPOSALS." UK USA+45 MARKET SANCTION CRIME LAW
...POLICY NEW/IDEA. PAGE 50 G0986 ADJUD
PROB/SOLV

S67
HARRIS F.R.,"POLITICAL SCIENCE AND THE PROPOSAL FOR PROF/ORG
A NATIONAL SOCIAL SCIENCE FOUNDATION." FUT CONSULT R+D
DELIB/GP PLAN PROB/SOLV BUDGET CONFER SANCTION CREATE
CRIME...POLICY SOC/WK 20 NSF NSSF. PAGE 25 G0484 NAT/G

CRIMINOLOGY....SEE CRIMLGY

CRIMLGY....CRIMINOLOGY

B67
US PRES COMN LAW ENFORCE-JUS,THE CHALLENGE OF CRIME CT/SYS
IN A FREE SOCIETY. LAW STRUCT CONSULT ACT/RES PUB/INST
TEC/DEV INGP/REL...SOC/WK 20. PAGE 59 G1160 CRIMLGY
CRIME

CRIMNL/LAW....CRIMINAL LAW

CROMWELL/O....OLIVER CROMWELL

CROSS-PRESSURES .... SEE ROLE

CROSSON F.J. G0263

CROWD....MOB BEHAVIOR, MASS BEHAVIOR

B45
MAYO E.,THE SOCIAL PROBLEMS OF AN INDUSTRIAL INDUS
CIVILIZATION. USA+45 SOCIETY LABOR CROWD PERS/REL GP/REL
LAISSEZ. PAGE 37 G0725 MGT
WORKER

S58
KLAPPER J.T.,"WHAT WE KNOW ABOUT THE EFFECTS OF ACT/RES
MASS COMMUNICATION: THE BRINK OF HOPE" (BMR)" PERCEPT
COM/IND KNOWL...METH/CNCPT GEN/LAWS BIBLIOG METH CROWD
20. PAGE 31 G0605 PHIL/SCI

C60
SCHRAMM W.,"MASS COMMUNICATIONS: A BOOK OF READINGS COM/IND
(2ND ED.)" LG/CO PRESS ADMIN CONTROL ROUTINE ATTIT EDU/PROP
ROLE SUPEGO...CHARTS ANTHOL BIBLIOG 20. PAGE 50 CROWD
G0977 MAJORIT

B67
UNIVERSAL REFERENCE SYSTEM,PUBLIC OPINION, MASS BIBLIOG/A
BEHAVIOR, AND POLITICAL PSYCHOLOGY (VOLUME VI). ATTIT
WOR+45 WOR-45 SOCIETY EDU/PROP PRESS PARTIC CHOOSE CROWD

PERSON...TREND COMPUT/IR GEN/METH. PAGE 56 G1098 PSY

CROWE S. G0264

CROWTHER J.G. G0265

CRUMP/ED....EDWARD H. CRUMP

CT/APPEALS....COURT OF APPEALS AND APPELLATE COURT SYSTEM

CT/SYS....COURT SYSTEMS

B14
CRAIG J.,ELEMENTS OF POLITICAL SCIENCE (3 VOLS.). PHIL/SCI
CONSTN AGRI INDUS SCHOOL FORCES TAX CT/SYS SUFF NAT/G
MORAL WEALTH...CONCPT 19 CIVIL/LIB. PAGE 13 G0259 ORD/FREE

N19
LAWRENCE S.A.,THE BATTERY ADDITIVE CONTROVERSY PHIL/SCI
(PAMPHLET). USA+45 LAW MARKET PROC/MFG R+D CAP/ISM LOBBY
CT/SYS GOV/REL OWN FTC CONGRESS BUR/STNDRD INSPECT
RITCHIE/JM. PAGE 33 G0645

B25
MATHEWS J.M.,AMERICAN STATE GOVERNMENT. USA-45 PROVS
LOC/G CHIEF EX/STRUC LEGIS ADJUD CONTROL CT/SYS ADMIN
ROUTINE GOV/REL PWR 20 GOVERNOR. PAGE 37 G0721 FEDERAL
CONSTN

B40
HELLMAN F.S.,THE NEW DEAL: SELECTED LIST OF BIBLIOG/A
REFERENCES. USA-45 FINAN LABOR EX/STRUC CREATE ECO/TAC
INT/TRADE ADMIN CT/SYS 20 SUPREME/CT. PAGE 26 G0505 PLAN
POLICY

B48
PUBLIC ADMINISTRATION SERVICE,SOURCE MATERIALS IN BIBLIOG/A
PUBLIC ADMINISTRATION: A SELECTED BIBLIOGRAPHY (PAS GOV/REL
PUBLICATION NO. 102). USA+45 LAW FINAN LOC/G MUNIC MGT
NAT/G PLAN RECEIVE EDU/PROP CT/SYS CHOOSE HEALTH ADMIN
20. PAGE 45 G0895

C50
WAGER P.W.,"COUNTY GOVERNMENT ACROSS THE NATION." LOC/G
USA+45 CONSTN COM/IND FINAN SCHOOL DOMIN CT/SYS PROVS
LEAD GOV/REL...STAT BIBLIOG 20. PAGE 61 G1204 ADMIN
ROUTINE

B52
APPADORAI A.,THE SUBSTANCE OF POLITICS (6TH ED.). PHIL/SCI
EX/STRUC LEGIS DIPLOM CT/SYS CHOOSE FASCISM MARXISM NAT/G
SOCISM...BIBLIOG T. PAGE 3 G0062

B54
TOMPKINS D.C.,STATE GOVERNMENT AND ADMINISTRATION: BIBLIOG/A
A BIBLIOGRAPHY. USA+45 USA-45 CONSTN LEGIS JUDGE LOC/G
BUDGET CT/SYS LOBBY...CHARTS 20. PAGE 55 G1077 PROVS
ADMIN

C54
CALDWELL L.K.,"THE GOVERNMENT AND ADMINISTRATION OF PROVS
NEW YORK." LOC/G MUNIC POL/PAR SCHOOL CHIEF LEGIS ADMIN
PLAN TAX CT/SYS...MGT SOC/WK BIBLIOG 20 NEWYORK/C. CONSTN
PAGE 10 G0202 EX/STRUC

B58
DAVIS K.C.,ADMINISTRATIVE LAW TREATISE (VOLS. I AND ADMIN
IV). NAT/G JUDGE PROB/SOLV ADJUD GP/REL 20 JURID
SUPREME/CT. PAGE 14 G0278 CT/SYS
EX/STRUC

S58
MCDOUGAL M.S.,"PERSPECTIVES FOR A LAW OF OUTER INT/ORG
SPACE." FUT WOR+45 AIR CONSULT DELIB/GP TEC/DEV SPACE
CT/SYS ORD/FREE...POLICY JURID 20 UN. PAGE 37 G0736 INT/LAW

B60
WEBSTER J.A.,A GENERAL STUDY OF THE DEPARTMENT OF ORD/FREE
DEFENSE INTERNAL SECURITY PROGRAM. USA+45 WORKER PLAN
TEC/DEV ADJUD CONTROL CT/SYS EXEC GOV/REL COST ADMIN
...POLICY DECISION MGT 20 DEPT/DEFEN SUPREME/CT. NAT/G
PAGE 62 G1221

S61
SCHILLING W.R.,"THE H-BOMB: HOW TO DECIDE WITHOUT PERSON
ACTUALLY CHOOSING." FUT USA+45 INTELL CONSULT ADMIN LEGIT
CT/SYS MORAL...JURID OBS 20 TRUMAN/HS. PAGE 49 NUC/PWR
G0966

B62
BOCK E.A.,CASE STUDIES IN AMERICAN GOVERNMENT. POLICY
USA+45 ECO/DEV CHIEF EDU/PROP CT/SYS RACE/REL LEGIS
ORD/FREE...JURID MGT PHIL/SCI PRESIDENT CASEBOOK. IDEA/COMP
PAGE 8 G0146 NAT/G

B65
US CONGRESS JT ATOM ENRGY COMM,PROPOSED AMENDMENT   LAW
TO SECTION 271 OF THE ATOMIC ENERGY ACT OF 1954.   LEGIS
USA+45 CONSTRUC PLAN INSPECT CONTROL CT/SYS 20   DELIB/GP
CONGRESS AEC. PAGE 57 G1115   NUC/PWR

B66
US HOUSE COMM ON JUDICIARY,CIVIL COMMITMENT AND   BIO/SOC
TREATMENT OF NARCOTIC ADDICTS. USA+45 SOCIETY FINAN   CRIME
LEGIS PROB/SOLV GIVE CT/SYS SANCTION HEALTH   IDEA/COMP
...POLICY HEAL 20. PAGE 58 G1141   CONTROL

B67
UNIVERSAL REFERENCE SYSTEM,LAW, JURISPRUDENCE, AND   BIBLIOG/A
JUDICIAL PROCESS (VOLUME VII). WOR+45 WOR-45 CONSTN   LAW
NAT/G LEGIS JUDGE CT/SYS...INT/LAW COMPUT/IR   JURID
GEN/METH METH. PAGE 56 G1101   ADJUD

B67
US PRES COMN LAW ENFORCE-JUS,THE CHALLENGE OF CRIME   CT/SYS
IN A FREE SOCIETY. LAW STRUCT CONSULT ACT/RES   PUB/INST
TEC/DEV INGP/REL...SOC/WK 20. PAGE 59 G1160   CRIMLGY
                                                         CRIME

B67
US SUPERINTENDENT OF DOCUMENTS,LIBRARY OF CONGRESS   BIBLIOG/A
(PRICE LIST 83). AFR ASIA EUR+WWI USA-45 USSR NAT/G   USA+45
DIPLOM CONFER CT/SYS WAR...DECISION PHIL/SCI   AUTOMAT
CLASSIF 19/20 CONGRESS PRESIDENT. PAGE 61 G1189   LAW

L67
NADER R.,"AUTOMOBILE DESIGN AND THE JUDICIAL   LAW
PROCESS." USA+45 CT/SYS SUPEGO JURID. PAGE 40 G0799   ADJUD
                                                         TEC/DEV
                                                         PROC/MFG

S67
KOMESAR N.K.,"SECURITY INTERESTS IN GOVERNMENT   POLICY
CONTRACTS* WHEREIN THE TORTOISE WINS THE RES."   CT/SYS
USA+45 INDUS NAT/G OP/RES SANCTION. PAGE 31 G0613   PRIVIL
                                                         JURID

CTS/WESTM....COURTS OF WESTMINSTER HALL

CUBA....SEE ALSO L/A+17C

B61
SCHMIDT H.,VERTEIDIGUNG ODER VERGELTUNG. COM CUBA   PLAN
GERMANY/W USSR FORCES DIPLOM ARMS/CONT DETER   WAR
NUC/PWR...POLICY CHARTS HYPO/EXP SIMUL BIBLIOG 20   BAL/PWR
NATO COLD/WAR. PAGE 49 G0970   ORD/FREE

B63
PACHTER H.M.,COLLISION COURSE; THE CUBAN MISSILE   WAR
CRISIS AND COEXISTENCE. CUBA USA+45 DIPLOM   BAL/PWR
ARMS/CONT PEACE MARXISM...DECISION INT/LAW 20   NUC/PWR
COLD/WAR KHRUSH/N KENNEDY/JF CASTRO/F. PAGE 43   DETER
G0854

B66
BRODIE B.,ESCALATION AND THE NUCLEAR OPTION. ASIA   NUC/PWR
CUBA EUR+WWI KOREA USA+45 USSR VIETNAM RISK ATTIT   GUERRILLA
DRIVE PERCEPT PROBABIL. PAGE 9 G0172   WAR
                                                         DETER

B67
WYLIE J.C.,MILITARY STRATEGY: GENERAL THEORY OF   FORCES
POWER CONTROL. CUBA USA+45 VIETNAM/N WOR+45 ELITES   PLAN
CONTROL WAR PWR...POLICY METH/COMP 20 MAO. PAGE 64   DECISION
G1260   IDEA/COMP

CUBAN CRISIS....SEE DIPLOM +APPROPRIATE NATIONS+COLD WAR

CULHAN R.H. G0289

CULTS....SEE SECT

CULTUR/REV....CULTURAL REVOLUTION IN CHINA

CULTURAL REVOLUTION IN CHINA....SEE CULTUR/REV

CULTURE....CULTURAL PATTERNS

N
FOREIGN AFFAIRS. SPACE WOR+45 WOR-45 CULTURE   BIBLIOG
ECO/UNDEV FINAN NAT/G TEC/DEV INT/TRADE ARMS/CONT   DIPLOM
NUC/PWR...POLICY 20 UN EURATOM ECSC EEC. PAGE 1   INT/ORG
G0004   INT/LAW

N
INDIA: A REFERENCE ANNUAL. INDIA CULTURE COM/IND   CONSTN
R+D FORCES PLAN RECEIVE EDU/PROP HEALTH...STAT   LABOR
CHARTS BIBLIOG 20. PAGE 1 G0005   INT/ORG

B28
SOROKIN P.,CONTEMPORARY SOCIOLOGICAL THEORIES.   CULTURE
MOD/EUR UNIV SOCIETY R+D SCHOOL ECO/TAC EDU/PROP   SOC
ROUTINE ATTIT DRIVE...PSY CONCPT TIME/SEQ TREND   WAR
GEN/LAWS 20. PAGE 52 G1021

B34
BOWMAN I.,GEOGRAPHY IN RELATION TO THE SOCIAL   GEOG
SCIENCES. UNIV...SOC CONCPT METH. PAGE 8 G0161   CULTURE
                                                        ROUTINE
                                                        PHIL/SCI

S38
LUNDBERG G.A.,"THE CONCEPT OF LAW IN THE SOCIAL   EPIST
SCIENCES"(BMR)" CULTURE INTELL SOCIETY STRUCT   GEN/LAWS
CREATE...NEW/IDEA 20. PAGE 34 G0678   CONCPT
                                                        PHIL/SCI

B45
REVES E.,THE ANATOMY OF PEACE. WOR-45 LAW CULTURE   ACT/RES
NAT/G PLAN TEC/DEV EDU/PROP WAR NAT/LISM ATTIT   CONCPT
ALL/VALS SOVEREIGN...POLICY HUM TIME/SEQ 20.   NUC/PWR
PAGE 46 G0914   PEACE

B47
BRYSON L.,SCIENCE AND FREEDOM. WOR+45 ACT/RES   CONCPT
CREATE TECHRACY...TECHNIC SOC/INTEG. PAGE 9 G0183   ORD/FREE
                                                        CULTURE
                                                        SOC

B47
LASSWELL H.D.,THE ANALYSIS OF POLITICAL BEHAVIOUR: R+D
AN EMPIRICAL APPROACH. WOR+45 CULTURE NAT/G FORCES   ACT/RES
EDU/PROP ADMIN ATTIT PERCEPT KNOWL...PHIL/SCI PSY   ELITES
SOC NEW/IDEA OBS INT GEN/METH NAZI 20. PAGE 32
G0639

B50
CANTRIL H.,TENSIONS THAT CAUSE WAR. UNIV CULTURE   SOCIETY
R+D CREATE EDU/PROP DRIVE PERSON KNOWL ORD/FREE   PHIL/SCI
...HUM PSY SOC OBS CENSUS TREND CON/ANAL SOC/EXP   PEACE
SIMUL GEN/METH ANTHOL COLD/WAR TOT/POP. PAGE 11
G0206

B51
HUXLEY J.,FREEDOM AND CULTURE. UNIV LAW SOCIETY R+D   CULTURE
ACADEM SCHOOL CREATE SANCTION ATTIT KNOWL...HUM   ORD/FREE
ANTHOL 20. PAGE 27 G0540   PHIL/SCI
                                                        IDEA/COMP

B52
CALLOT E.,LA SOCIETE ET SON ENVIRONNEMENT: ESSAI   SOCIETY
SUR LES PRINCIPES DES SCIENCES SOCIALES. GP/REL   PHIL/SCI
ADJUST CONSEN ISOLAT HABITAT PERCEPT PERSON   CULTURE
...BIBLIOG SOC/INTEG 20. PAGE 10 G0205

B52
DAY E.E.,EDUCATION FOR FREEDOM AND RESPONSIBILITY.   SCHOOL
FUT USA+45 CULTURE CONSULT EDU/PROP ATTIT SKILL   KNOWL
...MGT CONCPT OBS GEN/LAWS COLD/WAR 20. PAGE 14
G0282

S52
KECSKEMETI P.,"THE 'POLICY SCIENCES': ASPIRATION   CREATE
AND OUTLOOK." UNIV CULTURE INTELL SOCIETY STRUCT   NEW/IDEA
EDU/PROP ATTIT PERCEPT RIGID/FLEX KNOWL...PHIL/SCI
METH/CNCPT OBS 20. PAGE 30 G0589

B53
SAYLES L.R.,THE LOCAL UNION. CONSTN CULTURE   LABOR
DELIB/GP PARTIC CHOOSE GP/REL INGP/REL ATTIT ROLE   LEAD
...MAJORIT DECISION MGT. PAGE 49 G0958   ADJUD
                                                        ROUTINE

B54
KENWORTHY L.S.,FREE AND INEXPENSIVE MATERIALS ON   BIBLIOG/A
WORLD AFFAIRS (PAMPHLET). WOR+45 CULTURE ECO/UNDEV   NAT/G
INT/TRADE ARMS/CONT NUC/PWR UN. PAGE 30 G0594   INT/ORG
                                                        DIPLOM

B54
SPROTT W.J.H.,SCIENCE AND SOCIAL ACTION. STRUCT   SOC
ACT/RES CRIME GP/REL INGP/REL ANOMIE...PSY   CULTURE
SOC/INTEG 19/20. PAGE 52 G1027   PHIL/SCI

B54
WASHBURNE N.F.,INTERPRETING SOCIAL CHANGE IN   CULTURE
AMERICA. USA+45 STRATA FAM NAT/G SECT OP/RES   STRUCT
ECO/TAC EDU/PROP HABITAT...SOC TIME/SEQ TREND 20   CREATE
BUREAUCRCY. PAGE 62 G1217   TEC/DEV

S55
ANGELL R.,"GOVERNMENTS AND PEOPLES AS A FOCI FOR   FUT
PEACE-ORIENTED RESEARCH." WOR+45 CULTURE SOCIETY   SOC
FACE/GP ACT/RES CREATE PLAN DIPLOM EDU/PROP ROUTINE   PEACE
ATTIT PERCEPT SKILL...POLICY CONCPT OBS TREND

GEN/METH 20. PAGE 3 G0060

CROWE S.,THE LANDSCAPE OF POWER. UK CULTURE SERV/IND NAT/G CONSULT PARTIC NUC/PWR LEISURE...SOC EXHIBIT 20. PAGE 14 G0264
B58
HABITAT
TEC/DEV
PLAN
CONTROL

ORTEGA Y GASSET J.,MAN AND CRISIS. SECT CREATE PERSON CONSERVE...GEN/LAWS RENAISSAN. PAGE 43 G0846
B58
PHIL/SCI
CULTURE
CONCPT

JACOBS N.,CULTURE FOR THE MILLIONS? INTELL SOCIETY NAT/G...POLICY SOC OBS ANTHOL 20. PAGE 28 G0553
B59
CULTURE
COM/IND
PERF/ART
CONCPT

CARPENTER E.,EXPLORATIONS IN COMMUNICATION. USSR CULTURE SCHOOL SECT EDU/PROP PRESS TV AUTOMAT FEEDBACK ATTIT PERSON...ART/METH PSY 20. PAGE 11 G0211
B60
ANTHOL
COM/IND
TEC/DEV
WRITING

JANOWITZ M.,THE PROFESSIONAL SOLDIER. CULTURE STRATA STRUCT FAM PROB/SOLV TEC/DEV COERCE WAR CIVMIL/REL NAT/LISM AGE HEREDITY ALL/VALS CONSERVE ...MGT WORSHIP. PAGE 28 G0560
B60
FORCES
MYTH
LEAD
ELITES

LEYDER J.,BIBLIOGRAPHIE DE L'ENSEIGNEMENT SUPERIEUR ET DE LA RECHERCHE SCIENTIFIQUE EN AFRIQUE INTERTROPICALE (2 VOLS.). AFR CULTURE ECO/UNDEV AGRI PLAN EDU/PROP ADMIN COLONIAL...GEOG SOC/INTEG 20 NEGRO. PAGE 34 G0664
B60
BIBLIOG/A
ACT/RES
ACADEM
R+D

PENTONY D.E.,THE UNDERDEVELOPED LANDS. FUT WOR+45 CULTURE AGRI FINAN INDUS MARKET INT/ORG LABOR NAT/G VOL/ASSN CONSULT TEC/DEV ECO/TAC EDU/PROP COLONIAL ATTIT WEALTH...OBS RECORD SAMP TREND GEN/METH WORK UN 20. PAGE 44 G0867
B60
ECO/UNDEV
POLICY
FOR/AID
INT/TRADE

HOLTON G.,"ARMS CONTROL." FUT WOR+45 CULTURE INT/ORG NAT/G FORCES TOP/EX PLAN EDU/PROP COERCE ATTIT RIGID/FLEX ORD/FREE...POLICY PHIL/SCI SOC TREND COLD/WAR. PAGE 27 G0524
L60
ACT/RES
CONSULT
ARMS/CONT
NUC/PWR

HALSEY A.H.,"THE CHANGING FUNCTIONS OF UNIVERSITIES IN ADVANCED INDUSTRIAL SOCIETIES." R+D EDU/PROP REPRESENT ROLE ORD/FREE PWR TREND. PAGE 24 G0476
S60
ACADEM
CREATE
CULTURE
ADJUST

JAFFEE A.J.,"POPULATION TRENDS AND CONTROLS IN UNDERDEVELOPED COUNTRIES." AFR FUT ISLAM L/A+17C S/ASIA CULTURE R+D FAM ACT/RES PLAN EDU/PROP BIO/SOC RIGID/FLEX HEALTH...SOC STAT OBS CHARTS 20. PAGE 28 G0555
S60
ECO/UNDEV
GEOG

OSGOOD C.E.,"A CASE FOR GRADUATED UNILATERAL DISENGAGEMENT." FUT WOR+45 CULTURE SOCIETY NAT/G NUC/PWR WAR PERSON SUPEGO ALL/VALS...POLICY PSY CONCPT COLD/WAR TOT/POP VAL/FREE 20. PAGE 43 G0848
S60
ATTIT
EDU/PROP
ARMS/CONT

RIVKIN A.,"AFRICAN ECONOMIC DEVELOPMENT: ADVANCED TECHNOLOGY AND THE STAGES OF GROWTH." CULTURE ECO/UNDEV AGRI COM/IND EXTR/IND PLAN ECO/TAC ATTIT DRIVE RIGID/FLEX SKILL WEALTH...MGT SOC GEN/LAWS WORK TOT/POP 20. PAGE 47 G0923
S60
AFR
TEC/DEV
FOR/AID

LUNDBERG G.A.,CAN SCIENCE SAVE US. UNIV CULTURE INTELL SOCIETY ECO/DEV R+D PLAN EDU/PROP ROUTINE CHOOSE ATTIT PERCEPT ALL/VALS...TREND 20. PAGE 34 G0679
B61
ACT/RES
CONCPT
TOTALISM

BENNIS W.G.,THE PLANNING OF CHANGE: READINGS IN THE APPLIED BEHAVIORAL SCIENCES. CULTURE STRATA STRUCT PLAN GP/REL...SOC T. PAGE 6 G0123
B62
PROB/SOLV
CREATE
ACT/RES
OP/RES

CARSON R.,SILENT SPRING. USA+45 AIR CULTURE AGRI INDUS ADMIN ATTIT RIGID/FLEX ORD/FREE PWR...POLICY 20. PAGE 11 G0216
B62
HABITAT
TREND
SOCIETY
CONTROL

KARNJAHAPRAKORN C.,MUNICIPAL GOVERNMENT IN THAILAND AS AN INSTITUTION AND PROCESS OF SELF-GOVERNMENT. THAILAND CULTURE FINAN EX/STRUC LEGIS PLAN CONTROL GOV/REL EFFICIENCY ATTIT...POLICY 20. PAGE 29 G0578
B62
LOC/G
MUNIC
ORD/FREE
ADMIN

OSGOOD C.E.,AN ALTERNATIVE TO WAR OR SURRENDER. FUT UNIV CULTURE INTELL SOCIETY R+D INT/ORG CONSULT DELIB/GP ACT/RES PLAN CHOOSE ATTIT PERCEPT KNOWL ...PHIL/SCI PSY SOC TREND GEN/LAWS 20. PAGE 43 G0849
B62
ORD/FREE
EDU/PROP
PEACE
WAR

ROSS R.,SYMBOLS AND CIVILIZATION. UNIV CULTURE SECT CREATE ALL/VALS MORAL ART/METH. PAGE 48 G0939
B62
PHIL/SCI
KNOWL
EPIST
SOCIETY

WRIGHT Q.,PREVENTING WORLD WAR THREE. FUT WOR+45 CULTURE INT/ORG NAT/G CONSULT FORCES ADMIN ARMS/CONT DRIVE RIGID/FLEX ORD/FREE SOVEREIGN ...POLICY CONCPT TREND STERTYP COLD/WAR 20. PAGE 64 G1259
B62
CREATE
ATTIT

WALTER E.,"VERS UNE CLASSIFICATION SCIENTIFIQUE DE LA SOCIOLOGIA." UNIV CULTURE INTELL SOCIETY R+D ACT/RES LEGIT ROUTINE ATTIT KNOWL...JURID MGT TREND GEN/LAWS 20. PAGE 62 G1208
S62
PLAN
CONCPT

GEERTZ C.,OLD SOCIETIES AND NEW STATES: THE QUEST FOR MODERNITY IN ASIA AND AFRICA. AFR ASIA LAW CULTURE SECT EDU/PROP REV...GOV/COMP NAT/COMP 20. PAGE 21 G0415
B63
ECO/UNDEV
TEC/DEV
NAT/LISM
SOVEREIGN

HOFSTADTER R.,ANTI-INTELLECTUALISM IN AMERICAN LIFE. USA+45 AGRI INDUS ACADEM TEC/DEV EDU/PROP INGP/REL ATTIT...SOC WORSHIP 20 MCCARTHY/J STEVENSN/A. PAGE 26 G0522
B63
INTELL
EPIST
CULTURE
SOCIETY

MULLER H.J.,FREEDOM IN THE WESTERN WORLD. PREHIST CULTURE SECT CREATE TEC/DEV DOMIN PWR WEALTH ...MAJORIT SOC CONCPT. PAGE 40 G0793
B63
ORD/FREE
TIME/SEQ
SOCIETY

RUITENBEER H.M.,THE DILEMMA OF ORGANIZATIONAL SOCIETY. CULTURE ECO/DEV MUNIC SECT TEC/DEV EDU/PROP NAT/LISM ORD/FREE...NAT/COMP 20 RIESMAN/D WHYTE/WF MERTON/R MEAD/MARG JASPERS/K. PAGE 48 G0945
B63
PERSON
ROLE
ADMIN
WORKER

DE FOREST J.D.,"LOW LEVELS OF TECHNOLOGY AND ECONOMIC DEVELOPMENT PROSPECTS." WOR+45 WOR-45 CULTURE ACT/RES CREATE PLAN ECO/TAC ROUTINE PERCEPT WEALTH...METH/CNCPT GEN/LAWS 20. PAGE 15 G0284
S63
ECO/UNDEV
TEC/DEV

BRIGHT J.R.,RESEARCH, DEVELOPMENT AND TECHNOLOGICAL INNOVATION. CULTURE R+D CREATE PLAN PROB/SOLV AUTOMAT RISK PERSON...DECISION CONCPT PREDICT BIBLIOG. PAGE 9 G0168
B64
TEC/DEV
NEW/IDEA
INDUS
MGT

PETERSON W.,THE POLITICS OF POPULATION. COM EUR+WWI FUT MOD/EUR S/ASIA USA+45 USA-45 LAW CULTURE FAM SECT DOMIN EDU/PROP BIO/SOC HEALTH ORD/FREE ...GEOG STAT TIME/SEQ TREND VAL/FREE. PAGE 44 G0871
B64
PLAN
CENSUS
POLICY

BENTWICH J.S.,EDUCATION IN ISRAEL. ISRAEL CULTURE STRATA PROB/SOLV TEC/DEV ADJUST ALL/VALS 20 JEWS. PAGE 7 G0125
B65
SECT
EDU/PROP
ACADEM
SCHOOL

FOSTER P.,EDUCATION AND SOCIAL CHANGE IN GHANA. GHANA CULTURE STRUCT ECO/UNDEV TEC/DEV REGION EFFICIENCY LITERACY ALL/VALS SOVEREIGN...STAT METH/COMP 19/20 GOLD/COAST. PAGE 20 G0385
B65
SCHOOL
CREATE
SOCIETY

HALPERIN M.H.,COMMUNIST CHINA AND ARMS CONTROL. CHINA/COM FUT USA+45 CULTURE FORCES TEC/DEV ECO/TAC WAR PEACE ORD/FREE MARXISM 20 COLD/WAR. PAGE 24 G0473
B65
ATTIT
POLICY
ARMS/CONT
NUC/PWR

PYE L.W.,POLITICAL CULTURE AND DEVELOPMENT. WOR+45 WOR-45 CULTURE ECO/UNDEV NAT/G ALL/VALS ORD/FREE PWR WEALTH ALL/IDEOS...TRADIT TREND 20. PAGE 46
B65
PHIL/SCI
TEC/DEV
SOCIETY

G0897

REISS A.J. JR.,SCHOOLS IN A CHANGING SOCIETY. CULTURE PROB/SOLV INSPECT DOMIN CONFER INGP/REL RACE/REL AGE/C AGE/Y ALL/VALS...ANTHOL SOC/INTEG 20 NEWYORK/C. PAGE 46 G0912
B65
SCHOOL
EX/STRUC
ADJUST
ADMIN

TURNER A.N.,INDUSTRIAL JOBS AND THE WORKER. USA+45 CULTURE ECO/DEV LABOR MUNIC ACT/RES AUTOMAT TASK ...CHARTS BIBLIOG 20. PAGE 55 G1082
B65
WORKER
INDUS
ATTIT
TEC/DEV

VERMOT-GAUCHY M.,L'EDUCATION NATIONALE DANS LA FRANCE DE 1975. FRANCE FUT CULTURE ELITES R+D SCHOOL PLAN EDU/PROP EFFICIENCY...POLICY PREDICT CHARTS INDEX 20. PAGE 61 G1195
B65
ACADEM
CREATE
TREND
INTELL

LASSWELL H.D.,"THE POLICY SCIENCES OF DEVELOPMENT." CULTURE SOCIETY EX/STRUC CREATE ADMIN ATTIT KNOWL ...SOC CONCPT SIMUL GEN/METH. PAGE 33 G0644
L65
PWR
METH/CNCPT
DIPLOM

HOPKINS J.F.K.,ARABIC PERIODICAL LITERATURE, 1961. ISLAM LAW CULTURE SECT...GEOG HEAL PHIL/SCI PSY SOC 20. PAGE 27 G0528
B66
BIBLIOG/A
NAT/LISM
TEC/DEV
INDUS

SPULBER N.,THE STATE AND ECONOMIC DEVELOPMENT IN EASTERN EUROPE. BULGARIA COM CZECHOSLVK HUNGARY POLAND YUGOSLAVIA CULTURE PLAN CAP/ISM INT/TRADE CONTROL...POLICY CHARTS METH/COMP BIBLIOG/A 19/20. PAGE 52 G1028
B66
ECO/DEV
ECO/UNDEV
NAT/G
TOTALISM

BARANSON J.,TECHNOLOGY FOR UNDERDEVELOPED AREAS: AN ANNOTATED BIBLIOGRAPHY. FUT WOR+45 CULTURE INDUS INT/ORG CREATE PROB/SOLV INT/TRADE EDU/PROP AUTOMAT ...CONCPT METH. PAGE 5 G0092
B67
BIBLIOG/A
ECO/UNDEV
TEC/DEV
R+D

HOROWITZ I.L.,THE RISE AND FALL OF PROJECT CAMELOT: STUDIES IN THE RELATIONSHIP BETWEEN SOCIAL SCIENCE AND PRACTICAL POLITICS. USA+45 WOR+45 CULTURE FORCES LEGIS EXEC CIVMIL/REL KNOWL...POLICY SOC METH/CNCPT 20. PAGE 27 G0529
B67
NAT/G
ACADEM
ACT/RES
GP/REL

NASH M.,MACHINE AGE MAYA. GUATEMALA L/A+17C STRUCT AGRI WORKER CREATE INCOME ATTIT RIGID/FLEX ROLE ...IDEA/COMP SOC/EXP WORSHIP 20 INDIAN/AM. PAGE 41 G0806
B67
INDUS
CULTURE
SOC
MUNIC

LEVENSTEIN A.,"TECHNOLOGICAL CHANGE, WORK, AND HUMAN VALUES." WOR+45 SOCIETY AUTOMAT ROUTINE LEISURE INGP/REL ADJUST TECHRACY...MGT CONCPT. PAGE 33 G0660
S67
TEC/DEV
CULTURE
ALL/VALS
TIME/SEQ

SHARP G.,"THE NEED OF A FUNCTIONAL SUBSTITUTE FOR WAR." FUT UNIV WOR+45 CULTURE SOCIETY INT/ORG CONSULT DELIB/GP ACT/RES CREATE BAL/PWR CONFER ARMS/CONT NUC/PWR 20. PAGE 50 G0989
S67
PEACE
WAR
DIPLOM
PROB/SOLV

ASIAN STUDIES CENTER,FOUR ARTICLES ON POPULATION AND FAMILY LIFE IN TAIWAN (ASIAN STUDIES PAPERS, REPRINT SERIES NO. 2). CULTURE STRATA ECO/UNDEV AGRI INDUS R+D KIN MUNIC...GEOG SOC CHARTS 20. PAGE 4 G0072
N67
ASIA
FAM
CENSUS
ANTHOL

CURLEY/JM....JAMES M. CURLEY

CURRENT TRENDS IN PSYCHOLOGY G0266

CURZON/GN....GEORGE NATHANIEL CURZON

CYBERNETICS....SEE FEEDBACK, SIMUL, CONTROL

CYCLES....SEE TIME/SEQ

CYERT R.M. G0267

CYPRUS....SEE ALSO APPROPRIATE TIME/SPACE/CULTURE INDEX

CZECHOSLVK....CZECHOSLOVAKIA; SEE ALSO COM

REYNOLDS P.A.,BRITISH FOREIGN POLICY IN THE INTER-
B54
DIPLOM

WAR YEARS. CZECHOSLVK GERMANY POLAND UK USA-45 POL/PAR FORCES ECO/TAC ARMS/CONT WAR ATTIT 20. PAGE 46 G0915
POLICY
NAT/G

SPULBER N.,THE STATE AND ECONOMIC DEVELOPMENT IN EASTERN EUROPE. BULGARIA COM CZECHOSLVK HUNGARY POLAND YUGOSLAVIA CULTURE PLAN CAP/ISM INT/TRADE CONTROL...POLICY CHARTS METH/COMP BIBLIOG/A 19/20. PAGE 52 G1028
B66
ECO/DEV
ECO/UNDEV
NAT/G
TOTALISM

NATIONAL SCIENCE FOUNDATION,DIRECTORY OF SELECTED RESEARCH INSTITUTES IN EASTERN EUROPE. BULGARIA CZECHOSLVK HUNGARY POLAND ROMANIA INTELL ACADEM NAT/G ACT/RES 20. PAGE 41 G0814
B67
INDEX
R+D
COM
PHIL/SCI

---D---

D'AMATO D. G0268

DAC....DEVELOPMENT ASSISTANCE COMMITTEE (PART OF OECD)

DADDARIO E.Q. G0269

DAENIKER G. G0270

DAHOMEY....SEE ALSO AFR

DAHRENDORF R. G0271

DAKAR....DAKAR, SENEGAL

DALAND R.T. G0272

DALKEY N.C. G0273

DALTON G. G0274

DANIEL/Y....YULI DANIEL

DANTE....DANTE ALIGHIERI

DARWIN/C....CHARLES DARWIN

DATA ANALYSIS....SEE CON/ANAL, STAT, MATH, COMPUTER

DAVENPORT J. G0276

DAVIS E. G0277

DAVIS K.C. G0278

DAVIS P.C. G0279

DAVIS R.L. G0245

DAVIS V. G0280

DAVIS/JEFF....JEFFERSON DAVIS

DAVIS/W....WARREN DAVIS

DAWSON R.H. G0281

DAY E.E. G0282

DE BLIJ H.J. G0283

DE FOREST J.D. G0284

DE JOUVENEL B. G0285

DE NEUFVILLE R. G0286

DEAN A.L. G0287

DEAN B.V. G0288,G0289

DEATH....DEATH

BROWN W.M.,THE DESIGN AND PERFORMANCE OF "OPTIMUM" BLAST SHELTER PROGRAMS (PAMPHLET). USA+45 ACT/RES PLAN DEATH COST EFFICIENCY OPTIMAL...POLICY CHARTS 20. PAGE 9 G0180
N19
HABITAT
NUC/PWR
WAR
HEALTH

KOENIG L.W.,THE TRUMAN ADMINISTRATION: ITS PRINCIPLES AND PRACTICE. USA+45 POL/PAR CHIEF LEGIS DIPLOM DEATH NUC/PWR WAR CIVMIL/REL PEACE ...DECISION 20 TRUMAN/HS PRESIDENT TREATY. PAGE 31 G0610
B56
ADMIN
POLICY
EX/STRUC
GOV/REL

ELDRIDGE H.T.,THE MATERIALS OF DEMOGRAPHY: A SELECTED AND ANNOTATED BIBLIOGRAPHY. R+D DEATH ...SAMP METH/COMP NAT/COMP 20. PAGE 18 G0343
B59
BIBLIOG/A
GEOG
STAT

TREND

ROUTINE

B62

PERRE J.,LES MUTATIONS DE LA GUERRE MODERNE: DE LA   WAR
REVOLUTION FRANCAISE A LA REVOLUTION NUCLEAIRE.   FORCES
DIPLOM ARMS/CONT DEATH REV WEAPON GP/REL PEACE   NUC/PWR
ATTIT...STAT PREDICT BIBLIOG 18/20 WWI. PAGE 44
G0870

DEBATE....ORGANIZED COLLECTIVE ARGUMENT

S63

KOLDZIEF E.A.,"CONGRESSIONAL RESPONSIBILITY FOR THE   LEGIS
COMMON DEFENSE: THE MONEY PROBLEM." PLAN DEBATE   NAT/G
EFFICIENCY ATTIT PWR DECISION. PAGE 31 G0612   FORCES
                                                     POLICY

B65

JENKS C.W.,SPACE LAW. DIPLOM DEBATE CONTROL   SPACE
ORD/FREE TREATY 20 UN. PAGE 29 G0563   INT/LAW
                                                     JURID
                                                     INT/ORG

S67

CARY G.D.,"THE QUIET REVOLUTION IN COPYRIGHT* THE   COM/IND
END OF THE 'PUBLICATION' CONCEPT." USA+45 LAW   POLICY
OP/RES TEC/DEV CONFER DEBATE EFFICIENCY...JURID   LICENSE
CONGRESS. PAGE 11 G0217   PRESS

S67

MARTIN L.W.,"BALLISTIC MISSILE DEFENSE AND EUROPE."   ATTIT
EUR+WWI USA+45 FORCES PLAN BAL/PWR DEBATE PEACE   ARMS/CONT
...POLICY COLD/WAR NATO. PAGE 36 G0715   NUC/PWR
                                                     DETER

S67

ROBERTS W.,"DIVERSITY, CONSENSUS, AND ECLECTICISM   CONSEN
IN POLITICAL SCIENCE"...PHIL/SCI 20. PAGE 47 G0927   DEBATE
                                                     GEN/METH

S67

YOUNG O.R.,"ACTIVE DEFENSE AND INTERNATIONAL   ARMS/CONT
ORDER." FORCES BAL/PWR DEBATE GAMBLE COST PEACE.   DETER
PAGE 64 G1265   PLAN
                                                     DECISION

DEBS/E....EUGENE DEBS

DEBT....PUBLIC DEBT, INCLUDING NATIONAL DEBT

DECHERT C.R. G0290

DECISION....DECISION-MAKING AND GAME THEORY; SEE ALSO GAME

N

ADVANCED MANAGEMENT. INDUS EX/STRUC WORKER OP/RES   MGT
...DECISION BIBLIOG/A 20. PAGE 1 G0003   ADMIN
                                                     LABOR
                                                     GP/REL

S42

LASSWELL H.D.,"THE RELATION OF IDEOLOGICAL   ATTIT
INTELLIGENCE TO PUBLIC POLICY." WOR+45 WOR-45   DECISION
SOCIETY DELIB/GP ACT/RES CREATE PLAN DIPLOM
EDU/PROP CHOOSE KNOWL PWR...POLICY SOC TREND
GEN/LAWS 20. PAGE 32 G0638

B44

FULLER G.H.,MILITARY GOVERNMENT: A LIST OF   BIBLIOG
REFERENCES (A PAMPHLET). ITALY UK USA-45 WOR-45 LAW   DIPLOM
FORCES DOMIN ADMIN ARMS/CONT ORD/FREE PWR   CIVMIL/REL
...DECISION 20 CHINJAP. PAGE 21 G0404   SOVEREIGN

S49

SOUERS S.W.,"POLICY FORMULATION FOR NATIONAL   DELIB/GP
SECURITY." EX/STRUC FORCES PROB/SOLV DIPLOM CONFER   CHIEF
EXEC ARMS/CONT DETER NUC/PWR GOV/REL PEACE   DECISION
COLD/WAR. PAGE 52 G1022   POLICY

B50

KOENIG L.W.,THE SALE OF THE TANKERS. USA+45 SEA   NAT/G
DIST/IND POL/PAR DIPLOM ADMIN CIVMIL/REL ATTIT   POLICY
...DECISION 20 PRESIDENT DEPT/STATE. PAGE 31 G0609   PLAN
                                                     GOV/REL

B52

CURRENT TRENDS IN PSYCHOLOGY,PSYCHOLOGY IN THE   NAT/G
WORLD EMERGENCY. USA+45 CONSULT FORCES ACT/RES PLAN   PSY
SKILL...DECISION OBS APT/TEST KNO/TEST PERS/TEST
TREND CHARTS 20. PAGE 14 G0266

B53

SAYLES L.R.,THE LOCAL UNION. CONSTN CULTURE   LABOR
DELIB/GP PARTIC CHOOSE GP/REL INGP/REL ATTIT ROLE   LEAD
...MAJORIT DECISION MGT. PAGE 49 G0958   ADJUD

B54

COMBS C.H.,DECISION PROCESSES. INTELL SOCIETY   MATH
DELIB/GP CREATE TEC/DEV DOMIN LEGIT EXEC CHOOSE   DECISION
DRIVE RIGID/FLEX KNOWL PWR...PHIL/SCI SOC
METH/CNCPT CONT/OBS REC/INT PERS/TEST SAMP/SIZ BIOG
SOC/EXP WORK. PAGE 13 G0245

S54

BATES J.,"A MODEL FOR THE SCIENCE OF DECISION."   QUANT
UNIV ROUTINE...CONT/OBS CON/ANAL HYPO/EXP GAME.   DECISION
PAGE 5 G0101   PHIL/SCI
                                                     METH/CNCPT

S54

DEUTSCH K.W.,"GAME THEORY AND POLITICS: SOME   DECISION
PROBLEMS OF APPLICATION." FUT WOR+45 SOCIETY R+D   GEN/METH
KNOWL PWR...CONCPT METH/CNCPT MATH QUANT GAME SIMUL
VAL/FREE 20. PAGE 15 G0295

B55

SHUBIK M.,READINGS IN GAME THEORY AND POLITICAL   MATH
BEHAVIOR. WOR+45 FORCES CREATE ROUTINE WAR PEACE   DECISION
PERCEPT KNOWL PWR...PSY SOC CONCPT METH/CNCPT STAT   DIPLOM
CHARTS HYPO/EXP GAME METH VAL/FREE 20. PAGE 50
G0991

S55

DRUCKER P.F.,"'MANAGEMENT SCIENCE' AND THE   MGT
MANAGER." PLAN ROUTINE RIGID/FLEX...METH/CNCPT LOG   STRUCT
HYPO/EXP. PAGE 16 G0315   DECISION
                                                     RATIONAL

B56

ESTEP R.,AN AIR POWER BIBLIOGRAPHY. USA+45 TEC/DEV   BIBLIOG/A
BUDGET DIPLOM EDU/PROP DETER CIVMIL/REL...DECISION   FORCES
INT/LAW 20. PAGE 18 G0351   WEAPON
                                                     PLAN

B56

KOENIG L.W.,THE TRUMAN ADMINISTRATION: ITS   ADMIN
PRINCIPLES AND PRACTICE. USA+45 POL/PAR CHIEF LEGIS   POLICY
DIPLOM DEATH NUC/PWR WAR CIVMIL/REL PEACE   EX/STRUC
...DECISION 20 TRUMAN/HS PRESIDENT TREATY. PAGE 31   GOV/REL
G0610

S56

MILLER W.E.,"PRESIDENTIAL COATTAILS: A STUDY IN   CHIEF
POLITICAL MYTH AND METHODOLOGY" (BMR)" USA+45   CHOOSE
CREATE PARTIC ATTIT DRIVE PWR...DECISION CONCPT   POL/PAR
CHARTS SIMUL 20 PRESIDENT CONGRESS. PAGE 39 G0774   MYTH

B57

KIETH-LUCAS A.,DECISIONS ABOUT PEOPLE IN NEED, A   ADMIN
STUDY OF ADMINISTRATIVE RESPONSIVENESS IN PUBLIC   RIGID/FLEX
ASSISTANCE. USA+45 GIVE RECEIVE INGP/REL PERS/REL   SOC/WK
MORAL RESPECT WEALTH...SOC OBS BIBLIOG 20. PAGE 30   DECISION
G0595

B57

KISSINGER H.A.,NUCLEAR WEAPONS AND FOREIGN POLICY.   PLAN
FUT USA+45 WOR+45 INT/ORG FORCES ACT/RES TEC/DEV   DETER
DIPLOM ARMS/CONT COERCE ATTIT KNOWL PWR...DECISION   NUC/PWR
GEOG CHARTS 20. PAGE 31 G0602

B57

MCKINNEY E.R.,A BIBLIOGRAPHY OF CYBERNETICS AND   BIBLIOG/A
INFORMATION THEORY. COMPUTER OP/RES...DECISION   FEEDBACK
PHIL/SCI PSY LING LOG MATH PROBABIL GAME 20.   SIMUL
PAGE 38 G0743   CONTROL

S57

TAYLOR P.S.,"THE RELATION OF RESEARCH TO   DECISION
LEGISLATIVE AND ADMINISTRATIVE DECISIONS." ELITES   LEGIS
ACT/RES PLAN PROB/SOLV CONFER CHOOSE POLICY.   MGT
PAGE 54 G1059   PWR

B58

OPERATIONS RESEARCH SOCIETY,A COMPREHENSIVE   BIBLIOG/A
BIBLIOGRAPHY ON OPERATIONS RESEARCH: THROUGH 1956   COMPUT/IR
WITH SUPPLEMENT FOR 1957. COM/IND DIST/IND INDUS   OP/RES
ADMIN...DECISION MATH STAT METH 20. PAGE 43 G0840   MGT

L58

FORRESTER J.W.,"INDUSTRIAL DYNAMICS* A MAJOR   INDUS
BREAKTHROUGH FOR DECISION MAKERS." COMPUTER OP/RES   ACT/RES
...DECISION CONCPT NEW/IDEA. PAGE 20 G0382   MGT
                                                     PROB/SOLV

S58

DEAN B.V.,"APPLICATION OF OPERATIONS RESEARCH TO   DECISION
MANAGERIAL DECISION MAKING" STRATA ACT/RES   OP/RES
PROB/SOLV ROLE...SOC PREDICT SIMUL 20. PAGE 15   MGT
G0288   METH/CNCPT

PROB/SOLV

FOLDES L.,"UNCERTAINTY, PROBABILITY AND POTENTIAL
SURPRISE." MARKET PROB/SOLV RISK PERSON...DECISION
MGT HYPO/EXP GAME. PAGE 19 G0376
PROBABIL
ADMIN
ROUTINE
S58

LASSWELL H.D.,"THE SCIENTIFIC STUDY OF
INTERNATIONAL RELATIONS." USA+45 INT/ORG CREATE
EDU/PROP DETER ATTIT PERCEPT PWR...DECISION CONCPT
METH/CNCPT STYLE CON/ANAL 20. PAGE 33 G0642
PHIL/SCI
GEN/METH
DIPLOM
S58

SINGER J.D.,"THREAT PERCEPTION AND THE ARMAMENT
TENSION DILEMMA." WOR+45 WOR-45 ELITES INT/ORG
NAT/G DELIB/GP PLAN LEGIT COERCE DETER ATTIT
RIGID/FLEX PWR...DECISION PSY 20. PAGE 51 G1002
PERCEPT
ARMS/CONT
BAL/PWR
S58

AMRINE M.,THE GREAT DECISION: THE SECRET HISTORY OF
THE ATOMIC BOMB. USA+45 TOP/EX EDU/PROP LEGIT
PERCEPT ORD/FREE PWR VAL/FREE HIROSHIMA. PAGE 3
G0055
DECISION
NAT/G
NUC/PWR
FORCES
B59

MIKSCHE F.O.,THE FAILURE OF ATOMIC STRATEGY. COM
EUR+WWI INTELL POL/PAR FORCES PLAN ECO/TAC NUC/PWR
ATTIT DRIVE RIGID/FLEX PWR...DECISION GEOG PSY
CONCPT RECORD TREND CHARTS VAL/FREE 20. PAGE 39
G0766
ACT/RES
ORD/FREE
DIPLOM
ARMS/CONT
B59

BURNS A.L.,"THE RATIONALE OF CATALYTIC WAR." COM
USA+45 WOR+45 R+D NAT/G FORCES ACT/RES TEC/DEV PWR
...DECISION HYPO/EXP TOT/POP 20. PAGE 10 G0191
COERCE
NUC/PWR
WAR
L59

BURNS A.L.,"POWER POLITICS AND THE GROWING NUCLEAR
CLUB." FUT WOR+45 TEC/DEV EXEC ARMS/CONT COERCE
DETER...DECISION HYPO/EXP 20. PAGE 10 G0192
FORCES
BAL/PWR
NUC/PWR
L59

ADAMS E.W.,"A MODEL OF RISKLESS CHOICE." CREATE
PROB/SOLV UTIL...PROBABIL PREDICT HYPO/EXP. PAGE 2
G0029
GAME
SIMUL
RISK
DECISION
S59

BLOOMFIELD L.P.,"THREE EXPERIMENTS IN POLITICAL
GAMING." ACT/RES CREATE PWR...GAME GEN/METH METH.
PAGE 7 G0140
TEC/DEV
METH/CNCPT
DECISION
S59

CALKINS R.D.,"THE DECISION PROCESS IN
ADMINISTRATION." EX/STRUC PROB/SOLV ROUTINE MGT.
PAGE 10 G0204
ADMIN
OP/RES
DECISION
CON/ANAL
S59

CYERT R.M.,"MODELS IN A BEHAVIORAL THEORY OF THE
FIRM." ROUTINE...DECISION MGT METH/CNCPT MATH.
PAGE 14 G0267
SIMUL
GAME
PREDICT
INDUS
S59

GOLDHAMMER H.,"SOME OBSERVATIONS ON POLITICAL
GAMING." FUT WOR+45 R+D NAT/G ACT/RES CREATE CHOOSE
ATTIT PWR...POLICY CONCPT METH/CNCPT STYLE KNO/TEST
TREND HYPO/EXP GAME GEN/METH METH 20. PAGE 22 G0426
COMPUT/IR
DECISION
DIPLOM
S59

LEFTON M.,"DECISION MAKING IN A MENTAL HOSPITAL:
REAL, PERCEIVED, AND IDEAL." R+D PUB/INST CONSULT
CONFER INGP/REL PERCEPT...MODAL 20. PAGE 33 G0653
ACT/RES
PROB/SOLV
DECISION
PSY
S59

FRANCIS R.G.,THE PREDICTIVE PROCESS. PLAN MARXISM
...DECISION SOC CONCPT NAT/COMP 19/20. PAGE 20
G0390
PREDICT
PHIL/SCI
TREND
B60

KINGSTON-MCCLOUG E.,DEFENSE; POLICY AND STRATEGY.
UK SEA AIR TEC/DEV DIPLOM ADMIN LEAD WAR ORD/FREE
...CHARTS 20. PAGE 30 G0597
FORCES
PLAN
POLICY
DECISION
B60

LE GHAIT E.,NO CARTE BLANCHE TO CAPRICORN; THE
FOLLY OF NUCLEAR WAR. WOR+45 INT/ORG BAL/PWR DIPLOM
RISK COERCE...CENSUS 20 NATO. PAGE 33 G0647
DETER
NUC/PWR
PLAN
DECISION
B60

MORRIS W.T.,ENGINEERING ECONOMY. AUTOMAT RISK
RATIONAL...PROBABIL STAT CHARTS GAME SIMUL BIBLIOG
T 20. PAGE 40 G0785
OP/RES
DECISION
MGT
B60

RAPOPORT A.,FIGHTS, GAMES AND DEBATES. INTELL
SOCIETY R+D EX/STRUC PERCEPT PERSON SKILL...PSY SOC
GAME. PAGE 46 G0902
METH/CNCPT
MATH
DECISION
CON/ANAL
B60

SLUCKIN W.,MINDS AND MACHINES (REV. ED.). PROB/SOLV
TEC/DEV AUTOMAT TASK PERCEPT HEALTH KNOWL
...DECISION MATH PROBABIL COMPUT/IR GAME 20.
PAGE 51 G1012
PSY
COMPUTER
PERSON
SIMUL
B60

WEBSTER J.A.,A GENERAL STUDY OF THE DEPARTMENT OF
DEFENSE INTERNAL SECURITY PROGRAM. USA+45 WORKER
TEC/DEV ADJUD CONTROL CT/SYS EXEC GOV/REL COST
...POLICY DECISION MGT 20 DEPT/DEFEN SUPREME/CT.
PAGE 62 G1221
ORD/FREE
PLAN
ADMIN
NAT/G
B60

BRODY R.A.,"DETERRENCE STRATEGIES: AN ANNOTATED
BIBLIOGRAPHY." WOR+45 PLAN ARMS/CONT NUC/PWR WAR
WEAPON DECISION. PAGE 9 G0173
BIBLIOG/A
FORCES
DETER
DIPLOM
S60

DOTY P.M.,"THE ROLE OF THE SMALLER POWERS." FUT
WOR+45 NAT/G TEC/DEV BAL/PWR DOMIN LEGIT CHOOSE
DISPL DRIVE RESPECT...DECISION 20. PAGE 16 G0310
PWR
POLICY
ARMS/CONT
NUC/PWR
S60

DOUGHERTY J.E.,"KEY TO SECURITY: DISARMAMENT OR
ARMS STABILITY." COM USA+45 USSR INT/ORG NAT/G
CREATE EDU/PROP COERCE DETER ATTIT PWR...DECISION
CONCPT MYTH NEW/IDEA TREND 20 COLD/WAR. PAGE 16
G0311
FORCES
ORD/FREE
ARMS/CONT
NUC/PWR
S60

HUTCHINSON C.E.,"AN INSTITUTE FOR NATIONAL SECURITY
AFFAIRS." USA+45 R+D NAT/G CONSULT TOP/EX ACT/RES
CREATE PLAN TEC/DEV EDU/PROP ROUTINE NUC/PWR ATTIT
ORD/FREE PWR...DECISION MGT PHIL/SCI CONCPT RECORD
GEN/LAWS GEN/METH 20. PAGE 27 G0539
POLICY
METH/CNCPT
ELITES
DIPLOM
S60

SHUBIK M.,"BIBLIOGRAPHY ON SIMULATION, GAMING,
ARTIFICIAL INTELLIGENCE AND ALLIED TOPICS."
COMPUTER ROUTINE...DECISION MGT STAT 20. PAGE 50
G0992
BIBLIOG
SIMUL
GAME
OP/RES
S60

TAYLOR M.G.,"THE ROLE OF THE MEDICAL PROFESSION IN
THE FORMULATION AND EXECUTION OF PUBLIC POLICY"
(BMR)" CANADA NAT/G CONSULT ADMIN REPRESENT GP/REL
ROLE SOVEREIGN...DECISION 20 CMA. PAGE 54 G1058
PROF/ORG
HEALTH
LOBBY
POLICY
S60

BRADY R.A.,ORGANIZATION, AUTOMATION, AND SOCIETY.
USA+45 AGRI COM/IND DIST/IND MARKET CREATE
...DECISION MGT 20. PAGE 8 G0163
TEC/DEV
INDUS
AUTOMAT
ADMIN
B61

CHAPPLE E.D.,THE MEASURE OF MANAGEMENT. USA+45
WORKER ADMIN GP/REL EFFICIENCY...DECISION
ORG/CHARTS SIMUL 20. PAGE 11 G0221
MGT
OP/RES
PLAN
METH/CNCPT
B61

GORDON W.J.J.,SYNECTICS; THE DEVELOPMENT OF
CREATIVE CAPACITY. USA+45 PLAN TEC/DEV KNOWL WEALTH
...DECISION MGT 20. PAGE 22 G0436
CREATE
PROB/SOLV
ACT/RES
TOP/EX
B61

KRUPP S.,PATTERN IN ORGANIZATIONAL ANALYSIS: A
CRITICAL EXAMINATION. INGP/REL PERS/REL RATIONAL
ATTIT AUTHORIT DRIVE PWR...DECISION PHIL/SCI SOC
IDEA/COMP. PAGE 32 G0622
MGT
CONTROL
CONCPT
METH/CNCPT
B61

ROSENAU J.N.,INTERNATIONAL POLITICS AND FOREIGN
POLICY: A READER IN RESEARCH AND THEORY. ELITES
ATTIT SOVEREIGN...DECISION CHARTS HYPO/EXP GAME
SIMUL ANTHOL BIBLIOG METH 20. PAGE 48 G0936
ACT/RES
DIPLOM
CONCPT
POLICY
B61

COHEN K.J.,"THE ROLE OF MANAGEMENT GAMES IN
EDUCATION AND RESEARCH." INTELL ECO/DEV FINAN
ACT/RES ECO/TAC DECISION. PAGE 12 G0240
SOCIETY
GAME
MGT
EDU/PROP
L61

S61

BENNION E.G.,"ECONOMETRICS FOR MANAGEMENT." USA+45 ECOMETRIC
INDUS EX/STRUC ACT/RES COMPUTER UTIL...MATH STAT MGT
PREDICT METH/COMP HYPO/EXP. PAGE 6 G0122 SIMUL
DECISION

S61

COOKE E.F.,"RESEARCH: AN INSTRUMENT OF POWER." R+D
VOL/ASSN PLAN TEC/DEV TAX LOBBY INGP/REL ROLE PROVS
POLICY. PAGE 13 G0253 LOC/G
DECISION

S61

DEUTSCH K.W.,"A NOTE ON THE APPEARANCE OF WISDOM IN ADMIN
LARGE BUREAUCRATIC ORGANIZATIONS." ROUTINE PERSON PROBABIL
KNOWL SKILL...DECISION STAT. PAGE 15 G0299 PROB/SOLV
SIMUL

S61

DYKMAN J.W.,"REVIEW ARTICLE* PLANNING AND DECISION DECISION
THEORY." ELITES LOC/G MUNIC CONSULT ADMIN...POLICY PLAN
MGT. PAGE 17 G0327 RATIONAL

S61

FAIR M.L.,"PORT AUTHORITIES IN THE UNITED STATES." MUNIC
PROB/SOLV ADMIN LEAD REPRESENT PWR...DECISION GEOG. REGION
PAGE 18 G0357 LOC/G
GOV/REL

S61

MANGELSDORF J.E.,"HUMAN DECISIONS IN MISSILE DECISION
YSTEMS." OP/RES CHARTS. PAGE 35 G0699 PROB/SOLV
AUTOMAT
CONTROL

B62

BAKER G.W.,BEHAVIORAL SCIENCE AND CIVIL DEFENSE. NUC/PWR
USA+45 PROB/SOLV ADMIN GP/REL INGP/REL PERS/REL WAR
ANOMIE DRIVE PERSON...DECISION MGT SOC 20 POLICY
CIV/DEFENS. PAGE 4 G0085 ACT/RES

B62

BELLMAN R.,APPLIED DYNAMIC PROGRAMMING. OPTIMAL COMPUTER
...DECISION STAT SIMUL. PAGE 6 G0116 ECOMETRIC
GAME
MATH

B62

BLOOMFIELD L.P.,OUTER SPACE: A PATTERN OF WAR IN A CREATE
NEW DIMENSION. FUT USA+45 AIR TEC/DEV PWR ACT/RES
...DECISION CONCPT GEN/LAWS 20. PAGE 7 G0141 ARMS/CONT
SPACE

B62

BORKOF H.,COMPUTER APPLICATIONS IN THE BEHAVIORAL R+D
SCIENCES. AUTOMAT UTIL...DECISION PHIL/SCI PSY COMPUTER
METH/CNCPT LING LOG MATH STYLE NET/THEORY COMPUT/IR PROB/SOLV
PROG/TEAC SIMUL. PAGE 8 G0154 FEEDBACK

B62

BOULDING K.E.,CONFLICT AND DEFENSE: A GENERAL MATH
THEORY. FUT SOCIETY INT/ORG NAT/G CREATE BAL/PWR SIMUL
COERCE NAT/LISM DRIVE ALL/VALS...PLURIST DECISION PEACE
CONCPT METH/CNCPT TREND HYPO/EXP TOT/POP 20. PAGE 8 WAR
G0157

B62

CHANDLER A.D.,STRATEGY AND STRUCTURE: CHAPTERS IN LG/CO
THE HISTORY OF THE INDUSTRIAL ENTERPRISE. USA+45 PLAN
USA-45 ECO/DEV EX/STRUC ECO/TAC EXEC...DECISION 20. ADMIN
PAGE 11 G0220 FINAN

B62

DUCKWORTH W.E.,A GUIDE TO OPERATIONAL RESEARCH. OP/RES
INDUS PLAN PROB/SOLV EXEC EFFICIENCY PRODUC KNOWL GAME
...MGT MATH STAT SIMUL METH 20 MONTECARLO. PAGE 16 DECISION
G0319 ADMIN

B62

DUPRE S.,SCIENCE AND THE NATION. USA+45 ECO/DEV ARMS/CONT
ACADEM ORD/FREE TECHNIC. PAGE 17 G0323 DECISION
TEC/DEV
INDUS

B62

MARS D.,SUGGESTED LIBRARY IN PUBLIC ADMINISTRATION. BIBLIOG
FINAN DELIB/GP EX/STRUC WORKER COMPUTER ADJUD ADMIN
...DECISION PSY SOC METH/COMP 20. PAGE 36 G0710 METH
MGT

B62

RIKER W.H.,THE THEORY OF POLITICAL COALITIONS. FUT
WOR+45 INTELL NAT/G CREATE PLAN ATTIT DRIVE PERCEPT SIMUL
...DECISION PSY SOC METH/CNCPT NEW/IDEA MATH CHARTS
GAME TOT/POP 20. PAGE 47 G0921

B62

SNYDER R.C.,FOREIGN POLICY DECISION-MAKING. FUT TEC/DEV
KOREA WOR+45 R+D CREATE ADMIN ROUTINE PWR HYPO/EXP
...DECISION PSY SOC CONCPT METH/CNCPT CON/ANAL DIPLOM
CHARTS GEN/METH METH 20. PAGE 52 G1018

B62

STRAUSS L.L.,MEN AND DECISIONS. USA+45 USA-45 USSR DECISION
CONSULT FORCES TOP/EX WAR PEACE 20. PAGE 53 G1042 PWR
NUC/PWR
DIPLOM

B62

US SENATE COMM GOVT OPERATIONS,ADMINISTRATION OF ORD/FREE
NATIONAL SECURITY. USA+45 CHIEF PLAN PROB/SOLV ADMIN
TEC/DEV DIPLOM ATTIT...POLICY DECISION 20 NAT/G
KENNEDY/JF RUSK/D MCNAMARA/R BUNDY/M HERTER/C. CONTROL
PAGE 60 G1177

L62

LINS L.J.,"BASIS FOR DECISION: A COMPOSITE OF DECISION
CURRENT INSTITUTIONAL RESEARCH METHODS OF COLLEGES ACADEM
AND UNIVERSITIES" ADMIN MGT. PAGE 34 G0671 R+D
ACT/RES

S62

BETHE H.,"DISARMAMENT AND STRATEGY." COM USA+45 PLAN
USSR WOR+45 VOL/ASSN TEC/DEV PROP NUC/PWR ORD/FREE
CHOOSE PEACE...POLICY DECISION NEW/IDEA OBS ARMS/CONT
GEN/LAWS COLD/WAR 420. PAGE 7 G0133 DIPLOM

S62

FINKELSTEIN L.S.,"THE UNITED NATIONS AND INT/ORG
ORGANIZATIONS FOR CONTROL OF ARMAMENT." FUT WOR+45 PWR
VOL/ASSN DELIB/GP TOP/EX CREATE EDU/PROP LEGIT ARMS/CONT
ADJUD NUC/PWR ATTIT RIGID/FLEX ORD/FREE...POLICY
DECISION CONCPT OBS TREND GEN/LAWS TOT/POP
COLD/WAR. PAGE 19 G0368

S62

FLOOD M.M.,"STOCHASTIC LEARNING THEORY APPLIED TO DECISION
CHOICE EXPERIMENTS WITH RATS, DOGS, AND MEN."...PSY COMPUTER
LAB/EXP METH. PAGE 19 G0372 HYPO/EXP
TEC/DEV

S62

MARTIN L.W.,"THE MARKET FOR STRATEGIC IDEAS IN DIPLOM
BRITAIN: THE 'SANDYS ERA'" UK ARMS/CONT WAR GOV/REL COERCE
OPTIMAL...POLICY DECISION GOV/COMP COLD/WAR FORCES
CMN/WLTH. PAGE 36 G0714 PWR

B63

BONINI C.P.,SIMULATION OF INFORMATION AND DECISION INDUS
SYSTEMS IN THE FIRM. MARKET BUDGET DOMIN EDU/PROP SIMUL
ADMIN COST ATTIT HABITAT PERCEPT PWR...CONCPT DECISION
PROBABIL QUANT PREDICT HYPO/EXP BIBLIOG. PAGE 8 MGT
G0152

B63

BROUDE H.W.,STEEL DECISIONS AND THE NATIONAL PROC/MFG
ECONOMY. USA+45 LG/CO PLAN ADMIN COST DECISION. NAT/G
PAGE 9 G0176 CONTROL
ECO/TAC

B63

BURSK E.C.,NEW DECISION-MAKING TOOLS FOR MANAGERS. DECISION
COMPUTER PLAN PROB/SOLV ROUTINE COST. PAGE 10 G0194 MGT
MATH
RIGID/FLEX

B63

GREEN H.P.,GOVERNMENT OF THE ATOM. USA+45 LEGIS GOV/REL
PROB/SOLV ADMIN CONTROL PWR...POLICY DECISION 20 EX/STRUC
PRESIDENT CONGRESS. PAGE 22 G0443 NUC/PWR
DELIB/GP

B63

HERNDON J.,A SELECTED BIBLIOGRAPHY OF MATERIALS IN BIBLIOG
STATE GOVERNMENT AND POLITICS (PAMPHLET). USA+45 GOV/COMP
POL/PAR LEGIS ADMIN CHOOSE MGT. PAGE 26 G0507 PROVS
DECISION

B63

JACOB H.,GERMAN ADMINISTRATION SINCE BISMARCK: ADMIN
CENTRAL AUTHORITY VERSUS LOCAL AUTONOMY. GERMANY NAT/G
GERMANY/W LAW POL/PAR CONTROL CENTRAL TOTALISM LOC/G
FASCISM...MAJORIT DECISION STAT CHARTS GOV/COMP POLICY
19/20 BISMARCK/O HITLER/A WEIMAR/REP. PAGE 28 G0551

B63

MCDOUGAL M.S.,LAW AND PUBLIC ORDER IN SPACE. FUT SPACE
USA+45 ACT/RES TEC/DEV ADJUD...POLICY INT/LAW JURID ORD/FREE
20. PAGE 37 G0739 DIPLOM
DECISION

B63
MILBRATH L.W.,THE WASHINGTON LOBBYISTS. CONSTN   LOBBY
BAL/PWR CONTROL LEAD TASK CHOOSE SUPEGO...DECISION   POLICY
STAT CHARTS BIBLIOG. PAGE 39 G0767   PERS/REL

B63
PACHTER H.M.,COLLISION COURSE; THE CUBAN MISSILE   WAR
CRISIS AND COEXISTENCE. CUBA USA+45 DIPLOM   BAL/PWR
ARMS/CONT PEACE MARXISM...DECISION INT/LAW 20   NUC/PWR
COLD/WAR KHRUSH/N KENNEDY/JF CASTRO/F. PAGE 43   DETER
G0854

B63
PEABODY R.L.,NEW PERSPECTIVES ON THE HOUSE OF   NEW/IDEA
REPRESENTATIVES. AGRI FINAN SCHOOL FORCES CONFER   LEGIS
LEAD CHOOSE REPRESENT FEDERAL...POLICY DECISION   PWR
HOUSE/REP. PAGE 44 G0862   ADMIN

B63
THORELLI H.B.,INTOP: INTERNATIONAL OPERATIONS   GAME
SIMULATION: PLAYER'S MANUAL. BRAZIL FINAN OP/RES   INT/TRADE
ADMIN GP/REL INGP/REL PRODUC PERCEPT...DECISION MGT   EDU/PROP
EEC. PAGE 54 G1073   LG/CO

S63
BUNDY M.,"THE SCIENTIST AND NATIONAL POLICY."   NAT/G
PROF/ORG PLAN PARTIC POLICY. PAGE 10 G0186   PHIL/SCI
                                                       DECISION

S63
CLEVELAND H.,"CRISIS DIPLOMACY." USA+45 WOR+45 LAW   DECISION
FORCES TASK NUC/PWR PWR 20. PAGE 12 G0235   DIPLOM
                                                       PROB/SOLV
                                                       POLICY

S63
DUBRIDGE L.A.,"POLICY AND THE SCIENTISTS." ELITES   POLICY
PROB/SOLV ROLE KNOWL PWR. PAGE 16 G0318   PHIL/SCI
                                                       ACADEM
                                                       DECISION

S63
ENTHOVEN A.C.,"ECONOMIC ANALYSIS IN THE DEPARTMENT   PLAN
OF DEFENSE." USA+45 NAT/G DELIB/GP PROB/SOLV RATION   BUDGET
NUC/PWR WEAPON COST...DECISION 20 DEPT/DEFEN   ECO/TAC
RESOURCE/N. PAGE 18 G0349   FORCES

S63
KOLDZIEF E.A.,"CONGRESSIONAL RESPONSIBILITY FOR THE   LEGIS
COMMON DEFENSE: THE MONEY PROBLEM." PLAN DEBATE   NAT/G
EFFICIENCY ATTIT PWR DECISION. PAGE 31 G0612   FORCES
                                                       POLICY

S63
WOHLSTETTER A.,"SCIENTISTS, SEERS AND STRATEGY."   INTELL
USA+45 ELITES R+D NAT/G CONSULT FORCES TOP/EX   ACT/RES
EDU/PROP ARMS/CONT KNOWL ORD/FREE...DECISION MYTH
20. PAGE 64 G1253

B64
BRIGHT J.R.,RESEARCH, DEVELOPMENT AND TECHNOLOGICAL   TEC/DEV
INNOVATION. CULTURE R+D CREATE PLAN PROB/SOLV   NEW/IDEA
AUTOMAT RISK PERSON...DECISION CONCPT PREDICT   INDUS
BIBLIOG. PAGE 9 G0168   MGT

B64
FOGELMAN E.,HIROSHIMA: THE DECISION TO USE THE A-   INTELL
BOMB. USA-45 DIPLOM EFFICIENCY PEACE...ANTHOL   DECISION
BIBLIOG T 20 CHINJAP. PAGE 19 G0375   NUC/PWR
                                                       WAR

B64
MARTINO R.L.,PROJECT MANAGEMENT AND CONTROL: VOL. 2   DECISION
APPLIED OPERATIONAL PLANNING. COMPUTER...MATH   PLAN
CHARTS SIMUL METH TIME. PAGE 36 G0716   TEC/DEV
                                                       OP/RES

B64
RIES J.C.,THE MANAGEMENT OF DEFENSE: ORGANIZATION   FORCES
AND CONTROL OF THE US ARMED SERVICES. PROF/ORG   ACT/RES
DELIB/GP EX/STRUC LEGIS GOV/REL PERS/REL CENTRAL   DECISION
RATIONAL PWR...POLICY TREND GOV/COMP BIBLIOG.   CONTROL
PAGE 47 G0920

B64
SHUBIK M.,GAME THEORY AND RELATED APPROACHES TO   SOC
SOCIAL BEHAVIOR: SELECTIONS. INTELL SOCIETY ACT/RES   SIMUL
CREATE PLAN PROB/SOLV...DECISION MATH. PAGE 50   GAME
G0994   PWR

S64
ABT C.,"WAR GAMING." USA+45 NAT/G TOP/EX ACT/RES   FORCES
TEC/DEV COERCE KNOWL ORD/FREE PWR...DECISION MATH   SIMUL
TIME/SEQ COMPUT/IR CHARTS LAB/EXP VAL/FREE. PAGE 2   WAR
G0026

S64
GARDNER R.N.,"GATT AND THE UNITED NATIONS   INT/ORG
CONFERENCE ON TRADE AND DEVELOPMENT." USA+45 WOR+45   INT/TRADE
SOCIETY ECO/UNDEV MARKET NAT/G DELIB/GP ACT/RES
PLAN ECO/TAC TARIFFS EDU/PROP ROUTINE DRIVE
RIGID/FLEX WEALTH...DECISION MGT TREND UN TOT/POP
20 GATT. PAGE 21 G0411

S64
PILISUK M.,"STEPWISE DISARMAMENT & SUDDEN   PWR
DESTRUCTION IN A TWOPERSON GAME: A RESEARCH TOOL."   DECISION
NAT/G FORCES ACT/RES ECO/TAC EDU/PROP EXEC ROUTINE   ARMS/CONT
COERCE ORD/FREE...SIMUL GEN/LAWS VAL/FREE. PAGE 45
G0877

S64
STONE P.A.,"DECISION TECHNIQUES FOR TOWN   OP/RES
DEVELOPMENT." PLAN COST PROFIT...DECISION MGT   MUNIC
CON/ANAL CHARTS METH/COMP BIBLIOG 20. PAGE 53 G1039   ADMIN
                                                       PROB/SOLV

S64
UNRUH J.M.,"SCIENTIFIC INPUTS TO LEGISLATIVE   CREATE
DECISION-MAKING (SUPPLEMENT)" USA+45 ACADEM NAT/G   DECISION
PROVS GOV/REL GOV/COMP. PAGE 56 G1102   LEGIS
                                                       PARTIC

B65
ALKER H.R. JR.,MATHEMATICS AND POLITICS. PROB/SOLV   GEN/METH
...DECISION PHIL/SCI CLASSIF QUANT STAT GAME   CONCPT
GEN/LAWS INDEX. PAGE 2 G0042   MATH

B65
ANTHONY R.N.,PLANNING AND CONTROL SYSTEMS. UNIV   CONTROL
OP/RES...DECISION MGT LING. PAGE 3 G0061   PLAN
                                                       METH
                                                       HYPO/EXP

B65
BEAUFRE A.,AN INTRODUCTION TO STRATEGY, WITH   PLAN
PARTICULAR REFERENCE TO PROBLEMS OF DEFENSE,   NUC/PWR
POLITICS, ECONOMICS IN THE NUCLEAR AGE. WOR+45   WEAPON
FORCES DIPLOM DETER CIVMIL/REL GP/REL...NEW/IDEA   DECISION
IDEA/COMP 20. PAGE 6 G0111

B65
BOBROW D.B.,COMPONENTS OF DEFENSE POLICY. ASIA   DETER
EUR+WWI USA+45 WOR+45 INTELL INT/ORG NAT/G PROF/ORG   NUC/PWR
CONSULT LEGIS ACT/RES CREATE ARMS/CONT COERCE   PLAN
ORD/FREE...DECISION SIMUL. PAGE 7 G0145   FORCES

B65
HICKMAN B.G.,QUANTITATIVE PLANNING OF ECONOMIC   PROB/SOLV
POLICY. FRANCE NETHERLAND OP/RES PRICE ROUTINE UTIL   PLAN
...POLICY DECISION ECOMETRIC METH/CNCPT STAT STYLE   QUANT
CHINJAP. PAGE 26 G0511

B65
HITCH C.J.,DECISION-MAKING FOR DEFENSE. USA+45   DECISION
CREATE BUDGET COERCE WAR WEAPON EFFICIENCY...SIMUL   OP/RES
20. PAGE 26 G0515   PLAN
                                                       FORCES

B65
JANDA K.,DATA PROCESSING: APPLICATIONS TO POLITICAL   DECISION
RESEARCH....STAT CON/ANAL. PAGE 28 G0557   COMPUTER
                                                       TEC/DEV
                                                       METH

B65
KANTOROVICH L.V.,THE BEST USE OF ECONOMIC   PLAN
RESOURCES. USSR SOCIETY FINAN ACT/RES TEC/DEV   MATH
ECO/TAC PRICE CONTROL COST DEMAND EFFICIENCY   DECISION
OPTIMAL...MGT STAT. PAGE 29 G0572

B65
KENT A.,SPECIALIZED INFORMATION CENTERS. INTELL R+D   COMPUT/IR
VOL/ASSN CONSULT COMPUTER KNOWL...DECISION HUM   CREATE
PHIL/SCI METH/CNCPT TREND CHARTS 20. PAGE 30 G0593   TEC/DEV
                                                       METH/COMP

B65
KNORR K.,SCIENCE AND DEFENSE: SOME CRITICAL   CIVMIL/REL
THOUGHTS ON MILITARY RESEARCH AND DEVELOPMENT.   R+D
USA+45 ACT/RES CREATE BUDGET ECO/TAC DEMAND   FORCES
DECISION. PAGE 31 G0608   PLAN

B65
PHELPS E.S.,PRIVATE WANTS AND PUBLIC NEEDS - AN   NAT/G
INTRODUCTION TO A CURRENT ISSUE OF PUBLIC POLICY   POLICY
(REV. ED.). USA+45 PLAN CAP/ISM INGP/REL ROLE   DEMAND
...DECISION TIME/SEQ 20. PAGE 44 G0873

B65
SINGER J.D.,HUMAN BEHAVIOR AND INTERNATIONAL   DIPLOM
POLITICS* CONTRIBUTIONS FROM THE SOCIAL-   PHIL/SCI

PSYCHOLOGICAL SCIENCES. ACT/RES PLAN EDU/PROP ADMIN QUANT
KNOWL...DECISION PSY SOC NET/THEORY HYPO/EXP SIMUL
LAB/EXP SOC/EXP GEN/METH ANTHOL BIBLIOG. PAGE 51
G1006

B65
TYBOUT R.A.,ECONOMICS OF RESEARCH AND DEVELOPMENT. R+D
ECO/DEV ECO/UNDEV INDUS PROFIT DECISION. PAGE 55 FORCES
G1084 ADMIN
DIPLOM

B65
VEINOTT A.F. JR.,MATHEMATICAL STUDIES IN MANAGEMENT MATH
SCIENCE. UNIV INDUS COMPUTER ADMIN...DECISION MGT
NET/THEORY SIMUL 20. PAGE 61 G1193 PLAN
PRODUC

B65
WARNER A.W.,THE IMPACT OF SCIENCE ON TECHNOLOGY. DECISION
UNIV INTELL SOCIETY NAT/G ACT/RES PLAN PROB/SOLV TEC/DEV
BUDGET OPTIMAL GEN/METH. PAGE 62 G1214 CREATE
POLICY

S65
BIRNBAUM K.,"SWEDEN'S NUCLEAR POLICY." WOR+45 SWEDEN
POL/PAR CREATE TEC/DEV NEUTRAL RISK WAR ORD/FREE NUC/PWR
...DECISION IDEA/COMP NAT/COMP TIME. PAGE 7 G0137 DIPLOM
ARMS/CONT

S65
CHU K.,"A DYNAMIC MODEL OF THE FIRM." OP/RES INDUS
PROB/SOLV...DECISION ECOMETRIC NEW/IDEA STAT GAME COMPUTER
ORG/CHARTS SIMUL. PAGE 12 G0230 TEC/DEV

S65
DALKEY N.C.,"SOLVABLE NUCLEAR WAR MODELS." FORCES GAME
BAL/PWR DIPLOM COERCE PEACE DECISION. PAGE 14 G0273 SIMUL
WAR
NUC/PWR

S65
DECHERT C.R.,"THE DEVELOPMENT OF CYBERNETICS." SIMUL
ACT/RES CREATE SKILL...STERTYP METH. PAGE 15 G0290 COMPUT/IR
PLAN
DECISION

S65
GREGG P.M.,"DIMENSIONS OF POLITICAL SYSTEMS: FACTOR SIMUL
ANALYSIS OF A CROSS POLITY SURVEY." TEC/DEV GEN/METH
...DECISION PHIL/SCI CONCPT STAT IDEA/COMP CLASSIF
GEN/LAWS. PAGE 23 G0447

S65
GRENIEWSKI H.,"INTENTION AND PERFORMANCE: A PRIMER SIMUL
OF CYBERNETICS OF PLANNING." EFFICIENCY OPTIMAL GAME
KNOWL SKILL...DECISION MGT EQULIB. PAGE 23 G0448 GEN/METH
PLAN

S65
HOLSTI O.R.,"EAST-WEST CONFLICT AND SINO-SOVIET VOL/ASSN
RELATIONS" CHINA/COM USSR COMPUTER REGION DECISION. DIPLOM
PAGE 27 G0523 CON/ANAL
COM

S65
KREITH K.,"PEACE RESEARCH AND GOVERNMENT POLICY." PEACE
INTELL NAT/G DIPLOM ECO/TAC CONTROL ARMS/CONT WAR STYLE
PERCEPT...DECISION IDEA/COMP. PAGE 31 G0619 OBS

C65
US AIR FORCE ACADEMY,"AMERICAN DEFENSE POLICY." COM PLAN
INT/ORG TEC/DEV FOR/AID ARMS/CONT DETER NUC/PWR FORCES
...POLICY DECISION CONCPT ANTHOL BIBLIOG/A 20 WAR
COLD/WAR NATO. PAGE 56 G1103 COERCE

B66
GORDON G.,THE LEGISLATIVE PROCESS AND DIVIDED LEGIS
GOVERNMENT: A CASE STUDY OF THE 86TH CONGRESS. HABITAT
USA+45 POL/PAR PROVS PROB/SOLV BAL/PWR CHOOSE CHIEF
REPRESENT EFFICIENCY ATTIT...POLICY DECISION STAT NAT/G
20 CONGRESS EISNHWR/DD. PAGE 22 G0434

B66
GOULD J.M.,THE TECHNICAL ELITE. INDUS LABOR ECO/DEV
TECHRACY...POLICY DECISION STAT CHARTS 20. PAGE 22 TEC/DEV
G0437 ELITES
TECHNIC

B66
GREEN P.,DEADLY LOGIC* THE THEORY OF NUCLEAR DETER
DETERRENCE. USA+45 ACT/RES OP/RES NUC/PWR RATIONAL ACADEM
ALL/VALS PWR...DECISION MGT PHIL/SCI QUANT GEN/LAWS
IDEA/COMP GAME. PAGE 23 G0444 RECORD

B66
MARKHAM J.W.,AN ECONOMIC-MEDIA STUDY OF BOOK PRESS

PUBLISHING. USA+45 LAW COM/IND ACADEM SCHOOL ECO/TAC
EDU/PROP AUTOMAT CONTROL...DECISION STAT CHARTS 20 TEC/DEV
CONGRESS. PAGE 36 G0707 NAT/G

L66
RASER J.R.,"DETERRENCE RESEARCH* PAST PROGRESS AND DETER
FUTURE NEEDS." INTELL PLAN TEC/DEV NUC/PWR PERCEPT BIBLIOG/A
...DECISION PSY SOC NET/THEORY. PAGE 46 G0905 FUT

L66
ZOPPO C.E.,"NUCLEAR TECHNOLOGY, MULTIPOLARITY, AND NET/THEORY
INTERNATIONAL STABILITY." ASIA RUSSIA USA+45 STRUCT ORD/FREE
TOP/EX BAL/PWR DIPLOM DETER CIVMIL/REL NAT/COMP. DECISION
PAGE 65 G1270 NUC/PWR

S66
KAPLAN M.A.,"THE NEW GREAT DEBATE* TRADITIONALISM PHIL/SCI
VS SCIENCE IN INTERNATIONAL RELATIONS."...DECISION CONSERVE
HUM QUANT STYLE NET/THEORY CON/ANAL STERTYP DIPLOM
GEN/LAWS. PAGE 29 G0577 SIMUL

S66
RIZOS E.J.,"SCIENCE AND TECHNOLOGY IN COUNTRY ADMIN
DEVELOPMENT* TOWARDS AN UNDERSTANDING OF THE ROLE TEC/DEV
OF PUBLIC ADMINISTRATION." WOR+45 STRUCT INT/ORG ECO/UNDEV
EX/STRUC CREATE PLAN PROB/SOLV EFFICIENCY ROLE PHIL/SCI
DECISION. PAGE 47 G0924

B67
CHARLESWORTH J.C.,CONTEMPORARY POLITICAL ANALYSIS. R+D
INTELL...DECISION METH/CNCPT MATH STYLE CON/ANAL IDEA/COMP
GAME ANTHOL 20. PAGE 11 G0222 CONCPT
METH/COMP

B67
DE JOUVENAL B.,THE ART OF CONJECTURE. WOR+45 FUT
EFFICIENCY PERCEPT KNOWL...DECISION PHIL/SCI CONCPT PREDICT
METH/COMP BIBLIOG 20. PAGE 15 G0285 SIMUL
METH

B67
ENKE S.,DEFENSE MANAGEMENT. USA+45 R+D FORCES DECISION
WORKER PLAN ECO/TAC ADMIN NUC/PWR BAL/PAY UTIL DELIB/GP
WEALTH...MGT DEPT/DEFEN. PAGE 18 G0348 EFFICIENCY
BUDGET

B67
HARMAN H.H.,MODERN FACTOR ANALYSIS (2ND REV. ED.). CON/ANAL
COMPUTER...DECISION CHARTS BIBLIOG T. PAGE 24 G0482 METH/CNCPT
SIMUL
MATH

B67
PADELFORD N.J.,THE DYNAMICS OF INTERNATIONAL DIPLOM
POLITICS (2ND ED.). WOR+45 LAW INT/ORG FORCES NAT/G
TEC/DEV REGION NAT/LISM PEACE ATTIT PWR ALL/IDEOS POLICY
UN COLD/WAR NATO TREATY. PAGE 43 G0856 DECISION

B67
PORWIT K.,CENTRAL PLANNING: EVALUATION OF VARIANTS. PLAN
PRICE OPTIMAL PRODUC...DECISION MATH CHARTS SIMUL MGT
BIBLIOG 20. PAGE 45 G0886 ECOMETRIC

B67
SAPARINA Y.,CYBERNETICS WITHIN US. WOR+45 EDU/PROP COMPUTER
FEEDBACK PERCEPT HEALTH...DECISION METH/CNCPT METH/COMP
NEW/IDEA 20. PAGE 49 G0957 CONTROL
SIMUL

B67
UNIVERSAL REFERENCE SYSTEM,LEGISLATIVE PROCESS, BIBLIOG/A
REPRESENTATION, AND DECISION-MAKING (VOLUME II). LEGIS
WOR+45 WOR-45 CONSTN LOC/G NAT/G...POLICY CON/ANAL REPRESENT
COMPUT/IR GEN/METH. PAGE 56 G1094 DECISION

B67
US SENATE COMM ON FOREIGN REL,ARMS SALES TO NEAR WEAPON
EAST AND SOUTH ASIAN COUNTRIES. INDIA IRAN PAKISTAN FOR/AID
WOR+45 PROC/MFG BAL/PWR DIPLOM...DECISION SENATE. FORCES
PAGE 60 G1183 POLICY

B67
US SUPERINTENDENT OF DOCUMENTS,LIBRARY OF CONGRESS BIBLIOG/A
(PRICE LIST 83). AFR ASIA EUR+WWI USA-45 USSR NAT/G USA+45
DIPLOM CONFER CT/SYS WAR...DECISION PHIL/SCI AUTOMAT
CLASSIF 19/20 CONGRESS PRESIDENT. PAGE 61 G1189 LAW

B67
WYLIE J.C.,MILITARY STRATEGY: GENERAL THEORY OF FORCES
POWER CONTROL. CUBA USA+45 VIETNAM/N WOR+45 ELITES PLAN
CONTROL WAR PWR...POLICY METH/COMP 20 MAO. PAGE 64 DECISION
G1260 IDEA/COMP

B67
YAVITZ B.,AUTOMATION IN COMMERCIAL BANKING. USA+45 TEC/DEV
STRUCT WORKER CREATE OP/RES PLAN ROLE...DECISION FINAN

SAMP/SIZ. PAGE 64 G1263 — COMPUT/IR MGT

L67
"POLITICAL PARTIES ON FOREIGN POLICY IN THE INTER-ELECTION YEARS 1962-66." ASIA COM INDIA USA+45 PLAN ATTIT...DECISION 20. PAGE 1 G0023 — POL/PAR DIPLOM POLICY

L67
TRAVERS H. JR.,"AN EXAMINATION OF THE CAB'S MERGER POLICY." USA+45 USA-45 LAW NAT/G LEGIS PLAN ADMIN ...DECISION 20 CONGRESS. PAGE 55 G1078 — ADJUD LG/CO POLICY DIST/IND

S67
CLEMENS W.C.,"CHINESE NUCLEAR TESTS: TRENDS AND PORTENTS." CHINA/COM USA+45 USSR FORCES PLAN TEC/DEV ARMS/CONT WAR PWR...DECISION 20 MAO KHRUSH/N. PAGE 12 G0234 — NUC/PWR WEAPON POLICY DIPLOM

S67
CONWAY J.E.,"MAKING RESEARCH EFFECTIVE IN LEGISLATION." LAW R+D CONSULT EX/STRUC PLAN CONFER ADMIN LEAD ROUTINE TASK INGP/REL DECISION. PAGE 13 G0252 — ACT/RES POLICY LEGIS PROB/SOLV

S67
D'AMATO D.,"LEGAL ASPECTS OF THE FRENCH NUCLEAR TESTS." FRANCE WOR+45 ACT/RES COLONIAL RISK GOV/REL EQUILIB ORD/FREE PWR DECISION. PAGE 14 G0268 — INT/LAW DIPLOM NUC/PWR ADJUD

S67
DADDARIO E.Q.,"CONGRESS FACES SPACE POLICIES." R+D NAT/G FORCES CREATE LEAD...DECISION CONGRESS NASA. PAGE 14 G0269 — SPACE PLAN BUDGET POLICY

S67
JONES G.S.,"STRATEGIC PLANNING." USA+45 EX/STRUC FORCES DETER WAR 20 PRESIDENT. PAGE 29 G0566 — PLAN DECISION DELIB/GP POLICY

S67
LEWIS R.L.,"GOAL AND NO GOAL* A NEW POLICY IN SPACE." R+D BUDGET COST...POLICY DECISION PHIL/SCI. PAGE 34 G0662 — SPACE PLAN EFFICIENCY CREATE

S67
MACDONALD G.J.F.,"SCIENCE AND SPACE POLICY* HOW DOES IT GET PLANNED?" R+D CREATE TEC/DEV BUDGET ADMIN ROUTINE...DECISION NASA. PAGE 35 G0687 — SPACE PLAN MGT EX/STRUC

S67
SUINN R.M.,"THE DISARMAMENT FANTASY* PSYCHOLOGICAL FACTORS THAT MAY PRODUCE WARFARE." DIPLOM RISK ARMS/CONT DETER ANOMIE PERSON GAME. PAGE 53 G1046 — DECISION NUC/PWR WAR PSY

S67
TEKINER S.,"SINKIAN AND THE SINO-SOVIET CONFLICT." ASIA COM USSR FORCES PLAN BAL/PWR CONTROL NUC/PWR WAR WEAPON...DECISION 20. PAGE 54 G1060 — DIPLOM PWR MARXISM

S67
TIVEY L.,"THE POLITICAL CONSEQUENCES OF ECONOMIC PLANNING." UK CONSTN INDUS ACT/RES ADMIN CONTROL LOBBY REPRESENT EFFICIENCY SUPEGO SOVEREIGN ...DECISION 20. PAGE 55 G1074 — PLAN POLICY NAT/G

S67
VERGIN R.C.,"COMPUTER INDUCED ORGANIZATION CHANGES." FUT USA+45 R+D CREATE OP/RES TEC/DEV ADJUST CENTRAL...MGT INT CON/ANAL COMPUT/IR. PAGE 61 G1194 — COMPUTER DECISION AUTOMAT EX/STRUC

S67
WALTERS R.E.,"THE ROLE OF NUCLEAR WEAPONS FOR THE WEST." ASIA UK USA+45 USSR DIPLOM COERCE WAR PEACE ...POLICY DECISION 20. PAGE 62 G1209 — PLAN NUC/PWR WEAPON FORCES

S67
WEIL G.L.,"THE MERGER OF THE INSTITUTIONS OF THE EUROPEAN COMMUNITIES" EUR+WWI ECO/DEV INT/TRADE CONSEN PLURISM...DECISION MGT 20 EEC EURATOM ECSC TREATY. PAGE 62 G1223 — ECO/TAC INT/ORG CENTRAL INT/LAW

S67
YOUNG O.R.,"ACTIVE DEFENSE AND INTERNATIONAL ORDER." FORCES BAL/PWR DEBATE GAMBLE COST PEACE. PAGE 64 G1265 — ARMS/CONT DETER PLAN DECISION

B68
GALLAHER A. JR.,PERSPECTIVES IN DEVELOPMENTAL CHANGE. MUNIC PLAN INSPECT EDU/PROP...POLICY DECISION GEOG PSY SOC IDEA/COMP ANTHOL 20 MODERNIZE. PAGE 21 G0405 — TECHNIC TEC/DEV PROB/SOLV CREATE

DECISION-MAKING, DISIPLINE....SEE DECISION

DECISION-MAKING, INDIVIDUAL....SEE PROB/SOLV, PWR

DECISION-MAKING, PROCEDURAL....SEE PROB/SOLV

DECISION-MAKING, THEORY....SEE GAME

DECLAR/IND....DECLARATION OF INDEPENDENCE (U.S.)

DEEP/INT....DEPTH INTERVIEWS

N67
US HOUSE COMM APPROPRIATIONS,PUBLIC WORKS AND ATOMIC ENERGY COMMISSION APPROPRIATION BILL, 1968 (PAMPHLET). USA+45 ECO/DEV NAT/G...GEOG DEEP/INT CHARTS HOUSE/REP AEC DEPT/DEFEN TVA. PAGE 58 G1137 — BUDGET NUC/PWR PROVS PLAN

DEEP/QU....DEPTH QUESTIONNAIRES

DEES J.W. G0291

DEFENSE....SEE DETER, PLAN, FORCES, WAR, COERCE

DEFENSE DEPARTMENT....SEE DEPT/DEFEN

DEFINETT/B....BRUNO DEFINETTI

DEFLATION....DEFLATION

DEGAULLE/C....CHARLES DE GAULLE

S63
KAWALKOWSKI A.,"POUR UNE EUROPE INDEPENDENTE ET REUNIFIEE." EUR+WWI FUT USA+45 USSR WOR+45 ECO/DEV PROC/MFG INT/ORG NAT/G ACT/RES TEC/DEV FEDERAL RIGID/FLEX...CONCPT METH/CNCPT OEEC TOT/POP 20 DEGAULLE/C. PAGE 30 G0587 — R+D PLAN NUC/PWR

B65
SCHEINMAN L.,ATOMIC ENERGY POLICY IN FRANCE UNDER THE FOURTH REPUBLIC. FRANCE UK USA+45 ELITES POL/PAR PROB/SOLV DIPLOM LEAD GOV/REL ...BIBLIOG 20 DEGAULLE/C. PAGE 49 G0962 — NUC/PWR NAT/G DELIB/GP POLICY

DEGLER C.N. G0292

DEITY....DEITY: GOD AND GODS

DELAWARE....DELAWARE

DELEGATION OF POWER....SEE EX/STRUC

DELIB/GP....CONFERENCES, COMMITTEES, BOARDS, CABINETS

N
UNITED NATIONS,OFFICIAL RECORDS OF THE UNITED NATIONS' ATOMIC ENERGY COMMISSION - DISARMAMENT COMMISSION. WOR+45 TEC/DEV DIPLOM WRITING NUC/PWR 20 UN. PAGE 55 G1092 — ARMS/CONT INT/ORG DELIB/GP CONFER

N19
ATOMIC INDUSTRIAL FORUM,COMMENTARY ON LEGISLATION TO PERMIT PRIVATE OWNERSHIP OF SPECIAL NUCLEAR MATERIAL (PAMPHLET). USA+45 DELIB/GP LEGIS PLAN OWN ...POLICY 20 AEC CONGRESS. PAGE 4 G0076 — NUC/PWR MARKET INDUS LAW

N19
FOLSOM M.B.,BETTER MANAGEMENT OF THE PUBLIC'S BUSINESS (PAMPHLET). USA+45 DELIB/GP PAY CONFER CONTROL REGION GP/REL...METH/COMP ANTHOL 20. PAGE 19 G0377 — ADMIN NAT/G MGT PROB/SOLV

N19
MEZERIK AG,OUTER SPACE: UN, US, USSR (PAMPHLET). USSR DELIB/GP FORCES DETER NUC/PWR SOVEREIGN ...POLICY 20 UN TREATY. PAGE 39 G0763 — SPACE CONTROL DIPLOM INT/ORG

B41
FULLER G.H.,DEFENSE FINANCING: A SELECTED LIST OF REFERENCES (PAMPHLET). MOD/EUR USA-45 ECO/DEV NAT/G DELIB/GP RATION ARMS/CONT WEAPON COST PEACE PWR 20 CONGRESS. PAGE 20 G0401 — BIBLIOG/A FINAN FORCES BUDGET

B42
FULLER G.H.,DEFENSE FINANCING: A SUPPLEMENTARY LIST — BIBLIOG/A

OF REFERENCES (PAMPHLET). CANADA UK USA-45 ECO/DEV
NAT/G DELIB/GP BUDGET ADJUD ARMS/CONT WEAPON COST
PEACE PWR 20 AUSTRAL CHINJAP CONGRESS. PAGE 21
G0403
FINAN
FORCES
DIPLOM

S42
LASSWELL H.D.,"THE RELATION OF IDEOLOGICAL
INTELLIGENCE TO PUBLIC POLICY." WOR+45 WOR-45
SOCIETY DELIB/GP ACT/RES CREATE PLAN
EDU/PROP CHOOSE KNOWL PWR...POLICY SOC TREND
GEN/LAWS 20. PAGE 32 G0638
ATTIT
DECISION

B45
WHITE L.D.,CIVIL SERVICE IN WARTIME. CONSULT
DELIB/GP PARTIC WAR CHOOSE. PAGE 63 G1233
REPRESENT
ADMIN
INTELL
NAT/G

S45
WHITE L.D.,"CONGRESSIONAL CONTROL OF THE PUBLIC
SERVICE." USA-45 NAT/G CONSULT DELIB/GP PLAN SENIOR
CONGRESS. PAGE 63 G1232
LEGIS
EXEC
POLICY
CONTROL

C45
MCDIARMID J.,"THE MOBILIZATION OF SOCIAL
SCIENTISTS," IN L. WHITE'S CIVIL CIVIL SERVICE IN
WARTIME." USA-45 TEC/DEV CENTRAL...SOC 20
CIVIL/SERV. PAGE 37 G0733
INTELL
WAR
DELIB/GP
ADMIN

B46
BRODIE B.,THE OBSOLETE WEAPON: ATOMIC POWER AND
WORLD ORDER. COM USA+45 USSR WOR+45 DELIB/GP PLAN
ORD/FREE PWR...CONCPT TIME/SEQ TREND UN 20. PAGE 9
G0171
INT/ORG
TEC/DEV
ARMS/CONT
NUC/PWR

B46
VINER J.,SYMPOSIUM ON ATOMIC ENERGY AND ITS
IMPLICATIONS. USA+45 WOR+45 SOCIETY DELIB/GP...SOC
CONCPT TIME/SEQ TOT/POP 20. PAGE 61 G1200
R+D
RIGID/FLEX
NUC/PWR

B48
STEWART I.,ORGANIZING SCIENTIFIC RESEARCH FOR WAR:
ADMINISTRATIVE HISTORY OF OFFICE OF SCIENTIFIC
RESEARCH AND DEVELOPMENT. USA-45 INTELL R+D LABOR
WORKER CREATE BUDGET WEAPON CIVMIL/REL GP/REL
EFFICIENCY...POLICY 20. PAGE 53 G1036
DELIB/GP
ADMIN
WAR
TEC/DEV

B49
MCLEAN J.M.,THE PUBLIC SERVICE AND UNIVERSITY
EDUCATION. UK USA-45 DELIB/GP EX/STRUC TOP/EX ADMIN
...GOV/COMP METH/COMP NAT/COMP ANTHOL 20. PAGE 38
G0746
ACADEM
NAT/G
EXEC
EDU/PROP

S49
SOUERS S.W.,"POLICY FORMULATION FOR NATIONAL
SECURITY." EX/STRUC FORCES PROB/SOLV DIPLOM CONFER
EXEC ARMS/CONT DETER NUC/PWR GOV/REL PEACE
COLD/WAR. PAGE 52 G1022
DELIB/GP
CHIEF
DECISION
POLICY

B50
HUZAR E.,THE PURSE AND THE SWORD: CONTROL OF THE
ARMY BY CONGRESS THROUGH MILITARY APPROPRIATIONS
1933-1950. NAT/G DELIB/GP EX/STRUC FORCES PROB/SOLV
BARGAIN CONFER ADMIN ROUTINE GOV/REL EFFICIENCY
...POLICY COLD/WAR. PAGE 27 G0541
CIVMIL/REL
BUDGET
CONTROL
LEGIS

B53
SAYLES L.R.,THE LOCAL UNION. CONSTN CULTURE
DELIB/GP PARTIC CHOOSE GP/REL INGP/REL ATTIT ROLE
...MAJORIT DECISION MGT. PAGE 49 G0958
LABOR
LEAD
ADJUD
ROUTINE

B53
SCHAAF R.W.,DOCUMENTS OF INTERNATIONAL MEETINGS.
AGRI INDUS ACADEM DIPLOM NUC/PWR RACE/REL AGE/Y
HEALTH...SOC 20. PAGE 49 G0960
BIBLIOG/A
DELIB/GP
INT/ORG
POLICY

B54
COMBS C.H.,DECISION PROCESSES. INTELL SOCIETY
DELIB/GP CREATE TEC/DEV DOMIN LEGIT EXEC CHOOSE
DRIVE RIGID/FLEX KNOWL PWR...PHIL/SCI SOC
METH/CNCPT CONT/OBS REC/INT PERS/TEST SAMP/SIZ BIOG
SOC/EXP WORK. PAGE 13 G0245
MATH
DECISION

B55
MOCH J.,HUMAN FOLLY: DISARM OR PERISH. USA+45
WOR+45 SOCIETY INT/ORG NAT/G ACT/RES EDU/PROP ATTIT
PERSON KNOWL ORD/FREE PWR...MAJORIT TOT/POP
COLD/WAR 20. PAGE 39 G0776
FUT
DELIB/GP
ARMS/CONT
NUC/PWR

B55
OPPENHEIMER R.,THE OPEN MIND. USA+45 WOR+45 NAT/G
DELIB/GP DETER MORAL ORD/FREE...MYTH GEN/LAWS 20.
PAGE 43 G0842
CREATE
PWR
ARMS/CONT

NUC/PWR

B56
BLACKETT P.M.S.,ATOMIC WEAPONS AND EAST-WEST
RELATIONS. FUT WOR+45 INT/ORG DELIB/GP COERCE ATTIT
RIGID/FLEX KNOWL...RELATIV HIST/WRIT TREND GEN/METH
COLD/WAR 20. PAGE 7 G0138
FORCES
PWR
ARMS/CONT
NUC/PWR

S56
GORDON L.,"THE ORGANIZATION FOR EUROPEAN ECONOMIC
COOPERATION." EUR+WWI INDUS INT/ORG NAT/G CONSULT
DELIB/GP ACT/RES CREATE PLAN TEC/DEV EDU/PROP LEGIT
WEALTH OEEC 20. PAGE 22 G0435
VOL/ASSN
ECO/DEV

S56
KNAPP D.C.,"CONGRESSIONAL CONTROL OF AGRICULTURAL
CONSERVATION POLICY: A CASE STUDY OF THE
APPROPRIATIONS PROCESS." DELIB/GP PLAN PROB/SOLV
CONFER PARL/PROC...POLICY INT CONGRESS. PAGE 31
G0607
LEGIS
AGRI
BUDGET
CONTROL

B57
DUPREE A.H.,SCIENCE IN THE FEDERAL GOVERNMENT: A
HISTORY OF POLICIES AND ACTIVITIES TO 1940. USA-45
AGRI SCHOOL DELIB/GP WAR GOV/REL...PHIL/SCI BIBLIOG
18/20 DEPRESSION NEW/DEAL WWI JEFFERSN/T. PAGE 17
G0324
NAT/G
R+D
CREATE
TEC/DEV

B58
NOEL-BAKER D.,THE ARMS RACE. WOR+45 NAT/G DELIB/GP
ACT/RES TEC/DEV EDU/PROP NUC/PWR ATTIT KNOWL PWR
...CONCPT OBS LEAGUE/NAT 20 COLD/WAR. PAGE 42 G0823
FUT
INT/ORG
ARMS/CONT
PEACE

S58
ANDERSON N.,"INTERNATIONAL SEMINARS: AN ANALYSIS
AND AN EVALUATION." WOR+45 R+D ACT/RES CREATE PLAN
REGION ATTIT KNOWL SKILL...SOC REC/INT PERS/TEST
CHARTS 20. PAGE 3 G0057
INT/ORG
DELIB/GP

S58
MARCY C.,"THE RESEARCH PROGRAM OF THE SENATE
COMMITTEE ON FOREIGN RELATIONS." EUR+WWI ECO/UNDEV
ACT/RES PLAN PARL/PROC GOV/REL...GEOG CONFE
CONGRESS. PAGE 36 G0704
DELIB/GP
LEGIS
FOR/AID
POLICY

S58
MCDOUGAL M.S.,"PERSPECTIVES FOR A LAW OF OUTER
SPACE." FUT WOR+45 AIR CONSULT DELIB/GP TEC/DEV
CT/SYS ORD/FREE...POLICY JURID 20 UN. PAGE 37 G0736
INT/ORG
SPACE
INT/LAW

S58
SINGER J.D.,"THREAT PERCEPTION AND THE ARMAMENT
TENSION DILEMMA." WOR+45 WOR-45 ELITES INT/ORG
NAT/G DELIB/GP PLAN LEGIT COERCE DETER ATTIT
RIGID/FLEX PWR...DECISION PSY 20. PAGE 51 G1002
PERCEPT
ARMS/CONT
BAL/PWR

B59
GREENFIELD K.R.,COMMAND DECISIONS. ASIA EUR+WWI
S/ASIA USA+45 WOR-45 NAT/G CONSULT DELIB/GP COERCE
NUC/PWR PWR...OBS 20 CHINJAP. PAGE 23 G0446
PLAN
FORCES
WAR
WEAPON

B59
HARVARD UNIVERSITY LAW SCHOOL,INTERNATIONAL
PROBLEMS OF FINANCIAL PROTECTION AGAINST NUCLEAR
RISK. WOR+45 NAT/G DELIB/GP PROB/SOLV DIPLOM
CONTROL ATTIT...POLICY INT/LAW MATH 20. PAGE 25
G0488
NUC/PWR
ADJUD
INDUS
FINAN

B59
US CONGRESS JT ATOM ENRGY COMM,SELECTED MATERIALS
ON FEDERAL-STATE COOPERATION IN THE ATOMIC ENERGY
FIELD. USA+45 LAW LOC/G PROVS CONSULT LEGIS ADJUD
...POLICY BIBLIOG 20 AEC. PAGE 57 G1111
NAT/G
NUC/PWR
GOV/REL
DELIB/GP

S59
STOESSINGER J.G.,"THE INTERNATIONAL ATOMIC ENERGY
AGENCY: THE FIRST PHASE." FUT WOR+45 NAT/G VOL/ASSN
DELIB/GP BAL/PWR LEGIT ADMIN ROUTINE PWR...OBS
CON/ANAL GEN/LAWS VAL/FREE 20 IAEA. PAGE 53 G1037
INT/ORG
ECO/DEV
FOR/AID
NUC/PWR

B60
ARMS CONTROL. FUT UNIV WOR+45 INTELL R+D INT/ORG
NAT/G VOL/ASSN CONSULT CREATE EDU/PROP PEACE...HUM
GEN/LAWS TOT/POP 20. PAGE 1 G0015
DELIB/GP
ORD/FREE
ARMS/CONT
NUC/PWR

B60
CARPER E.T.,THE DEFENSE APPROPRIATIONS RIDER
(PAMPHLET). USA+45 CONSTN CHIEF DELIB/GP LEGIS
BUDGET LOBBY CIVMIL/REL...POLICY 20 CONGRESS
EISNHWR/DD DEPT/DEFEN PRESIDENT BOSTON. PAGE 11
G0212
GOV/REL
ADJUD
LAW
CONTROL

MCKINNEY R.,REVIEW OF THE INTERNATIONAL ATOMIC NUC/PWR
POLICIES AND PROGRAMS OF THE UNITED STATES (5   PEACE
VOLS.). COM FUT USA+45 ECO/DEV ECO/UNDEV INT/ORG DIPLOM
DELIB/GP PLAN ADMIN 20 THIRD/WRLD. PAGE 38 G0744 POLICY
B60

JACOB P.E.,"THE DISARMAMENT CONSENSUS." USA+45 USSR DELIB/GP
WOR+45 INT/ORG NAT/G ACT/RES TEC/DEV BAL/PWR   ATTIT
EDU/PROP ADMIN COERCE DETER NUC/PWR CONSEN   ARMS/CONT
RIGID/FLEX PWR...CONCPT RECORD CHARTS COLD/WAR 20.
PAGE 28 G0552
L60

DYSON F.J.,"THE FUTURE DEVELOPMENT OF NUCLEAR   INT/ORG
WEAPONS." FUT WOR+45 DELIB/GP ACT/RES PLAN DETER ARMS/CONT
WEAPON ATTIT PWR...POLICY 20. PAGE 17 G0328   NUC/PWR
S60

HAYTON R.D.,"THE ANTARCTIC SETTLEMENT OF 1959." FUT DELIB/GP
USA+45 WOR+45 WOR-45 STRUCT R+D INT/ORG EX/STRUC JURID
CREATE TEC/DEV LEGIT PEACE ATTIT SOVEREIGN   DIPLOM
...TIME/SEQ 20 TREATY IGY. PAGE 25 G0495   REGION
S60

HUNTINGTON S.P.,"STRATEGIC PLANNING AND THE   EXEC
POLITICAL PROCESS." USA+45 NAT/G DELIB/GP LEGIS FORCES
ACT/RES ECO/TAC LEGIT ROUTINE CHOOSE RIGID/FLEX PWR NUC/PWR
...POLICY MAJORIT MGT 20. PAGE 27 G0538   WAR
S60

IKLE F.C.,"NTH COUNTRIES AND DISARMAMENT." WOR+45 FUT
DELIB/GP ECO/TAC DOMIN EDU/PROP LEGIT ROUTINE   INT/ORG
COERCE RIGID/FLEX ORD/FREE...MARXIST TREND 20.   ARMS/CONT
PAGE 28 G0543   NUC/PWR
S60

SWIFT R.,"THE UNITED NATIONS AND ITS PUBLIC."   INT/ORG
WOR+45 CONSTN FINAN CONSULT DELIB/GP ACT/RES ADMIN EDU/PROP
ROUTINE RIGID/FLEX SKILL UN 20. PAGE 53 G1048
B61

HELLER D.,THE KENNEDY CABINET--AMERICA'S MEN OF EX/STRUC
DESTINY. NAT/G CHIEF CONSULT ADMIN CONTROL GOV/REL CONFER
...MGT 20 DEPT/LABOR DEPT/STATE DEPT/JUST   DELIB/GP
DEPT/DEFEN KENNEDY/J. PAGE 26 G0504   TOP/EX
B61

HENKIN L.,ARMS CONTROL: ISSUES FOR THE PUBLIC.   WOR+45
EUR+WWI FUT USA+45 USSR INT/ORG NAT/G DIPLOM   DELIB/GP
EDU/PROP DETER NUC/PWR ATTIT PWR...CONCPT RECORD ARMS/CONT
HIST/WRIT TIME/SEQ TOT/POP COLD/WAR 20. PAGE 26
G0506
B61

SMITH H.H.,THE CITIZEN'S GUIDE TO PLANNING. USA+45 MUNIC
LAW SCHOOL CREATE PROB/SOLV EDU/PROP GP/REL ROLE 20 PLAN
URBAN/RNWL OPEN/SPACE. PAGE 52 G1015   DELIB/GP
CONSULT
L61

HERRING P.,"RESEARCH FOR PUBLIC POLICY: BROOKINGS R+D
DEDICATION LECTURES." USA+45 CONSULT DELIB/GP   ACT/RES
ROUTINE PERCEPT SKILL...MGT 20. PAGE 26 G0508   DIPLOM
S61

HAINES G.,"THE COMPUTER AS A SMALL-GROUP MEMBER." INGP/REL
DELIB/GP BAL/PWR TASK 20. PAGE 24 G0467   COMPUTER
PROB/SOLV
EFFICIENCY
B62

CALDER R.,LIVING WITH THE ATOM. FUT USA+45 WOR+45 TEC/DEV
R+D INT/ORG VOL/ASSN DELIB/GP ARMS/CONT...STYLE 20. HEALTH
PAGE 10 G0200   NUC/PWR
B62

DODDS H.W.,THE ACADEMIC PRESIDENT "EDUCATOR OR   ACADEM
CARETAKER? FINAN DELIB/GP EDU/PROP PARTIC ATTIT ADMIN
ROLE PWR...POLICY RECORD INT. PAGE 16 G0304   LEAD
CONTROL
B62

MARS D.,SUGGESTED LIBRARY IN PUBLIC ADMINISTRATION. BIBLIOG
FINAN DELIB/GP EX/STRUC WORKER COMPUTER ADJUD   ADMIN
...DECISION PSY SOC METH/COMP 20. PAGE 36 G0710 METH
MGT
B62

MELMAN S.,DISARMAMENT: ITS POLITICS AND ECONOMICS. NAT/G
WOR+45 DELIB/GP FORCES ECO/TAC DOMIN EDU/PROP LEGIT ORD/FREE
COERCE PWR...POLICY CONCPT 20. PAGE 38 G0752   ARMS/CONT
NUC/PWR
B62

OSGOOD C.E.,AN ALTERNATIVE TO WAR OR SURRENDER. FUT ORD/FREE

UNIV CULTURE INTELL SOCIETY R+D INT/ORG CONSULT EDU/PROP
DELIB/GP ACT/RES PLAN CHOOSE ATTIT PERCEPT KNOWL PEACE
...PHIL/SCI PSY SOC TREND GEN/LAWS 20. PAGE 43   WAR
G0849
B62

SCHILLING W.R.,STRATEGY, POLITICS, AND DEFENSE   ROUTINE
BUDGETS. USA+45 R+D NAT/G CONSULT DELIB/GP FORCES POLICY
LEGIS ACT/RES PLAN BAL/PWR LEGIT EXEC NUC/PWR
RIGID/FLEX PWR...TREND COLD/WAR CONGRESS 20
EISNHWR/DD. PAGE 49 G0968
B62

YALEN R.,REGIONALISM AND WORLD ORDER. EUR+WWI   ORD/FREE
WOR+45 WOR-45 INT/ORG VOL/ASSN DELIB/GP FORCES   POLICY
TOP/EX BAL/PWR DIPLOM DOMIN REGION ARMS/CONT PWR
...JURID HYPO/EXP COLD/WAR 20. PAGE 64 G1261
L62

NEIBURG H.L.,"THE EISENHOWER AEC AND CONGRESS: A CHIEF
STUDY IN EXECUTIVE-LEGISLATIVE RELATIONS." USA+45 LEGIS
NAT/G POL/PAR DELIB/GP EX/STRUC TOP/EX ADMIN EXEC GOV/REL
LEAD ROUTINE PWR...POLICY COLD/WAR CONGRESS   NUC/PWR
PRESIDENT AEC. PAGE 41 G0816
L62

NIEBURG H.L.,"THE EISENHOWER ATOMIC ENERGY   NUC/PWR
COMMISSION AND CONGRESS" R+D INT/ORG OP/RES DIPLOM TOP/EX
ADMIN CONTROL 20 PRESIDENT CONGRESS AEC. PAGE 42 LOBBY
G0821   DELIB/GP
S62

FINKELSTEIN L.S.,"THE UNITED NATIONS AND   INT/ORG
ORGANIZATIONS FOR CONTROL OF ARMAMENT." FUT WOR+45 PWR
VOL/ASSN DELIB/GP TOP/EX CREATE EDU/PROP LEGIT   ARMS/CONT
ADJUD NUC/PWR ATTIT RIGID/FLEX ORD/FREE...POLICY
DECISION CONCPT OBS TREND GEN/LAWS TOT/POP
COLD/WAR. PAGE 19 G0368
S62

FOSTER R.B.,"UNILATERAL ARMS CONTROL MEASURES AND PLAN
DISARMAMENT NEGOTIATION." WOR+45 VOL/ASSN DELIB/GP ORD/FREE
ACT/RES ECO/TAC EDU/PROP ATTIT RIGID/FLEX...CONCPT ARMS/CONT
MYTH TIME/SEQ COLD/WAR 20. PAGE 20 G0386   DETER
S62

FOSTER W.C.,"ARMS CONTROL AND DISARMAMENT IN A   DELIB/GP
DIVIDED WORLD." COM FUT USA+45 USSR WOR+45 INTELL POLICY
INT/ORG NAT/G VOL/ASSN CONSULT CREATE PLAN TEC/DEV ARMS/CONT
EDU/PROP LEGIT NUC/PWR ATTIT RIGID/FLEX...CONCPT DIPLOM
TREND TOT/POP 20 UN. PAGE 20 G0387
S62

MORGENTHAU H.J.,"A POLITICAL THEORY OF FOREIGN   USA+45
AID." ECO/UNDEV NAT/G DELIB/GP PLAN ECO/TAC   PHIL/SCI
EDU/PROP EXEC ORD/FREE RESPECT WEALTH...METH/CNCPT FOR/AID
TREND 20. PAGE 40 G0783
S62

NANES A.,"DISARMAMENT: THE LAST SEVEN YEARS." COM DELIB/GP
EUR+WWI USA+45 USSR INT/ORG FORCES TOP/EX CREATE RIGID/FLEX
LEGIT NUC/PWR DISPL ORD/FREE...CONCPT TIME/SEQ   ARMS/CONT
CON/ANAL 20. PAGE 41 G0803
S62

THORELLI H.B.,"THE INTERNATIONAL OPERATIONS   ECO/TAC
SIMULATION AT THE UNIVERSITY OF CHICAGO." FUT   SIMUL
USA+45 WOR+45 ECO/DIST/IND FINAN INDUS INT/ORG   INT/TRADE
DELIB/GP ACT/RES CREATE TEC/DEV WEALTH...STAT
VAL/FREE 20. PAGE 54 G1072
B63

ABSHIRE D.M.,NATIONAL SECURITY: POLITICAL,   FUT
MILITARY, AND ECONOMIC STRATEGIES IN THE DECADE ACT/RES
AHEAD. ASIA COM USA+45 WOR+45 ECO/DEV ECO/UNDEV BAL/PWR
INT/ORG DELIB/GP FORCES ECO/TAC COERCE ATTIT
RIGID/FLEX HEALTH ORD/FREE PWR WEALTH...POLICY STAT
CHARTS ANTHOL COLD/WAR VAL/FREE. PAGE 1 G0024
B63

DEAN A.L.,FEDERAL AGENCY APPROACHES TO FIELD   ADMIN
MANAGEMENT (PAMPHLET). R+D DELIB/GP EX/STRUC   MGT
PROB/SOLV GOV/REL...CLASSIF BIBLIOG 20 FAA NASA NAT/G
DEPT/HEW POSTAL/SYS IRS. PAGE 15 G0287   OP/RES
B63

GREEN H.P.,GOVERNMENT OF THE ATOM. USA+45 LEGIS GOV/REL
PROB/SOLV ADMIN CONTROL PWR...POLICY DECISION 20 EX/STRUC
PRESIDENT CONGRESS. PAGE 22 G0443   NUC/PWR
DELIB/GP
B63

LILIENTHAL D.E.,CHANGE, HOPE, AND THE BOMB. USA+45 ATTIT
WOR+45 R+D INT/ORG NAT/G DELIB/GP FORCES ACT/RES MYTH
DETER RIGID/FLEX ORD/FREE...POLICY CONCPT OBS AEC ARMS/CONT
20. PAGE 34 G0666   NUC/PWR

MAYNE R.,THE COMMUNITY OF EUROPE. UK CONSTN NAT/G
CONSULT DELIB/GP CREATE PLAN ECO/TAC LEGIT ADMIN
ROUTINE ORD/FREE PWR WEALTH...CONCPT TIME/SEQ EEC
EURATOM 20. PAGE 37 G0724
EUR+WWI
INT/ORG
REGION
B63

MULLENBACH P.,CIVILIAN NUCLEAR POWER: ECONOMIC
ISSUES AND POLICY FORMATION. FINAN INT/ORG DELIB/GP
ACT/RES ECO/TAC ATTIT SUPEGO HEALTH ORD/FREE PWR
...POLICY CONCPT MATH STAT CHARTS VAL/FREE 20
COLD/WAR. PAGE 40 G0792
USA+45
ECO/DEV
NUC/PWR
B63

PANAMERICAN UNION,DOCUMENTOS OFICIALES DE LA
ORGANIZACION DE LOS ESTADOS AMERICANOS, INDICE Y
LISTA (VOL. III, 1962). L/A+17C DELIB/GP INT/TRADE
EDU/PROP REGION NUC/PWR...HEAL INT/LAW SOC/WK 20
OAS. PAGE 44 G0857
BIBLIOG
INT/ORG
DIPLOM
B63

REED E.,CHALLENGES TO DEMOCRACY: THE NEXT TEN
YEARS. FUT USA+45 ECO/DEV DELIB/GP TEC/DEV CONFER
GOV/REL KNOWL ORD/FREE...MAJORIT IDEA/COMP ANTHOL
20. PAGE 46 G0909
POLICY
EDU/PROP
ECO/TAC
NAT/G
B63

US SENATE COMM GOVT OPERATIONS,ADMINISTRATION OF
NATIONAL SECURITY (9 PARTS). ADMIN...INT REC/INT
CHARTS 20 SENATE CONGRESS. PAGE 60 G1178
DELIB/GP
NAT/G
OP/RES
ORD/FREE
B63

WILTZ J.E.,IN SEARCH OF PEACE: THE SENATE MUNITIONS
INQUIRY, 1934-36. EUR+WWI USA+45 ELITES INDUS LG/CO
LEGIS INT/TRADE LOBBY NEUTRAL ARMS/CONT...POLICY
CONGRESS 20 LEAGUE/NAT PRESIDENT SENATE CONSCRIPTN.
PAGE 64 G1246
DELIB/GP
PROFIT
WAR
WEAPON
B63

NIEBURG H.,"EURATOM: A STUDY IN COALITION
POLITICS." EUR+WWI UK USA+45 ELITES NAT/G DELIB/GP
LEGIS TOP/EX ECO/TAC NUC/PWR ATTIT ORD/FREE PWR
TOT/POP EEC OEEC 20 NATO EURATOM. PAGE 42 G0820
VOL/ASSN
ACT/RES
L63

ENTHOVEN A.C.,"ECONOMIC ANALYSIS IN THE DEPARTMENT
OF DEFENSE." USA+45 NAT/G DELIB/GP PROB/SOLV RATION
NUC/PWR WEAPON COST...DECISION 20 DEPT/DEFEN
RESOURCE/N. PAGE 18 G0349
PLAN
BUDGET
ECO/TAC
FORCES
S63

GARDNER R.N.,"COOPERATION IN OUTER SPACE." FUT USSR
WOR+45 AIR LAW COM/IND CONSULT DELIB/GP CREATE
KNOWL 20 TREATY. PAGE 21 G0410
INT/ORG
ACT/RES
PEACE
SPACE
S63

PHELPS J.,"INFORMATION AND ARMS CONTROL." COM SPACE
USA+45 USSR WOR+45 R+D INT/ORG NAT/G DELIB/GP
DIPLOM ORD/FREE...CONCPT 20. PAGE 45 G0875
KNOWL
ARMS/CONT
NUC/PWR
S63

SCHMITT H.A.,"THE EUROPEAN COMMUNITIES." EUR+WWI
FRANCE DELIB/GP EX/STRUC TOP/EX CREATE TEC/DEV
ECO/TAC LEGIT REGION COERCE DRIVE ALL/VALS
...METH/CNCPT EEC 20. PAGE 49 G0972
VOL/ASSN
ECO/DEV
S63

COMMITTEE ECONOMIC DEVELOPMENT,TAXES AND TRADE: 20
YEARS OF CED POLICY (PAMPHLET). USA+45 ECO/DEV PLAN
BUDGET LEAD...POLICY KENNEDY/JF PRESIDENT. PAGE 13
G0246
FINAN
ECO/TAC
NAT/G
DELIB/GP
N63

COHEN M.,LAW AND POLITICS IN SPACE: SPECIFIC AND
URGENT PROBLEMS IN THE LAW OF OUTER SPACE.
CHINA/COM COM USA+45 WOR+45 COM/IND INT/ORG
NAT/G LEGIT NUC/PWR ATTIT BIO/SOC...JURID CONCPT
CONGRESS 20 STALIN/J. PAGE 12 G0241
DELIB/GP
LAW
INT/LAW
SPACE
B64

NASA,PROCEEDINGS OF CONFERENCE ON THE LAW OF SPACE
AND OF SATELLITE COMMUNICATIONS: CHICAGO 1963. FUT
WOR+45 DELIB/GP PROB/SOLV TEC/DEV CONFER ADJUD
NUC/PWR...POLICY IDEA/COMP 20 NASA. PAGE 41 G0805
SPACE
COM/IND
LAW
DIPLOM
B64

RANSOM H.H.,CAN AMERICAN DEMOCRACY SURVIVE COLD
WAR. USA+45 CONSTN NAT/G CONSULT DELIB/GP LEGIS
ACT/RES LEGIT EXEC ATTIT KNOWL ORD/FREE PWR SKILL
...POLICY TIME/SEQ TREND GEN/LAWS 20 COLD/WAR.
PAGE 46 G0901
USA+45
ROUTINE
B64

RIES J.C.,THE MANAGEMENT OF DEFENSE: ORGANIZATION
AND CONTROL OF THE US ARMED SERVICES. PROF/ORG
DELIB/GP EX/STRUC LEGIS GOV/REL PERS/REL CENTRAL
RATIONAL PWR...POLICY TREND GOV/COMP BIBLIOG.
PAGE 47 G0920
FORCES
ACT/RES
DECISION
CONTROL
B64

ROSECRANCE R.N.,THE DISPERSION OF NUCLEAR WEAPONS:
STRATEGY AND POLITICS. ASIA COM FUT S/ASIA USA+45
INT/ORG NAT/G DELIB/GP FORCES ACT/RES TEC/DEV
BAL/PWR COERCE DETER ATTIT RIGID/FLEX ORD/FREE
...POLICY CHARTS VAL/FREE. PAGE 48 G0935
EUR+WWI
PWR
PEACE
B64

SCHERER F.M.,THE WEAPONS ACQUISITION PROCESS:
ECONOMIC INCENTIVES. BOSTON: DIVISION OF RESEARCH,
GRADUATE SCHOOL OF BUSINESS. USA+45 FINAN NAT/G
DELIB/GP ECO/TAC RIGID/FLEX WEALTH...MGT MATH STAT
CHARTS VAL/FREE 20. PAGE 49 G0965
INDUS
ACT/RES
WEAPON
B64

THANT U.,TOWARD WORLD PEACE. DELIB/GP TEC/DEV
EDU/PROP WAR SOVEREIGN...INT/LAW 20 UN MID/EAST.
PAGE 54 G1065
DIPLOM
BIOG
PEACE
COERCE
B64

US AIR FORCE ACADEMY ASSEMBLY,OUTER SPACE: FINAL
REPORT APRIL 1-4, 1964. FUT USA+45 WOR+45 LAW
DELIB/GP CONFER ARMS/CONT WAR PEACE ATTIT MORAL
...ANTHOL 20 NASA. PAGE 56 G1104
SPACE
CIVMIL/REL
NUC/PWR
DIPLOM
B64

VAN DYKE V.,PRIDE AND POWER: THE RATIONALE OF THE
SPACE PROGRAM. FUT USA+45 INTELL R+D NAT/G POL/PAR
DELIB/GP EX/STRUC LEGIS TOP/EX ACT/RES PLAN ECO/TAC
EDU/PROP ORD/FREE PWR RESPECT SKILL...TIME/SEQ
VAL/FREE. PAGE 61 G1191
TEC/DEV
ATTIT
POLICY
B64

CARNEGIE ENDOWMENT INT. PEACE,"POLITICAL QUESTIONS
(ISSUES BEFORE THE NINETEENTH GENERAL ASSEMBLY)."
SPACE WOR+45 CONSTN FINAN NAT/G CONSULT DELIB/GP
FORCES LEGIS TEC/DEV EDU/PROP LEGIT ARMS/CONT
COERCE NUC/PWR ATTIT ALL/VALS...CONCPT OBS UN
COLD/WAR 20. PAGE 11 G0208
INT/ORG
PEACE
L64

CARNEGIE ENDOWMENT INT. PEACE,"ECONOMIC AND SOCIAL
QUESTION (ISSUES BEFORE THE NINETEENTH GENERAL
ASSEMBLY)." WOR+45 ECO/DEV ECO/UNDEV INDUS R+D
DELIB/GP CREATE PLAN TEC/DEV ECO/TAC FOR/AID
BAL/PAY...RECORD UN 20. PAGE 11 G0209
INT/ORG
INT/TRADE
L64

HAAS E.B.,"ECONOMICS AND DIFFERENTIAL PATTERNS OF
POLITICAL INTEGRATION: PROJECTIONS ABOUT UNITY IN
LATIN AMERICA." SOCIETY NAT/G DELIB/GP ACT/RES
CREATE PLAN ECO/TAC REGION ROUTINE ATTIT DRIVE PWR
WEALTH...CONCPT TREND CHARTS LAFTA 20. PAGE 24
G0464
L/A+17C
INT/ORG
MARKET
L64

GARDNER R.N.,"GATT AND THE UNITED NATIONS
CONFERENCE ON TRADE AND DEVELOPMENT." USA+45 WOR+45
SOCIETY ECO/UNDEV MARKET NAT/G DELIB/GP ACT/RES
PLAN ECO/TAC TARIFFS EDU/PROP ROUTINE DRIVE
RIGID/FLEX WEALTH...DECISION MGT TREND UN TOT/POP
20 GATT. PAGE 21 G0411
INT/ORG
INT/TRADE
S64

ATOMIC INDUSTRIAL FORUM,SAFEGUARDS AGAINST
DIVERSION OF NUCLEAR MATERIALS FROM PEACEFUL TO
MILITARY PURPOSES. WOR+45 DELIB/GP FORCES PLAN
DIPLOM CONFER PEACE...ANTHOL 20 IAEA. PAGE 4 G0081
NUC/PWR
CIVMIL/REL
INSPECT
CONTROL
B65

NATIONAL ACADEMY OF SCIENCES,BASIC RESEARCH AND
NATIONAL GOALS. R+D ACADEM DELIB/GP PLAN EDU/PROP
...POLICY HEAL PHIL/SCI PSY SOC ANTHOL 20 CONGRESS
HOUSE/REP HS/SCIASTR. PAGE 41 G0809
LEGIS
BUDGET
NAT/G
CREATE
B65

SCHEINMAN L.,ATOMIC ENERGY POLICY IN FRANCE UNDER
THE FOURTH REPUBLIC. FRANCE UK USA+45 ELITES
POL/PAR PLAN PROB/SOLV DIPLOM LEAD GOV/REL
...BIBLIOG 20 DEGAULLE/C. PAGE 49 G0962
NUC/PWR
NAT/G
DELIB/GP
POLICY
B65

US CONGRESS JT ATOM ENRGY COMM,PEACEFUL
APPLICATIONS OF NUCLEAR EXPLOSIVES: PLOWSHARE,
HEARING. USA+45 LEGIS CREATE PLAN PEACE...CHARTS
EXHIBIT BIBLIOG CONGRESS PANAMA/CNL. PAGE 57 G1113
NUC/PWR
DELIB/GP
TEC/DEV
NAT/G
B65

US CONGRESS JT ATOM ENRGY COMM,ATOMIC ENERGY
LEGISLATION THROUGH 89TH CONGRESS, 1ST SESSION.
USA+45 LAW INT/ORG DELIB/GP BUDGET DIPLOM 20 AEC
CONGRESS CASEBOOK EURATOM IAEA. PAGE 57 G1114
NUC/PWR
FORCES
PEACE
LEGIS
B65

US CONGRESS JT ATOM ENRGY COMM,PROPOSED AMENDMENT
TO SECTION 271 OF THE ATOMIC ENERGY ACT OF 1954.
USA+45 CONSTRUC PLAN INSPECT CONTROL CT/SYS 20
CONGRESS AEC. PAGE 57 G1115
LAW
LEGIS
DELIB/GP
NUC/PWR
B65

US SENATE COMM AERO SPACE SCI,NATIONAL SPACE GOALS
FOR THE POST-APOLLO PERIOD. USA+45 CONSULT DELIB/GP
TEC/DEV BUDGET GP/REL ATTIT...CHARTS IDEA/COMP TIME
20 DEPT/DEFEN NASA CONGRESS. PAGE 59 G1166
SPACE
FUT
R+D
LEGIS
B65

US SENATE COMM AERO SPACE SCI,INTERNATIONAL
COOPERATION AND ORGANIZATION FOR OUTER SPACE. FUT
USA+45 WOR+45 PROF/ORG VOL/ASSN CONSULT DELIB/GP
PLAN TEC/DEV ARMS/CONT GP/REL PEACE 20 UN NASA.
PAGE 59 G1167
DIPLOM
SPACE
R+D
NAT/G
B65

BEAUFRE A.,"THE SHARING OF NUCLEAR
RESPONSIBILITIES* A PROBLEM IN NEED OF SOLUTION."
FRANCE USA+45 INT/ORG NAT/G DELIB/GP FORCES CONTROL
NUC/PWR RIGID/FLEX...CONCPT IDEA/COMP NATO. PAGE 6
G0110
DETER
RISK
ACT/RES
WAR
S65

FOX A.B.,"NATO AND CONGRESS." CONSTN DELIB/GP
EX/STRUC FORCES TOP/EX BUDGET NUC/PWR GOV/REL
...GP/COMP CONGRESS NATO TREATY. PAGE 20 G0388
CONTROL
DIPLOM
S65

CLARK G.,WORLD PEACE THROUGH WORLD LAW: TWO
ALTERNATIVE PLANS. WOR+45 DELIB/GP FORCES TAX
CONFER ADJUD SANCTION ARMS/CONT WAR CHOOSE PRIVIL
20 UN COLD/WAR. PAGE 12 G0231
INT/LAW
PEACE
PLAN
INT/ORG
B66

ONYEMELUKWE C.C.,PROBLEMS OF INDUSTRIAL PLANNING
AND MANAGEMENT IN NIGERIA. AFR FINAN LABOR DELIB/GP
TEC/DEV ADJUST...MGT TREND BIBLIOG. PAGE 43 G0839
ECO/UNDEV
ECO/TAC
INDUS
PLAN
B66

ROSHOLT R.L.,AN ADMINISTRATIVE HISTORY OF NASA,
1958-1963. SPACE USA+45 FINAN LEAD...MGT CHARTS
BIBLIOG 20 NASA. PAGE 48 G0938
ADMIN
EX/STRUC
ADJUST
DELIB/GP
B66

US PRES COMM ECO IMPACT DEFENS,REPORT* JULY 1965.
USA+45 ECO/DEV INDUS DELIB/GP FORCES OP/RES
ARMS/CONT NUC/PWR WEAPON BAL/PAY...PREDICT SIMUL.
PAGE 59 G1159
ACT/RES
STAT
WAR
BUDGET
B66

WHITNAH D.R.,SAFER SKYWAYS. DIST/IND DELIB/GP
FORCES TOP/EX WORKER TEC/DEV ROUTINE WAR CIVMIL/REL
COST...TIME/SEQ 20 FAA CAB. PAGE 63 G1235
ADMIN
NAT/G
AIR
GOV/REL
B66

US HOUSE COMM SCI ASTRONAUT,GOVERNMENT, SCIENCE,
AND PUBLIC POLICY (PAMPHLET). R+D ACADEM DELIB/GP
COMPUTER BUDGET CONFER ADMIN...PHIL/SCI PREDICT
TREND 20 CONGRESS HS/SCIASTR. PAGE 58 G1143
NAT/G
POLICY
TEC/DEV
CREATE
N66

US HOUSE COMM SCI ASTRONAUT,INQUIRIES, LEGISLATION,
POLICY STUDIES RE: SCIENCE AND TECHNOLOGY: REVIEW
AND FORECAST (PAMPHLET). FUT WOR+45 DELIB/GP
PROB/SOLV...POLICY JURID TREND 20 CONGRESS. PAGE 58
G1144
TEC/DEV
R+D
PLAN
LEGIS
N66

ENKE S.,DEFENSE MANAGEMENT. USA+:5 R+D FORCES
WORKER PLAN ECO/TAC ADMIN NUC/PWR BAL/PAY UTIL
WEALTH...MGT DEPT/DEFEN. PAGE 18 G0348
DECISION
DELIB/GP
EFFICIENCY
BUDGET
B67

MCBRIDE J.H.,THE TEST BAN TREATY: MILITARY,
TECHNOLOGICAL, AND POLITICAL IMPLICATIONS. USA+45
USSR DELIB/GP FORCES LEGIS TEC/DEV BAL/PWR TREATY.
PAGE 37 G0727
ARMS/CONT
DIPLOM
NUC/PWR
B67

US SENATE COMM AERO SPACE SCI,TREATY ON PRINCIPLES
GOVERNING ACTIVITIES OF STATES IN EXPLORATION AND
USE OF OUTER SPACE, INCLUDING...BODIES. DELIB/GP
SPACE
INT/LAW
ORD/FREE
B67

FORCES LEGIS DIPLOM...JURID 20 DEPT/STATE NASA
DEPT/DEFEN UN. PAGE 60 G1170
PEACE

US SENATE COMM AERO SPACE SCI,APOLLO ACCIDENT
(PARTS 1-7). USA+45 DELIB/GP LEGIS...INT CHARTS
NASA. PAGE 60 G1173
PROB/SOLV
SPACE
BUDGET
GOV/REL
B67

US SENATE COMM ON FOREIGN REL,FOREIGN ASSISTANCE
ACT OF 1967. VIETNAM WOR+45 DELIB/GP CONFER CONTROL
WAR WEAPON BAL/PAY...CENSUS CHARTS SENATE. PAGE 60
G1185
FOR/AID
LAW
DIPLOM
POLICY
B67

CARMICHAEL D.M.,"FORTY YEARS OF WATER POLLUTION
CONTROL IN WISCONSIN: A CASE STUDY." LAW EXTR/IND
INDUS MUNIC DELIB/GP PLAN PROB/SOLV SANCTION
...CENSUS CHARTS 20 WISCONSIN. PAGE 11 G0207
HEALTH
CONTROL
ADMIN
ADJUD
L67

FELD B.T.,"A PLEDGE* NO FIRST USE." DELIB/GP
BAL/PWR DOMIN DETER. PAGE 19 G0363
ARMS/CONT
NUC/PWR
DIPLOM
PEACE
S67

FOREIGN POLICY ASSOCIATION,"US CONCERN FOR WORLD
LAW." USA+45 WOR+45 DELIB/GP JUDGE BAL/PWR CONFER
PEACE ORD/FREE 20 UN. PAGE 19 G0379
INT/LAW
INT/ORG
DIPLOM
ARMS/CONT
S67

GANZ G.,"THE CONTROL OF INDUSTRY BY ADMINISTRATIVE
PROCESS." UK DELIB/GP WORKER 20. PAGE 21 G0408
INDUS
LAW
ADMIN
CONTROL
S67

HARRIS F.R.,"POLITICAL SCIENCE AND THE PROPOSAL FOR
A NATIONAL SOCIAL SCIENCE FOUNDATION." FUT CONSULT
DELIB/GP PLAN PROB/SOLV BUDGET CONFER SANCTION
CRIME...POLICY SOC/WK 20 NSF NSSF. PAGE 25 G0484
PROF/ORG
R+D
CREATE
NAT/G
S67

HAZARD J.N.,"POST-DISARMAMENT INTERNATIONAL LAW."
FUT USSR WOR+45 INT/ORG DELIB/GP FORCES DETER
EQUILIB SOVEREIGN MARXISM 20 UN. PAGE 25 G0496
INT/LAW
ARMS/CONT
PWR
PLAN
S67

JONES G.S.,"STRATEGIC PLANNING." USA+45 EX/STRUC
FORCES DETER WAR 20 PRESIDENT. PAGE 29 G0566
PLAN
DECISION
DELIB/GP
POLICY
S67

SHARP G.,"THE NEED OF A FUNCTIONAL SUBSTITUTE FOR
WAR." FUT UNIV WOR+45 CULTURE SOCIETY INT/ORG
CONSULT DELIB/GP ACT/RES CREATE BAL/PWR CONFER
ARMS/CONT NUC/PWR 20. PAGE 50 G0989
PEACE
WAR
DIPLOM
PROB/SOLV
S67

TELLER E.,"PLANNING FOR PEACE." CHINA/COM WOR+45
DELIB/GP TEC/DEV RISK COERCE DETER WAR ATTIT
ORD/FREE 20 NATO. PAGE 54 G1061
ARMS/CONT
NUC/PWR
PEACE
DOMIN
S67

WASHBURN A.M.,"NUCLEAR PROLIFERATION IN A
REVOLUTIONARY INTERNATIONAL SYSTEM." WOR+45 NAT/G
DELIB/GP PLAN TEC/DEV...POLICY 20. PAGE 62 G1216
ARMS/CONT
NUC/PWR
DIPLOM
CONFER
S67

US HOUSE COMM SCI ASTRONAUT,AMENDING NATIONAL
SCIENCE FOUNDATION ACT OF 1950 TO MAKE IMPROVEMENTS
IN ORGANIZATION AND OPERATION OF FOUNDAT'N(PAMPH).
USA+45 GIVE ADMIN...POLICY HOUSE/REP NSF. PAGE 58
G1147
PHIL/SCI
DELIB/GP
TEC/DEV
R+D
N67

US SENATE COMM AERO SPACE SCI,HEARINGS BEFORE THE
COMMITTEE ON AERONAUTICAL AND SPACE SCIENCES UNITED
STATES SENATE NINETIETH CONGRESS (PAMPHLET). USA+45
CONSULT PLAN CONFER EFFICIENCY SENATE. PAGE 60
G1172
NAT/G
DELIB/GP
SPACE
CREATE
N67

DELLIN L.A.D. G0293

DEMAND....ECONOMIC DEMAND

MEANS G.C.,ADMINISTRATIVE INFLATION AND PUBLIC
POLICY (PAMPHLET). USA+45 ECO/DEV FINAN INDUS
ECO/TAC
POLICY
B59

WORKER PLAN BUDGET GOV/REL COST DEMAND WEALTH 20   RATION
CONGRESS MONOPOLY GOLD/STAND. PAGE 38 G0749   CONTROL

B61
MCCRACKEN H.L.,KEYNESIAN ECONOMICS IN THE STREAM OF   ECO/TAC
ECONOMIC THOUGHT. FINAN MARKET BARGAIN EFFICIENCY   DEMAND
OPTIMAL...PHIL/SCI CONCPT IDEA/COMP BIBLIOG 18/20   ECOMETRIC
KEYNES/JM. PAGE 37 G0732

B62
GRANICK D.,THE EUROPEAN EXECUTIVE. BELGIUM FRANCE   MGT
GERMANY/W UK INDUS LABOR LG/CO SML/CO EX/STRUC PLAN   ECO/DEV
TEC/DEV CAP/ISM COST DEMAND...POLICY CHARTS 20.   ECO/TAC
PAGE 22 G0441   EXEC

B62
MARTINS A.F.,REVOLUCAO BRANCA NO CAMPO. L/A+17C   AGRI
SERV/IND DEMAND EFFICIENCY PRODUC...POLICY   ECO/UNDEV
METH/COMP. PAGE 36 G0717   TEC/DEV
   NAT/COMP

B64
BAUCHET P.,ECONOMIC PLANNING. FRANCE STRATA LG/CO   ECO/DEV
CAP/ISM ADMIN PARL/PROC DEMAND OPTIMAL ATTIT PWR   NAT/G
SOCISM...POLICY CHARTS 20. PAGE 5 G0102   PLAN
   ECO/TAC

B64
MARRIS R.,THE ECONOMIC THEORY OF "MANAGERIAL"   CAP/ISM
CAPITALISM. USA+45 ECO/DEV LG/CO ECO/TAC DEMAND   MGT
...CHARTS BIBLIOG 20. PAGE 36 G0709   CONTROL
   OP/RES

B64
PARANJAPE H.K.,THE FLIGHT OF TECHNICAL PERSONNEL IN   ADMIN
PUBLIC UNDERTAKINGS. INDIA PAY DEMAND HAPPINESS   NAT/G
ORD/FREE...MGT QU 20 MIGRATION. PAGE 44 G0858   WORKER
   PLAN

B65
KANTOROVICH L.V.,THE BEST USE OF ECONOMIC   PLAN
RESOURCES. USSR SOCIETY FINAN ACT/RES TEC/DEV   MATH
ECO/TAC PRICE CONTROL COST DEMAND EFFICIENCY   DECISION
OPTIMAL...MGT STAT. PAGE 29 G0572

B65
KNORR K.,SCIENCE AND DEFENSE: SOME CRITICAL   CIVMIL/REL
THOUGHTS ON MILITARY RESEARCH AND DEVELOPMENT.   R+D
USA+45 ACT/RES CREATE BUDGET ECO/TAC DEMAND   FORCES
DECISION. PAGE 31 G0608   PLAN

B65
OECD,THE MEDITERRANEAN REGIONAL PROJECT: GREECE;   EDU/PROP
EDUCATION AND DEVELOPMENT. FUT GREECE SOCIETY AGRI   SCHOOL
FINAN NAT/G PROF/ORG WORKER PLAN PROB/SOLV ADMIN   ACADEM
DEMAND ATTIT 20 OECD. PAGE 42 G0834   ECO/UNDEV

B65
ORG FOR ECO COOP AND DEVEL,THE MEDITERRANEAN   EDU/PROP
REGIONAL PROJECT: YUGOSLAVIA; EDUCATION AND   ACADEM
DEVELOPMENT. YUGOSLAVIA SOCIETY FINAN PROF/ORG PLAN   SCHOOL
ADMIN COST DEMAND MARXISM...STAT TREND CHARTS METH   ECO/UNDEV
20 OECD. PAGE 43 G0843

B65
PHELPS E.S.,PRIVATE WANTS AND PUBLIC NEEDS - AN   NAT/G
INTRODUCTION TO A CURRENT ISSUE OF PUBLIC POLICY   POLICY
(REV. ED.). USA+45 PLAN CAP/ISM INGP/REL ROLE   DEMAND
...DECISION TIME/SEQ 20. PAGE 44 G0873

B67
BAUMOL W.J.,BUSINESS BEHAVIOR, VALUE AND GROWTH   ALL/IDEOS
(REV. ED.). WOR+45 FINAN LG/CO TEC/DEV CAP/ISM   PHIL/SCI
DEMAND EQUILIB...METH/COMP SIMUL 20. PAGE 5 G0105   PLAN
   ECO/DEV

B67
GROSSMAN G.,ECONOMIC SYSTEMS. USA+45 USA-45 USSR   ECO/DEV
YUGOSLAVIA WORKER CAP/ISM PRICE GP/REL EQUILIB   PLAN
WEALTH MARXISM SOCISM...MGT METH/COMP 19/20.   TEC/DEV
PAGE 23 G0456   DEMAND

B67
HIRSCHMAN A.O.,DEVELOPMENT PROJECTS OBSERVED. INDUS   ECO/UNDEV
INT/ORG CONSULT EX/STRUC CREATE OP/RES ECO/TAC   R+D
DEMAND...POLICY MGT METH/COMP 20 WORLD/BANK.   FINAN
PAGE 26 G0513   PLAN

B67
MACAVOY P.W.,REGULATION OF TRANSPORT INNOVATION.   DIST/IND
ACT/RES ADJUD COST DEMAND...POLICY CHARTS 20.   CONTROL
PAGE 35 G0684   PRICE
   PROFIT

B67
MOORE J.R.,THE ECONOMIC IMPACT OF THE TVA. AGRI   ECO/UNDEV

INDUS PLAN BARGAIN CONTROL REGION GOV/REL DEMAND   ECO/DEV
EFFICIENCY SOCISM 20 TVA. PAGE 40 G0780   NAT/G
   CREATE

B67
SCHON D.A.,TECHNOLOGY AND CHANGE* THE NEW   INDUS
HERACLITUS. TEC/DEV CONTROL COST DEMAND EFFICIENCY   PROB/SOLV
RIGID/FLEX...MYTH 20. PAGE 49 G0975   R+D
   CREATE

L67
PASLEY R.S.,"ORGANIZATIONAL CONFLICTS OF INTEREST   NAT/G
IN GOVERNMENT CONTRACTS." ELITES R+D ROUTINE   ECO/TAC
NUC/PWR DEMAND EFFICIENCY 20. PAGE 44 G0860   RATION
   CONTROL

L67
RUTH J.M.,"THE ADMINISTRATION OF WATER RESOURCES IN   EFFICIENCY
GUATEMALA." GUATEMALA L/A+17C DIST/IND LOC/G NAT/G   ECO/UNDEV
EX/STRUC ADMIN GOV/REL DEMAND EQUILIB WEALTH...GEOG   PLAN
MGT 20. PAGE 48 G0952   ACT/RES

S67
BRUNHILD G.,"THEORY OF 'TECHNICAL UNEMPLOYMENT'."   WORKER
ECO/DEV ACT/RES PROB/SOLV DEMAND PRODUC...PHIL/SCI   TEC/DEV
20. PAGE 9 G0182   SKILL
   INDUS

S67
MORTON J.A.,"A SYSTEMS APPROACH TO THE INNOVATION   TEC/DEV
PROCESS: ITS USE IN THE BELL SYSTEM." USA+45 INTELL   GEN/METH
INDUS LG/CO CONSULT WORKER COMPUTER AUTOMAT DEMAND   R+D
...MGT CHARTS 20. PAGE 40 G0787   COM/IND

N67
US CONGRESS JT COMM ECO GOVT,BACKGROUND MATERIAL ON   BUDGET
ECONOMY IN GOVERNMENT 1967 (PAMPHLET). WOR+45   COST
ECO/DEV BARGAIN PRICE DEMAND OPTIMAL...STAT   MGT
DEPT/DEFEN. PAGE 57 G1116   NAT/G

DEMOCRACY....SEE MAJORIT, REPRESENT, CHOOSE, PWR
   POPULISM, NEW/LIB

DEMOCRAT....DEMOCRATIC PARTY (ALL NATIONS)

DEMOGRAPHY....SEE GEOG

DENMARK....SEE ALSO APPROPRIATE TIME/SPACE/CULTURE INDEX

DENVER....DENVER, COLORADO

DEPARTMENT HEADS...SEE EX/STRUC, TOP/EX

DEPORT....DEPORTATION

DEPRESSION....ECONOMIC DEPRESSION

B57
DUPREE A.H.,SCIENCE IN THE FEDERAL GOVERNMENT: A   NAT/G
HISTORY OF POLICIES AND ACTIVITIES TO 1940. USA+45   R+D
AGRI SCHOOL DELIB/GP WAR GOV/REL...PHIL/SCI BIBLIOG   CREATE
18/20 DEPRESSION NEW/DEAL WWI JEFFERSN/T. PAGE 17   TEC/DEV
G0324

DEPT/AGRI....U.S. DEPARTMENT OF AGRICULTURE

DEPT/COM....U.S. DEPARTMENT OF COMMERCE

DEPT/DEFEN....U.S. DEPARTMENT OF DEFENSE

B55
US OFFICE OF THE PRESIDENT,REPORT TO CONGRESS ON   DIPLOM
THE MUTUAL SECURITY PROGRAM FOR THE SIX MONTHS   FORCES
ENDED JUNE 30, 1955. ECO/DEV INT/ORG NAT/G CREATE   PLAN
TEC/DEV BAL/PWR ECO/TAC AGREE DETER COST ORD/FREE   FOR/AID
20 DEPT/STATE DEPT/DEFEN. PAGE 59 G1157

B56
US OFFICE OF THE PRESIDENT,REPORT TO CONGRESS ON   DIPLOM
THE MUTUAL SECURITY PROGRAM FOR THE SIX MONTHS   FORCES
ENDED DECEMBER 31, 1955. ASIA USSR ECO/DEV   PLAN
ECO/UNDEV INT/ORG CREATE TEC/DEV BAL/PWR ECO/TAC   FOR/AID
AGREE DETER COST ORD/FREE 20 DEPT/STATE DEPT/DEFEN
EISNHWR/DD. PAGE 59 G1158

B59
VAN WAGENEN R.W.,SOME VIEWS OF AMERICAN DEFENSE   INT/ORG
OFFICIALS ABOUT THE UNITED NATIONS (PAPER). FUT   LEAD
USA+45 NAT/G DIPLOM WAR EFFICIENCY PEACE...POLICY   ATTIT
INT 20 UN DEPT/DEFEN. PAGE 61 G1192   FORCES

B60
CARPER E.T.,THE DEFENSE APPROPRIATIONS RIDER   GOV/REL
(PAMPHLET). USA+45 CONSTN CHIEF DELIB/GP LEGIS   ADJUD
BUDGET LOBBY CIVMIL/REL...POLICY 20 CONGRESS   LAW
EISNHWR/DD DEPT/DEFEN PRESIDENT BOSTON. PAGE 11   CONTROL

G0212

B60
WEBSTER J.A.,A GENERAL STUDY OF THE DEPARTMENT OF   ORD/FREE
DEFENSE INTERNAL SECURITY PROGRAM. USA+45 WORKER   PLAN
TEC/DEV ADJUD CONTROL CT/SYS EXEC GOV/REL COST   ADMIN
...POLICY DECISION MGT 20 DEPT/DEFEN SUPREME/CT.   NAT/G
PAGE 62 G1221

B61
HELLER D.,THE KENNEDY CABINET--AMERICA'S MEN OF   EX/STRUC
DESTINY. NAT/G CHIEF CONSULT ADMIN CONTROL GOV/REL   CONFER
...MGT 20 DEPT/LABOR DEPT/STATE DEPT/JUST   DELIB/GP
DEPT/DEFEN KENNEDY/J. PAGE 26 G0504   TOP/EX

S63
ENTHOVEN A.C.,"ECONOMIC ANALYSIS IN THE DEPARTMENT   PLAN
OF DEFENSE." USA+45 NAT/G DELIB/GP PROB/SOLV RATION   BUDGET
NUC/PWR WEAPON COST...DECISION 20 DEPT/DEFEN   ECO/TAC
RESOURCE/N. PAGE 18 G0349   FORCES

B64
DUSCHA J.,ARMS, MONEY, AND POLITICS. USA+45 INDUS   NAT/G
POL/PAR ECO/TAC TAX DETER NUC/PWR WAR WEAPON   FORCES
GOV/REL ATTIT...BIBLIOG/A 20 CONGRESS MONEY   POLICY
DEPT/DEFEN. PAGE 17 G0326   BUDGET

B64
KAUFMANN W.W.,THE MC NAMARA STRATEGY. TOP/EX   FORCES
INSPECT BAL/PWR DIPLOM CONTROL DETER GUERRILLA   WAR
NUC/PWR WEAPON COST PWR...METH/COMP 20 MCNAMARA/R   PLAN
KENNEDY/JF JOHNSON/LB NATO DEPT/DEFEN. PAGE 30   PROB/SOLV
G0586

B65
THAYER F.C. JR.,AIR TRANSPORT POLICY AND NATIONAL   AIR
SECURITY: A POLITICAL, ECONOMIC, AND MILITARY   FORCES
ANALYSIS. DIST/IND OP/RES PLAN TEC/DEV DIPLOM DETER   CIVMIL/REL
WAR COST EFFICIENCY...POLICY BIBLIOG 20 DEPT/DEFEN   ORD/FREE
FAA CAB. PAGE 54 G1066

B65
US SENATE COMM AERO SPACE SCI,NATIONAL SPACE GOALS   SPACE
FOR THE POST-APOLLO PERIOD. USA+45 CONSULT DELIB/GP   FUT
TEC/DEV BUDGET GP/REL ATTIT...CHARTS IDEA/COMP TIME   R+D
20 DEPT/DEFEN NASA CONGRESS. PAGE 59 G1166   LEGIS

B66
STONE J.J.,CONTAINING THE ARMS RACE* SOME SPECIFIC   ARMS/CONT
PROPOSALS. ASIA USA+45 USSR PROB/SOLV BARGAIN   FEEDBACK
DIPLOM DETER NUC/PWR RATIONAL...GAME 20 DEPT/DEFEN   COST
TREATY. PAGE 53 G1038   ATTIT

B67
ENKE S.,DEFENSE MANAGEMENT. USA+45 R+D FORCES   DECISION
WORKER PLAN ECO/TAC ADMIN NUC/PWR BAL/PAY UTIL   DELIB/GP
WEALTH...MGT DEPT/DEFEN. PAGE 18 G0348   EFFICIENCY
                                                       BUDGET

B67
US SENATE COMM AERO SPACE SCI,TREATY ON PRINCIPLES   SPACE
GOVERNING ACTIVITIES OF STATES IN EXPLORATION AND   INT/LAW
USE OF OUTER SPACE, INCLUDING...BODIES. DELIB/GP   ORD/FREE
FORCES LEGIS DIPLOM...JURID 20 DEPT/STATE NASA   PEACE
DEPT/DEFEN UN. PAGE 60 G1170

N67
US CONGRESS JT COMM ECO GOVT,BACKGROUND MATERIAL ON   BUDGET
ECONOMY IN GOVERNMENT 1967 (PAMPHLET). WOR+45   COST
ECO/DEV BARGAIN PRICE DEMAND OPTIMAL...STAT   MGT
DEPT/DEFEN. PAGE 57 G1116   NAT/G

N67
US HOUSE COMM APPROPRIATIONS,PUBLIC WORKS AND   BUDGET
ATOMIC ENERGY COMMISSION APPROPRIATION BILL, 1968   NUC/PWR
(PAMPHLET). USA+45 ECO/DEV NAT/G...GEOG DEEP/INT   PROVS
CHARTS HOUSE/REP AEC DEPT/DEFEN TVA. PAGE 58 G1137   PLAN

N67
US SENATE,STATUS OF THE DEVELOPMENT OF THE ANTI-   FORCES
BALLISTIC MISSILE SYSTEMS IN THE UNITED STATES   NUC/PWR
(PAMPHLET). FUT USA+45 R+D PLAN TEC/DEV DEPT/DEFEN.   WAR
PAGE 59 G1165   UTIL

N67
US SENATE COMM AERO SPACE SCI,AERONAUTICAL RESEARCH   DIST/IND
AND DEVELOPMENT POLICY; HEARINGS, COMM ON   SPACE
AERONAUTICAL AND SPACE SCIENCES...1967 (PAMPHLET).   NAT/G
R+D PROB/SOLV EXEC GOV/REL 20 DEPT/DEFEN FAA NASA   PLAN
CONGRESS. PAGE 60 G1174

DEPT/HEW....U.S. DEPARTMENT OF HEALTH, EDUCATION,
   AND WELFARE

B63
DEAN A.L.,FEDERAL AGENCY APPROACHES TO FIELD   ADMIN

MANAGEMENT (PAMPHLET). R+D DELIB/GP EX/STRUC   MGT
PROB/SOLV GOV/REL...CLASSIF BIBLIOG 20 FAA NASA   NAT/G
DEPT/HEW POSTAL/SYS IRS. PAGE 15 G0287   OP/RES

DEPT/HUD....U.S. DEPARTMENT OF HOUSING AND URBAN DEVELOPMENT

DEPT/INTER....U.S. DEPARTMENT OF THE INTERIOR

DEPT/JUST....U.S. DEPARTMENT OF JUSTICE

B61
HELLER D.,THE KENNEDY CABINET--AMERICA'S MEN OF   EX/STRUC
DESTINY. NAT/G CHIEF CONSULT ADMIN CONTROL GOV/REL   CONFER
...MGT 20 DEPT/LABOR DEPT/STATE DEPT/JUST   DELIB/GP
DEPT/DEFEN KENNEDY/J. PAGE 26 G0504   TOP/EX

DEPT/LABOR....U.S. DEPARTMENT OF LABOR AND INDUSTRY

B61
HELLER D.,THE KENNEDY CABINET--AMERICA'S MEN OF   EX/STRUC
DESTINY. NAT/G CHIEF CONSULT ADMIN CONTROL GOV/REL   CONFER
...MGT 20 DEPT/LABOR DEPT/STATE DEPT/JUST   DELIB/GP
DEPT/DEFEN KENNEDY/J. PAGE 26 G0504   TOP/EX

DEPT/STATE....U.S. DEPARTMENT OF STATE

B48
CHILDS J.R.,AMERICAN FOREIGN SERVICE. USA+45   DIPLOM
SOCIETY NAT/G ROUTINE GOV/REL 20 DEPT/STATE   ADMIN
CIVIL/SERV. PAGE 12 G0227   GP/REL

B50
KOENIG L.W.,THE SALE OF THE TANKERS. USA+45 SEA   NAT/G
DIST/IND POL/PAR DIPLOM ADMIN CIVMIL/REL ATTIT   POLICY
...DECISION 20 PRESIDENT DEPT/STATE. PAGE 31 G0609   PLAN
                                                       GOV/REL

B54
US DEPARTMENT OF STATE,PUBLICATIONS OF THE   BIBLIOG
DEPARTMENT OF STATE, OCTOBER 1,1929 TO JANUARY 1,   DIPLOM
1953. AGRI INT/ORG FORCES FOR/AID EDU/PROP
ARMS/CONT NUC/PWR ATTIT 20 DEPT/STATE OAS UN NATO.
PAGE 57 G1122

B55
US OFFICE OF THE PRESIDENT,REPORT TO CONGRESS ON   DIPLOM
THE MUTUAL SECURITY PROGRAM FOR THE SIX MONTHS   FORCES
ENDED JUNE 30, 1955. ECO/DEV INT/ORG NAT/G CREATE   PLAN
TEC/DEV BAL/PWR ECO/TAC AGREE DETER COST ORD/FREE   FOR/AID
20 DEPT/STATE DEPT/DEFEN. PAGE 59 G1157

B56
US OFFICE OF THE PRESIDENT,REPORT TO CONGRESS ON   DIPLOM
THE MUTUAL SECURITY PROGRAM FOR THE SIX MONTHS   FORCES
ENDED DECEMBER 31, 1955. ASIA USSR ECO/DEV   PLAN
ECO/UNDEV INT/ORG CREATE TEC/DEV BAL/PWR ECO/TAC   FOR/AID
AGREE DETER COST ORD/FREE 20 DEPT/STATE DEPT/DEFEN
EISNHWR/DD. PAGE 59 G1158

B58
US DEPARTMENT OF STATE,PUBLICATIONS OF THE   BIBLIOG
DEPARTMENT OF STATE, JANUARY 1,1953 TO DECEMBER 31,   DIPLOM
1957. AGRI INT/ORG FORCES FOR/AID EDU/PROP
ARMS/CONT NUC/PWR ATTIT 20 DEPT/STATE OAS UN NATO.
PAGE 57 G1123

B61
HELLER D.,THE KENNEDY CABINET--AMERICA'S MEN OF   EX/STRUC
DESTINY. NAT/G CHIEF CONSULT ADMIN CONTROL GOV/REL   CONFER
...MGT 20 DEPT/LABOR DEPT/STATE DEPT/JUST   DELIB/GP
DEPT/DEFEN KENNEDY/J. PAGE 26 G0504   TOP/EX

B67
SKOLNIKOFF E.B.,SCIENCE, TECHNOLOGY, AND AMERICAN   PHIL/SCI
FOREIGN POLICY. SPACE USA+45 INT/ORG TEC/DEV   DIPLOM
ARMS/CONT NUC/PWR 29 DEPT/STATE. PAGE 51 G1010   NAT/G
                                                       EFFICIENCY

B67
US SENATE COMM AERO SPACE SCI,TREATY ON PRINCIPLES   SPACE
GOVERNING ACTIVITIES OF STATES IN EXPLORATION AND   INT/LAW
USE OF OUTER SPACE, INCLUDING...BODIES. DELIB/GP   ORD/FREE
FORCES LEGIS DIPLOM...JURID 20 DEPT/STATE NASA   PEACE
DEPT/DEFEN UN. PAGE 60 G1170

DEPT/TREAS....U.S. DEPARTMENT OF THE TREASURY

DESAI M.J. G0294

DESCARTE/R....RENE DESCARTES

B61
MCRAE R.,THE PROBLEM OF THE UNITY OF THE SCIENCES: PHIL/SCI
BACON TO KANT. CREATE TASK KNOWL...PERS/COMP 16/18   IDEA/COMP
BACON/F DESCARTE/R LEIBNITZ/G KANT/I DIDEROT/D.   PERSON
PAGE 38 G0748

DESEGREGATION....SEE NEGRO, SOUTH/US, RACE/REL, SOC/INTEG,
    CIV/RIGHTS, DISCRIM, MISCEGEN, ISOLAT, SCHOOL, STRANGE

DESSALIN/J....JEAN-JACQUES DESSALINES

DESTALIN....DE-STALINIZATION

DETER....DETERRENCE; SEE ALSO PWR, PLAN

MEZERIK A.G.,ATOM TESTS AND RADIATION HAZARDS   N19
(PAMPHLET). WOR+45 INT/ORG DIPLOM DETER 20 UN   NUC/PWR
TREATY. PAGE 39 G0761   ARMS/CONT
                                                    CONFER
                                                    HEALTH

MEZERIK AG,OUTER SPACE: UN, US, USSR (PAMPHLET).   N19
USSR DELIB/GP FORCES DETER NUC/PWR SOVEREIGN   SPACE
...POLICY 20 UN TREATY. PAGE 39 G0763   CONTROL
                                                    DIPLOM
                                                    INT/ORG

MASTERS D.,"ONE WORLD OR NONE." FUT WOR+45 INTELL   L46
INT/ORG ACT/RES EDU/PROP DETER ATTIT RIGID/FLEX   POLICY
SUPEGO KNOWL...STAT TREND ORG/CHARTS 20. PAGE 36   PHIL/SCI
G0719   ARMS/CONT
                                                    NUC/PWR

BRADLEY D.,NO PLACE TO HIDE. USA+45 SOCIETY NAT/G   B48
FORCES TEC/DEV EDU/PROP DETER PEACE BIO/SOC   R+D
ALL/VALS...POLICY PHIL/SCI OBS RECORD SAMP BIOG   LAB/EXP
GEN/METH COLD/WAR 20. PAGE 8 G0162   ARMS/CONT
                                                    NUC/PWR

SOUERS S.W.,"POLICY FORMULATION FOR NATIONAL   S49
SECURITY." EX/STRUC FORCES PROB/SOLV DIPLOM CONFER DELIB/GP
EXEC ARMS/CONT DETER NUC/PWR GOV/REL PEACE   CHIEF
COLD/WAR. PAGE 52 G1022   DECISION
                                                    POLICY

ARON R.,CENTURY OF TOTAL WAR. FUT WOR+45 WOR-45   B54
SOCIETY INT/ORG NAT/G FORCES TOP/EX CREATE BAL/PWR ATTIT
DOMIN EDU/PROP COERCE DETER PEACE TOTALISM PWR   WAR
...TIME/SEQ TREND COLD/WAR TOT/POP VAL/FREE
LEAGUE/NAT 20. PAGE 4 G0066

DAVIS E.,TWO MINUTES TO MIDNIGHT. WOR+45 PLAN   B55
CONTROL NEUTRAL ARMS/CONT ATTIT ORD/FREE...PSY 20   NUC/PWR
COLD/WAR. PAGE 14 G0277   WAR
                                                    DETER
                                                    DIPLOM

MIKSCHE F.O.,ATOMIC WEAPONS AND ARMIES. FUT WOR+45   B55
WOR-45 SOCIETY COERCE DETER WEAPON PWR...POLICY   TEC/DEV
WELF/ST PSY CONCPT INT SYS/QU KNO/TEST TOT/POP 20. FORCES
PAGE 39 G0765   NUC/PWR

OPPENHEIMER R.,THE OPEN MIND. USA+45 WOR+45 NAT/G   B55
DELIB/GP DETER MORAL ORD/FREE...MYTH GEN/LAWS 20.   CREATE
PAGE 43 G0842   PWR
                                                    ARMS/CONT
                                                    NUC/PWR

US OFFICE OF THE PRESIDENT,REPORT TO CONGRESS ON   B55
THE MUTUAL SECURITY PROGRAM FOR THE SIX MONTHS   DIPLOM
ENDED JUNE 30, 1955. ECO/DEV INT/ORG NAT/G CREATE   FORCES
TEC/DEV BAL/PWR ECO/TAC AGREE DETER COST ORD/FREE   PLAN
20 DEPT/STATE DEPT/DEFEN. PAGE 59 G1157   FOR/AID

ESTEP R.,AN AIR POWER BIBLIOGRAPHY. USA+45 TEC/DEV   B56
BUDGET DIPLOM EDU/PROP DETER CIVMIL/REL...DECISION BIBLIOG/A
INT/LAW 20. PAGE 18 G0351   FORCES
                                                    WEAPON
                                                    PLAN

US DEPARTMENT OF THE ARMY,RESEARCH AND DEVELOPMENT   B56
(AND RELATED ASPECTS) IN FOREIGN COUNTRIES. WOR+45 BIBLIOG/A
DIST/IND INDUS CONSULT FORCES CREATE EDU/PROP   R+D
AUTOMAT DETER WEAPON. PAGE 57 G1126   TEC/DEV
                                                    NUC/PWR

US OFFICE OF THE PRESIDENT,REPORT TO CONGRESS ON   B56
THE MUTUAL SECURITY PROGRAM FOR THE SIX MONTHS   DIPLOM
ENDED DECEMBER 31, 1955. ASIA USSR ECO/DEV   FORCES
ECO/UNDEV INT/ORG CREATE TEC/DEV BAL/PWR ECO/TAC   PLAN
AGREE DETER COST ORD/FREE 20 DEPT/STATE DEPT/DEFEN FOR/AID
EISNHWR/DD. PAGE 59 G1158

KISSINGER H.A.,NUCLEAR WEAPONS AND FOREIGN POLICY.   B57
FUT USA+45 WOR+45 INT/ORG FORCES ACT/RES TEC/DEV   PLAN
DIPLOM ARMS/CONT COERCE ATTIT KNOWL PWR...DECISION DETER
GEOG CHARTS 20. PAGE 31 G0602   NUC/PWR

GAVIN J.M.,WAR AND PEACE IN THE SPACE AGE. SPACE   B58
USA+45 USSR FORCES PLAN TEC/DEV BAL/PWR DIPLOM   WAR
ARMS/CONT WEAPON CIVMIL/REL...CHARTS GP/COMP 20   DETER
NATO COLD/WAR. PAGE 21 G0414   NUC/PWR
                                                    PEACE

NATIONAL PLANNING ASSOCIATION,1970 WITHOUT ARMS   B58
CONTROL (PAMPHLET). WOR+45 PROB/SOLV TEC/DEV DIPLOM ARMS/CONT
CONFER DETER NUC/PWR WAR...CHARTS 20 COLD/WAR.   ORD/FREE
PAGE 41 G0810   WEAPON
                                                    PREDICT

ROCKEFELLER BROTH FUND INC,INTERNATIONAL SECURITY -   B58
THE MILITARY ASPECT. USA+45 INT/ORG NAT/G BUDGET   NUC/PWR
ARMS/CONT WAR WEAPON PEACE ORD/FREE 20 NATO.   DETER
PAGE 47 G0932   FORCES
                                                    DIPLOM

US DEPARTMENT OF THE ARMY,BIBLIOGRAPHY ON LIMITED   B58
WAR (PAMPHLET). USA+45 TEC/DEV CONTROL RISK COERCE BIBLIOG/A
DETER NUC/PWR WEAPON ADJUST PEACE ALL/VALS ORD/FREE WAR
20. PAGE 57 G1127   FORCES
                                                    CIVMIL/REL

HUNTINGTON S.P.,"ARMS RACES: PREREQUISITES AND   S58
RESULTS." EUR+WWI MOD/EUR USA+45 WOR+45 WOR-45   FORCES
NAT/G TEC/DEV BAL/PWR COERCE DETER ATTIT...POLICY   PWR
TREND 20. PAGE 27 G0537   ARMS/CONT

LASSWELL H.D.,"THE SCIENTIFIC STUDY OF   S58
INTERNATIONAL RELATIONS." USA+45 INT/ORG CREATE   PHIL/SCI
EDU/PROP DETER ATTIT PERCEPT PWR...DECISION CONCPT GEN/METH
METH/CNCPT STYLE CON/ANAL 20. PAGE 33 G0642   DIPLOM

SINGER J.D.,"THREAT PERCEPTION AND THE ARMAMENT   S58
TENSION DILEMMA." WOR+45 WOR-45 ELITES INT/ORG   PERCEPT
NAT/G DELIB/GP PLAN LEGIT COERCE DETER ATTIT   ARMS/CONT
RIGID/FLEX PWR...DECISION PSY 20. PAGE 51 G1002   BAL/PWR

AIR FORCE ACADEMY ASSEMBLY '59,INTERNATIONAL   B59
STABILITY AND PROGRESS (PAMPHLET). USA+45 USSR   FOR/AID
ECO/UNDEV PROB/SOLV BUDGET DIPLOM ADMIN DETER COST FORCES
ATTIT...TREND 20. PAGE 2 G0030   WAR
                                                    PLAN

EMME E.M.,THE IMPACT OF AIR POWER - NATIONAL   B59
SECURITY AND WORLD POLITICS. USA+45 USSR FORCES   DETER
DIPLOM WEAPON PEACE TOTALISM...POLICY NAT/COMP 20   AIR
EUROPE. PAGE 18 G0346   WAR
                                                    ORD/FREE

POKROVSKY G.I.,SCIENCE AND TECHNOLOGY IN   B59
CONTEMPORARY WAR. SPACE USSR WOR+45 NAT/G CONSULT   TEC/DEV
ACT/RES PLAN DETER WEAPON...MARXIST METH/CNCPT   FORCES
CHARTS STERTYP COLD/WAR 20. PAGE 45 G0881   NUC/PWR
                                                    WAR

BURNS A.L.,"POWER POLITICS AND THE GROWING NUCLEAR   L59
CLUB." FUT WOR+45 TEC/DEV EXEC ARMS/CONT COERCE   FORCES
DETER...DECISION HYPO/EXP 20. PAGE 10 G0192   BAL/PWR
                                                    NUC/PWR

MILBURN T.W.,"WHAT CONSTITUTES EFFECTIVE   S59
DETERRENCE." USA+45 USSR WOR+45 STRUCT FORCES   INTELL
ACT/RES PLAN SUPEGO KNOWL ORD/FREE PWR...RELATIV   ATTIT
PSY CONCPT VAL/FREE 20 COLD/WAR. PAGE 39 G0768   DETER
                                                    NUC/PWR

BARNET R.,WHO WANTS DISARMAMENT. COM EUR+WWI USA+45   B60
USSR INT/ORG NAT/G BAL/PWR DIPLOM EDU/PROP COERCE   PLAN
DETER NUC/PWR WAR WEAPON ATTIT PWR...TIME/SEQ   FORCES
COLD/WAR CONGRESS 20. PAGE 5 G0096   ARMS/CONT

EINSTEIN A.,EINSTEIN ON PEACE. FUT WOR+45 WOR-45   B60
SOCIETY NAT/G PLAN BAL/PWR CAP/ISM DIPLOM ARMS/CONT INT/ORG
DETER NAT/LISM...POLICY RELATIV HUM PHIL/SCI CONCPT ATTIT
BIOG COLD/WAR LEAGUE/NAT NAZI. PAGE 17 G0338   NUC/PWR
                                                    PEACE

LE GHAIT E.,NO CARTE BLANCHE TO CAPRICORN; THE   B60
FOLLY OF NUCLEAR WAR. WOR+45 INT/ORG BAL/PWR DIPLOM DETER
RISK COERCE...CENSUS 20 NATO. PAGE 33 G0647   NUC/PWR
                                                    PLAN
                                                    DECISION

MCCLELLAND C.A.,NUCLEAR WEAPONS, MISSILES, AND   B60
FUTURE WAR: PROBLEM FOR THE SIXTIES. WOR+45 FORCES DIPLOM
ARMS/CONT DETER MARXISM...POLICY ANTHOL COLD/WAR.   NUC/PWR
PAGE 37 G0729   WAR
                                                    WEAPON

US DEPARTMENT OF THE ARMY.DISARMAMENT: A
BIBLIOGRAPHIC RECORD: 1916-1960. DETER WAR WEAPON
PEACE 20 UN LEAGUE/NAT COLD/WAR NATO. PAGE 57 G1128
B60 BIBLIOG/A ARMS/CONT NUC/PWR DIPLOM

BRENNAN D.G.,"SETTING AND GOALS OF ARMS CONTROL."
FUT USA+45 USSR WOR+45 INTELL INT/ORG NAT/G
VOL/ASSN CONSULT PLAN DIPLOM ECO/TAC ADMIN KNOWL
PWR...POLICY CONCPT TREND COLD/WAR 20. PAGE 8 G0164
L60 FORCES COERCE ARMS/CONT DETER

JACOB P.E.,"THE DISARMAMENT CONSENSUS." USA+45 USSR
WOR+45 INT/ORG NAT/G ACT/RES TEC/DEV ATTIT
EDU/PROP ADMIN COERCE DETER NUC/PWR CONSEN
RIGID/FLEX PWR...CONCPT RECORD CHARTS COLD/WAR 20.
PAGE 28 G0552
L60 DELIB/GP ATTIT ARMS/CONT

BRODY R.A.,"DETERRENCE STRATEGIES: AN ANNOTATED
BIBLIOGRAPHY." WOR+45 PLAN ARMS/CONT NUC/PWR WAR
WEAPON DECISION. PAGE 9 G0173
S60 BIBLIOG/A FORCES DETER DIPLOM

DOUGHERTY J.E.,"KEY TO SECURITY: DISARMAMENT OR
ARMS STABILITY." COM USA+45 USSR INT/ORG NAT/G
CREATE EDU/PROP COERCE DETER ATTIT PWR...DECISION
CONCPT MYTH NEW/IDEA TREND 20 COLD/WAR. PAGE 16
G0311
S60 FORCES ORD/FREE ARMS/CONT NUC/PWR

DYSON F.J.,"THE FUTURE DEVELOPMENT OF NUCLEAR
WEAPONS." FUT WOR+45 DELIB/GP ACT/RES PLAN DETER
WEAPON ATTIT PWR...POLICY 20. PAGE 17 G0328
S60 INT/ORG ARMS/CONT NUC/PWR

KISSINGER H.A.,"ARMS CONTROL, INSPECTION AND
SURPRISE ATTACK." COM USA+45 NAT/G ACT/RES PLAN
TEC/DEV DIPLOM EDU/PROP DETER WAR RIGID/FLEX
...CONCPT GEN/METH TOT/POP 20. PAGE 31 G0603
S60 FORCES ORD/FREE ARMS/CONT NUC/PWR

HADLEY A.T.,THE NATIONS SAFETY AND ARMS CONTROL.
FUT USA+45 WOR+45 TOP/EX PLAN TEC/DEV ATTIT DRIVE
...CONCPT OBS TIME/SEQ TREND 20. PAGE 24 G0466
B61 ACT/RES ROUTINE DETER NUC/PWR

HENKIN L.,ARMS CONTROL: ISSUES FOR THE PUBLIC.
EUR+WWI FUT USA+45 USSR INT/ORG NAT/G DIPLOM
EDU/PROP DETER NUC/PWR ATTIT PWR...CONCPT RECORD
HIST/WRIT TIME/SEQ TOT/POP COLD/WAR 20. PAGE 26
G0506
B61 WOR+45 DELIB/GP ARMS/CONT

KAHN H.,ON THERMONUCLEAR WAR. FUT UNIV WOR+45
ECO/DEV CONSULT EX/STRUC TOP/EX ACT/RES CREATE PLAN
COERCE WAR PERSON ALL/VALS...POLICY GEOG CONCPT
METH/CNCPT OBS TREND 20. PAGE 29 G0569
B61 DETER NUC/PWR SOCIETY

KISSINGER H.A.,THE NECESSITY FOR CHOICE. FUT USA+45
ECO/UNDEV NAT/G PLAN BAL/PWR ECO/TAC ARMS/CONT
DETER NUC/PWR ATTIT...POLICY CONCPT RECORD GEN/LAWS
COLD/WAR 20. PAGE 31 G0604
B61 TOP/EX TREND DIPLOM

SCHMIDT H.,VERTEIDIGUNG ODER VERGELTUNG. COM CUBA
GERMANY/W USSR FORCES DIPLOM ARMS/CONT DETER
NUC/PWR...POLICY CHARTS HYPO/EXP SIMUL BIBLIOG 20
NATO COLD/WAR. PAGE 49 G0970
B61 PLAN WAR BAL/PWR ORD/FREE

STEIN W.,NUCLEAR WEAPONS: A CATHOLIC RESPONSE.
WOR+45 FORCES ARMS/CONT DETER MURDER MORAL...POLICY
CATH IDEA/COMP ANTHOL 20. PAGE 52 G1033
B61 NUC/PWR WAR CATHISM ATTIT

US SENATE COMM GOVT OPERATIONS.ORGANIZING FOR
NATIONAL SECURITY. COM USA+45 BUDGET DIPLOM DETER
NUC/PWR WAR WEAPON ORD/FREE...BIBLIOG 20 COLD/WAR.
PAGE 60 G1176
B61 POLICY PLAN FORCES COERCE

MACHOWSKI K.,"SELECTED PROBLEMS OF NATIONAL
SOVEREIGNTY WITH REFERENCE TO THE LAW OF OUTER
SPACE." FUT WOR+45 AIR LAW INTELL SOCIETY ECO/DEV
PLAN EDU/PROP DETER DRIVE PERCEPT SOVEREIGN
...POLICY INT/LAW OBS TREND TOT/POP 20. PAGE 35
G0689
S61 UNIV ACT/RES NUC/PWR SPACE

WOHLSTETTER A.,"NUCLEAR SHARING: NATO AND THE NTH
S61 TREND

COUNTRY." EUR+WWI FUT SOCIETY DIPLOM EXEC DETER PWR
SKILL...POLICY TECHNIC CONCPT 20 NATO. PAGE 64
G1252
S61 TEC/DEV NUC/PWR ARMS/CONT

AIR FORCE ACADEMY LIBRARY.INTERNATIONAL
ORGANIZATIONS AND MILITARY SECURITY SYSTEMS
(PAMPHLET) (SPECIAL BIBLIOGRAPHY SERIES, NUMBER
25). DIPLOM FOR/AID INT/TRADE NUC/PWR PEACE 20 UN
NATO OAS SEATO LEAGUE/NAT. PAGE 2 G0031
B62 BIBLIOG INT/ORG FORCES DETER

FRYKLUND R.,100 MILLION LIVES: MAXIMUM SURVIVAL IN
A NUCLEAR WAR. USA+45 USSR CONTROL WEAPON
...IDEA/COMP NAT/COMP 20. PAGE 20 G0397
B62 NUC/PWR WAR PLAN DETER

GILPIN R.,AMERICAN SCIENTISTS AND NUCLEAR WEAPONS
POLICY. COM FUT USA+45 WOR+45 INT/ORG NAT/G
PROF/ORG CONSULT FORCES CREATE TEC/DEV BAL/PWR
EDU/PROP ARMS/CONT WAR PERCEPT KNOWL MORAL PWR
...PHIL/SCI SOC CONCPT GEN/LAWS 20. PAGE 21 G0417
B62 INTELL ATTIT DETER NUC/PWR

KAHN H.,THINKING ABOUT THE UNTHINKABLE. FUT USA+45
LAW NAT/G CONSULT FORCES ACT/RES CREATE PLAN
TEC/DEV BAL/PWR DIPLOM EDU/PROP ARMS/CONT DETER
ATTIT...CONCPT OBS TREND COLD/WAR 20. PAGE 29 G0570
B62 INT/ORG ORD/FREE NUC/PWR PEACE

SINGER J.D.,DETERRENCE, ARMS CONTROL AND
DISARMAMENT: TOWARD A SYNTHESIS IN NATIONAL
SECURITY POLICY. COM USA+45 INT/ORG BAL/PWR DETER
ORD/FREE...POLICY COLD/WAR 20. PAGE 51 G1003
B62 FUT ACT/RES ARMS/CONT

BETTEN J.K.,"ARMS CONTROL AND THE PROBLEM OF
EVASION." WOR+45 FORCES CREATE DIPLOM DETER PWR
...PSY TREND GEN/LAWS COLD/WAR 20. PAGE 7 G0134
L62 NAT/G PLAN ARMS/CONT

FOSTER R.B.,"UNILATERAL ARMS CONTROL MEASURES AND
DISARMAMENT NEGOTIATION." WOR+45 VOL/ASSN DELIB/GP
ACT/RES ECO/TAC EDU/PROP ATTIT RIGID/FLEX...CONCPT
MYTH TIME/SEQ COLD/WAR 20. PAGE 20 G0386
S62 PLAN ORD/FREE ARMS/CONT DETER

PHIPPS T.E.,"THE CASE FOR DETERRENCE." FUT WOR+45
SOCIETY EX/STRUC FORCES ACT/RES CREATE PLAN TEC/DEV
ROUTINE RIGID/FLEX ORD/FREE...POLICY MYTH NEW/IDEA
STERTYP COLD/WAR 20. PAGE 45 G0876
S62 ATTIT COERCE DETER ARMS/CONT

SINGER J.D.,"STABLE DETERRENCE AND ITS LIMITS." FUT
WOR+45 R+D INT/ORG CONSULT ACT/RES TEC/DEV
ARMS/CONT COERCE DRIVE PERCEPT RIGID/FLEX ORD/FREE
PWR...MYTH SIMUL TOT/POP 20. PAGE 51 G1004
S62 NAT/G FORCES DETER NUC/PWR

KAST F.E.,SCIENCE, TECHNOLOGY, AND MANAGEMENT.
SPACE USA+45 FORCES CONFER DETER NUC/PWR...PHIL/SCI
CHARTS ANTHOL BIBLIOG 20 NASA. PAGE 30 G0581
B63 MGT PLAN TEC/DEV PROB/SOLV

LILIENTHAL D.E.,CHANGE, HOPE, AND THE BOMB. USA+45
WOR+45 R+D INT/ORG NAT/G DELIB/GP FORCES ACT/RES
DETER RIGID/FLEX ORD/FREE...POLICY CONCPT OBS AEC
20. PAGE 34 G0666
B63 ATTIT MYTH ARMS/CONT NUC/PWR

PACHTER H.M.,COLLISION COURSE; THE CUBAN MISSILE
CRISIS AND COEXISTENCE. CUBA USA+45 DIPLOM
ARMS/CONT PEACE MARXISM...DECISION INT/LAW 20
COLD/WAR KHRUSH/N KENNEDY/JF CASTRO/F. PAGE 43
G0854
B63 WAR BAL/PWR NUC/PWR DETER

PERLO V.,MILITARISM AND INDUSTRY. USA+45 INT/TRADE
EDU/PROP DETER KNOWL...CHARTS MAPS 20. PAGE 44
G0869
B63 CIVMIL/REL INDUS LOBBY ARMS/CONT

US DEPARTMENT OF THE ARMY.US OVERSEAS BASES:
PRESENT STATUS AND FUTURE PROSPECTS (PAMPHLET).
USA+45 DIPLOM NUC/PWR ATTIT ORD/FREE...POLICY
CHARTS 20. PAGE 58 G1130
B63 BIBLIOG/A WAR BAL/PWR DETER

BRENNAN D.G.,"ARMS CONTROL AND CIVIL DEFENSE."
USA+45 WOR+45 NAT/G BAL/PWR ROUTINE ATTIT
RIGID/FLEX ORD/FREE...SOC TOT/POP 20. PAGE 8 G0165
L63 PLAN HEALTH ARMS/CONT DETER

PHELPS J.,"STUDIES IN DETERRENCE VIII: MILITARY STABILITY AND ARMS CONTROL: A CRITICAL SURVEY." FUT WOR+45 INT/ORG ACT/RES EDU/PROP COERCE NUC/PWR WAR HEALTH PWR...POLICY TECHNIC TREND SIMUL TOT/POP 20. PAGE 44 G0874
L63
FORCES
ORD/FREE
ARMS/CONT
DETER

BOULDING K.E.,"UNIVERSITY, SOCIETY, AND ARMS CONTROL." WOR+45 WOR-45 ACADEM NAT/G CONSULT FORCES ACT/RES PLAN TEC/DEV BAL/PWR ECO/TAC COERCE DETER WAR ATTIT RIGID/FLEX KNOWL ORD/FREE PWR WEALTH ...CONCPT COLD/WAR TOT/POP 20. PAGE 8 G0159
S63
SOCIETY
ARMS/CONT

SMITH D.O.,"WHAT IS A WAR DETERRENT." FUT GERMANY HUNGARY UK USA+45 WOR+45 WOR-45 NAT/G TEC/DEV BAL/PWR PWR...CONCPT GEN/LAWS COLD/WAR 20. PAGE 51 G1013
S63
ACT/RES
FORCES
ARMS/CONT
DETER

DUSCHA J.,ARMS, MONEY, AND POLITICS. USA+45 INDUS POL/PAR ECO/TAC TAX DETER NUC/PWR WAR WEAPON GOV/REL ATTIT...BIBLIOG/A 20 CONGRESS MONEY DEPT/DEFEN. PAGE 17 G0326
B64
NAT/G
FORCES
POLICY
BUDGET

HEKHUIS D.J.,INTERNATIONAL STABILITY: MILITARY, ECONOMIC AND POLITICAL DIMENSIONS. FUT WOR+45 LAW ECO/UNDEV INT/ORG NAT/G VOL/ASSN FORCES ACT/RES BAL/PWR PWR WEALTH...STAT UN 20. PAGE 25 G0503
B64
TEC/DEV
DETER
REGION

KAUFMANN W.W.,THE MC NAMARA STRATEGY. TOP/EX INSPECT BAL/PWR DIPLOM CONTROL DETER GUERRILLA NUC/PWR WEAPON COST PWR...METH/COMP 20 MCNAMARA/R KENNEDY/JF JOHNSON/LB NATO DEPT/DEFEN. PAGE 30 G0586
B64
FORCES
WAR
PLAN
PROB/SOLV

ROSECRANCE R.N.,THE DISPERSION OF NUCLEAR WEAPONS: STRATEGY AND POLITICS. ASIA COM FUT S/ASIA USA+45 INT/ORG NAT/G DELIB/GP FORCES ACT/RES TEC/DEV BAL/PWR COERCE DETER ATTIT RIGID/FLEX ORD/FREE ...POLICY CHARTS VAL/FREE. PAGE 48 G0935
B64
EUR+WWI
PWR
PEACE

ROTHSCHILD J.H.,TOMORROW'S WEAPONS: CHEMICAL AND BIOLOGICAL. FUT PROB/SOLV ARMS/CONT PEACE MORAL ...CHARTS BIBLIOG 20. PAGE 48 G0941
B64
WAR
WEAPON
BIO/SOC
DETER

GOLDBERG A.,"ATOMIC ORIGINS OF THE BRITISH NUCLEAR DETERRENT." EUR+WWI UK NAT/G TOP/EX PLAN BAL/PWR DOMIN DETER CHOOSE ATTIT DRIVE HEALTH ORD/FREE PWR RESPECT...CONCPT VAL/FREE COLD/WAR 20 CMN/WLTH. PAGE 22 G0425
L64
CREATE
FORCES
NUC/PWR

LERNER A.P.,"NUCLEAR SYMMETRY AS A FRAMEWORK FOR COEXISTENCE." COM FUT USA+45 NAT/G ACT/RES CREATE PLAN EDU/PROP COERCE WAR RIGID/FLEX PWR SKILL...CONCPT METH/CNCPT GEN/LAWS TOT/POP VAL/FREE COLD/WAR 20. PAGE 33 G0657
S64
FORCES
ORD/FREE
DETER
NUC/PWR

NATIONAL ACADEMY OF SCIENCES,CIVIL DEFENSE: PROJECT HARBOR SUMMARY REPORT (PAMPHLET). USA+45 MUNIC NAT/G ACT/RES BUDGET EDU/PROP DETER WEAPON EATING ...GEOG 20. PAGE 41 G0808
N64
NUC/PWR
FORCES
WAR
PLAN

BEAUFRE A.,AN INTRODUCTION TO STRATEGY, WITH PARTICULAR REFERENCE TO PROBLEMS OF DEFENSE, POLITICS, ECONOMICS IN THE NUCLEAR AGE. WOR+45 FORCES DIPLOM DETER CIVMIL/REL GP/REL...NEW/IDEA IDEA/COMP 20. PAGE 6 G0111
B65
PLAN
NUC/PWR
WEAPON
DECISION

BLOOMFIELD L.,SOVIET INTERESTS IN ARMS CONTROL AND DISARMAMENT* THE DECADE UNDER KHRUSHCHEV 1954-1964. ASIA FORCES ACT/RES EDU/PROP DETER NUC/PWR WEAPON COST ATTIT...PHIL/SCI CLASSIF STAT NET/THEORY GAME BIBLIOG. PAGE 7 G0139
B65
USSR
ARMS/CONT
DIPLOM
TREND

BOBROW D.B.,COMPONENTS OF DEFENSE POLICY. ASIA EUR+WWI USA+45 WOR+45 INTELL INT/ORG NAT/G PROF/ORG CONSULT LEGIS ACT/RES CREATE ARMS/CONT COERCE ORD/FREE...DECISION SIMUL. PAGE 7 G0145
B65
DETER
NUC/PWR
PLAN
FORCES

GRETTON P.,MARITIME STRATEGY - A STUDY OF DEFENSE PROBLEMS. ASIA UK USSR DIPLOM COERCE DETER NUC/PWR WEAPON...CONCPT NAT/COMP 20. PAGE 23 G0449
B65
FORCES
PLAN
WAR

SEA

HALPERIN M.H.,CHINA AND THE BOMB. USA+45 USSR INT/ORG FORCES ARMS/CONT DETER PRODUC ORD/FREE PWR TREND. PAGE 24 G0472
B65
ASIA
NUC/PWR
WAR
DIPLOM

MCGUIRE M.C.,SECRECY AND THE ARMS RACE* A THEORY OF THE ACCUMULATION OF STRATEGIC WEAPONS AND HOW SECRECY AFFECTS IT. DIPLOM NUC/PWR WEAPON ISOLAT RATIONAL ORD/FREE WEALTH...ECOMETRIC MATH GEN/LAWS. PAGE 38 G0742
B65
DETER
ARMS/CONT
SIMUL
GAME

MOSKOWITZ H.,US SECURITY, ARMS CONTROL, AND DISARMAMENT 1961-1965. FORCES DIPLOM DETER WAR WEAPON...CHARTS 20 UN COLD/WAR NATO. PAGE 40 G0790
B65
BIBLIOG/A
ARMS/CONT
NUC/PWR
PEACE

THAYER F.C. JR.,AIR TRANSPORT POLICY AND NATIONAL SECURITY: A POLITICAL, ECONOMIC, AND MILITARY ANALYSIS. DIST/IND OP/RES PLAN TEC/DEV DIPLOM DETER WAR COST EFFICIENCY...POLICY BIBLIOG 20 DEPT/DEFEN FAA CAB. PAGE 54 G1066
B65
AIR
FORCES
CIVMIL/REL
ORD/FREE

US DEPARTMENT OF DEFENSE,US SECURITY ARMS CONTROL, AND DISARMAMENT 1961-1965 (PAMPHLET). CHINA/COM COM GERMANY/W ISRAEL SPACE USA+45 USSR WOR+45 FORCES EDU/PROP DETER EQUILIB PEACE ALL/VALS...GOV/COMP 20 NATO. PAGE 57 G1118
B65
BIBLIOG/A
ARMS/CONT
NUC/PWR
DIPLOM

BEAUFRE A.,"THE SHARING OF NUCLEAR RESPONSIBILITIES* A PROBLEM IN NEED OF SOLUTION." FRANCE USA+45 INT/ORG NAT/G DELIB/GP FORCES CONTROL NUC/PWR RIGID/FLEX...CONCPT IDEA/COMP NATO. PAGE 6 G0110
S65
DETER
RISK
ACT/RES
WAR

FINK C.F.,"MORE CALCULATIONS ABOUT DETERRENCE." DRIVE...PHIL/SCI PSY STAT TIME/SEQ GAME GEN/LAWS. PAGE 19 G0367
S65
DETER
RECORD
PROBABIL
IDEA/COMP

HSIEH A.L.,"THE SINO-SOVIET NUCLEAR DIALOGUE* 1963." S/ASIA USA+45 RISK DETER REV WAR SOVEREIGN IDEA/COMP. PAGE 27 G0533
S65
ASIA
USSR
NUC/PWR

KRICKUS R.J.,"ON THE MORALITY OF CHEMICAL/BIOLOGICAL WAR." ECO/UNDEV ARMS/CONT DETER NUC/PWR RIGID/FLEX HEALTH INT/LAW. PAGE 31 G0621
S65
MORAL
BIO/SOC
WEAPON
WAR

KUZMACK A.M.,"TECHNOLOGICAL CHANGE AND STABLE DETERRENCE." CREATE EDU/PROP ARMS/CONT WEAPON CHOOSE COST DRIVE PERCEPT...RECORD STERTYP TIME. PAGE 32 G0627
S65
R+D
DETER
EQUILIB

RASER J.R.,"WEAPONS DESIGN AND ARMS CONTROL* THE POLARIS EXAMPLE." DETER NUC/PWR WEAPON CHOOSE PERCEPT...STERTYP TIME. PAGE 46 G0904
S65
ARMS/CONT
R+D
GEOG
ACT/RES

SCHELLING T.C.,"SIGNALS AND FEEDBACK IN THE ARMS DIALOGUE." USA+45 USSR R+D ACADEM FORCES ACT/RES ADJUST COST GEN/LAWS. PAGE 49 G0964
S65
FEEDBACK
DETER
EDU/PROP
ARMS/CONT

US AIR FORCE ACADEMY,"AMERICAN DEFENSE POLICY." COM INT/ORG TEC/DEV FOR/AID ARMS/CONT DETER NUC/PWR ...POLICY DECISION CONCPT ANTHOL BIBLIOG/A 20 COLD/WAR NATO. PAGE 56 G1103
C65
PLAN
FORCES
WAR
COERCE

BOLTON R.E.,DEFENSE AND DISARMAMENT: THE ECONOMICS OF TRANSITION. USA+45 R+D FORCES PLAN LOBBY DETER WAR COST PEACE...ANTHOL BIBLIOG 20. PAGE 8 G0150
B66
ARMS/CONT
POLICY
INDUS

BRODIE B.,ESCALATION AND THE NUCLEAR OPTION. ASIA CUBA EUR+WWI KOREA USA+45 USSR VIETNAM RISK ATTIT DRIVE PERCEPT PROBABIL. PAGE 9 G0172
B66
NUC/PWR
GUERRILLA
WAR
DETER

DAENIKER G.,STRATEGIE DES KLEIN STAATS. SWITZERLND
B66
NUC/PWR

ACT/RES CREATE DIPLOM NEUTRAL DETER WAR WEAPON PWR
SOVEREIGN...IDEA/COMP 20 COLD/WAR. PAGE 14 G0270
PLAN
FORCES
NAT/G

B66
GREEN P.,DEADLY LOGIC* THE THEORY OF NUCLEAR
DETERRENCE. USA+45 ACT/RES OP/RES NUC/PWR RATIONAL
ALL/VALS PWR...DECISION MGT PHIL/SCI QUANT
IDEA/COMP GAME. PAGE 23 G0444
DETER
ACADEM
GEN/LAWS
RECORD

B66
JACOBSON H.K.,DIPLOMATS, SCIENTISTS, AND
POLITICIANS* THE UNITED STATES AND THE NUCLEAR TEST
BAN NEGOTIATIONS. USA+45 USSR ACT/RES PLAN CONFER
DETER NUC/PWR CONSEN ORD/FREE...INT TREATY. PAGE 28
G0554
DIPLOM
ARMS/CONT
TECHRACY
INT/ORG

B66
KUENNE R.E.,THE POLARIS MISSILE STRIKE* A GENERAL
ECONOMIC SYSTEMS ANALYSIS. USA+45 USSR NAT/G
BAL/PWR ARMS/CONT WAR...MATH PROBABIL COMPUT/IR
CHARTS HYPO/EXP SIMUL. PAGE 32 G0625
NUC/PWR
FORCES
DETER
DIPLOM

B66
STONE J.J.,CONTAINING THE ARMS RACE* SOME SPECIFIC
PROPOSALS. ASIA USA+45 USSR PROB/SOLV BARGAIN
DIPLOM DETER NUC/PWR RATIONAL...GAME 20 DEPT/DEFEN
TREATY. PAGE 53 G1038
ARMS/CONT
FEEDBACK
COST
ATTIT

B66
WOLFERS A.,THE UNITED STATES IN A DISARMED WORLD: A
STUDY OF THE US OUTLINE FOR GENERAL AND COMPLETE
DISARMAMENT. USA+45 NAT/G CONTROL DETER NUC/PWR
EFFICIENCY...ANTHOL 20. PAGE 64 G1255
ARMS/CONT
POLICY
FORCES
PEACE

L66
DOUGHERTY J.E.,"THE CATHOLIC CHURCH, WAR AND
NUCLEAR WEAPONS." COM EUR+WWI SECT TOP/EX LEAD
DETER ALL/VALS. PAGE 16 G0312
CATHISM
MORAL
WAR
NUC/PWR

L66
RASER J.R.,"DETERRENCE RESEARCH* PAST PROGRESS AND
FUTURE NEEDS." INTELL PLAN TEC/DEV NUC/PWR PERCEPT
...DECISION PSY SOC NET/THEORY. PAGE 46 G0905
DETER
BIBLIOG/A
FUT

L66
ZOPPO C.E.,"NUCLEAR TECHNOLOGY, MULTIPOLARITY, AND
INTERNATIONAL STABILITY." ASIA RUSSIA USA+45 STRUCT
TOP/EX BAL/PWR DIPLOM DETER CIVMIL/REL NAT/COMP.
PAGE 65 G1270
NET/THEORY
ORD/FREE
DECISION
NUC/PWR

B67
AMERICAN FRIENDS SERVICE COMM,IN PLACE OF WAR.
NAT/G ACT/RES DIPLOM ADMIN NUC/PWR EFFICIENCY
...POLICY 20. PAGE 3 G0053
PEACE
PACIFISM
WAR
DETER

B67
ARON R.,THE GREAT DEBATE: THEORIES OF NUCLEAR
STRATEGY. FRANCE USA+45 INT/ORG PLAN TREND. PAGE 4
G0068
NUC/PWR
DETER
BAL/PWR
DIPLOM

B67
BURNS E.L.M.,MEGAMURDER. WOR+45 LAW INT/ORG NAT/G
BAL/PWR DIPLOM DETER MURDER WEAPON CIVMIL/REL PEACE
...INT/LAW TREND 20. PAGE 10 G0193
FORCES
PLAN
WAR
NUC/PWR

B67
KINTNER W.R.,PEACE AND THE STRATEGY CONFLICT. PLAN
BAL/PWR DIPLOM CONTROL ARMS/CONT DETER WEAPON 20.
PAGE 30 G0599
ROLE
PEACE
NUC/PWR
ORD/FREE

B67
ORLANS H.,CONTRACTING FOR ATOMS. USA+45 LAW INTELL
ACADEM LG/CO NAT/G PLAN TEC/DEV CONTROL DETER
...TREND 20 AEC. PAGE 43 G0845
NUC/PWR
R+D
PRODUC
PEACE

L67
DAVIS P.C.,"THE COMING CHINESE COMMUNIST NUCLEAR
THREAT AND U.S. SEA BASED ABM OPTIONS." ASIA
CHINA/COM FUT USA+45 SEA NAT/G FORCES PLAN TEC/DEV
LEAD ARMS/CONT...GEOG METH/COMP 20 ABM/DEFSYS.
PAGE 14 G0279
NUC/PWR
DETER
WEAPON
DIPLOM

S67
BRETNOR R.,"DESTRUCTIVE FORCE AND THE MILITARY
EQUATIONS." UNIV COMPUTER PLAN PROB/SOLV AUTOMAT
CONTROL COERCE DETER NUC/PWR WEAPON DRIVE PWR.
PAGE 9 G0166
FORCES
TEC/DEV
DOMIN
WAR

S67
CHRIST R.F.,"REORGANIZATION OF FRENCH ARMED
FORCES." FRANCE CREATE PLAN TEC/DEV BAL/PWR DOMIN
COERCE CENTRAL EFFICIENCY 20. PAGE 12 G0229
CHIEF
DETER
NUC/PWR
FORCES

S67
COFFEY J.I.,"THE ANTI-BALLISTIC MISSILE DEBATE."
USA+45 USSR TEC/DEV BAL/PWR 20. PAGE 12 G0238
ARMS/CONT
NUC/PWR
DETER
DIPLOM

S67
FELD B.T.,"A PLEDGE* NO FIRST USE." DELIB/GP
BAL/PWR DOMIN DETER. PAGE 19 G0363
ARMS/CONT
NUC/PWR
DIPLOM
PEACE

S67
HAZARD J.N.,"POST-DISARMAMENT INTERNATIONAL LAW."
FUT USSR WOR+45 INT/ORG DELIB/GP FORCES DETER
EQUILIB SOVEREIGN MARXISM 20 UN. PAGE 25 G0496
INT/LAW
ARMS/CONT
PWR
PLAN

S67
INGLIS D.R.,"MISSILE DEFENSE, NUCLEAR SPREAD, AND
VIETNAM." CHINA/COM USA+45 USSR VIETNAM INDUS
BAL/PWR DETER WAR COST NAT/LISM PEACE. PAGE 28
G0544
NUC/PWR
ARMS/CONT
DIPLOM
FORCES

S67
JACKSON W.G.F.,"NUCLEAR PROLIFERATION AND THE GREAT
POWERS." FUT UK WOR+45 INT/ORG DOMIN ARMS/CONT
DETER ORD/FREE PACIFIST. PAGE 28 G0550
NUC/PWR
ATTIT
BAL/PWR
NAT/LISM

S67
JONES G.S.,"STRATEGIC PLANNING." USA+45 EX/STRUC
FORCES DETER WAR 20 PRESIDENT. PAGE 29 G0566
PLAN
DECISION
DELIB/GP
POLICY

S67
KAHN H.,"CRITERIA FOR LONG-RANGE NUCLEAR CONTROL
POLICIES." WOR+45 INT/ORG TEC/DEV DOMIN DETER WAR
WEAPON ISOLAT ORD/FREE POLICY. PAGE 29 G0571
NUC/PWR
ARMS/CONT
BAL/PWR
DIPLOM

S67
LALL B.G.,"GAPS IN THE ABM DEBATE." NAT/G DIPLOM
DETER CIVMIL/REL 20. PAGE 32 G0630
NUC/PWR
ARMS/CONT
EX/STRUC
FORCES

S67
MARTIN L.,"THE AMERICAN ABM DECISION." ASIA COM
EUR+WWI UK USA+45 USSR FORCES DIPLOM PEACE...POLICY
20 ABM/DEFSYS. PAGE 36 G0713
WEAPON
DETER
NUC/PWR
WAR

S67
MARTIN L.W.,"BALLISTIC MISSILE DEFENSE AND EUROPE."
EUR+WWI USA+45 FORCES PLAN BAL/PWR DEBATE PEACE
...POLICY COLD/WAR NATO. PAGE 36 G0715
ATTIT
ARMS/CONT
NUC/PWR
DETER

S67
ROTHSTEIN R.L.,"NUCLEAR PROLIFERATION AND AMERICAN
POLICY." PROB/SOLV BAL/PWR DIPLOM ARMS/CONT
EFFICIENCY 20. PAGE 48 G0942
NUC/PWR
CONTROL
DETER
WOR+45

S67
SHULMAN M.D.,"'EUROPE' VERSUS 'DETENTE'." USA+45
USSR INT/ORG CONTROL ARMS/CONT DETER 20. PAGE 50
G0995
DIPLOM
BAL/PWR
NUC/PWR

S67
SUINN R.M.,"THE DISARMAMENT FANTASY* PSYCHOLOGICAL
FACTORS THAT MAY PRODUCE WARFARE." DIPLOM RISK
ARMS/CONT DETER ANOMIE PERSON GAME. PAGE 53 G1046
DECISION
NUC/PWR
WAR
PSY

S67
TELLER E.,"PLANNING FOR PEACE." CHINA/COM WOR+45
DELIB/GP TEC/DEV RISK COERCE DETER WAR ATTIT
ORD/FREE 20 NATO. PAGE 54 G1061
ARMS/CONT
NUC/PWR
PEACE
DOMIN

S67
YOUNG O.R.,"ACTIVE DEFENSE AND INTERNATIONAL
ORDER." FORCES BAL/PWR DEBATE GAMBLE COST PEACE.
PAGE 64 G1265
ARMS/CONT
DETER
PLAN
DECISION

DETERRENCE....SEE DETER

DETROIT....DETROIT, MICHIGAN

DEUTSCH K.W. G0295,G0297,G0298,G0299,G0300

DEV/ASSIST....DEVELOPMENT AND ASSISTANCE COMMITTEE

DEVELOPMENT....SEE CREATE+ECO/UNDEV·

DEVELOPMENT AND ASSISTANCE COMMITTEE....SEE DEV/ASSIST

DEVELOPMNT....HUMAN DEVELOPMENTAL CHANGE, PSYCHOLOGICAL
    AND PHYSIOLOGICAL

DEVIANT BEHAVIOR....SEE ANOMIE, CRIME

DEWEY J. G0301

DEWEY/JOHN....JOHN DEWEY

DEWEY/THOM....THOMAS DEWEY

DIAZ/P....PORFIRIO DIAZ

DIBBLE C. G0571

DICKSON P.G.M. G0302

DICTIONARY....DICTIONARY

US FOOD AND DRUG ADMIN,CIVIL DEFENSE INFORMATION
FOR FOOD AND DRUG OFFICIALS (2ND ED.) (PAMPHLET).
USA+45 PROB/SOLV RISK HABITAT...MATH CHARTS
DICTIONARY 20 CIV/DEFENS. PAGE 58 G1136
N19 NUC/PWR WAR EATING HEALTH

HISTORICAL ABSTRACTS. NAT/G CREATE DIPLOM ATTIT
...SOC DICTIONARY INDEX 18/20. PAGE 1 G0013
B56 WOR-45 COMPUT/IR BIBLIOG/A

RAWLINSON J.L.,CHINA'S STRUGGLE FOR NAVAL
DEVELOPMENT 1839-1895. ASIA DIPLOM ADMIN WAR
...BIBLIOG DICTIONARY 19 CHINJAP. PAGE 46 G0907
B67 SEA FORCES PWR

DIDEROT/D....DENIS DIDEROT

MCRAE R.,THE PROBLEM OF THE UNITY OF THE SCIENCES:
BACON TO KANT. CREATE TASK KNOWL...PERS/COMP 16/18
BACON/F DESCARTE/R LEIBNITZ/G KANT/I DIDEROT/D.
PAGE 38 G0748
B61 PHIL/SCI IDEA/COMP PERSON

DIEBOLD J. G0303

DIEM....NGO DINH DIEM

DIPLOM....DIPLOMACY

AMERICAN DOCUMENTATION INST,DOCUMENTATION
ABSTRACTS. WOR+45 NAT/G COMPUTER CREATE TEC/DEV
DIPLOM EDU/PROP REGION KNOWL...PHIL/SCI CLASSIF
LING. PAGE 3 G0051
N BIBLIOG/A AUTOMAT COMPUT/IR R+D

CURRENT THOUGHT ON PEACE AND WAR. WOR+45 INT/ORG
FORCES PROB/SOLV DIPLOM NUC/PWR PERCEPT...POLICY
SOC 20 UN NATO. PAGE 1 G0001
B BIBLIOG/A PEACE ATTIT WAR

JOURNAL OF CONFLICT RESOLUTION. FUT WOR+45 INT/ORG
NAT/G FORCES CREATE PROB/SOLV ARMS/CONT NUC/PWR
WEAPON SOC. PAGE 1 G0002
N BIBLIOG/A DIPLOM WAR

FOREIGN AFFAIRS. SPACE WOR+45 WOR-45 CULTURE
ECO/UNDEV FINAN NAT/G TEC/DEV INT/TRADE ARMS/CONT
NUC/PWR...POLICY 20 UN EURATOM ECSC EEC. PAGE 1
G0004
N BIBLIOG DIPLOM INT/ORG INT/LAW

AIR UNIVERSITY LIBRARY,INDEX TO MILITARY
PERIODICALS. FUT SPACE WOR+45 REGION ARMS/CONT
NUC/PWR WAR PEACE INT/LAW. PAGE 2 G0032
N BIBLIOG/A FORCES NAT/G DIPLOM

AMER COUNCIL OF LEARNED SOCIET,THE ACLS CONSTITUENT
SOCIETY JOURNAL PROJECT. FUT USA+45 LAW NAT/G PLAN
DIPLOM PHIL/SCI. PAGE 3 G0048
N BIBLIOG/A HUM COMPUT/IR COMPUTER

GT BRIT MIN OVERSEAS DEV, LIB, TECHNICAL CO-
OPERATION -- A BIBLIOGRAPHY. UK LAW SOCIETY DIPLOM
ECO/TAC FOR/AID...STAT 20 CMN/WLTH. PAGE 39 G0775
N BIBLIOG TEC/DEV ECO/DEV NAT/G

RAND SCHOOL OF SOCIAL SCIENCE,INDEX TO LABOR
ARTICLES. ECO/DEV INT/ORG LEGIS DIPLOM GP/REL
...NAT/COMP 20. PAGE 46 G0900
N BIBLIOG LABOR MGT ADJUD

UNITED NATIONS,OFFICIAL RECORDS OF THE UNITED
NATIONS' ATOMIC ENERGY COMMISSION - DISARMAMENT
COMMISSION. WOR+45 TEC/DEV DIPLOM WRITING NUC/PWR
20 UN. PAGE 55 G1092
N ARMS/CONT INT/ORG DELIB/GP CONFER

US SUPERINTENDENT OF DOCUMENTS,TRANSPORTATION:
HIGHWAYS, ROADS, AND POSTAL SERVICE (PRICE LIST
25). PANAMA USA+45 LAW FORCES DIPLOM ADMIN GOV/REL
HEALTH MGT. PAGE 61 G1188
N BIBLIOG/A DIST/IND SERV/IND NAT/G

MEZERIK A.G.,ATOM TESTS AND RADIATION HAZARDS
(PAMPHLET). WOR+45 INT/ORG DIPLOM DETER 20 UN
TREATY. PAGE 39 G0761
N19 NUC/PWR ARMS/CONT CONFER HEALTH

MEZERIK A.G.,INTERNATIONAL POLICY 1965 (PAMPHLET).
KASHMIR S/ASIA SPACE USA+45 VIETNAM WOR+45
ARMS/CONT RACE/REL DISCRIM PEACE PWR 20 UN. PAGE 39
G0762
N19 DIPLOM INT/ORG POLICY WAR

MEZERIK AG,OUTER SPACE: UN, US, USSR (PAMPHLET).
USSR DELIB/GP FORCES DETER NUC/PWR SOVEREIGN
...POLICY 20 UN TREATY. PAGE 39 G0763
N19 SPACE CONTROL DIPLOM INT/ORG

US SEN SPEC COMM SPACE ASTRO,SPACE LAW; A SYMPOSIUM
(PAMPHLET). USA+45 TEC/DEV CONFER CONTROL SOVEREIGN
...INT/LAW 20 SEN/SPACE. PAGE 59 G1161
N19 SPACE ADJUD DIPLOM INT/ORG

ZLOTNICK M.,WEAPONS IN SPACE (PAMPHLET). FUT WOR+45
TEC/DEV DIPLOM ARMS/CONT CIVMIL/REL PEACE HABITAT
...CONCPT NEW/IDEA CHARTS. PAGE 65 G1268
N19 SPACE WEAPON NUC/PWR WAR

MOON P.T.,"SYLLABUS ON INTERNATIONAL RELATIONS."
EUR+WWI MOD/EUR USA-45 FORCES COLONIAL WAR WEAPON
NAT/LISM...POLICY BIBLIOG T 19/20. PAGE 39 G0778
C25 INT/ORG DIPLOM NAT/G

EINSTEIN A.,THE WORLD AS I SEE IT. WOR-45 INTELL
R+D INT/ORG NAT/G SECT VOL/ASSN FORCES CREATE
EDU/PROP LEGIT ARMS/CONT WAR WEAPON NAT/LISM
ALL/VALS...POLICY CONCPT 20. PAGE 17 G0337
B34 SOCIETY PHIL/SCI DIPLOM PACIFISM

FOREIGN AFFAIRS BIBLIOGRAPHY: A SELECTED AND
ANNOTATED LIST OF BOOKS ON INTERNATIONAL RELATIONS
1919-1962 (4 VOLS.). CONSTN FORCES COLONIAL
ARMS/CONT WAR NAT/LISM PEACE ATTIT DRIVE...POLICY
INT/LAW 20. PAGE 1 G0011
B35 BIBLIOG/A DIPLOM INT/ORG

HARPER S.N.,THE GOVERNMENT OF THE SOVIET UNION. COM
USSR LAW CONSTN ECO/DEV PLAN TEC/DEV DIPLOM
INT/TRADE ADMIN REV NAT/LISM...POLICY 20. PAGE 24
G0483
B38 MARXISM NAT/G LEAD POL/PAR

FULLER G.H.,A SELECTED LIST OF REFERENCES ON THE
EXPANSION OF THE US NAVY, 1933-1939 (PAMPHLET).
MOD/EUR USA-45 NAT/G PLAN DIPLOM DOMIN RISK
ARMS/CONT EQUILIB PWR 20 NAVY. PAGE 20 G0399
B39 BIBLIOG FORCES WEAPON WAR

FULLER G.H.,DEFENSE FINANCING: A SUPPLEMENTARY LIST
OF REFERENCES (PAMPHLET). CANADA UK USA-45 ECO/DEV
NAT/G DELIB/GP BUDGET ADJUD ARMS/CONT WEAPON COST
PEACE PWR 20 AUSTRAL CHINJAP CONGRESS. PAGE 21
G0403
B42 BIBLIOG/A FINAN FORCES DIPLOM

LASSWELL H.D.,"THE RELATION OF IDEOLOGICAL
INTELLIGENCE TO PUBLIC POLICY." WOR+45 WOR-45
SOCIETY DELIB/GP ACT/RES CREATE PLAN DIPLOM
EDU/PROP CHOOSE KNOWL PWR...POLICY SOC TREND
S42 ATTIT DECISION

GEN/LAWS 20. PAGE 32 G0638

TREATY VERSAILLES STRESEMN/G. PAGE 9 G0167

B44
FULLER G.H.,MILITARY GOVERNMENT: A LIST OF
REFERENCES (A PAMPHLET). ITALY UK USA-45 WOR-45 LAW
FORCES DOMIN ADMIN ARMS/CONT ORD/FREE PWR
...DECISION 20 CHINJAP. PAGE 21 G0404
BIBLIOG
DIPLOM
CIVMIL/REL
SOVEREIGN

B53
LANGER W.L.,THE UNDECLARED WAR, 1940-1941. EUR+WWI
GERMANY USA-45 USSR AIR FORCES TEC/DEV CONFER
CONTROL COERCE PERCEPT ORD/FREE PWR 20 CHINJAP
EUROPE. PAGE 32 G0634
WAR
POLICY
DIPLOM

B44
MATTHEWS M.A.,INTERNATIONAL POLICE (PAMPHLET).
WOR-45 DIPLOM ARMS/CONT WAR 20. PAGE 37 G0722
BIBLIOG
INT/ORG
FORCES
PEACE

B53
LARSEN K.,NATIONAL BIBLIOGRAPHIC SERVICES: THEIR
CREATION AND OPERATION. WOR+45 COM/IND CREATE PLAN
DIPLOM PRESS ADMIN ROUTINE...MGT UNESCO. PAGE 32
G0636
BIBLIOG/A
INT/ORG
WRITING

B47
SOCIAL SCIENCE RESEARCH COUN,PUBLIC REACTION TO THE
ATOMIC BOMB AND WORLD AFFAIRS. SOCIETY CONFER
ARMS/CONT...STAT QU SAMP CHARTS 20. PAGE 52 G1019
ATTIT
NUC/PWR
DIPLOM
WAR

B53
ROBINSON E.A.G.,THE STRUCTURE OF COMPETITIVE
INDUSTRY. UK ECO/DEV DIST/IND MARKET TEC/DEV DIPLOM
EDU/PROP ADMIN EFFICIENCY WEALTH...MGT 19/20.
PAGE 47 G0929
INDUS
PRODUC
WORKER
OPTIMAL

N47
FOX W.T.R.,UNITED STATES POLICY IN A TWO POWER
WORLD. COM USA+45 USSR FORCES DOMIN AGREE NEUTRAL
NUC/PWR ORD/FREE SOVEREIGN 20 COLD/WAR TREATY
EUROPE/W INTERVENT. PAGE 20 G0389
DIPLOM
FOR/AID
POLICY

B53
SCHAAF R.W.,DOCUMENTS OF INTERNATIONAL MEETINGS.
AGRI INDUS ACADEM DIPLOM NUC/PWR RACE/REL AGE/Y
HEALTH...SOC 20. PAGE 49 G0960
BIBLIOG/A
DELIB/GP
INT/ORG
POLICY

B48
CHILDS J.R.,AMERICAN FOREIGN SERVICE. USA+45
SOCIETY NAT/G ROUTINE GOV/REL 20 DEPT/STATE
CIVIL/SERV. PAGE 12 G0227
DIPLOM
ADMIN
GP/REL

B54
BUTOW R.J.C.,JAPAN'S DECISION TO SURRENDER. USA-45
USSR CHIEF FORCES DOMIN NUC/PWR...BIBLIOG 20 TREATY
CHINJAP. PAGE 10 G0198
ELITES
DIPLOM
WAR
PEACE

B48
GRIFFITH E.S.,RESEARCH IN POLITICAL SCIENCE: THE
WORK OF PANELS OF RESEARCH COMMITTEE, APSA. WOR+45
WOR-45 COM/IND R+D FORCES ACT/RES WAR...GOV/COMP
ANTHOL 20. PAGE 23 G0451
BIBLIOG
PHIL/SCI
DIPLOM
JURID

B54
GERMANY FOREIGN MINISTRY,DOCUMENTS ON GERMAN
FOREIGN POLICY 1918-1945. SERIES C (1933-1937)
VOLS. I-V. GERMANY MOD/EUR FORCES PLAN ECO/TAC
...FASCIST CHARTS ANTHOL 20. PAGE 21 G0416
NAT/G
DIPLOM
POLICY

B49
OGBURN W.,TECHNOLOGY AND INTERNATIONAL RELATIONS.
WOR+45 WOR-45 ECO/DEV CREATE PLAN ECO/TAC EDU/PROP
COERCE PWR SKILL WEALTH...TECHNIC PSY SOC NEW/IDEA
CHARTS TOT/POP 20. PAGE 43 G0837
TEC/DEV
DIPLOM
INT/ORG

B54
KENWORTHY L.S.,FREE AND INEXPENSIVE MATERIALS ON
WORLD AFFAIRS (PAMPHLET). WOR+45 CULTURE ECO/UNDEV
INT/TRADE ARMS/CONT NUC/PWR UN. PAGE 30 G0594
BIBLIOG/A
NAT/G
INT/ORG
DIPLOM

B49
ROSENHAUPT H.W.,HOW TO WAGE PEACE. USA+45 SOCIETY
STRATA STRUCT R+D INT/ORG POL/PAR LEGIS ACT/RES
CREATE PLAN EDU/PROP ADMIN EXEC ATTIT ALL/VALS
...TIME/SEQ TREND COLD/WAR 20. PAGE 48 G0937
INTELL
CONCPT
DIPLOM

B54
REYNOLDS P.A.,BRITISH FOREIGN POLICY IN THE INTER-
WAR YEARS. CZECHOSLVK GERMANY POLAND UK USA-45
POL/PAR FORCES ECO/TAC ARMS/CONT WAR ATTIT 20.
PAGE 46 G0915
DIPLOM
POLICY
NAT/G

S49
MERTON R.,"THE ROLE OF APPLIED SOCIAL SCIENCE IN
THE FORMATION OF POLICY: A RESEARCH MEMORANDUM."
WOR+45 INDUS NAT/G EXEC ROUTINE CHOOSE ORD/FREE PWR
SKILL...POLICY MGT PSY METH/CNCPT TESTS CHARTS METH
VAL/FREE 20. PAGE 38 G0756
PLAN
SOC
DIPLOM

B54
US DEPARTMENT OF STATE,PUBLICATIONS OF THE
DEPARTMENT OF STATE. OCTOBER 1,1929 TO JANUARY 1,
1953. AGRI INT/ORG FORCES FOR/AID EDU/PROP
ARMS/CONT NUC/PWR ATTIT 20 DEPT/STATE OAS UN NATO.
PAGE 57 G1122
BIBLIOG
DIPLOM

S49
SOUERS S.W.,"POLICY FORMULATION FOR NATIONAL
SECURITY." EX/STRUC FORCES PROB/SOLV DIPLOM CONFER
EXEC ARMS/CONT DETER NUC/PWR GOV/REL PEACE
COLD/WAR. PAGE 52 G1022
DELIB/GP
CHIEF
DECISION
POLICY

B54
WRIGHT Q.,PROBLEMS OF STABILITY AND PROGRESS IN
INTERNATIONAL RELATIONSHIPS. FUT WOR+45 WOR-45
SOCIETY LEGIS CREATE TEC/DEV ECO/TAC EDU/PROP ADJUD
WAR PEACE ORD/FREE PWR...KNO/TEST TREND GEN/LAWS
20. PAGE 64 G1257
INT/ORG
CONCPT
DIPLOM

B50
KOENIG L.W.,THE SALE OF THE TANKERS. USA+45 SEA
DIST/IND POL/PAR DIPLOM ADMIN CIVMIL/REL ATTIT
...DECISION 20 PRESIDENT DEPT/STATE. PAGE 31 G0609
NAT/G
POLICY
PLAN
GOV/REL

S54
PYE L.W.,"EASTERN NATIONALISM AND WESTERN POLICY."
ASIA S/ASIA USA+45 USA-45 SOCIETY PLAN DIPLOM KNOWL
TOT/POP 20. PAGE 46 G0896
CREATE
ACT/RES
NAT/LISM

B50
US DEPARTMENT OF STATE,POINT FOUR: COOPERATIVE
PROGRAM FOR AID IN THE DEVELOPMENT OF ECONOMICALLY
UNDERDEVELOPED AREAS. WOR+45 AGRI INDUS INT/ORG
PLAN TEC/DEV DIPLOM EDU/PROP ADMIN PEACE PRODUC
WEALTH 20 CONGRESS UN. PAGE 57 G1121
ECO/UNDEV
FOR/AID
FINAN
INT/TRADE

B55
DAVIS E.,TWO MINUTES TO MIDNIGHT. WOR+45 PLAN
CONTROL NEUTRAL ARMS/CONT ATTIT ORD/FREE...PSY 20
COLD/WAR. PAGE 14 G0277
NUC/PWR
WAR
DETER
DIPLOM

S50
LENTZ T.F.,"REPORT ON A SURVEY OF SOCIAL SCIENTISTS
CONDUCTED BY THE ATTITUDE RESEARCH LABORATORY." FUT
WOR+45 CREATE EDU/PROP...PSY STAT RECORD SYS/QU
SAMP/SIZ CON/ANAL VAL/FREE 20. PAGE 33 G0655
ACT/RES
ATTIT
DIPLOM

B55
JONES J.M.,THE FIFTEEN WEEKS (FEBRUARY 21-JUNE 5,
1947). EUR+WWI USA+45 PROB/SOLV BAL/PWR...POLICY
TIME/SEQ 20 COLD/WAR MARSHL/PLN TRUMAN/HS
WASHING/DC. PAGE 29 G0567
DIPLOM
ECO/TAC
FOR/AID

S51
LERNER D.,"THE POLICY SCIENCES: RECENT DEVELOPMENTS
IN SCOPE AND METHODS." R+D SERV/IND CREATE DIPLOM
ROUTINE PWR...METH/CNCPT TREND GEN/LAWS METH 20.
PAGE 33 G0658
CONSULT
SOC

B55
SHUBIK M.,READINGS IN GAME THEORY AND POLITICAL
BEHAVIOR. WOR+45 FORCES CREATE ROUTINE WAR PEACE
PERCEPT KNOWL PWR...PSY SOC CONCPT METH/CNCPT STAT
CHARTS HYPO/EXP GAME METH VAL/FREE 20. PAGE 50
G0991
MATH
DECISION
DIPLOM

B52
APPADORAI A.,THE SUBSTANCE OF POLITICS (6TH ED.).
EX/STRUC LEGIS DIPLOM CT/SYS CHOOSE FASCISM MARXISM
SOCISM...BIBLIOG T. PAGE 3 G0062
PHIL/SCI
NAT/G

B55
US OFFICE OF THE PRESIDENT,REPORT TO CONGRESS ON
THE MUTUAL SECURITY PROGRAM FOR THE SIX MONTHS
ENDED JUNE 30, 1955. ECO/DEV INT/ORG NAT/G CREATE
TEC/DEV BAL/PWR ECO/TAC AGREE DETER COST ORD/FREE
20 DEPT/STATE DEPT/DEFEN. PAGE 59 G1157
DIPLOM
FORCES
PLAN
FOR/AID

B53
BRETTON H.L.,STRESEMANN AND THE REVISION OF
VERSAILLES: A FIGHT FOR REASON. EUR+WWI GERMANY
FORCES BUDGET ARMS/CONT WAR SUPEGO...BIBLIOG 20
POLICY
DIPLOM
BIOG

KISER M.,"ORGANIZATION OF AMERICAN STATES." L/A+17C VOL/ASSN
USA+45 ECO/UNDEV INT/ORG NAT/G PLAN TEC/DEV DIPLOM ECO/DEV
ECO/TAC INT/TRADE EDU/PROP ADMIN ALL/VALS...POLICY REGION
MGT RECORD ORG/CHARTS OAS 20. PAGE 30 G0601   L55

ANGELL R.,"GOVERNMENTS AND PEOPLES AS A FOCI FOR   FUT
PEACE-ORIENTED RESEARCH." WOR+45 CULTURE SOCIETY   SOC
FACE/GP ACT/RES CREATE PLAN DIPLOM EDU/PROP ROUTINE   PEACE
ATTIT PERCEPT SKILL...POLICY CONCPT OBS TREND
GEN/METH 20. PAGE 3 G0060   S55

HISTORICAL ABSTRACTS. NAT/G CREATE DIPLOM ATTIT   WOR-45
...SOC DICTIONARY INDEX 18/20. PAGE 1 G0013   COMPUT/IR
                                                     BIBLIOG/A
                                                     B56

ESTEP R.,AN AIR POWER BIBLIOGRAPHY. USA+45 TEC/DEV   BIBLIOG/A
BUDGET DIPLOM EDU/PROP DETER CIVMIL/REL...DECISION   FORCES
INT/LAW 20. PAGE 18 G0351   WEAPON
                                                     PLAN
                                                     B56

KOENIG L.W.,THE TRUMAN ADMINISTRATION: ITS   ADMIN
PRINCIPLES AND PRACTICE. USA+45 POL/PAR CHIEF LEGIS   POLICY
DIPLOM DEATH NUC/PWR WAR CIVMIL/REL PEACE   EX/STRUC
...DECISION 20 TRUMAN/HS PRESIDENT TREATY. PAGE 31   GOV/REL
G0610   B56

US DEPARTMENT OF THE ARMY,AMERICAN MILITARY   BIBLIOG
HISTORY. USA+45 USA-45 EX/STRUC PROB/SOLV TEC/DEV   FORCES
DIPLOM NUC/PWR REV WAR WEAPON...PSY 18/20. PAGE 57   NAT/G
G1125   B56

US OFFICE OF THE PRESIDENT,REPORT TO CONGRESS ON   DIPLOM
THE MUTUAL SECURITY PROGRAM FOR THE SIX MONTHS   FORCES
ENDED DECEMBER 31, 1955. ASIA USSR ECO/DEV   PLAN
ECO/UNDEV INT/ORG CREATE TEC/DEV BAL/PWR ECO/TAC   FOR/AID
AGREE DETER COST ORD/FREE 20 DEPT/STATE DEPT/DEFEN
EISNHWR/DD. PAGE 59 G1158   B56

ALMOND G.A.,"COMPARATIVE POLITICAL SYSTEMS" (BMR)"   GOV/COMP
WOR+45 WOR-45 PROB/SOLV DIPLOM EFFICIENCY   CONCPT
...PHIL/SCI SOC METH 17/20. PAGE 3 G0046   ALL/IDEOS
                                                     NAT/COMP
                                                     S56

DUPUY R.E.,"MILITARY HERITAGE OF AMERICA." USA+45   FORCES
USA-45 TEC/DEV DIPLOM ROUTINE...POLICY TREND CHARTS   WAR
IDEA/COMP BIBLIOG COLD/WAR. PAGE 17 G0325   CONCPT
                                                     C56

DRUCKER P.F.,AMERICA'S NEXT TWENTY YEARS. USA+45   WORKER
DIST/IND ACADEM MUNIC SCHOOL DIPLOM ECO/TAC AUTOMAT   FOR/AID
HABITAT HEALTH...SOC/WK TREND 20 URBAN/RNWL   CENSUS
PUB/TRANS. PAGE 16 G0316   GEOG
                                                     B57

KISSINGER H.A.,NUCLEAR WEAPONS AND FOREIGN POLICY.   PLAN
FUT USA+45 WOR+45 INT/ORG FORCES ACT/RES TEC/DEV   DETER
DIPLOM ARMS/CONT COERCE ATTIT KNOWL PWR...DECISION   NUC/PWR
GEOG CHARTS 20. PAGE 31 G0602   B57

FISHMAN B.G.,"PUBLIC POLICY AND POLITICAL   ECO/DEV
CONSIDERATIONS." USA+45 SOCIETY NAT/G ACT/RES   CONSULT
CREATE PLAN DIPLOM KNOWL ORD/FREE...CONCPT GEN/METH
20. PAGE 19 G0370   S57

MORTON L.,"THE DECISION TO USE THE BOMB." FORCES   NUC/PWR
TOP/EX DOMIN COERCE PEACE. PAGE 40 G0788   DIPLOM
                                                     WAR
                                                     S57

ANGELL N.,DEFENCE AND THE ENGLISH-SPEAKING ROLE.   DIPLOM
CHINA/COM UK USSR INT/ORG FORCES EDU/PROP NEUTRAL   WAR
NUC/PWR NAT/LISM PEACE TOTALISM 20 COLD/WAR   MARXISM
COEXIST. PAGE 3 G0059   ORD/FREE
                                                     B58

ARON R.,ON WAR: ATOMIC WEAPONS AND GLOBAL DIPLOMACY   ARMS/CONT
(TRANS. BY TERENCE KILMARTIN). WOR+45 SOCIETY   NUC/PWR
FORCES BAL/PWR WAR WEAPON PERSON...SOC 20. PAGE 4   COERCE
G0067   DIPLOM
                                                     B58

EHRHARD J.,LE DESTIN DU COLONIALISME. AFR FRANCE   COLONIAL
ECO/UNDEV AGRI FINAN MARKET CREATE PLAN TEC/DEV   FOR/AID
BUDGET DIPLOM PRICE 20. PAGE 17 G0335   INT/TRADE
                                                     INDUS

GANGE J.,UNIVERSITY RESEARCH ON INTERNATIONAL   R+D
AFFAIRS. USA+45 ACADEM INT/ORG CONSULT CREATE EXEC   MGT
ROUTINE...QUANT STAT INT STERTYP GEN/METH TOT/POP   DIPLOM
VAL/FREE 20. PAGE 21 G0407   B58

GAVIN J.M.,WAR AND PEACE IN THE SPACE AGE. SPACE   WAR
USA+45 USSR FORCES PLAN TEC/DEV BAL/PWR DIPLOM   DETER
ARMS/CONT WEAPON CIVMIL/REL...CHARTS GP/COMP 20   NUC/PWR
NATO COLD/WAR. PAGE 21 G0414   PEACE
                                                     B58

NATIONAL PLANNING ASSOCIATION,1970 WITHOUT ARMS   ARMS/CONT
CONTROL (PAMPHLET). WOR+45 PROB/SOLV TEC/DEV DIPLOM   ORD/FREE
CONFER DETER NUC/PWR WAR...CHARTS 20 COLD/WAR.   WEAPON
PAGE 41 G0810   PREDICT
                                                     B58

ROCKEFELLER BROTH FUND INC,INTERNATIONAL SECURITY -   NUC/PWR
THE MILITARY ASPECT. USA+45 INT/ORG NAT/G BUDGET   DETER
ARMS/CONT WAR WEAPON PEACE ORD/FREE 20 NATO.   FORCES
PAGE 47 G0932   DIPLOM
                                                     B58

UN INTL CONF ON PEACEFUL USE,PROGRESS IN ATOMIC   NUC/PWR
ENERGY (VOL. I). WOR+45 R+D PLAN TEC/DEV CONFER   DIPLOM
CONTROL PEACE SKILL...CHARTS ANTHOL 20 UN BAGHDAD.   WORKER
PAGE 55 G1088   EDU/PROP
                                                     B58

US DEPARTMENT OF STATE,PUBLICATIONS OF THE   BIBLIOG
DEPARTMENT OF STATE, JANUARY 1,1953 TO DECEMBER 31,   DIPLOM
1957. AGRI INT/ORG FORCES FOR/AID EDU/PROP
ARMS/CONT NUC/PWR ATTIT 20 DEPT/STATE OAS UN NATO.
PAGE 57 G1123   B58

BURNS A.L.,"THE NEW WEAPONS AND INTERNATIONAL   TEC/DEV
RELATIONS." SPACE WOR+45 NAT/G VOL/ASSN FORCES   ARMS/CONT
NUC/PWR 20. PAGE 10 G0190   DIPLOM
                                                     S58

LASSWELL H.D.,"THE SCIENTIFIC STUDY OF   PHIL/SCI
INTERNATIONAL RELATIONS." USA+45 INT/ORG CREATE   GEN/METH
EDU/PROP DETER ATTIT PERCEPT PWR...DECISION CONCPT   DIPLOM
METH/CNCPT STYLE CON/ANAL 20. PAGE 33 G0642   S58

THOMPSON K.W.,"NATIONAL SECURITY IN A NUCLEAR AGE."   FORCES
USA+45 WOR+45 SOCIETY INT/ORG NAT/G TOP/EX DIPLOM   PWR
DOMIN EDU/PROP LEGIT ARMS/CONT COERCE ORD/FREE   BAL/PWR
...TREND STERTYP TOT/POP VAL/FREE COLD/WAR 20.
PAGE 54 G1068   S58

AIR FORCE ACADEMY ASSEMBLY '59,INTERNATIONAL   FOR/AID
STABILITY AND PROGRESS (PAMPHLET). USA+45 USSR   FORCES
ECO/UNDEV PROB/SOLV BUDGET DIPLOM ADMIN DETER COST   WAR
ATTIT...TREND 20. PAGE 2 G0030   PLAN
                                                     B59

EMME E.M.,THE IMPACT OF AIR POWER - NATIONAL   DETER
SECURITY AND WORLD POLITICS. USA+45 USSR FORCES   AIR
DIPLOM WEAPON PEACE TOTALISM...POLICY NAT/COMP 20   WAR
EUROPE. PAGE 18 G0346   ORD/FREE
                                                     B59

GODDARD V.,THE ENIGMA OF MENACE. WOR+45 SECT LEAD   PEACE
NUC/PWR WAR WEAPON CHOOSE PERSON PWR...POLICY   ARMS/CONT
PHIL/SCI PACIFIST 20 COLD/WAR. PAGE 22 G0423   DIPLOM
                                                     ATTIT
                                                     B59

HARVARD UNIVERSITY LAW SCHOOL,INTERNATIONAL   NUC/PWR
PROBLEMS OF FINANCIAL PROTECTION AGAINST NUCLEAR   ADJUD
RISK. WOR+45 NAT/G DELIB/GP PROB/SOLV DIPLOM   INDUS
CONTROL ATTIT...POLICY INT/LAW MATH 20. PAGE 25   FINAN
G0488   B59

HUGHES E.M.,AMERICA THE VINCIBLE. USA+45 FOR/AID   ORD/FREE
ARMS/CONT NUC/PWR PERS/REL RATIONAL ATTIT ALL/VALS   DIPLOM
20 COLD/WAR. PAGE 27 G0534   WAR
                                                     B59

MIKSCHE F.O.,THE FAILURE OF ATOMIC STRATEGY. COM   ACT/RES
EUR+WWI INTELL POL/PAR FORCES PLAN ECO/TAC NUC/PWR   ORD/FREE
ATTIT DRIVE RIGID/FLEX PWR...DECISION GEOG PSY   DIPLOM
CONCPT RECORD TREND CHARTS VAL/FREE 20. PAGE 39   ARMS/CONT
G0766   B59

U OF MICHIGAN LAW SCHOOL,ATOMS AND THE LAW. USA+45   NUC/PWR
PROVS WORKER PROB/SOLV DIPLOM ADMIN GOV/REL ANTHOL.   NAT/G

CONTROL
LAW

PWR...POLICY CONCPT TREND COLD/WAR 20. PAGE 8 G0164 DETER

B59
VAN WAGENEN R.W.,SOME VIEWS OF AMERICAN DEFENSE
OFFICIALS ABOUT THE UNITED NATIONS (PAPER). FUT
USA+45 NAT/G DIPLOM WAR EFFICIENCY PEACE...POLICY
INT 20 UN DEPT/DEFEN. PAGE 61 G1192
INT/ORG
LEAD
ATTIT
FORCES

L60
MACPHERSON C.,"TECHNICAL CHANGE AND POLITICAL
DECISION." WOR+45 NAT/G CREATE CAP/ISM DIPLOM
ROUTINE RIGID/FLEX...CONCPT OBS GEN/METH 20.
PAGE 35 G0692
TEC/DEV
ADMIN

B59
WELTON H.,THE THIRD WORLD WAR; TRADE AND INDUSTRY,
THE NEW BATTLEGROUND. WOR+45 ECO/DEV INDUS MARKET
TASK...MGT IDEA/COMP COLD/WAR. PAGE 63 G1229
INT/TRADE
PLAN
DIPLOM

L60
MCCLELLAND C.A.,"THE FUNCTION OF THEORY IN
INTERNATIONAL RELATIONS." WOR+45 PLAN EDU/PROP
ROUTINE ORD/FREE...PHIL/SCI PSY SOC METH/CNCPT
NEW/IDEA OBS TREND GEN/METH 20. PAGE 37 G0728
INT/ORG
CONCPT
DIPLOM

L59
MCDOUGAL M.S.,"THE IDENTIFICATION AND APPRAISAL OF
DIVERSE SYSTEMS OF PUBLIC ORDER (BMR)" WOR+45 NAT/G
CONSULT EDU/PROP POLICY. PAGE 37 G0737
INT/LAW
DIPLOM
ALL/IDEOS

S60
BRODY R.A.,"DETERRENCE STRATEGIES: AN ANNOTATED
BIBLIOGRAPHY." WOR+45 PLAN ARMS/CONT NUC/PWR WAR
WEAPON DECISION. PAGE 9 G0173
BIBLIOG/A
FORCES
DETER
DIPLOM

S59
DEUTSCH K.W.,"THE IMPACT OF SCIENCE AND TECHNOLOGY
ON INTERNATIONAL POLITICS." UNIV INTELL NAT/G
ACT/RES CREATE TEC/DEV EDU/PROP EXEC KNOWL...CONCPT
TREND TOT/POP 20. PAGE 15 G0297
PHIL/SCI
MYTH
DIPLOM
NAT/LISM

S60
HAYTON R.D.,"THE ANTARCTIC SETTLEMENT OF 1959." FUT
USA+45 WOR+45 WOR-45 STRUCT R+D INT/ORG EX/STRUC
CREATE TEC/DEV LEGIT PEACE ATTIT SOVEREIGN
...TIME/SEQ 20 TREATY IGY. PAGE 25 G0495
DELIB/GP
JURID
DIPLOM
REGION

S59
GOLDHAMMER H.,"SOME OBSERVATIONS ON POLITICAL
GAMING." FUT WOR+45 R+D NAT/G ACT/RES CREATE CHOOSE
ATTIT PWR...POLICY CONCPT METH/CNCPT STYLE KNO/TEST
TREND HYPO/EXP GAME GEN/METH METH 20. PAGE 22 G0426
COMPUT/IR
DECISION
DIPLOM

S60
HUTCHINSON C.E.,"AN INSTITUTE FOR NATIONAL SECURITY
AFFAIRS." USA+45 R+D NAT/G CONSULT TOP/EX ACT/RES
CREATE PLAN TEC/DEV EDU/PROP ROUTINE NUC/PWR ATTIT
ORD/FREE PWR...DECISION MGT PHIL/SCI CONCPT RECORD
GEN/LAWS GEN/METH 20. PAGE 27 G0539
POLICY
METH/CNCPT
ELITES
DIPLOM

S59
WILLIAMS B.H.,"SCIENTIFIC METHOD IN FOREIGN
POLICY." WOR+45 NAT/G FORCES TOP/EX DOMIN LEGIT
COERCE PEACE ATTIT KNOWL ORD/FREE PWR...GEN/LAWS
GEN/METH TOT/POP COLD/WAR NAZI. PAGE 63 G1241
PLAN
PHIL/SCI
DIPLOM

S60
KAPLAN M.A.,"THEORETICAL ANALYSIS OF THE BALANCE OF
POWER." FUT USA+45 WOR+45 INTELL ECO/DEV INT/ORG
NAT/G CONSULT TOP/EX ACT/RES PLAN TEC/DEV ATTIT
ALL/VALS...METH/CNCPT TOT/POP 20. PAGE 29 G0576
CREATE
NEW/IDEA
DIPLOM
NUC/PWR

B60
BARNET R.,WHO WANTS DISARMAMENT. COM EUR+WWI USA+45
USSR INT/ORG NAT/G BAL/PWR DIPLOM EDU/PROP COERCE
DETER NUC/PWR WAR WEAPON ATTIT PWR...TIME/SEQ
COLD/WAR CONGRESS 20. PAGE 5 G0096
PLAN
FORCES
ARMS/CONT

S60
KISSINGER H.A.,"ARMS CONTROL, INSPECTION AND
SURPRISE ATTACK." COM USA+45 NAT/G ACT/RES PLAN
TEC/DEV DIPLOM EDU/PROP DETER WAR RIGID/FLEX
...CONCPT GEN/METH TOT/POP 20. PAGE 31 G0603
FORCES
ORD/FREE
ARMS/CONT
NUC/PWR

B60
BROOKINGS INSTITUTION,UNITED STATES FOREIGN POLICY:
STUDY NO 9: THE FORMULATION AND ADMINISTRATION OF
UNITED STATES FOREIGN POLICY. USA+45 WOR+45
EX/STRUC LEGIS BAL/PWR FOR/AID EDU/PROP CIVMIL/REL
GOV/REL...INT COLD/WAR. PAGE 9 G0174
DIPLOM
INT/ORG
CREATE

S60
SANDERS R.,"NUCLEAR DYNAMITE: A NEW DIMENSION IN
FOREIGN POLICY." FUT WOR+45 ECO/DEV CONSULT TEC/DEV
PERCEPT...CONT/OBS TIME/SEQ TREND GEN/LAWS TOT/POP
20 TREATY. PAGE 49 G0955
INDUS
PWR
DIPLOM
NUC/PWR

B60
CHASE S.,LIVE AND LET LIVE. USA+45 ECO/DEV
PROB/SOLV TEC/DEV ECO/TAC ARMS/CONT NUC/PWR WAR
NAT/LISM PEACE...GEOG TREND 20 COLD/WAR. PAGE 11
G0223
NAT/G
DIPLOM
SOCIETY
TASK

N60
US HOUSE COMM SCI ASTRONAUT,THE ORGANIZATION OF THE
US NATIONAL SPACE EFFORT. USA+45 WOR+45 AIR ECO/DEV
NAT/G PLAN TEC/DEV DIPLOM EDU/PROP ATTIT DRIVE PWR
...OBS TIME/SEQ TREND TOT/POP 20. PAGE 58 G1142
ACT/RES
SKILL
SPACE

B60
EINSTEIN A.,EINSTEIN ON PEACE. FUT WOR+45 WOR-45
SOCIETY BAL/PWR CAP/ISM DIPLOM ARMS/CONT ATTIT
DETER NAT/LISM...POLICY RELATIV HUM PHIL/SCI CONCPT
BIOG COLD/WAR LEAGUE/NAT NAZI. PAGE 17 G0338
INT/ORG
ATTIT
NUC/PWR
PEACE

B61
CARNELL F.,THE POLITICS OF THE NEW STATES: A SELECT
ANNOTATED BIBLIOGRAPHY WITH SPECIAL REFERENCE TO
THE COMMONWEALTH. CONSTN ELITES LABOR NAT/G POL/PAR
EX/STRUC DIPLOM ADJUD ADMIN...GOV/COMP 20
COMMONWLTH. PAGE 11 G0210
BIBLIOG/A
AFR
ASIA
COLONIAL

B60
KINGSTON-MCCLOUG E.,DEFENSE; POLICY AND STRATEGY.
UK SEA AIR TEC/DEV DIPLOM ADMIN LEAD WAR ORD/FREE
...CHARTS 20. PAGE 30 G0597
FORCES
PLAN
POLICY
DECISION

B61
FRISCH D.,ARMS REDUCTION: PROGRAM AND ISSUES.
USA+45 INT/ORG NAT/G ACT/RES REGION NUC/PWR ATTIT
PWR...POLICY 20. PAGE 20 G0395
PLAN
FORCES
ARMS/CONT
DIPLOM

B60
LE GHAIT E.,NO CARTE BLANCHE TO CAPRICORN; THE
FOLLY OF NUCLEAR WAR. WOR+45 INT/ORG BAL/PWR DIPLOM
RISK COERCE...CENSUS 20 NATO. PAGE 33 G0647
DETER
NUC/PWR
PLAN
DECISION

B61
HENKIN L.,ARMS CONTROL: ISSUES FOR THE PUBLIC.
EUR+WWI FUT USA+45 USSR INT/ORG NAT/G DIPLOM
EDU/PROP DETER NUC/PWR ATTIT PWR...CONCPT RECORD
HIST/WRIT TIME/SEQ TOT/POP COLD/WAR 20. PAGE 26
G0506
WOR+45
DELIB/GP
ARMS/CONT

B60
MCCLELLAND C.A.,NUCLEAR WEAPONS, MISSILES, AND
FUTURE WAR: PROBLEM FOR THE SIXTIES. WOR+45 FORCES
ARMS/CONT DETER MARXISM...POLICY ANTHOL COLD/WAR.
PAGE 37 G0729
DIPLOM
NUC/PWR
WAR
WEAPON

B61
KISSINGER H.A.,THE NECESSITY FOR CHOICE. FUT USA+45
ECO/UNDEV NAT/G PLAN BAL/PWR ECO/TAC ARMS/CONT
DETER NUC/PWR ATTIT...POLICY CONCPT RECORD GEN/LAWS
COLD/WAR 20. PAGE 31 G0604
TOP/EX
TREND
DIPLOM

B60
MCKINNEY R.,REVIEW OF THE INTERNATIONAL ATOMIC
POLICIES AND PROGRAMS OF THE UNITED STATES (5
VOLS.). COM FUT USA+45 ECO/DEV ECO/UNDEV INT/ORG
DELIB/GP PLAN ADMIN 20 THIRD/WRLD. PAGE 38 G0744
NUC/PWR
PEACE
DIPLOM
POLICY

B61
MICHAEL D.N.,PROPOSED STUDIES ON THE IMPLICATIONS
OF PEACEFUL SPACE ACTIVITIES FOR HUMAN AFFAIRS.
COM/IND INDUS FORCES DIPLOM PEACE PERSON...PSY SOC
20. PAGE 39 G0764
FUT
SPACE
ACT/RES
PROB/SOLV

B60
US DEPARTMENT OF THE ARMY,DISARMAMENT: A
BIBLIOGRAPHIC RECORD: 1916-1960. DETER WAR WEAPON
PEACE 20 UN LEAGUE/NAT COLD/WAR NATO. PAGE 57 G1128
BIBLIOG/A
ARMS/CONT
NUC/PWR
DIPLOM

B61
NOGEE J.L.,SOVIET POLICY TOWARD INTERNATIONAL
CONTROL OF ATOMIC ENERGY. COM USA+45 WOR+45 INTELL
NAT/G ACT/RES DIPLOM EDU/PROP NUC/PWR TOTALISM
PERCEPT KNOWL PWR...TIME/SEQ COLD/WAR 20. PAGE 42
G0824
INT/ORG
ATTIT
ARMS/CONT
USSR

L60
BRENNAN D.G.,"SETTING AND GOALS OF ARMS CONTROL."
FUT USA+45 USSR WOR+45 INTELL INT/ORG NAT/G
VOL/ASSN CONSULT PLAN DIPLOM ECO/TAC ADMIN KNOWL
FORCES
COERCE
ARMS/CONT

ROSENAU J.N.,INTERNATIONAL POLITICS AND FOREIGN POLICY: A READER IN RESEARCH AND THEORY. ELITES ATTIT SOVEREIGN...DECISION CHARTS HYPO/EXP GAME SIMUL ANTHOL BIBLIOG METH 20. PAGE 48 G0936
B61 ACT/RES DIPLOM CONCPT POLICY

SCHMIDT H.,VERTEIDIGUNG ODER VERGELTUNG. COM CUBA GERMANY/W USSR FORCES DIPLOM ARMS/CONT DETER NUC/PWR...POLICY CHARTS HYPO/EXP SIMUL BIBLIOG 20 NATO COLD/WAR. PAGE 49 G0970
B61 PLAN WAR BAL/PWR ORD/FREE

US SENATE COMM GOVT OPERATIONS,ORGANIZING FOR NATIONAL SECURITY. COM USA+45 BUDGET DIPLOM DETER NUC/PWR WAR WEAPON ORD/FREE...BIBLIOG 20 COLD/WAR. PAGE 60 G1176
B61 POLICY PLAN FORCES COERCE

HERRING P.,"RESEARCH FOR PUBLIC POLICY: BROOKINGS DEDICATION LECTURES." USA+45 CONSULT DELIB/GP ROUTINE PERCEPT SKILL...MGT 20. PAGE 26 G0508
L61 R+D ACT/RES DIPLOM

TAUBENFELD H.J.,"A TREATY FOR ANTARCTICA." FUT USA+45 INTELL INT/ORG LABOR 20 TREATY ANTARCTICA. PAGE 54 G1055
L61 R+D ACT/RES DIPLOM

LINDSAY F.A.,"PLANNING IN FOREIGN AFFAIRS: THE MISSING ELEMENT." FUT USA+45 ROUTINE SKILL...MGT TOT/POP 20. PAGE 34 G0669
S61 ECO/DEV PLAN DIPLOM

WOHLSTETTER A.,"NUCLEAR SHARING: NATO AND THE NTH COUNTRY." EUR+WWI FUT SOCIETY DIPLOM EXEC DETER PWR SKILL...POLICY TECHNIC CONCPT 20 NATO. PAGE 64 G1252
S61 TREND TEC/DEV NUC/PWR ARMS/CONT

AIR FORCE ACADEMY LIBRARY,INTERNATIONAL ORGANIZATIONS AND MILITARY SECURITY SYSTEMS (PAMPHLET) (SPECIAL BIBLIOGRAPHY SERIES, NUMBER 25). DIPLOM FOR/AID INT/TRADE NUC/PWR PEACE 20 UN NATO OAS SEATO LEAGUE/NAT. PAGE 2 G0031
B62 BIBLIOG INT/ORG FORCES DETER

BENNETT J.C.,NUCLEAR WEAPONS AND THE CONFLICT OF CONSCIENCE. WOR+45 PROB/SOLV DIPLOM WEAPON SUPEGO MORAL...ANTHOL WORSHIP 20. PAGE 6 G0120
B62 POLICY NUC/PWR WAR

BURKE A.E.,ENOUGH GOOD MEN. USA+45 WOR+45 ECO/UNDEV FORCES TEC/DEV GUERRILLA NUC/PWR REV WAR ORD/FREE MARXISM...GEOG 20 COLD/WAR. PAGE 10 G0189
B62 DIPLOM POLICY NAT/G TASK

FORBES H.W.,THE STRATEGY OF DISARMAMENT. FUT WOR+45 INT/ORG VOL/ASSN CONSULT ARMS/CONT COERCE NUC/PWR WAR DRIVE RIGID/FLEX ORD/FREE PWR...POLICY CONCPT OBS TREND STERTYP 20. PAGE 19 G0378
B62 PLAN FORCES DIPLOM

FRIEDRICH-EBERT-STIFTUNG,THE SOVIET BLOC AND DEVELOPING COUNTRIES. CHINA/COM COM GERMANY/E USSR WOR+45 ECO/UNDEV INT/ORG NAT/G TEC/DEV NEUTRAL PWR ...POLICY 20. PAGE 20 G0394
B62 MARXISM DIPLOM ECO/TAC FOR/AID

GOLOVINE M.N.,CONFLICT IN SPACE: A PATTERN OF WAR IN A NEW DIMENSION. FUT USA+45 WOR+45 AIR FORCES PLAN DIPLOM DOMIN ATTIT...STAT AUD/VIS CHARTS COLD/WAR 20. PAGE 22 G0432
B62 CREATE TEC/DEV NUC/PWR SPACE

KAHN H.,THINKING ABOUT THE UNTHINKABLE. FUT USA+45 LAW NAT/G CONSULT FORCES ACT/RES CREATE PLAN TEC/DEV BAL/PWR DIPLOM EDU/PROP ARMS/CONT DETER ATTIT...CONCPT OBS TREND COLD/WAR 20. PAGE 29 G0570
B62 INT/ORG ORD/FREE NUC/PWR PEACE

KENNEDY J.F.,TO TURN THE TIDE. SPACE AGRI INT/ORG FORCES TEC/DEV ADMIN NUC/PWR PEACE WEALTH...ANTHOL 20 KENNEDY/JF CIV/RIGHTS. PAGE 30 G0592
B62 DIPLOM CHIEF POLICY NAT/G

LEFEVER E.W.,ARMS AND ARMS CONTROL. COM USA+45 INT/ORG TEC/DEV DIPLOM ORD/FREE 20. PAGE 33 G0652
B62 ATTIT PWR ARMS/CONT BAL/PWR

PERRE J.,LES MUTATIONS DE LA GUERRE MODERNE: DE LA REVOLUTION FRANCAISE A LA REVOLUTION NUCLEAIRE.
B62 WAR FORCES

DIPLOM ARMS/CONT DEATH REV WEAPON GP/REL PEACE ATTIT...STAT PREDICT BIBLIOG 18/20 WWI. PAGE 44 G0870
NUC/PWR

SCHMITT H.A.,THE PATH TO EUROPEAN UNITY. EUR+WWI USA+45 PLAN TEC/DEV DIPLOM FOR/AID CONFER...INT/LAW 20 EEC EURCOALSTL MARSHL/PLN UNIFICA. PAGE 49 G0971
B62 INT/ORG INT/TRADE REGION ECO/DEV

SCHWARTZ L.E.,INTERNATIONAL ORGANIZATIONS AND SPACE COOPERATION. VOL/ASSN CONSULT CREATE TEC/DEV SANCTION...POLICY INT/LAW PHIL/SCI 20 UN. PAGE 50 G0982
B62 INT/ORG DIPLOM R+D SPACE

SNYDER R.C.,FOREIGN POLICY DECISION-MAKING. FUT KOREA WOR+45 R+D CREATE ADMIN ROUTINE PWR ...DECISION PSY SOC CONCPT METH/CNCPT CON/ANAL CHARTS GEN/METH METH 20. PAGE 52 G1018
B62 TEC/DEV HYPO/EXP DIPLOM

STRAUSS L.L.,MEN AND DECISIONS. USA+45 USA-45 USSR CONSULT FORCES TOP/EX WAR PEACE 20. PAGE 53 G1042
B62 DECISION PWR NUC/PWR DIPLOM

THOMSON G.P.,NUCLEAR ENERGY IN BRITAIN DURING THE LAST WAR: THE CHERWELL SIMON LECTURE (MONOGRAPH). UK R+D CONSULT FORCES PLAN DIPLOM TASK CIVMIL/REL ROLE...PHIL/SCI NEW/IDEA LAB/EXP 20 MAUD. PAGE 54 G1071
B62 CREATE TEC/DEV WAR NUC/PWR

US CONGRESS,COMMUNICATIONS SATELLITE LEGISLATION: HEARINGS BEFORE COMM ON AERON AND SPACE SCIENCES ON BILLS S2550 AND 2814. WOR+45 LAW VOL/ASSN PLAN DIPLOM CONTROL OWN PEACE...NEW/IDEA CONGRESS NASA. PAGE 56 G1110
B62 SPACE COM/IND ADJUD GOV/REL

US SENATE COMM GOVT OPERATIONS,ADMINISTRATION OF NATIONAL SECURITY. USA+45 CHIEF PLAN PROB/SOLV TEC/DEV DIPLOM ATTIT...POLICY DECISION 20 KENNEDY/JF RUSK/D MCNAMARA/R BUNDY/M HERTER/C. PAGE 60 G1177
B62 ORD/FREE ADMIN NAT/G CONTROL

YALEN R.,REGIONALISM AND WORLD ORDER. EUR+WWI WOR+45 WOR-45 INT/ORG VOL/ASSN DELIB/GP FORCES TOP/EX BAL/PWR DIPLOM DOMIN REGION ARMS/CONT PWR ...JURID HYPO/EXP COLD/WAR 20. PAGE 64 G1261
B62 ORD/FREE POLICY

BETTEN J.K.,"ARMS CONTROL AND THE PROBLEM OF EVASION." WOR+45 FORCES CREATE DIPLOM DETER PWR ...PSY TREND GEN/LAWS COLD/WAR 20. PAGE 7 G0134
L62 NAT/G PLAN ARMS/CONT

FINKELSTEIN L.S.,"ARMS INSPECTION." FUT WOR+45 NAT/G DIPLOM ATTIT PERCEPT RIGID/FLEX ORD/FREE COLD/WAR 20. PAGE 19 G0369
L62 FORCES PWR ARMS/CONT

NIEBURG H.L.,"THE EISENHOWER ATOMIC ENERGY COMMISSION AND CONGRESS" R+D INT/ORG OP/RES DIPLOM ADMIN CONTROL 20 PRESIDENT CONGRESS AEC. PAGE 42 G0821
L62 NUC/PWR TOP/EX LOBBY DELIB/GP

BETHE H.,"DISARMAMENT AND STRATEGY." COM USA+45 USSR WOR+45 VOL/ASSN TEC/DEV EDU/PROP NUC/PWR CHOOSE PEACE...POLICY DECISION NEW/IDEA OBS GEN/LAWS COLD/WAR 420. PAGE 7 G0133
S62 PLAN ORD/FREE ARMS/CONT DIPLOM

BOULDING K.E.,"THE PREVENTION OF WORLD WAR THREE." FUT WOR+45 INT/ORG PLAN BAL/PWR PEACE ORD/FREE PWR ...NEW/IDEA TREND TOT/POP COLD/WAR 20. PAGE 8 G0158
S62 VOL/ASSN NAT/G ARMS/CONT DIPLOM

FOSTER W.C.,"ARMS CONTROL AND DISARMAMENT IN A DIVIDED WORLD." COM FUT USA+45 USSR WOR+45 INTELL INT/ORG NAT/G VOL/ASSN CONSULT CREATE PLAN TEC/DEV EDU/PROP LEGIT NUC/PWR ATTIT RIGID/FLEX...CONCPT TREND TOT/POP 20 UN. PAGE 20 G0387
S62 DELIB/GP POLICY ARMS/CONT DIPLOM

MARTIN L.W.,"THE MARKET FOR STRATEGIC IDEAS IN BRITAIN: THE 'SANDYS ERA'" UK ARMS/CONT WAR GOV/REL OPTIMAL...POLICY DECISION GOV/COMP COLD/WAR CMN/WLTH. PAGE 36 G0714
S62 DIPLOM COERCE FORCES PWR

SCHILLING W.R.,"SCIENTISTS, FOREIGN POLICY AND
POLITICS." WOR+45 WOR-45 INTELL INT/ORG CONSULT
TOP/EX ACT/RES PLAN ADMIN KNOWL...CONCPT OBS TREND
LEAGUE/NAT 20. PAGE 49 G0967
S62
NAT/G
TEC/DEV
DIPLOM
NUC/PWR

FLORES E.,LAND REFORM AND THE ALLIANCE FOR PROGRESS
(PAMPHLET). L/A+17C USA+45 STRUCT ECO/UNDEV NAT/G
WORKER CREATE PLAN ECO/TAC COERCE REV 20. PAGE 19
G0373
B63
AGRI
INT/ORG
DIPLOM
POLICY

GOLDSEN J.M.,OUTER SPACE IN WORLD POLITICS. COM
USA+45 NAT/G FORCES ACT/RES PLAN DOMIN EDU/PROP
COERCE ORD/FREE PWR...TECHNIC STAT INT SAMP TREND
ANTHOL VAL/FREE 20. PAGE 22 G0428
B63
TEC/DEV
DIPLOM
SPACE

MCDOUGAL M.S.,LAW AND PUBLIC ORDER IN SPACE. FUT
USA+45 ACT/RES TEC/DEV ADJUD...POLICY INT/LAW JURID
20. PAGE 37 G0739
B63
SPACE
ORD/FREE
DIPLOM
DECISION

MENEZES A.J.,SUBDESENVOLVIMENTO E POLITICA
INTERNACIONAL. BRAZIL WOR+45 PLAN CONTROL LEAD
NAT/LISM ORD/FREE 20 THIRD/WRLD. PAGE 38 G0754
B63
ECO/UNDEV
DIPLOM
POLICY
BAL/PWR

OECD,SCIENCE AND THE POLICIES OF GOVERNMENTS: THE
IMPLICATIONS OF SCIENCE AND TECHNOLOGY FOR NATL AND
INTL AFFAIRS. WOR+45 INT/ORG EDU/PROP AUTOMAT
...POLICY PHIL/SCI 20. PAGE 42 G0830
B63
CREATE
TEC/DEV
DIPLOM
NAT/G

PACHTER H.M.,COLLISION COURSE; THE CUBAN MISSILE
CRISIS AND COEXISTENCE. CUBA USA+45 DIPLOM
ARMS/CONT PEACE MARXISM...DECISION INT/LAW 20
COLD/WAR KHRUSH/N KENNEDY/JF CASTRO/F. PAGE 43
G0854
B63
WAR
BAL/PWR
NUC/PWR
DETER

PANAMERICAN UNION,DOCUMENTOS OFICIALES DE LA
ORGANIZACION DE LOS ESTADOS AMERICANOS, INDICE Y
LISTA (VOL. III, 1962). L/A+17C DELIB/GP INT/TRADE
EDU/PROP REGION NUC/PWR...HEAL INT/LAW SOC/WK 20
OAS. PAGE 44 G0857
B63
BIBLIOG
INT/ORG
DIPLOM

SCHRADER R.,SCIENCE AND POLICY. WOR+45 ECO/DEV
ECO/UNDEV R+D FORCES PLAN DIPLOM GOV/REL TECHRACY
BIBLIOG. PAGE 50 G0976
B63
TEC/DEV
NAT/G
POLICY
ADMIN

US ATOMIC ENERGY COMMISSION,ATOMIC ENERGY IN THE
SOVIET UNION: TRIP REPORT OF THE US ATOMIC ENERGY
DELEGATION, MAY 1933. USSR R+D NAT/G CONSULT CREATE
DIPLOM ADMIN ROUTINE EFFICIENCY PRODUC KNOWL SKILL
...NAT/COMP 20 AEC TRAVEL TREATY. PAGE 56 G1107
B63
METH/COMP
OP/RES
TEC/DEV
NUC/PWR

US DEPARTMENT OF THE ARMY,SOVIET RUSSIA: STRATEGIC
SURVEY (PAMPHLET). USSR POL/PAR PLAN DOMIN EDU/PROP
ARMS/CONT GUERRILLA WAR WEAPON...TREND CHARTS
ORG/CHARTS 20. PAGE 57 G1129
B63
BIBLIOG/A
MARXISM
DIPLOM
COERCE

US DEPARTMENT OF THE ARMY,US OVERSEAS BASES:
PRESENT STATUS AND FUTURE PROSPECTS (PAMPHLET).
USA+45 DIPLOM NUC/PWR ATTIT ORD/FREE...POLICY
CHARTS 20. PAGE 58 G1130
B63
BIBLIOG/A
WAR
BAL/PWR
DETER

US SENATE,DOCUMENTS ON INTERNATIONAL AS"ECTS OF
EXPLORATION AND USE OF OUTER SPACE, 1954-62: STAFF
REPORT FOR COMM AERON SPACE SCI. USA+45 USSR LEGIS
LEAD CIVMIL/REL PEACE...POLICY INT/LAW ANTHOL 20
CONGRESS NASA KHRUSH/N. PAGE 59 G1162
B63
SPACE
UTIL
GOV/REL
DIPLOM

US SENATE COMM APPROPRIATIONS,PERSONNEL
ADMINISTRATION AND OPERATIONS OF AGENCY FOR
INTERNATIONAL DEVELOPMENT: SPECIAL HEARING. FINAN
LEAD COST UTIL SKILL...CHARTS 20 CONGRESS AID
CIVIL/SERV. PAGE 60 G1175
B63
ADMIN
FOR/AID
EFFICIENCY
DIPLOM

BEGUIN H.,"ASPECTS GEOGRAPHIQUE DE LA
POLARISATION." FUT WOR+45 SOCIETY STRUCT ECO/DEV
R+D BAL/PWR ADMIN ATTIT RIGID/FLEX HEALTH WEALTH
...CHARTS 20. PAGE 6 G0114
L63
ECO/UNDEV
GEOG
DIPLOM

CLEVELAND H.,"CRISIS DIPLOMACY." USA+45 WOR+45 LAW
FORCES TASK NUC/PWR PWR 20. PAGE 12 G0235
S6
DECISION
DIPLOM
PROB/SOLV
POLICY

HOSKINS H.L. "ARAB SOCIALISM IN THE UAR." ISLAM
USSR AGRI INDUS NAT/G TOP/EX CREATE DIPLOM EDU/PROP
DRIVE KNOWL PWR SOCISM...POLICY CONCPT TREND SUEZ
20. PAGE 27 G0530
S6
ECO/DEV
PLAN
UAR

PHELPS J.,"INFORMATION AND ARMS CONTROL." COM SPACE
USA+45 USSR WOR+45 R+D INT/ORG NAT/G DELIB/GP
DIPLOM ORD/FREE...CONCPT 20. PAGE 45 G0875
56'
KNOWL
ARMS/CONT
NUC/PWR

ETZIONI A.,THE MOON-DOGGLE: DOMESTIC AND
INTERNATIONAL IMPLICATIONS OF THE SPACE RACE. FUT
USA+45 WOR+45 INTELL ECO/DEV INDUS VOL/ASSN
EX/STRUC FORCES LEGIS TOP/EX PLAN TEC/DEV ECO/TAC
EDU/PROP KNOWL ORD/FREE PWR RESPECT WEALTH
TIME/SEQ. PAGE 18 G0352
B64
R+D
NAT/G
DIPLOM
SPACE

FOGELMAN E.,HIROSHIMA: THE DECISION TO USE THE A-
BOMB. USA-45 DIPLOM EFFICIENCY PEACE...ANTHOL
BIBLIOG T 20 CHINJAP. PAGE 19 G0375
B6
INTELL
DECISION
NUC/PWR
WAR

FREYMOND J.,WESTERN EUROPE SINCE THE WAR. COM
EUR+WWI USA+45 DIPLOM...BIBLIOG 20 NATO UN EEC.
PAGE 20 G0392
B64
INT/ORG
POLICY
ECO/DEV
ECO/TAC

GOWING M.,BRITAIN AND ATOMIC ENERGY 1939-1945.
FRANCE UK USA+45 USA-45 NAT/G CREATE...PHIL/SCI 20
AEA. PAGE 22 G0439
B64
NUC/PWR
DIPLOM
TEC/DEV

HASKINS C.P.,THE SCIENTIFIC REVOLUTION AND WORLD
POLITICS. COM FUT USA+45 ECO/DEV ECO/UNDEV ATTIT
...PHIL/SCI BIBLIOG 20 THIRD/WRLD. PAGE 25 G0489
B64
TEC/DEV
POLICY
DIPLOM
TREND

HAZLEWOOD A.,THE ECONOMICS OF DEVELOPMENT: AN
ANNOTATED LIST OF BOOKS AND ARTICLES PUBLISHED
1958-1962. AGRI FINAN INDUS LABOR NAT/G DIPLOM
INT/TRADE INCOME...MGT 20. PAGE 25 G0497
B64
BIBLIOG/A
ECO/UNDEV
TEC/DEV

KAUFMANN W.W.,THE MC NAMARA STRATEGY. TOP/EX
INSPECT BAL/PWR DIPLOM CONTROL DETER GUERRILLA
NUC/PWR WEAPON COST PWR...METH/COMP 20 MCNAMARA/R
KENNEDY/JF JOHNSON/LB NATO DEPT/DEFEN. PAGE 30
G0586
B64
FORCES
WAR
PLAN
PROB/SOLV

NASA,PROCEEDINGS OF CONFERENCE ON THE LAW OF SPACE
AND OF SATELLITE COMMUNICATIONS: CHICAGO 1963. FUT
WOR+45 DELIB/GP PROB/SOLV TEC/DEV CONFER ADJUD
NUC/PWR...POLICY IDEA/COMP 20 NASA. PAGE 41 G0805
B64
SPACE
COM/IND
LAW
DIPLOM

OSSENBECK F.J.,OPEN SPACE AND PEACE. CHINA/COM FUT
USA+45 USSR LAW PROB/SOLV TEC/DEV EDU/PROP NEUTRAL
PEACE...AUD/VIS ANTHOL 20. PAGE 43 G0850
B64
SPACE
ORD/FREE
DIPLOM
CREATE

POWELSON J.P.,LATIN AMERICA: TODAY'S ECONOMIC AND
SOCIAL REVOLUTION. L/A+17C INTELL SOCIETY STRUCT
AGRI INDUS NAT/G DIPLOM ECO/TAC REV...POLICY 20.
PAGE 45 G0887
B64
ECO/UNDEV
WEALTH
ADJUST
PLAN

ROBERTS HL,FOREIGN AFFAIRS BIBLIOGRAPHY, 1952-1962.
ECO/DEV SECT PLAN FOR/AID INT/TRADE ARMS/CONT
NAT/LISM ATTIT...INT/LAW GOV/COMP IDEA/COMP 20.
PAGE 47 G0928
B64
BIBLIOG/A
DIPLOM
INT/ORG
WAR

SCHWARTZ M.D.,CONFERENCE ON SPACE SCIENCE AND SPACE
LAW. FUT COM/IND NAT/G FORCES ACT/RES PLAN BUDGET
DIPLOM NUC/PWR WEAPON...POLICY ANTHOL 20. PAGE 50
G0983
B64
SPACE
LAW
PEACE
TEC/DEV

TAUBENFELD H.J.,SPACE AND SOCIETY. USA+45 LAW
FORCES CREATE TEC/DEV ADJUD CONTROL COST PEACE
...PREDICT ANTHOL 20. PAGE 54 G1057
B64
SPACE
SOCIETY
ADJUST
DIPLOM

THANT U.,TOWARD WORLD PEACE. DELIB/GP TEC/DEV
EDU/PROP WAR SOVEREIGN...INT/LAW 20 UN MID/EAST.
PAGE 54 G1065

B64

DIPLOM
BIOG
PEACE
COERCE

US AIR FORCE ACADEMY ASSEMBLY,OUTER SPACE: FINAL
REPORT APRIL 1-4, 1964. FUT USA+45 WOR+45 LAW
DELIB/GP CONFER ARMS/CONT WAR PEACE ATTIT MORAL
...ANTHOL 20 NASA. PAGE 56 G1104

B64

SPACE
CIVMIL/REL
NUC/PWR
DIPLOM

WILLIAMS S.P.,TOWARD A GENUINE WORLD SECURITY
SYSTEM (PAMPHLET). WOR+45 INT/ORG FORCES PLAN
NUC/PWR ORD/FREE...INT/LAW CONCPT UN PRESIDENT.
PAGE 63 G1243

B64

BIBLIOG/A
ARMS/CONT
DIPLOM
PEACE

"FURTHER READING." INDIA PAKISTAN SECT WAR PEACE
ATTIT...POLICY 20. PAGE 1 G0018

S64

BIBLIOG
GP/REL
DIPLOM
NAT/G

LERNER A.P.,"NUCLEAR SYMMETRY AS A FRAMEWORK FOR
COEXISTENCE." COM FUT USA+45 NAT/G ACT/RES CREATE
PLAN DIPLOM EDU/PROP COERCE WAR RIGID/FLEX PWR
SKILL...CONCPT METH/CNCPT GEN/LAWS TOT/POP VAL/FREE
COLD/WAR 20. PAGE 33 G0657

S64

FORCES
ORD/FREE
DETER
NUC/PWR

MAGGS P.B.,"SOVIET VIEWPOINT ON NUCLEAR WEAPONS IN
INTERNATIONAL LAW." USSR WOR+45 INT/ORG FORCES
DIPLOM ARMS/CONT ATTIT ORD/FREE PWR...POLICY JURID
CONCPT OBS TREND CON/ANAL GEN/LAWS VAL/FREE 20.
PAGE 35 G0694

S64

COM
LAW
INT/LAW
NUC/PWR

SCHRAMM W.,"MASS MEDIA AND NATIONAL DEVELOPMENT:
THE ROLE OF INFORMATION IN DEVELOPING COUNTRIES."
FINAN R+D ACT/RES PLAN TEC/DEV DIPLOM CHOOSE SUPEGO
ORD/FREE...BIBLIOG 20. PAGE 50 G0978

C64

ECO/UNDEV
COM/IND
EDU/PROP
MAJORIT

WHITE HOUSE CONFERENCE ON INTERNATIONAL
COOPERATION(VOL.II). SPACE WOR+45 EXTR/IND INT/ORG
LABOR WORKER NUC/PWR PEACE AGE/Y...CENSUS ANTHOL 20
RESOURCE/N URBAN/RNWL PUB/TRANS. PAGE 1 G0019

B65

R+D
CONFER
TEC/DEV
DIPLOM

PEACE RESEARCH ABSTRACTS. FUT WOR+45 R+D INT/ORG
NAT/G PLAN TEC/DEV BAL/PWR DIPLOM FOR/AID NUC/PWR
HEALTH. PAGE 1 G0020

B65

BIBLIOG/A
PEACE
ARMS/CONT
WAR

ALLEN S.,LETTER TO A CONSERVATIVE. SOCIETY NAT/G
DIPLOM EDU/PROP NUC/PWR GP/REL ATTIT MORAL
...MAJORIT CONCPT 20. PAGE 2 G0044

B65

ORD/FREE
MARXISM
POLICY
LAISSEZ

ATOMIC INDUSTRIAL FORUM,SAFEGUARDS AGAINST
DIVERSION OF NUCLEAR MATERIALS FROM PEACEFUL TO
MILITARY PURPOSES. WOR+45 DELIB/GP FORCES PLAN
DIPLOM CONFER PEACE...ANTHOL 20 IAEA. PAGE 4 G0081

B65

NUC/PWR
CIVMIL/REL
INSPECT
CONTROL

BAILEY S.K.,AMERICAN POLITICS AND GOVERNMENT.
USA+45 CONSTN FINAN LABOR POL/PAR DIPLOM ADMIN WAR
INGP/REL RACE/REL NEW/LIB 20 SUPREME/CT PRESIDENT
CONGRESS. PAGE 4 G0084

B65

ANTHOL
LEGIS
PWR

BEAUFRE A.,AN INTRODUCTION TO STRATEGY, WITH
PARTICULAR REFERENCE TO PROBLEMS OF DEFENSE,
POLITICS, ECONOMICS IN THE NUCLEAR AGE. WOR+45
FORCES DIPLOM DETER CIVMIL/REL GP/REL...NEW/IDEA
IDEA/COMP 20. PAGE 6 G0111

B65

PLAN
NUC/PWR
WEAPON
DECISION

BLOOMFIELD L.,SOVIET INTERESTS IN ARMS CONTROL AND
DISARMAMENT* THE DECADE UNDER KHRUSHCHEV 1954-1964.
ASIA FORCES ACT/RES EDU/PROP DETER NUC/PWR WEAPON
COST ATTIT...PHIL/SCI CLASSIF STAT NET/THEORY GAME
BIBLIOG. PAGE 7 G0139

B65

USSR
ARMS/CONT
DIPLOM
TREND

CORDIER A.W.,THE QUEST FOR PEACE. WOR+45 NAT/G PLAN
BAL/PWR ECO/TAC ARMS/CONT NUC/PWR PWR...ANTHOL UN
COLD/WAR. PAGE 13 G0256

B65

PEACE
DIPLOM
POLICY
INT/ORG

FRUTKIN A.W.,SPACE AND THE INTERNATIONAL
COOPERATION YEAR: A NATIONAL CHALLENGE (PAMPHLET).
EUR+WWI USA+45 FINAN TEC/DEV BUDGET...MGT 20 NASA.
PAGE 20 G0396

B65

SPACE
INDUS
NAT/G
DIPLOM

GRETTON P.,MARITIME STRATEGY - A STUDY OF DEFENSE
PROBLEMS. ASIA UK USSR DIPLOM COERCE DETER NUC/PWR
WEAPON...CONCPT NAT/COMP 20. PAGE 23 G0449

B65

FORCES
PLAN
WAR
SEA

HALPERIN M.H.,CHINA AND THE BOMB. USA+45 USSR
INT/ORG FORCES ARMS/CONT DETER PRODUC ORD/FREE PWR
TREND. PAGE 24 G0472

B65

ASIA
NUC/PWR
WAR
DIPLOM

JENKS C.W.,SPACE LAW. DIPLOM DEBATE CONTROL
ORD/FREE TREATY 20 UN. PAGE 29 G0563

B65

SPACE
INT/LAW
JURID
INT/ORG

LOWENSTEIN L.,GOVERNMENT RESOURCES AVAILABLE FOR
FOREIGN AFFAIRS RESEARCH. NAT/G DIPLOM GOV/REL.
PAGE 34 G0677

B65

R+D
ACADEM
ACT/RES
BIBLIOG/A

MCGUIRE M.C.,SECRECY AND THE ARMS RACE* A THEORY OF
THE ACCUMULATION OF STRATEGIC WEAPONS AND HOW
SECRECY AFFECTS IT. DIPLOM NUC/PWR WEAPON ISOLAT
RATIONAL ORD/FREE WEALTH...ECOMETRIC MATH GEN/LAWS.
PAGE 38 G0742

B65

DETER
ARMS/CONT
SIMUL
GAME

MOSKOWITZ H.,US SECURITY, ARMS CONTROL, AND
DISARMAMENT 1961-1965. FORCES DIPLOM DETER WAR
WEAPON...CHARTS 20 UN COLD/WAR NATO. PAGE 40 G0790

B65

BIBLIOG/A
ARMS/CONT
NUC/PWR
PEACE

SCHEINMAN L.,ATOMIC ENERGY POLICY IN FRANCE UNDER
THE FOURTH REPUBLIC. FRANCE UK USA+45 ELITES
POL/PAR PLAN PROB/SOLV DIPLOM LEAD GOV/REL
...BIBLIOG 20 DEGAULLE/C. PAGE 49 G0962

B65

NUC/PWR
NAT/G
DELIB/GP
POLICY

SINGER J.D.,HUMAN BEHAVIOR AND INTERNATIONAL
POLITICS* CONTRIBUTIONS FROM THE SOCIAL-
PSYCHOLOGICAL SCIENCES. ACT/RES PLAN EDU/PROP ADMIN
KNOWL...DECISION PSY SOC NET/THEORY HYPO/EXP
LAB/EXP SOC/EXP GEN/METH ANTHOL BIBLIOG. PAGE 51
G1006

B65

DIPLOM
PHIL/SCI
QUANT
SIMUL

THAYER F.C. JR.,AIR TRANSPORT POLICY AND NATIONAL
SECURITY: A POLITICAL, ECONOMIC, AND MILITARY
ANALYSIS. DIST/IND OP/RES PLAN TEC/DEV DIPLOM DETER
WAR COST EFFICIENCY...POLICY BIBLIOG 20 DEPT/DEFEN
FAA CAB. PAGE 54 G1066

B65

AIR
FORCES
CIVMIL/REL
ORD/FREE

TYBOUT R.A.,ECONOMICS OF RESEARCH AND DEVELOPMENT.
ECO/DEV ECO/UNDEV INDUS PROFIT DECISION. PAGE 55
G1084

B65

R+D
FORCES
ADMIN
DIPLOM

UN,SPACE ACTIVITIES AND RESOURCES: REVIEW OF UNITED
NATION'S NATIONAL AND INTERNATIONAL PROGRAMS.
INT/ORG LABOR PLAN TEC/DEV DIPLOM EFFICIENCY HEALTH
...GOV/COMP 20 UN. PAGE 55 G1086

B65

SPACE
NUC/PWR
FOR/AID
PEACE

UNESCO,HANDBOOK OF INTERNATIONAL EXCHANGES. COM/IND
R+D ACADEM PROF/ORG VOL/ASSN CREATE TEC/DEV
EDU/PROP AGREE 20 TREATY. PAGE 55 G1090

B65

INDEX
INT/ORG
DIPLOM
PRESS

US CONGRESS JT ATOM ENRGY COMM,ATOMIC ENERGY
LEGISLATION THROUGH 89TH CONGRESS, 1ST SESSION.
USA+45 LAW INT/ORG DELIB/GP BUDGET DIPLOM 20 AEC
CONGRESS CASEBOOK EURATOM IAEA. PAGE 57 G1114

B65

NUC/PWR
FORCES
PEACE
LEGIS

US DEPARTMENT OF DEFENSE,US SECURITY ARMS CONTROL,
AND DISARMAMENT 1961-1965 (PAMPHLET). CHINA/COM COM
GERMANY/W ISRAEL SPACE USA+45 USSR WOR+45 FORCES
EDU/PROP DETER EQUILIB PEACE ALL/VALS...GOV/COMP 20
NATO. PAGE 57 G1118

B65

BIBLIOG/A
ARMS/CONT
NUC/PWR
DIPLOM

US DEPARTMENT OF THE ARMY,NUCLEAR WEAPONS AND THE
ATLANTIC ALLIANCE: A BIBLIOGRAPHIC SURVEY. ASIA COM
EUR+WWI USA+45 FORCES DIPLOM WEAPON...STAT 20 NATO.
PAGE 58 G1131
B65
BIBLIOG/A
ARMS/CONT
NUC/PWR
BAL/PWR

US SENATE,US INTERNATIONAL SPACE PROGRAMS, 1959-65:
STAFF REPORT FOR COMM ON AERONAUTICAL AND SPACE
SCIENCES. WOR+45 VOL/ASSN CIVMIL/REL 20 CONGRESS
NASA TREATY. PAGE 59 G1163
B65
SPACE
DIPLOM
PLAN
GOV/REL

US SENATE COMM AERO SPACE SCI,INTERNATIONAL
COOPERATION AND ORGANIZATION FOR OUTER SPACE. FUT
USA+45 WOR+45 PROF/ORG VOL/ASSN CONSULT DELIB/GP
PLAN TEC/DEV ARMS/CONT GP/REL PEACE 20 UN NASA.
PAGE 59 G1167
B65
DIPLOM
SPACE
R+D
NAT/G

US SENATE COMM GOVT OPERATIONS,ORGANIZATION OF
FEDERAL EXECUTIVE DEPARTMENTS AND AGENCIES: REPORT
OF MARCH 23, 1965. USA+45 FORCES LEGIS DIPLOM
ROUTINE CIVMIL/REL EFFICIENCY FEDERAL...MGT STAT.
PAGE 60 G1179
B65
ADMIN
EX/STRUC
GOV/REL
ORG/CHARTS

WASKOW A.I.,KEEPING THE WORLD DISARMED. AFR
GERMANY/E DIPLOM CONTROL WAR 20 UN. PAGE 62 G1218
B65
ARMS/CONT
PEACE
FORCES
PROB/SOLV

WEISNER J.B.,WHERE SCIENCE AND POLITICS MEET.
USA+45 ECO/DEV R+D FORCES PROB/SOLV DIPLOM FOR/AID
CONTROL...PHIL/SCI PRESIDENT KENNEDY/JF JOHNSON/LB.
PAGE 63 G1228
B65
CHIEF
NAT/G
POLICY
TEC/DEV

LASSWELL H.D.,"THE POLICY SCIENCES OF DEVELOPMENT."
CULTURE SOCIETY EX/STRUC CREATE ADMIN ATTIT KNOWL
...SOC CONCPT SIMUL GEN/METH. PAGE 33 G0644
L65
PWR
METH/CNCPT
DIPLOM

ABT C.C.,"CONTROLLING FUTURE ARMS." USSR PLAN
BAL/PWR DIPLOM NUC/PWR COST...CLASSIF STAT CHARTS.
PAGE 2 G0027
S65
PREDICT
FUT
ARMS/CONT
TEC/DEV

BIRNBAUM K.,"SWEDEN'S NUCLEAR POLICY." WOR+45
POL/PAR CREATE TEC/DEV NEUTRAL RISK WAR ORD/FREE
...DECISION IDEA/COMP NAT/COMP TIME. PAGE 7 G0137
S65
SWEDEN
NUC/PWR
DIPLOM
ARMS/CONT

BLOOMFIELD L.P.,"ARMS CONTROL AND THE DEVELOPING
COUNTRIES." AFR ISLAM S/ASIA USA+45 VOL/ASSN
TEC/DEV DIPLOM REGION NUC/PWR...PREDICT TREND.
PAGE 7 G0142
S65
ARMS/CONT
ECO/UNDEV
HYPO/EXP
OBS

BOHN L.C.,"ATOMS FOR PEACE AND ATOMS FOR WAR."
WOR+45 INT/ORG TEC/DEV DIPLOM IDEA/COMP. PAGE 8
G0149
S65
NUC/PWR
ARMS/CONT
RECORD

DALKEY N.C.,"SOLVABLE NUCLEAR WAR MODELS." FORCES
BAL/PWR DIPLOM COERCE PEACE DECISION. PAGE 14 G0273
S65
GAME
SIMUL
WAR
NUC/PWR

DESAI M.J.,"INDIA AND NUCLEAR WEAPONS." ASIA
BAL/PWR DIPLOM NUC/PWR WEAPON PEACE RECORD. PAGE 15
G0294
S65
INDIA
ARMS/CONT

FOX A.B.,"NATO AND CONGRESS." CONSTN DELIB/GP
EX/STRUC FORCES TOP/EX BUDGET NUC/PWR GOV/REL
...GP/COMP CONGRESS NATO TREATY. PAGE 20 G0388
S65
CONTROL
DIPLOM

HARRISON S.L.,"NTH NATION CHALLENGES* THE PRESENT
PERSPECTIVE." EUR+WWI FUT USA+45 BAL/PWR CONTROL
RISK COERCE WAR...PREDICT COLD/WAR. PAGE 25 G0485
S65
ARMS/CONT
NUC/PWR
NAT/G
DIPLOM

HOLSTI O.R.,"EAST-WEST CONFLICT AND SINO-SOVIET
RELATIONS" CHINA/COM USSR COMPUTER REGION DECISION.
PAGE 27 G0523
S65
VOL/ASSN
DIPLOM
CON/ANAL
COM

HUGHES T.L.,"SCHOLARS AND FOREIGN POLICY* VARIETIES
S65
ACT/RES

OF RESEARCH EXPERIENCE." COM/IND DIPLOM ADMIN EXEC
ROUTINE...MGT OBS CONGRESS PRESIDENT CAMELOT.
PAGE 27 G0535
ACADEM
CONTROL
NAT/G

KOHL W.L.,"NUCLEAR SHARING IN NATO AND THE
MULTILATERAL FORCE." FUT USSR VOL/ASSN TEC/DEV
DIPLOM NUC/PWR WAR WEAPON NATO. PAGE 31 G0611
S65
ARMS/CONT
OBS
IDEA/COMP

KREITH K.,"PEACE RESEARCH AND GOVERNMENT POLICY."
INTELL NAT/G DIPLOM ECO/TAC CONTROL ARMS/CONT WAR
PERCEPT...DECISION IDEA/COMP. PAGE 31 G0619
S65
PEACE
STYLE
OBS

RUBINSTEIN A.Z.,"POLITICAL BARRIERS TO
DISARMAMENT." FUT DIPLOM COERCE NUC/PWR WAR
NAT/LISM ORD/FREE PREDICT. PAGE 48 G0944
S65
COM
USA+45
ARMS/CONT
ATTIT

MARK M.,"BEYOND SOVEREIGNTY." WOR+45 WOR-45
ECO/UNDEV BAL/PWR INT/TRADE NUC/PWR REV WAR MARXISM
NEW/LIB BIBLIOG. PAGE 36 G0706
C65
NAT/LISM
NAT/G
DIPLOM
INTELL

SCHWEBEL M.,"BEHAVIORAL SCIENCE AND HUMAN
SURVIVAL." FORCES ARMS/CONT COERCE NUC/PWR WAR
GP/REL NAT/LISM PERCEPT...POLICY PSY ANTHOL
BIBLIOG/A 20 COLD/WAR. PAGE 50 G0984
C65
PEACE
ACT/RES
DIPLOM
HEAL

SEARA M.V.,"COSMIC INTERNATIONAL LAW." LAW ACADEM
ACT/RES DIPLOM COLONIAL CONTROL NUC/PWR SOVEREIGN
...GEN/LAWS BIBLIOG UN. PAGE 50 G0987
C65
SPACE
INT/LAW
IDEA/COMP
INT/ORG

ALEXANDER Y.,INTERNATIONAL TECHNICAL ASSISTANCE
EXPERTS* A CASE STUDY OF THE U.N. EXPERIENCE.
ECO/UNDEV CONSULT EX/STRUC CREATE PLAN DIPLOM
FOR/AID TASK EFFICIENCY...ORG/CHARTS UN. PAGE 2
G0038
B66
ECO/TAC
INT/ORG
ADMIN
MGT

AMERICAN ASSEMBLY COLUMBIA U,A WORLD OF NUCLEAR
POWERS? FUT WOR+45 ECO/DEV BAL/PWR ECO/TAC CONTROL
RISK EFFICIENCY ATTIT PWR...METH/COMP ANTHOL 20.
PAGE 3 G0049
B66
NUC/PWR
DIPLOM
TEC/DEV
ARMS/CONT

BEATON L.,MUST THE BOMB SPREAD? WOR+45 TEC/DEV
DIPLOM DRIVE ORD/FREE PWR...CHARTS 20. PAGE 6 G0109
B66
NUC/PWR
ARMS/CONT
PLAN
PROB/SOLV

BLOOMFIELD L.P.,KHRUSHCHEV AND THE ARMS RACE.
USA+45 USSR ECO/DEV BAL/PWR EDU/PROP CONFER NUC/PWR
ATTIT...CHARTS 20 KHRUSH/N. PAGE 7 G0143
B66
ARMS/CONT
COM
POLICY
DIPLOM

DAENIKER G.,STRATEGIE DES KLEIN STAATS. SWITZERLND
ACT/RES CREATE DIPLOM NEUTRAL DETER WAR WEAPON PWR
SOVEREIGN...IDEA/COMP 20 COLD/WAR. PAGE 14 G0270
B66
NUC/PWR
PLAN
FORCES
NAT/G

ECKSTEIN A.,COMMUNIST CHINA'S ECONOMIC GROWTH AND
FOREIGN TRADE* IMPLICATIONS FOR US POLICY. COM
USA+45 USSR STRUCT INDUS MARKET DIPLOM ECO/TAC
FOR/AID INT/TRADE...STAT CHARTS. PAGE 17 G0332
B66
ASIA
ECO/UNDEV
CREATE
PWR

FALK R.A.,ON MINIMIZING THE USE OF NUCLEAR WEAPONS;
THREE ESSAYS; RESEARCH MONOGRAPH NO. 23. WOR+45
STRUCT CREATE NUC/PWR REV CONSERVE...POLICY
NET/THEORY IDEA/COMP GEN/LAWS GEN/METH. PAGE 18
G0359
B66
DIPLOM
EQUILIB
PHIL/SCI
PROB/SOLV

FEIS H.,THE ATOMIC BOMB AND THE END OF WORLD WAR
II. FORCES PLAN PROB/SOLV DIPLOM CONFER WAR
...TIME/SEQ TREND CHINJAP PRESIDENT TIME. PAGE 19
G0362
B66
USA+45
PEACE
NUC/PWR

FREIDEL F.,AMERICAN ISSUES IN THE TWENTIETH
CENTURY. SOCIETY FINAN ECO/TAC FOR/AID CONTROL
NUC/PWR WAR RACE/REL PEACE ATTIT...ANTHOL T 20
WILSON/W ROOSEVLT/F KENNEDY/JF TRUMAN/HS. PAGE 20
G0391
B66
DIPLOM
POLICY
NAT/G
ORD/FREE

B66
GLAZER M.,THE FEDERAL GOVERNMENT AND THE
UNIVERSITY. CHILE PROB/SOLV DIPLOM GIVE ADMIN WAR
...POLICY SOC 20. PAGE 21 G0421

BIBLIOG/A
NAT/G
PLAN
ACADEM

B66
HALPERIN M.H.,CHINA AND NUCLEAR PROLIFERATION
(PAMPHLET). CHINA/COM FUT INDIA USA+45 USSR
ARMS/CONT WAR 20 CHINJAP. PAGE 24 G0474

NUC/PWR
FORCES
POLICY
DIPLOM

B66
JACOBSON H.K.,DIPLOMATS, SCIENTISTS, AND
POLITICIANS* THE UNITED STATES AND THE NUCLEAR TEST
BAN NEGOTIATIONS. USA+45 USSR ACT/RES PLAN CONFER
DETER NUC/PWR CONSEN ORD/FREE...INT TREATY. PAGE 28
G0554

DIPLOM
ARMS/CONT
TECHRACY
INT/ORG

B66
KUENNE R.E.,THE POLARIS MISSILE STRIKE* A GENERAL
ECONOMIC SYSTEMS ANALYSIS. USA+45 USSR NAT/G
BAL/PWR ARMS/CONT WAR...MATH PROBABIL COMPUT/IR
CHARTS HYPO/EXP SIMUL. PAGE 32 G0625

NUC/PWR
FORCES
DETER
DIPLOM

B66
VON BORCH H,FRIEDE TROTZ KRIEG.GERMANY USSR
WOR+45 PEACE ANOMIE ATTIT 20. PAGE 43 G0853

DIPLOM
NUC/PWR
WAR
COERCE

B66
STONE J.J.,CONTAINING THE ARMS RACE* SOME SPECIFIC
PROPOSALS. ASIA USA+45 USSR PROB/SOLV BARGAIN
DIPLOM DETER NUC/PWR RATIONAL...GAME 20 DEPT/DEFEN
TREATY. PAGE 53 G1038

ARMS/CONT
FEEDBACK
COST
ATTIT

B66
UNITED NATIONS,INTERNATIONAL SPACE BIBLIOGRAPHY.
FUT INT/ORG TEC/DEV DIPLOM ARMS/CONT NUC/PWR
...JURID SOC UN. PAGE 56 G1093

BIBLIOG
SPACE
PEACE
R+D

B66
US DEPARTMENT OF THE ARMY,COMMUNIST CHINA: A
STRATEGIC SURVEY: A BIBLIOGRAPHY (PAMPHLET NO.
20-67). CHINA/COM COM INDIA USSR NAT/G POL/PAR
EX/STRUC FORCES NUC/PWR REV ATTIT...POLICY GEOG
CHARTS. PAGE 58 G1133

BIBLIOG/A
MARXISM
S/ASIA
DIPLOM

B66
US SENATE COMM AERO SPACE SCI,SOVIET SPACE
PROGRAMS, 1962-65; GOALS AND PURPOSES,
ACHIEVEMENTS, PLANS, AND INTERNATIONAL
IMPLICATIONS. USA+45 USSR R+D FORCES PLAN EDU/PROP
PRESS ADJUD ARMS/CONT ATTIT MARXISM. PAGE 60 G1168

CONSULT
SPACE
FUT
DIPLOM

B66
YOUNG W.,EXISTING MECHANISMS OF ARMS CONTROL.
PROC/MFG OP/RES DIPLOM TASK CENTRAL...MGT TREATY.
PAGE 65 G1266

ARMS/CONT
ADMIN
NUC/PWR
ROUTINE

L66
PACKENHAM R.A.,"POLITICAL-DEVELOPMENT DOCTRINES IN
THE AMERICAN FOREIGN AID PROGRAM." STRUCT R+D
CREATE DIPLOM AID. PAGE 43 G0855

FOR/AID
ECO/UNDEV
GEN/LAWS

L66
ZOPPO C.E.,"NUCLEAR TECHNOLOGY, MULTIPOLARITY, AND
INTERNATIONAL STABILITY." ASIA RUSSIA USA+45 STRUCT
TOP/EX BAL/PWR DIPLOM DETER CIVMIL/REL NAT/COMP.
PAGE 65 G1270

NET/THEORY
ORD/FREE
DECISION
NUC/PWR

S66
KAPLAN M.A.,"THE NEW GREAT DEBATE* TRADITIONALISM
VS SCIENCE IN INTERNATIONAL RELATIONS."...DECISION
HUM QUANT STYLE NET/THEORY CON/ANAL STERTYP
GEN/LAWS. PAGE 29 G0577

PHIL/SCI
CONSERVE
DIPLOM
SIMUL

S66
TURKEVICH J.,"SOVIET SCIENCE APPRAISED." USA+45 R+D
ACADEM FORCES DIPLOM EDU/PROP WAR EFFICIENCY PEACE
SKILL OBS. PAGE 55 G1081

USSR
TEC/DEV
NAT/COMP
ATTIT

B67
AMERICAN FRIENDS SERVICE COMM,IN PLACE OF WAR.
NAT/G ACT/RES DIPLOM ADMIN NUC/PWR EFFICIENCY
...POLICY 20. PAGE 3 G0053

PEACE
PACIFISM
WAR
DETER

B67
ARON R.,THE GREAT DEBATE: THEORIES OF NUCLEAR
STRATEGY. FRANCE USA+45 INT/ORG PLAN TREND. PAGE 4
G0068

NUC/PWR
DETER
BAL/PWR

DIPLOM

B67
BURNS E.L.M.,MEGAMURDER. WOR+45 LAW INT/ORG NAT/G
BAL/PWR DIPLOM DETER MURDER WEAPON CIVMIL/REL PEACE
...INT/LAW TREND 20. PAGE 10 G0193

FORCES
PLAN
WAR
NUC/PWR

B67
GARCIA ROBLES A.,THE DENUCLEARIZATION OF LATIN
AMERICA (TRANS. BY MARJORIE URQUIDI). LAW PLAN
DIPLOM...ANTHOL 20 TREATY UN. PAGE 21 G0409

NUC/PWR
ARMS/CONT
L/A+17C
INT/ORG

B67
HALLE L.J.,THE COLD WAR AS HISTORY. USSR WOR+45
ECO/TAC FOR/AID NUC/PWR WAR PEACE ORD/FREE
...MAJORIT TREND 20 COLD/WAR KENNEDY/JF KHRUSH/N
BERLIN/BLO. PAGE 24 G0470

DIPLOM
BAL/PWR

B67
KINTNER W.R.,PEACE AND THE STRATEGY CONFLICT. PLAN
BAL/PWR DIPLOM CONTROL ARMS/CONT DETER WEAPON 20.
PAGE 30 G0599

ROLE
PEACE
NUC/PWR
ORD/FREE

B67
LAMBERT J.,LATIN AMERICA: SOCIAL STRUCTURES AND
POLITICAL INSTITUTIONS. STRUCT TEC/DEV DIPLOM ADMIN
COLONIAL LEAD ATTIT...SOC CLASSIF NAT/COMP 17/20.
PAGE 32 G0631

L/A+17C
ECO/UNDEV
SOCIETY

B67
MCBRIDE J.H.,THE TEST BAN TREATY: MILITARY,
TECHNOLOGICAL, AND POLITICAL IMPLICATIONS. USA+45
USSR DELIB/GP FORCES LEGIS TEC/DEV BAL/PWR TREATY.
PAGE 37 G0727

ARMS/CONT
DIPLOM
NUC/PWR

B67
MCCLINTOCK R.,THE MEANING OF LIMITED WAR. FUT
WOR+45 NAT/G FORCES GUERRILLA REV...POLICY SAMP/SIZ
TREND NAT/COMP 45 COLD/WAR. PAGE 37 G0730

WAR
NUC/PWR
BAL/PWR
DIPLOM

B67
MCDOUGAL M.S.,THE INTERPRETATION OF AGREEMENTS AND
WORLD PUBLIC ORDER: PRINCIPLES OF CONTENT AND
PROCEDURE. WOR+45 CONSTN PROB/SOLV TEC/DEV
...CON/ANAL TREATY. PAGE 37 G0740

INT/LAW
STRUCT
ECO/UNDEV
DIPLOM

B67
OVERSEAS DEVELOPMENT INSTIT,EFFECTIVE AID. WOR+45
INT/ORG TEC/DEV DIPLOM INT/TRADE ADMIN. PAGE 43
G0852

FOR/AID
ECO/UNDEV
ECO/TAC
NAT/COMP

B67
PADELFORD N.J.,THE DYNAMICS OF INTERNATIONAL
POLITICS (2ND ED.). WOR+45 LAW INT/ORG FORCES
TEC/DEV REGION NAT/LISM PEACE ATTIT PWR ALL/IDEOS
UN COLD/WAR NATO TREATY. PAGE 43 G0856

DIPLOM
NAT/G
POLICY
DECISION

B67
PIPER D.C.,THE INTERNATIONAL LAW OF THE GREAT
LAKES. CANADA EXTR/IND MUNIC LICENSE ARMS/CONT
CRIME...GEOG 19/20. PAGE 45 G0879

CONCPT
DIPLOM
INT/LAW

B67
POMEROY W.J.,HALF A CENTURY OF SOCIALISM. USSR LAW
AGRI INDUS NAT/G CREATE DIPLOM EDU/PROP PERSON
ORD/FREE WEALTH...POLICY TREND 20. PAGE 45 G0884

SOCISM
MARXISM
COM
SOCIETY

B67
RAWLINSON J.L.,CHINA'S STRUGGLE FOR NAVAL
DEVELOPMENT 1839-1895. ASIA DIPLOM ADMIN WAR
...BIBLIOG DICTIONARY 19 CHINJAP. PAGE 46 G0907

SEA
FORCES
PWR

B67
ROACH J.R.,THE UNITED STATES AND THE ATLANTIC
COMMUNITY; ISSUES AND PROSPECTS. WOR+45 TEC/DEV
ECO/TAC COLONIAL REGION PEACE ROLE...ANTHOL NATO
COLD/WAR EEC. PAGE 47 G0925

INT/ORG
POLICY
ADJUST
DIPLOM

B67
RUSSELL B.,WAR CRIMES IN VIETNAM. USA+45 VIETNAM
FORCES DIPLOM WEAPON RACE/REL DISCRIM ISOLAT
BIO/SOC 20 COLD/WAR RUSSELL/B. PAGE 48 G0949

WAR
CRIME
ATTIT
POLICY

B67
RUSSETT B.M.,ARMS CONTROL IN EUROPE: PROPOSALS AND
POLITICAL CONSTRAINTS. GERMANY WOR+45 POL/PAR
BARGAIN DIPLOM...TREND CHARTS 20 COLD/WAR. PAGE 48
G0950

ARMS/CONT
REGION
METH/COMP

SCHEINMAN L.,EURATOM* NUCLEAR INTEGRATION IN
EUROPE. EX/STRUC LEAD 20 EURATOM. PAGE 49 G0963

B67
INT/ORG
NAT/LISM
NUC/PWR
DIPLOM

SKOLNIKOFF E.B.,SCIENCE, TECHNOLOGY, AND AMERICAN
FOREIGN POLICY. SPACE USA+45 INT/ORG TEC/DEV
ARMS/CONT NUC/PWR 29 DEPT/STATE. PAGE 51 G1010

B67
PHIL/SCI
DIPLOM
NAT/G
EFFICIENCY

UNIVERSAL REFERENCE SYSTEM,BIBLIOGRAPHY OF
BIBLIOGRAPHIES IN POLITICAL SCIENCE, GOVERNMENT,
AND PUBLIC POLICY (VOLUME III). WOR+45 WOR-45 LAW
ADMIN...SOC CON/ANAL COMPUT/IR GEN/METH. PAGE 56
G1095

B67
BIBLIOG/A
NAT/G
DIPLOM
POLICY

US DEPARTMENT OF STATE,FOREIGN AFFAIRS RESEARCH
(PAMPHLET). USA+45 WOR+45 ACADEM NAT/G...PSY SOC
CHARTS 20. PAGE 57 G1124

B67
BIBLIOG
INDEX
R+D
DIPLOM

US DEPARTMENT OF THE ARMY,CIVILIAN IN PEACE,
SOLDIER IN WAR: A BIBLIOGRAPHIC SURVEY OF THE ARMY
AND AIR NATIONAL GUARD (PAMPHLET, NOS. 130-2).
USA+45 USA-45 LOC/G NAT/G PROVS LEGIS PLAN ADMIN
ATTIT ORD/FREE...POLICY 19/20. PAGE 58 G1134

B67
BIBLIOG/A
FORCES
ROLE
DIPLOM

US HOUSE COMM SCI ASTRONAUT,GOVERNMENT, SCIENCE,
AND INTERNATIONAL POLICY. R+D OP/RES PLAN 20.
PAGE 58 G1146

B67
ADMIN
PHIL/SCI
ACT/RES
DIPLOM

US SENATE COMM AERO SPACE SCI,TREATY ON PRINCIPLES
GOVERNING ACTIVITIES OF STATES IN EXPLORATION AND
USE OF OUTER SPACE, INCLUDING...BODIES. DELIB/GP
FORCES LEGIS DIPLOM...JURID 20 DEPT/STATE NASA
DEPT/DEFEN UN. PAGE 60 G1170

B67
SPACE
INT/LAW
ORD/FREE
PEACE

US SENATE COMM ON FOREIGN REL,TREATY ON OUTER
SPACE. WOR+45 AIR FORCES PROB/SOLV NUC/PWR SENATE
TREATY UN. PAGE 60 G1182

B67
SPACE
DIPLOM
ARMS/CONT
LAW

US SENATE COMM ON FOREIGN REL,ARMS SALES TO NEAR
EAST AND SOUTH ASIAN COUNTRIES. INDIA IRAN PAKISTAN
WOR+45 PROC/MFG BAL/PWR DIPLOM...DECISION SENATE.
PAGE 60 G1183

B67
WEAPON
FOR/AID
FORCES
POLICY

US SENATE COMM ON FOREIGN REL,UNITED STATES
ARMAMENT AND DISARMAMENT PROBLEMS. USA+45 AIR
BAL/PWR DIPLOM FOR/AID NUC/PWR ORD/FREE SENATE
TREATY. PAGE 60 G1184

B67
ARMS/CONT
WEAPON
FORCES
PROB/SOLV

US SENATE COMM ON FOREIGN REL,FOREIGN ASSISTANCE
ACT OF 1967. VIETNAM WOR+45 DELIB/GP CONFER CONTROL
WAR WEAPON BAL/PAY...CENSUS CHARTS SENATE. PAGE 60
G1185

B67
FOR/AID
LAW
DIPLOM
POLICY

US SUPERINTENDENT OF DOCUMENTS,LIBRARY OF CONGRESS
(PRICE LIST 83). AFR ASIA EUR+WWI USA-45 USSR NAT/G
DIPLOM CONFER CT/SYS WAR...DECISION PHIL/SCI
CLASSIF 19/20 CONGRESS PRESIDENT. PAGE 61 G1189

B67
BIBLIOG/A
USA+45
AUTOMAT
LAW

YAMAMURA K.,ECONOMIC POLICY IN POSTWAR JAPAN. ASIA
FINAN POL/PAR DIPLOM LEAD NAT/LISM ATTIT NEW/LIB
POPULISM 20 CHINJAP. PAGE 64 G1262

B67
ECO/DEV
POLICY
NAT/G
TEC/DEV

ZUCKERMAN S.,SCIENTISTS AND WAR. ELITES INDUS
DIPLOM CENTRAL EFFICIENCY KNOWL 20. PAGE 65 G1271

B67
R+D
CONSULT
ACT/RES
GP/REL

"POLITICAL PARTIES ON FOREIGN POLICY IN THE INTER-
ELECTION YEARS 1962-66." ASIA COM INDIA USA+45 PLAN
ATTIT...DECISION 20. PAGE 1 G0023

L67
POL/PAR
DIPLOM
POLICY

DAVIS P.C.,"THE COMING CHINESE COMMUNIST NUCLEAR
THREAT AND U.S. SEA BASED ABM OPTIONS." ASIA
CHINA/COM FUT USA+45 SEA NAT/G FORCES PLAN TEC/DEV

L67
NUC/PWR
DETER
WEAPON

LEAD ARMS/CONT...GEOG METH/COMP 20 ABM/DEFSYS.
PAGE 14 G0279

DIPLOM

ROBINSON T.W.,"A NATIONAL INTEREST ANALYSIS OF
SINO-SOVIET RELATIONS." CHINA/COM USSR NAT/G
NUC/PWR ATTIT PWR...CONCPT CHARTS 20. PAGE 47 G0931

L67
MARXISM
DIPLOM
SOVEREIGN
GEN/LAWS

"CHINESE STATEMENT ON NUCLEAR PROLIFERATION."
CHINA/COM USA+45 USSR DOMIN COLONIAL PWR. PAGE 1
G0022

S67
NUC/PWR
BAL/PWR
ARMS/CONT
DIPLOM

BROWN N.,"BRITISH ARMS AND THE SWITCH TOWARD
EUROPE." EUR+WWI UK ARMS/CONT. PAGE 9 G0178

S67
FORCES
PLAN
DIPLOM
INT/ORG

CARROLL K.J.,"SECOND STEP TOWARD ARMS CONTROL."
WOR+45 INT/ORG VOL/ASSN FORCES PROB/SOLV RISK
WEAPON 20 COLD/WAR. PAGE 11 G0215

S67
ARMS/CONT
DIPLOM
PLAN
NUC/PWR

CHIU S.M.,"CHINA'S MILITARY POSTURE." CHINA/COM
ELITES NAT/G POL/PAR TEC/DEV ECO/TAC DOMIN CONTROL
LEAD REV MARXISM 20 MAO. PAGE 12 G0228

S67
FORCES
CIVMIL/REL
NUC/PWR
DIPLOM

CLEMENS W.C.,"CHINESE NUCLEAR TESTS: TRENDS AND
PORTENTS." CHINA/COM USA+45 USSR FORCES PLAN
TEC/DEV ARMS/CONT WAR PWR...DECISION 20 MAO
KHRUSH/N. PAGE 12 G0234

S67
NUC/PWR
WEAPON
POLICY
DIPLOM

COFFEY J.I.,"THE ANTI-BALLISTIC MISSILE DEBATE."
USA+45 USSR TEC/DEV BAL/PWR 20. PAGE 12 G0238

S67
ARMS/CONT
NUC/PWR
DETER
DIPLOM

D'AMATO D.,"LEGAL ASPECTS OF THE FRENCH NUCLEAR
TESTS." FRANCE WOR+45 ACT/RES COLONIAL RISK GOV/REL
EQUILIB ORD/FREE PWR DECISION. PAGE 14 G0268

S67
INT/LAW
DIPLOM
NUC/PWR
ADJUD

DEUTSCH K.W.,"ARMS CONTROL AND EUROPEAN UNITY* THE
NEXT TEN YEARS." USA+45 ELITES NAT/G BAL/PWR DIPLOM
NUC/PWR...INT KNO/TEST NATO EEC. PAGE 15 G0300

S67
ARMS/CONT
PEACE
REGION
PLAN

DOYLE S.E.,"COMMUNICATION SATELLITES* INTERNAL
ORGANIZATION FOR DEVELOPMENT AND CONTROL." USA+45
R+D ACT/RES DIPLOM NAT/LISM...POLICY INT/LAW
PREDICT UN. PAGE 16 G0313

S67
TEC/DEV
SPACE
COM/IND
INT/ORG

EDMONDS M.,"INTERNATIONAL COLLABORATION IN WEAPONS
PROCUREMENT* THE IMPLICATIONS OF THE ANGLO-FRENCH
CASE." FRANCE UK CONSULT OP/RES PROB/SOLV TEC/DEV
CONFER CONTROL EFFICIENCY 20. PAGE 17 G0334

S67
DIPLOM
VOL/ASSN
BAL/PWR
ARMS/CONT

EISENDRATH C.,"THE OUTER SPACE TREATY." CHINA/COM
COM USA+45 DIPLOM CONTROL NUC/PWR...INT/LAW 20 UN
COLD/WAR TREATY. PAGE 17 G0339

S67
SPACE
INT/ORG
PEACE
ARMS/CONT

FADDEYEV N.,"CMEA CO-OPERATION OF EQUAL NATIONS."
COM R+D PLAN CAP/ISM DIPLOM FOR/AID WEALTH...POLICY
MARXIST. PAGE 18 G0356

S67
MARXISM
ECO/TAC
INT/ORG
ECO/UNDEV

FELD B.T.,"A PLEDGE* NO FIRST USE." DELIB/GP
BAL/PWR DOMIN DETER. PAGE 19 G0363

S67
ARMS/CONT
NUC/PWR
DIPLOM
PEACE

FOREIGN POLICY ASSOCIATION,"US CONCERN FOR WORLD
LAW." USA+45 WOR+45 DELIB/GP JUDGE BAL/PWR CONFER
PEACE ORD/FREE 20 UN. PAGE 19 G0379

S67
INT/LAW
INT/ORG
DIPLOM
ARMS/CONT

FOREIGN POLICY ASSOCIATION,"HOW WORLD LAW DEVELOPS*
A CASE STUDY OF THE OUTER SPACE TREATY." SPACE

S67
INT/LAW
DIPLOM

WOR+45 BAL/PWR NEUTRAL NUC/PWR PEACE KNOWL 20 UN   ARMS/CONT
TREATY. PAGE 19 G0380   INT/ORG

S67
GRIFFITHS F.,"THE POLITICAL SIDE OF 'DISARMAMENT'." ARMS/CONT
FUT WOR+45 NUC/PWR NAT/LISM PEACE...NEW/IDEA   DIPLOM
PREDICT METH/COMP GEN/LAWS 20. PAGE 23 G0453

S67
HARTIGAN R.S.,"NONCOMBAT IMMUNITY* REFLECTIONS ON   INT/LAW
ITS ORIGINS AND PRESENT STATUS." WOR+45 PROB/SOLV   NUC/PWR
WAR PRIVIL MORAL...POLICY 20. PAGE 25 G0487   ARMS/CONT
                                                     DIPLOM

S67
HULL E.W.S.,"THE POLITICAL OCEAN." FUT UNIV WOR+45   DIPLOM
EXTR/IND R+D VOL/ASSN PLAN BAL/PWR ECO/TAC PEACE   ECO/UNDEV
WEALTH 20 UN. PAGE 27 G0536   INT/ORG
                                                     INT/LAW

S67
INGLIS D.R.,"MISSILE DEFENSE, NUCLEAR SPREAD, AND   NUC/PWR
VIETNAM." CHINA/COM USA+45 USSR VIETNAM INDUS   ARMS/CONT
BAL/PWR DETER WAR COST NAT/LISM PEACE. PAGE 28   DIPLOM
G0544   FORCES

S67
JAIN G.,"INDIA REJECTS THE POWER RACE* REALISM   INDIA
ABOUT NUCLEAR WEAPONS." FORCES PROB/SOLV FOR/AID   CHINA/COM
ARMS/CONT COST PWR...GOV/COMP 20. PAGE 28 G0556   NUC/PWR
                                                     DIPLOM

S67
JOHNSTON D.M.,"LAW, TECHNOLOGY AND THE SEA." WOR+45 INT/LAW
PLAN PROB/SOLV TEC/DEV CONFER ADJUD ORD/FREE   INT/ORG
...POLICY JURID. PAGE 29 G0564   DIPLOM
                                                     NEUTRAL

S67
KAHN H.,"CRITERIA FOR LONG-RANGE NUCLEAR CONTROL   NUC/PWR
POLICIES." WOR+45 INT/ORG TEC/DEV DOMIN DETER WAR   ARMS/CONT
WEAPON ISOLAT ORD/FREE POLICY. PAGE 29 G0571   BAL/PWR
                                                     DIPLOM

S67
KRAUS J.,"A MARXIST IN GHANA." GHANA ELITES CHIEF   MARXISM
PROB/SOLV TEC/DEV DIPLOM ECO/TAC COLONIAL PARTIC   PLAN
PWR 20 NKRUMAH/K. PAGE 31 G0618   ATTIT
                                                     CREATE

S67
KRUSCHE H.,"THE STRIVING OF THE KIESINGER-STRAUS   ARMS/CONT
GOVERNMENT FOR NUCLEAR WEAPONS IS A THREAT TO   INT/ORG
EUROPEAN SECURITY." EUR+WWI GERMANY BAL/PWR   NUC/PWR
SANCTION WEAPON PEACE ORD/FREE...MARXIST 20 NATO   DIPLOM
COLD/WAR. PAGE 32 G0623

S67
LALL B.G.,"GAPS IN THE ABM DEBATE." NAT/G DIPLOM   NUC/PWR
DETER CIVMIL/REL 20. PAGE 32 G0630   ARMS/CONT
                                                     EX/STRUC
                                                     FORCES

S67
MARTIN L.,"THE AMERICAN ABM DECISION." ASIA COM   WEAPON
EUR+WWI UK USA+45 USSR FORCES DIPLOM PEACE...POLICY DETER
20 ABM/DEFSYS. PAGE 36 G0713   NUC/PWR
                                                     WAR

S67
RAMSEY J.A.,"THE STATUS OF INTERNATIONAL   INT/LAW
COPYRIGHTS." WOR+45 CREATE TEC/DEV DIPLOM CONFER   INT/ORG
CONTROL SANCTION OWN...POLICY JURID. PAGE 46 G0899   COM/IND
                                                     PRESS

S67
REINTANZ G.,"THE SPACE TREATY." WOR+45 DIPLOM   SPACE
CONTROL ARMS/CONT NUC/PWR WAR...MARXIST 20 COLD/WAR INT/LAW
UN TREATY. PAGE 46 G0911   INT/ORG
                                                     PEACE

S67
ROMANIECKI L.,"THE ATOM AND INTERNATIONAL   INT/ORG
COOPERATION." PROB/SOLV DIPLOM PEACE ORD/FREE 20.   NUC/PWR
PAGE 47 G0933   ARMS/CONT
                                                     CONTROL

S67
ROTHSTEIN R.L.,"NUCLEAR PROLIFERATION AND AMERICAN   NUC/PWR
POLICY." PROB/SOLV BAL/PWR DIPLOM ARMS/CONT   CONTROL
EFFICIENCY 20. PAGE 48 G0942   DETER
                                                     WOR+45

S67
SALISBURY H.E.,"THE WAR IN VIETNAM." USA+45   POLICY
VIETNAM/N DIPLOM MURDER 20. PAGE 48 G0953   WAR

FORCES
OBS

S67
SHARP G.,"THE NEED OF A FUNCTIONAL SUBSTITUTE FOR   PEACE
WAR." FUT UNIV WOR+45 CULTURE SOCIETY INT/ORG   WAR
CONSULT DELIB/GP ACT/RES CREATE BAL/PWR CONFER   DIPLOM
ARMS/CONT NUC/PWR 20. PAGE 50 G0989   PROB/SOLV

S67
SHULMAN M.D.,"'EUROPE' VERSUS 'DETENTE'." USA+45   DIPLOM
USSR INT/ORG CONTROL ARMS/CONT DETER 20. PAGE 50   BAL/PWR
G0995   NUC/PWR

S67
SUINN R.M.,"THE DISARMAMENT FANTASY* PSYCHOLOGICAL   DECISION
FACTORS THAT MAY PRODUCE WARFARE." DIPLOM RISK   NUC/PWR
ARMS/CONT DETER ANOMIE PERSON GAME. PAGE 53 G1046   WAR
                                                     PSY

S67
TEKINER S.,"SINKIAN AND THE SINO-SOVIET CONFLICT."   DIPLOM
ASIA COM USSR FORCES PLAN BAL/PWR CONTROL NUC/PWR   PWR
WAR WEAPON...DECISION 20. PAGE 54 G1060   MARXISM

S67
VLASCIC I.A.,"THE SPACE TREATY* A PRELIMINARY   SPACE
EVALUATION." FUT USSR WOR+45 R+D ACT/RES TEC/DEV   INT/LAW
DIPLOM CONFER ARMS/CONT PEACE...PREDICT UN TREATY.   INT/ORG
PAGE 61 G1201   NEUTRAL

S67
WALTERS R.E.,"THE ROLE OF NUCLEAR WEAPONS FOR THE   PLAN
WEST." ASIA UK USA+45 USSR DIPLOM COERCE WAR PEACE   NUC/PWR
...POLICY DECISION 20. PAGE 62 G1209   WEAPON
                                                     FORCES

S67
WASHBURN A.M.,"NUCLEAR PROLIFERATION IN A   ARMS/CONT
REVOLUTIONARY INTERNATIONAL SYSTEM." WOR+45 NAT/G   NUC/PWR
DELIB/GP PLAN TEC/DEV...POLICY 20. PAGE 62 G1216   DIPLOM
                                                     CONFER

N67
US SUPERINTENDENT OF DOCUMENTS,SPACE: MISSILES, THE BIBLIOG/A
MOON, NASA, AND SATELLITES (PRICE LIST 79A). USA+45 SPACE
COM/IND R+D NAT/G DIPLOM EDU/PROP ADMIN CONTROL   TEC/DEV
HEALTH...POLICY SIMUL NASA CONGRESS. PAGE 61 G1190   PEACE

N67
US HOUSE COMM FOREIGN AFFAIRS,REPORT OF SPECIAL   ISLAM
STUDY MISSION TO THE NEAR EAST (PAMPHLET). ISRAEL   DIPLOM
USA+45 YEMEN ECO/UNDEV INT/ORG FOR/AID ARMS/CONT   FORCES
WAR WEAPON NAT/LISM PEACE...GEOG 20 UN HOUSE/REP.
PAGE 58 G1138

N67
US HOUSE COMM SCI ASTRONAUT,GOVERNMENT, SCIENCE,   NAT/G
AND INTERNATIONAL POLICY (PAMPHLET). INDIA   POLICY
NETHERLAND ECO/DEV ECO/UNDEV R+D ACADEM PLAN DIPLOM CREATE
FOR/AID CONFER...PREDICT 20 CHINJAP. PAGE 59 G1152   TEC/DEV

N67
US SENATE COMM ON FOREIGN REL,ARMS SALES AND   ARMS/CONT
FOREIGN POLICY (PAMPHLET). FINAN FOR/AID CONTROL   ADMIN
20. PAGE 60 G1181   OP/RES
                                                     DIPLOM

N67
US SENATE COMM ON FOREIGN REL,SURVEY OF THE   L/A+17C
ALLIANCE FOR PROGRESS; THE POLITICAL ASPECTS   POLICY
(PAMPHLET). CONSTN SOCIETY ECO/UNDEV INT/ORG   PROB/SOLV
TEC/DEV DIPLOM...CENSUS 20. PAGE 60 G1186

DIPLOMACY....SEE DIPLOM

DIRECT/NAT....DIRECTORY NATIONAL (IRELAND)

DIRECTORY NATIONAL (IRELAND)....SEE DIRECT/NAT

DIRKSEN/E....EVERETT DIRKSEN

DISARMAMENT....SEE ARMS/CONT

DISCIPLINE....SEE EDU/PROP, CONTROL

DISCRIM....DISCRIMINATION; SEE ALSO GP/REL, RACE/REL,
   ISOLAT

N19
MEZERIK A.G.,INTERNATIONAL POLICY 1965 (PAMPHLET).   DIPLOM
KASHMIR S/ASIA SPACE USA+45 VIETNAM WOR+45   INT/ORG
ARMS/CONT RACE/REL DISCRIM PEACE PWR 20 UN. PAGE 39 POLICY
G0762   WAR

BECK H.P.,MEN WHO CONTROL OUR UNIVERSITIES. EX/STRUC CHOOSE INGP/REL DISCRIM PERSON WEALTH ...POLICY TREND CON/ANAL CHARTS BIBLIOG. PAGE 6 G0112
B47
EDU/PROP
ACADEM
CONTROL
LEAD

OGDEN F.D.,THE POLL TAX IN THE SOUTH. USA+45 USA-45 CONSTN ADJUD ADMIN PARTIC CRIME...TIME/SEQ GOV/COMP METH/COMP 18/20 SOUTH/US. PAGE 43 G0838
B58
TAX
CHOOSE
RACE/REL
DISCRIM

RUSSELL B.,WAR CRIMES IN VIETNAM. USA+45 VIETNAM FORCES DIPLOM WEAPON RACE/REL DISCRIM ISOLAT BIO/SOC 20 COLD/WAR RUSSELL/B. PAGE 48 G0949
B67
WAR
CRIME
ATTIT
POLICY

ARONOWITZ D.S.,"CIVIL COMMITMENT OF NARCOTIC ADDICTS." USA+45 LAW INGP/REL DISCRIM MORAL...TREND 20. PAGE 4 G0069
S67
PUB/INST
ACT/RES
POLICY

DISCRIMINATION....SEE DISCRIM

DISEASE....SEE HEALTH

DISPL....DISPLACEMENT AND PROJECTION

DOTY P.M.,"THE ROLE OF THE SMALLER POWERS." FUT WOR+45 NAT/G TEC/DEV BAL/PWR DOMIN LEGIT CHOOSE DISPL DRIVE RESPECT...DECISION 20. PAGE 16 G0310
S60
PWR
POLICY
ARMS/CONT
NUC/PWR

NANES A.,"DISARMAMENT: THE LAST SEVEN YEARS." COM EUR+WWI USA+45 USSR INT/ORG FORCES TOP/EX CREATE LEGIT NUC/PWR DISPL ORD/FREE...CONCPT TIME/SEQ CON/ANAL 20. PAGE 41 G0803
S62
DELIB/GP
RIGID/FLEX
ARMS/CONT

GROSSER G.H.,THE THREAT OF IMPENDING DISASTER: CONTRIBUTIONS TO THE PSYCHOLOGY OF STRESS. SPACE UNIV SOCIETY R+D TEC/DEV EDU/PROP PERCEPT PERSON BIO/SOC DISPL PERCEPT PERSON...SOC MYTH SELF/OBS CONT/OBS BIOG CON/ANAL TOT/POP 20. PAGE 23 G0455
B64
HEALTH
PSY
NUC/PWR

BYRNES F.C.,"ASSIGNMENT TO AMBIGUITY: WORK PERFORMANCE IN CROSSCULTURAL TECHNICAL ASSISTANCE." USA+45 WOR+45 PROF/ORG CONSULT PLAN EDU/PROP ATTIT DISPL PERCEPT PERSON ALL/VALS...POLICY INT CHARTS NATO 20. PAGE 10 G0199
S64
INTELL
QU

DISPLACEMENT....SEE DISPL

DISPUTE, RESOLUTION OF....SEE ADJUD

DISRAELI/B....BENJAMIN DISRAELI

DIST/IND....DISTRIBUTIVE SYSTEM

MARKETING INFORMATION GUIDE. USA+45 ECO/DEV FINAN ADMIN GP/REL. PAGE 1 G0008
N
BIBLIOG/A
DIST/IND
MARKET
ECO/TAC

US SUPERINTENDENT OF DOCUMENTS,TRANSPORTATION: HIGHWAYS, ROADS, AND POSTAL SERVICE (PRICE LIST 25). PANAMA USA+45 LAW FORCES DIPLOM ADMIN GOV/REL HEALTH MGT. PAGE 61 G1188
N
BIBLIOG/A
DIST/IND
SERV/IND
NAT/G

DOTSON A.,PRODUCTION PLANNING IN THE PATENT OFFICE (PAMPHLET). USA+45 DIST/IND PROB/SOLV PRODUC...MGT PHIL/SCI 20 BUR/BUDGET PATENT/OFF. PAGE 16 G0309
N19
EFFICIENCY
PLAN
NAT/G
ADMIN

TURNER R.H.,"THE NAVY DISBURSING OFFICER AS A BUREAUCRAT" (BMR)" USA-45 LAW STRATA DIST/IND WAR PWR...SOC 20 BUREAUCRCY. PAGE 55 G1083
S47
FORCES
ADMIN
PERSON
ROLE

KOENIG L.W.,THE SALE OF THE TANKERS. USA+45 SEA DIST/IND POL/PAR DIPLOM ADMIN CIVMIL/REL ATTIT ...DECISION 20 PRESIDENT DEPT/STATE. PAGE 31 G0609
B50
NAT/G
POLICY
PLAN
GOV/REL

ROBINSON E.A.G.,THE STRUCTURE OF COMPETITIVE INDUSTRY. UK ECO/DEV DIST/IND MARKET TEC/DEV DIPLOM
B53
INDUS
PRODUC

EDU/PROP ADMIN EFFICIENCY WEALTH...MGT 19/20. PAGE 47 G0929
WORKER
OPTIMAL

LOCKLIN D.P.,ECONOMICS OF TRANSPORTATION (4TH ED.). USA+45 USA-45 SEA AIR LAW FINAN LG/CO EX/STRUC ADMIN CONTROL...STAT CHARTS 19/20 RAILROAD PUB/TRANS. PAGE 34 G0675
B54
ECO/DEV
DIST/IND
ECO/TAC
TEC/DEV

US DEPARTMENT OF THE ARMY,RESEARCH AND DEVELOPMENT (AND RELATED ASPECTS) IN FOREIGN COUNTRIES. WOR+45 DIST/IND INDUS CONSULT FORCES CREATE EDU/PROP AUTOMAT DETER WEAPON. PAGE 57 G1126
B56
BIBLIOG/A
R+D
TEC/DEV
NUC/PWR

DRUCKER P.F.,AMERICA'S NEXT TWENTY YEARS. USA+45 DIST/IND ACADEM MUNIC DIPLOM ECO/TAC AUTOMAT HABITAT HEALTH...SOC/WK TREND 20 URBAN/RNWL PUB/TRANS. PAGE 16 G0316
B57
WORKER
FOR/AID
CENSUS
GEOG

OPERATIONS RESEARCH SOCIETY,A COMPREHENSIVE BIBLIOGRAPHY ON OPERATIONS RESEARCH; THROUGH 1956 WITH SUPPLEMENT FOR 1957. COM/IND DIST/IND INDUS ADMIN...DECISION MATH STAT METH 20. PAGE 43 G0840
B58
BIBLIOG/A
COMPUT/IR
OP/RES
MGT

APTHEKER H.,DISARMAMENT AND THE AMERICAN ECONOMY: A SYMPOSIUM. FUT USA+45 ECO/DEV DIST/IND FINAN INDUS PROC/MFG LABOR NAT/G POL/PAR CONSULT PLAN CAP/ISM INT/TRADE PEACE ATTIT MORAL WEALTH...TREND GEN/LAWS TOT/POP 20. PAGE 3 G0063
B60
MARXIST
ARMS/CONT

US SENATE COMM ON COMMERCE,URBAN MASS TRANSPORTATION. FUT USA+45 AIR ECO/DEV FINAN LOC/G MUNIC LEGIS CREATE PROB/SOLV TEC/DEV 20 PUB/TRANS. PAGE 60 G1180
B60
DIST/IND
PLAN
NAT/G
LAW

BECKER A.S.,"COMPARISIONS OF UNITED STATES AND USSR NATIONAL OUTPUT: SOME RULES OF THE GAME." COM USA+45 ECO/DEV AGRI DIST/IND INDUS R+D CONSULT PLAN ECO/TAC RIGID/FLEX KNOWL...METH/CNCPT CHARTS 20. PAGE 6 G0113
S60
STAT
USSR

BRADY R.A.,ORGANIZATION, AUTOMATION, AND SOCIETY. USA+45 AGRI COM/IND DIST/IND MARKET CREATE ...DECISION MGT 20. PAGE 8 G0163
B61
TEC/DEV
INDUS
AUTOMAT
ADMIN

LAHAYE R.,LES ENTREPRISES PUBLIQUES AU MAROC. FRANCE MOROCCO LAW DIST/IND EXTR/IND FINAN CONSULT PLAN TEC/DEV ADMIN AGREE CONTROL OWN...POLICY 20. PAGE 32 G0629
B61
NAT/G
INDUS
ECO/UNDEV
ECO/TAC

RAMO S.,PEACETIME USES OF OUTER SPACE. FUT DIST/IND INT/ORG CONSULT NUC/PWR...AUD/VIS ANTHOL 20. PAGE 46 G0898
B61
PEACE
TEC/DEV
SPACE
CREATE

CLARKE A.C.,PROFILES OF THE FUTURE; AN INQUIRY INTO THE LIMITS OF THE POSSIBLE. COM/IND DIST/IND PRODUC AGE PERCEPT...TECHNIC NEW/IDEA TIME. PAGE 12 G0232
B62
FUT
TEC/DEV
PREDICT
SPACE

THORELLI H.B.,"THE INTERNATIONAL OPERATIONS SIMULATION AT THE UNIVERSITY OF CHICAGO." FUT USA+45 WOR+45 ECO/DEV DIST/IND FINAN INDUS INT/ORG DELIB/GP ACT/RES CREATE TEC/DEV WEALTH...STAT VAL/FREE 20. PAGE 54 G1072
S62
ECO/TAC
SIMUL
INT/TRADE

KATZ S.M.,A SELECTED LIST OF US READINGS ON DEVELOPMENT. AGRI COM/IND DIST/IND INDUS LABOR PLAN FOR/AID EDU/PROP HEALTH...POLICY SOC/WK 20. PAGE 30 G0582
B63
BIBLIOG/A
ECO/UNDEV
TEC/DEV
ACT/RES

WILES P.J.D.,"WILL CAPITALISM AND COMMUNISM SPONTANEOUSLY CONVERGE." COM FUT USA+45 ECO/DEV DIST/IND MARKET CAP/ISM ECO/TAC RIGID/FLEX WEALTH MARXISM SOCISM...MATH STAT TREND COMPUT/IR 20. PAGE 63 G1240
S63
PLAN
TEC/DEV
USSR

LANG A.S.,URBAN RAIL TRANSIT. OP/RES PLAN PROB/SOLV TEC/DEV AUTOMAT COST...TECHNIC MATH CON/ANAL CHARTS METH/COMP SIMUL 20 RAILROAD PUB/TRANS. PAGE 32 G0632
B64
MUNIC
DIST/IND
ECOMETRIC

B64
ORGANIZATION AMERICAN STATES,ECONOMIC SURVEY OF   ECO/UNDEV
LATIN AMERICA, 1962. L/A+17C AGRI DIST/IND INDUS   CHARTS
MARKET PROC/MFG R+D PLAN TEC/DEV ECO/TAC REGION
BAL/PAY ALL/VALS...CON/ANAL ORG/CHARTS GEN/METH OAS
20. PAGE 43 G0844

S64
MAHALANOBIS P.C.,"PERSPECTIVE PLANNING IN INDIA: PLAN
STATISTICAL TOOLS." INDIA S/ASIA STRATA AGRI   STAT
DIST/IND FINAN INDUS SERV/IND NAT/G ECO/TAC
ORD/FREE WEALTH...POLICY TREND SIMUL VAL/FREE 20.
PAGE 35 G0695

B65
KOROL A.G.,SOVIET RESEARCH AND DEVELOPMENT. USSR   COM
ACADEM SCHOOL WORKER ROUTINE COST...STAT T 20.   R+D
PAGE 31 G0615   FINAN
                                                        DIST/IND

B65
THAYER F.C. JR.,AIR TRANSPORT POLICY AND NATIONAL   AIR
SECURITY: A POLITICAL, ECONOMIC, AND MILITARY   FORCES
ANALYSIS. DIST/IND OP/RES PLAN TEC/DEV DIPLOM DETER   CIVMIL/REL
WAR COST EFFICIENCY...POLICY BIBLIOG 20 DEPT/DEFEN   ORD/FREE
FAA CAB. PAGE 54 G1066

S65
TENDLER J.D.,"TECHNOLOGY AND ECONOMIC DEVELOPMENT*   BRAZIL
THE CASE OF HYDRO VS THERMAL POWER." CONSTRUC   INDUS
DIST/IND CREATE TEC/DEV INT/TRADE CENTRAL PWR SKILL   ECO/UNDEV
WEALTH...MGT NAT/COMP ARGEN. PAGE 54 G1063

B66
RUPPENTHAL K.M.,TRANSPORTATION AND TOMORROW. FUT   DIST/IND
SPACE USA+45 SEA AIR FORCES TEC/DEV INT/TRADE   PLAN
...ANTHOL 20 RAILROAD. PAGE 48 G0946   CIVMIL/REL
                                                        PREDICT

B66
US SENATE,POLICY PLANNING FOR AERONAUTICAL RESEARCH   SPACE
AND DEVELOPMENT: STAFF REPORT FOR COMM ON   CIVMIL/REL
AERONAUTICAL AND SPACE SCIENCES. USA+45 AIR   GOV/REL
DIST/IND PLAN...POLICY CHARTS 20 CONGRESS NASA.   R+D
PAGE 59 G1164

B66
WHITNAH D.R.,SAFER SKYWAYS. DIST/IND DELIB/GP   ADMIN
FORCES TOP/EX WORKER TEC/DEV ROUTINE WAR CIVMIL/REL   NAT/G
COST...TIME/SEQ 20 FAA CAB. PAGE 63 G1235   AIR
                                                        GOV/REL

B67
BUDER S.,PULLMAN: AN EXPERIMENT IN INDUSTRIAL ORDER   DIST/IND
AND COMMUNITY PLANNING, 1880-1930. USA-45 SOCIETY   INDUS
LABOR LG/CO CREATE PROB/SOLV CONTROL GP/REL   MUNIC
EFFICIENCY ATTIT...MGT BIBLIOG 19/20 PULLMAN.   PLAN
PAGE 9 G0184

B67
MACAVOY P.W.,REGULATION OF TRANSPORT INNOVATION.   DIST/IND
ACT/RES ADJUD COST DEMAND...POLICY CHARTS 20.   CONTROL
PAGE 35 G0684   PRICE
                                                        PROFIT

B67
NORTHRUP H.R.,RESTRICTIVE LABOR PRACTICES IN THE   DIST/IND
SUPERMARKET INDUSTRY. USA+45 INDUS WORKER TEC/DEV   MARKET
BARGAIN PAY CONTROL GP/REL COST...STAT CHARTS NLRB.   LABOR
PAGE 42 G0827   MGT

L67
RUTH J.M.,"THE ADMINISTRATION OF WATER RESOURCES IN   EFFICIENCY
GUATEMALA." GUATEMALA L/A+17C DIST/IND LOC/G NAT/G   ECO/UNDEV
EX/STRUC ADMIN GOV/REL DEMAND EQUILIB WEALTH...GEOG   PLAN
MGT 20. PAGE 48 G0952   ACT/RES

L67
TRAVERS H. JR.,"AN EXAMINATION OF THE CAB'S MERGER   ADJUD
POLICY." USA+45 USA-45 LAW NAT/G LEGIS PLAN ADMIN   LG/CO
...DECISION 20 CONGRESS. PAGE 55 G1078   POLICY
                                                        DIST/IND

S67
MYERS S.,"TECHNOLOGY AND URBAN TRANSIT: THE   R+D
ENORMOUS POTENTIAL OF BUS AND RAIL SYSTEMS." USA+45   TEC/DEV
FINAN LOC/G MUNIC WORKER PLAN PROB/SOLV PRICE   DIST/IND
AUTOMAT 20. PAGE 40 G0798   ACT/RES

S67
WILLIAMS C.,"REGIONAL MANAGEMENT OVERSEAS." USA+45   MGT
WOR+45 DIST/IND LG/CO EX/STRUC INT/TRADE TARIFFS   EUR+WWI
ADMIN TASK CENTRAL. PAGE 63 G1242   ECO/DEV
                                                        PLAN

N67
US SENATE COMM AERO SPACE SCI,AERONAUTICAL RESEARCH   DIST/IND
AND DEVELOPMENT POLICY; HEARINGS, COMM ON   SPACE
AERONAUTICAL AND SPACE SCIENCES...1967 (PAMPHLET).   NAT/G
R+D PROB/SOLV EXEC GOV/REL 20 DEPT/DEFEN FAA NASA   PLAN
CONGRESS. PAGE 60 G1174

DISTRIBUTIVE SYSTEM....SEE DIST/IND

DISTRICT OF COLUMBIA....SEE WASHING/DC

DISTRICTING...SEE APPORT

DIVORCE....DIVORCE

DIXON/YATE....DIXON-YATES BILL

DOC/ANAL....CONVENTIONAL CONTENT ANALYSIS

DODD/TJ....SENATOR THOMAS J. DODD

DODDS H.W. G0304

DOMIN....DOMINATION THROUGH USE OF ESTABLISHED POWER

B39
FULLER G.H.,A SELECTED LIST OF REFERENCES ON THE   BIBLIOG
EXPANSION OF THE US NAVY, 1933-1939 (PAMPHLET).   FORCES
MOD/EUR USA-45 NAT/G PLAN DIPLOM DOMIN RISK   WEAPON
ARMS/CONT EQUILIB PWR 20 NAVY. PAGE 20 G0399   WAR

B44
FULLER G.H.,MILITARY GOVERNMENT: A LIST OF   BIBLIOG
REFERENCES (A PAMPHLET). ITALY UK USA-45 WOR-45 LAW   DIPLOM
FORCES DOMIN ADMIN ARMS/CONT ORD/FREE PWR   CIVMIL/REL
...DECISION 20 CHINJAP. PAGE 21 G0404   SOVEREIGN

N47
FOX W.T.R.,UNITED STATES POLICY IN A TWO POWER   DIPLOM
WORLD. COM USA+45 USSR FORCES DOMIN AGREE NEUTRAL   FOR/AID
NUC/PWR ORD/FREE SOVEREIGN 20 COLD/WAR TREATY   POLICY
EUROPE/W INTERVENT. PAGE 20 G0389

B48
KILE O.M.,THE FARM BUREAU MOVEMENT: THE FARM BUREAU   AGRI
THROUGH THREE DECADES. NAT/G LEGIS LEAD LOBBY   STRUCT
GP/REL INCOME POLICY. PAGE 30 G0596   VOL/ASSN
                                                        DOMIN

B50
CROWTHER J.G.,SCIENCE AT WAR. EUR+WWI PLAN TEC/DEV   R+D
DOMIN COERCE NUC/PWR WEAPON KNOWL PWR...CONCPT OBS   FORCES
TREND VAL/FREE 20. PAGE 14 G0265   WAR
                                                        UK

C50
WAGER P.W.,"COUNTY GOVERNMENT ACROSS THE NATION."   LOC/G
USA+45 CONSTN COM/IND FINAN SCHOOL DOMIN CT/SYS   PROVS
LEAD GOV/REL...STAT BIBLIOG 20. PAGE 61 G1204   ADMIN
                                                        ROUTINE

B54
ARON R.,CENTURY OF TOTAL WAR. FUT WOR+45 WOR-45   ATTIT
SOCIETY INT/ORG NAT/G FORCES TOP/EX CREATE BAL/PWR   WAR
DOMIN EDU/PROP COERCE DETER PEACE TOTALISM PWR
...TIME/SEQ TREND COLD/WAR TOT/POP VAL/FREE
LEAGUE/NAT 20. PAGE 4 G0066

B54
BUTOW R.J.C.,JAPAN'S DECISION TO SURRENDER. USA-45   ELITES
USSR CHIEF FORCES DOMIN NUC/PWR...BIBLIOG 20 TREATY   DIPLOM
CHINJAP. PAGE 10 G0198   WAR
                                                        PEACE

B54
COMBS C.H.,DECISION PROCESSES. INTELL SOCIETY   MATH
DELIB/GP CREATE TEC/DEV DOMIN LEGIT EXEC CHOOSE   DECISION
DRIVE RIGID/FLEX KNOWL PWR...PHIL/SCI SOC
METH/CNCPT CONT/OBS REC/INT PERS/TEST SAMP/SIZ BIOG
SOC/EXP WORK. PAGE 13 G0245

S57
JANOWITZ M.,"MILITARY ELITES AND THE STUDY OF WAR."   FORCES
USA+45 WOR-45 STRATA NAT/G PROF/ORG TEC/DEV DOMIN   ELITES
EDU/PROP COERCE WAR ATTIT RIGID/FLEX PWR RESPECT
...MGT TREND STERTYP GEN/METH 20. PAGE 28 G0558

S57
MORTON L.,"THE DECISION TO USE THE BOMB." FORCES   NUC/PWR
TOP/EX DOMIN COERCE PEACE. PAGE 40 G0788   DIPLOM
                                                        WAR

S58
DAVENPORT J.,"ARMS AND THE WELFARE STATE." INTELL   USA+45

STRUCT FORCES CREATE ECO/TAC FOR/AID DOMIN LEGIT ADMIN WAR ORD/FREE PWR...POLICY SOC CONCPT MYTH OBS TREND COLD/WAR TOT/POP 20. PAGE 14 G0276 — NAT/G USSR

S58
THOMPSON K.W.,"NATIONAL SECURITY IN A NUCLEAR AGE." USA+45 WOR+45 SOCIETY INT/ORG NAT/G TOP/EX DIPLOM DOMIN EDU/PROP LEGIT ARMS/CONT COERCE ORD/FREE ...TREND STERTYP TOT/POP VAL/FREE COLD/WAR 20. PAGE 54 G1068 — FORCES PWR BAL/PWR

S59
JANOWITZ M.,"CHANGING PATTERNS OF ORGANIZATIONAL AUTHORITY: THE MILITARY ESTABLISHMENT" (BMR)" USA+45 ELITES STRUCT EX/STRUC PLAN DOMIN AUTOMAT NUC/PWR WEAPON 20. PAGE 28 G0559 — FORCES AUTHORIT ADMIN TEC/DEV

S59
WILLIAMS B.H.,"SCIENTIFIC METHOD IN FOREIGN POLICY." WOR+45 NAT/G FORCES TOP/EX DOMIN LEGIT COERCE PEACE ATTIT KNOWL ORD/FREE PWR...GEN/LAWS GEN/METH TOT/POP COLD/WAR NAZI. PAGE 63 G1241 — PLAN PHIL/SCI DIPLOM

S60
DOTY P.M.,"THE ROLE OF THE SMALLER POWERS." FUT WOR+45 NAT/G TEC/DEV BAL/PWR DOMIN LEGIT CHOOSE DISPL DRIVE RESPECT...DECISION 20. PAGE 16 G0310 — PWR POLICY ARMS/CONT NUC/PWR

S60
IKLE F.C.,"NTH COUNTRIES AND DISARMAMENT." WOR+45 DELIB/GP ECO/TAC DOMIN EDU/PROP LEGIT ROUTINE COERCE RIGID/FLEX ORD/FREE...MARXIST TREND 20. PAGE 28 G0543 — FUT INT/ORG ARMS/CONT NUC/PWR

B62
GOLOVINE M.N.,CONFLICT IN SPACE: A PATTERN OF WAR IN A NEW DIMENSION. FUT USA+45 WOR+45 AIR FORCES PLAN DIPLOM DOMIN ATTIT...STAT AUD/VIS CHARTS COLD/WAR 20. PAGE 22 G0432 — CREATE TEC/DEV NUC/PWR SPACE

B62
MELMAN S.,DISARMAMENT: ITS POLITICS AND ECONOMICS. WOR+45 DELIB/GP FORCES ECO/TAC DOMIN EDU/PROP LEGIT COERCE PWR...POLICY CONCPT 20. PAGE 38 G0752 — NAT/G ORD/FREE ARMS/CONT NUC/PWR

B62
YALEN R.,REGIONALISM AND WORLD ORDER. EUR+WWI WOR+45 WOR-45 INT/ORG VOL/ASSN DELIB/GP FORCES TOP/EX BAL/PWR DIPLOM DOMIN REGION ARMS/CONT PWR ...JURID HYPO/EXP COLD/WAR 20. PAGE 64 G1261 — ORD/FREE POLICY

B63
BONINI C.P.,SIMULATION OF INFORMATION AND DECISION SYSTEMS IN THE FIRM. MARKET BUDGET DOMIN EDU/PROP ADMIN COST ATTIT HABITAT PERCEPT PWR...CONCPT PROBABIL QUANT PREDICT HYPO/EXP BIBLIOG. PAGE 8 G0152 — INDUS SIMUL DECISION MGT

B63
GOLDSEN J.M.,OUTER SPACE IN WORLD POLITICS. COM USA+45 NAT/G FORCES ACT/RES PLAN DOMIN EDU/PROP COERCE ORD/FREE PWR...TECHNIC STAT INT SAMP TREND ANTHOL VAL/FREE 20. PAGE 22 G0428 — TEC/DEV DIPLOM SPACE

B63
LITTERER J.A.,ORGANIZATIONS: STRUCTURE AND BEHAVIOR. PLAN DOMIN CONTROL LEAD ROUTINE SANCTION INGP/REL EFFICIENCY PRODUC DRIVE RIGID/FLEX PWR. PAGE 34 G0674 — ADMIN CREATE MGT ADJUST

B63
MULLER H.J.,FREEDOM IN THE WESTERN WORLD. PREHIST CULTURE SECT CREATE TEC/DEV DOMIN PWR WEALTH ...MAJORIT SOC CONCPT. PAGE 40 G0793 — ORD/FREE TIME/SEQ SOCIETY

B63
NORTH R.C.,CONTENT ANALYSIS: A HANDBOOK WITH APPLICATIONS FOR THE STUDY OF INTERNATIONAL CRISIS. ASIA COM EUR+WWI MOD/EUR INT/ORG TEC/DEV DOMIN EDU/PROP ROUTINE COERCE PERCEPT RIGID/FLEX ALL/VALS ...QUANT TESTS CON/ANAL SIMUL GEN/LAWS VAL/FREE. PAGE 42 G0825 — METH/CNCPT COMPUT/IR USSR

B63
US DEPARTMENT OF THE ARMY,SOVIET RUSSIA: STRATEGIC SURVEY (PAMPHLET). USSR POL/PAR PLAN DOMIN EDU/PROP ARMS/CONT GUERRILLA WAR WEAPON...TREND CHARTS ORG/CHARTS 20. PAGE 57 G1129 — BIBLIOG/A MARXISM DIPLOM COERCE

S63
TASHJEAN J.E.,"RESEARCH ON ARMS CONTROL." COM USA+45 USSR FORCES ACT/RES PLAN DOMIN COERCE ORD/FREE PWR...TIME/SEQ GEN/LAWS 20 COLD/WAR. PAGE 53 G1053 — NAT/G POLICY ARMS/CONT

B64
MASTERS N.A.,STATE POLITICS AND THE PUBLIC SCHOOLS. STRUCT FINAN ADMIN LOBBY GP/REL PWR BIBLIOG. PAGE 36 G0720 — EDU/PROP PROVS DOMIN

B64
PETERSON W.,THE POLITICS OF POPULATION. COM EUR+WWI FUT MOD/EUR S/ASIA USA+45 USA-45 WOR+45 LAW CULTURE FAM SECT DOMIN EDU/PROP BIO/SOC HEALTH ORD/FREE ...GEOG STAT TIME/SEQ TREND VAL/FREE. PAGE 44 G0871 — PLAN CENSUS POLICY

B64
RUSHING W.A.,THE PSYCHIATRIC PROFESSIONS. DOMIN INGP/REL DRIVE RIGID/FLEX ROLE HEALTH PWR...POLICY GP/COMP. PAGE 48 G0947 — ATTIT PUB/INST PROF/ORG BAL/PWR

L64
GOLDBERG A.,"ATOMIC ORIGINS OF THE BRITISH NUCLEAR DETERRENT." EUR+WWI UK NAT/G TOP/EX PLAN BAL/PWR DOMIN DETER CHOOSE ATTIT DRIVE HEALTH ORD/FREE PWR RESPECT...CONCPT VAL/FREE COLD/WAR 20 CMN/WLTH. PAGE 22 G0425 — CREATE FORCES NUC/PWR

L64
WARD C.,"THE 'NEW MYTHS' AND 'OLD REALITIES' OF NUCLEAR WAR." COM FUT USA+45 USSR WOR+45 INT/ORG NAT/G DOMIN LEGIT EXEC ATTIT PERCEPT ALL/VALS ...POLICY RELATIV PSY MYTH TREND 20. PAGE 62 G1212 — FORCES COERCE ARMS/CONT NUC/PWR

S64
KASSOF A.,"THE ADMINISTERED SOCIETY: TOTALITARIANISM WITHOUT TERROR." COM USSR STRATA AGRI INDUS NAT/G PERF/ART SCHOOL TOP/EX EDU/PROP ADMIN ORD/FREE PWR...POLICY SOC TIME/SEQ GEN/LAWS VAL/FREE 20. PAGE 29 G0580 — SOCIETY DOMIN TOTALISM

S64
THOMPSON V.A.,"ADMINISTRATIVE OBJECTIVES FOR DEVELOPMENT ADMINISTRATION." WOR+45 CREATE PLAN DOMIN EDU/PROP EXEC ROUTINE ATTIT ORD/FREE PWR ...POLICY GEN/LAWS VAL/FREE. PAGE 54 G1070 — ECO/UNDEV MGT

B65
REISS A.J. JR.,SCHOOLS IN A CHANGING SOCIETY. CULTURE PROB/SOLV INSPECT DOMIN CONFER INGP/REL RACE/REL AGE/C AGE/Y ALL/VALS...ANTHOL SOC/INTEG 20 NEWYORK/C. PAGE 46 G0912 — SCHOOL EX/STRUC ADJUST ADMIN

S65
GRIFFITH S.B.,"COMMUNIST CHINA'S CAPACITY TO MAKE WAR." CHINA/COM COM NAT/G TOP/EX PLAN DOMIN COERCE NUC/PWR ATTIT RESPECT SKILL...CONCPT MYTH TIME/SEQ TREND COLD/WAR 20. PAGE 23 G0452 — FORCES PWR WEAPON ASIA

S66
FLEMING W.G.,"AUTHORITY, EFFICIENCY, AND ROLE STRESS: PROBLEMS IN THE DEVELOPMENT OF EAST AFRICAN BUREAUCRACIES." AFR UGANDA STRUCT PROB/SOLV ROUTINE INGP/REL ROLE...MGT SOC GP/COMP GOV/COMP 20 TANGANYIKA AFRICA/E. PAGE 19 G0371 — DOMIN EFFICIENCY COLONIAL ADMIN

B67
BERNAL J.D.,THE SOCIAL FUNCTION OF SCIENCE. WOR+45 WOR-45 R+D NAT/G PROB/SOLV DOMIN WAR...PHIL/SCI 20. PAGE 7 G0130 — ROLE TEC/DEV SOCIETY ADJUST

B67
GOLEMBIEWSKI R.T.,ORGANIZING MEN AND POWER: PATTERNS OF BEHAVIOR AND LINESTAFF MODELS. WOR+45 EX/STRUC ACT/RES DOMIN PERS/REL...NEW/IDEA 20. PAGE 22 G0431 — ADMIN CONTROL SIMUL MGT

L67
EINAUDI L.,"ANNOTATED BIBLIOGRAPHY OF LATIN AMERICAN MILITARY JOURNALS" LAW TEC/DEV DOMIN EDU/PROP COERCE WAR CIVMIL/REL 20. PAGE 17 G0336 — BIBLIOG/A NAT/G FORCES L/A+17C

S67
"CHINESE STATEMENT ON NUCLEAR PROLIFERATION." CHINA/COM USA+45 USSR DOMIN COLONIAL PWR. PAGE 1 G0022 — NUC/PWR BAL/PWR ARMS/CONT DIPLOM

S67
BRETNOR R.,"DESTRUCTIVE FORCE AND THE MILITARY EQUATIONS." UNIV COMPUTER PLAN PROB/SOLV AUTOMAT CONTROL COERCE DETER NUC/PWR WEAPON DRIVE PWR. PAGE 9 G0166 — FORCES TEC/DEV DOMIN WAR

S67
CARR E.H.,"REVOLUTION FROM ABOVE." USSR STRATA FINAN INDUS NAT/G DOMIN LEAD GP/REL INGP/REL OWN — AGRI POLICY

PRODUC PWR 20 STALIN/J. PAGE 11 G0214 — COM EFFICIENCY

S67
CHIU S.M.,"CHINA'S MILITARY POSTURE." CHINA/COM ELITES NAT/G POL/PAR TEC/DEV ECO/TAC DOMIN CONTROL LEAD REV MARXISM 20 MAO. PAGE 12 G0228 — FORCES CIVMIL/REL NUC/PWR DIPLOM

S67
CHRIST R.F.,"REORGANIZATION OF FRENCH ARMED FORCES." FRANCE CREATE PLAN TEC/DEV BAL/PWR DOMIN COERCE CENTRAL EFFICIENCY 20. PAGE 12 G0229 — CHIEF DETER NUC/PWR FORCES

S67
FELD B.T.,"A PLEDGE* NO FIRST USE." DELIB/GP BAL/PWR DOMIN DETER. PAGE 19 G0363 — ARMS/CONT NUC/PWR DIPLOM PEACE

S67
JACKSON W.G.F.,"NUCLEAR PROLIFERATION AND THE GREAT POWERS." FUT UK WOR+45 INT/ORG DOMIN ARMS/CONT DETER ORD/FREE PACIFIST. PAGE 28 G0550 — NUC/PWR ATTIT BAL/PWR NAT/LISM

S67
KAHN H.,"CRITERIA FOR LONG-RANGE NUCLEAR CONTROL POLICIES." WOR+45 INT/ORG TEC/DEV DOMIN DETER WAR WEAPON ISOLAT ORD/FREE POLICY. PAGE 29 G0571 — NUC/PWR ARMS/CONT BAL/PWR DIPLOM

S67
TELLER E.,"PLANNING FOR PEACE." CHINA/COM WOR+45 DELIB/GP TEC/DEV RISK COERCE DETER WAR ATTIT ORD/FREE 20 NATO. PAGE 54 G1061 — ARMS/CONT NUC/PWR PEACE DOMIN

DOMIN/REP....DOMINICAN REPUBLIC; SEE ALSO L/A + 17C

DOMINATION....SEE DOMIN

DOMINICAN REPUBLIC....SEE DOMIN/REP

DOMINO....THE DOMINO THEORY

DONAHO J.A. G0305

DONALD A.G. G0306

DONNELLY D. G0307

DONNELLY/I....IGNATIUS DONNELLY

DORFMAN R. G0308

DOSTOYEV/F....FYODOR DOSTOYEVSKY

DOTSON A. G0309

DOTY P.M. G0310

DOUGHERTY J.E. G0311,G0312

DOUGLAS/P....PAUL DOUGLAS

DOUGLAS/WO....WILLIAM O. DOUGLAS

DOYLE S.E. G0313

DRAPER J.W. G0314

DRAPER/HAL....HAL DRAPER

DREAM....DREAMING

DREYFUS S.E. G0116

DREYFUS/A....ALFRED DREYFUS OR DREYFUS AFFAIR

DRIVE....DRIVE AND MORALE

B28
SOROKIN P.,CONTEMPORARY SOCIOLOGICAL THEORIES. MOD/EUR UNIV SOCIETY R+D SCHOOL ECO/TAC EDU/PROP ROUTINE ATTIT DRIVE...PSY CONCPT TIME/SEQ TREND GEN/LAWS 20. PAGE 52 G1021 — CULTURE SOC WAR

B35
FOREIGN AFFAIRS BIBLIOGRAPHY: A SELECTED AND ANNOTATED LIST OF BOOKS ON INTERNATIONAL RELATIONS 1919-1962 (4 VOLS.). CONSTN FORCES COLONIAL ARMS/CONT WAR NAT/LISM PEACE ATTIT DRIVE...POLICY INT/LAW 20. PAGE 1 G0011 — BIBLIOG/A DIPLOM INT/ORG

B46
BUSH V.,ENDLESS HORIZONS. FUT USA-45 INTELL NAT/G CONSULT ACT/RES CREATE PLAN EDU/PROP DRIVE ...MAJORIT HEAL MGT PHIL/SCI CONCPT OBS TREND GEN/METH TOT/POP 20. PAGE 10 G0196 — R+D KNOWL PEACE

B46
NORTHROP F.S.C.,THE MEETING OF EAST AND WEST. EUR+WWI FUT MOD/EUR UNIV WOR+45 WOR-45 INTELL SOCIETY EX/STRUC TOP/EX ACT/RES LEGIT CHOOSE ATTIT PERCEPT RIGID/FLEX ALL/VALS...POLICY JURID OBS TOT/POP. PAGE 42 G0826 — DRIVE TREND PEACE

B47
WHITEHEAD T.N.,LEADERSHIP IN A FREE SOCIETY; A STUDY IN HUMAN RELATIONS BASED ON AN ANALYSIS OF PRESENT-DAY INDUSTRIAL CIVILIZATION. WOR-45 STRUCT R+D LABOR LG/CO SML/CO WORKER PLAN PROB/SOLV TEC/DEV DRIVE...MGT 20. PAGE 63 G1234 — INDUS LEAD ORD/FREE SOCIETY

B50
CANTRIL H.,TENSIONS THAT CAUSE WAR. UNIV CULTURE R+D CREATE DRIVE PERSON KNOWL ORD/FREE ...HUM PSY SOC OBS CENSUS TREND CON/ANAL SOC/EXP SIMUL GEN/METH ANTHOL COLD/WAR TOT/POP. PAGE 11 G0206 — SOCIETY PHIL/SCI PEACE

B50
MANNHEIM K.,FREEDOM, POWER, AND DEMOCRATIC PLANNING. FUT USSR WOR+45 ELITES INTELL SOCIETY NAT/G EDU/PROP ROUTINE ATTIT DRIVE SUPEGO SKILL ...POLICY PSY CONCPT TREND GEN/LAWS 20. PAGE 35 G0700 — TEC/DEV PLAN CAP/ISM UK

B50
SURANYI-UNGER T.,PRIVATE ENTERPRISE AND GOVERNMENTAL PLANNING. STRUCT FINAN BAL/PWR HAPPINESS DRIVE NEW/LIB PLURISM...MATH QUANT STAT TREND BIBLIOG. PAGE 53 G1047 — PLAN NAT/G LAISSEZ POLICY

B51
LEWIN K.,FIELD THEORY IN SOCIAL SCIENCE: SELECTED THEORETICAL PAPERS. UNIV CREATE DRIVE PERCEPT KNOWL ...METH/CNCPT CONT/OBS CHARTS GEN/METH METH VAL/FREE 20. PAGE 33 G0661 — PHIL/SCI HYPO/EXP

C51
HOMANS G.C.,"THE WESTERN ELECTRIC RESEARCHES" IN S. HOSLETT, ED., HUMAN FACTORS IN MANAGEMENT (BMR)" ACT/RES GP/REL HAPPINESS PRODUC DRIVE...MGT OBS 20. PAGE 27 G0526 — OP/RES EFFICIENCY SOC/EXP WORKER

B54
COMBS C.H.,DECISION PROCESSES. INTELL SOCIETY DELIB/GP CREATE EXEC TEC/DEV DOMIN LEGIT CHOOSE DRIVE RIGID/FLEX KNOWL PWR...PHIL/SCI SOC METH/CNCPT CONT/OBS REC/INT PERS/TEST SAMP/SIZ BIOG SOC/EXP WORK. PAGE 13 G0245 — MATH DECISION

C54
GOULDNER A.W.,"PATTERNS OF INDUSTRIAL BUREAUCRACY." GP/REL CONSEN ATTIT DRIVE...BIBLIOG 20. PAGE 22 G0438 — ADMIN INDUS OP/RES WORKER

S56
MILLER W.E.,"PRESIDENTIAL COATTAILS: A STUDY IN POLITICAL MYTH AND METHODOLOGY" (BMR)" USA+45 CREATE PARTIC ATTIT DRIVE PWR...DECISION CONCPT CHARTS SIMUL 20 PRESIDENT CONGRESS. PAGE 39 G0774 — CHIEF CHOOSE POL/PAR MYTH

B58
BIDWELL P.W.,RAW MATERIALS: A STUDY OF AMERICAN POLICY. USA+45 USA-45 ECO/UNDEV AGRI INDUS KIN CREATE PLAN ECO/TAC WAR PEACE ATTIT DRIVE WEALTH ...STAT CHARTS CONGRESS VAL/FREE. PAGE 7 G0135 — EXTR/IND ECO/DEV

B58
DUBIN R.,THE WORLD OF WORK: INDUSTRIAL SOCIETY AND HUMAN RELATIONS. MARKET PROC/MFG LABOR TEC/DEV CAP/ISM AUTOMAT TASK GP/REL EFFICIENCY...CONCPT CHARTS BIBLIOG 20. PAGE 16 G0317 — WORKER ECO/TAC PRODUC DRIVE

B58
JUNGK R.,BRIGHTER THAN A THOUSAND SUNS: THE MORAL AND POLITICAL HISTORY OF THE ATOMIC SCIENTISTS. WOR+45 WOR-45 CONSULT CREATE RISK UTIL DRIVE PERCEPT PWR...INT 20. PAGE 29 G0568 — NUC/PWR MORAL GOV/REL PERSON

B59
MIKSCHE F.O.,THE FAILURE OF ATOMIC STRATEGY. COM EUR+WWI INTELL POL/PAR FORCES PLAN ECO/TAC NUC/PWR ATTIT DRIVE RIGID/FLEX PWR...DECISION GEOG PSY CONCPT RECORD TREND CHARTS VAL/FREE 20. PAGE 39 G0766 — ACT/RES ORD/FREE DIPLOM ARMS/CONT

B59
WARD B.,5 IDEAS THAT CHANGE THE WORLD. WOR+45 ECO/UNDEV
WOR-45 SOCIETY STRUCT AGRI INDUS INT/ORG NAT/G ALL/VALS
FORCES ACT/RES ARMS/CONT TOTALISM ATTIT DRIVE NAT/LISM
GEN/LAWS. PAGE 62 G1210 COLONIAL

B60
GRANICK D.,THE RED EXECUTIVE. COM USA+45 SOCIETY PWR
ECO/DEV INDUS NAT/G POL/PAR EX/STRUC PLAN ECO/TAC STRATA
EDU/PROP ADMIN EXEC ATTIT DRIVE...GP/COMP 20. USSR
PAGE 22 G0440 ELITES

B60
LINDVEIT E.N.,SCIENTISTS IN GOVERNMENT. USA+45 PAY TEC/DEV
EDU/PROP ADMIN DRIVE HABITAT ROLE...TECHNIC BIBLIOG ECO/TAC
20. PAGE 34 G0670 PHIL/SCI
GOV/REL

S60
BARNETT H.J.,"RESEARCH AND DEVELOPMENT, ECONOMIC ACT/RES
GROWTH, AND NATIONAL SECURITY." USA+45 R+D CREATE PLAN
ECO/TAC ATTIT DRIVE PWR...POLICY SOC METH/CNCPT
QUANT STAT TIME/SEQ ORG/CHARTS COLD/WAR 20. PAGE 5
G0097

S60
DOTY P.M.,"THE ROLE OF THE SMALLER POWERS." FUT PWR
WOR+45 NAT/G TEC/DEV BAL/PWR DOMIN LEGIT CHOOSE POLICY
DISPL DRIVE RESPECT...DECISION 20. PAGE 16 G0310 ARMS/CONT
NUC/PWR

S60
RIVKIN A.,"AFRICAN ECONOMIC DEVELOPMENT: ADVANCED AFR
TECHNOLOGY AND THE STAGES OF GROWTH." CULTURE TEC/DEV
ECO/UNDEV AGRI COM/IND EXTR/IND PLAN ECO/TAC ATTIT FOR/AID
DRIVE RIGID/FLEX SKILL WEALTH...MGT SOC GEN/LAWS
WORK TOT/POP 20. PAGE 47 G0923

N60
US HOUSE COMM SCI ASTRONAUT,THE ORGANIZATION OF THE ACT/RES
US NATIONAL SPACE EFFORT. USA+45 WOR+45 AIR ECO/DEV SKILL
NAT/G PLAN TEC/DEV DIPLOM EDU/PROP ATTIT DRIVE PWR SPACE
...OBS TIME/SEQ TREND TOT/POP 20. PAGE 58 G1142

B61
HADLEY A.T.,THE NATIONS SAFETY AND ARMS CONTROL. ACT/RES
FUT USA+45 WOR+45 TOP/EX PLAN TEC/DEV ATTIT DRIVE ROUTINE
...CONCPT OBS TIME/SEQ TREND 20. PAGE 24 G0466 DETER
NUC/PWR

B61
KRUPP S.,PATTERN IN ORGANIZATIONAL ANALYSIS: A MGT
CRITICAL EXAMINATION. INGP/REL PERS/REL RATIONAL CONTROL
ATTIT AUTHORIT DRIVE PWR...DECISION PHIL/SCI SOC CONCPT
IDEA/COMP. PAGE 32 G0622 METH/CNCPT

S61
MACHOWSKI K.,"SELECTED PROBLEMS OF NATIONAL UNIV
SOVEREIGNTY WITH REFERENCE TO THE LAW OF OUTER ACT/RES
SPACE." FUT WOR+45 AIR LAW INTELL SOCIETY ECO/DEV NUC/PWR
PLAN EDU/PROP DETER DRIVE PERCEPT SOVEREIGN SPACE
...POLICY INT/LAW OBS TREND TOT/POP 20. PAGE 35
G0689

S61
MORGENSTERN O.,"THE N-COUNTRY PROBLEM." EUR+WWI FUT
UNIV USA+45 WOR+45 SOCIETY CONSULT TOP/EX ACT/RES BAL/PWR
PLAN EDU/PROP ATTIT DRIVE...POLICY OBS TREND NUC/PWR
TOT/POP 20. PAGE 40 G0781 TEC/DEV

S61
TAUBENFELD H.J.,"OUTER SPACE--PAST POLITICS AND PLAN
FUTURE POLICY." FUT USA+45 USA-45 WOR+45 AIR INTELL SPACE
STRUC NAT/G TOP/EX ACT/RES ADMIN ROUTINE INT/ORG
NUC/PWR ATTIT DRIVE...CONCPT TIME/SEQ TREND TOT/POP
20. PAGE 54 G1054

B62
BAKER G.W.,BEHAVIORAL SCIENCE AND CIVIL DEFENSE. NUC/PWR
USA+45 PROB/SOLV ADMIN GP/REL INGP/REL PERS/REL WAR
ANOMIE DRIVE PERSON...DECISION MGT SOC 20 POLICY
CIV/DEFENS. PAGE 4 G0085 ACT/RES

B62
BOULDING K.E.,CONFLICT AND DEFENSE: A GENERAL MATH
THEORY. FUT SOCIETY INT/ORG NAT/G CREATE BAL/PWR SIMUL
COERCE NAT/LISM DRIVE ALL/VALS...PLURIST DECISION PEACE
CONCPT METH/CNCPT TREND HYPO/EXP TOT/POP 20. PAGE 8 WAR
G0157

B62
FORBES H.W.,THE STRATEGY OF DISARMAMENT. FUT WOR+45 PLAN
INT/ORG VOL/ASSN CONSULT ARMS/CONT COERCE NUC/PWR FORCES
WAR DRIVE RIGID/FLEX ORD/FREE PWR...POLICY CONCPT DIPLOM
OBS TREND STERTYP 20. PAGE 19 G0378

B62
KRAFT J.,THE GRAND DESIGN. EUR+WWI USA+45 AGRI VOL/ASSN
FINAN INDUS MARKET INT/ORG NAT/G PLAN ECO/TAC ECO/DEV
TARIFFS REGION DRIVE ORD/FREE WEALTH...POLICY OBS INT/TRADE
TREND EEC 20. PAGE 31 G0616

B62
RIKER W.H.,THE THEORY OF POLITICAL COALITIONS. FUT
WOR+45 INTELL NAT/G CREATE PLAN ATTIT DRIVE PERCEPT SIMUL
...DECISION PSY SOC METH/CNCPT NEW/IDEA MATH CHARTS
GAME TOT/POP 20. PAGE 47 G0921

B62
WRIGHT Q.,PREVENTING WORLD WAR THREE. FUT WOR+45 CREATE
CULTURE INT/ORG NAT/G CONSULT FORCES ADMIN ATTIT
ARMS/CONT DRIVE RIGID/FLEX ORD/FREE SOVEREIGN
...POLICY CONCPT TREND STERTYP COLD/WAR 20. PAGE 64
G1259

S62
SINGER J.D.,"STABLE DETERRENCE AND ITS LIMITS." FUT NAT/G
WOR+45 R+D INT/ORG CONSULT ACT/RES TEC/DEV FORCES
ARMS/CONT COERCE DRIVE PERCEPT RIGID/FLEX ORD/FREE DETER
PWR...MYTH SIMUL TOT/POP 20. PAGE 51 G1004 NUC/PWR

S62
STORER N.W.,"SOME SOCIOLOGICAL ASPECTS OF FEDERAL POLICY
SCIENCE POLICY." USA+45 INTELL PUB/INST PLAN GP/REL CREATE
PERS/REL DRIVE PERSON ROLE...PSY SOC SIMUL 20 NIH NAT/G
NSF. PAGE 53 G1040 ALL/VALS

B63
HOWER R.M.,MANAGERS AND SCIENTISTS. EX/STRUC CREATE R+D
ADMIN REPRESENT ATTIT DRIVE ROLE PWR SKILL...SOC MGT
INT. PAGE 27 G0532 PERS/REL
INGP/REL

B63
LITTERER J.A.,ORGANIZATIONS: STRUCTURE AND ADMIN
BEHAVIOR. PLAN DOMIN CONTROL LEAD ROUTINE SANCTION CREATE
INGP/REL EFFICIENCY PRODUC DRIVE RIGID/FLEX PWR. MGT
PAGE 34 G0674 ADJUST

S63
HOSKINS H.L.,"ARAB SOCIALISM IN THE UAR." ISLAM ECO/DEV
USSR AGRI INDUS NAT/G TOP/EX CREATE DIPLOM EDU/PROP PLAN
DRIVE KNOWL PWR SOCISM...POLICY CONCPT TREND SUEZ UAR
20. PAGE 27 G0530

S63
SCHMITT H.A.,"THE EUROPEAN COMMUNITIES." EUR+WWI VOL/ASSN
FRANCE DELIB/GP EX/STRUC TOP/EX CREATE TEC/DEV ECO/DEV
ECO/TAC REGION COERCE DRIVE ALL/VALS
...METH/CNCPT EEC 20. PAGE 49 G0972

B64
RUSHING W.A.,THE PSYCHIATRIC PROFESSIONS. DOMIN ATTIT
INGP/REL DRIVE RIGID/FLEX ROLE HEALTH PWR...POLICY PUB/INST
GP/COMP. PAGE 48 G0947 PROF/ORG
BAL/PWR

L64
GOLDBERG A.,"ATOMIC ORIGINS OF THE BRITISH NUCLEAR CREATE
DETERRENT." EUR+WWI UK NAT/G TOP/EX PLAN BAL/PWR FORCES
DOMIN DETER CHOOSE ATTIT DRIVE HEALTH ORD/FREE PWR NUC/PWR
RESPECT...CONCPT VAL/FREE COLD/WAR 20 CMN/WLTH.
PAGE 22 G0425

L64
HAAS E.B.,"ECONOMICS AND DIFFERENTIAL PATTERNS OF L/A+17C
POLITICAL INTEGRATION: PROJECTIONS ABOUT UNITY IN INT/ORG
LATIN AMERICA." SOCIETY NAT/G DELIB/GP ACT/RES MARKET
CREATE PLAN ECO/TAC REGION ROUTINE ATTIT DRIVE PWR
WEALTH...CONCPT TREND CHARTS LAFTA 20. PAGE 24
G0464

S64
GARDNER R.N.,"GATT AND THE UNITED NATIONS INT/ORG
CONFERENCE ON TRADE AND DEVELOPMENT." USA+45 WOR+45 INT/TRADE
SOCIETY ECO/UNDEV MARKET NAT/G DELIB/GP ACT/RES
PLAN ECO/TAC TARIFFS EDU/PROP ROUTINE DRIVE
RIGID/FLEX WEALTH...DECISION MGT TREND UN TOT/POP
20 GATT. PAGE 21 G0411

S65
FINK C.F.,"MORE CALCULATIONS ABOUT DETERRENCE." DETER
DRIVE...PHIL/SCI PSY STAT TIME/SEQ GAME GEN/LAWS. RECORD
PAGE 19 G0367 PROBABIL
IDEA/COMP

S65
KUZMACK A.M.,"TECHNOLOGICAL CHANGE AND STABLE R+D
DETERRENCE." CREATE EDU/PROP ARMS/CONT WEAPON DETER
CHOOSE COST DRIVE PERCEPT...RECORD STERTYP TIME. EQUILIB
PAGE 32 G0627

B66
BEATON L.,MUST THE BOMB SPREAD? WOR+45 TEC/DEV
DIPLOM DRIVE ORD/FREE PWR...CHARTS 20. PAGE 6 G0109
NUC/PWR
ARMS/CONT
PLAN
PROB/SOLV

B66
BRODIE B.,ESCALATION AND THE NUCLEAR OPTION. ASIA
CUBA EUR+WWI KOREA USA+45 USSR VIETNAM RISK ATTIT
DRIVE PERCEPT PROBABIL. PAGE 9 G0172
NUC/PWR
GUERRILLA
WAR
DETER

S66
MALENBAUM W.,"GOVERNMENT, ENTREPRENEURSHIP, AND
ECONOMIC GROWTH IN POOR LANDS." ELITES ECO/UNDEV
INDUS CREATE DRIVE. PAGE 35 G0697
ECO/TAC
PLAN
CONSERVE
NAT/G

S67
BRETNOR R.,"DESTRUCTIVE FORCE AND THE MILITARY
EQUATIONS." UNIV COMPUTER PLAN PROB/SOLV AUTOMAT
CONTROL COERCE DETER NUC/PWR WEAPON DRIVE PWR.
PAGE 9 G0166
FORCES
TEC/DEV
DOMIN
WAR

S67
HILL R.,"SOCIAL ASPECTS OF FAMILY PLANNING." INDIA
KOREA TAIWAN ECO/UNDEV PLAN PROB/SOLV TEC/DEV
EDU/PROP CONTROL ATTIT DRIVE...HEAL PSY SOC 20
BIRTH/CON UN. PAGE 26 G0512
FAM
BIO/SOC
GEOG
MARRIAGE

DRUCKER P.F. G0315,G0316

DRUG ADDICTION....SEE BIO/SOC, ANOMIE, CRIME

DUBCEK/A....ALEXANDER DUBCEK

DUBIN R. G0317

DUBOIS/J....JULES DUBOIS

DUBOIS/WEB....W.E.B. DUBOIS

DUBRIDGE L.A. G0318

DUCKWORTH W.E. G0319

DUGUIT/L....LEON DUGUIT

DUHRING/E....EUGEN DUHRING

DULLES/JF....JOHN FOSTER DULLES

DUNBAR L.W. G0320

DUNCAN O.D. G0321

DUPONT....DUPONT CORPORATION (E.I. DUPONT DE NEMOURS)

DUPRE J.S. G0322

DUPRE S. G0323

DUPREE A.H. G0324

DUPUY R.E. G0325

DUPUY T.N. G0325

DURKHEIM/E....EMILE DURKHEIM

DUSCHA J. G0326

DUTY....SEE SUPEGO

DUVERGER/M....MAURICE DUVERGER

DYKMAN J.W. G0327

DYSON F.J. G0328

——————————————————— E ———————————————————

EACM....EAST AFRICAN COMMON MARKET

EAST AFRICA....SEE AFRICA/E

EAST GERMANY....SEE GERMANY/E

EASTON D. G0329,G0330,G0331

EATING....EATING, CUISINE

N19
US FOOD AND DRUG ADMIN,CIVIL DEFENSE INFORMATION
FOR FOOD AND DRUG OFFICIALS (2ND ED.) (PAMPHLET).
USA+45 PROB/SOLV RISK HABITAT...MATH CHARTS
NUC/PWR
WAR
EATING

DICTIONARY 20 CIV/DEFENS. PAGE 58 G1136
HEALTH

N64
NATIONAL ACADEMY OF SCIENCES,CIVIL DEFENSE: PROJECT
HARBOR SUMMARY REPORT (PAMPHLET). USA+45 MUNIC
NAT/G ACT/RES BUDGET EDU/PROP DETER WEAPON EATING
...GEOG 20. PAGE 41 G0808
NUC/PWR
FORCES
WAR
PLAN

ECAFE

B63
WIGHTMAN D.,TOWARD ECONOMIC CO-OPERATION IN ASIA.
ASIA S/ASIA VOL/ASSN ACT/RES PLAN TEC/DEV ECO/TAC
EDU/PROP RIGID/FLEX SKILL...POLICY METH/CNCPT OBS
INT GEN/LAWS UN 20 ECAFE. PAGE 63 G1237
ECO/UNDEV
CREATE

ECHR....EUROPEAN CONVENTION ON HUMAN RIGHTS

ECKSTEIN A. G0332

ECO....ECONOMICS

ECO/DEV....ECONOMIC SYSTEM IN DEVELOPED COUNTRIES

ECO/TAC....ECONOMIC MEASURES

N
FULLER G.A.,DEMOBILIZATION: A SELECTED LIST OF
REFERENCES. USA+45 LAW AGRI LABOR WORKER ECO/TAC
RATION RECEIVE EDU/PROP ROUTINE ARMS/CONT ALL/VALS
20. PAGE 20 G0398
BIBLIOG/A
INDUS
FORCES
NAT/G

N
MARKETING INFORMATION GUIDE. USA+45 ECO/DEV FINAN
ADMIN GP/REL. PAGE 1 G0008
BIBLIOG/A
DIST/IND
MARKET
ECO/TAC

N
GT BRIT MIN OVERSEAS DEV, LIB, TECHNICAL CO-
OPERATION -- A BIBLIOGRAPHY. UK LAW SOCIETY DIPLOM
ECO/TAC FOR/AID...STAT 20 CMN/WLTH. PAGE 39 G0775
BIBLIOG
TEC/DEV
ECO/DEV
NAT/G

B28
SOROKIN P.,CONTEMPORARY SOCIOLOGICAL THEORIES.
MOD/EUR UNIV SOCIETY R+D SCHOOL ECO/TAC EDU/PROP
ROUTINE ATTIT DRIVE...PSY CONCPT TIME/SEQ TREND
GEN/LAWS 20. PAGE 52 G1021
CULTURE
SOC
WAR

B37
STAMP S.,THE SCIENCE OF SOCIAL ADJUSTMENT. WOR-45
ACT/RES CREATE PLAN PROB/SOLV TEC/DEV ECO/TAC
EFFICIENCY SOC/INTEG 20. PAGE 52 G1031
ADJUST
ORD/FREE
PHIL/SCI

S39
HECKSCHER G.,"GROUP ORGANIZATION IN SWEDEN." SWEDEN
STRATA ECO/DEV AGRI INDUS LABOR NAT/G PROF/ORG
ECO/TAC CENTRAL SOCISM...MGT 19/20. PAGE 25 G0499
LAISSEZ
SOC

B40
HELLMAN F.S.,THE NEW DEAL: SELECTED LIST OF
REFERENCES. USA-45 FINAN LABOR EX/STRUC CREATE
INT/TRADE ADMIN CT/SYS 20 SUPREME/CT. PAGE 26 G0505
BIBLIOG/A
ECO/TAC
PLAN
POLICY

B43
LASKI H.J.,REFLECTIONS ON THE REVOLUTIONS OF OUR
TIME. COM USSR NAT/G WORKER UTOPIA ORD/FREE WEALTH
MARXISM SOCISM 19/20. PAGE 32 G0637
CAP/ISM
WELF/ST
ECO/TAC
POLICY

B45
SCHULTZ T.H.,FOOD FOR THE WORLD. UNIV SOCIETY INDUS
R+D ECO/TAC...GEOG TREND GEN/LAWS 20. PAGE 50 G0979
AGRI
TEC/DEV

B48
METZLER L.A.,INCOME, EMPLOYMENT, AND PUBLIC POLICY.
FINAN INDUS LOC/G NAT/G TAX GIVE PAY COST PRODUC
...MGT TIME/SEQ 20. PAGE 38 G0760
INCOME
WEALTH
POLICY
ECO/TAC

S48
HARDIN L.M.,"REFLECTIONS ON AGRICULTURAL POLICY
FORMATION IN THE UNITED STATES." LEGIS PLAN BUDGET
ECO/TAC LEAD CENTRAL...MGT SOC NEW/IDEA STAT FAO.
PAGE 24 G0480
AGRI
POLICY
ADMIN
NEW/LIB

B49
OGBURN W.,TECHNOLOGY AND INTERNATIONAL RELATIONS.
WOR+45 WOR-45 ECO/DEV CREATE PLAN ECO/TAC EDU/PROP
COERCE PWR SKILL WEALTH...TECHNIC PSY SOC NEW/IDEA
CHARTS TOT/POP 20. PAGE 43 G0837
TEC/DEV
DIPLOM
INT/ORG

B53
MACK R.T.,RAISING THE WORLDS STANDARD OF LIVING.
WOR+45

IRAN INT/ORG VOL/ASSN EX/STRUC ECO/TAC WEALTH...MGT FOR/AID
METH/CNCPT STAT CONT/OBS INT TOT/POP VAL/FREE 20 INT/TRADE
UN. PAGE 35 G0690

B54

GERMANY FOREIGN MINISTRY,DOCUMENTS ON GERMAN NAT/G
FOREIGN POLICY 1918-1945. SERIES C (1933-1937) DIPLOM
VOLS. I-V. GERMANY MOD/EUR FORCES PLAN ECO/TAC POLICY
...FASCIST CHARTS ANTHOL 20. PAGE 21 G0416

B54

LOCKLIN D.P.,ECONOMICS OF TRANSPORTATION (4TH ED.). ECO/DEV
USA+45 USA-45 SEA AIR LAW FINAN LG/CO EX/STRUC DIST/IND
ADMIN CONTROL...STAT CHARTS 19/20 RAILROAD ECO/TAC
PUB/TRANS. PAGE 34 G0675 TEC/DEV

B54

REYNOLDS P.A.,BRITISH FOREIGN POLICY IN THE INTER- DIPLOM
WAR YEARS. CZECHOSLVK GERMANY POLAND UK USA-45 POLICY
POL/PAR FORCES ECO/TAC ARMS/CONT WAR ATTIT 20. NAT/G
PAGE 46 G0915

B54

WASHBURNE N.F.,INTERPRETING SOCIAL CHANGE IN CULTURE
AMERICA. USA+45 STRATA FAM NAT/G SECT OP/RES STRUCT
ECO/TAC EDU/PROP HABITAT...SOC TIME/SEQ TREND 20 CREATE
BUREAUCRCY. PAGE 62 G1217 TEC/DEV

B54

WRIGHT Q.,PROBLEMS OF STABILITY AND PROGRESS IN INT/ORG
INTERNATIONAL RELATIONSHIPS. FUT WOR+45 WOR-45 CONCPT
SOCIETY LEGIS CREATE TEC/DEV ECO/TAC EDU/PROP ADJUD DIPLOM
WAR PEACE ORD/FREE PWR...KNO/TEST TREND GEN/LAWS
20. PAGE 64 G1257

B55

JONES J.M.,THE FIFTEEN WEEKS (FEBRUARY 21-JUNE 5, DIPLOM
1947). EUR+WWI USA+45 PROB/SOLV BAL/PWR...POLICY ECO/TAC
TIME/SEQ 20 COLD/WAR MARSHL/PLN TRUMAN/HS FOR/AID
WASHING/DC. PAGE 29 G0567

B55

US OFFICE OF THE PRESIDENT,REPORT TO CONGRESS ON DIPLOM
THE MUTUAL SECURITY PROGRAM FOR THE SIX MONTHS FORCES
ENDED JUNE 30, 1955. ECO/DEV INT/ORG NAT/G CREATE PLAN
TEC/DEV BAL/PWR ECO/TAC AGREE DETER COST ORD/FREE FOR/AID
20 DEPT/STATE DEPT/DEFEN. PAGE 59 G1157

L55

KISER M.,"ORGANIZATION OF AMERICAN STATES." L/A+17C VOL/ASSN
USA+45 ECO/UNDEV INT/ORG NAT/G PLAN TEC/DEV DIPLOM ECO/DEV
ECO/TAC INT/TRADE EDU/PROP ADMIN ALL/VALS...POLICY REGION
MGT RECORD ORG/CHARTS OAS 20. PAGE 30 G0601

B56

US OFFICE OF THE PRESIDENT,REPORT TO CONGRESS ON DIPLOM
THE MUTUAL SECURITY PROGRAM FOR THE SIX MONTHS FORCES
ENDED DECEMBER 31, 1955. USA+45 USSR ECO/DEV PLAN
ECO/UNDEV INT/ORG CREATE TEC/DEV BAL/PWR ECO/TAC FOR/AID
AGREE DETER COST ORD/FREE 20 DEPT/STATE DEPT/DEFEN
EISNHWR/DD. PAGE 59 G1158

B57

DRUCKER P.F.,AMERICA'S NEXT TWENTY YEARS. USA+45 WORKER
DIST/IND ACADEM MUNIC SCHOOL DIPLOM ECO/TAC AUTOMAT FOR/AID
HABITAT HEALTH...SOC/WK TREND 20 URBAN/RNWL CENSUS
PUB/TRANS. PAGE 16 G0316 GEOG

B58

ATOMIC INDUSTRIAL FORUM,MANAGEMENT AND ATOMIC NUC/PWR
ENERGY. WOR+45 SEA LAW MARKET NAT/G TEC/DEV INSPECT INDUS
INT/TRADE CONFER PEACE HEALTH...ANTHOL 20. PAGE 4 MGT
G0078 ECO/TAC

B58

BIDWELL P.W.,RAW MATERIALS: A STUDY OF AMERICAN EXTR/IND
POLICY. USA+45 USA-45 ECO/UNDEV AGRI INDUS KIN ECO/DEV
CREATE PLAN ECO/TAC WAR PEACE ATTIT DRIVE WEALTH
...STAT CHARTS CONGRESS VAL/FREE. PAGE 7 G0135

B58

DUBIN R.,THE WORLD OF WORK: INDUSTRIAL SOCIETY AND WORKER
HUMAN RELATIONS. MARKET PROC/MFG LABOR TEC/DEV ECO/TAC
CAP/ISM AUTOMAT TASK GP/REL EFFICIENCY...CONCPT PRODUC
CHARTS BIBLIOG 20. PAGE 16 G0317 DRIVE

B58

MECRENSKY E.,SCIENTIFIC MANPOWER IN EUROPE. WOR+45 ECO/TAC
EDU/PROP GOV/REL SKILL...TECHNIC PHIL/SCI INT TEC/DEV
CHARTS BIBLIOG 20. PAGE 38 G0750 METH/COMP
NAT/COMP

S58

DAVENPORT J.,"ARMS AND THE WELFARE STATE." INTELL USA+45
STRUCT FORCES CREATE ECO/TAC FOR/AID DOMIN LEGIT NAT/G
ADMIN WAR ORD/FREE PWR...POLICY SOC CONCPT MYTH OBS USSR

TREND COLD/WAR TOT/POP 20. PAGE 14 G0276

B59

MEANS G.C.,ADMINISTRATIVE INFLATION AND PUBLIC ECO/TAC
POLICY (PAMPHLET). USA+45 ECO/DEV FINAN INDUS POLICY
WORKER PLAN BUDGET GOV/REL COST DEMAND WEALTH 20 RATION
CONGRESS MONOPOLY GOLD/STAND. PAGE 38 G0749 CONTROL

B59

MIKSCHE F.O.,THE FAILURE OF ATOMIC STRATEGY. COM ACT/RES
EUR+WWI INTELL POL/PAR FORCES PLAN ECO/TAC NUC/PWR ORD/FREE
ATTIT DRIVE RIGID/FLEX PWR...DECISION GEOG PSY DIPLOM
CONCPT RECORD TREND CHARTS VAL/FREE 20. PAGE 39 ARMS/CONT
G0766

B59

WASSERMAN P.,MEASUREMENT AND ANALYSIS OF BIBLIOG/A
ORGANIZATIONAL PERFORMANCE. FINAN MARKET EX/STRUC ECO/TAC
TEC/DEV EDU/PROP CONTROL ROUTINE TASK...MGT 20. OP/RES
PAGE 62 G1220 EFFICIENCY

S59

CORY R.H. JR.,"INTERNATIONAL INSPECTION FROM STRUCT
PROPOSALS TO REALIZATION." WOR+45 TEC/DEV ECO/TAC PSY
ADJUD ORD/FREE PWR WEALTH...RECORD VAL/FREE 20. ARMS/CONT
PAGE 13 G0258 NUC/PWR

S59

SIMONS H.,"WORLD-WIDE CAPABILITIES FOR PRODUCTION TEC/DEV
AND CONTROL OF NUCLEAR WEAPONS." FUT WOR+45 INDUS ARMS/CONT
INT/ORG NAT/G ECO/TAC ATTIT PWR SKILL...TREND NUC/PWR
CHARTS VAL/FREE 20. PAGE 51 G1001

B60

CHASE S.,LIVE AND LET LIVE. USA+45 ECO/DEV NAT/G
PROB/SOLV TEC/DEV ECO/TAC ARMS/CONT NUC/PWR WAR DIPLOM
NAT/LISM PEACE...GEOG TREND 20 COLD/WAR. PAGE 11 SOCIETY
G0223 TASK

B60

GRANICK D.,THE RED EXECUTIVE. COM USA+45 SOCIETY PWR
ECO/DEV INDUS NAT/G POL/PAR EX/STRUC PLAN ECO/TAC STRATA
EDU/PROP ADMIN EXEC ATTIT DRIVE...GP/COMP 20. USSR
PAGE 22 G0440 ELITES

B60

LINDVEIT E.N.,SCIENTISTS IN GOVERNMENT. USA+45 PAY TEC/DEV
EDU/PROP ADMIN DRIVE HABITAT ROLE...TECHNIC BIBLIOG ECO/TAC
20. PAGE 34 G0670 PHIL/SCI
GOV/REL

B60

PENTONY D.E.,THE UNDERDEVELOPED LANDS. FUT WOR+45 ECO/UNDEV
CULTURE AGRI FINAN INDUS MARKET INT/ORG LABOR NAT/G POLICY
VOL/ASSN CONSULT TEC/DEV ECO/TAC EDU/PROP COLONIAL FOR/AID
ATTIT WEALTH...OBS RECORD SAMP TREND GEN/METH WORK INT/TRADE
UN 20. PAGE 44 G0867

B60

SILK L.S.,THE RESEARCH REVOLUTION. USA+45 FINAN ECO/DEV
CAP/ISM ECO/TAC PRICE EQUILIB PRODUC...STAT TREND R+D
CHARTS. PAGE 51 G0997 TEC/DEV
PROB/SOLV

B60

US HOUSE COMM. SCI. ASTRONAUT.,OCEAN SCIENCES AND R+D
NATIONAL SECURITY. FUT SEA ECO/DEV EXTR/IND INT/ORG ORD/FREE
NAT/G FORCES ACT/RES TEC/DEV ECO/TAC COERCE WAR
BIO/SOC KNOWL PWR...CONCPT RECORD LAB/EXP 20.
PAGE 59 G1153

L60

BRENNAN D.G.,"SETTING AND GOALS OF ARMS CONTROL." FORCES
FUT USA+45 USSR WOR+45 INTELL INT/ORG NAT/G COERCE
VOL/ASSN CONSULT PLAN DIPLOM ECO/TAC ADMIN KNOWL ARMS/CONT
PWR...POLICY CONCPT TREND COLD/WAR 20. PAGE 8 G0164 DETER

S60

BARNETT H.J.,"RESEARCH AND DEVELOPMENT, ECONOMIC ACT/RES
GROWTH, AND NATIONAL SECURITY." USA+45 R+D CREATE PLAN
ECO/TAC ATTIT DRIVE PWR...POLICY SOC METH/CNCPT
QUANT STAT TIME/SEQ ORG/CHARTS COLD/WAR 20. PAGE 5
G0097

S60

BECKER A.S.,"COMPARISIONS OF UNITED STATES AND USSR STAT
NATIONAL OUTPUT: SOME RULES OF THE GAME." COM USSR
USA+45 ECO/DEV AGRI DIST/IND INDUS R+D CONSULT PLAN
ECO/TAC RIGID/FLEX KNOWL...METH/CNCPT CHARTS 20.
PAGE 6 G0113

S60

HUNTINGTON S.P.,"STRATEGIC PLANNING AND THE EXEC
POLITICAL PROCESS." USA+45 NAT/G DELIB/GP LEGIS FORCES
ACT/RES ECO/TAC LEGIT ROUTINE CHOOSE RIGID/FLEX PWR NUC/PWR
...POLICY MAJORIT MGT 20. PAGE 27 G0538 WAR

IKLE F.C.,"NTH COUNTRIES AND DISARMAMENT." WOR+45   S60
DELIB/GP ECO/TAC DOMIN EDU/PROP LEGIT ROUTINE   FUT
COERCE RIGID/FLEX ORD/FREE...MARXIST TREND 20.   INT/ORG
PAGE 28 G0543   ARMS/CONT
                                                        NUC/PWR

RIVKIN A.,"AFRICAN ECONOMIC DEVELOPMENT: ADVANCED   S60
TECHNOLOGY AND THE STAGES OF GROWTH." CULTURE   AFR
ECO/UNDEV AGRI COM/IND EXTR/IND PLAN ECO/TAC ATTIT   TEC/DEV
DRIVE RIGID/FLEX SKILL WEALTH...MGT SOC GEN/LAWS   FOR/AID
WORK TOT/POP 20. PAGE 47 G0923

BONNEFOUS M.,EUROPE ET TIERS MONDE. EUR+WWI SOCIETY   B61
INT/ORG NAT/G VOL/ASSN ACT/RES TEC/DEV CAP/ISM   AFR
ECO/TAC ATTIT ORD/FREE SOVEREIGN...POLICY CONCPT   ECO/UNDEV
TREND 20. PAGE 8 G0153   FOR/AID
                                                        INT/TRADE

KISSINGER H.A.,THE NECESSITY FOR CHOICE. FUT USA+45   B61
ECO/UNDEV NAT/G PLAN BAL/PWR ECO/TAC ARMS/CONT   TOP/EX
DETER NUC/PWR ATTIT...POLICY CONCPT RECORD GEN/LAWS   TREND
COLD/WAR 20. PAGE 31 G0604   DIPLOM

LAHAYE R.,LES ENTREPRISES PUBLIQUES AU MAROC.   B61
FRANCE MOROCCO LAW DIST/IND EXTR/IND FINAN CONSULT   NAT/G
PLAN TEC/DEV ADMIN AGREE CONTROL OWN...POLICY 20.   INDUS
PAGE 32 G0629   ECO/UNDEV
                                                        ECO/TAC

MCCRACKEN H.L.,KEYNESIAN ECONOMICS IN THE STREAM OF   B61
ECONOMIC THOUGHT. FINAN MARKET BARGAIN EFFICIENCY   ECO/TAC
OPTIMAL...PHIL/SCI CONCPT IDEA/COMP BIBLIOG 18/20   DEMAND
KEYNES/JM. PAGE 37 G0732   ECOMETRIC

NOVE A.,THE SOVIET ECONOMY. USSR ECO/DEV FINAN   B61
NAT/G ECO/TAC PRICE ADMIN EFFICIENCY MARXISM   PLAN
...TREND BIBLIOG 20. PAGE 42 G0828   PRODUC
                                                        POLICY

COHEN K.J.,"THE ROLE OF MANAGEMENT GAMES IN   L61
EDUCATION AND RESEARCH." INTELL ECO/DEV FINAN   SOCIETY
ACT/RES ECO/TAC DECISION. PAGE 12 G0240   GAME
                                                        MGT
                                                        EDU/PROP

DALTON G.,"ECONOMIC THEORY AND PRIMITIVE SOCIETY"   S61
(BMR)" UNIV AGRI KIN TEC/DEV ECO/TAC REGION HABITAT   ECO/UNDEV
SKILL...METH/COMP BIBLIOG. PAGE 14 G0274   METH
                                                        PHIL/SCI
                                                        SOC

CHANDLER A.D.,STRATEGY AND STRUCTURE: CHAPTERS IN   B62
THE HISTORY OF THE INDUSTRIAL ENTERPRISE. USA+45   LG/CO
USA-45 ECO/DEV EX/STRUC ECO/TAC EXEC...DECISION 20.   PLAN
PAGE 11 G0220   ADMIN
                                                        FINAN

FERBER R.,RESEARCH METHODS IN ECONOMICS AND   B62
BUSINESS. ECO/DEV FINAN MARKET LG/CO SML/CO CONSULT   ACT/RES
CONTROL COST...STAT METH/COMP 20. PAGE 19 G0364   PROB/SOLV
                                                        ECO/TAC
                                                        MGT

FRIEDRICH-EBERT-STIFTUNG,THE SOVIET BLOC AND   B62
DEVELOPING COUNTRIES. CHINA/COM COM GERMANY/E USSR   MARXISM
WOR+45 ECO/UNDEV INT/ORG NAT/G TEC/DEV NEUTRAL PWR   DIPLOM
...POLICY 20. PAGE 20 G0394   ECO/TAC
                                                        FOR/AID

GRANICK D.,THE EUROPEAN EXECUTIVE. BELGIUM FRANCE   B62
GERMANY/W UK INDUS LABOR LG/CO SML/CO EX/STRUC PLAN   MGT
TEC/DEV CAP/ISM COST DEMAND...POLICY CHARTS 20.   ECO/DEV
PAGE 22 G0441   ECO/TAC
                                                        EXEC

KRAFT J.,THE GRAND DESIGN. EUR+WWI USA+45 AGRI   B62
FINAN INDUS MARKET INT/ORG NAT/G PLAN ECO/TAC   VOL/ASSN
TARIFFS REGION DRIVE ORD/FREE WEALTH...POLICY OBS   ECO/DEV
TREND EEC 20. PAGE 31 G0616   INT/TRADE

MELMAN S.,DISARMAMENT: ITS POLITICS AND ECONOMICS.   B62
WOR+45 DELIB/GP FORCES ECO/TAC DOMIN EDU/PROP LEGIT   NAT/G
COERCE PWR...POLICY CONCPT 20. PAGE 38 G0752   ORD/FREE
                                                        ARMS/CONT
                                                        NUC/PWR

THANT U.,THE UNITED NATIONS' DEVELOPMENT DECADE: B62
PROPOSALS FOR ACTION. WOR+45 SOCIETY ECO/UNDEV AGRI   INT/ORG
COM/IND FINAN R+D MUNIC SCHOOL VOL/ASSN CONSULT   ALL/VALS
PLAN TEC/DEV ECO/TAC EDU/PROP ADMIN ROUTINE

RIGID/FLEX...MGT SOC CONCPT UNESCO UN TOT/POP
VAL/FREE. PAGE 54 G1064

ALBONETTI A.,"IL SECONDO PROGRAMMA QUINQUENNALE   S62
1963-67 ED IL BILANCIO RICERCHE ED INVESTIMENTI PER   R+D
IL 1963 DELL'ERATOM." EUR+WWI FUT ITALY WOR+45   PLAN
ECO/DEV SERV/IND INT/ORG TEC/DEV ECO/TAC ATTIT   NUC/PWR
SKILL WEALTH...MGT TIME/SEQ OEEC 20. PAGE 2 G0035

FOSTER R.B.,"UNILATERAL ARMS CONTROL MEASURES AND   S62
DISARMAMENT NEGOTIATION." WOR+45 VOL/ASSN DELIB/GP   PLAN
ACT/RES ECO/TAC EDU/PROP ATTIT RIGID/FLEX...CONCPT   ORD/FREE
MYTH TIME/SEQ COLD/WAR 20. PAGE 20 G0386   ARMS/CONT
                                                        DETER

MORGENTHAU H.J.,"A POLITICAL THEORY OF FOREIGN   S62
AID." ECO/UNDEV NAT/G DELIB/GP PLAN ECO/TAC   USA+45
EDU/PROP EXEC ORD/FREE RESPECT WEALTH...METH/CNCPT   PHIL/SCI
TREND 20. PAGE 40 G0783   FOR/AID

THORELLI H.B.,"THE INTERNATIONAL OPERATIONS   S62
SIMULATION AT THE UNIVERSITY OF CHICAGO." FUT   ECO/TAC
USA+45 WOR+45 ECO/DEV DIST/IND FINAN INDUS INT/ORG   SIMUL
DELIB/GP ACT/RES CREATE TEC/DEV WEALTH...STAT   INT/TRADE
VAL/FREE 20. PAGE 54 G1072

ABSHIRE D.M.,NATIONAL SECURITY: POLITICAL,   B63
MILITARY, AND ECONOMIC STRATEGIES IN THE DECADE   FUT
AHEAD. ASIA COM USA+45 WOR+45 ECO/DEV ECO/UNDEV   ACT/RES
INT/ORG DELIB/GP FORCES ECO/TAC COERCE ATTIT   BAL/PWR
RIGID/FLEX HEALTH ORD/FREE PWR WEALTH...POLICY STAT
CHARTS ANTHOL COLD/WAR VAL/FREE. PAGE 1 G0024

BROUDE H.W.,STEEL DECISIONS AND THE NATIONAL   B63
ECONOMY. USA+45 LG/CO PLAN ADMIN COST DECISION.   PROC/MFG
PAGE 9 G0176   NAT/G
                                                        CONTROL
                                                        ECO/TAC

FLORES E.,LAND REFORM AND THE ALLIANCE FOR PROGRESS   B63
(PAMPHLET). L/A+17C USA+45 STRUCT ECO/UNDEV NAT/G   AGRI
WORKER CREATE PLAN ECO/TAC COERCE REV 20. PAGE 19   INT/ORG
G0373   DIPLOM
                                                        POLICY

MAYNE R.,THE COMMUNITY OF EUROPE. UK CONSTN NAT/G   B63
CONSULT DELIB/GP CREATE PLAN ECO/TAC LEGIT ADMIN   EUR+WWI
ROUTINE ORD/FREE PWR WEALTH...CONCPT TIME/SEQ EEC   INT/ORG
EURATOM 20. PAGE 37 G0724   REGION

MULLENBACH P.,CIVILIAN NUCLEAR POWER: ECONOMIC   B63
ISSUES AND POLICY FORMATION. FINAN INT/ORG DELIB/GP   USA+45
ACT/RES ECO/TAC ATTIT SUPEGO HEALTH ORD/FREE PWR   ECO/DEV
...POLICY CONCPT MATH STAT CHARTS VAL/FREE 20   NUC/PWR
COLD/WAR. PAGE 40 G0792

NASA,CONFERENCE ON SPACE, SCIENCE, AND URBAN LIFE.   B63
USA+45 SOCIETY INDUS ACADEM ACT/RES ECO/TAC ADMIN   MUNIC
20. PAGE 41 G0804   SPACE
                                                        TEC/DEV
                                                        PROB/SOLV

RAUDSEPP E.,MANAGING CREATIVE SCIENTISTS AND   B63
ENGINEERS. USA+45 ECO/DEV LG/CO GP/REL PERS/REL   MGT
PRODUC. PAGE 46 G0906   CREATE
                                                        R+D
                                                        ECO/TAC

REED E.,CHALLENGES TO DEMOCRACY: THE NEXT TEN   B63
YEARS. FUT USA+45 ECO/DEV DELIB/GP TEC/DEV CONFER   POLICY
GOV/REL KNOWL ORD/FREE...MAJORIT IDEA/COMP ANTHOL   EDU/PROP
20. PAGE 46 G0909   ECO/TAC
                                                        NAT/G

SCHOECK H.,THE NEW ARGUMENT IN ECONOMICS. UK USA+45   B63
INDUS MARKET LABOR NAT/G ECO/TAC ADMIN ROUTINE   WELF/ST
BAL/PAY PWR...POLICY BOLIV. PAGE 49 G0973   FOR/AID
                                                        ECO/DEV
                                                        ALL/IDEOS

UN SECRETARY GENERAL,PLANNING FOR ECONOMIC   B63
DEVELOPMENT. ECO/UNDEV FINAN BUDGET INT/TRADE   PLAN
TARIFFS TAX ADMIN 20 UN. PAGE 55 G1089   ECO/TAC
                                                        MGT
                                                        NAT/COMP

WIGHTMAN D.,TOWARD ECONOMIC CO-OPERATION IN ASIA.   B63
ASIA S/ASIA VOL/ASSN ACT/RES PLAN TEC/DEV ECO/TAC   ECO/UNDEV
EDU/PROP RIGID/FLEX SKILL...POLICY METH/CNCPT OBS   CREATE

INT GEN/LAWS UN 20 ECAFE. PAGE 63 G1237

L63

MCDOUGAL M.S.,"THE ENJOYMENT AND ACQUISITION OF
RESOURCES IN OUTER SPACE." CHRIST-17C FUT WOR+45
WOR-45 LAW EXTR/IND INT/ORG ACT/RES CREATE TEC/DEV
ECO/TAC LEGIT COERCE HEALTH KNOWL ORD/FREE PWR
WEALTH...JURID HIST/WRIT VAL/FREE. PAGE 37 G0738
   PLAN
   TREND

L63

NIEBURG H.,"EURATOM: A STUDY IN COALITION
POLITICS." EUR+WWI UK USA+45 ELITES NAT/G DELIB/GP
LEGIS TOP/EX ECO/TAC NUC/PWR ATTIT ORD/FREE PWR
TOT/POP EEC OEEC 20 NATO EURATOM. PAGE 42 G0820
   VOL/ASSN
   ACT/RES

S63

BOULDING K.E.,"UNIVERSITY, SOCIETY, AND ARMS
CONTROL." WOR+45 WOR-45 ACADEM NAT/G CONSULT FORCES
ACT/RES PLAN TEC/DEV BAL/PWR ECO/TAC COERCE DETER
WAR ATTIT RIGID/FLEX KNOWL ORD/FREE PWR WEALTH
...CONCPT COLD/WAR TOT/POP 20. PAGE 8 G0159
   SOCIETY
   ARMS/CONT

S63

DE FOREST J.D.,"LOW LEVELS OF TECHNOLOGY AND
ECONOMIC DEVELOPMENT PROSPECTS." WOR+45 WOR-45
CULTURE ACT/RES CREATE PLAN ECO/TAC ROUTINE PERCEPT
WEALTH...METH/CNCPT GEN/LAWS 20. PAGE 15 G0284
   ECO/UNDEV
   TEC/DEV

S63

ENTHOVEN A.C.,"ECONOMIC ANALYSIS IN THE DEPARTMENT
OF DEFENSE." USA+45 NAT/G DELIB/GP PROB/SOLV RATION
NUC/PWR WEAPON COST...DECISION 20 DEPT/DEFEN
RESOURCE/N. PAGE 18 G0349
   PLAN
   BUDGET
   ECO/TAC
   FORCES

S63

NADLER E.B.,"SOME ECONOMIC DISADVANTAGES OF THE
ARMS RACE." USA+45 INDUS R+D FORCES PLAN TEC/DEV
ECO/TAC FOR/AID EDU/PROP PWR WEALTH...TREND
COLD/WAR 20. PAGE 41 G0800
   ECO/DEV
   MGT
   BAL/PAY

S63

SCHMITT H.A.,"THE EUROPEAN COMMUNITIES." EUR+WWI
FRANCE DELIB/GP EX/STRUC TOP/EX CREATE TEC/DEV
ECO/TAC LEGIT REGION COERCE DRIVE ALL/VALS
...METH/CNCPT EEC 20. PAGE 49 G0972
   VOL/ASSN
   ECO/DEV

S63

WILES P.J.D.,"WILL CAPITALISM AND COMMUNISM
SPONTANEOUSLY CONVERGE." COM FUT USA+45 ECO/DEV
DIST/IND MARKET CAP/ISM ECO/TAC RIGID/FLEX WEALTH
MARXISM SOCISM...MATH STAT TREND COMPUT/IR 20.
PAGE 63 G1240
   PLAN
   TEC/DEV
   USSR

N63

COMMITTEE ECONOMIC DEVELOPMENT,TAXES AND TRADE: 20
YEARS OF CED POLICY (PAMPHLET). USA+45 ECO/DEV PLAN
BUDGET LEAD...POLICY KENNEDY/JF PRESIDENT. PAGE 13
G0246
   FINAN
   ECO/TAC
   NAT/G
   DELIB/GP

B64

BAUCHET P.,ECONOMIC PLANNING. FRANCE STRATA LG/CO
CAP/ISM ADMIN PARL/PROC DEMAND OPTIMAL ATTIT PWR
SOCISM...POLICY CHARTS 20. PAGE 5 G0102
   ECO/DEV
   NAT/G
   PLAN
   ECO/TAC

B64

COENEN E.,LA "KONJUNKTURFORSCHUNG" EN ALLEMAGNE ET
EN AUTRICHE, 1925-1935. AUSTRIA GERMANY OP/RES PLAN
COST PERCEPT...METH/CNCPT BIBLIOG 20. PAGE 12 G0237
   METH/COMP
   R+D
   ECO/TAC

B64

DIEBOLD J.,BEYOND AUTOMATION: MANAGERIAL PROBLEMS
OF AN EXPLODING TECHNOLOGY. SOCIETY ECO/DEV CREATE
ECO/TAC AUTOMAT SKILL...TECHNIC MGT WORK. PAGE 16
G0303
   FUT
   INDUS
   PROVS
   NAT/G

B64

DUSCHA J.,ARMS, MONEY, AND POLITICS. USA+45 INDUS
POL/PAR ECO/TAC TAX DETER NUC/PWR WAR WEAPON
GOV/REL ATTIT...BIBLIOG/A 20 CONGRESS MONEY
DEPT/DEFEN. PAGE 17 G0326
   NAT/G
   FORCES
   POLICY
   BUDGET

B64

ETZIONI A.,THE MOON-DOGGLE: DOMESTIC AND
INTERNATIONAL IMPLICATIONS OF THE SPACE RACE. FUT
USA+45 WOR+45 INTELL ECO/DEV INDUS VOL/ASSN
EX/STRUC FORCES LEGIS TOP/EX PLAN TEC/DEV ECO/TAC
EDU/PROP KNOWL ORD/FREE PWR RESPECT WEALTH
TIME/SEQ. PAGE 18 G0352
   R+D
   NAT/G
   DIPLOM
   SPACE

B64

FEI J.C.H.,DEVELOPMENT OF THE LABOR SURPLUS
ECONOMY: THEORY AND POLICY. WOR+45 AGRI INDUS
MARKET PROB/SOLV TEC/DEV...STAT CHARTS GEN/LAWS
METH 20 THIRD/WRLD. PAGE 18 G0361
   ECO/TAC
   POLICY
   WORKER
   ECO/UNDEV

B64

FREYMOND J.,WESTERN EUROPE SINCE THE WAR. COM
EUR+WWI USA+45 DIPLOM...BIBLIOG 20 NATO UN EEC.
PAGE 20 G0392
   INT/ORG
   POLICY
   ECO/DEV
   ECO/TAC

B64

LI C.M.,INDUSTRIAL DEVELOPMENT IN COMMUNIST CHINA.
CHINA/COM ECO/DEV ECO/UNDEV AGRI FINAN INDUS MARKET
LABOR NAT/G ECO/TAC INT/TRADE EXEC ALL/VALS
...POLICY RELATIV TREND WORK TOT/POP VAL/FREE 20.
PAGE 34 G0665
   ASIA
   TEC/DEV

B64

MANSFIELD E.,MONOPOLY POWER AND ECONOMIC
PERFORMANCE: AN INTRODUCTION TO A CURRENT ISSUE OF
PUBLIC POLICY. ECO/DEV INDUS NAT/G PLAN CAP/ISM
PRICE CONTROL LOBBY EFFICIENCY PRODUC...POLICY 20
CONGRESS KENNEDY/JF MONOPOLY. PAGE 36 G0701
   LG/CO
   PWR
   ECO/TAC
   MARKET

B64

MARRIS R.,THE ECONOMIC THEORY OF "MANAGERIAL"
CAPITALISM. USA+45 ECO/DEV LG/CO ECO/TAC DEMAND
...CHARTS BIBLIOG 20. PAGE 36 G0709
   CAP/ISM
   MGT
   CONTROL
   OP/RES

B64

MILIBAND R.,THE SOCIALIST REGISTER: 1964. GERMANY/W
ITALY UK LABOR POL/PAR ECO/TAC FOR/AID NUC/PWR
...POLICY SOCIALIST IDEA/COMP 20 MAO NASSER/G.
PAGE 39 G0769
   MARXISM
   SOCISM
   CAP/ISM
   PROB/SOLV

B64

ORGANIZATION AMERICAN STATES,ECONOMIC SURVEY OF
LATIN AMERICA, 1962. L/A+17C AGRI DIST/IND INDUS
MARKET PROC/MFG R+D PLAN TEC/DEV ECO/TAC REGION
BAL/PAY ALL/VALS...CON/ANAL ORG/CHARTS GEN/METH OAS
20. PAGE 43 G0844
   ECO/UNDEV
   CHARTS

B64

POWELSON J.P.,LATIN AMERICA: TODAY'S ECONOMIC AND
SOCIAL REVOLUTION. L/A+17C INTELL SOCIETY STRUCT
AGRI INDUS NAT/G DIPLOM ECO/TAC REV...POLICY 20.
PAGE 45 G0887
   ECO/UNDEV
   WEALTH
   ADJUST
   PLAN

B64

SCHERER F.M.,THE WEAPONS ACQUISITION PROCESS:
ECONOMIC INCENTIVES. BOSTON: DIVISION OF RESEARCH,
GRADUATE SCHOOL OF BUSINESS. USA+45 FINAN NAT/G
DELIB/GP ECO/TAC RIGID/FLEX WEALTH...MGT MATH STAT
CHARTS VAL/FREE 20. PAGE 49 G0965
   INDUS
   ACT/RES
   WEAPON

B64

SCHOECK H.,CENTRAL PLANNING AND NEOMERCANTILISM.
L/A+17C UK WOR+45 BUDGET ECO/TAC PRICE CONTROL
GOV/REL UTOPIA 20. PAGE 49 G0974
   PLAN
   CENTRAL
   NAT/G
   POLICY

B64

VAN DYKE V.,PRIDE AND POWER: THE RATIONALE OF THE
SPACE PROGRAM. FUT USA+45 INTELL R+D NAT/G POL/PAR
DELIB/GP EX/STRUC LEGIS TOP/EX ACT/RES PLAN ECO/TAC
EDU/PROP ORD/FREE PWR RESPECT SKILL...TIME/SEQ
VAL/FREE. PAGE 61 G1191
   TEC/DEV
   ATTIT
   POLICY

L64

CARNEGIE ENDOWMENT INT. PEACE,"ECONOMIC AND SOCIAL
QUESTION (ISSUES BEFORE THE NINETEENTH GENERAL
ASSEMBLY)." WOR+45 ECO/DEV ECO/UNDEV INDUS R+D
DELIB/GP CREATE PLAN TEC/DEV ECO/TAC FOR/AID
BAL/PAY...RECORD UN 20. PAGE 11 G0209
   INT/ORG
   INT/TRADE

L64

HAAS E.B.,"ECONOMICS AND DIFFERENTIAL PATTERNS OF
POLITICAL INTEGRATION: PROJECTIONS ABOUT UNITY IN
LATIN AMERICA." SOCIETY NAT/G DELIB/GP ACT/RES
CREATE PLAN ECO/TAC REGION ROUTINE ATTIT DRIVE PWR
WEALTH...CONCPT TREND CHARTS LAFTA 20. PAGE 24
G0464
   L/A+17C
   INT/ORG
   MARKET

S64

FLORINSKY M.T.,"TRENDS IN THE SOVIET ECONOMY." COM
USA+45 USSR INDUS LABOR NAT/G PLAN TEC/DEV ECO/TAC
ALL/VALS SOCISM...MGT METH/CNCPT STYLE CON/ANAL
GEN/METH WORK 20. PAGE 19 G0374
   ECO/DEV
   AGRI

S64

GARDNER R.N.,"GATT AND THE UNITED NATIONS
CONFERENCE ON TRADE AND DEVELOPMENT." USA+45 WOR+45
SOCIETY ECO/UNDEV MARKET NAT/G DELIB/GP ACT/RES
PLAN ECO/TAC TARIFFS EDU/PROP ROUTINE DRIVE
RIGID/FLEX WEALTH...DECISION MGT TREND UN TOT/POP
20 GATT. PAGE 21 G0411
   INT/ORG
   INT/TRADE

S64

MAHALANOBIS P.C.,"PERSPECTIVE PLANNING IN INDIA:
   PLAN

STATISTICAL TOOLS." INDIA S/ASIA STRATA AGRI
DIST/IND FINAN INDUS SERV/IND NAT/G ECO/TAC
ORD/FREE WEALTH...POLICY TREND SIMUL VAL/FREE 20.
PAGE 35 G0695 — STAT

S64
MARES V.E.,"EAST EUROPE'S SECOND CHANCE." COM
EUR+WWI HUNGARY ROMANIA USSR YUGOSLAVIA ECO/UNDEV
NAT/G TOP/EX CREATE PLAN TEC/DEV REGION NAT/LISM
RIGID/FLEX PWR...CONCPT STAT COMECON 20. PAGE 36
G0705 — VOL/ASSN ECO/TAC

S64
PILISUK M.,"STEPWISE DISARMAMENT & SUDDEN
DESTRUCTION IN A TWOPERSON GAME: A RESEARCH TOOL."
NAT/G FORCES ACT/RES ECO/TAC EDU/PROP EXEC ROUTINE
COERCE ORD/FREE...SIMUL GEN/LAWS VAL/FREE. PAGE 45
G0877 — PWR DECISION ARMS/CONT

B65
ANDERSON C.A.,EDUCATION AND ECONOMIC DEVELOPMENT.
INDUS R+D SCHOOL TEC/DEV ECO/TAC EDU/PROP AGE
HEREDITY PERCEPT SKILL 20. PAGE 3 G0056 — ANTHOL ECO/DEV ECO/UNDEV WORKER

B65
CORDIER A.W.,THE QUEST FOR PEACE. WOR+45 NAT/G PLAN
BAL/PWR ECO/TAC ARMS/CONT NUC/PWR PWR...ANTHOL UN
COLD/WAR. PAGE 13 G0256 — PEACE DIPLOM POLICY INT/ORG

B65
DORFMAN R.,MEASURING BENEFITS OF GOVERNMENT
INVESTMENTS. ECO/DEV R+D ECO/TAC PROFIT UTIL...MGT
GEN/METH. PAGE 16 G0308 — PLAN RATION EFFICIENCY OPTIMAL

B65
HALPERIN M.H.,COMMUNIST CHINA AND ARMS CONTROL.
CHINA/COM FUT USA+45 CULTURE FORCES TEC/DEV ECO/TAC
WAR PEACE ORD/FREE MARXISM 20 COLD/WAR. PAGE 24
G0473 — ATTIT POLICY ARMS/CONT NUC/PWR

B65
IANNI O.,ESTADO E CAPITALISMO. L/A+17C FINAN
TEC/DEV ECO/TAC ORD/FREE WEALTH POLICY. PAGE 28
G0542 — ECO/UNDEV STRUCT INDUS NAT/G

B65
INT. BANK RECONSTR. DEVELOP.,ECONOMIC DEVELOPMENT
OF KUWAIT. ISLAM KUWAIT AGRI FINAN MARKET EX/STRUC
TEC/DEV ECO/TAC ADMIN WEALTH...OBS CON/ANAL CHARTS
20. PAGE 28 G0548 — INDUS NAT/G

B65
JASNY H.,KHRUSHCHEV'S CROP POLICY. USSR ECO/DEV
PLAN MARXISM...STAT 20 KHRUSH/N RESOURCE/N. PAGE 29
G0562 — AGRI NAT/G POLICY ECO/TAC

B65
KANTOROVICH L.V.,THE BEST USE OF ECONOMIC
RESOURCES. USSR SOCIETY FINAN ACT/RES TEC/DEV
ECO/TAC PRICE CONTROL COST DEMAND EFFICIENCY
OPTIMAL...MGT STAT. PAGE 29 G0572 — PLAN MATH DECISION

B65
KNORR K.,SCIENCE AND DEFENSE: SOME CRITICAL
THOUGHTS ON MILITARY RESEARCH AND DEVELOPMENT.
USA+45 ACT/RES CREATE BUDGET ECO/TAC DEMAND
DECISION. PAGE 31 G0608 — CIVMIL/REL R+D FORCES PLAN

B65
MELMANS S.,OUR DEPLETED SOCIETY. SPACE USA+45
ECO/DEV FORCES BUDGET ECO/TAC ADMIN WEAPON
EFFICIENCY 20 COLD/WAR. PAGE 38 G0753 — CIVMIL/REL INDUS EDU/PROP CONTROL

S65
DEAN B.V.,"CONTRACT RESEARCH PROPOSAL PREPARATION
STRATEGIES." ECO/TAC WEALTH...MGT SIMUL. PAGE 15
G0289 — USA+45 PROC/MFG R+D PLAN

S65
KREITH K.,"PEACE RESEARCH AND GOVERNMENT POLICY."
INTELL NAT/G DIPLOM ECO/TAC CONTROL ARMS/CONT WAR
PERCEPT...DECISION IDEA/COMP. PAGE 31 G0619 — PEACE STYLE OBS

S65
LECLERCQ H.,"ECONOMIC RESEARCH AND DEVELOPMENT IN
TROPICAL AFRICA." ECO/UNDEV INT/ORG CREATE PLAN UN.
PAGE 33 G0650 — AFR R+D ACADEM ECO/TAC

S65
STAAR R.F.,"RETROGRESSION IN POLAND." COM USSR AGRI
INDUS NAT/G CREATE EDU/PROP TOTALISM RIGID/FLEX
ORD/FREE PWR SOCISM...RECORD CHARTS 20. PAGE 52
G1029 — TOP/EX ECO/TAC POLAND

B66
ALEXANDER Y.,INTERNATIONAL TECHNICAL ASSISTANCE
EXPERTS* A CASE STUDY OF THE U.N. EXPERIENCE.
ECO/UNDEV CONSULT EX/STRUC CREATE PLAN DIPLOM
FOR/AID TASK EFFICIENCY...ORG/CHARTS UN. PAGE 2
G0038 — ECO/TAC INT/ORG ADMIN MGT

B66
ALEXANDER Y.,INTERNATIONAL TECHNICAL ASSISTANCE
EXPERTS: A CASE STUDY OF THE U.N. EXPERIENCE.
USA+45 WOR+45 WORKER CREATE PLAN PROB/SOLV ECO/TAC
FOR/AID GIVE EDU/PROP...CHARTS BIBLIOG 20 UN.
PAGE 2 G0039 — SKILL INT/ORG TEC/DEV CONSULT

B66
AMERICAN ASSEMBLY COLUMBIA U,A WORLD OF NUCLEAR
POWERS? FUT WOR+45 ECO/DEV BAL/PWR ECO/TAC CONTROL
RISK EFFICIENCY ATTIT PWR...METH/COMP ANTHOL 20.
PAGE 3 G0049 — NUC/PWR DIPLOM TEC/DEV ARMS/CONT

B66
ECKSTEIN A.,COMMUNIST CHINA'S ECONOMIC GROWTH AND
FOREIGN TRADE* IMPLICATIONS FOR US POLICY. COM
USA+45 USSR STRUCT INDUS MARKET DIPLOM ECO/TAC
FOR/AID INT/TRADE...STAT CHARTS. PAGE 17 G0332 — ASIA ECO/UNDEV CREATE PWR

B66
FREIDEL F.,AMERICAN ISSUES IN THE TWENTIETH
CENTURY. SOCIETY FINAN ECO/TAC FOR/AID CONTROL
NUC/PWR WAR RACE/REL PEACE ATTIT...ANTHOL T 20
WILSON/W ROOSEVLT/F KENNEDY/JF TRUMAN/HS. PAGE 20
G0391 — DIPLOM POLICY NAT/G ORD/FREE

B66
KURAKOV I.G.,SCIENCE, TECHNOLOGY AND COMMUNISM;
SOME QUESTIONS OF DEVELOPMENT (TRANS. BY CARIN
DEDIJER). USSR INDUS PLAN PROB/SOLV COST PRODUC
...MGT MATH CHARTS METH 20. PAGE 32 G0626 — CREATE TEC/DEV MARXISM ECO/TAC

B66
MARKHAM J.W.,AN ECONOMIC-MEDIA STUDY OF BOOK
PUBLISHING. USA+45 LAW COM/IND ACADEM SCHOOL
EDU/PROP AUTOMAT CONTROL...DECISION STAT CHARTS 20
CONGRESS. PAGE 36 G0707 — PRESS ECO/TAC TEC/DEV NAT/G

B66
ONYEMELUKWE C.C.,PROBLEMS OF INDUSTRIAL PLANNING
AND MANAGEMENT IN NIGERIA. AFR FINAN LABOR DELIB/GP
TEC/DEV ADJUST...MGT TREND BIBLIOG. PAGE 43 G0839 — ECO/TAC ECO/UNDEV INDUS PLAN

B66
PEIRCE W.S.,SELECTIVE MANPOWER POLICIES AND THE
TRADE-OFF BETWEEN RISING PRICES AND UNEMPLOYMENT
(DISSERTATION). ECO/DEV WORKER ACT/RES...PHIL/SCI
20. PAGE 44 G0865 — PRICE LABOR POLICY ECO/TAC

B66
SCHURMANN F.,IDEOLOGY AND ORGANIZATION IN COMMUNIST
CHINA. CHINA/COM LOC/G MUNIC POL/PAR ECO/TAC
CONTROL ATTIT...MGT STERTYP 20 COM/PARTY. PAGE 50
G0981 — MARXISM STRUCT ADMIN NAT/G

S66
COHEN A.,"THE TECHNOLOGY/ELITE APPROACH TO THE
DEVELOPMENTAL PROCESS* PERUVIAN CASE STUDY."
L/A+17C STRUCT CREATE ECO/TAC FOR/AID CIVMIL/REL
MARXISM TECHRACY HYPO/EXP. PAGE 12 G0239 — ECO/UNDEV ELITES PERU

S66
MALENBAUM W.,"GOVERNMENT, ENTREPRENEURSHIP, AND
ECONOMIC GROWTH IN POOR LANDS." ELITES ECO/UNDEV
INDUS CREATE DRIVE. PAGE 35 G0697 — ECO/TAC PLAN CONSERVE NAT/G

N66
PRINCETON U INDUSTRIAL REL SEC,RECENT MATERIAL ON
COLLECTIVE BARGAINING IN GOVERNMENT (PAMPHLET NO.
130). USA+45 ECO/DEV LABOR WORKER ECO/TAC GOV/REL
...MGT 20. PAGE 45 G0890 — BIBLIOG/A BARGAIN NAT/G GP/REL

B67
COLEMAN J.R.,THE CHANGING AMERICAN ECONOMY. USA+45
AGRI FINAN LABOR FOR/AID INT/TRADE AUTOMAT GP/REL
INGP/REL ANTHOL. PAGE 13 G0243 — BUDGET ECO/TAC ECO/DEV WEALTH

B67
COLM G.,THE ECONOMY OF THE AMERICAN PEOPLE. USA+45
ECO/DEV FINAN WORKER INT/TRADE AUTOMAT GP/REL. — ECO/TAC PRODUC

PAGE 13 G0244   TREND
TEC/DEV

B67

DEGLER C.N.,THE AGE OF THE ECONOMIC REVOLUTION   INDUS
1876-1900. USA-45 AGRI MUNIC POL/PAR SECT ECO/TAC   SOCIETY
CHOOSE...PHIL/SCI CHARTS NAT/COMP 19 NEGRO. PAGE 15   ECO/DEV
G0292   TEC/DEV

B67

EISENMENGER R.W.,THE DYNAMICS OF GROWTH IN NEW   ECO/DEV
ENGLAND'S ECONOMY. 1870-1964. USA+45 USA-45 ECO/TAC   AGRI
TAX PAY AUTOMAT GOV/REL ADJUST HABITAT...STAT   INDUS
19/20. PAGE 17 G0340   CAP/ISM

B67

ENKE S.,DEFENSE MANAGEMENT. USA+45 R+D FORCES   DECISION
WORKER PLAN ECO/TAC ADMIN NUC/PWR BAL/PAY UTIL   DELIB/GP
WEALTH...MGT DEPT/DEFEN. PAGE 18 G0348   EFFICIENCY
BUDGET

B67

HALLE L.J.,THE COLD WAR AS HISTORY. USSR WOR+45   DIPLOM
ECO/TAC FOR/AID NUC/PWR WAR PEACE ORD/FREE   BAL/PWR
...MAJORIT TREND 20 COLD/WAR KENNEDY/JF KHRUSH/N
BERLIN/BLO. PAGE 24 G0470

B67

HIRSCHMAN A.O.,DEVELOPMENT PROJECTS OBSERVED. INDUS   ECO/UNDEV
INT/ORG CONSULT EX/STRUC CREATE OP/RES ECO/TAC   R+D
DEMAND...POLICY MGT METH/COMP 20 WORLD/BANK.   FINAN
PAGE 26 G0513   PLAN

B67

MAZOUR A.G.,SOVIET ECONOMIC DEVELOPMENT: OPERATION   ECO/TAC
OUTSTRIP: 1921-1965. USSR ECO/UNDEV FINAN CHIEF   AGRI
WORKER PROB/SOLV CONTROL PRODUC MARXISM...CHARTS   INDUS
ORG/CHARTS 20 STALIN/J. PAGE 37 G0726   PLAN

B67

OVERSEAS DEVELOPMENT INSTIT,EFFECTIVE AID. WOR+45   FOR/AID
INT/ORG TEC/DEV DIPLOM INT/TRADE ADMIN. PAGE 43   ECO/UNDEV
G0852   ECO/TAC
NAT/COMP

B67

ROACH J.R.,THE UNITED STATES AND THE ATLANTIC   INT/ORG
COMMUNITY; ISSUES AND PROSPECTS. WOR+45 TEC/DEV   POLICY
ECO/TAC COLONIAL REGION PEACE ROLE...ANTHOL NATO   ADJUST
COLD/WAR EEC. PAGE 47 G0925   DIPLOM

B67

SALMOND J.A.,THE CIVILIAN CONSERVATION CORPS,   ADMIN
1933-1942. USA-45 NAT/G CREATE EXEC EFFICIENCY   ECO/TAC
WEALTH...BIBLIOG 20 ROOSEVLT/F. PAGE 48 G0954   TASK
AGRI

B67

UNIVERSAL REFERENCE SYSTEM,ECONOMIC REGULATION,   BIBLIOG/A
BUSINESS, AND GOVERNMENT (VOLUME VIII). WOR+45   CONTROL
WOR-45 ECO/DEV ECO/UNDEV FINAN LABOR TEC/DEV   NAT/G
ECO/TAC INT/TRADE GOV/REL...POLICY COMPUT/IR.
PAGE 56 G1099

L67

PASLEY R.S.,"ORGANIZATIONAL CONFLICTS OF INTEREST   NAT/G
IN GOVERNMENT CONTRACTS." ELITES R+D ROUTINE   ECO/TAC
NUC/PWR DEMAND EFFICIENCY 20. PAGE 44 G0860   RATION
CONTROL

S67

BARRO S.,"ECONOMIC IMPACT OF SPACE EXPENDITURES: SPACE
SOME BROAD ISSUES DEALING WITH COSTS AND BENEFITS."   FINAN
USA+45 PROC/MFG R+D LG/CO CONSULT COST PRODUC 20.   ECO/TAC
PAGE 5 G0098   NAT/G

S67

CHIU S.M.,"CHINA'S MILITARY POSTURE." CHINA/COM   FORCES
ELITES NAT/G POL/PAR TEC/DEV ECO/TAC DOMIN CONTROL   CIVMIL/REL
LEAD REV MARXISM 20 MAO. PAGE 12 G0228   NUC/PWR
DIPLOM

S67

FADDEYEV N.,"CMEA CO-OPERATION OF EQUAL NATIONS."   MARXISM
COM R+D PLAN CAP/ISM DIPLOM FOR/AID WEALTH...POLICY   ECO/TAC
MARXIST. PAGE 18 G0356   INT/ORG
ECO/UNDEV

S67

HULL E.W.S.,"THE POLITICAL OCEAN." FUT UNIV WOR+45   DIPLOM
EXTR/IND R+D VOL/ASSN PLAN BAL/PWR ECO/TAC PEACE   ECO/UNDEV
WEALTH 20 UN. PAGE 27 G0536   INT/ORG
INT/LAW

S67

KRAUS J.,"A MARXIST IN GHANA." GHANA ELITES CHIEF   MARXISM

PROB/SOLV TEC/DEV DIPLOM ECO/TAC COLONIAL PARTIC   PLAN
PWR 20 NKRUMAH/K. PAGE 31 G0618   ATTIT
CREATE

S67

MEHTA A.,"INDIA* POVERTY AND CHANGE." STRATA INDUS   INDIA
CREATE ECO/TAC FOR/AID NEUTRAL GP/REL ADJUST INCOME   SOCIETY
...NEW/IDEA 20. PAGE 38 G0751   ECO/UNDEV
TEC/DEV

S67

SINGH B.,"ITALIAN EXPERIENCE IN REGIONAL ECONOMIC   ECO/UNDEV
DEVELOPMENT AND LESSONS FOR OTHER COUNTRIES."   PLAN
EUR+WWI ITALY INDUS NAT/G ACT/RES REGION GP/REL   ECO/TAC
EFFICIENCY EQUILIB PRODUC WEALTH. PAGE 51 G1007   CONTROL

S67

WEIL G.L.,"THE MERGER OF THE INSTITUTIONS OF THE   ECO/TAC
EUROPEAN COMMUNITIES" EUR+WWI ECO/DEV INT/TRADE   INT/ORG
CONSEN PLURISM...DECISION MGT 20 EEC EURATOM ECSC   CENTRAL
TREATY. PAGE 62 G1223   INT/LAW

S67

WHITTIER J.M.,"COMPULSORY POOLING AND UNITIZATION*   LEGIS
DIE-HARD KANSAS." LAW PLAN EDU/PROP ATTIT...POLICY   MUNIC
JURID PREDICT TREND METH/COMP 20. PAGE 63 G1236   INDUS
ECO/TAC

B88

BENTHAM J.,DEFENCE OF USURY (1787). UK LAW NAT/G   TAX
TEC/DEV ECO/TAC CONTROL ATTIT...CONCPT IDEA/COMP 18   FINAN
SMITH/ADAM. PAGE 6 G0124   ECO/DEV
POLICY

ECO/UNDEV....ECONOMIC SYSTEM IN DEVELOPING COUNTRIES

N

FOREIGN AFFAIRS. SPACE WOR+45 WOR-45 CULTURE   BIBLIOG
ECO/UNDEV FINAN NAT/G TEC/DEV INT/TRADE ARMS/CONT   DIPLOM
NUC/PWR...POLICY 20 UN EURATOM ECSC EEC. PAGE 1   INT/ORG
G0004   INT/LAW

N

PUBLIC ADMINISTRATION ABSTRACTS AND INDEX OF   BIBLIOG/A
ARTICLES. WOR+45 PLAN PROB/SOLV...POLICY 20. PAGE 1   ADMIN
G0009   ECO/UNDEV
NAT/G

B50

US DEPARTMENT OF STATE,POINT FOUR: COOPERATIVE   ECO/UNDEV
PROGRAM FOR AID IN THE DEVELOPMENT OF ECONOMICALLY   FOR/AID
UNDERDEVELOPED AREAS. WOR+45 AGRI INDUS INT/ORG   FINAN
PLAN TEC/DEV DIPLOM EDU/PROP ADMIN PEACE PRODUC   INT/TRADE
WEALTH 20 CONGRESS UN. PAGE 57 G1121

B54

KENWORTHY L.S.,FREE AND INEXPENSIVE MATERIALS ON   BIBLIOG/A
WORLD AFFAIRS (PAMPHLET). WOR+45 CULTURE ECO/UNDEV   NAT/G
INT/TRADE ARMS/CONT NUC/PWR UN. PAGE 30 G0594   INT/ORG
DIPLOM

B54

MOSK S.A.,INDUSTRIAL REVOLUTION IN MEXICO. MARKET   INDUS
LABOR CREATE CAP/ISM ADMIN ATTIT SOCISM...POLICY 20   TEC/DEV
MEXIC/AMER. PAGE 40 G0789   ECO/UNDEV
NAT/G

L55

KISER M.,"ORGANIZATION OF AMERICAN STATES." L/A+17C   VOL/ASSN
USA+45 ECO/UNDEV INT/ORG NAT/G PLAN TEC/DEV DIPLOM   ECO/DEV
ECO/TAC INT/TRADE EDU/PROP ADMIN ALL/VALS...POLICY   REGION
MGT RECORD ORG/CHARTS OAS 20. PAGE 30 G0601

B56

UN HEADQUARTERS LIBRARY,BIBLIOGRAPHY OF   BIBLIOG
INDUSTRIALIZATION IN UNDERDEVELOPED COUNTRIES   ECO/UNDEV
(BIBLIOGRAPHICAL SERIES NO. 6). WOR+45 R+D ACADEM   TEC/DEV
INT/ORG NAT/G. PAGE 55 G1087

B56

US OFFICE OF THE PRESIDENT,REPORT TO CONGRESS ON   DIPLOM
THE MUTUAL SECURITY PROGRAM FOR THE SIX MONTHS   FORCES
ENDED DECEMBER 31, 1955. ASIA USSR ECO/DEV   PLAN
ECO/UNDEV INT/ORG CREATE TEC/DEV BAL/PWR ECO/TAC   FOR/AID
AGREE DETER COST ORD/FREE 20 DEPT/STATE DEPT/DEFEN
EISNHWR/DD. PAGE 59 G1158

B57

BAUER P.T.,ECONOMIC ANALYSIS AND POLICY IN   ECO/UNDEV
UNDERDEVELOPED COUNTRIES. WOR+45 AGRI INT/TRADE TAX   METH/COMP
PRICE...GEN/METH BIBLIOG/A 20 COMMONWLTH. PAGE 5   POLICY
G0103

B57

GOLD N.L.,REGIONAL ECONOMIC DEVELOPMENT AND NUCLEAR   ECO/UNDEV
POWER IN INDIA. FUT INDIA FINAN FOR/AID INT/TRADE   TEC/DEV

BAL/PAY EFFICIENCY OPTIMAL PRODUC WEALTH...PREDICT NUC/PWR
20. PAGE 22 G0424   INDUS

B58
LIST OF PUBLICATIONS (PERIODICAL OR AD HOC) ISSUED   BIBLIOG
BY VARIOUS MINISTRIES OF THE GOVERNMENT OF INDIA   NAT/G
(3RD ED.). INDIA ECO/UNDEV PLAN...POLICY MGT 20.   ADMIN
PAGE 1 G0014

BIDWELL P.W.,RAW MATERIALS: A STUDY OF AMERICAN   EXTR/IND
POLICY. USA+45 USA-45 ECO/UNDEV AGRI INDUS KIN   ECO/DEV
CREATE PLAN ECO/TAC WAR PEACE ATTIT DRIVE WEALTH
...STAT CHARTS CONGRESS VAL/FREE. PAGE 7 G0135

B58
EHRHARD J.,LE DESTIN DU COLONIALISME. AFR FRANCE   COLONIAL
ECO/UNDEV AGRI FINAN MARKET CREATE PLAN TEC/DEV   FOR/AID
BUDGET DIPLOM PRICE 20. PAGE 17 G0335   INT/TRADE
                                                     INDUS

S58
MARCY C.,"THE RESEARCH PROGRAM OF THE SENATE   DELIB/GP
COMMITTEE ON FOREIGN RELATIONS." EUR+WWI ECO/UNDEV   LEGIS
ACT/RES PLAN PARL/PROC GOV/REL...GEOG CONFE   FOR/AID
CONGRESS. PAGE 36 G0704   POLICY

B59
AIR FORCE ACADEMY ASSEMBLY '59,INTERNATIONAL   FOR/AID
STABILITY AND PROGRESS (PAMPHLET). USA+45 USSR   FORCES
ECO/UNDEV PROB/SOLV BUDGET DIPLOM ADMIN DETER COST   WAR
ATTIT...TREND 20. PAGE 2 G0030   PLAN

B59
MAYDA J.,ATOMIC ENERGY AND LAW. ECO/UNDEV FINAN   NUC/PWR
TEC/DEV FOR/AID EFFICIENCY PRODUC WEALTH...POLICY   L/A+17C
TECHNIC 20. PAGE 37 G0723   LAW
                                                     ADMIN

B59
WARD B.,5 IDEAS THAT CHANGE THE WORLD. WOR+45   ECO/UNDEV
WOR-45 SOCIETY STRUCT AGRI INDUS INT/ORG NAT/G   ALL/VALS
FORCES ACT/RES ARMS/CONT TOTALISM ATTIT DRIVE   NAT/LISM
GEN/LAWS. PAGE 62 G1210   COLONIAL

B60
HEILBRONER R.L.,THE FUTURE AS HISTORY. USA+45   TEC/DEV
WOR+45 WOR-45 SOCIETY ECO/DEV ECO/UNDEV VOL/ASSN   TREND
PLAN CAP/ISM NUC/PWR CHOOSE NAT/LISM ATTIT ORD/FREE
RESPECT WEALTH SOCISM 20. PAGE 25 G0501

B60
LEYDER J.,BIBLIOGRAPHIE DE L'ENSEIGNEMENT SUPERIEUR BIBLIOG/A
ET DE LA RECHERCHE SCIENTIFIQUE EN AFRIQUE   ACT/RES
INTERTROPICALE (2 VOLS.). AFR CULTURE ECO/UNDEV   ACADEM
AGRI PLAN EDU/PROP ADMIN COLONIAL...GEOG SOC/INTEG   R+D
20 NEGRO. PAGE 34 G0664

B60
MCKINNEY R.,REVIEW OF THE INTERNATIONAL ATOMIC   NUC/PWR
POLICIES AND PROGRAMS OF THE UNITED STATES (5   PEACE
VOLS.). COM FUT USA+45 ECO/DEV ECO/UNDEV INT/ORG   DIPLOM
DELIB/GP PLAN ADMIN 20 THIRD/WRLD. PAGE 38 G0744   POLICY

B60
PENTONY D.E.,THE UNDERDEVELOPED LANDS. FUT WOR+45   ECO/UNDEV
CULTURE AGRI FINAN INDUS MARKET INT/ORG LABOR NAT/G POLICY
VOL/ASSN CONSULT TEC/DEV ECO/TAC EDU/PROP COLONIAL   FOR/AID
ATTIT WEALTH...OBS RECORD SAMP TREND GEN/METH WORK   INT/TRADE
UN 20. PAGE 44 G0867

S60
JAFFEE A.J.,"POPULATION TRENDS AND CONTROLS IN   ECO/UNDEV
UNDERDEVELOPED COUNTRIES." AFR FUT ISLAM L/A+17C   GEOG
S/ASIA CULTURE R+D FAM ACT/RES PLAN EDU/PROP
BIO/SOC RIGID/FLEX HEALTH...SOC STAT OBS CHARTS 20.
PAGE 28 G0555

S60
RIVKIN A.,"AFRICAN ECONOMIC DEVELOPMENT: ADVANCED   AFR
TECHNOLOGY AND THE STAGES OF GROWTH." CULTURE   TEC/DEV
ECO/UNDEV AGRI COM/IND EXTR/IND PLAN ECO/TAC ATTIT   FOR/AID
DRIVE RIGID/FLEX SKILL WEALTH...MGT SOC GEN/LAWS
WORK TOT/POP 20. PAGE 47 G0923

B61
BONNEFOUS M.,EUROPE ET TIERS MONDE. EUR+WWI SOCIETY AFR
INT/ORG NAT/G VOL/ASSN ACT/RES TEC/DEV CAP/ISM   ECO/UNDEV
ECO/TAC ATTIT ORD/FREE SOVEREIGN...POLICY CONCPT   FOR/AID
TREND 20. PAGE 8 G0153   INT/TRADE

B61
GRUBER R.,SCIENCE AND THE NEW NATIONS. WOR+45 NAT/G ECO/UNDEV
CREATE SKILL...CONCPT GEN/LAWS 20. PAGE 23 G0457   KNOWL

B61
KISSINGER H.A.,THE NECESSITY FOR CHOICE. FUT USA+45 TOP/EX
ECO/UNDEV NAT/G PLAN BAL/PWR ECO/TAC ARMS/CONT   TREND
DETER NUC/PWR ATTIT...POLICY CONCPT RECORD GEN/LAWS DIPLOM
COLD/WAR 20. PAGE 31 G0604

B61
LAHAYE R.,LES ENTREPRISES PUBLIQUES AU MAROC.   NAT/G
FRANCE MOROCCO LAW DIST/IND EXTR/IND FINAN CONSULT   INDUS
PLAN TEC/DEV ADMIN AGREE CONTROL OWN...POLICY 20.   ECO/UNDEV
PAGE 32 G0629   ECO/TAC

S61
DALTON G.,"ECONOMIC THEORY AND PRIMITIVE SOCIETY"   ECO/UNDEV
(BMR)" UNIV AGRI KIN TEC/DEV ECO/TAC REGION HABITAT METH
SKILL...METH/COMP BIBLIOG. PAGE 14 G0274   PHIL/SCI
                                                     SOC

B62
BROOKINGS INSTITUTION,DEVELOPMENT OF THE EMERGING   ECO/UNDEV
COUNTRIES; AN AGENDA FOR RESEARCH. WOR+45 AGRI   R+D
TEC/DEV FOR/AID EDU/PROP ADJUST HABITAT KNOWL...PSY SOCIETY
SOC ANTHOL 20 THIRD/WRLD. PAGE 9 G0175   PROB/SOLV

B62
BURKE A.E.,ENOUGH GOOD MEN. USA+45 WOR+45 ECO/UNDEV DIPLOM
FORCES TEC/DEV GUERRILLA NUC/PWR REV WAR ORD/FREE   POLICY
MARXISM...GEOG 20 COLD/WAR. PAGE 10 G0189   NAT/G
                                                     TASK

B62
FRIEDRICH-EBERT-STIFTUNG,THE SOVIET BLOC AND   MARXISM
DEVELOPING COUNTRIES. CHINA/COM COM GERMANY/E USSR   DIPLOM
WOR+45 ECO/UNDEV INT/ORG NAT/G TEC/DEV NEUTRAL PWR   ECO/TAC
...POLICY 20. PAGE 20 G0394   FOR/AID

B62
MARTINS A.F.,REVOLUCAO BRANCA NO CAMPO. L/A+17C   AGRI
SERV/IND DEMAND EFFICIENCY PRODUC...POLICY   ECO/UNDEV
METH/COMP. PAGE 36 G0717   TEC/DEV
                                                     NAT/COMP

B62
THANT U.,THE UNITED NATIONS' DEVELOPMENT DECADE: INT/ORG
PROPOSALS FOR ACTION. WOR+45 SOCIETY ECO/UNDEV AGRI ALL/VALS
COM/IND FINAN R+D MUNIC SCHOOL VOL/ASSN CONSULT
PLAN TEC/DEV ECO/TAC EDU/PROP ADMIN ROUTINE
RIGID/FLEX...MGT SOC CONCPT UNESCO UN TOT/POP
VAL/FREE. PAGE 54 G1064

S62
MORGENTHAU H.J.,"A POLITICAL THEORY OF FOREIGN   USA+45
AID." ECO/UNDEV NAT/G DELIB/GP PLAN ECO/TAC   PHIL/SCI
EDU/PROP EXEC ORD/FREE RESPECT WEALTH...METH/CNCPT   FOR/AID
TREND 20. PAGE 40 G0783

S62
VIETORISZ T.,"PRELIMINARY BIBLIOGRAPHY FOR   BIBLIOG/A
INDUSTRIAL DEVELOPMENT PROGRAMMING." ECO/DEV   TEC/DEV
ECO/UNDEV R+D LABOR PROB/SOLV AUTOMAT PRODUC.   ACT/RES
PAGE 61 G1198   PLAN

B63
ABSHIRE D.M.,NATIONAL SECURITY: POLITICAL,   FUT
MILITARY, AND ECONOMIC STRATEGIES IN THE DECADE   ACT/RES
AHEAD. ASIA COM USA+45 WOR+45 ECO/DEV ECO/UNDEV   BAL/PWR
INT/ORG DELIB/GP FORCES ECO/TAC COERCE ATTIT
RIGID/FLEX HEALTH ORD/FREE PWR WEALTH...POLICY STAT
CHARTS ANTHOL COLD/WAR VAL/FREE. PAGE 1 G0024

B63
DALAND R.T.,PERSPECTIVES OF BRAZILIAN PUBLIC   ADMIN
ADMINISTRATION (VOL. I). BRAZIL LAW ECO/UNDEV   NAT/G
SCHOOL CHIEF TEC/DEV CONFER CONTROL GP/REL ATTIT   PLAN
ROLE PWR...ANTHOL 20. PAGE 14 G0272   GOV/REL

B63
FLORES E.,LAND REFORM AND THE ALLIANCE FOR PROGRESS AGRI
(PAMPHLET). L/A+17C USA+45 STRUCT ECO/UNDEV NAT/G   INT/ORG
WORKER CREATE PLAN ECO/TAC COERCE REV 20. PAGE 19   DIPLOM
G0373   POLICY

B63
GEERTZ C.,OLD SOCIETIES AND NEW STATES: THE QUEST   ECO/UNDEV
FOR MODERNITY IN ASIA AND AFRICA. AFR ASIA LAW   TEC/DEV
CULTURE SECT EDU/PROP REV...GOV/COMP NAT/COMP 20.   NAT/LISM
PAGE 21 G0415   SOVEREIGN

B63
HAUSMAN W.H.,MANAGING ECONOMIC DEVELOPMENT IN   ECO/UNDEV
AFRICA. AFR USA+45 LAW FINAN WORKER TEC/DEV WEALTH   PLAN
...ANTHOL 20. PAGE 25 G0492   FOR/AID
                                                     MGT

B63
KATZ S.M.,A SELECTED LIST OF US READINGS ON   BIBLIOG/A

DEVELOPMENT. AGRI COM/IND DIST/IND INDUS LABOR PLAN ECO/UNDEV
FOR/AID EDU/PROP HEALTH...POLICY SOC/WK 20. PAGE 30 TEC/DEV
G0582   ACT/RES

B63
MENEZES A.J.,SUBDESENVOLVIMENTO E POLITICA   ECO/UNDEV
INTERNACIONAL. BRAZIL WOR+45 PLAN CONTROL LEAD   DIPLOM
NAT/LISM ORD/FREE 20 THIRD/WRLD. PAGE 38 G0754   POLICY
                                                   BAL/PWR

B63
SCHRADER R.,SCIENCE AND POLICY. WOR+45 ECO/DEV   TEC/DEV
ECO/UNDEV R+D FORCES PLAN DIPLOM GOV/REL TECHRACY   NAT/G
BIBLIOG. PAGE 50 G0976   POLICY
                                                   ADMIN

B63
UN SECRETARY GENERAL,PLANNING FOR ECONOMIC   PLAN
DEVELOPMENT. ECO/UNDEV FINAN BUDGET INT/TRADE   ECO/TAC
TARIFFS TAX ADMIN 20 UN. PAGE 55 G1089   MGT
                                                   NAT/COMP

B63
WIGHTMAN D.,TOWARD ECONOMIC CO-OPERATION IN ASIA.   ECO/UNDEV
ASIA S/ASIA VOL/ASSN ACT/RES PLAN TEC/DEV ECO/TAC   CREATE
EDU/PROP RIGID/FLEX SKILL...POLICY METH/CNCPT OBS
INT GEN/LAWS UN 20 ECAFE. PAGE 63 G1237

L63
BEGUIN H.,"ASPECTS GEOGRAPHIQUE DE LA   ECO/UNDEV
POLARISATION." FUT WOR+45 SOCIETY STRUCT ECO/DEV   GEOG
R+D BAL/PWR ADMIN ATTIT RIGID/FLEX HEALTH WEALTH   DIPLOM
...CHARTS 20. PAGE 6 G0114

S63
DE FOREST J.D.,"LOW LEVELS OF TECHNOLOGY AND   ECO/UNDEV
ECONOMIC DEVELOPMENT PROSPECTS." WOR+45 WOR-45   TEC/DEV
CULTURE ACT/RES CREATE PLAN ECO/TAC ROUTINE PERCEPT
WEALTH...METH/CNCPT GEN/LAWS 20. PAGE 15 G0284

S63
GANDILHON J.,"LA SCIENCE ET LA TECHNIQUE A L'AIDE   ECO/UNDEV
DES REGIONS PEU DEVELOPPEES." FRANCE FUT WOR+45   TEC/DEV
ECO/DEV R+D PROF/ORG ACT/RES PLAN...MGT TOT/POP   FOR/AID
VAL/FREE 20 UN. PAGE 21 G0406

S63
VIETORISZ T.,"PRELIMINARY BIBLIOGRAPHY FOR   BIBLIOG/A
INDUSTRIAL DEVELOPMENT PROGRAMMING." ECO/DEV   TEC/DEV
ECO/UNDEV R+D LABOR PROB/SOLV AUTOMAT PRODUC.   ACT/RES
PAGE 61 G1199   PLAN

B64
BALASSA B.,TRADE PROSPECTS FOR DEVELOPING   INT/TRADE
COUNTRIES. WOR+45 ECO/DEV AGRI EXTR/IND INDUS   ECO/UNDEV
CREATE PLAN PRICE...ECOMETRIC CLASSIF TIME/SEQ   TREND
GEN/METH. PAGE 5 G0087   STAT

B64
FEI J.C.H.,DEVELOPMENT OF THE LABOR SURPLUS   ECO/TAC
ECONOMY: THEORY AND POLICY. WOR+45 AGRI INDUS   POLICY
MARKET PROB/SOLV TEC/DEV...STAT CHARTS GEN/LAWS   WORKER
METH 20 THIRD/WRLD. PAGE 18 G0361   ECO/UNDEV

B64
HASKINS C.P.,THE SCIENTIFIC REVOLUTION AND WORLD   TEC/DEV
POLITICS. COM FUT USA+45 ECO/DEV ECO/UNDEV ATTIT   POLICY
...PHIL/SCI BIBLIOG 20 THIRD/WRLD. PAGE 25 G0489   DIPLOM
                                                   TREND

B64
HAZLEWOOD A.,THE ECONOMICS OF DEVELOPMENT: AN   BIBLIOG/A
ANNOTATED LIST OF BOOKS AND ARTICLES PUBLISHED   ECO/UNDEV
1958-1962. AGRI FINAN INDUS LABOR NAT/G DIPLOM   TEC/DEV
INT/TRADE INCOME...MGT 20. PAGE 25 G0497

B64
HEKHUIS D.J.,INTERNATIONAL STABILITY: MILITARY,   TEC/DEV
ECONOMIC AND POLITICAL DIMENSIONS. FUT WOR+45 LAW   DETER
ECO/UNDEV INT/ORG NAT/G VOL/ASSN FORCES ACT/RES   REGION
BAL/PWR PWR WEALTH...STAT UN 20. PAGE 25 G0503

B64
LI C.M.,INDUSTRIAL DEVELOPMENT IN COMMUNIST CHINA. ASIA
CHINA/COM ECO/DEV ECO/UNDEV AGRI FINAN INDUS MARKET TEC/DEV
LABOR NAT/G ECO/TAC INT/TRADE EXEC ALL/VALS
...POLICY RELATIV TREND WORK TOT/POP VAL/FREE 20.
PAGE 34 G0665

B64
ORGANIZATION AMERICAN STATES,ECONOMIC SURVEY OF   ECO/UNDEV
LATIN AMERICA, 1962. L/A+17C AGRI DIST/IND INDUS   CHARTS
MARKET PROC/MFG R+D PLAN TEC/DEV ECO/TAC REGION
BAL/PAY ALL/VALS...CON/ANAL ORG/CHARTS GEN/METH OAS
20. PAGE 43 G0844

B64
POWELSON J.P.,LATIN AMERICA: TODAY'S ECONOMIC AND   ECO/UNDEV
SOCIAL REVOLUTION. L/A+17C INTELL SOCIETY STRUCT   WEALTH
AGRI INDUS NAT/G DIPLOM ECO/TAC REV...POLICY 20.   ADJUST
PAGE 45 G0887   PLAN

L64
CARNEGIE ENDOWMENT INT. PEACE,"ECONOMIC AND SOCIAL INT/ORG
QUESTION (ISSUES BEFORE THE NINETEENTH GENERAL   INT/TRADE
ASSEMBLY)." WOR+45 ECO/DEV ECO/UNDEV INDUS R+D
DELIB/GP CREATE PLAN TEC/DEV ECO/TAC FOR/AID
BAL/PAY...RECORD UN 20. PAGE 11 G0209

S64
GARDNER R.N.,"GATT AND THE UNITED NATIONS   INT/ORG
CONFERENCE ON TRADE AND DEVELOPMENT." USA+45 WOR+45 INT/TRADE
SOCIETY ECO/UNDEV MARKET NAT/G DELIB/GP ACT/RES
PLAN ECO/TAC TARIFFS EDU/PROP ROUTINE DRIVE
RIGID/FLEX WEALTH...DECISION MGT TREND UN TOT/POP
20 GATT. PAGE 21 G0411

S64
MARES V.E.,"EAST EUROPE'S SECOND CHANCE." COM   VOL/ASSN
EUR+WWI HUNGARY ROMANIA USSR YUGOSLAVIA ECO/UNDEV   ECO/TAC
NAT/G TOP/EX CREATE PLAN TEC/DEV REGION NAT/LISM
RIGID/FLEX PWR...CONCPT STAT COMECON 20. PAGE 36
G0705

S64
THOMPSON V.A.,"ADMINISTRATIVE OBJECTIVES FOR   ECO/UNDEV
DEVELOPMENT ADMINISTRATION." WOR+45 CREATE PLAN   MGT
DOMIN EDU/PROP EXEC ROUTINE ATTIT ORD/FREE PWR
...POLICY GEN/LAWS VAL/FREE. PAGE 54 G1070

C64
SCHRAMM W.,"MASS MEDIA AND NATIONAL DEVELOPMENT: ECO/UNDEV
THE ROLE OF INFORMATION IN DEVELOPING COUNTRIES."   COM/IND
FINAN R+D ACT/RES PLAN TEC/DEV DIPLOM CHOOSE SUPEGO EDU/PROP
ORD/FREE...BIBLIOG 20. PAGE 50 G0978   MAJORIT

B65
ANDERSON C.A.,EDUCATION AND ECONOMIC DEVELOPMENT.   ANTHOL
INDUS R+D SCHOOL TEC/DEV ECO/TAC EDU/PROP AGE   ECO/DEV
HEREDITY PERCEPT SKILL 20. PAGE 3 G0056   ECO/UNDEV
                                                   WORKER

B65
BARISH N.N.,MANAGEMENT SCIENCES IN THE EMERGING   ECO/UNDEV
COUNTRIES. AFR CHINA/COM WOR+45 FINAN INDUS PLAN   OP/RES
PRODUC HABITAT...ANTHOL 20. PAGE 5 G0093   MGT
                                                   TEC/DEV

B65
FOSTER P.,EDUCATION AND SOCIAL CHANGE IN GHANA.   SCHOOL
GHANA CULTURE STRUCT ECO/UNDEV TEC/DEV REGION   CREATE
EFFICIENCY LITERACY ALL/VALS SOVEREIGN...STAT   SOCIETY
METH/COMP 19/20 GOLD/COAST. PAGE 20 G0385

B65
IANNI O.,ESTADO E CAPITALISMO. L/A+17C FINAN   ECO/UNDEV
TEC/DEV ECO/TAC ORD/FREE WEALTH POLICY. PAGE 28   STRUCT
G0542   INDUS
                                                   NAT/G

B65
MORRIS M.D.,THE EMERGENCE OF AN INDUSTRIAL LABOR   INDUS
FORCE IN INDIA: A STUDY OF THE BOMBAY COTTON MILLS, LABOR
1854-1947. INDIA WORKER OP/RES ADMIN 19/20. PAGE 40 ECO/UNDEV
G0784   CAP/ISM

B65
OECD,MEDITERRANEAN REGIONAL PROJECT: TURKEY;   EDU/PROP
EDUCATION AND DEVELOPMENT. FUT TURKEY SOCIETY   ACADEM
STRATA FINAN NAT/G PROF/ORG PLAN PROB/SOLV ADMIN   SCHOOL
COST...STAT CHARTS 20 OECD. PAGE 42 G0831   ECO/UNDEV

B65
OECD,THE MEDITERRANEAN REGIONAL PROJECT: PORTUGAL; EDU/PROP
EDUCATION AND DEVELOPMENT. PORTUGAL SOCIETY STRATA SCHOOL
FINAN PROF/ORG WORKER PLAN PROB/SOLV ADMIN...POLICY ACADEM
STAT CHARTS METH 20 OECD. PAGE 42 G0832   ECO/UNDEV

B65
OECD,THE MEDITERRANEAN REGIONAL PROJECT: ITALY;   SCHOOL
EDUCATION AND DEVELOPMENT. ITALY SOCIETY STRATA   EDU/PROP
FINAN NAT/G PROF/ORG WORKER PLAN PROB/SOLV ADMIN   ECO/UNDEV
...STAT CHARTS METH 20 OECD. PAGE 42 G0833   ACADEM

B65
OECD,THE MEDITERRANEAN REGIONAL PROJECT: GREECE;   EDU/PROP
EDUCATION AND DEVELOPMENT. FUT GREECE SOCIETY AGRI SCHOOL
FINAN NAT/G PROF/ORG WORKER PLAN PROB/SOLV ADMIN   ACADEM
DEMAND ATTIT 20 OECD. PAGE 42 G0834   ECO/UNDEV

B65
OECD,THE MEDITERRANEAN REGIONAL PROJECT: SPAIN;   ECO/UNDEV

PLAN

EDUCATION AND DEVELOPMENT. FUT SPAIN STRATA FINAN NAT/G WORKER PLAN PROB/SOLV ADMIN COST...POLICY STAT CHARTS 20 OECD. PAGE 42 G0835
EDU/PROP
ACADEM
SCHOOL

B65
ORG FOR ECO COOP AND DEVEL,THE MEDITERRANEAN REGIONAL PROJECT: YUGOSLAVIA; EDUCATION AND DEVELOPMENT. YUGOSLAVIA SOCIETY FINAN PROF/ORG PLAN ADMIN COST DEMAND MARXISM...STAT TREND CHARTS METH 20 OECD. PAGE 43 G0843
EDU/PROP
ACADEM
SCHOOL
ECO/UNDEV

B65
PYE L.W.,POLITICAL CULTURE AND DEVELOPMENT. WOR+45 WOR-45 CULTURE ECO/UNDEV NAT/G ALL/VALS ORD/FREE PWR WEALTH ALL/IDEOS...TRADIT TREND 20. PAGE 46 G0897
PHIL/SCI
TEC/DEV
SOCIETY

B65
TYBOUT R.A.,ECONOMICS OF RESEARCH AND DEVELOPMENT. ECO/DEV ECO/UNDEV INDUS PROFIT DECISION. PAGE 55 G1084
R+D
FORCES
ADMIN
DIPLOM

B65
WISH J.R.,ECONOMIC DEVELOPMENT IN LATIN AMERICA: AN ANNOTATED BIBLIOGRAPHY. L/A+17C COM/IND MARKET R+D CREATE CAP/ISM ATTIT...STAT METH 20. PAGE 64 G1250
BIBLIOG/A
ECO/UNDEV
TEC/DEV
AGRI

S65
BLOOMFIELD L.P.,"ARMS CONTROL AND THE DEVELOPING COUNTRIES." AFR ISLAM S/ASIA USA+45 VOL/ASSN TEC/DEV DIPLOM REGION NUC/PWR...PREDICT TREND. PAGE 7 G0142
ARMS/CONT
ECO/UNDEV
HYPO/EXP
OBS

S65
GOLDSTEIN W.,"KEEPING THE GENIE IN THE BOTTLE* THE FEASIBILITY OF A NUCLEAR NON-PROLIFERATION AGREEMENT." ASIA FRANCE UK USA+45 USSR WOR+45 ECO/UNDEV VOL/ASSN ACT/RES PLAN RISK ARMS/CONT WAR PEACE ATTIT PERCEPT...RECORD TREND TIME. PAGE 22 G0429
NUC/PWR
CREATE
COST

S65
KRICKUS R.J.,"ON THE MORALITY OF CHEMICAL/BIOLOGICAL WAR." ECO/UNDEV ARMS/CONT DETER NUC/PWR RIGID/FLEX HEALTH INT/LAW. PAGE 31 G0621
MORAL
BIO/SOC
WEAPON
WAR

S65
LECLERCQ H.,"ECONOMIC RESEARCH AND DEVELOPMENT IN TROPICAL AFRICA." ECO/UNDEV INT/ORG CREATE PLAN UN. PAGE 33 G0650
AFR
R+D
ACADEM
ECO/TAC

S65
TENDLER J.D.,"TECHNOLOGY AND ECONOMIC DEVELOPMENT* THE CASE OF HYDRO VS THERMAL POWER." CONSTRUC DIST/IND CREATE TEC/DEV INT/TRADE CENTRAL PWR SKILL WEALTH...MGT NAT/COMP ARGEN. PAGE 54 G1063
BRAZIL
INDUS
ECO/UNDEV

C65
MARK M.,"BEYOND SOVEREIGNTY." WOR+45 WOR-45 ECO/UNDEV BAL/PWR INT/TRADE NUC/PWR REV WAR MARXISM NEW/LIB BIBLIOG. PAGE 36 G0706
NAT/LISM
NAT/G
DIPLOM
INTELL

B66
ALEXANDER Y.,INTERNATIONAL TECHNICAL ASSISTANCE EXPERTS* A CASE STUDY OF THE U.N. EXPERIENCE. ECO/UNDEV CONSULT EX/STRUC CREATE PLAN DIPLOM FOR/AID TASK EFFICIENCY...ORG/CHARTS UN. PAGE 2 G0038
ECO/TAC
INT/ORG
ADMIN
MGT

B66
ALI S.,PLANNING, DEVELOPMENT AND CHANGE: AN ANNOTATED BIBLIOGRAPHY ON DEVELOPMENTAL ADMINISTRATION. PAKISTAN SOCIETY ORD/FREE 20. PAGE 2 G0041
BIBLIOG/A
ADMIN
ECO/UNDEV
PLAN

B66
ECKSTEIN A.,COMMUNIST CHINA'S ECONOMIC GROWTH AND FOREIGN TRADE* IMPLICATIONS FOR US POLICY. COM USA+45 USSR STRUCT INDUS MARKET DIPLOM ECO/TAC FOR/AID INT/TRADE...STAT CHARTS. PAGE 17 G0332
ASIA
ECO/UNDEV
CREATE
PWR

B66
OECD DEVELOPMENT CENTRE,CATALOGUE OF SOCIAL AND ECONOMIC DEVELOPMENT INSTITUTES AND PROGRAMMES* RESEARCH. ACT/RES PLAN TEC/DEV EDU/PROP...SOC GP/COMP NAT/COMP. PAGE 43 G0836
ECO/UNDEV
ECO/DEV
R+D
ACADEM

B66
ONYEMELUKWE C.C.,PROBLEMS OF INDUSTRIAL PLANNING AND MANAGEMENT IN NIGERIA. AFR FINAN LABOR DELIB/GP TEC/DEV ADJUST...MGT TREND BIBLIOG. PAGE 43 G0839
ECO/UNDEV
ECO/TAC
INDUS

B66
SPULBER N.,THE STATE AND ECONOMIC DEVELOPMENT IN EASTERN EUROPE. BULGARIA COM CZECHOSLVK HUNGARY POLAND YUGOSLAVIA CULTURE PLAN CAP/ISM INT/TRADE CONTROL...POLICY CHARTS METH/COMP BIBLIOG/A 19/20. PAGE 52 G1028
ECO/DEV
ECO/UNDEV
NAT/G
TOTALISM

B66
WARD B.,NATIONALISM AND IDEOLOGY. ECO/UNDEV KIN CREATE CAP/ISM FOR/AID ALL/VALS MARXISM...POLICY SOC. PAGE 62 G1211
IDEA/COMP
NAT/LISM
ATTIT

L66
PACKENHAM R.A.,"POLITICAL-DEVELOPMENT DOCTRINES IN THE AMERICAN FOREIGN AID PROGRAM." STRUCT R+D CREATE DIPLOM AID. PAGE 43 G0855
FOR/AID
ECO/UNDEV
GEN/LAWS

S66
"FURTHER READING." INDIA LOC/G NAT/G PLAN ADMIN WEALTH...GEOG SOC CONCPT CENSUS 20. PAGE 1 G0021
BIBLIOG
ECO/UNDEV
TEC/DEV
PROVS

S66
BROWNLIE I.,"NUCLEAR PROLIFERATION* SOME PROBLEMS OF CONTROL." USA+45 USSR ECO/UNDEV INT/ORG FORCES TEC/DEV REGION CONSEN...RECORD TREATY. PAGE 9 G0181
NUC/PWR
ARMS/CONT
VOL/ASSN
ORD/FREE

S66
COHEN A.,"THE TECHNOLOGY/ELITE APPROACH TO THE DEVELOPMENTAL PROCESS* PERUVIAN CASE STUDY." L/A+17C STRUCT CREATE ECO/TAC FOR/AID CIVMIL/REL MARXISM TECHRACY HYPO/EXP. PAGE 12 G0239
ECO/UNDEV
ELITES
PERU

S66
MALENBAUM W.,"GOVERNMENT, ENTREPRENEURSHIP, AND ECONOMIC GROWTH IN POOR LANDS." ELITES ECO/UNDEV INDUS CREATE DRIVE. PAGE 35 G0697
ECO/TAC
PLAN
CONSERVE
NAT/G

S66
RIZOS E.J.,"SCIENCE AND TECHNOLOGY IN COUNTRY DEVELOPMENT* TOWARDS AN UNDERSTANDING OF THE ROLE OF PUBLIC ADMINISTRATION." WOR+45 STRUCT INT/ORG EX/STRUC CREATE PLAN PROB/SOLV EFFICIENCY ROLE DECISION. PAGE 47 G0924
ADMIN
TEC/DEV
ECO/UNDEV
PHIL/SCI

B67
BARANSON J.,TECHNOLOGY FOR UNDERDEVELOPED AREAS: AN ANNOTATED BIBLIOGRAPHY. FUT WOR+45 CULTURE INDUS INT/ORG CREATE PROB/SOLV INT/TRADE EDU/PROP AUTOMAT ...CONCPT METH. PAGE 5 G0092
BIBLIOG/A
ECO/UNDEV
TEC/DEV
R+D

B67
ELDREDGE H.W.,TAMING MEGALOPOLIS: HOW TO MANAGE AN URBANIZED WORLD. WOR+45 SOCIETY ECO/DEV ECO/UNDEV NAT/G COMPUTER CREATE PARTIC EFFICIENCY WEALTH ...MGT ANTHOL. PAGE 17 G0342
MUNIC
TEC/DEV
PLAN
PROB/SOLV

B67
HIRSCHMAN A.O.,DEVELOPMENT PROJECTS OBSERVED. INDUS INT/ORG CONSULT EX/STRUC CREATE OP/RES ECO/TAC DEMAND...POLICY MGT METH/COMP 20 WORLD/BANK. PAGE 26 G0513
ECO/UNDEV
R+D
FINAN
PLAN

B67
LAMBERT J.,LATIN AMERICA: SOCIAL STRUCTURES AND POLITICAL INSTITUTIONS. STRUCT TEC/DEV DIPLOM ADMIN COLONIAL LEAD ATTIT...SOC CLASSIF NAT/COMP 17/20. PAGE 32 G0631
L/A+17C
NAT/G
ECO/UNDEV
SOCIETY

B67
LERNER D.,COMMUNICATION AND CHANGE IN DEVELOPING COUNTRIES. CHINA/COM INDIA PHILIPPINE COM/IND CREATE TEC/DEV...ANTHOL 20. PAGE 33 G0659
EDU/PROP
ORD/FREE
PERCEPT
ECO/UNDEV

B67
MAZOUR A.G.,SOVIET ECONOMIC DEVELOPMENT: OPERATION OUTSTRIP: 1921-1965. USSR ECO/UNDEV FINAN CHIEF WORKER PROB/SOLV CONTROL PRODUC MARXISM...CHARTS ORG/CHARTS 20 STALIN/J. PAGE 37 G0726
ECO/TAC
AGRI
INDUS
PLAN

B67
MCDOUGAL M.S.,THE INTERPRETATION OF AGREEMENTS AND WORLD PUBLIC ORDER: PRINCIPLES OF CONTENT AND PROCEDURE. WOR+45 CONSTN PROB/SOLV TEC/DEV ...CON/ANAL TREATY. PAGE 37 G0740
INT/LAW
STRUCT
ECO/UNDEV
DIPLOM

B67
MOORE J.R.,THE ECONOMIC IMPACT OF THE TVA. AGRI INDUS PLAN BARGAIN CONTROL REGION GOV/REL DEMAND EFFICIENCY SOCISM 20 TVA. PAGE 40 G0780
ECO/UNDEV
ECO/DEV
NAT/G

CREATE

OVERSEAS DEVELOPMENT INSTIT,EFFECTIVE AID. WOR+45   FOR/AID
INT/ORG TEC/DEV DIPLOM INT/TRADE ADMIN. PAGE 43   ECO/UNDEV
G0852   ECO/TAC
   NAT/COMP

                        B67
UNESCO,PRINCIPLES AND PROBLEMS OF NATIONAL SCIENCE   NAT/COMP
POLICIES. WOR+45 ECO/DEV ECO/UNDEV R+D INT/ORG   POLICY
PROB/SOLV CONFER...PHIL/SCI CHARTS 20 UNESCO UN.   TEC/DEV
PAGE 55 G1091   CREATE

                        B67
UNIVERSAL REFERENCE SYSTEM,ECONOMIC REGULATION,   BIBLIOG/A
BUSINESS, AND GOVERNMENT (VOLUME VIII). WOR+45   CONTROL
WOR-45 ECO/DEV ECO/UNDEV FINAN LABOR TEC/DEV   NAT/G
ECO/TAC INT/TRADE GOV/REL...POLICY COMPUT/IR.
PAGE 56 G1099

                        L67
RUTH J.M.,"THE ADMINISTRATION OF WATER RESOURCES IN   EFFICIENCY
GUATEMALA." GUATEMALA L/A+17C DIST/IND LOC/G NAT/G   ECO/UNDEV
EX/STRUC ADMIN GOV/REL DEMAND EQUILIB WEALTH...GEOG   PLAN
MGT 20. PAGE 48 G0952   ACT/RES

                        S67
FADDEYEV N.,"CMEA CO-OPERATION OF EQUAL NATIONS."   MARXISM
COM R+D PLAN CAP/ISM DIPLOM FOR/AID WEALTH...POLICY   ECO/TAC
MARXIST. PAGE 18 G0356   INT/ORG
   ECO/UNDEV

                        S67
HILL R.,"SOCIAL ASPECTS OF FAMILY PLANNING." INDIA   FAM
KOREA TAIWAN ECO/UNDEV PLAN PROB/SOLV TEC/DEV   BIO/SOC
EDU/PROP CONTROL ATTIT DRIVE...HEAL PSY SOC 20   GEOG
BIRTH/CON UN. PAGE 26 G0512   MARRIAGE

                        S67
HULL E.W.S.,"THE POLITICAL OCEAN." FUT UNIV WOR+45   DIPLOM
EXTR/IND R+D VOL/ASSN PLAN BAL/PWR ECO/TAC PEACE   ECO/UNDEV
WEALTH 20 UN. PAGE 27 G0536   INT/ORG
   INT/LAW

                        S67
MCNAMARA R.L.,"THE NEED FOR INNOVATIVENESS IN   PROB/SOLV
DEVELOPING SOCIETIES." L/A+17C EDU/PROP ADMIN LEAD   PLAN
WEALTH...POLICY PSY SOC METH 20 COLOMB. PAGE 38   ECO/UNDEV
G0747   NEW/IDEA

                        S67
MEHTA A.,"INDIA* POVERTY AND CHANGE." STRATA INDUS   INDIA
CREATE ECO/TAC FOR/AID NEUTRAL GP/REL ADJUST INCOME   SOCIETY
...NEW/IDEA 20. PAGE 38 G0751   ECO/UNDEV
   TEC/DEV

                        S67
PONTECORVO G.,"THE LAW OF THE SEA." ECO/DEV   CONFER
ECO/UNDEV TEC/DEV GEOG. PAGE 45 G0885   INT/LAW
   EXTR/IND
   SEA

                        S67
SINGH B.,"ITALIAN EXPERIENCE IN REGIONAL ECONOMIC   ECO/UNDEV
DEVELOPMENT AND LESSONS FOR OTHER COUNTRIES."   PLAN
EUR+WWI ITALY INDUS NAT/G ACT/RES REGION GP/REL   ECO/TAC
EFFICIENCY EQUILIB PRODUC WEALTH. PAGE 51 G1007   CONTROL

                        S67
WARE R.S.,"FORECAST A.D. 2000." SOCIETY STRATA   NUC/PWR
ECO/UNDEV INDUS FORCES EDU/PROP AUTOMAT COERCE REV   GEOG
WEAPON ATTIT PREDICT. PAGE 62 G1213   TEC/DEV
   WAR

                        N67
ASIAN STUDIES CENTER,FOUR ARTICLES ON POPULATION   ASIA
AND FAMILY LIFE IN TAIWAN (ASIAN STUDIES PAPERS,   FAM
REPRINT SERIES NO. 2). CULTURE STRATA ECO/UNDEV   CENSUS
AGRI INDUS R+D KIN MUNIC...GEOG SOC CHARTS 20.   ANTHOL
PAGE 4 G0072

                        N67
US HOUSE COMM FOREIGN AFFAIRS,REPORT OF SPECIAL   ISLAM
STUDY MISSION TO THE NEAR EAST (PAMPHLET). ISRAEL   DIPLOM
USA+45 YEMEN ECO/UNDEV INT/ORG FOR/AID ARMS/CONT   FORCES
WAR WEAPON NAT/LISM PEACE...GEOG 20 UN HOUSE/REP.
PAGE 58 G1138

                        N67
US HOUSE COMM SCI ASTRONAUT,GOVERNMENT, SCIENCE,   NAT/G
AND INTERNATIONAL POLICY (PAMPHLET). INDIA   POLICY
NETHERLAND ECO/DEV ECO/UNDEV R+D ACADEM PLAN DIPLOM   CREATE
FOR/AID CONFER...PREDICT 20 CHINJAP. PAGE 59 G1152   TEC/DEV

                        N67
US SENATE COMM ON FOREIGN REL,SURVEY OF THE   L/A+17C
ALLIANCE FOR PROGRESS; THE POLITICAL ASPECTS   POLICY
(PAMPHLET). CONSTN SOCIETY ECO/UNDEV INT/ORG   PROB/SOLV
TEC/DEV DIPLOM...CENSUS 20. PAGE 60 G1186

ECOLOGY....SEE HABITAT

ECOMETRIC....MATHEMATICAL ECONOMICS, ECONOMETRICS

                        B61
MCCRACKEN H.L.,KEYNESIAN ECONOMICS IN THE STREAM OF   ECO/TAC
ECONOMIC THOUGHT. FINAN MARKET BARGAIN EFFICIENCY   DEMAND
OPTIMAL...PHIL/SCI CONCPT IDEA/COMP BIBLIOG 18/20   ECOMETRIC
KEYNES/JM. PAGE 37 G0732

                        S61
ANDREWS R.B.,"URBAN ECONOMICS: AN APPRAISAL OF   MUNIC
PROGRESS." LOC/G PROB/SOLV TEC/DEV...CONCPT   PHIL/SCI
OBS/ENVIR METH/COMP HYPO/EXP SOC/EXP SIMUL GEN/METH   ECOMETRIC
METH 20. PAGE 3 G0058

                        S61
BENNION E.G.,"ECONOMETRICS FOR MANAGEMENT." USA+45   ECOMETRIC
INDUS EX/STRUC ACT/RES COMPUTER UTIL...MATH STAT   MGT
PREDICT METH/COMP HYPO/EXP. PAGE 6 G0122   SIMUL
   DECISION

                        B62
BELLMAN R.,APPLIED DYNAMIC PROGRAMMING. OPTIMAL   COMPUTER
...DECISION STAT SIMUL. PAGE 6 G0116   ECOMETRIC
   GAME
   MATH

                        B64
BALASSA B.,TRADE PROSPECTS FOR DEVELOPING   INT/TRADE
COUNTRIES. WOR+45 ECO/DEV AGRI EXTR/IND INDUS   ECO/UNDEV
CREATE PLAN PRICE...ECOMETRIC CLASSIF TIME/SEQ   TREND
GEN/METH. PAGE 5 G0087   STAT

                        B64
LANG A.S.,URBAN RAIL TRANSIT. OP/RES PLAN PROB/SOLV   MUNIC
TEC/DEV AUTOMAT COST...TECHNIC MATH CON/ANAL CHARTS   DIST/IND
METH/COMP SIMUL 20 RAILROAD PUB/TRANS. PAGE 32   ECOMETRIC
G0632

                        B65
HICKMAN B.G.,QUANTITATIVE PLANNING OF ECONOMIC   PROB/SOLV
POLICY. FRANCE NETHERLAND OP/RES PRICE ROUTINE UTIL   PLAN
...POLICY DECISION ECOMETRIC METH/CNCPT STAT STYLE   QUANT
CHINJAP. PAGE 26 G0511

                        B65
MCGUIRE M.C.,SECRECY AND THE ARMS RACE* A THEORY OF   DETER
THE ACCUMULATION OF STRATEGIC WEAPONS AND HOW   ARMS/CONT
SECRECY AFFECTS IT. DIPLOM NUC/PWR WEAPON ISOLAT   SIMUL
RATIONAL ORD/FREE WEALTH...ECOMETRIC MATH GEN/LAWS.   GAME
PAGE 38 G0742

                        S65
CHU K.,"A DYNAMIC MODEL OF THE FIRM." OP/RES   INDUS
PROB/SOLV...DECISION ECOMETRIC NEW/IDEA STAT GAME   COMPUTER
ORG/CHARTS SIMUL. PAGE 12 G0230   TEC/DEV

                        B67
PORWIT K.,CENTRAL PLANNING: EVALUATION OF VARIANTS.   PLAN
PRICE OPTIMAL PRODUC...DECISION MATH CHARTS SIMUL   MGT
BIBLIOG 20. PAGE 45 G0886   ECOMETRIC

                        S67
DONAHO J.A.,"PLANNING-PROGRAMMING-BUDGETING   PLAN
SYSTEMS." USA+45 LOC/G NAT/G ROUTINE. PAGE 16 G0305   BUDGET
   ADMIN
   ECOMETRIC

ECONOMIC WARFARE....SEE ECO/TAC

ECOSOC....UNITED NATIONS ECONOMIC AND SOCIAL COUNCIL

ECSC....EUROPEAN COAL AND STEEL COMMUNITY. SEE ALSO VOL/ASSN,
     INT/ORG

                        N
FOREIGN AFFAIRS. SPACE WOR+45 WOR-45 CULTURE   BIBLIOG
ECO/UNDEV FINAN NAT/G TEC/DEV INT/TRADE ARMS/CONT   DIPLOM
NUC/PWR...POLICY 20 UN EURATOM ECSC EEC. PAGE 1   INT/ORG
G0004   INT/LAW

                        S67
WEIL G.L.,"THE MERGER OF THE INSTITUTIONS OF THE   ECO/TAC

EUROPEAN COMMUNITIES" EUR+WWI ECO/DEV INT/TRADE CONSEN PLURISM...DECISION MGT 20 EEC EURATOM ECSC TREATY. PAGE 62 G1223 — INT/ORG CENTRAL INT/LAW

ECUADOR....SEE ALSO L/A+17C

ECUMENIC....ECUMENICAL MOVEMENT OF CHURCHES

EDELMAN M. G0333

EDEN/A....ANTHONY EDEN

EDMONDS M. G0334

EDSEL....EDSEL (AUTOMOBILE)

EDU/PROP....EDUCATION, PROPAGANDA, PERSUASION

N
AMERICAN DOCUMENTATION INST,DOCUMENTATION ABSTRACTS. WOR+45 NAT/G COMPUTER CREATE TEC/DEV DIPLOM EDU/PROP REGION KNOWL...PHIL/SCI CLASSIF LING. PAGE 3 G0051 — BIBLIOG/A AUTOMAT COMPUT/IR R+D

N
FULLER G.A.,DEMOBILIZATION: A SELECTED LIST OF REFERENCES. USA+45 LAW AGRI LABOR WORKER ECO/TAC RATION RECEIVE EDU/PROP ROUTINE ARMS/CONT ALL/VALS 20. PAGE 20 G0398 — BIBLIOG/A INDUS FORCES NAT/G

N
KRUTILIA J.V.,CONSERVATION RECONSIDERED. USA+45 CREATE EDU/PROP. PAGE 32 G0624 — PROB/SOLV POLICY HABITAT GEOG

N
INDIA: A REFERENCE ANNUAL. INDIA CULTURE COM/IND R+D FORCES PLAN RECEIVE EDU/PROP HEALTH...STAT CHARTS BIBLIOG 20. PAGE 1 G0005 — CONSTN LABOR INT/ORG

N19
GINZBERG E.,MANPOWER FOR GOVERNMENT (PAMPHLET). USA+45 FORCES PLAN PROB/SOLV PAY EDU/PROP ADMIN GP/REL COST...MGT PREDICT TREND 20 CIVIL/SERV. PAGE 21 G0418 — WORKER CONSULT NAT/G LOC/G

B23
DRAPER J.W.,HISTORY OF THE CONFLICT BETWEEN RELIGION AND SCIENCE. WOR-45 INTELL SOCIETY R+D CREATE PLAN TEC/DEV EDU/PROP ATTIT PWR...PHIL/SCI CONCPT OBS TIME/SEQ TREND GEN/LAWS TOT/POP. PAGE 16 G0314 — SECT KNOWL

B28
SOROKIN P.,CONTEMPORARY SOCIOLOGICAL THEORIES. MOD/EUR UNIV SOCIETY R+D SCHOOL ECO/TAC EDU/PROP ROUTINE ATTIT DRIVE...PSY CONCPT TIME/SEQ TREND GEN/LAWS 20. PAGE 52 G1021 — CULTURE SOC WAR

B34
EINSTEIN A.,THE WORLD AS I SEE IT. WOR-45 INTELL R+D INT/ORG NAT/G SECT VOL/ASSN FORCES CREATE EDU/PROP LEGIT ARMS/CONT WAR WEAPON NAT/LISM ALL/VALS...POLICY CONCPT 20. PAGE 17 G0337 — SOCIETY PHIL/SCI DIPLOM PACIFISM

B42
US LIBRARY OF CONGRESS,CONDUCT OF THE WAR (APRIL 1941-MARCH 1942). USA-45 WOR-45 LAW INDUS PUB/INST TEC/DEV EDU/PROP CIVMIL/REL 20. PAGE 59 G1155 — BIBLIOG/A WAR FORCES PLAN

S42
LASSWELL H.D.,"THE RELATION OF IDEOLOGICAL INTELLIGENCE TO PUBLIC POLICY." WOR+45 WOR-45 SOCIETY DELIB/GP ACT/RES CREATE PLAN DIPLOM EDU/PROP CHOOSE KNOWL PWR...POLICY SOC TREND GEN/LAWS 20. PAGE 32 G0638 — ATTIT DECISION

B44
MERRIAM C.E.,PUBLIC AND PRIVATE GOVERNMENT. VOL/ASSN EDU/PROP ADMIN REPRESENT EFFICIENCY PWR PLURISM...MAJORIT CONCPT. PAGE 38 G0755 — NAT/G NEIGH MGT POLICY

B45
BUSH V.,SCIENCE, THE ENDLESS FRONTIER. FUT USA-45 INTELL STRATA ACT/RES CREATE PLAN EDU/PROP ADMIN NUC/PWR PEACE ATTIT HEALTH KNOWL...MAJORIT HEAL MGT PHIL/SCI CONCPT OBS TREND 20. PAGE 10 G0195 — R+D NAT/G

B45
REVES E.,THE ANATOMY OF PEACE. WOR-45 LAW CULTURE NAT/G PLAN TEC/DEV EDU/PROP WAR NAT/LISM ATTIT — ACT/RES CONCPT

ALL/VALS SOVEREIGN...POLICY HUM TIME/SEQ 20. PAGE 46 G0914 — NUC/PWR PEACE

B46
AMERICAN DOCUMENTATION INST,CATALOGUE OF AUXILIARY PUBLICATIONS IN MICROFILMS AND PHOTOPRINTS. USA-45 LAW AGRI CREATE TEC/DEV ADMIN...GEOG LING MATH 20. PAGE 3 G0052 — BIBLIOG EDU/PROP PSY

B46
BUSH V.,ENDLESS HORIZONS. FUT USA-45 INTELL NAT/G CONSULT ACT/RES CREATE PLAN EDU/PROP DRIVE ...MAJORIT HEAL MGT PHIL/SCI CONCPT OBS TREND GEN/METH TOT/POP 20. PAGE 10 G0196 — R+D KNOWL PEACE

B46
MORGENTHAU H.J.,SCIENTIFIC MAN VS POWER POLITICS. USA+45 WOR+45 INTELL SOCIETY ACT/RES CREATE PLAN EDU/PROP...CONCPT TREND TOT/POP 20. PAGE 40 G0782 — UNIV MORAL PEACE

L46
MASTERS D.,"ONE WORLD OR NONE." FUT WOR+45 INTELL INT/ORG ACT/RES EDU/PROP DETER ATTIT RIGID/FLEX SUPEGO KNOWL...STAT TREND ORG/CHARTS 20. PAGE 36 G0719 — POLICY PHIL/SCI ARMS/CONT NUC/PWR

B47
BECK H.P.,MEN WHO CONTROL OUR UNIVERSITIES. EX/STRUC CHOOSE INGP/REL DISCRIM PERSON WEALTH ...POLICY TREND CON/ANAL CHARTS BIBLIOG. PAGE 6 G0112 — EDU/PROP ACADEM CONTROL LEAD

B47
LASSWELL H.D.,THE ANALYSIS OF POLITICAL BEHAVIOUR: AN EMPIRICAL APPROACH. WOR+45 CULTURE NAT/G FORCES EDU/PROP ADMIN ATTIT PERCEPT KNOWL...PHIL/SCI PSY SOC NEW/IDEA OBS INT GEN/METH NAZI 20. PAGE 32 G0639 — R+D ACT/RES ELITES

B48
BRADLEY D.,NO PLACE TO HIDE. USA+45 SOCIETY NAT/G FORCES TEC/DEV EDU/PROP DETER PEACE BIO/SOC ALL/VALS...POLICY PHIL/SCI OBS RECORD SAMP BIOG GEN/METH COLD/WAR 20. PAGE 8 G0162 — R+D LAB/EXP ARMS/CONT NUC/PWR

B48
PUBLIC ADMINISTRATION SERVICE,SOURCE MATERIALS IN PUBLIC ADMINISTRATION: A SELECTED BIBLIOGRAPHY (PAS PUBLICATION NO. 102). USA+45 LAW FINAN LOC/G MUNIC NAT/G PLAN RECEIVE EDU/PROP CT/SYS CHOOSE HEALTH 20. PAGE 45 G0895 — BIBLIOG/A GOV/REL MGT ADMIN

B49
MCLEAN J.M.,THE PUBLIC SERVICE AND UNIVERSITY EDUCATION. UK USA-45 DELIB/GP EX/STRUC TOP/EX ADMIN ...GOV/COMP METH/COMP NAT/COMP ANTHOL 20. PAGE 38 G0746 — ACADEM NAT/G EXEC EDU/PROP

B49
OGBURN W.,TECHNOLOGY AND INTERNATIONAL RELATIONS. WOR+45 WOR-45 ECO/DEV CREATE PLAN ECO/TAC EDU/PROP COERCE PWR SKILL WEALTH...TECHNIC PSY SOC NEW/IDEA CHARTS TOT/POP 20. PAGE 43 G0837 — TEC/DEV DIPLOM INT/ORG

B49
ROSENHAUPT H.W.,HOW TO WAGE PEACE. USA+45 SOCIETY STRATA STRUCT R+D INT/ORG POL/PAR LEGIS ACT/RES CREATE PLAN EDU/PROP ADMIN EXEC ATTIT ALL/VALS ...TIME/SEQ TREND COLD/WAR 20. PAGE 48 G0937 — INTELL CONCPT DIPLOM

B50
CANTRIL H.,TENSIONS THAT CAUSE WAR. UNIV CULTURE R+D CREATE EDU/PROP DRIVE PERSON KNOWL ORD/FREE ...HUM PSY SOC OBS CENSUS TREND CON/ANAL SOC/EXP SIMUL GEN/METH ANTHOL COLD/WAR TOT/POP. PAGE 11 G0206 — SOCIETY PHIL/SCI PEACE

B50
MANNHEIM K.,FREEDOM, POWER, AND DEMOCRATIC PLANNING. FUT USSR WOR+45 ELITES INTELL SOCIETY NAT/G EDU/PROP ROUTINE ATTIT DRIVE SUPEGO SKILL ...POLICY PSY CONCPT TREND GEN/LAWS 20. PAGE 35 G0700 — TEC/DEV PLAN CAP/ISM UK

B50
US DEPARTMENT OF STATE,POINT FOUR: COOPERATIVE PROGRAM FOR AID IN THE DEVELOPMENT OF ECONOMICALLY UNDERDEVELOPED AREAS. WOR+45 AGRI INDUS INT/ORG PLAN TEC/DEV DIPLOM EDU/PROP ADMIN PEACE PRODUC WEALTH 20 CONGRESS UN. PAGE 57 G1121 — ECO/UNDEV FOR/AID FINAN INT/TRADE

S50
LENTZ T.F.,"REPORT ON A SURVEY OF SOCIAL SCIENTISTS CONDUCTED BY THE ATTITUDE RESEARCH LABORATORY." FUT WOR+45 CREATE EDU/PROP...PSY STAT RECORD SYS/QU SAMP/SIZ CON/ANAL VAL/FREE 20. PAGE 33 G0655 — ACT/RES ATTIT DIPLOM

B51
CONANT J.B.,.SCIENCE AND COMMON SENSE. WOR+45 WOR-45 CREATE
R+D SCHOOL CONSULT TEC/DEV EDU/PROP SKILL...PLURIST PHIL/SCI
METH/CNCPT RECORD TIME/SEQ SIMUL GEN/METH METH.
PAGE 13 G0248

B52
DAY E.E.,EDUCATION FOR FREEDOM AND RESPONSIBILITY. SCHOOL
FUT USA+45 CULTURE CONSULT EDU/PROP ATTIT SKILL KNOWL
...MGT CONCPT OBS GEN/LAWS COLD/WAR 20. PAGE 14
G0282

B52
HAYEK F.A.,THE COUNTER-REVOLUTION OF SCIENCE. UNIV PERCEPT
INTELL R+D VOL/ASSN CREATE EDU/PROP...PHIL/SCI SOC KNOWL
OBS TIME/SEQ TREND GEN/METH. PAGE 25 G0494

L52
ROYAL INST. INT. AFF.,"ANNUAL REPORT OF THE R+D
COUNCIL: 1951-1952." WOR+45 CREATE KNOWL...MGT EDU/PROP
COLD/WAR CMN/WLTH TOT/POP VAL/FREE 20. PAGE 48
G0943

S52
"SELECTED CRITICAL BIBLIOGRAPHY ON THE METHODS AND BIBLIOG/A
TECHNIQUES OF POLITICAL BEHAVIOR RESEARCH." METH
...PHIL/SCI OBS QU SYS/QU TESTS CON/ANAL. PAGE 1 SOC
G0012 EDU/PROP

S52
KECSKEMETI P.,"THE 'POLICY SCIENCES': ASPIRATION CREATE
AND OUTLOOK." UNIV CULTURE INTELL SOCIETY STRUCT NEW/IDEA
EDU/PROP ATTIT PERCEPT RIGID/FLEX KNOWL...PHIL/SCI
METH/CNCPT OBS 20. PAGE 30 G0589

B53
EASTON D.,THE POLITICAL SYSTEM, AN INQUIRY INTO THE R+D
STATE POLITICAL SCIENCE. USA+45 INTELL CREATE PERCEPT
EDU/PROP RIGID/FLEX KNOWL SKILL...PHIL/SCI NEW/IDEA
STERTYP TOT/POP 20. PAGE 17 G0329

B53
HOVLAND C.I.,COMMUNICATION AND PERSUASION: PSY
PSYCHOLOGICAL STUDIES OF OPINION CHANGE. INTELL EDU/PROP
SOCIETY ECO/DEV COM/IND R+D SERV/IND CREATE TEC/DEV
ATTIT RIGID/FLEX KNOWL NEW/IDEA. PAGE 27 G0531

B53
ROBINSON E.A.G.,THE STRUCTURE OF COMPETITIVE INDUS
INDUSTRY. UK ECO/DEV DIST/IND MARKET TEC/DEV DIPLOM PRODUC
EDU/PROP ADMIN EFFICIENCY WEALTH...MGT 19/20. WORKER
PAGE 47 G0929 OPTIMAL

S53
CORY R.H. JR.,"FORGING A PUBLIC INFORMATION POLICY INT/ORG
FOR THE UNITED NATIONS." FUT WOR+45 SOCIETY ADMIN EDU/PROP
PEACE ATTIT PERSON SKILL...CONCPT 20 UN. PAGE 13 BAL/PWR
G0257

B54
ARON R.,CENTURY OF TOTAL WAR. FUT WOR+45 WOR-45 ATTIT
SOCIETY INT/ORG NAT/G FORCES TOP/EX CREATE BAL/PWR WAR
DOMIN EDU/PROP COERCE DETER PEACE TOTALISM PWR
...TIME/SEQ TREND COLD/WAR TOT/POP VAL/FREE
LEAGUE/NAT 20. PAGE 4 G0066

B54
US DEPARTMENT OF STATE,PUBLICATIONS OF THE BIBLIOG
DEPARTMENT OF STATE, OCTOBER 1,1929 TO JANUARY 1, DIPLOM
1953. AGRI INT/ORG FORCES FOR/AID EDU/PROP
ARMS/CONT NUC/PWR ATTIT 20 DEPT/STATE OAS UN NATO.
PAGE 57 G1122

B54
WASHBURNE N.F.,INTERPRETING SOCIAL CHANGE IN CULTURE
AMERICA. USA+45 STRATA FAM NAT/G SECT OP/RES STRUCT
ECO/TAC EDU/PROP HABITAT...SOC TIME/SEQ TREND 20 CREATE
BUREAUCRCY. PAGE 62 G1217 TEC/DEV

B54
WRIGHT Q.,PROBLEMS OF STABILITY AND PROGRESS IN INT/ORG
INTERNATIONAL RELATIONSHIPS. FUT WOR+45 WOR-45 CONCPT
SOCIETY LEGIS CREATE TEC/DEV ECO/TAC EDU/PROP ADJUD DIPLOM
WAR PEACE ORD/FREE PWR...KNO/TEST TREND GEN/LAWS
20. PAGE 64 G1257

L54
OPLER M.E.,"SOCIAL ASPECTS OF TECHNICAL ASSISTANCE INT/ORG
IN OPERATION." WOR+45 VOL/ASSN CREATE PLAN TEC/DEV CONSULT
EDU/PROP ALL/VALS...METH/CNCPT OBS RECORD TREND UN FOR/AID
20. PAGE 43 G0841

B55
MOCH J.,HUMAN FOLLY: DISARM OR PERISH. USA+45 FUT
WOR+45 SOCIETY INT/ORG NAT/G ACT/RES EDU/PROP ATTIT DELIB/GP

PERSON KNOWL ORD/FREE PWR...MAJORIT TOT/POP ARMS/CONT
COLD/WAR 20. PAGE 39 G0776 NUC/PWR

L55
KISER M.,"ORGANIZATION OF AMERICAN STATES." L/A+17C VOL/ASSN
USA+45 ECO/UNDEV INT/ORG NAT/G PLAN TEC/DEV DIPLOM ECO/DEV
ECO/TAC INT/TRADE EDU/PROP ADMIN ALL/VALS...POLICY REGION
MGT RECORD ORG/CHARTS OAS 20. PAGE 30 G0601

S55
ANGELL R.,"GOVERNMENTS AND PEOPLES AS A FOCI FOR FUT
PEACE-ORIENTED RESEARCH." WOR+45 CULTURE SOCIETY SOC
FACE/GP ACT/RES CREATE PLAN DIPLOM EDU/PROP ROUTINE PEACE
ATTIT PERCEPT SKILL...POLICY CONCPT OBS TREND
GEN/METH 20. PAGE 3 G0060

S55
GLADSTONE A.E.,"THE POSSIBILITY OF PREDICTING PHIL/SCI
REACTIONS TO INTERNATIONAL EVENTS." UNIV SOCIETY CONCPT
NAT/G FORCES CREATE EDU/PROP COERCE WAR ATTIT
PERSON KNOWL PWR SKILL...METH/CNCPT NEW/IDEA
ORG/CHARTS. PAGE 21 G0420

S55
WRIGHT Q.,"THE PEACEFUL ADJUSTMENT OF INTERNATIONAL R+D
RELATIONS: PROBLEMS AND RESEARCH APPROACHES." METH/CNCPT
INTELL EDU/PROP ADJUD ROUTINE KNOWL SKILL...INT/LAW PEACE
JURID PHIL/SCI CLASSIF 20. PAGE 64 G1258

B56
ATOMIC INDUSTRIAL FORUM,PUBLIC RELATIONS FOR THE NUC/PWR
ATOMIC INDUSTRY. WOR+45 PLAN PROB/SOLV EDU/PROP INDUS
PRESS CONFER...AUD/VIS ANTHOL 20. PAGE 4 G0077 GP/REL
ATTIT

B56
ESTEP R.,AN AIR POWER BIBLIOGRAPHY. USA+45 TEC/DEV BIBLIOG/A
BUDGET DIPLOM EDU/PROP DETER CIVMIL/REL...DECISION FORCES
INT/LAW 20. PAGE 18 G0351 WEAPON
PLAN

B56
THOMAS M.,ATOMIC ENERGY AND CONGRESS. USA+45 NAT/G LEGIS
ACT/RES PLAN TEC/DEV EDU/PROP ROUTINE KNOWL PWR ADMIN
SKILL...PHIL/SCI NEW/IDEA TIME/SEQ CHARTS METH NUC/PWR
CONGRESS VAL/FREE 20 AEC. PAGE 54 G1067

B56
US DEPARTMENT OF THE ARMY,RESEARCH AND DEVELOPMENT BIBLIOG/A
(AND RELATED ASPECTS) IN FOREIGN COUNTRIES. WOR+45 R+D
DIST/IND INDUS CONSULT FORCES CREATE EDU/PROP TEC/DEV
AUTOMAT DETER WEAPON. PAGE 57 G1126 NUC/PWR

B56
VUCINICH A.,THE SOVIET ACADEMY OF SCIENCES. USSR PHIL/SCI
STRUCT ACADEM NAT/G EDU/PROP ADMIN LEAD ROLE CREATE
...BIBLIOG 20 ACADEM/SCI. PAGE 61 G1203 INTELL
PROF/ORG

B56
WASSERMAN P.,INFORMATION FOR ADMINISTRATORS: A BIBLIOG
GUIDE TO PUBLICATIONS AND SERVICES FOR MANAGEMENT MGT
IN BUSINESS AND GOVERNMENT. R+D LOC/G NAT/G KNOWL
PROF/ORG VOL/ASSN PRESS...PSY SOC STAT 20. PAGE 62 EDU/PROP
G1219

S56
GORDON L.,"THE ORGANIZATION FOR EUROPEAN ECONOMIC VOL/ASSN
COOPERATION." EUR+WWI INDUS INT/ORG NAT/G CONSULT ECO/DEV
DELIB/GP ACT/RES CREATE PLAN TEC/DEV EDU/PROP LEGIT
WEALTH OEEC 20. PAGE 22 G0435

B57
MERTON R.K.,SOCIAL THEORY AND SOCIAL STRUCTURE SOC
(REV. ED.). INTELL SECT WORKER OP/RES EDU/PROP GEN/LAWS
ADMIN INGP/REL ANOMIE PERSON...AUD/VIS T 20 SOCIETY
BUREAUCRCY. PAGE 38 G0759 STRUCT

S57
EASTON D.,"AN APPROACH TO THE ANALYSIS OF POLITICAL STRUCT
SYSTEMS." R+D EDU/PROP KNOWL SKILL...POLICY SOC PHIL/SCI
METH/CNCPT NEW/IDEA SELF/OBS CHARTS GEN/METH
TOT/POP. PAGE 17 G0331

S57
JANOWITZ M.,"MILITARY ELITES AND THE STUDY OF WAR." FORCES
USA+45 WOR-45 STRATA NAT/G PROF/ORG TEC/DEV DOMIN ELITES
EDU/PROP COERCE WAR ATTIT RIGID/FLEX PWR RESPECT
...MGT TREND STERTYP GEN/METH 20. PAGE 28 G0558

B58
ANGELL N.,DEFENCE AND THE ENGLISH-SPEAKING ROLE. DIPLOM
CHINA/COM UK USSR INT/ORG FORCES EDU/PROP NEUTRAL WAR
NUC/PWR NAT/LISM PEACE TOTALISM 20 COLD/WAR MARXISM
COEXIST. PAGE 3 G0059 ORD/FREE

B58
MECRENSKY E.,SCIENTIFIC MANPOWER IN EUROPE. WOR+45   ECO/TAC
EDU/PROP GOV/REL SKILL...TECHNIC PHIL/SCI INT   TEC/DEV
CHARTS BIBLIOG 20. PAGE 38 G0750   METH/COMP
                                                        NAT/COMP

B58
NOEL-BAKER D.,THE ARMS RACE. WOR+45 NAT/G DELIB/GP   FUT
ACT/RES TEC/DEV EDU/PROP NUC/PWR ATTIT KNOWL PWR   INT/ORG
...CONCPT OBS LEAGUE/NAT 20 COLD/WAR. PAGE 42 G0823   ARMS/CONT
                                                        PEACE

B58
TELLER E.A.,OUR NUCLEAR FUTURE. SOCIETY FORCES   FUT
TEC/DEV EDU/PROP KNOWL ORD/FREE...STAND/INT SYS/QU   PHIL/SCI
KNO/TEST AUD/VIS CHARTS SIMUL 20. PAGE 54 G1062   NUC/PWR
                                                        WAR

B58
UN INTL CONF ON PEACEFUL USE,PROGRESS IN ATOMIC   NUC/PWR
ENERGY (VOL. I). WOR+45 R+D PLAN TEC/DEV CONFER   DIPLOM
CONTROL PEACE SKILL...CHARTS ANTHOL 20 UN BAGHDAD.   WORKER
PAGE 55 G1088   EDU/PROP

B58
US DEPARTMENT OF STATE,PUBLICATIONS OF THE   BIBLIOG
DEPARTMENT OF STATE, JANUARY 1,1953 TO DECEMBER 31,   DIPLOM
1957. AGRI INT/ORG FORCES FOR/AID EDU/PROP
ARMS/CONT NUC/PWR ATTIT 20 DEPT/STATE OAS UN NATO.
PAGE 57 G1123

S58
LASSWELL H.D.,"THE SCIENTIFIC STUDY OF   PHIL/SCI
INTERNATIONAL RELATIONS." USA+45 INT/ORG CREATE   GEN/METH
EDU/PROP DETER ATTIT PERCEPT PWR...DECISION CONCPT   DIPLOM
METH/CNCPT STYLE CON/ANAL 20. PAGE 33 G0642

S58
THOMPSON K.W.,"NATIONAL SECURITY IN A NUCLEAR AGE."   FORCES
USA+45 WOR+45 SOCIETY INT/ORG NAT/G TOP/EX DIPLOM   PWR
DOMIN EDU/PROP LEGIT ARMS/CONT COERCE ORD/FREE   BAL/PWR
...TREND STERTYP TOT/POP VAL/FREE COLD/WAR 20.
PAGE 54 G1068

B59
AMRINE M.,THE GREAT DECISION: THE SECRET HISTORY OF   DECISION
THE ATOMIC BOMB. USA+45 TOP/EX EDU/PROP LEGIT   NAT/G
PERCEPT ORD/FREE PWR VAL/FREE HIROSHIMA. PAGE 3   NUC/PWR
G0055   FORCES

B59
RUSSELL B.,COMMON SENSE AND NUCLEAR WARFARE. WOR+45   ORD/FREE
INTELL SOCIETY STRATA NAT/G TOP/EX EDU/PROP ATTIT   ARMS/CONT
PERSON KNOWL MORAL PWR...POLICY CONCPT MYTH   NUC/PWR
CON/ANAL COLD/WAR 20. PAGE 48 G0948

B59
WASSERMAN P.,MEASUREMENT AND ANALYSIS OF   BIBLIOG/A
ORGANIZATIONAL PERFORMANCE. FINAN MARKET EX/STRUC   ECO/TAC
TEC/DEV EDU/PROP CONTROL ROUTINE TASK...MGT 20.   OP/RES
PAGE 62 G1220   EFFICIENCY

L59
MCDOUGAL M.S.,"THE IDENTIFICATION AND APPRAISAL OF   INT/LAW
DIVERSE SYSTEMS OF PUBLIC ORDER (BMR)" WOR+45 NAT/G   DIPLOM
CONSULT EDU/PROP POLICY. PAGE 37 G0737   ALL/IDEOS

S59
DEUTSCH K.W.,"THE IMPACT OF SCIENCE AND TECHNOLOGY   PHIL/SCI
ON INTERNATIONAL POLITICS." UNIV INTELL NAT/G   MYTH
ACT/RES CREATE TEC/DEV EDU/PROP EXEC KNOWL...CONCPT   DIPLOM
TREND TOT/POP 20. PAGE 15 G0297   NAT/LISM

B60
ARMS CONTROL. FUT UNIV WOR+45 INTELL R+D INT/ORG   DELIB/GP
NAT/G VOL/ASSN CONSULT CREATE EDU/PROP PEACE...HUM   ORD/FREE
GEN/LAWS TOT/POP 20. PAGE 1 G0015   ARMS/CONT
                                                        NUC/PWR

B60
BARNET R.,WHO WANTS DISARMAMENT. COM EUR+WWI USA+45   PLAN
USSR INT/ORG NAT/G BAL/PWR DIPLOM EDU/PROP COERCE   FORCES
DETER NUC/PWR WAR WEAPON ATTIT PWR...TIME/SEQ   ARMS/CONT
COLD/WAR CONGRESS 20. PAGE 5 G0096

B60
BROOKINGS INSTITUTION,UNITED STATES FOREIGN POLICY: DIPLOM
STUDY NO 9: THE FORMULATION AND ADMINISTRATION OF   INT/ORG
UNITED STATES FOREIGN POLICY. USA+45 WOR+45   CREATE
EX/STRUC LEGIS BAL/PWR FOR/AID EDU/PROP CIVMIL/REL
GOV/REL...INT COLD/WAR. PAGE 9 G0174

B60
CARPENTER E.,EXPLORATIONS IN COMMUNICATION. USSR   ANTHOL
CULTURE SCHOOL SECT EDU/PROP PRESS TV AUTOMAT   COM/IND
FEEDBACK ATTIT PERSON...ART/METH PSY 20. PAGE 11   TEC/DEV

G0211   WRITING

B60
GRANICK D.,THE RED EXECUTIVE. COM USA+45 SOCIETY   PWR
ECO/DEV INDUS NAT/G POL/PAR EX/STRUC PLAN ECO/TAC   STRATA
EDU/PROP ADMIN EXEC ATTIT DRIVE...GP/COMP 20.   USSR
PAGE 22 G0440   ELITES

B60
LEYDER J.,BIBLIOGRAPHIE DE L'ENSEIGNEMENT SUPERIEUR   BIBLIOG/A
ET DE LA RECHERCHE SCIENTIFIQUE EN AFRIQUE   ACT/RES
INTERTROPICALE (2 VOLS.). AFR CULTURE ECO/UNDEV   ACADEM
AGRI PLAN EDU/PROP ADMIN COLONIAL...GEOG SOC/INTEG   R+D
20 NEGRO. PAGE 34 G0664

B60
LINDVEIT E.N.,SCIENTISTS IN GOVERNMENT. USA+45 PAY   TEC/DEV
EDU/PROP ADMIN DRIVE HABITAT ROLE...TECHNIC BIBLIOG   ECO/TAC
20. PAGE 34 G0670   PHIL/SCI
                                                        GOV/REL

B60
MCGREGOR D.,THE HUMAN SIDE OF ENTERPRISE. USA+45   MGT
LEAD ROUTINE GP/REL INGP/REL...CONCPT GEN/LAWS 20.   ATTIT
PAGE 38 G0741   SKILL
                                                        EDU/PROP

B60
PENTONY D.E.,THE UNDERDEVELOPED LANDS. FUT WOR+45   ECO/UNDEV
CULTURE AGRI FINAN INDUS MARKET INT/ORG LABOR NAT/G   POLICY
VOL/ASSN CONSULT TEC/DEV ECO/TAC EDU/PROP COLONIAL   FOR/AID
ATTIT WEALTH...OBS RECORD SAMP TREND GEN/METH WORK   INT/TRADE
UN 20. PAGE 44 G0867

B60
WILLIAUS T.H.,AMERICANS AT WAR: THE DEVELOPMENT OF   FORCES
THE AMERICAN MILITARY SYSTEM. USA+45 USA-45   WAR
EDU/PROP LEAD REV...GP/COMP BIBLIOG/A 18/20   NAT/G
PRESIDENT. PAGE 63 G1244   POLICY

L60
DEUTSCH K.W.,"TOWARD AN INVENTORY OF BASIC TRENDS   R+D
AND PATTERNS IN COMPARATIVE AND INTERNATIONAL   PERCEPT
POLITICS." UNIV WOR+45 SOCIETY STRUCT INT/ORG NAT/G
CREATE PLAN EDU/PROP KNOWL...PHIL/SCI METH/CNCPT
STAT SELF/OBS OBS/ENVIR SAMP TREND CON/ANAL CHARTS
SOC/EXP GEN/METH 20. PAGE 15 G0298

L60
HOLTON G.,"ARMS CONTROL." FUT WOR+45 CULTURE   ACT/RES
INT/ORG NAT/G FORCES TOP/EX PLAN EDU/PROP COERCE   CONSULT
ATTIT RIGID/FLEX ORD/FREE...POLICY PHIL/SCI SOC   ARMS/CONT
TREND COLD/WAR. PAGE 27 G0524   NUC/PWR

L60
HOLZMAN B.G.,"BASIC RESEARCH FOR NATIONAL   FORCES
SURVIVAL." FUT USA+45 INTELL R+D ACT/RES OP/RES   STAT
PLAN TEC/DEV EDU/PROP PERCEPT PERSON...PHIL/SCI
METH/CNCPT NEW/IDEA MATH OBS RECORD TREND LAB/EXP
20. PAGE 27 G0525

L60
JACOB P.E.,"THE DISARMAMENT CONSENSUS." USA+45 USSR   DELIB/GP
WOR+45 INT/ORG NAT/G ACT/RES TEC/DEV BAL/PWR   ATTIT
EDU/PROP ADMIN COERCE DETER NUC/PWR CONSEN   ARMS/CONT
RIGID/FLEX PWR...CONCPT RECORD CHARTS COLD/WAR 20.
PAGE 28 G0552

L60
MCCLELLAND C.A.,"THE FUNCTION OF THEORY IN   INT/ORG
INTERNATIONAL RELATIONS." WOR+45 PLAN EDU/PROP   CONCPT
ROUTINE ORD/FREE...PHIL/SCI PSY SOC METH/CNCPT   DIPLOM
NEW/IDEA OBS TREND GEN/METH 20. PAGE 37 G0728

S60
DOUGHERTY J.E.,"KEY TO SECURITY: DISARMAMENT OR   FORCES
ARMS STABILITY." COM USA+45 USSR INT/ORG NAT/G   ORD/FREE
CREATE EDU/PROP COERCE DETER ATTIT PWR...DECISION   ARMS/CONT
CONCPT MYTH NEW/IDEA TREND 20 COLD/WAR. PAGE 16   NUC/PWR
G0311

S60
HALSEY A.H.,"THE CHANGING FUNCTIONS OF UNIVERSITIES   ACADEM
IN ADVANCED INDUSTRIAL SOCIETIES." R+D EDU/PROP   CREATE
REPRESENT ROLE ORD/FREE PWR TREND. PAGE 24 G0476   CULTURE
                                                      ADJUST

S60
HUTCHINSON C.E.,"AN INSTITUTE FOR NATIONAL SECURITY   POLICY
AFFAIRS." USA+45 R+D NAT/G CONSULT TOP/EX ACT/RES   METH/CNCPT
CREATE PLAN TEC/DEV EDU/PROP ROUTINE NUC/PWR ATTIT   ELITES
ORD/FREE PWR...DECISION MGT PHIL/SCI CONCPT RECORD   DIPLOM
GEN/LAWS GEN/METH 20. PAGE 27 G0539

S60
IKLE F.C.,"NTH COUNTRIES AND DISARMAMENT." WOR+45   FUT

DELIB/GP ECO/TAC DOMIN EDU/PROP LEGIT ROUTINE INT/ORG
COERCE RIGID/FLEX ORD/FREE...MARXIST TREND 20. ARMS/CONT
PAGE 28 G0543 NUC/PWR

S60
JAFFEE A.J.,"POPULATION TRENDS AND CONTROLS IN ECO/UNDEV
UNDERDEVELOPED COUNTRIES." AFR FUT ISLAM L/A+17C GEOG
S/ASIA CULTURE R+D FAM ACT/RES PLAN EDU/PROP
BIO/SOC RIGID/FLEX HEALTH...SOC STAT OBS CHARTS 20.
PAGE 28 G0555

S60
KISSINGER H.A.,"ARMS CONTROL, INSPECTION AND FORCES
SURPRISE ATTACK." COM USA+45 NAT/G ACT/RES PLAN ORD/FREE
TEC/DEV DIPLOM EDU/PROP DETER WAR RIGID/FLEX ARMS/CONT
...CONCPT GEN/METH TOT/POP 20. PAGE 31 G0603 NUC/PWR

S60
LEAR J.,"PEACE: SCIENCE'S NEXT GREAT EXPLORATION." EX/STRUC
USA+45 INT/ORG TOP/EX TEC/DEV EDU/PROP ROUTINE ARMS/CONT
PEACE KNOWL SKILL 20. PAGE 33 G0648 NUC/PWR

S60
OSGOOD C.E.,"A CASE FOR GRADUATED UNILATERAL ATTIT
DISENGAGEMENT." FUT WOR+45 CULTURE SOCIETY NAT/G EDU/PROP
NUC/PWR WAR PERSON SUPEGO ALL/VALS...POLICY PSY ARMS/CONT
CONCPT COLD/WAR TOT/POP VAL/FREE 20. PAGE 43 G0848

S60
SWIFT R.,"THE UNITED NATIONS AND ITS PUBLIC." INT/ORG
WOR+45 CONSTN FINAN CONSULT DELIB/GP ACT/RES ADMIN EDU/PROP
ROUTINE RIGID/FLEX SKILL UN 20. PAGE 53 G1048

S60
YEMELYANOV V.S.,"ATOMIC ENERGY FOR PEACE: THE USSR VOL/ASSN
AND INTERNATIONAL CO-OPERATION." FUT USSR WOR+45 TEC/DEV
R+D CREATE EDU/PROP...CONCPT GEN/LAWS 20. PAGE 64 ARMS/CONT
G1264 NUC/PWR

C60
SCHRAMM W.,"MASS COMMUNICATIONS: A BOOK OF READINGS COM/IND
(2ND ED.)" LG/CO PRESS ADMIN CONTROL ROUTINE ATTIT EDU/PROP
ROLE SUPEGO...CHARTS ANTHOL BIBLIOG 20. PAGE 50 CROWD
G0977 MAJORIT

N60
US HOUSE COMM SCI ASTRONAUT,THE ORGANIZATION OF THE ACT/RES
US NATIONAL SPACE EFFORT. USA+45 WOR+45 AIR ECO/DEV SKILL
NAT/G PLAN TEC/DEV DIPLOM EDU/PROP ATTIT DRIVE PWR SPACE
...OBS TIME/SEQ TREND TOT/POP 20. PAGE 58 G1142

B61
HENKIN L.,ARMS CONTROL: ISSUES FOR THE PUBLIC. WOR+45
EUR+WWI FUT USA+45 USSR INT/ORG NAT/G DIPLOM DELIB/GP
EDU/PROP DETER NUC/PWR ATTIT PWR...CONCPT RECORD ARMS/CONT
HIST/WRIT TIME/SEQ TOT/POP COLD/WAR 20. PAGE 26
G0506

B61
INSTITUTE PSYCHOLOGICAL RES,HUMAN ENGINEERING BIBLIOG/A
BIBLIOGRAPHY, 1959-1960. USA+45 WORKER EDU/PROP METH
PERSON METH/COMP. PAGE 28 G0547 PSY
R+D

B61
LUNDBERG G.A.,CAN SCIENCE SAVE US. UNIV CULTURE ACT/RES
INTELL SOCIETY ECO/DEV R+D PLAN EDU/PROP ROUTINE CONCPT
CHOOSE ATTIT PERCEPT ALL/VALS...TREND 20. PAGE 34 TOTALISM
G0679

B61
NOGEE J.L.,SOVIET POLICY TOWARD INTERNATIONAL INT/ORG
CONTROL OF ATOMIC ENERGY. COM USA+45 WOR+45 INTELL ATTIT
NAT/G ACT/RES DIPLOM EDU/PROP NUC/PWR TOTALISM ARMS/CONT
PERCEPT KNOWL PWR...TIME/SEQ COLD/WAR 20. PAGE 42 USSR
G0824

B61
SMITH H.H.,THE CITIZEN'S GUIDE TO PLANNING. USA+45 MUNIC
LAW SCHOOL CREATE PROB/SOLV EDU/PROP GP/REL ROLE 20 PLAN
URBAN/RNWL OPEN/SPACE. PAGE 52 G1015 DELIB/GP
CONSULT

L61
COHEN K.J.,"THE ROLE OF MANAGEMENT GAMES IN SOCIETY
EDUCATION AND RESEARCH." INTELL ECO/DEV FINAN GAME
ACT/RES ECO/TAC DECISION. PAGE 12 G0240 MGT
EDU/PROP

S61
MACHOWSKI K.,"SELECTED PROBLEMS OF NATIONAL UNIV
SOVEREIGNTY WITH REFERENCE TO THE LAW OF OUTER ACT/RES
SPACE." FUT WOR+45 AIR LAW INTELL SOCIETY ECO/DEV NUC/PWR
PLAN EDU/PROP DETER DRIVE PERCEPT SOVEREIGN SPACE
...POLICY INT/LAW OBS TREND TOT/POP 20. PAGE 35
G0689

S61
MORGENSTERN O.,"THE N-COUNTRY PROBLEM." EUR+WWI FUT
UNIV USA+45 WOR+45 SOCIETY CONSULT TOP/EX ACT/RES BAL/PWR
PLAN EDU/PROP ATTIT DRIVE...POLICY OBS TREND NUC/PWR
TOT/POP 20. PAGE 40 G0781 TEC/DEV

B62
ASTIA,HUMAN ENGINEERING: A REPORT BIBLIOGRAPHY. BIBLIOG/A
USA+45 R+D FORCES ACT/RES COMPUTER CREATE OP/RES COM/IND
EDU/PROP CONTROL WEAPON...SOC NEW/IDEA. PAGE 4 COMPUT/IR
G0073 METH

B62
BOCK E.A.,CASE STUDIES IN AMERICAN GOVERNMENT. POLICY
USA+45 ECO/DEV CHIEF EDU/PROP CT/SYS RACE/REL LEGIS
ORD/FREE...JURID MGT PHIL/SCI PRESIDENT CASEBOOK. IDEA/COMP
PAGE 8 G0146 NAT/G

B62
BROOKINGS INSTITUTION,DEVELOPMENT OF THE EMERGING ECO/UNDEV
COUNTRIES: AN AGENDA FOR RESEARCH. WOR+45 AGRI R+D
TEC/DEV FOR/AID EDU/PROP ADJUST HABITAT KNOWL...PSY SOCIETY
SOC ANTHOL 20 THIRD/WRLD. PAGE 9 G0175 PROB/SOLV

B62
DODDS H.W.,THE ACADEMIC PRESIDENT "EDUCATOR OR ACADEM
CARETAKER? FINAN DELIB/GP EDU/PROP PARTIC ATTIT ADMIN
ROLE PWR...POLICY RECORD INT. PAGE 16 G0304 LEAD
CONTROL

B62
GILPIN R.,AMERICAN SCIENTISTS AND NUCLEAR WEAPONS INTELL
POLICY. COM FUT USA+45 WOR+45 INT/ORG NAT/G ATTIT
PROF/ORG CONSULT FORCES CREATE TEC/DEV BAL/PWR DETER
EDU/PROP ARMS/CONT WAR PERCEPT KNOWL MORAL PWR NUC/PWR
...PHIL/SCI SOC CONCPT GEN/LAWS 20. PAGE 21 G0417

B62
KAHN H.,THINKING ABOUT THE UNTHINKABLE. FUT USA+45 INT/ORG
LAW NAT/G CONSULT FORCES ACT/RES CREATE PLAN ORD/FREE
TEC/DEV BAL/PWR DIPLOM EDU/PROP ARMS/CONT DETER NUC/PWR
ATTIT...CONCPT OBS TREND COLD/WAR 20. PAGE 29 G0570 PEACE

B62
MACHLUP F.,THE PRODUCTION AND DISTRIBUTION OF ACADEM
KNOWLEDGE IN THE UNITED STATES. USA+45 COM/IND TEC/DEV
INDUS SCHOOL SECT WORKER COMPUTER CREATE CIVMIL/REL EDU/PROP
COST EFFICIENCY WEALTH 20. PAGE 35 G0688 R+D

B62
MELMAN S.,DISARMAMENT: ITS POLITICS AND ECONOMICS. NAT/G
WOR+45 DELIB/GP FORCES ECO/TAC DOMIN EDU/PROP LEGIT ORD/FREE
COERCE PWR...POLICY CONCPT 20. PAGE 38 G0752 ARMS/CONT
NUC/PWR

B62
OSGOOD C.E.,AN ALTERNATIVE TO WAR OR SURRENDER. FUT ORD/FREE
UNIV CULTURE INTELL SOCIETY R+D INT/ORG CONSULT EDU/PROP
DELIB/GP ACT/RES PLAN CHOOSE ATTIT PERCEPT KNOWL PEACE
...PHIL/SCI PSY SOC TREND GEN/LAWS 20. PAGE 43 WAR
G0849

B62
THANT U.,THE UNITED NATIONS' DEVELOPMENT DECADE: INT/ORG
PROPOSALS FOR ACTION. WOR+45 SOCIETY ECO/UNDEV AGRI ALL/VALS
COM/IND FINAN R+D MUNIC SCHOOL VOL/ASSN CONSULT
PLAN TEC/DEV ECO/TAC EDU/PROP ADMIN ROUTINE
RIGID/FLEX...MGT SOC CONCPT UNESCO UN TOT/POP
VAL/FREE. PAGE 54 G1064

S62
BETHE H.,"DISARMAMENT AND STRATEGY." COM USA+45 PLAN
USSR WOR+45 VOL/ASSN TEC/DEV EDU/PROP NUC/PWR ORD/FREE
CHOOSE PEACE...POLICY DECISION NEW/IDEA OBS ARMS/CONT
GEN/LAWS COLD/WAR 420. PAGE 7 G0133 DIPLOM

S62
FINKELSTEIN L.S.,"THE UNITED NATIONS AND INT/ORG
ORGANIZATIONS FOR CONTROL OF ARMAMENT." FUT WOR+45 PWR
VOL/ASSN DELIB/GP TOP/EX CREATE EDU/PROP LEGIT ARMS/CONT
ADJUD NUC/PWR ATTIT RIGID/FLEX ORD/FREE...POLICY
DECISION CONCPT OBS TREND GEN/LAWS TOT/POP
COLD/WAR. PAGE 19 G0368

S62
FOSTER R.B.,"UNILATERAL ARMS CONTROL MEASURES AND PLAN
DISARMAMENT NEGOTIATION." WOR+45 VOL/ASSN DELIB/GP ORD/FREE
ACT/RES ECO/TAC EDU/PROP ATTIT RIGID/FLEX...CONCPT ARMS/CONT
MYTH TIME/SEQ COLD/WAR 20. PAGE 20 G0386 DETER

S62
FOSTER W.C.,"ARMS CONTROL AND DISARMAMENT IN A DELIB/GP
DIVIDED WORLD." COM FUT USA+45 USSR WOR+45 INTELL POLICY
INT/ORG NAT/G VOL/ASSN CONSULT CREATE PLAN TEC/DEV ARMS/CONT
EDU/PROP LEGIT NUC/PWR ATTIT RIGID/FLEX...CONCPT DIPLOM

TREND TOT/POP 20 UN. PAGE 20 G0387

MORGENTHAU H.J.,"A POLITICAL THEORY OF FOREIGN
AID." ECO/UNDEV NAT/G DELIB/GP PLAN ECO/TAC
EDU/PROP EXEC ORD/FREE RESPECT WEALTH...METH/CNCPT
TREND 20. PAGE 40 G0783
    S62
USA+45
PHIL/SCI
FOR/AID

PAULING L.,"GENETIC EFFECTS OF WEAPONS TESTS."
WOR+45 SOCIETY FAM ACT/RES EDU/PROP AGE/C HEALTH
ORD/FREE...GEOG STAT CONT/OBS PROJ/TEST CHARTS
TOT/POP 20. PAGE 44 G0861
    S62
HEAL
ARMS/CONT
NUC/PWR

BONINI C.P.,SIMULATION OF INFORMATION AND DECISION
SYSTEMS IN THE FIRM. MARKET BUDGET DOMIN EDU/PROP
ADMIN COST ATTIT HABITAT PERCEPT PWR...CONCPT
PROBABIL QUANT PREDICT HYPO/EXP BIBLIOG. PAGE 8
G0152
    B63
INDUS
SIMUL
DECISION
MGT

GEERTZ C.,OLD SOCIETIES AND NEW STATES: THE QUEST
FOR MODERNITY IN ASIA AND AFRICA. AFR ASIA LAW
CULTURE SECT EDU/PROP REV...GOV/COMP NAT/COMP 20.
PAGE 21 G0415
    B63
ECO/UNDEV
TEC/DEV
NAT/LISM
SOVEREIGN

GOLDSEN J.M.,OUTER SPACE IN WORLD POLITICS. COM
USA+45 NAT/G FORCES ACT/RES PLAN DOMIN EDU/PROP
COERCE ORD/FREE PWR...TECHNIC STAT INT SAMP TREND
ANTHOL VAL/FREE 20. PAGE 22 G0428
    B63
TEC/DEV
DIPLOM
SPACE

HOFSTADTER R.,ANTI-INTELLECTUALISM IN AMERICAN
LIFE. USA+45 AGRI INDUS ACADEM TEC/DEV EDU/PROP
INGP/REL ATTIT...SOC WORSHIP 20 MCCARTHY/J
STEVENSN/A. PAGE 26 G0522
    B63
INTELL
EPIST
CULTURE
SOCIETY

KATZ S.M.,A SELECTED LIST OF US READINGS ON
DEVELOPMENT. AGRI COM/IND DIST/IND INDUS LABOR PLAN
FOR/AID EDU/PROP HEALTH...POLICY SOC/WK 20. PAGE 30
G0582
    B63
BIBLIOG/A
ECO/UNDEV
TEC/DEV
ACT/RES

MARSCH P.E.,FEDERAL AID TO SCIENCE EDUCATION: TWO
PROGRAMS. USA+45 SCHOOL RECEIVE EFFICIENCY 20.
PAGE 36 G0711
    B63
EDU/PROP
PHIL/SCI
NAT/G
METH/COMP

NORTH R.C.,CONTENT ANALYSIS: A HANDBOOK WITH
APPLICATIONS FOR THE STUDY OF INTERNATIONAL CRISIS.
ASIA COM EUR+WWI MOD/EUR INT/ORG TEC/DEV DOMIN
EDU/PROP ROUTINE COERCE PERCEPT RIGID/FLEX ALL/VALS
...QUANT TESTS CON/ANAL SIMUL GEN/LAWS VAL/FREE.
PAGE 42 G0825
    B63
METH/CNCPT
COMPUT/IR
USSR

OECD,SCIENCE AND THE POLICIES OF GOVERNMENTS: THE
IMPLICATIONS OF SCIENCE AND TECHNOLOGY FOR NATL AND
INTL AFFAIRS. WOR+45 INT/ORG EDU/PROP AUTOMAT
...POLICY PHIL/SCI 20. PAGE 42 G0830
    B63
CREATE
TEC/DEV
DIPLOM
NAT/G

PANAMERICAN UNION,DOCUMENTOS OFICIALES DE LA
ORGANIZACION DE LOS ESTADOS AMERICANOS. INDICE Y
LISTA (VOL. III, 1962). L/A+17C DELIB/GP INT/TRADE
EDU/PROP REGION NUC/PWR...HEAL INT/LAW SOC/WK 20
OAS. PAGE 44 G0857
    B63
BIBLIOG
INT/ORG
DIPLOM

PERLO V.,MILITARISM AND INDUSTRY. USA+45 INT/TRADE
EDU/PROP DETER KNOWL...CHARTS MAPS 20. PAGE 44
G0869
    B63
CIVMIL/REL
INDUS
LOBBY
ARMS/CONT

REED E.,CHALLENGES TO DEMOCRACY: THE NEXT TEN
YEARS. FUT USA+45 ECO/DEV DELIB/GP TEC/DEV CONFER
GOV/REL KNOWL ORD/FREE...MAJORIT IDEA/COMP ANTHOL
20. PAGE 46 G0909
    B63
POLICY
EDU/PROP
ECO/TAC
NAT/G

RUITENBEER H.M.,THE DILEMMA OF ORGANIZATIONAL
SOCIETY. CULTURE ECO/DEV MUNIC SECT TEC/DEV
EDU/PROP NAT/LISM ORD/FREE...NAT/COMP 20 RIESMAN/D
WHYTE/WF MERTON/R MEAD/MARG JASPERS/K. PAGE 48
G0945
    B63
PERSON
ROLE
ADMIN
WORKER

THORELLI H.B.,INTOP: INTERNATIONAL OPERATIONS
SIMULATION: PLAYER'S MANUAL. BRAZIL FINAN OP/RES
ADMIN GP/REL INGP/REL PRODUC PERCEPT...DECISION MGT
EEC. PAGE 54 G1073
    B63
GAME
INT/TRADE
EDU/PROP
LG/CO

US DEPARTMENT OF THE ARMY,SOVIET RUSSIA: STRATEGIC
SURVEY (PAMPHLET). USSR POL/PAR PLAN DOMIN EDU/PROP
ARMS/CONT GUERRILLA WAR WEAPON...TREND CHARTS
ORG/CHARTS 20. PAGE 57 G1129
    B63
BIBLIOG/A
MARXISM
DIPLOM
COERCE

WIGHTMAN D.,TOWARD ECONOMIC CO-OPERATION IN ASIA.
ASIA S/ASIA VOL/ASSN ACT/RES PLAN TEC/DEV ECO/TAC
EDU/PROP RIGID/FLEX SKILL...POLICY METH/CNCPT OBS
INT GEN/LAWS UN 20 ECAFE. PAGE 63 G1237
    B63
ECO/UNDEV
CREATE

PHELPS J.,"STUDIES IN DETERRENCE VIII: MILITARY
STABILITARY AND ARMS CONTROL: A CRITICAL SURVEY."
FUT WOR+45 INT/ORG ACT/RES EDU/PROP COERCE NUC/PWR
WAR HEALTH PWR...POLICY TECHNIC TREND SIMUL TOT/POP
20. PAGE 44 G0874
    L63
FORCES
ORD/FREE
ARMS/CONT
DETER

ABT C.,"THE PROBLEMS AND POSSIBILITIES OF SPACE
ARMS CONTROL." FUT USA+45 WOR+45 AIR SOCIETY NAT/G
BAL/PWR EDU/PROP ATTIT PWR WEALTH...HYPO/EXP
TOT/POP 20. PAGE 2 G0025
    S63
ACT/RES
ORD/FREE
ARMS/CONT
SPACE

HOSKINS H.L.,"ARAB SOCIALISM IN THE UAR." ISLAM
USSR AGRI INDUS NAT/G TOP/EX CREATE DIPLOM EDU/PROP
DRIVE KNOWL PWR SOCISM...POLICY CONCPT TREND SUEZ
20. PAGE 27 G0530
    S63
ECO/DEV
PLAN
UAR

MASSART L.,"L'ORGANISATION DE LA RECHERCHE
SCIENTIFIQUE EN EUROPE." EUR+WWI WOR+45 ACT/RES
PLAN TEC/DEV EDU/PROP EXEC KNOWL...METH/CNCPT EEC
20. PAGE 36 G0718
    S6?
R+D
CREATE

NADLER E.B.,"SOME ECONOMIC DISADVANTAGES OF THE
ARMS RACE." USA+45 INDUS R+D FORCES PLAN TEC/DEV
ECO/TAC FOR/AID EDU/PROP PWR WEALTH...TREND
COLD/WAR 20. PAGE 41 G0800
    S63
ECO/DEV
MGT
BAL/PAY

WOHLSTETTER A.,"SCIENTISTS, SEERS AND STRATEGY."
USA+45 ELITES R+D NAT/G CONSULT FORCES TOP/EX
EDU/PROP ARMS/CONT KNOWL ORD/FREE...DECISION MYTH
20. PAGE 64 G1253
    S63
INTELL
ACT/RES

RECENT PUBLICATIONS ON GOVERNMENTAL PROBLEMS. FINAN
INDUS ACADEM PLAN PROB/SOLV EDU/PROP ADJUD ADMIN
BIO/SOC...MGT SOC. PAGE 1 G0017
    B64
BIBLIOG
AUTOMAT
LEGIS
JURID

ETZIONI A.,THE MOON-DOGGLE: DOMESTIC AND
INTERNATIONAL IMPLICATIONS OF THE SPACE RACE. FUT
USA+45 WOR+45 INTELL ECO/DEV INDUS VOL/ASSN
EX/STRUC FORCES LEGIS TOP/EX PLAN TEC/DEV ECO/TAC
EDU/PROP KNOWL ORD/FREE PWR RESPECT WEALTH
TIME/SEQ. PAGE 18 G0352
    B64
R+D
NAT/G
DIPLOM
SPACE

GRODZINS M.,THE ATOMIC AGE: FORTY-FIVE SCIENTISTS
AND SCHOLARS SPEAK ON NATIONAL AND WORLD AFFAIRS.
FUT USA+45 WOR+45 R+D INT/ORG NAT/G CONSULT TEC/DEV
EDU/PROP ATTIT PERSON ORD/FREE...HUM CONCPT
TIME/SEQ CON/ANAL. PAGE 23 G0454
    B64
INTELL
ARMS/CONT
NUC/PWR

GROSSER G.H.,THE THREAT OF IMPENDING DISASTER:
CONTRIBUTIONS TO THE PSYCHOLOGY OF STRESS. SPACE
UNIV SOCIETY R+D TEC/DEV EDU/PROP COERCE WAR ATTIT
BIO/SOC DISPL PERCEPT PERSON...SOC MYTH SELF/OBS
CONT/OBS BIOG CON/ANAL TOT/POP 20. PAGE 23 G0455
    B64
HEALTH
PSY
NUC/PWR

MASTERS N.A.,STATE POLITICS AND THE PUBLIC SCHOOLS.
STRUCT FINAN ADMIN LOBBY GP/REL PWR BIBLIOG.
PAGE 36 G0720
    B64
EDU/PROP
PROVS
DOMIN

OSSENBECK F.J.,OPEN SPACE AND PEACE. CHINA/COM FUT
USA+45 USSR LAW PROB/SOLV TEC/DEV EDU/PROP NEUTRAL
PEACE...AUD/VIS ANTHOL 20. PAGE 43 G0850
    B64
SPACE
ORD/FREE
DIPLOM
CREATE

PETERSON W.,THE POLITICS OF POPULATION. COM EUR+WWI
FUT MOD/EUR S/ASIA USA+45 USA-45 WOR+45 LAW CULTURE
FAM SECT DOMIN EDU/PROP BIO/SOC HEALTH ORD/FREE
...GEOG STAT TIME/SEQ TREND VAL/FREE. PAGE 44 G0871
    B64
PLAN
CENSUS
POLICY

B64
THANT U.,TOWARD WORLD PEACE. DELIB/GP TEC/DEV   DIPLOM
EDU/PROP WAR SOVEREIGN...INT/LAW 20 UN MID/EAST.   BIOG
PAGE 54 G1065   PEACE
                                                   COERCE

B64
VAN DYKE V.,PRIDE AND POWER: THE RATIONALE OF THE TEC/DEV
SPACE PROGRAM. FUT USA+45 INTELL R+D NAT/G POL/PAR ATTIT
DELIB/GP EX/STRUC LEGIS TOP/EX ACT/RES PLAN ECO/TAC POLICY
EDU/PROP ORD/FREE PWR RESPECT SKILL...TIME/SEQ
VAL/FREE. PAGE 61 G1191

L64
CARNEGIE ENDOWMENT INT. PEACE,"POLITICAL QUESTIONS INT/ORG
(ISSUES BEFORE THE NINETEENTH GENERAL ASSEMBLY)." PEACE
SPACE WOR+45 CONSTN FINAN NAT/G CONSULT DELIB/GP
FORCES LEGIS TEC/DEV LEGIT ARMS/CONT
COERCE NUC/PWR ATTIT ALL/VALS...CONCPT OBS UN
COLD/WAR 20. PAGE 11 G0208

S64
BYRNES F.C.,"ASSIGNMENT TO AMBIGUITY: WORK   INTELL
PERFORMANCE IN CROSSCULTURAL TECHNICAL ASSISTANCE." QU
USA+45 WOR+45 PROF/ORG CONSULT PLAN EDU/PROP ATTIT
DISPL PERCEPT PERSON ALL/VALS...POLICY INT CHARTS
NATO 20. PAGE 10 G0199

S64
CALDWELL L.K.,"BIOPOLITICS: SCIENCE, ETHICS, AND   TEC/DEV
PUBLIC POLICY." FUT USA+45 WOR+45 INTELL STRATA R+D POLICY
NAT/G CONSULT PLAN EDU/PROP ALL/VALS...RELATIV
PHIL/SCI 20. PAGE 10 G0203

S64
GARDNER R.N.,"GATT AND THE UNITED NATIONS   INT/ORG
CONFERENCE ON TRADE AND DEVELOPMENT." USA+45 WOR+45 INT/TRADE
SOCIETY ECO/UNDEV MARKET NAT/G DELIB/GP ACT/RES
PLAN ECO/TAC TARIFFS EDU/PROP ROUTINE DRIVE
RIGID/FLEX WEALTH...DECISION MGT TREND UN TOT/POP
20 GATT. PAGE 21 G0411

S64
KASSOF A.,"THE ADMINISTERED SOCIETY: SOCIETY
TOTALITARIANISM WITHOUT TERROR." COM USSR STRATA   DOMIN
AGRI INDUS NAT/G PERF/ART SCHOOL TOP/EX EDU/PROP   TOTALISM
ADMIN ORD/FREE PWR...POLICY SOC TIME/SEQ GEN/LAWS
VAL/FREE 20. PAGE 29 G0580

S64
LERNER A.P.,"NUCLEAR SYMMETRY AS A FRAMEWORK FOR   FORCES
COEXISTENCE." COM FUT USA+45 NAT/G ACT/RES CREATE ORD/FREE
PLAN DIPLOM EDU/PROP COERCE WAR RIGID/FLEX PWR   DETER
SKILL...CONCPT METH/CNCPT GEN/LAWS TOT/POP VAL/FREE NUC/PWR
COLD/WAR 20. PAGE 33 G0657

S64
NEEDHAM T.,"SCIENCE AND SOCIETY IN EAST AND WEST." ASIA
INTELL STRATA R+D LOC/G NAT/G PROVS CONSULT ACT/RES STRUCT
CREATE PLAN TEC/DEV EDU/PROP ADMIN ATTIT ALL/VALS
...POLICY RELATIV MGT CONCPT NEW/IDEA TIME/SEQ WORK
WORK. PAGE 41 G0815

S64
PILISUK M.,"STEPWISE DISARMAMENT & SUDDEN   PWR
DESTRUCTION IN A TWOPERSON GAME: A RESEARCH TOOL." DECISION
NAT/G FORCES ACT/RES ECO/TAC EDU/PROP EXEC ROUTINE ARMS/CONT
COERCE ORD/FREE...SIMUL GEN/LAWS VAL/FREE. PAGE 45
G0877

S64
THOMPSON V.A.,"ADMINISTRATIVE OBJECTIVES FOR   ECO/UNDEV
DEVELOPMENT ADMINISTRATION." WOR+45 CREATE PLAN   MGT
DOMIN EDU/PROP EXEC ROUTINE ATTIT ORD/FREE PWR
...POLICY GEN/LAWS VAL/FREE. PAGE 54 G1070

C64
SCHRAMM W.,"MASS MEDIA AND NATIONAL DEVELOPMENT: ECO/UNDEV
THE ROLE OF INFORMATION IN DEVELOPING COUNTRIES." COM/IND
FINAN R+D ACT/RES PLAN TEC/DEV DIPLOM CHOOSE SUPEGO EDU/PROP
ORD/FREE...BIBLIOG 20. PAGE 50 G0978   MAJORIT

N64
NATIONAL ACADEMY OF SCIENCES,CIVIL DEFENSE: PROJECT NUC/PWR
HARBOR SUMMARY REPORT (PAMPHLET). USA+45 MUNIC   FORCES
NAT/G ACT/RES BUDGET EDU/PROP DETER WEAPON EATING WAR
...GEOG 20. PAGE 41 G0808   PLAN

B65
ALLEN S.,LETTER TO A CONSERVATIVE. SOCIETY NAT/G   ORD/FREE
DIPLOM EDU/PROP NUC/PWR GP/REL ATTIT MORAL   MARXISM
...MAJORIT CONCPT 20. PAGE 2 G0044   POLICY
                                                   LAISSEZ

B65
ANDERSON C.A.,EDUCATION AND ECONOMIC DEVELOPMENT. ANTHOL

INDUS R+D SCHOOL TEC/DEV ECO/TAC EDU/PROP AGE   ECO/DEV
HEREDITY PERCEPT SKILL 20. PAGE 3 G0056   ECO/UNDEV
                                                   WORKER

B65
BENJAMIN A.C.,SCIENCE, TECHNOLOGY, AND HUMAN   PHIL/SCI
VALUES. WOR+45 SECT EDU/PROP GP/REL ATTIT...TECHNIC CREATE
LING IDEA/COMP WORSHIP 20. PAGE 6 G0118   ROLE
                                                   SOCIETY

B65
BENTWICH J.S.,EDUCATION IN ISRAEL. ISRAEL CULTURE SECT
STRATA PROB/SOLV TEC/DEV ADJUST ALL/VALS 20 JEWS. EDU/PROP
PAGE 7 G0125   ACADEM
                                                   SCHOOL

B65
BLOOMFIELD L.,SOVIET INTERESTS IN ARMS CONTROL AND USSR
DISARMAMENT* THE DECADE UNDER KHRUSHCHEV 1954-1964. ARMS/CONT
ASIA FORCES ACT/RES EDU/PROP DETER NUC/PWR WEAPON DIPLOM
COST ATTIT...PHIL/SCI CLASSIF STAT NET/THEORY GAME TREND
BIBLIOG. PAGE 7 G0139

B65
CHENG C.-Y.,SCIENTIFIC AND ENGINEERING MANPOWER IN WORKER
COMMUNIST CHINA, 1949-1963. CHINA/COM USSR ELITES CONSULT
ECO/DEV R+D ACADEM LABOR NAT/G EDU/PROP CONTROL   MARXISM
UTIL...POLICY BIBLIOG 20. PAGE 12 G0226   BIOG

B65
MELMANS S.,OUR DEPLETED SOCIETY. SPACE USA+45   CIVMIL/REL
ECO/DEV FORCES BUDGET ECO/TAC ADMIN WEAPON   INDUS
EFFICIENCY 20 COLD/WAR. PAGE 38 G0753   EDU/PROP
                                                   CONTROL

B65
NATIONAL ACADEMY OF SCIENCES,BASIC RESEARCH AND   LEGIS
NATIONAL GOALS. R+D ACADEM DELIB/GP PLAN EDU/PROP BUDGET
...POLICY HEAL PHIL/SCI PSY SOC ANTHOL 20 CONGRESS NAT/G
HOUSE/REP HS/SCIASTR. PAGE 41 G0809   CREATE

B65
OECD,MEDITERRANEAN REGIONAL PROJECT: TURKEY;   EDU/PROP
EDUCATION AND DEVELOPMENT. FUT TURKEY SOCIETY   ACADEM
STRATA FINAN NAT/G PROF/ORG PLAN PROB/SOLV ADMIN   SCHOOL
COST...STAT CHARTS 20 OECD. PAGE 42 G0831   ECO/UNDEV

B65
OECD,THE MEDITERRANEAN REGIONAL PROJECT: PORTUGAL; EDU/PROP
EDUCATION AND DEVELOPMENT. PORTUGAL SOCIETY STRATA SCHOOL
FINAN PROF/ORG WORKER PLAN PROB/SOLV ADMIN...POLICY ACADEM
STAT CHARTS METH 20 OECD. PAGE 42 G0832   ECO/UNDEV

B65
OECD,THE MEDITERRANEAN REGIONAL PROJECT: ITALY;   SCHOOL
EDUCATION AND DEVELOPMENT. ITALY SOCIETY STRATA   EDU/PROP
FINAN NAT/G PROF/ORG WORKER PLAN PROB/SOLV ADMIN   ECO/UNDEV
...STAT CHARTS METH 20 OECD. PAGE 42 G0833   ACADEM

B65
OECD,THE MEDITERRANEAN REGIONAL PROJECT: GREECE;   EDU/PROP
EDUCATION AND DEVELOPMENT. FUT GREECE SOCIETY AGRI SCHOOL
FINAN NAT/G PROF/ORG WORKER PLAN PROB/SOLV ADMIN   ACADEM
DEMAND ATTIT 20 OECD. PAGE 42 G0834   ECO/UNDEV

B65
OECD,THE MEDITERRANEAN REGIONAL PROJECT: SPAIN;   ECO/UNDEV
EDUCATION AND DEVELOPMENT. FUT SPAIN STRATA FINAN EDU/PROP
NAT/G WORKER PLAN PROB/SOLV ADMIN COST...POLICY   ACADEM
STAT CHARTS 20 OECD. PAGE 42 G0835   SCHOOL

B65
ORG FOR ECO COOP AND DEVEL,THE MEDITERRANEAN   EDU/PROP
REGIONAL PROJECT: YUGOSLAVIA; EDUCATION AND   ACADEM
DEVELOPMENT. YUGOSLAVIA SOCIETY FINAN PROF/ORG PLAN SCHOOL
ADMIN COST DEMAND MARXISM...STAT TREND CHARTS METH ECO/UNDEV
20 OECD. PAGE 43 G0843

B65
SINGER J.D.,HUMAN BEHAVIOR AND INTERNATINAL   DIPLOM
POLITICS* CONTRIBUTIONS FROM THE SOCIAL-   PHIL/SCI
PSYCHOLOGICAL SCIENCES. ACT/RES PLAN EDU/PROP ADMIN QUANT
KNOWL...DECISION PSY SOC NET/THEORY HYPO/EXP   SIMUL
LAB/EXP SOC/EXP GEN/METH ANTHOL BIBLIOG. PAGE 51
G1006

B65
UNESCO,HANDBOOK OF INTERNATIONAL EXCHANGES. COM/IND INDEX
R+D ACADEM PROF/ORG VOL/ASSN CREATE TEC/DEV   INT/ORG
EDU/PROP AGREE 20 TREATY. PAGE 55 G1090   DIPLOM
                                                   PRESS

B65
US DEPARTMENT OF DEFENSE,US SECURITY ARMS CONTROL, BIBLIOG/A
AND DISARMAMENT 1961-1965 (PAMPHLET). CHINA/COM COM ARMS/CONT
GERMANY/W ISRAEL SPACE USA+45 USSR WOR+45 FORCES   NUC/PWR

EDU/PROP DETER EQUILIB PEACE ALL/VALS...GOV/COMP 20 DIPLOM
NATO. PAGE 57 G1118

B65

VERMOT-GAUCHY M.,L'EDUCATION NATIONALE DANS LA   ACADEM
FRANCE DE 1975. FRANCE FUT CULTURE ELITES R+D   CREATE
SCHOOL PLAN EDU/PROP EFFICIENCY...POLICY PREDICT   TREND
CHARTS INDEX 20. PAGE 61 G1195   INTELL

S65

KUZMACK A.M.,"TECHNOLOGICAL CHANGE AND STABLE   R+D
DETERRENCE." CREATE EDU/PROP ARMS/CONT WEAPON   DETER
CHOOSE COST DRIVE PERCEPT...RECORD STERTYP TIME.   EQUILIB
PAGE 32 G0627

S65

SCHELLING T.C.,"SIGNALS AND FEEDBACK IN THE ARMS   FEEDBACK
DIALOGUE." USA+45 USSR R+D ACADEM FORCES ACT/RES   DETER
ADJUST COST GEN/LAWS. PAGE 49 G0964   EDU/PROP
                                                        ARMS/CONT

S65

STAAR R.F.,"RETROGRESSION IN POLAND." COM USSR AGRI   TOP/EX
INDUS NAT/G CREATE EDU/PROP TOTALISM RIGID/FLEX   ECO/TAC
ORD/FREE PWR SOCISM...RECORD CHARTS 20. PAGE 52   POLAND
G1029

B66

ALEXANDER Y.,INTERNATIONAL TECHNICAL ASSISTANCE   SKILL
EXPERTS: A CASE STUDY OF THE U.N. EXPERIENCE.   INT/ORG
USA+45 WOR+45 WORKER CREATE PLAN PROB/SOLV ECO/TAC   TEC/DEV
FOR/AID GIVE EDU/PROP...CHARTS BIBLIOG 20 UN.   CONSULT
PAGE 2 G0039

B66

BLOOMFIELD L.P.,KHRUSHCHEV AND THE ARMS RACE.   ARMS/CONT
USA+45 USSR ECO/DEV BAL/PWR EDU/PROP CONFER NUC/PWR   COM
ATTIT...CHARTS 20 KHRUSH/N. PAGE 7 G0143   POLICY
                                                        DIPLOM

B66

HALPIN A.W.,THEORY AND RESEARCH IN ADMINISTRATION.   GEN/LAWS
ACT/RES LEAD...MGT IDEA/COMP METH/COMP. PAGE 24   EDU/PROP
G0475   ADMIN
                                                        PHIL/SCI

B66

MARKHAM J.W.,AN ECONOMIC-MEDIA STUDY OF BOOK   PRESS
PUBLISHING. USA+45 LAW COM/IND ACADEM SCHOOL   ECO/TAC
EDU/PROP AUTOMAT CONTROL...DECISION STAT CHARTS 20   TEC/DEV
CONGRESS. PAGE 36 G0707   NAT/G

B66

NATIONAL SCIENCE FOUNDATION,SIXTEENTH ANNUAL REPORT   NAT/G
FOR THE FISCAL YEAR ENDED JUNE 30, 1966. USA+45   EDU/PROP
CREATE BUDGET SKILL 20 NSF. PAGE 41 G0813   ACADEM
                                                        KNOWL

B66

OECD DEVELOPMENT CENTRE,CATALOGUE OF SOCIAL AND   ECO/UNDEV
ECONOMIC DEVELOPMENT INSTITUTES AND PROGRAMMES*   ECO/DEV
RESEARCH. ACT/RES PLAN TEC/DEV EDU/PROP...SOC   R+D
GP/COMP NAT/COMP. PAGE 43 G0836   ACADEM

B66

SANFORD T.,BUT WHAT ABOUT THE PEOPLE? ACADEM SCHOOL EDU/PROP
BUDGET TAX CONTROL SKILL WEALTH 20 NORTH/CAR.   PROB/SOLV
PAGE 49 G0956   POLICY
                                                        PROVS

B66

US SENATE COMM AERO SPACE SCI,SOVIET SPACE   CONSULT
PROGRAMS, 1962-65: GOALS AND PURPOSES,   SPACE
ACHIEVEMENTS, PLANS, AND INTERNATIONAL   FUT
IMPLICATIONS. USA+45 USSR R+D FORCES PLAN EDU/PROP   DIPLOM
PRESS ADJUD ARMS/CONT ATTIT MARXISM. PAGE 60 G1168

S66

TURKEVICH J.,"SOVIET SCIENCE APPRAISED." USA+45 R+D   USSR
ACADEM FORCES DIPLOM EDU/PROP WAR EFFICIENCY PEACE   TEC/DEV
SKILL OBS. PAGE 55 G1081   NAT/COMP
                                                        ATTIT

B67

BARANSON J.,TECHNOLOGY FOR UNDERDEVELOPED AREAS: AN   BIBLIOG/A
ANNOTATED BIBLIOGRAPHY. FUT WOR+45 CULTURE INDUS   ECO/UNDEV
INT/ORG CREATE PROB/SOLV INT/TRADE EDU/PROP AUTOMAT   TEC/DEV
...CONCPT METH. PAGE 5 G0092   R+D

B67

DE BLIJ H.J.,SYSTEMATIC POLITICAL GEOGRAPHY. WOR+45   GEOG
STRUCT INT/ORG NAT/G EDU/PROP ADMIN COLONIAL   CONCPT
ROUTINE ORD/FREE PWR...IDEA/COMP T 20. PAGE 15   METH
G0283

B67

GULICK M.C.,NONCONVENTIONAL INFORMATION SYSTEMS   BIBLIOG/A
SERVING THE SOCIAL SCIENCES AND THE HUMANITIES; A   R+D
BIBLIOGRAPHIC ESSAY (PAPER). USA+45 COMPUTER CREATE   COMPUT/IR
EDU/PROP KNOWL...SOC METH 20. PAGE 23 G0462   HUM

B67

LERNER D.,COMMUNICATION AND CHANGE IN DEVELOPING   EDU/PROP
COUNTRIES. CHINA/COM INDIA PHILIPPINE COM/IND   ORD/FREE
CREATE TEC/DEV...ANTHOL 20. PAGE 33 G0659   PERCEPT
                                                        ECO/UNDEV

B67

MCLAUGHLIN M.R.,RELIGIOUS EDUCATION AND THE STATE: SECT
DEMOCRACY FINDS A WAY. CANADA EUR+WWI GP/REL   NAT/G
POPULISM...CATH NAT/COMP 20 AUSTRAL. PAGE 38 G0745   EDU/PROP
                                                        POLICY

B67

POMEROY W.J.,HALF A CENTURY OF SOCIALISM. USSR LAW   SOCISM
AGRI INDUS NAT/G CREATE DIPLOM EDU/PROP PERSON   MARXISM
ORD/FREE WEALTH...POLICY TREND 20. PAGE 45 G0884   COM
                                                        SOCIETY

B67

SAPARINA Y.,CYBERNETICS WITHIN US. WOR+45 EDU/PROP   COMPUTER
FEEDBACK PERCEPT HEALTH...DECISION METH/CNCPT   METH/COMP
NEW/IDEA 20. PAGE 49 G0957   CONTROL
                                                        SIMUL

B67

UNIVERSAL REFERENCE SYSTEM,CURRENT EVENTS AND   BIBLIOG/A
PROBLEMS OF MODERN SOCIETY (VOLUME V). WOR+45 LOC/G   SOCIETY
MUNIC NAT/G EDU/PROP CRIME RACE/REL WEALTH   PROB/SOLV
...COMPUT/IR GEN/METH. PAGE 56 G1097   ATTIT

B67

UNIVERSAL REFERENCE SYSTEM,PUBLIC OPINION, MASS   BIBLIOG/A
BEHAVIOR, AND POLITICAL PSYCHOLOGY (VOLUME VI).   ATTIT
WOR+45 WOR-45 SOCIETY EDU/PROP PRESS PARTIC CHOOSE   CROWD
PERSON...TREND COMPUT/IR GEN/METH. PAGE 56 G1098   PSY

B67

US HOUSE COMM SCI ASTRONAUT,THE JUNIOR COLLEGE AND   ACADEM
EDUCATION IN THE SCIENCES (PAMPHLET). USA+45 AGE/Y   EDU/PROP
...CHARTS SIMUL HOUSE/REP. PAGE 58 G1148   PHIL/SCI
                                                        R+D

B67

WEINBERG A.M.,REFLECTIONS ON BIG SCIENCE. FUT   ACADEM
USA+45 NAT/G EDU/PROP CHOOSE PERS/REL COST OPTIMAL   KNOWL
...PHIL/SCI TREND. PAGE 62 G1225   R+D
                                                        PLAN

L67

BARRON J.A.,"ACCESS TO THE PRESS." USA+45 TEC/DEV   ORD/FREE
PRESS TV ADJUD AUD/VIS. PAGE 5 G0099   COM/IND
                                                        EDU/PROP
                                                        LAW

L67

EINAUDI L.,"ANNOTATED BIBLIOGRAPHY OF LATIN   BIBLIOG/A
AMERICAN MILITARY JOURNALS" LAW TEC/DEV DOMIN   NAT/G
EDU/PROP COERCE WAR CIVMIL/REL 20. PAGE 17 G0336   FORCES
                                                        L/A+17C

S67

BENN W.,"TECHNOLOGY HAS AN INEXORABLE EFFECT." FUT   R+D
UK ECO/DEV INT/ORG CONSULT PLAN EDU/PROP ADMIN LEAD   LG/CO
GP/REL PRODUC...INT 20 EEC. PAGE 6 G0119   TEC/DEV
                                                        INDUS

S67

CRANBERG L.,"SCIENCE, ETHICS, AND LAW." UNIV CREATE   LAW
PLAN EDU/PROP INGP/REL PERS/REL ADJUST RATIONAL   PHIL/SCI
KNOWL MORAL...CONCPT IDEA/COMP 20. PAGE 13 G0260   INTELL

S67

HILL R.,"SOCIAL ASPECTS OF FAMILY PLANNING." INDIA   FAM
KOREA TAIWAN ECO/UNDEV PLAN PROB/SOLV TEC/DEV   BIO/SOC
EDU/PROP CONTROL ATTIT DRIVE...HEAL PSY SOC 20   GEOG
BIRTH/CON UN. PAGE 26 G0512   MARRIAGE

S67

MCNAMARA R.L.,"THE NEED FOR INNOVATIVENESS IN   PROB/SOLV
DEVELOPING SOCIETIES." L/A+17C EDU/PROP ADMIN LEAD   PLAN
WEALTH...POLICY PSY SOC METH 20 COLOMB. PAGE 38   ECO/UNDEV
G0747   NEW/IDEA

S67

SLOAN P.,"FIFTY YEARS OF SOVIET RULE." USSR INDUS   CREATE
EDU/PROP EFFICIENCY PRODUC HEALTH KNOWL MORAL   NAT/G
WEALTH MARXISM...POLICY 20. PAGE 51 G1011   PLAN
                                                        INSPECT

S67
WARE R.S.,"FORECAST A.D. 2000." SOCIETY STRATA   NUC/PWR
ECO/UNDEV INDUS FORCES EDU/PROP AUTOMAT COERCE REV   GEOG
WEAPON ATTIT PREDICT. PAGE 62 G1213   TEC/DEV
                                                         WAR

S67
WHITTIER J.M.,"COMPULSORY POOLING AND UNITIZATION*   LEGIS
DIE-HARD KANSAS." LAW PLAN EDU/PROP ATTIT...POLICY   MUNIC
JURID PREDICT TREND METH/COMP 20. PAGE 63 G1236   INDUS
                                                         ECO/TAC

N67
US SUPERINTENDENT OF DOCUMENTS,SPACE: MISSILES, THE   BIBLIOG/A
MOON, NASA, AND SATELLITES (PRICE LIST 79A). USA+45   SPACE
COM/IND R+D NAT/G DIPLOM EDU/PROP ADMIN CONTROL   TEC/DEV
HEALTH...POLICY SIMUL NASA CONGRESS. PAGE 61 G1190   PEACE

B68
GALLAHER A. JR.,PERSPECTIVES IN DEVELOPMENTAL   TECHNIC
CHANGE. MUNIC PLAN INSPECT EDU/PROP...POLICY   TEC/DEV
DECISION GEOG PSY SOC IDEA/COMP ANTHOL 20   PROB/SOLV
MODERNIZE. PAGE 21 G0405   CREATE

S68
BARAGWANATH L.E.,"SCIENTIFIC CO-OPERATION BETWEEN   R+D
THE UNIVERSITIES AND INDUSTRY - A RESEARCH NOTE."   ACADEM
UK LG/CO CREATE TEC/DEV EDU/PROP ATTIT...PHIL/SCI   INDUS
STAT QU 20. PAGE 5 G0090   GP/REL

EDUCATION....SEE EDU/PROP

EDUCATIONAL INSTITUTIONS....SEE ACADEM, SCHOOL

EEC....EUROPEAN ECONOMIC COMMUNITY; SEE ALSO VOL/ASSN,
  INT/ORG

N
FOREIGN AFFAIRS. SPACE WOR+45 WOR-45 CULTURE   BIBLIOG
ECO/UNDEV FINAN NAT/G TEC/DEV INT/TRADE ARMS/CONT   DIPLOM
NUC/PWR...POLICY 20 UN EURATOM ECSC EEC. PAGE 1   INT/ORG
G0004   INT/LAW

B62
KRAFT J.,THE GRAND DESIGN. EUR+WWI USA+45 AGRI   VOL/ASSN
FINAN INDUS MARKET INT/ORG NAT/G PLAN ECO/TAC   ECO/DEV
TARIFFS REGION DRIVE ORD/FREE WEALTH...POLICY OBS   INT/TRADE
TREND EEC 20. PAGE 31 G0616

B62
SCHMITT H.A.,THE PATH TO EUROPEAN UNITY. EUR+WWI   INT/ORG
USA+45 PLAN TEC/DEV DIPLOM FOR/AID CONFER...INT/LAW   INT/TRADE
20 EEC EURCOALSTL MARSHL/PLN UNIFICA. PAGE 49 G0971   REGION
                                                         ECO/DEV

B63
MAYNE R.,THE COMMUNITY OF EUROPE. UK CONSTN NAT/G   EUR+WWI
CONSULT DELIB/GP CREATE PLAN ECO/TAC LEGIT ADMIN   INT/ORG
ROUTINE ORD/FREE PWR WEALTH...CONCPT TIME/SEQ EEC   REGION
EURATOM 20. PAGE 37 G0724

B63
THORELLI H.B.,INTOP: INTERNATIONAL OPERATIONS   GAME
SIMULATION: PLAYER'S MANUAL. BRAZIL FINAN OP/RES   INT/TRADE
ADMIN GP/REL INGP/REL PRODUC PERCEPT...DECISION MGT   EDU/PROP
EEC. PAGE 54 G1073   LG/CO

L63
NIEBURG H.,"EURATOM: A STUDY IN COALITION   VOL/ASSN
POLITICS." EUR+WWI UK USA+45 ELITES NAT/G DELIB/GP   ACT/RES
LEGIS TOP/EX ECO/TAC NUC/PWR ATTIT ORD/FREE PWR
TOT/POP EEC OEEC 20 NATO EURATOM. PAGE 42 G0820

S63
MASSART L.,"L'ORGANISATION DE LA RECHERCHE   R+D
SCIENTIFIQUE EN EUROPE." EUR+WWI WOR+45 ACT/RES   CREATE
PLAN TEC/DEV EDU/PROP EXEC KNOWL...METH/CNCPT EEC
20. PAGE 36 G0718

S63
SCHMITT H.A.,"THE EUROPEAN COMMUNITIES." EUR+WWI   VOL/ASSN
FRANCE DELIB/GP EX/STRUC TOP/EX CREATE TEC/DEV   ECO/DEV
ECO/TAC LEGIT REGION COERCE DRIVE ALL/VALS
...METH/CNCPT EEC 20. PAGE 49 G0972

B64
FREYMOND J.,WESTERN EUROPE SINCE THE WAR. COM   INT/ORG
EUR+WWI USA+45 DIPLOM...BIBLIOG 20 NATO UN EEC.   POLICY
PAGE 20 G0392   ECO/DEV
                                                         ECO/TAC

B67
ROACH J.R.,THE UNITED STATES AND THE ATLANTIC   INT/ORG
COMMUNITY; ISSUES AND PROSPECTS. WOR+45 TEC/DEV   POLICY
ECO/TAC COLONIAL REGION PEACE ROLE...ANTHOL NATO   ADJUST
COLD/WAR EEC. PAGE 47 G0925   DIPLOM

S67
BENN W.,"TECHNOLOGY HAS AN INEXORABLE EFFECT." FUT   R+D
UK ECO/DEV INT/ORG CONSULT PLAN EDU/PROP ADMIN LEAD   LG/CO
GP/REL PRODUC...INT 20 EEC. PAGE 6 G0119   TEC/DEV
                                                         INDUS

S67
DEUTSCH K.W.,"ARMS CONTROL AND EUROPEAN UNITY* THE   ARMS/CONT
NEXT TEN YEARS." USA+45 ELITES NAT/G BAL/PWR DIPLOM   PEACE
NUC/PWR...INT KNO/TEST NATO EEC. PAGE 15 G0300   REGION
                                                         PLAN

S67
WEIL G.L.,"THE MERGER OF THE INSTITUTIONS OF THE   ECO/TAC
EUROPEAN COMMUNITIES" EUR+WWI ECO/DEV INT/TRADE   INT/ORG
CONSEN PLURISM...DECISION MGT 20 EEC EURATOM ECSC   CENTRAL
TREATY. PAGE 62 G1223   INT/LAW

EFFECTIVENESS....SEE EFFICIENCY, PRODUC

EFFICIENCY....EFFECTIVENESS

N19
BROWN W.M.,THE DESIGN AND PERFORMANCE OF "OPTIMUM"   HABITAT
BLAST SHELTER PROGRAMS (PAMPHLET). USA+45 ACT/RES   NUC/PWR
PLAN DEATH COST EFFICIENCY OPTIMAL...POLICY CHARTS   WAR
20. PAGE 9 G0180   HEALTH

N19
DOTSON A.,PRODUCTION PLANNING IN THE PATENT OFFICE   EFFICIENCY
(PAMPHLET). USA+45 DIST/IND PROB/SOLV PRODUC...MGT   PLAN
PHIL/SCI 20 BUR/BUDGET PATENT/OFF. PAGE 16 G0309   NAT/G
                                                         ADMIN

N19
US ATOMIC ENERGY COMMISSION,ATOMIC ENERGY IN USE   OP/RES
(PAMPHLET). R+D RISK EFFICIENCY HEALTH KNOWL   TEC/DEV
ORD/FREE...PHIL/SCI CONCPT METH/CNCPT CHARTS   NUC/PWR
LAB/EXP 20 AEC. PAGE 56 G1106   CREATE

B37
GULICK L.,PAPERS ON THE SCIENCE OF ADMINISTRATION.   OP/RES
INDUS PROB/SOLV TEC/DEV COST EFFICIENCY PRODUC   CONTROL
HABITAT...PHIL/SCI METH/COMP 20. PAGE 23 G0461   ADMIN
                                                         MGT

B37
STAMP S.,THE SCIENCE OF SOCIAL ADJUSTMENT. WOR-45   ADJUST
ACT/RES CREATE PLAN PROB/SOLV TEC/DEV ECO/TAC   ORD/FREE
EFFICIENCY SOC/INTEG 20. PAGE 52 G1031   PHIL/SCI

B44
MERRIAM C.E.,PUBLIC AND PRIVATE GOVERNMENT.   NAT/G
VOL/ASSN EDU/PROP ADMIN REPRESENT EFFICIENCY PWR   NEIGH
PLURISM...MAJORIT CONCPT. PAGE 38 G0755   MGT
                                                         POLICY

B46
WILCOX J.K.,OFFICIAL DEFENSE PUBLICATIONS.   BIBLIOG/A
1941-1945 (NINE VOLS.). USA-45 AGRI INDUS R+D LABOR   WAR
FORCES TEC/DEV EFFICIENCY PRODUC SKILL WEALTH 20.   CIVMIL/REL
PAGE 63 G1238   ADMIN

B48
STEWART I.,ORGANIZING SCIENTIFIC RESEARCH FOR WAR: DELIB/GP
ADMINISTRATIVE HISTORY OF OFFICE OF SCIENTIFIC   ADMIN
RESEARCH AND DEVELOPMENT. USA-45 INTELL R+D LABOR   WAR
WORKER CREATE BUDGET WEAPON CIVMIL/REL GP/REL   TEC/DEV
EFFICIENCY...POLICY 20. PAGE 53 G1036

B48
WEINER N.,CYBERNETICS. SOCIETY COMPUTER ADJUST   FEEDBACK
EFFICIENCY UTIL PERCEPT...PSY MATH REGRESS TIME.   AUTOMAT
PAGE 63 G1226   CONTROL
                                                         TEC/DEV

S48
COCH L.,"OVERCOMING RESISTANCE TO CHANGE" (BMR)"   WORKER
USA+45 CONSULT ADMIN ROUTINE GP/REL EFFICIENCY   OP/RES
PRODUC PERCEPT SKILL...CHARTS SOC/EXP 20. PAGE 12   PROC/MFG
G0236   RIGID/FLEX

S48
MARQUIS D.G.,"RESEARCH PLANNING AT THE FRONTIERS OF   PLAN
SCIENCE" (BMR)" INTELL ACADEM CREATE UTIL...PSY 20.   ACT/RES
PAGE 36 G0708   EFFICIENCY
                                                         GEN/METH

B49
LEPAWSKY A.,ADMINISTRATION. FINAN INDUS LG/CO   ADMIN
SML/CO INGP/REL PERS/REL COST EFFICIENCY OPTIMAL   MGT
SKILL 20. PAGE 33 G0656   WORKER
                                                         EX/STRUC

METH/CNCPT

HUZAR E.,THE PURSE AND THE SWORD: CONTROL OF THE
ARMY BY CONGRESS THROUGH MILITARY APPROPRIATIONS
1933-1950. NAT/G DELIB/GP EX/STRUC FORCES PROB/SOLV
BARGAIN CONFER ADMIN ROUTINE GOV/REL EFFICIENCY
...POLICY COLD/WAR. PAGE 27 G0541
B50
CIVMIL/REL
BUDGET
CONTROL
LEGIS

BAVELAS A.,"COMMUNICATION PATTERNS IN TASK-ORIENTED
GROUPS" (BMR)" R+D OP/RES INSPECT LEAD CENTRAL
EFFICIENCY HAPPINESS RIGID/FLEX...PROBABIL 20.
PAGE 6 G0106
S50
ACT/RES
PERS/REL
TASK
INGP/REL

HOMANS G.C.,"THE WESTERN ELECTRIC RESEARCHES" IN S.
HOSLETT, ED., HUMAN FACTORS IN MANAGEMENT (BMR)"
ACT/RES GP/REL HAPPINESS PRODUC DRIVE...MGT OBS 20.
PAGE 27 G0526
C51
EFFICIENCY
SOC/EXP
WORKER

ROBINSON E.A.G.,THE STRUCTURE OF COMPETITIVE
INDUSTRY. UK ECO/DEV DIST/IND MARKET TEC/DEV DIPLOM
EDU/PROP ADMIN EFFICIENCY WEALTH...MGT 19/20.
PAGE 47 G0929
B53
INDUS
PRODUC
WORKER
OPTIMAL

SMITHIES A.,THE BUDGETARY PROCESS IN THE UNITED
STATES. ECO/DEV AGRI EX/STRUC FORCES LEGIS
PROB/SOLV TAX ROUTINE EFFICIENCY...MGT CONGRESS
PRESIDENT. PAGE 52 G1016
B55
NAT/G
ADMIN
BUDGET
GOV/REL

ALMOND G.A.,"COMPARATIVE POLITICAL SYSTEMS" (BMR)"
WOR+45 WOR-45 PROB/SOLV DIPLOM EFFICIENCY
...PHIL/SCI SOC METH 17/20. PAGE 3 G0046
S56
GOV/COMP
CONCPT
ALL/IDEOS
NAT/COMP

GOLD N.L.,REGIONAL ECONOMIC DEVELOPMENT AND NUCLEAR
POWER IN INDIA. FUT INDIA FINAN FOR/AID INT/TRADE
BAL/PAY EFFICIENCY OPTIMAL PRODUC WEALTH...PREDICT
20. PAGE 22 G0424
B57
ECO/UNDEV
TEC/DEV
NUC/PWR
INDUS

CHEEK G.,ECONOMIC AND SOCIAL IMPLICATIONS OF
AUTOMATION: A BIBLIOGRAPHIC REVIEW (PAMPHLET).
USA+45 LG/CO WORKER CREATE PLAN CONTROL ROUTINE
PERS/REL EFFICIENCY PRODUC...METH/COMP 20. PAGE 12
G0225
B58
BIBLIOG/A
SOCIETY
INDUS
AUTOMAT

DUBIN R.,THE WORLD OF WORK: INDUSTRIAL SOCIETY AND
HUMAN RELATIONS. MARKET PROC/MFG LABOR TEC/DEV
CAP/ISM AUTOMAT TASK GP/REL EFFICIENCY...CONCPT
CHARTS BIBLIOG 20. PAGE 16 G0317
B58
WORKER
ECO/TAC
PRODUC
DRIVE

MAYDA J.,ATOMIC ENERGY AND LAW. ECO/UNDEV FINAN
TEC/DEV FOR/AID EFFICIENCY PRODUC WEALTH...POLICY
TECHNIC 20. PAGE 37 G0723
B59
NUC/PWR
L/A+17C
LAW
ADMIN

VAN WAGENEN R.W.,SOME VIEWS OF AMERICAN DEFENSE
OFFICIALS ABOUT THE UNITED NATIONS (PAPER). FUT
USA+45 NAT/G DIPLOM WAR EFFICIENCY PEACE...POLICY
INT 20 UN DEPT/DEFEN. PAGE 61 G1192
B59
INT/ORG
LEAD
ATTIT
FORCES

WASSERMAN P.,MEASUREMENT AND ANALYSIS OF
ORGANIZATIONAL PERFORMANCE. FINAN MARKET EX/STRUC
TEC/DEV EDU/PROP CONTROL ROUTINE TASK...MGT 20.
PAGE 62 G1220
B59
BIBLIOG/A
ECO/TAC
OP/RES
EFFICIENCY

TARKOWSKI Z.M.,"SCIENTISTS VERSUS ADMINISTRATORS:
AN APPROACH TOWARD ACHIEVING GREATER
UNDERSTANDING." UK EXEC EFFICIENCY 20. PAGE 53
G1052
L59
INGP/REL
GP/REL
ADMIN
EX/STRUC

BENDIX R.,"INDUSTRIALIZATION, IDEOLOGIES, AND
SOCIAL STRUCTURE" (BMR)" UK USA-45 USSR STRUCT
WORKER GP/REL EFFICIENCY...IDEA/COMP 20. PAGE 6
G0117
S59
INDUS
ATTIT
MGT
ADMIN

SHEENAN D.,"PUBLIC CORPORATIONS AND PUBLIC ACTION."
UK ADMIN CONTROL REPRESENT SOCISM 20. PAGE 50 G0990
S59
ECO/DEV
EFFICIENCY
EX/STRUC
EXEC

CHAPPLE E.D.,THE MEASURE OF MANAGEMENT. USA+45
WORKER ADMIN GP/REL EFFICIENCY...DECISION
ORG/CHARTS SIMUL 20. PAGE 11 G0221
B61
MGT
OP/RES
PLAN

GLADDEN E.N.,BRITISH PUBLIC SERVICE ADMINISTRATION.
UK...CHARTS 20. PAGE 21 G0419
B61
EFFICIENCY
ADMIN
EX/STRUC
EXEC

MCCRACKEN H.L.,KEYNESIAN ECONOMICS IN THE STREAM OF
ECONOMIC THOUGHT. FINAN MARKET BARGAIN EFFICIENCY
OPTIMAL...PHIL/SCI CONCPT IDEA/COMP BIBLIOG 18/20
KEYNES/JM. PAGE 37 G0732
B61
ECO/TAC
DEMAND
ECOMETRIC

NAKICENOVIC S.,NUCLEAR ENERGY IN YUGOSLAVIA.
YUGOSLAVIA AGRI INDUS CREATE OP/RES ROUTINE
EFFICIENCY KNOWL...HEAL STAT CHARTS LAB/EXP BIBLIOG
20. PAGE 41 G0802
B61
R+D
ECO/DEV
TEC/DEV
NUC/PWR

NOVE A.,THE SOVIET ECONOMY. USSR ECO/DEV FINAN
NAT/G ECO/TAC PRICE ADMIN EFFICIENCY MARXISM
...TREND BIBLIOG 20. PAGE 42 G0828
B61
PLAN
PRODUC
POLICY

HAINES G.,"THE COMPUTER AS A SMALL-GROUP MEMBER."
DELIB/GP BAL/PWR TASK 20. PAGE 24 G0467
S61
INGP/REL
COMPUTER
PROB/SOLV
EFFICIENCY

BERKELEY E.C.,THE COMPUTER REVOLUTION. WOR+45
CREATE TEC/DEV EFFICIENCY TECHRACY...SOC TREND 20.
PAGE 7 G0128
B62
COMPUTER
CONTROL
AUTOMAT
SOCIETY

DUCKWORTH W.E.,A GUIDE TO OPERATIONAL RESEARCH.
INDUS PLAN PROB/SOLV EXEC EFFICIENCY PRODUC KNOWL
...MGT MATH STAT SIMUL METH 20 MONTECARLO. PAGE 16
G0319
B62
OP/RES
GAME
DECISION
ADMIN

DUPRE J.S.,SCIENCE AND THE NATION: POLICY AND
POLITICS. USA+45 LAW ACADEM FORCES ADMIN CIVMIL/REL
GOV/REL EFFICIENCY PEACE...TREND 20 SCI/ADVSRY.
PAGE 16 G0322
B62
R+D
INDUS
TEC/DEV
NUC/PWR

KARNJAHAPRAKORN C.,MUNICIPAL GOVERNMENT IN THAILAND
AS AN INSTITUTION AND PROCESS OF SELF-GOVERNMENT.
THAILAND CULTURE FINAN EX/STRUC LEGIS PLAN CONTROL
GOV/REL EFFICIENCY ATTIT...POLICY 20. PAGE 29 G0578
B62
LOC/G
MUNIC
ORD/FREE
ADMIN

MACHLUP F.,THE PRODUCTION AND DISTRIBUTION OF
KNOWLEDGE IN THE UNITED STATES. USA+45 COM/IND
INDUS SCHOOL SECT WORKER COMPUTER CREATE CIVMIL/REL
COST EFFICIENCY WEALTH 20. PAGE 35 G0688
B62
ACADEM
TEC/DEV
EDU/PROP
R+D

MARTINS A.F.,REVOLUCAO BRANCA NO CAMPO. L/A+17C
SERV/IND DEMAND EFFICIENCY PRODUC...POLICY
METH/COMP. PAGE 36 G0717
B62
AGRI
ECO/UNDEV
TEC/DEV
NAT/COMP

DAWSON R.H.,"CONGRESSIONAL INNOVATION AND
INTERVENTION IN DEFENSE POLICY: LEGISLATIVE
AUTHORIZATION OF WEAPONS SYSTEMS." CONSTN PLAN
ARMS/CONT GOV/REL EFFICIENCY PEACE NEW/LIB OLD/LIB.
PAGE 14 G0281
S62
LEGIS
PWR
CONTROL
WEAPON

DONNELLY D.,"THE POLITICS AND ADMINISTRATION OF
PLANNING." UK ROUTINE FEDERAL 20. PAGE 16 G0307
S62
GOV/REL
EFFICIENCY
ADMIN
EX/STRUC

LITTERER J.A.,ORGANIZATIONS: STRUCTURE AND
BEHAVIOR. PLAN DOMIN CONTROL LEAD ROUTINE SANCTION
INGP/REL EFFICIENCY PRODUC DRIVE RIGID/FLEX PWR.
PAGE 34 G0674
B63
ADMIN
CREATE
MGT
ADJUST

MARSCH P.E.,FEDERAL AID TO SCIENCE EDUCATION: TWO
PROGRAMS. USA+45 SCHOOL RECEIVE EFFICIENCY 20.
PAGE 36 G0711
B63
EDU/PROP
PHIL/SCI
NAT/G
METH/COMP

MCDONOUGH A.M.,INFORMATION ECONOMICS AND MANAGEMENT
SYSTEMS. ECO/DEV OP/RES AUTOMAT EFFICIENCY 20.
PAGE 37 G0735
B63
COMPUT/IR
MGT
CONCPT

COMPUTER

B63

US ATOMIC ENERGY COMMISSION.ATOMIC ENERGY IN THE METH/COMP
SOVIET UNION: TRIP REPORT OF THE US ATOMIC ENERGY OP/RES
DELEGATION, MAY 1933. USSR R+D NAT/G CONSULT CREATE TEC/DEV
DIPLOM ADMIN ROUTINE EFFICIENCY PRODUC KNOWL SKILL NUC/PWR
...NAT/COMP 20 AEC TRAVEL TREATY. PAGE 56 G1107

B63

US SENATE COMM APPROPRIATIONS.PERSONNEL ADMIN
ADMINISTRATION AND OPERATIONS OF AGENCY FOR FOR/AID
INTERNATIONAL DEVELOPMENT: SPECIAL HEARING. FINAN EFFICIENCY
LEAD COST UTIL SKILL...CHARTS 20 CONGRESS AID DIPLOM
CIVIL/SERV. PAGE 60 G1175

S63

KOLDZIEF E.A.."CONGRESSIONAL RESPONSIBILITY FOR THE LEGIS
COMMON DEFENSE: THE MONEY PROBLEM." PLAN DEBATE NAT/G
EFFICIENCY ATTIT PWR DECISION. PAGE 31 G0612 FORCES
POLICY

B64

FOGELMAN E..HIROSHIMA: THE DECISION TO USE THE A- INTELL
BOMB. USA-45 DIPLOM EFFICIENCY PEACE...ANTHOL DECISION
BIBLIOG T 20 CHINJAP. PAGE 19 G0375 NUC/PWR
WAR

B64

HAMMOND P.E..SOCIOLOGISTS AT WORK. VOL/ASSN OP/RES R+D
TEC/DEV CONFER ROUTINE TASK EFFICIENCY...MGT BIOG
NEW/IDEA STYLE SAMP. PAGE 24 G0478 SOC

B64

MANSFIELD E..MONOPOLY POWER AND ECONOMIC LG/CO
PERFORMANCE: AN INTRODUCTION TO A CURRENT ISSUE OF PWR
PUBLIC POLICY. ECO/DEV INDUS NAT/G PLAN CAP/ISM ECO/TAC
PRICE CONTROL LOBBY EFFICIENCY PRODUC...POLICY 20 MARKET
CONGRESS KENNEDY/JF MONOPOLY. PAGE 36 G0701

B65

DORFMAN R..MEASURING BENEFITS OF GOVERNMENT PLAN
INVESTMENTS. ECO/DEV R+D ECO/TAC PROFIT UTIL...MGT RATION
GEN/METH. PAGE 16 G0308 EFFICIENCY
OPTIMAL

B65

FOSTER P..EDUCATION AND SOCIAL CHANGE IN GHANA. SCHOOL
GHANA CULTURE STRUCT ECO/UNDEV TEC/DEV REGION CREATE
EFFICIENCY LITERACY ALL/VALS SOVEREIGN...STAT SOCIETY
METH/COMP 19/20 GOLD/COAST. PAGE 20 G0385

B65

HITCH C.J..DECISION-MAKING FOR DEFENSE. USA+45 DECISION
CREATE BUDGET COERCE WAR WEAPON EFFICIENCY...SIMUL OP/RES
20. PAGE 26 G0515 PLAN
FORCES

B65

KANTOROVICH L.V..THE BEST USE OF ECONOMIC PLAN
RESOURCES. USSR SOCIETY FINAN ACT/RES TEC/DEV MATH
ECO/TAC PRICE CONTROL COST DEMAND EFFICIENCY DECISION
OPTIMAL...MGT STAT. PAGE 29 G0572

B65

MELMANS S..OUR DEPLETED SOCIETY. SPACE USA+45 CIVMIL/REL
ECO/DEV FORCES BUDGET ECO/TAC ADMIN WEAPON INDUS
EFFICIENCY 20 COLD/WAR. PAGE 38 G0753 EDU/PROP
CONTROL

B65

THAYER F.C. JR..AIR TRANSPORT POLICY AND NATIONAL AIR
SECURITY: A POLITICAL, ECONOMIC, AND MILITARY FORCES
ANALYSIS. DIST/IND OP/RES PLAN TEC/DEV DIPLOM DETER CIVMIL/REL
WAR COST EFFICIENCY...POLICY BIBLIOG 20 DEPT/DEFEN ORD/FREE
FAA CAB. PAGE 54 G1066

B65

UN.SPACE ACTIVITIES AND RESOURCES: REVIEW OF UNITED SPACE
NATION'S NATIONAL AND INTERNATIONAL PROGRAMS. NUC/PWR
INT/ORG LABOR PLAN TEC/DEV DIPLOM EFFICIENCY HEALTH FOR/AID
...GOV/COMP 20 UN. PAGE 55 G1086 PEACE

B65

US DEPARTMENT OF ARMY.MILITARY PROTECTIVE FORCES
CONSTRUCTION: NUCLEAR WARFARE AND CHEMICAL AND CONSTRUC
BIOLOGICAL OPERATIONS (MANUAL). OP/RES TEC/DEV RISK TASK
COERCE NUC/PWR WAR WEAPON EFFICIENCY UTIL BIO/SOC HEALTH
HABITAT ORD/FREE 20. PAGE 57 G1117

B65

US SENATE COMM GOVT OPERATIONS.ORGANIZATION OF ADMIN
FEDERAL EXECUTIVE DEPARTMENTS AND AGENCIES: REPORT EX/STRUC
OF MARCH 23, 1965. USA+45 FORCES LEGIS DIPLOM GOV/REL
ROUTINE CIVMIL/REL EFFICIENCY FEDERAL...MGT STAT. ORG/CHARTS
PAGE 60 G1179

B65

VERMOT-GAUCHY M..L'EDUCATION NATIONALE DANS LA ACADEM
FRANCE DE 1975. FRANCE FUT CULTURE ELITES R+D CREATE
SCHOOL PLAN EDU/PROP EFFICIENCY...POLICY PREDICT TREND
CHARTS INDEX 20. PAGE 61 G1195 INTELL

S65

BALDWIN H.."SLOW-DOWN IN THE PENTAGON." USA+45 RECORD
CREATE PLAN GOV/REL CENTRAL COST EFFICIENCY PWR R+D
...MGT MCNAMARA/R. PAGE 5 G0088 WEAPON
ADMIN

S65

ETZIONI A.."ON THE NATIONAL GUIDANCE OF SCIENCE." PHIL/SCI
USA+45 FINAN NAT/G LEGIS GIVE 20. PAGE 18 G0353 CREATE
POLICY
EFFICIENCY

S65

GRENIEWSKI H.."INTENTION AND PERFORMANCE: A PRIMER SIMUL
OF CYBERNETICS OF PLANNING." EFFICIENCY OPTIMAL GAME
KNOWL SKILL...DECISION MGT EQUILB. PAGE 23 G0448 GEN/METH
PLAN

S65

HIBBS A.R.."SPACE TECHNOLOGY* THE THREAT AND THE SPACE
PROMISE." FUT VOL/ASSN TEC/DEV NUC/PWR COST ARMS/CONT
EFFICIENCY UTIL UN TREATY. PAGE 26 G0510 PREDICT

B66

ALEXANDER Y..INTERNATIONAL TECHNICAL ASSISTANCE ECO/TAC
EXPERTS* A CASE STUDY OF THE U.N. EXPERIENCE. INT/ORG
ECO/UNDEV CONSULT EX/STRUC CREATE PLAN DIPLOM ADMIN
FOR/AID TASK EFFICIENCY...ORG/CHARTS UN. PAGE 2 MGT
G0038

B66

AMERICAN ASSEMBLY COLUMBIA U.A WORLD OF NUCLEAR NUC/PWR
POWERS? FUT WOR+45 ECO/DEV BAL/PWR ECO/TAC CONTROL DIPLOM
RISK EFFICIENCY ATTIT PWR...METH/COMP ANTHOL 20. TEC/DEV
PAGE 3 G0049 ARMS/CONT

B66

GORDON G..THE LEGISLATIVE PROCESS AND DIVIDED LEGIS
GOVERNMENT; A CASE STUDY OF THE 86TH CONGRESS. HABITAT
USA+45 POL/PAR PROVS PROB/SOLV BAL/PWR CHOOSE CHIEF
REPRESENT EFFICIENCY ATTIT...POLICY DECISION STAT NAT/G
20 CONGRESS EISNHWR/DD. PAGE 22 G0434

B66

WOLFERS A..THE UNITED STATES IN A DISARMED WORLD: A ARMS/CONT
STUDY OF THE US OUTLINE FOR GENERAL AND COMPLETE POLICY
DISARMAMENT. USA+45 NAT/G CONTROL DETER NUC/PWR FORCES
EFFICIENCY...ANTHOL 20. PAGE 64 G1255 PEACE

S66

FLEMING W.G.."AUTHORITY, EFFICIENCY, AND ROLE DOMIN
STRESS: PROBLEMS IN THE DEVELOPMENT OF EAST AFRICAN EFFICIENCY
BUREAUCRACIES." AFR UGANDA STRUCT PROB/SOLV ROUTINE COLONIAL
INGP/REL ROLE...MGT SOC GP/COMP GOV/COMP 20 ADMIN
TANGANYIKA AFRICA/E. PAGE 19 G0371

S66

RIZOS E.J.."SCIENCE AND TECHNOLOGY IN COUNTRY ADMIN
DEVELOPMENT* TOWARDS AN UNDERSTANDING OF THE ROLE TEC/DEV
OF PUBLIC ADMINISTRATION." WOR+45 STRUCT INT/ORG ECO/UNDEV
EX/STRUC CREATE PLAN PROB/SOLV EFFICIENCY ROLE PHIL/SCI
DECISION. PAGE 47 G0924

S66

TURKEVICH J.."SOVIET SCIENCE APPRAISED." USA+45 R+D USSR
ACADEM FORCES DIPLOM EDU/PROP WAR EFFICIENCY PEACE TEC/DEV
SKILL OBS. PAGE 55 G1081 NAT/COMP
ATTIT

B67

AMERICAN FRIENDS SERVICE COMM.IN PLACE OF WAR. PEACE
NAT/G ACT/RES DIPLOM ADMIN NUC/PWR EFFICIENCY PACIFISM
...POLICY 20. PAGE 3 G0053 WAR
DETER

B67

BUDER S..PULLMAN: AN EXPERIMENT IN INDUSTRIAL ORDER DIST/IND
AND COMMUNITY PLANNING, 1880-1930. USA-45 SOCIETY INDUS
LABOR LG/CO CREATE PROB/SOLV CONTROL GP/REL MUNIC
EFFICIENCY ATTIT...MGT BIBLIOG 19/20 PULLMAN. PLAN
PAGE 9 G0184

B67

DE JOUVENAL B..THE ART OF CONJECTURE. WOR+45 FUT
EFFICIENCY PERCEPT KNOWL...DECISION PHIL/SCI CONCPT PREDICT
METH/COMP BIBLIOG 20. PAGE 15 G0285 SIMUL
METH

ELDREDGE H.W.,TAMING MEGALOPOLIS; HOW TO MANAGE AN
URBANIZED WORLD. WOR+45 SOCIETY ECO/DEV ECO/UNDEV
NAT/G COMPUTER CREATE PARTIC EFFICIENCY WEALTH
...MGT ANTHOL. PAGE 17 G0342
B67
MUNIC
TEC/DEV
PLAN
PROB/SOLV

ENKE S.,DEFENSE MANAGEMENT. USA+45 R+D FORCES
WORKER PLAN ECO/TAC ADMIN NUC/PWR BAL/PAY UTIL
WEALTH...MGT DEPT/DEFEN. PAGE 18 G0348
B67
DECISION
DELIB/GP
EFFICIENCY
BUDGET

HODGKINSON R.G.,THE ORIGINS OF THE NATIONAL HEALTH
SERVICE: THE MEDICAL SERVICES OF THE NEW POOR LAW,
1834-1871. UK INDUS MUNIC WORKER PROB/SOLV
EFFICIENCY ATTIT HEALTH WEALTH SOCISM...JURID
SOC/WK 19/20. PAGE 26 G0519
B67
HEAL
NAT/G
POLICY
LAW

MOORE J.R.,THE ECONOMIC IMPACT OF THE TVA. AGRI
INDUS PLAN BARGAIN CONTROL REGION GOV/REL DEMAND
EFFICIENCY SOCISM 20 TVA. PAGE 40 G0780
B67
ECO/UNDEV
ECO/DEV
NAT/G
CREATE

SALMOND J.A.,THE CIVILIAN CONSERVATION CORPS,
1933-1942. USA-45 NAT/G CREATE EXEC EFFICIENCY
WEALTH...BIBLIOG 20 ROOSEVLT/F. PAGE 48 G0954
B67
ADMIN
ECO/TAC
TASK
AGRI

SCHON D.A.,TECHNOLOGY AND CHANGE* THE NEW
HERACLITUS. TEC/DEV CONTROL COST DEMAND EFFICIENCY
RIGID/FLEX...MYTH 20. PAGE 49 G0975
B67
INDUS
PROB/SOLV
R+D
CREATE

SKOLNIKOFF E.B.,SCIENCE, TECHNOLOGY, AND AMERICAN
FOREIGN POLICY. SPACE USA+45 INT/ORG TEC/DEV
ARMS/CONT NUC/PWR 29 DEPT/STATE. PAGE 51 G1010
B67
PHIL/SCI
DIPLOM
NAT/G
EFFICIENCY

ZUCKERMAN S.,SCIENTISTS AND WAR. ELITES INDUS
DIPLOM CENTRAL EFFICIENCY KNOWL 20. PAGE 65 G1271
B67
R+D
CONSULT
ACT/RES
GP/REL

PASLEY R.S.,"ORGANIZATIONAL CONFLICTS OF INTEREST
IN GOVERNMENT CONTRACTS." ELITES R+D ROUTINE
NUC/PWR DEMAND EFFICIENCY 20. PAGE 44 G0860
L67
NAT/G
ECO/TAC
RATION
CONTROL

RUTH J.M.,"THE ADMINISTRATION OF WATER RESOURCES IN
GUATEMALA." GUATEMALA L/A+17C DIST/IND LOC/G NAT/G
EX/STRUC ADMIN GOV/REL DEMAND EQUILIB WEALTH...GEOG
MGT 20. PAGE 48 G0952
L67
EFFICIENCY
ECO/UNDEV
PLAN
ACT/RES

ALBAUM G.,"INFORMATION FLOW AND DECENTRALIZED
DECISION MAKING IN MARKETING." EX/STRUC COMPUTER
OP/RES PROB/SOLV EFFICIENCY OPTIMAL...METH/COMP
ORG/CHARTS 20. PAGE 2 G0033
S67
LG/CO
ROUTINE
KNOWL
MARKET

ALLEE D.,"AMERICAN AGRICULTURE - ITS RESOURCE
ISSUES FOR THE COMING YEARS." FUT USA+45 PLAN
PROB/SOLV 20. PAGE 2 G0043
S67
AGRI
SOCIETY
EFFICIENCY
AUTOMAT

ATKIN J.M.,"THE FEDERAL GOVERNMENT, BIG BUSINESS,
AND COLLEGES OF EDUCATION." PROF/ORG CONSULT CREATE
PLAN PROB/SOLV ADMIN EFFICIENCY. PAGE 4 G0075
S67
SCHOOL
ACADEM
NAT/G
INDUS

CARR E.H.,"REVOLUTION FROM ABOVE." USSR STRATA
FINAN INDUS NAT/G DOMIN LEAD GP/REL INGP/REL OWN
PRODUC PWR 20 STALIN/J. PAGE 11 G0214
S67
AGRI
POLICY
COM
EFFICIENCY

CARY G.D.,"THE QUIET REVOLUTION IN COPYRIGHT* THE
END OF THE 'PUBLICATION' CONCEPT." USA+45 LAW
OP/RES TEC/DEV CONFER DEBATE EFFICIENCY...JURID
CONGRESS. PAGE 11 G0217
S67
COM/IND
POLICY
LICENSE
PRESS

CHRIST R.F.,"REORGANIZATION OF FRENCH ARMED
FORCES." FRANCE CREATE PLAN TEC/DEV BAL/PWR DOMIN
COERCE CENTRAL EFFICIENCY 20. PAGE 12 G0229
S67
CHIEF
DETER
NUC/PWR
FORCES

EDMONDS M.,"INTERNATIONAL COLLABORATION IN WEAPONS
PROCUREMENT* THE IMPLICATIONS OF THE ANGLO-FRENCH
CASE." FRANCE UK CONSULT OP/RES PROB/SOLV TEC/DEV
CONFER CONTROL EFFICIENCY 20. PAGE 17 G0334
S67
DIPLOM
VOL/ASSN
BAL/PWR
ARMS/CONT

GAUSSENS J.,"THE APPLICATIONS OF NUCLEAR ENERGY -
TECHNICAL, ECONOMIC AND SOCIAL ASPECTS." WOR+45
INDUS R+D ACT/RES EFFICIENCY PRODUC SKILL PREDICT.
PAGE 21 G0413
S67
NUC/PWR
TEC/DEV
ECO/DEV
ADJUST

HODGE G.,"THE RISE AND DEMISE OF THE UN TECHNICAL
ASSISTANCE ADMINISTRATION." RISK TASK INGP/REL
CONSEN EFFICIENCY 20 UN. PAGE 26 G0516
S67
ADMIN
TEC/DEV
EX/STRUC
INT/ORG

KAYSEN C.,"DATA BANKS AND DOSSIERS." FUT USA+45
COM/IND NAT/G PLAN PROB/SOLV TEC/DEV BUDGET ADMIN
ROUTINE. PAGE 30 G0588
S67
CENTRAL
EFFICIENCY
CENSUS
ACT/RES

LEWIS R.L.,"GOAL AND NO GOAL* A NEW POLICY IN
SPACE." R+D BUDGET COST...POLICY DECISION PHIL/SCI.
PAGE 34 G0662
S67
SPACE
PLAN
EFFICIENCY
CREATE

MOOR E.J.,"THE INTERNATIONAL IMPACT OF AUTOMATION."
WOR+45 ACT/RES COMPUTER CREATE PLAN CAP/ISM ROUTINE
EFFICIENCY PREDICT. PAGE 39 G0779
S67
TEC/DEV
OP/RES
AUTOMAT
INDUS

PENNEY N.,"BANK STATEMENTS, CANCELLED CHECKS, AND
ARTICLE FOUR IN THE ELECTRONIC AGE." USA+45 TEC/DEV
COST EFFICIENCY WEALTH. PAGE 44 G0866
S67
CREATE
LAW
ADJUD
FINAN

RICH G.S.,"THE PROPOSED PATENT LEGISLATION* SOME
COMMENTS." USA+45 LAW R+D ACT/RES TEC/DEV CONFER
EFFICIENCY OWN JURID. PAGE 46 G0916
S67
LICENSE
POLICY
CREATE
CAP/ISM

RICHMAN B.M.,"SOVIET MANAGEMENT IN TRANSITION."
USSR FINAN MARKET EX/STRUC PLAN PROB/SOLV TEC/DEV
CONTROL LEAD CENTRAL EFFICIENCY...METH/COMP 20
REFORMERS. PAGE 47 G0917
S67
MGT
MARXISM
POLICY
AUTHORIT

ROBERTS E.B.,"THE PROBLEM OF AGING ORGANIZATIONS."
INTELL PROB/SOLV ADMIN EXEC FEEDBACK EFFICIENCY
PRODUC...GEN/LAWS 20. PAGE 47 G0926
S67
INDUS
R+D
MGT
PLAN

ROTHSTEIN R.L.,"NUCLEAR PROLIFERATION AND AMERICAN
POLICY." PROB/SOLV BAL/PWR DIPLOM ARMS/CONT
EFFICIENCY 20. PAGE 48 G0942
S67
NUC/PWR
CONTROL
DETER
WOR+45

SINGH B.,"ITALIAN EXPERIENCE IN REGIONAL ECONOMIC
DEVELOPMENT AND LESSONS FOR OTHER COUNTRIES."
EUR+WWI ITALY INDUS NAT/G ACT/RES REGION GP/REL
EFFICIENCY EQUILIB PRODUC WEALTH. PAGE 51 G1007
S67
ECO/UNDEV
PLAN
ECO/TAC
CONTROL

SKOLNIKOFF E.B.,"MAKING FOREIGN POLICY" PROB/SOLV
EFFICIENCY PERCEPT PWR...MGT METH/CNCPT CLASSIF 20.
PAGE 51 G1009
S67
TEC/DEV
CONTROL
USA+45
NAT/G

SLOAN P.,"FIFTY YEARS OF SOVIET RULE." USSR INDUS
EDU/PROP EFFICIENCY PRODUC HEALTH KNOWL MORAL
WEALTH MARXISM...POLICY 20. PAGE 51 G1011
S67
CREATE
NAT/G
PLAN
INSPECT

TIVEY L.,"THE POLITICAL CONSEQUENCES OF ECONOMIC
PLANNING." UK CONSTN INDUS ACT/RES ADMIN CONTROL
LOBBY REPRESENT EFFICIENCY SUPEGO SOVEREIGN
...DECISION 20. PAGE 55 G1074
S67
PLAN
POLICY
NAT/G

US SENATE COMM AERO SPACE SCI,POLICY PLANNING FOR
TECHNOLOGY TRANSFER (PAMPHLET). WOR+45 INDUS CREATE
PLAN EFFICIENCY ATTIT. PAGE 60 G1171
N67
TEC/DEV
POLICY
NAT/G
ECO/DEV

US SENATE COMM AERO SPACE SCI.HEARINGS BEFORE THE
COMMITTEE ON AERONAUTICAL AND SPACE SCIENCES UNITED
STATES SENATE NINETIETH CONGRESS (PAMPHLET). USA+45
CONSULT PLAN CONFER EFFICIENCY SENATE. PAGE 60
G1172
N67 NAT/G DELIB/GP SPACE CREATE

EFTA....EUROPEAN FREE TRADE ASSOCIATION

EGYPT....SEE ALSO ISLAM, UAR, EGYPT/ANC

EGYPT/ANC....ANCIENT EGYPT

EHRHARD J. G0335

EIB....EUROPEAN INVESTMENT BANK

EICHMANN/A....ADOLF EICHMANN

EICHNER A.S. G1214

EINAUDI L. G0336

EINSTEIN A. G0337,G0338

EINSTEIN/A....ALBERT EINSTEIN

NATHAN O..EINSTEIN ON PEACE. WOR+45 WOR-45 INTELL
NUC/PWR WAR PERSON MORAL...BIOG VAL/FREE NAZI 20
EINSTEIN/A. PAGE 41 G0807
B61 CONCPT PEACE

EISENDRATH C. G0339

EISENMENGER R.W. G0340

EISNHWR/DD....PRESIDENT DWIGHT DAVID EISENHOWER

US OFFICE OF THE PRESIDENT,REPORT TO CONGRESS ON
THE MUTUAL SECURITY PROGRAM FOR THE SIX MONTHS
ENDED DECEMBER 31, 1955. ASIA USSR ECO/DEV
ECO/UNDEV INT/ORG CREATE TEC/DEV BAL/PWR ECO/TAC
AGREE DETER COST ORD/FREE 20 DEPT/STATE DEPT/DEFEN
EISNHWR/DD. PAGE 59 G1158
B56 DIPLOM FORCES PLAN FOR/AID

CARPER E.T..THE DEFENSE APPROPRIATIONS RIDER
(PAMPHLET). USA+45 CONSTN CHIEF DELIB/GP LEGIS
BUDGET LOBBY CIVMIL/REL...POLICY 20 CONGRESS
EISNHWR/DD DEPT/DEFEN PRESIDENT BOSTON. PAGE 11
G0212
B60 GOV/REL ADJUD LAW CONTROL

SCHILLING W.R.,STRATEGY, POLITICS, AND DEFENSE
BUDGETS. USA+45 R+D NAT/G CONSULT DELIB/GP FORCES
LEGIS ACT/RES PLAN BAL/PWR LEGIT EXEC NUC/PWR
RIGID/FLEX PWR...TREND COLD/WAR CONGRESS 20
EISNHWR/DD. PAGE 49 G0968
B62 ROUTINE POLICY

GORDON G..THE LEGISLATIVE PROCESS AND DIVIDED
GOVERNMENT; A CASE STUDY OF THE 86TH CONGRESS.
USA+45 POL/PAR PROVS PROB/SOLV BAL/PWR CHOOSE
REPRESENT EFFICIENCY ATTIT...POLICY DECISION STAT
20 CONGRESS EISNHWR/DD. PAGE 22 G0434
B66 LEGIS HABITAT CHIEF NAT/G

EL/SALVADR....EL SALVADOR; SEE ALSO L/A+17C

ELDERSVELD S.J. G0341

ELDREDGE H.W. G0342

ELDRIDGE H.T. G0343

ELECT/COLL....ELECTORAL COLLEGE

ELECTIONS....SEE CHOOSE

ELECTORAL COLLEGE....SEE ELECT/COLL

ELIOT T.H. G0720

ELITES....POWER-DOMINANT GROUPINGS OF A SOCIETY

LASSWELL H.D.,THE ANALYSIS OF POLITICAL BEHAVIOUR:
AN EMPIRICAL APPROACH. WOR+45 CULTURE NAT/G FORCES
EDU/PROP ADMIN ATTIT PERCEPT KNOWL...PHIL/SCI PSY
SOC NEW/IDEA OBS INT GEN/METH NAZI 20. PAGE 32
G0639
B47 R+D ACT/RES ELITES

MANNHEIM K.,FREEDOM, POWER, AND DEMOCRATIC
PLANNING. FUT USSR WOR+45 ELITES INTELL SOCIETY
B50 TEC/DEV PLAN

NAT/G EDU/PROP ROUTINE ATTIT DRIVE SUPEGO SKILL
...POLICY PSY CONCPT TREND GEN/LAWS 20. PAGE 35
G0700
CAP/ISM UK

BUTOW R.J.C.,JAPAN'S DECISION TO SURRENDER. USA-45
USSR CHIEF FORCES DOMIN NUC/PWR...BIBLIOG 20 TREATY
CHINJAP. PAGE 10 G0198
B54 ELITES DIPLOM WAR PEACE

JANOWITZ M.,"MILITARY ELITES AND THE STUDY OF WAR."
USA+45 WOR-45 STRATA NAT/G PROF/ORG TEC/DEV DOMIN
EDU/PROP COERCE WAR ATTIT RIGID/FLEX PWR RESPECT
...MGT TREND STERTYP GEN/METH 20. PAGE 28 G0558
S57 FORCES ELITES

TAYLOR P.S.,"THE RELATION OF RESEARCH TO
LEGISLATIVE AND ADMINISTRATIVE DECISIONS." ELITES
ACT/RES PLAN PROB/SOLV CONFER CHOOSE POLICY.
PAGE 54 G1059
S57 DECISION LEGIS MGT PWR

KEISER N.F.,"PUBLIC RESPONSIBILITY AND FEDERAL
ADVISORY GROUPS: A CASE STUDY." NAT/G ADMIN CONTROL
LOBBY...POLICY 20. PAGE 30 G0590
S58 REPRESENT ELITES GP/REL EX/STRUC

SINGER J.D.,"THREAT PERCEPTION AND THE ARMAMENT
TENSION DILEMMA." WOR+45 WOR-45 ELITES INT/ORG
NAT/G DELIB/GP PLAN LEGIT COERCE DETER ATTIT
RIGID/FLEX PWR...DECISION PSY 20. PAGE 51 G1002
S58 PERCEPT ARMS/CONT BAL/PWR

COLUMBIA U BUREAU APPL SOC R, ATTITUDES OF
PROMINENT AMERICANS TOWARD "WORLD PEACE THROUGH
WORLD LAW" (SUPRA-NATL ORGANIZATION FOR WAR
PREVENTION). USA+45 USSR ELITES FORCES PLAN
PROB/SOLV CONTROL WAR PWR...POLICY SOC QU IDEA/COMP
20 UN. PAGE 45 G0888
B59 ATTIT ACT/RES INT/LAW STAT

JANOWITZ M.,"CHANGING PATTERNS OF ORGANIZATIONAL
AUTHORITY: THE MILITARY ESTABLISHMENT" (BMR)"
USA+45 ELITES STRUCT EX/STRUC PLAN DOMIN AUTOMAT
NUC/PWR WEAPON 20. PAGE 28 G0559
S59 FORCES AUTHORIT ADMIN TEC/DEV

GRANICK D.,THE RED EXECUTIVE. COM USA+45 SOCIETY
ECO/DEV INDUS NAT/G POL/PAR EX/STRUC PLAN ECO/TAC
EDU/PROP ADMIN EXEC ATTIT DRIVE...GP/COMP 20.
PAGE 22 G0440
B60 PWR STRATA USSR ELITES

JANOWITZ M.,THE PROFESSIONAL SOLDIER. CULTURE
STRATA STRUCT FAM PROB/SOLV TEC/DEV COERCE WAR
CIVMIL/REL NAT/LISM AGE HEREDITY ALL/VALS CONSERVE
...MGT WORSHIP. PAGE 28 G0560
B60 FORCES MYTH LEAD ELITES

HUTCHINSON C.E.,"AN INSTITUTE FOR NATIONAL SECURITY
AFFAIRS." USA+45 R+D NAT/G CONSULT TOP/EX ACT/RES
CREATE PLAN TEC/DEV EDU/PROP ROUTINE NUC/PWR ATTIT
ORD/FREE PWR...DECISION MGT PHIL/SCI CONCPT RECORD
GEN/LAWS GEN/METH 20. PAGE 27 G0539
S60 POLICY METH/CNCPT ELITES DIPLOM

CARNELL F..THE POLITICS OF THE NEW STATES: A SELECT
ANNOTATED BIBLIOGRAPHY WITH SPECIAL REFERENCE TO
THE COMMONWEALTH. CONSTN ELITES LABOR NAT/G POL/PAR
EX/STRUC DIPLOM ADJUD ADMIN...GOV/COMP 20
COMMONWLTH. PAGE 11 G0210
B61 BIBLIOG/A AFR ASIA COLONIAL

ROSENAU J.N.,INTERNATIONAL POLITICS AND FOREIGN
POLICY: A READER IN RESEARCH AND THEORY. ELITES
ATTIT SOVEREIGN...DECISION CHARTS HYPO/EXP GAME
SIMUL ANTHOL BIBLIOG METH 20. PAGE 48 G0936
B61 ACT/RES DIPLOM CONCPT POLICY

DYKMAN J.W.,"REVIEW ARTICLE* PLANNING AND DECISION
THEORY." ELITES LOC/G MUNIC CONSULT ADMIN...POLICY
MGT. PAGE 17 G0327
S61 DECISION PLAN RATIONAL

WILTZ J.E.,IN SEARCH OF PEACE: THE SENATE MUNITIONS
INQUIRY, 1934-36. EUR+WWI USA-45 ELITES INDUS LG/CO
LEGIS INT/TRADE LOBBY NEUTRAL ARMS/CONT...POLICY
CONGRESS 20 LEAGUE/NAT PRESIDENT SENATE CONSCRIPTN.
PAGE 64 G1246
B63 DELIB/GP PROFIT WAR WEAPON

NIEBURG H.,"EURATOM: A STUDY IN COALITION
POLITICS." EUR+WWI UK USA+45 ELITES NAT/G DELIB/GP
LEGIS TOP/EX ECO/TAC NUC/PWR ATTIT ORD/FREE PWR
L63 VOL/ASSN ACT/RES

TOT/POP EEC OEEC 20 NATO EURATOM. PAGE 42 G0820

S63
DUBRIDGE L.A.,"POLICY AND THE SCIENTISTS." ELITES   POLICY
PROB/SOLV ROLE KNOWL PWR. PAGE 16 G0318   PHIL/SCI
  ACADEM
  DECISION

S63
WOHLSTETTER A.,"SCIENTISTS, SEERS AND STRATEGY."   INTELL
USA+45 ELITES R+D NAT/G CONSULT FORCES TOP/EX   ACT/RES
EDU/PROP ARMS/CONT KNOWL ORD/FREE...DECISION MYTH
20. PAGE 64 G1253

B64
EDELMAN M.,THE SYMBOLIC USES OF POWER. USA+45   CLIENT
EX/STRUC CONTROL GP/REL INGP/REL...MGT T. PAGE 17   PWR
G0333   EXEC
  ELITES

B65
CHENG C.-Y.,SCIENTIFIC AND ENGINEERING MANPOWER IN   WORKER
COMMUNIST CHINA, 1949-1963. CHINA/COM USSR ELITES   CONSULT
ECO/DEV R+D ACADEM LABOR NAT/G EDU/PROP CONTROL   MARXISM
UTIL...POLICY BIBLIOG 20. PAGE 12 G0226   BIOG

B65
LAPP R.E.,THE NEW PRIESTHOOD; THE SCIENTIFIC ELITE   TEC/DEV
AND THE USES OF POWER. USA+45 ELITES INTELL SOCIETY   TECHRACY
R+D NAT/G CHIEF LEGIS CIVMIL/REL GP/REL PWR 20   CONTROL
PRESIDENT CONGRESS. PAGE 32 G0635   POPULISM

B65
SCHEINMAN L.,ATOMIC ENERGY POLICY IN FRANCE UNDER   NUC/PWR
THE FOURTH REPUBLIC. FRANCE UK USA+45 ELITES   NAT/G
POL/PAR PLAN PROB/SOLV DIPLOM LEAD GOV/REL   DELIB/GP
...BIBLIOG 20 DEGAULLE/C. PAGE 49 G0962   POLICY

B65
STEINER G.A.,THE CREATIVE ORGANIZATION. ELITES   CREATE
LG/CO PLAN PROB/SOLV TEC/DEV INSPECT CAP/ISM   MGT
CONTROL EXEC PERSON...METH/COMP HYPO/EXP 20.   ADMIN
PAGE 52 G1034   SOC

B65
VERMOT-GAUCHY M.,L'EDUCATION NATIONALE DANS LA   ACADEM
FRANCE DE 1975. FRANCE FUT CULTURE ELITES R+D   CREATE
SCHOOL PLAN EDU/PROP EFFICIENCY...POLICY PREDICT   TREND
CHARTS INDEX 20. PAGE 61 G1195   INTELL

L65
PILISUK M.,"IS THERE A MILITARY INDUSTRIAL COMPLEX   ELITES
WHICH PREVENTS PEACE CONSENSUS; COUNTERVAILING   WEAPON
POWER IN PLURALIST SYSTEMS." INDUS R+D ACADEM   PEACE
FEEDBACK CIVMIL/REL ADJUST CONSEN ATTIT RIGID/FLEX   ARMS/CONT
...CENSUS IDEA/COMP BIBLIOG. PAGE 45 G0878

B66
GOULD J.M.,THE TECHNICAL ELITE. INDUS LABOR   ECO/DEV
TECHRACY...POLICY DECISION STAT CHARTS 20. PAGE 22   TEC/DEV
G0437   ELITES
  TECHNIC

B66
MILLAR R.,THE NEW CLASSES. UK ELITES SOCIETY INDUS   STRUCT
AUTOMAT GP/REL SOC/INTEG 20 INDUS/REV. PAGE 39   STRATA
G0770   TEC/DEV
  CREATE

S66
COHEN A.,"THE TECHNOLOGY/ELITE APPROACH TO THE   ECO/UNDEV
DEVELOPMENTAL PROCESS* PERUVIAN CASE STUDY."   ELITES
L/A+17C STRUCT CREATE ECO/TAC FOR/AID CIVMIL/REL   PERU
MARXISM TECHRACY HYPO/EXP. PAGE 12 G0239

S66
MALENBAUM W.,"GOVERNMENT, ENTREPRENEURSHIP, AND   ECO/TAC
ECONOMIC GROWTH IN POOR LANDS." ELITES ECO/UNDEV   PLAN
INDUS CREATE DRIVE. PAGE 35 G0697   CONSERVE
  NAT/G

B67
CONNOLLY W.E.,POLITICAL SCIENCE AND IDEOLOGY.   PWR
UTOPIA ATTIT KNOWL...MAJORIT EPIST PHIL/SCI SOC   PLURISM
IDEA/COMP HYPO/EXP GEN/LAWS METH HUME/D MARX/KARL.   ELITES
PAGE 13 G0250   CONCPT

B67
HEILBRONER R.L.,THE LIMITS OF AMERICAN CAPITALISM.   ELITES
FUT ECO/DEV INDUS LG/CO EX/STRUC LEAD PWR TECHRACY   CREATE
20. PAGE 25 G0502   TEC/DEV
  CAP/ISM

B67
WYLIE J.C.,MILITARY STRATEGY: GENERAL THEORY OF   FORCES
POWER CONTROL. CUBA USA+45 VIETNAM/N WOR+45 ELITES   PLAN

CONTROL WAR PWR...POLICY METH/COMP 20 MAO. PAGE 64   DECISION
G1260   IDEA/COMP

B67
ZUCKERMAN S.,SCIENTISTS AND WAR. ELITES INDUS   R+D
DIPLOM CENTRAL EFFICIENCY KNOWL 20. PAGE 65 G1271   CONSULT
  ACT/RES
  GP/REL

L67
PASLEY R.S.,"ORGANIZATIONAL CONFLICTS OF INTEREST   NAT/G
IN GOVERNMENT CONTRACTS." ELITES R+D ROUTINE   ECO/TAC
NUC/PWR DEMAND EFFICIENCY 20. PAGE 44 G0860   RATION
  CONTROL

S67
CHIU S.M.,"CHINA'S MILITARY POSTURE." CHINA/COM   FORCES
ELITES NAT/G POL/PAR TEC/DEV ECO/TAC DOMIN CONTROL   CIVMIL/REL
LEAD REV MARXISM 20 MAO. PAGE 12 G0228   NUC/PWR
  DIPLOM

S67
DE NEUFVILLE R.,"EDUCATION AT THE ACADEMIES."   FORCES
USA+45 ELITES CONSULT EX/STRUC COMPUTER PLAN   ACADEM
PROB/SOLV TASK CIVMIL/REL ORD/FREE 20. PAGE 15   TEC/DEV
G0286   SKILL

S67
DEUTSCH K.W.,"ARMS CONTROL AND EUROPEAN UNITY* THE   ARMS/CONT
NEXT TEN YEARS." USA+45 ELITES NAT/G BAL/PWR DIPLOM   PEACE
NUC/PWR...INT KNO/TEST NATO EEC. PAGE 15 G0300   REGION
  PLAN

S67
KRAUS J.,"A MARXIST IN GHANA." GHANA ELITES CHIEF   MARXISM
PROB/SOLV TEC/DEV DIPLOM ECO/TAC COLONIAL PARTIC   PLAN
PWR 20 NKRUMAH/K. PAGE 31 G0618   ATTIT
  CREATE

S67
MALONE D.K.,"THE COMMANDER AND THE COMPUTER."   COMPUTER
USA+45 OP/RES PROB/SOLV TEC/DEV AUTOMAT CENTRAL 20.   FORCES
PAGE 35 G0698   ELITES
  PLAN

S38
LUNDBERG G.A.,"THE CONCEPT OF LAW IN THE SOCIAL   EPIST
SCIENCES"(BMR)" CULTURE INTELL SOCIETY STRUCT   GEN/LAWS
CREATE...NEW/IDEA 20. PAGE 34 G0678   CONCPT
  PHIL/SCI

B40
ZNANIECKI F.,THE SOCIAL ROLE OF THE MAN OF   ROLE
KNOWLEDGE. UNIV SOCIETY STRUCT TEC/DEV...EPIST   INTELL
PHIL/SCI SOC NEW/IDEA 20. PAGE 65 G1269   KNOWL
  INGP/REL

PLAN

B62
ROSS R.,SYMBOLS AND CIVILIZATION. UNIV CULTURE SECT PHIL/SCI
CREATE ALL/VALS MORAL ART/METH. PAGE 48 G0939   KNOWL
                                                       EPIST
                                                       SOCIETY

S67
SINGH B.,"ITALIAN EXPERIENCE IN REGIONAL ECONOMIC   ECO/UNDEV
DEVELOPMENT AND LESSONS FOR OTHER COUNTRIES."   PLAN
EUR+WWI ITALY INDUS NAT/G ACT/RES REGION GP/REL   ECO/TAC
EFFICIENCY EQUILIB PRODUC WEALTH. PAGE 51 G1007   CONTROL

B63
HOFSTADTER R.,ANTI-INTELLECTUALISM IN AMERICAN   INTELL
LIFE. USA+45 AGRI INDUS ACADEM TEC/DEV EDU/PROP   EPIST
INGP/REL ATTIT...SOC WORSHIP 20 MCCARTHY/J   CULTURE
STEVENSN/A. PAGE 26 G0522   SOCIETY

S65
GRENIEWSKI H.,"INTENTION AND PERFORMANCE: A PRIMER   SIMUL
OF CYBERNETICS OF PLANNING." EFFICIENCY OPTIMAL   GAME
KNOWL SKILL...DECISION MGT EQULIB. PAGE 23 G0448   GEN/METH
                                                      PLAN

B66
MUMFORD L.,THE MYTH OF THE MACHINE: TECHNICS AND   WORKER
HUMAN DEVELOPMENT. UNIV WOR-45 CREATE AUTOMAT   TEC/DEV
PERCEPT KNOWL...EPIST PHIL/SCI SOC LING TREND   SOCIETY
SOC/INTEG 20 MARX/KARL. PAGE 40 G0795

ERDEMLI....ERDEMLI, TURKEY

B67
CONNOLLY W.E.,POLITICAL SCIENCE AND IDEOLOGY.   PWR
UTOPIA ATTIT KNOWL...MAJORIT EPIST PHIL/SCI SOC   PLURISM
IDEA/COMP HYPO/EXP GEN/LAWS METH HUME/D MARX/KARL.   ELITES
PAGE 13 G0250   CONCPT

ERSKINE H.G. G0350

ESPIONAGE....ESPIONAGE

EPISTEMOLOGY....SEE EPIST

ESTEP R. G0351

EPTA....EXPANDED PROGRAM OF TECHNICAL ASSISTANCE

ESTIMATION....SEE COST

EQUILIB....EQUILIBRIUM; SEE ALSO BAL/PWR

ESTONIA....SEE ALSO USSR

ESTRANGEMENT....SEE STRANGE

B39
FULLER G.H.,A SELECTED LIST OF REFERENCES ON THE   BIBLIOG
EXPANSION OF THE US NAVY, 1933-1939 (PAMPHLET).   FORCES
MOD/EUR USA-45 NAT/G PLAN DIPLOM DOMIN RISK   WEAPON
ARMS/CONT EQUILIB PWR 20 NAVY. PAGE 20 G0399   WAR

ETHIC....PERSONAL ETHICS

ETHIOPIA....SEE ALSO AFR

B60
SILK L.S.,THE RESEARCH REVOLUTION. USA+45 FINAN   ECO/DEV
CAP/ISM ECO/TAC PRICE EQUILIB PRODUC...STAT TREND   R+D
CHARTS. PAGE 51 G0997   TEC/DEV
                                                      PROB/SOLV

ETHNICITY....SEE RACE/REL, CULTURE

ETHNOGRAPHY....SEE CULTURE

ETIQUET....ETIQUETTE, STYLING, FASHION, MANNERS

B65
US DEPARTMENT OF DEFENSE.US SECURITY ARMS CONTROL,   BIBLIOG/A
AND DISARMAMENT 1961-1965 (PAMPHLET). CHINA/COM COM   ARMS/CONT
GERMANY/W ISRAEL SPACE USA+45 USSR WOR+45 FORCES   NUC/PWR
EDU/PROP DETER EQUILIB PEACE ALL/VALS...GOV/COMP 20   DIPLOM
NATO. PAGE 57 G1118

ETZIONI A. G0352,G0353

EUGENICS....SEE BIO/SOC+GEOG

EUGENIE....EMPRESS EUGENIE (FRANCE)

S65
KUZMACK A.M.,"TECHNOLOGICAL CHANGE AND STABLE   R+D
DETERRENCE." CREATE EDU/PROP ARMS/CONT WEAPON   DETER
CHOOSE COST DRIVE PERCEPT...RECORD STERTYP TIME.   EQUILIB
PAGE 32 G0627

EUR+WWI....EUROPE SINCE WORLD WAR I

EURATOM....EUROPEAN ATOMIC ENERGY COMMUNITY

B66
FALK R.A.,ON MINIMIZING THE USE OF NUCLEAR WEAPONS;   DIPLOM
THREE ESSAYS; RESEARCH MONOGRAPH NO. 23. WOR+45   EQUILIB
STRUCT CREATE NUC/PWR REV CONSERVE...POLICY   PHIL/SCI
NET/THEORY IDEA/COMP GEN/LAWS GEN/METH. PAGE 18   PROB/SOLV
G0359

N
FOREIGN AFFAIRS. SPACE WOR+45 WOR-45 CULTURE   BIBLIOG
ECO/UNDEV FINAN NAT/G TEC/DEV INT/TRADE ARMS/CONT   DIPLOM
NUC/PWR...POLICY 20 UN EURATOM ECSC EEC. PAGE 1   INT/ORG
G0004   INT/LAW

B67
BAUMOL W.J.,BUSINESS BEHAVIOR, VALUE AND GROWTH   ALL/IDEOS
(REV. ED.). WOR+45 FINAN LG/CO TEC/DEV CAP/ISM   PHIL/SCI
DEMAND EQUILIB...METH/COMP SIMUL 20. PAGE 5 G0105   PLAN
                                                      ECO/DEV

B63
MAYNE R.,THE COMMUNITY OF EUROPE. UK CONSTN NAT/G   EUR+WWI
CONSULT DELIB/GP CREATE PLAN ECO/TAC ADMIN   INT/ORG
ROUTINE ORD/FREE PWR WEALTH...CONCPT TIME/SEQ EEC   REGION
EURATOM 20. PAGE 37 G0724

B67
COMMONER B.,SCIENCE AND SURVIVAL. SOCIETY INDUS   PHIL/SCI
PLAN NUC/PWR KNOWL PWR...SOC 20 AEC. PAGE 13 G0247   CONTROL
                                                     PROB/SOLV
                                                     EQUILIB

L63
NIEBURG H.,"EURATOM: A STUDY IN COALITION   VOL/ASSN
POLITICS." EUR+WWI UK USA+45 ELITES NAT/G DELIB/GP   ACT/RES
LEGIS TOP/EX ECO/TAC NUC/PWR ATTIT ORD/FREE PWR
TOT/POP EEC OEEC 20 NATO EURATOM. PAGE 42 G0820

B67
GROSSMAN G.,ECONOMIC SYSTEMS. USA+45 USA-45 USSR   ECO/DEV
YUGOSLAVIA WORKER CAP/ISM PRICE GP/REL EQUILIB   PLAN
WEALTH MARXISM SOCISM...MGT METH/COMP 19/20.   TEC/DEV
PAGE 23 G0456   DEMAND

B65
HASSON J.A.,THE ECONOMICS OF NUCLEAR POWER. INDIA   NUC/PWR
UK USA+45 WOR+45 INT/ORG TEC/DEV COST...SOC STAT   INDUS
CHARTS 20 EURATOM. PAGE 25 G0490   ECO/DEV
                                                     METH

L67
RUTH J.M.,"THE ADMINISTRATION OF WATER RESOURCES IN   EFFICIENCY
GUATEMALA." GUATEMALA L/A+17C DIST/IND LOC/G NAT/G   ECO/UNDEV
EX/STRUC ADMIN GOV/REL DEMAND EQUILIB WEALTH...GEOG   PLAN
MGT 20. PAGE 48 G0952   ACT/RES

B65
US CONGRESS JT ATOM ENRGY COMM.ATOMIC ENERGY   NUC/PWR
LEGISLATION THROUGH 89TH CONGRESS, 1ST SESSION.   FORCES
USA+45 LAW INT/ORG DELIB/GP BUDGET DIPLOM 20 AEC   PEACE
CONGRESS CASEBOOK EURATOM IAEA. PAGE 57 G1114   LEGIS

S67
D'AMATO D.,"LEGAL ASPECTS OF THE FRENCH NUCLEAR   INT/LAW
TESTS." FRANCE WOR+45 ACT/RES COLONIAL RISK GOV/REL   DIPLOM
EQUILIB ORD/FREE PWR DECISION. PAGE 14 G0268   NUC/PWR
                                                     ADJUD

B67
SCHEINMAN L.,EURATOM; NUCLEAR INTEGRATION IN   INT/ORG
EUROPE. EX/STRUC LEAD 20 EURATOM. PAGE 49 G0963   NAT/LISM
                                                     NUC/PWR
                                                     DIPLOM

S67
HAZARD J.N.,"POST-DISARMAMENT INTERNATIONAL LAW."   INT/LAW
FUT USSR WOR+45 INT/ORG DELIB/GP FORCES DETER   ARMS/CONT
EQUILIB SOVEREIGN MARXISM 20 UN. PAGE 25 G0496   PWR

S67
EYRAUD M.,"LA FRANCE FACE A UN EVENTUEL TRAITE DE   NUC/PWR
NON DISSEMINATION DES ARMES NUCLEAIRES." FRANCE   ARMS/CONT
USA+45 EXTR/IND INDUS R+D INT/ORG ACT/RES TEC/DEV   POLICY
AGREE PRODUC ATTIT 20 TREATY AEC EURATOM. PAGE 18
G0355

S67
WEIL G.L.,"THE MERGER OF THE INSTITUTIONS OF THE   ECO/TAC
EUROPEAN COMMUNITIES" EUR+WWI ECO/DEV INT/TRADE   INT/ORG
CONSEN PLURISM...DECISION MGT 20 EEC EURATOM ECSC   CENTRAL
TREATY. PAGE 62 G1223   INT/LAW

EURCOALSTL....EUROPEAN COAL AND STEEL COMMUNITY; SEE ALSO
    VOL/ASSN, INT/ORG

B62
SCHMITT H.A.,THE PATH TO EUROPEAN UNITY. EUR+WWI   INT/ORG
USA+45 PLAN TEC/DEV DIPLOM FOR/AID CONFER...INT/LAW   INT/TRADE
20 EEC EURCOALSTL MARSHL/PLN UNIFICA. PAGE 49 G0971   REGION
   ECO/DEV

EURCT/JUST....EUROPEAN COURT OF JUSTICE

EUROPE....SEE EUR+WWI, MOD/EUR

B53
LANGER W.L.,THE UNDECLARED WAR, 1940-1941. EUR+WWI   WAR
GERMANY USA-45 USSR AIR FORCES TEC/DEV CONFER   POLICY
CONTROL COERCE PERCEPT ORD/FREE PWR 20 CHINJAP   DIPLOM
EUROPE. PAGE 32 G0634

B59
EMME E.M.,THE IMPACT OF AIR POWER - NATIONAL   DETER
SECURITY AND WORLD POLITICS. USA+45 USSR FORCES   AIR
DIPLOM WEAPON PEACE TOTALISM...POLICY NAT/COMP 20   WAR
EUROPE. PAGE 18 G0346   ORD/FREE

EUROPE/E....EASTERN EUROPE (ALL EUROPEAN COMMUNIST NATIONS)

EUROPE/W....WESTERN EUROPE (NON-COMMUNIST EUROPE, EXCLUDING
    GREECE, TURKEY, SCANDINAVIA, AND THE BRITISH ISLES)

N47
FOX W.T.R.,UNITED STATES POLICY IN A TWO POWER   DIPLOM
WORLD. COM USA+45 USSR FORCES DOMIN AGREE NEUTRAL   FOR/AID
NUC/PWR ORD/FREE SOVEREIGN 20 COLD/WAR TREATY   POLICY
EUROPE/W INTERVENT. PAGE 20 G0389

EUROPEAN ATOMIC ENERGY COMMUNITY....SEE EURATOM

EUROPEAN COAL AND STEEL COMMUNITY....SEE EURCOALSTL

EUROPEAN CONVENTION ON HUMAN RIGHTS....SEE ECHR

EUROPEAN COURT OF JUSTICE....SEE EURCT/JUST

EUROPEAN ECONOMIC COMMUNITY....SEE EEC

EUROPEAN FREE TRADE ASSOCIATION....SEE EFTA

EUROPEAN INVESTMENT BANK....SEE EIB

EVERS/MED....MEDGAR EVERS

EWALD R.F. G0354

EX POST FACTO LAWS....SEE EXPOSTFACT

EX/IM/BANK....EXPORT-IMPORT BANK

EX/STRUC....EXECUTIVE ESTABLISHMENTS

N
ADVANCED MANAGEMENT. INDUS EX/STRUC WORKER OP/RES   MGT
...DECISION BIBLIOG/A 20. PAGE 1 G0003   ADMIN
   LABOR
   GP/REL

N
THE MANAGEMENT REVIEW. FINAN EX/STRUC PROFIT   LABOR
BIBLIOG/A. PAGE 1 G0007   MGT
   ADMIN
   MARKET

N
PRINCETON UNIVERSITY.SELECTED REFERENCES: BIBLIOG/A
INDUSTRIAL RELATIONS SECTION. USA+45 EX/STRUC   LABOR
WORKER TEC/DEV...MGT 20. PAGE 45 G0892   INDUS
   GP/REL

B25
MATHEWS J.M.,AMERICAN STATE GOVERNMENT. USA-45   PROVS
LOC/G CHIEF EX/STRUC LEGIS ADJUD CONTROL CT/SYS   ADMIN
ROUTINE GOV/REL PWR 20 GOVERNOR. PAGE 37 G0721   FEDERAL
   CONSTN

B40
HELLMAN F.S.,THE NEW DEAL: SELECTED LIST OF   BIBLIOG/A
REFERENCES. USA-45 FINAN LABOR EX/STRUC CREATE   ECO/TAC
INT/TRADE ADMIN CT/SYS 20 SUPREME/CT. PAGE 26 G0505   PLAN
   POLICY

B40
MORSTEIN-MARX F.,PUBLIC MANAGEMENT IN THE NEW   EX/STRUC
DEMOCRACY. REPRESENT...MGT 20. PAGE 40 G0786   ADMIN
   EXEC
   PWR

B44
BARKER E.,THE DEVELOPMENT OF PUBLIC SERVICES IN   GOV/COMP
WESTERN WUROPE: 1660-1930. FRANCE GERMANY UK SCHOOL   ADMIN
CONTROL REPRESENT ROLE...WELF/ST 17/20. PAGE 5   EX/STRUC
G0095

B46
NORTHROP F.S.C.,THE MEETING OF EAST AND WEST.   DRIVE
EUR+WWI FUT MOD/EUR UNIV WOR+45 WOR-45 INTELL   TREND
SOCIETY EX/STRUC TOP/EX ACT/RES LEGIT CHOOSE ATTIT   PEACE
PERCEPT RIGID/FLEX ALL/VALS...POLICY JURID OBS
TOT/POP. PAGE 42 G0826

B47
BECK H.P.,MEN WHO CONTROL OUR UNIVERSITIES.   EDU/PROP
EX/STRUC CHOOSE INGP/REL DISCRIM PERSON WEALTH   ACADEM
...POLICY TREND CON/ANAL CHARTS BIBLIOG. PAGE 6   CONTROL
G0112   LEAD

B49
LEPAWSKY A.,ADMINISTRATION. FINAN INDUS LG/CO   ADMIN
SML/CO INGP/REL PERS/REL COST EFFICIENCY OPTIMAL   MGT
SKILL 20. PAGE 33 G0656   WORKER
   EX/STRUC

B49
MCLEAN J.M.,THE PUBLIC SERVICE AND UNIVERSITY   ACADEM
EDUCATION. UK USA-45 DELIB/GP EX/STRUC TOP/EX ADMIN   NAT/G
...GOV/COMP METH/COMP NAT/COMP ANTHOL 20. PAGE 38   EXEC
G0746   EDU/PROP

S49
SOUERS S.W.,"POLICY FORMULATION FOR NATIONAL   DELIB/GP
SECURITY." EX/STRUC FORCES PROB/SOLV DIPLOM CONFER   CHIEF
EXEC ARMS/CONT DETER NUC/PWR GOV/REL PEACE   DECISION
COLD/WAR. PAGE 52 G1022   POLICY

B50
HUZAR E.,THE PURSE AND THE SWORD: CONTROL OF THE   CIVMIL/REL
ARMY BY CONGRESS THROUGH MILITARY APPROPRIATIONS   BUDGET
1933-1950. NAT/G DELIB/GP EX/STRUC FORCES PROB/SOLV   CONTROL
BARGAIN CONFER ADMIN ROUTINE GOV/REL EFFICIENCY   LEGIS
...POLICY COLD/WAR. PAGE 27 G0541

B52
APPADORAI A.,THE SUBSTANCE OF POLITICS (6TH ED.).   PHIL/SCI
EX/STRUC LEGIS DIPLOM CT/SYS CHOOSE FASCISM MARXISM   NAT/G
SOCISM...BIBLIOG T. PAGE 3 G0062

B53
MACK R.T.,RAISING THE WORLDS STANDARD OF LIVING.   WOR+45
IRAN INT/ORG VOL/ASSN EX/STRUC ECO/TAC WEALTH...MGT   FOR/AID
METH/CNCPT STAT CONT/OBS INT TOT/POP VAL/FREE 20   INT/TRADE
UN. PAGE 35 G0690

S53
PERKINS J.A.,"ADMINISTRATION OF THE NATIONAL   CONTROL
SECURITY PROGRAM." USA+45 EX/STRUC FORCES ADMIN   GP/REL
CIVMIL/REL ORD/FREE 20. PAGE 44 G0868   REPRESENT
   PROB/SOLV

B54
LOCKLIN D.P.,ECONOMICS OF TRANSPORTATION (4TH ED.).   ECO/DEV
USA+45 USA-45 SEA AIR LAW FINAN LG/CO EX/STRUC   DIST/IND
ADMIN CONTROL...STAT CHARTS 19/20 RAILROAD   ECO/TAC
PUB/TRANS. PAGE 34 G0675   TEC/DEV

S54
LONG N.E.,"PUBLIC POLICY AND ADMINISTRATION: THE   PROB/SOLV
GOALS OF RATIONALITY AND RESPONSIBILITY." EX/STRUC   EXEC
ADMIN LEAD 20. PAGE 34 G0676   REPRESENT

C54
CALDWELL L.K.,"THE GOVERNMENT AND ADMINISTRATION OF   PROVS
NEW YORK." LOC/G MUNIC POL/PAR SCHOOL CHIEF LEGIS   ADMIN
PLAN TAX CT/SYS...MGT SOC/WK BIBLIOG 20 NEWYORK/C.   CONSTN
PAGE 10 G0202   EX/STRUC

C54
ZELLER B.,"AMERICAN STATE LEGISLATURES: REPORT ON   REPRESENT
THE COMMITTEE ON AMERICAN LEGISLATURES." CONSTN   LEGIS
POL/PAR EX/STRUC CONFER ADMIN CONTROL EXEC LOBBY   PROVS
ROUTINE GOV/REL...POLICY BIBLIOG 20. PAGE 65 G1267   APPORT

B55
LIPPMAN W.,THE PUBLIC PHILOSOPHY. EX/STRUC TOP/EX   MAJORIT
LOBBY RATIONAL POPULISM...POLICY SOC CONCPT PREDICT   STRUCT
GP/COMP IDEA/COMP. PAGE 34 G0673   PWR
   TOTALISM

SMITHIES A.,THE BUDGETARY PROCESS IN THE UNITED
STATES. ECO/DEV AGRI EX/STRUC FORCES LEGIS
PROB/SOLV TAX ROUTINE EFFICIENCY...MGT CONGRESS
PRESIDENT. PAGE 52 G1016
B55
NAT/G
ADMIN
BUDGET
GOV/REL

KOENIG L.W.,THE TRUMAN ADMINISTRATION: ITS
PRINCIPLES AND PRACTICE. USA+45 POL/PAR CHIEF LEGIS
DIPLOM DEATH NUC/PWR WAR CIVMIL/REL PEACE
...DECISION 20 TRUMAN/HS PRESIDENT TREATY. PAGE 31
G0610
B56
ADMIN
POLICY
EX/STRUC
GOV/REL

REDFORD E.S.,PUBLIC ADMINISTRATION AND POLICY
FORMATION: STUDIES IN OIL, GAS, BANKING, RIVER
DEVELOPMENT AND CORPORATE INVESTIGATIONS. USA+45
CLIENT NAT/G ADMIN LOBBY REPRESENT GOV/REL INGP/REL
20. PAGE 46 G0908
B56
EX/STRUC
PROB/SOLV
CONTROL
EXEC

US DEPARTMENT OF THE ARMY,AMERICAN MILITARY
HISTORY. USA+45 USA-45 EX/STRUC PROB/SOLV TEC/DEV
DIPLOM NUC/PWR REV WAR WEAPON...PSY 18/20. PAGE 57
G1125
B56
BIBLIOG
FORCES
NAT/G

SCARROW H.A.,THE HIGHER PUBLIC SERVICE OF THE
COMMONWEALTH OF AUSTRALIA. LAW SENIOR LOBBY ROLE 20
AUSTRAL CIVIL/SERV COMMONWLTH. PAGE 49 G0959
B57
ADMIN
NAT/G
EX/STRUC
GOV/COMP

DAVIS K.C.,ADMINISTRATIVE LAW TREATISE (VOLS. I AND
IV). NAT/G JUDGE PROB/SOLV ADJUD GP/REL 20
SUPREME/CT. PAGE 14 G0278
B58
ADMIN
JURID
CT/SYS
EX/STRUC

ARGYRIS C.,"SOME PROBLEMS IN CONCEPTUALIZING
ORGANIZATIONAL CLIMATE: A CASE STUDY OF A BANK"
(BMR)" USA+45 EX/STRUC ADMIN PERS/REL ADJUST PERSON
...POLICY HYPO/EXP SIMUL 20. PAGE 3 G0064
S58
FINAN
CONCPT
LG/CO
INGP/REL

KEISER N.F.,"PUBLIC RESPONSIBILITY AND FEDERAL
ADVISORY GROUPS: A CASE STUDY." NAT/G ADMIN CONTROL
LOBBY...POLICY 20. PAGE 30 G0590
S58
REPRESENT
ELITES
GP/REL
EX/STRUC

WASSERMAN P.,MEASUREMENT AND ANALYSIS OF
ORGANIZATIONAL PERFORMANCE. FINAN MARKET EX/STRUC
TEC/DEV EDU/PROP CONTROL ROUTINE TASK...MGT 20.
PAGE 62 G1220
B59
BIBLIOG/A
ECO/TAC
OP/RES
EFFICIENCY

TARKOWSKI Z.M.,"SCIENTISTS VERSUS ADMINISTRATORS:
AN APPROACH TOWARD ACHIEVING GREATER
UNDERSTANDING." UK EXEC EFFICIENCY 20. PAGE 53
G1052
L59
INGP/REL
GP/REL
ADMIN
EX/STRUC

CALKINS R.D.,"THE DECISION PROCESS IN
ADMINISTRATION." EX/STRUC PROB/SOLV ROUTINE MGT.
PAGE 10 G0204
S59
ADMIN
OP/RES
DECISION
CON/ANAL

JANOWITZ M.,"CHANGING PATTERNS OF ORGANIZATIONAL
AUTHORITY: THE MILITARY ESTABLISHMENT" (BMR)"
USA+45 ELITES STRUCT EX/STRUC PLAN DOMIN AUTOMAT
NUC/PWR WEAPON 20. PAGE 28 G0559
S59
FORCES
AUTHORIT
ADMIN
TEC/DEV

SEIDMAN H.,"THE GOVERNMENT CORPORATION IN THE
UNITED STATES." USA+45 LEGIS ADMIN PLURISM 20.
PAGE 50 G0988
S59
CONTROL
GOV/REL
EX/STRUC
EXEC

SHEENAN D.,"PUBLIC CORPORATIONS AND PUBLIC ACTION."
UK ADMIN CONTROL REPRESENT SOCISM 20. PAGE 50 G0990
S59
ECO/DEV
EFFICIENCY
EX/STRUC
EXEC

STREAT R.,"GOVERNMENT CONSULTATION WITH INDUSTRY."
UK 20. PAGE 53 G1043
S59
REPRESENT
ADMIN
EX/STRUC
INDUS

BROOKINGS INSTITUTION,UNITED STATES FOREIGN POLICY:
STUDY NO 9: THE FORMULATION AND ADMINISTRATION OF
UNITED STATES FOREIGN POLICY. USA+45 WOR+45
B60
DIPLOM
INT/ORG
CREATE

EX/STRUC LEGIS BAL/PWR FOR/AID EDU/PROP CIVMIL/REL
GOV/REL...INT COLD/WAR. PAGE 9 G0174

GRANICK D.,THE RED EXECUTIVE. COM USA+45 SOCIETY
ECO/DEV INDUS NAT/G POL/PAR EX/STRUC PLAN ECO/TAC
EDU/PROP ADMIN EXEC ATTIT DRIVE...GP/COMP 20.
PAGE 22 G0440
B60
PWR
STRATA
USSR
ELITES

RAPOPORT A.,FIGHTS, GAMES AND DEBATES. INTELL
SOCIETY R+D EX/STRUC PERCEPT PERSON SKILL...PSY SOC
GAME. PAGE 46 G0902
B60
METH/CNCPT
MATH
DECISION
CON/ANAL

HAYTON R.D.,"THE ANTARCTIC SETTLEMENT OF 1959." FUT
USA+45 WOR+45 WOR-45 STRUCT R+D INT/ORG EX/STRUC
CREATE TEC/DEV LEGIT PEACE ATTIT SOVEREIGN
...TIME/SEQ 20 TREATY IGY. PAGE 25 G0495
S60
DELIB/GP
JURID
DIPLOM
REGION

LEAR J.,"PEACE: SCIENCE'S NEXT GREAT EXPLORATION."
USA+45 INT/ORG TOP/EX TEC/DEV EDU/PROP ROUTINE
PEACE KNOWL SKILL 20. PAGE 33 G0648
S60
EX/STRUC
ARMS/CONT
NUC/PWR

RAPP W.F.,"MANAGEMENT ANALYSIS AT THE HEADQUARTERS
OF FEDERAL AGENCIES." USA+45 NAT/G 20. PAGE 46
G0903
S60
INGP/REL
ADMIN
EX/STRUC
MGT

CARNELL F.,THE POLITICS OF THE NEW STATES: A SELECT
ANNOTATED BIBLIOGRAPHY WITH SPECIAL REFERENCE TO
THE COMMONWEALTH. CONSTN ELITES LABOR NAT/G POL/PAR
EX/STRUC DIPLOM ADJUD ADMIN...GOV/COMP 20
COMMONWLTH. PAGE 11 G0210
B61
BIBLIOG/A
AFR
ASIA
COLONIAL

GLADDEN E.N.,BRITISH PUBLIC SERVICE ADMINISTRATION.
UK...CHARTS 20. PAGE 21 G0419
B61
EFFICIENCY
ADMIN
EX/STRUC
EXEC

HELLER D.,THE KENNEDY CABINET--AMERICA'S MEN OF
DESTINY. NAT/G CHIEF CONSULT ADMIN CONTROL GOV/REL
...MGT 20 DEPT/LABOR DEPT/STATE DEPT/JUST
DEPT/DEFEN KENNEDY/J. PAGE 26 G0504
B61
EX/STRUC
CONFER
DELIB/GP
TOP/EX

KAHN H.,ON THERMONUCLEAR WAR. FUT UNIV WOR+45
ECO/DEV CONSULT EX/STRUC TOP/EX ACT/RES CREATE PLAN
COERCE WAR PERSON ALL/VALS...POLICY GEOG CONCPT
METH/CNCPT OBS TREND 20. PAGE 29 G0569
B61
DETER
NUC/PWR
SOCIETY

THOMPSON V.A.,"HIERARCHY, SPECIALIZATION, AND
ORGANIZATIONAL CONFLICT" (BMR)" WOR+45 STRATA
STRUCT WORKER TEC/DEV GP/REL INGP/REL ATTIT
AUTHORIT 20 BUREAUCRCY. PAGE 54 G1069
L61
PERS/REL
PROB/SOLV
ADMIN
EX/STRUC

BENNION E.G.,"ECONOMETRICS FOR MANAGEMENT." USA+45
INDUS EX/STRUC ACT/RES COMPUTER UTIL...MATH STAT
PREDICT METH/COMP HYPO/EXP. PAGE 6 G0122
S61
ECOMETRIC
MGT
SIMUL
DECISION

LYONS G.M.,"THE NEW CIVIL-MILITARY RELATIONS."
USA+45 NAT/G EX/STRUC TOP/EX PROB/SOLV ADMIN EXEC
PARTIC 20. PAGE 35 G0681
S61
CIVMIL/REL
PWR
REPRESENT

CHANDLER A.D.,STRATEGY AND STRUCTURE: CHAPTERS IN
THE HISTORY OF THE INDUSTRIAL ENTERPRISE. USA+45
USA-45 ECO/DEV EX/STRUC ECO/TAC EXEC...DECISION 20.
PAGE 11 G0220
B62
LG/CO
PLAN
ADMIN
FINAN

GRANICK D.,THE EUROPEAN EXECUTIVE. BELGIUM FRANCE
GERMANY/W UK INDUS LABOR LG/CO SML/CO EX/STRUC PLAN
TEC/DEV CAP/ISM COST DEMAND...POLICY CHARTS 20.
PAGE 22 G0441
B62
MGT
ECO/DEV
ECO/TAC
EXEC

KARNJAHAPRAKORN C.,MUNICIPAL GOVERNMENT IN THAILAND
AS AN INSTITUTION AND PROCESS OF SELF-GOVERNMENT.
THAILAND CULTURE FINAN EX/STRUC LEGIS PLAN CONTROL
GOV/REL EFFICIENCY ATTIT...POLICY 20. PAGE 29 G0578
B62
LOC/G
MUNIC
ORD/FREE
ADMIN

MARS D.,SUGGESTED LIBRARY IN PUBLIC ADMINISTRATION.
FINAN DELIB/GP EX/STRUC WORKER COMPUTER ADJUD
...DECISION PSY SOC METH/COMP 20. PAGE 36 G0710
B62
BIBLIOG
ADMIN
METH

MGT

B62
NEW ZEALAND COMM OF ST SERVICE,THE STATE SERVICES   ADMIN
IN NEW ZEALAND. NEW/ZEALND CONSULT EX/STRUC ACT/RES WORKER
...BIBLIOG 20. PAGE 42 G0818   TEC/DEV
                                                     NAT/G

B62
REICH C.A.,BUREAUCRACY AND THE FORESTS (PAMPHLET).   ADMIN
USA+45 LOBBY...POLICY MGT 20. PAGE 46 G0910   CONTROL
                                                     EX/STRUC
                                                     REPRESENT

B62
STAHL O.G.,PUBLIC PERSONNEL ADMINISTRATION. LOC/G   ADMIN
TOP/EX CREATE PLAN ROUTINE...TECHNIC MGT T. PAGE 52 WORKER
G1030   EX/STRUC
                                                     NAT/G

B62
STOVER C.F.,THE GOVERNMENT OF SCIENCE (PAMPHLET).   PHIL/SCI
USA+45 SOCIETY PROF/ORG EX/STRUC CREATE CONTROL   TEC/DEV
NUC/PWR WAR GOV/REL PEACE ORD/FREE 20. PAGE 53   LAW
G1041   NAT/G

L62
NEIBURG H.L.,"THE EISENHOWER AEC AND CONGRESS: A   CHIEF
STUDY IN EXECUTIVE-LEGISLATIVE RELATIONS." USA+45   LEGIS
NAT/G POL/PAR DELIB/GP EX/STRUC TOP/EX ADMIN EXEC   GOV/REL
LEAD ROUTINE PWR...POLICY COLD/WAR CONGRESS   NUC/PWR
PRESIDENT AEC. PAGE 41 G0816

S62
DONNELLY D.,"THE POLITICS AND ADMINISTRATION OF   GOV/REL
PLANNING." UK ROUTINE FEDERAL 20. PAGE 16 G0307   EFFICIENCY
                                                     ADMIN
                                                     EX/STRUC

S62
PHIPPS T.E.,"THE CASE FOR DETERRENCE." FUT WOR+45   ATTIT
SOCIETY EX/STRUC FORCES ACT/RES CREATE PLAN TEC/DEV COERCE
ROUTINE RIGID/FLEX ORD/FREE...POLICY MYTH NEW/IDEA   DETER
STERTYP COLD/WAR 20. PAGE 45 G0876   ARMS/CONT

B63
DEAN A.L.,FEDERAL AGENCY APPROACHES TO FIELD   ADMIN
MANAGEMENT (PAMPHLET). R+D DELIB/GP EX/STRUC   MGT
PROB/SOLV GOV/REL...CLASSIF BIBLIOG 20 FAA NASA   NAT/G
DEPT/HEW POSTAL/SYS IRS. PAGE 15 G0287   OP/RES

B63
GREEN H.P.,GOVERNMENT OF THE ATOM. USA+45 LEGIS   GOV/REL
PROB/SOLV ADMIN CONTROL PWR...POLICY DECISION 20   EX/STRUC
PRESIDENT CONGRESS. PAGE 22 G0443   NUC/PWR
                                                     DELIB/GP

B63
HATHAWAY D.A.,GOVERNMENT AND AGRICULTURE: PUBLIC   AGRI
POLICY IN A DEMOCRATIC SOCIETY. USA+45 LEGIS ADMIN   GOV/REL
EXEC LOBBY REPRESENT PWR 20. PAGE 25 G0491   PROB/SOLV
                                                     EX/STRUC

B63
HOWER R.M.,MANAGERS AND SCIENTISTS. EX/STRUC CREATE R+D
ADMIN REPRESENT ATTIT DRIVE ROLE PWR SKILL...SOC   MGT
INT. PAGE 27 G0532   PERS/REL
                                                     INGP/REL

S63
DELLIN L.A.D.,"BULGARIA UNDER SOVIET LEADERSHIP."   AGRI
BULGARIA COM USA+45 USSR ECO/DEV INDUS POL/PAR   NAT/G
EX/STRUC TOP/EX COERCE ATTIT RIGID/FLEX...POLICY   TOTALISM
TIME/SEQ 20. PAGE 15 G0293

S63
SCHMITT H.A.,"THE EUROPEAN COMMUNITIES." EUR+WWI   VOL/ASSN
FRANCE DELIB/GP EX/STRUC TOP/EX CREATE TEC/DEV   ECO/DEV
ECO/TAC LEGIT REGION COERCE DRIVE ALL/VALS
...METH/CNCPT EEC 20. PAGE 49 G0972

B64
EDELMAN M.,THE SYMBOLIC USES OF POWER. USA+45   CLIENT
EX/STRUC CONTROL GP/REL INGP/REL...MGT T. PAGE 17   PWR
G0333   EXEC
                                                     ELITES

B64
ETZIONI A.,THE MOON-DOGGLE: DOMESTIC AND   R+D
INTERNATIONAL IMPLICATIONS OF THE SPACE RACE. FUT   NAT/G
USA+45 WOR+45 INTELL ECO/DEV INDUS VOL/ASSN   DIPLOM
EX/STRUC FORCES LEGIS TOP/EX PLAN TEC/DEV ECO/TAC   SPACE
EDU/PROP KNOWL ORD/FREE PWR RESPECT WEALTH
TIME/SEQ. PAGE 18 G0352

B64
RIES J.C.,THE MANAGEMENT OF DEFENSE: ORGANIZATION   FORCES
AND CONTROL OF THE US ARMED SERVICES. PROF/ORG   ACT/RES
DELIB/GP EX/STRUC LEGIS GOV/REL PERS/REL CENTRAL   DECISION
RATIONAL PWR...POLICY TREND GOV/COMP BIBLIOG.   CONTROL
PAGE 47 G0920

B64
VAN DYKE V.,PRIDE AND POWER: THE RATIONALE OF THE   TEC/DEV
SPACE PROGRAM. FUT USA+45 INTELL R+D NAT/G POL/PAR   ATTIT
DELIB/GP EX/STRUC LEGIS TOP/EX ACT/RES PLAN ECO/TAC POLICY
EDU/PROP ORD/FREE PWR RESPECT SKILL...TIME/SEQ
VAL/FREE. PAGE 61 G1191

B65
INT. BANK RECONSTR. DEVELOP.,ECONOMIC DEVELOPMENT   INDUS
OF KUWAIT. ISLAM KUWAIT AGRI FINAN MARKET EX/STRUC   NAT/G
TEC/DEV ECO/TAC ADMIN WEALTH...OBS CON/ANAL CHARTS
20. PAGE 28 G0548

B65
REISS A.J. JR.,SCHOOLS IN A CHANGING SOCIETY.   SCHOOL
CULTURE PROB/SOLV INSPECT DOMIN CONFER INGP/REL   EX/STRUC
RACE/REL AGE/C AGE/Y ALL/VALS...ANTHOL SOC/INTEG 20 ADJUST
NEWYORK/C. PAGE 46 G0912   ADMIN

B65
US SENATE COMM GOVT OPERATIONS,ORGANIZATION OF   ADMIN
FEDERAL EXECUTIVE DEPARTMENTS AND AGENCIES: REPORT   EX/STRUC
OF MARCH 23, 1965. USA+45 FORCES LEGIS DIPLOM   GOV/REL
ROUTINE CIVMIL/REL EFFICIENCY FEDERAL...MGT STAT.   ORG/CHARTS
PAGE 60 G1179

L65
LASSWELL H.D.,"THE POLICY SCIENCES OF DEVELOPMENT." PWR
CULTURE SOCIETY EX/STRUC CREATE ADMIN ATTIT KNOWL   METH/CNCPT
...SOC CONCPT SIMUL GEN/METH. PAGE 33 G0644   DIPLOM

S65
FOX A.B.,"NATO AND CONGRESS." CONSTN DELIB/GP   CONTROL
EX/STRUC FORCES TOP/EX BUDGET NUC/PWR GOV/REL   DIPLOM
...GP/COMP CONGRESS NATO TREATY. PAGE 20 G0388

S65
LEISERSON A.,"SCIENTISTS AND THE POLICY PROCESS."   PHIL/SCI
USA+45 NAT/G LEAD PARTIC REPRESENT. PAGE 33 G0654   ADMIN
                                                     EX/STRUC
                                                     EXEC

B66
ALEXANDER Y.,INTERNATIONAL TECHNICAL ASSISTANCE   ECO/TAC
EXPERTS* A CASE STUDY OF THE U.N. EXPERIENCE.   INT/ORG
ECO/UNDEV CONSULT EX/STRUC CREATE PLAN DIPLOM   ADMIN
FOR/AID TASK EFFICIENCY...ORG/CHARTS UN. PAGE 2   MGT
G0038

B66
NIEBURG H.L.,IN THE NAME OF SCIENCE. USA+45   NAT/G
EX/STRUC LEGIS TEC/DEV BUDGET PAY AUTOMAT LOBBY PWR INDUS
...OBS 20. PAGE 42 G0822   TECHRACY

B66
ROSHOLT R.L.,AN ADMINISTRATIVE HISTORY OF NASA,   ADMIN
1958-1963. SPACE USA+45 FINAN LEAD...MGT CHARTS   EX/STRUC
BIBLIOG 20 NASA. PAGE 48 G0938   ADJUST
                                                     DELIB/GP

B66
US DEPARTMENT OF THE ARMY,COMMUNIST CHINA: A   BIBLIOG/A
STRATEGIC SURVEY: A BIBLIOGRAPHY (PAMPHLET NO.   MARXISM
20-67). CHINA/COM COM INDIA USSR NAT/G POL/PAR   S/ASIA
EX/STRUC FORCES NUC/PWR REV ATTIT...POLICY GEOG   DIPLOM
CHARTS. PAGE 58 G1133

S66
RIZOS E.J.,"SCIENCE AND TECHNOLOGY IN COUNTRY   ADMIN
DEVELOPMENT* TOWARDS AN UNDERSTANDING OF THE ROLE   TEC/DEV
OF PUBLIC ADMINISTRATION." WOR+45 STRUCT INT/ORG   ECO/UNDEV
EX/STRUC CREATE PLAN PROB/SOLV EFFICIENCY ROLE   PHIL/SCI
DECISION. PAGE 47 G0924

B67
GOLEMBIEWSKI R.T.,ORGANIZING MEN AND POWER: ADMIN
PATTERNS OF BEHAVIOR AND LINESTAFF MODELS. WOR+45   CONTROL
EX/STRUC ACT/RES DOMIN PERS/REL...NEW/IDEA 20.   SIMUL
PAGE 22 G0431   MGT

B67
HEILBRONER R.L.,THE LIMITS OF AMERICAN CAPITALISM.   ELITES
FUT ECO/DEV INDUS LG/CO EX/STRUC LEAD PWR TECHRACY   CREATE
20. PAGE 25 G0502   TEC/DEV
                                                     CAP/ISM

B67
HIRSCHMAN A.O.,DEVELOPMENT PROJECTS OBSERVED. INDUS ECO/UNDEV
INT/ORG CONSULT EX/STRUC CREATE OP/RES ECO/TAC   R+D

DEMAND...POLICY MGT METH/COMP 20 WORLD/BANK.   FINAN
PAGE 26 G0513   PLAN

                                                     B67
SCHEINMAN L.,EURATOM* NUCLEAR INTEGRATION IN   INT/ORG
EUROPE. EX/STRUC LEAD 20 EURATOM. PAGE 49 G0963   NAT/LISM
                                                     NUC/PWR
                                                     DIPLOM

                                                     B67
WARNER W.L.,THE EMERGENT AMERICAN SOCIETY VOL I,   ANTHOL
LARGE-SCALE ORGANIZATIONS. USA+45 USA-45 ACADEM   NAT/G
PROF/ORG SCHOOL SECT EX/STRUC TEC/DEV GP/REL   LABOR
...TREND CHARTS. PAGE 62 G1215   LG/CO

                                                     L67
RUTH J.M.,"THE ADMINISTRATION OF WATER RESOURCES IN EFFICIENCY
GUATEMALA." GUATEMALA L/A+17C DIST/IND LOC/G NAT/G   ECO/UNDEV
EX/STRUC ADMIN GOV/REL DEMAND EQUILIB WEALTH...GEOG PLAN
MGT 20. PAGE 48 G0952   ACT/RES

                                                     S67
ALBAUM G.,"INFORMATION FLOW AND DECENTRALIZED   LG/CO
DECISION MAKING IN MARKETING." EX/STRUC COMPUTER   ROUTINE
OP/RES PROB/SOLV EFFICIENCY OPTIMAL...METH/COMP   KNOWL
ORG/CHARTS 20. PAGE 2 G0033   MARKET

                                                     S67
CONWAY J.E.,"MAKING RESEARCH EFFECTIVE IN   ACT/RES
LEGISLATION." LAW R+D CONSULT EX/STRUC PLAN CONFER   POLICY
ADMIN LEAD ROUTINE TASK INGP/REL DECISION. PAGE 13   LEGIS
G0252   PROB/SOLV

                                                     S67
DE WEUFVILLE R.,"EDUCATION AT THE ACADEMIES."   FORCES
USA+45 ELITES CONSULT EX/STRUC COMPUTER PLAN   ACADEM
PROB/SOLV TASK CIVMIL/REL ORD/FREE 20. PAGE 15   TEC/DEV
G0286   SKILL

                                                     S67
HODGE G.,"THE RISE AND DEMISE OF THE UN TECHNICAL   ADMIN
ASSISTANCE ADMINISTRATION." RISK TASK INGP/REL   TEC/DEV
CONSEN EFFICIENCY 20 UN. PAGE 26 G0516   EX/STRUC
                                                     INT/ORG

                                                     S67
JONES G.S.,"STRATEGIC PLANNING." USA+45 EX/STRUC   PLAN
FORCES DETER WAR 20 PRESIDENT. PAGE 29 G0566   DECISION
                                                     DELIB/GP
                                                     POLICY

                                                     S67
LALL B.G.,"GAPS IN THE ABM DEBATE." NAT/G DIPLOM   NUC/PWR
DETER CIVMIL/REL 20. PAGE 32 G0630   ARMS/CONT
                                                     EX/STRUC
                                                     FORCES

                                                     S67
MACDONALD G.J.F.,"SCIENCE AND SPACE POLICY* HOW   SPACE
DOES IT GET PLANNED?" R+D CREATE TEC/DEV BUDGET   PLAN
ADMIN ROUTINE...DECISION NASA. PAGE 35 G0687   MGT
                                                     EX/STRUC

                                                     S67
RICHMAN B.M.,"SOVIET MANAGEMENT IN TRANSITION."   MGT
USSR FINAN MARKET EX/STRUC PLAN PROB/SOLV TEC/DEV   MARXISM
CONTROL LEAD CENTRAL EFFICIENCY...METH/COMP 20   POLICY
REFORMERS. PAGE 47 G0917   AUTHORIT

                                                     S67
VERGIN R.C.,"COMPUTER INDUCED ORGANIZATION   COMPUTER
CHANGES." FUT USA+45 R+D CREATE OP/RES TEC/DEV   DECISION
ADJUST CENTRAL...MGT INT CON/ANAL COMPUT/IR.   AUTOMAT
PAGE 61 G1194   EX/STRUC

                                                     S67
WILLIAMS C.,"REGIONAL MANAGEMENT OVERSEAS." USA+45   MGT
WOR+45 DIST/IND LG/CO EX/STRUC INT/TRADE TARIFFS   EUR+WWI
ADMIN TASK CENTRAL. PAGE 63 G1242   ECO/DEV
                                                     PLAN

EXEC....EXECUTIVE PROCESS

                                                     B40
MORSTEIN-MARX F.,PUBLIC MANAGEMENT IN THE NEW   EX/STRUC
DEMOCRACY. REPRESENT...MGT 20. PAGE 40 G0786   ADMIN
                                                     EXEC
                                                     PWR

                                                     S45
WHITE L.D.,"CONGRESSIONAL CONTROL OF THE PUBLIC   LEGIS
SERVICE." USA-45 NAT/G CONSULT DELIB/GP PLAN SENIOR EXEC
CONGRESS. PAGE 63 G1232   POLICY
                                                     CONTROL

                                                     B49
MCLEAN J.M.,THE PUBLIC SERVICE AND UNIVERSITY   ACADEM
EDUCATION. UK USA-45 DELIB/GP EX/STRUC TOP/EX ADMIN NAT/G
...GOV/COMP METH/COMP NAT/COMP ANTHOL 20. PAGE 38   EXEC
G0746   EDU/PROP

                                                     B49
ROSENHAUPT H.W.,HOW TO WAGE PEACE. USA+45 SOCIETY   INTELL
STRATA STRUCT R+D INT/ORG POL/PAR LEGIS ACT/RES   CONCPT
CREATE PLAN EDU/PROP ADMIN EXEC ATTIT ALL/VALS   DIPLOM
...TIME/SEQ TREND COLD/WAR 20. PAGE 48 G0937

                                                     S49
MERTON R.,"THE ROLE OF APPLIED SOCIAL SCIENCE IN   PLAN
THE FORMATION OF POLICY: A RESEARCH MEMORANDUM."   SOC
WOR+45 INDUS NAT/G EXEC ROUTINE CHOOSE ORD/FREE PWR DIPLOM
SKILL...POLICY MGT PSY METH/CNCPT TESTS CHARTS METH
VAL/FREE 20. PAGE 38 G0756

                                                     S49
SOUERS S.W.,"POLICY FORMULATION FOR NATIONAL   DELIB/GP
SECURITY." EX/STRUC FORCES PROB/SOLV DIPLOM CONFER   CHIEF
EXEC ARMS/CONT DETER NUC/PWR GOV/REL PEACE   DECISION
COLD/WAR. PAGE 52 G1022   POLICY

                                                     B51
MAASS A.,MUDDY WATERS: THE ARMY ENGINEERS AND THE   FORCES
NATIONS RIVERS. USA-45 PROF/ORG CONSULT LEGIS ADMIN GP/REL
EXEC ROLE PWR...SOC PRESIDENT 20. PAGE 35 G0682   LOBBY
                                                     CONSTRUC

                                                     B54
COMBS C.H.,DECISION PROCESSES. INTELL SOCIETY   MATH
DELIB/GP CREATE TEC/DEV DOMIN LEGIT EXEC CHOOSE   DECISION
DRIVE RIGID/FLEX KNOWL PWR...PHIL/SCI SOC
METH/CNCPT CONT/OBS REC/INT PERS/TEST SAMP/SIZ BIOG
SOC/EXP WORK. PAGE 13 G0245

                                                     S54
LONG N.E.,"PUBLIC POLICY AND ADMINISTRATION: THE   PROB/SOLV
GOALS OF RATIONALITY AND RESPONSIBILITY." EX/STRUC   EXEC
ADMIN LEAD 20. PAGE 34 G0676   REPRESENT

                                                     C54
ZELLER B.,"AMERICAN STATE LEGISLATURES: REPORT ON   REPRESENT
THE COMMITTEE ON AMERICAN LEGISLATURES." CONSTN   LEGIS
POL/PAR EX/STRUC CONFER ADMIN CONTROL EXEC LOBBY   PROVS
ROUTINE GOV/REL...POLICY BIBLIOG 20. PAGE 65 G1267   APPORT

                                                     B56
REDFORD E.S.,PUBLIC ADMINISTRATION AND POLICY   EX/STRUC
FORMATION: STUDIES IN OIL, GAS, BANKING, RIVER   PROB/SOLV
DEVELOPMENT AND CORPORATE INVESTIGATIONS. USA+45   CONTROL
CLIENT NAT/G ADMIN LOBBY REPRESENT GOV/REL INGP/REL EXEC
20. PAGE 46 G0908

                                                     S57
BAUMGARTEL H.,"LEADERSHIP STYLE AS A VARIABLE IN   LEAD
RESEARCH ADMINISTRATION." USA+45 ADMIN REPRESENT   EXEC
PERS/REL 20. PAGE 5 G0104   MGT
                                                     INGP/REL

                                                     B58
GANGE J.,UNIVERSITY RESEARCH ON INTERNATIONAL   R+D
AFFAIRS. USA+45 ACADEM INT/ORG CONSULT CREATE EXEC   MGT
ROUTINE...QUANT STAT INT STERTYP GEN/METH TOT/POP   DIPLOM
VAL/FREE 20. PAGE 21 G0407

                                                     L59
BURNS A.L.,"POWER POLITICS AND THE GROWING NUCLEAR   FORCES
CLUB." FUT WOR+45 TEC/DEV EXEC ARMS/CONT COERCE   BAL/PWR
DETER...DECISION HYPO/EXP 20. PAGE 10 G0192   NUC/PWR

                                                     L59
TARKOWSKI Z.M.,"SCIENTISTS VERSUS ADMINISTRATORS: INGP/REL
AN APPROACH TOWARD ACHIEVING GREATER   GP/REL
UNDERSTANDING." UK EXEC EFFICIENCY 20. PAGE 53   ADMIN
G1052   EX/STRUC

                                                     S59
DEUTSCH K.W.,"THE IMPACT OF SCIENCE AND TECHNOLOGY   PHIL/SCI
ON INTERNATIONAL POLITICS." UNIV INTELL NAT/G   MYTH
ACT/RES CREATE TEC/DEV EDU/PROP EXEC KNOWL...CONCPT DIPLOM
TREND TOT/POP 20. PAGE 15 G0297   NAT/LISM

                                                     S59
SEIDMAN H.,"THE GOVERNMENT CORPORATION IN THE   CONTROL
UNITED STATES." USA+45 LEGIS ADMIN PLURISM 20.   GOV/REL
PAGE 50 G0988   EX/STRUC
                                                     EXEC

                                                     S59
SHEENAN D.,"PUBLIC CORPORATIONS AND PUBLIC ACTION." ECO/DEV
UK ADMIN CONTROL REPRESENT SOCISM 20. PAGE 50 G0990 EFFICIENCY
                                                     EX/STRUC
                                                     EXEC

B60
ALBI F.,TRATADO DE LOS MODOS DE GESTION DE LAS   LOC/G
CORPORACIONES LOCALES. SPAIN FINAN NAT/G BUDGET   LAW
CONTROL EXEC ROUTINE GOV/REL ORD/FREE SOVEREIGN   ADMIN
...MGT 20. PAGE 2 G0034   MUNIC

B60
GRANICK D.,THE RED EXECUTIVE. COM USA+45 SOCIETY   PWR
ECO/DEV INDUS NAT/G POL/PAR EX/STRUC PLAN ECO/TAC   STRATA
EDU/PROP ADMIN EXEC ATTIT DRIVE...GP/COMP 20.   USSR
PAGE 22 G0440   ELITES

B60
WEBSTER J.A.,A GENERAL STUDY OF THE DEPARTMENT OF   ORD/FREE
DEFENSE INTERNAL SECURITY PROGRAM. USA+45 WORKER   PLAN
TEC/DEV ADJUD CONTROL CT/SYS EXEC GOV/REL COST   ADMIN
...POLICY DECISION MGT 20 DEPT/DEFEN SUPREME/CT.   NAT/G
PAGE 62 G1221

S60
HUNTINGTON S.P.,"STRATEGIC PLANNING AND THE   EXEC
POLITICAL PROCESS." USA+45 NAT/G DELIB/GP LEGIS   FORCES
ACT/RES ECO/TAC LEGIT ROUTINE CHOOSE RIGID/FLEX PWR   NUC/PWR
...POLICY MAJORIT MGT 20. PAGE 27 G0538   WAR

B61
GLADDEN E.N.,BRITISH PUBLIC SERVICE ADMINISTRATION.   EFFICIENCY
UK...CHARTS 20. PAGE 21 G0419   ADMIN
                                                          EX/STRUC
                                                          EXEC

S61
LYONS G.M.,"THE NEW CIVIL-MILITARY RELATIONS."   CIVMIL/REL
USA+45 NAT/G EX/STRUC TOP/EX PROB/SOLV ADMIN EXEC   PWR
PARTIC 20. PAGE 35 G0681   REPRESENT

S61
WOHLSTETTER A.,"NUCLEAR SHARING: NATO AND THE NTH   TREND
COUNTRY." EUR+WWI FUT SOCIETY DIPLOM EXEC DETER PWR   TEC/DEV
SKILL...POLICY TECHNIC CONCPT 20 NATO. PAGE 64   NUC/PWR
G1252   ARMS/CONT

B62
CHANDLER A.D.,STRATEGY AND STRUCTURE: CHAPTERS IN   LG/CO
THE HISTORY OF THE INDUSTRIAL ENTERPRISE. USA+45   PLAN
USA-45 ECO/DEV EX/STRUC ECO/TAC EXEC...DECISION 20.   ADMIN
PAGE 11 G0220   FINAN

B62
DUCKWORTH W.E.,A GUIDE TO OPERATIONAL RESEARCH.   OP/RES
INDUS PLAN PROB/SOLV EXEC EFFICIENCY PRODUC KNOWL   GAME
...MGT MATH STAT SIMUL METH 20 MONTECARLO. PAGE 16   DECISION
G0319   ADMIN

B62
GRANICK D.,THE EUROPEAN EXECUTIVE. BELGIUM FRANCE   MGT
GERMANY/W UK INDUS LABOR LG/CO SML/CO EX/STRUC PLAN   ECO/DEV
TEC/DEV CAP/ISM COST DEMAND...POLICY CHARTS 20.   ECO/TAC
PAGE 22 G0441   EXEC

B62
SCHILLING W.R.,STRATEGY, POLITICS, AND DEFENSE   ROUTINE
BUDGETS. USA+45 R+D NAT/G CONSULT DELIB/GP FORCES   POLICY
LEGIS ACT/RES PLAN BAL/PWR LEGIT EXEC NUC/PWR
RIGID/FLEX PWR...TREND COLD/WAR CONGRESS 20
EISNHWR/DD. PAGE 49 G0968

L62
CAVERS D.F.,"ADMINISTRATIVE DECISION-MAKING IN   REPRESENT
NUCLEAR FACILITIES LICENSING." USA+45 CLIENT ADMIN   LOBBY
EXEC 20 AEC. PAGE 11 G0218   PWR
                                                          CONTROL

L62
NEIBURG H.L.,"THE EISENHOWER AEC AND CONGRESS: A   CHIEF
STUDY IN EXECUTIVE-LEGISLATIVE RELATIONS." USA+45   LEGIS
NAT/G POL/PAR DELIB/GP EX/STRUC TOP/EX ADMIN EXEC   GOV/REL
LEAD ROUTINE PWR...POLICY COLD/WAR CONGRESS   NUC/PWR
PRESIDENT AEC. PAGE 41 G0816

S62
MORGENTHAU H.J.,"A POLITICAL THEORY OF FOREIGN   USA+45
AID." ECO/UNDEV NAT/G DELIB/GP PLAN ECO/TAC   PHIL/SCI
EDU/PROP EXEC ORD/FREE RESPECT WEALTH...METH/CNCPT   FOR/AID
TREND 20. PAGE 40 G0783

B63
HATHAWAY D.A.,GOVERNMENT AND AGRICULTURE: PUBLIC   AGRI
POLICY IN A DEMOCRATIC SOCIETY. USA+45 LEGIS ADMIN   GOV/REL
EXEC LOBBY REPRESENT PWR 20. PAGE 25 G0491   PROB/SOLV
                                                          EX/STRUC

S63
FERRETTI B.,"IMPORTANZA E PROSPETTIVE DELL ENERGIA   TEC/DEV
DI ORIGINE NUCLEARE." FUT ITALY WOR+45 INTELL R+D   EXEC

ACT/RES CREATE HEALTH WEALTH...METH/CNCPT TIME/SEQ   NUC/PWR
20. PAGE 19 G0365

S63
MASSART L.,"L'ORGANISATION DE LA RECHERCHE   R+D
SCIENTIFIQUE EN EUROPE." EUR+WWI WOR+45 ACT/RES   CREATE
PLAN TEC/DEV EDU/PROP EXEC KNOWL...METH/CNCPT EEC
20. PAGE 36 G0718

B64
EDELMAN M.,THE SYMBOLIC USES OF POWER. USA+45   CLIENT
EX/STRUC CONTROL GP/REL INGP/REL...MGT T. PAGE 17   PWR
G0333   EXEC
                                                          ELITES

B64
LI C.M.,INDUSTRIAL DEVELOPMENT IN COMMUNIST CHINA.   ASIA
CHINA/COM ECO/DEV ECO/UNDEV AGRI FINAN INDUS MARKET   TEC/DEV
LABOR NAT/G ECO/TAC INT/TRADE EXEC ALL/VALS
...POLICY RELATIV TREND WORK TOT/POP VAL/FREE 20.
PAGE 34 G0665

B64
RANSOM H.H.,CAN AMERICAN DEMOCRACY SURVIVE COLD   USA+45
WAR. USA+45 CONSTN NAT/G CONSULT DELIB/GP LEGIS   ROUTINE
ACT/RES LEGIT EXEC ATTIT KNOWL ORD/FREE PWR SKILL
...POLICY TIME/SEQ TREND GEN/LAWS 20 COLD/WAR.
PAGE 46 G0901

L64
BERKS R.N.,"THE US AND WEAPONS CONTROL." WOR+45 LAW   USA+45
INT/ORG NAT/G LEGIS EXEC COERCE PEACE ATTIT   PLAN
RIGID/FLEX ALL/VALS PWR...POLICY TOT/POP 20. PAGE 7   ARMS/CONT
G0129

L64
WARD C.,"THE 'NEW MYTHS' AND 'OLD REALITIES' OF   FORCES
NUCLEAR WAR." COM FUT USA+45 USSR WOR+45 INT/ORG   COERCE
NAT/G DOMIN LEGIT EXEC ATTIT PERCEPT ALL/VALS   ARMS/CONT
...POLICY RELATIV PSY MYTH TREND 20. PAGE 62 G1212   NUC/PWR

S64
PILISUK M.,"STEPWISE DISARMAMENT & SUDDEN   PWR
DESTRUCTION IN A TWOPERSON GAME: A RESEARCH TOOL."   DECISION
NAT/G FORCES ACT/RES ECO/TAC EDU/PROP EXEC ROUTINE   ARMS/CONT
COERCE ORD/FREE...SIMUL GEN/LAWS VAL/FREE. PAGE 45
G0877

S64
THOMPSON V.A.,"ADMINISTRATIVE OBJECTIVES FOR   ECO/UNDEV
DEVELOPMENT ADMINISTRATION." WOR+45 CREATE PLAN   MGT
DOMIN EDU/PROP EXEC ROUTINE ATTIT ORD/FREE PWR
...POLICY GEN/LAWS VAL/FREE. PAGE 54 G1070

B65
STEINER G.A.,THE CREATIVE ORGANIZATION. ELITES   CREATE
LG/CO PLAN PROB/SOLV TEC/DEV INSPECT CAP/ISM   MGT
CONTROL EXEC PERSON...METH/COMP HYPO/EXP 20.   ADMIN
PAGE 52 G1034   SOC

B65
US DEPARTMENT OF THE ARMY,MILITARY MANPOWER POLICY.   BIBLIOG/A
USA+45 LEGIS EXEC WAR 20 CONGRESS. PAGE 58 G1132   POLICY
                                                          FORCES
                                                          TREND

S65
HUGHES T.L.,"SCHOLARS AND FOREIGN POLICY* VARIETIES   ACT/RES
OF RESEARCH EXPERIENCE." COM/IND DIPLOM ADMIN EXEC   ACADEM
ROUTINE...MGT OBS CONGRESS PRESIDENT CAMELOT.   CONTROL
PAGE 27 G0535   NAT/G

S65
LEISERSON A.,"SCIENTISTS AND THE POLICY PROCESS."   PHIL/SCI
USA+45 NAT/G LEAD PARTIC REPRESENT. PAGE 33 G0654   ADMIN
                                                          EX/STRUC
                                                          EXEC

B67
HOROWITZ I.L.,THE RISE AND FALL OF PROJECT CAMELOT: NAT/G
STUDIES IN THE RELATIONSHIP BETWEEN SOCIAL SCIENCE   ACADEM
AND PRACTICAL POLITICS. USA+45 WOR+45 CULTURE   ACT/RES
FORCES LEGIS EXEC CIVMIL/REL KNOWL...POLICY SOC   GP/REL
METH/CNCPT 20. PAGE 27 G0529

B67
SALMOND J.A.,THE CIVILIAN CONSERVATION CORPS.   ADMIN
1933-1942. USA-45 NAT/G CREATE EXEC EFFICIENCY   ECO/TAC
WEALTH...BIBLIOG 20 ROOSEVLT/F. PAGE 48 G0954   TASK
                                                          AGRI

S67
ROBERTS E.B.,"THE PROBLEM OF AGING ORGANIZATIONS."   INDUS
INTELL PROB/SOLV ADMIN EXEC FEEDBACK EFFICIENCY   R+D
PRODUC...GEN/LAWS 20. PAGE 47 G0926   MGT
                                                          PLAN

N67
US SENATE COMM AERO SPACE SCI,AERONAUTICAL RESEARCH DIST/IND
AND DEVELOPMENT POLICY; HEARINGS, COMM ON SPACE
AERONAUTICAL AND SPACE SCIENCES...1967 (PAMPHLET). NAT/G
R+D PROB/SOLV EXEC GOV/REL 20 DEPT/DEFEN FAA NASA PLAN
CONGRESS. PAGE 60 G1174

EXECUTIVE....SEE TOP/EX

EXECUTIVE ESTABLISHMENTS....SEE EX/STRUC

EXECUTIVE PROCESS....SEE EXEC

EXHIBIT....DISPLAY

EXPECTATIONS....SEE PROBABIL, SUPEGO, PREDICT

EXPERIMENTATION....SEE EXPERIMENTATION INDEX, P. XIV

EXPOSTFACT....EX POST FACTO LAWS

EXPROPRIAT....EXPROPRIATION

EXTR/IND....EXTRACTIVE INDUSTRY (FISHING, LUMBERING, ETC.)

B58
BIDWELL P.W.,RAW MATERIALS: A STUDY OF AMERICAN EXTR/IND
POLICY. USA+45 USA-45 ECO/UNDEV AGRI INDUS KIN ECO/DEV
CREATE PLAN ECO/TAC WAR PEACE ATTIT DRIVE WEALTH
...STAT CHARTS CONGRESS VAL/FREE. PAGE 7 G0135

B59
CLEAVELAND F.N.,SCIENCE AND STATE GOVERNMENT. AGRI TEC/DEV
EXTR/IND FINAN INDUS PROVS...METH/CNCPT STAT CHARTS PHIL/SCI
20 NEW/YORK CONNECTICT WISCONSIN CALIFORNIA GOV/REL
NEW/MEXICO. PAGE 12 G0233 METH/COMP

B60
US HOUSE COMM. SCI. ASTRONAUT.,OCEAN SCIENCES AND R+D
NATIONAL SECURITY. FUT SEA ECO/DEV EXTR/IND INT/ORG ORD/FREE
NAT/G FORCES ACT/RES TEC/DEV ECO/TAC COERCE WAR
BIO/SOC KNOWL PWR...CONCPT RECORD LAB/EXP 20.
PAGE 59 G1153

S60
RIVKIN A.,"AFRICAN ECONOMIC DEVELOPMENT: ADVANCED AFR
TECHNOLOGY AND THE STAGES OF GROWTH." CULTURE TEC/DEV
ECO/UNDEV AGRI COM/IND EXTR/IND PLAN ECO/TAC ATTIT FOR/AID
DRIVE RIGID/FLEX SKILL WEALTH...MGT SOC GEN/LAWS
WORK TOT/POP 20. PAGE 47 G0923

B61
HODGKINS J.A.,SOVIET POWER: ENERGY RESOURCES, GEOG
PRODUCTION AND POTENTIALS. USSR ECO/DEV INDUS EXTR/IND
MARKET...POLICY STAT CHARTS 20 RESOURCE/N. PAGE 26 TEC/DEV
G0518

B61
LAHAYE R.,LES ENTREPRISES PUBLIQUES AU MAROC. NAT/G
FRANCE MOROCCO LAW DIST/IND EXTR/IND FINAN CONSULT INDUS
PLAN TEC/DEV ADMIN AGREE CONTROL OWN...POLICY 20. ECO/UNDEV
PAGE 32 G0629 ECO/TAC

L63
MCDOUGAL M.S.,"THE ENJOYMENT AND ACQUISITION OF PLAN
RESOURCES IN OUTER SPACE." CHRIST-17C FUT WOR+45 TREND
WOR-45 LAW EXTR/IND INT/ORG ACT/RES CREATE TEC/DEV
ECO/TAC LEGIT COERCE HEALTH KNOWL ORD/FREE PWR
WEALTH...JURID HIST/WRIT VAL/FREE. PAGE 37 G0738

B64
BALASSA B.,TRADE PROSPECTS FOR DEVELOPING INT/TRADE
COUNTRIES. WOR+45 ECO/DEV AGRI EXTR/IND INDUS ECO/UNDEV
CREATE PLAN PRICE...ECOMETRIC CLASSIF TIME/SEQ TREND
GEN/METH. PAGE 5 G0087 STAT

B65
WHITE HOUSE CONFERENCE ON INTERNATIONAL R+D
COOPERATION(VOL.II). SPACE WOR+45 EXTR/IND INT/ORG CONFER
LABOR WORKER NUC/PWR PEACE AGE/Y...CENSUS ANTHOL 20 TEC/DEV
RESOURCE/N URBAN/RNWL PUB/TRANS. PAGE 1 G0019 DIPLOM

B67
ALEXANDER L.M.,THE LAW OF THE SEA: OFFSHORE SEA
BOUNDARIES AND ZONES. WOR+45 INT/ORG TEC/DEV INT/LAW
CONTROL PRIVIL HABITAT SOVEREIGN...CON/ANAL CHARTS EXTR/IND
ANTHOL. PAGE 2 G0037

B67
PIPER D.C.,THE INTERNATIONAL LAW OF THE GREAT CONCPT
LAKES. CANADA EXTR/IND MUNIC LICENSE ARMS/CONT DIPLOM
CRIME...GEOG 19/20. PAGE 45 G0879 INT/LAW

L67
CARMICHAEL D.M.,"FORTY YEARS OF WATER POLLUTION HEALTH

CONTROL IN WISCONSIN: A CASE STUDY." LAW EXTR/IND CONTROL
INDUS MUNIC DELIB/GP PLAN PROB/SOLV SANCTION ADMIN
...CENSUS CHARTS 20 WISCONSIN. PAGE 11 G0207 ADJUD

S67
EYRAUD M.,"LA FRANCE FACE A UN EVENTUEL TRAITE DE NUC/PWR
NON DISSEMINATION DES ARMES NUCLEAIRES." FRANCE ARMS/CONT
USA+45 EXTR/IND INDUS R+D INT/ORG ACT/RES TEC/DEV POLICY
AGREE PRODUC ATTIT 20 TREATY AEC EURATOM. PAGE 18
G0355

S67
HULL E.W.S.,"THE POLITICAL OCEAN." FUT UNIV WOR+45 DIPLOM
EXTR/IND R+D VOL/ASSN PLAN BAL/PWR ECO/TAC PEACE ECO/UNDEV
WEALTH 20 UN. PAGE 27 G0536 INT/ORG
INT/LAW

S67
INGLIS D.R.,"PROSPECTS AND PROBLEMS: THE NUC/PWR
NONMILITARY USES OF NUCLEAR EXPLOSIVES." CREATE INDUS
PROB/SOLV TEC/DEV AGREE PEACE...INT/LAW PHIL/SCI ARMS/CONT
NEW/IDEA 20 TREATY. PAGE 28 G0545 EXTR/IND

S67
PONTECORVO G.,"THE LAW OF THE SEA." ECO/DEV CONFER
ECO/UNDEV TEC/DEV GEOG. PAGE 45 G0885 INT/LAW
EXTR/IND
SEA

EXTRACTIVE INDUSTRY....SEE EXTR/IND

EYRAUD M. G0355
_____ F _____
FAA....U.S. FEDERAL AVIATION AGENCY

B63
DEAN A.L.,FEDERAL AGENCY APPROACHES TO FIELD ADMIN
MANAGEMENT (PAMPHLET). R+D DELIB/GP EX/STRUC MGT
PROB/SOLV GOV/REL...CLASSIF BIBLIOG 20 FAA NASA NAT/G
DEPT/HEW POSTAL/SYS IRS. PAGE 15 G0287 OP/RES

B65
THAYER F.C. JR.,AIR TRANSPORT POLICY AND NATIONAL AIR
SECURITY: A POLITICAL, ECONOMIC, AND MILITARY FORCES
ANALYSIS. DIST/IND OP/RES PLAN TEC/DEV DIPLOM DETER CIVMIL/REL
WAR COST EFFICIENCY...POLICY BIBLIOG 20 DEPT/DEFEN ORD/FREE
FAA CAB. PAGE 54 G1066

B66
WHITNAH D.R.,SAFER SKYWAYS. DIST/IND DELIB/GP ADMIN
FORCES TOP/EX WORKER TEC/DEV ROUTINE WAR CIVMIL/REL NAT/G
COST...TIME/SEQ 20 FAA CAB. PAGE 63 G1235 AIR
GOV/REL

N67
US SENATE COMM AERO SPACE SCI,AERONAUTICAL RESEARCH DIST/IND
AND DEVELOPMENT POLICY; HEARINGS, COMM ON SPACE
AERONAUTICAL AND SPACE SCIENCES...1967 (PAMPHLET). NAT/G
R+D PROB/SOLV EXEC GOV/REL 20 DEPT/DEFEN FAA NASA PLAN
CONGRESS. PAGE 60 G1174

FABIAN....FABIANS: MEMBERS AND/OR SUPPORTERS OF FABIAN
SOCIETY

FACE/GP....ACQUAINTANCE GROUP

S55
ANGELL R.,"GOVERNMENTS AND PEOPLES AS A FOCI FOR FUT
PEACE-ORIENTED RESEARCH." WOR+45 CULTURE SOCIETY SOC
FACE/GP ACT/RES CREATE PLAN DIPLOM EDU/PROP ROUTINE PEACE
ATTIT PERCEPT SKILL...POLICY CONCPT OBS TREND
GEN/METH 20. PAGE 3 G0060

FACTION....FACTION

FACTOR ANALYSIS....SEE CON/ANAL

FADDEYEV N. G0356

FAGOT R. G0029

FAIR M.L. G0357

FAIR/LABOR....FAIR LABOR STANDARD ACT

FAIRNESS, JUSTICE....SEE VALUES INDEX

FALANGE....FALANGE PARTY (SPAIN)

FALK L.A. G0358

FALK R.A. G0359

FALK S.L. G0360

FALKLAND/I....FALKLAND ISLANDS

FAM....FAMILY

B54
WASHBURNE N.F.,INTERPRETING SOCIAL CHANGE IN CULTURE
AMERICA. USA+45 STRATA FAM NAT/G SECT OP/RES STRUCT
ECO/TAC EDU/PROP HABITAT...SOC TIME/SEQ TREND 20 CREATE
BUREAUCRCY. PAGE 62 G1217 TEC/DEV

C55
BONER H.A.,"HUNGRY GENERATIONS." UK WOR+45 WOR-45 ECO/DEV
STRATA INDUS FAM LABOR CAP/ISM...MGT BIBLIOG 19/20. PHIL/SCI
PAGE 8 G0151 CONCPT
WEALTH

B60
JANOWITZ M.,THE PROFESSIONAL SOLDIER. CULTURE FORCES
STRATA STRUCT FAM PROB/SOLV TEC/DEV COERCE WAR MYTH
CIVMIL/REL NAT/LISM AGE HEREDITY ALL/VALS CONSERVE LEAD
...MGT WORSHIP. PAGE 28 G0560 ELITES

S60
JAFFEE A.J.,"POPULATION TRENDS AND CONTROLS IN ECO/UNDEV
UNDERDEVELOPED COUNTRIES." AFR FUT ISLAM L/A+17C GEOG
S/ASIA CULTURE R+D FAM ACT/RES PLAN EDU/PROP
BIO/SOC RIGID/FLEX HEALTH...SOC STAT OBS CHARTS 20.
PAGE 28 G0555

S62
PAULING L.,"GENETIC EFFECTS OF WEAPONS TESTS." HEAL
WOR+45 SOCIETY FAM ACT/RES EDU/PROP AGE/C HEALTH ARMS/CONT
ORD/FREE...GEOG STAT CONT/OBS PROJ/TEST CHARTS NUC/PWR
TOT/POP 20. PAGE 44 G0861

B64
PETERSON W.,THE POLITICS OF POPULATION. COM EUR+WWI PLAN
FUT MOD/EUR S/ASIA USA+45 USA-45 WOR+45 LAW CULTURE CENSUS
FAM SECT DOMIN EDU/PROP BIO/SOC HEALTH ORD/FREE POLICY
...GEOG STAT TIME/SEQ TREND VAL/FREE. PAGE 44 G0871

B67
BENNETT J.W.,HUTTERIAN BRETHREN; THE AGRICULTURAL SECT
ECONOMY AND SOCIAL ORGANIZATION OF A COMMUNAL AGRI
PEOPLE. USA+45 SOCIETY FAM KIN TEC/DEV ADJUST...MGT STRUCT
AUD/VIS GP/COMP 20. PAGE 6 G0121 GP/REL

S67
HILL R.,"SOCIAL ASPECTS OF FAMILY PLANNING." INDIA FAM
KOREA TAIWAN ECO/UNDEV PLAN PROB/SOLV TEC/DEV BIO/SOC
EDU/PROP CONTROL ATTIT DRIVE...HEAL PSY SOC 20 GEOG
BIRTH/CON UN. PAGE 26 G0512 MARRIAGE

S67
STYCOS J.M.,"POLITICS AND POPULATION CONTROL IN PLAN
LATIN AMERICA." USA+45 FAM NAT/G GP/REL AGE/C ATTIT CENSUS
CATHISM MARXISM...POLICY UN WHO. PAGE 53 G1045 CONTROL
L/A+17C

N67
ASIAN STUDIES CENTER,FOUR ARTICLES ON POPULATION ASIA
AND FAMILY LIFE IN TAIWAN (ASIAN STUDIES PAPERS, FAM
REPRINT SERIES NO. 2). CULTURE STRATA ECO/UNDEV CENSUS
AGRI INDUS R+D KIN MUNIC...GEOG SOC CHARTS 20. ANTHOL
PAGE 4 G0072

FAMILY....SEE FAM

FAMINE....SEE AGRI, HEALTH

FAO....FOOD AND AGRICULTURE ORGANIZATION; SEE ALSO UN,
INT/ORG

S48
HARDIN L.M.,"REFLECTIONS ON AGRICULTURAL POLICY AGRI
FORMATION IN THE UNITED STATES." LEGIS PLAN BUDGET POLICY
ECO/TAC LEAD CENTRAL...MGT SOC NEW/IDEA STAT FAO. ADMIN
PAGE 24 G0480 NEW/LIB

FARM/BUR....FARM BUREAU

FARMING....SEE AGRI

FASCISM....FASCISM; SEE ALSO TOTALISM, FASCIST

B52
APPADORAI A.,THE SUBSTANCE OF POLITICS (6TH ED.). PHIL/SCI
EX/STRUC LEGIS DIPLOM CT/SYS CHOOSE FASCISM MARXISM NAT/G
SOCISM...BIBLIOG T. PAGE 3 G0062

B63
JACOB H.,GERMAN ADMINISTRATION SINCE BISMARCK: ADMIN
CENTRAL AUTHORITY VERSUS LOCAL AUTONOMY. GERMANY NAT/G
GERMANY/W LAW POL/PAR CONTROL CENTRAL TOTALISM LOC/G
FASCISM...MAJORIT DECISION STAT CHARTS GOV/COMP POLICY
19/20 BISMARCK/O HITLER/A WEIMAR/REP. PAGE 28 G0551

B64
WHEELER-BENNETT J.W.,THE NEMESIS OF POWER (2ND FORCES
ED.). EUR+WWI GERMANY TOP/EX TEC/DEV ADMIN WAR NAT/G
PERS/REL RIGID/FLEX ROLE ORD/FREE PWR FASCISM 20 GP/REL
HITLER/A. PAGE 63 G1231 STRUCT

FASCIST....FASCIST

B54
GERMANY FOREIGN MINISTRY,DOCUMENTS ON GERMAN NAT/G
FOREIGN POLICY 1918-1945, SERIES C (1933-1937) DIPLOM
VOLS. I-V. GERMANY MOD/EUR FORCES PLAN ECO/TAC POLICY
...FASCIST CHARTS ANTHOL 20. PAGE 21 G0416

FASHION....SEE MODAL

FATHER/DIV....FATHER DIVINE AND HIS FOLLOWERS

FATIGUE....SEE SLEEP

FBI....U.S. FEDERAL BUREAU OF INVESTIGATION

FCC....U.S. FEDERAL COMMUNICATIONS COMMISSION

FDA....U.S. FOOD AND DRUG ADMINISTRATION

FDR....FRANKLIN D. ROOSEVELT

FEARS....SEE ANOMIE

FECHNER/GT....GUSTAV THEODOR FECHNER

FED/OPNMKT....FEDERAL OPEN MARKET COMMITTEE

FED/RESERV....U.S. FEDERAL RESERVE SYSTEM (INCLUDES FEDERAL
RESERVE BANK)

FEDERAL AVIATION AGENCY....SEE FAA

FEDERAL COMMUNICATIONS COMMISSION....SEE FCC

FEDERAL COUNCIL FOR SCIENCE + TECHNOLOGY....SEE FEDSCI/TEC

FEDERAL HOUSING ADMINISTRATION...SEE FHA

FEDERAL RESERVE SYSTEM....SEE FED/RESERV

FEDERAL TRADE COMMISSION....SEE FTC

FEDERAL....FEDERALISM

B25
MATHEWS J.M.,AMERICAN STATE GOVERNMENT. USA-45 PROVS
LOC/G CHIEF EX/STRUC LEGIS ADJUD CONTROL CT/SYS ADMIN
ROUTINE GOV/REL PWR 20 GOVERNOR. PAGE 37 G0721 FEDERAL
CONSTN

S62
DONNELLY D.,"THE POLITICS AND ADMINISTRATION OF GOV/REL
PLANNING." UK ROUTINE FEDERAL 20. PAGE 16 G0307 EFFICIENCY
ADMIN
EX/STRUC

B63
PEABODY R.L.,NEW PERSPECTIVES ON THE HOUSE OF NEW/IDEA
REPRESENTATIVES. AGRI FINAN SCHOOL FORCES CONFER LEGIS
LEAD CHOOSE REPRESENT FEDERAL...POLICY DECISION PWR
HOUSE/REP. PAGE 44 G0862 ADMIN

S63
KAWALKOWSKI A.,"POUR UNE EUROPE INDEPENDENTE ET R+D
REUNIFIEE." EUR+WWI FUT USA+45 USSR WOR+45 ECO/DEV PLAN
PROC/MFG INT/ORG NAT/G ACT/RES TEC/DEV FEDERAL NUC/PWR
RIGID/FLEX...CONCPT METH/CNCPT OEEC TOT/POP 20
DEGAULLE/C. PAGE 30 G0587

B65
US SENATE COMM GOVT OPERATIONS,ORGANIZATION OF ADMIN
FEDERAL EXECUTIVE DEPARTMENTS AND AGENCIES: REPORT EX/STRUC
OF MARCH 23, 1965. USA+45 FORCES LEGIS DIPLOM GOV/REL
ROUTINE CIVMIL/REL EFFICIENCY FEDERAL...MGT STAT. ORG/CHARTS
PAGE 60 G1179

B66
DUNBAR L.W.,A REPUBLIC OF EQUALS. USA+45 CREATE LAW
ADJUD PEACE NEW/LIB...POLICY 20 SOUTH/US CONSTN
CIV/RIGHTS. PAGE 16 G0320 FEDERAL
RACE/REL

S67
GOBER J.L.,"FEDERALISM AT WORK." USA+45 NAT/G MUNIC
CONSULT ACT/RES PLAN CONFER ADMIN LEAD PARTIC TEC/DEV
FEDERAL ATTIT. PAGE 21 G0422 R+D

GOV/REL

FEDERALIST....FEDERALIST PARTY (ALL NATIONS)

FEDSCI/TEC....FEDERAL COUNCIL FOR SCIENCE AND TECHNOLOGY

FEEDBACK....FEEDBACK PHENOMENA

WEINER N.,CYBERNETICS. SOCIETY COMPUTER ADJUST EFFICIENCY UTIL PERCEPT...PSY MATH REGRESS TIME. PAGE 63 G1226	B48 FEEDBACK AUTOMAT CONTROL TEC/DEV	

MCKINNEY E.R.,A BIBLIOGRAPHY OF CYBERNETICS AND INFORMATION THEORY. COMPUTER OP/RES...DECISION PHIL/SCI PSY LING LOG MATH PROBABIL GAME 20. PAGE 38 G0743
B57 BIBLIOG/A FEEDBACK SIMUL CONTROL

GUILBAUD G.T.,WHAT IS CYBERNETICS? COMPUTER OP/RES TEC/DEV AUTOMAT ROUTINE PERS/REL PERCEPT...PSY MATH COMPUT/IR SIMUL GEN/METH. PAGE 23 G0460
B59 CONTROL COM/IND FEEDBACK NET/THEORY

CARPENTER E.,EXPLORATIONS IN COMMUNICATION. USSR CULTURE SCHOOL SECT EDU/PROP PRESS TV AUTOMAT FEEDBACK ATTIT PERSON...ART/METH PSY 20. PAGE 11 G0211
B60 ANTHOL COM/IND TEC/DEV WRITING

BORKOF H.,COMPUTER APPLICATIONS IN THE BEHAVIORAL SCIENCES. AUTOMAT UTIL...DECISION PHIL/SCI PSY METH/CNCPT LING LOG MATH STYLE NET/THEORY COMPUT/IR PROG/TEAC SIMUL. PAGE 8 G0154
B62 R+D COMPUTER PROB/SOLV FEEDBACK

GUETZKOW H.,SIMULATION IN SOCIAL SCIENCE: READINGS. STRUCT OP/RES ADMIN AUTOMAT FEEDBACK...MGT PSY SOC STYLE BIBLIOG. PAGE 23 G0459
B62 SIMUL TEC/DEV COMPUTER GAME

TOMKINS S.S.,COMPUTER SIMULATION OF PERSONALITY. R+D TEC/DEV AUTOMAT FEEDBACK ANOMIE PERCEPT...STYLE PERS/TEST PREDICT COMPUT/IR GP/COMP. PAGE 55 G1075
B63 COMPUTER PERSON SIMUL PROG/TEAC

PILISUK M.,"IS THERE A MILITARY INDUSTRIAL COMPLEX WHICH PREVENTS PEACE CONSENSUS: COUNTERVAILING POWER IN PLURALIST SYSTEMS." INDUS R+D ACADEM FEEDBACK CIVMIL/REL ADJUST CONSEN ATTIT RIGID/FLEX ...CENSUS IDEA/COMP BIBLIOG. PAGE 45 G0878
L65 ELITES WEAPON PEACE ARMS/CONT

SCHELLING T.C.,"SIGNALS AND FEEDBACK IN THE ARMS DIALOGUE." USA+45 USSR R+D ACADEM FORCES ACT/RES ADJUST COST GEN/LAWS. PAGE 49 G0964
S65 FEEDBACK DETER EDU/PROP ARMS/CONT

STONE J.J.,CONTAINING THE ARMS RACE* SOME SPECIFIC PROPOSALS. ASIA USA+45 USSR PROB/SOLV BARGAIN DIPLOM DETER NUC/PWR RATIONAL...GAME 20 DEPT/DEFEN TREATY. PAGE 53 G1038
B66 ARMS/CONT FEEDBACK COST ATTIT

DONALD A.G.,MANAGEMENT, INFORMATION, AND SYSTEMS. WOR+45 LG/CO PROB/SOLV CONTROL FEEDBACK KNOWL MGT. PAGE 16 G0306
B67 ROUTINE TEC/DEV CONCPT ADMIN

RUTGERS U GRADUATE SCH LIB SCI,BIBLIOGRAPHY OF RESEARCH RELATING TO THE COMMUNICATION OF SCIENTIFIC AND TECHNICAL INFORMATION. FUT CREATE FEEDBACK...PHIL/SCI NEW/IDEA COMPUT/IR HYPO/EXP. PAGE 48 G0951
B67 BIBLIOG/A COM/IND R+D TEC/DEV

SAPARINA Y.,CYBERNETICS WITHIN US. WOR+45 EDU/PROP FEEDBACK PERCEPT HEALTH...DECISION METH/CNCPT NEW/IDEA 20. PAGE 49 G0957
B67 COMPUTER METH/COMP CONTROL SIMUL

BROWN W.B.,"MODEL-BUILDING AND ORGANIZATIONS." CONTROL FEEDBACK...PROBABIL CHARTS METH/COMP. PAGE 9 G0179
S67 MGT ADMIN GAME COMPUTER

ROBERTS E.B.,"THE PROBLEM OF AGING ORGANIZATIONS."
S67 INDUS

INTELL PROB/SOLV ADMIN EXEC FEEDBACK EFFICIENCY PRODUC...GEN/LAWS 20. PAGE 47 G0926
R+D MGT PLAN

FEI J.C.H. G0361

FEIGENBAUM E.A. G0267

FEIS H. G0362

FELD B.T. G0363

FEMALE/SEX....FEMALE SEX

FENDER B.E.F. G0090

FEPC....FAIR EMPLOYMENT PRACTICES COMMISSION

FERBER R. G0364,G1206

FERRETTI B. G0365

FEUDALISM....FEUDALISM

FHA....U.S. FEDERAL HOUSING ADMINISTRATION

FICHTE/JG....JOHANN GOTTLIEB FICHTE

FICTIONS....SEE MYTH

FIELD M.G. G0366

FIELD/S....STEVEN FIELD

FILLMORE/M....PRESIDENT MILLARD FILLMORE

FILM....FILM AND CINEMA

FINAN....FINANCIAL SERVICE, BANKS, INSURANCE SYSTEMS, SECURITIES, EXCHANGES

FOREIGN AFFAIRS. SPACE WOR+45 WOR-45 CULTURE ECO/UNDEV FINAN NAT/G TEC/DEV INT/TRADE ARMS/CONT NUC/PWR...POLICY 20 UN EURATOM ECSC EEC. PAGE 1 G0004
N BIBLIOG DIPLOM INT/ORG INT/LAW

THE MANAGEMENT REVIEW. FINAN EX/STRUC PROFIT BIBLIOG/A. PAGE 1 G0007
N LABOR MGT ADMIN MARKET

MARKETING INFORMATION GUIDE. USA+45 ECO/DEV FINAN ADMIN GP/REL. PAGE 1 G0008
N BIBLIOG/A DIST/IND MARKET ECO/TAC

US CHAMBER OF COMMERCE,THE SIGNIFICANCE OF CONCENTRATION RATIOS (PAMPHLET). USA+45 FINAN INDUS ADMIN...METH/CNCPT SAMP CHARTS 20. PAGE 56 G1109
N19 MARKET PREDICT LG/CO CONTROL

FULLER G.H.,SELECTED LIST OF RECENT REFERENCES ON AMERICAN NATIONAL DEFENSE (PAMPHLET). USA-45 FINAN NAT/G ARMS/CONT WAR GOV/REL CENTRAL COST PEACE PWR 20. PAGE 20 G0400
B40 BIBLIOG CIVMIL/REL FORCES WEAPON

HELLMAN F.S.,THE NEW DEAL: SELECTED LIST OF REFERENCES. USA-45 FINAN LABOR EX/STRUC CREATE INT/TRADE ADMIN CT/SYS 20 SUPREME/CT. PAGE 26 G0505
B40 BIBLIOG/A ECO/TAC PLAN POLICY

FULLER G.H.,DEFENSE FINANCING: A SELECTED LIST OF REFERENCES (PAMPHLET). MOD/EUR USA-45 ECO/DEV NAT/G DELIB/GP RATION ARMS/CONT WEAPON COST PEACE PWR 20 CONGRESS. PAGE 20 G0401
B41 BIBLIOG/A FINAN FORCES BUDGET

FULLER G.H.,DEFENSE FINANCING: A SUPPLEMENTARY LIST OF REFERENCES (PAMPHLET). CANADA UK USA-45 ECO/DEV NAT/G DELIB/GP BUDGET ADJUD ARMS/CONT WEAPON COST PEACE PWR 20 AUSTRAL CHINJAP CONGRESS. PAGE 21 G0403
B42 BIBLIOG/A FINAN FORCES DIPLOM

PUBLIC ADMINISTRATION SERVICE,YOUR BUSINESS OF GOVERNMENT: A CATALOG OF PUBLICATIONS IN THE FIELD OF PUBLIC ADMINISTRATION (PAMPHLET). FINAN R+D LOC/G ACT/RES OP/RES PLAN 20. PAGE 45 G0894
B44 BIBLIOG ADMIN NAT/G MUNIC

S44
GRIFFITH E.S.,"THE CHANGING PATTERN OF PUBLIC   LAW
POLICY FORMATION." MOD/EUR WOR+45 FINAN CHIEF   POLICY
CONFER ADMIN LEAD CONSERVE SOCISM TECHRACY...SOC   TEC/DEV
CHARTS CONGRESS. PAGE 23 G0450

B48
METZLER L.A.,INCOME, EMPLOYMENT, AND PUBLIC POLICY.   INCOME
FINAN INDUS LOC/G NAT/G TAX GIVE PAY COST PRODUC   WEALTH
...MGT TIME/SEQ 20. PAGE 38 G0760   POLICY
ECO/TAC

B48
PUBLIC ADMINISTRATION SERVICE,SOURCE MATERIALS IN   BIBLIOG/A
PUBLIC ADMINISTRATION: A SELECTED BIBLIOGRAPHY (PAS   GOV/REL
PUBLICATION NO. 102). USA+45 LAW FINAN LOC/G MUNIC   MGT
NAT/G PLAN RECEIVE EDU/PROP CT/SYS CHOOSE HEALTH   ADMIN
20. PAGE 45 G0895

B49
LEPAWSKY A.,ADMINISTRATION. FINAN INDUS LG/CO   ADMIN
SML/CO INGP/REL PERS/REL COST EFFICIENCY OPTIMAL   MGT
SKILL 20. PAGE 33 G0656   WORKER
EX/STRUC

B50
SURANYI-UNGER T.,PRIVATE ENTERPRISE AND   PLAN
GOVERNMENTAL PLANNING. STRUCT FINAN BAL/PWR   NAT/G
HAPPINESS DRIVE NEW/LIB PLURISM...MATH QUANT STAT   LAISSEZ
TREND BIBLIOG. PAGE 53 G1047   POLICY

B50
US DEPARTMENT OF STATE,POINT FOUR: COOPERATIVE   ECO/UNDEV
PROGRAM FOR AID IN THE DEVELOPMENT OF ECONOMICALLY   FOR/AID
UNDERDEVELOPED AREAS. WOR+45 AGRI INDUS INT/ORG   FINAN
PLAN TEC/DEV DIPLOM EDU/PROP ADMIN PEACE PRODUC   INT/TRADE
WEALTH 20 CONGRESS UN. PAGE 57 G1121

C50
WAGER P.W.,"COUNTY GOVERNMENT ACROSS THE NATION."   LOC/G
USA+45 CONSTN COM/IND FINAN SCHOOL DOMIN CT/SYS   PROVS
LEAD GOV/REL...STAT BIBLIOG 20. PAGE 61 G1204   ADMIN
ROUTINE

B54
LOCKLIN D.P.,ECONOMICS OF TRANSPORTATION (4TH ED.).   ECO/DEV
USA+45 USA-45 SEA AIR LAW FINAN LG/CO EX/STRUC   DIST/IND
ADMIN CONTROL...STAT CHARTS 19/20 RAILROAD   ECO/TAC
PUB/TRANS. PAGE 34 G0675   TEC/DEV

B57
GOLD N.L.,REGIONAL ECONOMIC DEVELOPMENT AND NUCLEAR   ECO/UNDEV
POWER IN INDIA. FUT INDIA FINAN FOR/AID INT/TRADE   TEC/DEV
BAL/PAY EFFICIENCY OPTIMAL PRODUC WEALTH...PREDICT   NUC/PWR
20. PAGE 22 G0424   INDUS

B58
EHRHARD J.,LE DESTIN DU COLONIALISME. AFR FRANCE   COLONIAL
ECO/UNDEV AGRI FINAN MARKET CREATE PLAN TEC/DEV   FOR/AID
BUDGET DIPLOM PRICE 20. PAGE 17 G0335   INT/TRADE
INDUS

S58
ARGYRIS C.,"SOME PROBLEMS IN CONCEPTUALIZING   FINAN
ORGANIZATIONAL CLIMATE: A CASE STUDY OF A BANK"   CONCPT
(BMR)" USA+45 EX/STRUC ADMIN PERS/REL ADJUST PERSON   LG/CO
...POLICY HYPO/EXP SIMUL 20. PAGE 3 G0064   INGP/REL

B59
CLEAVELAND F.N.,SCIENCE AND STATE GOVERNMENT. AGRI   TEC/DEV
EXTR/IND FINAN INDUS PROVS...METH/CNCPT STAT CHARTS   PHIL/SCI
20 NEW/YORK CONNECTICT WISCONSIN CALIFORNIA   GOV/REL
NEW/MEXICO. PAGE 12 G0233   METH/COMP

B59
HARVARD UNIVERSITY LAW SCHOOL,INTERNATIONAL   NUC/PWR
PROBLEMS OF FINANCIAL PROTECTION AGAINST NUCLEAR   ADJUD
RISK. WOR+45 NAT/G DELIB/GP PROB/SOLV DIPLOM   INDUS
CONTROL ATTIT...POLICY INT/LAW MATH 20. PAGE 25   FINAN
G0488

B59
MAYDA J.,ATOMIC ENERGY AND LAW. ECO/UNDEV FINAN   NUC/PWR
TEC/DEV FOR/AID EFFICIENCY PRODUC WEALTH...POLICY   L/A+17C
TECHNIC 20. PAGE 37 G0723   LAW
ADMIN

B59
MEANS G.C.,ADMINISTRATIVE INFLATION AND PUBLIC   ECO/TAC
POLICY (PAMPHLET). USA+45 ECO/DEV FINAN INDUS   POLICY
WORKER PLAN BUDGET GOV/REL COST DEMAND WEALTH 20   RATION
CONGRESS MONOPOLY GOLD/STAND. PAGE 38 G0749   CONTROL

B59
WASSERMAN P.,MEASUREMENT AND ANALYSIS OF   BIBLIOG/A
ORGANIZATIONAL PERFORMANCE. FINAN MARKET EX/STRUC   ECO/TAC

TEC/DEV EDU/PROP CONTROL ROUTINE TASK...MGT 20.   OP/RES
PAGE 62 G1220   EFFICIENCY

B60
ALBI F.,TRATADO DE LOS MODOS DE GESTION DE LAS   LOC/G
CORPORACIONES LOCALES. SPAIN FINAN NAT/G BUDGET   LAW
CONTROL EXEC ROUTINE GOV/REL ORD/FREE SOVEREIGN   ADMIN
...MGT 20. PAGE 2 G0034   MUNIC

B60
APTHEKER H.,DISARMAMENT AND THE AMERICAN ECONOMY: A   MARXIST
SYMPOSIUM. FUT USA+45 ECO/DEV DIST/IND FINAN INDUS   ARMS/CONT
PROC/MFG LABOR NAT/G POL/PAR CONSULT PLAN CAP/ISM
INT/TRADE PEACE ATTIT MORAL WEALTH...TREND GEN/LAWS
TOT/POP 20. PAGE 3 G0063

B60
ATOMIC INDUSTRIAL FORUM,ATOMS FOR INDUSTRY: WORLD   NUC/PWR
FORUM. WOR+45 FINAN COST UTIL...JURID ANTHOL 20.   INDUS
PAGE 4 G0080   PLAN
PROB/SOLV

B60
CRAUMER L.V.,BUSINESS PERIODICALS INDEX (8VOLS.).   BIBLIOG/A
USA+45 LABOR TAX 20. PAGE 13 G0262   FINAN
ECO/DEV
MGT

B60
PENTONY D.E.,THE UNDERDEVELOPED LANDS. FUT WOR+45   ECO/UNDEV
CULTURE AGRI FINAN INDUS MARKET INT/ORG LABOR NAT/G   POLICY
VOL/ASSN CONSULT TEC/DEV ECO/TAC EDU/PROP COLONIAL   FOR/AID
ATTIT WEALTH...OBS RECORD SAMP TREND GEN/METH WORK   INT/TRADE
UN 20. PAGE 44 G0867

B60
SILK L.S.,THE RESEARCH REVOLUTION. USA+45 FINAN   ECO/DEV
CAP/ISM ECO/TAC PRICE EQUILIB PRODUC...STAT TREND   R+D
CHARTS. PAGE 51 G0997   TEC/DEV
PROB/SOLV

B60
US SENATE COMM ON COMMERCE,URBAN MASS   DIST/IND
TRANSPORTATION. FUT USA+45 AIR ECO/DEV FINAN LOC/G   PLAN
MUNIC LEGIS CREATE PROB/SOLV TEC/DEV 20 PUB/TRANS.   NAT/G
PAGE 60 G1180   LAW

B60
WALDO D.,THE RESEARCH FUNCTION OF UNIVERSITY   ADMIN
BUREAUS AND INSTITUTES FOR GOVERNMENTAL-RELATED   R+D
RESEARCH. FINAN ACADEM NAT/G INGP/REL ROLE...POLICY   MUNIC
CLASSIF GOV/COMP. PAGE 61 G1205

S60
SWIFT R.,"THE UNITED NATIONS AND ITS PUBLIC."   INT/ORG
WOR+45 CONSTN FINAN CONSULT DELIB/GP ACT/RES ADMIN   EDU/PROP
ROUTINE RIGID/FLEX SKILL UN 20. PAGE 53 G1048

B61
LAHAYE R.,LES ENTREPRISES PUBLIQUES AU MAROC.   NAT/G
FRANCE MOROCCO LAW DIST/IND EXTR/IND FINAN CONSULT   INDUS
PLAN TEC/DEV ADMIN AGREE CONTROL OWN...POLICY 20.   ECO/UNDEV
PAGE 32 G0629   ECO/TAC

B61
LEE R.R.,ENGINEERING-ECONOMIC PLANNING   BIBLIOG/A
MISCELLANEOUS SUBJECTS: A SELECTED BIBLIOGRAPHY   PLAN
(MIMEOGRAPHED). FINAN LOC/G MUNIC NEIGH ADMIN   REGION
CONTROL INGP/REL HABITAT...GEOG MGT SOC/WK 20
RESOURCE/N. PAGE 33 G0651

B61
MCCRACKEN H.L.,KEYNESIAN ECONOMICS IN THE STREAM OF   ECO/TAC
ECONOMIC THOUGHT. FINAN MARKET BARGAIN EFFICIENCY   DEMAND
OPTIMAL...PHIL/SCI CONCPT IDEA/COMP BIBLIOG 18/20   ECOMETRIC
KEYNES/JM. PAGE 37 G0732

B61
NOVE A.,THE SOVIET ECONOMY. USSR ECO/DEV FINAN   PLAN
NAT/G ECO/TAC PRICE ADMIN EFFICIENCY MARXISM   PRODUC
...TREND BIBLIOG 20. PAGE 42 G0828   POLICY

L61
COHEN K.J.,"THE ROLE OF MANAGEMENT GAMES IN   SOCIETY
EDUCATION AND RESEARCH." INTELL ECO/DEV FINAN   GAME
ACT/RES ECO/TAC DECISION. PAGE 12 G0240   MGT
EDU/PROP

B62
CHANDLER A.D.,STRATEGY AND STRUCTURE: CHAPTERS IN   LG/CO
THE HISTORY OF THE INDUSTRIAL ENTERPRISE. USA+45   PLAN
USA-45 ECO/DEV EX/STRUC ECO/TAC EXEC...DECISION 20.   ADMIN
PAGE 11 G0220   FINAN

B62
DODDS H.W.,THE ACADEMIC PRESIDENT "EDUCATOR OR   ACADEM

CARETAKER? FINAN DELIB/GP EDU/PROP PARTIC ATTIT   ADMIN
ROLE PWR...POLICY RECORD INT. PAGE 16 G0304   LEAD
                                                        CONTROL

                                                        B62
FERBER R.,RESEARCH METHODS IN ECONOMICS AND   ACT/RES
BUSINESS. ECO/DEV FINAN MARKET LG/CO SML/CO CONSULT   PROB/SOLV
CONTROL COST...STAT METH/COMP 20. PAGE 19 G0364   ECO/TAC
                                                        MGT

                                                        B62
FORTUNE EDITORS,THE SPACE INDUSTRY: AMERICA'S   SPACE
NEWEST GIANT. USA+45 FINAN NAT/G BUDGET 20. PAGE 20   INDUS
G0383   TEC/DEV
                                                        MGT

                                                        B62
KARNJAHAPRAKORN C.,MUNICIPAL GOVERNMENT IN THAILAND   LOC/G
AS AN INSTITUTION AND PROCESS OF SELF-GOVERNMENT.   MUNIC
THAILAND CULTURE FINAN EX/STRUC LEGIS PLAN CONTROL   ORD/FREE
GOV/REL EFFICIENCY ATTIT...POLICY 20. PAGE 29 G0578   ADMIN

                                                        B62
KRAFT J.,THE GRAND DESIGN. EUR+WWI USA+45 AGRI   VOL/ASSN
FINAN INDUS MARKET INT/ORG NAT/G PLAN ECO/TAC   ECO/DEV
TARIFFS REGION DRIVE ORD/FREE WEALTH...POLICY OBS   INT/TRADE
TREND EEC 20. PAGE 31 G0616

                                                        B62
MARS D.,SUGGESTED LIBRARY IN PUBLIC ADMINISTRATION.   BIBLIOG
FINAN DELIB/GP EX/STRUC WORKER COMPUTER ADJUD   ADMIN
...DECISION PSY SOC METH/COMP 20. PAGE 36 G0710   METH
                                                        MGT

                                                        B62
THANT U.,THE UNITED NATIONS' DEVELOPMENT DECADE: INT/ORG
PROPOSALS FOR ACTION. WOR+45 SOCIETY ECO/UNDEV AGRI   ALL/VALS
COM/IND FINAN R+D MUNIC SCHOOL VOL/ASSN CONSULT
PLAN TEC/DEV ECO/TAC EDU/PROP ADMIN ROUTINE
RIGID/FLEX...MGT SOC CONCPT UNESCO UN TOT/POP
VAL/FREE. PAGE 54 G1064

                                                        S62
THORELLI H.B.,"THE INTERNATIONAL OPERATIONS   ECO/TAC
SIMULATION AT THE UNIVERSITY OF CHICAGO." FUT   SIMUL
USA+45 WOR+45 ECO/DEV DIST/IND FINAN INDUS INT/ORG   INT/TRADE
DELIB/GP ACT/RES CREATE TEC/DEV WEALTH...STAT
VAL/FREE 20. PAGE 54 G1072

                                                        B63
BASS M.E.,SELECTIVE BIBLIOGRAPHY ON MUNICIPAL   BIBLIOG
GOVERNMENT FROM THE FILES OF THE MUNICIPAL   LOC/G
TECHNICAL ADVISORY SERVICE. USA+45 FINAN SERV/IND   ADMIN
PLAN 20. PAGE 5 G0100   MUNIC

                                                        B63
HAUSMAN W.H.,MANAGING ECONOMIC DEVELOPMENT IN   ECO/UNDEV
AFRICA. AFR USA+45 LAW FINAN WORKER TEC/DEV WEALTH   PLAN
...ANTHOL 20. PAGE 25 G0492   FOR/AID
                                                        MGT

                                                        B63
HEYEL C.,THE ENCYCLOPEDIA OF MANAGEMENT. WOR+45   MGT
MARKET TOP/EX TEC/DEV AUTOMAT LEAD ADJUST...STAT   INDUS
CHARTS GAME ANTHOL BIBLIOG. PAGE 26 G0509   ADMIN
                                                        FINAN

                                                        B63
MULLENBACH P.,CIVILIAN NUCLEAR POWER: ECONOMIC   USA+45
ISSUES AND POLICY FORMATION. FINAN INT/ORG DELIB/GP   ECO/DEV
ACT/RES ECO/TAC ATTIT SUPEGO HEALTH ORD/FREE PWR   NUC/PWR
...POLICY CONCPT MATH STAT CHARTS VAL/FREE 20
COLD/WAR. PAGE 40 G0792

                                                        B63
PEABODY R.L.,NEW PERSPECTIVES ON THE HOUSE OF   NEW/IDEA
REPRESENTATIVES. AGRI FINAN SCHOOL FORCES CONFER   LEGIS
LEAD CHOOSE REPRESENT FEDERAL...POLICY DECISION   PWR
HOUSE/REP. PAGE 44 G0862   ADMIN

                                                        B63
THORELLI H.B.,INTOP: INTERNATIONAL OPERATIONS   GAME
SIMULATION: PLAYER'S MANUAL. BRAZIL FINAN OP/RES   INT/TRADE
ADMIN GP/REL INGP/REL PRODUC PERCEPT...DECISION MGT   EDU/PROP
EEC. PAGE 54 G1073   LG/CO

                                                        B63
UN SECRETARY GENERAL,PLANNING FOR ECONOMIC   PLAN
DEVELOPMENT. ECO/UNDEV FINAN BUDGET INT/TRADE   ECO/TAC
TARIFFS TAX ADMIN 20 UN. PAGE 55 G1089   MGT
                                                        NAT/COMP

                                                        B63
US SENATE COMM APPROPRIATIONS,PERSONNEL   ADMIN
ADMINISTRATION AND OPERATIONS OF AGENCY FOR   FOR/AID
INTERNATIONAL DEVELOPMENT: SPECIAL HEARING. FINAN   EFFICIENCY

LEAD COST UTIL SKILL...CHARTS 20 CONGRESS AID   DIPLOM
CIVIL/SERV. PAGE 60 G1175

                                                        N63
COMMITTEE ECONOMIC DEVELOPMENT,TAXES AND TRADE: 20   FINAN
YEARS OF CED POLICY (PAMPHLET). USA+45 ECO/DEV PLAN   ECO/TAC
BUDGET LEAD...POLICY KENNEDY/JF PRESIDENT. PAGE 13   NAT/G
G0246   DELIB/GP

                                                        B64
RECENT PUBLICATIONS ON GOVERNMENTAL PROBLEMS. FINAN   BIBLIOG
INDUS ACADEM PLAN PROB/SOLV EDU/PROP ADJUD ADMIN   AUTOMAT
BIO/SOC...MGT SOC. PAGE 1 G0017   LEGIS
                                                        JURID

                                                        B64
FALK L.A.,ADMINISTRATIVE ASPECTS OF GROUP PRACTICE.   BIBLIOG/A
USA+45 FINAN PROF/ORG PLAN MGT. PAGE 18 G0358   HEAL
                                                        ADMIN
                                                        SERV/IND

                                                        B64
GUTMANN P.M.,ECONOMIC GROWTH: AN AMERICAN PROBLEM.   WEALTH
USA+45 FINAN R+D...POLICY NAT/COMP ANTHOL BIBLIOG   ECO/DEV
20. PAGE 24 G0463   CAP/ISM
                                                        ORD/FREE

                                                        B64
HAZLEWOOD A.,THE ECONOMICS OF DEVELOPMENT: AN   BIBLIOG/A
ANNOTATED LIST OF BOOKS AND ARTICLES PUBLISHED   ECO/UNDEV
1958-1962. AGRI FINAN INDUS LABOR NAT/G DIPLOM   TEC/DEV
INT/TRADE INCOME...MGT 20. PAGE 25 G0497

                                                        B64
LI C.M.,INDUSTRIAL DEVELOPMENT IN COMMUNIST CHINA.   ASIA
CHINA/COM ECO/DEV ECO/UNDEV AGRI FINAN INDUS MARKET   TEC/DEV
LABOR NAT/G ECO/TAC INT/TRADE EXEC ALL/VALS
...POLICY RELATIV TREND WORK TOT/POP VAL/FREE 20.
PAGE 34 G0665

                                                        B64
MASTERS N.A.,STATE POLITICS AND THE PUBLIC SCHOOLS.   EDU/PROP
STRUCT FINAN ADMIN LOBBY GP/REL PWR BIBLIOG.   PROVS
PAGE 36 G0720   DOMIN

                                                        B64
ORTH C.D.,ADMINISTERING RESEARCH AND DEVELOPMENT.   MGT
FINAN PLAN PROB/SOLV ADMIN ROUTINE...METH/CNCPT   R+D
STAT CHARTS METH 20. PAGE 43 G0847   LG/CO
                                                        INDUS

                                                        B64
SCHERER F.M.,THE WEAPONS ACQUISITION PROCESS: INDUS
ECONOMIC INCENTIVES. BOSTON: DIVISION OF RESEARCH,   ACT/RES
GRADUATE SCHOOL OF BUSINESS. USA+45 FINAN NAT/G   WEAPON
DELIB/GP ECO/TAC RIGID/FLEX WEALTH...MGT MATH STAT
CHARTS VAL/FREE 20. PAGE 49 G0965

                                                        L64
CARNEGIE ENDOWMENT INT. PEACE,"POLITICAL QUESTIONS   INT/ORG
(ISSUES BEFORE THE NINETEENTH GENERAL ASSEMBLY)."   PEACE
SPACE WOR+45 CONSTN FINAN NAT/G CONSULT DELIB/GP
FORCES LEGIS TEC/DEV EDU/PROP LEGIT ARMS/CONT
COERCE NUC/PWR ATTIT ALL/VALS...CONCPT OBS UN
COLD/WAR 20. PAGE 11 G0208

                                                        S64
MAHALANOBIS P.C.,"PERSPECTIVE PLANNING IN INDIA: PLAN
STATISTICAL TOOLS." INDIA S/ASIA STRATA AGRI   STAT
DIST/IND FINAN INDUS SERV/IND NAT/G ECO/TAC
ORD/FREE WEALTH...POLICY TREND SIMUL VAL/FREE 20.
PAGE 35 G0695

                                                        C64
SCHRAMM W.,"MASS MEDIA AND NATIONAL DEVELOPMENT: ECO/UNDEV
THE ROLE OF INFORMATION IN DEVELOPING COUNTRIES."   COM/IND
FINAN R+D ACT/RES PLAN TEC/DEV DIPLOM CHOOSE SUPEGO   EDU/PROP
ORD/FREE...BIBLIOG 20. PAGE 50 G0978   MAJORIT

                                                        B65
ARTHUR D LITTLE INC,SAN FRANCISCO COMMUNITY RENEWAL   HABITAT
PROGRAM. USA+45 FINAN PROVS ADMIN INCOME...CHARTS   MUNIC
20 CALIFORNIA SAN/FRAN URBAN/RNWL. PAGE 4 G0071   PLAN
                                                        PROB/SOLV

                                                        B65
BAILEY S.K.,AMERICAN POLITICS AND GOVERNMENT.   ANTHOL
USA+45 CONSTN FINAN LABOR POL/PAR DIPLOM ADMIN WAR   LEGIS
INGP/REL RACE/REL NEW/LIB 20 SUPREME/CT PRESIDENT   PWR
CONGRESS. PAGE 4 G0084

                                                        B65
BARISH N.N.,MANAGEMENT SCIENCES IN THE EMERGING   ECO/UNDEV
COUNTRIES. AFR CHINA/COM WOR+45 FINAN INDUS PLAN   OP/RES
PRODUC HABITAT...ANTHOL 20. PAGE 5 G0093   MGT
                                                        TEC/DEV

FRUTKIN A.W.,SPACE AND THE INTERNATIONAL
COOPERATION YEAR: A NATIONAL CHALLENGE (PAMPHLET).
EUR+WWI USA+45 FINAN TEC/DEV BUDGET...MGT 20 NASA.
PAGE 20 G0396

B65
SPACE
INDUS
NAT/G
DIPLOM

IANNI O.,ESTADO E CAPITALISMO. L/A+17C FINAN
TEC/DEV ECO/TAC ORD/FREE WEALTH POLICY. PAGE 28
G0542

B65
ECO/UNDEV
STRUCT
INDUS
NAT/G

INT. BANK RECONSTR. DEVELOP.,ECONOMIC DEVELOPMENT
OF KUWAIT. ISLAM KUWAIT AGRI FINAN MARKET EX/STRUC
TEC/DEV ECO/TAC ADMIN WEALTH...OBS CON/ANAL CHARTS
20. PAGE 28 G0548

B65
INDUS
NAT/G

KANTOROVICH L.V.,THE BEST USE OF ECONOMIC
RESOURCES. USSR SOCIETY FINAN ACT/RES TEC/DEV
ECO/TAC PRICE CONTROL COST DEMAND EFFICIENCY
OPTIMAL...MGT STAT. PAGE 29 G0572

B65
PLAN
MATH
DECISION

KOROL A.G.,SOVIET RESEARCH AND DEVELOPMENT. USSR
ACADEM SCHOOL WORKER ROUTINE COST...STAT T 20.
PAGE 31 G0615

B65
COM
R+D
FINAN
DIST/IND

OECD,MEDITERRANEAN REGIONAL PROJECT: TURKEY;
EDUCATION AND DEVELOPMENT. FUT TURKEY SOCIETY
STRATA FINAN NAT/G PROF/ORG PLAN PROB/SOLV ADMIN
COST...STAT CHARTS 20 OECD. PAGE 42 G0831

B65
EDU/PROP
ACADEM
SCHOOL
ECO/UNDEV

OECD,THE MEDITERRANEAN REGIONAL PROJECT: PORTUGAL;
EDUCATION AND DEVELOPMENT. PORTUGAL SOCIETY STRATA
FINAN PROF/ORG WORKER PLAN PROB/SOLV ADMIN...POLICY
STAT CHARTS METH 20 OECD. PAGE 42 G0832

B65
EDU/PROP
SCHOOL
ACADEM
ECO/UNDEV

OECD,THE MEDITERRANEAN REGIONAL PROJECT: ITALY;
EDUCATION AND DEVELOPMENT. ITALY SOCIETY STRATA
FINAN NAT/G PROF/ORG WORKER PLAN PROB/SOLV ADMIN
...STAT CHARTS METH 20 OECD. PAGE 42 G0833

B65
SCHOOL
EDU/PROP
ECO/UNDEV
ACADEM

OECD,THE MEDITERRANEAN REGIONAL PROJECT: GREECE;
EDUCATION AND DEVELOPMENT. FUT GREECE SOCIETY AGRI
FINAN NAT/G PROF/ORG WORKER PLAN PROB/SOLV ADMIN
DEMAND ATTIT 20 OECD. PAGE 42 G0834

B65
EDU/PROP
SCHOOL
ACADEM
ECO/UNDEV

OECD,THE MEDITERRANEAN REGIONAL PROJECT: SPAIN;
EDUCATION AND DEVELOPMENT. FUT SPAIN STRATA FINAN
NAT/G WORKER PLAN PROB/SOLV ADMIN COST...POLICY
STAT CHARTS 20 OECD. PAGE 42 G0835

B65
ECO/UNDEV
EDU/PROP
ACADEM
SCHOOL

ORG FOR ECO COOP AND DEVEL,THE MEDITERRANEAN
REGIONAL PROJECT: YUGOSLAVIA; EDUCATION AND
DEVELOPMENT. YUGOSLAVIA SOCIETY FINAN PROF/ORG PLAN
ADMIN COST DEMAND MARXISM...STAT TREND CHARTS METH
20 OECD. PAGE 43 G0843

B65
EDU/PROP
ACADEM
SCHOOL
ECO/UNDEV

ETZIONI A.,"ON THE NATIONAL GUIDANCE OF SCIENCE."
USA+45 FINAN NAT/G LEGIS GIVE 20. PAGE 18 G0353

S65
PHIL/SCI
CREATE
POLICY
EFFICIENCY

SILVERT K.H.,"AMERICAN ACADEMIC ETHICS AND SOCIAL
RESEARCH ABROAD* THE LESSON OF PROJECT CAMELOT."
CHILE L/A+17C USA+45 FINAN ADMIN...PHIL/SCI SOC
GEN/LAWS CAMELOT. PAGE 51 G0998

S65
ACADEM
NAT/G
ACT/RES
POLICY

FREIDEL F.,AMERICAN ISSUES IN THE TWENTIETH
CENTURY. SOCIETY FINAN ECO/TAC FOR/AID CONTROL
NUC/PWR WAR RACE/REL PEACE ATTIT...ANTHOL T 20
WILSON/W ROOSEVLT/F KENNEDY/JF TRUMAN/HS. PAGE 20
G0391

B66
DIPLOM
POLICY
NAT/G
ORD/FREE

LEWIS W.A.,DEVELOPMENT PLANNING; THE ESSENTIALS OF
ECONOMIC POLICY. USA+45 FINAN INDUS NAT/G WORKER
FOR/AID INT/TRADE ADMIN ROUTINE WEALTH...CONCPT
STAT. PAGE 34 G0663

B66
PLAN
ECO/DEV
POLICY
CREATE

LINDFORS G.V.,INTERCOLLEGIATE BIBLIOGRAPHY; CASES
IN BUSINESS ADMINISTRATION (VOL. X). FINAN MARKET

B66
BIBLIOG/A
ADMIN

LABOR CONSULT PLAN GP/REL PRODUC 20. PAGE 34 G0668

MGT
OP/RES

MURDOCK J.C.,RESEARCH AND REGIONS. AGRI FINAN INDUS
LOC/G MUNIC NAT/G PROB/SOLV TEC/DEV ADMIN REGION
20. PAGE 40 G0796

B66
BIBLIOG
ECO/DEV
COMPUT/IR
R+D

ONYEMELUKWE C.C.,PROBLEMS OF INDUSTRIAL PLANNING
AND MANAGEMENT IN NIGERIA. AFR FINAN LABOR DELIB/GP
TEC/DEV ADJUST...MGT TREND BIBLIOG. PAGE 43 G0839

B66
ECO/UNDEV
ECO/TAC
INDUS
PLAN

ROSHOLT R.L.,AN ADMINISTRATIVE HISTORY OF NASA,
1958-1963. SPACE USA+45 FINAN LEAD...MGT CHARTS
BIBLIOG 20 NASA. PAGE 48 G0938

B66
ADMIN
EX/STRUC
ADJUST
DELIB/GP

US HOUSE COMM ON JUDICIARY,CIVIL COMMITMENT AND
TREATMENT OF NARCOTIC ADDICTS. USA+45 SOCIETY FINAN
LEGIS PROB/SOLV GIVE CT/SYS SANCTION HEALTH
...POLICY HEAL 20. PAGE 58 G1141

B66
BIO/SOC
CRIME
IDEA/COMP
CONTROL

BAUMOL W.J.,BUSINESS BEHAVIOR, VALUE AND GROWTH
(REV. ED.). WOR+45 FINAN LG/CO TEC/DEV CAP/ISM
DEMAND EQUILIB...METH/COMP SIMUL 20. PAGE 5 G0105

B67
ALL/IDEOS
PHIL/SCI
PLAN
ECO/DEV

COLEMAN J.R.,THE CHANGING AMERICAN ECONOMY. USA+45
AGRI FINAN LABOR FOR/AID INT/TRADE AUTOMAT GP/REL
INGP/REL ANTHOL. PAGE 13 G0243

B67
BUDGET
ECO/TAC
ECO/DEV
WEALTH

COLM G.,THE ECONOMY OF THE AMERICAN PEOPLE. USA+45
ECO/DEV FINAN WORKER INT/TRADE AUTOMAT GP/REL.
PAGE 13 G0244

B67
ECO/TAC
PRODUC
TREND
TEC/DEV

DICKSON P.G.M.,THE FINANCIAL REVOLUTION IN ENGLAND.
UK NAT/G TEC/DEV ADMIN GOV/REL...SOC METH/CNCPT
CHARTS GP/COMP BIBLIOG 17/18. PAGE 15 G0302

B67
ECO/DEV
FINAN
CAP/ISM
MGT

FIELD M.G.,SOVIET SOCIALIZED MEDICINE. USSR FINAN
R+D PROB/SOLV ADMIN SOCISM...MGT SOC CONCPT 20.
PAGE 19 G0366

B67
PUB/INST
HEALTH
NAT/G
MARXISM

HIRSCHMAN A.O.,DEVELOPMENT PROJECTS OBSERVED. INDUS
INT/ORG CONSULT EX/STRUC CREATE OP/RES ECO/TAC
DEMAND...POLICY MGT METH/COMP 20 WORLD/BANK.
PAGE 26 G0513

B67
ECO/UNDEV
R+D
FINAN
PLAN

MACBRIDE R.,THE AUTOMATED STATE; COMPUTER SYSTEMS
AS A NEW FORCE IN SOCIETY. FUT WOR+45 FINAN MUNIC
NAT/G WORKER PLAN TEC/DEV CONTROL PERS/REL RACE/REL
ADJUST. PAGE 35 G0685

B67
COMPUTER
AUTOMAT
PROB/SOLV
SOCIETY

MAZOUR A.G.,SOVIET ECONOMIC DEVELOPMENT: OPERATION
OUTSTRIP: 1921-1965. USSR ECO/UNDEV FINAN CHIEF
WORKER PROB/SOLV CONTROL PRODUC MARXISM...CHARTS
ORG/CHARTS 20 STALIN/J. PAGE 37 G0726

B67
ECO/TAC
AGRI
INDUS
PLAN

UNIVERSAL REFERENCE SYSTEM,ECONOMIC REGULATION,
BUSINESS, AND GOVERNMENT (VOLUME VIII). WOR+45
WOR-45 ECO/DEV ECO/UNDEV FINAN LABOR TEC/DEV
ECO/TAC INT/TRADE GOV/REL...POLICY COMPUT/IR.
PAGE 56 G1099

B67
BIBLIOG/A
CONTROL
NAT/G

YAMAMURA K.,ECONOMIC POLICY IN POSTWAR JAPAN. ASIA
FINAN POL/PAR DIPLOM LEAD NAT/LISM ATTIT NEW/LIB
POPULISM 20 CHINJAP. PAGE 64 G1262

B67
ECO/DEV
POLICY
NAT/G
TEC/DEV

YAVITZ B.,AUTOMATION IN COMMERCIAL BANKING. USA+45
STRUCT WORKER CREATE OP/RES PLAN ROLE...DECISION
SAMP/SIZ. PAGE 64 G1263

B67
TEC/DEV
FINAN
COMPUT/IR
MGT

BARRO S.,"ECONOMIC IMPACT OF SPACE EXPENDITURES:

S67
SPACE

SOME BROAD ISSUES DEALING WITH COSTS AND BENEFITS." FINAN
USA+45 PROC/MFG R+D LG/CO CONSULT COST PRODUC 20.   ECO/TAC
PAGE 5 G0098   NAT/G

                                                          S67
CARR E.H.,"REVOLUTION FROM ABOVE." USSR STRATA   AGRI
FINAN INDUS NAT/G DOMIN LEAD GP/REL INGP/REL OWN   POLICY
PRODUC PWR 20 STALIN/J. PAGE 11 G0214   COM
                                                          EFFICIENCY

                                                          S67
ENKE S.,"GOVERNMENT-INDUSTRY DEVELOPMENT OF A   INDUS
COMMERCIAL SUPERSONIC TRANSPORT." USA+45 ECO/DEV   FINAN
R+D LG/CO NAT/G TEC/DEV PRICE RISK COST PROFIT.   SERV/IND
PAGE 18 G0347   CAP/ISM

                                                          S67
LAY S.H.,"EXCLUSIVE GOVERNMENTAL LIABILITY FOR   NAT/G
SPACE ACCIDENTS." USA+45 LAW FINAN SERV/IND TEC/DEV   SUPEGO
ADJUD. PAGE 33 G0646   SPACE
                                                          PROB/SOLV

                                                          S67
MYERS S.,"TECHNOLOGY AND URBAN TRANSIT: THE   R+D
ENORMOUS POTENTIAL OF BUS AND RAIL SYSTEMS." USA+45   TEC/DEV
FINAN LOC/G MUNIC WORKER PLAN PROB/SOLV PRICE   DIST/IND
AUTOMAT 20. PAGE 40 G0798   ACT/RES

                                                          S67
PENNEY N.,"BANK STATEMENTS, CANCELLED CHECKS, AND   CREATE
ARTICLE FOUR IN THE ELECTRONIC AGE." USA+45 TEC/DEV   LAW
COST EFFICIENCY WEALTH. PAGE 44 G0866   ADJUD
                                                          FINAN

                                                          S67
RICHMAN B.M.,"SOVIET MANAGEMENT IN TRANSITION."   MGT
USSR FINAN MARKET EX/STRUC PLAN PROB/SOLV TEC/DEV   MARXISM
CONTROL LEAD CENTRAL EFFICIENCY...METH/COMP 20   POLICY
REFORMERS. PAGE 47 G0917   AUTHORIT

                                                          S67
SCOVILLE W.J.,"GOVERNMENT REGULATION AND GROWTH IN   NAT/G
THE FRENCH PAPER INDUSTRY DURING THE EIGHTEENTH   PROC/MFG
CENTURY." FRANCE MOD/EUR FINAN CAP/ISM TAX ADMIN   ECO/DEV
CONTROL PRIVIL LAISSEZ...POLICY 18. PAGE 50 G0985   INGP/REL

                                                          N67
US SENATE COMM ON FOREIGN REL,ARMS SALES AND   ARMS/CONT
FOREIGN POLICY (PAMPHLET). FINAN FOR/AID CONTROL   ADMIN
20. PAGE 60 G1181   OP/RES
                                                          DIPLOM

                                                          B88
BENTHAM J.,DEFENCE OF USURY (1787). UK LAW NAT/G   TAX
TEC/DEV ECO/TAC CONTROL ATTIT...CONCPT IDEA/COMP 18   FINAN
SMITH/ADAM. PAGE 6 G0124   ECO/DEV
                                                          POLICY

FINANCE....SEE FINAN

FINCH/D....DANIEL FINCH

FINCH/ER....E.R. FINCH

FINE ARTS....SEE ART/METH

FINK C.F. G0367

FINKELSTEIN L.S. G0368,G0369

FINLAND....SEE ALSO APPROPRIATE TIME/SPACE/CULTURE INDEX

FIRM....SEE INDUS

FISCAL POLICY....SEE BUDGET

FISHING INDUSTRY....SEE EXTR/IND

FISHMAN B.G. G0370

FISHMAN L. G0370

FLANDERS....FLANDERS

FLEISCHER G.A. G0651

FLEMING W.G. G0371

FLOOD M.M. G0372

FLORENCE....MEDIEVAL AND RENAISSANCE

FLORES E. G0373

FLORIDA....FLORIDA

FLORINSKY M.T. G0374

FLYNN/BOSS....BOSS FLYNN

FNMA....FEDERAL NATIONAL MORTGAGE ASSOCIATION

FOCH/F....FERDINAND FOCH

FOGELMAN E. G0375

FOLDES L. G0376

FOLKLORE....SEE MYTH

FOLSOM M.B. G0377

FONTANE/T....THEODORE FONTANE

FOOD....SEE AGRI, ALSO EATING

FOOD AND AGRICULTURAL ORGANIZATION....SEE FAO

FOOD/PEACE....OFFICE OF FOOD FOR PEACE

FOOTE W. G0256

FOR/AID....FOREIGN AID

                                                          N
GT BRIT MIN OVERSEAS DEV, LIB, TECHNICAL CO-   BIBLIOG
OPERATION -- A BIBLIOGRAPHY. UK LAW SOCIETY DIPLOM   TEC/DEV
ECO/TAC FOR/AID...STAT 20 CMN/WLTH. PAGE 39 G0775   ECO/DEV
                                                        NAT/G

                                                          N47
FOX W.T.R.,UNITED STATES POLICY IN A TWO POWER   DIPLOM
WORLD. COM USA+45 USSR FORCES DOMIN AGREE NEUTRAL   FOR/AID
NUC/PWR ORD/FREE SOVEREIGN 20 COLD/WAR TREATY   POLICY
EUROPE/W INTERVENT. PAGE 20 G0389

                                                          B50
US DEPARTMENT OF STATE,POINT FOUR: COOPERATIVE   ECO/UNDEV
PROGRAM FOR AID IN THE DEVELOPMENT OF ECONOMICALLY   FOR/AID
UNDERDEVELOPED AREAS. WOR+45 AGRI INDUS INT/ORG   FINAN
PLAN TEC/DEV DIPLOM EDU/PROP ADMIN PEACE PRODUC   INT/TRADE
WEALTH 20 CONGRESS UN. PAGE 57 G1121

                                                          B53
MACK R.T.,RAISING THE WORLDS STANDARD OF LIVING.   WOR+45
IRAN INT/ORG VOL/ASSN EX/STRUC ECO/TAC WEALTH...MGT   FOR/AID
METH/CNCPT STAT CONT/OBS INT TOT/POP VAL/FREE 20   INT/TRADE
UN. PAGE 35 G0690

                                                          B54
US DEPARTMENT OF STATE,PUBLICATIONS OF THE   BIBLIOG
DEPARTMENT OF STATE, OCTOBER 1,1929 TO JANUARY 1,   DIPLOM
1953. AGRI INT/ORG FORCES FOR/AID EDU/PROP
ARMS/CONT NUC/PWR ATTIT 20 DEPT/STATE OAS UN NATO.
PAGE 57 G1122

                                                          L54
OPLER M.E.,"SOCIAL ASPECTS OF TECHNICAL ASSISTANCE   INT/ORG
IN OPERATION." WOR+45 VOL/ASSN CREATE PLAN TEC/DEV   CONSULT
EDU/PROP ALL/VALS...METH/CNCPT OBS RECORD TREND UN   FOR/AID
20. PAGE 43 G0841

                                                          B55
JONES J.M.,THE FIFTEEN WEEKS (FEBRUARY 21-JUNE 5,   DIPLOM
1947). DIPLOM USA+45 PROB/SOLV BAL/PWR...POLICY   ECO/TAC
TIME/SEQ 20 COLD/WAR MARSHL/PLN TRUMAN/HS   FOR/AID
WASHING/DC. PAGE 29 G0567

                                                          B55
US OFFICE OF THE PRESIDENT,REPORT TO CONGRESS ON   DIPLOM
THE MUTUAL SECURITY PROGRAM FOR THE SIX MONTHS   FORCES
ENDED JUNE 30, 1955. ECO/DEV INT/ORG NAT/G CREATE   PLAN
TEC/DEV BAL/PWR ECO/TAC AGREE DETER COST ORD/FREE   FOR/AID
20 DEPT/STATE DEPT/DEFEN. PAGE 59 G1157

                                                          B56
US OFFICE OF THE PRESIDENT,REPORT TO CONGRESS ON   DIPLOM
THE MUTUAL SECURITY PROGRAM FOR THE SIX MONTHS   FORCES
ENDED DECEMBER 31, 1955. ASIA USSR ECO/DEV   PLAN
ECO/UNDEV INT/ORG CREATE TEC/DEV BAL/PWR ECO/TAC   FOR/AID
AGREE DETER COST ORD/FREE 20 DEPT/STATE DEPT/DEFEN
EISNHWR/DD. PAGE 59 G1158

                                                          B57
DRUCKER P.F.,AMERICA'S NEXT TWENTY YEARS. USA+45   WORKER
DIST/IND ACADEM MUNIC SCHOOL DIPLOM ECO/TAC AUTOMAT   FOR/AID
HABITAT HEALTH...SOC/WK TREND 20 URBAN/RNWL   CENSUS
PUB/TRANS. PAGE 16 G0316   GEOG

B57
GOLD N.L.,REGIONAL ECONOMIC DEVELOPMENT AND NUCLEAR ECO/UNDEV
POWER IN INDIA. FUT INDIA FINAN FOR/AID INT/TRADE TEC/DEV
BAL/PAY EFFICIENCY OPTIMAL PRODUC WEALTH...PREDICT NUC/PWR
20. PAGE 22 G0424 INDUS

B58
EHRHARD J.,LE DESTIN DU COLONIALISME. AFR FRANCE COLONIAL
ECO/UNDEV AGRI FINAN MARKET CREATE PLAN TEC/DEV FOR/AID
BUDGET DIPLOM PRICE 20. PAGE 17 G0335 INT/TRADE
INDUS

B58
US DEPARTMENT OF STATE,PUBLICATIONS OF THE BIBLIOG
DEPARTMENT OF STATE, JANUARY 1,1953 TO DECEMBER 31, DIPLOM
1957. AGRI INT/ORG FORCES FOR/AID EDU/PROP
ARMS/CONT NUC/PWR ATTIT 20 DEPT/STATE OAS UN NATO.
PAGE 57 G1123

S58
DAVENPORT J.,"ARMS AND THE WELFARE STATE." INTELL USA+45
STRUCT FORCES CREATE ECO/TAC FOR/AID DOMIN LEGIT NAT/G
ADMIN WAR ORD/FREE PWR...POLICY SOC CONCPT MYTH OBS USSR
TREND COLD/WAR TOT/POP 20. PAGE 14 G0276

S58
MARCY C.,"THE RESEARCH PROGRAM OF THE SENATE DELIB/GP
COMMITTEE ON FOREIGN RELATIONS." EUR+WWI ECO/UNDEV LEGIS
ACT/RES PLAN PARL/PROC GOV/REL...GEOG CONFE FOR/AID
CONGRESS. PAGE 36 G0704 POLICY

B59
AIR FORCE ACADEMY ASSEMBLY '59,INTERNATIONAL FOR/AID
STABILITY AND PROGRESS (PAMPHLET). USA+45 USSR FORCES
ECO/UNDEV PROB/SOLV BUDGET DIPLOM ADMIN DETER COST WAR
ATTIT...TREND 20. PAGE 2 G0030 PLAN

B59
HUGHES E.M.,AMERICA THE VINCIBLE. USA+45 FOR/AID ORD/FREE
ARMS/CONT NUC/PWR PERS/REL RATIONAL ATTIT ALL/VALS DIPLOM
20 COLD/WAR. PAGE 27 G0534 WAR

B59
MAYDA J.,ATOMIC ENERGY AND LAW. ECO/UNDEV FINAN NUC/PWR
TEC/DEV FOR/AID EFFICIENCY PRODUC WEALTH...POLICY L/A+17C
TECHNIC 20. PAGE 37 G0723 LAW
ADMIN

S59
STOESSINGER J.G.,"THE INTERNATIONAL ATOMIC ENERGY INT/ORG
AGENCY: THE FIRST PHASE." FUT WOR+45 NAT/G VOL/ASSN ECO/DEV
DELIB/GP BAL/PWR LEGIT ADMIN ROUTINE PWR...OBS FOR/AID
CON/ANAL GEN/LAWS VAL/FREE 20 IAEA. PAGE 53 G1037 NUC/PWR

B60
BROOKINGS INSTITUTION,UNITED STATES FOREIGN POLICY: DIPLOM
STUDY NO 9: THE FORMULATION AND ADMINISTRATION OF INT/ORG
UNITED STATES FOREIGN POLICY. USA+45 WOR+45 CREATE
EX/STRUC LEGIS BAL/PWR FOR/AID EDU/PROP CIVMIL/REL
GOV/REL...INT COLD/WAR. PAGE 9 G0174

B60
PENTONY D.E.,THE UNDERDEVELOPED LANDS. FUT WOR+45 ECO/UNDEV
CULTURE AGRI FINAN INDUS MARKET INT/ORG LABOR NAT/G POLICY
VOL/ASSN CONSULT TEC/DEV ECO/TAC EDU/PROP COLONIAL FOR/AID
ATTIT WEALTH...OBS RECORD SAMP TREND GEN/METH WORK INT/TRADE
UN 20. PAGE 44 G0867

S60
RIVKIN A.,"AFRICAN ECONOMIC DEVELOPMENT: ADVANCED AFR
TECHNOLOGY AND THE STAGES OF GROWTH." CULTURE TEC/DEV
ECO/UNDEV AGRI COM/IND EXTR/IND PLAN ECO/TAC ATTIT FOR/AID
DRIVE RIGID/FLEX SKILL WEALTH...MGT SOC GEN/LAWS
WORK TOT/POP 20. PAGE 47 G0923

B61
BONNEFOUS M.,EUROPE ET TIERS MONDE. EUR+WWI SOCIETY AFR
INT/ORG NAT/G VOL/ASSN ACT/RES TEC/DEV CAP/ISM ECO/UNDEV
ECO/TAC ATTIT ORD/FREE SOVEREIGN...POLICY CONCPT FOR/AID
TREND 20. PAGE 8 G0153 INT/TRADE

B62
AIR FORCE ACADEMY LIBRARY,INTERNATIONAL BIBLIOG
ORGANIZATIONS AND MILITARY SECURITY SYSTEMS INT/ORG
(PAMPHLET) (SPECIAL BIBLIOGRAPHY SERIES, NUMBER FORCES
25). DIPLOM FOR/AID INT/TRADE NUC/PWR PEACE 20 UN DETER
NATO OAS SEATO LEAGUE/NAT. PAGE 2 G0031

B62
BROOKINGS INSTITUTION,DEVELOPMENT OF THE EMERGING ECO/UNDEV
COUNTRIES: AN AGENDA FOR RESEARCH. WOR+45 AGRI R+D
TEC/DEV FOR/AID EDU/PROP ADJUST HABITAT KNOWL...PSY SOCIETY
SOC ANTHOL 20 THIRD/WRLD. PAGE 9 G0175 PROB/SOLV

B62
FRIEDRICH-EBERT-STIFTUNG,THE SOVIET BLOC AND MARXISM

DEVELOPING COUNTRIES. CHINA/COM COM GERMANY/E USSR DIPLOM
WOR+45 ECO/UNDEV INT/ORG NAT/G TEC/DEV NEUTRAL PWR ECO/TAC
...POLICY 20. PAGE 20 G0394 FOR/AID

B62
SCHMITT H.A.,THE PATH TO EUROPEAN UNITY. EUR+WWI INT/ORG
USA+45 PLAN TEC/DEV DIPLOM FOR/AID CONFER...INT/LAW INT/TRADE
20 EEC EURCOALSTL MARSHL/PLN UNIFICA. PAGE 49 G0971 REGION
ECO/DEV

S62
MORGENTHAU H.J.,"A POLITICAL THEORY OF FOREIGN USA+45
AID." ECO/UNDEV NAT/G DELIB/GP PLAN ECO/TAC PHIL/SCI
EDU/PROP EXEC ORD/FREE RESPECT WEALTH...METH/CNCPT FOR/AID
TREND 20. PAGE 40 G0783

B63
HAUSMAN W.H.,MANAGING ECONOMIC DEVELOPMENT IN ECO/UNDEV
AFRICA. AFR USA+45 LAW FINAN WORKER TEC/DEV WEALTH PLAN
...ANTHOL 20. PAGE 25 G0492 FOR/AID
MGT

B63
KATZ S.M.,A SELECTED LIST OF US READINGS ON BIBLIOG/A
DEVELOPMENT. AGRI COM/IND DIST/IND INDUS LABOR PLAN ECO/UNDEV
FOR/AID EDU/PROP HEALTH...POLICY SOC/WK 20. PAGE 30 TEC/DEV
G0582 ACT/RES

B63
SCHOECK H.,THE NEW ARGUMENT IN ECONOMICS. UK USA+45 WELF/ST
INDUS MARKET LABOR NAT/G ECO/TAC ADMIN ROUTINE FOR/AID
BAL/PAY PWR...POLICY BOLIV. PAGE 49 G0973 ECO/DEV
ALL/IDEOS

B63
US SENATE COMM APPROPRIATIONS,PERSONNEL ADMIN
ADMINISTRATION AND OPERATIONS OF AGENCY FOR FOR/AID
INTERNATIONAL DEVELOPMENT: SPECIAL HEARING. FINAN EFFICIENCY
LEAD COST UTIL SKILL...CHARTS 20 CONGRESS AID DIPLOM
CIVIL/SERV. PAGE 60 G1175

S63
GANDILHON J.,"LA SCIENCE ET LA TECHNIQUE A L'AIDE ECO/UNDEV
DES REGIONS PEU DEVELOPPEES." FRANCE FUT WOR+45 TEC/DEV
ECO/DEV R+D PROF/ORG ACT/RES PLAN...MGT TOT/POP FOR/AID
VAL/FREE 20 UN. PAGE 21 G0406

S63
NADLER E.B.,"SOME ECONOMIC DISADVANTAGES OF THE ECO/DEV
ARMS RACE." USA+45 INDUS R+D FORCES PLAN TEC/DEV MGT
ECO/TAC FOR/AID EDU/PROP PWR WEALTH...TREND BAL/PAY
COLD/WAR 20. PAGE 41 G0800

B64
MILIBAND R.,THE SOCIALIST REGISTER: 1964. GERMANY/W MARXISM
ITALY UK LABOR POL/PAR ECO/TAC FOR/AID NUC/PWR SOCISM
...POLICY SOCIALIST IDEA/COMP 20 MAO NASSER/G. CAP/ISM
PAGE 39 G0769 PROB/SOLV

B64
ROBERTS HL,FOREIGN AFFAIRS BIBLIOGRAPHY, 1952-1962. BIBLIOG/A
ECO/DEV SECT PLAN FOR/AID INT/TRADE ARMS/CONT DIPLOM
NAT/LISM ATTIT...INT/LAW GOV/COMP IDEA/COMP 20. INT/ORG
PAGE 47 G0928 WAR

L64
CARNEGIE ENDOWMENT INT. PEACE,"ECONOMIC AND SOCIAL INT/ORG
QUESTION BEFORE THE NINETEENTH GENERAL INT/TRADE
ASSEMBLY)." WOR+45 ECO/DEV ECO/UNDEV INDUS R+D
DELIB/GP CREATE PLAN TEC/DEV ECO/TAC FOR/AID
BAL/PAY...RECORD UN 20. PAGE 11 G0209

B65
PEACE RESEARCH ABSTRACTS. FUT WOR+45 R+D INT/ORG BIBLIOG/A
NAT/G PLAN TEC/DEV BAL/PWR DIPLOM FOR/AID NUC/PWR PEACE
HEALTH. PAGE 1 G0020 ARMS/CONT
WAR

B65
UN,SPACE ACTIVITIES AND RESOURCES: REVIEW OF UNITED SPACE
NATION'S NATIONAL AND INTERNATIONAL PROGRAMS. NUC/PWR
INT/ORG LABOR PLAN TEC/DEV DIPLOM EFFICIENCY HEALTH FOR/AID
...GOV/COMP 20 UN. PAGE 55 G1086 PEACE

B65
WEISNER J.B.,WHERE SCIENCE AND POLITICS MEET. CHIEF
USA+45 ECO/DEV R+D FORCES PROB/SOLV DIPLOM FOR/AID NAT/G
CONTROL...PHIL/SCI PRESIDENT KENNEDY/JF JOHNSON/LB. POLICY
PAGE 63 G1228 TEC/DEV

C65
US AIR FORCE ACADEMY,"AMERICAN DEFENSE POLICY." COM PLAN
INT/ORG TEC/DEV FOR/AID ARMS/CONT DETER NUC/PWR FORCES
...POLICY DECISION CONCPT ANTHOL BIBLIOG/A 20 WAR
COLD/WAR NATO. PAGE 56 G1103 COERCE

ALEXANDER Y.,INTERNATIONAL TECHNICAL ASSISTANCE   B66
EXPERTS* A CASE STUDY OF THE U.N. EXPERIENCE.   ECO/TAC
ECO/UNDEV CONSULT EX/STRUC CREATE PLAN DIPLOM   INT/ORG
FOR/AID TASK EFFICIENCY...ORG/CHARTS UN. PAGE 2   ADMIN
G0038   MGT

ALEXANDER Y.,INTERNATIONAL TECHNICAL ASSISTANCE   B66
EXPERTS: A CASE STUDY OF THE U.N. EXPERIENCE.   SKILL
USA+45 WOR+45 WORKER CREATE PLAN PROB/SOLV ECO/TAC   INT/ORG
FOR/AID GIVE EDU/PROP...CHARTS BIBLIOG 20 UN.   TEC/DEV
PAGE 2 G0039   CONSULT

ECKSTEIN A.,COMMUNIST CHINA'S ECONOMIC GROWTH AND   B66
FOREIGN TRADE* IMPLICATIONS FOR US POLICY. COM   ASIA
USA+45 USSR INDUS MARKET DIPLOM ECO/TAC   ECO/UNDEV
FOR/AID INT/TRADE...STAT CHARTS. PAGE 17 G0332   CREATE
                                                      PWR

FREIDEL F.,AMERICAN ISSUES IN THE TWENTIETH   B66
CENTURY. SOCIETY FINAN ECO/TAC FOR/AID CONTROL   DIPLOM
NUC/PWR WAR RACE/REL PEACE ATTIT...ANTHOL T 20   POLICY
WILSON/W ROOSEVLT/F KENNEDY/JF TRUMAN/HS. PAGE 20   NAT/G
G0391   ORD/FREE

LECHT L.,GOAL, PRIORITIES, AND DOLLARS: THE NEXT   B66
DECADE. SPACE USA+45 SOCIETY AGRI BUDGET FOR/AID   IDEA/COMP
...HEAL SOC/WK STAT CHARTS 20 URBAN/RNWL PUB/TRANS.   POLICY
PAGE 33 G0649   CONSEN
                                                      PLAN

LEWIS W.A.,DEVELOPMENT PLANNING; THE ESSENTIALS OF   B66
ECONOMIC POLICY. USA+45 FINAN INDUS NAT/G WORKER   PLAN
FOR/AID INT/TRADE ADMIN ROUTINE WEALTH...CONCPT   ECO/DEV
STAT. PAGE 34 G0663   POLICY
                                                      CREATE

WARD B.,NATIONALISM AND IDEOLOGY. ECO/UNDEV KIN   B66
CREATE CAP/ISM FOR/AID ALL/VALS MARXISM...POLICY   IDEA/COMP
SOC. PAGE 62 G1211   NAT/LISM
                                                      ATTIT

PACKENHAM R.A.,"POLITICAL-DEVELOPMENT DOCTRINES IN   L66
THE AMERICAN FOREIGN AID PROGRAM." STRUCT R+D   FOR/AID
CREATE DIPLOM AID. PAGE 43 G0855   ECO/UNDEV
                                                      GEN/LAWS

COHEN A.,"THE TECHNOLOGY/ELITE APPROACH TO THE   S66
DEVELOPMENTAL PROCESS* PERUVIAN CASE STUDY."   ECO/UNDEV
L/A+17C STRUCT CREATE ECO/TAC FOR/AID CIVMIL/REL   ELITES
MARXISM TECHRACY HYPO/EXP. PAGE 12 G0239   PERU

COLEMAN J.R.,THE CHANGING AMERICAN ECONOMY. USA+45   B67
AGRI FINAN LABOR FOR/AID INT/TRADE AUTOMAT GP/REL   BUDGET
INGP/REL ANTHOL. PAGE 13 G0243   ECO/TAC
                                                      ECO/DEV
                                                      WEALTH

HALLE L.J.,THE COLD WAR AS HISTORY. USSR WOR+45   B67
ECO/TAC FOR/AID NUC/PWR WAR PEACE ORD/FREE   DIPLOM
...MAJORIT TREND 20 COLD/WAR KENNEDY/JF KHRUSH/N   BAL/PWR
BERLIN/BLO. PAGE 24 G0470

OVERSEAS DEVELOPMENT INSTIT.EFFECTIVE AID. WOR+45   B67
INT/ORG TEC/DEV DIPLOM INT/TRADE ADMIN. PAGE 43   FOR/AID
G0852   ECO/UNDEV
                                                      ECO/TAC
                                                      NAT/COMP

US SENATE COMM ON FOREIGN REL.ARMS SALES TO NEAR   B67
EAST AND SOUTH ASIAN COUNTRIES. INDIA IRAN PAKISTAN   WEAPON
WOR+45 PROC/MFG BAL/PWR DIPLOM...DECISION SENATE.   FOR/AID
PAGE 60 G1183   FORCES
                                                      POLICY

US SENATE COMM ON FOREIGN REL.UNITED STATES   B67
ARMAMENT AND DISARMAMENT PROBLEMS. USA+45 AIR   ARMS/CONT
BAL/PWR DIPLOM FOR/AID NUC/PWR ORD/FREE SENATE   WEAPON
TREATY. PAGE 60 G1184   FORCES
                                                      PROB/SOLV

US SENATE COMM ON FOREIGN REL.FOREIGN ASSISTANCE   B67
ACT OF 1967. VIETNAM WOR+45 DELIB/GP CONFER CONTROL   FOR/AID
WAR WEAPON BAL/PAY...CENSUS CHARTS SENATE. PAGE 60   LAW
G1185   DIPLOM
                                                      POLICY

FADDEYEV N.,"CMEA CO-OPERATION OF EQUAL NATIONS."   S67
COM R+D PLAN CAP/ISM DIPLOM FOR/AID WEALTH...POLICY   MARXISM
MARXIST. PAGE 18 G0356   ECO/TAC
                                                      INT/ORG
                                                      ECO/UNDEV

JAIN G.,"INDIA REJECTS THE POWER RACE* REALISM   S67
ABOUT NUCLEAR WEAPONS." FORCES PROB/SOLV FOR/AID   INDIA
ARMS/CONT COST PWR...GOV/COMP 20. PAGE 28 G0556   CHINA/COM
                                                      NUC/PWR
                                                      DIPLOM

MEHTA A.,"INDIA* POVERTY AND CHANGE." STRATA INDUS   S67
CREATE ECO/TAC FOR/AID NEUTRAL GP/REL ADJUST INCOME   INDIA
...NEW/IDEA 20. PAGE 38 G0751   SOCIETY
                                                      ECO/UNDEV
                                                      TEC/DEV

US HOUSE COMM FOREIGN AFFAIRS.REPORT OF SPECIAL   N67
STUDY MISSION TO THE NEAR EAST (PAMPHLET). ISRAEL   ISLAM
USA+45 YEMEN ECO/UNDEV INT/ORG FOR/AID ARMS/CONT   DIPLOM
WAR WEAPON NAT/LISM PEACE...GEOG 20 UN HOUSE/REP.   FORCES
PAGE 58 G1138

US HOUSE COMM SCI ASTRONAUT.GOVERNMENT, SCIENCE,   N67
AND INTERNATIONAL POLICY (PAMPHLET). INDIA   NAT/G
NETHERLAND ECO/DEV ECO/UNDEV R+D ACADEM PLAN DIPLOM   POLICY
FOR/AID CONFER...PREDICT 20 CHINJAP. PAGE 59 G1152   CREATE
                                                      TEC/DEV

US SENATE COMM ON FOREIGN REL.ARMS SALES AND   N67
FOREIGN POLICY (PAMPHLET). FINAN FOR/AID CONTROL   ARMS/CONT
20. PAGE 60 G1181   ADMIN
                                                      OP/RES
                                                      DIPLOM

FORBES H.W. G0378

FORCE AND VIOLENCE....SEE COERCE

FORCES....ARMED FORCES AND POLICE

FULLER G.A.,DEMOBILIZATION: A SELECTED LIST OF   N
REFERENCES. USA+45 LAW AGRI LABOR WORKER ECO/TAC   BIBLIOG/A
RATION RECEIVE EDU/PROP ROUTINE ARMS/CONT ALL/VALS   INDUS
20. PAGE 20 G0398   FORCES
                                                      NAT/G

WEIGLEY R.F.,HISTORY OF THE UNITED STATES ARMY.   N
USA+45 USA-45 SOCIETY NAT/G LEAD WAR GP/REL PWR   FORCES
...SOC METH/COMP COLD/WAR. PAGE 62 G1222   ADMIN
                                                      ROLE
                                                      CIVMIL/REL

CURRENT THOUGHT ON PEACE AND WAR. WOR+45 INT/ORG   B
FORCES PROB/SOLV DIPLOM NUC/PWR PERCEPT...POLICY   BIBLIOG/A
SOC 20 UN NATO. PAGE 1 G0001   PEACE
                                                      ATTIT
                                                      WAR

JOURNAL OF CONFLICT RESOLUTION. FUT WOR+45 INT/ORG   N
NAT/G FORCES CREATE PROB/SOLV ARMS/CONT NUC/PWR   BIBLIOG/A
WEAPON SOC. PAGE 1 G0002   DIPLOM
                                                      WAR

INDIA: A REFERENCE ANNUAL. INDIA CULTURE COM/IND   N
R+D FORCES PLAN RECEIVE EDU/PROP HEALTH...STAT   CONSTN
CHARTS BIBLIOG 20. PAGE 1 G0005   LABOR
                                                      INT/ORG

AIR UNIVERSITY LIBRARY.INDEX TO MILITARY   N
PERIODICALS. FUT SPACE WOR+45 REGION ARMS/CONT   BIBLIOG/A
NUC/PWR WAR PEACE INT/LAW. PAGE 2 G0032   FORCES
                                                      NAT/G
                                                      DIPLOM

US SUPERINTENDENT OF DOCUMENTS.TRANSPORTATION: N
HIGHWAYS, ROADS, AND POSTAL SERVICE (PRICE LIST   BIBLIOG/A
25). PANAMA USA+45 LAW FORCES DIPLOM ADMIN GOV/REL   DIST/IND
HEALTH MGT. PAGE 61 G1188   SERV/IND
                                                      NAT/G

CRAIG J.,ELEMENTS OF POLITICAL SCIENCE (3 VOLS.).   B14
CONSTN AGRI INDUS SCHOOL FORCES TAX CT/SYS SUFF   PHIL/SCI
MORAL WEALTH...CONCPT 19 CIVIL/LIB. PAGE 13 G0259   NAT/G
                                                      ORD/FREE

GINZBERG E.,MANPOWER FOR GOVERNMENT (PAMPHLET).   N19
USA+45 FORCES PLAN PROB/SOLV PAY EDU/PROP ADMIN   WORKER
GP/REL COST...MGT PREDICT TREND 20 CIVIL/SERV.   CONSULT
PAGE 21 G0418   NAT/G
                                                      LOC/G

MEZERIK AG.OUTER SPACE: UN, US, USSR (PAMPHLET).   N19
USSR DELIB/GP FORCES DETER NUC/PWR SOVEREIGN   SPACE
...POLICY 20 UN TREATY. PAGE 39 G0763   CONTROL
                                                      DIPLOM
                                                      INT/ORG

MOON P.T.,"SYLLABUS ON INTERNATIONAL RELATIONS."
EUR+WWI MOD/EUR USA-45 FORCES COLONIAL WAR WEAPON
NAT/LISM...POLICY BIBLIOG T 19/20. PAGE 39 G0778
C25
INT/ORG
DIPLOM
NAT/G

EINSTEIN A.,THE WORLD AS I SEE IT. WOR-45 INTELL
R+D INT/ORG NAT/G SECT VOL/ASSN FORCES CREATE
EDU/PROP LEGIT ARMS/CONT WAR WEAPON NAT/LISM
ALL/VALS...POLICY CONCPT 20. PAGE 17 G0337
B34
SOCIETY
PHIL/SCI
DIPLOM
PACIFISM

FOREIGN AFFAIRS BIBLIOGRAPHY: A SELECTED AND
ANNOTATED LIST OF BOOKS ON INTERNATIONAL RELATIONS
1919-1962 (4 VOLS.). CONSTN FORCES COLONIAL
ARMS/CONT WAR NAT/LISM PEACE ATTIT DRIVE...POLICY
INT/LAW 20. PAGE 1 G0011
B35
BIBLIOG/A
DIPLOM
INT/ORG

FULLER G.H.,A SELECTED LIST OF REFERENCES ON THE
EXPANSION OF THE US NAVY, 1933-1939 (PAMPHLET).
MOD/EUR USA-45 NAT/G PLAN DIPLOM DOMIN RISK
ARMS/CONT EQUILIB PWR 20 NAVY. PAGE 20 G0399
B39
BIBLIOG
FORCES
WEAPON
WAR

FULLER G.H.,SELECTED LIST OF RECENT REFERENCES ON
AMERICAN NATIONAL DEFENSE (PAMPHLET). USA-45 FINAN
NAT/G ARMS/CONT WAR GOV/REL CENTRAL COST PEACE PWR
20. PAGE 20 G0400
B40
BIBLIOG
CIVMIL/REL
FORCES
WEAPON

FULLER G.H.,DEFENSE FINANCING: A SELECTED LIST OF
REFERENCES (PAMPHLET). MOD/EUR USA-45 ECO/DEV FINAN
DELIB/GP RATION ARMS/CONT WEAPON COST PEACE PWR 20
CONGRESS. PAGE 20 G0401
B41
BIBLIOG/A
FINAN
FORCES
BUDGET

FULLER G.H.,A LIST OF BIBLIOGRAPHIES ON QUESTIONS
RELATING TO NATIONAL DEFENSE (PAMPHLET). USA-45
NAT/G ARMS/CONT WAR GOV/REL COST PEACE 20. PAGE 20
G0402
B41
BIBLIOG/A
FORCES
CIVMIL/REL
WEAPON

FULLER G.H.,DEFENSE FINANCING: A SUPPLEMENTARY LIST
OF REFERENCES (PAMPHLET). CANADA UK USA-45 ECO/DEV
NAT/G DELIB/GP BUDGET ADJUD ARMS/CONT WEAPON COST
PEACE PWR 20 AUSTRAL CHINJAP CONGRESS. PAGE 21
G0403
B42
BIBLIOG/A
FINAN
FORCES
DIPLOM

US LIBRARY OF CONGRESS,CONDUCT OF THE WAR (APRIL
1941-MARCH 1942). USA-45 WOR-45 LAW INDUS PUB/INST
TEC/DEV EDU/PROP CIVMIL/REL 20. PAGE 59 G1155
B42
BIBLIOG/A
WAR
FORCES
PLAN

FULLER G.H.,MILITARY GOVERNMENT: A LIST OF
REFERENCES (A PAMPHLET). ITALY UK USA-45 WOR-45 LAW
FORCES DOMIN ADMIN ARMS/CONT ORD/FREE PWR
...DECISION 20 CHINJAP. PAGE 21 G0404
B44
BIBLIOG
DIPLOM
CIVMIL/REL
SOVEREIGN

MATTHEWS M.A.,INTERNATIONAL POLICE (PAMPHLET).
WOR-45 DIPLOM ARMS/CONT WAR 20. PAGE 37 G0722
B44
BIBLIOG
INT/ORG
FORCES
PEACE

TRYTTEN M.H.,"THE MOBILIZATION OF SCIENTISTS," IN
L. WHITE, CIVIL SERVICE IN WARTIME." USA-45 R+D
FORCES ACT/RES PERSON ROLE 20. PAGE 55 G1080
C45
INTELL
WAR
TEC/DEV
NAT/G

BAXTER J.P.,SCIENTISTS AGAINST TIME. EUR+WWI
MOD/EUR USA-45 WOR-45 WOR-45 R+D NAT/G PLAN
ATTIT PWR...PHIL/SCI RECORD CON/ANAL 17/20. PAGE 6
G0107
B46
FORCES
WAR
NUC/PWR

WILCOX J.K.,OFFICIAL DEFENSE PUBLICATIONS,
1941-1945 (NINE VOLS.). USA-45 AGRI INDUS R+D LABOR
FORCES TEC/DEV EFFICIENCY PRODUC SKILL WEALTH 20.
PAGE 63 G1238
B46
BIBLIOG/A
WAR
CIVMIL/REL
ADMIN

BALDWIN H.W.,THE PRICE OF POWER. USA+45 FORCES PLAN
NUC/PWR ADJUST COST ORD/FREE...POLICY PSY BIBLIOG
20. PAGE 5 G0089
B47
PROB/SOLV
PWR
POPULISM
PRICE

LASSWELL H.D.,THE ANALYSIS OF POLITICAL BEHAVIOUR:
AN EMPIRICAL APPROACH. WOR+45 CULTURE NAT/G FORCES
EDU/PROP ADMIN ATTIT PERCEPT KNOWL...PHIL/SCI PSY
SOC NEW/IDEA OBS INT GEN/METH NAZI 20. PAGE 32
B47
R+D
ACT/RES
ELITES

G0639

TURNER R.H.,"THE NAVY DISBURSING OFFICER AS A
BUREAUCRAT" (BMR)" USA-45 LAW STRATA DIST/IND WAR
PWR...SOC 20 BUREAUCRCY. PAGE 55 G1083
S47
FORCES
ADMIN
PERSON
ROLE

FOX W.T.R.,UNITED STATES POLICY IN A TWO POWER
WORLD. COM USA+45 USSR FORCES DOMIN AGREE NEUTRAL
NUC/PWR ORD/FREE SOVEREIGN 20 COLD/WAR TREATY
EUROPE/W INTERVENT. PAGE 20 G0389
N47
DIPLOM
FOR/AID
POLICY

BRADLEY D.,NO PLACE TO HIDE. USA+45 SOCIETY NAT/G
FORCES TEC/DEV EDU/PROP DETER PEACE BIO/SOC
ALL/VALS...POLICY PHIL/SCI OBS RECORD SAMP BIOG
GEN/METH COLD/WAR 20. PAGE 8 G0162
B48
R+D
LAB/EXP
ARMS/CONT
NUC/PWR

GRIFFITH E.S.,RESEARCH IN POLITICAL SCIENCE: THE
WORK OF PANELS OF RESEARCH COMMITTEE, APSA. WOR+45
WOR-45 COM/IND R+D FORCES ACT/RES WAR...GOV/COMP
ANTHOL 20. PAGE 23 G0451
B48
BIBLIOG
PHIL/SCI
DIPLOM
JURID

SOUERS S.W.,"POLICY FORMULATION FOR NATIONAL
SECURITY." EX/STRUC FORCES PROB/SOLV DIPLOM CONFER
EXEC ARMS/CONT DETER NUC/PWR GOV/REL PEACE
COLD/WAR. PAGE 52 G1022
S49
DELIB/GP
CHIEF
DECISION
POLICY

CROWTHER J.G.,SCIENCE AT WAR. EUR+WWI PLAN TEC/DEV
DOMIN COERCE NUC/PWR WEAPON KNOWL PWR...CONCPT OBS
TREND VAL/FREE 20. PAGE 14 G0265
B50
R+D
FORCES
WAR
UK

HUZAR E.,THE PURSE AND THE SWORD: CONTROL OF THE
ARMY BY CONGRESS THROUGH MILITARY APPROPRIATIONS
1933-1950. NAT/G DELIB/GP EX/STRUC FORCES PROB/SOLV
BARGAIN CONFER ADMIN ROUTINE GOV/REL EFFICIENCY
...POLICY COLD/WAR. PAGE 27 G0541
B50
CIVMIL/REL
BUDGET
CONTROL
LEGIS

CONTINUITIES IN SOCIAL RESEARCH; STUDIES IN SCOPE
AND METHOD OF "THE AMERICAN SOLDIER" USA+45 FORCES
INGP/REL ATTIT...PSY SAMP CON/ANAL CHARTS GEN/LAWS
ANTHOL 20. PAGE 38 G0758
B50
SOC
PHIL/SCI
METH

MAASS A.,MUDDY WATERS: THE ARMY ENGINEERS AND THE
NATIONS RIVERS. USA-45 PROF/ORG CONSULT LEGIS ADMIN
EXEC ROLE PWR...SOC PRESIDENT 20. PAGE 35 G0682
B51
FORCES
GP/REL
LOBBY
CONSTRUC

CURRENT TRENDS IN PSYCHOLOGY,PSYCHOLOGY IN THE
WORLD EMERGENCY. USA+45 CONSULT FORCES ACT/RES PLAN
SKILL...DECISION OBS APT/TEST KNO/TEST PERS/TEST
TREND CHARTS 20. PAGE 14 G0266
B52
NAT/G
PSY

BRETTON H.L.,STRESEMANN AND THE REVISION OF
VERSAILLES: A FIGHT FOR REASON. EUR+WWI GERMANY
FORCES BUDGET ARMS/CONT WAR SUPEGO...BIBLIOG 20
TREATY VERSAILLES STRESEMN/G. PAGE 9 G0167
B53
POLICY
DIPLOM
BIOG

LANGER W.L.,THE UNDECLARED WAR, 1940-1941. EUR+WWI
GERMANY USA-45 USSR AIR FORCES TEC/DEV CONFER
CONTROL COERCE PERCEPT ORD/FREE PWR 20 CHINJAP
EUROPE. PAGE 32 G0634
B53
WAR
POLICY
DIPLOM

PERKINS J.A.,"ADMINISTRATION OF THE NATIONAL
SECURITY PROGRAM." USA+45 EX/STRUC FORCES ADMIN
CIVMIL/REL ORD/FREE 20. PAGE 44 G0868
S53
CONTROL
GP/REL
REPRESENT
PROB/SOLV

ARON R.,CENTURY OF TOTAL WAR. FUT WOR+45 WOR-45
SOCIETY INT/ORG NAT/G FORCES TOP/EX CREATE BAL/PWR
DOMIN EDU/PROP COERCE DETER PEACE TOTALISM PWR
...TIME/SEQ TREND COLD/WAR TOT/POP VAL/FREE
LEAGUE/NAT 20. PAGE 4 G0066
B54
ATTIT
WAR

BUTOW R.J.C.,JAPAN'S DECISION TO SURRENDER. USA-45
USSR CHIEF FORCES DOMIN NUC/PWR...BIBLIOG 20 TREATY
CHINJAP. PAGE 10 G0198
B54
ELITES
DIPLOM
WAR
PEACE

GERMANY FOREIGN MINISTRY,DOCUMENTS ON GERMAN
B54
NAT/G

FOREIGN POLICY 1918-1945, SERIES C (1933-1937) DIPLOM
VOLS. I-V. GERMANY MOD/EUR FORCES PLAN ECO/TAC POLICY
...FASCIST CHARTS ANTHOL 20. PAGE 21 G0416

B54
HART B.H.L.,STRATEGY (REV. ED.). CHRIST-17C EUR+WWI WAR
MEDIT-7 MOD/EUR TEC/DEV LEAD REV WEAPON...POLICY PLAN
CHARTS. PAGE 25 G0486 FORCES
PHIL/SCI

B54
REYNOLDS P.A.,BRITISH FOREIGN POLICY IN THE INTER- DIPLOM
WAR YEARS. CZECHOSLVK GERMANY POLAND UK USA-45 POLICY
POL/PAR FORCES ECO/TAC ARMS/CONT WAR ATTIT 20. NAT/G
PAGE 46 G0915

B54
US DEPARTMENT OF STATE,PUBLICATIONS OF THE BIBLIOG
DEPARTMENT OF STATE, OCTOBER 1,1929 TO JANUARY 1, DIPLOM
1953. AGRI INT/ORG FORCES FOR/AID EDU/PROP
ARMS/CONT NUC/PWR ATTIT 20 DEPT/STATE OAS UN NATO.
PAGE 57 G1122

S54
HOOPES T.,"CIVILIAN-MILITARY BALANCE." USA+45 CHIEF CIVMIL/REL
FORCES PLAN CONTROL WAR GOV/REL GP/REL INGP/REL LEAD
...POLICY 19/20. PAGE 27 G0527 PWR
NAT/G

B55
MIKSCHE F.O.,ATOMIC WEAPONS AND ARMIES. FUT WOR+45 TEC/DEV
WOR-45 SOCIETY COERCE DETER WEAPON PWR...POLICY FORCES
WELF/ST PSY CONCPT INT SYS/QU KNO/TEST TOT/POP 20. NUC/PWR
PAGE 39 G0765

B55
SHUBIK M.,READINGS IN GAME THEORY AND POLITICAL MATH
BEHAVIOR. WOR+45 FORCES CREATE ROUTINE WAR PEACE DECISION
PERCEPT KNOWL PWR...PSY SOC CONCPT METH/CNCPT STAT DIPLOM
CHARTS HYPO/EXP GAME METH VAL/FREE 20. PAGE 50
G0991

B55
SMITHIES A.,THE BUDGETARY PROCESS IN THE UNITED NAT/G
STATES. ECO/DEV AGRI EX/STRUC FORCES LEGIS ADMIN
PROB/SOLV TAX ROUTINE EFFICIENCY...MGT CONGRESS BUDGET
PRESIDENT. PAGE 52 G1016 GOV/REL

B55
US OFFICE OF THE PRESIDENT,REPORT TO CONGRESS ON DIPLOM
THE MUTUAL SECURITY PROGRAM FOR THE SIX MONTHS FORCES
ENDED JUNE 30, 1955. ECO/DEV INT/ORG NAT/G CREATE PLAN
TEC/DEV BAL/PWR ECO/TAC AGREE DETER COST ORD/FREE FOR/AID
20 DEPT/STATE DEPT/DEFEN. PAGE 59 G1157

S55
GLADSTONE A.E.,"THE POSSIBILITY OF PREDICTING PHIL/SCI
REACTIONS TO INTERNATIONAL EVENTS." UNIV SOCIETY CONCPT
NAT/G FORCES CREATE EDU/PROP COERCE WAR ATTIT
PERSON KNOWL PWR SKILL...METH/CNCPT NEW/IDEA
ORG/CHARTS. PAGE 21 G0420

B56
BLACKETT P.M.S.,ATOMIC WEAPONS AND EAST-WEST FORCES
RELATIONS. FUT WOR+45 INT/ORG DELIB/GP COERCE ATTIT PWR
RIGID/FLEX KNOWL...RELATIV HIST/WRIT TREND GEN/METH ARMS/CONT
COLD/WAR 20. PAGE 7 G0138 NUC/PWR

B56
ESTEP R.,AN AIR POWER BIBLIOGRAPHY. USA+45 TEC/DEV BIBLIOG/A
BUDGET DIPLOM EDU/PROP DETER CIVMIL/REL...DECISION FORCES
INT/LAW 20. PAGE 18 G0351 WEAPON
PLAN

B56
US DEPARTMENT OF THE ARMY,AMERICAN MILITARY BIBLIOG
HISTORY. USA+45 USA-45 EX/STRUC PROB/SOLV TEC/DEV FORCES
DIPLOM NUC/PWR REV WAR WEAPON...PSY 18/20. PAGE 57 NAT/G
G1125

B56
US DEPARTMENT OF THE ARMY,RESEARCH AND DEVELOPMENT BIBLIOG/A
(AND RELATED ASPECTS) IN FOREIGN COUNTRIES. WOR+45 R+D
DIST/IND INDUS CONSULT FORCES CREATE EDU/PROP TEC/DEV
AUTOMAT DETER WEAPON. PAGE 57 G1126 NUC/PWR

B56
US OFFICE OF THE PRESIDENT,REPORT TO CONGRESS ON DIPLOM
THE MUTUAL SECURITY PROGRAM FOR THE SIX MONTHS FORCES
ENDED DECEMBER 31, 1955. ASIA USSR ECO/DEV PLAN
ECO/UNDEV INT/ORG CREATE TEC/DEV BAL/PWR ECO/TAC FOR/AID
AGREE DETER COST ORD/FREE 20 DEPT/STATE DEPT/DEFEN
EISNHWR/DD. PAGE 59 G1158

C56
DUPUY R.E.,"MILITARY HERITAGE OF AMERICA." USA+45 FORCES

USA-45 TEC/DEV DIPLOM ROUTINE...POLICY TREND CHARTS WAR
IDEA/COMP BIBLIOG COLD/WAR. PAGE 17 G0325 CONCPT

B57
KISSINGER H.A.,NUCLEAR WEAPONS AND FOREIGN POLICY. PLAN
FUT USA+45 WOR+45 INT/ORG FORCES ACT/RES TEC/DEV DETER
DIPLOM ARMS/CONT COERCE ATTIT KNOWL PWR...DECISION NUC/PWR
GEOG CHARTS 20. PAGE 31 G0602

B57
SPEIER H.,GERMAN REARMAMENT AND ATOMIC WAR: THE TOP/EX
VIEWS OF GERMAN MILITARY AND POLITICAL LEADERS. FUT FORCES
WOR+45 INT/ORG NAT/G WEAPON ATTIT PWR...INT QU NUC/PWR
TOT/POP VAL/FREE COLD/WAR 20. PAGE 52 G1024 GERMANY

S57
JANOWITZ M.,"MILITARY ELITES AND THE STUDY OF WAR." FORCES
USA+45 WOR+45 STRATA NAT/G PROF/ORG TEC/DEV DOMIN ELITES
EDU/PROP COERCE WAR ATTIT RIGID/FLEX PWR RESPECT
...MGT TREND STERTYP GEN/METH 20. PAGE 28 G0558

S57
MORTON L.,"THE DECISION TO USE THE BOMB." FORCES NUC/PWR
TOP/EX DOMIN COERCE PEACE. PAGE 40 G0788 DIPLOM
WAR

N57
US ARMY LIBRARY,THESES AND DISSERTATIONS IN THE BIBLIOG
HOLDINGS OF THE ARMY LIBRARY (PAMPHLET). USA+45 FORCES
...INT/LAW PSY SOC 20. PAGE 56 G1105 MGT
CONTROL

B58
ANGELL N.,DEFENCE AND THE ENGLISH-SPEAKING ROLE. DIPLOM
CHINA/COM UK USSR INT/ORG FORCES EDU/PROP NEUTRAL WAR
NUC/PWR NAT/LISM PEACE TOTALISM 20 COLD/WAR MARXISM
COEXIST. PAGE 3 G0059 ORD/FREE

B58
ARON R.,ON WAR: ATOMIC WEAPONS AND GLOBAL DIPLOMACY ARMS/CONT
(TRANS. BY TERENCE KILMARTIN). WOR+45 SOCIETY NUC/PWR
FORCES BAL/PWR WAR WEAPON PERSON...SOC 20. PAGE 4 COERCE
G0067 DIPLOM

B58
GAVIN J.M.,WAR AND PEACE IN THE SPACE AGE. SPACE WAR
USA+45 USSR FORCES PLAN TEC/DEV BAL/PWR DIPLOM DETER
ARMS/CONT WEAPON CIVMIL/REL...CHARTS GP/COMP 20 NUC/PWR
NATO COLD/WAR. PAGE 21 G0414 PEACE

B58
ROCKEFELLER BROTH FUND INC,INTERNATIONAL SECURITY - NUC/PWR
THE MILITARY ASPECT. USA+45 INT/ORG NAT/G BUDGET DETER
ARMS/CONT WAR WEAPON PEACE ORD/FREE 20 NATO. FORCES
PAGE 47 G0932 DIPLOM

B58
TELLER E.A.,OUR NUCLEAR FUTURE. SOCIETY FORCES FUT
TEC/DEV EDU/PROP KNOWL ORD/FREE...STAND/INT SYS/QU PHIL/SCI
KNO/TEST AUD/VIS CHARTS SIMUL 20. PAGE 54 G1062 NUC/PWR
WAR

B58
US DEPARTMENT OF STATE,PUBLICATIONS OF THE BIBLIOG
DEPARTMENT OF STATE, JANUARY 1,1953 TO DECEMBER 31, DIPLOM
1957. AGRI INT/ORG FORCES FOR/AID EDU/PROP
ARMS/CONT NUC/PWR ATTIT 20 DEPT/STATE OAS UN NATO.
PAGE 57 G1123

B58
US DEPARTMENT OF THE ARMY,BIBLIOGRAPHY ON LIMITED BIBLIOG/A
WAR (PAMPHLET). USA+45 TEC/DEV CONTROL RISK COERCE WAR
DETER NUC/PWR WEAPON ADJUST PEACE ALL/VALS ORD/FREE FORCES
20. PAGE 57 G1127 CIVMIL/REL

B58
US HOUSE COMM GOVT OPERATIONS,CIVIL DEFENSE. USA+45 NUC/PWR
FORCES...CHARTS 20 CONGRESS CIV/DEFENS HOLIFLD/C. WAR
PAGE 58 G1139 PLAN
ADJUST

S58
BURNS A.L.,"THE NEW WEAPONS AND INTERNATIONAL TEC/DEV
RELATIONS." SPACE WOR+45 NAT/G VOL/ASSN FORCES ARMS/CONT
NUC/PWR 20. PAGE 10 G0190 DIPLOM

S58
DAVENPORT J.,"ARMS AND THE WELFARE STATE." INTELL USA+45
STRUCT FORCES CREATE ECO/TAC FOR/AID DOMIN LEGIT NAT/G
ADMIN WAR ORD/FREE PWR...POLICY SOC CONCPT MYTH OBS USSR
TREND COLD/WAR TOT/POP 20. PAGE 14 G0276

S58
HUNTINGTON S.P.,"ARMS RACES: PREREQUISITES AND FORCES
RESULTS." EUR+WWI MOD/EUR USA+45 WOR+45 WOR-45 PWR
NAT/G TEC/DEV BAL/PWR COERCE DETER ATTIT...POLICY ARMS/CONT

TREND 20. PAGE 27 G0537

S58
THOMPSON K.W.,"NATIONAL SECURITY IN A NUCLEAR AGE." FORCES
USA+45 WOR+45 SOCIETY INT/ORG NAT/G TOP/EX DIPLOM   PWR
DOMIN EDU/PROP LEGIT ARMS/CONT COERCE ORD/FREE   BAL/PWR
...TREND STERTYP TOT/POP VAL/FREE COLD/WAR 20.
PAGE 54 G1068

B59
AIR FORCE ACADEMY ASSEMBLY '59,INTERNATIONAL   FOR/AID
STABILITY AND PROGRESS (PAMPHLET). USA+45 USSR   FORCES
ECO/UNDEV PROB/SOLV BUDGET DIPLOM ADMIN DETER COST   WAR
ATTIT...TREND 20. PAGE 2 G0030   PLAN

B59
AMRINE M.,THE GREAT DECISION: THE SECRET HISTORY OF DECISION
THE ATOMIC BOMB. USA+45 TOP/EX EDU/PROP LEGIT   NAT/G
PERCEPT ORD/FREE PWR VAL/FREE HIROSHIMA. PAGE 3   NUC/PWR
G0055   FORCES

B59
EMME E.M.,THE IMPACT OF AIR POWER - NATIONAL   DETER
SECURITY AND WORLD POLITICS. USA+45 USSR FORCES   AIR
DIPLOM WEAPON PEACE TOTALISM...POLICY NAT/COMP 20   WAR
EUROPE. PAGE 18 G0346   ORD/FREE

B59
GREENFIELD K.R.,COMMAND DECISIONS. ASIA EUR+WWI   PLAN
S/ASIA USA-45 WOR-45 NAT/G CONSULT DELIB/GP COERCE   FORCES
NUC/PWR PWR...OBS 20 CHINJAP. PAGE 23 G0446   WAR
                                                     WEAPON

B59
MIKSCHE F.O.,THE FAILURE OF ATOMIC STRATEGY. COM   ACT/RES
EUR+WWI INTELL POL/PAR FORCES PLAN ECO/TAC NUC/PWR   ORD/FREE
ATTIT DRIVE RIGID/FLEX PWR...DECISION GEOG PSY   DIPLOM
CONCPT RECORD TREND CHARTS VAL/FREE 20. PAGE 39   ARMS/CONT
G0766

B59
MODELSKI G.,ATOMIC ENERGY IN THE COMMUNIST BLOC.   TEC/DEV
FUT INT/ORG CONSULT FORCES ACT/RES PLAN KNOWL SKILL NUC/PWR
...PHIL/SCI STAT CHARTS 20. PAGE 39 G0777   USSR
                                                     COM

B59
POKROVSKY G.I.,SCIENCE AND TECHNOLOGY IN   TEC/DEV
CONTEMPORARY WAR. SPACE USSR WOR+45 NAT/G CONSULT   FORCES
ACT/RES PLAN DETER WEAPON...MARXIST METH/CNCPT   NUC/PWR
CHARTS STERTYP COLD/WAR 20. PAGE 45 G0881   WAR

B59
COLUMBIA U BUR APPL SOC RES, ATTITUDES OF   ATTIT
PROMINENT AMERICANS TOWARD "WORLD PEACE THROUGH   ACT/RES
WORLD LAW" (SUPRA-NATL ORGANIZATION FOR WAR   INT/LAW
PREVENTION). USA+45 USSR ELITES FORCES PLAN   STAT
PROB/SOLV CONTROL WAR PWR...POLICY SOC QU IDEA/COMP
20 UN. PAGE 45 G0888

B59
SPANIER J.W.,THE TRUMAN-MACARTHUR CONTROVERSY AND   CIVMIL/REL
THE KOREAN WAR. USA+45 TOP/EX PROB/SOLV LEAD ATTIT   FORCES
PWR...POLICY BIBLIOG/A UN. PAGE 52 G1023   CHIEF
                                                     WAR

B59
VAN WAGENEN R.W.,SOME VIEWS OF AMERICAN DEFENSE   INT/ORG
OFFICIALS ABOUT THE UNITED NATIONS (PAPER). FUT   LEAD
USA+45 NAT/G DIPLOM WAR EFFICIENCY PEACE...POLICY   ATTIT
INT 20 UN DEPT/DEFEN. PAGE 61 G1192   FORCES

B59
WARD B.,5 IDEAS THAT CHANGE THE WORLD. WOR+45   ECO/UNDEV
WOR-45 SOCIETY STRUCT AGRI INDUS INT/ORG NAT/G   ALL/VALS
FORCES ACT/RES ARMS/CONT TOTALISM ATTIT DRIVE   NAT/LISM
GEN/LAWS. PAGE 62 G1210   COLONIAL

L59
BURNS A.L.,"THE RATIONALE OF CATALYTIC WAR." COM   COERCE
USA+45 WOR+45 R+D NAT/G FORCES ACT/RES TEC/DEV PWR   NUC/PWR
...DECISION HYPO/EXP TOT/POP 20. PAGE 10 G0191   WAR

L59
BURNS A.L.,"POWER POLITICS AND THE GROWING NUCLEAR   FORCES
CLUB." FUT WOR+45 TEC/DEV EXEC ARMS/CONT COERCE   BAL/PWR
DETER...DECISION HYPO/EXP 20. PAGE 10 G0192   NUC/PWR

S59
JANOWITZ M.,"CHANGING PATTERNS OF ORGANIZATIONAL   FORCES
AUTHORITY: THE MILITARY ESTABLISHMENT" (BMR)"   AUTHORIT
USA+45 ELITES STRUCT EX/STRUC PLAN DOMIN AUTOMAT   ADMIN
NUC/PWR WEAPON 20. PAGE 28 G0559   TEC/DEV

S59
MILBURN T.W.,"WHAT CONSTITUTES EFFECTIVE   INTELL

DETERRENCE." USA+45 USSR WOR+45 STRUCT FORCES   ATTIT
ACT/RES PLAN SUPEGO KNOWL ORD/FREE PWR...RELATIV   DETER
PSY CONCPT VAL/FREE 20 COLD/WAR. PAGE 39 G0768   NUC/PWR

S59
WILLIAMS B.H.,"SCIENTIFIC METHOD IN FOREIGN   PLAN
POLICY." WOR+45 NAT/G FORCES TOP/EX DOMIN LEGIT   PHIL/SCI
COERCE PEACE ATTIT KNOWL ORD/FREE PWR...GEN/LAWS   DIPLOM
GEN/METH TOT/POP COLD/WAR NAZI. PAGE 63 G1241

B60
BARNET R.,WHO WANTS DISARMAMENT. COM EUR+WWI USA+45 PLAN
USSR INT/ORG NAT/G BAL/PWR DIPLOM EDU/PROP COERCE   FORCES
DETER NUC/PWR WAR WEAPON ATTIT PWR...TIME/SEQ   ARMS/CONT
COLD/WAR CONGRESS 20. PAGE 5 G0096

B60
HITCH C.J.,THE ECONOMICS OF DEFENSE IN THE NUCLEAR   R+D
AGE. USA+45 WOR+45 CREATE PLAN NUC/PWR ATTIT   FORCES
...CON/ANAL CHARTS HYPO/EXP NATO 20. PAGE 26 G0514

B60
JANOWITZ M.,THE PROFESSIONAL SOLDIER. CULTURE   FORCES
STRATA STRUCT FAM PROB/SOLV TEC/DEV COERCE WAR   MYTH
CIVMIL/REL NAT/LISM AGE HEREDITY ALL/VALS CONSERVE   LEAD
...MGT WORSHIP. PAGE 28 G0560   ELITES

B60
KINGSTON-MCCLOUG E.,DEFENSE: POLICY AND STRATEGY.   FORCES
UK SEA AIR TEC/DEV DIPLOM ADMIN LEAD WAR ORD/FREE   PLAN
...CHARTS 20. PAGE 30 G0597   POLICY
                                                     DECISION

B60
MCCLELLAND C.A.,NUCLEAR WEAPONS, MISSILES, AND   DIPLOM
FUTURE WAR: PROBLEM FOR THE SIXTIES. WOR+45 FORCES   NUC/PWR
ARMS/CONT DETER MARXISM...POLICY ANTHOL COLD/WAR.   WAR
PAGE 37 G0729   WEAPON

B60
US HOUSE COMM. SCI. ASTRONAUT.,OCEAN SCIENCES AND   R+D
NATIONAL SECURITY. FUT SEA ECO/DEV EXTR/IND INT/ORG ORD/FREE
NAT/G FORCES ACT/RES TEC/DEV ECO/TAC COERCE WAR
BIO/SOC KNOWL PWR...CONCPT RECORD LAB/EXP 20.
PAGE 59 G1153

B60
WILLIAUS T.H.,AMERICANS AT WAR: THE DEVELOPMENT OF   FORCES
THE AMERICAN MILITARY SYSTEM. USA+45 USA-45   WAR
EDU/PROP LEAD REV...GP/COMP BIBLIOG/A 18/20   NAT/G
PRESIDENT. PAGE 63 G1244   POLICY

L60
BRENNAN D.G.,"SETTING AND GOALS OF ARMS CONTROL."   FORCES
FUT USA+45 USSR WOR+45 INTELL INT/ORG NAT/G   COERCE
VOL/ASSN CONSULT PLAN DIPLOM ECO/TAC ADMIN KNOWL   ARMS/CONT
PWR...POLICY CONCPT TREND COLD/WAR 20. PAGE 8 G0164 DETER

L60
HOLTON G.,"ARMS CONTROL." FUT WOR+45 CULTURE   ACT/RES
INT/ORG NAT/G FORCES TOP/EX PLAN EDU/PROP COERCE   CONSULT
ATTIT RIGID/FLEX ORD/FREE...POLICY PHIL/SCI SOC   ARMS/CONT
TREND COLD/WAR. PAGE 27 G0524   NUC/PWR

L60
HOLZMAN B.G.,"BASIC RESEARCH FOR NATIONAL   FORCES
SURVIVAL." FUT USA+45 INTELL R+D ACT/RES OP/RES   STAT
PLAN TEC/DEV EDU/PROP PERCEPT PERSON...PHIL/SCI
METH/CNCPT NEW/IDEA MATH OBS RECORD TREND LAB/EXP
20. PAGE 27 G0525

S60
BRODY R.A.,"DETERRENCE STRATEGIES: AN ANNOTATED   BIBLIOG/A
BIBLIOGRAPHY." WOR+45 PLAN ARMS/CONT NUC/PWR WAR   FORCES
WEAPON DECISION. PAGE 9 G0173   DETER
                                                     DIPLOM

S60
DOUGHERTY J.E.,"KEY TO SECURITY: DISARMAMENT OR   FORCES
ARMS STABILITY." COM USA+45 USSR INT/ORG NAT/G   ORD/FREE
CREATE EDU/PROP COERCE DETER ATTIT PWR...DECISION   ARMS/CONT
CONCPT MYTH NEW/IDEA TREND 20 COLD/WAR. PAGE 16   NUC/PWR
G0311

S60
HUNTINGTON S.P.,"STRATEGIC PLANNING AND THE   EXEC
POLITICAL PROCESS." USA+45 NAT/G DELIB/GP LEGIS   FORCES
ACT/RES ECO/TAC LEGIT ROUTINE CHOOSE RIGID/FLEX PWR NUC/PWR
...POLICY MAJORIT MGT 20. PAGE 27 G0538   WAR

S60
KELLEY G.A.,"THE POLITICAL BACKGROUND OF THE FRENCH NAT/G
A-BOMB." EUR+WWI USSR FORCES TOP/EX TEC/DEV NUC/PWR RESPECT
ATTIT PWR...CONCPT OBS/ENVIR TREND 20. PAGE 30   NAT/LISM
G0591   FRANCE

KISSINGER H.A.,"ARMS CONTROL, INSPECTION AND SURPRISE ATTACK." COM USA+45 NAT/G ACT/RES PLAN TEC/DEV DIPLOM EDU/PROP DETER WAR RIGID/FLEX ...CONCPT GEN/METH TOT/POP 20. PAGE 31 G0603
S60 FORCES ORD/FREE ARMS/CONT NUC/PWR

FRISCH D.,ARMS REDUCTION: PROGRAM AND ISSUES. USA+45 INT/ORG NAT/G ACT/RES REGION NUC/PWR ATTIT PWR...POLICY 20. PAGE 20 G0395
B61 PLAN FORCES ARMS/CONT DIPLOM

MICHAEL D.N.,PROPOSED STUDIES ON THE IMPLICATIONS OF PEACEFUL SPACE ACTIVITIES FOR HUMAN AFFAIRS. COM/IND INDUS FORCES DIPLOM PEACE PERSON...PSY SOC 20. PAGE 39 G0764
B61 FUT SPACE ACT/RES PROB/SOLV

SCHMIDT H.,VERTEIDIGUNG ODER VERGELTUNG. COM CUBA GERMANY/W USSR FORCES DIPLOM ARMS/CONT DETER NUC/PWR...POLICY CHARTS HYPO/EXP SIMUL BIBLIOG 20 NATO COLD/WAR. PAGE 49 G0970
B61 PLAN WAR BAL/PWR ORD/FREE

STEIN W.,NUCLEAR WEAPONS: A CATHOLIC RESPONSE. WOR+45 FORCES ARMS/CONT DETER MURDER MORAL...POLICY CATH IDEA/COMP ANTHOL 20. PAGE 52 G1033
B61 NUC/PWR WAR CATHISM ATTIT

US SENATE COMM GOVT OPERATIONS,ORGANIZING FOR NATIONAL SECURITY. COM USA+45 BUDGET DIPLOM DETER NUC/PWR WAR WEAPON ORD/FREE...BIBLIOG 20 COLD/WAR. PAGE 60 G1176
B61 POLICY PLAN FORCES COERCE

RICHSTEIN A.R.,"LEGAL RULES IN NUCLEAR WEAPONS EMPLOYMENTS." FUT WOR+45 LAW SOCIETY FORCES PLAN WEAPON RIGID/FLEX...HEAL CONCPT TREND VAL/FREE 20. PAGE 47 G0918
S61 NUC/PWR TEC/DEV MORAL ARMS/CONT

AIR FORCE ACADEMY LIBRARY,INTERNATIONAL ORGANIZATIONS AND MILITARY SECURITY SYSTEMS (PAMPHLET) (SPECIAL BIBLIOGRAPHY SERIES, NUMBER 25). DIPLOM FOR/AID INT/TRADE NUC/PWR PEACE 20 UN NATO OAS SEATO LEAGUE/NAT. PAGE 2 G0031
B62 BIBLIOG INT/ORG FORCES DETER

ASTIA,HUMAN ENGINEERING: A REPORT BIBLIOGRAPHY. USA+45 R+D FORCES ACT/RES COMPUTER CREATE OP/RES EDU/PROP CONTROL WEAPON...SOC NEW/IDEA. PAGE 4 G0073
B62 BIBLIOG/A COM/IND COMPUT/IR METH

ASTIA,INFORMATION THEORY: A REPORT BIBLIOGRAPHY. USA+45 COMPUTER CREATE OP/RES PLAN TEC/DEV CONTROL ...CONCPT METH/COMP. PAGE 4 G0074
B62 BIBLIOG/A COM/IND FORCES METH

BURKE A.E.,ENOUGH GOOD MEN. USA+45 WOR+45 ECO/UNDEV FORCES TEC/DEV GUERRILLA NUC/PWR REV WAR ORD/FREE MARXISM...GEOG 20 COLD/WAR. PAGE 10 G0189
B62 DIPLOM POLICY NAT/G TASK

DUPRE J.S.,SCIENCE AND THE NATION: POLICY AND POLITICS. USA+45 LAW ACADEM FORCES ADMIN CIVMIL/REL GOV/REL EFFICIENCY PEACE...TREND 20 SCI/ADVSRY. PAGE 16 G0322
B62 R+D INDUS TEC/DEV NUC/PWR

FORBES H.W.,THE STRATEGY OF DISARMAMENT. FUT WOR+45 INT/ORG VOL/ASSN CONSULT ARMS/CONT COERCE NUC/PWR WAR DRIVE RIGID/FLEX ORD/FREE PWR...POLICY CONCPT OBS TREND STERTYP 20. PAGE 19 G0378
B62 PLAN FORCES DIPLOM

GILPIN R.,AMERICAN SCIENTISTS AND NUCLEAR WEAPONS POLICY. COM FUT USA+45 WOR+45 INT/ORG NAT/G PROF/ORG CONSULT FORCES CREATE TEC/DEV BAL/PWR EDU/PROP ARMS/CONT WAR PERCEPT KNOWL MORAL PWR ...PHIL/SCI SOC CONCPT GEN/LAWS 20. PAGE 21 G0417
B62 INTELL ATTIT DETER NUC/PWR

GOLOVINE M.N.,CONFLICT IN SPACE: A PATTERN OF WAR IN A NEW DIMENSION. FUT USA+45 WOR+45 AIR FORCES PLAN DIPLOM DOMIN ATTIT...STAT AUD/VIS CHARTS COLD/WAR 20. PAGE 22 G0432
B62 CREATE TEC/DEV NUC/PWR SPACE

HALPERIN M.H.,LIMITED WAR; AN ESSAY ON THE DEVELOPMENT OF THE THEORY AND AN ANNOTATED BIBLIOGRAPHY (OCCASIONAL PAPER NO. 3). WOR+45
B62 BIBLIOG/A WAR ARMS/CONT

WOR-45 NUC/PWR...CONCPT IDEA/COMP METH/COMP 19/20. PAGE 24 G0471
FORCES

KAHN H.,THINKING ABOUT THE UNTHINKABLE. FUT USA+45 LAW NAT/G CONSULT FORCES ACT/RES CREATE PLAN TEC/DEV BAL/PWR DIPLOM EDU/PROP ARMS/CONT DETER ATTIT...CONCPT OBS TREND COLD/WAR 20. PAGE 29 G0570
B62 INT/ORG ORD/FREE NUC/PWR PEACE

KENNEDY J.F.,TO TURN THE TIDE. SPACE AGRI INT/ORG FORCES TEC/DEV ADMIN NUC/PWR PEACE WEALTH...ANTHOL 20 KENNEDY/JF CIV/RIGHTS. PAGE 30 G0592
B62 DIPLOM CHIEF POLICY NAT/G

MELMAN S.,DISARMAMENT: ITS POLITICS AND ECONOMICS. WOR+45 DELIB/GP FORCES ECO/TAC DOMIN EDU/PROP LEGIT COERCE PWR...POLICY CONCPT 20. PAGE 38 G0752
B62 NAT/G ORD/FREE ARMS/CONT NUC/PWR

PERRE J.,LES MUTATIONS DE LA GUERRE MODERNE: DE LA REVOLUTION FRANCAISE A LA REVOLUTION NUCLEAIRE. DIPLOM ARMS/CONT DEATH REV WEAPON GP/REL PEACE ATTIT...STAT PREDICT BIBLIOG 18/20 WWI. PAGE 44 G0870
B62 WAR FORCES NUC/PWR

SCHILLING W.R.,STRATEGY, POLITICS, AND DEFENSE BUDGETS. USA+45 R+D NAT/G CONSULT DELIB/GP FORCES LEGIS ACT/RES PLAN BAL/PWR LEGIT EXEC NUC/PWR RIGID/FLEX PWR...TREND COLD/WAR CONGRESS 20 EISNHWR/DD. PAGE 49 G0968
B62 ROUTINE POLICY

STRAUSS L.L.,MEN AND DECISIONS. USA+45 USA-45 USSR CONSULT FORCES TOP/EX WAR PEACE 20. PAGE 53 G1042
B62 DECISION PWR NUC/PWR DIPLOM

THOMSON G.P.,NUCLEAR ENERGY IN BRITAIN DURING THE LAST WAR: THE CHERWELL SIMON LECTURE (MONOGRAPH). UK R+D CONSULT FORCES PLAN DIPLOM TASK CIVMIL/REL ROLE...PHIL/SCI NEW/IDEA LAB/EXP 20 MAUD. PAGE 54 G1071
B62 CREATE TEC/DEV WAR NUC/PWR

WRIGHT Q.,PREVENTING WORLD WAR THREE. FUT WOR+45 CULTURE INT/ORG NAT/G CONSULT FORCES ADMIN ARMS/CONT DRIVE RIGID/FLEX ORD/FREE SOVEREIGN ...POLICY CONCPT TREND STERTYP COLD/WAR 20. PAGE 64 G1259
B62 CREATE ATTIT

YALEN R.,REGIONALISM AND WORLD ORDER. EUR+WWI WOR+45 WOR-45 INT/ORG VOL/ASSN DELIB/GP FORCES TOP/EX BAL/PWR DIPLOM DOMIN REGION ARMS/CONT PWR ...JURID HYPO/EXP COLD/WAR 20. PAGE 64 G1261
B62 ORD/FREE POLICY

BETTEN J.K.,"ARMS CONTROL AND THE PROBLEM OF EVASION." WOR+45 FORCES CREATE DIPLOM DETER PWR ...PSY TREND GEN/LAWS COLD/WAR 20. PAGE 7 G0134
L62 NAT/G PLAN ARMS/CONT

FINKELSTEIN L.S.,"ARMS INSPECTION." FUT WOR+45 NAT/G DIPLOM ATTIT PERCEPT RIGID/FLEX ORD/FREE COLD/WAR 20. PAGE 19 G0369
L62 FORCES PWR ARMS/CONT

CRANE R.D.,"LAW AND STRATEGY IN SPACE." FUT USA+45 WOR+45 AIR LAW INT/ORG NAT/G FORCES ACT/RES PLAN BAL/PWR LEGIT ARMS/CONT COERCE ORD/FREE...POLICY INT/LAW JURID SOC/EXP 20 TREATY. PAGE 13 G0261
S62 CONCPT SPACE

GORDON B.K.,"NUCLEAR WEAPONS: RUSSIAN AND AMERICAN." COM FUT USA+45 WOR+45 USSR NAT/G ACT/RES TEC/DEV PERCEPT RIGID/FLEX PWR SKILL...MGT METH/CNCPT QUANT OBS TIME/SEQ CON/ANAL GEN/METH TOT/POP VAL/FREE 20. PAGE 22 G0433
S62 ORD/FREE COERCE NUC/PWR

MARTIN L.W.,"THE MARKET FOR STRATEGIC IDEAS IN BRITAIN: THE 'SANDYS ERA'" UK ARMS/CONT WAR GOV/REL OPTIMAL...POLICY DECISION GOV/COMP COLD/WAR CMN/WLTH. PAGE 36 G0714
S62 DIPLOM COERCE FORCES PWR

NANES A.,"DISARMAMENT: THE LAST SEVEN YEARS." COM EUR+WWI USA+45 USSR INT/ORG FORCES TOP/EX CREATE LEGIT NUC/PWR DISPL ORD/FREE...CONCPT TIME/SEQ CON/ANAL 20. PAGE 41 G0803
S62 DELIB/GP RIGID/FLEX ARMS/CONT

PHIPPS T.E.,"THE CASE FOR DETERRENCE." FUT WOR+45 | S62
SOCIETY EX/STRUC FORCES ACT/RES CREATE PLAN TEC/DEV | ATTIT
ROUTINE RIGID/FLEX ORD/FREE...POLICY MYTH NEW/IDEA | COERCE
STERTYP COLD/WAR 20. PAGE 45 G0876 | DETER
| ARMS/CONT

SINGER J.D.,"STABLE DETERRENCE AND ITS LIMITS." FUT | S62
WOR+45 R+D INT/ORG CONSULT ACT/RES TEC/DEV | NAT/G
ARMS/CONT COERCE DRIVE PERCEPT RIGID/FLEX ORD/FREE | FORCES
PWR...MYTH SIMUL TOT/POP 20. PAGE 51 G1004 | DETER
| NUC/PWR

JOINT ECONOMIC COMMITTEE,"DIMENSIONS OF SOVIET | C62
ECONOMIC POWER." USSR R+D FORCES ACT/RES OP/RES | ECO/DEV
TEC/DEV...GEOG STAT BIBLIOG 20. PAGE 29 G0565 | PLAN
| PRODUC
| LABOR

ABSHIRE D.M.,NATIONAL SECURITY: POLITICAL, | B63
MILITARY, AND ECONOMIC STRATEGIES IN THE DECADE | FUT
AHEAD. ASIA COM USA+45 WOR+45 ECO/DEV ECO/UNDEV | ACT/RES
INT/ORG DELIB/GP FORCES ECO/TAC COERCE ATTIT | BAL/PWR
RIGID/FLEX HEALTH ORD/FREE PWR WEALTH...POLICY STAT
CHARTS ANTHOL COLD/WAR VAL/FREE. PAGE 1 G0024

GOLDSEN J.M.,OUTER SPACE IN WORLD POLITICS. COM | B63
USA+45 NAT/G FORCES ACT/RES PLAN DOMIN EDU/PROP | TEC/DEV
COERCE ORD/FREE PWR...TECHNIC STAT INT SAMP TREND | DIPLOM
ANTHOL VAL/FREE 20. PAGE 22 G0428 | SPACE

KAST F.E.,SCIENCE, TECHNOLOGY, AND MANAGEMENT. | B63
SPACE USA+45 FORCES CONFER DETER NUC/PWR...PHIL/SCI | MGT
CHARTS ANTHOL BIBLIOG 20 NASA. PAGE 30 G0581 | PLAN
| TEC/DEV
| PROB/SOLV

LILIENTHAL D.E.,CHANGE, HOPE, AND THE BOMB. USA+45 | B63
WOR+45 R+D INT/ORG NAT/G DELIB/GP FORCES ACT/RES | ATTIT
DETER RIGID/FLEX ORD/FREE...POLICY CONCPT OBS AEC | MYTH
20. PAGE 34 G0666 | ARMS/CONT
| NUC/PWR

PEABODY R.L.,NEW PERSPECTIVES ON THE HOUSE OF | B63
REPRESENTATIVES. AGRI FINAN SCHOOL FORCES CONFER | NEW/IDEA
LEAD CHOOSE REPRESENT FEDERAL...POLICY DECISION | LEGIS
HOUSE/REP. PAGE 44 G0862 | PWR
| ADMIN

SCHRADER R.,SCIENCE AND POLICY. WOR+45 ECO/DEV | B63
ECO/UNDEV R+D FORCES PLAN DIPLOM GOV/REL TECHRACY | TEC/DEV
BIBLIOG. PAGE 50 G0976 | NAT/G
| POLICY
| ADMIN

PHELPS J.,"STUDIES IN DETERRENCE VIII: MILITARY | L63
STABILITY AND ARMS CONTROL: A CRITICAL SURVEY." | FORCES
FUT WOR+45 INT/ORG ACT/RES EDU/PROP COERCE NUC/PWR | ORD/FREE
WAR HEALTH PWR...POLICY TECHNIC TREND SIMUL TOT/POP | ARMS/CONT
20. PAGE 44 G0874 | DETER

BOULDING K.E.,"UNIVERSITY, SOCIETY, AND ARMS | S63
CONTROL." WOR+45 WOR-45 ACADEM NAT/G CONSULT FORCES | SOCIETY
ACT/RES PLAN TEC/DEV BAL/PWR ECO/TAC COERCE DETER | ARMS/CONT
WAR ATTIT RIGID/FLEX KNOWL ORD/FREE PWR WEALTH
...CONCPT COLD/WAR TOT/POP 20. PAGE 8 G0159

CLEVELAND H.,"CRISIS DIPLOMACY." USA+45 WOR+45 LAW | S63
FORCES TASK NUC/PWR PWR 20. PAGE 12 G0235 | DECISION
| DIPLOM
| PROB/SOLV
| POLICY

ENTHOVEN A.C.,"ECONOMIC ANALYSIS IN THE DEPARTMENT | S63
OF DEFENSE." USA+45 NAT/G DELIB/GP PROB/SOLV RATION | PLAN
NUC/PWR WEAPON COST...DECISION 20 DEPT/DEFEN | BUDGET
RESOURCE/N. PAGE 18 G0349 | ECO/TAC
| FORCES

KOLDZIEF E.A.,"CONGRESSIONAL RESPONSIBILITY FOR THE | S63
COMMON DEFENSE: THE MONEY PROBLEM." PLAN DEBATE | LEGIS
EFFICIENCY ATTIT PWR DECISION. PAGE 31 G0612 | NAT/G
| FORCES
| POLICY

NADLER E.B.,"SOME ECONOMIC DISADVANTAGES OF THE | S63
ARMS RACE." USA+45 INDUS R+D FORCES PLAN TEC/DEV | ECO/DEV
ECO/TAC FOR/AID EDU/PROP PWR WEALTH...TREND | MGT
COLD/WAR 20. PAGE 41 G0800 | BAL/PAY

SMITH D.O.,"WHAT IS A WAR DETERRENT." FUT GERMANY | S63
| ACT/RES

HUNGARY UK USA+45 WOR+45 WOR-45 NAT/G TEC/DEV | FORCES
BAL/PWR PWR...CONCPT GEN/LAWS COLD/WAR 20. PAGE 51 | ARMS/CONT
G1013 | DETER

TASHJEAN J.E.,"RESEARCH ON ARMS CONTROL." COM | S63
USA+45 USSR FORCES ACT/RES PLAN DOMIN COERCE | NAT/G
ORD/FREE PWR...TIME/SEQ GEN/LAWS 20 COLD/WAR. | POLICY
PAGE 53 G1053 | ARMS/CONT

WOHLSTETTER A.,"SCIENTISTS, SEERS AND STRATEGY." | S63
USA+45 ELITES R+D NAT/G CONSULT FORCES TOP/EX | INTELL
EDU/PROP ARMS/CONT KNOWL ORD/FREE...DECISION MYTH | ACT/RES
20. PAGE 64 G1253

BROWN N.,NUCLEAR WAR* THE IMPENDING STRATEGIC | B64
DEADLOCK. USA+45 USSR TEC/DEV BUDGET RISK ARMS/CONT | FORCES
NUC/PWR WEAPON COST BIO/SOC...GEOG IDEA/COMP | OP/RES
NAT/COMP GAME NATO WARSAW/P. PAGE 9 G0177 | WAR
| GEN/LAWS

DUSCHA J.,ARMS, MONEY, AND POLITICS. USA+45 INDUS | B64
POL/PAR ECO/TAC TAX DETER NUC/PWR WAR WEAPON | NAT/G
GOV/REL ATTIT...BIBLIOG/A 20 CONGRESS MONEY | FORCES
DEPT/DEFEN. PAGE 17 G0326 | POLICY
| BUDGET

ETZIONI A.,THE MOON-DOGGLE: DOMESTIC AND | B64
INTERNATIONAL IMPLICATIONS OF THE SPACE RACE. FUT | R+D
USA+45 WOR+45 INTELL ECO/DEV INDUS VOL/ASSN | NAT/G
EX/STRUC FORCES LEGIS TOP/EX PLAN TEC/DEV ECO/TAC | DIPLOM
EDU/PROP KNOWL ORD/FREE PWR RESPECT WEALTH | SPACE
TIME/SEQ. PAGE 18 G0352

HEKHUIS D.J.,INTERNATIONAL STABILITY: MILITARY, | B64
ECONOMIC AND POLITICAL DIMENSIONS. FUT WOR+45 LAW | TEC/DEV
ECO/UNDEV INT/ORG NAT/G VOL/ASSN FORCES ACT/RES | DETER
BAL/PWR PWR WEALTH...STAT UN 20. PAGE 25 G0503 | REGION

KAUFMANN W.W.,THE MC NAMARA STRATEGY. TOP/EX | B64
INSPECT BAL/PWR DIPLOM CONTROL DETER GUERRILLA | FORCES
NUC/PWR WEAPON COST PWR...METH/COMP 20 MCNAMARA/R | WAR
KENNEDY/JF JOHNSON/LB NATO DEPT/DEFEN. PAGE 30 | PLAN
G0586 | PROB/SOLV

RIES J.C.,THE MANAGEMENT OF DEFENSE: ORGANIZATION | B64
AND CONTROL OF THE US ARMED SERVICES. PROF/ORG | FORCES
DELIB/GP EX/STRUC LEGIS GOV/REL PERS/REL CENTRAL | ACT/RES
RATIONAL PWR...POLICY TREND GOV/COMP BIBLIOG. | DECISION
PAGE 47 G0920 | CONTROL

ROSECRANCE R.N.,THE DISPERSION OF NUCLEAR WEAPONS: | B64
STRATEGY AND POLITICS. ASIA COM FUT S/ASIA USA+45 | EUR+WWI
INT/ORG NAT/G DELIB/GP FORCES ACT/RES TEC/DEV | PWR
BAL/PWR COERCE DETER ATTIT RIGID/FLEX ORD/FREE | PEACE
...POLICY CHARTS VAL/FREE. PAGE 48 G0935

SCHWARTZ M.D.,CONFERENCE ON SPACE SCIENCE AND SPACE | B64
LAW. FUT COM/IND NAT/G FORCES ACT/RES PLAN BUDGET | SPACE
DIPLOM NUC/PWR WEAPON...POLICY ANTHOL 20. PAGE 50 | LAW
G0983 | PEACE
| TEC/DEV

TAUBENFELD H.J.,SPACE AND SOCIETY. USA+45 LAW | B64
FORCES CREATE TEC/DEV ADJUD CONTROL COST PEACE | SPACE
...PREDICT ANTHOL 20. PAGE 54 G1057 | SOCIETY
| ADJUST
| DIPLOM

WHEELER-BENNETT J.W.,THE NEMESIS OF POWER (2ND | B64
ED.). EUR+WWI GERMANY TOP/EX TEC/DEV ADMIN WAR | FORCES
PERS/REL RIGID/FLEX ROLE ORD/FREE PWR FASCISM 20 | NAT/G
HITLER/A. PAGE 63 G1231 | GP/REL
| STRUCT

WILLIAMS S.P.,TOWARD A GENUINE WORLD SECURITY | B64
SYSTEM (PAMPHLET). WOR+45 INT/ORG FORCES PLAN | BIBLIOG/A
NUC/PWR ORD/FREE...INT/LAW CONCPT UN PRESIDENT. | ARMS/CONT
PAGE 63 G1243 | DIPLOM
| PEACE

CARNEGIE ENDOWMENT INT. PEACE,"POLITICAL QUESTIONS | L64
(ISSUES BEFORE THE NINETEENTH GENERAL ASSEMBLY)." | INT/ORG
SPACE WOR+45 CONSTN FINAN NAT/G CONSULT DELIB/GP | PEACE
FORCES LEGIS TEC/DEV EDU/PROP LEGIT ARMS/CONT
COERCE NUC/PWR ATTIT ALL/VALS...CONCPT OBS UN
COLD/WAR 20. PAGE 11 G0208

GOLDBERG A.,"ATOMIC ORIGINS OF THE BRITISH NUCLEAR DETERRENT." EUR+WWI UK NAT/G TOP/EX PLAN BAL/PWR DOMIN DETER CHOOSE ATTIT DRIVE HEALTH ORD/FREE PWR RESPECT...CONCPT VAL/FREE COLD/WAR 20 CMN/WLTH. PAGE 22 G0425
L64 CREATE FORCES NUC/PWR

WARD C.,"THE 'NEW MYTHS' AND 'OLD REALITIES' OF NUCLEAR WAR." COM FUT USA+45 USSR WOR+45 INT/ORG NAT/G DOMIN LEGIT EXEC ATTIT PERCEPT ALL/VALS ...POLICY RELATIV PSY MYTH TREND 20. PAGE 62 G1212
FORCES COERCE ARMS/CONT NUC/PWR

ABT C.,"WAR GAMING." USA+45 NAT/G TOP/EX ACT/RES TEC/DEV COERCE KNOWL ORD/FREE PWR...DECISION MATH TIME/SEQ COMPUT/IR CHARTS LAB/EXP VAL/FREE. PAGE 2 G0026
S64 FORCES SIMUL WAR

LERNER A.P.,"NUCLEAR SYMMETRY AS A FRAMEWORK FOR COEXISTENCE." COM FUT USA+45 NAT/G ACT/RES CREATE PLAN DIPLOM EDU/PROP COERCE WAR RIGID/FLEX PWR SKILL...CONCPT METH/CNCPT GEN/LAWS TOT/POP VAL/FREE COLD/WAR 20. PAGE 33 G0657
S64 FORCES ORD/FREE DETER NUC/PWR

MAGGS P.B.,"SOVIET VIEWPOINT ON NUCLEAR WEAPONS IN INTERNATIONAL LAW." USSR WOR+45 INT/ORG FORCES DIPLOM ARMS/CONT ATTIT ORD/FREE PWR...POLICY JURID CONCPT OBS TREND CON/ANAL GEN/LAWS VAL/FREE 20. PAGE 35 G0694
S64 COM LAW INT/LAW NUC/PWR

PILISUK M.,"STEPWISE DISARMAMENT & SUDDEN DESTRUCTION IN A TWOPERSON GAME: A RESEARCH TOOL." NAT/G FORCES ACT/RES ECO/TAC EDU/PROP EXEC ROUTINE COERCE ORD/FREE...SIMUL GEN/LAWS VAL/FREE. PAGE 45 G0877
S64 PWR DECISION ARMS/CONT

SPONSLER G.C.,"THE MILITARY ROLE IN SPACE." FUT USA+45 SEA AIR NAT/G ACT/RES PLAN COERCE NUC/PWR WEAPON KNOWL ORD/FREE PWR RESPECT...TREND 20. PAGE 52 G1026
S64 TEC/DEV FORCES SPACE

NATIONAL ACADEMY OF SCIENCES,CIVIL DEFENSE: PROJECT HARBOR SUMMARY REPORT (PAMPHLET). USA+45 MUNIC NAT/G ACT/RES BUDGET EDU/PROP DETER WEAPON EATING ...GEOG 20. PAGE 41 G0808
N64 NUC/PWR FORCES WAR PLAN

ATOMIC INDUSTRIAL FORUM,SAFEGUARDS AGAINST DIVERSION OF NUCLEAR MATERIALS FROM PEACEFUL TO MILITARY PURPOSES. WOR+45 DELIB/GP FORCES PLAN DIPLOM CONFER PEACE...ANTHOL 20 IAEA. PAGE 4 G0081
B65 NUC/PWR CIVMIL/REL INSPECT CONTROL

BEAUFRE A.,AN INTRODUCTION TO STRATEGY, WITH PARTICULAR REFERENCE TO PROBLEMS OF DEFENSE, POLITICS, ECONOMICS IN THE NUCLEAR AGE. WOR+45 FORCES DIPLOM DETER CIVMIL/REL GP/REL...NEW/IDEA IDEA/COMP 20. PAGE 6 G0111
B65 PLAN NUC/PWR WEAPON DECISION

BLOOMFIELD L.,SOVIET INTERESTS IN ARMS CONTROL AND DISARMAMENT* THE DECADE UNDER KHRUSHCHEV 1954-1964. ASIA FORCES ACT/RES EDU/PROP DETER NUC/PWR WEAPON COST ATTIT...PHIL/SCI CLASSIF STAT NET/THEORY GAME BIBLIOG. PAGE 7 G0139
B65 USSR ARMS/CONT DIPLOM TREND

BOBROW D.B.,COMPONENTS OF DEFENSE POLICY. ASIA EUR+WWI USA+45 WOR+45 INTELL INT/ORG NAT/G PROF/ORG CONSULT LEGIS ACT/RES CREATE ARMS/CONT COERCE ORD/FREE...DECISION SIMUL. PAGE 7 G0145
B65 DETER NUC/PWR PLAN FORCES

GRETTON P.,MARITIME STRATEGY - A STUDY OF DEFENSE PROBLEMS. ASIA UK USSR DIPLOM COERCE DETER NUC/PWR WEAPON...CONCPT NAT/COMP 20. PAGE 23 G0449
B65 FORCES PLAN WAR SEA

HALPERIN M.H.,CHINA AND THE BOMB. USA+45 USSR INT/ORG FORCES ARMS/CONT DETER PRODUC ORD/FREE PWR TREND. PAGE 24 G0472
B65 ASIA NUC/PWR WAR DIPLOM

HALPERIN M.H.,COMMUNIST CHINA AND ARMS CONTROL. CHINA/COM FUT USA+45 CULTURE FORCES TEC/DEV ECO/TAC WAR PEACE ORD/FREE MARXISM 20 COLD/WAR. PAGE 24 G0473
B65 ATTIT POLICY ARMS/CONT NUC/PWR

HITCH C.J.,DECISION-MAKING FOR DEFENSE. USA+45 CREATE BUDGET COERCE WAR WEAPON EFFICIENCY...SIMUL 20. PAGE 26 G0515
B65 DECISION OP/RES PLAN FORCES

KNORR K.,SCIENCE AND DEFENSE: SOME CRITICAL THOUGHTS ON MILITARY RESEARCH AND DEVELOPMENT. USA+45 ACT/RES CREATE BUDGET ECO/TAC DEMAND DECISION. PAGE 31 G0608
B65 CIVMIL/REL R+D FORCES PLAN

MELMANS S.,OUR DEPLETED SOCIETY. SPACE USA+45 ECO/DEV FORCES BUDGET ECO/TAC ADMIN WEAPON EFFICIENCY 20 COLD/WAR. PAGE 38 G0753
B65 CIVMIL/REL INDUS EDU/PROP CONTROL

MOSKOWITZ H.,US SECURITY, ARMS CONTROL, AND DISARMAMENT 1961-1965. FORCES DIPLOM DETER WAR WEAPON...CHARTS 20 UN COLD/WAR NATO. PAGE 40 G0790
B65 BIBLIOG/A ARMS/CONT NUC/PWR PEACE

THAYER F.C. JR.,AIR TRANSPORT POLICY AND NATIONAL SECURITY: A POLITICAL, ECONOMIC, AND MILITARY ANALYSIS. DIST/IND OP/RES PLAN TEC/DEV DIPLOM DETER WAR COST EFFICIENCY...POLICY BIBLIOG 20 DEPT/DEFEN FAA CAB. PAGE 54 G1066
B65 AIR FORCES CIVMIL/REL ORD/FREE

TYBOUT R.A.,ECONOMICS OF RESEARCH AND DEVELOPMENT. ECO/DEV ECO/UNDEV INDUS PROFIT DECISION. PAGE 55 G1084
B65 R+D FORCES ADMIN DIPLOM

US CONGRESS JT ATOM ENRGY COMM,ATOMIC ENERGY LEGISLATION THROUGH 89TH CONGRESS, 1ST SESSION. USA+45 LAW INT/ORG DELIB/GP BUDGET DIPLOM 20 AEC CONGRESS CASEBOOK EURATOM IAEA. PAGE 57 G1114
B65 NUC/PWR FORCES PEACE LEGIS

US DEPARTMENT OF ARMY,MILITARY PROTECTIVE CONSTRUCTION: NUCLEAR WARFARE AND CHEMICAL AND BIOLOGICAL OPERATIONS (MANUAL). OP/RES TEC/DEV RISK COERCE NUC/PWR WAR WEAPON EFFICIENCY UTIL BIO/SOC HABITAT ORD/FREE 20. PAGE 57 G1117
B65 FORCES CONSTRUC TASK HEALTH

US DEPARTMENT OF DEFENSE,US SECURITY ARMS CONTROL, AND DISARMAMENT 1961-1965 (PAMPHLET). CHINA/COM COM GERMANY/W ISRAEL SPACE USA+45 USSR WOR+45 FORCES EDU/PROP DETER EQUILIB PEACE ALL/VALS...GOV/COMP 20 NATO. PAGE 57 G1118
B65 BIBLIOG/A ARMS/CONT NUC/PWR DIPLOM

US DEPARTMENT OF THE ARMY,NUCLEAR WEAPONS AND THE ATLANTIC ALLIANCE: A BIBLIOGRAPHIC SURVEY. ASIA COM EUR+WWI USA+45 FORCES DIPLOM WEAPON...STAT 20 NATO. PAGE 58 G1131
B65 BIBLIOG/A ARMS/CONT NUC/PWR BAL/PWR

US DEPARTMENT OF THE ARMY,MILITARY MANPOWER POLICY. USA+45 LEGIS EXEC WAR 20 CONGRESS. PAGE 58 G1132
B65 BIBLIOG/A POLICY FORCES TREND

US SENATE COMM GOVT OPERATIONS,ORGANIZATION OF FEDERAL EXECUTIVE DEPARTMENTS AND AGENCIES: REPORT OF MARCH 23, 1965. USA+45 FORCES LEGIS DIPLOM ROUTINE CIVMIL/REL EFFICIENCY FEDERAL...MGT STAT. PAGE 60 G1179
B65 ADMIN EX/STRUC GOV/REL ORG/CHARTS

WASKOW A.I.,KEEPING THE WORLD DISARMED. AFR GERMANY/E DIPLOM CONTROL WAR 20 UN. PAGE 62 G1218
B65 ARMS/CONT PEACE FORCES PROB/SOLV

WEISNER J.B.,WHERE SCIENCE AND POLITICS MEET. USA+45 ECO/DEV R+D FORCES PROB/SOLV DIPLOM FOR/AID CONTROL...PHIL/SCI PRESIDENT KENNEDY/JF JOHNSON/LB. PAGE 63 G1228
B65 CHIEF NAT/G POLICY TEC/DEV

BEAUFRE A.,"THE SHARING OF NUCLEAR RESPONSIBILITIES* A PROBLEM IN NEED OF SOLUTION." FRANCE USA+45 INT/ORG NAT/G DELIB/GP FORCES CONTROL NUC/PWR RIGID/FLEX...CONCPT IDEA/COMP NATO. PAGE 6 G0110
S65 DETER RISK ACT/RES WAR

DALKEY N.C.,"SOLVABLE NUCLEAR WAR MODELS." FORCES
BAL/PWR DIPLOM COERCE PEACE DECISION. PAGE 14 G0273

S65
GAME
SIMUL
WAR
NUC/PWR

FOX A.B.,"NATO AND CONGRESS." CONSTN DELIB/GP
EX/STRUC FORCES TOP/EX BUDGET NUC/PWR GOV/REL
...GP/COMP CONGRESS NATO TREATY. PAGE 20 G0388

S65
CONTROL
DIPLOM

GRIFFITH S.B.,"COMMUNIST CHINA'S CAPACITY TO MAKE
WAR." CHINA/COM NAT/G TOP/EX PLAN DOMIN COERCE
NUC/PWR ATTIT RESPECT SKILL...CONCPT MYTH TIME/SEQ
TREND COLD/WAR 20. PAGE 23 G0452

S65
FORCES
PWR
WEAPON
ASIA

SCHELLING T.C.,"SIGNALS AND FEEDBACK IN THE ARMS
DIALOGUE." USA+45 USSR R+D ACADEM FORCES ACT/RES
ADJUST COST GEN/LAWS. PAGE 49 G0964

S65
FEEDBACK
DETER
EDU/PROP
ARMS/CONT

SCHWEBEL M.,"BEHAVIORAL SCIENCE AND HUMAN
SURVIVAL." FORCES ARMS/CONT COERCE NUC/PWR WAR
GP/REL NAT/LISM PERCEPT...POLICY PSY ANTHOL
BIBLIOG/A 20 COLD/WAR. PAGE 50 G0984

C65
PEACE
ACT/RES
DIPLOM
HEAL

US AIR FORCE ACADEMY,"AMERICAN DEFENSE POLICY." COM
INT/ORG TEC/DEV FOR/AID ARMS/CONT DETER NUC/PWR
...POLICY DECISION CONCPT ANTHOL BIBLIOG/A 20
COLD/WAR NATO. PAGE 56 G1103

C65
PLAN
FORCES
WAR
COERCE

BOLTON R.E.,DEFENSE AND DISARMAMENT: THE ECONOMICS
OF TRANSITION. USA+45 R+D FORCES PLAN LOBBY DETER
WAR COST PEACE...ANTHOL BIBLIOG 20. PAGE 8 G0150

B66
ARMS/CONT
POLICY
INDUS

CLARK G.,WORLD PEACE THROUGH WORLD LAW: TWO
ALTERNATIVE PLANS. WOR+45 DELIB/GP FORCES TAX
CONFER ADJUD SANCTION ARMS/CONT WAR CHOOSE PRIVIL
20 UN COLD/WAR. PAGE 12 G0231

B66
INT/LAW
PEACE
PLAN
INT/ORG

DAENIKER G.,STRATEGIE DES KLEIN STAATS. SWITZERLND
ACT/RES CREATE DIPLOM NEUTRAL DETER WAR WEAPON PWR
SOVEREIGN...IDEA/COMP 20 COLD/WAR. PAGE 14 G0270

B66
NUC/PWR
PLAN
FORCES
NAT/G

FEIS H.,THE ATOMIC BOMB AND THE END OF WORLD WAR
II. FORCES PLAN PROB/SOLV DIPLOM CONFER WAR
...TIME/SEQ TREND CHINJAP PRESIDENT TIME. PAGE 19
G0362

B66
USA+45
PEACE
NUC/PWR

HALPERIN M.H.,CHINA AND NUCLEAR PROLIFERATION
(PAMPHLET). CHINA/COM FUT INDIA USA+45 USSR
ARMS/CONT WAR 20 CHINJAP. PAGE 24 G0474

B66
NUC/PWR
FORCES
POLICY
DIPLOM

KUENNE R.E.,THE POLARIS MISSILE STRIKE* A GENERAL
ECONOMIC SYSTEMS ANALYSIS. USA+45 USSR NAT/G
BAL/PWR ARMS/CONT WAR...MATH PROBABIL COMPUT/IR
CHARTS HYPO/EXP SIMUL. PAGE 32 G0625

B66
NUC/PWR
FORCES
DETER
DIPLOM

RUPPENTHAL K.M.,TRANSPORTATION AND TOMORROW. FUT
SPACE USA+45 SEA AIR FORCES TEC/DEV INT/TRADE
...ANTHOL 20 RAILROAD. PAGE 48 G0946

B66
DIST/IND
PLAN
CIVMIL/REL
PREDICT

US DEPARTMENT OF THE ARMY,COMMUNIST CHINA: A
STRATEGIC SURVEY: A BIBLIOGRAPHY (PAMPHLET NO.
20-67). CHINA/COM COM INDIA USSR NAT/G POL/PAR
EX/STRUC FORCES NUC/PWR REV ATTIT...POLICY GEOG
CHARTS. PAGE 58 G1133

B66
BIBLIOG/A
MARXISM
S/ASIA
DIPLOM

US PRES COMM ECO IMPACT DEFENS,REPORT* JULY 1965.
USA+45 ECO/DEV INDUS DELIB/GP FORCES OP/RES
ARMS/CONT NUC/PWR WEAPON BAL/PAY...PREDICT SIMUL.
PAGE 59 G1159

B66
ACT/RES
STAT
WAR
BUDGET

US SENATE COMM AERO SPACE SCI,SOVIET SPACE
PROGRAMS, 1962-65; GOALS AND PURPOSES,
ACHIEVEMENTS, PLANS, AND INTERNATIONAL
IMPLICATIONS. USA+45 USSR R+D FORCES PLAN EDU/PROP
PRESS ADJUD ARMS/CONT ATTIT MARXISM. PAGE 60 G1168

B66
CONSULT
SPACE
FUT
DIPLOM

WHITNAH D.R.,SAFER SKYWAYS. DIST/IND DELIB/GP
FORCES TOP/EX WORKER TEC/DEV ROUTINE WAR CIVMIL/REL
COST...TIME/SEQ 20 FAA CAB. PAGE 63 G1235

B66
ADMIN
NAT/G
AIR
GOV/REL

WOLFERS A.,THE UNITED STATES IN A DISARMED WORLD: A
STUDY OF THE US OUTLINE FOR GENERAL AND COMPLETE
DISARMAMENT. USA+45 NAT/G CONTROL DETER NUC/PWR
EFFICIENCY...ANTHOL 20. PAGE 64 G1255

B66
ARMS/CONT
POLICY
FORCES
PEACE

BROWNLIE I.,"NUCLEAR PROLIFERATION* SOME PROBLEMS
OF CONTROL." USA+45 USSR ECO/UNDEV INT/ORG FORCES
TEC/DEV REGION CONSEN...RECORD TREATY. PAGE 9 G0181

S66
NUC/PWR
ARMS/CONT
VOL/ASSN
ORD/FREE

TURKEVICH J.,"SOVIET SCIENCE APPRAISED." USA+45 R+D
ACADEM FORCES DIPLOM EDU/PROP WAR EFFICIENCY PEACE
SKILL OBS. PAGE 55 G1081

S66
USSR
TEC/DEV
NAT/COMP
ATTIT

BURNS E.L.M.,MEGAMURDER. WOR+45 LAW INT/ORG NAT/G
BAL/PWR DIPLOM DETER MURDER WEAPON CIVMIL/REL PEACE
...INT/LAW TREND 20. PAGE 10 G0193

B67
FORCES
PLAN
WAR
NUC/PWR

DAVIS V.,THE POLITICS OF INNOVATION: PATTERNS IN
NAVY CASES (PAMPHLET). WOR+45 NAT/G CREATE WEAPON
INGP/REL ATTIT...POLICY SOC METH/COMP METH. PAGE 14
G0280

B67
BIBLIOG
FORCES
NUC/PWR
TEC/DEV

ENKE S.,DEFENSE MANAGEMENT. USA+45 R+D FORCES
WORKER PLAN ECO/TAC ADMIN NUC/PWR BAL/PAY UTIL
WEALTH...MGT DEPT/DEFEN. PAGE 18 G0348

B67
DECISION
DELIB/GP
EFFICIENCY
BUDGET

HOROWITZ I.L.,THE RISE AND FALL OF PROJECT CAMELOT:
STUDIES IN THE RELATIONSHIP BETWEEN SOCIAL SCIENCE
AND PRACTICAL POLITICS. USA+45 WOR+45 CULTURE
FORCES LEGIS EXEC CIVMIL/REL KNOWL...POLICY SOC
METH/CNCPT 20. PAGE 27 G0529

B67
NAT/G
ACADEM
ACT/RES
GP/REL

MACKINTOSH J.M.,JUGGERNAUT. USSR NAT/G POL/PAR
ADMIN LEAD CIVMIL/REL COST TOTALISM PWR MARXISM
...GOV/COMP 20. PAGE 35 G0691

B67
WAR
FORCES
COM
PROF/ORG

MCBRIDE J.H.,THE TEST BAN TREATY: MILITARY,
TECHNOLOGICAL, AND POLITICAL IMPLICATIONS. USA+45
USSR DELIB/GP FORCES LEGIS TEC/DEV BAL/PWR TREATY.
PAGE 37 G0727

B67
ARMS/CONT
DIPLOM
NUC/PWR

MCCLINTOCK R.,THE MEANING OF LIMITED WAR. FUT
WOR+45 NAT/G FORCES GUERRILLA REV...POLICY SAMP/SIZ
TREND NAT/COMP 45 COLD/WAR. PAGE 37 G0730

B67
WAR
NUC/PWR
BAL/PWR
DIPLOM

PADELFORD N.J.,THE DYNAMICS OF INTERNATIONAL
POLITICS (2ND ED.). WOR+45 LAW INT/ORG FORCES
TEC/DEV REGION NAT/LISM PEACE ATTIT PWR ALL/IDEOS
UN COLD/WAR NATO TREATY. PAGE 43 G0856

B67
DIPLOM
NAT/G
POLICY
DECISION

RAWLINSON J.L.,CHINA'S STRUGGLE FOR NAVAL
DEVELOPMENT 1839-1895. ASIA DIPLOM ADMIN WAR
...BIBLIOG DICTIONARY 19 CHINJAP. PAGE 46 G0907

B67
SEA
FORCES
PWR

RUSSELL B.,WAR CRIMES IN VIETNAM. USA+45 VIETNAM
FORCES DIPLOM WEAPON RACE/REL DISCRIM ISOLAT
BIO/SOC 20 COLD/WAR RUSSELL/B. PAGE 48 G0949

B67
WAR
CRIME
ATTIT
POLICY

US DEPARTMENT OF THE ARMY,CIVILIAN IN PEACE,
SOLDIER IN WAR: A BIBLIOGRAPHIC SURVEY OF THE ARMY
AND AIR NATIONAL GUARD (PAMPHLET NOS. 130-2).
USA+45 USA-45 LOC/G NAT/G PROVS LEGIS PLAN ADMIN
ATTIT ORD/FREE...POLICY 19/20. PAGE 58 G1134

B67
BIBLIOG/A
FORCES
ROLE
DIPLOM

US SENATE COMM AERO SPACE SCI,TREATY ON PRINCIPLES
GOVERNING ACTIVITIES OF STATES IN EXPLORATION AND
USE OF OUTER SPACE, INCLUDING...BODIES. DELIB/GP
FORCES LEGIS DIPLOM...JURID 20 DEPT/STATE NASA

B67
SPACE
INT/LAW
ORD/FREE
PEACE

DEPT/DEFEN UN. PAGE 60 G1170

EQUILIB SOVEREIGN MARXISM 20 UN. PAGE 25 G0496   PWR
PLAN

B67

US SENATE COMM ON FOREIGN REL,TREATY ON OUTER
SPACE. WOR+45 AIR FORCES PROB/SOLV NUC/PWR SENATE
TREATY UN. PAGE 60 G1182   SPACE DIPLOM ARMS/CONT LAW

S67

INGLIS D.R.,"MISSILE DEFENSE, NUCLEAR SPREAD, AND
VIETNAM." CHINA/COM USA+45 USSR VIETNAM INDUS
BAL/PWR DETER WAR COST NAT/LISM PEACE. PAGE 28
G0544   NUC/PWR ARMS/CONT DIPLOM FORCES

B67

US SENATE COMM ON FOREIGN REL,ARMS SALES TO NEAR
EAST AND SOUTH ASIAN COUNTRIES. INDIA IRAN PAKISTAN
WOR+45 PROC/MFG BAL/PWR DIPLOM...DECISION SENATE.
PAGE 60 G1183   WEAPON FOR/AID FORCES POLICY

S67

JAIN G.,"INDIA REJECTS THE POWER RACE* REALISM
ABOUT NUCLEAR WEAPONS." FORCES PROB/SOLV FOR/AID
ARMS/CONT COST PWR...GOV/COMP 20. PAGE 28 G0556   INDIA CHINA/COM NUC/PWR DIPLOM

B67

US SENATE COMM ON FOREIGN REL,UNITED STATES
ARMAMENT AND DISARMAMENT PROBLEMS. USA+45 AIR
BAL/PWR DIPLOM FOR/AID NUC/PWR ORD/FREE SENATE
TREATY. PAGE 60 G1184   ARMS/CONT WEAPON FORCES PROB/SOLV

S67

JONES G.S.,"STRATEGIC PLANNING." USA+45 EX/STRUC
FORCES DETER WAR 20 PRESIDENT. PAGE 29 G0566   PLAN DECISION DELIB/GP POLICY

B67

WYLIE J.C.,MILITARY STRATEGY: GENERAL THEORY OF
POWER CONTROL. CUBA USA+45 VIETNAM/N WOR+45 ELITES
CONTROL WAR PWR...POLICY METH/COMP 20 MAO. PAGE 64
G1260   FORCES PLAN DECISION IDEA/COMP

S67

LALL B.G.,"GAPS IN THE ABM DEBATE." NAT/G DIPLOM
DETER CIVMIL/REL 20. PAGE 32 G0630   NUC/PWR ARMS/CONT EX/STRUC FORCES

L67

DAVIS P.C.,"THE COMING CHINESE COMMUNIST NUCLEAR
THREAT AND U.S. SEA BASED ABM OPTIONS." ASIA
CHINA/COM FUT USA+45 SEA NAT/G FORCES PLAN TEC/DEV
LEAD ARMS/CONT...GEOG METH/COMP 20 ABM/DEFSYS.
PAGE 14 G0279   NUC/PWR DETER WEAPON DIPLOM

S67

MALONE D.K.,"THE COMMANDER AND THE COMPUTER."
USA+45 OP/RES PROB/SOLV TEC/DEV AUTOMAT CENTRAL 20.
PAGE 35 G0698   COMPUTER FORCES ELITES PLAN

L67

EINAUDI L.,"ANNOTATED BIBLIOGRAPHY OF LATIN
AMERICAN MILITARY JOURNALS" LAW TEC/DEV DOMIN
EDU/PROP COERCE WAR CIVMIL/REL 20. PAGE 17 G0336   BIBLIOG/A NAT/G FORCES L/A+17C

S67

MARTIN L.,"THE AMERICAN ABM DECISION." ASIA COM
EUR+WWI UK USA+45 USSR FORCES DIPLOM PEACE...POLICY
20 ABM/DEFSYS. PAGE 36 G0713   WEAPON DETER NUC/PWR WAR

S67

BRETNOR R.,"DESTRUCTIVE FORCE AND THE MILITARY
EQUATIONS." UNIV COMPUTER PLAN PROB/SOLV AUTOMAT
CONTROL COERCE DETER NUC/PWR WEAPON DRIVE PWR.
PAGE 9 G0166   FORCES TEC/DEV DOMIN WAR

S67

MARTIN L.W.,"BALLISTIC MISSILE DEFENSE AND EUROPE."
EUR+WWI USA+45 FORCES PLAN BAL/PWR DEBATE PEACE
...POLICY COLD/WAR NATO. PAGE 36 G0715   ATTIT ARMS/CONT NUC/PWR DETER

S67

BROWN N.,"BRITISH ARMS AND THE SWITCH TOWARD
EUROPE." EUR+WWI UK ARMS/CONT. PAGE 9 G0178   FORCES PLAN DIPLOM INT/ORG

S67

SALISBURY H.E.,"THE WAR IN VIETNAM." USA+45
VIETNAM/N DIPLOM MURDER 20. PAGE 48 G0953   POLICY WAR FORCES OBS

S67

CARROLL K.J.,"SECOND STEP TOWARD ARMS CONTROL."
WOR+45 INT/ORG VOL/ASSN FORCES PROB/SOLV RISK
WEAPON 20 COLD/WAR. PAGE 11 G0215   ARMS/CONT DIPLOM PLAN NUC/PWR

S67

TEKINER S.,"SINKIANG AND THE SINO-SOVIET CONFLICT."
ASIA COM USSR FORCES PLAN BAL/PWR CONTROL NUC/PWR
WAR WEAPON...DECISION 20. PAGE 54 G1060   DIPLOM PWR MARXISM

S67

CETRON M.J.,"FORECASTING TECHNOLOGY." INDUS FORCES
TASK UTIL...PHIL/SCI CONCPT CHARTS METH/COMP TIME.
PAGE 11 G0219   TEC/DEV FUT R+D PLAN

S67

WALTERS R.E.,"THE ROLE OF NUCLEAR WEAPONS FOR THE
WEST." ASIA UK USA+45 USSR DIPLOM COERCE WAR PEACE
...POLICY DECISION 20. PAGE 62 G1209   PLAN NUC/PWR WEAPON FORCES

S67

CHIU S.M.,"CHINA'S MILITARY POSTURE." CHINA/COM
ELITES NAT/G POL/PAR TEC/DEV ECO/TAC DOMIN CONTROL
LEAD REV MARXISM 20 MAO. PAGE 12 G0228   FORCES CIVMIL/REL NUC/PWR DIPLOM

S67

WARE R.S.,"FORECAST A.D. 2000." SOCIETY STRATA
ECO/UNDEV INDUS FORCES EDU/PROP AUTOMAT COERCE REV
WEAPON ATTIT PREDICT. PAGE 62 G1213   NUC/PWR GEOG TEC/DEV WAR

S67

CHRIST R.F.,"REORGANIZATION OF FRENCH ARMED
FORCES." FRANCE CREATE PLAN TEC/DEV BAL/PWR DOMIN
COERCE CENTRAL EFFICIENCY 20. PAGE 12 G0229   CHIEF DETER NUC/PWR FORCES

S67

WOLFE T.W.,"SOVIET MILITARY POLICY AT THE FIFTY
YEAR MARK." USSR VIETNAM WOR+45 RATION AGREE WAR
WEAPON CIVMIL/REL TREATY. PAGE 64 G1254   FORCES POLICY TIME/SEQ PLAN

S67

CLEMENS W.C.,"CHINESE NUCLEAR TESTS: TRENDS AND
PORTENTS." CHINA/COM USA+45 USSR FORCES PLAN
TEC/DEV ARMS/CONT WAR PWR...DECISION 20 MAO
KHRUSH/N. PAGE 12 G0234   NUC/PWR WEAPON POLICY DIPLOM

S67

YOUNG O.R.,"ACTIVE DEFENSE AND INTERNATIONAL
ORDER." FORCES BAL/PWR DEBATE GAMBLE COST PEACE.
PAGE 64 G1265   ARMS/CONT DETER PLAN DECISION

S67

DADDARIO E.Q.,"CONGRESS FACES SPACE POLICIES." R+D
NAT/G FORCES CREATE LEAD...DECISION CONGRESS NASA.
PAGE 14 G0269   SPACE PLAN BUDGET POLICY

N67

US HOUSE COMM FOREIGN AFFAIRS,REPORT OF SPECIAL
STUDY MISSION TO THE NEAR EAST (PAMPHLET). ISRAEL
USA+45 YEMEN ECO/UNDEV INT/ORG FOR/AID ARMS/CONT
WAR WEAPON NAT/LISM PEACE...GEOG 20 UN HOUSE/REP.
PAGE 58 G1138   ISLAM DIPLOM FORCES

S67

DE WEUFVILLE R.,"EDUCATION AT THE ACADEMIES."
USA+45 ELITES CONSULT EX/STRUC COMPUTER PLAN
PROB/SOLV TASK CIVMIL/REL ORD/FREE 20. PAGE 15
G0286   FORCES ACADEM TEC/DEV SKILL

N67

US SENATE,STATUS OF THE DEVELOPMENT OF THE ANTI-
BALLISTIC MISSILE SYSTEMS IN THE UNITED STATES
(PAMPHLET). FUT USA+45 R+D PLAN TEC/DEV DEPT/DEFEN.
PAGE 59 G1165   FORCES NUC/PWR WAR UTIL

S67

HAZARD J.N.,"POST-DISARMAMENT INTERNATIONAL LAW."
FUT USSR WOR+45 INT/ORG DELIB/GP FORCES DETER   INT/LAW ARMS/CONT

FORD FOUNDATION....SEE FORD/FOUND

FORD/FOUND....FORD FOUNDATION

PUBLIC POLICY AND THE MANAGEMENT OF SCIENCE

FOREIGN AID....SEE FOR/AID

FOREIGN TRADE....SEE INT/TRADE

FOREIGN POLICY ASSOCIATION G0379,G0380

FOREIGNREL....UNITED STATES SENATE COMMITTEE ON FOREIGN
    RELATIONS

FORGN/SERV....FOREIGN SERVICE

FORM W.H. G0381

FORMOSA....FORMOSA, PRE-1949; FOR POST-1949, SEE TAIWAN;
    SEE ALSO ASIA, CHINA

FORRESTER J.W. G0382

FORTRAN....FORTRAN - COMPUTER LANGUAGE

FORTUNE EDITORS G0383

FOSKETT D.J. G0384

FOSTER P. G0385

FOSTER R.B. G0386

FOSTER W.C. G0387

FOSTER/G....G. FOSTER

FOURIER/FM....FRANCOIS MARIE CHARLES FOURIER

FOX A.B. G0388

FOX W.T.R. G0389

FOX/CJ....CHARLES J. FOX

FOX/INDIAN....FOX INDIANS

FPC....U.S. FEDERAL POWER COMMISSION

FRANCE....SEE ALSO APPROPRIATE TIME/SPACE/CULTURE INDEX

B44
BARKER E.,THE DEVELOPMENT OF PUBLIC SERVICES IN   GOV/COMP
WESTERN WUROPE: 1660-1930. FRANCE GERMANY UK SCHOOL   ADMIN
CONTROL REPRESENT ROLE...WELF/ST 17/20. PAGE 5   EX/STRUC
G0095

B58
EHRHARD J.,LE DESTIN DU COLONIALISME. AFR FRANCE   COLONIAL
ECO/UNDEV AGRI FINAN MARKET CREATE PLAN TEC/DEV   FOR/AID
BUDGET DIPLOM PRICE 20. PAGE 17 G0335   INT/TRADE
                                                      INDUS

S60
KELLEY G.A.,"THE POLITICAL BACKGROUND OF THE FRENCH   NAT/G
A-BOMB." EUR+WWI USSR FORCES TOP/EX TEC/DEV NUC/PWR   RESPECT
ATTIT PWR...CONCPT OBS/ENVIR TREND 20. PAGE 30   NAT/LISM
G0591   FRANCE

B61
LAHAYE R.,LES ENTREPRISES PUBLIQUES AU MAROC.   NAT/G
FRANCE MOROCCO LAW DIST/IND EXTR/IND FINAN CONSULT   INDUS
PLAN TEC/DEV ADMIN AGREE CONTROL OWN...POLICY 20.   ECO/UNDEV
PAGE 32 G0629   ECO/TAC

B62
GRANICK D.,THE EUROPEAN EXECUTIVE. BELGIUM FRANCE   MGT
GERMANY/W UK INDUS LABOR LG/CO SML/CO EX/STRUC PLAN   ECO/DEV
TEC/DEV CAP/ISM COST DEMAND...POLICY CHARTS 20.   ECO/TAC
PAGE 22 G0441   EXEC

S63
GANDILHON J.,"LA SCIENCE ET LA TECHNIQUE A L'AIDE   ECO/UNDEV
DES REGIONS PEU DEVELOPPEES." FRANCE FUT WOR+45   TEC/DEV
ECO/DEV R+D PROF/ORG ACT/RES PLAN...MGT TOT/POP   FOR/AID
VAL/FREE 20 UN. PAGE 21 G0406

S63
SCHMITT H.A.,"THE EUROPEAN COMMUNITIES." EUR+WWI   VOL/ASSN
FRANCE DELIB/GP EX/STRUC TOP/EX CREATE TEC/DEV   ECO/DEV
ECO/TAC LEGIT REGION COERCE DRIVE ALL/VALS
...METH/CNCPT EEC 20. PAGE 49 G0972

B64
BAUCHET P.,ECONOMIC PLANNING. FRANCE STRATA LG/CO   ECO/DEV
CAP/ISM ADMIN PARL/PROC DEMAND OPTIMAL ATTIT PWR   NAT/G
SOCISM...POLICY CHARTS 20. PAGE 5 G0102   PLAN
                                                      ECO/TAC

B64
GOWING M.,BRITAIN AND ATOMIC ENERGY 1939-1945.   NUC/PWR

FRANCE UK USA+45 USA-45 NAT/G CREATE...PHIL/SCI 20   DIPLOM
AEA. PAGE 22 G0439   TEC/DEV

B64
GRAVIER J.F.,AMENAGEMENT DU TERRITOIRE ET L'AVENIR   PLAN
DES REGIONS FRANCAISES. FRANCE ECO/DEV AGRI INDUS   MUNIC
CREATE...GEOG CHARTS 20. PAGE 22 G0442   NEIGH
                                                      ADMIN

B64
INST D'ETUDE POL L'U GRENOBLE,ADMINISTRATION   ADMIN
TRADITIONELLE ET PLANIFICATION REGIONALE. FRANCE   MUNIC
LAW POL/PAR PROB/SOLV ADJUST RIGID/FLEX...CHARTS   PLAN
ANTHOL BIBLIOG T 20 REFORMERS. PAGE 28 G0546   CREATE

B65
HICKMAN B.G.,QUANTITATIVE PLANNING OF ECONOMIC   PROB/SOLV
POLICY. FRANCE NETHERLAND OP/RES PRICE ROUTINE UTIL   PLAN
...POLICY DECISION ECOMETRIC METH/CNCPT STAT STYLE   QUANT
CHINJAP. PAGE 26 G0511

B65
LUTZ V.,FRENCH PLANNING. FRANCE TEC/DEV RIGID/FLEX   PLAN
ORD/FREE 20. PAGE 34 G0680   ADMIN
                                                      FUT

B65
SCHEINMAN L.,ATOMIC ENERGY POLICY IN FRANCE UNDER   NUC/PWR
THE FOURTH REPUBLIC. FRANCE UK USA+45 ELITES   NAT/G
POL/PAR PLAN PROB/SOLV DIPLOM LEAD GOV/REL   DELIB/GP
...BIBLIOG 20 DEGAULLE/C. PAGE 49 G0962   POLICY

B65
VERMOT-GAUCHY M.,L'EDUCATION NATIONALE DANS LA   ACADEM
FRANCE DE 1975. FRANCE FUT CULTURE ELITES R+D   CREATE
SCHOOL PLAN EDU/PROP EFFICIENCY...POLICY PREDICT   TREND
CHARTS INDEX 20. PAGE 61 G1195   INTELL

S65
BEAUFRE A.,"THE SHARING OF NUCLEAR   DETER
RESPONSIBILITIES* A PROBLEM IN NEED OF SOLUTION."   RISK
FRANCE USA+45 INT/ORG NAT/G DELIB/GP FORCES CONTROL   ACT/RES
NUC/PWR RIGID/FLEX...CONCPT IDEA/COMP NATO. PAGE 6   WAR
G0110

S65
GOLDSTEIN W.,"KEEPING THE GENIE IN THE BOTTLE* THE   NUC/PWR
FEASIBILITY OF A NUCLEAR NON-PROLIFERATION   CREATE
AGREEMENT." ASIA FRANCE UK USA+45 USSR WOR+45   COST
ECO/UNDEV VOL/ASSN ACT/RES PLAN RISK ARMS/CONT WAR
PEACE ATTIT PERCEPT...RECORD TREND TIME. PAGE 22
G0429

S65
KINTNER W.P.,"THE PROSPECTS FOR WESTERN SCIENCE AND   TEC/DEV
TECHNOLOGY." EUR+WWI FRANCE USA+45 USSR R+D NUC/PWR   VOL/ASSN
NATO. PAGE 30 G0598   STAT
                                                      RECORD

B67
ARON R.,THE GREAT DEBATE: THEORIES OF NUCLEAR   NUC/PWR
STRATEGY. FRANCE USA+45 INT/ORG PLAN TREND. PAGE 4   DETER
G0068   BAL/PWR
                                                      DIPLOM

S67
CHRIST R.F.,"REORGANIZATION OF FRENCH ARMED   CHIEF
FORCES." FRANCE CREATE PLAN TEC/DEV BAL/PWR DOMIN   DETER
COERCE CENTRAL EFFICIENCY 20. PAGE 12 G0229   NUC/PWR
                                                      FORCES

S67
D'AMATO D.,"LEGAL ASPECTS OF THE FRENCH NUCLEAR   INT/LAW
TESTS." FRANCE WOR+45 ACT/RES COLONIAL RISK GOV/REL   DIPLOM
EQUILIB ORD/FREE PWR DECISION. PAGE 14 G0268   NUC/PWR
                                                      ADJUD

S67
EDMONDS M.,"INTERNATIONAL COLLABORATION IN WEAPONS   DIPLOM
PROCUREMENT* THE IMPLICATIONS OF THE ANGLO-FRENCH   VOL/ASSN
CASE." FRANCE UK CONSULT OP/RES PROB/SOLV TEC/DEV   BAL/PWR
CONFER CONTROL EFFICIENCY 20. PAGE 17 G0334   ARMS/CONT

S67
EYRAUD M.,"LA FRANCE FACE A UN EVENTUEL TRAITE DE   NUC/PWR
NON DISSEMINATION DES ARMES NUCLEAIRES." FRANCE   ARMS/CONT
USA+45 EXTR/IND INDUS R+D INT/ORG ACT/RES TEC/DEV   POLICY
AGREE PRODUC ATTIT 20 TREATY AEC EURATOM. PAGE 18
G0355

S67
SCOVILLE W.J.,"GOVERNMENT REGULATION AND GROWTH IN   NAT/G
THE FRENCH PAPER INDUSTRY DURING THE EIGHTEENTH   PROC/MFG
CENTURY." FRANCE MOD/EUR FINAN CAP/ISM TAX ADMIN   ECO/DEV
CONTROL PRIVIL LAISSEZ...POLICY 18. PAGE 50 G0985   INGP/REL

FRANCHISE-FUT

FRANCHISE....FRANCHISE

FRANCIS R.G. G0390

FRANCO/F....FRANCISCO FRANCO

FRANCO-PRUSSIAN WAR....SEE FRNCO/PRUS

FRANK/PARL....FRANKFURT PARLIAMENT

FRANKFUR/F....FELIX FRANKFURTER

FRANKFURT PARLIAMENT....SEE FRANK/PARL

FRANKLIN/B....BENJAMIN FRANKLIN

FREDERICK....FREDERICK THE GREAT

FREDRKSBRG....FREDERICKSBURG, VIRGINIA

FREE/SOIL....FREE-SOIL DEBATE (U.S.)

FREE/SPEE....FREE SPEECH MOVEMENT; SEE ALSO AMEND/I

FREEDOM....SEE ORD/FREE

FREEDOM/HS....FREEDOM HOUSE

FREIDEL F. G0391

FRELIMO....MOZAMBIQUE LIBERATION FRONT

FRENCH J.R.P. G0236

FRENCH/CAN....FRENCH CANADA

FREUD/S....SIGMUND FREUD

FREYMOND J. G0392

FRIED M. G0393

FRIEDRICH-EBERT-STIFTUNG G0394

FRISCH D. G0395

FRNCO/PRUS....FRANCO-PRUSSIAN WAR

FROMM/E....ERICH FROMM

FRONTIER....FRONTIER

FRUSTRATION....SEE BIO/SOC, ANOMIE, DRIVE

FRUTKIN A.W. G0396

FRYKLUND R. G0397

FTC....FEDERAL TRADE COMMISSION

LAWRENCE S.A.,THE BATTERY ADDITIVE CONTROVERSY   PHIL/SCI
(PAMPHLET). USA+45 LAW MARKET PROC/MFG R+D CAP/ISM LOBBY
CT/SYS GOV/REL OWN FTC CONGRESS BUR/STNDRD   INSPECT
RITCHIE/JM. PAGE 33 G0645

FULBRGHT/J....J. WILLIAM FULBRIGHT

FULLER G.A. G0398

FULLER G.H. G0399,G0400,G0401,G0402,G0403,G0404

FULLER/MW....MELVILLE WESTON FULLER

FUNCTIONAL ANALYSIS....SEE OP/RES

FUNCTIONALISM (THEORY)....SEE GEN/LAWS

FURNIVAL/J....J.S. FURNIVAL

FUT....FUTURE (PAST AND PRESENT ATTEMPTS TO DEPICT IT)

                  N
JOURNAL OF CONFLICT RESOLUTION. FUT WOR+45 INT/ORG BIBLIOG/A
NAT/G FORCES CREATE PROB/SOLV ARMS/CONT NUC/PWR DIPLOM
WEAPON SOC. PAGE 1 G0002   WAR

                  N
AIR UNIVERSITY LIBRARY,INDEX TO MILITARY   BIBLIOG/A
PERIODICALS. FUT SPACE WOR+45 REGION ARMS/CONT FORCES

NUC/PWR WAR PEACE INT/LAW. PAGE 2 G0032   NAT/G
                  DIPLOM

                  N
AMER COUNCIL OF LEARNED SOCIET,THE ACLS CONSTITUENT BIBLIOG/A
SOCIETY JOURNAL PROJECT. FUT USA+45 LAW NAT/G PLAN HUM
DIPLOM PHIL/SCI. PAGE 3 G0048   COMPUT/IR
                  COMPUTER

                  B11
BERGSON H.,CREATIVE EVOLUTION. FUT WOR+45 WOR-45 BIO/SOC
INTELL AGRI R+D ATTIT PERCEPT PERSON RIGID/FLEX KNOWL
...RELATIV PHIL/SCI PSY METH/CNCPT MATH HIST/WRIT
TREND HYPO/EXP TOT/POP. PAGE 7 G0127

                  N19
ZLOTNICK M.,WEAPONS IN SPACE (PAMPHLET). FUT WOR+45 SPACE
TEC/DEV DIPLOM ARMS/CONT CIVMIL/REL PEACE HABITAT WEAPON
...CONCPT NEW/IDEA CHARTS. PAGE 65 G1268   NUC/PWR
                  WAR

                  B45
BUSH V.,SCIENCE, THE ENDLESS FRONTIER. FUT USA-45 R+D
INTELL STRATA ACT/RES CREATE PLAN EDU/PROP ADMIN NAT/G
NUC/PWR PEACE ATTIT HEALTH KNOWL...MAJORIT HEAL MGT
PHIL/SCI CONCPT OBS TREND 20. PAGE 10 G0195

                  B46
BUSH V.,ENDLESS HORIZONS. FUT USA-45 INTELL NAT/G R+D
CONSULT ACT/RES CREATE PLAN EDU/PROP DRIVE   KNOWL
...MAJORIT HEAL MGT PHIL/SCI CONCPT OBS TREND   PEACE
GEN/METH TOT/POP 20. PAGE 10 G0196

                  B46
NORTHROP F.S.C.,THE MEETING OF EAST AND WEST.   DRIVE
EUR+WWI FUT MOD/EUR UNIV WOR+45 WOR-45 INTELL TREND
SOCIETY EX/STRUC TOP/EX ACT/RES LEGIT CHOOSE ATTIT PEACE
PERCEPT RIGID/FLEX ALL/VALS...POLICY JURID OBS
TOT/POP. PAGE 42 G0826

                  L46
MASTERS D.,"ONE WORLD OR NONE." FUT WOR+45 INTELL POLICY
INT/ORG ACT/RES EDU/PROP DETER ATTIT RIGID/FLEX PHIL/SCI
SUPEGO KNOWL...STAT TREND ORG/CHARTS 20. PAGE 36 ARMS/CONT
G0719   NUC/PWR

                  B50
MANNHEIM K.,FREEDOM, POWER, AND DEMOCRATIC   TEC/DEV
PLANNING. FUT USSR WOR+45 ELITES INTELL SOCIETY PLAN
NAT/G EDU/PROP ROUTINE ATTIT DRIVE SUPEGO SKILL CAP/ISM
...POLICY PSY CONCPT TREND GEN/LAWS 20. PAGE 35 UK
G0700

                  S50
LENTZ T.F.,"REPORT ON A SURVEY OF SOCIAL SCIENTISTS ACT/RES
CONDUCTED BY THE ATTITUDE RESEARCH LABORATORY." FUT ATTIT
WOR+45 CREATE EDU/PROP...PSY STAT RECORD SYS/QU DIPLOM
SAMP/SIZ CON/ANAL VAL/FREE 20. PAGE 33 G0655

                  B52
DAY E.E.,EDUCATION FOR FREEDOM AND RESPONSIBILITY. SCHOOL
FUT USA+45 CULTURE CONSULT EDU/PROP ATTIT SKILL KNOWL
...MGT CONCPT OBS GEN/LAWS COLD/WAR 20. PAGE 14
G0282

                  S53
CORY R.H. JR.,"FORGING A PUBLIC INFORMATION POLICY INT/ORG
FOR THE UNITED NATIONS." FUT WOR+45 SOCIETY ADMIN EDU/PROP
PEACE ATTIT PERSON SKILL...CONCPT 20 UN. PAGE 13 BAL/PWR
G0257

                  B54
ARON R.,CENTURY OF TOTAL WAR. FUT WOR+45 WOR-45 ATTIT
SOCIETY INT/ORG NAT/G FORCES TOP/EX CREATE BAL/PWR WAR
DOMIN EDU/PROP COERCE DETER PEACE TOTALISM PWR
...TIME/SEQ TREND COLD/WAR TOT/POP VAL/FREE
LEAGUE/NAT 20. PAGE 4 G0066

                  B54
WRIGHT Q.,PROBLEMS OF STABILITY AND PROGRESS IN INT/ORG
INTERNATIONAL RELATIONSHIPS. FUT WOR+45 WOR-45 CONCPT
SOCIETY LEGIS CREATE TEC/DEV ECO/TAC EDU/PROP ADJUD DIPLOM
WAR PEACE ORD/FREE PWR...KNO/TEST TREND GEN/LAWS
20. PAGE 64 G1257

                  S54
DEUTSCH K.W.,"GAME THEORY AND POLITICS: SOME DECISION
PROBLEMS OF APPLICATION." FUT WOR+45 SOCIETY R+D GEN/METH
KNOWL PWR...CONCPT METH/CNCPT MATH QUANT GAME SIMUL
VAL/FREE 20. PAGE 15 G0295

                  S54
POLANYI M.,"ON THE INTRODUCTION OF SCIENCE INTO INTELL
MORAL SUBJECTS." FUT WOR+45 ACT/RES ATTIT KNOWL PHIL/SCI
...CONCPT NEW/IDEA 20. PAGE 45 G0882

MIKSCHE F.O.,ATOMIC WEAPONS AND ARMIES. FUT WOR+45 TEC/DEV
WOR-45 SOCIETY COERCE DETER WEAPON PWR...POLICY FORCES
WELF/ST PSY CONCPT INT SYS/QU KNO/TEST TOT/POP 20. NUC/PWR
PAGE 39 G0765

B55

MOCH J.,HUMAN FOLLY: DISARM OR PERISH. USA+45 FUT
WOR+45 SOCIETY INT/ORG NAT/G ACT/RES EDU/PROP ATTIT DELIB/GP
PERSON KNOWL ORD/FREE PWR...MAJORIT TOT/POP ARMS/CONT
COLD/WAR 20. PAGE 39 G0776 NUC/PWR

B55

ANGELL R.,"GOVERNMENTS AND PEOPLES AS A FOCI FOR FUT
PEACE-ORIENTED RESEARCH." WOR+45 CULTURE SOCIETY SOC
FACE/GP ACT/RES CREATE PLAN DIPLOM EDU/PROP ROUTINE PEACE
ATTIT PERCEPT SKILL...POLICY CONCPT OBS TREND
GEN/METH 20. PAGE 3 G0060

S55

SKINNER B.F.,"FREEDOM AND THE CONTROL OF MEN" ORD/FREE
(BMR)" FUT WOR+45 CONTROL CHOOSE GP/REL ATTIT MORAL TEC/DEV
PWR POPULISM...POLICY 20. PAGE 51 G1008 PHIL/SCI
INTELL

S55

VON NEUMANN J.,"CAN WE SURVIVE TECHNOLOGY?" WOR+45 TEC/DEV
AIR INDUS ADMIN ADJUST RIGID/FLEX...GEOG PHIL/SCI NUC/PWR
NEW/IDEA 20. PAGE 61 G1202 FUT
HABITAT

S55

BLACKETT P.M.S.,ATOMIC WEAPONS AND EAST-WEST FORCES
RELATIONS. FUT WOR+45 INT/ORG DELIB/GP COERCE ATTIT PWR
RIGID/FLEX KNOWL...RELATIV HIST/WRIT TREND GEN/METH ARMS/CONT
COLD/WAR 20. PAGE 7 G0138 NUC/PWR

B56

GOLD N.L.,REGIONAL ECONOMIC DEVELOPMENT AND NUCLEAR ECO/UNDEV
POWER IN INDIA. FUT INDIA FINAN FOR/AID INT/TRADE TEC/DEV
BAL/PAY EFFICIENCY OPTIMAL PRODUC WEALTH...PREDICT NUC/PWR
20. PAGE 22 G0424 INDUS

B57

KISSINGER H.A.,NUCLEAR WEAPONS AND FOREIGN POLICY. PLAN
FUT USA+45 WOR+45 INT/ORG FORCES ACT/RES TEC/DEV DETER
DIPLOM ARMS/CONT COERCE ATTIT KNOWL PWR...DECISION NUC/PWR
GEOG CHARTS 20. PAGE 31 G0602

B57

SPEIER H.,GERMAN REARMAMENT AND ATOMIC WAR: THE TOP/EX
VIEWS OF GERMAN MILITARY AND POLITICAL LEADERS. FUT FORCES
WOR+45 INT/ORG NAT/G WEAPON ATTIT PWR...INT QU NUC/PWR
TOT/POP VAL/FREE COLD/WAR 20. PAGE 52 G1024 GERMANY

B57

NOEL-BAKER D.,THE ARMS RACE. WOR+45 NAT/G DELIB/GP FUT
ACT/RES TEC/DEV EDU/PROP NUC/PWR ATTIT KNOWL PWR INT/ORG
...CONCPT OBS LEAGUE/NAT 20 COLD/WAR. PAGE 42 G0823 ARMS/CONT
PEACE

B58

TELLER E.A.,OUR NUCLEAR FUTURE. SOCIETY FORCES FUT
TEC/DEV EDU/PROP KNOWL ORD/FREE...STAND/INT SYS/QU PHIL/SCI
KNO/TEST AUD/VIS CHARTS SIMUL 20. PAGE 54 G1062 NUC/PWR
WAR

B58

MCDOUGAL M.S.,"PERSPECTIVES FOR A LAW OF OUTER INT/ORG
SPACE." FUT WOR+45 AIR CONSULT DELIB/GP TEC/DEV SPACE
CT/SYS ORD/FREE...POLICY JURID 20 UN. PAGE 37 G0736 INT/LAW

S58

MODELSKI G.,ATOMIC ENERGY IN THE COMMUNIST BLOC. TEC/DEV
FUT INT/ORG CONSULT FORCES ACT/RES PLAN KNOWL SKILL NUC/PWR
...PHIL/SCI STAT CHARTS 20. PAGE 39 G0777 USSR
COM

B59

STANFORD RESEARCH INSTITUTE,POSSIBLE NONMILITARY R+D
SCIENTIFIC DEVELOPMENTS AND THEIR POTENTIAL IMPACT TEC/DEV
ON FOREIGN POLICY PROBLEMS OF THE UNITED. FUT
USA+45 INT/ORG PROF/ORG CONSULT ACT/RES CREATE PLAN
PEACE KNOWL SKILL...TECHNIC PHIL/SCI NEW/IDEA
UNESCO 20. PAGE 52 G1032

B59

VAN WAGENEN R.W.,SOME VIEWS OF AMERICAN DEFENSE INT/ORG
OFFICIALS ABOUT THE UNITED NATIONS (PAPER). FUT LEAD
USA+45 NAT/G DIPLOM WAR EFFICIENCY PEACE...POLICY ATTIT
INT 20 UN DEPT/DEFEN. PAGE 61 G1192 FORCES

B59

VERNEY D.V.,PUBLIC ENTERPRISE IN SWEDEN. FUT SWEDEN ECO/DEV
UK INDUS POL/PAR LEGIS PROB/SOLV CAP/ISM INT/TRADE POLICY
CONTROL SOCISM...MGT CONCPT NAT/COMP 20 SOCDEM/PAR LG/CO

B59

CIVIL/SERV. PAGE 61 G1196 NAT/G

BURNS A.L.,"POWER POLITICS AND THE GROWING NUCLEAR FORCES
CLUB." FUT WOR+45 TEC/DEV EXEC ARMS/CONT COERCE BAL/PWR
DETER...DECISION HYPO/EXP 20. PAGE 10 G0192 NUC/PWR

L59

GOLDHAMMER H.,"SOME OBSERVATIONS ON POLITICAL COMPUT/IR
GAMING." FUT WOR+45 R+D NAT/G ACT/RES CREATE CHOOSE DECISION
ATTIT PWR...POLICY CONCPT METH/CNCPT STYLE KNO/TEST DIPLOM
TREND HYPO/EXP GAME GEN/METH METH 20. PAGE 22 G0426

S59

SIMONS H.,"WORLD-WIDE CAPABILITIES FOR PRODUCTION TEC/DEV
AND CONTROL OF NUCLEAR WEAPONS." FUT WOR+45 INDUS ARMS/CONT
INT/ORG NAT/G ECO/TAC ATTIT PWR SKILL...TREND NUC/PWR
CHARTS VAL/FREE 20. PAGE 51 G1001

S59

STOESSINGER J.G.,"THE INTERNATIONAL ATOMIC ENERGY INT/ORG
AGENCY: THE FIRST PHASE." FUT WOR+45 NAT/G VOL/ASSN ECO/DEV
DELIB/GP BAL/PWR LEGIT ADMIN ROUTINE PWR...OBS FOR/AID
CON/ANAL GEN/LAWS VAL/FREE 20 IAEA. PAGE 53 G1037 NUC/PWR

S59

ARMS CONTROL. FUT UNIV WOR+45 INTELL R+D INT/ORG DELIB/GP
NAT/G VOL/ASSN CONSULT CREATE EDU/PROP PEACE...HUM ORD/FREE
GEN/LAWS TOT/POP 20. PAGE 1 G0015 ARMS/CONT
NUC/PWR

B60

APTHEKER H.,DISARMAMENT AND THE AMERICAN ECONOMY: A MARXIST
SYMPOSIUM. FUT USA+45 DIST/IND FINAN INDUS ARMS/CONT
PROC/MFG LABOR NAT/G POL/PAR CONSULT PLAN CAP/ISM
INT/TRADE PEACE ATTIT MORAL WEALTH...TREND GEN/LAWS
TOT/POP 20. PAGE 3 G0063

B60

EINSTEIN A.,EINSTEIN ON PEACE. FUT WOR+45 WOR-45 INT/ORG
SOCIETY NAT/G PLAN BAL/PWR CAP/ISM DIPLOM ARMS/CONT ATTIT
DETER NAT/LISM...POLICY RELATIV HUM PHIL/SCI CONCPT NUC/PWR
BIOG COLD/WAR LEAGUE/NAT NAZI. PAGE 17 G0338 PEACE

B60

GOLDSEN J.M.,INTERNATIONAL POLITICAL IMPLICATIONS R+D
OF ACTIVITIES IN OUTER SPACE. FUT USA+45 WOR+45 AIR SPACE
LAW ACT/RES LEGIT ATTIT KNOWL ORD/FREE PWR...CONCPT
20. PAGE 22 G0427

B60

MCKINNEY R.,REVIEW OF THE INTERNATIONAL ATOMIC NUC/PWR
POLICIES AND PROGRAMS OF THE UNITED STATES (5 PEACE
VOLS.). COM FUT USA+45 ECO/DEV ECO/UNDEV INT/ORG DIPLOM
DELIB/GP PLAN ADMIN 20 THIRD/WRLD. PAGE 38 G0744 POLICY

B60

PARRY A.,RUSSIA'S ROCKETS AND MISSILES. COM FUT PLAN
GERMANY USA+45 WOR+45 INTELL ECO/DEV ACT/RES TEC/DEV
NUC/PWR WEAPON ATTIT ALL/VALS...OBS TIME/SEQ SPACE
COLD/WAR 20. PAGE 44 G0859 USSR

B60

PENTONY D.E.,THE UNDERDEVELOPED LANDS. FUT WOR+45 ECO/UNDEV
CULTURE AGRI FINAN INDUS MARKET INT/ORG LABOR NAT/G POLICY
VOL/ASSN CONSULT TEC/DEV ECO/TAC EDU/PROP COLONIAL FOR/AID
ATTIT WEALTH...OBS RECORD SAMP TREND GEN/METH WORK INT/TRADE
UN 20. PAGE 44 G0867

B60

US HOUSE COMM. SCI. ASTRONAUT.,OCEAN SCIENCES AND R+D
NATIONAL SECURITY. FUT SEA ECO/DEV EXTR/IND INT/ORG ORD/FREE
NAT/G FORCES ACT/RES TEC/DEV ECO/TAC COERCE WAR
BIO/SOC KNOWL PWR...CONCPT RECORD LAB/EXP 20.
PAGE 59 G1153

B60

US SENATE COMM ON COMMERCE,URBAN MASS DIST/IND
TRANSPORTATION. FUT USA+45 AIR ECO/DEV FINAN LOC/G PLAN
MUNIC LEGIS CREATE PROB/SOLV TEC/DEV 20 PUB/TRANS. NAT/G
PAGE 60 G1180 LAW

B60

WOETZEL R.K.,THE INTERNATIONAL CONTROL OF AIRSPACE INT/ORG
AND OUTERSPACE. FUT WOR+45 AIR CONSTN STRUCT JURID
CONSULT PLAN TEC/DEV ADJUD RIGID/FLEX KNOWL SPACE
ORD/FREE PWR...TECHNIC GEOG MGT NEW/IDEA TREND INT/LAW
COMPUT/IR VAL/FREE 20 TREATY. PAGE 64 G1251

B60

BRENNAN D.G.,"SETTING AND GOALS OF ARMS CONTROL." FORCES
FUT USA+45 USSR WOR+45 INTELL INT/ORG NAT/G COERCE
VOL/ASSN CONSULT PLAN DIPLOM ECO/TAC ADMIN KNOWL ARMS/CONT
PWR...POLICY CONCPT TREND COLD/WAR 20. PAGE 8 G0164 DETER

L60

HOLTON G.,"ARMS CONTROL." FUT WOR+45 CULTURE
INT/ORG NAT/G FORCES TOP/EX PLAN EDU/PROP COERCE
ATTIT RIGID/FLEX ORD/FREE...POLICY PHIL/SCI SOC
TREND COLD/WAR. PAGE 27 G0524
   L60 ACT/RES CONSULT ARMS/CONT NUC/PWR

HOLZMAN B.G.,"BASIC RESEARCH FOR NATIONAL
SURVIVAL." FUT USA+45 INTELL R+D ACT/RES OP/RES
PLAN TEC/DEV EDU/PROP PERCEPT PERSON...PHIL/SCI
METH/CNCPT NEW/IDEA MATH OBS RECORD TREND LAB/EXP
20. PAGE 27 G0525
   L60 FORCES STAT

DOTY P.M.,"THE ROLE OF THE SMALLER POWERS." FUT
WOR+45 NAT/G TEC/DEV BAL/PWR DOMIN LEGIT CHOOSE
DISPL DRIVE RESPECT...DECISION 20. PAGE 16 G0310
   S60 PWR POLICY ARMS/CONT NUC/PWR

DYSON F.J.,"THE FUTURE DEVELOPMENT OF NUCLEAR
WEAPONS." FUT WOR+45 DELIB/GP ACT/RES PLAN DETER
WEAPON ATTIT PWR...POLICY 20. PAGE 17 G0328
   S60 INT/ORG ARMS/CONT NUC/PWR

HAYTON R.D.,"THE ANTARCTIC SETTLEMENT OF 1959." FUT
USA+45 WOR+45 WOR+45 STRUCT R+D INT/ORG EX/STRUC
CREATE TEC/DEV LEGIT PEACE ATTIT SOVEREIGN
...TIME/SEQ 20 TREATY IGY. PAGE 25 G0495
   S60 DELIB/GP JURID DIPLOM REGION

IKLE F.C.,"NTH COUNTRIES AND DISARMAMENT." WOR+45
DELIB/GP ECO/TAC DOMIN EDU/PROP LEGIT ROUTINE
COERCE RIGID/FLEX ORD/FREE...MARXIST TREND 20.
PAGE 28 G0543
   S60 FUT INT/ORG ARMS/CONT NUC/PWR

JAFFEE A.J.,"POPULATION TRENDS AND CONTROLS IN
UNDERDEVELOPED COUNTRIES." AFR FUT ISLAM L/A+17C
S/ASIA CULTURE R+D FAM ACT/RES PLAN EDU/PROP
BIO/SOC RIGID/FLEX HEALTH...SOC STAT OBS CHARTS 20.
PAGE 28 G0555
   S60 ECO/UNDEV GEOG

KAPLAN M.A.,"THEORETICAL ANALYSIS OF THE BALANCE OF
POWER." FUT USA+45 WOR+45 INTELL ECO/DEV INT/ORG
NAT/G CONSULT TOP/EX ACT/RES PLAN TEC/DEV ATTIT
ALL/VALS...METH/CNCPT TOT/POP 20. PAGE 29 G0576
   S60 CREATE NEW/IDEA DIPLOM NUC/PWR

OSGOOD C.E.,"A CASE FOR GRADUATED UNILATERAL
DISENGAGEMENT." FUT WOR+45 CULTURE SOCIETY NAT/G
NUC/PWR WAR PERSON SUPEGO ALL/VALS...POLICY PSY
CONCPT COLD/WAR TOT/POP VAL/FREE 20. PAGE 43 G0848
   S60 ATTIT EDU/PROP ARMS/CONT

SANDERS R.,"NUCLEAR DYNAMITE: A NEW DIMENSION IN
FOREIGN POLICY." FUT WOR+45 ECO/DEV CONSULT TEC/DEV
PERCEPT...CONT/OBS TIME/SEQ TREND GEN/LAWS TOT/POP
20 TREATY. PAGE 49 G0955
   S60 INDUS PWR DIPLOM NUC/PWR

YEMELYANOV V.S.,"ATOMIC ENERGY FOR PEACE: THE USSR
AND INTERNATIONAL CO-OPERATION." FUT USSR WOR+45
R+D CREATE EDU/PROP...CONCPT GEN/LAWS 20. PAGE 64
G1264
   S60 VOL/ASSN TEC/DEV ARMS/CONT NUC/PWR

HADLEY A.T.,THE NATIONS SAFETY AND ARMS CONTROL.
FUT USA+45 WOR+45 TOP/EX PLAN TEC/DEV ATTIT DRIVE
...CONCPT OBS TIME/SEQ TREND 20. PAGE 24 G0466
   B61 ACT/RES ROUTINE DETER NUC/PWR

HENKIN L.,ARMS CONTROL: ISSUES FOR THE PUBLIC.
EUR+WWI FUT USA+45 USSR INT/ORG NAT/G DIPLOM
EDU/PROP DETER NUC/PWR ATTIT PWR...CONCPT RECORD
HIST/WRIT TIME/SEQ TOT/POP COLD/WAR 20. PAGE 26
G0506
   B61 WOR+45 DELIB/GP ARMS/CONT

KAHN H.,ON THERMONUCLEAR WAR. FUT UNIV WOR+45
ECO/DEV CONSULT EX/STRUC TOP/EX ACT/RES CREATE PLAN
COERCE WAR PERSON ALL/VALS...POLICY GEOG CONCPT
METH/CNCPT OBS TREND 20. PAGE 29 G0569
   B61 DETER NUC/PWR SOCIETY

KISSINGER H.A.,THE NECESSITY FOR CHOICE. FUT USA+45
ECO/UNDEV NAT/G PLAN BAL/PWR ECO/TAC ARMS/CONT
DETER NUC/PWR ATTIT...POLICY CONCPT RECORD GEN/LAWS
COLD/WAR 20. PAGE 31 G0604
   B61 TOP/EX TREND DIPLOM

MICHAEL D.N.,PROPOSED STUDIES ON THE IMPLICATIONS
OF PEACEFUL SPACE ACTIVITIES FOR HUMAN AFFAIRS.
COM/IND INDUS FORCES DIPLOM PEACE PERSON...PSY SOC
   B61 FUT SPACE ACT/RES

20. PAGE 39 G0764
   PROB/SOLV

RAMO S.,PEACETIME USES OF OUTER SPACE. FUT DIST/IND
INT/ORG CONSULT NUC/PWR...AUD/VIS ANTHOL 20.
PAGE 46 G0898
   B61 PEACE TEC/DEV SPACE CREATE

TAUBENFELD H.J.,"A TREATY FOR ANTARCTICA." FUT
USA+45 INTELL INT/ORG LABOR 20 TREATY ANTARCTICA.
PAGE 54 G1055
   L61 R+D ACT/RES DIPLOM

TAUBENFELD H.J.,"A REGIME FOR OUTER SPACE." FUT
UNIV R+D ACT/RES PLAN BAL/PWR LEGIT ARMS/CONT
ORD/FREE...POLICY JURID TREND UN TOT/POP 20
COLD/WAR. PAGE 54 G1056
   L61 INT/ORG ADJUD SPACE

LINDSAY F.A.,"PLANNING IN FOREIGN AFFAIRS: THE
MISSING ELEMENT." FUT USA+45 ROUTINE SKILL...MGT
TOT/POP 20. PAGE 34 G0669
   S61 ECO/DEV PLAN DIPLOM

MACHOWSKI K.,"SELECTED PROBLEMS OF NATIONAL
SOVEREIGNTY WITH REFERENCE TO THE LAW OF OUTER
SPACE." FUT WOR+45 AIR LAW INTELL SOCIETY ECO/DEV
PLAN EDU/PROP DETER DRIVE PERCEPT SOVEREIGN
...POLICY INT/LAW OBS TREND TOT/POP 20. PAGE 35
G0689
   S61 UNIV ACT/RES NUC/PWR SPACE

MORGENSTERN O.,"THE N-COUNTRY PROBLEM." EUR+WWI
UNIV USA+45 WOR+45 SOCIETY CONSULT TOP/EX ACT/RES
PLAN EDU/PROP ATTIT DRIVE...POLICY OBS TREND
TOT/POP 20. PAGE 40 G0781
   S61 FUT BAL/PWR NUC/PWR TEC/DEV

RICHSTEIN A.R.,"LEGAL RULES IN NUCLEAR WEAPONS
EMPLOYMENTS." FUT WOR+45 LAW SOCIETY FORCES PLAN
WEAPON RIGID/FLEX...HEAL CONCPT TREND VAL/FREE 20.
PAGE 47 G0918
   S61 NUC/PWR TEC/DEV MORAL ARMS/CONT

SCHILLING W.R.,"THE H-BOMB: HOW TO DECIDE WITHOUT
ACTUALLY CHOOSING." FUT USA+45 INTELL CONSULT ADMIN
CT/SYS MORAL...JURID OBS 20 TRUMAN/HS. PAGE 49
G0966
   S61 PERSON LEGIT NUC/PWR

TAUBENFELD H.J.,"OUTER SPACE--PAST POLITICS AND
FUTURE POLICY." FUT USA+45 USA-45 WOR+45 AIR INTELL
STRUCT ECO/DEV NAT/G TOP/EX ACT/RES ADMIN ROUTINE
NUC/PWR ATTIT DRIVE...CONCPT TIME/SEQ TREND TOT/POP
20. PAGE 54 G1054
   S61 PLAN SPACE INT/ORG

WOHLSTETTER A.,"NUCLEAR SHARING: NATO AND THE NTH
COUNTRY." EUR+WWI FUT SOCIETY DIPLOM EXEC DETER PWR
SKILL...POLICY TECHNIC CONCPT 20 NATO. PAGE 64
G1252
   S61 TREND TEC/DEV NUC/PWR ARMS/CONT

SOVIET STAND ON DISARMAMENT. COM EUR+WWI FUT USA+45
NAT/G TOP/EX NUC/PWR PEACE ATTIT...POLICY CONCPT
TOT/POP 20. PAGE 1 G0016
   B62 ACT/RES ORD/FREE ARMS/CONT USSR

BLOOMFIELD L.P.,OUTER SPACE: A PATTERN OF WAR IN A
NEW DIMENSION. FUT USA+45 AIR TEC/DEV PWR
...DECISION CONCPT GEN/LAWS 20. PAGE 7 G0141
   B62 CREATE ACT/RES ARMS/CONT SPACE

BOULDING K.E.,CONFLICT AND DEFENSE: A GENERAL
THEORY. FUT SOCIETY INT/ORG NAT/G CREATE BAL/PWR
COERCE NAT/LISM DRIVE ALL/VALS...PLURIST DECISION
CONCPT METH/CNCPT TREND HYPO/EXP TOT/POP 20. PAGE 8
G0157
   B62 MATH SIMUL PEACE WAR

CALDER R.,LIVING WITH THE ATOM. FUT USA+45 WOR+45
R+D INT/ORG VOL/ASSN DELIB/GP ARMS/CONT...STYLE 20.
PAGE 10 G0200
   B62 TEC/DEV HEALTH NUC/PWR

CLARKE A.C.,PROFILES OF THE FUTURE; AN INQUIRY INTO
THE LIMITS OF THE POSSIBLE. COM/IND DIST/IND PRODUC
AGE PERCEPT...TECHNIC NEW/IDEA TIME. PAGE 12 G0232
   B62 FUT TEC/DEV PREDICT SPACE

FORBES H.W.,THE STRATEGY OF DISARMAMENT. FUT WOR+45
INT/ORG VOL/ASSN CONSULT ARMS/CONT COERCE NUC/PWR
   B62 PLAN FORCES

WAR DRIVE RIGID/FLEX ORD/FREE PWR...POLICY CONCPT   DIPLOM
OBS TREND STERTYP 20. PAGE 19 G0378

B62
GILPIN R.,AMERICAN SCIENTISTS AND NUCLEAR WEAPONS   INTELL
POLICY. COM FUT USA+45 WOR+45 INT/ORG NAT/G   ATTIT
PROF/ORG CONSULT FORCES CREATE TEC/DEV BAL/PWR   DETER
EDU/PROP ARMS/CONT WAR PERCEPT KNOWL MORAL PWR   NUC/PWR
...PHIL/SCI SOC CONCPT GEN/LAWS 20. PAGE 21 G0417

B62
GOLOVINE M.N.,CONFLICT IN SPACE: A PATTERN OF WAR   CREATE
IN A NEW DIMENSION. FUT USA+45 WOR+45 AIR FORCES   TEC/DEV
PLAN DIPLOM DOMIN ATTIT...STAT AUD/VIS CHARTS   NUC/PWR
COLD/WAR 20. PAGE 22 G0432   SPACE

B62
KAHN H.,THINKING ABOUT THE UNTHINKABLE. FUT USA+45   INT/ORG
LAW NAT/G CONSULT FORCES ACT/RES CREATE PLAN   ORD/FREE
TEC/DEV BAL/PWR DIPLOM EDU/PROP ARMS/CONT DETER   NUC/PWR
ATTIT...CONCPT OBS TREND COLD/WAR 20. PAGE 29 G0570   PEACE

B62
OSGOOD C.E.,AN ALTERNATIVE TO WAR OR SURRENDER. FUT   ORD/FREE
UNIV CULTURE INTELL SOCIETY R+D INT/ORG CONSULT   EDU/PROP
DELIB/GP ACT/RES PLAN CHOOSE ATTIT PERCEPT KNOWL   PEACE
...PHIL/SCI PSY SOC TREND GEN/LAWS 20. PAGE 43   WAR
G0849

B62
RIKER W.H.,THE THEORY OF POLITICAL COALITIONS.   FUT
WOR+45 INTELL NAT/G CREATE PLAN ATTIT DRIVE PERCEPT   SIMUL
...DECISION PSY SOC METH/CNCPT NEW/IDEA MATH CHARTS
GAME TOT/POP 20. PAGE 47 G0921

B62
SINGER J.D.,DETERRENCE, ARMS CONTROL AND   FUT
DISARMAMENT: TOWARD A SYNTHESIS IN NATIONAL   ACT/RES
SECURITY POLICY. COM USA+45 INT/ORG BAL/PWR DETER   ARMS/CONT
ORD/FREE...POLICY COLD/WAR 20. PAGE 51 G1003

B62
SNYDER R.C.,FOREIGN POLICY DECISION-MAKING. FUT   TEC/DEV
KOREA WOR+45 R+D CREATE ADMIN ROUTINE PWR   HYPO/EXP
...DECISION PSY SOC CONCPT METH/CNCPT CON/ANAL   DIPLOM
CHARTS GEN/METH METH 20. PAGE 52 G1018

B62
SOHN L.B.,ZONAL DISARMAMENT: VARIATIONS ON A THEME.   ORD/FREE
FUT WOR+45 SOCIETY ACT/RES PLAN NUC/PWR PEACE ATTIT   NEW/IDEA
...POLICY GEOG CONT/OBS HYPO/EXP 20. PAGE 52 G1020   ARMS/CONT

B62
WRIGHT Q.,PREVENTING WORLD WAR THREE. FUT WOR+45   CREATE
CULTURE INT/ORG NAT/G CONSULT FORCES ADMIN   ATTIT
ARMS/CONT DRIVE RIGID/FLEX ORD/FREE SOVEREIGN
...POLICY CONCPT TREND STERTYP COLD/WAR 20. PAGE 64
G1259

L62
FINKELSTEIN L.S.,"ARMS INSPECTION." FUT WOR+45   FORCES
NAT/G DIPLOM ATTIT PERCEPT RIGID/FLEX ORD/FREE   PWR
COLD/WAR 20. PAGE 19 G0369   ARMS/CONT

S62
ALBONETTI A.,"IL SECONDO PROGRAMMA QUINQUENNALE   R+D
1963-67 ED IL BILANCIO RICERCHE ED INVESTIMENTI PER   PLAN
IL 1963 DELL'ERATOM." EUR+WWI FUT ITALY WOR+45   NUC/PWR
ECO/DEV SERV/IND INT/ORG TEC/DEV ECO/TAC ATTIT
SKILL WEALTH...MGT TIME/SEQ OEEC 20. PAGE 2 G0035

S62
BOULDING K.E.,"THE PREVENTION OF WORLD WAR THREE."   VOL/ASSN
FUT WOR+45 INT/ORG PLAN BAL/PWR PEACE ORD/FREE PWR   NAT/G
...NEW/IDEA TREND TOT/POP COLD/WAR 20. PAGE 8 G0158   ARMS/CONT
    DIPLOM

S62
CRANE R.D.,"LAW AND STRATEGY IN SPACE." FUT USA+45   CONCPT
WOR+45 AIR LAW INT/ORG NAT/G FORCES ACT/RES PLAN   SPACE
BAL/PWR LEGIT ARMS/CONT COERCE ORD/FREE...POLICY
INT/LAW JURID SOC/EXP 20 TREATY. PAGE 13 G0261

S62
FINKELSTEIN L.S.,"THE UNITED NATIONS AND   INT/ORG
ORGANIZATIONS FOR CONTROL OF ARMAMENT." FUT WOR+45   PWR
VOL/ASSN DELIB/GP TOP/EX CREATE EDU/PROP LEGIT   ARMS/CONT
ADJUD NUC/PWR ATTIT RIGID/FLEX ORD/FREE...POLICY
DECISION CONCPT OBS TREND GEN/LAWS TOT/POP
COLD/WAR. PAGE 19 G0368

S62
FOSTER W.C.,"ARMS CONTROL AND DISARMAMENT IN A   DELIB/GP
DIVIDED WORLD." COM FUT USA+45 USSR WOR+45 INTELL   POLICY
INT/ORG NAT/G VOL/ASSN CONSULT CREATE PLAN TEC/DEV   ARMS/CONT
EDU/PROP LEGIT NUC/PWR ATTIT RIGID/FLEX...CONCPT   DIPLOM

TREND TOT/POP 20 UN. PAGE 20 G0387

S62
PHIPPS T.E.,"THE CASE FOR DETERRENCE." FUT WOR+45   ATTIT
SOCIETY EX/STRUC FORCES ACT/RES CREATE PLAN TEC/DEV   COERCE
ROUTINE RIGID/FLEX ORD/FREE...POLICY MYTH NEW/IDEA   DETER
STERTYP COLD/WAR 20. PAGE 45 G0876   ARMS/CONT

S62
SINGER J.D.,"STABLE DETERRENCE AND ITS LIMITS." FUT   NAT/G
WOR+45 R+D INT/ORG CONSULT ACT/RES TEC/DEV   FORCES
ARMS/CONT COERCE DRIVE PERCEPT RIGID/FLEX ORD/FREE   DETER
PWR...MYTH SIMUL TOT/POP 20. PAGE 51 G1004   NUC/PWR

S62
THORELLI H.B.,"THE INTERNATIONAL OPERATIONS   ECO/TAC
SIMULATION AT THE UNIVERSITY OF CHICAGO." FUT   SIMUL
USA+45 WOR+45 DIST/IND FINAN INDUS INT/ORG   INT/TRADE
DELIB/GP ACT/RES CREATE TEC/DEV WEALTH...STAT
VAL/FREE 20. PAGE 54 G1072

B63
ABSHIRE D.M.,NATIONAL SECURITY: POLITICAL,   FUT
MILITARY, AND ECONOMIC STRATEGIES IN THE DECADE   ACT/RES
AHEAD. ASIA COM USA+45 WOR+45 ECO/DEV ECO/UNDEV   BAL/PWR
INT/ORG DELIB/GP FORCES ECO/TAC COERCE ATTIT
RIGID/FLEX HEALTH ORD/FREE PWR WEALTH...POLICY STAT
CHARTS ANTHOL COLD/WAR VAL/FREE. PAGE 1 G0024

B63
HALEY A.G.,SPACE LAW AND GOVERNMENT. FUT USA+45   INT/ORG
WOR+45 LEGIS ACT/RES CREATE ATTIT RIGID/FLEX   LAW
ORD/FREE PWR SOVEREIGN...POLICY JURID CONCPT CHARTS   SPACE
VAL/FREE 20. PAGE 24 G0469

B63
LASSWELL H.D.,THE FUTURE OF POLITICAL SCIENCE.   CREATE
SOCIETY ECO/DEV ACADEM NAT/G PROB/SOLV...OBS   ACT/RES
SOC/INTEG. PAGE 33 G0643   FUT

B63
MCDOUGAL M.S.,LAW AND PUBLIC ORDER IN SPACE. FUT   SPACE
USA+45 ACT/RES TEC/DEV ADJUD...POLICY INT/LAW JURID   ORD/FREE
20. PAGE 37 G0739   DIPLOM
    DECISION

B63
REED E.,CHALLENGES TO DEMOCRACY: THE NEXT TEN   POLICY
YEARS. FUT USA+45 ECO/DEV DELIB/GP TEC/DEV CONFER   EDU/PROP
GOV/REL KNOWL ORD/FREE...MAJORIT IDEA/COMP ANTHOL   ECO/TAC
20. PAGE 46 G0909   NAT/G

L63
BEGUIN H.,"ASPECTS GEOGRAPHIQUE DE LA   ECO/UNDEV
POLARISATION." FUT WOR+45 SOCIETY STRUCT ECO/DEV   GEOG
R+D BAL/PWR ADMIN ATTIT RIGID/FLEX HEALTH WEALTH   DIPLOM
...CHARTS 20. PAGE 6 G0114

L63
MCDOUGAL M.S.,"THE ENJOYMENT AND ACQUISITION OF   PLAN
RESOURCES IN OUTER SPACE." CHRIST-17C FUT WOR+45   TREND
WOR-45 LAW EXTR/IND INT/ORG ACT/RES CREATE TEC/DEV
ECO/TAC LEGIT COERCE HEALTH KNOWL ORD/FREE PWR
WEALTH...JURID HIST/WRIT VAL/FREE. PAGE 37 G0738

L63
PHELPS J.,"STUDIES IN DETERRENCE VIII: MILITARY   FORCES
STABILITARY AND ARMS CONTROL: A CRITICAL SURVEY."   ORD/FREE
FUT WOR+45 INT/ORG ACT/RES EDU/PROP COERCE NUC/PWR   ARMS/CONT
WAR HEALTH PWR...POLICY TECHNIC TREND SIMUL TOT/POP   DETER
20. PAGE 44 G0874

S63
ABT C.,"THE PROBLEMS AND POSSIBILITIES OF SPACE   ACT/RES
ARMS CONTROL." FUT USA+45 WOR+45 AIR SOCIETY NAT/G   ORD/FREE
BAL/PWR EDU/PROP ATTIT PWR WEALTH...HYPO/EXP   ARMS/CONT
TOT/POP 20. PAGE 2 G0025   SPACE

S63
FERRETTI B.,"IMPORTANZA E PROSPETTIVE DELL ENERGIA   TEC/DEV
DI ORIGINE NUCLEARE." FUT ITALY WOR+45 INTELL R+D   EXEC
ACT/RES CREATE HEALTH WEALTH...METH/CNCPT TIME/SEQ   NUC/PWR
20. PAGE 19 G0365

S63
GANDILHON J.,"LA SCIENCE ET LA TECHNIQUE A L'AIDE   ECO/UNDEV
DES REGIONS PEU DEVELOPPEES." FRANCE FUT WOR+45   TEC/DEV
ECO/DEV R+D PROF/ORG ACT/RES PLAN...MGT TOT/POP   FOR/AID
VAL/FREE 20 UN. PAGE 21 G0406

S63
GARDNER R.N.,"COOPERATION IN OUTER SPACE." FUT USSR   INT/ORG
WOR+45 AIR LAW COM/IND CONSULT DELIB/GP CREATE   ACT/RES
KNOWL 20 TREATY. PAGE 21 G0410   PEACE
    SPACE

KAWALKOWSKI A.,"POUR UNE EUROPE INDEPENDENTE ET REUNIFIEE." EUR+WWI FUT USA+45 USSR WOR+45 ECO/DEV PROC/MFG INT/ORG NAT/G ACT/RES TEC/DEV FEDERAL RIGID/FLEX...CONCPT METH/CNCPT OEEC TOT/POP 20 DEGAULLE/C. PAGE 30 G0587
S63
R+D
PLAN
NUC/PWR

SMITH D.O.,"WHAT IS A WAR DETERRENT." FUT GERMANY HUNGARY UK USA+45 WOR+45 WOR-45 NAT/G TEC/DEV BAL/PWR PWR...CONCPT GEN/LAWS COLD/WAR 20. PAGE 51 G1013
S63
ACT/RES
FORCES
ARMS/CONT
DETER

WILES P.J.D.,"WILL CAPITALISM AND COMMUNISM SPONTANEOUSLY CONVERGE." COM FUT USA+45 ECO/DEV DIST/IND MARKET CAP/ISM ECO/TAC RIGID/FLEX WEALTH MARXISM SOCISM...MATH STAT TREND COMPUT/IR 20. PAGE 63 G1240
S63
PLAN
TEC/DEV
USSR

DIEBOLD J.,BEYOND AUTOMATION: MANAGERIAL PROBLEMS OF AN EXPLODING TECHNOLOGY. SOCIETY ECO/DEV CREATE ECO/TAC AUTOMAT SKILL...TECHNIC MGT WORK. PAGE 16 G0303
B64
FUT
INDUS
PROVS
NAT/G

ELLUL J.,THE TECHNOLOGICAL SOCIETY. FUT STRUCT CREATE AUTOMAT ROUTINE STRANGE ANOMIE MORAL PHIL/SCI. PAGE 18 G0344
B64
SOC
SOCIETY
TECHNIC
TEC/DEV

ETZIONI A.,THE MOON-DOGGLE: DOMESTIC AND INTERNATIONAL IMPLICATIONS OF THE SPACE RACE. FUT USA+45 WOR+45 INTELL ECO/DEV INDUS VOL/ASSN EX/STRUC FORCES LEGIS TOP/EX PLAN TEC/DEV ECO/TAC EDU/PROP KNOWL ORD/FREE PWR RESPECT WEALTH TIME/SEQ. PAGE 18 G0352
B64
R+D
NAT/G
DIPLOM
SPACE

GRODZINS M.,THE ATOMIC AGE: FORTY-FIVE SCIENTISTS AND SCHOLARS SPEAK ON NATIONAL AND WORLD AFFAIRS. FUT USA+45 WOR+45 R+D INT/ORG NAT/G CONSULT TEC/DEV EDU/PROP ATTIT PERSON ORD/FREE...HUM CONCPT TIME/SEQ CON/ANAL. PAGE 23 G0454
B64
INTELL
ARMS/CONT
NUC/PWR

HASKINS C.P.,THE SCIENTIFIC REVOLUTION AND WORLD POLITICS. COM FUT USA+45 ECO/DEV ECO/UNDEV ATTIT ...PHIL/SCI BIBLIOG 20 THIRD/WRLD. PAGE 25 G0489
B64
TEC/DEV
POLICY
DIPLOM
TREND

HEKHUIS D.J.,INTERNATIONAL STABILITY: MILITARY, ECONOMIC AND POLITICAL DIMENSIONS. FUT WOR+45 LAW ECO/UNDEV INT/ORG NAT/G VOL/ASSN FORCES ACT/RES BAL/PWR PWR WEALTH...STAT UN 20. PAGE 25 G0503
B64
TEC/DEV
DETER
REGION

NASA,PROCEEDINGS OF CONFERENCE ON THE LAW OF SPACE AND OF SATELLITE COMMUNICATIONS: CHICAGO 1963. FUT WOR+45 DELIB/GP PROB/SOLV TEC/DEV CONFER ADJUD NUC/PWR...POLICY IDEA/COMP 20 NASA. PAGE 41 G0805
B64
SPACE
COM/IND
LAW
DIPLOM

OSSENBECK F.J.,OPEN SPACE AND PEACE. CHINA/COM FUT USA+45 USSR LAW PROB/SOLV TEC/DEV EDU/PROP NEUTRAL PEACE...AUD/VIS ANTHOL 20. PAGE 43 G0850
B64
SPACE
ORD/FREE
DIPLOM
CREATE

PEDERSEN E.S.,NUCLEAR ENERGY IN SPACE. FUT INTELL R+D CONSULT...NEW/IDEA CHARTS METH T 20. PAGE 44 G0864
B64
SPACE
TEC/DEV
NUC/PWR
LAB/EXP

PETERSON W.,THE POLITICS OF POPULATION. COM EUR+WWI FUT MOD/EUR S/ASIA USA+45 USA-45 WOR+45 LAW CULTURE FAM SECT DOMIN EDU/PROP BIO/SOC HEALTH ORD/FREE ...GEOG STAT TIME/SEQ TREND VAL/FREE. PAGE 44 G0871
B64
PLAN
CENSUS
POLICY

ROSECRANCE R.N.,THE DISPERSION OF NUCLEAR WEAPONS: STRATEGY AND POLITICS. ASIA COM FUT S/ASIA USA+45 INT/ORG NAT/G DELIB/GP FORCES ACT/RES TEC/DEV BAL/PWR COERCE DETER ATTIT RIGID/FLEX ORD/FREE ...POLICY CHARTS VAL/FREE. PAGE 48 G0935
B64
EUR+WWI
PWR
PEACE

ROTHSCHILD J.H.,TOMORROW'S WEAPONS: CHEMICAL AND BIOLOGICAL. FUT PROB/SOLV ARMS/CONT PEACE MORAL ...CHARTS BIBLIOG 20. PAGE 48 G0941
B64
WAR
WEAPON
BIO/SOC
DETER

SCHWARTZ M.D.,CONFERENCE ON SPACE SCIENCE AND SPACE LAW. FUT COM/IND NAT/G FORCES ACT/RES PLAN BUDGET DIPLOM NUC/PWR WEAPON...POLICY ANTHOL 20. PAGE 50 G0983
B64
SPACE
LAW
PEACE
TEC/DEV

US AIR FORCE ACADEMY ASSEMBLY,OUTER SPACE: FINAL REPORT APRIL 1-4, 1964. FUT USA+45 WOR+45 LAW DELIB/GP CONFER ARMS/CONT WAR PEACE ATTIT MORAL ...ANTHOL 20 NASA. PAGE 56 G1104
B64
SPACE
CIVMIL/REL
NUC/PWR
DIPLOM

VAN DYKE V.,PRIDE AND POWER: THE RATIONALE OF THE SPACE PROGRAM. FUT USA+45 INTELL R+D NAT/G POL/PAR DELIB/GP EX/STRUC LEGIS TOP/EX ACT/RES PLAN ECO/TAC EDU/PROP ORD/FREE PWR RESPECT SKILL...TIME/SEQ VAL/FREE. PAGE 61 G1191
B64
TEC/DEV
ATTIT
POLICY

WARD C.,"THE 'NEW MYTHS' AND 'OLD REALITIES' OF NUCLEAR WAR." COM FUT USA+45 USSR WOR+45 INT/ORG NAT/G DOMIN LEGIT EXEC ATTIT PERCEPT ALL/VALS ...POLICY RELATIV PSY MYTH TREND 20. PAGE 62 G1212
L64
FORCES
COERCE
ARMS/CONT
NUC/PWR

CALDWELL L.K.,"BIOPOLITICS: SCIENCE, ETHICS, AND PUBLIC POLICY." COM FUT USA+45 WOR+45 INTELL STRATA R+D NAT/G CONSULT PLAN EDU/PROP ALL/VALS...RELATIV PHIL/SCI 20. PAGE 10 G0203
S64
TEC/DEV
POLICY

LERNER A.P.,"NUCLEAR SYMMETRY AS A FRAMEWORK FOR COEXISTENCE." COM FUT USA+45 NAT/G ACT/RES CREATE PLAN DIPLOM EDU/PROP COERCE WAR RIGID/FLEX PWR SKILL...CONCPT METH/CNCPT GEN/LAWS TOT/POP VAL/FREE COLD/WAR 20. PAGE 33 G0657
S64
FORCES
ORD/FREE
DETER
NUC/PWR

SPONSLER G.C.,"THE MILITARY ROLE IN SPACE." FUT USA+45 SEA AIR NAT/G ACT/RES PLAN COERCE NUC/PWR WEAPON KNOWL ORD/FREE PWR RESPECT...TREND 20. PAGE 52 G1026
TEC/DEV
FORCES
SPACE

PEACE RESEARCH ABSTRACTS. FUT WOR+45 R+D INT/ORG NAT/G PLAN TEC/DEV BAL/PWR DIPLOM FOR/AID NUC/PWR HEALTH. PAGE 1 G0020
B65
BIBLIOG/A
PEACE
ARMS/CONT
WAR

CARPER E.T.,REORGANIZATION OF THE U.S. PUBLIC HEALTH SERVICE. FUT USA+45 INTELL R+D LOBBY GP/REL INGP/REL PERS/REL RIGID/FLEX ROLE HEALTH...PHIL/SCI 20 CONGRESS PHS. PAGE 11 G0213
B65
HEAL
PLAN
NAT/G
OP/RES

HALPERIN M.H.,COMMUNIST CHINA AND ARMS CONTROL. CHINA/COM FUT USA+45 CULTURE FORCES TEC/DEV ECO/TAC WAR PEACE ORD/FREE MARXISM 20 COLD/WAR. PAGE 24 G0473
B65
ATTIT
POLICY
ARMS/CONT
NUC/PWR

LUTZ V.,FRENCH PLANNING. FRANCE TEC/DEV RIGID/FLEX ORD/FREE 20. PAGE 34 G0680
B65
PLAN
ADMIN
FUT

OECD,MEDITERRANEAN REGIONAL PROJECT: TURKEY; EDUCATION AND DEVELOPMENT. FUT TURKEY SOCIETY STRATA FINAN NAT/G PROF/ORG PLAN PROB/SOLV ADMIN COST...STAT CHARTS 20 OECD. PAGE 42 G0831
B65
EDU/PROP
ACADEM
SCHOOL
ECO/UNDEV

OECD,THE MEDITERRANEAN REGIONAL PROJECT: GREECE; EDUCATION AND DEVELOPMENT. FUT GREECE SOCIETY AGRI FINAN NAT/G PROF/ORG WORKER PLAN PROB/SOLV ADMIN DEMAND ATTIT 20 OECD. PAGE 42 G0834
B65
EDU/PROP
SCHOOL
ACADEM
ECO/UNDEV

OECD,THE MEDITERRANEAN REGIONAL PROJECT: SPAIN; EDUCATION AND DEVELOPMENT. FUT SPAIN STRATA FINAN NAT/G WORKER PLAN PROB/SOLV ADMIN COST...POLICY STAT CHARTS 20 OECD. PAGE 42 G0835
B65
ECO/UNDEV
EDU/PROP
ACADEM
SCHOOL

US SENATE COMM AERO SPACE SCI,NATIONAL SPACE GOALS FOR THE POST-APOLLO PERIOD. USA+45 CONSULT DELIB/GP TEC/DEV BUDGET GP/REL ATTIT...CHARTS IDEA/COMP TIME 20 DEPT/DEFEN NASA CONGRESS. PAGE 59 G1166
B65
SPACE
FUT
R+D
LEGIS

US SENATE COMM AERO SPACE SCI,INTERNATIONAL COOPERATION AND ORGANIZATION FOR OUTER SPACE. FUT USA+45 WOR+45 PROF/ORG VOL/ASSN CONSULT DELIB/GP PLAN TEC/DEV ARMS/CONT GP/REL PEACE 20 UN NASA.
B65
DIPLOM
SPACE
R+D
NAT/G

VERMOT-GAUCHY M.,L'EDUCATION NATIONALE DANS LA
FRANCE DE 1975. FRANCE FUT CULTURE ELITES R+D
SCHOOL PLAN EDU/PROP EFFICIENCY...POLICY PREDICT
CHARTS INDEX 20. PAGE 61 G1195

B65
ACADEM
CREATE
TREND
INTELL

ABT C.C.,"CONTROLLING FUTURE ARMS." USSR PLAN
BAL/PWR DIPLOM NUC/PWR COST...CLASSIF STAT CHARTS.
PAGE 2 G0027

S65
PREDICT
FUT
ARMS/CONT
TEC/DEV

HARRISON S.L.,"NTH NATION CHALLENGES* THE PRESENT
PERSPECTIVE." EUR+WWI FUT USA+45 BAL/PWR CONTROL
RISK COERCE WAR...PREDICT COLD/WAR. PAGE 25 G0485

S65
ARMS/CONT
NUC/PWR
NAT/G
DIPLOM

HIBBS A.R.,"SPACE TECHNOLOGY* THE THREAT AND THE
PROMISE." FUT VOL/ASSN TEC/DEV NUC/PWR COST
EFFICIENCY UTIL UN TREATY. PAGE 26 G0510

S65
SPACE
ARMS/CONT
PREDICT

KOHL W.L.,"NUCLEAR SHARING IN NATO AND THE
MULTILATERAL FORCE." FUT USSR VOL/ASSN TEC/DEV
DIPLOM NUC/PWR WAR WEAPON NATO. PAGE 31 G0611

S65
ARMS/CONT
OBS
IDEA/COMP

MARTIN A.,"PROLIFERATION." FUT WOR+45 PROB/SOLV
REGION ADJUST...PREDICT NAT/COMP UN TREATY. PAGE 36
G0712

S65
RECORD
NUC/PWR
ARMS/CONT
VOL/ASSN

RUBINSTEIN A.Z.,"POLITICAL BARRIERS TO
DISARMAMENT." FUT DIPLOM COERCE NUC/PWR WAR
NAT/LISM ORD/FREE PREDICT. PAGE 48 G0944

S65
COM
USA+45
ARMS/CONT
ATTIT

AMERICAN ASSEMBLY COLUMBIA U,A WORLD OF NUCLEAR
POWERS? FUT WOR+45 ECO/DEV BAL/PWR ECO/TAC CONTROL
RISK EFFICIENCY ATTIT PWR...METH/COMP ANTHOL 20.
PAGE 3 G0049

B66
NUC/PWR
DIPLOM
TEC/DEV
ARMS/CONT

HALPERIN M.H.,CHINA AND NUCLEAR PROLIFERATION
(PAMPHLET). CHINA/COM FUT INDIA USA+45 USSR
ARMS/CONT WAR 20 CHINJAP. PAGE 24 G0474

B66
NUC/PWR
FORCES
POLICY
DIPLOM

KLOTSCHE J.M.,THE URBAN UNIVERSITY AND THE FUTURE
OF OUR CITIES. FUT USA+45 USA-45 LOC/G NEIGH GIVE
19/20. PAGE 31 G0606

B66
ACADEM
MUNIC
PROB/SOLV
TEC/DEV

RUPPENTHAL K.M.,TRANSPORTATION AND TOMORROW. FUT
SPACE USA+45 SEA AIR FORCES TEC/DEV INT/TRADE
...ANTHOL 20 RAILROAD. PAGE 48 G0946

B66
DIST/IND
PLAN
CIVMIL/REL
PREDICT

UNITED NATIONS,INTERNATIONAL SPACE BIBLIOGRAPHY.
FUT INT/ORG TEC/DEV DIPLOM ARMS/CONT NUC/PWR
...JURID SOC UN. PAGE 56 G1093

B66
BIBLIOG
SPACE
PEACE
R+D

US SENATE COMM AERO SPACE SCI,SOVIET SPACE
PROGRAMS, 1962-65; GOALS AND PURPOSES,
ACHIEVEMENTS, PLANS, AND INTERNATIONAL
IMPLICATIONS. USA+45 USSR R+D FORCES PLAN EDU/PROP
PRESS ADJUD ARMS/CONT ATTIT MARXISM. PAGE 60 G1168

B66
CONSULT
SPACE
FUT
DIPLOM

RASER J.R.,"DETERRENCE RESEARCH* PAST PROGRESS AND
FUTURE NEEDS." INTELL PLAN TEC/DEV NUC/PWR PERCEPT
...DECISION PSY SOC NET/THEORY. PAGE 46 G0905

L66
DETER
BIBLIOG/A
FUT

US HOUSE COMM SCI ASTRONAUT,INQUIRIES, LEGISLATION,
POLICY STUDIES RE: SCIENCE AND TECHNOLOGY: REVIEW
AND FORECAST (PAMPHLET). FUT WOR+45 DELIB/GP
PROB/SOLV...POLICY JURID TREND 20 CONGRESS. PAGE 58
G1144

N66
TEC/DEV
R+D
PLAN
LEGIS

BARANSON J.,TECHNOLOGY FOR UNDERDEVELOPED AREAS: AN
ANNOTATED BIBLIOGRAPHY. FUT WOR+45 CULTURE INDUS
INT/ORG CREATE PROB/SOLV INT/TRADE EDU/PROP AUTOMAT
...CONCPT METH. PAGE 5 G0092

B67
BIBLIOG/A
ECO/UNDEV
TEC/DEV
R+D

CROSSON F.J.,SCIENCE AND CONTEMPORARY SOCIETY. FUT
WOR+45 SECT CREATE PROB/SOLV...HUM PREDICT TREND
IDEA/COMP ANTHOL. PAGE 14 G0263

B67
PHIL/SCI
SOCIETY
TEC/DEV
CONCPT

DE JOUVENAL B.,THE ART OF CONJECTURE. WOR+45
EFFICIENCY PERCEPT KNOWL...DECISION PHIL/SCI CONCPT
METH/COMP BIBLIOG 20. PAGE 15 G0285

B67
FUT
PREDICT
SIMUL
METH

HEILBRONER R.L.,THE LIMITS OF AMERICAN CAPITALISM.
FUT ECO/DEV INDUS LG/CO EX/STRUC LEAD PWR TECHRACY
20. PAGE 25 G0502

B67
ELITES
CREATE
TEC/DEV
CAP/ISM

KAPLAN B.,AN UNHURRIED VIEW OF COPYRIGHT. FUT
...JURID 20. PAGE 29 G0575

B67
TEC/DEV
LAW
LICENSE

MACBRIDE R.,THE AUTOMATED STATE; COMPUTER SYSTEMS
AS A NEW FORCE IN SOCIETY. FUT WOR+45 FINAN MUNIC
NAT/G WORKER PLAN TEC/DEV CONTROL PERS/REL RACE/REL
ADJUST. PAGE 35 G0685

B67
COMPUTER
AUTOMAT
PROB/SOLV
SOCIETY

MCCLINTOCK R.,THE MEANING OF LIMITED WAR. FUT
WOR+45 NAT/G FORCES GUERRILLA REV...POLICY SAMP/SIZ
TREND NAT/COMP 45 COLD/WAR. PAGE 37 G0730

B67
WAR
NUC/PWR
BAL/PWR
DIPLOM

RUTGERS U GRADUATE SCH LIB SCI,BIBLIOGRAPHY OF
RESEARCH RELATING TO THE COMMUNICATION OF
SCIENTIFIC AND TECHNICAL INFORMATION. FUT CREATE
FEEDBACK...PHIL/SCI NEW/IDEA COMPUT/IR HYPO/EXP.
PAGE 48 G0951

B67
BIBLIOG/A
COM/IND
R+D
TEC/DEV

UNIVERSAL REFERENCE SYSTEM,PUBLIC POLICY AND THE
MANAGEMENT OF SCIENCE (VOLUME IX). FUT SPACE WOR+45
LAW NAT/G TEC/DEV CONTROL NUC/PWR GOV/REL
...COMPUT/IR GEN/METH. PAGE 56 G1100

B67
BIBLIOG/A
POLICY
MGT
PHIL/SCI

WEINBERG A.M.,REFLECTIONS ON BIG SCIENCE. FUT
USA+45 NAT/G EDU/PROP CHOOSE PERS/REL COST OPTIMAL
...PHIL/SCI TREND. PAGE 62 G1225

B67
ACADEM
KNOWL
R+D
PLAN

DAVIS P.C.,"THE COMING CHINESE COMMUNIST NUCLEAR
THREAT AND U.S. SEA BASED ABM OPTIONS." ASIA
CHINA/COM FUT USA+45 SEA NAT/G FORCES PLAN TEC/DEV
LEAD ARMS/CONT...GEOG METH/COMP 20 ABM/DEFSYS.
PAGE 14 G0279

L67
NUC/PWR
DETER
WEAPON
DIPLOM

ALLEE D.,"AMERICAN AGRICULTURE - ITS RESOURCE
ISSUES FOR THE COMING YEARS." FUT USA+45 PLAN
PROB/SOLV 20. PAGE 2 G0043

S67
AGRI
SOCIETY
EFFICIENCY
AUTOMAT

BARAN P.,"THE FUTURE COMPUTER UTILITY." USA+45
NAT/G PLAN CONTROL COST...POLICY 20. PAGE 5 G0091

S67
COMPUTER
UTIL
FUT
TEC/DEV

BENN W.,"TECHNOLOGY HAS AN INEXORABLE EFFECT." FUT
UK ECO/DEV INT/ORG CONSULT PLAN EDU/PROP ADMIN LEAD
GP/REL PRODUC...INT 20 EEC. PAGE 6 G0119

S67
R+D
LG/CO
TEC/DEV
INDUS

BULMER-THOMAS I.,"SO, ON TO THE GREAT SOCIETY." FUT
UNIV TEC/DEV BAL/PWR WAR BIO/SOC KNOWL...ART/METH
SOC PREDICT TREND WORSHIP 20 GREAT/SOC. PAGE 9
G0185

S67
PHIL/SCI
SOCIETY
CREATE

CETRON M.J.,"FORECASTING TECHNOLOGY." INDUS FORCES
TASK UTIL...PHIL/SCI CONCPT CHARTS METH/COMP TIME.
PAGE 11 G0219

S67
TEC/DEV
FUT
R+D
PLAN

GRIFFITHS F.,"THE POLITICAL SIDE OF 'DISARMAMENT'."
FUT WOR+45 NUC/PWR NAT/LISM PEACE...NEW/IDEA
PREDICT METH/COMP GEN/LAWS 20. PAGE 23 G0453

S67
ARMS/CONT
DIPLOM

HARRIS F.R.,"POLITICAL SCIENCE AND THE PROPOSAL FOR PROF/ORG
A NATIONAL SOCIAL SCIENCE FOUNDATION." FUT CONSULT R+D
DELIB/GP PLAN PROB/SOLV BUDGET CONFER SANCTION CREATE
CRIME...POLICY SOC/WK 20 NSF NSSF. PAGE 25 G0484 NAT/G
                                                                    S67

HAZARD J.N.,"POST-DISARMAMENT INTERNATIONAL LAW." INT/LAW
FUT USSR WOR+45 INT/ORG DELIB/GP FORCES DETER ARMS/CONT
EQUILIB SOVEREIGN MARXISM 20 UN. PAGE 25 G0496 PWR
                                                                    PLAN
                                                                    S67

HULL E.W.S.,"THE POLITICAL OCEAN." FUT UNIV WOR+45 DIPLOM
EXTR/IND R+D VOL/ASSN PLAN BAL/PWR ECO/TAC PEACE ECO/UNDEV
WEALTH 20 UN. PAGE 27 G0536 INT/ORG
                                                                    INT/LAW
                                                                    S67

JACKSON W.G.F.,"NUCLEAR PROLIFERATION AND THE GREAT NUC/PWR
POWERS." FUT UK WOR+45 INT/ORG DOMIN ARMS/CONT ATTIT
DETER ORD/FREE PACIFIST. PAGE 28 G0550 BAL/PWR
                                                                    NAT/LISM
                                                                    S67

KAYSEN C.,"DATA BANKS AND DOSSIERS." FUT USA+45 CENTRAL
COM/IND NAT/G PLAN PROB/SOLV TEC/DEV BUDGET ADMIN EFFICIENCY
ROUTINE. PAGE 30 G0588 CENSUS
                                                                    ACT/RES
                                                                    S67

SCHACTER O.,"SCIENTIFIC ADVANCES AND INTERNATIONAL TEC/DEV
LAWMAKING." FUT R+D PLAN PROB/SOLV CONFER CONTROL INT/LAW
...POLICY PREDICT 20 UN. PAGE 49 G0961 INT/ORG
                                                                    ACT/RES
                                                                    S67

SHARP G.,"THE NEED OF A FUNCTIONAL SUBSTITUTE FOR PEACE
WAR." FUT UNIV WOR+45 CULTURE SOCIETY INT/ORG WAR
CONSULT DELIB/GP ACT/RES CREATE BAL/PWR CONFER DIPLOM
ARMS/CONT NUC/PWR 20. PAGE 50 G0989 PROB/SOLV
                                                                    S67

VERGIN R.C.,"COMPUTER INDUCED ORGANIZATION COMPUTER
CHANGES." FUT USA+45 R+D CREATE OP/RES TEC/DEV DECISION
ADJUST CENTRAL...MGT INT CON/ANAL COMPUT/IR. AUTOMAT
PAGE 61 G1194 EX/STRUC
                                                                    S67

VLASCIC I.A.,"THE SPACE TREATY* A PRELIMINARY SPACE
EVALUATION." FUT USSR WOR+45 R+D ACT/RES TEC/DEV INT/LAW
DIPLOM CONFER ARMS/CONT PEACE...PREDICT UN TREATY. INT/ORG
PAGE 61 G1201 NEUTRAL
                                                                    S67

WINSTON O.,"AN URBANIZATION PATTERN FOR THE US* USA+45
SOME CONSIDERATIONS FOR THE DECENTRALIZATION OF MUNIC
EXCELLENCE." FUT SOCIETY ECO/DEV R+D NEIGH ACT/RES PLAN
PROB/SOLV TEC/DEV. PAGE 64 G1247 HABITAT
                                                                    S67

WINTHROP H.,"THE MEANING OF DECENTRALIZATION FOR ADMIN
TWENTIETH-CENTURY MAN." FUT WOR+45 SOCIETY TEC/DEV. STRUCT
PAGE 64 G1248 CENTRAL
                                                                    PROB/SOLV
                                                                    N67

US SENATE,STATUS OF THE DEVELOPMENT OF THE ANTI- FORCES
BALLISTIC MISSILE SYSTEMS IN THE UNITED STATES NUC/PWR
(PAMPHLET). FUT USA+45 R+D PLAN TEC/DEV DEPT/DEFEN. WAR
PAGE 59 G1165 UTIL

FUTURE....SEE FUT
————————————————————— G —————————————————————
GABON....SEE ALSO AFR

GALBRAITH, JOHN KENNETH....SEE GALBRTH/JK

GALBRTH/JK....JOHN KENNETH GALBRAITH

GALLAHER A. G0405

GAMBIA....SEE ALSO AFR

GAMBLE....SPECULATION ON AN UNCERTAIN EVENT
                                                                    S67

YOUNG O.R.,"ACTIVE DEFENSE AND INTERNATIONAL ARMS/CONT
ORDER." FORCES BAL/PWR DEBATE GAMBLE COST PEACE. DETER
PAGE 64 G1265 PLAN
                                                                    DECISION

GAMBLING....SEE RISK, GAMBLE

GAME....GAME THEORY AND DECISION THEORY IN MODELS

BATES J.,"A MODEL FOR THE SCIENCE OF DECISION." QUANT
UNIV ROUTINE...CONT/OBS CON/ANAL HYPO/EXP GAME. DECISION
PAGE 5 G0101 PHIL/SCI
                                                                    METH/CNCPT
                                                                    S54

DEUTSCH K.W.,"GAME THEORY AND POLITICS: SOME DECISION
PROBLEMS OF APPLICATION." FUT WOR+45 SOCIETY R+D GEN/METH
KNOWL PWR...CONCPT METH/CNCPT MATH QUANT GAME SIMUL
VAL/FREE 20. PAGE 15 G0295
                                                                    S54

SHUBIK M.,READINGS IN GAME THEORY AND POLITICAL MATH
BEHAVIOR. WOR+45 FORCES CREATE ROUTINE WAR PEACE DECISION
PERCEPT KNOWL PWR...PSY SOC CONCPT METH/CNCPT STAT DIPLOM
CHARTS HYPO/EXP GAME METH VAL/FREE 20. PAGE 50
G0991
                                                                    B55

MCKINNEY E.R.,A BIBLIOGRAPHY OF CYBERNETICS AND BIBLIOG/A
INFORMATION THEORY. COMPUTER OP/RES...DECISION FEEDBACK
PHIL/SCI PSY LING LOG MATH PROBABIL GAME 20. SIMUL
PAGE 38 G0743 CONTROL
                                                                    B57

FOLDES L.,"UNCERTAINTY, PROBABILITY AND POTENTIAL PROBABIL
SURPRISE." MARKET PROB/SOLV RISK PERSON...DECISION ADMIN
MGT HYPO/EXP GAME. PAGE 19 G0376 ROUTINE
                                                                    S58

ADAMS E.W.,"A MODEL OF RISKLESS CHOICE." CREATE GAME
PROB/SOLV UTIL...PROBABIL PREDICT HYPO/EXP. PAGE 2 SIMUL
G0029 RISK
                                                                    DECISION
                                                                    S59

BLOOMFIELD L.P.,"THREE EXPERIMENTS IN POLITICAL TEC/DEV
GAMING." ACT/RES CREATE PWR...GAME GEN/METH METH. METH/CNCPT
PAGE 7 G0140 DECISION
                                                                    S59

CYERT R.M.,"MODELS IN A BEHAVIORAL THEORY OF THE SIMUL
FIRM." ROUTINE...DECISION MGT METH/CNCPT MATH. GAME
PAGE 14 G0267 PREDICT
                                                                    INDUS
                                                                    S59

GOLDHAMMER H.,"SOME OBSERVATIONS ON POLITICAL COMPUT/IR
GAMING." FUT WOR+45 R+D NAT/G ACT/RES CREATE CHOOSE DECISION
ATTIT PWR...POLICY CONCPT METH/CNCPT STYLE KNO/TEST DIPLOM
TREND HYPO/EXP GAME GEN/METH METH 20. PAGE 22 G0426
                                                                    B60

ARROW K.J.,MATHEMATICAL METHODS IN THE SOCIAL MATH
SCIENCES, 1959. TEC/DEV CHOOSE UTIL PERCEPT PSY
...KNO/TEST GAME SIMUL ANTHOL. PAGE 4 G0070 MGT
                                                                    B60

MORRIS W.T.,ENGINEERING ECONOMY. AUTOMAT RISK OP/RES
RATIONAL...PROBABIL STAT CHARTS GAME SIMUL BIBLIOG DECISION
T 20. PAGE 40 G0785 MGT
                                                                    PROB/SOLV
                                                                    B60

RAPOPORT A.,FIGHTS, GAMES AND DEBATES. INTELL METH/CNCPT
SOCIETY R+D EX/STRUC PERCEPT PERSON SKILL...PSY SOC MATH
GAME. PAGE 46 G0902 DECISION
                                                                    CON/ANAL
                                                                    B60

SLUCKIN W.,MINDS AND MACHINES (REV. ED.). PROB/SOLV PSY
TEC/DEV AUTOMAT TASK PERCEPT HEALTH KNOWL COMPUTER
...DECISION MATH PROBABIL COMPUT/IR GAME 20. PERSON
PAGE 51 G1012 SIMUL
                                                                    S60

SHUBIK M.,"BIBLIOGRAPHY ON SIMULATION, GAMING, BIBLIOG
ARTIFICIAL INTELLIGENCE AND ALLIED TOPICS." SIMUL
COMPUTER ROUTINE...DECISION MGT STAT 20. PAGE 50 GAME
G0992 OP/RES
                                                                    B61

ROSENAU J.N.,INTERNATIONAL POLITICS AND FOREIGN ACT/RES
POLICY: A READER IN RESEARCH AND THEORY. ELITES DIPLOM
ATTIT SOVEREIGN...DECISION CHARTS HYPO/EXP GAME CONCPT
SIMUL ANTHOL BIBLIOG METH 20. PAGE 48 G0936 POLICY
                                                                    L61

COHEN K.J.,"THE ROLE OF MANAGEMENT GAMES IN SOCIETY
EDUCATION AND RESEARCH." INTELL ECO/DEV FINAN GAME
ACT/RES ECO/TAC DECISION. PAGE 12 G0240 MGT
                                                                    EDU/PROP
                                                                    B62

BELLMAN R.,APPLIED DYNAMIC PROGRAMMING. OPTIMAL COMPUTER

...DECISION STAT SIMUL. PAGE 6 G0116 — ECOMETRIC GAME MATH

B62
DUCKWORTH W.E.,A GUIDE TO OPERATIONAL RESEARCH. OP/RES
INDUS PLAN PROB/SOLV EXEC EFFICIENCY PRODUC KNOWL GAME
...MGT MATH STAT SIMUL METH 20 MONTECARLO. PAGE 16 DECISION
G0319 ADMIN

B62
GUETZKOW H.,SIMULATION IN SOCIAL SCIENCE: READINGS. SIMUL
STRUCT OP/RES ADMIN AUTOMAT FEEDBACK...MGT PSY SOC TEC/DEV
STYLE BIBLIOG. PAGE 23 G0459 COMPUTER GAME

B62
RIKER W.H.,THE THEORY OF POLITICAL COALITIONS. FUT
WOR+45 INTELL NAT/G CREATE PLAN ATTIT DRIVE PERCEPT SIMUL
...DECISION PSY SOC METH/CNCPT NEW/IDEA MATH CHARTS
GAME TOT/POP 20. PAGE 47 G0921

B63
HEYEL C.,THE ENCYCLOPEDIA OF MANAGEMENT. WOR+45 MGT
MARKET TOP/EX TEC/DEV AUTOMAT LEAD ADJUST...STAT INDUS
CHARTS GAME ANTHOL BIBLIOG. PAGE 26 G0509 ADMIN FINAN

B63
THORELLI H.B.,INTOP: INTERNATIONAL OPERATIONS GAME
SIMULATION: PLAYER'S MANUAL. BRAZIL FINAN OP/RES INT/TRADE
ADMIN GP/REL INGP/REL PRODUC PERCEPT...DECISION MGT EDU/PROP
EEC. PAGE 54 G1073 LG/CO

B64
BROWN N.,NUCLEAR WAR* THE IMPENDING STRATEGIC FORCES
DEADLOCK. USA+45 USSR TEC/DEV BUDGET RISK ARMS/CONT OP/RES
NUC/PWR WEAPON COST BIO/SOC...GEOG IDEA/COMP WAR
NAT/COMP GAME NATO WARSAW/P. PAGE 9 G0177 GEN/LAWS

B64
SHUBIK M.,GAME THEORY AND RELATED APPROACHES TO SOC
SOCIAL BEHAVIOR: SELECTIONS. INTELL SOCIETY ACT/RES SIMUL
CREATE PLAN PROB/SOLV...DECISION MATH. PAGE 50 GAME
G0994 PWR

B65
ALKER H.R. JR.,MATHEMATICS AND POLITICS. PROB/SOLV GEN/METH
...DECISION PHIL/SCI CLASSIF QUANT STAT GAME CONCPT
GEN/LAWS INDEX. PAGE 2 G0042 MATH

B65
BLOOMFIELD L.,SOVIET INTERESTS IN ARMS CONTROL AND USSR
DISARMAMENT* THE DECADE UNDER KHRUSHCHEV 1954-1964. ARMS/CONT
ASIA FORCES ACT/RES EDU/PROP DETER NUC/PWR WEAPON DIPLOM
COST ATTIT...PHIL/SCI CLASSIF STAT NET/THEORY GAME TREND
BIBLIOG. PAGE 7 G0139

B65
MCGUIRE M.C.,SECRECY AND THE ARMS RACE* A THEORY OF DETER
THE ACCUMULATION OF STRATEGIC WEAPONS AND HOW ARMS/CONT
SECRECY AFFECTS IT. DIPLOM NUC/PWR WEAPON ISOLAT SIMUL
RATIONAL ORD/FREE WEALTH...ECOMETRIC MATH GEN/LAWS. GAME
PAGE 38 G0742

S65
CHU K.,"A DYNAMIC MODEL OF THE FIRM." OP/RES INDUS
PROB/SOLV...DECISION ECOMETRIC NEW/IDEA STAT GAME COMPUTER
ORG/CHARTS SIMUL. PAGE 12 G0230 TEC/DEV

S65
DALKEY N.C.,"SOLVABLE NUCLEAR WAR MODELS." FORCES GAME
BAL/PWR DIPLOM COERCE PEACE DECISION. PAGE 14 G0273 SIMUL
WAR
NUC/PWR

S65
FINK C.F.,"MORE CALCULATIONS ABOUT DETERRENCE." DETER
DRIVE...PHIL/SCI PSY STAT TIME/SEQ GAME GEN/LAWS. RECORD
PAGE 19 G0367 PROBABIL
IDEA/COMP

S65
GRENIEWSKI H.,"INTENTION AND PERFORMANCE: A PRIMER SIMUL
OF CYBERNETICS OF PLANNING." EFFICIENCY OPTIMAL GAME
KNOWL SKILL...DECISION MGT EQULIB. PAGE 23 G0448 GEN/METH
PLAN

B66
GREEN P.,DEADLY LOGIC* THE THEORY OF NUCLEAR DETER
DETERRENCE. USA+45 ACT/RES OP/RES NUC/PWR RATIONAL ACADEM
ALL/VALS PWR...DECISION MGT PHIL/SCI QUANT GEN/LAWS
IDEA/COMP GAME. PAGE 23 G0444 RECORD

B66
STONE J.J.,CONTAINING THE ARMS RACE* SOME SPECIFIC ARMS/CONT

PROPOSALS. ASIA USA+45 USSR PROB/SOLV BARGAIN FEEDBACK
DIPLOM DETER NUC/PWR RATIONAL...GAME 20 DEPT/DEFEN COST
TREATY. PAGE 53 G1038 ATTIT

S66
EWALD R.F.,"ONE OF MANY POSSIBLE GAMES." ACADEM SIMUL
INT/ORG ARMS/CONT...INT/LAW GAME. PAGE 18 G0354 HYPO/EXP
PROG/TEAC
RECORD

B67
CHARLESWORTH J.C.,CONTEMPORARY POLITICAL ANALYSIS. R+D
INTELL...DECISION METH/CNCPT MATH STYLE CON/ANAL IDEA/COMP
GAME ANTHOL 20. PAGE 11 G0222 CONCPT
METH/COMP

S67
BROWN W.B.,"MODEL-BUILDING AND ORGANIZATIONS." MGT
CONTROL FEEDBACK...PROBABIL CHARTS METH/COMP. ADMIN
PAGE 9 G0179 GAME
COMPUTER

S67
SUINN R.M.,"THE DISARMAMENT FANTASY* PSYCHOLOGICAL DECISION
FACTORS THAT MAY PRODUCE WARFARE." DIPLOM RISK NUC/PWR
ARMS/CONT DETER ANOMIE PERSON GAME. PAGE 53 G1046 WAR
PSY

GANDHI/I....MME. INDIRA GANDHI

GANDHI/M....MAHATMA GANDHI

GANDILHON J. G0406

GANGE J. G0407

GANZ G. G0408

GAO....THE EMPIRE OF GAO

GARCIA ROBLES A. G0409

GARDNER R.N. G0410,G0411

GARFIELD/J....PRESIDENT JAMES A. GARFIELD

GARFINKEL H. G0412

GARIBALD/G....GUISEPPE GARIBALDI

GARY....GARY, INDIANA

GAS/NATURL....GAS, NATURAL

GATT....GENERAL AGREEMENT ON TARIFFS AND TRADE; SEE ALSO
VOL/ASSN, INT/ORG

S64
GARDNER R.N.,"GATT AND THE UNITED NATIONS INT/ORG
CONFERENCE ON TRADE AND DEVELOPMENT." USA+45 WOR+45 INT/TRADE
SOCIETY ECO/UNDEV MARKET NAT/G DELIB/GP ACT/RES
PLAN ECO/TAC TARIFFS EDU/PROP ROUTINE DRIVE
RIGID/FLEX WEALTH...DECISION MGT TREND UN TOT/POP
20 GATT. PAGE 21 G0411

GAUSSENS J. G0413

GAVIN J.M. G0414

GEARY....GEARY ACT

GEERTZ C. G0415

GEIGER T. G0244

GEN/DYNMCS....GENERAL DYNAMICS CORPORATION

GEN/ELCTRC....GENERAL ELECTRIC CO.

GEN/LAWS....SYSTEMS AND APPROACHES BASED ON SUBSTANTIVE
RELATIONS

GEN/METH....SYSTEMS BASED ON METHODOLGY

GEN/MOTORS....GENERAL MOTORS CORPORATION

GENACCOUNT....GENERAL ACCOUNTING OFFICE

GENERAL ACCOUNTING OFFICE....SEE GENACCOUNT

GENERAL AGREEMENT ON TARIFFS AND TRADE....SEE GATT

GENERAL AND COMPLETE DISARMAMENT....SEE ARMS/CONT

GENERAL ASSEMBLY....SEE UN+LEGIS

GENERAL DYNAMICS CORPORATION....SEE GEN/DYNMCS

GENERAL ELECTRIC COMPANY....SEE GEN/ELCTRC

GENERAL MOTORS CORPORATION....SEE GEN/MOTORS

GENEVA/CON....GENEVA CONFERENCES (ANY OR ALL)

GEOG....DEMOGRAPHY AND GEOGRAPHY

KRUTILIA J.V.,CONSERVATION RECONSIDERED. USA+45
CREATE EDU/PROP. PAGE 32 G0624
    N
PROB/SOLV
POLICY
HABITAT
GEOG

BRITISH COMMONWEALTH BUR AGRI,WORLD AGRICULTURAL
ECONOMICS AND RURAL SOCIOLOGY ABSTRACTS. NAT/G
OP/RES PLAN TEC/DEV LEAD PRODUC...GEOG MGT NAT/COMP
20. PAGE 9 G0170
    B
BIBLIOG/A
AGRI
SOC
WORKER

BOWMAN I.,GEOGRAPHY IN RELATION TO THE SOCIAL
SCIENCES. UNIV...SOC CONCPT METH. PAGE 8 G0161
    B34
GEOG
CULTURE
ROUTINE
PHIL/SCI

HAWLEY A.H.,"ECOLOGY AND HUMAN ECOLOGY" WOR+45
INTELL ACADEM PLAN GP/REL ADJUST PERSON...PHIL/SCI
SOC METH/CNCPT METH 20. PAGE 25 G0493
    S44
HABITAT
GEOG
GEN/LAWS
METH/COMP

SCHULTZ T.H.,FOOD FOR THE WORLD. UNIV SOCIETY INDUS
R+D ECO/TAC...GEOG TREND GEN/LAWS 20. PAGE 50 G0979
    B45
AGRI
TEC/DEV

AMERICAN DOCUMENTATION INST,CATALOGUE OF AUXILIARY
PUBLICATIONS IN MICROFILMS AND PHOTOPRINTS. USA-45
LAW AGRI CREATE TEC/DEV ADMIN...GEOG LING MATH 20.
PAGE 3 G0052
    B46
BIBLIOG
EDU/PROP
PSY

MAASS A.A.,"CONGRESS AND WATER RESOURCES." LOC/G
TEC/DEV CONTROL SANCTION...WELF/ST GEOG CONGRESS.
PAGE 35 G0683
    L50
REGION
AGRI
PLAN

SPENCER R.F.,METHOD AND PERSPECTIVE IN ANTHROPOLOGY
....GEOG LING QUANT STAT TESTS SAMP/SIZ CON/ANAL
IDEA/COMP METH/COMP ANTHOL BIBLIOG 20. PAGE 52
G1025
    B54
PHIL/SCI
SOC
PSY
METH

FORM W.H.,"THE PLACE OF SOCIAL STRUCTURE IN THE
DETERMINATION OF LAND USE: SOME IMPLICATIONS FOR A
THEORY OF URBAN ECOLOGY" (BMR)" STRUCT...GEOG
PHIL/SCI SOC 20. PAGE 19 G0381
    S54
HABITAT
MARKET
ORD/FREE
MUNIC

VON NEUMANN J.,"CAN WE SURVIVE TECHNOLOGY?" WOR+45
AIR INDUS ADMIN ADJUST RIGID/FLEX...GEOG PHIL/SCI
NEW/IDEA 20. PAGE 61 G1202
    S55
TEC/DEV
NUC/PWR
FUT
HABITAT

DRUCKER P.F.,AMERICA'S NEXT TWENTY YEARS. USA+45
DIST/IND ACADEM MUNIC SCHOOL DIPLOM ECO/TAC AUTOMAT
HABITAT HEALTH...SOC/WK TREND 20 URBAN/RNWL
PUB/TRANS. PAGE 16 G0316
    B57
WORKER
FOR/AID
CENSUS
GEOG

KISSINGER H.A.,NUCLEAR WEAPONS AND FOREIGN POLICY.
FUT USA+45 WOR+45 INT/ORG FORCES ACT/RES TEC/DEV
DIPLOM ARMS/CONT COERCE ATTIT KNOWL PWR...DECISION
GEOG CHARTS 20. PAGE 31 G0602
    B57
PLAN
DETER
NUC/PWR

DUNCAN O.D.,"THE MEASUREMENT OF POPULATION
DISTRIBUTION" (BMR)" WOR+45...QUANT STAT CENSUS
CHARTS 20. PAGE 16 G0321
    S57
GEOG
PHIL/SCI
PROB/SOLV
CLASSIF

MARCY C.,"THE RESEARCH PROGRAM OF THE SENATE
COMMITTEE ON FOREIGN RELATIONS." EUR+WWI ECO/UNDEV
ACT/RES PLAN PARL/PROC GOV/REL...GEOG CONFE
CONGRESS. PAGE 36 G0704
    S58
DELIB/GP
LEGIS
FOR/AID
POLICY

ELDRIDGE H.T.,THE MATERIALS OF DEMOGRAPHY: A
SELECTED AND ANNOTATED BIBLIOGRAPHY. R+D DEATH
...SAMP METH/COMP NAT/COMP 20. PAGE 18 G0343
    B59
BIBLIOG/A
GEOG
STAT
TREND

MIKSCHE F.O.,THE FAILURE OF ATOMIC STRATEGY. COM
EUR+WWI INTELL POL/PAR FORCES PLAN ECO/TAC NUC/PWR
ATTIT DRIVE RIGID/FLEX PWR...DECISION GEOG PSY
CONCPT RECORD TREND CHARTS VAL/FREE 20. PAGE 39
G0766
    B59
ACT/RES
ORD/FREE
DIPLOM
ARMS/CONT

CHASE S.,LIVE AND LET LIVE. USA+45 ECO/DEV
PROB/SOLV TEC/DEV ECO/TAC ARMS/CONT NUC/PWR WAR
NAT/LISM PEACE...GEOG TREND 20 COLD/WAR. PAGE 11
G0223
    B60
NAT/G
DIPLOM
SOCIETY
TASK

LEYDER J.,BIBLIOGRAPHIE DE L'ENSEIGNEMENT SUPERIEUR
ET DE LA RECHERCHE SCIENTIFIQUE EN AFRIQUE
INTERTROPICALE (2 VOLS.). AFR CULTURE ECO/UNDEV
AGRI PLAN EDU/PROP ADMIN COLONIAL...GEOG SOC/INTEG
20 NEGRO. PAGE 34 G0664
    B60
BIBLIOG/A
ACT/RES
ACADEM
R+D

WOETZEL R.K.,THE INTERNATIONAL CONTROL OF AIRSPACE
AND OUTERSPACE. FUT WOR+45 AIR CONSTN STRUCT
CONSULT PLAN TEC/DEV ADJUD RIGID/FLEX KNOWL
ORD/FREE PWR...TECHNIC GEOG MGT NEW/IDEA TREND
COMPUT/IR VAL/FREE 20 TREATY. PAGE 64 G1251
    B60
INT/ORG
JURID
SPACE
INT/LAW

JAFFEE A.J.,"POPULATION TRENDS AND CONTROLS IN
UNDERDEVELOPED COUNTRIES." AFR FUT ISLAM L/A+17C
S/ASIA CULTURE R+D FAM ACT/RES PLAN EDU/PROP
BIO/SOC RIGID/FLEX HEALTH...SOC STAT OBS CHARTS 20.
PAGE 28 G0555
    S60
ECO/UNDEV
GEOG

HODGKINS J.A.,SOVIET POWER: ENERGY RESOURCES,
PRODUCTION AND POTENTIALS. USSR ECO/DEV INDUS
MARKET...POLICY STAT CHARTS 20 RESOURCE/N. PAGE 26
G0518
    B61
GEOG
EXTR/IND
TEC/DEV

KAHN H.,ON THERMONUCLEAR WAR. FUT UNIV WOR+45
ECO/DEV CONSULT EX/STRUC TOP/EX ACT/RES CREATE PLAN
COERCE WAR PERSON ALL/VALS...POLICY GEOG CONCPT
METH/CNCPT OBS TREND 20. PAGE 29 G0569
    B61
DETER
NUC/PWR
SOCIETY

LEE R.R.,ENGINEERING-ECONOMIC PLANNING
MISCELLANEOUS SUBJECTS: A SELECTED BIBLIOGRAPHY
(MIMEOGRAPHED). FINAN LOC/G MUNIC NEIGH ADMIN
CONTROL INGP/REL HABITAT...GEOG MGT SOC/WK 20
RESOURCE/N. PAGE 33 G0651
    B61
BIBLIOG/A
PLAN
REGION

FAIR M.L.,"PORT AUTHORITIES IN THE UNITED STATES."
PROB/SOLV ADMIN LEAD REPRESENT PWR...DECISION GEOG.
PAGE 18 G0357
    S61
MUNIC
REGION
LOC/G
GOV/REL

BURKE A.E.,ENOUGH GOOD MEN. USA+45 WOR+45 ECO/UNDEV
FORCES TEC/DEV GUERRILLA NUC/PWR REV WAR ORD/FREE
MARXISM...GEOG 20 COLD/WAR. PAGE 10 G0189
    B62
DIPLOM
POLICY
NAT/G
TASK

SOHN L.B.,ZONAL DISARMAMENT: VARIATIONS ON A THEME.
FUT WOR+45 SOCIETY ACT/RES PLAN NUC/PWR PEACE ATTIT
...POLICY GEOG CONT/OBS HYPO/EXP 20. PAGE 52 G1020
    B62
ORD/FREE
NEW/IDEA
ARMS/CONT

PAULING L.,"GENETIC EFFECTS OF WEAPONS TESTS."
WOR+45 SOCIETY FAM ACT/RES EDU/PROP AGE/C HEALTH
ORD/FREE...GEOG STAT CONT/OBS PROJ/TEST CHARTS
TOT/POP 20. PAGE 44 G0861
    S62
HEAL
ARMS/CONT
NUC/PWR

JOINT ECONOMIC COMMITTEE,"DIMENSIONS OF SOVIET
ECONOMIC POWER." USSR R+D FORCES ACT/RES OP/RES
TEC/DEV...GEOG STAT BIBLIOG 20. PAGE 29 G0565
    C62
ECO/DEV
PLAN
PRODUC
LABOR

BEGUIN H.,"ASPECTS GEOGRAPHIQUE DE LA
POLARISATION." FUT WOR+45 SOCIETY STRUCT ECO/DEV
R+D BAL/PWR ADMIN ATTIT RIGID/FLEX HEALTH WEALTH
...CHARTS 20. PAGE 6 G0114
    L63
ECO/UNDEV
GEOG
DIPLOM

BROWN N.,NUCLEAR WAR* THE IMPENDING STRATEGIC
DEADLOCK. USA+45 USSR TEC/DEV BUDGET RISK ARMS/CONT
NUC/PWR WEAPON COST BIO/SOC...GEOG IDEA/COMP
NAT/COMP GAME NATO WARSAW/P. PAGE 9 G0177
    B64
FORCES
OP/RES
WAR
GEN/LAWS

GRAVIER J.F.,AMENAGEMENT DU TERRITOIRE ET L'AVENIR DES REGIONS FRANCAISES. FRANCE ECO/DEV AGRI INDUS CREATE...GEOG CHARTS 20. PAGE 22 G0442
B64
PLAN
MUNIC
NEIGH
ADMIN

PETERSON W.,THE POLITICS OF POPULATION. COM EUR+WWI FUT MOD/EUR S/ASIA USA-45 WOR+45 LAW CULTURE FAM SECT DOMIN EDU/PROP BIO/SOC HEALTH ORD/FREE ...GEOG STAT TIME/SEQ TREND VAL/FREE. PAGE 44 G0871
B64
PLAN
CENSUS
POLICY

NATIONAL ACADEMY OF SCIENCES,CIVIL DEFENSE: PROJECT HARBOR SUMMARY REPORT (PAMPHLET). USA+45 MUNIC NAT/G ACT/RES BUDGET EDU/PROP DETER WEAPON EATING ...GEOG 20. PAGE 41 G0808
N64
NUC/PWR
FORCES
WAR
PLAN

ALTSHULER A.,A LAND-USE PLAN FOR ST. PAUL (PAMPHLET). USA+45 CREATE CAP/ISM RIGID/FLEX ROLE ...NEW/IDEA 20 ST/PAUL. PAGE 3 G0047
B65
MUNIC
PLAN
ECO/DEV
GEOG

HEER D.M.,AFTER NUCLEAR ATTACK: A DEMOGRAPHIC INQUIRY. USA+45 ECO/DEV SECT WORKER SEX...HEAL SOC STAT PREDICT CHARTS 20 NEGRO. PAGE 25 G0500
B65
GEOG
NUC/PWR
CENSUS
WAR

RASER J.R.,"WEAPONS DESIGN AND ARMS CONTROL* THE POLARIS EXAMPLE." DETER NUC/PWR WEAPON CHOOSE PERCEPT...STERTYP TIME. PAGE 46 G0904
S65
ARMS/CONT
R+D
GEOG
ACT/RES

HOPKINS J.F.K.,ARABIC PERIODICAL LITERATURE, 1961. ISLAM LAW CULTURE SECT...GEOG HEAL PHIL/SCI PSY SOC 20. PAGE 27 G0528
B66
BIBLIOG/A
NAT/LISM
TEC/DEV
INDUS

ODEGARD P.H.,POLITICAL POWER AND SOCIAL CHANGE. UNIV NAT/G CREATE ALL/IDEOS...POLICY GEOG SOC CENSUS TREND. PAGE 42 G0829
B66
PWR
TEC/DEV
IDEA/COMP

US DEPARTMENT OF THE ARMY,COMMUNIST CHINA: A STRATEGIC SURVEY: A BIBLIOGRAPHY (PAMPHLET NO. 20-67). CHINA/COM COM INDIA USSR NAT/G POL/PAR EX/STRUC FORCES NUC/PWR REV ATTIT...POLICY GEOG CHARTS. PAGE 58 G1133
B66
BIBLIOG/A
MARXISM
S/ASIA
DIPLOM

"FURTHER READING." INDIA LOC/G NAT/G PLAN ADMIN WEALTH...GEOG SOC CONCPT CENSUS 20. PAGE 1 G0021
S66
BIBLIOG
ECO/UNDEV
TEC/DEV
PROVS

DE BLIJ H.J.,SYSTEMATIC POLITICAL GEOGRAPHY. WOR+45 STRUCT INT/ORG NAT/G EDU/PROP ADMIN COLONIAL ROUTINE ORD/FREE PWR...IDEA/COMP T 20. PAGE 15 G0283
B67
GEOG
CONCPT
METH

MOSS F.M.,THE WATER CRISIS. PROB/SOLV CONTROL ...POLICY NEW/IDEA. PAGE 40 G0791
B67
GEOG
ACT/RES
PRODUC
WEALTH

PIPER D.C.,THE INTERNATIONAL LAW OF THE GREAT LAKES. CANADA EXTR/IND MUNIC LICENSE ARMS/CONT CRIME...GEOG 19/20. PAGE 45 G0879
B67
CONCPT
DIPLOM
INT/LAW

DAVIS P.C.,"THE COMING CHINESE COMMUNIST NUCLEAR THREAT AND U.S. SEA BASED ABM OPTIONS." ASIA CHINA/COM FUT USA+45 SEA NAT/G FORCES PLAN TEC/DEV LEAD ARMS/CONT...GEOG METH/COMP 20 ABM/DEFSYS. PAGE 14 G0279
L67
NUC/PWR
DETER
WEAPON
DIPLOM

RUTH J.M.,"THE ADMINISTRATION OF WATER RESOURCES IN GUATEMALA." GUATEMALA L/A+17C DIST/IND LOC/G NAT/G EX/STRUC ADMIN GOV/REL DEMAND EQUILIB WEALTH...GEOG MGT 20. PAGE 48 G0952
L67
EFFICIENCY
ECO/UNDEV
PLAN
ACT/RES

HILL R.,"SOCIAL ASPECTS OF FAMILY PLANNING." INDIA KOREA TAIWAN ECO/UNDEV PLAN PROB/SOLV TEC/DEV EDU/PROP CONTROL ATTIT DRIVE...HEAL PSY SOC 20 BIRTH/CON UN. PAGE 26 G0512
S67
FAM
BIO/SOC
GEOG
MARRIAGE

PONTECORVO G.,"THE LAW OF THE SEA." ECO/DEV ECO/UNDEV TEC/DEV GEOG. PAGE 45 G0885
S67
CONFER
INT/LAW
EXTR/IND
SEA

WARE R.S.,"FORECAST A.D. 2000." SOCIETY STRATA ECO/UNDEV INDUS FORCES EDU/PROP AUTOMAT COERCE REV WEAPON ATTIT PREDICT. PAGE 62 G1213
S67
NUC/PWR
GEOG
TEC/DEV
WAR

ASIAN STUDIES CENTER,FOUR ARTICLES ON POPULATION AND FAMILY LIFE IN TAIWAN (ASIAN STUDIES PAPERS, REPRINT SERIES NO. 2). CULTURE STRATA ECO/UNDEV AGRI INDUS R+D KIN MUNIC...GEOG SOC CHARTS 20. PAGE 4 G0072
N67
ASIA
FAM
CENSUS
ANTHOL

US HOUSE COMM APPROPRIATIONS,PUBLIC WORKS AND ATOMIC ENERGY COMMISSION APPROPRIATION BILL, 1968 (PAMPHLET). USA+45 ECO/DEV NAT/G...GEOG DEEP/INT CHARTS HOUSE/REP AEC DEPT/DEFEN TVA. PAGE 58 G1137
N67
BUDGET
NUC/PWR
PROVS
PLAN

US HOUSE COMM FOREIGN AFFAIRS,REPORT OF SPECIAL STUDY MISSION TO THE NEAR EAST (PAMPHLET). ISRAEL USA+45 YEMEN ECO/UNDEV INT/ORG FOR/AID ARMS/CONT WAR WEAPON NAT/LISM PEACE...GEOG 20 UN HOUSE/REP. PAGE 58 G1138
N67
ISLAM
DIPLOM
FORCES

GALLAHER A. JR.,PERSPECTIVES IN DEVELOPMENTAL CHANGE. MUNIC PLAN INSPECT EDU/PROP...POLICY DECISION GEOG PSY SOC IDEA/COMP ANTHOL 20 MODERNIZE. PAGE 21 G0405
B68
TECHNIC
TEC/DEV
PROB/SOLV
CREATE

GEOGRAPHY....SEE GEOG

GEOPOLITIC....GEOPOLITICS

GEOPOLITICS....SEE GEOG

GEORGE/DL....DAVID LLOYD GEORGE

GEORGE/III....GEORGE THE THIRD OF ENGLAND

GEORGIA....GEORGIA(U.S.A.)

GER/CONFED....GERMAN CONFEDERATION

GERMAN CONFEDERATION....SEE GER/CONFED

GERMAN/AM....GERMAN-AMERICANS

GERMANS/PA....GERMANS IN PENNSYLVANIA

GERMANY....GERMANY IN GENERAL; SEE ALSO APPROPRIATE TIME/ SPACE/CULTURE INDEX

BARKER E.,THE DEVELOPMENT OF PUBLIC SERVICES IN WESTERN WUROPE: 1660-1930. FRANCE GERMANY UK SCHOOL CONTROL REPRESENT ROLE...WELF/ST 17/20. PAGE 5 G0095
B44
GOV/COMP
ADMIN
EX/STRUC

BRETTON H.L.,STRESEMANN AND THE REVISION OF VERSAILLES: A FIGHT FOR REASON. EUR+WWI GERMANY FORCES BUDGET ARMS/CONT WAR SUPEGO...BIBLIOG 20 TREATY VERSAILLES STRESEMN/G. PAGE 9 G0167
B53
POLICY
DIPLOM
BIOG

LANGER W.L.,THE UNDECLARED WAR, 1940-1941. EUR+WWI GERMANY USA-45 USSR AIR FORCES TEC/DEV CONFER CONTROL COERCE PERCEPT ORD/FREE PWR 20 CHINJAP EUROPE. PAGE 32 G0634
B53
WAR
POLICY
DIPLOM

GERMANY FOREIGN MINISTRY,DOCUMENTS ON GERMAN FOREIGN POLICY 1918-1945, SERIES C (1933-1937) VOLS. I-V. GERMANY MOD/EUR FORCES PLAN ECO/TAC ...FASCIST CHARTS ANTHOL 20. PAGE 21 G0416
B54
NAT/G
DIPLOM
POLICY

REYNOLDS P.A.,BRITISH FOREIGN POLICY IN THE INTER- WAR YEARS. CZECHOSLVK GERMANY POLAND UK USA-45 POL/PAR FORCES ECO/TAC ARMS/CONT WAR ATTIT 20. PAGE 46 G0915
B54
DIPLOM
POLICY
NAT/G

SPEIER H.,GERMAN REARMAMENT AND ATOMIC WAR: THE VIEWS OF GERMAN MILITARY AND POLITICAL LEADERS. FUT WOR+45 INT/ORG NAT/G WEAPON ATTIT PWR...INT QU TOT/POP VAL/FREE COLD/WAR 20. PAGE 52 G1024
B57
TOP/EX
FORCES
NUC/PWR
GERMANY

B60

PARRY A.,RUSSIA'S ROCKETS AND MISSILES. COM FUT   PLAN
GERMANY USA+45 WOR+45 INTELL ECO/DEV ACT/RES   TEC/DEV
NUC/PWR WEAPON ATTIT ALL/VALS...OBS TIME/SEQ   SPACE
COLD/WAR 20. PAGE 44 G0859   USSR

B63

JACOB H.,GERMAN ADMINISTRATION SINCE BISMARCK: ADMIN
CENTRAL AUTHORITY VERSUS LOCAL AUTONOMY. GERMANY   NAT/G
GERMANY/W LAW POL/PAR CONTROL CENTRAL TOTALISM   LOC/G
FASCISM...MAJORIT DECISION STAT CHARTS GOV/COMP   POLICY
19/20 BISMARCK/O HITLER/A WEIMAR/REP. PAGE 28 G0551

S63

SMITH D.O.,"WHAT IS A WAR DETERRENT." FUT GERMANY   ACT/RES
HUNGARY UK USA+45 WOR+45 WOR-45 NAT/G TEC/DEV   FORCES
BAL/PWR PWR...CONCPT GEN/LAWS COLD/WAR 20. PAGE 51   ARMS/CONT
G1013   DETER

B64

COENEN E.,LA "KONJUNKTURFORSCHUNG" EN ALLEMAGNE ET   METH/COMP
EN AUTRICHE, 1925-1935. AUSTRIA GERMANY OP/RES PLAN   R+D
COST PERCEPT...METH/CNCPT BIBLIOG 20. PAGE 12 G0237   ECO/TAC

B64

WHEELER-BENNETT J.W.,THE NEMESIS OF POWER (2ND   FORCES
ED.). EUR+WWI GERMANY TOP/EX TEC/DEV ADMIN WAR   NAT/G
PERS/REL RIGID/FLEX ROLE ORD/FREE PWR FASCISM 20   GP/REL
HITLER/A. PAGE 63 G1231   STRUCT

B66

VON BORCH H,FRIEDE TROTZ KRIEG. GERMANY USSR   DIPLOM
WOR+45 PEACE ANOMIE ATTIT 20. PAGE 43 G0853   NUC/PWR
                                                     WAR
                                                     COERCE

B67

RUSSETT B.M.,ARMS CONTROL IN EUROPE: PROPOSALS AND   ARMS/CONT
POLITICAL CONSTRAINTS. GERMANY WOR+45 POL/PAR   REGION
BARGAIN DIPLOM...TREND CHARTS 20 COLD/WAR. PAGE 48   METH/COMP
G0950

S67

KRUSCHE H.,"THE STRIVING OF THE KIESINGER-STRAUS   ARMS/CONT
GOVERNMENT FOR NUCLEAR WEAPONS IS A THREAT TO   INT/ORG
EUROPEAN SECURITY." EUR+WWI GERMANY BAL/PWR   NUC/PWR
SANCTION WEAPON PEACE ORD/FREE...MARXIST 20 NATO   DIPLOM
COLD/WAR. PAGE 32 G0623

S67

TAGIL S.,"WEGENER, RAEDER, AND THE GERMAN NAVAL   SEA
STRATEGY: VIEWPOINTS ON THE CONDITIONS FOR THE   POLICY
INFLUENCE OF IDEAS." GERMANY WOR-45...IDEA/COMP   HIST/WRIT
METH 20. PAGE 53 G1049   CIVMIL/REL

GERMANY FOREIGN MINISTRY G0416

GERMANY/E....EAST GERMANY; SEE ALSO COM

B62

FRIEDRICH-EBERT-STIFTUNG,THE SOVIET BLOC AND   MARXISM
DEVELOPING COUNTRIES. CHINA/COM COM GERMANY/E USSR   DIPLOM
WOR+45 ECO/UNDEV INT/ORG NAT/G TEC/DEV NEUTRAL PWR   ECO/TAC
...POLICY 20. PAGE 20 G0394   FOR/AID

B65

WASKOW A.I.,KEEPING THE WORLD DISARMED. AFR   ARMS/CONT
GERMANY/E DIPLOM CONTROL WAR 20 UN. PAGE 62 G1218   PEACE
                                                     FORCES
                                                     PROB/SOLV

GERMANY/W....WEST GERMANY

B61

SCHMIDT H.,VERTEIDIGUNG ODER VERGELTUNG. COM CUBA   PLAN
GERMANY/W USSR FORCES DIPLOM ARMS/CONT DETER   WAR
NUC/PWR...POLICY CHARTS HYPO/EXP SIMUL BIBLIOG 20   BAL/PWR
NATO COLD/WAR. PAGE 49 G0970   ORD/FREE

B62

GRANICK D.,THE EUROPEAN EXECUTIVE. BELGIUM FRANCE   MGT
GERMANY/W UK INDUS LABOR LG/CO SML/CO EX/STRUC PLAN   ECO/DEV
TEC/DEV CAP/ISM COST DEMAND...POLICY CHARTS 20.   ECO/TAC
PAGE 22 G0441   EXEC

B62

WENDT P.F.,HOUSING POLICY - THE SEARCH FOR   PLAN
SOLUTIONS. GERMANY/W SWEDEN UK USA+45 OP/RES   ADMIN
HABITAT WEALTH...SOC/WK CHARTS 20. PAGE 63 G1230   METH/COMP
                                                     NAT/G

B63

JACOB H.,GERMAN ADMINISTRATION SINCE BISMARCK: ADMIN
CENTRAL AUTHORITY VERSUS LOCAL AUTONOMY. GERMANY   NAT/G
GERMANY/W LAW POL/PAR CONTROL CENTRAL TOTALISM   LOC/G

FASCISM...MAJORIT DECISION STAT CHARTS GOV/COMP   POLICY
19/20 BISMARCK/O HITLER/A WEIMAR/REP. PAGE 28 G0551

B64

MILIBAND R.,THE SOCIALIST REGISTER: 1964. GERMANY/W   MARXISM
ITALY UK LABOR POL/PAR ECO/TAC FOR/AID NUC/PWR   SOCISM
...POLICY SOCIALIST IDEA/COMP 20 MAO NASSER/G.   CAP/ISM
PAGE 39 G0769   PROB/SOLV

B65

US DEPARTMENT OF DEFENSE,US SECURITY ARMS CONTROL,   BIBLIOG/A
AND DISARMAMENT 1961-1965 (PAMPHLET). CHINA/COM COM   ARMS/CONT
GERMANY/W ISRAEL SPACE USA+45 USSR WOR+45 FORCES   NUC/PWR
EDU/PROP DETER EQUILIB PEACE ALL/VALS...GOV/COMP 20   DIPLOM
NATO. PAGE 57 G1118

GETTYSBURG....BATTLE OF GETTYSBURG

GHANA....SEE ALSO AFR

B65

FOSTER P.,EDUCATION AND SOCIAL CHANGE IN GHANA.   SCHOOL
GHANA CULTURE STRUCT ECO/UNDEV TEC/DEV REGION   CREATE
EFFICIENCY LITERACY ALL/VALS SOVEREIGN...STAT   SOCIETY
METH/COMP 19/20 GOLD/COAST. PAGE 20 G0385

S67

KRAUS J.,"A MARXIST IN GHANA." GHANA ELITES CHIEF   MARXISM
PROB/SOLV TEC/DEV DIPLOM ECO/TAC COLONIAL PARTIC   PLAN
PWR 20 NKRUMAH/K. PAGE 31 G0618   ATTIT
                                                     CREATE

GIBBON/EDW....EDWARD GIBBON

GIBRALTAR....SEE UK

GILPIN R. G0417

GINZBERG E. G0418

GIRSHICK M.A. G0574

GIVE....GIVING, PHILANTHROPY

B48

METZLER L.A.,INCOME, EMPLOYMENT, AND PUBLIC POLICY.   INCOME
FINAN INDUS LOC/G NAT/G TAX GIVE PAY COST PRODUC   WEALTH
...MGT TIME/SEQ 20. PAGE 38 G0760   POLICY
                                                     ECO/TAC

B57

KIETH-LUCAS A.,DECISIONS ABOUT PEOPLE IN NEED, A   ADMIN
STUDY OF ADMINISTRATIVE RESPONSIVENESS IN PUBLIC   RIGID/FLEX
ASSISTANCE. USA+45 GIVE RECEIVE INGP/REL PERS/REL   SOC/WK
MORAL RESPECT WEALTH...SOC OBS BIBLIOG 20. PAGE 30   DECISION
G0595

S65

ETZIONI A.,"ON THE NATIONAL GUIDANCE OF SCIENCE."   PHIL/SCI
USA+45 FINAN NAT/G LEGIS GIVE 20. PAGE 18 G0353   CREATE
                                                     POLICY
                                                     EFFICIENCY

B66

ALEXANDER Y.,INTERNATIONAL TECHNICAL ASSISTANCE   SKILL
EXPERTS: A CASE STUDY OF THE U.N. EXPERIENCE.   INT/ORG
USA+45 WOR+45 WORKER CREATE PLAN PROB/SOLV ECO/TAC   TEC/DEV
FOR/AID GIVE EDU/PROP...CHARTS BIBLIOG 20 UN.   CONSULT
PAGE 2 G0039

B66

GLAZER M.,THE FEDERAL GOVERNMENT AND THE   BIBLIOG/A
UNIVERSITY. CHILE PROB/SOLV DIPLOM GIVE ADMIN WAR   NAT/G
...POLICY SOC 20. PAGE 21 G0421   PLAN
                                                     ACADEM

B66

KLOTSCHE J.M.,THE URBAN UNIVERSITY AND THE FUTURE   ACADEM
OF OUR CITIES. FUT USA+45 USA-45 LOC/G NEIGH GIVE   MUNIC
19/20. PAGE 31 G0606   PROB/SOLV
                                                     TEC/DEV

B66

US HOUSE COMM ON JUDICIARY,CIVIL COMMITMENT AND   BIO/SOC
TREATMENT OF NARCOTIC ADDICTS. USA+45 SOCIETY FINAN   CRIME
LEGIS PROB/SOLV GIVE CT/SYS SANCTION HEALTH   IDEA/COMP
...POLICY HEAL 20. PAGE 58 G1141   CONTROL

S66

GREENBERG D.S.,"THE SCIENTIFIC PORK BARREL." USA+45   R+D
ECO/DEV PUB/INST CHIEF LEGIS BUDGET GIVE GP/REL PWR   NAT/G
WEALTH 20. PAGE 23 G0445   ACADEM
                                                     ATTIT

N67

US HOUSE COMM SCI ASTRONAUT,AMENDING NATIONAL   PHIL/SCI

SCIENCE FOUNDATION ACT OF 1950 TO MAKE IMPROVEMENTS DELIB/GP
IN ORGANIZATION AND OPERATION OF FOUNDAT'N(PAMPH).   TEC/DEV
USA+45 GIVE ADMIN...POLICY HOUSE/REP NSF. PAGE 58   R+D
G1147

GLADDEN E.N. G0419

GLADSTON/W....WILLIAM GLADSTONE

GLADSTONE A.E. G0420

GLAZER M. G0421

GLEASON S.E. G0634

GMP/REG....GOOD MANUFACTURING PRACTICE REGULATIONS

GOBER J.L. G0422

GODDARD V. G0423

GOEBBELS/J....JOSEPH GOEBBELS

GOETHE/J....JOHANN WOLFGANG VON GOETHE

GOLD N.L. G0424

GOLD....GOLD

GOLD/COAST....GOLD COAST (PRE-GHANA)

                                                          B65
FOSTER P.,EDUCATION AND SOCIAL CHANGE IN GHANA.   SCHOOL
GHANA CULTURE STRUCT ECO/UNDEV TEC/DEV REGION   CREATE
EFFICIENCY LITERACY ALL/VALS SOVEREIGN...STAT   SOCIETY
METH/COMP 19/20 GOLD/COAST. PAGE 20 G0385

GOLD/STAND....GOLD STANDARD

                                                          B59
MEANS G.C.,ADMINISTRATIVE INFLATION AND PUBLIC   ECO/TAC
POLICY (PAMPHLET). USA+45 ECO/DEV FINAN INDUS   POLICY
WORKER PLAN BUDGET GOV/REL COST DEMAND WEALTH 20   RATION
CONGRESS MONOPOLY GOLD/STAND. PAGE 38 G0749   CONTROL

GOLDBERG A. G0425

GOLDHAMER H. G0336

GOLDHAMMER H. G0426

GOLDMAN/E....ERIC GOLDMAN

GOLDSEN J.M. G0427,G0428

GOLDSTEIN W. G0429,G0430

GOLDWATR/B....BARRY GOLDWATER

GOLEMBIEWSKI R.T. G0431

GOLOVINE M.N. G0432

GOMILLN/CG....C.G. GOMILLION

GOOD MANUFACTURING PRACTICE REGULATIONS....SEE GMP/REG

GORDON B.K. G0433

GORDON G. G0434

GORDON L. G0435

GORDON W.J.J. G0436

GORDON/K....K. GORDON

GORDON/W....WILLIAM GORDON

GORTNER R.A. G0711

GOULD J.M. G0437

GOULDNER A.W. G0438

GOV/COMP....COMPARISON OF GOVERNMENTS

                                                          B44
BARKER E.,THE DEVELOPMENT OF PUBLIC SERVICES IN   GOV/COMP
WESTERN WUROPE: 1660-1930. FRANCE GERMANY UK SCHOOL ADMIN
CONTROL REPRESENT ROLE...WELF/ST 17/20. PAGE 5   EX/STRUC
G0095

                                                          B48
GRIFFITH E.S.,RESEARCH IN POLITICAL SCIENCE: THE   BIBLIOG
WORK OF PANELS OF RESEARCH COMMITTEE, APSA. WOR+45 PHIL/SCI
WOR-45 COM/IND R+D FORCES ACT/RES WAR...GOV/COMP   DIPLOM
ANTHOL 20. PAGE 23 G0451   JURID

                                                          B49
MCLEAN J.M.,THE PUBLIC SERVICE AND UNIVERSITY   ACADEM
EDUCATION. UK USA-45 DELIB/GP EX/STRUC TOP/EX ADMIN NAT/G
...GOV/COMP METH/COMP NAT/COMP ANTHOL 20. PAGE 38   EXEC
G0746   EDU/PROP

                                                          S56
ALMOND G.A.,"COMPARATIVE POLITICAL SYSTEMS" (BMR)" GOV/COMP
WOR+45 WOR-45 PROB/SOLV DIPLOM EFFICIENCY   CONCPT
...PHIL/SCI SOC METH 17/20. PAGE 3 G0046   ALL/IDEOS
                                                    NAT/COMP

                                                          B57
SCARROW H.A.,THE HIGHER PUBLIC SERVICE OF THE   ADMIN
COMMONWEALTH OF AUSTRALIA. LAW SENIOR LOBBY ROLE 20 NAT/G
AUSTRAL CIVIL/SERV COMMONWLTH. PAGE 49 G0959   EX/STRUC
                                                    GOV/COMP

                                                          B58
OGDEN F.D.,THE POLL TAX IN THE SOUTH. USA+45 USA-45 TAX
CONSTN ADJUD ADMIN PARTIC CRIME...TIME/SEQ GOV/COMP CHOOSE
METH/COMP 18/20 SOUTH/US. PAGE 43 G0838   RACE/REL
                                                    DISCRIM

                                                          B60
WALDO D.,THE RESEARCH FUNCTION OF UNIVERSITY   ADMIN
BUREAUS AND INSTITUTES FOR GOVERNMENTAL-RELATED   R+D
RESEARCH. FINAN ACADEM NAT/G INGP/REL ROLE...POLICY MUNIC
CLASSIF GOV/COMP. PAGE 61 G1205

                                                          B61
CARNELL F.,THE POLITICS OF THE NEW STATES: A SELECT BIBLIOG/A
ANNOTATED BIBLIOGRAPHY WITH SPECIAL REFERENCE TO   AFR
THE COMMONWEALTH. CONSTN ELITES LABOR NAT/G POL/PAR ASIA
EX/STRUC DIPLOM ADJUD ADMIN...GOV/COMP 20   COLONIAL
COMMONWLTH. PAGE 11 G0210

                                                          S62
MARTIN L.W.,"THE MARKET FOR STRATEGIC IDEAS IN   DIPLOM
BRITAIN: THE 'SANDYS ERA'" UK ARMS/CONT WAR GOV/REL COERCE
OPTIMAL...POLICY DECISION GOV/COMP COLD/WAR   FORCES
CMN/WLTH. PAGE 36 G0714   PWR

                                                          B63
GEERTZ C.,OLD SOCIETIES AND NEW STATES: THE QUEST   ECO/UNDEV
FOR MODERNITY IN ASIA AND AFRICA. AFR ASIA LAW   TEC/DEV
CULTURE SECT EDU/PROP REV...GOV/COMP NAT/COMP 20.   NAT/LISM
PAGE 21 G0415   SOVEREIGN

                                                          B63
HERNDON J.,A SELECTED BIBLIOGRAPHY OF MATERIALS IN BIBLIOG
STATE GOVERNMENT AND POLITICS (PAMPHLET). USA+45   GOV/COMP
POL/PAR LEGIS ADMIN CHOOSE MGT. PAGE 26 G0507   PROVS
                                                    DECISION

                                                          B63
JACOB H.,GERMAN ADMINISTRATION SINCE BISMARCK: ADMIN
CENTRAL AUTHORITY VERSUS LOCAL AUTONOMY. GERMANY   NAT/G
GERMANY/W LAW POL/PAR CONTROL CENTRAL TOTALISM   LOC/G
FASCISM...MAJORIT DECISION STAT CHARTS GOV/COMP   POLICY
19/20 BISMARCK/O HITLER/A WEIMAR/REP. PAGE 28 G0551

                                                          B64
RIES J.C.,THE MANAGEMENT OF DEFENSE: ORGANIZATION   FORCES
AND CONTROL OF THE US ARMED SERVICES. PROF/ORG   ACT/RES
DELIB/GP EX/STRUC LEGIS GOV/REL PERS/REL CENTRAL   DECISION
RATIONAL PWR...POLICY TREND GOV/COMP BIBLIOG.   CONTROL
PAGE 47 G0920

                                                          B64
ROBERTS HL,FOREIGN AFFAIRS BIBLIOGRAPHY, 1952-1962. BIBLIOG/A
ECO/DEV SECT PLAN FOR/AID INT/TRADE ARMS/CONT   DIPLOM
NAT/LISM ATTIT...INT/LAW GOV/COMP IDEA/COMP 20.   INT/ORG
PAGE 47 G0928   WAR

                                                          S64
UNRUH J.M.,"SCIENTIFIC INPUTS TO LEGISLATIVE   CREATE
DECISION-MAKING (SUPPLEMENT)" USA+45 ACADEM NAT/G   DECISION
PROVS GOV/REL GOV/COMP. PAGE 56 G1102   LEGIS
                                                    PARTIC

                                                          B65
UN,SPACE ACTIVITIES AND RESOURCES: REVIEW OF UNITED SPACE
NATION'S NATIONAL AND INTERNATIONAL PROGRAMS.   NUC/PWR
INT/ORG LABOR PLAN TEC/DEV DIPLOM EFFICIENCY HEALTH FOR/AID
...GOV/COMP 20 UN. PAGE 55 G1086   PEACE

                                                          B65
US DEPARTMENT OF DEFENSE,US SECURITY ARMS CONTROL. BIBLIOG/A
AND DISARMAMENT 1961-1965 (PAMPHLET). CHINA/COM COM ARMS/CONT

GERMANY/W ISRAEL SPACE USA+45 USSR WOR+45 FORCES NUC/PWR
EDU/PROP DETER EQUILIB PEACE ALL/VALS...GOV/COMP 20 DIPLOM
NATO. PAGE 57 G1118

S66
FLEMING W.G.,"AUTHORITY, EFFICIENCY, AND ROLE DOMIN
STRESS: PROBLEMS IN THE DEVELOPMENT OF EAST AFRICAN EFFICIENCY
BUREAUCRACIES." AFR UGANDA STRUCT PROB/SOLV ROUTINE COLONIAL
INGP/REL ROLE...MGT SOC GP/COMP GOV/COMP 20 ADMIN
TANGANYIKA AFRICA/E. PAGE 19 G0371

B67
MACKINTOSH J.M.,JUGGERNAUT. USSR NAT/G POL/PAR WAR
ADMIN LEAD CIVMIL/REL COST TOTALISM PWR MARXISM FORCES
...GOV/COMP 20. PAGE 35 G0691 COM
PROF/ORG

B67
WOODRUFF W.,IMPACT OF WESTERN MAN. ECO/DEV INDUS EUR+WWI
CREATE PLAN PROB/SOLV COLONIAL GOV/REL...CHARTS MOD/EUR
GOV/COMP BIBLIOG 18/20. PAGE 64 G1256 CAP/ISM

S67
JAIN G.,"INDIA REJECTS THE POWER RACE* REALISM INDIA
ABOUT NUCLEAR WEAPONS." FORCES PROB/SOLV FOR/AID CHINA/COM
ARMS/CONT COST PWR...GOV/COMP 20. PAGE 28 G0556 NUC/PWR
DIPLOM

B91
RENAN E.,THE FUTURE OF SCIENCE. WAR ORD/FREE WEALTH PHIL/SCI
...GOV/COMP IDEA/COMP GEN/LAWS 19. PAGE 46 G0913 KNOWL
SECT
PREDICT

GOV/REL....RELATIONS BETWEEN GOVERNMENTS

N
CONOVER H.L.,CIVILIAN DEFENSE: A SELECTED LIST OF BIBLIOG
RECENT REFERENCES (PAMPHLET). USA+45 LOC/G MUNIC PLAN
PROB/SOLV ADMIN LEAD TASK WEAPON GOV/REL...POLICY WAR
CON/ANAL 20 CIV/DEFENS. PAGE 13 G0251 CIVMIL/REL

N
PERSONNEL. USA+45 LAW LABOR LG/CO WORKER CREATE BIBLIOG/A
GOV/REL PERS/REL ATTIT WEALTH. PAGE 1 G0010 ADMIN
MGT
GP/REL

N
US SUPERINTENDENT OF DOCUMENTS,TRANSPORTATION: BIBLIOG/A
HIGHWAYS, ROADS, AND POSTAL SERVICE (PRICE LIST DIST/IND
25). PANAMA USA+45 LAW FORCES DIPLOM ADMIN GOV/REL SERV/IND
HEALTH MGT. PAGE 61 G1188 NAT/G

N19
LAWRENCE S.A.,THE BATTERY ADDITIVE CONTROVERSY PHIL/SCI
(PAMPHLET). USA+45 LAW MARKET PROC/MFG R+D CAP/ISM LOBBY
CT/SYS GOV/REL OWN FTC CONGRESS BUR/STNDRD INSPECT
RITCHIE/JM. PAGE 33 G0645

B25
MATHEWS J.M.,AMERICAN STATE GOVERNMENT. USA-45 PROVS
LOC/G CHIEF EX/STRUC LEGIS ADJUD CONTROL CT/SYS ADMIN
ROUTINE GOV/REL PWR 20 GOVERNOR. PAGE 37 G0721 FEDERAL
CONSTN

B40
FULLER G.H.,SELECTED LIST OF RECENT REFERENCES ON BIBLIOG
AMERICAN NATIONAL DEFENSE (PAMPHLET). USA-45 FINAN CIVMIL/REL
NAT/G ARMS/CONT WAR GOV/REL CENTRAL COST PEACE PWR FORCES
20. PAGE 20 G0400 WEAPON

B41
FULLER G.H.,A LIST OF BIBLIOGRAPHIES ON QUESTIONS BIBLIOG/A
RELATING TO NATIONAL DEFENSE (PAMPHLET). USA-45 FORCES
NAT/G ARMS/CONT WAR GOV/REL COST PEACE 20. PAGE 20 CIVMIL/REL
G0402 WEAPON

B48
CHILDS J.R.,AMERICAN FOREIGN SERVICE. USA+45 DIPLOM
SOCIETY NAT/G ROUTINE GOV/REL 20 DEPT/STATE ADMIN
CIVIL/SERV. PAGE 12 G0227 GP/REL

B48
PUBLIC ADMINISTRATION SERVICE,SOURCE MATERIALS IN BIBLIOG/A
PUBLIC ADMINISTRATION: A SELECTED BIBLIOGRAPHY (PAS GOV/REL
PUBLICATION NO. 102). USA+45 LAW FINAN LOC/G MUNIC MGT
NAT/G PLAN RECEIVE EDU/PROP CT/SYS CHOOSE HEALTH ADMIN
20. PAGE 45 G0895

S49
SOUERS S.W.,"POLICY FORMULATION FOR NATIONAL DELIB/GP
SECURITY." EX/STRUC FORCES PROB/SOLV DIPLOM CONFER CHIEF
EXEC ARMS/CONT DETER NUC/PWR GOV/REL PEACE DECISION
COLD/WAR. PAGE 52 G1022 POLICY

B50
BERNSTEIN I.,THE NEW DEAL COLLECTIVE BARGAINING LABOR
PROCESS. USA-45 GOV/REL ATTIT...BIBLIOG 20 LEGIS
ROOSEVLT/F. PAGE 7 G0132 POLICY
NEW/LIB

B50
HUZAR E.,THE PURSE AND THE SWORD: CONTROL OF THE CIVMIL/REL
ARMY BY CONGRESS THROUGH MILITARY APPROPRIATIONS BUDGET
1933-1950. NAT/G DELIB/GP EX/STRUC FORCES PROB/SOLV CONTROL
BARGAIN CONFER ADMIN ROUTINE GOV/REL EFFICIENCY LEGIS
...POLICY COLD/WAR. PAGE 27 G0541

B50
KOENIG L.W.,THE SALE OF THE TANKERS. USA+45 SEA NAT/G
DIST/IND POL/PAR DIPLOM ADMIN CIVMIL/REL ATTIT POLICY
...DECISION 20 PRESIDENT DEPT/STATE. PAGE 31 G0609 PLAN
GOV/REL

C50
WAGER P.W.,"COUNTY GOVERNMENT ACROSS THE NATION." LOC/G
USA+45 CONSTN COM/IND FINAN SCHOOL DOMIN CT/SYS PROVS
LEAD GOV/REL...STAT BIBLIOG 20. PAGE 61 G1204 ADMIN
ROUTINE

S54
HOOPES T.,"CIVILIAN-MILITARY BALANCE." USA+45 CHIEF CIVMIL/REL
FORCES PLAN CONTROL WAR GOV/REL GP/REL INGP/REL LEAD
...POLICY 19/20. PAGE 27 G0527 PWR
NAT/G

C54
ZELLER B.,"AMERICAN STATE LEGISLATURES: REPORT ON REPRESENT
THE COMMITTEE ON AMERICAN LEGISLATURES." CONSTN LEGIS
POL/PAR EX/STRUC CONFER ADMIN CONTROL EXEC LOBBY PROVS
ROUTINE GOV/REL...POLICY BIBLIOG 20. PAGE 65 G1267 APPORT

B55
SMITHIES A.,THE BUDGETARY PROCESS IN THE UNITED NAT/G
STATES. ECO/DEV AGRI EX/STRUC FORCES LEGIS ADMIN
PROB/SOLV TAX ROUTINE EFFICIENCY...MGT CONGRESS BUDGET
PRESIDENT. PAGE 52 G1016 GOV/REL

B56
KOENIG L.W.,THE TRUMAN ADMINISTRATION: ITS ADMIN
PRINCIPLES AND PRACTICE. USA+45 POL/PAR CHIEF LEGIS POLICY
DIPLOM DEATH NUC/PWR WAR CIVMIL/REL PEACE EX/STRUC
...DECISION 20 TRUMAN/HS PRESIDENT TREATY. PAGE 31 GOV/REL
G0610

B56
REDFORD E.S.,PUBLIC ADMINISTRATION AND POLICY EX/STRUC
FORMATION: STUDIES IN OIL, GAS, BANKING, RIVER PROB/SOLV
DEVELOPMENT AND CORPORATE INVESTIGATIONS. USA+45 CONTROL
CLIENT NAT/G ADMIN LOBBY REPRESENT GOV/REL INGP/REL EXEC
20. PAGE 46 G0908

B57
DUPREE A.H.,SCIENCE IN THE FEDERAL GOVERNMENT; A NAT/G
HISTORY OF POLICIES AND ACTIVITIES TO 1940. USA-45 R+D
AGRI SCHOOL DELIB/GP WAR GOV/REL...PHIL/SCI BIBLIOG CREATE
18/20 DEPRESSION NEW/DEAL WWI JEFFERSN/T. PAGE 17 TEC/DEV
G0324

B58
JUNGK R.,BRIGHTER THAN A THOUSAND SUNS: THE MORAL NUC/PWR
AND POLITICAL HISTORY OF THE ATOMIC SCIENTISTS. MORAL
WOR+45 WOR-45 CONSULT CREATE RISK UTIL DRIVE GOV/REL
PERCEPT PWR...INT 20. PAGE 29 G0568 PERSON

B58
MECRENSKY E.,SCIENTIFIC MANPOWER IN EUROPE. WOR+45 ECO/TAC
EDU/PROP GOV/REL SKILL...TECHNIC PHIL/SCI INT TEC/DEV
CHARTS BIBLIOG 20. PAGE 38 G0750 METH/COMP
NAT/COMP

S58
MARCY C.,"THE RESEARCH PROGRAM OF THE SENATE DELIB/GP
COMMITTEE ON FOREIGN RELATIONS." EUR+WWI ECO/UNDEV LEGIS
ACT/RES PLAN PARL/PROC GOV/REL...GEOG CONFE FOR/AID
CONGRESS. PAGE 36 G0704 POLICY

B59
ATOMIC INDUSTRIAL FORUM,THE IMPACT OF THE PEACEFUL PROVS
USES OF ATOMIC ENERGY ON STATE AND LOCAL LOC/G
GOVERNMENT. USA+45 INDUS NAT/G LEGIS PLAN CONTROL NUC/PWR
GOV/REL. PAGE 4 G0079 PEACE

B59
CLEAVELAND F.N.,SCIENCE AND STATE GOVERNMENT. AGRI TEC/DEV
EXTR/IND FINAN INDUS PROVS...METH/CNCPT STAT CHARTS PHIL/SCI
20 NEW/YORK CONNECTICT WISCONSIN CALIFORNIA GOV/REL
NEW/MEXICO. PAGE 12 G0233 METH/COMP

B59
MEANS G.C.,ADMINISTRATIVE INFLATION AND PUBLIC ECO/TAC

POLICY (PAMPHLET). USA+45 ECO/DEV FINAN INDUS
WORKER PLAN BUDGET GOV/REL COST DEMAND WEALTH 20
CONGRESS MONOPOLY GOLD/STAND. PAGE 38 G0749
POLICY
RATION
CONTROL

B59
U OF MICHIGAN LAW SCHOOL,ATOMS AND THE LAW. USA+45
PROVS WORKER PROB/SOLV DIPLOM ADMIN GOV/REL ANTHOL.
PAGE 55 G1085
NUC/PWR
NAT/G
CONTROL
LAW

B59
US CONGRESS JT ATOM ENRGY COMM,SELECTED MATERIALS
ON FEDERAL-STATE COOPERATION IN THE ATOMIC ENERGY
FIELD. USA+45 LAW LOC/G PROVS CONSULT LEGIS ADJUD
...POLICY BIBLIOG 20 AEC. PAGE 57 G1111
NAT/G
NUC/PWR
GOV/REL
DELIB/GP

S59
SEIDMAN H.,"THE GOVERNMENT CORPORATION IN THE
UNITED STATES." USA+45 LEGIS ADMIN PLURISM 20.
PAGE 50 G0988
CONTROL
GOV/REL
EX/STRUC
EXEC

B60
ALBI F.,TRATADO DE LOS MODOS DE GESTION DE LAS
CORPORACIONES LOCALES. SPAIN FINAN NAT/G BUDGET
CONTROL EXEC ROUTINE GOV/REL ORD/FREE SOVEREIGN
...MGT 20. PAGE 2 G0034
LOC/G
LAW
ADMIN
MUNIC

B60
BROOKINGS INSTITUTION,UNITED STATES FOREIGN POLICY:
STUDY NO 9: THE FORMULATION AND ADMINISTRATION OF
UNITED STATES FOREIGN POLICY. USA+45 WOR+45
EX/STRUC LEGIS BAL/PWR FOR/AID EDU/PROP CIVMIL/REL
GOV/REL...INT COLD/WAR. PAGE 9 G0174
DIPLOM
INT/ORG
CREATE

B60
CARPER E.T.,THE DEFENSE APPROPRIATIONS RIDER
(PAMPHLET). USA+45 CONSTN CHIEF DELIB/GP LEGIS
BUDGET LOBBY CIVMIL/REL...POLICY 20 CONGRESS
EISNHWR/DD DEPT/DEFEN PRESIDENT BOSTON. PAGE 11
G0212
GOV/REL
ADJUD
LAW
CONTROL

B60
LINDVEIT E.N.,SCIENTISTS IN GOVERNMENT. USA+45 PAY
EDU/PROP ADMIN DRIVE HABITAT ROLE...TECHNIC BIBLIOG
20. PAGE 34 G0670
TEC/DEV
ECO/TAC
PHIL/SCI
GOV/REL

B60
WEBSTER J.A.,A GENERAL STUDY OF THE DEPARTMENT OF
DEFENSE INTERNAL SECURITY PROGRAM. USA+45 WORKER
TEC/DEV ADJUD CONTROL CT/SYS EXEC GOV/REL COST
...POLICY DECISION MGT 20 DEPT/DEFEN SUPREME/CT.
PAGE 62 G1221
ORD/FREE
PLAN
ADMIN
NAT/G

B61
HELLER D.,THE KENNEDY CABINET--AMERICA'S MEN OF
DESTINY. NAT/G CHIEF CONSULT ADMIN CONTROL GOV/REL
...MGT 20 DEPT/LABOR DEPT/STATE DEPT/JUST
DEPT/DEFEN KENNEDY/J. PAGE 26 G0504
EX/STRUC
CONFER
DELIB/GP
TOP/EX

S61
FAIR M.L.,"PORT AUTHORITIES IN THE UNITED STATES."
PROB/SOLV ADMIN LEAD REPRESENT PWR...DECISION GEOG.
PAGE 18 G0357
MUNIC
REGION
LOC/G
GOV/REL

B62
DUPRE J.S.,SCIENCE AND THE NATION: POLICY AND
POLITICS. USA+45 LAW ACADEM FORCES ADMIN CIVMIL/REL
GOV/REL EFFICIENCY PEACE...TREND 20 SCI/ADVSRY.
PAGE 16 G0322
R+D
INDUS
TEC/DEV
NUC/PWR

B62
KARNJAHAPRAKORN C.,MUNICIPAL GOVERNMENT IN THAILAND
AS AN INSTITUTION AND PROCESS OF SELF-GOVERNMENT.
THAILAND CULTURE FINAN EX/STRUC LEGIS PLAN CONTROL
GOV/REL EFFICIENCY ATTIT...POLICY 20. PAGE 29 G0578
LOC/G
MUNIC
ORD/FREE
ADMIN

B62
STOVER C.F.,THE GOVERNMENT OF SCIENCE (PAMPHLET).
USA+45 SOCIETY PROF/ORG EX/STRUC CREATE CONTROL
NUC/PWR WAR GOV/REL PEACE ORD/FREE 20. PAGE 53
G1041
PHIL/SCI
TEC/DEV
LAW
NAT/G

B62
US CONGRESS,COMMUNICATIONS SATELLITE LEGISLATION:
HEARINGS BEFORE COMM ON AERON AND SPACE SCIENCES ON
BILLS S2550 AND 2814. WOR+45 LAW VOL/ASSN PLAN
DIPLOM CONTROL OWN PEACE...NEW/IDEA CONGRESS NASA.
PAGE 56 G1110
SPACE
COM/IND
ADJUD
GOV/REL

L62
NEIBURG H.L.,"THE EISENHOWER AEC AND CONGRESS: A
STUDY IN EXECUTIVE-LEGISLATIVE RELATIONS." USA+45
NAT/G POL/PAR DELIB/GP EX/STRUC TOP/EX ADMIN EXEC
CHIEF
LEGIS
GOV/REL

LEAD ROUTINE PWR...POLICY COLD/WAR CONGRESS
PRESIDENT AEC. PAGE 41 G0816
NUC/PWR

S62
DAWSON R.H.,"CONGRESSIONAL INNOVATION AND
INTERVENTION IN DEFENSE POLICY: LEGISLATIVE
AUTHORIZATION OF WEAPONS SYSTEMS." CONSTN PLAN
ARMS/CONT GOV/REL EFFICIENCY PEACE NEW/LIB OLD/LIB.
PAGE 14 G0281
LEGIS
PWR
CONTROL
WEAPON

S62
DONNELLY D.,"THE POLITICS AND ADMINISTRATION OF
PLANNING." UK ROUTINE FEDERAL 20. PAGE 16 G0307
GOV/REL
EFFICIENCY
ADMIN
EX/STRUC

S62
MARTIN L.W.,"THE MARKET FOR STRATEGIC IDEAS IN
BRITAIN: THE 'SANDYS ERA'" UK ARMS/CONT WAR GOV/REL
OPTIMAL...POLICY DECISION GOV/COMP COLD/WAR
CMN/WLTH. PAGE 36 G0714
DIPLOM
COERCE
FORCES
PWR

B63
DALAND R.T.,PERSPECTIVES OF BRAZILIAN PUBLIC
ADMINISTRATION (VOL. I). BRAZIL LAW ECO/UNDEV
SCHOOL CHIEF TEC/DEV CONFER CONTROL GP/REL ATTIT
ROLE PWR...ANTHOL 20. PAGE 14 G0272
ADMIN
NAT/G
PLAN
GOV/REL

B63
DEAN A.L.,FEDERAL AGENCY APPROACHES TO FIELD
MANAGEMENT (PAMPHLET). R+D DELIB/GP EX/STRUC
PROB/SOLV GOV/REL...CLASSIF BIBLIOG 20 FAA NASA
DEPT/HEW POSTAL/SYS IRS. PAGE 15 G0287
ADMIN
MGT
NAT/G
OP/RES

B63
GREEN H.P.,GOVERNMENT OF THE ATOM. USA+45 LEGIS
PROB/SOLV ADMIN CONTROL PWR...POLICY DECISION 20
PRESIDENT CONGRESS. PAGE 22 G0443
GOV/REL
EX/STRUC
NUC/PWR
DELIB/GP

B63
HATHAWAY D.A.,GOVERNMENT AND AGRICULTURE: PUBLIC
POLICY IN A DEMOCRATIC SOCIETY. USA+45 LEGIS ADMIN
EXEC LOBBY REPRESENT PWR 20. PAGE 25 G0491
AGRI
GOV/REL
PROB/SOLV
EX/STRUC

B63
REED E.,CHALLENGES TO DEMOCRACY: THE NEXT TEN
YEARS. FUT USA+45 ECO/DEV DELIB/GP TEC/DEV CONFER
GOV/REL KNOWL ORD/FREE...MAJORIT IDEA/COMP ANTHOL
20. PAGE 46 G0909
POLICY
EDU/PROP
ECO/TAC
NAT/G

B63
SCHRADER R.,SCIENCE AND POLICY. WOR+45 ECO/DEV
ECO/UNDEV R+D FORCES PLAN DIPLOM GOV/REL TECHRACY
BIBLIOG. PAGE 50 G0976
TEC/DEV
NAT/G
POLICY
ADMIN

B63
US SENATE,DOCUMENTS ON INTERNATIONAL ASPECTS OF
EXPLORATION AND USE OF OUTER SPACE, 1954-62: STAFF
REPORT FOR COMM AERON SPACE SCI. USA+45 USSR LEGIS
LEAD CIVMIL/REL PEACE...POLICY INT/LAW ANTHOL 20
CONGRESS NASA KHRUSH/N. PAGE 59 G1162
SPACE
UTIL
GOV/REL
DIPLOM

B64
DUSCHA J.,ARMS, MONEY, AND POLITICS. USA+45 INDUS
POL/PAR ECO/TAC TAX DETER NUC/PWR WAR WEAPON
GOV/REL ATTIT...BIBLIOG/A 20 CONGRESS MONEY
DEPT/DEFEN. PAGE 17 G0326
NAT/G
FORCES
POLICY
BUDGET

B64
RIES J.C.,THE MANAGEMENT OF DEFENSE: ORGANIZATION
AND CONTROL OF THE US ARMED SERVICES. PROF/ORG
DELIB/GP EX/STRUC LEGIS GOV/REL PERS/REL CENTRAL
RATIONAL PWR...POLICY TREND GOV/COMP BIBLIOG.
PAGE 47 G0920
FORCES
ACT/RES
DECISION
CONTROL

B64
SCHOECK H.,CENTRAL PLANNING AND NEOMERCANTILISM.
L/A+17C UK WOR+45 BUDGET ECO/TAC PRICE CONTROL
GOV/REL UTOPIA 20. PAGE 49 G0974
PLAN
CENTRAL
NAT/G
POLICY

S64
UNRUH J.M.,"SCIENTIFIC INPUTS TO LEGISLATIVE
DECISION-MAKING (SUPPLEMENT)" USA+45 ACADEM NAT/G
PROVS GOV/REL GOV/COMP. PAGE 56 G1102
CREATE
DECISION
LEGIS
PARTIC

B65
INTERNATIONAL CITY MGRS ASSN,COUNCIL-MANAGER
GOVERNMENT, 1940-64: AN ANNOTATED BIBLIOGRAPHY.
USA+45 ADMIN GOV/REL ROLE...MGT 20. PAGE 28 G0549
BIBLIOG/A
MUNIC
CONSULT
PLAN

B65
LOWENSTEIN L.,GOVERNMENT RESOURCES AVAILABLE FOR   R+D
FOREIGN AFFAIRS RESEARCH. NAT/G DIPLOM GOV/REL.   ACADEM
PAGE 34 G0677   ACT/RES
                                                       BIBLIOG/A

B65
SCHEINMAN L.,ATOMIC ENERGY POLICY IN FRANCE UNDER   NUC/PWR
THE FOURTH REPUBLIC. FRANCE UK USA+45 ELITES   NAT/G
POL/PAR PLAN PROB/SOLV DIPLOM LEAD GOV/REL   DELIB/GP
...BIBLIOG 20 DEGAULLE/C. PAGE 49 G0962   POLICY

B65
US SENATE,US INTERNATIONAL SPACE PROGRAMS, 1959-65:   SPACE
STAFF REPORT FOR COMM ON AERONAUTICAL AND SPACE   DIPLOM
SCIENCES. WOR+45 VOL/ASSN CIVMIL/REL 20 CONGRESS   PLAN
NASA TREATY. PAGE 59 G1163   GOV/REL

B65
US SENATE COMM GOVT OPERATIONS,ORGANIZATION OF   ADMIN
FEDERAL EXECUTIVE DEPARTMENTS AND AGENCIES: REPORT   EX/STRUC
OF MARCH 23, 1965. USA+45 FORCES LEGIS DIPLOM   GOV/REL
ROUTINE CIVMIL/REL EFFICIENCY FEDERAL...MGT STAT.   ORG/CHARTS
PAGE 60 G1179

S65
BALDWIN H.,"SLOW-DOWN IN THE PENTAGON." USA+45   RECORD
CREATE PLAN GOV/REL CENTRAL COST EFFICIENCY PWR   R+D
...MGT MCNAMARA/R. PAGE 5 G0088   WEAPON
                                                       ADMIN

S65
FOX A.B.,"NATO AND CONGRESS." CONSTN DELIB/GP   CONTROL
EX/STRUC FORCES TOP/EX BUDGET NUC/PWR GOV/REL   DIPLOM
...GP/COMP CONGRESS NATO TREATY. PAGE 20 G0388

B66
US SENATE,POLICY PLANNING FOR AERONAUTICAL RESEARCH   SPACE
AND DEVELOPMENT: STAFF REPORT FOR COMM ON   CIVMIL/REL
AERONAUTICAL AND SPACE SCIENCES. USA+45 AIR   GOV/REL
DIST/IND PLAN...POLICY CHARTS 20 CONGRESS NASA.   R+D
PAGE 59 G1164

B66
WHITNAH D.R.,SAFER SKYWAYS. DIST/IND DELIB/GP   ADMIN
FORCES TOP/EX WORKER TEC/DEV ROUTINE WAR CIVMIL/REL   NAT/G
COST...TIME/SEQ 20 FAA CAB. PAGE 63 G1235   AIR
                                                       GOV/REL

N66
PRINCETON U INDUSTRIAL REL SEC,RECENT MATERIAL ON   BIBLIOG/A
COLLECTIVE BARGAINING IN GOVERNMENT (PAMPHLET NO.   BARGAIN
130). USA+45 ECO/DEV LABOR WORKER ECO/TAC GOV/REL   NAT/G
...MGT 20. PAGE 45 G0890   GP/REL

B67
DICKSON P.G.M.,THE FINANCIAL REVOLUTION IN ENGLAND.   ECO/DEV
UK NAT/G TEC/DEV ADMIN GOV/REL...SOC METH/CNCPT   FINAN
CHARTS GP/COMP BIBLIOG 17/18. PAGE 15 G0302   CAP/ISM
                                                       MGT

B67
EISENMENGER R.W.,THE DYNAMICS OF GROWTH IN NEW   ECO/DEV
ENGLAND'S ECONOMY, 1870-1964. USA+45 USA-45 ECO/TAC   AGRI
TAX PAY AUTOMAT GOV/REL ADJUST HABITAT...STAT   INDUS
19/20. PAGE 17 G0340   CAP/ISM

B67
HEADLEY J.C.,PESTICIDE PROBLEM: AN ECONOMIC   HABITAT
APPROACH TO PUBLIC POLICY. AGRI TEC/DEV GOV/REL   POLICY
COST ATTIT CHARTS. PAGE 25 G0498   BIO/SOC
                                                       CONTROL

B67
MOORE J.R.,THE ECONOMIC IMPACT OF THE TVA. AGRI   ECO/UNDEV
INDUS PLAN BARGAIN CONTROL REGION GOV/REL DEMAND   ECO/DEV
EFFICIENCY SOCISM 20 TVA. PAGE 40 G0780   NAT/G
                                                       CREATE

B67
UNIVERSAL REFERENCE SYSTEM,ADMINISTRATIVE   BIBLIOG/A
MANAGEMENT: PUBLIC AND PRIVATE BUREAUCRACY (VOLUME   MGT
IV). WOR+45 WOR-45 ECO/DEV LG/CO LOC/G PUB/INST   ADMIN
VOL/ASSN GOV/REL...COMPUT/IR GEN/METH. PAGE 56   NAT/G
G1096

B67
UNIVERSAL REFERENCE SYSTEM,ECONOMIC REGULATION,   BIBLIOG/A
BUSINESS, AND GOVERNMENT (VOLUME VIII). WOR+45   CONTROL
WOR-45 ECO/DEV ECO/UNDEV FINAN LABOR TEC/DEV   NAT/G
ECO/TAC INT/TRADE GOV/REL...POLICY COMPUT/IR.
PAGE 56 G1099

B67
UNIVERSAL REFERENCE SYSTEM,PUBLIC POLICY AND THE   BIBLIOG/A
MANAGEMENT OF SCIENCE (VOLUME IX). FUT SPACE WOR+45   POLICY

LAW NAT/G TEC/DEV CONTROL NUC/PWR GOV/REL   MGT
...COMPUT/IR GEN/METH. PAGE 56 G1100   PHIL/SCI

B67
US SENATE COMM AERO SPACE SCI,APOLLO ACCIDENT   PROB/SOLV
(PARTS 1-7). USA+45 DELIB/GP LEGIS...INT CHARTS   SPACE
NASA. PAGE 60 G1173   BUDGET
                                                       GOV/REL

B67
WOODRUFF W.,IMPACT OF WESTERN MAN. ECO/DEV INDUS   EUR+WWI
CREATE PLAN PROB/SOLV COLONIAL GOV/REL...CHARTS   MOD/EUR
GOV/COMP BIBLIOG 18/20. PAGE 64 G1256   CAP/ISM

L67
RUTH J.M.,"THE ADMINISTRATION OF WATER RESOURCES IN   EFFICIENCY
GUATEMALA." GUATEMALA L/A+17C DIST/IND LOC/G NAT/G   ECO/UNDEV
EX/STRUC ADMIN GOV/REL DEMAND EQUILIB WEALTH...GEOG   PLAN
MGT 20. PAGE 48 G0952   ACT/RES

S67
D'AMATO D.,"LEGAL ASPECTS OF THE FRENCH NUCLEAR   INT/LAW
TESTS." FRANCE WOR+45 ACT/RES COLONIAL RISK GOV/REL   DIPLOM
EQUILIB ORD/FREE PWR DECISION. PAGE 14 G0268   NUC/PWR
                                                       ADJUD

S67
GOBER J.L.,"FEDERALISM AT WORK." USA+45 NAT/G   MUNIC
CONSULT ACT/RES PLAN CONFER ADMIN LEAD PARTIC   TEC/DEV
FEDERAL ATTIT. PAGE 21 G0422   R+D
                                                       GOV/REL

N67
US SENATE COMM AERO SPACE SCI,AERONAUTICAL RESEARCH   DIST/IND
AND DEVELOPMENT POLICY; HEARINGS, COMM ON   SPACE
AERONAUTICAL AND SPACE SCIENCES...1967 (PAMPHLET).   NAT/G
R+D PROB/SOLV EXEC GOV/REL 20 DEPT/DEFEN FAA NASA   PLAN
CONGRESS. PAGE 60 G1174

GOVERNMENT.... LOC/G

GOVERNOR.... GOVERNOR; SEE ALSO PROVS, CHIEF, LEAD

B25
MATHEWS J.M.,AMERICAN STATE GOVERNMENT. USA-45   PROVS
LOC/G CHIEF EX/STRUC LEGIS ADJUD CONTROL CT/SYS   ADMIN
ROUTINE GOV/REL PWR 20 GOVERNOR. PAGE 37 G0721   FEDERAL
                                                       CONSTN

GOWING M. G0439

GP/COMP.... COMPARISON OF GROUPS

B54
ROSE A.M.,THEORY AND METHOD IN THE SOCIAL SCIENCES.   CONCPT
STRATA R+D NEIGH PARTIC...METH/CNCPT GP/COMP.   SOC
PAGE 47 G0934   VOL/ASSN
                                                       ROLE

B55
LIPPMAN W.,THE PUBLIC PHILOSOPHY. EX/STRUC TOP/EX   MAJORIT
LOBBY RATIONAL POPULISM...POLICY SOC CONCPT PREDICT   STRUCT
GP/COMP IDEA/COMP. PAGE 34 G0673   PWR
                                                       TOTALISM

B58
GAVIN J.M.,WAR AND PEACE IN THE SPACE AGE. SPACE   WAR
USA+45 USSR FORCES PLAN TEC/DEV BAL/PWR DIPLOM   DETER
ARMS/CONT WEAPON CIVMIL/REL...CHARTS GP/COMP 20   NUC/PWR
NATO COLD/WAR. PAGE 21 G0414   PEACE

B60
GRANICK D.,THE RED EXECUTIVE. COM USA+45 SOCIETY   PWR
ECO/DEV INDUS NAT/G POL/PAR EX/STRUC PLAN ECO/TAC   STRATA
EDU/PROP ADMIN EXEC ATTIT DRIVE...GP/COMP 20.   USSR
PAGE 22 G0440   ELITES

B60
WILLIAUS T.H.,AMERICANS AT WAR: THE DEVELOPMENT OF   FORCES
THE AMERICAN MILITARY SYSTEM. USA+45 USA-45   WAR
EDU/PROP LEAD REV...GP/COMP BIBLIOG/A 18/20   NAT/G
PRESIDENT. PAGE 63 G1244   POLICY

B63
TOMKINS S.S.,COMPUTER SIMULATION OF PERSONALITY.   COMPUTER
R+D TEC/DEV AUTOMAT FEEDBACK ANOMIE PERCEPT...STYLE   PERSON
PERS/TEST PREDICT COMPUT/IR GP/COMP. PAGE 55 G1075   SIMUL
                                                       PROG/TEAC

B64
RUSHING W.A.,THE PSYCHIATRIC PROFESSIONS. DOMIN   ATTIT
INGP/REL DRIVE RIGID/FLEX ROLE HEALTH PWR...POLICY   PUB/INST
GP/COMP. PAGE 48 G0947   PROF/ORG
                                                       BAL/PWR

COOPER A.C.,"R&D IS MORE EFFICIENT IN SMALL COMPANIES." USA+45 LG/CO SML/CO WEALTH...RECORD INT LAB/EXP 20. PAGE 13 G0255
S64
R+D
INDUS
CREATE
GP/COMP

FOX A.B.,"NATO AND CONGRESS." CONSTN DELIB/GP EX/STRUC FORCES TOP/EX BUDGET NUC/PWR GOV/REL ...GP/COMP CONGRESS NATO TREATY. PAGE 20 G0388
S65
CONTROL
DIPLOM

OECD DEVELOPMENT CENTRE,CATALOGUE OF SOCIAL AND ECONOMIC DEVELOPMENT INSTITUTES AND PROGRAMMES* RESEARCH. ACT/RES PLAN TEC/DEV EDU/PROP...SOC GP/COMP NAT/COMP. PAGE 43 G0836
B66
ECO/UNDEV
ECO/DEV
R+D
ACADEM

STREET D.,ORGANIZATION FOR TREATMENT. CLIENT PROVS PUB/INST PLAN CONTROL PARTIC REPRESENT ATTIT PWR ...POLICY BIBLIOG. PAGE 53 G1044
B66
GP/COMP
AGE/Y
ADMIN
VOL/ASSN

FLEMING W.G.,"AUTHORITY, EFFICIENCY, AND ROLE STRESS: PROBLEMS IN THE DEVELOPMENT OF EAST AFRICAN BUREAUCRACIES." AFR UGANDA STRUCT PROB/SOLV ROUTINE INGP/REL ROLE...MGT SOC GP/COMP GOV/COMP 20 TANGANYIKA AFRICA/E. PAGE 19 G0371
S66
DOMIN
EFFICIENCY
COLONIAL
ADMIN

BENNETT J.W.,HUTTERIAN BRETHREN; THE AGRICULTURAL ECONOMY AND SOCIAL ORGANIZATION OF A COMMUNAL PEOPLE. USA+45 SOCIETY FAM KIN TEC/DEV ADJUST...MGT AUD/VIS GP/COMP 20. PAGE 6 G0121
B67
SECT
AGRI
STRUCT
GP/REL

DICKSON P.G.M.,THE FINANCIAL REVOLUTION IN ENGLAND. UK NAT/G TEC/DEV ADMIN GOV/REL...SOC METH/CNCPT CHARTS GP/COMP BIBLIOG 17/18. PAGE 15 G0302
B67
ECO/DEV
FINAN
CAP/ISM
MGT

GP/REL....RELATIONS AMONG GROUPS

WEIGLEY R.F.,HISTORY OF THE UNITED STATES ARMY. USA+45 USA-45 SOCIETY NAT/G LEAD WAR GP/REL PWR ...SOC METH/COMP COLD/WAR. PAGE 62 G1222
N
FORCES
ADMIN
ROLE
CIVMIL/REL

ADVANCED MANAGEMENT. INDUS EX/STRUC WORKER OP/RES ...DECISION BIBLIOG/A 20. PAGE 1 G0003
N
MGT
ADMIN
LABOR
GP/REL

JOURNAL OF PUBLIC ADMINISTRATION: JOURNAL OF THE ROYAL INSTITUTE OF PUBLIC ADMINISTRATION. UK PLAN GP/REL INGP/REL 20. PAGE 1 G0006
N
BIBLIOG/A
ADMIN
NAT/G
MGT

MARKETING INFORMATION GUIDE. USA+45 ECO/DEV FINAN ADMIN GP/REL. PAGE 1 G0008
N
BIBLIOG/A
DIST/IND
MARKET
ECO/TAC

PERSONNEL. USA+45 LAW LABOR LG/CO WORKER CREATE GOV/REL PERS/REL ATTIT WEALTH. PAGE 1 G0010
N
BIBLIOG/A
ADMIN
MGT
GP/REL

PRINCETON UNIVERSITY,SELECTED REFERENCES: INDUSTRIAL RELATIONS SECTION. USA+45 EX/STRUC WORKER TEC/DEV...MGT 20. PAGE 45 G0892
N
BIBLIOG/A
LABOR
INDUS
GP/REL

RAND SCHOOL OF SOCIAL SCIENCE,INDEX TO LABOR ARTICLES. ECO/DEV INT/ORG LEGIS DIPLOM GP/REL ...NAT/COMP 20. PAGE 46 G0900
N
BIBLIOG
LABOR
MGT
ADJUD

FOLSOM M.B.,BETTER MANAGEMENT OF THE PUBLIC'S BUSINESS (PAMPHLET). USA+45 DELIB/GP PAY CONFER CONTROL REGION GP/REL...METH/COMP ANTHOL 20. PAGE 19 G0377
N19
ADMIN
NAT/G
MGT
PROB/SOLV

GINZBERG E.,MANPOWER FOR GOVERNMENT (PAMPHLET). USA+45 FORCES PLAN PROB/SOLV PAY EDU/PROP ADMIN GP/REL COST...MGT PREDICT TREND 20 CIVIL/SERV.
N19
WORKER
CONSULT
NAT/G

PAGE 21 G0418   LOC/G

DEWEY J.,THE QUEST FOR CERTAINTY. GP/REL RATIONAL UTOPIA ATTIT MORAL ORD/FREE PWR...MYTH HIST/WRIT. PAGE 15 G0301
B29
PHIL/SCI
PERSON
PERCEPT
KNOWL

HAWLEY A.H.,"ECOLOGY AND HUMAN ECOLOGY" WOR+45 INTELL ACADEM PLAN GP/REL ADJUST PERSON...PHIL/SCI SOC METH/CNCPT METH 20. PAGE 25 G0493
S44
HABITAT
GEOG
GEN/LAWS
METH/COMP

MAYO E.,THE SOCIAL PROBLEMS OF AN INDUSTRIAL CIVILIZATION. USA+45 SOCIETY LABOR CROWD PERS/REL LAISSEZ. PAGE 37 G0725
B45
INDUS
GP/REL
MGT
WORKER

CHILDS J.R.,AMERICAN FOREIGN SERVICE. USA+45 SOCIETY NAT/G ROUTINE GOV/REL 20 DEPT/STATE CIVIL/SERV. PAGE 12 G0227
B48
DIPLOM
ADMIN
GP/REL

KILE O.M.,THE FARM BUREAU MOVEMENT: THE FARM BUREAU THROUGH THREE DECADES. NAT/G LEGIS LEAD LOBBY GP/REL INCOME POLICY. PAGE 30 G0596
B48
AGRI
STRUCT
VOL/ASSN
DOMIN

STEWART I.,ORGANIZING SCIENTIFIC RESEARCH FOR WAR: ADMINISTRATIVE HISTORY OF OFFICE OF SCIENTIFIC RESEARCH AND DEVELOPMENT. USA-45 INTELL R+D LABOR WORKER CREATE BUDGET WEAPON CIVMIL/REL GP/REL EFFICIENCY...POLICY 20. PAGE 53 G1036
B48
DELIB/GP
ADMIN
WAR
TEC/DEV

COCH L.,"OVERCOMING RESISTANCE TO CHANGE" (BMR)" USA+45 CONSULT ADMIN ROUTINE GP/REL EFFICIENCY PRODUC PERCEPT SKILL...CHARTS SOC/EXP 20. PAGE 12 G0236
S48
WORKER
OP/RES
PROC/MFG
RIGID/FLEX

MAASS A.,MUDDY WATERS: THE ARMY ENGINEERS AND THE NATIONS RIVERS. USA-45 PROF/ORG CONSULT LEGIS ADMIN EXEC ROLE PWR...SOC PRESIDENT 20. PAGE 35 G0682
B51
FORCES
GP/REL
LOBBY
CONSTRUC

HOMANS G.C.,"THE WESTERN ELECTRIC RESEARCHES" IN S. HOSLETT, ED., HUMAN FACTORS IN MANAGEMENT (BMR)" ACT/RES GP/REL HAPPINESS PRODUC DRIVE...MGT OBS 20. PAGE 27 G0526
C51
OP/RES
EFFICIENCY
SOC/EXP
WORKER

CALLOT E.,LA SOCIETE ET SON ENVIRONNEMENT: ESSAI SUR LES PRINCIPES DES SCIENCES SOCIALES. GP/REL ADJUST CONSEN ISOLAT HABITAT PERCEPT PERSON ...BIBLIOG SOC/INTEG 20. PAGE 10 G0205
B52
SOCIETY
PHIL/SCI
CULTURE

SAYLES L.R.,THE LOCAL UNION. CONSTN CULTURE DELIB/GP PARTIC CHOOSE GP/REL INGP/REL ATTIT ROLE ...MAJORIT DECISION MGT. PAGE 49 G0958
B53
LABOR
LEAD
ADJUD
ROUTINE

PERKINS J.A.,"ADMINISTRATION OF THE NATIONAL SECURITY PROGRAM." USA+45 EX/STRUC FORCES ADMIN CIVMIL/REL ORD/FREE 20. PAGE 44 G0868
S53
CONTROL
GP/REL
REPRESENT
PROB/SOLV

SPROTT W.J.H.,SCIENCE AND SOCIAL ACTION. STRUCT ACT/RES CRIME GP/REL INGP/REL ANOMIE...PSY SOC/INTEG 19/20. PAGE 52 G1027
B54
SOC
CULTURE
PHIL/SCI

HOOPES T.,"CIVILIAN-MILITARY BALANCE." USA+45 CHIEF FORCES PLAN CONTROL WAR GOV/REL GP/REL INGP/REL ...POLICY 19/20. PAGE 27 G0527
S54
CIVMIL/REL
LEAD
PWR
NAT/G

GOULDNER A.W.,"PATTERNS OF INDUSTRIAL BUREAUCRACY." GP/REL CONSEN ATTIT DRIVE...BIBLIOG 20. PAGE 22 G0438
C54
ADMIN
INDUS
OP/RES
WORKER

SKINNER B.F.,"FREEDOM AND THE CONTROL OF MEN" (BMR)" FUT WOR+45 CONTROL CHOOSE GP/REL ATTIT MORAL PWR POPULISM...POLICY 20. PAGE 51 G1008
S55
ORD/FREE
TEC/DEV
PHIL/SCI
INTELL

ATOMIC INDUSTRIAL FORUM,PUBLIC RELATIONS FOR THE ATOMIC INDUSTRY. WOR+45 PLAN PROB/SOLV EDU/PROP PRESS CONFER...AUD/VIS ANTHOL 20. PAGE 4 G0077
NUC/PWR
INDUS
GP/REL
ATTIT
B56

EASTON D.,"LIMITS OF THE EQUILIBRIUM MODEL IN SOCIAL RESEARCH." STRUCT GP/REL PWR...PHIL/SCI CLASSIF. PAGE 17 G0330
METH/CNCPT
GEN/METH
R+D
QUANT
S56

DAVIS K.C.,ADMINISTRATIVE LAW TREATISE (VOLS. I AND IV). NAT/G JUDGE PROB/SOLV ADJUD GP/REL 20 SUPREME/CT. PAGE 14 G0278
ADMIN
JURID
CT/SYS
EX/STRUC
B58

DUBIN R.,THE WORLD OF WORK: INDUSTRIAL SOCIETY AND HUMAN RELATIONS. MARKET PROC/MFG LABOR TEC/DEV CAP/ISM AUTOMAT TASK GP/REL EFFICIENCY...CONCPT CHARTS BIBLIOG 20. PAGE 16 G0317
WORKER
ECO/TAC
PRODUC
DRIVE
B58

KEISER N.F.,"PUBLIC RESPONSIBILITY AND FEDERAL ADVISORY GROUPS: A CASE STUDY." NAT/G ADMIN CONTROL LOBBY...POLICY 20. PAGE 30 G0590
REPRESENT
ELITES
GP/REL
EX/STRUC
S58

DAHRENDORF R.,CLASS AND CLASS CONFLICT IN INDUSTRIAL SOCIETY. LABOR NAT/G COERCE ROLE PLURISM ...POLICY MGT CONCPT CLASSIF. PAGE 14 G0271
VOL/ASSN
STRUCT
SOC
GP/REL
B59

TARKOWSKI Z.M.,"SCIENTISTS VERSUS ADMINISTRATORS: AN APPROACH TOWARD ACHIEVING GREATER UNDERSTANDING." UK EXEC EFFICIENCY 20. PAGE 53 G1052
INGP/REL
GP/REL
ADMIN
EX/STRUC
L59

BENDIX R.,"INDUSTRIALIZATION, IDEOLOGIES, AND SOCIAL STRUCTURE" (BMR)" UK USA-45 USSR STRUCT WORKER GP/REL EFFICIENCY...IDEA/COMP 20. PAGE 6 G0117
INDUS
ATTIT
MGT
ADMIN
S59

MCGREGOR D.,THE HUMAN SIDE OF ENTERPRISE. USA+45 LEAD ROUTINE GP/REL INGP/REL...CONCPT GEN/LAWS 20. PAGE 38 G0741
MGT
ATTIT
SKILL
EDU/PROP
B60

TAYLOR M.G.,"THE ROLE OF THE MEDICAL PROFESSION IN THE FORMULATION AND EXECUTION OF PUBLIC POLICY" (BMR)" CANADA NAT/G CONSULT ADMIN REPRESENT GP/REL ROLE SOVEREIGN...DECISION 20 CMA. PAGE 54 G1058
PROF/ORG
HEALTH
LOBBY
POLICY
S60

CHAPPLE E.D.,THE MEASURE OF MANAGEMENT. USA+45 WORKER ADMIN GP/REL EFFICIENCY...DECISION ORG/CHARTS SIMUL 20. PAGE 11 G0221
MGT
OP/RES
PLAN
METH/CNCPT
B61

MURPHY E.F.,WATER PURITY: A STUDY IN LEGAL CONTROL OF NATURAL RESOURCES. LOC/G ACT/RES PLAN TEC/DEV LOBBY GP/REL COST ATTIT HEALTH ORD/FREE...HEAL JURID 20 WISCONSIN WATER. PAGE 40 G0797
SEA
LAW
PROVS
CONTROL
B61

SMITH H.H.,THE CITIZEN'S GUIDE TO PLANNING. USA+45 LAW SCHOOL CREATE PROB/SOLV EDU/PROP GP/REL ROLE 20 URBAN/RNWL OPEN/SPACE. PAGE 52 G1015
MUNIC
PLAN
DELIB/GP
CONSULT
B61

THOMPSON V.A.,"HIERARACHY, SPECIALIZATION, AND ORGANIZATIONAL CONFLICT" (BMR)" WOR+45 STRATA STRUCT WORKER TEC/DEV GP/REL INGP/REL ATTIT AUTHORIT 20 BUREAUCRCY. PAGE 54 G1069
PERS/REL
PROB/SOLV
ADMIN
EX/STRUC
L61

BAKER G.W.,BEHAVIORAL SCIENCE AND CIVIL DEFENSE. USA+45 PROB/SOLV ADMIN GP/REL INGP/REL PERS/REL ANOMIE DRIVE PERSON...DECISION MGT SOC 20 CIV/DEFENS. PAGE 4 G0085
NUC/PWR
WAR
POLICY
ACT/RES
B62

BENNIS W.G.,THE PLANNING OF CHANGE: READINGS IN THE APPLIED BEHAVIORAL SCIENCES. CULTURE STRATA STRUCT PLAN GP/REL...SOC T. PAGE 6 G0123
PROB/SOLV
CREATE
ACT/RES
OP/RES
B62

PERRE J.,LES MUTATIONS DE LA GUERRE MODERNE: DE LA REVOLUTION FRANCAISE A LA REVOLUTION NUCLEAIRE. DIPLOM ARMS/CONT DEATH REV WEAPON GP/REL PEACE ATTIT...STAT PREDICT BIBLIOG 18/20 WWI. PAGE 44 G0870
WAR
FORCES
NUC/PWR
B62

STORER N.W.,"SOME SOCIOLOGICAL ASPECTS OF FEDERAL SCIENCE POLICY." USA+45 INTELL PUB/INST PLAN GP/REL PERS/REL DRIVE PERSON ROLE...PSY SOC SIMUL 20 NIH NSF. PAGE 53 G1040
POLICY
CREATE
NAT/G
ALL/VALS
S62

ACKOFF R.L.,A MANAGER'S GUIDE TO OPERATIONS RESEARCH. STRUCT INDUS PROB/SOLV ROUTINE 20. PAGE 2 G0028
OP/RES
MGT
GP/REL
ADMIN
B63

DALAND R.T.,PERSPECTIVES OF BRAZILIAN PUBLIC ADMINISTRATION (VOL. I). BRAZIL LAW ECO/UNDEV SCHOOL CHIEF TEC/DEV CONFER CONTROL GP/REL ATTIT ROLE PWR...ANTHOL 20. PAGE 14 G0272
ADMIN
NAT/G
PLAN
GOV/REL
B63

KORNHAUSER W.,SCIENTISTS IN INDUSTRY: CONFLICT AND ACCOMMODATION. USA+45 R+D LG/CO NAT/G TEC/DEV CONTROL ADJUST ATTIT...MGT STAT INT BIBLIOG 20. PAGE 31 G0614
CREATE
INDUS
PROF/ORG
GP/REL
B63

OTTOSON H.W.,LAND USE POLICY AND PROBLEMS IN THE UNITED STATES. USA+45 USA-45 LAW AGRI INDUS NAT/G GP/REL...CHARTS ANTHOL 19/20 HOMEST/ACT. PAGE 43 G0851
PROB/SOLV
UTIL
HABITAT
POLICY
B63

RAUDSEPP E.,MANAGING CREATIVE SCIENTISTS AND ENGINEERS. USA+45 ECO/DEV LG/CO GP/REL PERS/REL PRODUC. PAGE 46 G0906
MGT
CREATE
R+D
ECO/TAC
B63

THORELLI H.B.,INTOP: INTERNATIONAL OPERATIONS SIMULATION: PLAYER'S MANUAL. BRAZIL FINAN OP/RES ADMIN GP/REL INGP/REL PRODUC PERCEPT...DECISION MGT EEC. PAGE 54 G1073
GAME
INT/TRADE
EDU/PROP
LG/CO
B63

BLOUSTEIN E.J.,NUCLEAR ENERGY, PUBLIC POLICY, AND THE LAW. USA+45 NAT/G ADJUD ADMIN GP/REL OWN PEACE ATTIT HEALTH...ANTHOL 20. PAGE 7 G0144
TEC/DEV
LAW
POLICY
NUC/PWR
B64

EDELMAN M.,THE SYMBOLIC USES OF POWER. USA+45 EX/STRUC CONTROL GP/REL INGP/REL...MGT T. PAGE 17 G0333
CLIENT
PWR
EXEC
ELITES
B64

MASTERS N.A.,STATE POLITICS AND THE PUBLIC SCHOOLS. STRUCT FINAN ADMIN LOBBY GP/REL PWR BIBLIOG. PAGE 36 G0720
EDU/PROP
PROVS
DOMIN
B64

WHEELER-BENNETT J.W.,THE NEMESIS OF POWER (2ND ED.). EUR+WWI GERMANY TOP/EX TEC/DEV ADMIN WAR PERS/REL RIGID/FLEX ROLE ORD/FREE PWR FASCISM 20 HITLER/A. PAGE 63 G1231
FORCES
NAT/G
GP/REL
STRUCT
B64

"FURTHER READING." INDIA PAKISTAN SECT WAR PEACE ATTIT...POLICY 20. PAGE 1 G0018
BIBLIOG
GP/REL
DIPLOM
NAT/G
S64

PLATT J.R.,"RESEARCH AND DEVELOPMENT FOR SOCIAL PROBLEMS." INTELL SOCIETY PROB/SOLV GP/REL ATTIT ALL/VALS CONT/OBS. PAGE 45 G0880
R+D
ACT/RES
PLAN
SOC
S64

ALLEN S.,LETTER TO A CONSERVATIVE. SOCIETY NAT/G DIPLOM EDU/PROP NUC/PWR GP/REL ATTIT MORAL ...MAJORIT CONCPT 20. PAGE 2 G0044
ORD/FREE
MARXISM
POLICY
LAISSEZ
B65

BEAUFRE A.,AN INTRODUCTION TO STRATEGY, WITH PARTICULAR REFERENCE TO PROBLEMS OF DEFENSE, POLITICS, ECONOMICS IN THE NUCLEAR AGE. WOR+45 FORCES DIPLOM DETER CIVMIL/REL GP/REL...NEW/IDEA
PLAN
NUC/PWR
WEAPON
DECISION
B65

IDEA/COMP 20. PAGE 6 G0111

B65
BENJAMIN A.C.,SCIENCE, TECHNOLOGY, AND HUMAN   PHIL/SCI
VALUES. WOR+45 SECT EDU/PROP GP/REL ATTIT...TECHNIC CREATE
LING IDEA/COMP WORSHIP 20. PAGE 6 G0118   ROLE
                                                    SOCIETY

B65
CARPER E.T.,REORGANIZATION OF THE U.S. PUBLIC   HEAL
HEALTH SERVICE. FUT USA+45 INTELL R+D LOBBY GP/REL   PLAN
INGP/REL PERS/REL RIGID/FLEX ROLE HEALTH...PHIL/SCI NAT/G
20 CONGRESS PHS. PAGE 11 G0213   OP/RES

B65
LAPP R.E.,THE NEW PRIESTHOOD; THE SCIENTIFIC ELITE   TEC/DEV
AND THE USES OF POWER. USA+45 ELITES INTELL SOCIETY TECHRACY
R+D NAT/G CHIEF LEGIS CIVMIL/REL GP/REL PWR 20   CONTROL
PRESIDENT CONGRESS. PAGE 32 G0635   POPULISM

B65
SMITH E.A.,SOCIAL WELFARE: PRINCIPLES AND CONCEPTS. CONCPT
STRATA STRUCT CONSULT WORKER ACT/RES CREATE PLAN   SOC/WK
TEC/DEV ROUTINE GP/REL UTOPIA...SOC 20. PAGE 51   RECEIVE
G1014   ORD/FREE

B65
US SENATE COMM AERO SPACE SCI,NATIONAL SPACE GOALS   SPACE
FOR THE POST-APOLLO PERIOD. USA+45 CONSULT DELIB/GP FUT
TEC/DEV BUDGET GP/REL ATTIT...CHARTS IDEA/COMP TIME R+D
20 DEPT/DEFEN NASA CONGRESS. PAGE 59 G1166   LEGIS

B65
US SENATE COMM AERO SPACE SCI,INTERNATIONAL   DIPLOM
COOPERATION AND ORGANIZATION FOR OUTER SPACE. FUT   SPACE
USA+45 WOR+45 PROF/ORG VOL/ASSN CONSULT DELIB/GP   P+D
PLAN TEC/DEV ARMS/CONT GP/REL PEACE 20 UN NASA.   NAT/G
PAGE 59 G1167

C65
SCHWEBEL M.,"BEHAVIORAL SCIENCE AND HUMAN   PEACE
SURVIVAL." FORCES ARMS/CONT COERCE NUC/PWR WAR   ACT/RES
GP/REL NAT/LISM PERCEPT...POLICY PSY ANTHOL   DIPLOM
BIBLIOG/A 20 COLD/WAR. PAGE 50 G0984   HEAL

B66
LINDFORS G.V.,INTERCOLLEGIATE BIBLIOGRAPHY; CASES   BIBLIOG/A
IN BUSINESS ADMINISTRATION (VOL. X). FINAN MARKET   ADMIN
LABOR CONSULT PLAN GP/REL PRODUC 20. PAGE 34 G0668   MGT
                                                    OP/RES

B66
MILLAR R.,THE NEW CLASSES. UK ELITES SOCIETY INDUS   STRUCT
AUTOMAT GP/REL SOC/INTEG 20 INDUS/REV. PAGE 39   STRATA
G0770   TEC/DEV
                                                    CREATE

B66
POLLARD W.G.,ATOMIC ENERGY AND SOUTHERN SCIENCE.   NUC/PWR
USA+45 HEALTH. PAGE 45 G0883   GP/REL
                                                    PHIL/SCI
                                                    CREATE

B66
PRINCETON U INDUSTRIAL REL SEC,THE FEDERAL   BIBLIOG/A
GOVERNMENT AND THE UNIVERSITY: SUPPORT FOR SOCIAL   NAT/G
SCIENCE RESEARCH AND THE IMPACT OF PROJECT CAMELOT. ACADEM
USA+45 ACT/RES CONTROL GP/REL PWR...POLICY 20.   PLAN
PAGE 45 G0889

B66
US BUREAU OF THE BUDGET,THE ADMINISTRATION OF   ACT/RES
GOVERNMENT SUPPORTED RESEARCH AT UNIVERSITIES   NAT/G
(PAMPHLET). USA+45 CONSULT TOP/EX ADMIN INCOME   ACADEM
WEALTH...MGT PHIL/SCI INT. PAGE 56 G1108   GP/REL

B66
US DEPARTMENT OF LABOR,TECHNOLOGICAL TRENDS IN   TEC/DEV
MAJOR AMERICAN INDUSTRIES. USA+45 R+D LABOR GP/REL   INDUS
PRODUC...MGT BIBLIOG 20. PAGE 57 G1120   TREND
                                                    AUTOMAT

S66
GREENBERG D.S.,"THE SCIENTIFIC PORK BARREL." USA+45 R+D
ECO/DEV PUB/INST CHIEF LEGIS BUDGET GIVE GP/REL PWR NAT/G
WEALTH 20. PAGE 23 G0445   ACADEM
                                                    ATTIT

S66
SIMON R.,"THE STATE OF PUBLIC RELATIONS SCHOLARLY   ACADEM
RESEARCH." TEC/DEV TASK MAJORITY PRODUC...TREND   CREATE
CHARTS BIBLIOG 20. PAGE 51 G1000   STAT
                                                    GP/REL

N66
PRINCETON U INDUSTRIAL REL SEC,RECENT MATERIAL ON   BIBLIOG/A

COLLECTIVE BARGAINING IN GOVERNMENT (PAMPHLET NO.   BARGAIN
130). USA+45 ECO/DEV LABOR WORKER ECO/TAC GOV/REL   NAT/G
...MGT 20. PAGE 45 G0890   GP/REL

B67
BENNETT J.W.,HUTTERIAN BRETHREN; THE AGRICULTURAL   SECT
ECONOMY AND SOCIAL ORGANIZATION OF A COMMUNAL   AGRI
PEOPLE. USA+45 SOCIETY FAM KIN TEC/DEV ADJUST...MGT STRUCT
AUD/VIS GP/COMP 20. PAGE 6 G0121   GP/REL

B67
BUDER S.,PULLMAN: AN EXPERIMENT IN INDUSTRIAL ORDER DIST/IND
AND COMMUNITY PLANNING, 1880-1930. USA-45 SOCIETY   INDUS
LABOR LG/CO CREATE PROB/SOLV CONTROL GP/REL   MUNIC
EFFICIENCY ATTIT...MGT BIBLIOG 19/20 PULLMAN.   PLAN
PAGE 9 G0184

B67
COLEMAN J.R.,THE CHANGING AMERICAN ECONOMY. USA+45   BUDGET
AGRI FINAN LABOR FOR/AID INT/TRADE AUTOMAT GP/REL   ECO/TAC
INGP/REL ANTHOL. PAGE 13 G0243   ECO/DEV
                                                    WEALTH

B67
COLM G.,THE ECONOMY OF THE AMERICAN PEOPLE. USA+45   ECO/TAC
ECO/DEV FINAN WORKER INT/TRADE AUTOMAT GP/REL.   PRODUC
PAGE 13 G0244   TREND
                                                    TEC/DEV

B67
GROSSMAN G.,ECONOMIC SYSTEMS. USA+45 USA-45 USSR   ECO/DEV
YUGOSLAVIA WORKER CAP/ISM PRICE GP/REL EQUILIB   PLAN
WEALTH MARXISM SOCISM...MGT METH/COMP 19/20.   TEC/DEV
PAGE 23 G0456   DEMAND

B67
HOROWITZ I.L.,THE RISE AND FALL OF PROJECT CAMELOT: NAT/G
STUDIES IN THE RELATIONSHIP BETWEEN SOCIAL SCIENCE   ACADEM
AND PRACTICAL POLITICS. USA+45 WOR+45 CULTURE   ACT/RES
FORCES LEGIS EXEC CIVMIL/REL KNOWL...POLICY SOC   GP/REL
METH/CNCPT 20. PAGE 27 G0529

B67
MCLAUGHLIN M.R.,RELIGIOUS EDUCATION AND THE STATE: SECT
DEMOCRACY FINDS A WAY. CANADA EUR+WWI GP/REL   NAT/G
POPULISM...CATH NAT/COMP 20 AUSTRAL. PAGE 38 G0745   EDU/PROP
                                                    POLICY

B67
NELSON R.R.,TECHNOLOGY, ECONOMIC GROWTH, AND PUBLIC R+D
POLICY. USA+45 PLAN GP/REL UTIL KNOWL...POLICY   CONSULT
PHIL/SCI CHARTS BIBLIOG 20. PAGE 41 G0817   CREATE
                                                    ACT/RES

B67
NORTHRUP H.R.,RESTRICTIVE LABOR PRACTICES IN THE   DIST/IND
SUPERMARKET INDUSTRY. USA+45 INDUS WORKER TEC/DEV   MARKET
BARGAIN PAY CONTROL GP/REL COST...STAT CHARTS NLRB. LABOR
PAGE 42 G0827   MGT

B67
RIDKER R.G.,ECONOMIC COSTS OF AIR POLLUTION*   OP/RES
STUDIES IN MEASUREMENT. R+D MUNIC GP/REL KNOWL   HABITAT
...OBS 20. PAGE 47 G0919   PHIL/SCI

B67
WARNER W.L.,THE EMERGENT AMERICAN SOCIETY VOL I,   ANTHOL
LARGE-SCALE ORGANIZATIONS. USA+45 USA-45 ACADEM   NAT/G
PROF/ORG SCHOOL SECT EX/STRUC TEC/DEV GP/REL   LABOR
...TREND CHARTS. PAGE 62 G1215   LG/CO

B67
ZUCKERMAN S.,SCIENTISTS AND WAR. ELITES INDUS   R+D
DIPLOM CENTRAL EFFICIENCY KNOWL 20. PAGE 65 G1271   CONSULT
                                                    ACT/RES
                                                    GP/REL

S67
BENN W.,"TECHNOLOGY HAS AN INEXORABLE EFFECT." FUT   R+D
UK ECO/DEV INT/ORG CONSULT PLAN EDU/PROP ADMIN LEAD LG/CO
GP/REL PRODUC...INT 20 EEC. PAGE 6 G0119   TEC/DEV
                                                    INDUS

S67
CARR E.H.,"REVOLUTION FROM ABOVE." USSR STRATA   AGRI
FINAN INDUS NAT/G DOMIN LEAD GP/REL INGP/REL OWN   POLICY
PRODUC PWR 20 STALIN/J. PAGE 11 G0214   COM
                                                    EFFICIENCY

S67
FRIED M.,"FUNCTIONS OF THE WORKING CLASS COMMUNITY   CLASSIF
IN MODERN URBAN SOCIETY* IMPLICATIONS FOR FORCED   WORKER
RELOCATION." USA+45 INDUS R+D NEIGH PLAN TEC/DEV   MUNIC
PARTIC GP/REL ATTIT...SOC STAT CHARTS. PAGE 20   ADJUST
G0393

S67
GOLDSTEIN W.,"THE SCIENCE ESTABLISHMENT AND ITS   CREATE
POLITICAL CONTROL." WOR+45 SOCIETY GP/REL RATIONAL   ADJUST
ORD/FREE. PAGE 22 G0430   CONTROL

S67
HOFFER J.R.,"RELATIONSHIP OF NATURAL AND SOCIAL   PROB/SOLV
SCIENCES TO SOCIAL PROBLEMS AND CONTRIBUTION OF...   SOCIETY
SCIENTISTS TO SOLUTIONS." USA+45 COMPUTER TEC/DEV   INTELL
GP/REL KNOWL...SOC TREND. PAGE 26 G0521   ACT/RES

S67
LA PORTE T.,"DIFFUSION AND DISCONTINUITY IN   INTELL
SCIENCE, TECHNOLOGY AND PUBLIC AFFAIRS: RESULTS OF   ADMIN
A SEARCH IN THE FIELD." USA+45 ACT/RES TEC/DEV   ACADEM
PERS/REL ATTIT PHIL/SCI. PAGE 32 G0628   GP/REL

S67
MEHTA A.,"INDIA* POVERTY AND CHANGE." STRATA INDUS   INDIA
CREATE ECO/TAC FOR/AID NEUTRAL GP/REL ADJUST INCOME   SOCIETY
...NEW/IDEA 20. PAGE 38 G0751   ECO/UNDEV
                                                        TEC/DEV

S67
SINGH B.,"ITALIAN EXPERIENCE IN REGIONAL ECONOMIC   ECO/UNDEV
DEVELOPMENT AND LESSONS FOR OTHER COUNTRIES."   PLAN
EUR+WWI ITALY INDUS NAT/G ACT/RES REGION GP/REL   ECO/TAC
EFFICIENCY EQUILIB PRODUC WEALTH. PAGE 51 G1007   CONTROL

S67
STYCOS J.M.,"POLITICS AND POPULATION CONTROL IN   PLAN
LATIN AMERICA." USA+45 FAM NAT/G GP/REL AGE/C ATTIT   CENSUS
CATHISM MARXISM...POLICY UN WHO. PAGE 53 G1045   CONTROL
                                                        L/A+17C

S67
WEINBERG A.M.,"CAN TECHNOLOGY REPLACE SOCIAL   TEC/DEV
ENGINEERING?" SPACE USA+45 SOCIETY ACADEM GP/REL.   ACT/RES
PAGE 62 G1224   PROB/SOLV
                                                        INTELL

N67
PRINCETON U INDUSTRIAL REL SEC,COLLECTIVE   BIBLIOG/A
BARGAINING IN THE PUBLIC SCHOOLS (PAMPHLET NO. 33).   SCHOOL
USA+45 LABOR PROB/SOLV PWR MGT. PAGE 45 G0891   BARGAIN
                                                        GP/REL

S68
BARAGWANATH L.E.,"SCIENTIFIC CO-OPERATION BETWEEN   R+D
THE UNIVERSITIES AND INDUSTRY - A RESEARCH NOTE."   ACADEM
UK LG/CO CREATE TEC/DEV EDU/PROP ATTIT...PHIL/SCI   INDUS
STAT QU 20. PAGE 5 G0090   GP/REL

GRAFT....SEE TRIBUTE

GRAND/JURY....GRAND JURIES

GRANGE....GRANGE AND GRANGERS

GRANICK D. G0440,G0441

GRANT/US....PRESIDENT ULYSSES S. GRANT

GRANTS....SEE GIVE+FOR/AID

GRAPHIC PRESENTATION....SEE CHARTS

GRAVES J. G0796

GRAVES R.L. G1072,G1073

GRAVIER J.F. G0442

GREAT BRITAIN....SEE UK

GREAT/SOC....GREAT SOCIETY

S67
BULMER-THOMAS I.,"SO, ON TO THE GREAT SOCIETY." FUT   PHIL/SCI
UNIV TEC/DEV BAL/PWR WAR BIO/SOC KNOWL...ART/METH   SOCIETY
SOC PREDICT TREND WORSHIP 20 GREAT/SOC. PAGE 9   CREATE
G0185

GRECO/ROMN....GRECO-ROMAN CIVILIZATION

GREECE....MODERN GREECE

B65
OECD,THE MEDITERRANEAN REGIONAL PROJECT: GREECE;   EDU/PROP
EDUCATION AND DEVELOPMENT. FUT GREECE SOCIETY AGRI   SCHOOL
FINAN NAT/G PROF/ORG WORKER PLAN PROB/SOLV ADMIN   ACADEM
DEMAND ATTIT 20 OECD. PAGE 42 G0834   ECO/UNDEV

GREECE/ANC....ANCIENT GREECE

GREEN H.P. G0443

GREEN P. G0444

GREEN/TH....T.H. GREEN

B28
BARKER E.,POLITICAL THOUGHT IN ENGLAND: FROM   INTELL
HERBERT SPENCER TO THE PRESENT DAY. UK ALL/IDEOS   GEN/LAWS
...PHIL/SCI 19/20 SPENCER/H GREEN/TH BENTHAM/J   IDEA/COMP
MAITLAND/F. PAGE 5 G0094

GREENBACK....GREENBACK PARTY

GREENBERG D.S. G0445

GREENFIELD K.R. G0446

GREENWICH VILLAGE....SEE GRNWCH/VIL

GREENWICH....GREENWICH, ENGLAND

GREGG P.M. G0447

GRENADA....GRENADA (WEST INDIES)

GRENIEWSKI H. G0448

GRENVILLES....GRENVILLES - ENGLISH FAMILY; SEE ALSO UK

GRESHAM-YANG TREATY....SEE GRESHMYANG

GRESHAM'S LAW....SEE GRESHM/LAW

GRESHM/LAW....GRESHAM'S LAW

GRESHMYANG....GRESHAM-YANG TREATY

GRETTON P. G0449

GRIFFITH E.S. G0450,G0451

GRIFFITH S.B. G0452

GRIFFITHS F. G0139,G0143,G0453

GRNWCH/VIL....GREENWICH VILLAGE

GRODZINS M. G0454

GROSS NATIONAL PRODUCT....WEALTH+ECO+PRODUC

GROSSER G.H. G0455

GROSSMAN G. G0456

GROUP RELATIONS....SEE GP/REL

GROWTH....SEE CREATE+ECO/UNDEV

GRUBER R. G0457

GRUNEWALD D. G0458
GT BRIT MIN OVERSEAS DEV, LIB G0775
GUAM....GUAM

GUATEMALA....SEE ALSO L/A+17C

B67
NASH M.,MACHINE AGE MAYA. GUATEMALA L/A+17C STRUCT   INDUS
AGRI WORKER CREATE INCOME ATTIT RIGID/FLEX ROLE   CULTURE
...IDEA/COMP SOC/EXP WORSHIP 20 INDIAN/AM. PAGE 41   SOC
G0806   MUNIC

L67
RUTH J.M.,"THE ADMINISTRATION OF WATER RESOURCES IN   EFFICIENCY
GUATEMALA." GUATEMALA L/A+17C DIST/IND LOC/G NAT/G   ECO/UNDEV
EX/STRUC ADMIN GOV/REL DEMAND EQUILIB WEALTH...GEOG   PLAN
MGT 20. PAGE 48 G0952   ACT/RES

GUEMES/M....MARTIN GUEMES

GUERRILLA....GUERRILLA WARFARE

B62
BURKE A.E.,ENOUGH GOOD MEN. USA+45 WOR+45 ECO/UNDEV   DIPLOM
FORCES TEC/DEV GUERRILLA NUC/PWR REV WAR ORD/FREE   POLICY
MARXISM...GEOG 20 COLD/WAR. PAGE 10 G0189   NAT/G
                                                        TASK

B63
US DEPARTMENT OF THE ARMY,SOVIET RUSSIA: STRATEGIC   BIBLIOG/A
SURVEY (PAMPHLET). USSR POL/PAR PLAN DOMIN EDU/PROP   MARXISM
ARMS/CONT GUERRILLA WAR WEAPON...TREND CHARTS   DIPLOM
ORG/CHARTS 20. PAGE 57 G1129   COERCE

KAUFMANN W.W.,THE MC NAMARA STRATEGY. TOP/EX
INSPECT BAL/PWR DIPLOM CONTROL DETER GUERRILLA
NUC/PWR WEAPON COST PWR...METH/COMP 20 MCNAMARA/R
KENNEDY/JF JOHNSON/LB NATO DEPT/DEFEN. PAGE 30
G0586
B64
FORCES
WAR
PLAN
PROB/SOLV

BRODIE B.,ESCALATION AND THE NUCLEAR OPTION. ASIA
CUBA EUR+WWI KOREA USA+45 USSR VIETNAM RISK ATTIT
DRIVE PERCEPT PROBABIL. PAGE 9 G0172
B66
NUC/PWR
GUERRILLA
WAR
DETER

MCCLINTOCK R.,THE MEANING OF LIMITED WAR. FUT
WOR+45 NAT/G FORCES GUERRILLA REV...POLICY SAMP/SIZ
TREND NAT/COMP 45 COLD/WAR. PAGE 37 G0730
B67
WAR
NUC/PWR
BAL/PWR
DIPLOM

GUETZKOW H. G0459

GUEVARA/E....ERNESTO GUEVARA

GUIANA/BR....BRITISH GUIANA; SEE ALSO GUYANA

GUIANA/FR....FRENCH GUIANA

GUILBAUD G.T. G0460

GUILDS....SEE PROF/ORG

GUINEA....SEE ALSO AFR

GUJARAT....GUJARAT (STATE OF INDIA)

GULICK L. G0461

GULICK M.C. G0462

GUTMANN P.M. G0463

GUTTMAN/L....LOUIS GUTTMAN (AND GUTTMAN SCALE)

GUYANA....GUYANA; SEE ALSO GUIANA/BR, L/A+17C

H

HAAS E.B. G0464

HABERER J. G0465

HABITAT....ECOLOGY

KRUTILIA J.V.,CONSERVATION RECONSIDERED. USA+45
CREATE EDU/PROP. PAGE 32 G0624
N
PROB/SOLV
POLICY
HABITAT
GEOG

BROWN W.M.,THE DESIGN AND PERFORMANCE OF "OPTIMUM"
BLAST SHELTER PROGRAMS (PAMPHLET). USA+45 ACT/RES
PLAN DEATH COST EFFICIENCY OPTIMAL...POLICY CHARTS
20. PAGE 9 G0180
N19
HABITAT
NUC/PWR
WAR
HEALTH

US FOOD AND DRUG ADMIN.CIVIL DEFENSE INFORMATION
FOR FOOD AND DRUG OFFICIALS (2ND ED.) (PAMPHLET).
USA+45 PROB/SOLV RISK HABITAT...MATH CHARTS
DICTIONARY 20 CIV/DEFENS. PAGE 58 G1136
N19
NUC/PWR
WAR
EATING
HEALTH

VERNON R.,THE MYTH AND REALITY OF OUR URBAN
PROBLEMS (PAMPHLET). USA+45 SOCIETY LOC/G ADMIN
COST 20 PRINCETN/U INTERVENT URBAN/RNWL. PAGE 61
G1197
N19
PLAN
MUNIC
HABITAT
PROB/SOLV

ZLOTNICK M.,WEAPONS IN SPACE (PAMPHLET). FUT WOR+45
TEC/DEV DIPLOM ARMS/CONT CIVMIL/REL PEACE HABITAT
...CONCPT NEW/IDEA CHARTS. PAGE 65 G1268
N19
SPACE
WEAPON
NUC/PWR
WAR

GULICK L.,PAPERS ON THE SCIENCE OF ADMINISTRATION.
INDUS PROB/SOLV TEC/DEV COST EFFICIENCY PRODUC
HABITAT...PHIL/SCI METH/COMP 20. PAGE 23 G0461
B37
OP/RES
CONTROL
ADMIN
MGT

HAWLEY A.H.,"ECOLOGY AND HUMAN ECOLOGY" WOR+45
INTELL ACADEM PLAN GP/REL ADJUST PERSON...PHIL/SCI
SOC METH/CNCPT METH 20. PAGE 25 G0493
S44
HABITAT
GEOG
GEN/LAWS
METH/COMP

DEES J.W. JR.,URBAN SOCIOLOGY AND THE EMERGING
ATOMIC MEGALOPOLIS. PART I. USA+45 TEC/DEV ADMIN
B50
PLAN
NEIGH

NUC/PWR HABITAT...SOC AUD/VIS CHARTS GEN/LAWS 20
WATER. PAGE 15 G0291
MUNIC
PROB/SOLV

CALLOT E.,LA SOCIETE ET SON ENVIRONNEMENT: ESSAI
SUR LES PRINCIPES DES SCIENCES SOCIALES. GP/REL
ADJUST CONSEN ISOLAT HABITAT PERCEPT PERSON
...BIBLIOG SOC/INTEG 20. PAGE 10 G0205
B52
SOCIETY
PHIL/SCI
CULTURE

SIMMONS L.W.,SOCIAL SCIENCE IN MEDICINE. USA+45
USA-45 SOCIETY CONSULT PLAN PROB/SOLV CONTROL
PERS/REL...POLICY HEAL TREND BIBLIOG 20. PAGE 51
G0999
B54
PUB/INST
HABITAT
HEALTH
BIO/SOC

WASHBURNE N.F.,INTERPRETING SOCIAL CHANGE IN
AMERICA. USA+45 STRATA FAM NAT/G SECT OP/RES
ECO/TAC EDU/PROP HABITAT...SOC TIME/SEQ TREND 20
BUREAUCRCY. PAGE 62 G1217
B54
CULTURE
STRUCT
CREATE
TEC/DEV

FORM W.H.,"THE PLACE OF SOCIAL STRUCTURE IN THE
DETERMINATION OF LAND USE: SOME IMPLICATIONS FOR A
THEORY OF URBAN ECOLOGY" (BMR)" STRUCT...GEOG
PHIL/SCI SOC 20. PAGE 19 G0381
S54
HABITAT
MARKET
ORD/FREE
MUNIC

VON NEUMANN J.,"CAN WE SURVIVE TECHNOLOGY?" WOR+45
AIR INDUS ADMIN ADJUST RIGID/FLEX...GEOG PHIL/SCI
NEW/IDEA 20. PAGE 61 G1202
S55
TEC/DEV
NUC/PWR
FUT
HABITAT

DRUCKER P.F.,AMERICA'S NEXT TWENTY YEARS. USA+45
DIST/IND ACADEM MUNIC SCHOOL DIPLOM ECO/TAC AUTOMAT
HABITAT HEALTH...SOC/WK TREND 20 URBAN/RNWL
PUB/TRANS. PAGE 16 G0316
B57
WORKER
FOR/AID
CENSUS
GEOG

CROWE S.,THE LANDSCAPE OF POWER. UK CULTURE
SERV/IND NAT/G CONSULT PARTIC NUC/PWR LEISURE...SOC
EXHIBIT 20. PAGE 14 G0264
B58
HABITAT
TEC/DEV
PLAN
CONTROL

LANG D.,FROM HIROSHIMA TO THE MOON: CHRONICLES OF
LIFE IN THE ATOMIC AGE. USA+45 OP/RES CONTROL
ARMS/CONT WAR CIVMIL/REL PEACE HABITAT MORAL PWR
...OBS INT 20 AEC. PAGE 32 G0633
B59
NUC/PWR
SPACE
HEALTH
TEC/DEV

LINDVEIT E.N.,SCIENTISTS IN GOVERNMENT. USA+45 PAY
EDU/PROP ADMIN DRIVE HABITAT ROLE...TECHNIC BIBLIOG
20. PAGE 34 G0670
B60
TEC/DEV
ECO/TAC
PHIL/SCI
GOV/REL

LEE R.R.,ENGINEERING-ECONOMIC PLANNING
MISCELLANEOUS SUBJECTS: A SELECTED BIBLIOGRAPHY
(MIMEOGRAPHED). FINAN LOC/G MUNIC NEIGH ADMIN
CONTROL INGP/REL HABITAT...GEOG MGT SOC/WK 20
RESOURCE/N. PAGE 33 G0651
B61
BIBLIOG/A
PLAN
REGION

WEISBROD B.A.,ECONOMICS OF PUBLIC HEALTH. USA+45
INGP/REL HABITAT...POLICY STAT 20. PAGE 63 G1227
B61
SOCIETY
HEALTH
NEW/IDEA
ECO/DEV

DALTON G.,"ECONOMIC THEORY AND PRIMITIVE SOCIETY"
(BMR)" UNIV AGRI KIN TEC/DEV ECO/TAC REGION HABITAT
SKILL...METH/COMP BIBLIOG. PAGE 14 G0274
S61
ECO/UNDEV
METH
PHIL/SCI
SOC

BROOKINGS INSTITUTION.DEVELOPMENT OF THE EMERGING
COUNTRIES; AN AGENDA FOR RESEARCH. WOR+45 AGRI
TEC/DEV FOR/AID EDU/PROP ADJUST HABITAT KNOWL...PSY
SOC ANTHOL 20 THIRD/WRLD. PAGE 9 G0175
B62
ECO/UNDEV
R+D
SOCIETY
PROB/SOLV

CARSON R.,SILENT SPRING. USA+45 AIR CULTURE AGRI
INDUS ADMIN ATTIT RIGID/FLEX ORD/FREE PWR...POLICY
20. PAGE 11 G0216
B62
HABITAT
TREND
SOCIETY
CONTROL

STERN A.C.,AIR POLLUTION (2 VOLS.). LAW INDUS
PROB/SOLV TEC/DEV INSPECT RISK BIO/SOC HABITAT
...OBS/ENVIR TESTS SAMP 20 POLLUTION. PAGE 53 G1035
B62
AIR
OP/RES
CONTROL
HEALTH

WENDT P.F.,HOUSING POLICY - THE SEARCH FOR
B62
PLAN

SOLUTIONS. GERMANY/W SWEDEN UK USA+45 OP/RES   ADMIN
HABITAT WEALTH...SOC/WK CHARTS 20. PAGE 63 G1230   METH/COMP
                                                        NAT/G

                                                        B63
BONINI C.P.,SIMULATION OF INFORMATION AND DECISION   INDUS
SYSTEMS IN THE FIRM. MARKET BUDGET DOMIN EDU/PROP   SIMUL
ADMIN COST ATTIT HABITAT PERCEPT PWR...CONCPT   DECISION
PROBABIL QUANT PREDICT HYPO/EXP BIBLIOG. PAGE 8   MGT
G0152

                                                        B63
OTTOSON H.W.,LAND USE POLICY AND PROBLEMS IN THE   PROB/SOLV
UNITED STATES. USA+45 USA-45 LAW AGRI INDUS NAT/G   UTIL
GP/REL...CHARTS ANTHOL 19/20 HOMEST/ACT. PAGE 43   HABITAT
G0851   POLICY

                                                        B64
WIRTH L.,ON CITIES AND SOCIAL LIFE: SELECTED   GEN/LAWS
PAPERS. PLAN PROB/SOLV RACE/REL CONSEN ATTIT   SOCIETY
HABITAT PERSON...POLICY SOC CONCPT ANTHOL BIBLIOG   NEIGH
20. PAGE 64 G1249   STRUCT

                                                        B65
ARTHUR D LITTLE INC,SAN FRANCISCO COMMUNITY RENEWAL   HABITAT
PROGRAM. USA+45 FINAN PROVS ADMIN INCOME...CHARTS   MUNIC
20 CALIFORNIA SAN/FRAN URBAN/RNWL. PAGE 4 G0071   PLAN
                                                        PROB/SOLV

                                                        B65
BARISH N.N.,MANAGEMENT SCIENCES IN THE EMERGING   ECO/UNDEV
COUNTRIES. AFR CHINA/COM WOR+45 FINAN INDUS PLAN   OP/RES
PRODUC HABITAT...ANTHOL 20. PAGE 5 G0093   MGT
                                                        TEC/DEV

                                                        B65
US DEPARTMENT OF ARMY,MILITARY PROTECTIVE   FORCES
CONSTRUCTION: NUCLEAR WARFARE AND CHEMICAL AND   CONSTRUC
BIOLOGICAL OPERATIONS (MANUAL). OP/RES TEC/DEV RISK   TASK
COERCE NUC/PWR WAR WEAPON EFFICIENCY UTIL BIO/SOC   HEALTH
HABITAT ORD/FREE 20. PAGE 57 G1117

                                                        B66
GORDON G.,THE LEGISLATIVE PROCESS AND DIVIDED   LEGIS
GOVERNMENT; A CASE STUDY OF THE 86TH CONGRESS.   HABITAT
USA+45 POL/PAR PROVS PROB/SOLV BAL/PWR CHOOSE   CHIEF
REPRESENT EFFICIENCY ATTIT...POLICY DECISION STAT   NAT/G
20 CONGRESS EISNHWR/DD. PAGE 22 G0434

                                                        B67
ALEXANDER L.M.,THE LAW OF THE SEA: OFFSHORE   SEA
BOUNDARIES AND ZONES. WOR+45 INT/ORG TEC/DEV   INT/LAW
CONTROL PRIVIL HABITAT SOVEREIGN...CON/ANAL CHARTS   EXTR/IND
ANTHOL. PAGE 2 G0037

                                                        B67
EISENMENGER R.W.,THE DYNAMICS OF GROWTH IN NEW   ECO/DEV
ENGLAND'S ECONOMY, 1870-1964. USA+45 USA-45 ECO/TAC   AGRI
TAX PAY AUTOMAT GOV/REL ADJUST HABITAT...STAT   INDUS
19/20. PAGE 17 G0340   CAP/ISM

                                                        B67
HEADLEY J.C.,PESTICIDE PROBLEM: AN ECONOMIC   HABITAT
APPROACH TO PUBLIC POLICY. AGRI TEC/DEV GOV/REL   POLICY
COST ATTIT CHARTS. PAGE 25 G0498   BIO/SOC
                                                        CONTROL

                                                        B67
RIDKER R.G.,ECONOMIC COSTS OF AIR POLLUTION*   OP/RES
STUDIES IN MEASUREMENT. R+D MUNIC GP/REL KNOWL   HABITAT
...OBS 20. PAGE 47 G0919   PHIL/SCI

                                                        S67
WINSTON O.,"AN URBANIZATION PATTERN FOR THE US*   USA+45
SOME CONSIDERATIONS FOR THE DECENTRALIZATION OF   MUNIC
EXCELLENCE." FUT SOCIETY ECO/DEV R+D NEIGH ACT/RES   PLAN
PROB/SOLV TEC/DEV. PAGE 64 G1247   HABITAT

                                                        N67
US SENATE COMM ON PUBLIC WORKS,AIR QUALITY ACT OF   HEALTH
1967 (PAMPHLET). USA+45 INDUS R+D LEGIS SENATE.   AIR
PAGE 61 G1187   HABITAT
                                                        CONTROL

HADLEY A.T. G0466

HAGUE/F....FRANK HAGUE

HAINES G. G0467

HAITI....SEE ALSO L/A+17C

HAKLUYT/R....RICHARD HAKLUYT

HALEY A.G. G0468,G0469

HALLE L.J. G0470

HALLECK/C....CHARLES HALLECK

HALPERIN M.H. G0471,G0472,G0473,G0474

HALPIN A.W. G0475

HALSEY A.H. G0476

HAMBERG D. G0477

HAMBURG....HAMBURG, GERMANY

HAMILTON/A....ALEXANDER HAMILTON

HAMMARSK/D....DAG HAMMARSKJOLD

HAMMARSKJOLD, DAG....SEE HAMMARSK/D

HAMMOND P.E. G0478

HAMMOND P.Y. G0968

HANNA/MARK....MARK HANNA

HANSON A.H. G0479

HAPPINESS.... HAPPINESS AS A CONDITION (UNHAPPINESS)

                                                        B50
SURANYI-UNGER T.,PRIVATE ENTERPRISE AND   PLAN
GOVERNMENTAL PLANNING. STRUCT FINAN BAL/PWR   NAT/G
HAPPINESS DRIVE NEW/LIB PLURISM...MATH QUANT STAT   LAISSEZ
TREND BIBLIOG. PAGE 53 G1047   POLICY

                                                        S50
BAVELAS A.,"COMMUNICATION PATTERNS IN TASK-ORIENTED   ACT/RES
GROUPS" (BMR)" R+D OP/RES INSPECT LEAD CENTRAL   PERS/REL
EFFICIENCY HAPPINESS RIGID/FLEX...PROBABIL 20.   TASK
PAGE 6 G0106   INGP/REL

                                                        C51
HOMANS G.C.,"THE WESTERN ELECTRIC RESEARCHES" IN S.   OP/RES
HOSLETT. ED., HUMAN FACTORS IN MANAGEMENT (BMR)"   EFFICIENCY
ACT/RES GP/REL HAPPINESS PRODUC DRIVE...MGT OBS 20.   SOC/EXP
PAGE 27 G0526   WORKER

                                                        B62
WALSTON H.,AGRICULTURE UNDER COMMUNISM. CHINA/COM   AGRI
COM PROB/SOLV HAPPINESS RIGID/FLEX...POLICY   MARXISM
METH/COMP 20. PAGE 62 G1207   PLAN
                                                        CREATE

                                                        B64
PARANJAPE H.K.,THE FLIGHT OF TECHNICAL PERSONNEL IN   ADMIN
PUBLIC UNDERTAKINGS. INDIA PAY DEMAND HAPPINESS   NAT/G
ORD/FREE...MGT QU 20 MIGRATION. PAGE 44 G0858   WORKER
                                                        PLAN

HAPSBURG....HAPSBURG MONARCHY

HAPTHEKER....HAPTHEKER THEORY

HARDIN L.M. G0480

HARDING/WG....PRESIDENT WARREN G. HARDING

HARDT J.P. G0481

HARGIS/BJ....BILLY JAMES HARGIS

HARLAN/JM....JOHN MARSHALL HARLAN

HARLEM....HARLEM

HARMAN H.H. G0482

HARPER S.N. G0483

HARRIMAN/A....AVERILL HARRIMAN

HARRIS F.R. G0484

HARRISN/WH....PRESIDENT WILLIAM HENRY HARRISON

HARRISON S.L. G0485

HARRISON/B....PRESIDENT BENJAMIN HARRISON

HART B.H.L. G0486

HARTIGAN R.S. G0487

HARVARD UNIVERSITY LAW SCHOOL G0488

HODGSON J.G.,THE OFFICIAL PUBLICATIONS OF AMERICAN COUNTIES: A UNION LIST. SCHOOL BUDGET...HEAL MGT SOC/WK 19/20. PAGE 26 G0520
BIBLIOG LOC/G PUB/INST
B37

BUSH V.,SCIENCE, THE ENDLESS FRONTIER. FUT USA-45 INTELL STRATA ACT/RES CREATE PLAN EDU/PROP ADMIN NUC/PWR PEACE ATTIT HEALTH KNOWL...MAJORIT HEAL MGT PHIL/SCI CONCPT OBS TREND 20. PAGE 10 G0195
R+D NAT/G
B45

BUSH V.,ENDLESS HORIZONS. FUT USA-45 INTELL NAT/G CONSULT ACT/RES CREATE PLAN EDU/PROP DRIVE ...MAJORIT HEAL MGT PHIL/SCI CONCPT OBS TREND GEN/METH TOT/POP 20. PAGE 10 G0196
R+D KNOWL PEACE
B46

SIMMONS L.W.,SOCIAL SCIENCE IN MEDICINE. USA+45 USA-45 SOCIETY CONSULT PLAN PROB/SOLV CONTROL PERS/REL...POLICY HEAL TREND BIBLIOG 20. PAGE 51 G0999
PUB/INST HABITAT HEALTH BIO/SOC
B54

MURPHY E.F.,WATER PURITY: A STUDY IN LEGAL CONTROL OF NATURAL RESOURCES. LOC/G ACT/RES PLAN TEC/DEV LOBBY GP/REL COST ATTIT HEALTH ORD/FREE...HEAL JURID 20 WISCONSIN WATER. PAGE 40 G0797
SEA LAW PROVS CONTROL
B61

NAKICENOVIC S.,NUCLEAR ENERGY IN YUGOSLAVIA. YUGOSLAVIA AGRI INDUS CREATE OP/RES ROUTINE EFFICIENCY KNOWL...HEAL STAT CHARTS LAB/EXP BIBLIOG 20. PAGE 41 G0802
R+D ECO/DEV TEC/DEV NUC/PWR
B61

RICHSTEIN A.R.,"LEGAL RULES IN NUCLEAR WEAPONS EMPLOYMENTS." FUT WOR+45 LAW SOCIETY FORCES PLAN WEAPON RIGID/FLEX...HEAL CONCPT TREND VAL/FREE 20. PAGE 47 G0918
NUC/PWR TEC/DEV MORAL ARMS/CONT
S61

PAULING L.,"GENETIC EFFECTS OF WEAPONS TESTS." WOR+45 SOCIETY FAM ACT/RES EDU/PROP AGE/C HEALTH ORD/FREE...GEOG STAT CONT/OBS PROJ/TEST CHARTS TOT/POP 20. PAGE 44 G0861
HEAL ARMS/CONT NUC/PWR
S62

PANAMERICAN UNION,DOCUMENTOS OFICIALES DE LA ORGANIZACION DE LOS ESTADOS AMERICANOS, INDICE Y LISTA (VOL. III, 1962). L/A+17C DELIB/GP INT/TRADE EDU/PROP REGION NUC/PWR...HEAL INT/LAW SOC/WK 20 OAS. PAGE 44 G0857
BIBLIOG INT/ORG DIPLOM
B63

FALK L.A.,ADMINISTRATIVE ASPECTS OF GROUP PRACTICE. USA+45 FINAN PROF/ORG PLAN MGT. PAGE 18 G0358
BIBLIOG/A HEAL ADMIN
B64

CARPER E.T.,REORGANIZATION OF THE U.S. PUBLIC HEALTH SERVICE. FUT USA+45 INTELL R+D LOBBY GP/REL INGP/REL PERS/REL RIGID/FLEX ROLE HEALTH...PHIL/SCI 20 CONGRESS PHS. PAGE 11 G0213
HEAL PLAN NAT/G OP/RES
B65

HEER D.M.,AFTER NUCLEAR ATTACK: A DEMOGRAPHIC INQUIRY. USA+45 ECO/DEV SECT WORKER SEX...HEAL SOC STAT PREDICT CHARTS 20 NEGRO. PAGE 25 G0500
GEOG NUC/PWR CENSUS WAR
B65

NATIONAL ACADEMY OF SCIENCES,BASIC RESEARCH AND NATIONAL GOALS. R+D ACADEM DELIB/GP PLAN EDU/PROP ...POLICY HEAL PHIL/SCI PSY SOC ANTHOL 20 CONGRESS HOUSE/REP HS/SCIASTR. PAGE 41 G0809
LEGIS BUDGET NAT/G CREATE
B65

SCHWEBEL M.,"BEHAVIORAL SCIENCE AND HUMAN SURVIVAL." FORCES ARMS/CONT COERCE NUC/PWR WAR GP/REL NAT/LISM PERCEPT...POLICY PSY ANTHOL BIBLIOG/A 20 COLD/WAR. PAGE 50 G0984
PEACE ACT/RES DIPLOM HEAL
C65

HOPKINS J.F.K.,ARABIC PERIODICAL LITERATURE, 1961. ISLAM LAW CULTURE SECT...GEOG HEAL PHIL/SCI PSY SOC 20. PAGE 27 G0528
BIBLIOG/A NAT/LISM TEC/DEV INDUS
B66

LECHT L.,GOAL, PRIORITIES, AND DOLLARS: THE NEXT DECADE. SPACE USA+45 SOCIETY AGRI BUDGET FOR/AID ...HEAL SOC/WK STAT CHARTS 20 URBAN/RNWL PUB/TRANS. PAGE 33 G0649
IDEA/COMP POLICY CONSEN PLAN
B66

US HOUSE COMM ON JUDICIARY,CIVIL COMMITMENT AND TREATMENT OF NARCOTIC ADDICTS. USA+45 SOCIETY FINAN LEGIS PROB/SOLV GIVE CT/SYS SANCTION HEALTH ...POLICY HEAL 20. PAGE 58 G1141
BIO/SOC CRIME IDEA/COMP CONTROL
B66

HODGKINSON R.G.,THE ORIGINS OF THE NATIONAL HEALTH SERVICE: THE MEDICAL SERVICES OF THE NEW POOR LAW, 1834-1871. UK INDUS MUNIC WORKER PROB/SOLV EFFICIENCY ATTIT HEALTH WEALTH SOCISM...JURID SOC/WK 19/20. PAGE 26 G0519
HEAL NAT/G POLICY LAW
B67

HILL R.,"SOCIAL ASPECTS OF FAMILY PLANNING." INDIA KOREA TAIWAN ECO/UNDEV PLAN PROB/SOLV TEC/DEV EDU/PROP CONTROL ATTIT DRIVE...HEAL PSY SOC 20 BIRTH/CON UN. PAGE 26 G0512
FAM BIO/SOC GEOG MARRIAGE
S67

INDIA: A REFERENCE ANNUAL. INDIA CULTURE COM/IND R+D FORCES PLAN RECEIVE EDU/PROP HEALTH...STAT CHARTS BIBLIOG 20. PAGE 1 G0005
CONSTN LABOR INT/ORG
N

US SUPERINTENDENT OF DOCUMENTS,TRANSPORTATION: HIGHWAYS, ROADS, AND POSTAL SERVICE (PRICE LIST 25). PANAMA USA+45 LAW FORCES DIPLOM ADMIN GOV/REL HEALTH MGT. PAGE 61 G1188
BIBLIOG/A DIST/IND SERV/IND NAT/G
N

BROWN W.M.,THE DESIGN AND PERFORMANCE OF "OPTIMUM" BLAST SHELTER PROGRAMS (PAMPHLET). USA+45 ACT/RES PLAN DEATH COST EFFICIENCY OPTIMAL...POLICY CHARTS 20. PAGE 9 G0180
HABITAT NUC/PWR WAR HEALTH
N19

MEZERIK A.G.,ATOM TESTS AND RADIATION HAZARDS (PAMPHLET). WOR+45 INT/ORG DIPLOM DETER 20 UN TREATY. PAGE 39 G0761
NUC/PWR ARMS/CONT CONFER HEALTH
N19

US ATOMIC ENERGY COMMISSION,ATOMIC ENERGY IN USE (PAMPHLET). R+D RISK EFFICIENCY HEALTH KNOWL ORD/FREE...PHIL/SCI CONCPT METH/CNCPT CHARTS LAB/EXP 20 AEC. PAGE 56 G1106
OP/RES TEC/DEV NUC/PWR CREATE
N19

US FOOD AND DRUG ADMIN,CIVIL DEFENSE INFORMATION FOR FOOD AND DRUG OFFICIALS (2ND ED.) (PAMPHLET). USA+45 PROB/SOLV RISK HABITAT...MATH CHARTS DICTIONARY 20 CIV/DEFENS. PAGE 58 G1136
NUC/PWR WAR EATING HEALTH
N19

B45

BUSH V.,SCIENCE, THE ENDLESS FRONTIER. FUT USA-45   R+D
INTELL STRATA ACT/RES CREATE PLAN EDU/PROP ADMIN   NAT/G
NUC/PWR PEACE ATTIT HEALTH KNOWL...MAJORIT HEAL MGT
PHIL/SCI CONCPT OBS TREND 20. PAGE 10 G0195

B48

PUBLIC ADMINISTRATION SERVICE,SOURCE MATERIALS IN   BIBLIOG/A
PUBLIC ADMINISTRATION: A SELECTED BIBLIOGRAPHY (PAS GOV/REL
PUBLICATION NO. 102). USA+45 LAW FINAN LOC/G MUNIC   MGT
NAT/G PLAN RECEIVE EDU/PROP CT/SYS CHOOSE HEALTH   ADMIN
20. PAGE 45 G0895

B53

SCHAAF R.W.,DOCUMENTS OF INTERNATIONAL MEETINGS.   BIBLIOG/A
AGRI INDUS ACADEM DIPLOM NUC/PWR RACE/REL AGE/Y   DELIB/GP
HEALTH...SOC 20. PAGE 49 G0960   INT/ORG
                                                     POLICY

B54

SIMMONS L.W.,SOCIAL SCIENCE IN MEDICINE. USA+45   PUB/INST
USA-45 SOCIETY CONSULT PLAN PROB/SOLV CONTROL   HABITAT
PERS/REL...POLICY HEAL TREND BIBLIOG 20. PAGE 51   HEALTH
G0999   BIO/SOC

B57

DRUCKER P.F.,AMERICA'S NEXT TWENTY YEARS. USA+45   WORKER
DIST/IND ACADEM MUNIC SCHOOL DIPLOM ECO/TAC AUTOMAT FOR/AID
HABITAT HEALTH...SOC/WK TREND 20 URBAN/RNWL   CENSUS
PUB/TRANS. PAGE 16 G0316   GEOG

B58

ATOMIC INDUSTRIAL FORUM,MANAGEMENT AND ATOMIC   NUC/PWR
ENERGY. WOR+45 SEA LAW MARKET NAT/G TEC/DEV INSPECT INDUS
INT/TRADE CONFER PEACE HEALTH...ANTHOL 20. PAGE 4   MGT
G0078   ECO/TAC

B59

LANG D.,FROM HIROSHIMA TO THE MOON: CHRONICLES OF   NUC/PWR
LIFE IN THE ATOMIC AGE. USA+45 OP/RES CONTROL   SPACE
ARMS/CONT WAR CIVMIL/REL PEACE HABITAT MORAL PWR   HEALTH
...OBS INT 20 AEC. PAGE 32 G0633   TEC/DEV

B60

SLUCKIN W.,MINDS AND MACHINES (REV. ED.). PROB/SOLV PSY
TEC/DEV AUTOMAT TASK PERCEPT HEALTH KNOWL   COMPUTER
...DECISION MATH PROBABIL COMPUT/IR GAME 20.   PERSON
PAGE 51 G1012   SIMUL

S60

JAFFEE A.J.,"POPULATION TRENDS AND CONTROLS IN   ECO/UNDEV
UNDERDEVELOPED COUNTRIES." AFR FUT ISLAM L/A+17C   GEOG
S/ASIA CULTURE R+D FAM ACT/RES PLAN EDU/PROP
BIO/SOC RIGID/FLEX HEALTH...SOC STAT OBS CHARTS 20.
PAGE 28 G0555

S60

TAYLOR M.G.,"THE ROLE OF THE MEDICAL PROFESSION IN   PROF/ORG
THE FORMULATION AND EXECUTION OF PUBLIC POLICY"   HEALTH
(BMR)" CANADA NAT/G CONSULT ADMIN REPRESENT GP/REL   LOBBY
ROLE SOVEREIGN...DECISION 20 CMA. PAGE 54 G1058   POLICY

B61

MURPHY E.F.,WATER PURITY: A STUDY IN LEGAL CONTROL   SEA
OF NATURAL RESOURCES. LOC/G ACT/RES PLAN TEC/DEV   LAW
LOBBY GP/REL COST ATTIT HEALTH ORD/FREE...HEAL   PROVS
JURID 20 WISCONSIN WATER. PAGE 40 G0797   CONTROL

B61

WEISBROD B.A.,ECONOMICS OF PUBLIC HEALTH. USA+45   SOCIETY
INGP/REL HABITAT...POLICY STAT 20. PAGE 63 G1227   HEALTH
                                                     NEW/IDEA
                                                     ECO/DEV

B62

CALDER R.,LIVING WITH THE ATOM. FUT USA+45 WOR+45   TEC/DEV
R+D INT/ORG VOL/ASSN DELIB/GP ARMS/CONT...STYLE 20. HEALTH
PAGE 10 G0200   NUC/PWR

B62

STERN A.C.,AIR POLLUTION (2 VOLS.). LAW INDUS   AIR
PROB/SOLV TEC/DEV INSPECT RISK BIO/SOC HABITAT   OP/RES
...OBS/ENVIR TESTS SAMP 20 POLLUTION. PAGE 53 G1035 CONTROL
                                                     HEALTH

S62

PAULING L.,"GENETIC EFFECTS OF WEAPONS TESTS."   HEAL
WOR+45 SOCIETY FAM ACT/RES EDU/PROP AGE/C HEALTH   ARMS/CONT
ORD/FREE...GEOG STAT CONT/OBS PROJ/TEST CHARTS   NUC/PWR
TOT/POP 20. PAGE 44 G0861

B63

ABSHIRE D.M.,NATIONAL SECURITY: POLITICAL,   FUT
MILITARY, AND ECONOMIC STRATEGIES IN THE DECADE   ACT/RES
AHEAD. ASIA COM USA+45 WOR+45 ECO/DEV ECO/UNDEV   BAL/PWR
INT/ORG DELIB/GP FORCES ECO/TAC COERCE ATTIT

RIGID/FLEX HEALTH ORD/FREE PWR WEALTH...POLICY STAT
CHARTS ANTHOL COLD/WAR VAL/FREE. PAGE 1 G0024

B63

KATZ S.M.,A SELECTED LIST OF US READINGS ON   BIBLIOG/A
DEVELOPMENT. AGRI COM/IND DIST/IND INDUS LABOR PLAN ECO/UNDEV
FOR/AID EDU/PROP HEALTH...POLICY SOC/WK 20. PAGE 30 TEC/DEV
G0582   ACT/RES

B63

MULLENBACH P.,CIVILIAN NUCLEAR POWER: ECONOMIC   USA+45
ISSUES AND POLICY FORMATION. FINAN INT/ORG DELIB/GP ECO/DEV
ACT/RES ECO/TAC ATTIT SUPEGO HEALTH ORD/FREE PWR   NUC/PWR
...POLICY CONCPT MATH STAT CHARTS VAL/FREE 20
COLD/WAR. PAGE 40 G0792

B63

PEARSELL M.,MEDICAL BEHAVIORAL SCIENCE: A SELECTED   BIBLIOG
BIBLIOGRAPHY OF CULTURAL ANTHROPOLOGY, SOCIAL   SOC
PSYCHOLOGY, AND SOCIOLOGY... USA+45 USA-45 R+D   PSY
ATTIT ROLE 20. PAGE 44 G0863   HEALTH

L63

BEGUIN H.,"ASPECTS GEOGRAPHIQUE DE LA   ECO/UNDEV
POLARISATION." FUT WOR+45 SOCIETY STRUCT ECO/DEV   GEOG
R+D BAL/PWR ADMIN ATTIT RIGID/FLEX HEALTH WEALTH   DIPLOM
...CHARTS 20. PAGE 6 G0114

L63

BRENNAN D.G.,"ARMS CONTROL AND CIVIL DEFENSE."   PLAN
USA+45 WOR+45 NAT/G BAL/PWR ROUTINE ATTIT   HEALTH
RIGID/FLEX ORD/FREE...SOC TOT/POP 20. PAGE 8 G0165   ARMS/CONT
                                                     DETER

L63

MCDOUGAL M.S.,"THE ENJOYMENT AND ACQUISITION OF   PLAN
RESOURCES IN OUTER SPACE." CHRIST-17C FUT WOR+45   TREND
WOR-45 LAW EXTR/IND INT/ORG ACT/RES CREATE TEC/DEV
ECO/TAC LEGIT COERCE HEALTH KNOWL ORD/FREE PWR
WEALTH...JURID HIST/WRIT VAL/FREE. PAGE 37 G0738

L63

PHELPS J.,"STUDIES IN DETERRENCE VIII: MILITARY   FORCES
STABILITARY AND ARMS CONTROL: A CRITICAL SURVEY."   ORD/FREE
FUT WOR+45 INT/ORG ACT/RES EDU/PROP COERCE NUC/PWR   ARMS/CONT
WAR HEALTH PWR...POLICY TECHNIC TREND SIMUL TOT/POP DETER
20. PAGE 44 G0874

S63

FERRETTI B.,"IMPORTANZA E PROSPETTIVE DELL ENERGIA   TEC/DEV
DI ORIGINE NUCLEARE." FUT ITALY WOR+45 INTELL R+D   EXEC
ACT/RES CREATE HEALTH WEALTH...METH/CNCPT TIME/SEQ   NUC/PWR
20. PAGE 19 G0365

B64

BLOUSTEIN E.J.,NUCLEAR ENERGY, PUBLIC POLICY, AND   TEC/DEV
THE LAW. USA+45 NAT/G ADJUD ADMIN GP/REL OWN PEACE   LAW
ATTIT HEALTH...ANTHOL 20. PAGE 7 G0144   POLICY
                                                     NUC/PWR

B64

GROSSER G.H.,THE THREAT OF IMPENDING DISASTER: HEALTH
CONTRIBUTIONS TO THE PSYCHOLOGY OF STRESS. SPACE   PSY
UNIV SOCIETY R+D TEC/DEV EDU/PROP COERCE WAR ATTIT   NUC/PWR
BIO/SOC DISPL PERCEPT PERSON...SOC MYTH SELF/OBS
CONT/OBS BIOG CON/ANAL TOT/POP 20. PAGE 23 G0455

B64

PETERSON W.,THE POLITICS OF POPULATION. COM EUR+WWI PLAN
FUT MOD/EUR S/ASIA USA+45 USA-45 WOR+45 LAW CULTURE CENSUS
FAM SECT DOMIN EDU/PROP BIO/SOC HEALTH ORD/FREE   POLICY
...GEOG STAT TIME/SEQ TREND VAL/FREE. PAGE 44 G0871

B64

RUSHING W.A.,THE PSYCHIATRIC PROFESSIONS. DOMIN   ATTIT
INGP/REL DRIVE RIGID/FLEX ROLE HEALTH PWR...POLICY   PUB/INST
GP/COMP. PAGE 48 G0947   PROF/ORG
                                                     BAL/PWR

L64

GOLDBERG A.,"ATOMIC ORIGINS OF THE BRITISH NUCLEAR   CREATE
DETERRENT." EUR+WWI UK NAT/G TOP/EX PLAN BAL/PWR   FORCES
DOMIN DETER CHOOSE ATTIT DRIVE HEALTH ORD/FREE PWR   NUC/PWR
RESPECT...CONCPT VAL/FREE COLD/WAR 20 CMN/WLTH.
PAGE 22 G0425

B65

PEACE RESEARCH ABSTRACTS. FUT WOR+45 R+D INT/ORG   BIBLIOG/A
NAT/G PLAN TEC/DEV BAL/PWR DIPLOM FOR/AID NUC/PWR   PEACE
HEALTH. PAGE 1 G0020   ARMS/CONT
                                                     WAR

B65

CARPER E.T.,REORGANIZATION OF THE U.S. PUBLIC   HEAL
HEALTH SERVICE. FUT USA+45 INTELL R+D LOBBY GP/REL   PLAN
INGP/REL PERS/REL RIGID/FLEX ROLE HEALTH...PHIL/SCI NAT/G

20 CONGRESS PHS. PAGE 11 G0213 — OP/RES

B65
UN,SPACE ACTIVITIES AND RESOURCES: REVIEW OF UNITED NATION'S NATIONAL AND INTERNATIONAL PROGRAMS. INT/ORG LABOR PLAN TEC/DEV DIPLOM EFFICIENCY HEALTH ...GOV/COMP 20 UN. PAGE 55 G1086 — SPACE NUC/PWR FOR/AID PEACE

B65
US DEPARTMENT OF ARMY,MILITARY PROTECTIVE CONSTRUCTION: NUCLEAR WARFARE AND CHEMICAL AND BIOLOGICAL OPERATIONS (MANUAL). OP/RES TEC/DEV RISK COERCE NUC/PWR WAR WEAPON EFFICIENCY UTIL BIO/SOC HABITAT ORD/FREE 20. PAGE 57 G1117 — FORCES CONSTRUC TASK HEALTH

S65
KRICKUS R.J.,"ON THE MORALITY OF CHEMICAL/BIOLOGICAL WAR." ECO/UNDEV ARMS/CONT DETER NUC/PWR RIGID/FLEX HEALTH INT/LAW. PAGE 31 G0621 — MORAL BIO/SOC WEAPON WAR

B66
POLLARD W.G.,ATOMIC ENERGY AND SOUTHERN SCIENCE. USA+45 HEALTH. PAGE 45 G0883 — NUC/PWR GP/REL PHIL/SCI CREATE

B66
US HOUSE COMM ON JUDICIARY,CIVIL COMMITMENT AND TREATMENT OF NARCOTIC ADDICTS. USA+45 SOCIETY FINAN LEGIS PROB/SOLV GIVE CT/SYS SANCTION HEALTH ...POLICY HEAL 20. PAGE 58 G1141 — BIO/SOC CRIME IDEA/COMP CONTROL

N66
US HOUSE COMM SCI ASTRONAUT,THE ADEQUACY OF TECHNOLOGY FOR POLLUTION ABATEMENT (PAMPHLET). WOR+45 PLAN PROB/SOLV CONFER ADMIN...JURID 20 POLLUTION. PAGE 58 G1145 — HEALTH POLICY TEC/DEV LEGIS

B67
FIELD M.G.,SOVIET SOCIALIZED MEDICINE. USSR FINAN R+D PROB/SOLV ADMIN SOCISM...MGT SOC CONCPT 20. PAGE 19 G0366 — PUB/INST HEALTH NAT/G MARXISM

B67
HODGKINSON R.G.,THE ORIGINS OF THE NATIONAL HEALTH SERVICE: THE MEDICAL SERVICES OF THE NEW POOR LAW, 1834-1871. UK INDUS MUNIC WORKER PROB/SOLV EFFICIENCY ATTIT HEALTH WEALTH SOCISM...JURID SOC/WK 19/20. PAGE 26 G0519 — HEAL NAT/G POLICY LAW

B67
SAPARINA Y.,CYBERNETICS WITHIN US. WOR+45 EDU/PROP FEEDBACK PERCEPT HEALTH...DECISION METH/CNCPT NEW/IDEA 20. PAGE 49 G0957 — COMPUTER METH/COMP CONTROL SIMUL

L67
CARMICHAEL D.M.,"FORTY YEARS OF WATER POLLUTION CONTROL IN WISCONSIN: A CASE STUDY." LAW EXTR/IND INDUS MUNIC DELIB/GP PLAN PROB/SOLV SANCTION ...CENSUS CHARTS 20 WISCONSIN. PAGE 11 G0207 — HEALTH CONTROL ADMIN ADJUD

S67
ROBINSON J.A.T.,"ABORTION* THE CASE FOR A FREE DECISION." LAW PROB/SOLV SANCTION ATTIT MORAL...PSY IDEA/COMP 20 ABORTION. PAGE 47 G0930 — PLAN ILLEGIT SEX HEALTH

S67
SLOAN P.,"FIFTY YEARS OF SOVIET RULE." USSR INDUS EDU/PROP EFFICIENCY PRODUC HEALTH KNOWL MORAL WEALTH MARXISM...POLICY 20. PAGE 51 G1011 — CREATE NAT/G PLAN INSPECT

N67
US SUPERINTENDENT OF DOCUMENTS,SPACE: MISSILES, THE MOON, NASA, AND SATELLITES (PRICE LIST 79A). USA+45 COM/IND R+D NAT/G DIPLOM EDU/PROP ADMIN CONTROL HEALTH...POLICY SIMUL NASA CONGRESS. PAGE 61 G1190 — BIBLIOG/A SPACE TEC/DEV PEACE

N67
US SENATE COMM ON PUBLIC WORKS,AIR QUALITY ACT OF 1967 (PAMPHLET). USA+45 INDUS R+D LEGIS SENATE. PAGE 61 G1187 — HEALTH AIR HABITAT CONTROL

HEARD A. G0341

HECKSCHER G. G0499

HEER D.M. G0500

HEGEL/G....GEORG WILHELM FRIEDRICH HEGEL

HEIDER F. G0467

HEILBRNR/R....ROBERT HEILBRONER

HEILBRONER R.L. G0501,G0502

HEINRICH W. G0468

HEKHUIS D.J. G0503

HELLER D. G0504

HELLMAN F.S. G0505

HENKIN L. G0506

HERDER/J....JOHANN GOTTFRIED VON HERDER

HEREDITY....GENETIC INFLUENCES ON PERSONALITY DEVELOPMENT AND SOCIAL GROWTH

B60
JANOWITZ M.,THE PROFESSIONAL SOLDIER. CULTURE STRATA STRUCT FAM PROB/SOLV TEC/DEV COERCE WAR CIVMIL/REL NAT/LISM AGE HEREDITY ALL/VALS CONSERVE ...MGT WORSHIP. PAGE 28 G0560 — FORCES MYTH LEAD ELITES

B65
ANDERSON C.A.,EDUCATION AND ECONOMIC DEVELOPMENT. INDUS R+D SCHOOL TEC/DEV ECO/TAC EDU/PROP AGE HEREDITY PERCEPT SKILL 20. PAGE 3 G0056 — ANTHOL ECO/DEV ECO/UNDEV WORKER

HERESY....HERESY

HERNDON J. G0507

HERRING P. G0508

HERTER/C ....CHRISTIAN HERTER

B62
US SENATE COMM GOVT OPERATIONS,ADMINISTRATION OF NATIONAL SECURITY. USA+45 CHIEF PLAN PROB/SOLV TEC/DEV DIPLOM ATTIT...POLICY DECISION 20 KENNEDY/JF RUSK/D MCNAMARA/R BUNDY/M HERTER/C. PAGE 60 G1177 — ORD/FREE ADMIN NAT/G CONTROL

HEYEL C. G0509

HIBBS A.R. G0510

HICKMAN B.G. G0511

HIESTAND/F....FRED J. HIESTAND

HIGGINS/G....GODFREY HIGGINS

HIGHWAY PLANNING AND DEVELOPMENT....SEE HIGHWAY

HIGHWAY....HIGHWAY PLANNING AND DEVELOPMENT

HILL R. G0512

HINDU....HINDUISM AND HINDU PEOPLE

HIROSHIMA....SEE WAR, NUC/PWR, PLAN, PROB/SOLV, CONSULT

B59
AMRINE M.,THE GREAT DECISION: THE SECRET HISTORY OF THE ATOMIC BOMB. USA+45 TOP/EX EDU/PROP LEGIT PERCEPT ORD/FREE PWR VAL/FREE HIROSHIMA. PAGE 3 G0055 — DECISION NAT/G NUC/PWR FORCES

HIRSCHMAN A.O. G0513

HISS/ALGER....ALGER HISS

HIST....HISTORY, INCLUDING CURRENT EVENTS

HIST/WRIT....HISTORIOGRAPHY

B11
BERGSON H.,CREATIVE EVOLUTION. FUT WOR+45 WOR-45 INTELL AGRI R+D ATTIT PERCEPT PERSON RIGID/FLEX ...RELATIV PHIL/SCI PSY METH/CNCPT MATH HIST/WRIT TREND HYPO/EXP TOT/POP. PAGE 7 G0127 — BIO/SOC KNOWL

B29
DEWEY J.,THE QUEST FOR CERTAINTY. GP/REL RATIONAL UTOPIA ATTIT MORAL ORD/FREE PWR...MYTH HIST/WRIT. PAGE 15 G0301 — PHIL/SCI PERSON PERCEPT KNOWL

B56
BLACKETT P.M.S.,ATOMIC WEAPONS AND EAST-WEST — FORCES

RELATIONS. FUT WOR+45 INT/ORG DELIB/GP COERCE ATTIT PWR
RIGID/FLEX KNOWL...RELATIV HIST/WRIT TREND GEN/METH ARMS/CONT
COLD/WAR 20. PAGE 7 G0138   NUC/PWR

B61
HENKIN L.,ARMS CONTROL: ISSUES FOR THE PUBLIC.   WOR+45
EUR+WWI FUT USA+45 USSR INT/ORG NAT/G DIPLOM   DELIB/GP
EDU/PROP DETER NUC/PWR ATTIT PWR...CONCPT RECORD   ARMS/CONT
HIST/WRIT TIME/SEQ TOT/POP COLD/WAR 20. PAGE 26
G0506

L63
MCDOUGAL M.S.,"THE ENJOYMENT AND ACQUISITION OF   PLAN
RESOURCES IN OUTER SPACE." CHRIST-17C FUT WOR+45   TREND
WOR-45 LAW EXTR/IND INT/ORG NAT/G ACT/RES CREATE TEC/DEV
ECO/TAC LEGIT COERCE HEALTH KNOWL ORD/FREE PWR
WEALTH...JURID HIST/WRIT VAL/FREE. PAGE 37 G0738

B67
ELSNER H.,THE TECHNOCRATS, PROPHETS OF AUTOMATION.   AUTOMAT
SOCIETY INDUS VOL/ASSN COST INCOME ATTIT 20.   TECHRACY
PAGE 18 G0345   PRODUC
                                                       HIST/WRIT

S67
TAGIL S.,"WEGENER, RAEDER, AND THE GERMAN NAVAL   SEA
STRATEGY: VIEWPOINTS ON THE CONDITIONS FOR THE   POLICY
INFLUENCE OF IDEAS." GERMANY WOR-45...IDEA/COMP   HIST/WRIT
METH 20. PAGE 53 G1049   CIVMIL/REL

HITCH C.J. G0508,G0514,G0515

HITLER/A....ADOLF HITLER

B63
JACOB H.,GERMAN ADMINISTRATION SINCE BISMARCK: ADMIN
CENTRAL AUTHORITY VERSUS LOCAL AUTONOMY. GERMANY   NAT/G
GERMANY/W LAW POL/PAR CONTROL CENTRAL TOTALISM   LOC/G
FASCISM...MAJORIT DECISION STAT CHARTS GOV/COMP   POLICY
19/20 BISMARCK/O HITLER/A WEIMAR/REP. PAGE 28 G0551

B64
WHEELER-BENNETT J.W.,THE NEMESIS OF POWER (2ND   FORCES
ED.). EUR+WWI GERMANY TOP/EX TEC/DEV ADMIN WAR   NAT/G
PERS/REL RIGID/FLEX ROLE ORD/FREE PWR FASCISM 20   GP/REL
HITLER/A. PAGE 63 G1231   STRUCT

HO/CHI/MIN....HO CHI MINH

HOBBES/T....THOMAS HOBBES

HODGE G. G0516

HODGETTS J.E. G0517

HODGKINS J.A. G0518

HODGKINSON R.G. G0519

HODGSON J.G. G0520

HOFFA/J....JAMES HOFFA

HOFFENBERG M. G0481

HOFFER J.R. G0521

HOFSTADTER R. G0522

HOLIFLD/C....CHET HOLIFIELD

B58
US HOUSE COMM GOVT OPERATIONS,CIVIL DEFENSE. USA+45 NUC/PWR
FORCES...CHARTS 20 CONGRESS CIV/DEFENS HOLIFLD/C.   WAR
PAGE 58 G1139   PLAN
                                                       ADJUST

HOLLAND....SEE NETHERLAND

HOLMES/OW....OLIVER WENDELL HOLMES

HOLMES/OWJ....OLIVER WENDELL HOLMES, JR.

HOLSTI O.R. G0523

HOLSTI/KJ....K.J. HOLSTI

HOLTON G. G0524

HOLZMAN B.G. G0525

HOMANS G.C. G0526

HOMEOSTASIS....SEE FEEDBACK

HOMER....HOMER

HOMEST/ACT....HOMESTEAD ACT OF 1862

B63
OTTOSON H.W.,LAND USE POLICY AND PROBLEMS IN THE   PROB/SOLV
UNITED STATES. USA+45 USA-45 LAW AGRI INDUS NAT/G   UTIL
GP/REL...CHARTS ANTHOL 19/20 HOMEST/ACT. PAGE 43   HABITAT
G0851   POLICY

HOMESTEAD ACT OF 1862....SEE HOMEST/ACT

HOMICIDE....SEE MURDER

HOMOSEXUAL....HOMOSEXUALITY; SEE ALSO BIO/SOC, CRIME, SEX

HOMOSEXUALITY....SEE BIO/SOC, SEX, CRIME, HOMOSEXUAL

HONDURAS....SEE ALSO L/A+17C

HONG/KONG....HONG KONG

HOOPES T. G0527

HOOVER/H....HERBERT HOOVER

HOPI....HOPI INDIANS

HOPKINS J.F.K. G0528

HOPKINS/H....HARRY HOPKINS

HOROWITZ I.L. G0529

HOSKINS H.L. G0530

HOSPITALS....SEE PUB/INST

HOUSE COMMITTEE ON SCIENCE AND ASTRONAUTICS....SEE
    HS/SCIASTR

HOUSE OF REPRESENTATIVES....SEE HOUSE/REP

HOUSE RULES COMMITTEE....SEE RULES/COMM, HOUSE/REP

HOUSE UNAMERICAN ACTIVITIES COMMITTEE....SEE HUAC

HOUSE/CMNS....HOUSE OF COMMONS (ALL NATIONS)

HOUSE/LORD....HOUSE OF LORDS (ALL NATIONS)

HOUSE/REP....HOUSE OF REPRESENTATIVES (ALL NATIONS); SEE
    ALSO CONGRESS, LEGIS

B63
PEABODY R.L.,NEW PERSPECTIVES ON THE HOUSE OF   NEW/IDEA
REPRESENTATIVES. AGRI FINAN SCHOOL FORCES CONFER   LEGIS
LEAD CHOOSE REPRESENT FEDERAL...POLICY DECISION   PWR
HOUSE/REP. PAGE 44 G0862   ADMIN

B65
NATIONAL ACADEMY OF SCIENCES,BASIC RESEARCH AND   LEGIS
NATIONAL GOALS. R+D ACADEM DELIB/GP PLAN EDU/PROP   BUDGET
...POLICY HEAL PHIL/SCI PSY SOC ANTHOL 20 CONGRESS   NAT/G
HOUSE/REP HS/SCIASTR. PAGE 41 G0809   CREATE

B66
US HOUSE COMM GOVT OPERATIONS,THE COMPUTER AND   ORD/FREE
INVASION OF PRIVACY. USA+45 SOCIETY ALL/VALS...PSY   COMPUTER
SOC CHARTS HOUSE/REP PRIVACY. PAGE 58 G1140   TEC/DEV
                                                      NAT/G

B67
US HOUSE COMM SCI ASTRONAUT,THE JUNIOR COLLEGE AND   ACADEM
EDUCATION IN THE SCIENCES (PAMPHLET). USA+45 AGE/Y   EDU/PROP
...CHARTS SIMUL HOUSE/REP. PAGE 58 G1148   PHIL/SCI
                                                      R+D

B67
US HOUSE COMM SCI ASTRONAUT,AUTHORIZING SECY OF   PHIL/SCI
COMMERCE TO PROVIDE FOR COLLECTION, COMPILATION,   CON/ANAL
CRIT EVALUATION, PUBLICATION, SALE OF STD REF DATA.   STAT
USA+45 TEC/DEV...COMPUT/IR HOUSE/REP. PAGE 59 G1150   R+D

N67
US HOUSE COMM APPROPRIATIONS,PUBLIC WORKS AND   BUDGET
ATOMIC ENERGY COMMISSION APPROPRIATION BILL, 1968   NUC/PWR
(PAMPHLET). USA+45 ECO/DEV NAT/G...GEOG DEEP/INT   PROVS
CHARTS HOUSE/REP AEC DEPT/DEFEN TVA. PAGE 58 G1137   PLAN

N67
US HOUSE COMM FOREIGN AFFAIRS,REPORT OF SPECIAL   ISLAM
STUDY MISSION TO THE NEAR EAST (PAMPHLET). ISRAEL   DIPLOM
USA+45 YEMEN ECO/UNDEV INT/ORG FOR/AID ARMS/CONT   FORCES
WAR WEAPON NAT/LISM PEACE...GEOG 20 UN HOUSE/REP.
PAGE 58 G1138

N67
US HOUSE COMM SCI ASTRONAUT.AMENDING NATIONAL PHIL/SCI
SCIENCE FOUNDATION ACT OF 1950 TO MAKE IMPROVEMENTS DELIB/GP
IN ORGANIZATION AND OPERATION OF FOUNDAT'N(PAMPH). TEC/DEV
USA+45 GIVE ADMIN...POLICY HOUSE/REP NSF. PAGE 58 R+D
G1147

N67
US HOUSE COMM SCI ASTRONAUT.AUTHORIZING SPACE
APPROPRIATIONS TO THE NATIONAL AERONAUTICS AND R+D
SPACE ADMINISTRATION (PAMPHLET). USA+45 NAT/G PHIL/SCI
OP/RES TEC/DEV BUDGET NASA HOUSE/REP. PAGE 58 G1149 NUC/PWR

HOUSTON....HOUSTON, TEXAS

HOVLAND C.I. G0531

HOWELLS L.T. G1072,G1073

HOWER R.M. G0532

HS/SCIASTR....HOUSE COMMITTEE ON SCIENCE AND ASTRONAUTICS

B65
NATIONAL ACADEMY OF SCIENCES.BASIC RESEARCH AND LEGIS
NATIONAL GOALS. R+D ACADEM DELIB/GP PLAN EDU/PROP BUDGET
...POLICY HEAL PHIL/SCI PSY SOC ANTHOL 20 CONGRESS NAT/G
HOUSE/REP HS/SCIASTR. PAGE 41 G0809 CREATE

N66
US HOUSE COMM SCI ASTRONAUT.GOVERNMENT, SCIENCE, NAT/G
AND PUBLIC POLICY (PAMPHLET). R+D ACADEM DELIB/GP POLICY
COMPUTER BUDGET CONFER ADMIN...PHIL/SCI PREDICT TEC/DEV
TREND 20 CONGRESS HS/SCIASTR. PAGE 58 G1143 CREATE

HSIEH A.L. G0533

HU/FENG....HU FENG

HUAC....HOUSE UNAMERICAN ACTIVITIES COMMITTEE

HUGHES E.M. G0534

HUGHES T.L. G0535

HUKS....HUKS (PHILIPPINES)

HULL E.W.S. G0536

HUM....METHODS OF HUMANITIES, LITERARY ANALYSIS

N
AMER COUNCIL OF LEARNED SOCIET.THE ACLS CONSTITUENT BIBLIOG/A
SOCIETY JOURNAL PROJECT. FUT USA+45 LAW NAT/G PLAN HUM
DIPLOM PHIL/SCI. PAGE 3 G0048 COMPUT/IR
COMPUTER

B45
REVES E..THE ANATOMY OF PEACE. WOR-45 LAW CULTURE ACT/RES
NAT/G PLAN TEC/DEV EDU/PROP WAR NAT/LISM ATTIT CONCPT
ALL/VALS SOVEREIGN...POLICY HUM TIME/SEQ 20. NUC/PWR
PAGE 46 G0914 PEACE

B50
CANTRIL H..TENSIONS THAT CAUSE WAR. UNIV CULTURE SOCIETY
R+D CREATE EDU/PROP DRIVE PERSON KNOWL ORD/FREE PHIL/SCI
...HUM PSY SOC OBS CENSUS TREND CON/ANAL SOC/EXP PEACE
SIMUL GEN/METH ANTHOL COLD/WAR TOT/POP. PAGE 11
G0206

B51
HUXLEY J..FREEDOM AND CULTURE. UNIV LAW SOCIETY R+D CULTURE
ACADEM SCHOOL CREATE SANCTION ATTIT KNOWL...HUM ORD/FREE
ANTHOL 20. PAGE 27 G0540 PHIL/SCI
IDEA/COMP

B60
ARMS CONTROL. FUT UNIV WOR+45 INTELL R+D INT/ORG DELIB/GP
NAT/G VOL/ASSN CONSULT CREATE EDU/PROP PEACE...HUM ORD/FREE
GEN/LAWS TOT/POP 20. PAGE 1 G0015 ARMS/CONT
NUC/PWR

B60
EINSTEIN A..EINSTEIN ON PEACE. FUT WOR+45 WOR-45 INT/ORG
SOCIETY NAT/G PLAN BAL/PWR CAP/ISM DIPLOM ARMS/CONT NUC/PWR
DETER NAT/LISM...POLICY RELATIV HUM PHIL/SCI CONCPT PEACE
BIOG COLD/WAR LEAGUE/NAT NAZI. PAGE 17 G0338

B64
GRODZINS M..THE ATOMIC AGE: FORTY-FIVE SCIENTISTS INTELL
AND SCHOLARS SPEAK ON NATIONAL AND WORLD AFFAIRS. ARMS/CONT
FUT USA+45 WOR+45 R+D INT/ORG NAT/G CONSULT TEC/DEV NUC/PWR
EDU/PROP ATTIT PERSON ORD/FREE...HUM CONCPT ATTIT
TIME/SEQ CON/ANAL. PAGE 23 G0454

B65
KENT A..SPECIALIZED INFORMATION CENTERS. INTELL R+D COMPUT/IR
VOL/ASSN CONSULT COMPUTER KNOWL...DECISION HUM CREATE
PHIL/SCI METH/CNCPT TREND CHARTS 20. PAGE 30 G0593 TEC/DEV
METH/COMP

B66
AMERICAN LIBRARY ASSN.GUIDE TO JAPANESE REFERENCE BIBLIOG/A
BOOKS....HUM 20 CHINJAP. PAGE 3 G0054 SOC
TEC/DEV
PHIL/SCI

S66
KAPLAN M.A.,"THE NEW GREAT DEBATE* TRADITIONALISM PHIL/SCI
VS SCIENCE IN INTERNATIONAL RELATIONS."...DECISION CONSERVE
HUM QUANT STYLE NET/THEORY CON/ANAL STERTYP DIPLOM
GEN/LAWS. PAGE 29 G0577 SIMUL

B67
CROSSON F.J..SCIENCE AND CONTEMPORARY SOCIETY. FUT PHIL/SCI
WOR+45 SECT CREATE PROB/SOLV...HUM PREDICT TREND SOCIETY
IDEA/COMP ANTHOL. PAGE 14 G0263 TEC/DEV
CONCPT

B67
GULICK M.C.,NONCONVENTIONAL INFORMATION SYSTEMS BIBLIOG/A
SERVING THE SOCIAL SCIENCES AND THE HUMANITIES; A R+D
BIBLIOGRAPHIC ESSAY (PAPER). USA+45 COMPUTER CREATE COMPUT/IR
EDU/PROP KNOWL...SOC METH 20. PAGE 23 G0462 HUM

HUM/RIGHTS....HUMAN RIGHTS, DECLARATIONS OF HUMAN RIGHTS,
AND HUMAN RIGHTS COMMISSIONS (OFFICIAL ORGANIZATIONS)

HUMAN DEVELOPMENTAL CHANGE....SEE DEVELOPMNT

HUMAN NATURE....SEE PERSON

HUMAN RELATIONS....SEE RELATIONS INDEX

HUMAN RIGHTS, DECLARATIONS OF HUMAN RIGHTS, AND HUMAN
RIGHTS COMMISSIONS (OFFICIAL ORGANIZATIONS)....SEE
HUM/RIGHTS

HUMANISM....HUMANISM AND HUMANISTS

HUMANITARIANISM....SEE HUMANISM

HUMANITIES....SEE HUM

HUME/D....DAVID HUME

B67
CONNOLLY W.E.,POLITICAL SCIENCE AND IDEOLOGY. PWR
UTOPIA ATTIT KNOWL...MAJORIT EPIST PHIL/SCI SOC PLURISM
IDEA/COMP HYPO/EXP GEN/LAWS METH HUME/D MARX/KARL. ELITES
PAGE 13 G0250 CONCPT

HUMPHREY/H....HUBERT HORATIO HUMPHREY

HUNGARY....SEE ALSO COM

S63
SMITH D.O.,"WHAT IS A WAR DETERRENT." FUT GERMANY ACT/RES
HUNGARY UK USA+45 WOR+45 WOR-45 NAT/G TEC/DEV FORCES
BAL/PWR PWR...CONCPT GEN/LAWS COLD/WAR 20. PAGE 51 ARMS/CONT
G1013 DETER

S64
MARES V.E.,"EAST EUROPE'S SECOND CHANCE." COM VOL/ASSN
EUR+WWI HUNGARY ROMANIA USSR YUGOSLAVIA ECO/UNDEV ECO/TAC
NAT/G TOP/EX CREATE PLAN TEC/DEV REGION NAT/LISM
RIGID/FLEX PWR...CONCPT STAT COMECON 20. PAGE 36
G0705

B66
SPULBER N..THE STATE AND ECONOMIC DEVELOPMENT IN ECO/DEV
EASTERN EUROPE. BULGARIA COM CZECHOSLVK HUNGARY ECO/UNDEV
POLAND YUGOSLAVIA CULTURE PLAN CAP/ISM INT/TRADE NAT/G
CONTROL...POLICY CHARTS METH/COMP BIBLIOG/A 19/20. TOTALISM
PAGE 52 G1028

B67
NATIONAL SCIENCE FOUNDATION.DIRECTORY OF SELECTED INDEX
RESEARCH INSTITUTES IN EASTERN EUROPE. BULGARIA R+D
CZECHOSLVK HUNGARY POLAND ROMANIA INTELL ACADEM COM
NAT/G ACT/RES 20. PAGE 41 G0814 PHIL/SCI

HUNTINGTON S.P. G0537,G0538

HUNTNGTN/S....SAMUEL P. HUNTINGTON

HUNTON/P....PHILIP HUNTON

HURLEY/PJ....PATRICK J. HURLEY

HUSSEIN....KING HUSSEIN I, KING OF JORDAN

HUTCHINS/R....ROBERT HUTCHINS

HUTCHINSON C.E. G0539

HUXLEY J. G0540

HUZAR E. G0541

HYPO/EXP....INTELLECTUAL CONSTRUCTS

B11
BERGSON H.,CREATIVE EVOLUTION. FUT WOR+45 WOR-45   BIO/SOC
INTELL AGRI R+D ATTIT PERCEPT PERSON RIGID/FLEX   KNOWL
...RELATIV PHIL/SCI PSY METH/CNCPT MATH HIST/WRIT
TREND HYPO/EXP TOT/POP. PAGE 7 G0127

S48
MACCORQUODALE K.,"ON A DISTINCTION BETWEEN   PSY
HYPOTHETICAL CONSTRUCTS AND INTERVENING VARIABLES."   PHIL/SCI
...METH/CNCPT LING IDEA/COMP HYPO/EXP SOC/EXP   CONCPT
BIBLIOG 20. PAGE 35 G0686   GEN/METH

S48
MERTON R.K.,"THE BEARING OF EMPIRICAL RESEARCH UPON ACT/RES
THE DEVELOPMENT OF SOCIAL THEORY" (BMR)"...SOC   SOC/EXP
CONCPT QUANT METH/COMP HYPO/EXP 20. PAGE 38 G0757 OBS
  PHIL/SCI

B51
LEWIN K.,FIELD THEORY IN SOCIAL SCIENCE: SELECTED PHIL/SCI
THEORETICAL PAPERS. UNIV CREATE DRIVE PERCEPT KNOWL HYPO/EXP
...METH/CNCPT CONT/OBS CHARTS GEN/METH METH
VAL/FREE 20. PAGE 33 G0661

S54
BATES J.,"A MODEL FOR THE SCIENCE OF DECISION."   QUANT
UNIV ROUTINE...CONT/OBS CON/ANAL HYPO/EXP GAME. DECISION
PAGE 5 G0101   PHIL/SCI
  METH/CNCPT

B55
SHUBIK M.,READINGS IN GAME THEORY AND POLITICAL MATH
BEHAVIOR. WOR+45 FORCES CREATE ROUTINE WAR PEACE DECISION
PERCEPT KNOWL PWR...PSY SOC CONCPT METH/CNCPT STAT DIPLOM
CHARTS HYPO/EXP GAME METH VAL/FREE 20. PAGE 50
G0991

S55
DRUCKER P.F.,"'MANAGEMENT SCIENCE' AND THE   MGT
MANAGER." PLAN ROUTINE RIGID/FLEX...METH/CNCPT LOG STRUCT
HYPO/EXP. PAGE 16 G0315   DECISION
  RATIONAL

S55
MILLER J.G.,"TOWARD A GENERAL THEORY FOR THE   CONCPT
BEHAVIORAL SCIENCES" (BMR)" CREATE ALL/VALS KNOWL OP/RES
...CON/ANAL CHARTS HYPO/EXP SIMUL BIBLIOG 20. METH/CNCPT
PAGE 39 G0773   COMPUTER

S58
ARGYRIS C.,"SOME PROBLEMS IN CONCEPTUALIZING FINAN
ORGANIZATIONAL CLIMATE: A CASE STUDY OF A BANK" CONCPT
(BMR)" USA+45 EX/STRUC ADMIN PERS/REL ADJUST PERSON LG/CO
...POLICY HYPO/EXP SIMUL 20. PAGE 3 G0064   INGP/REL

S58
FOLDES L.,"UNCERTAINTY, PROBABILITY AND POTENTIAL PROBABIL
SURPRISE." MARKET PROB/SOLV RISK PERSON...DECISION ADMIN
MGT HYPO/EXP GAME. PAGE 19 G0376   ROUTINE

L59
BURNS A.L.,"THE RATIONALE OF CATALYTIC WAR." COM COERCE
USA+45 WOR+45 R+D NAT/G FORCES ACT/RES TEC/DEV PWR NUC/PWR
...DECISION HYPO/EXP TOT/POP 20. PAGE 10 G0191 WAR

L59
BURNS A.L.,"POWER POLITICS AND THE GROWING NUCLEAR FORCES
CLUB." FUT WOR+45 TEC/DEV EXEC ARMS/CONT COERCE BAL/PWR
DETER...DECISION HYPO/EXP 20. PAGE 10 G0192 NUC/PWR

S59
ADAMS E.W.,"A MODEL OF RISKLESS CHOICE." CREATE GAME
PROB/SOLV UTIL...PROBABIL PREDICT HYPO/EXP. PAGE 2 SIMUL
G0029   RISK
  DECISION

S59
GOLDHAMMER H.,"SOME OBSERVATIONS ON POLITICAL COMPUT/IR
GAMING." FUT WOR+45 R+D NAT/G ACT/RES CREATE CHOOSE DECISION
ATTIT PWR...POLICY CONCPT METH/CNCPT STYLE KNO/TEST DIPLOM
TREND HYPO/EXP GAME GEN/METH METH 20. PAGE 22 G0426

B60
HITCH C.J.,THE ECONOMICS OF DEFENSE IN THE NUCLEAR R+D

AGE. USA+45 WOR+45 CREATE PLAN NUC/PWR ATTIT FORCES
...CON/ANAL CHARTS HYPO/EXP NATO 20. PAGE 26 G0514

B61
ROSENAU J.N.,INTERNATIONAL POLITICS AND FOREIGN ACT/RES
POLICY: A READER IN RESEARCH AND THEORY. ELITES DIPLOM
ATTIT SOVEREIGN...DECISION CHARTS HYPO/EXP GAME CONCPT
SIMUL ANTHOL BIBLIOG METH 20. PAGE 48 G0936 POLICY

B61
SCHMIDT H.,VERTEIDIGUNG ODER VERGELTUNG. COM CUBA PLAN
GERMANY/W USSR FORCES DIPLOM ARMS/CONT DETER WAR
NUC/PWR...POLICY CHARTS HYPO/EXP SIMUL BIBLIOG 20 BAL/PWR
NATO COLD/WAR. PAGE 49 G0970   ORD/FREE

S61
ANDREWS R.B.,"URBAN ECONOMICS: AN APPRAISAL OF MUNIC
PROGRESS." LOC/G PROB/SOLV TEC/DEV...CONCPT PHIL/SCI
OBS/ENVIR METH/COMP HYPO/EXP SOC/EXP SIMUL GEN/METH ECOMETRIC
METH 20. PAGE 3 G0058

S61
BENNION E.G.,"ECONOMETRICS FOR MANAGEMENT." USA+45 ECOMETRIC
INDUS EX/STRUC ACT/RES COMPUTER UTIL...MATH STAT MGT
PREDICT METH/COMP HYPO/EXP. PAGE 6 G0122   SIMUL
  DECISION

B62
BOULDING K.E.,CONFLICT AND DEFENSE: A GENERAL MATH
THEORY. FUT SOCIETY INT/ORG NAT/G CREATE BAL/PWR SIMUL
COERCE NAT/LISM DRIVE ALL/VALS...PLURIST DECISION PEACE
CONCPT METH/CNCPT TREND HYPO/EXP TOT/POP 20. PAGE 8 WAR
G0157

B62
SNYDER R.C.,FOREIGN POLICY DECISION-MAKING. FUT TEC/DEV
KOREA WOR+45 R+D CREATE ADMIN ROUTINE PWR HYPO/EXP
...DECISION PSY SOC CONCPT METH/CNCPT CON/ANAL DIPLOM
CHARTS GEN/METH METH 20. PAGE 52 G1018

B62
SOHN L.B.,ZONAL DISARMAMENT: VARIATIONS ON A THEME. ORD/FREE
FUT WOR+45 SOCIETY ACT/RES PLAN NUC/PWR PEACE ATTIT NEW/IDEA
...POLICY GEOG CONT/OBS HYPO/EXP 20. PAGE 52 G1020 ARMS/CONT

B62
YALEN R.,REGIONALISM AND WORLD ORDER. EUR+WWI ORD/FREE
WOR+45 WOR-45 INT/ORG VOL/ASSN DELIB/GP FORCES POLICY
TOP/EX BAL/PWR DIPLOM DOMIN REGION ARMS/CONT PWR
...JURID HYPO/EXP COLD/WAR 20. PAGE 64 G1261

S62
FLOOD M.M.,"STOCHASTIC LEARNING THEORY APPLIED TO DECISION
CHOICE EXPERIMENTS WITH RATS, DOGS, AND MEN."...PSY COMPUTER
LAB/EXP METH. PAGE 19 G0372   HYPO/EXP
  TEC/DEV

B63
BONINI C.P.,SIMULATION OF INFORMATION AND DECISION INDUS
SYSTEMS IN THE FIRM. MARKET BUDGET DOMIN EDU/PROP SIMUL
ADMIN COST ATTIT HABITAT PERCEPT PWR...CONCPT DECISION
PROBABIL QUANT PREDICT HYPO/EXP BIBLIOG. PAGE 8 MGT
G0152

S63
ABT C.,"THE PROBLEMS AND POSSIBILITIES OF SPACE ACT/RES
ARMS CONTROL." FUT USA+45 WOR+45 AIR SOCIETY NAT/G ORD/FREE
BAL/PWR EDU/PROP ATTIT PWR WEALTH...HYPO/EXP ARMS/CONT
TOT/POP 20. PAGE 2 G0025   SPACE

B65
ANTHONY R.N.,PLANNING AND CONTROL SYSTEMS. UNIV CONTROL
OP/RES...DECISION MGT LING. PAGE 3 G0061 PLAN
  METH
  HYPO/EXP

B65
SINGER J.D.,HUMAN BEHAVIOR AND INTERNATIONAL DIPLOM
POLITICS* CONTRIBUTIONS FROM THE SOCIAL- PHIL/SCI
PSYCHOLOGICAL SCIENCES. ACT/RES PLAN EDU/PROP ADMIN QUANT
KNOWL...DECISION PSY SOC NET/THEORY HYPO/EXP SIMUL
LAB/EXP SOC/EXP GEN/METH ANTHOL BIBLIOG. PAGE 51
G1006

B65
STEINER G.A.,THE CREATIVE ORGANIZATION. ELITES CREATE
LG/CO PLAN PROB/SOLV TEC/DEV INSPECT CAP/ISM MGT
CONTROL EXEC PERSON...METH/COMP HYPO/EXP 20. ADMIN
PAGE 52 G1034   SOC

S65
BLOOMFIELD L.P.,"ARMS CONTROL AND THE DEVELOPING ARMS/CONT
COUNTRIES." AFR ISLAM S/ASIA USA+45 VOL/ASSN ECO/UNDEV
TEC/DEV DIPLOM REGION NUC/PWR...PREDICT TREND. HYPO/EXP
PAGE 7 G0142   OBS

KUENNE R.E.,THE POLARIS MISSILE STRIKE* A GENERAL ECONOMIC SYSTEMS ANALYSIS. USA+45 USSR NAT/G BAL/PWR ARMS/CONT WAR...MATH PROBABIL COMPUT/IR CHARTS HYPO/EXP SIMUL. PAGE 32 G0625
B66 NUC/PWR FORCES DETER DIPLOM

COHEN A.,"THE TECHNOLOGY/ELITE APPROACH TO THE DEVELOPMENTAL PROCESS* PERUVIAN CASE STUDY." L/A+17C STRUCT CREATE ECO/TAC FOR/AID CIVMIL/REL MARXISM TECHRACY HYPO/EXP. PAGE 12 G0239
S66 ECO/UNDEV ELITES PERU

EWALD R.F.,"ONE OF MANY POSSIBLE GAMES." ACADEM INT/ORG ARMS/CONT...INT/LAW GAME. PAGE 18 G0354
S66 SIMUL HYPO/EXP PROG/TEAC RECORD

CONNOLLY W.E.,POLITICAL SCIENCE AND IDEOLOGY. UTOPIA ATTIT KNOWL...MAJORIT EPIST PHIL/SCI SOC IDEA/COMP HYPO/EXP GEN/LAWS METH HUME/D MARX/KARL. PAGE 13 G0250
B67 PWR PLURISM ELITES CONCPT

RUTGERS U GRADUATE SCH LIB SCI,BIBLIOGRAPHY OF RESEARCH RELATING TO THE COMMUNICATION OF SCIENTIFIC AND TECHNICAL INFORMATION. FUT CREATE FEEDBACK...PHIL/SCI NEW/IDEA COMPUT/IR HYPO/EXP. PAGE 48 G0951
B67 BIBLIOG/A COM/IND R+D TEC/DEV

HYPOTHETICAL EXPERIMENTS....SEE HYPO/EXP

IADB....INTER-ASIAN DEVELOPMENT BANK

IAEA....INTERNATIONAL ATOMIC ENERGY AGENCY

STOESSINGER J.G.,"THE INTERNATIONAL ATOMIC ENERGY AGENCY: THE FIRST PHASE." FUT WOR+45 NAT/G VOL/ASSN DELIB/GP BAL/PWR LEGIT ADMIN ROUTINE PWR...OBS CON/ANAL GEN/LAWS VAL/FREE 20 IAEA. PAGE 53 G1037
S59 INT/ORG ECO/DEV FOR/AID NUC/PWR

ATOMIC INDUSTRIAL FORUM,SAFEGUARDS AGAINST DIVERSION OF NUCLEAR MATERIALS FROM PEACEFUL TO MILITARY PURPOSES. WOR+45 DELIB/GP FORCES PLAN DIPLOM CONFER PEACE...ANTHOL 20 IAEA. PAGE 4 G0081
B65 NUC/PWR CIVMIL/REL INSPECT CONTROL

US CONGRESS JT ATOM ENRGY COMM,ATOMIC ENERGY LEGISLATION THROUGH 89TH CONGRESS, 1ST SESSION. USA+45 LAW INT/ORG DELIB/GP BUDGET DIPLOM 20 AEC CONGRESS CASEBOOK EURATOM IAEA. PAGE 57 G1114
B65 NUC/PWR FORCES PEACE LEGIS

IANNI O. G0542

IBO....IBO TRIBE

IBRD....INTERNATIONAL BANK FOR RECONSTRUCTION AND DEVELOPMENT

ICA....INTERNATIONAL COOPERATION ADMINISTRATION

ICC....U.S. INTERSTATE COMMERCE COMMISSION

ICELAND....ICELAND

ICJ....INTERNATIONAL COURT OF JUSTICE; SEE ALSO WORLD/CT

ICSU....INTERNATIONAL COUNCIL OF SCIENTIFIC UNIONS

IDA....INTERNATIONAL DEVELOPMENT ASSOCIATION

IDAHO....IDAHO

IDEA....SEE NEW/IDEA

IDEA/COMP....COMPARISON OF IDEAS

BARKER E.,POLITICAL THOUGHT IN ENGLAND: FROM HERBERT SPENCER TO THE PRESENT DAY. UK ALL/IDEOS ...PHIL/SCI 19/20 SPENCER/H GREEN/TH BENTHAM/J MAITLAND/F. PAGE 5 G0094
B28 INTELL GEN/LAWS IDEA/COMP

KAPLAN A.,"CONTENT ANALYSIS AND THE THEORY OF SIGNS" (BMR)" PERS/REL...PSY CONCPT LING IDEA/COMP SIMUL BIBLIOG 20 MORRIS/CW. PAGE 29 G0573
S43 LOG CON/ANAL STAT PHIL/SCI

MACCORQUODALE K.,"ON A DISTINCTION BETWEEN HYPOTHETICAL CONSTRUCTS AND INTERVENING VARIABLES." ...METH/CNCPT LING IDEA/COMP HYPO/EXP SOC/EXP
S48 PSY PHIL/SCI CONCPT

BIBLIOG 20. PAGE 35 G0686
GEN/METH

HUXLEY J.,FREEDOM AND CULTURE. UNIV LAW SOCIETY R+D ACADEM SCHOOL CREATE SANCTION ATTIT KNOWL...HUM ANTHOL 20. PAGE 27 G0540
B51 CULTURE ORD/FREE PHIL/SCI IDEA/COMP

BERGMANN G.,"IDEOLOGY" (BMR)" UNIV PERCEPT KNOWL ...IDEA/COMP METH. PAGE 7 G0126
S51 PHIL/SCI CONCPT LOG ALL/IDEOS

SPENCER R.F.,METHOD AND PERSPECTIVE IN ANTHROPOLOGY ....GEOG LING QUANT STAT TESTS SAMP/SIZ CON/ANAL IDEA/COMP METH/COMP ANTHOL BIBLIOG 20. PAGE 52 G1025
B54 PHIL/SCI SOC PSY METH

LIPPMAN W.,THE PUBLIC PHILOSOPHY. EX/STRUC TOP/EX LOBBY RATIONAL POPULISM...POLICY SOC CONCPT PREDICT GP/COMP IDEA/COMP. PAGE 34 G0673
B55 MAJORIT STRUCT PWR TOTALISM

DUPUY R.E.,"MILITARY HERITAGE OF AMERICA." USA+45 USA-45 TEC/DEV DIPLOM ROUTINE...POLICY TREND CHARTS IDEA/COMP BIBLIOG COLD/WAR. PAGE 17 G0325
C56 FORCES WAR CONCPT

MARCUSE H.,SOVIET MARXISM. A CRITICAL ANALYSIS. USSR CONSTN PLAN PRODUC RATIONAL SOCISM...IDEA/COMP 20 COM/PARTY. PAGE 36 G0703
B58 MARXISM ATTIT POLICY

COLUMBIA U BUREAU APPL SOC R, ATTITUDES OF PROMINENT AMERICANS TOWARD "WORLD PEACE THROUGH WORLD LAW" (SUPRA-NATL ORGANIZATION FOR WAR PREVENTION). USA+45 USSR ELITES FORCES PLAN PROB/SOLV CONTROL WAR PWR...POLICY SOC QU IDEA/COMP 20 UN. PAGE 45 G0888
B59 ATTIT ACT/RES INT/LAW STAT

WELTON H.,THE THIRD WORLD WAR; TRADE AND INDUSTRY, THE NEW BATTLEGROUND. WOR+45 ECO/DEV INDUS MARKET TASK...MGT IDEA/COMP COLD/WAR. PAGE 63 G1229
B59 INT/TRADE PLAN DIPLOM

BENDIX R.,"INDUSTRIALIZATION, IDEOLOGIES, AND SOCIAL STRUCTURE" (BMR)" UK USA-45 USSR STRUCT WORKER GP/REL EFFICIENCY...IDEA/COMP 20. PAGE 6 G0117
S59 INDUS ATTIT MGT ADMIN

KRUPP S.,PATTERN IN ORGANIZATIONAL ANALYSIS: A CRITICAL EXAMINATION. INGP/REL PERS/REL RATIONAL ATTIT AUTHORIT DRIVE PWR...DECISION PHIL/SCI SOC IDEA/COMP. PAGE 32 G0622
B61 MGT CONTROL CONCPT METH/CNCPT

MCCRACKEN H.L.,KEYNESIAN ECONOMICS IN THE STREAM OF ECONOMIC THOUGHT. FINAN MARKET BARGAIN EFFICIENCY OPTIMAL...PHIL/SCI CONCPT IDEA/COMP BIBLIOG 18/20 KEYNES/JM. PAGE 37 G0732
B61 ECO/TAC DEMAND ECOMETRIC

MCRAE R.,THE PROBLEM OF THE UNITY OF THE SCIENCES: BACON TO KANT. CREATE TASK KNOWL...PERS/COMP 16/18 BACON/F DESCARTE/R LEIBNITZ/G KANT/I DIDEROT/D. PAGE 38 G0748
B61 PHIL/SCI IDEA/COMP PERSON

STEIN W.,NUCLEAR WEAPONS: A CATHOLIC RESPONSE. WOR+45 FORCES ARMS/CONT DETER MURDER MORAL...POLICY CATH IDEA/COMP ANTHOL 20. PAGE 52 G1033
B61 NUC/PWR WAR CATHISM ATTIT

BOCK E.A.,CASE STUDIES IN AMERICAN GOVERNMENT. USA+45 ECO/DEV CHIEF EDU/PROP CT/SYS RACE/REL ORD/FREE...JURID MGT PHIL/SCI PRESIDENT CASEBOOK. PAGE 8 G0146
B62 POLICY LEGIS IDEA/COMP NAT/G

FRYKLUND R.,100 MILLION LIVES: MAXIMUM SURVIVAL IN A NUCLEAR WAR. USA+45 USSR CONTROL WEAPON ...IDEA/COMP NAT/COMP 20. PAGE 20 G0397
B62 NUC/PWR WAR PLAN DETER

HALPERIN M.H.,LIMITED WAR; AN ESSAY ON THE DEVELOPMENT OF THE THEORY AND AN ANNOTATED BIBLIOGRAPHY (OCCASIONAL PAPER NO. 3). WOR+45 WOR-45 NUC/PWR...CONCPT IDEA/COMP METH/COMP 19/20.
B62 BIBLIOG/A WAR ARMS/CONT FORCES

ANALYSIS OF A CROSS POLITY SURVEY." TEC/DEV
...DECISION PHIL/SCI CONCPT STAT IDEA/COMP
GEN/LAWS. PAGE 23 G0447
GEN/METH
CLASSIF

B63
REED E.,CHALLENGES TO DEMOCRACY: THE NEXT TEN
YEARS. FUT USA+45 ECO/DEV DELIB/GP TEC/DEV CONFER
GOV/REL KNOWL ORD/FREE...MAJORIT IDEA/COMP ANTHOL
20. PAGE 46 G0909
POLICY
EDU/PROP
ECO/TAC
NAT/G

S65
HSIEH A.L.,"THE SINO-SOVIET NUCLEAR DIALOGUE*
1963." S/ASIA USA+45 RISK DETER REV WAR SOVEREIGN
IDEA/COMP. PAGE 27 G0533
ASIA
USSR
NUC/PWR

B64
BRILLOUIN L.,SCIENTIFIC UNCERTAINTY AND
INFORMATION. PROB/SOLV AUTOMAT PERCEPT ORD/FREE
...MATH REGRESS STAT STYLE OBS IDEA/COMP SIMUL
TIME. PAGE 9 G0169
PHIL/SCI
NEW/IDEA
METH/CNCPT
CREATE

S65
KOHL W.L.,"NUCLEAR SHARING IN NATO AND THE
MULTILATERAL FORCE." FUT USSR VOL/ASSN TEC/DEV
DIPLOM NUC/PWR WAR WEAPON NATO. PAGE 31 G0611
ARMS/CONT
OBS
IDEA/COMP

B64
BROWN N.,NUCLEAR WAR* THE IMPENDING STRATEGIC
DEADLOCK. USA+45 USSR TEC/DEV BUDGET RISK ARMS/CONT
NUC/PWR WEAPON COST BIO/SOC...GEOG IDEA/COMP
NAT/COMP GAME NATO WARSAW/P. PAGE 9 G0177
FORCES
OP/RES
WAR
GEN/LAWS

S65
KREITH K.,"PEACE RESEARCH AND GOVERNMENT POLICY."
INTELL NAT/G DIPLOM ECO/TAC CONTROL ARMS/CONT WAR
PERCEPT...DECISION IDEA/COMP. PAGE 31 G0619
PEACE
STYLE
OBS

B64
HODGETTS J.E.,ADMINISTERING THE ATOM FOR PEACE.
OP/RES TEC/DEV ADMIN...IDEA/COMP METH/COMP 20.
PAGE 26 G0517
PROB/SOLV
NUC/PWR
PEACE
MGT

C65
SEARA M.V.,"COSMIC INTERNATIONAL LAW." LAW ACADEM
ACT/RES DIPLOM COLONIAL CONTROL NUC/PWR SOVEREIGN
...GEN/LAWS BIBLIOG UN. PAGE 50 G0987
SPACE
INT/LAW
IDEA/COMP
INT/ORG

B64
MILIBAND R.,THE SOCIALIST REGISTER: 1964. GERMANY/W
ITALY UK LABOR POL/PAR ECO/TAC FOR/AID NUC/PWR
...POLICY SOCIALIST IDEA/COMP 20 MAO NASSER/G.
PAGE 39 G0769
MARXISM
SOCISM
CAP/ISM
PROB/SOLV

B66
DAENIKER G.,STRATEGIE DES KLEIN STAATS. SWITZERLND
ACT/RES CREATE DIPLOM NEUTRAL DETER WAR WEAPON PWR
SOVEREIGN...IDEA/COMP 20 COLD/WAR. PAGE 14 G0270
NUC/PWR
PLAN
FORCES
NAT/G

B64
NASA,PROCEEDINGS OF CONFERENCE ON THE LAW OF SPACE
AND OF SATELLITE COMMUNICATIONS: CHICAGO 1963. FUT
WOR+45 DELIB/GP PROB/SOLV TEC/DEV CONFER ADJUD
NUC/PWR...POLICY IDEA/COMP 20 NASA. PAGE 41 G0805
SPACE
COM/IND
LAW
DIPLOM

B66
FALK R.A.,ON MINIMIZING THE USE OF NUCLEAR WEAPONS;
THREE ESSAYS; RESEARCH MONOGRAPH NO. 23. WOR+45
STRUCT CREATE NUC/PWR REV CONSERVE...POLICY
NET/THEORY IDEA/COMP GEN/LAWS GEN/METH. PAGE 18
G0359
DIPLOM
EQUILIB
PHIL/SCI
PROB/SOLV

B64
ROBERTS HL,FOREIGN AFFAIRS BIBLIOGRAPHY, 1952-1962.
ECO/DEV SECT PLAN FOR/AID INT/TRADE ARMS/CONT
NAT/LISM ATTIT...INT/LAW GOV/COMP IDEA/COMP 20.
PAGE 47 G0928
BIBLIOG/A
DIPLOM
INT/ORG
WAR

B66
GREEN P.,DEADLY LOGIC* THE THEORY OF NUCLEAR
DETERRENCE. USA+45 ACT/RES OP/RES NUC/PWR RATIONAL
ALL/VALS PWR...DECISION MGT PHIL/SCI QUANT
IDEA/COMP GAME. PAGE 23 G0444
DETER
ACADEM
GEN/LAWS
RECORD

B65
BEAUFRE A.,AN INTRODUCTION TO STRATEGY, WITH
PARTICULAR REFERENCE TO PROBLEMS OF DEFENSE,
POLITICS, ECONOMICS IN THE NUCLEAR AGE. WOR+45
FORCES DIPLOM DETER CIVMIL/REL GP/REL...NEW/IDEA
IDEA/COMP 20. PAGE 6 G0111
PLAN
NUC/PWR
WEAPON
DECISION

B66
HALPIN A.W.,THEORY AND RESEARCH IN ADMINISTRATION.
ACT/RES LEAD...MGT IDEA/COMP METH/COMP. PAGE 24
G0475
GEN/LAWS
EDU/PROP
ADMIN
PHIL/SCI

B65
BENJAMIN A.C.,SCIENCE, TECHNOLOGY, AND HUMAN
VALUES. WOR+45 SECT EDU/PROP GP/REL ATTIT...TECHNIC
LING IDEA/COMP WORSHIP 20. PAGE 6 G0118
PHIL/SCI
CREATE
ROLE
SOCIETY

B66
LECHT L.,GOAL, PRIORITIES, AND DOLLARS: THE NEXT
DECADE. SPACE USA+45 SOCIETY AGRI BUDGET FOR/AID
...HEAL SOC/WK STAT CHARTS 20 URBAN/RNWL PUB/TRANS.
PAGE 33 G0649
IDEA/COMP
POLICY
CONSEN
PLAN

B65
US SENATE COMM AERO SPACE SCI,NATIONAL SPACE GOALS
FOR THE POST-APOLLO PERIOD. USA+45 CONSULT DELIB/GP
TEC/DEV BUDGET GP/REL ATTIT...CHARTS IDEA/COMP TIME
20 DEPT/DEFEN NASA CONGRESS. PAGE 59 G1166
SPACE
FUT
R+D
LEGIS

B66
ODEGARD P.H.,POLITICAL POWER AND SOCIAL CHANGE.
UNIV NAT/G CREATE ALL/IDEOS...POLICY GEOG SOC
CENSUS TREND. PAGE 42 G0829
PWR
TEC/DEV
IDEA/COMP

L65
PILISUK M.,"IS THERE A MILITARY INDUSTRIAL COMPLEX
WHICH PREVENTS PEACE CONSENSUS; COUNTERVAILING
POWER IN PLURALIST SYSTEMS." INDUS R+D ACADEM
FEEDBACK CIVMIL/REL ADJUST CONSEN ATTIT RIGID/FLEX
...CENSUS IDEA/COMP BIBLIOG. PAGE 45 G0878
ELITES
WEAPON
PEACE
ARMS/CONT

B66
US HOUSE COMM ON JUDICIARY,CIVIL COMMITMENT AND
TREATMENT OF NARCOTIC ADDICTS. USA+45 SOCIETY FINAN
LEGIS PROB/SOLV GIVE CT/SYS SANCTION HEALTH
...POLICY HEAL 20. PAGE 58 G1141
BIO/SOC
CRIME
IDEA/COMP
CONTROL

S65
BEAUFRE A.,"THE SHARING OF NUCLEAR
RESPONSIBILITIES* A PROBLEM IN NEED OF SOLUTION."
FRANCE USA+45 INT/ORG NAT/G DELIB/GP FORCES CONTROL
NUC/PWR RIGID/FLEX...CONCPT IDEA/COMP NATO. PAGE 6
G0110
DETER
RISK
ACT/RES
WAR

B66
WARD B.,NATIONALISM AND IDEOLOGY. ECO/UNDEV KIN
CREATE CAP/ISM FOR/AID ALL/VALS MARXISM...POLICY
SOC. PAGE 62 G1211
IDEA/COMP
NAT/LISM
ATTIT

S65
BIRNBAUM K.,"SWEDEN'S NUCLEAR POLICY." WOR+45
POL/PAR CREATE TEC/DEV NEUTRAL RISK WAR ORD/FREE
...DECISION IDEA/COMP NAT/COMP TIME. PAGE 7 G0137
SWEDEN
NUC/PWR
DIPLOM
ARMS/CONT

B67
BUTLER J.,BOSTON UNIVERSITY PAPERS ON AFRICA*
TRANSITION IN AFRICAN POLITICS. AFR LAW CONSTN
LABOR POL/PAR TEC/DEV 20. PAGE 10 G0197
IDEA/COMP
NAT/G
PWR

S65
BOHN L.C.,"ATOMS FOR PEACE AND ATOMS FOR WAR."
WOR+45 INT/ORG TEC/DEV DIPLOM IDEA/COMP. PAGE 8
G0149
NUC/PWR
ARMS/CONT
RECORD

B67
CHARLESWORTH J.C.,CONTEMPORARY POLITICAL ANALYSIS.
INTELL...DECISION METH/CNCPT MATH STYLE CON/ANAL
GAME ANTHOL 20. PAGE 11 G0222
R+D
IDEA/COMP
CONCPT
METH/COMP

S65
FINK C.F.,"MORE CALCULATIONS ABOUT DETERRENCE."
DRIVE...PHIL/SCI PSY STAT TIME/SEQ GAME GEN/LAWS.
PAGE 19 G0367
DETER
RECORD
PROBABIL
IDEA/COMP

B67
CONNOLLY W.E.,POLITICAL SCIENCE AND IDEOLOGY.
UTOPIA ATTIT KNOWL...MAJORIT EPIST PHIL/SCI SOC
IDEA/COMP HYPO/EXP GEN/LAWS METH HUME/D MARX/KARL.
PAGE 13 G0250
PWR
PLURISM
ELITES
CONCPT

S65
GREGG P.M.,"DIMENSIONS OF POLITICAL SYSTEMS: FACTOR
SIMUL

B67
CROSSON F.J.,SCIENCE AND CONTEMPORARY SOCIETY. FUT
WOR+45 SECT CREATE PROB/SOLV...HUM PREDICT TREND
IDEA/COMP ANTHOL. PAGE 14 G0263
PHIL/SCI
SOCIETY
TEC/DEV
CONCPT

EDU/PROP AGREE 20 TREATY. PAGE 55 G1090
DIPLOM
PRESS

B65
VERMOT-GAUCHY M.,L'EDUCATION NATIONALE DANS LA
FRANCE DE 1975. FRANCE FUT CULTURE ELITES R+D
SCHOOL PLAN EDU/PROP EFFICIENCY...POLICY PREDICT
CHARTS INDEX 20. PAGE 61 G1195
ACADEM
CREATE
TREND
INTELL

B67
NATIONAL SCIENCE FOUNDATION,DIRECTORY OF SELECTED
RESEARCH INSTITUTES IN EASTERN EUROPE. BULGARIA
CZECHOSLVK HUNGARY POLAND ROMANIA INTELL ACADEM
NAT/G ACT/RES 20. PAGE 41 G0814
INDEX
R+D
COM
PHIL/SCI

B67
US DEPARTMENT OF STATE,FOREIGN AFFAIRS RESEARCH
(PAMPHLET). USA+45 WOR+45 ACADEM NAT/G...PSY SOC
CHARTS 20. PAGE 57 G1124
BIBLIOG
INDEX
R+D
DIPLOM

INDIA....SEE ALSO S/ASIA

N
INDIA: A REFERENCE ANNUAL. INDIA CULTURE COM/IND
R+D FORCES PLAN RECEIVE EDU/PROP HEALTH...STAT
CHARTS BIBLIOG 20. PAGE 1 G0005
CONSTN
LABOR
INT/ORG

B57
GOLD N.L.,REGIONAL ECONOMIC DEVELOPMENT AND NUCLEAR
POWER IN INDIA. FUT INDIA FINAN FOR/AID INT/TRADE
BAL/PAY EFFICIENCY OPTIMAL PRODUC WEALTH...PREDICT
20. PAGE 22 G0424
ECO/UNDEV
TEC/DEV
NUC/PWR
INDUS

B58
LIST OF PUBLICATIONS (PERIODICAL OR AD HOC) ISSUED
BY VARIOUS MINISTRIES OF THE GOVERNMENT OF INDIA
(3RD ED.). INDIA ECO/UNDEV PLAN...POLICY MGT 20.
PAGE 1 G0014
BIBLIOG
NAT/G
ADMIN

B64
PARANJAPE H.K.,THE FLIGHT OF TECHNICAL PERSONNEL IN
PUBLIC UNDERTAKINGS. INDIA PAY DEMAND HAPPINESS
ORD/FREE...MGT QU 20 MIGRATION. PAGE 44 G0858
ADMIN
NAT/G
WORKER
PLAN

S64
"FURTHER READING." INDIA PAKISTAN SECT WAR PEACE
ATTIT...POLICY 20. PAGE 1 G0018
BIBLIOG
GP/REL
DIPLOM
NAT/G

S64
MAHALANOBIS P.C.,"PERSPECTIVE PLANNING IN INDIA:
STATISTICAL TOOLS." INDIA S/ASIA STRATA AGRI
DIST/IND FINAN INDUS SERV/IND NAT/G ECO/TAC
ORD/FREE WEALTH...POLICY TREND SIMUL VAL/FREE 20.
PAGE 35 G0695
PLAN
STAT

B65
HASSON J.A.,THE ECONOMICS OF NUCLEAR POWER. INDIA
UK USA+45 WOR+45 INT/ORG TEC/DEV COST...SOC STAT
CHARTS 20 EURATOM. PAGE 25 G0490
NUC/PWR
INDUS
ECO/DEV
METH

B65
MORRIS M.D.,THE EMERGENCE OF AN INDUSTRIAL LABOR
FORCE IN INDIA: A STUDY OF THE BOMBAY COTTON MILLS.
1854-1947. INDIA WORKER OP/RES ADMIN 19/20. PAGE 40
G0784
INDUS
LABOR
ECO/UNDEV
CAP/ISM

S65
DESAI M.J.,"INDIA AND NUCLEAR WEAPONS." ASIA
BAL/PWR DIPLOM NUC/PWR WEAPON PEACE RECORD. PAGE 15
G0294
INDIA
ARMS/CONT

B66
HALPERIN M.H.,CHINA AND NUCLEAR PROLIFERATION
(PAMPHLET). CHINA/COM FUT INDIA USA+45 USSR
ARMS/CONT WAR 20 CHINJAP. PAGE 24 G0474
NUC/PWR
FORCES
POLICY
DIPLOM

B66
US DEPARTMENT OF THE ARMY,COMMUNIST CHINA: A
STRATEGIC SURVEY: A BIBLIOGRAPHY (PAMPHLET NO.
20-67). CHINA/COM COM INDIA USSR NAT/G POL/PAR
EX/STRUC FORCES NUC/PWR REV ATTIT...POLICY GEOG
CHARTS. PAGE 58 G1133
BIBLIOG/A
MARXISM
S/ASIA
DIPLOM

S66
"FURTHER READING." INDIA LOC/G NAT/G PLAN ADMIN
WEALTH...GEOG SOC CONCPT CENSUS 20. PAGE 1 G0021
BIBLIOG
ECO/UNDEV
TEC/DEV
PROVS

B6
LERNER D.,COMMUNICATION AND CHANGE IN DEVELOPING
COUNTRIES. CHINA/COM INDIA PHILIPPINE COM/IND
CREATE TEC/DEV...ANTHOL 20. PAGE 33 G0659
EDU/PROP
ORD/FREE
PERCEPT
ECO/UNDEV

B67
US SENATE COMM ON FOREIGN REL,ARMS SALES TO NEAR
EAST AND SOUTH ASIAN COUNTRIES. INDIA IRAN PAKISTAN
WOR+45 PROC/MFG BAL/PWR DIPLOM...DECISION SENATE.
PAGE 60 G1183
WEAPON
FOR/AID
FORCES
POLICY

L67
"POLITICAL PARTIES ON FOREIGN POLICY IN THE INTER-
ELECTION YEARS 1962-66." ASIA COM INDIA USA+45 PLAN
ATTIT...DECISION 20. PAGE 1 G0023
POL/PAR
DIPLOM
POLICY

S67
HILL R.,"SOCIAL ASPECTS OF FAMILY PLANNING." INDIA
KOREA TAIWAN ECO/UNDEV PLAN PROB/SOLV TEC/DEV
EDU/PROP CONTROL ATTIT DRIVE...HEAL PSY SOC 20
BIRTH/CON UN. PAGE 26 G0512
FAM
BIO/SOC
GEOG
MARRIAGE

S67
JAIN G.,"INDIA REJECTS THE POWER RACE* REALISM
ABOUT NUCLEAR WEAPONS." FORCES PROB/SOLV FOR/AID
ARMS/CONT COST PWR...GOV/COMP 20. PAGE 28 G0556
INDIA
CHINA/COM
NUC/PWR
DIPLOM

S67
MEHTA A.,"INDIA* POVERTY AND CHANGE." STRATA INDUS
CREATE ECO/TAC FOR/AID NEUTRAL GP/REL ADJUST INCOME
...NEW/IDEA 20. PAGE 38 G0751
INDIA
SOCIETY
ECO/UNDEV
TEC/DEV

N67
US HOUSE COMM SCI ASTRONAUT,GOVERNMENT, SCIENCE,
AND INTERNATIONAL POLICY (PAMPHLET). INDIA
NETHERLAND ECO/DEV ECO/UNDEV R+D ACADEM PLAN DIPLOM
FOR/AID CONFER...PREDICT 20 CHINJAP. PAGE 59 G1152
NAT/G
POLICY
CREATE
TEC/DEV

INDIAN/AM....AMERICAN INDIANS

B67
NASH M.,MACHINE AGE MAYA. GUATEMALA L/A+17C STRUCT
AGRI WORKER CREATE INCOME ATTIT RIGID/FLEX ROLE
...IDEA/COMP SOC/EXP WORSHIP 20 INDIAN/AM. PAGE 41
G0806
INDUS
CULTURE
SOC
MUNIC

INDIANA....INDIANA

INDICATOR....NUMERICAL INDICES AND INDICATORS

INDIVIDUAL....SEE PERSON

INDOCTRINATION....SEE EDU/PROP

INDONESIA....SEE ALSO S/ASIA

INDUS....ALL OR MOST INDUSTRY; SEE ALSO SPECIFIC
    INDUSTRIES, INSTITUTIONAL INDEX, PART C, P. XII

N
FULLER G.A.,DEMOBILIZATION: A SELECTED LIST OF
REFERENCES. USA+45 LAW AGRI LABOR WORKER ECO/TAC
RATION RECEIVE EDU/PROP ROUTINE ARMS/CONT ALL/VALS
20. PAGE 20 G0398
BIBLIOG/A
INDUS
FORCES
NAT/G

B
US DEPT COMMERCE OFF TECH SERV,TECHNICAL
TRANSLATIONS. WOR+45 INDUS COMPUTER CREATE NUC/PWR
...PHIL/SCI COMPUT/IR METH/COMP METH. PAGE 58 G1135
BIBLIOG
R+D
TEC/DEV
AUTOMAT

N
ADVANCED MANAGEMENT. INDUS EX/STRUC WORKER OP/RES
...DECISION BIBLIOG/A 20. PAGE 1 G0003
MGT
ADMIN
LABOR
GP/REL

N
PRINCETON UNIVERSITY,SELECTED REFERENCES:
INDUSTRIAL RELATIONS SECTION. USA+45 EX/STRUC
WORKER TEC/DEV...MGT 20. PAGE 45 G0892
BIBLIOG/A
LABOR
INDUS
GP/REL

B14
CRAIG J.,ELEMENTS OF POLITICAL SCIENCE (3 VOLS.).
CONSTN AGRI INDUS SCHOOL FORCES TAX CT/SYS SUFF
MORAL WEALTH...CONCPT 19 CIVIL/LIB. PAGE 13 G0259
PHIL/SCI
NAT/G
ORD/FREE

N19
ATOMIC INDUSTRIAL FORUM,COMMENTARY ON LEGISLATION
TO PERMIT PRIVATE OWNERSHIP OF SPECIAL NUCLEAR
MATERIAL (PAMPHLET). USA+45 DELIB/GP LEGIS PLAN OWN
...POLICY 20 AEC CONGRESS. PAGE 4 G0076
NUC/PWR
MARKET
INDUS
LAW

US CHAMBER OF COMMERCE,THE SIGNIFICANCE OF CONCENTRATION RATIOS (PAMPHLET). USA+45 FINAN INDUS ADMIN...METH/CNCPT SAMP CHARTS 20. PAGE 56 G1109 — N19 — MARKET PREDICT LG/CO CONTROL

GULICK L.,PAPERS ON THE SCIENCE OF ADMINISTRATION. INDUS PROB/SOLV TEC/DEV COST EFFICIENCY PRODUC HABITAT...PHIL/SCI METH/COMP 20. PAGE 23 G0461 — B37 — OP/RES CONTROL ADMIN MGT

HECKSCHER G.,"GROUP ORGANIZATION IN SWEDEN." SWEDEN STRATA ECO/DEV AGRI INDUS LABOR NAT/G PROF/ORG ECO/TAC CENTRAL SOCISM...MGT 19/20. PAGE 25 G0499 — S39 — LAISSEZ SOC

US LIBRARY OF CONGRESS,CONDUCT OF THE WAR (APRIL 1941-MARCH 1942). USA-45 WOR-45 LAW INDUS PUB/INST TEC/DEV EDU/PROP CIVMIL/REL 20. PAGE 59 G1155 — B42 — BIBLIOG/A WAR FORCES PLAN

BAKER H.,PROBLEMS OF REEMPLOYMENT AND RETRAINING OF MANPOWER DURING THE TRANSITION FROM WAR TO PEACE. USA+45 INDUS LABOR LG/CO NAT/G PLAN ADMIN PEACE ...POLICY MGT 20. PAGE 5 G0086 — B45 — BIBLIOG/A ADJUST WAR PROB/SOLV

MAYO E.,THE SOCIAL PROBLEMS OF AN INDUSTRIAL CIVILIZATION. USA+45 SOCIETY LABOR CROWD PERS/REL LAISSEZ. PAGE 37 G0725 — B45 — INDUS GP/REL MGT WORKER

SCHULTZ T.H.,FOOD FOR THE WORLD. UNIV SOCIETY INDUS AGRI R+D ECO/TAC...GEOG TREND GEN/LAWS 20. PAGE 50 G0979 — B45 — TEC/DEV

WILCOX J.K.,OFFICIAL DEFENSE PUBLICATIONS, 1941-1945 (NINE VOLS.). USA-45 AGRI INDUS R+D LABOR FORCES TEC/DEV EFFICIENCY PRODUC SKILL WEALTH 20. PAGE 63 G1238 — B46 — BIBLIOG/A WAR CIVMIL/REL ADMIN

WHITEHEAD T.N.,LEADERSHIP IN A FREE SOCIETY; A STUDY IN HUMAN RELATIONS BASED ON AN ANALYSIS OF PRESENT-DAY INDUSTRIAL CIVILIZATION. WOR-45 STRUCT R+D LABOR LG/CO SML/CO WORKER PLAN PROB/SOLV TEC/DEV DRIVE...MGT 20. PAGE 63 G1234 — B47 — INDUS LEAD ORD/FREE SOCIETY

METZLER L.A.,INCOME, EMPLOYMENT, AND PUBLIC POLICY. FINAN INDUS LOC/G NAT/G TAX GIVE PAY COST PRODUC ...MGT TIME/SEQ 20. PAGE 38 G0760 — B48 — INCOME WEALTH POLICY ECO/TAC

LEPAWSKY A.,ADMINISTRATION. FINAN INDUS LG/CO SML/CO INGP/REL PERS/REL COST EFFICIENCY OPTIMAL SKILL 20. PAGE 33 G0656 — B49 — ADMIN MGT WORKER EX/STRUC

MERTON R.,"THE ROLE OF APPLIED SOCIAL SCIENCE IN THE FORMATION OF POLICY: A RESEARCH MEMORANDUM." WOR+45 INDUS NAT/G EXEC ROUTINE CHOOSE ORD/FREE PWR SKILL...POLICY MGT PSY METH/CNCPT TESTS CHARTS METH VAL/FREE 20. PAGE 38 G0756 — S49 — PLAN SOC DIPLOM

US DEPARTMENT OF STATE,POINT FOUR: COOPERATIVE PROGRAM FOR AID IN THE DEVELOPMENT OF ECONOMICALLY UNDERDEVELOPED AREAS. WOR+45 AGRI INDUS INT/ORG PLAN TEC/DEV DIPLOM EDU/PROP ADMIN PEACE PRODUC WEALTH 20 CONGRESS UN. PAGE 57 G1121 — B50 — ECO/UNDEV FOR/AID FINAN INT/TRADE

ROBINSON E.A.G.,THE STRUCTURE OF COMPETITIVE INDUSTRY. UK ECO/DEV DIST/IND MARKET TEC/DEV DIPLOM EDU/PROP ADMIN EFFICIENCY WEALTH...MGT 19/20. PAGE 47 G0929 — B53 — INDUS PRODUC WORKER OPTIMAL

SCHAAF R.W.,DOCUMENTS OF INTERNATIONAL MEETINGS. AGRI INDUS ACADEM DIPLOM NUC/PWR RACE/REL AGE/Y HEALTH...SOC 20. PAGE 49 G0960 — B53 — BIBLIOG/A DELIB/GP INT/ORG POLICY

MOSK S.A.,INDUSTRIAL REVOLUTION IN MEXICO. MARKET LABOR CREATE CAP/ISM ADMIN ATTIT SOCISM...POLICY 20 MEXIC/AMER. PAGE 40 G0789 — B54 — INDUS TEC/DEV ECO/UNDEV NAT/G

WILENSKY H.L.,SYLLABUS OF INDUSTRIAL RELATIONS: A GUIDE TO READING AND RESEARCH. USA+45 MUNIC ADMIN INGP/REL...POLICY MGT PHIL/SCI 20. PAGE 63 G1239 — B54 — BIBLIOG INDUS LABOR WORKER

GOULDNER A.W.,"PATTERNS OF INDUSTRIAL BUREAUCRACY." GP/REL CONSEN ATTIT DRIVE...BIBLIOG 20. PAGE 22 G0438 — C54 — ADMIN INDUS OP/RES WORKER

VON NEUMANN J.,"CAN WE SURVIVE TECHNOLOGY?" WOR+45 AIR INDUS ADMIN ADJUST RIGID/FLEX...GEOG PHIL/SCI NEW/IDEA 20. PAGE 61 G1202 — S55 — TEC/DEV NUC/PWR FUT HABITAT

BONER H.A.,"HUNGRY GENERATIONS." UK WOR+45 WOR-45 STRATA INDUS FAM LABOR CAP/ISM...MGT BIBLIOG 19/20. PAGE 8 G0151 — C55 — ECO/DEV PHIL/SCI CONCPT WEALTH

ATOMIC INDUSTRIAL FORUM,PUBLIC RELATIONS FOR THE ATOMIC INDUSTRY. WOR+45 PLAN PROB/SOLV EDU/PROP PRESS CONFER...AUD/VIS ANTHOL 20. PAGE 4 G0077 — B56 — NUC/PWR INDUS GP/REL ATTIT

US DEPARTMENT OF THE ARMY,RESEARCH AND DEVELOPMENT (AND RELATED ASPECTS) IN FOREIGN COUNTRIES. WOR+45 DIST/IND INDUS CONSULT FORCES CREATE EDU/PROP AUTOMAT DETER WEAPON. PAGE 57 G1126 — B56 — BIBLIOG/A R+D TEC/DEV NUC/PWR

GORDON L.,"THE ORGANIZATION FOR EUROPEAN ECONOMIC COOPERATION." EUR+WWI INDUS INT/ORG NAT/G CONSULT DELIB/GP ACT/RES CREATE PLAN TEC/DEV EDU/PROP LEGIT WEALTH OEEC 20. PAGE 22 G0435 — S56 — VOL/ASSN ECO/DEV

GOLD N.L.,REGIONAL ECONOMIC DEVELOPMENT AND NUCLEAR POWER IN INDIA. FUT INDIA FINAN FOR/AID INT/TRADE BAL/PAY EFFICIENCY OPTIMAL PRODUC WEALTH...PREDICT 20. PAGE 22 G0424 — B57 — ECO/UNDEV TEC/DEV NUC/PWR INDUS

ATOMIC INDUSTRIAL FORUM,MANAGEMENT AND ATOMIC ENERGY. WOR+45 SEA LAW MARKET NAT/G TEC/DEV INSPECT INT/TRADE CONFER PEACE HEALTH...ANTHOL 20. PAGE 4 G0078 — B58 — NUC/PWR INDUS MGT ECO/TAC

BIDWELL P.W.,RAW MATERIALS: A STUDY OF AMERICAN POLICY. USA+45 USA-45 ECO/UNDEV AGRI INDUS KIN CREATE PLAN ECO/TAC WAR PEACE ATTIT DRIVE WEALTH ...STAT CHARTS CONGRESS VAL/FREE. PAGE 7 G0135 — B58 — EXTR/IND ECO/DEV

CHEEK G.,ECONOMIC AND SOCIAL IMPLICATIONS OF AUTOMATION: A BIBLIOGRAPHIC REVIEW (PAMPHLET). USA+45 LG/CO WORKER CREATE PLAN CONTROL ROUTINE PERS/REL EFFICIENCY PRODUC...METH/COMP 20. PAGE 12 G0225 — B58 — BIBLIOG/A SOCIETY INDUS AUTOMAT

EHRHARD J.,LE DESTIN DU COLONIALISME. AFR FRANCE ECO/UNDEV AGRI FINAN MARKET CREATE PLAN TEC/DEV BUDGET DIPLOM PRICE 20. PAGE 17 G0335 — B58 — COLONIAL FOR/AID INT/TRADE INDUS

OPERATIONS RESEARCH SOCIETY,A COMPREHENSIVE BIBLIOGRAPHY ON OPERATIONS RESEARCH; THROUGH 1956 WITH SUPPLEMENT FOR 1957. COM/IND DIST/IND INDUS ADMIN...DECISION MATH STAT METH 20. PAGE 43 G0840 — B58 — BIBLIOG/A COMPUT/IR OP/RES MGT

FORRESTER J.W.,"INDUSTRIAL DYNAMICS* A MAJOR BREAKTHROUGH FOR DECISION MAKERS." COMPUTER OP/RES ...DECISION CONCPT NEW/IDEA. PAGE 20 G0382 — L58 — INDUS ACT/RES MGT PROB/SOLV

ATOMIC INDUSTRIAL FORUM,THE IMPACT OF THE PEACEFUL USES OF ATOMIC ENERGY ON STATE AND LOCAL GOVERNMENT. USA+45 INDUS NAT/G LEGIS PLAN CONTROL GOV/REL. PAGE 4 G0079 — B59 — PROVS LOC/G NUC/PWR PEACE

CLEAVELAND F.N.,SCIENCE AND STATE GOVERNMENT. AGRI EXTR/IND FINAN INDUS PROVS...METH/CNCPT STAT CHARTS 20 NEW/YORK CONNECTICT WISCONSIN CALIFORNIA — B59 — TEC/DEV PHIL/SCI GOV/REL

NEW/MEXICO. PAGE 12 G0233 | METH/COMP

B59

HARVARD UNIVERSITY LAW SCHOOL,INTERNATIONAL
PROBLEMS OF FINANCIAL PROTECTION AGAINST NUCLEAR
RISK. WOR+45 NAT/G DELIB/GP PROB/SOLV DIPLOM
CONTROL ATTIT...POLICY INT/LAW MATH 20. PAGE 25
G0488 | NUC/PWR ADJUD INDUS FINAN

B59

MEANS G.C.,ADMINISTRATIVE INFLATION AND PUBLIC
POLICY (PAMPHLET). USA+45 ECO/DEV FINAN INDUS
WORKER PLAN BUDGET GOV/REL COST DEMAND WEALTH 20
CONGRESS MONOPOLY GOLD/STAND. PAGE 38 G0749 | ECO/TAC POLICY RATION CONTROL

B59

VERNEY D.V.,PUBLIC ENTERPRISE IN SWEDEN. FUT SWEDEN
UK INDUS POL/PAR LEGIS PROB/SOLV CAP/ISM INT/TRADE
CONTROL SOCISM...MGT CONCPT NAT/COMP 20 SOCDEM/PAR
CIVIL/SERV. PAGE 61 G1196 | ECO/DEV POLICY LG/CO NAT/G

B59

WARD B.,5 IDEAS THAT CHANGE THE WORLD. WOR+45
WOR-45 SOCIETY STRUCT AGRI INDUS INT/ORG NAT/G
FORCES ACT/RES ARMS/CONT TOTALISM ATTIT DRIVE
GEN/LAWS. PAGE 62 G1210 | ECO/UNDEV ALL/VALS NAT/LISM COLONIAL

B59

WELTON H.,THE THIRD WORLD WAR: TRADE AND INDUSTRY,
THE NEW BATTLEGROUND. WOR+45 ECO/DEV INDUS MARKET
TASK...MGT IDEA/COMP COLD/WAR. PAGE 63 G1229 | INT/TRADE PLAN DIPLOM

S59

BENDIX R.,"INDUSTRIALIZATION, IDEOLOGIES, AND
SOCIAL STRUCTURE" (BMR)" UK USA-45 USSR STRUCT
WORKER GP/REL EFFICIENCY...IDEA/COMP 20. PAGE 6
G0117 | INDUS ATTIT MGT ADMIN

S59

CYERT R.M.,"MODELS IN A BEHAVIORAL THEORY OF THE
FIRM." ROUTINE...DECISION MGT METH/CNCPT MATH.
PAGE 14 G0267 | SIMUL GAME PREDICT INDUS

S59

SIMONS H.,"WORLD-WIDE CAPABILITIES FOR PRODUCTION
AND CONTROL OF NUCLEAR WEAPONS." FUT WOR+45 INDUS
INT/ORG NAT/G ECO/TAC ATTIT PWR SKILL...TREND
CHARTS VAL/FREE 20. PAGE 51 G1001 | TEC/DEV ARMS/CONT NUC/PWR

S59

STREAT R.,"GOVERNMENT CONSULTATION WITH INDUSTRY."
UK 20. PAGE 53 G1043 | REPRESENT ADMIN EX/STRUC INDUS

B60

APTHEKER H.,DISARMAMENT AND THE AMERICAN ECONOMY: A
SYMPOSIUM. FUT USA+45 ECO/DEV DIST/IND FINAN INDUS
PROC/MFG LABOR NAT/G POL/PAR CONSULT PLAN CAP/ISM
INT/TRADE PEACE ATTIT MORAL WEALTH...TREND GEN/LAWS
TOT/POP 20. PAGE 3 G0063 | MARXIST ARMS/CONT

B60

ATOMIC INDUSTRIAL FORUM,ATOMS FOR INDUSTRY: WORLD
FORUM. WOR+45 FINAN COST UTIL...JURID ANTHOL 20.
PAGE 4 G0080 | NUC/PWR INDUS PLAN PROB/SOLV

B60

GRANICK D.,THE RED EXECUTIVE. COM USA+45 SOCIETY
ECO/DEV INDUS NAT/G POL/PAR EX/STRUC PLAN ECO/TAC
EDU/PROP ADMIN EXEC ATTIT DRIVE...GP/COMP 20.
PAGE 22 G0440 | PWR STRATA USSR ELITES

B60

PENTONY D.E.,THE UNDERDEVELOPED LANDS. FUT WOR+45
CULTURE AGRI FINAN INDUS MARKET INT/ORG LABOR NAT/G
VOL/ASSN CONSULT TEC/DEV ECO/TAC EDU/PROP COLONIAL
ATTIT WEALTH...OBS RECORD SAMP TREND GEN/METH WORK
UN 20. PAGE 44 G0867 | ECO/UNDEV POLICY FOR/AID INT/TRADE

S60

BECKER A.S.,"COMPARISONS OF UNITED STATES AND USSR
NATIONAL OUTPUT: SOME RULES OF THE GAME." COM
USA+45 ECO/DEV AGRI DIST/IND INDUS R+D CONSULT PLAN
ECO/TAC RIGID/FLEX KNOWL...METH/CNCPT CHARTS 20.
PAGE 6 G0113 | STAT USSR

S60

SANDERS R.,"NUCLEAR DYNAMITE: A NEW DIMENSION IN
FOREIGN POLICY." FUT WOR+45 ECO/DEV CONSULT TEC/DEV
PERCEPT...CONT/OBS TIME/SEQ TREND GEN/LAWS TOT/POP
20 TREATY. PAGE 49 G0955 | INDUS PWR DIPLOM NUC/PWR

B61

BRADY R.A.,ORGANIZATION, AUTOMATION, AND SOCIETY.
USA+45 AGRI COM/IND DIST/IND MARKET CREATE
...DECISION MGT 20. PAGE 8 G0163 | TEC/DEV INDUS AUTOMAT ADMIN

B61

HODGKINS J.A.,SOVIET POWER: ENERGY RESOURCES,
PRODUCTION AND POTENTIALS. USSR ECO/DEV INDUS
MARKET...POLICY STAT CHARTS 20 RESOURCE/N. PAGE 26
G0518 | GEOG EXTR/IND TEC/DEV

B61

JANOWITZ M.,COMMUNITY POLITICAL SYSTEMS. USA+45
SOCIETY INDUS VOL/ASSN TEC/DEV ADMIN LEAD CHOOSE
...SOC SOC/WK 20. PAGE 29 G0561 | MUNIC STRUCT POL/PAR

B61

LAHAYE R.,LES ENTREPRISES PUBLIQUES AU MAROC.
FRANCE MOROCCO LAW DIST/IND EXTR/IND FINAN CONSULT
PLAN TEC/DEV ADMIN AGREE CONTROL OWN...POLICY 20.
PAGE 32 G0629 | NAT/G INDUS ECO/UNDEV ECO/TAC

B61

MICHAEL D.N.,PROPOSED STUDIES ON THE IMPLICATIONS
OF PEACEFUL SPACE ACTIVITIES FOR HUMAN AFFAIRS.
COM/IND INDUS FORCES DIPLOM PEACE PERSON...PSY SOC
20. PAGE 39 G0764 | FUT SPACE ACT/RES PROB/SOLV

B61

NAKICENOVIC S.,NUCLEAR ENERGY IN YUGOSLAVIA.
YUGOSLAVIA AGRI INDUS CREATE OP/RES ROUTINE
EFFICIENCY KNOWL...HEAL STAT CHARTS LAB/EXP BIBLIOG
20. PAGE 41 G0802 | R+D ECO/DEV TEC/DEV NUC/PWR

S61

BENNION E.G.,"ECONOMETRICS FOR MANAGEMENT." USA+45
INDUS EX/STRUC ACT/RES COMPUTER UTIL...MATH STAT
PREDICT METH/COMP HYPO/EXP. PAGE 6 G0122 | ECOMETRIC MGT SIMUL DECISION

B62

CARSON R.,SILENT SPRING. USA+45 AIR CULTURE AGRI
INDUS ADMIN ATTIT RIGID/FLEX ORD/FREE PWR...POLICY
20. PAGE 11 G0216 | HABITAT TREND SOCIETY CONTROL

B62

DUCKWORTH W.E.,A GUIDE TO OPERATIONAL RESEARCH.
INDUS PLAN PROB/SOLV EXEC EFFICIENCY PRODUC KNOWL
...MGT MATH STAT SIMUL METH 20 MONTECARLO. PAGE 16
G0319 | OP/RES GAME DECISION ADMIN

B62

DUPRE J.S.,SCIENCE AND THE NATION: POLICY AND
POLITICS. USA+45 LAW ACADEM FORCES ADMIN CIVMIL/REL
GOV/REL EFFICIENCY PEACE...TREND 20 SCI/ADVSRY.
PAGE 16 G0322 | R+D INDUS TEC/DEV NUC/PWR

B62

DUPRE S.,SCIENCE AND THE NATION. USA+45 ECO/DEV
ACADEM ORD/FREE TECHNIC. PAGE 17 G0323 | ARMS/CONT DECISION TEC/DEV INDUS

B62

FORTUNE EDITORS,THE SPACE INDUSTRY: AMERICA'S
NEWEST GIANT. USA+45 FINAN NAT/G BUDGET 20. PAGE 20
G0383 | SPACE INDUS TEC/DEV MGT

B62

GRANICK D.,THE EUROPEAN EXECUTIVE. BELGIUM FRANCE
GERMANY/W UK INDUS LABOR LG/CO SML/CO EX/STRUC PLAN
TEC/DEV CAP/ISM COST DEMAND...POLICY CHARTS 20.
PAGE 22 G0441 | MGT ECO/DEV ECO/TAC EXEC

B62

KRAFT J.,THE GRAND DESIGN. EUR+WWI USA+45 AGRI
FINAN INDUS MARKET INT/ORG NAT/G PLAN ECO/TAC
TARIFFS REGION DRIVE ORD/FREE WEALTH...POLICY OBS
TREND EEC 20. PAGE 31 G0616 | VOL/ASSN ECO/DEV INT/TRADE

B62

MACHLUP F.,THE PRODUCTION AND DISTRIBUTION OF
KNOWLEDGE IN THE UNITED STATES. USA+45 COM/IND
INDUS SCHOOL SECT WORKER COMPUTER CREATE CIVMIL/REL
COST EFFICIENCY WEALTH 20. PAGE 35 G0688 | ACADEM TEC/DEV EDU/PROP R+D

B62

STERN A.C.,AIR POLLUTION (2 VOLS.). LAW INDUS
PROB/SOLV TEC/DEV INSPECT RISK BIO/SOC HABITAT
...OBS/ENVIR TESTS SAMP 20 POLLUTION. PAGE 53 G1035 | AIR OP/RES CONTROL HEALTH

THORELLI H.B.,"THE INTERNATIONAL OPERATIONS SIMULATION AT THE UNIVERSITY OF CHICAGO." FUT USA+45 WOR+45 ECO/DEV DIST/IND FINAN INDUS INT/ORG DELIB/GP ACT/RES CREATE TEC/DEV WEALTH...STAT VAL/FREE 20. PAGE 54 G1072
S62
ECO/TAC
SIMUL
INT/TRADE

ACKOFF R.L.,A MANAGER'S GUIDE TO OPERATIONS RESEARCH. STRUCT INDUS PROB/SOLV ROUTINE 20. PAGE 2 G0028
B63
OP/RES
MGT
GP/REL
ADMIN

BONINI C.P.,SIMULATION OF INFORMATION AND DECISION SYSTEMS IN THE FIRM. MARKET BUDGET DOMIN EDU/PROP ADMIN COST ATTIT HABITAT PERCEPT PWR...CONCPT PROBABIL QUANT PREDICT HYPO/EXP BIBLIOG. PAGE 8 G0152
B63
INDUS
SIMUL
DECISION
MGT

HEYEL C.,THE ENCYCLOPEDIA OF MANAGEMENT. WOR+45 MARKET TOP/EX TEC/DEV AUTOMAT LEAD ADJUST...STAT CHARTS GAME ANTHOL BIBLIOG. PAGE 26 G0509
B63
MGT
INDUS
ADMIN
FINAN

HOFSTADTER R.,ANTI-INTELLECTUALISM IN AMERICAN LIFE. USA+45 AGRI INDUS ACADEM TEC/DEV EDU/PROP INGP/REL ATTIT...SOC WORSHIP 20 MCCARTHY/J STEVENSN/A. PAGE 26 G0522
B63
INTELL
EPIST
CULTURE
SOCIETY

KATZ S.M.,A SELECTED LIST OF US READINGS ON DEVELOPMENT. AGRI COM/IND DIST/IND INDUS LABOR PLAN FOR/AID EDU/PROP HEALTH...POLICY SOC/WK 20. PAGE 30 G0582
B63
BIBLIOG/A
ECO/UNDEV
TEC/DEV
ACT/RES

KORNHAUSER W.,SCIENTISTS IN INDUSTRY: CONFLICT AND ACCOMMODATION. USA+45 R+D LG/CO NAT/G TEC/DEV CONTROL ADJUST ATTIT...MGT STAT INT BIBLIOG 20. PAGE 31 G0614
B63
CREATE
INDUS
PROF/ORG
GP/REL

KREPS J.,AUTOMATION AND THE OLDER WORKER: AN ANNOTATED BIBLIOGRAPHY (PAMPHLET). USA+45 STRUCT ECO/DEV INDUS TEC/DEV. PAGE 31 G0620
B63
BIBLIOG/A
WORKER
AGE/O
AUTOMAT

NASA,CONFERENCE ON SPACE, SCIENCE, AND URBAN LIFE. USA+45 SOCIETY INDUS ACADEM ACT/RES ECO/TAC ADMIN 20. PAGE 41 G0804
B63
MUNIC
SPACE
TEC/DEV
PROB/SOLV

OTTOSON H.W.,LAND USE POLICY AND PROBLEMS IN THE UNITED STATES. USA+45 USA-45 LAW AGRI INDUS NAT/G GP/REL...CHARTS ANTHOL 19/20 HOMEST/ACT. PAGE 43 G0851
B63
PROB/SOLV
UTIL
HABITAT
POLICY

PERLO V.,MILITARISM AND INDUSTRY. USA+45 INT/TRADE EDU/PROP DETER KNOWL...CHARTS MAPS 20. PAGE 44 G0869
B63
CIVMIL/REL
INDUS
LOBBY
ARMS/CONT

SCHOECK H.,THE NEW ARGUMENT IN ECONOMICS. UK USA+45 INDUS MARKET LABOR NAT/G ECO/TAC ADMIN ROUTINE BAL/PAY PWR...POLICY BOLIV. PAGE 49 G0973
B63
WELF/ST
FOR/AID
ECO/DEV
ALL/IDEOS

WILTZ J.E.,IN SEARCH OF PEACE: THE SENATE MUNITIONS INQUIRY, 1934-36. EUR+WWI USA-45 ELITES INDUS LG/CO LEGIS INT/TRADE LOBBY NEUTRAL ARMS/CONT...POLICY CONGRESS 20 LEAGUE/NAT PRESIDENT SENATE CONSCRIPTN. PAGE 64 G1246
B63
DELIB/GP
PROFIT
WAR
WEAPON

DELLIN L.A.D.,"BULGARIA UNDER SOVIET LEADERSHIP." BULGARIA COM USA+45 USSR ECO/DEV INDUS POL/PAR EX/STRUC TOP/EX COERCE ATTIT RIGID/FLEX...POLICY TIME/SEQ 20. PAGE 15 G0293
S63
AGRI
NAT/G
TOTALISM

HOSKINS H.L.,"ARAB SOCIALISM IN THE UAR." ISLAM USSR AGRI INDUS NAT/G TOP/EX CREATE DIPLOM EDU/PROP DRIVE KNOWL PWR SOCISM...POLICY CONCPT TREND SUEZ 20. PAGE 27 G0530
S63
ECO/DEV
PLAN
UAR

NADLER E.B.,"SOME ECONOMIC DISADVANTAGES OF THE ARMS RACE." USA+45 INDUS R+D FORCES PLAN TEC/DEV
S63
ECO/DEV
MGT

ECO/TAC FOR/AID EDU/PROP PWR WEALTH...TREND COLD/WAR 20. PAGE 41 G0800
BAL/PAY

RECENT PUBLICATIONS ON GOVERNMENTAL PROBLEMS. FINAN INDUS ACADEM PLAN PROB/SOLV EDU/PROP ADJUD ADMIN BIO/SOC...MGT SOC. PAGE 1 G0017
B64
BIBLIOG
AUTOMAT
LEGIS
JURID

BALASSA B.,TRADE PROSPECTS FOR DEVELOPING COUNTRIES. WOR+45 ECO/DEV AGRI EXTR/IND INDUS CREATE PLAN PRICE...ECOMETRIC CLASSIF TIME/SEQ GEN/METH. PAGE 5 G0087
B64
INT/TRADE
ECO/UNDEV
TREND
STAT

BRIGHT J.R.,RESEARCH, DEVELOPMENT AND TECHNOLOGICAL INNOVATION. CULTURE R+D CREATE PLAN PROB/SOLV AUTOMAT RISK PERSON...DECISION CONCPT PREDICT BIBLIOG. PAGE 9 G0168
B64
TEC/DEV
NEW/IDEA
INDUS
MGT

DIEBOLD J.,BEYOND AUTOMATION: MANAGERIAL PROBLEMS OF AN EXPLODING TECHNOLOGY. SOCIETY ECO/DEV CREATE ECO/TAC AUTOMAT SKILL...TECHNIC MGT WORK. PAGE 16 G0303
B64
FUT
INDUS
PROVS
NAT/G

DUSCHA J.,ARMS, MONEY, AND POLITICS. USA+45 INDUS POL/PAR ECO/TAC TAX DETER NUC/PWR WAR WEAPON GOV/REL ATTIT...BIBLIOG/A 20 CONGRESS MONEY DEPT/DEFEN. PAGE 17 G0326
B64
NAT/G
FORCES
POLICY
BUDGET

ETZIONI A.,THE MOON-DOGGLE: DOMESTIC AND INTERNATIONAL IMPLICATIONS OF THE SPACE RACE. FUT USA+45 WOR+45 INTELL ECO/DEV INDUS VOL/ASSN EX/STRUC FORCES LEGIS TOP/EX PLAN TEC/DEV ECO/TAC EDU/PROP KNOWL ORD/FREE PWR RESPECT WEALTH TIME/SEQ. PAGE 18 G0352
B64
R+D
NAT/G
DIPLOM
SPACE

FEI J.C.H.,DEVELOPMENT OF THE LABOR SURPLUS ECONOMY: THEORY AND POLICY. WOR+45 AGRI INDUS MARKET PROB/SOLV TEC/DEV...STAT CHARTS GEN/LAWS METH 20 THIRD/WRLD. PAGE 18 G0361
B64
ECO/TAC
POLICY
WORKER
ECO/UNDEV

GRAVIER J.F.,AMENAGEMENT DU TERRITOIRE ET L'AVENIR DES REGIONS FRANCAISES. FRANCE ECO/DEV AGRI INDUS CREATE...GEOG CHARTS 20. PAGE 22 G0442
B64
PLAN
MUNIC
NEIGH
ADMIN

HAZLEWOOD A.,THE ECONOMICS OF DEVELOPMENT: AN ANNOTATED LIST OF BOOKS AND ARTICLES PUBLISHED 1958-1962. AGRI FINAN INDUS LABOR NAT/G DIPLOM INT/TRADE INCOME...MGT 20. PAGE 25 G0497
B64
BIBLIOG/A
ECO/UNDEV
TEC/DEV

LI C.M.,INDUSTRIAL DEVELOPMENT IN COMMUNIST CHINA. CHINA/COM ECO/DEV ECO/UNDEV AGRI FINAN INDUS MARKET LABOR NAT/G ECO/TAC INT/TRADE EXEC ALL/VALS ...POLICY RELATIV TREND WORK TOT/POP VAL/FREE 20. PAGE 34 G0665
B64
ASIA
TEC/DEV

MANSFIELD E.,MONOPOLY POWER AND ECONOMIC PERFORMANCE: AN INTRODUCTION TO A CURRENT ISSUE OF PUBLIC POLICY. ECO/DEV INDUS NAT/G PLAN CAP/ISM PRICE CONTROL LOBBY EFFICIENCY PRODUC...POLICY 20 CONGRESS KENNEDY/JF MONOPOLY. PAGE 36 G0701
B64
LG/CO
PWR
ECO/TAC
MARKET

ORGANIZATION AMERICAN STATES,ECONOMIC SURVEY OF LATIN AMERICA, 1962. L/A+17C AGRI DIST/IND INDUS MARKET PROC/MFG R+D PLAN TEC/DEV ECO/TAC REGION BAL/PAY ALL/VALS...CON/ANAL ORG/CHARTS GEN/METH OAS 20. PAGE 43 G0844
B64
ECO/UNDEV
CHARTS

ORTH C.D.,ADMINISTERING RESEARCH AND DEVELOPMENT. FINAN PLAN PROB/SOLV ADMIN ROUTINE...METH/CNCPT STAT CHARTS METH 20. PAGE 43 G0847
B64
MGT
R+D
LG/CO
INDUS

POWELSON J.P.,LATIN AMERICA: TODAY'S ECONOMIC AND SOCIAL REVOLUTION. L/A+17C INTELL SOCIETY STRUCT AGRI INDUS NAT/G DIPLOM ECO/TAC REV...POLICY 20. PAGE 45 G0887
B64
ECO/UNDEV
WEALTH
ADJUST
PLAN

SCHERER F.M.,THE WEAPONS ACQUISITION PROCESS: ECONOMIC INCENTIVES. BOSTON: DIVISION OF RESEARCH, GRADUATE SCHOOL OF BUSINESS. USA+45 FINAN NAT/G
B64
INDUS
ACT/RES
WEAPON

DELIB/GP ECO/TAC RIGID/FLEX WEALTH...MGT MATH STAT
CHARTS VAL/FREE 20. PAGE 49 G0965

L64

CARNEGIE ENDOWMENT INT. PEACE,"ECONOMIC AND SOCIAL
QUESTION (ISSUES BEFORE THE NINETEENTH GENERAL
ASSEMBLY)." WOR+45 ECO/DEV ECO/UNDEV INDUS R+D
DELIB/GP CREATE PLAN TEC/DEV ECO/TAC FOR/AID
BAL/PAY...RECORD UN 20. PAGE 11 G0209

INT/ORG
INT/TRADE

S64

COOPER A.C.,"R&D IS MORE EFFICIENT IN SMALL
COMPANIES." USA+45 LG/CO SML/CO WEALTH...RECORD INT
LAB/EXP 20. PAGE 13 G0255

R+D
INDUS
CREATE
GP/COMP

S64

FLORINSKY M.T.,"TRENDS IN THE SOVIET ECONOMY." COM
USA+45 USSR INDUS LABOR NAT/G PLAN TEC/DEV ECO/TAC
ALL/VALS SOCISM...MGT METH/CNCPT STYLE CON/ANAL
GEN/METH WORK 20. PAGE 19 G0374

ECO/DEV
AGRI

S64

KASSOF A.,"THE ADMINISTERED SOCIETY:
TOTALITARIANISM WITHOUT TERROR." COM USSR STRATA
AGRI INDUS NAT/G PERF/ART SCHOOL TOP/EX EDU/PROP
ADMIN ORD/FREE PWR...POLICY SOC TIME/SEQ GEN/LAWS
VAL/FREE 20. PAGE 29 G0580

SOCIETY
DOMIN
TOTALISM

S64

MAHALANOBIS P.C.,"PERSPECTIVE PLANNING IN INDIA:
STATISTICAL TOOLS." INDIA S/ASIA STRATA AGRI
DIST/IND FINAN INDUS SERV/IND NAT/G ECO/TAC
ORD/FREE WEALTH...POLICY TREND SIMUL VAL/FREE 20.
PAGE 35 G0695

PLAN
STAT

S64

MUMFORD L.,"AUTHORITARIAN AND DEMOCRATIC
TECHNIQUES." INDUS PROC/MFG LG/CO SML/CO CREATE
PLAN KNOWL...POLICY TREND WORK 20. PAGE 40 G0794

ECO/DEV
TEC/DEV

B65

ANDERSON C.A.,EDUCATION AND ECONOMIC DEVELOPMENT.
INDUS R+D SCHOOL TEC/DEV ECO/TAC EDU/PROP AGE
HEREDITY PERCEPT SKILL 20. PAGE 3 G0056

ANTHOL
ECO/DEV
ECO/UNDEV
WORKER

B65

BARISH N.N.,MANAGEMENT SCIENCES IN THE EMERGING
COUNTRIES. AFR CHINA/COM WOR+45 FINAN INDUS PLAN
PRODUC HABITAT...ANTHOL 20. PAGE 5 G0093

ECO/UNDEV
OP/RES
MGT
TEC/DEV

B65

FRUTKIN A.W.,SPACE AND THE INTERNATIONAL
COOPERATION YEAR: A NATIONAL CHALLENGE (PAMPHLET).
EUR+WWI USA+45 FINAN TEC/DEV BUDGET...MGT 20 NASA.
PAGE 20 G0396

SPACE
INDUS
NAT/G
DIPLOM

B65

HASSON J.A.,THE ECONOMICS OF NUCLEAR POWER. INDIA
UK USA+45 WOR+45 INT/ORG TEC/DEV COST...SOC STAT
CHARTS 20 EURATOM. PAGE 25 G0490

NUC/PWR
INDUS
ECO/DEV
METH

B65

IANNI O.,ESTADO E CAPITALISMO. L/A+17C FINAN
TEC/DEV ECO/TAC ORD/FREE WEALTH POLICY. PAGE 28
G0542

ECO/UNDEV
STRUCT
INDUS
NAT/G

B65

INT. BANK RECONSTR. DEVELOP.,ECONOMIC DEVELOPMENT
OF KUWAIT. ISLAM KUWAIT AGRI FINAN MARKET EX/STRUC
TEC/DEV ECO/TAC ADMIN WEALTH...OBS CON/ANAL CHARTS
20. PAGE 28 G0548

INDUS
NAT/G

B65

MELMANS S.,OUR DEPLETED SOCIETY. SPACE USA+45
ECO/DEV FORCES BUDGET ECO/TAC ADMIN WEAPON
EFFICIENCY 20 COLD/WAR. PAGE 38 G0753

CIVMIL/REL
INDUS
EDU/PROP
CONTROL

B65

MORRIS M.D.,THE EMERGENCE OF AN INDUSTRIAL LABOR
FORCE IN INDIA: A STUDY OF THE BOMBAY COTTON MILLS,
1854-1947. INDIA WORKER OP/RES ADMIN 19/20. PAGE 40
G0784

INDUS
LABOR
ECO/UNDEV
CAP/ISM

B65

TURNER A.N.,INDUSTRIAL JOBS AND THE WORKER. USA+45
CULTURE ECO/DEV LABOR MUNIC ACT/RES AUTOMAT TASK
...CHARTS BIBLIOG 20. PAGE 55 G1082

WORKER
INDUS
ATTIT
TEC/DEV

B65

TYBOUT R.A.,ECONOMICS OF RESEARCH AND DEVELOPMENT.
ECO/DEV ECO/UNDEV INDUS PROFIT DECISION. PAGE 55
G1084

R+D
FORCES
ADMIN
DIPLOM

B65

VEINOTT A.F. JR.,MATHEMATICAL STUDIES IN MANAGEMENT
SCIENCE. UNIV INDUS COMPUTER ADMIN...DECISION
NET/THEORY SIMUL 20. PAGE 61 G1193

MATH
MGT
PLAN
PRODUC

L65

PILISUK M.,"IS THERE A MILITARY INDUSTRIAL COMPLEX
WHICH PREVENTS PEACE CONSENSUS; COUNTERVAILING
POWER IN PLURALIST SYSTEMS." INDUS R+D ACADEM
FEEDBACK CIVMIL/REL ADJUST CONSEN ATTIT RIGID/FLEX
...CENSUS IDEA/COMP BIBLIOG. PAGE 45 G0878

ELITES
WEAPON
PEACE
ARMS/CONT

S65

CHU K.,"A DYNAMIC MODEL OF THE FIRM." OP/RES
PROB/SOLV...DECISION ECOMETRIC NEW/IDEA STAT GAME
ORG/CHARTS SIMUL. PAGE 12 G0230

INDUS
COMPUTER
TEC/DEV

S65

STAAR R.F.,"RETROGRESSION IN POLAND." COM USSR AGRI
INDUS NAT/G CREATE EDU/PROP TOTALISM RIGID/FLEX
ORD/FREE PWR SOCISM...RECORD CHARTS 20. PAGE 52
G1029

TOP/EX
ECO/TAC
POLAND

S65

TENDLER J.D.,"TECHNOLOGY AND ECONOMIC DEVELOPMENT*
THE CASE OF HYDRO VS THERMAL POWER." CONSTRUC
DIST/IND CREATE TEC/DEV INT/TRADE CENTRAL PWR SKILL
WEALTH...MGT NAT/COMP ARGEN. PAGE 54 G1063

BRAZIL
INDUS
ECO/UNDEV

B66

BOLTON R.E.,DEFENSE AND DISARMAMENT: THE ECONOMICS
OF TRANSITION. USA+45 R+D FORCES PLAN LOBBY DETER
WAR COST PEACE...ANTHOL BIBLIOG 20. PAGE 8 G0150

ARMS/CONT
POLICY
INDUS

B66

ECKSTEIN A.,COMMUNIST CHINA'S ECONOMIC GROWTH AND
FOREIGN TRADE* IMPLICATIONS FOR US POLICY. COM
USA+45 USSR STRUCT INDUS MARKET DIPLOM ECO/TAC
FOR/AID INT/TRADE...STAT CHARTS. PAGE 17 G0332

ASIA
ECO/UNDEV
CREATE
PWR

B66

GOULD J.M.,THE TECHNICAL ELITE. INDUS LABOR
TECHRACY...POLICY DECISION STAT CHARTS 20. PAGE 22
G0437

ECO/DEV
TEC/DEV
ELITES
TECHNIC

B66

HOPKINS J.F.K.,ARABIC PERIODICAL LITERATURE, 1961.
ISLAM LAW CULTURE SECT...GEOG HEAL PHIL/SCI PSY SOC
20. PAGE 27 G0528

BIBLIOG/A
NAT/LISM
TEC/DEV
INDUS

B66

KURAKOV I.G.,SCIENCE, TECHNOLOGY AND COMMUNISM;
SOME QUESTIONS OF DEVELOPMENT (TRANS. BY CARIN
DEDIJER). USSR INDUS PLAN PROB/SOLV COST PRODUC
...MGT MATH CHARTS METH 20. PAGE 32 G0626

CREATE
TEC/DEV
MARXISM
ECO/TAC

B66

LEWIS W.A.,DEVELOPMENT PLANNING; THE ESSENTIALS OF
ECONOMIC POLICY. USA+45 FINAN INDUS NAT/G WORKER
FOR/AID INT/TRADE ADMIN ROUTINE WEALTH...CONCPT
STAT. PAGE 34 G0663

PLAN
ECO/DEV
POLICY
CREATE

B66

MILLAR R.,THE NEW CLASSES. UK ELITES SOCIETY INDUS
AUTOMAT GP/REL SOC/INTEG 20 INDUS/REV. PAGE 39
G0770

STRUCT
STRATA
TEC/DEV
CREATE

B66

MURDOCK J.C.,RESEARCH AND REGIONS. AGRI FINAN INDUS
LOC/G MUNIC NAT/G PROB/SOLV TEC/DEV ADMIN REGION
20. PAGE 40 G0796

BIBLIOG
ECO/DEV
COMPUT/IR
R+D

B66

NIEBURG H.L.,IN THE NAME OF SCIENCE. USA+45
EX/STRUC LEGIS TEC/DEV BUDGET PAY AUTOMAT LOBBY PWR
...OBS 20. PAGE 42 G0822

NAT/G
INDUS
TECHRACY

B66

ONYEMELUKWE C.C.,PROBLEMS OF INDUSTRIAL PLANNING
AND MANAGEMENT IN NIGERIA. AFR FINAN LABOR DELIB/GP
TEC/DEV ADJUST...MGT TREND BIBLIOG. PAGE 43 G0839

ECO/UNDEV
ECO/TAC
INDUS
PLAN

B66

US DEPARTMENT OF LABOR,PRODUCTIVITY: A

BIBLIOG/A

BIBLIOGRAPHY. ECO/DEV INDUS MARKET OP/RES AUTOMAT COST...STAT 20. PAGE 57 G1119 — PRODUC LABOR PLAN

B66
US DEPARTMENT OF LABOR,TECHNOLOGICAL TRENDS IN MAJOR AMERICAN INDUSTRIES. USA+45 R+D LABOR GP/REL PRODUC...MGT BIBLIOG 20. PAGE 57 G1120 — TEC/DEV INDUS TREND AUTOMAT

B66
US PRES COMM ECO IMPACT DEFENS,REPORT* JULY 1965. USA+45 ECO/DEV INDUS DELIB/GP FORCES OP/RES ARMS/CONT NUC/PWR WEAPON BAL/PAY...PREDICT SIMUL. PAGE 59 G1159 — ACT/RES STAT WAR BUDGET

S66
MALENBAUM W.,"GOVERNMENT, ENTREPRENEURSHIP, AND ECONOMIC GROWTH IN POOR LANDS." ELITES ECO/UNDEV INDUS CREATE DRIVE. PAGE 35 G0697 — ECO/TAC PLAN CONSERVE NAT/G

B67
BARANSON J.,TECHNOLOGY FOR UNDERDEVELOPED AREAS: AN ANNOTATED BIBLIOGRAPHY. FUT WOR+45 CULTURE INDUS INT/ORG CREATE PROB/SOLV INT/TRADE EDU/PROP AUTOMAT ...CONCPT METH. PAGE 5 G0092 — BIBLIOG/A ECO/UNDEV TEC/DEV R+D

B67
BUDER S.,PULLMAN: AN EXPERIMENT IN INDUSTRIAL ORDER AND COMMUNITY PLANNING, 1880-1930. USA-45 SOCIETY LABOR LG/CO CREATE PROB/SOLV CONTROL GP/REL EFFICIENCY ATTIT...MGT BIBLIOG 19/20 PULLMAN. PAGE 9 G0184 — DIST/IND INDUS MUNIC PLAN

B67
COMMONER B.,SCIENCE AND SURVIVAL. SOCIETY INDUS PLAN NUC/PWR KNOWL PWR...SOC 20 AEC. PAGE 13 G0247 — PHIL/SCI CONTROL PROB/SOLV EQUILIB

B67
DEGLER C.N.,THE AGE OF THE ECONOMIC REVOLUTION 1876-1900. USA-45 AGRI MUNIC POL/PAR SECT ECO/TAC CHOOSE...PHIL/SCI CHARTS NAT/COMP 19 NEGRO. PAGE 15 G0292 — INDUS SOCIETY ECO/DEV TEC/DEV

B67
EISENMENGER R.W.,THE DYNAMICS OF GROWTH IN NEW ENGLAND'S ECONOMY, 1870-1964. USA+45 USA-45 ECO/TAC TAX PAY AUTOMAT GOV/REL ADJUST HABITAT...STAT 19/20. PAGE 17 G0340 — ECO/DEV AGRI INDUS CAP/ISM

B67
ELSNER H.,THE TECHNOCRATS, PROPHETS OF AUTOMATION. SOCIETY INDUS VOL/ASSN COST INCOME ATTIT 20. PAGE 18 G0345 — AUTOMAT TECHRACY PRODUC HIST/WRIT

B67
HEILBRONER R.L.,THE LIMITS OF AMERICAN CAPITALISM. FUT ECO/DEV INDUS LG/CO EX/STRUC LEAD PWR TECHRACY 20. PAGE 25 G0502 — ELITES CREATE TEC/DEV CAP/ISM

B67
HIRSCHMAN A.O.,DEVELOPMENT PROJECTS OBSERVED. INDUS INT/ORG CONSULT EX/STRUC CREATE OP/RES ECO/TAC DEMAND...POLICY MGT METH/COMP 20 WORLD/BANK. PAGE 26 G0513 — ECO/UNDEV R+D FINAN PLAN

B67
HODGKINSON R.G.,THE ORIGINS OF THE NATIONAL HEALTH SERVICE: THE MEDICAL SERVICES OF THE NEW POOR LAW, 1834-1871. UK INDUS MUNIC WORKER PROB/SOLV EFFICIENCY ATTIT HEALTH WEALTH SOCISM...JURID SOC/WK 19/20. PAGE 26 G0519 — HEAL NAT/G POLICY LAW

B67
KRANZBERG M.,TECHNOLOGY IN WESTERN CIVILIZATION VOLUME ONE. UNIV INDUS SKILL. PAGE 31 G0617 — TEC/DEV ACT/RES AUTOMAT POLICY

B67
MAZOUR A.G.,SOVIET ECONOMIC DEVELOPMENT: OPERATION OUTSTRIP: 1921-1965. USSR ECO/UNDEV FINAN CHIEF WORKER PROB/SOLV CONTROL PRODUC MARXISM...CHARTS ORG/CHARTS 20 STALIN/J. PAGE 37 G0726 — ECO/TAC AGRI INDUS PLAN

B67
MOORE J.R.,THE ECONOMIC IMPACT OF THE TVA. AGRI INDUS PLAN BARGAIN CONTROL REGION GOV/REL DEMAND EFFICIENCY SOCISM 20 TVA. PAGE 40 G0780 — ECO/UNDEV ECO/DEV NAT/G CREATE

B67
NASH M.,MACHINE AGE MAYA. GUATEMALA L/A+17C STRUCT AGRI WORKER CREATE INCOME ATTIT RIGID/FLEX ROLE ...IDEA/COMP SOC/EXP WORSHIP 20 INDIAN/AM. PAGE 41 G0806 — INDUS CULTURE SOC MUNIC

B67
NORTHRUP H.R.,RESTRICTIVE LABOR PRACTICES IN THE SUPERMARKET INDUSTRY. USA+45 INDUS WORKER TEC/DEV BARGAIN PAY CONTROL GP/REL COST...STAT CHARTS NLRB. PAGE 42 G0827 — DIST/IND MARKET LABOR MGT

B67
POMEROY W.J.,HALF A CENTURY OF SOCIALISM. USSR LAW AGRI INDUS NAT/G CREATE DIPLOM EDU/PROP PERSON ORD/FREE WEALTH...POLICY TREND 20. PAGE 45 G0884 — SOCISM MARXISM COM SOCIETY

B67
SCHON D.A.,TECHNOLOGY AND CHANGE* THE NEW HERACLITUS. TEC/DEV CONTROL COST DEMAND EFFICIENCY RIGID/FLEX...MYTH 20. PAGE 49 G0975 — INDUS PROB/SOLV R+D CREATE

B67
SILBERMAN C.E.,THE MYTHS OF AUTOMATION. INDUS WORKER COST PRODUC AGE WEALTH 20. PAGE 51 G0996 — MYTH AUTOMAT CHARTS TEC/DEV

B67
WOODRUFF W.,IMPACT OF WESTERN MAN. ECO/DEV INDUS CREATE PLAN PROB/SOLV COLONIAL GOV/REL...CHARTS GOV/COMP BIBLIOG 18/20. PAGE 64 G1256 — EUR+WWI MOD/EUR CAP/ISM

B67
ZUCKERMAN S.,SCIENTISTS AND WAR. ELITES INDUS DIPLOM CENTRAL EFFICIENCY KNOWL 20. PAGE 65 G1271 — R+D CONSULT ACT/RES GP/REL

L67
CARMICHAEL D.M.,"FORTY YEARS OF WATER POLLUTION CONTROL IN WISCONSIN: A CASE STUDY." LAW EXTR/IND INDUS MUNIC DELIB/GP PLAN PROB/SOLV SANCTION ...CENSUS CHARTS 20 WISCONSIN. PAGE 11 G0207 — HEALTH CONTROL ADMIN ADJUD

S67
ALLISON D.,"THE GROWTH OF IDEAS." USA+45 LG/CO ADMIN. PAGE 3 G0045 — R+D OP/RES INDUS TEC/DEV

S67
ATKIN J.M.,"THE FEDERAL GOVERNMENT, BIG BUSINESS, AND COLLEGES OF EDUCATION." PROF/ORG CONSULT CREATE PLAN PROB/SOLV ADMIN EFFICIENCY. PAGE 4 G0075 — SCHOOL ACADEM NAT/G INDUS

S67
BENN W.,"TECHNOLOGY HAS AN INEXORABLE EFFECT." FUT UK ECO/DEV INT/ORG CONSULT PLAN EDU/PROP ADMIN LEAD GP/REL PRODUC...INT 20 EEC. PAGE 6 G0119 — R+D LG/CO TEC/DEV INDUS

S67
BRUNHILD G.,"THEORY OF 'TECHNICAL UNEMPLOYMENT'." ECO/DEV ACT/RES PROB/SOLV DEMAND PRODUC...PHIL/SCI 20. PAGE 9 G0182 — WORKER TEC/DEV SKILL INDUS

S67
CARR E.H.,"REVOLUTION FROM ABOVE." USSR STRATA FINAN INDUS NAT/G DOMIN LEAD GP/REL INGP/REL OWN PRODUC PWR 20 STALIN/J. PAGE 11 G0214 — AGRI POLICY COM EFFICIENCY

S67
CETRON M.J.,"FORECASTING TECHNOLOGY." INDUS FORCES TASK UTIL...PHIL/SCI CONCPT CHARTS METH/COMP TIME. PAGE 11 G0219 — TEC/DEV FUT R+D PLAN

S67
ENKE S.,"GOVERNMENT-INDUSTRY DEVELOPMENT OF A COMMERCIAL SUPERSONIC TRANSPORT." USA+45 ECO/DEV R+D LG/CO NAT/G TEC/DEV PRICE RISK COST PROFIT. PAGE 18 G0347 — INDUS FINAN SERV/IND CAP/ISM

S67
EYRAUD M.,"LA FRANCE FACE A UN EVENTUEL TRAITE DE NON DISSEMINATION DES ARMES NUCLEAIRES." FRANCE USA+45 EXTR/IND INDUS R+D INT/ORG ACT/RES TEC/DEV AGREE PRODUC ATTIT 20 TREATY AEC EURATOM. PAGE 18 G0355 — NUC/PWR ARMS/CONT POLICY

FRIED M.,"FUNCTIONS OF THE WORKING CLASS COMMUNITY CLASSIF
IN MODERN URBAN SOCIETY* IMPLICATIONS FOR FORCED WORKER
RELOCATION." USA+45 INDUS R+D NEIGH PLAN TEC/DEV MUNIC
PARTIC GP/REL ATTIT...SOC STAT CHARTS. PAGE 20 ADJUST
G0393
                                                    S67

GANZ G.,"THE CONTROL OF INDUSTRY BY ADMINISTRATIVE INDUS
PROCESS." UK DELIB/GP WORKER 20. PAGE 21 G0408 LAW
                                              ADMIN
                                              CONTROL
                                                    S67

GAUSSENS J.,"THE APPLICATIONS OF NUCLEAR ENERGY - NUC/PWR
TECHNICAL, ECONOMIC AND SOCIAL ASPECTS." WOR+45 TEC/DEV
INDUS R+D ACT/RES EFFICIENCY PRODUC SKILL PREDICT. ECO/DEV
PAGE 21 G0413 ADJUST
                                                    S67

HAMBERG D.,"SIZE OF ENTERPRISE AND TECHNICAL TEC/DEV
CHANGE." USA+45 LG/CO SML/CO CREATE OP/RES PROFIT INDUS
...TREND 20. PAGE 24 G0477 R+D
                                              WEALTH
                                                    S67

INGLIS D.R.,"MISSILE DEFENSE, NUCLEAR SPREAD, AND NUC/PWR
VIETNAM." CHINA/COM USA+45 USSR VIETNAM INDUS ARMS/CONT
BAL/PWR DETER WAR COST NAT/LISM PEACE. PAGE 28 DIPLOM
G0544 FORCES
                                                    S67

INGLIS D.R.,"PROSPECTS AND PROBLEMS: THE NUC/PWR
NONMILITARY USES OF NUCLEAR EXPLOSIVES." CREATE INDUS
PROB/SOLV TEC/DEV AGREE PEACE...INT/LAW PHIL/SCI ARMS/CONT
NEW/IDEA 20 TREATY. PAGE 28 G0545 EXTR/IND
                                                    S67

KOMESAR N.K.,"SECURITY INTERESTS IN GOVERNMENT POLICY
CONTRACTS* WHEREIN THE TORTOISE WINS THE RES." CT/SYS
USA+45 INDUS NAT/G OP/RES SANCTION. PAGE 31 G0613 PRIVIL
                                              JURID
                                                    S67

MEHTA A.,"INDIA* POVERTY AND CHANGE." STRATA INDUS INDIA
CREATE ECO/TAC FOR/AID NEUTRAL GP/REL ADJUST INCOME SOCIETY
...NEW/IDEA 20. PAGE 38 G0751 ECO/UNDEV
                                              TEC/DEV
                                                    S67

MOOR E.J.,"THE INTERNATIONAL IMPACT OF AUTOMATION." TEC/DEV
WOR+45 ACT/RES COMPUTER CREATE PLAN CAP/ISM ROUTINE OP/RES
EFFICIENCY PREDICT. PAGE 39 G0779 AUTOMAT
                                              INDUS
                                                    S67

MORTON J.A.,"A SYSTEMS APPROACH TO THE INNOVATION TEC/DEV
PROCESS: ITS USE IN THE BELL SYSTEM." USA+45 INTELL GEN/METH
INDUS LG/CO CONSULT WORKER COMPUTER AUTOMAT DEMAND R+D
...MGT CHARTS 20. PAGE 40 G0787 COM/IND
                                                    S67

ROBERTS E.B.,"THE PROBLEM OF AGING ORGANIZATIONS." INDUS
INTELL PROB/SOLV ADMIN EXEC FEEDBACK EFFICIENCY R+D
PRODUC...GEN/LAWS 20. PAGE 47 G0926 MGT
                                              PLAN
                                                    S67

SINGH B.,"ITALIAN EXPERIENCE IN REGIONAL ECONOMIC ECO/UNDEV
DEVELOPMENT AND LESSONS FOR OTHER COUNTRIES." PLAN
EUR+WWI ITALY INDUS NAT/G ACT/RES REGION GP/REL ECO/TAC
EFFICIENCY EQUILIB PRODUC WEALTH. PAGE 51 G1007 CONTROL
                                                    S67

SLOAN P.,"FIFTY YEARS OF SOVIET RULE." USSR INDUS CREATE
EDU/PROP EFFICIENCY PRODUC HEALTH KNOWL MORAL NAT/G
WEALTH MARXISM...POLICY 20. PAGE 51 G1011 PLAN
                                              INSPECT
                                                    S67

TIVEY L.,"THE POLITICAL CONSEQUENCES OF ECONOMIC PLAN
PLANNING." UK CONSTN INDUS ACT/RES ADMIN CONTROL POLICY
LOBBY REPRESENT EFFICIENCY SUPEGO SOVEREIGN NAT/G
...DECISION 20. PAGE 55 G1074
                                                    S67

WARE R.S.,"FORECAST A.D. 2000." SOCIETY STRATA NUC/PWR
ECO/UNDEV INDUS FORCES EDU/PROP AUTOMAT COERCE REV GEOG
WEAPON ATTIT PREDICT. PAGE 62 G1213 TEC/DEV
                                              WAR
                                                    S67

WHITTIER J.M.,"COMPULSORY POOLING AND UNITIZATION* LEGIS
DIE-HARD KANSAS." LAW PLAN EDU/PROP ATTIT...POLICY MUNIC
JURID PREDICT TREND METH/COMP 20. PAGE 63 G1236 INDUS
                                              ECO/TAC

ASIAN STUDIES CENTER,FOUR ARTICLES ON POPULATION ASIA
AND FAMILY LIFE IN TAIWAN (ASIAN STUDIES PAPERS, FAM
REPRINT SERIES NO. 2). CULTURE STRATA ECO/UNDEV CENSUS
AGRI INDUS R+D KIN MUNIC...GEOG SOC CHARTS 20. ANTHOL
PAGE 4 G0072
                                                    N67

US SENATE COMM AERO SPACE SCI,AERONAUTICAL RESEARCH AIR
AND DEVELOPMENT POLICY (PAMPHLET). SPACE USA+45 R+D
INDUS CIVMIL/REL CONGRESS PRESIDENT NASA SENATE. POLICY
PAGE 60 G1169 PLAN
                                                    N67

US SENATE COMM AERO SPACE SCI,POLICY PLANNING FOR TEC/DEV
TECHNOLOGY TRANSFER (PAMPHLET). WOR+45 INDUS CREATE POLICY
PLAN EFFICIENCY ATTIT. PAGE 60 G1171 NAT/G
                                              ECO/DEV
                                                    N67

US SENATE COMM ON PUBLIC WORKS,AIR QUALITY ACT OF HEALTH
1967 (PAMPHLET). USA+45 INDUS R+D LEGIS SENATE. AIR
PAGE 61 G1187 HABITAT
                                              CONTROL
                                                    S68

BARAGWANATH L.E.,"SCIENTIFIC CO-OPERATION BETWEEN R+D
THE UNIVERSITIES AND INDUSTRY - A RESEARCH NOTE." ACADEM
UK LG/CO CREATE TEC/DEV EDU/PROP ATTIT...PHIL/SCI INDUS
STAT QU 20. PAGE 5 G0090 GP/REL

INDUS/REV....INDUSTRIAL REVOLUTION
                                                    B66

MILLAR R.,THE NEW CLASSES. UK ELITES SOCIETY INDUS STRUCT
AUTOMAT GP/REL SOC/INTEG 20 INDUS/REV. PAGE 39 STRATA
G0770 TEC/DEV
                                              CREATE

INDUSTRIAL AND WORKERS' COMMERCIAL UNION OF AFRICA....SEE
IND/WK/AFR

INDUSTRIAL RELATIONS....SEE LABOR, MGT, INDUS

INDUSTRIALIZATION....SEE ECO/DEV, ECO/UNDEV

INDUSTRY....SEE INDUS

INDUSTRY, COMMUNICATION....SEE COM/IND

INDUSTRY, CONSTRUCTION....SEE CONSTRUC

INDUSTRY, EXTRACTIVE....SEE EXTR/IND

INDUSTRY, MANUFACTURING....SEE PROC/MFG

INDUSTRY, PROCESSING....SEE PROC/MFG

INDUSTRY, SERVICE....SEE SERV/IND

INDUSTRY, TRANSPORTATION....SEE DIST/IND

INDUSTRY, WAREHOUSING....SEE DIST/IND

INFLATION....INFLATION

INFLUENCING....SEE MORE SPECIFIC FORMS, E.G., DOMIN, PWR,
WEALTH, EDU/PROP, SKILL, CHANGE, LOBBY

INGLIS D.R. G0544,G0545

INGP/REL....INTRAGROUP RELATIONS
                                                    N

JOURNAL OF PUBLIC ADMINISTRATION: JOURNAL OF THE BIBLIOG/A
ROYAL INSTITUTE OF PUBLIC ADMINISTRATION. UK PLAN ADMIN
GP/REL INGP/REL 20. PAGE 1 G0006 NAT/G
                                              MGT
                                                    B40

ZNANIECKI F.,THE SOCIAL ROLE OF THE MAN OF ROLE
KNOWLEDGE. UNIV SOCIETY STRUCT TEC/DEV...EPIST INTELL
PHIL/SCI SOC NEW/IDEA 20. PAGE 65 G1269 KNOWL
                                              INGP/REL
                                                    B47

BECK H.P.,MEN WHO CONTROL OUR UNIVERSITIES. EDU/PROP
EX/STRUC CHOOSE INGP/REL DISCRIM PERSON WEALTH ACADEM
...POLICY TREND CON/ANAL CHARTS BIBLIOG. PAGE 6 CONTROL
G0112 LEAD
                                                    B49

LEPAWSKY A.,ADMINISTRATION. FINAN INDUS LG/CO ADMIN
SML/CO INGP/REL PERS/REL COST EFFICIENCY OPTIMAL MGT
SKILL 20. PAGE 33 G0656 WORKER

EX/STRUC

B50
CONTINUITIES IN SOCIAL RESEARCH; STUDIES IN SCOPE SOC
AND METHOD OF "THE AMERICAN SOLDIER" USA+45 FORCES PHIL/SCI
INGP/REL ATTIT...PSY SAMP CON/ANAL CHARTS GEN/LAWS METH
ANTHOL 20. PAGE 38 G0758

S50
BAVELAS A.,"COMMUNICATION PATTERNS IN TASK-ORIENTED ACT/RES
GROUPS" (BMR)" R+D OP/RES INSPECT LEAD CENTRAL PERS/REL
EFFICIENCY HAPPINESS RIGID/FLEX...PROBABIL 20. TASK
PAGE 6 G0106 INGP/REL

B53
SAYLES L.R.,THE LOCAL UNION. CONSTN CULTURE LABOR
DELIB/GP PARTIC CHOOSE GP/REL INGP/REL ATTIT ROLE LEAD
...MAJORIT DECISION MGT. PAGE 49 G0958 ADJUD
ROUTINE

B54
SPROTT W.J.H.,SCIENCE AND SOCIAL ACTION. STRUCT SOC
ACT/RES CRIME GP/REL INGP/REL ANOMIE...PSY CULTURE
SOC/INTEG 19/20. PAGE 52 G1027 PHIL/SCI

B54
WILENSKY H.L.,SYLLABUS OF INDUSTRIAL RELATIONS: A BIBLIOG
GUIDE TO READING AND RESEARCH. USA+45 MUNIC ADMIN INDUS
INGP/REL...POLICY MGT PHIL/SCI 20. PAGE 63 G1239 LABOR
WORKER

S54
HOOPES T.,"CIVILIAN-MILITARY BALANCE." USA+45 CHIEF CIVMIL/REL
FORCES PLAN CONTROL WAR GOV/REL GP/REL INGP/REL LEAD
...POLICY 19/20. PAGE 27 G0527 PWR
NAT/G

B56
REDFORD E.S.,PUBLIC ADMINISTRATION AND POLICY EX/STRUC
FORMATION: STUDIES IN OIL, GAS, BANKING, RIVER PROB/SOLV
DEVELOPMENT AND CORPORATE INVESTIGATIONS. USA+45 CONTROL
CLIENT NAT/G ADMIN LOBBY REPRESENT GOV/REL INGP/REL EXEC
20. PAGE 46 G0908

B57
KIETH-LUCAS A.,DECISIONS ABOUT PEOPLE IN NEED. A ADMIN
STUDY OF ADMINISTRATIVE RESPONSIVENESS IN PUBLIC RIGID/FLEX
ASSISTANCE. USA+45 GIVE RECEIVE INGP/REL PERS/REL SOC/WK
MORAL RESPECT WEALTH...SOC OBS BIBLIOG 20. PAGE 30 DECISION
G0595

B57
MERTON R.K.,SOCIAL THEORY AND SOCIAL STRUCTURE SOC
(REV. ED.). INTELL SECT WORKER OP/RES EDU/PROP GEN/LAWS
ADMIN INGP/REL ANOMIE PERSON...AUD/VIS T 20 SOCIETY
BUREAUCRCY. PAGE 38 G0759 STRUCT

S57
BAUMGARTEL H.,"LEADERSHIP STYLE AS A VARIABLE IN LEAD
RESEARCH ADMINISTRATION." USA+45 ADMIN REPRESENT EXEC
PERS/REL 20. PAGE 5 G0104 MGT
INGP/REL

B58
LIPPITT R.,DYNAMICS OF PLANNED CHANGE. STRUCT VOL/ASSN
ACT/RES ROUTINE INGP/REL PWR...POLICY METH/CNCPT ORD/FREE
BIBLIOG. PAGE 34 G0672 PLAN
CREATE

S58
ARGYRIS C.,"SOME PROBLEMS IN CONCEPTUALIZING FINAN
ORGANIZATIONAL CLIMATE: A CASE STUDY OF A BANK" CONCPT
(BMR)" USA+45 EX/STRUC ADMIN PERS/REL ADJUST PERSON LG/CO
...POLICY HYPO/EXP SIMUL 20. PAGE 3 G0064 INGP/REL

L59
TARKOWSKI Z.M.,"SCIENTISTS VERSUS ADMINISTRATORS: INGP/REL
AN APPROACH TOWARD ACHIEVING GREATER GP/REL
UNDERSTANDING." UK EXEC EFFICIENCY 20. PAGE 53 ADMIN
G1052 EX/STRUC

S59
LEFTON M.,"DECISION MAKING IN A MENTAL HOSPITAL: ACT/RES
REAL, PERCEIVED, AND IDEAL." R+D PUB/INST CONSULT PROB/SOLV
CONFER INGP/REL PERCEPT...MODAL 20. PAGE 33 G0653 DECISION
PSY

B60
MCGREGOR D.,THE HUMAN SIDE OF ENTERPRISE. USA+45 MGT
LEAD ROUTINE GP/REL INGP/REL...CONCPT GEN/LAWS 20. ATTIT
PAGE 38 G0741 SKILL
EDU/PROP

B60
WALDO D.,THE RESEARCH FUNCTION OF UNIVERSITY ADMIN
BUREAUS AND INSTITUTES FOR GOVERNMENTAL-RELATED R+D

RESEARCH. FINAN ACADEM NAT/G INGP/REL ROLE...POLICY MUNIC
CLASSIF GOV/COMP. PAGE 61 G1205

S60
RAPP W.F.,"MANAGEMENT ANALYSIS AT THE HEADQUARTERS INGP/REL
OF FEDERAL AGENCIES." USA+45 NAT/G 20. PAGE 46 ADMIN
G0903 EX/STRUC
MGT

B61
KRUPP S.,PATTERN IN ORGANIZATIONAL ANALYSIS: A MGT
CRITICAL EXAMINATION. INGP/REL PERS/REL RATIONAL CONTROL
ATTIT AUTHORIT DRIVE PWR...DECISION PHIL/SCI SOC CONCPT
IDEA/COMP. PAGE 32 G0622 METH/CNCPT

B61
LEE R.R.,ENGINEERING-ECONOMIC PLANNING BIBLIOG/A
MISCELLANEOUS SUBJECTS: A SELECTED BIBLIOGRAPHY PLAN
(MIMEOGRAPHED). FINAN LOC/G MUNIC NEIGH ADMIN REGION
CONTROL INGP/REL HABITAT...GEOG MGT SOC/WK 20
RESOURCE/N. PAGE 33 G0651

B61
WEISBROD B.A.,ECONOMICS OF PUBLIC HEALTH. USA+45 SOCIETY
INGP/REL HABITAT...POLICY STAT 20. PAGE 63 G1227 HEALTH
NEW/IDEA
ECO/DEV

L61
THOMPSON V.A.,"HIERARCHY, SPECIALIZATION, AND PERS/REL
ORGANIZATIONAL CONFLICT" (BMR)" WOR+45 STRATA PROB/SOLV
STRUCT WORKER TEC/DEV GP/REL INGP/REL ATTIT ADMIN
AUTHORIT 20 BUREAUCRCY. PAGE 54 G1069 EX/STRUC

S61
COOKE E.F.,"RESEARCH: AN INSTRUMENT OF POWER." R+D
VOL/ASSN PLAN TEC/DEV TAX LOBBY INGP/REL ROLE PROVS
POLICY. PAGE 13 G0253 LOC/G
DECISION

S61
HAINES G.,"THE COMPUTER AS A SMALL-GROUP MEMBER." INGP/REL
DELIB/GP BAL/PWR TASK 20. PAGE 24 G0467 COMPUTER
PROB/SOLV
EFFICIENCY

B62
BAKER G.W.,BEHAVIORAL SCIENCE AND CIVIL DEFENSE. NUC/PWR
USA+45 PROB/SOLV ADMIN GP/REL INGP/REL PERS/REL WAR
ANOMIE DRIVE PERSON...DECISION MGT SOC 20 POLICY
CIV/DEFENS. PAGE 4 G0085 ACT/RES

B63
HOFSTADTER R.,ANTI-INTELLECTUALISM IN AMERICAN INTELL
LIFE. USA+45 AGRI INDUS ACADEM TEC/DEV EDU/PROP EPIST
INGP/REL ATTIT...SOC WORSHIP 20 MCCARTHY/J CULTURE
STEVENSN/A. PAGE 26 G0522 SOCIETY

B63
HOWER R.M.,MANAGERS AND SCIENTISTS. EX/STRUC CREATE R+D
ADMIN REPRESENT ATTIT DRIVE ROLE PWR SKILL...SOC MGT
INT. PAGE 27 G0532 PERS/REL
INGP/REL

B63
LITTERER J.A.,ORGANIZATIONS: STRUCTURE AND ADMIN
BEHAVIOR. PLAN DOMIN CONTROL LEAD ROUTINE SANCTION CREATE
INGP/REL EFFICIENCY PRODUC DRIVE RIGID/FLEX PWR. MGT
PAGE 34 G0674 ADJUST

B63
THORELLI H.B.,INTOP: INTERNATIONAL OPERATIONS GAME
SIMULATION: PLAYER'S MANUAL. BRAZIL FINAN OP/RES INT/TRADE
ADMIN GP/REL INGP/REL PRODUC PERCEPT...DECISION MGT EDU/PROP
EEC. PAGE 54 G1073 LG/CO

B64
EDELMAN M.,THE SYMBOLIC USES OF POWER. USA+45 CLIENT
EX/STRUC CONTROL GP/REL INGP/REL...MGT T. PAGE 17 PWR
G0333 EXEC
ELITES

B64
RUSHING W.A.,THE PSYCHIATRIC PROFESSIONS. DOMIN ATTIT
INGP/REL DRIVE RIGID/FLEX ROLE HEALTH PWR...POLICY PUB/INST
GP/COMP. PAGE 48 G0947 PROF/ORG
BAL/PWR

B65
BAILEY S.K.,AMERICAN POLITICS AND GOVERNMENT. ANTHOL
USA+45 CONSTN FINAN LABOR POL/PAR DIPLOM ADMIN WAR LEGIS
INGP/REL RACE/REL NEW/LIB 20 SUPREME/CT PRESIDENT PWR
CONGRESS. PAGE 4 G0084

B65
CARPER E.T.,REORGANIZATION OF THE U.S. PUBLIC HEAL

HEALTH SERVICE. FUT USA+45 INTELL R+D LOBBY GP/REL   PLAN
INGP/REL PERS/REL RIGID/FLEX ROLE HEALTH...PHIL/SCI   NAT/G
20 CONGRESS PHS. PAGE 11 G0213   OP/RES

B65
PHELPS E.S.,PRIVATE WANTS AND PUBLIC NEEDS - AN   NAT/G
INTRODUCTION TO A CURRENT ISSUE OF PUBLIC POLICY   POLICY
(REV. ED.). USA+45 PLAN CAP/ISM INGP/REL ROLE   DEMAND
...DECISION TIME/SEQ 20. PAGE 44 G0873

B65
REISS A.J. JR.,SCHOOLS IN A CHANGING SOCIETY.   SCHOOL
CULTURE PROB/SOLV INSPECT DOMIN CONFER INGP/REL   EX/STRUC
RACE/REL AGE/C AGE/Y ALL/VALS...ANTHOL SOC/INTEG 20   ADJUST
NEWYORK/C. PAGE 46 G0912   ADMIN

S66
FLEMING W.G.,"AUTHORITY, EFFICIENCY, AND ROLE   DOMIN
STRESS: PROBLEMS IN THE DEVELOPMENT OF EAST AFRICAN   EFFICIENCY
BUREAUCRACIES." AFR UGANDA STRUCT PROB/SOLV ROUTINE   COLONIAL
INGP/REL ROLE...MGT SOC GP/COMP GOV/COMP 20   ADMIN
TANGANYIKA AFRICA/E. PAGE 19 G0371

B67
COLEMAN J.R.,THE CHANGING AMERICAN ECONOMY. USA+45   BUDGET
AGRI FINAN LABOR FOR/AID INT/TRADE AUTOMAT GP/REL   ECO/TAC
INGP/REL ANTHOL. PAGE 13 G0243   ECO/DEV
                                                      WEALTH

B67
DAVIS V.,THE POLITICS OF INNOVATION: PATTERNS IN   BIBLIOG
NAVY CASES (PAMPHLET). WOR+45 NAT/G CREATE WEAPON   FORCES
INGP/REL ATTIT...POLICY SOC METH/COMP METH. PAGE 14   NUC/PWR
G0280   TEC/DEV

B67
US PRES COMN LAW ENFORCE-JUS,THE CHALLENGE OF CRIME   CT/SYS
IN A FREE SOCIETY. LAW STRUCT CONSULT ACT/RES   PUB/INST
TEC/DEV INGP/REL...SOC/WK 20. PAGE 59 G1160   CRIMLGY
                                                      CRIME

S67
ARONOWITZ D.S.,"CIVIL COMMITMENT OF NARCOTIC   PUB/INST
ADDICTS." USA+45 LAW INGP/REL DISCRIM MORAL...TREND   ACT/RES
20. PAGE 4 G0069   POLICY

S67
CARR E.H.,"REVOLUTION FROM ABOVE." USSR STRATA   AGRI
FINAN INDUS NAT/G DOMIN LEAD GP/REL INGP/REL OWN   POLICY
PRODUC PWR 20 STALIN/J. PAGE 11 G0214   COM
                                                      EFFICIENCY

S67
CONWAY J.E.,"MAKING RESEARCH EFFECTIVE IN   ACT/RES
LEGISLATION." LAW R+D CONSULT EX/STRUC PLAN CONFER   POLICY
ADMIN LEAD ROUTINE TASK INGP/REL DECISION. PAGE 13   LEGIS
G0252   PROB/SOLV

S67
CRANBERG L.,"SCIENCE, ETHICS, AND LAW." UNIV CREATE   LAW
PLAN EDU/PROP INGP/REL PERS/REL ADJUST RATIONAL   PHIL/SCI
KNOWL MORAL...CONCPT IDEA/COMP 20. PAGE 13 G0260   INTELL

S67
HODGE G.,"THE RISE AND DEMISE OF THE UN TECHNICAL   ADMIN
ASSISTANCE ADMINISTRATION." RISK TASK INGP/REL   TEC/DEV
CONSEN EFFICIENCY 20 UN. PAGE 26 G0516   EX/STRUC
                                                      INT/ORG

S67
LEVENSTEIN A.,"TECHNOLOGICAL CHANGE, WORK, AND   TEC/DEV
HUMAN VALUES." WOR+45 SOCIETY AUTOMAT ROUTINE   CULTURE
LEISURE INGP/REL ADJUST TECHRACY...MGT CONCPT.   ALL/VALS
PAGE 33 G0660   TIME/SEQ

S67
SCOVILLE W.J.,"GOVERNMENT REGULATION AND GROWTH IN   NAT/G
THE FRENCH PAPER INDUSTRY DURING THE EIGHTEENTH   PROC/MFG
CENTURY." FRANCE MOD/EUR FINAN CAP/ISM TAX ADMIN   ECO/DEV
CONTROL PRIVIL LAISSEZ...POLICY 18. PAGE 50 G0985   INGP/REL

INNIS/H....HAROLD ADAMS INNIS

INNOVATION....SEE CREATE

INONU/I....ISMET INONU

INSPECT....EXAMINING FOR QUALITY, OUTPUT, LEGALITY

N19
LAWRENCE S.A.,THE BATTERY ADDITIVE CONTROVERSY   PHIL/SCI
(PAMPHLET). USA+45 LAW MARKET PROC/MFG R+D CAP/ISM   LOBBY
CT/SYS GOV/REL OWN FTC CONGRESS BUR/STNDRD   INSPECT
RITCHIE/JM. PAGE 33 G0645

S50
BAVELAS A.,"COMMUNICATION PATTERNS IN TASK-ORIENTED   ACT/RES
GROUPS" (BMR)" R+D OP/RES INSPECT LEAD CENTRAL   PERS/REL
EFFICIENCY HAPPINESS RIGID/FLEX...PROBABIL 20.   TASK
PAGE 6 G0106   INGP/REL

B58
ATOMIC INDUSTRIAL FORUM,MANAGEMENT AND ATOMIC   NUC/PWR
ENERGY. WOR+45 SEA LAW MARKET NAT/G TEC/DEV INSPECT   INDUS
INT/TRADE CONFER PEACE HEALTH...ANTHOL 20. PAGE 4   MGT
G0078   ECO/TAC

B62
STERN A.C.,AIR POLLUTION (2 VOLS.). LAW INDUS   AIR
PROB/SOLV TEC/DEV INSPECT RISK BIO/SOC HABITAT   OP/RES
...OBS/ENVIR TESTS SAMP 20 POLLUTION. PAGE 53 G1035   CONTROL
                                                      HEALTH

B64
KAUFMANN W.W.,THE MC NAMARA STRATEGY. TOP/EX   FORCES
INSPECT BAL/PWR DIPLOM CONTROL DETER GUERRILLA   WAR
NUC/PWR WEAPON COST PWR...METH/COMP 20 MCNAMARA/R   PLAN
KENNEDY/JF JOHNSON/LB NATO DEPT/DEFEN. PAGE 30   PROB/SOLV
G0586

B65
ATOMIC INDUSTRIAL FORUM,SAFEGUARDS AGAINST   NUC/PWR
DIVERSION OF NUCLEAR MATERIALS FROM PEACEFUL TO   CIVMIL/REL
MILITARY PURPOSES. WOR+45 DELIB/GP FORCES PLAN   INSPECT
DIPLOM CONFER PEACE...ANTHOL 20 IAEA. PAGE 4 G0081   CONTROL

B65
REISS A.J. JR.,SCHOOLS IN A CHANGING SOCIETY.   SCHOOL
CULTURE PROB/SOLV INSPECT DOMIN CONFER INGP/REL   EX/STRUC
RACE/REL AGE/C AGE/Y ALL/VALS...ANTHOL SOC/INTEG 20   ADJUST
NEWYORK/C. PAGE 46 G0912   ADMIN

B65
STEINER G.A.,THE CREATIVE ORGANIZATION. ELITES   CREATE
LG/CO PLAN PROB/SOLV TEC/DEV INSPECT CAP/ISM   MGT
CONTROL EXEC PERSON...METH/COMP HYPO/EXP 20.   ADMIN
PAGE 52 G1034   SOC

B65
US CONGRESS JT ATOM ENRGY COMM,PROPOSED AMENDMENT   LAW
TO SECTION 271 OF THE ATOMIC ENERGY ACT OF 1954.   LEGIS
USA+45 CONSTRUC PLAN INSPECT CONTROL CT/SYS 20   DELIB/GP
CONGRESS AEC. PAGE 57 G1115   NUC/PWR

S67
SLOAN P.,"FIFTY YEARS OF SOVIET RULE." USSR INDUS   CREATE
EDU/PROP EFFICIENCY PRODUC HEALTH KNOWL MORAL   NAT/G
WEALTH MARXISM...POLICY 20. PAGE 51 G1011   PLAN
                                                      INSPECT

B68
GALLAHER A. JR.,PERSPECTIVES IN DEVELOPMENTAL   TECHNIC
CHANGE. MUNIC PLAN INSPECT EDU/PROP...POLICY   TEC/DEV
DECISION GEOG PSY SOC IDEA/COMP ANTHOL 20   PROB/SOLV
MODERNIZE. PAGE 21 G0405   CREATE

INST D'ETUDE POL L'U GRENOBLE G0546

INSTITUTE PSYCHOLOGICAL RES G0547

INSTITUTION, EDUCATIONAL....SEE SCHOOL, ACADEM

INSTITUTION, MENTAL....SEE PUB/INST

INSTITUTION, RELIGIOUS....SEE SECT

INSTITUTIONS....SEE DESCRIPTORS IN INSTITUTIONAL INDEX
   (TOPICAL INDEX, NO. 2)

INSURANCE....SEE FINAN, SERV/IND

INSURRECTION....SEE REV

INT....INTERVIEW; SEE ALSO INTERVIEWS INDEX, P. XIV

B40
PFIFFNER J.M.,RESEARCH METHODS IN PUBLIC   ADMIN
ADMINISTRATION. USA-45 R+D...MGT STAT INT QU T 20.   OP/RES
PAGE 44 G0872   METH
                                                     TEC/DEV

B47
LASSWELL H.D.,THE ANALYSIS OF POLITICAL BEHAVIOUR: R+D
AN EMPIRICAL APPROACH. WOR+45 CULTURE NAT/G FORCES   ACT/RES
EDU/PROP ADMIN ATTIT PERCEPT KNOWL...PHIL/SCI PSY   ELITES
SOC NEW/IDEA OBS INT GEN/METH NAZI 20. PAGE 32
G0639

S52
TRUMAN D.B.,"SELECTED CRITICAL BIBLIOGRAPHY ON THE   BIBLIOG/A
METHODS AND TECHNIQUES OF POLITICAL BEHAVIOR   ACT/RES

RESEARCH." R+D PARTIC...SOC OBS RECORD INT. PAGE 55 METH/CNCPT
G1079

B53
MACK R.T..RAISING THE WORLDS STANDARD OF LIVING. WOR+45
IRAN INT/ORG VOL/ASSN EX/STRUC ECO/TAC WEALTH...MGT FOR/AID
METH/CNCPT STAT CONT/OBS INT TOT/POP VAL/FREE 20 INT/TRADE
UN. PAGE 35 G0690

B55
MIKSCHE F.O..ATOMIC WEAPONS AND ARMIES. FUT WOR+45 TEC/DEV
WOR-45 SOCIETY COERCE DETER WEAPON PWR...POLICY FORCES
WELF/ST PSY CONCPT INT SYS/QU KNO/TEST TOT/POP 20. NUC/PWR
PAGE 39 G0765

S56
KNAPP D.C.."CONGRESSIONAL CONTROL OF AGRICULTURAL LEGIS
CONSERVATION POLICY: A CASE STUDY OF THE AGRI
APPROPRIATIONS PROCESS." DELIB/GP PLAN PROB/SOLV BUDGET
CONFER PARL/PROC...POLICY INT CONGRESS. PAGE 31 CONTROL
G0607

B57
SPEIER H..GERMAN REARMAMENT AND ATOMIC WAR: THE TOP/EX
VIEWS OF GERMAN MILITARY AND POLITICAL LEADERS. FUT FORCES
WOR+45 INT/ORG NAT/G WEAPON ATTIT PWR...INT QU NUC/PWR
TOT/POP VAL/FREE COLD/WAR 20. PAGE 52 G1024 GERMANY

B58
GANGE J..UNIVERSITY RESEARCH ON INTERNATIONAL R+D
AFFAIRS. USA+45 ACADEM INT/ORG CONSULT CREATE EXEC MGT
ROUTINE...QUANT STAT INT STERTYP GEN/METH TOT/POP DIPLOM
VAL/FREE 20. PAGE 21 G0407

B58
JUNGK R..BRIGHTER THAN A THOUSAND SUNS: THE MORAL NUC/PWR
AND POLITICAL HISTORY OF THE ATOMIC SCIENTISTS. MORAL
WOR+45 WOR-45 CONSULT CREATE RISK UTIL DRIVE GOV/REL
PERCEPT PWR...INT 20. PAGE 29 G0568 PERSON

B58
MECRENSKY E..SCIENTIFIC MANPOWER IN EUROPE. WOR+45 ECO/TAC
EDU/PROP GOV/REL SKILL...TECHNIC PHIL/SCI INT TEC/DEV
CHARTS BIBLIOG 20. PAGE 38 G0750 METH/COMP
NAT/COMP

B59
LANG D..FROM HIROSHIMA TO THE MOON: CHRONICLES OF NUC/PWR
LIFE IN THE ATOMIC AGE. USA+45 OP/RES CONTROL SPACE
ARMS/CONT WAR CIVMIL/REL PEACE HABITAT MORAL PWR HEALTH
...OBS INT 20 AEC. PAGE 32 G0633 TEC/DEV

B59
VAN WAGENEN R.W..SOME VIEWS OF AMERICAN DEFENSE INT/ORG
OFFICIALS ABOUT THE UNITED NATIONS (PAPER). FUT LEAD
USA+45 NAT/G DIPLOM WAR EFFICIENCY PEACE...POLICY ATTIT
INT 20 UN DEPT/DEFEN. PAGE 61 G1192 FORCES

B60
BROOKINGS INSTITUTION.UNITED STATES FOREIGN POLICY: DIPLOM
STUDY NO 9: THE FORMULATION AND ADMINISTRATION OF INT/ORG
UNITED STATES FOREIGN POLICY. USA+45 WOR+45 CREATE
EX/STRUC LEGIS BAL/PWR FOR/AID EDU/PROP CIVMIL/REL
GOV/REL...INT COLD/WAR. PAGE 9 G0174

B62
DODDS H.W..THE ACADEMIC PRESIDENT "EDUCATOR OR ACADEM
CARETAKER? FINAN DELIB/GP EDU/PROP PARTIC ATTIT ADMIN
ROLE PWR...POLICY RECORD INT. PAGE 16 G0304 LEAD
CONTROL

B63
GOLDSEN J.M..OUTER SPACE IN WORLD POLITICS. COM TEC/DEV
USA+45 NAT/G FORCES ACT/RES PLAN COERCE ORD/FREE DIPLOM
COERCE ORD/FREE PWR...TECHNIC STAT INT SAMP TREND SPACE
ANTHOL VAL/FREE 20. PAGE 22 G0428

B63
HOWER R.M..MANAGERS AND SCIENTISTS. EX/STRUC CREATE R+D
ADMIN REPRESENT ATTIT DRIVE ROLE PWR SKILL...SOC MGT
INT. PAGE 27 G0532 PERS/REL
INGP/REL

B63
KORNHAUSER W..SCIENTISTS IN INDUSTRY: CONFLICT AND CREATE
ACCOMMODATION. USA+45 R+D LG/CO NAT/G TEC/DEV INDUS
CONTROL ADJUST ATTIT...MGT STAT INT BIBLIOG 20. PROF/ORG
PAGE 31 G0614 GP/REL

B63
US SENATE COMM GOVT OPERATIONS.ADMINISTRATION OF DELIB/GP
NATIONAL SECURITY (9 PARTS). ADMIN...INT REC/INT NAT/G
CHARTS 20 SENATE CONGRESS. PAGE 60 G1178 OP/RES
ORD/FREE

B63
WALES H.G..A BASIC BIBLIOGRAPHY ON MARKETING BIBLIOG/A
RESEARCH (REV. ED.). ATTIT...MGT STAT INT QU SAMP MARKET
TREND 20. PAGE 62 G1206 OP/RES
METH/COMP

B63
WIGHTMAN D..TOWARD ECONOMIC CO-OPERATION IN ASIA. ECO/UNDEV
ASIA S/ASIA VOL/ASSN ACT/RES PLAN TEC/DEV ECO/TAC CREATE
EDU/PROP RIGID/FLEX SKILL...POLICY METH/CNCPT OBS
INT GEN/LAWS UN 20 ECAFE. PAGE 63 G1237

S63
ERSKINE H.G.."THE POLLS: ATOMIC WEAPONS AND NUCLEAR ATTIT
ENERGY." USA+45 COERCE ORD/FREE...POLICY SOC STAT INT
CENSUS SAMP VAL/FREE 20. PAGE 18 G0350 NUC/PWR

S64
BYRNES F.C.."ASSIGNMENT TO AMBIGUITY: WORK INTELL
PERFORMANCE IN CROSSCULTURAL TECHNICAL ASSISTANCE." QU
USA+45 WOR+45 PROF/ORG CONSULT PLAN EDU/PROP ATTIT
DISPL PERCEPT PERSON ALL/VALS...POLICY INT CHARTS
NATO 20. PAGE 10 G0199

S64
COOPER A.C.."R&D IS MORE EFFICIENT IN SMALL R+D
COMPANIES." USA+45 LG/CO SML/CO WEALTH...RECORD INT INDUS
LAB/EXP 20. PAGE 13 G0255 CREATE
GP/COMP

B66
JACOBSON H.K..DIPLOMATS, SCIENTISTS, AND DIPLOM
POLITICIANS* THE UNITED STATES AND THE NUCLEAR TEST ARMS/CONT
BAN NEGOTIATIONS. USA+45 USSR ACT/RES PLAN CONFER TECHRACY
DETER NUC/PWR CONSEN ORD/FREE...INT TREATY. PAGE 28 INT/ORG
G0554

B66
US BUREAU OF THE BUDGET.THE ADMINISTRATION OF ACT/RES
GOVERNMENT SUPPORTED RESEARCH AT UNIVERSITIES NAT/G
(PAMPHLET). USA+45 CONSULT TOP/EX ADMIN INCOME ACADEM
WEALTH...MGT PHIL/SCI INT. PAGE 56 G1108 GP/REL

B67
US SENATE COMM AERO SPACE SCI.APOLLO ACCIDENT PROB/SOLV
(PARTS 1-7). USA+45 DELIB/GP LEGIS...INT CHARTS SPACE
NASA. PAGE 60 G1173 BUDGET
GOV/REL

S67
ALEXANDER L.."PROTECTION OF PRIVACY IN BEHAVIORAL ACT/RES
RESEARCH." WOR+45 ADJUD SANCTION ORD/FREE...JURID POLICY
INT. PAGE 2 G0036 OBS/ENVIR

S67
BENN W.."TECHNOLOGY HAS AN INEXORABLE EFFECT." FUT R+D
UK ECO/DEV INT/ORG CONSULT PLAN EDU/PROP ADMIN LEAD LG/CO
GP/REL PRODUC...INT 20 EEC. PAGE 6 G0119 TEC/DEV
INDUS

S67
DEUTSCH K.W.."ARMS CONTROL AND EUROPEAN UNITY* THE ARMS/CONT
NEXT TEN YEARS." USA+45 ELITES NAT/G BAL/PWR DIPLOM PEACE
NUC/PWR...INT KNO/TEST NATO EEC. PAGE 15 G0300 REGION
PLAN

S67
VERGIN R.C.."COMPUTER INDUCED ORGANIZATION COMPUTER
CHANGES." FUT USA+45 R+D CREATE OP/RES TEC/DEV DECISION
ADJUST CENTRAL...MGT INT CON/ANAL COMPUT/IR. AUTOMAT
PAGE 61 G1194 EX/STRUC

N
FOREIGN AFFAIRS. SPACE WOR+45 WOR-45 CULTURE BIBLIOG
ECO/UNDEV FINAN NAT/G TEC/DEV INT/TRADE ARMS/CONT DIPLOM
NUC/PWR...POLICY 20 UN EURATOM ECSC EEC. PAGE 1 INT/ORG
G0004 INT/LAW

N
AIR UNIVERSITY LIBRARY.INDEX TO MILITARY BIBLIOG/A
PERIODICALS. FUT SPACE WOR+45 REGION ARMS/CONT FORCES
NUC/PWR WAR PEACE INT/LAW. PAGE 2 G0032 NAT/G
DIPLOM

N19
US SEN SPEC COMM SPACE ASTRO.SPACE LAW: A SYMPOSIUM SPACE
(PAMPHLET). USA+45 TEC/DEV CONFER CONTROL SOVEREIGN ADJUD
...INT/LAW 20 SEN/SPACE. PAGE 59 G1161 DIPLOM

INT/ORG

G0854

B35

FOREIGN AFFAIRS BIBLIOGRAPHY: A SELECTED AND
ANNOTATED LIST OF BOOKS ON INTERNATIONAL RELATIONS
1919-1962 (4 VOLS.). CONSTN FORCES COLONIAL
ARMS/CONT WAR NAT/LISM PEACE ATTIT DRIVE...POLICY
INT/LAW 20. PAGE 1 G0011

BIBLIOG/A
DIPLOM
INT/ORG

S55

WRIGHT Q.,"THE PEACEFUL ADJUSTMENT OF INTERNATIONAL
RELATIONS: PROBLEMS AND RESEARCH APPROACHES." UNIV
INTELL EDU/PROP ADJUD ROUTINE KNOWL SKILL...INT/LAW
JURID PHIL/SCI CLASSIF 20. PAGE 64 G1258

R+D
METH/CNCPT
PEACE

B56

ESTEP R.,AN AIR POWER BIBLIOGRAPHY. USA+45 TEC/DEV
BUDGET DIPLOM EDU/PROP DETER CIVMIL/REL...DECISION
INT/LAW 20. PAGE 18 G0351

BIBLIOG/A
FORCES
WEAPON
PLAN

N57

US ARMY LIBRARY,THESES AND DISSERTATIONS IN THE
HOLDINGS OF THE ARMY LIBRARY (PAMPHLET). USA+45
...INT/LAW PSY SOC 20. PAGE 56 G1105

BIBLIOG
FORCES
MGT
CONTROL

S58

MCDOUGAL M.S.,"PERSPECTIVES FOR A LAW OF OUTER
SPACE." FUT WOR+45 AIR CONSULT DELIB/GP TEC/DEV
CT/SYS ORD/FREE...POLICY JURID 20 UN. PAGE 37 G0736

INT/ORG
SPACE
INT/LAW

B59

HARVARD UNIVERSITY LAW SCHOOL,INTERNATIONAL
PROBLEMS OF FINANCIAL PROTECTION AGAINST NUCLEAR
RISK. WOR+45 NAT/G DELIB/GP PROB/SOLV DIPLOM
CONTROL ATTIT...POLICY INT/LAW MATH 20. PAGE 25
G0488

NUC/PWR
ADJUD
INDUS
FINAN

B59

COLUMBIA U BUREAU APPL SOC R, ATTITUDES OF
PROMINENT AMERICANS TOWARD "WORLD PEACE THROUGH
WORLD LAW" (SUPRA-NATL ORGANIZATION FOR WAR
PREVENTION). USA+45 USSR ELITES FORCES PLAN
PROB/SOLV CONTROL WAR PWR...POLICY SOC QU IDEA/COMP
20 UN. PAGE 45 G0888

ATTIT
ACT/RES
INT/LAW
STAT

L59

MCDOUGAL M.S.,"THE IDENTIFICATION AND APPRAISAL OF
DIVERSE SYSTEMS OF PUBLIC ORDER (BMR)" WOR+45 NAT/G
CONSULT EDU/PROP POLICY. PAGE 37 G0737

INT/LAW
DIPLOM
ALL/IDEOS

B60

WOETZEL R.K.,THE INTERNATIONAL CONTROL OF AIRSPACE
AND OUTERSPACE. FUT WOR+45 AIR CONSTN STRUCT
CONSULT PLAN TEC/DEV ADJUD RIGID/FLEX KNOWL
ORD/FREE PWR...TECHNIC GEOG MGT NEW/IDEA TREND
COMPUT/IR VAL/FREE 20 TREATY. PAGE 64 G1251

INT/ORG
JURID
SPACE
INT/LAW

S61

MACHOWSKI K.,"SELECTED PROBLEMS OF NATIONAL
SOVEREIGNTY WITH REFERENCE TO THE LAW OF OUTER
SPACE." FUT WOR+45 AIR LAW INTELL SOCIETY ECO/DEV
PLAN EDU/PROP DETER DRIVE PERCEPT SOVEREIGN
...POLICY INT/LAW OBS TREND TOT/POP 20. PAGE 35
G0689

UNIV
ACT/RES
NUC/PWR
SPACE

B62

SCHMITT H.A.,THE PATH TO EUROPEAN UNITY. EUR+WWI
USA+45 PLAN TEC/DEV DIPLOM FOR/AID CONFER...INT/LAW
20 EEC EURCOALSTL MARSHL/PLN UNIFICA. PAGE 49 G0971

INT/ORG
INT/TRADE
REGION
ECO/DEV

B62

SCHWARTZ L.E.,INTERNATIONAL ORGANIZATIONS AND SPACE
COOPERATION. VOL/ASSN CONSULT CREATE TEC/DEV
SANCTION...POLICY INT/LAW PHIL/SCI 20 UN. PAGE 50
G0982

INT/ORG
DIPLOM
R+D
SPACE

S62

CRANE R.D.,"LAW AND STRATEGY IN SPACE." FUT USA+45
WOR+45 AIR LAW INT/ORG NAT/G FORCES ACT/RES PLAN
BAL/PWR LEGIT ARMS/CONT COERCE ORD/FREE...POLICY
INT/LAW JURID SOC/EXP 20 TREATY. PAGE 13 G0261

CONCPT
SPACE

B63

MCDOUGAL M.S.,LAW AND PUBLIC ORDER IN SPACE. FUT
USA+45 ACT/RES TEC/DEV ADJUD...POLICY INT/LAW JURID
20. PAGE 37 G0739

SPACE
ORD/FREE
DIPLOM
DECISION

B63

PACHTER H.M.,COLLISION COURSE; THE CUBAN MISSILE
CRISIS AND COEXISTENCE. CUBA USA+45 DIPLOM
ARMS/CONT PEACE MARXISM...DECISION INT/LAW 20
COLD/WAR KHRUSH/N KENNEDY/JF CASTRO/F. PAGE 43

WAR
BAL/PWR
NUC/PWR
DETER

B6

PANAMERICAN UNION,DOCUMENTOS OFICIALES DE LA
ORGANIZACION DE LOS ESTADOS AMERICANOS, INDICE Y
LISTA (VOL. III, 1962). L/A+17C DELIB/GP INT/TRADE
EDU/PROP REGION NUC/PWR...HEAL INT/LAW SOC/WK 20
OAS. PAGE 44 G0857

BIBLIOG
INT/ORG
DIPLOM

B6

US SENATE,DOCUMENTS ON INTERNATIONAL AS"ECTS OF
EXPLORATION AND USE OF OUTER SPACE, 1954-62: STAFF
REPORT FOR COMM AERON SPACE SCI. USA+45 USSR LEGIS
LEAD CIVMIL/REL PEACE...POLICY INT/LAW ANTHOL 20
CONGRESS NASA KHRUSH/N. PAGE 59 G1162

SPACE
UTIL
GOV/REL
DIPLOM

B6

COHEN M.,LAW AND POLITICS IN SPACE: SPECIFIC AND
URGENT PROBLEMS IN THE LAW OF OUTER SPACE.
CHINA/COM COM USA+45 USSR WOR+45 COM/IND INT/ORG
NAT/G LEGIT NUC/PWR ATTIT BIO/SOC...JURID CONCPT
CONGRESS 20 STALIN/J. PAGE 12 G0241

DELIB/GP
LAW
INT/LAW
SPACE

B6

ROBERTS HL,FOREIGN AFFAIRS BIBLIOGRAPHY, 1952-1962.
ECO/DEV SECT PLAN FOR/AID INT/TRADE ARMS/CONT
NAT/LISM ATTIT...INT/LAW GOV/COMP IDEA/COMP 20.
PAGE 47 G0928

BIBLIOG/A
DIPLOM
INT/ORG
WAR

B6

THANT U.,TOWARD WORLD PEACE. DELIB/GP TEC/DEV
EDU/PROP WAR SOVEREIGN...INT/LAW 20 UN MID/EAST.
PAGE 54 G1065

DIPLOM
BIOG
PEACE
COERCE

B6

WILLIAMS S.P.,TOWARD A GENUINE WORLD SECURITY
SYSTEM (PAMPHLET). WOR+45 INT/ORG FORCES PLAN
NUC/PWR ORD/FREE...INT/LAW CONCPT UN PRESIDENT.
PAGE 63 G1243

BIBLIOG/A
ARMS/CONT
DIPLOM
PEACE

S64

MAGGS P.B.,"SOVIET VIEWPOINT ON NUCLEAR WEAPONS IN
INTERNATIONAL LAW." USSR WOR+45 INT/ORG FORCES
DIPLOM ARMS/CONT ATTIT ORD/FREE PWR...POLICY JURID
CONCPT OBS TREND CON/ANAL GEN/LAWS VAL/FREE 20.
PAGE 35 G0694

COM
LAW
INT/LAW
NUC/PWR

B65

JENKS C.W.,SPACE LAW. DIPLOM DEBATE CONTROL
ORD/FREE TREATY 20 UN. PAGE 29 G0563

SPACE
INT/LAW
JURID
INT/ORG

S65

KRICKUS R.J.,"ON THE MORALITY OF
CHEMICAL/BIOLOGICAL WAR." ECO/UNDEV ARMS/CONT DETER
NUC/PWR RIGID/FLEX HEALTH INT/LAW. PAGE 31 G0621

MORAL
BIO/SOC
WEAPON
WAR

C65

SEARA M.V.,"COSMIC INTERNATIONAL LAW." LAW ACADEM
ACT/RES DIPLOM COLONIAL CONTROL NUC/PWR SOVEREIGN
...GEN/LAWS BIBLIOG UN. PAGE 50 G0987

SPACE
INT/LAW
IDEA/COMP
INT/ORG

B66

CLARK G.,WORLD PEACE THROUGH WORLD LAW; TWO
ALTERNATIVE PLANS. WOR+45 DELIB/GP FORCES TAX
CONFER ADJUD SANCTION ARMS/CONT WAR CHOOSE PRIVIL
20 UN COLD/WAR. PAGE 12 G0231

INT/LAW
PEACE
PLAN
INT/ORG

S66

EWALD R.F.,"ONE OF MANY POSSIBLE GAMES." ACADEM
INT/ORG ARMS/CONT...INT/LAW GAME. PAGE 18 G0354

SIMUL
HYPO/EXP
PROG/TEAC
RECORD

B67

ALEXANDER L.M.,THE LAW OF THE SEA: OFFSHORE
BOUNDARIES AND ZONES. WOR+45 INT/ORG TEC/DEV
CONTROL PRIVIL HABITAT SOVEREIGN...CON/ANAL CHARTS
ANTHOL. PAGE 2 G0037

SEA
INT/LAW
EXTR/IND

B67

BURNS E.L.M.,MEGAMURDER. WOR+45 LAW INT/ORG NAT/G
BAL/PWR DIPLOM DETER MURDER WEAPON CIVMIL/REL PEACE
...INT/LAW TREND 20. PAGE 10 G0193

FORCES
PLAN
WAR
NUC/PWR

B67

MCDOUGAL M.S.,THE INTERPRETATION OF AGREEMENTS AND
WORLD PUBLIC ORDER: PRINCIPLES OF CONTENT AND
PROCEDURE. WOR+45 CONSTN PROB/SOLV TEC/DEV
...CON/ANAL TREATY. PAGE 37 G0740

INT/LAW
STRUCT
ECO/UNDEV
DIPLOM

PIPER D.C.,THE INTERNATIONAL LAW OF THE GREAT
LAKES. CANADA EXTR/IND MUNIC LICENSE ARMS/CONT
CRIME...GEOG 19/20. PAGE 45 G0879
B67
CONCPT
DIPLOM
INT/LAW

UNIVERSAL REFERENCE SYSTEM,LAW, JURISPRUDENCE, AND
JUDICIAL PROCESS (VOLUME VII). WOR+45 WOR-45 CONSTN
NAT/G LEGIS JUDGE CT/SYS...INT/LAW COMPUT/IR
GEN/METH METH. PAGE 56 G1101
B67
BIBLIOG/A
LAW
JURID
ADJUD

US SENATE COMM AERO SPACE SCI,TREATY ON PRINCIPLES
GOVERNING ACTIVITIES OF STATES IN EXPLORATION AND
USE OF OUTER SPACE, INCLUDING...BODIES. DELIB/GP
FORCES LEGIS DIPLOM...JURID 20 DEPT/STATE NASA
DEPT/DEFEN UN. PAGE 60 G1170
B67
SPACE
INT/LAW
ORD/FREE
PEACE

D'AMATO D.,"LEGAL ASPECTS OF THE FRENCH NUCLEAR
TESTS." FRANCE WOR+45 ACT/RES COLONIAL RISK GOV/REL
EQUILIB ORD/FREE PWR DECISION. PAGE 14 G0268
S67
INT/LAW
DIPLOM
NUC/PWR
ADJUD

DOYLE S.E.,"COMMUNICATION SATELLITES* INTERNAL
ORGANIZATION FOR DEVELOPMENT AND CONTROL." USA+45
R+D ACT/RES DIPLOM NAT/LISM...POLICY INT/LAW
PREDICT UN. PAGE 16 G0313
S67
TEC/DEV
SPACE
COM/IND
INT/ORG

EISENDRATH C.,"THE OUTER SPACE TREATY." CHINA/COM
COM USA+45 DIPLOM CONTROL NUC/PWR...INT/LAW 20 UN
COLD/WAR TREATY. PAGE 17 G0339
S67
SPACE
INT/ORG
PEACE
ARMS/CONT

FOREIGN POLICY ASSOCIATION,"US CONCERN FOR WORLD
LAW." USA+45 WOR+45 DELIB/GP JUDGE BAL/PWR CONFER
PEACE ORD/FREE 20 UN. PAGE 19 G0379
S67
INT/LAW
INT/ORG
DIPLOM
ARMS/CONT

FOREIGN POLICY ASSOCIATION,"HOW WORLD LAW DEVELOPS*
A CASE STUDY OF THE OUTER SPACE TREATY." SPACE
WOR+45 BAL/PWR NEUTRAL NUC/PWR PEACE KNOWL 20 UN
TREATY. PAGE 19 G0380
S67
INT/LAW
DIPLOM
ARMS/CONT
INT/ORG

HARTIGAN R.S.,"NONCOMBAT IMMUNITY* REFLECTIONS ON
ITS ORIGINS AND PRESENT STATUS." WOR+45 PROB/SOLV
WAR PRIVIL MORAL...POLICY 20. PAGE 25 G0487
S67
INT/LAW
NUC/PWR
ARMS/CONT
DIPLOM

HAZARD J.N.,"POST-DISARMAMENT INTERNATIONAL LAW."
FUT USSR WOR+45 INT/ORG DELIB/GP FORCES DETER
EQUILIB SOVEREIGN MARXISM 20 UN. PAGE 25 G0496
S67
INT/LAW
ARMS/CONT
PWR
PLAN

HULL E.W.S.,"THE POLITICAL OCEAN." FUT UNIV WOR+45
EXTR/IND R+D VOL/ASSN PLAN BAL/PWR ECO/TAC PEACE
WEALTH 20 UN. PAGE 27 G0536
S67
DIPLOM
ECO/UNDEV
INT/ORG
INT/LAW

INGLIS D.R.,"PROSPECTS AND PROBLEMS: THE
NONMILITARY USES OF NUCLEAR EXPLOSIVES." CREATE
PROB/SOLV TEC/DEV AGREE PEACE...INT/LAW PHIL/SCI
NEW/IDEA 20 TREATY. PAGE 28 G0545
S67
NUC/PWR
INDUS
ARMS/CONT
EXTR/IND

JOHNSTON D.M.,"LAW, TECHNOLOGY AND THE SEA." WOR+45
PLAN PROB/SOLV TEC/DEV CONFER ADJUD ORD/FREE
...POLICY JURID. PAGE 29 G0564
S67
INT/LAW
INT/ORG
DIPLOM
NEUTRAL

PONTECORVO G.,"THE LAW OF THE SEA." ECO/DEV
ECO/UNDEV TEC/DEV GEOG. PAGE 45 G0885
S67
CONFER
INT/LAW
EXTR/IND
SEA

RAMSEY J.A.,"THE STATUS OF INTERNATIONAL
COPYRIGHTS." WOR+45 CREATE TEC/DEV DIPLOM CONFER
CONTROL SANCTION OWN...POLICY JURID. PAGE 46 G0899
S67
INT/LAW
INT/ORG
COM/IND
PRESS

REINTANZ G.,"THE SPACE TREATY." WOR+45 DIPLOM
CONTROL ARMS/CONT NUC/PWR WAR...MARXIST 20 COLD/WAR
UN TREATY. PAGE 46 G0911
S67
SPACE
INT/LAW
INT/ORG
PEACE

SCHACTER O.,"SCIENTIFIC ADVANCES AND INTERNATIONAL
LAWMAKING." FUT R+D PLAN PROB/SOLV CONFER CONTROL
...POLICY PREDICT 20 UN. PAGE 49 G0961
S67
TEC/DEV
INT/LAW
INT/ORG
ACT/RES

VLASCIC I.A.,"THE SPACE TREATY* A PRELIMINARY
EVALUATION." FUT USSR WOR+45 R+D ACT/RES TEC/DEV
DIPLOM CONFER ARMS/CONT PEACE...PREDICT UN TREATY.
PAGE 61 G1201
S67
SPACE
INT/LAW
INT/ORG
NEUTRAL

WEIL G.L.,"THE MERGER OF THE INSTITUTIONS OF THE
EUROPEAN COMMUNITIES" EUR+WWI ECO/DEV INT/TRADE
CONSEN PLURISM...DECISION MGT 20 EEC EURATOM ECSC
TREATY. PAGE 62 G1223
S67
ECO/TAC
INT/ORG
CENTRAL
INT/LAW

INT/ORG....INTERNATIONAL ORGANIZATIONS; SEE ALSO VOL/ASSN
AND APPROPRIATE ORGANIZATION

CURRENT THOUGHT ON PEACE AND WAR. WOR+45 INT/ORG
FORCES PROB/SOLV DIPLOM NUC/PWR PERCEPT...POLICY
SOC 20 UN NATO. PAGE 1 G0001
B
BIBLIOG/A
PEACE
ATTIT
WAR

JOURNAL OF CONFLICT RESOLUTION. FUT WOR+45 INT/ORG
NAT/G FORCES CREATE PROB/SOLV ARMS/CONT NUC/PWR
WEAPON SOC. PAGE 1 G0002
N
BIBLIOG/A
DIPLOM
WAR

FOREIGN AFFAIRS. SPACE WOR+45 WOR-45 CULTURE
ECO/UNDEV FINAN NAT/G TEC/DEV INT/TRADE ARMS/CONT
NUC/PWR...POLICY 20 UN EURATOM ECSC EEC. PAGE 1
G0004
N
BIBLIOG
DIPLOM
INT/ORG
INT/LAW

INDIA: A REFERENCE ANNUAL. INDIA CULTURE COM/IND
R+D FORCES PLAN RECEIVE EDU/PROP HEALTH...STAT
CHARTS BIBLIOG 20. PAGE 1 G0005
N
CONSTN
LABOR
INT/ORG

RAND SCHOOL OF SOCIAL SCIENCE,INDEX TO LABOR
ARTICLES. ECO/DEV INT/ORG LEGIS DIPLOM GP/REL
...NAT/COMP 20. PAGE 46 G0900
N
BIBLIOG
LABOR
MGT
ADJUD

UNITED NATIONS,OFFICIAL RECORDS OF THE UNITED
NATIONS' ATOMIC ENERGY COMMISSION - DISARMAMENT
COMMISSION. WOR+45 TEC/DEV DIPLOM WRITING NUC/PWR
20 UN. PAGE 55 G1092
N
ARMS/CONT
INT/ORG
DELIB/GP
CONFER

MEZERIK A.G.,ATOM TESTS AND RADIATION HAZARDS
(PAMPHLET). WOR+45 INT/ORG DIPLOM DETER 20 UN
TREATY. PAGE 39 G0761
N19
NUC/PWR
ARMS/CONT
CONFER
HEALTH

MEZERIK A.G.,INTERNATIONAL POLICY 1965 (PAMPHLET).
KASHMIR S/ASIA SPACE USA+45 VIETNAM WOR+45
ARMS/CONT RACE/REL DISCRIM PEACE PWR 20 UN. PAGE 39
G0762
N19
DIPLOM
INT/ORG
POLICY
WAR

MEZERIK AG,OUTER SPACE: UN, US, USSR (PAMPHLET).
USSR DELIB/GP FORCES DETER NUC/PWR SOVEREIGN
...POLICY 20 UN TREATY. PAGE 39 G0763
N19
SPACE
CONTROL
DIPLOM
INT/ORG

US SEN SPEC COMM SPACE ASTRO,SPACE LAW; A SYMPOSIUM
(PAMPHLET). USA+45 TEC/DEV CONFER CONTROL SOVEREIGN
...INT/LAW 20 SEN/SPACE. PAGE 59 G1161
N19
SPACE
ADJUD
DIPLOM
INT/ORG

MOON P.T.,"SYLLABUS ON INTERNATIONAL RELATIONS."
EUR+WWI MOD/EUR USA-45 FORCES COLONIAL WAR WEAPON
NAT/LISM...POLICY BIBLIOG T 19/20. PAGE 39 G0778
C25
INT/ORG
DIPLOM
NAT/G

EINSTEIN A.,THE WORLD AS I SEE IT. WOR-45 INTELL
R+D INT/ORG NAT/G SECT VOL/ASSN FORCES CREATE
EDU/PROP LEGIT ARMS/CONT WAR WEAPON NAT/LISM
ALL/VALS...POLICY CONCPT 20. PAGE 17 G0337
B34
SOCIETY
PHIL/SCI
DIPLOM
PACIFISM

FOREIGN AFFAIRS BIBLIOGRAPHY: A SELECTED AND
ANNOTATED LIST OF BOOKS ON INTERNATIONAL RELATIONS
1919-1962 (4 VOLS.). CONSTN FORCES COLONIAL
ARMS/CONT WAR NAT/LISM PEACE ATTIT DRIVE...POLICY
INT/LAW 20. PAGE 1 G0011
B35
BIBLIOG/A
DIPLOM
INT/ORG

B44

MATTHEWS M.A.,INTERNATIONAL POLICE (PAMPHLET). BIBLIOG
WOR-45 DIPLOM ARMS/CONT WAR 20. PAGE 37 G0722 INT/ORG
FORCES
PEACE

B46

BRODIE B.,THE OBSOLETE WEAPON: ATOMIC POWER AND INT/ORG
WORLD ORDER. COM USA+45 USSR WOR+45 DELIB/GP PLAN TEC/DEV
ORD/FREE PWR...CONCPT TIME/SEQ TREND UN 20. PAGE 9 ARMS/CONT
G0171 NUC/PWR

L46

MASTERS D.,"ONE WORLD OR NONE." FUT WOR+45 INTELL POLICY
INT/ORG ACT/RES EDU/PROP DETER ATTIT RIGID/FLEX PHIL/SCI
SUPEGO KNOWL...STAT TREND ORG/CHARTS 20. PAGE 36 ARMS/CONT
G0719 NUC/PWR

B49

OGBURN W.,TECHNOLOGY AND INTERNATIONAL RELATIONS. TEC/DEV
WOR+45 WOR-45 ECO/DEV CREATE PLAN ECO/TAC EDU/PROP DIPLOM
COERCE PWR SKILL WEALTH...TECHNIC PSY SOC NEW/IDEA INT/ORG
CHARTS TOT/POP 20. PAGE 43 G0837

B49

ROSENHAUPT H.W.,HOW TO WAGE PEACE. USA+45 SOCIETY INTELL
STRATA STRUCT R+D INT/ORG POL/PAR LEGIS ACT/RES CONCPT
CREATE PLAN EDU/PROP ADMIN EXEC ATTIT ALL/VALS DIPLOM
...TIME/SEQ TREND COLD/WAR 20. PAGE 48 G0937

B50

US DEPARTMENT OF STATE,POINT FOUR: COOPERATIVE ECO/UNDEV
PROGRAM FOR AID IN THE DEVELOPMENT OF ECONOMICALLY FOR/AID
UNDERDEVELOPED AREAS. WOR+45 AGRI INDUS INT/ORG FINAN
PLAN TEC/DEV DIPLOM EDU/PROP ADMIN PEACE PRODUC INT/TRADE
WEALTH 20 CONGRESS UN. PAGE 57 G1121

B53

LARSEN K.,NATIONAL BIBLIOGRAPHIC SERVICES: THEIR BIBLIOG/A
CREATION AND OPERATION. WOR+45 COM/IND CREATE PLAN INT/ORG
DIPLOM PRESS ADMIN ROUTINE...MGT UNESCO. PAGE 32 WRITING
G0636

B53

MACK R.T.,RAISING THE WORLDS STANDARD OF LIVING. WOR+45
IRAN INT/ORG VOL/ASSN EX/STRUC ECO/TAC WEALTH...MGT FOR/AID
METH/CNCPT STAT CONT/OBS INT TOT/POP VAL/FREE 20 INT/TRADE
UN. PAGE 35 G0690

B53

SCHAAF R.W.,DOCUMENTS OF INTERNATIONAL MEETINGS. BIBLIOG/A
AGRI INDUS ACADEM DIPLOM NUC/PWR RACE/REL AGE/Y DELIB/GP
HEALTH...SOC 20. PAGE 49 G0960 INT/ORG
POLICY

S53

CORY R.H. JR.,"FORGING A PUBLIC INFORMATION POLICY INT/ORG
FOR THE UNITED NATIONS." FUT WOR+45 SOCIETY ADMIN EDU/PROP
PEACE ATTIT PERSON SKILL...CONCPT 20 UN. PAGE 13 BAL/PWR
G0257

B54

ARON R.,CENTURY OF TOTAL WAR. FUT WOR+45 WOR-45 ATTIT
SOCIETY INT/ORG NAT/G FORCES TOP/EX CREATE BAL/PWR WAR
DOMIN EDU/PROP COERCE DETER PEACE TOTALISM PWR
...TIME/SEQ TREND COLD/WAR TOT/POP VAL/FREE
LEAGUE/NAT 20. PAGE 4 G0066

B54

KENWORTHY L.S.,FREE AND INEXPENSIVE MATERIALS ON BIBLIOG/A
WORLD AFFAIRS (PAMPHLET). WOR+45 CULTURE ECO/UNDEV NAT/G
INT/TRADE ARMS/CONT NUC/PWR UN. PAGE 30 G0594 INT/ORG
DIPLOM

B54

US DEPARTMENT OF STATE,PUBLICATIONS OF THE BIBLIOG
DEPARTMENT OF STATE, OCTOBER 1,1929 TO JANUARY 1, DIPLOM
1953. AGRI INT/ORG FORCES FOR/AID EDU/PROP
ARMS/CONT NUC/PWR ATTIT 20 DEPT/STATE OAS UN NATO.
PAGE 57 G1122

B54

WRIGHT Q.,PROBLEMS OF STABILITY AND PROGRESS IN INT/ORG
INTERNATIONAL RELATIONSHIPS. FUT WOR+45 WOR-45 CONCPT
SOCIETY LEGIS CREATE TEC/DEV ECO/TAC EDU/PROP ADJUD DIPLOM
WAR PEACE ORD/FREE PWR...KNO/TEST TREND GEN/LAWS
20. PAGE 64 G1257

L54

OPLER M.E.,"SOCIAL ASPECTS OF TECHNICAL ASSISTANCE INT/ORG
IN OPERATION." WOR+45 VOL/ASSN CREATE PLAN TEC/DEV CONSULT
EDU/PROP ALL/VALS...METH/CNCPT OBS RECORD TREND UN FOR/AID
20. PAGE 43 G0841

B55

MOCH J.,HUMAN FOLLY: DISARM OR PERISH. USA+45 FUT
WOR+45 SOCIETY INT/ORG NAT/G ACT/RES EDU/PROP ATTIT DELIB/GP
PERSON KNOWL ORD/FREE PWR...MAJORIT TOT/POP ARMS/CONT
COLD/WAR 20. PAGE 39 G0776 NUC/PWR

B55

US OFFICE OF THE PRESIDENT,REPORT TO CONGRESS ON DIPLOM
THE MUTUAL SECURITY PROGRAM FOR THE SIX MONTHS FORCES
ENDED JUNE 30, 1955. ECO/DEV INT/ORG NAT/G CREATE PLAN
TEC/DEV BAL/PWR ECO/TAC AGREE DETER COST ORD/FREE FOR/AID
20 DEPT/STATE DEPT/DEFEN. PAGE 59 G1157

L55

KISER M.,"ORGANIZATION OF AMERICAN STATES." L/A+17C VOL/ASSN
USA+45 ECO/UNDEV INT/ORG NAT/G PLAN DIPLOM ECO/DEV
ECO/TAC INT/TRADE EDU/PROP ADMIN ALL/VALS...POLICY REGION
MGT RECORD ORG/CHARTS OAS 20. PAGE 30 G0601

B56

BLACKETT P.M.S.,ATOMIC WEAPONS AND EAST-WEST FORCES
RELATIONS. FUT WOR+45 INT/ORG DELIB/GP COERCE ATTIT PWR
RIGID/FLEX KNOWL...RELATIV HIST/WRIT TREND GEN/METH ARMS/CONT
COLD/WAR 20. PAGE 7 G0138 NUC/PWR

B56

UN HEADQUARTERS LIBRARY,BIBLIOGRAPHY OF BIBLIOG
INDUSTRIALIZATION IN UNDERDEVELOPED COUNTRIES ECO/UNDEV
(BIBLIOGRAPHICAL SERIES NO. 6). WOR+45 R+D ACADEM TEC/DEV
INT/ORG NAT/G. PAGE 55 G1087

B56

US OFFICE OF THE PRESIDENT,REPORT TO CONGRESS ON DIPLOM
THE MUTUAL SECURITY PROGRAM FOR THE SIX MONTHS FORCES
ENDED DECEMBER 31, 1955. ASIA USSR ECO/DEV PLAN
ECO/UNDEV INT/ORG CREATE TEC/DEV BAL/PWR ECO/TAC FOR/AID
AGREE DETER COST ORD/FREE 20 DEPT/STATE DEPT/DEFEN
EISNHWR/DD. PAGE 59 G1158

S56

GORDON L.,"THE ORGANIZATION FOR EUROPEAN ECONOMIC VOL/ASSN
COOPERATION." EUR+WWI INDUS INT/ORG NAT/G CONSULT ECO/DEV
DELIB/GP ACT/RES CREATE PLAN TEC/DEV EDU/PROP LEGIT
WEALTH OEEC 20. PAGE 22 G0435

B57

KISSINGER H.A.,NUCLEAR WEAPONS AND FOREIGN POLICY. PLAN
FUT USA+45 WOR+45 INT/ORG FORCES ACT/RES TEC/DEV DETER
DIPLOM ARMS/CONT COERCE ATTIT KNOWL PWR...DECISION NUC/PWR
GEOG CHARTS 20. PAGE 31 G0602

B57

SPEIER H.,GERMAN REARMAMENT AND ATOMIC WAR: THE TOP/EX
VIEWS OF GERMAN MILITARY AND POLITICAL LEADERS. FUT FORCES
WOR+45 INT/ORG NAT/G WEAPON ATTIT PWR...INT QU NUC/PWR
TOT/POP VAL/FREE COLD/WAR 20. PAGE 52 G1024 GERMANY

B58

ANGELL N.,DEFENCE AND THE ENGLISH-SPEAKING ROLE. DIPLOM
CHINA/COM UK USSR INT/ORG FORCES EDU/PROP NEUTRAL WAR
NUC/PWR NAT/LISM PEACE TOTALISM 20 COLD/WAR MARXISM
COEXIST. PAGE 3 G0059 ORD/FREE

B58

GANGE J.,UNIVERSITY RESEARCH ON INTERNATIONAL R+D
AFFAIRS. USA+45 ACADEM INT/ORG CONSULT CREATE EXEC MGT
ROUTINE...QUANT STAT INT STERTYP GEN/METH TOT/POP DIPLOM
VAL/FREE 20. PAGE 21 G0407

B58

NOEL-BAKER D.,THE ARMS RACE. WOR+45 NAT/G DELIB/GP FUT
ACT/RES TEC/DEV EDU/PROP NUC/PWR ATTIT KNOWL PWR INT/ORG
...CONCPT OBS LEAGUE/NAT 20 COLD/WAR. PAGE 42 G0823 ARMS/CONT
PEACE

B58

ROCKEFELLER BROTH FUND INC,INTERNATIONAL SECURITY - NUC/PWR
THE MILITARY ASPECT. USA+45 INT/ORG NAT/G BUDGET DETER
ARMS/CONT WAR WEAPON PEACE ORD/FREE 20 NATO. FORCES
PAGE 47 G0932 DIPLOM

B58

US DEPARTMENT OF STATE,PUBLICATIONS OF THE BIBLIOG
DEPARTMENT OF STATE, JANUARY 1,1953 TO DECEMBER 31, DIPLOM
1957. AGRI INT/ORG FORCES FOR/AID EDU/PROP
ARMS/CONT NUC/PWR ATTIT 20 DEPT/STATE OAS UN NATO.
PAGE 57 G1123

S58

ANDERSON N.,"INTERNATIONAL SEMINARS: AN ANALYSIS INT/ORG
AND AN EVALUATION." WOR+45 R+D ACT/RES CREATE PLAN DELIB/GP
REGION ATTIT KNOWL SKILL...SOC REC/INT PERS/TEST
CHARTS 20. PAGE 3 G0057

S58

LASSWELL H.D.,"THE SCIENTIFIC STUDY OF PHIL/SCI

INTERNATIONAL RELATIONS." USA+45 INT/ORG CREATE   GEN/METH
EDU/PROP DETER ATTIT PERCEPT PWR...DECISION CONCPT DIPLOM
METH/CNCPT STYLE CON/ANAL 20. PAGE 33 G0642

S58
MCDOUGAL M.S.,"PERSPECTIVES FOR A LAW OF OUTER   INT/ORG
SPACE." FUT WOR+45 AIR CONSULT DELIB/GP TEC/DEV   SPACE
CT/SYS ORD/FREE...POLICY JURID 20 UN. PAGE 37 G0736 INT/LAW

S58
SINGER J.D.,"THREAT PERCEPTION AND THE ARMAMENT   PERCEPT
TENSION DILEMMA." WOR+45 WOR-45 ELITES INT/ORG   ARMS/CONT
NAT/G DELIB/GP PLAN LEGIT COERCE DETER ATTIT   BAL/PWR
RIGID/FLEX PWR...DECISION PSY 20. PAGE 51 G1002

S58
THOMPSON K.W.,"NATIONAL SECURITY IN A NUCLEAR AGE." FORCES
USA+45 WOR+45 SOCIETY INT/ORG NAT/G TOP/EX DIPLOM   PWR
DOMIN EDU/PROP LEGIT ARMS/CONT COERCE ORD/FREE   BAL/PWR
...TREND STERTYP TOT/POP VAL/FREE COLD/WAR 20.
PAGE 54 G1068

B59
HALEY A.G.,FIRST COLLOQUIUM ON THE LAW OF OUTER   SPACE
SPACE. WOR+45 INT/ORG ACT/RES PLAN BAL/PWR CONFER   LAW
ATTIT PWR...POLICY JURID CHARTS ANTHOL 20. PAGE 24   SOVEREIGN
G0468   CONTROL

B59
MODELSKI G.,ATOMIC ENERGY IN THE COMMUNIST BLOC.   TEC/DEV
FUT INT/ORG CONSULT FORCES ACT/RES PLAN KNOWL SKILL NUC/PWR
...PHIL/SCI STAT CHARTS 20. PAGE 39 G0777   USSR
                                                     COM

B59
STANFORD RESEARCH INSTITUTE.POSSIBLE NONMILITARY   R+D
SCIENTIFIC DEVELOPMENTS AND THEIR POTENTIAL IMPACT   TEC/DEV
ON FOREIGN POLICY PROBLEMS OF THE UNITED. FUT
USA+45 INT/ORG PROF/ORG CONSULT ACT/RES CREATE PLAN
PEACE KNOWL SKILL...TECHNIC PHIL/SCI NEW/IDEA
UNESCO 20. PAGE 52 G1032

B59
VAN WAGENEN R.W.,SOME VIEWS OF AMERICAN DEFENSE   INT/ORG
OFFICIALS ABOUT THE UNITED NATIONS (PAPER). FUT   LEAD
USA+45 NAT/G DIPLOM WAR EFFICIENCY PEACE...POLICY   ATTIT
INT 20 UN DEPT/DEFEN. PAGE 61 G1192   FORCES

B59
WARD B.,5 IDEAS THAT CHANGE THE WORLD. WOR+45   ECO/UNDEV
WOR-45 SOCIETY STRUCT AGRI INDUS INT/ORG NAT/G   ALL/VALS
FORCES ACT/RES ARMS/CONT TOTALISM ATTIT DRIVE   NAT/LISM
GEN/LAWS. PAGE 62 G1210   COLONIAL

S59
SIMONS H.,"WORLD-WIDE CAPABILITIES FOR PRODUCTION   TEC/DEV
AND CONTROL OF NUCLEAR WEAPONS." FUT WOR+45 INDUS   ARMS/CONT
INT/ORG NAT/G ECO/TAC ATTIT PWR SKILL...TREND   NUC/PWR
CHARTS VAL/FREE 20. PAGE 51 G1001

S59
STOESSINGER J.G.,"THE INTERNATIONAL ATOMIC ENERGY   INT/ORG
AGENCY: THE FIRST PHASE." FUT WOR+45 NAT/G VOL/ASSN ECO/DEV
DELIB/GP BAL/PWR LEGIT ADMIN ROUTINE PWR...OBS   FOR/AID
CON/ANAL GEN/LAWS VAL/FREE 20 IAEA. PAGE 53 G1037   NUC/PWR

B60
ARMS CONTROL. FUT UNIV WOR+45 INTELL R+D INT/ORG   DELIB/GP
NAT/G VOL/ASSN CONSULT CREATE EDU/PROP PEACE...HUM   ORD/FREE
GEN/LAWS TOT/POP 20. PAGE 1 G0015   ARMS/CONT
                                                     NUC/PWR

B60
BARNET R.,WHO WANTS DISARMAMENT. COM EUR+WWI USA+45 PLAN
USSR INT/ORG NAT/G BAL/PWR DIPLOM EDU/PROP COERCE   FORCES
DETER NUC/PWR WAR WEAPON ATTIT PWR...TIME/SEQ   ARMS/CONT
COLD/WAR CONGRESS 20. PAGE 5 G0096

B60
BROOKINGS INSTITUTION.UNITED STATES FOREIGN POLICY: DIPLOM
STUDY NO 9: THE FORMULATION AND ADMINISTRATION OF   INT/ORG
UNITED STATES FOREIGN POLICY. USA+45 WOR+45   CREATE
EX/STRUC LEGIS BAL/PWR FOR/AID EDU/PROP CIVMIL/REL
GOV/REL...INT COLD/WAR. PAGE 9 G0174

B60
EINSTEIN A.,EINSTEIN ON PEACE. FUT WOR+45 WOR-45   INT/ORG
SOCIETY NAT/G PLAN BAL/PWR CAP/ISM DIPLOM ARMS/CONT ATTIT
DETER NAT/LISM...POLICY RELATIV HUM PHIL/SCI CONCPT NUC/PWR
BIOG COLD/WAR LEAGUE/NAT NAZI. PAGE 17 G0338   PEACE

B60
LE GHAIT E.,NO CARTE BLANCHE TO CAPRICORN; THE   DETER
FOLLY OF NUCLEAR WAR. WOR+45 INT/ORG BAL/PWR DIPLOM NUC/PWR
RISK COERCE...CENSUS 20 NATO. PAGE 33 G0647   PLAN
                                                     DECISION

B60
MCKINNEY R.,REVIEW OF THE INTERNATIONAL ATOMIC   NUC/PWR
POLICIES AND PROGRAMS OF THE UNITED STATES (5   PEACE
VOLS.). COM FUT USA+45 ECO/DEV ECO/UNDEV INT/ORG   DIPLOM
DELIB/GP PLAN ADMIN 20 THIRD/WRLD. PAGE 38 G0744   POLICY

B60
PENTONY D.E.,THE UNDERDEVELOPED LANDS. FUT WOR+45   ECO/UNDEV
CULTURE AGRI FINAN INDUS MARKET INT/ORG LABOR NAT/G POLICY
VOL/ASSN CONSULT TEC/DEV ECO/TAC EDU/PROP COLONIAL   FOR/AID
ATTIT WEALTH...OBS RECORD SAMP TREND GEN/METH WORK   INT/TRADE
UN 20. PAGE 44 G0867

B60
US HOUSE COMM. SCI. ASTRONAUT.,OCEAN SCIENCES AND   R+D
NATIONAL SECURITY. FUT SEA ECO/DEV EXTR/IND INT/ORG ORD/FREE
NAT/G FORCES ACT/RES TEC/DEV ECO/TAC COERCE WAR
BIO/SOC KNOWL PWR...CONCPT RECORD LAB/EXP 20.
PAGE 59 G1153

B60
WOETZEL R.K.,THE INTERNATIONAL CONTROL OF AIRSPACE   INT/ORG
AND OUTERSPACE. FUT WOR+45 AIR CONSTN STRUCT   JURID
CONSULT PLAN TEC/DEV ADJUD RIGID/FLEX KNOWL   SPACE
ORD/FREE PWR...TECHNIC GEOG MGT NEW/IDEA TREND   INT/LAW
COMPUT/IR VAL/FREE 20 TREATY. PAGE 64 G1251

L60
BRENNAN D.G.,"SETTING AND GOALS OF ARMS CONTROL."   FORCES
FUT USA+45 USSR WOR+45 INTELL INT/ORG NAT/G   COERCE
VOL/ASSN CONSULT PLAN DIPLOM ECO/TAC ADMIN KNOWL   ARMS/CONT
PWR...POLICY CONCPT TREND COLD/WAR 20. PAGE 8 G0164 DETER

L60
DEUTSCH K.W.,"TOWARD AN INVENTORY OF BASIC TRENDS   R+D
AND PATTERNS IN COMPARATIVE AND INTERNATIONAL   PERCEPT
POLITICS." UNIV WOR+45 SOCIETY STRUCT INT/ORG NAT/G
CREATE PLAN EDU/PROP KNOWL...PHIL/SCI METH/CNCPT
STAT SELF/OBS OBS/ENVIR SAMP TREND CON/ANAL CHARTS
SOC/EXP GEN/METH 20. PAGE 15 G0298

L60
HOLTON G.,"ARMS CONTROL." FUT WOR+45 CULTURE   ACT/RES
INT/ORG NAT/G FORCES TOP/EX PLAN EDU/PROP COERCE   CONSULT
ATTIT RIGID/FLEX ORD/FREE...POLICY PHIL/SCI SOC   ARMS/CONT
TREND COLD/WAR. PAGE 27 G0524   NUC/PWR

L60
JACOB P.E.,"THE DISARMAMENT CONSENSUS." USA+45 USSR DELIB/GP
WOR+45 INT/ORG NAT/G ACT/RES TEC/DEV BAL/PWR   ATTIT
EDU/PROP ADMIN COERCE DETER NUC/PWR CONSEN   ARMS/CONT
RIGID/FLEX PWR...CONCPT RECORD CHARTS COLD/WAR 20.
PAGE 28 G0552

L60
MCCLELLAND C.A.,"THE FUNCTION OF THEORY IN   INT/ORG
INTERNATIONAL RELATIONS." WOR+45 PLAN EDU/PROP   CONCPT
ROUTINE ORD/FREE...PHIL/SCI PSY SOC METH/CNCPT   DIPLOM
NEW/IDEA OBS TREND GEN/METH 20. PAGE 37 G0728

S60
DOUGHERTY J.E.,"KEY TO SECURITY: DISARMAMENT OR   FORCES
ARMS STABILITY." COM USA+45 USSR INT/ORG NAT/G   ORD/FREE
CREATE EDU/PROP COERCE DETER ATTIT PWR...DECISION   ARMS/CONT
CONCPT MYTH NEW/IDEA TREND 20 COLD/WAR. PAGE 16   NUC/PWR
G0311

S60
DYSON F.J.,"THE FUTURE DEVELOPMENT OF NUCLEAR   INT/ORG
WEAPONS." FUT WOR+45 DELIB/GP ACT/RES PLAN DETER   ARMS/CONT
WEAPON ATTIT PWR...POLICY 20. PAGE 17 G0328   NUC/PWR

S60
HAYTON R.D.,"THE ANTARCTIC SETTLEMENT OF 1959." FUT DELIB/GP
USA+45 WOR+45 WOR-45 STRUCT R+D INT/ORG EX/STRUC   JURID
CREATE TEC/DEV LEGIT PEACE ATTIT SOVEREIGN   DIPLOM
...TIME/SEQ 20 TREATY IGY. PAGE 25 G0495   REGION

S60
IKLE F.C.,"NTH COUNTRIES AND DISARMAMENT." WOR+45   FUT
DELIB/GP ECO/TAC DOMIN EDU/PROP LEGIT ROUTINE   INT/ORG
COERCE RIGID/FLEX ORD/FREE...MARXIST TREND 20.   ARMS/CONT
PAGE 28 G0543   NUC/PWR

S60
KAPLAN M.A.,"THEORETICAL ANALYSIS OF THE BALANCE OF CREATE
POWER." FUT USA+45 WOR+45 INTELL ECO/DEV INT/ORG   NEW/IDEA
NAT/G CONSULT TOP/EX ACT/RES PLAN TEC/DEV ATTIT   DIPLOM
ALL/VALS...METH/CNCPT TOT/POP 20. PAGE 29 G0576   NUC/PWR

S60
LEAR J.,"PEACE: SCIENCE'S NEXT GREAT EXPLORATION."   EX/STRUC
USA+45 INT/ORG TOP/EX TEC/DEV EDU/PROP ROUTINE   ARMS/CONT
PEACE KNOWL SKILL 20. PAGE 33 G0648   NUC/PWR

SWIFT R.,"THE UNITED NATIONS AND ITS PUBLIC." WOR+45 CONSTN FINAN CONSULT DELIB/GP ACT/RES ADMIN ROUTINE RIGID/FLEX SKILL UN 20. PAGE 53 G1048
S60
INT/ORG
EDU/PROP

BONNEFOUS M.,EUROPE ET TIERS MONDE. EUR+WWI SOCIETY INT/ORG NAT/G VOL/ASSN ACT/RES TEC/DEV CAP/ISM ECO/TAC ATTIT ORD/FREE SOVEREIGN...POLICY CONCPT TREND 20. PAGE 8 G0153
B61
AFR
ECO/UNDEV
FOR/AID
INT/TRADE

FRISCH D.,ARMS REDUCTION: PROGRAM AND ISSUES. USA+45 INT/ORG NAT/G ACT/RES REGION NUC/PWR ATTIT PWR...POLICY 20. PAGE 20 G0395
B61
PLAN
FORCES
ARMS/CONT
DIPLOM

HENKIN L.,ARMS CONTROL: ISSUES FOR THE PUBLIC. EUR+WWI FUT USA+45 USSR INT/ORG NAT/G DIPLOM EDU/PROP DETER NUC/PWR ATTIT PWR...CONCPT RECORD HIST/WRIT TIME/SEQ TOT/POP COLD/WAR 20. PAGE 26 G0506
B61
WOR+45
DELIB/GP
ARMS/CONT

NOGEE J.L.,SOVIET POLICY TOWARD INTERNATIONAL CONTROL OF ATOMIC ENERGY. COM USA+45 WOR+45 INTELL NAT/G ACT/RES DIPLOM EDU/PROP NUC/PWR TOTALISM PERCEPT KNOWL PWR...TIME/SEQ COLD/WAR 20. PAGE 42 G0824
B61
INT/ORG
ATTIT
ARMS/CONT
USSR

RAMO S.,PEACETIME USES OF OUTER SPACE. FUT DIST/IND INT/ORG CONSULT NUC/PWR...AUD/VIS ANTHOL 20. PAGE 46 G0898
B61
PEACE
TEC/DEV
SPACE
CREATE

TAUBENFELD H.J.,"A TREATY FOR ANTARCTICA." FUT USA+45 INTELL INT/ORG LABOR 20 TREATY ANTARCTICA. PAGE 54 G1055
L61
R+D
ACT/RES
DIPLOM

TAUBENFELD H.J.,"A REGIME FOR OUTER SPACE." FUT UNIV R+D ACT/RES PLAN BAL/PWR LEGIT ARMS/CONT ORD/FREE...POLICY JURID TREND UN TOT/POP 20 COLD/WAR. PAGE 54 G1056
L61
INT/ORG
ADJUD
SPACE

TAUBENFELD H.J.,"OUTER SPACE--PAST POLITICS AND FUTURE POLICY." FUT USA+45 USA-45 WOR+45 AIR INTELL STRUCT ECO/DEV NAT/G TOP/EX ACT/RES ADMIN ROUTINE NUC/PWR ATTIT DRIVE...CONCPT TIME/SEQ TREND TOT/POP 20. PAGE 54 G1054
S61
PLAN
SPACE
INT/ORG

AIR FORCE ACADEMY LIBRARY,INTERNATIONAL ORGANIZATIONS AND MILITARY SECURITY SYSTEMS (PAMPHLET) (SPECIAL BIBLIOGRAPHY SERIES, NUMBER 25). DIPLOM FOR/AID INT/TRADE NUC/PWR PEACE 20 UN NATO OAS SEATO LEAGUE/NAT. PAGE 2 G0031
B62
BIBLIOG
INT/ORG
FORCES
DETER

BOULDING K.E.,CONFLICT AND DEFENSE: A GENERAL THEORY. FUT SOCIETY INT/ORG NAT/G CREATE BAL/PWR COERCE NAT/LISM DRIVE ALL/VALS...PLURIST DECISION CONCPT METH/CNCPT TREND HYPO/EXP TOT/POP 20. PAGE 8 G0157
B62
MATH
SIMUL
PEACE
WAR

CALDER R.,LIVING WITH THE ATOM. FUT USA+45 WOR+45 R+D INT/ORG VOL/ASSN DELIB/GP ARMS/CONT...STYLE 20. PAGE 10 G0200
B62
TEC/DEV
HEALTH
NUC/PWR

FORBES H.W.,THE STRATEGY OF DISARMAMENT. FUT WOR+45 INT/ORG VOL/ASSN CONSULT ARMS/CONT COERCE NUC/PWR WAR DRIVE RIGID/FLEX ORD/FREE PWR...POLICY CONCPT OBS TREND STERTYP 20. PAGE 19 G0378
B62
PLAN
FORCES
DIPLOM

FRIEDRICH-EBERT-STIFTUNG,THE SOVIET BLOC AND DEVELOPING COUNTRIES. CHINA/COM COM GERMANY/E USSR WOR+45 ECO/UNDEV INT/ORG NAT/G TEC/DEV NEUTRAL PWR ...POLICY 20. PAGE 20 G0394
B62
MARXISM
DIPLOM
ECO/TAC
FOR/AID

GILPIN R.,AMERICAN SCIENTISTS AND NUCLEAR WEAPONS POLICY. COM FUT USA+45 WOR+45 INT/ORG NAT/G PROF/ORG CONSULT FORCES CREATE TEC/DEV BAL/PWR EDU/PROP ARMS/CONT WAR PERCEPT KNOWL MORAL PWR ...PHIL/SCI SOC CONCPT GEN/LAWS 20. PAGE 21 G0417
B62
INTELL
ATTIT
DETER
NUC/PWR

KAHN H.,THINKING ABOUT THE UNTHINKABLE. FUT USA+45 LAW NAT/G CONSULT FORCES ACT/RES CREATE PLAN
B62
INT/ORG
ORD/FREE

TEC/DEV BAL/PWR DIPLOM EDU/PROP ARMS/CONT DETER ATTIT...CONCPT OBS TREND COLD/WAR 20. PAGE 29 G0570
NUC/PWR
PEACE

KENNEDY J.F.,TO TURN THE TIDE. SPACE AGRI INT/ORG FORCES TEC/DEV ADMIN NUC/PWR PEACE WEALTH...ANTHOL 20 KENNEDY/JF CIV/RIGHTS. PAGE 30 G0592
B62
DIPLOM
CHIEF
POLICY
NAT/G

KRAFT J.,THE GRAND DESIGN. EUR+WWI USA+45 AGRI FINAN INDUS MARKET INT/ORG NAT/G PLAN ECO/TAC TARIFFS REGION DRIVE ORD/FREE WEALTH...POLICY OBS TREND EEC 20. PAGE 31 G0616
B62
VOL/ASSN
ECO/DEV
INT/TRADE

LEFEVER E.W.,ARMS AND ARMS CONTROL. COM USA+45 INT/ORG TEC/DEV DIPLOM ORD/FREE 20. PAGE 33 G0652
B62
ATTIT
PWR
ARMS/CONT
BAL/PWR

OSGOOD C.E.,AN ALTERNATIVE TO WAR OR SURRENDER. FUT UNIV CULTURE INTELL SOCIETY R+D INT/ORG CONSULT DELIB/GP ACT/RES PLAN CHOOSE ATTIT PERCEPT KNOWL ...PHIL/SCI PSY SOC TREND GEN/LAWS 20. PAGE 43 G0849
B62
ORD/FREE
EDU/PROP
PEACE
WAR

SCHMITT H.A.,THE PATH TO EUROPEAN UNITY. EUR+WWI USA+45 PLAN TEC/DEV DIPLOM FOR/AID CONFER...INT/LAW 20 EEC EURCOALSTL MARSHL/PLN UNIFICA. PAGE 49 G0971
B62
INT/ORG
INT/TRADE
REGION
ECO/DEV

SCHWARTZ L.E.,INTERNATIONAL ORGANIZATIONS AND SPACE COOPERATION. VOL/ASSN CONSULT CREATE TEC/DEV SANCTION...POLICY INT/LAW PHIL/SCI 20 UN. PAGE 50 G0982
B62
INT/ORG
DIPLOM
R+D
SPACE

SINGER J.D.,DETERRENCE, ARMS CONTROL AND DISARMAMENT: TOWARD A SYNTHESIS IN NATIONAL SECURITY POLICY. COM USA+45 INT/ORG BAL/PWR DETER ORD/FREE...POLICY COLD/WAR 20. PAGE 51 G1003
B62
FUT
ACT/RES
ARMS/CONT

THANT U.,THE UNITED NATIONS' DEVELOPMENT DECADE: PROPOSALS FOR ACTION. WOR+45 SOCIETY ECO/UNDEV AGRI COM/IND FINAN R+D MUNIC SCHOOL VOL/ASSN CONSULT PLAN TEC/DEV ECO/TAC EDU/PROP ADMIN ROUTINE RIGID/FLEX...MGT SOC CONCPT UNESCO UN TOT/POP VAL/FREE. PAGE 54 G1064
B62
INT/ORG
ALL/VALS

WRIGHT Q.,PREVENTING WORLD WAR THREE. FUT WOR+45 CULTURE INT/ORG NAT/G CONSULT FORCES ADMIN ARMS/CONT DRIVE RIGID/FLEX ORD/FREE SOVEREIGN ...POLICY CONCPT TREND STERTYP COLD/WAR 20. PAGE 64 G1259
B62
CREATE
ATTIT

YALEN R.,REGIONALISM AND WORLD ORDER. EUR+WWI WOR+45 WOR-45 INT/ORG VOL/ASSN DELIB/GP FORCES TOP/EX BAL/PWR DIPLOM DOMIN REGION ARMS/CONT PWR ...JURID HYPO/EXP COLD/WAR 20. PAGE 64 G1261
B62
ORD/FREE
POLICY

NIEBURG H.L.,"THE EISENHOWER ATOMIC ENERGY COMMISSION AND CONGRESS" R+D INT/ORG OP/RES DIPLOM ADMIN CONTROL 20 PRESIDENT CONGRESS AEC. PAGE 42 G0821
L62
NUC/PWR
TOP/EX
LOBBY
DELIB/GP

ALBONETTI A.,"IL SECONDO PROGRAMMA QUINQUENNALE 1963-67 ED IL BILANCIO RICERCHE ED INVESTIMENTI PER IL 1963 DELL'ERATOM." EUR+WWI FUT ITALY WOR+45 ECO/DEV SERV/IND INT/ORG TEC/DEV ECO/TAC ATTIT SKILL WEALTH...MGT TIME/SEQ OEEC 20. PAGE 2 G0035
S62
R+D
PLAN
NUC/PWR

BOULDING K.E.,"THE PREVENTION OF WORLD WAR THREE." FUT WOR+45 INT/ORG PLAN BAL/PWR PEACE ORD/FREE PWR ...NEW/IDEA TREND TOT/POP COLD/WAR 20. PAGE 8 G0158
S62
VOL/ASSN
NAT/G
ARMS/CONT
DIPLOM

CRANE R.D.,"LAW AND STRATEGY IN SPACE." FUT USA+45 WOR+45 AIR LAW INT/ORG NAT/G FORCES BAL/PWR LEGIT ARMS/CONT COERCE ORD/FREE...POLICY INT/LAW JURID SOC/EXP 20 TREATY. PAGE 13 G0261
S62
CONCPT
SPACE

FINKELSTEIN L.S.,"THE UNITED NATIONS AND ORGANIZATIONS FOR CONTROL OF ARMAMENT." FUT WOR+45 VOL/ASSN DELIB/GP TOP/EX CREATE EDU/PROP LEGIT
S62
INT/ORG
PWR
ARMS/CONT

ADJUD NUC/PWR ATTIT RIGID/FLEX ORD/FREE...POLICY
DECISION CONCPT OBS TREND GEN/LAWS TOT/POP
COLD/WAR. PAGE 19 G0368

FOSTER W.C.,"ARMS CONTROL AND DISARMAMENT IN A   DELIB/GP
DIVIDED WORLD." COM FUT USA+45 USSR WOR+45 INTELL   POLICY
INT/ORG NAT/G VOL/ASSN CONSULT CREATE PLAN TEC/DEV   ARMS/CONT
EDU/PROP LEGIT NUC/PWR ATTIT RIGID/FLEX...CONCPT   DIPLOM
TREND TOT/POP 20 UN. PAGE 20 G0387
  S62

NANES A.,"DISARMAMENT: THE LAST SEVEN YEARS." COM   DELIB/GP
EUR+WWI USA+45 USSR INT/ORG FORCES TOP/EX CREATE   RIGID/FLEX
LEGIT NUC/PWR DISPL ORD/FREE...CONCPT TIME/SEQ   ARMS/CONT
CON/ANAL 20. PAGE 41 G0803
  S62

SCHILLING W.R.,"SCIENTISTS, FOREIGN POLICY AND   NAT/G
POLITICS." WOR+45 WOR-45 INTELL INT/ORG CONSULT   TEC/DEV
TOP/EX ACT/RES PLAN ADMIN KNOWL...CONCPT OBS TREND   DIPLOM
LEAGUE/NAT 20. PAGE 49 G0967   NUC/PWR
  S62

SINGER J.D.,"STABLE DETERRENCE AND ITS LIMITS." FUT   NAT/G
WOR+45 R+D INT/ORG CONSULT ACT/RES TEC/DEV   FORCES
ARMS/CONT COERCE DRIVE PERCEPT RIGID/FLEX ORD/FREE   DETER
PWR...MYTH SIMUL TOT/POP 20. PAGE 51 G1004   NUC/PWR
  S62

THORELLI H.B.,"THE INTERNATIONAL OPERATIONS   ECO/TAC
SIMULATION AT THE UNIVERSITY OF CHICAGO." FUT   SIMUL
USA+45 WOR+45 ECO/DEV DIST/IND FINAN INDUS INT/ORG   INT/TRADE
DELIB/GP ACT/RES CREATE TEC/DEV WEALTH...STAT
VAL/FREE 20. PAGE 54 G1072
  B63

ABSHIRE D.M.,NATIONAL SECURITY: POLITICAL,   FUT
MILITARY, AND ECONOMIC STRATEGIES IN THE DECADE   ACT/RES
AHEAD. ASIA COM USA+45 WOR+45 ECO/DEV ECO/UNDEV   BAL/PWR
INT/ORG DELIB/GP FORCES ECO/TAC COERCE ATTIT
RIGID/FLEX HEALTH ORD/FREE PWR WEALTH...POLICY STAT
CHARTS ANTHOL COLD/WAR VAL/FREE. PAGE 1 G0024
  B63

FLORES E.,LAND REFORM AND THE ALLIANCE FOR PROGRESS   AGRI
(PAMPHLET). L/A+17C USA+45 STRUCT ECO/UNDEV NAT/G   INT/ORG
WORKER CREATE PLAN ECO/TAC COERCE REV 20. PAGE 19   DIPLOM
G0373   POLICY
  B63

HALEY A.G.,SPACE LAW AND GOVERNMENT. FUT USA+45   INT/ORG
WOR+45 LEGIS ACT/RES CREATE ATTIT RIGID/FLEX   LAW
ORD/FREE PWR SOVEREIGN...POLICY JURID CONCPT CHARTS   SPACE
VAL/FREE 20. PAGE 24 G0469
  B63

LILIENTHAL D.E.,CHANGE, HOPE, AND THE BOMB. USA+45   ATTIT
WOR+45 R+D INT/ORG NAT/G DELIB/GP FORCES ACT/RES   MYTH
DETER RIGID/FLEX ORD/FREE...POLICY CONCPT OBS AEC   ARMS/CONT
20. PAGE 34 G0666   NUC/PWR
  B63

MAYNE R.,THE COMMUNITY OF EUROPE. UK CONSTN NAT/G   EUR+WWI
CONSULT DELIB/GP CREATE PLAN ECO/TAC LEGIT ADMIN   INT/ORG
ROUTINE ORD/FREE PWR WEALTH...CONCPT TIME/SEQ EEC   REGION
EURATOM 20. PAGE 37 G0724
  B63

MULLENBACH P.,CIVILIAN NUCLEAR POWER: ECONOMIC   USA+45
ISSUES AND POLICY FORMATION. FINAN INT/ORG DELIB/GP   ECO/DEV
ACT/RES ECO/TAC ATTIT SUPEGO HEALTH ORD/FREE PWR   NUC/PWR
...POLICY CONCPT MATH STAT CHARTS VAL/FREE 20
COLD/WAR. PAGE 40 G0792
  B63

NORTH R.C.,CONTENT ANALYSIS: A HANDBOOK WITH   METH/CNCPT
APPLICATIONS FOR THE STUDY OF INTERNATIONAL CRISIS.   COMPUT/IR
ASIA COM EUR+WWI MOD/EUR INT/ORG TEC/DEV DOMIN   USSR
EDU/PROP ROUTINE COERCE PERCEPT RIGID/FLEX ALL/VALS
...QUANT TESTS CON/ANAL SIMUL GEN/LAWS VAL/FREE.
PAGE 42 G0825
  B63

OECD,SCIENCE AND THE POLICIES OF GOVERNMENTS: THE   CREATE
IMPLICATIONS OF SCIENCE AND TECHNOLOGY FOR NATL AND   TEC/DEV
INTL AFFAIRS. WOR+45 INT/ORG EDU/PROP AUTOMAT   DIPLOM
...POLICY PHIL/SCI 20. PAGE 42 G0830   NAT/G
  B63

PANAMERICAN UNION,DOCUMENTOS OFICIALES DE LA   BIBLIOG
ORGANIZACION DE LOS ESTADOS AMERICANOS, INDICE Y   INT/ORG
LISTA (VOL. III, 1962). L/A+17C DELIB/GP INT/TRADE   DIPLOM
EDU/PROP REGION NUC/PWR...HEAL INT/LAW SOC/WK 20
OAS. PAGE 44 G0857

MCDOUGAL M.S.,"THE ENJOYMENT AND ACQUISITION OF   PLAN
RESOURCES IN OUTER SPACE." CHRIST-17C FUT WOR+45   TREND
WOR-45 LAW EXTR/IND INT/ORG ACT/RES CREATE TEC/DEV
ECO/TAC LEGIT COERCE HEALTH KNOWL ORD/FREE PWR
WEALTH...JURID HIST/WRIT VAL/FREE. PAGE 37 G0738
  L63

PHELPS J.,"STUDIES IN DETERRENCE VIII: MILITARY   FORCES
STABILITY AND ARMS CONTROL: A CRITICAL SURVEY."   ORD/FREE
FUT WOR+45 INT/ORG ACT/RES EDU/PROP COERCE NUC/PWR   ARMS/CONT
WAR HEALTH PWR...POLICY TECHNIC TREND SIMUL TOT/POP   DETER
20. PAGE 44 G0874
  S63

BOHN L.,"WHOSE NUCLEAR TEST: NON-PHYSICAL   ADJUD
INSPECTION AND TEST BAN." WOR+45 R+D INT/ORG   ARMS/CONT
VOL/ASSN ORD/FREE...GEN/LAWS GEN/METH COLD/WAR 20.   TEC/DEV
PAGE 8 G0148   NUC/PWR
  S63

GARDNER R.N.,"COOPERATION IN OUTER SPACE." FUT USSR   INT/ORG
WOR+45 AIR LAW COM/IND CONSULT DELIB/GP CREATE   ACT/RES
KNOWL 20 TREATY. PAGE 21 G0410   PEACE
  SPACE
  S63

KAWALKOWSKI A.,"POUR UNE EUROPE INDEPENDENTE ET   R+D
REUNIFIEE." EUR+WWI FUT USA+45 USSR WOR+45 ECO/DEV   PLAN
PROC/MFG INT/ORG NAT/G ACT/RES TEC/DEV FEDERAL   NUC/PWR
RIGID/FLEX...CONCPT METH/CNCPT OEEC TOT/POP 20
DEGAULLE/C. PAGE 30 G0587
  S63

PHELPS J.,"INFORMATION AND ARMS CONTROL." COM SPACE   KNOWL
USA+45 USSR WOR+45 R+D INT/ORG NAT/G DELIB/GP   ARMS/CONT
DIPLOM ORD/FREE...CONCPT 20. PAGE 45 G0875   NUC/PWR
  B64

COHEN M.,LAW AND POLITICS IN SPACE: SPECIFIC AND   DELIB/GP
URGENT PROBLEMS IN THE LAW OF OUTER SPACE.   LAW
CHINA/COM COM USA+45 USSR WOR+45 COM/IND INT/ORG   INT/LAW
NAT/G LEGIT NUC/PWR ATTIT BIO/SOC...JURID CONCPT   SPACE
CONGRESS 20 STALIN/J. PAGE 12 G0241
  B64

FREYMOND J.,WESTERN EUROPE SINCE THE WAR. COM   INT/ORG
EUR+WWI USA+45 DIPLOM...BIBLIOG 20 NATO UN EEC.   POLICY
PAGE 20 G0392   ECO/DEV
  ECO/TAC
  B64

GRODZINS M.,THE ATOMIC AGE: FORTY-FIVE SCIENTISTS   INTELL
AND SCHOLARS SPEAK ON NATIONAL AND WORLD AFFAIRS.   ARMS/CONT
FUT USA+45 WOR+45 R+D INT/ORG NAT/G CONSULT TEC/DEV   NUC/PWR
EDU/PROP ATTIT PERSON ORD/FREE...HUM CONCPT
TIME/SEQ CON/ANAL. PAGE 23 G0454
  B64

HEKHUIS D.J.,INTERNATIONAL STABILITY: MILITARY,   TEC/DEV
ECONOMIC AND POLITICAL DIMENSIONS. FUT WOR+45 LAW   DETER
ECO/UNDEV INT/ORG NAT/G VOL/ASSN FORCES ACT/RES   REGION
BAL/PWR PWR WEALTH...STAT UN 20. PAGE 25 G0503
  B64

ROBERTS HL,FOREIGN AFFAIRS BIBLIOGRAPHY, 1952-1962.   BIBLIOG/A
ECO/DEV SECT PLAN FOR/AID INT/TRADE ARMS/CONT   DIPLOM
NAT/LISM ATTIT...INT/LAW GOV/COMP IDEA/COMP 20.   INT/ORG
PAGE 47 G0928   WAR
  B64

ROSECRANCE R.N.,THE DISPERSION OF NUCLEAR WEAPONS: EUR+WWI
STRATEGY AND POLITICS. ASIA COM FUT S/ASIA USA+45   PWR
INT/ORG NAT/G DELIB/GP FORCES ACT/RES TEC/DEV   PEACE
BAL/PWR COERCE DETER ATTIT RIGID/FLEX ORD/FREE
...POLICY CHARTS VAL/FREE. PAGE 48 G0935
  B64

WILLIAMS S.P.,TOWARD A GENUINE WORLD SECURITY   BIBLIOG/A
SYSTEM (PAMPHLET). WOR+45 INT/ORG FORCES PLAN   ARMS/CONT
NUC/PWR ORD/FREE...INT/LAW CONCPT UN PRESIDENT.   DIPLOM
PAGE 63 G1243   PEACE
  L64

BERKS R.N.,"THE US AND WEAPONS CONTROL." WOR+45 LAW   USA+45
INT/ORG NAT/G LEGIS EXEC COERCE PEACE ATTIT   PLAN
RIGID/FLEX ALL/VALS PWR...POLICY TOT/POP 20. PAGE 7   ARMS/CONT
G0129
  L64

CARNEGIE ENDOWMENT INT. PEACE,"POLITICAL QUESTIONS   INT/ORG
(ISSUES BEFORE THE NINETEENTH GENERAL ASSEMBLY)."   PEACE
SPACE WOR+45 CONSTN FINAN NAT/G CONSULT DELIB/GP
FORCES LEGIS TEC/DEV EDU/PROP LEGIT ARMS/CONT
COERCE NUC/PWR ATTIT ALL/VALS...CONCPT OBS UN
COLD/WAR 20. PAGE 11 G0208

CARNEGIE ENDOWMENT INT. PEACE,"ECONOMIC AND SOCIAL QUESTION (ISSUES BEFORE THE NINETEENTH GENERAL ASSEMBLY)." WOR+45 ECO/DEV ECO/UNDEV INDUS R+D DELIB/GP CREATE PLAN TEC/DEV ECO/TAC FOR/AID BAL/PAY...RECORD UN 20. PAGE 11 G0209
`L64` INT/ORG INT/TRADE

HAAS E.B.,"ECONOMICS AND DIFFERENTIAL PATTERNS OF POLITICAL INTEGRATION: PROJECTIONS ABOUT UNITY IN LATIN AMERICA." SOCIETY NAT/G DELIB/GP ACT/RES CREATE PLAN ECO/TAC REGION ROUTINE ATTIT DRIVE PWR WEALTH...CONCPT TREND CHARTS LAFTA 20. PAGE 24 G0464
`L/A+17C` INT/ORG MARKET

WARD C.,"THE 'NEW MYTHS' AND 'OLD REALITIES' OF NUCLEAR WAR." COM FUT USA+45 USSR WOR+45 INT/ORG NAT/G DOMIN LEGIT EXEC ATTIT PERCEPT ALL/VALS ...POLICY RELATIV PSY MYTH TREND 20. PAGE 62 G1212
`L64` FORCES COERCE ARMS/CONT NUC/PWR

FALK S.L.,"DISARMAMENT IN HISTORICAL PERSPECTIVE." WOR-45 NAT/G PLAN NUC/PWR PEACE ORD/FREE PWR ...TIME/SEQ AUD/VIS VAL/FREE LEAGUE/NAT 20. PAGE 18 G0360
`S64` INT/ORG COERCE ARMS/CONT

GARDNER R.N.,"GATT AND THE UNITED NATIONS CONFERENCE ON TRADE AND DEVELOPMENT." USA+45 WOR+45 SOCIETY ECO/UNDEV MARKET NAT/G DELIB/GP ACT/RES PLAN ECO/TAC TARIFFS EDU/PROP ROUTINE DRIVE RIGID/FLEX WEALTH...DECISION MGT TREND UN TOT/POP 20 GATT. PAGE 21 G0411
`S64` INT/ORG INT/TRADE

MAGGS P.B.,"SOVIET VIEWPOINT ON NUCLEAR WEAPONS IN INTERNATIONAL LAW." USSR WOR+45 INT/ORG FORCES DIPLOM ARMS/CONT ATTIT ORD/FREE PWR...POLICY JURID CONCPT OBS TREND CON/ANAL GEN/LAWS VAL/FREE 20. PAGE 35 G0694
`S64` COM LAW INT/LAW NUC/PWR

WHITE HOUSE CONFERENCE ON INTERNATIONAL COOPERATION(VOL.II). SPACE WOR+45 EXTR/IND INT/ORG LABOR WORKER NUC/PWR PEACE AGE/Y...CENSUS ANTHOL 20 RESOURCE/N URBAN/RNWL PUB/TRANS. PAGE 1 G0019
`B65` R+D CONFER TEC/DEV DIPLOM

PEACE RESEARCH ABSTRACTS. FUT WOR+45 R+D INT/ORG NAT/G PLAN TEC/DEV BAL/PWR DIPLOM FOR/AID NUC/PWR HEALTH. PAGE 1 G0020
`B65` BIBLIOG/A PEACE ARMS/CONT WAR

BOBROW D.B.,COMPONENTS OF DEFENSE POLICY. ASIA EUR+WWI USA+45 WOR+45 INTELL INT/ORG NAT/G PROF/ORG CONSULT LEGIS ACT/RES CREATE ARMS/CONT COERCE ORD/FREE...DECISION SIMUL. PAGE 7 G0145
`B65` DETER NUC/PWR PLAN FORCES

CORDIER A.W.,THE QUEST FOR PEACE. WOR+45 NAT/G PLAN BAL/PWR ECO/TAC ARMS/CONT NUC/PWR PWR...ANTHOL UN COLD/WAR. PAGE 13 G0256
`B65` PEACE DIPLOM POLICY INT/ORG

HALPERIN M.H.,CHINA AND THE BOMB. USA+45 USSR INT/ORG FORCES ARMS/CONT DETER PRODUC ORD/FREE PWR TREND. PAGE 24 G0472
`B65` ASIA NUC/PWR WAR DIPLOM

HASSON J.A.,THE ECONOMICS OF NUCLEAR POWER. INDIA UK USA+45 WOR+45 INT/ORG TEC/DEV COST...SOC STAT CHARTS 20 EURATOM. PAGE 25 G0490
`B65` NUC/PWR INDUS ECO/DEV METH

JENKS C.W.,SPACE LAW. DIPLOM DEBATE CONTROL ORD/FREE TREATY 20 UN. PAGE 29 G0563
`B65` SPACE INT/LAW JURID INT/ORG

KASER M.,COMECON* INTEGRATION PROBLEMS OF THE PLANNED ECONOMIES. INT/ORG TEC/DEV INT/TRADE PRICE ADMIN ADJUST CENTRAL...STAT TIME/SEQ ORG/CHARTS COMECON. PAGE 29 G0579
`B65` PLAN ECO/DEV COM REGION

UN,SPACE ACTIVITIES AND RESOURCES: REVIEW OF UNITED NATION'S NATIONAL AND INTERNATIONAL PROGRAMS. INT/ORG LABOR PLAN TEC/DEV DIPLOM EFFICIENCY HEALTH ...GOV/COMP 20 UN. PAGE 55 G1086
`B65` SPACE NUC/PWR FOR/AID PEACE

UNESCO,HANDBOOK OF INTERNATIONAL EXCHANGES. COM/IND R+D ACADEM PROF/ORG VOL/ASSN CREATE TEC/DEV EDU/PROP AGREE 20 TREATY. PAGE 55 G1090
`B65` INDEX INT/ORG DIPLOM PRESS

US CONGRESS JT ATOM ENRGY COMM,ATOMIC ENERGY LEGISLATION THROUGH 89TH CONGRESS, 1ST SESSION. USA+45 LAW INT/ORG DELIB/GP BUDGET DIPLOM 20 AEC CONGRESS CASEBOOK EURATOM IAEA. PAGE 57 G1114
`B65` NUC/PWR FORCES PEACE LEGIS

US LIBRARY OF CONGRESS,A DIRECTORY OF INFORMATION RESOURCES IN THE UNITED STATES: SOCIAL SCIENCES. USA+45 ACADEM INT/ORG LABOR PROF/ORG PUB/INST SCHOOL SECT 20. PAGE 59 G1156
`B65` BIBLIOG R+D COMPUT/IR

BEAUFRE A.,"THE SHARING OF NUCLEAR RESPONSIBILITIES* A PROBLEM IN NEED OF SOLUTION." FRANCE USA+45 INT/ORG NAT/G DELIB/GP FORCES CONTROL NUC/PWR RIGID/FLEX...CONCPT IDEA/COMP NATO. PAGE 6 G0110
`S65` DETER RISK ACT/RES WAR

BOHN L.C.,"ATOMS FOR PEACE AND ATOMS FOR WAR." WOR+45 INT/ORG TEC/DEV DIPLOM IDEA/COMP. PAGE 8 G0149
`S65` NUC/PWR ARMS/CONT RECORD

LECLERCQ H.,"ECONOMIC RESEARCH AND DEVELOPMENT IN TROPICAL AFRICA." ECO/UNDEV INT/ORG CREATE PLAN UN. PAGE 33 G0650
`S65` AFR R+D ACADEM ECO/TAC

SEARA M.V.,"COSMIC INTERNATIONAL LAW." LAW ACADEM ACT/RES DIPLOM COLONIAL CONTROL NUC/PWR SOVEREIGN ...GEN/LAWS BIBLIOG UN. PAGE 50 G0987
`C65` SPACE INT/LAW IDEA/COMP INT/ORG

US AIR FORCE ACADEMY,"AMERICAN DEFENSE POLICY." COM INT/ORG TEC/DEV FOR/AID ARMS/CONT DETER NUC/PWR ...POLICY DECISION CONCPT ANTHOL 20 COLD/WAR NATO. PAGE 56 G1103
`C65` PLAN FORCES WAR COERCE

ALEXANDER Y.,INTERNATIONAL TECHNICAL ASSISTANCE EXPERTS* A CASE STUDY OF THE U.N. EXPERIENCE. ECO/UNDEV CONSULT EX/STRUC CREATE PLAN DIPLOM FOR/AID TASK EFFICIENCY...ORG/CHARTS UN. PAGE 2 G0038
`B66` ECO/TAC INT/ORG ADMIN MGT

ALEXANDER Y.,INTERNATIONAL TECHNICAL ASSISTANCE EXPERTS: A CASE STUDY OF THE U.N. EXPERIENCE. USA+45 WOR+45 WORKER CREATE PLAN PROB/SOLV ECO/TAC FOR/AID GIVE EDU/PROP...CHARTS BIBLIOG 20 UN. PAGE 2 G0039
`B66` SKILL INT/ORG TEC/DEV CONSULT

CLARK G.,WORLD PEACE THROUGH WORLD LAW: TWO ALTERNATIVE PLANS. WOR+45 DELIB/GP FORCES TAX CONFER ADJUD SANCTION ARMS/CONT WAR CHOOSE PRIVIL 20 UN COLD/WAR. PAGE 12 G0231
`B66` INT/LAW PEACE PLAN INT/ORG

JACOBSON H.K.,DIPLOMATS, SCIENTISTS, AND POLITICIANS* THE UNITED STATES AND THE NUCLEAR TEST BAN NEGOTIATIONS. USA+45 USSR ACT/RES PLAN CONFER DETER NUC/PWR CONSEN ORD/FREE...INT TREATY. PAGE 28 G0554
`B66` DIPLOM ARMS/CONT TECHRACY INT/ORG

UNITED NATIONS,INTERNATIONAL SPACE BIBLIOGRAPHY. FUT INT/ORG TEC/DEV DIPLOM ARMS/CONT NUC/PWR ...JURID SOC UN. PAGE 56 G1093
`B66` BIBLIOG SPACE PEACE R+D

BROWNLIE I.,"NUCLEAR PROLIFERATION* SOME PROBLEMS OF CONTROL." USA+45 USSR ECO/UNDEV INT/ORG FORCES TEC/DEV REGION CONSEN...RECORD TREATY. PAGE 9 G0181
`S66` NUC/PWR ARMS/CONT VOL/ASSN ORD/FREE

EWALD R.F.,"ONE OF MANY POSSIBLE GAMES." ACADEM INT/ORG ARMS/CONT...INT/LAW GAME. PAGE 18 G0354
`S66` SIMUL HYPO/EXP PROG/TEAC RECORD

RIZOS E.J.,"SCIENCE AND TECHNOLOGY IN COUNTRY
`S66` ADMIN

DEVELOPMENT* TOWARDS AN UNDERSTANDING OF THE ROLE OF PUBLIC ADMINISTRATION." WOR+45 STRUCT INT/ORG EX/STRUC CREATE PLAN PROB/SOLV EFFICIENCY ROLE DECISION. PAGE 47 G0924 — TEC/DEV ECO/UNDEV PHIL/SCI

B67
ALEXANDER L.M.,THE LAW OF THE SEA: OFFSHORE BOUNDARIES AND ZONES. WOR+45 INT/ORG TEC/DEV CONTROL PRIVIL HABITAT SOVEREIGN...CON/ANAL CHARTS ANTHOL. PAGE 2 G0037 — SEA INT/LAW EXTR/IND

B67
ARON R.,THE GREAT DEBATE: THEORIES OF NUCLEAR STRATEGY. FRANCE USA+45 INT/ORG PLAN TREND. PAGE 4 G0068 — NUC/PWR DETER BAL/PWR DIPLOM

B67
BARANSON J.,TECHNOLOGY FOR UNDERDEVELOPED AREAS: AN ANNOTATED BIBLIOGRAPHY. FUT WOR+45 CULTURE INDUS INT/ORG CREATE PROB/SOLV INT/TRADE EDU/PROP AUTOMAT ...CONCPT METH. PAGE 5 G0092 — BIBLIOG/A ECO/UNDEV TEC/DEV R+D

B67
BURNS E.L.M.,MEGAMURDER. WOR+45 LAW INT/ORG NAT/G BAL/PWR DIPLOM DETER MURDER WEAPON CIVMIL/REL PEACE ...INT/LAW TREND 20. PAGE 10 G0193 — FORCES PLAN WAR NUC/PWR

B67
DE BLIJ H.J.,SYSTEMATIC POLITICAL GEOGRAPHY. WOR+45 STRUCT INT/ORG NAT/G EDU/PROP ADMIN COLONIAL ROUTINE ORD/FREE PWR...IDEA/COMP T 20. PAGE 15 G0283 — GEOG CONCPT METH

B67
GARCIA ROBLES A.,THE DENUCLEARIZATION OF LATIN AMERICA (TRANS. BY MARJORIE URQUIDI). LAW PLAN DIPLOM...ANTHOL 20 TREATY UN. PAGE 21 G0409 — NUC/PWR ARMS/CONT L/A+17C INT/ORG

B67
HIRSCHMAN A.O.,DEVELOPMENT PROJECTS OBSERVED. INDUS INT/ORG CONSULT EX/STRUC CREATE OP/RES ECO/TAC DEMAND...POLICY MGT METH/COMP 20 WORLD/BANK. PAGE 26 G0513 — ECO/UNDEV R+D FINAN PLAN

B67
OVERSEAS DEVELOPMENT INSTIT,EFFECTIVE AID. WOR+45 INT/ORG TEC/DEV DIPLOM INT/TRADE ADMIN. PAGE 43 G0852 — FOR/AID ECO/UNDEV ECO/TAC NAT/COMP

B67
PADELFORD N.J.,THE DYNAMICS OF INTERNATIONAL POLITICS (2ND ED.). WOR+45 LAW INT/ORG FORCES TEC/DEV REGION NAT/LISM PEACE ATTIT PWR ALL/IDEOS UN COLD/WAR NATO TREATY. PAGE 43 G0856 — DIPLOM NAT/G POLICY DECISION

B67
ROACH J.R.,THE UNITED STATES AND THE ATLANTIC COMMUNITY; ISSUES AND PROSPECTS. WOR+45 TEC/DEV ECO/TAC COLONIAL REGION PEACE ROLE...ANTHOL NATO COLD/WAR EEC. PAGE 47 G0925 — INT/ORG POLICY ADJUST DIPLOM

B67
SCHEINMAN L.,EURATOM* NUCLEAR INTEGRATION IN EUROPE. EX/STRUC LEAD 20 EURATOM. PAGE 49 G0963 — INT/ORG NAT/LISM NUC/PWR DIPLOM

B67
SKOLNIKOFF E.B.,SCIENCE, TECHNOLOGY, AND AMERICAN FOREIGN POLICY. SPACE USA+45 INT/ORG TEC/DEV ARMS/CONT NUC/PWR 29 DEPT/STATE. PAGE 51 G1010 — PHIL/SCI DIPLOM NAT/G EFFICIENCY

B67
UNESCO,PRINCIPLES AND PROBLEMS OF NATIONAL SCIENCE POLICIES. WOR+45 ECO/DEV ECO/UNDEV R+D INT/ORG PROB/SOLV CONFER...PHIL/SCI CHARTS 20 UNESCO UN. PAGE 55 G1091 — NAT/COMP POLICY TEC/DEV CREATE

S67
BENN W.,"TECHNOLOGY HAS AN INEXORABLE EFFECT." FUT UK ECO/DEV INT/ORG CONSULT PLAN EDU/PROP ADMIN LEAD GP/REL PRODUC...INT 20 EEC. PAGE 6 G0119 — R+D LG/CO TEC/DEV INDUS

S67
BROWN N.,"BRITISH ARMS AND THE SWITCH TOWARD EUROPE." EUR+WWI UK ARMS/CONT. PAGE 9 G0178 — FORCES PLAN DIPLOM INT/ORG

S67
CARROLL K.J.,"SECOND STEP TOWARD ARMS CONTROL." WOR+45 INT/ORG VOL/ASSN FORCES PROB/SOLV RISK WEAPON 20 COLD/WAR. PAGE 11 G0215 — ARMS/CONT DIPLOM PLAN NUC/PWR

S67
DOYLE S.E.,"COMMUNICATION SATELLITES* INTERNAL ORGANIZATION FOR DEVELOPMENT AND CONTROL." USA+45 R+D ACT/RES DIPLOM NAT/LISM...POLICY INT/LAW PREDICT UN. PAGE 16 G0313 — TEC/DEV SPACE COM/IND INT/ORG

S67
EISENDRATH C.,"THE OUTER SPACE TREATY." CHINA/COM COM USA+45 DIPLOM CONTROL NUC/PWR...INT/LAW 20 UN COLD/WAR TREATY. PAGE 17 G0339 — SPACE INT/ORG PEACE ARMS/CONT

S67
EYRAUD M.,"LA FRANCE FACE A UN EVENTUEL TRAITE DE NON DISSEMINATION DES ARMES NUCLEAIRES." FRANCE USA+45 EXTR/IND INDUS R+D INT/ORG ACT/RES TEC/DEV AGREE PRODUC ATTIT 20 TREATY AEC EURATOM. PAGE 18 G0355 — NUC/PWR ARMS/CONT POLICY

S67
FADDEYEV N.,"CMEA CO-OPERATION OF EQUAL NATIONS." COM R+D PLAN CAP/ISM DIPLOM FOR/AID WEALTH...POLICY MARXIST. PAGE 18 G0356 — MARXISM ECO/TAC INT/ORG ECO/UNDEV

S67
FOREIGN POLICY ASSOCIATION,"US CONCERN FOR WORLD LAW." USA+45 WOR+45 DELIB/GP JUDGE BAL/PWR CONFER PEACE ORD/FREE 20 UN. PAGE 19 G0379 — INT/LAW INT/ORG DIPLOM ARMS/CONT

S67
FOREIGN POLICY ASSOCIATION,"HOW WORLD LAW DEVELOPS* A CASE STUDY OF THE OUTER SPACE TREATY." SPACE WOR+45 BAL/PWR NEUTRAL NUC/PWR PEACE KNOWL 20 UN TREATY. PAGE 19 G0380 — INT/LAW DIPLOM ARMS/CONT INT/ORG

S67
HAZARD J.N.,"POST-DISARMAMENT INTERNATIONAL LAW." FUT USSR WOR+45 INT/ORG DELIB/GP FORCES DETER EQUILIB SOVEREIGN MARXISM 20 UN. PAGE 25 G0496 — INT/LAW ARMS/CONT PWR PLAN

S67
HODGE G.,"THE RISE AND DEMISE OF THE UN TECHNICAL ASSISTANCE ADMINISTRATION." RISK TASK INGP/REL CONSEN EFFICIENCY 20 UN. PAGE 26 G0516 — ADMIN TEC/DEV EX/STRUC INT/ORG

S67
HULL E.W.S.,"THE POLITICAL OCEAN." FUT UNIV WOR+45 EXTR/IND R+D VOL/ASSN PLAN BAL/PWR ECO/TAC PEACE WEALTH 20 UN. PAGE 27 G0536 — DIPLOM ECO/UNDEV INT/ORG INT/LAW

S67
JACKSON W.G.F.,"NUCLEAR PROLIFERATION AND THE GREAT POWERS." FUT UK WOR+45 INT/ORG DOMIN ARMS/CONT DETER ORD/FREE PACIFIST. PAGE 28 G0550 — NUC/PWR ATTIT BAL/PWR NAT/LISM

S67
JOHNSTON D.M.,"LAW, TECHNOLOGY AND THE SEA." WOR+45 PLAN PROB/SOLV TEC/DEV CONFER ADJUD ORD/FREE ...POLICY JURID. PAGE 29 G0564 — INT/LAW INT/ORG DIPLOM NEUTRAL

S67
KAHN H.,"CRITERIA FOR LONG-RANGE NUCLEAR CONTROL POLICIES." WOR+45 INT/ORG TEC/DEV DOMIN DETER WAR WEAPON ISOLAT ORD/FREE POLICY. PAGE 29 G0571 — NUC/PWR ARMS/CONT BAL/PWR DIPLOM

S67
KRUSCHE H.,"THE STRIVING OF THE KIESINGER-STRAUS GOVERNMENT FOR NUCLEAR WEAPONS IS A THREAT TO EUROPEAN SECURITY." EUR+WWI GERMANY BAL/PWR SANCTION WEAPON PEACE ORD/FREE...MARXIST 20 NATO COLD/WAR. PAGE 32 G0623 — ARMS/CONT INT/ORG NUC/PWR DIPLOM

S67
RAMSEY J.A.,"THE STATUS OF INTERNATIONAL COPYRIGHTS." WOR+45 CREATE TEC/DEV DIPLOM CONFER CONTROL SANCTION OWN...POLICY JURID. PAGE 46 G0899 — INT/LAW INT/ORG COM/IND PRESS

S67
REINTANZ G.,"THE SPACE TREATY." WOR+45 DIPLOM CONTROL ARMS/CONT NUC/PWR WAR...MARXIST 20 COLD/WAR UN TREATY. PAGE 46 G0911 — SPACE INT/LAW INT/ORG

PEACE

S67
ROMANIECKI L.,"THE ATOM AND INTERNATIONAL
COOPERATION." PROB/SOLV DIPLOM PEACE ORD/FREE 20.
PAGE 47 G0933
INT/ORG
NUC/PWR
ARMS/CONT
CONTROL

S67
SCHACTER O.,"SCIENTIFIC ADVANCES AND INTERNATIONAL
LAWMAKING." FUT R+D PLAN PROB/SOLV CONFER CONTROL
...POLICY PREDICT 20 UN. PAGE 49 G0961
TEC/DEV
INT/LAW
INT/ORG
ACT/RES

S67
SHARP G.,"THE NEED OF A FUNCTIONAL SUBSTITUTE FOR
WAR." FUT UNIV WOR+45 CULTURE SOCIETY INT/ORG
CONSULT DELIB/GP ACT/RES CREATE BAL/PWR CONFER
ARMS/CONT NUC/PWR 20. PAGE 50 G0989
PEACE
WAR
DIPLOM
PROB/SOLV

S67
SHULMAN M.D.,"'EUROPE' VERSUS 'DETENTE'." USA+45
USSR INT/ORG CONTROL ARMS/CONT DETER 20. PAGE 50
G0995
DIPLOM
BAL/PWR
NUC/PWR

S67
VLASCIC I.A.,"THE SPACE TREATY* A PRELIMINARY
EVALUATION." FUT USSR WOR+45 R+D ACT/RES TEC/DEV
DIPLOM CONFER ARMS/CONT PEACE...PREDICT UN TREATY.
PAGE 61 G1201
SPACE
INT/LAW
INT/ORG
NEUTRAL

S67
WEIL G.L.,"THE MERGER OF THE INSTITUTIONS OF THE
EUROPEAN COMMUNITIES" EUR+WWI ECO/DEV INT/TRADE
CONSEN PLURISM...DECISION MGT 20 EEC EURATOM ECSC
TREATY. PAGE 62 G1223
ECO/TAC
INT/ORG
CENTRAL
INT/LAW

N67
US HOUSE COMM FOREIGN AFFAIRS,REPORT OF SPECIAL
STUDY MISSION TO THE NEAR EAST (PAMPHLET). ISRAEL
USA+45 YEMEN ECO/UNDEV INT/ORG FOR/AID ARMS/CONT
WAR WEAPON NAT/LISM PEACE...GEOG 20 UN HOUSE/REP.
PAGE 58 G1138
ISLAM
DIPLOM
FORCES

N67
US SENATE COMM ON FOREIGN REL,SURVEY OF THE
ALLIANCE FOR PROGRESS; THE POLITICAL ASPECTS
(PAMPHLET). CONSTN SOCIETY ECO/UNDEV INT/ORG
TEC/DEV DIPLOM...CENSUS 20. PAGE 60 G1186
L/A+17C
POLICY
PROB/SOLV

INT/REL....INTERNATIONAL RELATIONS

INT/TRADE....INTERNATIONAL TRADE

N
FOREIGN AFFAIRS. SPACE WOR+45 WOR-45 CULTURE
ECO/UNDEV FINAN NAT/G TEC/DEV INT/TRADE ARMS/CONT
NUC/PWR...POLICY 20 UN EURATOM ECSC EEC. PAGE 1
G0004
BIBLIOG
DIPLOM
INT/ORG
INT/LAW

B38
HARPER S.N.,THE GOVERNMENT OF THE SOVIET UNION. COM
USSR LAW CONSTN ECO/DEV PLAN TEC/DEV DIPLOM
INT/TRADE ADMIN REV NAT/LISM...POLICY 20. PAGE 24
G0483
MARXISM
NAT/G
LEAD
POL/PAR

B40
HELLMAN F.S.,THE NEW DEAL: SELECTED LIST OF
REFERENCES. USA-45 FINAN LABOR EX/STRUC CREATE
INT/TRADE ADMIN CT/SYS 20 SUPREME/CT. PAGE 26 G0505
BIBLIOG/A
ECO/TAC
PLAN
POLICY

B50
US DEPARTMENT OF STATE,POINT FOUR: COOPERATIVE
PROGRAM FOR AID IN THE DEVELOPMENT OF ECONOMICALLY
UNDERDEVELOPED AREAS. WOR+45 AGRI INDUS INT/ORG
PLAN TEC/DEV DIPLOM EDU/PROP ADMIN PEACE PRODUC
WEALTH 20 CONGRESS UN. PAGE 57 G1121
ECO/UNDEV
FOR/AID
FINAN
INT/TRADE

B53
MACK R.T.,RAISING THE WORLDS STANDARD OF LIVING.
IRAN INT/ORG VOL/ASSN EX/STRUC ECO/TAC WEALTH...MGT
METH/CNCPT STAT CONT/OBS INT TOT/POP VAL/FREE 20
UN. PAGE 35 G0690
WOR+45
FOR/AID
INT/TRADE

B54
KENWORTHY L.S.,FREE AND INEXPENSIVE MATERIALS ON
WORLD AFFAIRS (PAMPHLET). WOR+45 CULTURE ECO/UNDEV
INT/TRADE ARMS/CONT NUC/PWR UN. PAGE 30 G0594
BIBLIOG/A
NAT/G
INT/ORG
DIPLOM

L55
KISER M.,"ORGANIZATION OF AMERICAN STATES." L/A+17C
USA+45 ECO/UNDEV INT/ORG NAT/G PLAN TEC/DEV DIPLOM
ECO/TAC INT/TRADE EDU/PROP ADMIN ALL/VALS...POLICY
MGT RECORD ORG/CHARTS OAS 20. PAGE 30 G0601
VOL/ASSN
ECO/DEV
REGION

B57
BAUER P.T.,ECONOMIC ANALYSIS AND POLICY IN
UNDERDEVELOPED COUNTRIES. WOR+45 AGRI INT/TRADE TAX
PRICE...GEN/METH BIBLIOG/A 20 COMMONWLTH. PAGE 5
G0103
ECO/UNDEV
METH/COMP
POLICY

B57
GOLD N.L.,REGIONAL ECONOMIC DEVELOPMENT AND NUCLEAR
POWER IN INDIA. FUT INDIA FINAN FOR/AID INT/TRADE
BAL/PAY EFFICIENCY OPTIMAL PRODUC WEALTH...PREDICT
20. PAGE 22 G0424
ECO/UNDEV
TEC/DEV
NUC/PWR
INDUS

B58
ATOMIC INDUSTRIAL FORUM,MANAGEMENT AND ATOMIC
ENERGY. WOR+45 SEA LAW MARKET NAT/G TEC/DEV INSPECT
INT/TRADE CONFER PEACE HEALTH...ANTHOL 20. PAGE 4
G0078
NUC/PWR
INDUS
MGT
ECO/TAC

B58
EHRHARD J.,LE DESTIN DU COLONIALISME. AFR FRANCE
ECO/UNDEV AGRI FINAN MARKET CREATE PLAN TEC/DEV
BUDGET DIPLOM PRICE 20. PAGE 17 G0335
COLONIAL
FOR/AID
INT/TRADE
INDUS

B59
VERNEY D.V.,PUBLIC ENTERPRISE IN SWEDEN. FUT SWEDEN
UK INDUS POL/PAR LEGIS PROB/SOLV CAP/ISM INT/TRADE
CONTROL SOCISM...MGT CONCPT NAT/COMP 20 SOCDEM/PAR
CIVIL/SERV. PAGE 61 G1196
ECO/DEV
POLICY
LG/CO
NAT/G

B59
WELTON H.,THE THIRD WORLD WAR; TRADE AND INDUSTRY,
THE NEW BATTLEGROUND. WOR+45 ECO/DEV INDUS MARKET
TASK...MGT IDEA/COMP COLD/WAR. PAGE 63 G1229
INT/TRADE
PLAN
DIPLOM

B60
APTHEKER H.,DISARMAMENT AND THE AMERICAN ECONOMY: A
SYMPOSIUM. FUT USA+45 ECO/DEV DIST/IND FINAN INDUS
PROC/MFG LABOR NAT/G POL/PAR CONSULT PLAN CAP/ISM
INT/TRADE PEACE ATTIT MORAL WEALTH...TREND GEN/LAWS
TOT/POP 20. PAGE 3 G0063
MARXIST
ARMS/CONT

B60
PENTONY D.E.,THE UNDERDEVELOPED LANDS. FUT WOR+45
CULTURE AGRI FINAN INDUS MARKET INT/ORG LABOR NAT/G
VOL/ASSN CONSULT TEC/DEV ECO/TAC EDU/PROP COLONIAL
ATTIT WEALTH...OBS RECORD SAMP TREND GEN/METH WORK
UN 20. PAGE 44 G0867
ECO/UNDEV
POLICY
FOR/AID
INT/TRADE

B61
BONNEFOUS M.,EUROPE ET TIERS MONDE. EUR+WWI SOCIETY
INT/ORG NAT/G VOL/ASSN ACT/RES TEC/DEV CAP/ISM
ECO/TAC ATTIT ORD/FREE SOVEREIGN...POLICY CONCPT
TREND 20. PAGE 8 G0153
AFR
ECO/UNDEV
FOR/AID
INT/TRADE

B62
AIR FORCE ACADEMY LIBRARY,INTERNATIONAL
ORGANIZATIONS AND MILITARY SECURITY SYSTEMS
(PAMPHLET) (SPECIAL BIBLIOGRAPHY SERIES, NUMBER
25). DIPLOM FOR/AID INT/TRADE NUC/PWR PEACE 20 UN
NATO OAS SEATO LEAGUE/NAT. PAGE 2 G0031
BIBLIOG
INT/ORG
FORCES
DETER

B62
KRAFT J.,THE GRAND DESIGN. EUR+WWI USA+45 AGRI
FINAN INDUS MARKET INT/ORG NAT/G PLAN ECO/TAC
TARIFFS REGION DRIVE ORD/FREE WEALTH...POLICY OBS
TREND EEC 20. PAGE 31 G0616
VOL/ASSN
ECO/DEV
INT/TRADE

B62
SCHMITT H.A.,THE PATH TO EUROPEAN UNITY. EUR+WWI
USA+45 PLAN TEC/DEV DIPLOM FOR/AID CONFER...INT/LAW
20 EEC EURCOALSTL MARSHL/PLN UNIFICA. PAGE 49 G0971
INT/ORG
INT/TRADE
REGION
ECO/DEV

S62
THORELLI H.B.,"THE INTERNATIONAL OPERATIONS
SIMULATION AT THE UNIVERSITY OF CHICAGO." FUT
USA+45 ECO/DEV DIST/IND FINAN INDUS INT/ORG
DELIB/GP ACT/RES CREATE TEC/DEV WEALTH...STAT
VAL/FREE 20. PAGE 54 G1072
ECO/TAC
SIMUL
INT/TRADE

B63
PANAMERICAN UNION,DOCUMENTOS OFICIALES DE LA
ORGANIZACION DE LOS ESTADOS AMERICANOS, INDICE Y
LISTA (VOL. III, 1962). L/A+17C DELIB/GP INT/TRADE
EDU/PROP REGION NUC/PWR...HEAL INT/LAW SOC/WK 20
OAS. PAGE 44 G0857
BIBLIOG
INT/ORG
DIPLOM

B63
PERLO V.,MILITARISM AND INDUSTRY. USA+45 INT/TRADE
EDU/PROP DETER KNOWL...CHARTS MAPS 20. PAGE 44
G0869
CIVMIL/REL
INDUS
LOBBY
ARMS/CONT

THORELLI H.B.,,INTOP: INTERNATIONAL OPERATIONS
SIMULATION: PLAYER'S MANUAL. BRAZIL FINAN OP/RES
ADMIN GP/REL INGP/REL PRODUC PERCEPT...DECISION MGT
EEC. PAGE 54 G1073
B63
GAME
INT/TRADE
EDU/PROP
LG/CO

UN SECRETARY GENERAL,PLANNING FOR ECONOMIC
DEVELOPMENT. ECO/UNDEV FINAN BUDGET INT/TRADE
TARIFFS TAX ADMIN 20 UN. PAGE 55 G1089
B63
PLAN
ECO/TAC
MGT
NAT/COMP

WILTZ J.E.,,IN SEARCH OF PEACE: THE SENATE MUNITIONS
INQUIRY, 1934-36. EUR+WWI USA-45 ELITES INDUS LG/CO
LEGIS INT/TRADE LOBBY NEUTRAL ARMS/CONT...POLICY
CONGRESS 20 LEAGUE/NAT PRESIDENT SENATE CONSCRIPTN.
PAGE 64 G1246
B63
DELIB/GP
PROFIT
WAR
WEAPON

BALASSA B.,TRADE PROSPECTS FOR DEVELOPING
COUNTRIES. WOR+45 ECO/DEV AGRI EXTR/IND INDUS
CREATE PLAN PRICE...ECOMETRIC CLASSIF TIME/SEQ
GEN/METH. PAGE 5 G0087
B64
INT/TRADE
ECO/UNDEV
TREND
STAT

HAZLEWOOD A.,THE ECONOMICS OF DEVELOPMENT: AN
ANNOTATED LIST OF BOOKS AND ARTICLES PUBLISHED
1958-1962. AGRI FINAN INDUS LABOR NAT/G DIPLOM
INT/TRADE INCOME...MGT 20. PAGE 25 G0497
B64
BIBLIOG/A
ECO/UNDEV
TEC/DEV

LI C.M.,INDUSTRIAL DEVELOPMENT IN COMMUNIST CHINA.
CHINA/COM ECO/DEV ECO/UNDEV AGRI FINAN INDUS MARKET
LABOR NAT/G ECO/TAC INT/TRADE EXEC ALL/VALS
...POLICY RELATIV TREND WORK TOT/POP VAL/FREE 20.
PAGE 34 G0665
B64
ASIA
TEC/DEV

ROBERTS HL,FOREIGN AFFAIRS BIBLIOGRAPHY, 1952-1962.
ECO/DEV SECT PLAN FOR/AID INT/TRADE ARMS/CONT
NAT/LISM ATTIT...INT/LAW GOV/COMP IDEA/COMP 20.
PAGE 47 G0928
B64
BIBLIOG/A
DIPLOM
INT/ORG
WAR

CARNEGIE ENDOWMENT INT. PEACE,"ECONOMIC AND SOCIAL
QUESTION (ISSUES BEFORE THE NINETEENTH GENERAL
ASSEMBLY)." WOR+45 ECO/DEV ECO/UNDEV INDUS R+D
DELIB/GP CREATE PLAN TEC/DEV ECO/TAC FOR/AID
BAL/PAY...RECORD UN 20. PAGE 11 G0209
L64
INT/ORG
INT/TRADE

GARDNER R.N.,"GATT AND THE UNITED NATIONS
CONFERENCE ON TRADE AND DEVELOPMENT." USA+45 WOR+45
SOCIETY ECO/UNDEV MARKET NAT/G DELIB/GP ACT/RES
PLAN ECO/TAC TARIFFS EDU/PROP ROUTINE DRIVE
RIGID/FLEX WEALTH...DECISION MGT TREND UN TOT/POP
20 GATT. PAGE 21 G0411
S64
INT/ORG
INT/TRADE

KASER M.,COMECON* INTEGRATION PROBLEMS OF THE
PLANNED ECONOMIES. INT/ORG TEC/DEV INT/TRADE PRICE
ADMIN ADJUST CENTRAL...STAT TIME/SEQ ORG/CHARTS
COMECON. PAGE 29 G0579
B65
PLAN
ECO/DEV
COM
REGION

TENDLER J.D.,"TECHNOLOGY AND ECONOMIC DEVELOPMENT*
THE CASE OF HYDRO VS THERMAL POWER." CONSTRUC
DIST/IND CREATE TEC/DEV INT/TRADE CENTRAL PWR SKILL
WEALTH...MGT NAT/COMP ARGEN. PAGE 54 G1063
S65
BRAZIL
INDUS
ECO/UNDEV

MARK M.,"BEYOND SOVEREIGNTY." WOR+45 WOR-45
ECO/UNDEV BAL/PWR INT/TRADE NUC/PWR REV WAR MARXISM
NEW/LIB BIBLIOG. PAGE 36 G0706
C65
NAT/LISM
NAT/G
DIPLOM
INTELL

ECKSTEIN A.,COMMUNIST CHINA'S ECONOMIC GROWTH AND
FOREIGN TRADE* IMPLICATIONS FOR US POLICY. COM
USA+45 USSR STRUCT INDUS MARKET DIPLOM ECO/TAC
FOR/AID INT/TRADE...STAT CHARTS. PAGE 17 G0332
B66
ASIA
ECO/UNDEV
CREATE
PWR

GRUNEWALD D.,,PUBLIC POLICY AND THE MODERN
COOPERATION: SELECTED READINGS. USA+45 LAW MARKET
VOL/ASSN CAP/ISM INT/TRADE CENTRAL OWN...SOC ANTHOL
20. PAGE 23 G0458
B66
LG/CO
POLICY
NAT/G
CONTROL

LEWIS W.A.,,DEVELOPMENT PLANNING: THE ESSENTIALS OF
ECONOMIC POLICY. USA+45 FINAN INDUS NAT/G WORKER
FOR/AID INT/TRADE ADMIN ROUTINE WEALTH...CONCPT
STAT. PAGE 34 G0663
B66
PLAN
ECO/DEV
POLICY
CREATE

RUPPENTHAL K.M.,,TRANSPORTATION AND TOMORROW. FUT
SPACE USA+45 SEA AIR FORCES TEC/DEV INT/TRADE
...ANTHOL 20 RAILROAD. PAGE 48 G0946
B66
DIST/IND
PLAN
CIVMIL/REL
PREDICT

SPULBER N.,THE STATE AND ECONOMIC DEVELOPMENT IN
EASTERN EUROPE. BULGARIA COM CZECHOSLVK HUNGARY
POLAND YUGOSLAVIA CULTURE PLAN CAP/ISM INT/TRADE
CONTROL...POLICY CHARTS METH/COMP BIBLIOG/A 19/20.
PAGE 52 G1028
B66
ECO/DEV
ECO/UNDEV
NAT/G
TOTALISM

BARANSON J.,TECHNOLOGY FOR UNDERDEVELOPED AREAS: AN
ANNOTATED BIBLIOGRAPHY. FUT WOR+45 CULTURE INDUS
INT/ORG CREATE PROB/SOLV INT/TRADE EDU/PROP AUTOMAT
...CONCPT METH. PAGE 5 G0092
B67
BIBLIOG/A
ECO/UNDEV
TEC/DEV
R+D

COLEMAN J.R.,THE CHANGING AMERICAN ECONOMY. USA+45
AGRI FINAN LABOR FOR/AID INT/TRADE AUTOMAT GP/REL
INGP/REL ANTHOL. PAGE 13 G0243
B67
BUDGET
ECO/TAC
ECO/DEV
WEALTH

COLM G.,THE ECONOMY OF THE AMERICAN PEOPLE. USA+45
ECO/DEV FINAN WORKER INT/TRADE AUTOMAT GP/REL.
PAGE 13 G0244
B67
ECO/TAC
PRODUC
TREND
TEC/DEV

OVERSEAS DEVELOPMENT INSTIT,EFFECTIVE AID. WOR+45
INT/ORG TEC/DEV DIPLOM INT/TRADE ADMIN. PAGE 43
G0852
B67
FOR/AID
ECO/UNDEV
ECO/TAC
NAT/COMP

UNIVERSAL REFERENCE SYSTEM,ECONOMIC REGULATION,
BUSINESS, AND GOVERNMENT (VOLUME VIII). WOR+45
WOR-45 ECO/DEV ECO/UNDEV FINAN LABOR TEC/DEV
ECO/TAC INT/TRADE GOV/REL...POLICY COMPUT/IR.
PAGE 56 G1099
B67
BIBLIOG/A
CONTROL
NAT/G

WEIL G.L.,,"THE MERGER OF THE INSTITUTIONS OF THE
EUROPEAN COMMUNITIES" EUR+WWI ECO/DEV INT/TRADE
CONSEN PLURISM...DECISION MGT 20 EEC EURATOM ECSC
TREATY. PAGE 62 G1223
S67
ECO/TAC
INT/ORG
CENTRAL
INT/LAW

WILLIAMS C.,"REGIONAL MANAGEMENT OVERSEAS." USA+45
WOR+45 DIST/IND LG/CO EX/STRUC INT/TRADE TARIFFS
ADMIN TASK CENTRAL. PAGE 63 G1242
S67
MGT
EUR+WWI
ECO/DEV
PLAN

INTEGRATION....SEE NEGRO, SOUTH/US, RACE/REL, SOC/INTEG,
CIV/RIGHTS, DISCRIM, ISOLAT, SCHOOL, STRANGE

INTEGRATION, POLITICAL+ECONOMIC....SEE REGION+INT/ORG+
VOL/ASSN+CENTRAL

INTELL....INTELLIGENTSIA

BERGSON H.,CREATIVE EVOLUTION. FUT WOR+45 WOR-45
INTELL AGRI R+D ATTIT PERCEPT PERSON RIGID/FLEX
...RELATIV PHIL/SCI PSY METH/CNCPT MATH HIST/WRIT
TREND HYPO/EXP TOT/POP. PAGE 7 G0127
B11
BIO/SOC
KNOWL

DRAPER J.W.,HISTORY OF THE CONFLICT BETWEEN
RELIGION AND SCIENCE. WOR-45 INTELL SOCIETY R+D
CREATE PLAN TEC/DEV EDU/PROP ATTIT PWR...PHIL/SCI
CONCPT OBS TIME/SEQ TREND GEN/LAWS TOT/POP. PAGE 16
G0314
B23
SECT
KNOWL

BARKER E.,POLITICAL THOUGHT IN ENGLAND: FROM
HERBERT SPENCER TO THE PRESENT DAY. UK ALL/IDEOS
...PHIL/SCI 19/20 SPENCER/H GREEN/TH BENTHAM/J
MAITLAND/F. PAGE 5 G0094
B28
INTELL
GEN/LAWS
IDEA/COMP

EINSTEIN A.,THE WORLD AS I SEE IT. WOR-45 INTELL
R+D INT/ORG NAT/G SECT VOL/ASSN FORCES CREATE
EDU/PROP LEGIT ARMS/CONT WAR WEAPON NAT/LISM
ALL/VALS...POLICY CONCPT 20. PAGE 17 G0337
B34
SOCIETY
PHIL/SCI
DIPLOM
PACIFISM

LUNDBERG G.A.,,"THE CONCEPT OF LAW IN THE SOCIAL
SCIENCES"(BMR)" CULTURE INTELL SOCIETY STRUCT
CREATE...NEW/IDEA 20. PAGE 34 G0678
S38
EPIST
GEN/LAWS
CONCPT
PHIL/SCI

ZNANIECKI F.,THE SOCIAL ROLE OF THE MAN OF
KNOWLEDGE. UNIV SOCIETY STRUCT TEC/DEV...EPIST
PHIL/SCI SOC NEW/IDEA 20. PAGE 65 G1269
B40 ROLE INTELL KNOWL INGP/REL

HAWLEY A.H.,"ECOLOGY AND HUMAN ECOLOGY" WOR+45
INTELL ACADEM PLAN GP/REL ADJUST PERSON...PHIL/SCI
SOC METH/CNCPT METH 20. PAGE 25 G0493
S44 HABITAT GEOG GEN/LAWS METH/COMP

BUSH V.,SCIENCE, THE ENDLESS FRONTIER. FUT USA-45
INTELL STRATA ACT/RES CREATE PLAN EDU/PROP ADMIN
NUC/PWR PEACE ATTIT HEALTH KNOWL...MAJORIT HEAL MGT
PHIL/SCI CONCPT OBS TREND 20. PAGE 10 G0195
B45 R+D NAT/G

WHITE L.D.,CIVIL SERVICE IN WARTIME. CONSULT
DELIB/GP PARTIC WAR CHOOSE. PAGE 63 G1233
B45 REPRESENT ADMIN INTELL NAT/G

MCDIARMID J.,"THE MOBILIZATION OF SOCIAL
SCIENTISTS," IN L. WHITE'S CIVIL CIVIL SERVICE IN
WARTIME." USA-45 TEC/DEV CENTRAL...SOC 20
CIVIL/SERV. PAGE 37 G0733
C45 INTELL WAR DELIB/GP ADMIN

TRYTTEN M.H.,"THE MOBILIZATION OF SCIENTISTS," IN
L. WHITE, CIVIL SERVICE IN WARTIME." USA-45 R+D
FORCES ACT/RES PERSON ROLE 20. PAGE 55 G1080
C45 INTELL WAR TEC/DEV NAT/G

BUSH V.,ENDLESS HORIZONS. FUT USA-45 INTELL NAT/G
CONSULT ACT/RES CREATE PLAN EDU/PROP DRIVE
...MAJORIT HEAL MGT PHIL/SCI CONCPT OBS TREND
GEN/METH TOT/POP 20. PAGE 10 G0196
B46 R+D KNOWL PEACE

MORGENTHAU H.J.,SCIENTIFIC MAN VS POWER POLITICS.
USA+45 WOR+45 INTELL SOCIETY ACT/RES CREATE PLAN
EDU/PROP...CONCPT TREND TOT/POP 20. PAGE 40 G0782
B46 UNIV MORAL PEACE

NORTHROP F.S.C.,THE MEETING OF EAST AND WEST.
EUR+WWI FUT MOD/EUR UNIV WOR+45 WOR-45 INTELL
SOCIETY EX/STRUC TOP/EX ACT/RES LEGIT CHOOSE ATTIT
PERCEPT RIGID/FLEX ALL/VALS...POLICY JURID OBS
TOT/POP. PAGE 42 G0826
B46 DRIVE TREND PEACE

MASTERS D.,"ONE WORLD OR NONE." FUT WOR+45 INTELL
INT/ORG ACT/RES EDU/PROP DETER ATTIT RIGID/FLEX
SUPEGO KNOWL...STAT TREND ORG/CHARTS 20. PAGE 36
G0719
L46 POLICY PHIL/SCI ARMS/CONT NUC/PWR

STEWART I.,ORGANIZING SCIENTIFIC RESEARCH FOR WAR:
ADMINISTRATIVE HISTORY OF OFFICE OF SCIENTIFIC
RESEARCH AND DEVELOPMENT. USA-45 INTELL R+D LABOR
WORKER CREATE BUDGET WEAPON CIVMIL/REL GP/REL
EFFICIENCY...POLICY 20. PAGE 53 G1036
B48 DELIB/GP ADMIN WAR TEC/DEV

MARQUIS D.G.,"RESEARCH PLANNING AT THE FRONTIERS OF
SCIENCE" (BMR)" INTELL ACADEM CREATE UTIL...PSY 20.
PAGE 36 G0708
S48 PLAN ACT/RES EFFICIENCY GEN/METH

ROSENHAUPT H.W.,HOW TO WAGE PEACE. USA+45 SOCIETY
STRATA STRUCT R+D INT/ORG POL/PAR LEGIS ACT/RES
CREATE PLAN EDU/PROP ADMIN EXEC ATTIT ALL/VALS
...TIME/SEQ TREND COLD/WAR 20. PAGE 48 G0937
B49 INTELL CONCPT DIPLOM

MANNHEIM K.,FREEDOM, POWER, AND DEMOCRATIC
PLANNING. FUT USSR WOR+45 ELITES INTELL SOCIETY
NAT/G EDU/PROP ROUTINE ATTIT DRIVE SUPEGO SKILL
...POLICY PSY CONCPT TREND GEN/LAWS 20. PAGE 35
G0700
B50 TEC/DEV PLAN CAP/ISM UK

MACRAE D.G.,"THE BOLSHEVIK IDEOLOGY: THE
INTELLECTUAL AND EMOTIONAL FACTORS IN COMMUNIST
AFFILIATION" (BMR)" COM LEAD REV ATTIT ORD/FREE
...SOC CON/ANAL 20 BOLSHEVISM. PAGE 35 G0693
S51 MARXISM INTELL PHIL/SCI SECT

HAYEK F.A.,THE COUNTER-REVOLUTION OF SCIENCE. UNIV
INTELL R+D VOL/ASSN CREATE EDU/PROP...PHIL/SCI SOC
OBS TIME/SEQ TREND GEN/METH. PAGE 25 G0494
B52 PERCEPT KNOWL

KECSKEMETI P.,"THE 'POLICY SCIENCES': ASPIRATION
AND OUTLOOK." UNIV CULTURE INTELL SOCIETY STRUCT
EDU/PROP ATTIT PERCEPT RIGID/FLEX KNOWL...PHIL/SCI
METH/CNCPT OBS 20. PAGE 30 G0589
S52 CREATE NEW/IDEA

EASTON D.,THE POLITICAL SYSTEM, AN INQUIRY INTO THE
STATE POLITICAL SCIENCE. USA+45 INTELL CREATE
EDU/PROP RIGID/FLEX KNOWL SKILL...PHIL/SCI NEW/IDEA
STERTYP TOT/POP 20. PAGE 17 G0329
B53 R+D PERCEPT

HOVLAND C.I.,COMMUNICATION AND PERSUASION:
PSYCHOLOGICAL STUDIES OF OPINION CHANGE. INTELL
SOCIETY ECO/DEV COM/IND R+D SERV/IND CREATE TEC/DEV
ATTIT RIGID/FLEX KNOWL NEW/IDEA. PAGE 27 G0531
B53 PSY EDU/PROP

COMBS C.H.,DECISION PROCESSES. INTELL SOCIETY
DELIB/GP CREATE TEC/DEV DOMIN LEGIT EXEC CHOOSE
DRIVE RIGID/FLEX KNOWL PWR...PHIL/SCI SOC
METH/CNCPT CONT/OBS REC/INT PERS/TEST SAMP/SIZ BIOG
SOC/EXP WORK. PAGE 13 G0245
B54 MATH DECISION

POLANYI M.,"ON THE INTRODUCTION OF SCIENCE INTO
MORAL SUBJECTS." FUT WOR+45 ACT/RES ATTIT KNOWL
...CONCPT NEW/IDEA 20. PAGE 45 G0882
S54 INTELL PHIL/SCI

SKINNER B.F.,"FREEDOM AND THE CONTROL OF MEN"
(BMR)" FUT WOR+45 CONTROL CHOOSE GP/REL ATTIT MORAL
PWR POPULISM...POLICY 20. PAGE 51 G1008
S55 ORD/FREE TEC/DEV PHIL/SCI INTELL

WRIGHT Q.,"THE PEACEFUL ADJUSTMENT OF INTERNATIONAL
RELATIONS: PROBLEMS AND RESEARCH APPROACHES." UNIV
INTELL EDU/PROP ADJUD ROUTINE KNOWL SKILL...INT/LAW
JURID PHIL/SCI CLASSIF 20. PAGE 64 G1258
S55 R+D METH/CNCPT PEACE

VUCINICH A.,THE SOVIET ACADEMY OF SCIENCES. USSR
STRUCT ACADEM NAT/G EDU/PROP ADMIN LEAD ROLE
...BIBLIOG 20 ACADEM/SCI. PAGE 61 G1203
B56 PHIL/SCI CREATE INTELL PROF/ORG

MERTON R.K.,SOCIAL THEORY AND SOCIAL STRUCTURE
(REV. ED.). INTELL SECT WORKER OP/RES EDU/PROP
ADMIN INGP/REL ANOMIE PERSON...AUD/VIS T 20
BUREAUCRCY. PAGE 38 G0759
B57 SOC GEN/LAWS SOCIETY STRUCT

MCDONALD L.C.,"VOEGELIN AND THE POSITIVISTS: A NEW
SCIENCE OF POLITICS." WOR+45 WOR-45 INTELL CREATE
PLAN ATTIT...METH/CNCPT NEW/IDEA OBS VAL/FREE 20.
PAGE 37 G0734
S57 PHIL/SCI CONCPT GEN/METH

DAVENPORT J.,"ARMS AND THE WELFARE STATE." INTELL
STRUCT FORCES CREATE ECO/TAC FOR/AID DOMIN LEGIT
ADMIN WAR ORD/FREE PWR...POLICY SOC CONCPT MYTH OBS
TREND COLD/WAR TOT/POP 20. PAGE 14 G0276
S58 USA+45 NAT/G USSR

JACOBS N.,CULTURE FOR THE MILLIONS? INTELL SOCIETY
NAT/G...POLICY SOC OBS ANTHOL 20. PAGE 28 G0553
B59 CULTURE COM/IND PERF/ART CONCPT

MIKSCHE F.O.,THE FAILURE OF ATOMIC STRATEGY. COM
EUR+WWI INTELL POL/PAR FORCES PLAN ECO/TAC NUC/PWR
ATTIT DRIVE RIGID/FLEX PWR...DECISION GEOG PSY
CONCPT RECORD TREND CHARTS VAL/FREE 20. PAGE 39
G0766
B59 ACT/RES ORD/FREE DIPLOM ARMS/CONT

RUSSELL B.,COMMON SENSE AND NUCLEAR WARFARE. WOR+45
INTELL SOCIETY STRATA NAT/G TOP/EX EDU/PROP ATTIT
PERSON KNOWL MORAL PWR...POLICY CONCPT MYTH
CON/ANAL COLD/WAR 20. PAGE 48 G0948
B59 ORD/FREE ARMS/CONT NUC/PWR

DEUTSCH K.W.,"THE IMPACT OF SCIENCE AND TECHNOLOGY
ON INTERNATIONAL POLITICS." UNIV INTELL NAT/G
ACT/RES CREATE TEC/DEV EDU/PROP EXEC KNOWL...CONCPT
TREND TOT/POP 20. PAGE 15 G0297
S59 PHIL/SCI MYTH DIPLOM NAT/LISM

MILBURN T.W.,"WHAT CONSTITUTES EFFECTIVE
DETERRENCE." USA+45 USSR WOR+45 STRUCT FORCES
ACT/RES PLAN SUPEGO KNOWL ORD/FREE PWR...RELATIV
S59 INTELL ATTIT DETER

PSY CONCPT VAL/FREE 20 COLD/WAR. PAGE 39 G0768   NUC/PWR

B60
ARMS CONTROL. FUT UNIV WOR+45 INTELL R+D INT/ORG   DELIB/GP
NAT/G VOL/ASSN CONSULT CREATE EDU/PROP PEACE...HUM   ORD/FREE
GEN/LAWS TOT/POP 20. PAGE 1 G0015   ARMS/CONT
NUC/PWR

B60
PARRY A.,RUSSIA'S ROCKETS AND MISSILES. COM FUT   PLAN
GERMANY USA+45 WOR+45 INTELL ECO/DEV ACT/RES   TEC/DEV
NUC/PWR WEAPON ATTIT ALL/VALS...OBS TIME/SEQ   SPACE
COLD/WAR 20. PAGE 44 G0859   USSR

B60
RAPOPORT A.,FIGHTS, GAMES AND DEBATES. INTELL   METH/CNCPT
SOCIETY R+D EX/STRUC PERCEPT PERSON SKILL...PSY SOC   MATH
GAME. PAGE 46 G0902   DECISION
CON/ANAL

L60
BRENNAN D.G.,"SETTING AND GOALS OF ARMS CONTROL."   FORCES
FUT USA+45 USSR WOR+45 INTELL INT/ORG NAT/G   COERCE
VOL/ASSN CONSULT PLAN DIPLOM ECO/TAC ADMIN KNOWL   ARMS/CONT
PWR...POLICY CONCPT TREND COLD/WAR 20. PAGE 8 G0164   DETER

L60
HOLZMAN B.G.,"BASIC RESEARCH FOR NATIONAL   FORCES
SURVIVAL." FUT USA+45 INTELL R+D ACT/RES OP/RES   STAT
PLAN TEC/DEV EDU/PROP PERCEPT PERSON...PHIL/SCI
METH/CNCPT NEW/IDEA MATH OBS RECORD TREND LAB/EXP
20. PAGE 27 G0525

S60
KAPLAN M.A.,"THEORETICAL ANALYSIS OF THE BALANCE OF   CREATE
POWER." FUT USA+45 WOR+45 INTELL ECO/DEV INT/ORG   NEW/IDEA
NAT/G CONSULT TOP/EX ACT/RES PLAN TEC/DEV ATTIT   DIPLOM
ALL/VALS...METH/CNCPT TOT/POP 20. PAGE 29 G0576   NUC/PWR

B61
LUNDBERG G.A.,CAN SCIENCE SAVE US. UNIV CULTURE   ACT/RES
INTELL SOCIETY ECO/DEV R+D PLAN EDU/PROP ROUTINE   CONCPT
CHOOSE ATTIT PERCEPT ALL/VALS...TREND 20. PAGE 34   TOTALISM
G0679

B61
NATHAN O.,EINSTEIN ON PEACE. WOR+45 WOR-45 INTELL   CONCPT
NUC/PWR WAR PERSON MORAL...BIOG VAL/FREE NAZI 20   PEACE
EINSTEIN/A. PAGE 41 G0807

B61
NOGEE J.L.,SOVIET POLICY TOWARD INTERNATIONAL   INT/ORG
CONTROL OF ATOMIC ENERGY. COM USA+45 WOR+45 INTELL   ATTIT
NAT/G ACT/RES DIPLOM EDU/PROP NUC/PWR TOTALISM   ARMS/CONT
PERCEPT KNOWL PWR...TIME/SEQ COLD/WAR 20. PAGE 42   USSR
G0824

L61
COHEN K.J.,"THE ROLE OF MANAGEMENT GAMES IN   SOCIETY
EDUCATION AND RESEARCH." INTELL ECO/DEV FINAN   GAME
ACT/RES ECO/TAC DECISION. PAGE 12 G0240   MGT
EDU/PROP

L61
TAUBENFELD H.J.,"A TREATY FOR ANTARCTICA." FUT   R+D
USA+45 INTELL INT/ORG LABOR 20 TREATY ANTARCTICA.   ACT/RES
PAGE 54 G1055   DIPLOM

S61
MACHOWSKI K.,"SELECTED PROBLEMS OF NATIONAL   UNIV
SOVEREIGNTY WITH REFERENCE TO THE LAW OF OUTER   ACT/RES
SPACE." FUT WOR+45 AIR LAW INTELL SOCIETY ECO/DEV   NUC/PWR
PLAN EDU/PROP DETER DRIVE PERCEPT SOVEREIGN   SPACE
...POLICY INT/LAW OBS TREND TOT/POP 20. PAGE 35
G0689

S61
MAINZER L.C.,"SCIENTIFIC FREEDOM IN GOVERNMENT-   CREATE
SPONSORED RESEARCH." USA+45 INTELL PUB/INST BUDGET   ORD/FREE
LOBBY AUTHORIT PWR...POLICY PHIL/SCI 20 NIH NSF.   NAT/G
PAGE 35 G0696   R+D

S61
SCHILLING W.R.,"THE H-BOMB: HOW TO DECIDE WITHOUT   PERSON
ACTUALLY CHOOSING." FUT USA+45 INTELL CONSULT ADMIN   LEGIT
CT/SYS MORAL...JURID OBS 20 TRUMAN/HS. PAGE 49   NUC/PWR
G0966

S61
TAUBENFELD H.J.,"OUTER SPACE--PAST POLITICS AND   PLAN
FUTURE POLICY." FUT USA+45 USA-45 WOR+45 AIR INTELL   SPACE
STRUCT ECO/DEV NAT/G TOP/EX ACT/RES ADMIN ROUTINE   INT/ORG
NUC/PWR ATTIT DRIVE...CONCPT TIME/SEQ TREND TOT/POP
20. PAGE 54 G1054

B62
CHASE S.,THE PROPER STUDY OF MANKIND (2ND REV.   PHIL/SCI
ED.). WOR+45 WOR-45 INTELL WAR...METH/CNCPT   SOC
SAMP/SIZ GEN/LAWS BIBLIOG METH 16/20. PAGE 11 G0224   PROB/SOLV
PERSON

B62
GILPIN R.,AMERICAN SCIENTISTS AND NUCLEAR WEAPONS   INTELL
POLICY. COM FUT USA+45 WOR+45 INT/ORG NAT/G   ATTIT
PROF/ORG CONSULT FORCES CREATE TEC/DEV BAL/PWR   DETER
EDU/PROP ARMS/CONT WAR PERCEPT KNOWL MORAL PWR   NUC/PWR
...PHIL/SCI SOC CONCPT GEN/LAWS 20. PAGE 21 G0417

B62
OSGOOD C.E.,AN ALTERNATIVE TO WAR OR SURRENDER. FUT   ORD/FREE
UNIV CULTURE INTELL SOCIETY R+D INT/ORG CONSULT   EDU/PROP
DELIB/GP ACT/RES PLAN CHOOSE ATTIT PERCEPT KNOWL   PEACE
...PHIL/SCI PSY SOC TREND GEN/LAWS 20. PAGE 43   WAR
G0849

B62
RIKER W.H.,THE THEORY OF POLITICAL COALITIONS.   FUT
WOR+45 INTELL NAT/G CREATE PLAN DRIVE PERCEPT   SIMUL
...DECISION PSY SOC METH/CNCPT NEW/IDEA MATH CHARTS
GAME TOT/POP 20. PAGE 47 G0921

S62
FOSTER W.C.,"ARMS CONTROL AND DISARMAMENT IN A   DELIB/GP
DIVIDED WORLD." COM FUT USA+45 USSR WOR+45 INTELL   POLICY
INT/ORG NAT/G VOL/ASSN CONSULT CREATE PLAN TEC/DEV   ARMS/CONT
EDU/PROP LEGIT NUC/PWR ATTIT RIGID/FLEX...CONCPT   DIPLOM
TREND TOT/POP 20 UN. PAGE 20 G0387

S62
SCHILLING W.R.,"SCIENTISTS, FOREIGN POLICY AND   NAT/G
POLITICS." WOR+45 INTELL INT/ORG CONSULT   TEC/DEV
TOP/EX ACT/RES PLAN ADMIN KNOWL...CONCPT OBS TREND   DIPLOM
LEAGUE/NAT 20. PAGE 49 G0967   NUC/PWR

S62
STORER N.W.,"SOME SOCIOLOGICAL ASPECTS OF FEDERAL   POLICY
SCIENCE POLICY." USA+45 INTELL PUB/INST PLAN GP/REL   CREATE
PERS/REL DRIVE PERSON ROLE...PSY SOC SIMUL 20 NIH   NAT/G
NSF. PAGE 53 G1040   ALL/VALS

S62
WALTER E.,"VERS UNE CLASSIFICATION SCIENTIFIQUE DE   PLAN
LA SOCIOLOGIA." UNIV CULTURE INTELL SOCIETY R+D   CONCPT
ACT/RES LEGIT ROUTINE ATTIT KNOWL...JURID MGT TREND
GEN/LAWS 20. PAGE 62 G1208

B63
HOFSTADTER R.,ANTI-INTELLECTUALISM IN AMERICAN   INTELL
LIFE. USA+45 AGRI INDUS ACADEM TEC/DEV EDU/PROP   EPIST
INGP/REL ATTIT...SOC WORSHIP 20 MCCARTHY/J   CULTURE
STEVENSN/A. PAGE 26 G0522   SOCIETY

S63
FERRETTI B.,"IMPORTANZA E PROSPETTIVE DELL ENERGIA   TEC/DEV
DI ORIGINE NUCLEARE." FUT ITALY WOR+45 INTELL R+D   EXEC
ACT/RES CREATE HEALTH WEALTH...METH/CNCPT TIME/SEQ   NUC/PWR
20. PAGE 19 G0365

S63
WOHLSTETTER A.,"SCIENTISTS, SEERS AND STRATEGY."   INTELL
USA+45 ELITES R+D NAT/G CONSULT FORCES TOP/EX   ACT/RES
EDU/PROP ARMS/CONT KNOWL ORD/FREE...DECISION MYTH
20. PAGE 64 G1253

B64
ETZIONI A.,THE MOON-DOGGLE: DOMESTIC AND   R+D
INTERNATIONAL IMPLICATIONS OF THE SPACE RACE. FUT   NAT/G
USA+45 WOR+45 INTELL ECO/DEV INDUS VOL/ASSN   DIPLOM
EX/STRUC FORCES LEGIS TOP/EX PLAN TEC/DEV ECO/TAC   SPACE
EDU/PROP KNOWL ORD/FREE PWR RESPECT WEALTH
TIME/SEQ. PAGE 18 G0352

B64
FOGELMAN E.,HIROSHIMA: THE DECISION TO USE THE A-   INTELL
BOMB. USA-45 DIPLOM EFFICIENCY PEACE...ANTHOL   DECISION
BIBLIOG T 20 CHINJAP. PAGE 19 G0375   NUC/PWR
WAR

B64
GRODZINS M.,THE ATOMIC AGE: FORTY-FIVE SCIENTISTS   INTELL
AND SCHOLARS SPEAK ON NATIONAL AND WORLD AFFAIRS.   ARMS/CONT
FUT USA+45 WOR+45 R+D INT/ORG NAT/G CONSULT TEC/DEV   NUC/PWR
EDU/PROP ATTIT PERSON ORD/FREE...HUM CONCPT
TIME/SEQ CON/ANAL. PAGE 23 G0454

B64
PEDERSEN E.S.,NUCLEAR ENERGY IN SPACE. FUT INTELL   SPACE
R+D CONSULT...NEW/IDEA CHARTS METH T 20. PAGE 44   TEC/DEV
G0864   NUC/PWR
LAB/EXP

POWELSON J.P.,LATIN AMERICA: TODAY'S ECONOMIC AND SOCIAL REVOLUTION. L/A+17C INTELL SOCIETY STRUCT AGRI INDUS NAT/G DIPLOM ECO/TAC REV...POLICY 20. PAGE 45 G0887
B64 ECO/UNDEV WEALTH ADJUST PLAN

SHUBIK M.,GAME THEORY AND RELATED APPROACHES TO SOCIAL BEHAVIOR: SELECTIONS. INTELL SOCIETY ACT/RES CREATE PLAN PROB/SOLV...DECISION MATH. PAGE 50 G0994
B64 SOC SIMUL GAME PWR

VAN DYKE V.,PRIDE AND POWER: THE RATIONALE OF THE SPACE PROGRAM. FUT USA+45 INTELL R+D NAT/G POL/PAR DELIB/GP EX/STRUC LEGIS TOP/EX ACT/RES PLAN ECO/TAC EDU/PROP ORD/FREE PWR RESPECT SKILL...TIME/SEQ VAL/FREE. PAGE 61 G1191
B64 TEC/DEV ATTIT POLICY

BYRNES F.C.,"ASSIGNMENT TO AMBIGUITY: WORK PERFORMANCE IN CROSSCULTURAL TECHNICAL ASSISTANCE." USA+45 WOR+45 PROF/ORG CONSULT PLAN EDU/PROP ATTIT DISPL PERCEPT PERSON ALL/VALS...POLICY INT CHARTS NATO 20. PAGE 10 G0199
S64 INTELL QU

CALDWELL L.K.,"BIOPOLITICS: SCIENCE, ETHICS, AND PUBLIC POLICY." FUT USA+45 WOR+45 INTELL STRATA R+D NAT/G CONSULT PLAN EDU/PROP ALL/VALS...RELATIV PHIL/SCI 20. PAGE 10 G0203
S64 TEC/DEV POLICY

NEEDHAM T.,"SCIENCE AND SOCIETY IN EAST AND WEST." INTELL STRATA R+D LOC/G NAT/G PROVS CONSULT ACT/RES CREATE PLAN TEC/DEV EDU/PROP ADMIN ATTIT ALL/VALS ...POLICY RELATIV MGT CONCPT NEW/IDEA TIME/SEQ WORK WORK. PAGE 41 G0815
S64 ASIA STRUCT

PLATT J.R.,"RESEARCH AND DEVELOPMENT FOR SOCIAL PROBLEMS." INTELL SOCIETY PROB/SOLV GP/REL ATTIT ALL/VALS CONT/OBS. PAGE 45 G0880
S64 R+D ACT/RES PLAN SOC

BOBROW D.B.,COMPONENTS OF DEFENSE POLICY. ASIA EUR+WWI USA+45 WOR+45 INTELL INT/ORG NAT/G PROF/ORG CONSULT LEGIS ACT/RES CREATE ARMS/CONT COERCE ORD/FREE...DECISION SIMUL. PAGE 7 G0145
B65 DETER NUC/PWR PLAN FORCES

CARPER E.T.,REORGANIZATION OF THE U.S. PUBLIC HEALTH SERVICE. FUT USA+45 INTELL R+D LOBBY GP/REL INGP/REL PERS/REL RIGID/FLEX ROLE HEALTH...PHIL/SCI 20 CONGRESS PHS. PAGE 11 G0213
B65 HEAL PLAN NAT/G OP/RES

KENT A.,SPECIALIZED INFORMATION CENTERS. INTELL R+D VOL/ASSN CONSULT COMPUTER KNOWL...DECISION HUM PHIL/SCI METH/CNCPT TREND CHARTS 20. PAGE 30 G0593
B65 COMPUT/IR CREATE TEC/DEV METH/COMP

LAPP R.E.,THE NEW PRIESTHOOD: THE SCIENTIFIC ELITE AND THE USES OF POWER. USA+45 ELITES INTELL SOCIETY R+D NAT/G CHIEF LEGIS CIVMIL/REL GP/REL PWR 20 PRESIDENT CONGRESS. PAGE 32 G0635
B65 TEC/DEV TECHRACY CONTROL POPULISM

NATIONAL SCIENCE FOUNDATION,CURRENT RESEARCH AND DEVELOPMENT IN SCIENTIFIC DOCUMENTATION - NO. 12. WOR+45 INTELL COM/IND NAT/G COMPUTER TEC/DEV AUTOMAT KNOWL...PSY LING 20. PAGE 41 G0812
B65 BIBLIOG COMPUT/IR R+D PHIL/SCI

VERMOT-GAUCHY M.,L'EDUCATION NATIONALE DANS LA FRANCE DE 1975. FRANCE FUT CULTURE ELITES R+D SCHOOL PLAN EDU/PROP EFFICIENCY...POLICY PREDICT CHARTS INDEX 20. PAGE 61 G1195
B65 ACADEM CREATE TREND INTELL

WARNER A.W.,THE IMPACT OF SCIENCE ON TECHNOLOGY. UNIV INTELL SOCIETY NAT/G ACT/RES PLAN PROB/SOLV BUDGET OPTIMAL GEN/METH. PAGE 62 G1214
B65 DECISION TEC/DEV CREATE POLICY

KREITH K.,"PEACE RESEARCH AND GOVERNMENT POLICY." INTELL NAT/G DIPLOM ECO/TAC CONTROL ARMS/CONT WAR PERCEPT...DECISION IDEA/COMP. PAGE 31 G0619
S65 PEACE STYLE OBS

MARK M.,"BEYOND SOVEREIGNTY." WOR+45 WOR-45 ECO/UNDEV BAL/PWR INT/TRADE NUC/PWR REV WAR MARXISM NEW/LIB BIBLIOG. PAGE 36 G0706
C65 NAT/LISM NAT/G DIPLOM

RASER J.R.,"DETERRENCE RESEARCH* PAST PROGRESS AND FUTURE NEEDS." INTELL PLAN TEC/DEV NUC/PWR PERCEPT ...DECISION PSY SOC NET/THEORY. PAGE 46 G0905
L66 DETER BIBLIOG/A FUT

BUNGE M.,THE SEARCH FOR SYSTEM. VOL. 3, PART 1 OF STUDIES IN THE FOUNDATIONS METHODOLOGY, AND PHILOSOPHY OF SCIENCE. UNIV LAW INTELL KNOWL. PAGE 10 G0187
B67 PHIL/SCI METH GEN/LAWS CONCPT

BUNGE M.,THE SEARCH FOR TRUTH, VOL. 3, PART 2 OF STUDIES IN THE FOUNDATIONS, METHODOLOGY, AND PHILOSOPHY OF SCIENCE. UNIV INTELL KNOWL...CONCPT OBS PREDICT METH. PAGE 10 G0188
B67 PHIL/SCI TESTS GEN/LAWS RATIONAL

CHARLESWORTH J.C.,CONTEMPORARY POLITICAL ANALYSIS. INTELL...DECISION METH/CNCPT MATH STYLE CON/ANAL GAME ANTHOL 20. PAGE 11 G0222
B67 R+D IDEA/COMP CONCPT METH/COMP

NATIONAL SCIENCE FOUNDATION,DIRECTORY OF SELECTED RESEARCH INSTITUTES IN EASTERN EUROPE. BULGARIA CZECHOSLVK HUNGARY POLAND ROMANIA INTELL ACADEM NAT/G ACT/RES 20. PAGE 41 G0814
B67 INDEX R+D COM PHIL/SCI

ORLANS H.,CONTRACTING FOR ATOMS. USA+45 LAW INTELL ACADEM LG/CO NAT/G PLAN TEC/DEV CONTROL DETER ...TREND 20 AEC. PAGE 43 G0845
B67 NUC/PWR R+D PRODUC PEACE

CRANBERG L.,"SCIENCE, ETHICS, AND LAW." UNIV CREATE PLAN EDU/PROP INGP/REL PERS/REL ADJUST RATIONAL KNOWL MORAL...CONCPT IDEA/COMP 20. PAGE 13 G0260
S67 LAW PHIL/SCI INTELL

HABERER J.,"POLITICS AND THE COMMUNITY OF SCIENCE." USA+45 SOCIETY ACT/RES PARTIC ATTIT PHIL/SCI. PAGE 24 G0465
S67 LEAD SUPEGO INTELL LOBBY

HOFFER J.R.,"RELATIONSHIP OF NATURAL AND SOCIAL SCIENCES TO SOCIAL PROBLEMS AND CONTRIBUTION OF... SCIENTISTS TO SOLUTIONS." USA+45 COMPUTER TEC/DEV GP/REL KNOWL...SOC TREND. PAGE 26 G0521
S67 PROB/SOLV SOCIETY INTELL ACT/RES

LA PORTE T.,"DIFFUSION AND DISCONTINUITY IN SCIENCE, TECHNOLOGY AND PUBLIC AFFAIRS: RESULTS OF A SEARCH IN THE FIELD." USA+45 ACT/RES TEC/DEV PERS/REL ATTIT PHIL/SCI. PAGE 32 G0628
S67 INTELL ADMIN ACADEM GP/REL

MORTON J.A.,"A SYSTEMS APPROACH TO THE INNOVATION PROCESS: ITS USE IN THE BELL SYSTEM." USA+45 INTELL INDUS LG/CO CONSULT WORKER COMPUTER AUTOMAT DEMAND ...MGT CHARTS 20. PAGE 40 G0787
S67 TEC/DEV GEN/METH R+D COM/IND

ROBERTS E.B.,"THE PROBLEM OF AGING ORGANIZATIONS." INTELL PROB/SOLV ADMIN EXEC FEEDBACK EFFICIENCY PRODUC...GEN/LAWS 20. PAGE 47 G0926
S67 INDUS R+D MGT PLAN

WEINBERG A.M.,"CAN TECHNOLOGY REPLACE SOCIAL ENGINEERING?" SPACE USA+45 SOCIETY ACADEM GP/REL. PAGE 62 G1224
S67 TEC/DEV ACT/RES PROB/SOLV INTELL

INTERNATIONAL BANK FOR RECONSTRUCT. AND DEV....SEE IBRD

INTERNATIONAL CIVIL AVIATION ORGANIZATION....SEE INT/AVIATN

INTERNATIONAL COOPERATION ADMINISTRATION....SEE ICA

INTERNATIONAL COUNCIL OF SCIENTIFIC UNIONS....SEE ICSU

INTERNATIONAL COURT OF JUSTICE....SEE ICJ

INTERNATIONAL DEVELOPMENT ASSOCIATION....SEE INTL/DEV

INTERNATIONAL ECONOMIC ASSOCIATION....SEE INTL/ECON

INTERNATIONAL FINANCE CORPORATION....SEE INTL/FINAN

INTERNATIONAL GEOPHYSICAL YEAR....SEE IGY

INTERNATIONAL INTEGRATION....SEE INT/ORG, INT/REL

INTERNATIONAL LABOR ORGANIZATION....SEE ILO

INTERNATIONAL LAW....SEE INT/LAW

INTERNATIONAL MONETARY FUND....SEE IMF

INTERNATIONAL ORGANIZATIONS....SEE INT/ORG

INTERNATIONAL RELATIONS....SEE INT/REL

INTERNATIONAL SYSTEMS....SEE NET/THEORY+INT/REL+WOR+45

INTERNATIONAL TELECOMMUNICATIONS UNION....SEE ITU

INTERNATIONAL TRADE....SEE INT/TRADE

INTERNATIONAL WORKERS OF THE WORLD....SEE IWW

INTERSTATE COMMERCE COMMISSION....SEE ICC

INTERSTATE COMMISSION ON CRIME....SEE INTST/CRIM

INTERVENT....INTERVENTIONISM (MILITARY, POLITICAL, AND/OR
    ECONOMIC INTERFERENCE BY A SOVEREIGN STATE OR AN
    INTERNATIONAL AGENCY IN THE AFFAIRS OF ANOTHER
    SOVEREIGN STATE)

                                                          N19
VERNON R.,THE MYTH AND REALITY OF OUR URBAN   PLAN
PROBLEMS (PAMPHLET). USA+45 SOCIETY LOC/G ADMIN   MUNIC
COST 20 PRINCETN/U INTERVENT URBAN/RNWL. PAGE 61   HABITAT
G1197   PROB/SOLV

                                                          N47
FOX W.T.R.,UNITED STATES POLICY IN A TWO POWER   DIPLOM
WORLD. COM USA+45 USSR FORCES DOMIN AGREE NEUTRAL   FOR/AID
NUC/PWR ORD/FREE SOVEREIGN 20 COLD/WAR TREATY   POLICY
EUROPE/W INTERVENT. PAGE 20 G0389

INTERVIEWING....SEE INT, REC/INT

INTERVIEWS....SEE INTERVIEWS INDEX, P. XIV

INTGOV/REL....ADVISORY COMMISSION ON INTERGOVERNMENTAL
    RELATIONS

INTL/DEV....INTERNATIONAL DEVELOPMENT ASSOCIATION

INTL/ECON....INTERNATIONAL ECONOMIC ASSOCIATION

INTL/FINAN....INTERNATIONAL FINANCE CORPORATION

INTRAGROUP RELATIONS....SEE INGP/REL

INTRVN/ECO....INTERVENTION (ECONOMIC) - PHILOSOPHY OF
    GOVERNMENTAL INTERFERENCE IN DOMESTIC ECONOMIC AFFAIRS

INTST/CRIM....U.S. INTERSTATE COMMISSION ON CRIME

INVENTION....SEE CREATE

INVESTMENT....SEE FINAN

IOWA....IOWA

IRAN....SEE ALSO ISLAM

                                                          B53
MACK R.T.,RAISING THE WORLDS STANDARD OF LIVING.   WOR+45
IRAN INT/ORG VOL/ASSN EX/STRUC ECO/TAC WEALTH...MGT FOR/AID
METH/CNCPT STAT CONT/OBS INT TOT/POP VAL/FREE 20   INT/TRADE
UN. PAGE 35 G0690

                                                          B67
US SENATE COMM ON FOREIGN REL,ARMS SALES TO NEAR   WEAPON
EAST AND SOUTH ASIAN COUNTRIES. INDIA IRAN PAKISTAN FOR/AID

                                                          FORCES
WOR+45 PROC/MFG BAL/PWR DIPLOM...DECISION SENATE.   POLICY
PAGE 60 G1183

IRAQ....SEE ALSO ISLAM

IRELAND....SEE ALSO UK

IRGUN....IRGUN - PALESTINE REVOLUTIONARY ORGANIZATION

IRISH/AMER....IRISH AMERICANS

IRS....U.S. INTERNAL REVENUE SERVICE

                                                          B63
DEAN A.L.,FEDERAL AGENCY APPROACHES TO FIELD   ADMIN
MANAGEMENT (PAMPHLET). R+D DELIB/GP EX/STRUC   MGT
PROB/SOLV GOV/REL...CLASSIF BIBLIOG 20 FAA NASA   NAT/G
DEPT/HEW POSTAL/SYS IRS. PAGE 15 G0287   OP/RES

ISLAM....ISLAMIC WORLD; SEE ALSO APPROPRIATE NATIONS

                                                          S60
JAFFEE A.J.,"POPULATION TRENDS AND CONTROLS IN   ECO/UNDEV
UNDERDEVELOPED COUNTRIES." AFR FUT ISLAM L/A+17C   GEOG
S/ASIA CULTURE R+D FAM ACT/RES PLAN EDU/PROP
BIO/SOC RIGID/FLEX HEALTH...SOC STAT OBS CHARTS 20.
PAGE 28 G0555

                                                          S63
HOSKINS H.L.,"ARAB SOCIALISM IN THE UAR." ISLAM   ECO/DEV
USSR AGRI INDUS NAT/G TOP/EX CREATE DIPLOM EDU/PROP PLAN
DRIVE KNOWL PWR SOCISM...POLICY CONCPT TREND SUEZ   UAR
20. PAGE 27 G0530

                                                          B65
INT. BANK RECONSTR. DEVELOP.,ECONOMIC DEVELOPMENT   INDUS
OF KUWAIT. ISLAM KUWAIT AGRI FINAN MARKET EX/STRUC NAT/G
TEC/DEV ECO/TAC ADMIN WEALTH...OBS CON/ANAL CHARTS
20. PAGE 28 G0548

                                                          S65
BLOOMFIELD L.P.,"ARMS CONTROL AND THE DEVELOPING   ARMS/CONT
COUNTRIES." AFR ISLAM S/ASIA USA+45 VOL/ASSN   ECO/UNDEV
TEC/DEV DIPLOM REGION NUC/PWR...PREDICT TREND.   HYPO/EXP
PAGE 7 G0142   OBS

                                                          B66
HOPKINS J.F.K.,ARABIC PERIODICAL LITERATURE, 1961. BIBLIOG/A
ISLAM LAW CULTURE SECT...GEOG HEAL PHIL/SCI PSY SOC NAT/LISM
20. PAGE 27 G0528   TEC/DEV
                                                    INDUS

                                                          N67
US HOUSE COMM FOREIGN AFFAIRS,REPORT OF SPECIAL   ISLAM
STUDY MISSION TO THE NEAR EAST (PAMPHLET). ISRAEL   DIPLOM
USA+45 YEMEN ECO/UNDEV INT/ORG FOR/AID ARMS/CONT   FORCES
WAR WEAPON NAT/LISM PEACE...GEOG 20 UN HOUSE/REP.
PAGE 58 G1138

ISOLAT....ISOLATION AND COMMUNITY, CONDITIONS OF HIGH
    GROUP SEGREGATION

                                                          B52
CALLOT E.,LA SOCIETE ET SON ENVIRONNEMENT: ESSAI   SOCIETY
SUR LES PRINCIPES DES SCIENCES SOCIALES. GP/REL   PHIL/SCI
ADJUST CONSEN ISOLAT HABITAT PERCEPT PERSON   CULTURE
...BIBLIOG SOC/INTEG 20. PAGE 10 G0205

                                                          B65
MCGUIRE M.C.,SECRECY AND THE ARMS RACE* A THEORY OF DETER
THE ACCUMULATION OF STRATEGIC WEAPONS AND HOW   ARMS/CONT
SECRECY AFFECTS IT. DIPLOM NUC/PWR WEAPON ISOLAT   SIMUL
RATIONAL ORD/FREE WEALTH...ECOMETRIC MATH GEN/LAWS. GAME
PAGE 38 G0742

                                                          B67
RUSSELL B.,WAR CRIMES IN VIETNAM. USA+45 VIETNAM   WAR
FORCES DIPLOM WEAPON RACE/REL DISCRIM ISOLAT   CRIME
BIO/SOC 20 COLD/WAR RUSSELL/B. PAGE 48 G0949   ATTIT
                                                    POLICY

                                                          S67
KAHN H.,"CRITERIA FOR LONG-RANGE NUCLEAR CONTROL   NUC/PWR
POLICIES." WOR+45 INT/ORG TEC/DEV DOMIN DETER WAR   ARMS/CONT
WEAPON ISOLAT ORD/FREE POLICY. PAGE 29 G0571   BAL/PWR
                                                    DIPLOM

ISOLATION....SEE ISOLAT

ISRAEL....SEE ALSO JEWS, ISLAM

                                                          B65
BENTWICH J.S.,EDUCATION IN ISRAEL. ISRAEL CULTURE   SECT
STRATA PROB/SOLV TEC/DEV ADJUST ALL/VALS 20 JEWS.   EDU/PROP
PAGE 7 G0125   ACADEM
                                                    SCHOOL

B65
US DEPARTMENT OF DEFENSE,US SECURITY ARMS CONTROL, BIBLIOG/A
AND DISARMAMENT 1961-1965 (PAMPHLET). CHINA/COM COM ARMS/CONT
GERMANY/W ISRAEL SPACE USA+45 USSR WOR+45 FORCES NUC/PWR
EDU/PROP DETER EQUILIB PEACE ALL/VALS...GOV/COMP 20 DIPLOM
NATO. PAGE 57 G1118

N67
US HOUSE COMM FOREIGN AFFAIRS,REPORT OF SPECIAL ISLAM
STUDY MISSION TO THE NEAR EAST (PAMPHLET). ISRAEL DIPLOM
USA+45 YEMEN ECO/UNDEV INT/ORG FOR/AID ARMS/CONT FORCES
WAR WEAPON NAT/LISM PEACE...GEOG 20 UN HOUSE/REP.
PAGE 58 G1138

ISSUES (CURRENT SUBJECTS OF DISCOURSE)....SEE CONCPT, POLICY

ITAL/AMER....ITALIAN-AMERICANS

ITALY....SEE ALSO APPROPRIATE TIME/SPACE/CULTURE INDEX

B44
FULLER G.H.,MILITARY GOVERNMENT: A LIST OF BIBLIOG
REFERENCES (A PAMPHLET). ITALY UK USA-45 WOR-45 LAW DIPLOM
FORCES DOMIN ADMIN ARMS/CONT ORD/FREE PWR CIVMIL/REL
...DECISION 20 CHINJAP. PAGE 21 G0404 SOVEREIGN

S62
ALBONETTI A.,"IL SECONDO PROGRAMMA QUINQUENNALE R+D
1963-67 ED IL BILANCIO RICERCHE ED INVESTIMENTI PER PLAN
IL 1963 DELL'ERATOM." EUR+WWI FUT ITALY WOR+45 NUC/PWR
ECO/DEV SERV/IND INT/ORG TEC/DEV ECO/TAC ATTIT
SKILL WEALTH...MGT TIME/SEQ OEEC 20. PAGE 2 G0035

S63
FERRETTI B.,"IMPORTANZA E PROSPETTIVE DELL ENERGIA TEC/DEV
DI ORIGINE NUCLEARE." FUT ITALY WOR+45 INTELL R+D EXEC
ACT/RES CREATE HEALTH WEALTH...METH/CNCPT TIME/SEQ NUC/PWR
20. PAGE 19 G0365

B64
MILIBAND R.,THE SOCIALIST REGISTER: 1964. GERMANY/W MARXISM
ITALY UK LABOR POL/PAR ECO/TAC FOR/AID NUC/PWR SOCISM
...POLICY SOCIALIST IDEA/COMP 20 MAO NASSER/G. CAP/ISM
PAGE 39 G0769 PROB/SOLV

B65
OECD,THE MEDITERRANEAN REGIONAL PROJECT: ITALY; SCHOOL
EDUCATION AND DEVELOPMENT. ITALY SOCIETY STRATA EDU/PROP
FINAN NAT/G PROF/ORG WORKER PLAN PROB/SOLV ADMIN ECO/UNDEV
...STAT CHARTS METH 20 OECD. PAGE 42 G0833 ACADEM

S67
SINGH B.,"ITALIAN EXPERIENCE IN REGIONAL ECONOMIC ECO/UNDEV
DEVELOPMENT AND LESSONS FOR OTHER COUNTRIES." PLAN
EUR+WWI ITALY INDUS NAT/G ACT/RES REGION GP/REL ECO/TAC
EFFICIENCY EQUILIB PRODUC WEALTH. PAGE 51 G1007 CONTROL

ITO....INTERNATIONAL TRADE ORGANIZATION

ITU....INTERNATIONAL TELECOMMUNICATIONS UNION

IVORY COAST....SEE IVORY/CST

IVORY/CST....IVORY COAST; SEE ALSO AFR

IWW....INTERNATIONAL WORKERS OF THE WORLD

J

JACKSON W.G.F. G0550

JACKSON/A....PRESIDENT ANDREW JACKSON

JACKSON/RH....R.H. JACKSON

JACOB H. G0551

JACOB P.E. G0552

JACOBINISM....JACOBINISM: FRENCH DEMOCRATIC REVOLUTIONARY
DOCTRINE, 1789

JACOBS N. G0553

JACOBSON H.K. G0554

JAFFA/HU....H.U. JAFFA

JAFFEE A.J. G0555

JAIN G. G0556

JAKARTA....JAKARTA, INDONESIA

JAMAICA....SEE ALSO L/A+17C

JANDA K. G0557

JANET/P....PIERRE JANET

JANIS I.L. G0531

JANOWITZ M. G0558,G0559,G0560,G0561

JAPAN....SEE ALSO ASIA

JAPANESE AMERICANS....SEE NISEI

JARMO....JARMO, A PRE- OR EARLY HISTORIC SOCIETY

JASNY H. G0562

JASPERS/K....KARL JASPERS

B63
RUITENBEER H.M.,THE DILEMMA OF ORGANIZATIONAL PERSON
SOCIETY. CULTURE ECO/DEV MUNIC SECT TEC/DEV ROLE
EDU/PROP NAT/LISM ORD/FREE...NAT/COMP 20 RIESMAN/D ADMIN
WHYTE/WF MERTON/R MEAD/MARG JASPERS/K. PAGE 48 WORKER
G0945

JAT....A POLITICAL SYSTEM OF INDIA

JAURES/JL....JEAN LEON JAURES (FRENCH SOCIALIST 1859-1914)

JAVA....JAVA, INDONESIA; SEE ALSO INDONESIA

JEFFERSN/T....PRESIDENT THOMAS JEFFERSON

B57
DUPREE A.H.,SCIENCE IN THE FEDERAL GOVERNMENT; A NAT/G
HISTORY OF POLICIES AND ACTIVITIES TO 1940. USA-45 R+D
AGRI SCHOOL DELIB/GP WAR GOV/REL...PHIL/SCI BIBLIOG CREATE
18/20 DEPRESSION NEW/DEAL WWI JEFFERSN/T. PAGE 17 TEC/DEV
G0324

JEHOVA/WIT....JEHOVAHOS WITNESSES

JENCKS/C....C. JENCKS

JENKS C.W. G0563

JEWS....JEWS, JUDAISM

B65
BENTWICH J.S.,EDUCATION IN ISRAEL. ISRAEL CULTURE SECT
STRATA PROB/SOLV TEC/DEV ADJUST ALL/VALS 20 JEWS. EDU/PROP
PAGE 7 G0125 ACADEM
SCHOOL

JOHN BIRCH SOCIETY....SEE BIRCH/SOC

JOHN/XXII....POPE JOHN XXII

JOHN/XXIII....POPE JOHN XXIII

JOHNSN/ALB....ALBERT JOHNSON

JOHNSN/AND....PRESIDENT ANDREW JOHNSON

JOHNSON/D....D. JOHNSON

JOHNSON/LB ....PRESIDENT LYNDON BAINES JOHNSON

B64
KAUFMANN W.W.,THE MC NAMARA STRATEGY. TOP/EX FORCES
INSPECT BAL/PWR DIPLOM CONTROL DETER GUERRILLA WAR
NUC/PWR WEAPON COST PWR...METH/COMP 20 MCNAMARA/R PLAN
KENNEDY/JF JOHNSON/LB NATO DEPT/DEFEN. PAGE 30 PROB/SOLV
G0586

B65
WEISNER J.B.,WHERE SCIENCE AND POLITICS MEET. CHIEF
USA+45 ECO/DEV R+D FORCES PROB/SOLV DIPLOM FOR/AID NAT/G
CONTROL...PHIL/SCI PRESIDENT KENNEDY/JF JOHNSON/LB. POLICY
PAGE 63 G1228 TEC/DEV

JOHNSTN/GD....GEORGE D. JOHNSTON

JOHNSTON D.M. G0564

JOINT ECONOMIC COMMITTEE G0565

JONES G.N. G0041

JONES G.S. G0566

JONES J.M. G0567

JONESVILLE....JONESVILLE: LOCATION OF W.L. WARNEROS
"DEMOCRACY IN JONESVILLE"

JORDAN....SEE ALSO ISLAM

JOURNALISM....SEE PRESS

JUDGE....JUDGES; SEE ALSO ADJUD

TOMPKINS D.C.,STATE GOVERNMENT AND ADMINISTRATION: BIBLIOG/A **B54**
A BIBLIOGRAPHY. USA+45 USA-45 CONSTN LEGIS JUDGE LOC/G
BUDGET CT/SYS LOBBY...CHARTS 20. PAGE 55 G1077 PROVS
ADMIN

DAVIS K.C.,ADMINISTRATIVE LAW TREATISE (VOLS. I AND ADMIN **B58**
IV). NAT/G JUDGE PROB/SOLV ADJUD GP/REL 20 JURID
SUPREME/CT. PAGE 14 G0278 CT/SYS
EX/STRUC

UNIVERSAL REFERENCE SYSTEM,LAW, JURISPRUDENCE, AND BIBLIOG/A **B67**
JUDICIAL PROCESS (VOLUME VII). WOR+45 WOR-45 CONSTN LAW
NAT/G LEGIS JUDGE CT/SYS...INT/LAW COMPUT/IR JURID
GEN/METH METH. PAGE 56 G1101 ADJUD

FOREIGN POLICY ASSOCIATION,"US CONCERN FOR WORLD INT/LAW **S67**
LAW." USA+45 WOR+45 DELIB/GP JUDGE BAL/PWR CONFER INT/ORG
PEACE ORD/FREE 20 UN. PAGE 19 G0379 DIPLOM
ARMS/CONT

JUDICIAL PROCESS....SEE ADJUD

JUGOSLAVIA....SEE YUGOSLAVIA

JUNGK R. G0568

JUNKER ....JUNKER: REACTIONARY PRUSSIAN ARISTOCRACY

JURID....LAW

NORTHROP F.S.C.,THE MEETING OF EAST AND WEST. DRIVE **B46**
EUR+WWI FUT MOD/EUR UNIV WOR+45 WOR-45 INTELL TREND
SOCIETY EX/STRUC TOP/EX ACT/RES LEGIT CHOOSE ATTIT PEACE
PERCEPT RIGID/FLEX ALL/VALS...POLICY JURID OBS
TOT/POP. PAGE 42 G0826

GRIFFITH E.S.,RESEARCH IN POLITICAL SCIENCE: THE BIBLIOG **B48**
WORK OF PANELS OF RESEARCH COMMITTEE. APSA. WOR+45 PHIL/SCI
WOR-45 COM/IND R+D FORCES ACT/RES WAR...GOV/COMP DIPLOM
ANTHOL 20. PAGE 23 G0451 JURID

WRIGHT Q.,"THE PEACEFUL ADJUSTMENT OF INTERNATIONAL R+D **S55**
RELATIONS: PROBLEMS AND RESEARCH APPROACHES." UNIV METH/CNCPT
INTELL EDU/PROP ADJUD ROUTINE KNOWL SKILL...INT/LAW PEACE
JURID PHIL/SCI CLASSIF 20. PAGE 64 G1258

DAVIS K.C.,ADMINISTRATIVE LAW TREATISE (VOLS. I AND ADMIN **B58**
IV). NAT/G JUDGE PROB/SOLV ADJUD GP/REL 20 JURID
SUPREME/CT. PAGE 14 G0278 CT/SYS
EX/STRUC

MCDOUGAL M.S.,"PERSPECTIVES FOR A LAW OF OUTER INT/ORG **S58**
SPACE." FUT WOR+45 AIR CONSULT DELIB/GP TEC/DEV SPACE
CT/SYS ORD/FREE...POLICY JURID 20 UN. PAGE 37 G0736 INT/LAW

HALEY A.G.,FIRST COLLOQUIUM ON THE LAW OF OUTER SPACE **B59**
SPACE. WOR+45 INT/ORG ACT/RES PLAN BAL/PWR CONFER LAW
ATTIT PWR...POLICY JURID CHARTS ANTHOL 20. PAGE 24 SOVEREIGN
G0468 CONTROL

ATOMIC INDUSTRIAL FORUM,ATOMS FOR INDUSTRY: WORLD NUC/PWR **B60**
FORUM. WOR+45 FINAN COST UTIL...JURID ANTHOL 20. INDUS
PAGE 4 G0080 PLAN
PROB/SOLV

WOETZEL R.K.,THE INTERNATIONAL CONTROL OF AIRSPACE INT/ORG **B60**
AND OUTERSPACE. FUT WOR+45 AIR CONSTN STRUCT JURID
CONSULT PLAN TEC/DEV ADJUD RIGID/FLEX KNOWL SPACE
ORD/FREE PWR...TECHNIC GEOG MGT NEW/IDEA TREND INT/LAW
COMPUT/IR VAL/FREE 20 TREATY. PAGE 64 G1251

HAYTON R.D.,"THE ANTARCTIC SETTLEMENT OF 1959." FUT DELIB/GP **S60**
USA+45 WOR+45 WOR-45 STRUCT R+D INT/ORG EX/STRUC JURID
CREATE TEC/DEV LEGIT PEACE ATTIT SOVEREIGN DIPLOM
...TIME/SEQ 20 TREATY IGY. PAGE 25 G0495 REGION

MURPHY E.F.,WATER PURITY: A STUDY IN LEGAL CONTROL SEA **B61**
OF NATURAL RESOURCES. LOC/G ACT/RES PLAN TEC/DEV LAW
LOBBY GP/REL COST ATTIT HEALTH ORD/FREE...HEAL PROVS
JURID 20 WISCONSIN WATER. PAGE 40 G0797 CONTROL

TAUBENFELD H.J.,"A REGIME FOR OUTER SPACE." FUT INT/ORG **L61**
UNIV R+D ACT/RES PLAN BAL/PWR LEGIT ARMS/CONT ADJUD
ORD/FREE...POLICY JURID TREND UN TOT/POP 20 SPACE
COLD/WAR. PAGE 54 G1056

SCHILLING W.R.,"THE H-BOMB: HOW TO DECIDE WITHOUT PERSON **S61**
ACTUALLY CHOOSING." FUT USA+45 INTELL CONSULT ADMIN LEGIT
CT/SYS MORAL...JURID OBS 20 TRUMAN/HS. PAGE 49 NUC/PWR
G0966

BOCK E.A.,CASE STUDIES IN AMERICAN GOVERNMENT. POLICY **B62**
USA+45 ECO/DEV CHIEF EDU/PROP CT/SYS RACE/REL LEGIS
ORD/FREE...JURID MGT PHIL/SCI PRESIDENT CASEBOOK. IDEA/COMP
PAGE 8 G0146 NAT/G

YALEN R.,REGIONALISM AND WORLD ORDER. EUR+WWI ORD/FREE **B62**
WOR+45 WOR-45 INT/ORG VOL/ASSN DELIB/GP FORCES POLICY
TOP/EX BAL/PWR DIPLOM DOMIN REGION ARMS/CONT PWR
...JURID HYPO/EXP COLD/WAR 20. PAGE 64 G1261

CRANE R.D.,"LAW AND STRATEGY IN SPACE." FUT USA+45 CONCPT **S62**
WOR+45 AIR LAW INT/ORG NAT/G FORCES ACT/RES PLAN SPACE
BAL/PWR LEGIT ARMS/CONT COERCE ORD/FREE...POLICY
INT/LAW JURID SOC/EXP 20 TREATY. PAGE 13 G0261

WALTER E.,"VERS UNE CLASSIFICATION SCIENTIFIQUE DE PLAN **S62**
LA SOCIOLOGIA." UNIV CULTURE INTELL SOCIETY R+D CONCPT
ACT/RES LEGIT ROUTINE ATTIT KNOWL...JURID MGT TREND
GEN/LAWS 20. PAGE 62 G1208

HALEY A.G.,SPACE LAW AND GOVERNMENT. FUT USA+45 INT/ORG **B63**
WOR+45 LEGIS ACT/RES CREATE ATTIT RIGID/FLEX LAW
ORD/FREE PWR SOVEREIGN...POLICY JURID CONCPT CHARTS SPACE
VAL/FREE 20. PAGE 24 G0469

MCDOUGAL M.S.,LAW AND PUBLIC ORDER IN SPACE. FUT SPACE **B63**
USA+45 ACT/RES TEC/DEV ADJUD...POLICY INT/LAW JURID ORD/FREE
20. PAGE 37 G0739 DIPLOM
DECISION

MCDOUGAL M.S.,"THE ENJOYMENT AND ACQUISITION OF PLAN **L63**
RESOURCES IN OUTER SPACE." CHRIST-17C FUT WOR+45 TREND
WOR-45 LAW EXTR/IND INT/ORG ACT/RES CREATE TEC/DEV
ECO/TAC LEGIT COERCE HEALTH KNOWL ORD/FREE PWR
WEALTH...JURID HIST/WRIT VAL/FREE. PAGE 37 G0738

RECENT PUBLICATIONS ON GOVERNMENTAL PROBLEMS. FINAN BIBLIOG **B64**
INDUS ACADEM PLAN PROB/SOLV EDU/PROP ADJUD ADMIN AUTOMAT
BIO/SOC...MGT SOC. PAGE 1 G0017 LEGIS
JURID

COHEN M.,LAW AND POLITICS IN SPACE: SPECIFIC AND DELIB/GP **B64**
URGENT PROBLEMS IN THE LAW OF OUTER SPACE. LAW
CHINA/COM COM USA+45 USSR WOR+45 COM/IND INT/ORG INT/LAW
NAT/G LEGIT NUC/PWR ATTIT BIO/SOC...JURID CONCPT SPACE
CONGRESS 20 STALIN/J. PAGE 12 G0241

CONANT J.B.,TWO MODES OF THOUGHT: MY ENCOUNTERS PHIL/SCI **B64**
WITH SCIENCE AND EDUCATION....ART/METH JURID SOC SKILL
TREND. PAGE 13 G0249 MYTH
STYLE

MAGGS P.B.,"SOVIET VIEWPOINT ON NUCLEAR WEAPONS IN COM **S64**
INTERNATIONAL LAW." USSR WOR+45 INT/ORG FORCES LAW
DIPLOM ARMS/CONT ATTIT ORD/FREE PWR...POLICY JURID INT/LAW
CONCPT OBS TREND CON/ANAL GEN/LAWS VAL/FREE 20. NUC/PWR
PAGE 35 G0694

JENKS C.W.,SPACE LAW. DIPLOM DEBATE CONTROL SPACE **B65**
ORD/FREE TREATY 20 UN. PAGE 29 G0563 INT/LAW
JURID
INT/ORG

UNITED NATIONS,INTERNATIONAL SPACE BIBLIOGRAPHY. BIBLIOG **B66**
FUT INT/ORG TEC/DEV DIPLOM ARMS/CONT NUC/PWR SPACE

...JURID SOC UN. PAGE 56 G1093

PEACE
R+D

N66

US HOUSE COMM SCI ASTRONAUT,INQUIRIES, LEGISLATION, POLICY STUDIES RE: SCIENCE AND TECHNOLOGY: REVIEW AND FORECAST (PAMPHLET). FUT WOR+45 DELIB/GP PROB/SOLV...POLICY JURID TREND 20 CONGRESS. PAGE 58 G1144

TEC/DEV
R+D
PLAN
LEGIS

N66

US HOUSE COMM SCI ASTRONAUT,THE ADEQUACY OF TECHNOLOGY FOR POLLUTION ABATEMENT (PAMPHLET). WOR+45 PLAN PROB/SOLV CONFER ADMIN...JURID 20 POLLUTION. PAGE 58 G1145

HEALTH
POLICY
TEC/DEV
LEGIS

B67

HODGKINSON R.G.,THE ORIGINS OF THE NATIONAL HEALTH SERVICE: THE MEDICAL SERVICES OF THE NEW POOR LAW, 1834-1871. UK INDUS MUNIC WORKER PROB/SOLV EFFICIENCY ATTIT HEALTH WEALTH SOCISM...JURID SOC/WK 19/20. PAGE 26 G0519

HEAL
NAT/G
POLICY
LAW

B67

KAPLAN B.,AN UNHURRIED VIEW OF COPYRIGHT. FUT ...JURID 20. PAGE 29 G0575

TEC/DEV
LAW
LICENSE

B67

UNIVERSAL REFERENCE SYSTEM,LAW, JURISPRUDENCE, AND JUDICIAL PROCESS (VOLUME VII). WOR+45 WOR-45 CONSTN NAT/G LEGIS JUDGE CT/SYS...INT/LAW COMPUT/IR GEN/METH METH. PAGE 56 G1101

BIBLIOG/A
LAW
JURID
ADJUD

B67

US SENATE COMM AERO SPACE SCI,TREATY ON PRINCIPLES GOVERNING ACTIVITIES OF STATES IN EXPLORATION AND USE OF OUTER SPACE, INCLUDING...BODIES. DELIB/GP FORCES LEGIS DIPLOM...JURID 20 DEPT/STATE NASA DEPT/DEFEN UN. PAGE 60 G1170

SPACE
INT/LAW
ORD/FREE
PEACE

L67

NADER R.,"AUTOMOBILE DESIGN AND THE JUDICIAL PROCESS." USA+45 CT/SYS SUPEGO JURID. PAGE 40 G0799

LAW
ADJUD
TEC/DEV
PROC/MFG

S67

ALEXANDER L.,"PROTECTION OF PRIVACY IN BEHAVIORAL RESEARCH." WOR+45 ADJUD SANCTION ORD/FREE...JURID INT. PAGE 2 G0036

ACT/RES
POLICY
OBS/ENVIR

S67

CARY G.D.,"THE QUIET REVOLUTION IN COPYRIGHT* THE END OF THE 'PUBLICATION' CONCEPT." USA+45 LAW OP/RES TEC/DEV CONFER DEBATE EFFICIENCY...JURID CONGRESS. PAGE 11 G0217

COM/IND
POLICY
LICENSE
PRESS

S67

JOHNSTON D.M.,"LAW, TECHNOLOGY AND THE SEA." WOR+45 PLAN PROB/SOLV TEC/DEV CONFER ADJUD ORD/FREE ...POLICY JURID. PAGE 29 G0564

INT/LAW
INT/ORG
DIPLOM
NEUTRAL

S67

KOMESAR N.K.,"SECURITY INTERESTS IN GOVERNMENT CONTRACTS* WHEREIN THE TORTOISE WINS THE RES." USA+45 INDUS NAT/G OP/RES SANCTION. PAGE 31 G0613

POLICY
CT/SYS
PRIVIL
JURID

S67

RAMSEY J.A.,"THE STATUS OF INTERNATIONAL COPYRIGHTS." WOR+45 CREATE TEC/DEV DIPLOM CONFER CONTROL SANCTION OWN...POLICY JURID. PAGE 46 G0899

INT/LAW
INT/ORG
COM/IND
PRESS

S67

RICH G.S.,"THE PROPOSED PATENT LEGISLATION* SOME COMMENTS." USA+45 LAW R+D ACT/RES TEC/DEV CONFER EFFICIENCY OWN JURID. PAGE 46 G0916

LICENSE
POLICY
CREATE
CAP/ISM

S67

WHITTIER J.M.,"COMPULSORY POOLING AND UNITIZATION* DIE-HARD KANSAS." LAW PLAN EDU/PROP ATTIT...POLICY JURID PREDICT TREND METH/COMP 20. PAGE 63 G1236

LEGIS
MUNIC
INDUS
ECO/TAC

JURISPRUDENCE....SEE LAW

JURY....JURIES AND JURY BEHAVIOR; SEE ALSO DELIB/GP, ADJUD

JUSTICE DEPARTMENT....SEE DEPT/JUST

K

KADALIE/C....CLEMENTS KADALIE

KAHN H. G0569,G0570,G0571

KAISR/ALUM....KAISER ALUMINUM

KALACHEK E.D. G0817

KAMCHATKA....KAMCHATKA, U.S.S.R.

KANSAS....KANSAS

KANT/I....IMMANUEL KANT

B61

MCRAE R.,THE PROBLEM OF THE UNITY OF THE SCIENCES: BACON TO KANT. CREATE TASK KNOWL...PERS/COMP 16/18 BACON/F DESCARTE/R LEIBNITZ/G KANT/I DIDEROT/D. PAGE 38 G0748

PHIL/SCI
IDEA/COMP
PERSON

KANTOROVICH L.V. G0572

KAPINGAMAR....KAPINGAMARANGI

KAPLAN A. G0573,G0574

KAPLAN B. G0575

KAPLAN M.A. G0576,G0577

KARLIN S. G0070

KARNJAHAPRAKORN C. G0578

KASER M. G0579

KASHMIR....SEE ALSO S/ASIA

N19

MEZERIK A.G.,INTERNATIONAL POLICY 1965 (PAMPHLET). KASHMIR S/ASIA SPACE USA+45 VIETNAM WOR+45 ARMS/CONT RACE/REL DISCRIM PEACE PWR 20 UN. PAGE 39 G0762

DIPLOM
INT/ORG
POLICY
WAR

KASSOF A. G0580

KAST F.E. G0581

KATANGA....SEE ALSO AFR

KATZ S.M. G0582

KAUFMAN J.L. G0584

KAUFMANN F. G0585

KAUFMANN W.W. G0586

KAUNDA/K....KENNETH KAUNDA, PRESIDENT OF ZAMBIA

KAWALKOWSKI A. G0587

KAYSEN C. G0588

KECSKEMETI P. G0589

KEFAUVER/E....ESTES KEFAUVER

KEISER N.F. G0590

KEITA/M....MOBIDO KEITA

KEL/BRIAND....KELLOGG BRIAND PEACE PACT

KELLEY G.A. G0591

KELLEY H.H. G0531

KELLOG BRIAND PEACE PACT....SEE KEL/BRIAND

KELSEN/H....HANS KELSEN

KENNAN/G....GEORGE KENNAN

KENNEDY J.F. G0592

KENNEDY/J F....PRESIDENT JOHN F. KENNEDY

B61

HELLER D.,THE KENNEDY CABINET--AMERICA'S MEN OF DESTINY. NAT/G CHIEF CONSULT ADMIN CONTROL GOV/REL ...MGT 20 DEPT/LABOR DEPT/STATE DEPT/JUST DEPT/DEFEN KENNEDY/J. PAGE 26 G0504

EX/STRUC
CONFER
DELIB/GP
TOP/EX

B62

KENNEDY J.F.,TO TURN THE TIDE. SPACE AGRI INT/ORG

DIPLOM

FORCES TEC/DEV ADMIN NUC/PWR PEACE WEALTH...ANTHOL CHIEF
20 KENNEDY/JF CIV/RIGHTS. PAGE 30 G0592 POLICY
NAT/G

B62
US SENATE COMM GOVT OPERATIONS.ADMINISTRATION OF ORD/FREE
NATIONAL SECURITY. USA+45 CHIEF PLAN PROB/SOLV ADMIN
TEC/DEV DIPLOM ATTIT...POLICY DECISION 20 NAT/G
KENNEDY/JF RUSK/D MCNAMARA/R BUNDY/M HERTER/C. CONTROL
PAGE 60 G1177

B63
PACHTER H.M.,COLLISION COURSE; THE CUBAN MISSILE WAR
CRISIS AND COEXISTENCE. CUBA USA+45 DIPLOM BAL/PWR
ARMS/CONT PEACE MARXISM...DECISION INT/LAW 20 NUC/PWR
COLD/WAR KHRUSH/N KENNEDY/JF CASTRO/F. PAGE 43 DETER
G0854

N63
COMMITTEE ECONOMIC DEVELOPMENT.TAXES AND TRADE: 20 FINAN
YEARS OF CED POLICY (PAMPHLET). USA+45 ECO/DEV PLAN ECO/TAC
BUDGET LEAD...POLICY KENNEDY/JF PRESIDENT. PAGE 13 NAT/G
G0246 DELIB/GP

B64
KAUFMANN W.W.,THE MC NAMARA STRATEGY. TOP/EX FORCES
INSPECT BAL/PWR DIPLOM CONTROL DETER GUERRILLA WAR
NUC/PWR WEAPON COST PWR...METH/COMP 20 MCNAMARA/R PLAN
KENNEDY/JF JOHNSON/LB NATO DEPT/DEFEN. PAGE 30 PROB/SOLV
G0586

B64
MANSFIELD E.,MONOPOLY POWER AND ECONOMIC LG/CO
PERFORMANCE: AN INTRODUCTION TO A CURRENT ISSUE OF PWR
PUBLIC POLICY. ECO/DEV INDUS NAT/G PLAN CAP/ISM ECO/TAC
PRICE CONTROL LOBBY EFFICIENCY PRODUC...POLICY 20 MARKET
CONGRESS KENNEDY/JF MONOPOLY. PAGE 36 G0701

B65
WEISNER J.B.,WHERE SCIENCE AND POLITICS MEET. CHIEF
USA+45 ECO/DEV R+D FORCES PROB/SOLV DIPLOM FOR/AID NAT/G
CONTROL...PHIL/SCI PRESIDENT KENNEDY/JF JOHNSON/LB. POLICY
PAGE 63 G1228 TEC/DEV

B66
FREIDEL F.,AMERICAN ISSUES IN THE TWENTIETH DIPLOM
CENTURY. SOCIETY FINAN ECO/TAC FOR/AID CONTROL POLICY
NUC/PWR WAR RACE/REL PEACE ATTIT...ANTHOL T 20 NAT/G
WILSON/W ROOSEVLT/F KENNEDY/JF TRUMAN/HS. PAGE 20 ORD/FREE
G0391

B67
HALLE L.J.,THE COLD WAR AS HISTORY. USSR WOR+45 DIPLOM
ECO/TAC FOR/AID NUC/PWR WAR PEACE ORD/FREE BAL/PWR
...MAJORIT TREND 20 COLD/WAR KENNEDY/JF KHRUSH/N
BERLIN/BLO. PAGE 24 G0470

KENNEDY/RF....ROBERT F. KENNEDY

KENT A. G0593

KENTUCKY....KENTUCKY

KENWORTHY L.S. G0594

KENYA....KENYA

KENYATTA....JOMO KENYATTA

KEYNES/G....GEOFFREY KEYNES

KEYNES/JM....JOHN MAYNARD KEYNES

B61
MCCRACKEN H.L.,KEYNESIAN ECONOMICS IN THE STREAM OF ECO/TAC
ECONOMIC THOUGHT. FINAN MARKET BARGAIN EFFICIENCY DEMAND
OPTIMAL...PHIL/SCI CONCPT IDEA/COMP BIBLIOG 18/20 ECOMETRIC
KEYNES/JM. PAGE 37 G0732

KHASAS....KHASAS (ANCIENT COMMUNITY)

KHRUSH/N....NIKITA KHRUSHCHEV

B63
PACHTER H.M.,COLLISION COURSE; THE CUBAN MISSILE WAR
CRISIS AND COEXISTENCE. CUBA USA+45 DIPLOM BAL/PWR
ARMS/CONT PEACE MARXISM...DECISION INT/LAW 20 NUC/PWR
COLD/WAR KHRUSH/N KENNEDY/JF CASTRO/F. PAGE 43 DETER
G0854

B63
US SENATE.DOCUMENTS ON INTERNATIONAL AS"ECTS OF SPACE
EXPLORATION AND USE OF OUTER SPACE, 1954-62: STAFF UTIL
REPORT FOR COMM AERON SPACE SCI. USA+45 USSR LEGIS GOV/REL
LEAD CIVMIL/REL PEACE...POLICY INT/LAW ANTHOL 20 DIPLOM
CONGRESS NASA KHRUSH/N. PAGE 59 G1162

B65
JASNY H.,KHRUSHCHEV'S CROP POLICY. USSR ECO/DEV AGRI
PLAN MARXISM...STAT 20 KHRUSH/N RESOURCE/N. PAGE 29 NAT/G
G0562 POLICY
ECO/TAC

B66
BLOOMFIELD L.P.,KHRUSHCHEV AND THE ARMS RACE. ARMS/CONT
USA+45 USSR ECO/DEV BAL/PWR EDU/PROP CONFER NUC/PWR COM
ATTIT...CHARTS 20 KHRUSH/N. PAGE 7 G0143 POLICY
DIPLOM

B67
HALLE L.J.,THE COLD WAR AS HISTORY. USSR WOR+45 DIPLOM
ECO/TAC FOR/AID NUC/PWR WAR PEACE ORD/FREE BAL/PWR
...MAJORIT TREND 20 COLD/WAR KENNEDY/JF KHRUSH/N
BERLIN/BLO. PAGE 24 G0470

S67
AVTORKHANOV A.,"A NEW AGRARIAN REVOLUTION." COM AGRI
USSR ECO/DEV PLAN TEC/DEV ADMIN CONTROL OPTIMAL METH/COMP
WEALTH SOCISM 20 KHRUSH/N STALIN/J. PAGE 4 G0082 MARXISM
OWN

S67
CLEMENS W.C.,"CHINESE NUCLEAR TESTS: TRENDS AND NUC/PWR
PORTENTS." CHINA/COM USA+45 USSR FORCES PLAN WEAPON
TEC/DEV ARMS/CONT WAR PWR...DECISION 20 MAO POLICY
KHRUSH/N. PAGE 12 G0234 DIPLOM

KIERKE/S....SOREN KIERKEGAARD

KIETH-LUCAS A. G0595

KILE O.M. G0596

KIM/IL-SON....IL-SON KIM

KIN....KINSHIP (EXCEPT NUCLEAR FAMILY)

B58
BIDWELL P.W.,RAW MATERIALS: A STUDY OF AMERICAN EXTR/IND
POLICY. USA+45 USA-45 ECO/UNDEV AGRI INDUS KIN ECO/DEV
CREATE PLAN ECO/TAC WAR PEACE ATTIT DRIVE WEALTH
...STAT CHARTS CONGRESS VAL/FREE. PAGE 7 G0135

S61
DALTON G.,"ECONOMIC THEORY AND PRIMITIVE SOCIETY" ECO/UNDEV
(BMR)" UNIV AGRI KIN TEC/DEV ECO/TAC REGION HABITAT METH
SKILL...METH/COMP BIBLIOG. PAGE 14 G0274 PHIL/SCI
SOC

B66
WARD B.,NATIONALISM AND IDEOLOGY. ECO/UNDEV KIN IDEA/COMP
CREATE CAP/ISM FOR/AID ALL/VALS MARXISM...POLICY NAT/LISM
SOC. PAGE 62 G1211 ATTIT

B67
BENNETT J.W.,HUTTERIAN BRETHREN; THE AGRICULTURAL SECT
ECONOMY AND SOCIAL ORGANIZATION OF A COMMUNAL AGRI
PEOPLE. USA+45 SOCIETY FAM KIN TEC/DEV ADJUST...MGT STRUCT
AUD/VIS GP/COMP 20. PAGE 6 G0121 GP/REL

N67
ASIAN STUDIES CENTER.FOUR ARTICLES ON POPULATION ASIA
AND FAMILY LIFE IN TAIWAN (ASIAN STUDIES PAPERS, FAM
REPRINT SERIES NO. 2). CULTURE STRATA ECO/UNDEV CENSUS
AGRI INDUS R+D KIN MUNIC...GEOG SOC CHARTS 20. ANTHOL
PAGE 4 G0072

KING....KING AND KINGSHIP; SEE ALSO CHIEF, CONSERVE, TRADIT

KING/MAR/L....REVEREND MARTIN LUTHER KING

KINGSTON-MCCLOUG E. G0597

KINSEY/A....ALFRED KINSEY

KINTNER W.R. G0598,G0599

KIPLING/R....RUDYARD KIPLING

KIRK/GRAY....GRAYSON KIRK

KISER M. G0601

KISSINGER H.A. G0602,G0603,G0604

KKK....KU KLUX KLAN

KLAPPER J.T. G0605

KLOTSCHE J.M. G0606

KLUCKHN/C....CLYDE KLUCKHOHN

KNAPP D.C. G0607

KNO/TEST....TESTS FOR FACTUAL KNOWLEDGE

S50
KAPLAN A.,"THE PREDICTION OF SOCIAL AND   PWR
TECHNOLOGICAL EVENTS." VOL/ASSN CONSULT ACT/RES   KNO/TEST
CREATE OP/RES PLAN ROUTINE PERSON...POLICY
METH/CNCPT STAT QU/SEMANT SYS/QU TESTS CENSUS TREND
20. PAGE 29 G0574

B52
CURRENT TRENDS IN PSYCHOLOGY,PSYCHOLOGY IN THE   NAT/G
WORLD EMERGENCY. USA+45 CONSULT FORCES ACT/RES PLAN   PSY
SKILL...DECISION OBS APT/TEST KNO/TEST PERS/TEST
TREND CHARTS 20. PAGE 14 G0266

B54
WRIGHT Q.,PROBLEMS OF STABILITY AND PROGRESS IN   INT/ORG
INTERNATIONAL RELATIONSHIPS. FUT WOR+45 WOR-45   CONCPT
SOCIETY LEGIS CREATE TEC/DEV ECO/TAC EDU/PROP ADJUD   DIPLOM
WAR PEACE ORD/FREE PWR...KNO/TEST TREND GEN/LAWS
20. PAGE 64 G1257

B55
MIKSCHE F.O.,ATOMIC WEAPONS AND ARMIES. FUT WOR+45   TEC/DEV
WOR-45 SOCIETY COERCE DETER WEAPON PWR...POLICY   FORCES
WELF/ST PSY CONCPT INT SYS/QU KNO/TEST TOT/POP 20.   NUC/PWR
PAGE 39 G0765

B58
TELLER E.A.,OUR NUCLEAR FUTURE. SOCIETY FORCES   FUT
TEC/DEV EDU/PROP KNOWL ORD/FREE...STAND/INT SYS/QU   PHIL/SCI
KNO/TEST AUD/VIS CHARTS SIMUL 20. PAGE 54 G1062   NUC/PWR
                                                       WAR

S59
GOLDHAMMER H.,"SOME OBSERVATIONS ON POLITICAL   COMPUT/IR
GAMING." FUT WOR+45 R+D NAT/G ACT/RES CREATE CHOOSE   DECISION
ATTIT PWR...POLICY CONCPT METH/CNCPT STYLE KNO/TEST   DIPLOM
TREND HYPO/EXP GAME GEN/METH METH 20. PAGE 22 G0426

B60
ARROW K.J.,MATHEMATICAL METHODS IN THE SOCIAL   MATH
SCIENCES, 1959. TEC/DEV CHOOSE UTIL PERCEPT   PSY
...KNO/TEST GAME SIMUL ANTHOL. PAGE 4 G0070   MGT

S67
DEUTSCH K.W.,"ARMS CONTROL AND EUROPEAN UNITY* THE   ARMS/CONT
NEXT TEN YEARS." USA+45 ELITES NAT/G BAL/PWR DIPLOM   PEACE
NUC/PWR...INT KNO/TEST NATO EEC. PAGE 15 G0300   REGION
                                                       PLAN

KNORR K. G0608

KNOWL....ENLIGHTENMENT, KNOWLEDGE

N
AMERICAN DOCUMENTATION INST,DOCUMENTATION   BIBLIOG/A
ABSTRACTS. WOR+45 NAT/G COMPUTER CREATE TEC/DEV   AUTOMAT
DIPLOM EDU/PROP REGION KNOWL...PHIL/SCI CLASSIF   COMPUT/IR
LING. PAGE 3 G0051   R+D

B11
BERGSON H.,CREATIVE EVOLUTION. FUT WOR+45 WOR-45   BIO/SOC
INTELL AGRI R+D ATTIT PERCEPT PERSON RIGID/FLEX   KNOWL
...RELATIV PHIL/SCI PSY METH/CNCPT MATH HIST/WRIT
TREND HYPO/EXP TOT/POP. PAGE 7 G0127

N19
US ATOMIC ENERGY COMMISSION,ATOMIC ENERGY IN USE   OP/RES
(PAMPHLET). R+D RISK EFFICIENCY HEALTH KNOWL   TEC/DEV
ORD/FREE...PHIL/SCI CONCPT METH/CNCPT CHARTS   NUC/PWR
LAB/EXP 20 AEC. PAGE 56 G1106   CREATE

B23
DRAPER J.W.,HISTORY OF THE CONFLICT BETWEEN   SECT
RELIGION AND SCIENCE. WOR-45 INTELL SOCIETY R+D   KNOWL
CREATE PLAN TEC/DEV EDU/PROP ATTIT PWR...PHIL/SCI
CONCPT OBS TIME/SEQ TREND GEN/LAWS TOT/POP. PAGE 16
G0314

B29
DEWEY J.,THE QUEST FOR CERTAINTY. GP/REL RATIONAL   PHIL/SCI
UTOPIA ATTIT MORAL ORD/FREE PWR...MYTH HIST/WRIT.   PERSON
PAGE 15 G0301   PERCEPT
                                                       KNOWL

B40
ZNANIECKI F.,THE SOCIAL ROLE OF THE MAN OF   ROLE
KNOWLEDGE. UNIV SOCIETY STRUCT TEC/DEV...EPIST   INTELL
PHIL/SCI SOC NEW/IDEA 20. PAGE 65 G1269   KNOWL
                                                       INGP/REL

S42
LASSWELL H.D.,"THE RELATION OF IDEOLOGICAL   ATTIT
INTELLIGENCE TO PUBLIC POLICY." WOR+45 WOR-45   DECISION
SOCIETY DELIB/GP ACT/RES CREATE PLAN DIPLOM
EDU/PROP CHOOSE KNOWL PWR...POLICY SOC TREND
GEN/LAWS 20. PAGE 32 G0638

B45
BUSH V.,SCIENCE, THE ENDLESS FRONTIER. FUT USA-45   R+D
INTELL STRATA ACT/RES CREATE PLAN EDU/PROP ADMIN   NAT/G
NUC/PWR PEACE ATTIT HEALTH KNOWL...MAJORIT HEAL MGT
PHIL/SCI CONCPT OBS TREND 20. PAGE 10 G0195

B45
SMYTH H.D.,ATOMIC ENERGY FOR MILITARY PURPOSES.   R+D
USA-45 NAT/G PLAN TEC/DEV KNOWL...MATH CON/ANAL   TIME/SEQ
CHARTS LAB/EXP SIMUL 20. PAGE 52 G1017   NUC/PWR

B46
BUSH V.,ENDLESS HORIZONS. FUT USA-45 INTELL NAT/G   R+D
CONSULT ACT/RES CREATE PLAN EDU/PROP DRIVE   KNOWL
...MAJORIT HEAL MGT PHIL/SCI CONCPT OBS TREND   PEACE
GEN/METH TOT/POP 20. PAGE 10 G0196

L46
MASTERS D.,"ONE WORLD OR NONE." FUT WOR+45 INTELL   POLICY
INT/ORG ACT/RES EDU/PROP DETER ATTIT RIGID/FLEX   PHIL/SCI
SUPEGO KNOWL...STAT TREND ORG/CHARTS 20. PAGE 36   ARMS/CONT
G0719   NUC/PWR

B47
LASSWELL H.D.,THE ANALYSIS OF POLITICAL BEHAVIOUR: R+D
AN EMPIRICAL APPROACH. WOR+45 CULTURE NAT/G FORCES   ACT/RES
EDU/PROP ADMIN ATTIT PERCEPT KNOWL...PHIL/SCI PSY   ELITES
SOC NEW/IDEA OBS INT GEN/METH NAZI 20. PAGE 32
G0639

B50
CANTRIL H.,TENSIONS THAT CAUSE WAR. UNIV CULTURE   SOCIETY
R+D CREATE EDU/PROP DRIVE PERSON KNOWL ORD/FREE   PHIL/SCI
...HUM PSY SOC OBS CENSUS TREND CON/ANAL SOC/EXP   PEACE
SIMUL GEN/METH ANTHOL COLD/WAR TOT/POP. PAGE 11
G0206

B50
CROWTHER J.G.,SCIENCE AT WAR. EUR+WWI PLAN TEC/DEV   R+D
DOMIN COERCE NUC/PWR WEAPON KNOWL PWR...CONCPT OBS   FORCES
TREND VAL/FREE 20. PAGE 14 G0265   WAR
                                                       UK

B51
HUXLEY J.,FREEDOM AND CULTURE. UNIV LAW SOCIETY R+D   CULTURE
ACADEM SCHOOL CREATE SANCTION ATTIT KNOWL...HUM   ORD/FREE
ANTHOL 20. PAGE 27 G0540   PHIL/SCI
                                                       IDEA/COMP

B51
LEWIN K.,FIELD THEORY IN SOCIAL SCIENCE: SELECTED   PHIL/SCI
THEORETICAL PAPERS. UNIV CREATE DRIVE PERCEPT KNOWL   HYPO/EXP
...METH/CNCPT CONT/OBS CHARTS GEN/METH METH
VAL/FREE 20. PAGE 33 G0661

S51
BERGMANN G.,"IDEOLOGY" (BMR)" UNIV PERCEPT KNOWL   PHIL/SCI
...IDEA/COMP METH. PAGE 7 G0126   CONCPT
                                                       LOG
                                                       ALL/IDEOS

B52
DAY E.E.,EDUCATION FOR FREEDOM AND RESPONSIBILITY.   SCHOOL
FUT USA+45 CULTURE CONSULT EDU/PROP ATTIT SKILL   KNOWL
...MGT CONCPT OBS GEN/LAWS COLD/WAR 20. PAGE 14
G0282

B52
HAYEK F.A.,THE COUNTER-REVOLUTION OF SCIENCE. UNIV   PERCEPT
INTELL R+D VOL/ASSN CREATE EDU/PROP...PHIL/SCI SOC   KNOWL
OBS TIME/SEQ TREND GEN/METH. PAGE 25 G0494

L52
ROYAL INST. INT. AFF.,"ANNUAL REPORT OF THE   R+D
COUNCIL: 1951-1952." WOR+45 CREATE KNOWL...MGT   EDU/PROP
COLD/WAR CMN/WLTH TOT/POP VAL/FREE 20. PAGE 48
G0943

S52
KECSKEMETI P.,"THE 'POLICY SCIENCES': ASPIRATION   CREATE
AND OUTLOOK." UNIV CULTURE INTELL SOCIETY STRUCT   NEW/IDEA
EDU/PROP ATTIT PERCEPT RIGID/FLEX KNOWL...PHIL/SCI
METH/CNCPT OBS 20. PAGE 30 G0589

B53
CALDWELL L.K.,RESEARCH METHODS IN PUBLIC   BIBLIOG/A
ADMINISTRATION: AN OUTLINE OF TOPICS AND READINGS   METH/COMP
(PAMPHLET). LAW ACT/RES COMPUTER KNOWL...SOC STAT   ADMIN
GEN/METH 20. PAGE 10 G0201   OP/RES

B53
EASTON D.,THE POLITICAL SYSTEM, AN INQUIRY INTO THE R+D
STATE POLITICAL SCIENCE. USA+45 INTELL CREATE   PERCEPT
EDU/PROP RIGID/FLEX KNOWL SKILL...PHIL/SCI NEW/IDEA
STERTYP TOT/POP 20. PAGE 17 G0329

B53
HOVLAND C.I.,COMMUNICATION AND PERSUASION: PSY
PSYCHOLOGICAL STUDIES OF OPINION CHANGE. INTELL   EDU/PROP
SOCIETY ECO/DEV COM/IND R+D SERV/IND CREATE TEC/DEV
ATTIT RIGID/FLEX KNOWL NEW/IDEA. PAGE 27 G0531

B54
COMBS C.H.,DECISION PROCESSES. INTELL SOCIETY   MATH
DELIB/GP CREATE TEC/DEV DOMIN LEGIT EXEC CHOOSE   DECISION
DRIVE RIGID/FLEX KNOWL PWR...PHIL/SCI SOC
METH/CNCPT CONT/OBS REC/INT PERS/TEST SAMP/SIZ BIOG
SOC/EXP WORK. PAGE 13 G0245

S54
DEUTSCH K.W.,"GAME THEORY AND POLITICS: SOME   DECISION
PROBLEMS OF APPLICATION." FUT WOR+45 SOCIETY R+D   GEN/METH
KNOWL PWR...CONCPT METH/CNCPT MATH QUANT GAME SIMUL
VAL/FREE 20. PAGE 15 G0295

S54
POLANYI M.,"ON THE INTRODUCTION OF SCIENCE INTO   INTELL
MORAL SUBJECTS." FUT WOR+45 ACT/RES ATTIT KNOWL   PHIL/SCI
...CONCPT NEW/IDEA 20. PAGE 45 G0882

S54
PYE L.W.,"EASTERN NATIONALISM AND WESTERN POLICY."   CREATE
ASIA S/ASIA USA+45 USA-45 SOCIETY PLAN DIPLOM KNOWL   ACT/RES
TOT/POP 20. PAGE 46 G0896   NAT/LISM

B55
MOCH J.,HUMAN FOLLY: DISARM OR PERISH. USA+45   FUT
WOR+45 SOCIETY INT/ORG NAT/G ACT/RES EDU/PROP ATTIT   DELIB/GP
PERSON KNOWL ORD/FREE PWR...MAJORIT TOT/POP   ARMS/CONT
COLD/WAR 20. PAGE 39 G0776   NUC/PWR

B55
SHUBIK M.,READINGS IN GAME THEORY AND POLITICAL   MATH
BEHAVIOR. WOR+45 FORCES CREATE ROUTINE WAR PEACE   DECISION
PERCEPT KNOWL PWR...PSY SOC CONCPT METH/CNCPT STAT   DIPLOM
CHARTS HYPO/EXP GAME METH VAL/FREE 20. PAGE 50
G0991

S55
GLADSTONE A.E.,"THE POSSIBILITY OF PREDICTING   PHIL/SCI
REACTIONS TO INTERNATIONAL EVENTS." UNIV SOCIETY   CONCPT
NAT/G FORCES CREATE EDU/PROP COERCE WAR ATTIT
PERSON KNOWL PWR SKILL...METH/CNCPT NEW/IDEA
ORG/CHARTS. PAGE 21 G0420

S55
MILLER J.G.,"TOWARD A GENERAL THEORY FOR THE   CONCPT
BEHAVIORAL SCIENCES" (BMR)" CREATE ALL/VALS KNOWL   OP/RES
...CON/ANAL CHARTS HYPO/EXP SIMUL BIBLIOG 20.   METH/CNCPT
PAGE 39 G0773   COMPUTER

S55
WRIGHT Q.,"THE PEACEFUL ADJUSTMENT OF INTERNATIONAL   R+D
RELATIONS: PROBLEMS AND RESEARCH APPROACHES." UNIV   METH/CNCPT
INTELL EDU/PROP ADJUD ROUTINE KNOWL SKILL...INT/LAW   PEACE
JURID PHIL/SCI CLASSIF 20. PAGE 64 G1258

B56
BLACKETT P.M.S.,ATOMIC WEAPONS AND EAST-WEST   FORCES
RELATIONS. FUT WOR+45 INT/ORG DELIB/GP COERCE ATTIT   PWR
RIGID/FLEX KNOWL...RELATIV HIST/WRIT TREND GEN/METH   ARMS/CONT
COLD/WAR 20. PAGE 7 G0138   NUC/PWR

B56
THOMAS M.,ATOMIC ENERGY AND CONGRESS. USA+45 NAT/G   LEGIS
ACT/RES PLAN TEC/DEV EDU/PROP ROUTINE KNOWL PWR   ADMIN
SKILL...PHIL/SCI NEW/IDEA TIME/SEQ CHARTS METH   NUC/PWR
CONGRESS VAL/FREE 20 AEC. PAGE 54 G1067

B56
WASSERMAN P.,INFORMATION FOR ADMINISTRATORS: A   BIBLIOG
GUIDE TO PUBLICATIONS AND SERVICES FOR MANAGEMENT   MGT
IN BUSINESS AND GOVERNMENT. R+D LOC/G NAT/G   KNOWL
PROF/ORG VOL/ASSN PRESS...PSY SOC STAT 20. PAGE 62   EDU/PROP
G1219

S56
MILLER G.A.,"THE MAGICAL NUMBER SEVEN, PLUS OR   LAB/EXP
MINUS TWO: SOME LIMITS ON OUR CAPACITY FOR   KNOWL
PROCESSING INFORMATION." PERS/REL...PSY METH/CNCPT   PERCEPT
LING CHARTS BIBLIOG 20. PAGE 39 G0772   COMPUT/IR

B57
KISSINGER H.A.,NUCLEAR WEAPONS AND FOREIGN POLICY.   PLAN
FUT USA+45 WOR+45 INT/ORG FORCES ACT/RES TEC/DEV   DETER

DIPLOM ARMS/CONT COERCE ATTIT KNOWL PWR...DECISION   NUC/PWR
GEOG CHARTS 20. PAGE 31 G0602

S57
EASTON D.,"AN APPROACH TO THE ANALYSIS OF POLITICAL   STRUCT
SYSTEMS." R+D EDU/PROP KNOWL SKILL...POLICY SOC   PHIL/SCI
METH/CNCPT NEW/IDEA SELF/OBS CHARTS GEN/METH
TOT/POP. PAGE 17 G0331

S57
FISHMAN B.G.,"PUBLIC POLICY AND POLITICAL   ECO/DEV
CONSIDERATIONS." USA+45 SOCIETY NAT/G ACT/RES   CONSULT
CREATE PLAN DIPLOM KNOWL ORD/FREE...CONCPT GEN/METH
20. PAGE 19 G0370

B58
NOEL-BAKER D.,THE ARMS RACE. WOR+45 NAT/G DELIB/GP   FUT
ACT/RES TEC/DEV EDU/PROP NUC/PWR ATTIT KNOWL PWR   INT/ORG
...CONCPT OBS LEAGUE/NAT 20 COLD/WAR. PAGE 42 G0823   ARMS/CONT
                                                      PEACE

B58
TELLER E.A.,OUR NUCLEAR FUTURE. SOCIETY FORCES   FUT
TEC/DEV EDU/PROP KNOWL ORD/FREE...STAND/INT SYS/QU   PHIL/SCI
KNO/TEST AUD/VIS CHARTS SIMUL 20. PAGE 54 G1062   NUC/PWR
                                                      WAR

S58
ANDERSON N.,"INTERNATIONAL SEMINARS: AN ANALYSIS   INT/ORG
AND AN EVALUATION." WOR+45 R+D ACT/RES CREATE PLAN   DELIB/GP
REGION ATTIT KNOWL SKILL...SOC REC/INT PERS/TEST
CHARTS 20. PAGE 3 G0057

S58
KLAPPER J.T.,"WHAT WE KNOW ABOUT THE EFFECTS OF   ACT/RES
MASS COMMUNICATION: THE BRINK OF HOPE" (BMR)"   PERCEPT
COM/IND KNOWL...METH/CNCPT GEN/LAWS BIBLIOG METH   CROWD
20. PAGE 31 G0605   PHIL/SCI

B59
MODELSKI G.,ATOMIC ENERGY IN THE COMMUNIST BLOC.   TEC/DEV
FUT INT/ORG CONSULT FORCES ACT/RES PLAN KNOWL SKILL   NUC/PWR
...PHIL/SCI STAT CHARTS 20. PAGE 39 G0777   USSR
                                                      COM

B59
RUSSELL B.,COMMON SENSE AND NUCLEAR WARFARE. WOR+45   ORD/FREE
INTELL SOCIETY STRATA NAT/G TOP/EX EDU/PROP ATTIT   ARMS/CONT
PERSON KNOWL MORAL PWR...POLICY CONCPT MYTH   NUC/PWR
CON/ANAL COLD/WAR 20. PAGE 48 G0948

B59
STANFORD RESEARCH INSTITUTE,POSSIBLE NONMILITARY   R+D
SCIENTIFIC DEVELOPMENTS AND THEIR POTENTIAL IMPACT   TEC/DEV
ON FOREIGN POLICY PROBLEMS OF THE UNITED. FUT
USA+45 INT/ORG PROF/ORG CONSULT ACT/RES CREATE PLAN
PEACE KNOWL SKILL...TECHNIC PHIL/SCI NEW/IDEA
UNESCO 20. PAGE 52 G1032

S59
DEUTSCH K.W.,"THE IMPACT OF SCIENCE AND TECHNOLOGY   PHIL/SCI
ON INTERNATIONAL POLITICS." UNIV INTELL NAT/G   MYTH
ACT/RES CREATE TEC/DEV EDU/PROP EXEC KNOWL...CONCPT   DIPLOM
TREND TOT/POP 20. PAGE 15 G0297   NAT/LISM

S59
MILBURN T.W.,"WHAT CONSTITUTES EFFECTIVE   INTELL
DETERRENCE." USA+45 USSR WOR+45 STRUCT FORCES   ATTIT
ACT/RES PLAN SUPEGO KNOWL ORD/FREE PWR...RELATIV   DETER
PSY CONCPT VAL/FREE 20 COLD/WAR. PAGE 39 G0768   NUC/PWR

S59
WILLIAMS B.H.,"SCIENTIFIC METHOD IN FOREIGN   PLAN
POLICY." WOR+45 NAT/G FORCES TOP/EX DOMIN LEGIT   PHIL/SCI
COERCE PEACE ATTIT KNOWL ORD/FREE PWR...GEN/LAWS   DIPLOM
GEN/METH TOT/POP COLD/WAR NAZI. PAGE 63 G1241

B60
GOLDSEN J.M.,INTERNATIONAL POLITICAL IMPLICATIONS   R+D
OF ACTIVITIES IN OUTER SPACE. FUT USA+45 WOR+45 AIR   SPACE
LAW ACT/RES LEGIT ATTIT KNOWL ORD/FREE PWR...CONCPT
20. PAGE 22 G0427

B60
SLUCKIN W.,MINDS AND MACHINES (REV. ED.). PROB/SOLV   PSY
TEC/DEV AUTOMAT TASK PERCEPT HEALTH KNOWL   COMPUTER
...DECISION MATH PROBABIL COMPUT/IR GAME 20.   PERSON
PAGE 51 G1012   SIMUL

B60
US HOUSE COMM. SCI. ASTRONAUT.,OCEAN SCIENCES AND   R+D
NATIONAL SECURITY. FUT SEA ECO/DEV EXTR/IND INT/ORG   ORD/FREE
NAT/G FORCES ACT/RES TEC/DEV ECO/TAC COERCE WAR
BIO/SOC KNOWL PWR...CONCPT RECORD LAB/EXP 20.
PAGE 59 G1153

WOETZEL R.K.,THE INTERNATIONAL CONTROL OF AIRSPACE
AND OUTERSPACE. FUT WOR+45 AIR CONSTN STRUCT
CONSULT PLAN TEC/DEV ADJUD RIGID/FLEX KNOWL
ORD/FREE PWR...TECHNIC GEOG MGT NEW/IDEA TREND
COMPUT/IR VAL/FREE 20 TREATY. PAGE 64 G1251
 B60 INT/ORG JURID SPACE INT/LAW

BRENNAN D.G.,"SETTING AND GOALS OF ARMS CONTROL."
FUT USA+45 USSR WOR+45 INTELL INT/ORG NAT/G
VOL/ASSN CONSULT PLAN DIPLOM ECO/TAC ADMIN KNOWL
PWR...POLICY CONCPT TREND COLD/WAR 20. PAGE 8 G0164
 L60 FORCES COERCE ARMS/CONT DETER

DEUTSCH K.W.,"TOWARD AN INVENTORY OF BASIC TRENDS
AND PATTERNS IN COMPARATIVE AND INTERNATIONAL
POLITICS." UNIV WOR+45 SOCIETY STRUCT INT/ORG NAT/G
CREATE PLAN EDU/PROP KNOWL...PHIL/SCI METH/CNCPT
STAT SELF/OBS OBS/ENVIR SAMP TREND CON/ANAL CHARTS
SOC/EXP GEN/METH 20. PAGE 15 G0298
 L60 R+D PERCEPT

BECKER A.S.,"COMPARISIONS OF UNITED STATES AND USSR
NATIONAL OUTPUT: SOME RULES OF THE GAME." COM
USA+45 ECO/DEV AGRI DIST/IND INDUS R+D CONSULT PLAN
ECO/TAC RIGID/FLEX KNOWL...METH/CNCPT CHARTS 20.
PAGE 6 G0113
 S60 STAT USSR

LEAR J.,"PEACE: SCIENCE'S NEXT GREAT EXPLORATION."
USA+45 INT/ORG TOP/EX TEC/DEV EDU/PROP ROUTINE
PEACE KNOWL SKILL 20. PAGE 33 G0648
 S60 EX/STRUC ARMS/CONT NUC/PWR

GORDON W.J.J.,SYNECTICS; THE DEVELOPMENT OF
CREATIVE CAPACITY. USA+45 PLAN TEC/DEV KNOWL WEALTH
...DECISION MGT 20. PAGE 22 G0436
 B61 CREATE PROB/SOLV ACT/RES TOP/EX

GRUBER R.,SCIENCE AND THE NEW NATIONS. WOR+45 NAT/G
CREATE SKILL...CONCPT GEN/LAWS 20. PAGE 23 G0457
 B61 ECO/UNDEV KNOWL

MCRAE R.,THE PROBLEM OF THE UNITY OF THE SCIENCES:
BACON TO KANT. CREATE TASK KNOWL...PERS/COMP 16/18
BACON/F DESCARTE/R LEIBNITZ/G KANT/I DIDEROT/D.
PAGE 38 G0748
 B61 PHIL/SCI IDEA/COMP PERSON

NAKICENOVIC S.,NUCLEAR ENERGY IN YUGOSLAVIA.
YUGOSLAVIA AGRI INDUS CREATE OP/RES ROUTINE
EFFICIENCY KNOWL...HEAL STAT CHARTS LAB/EXP BIBLIOG
20. PAGE 41 G0802
 B61 R+D ECO/DEV TEC/DEV NUC/PWR

NOGEE J.L.,SOVIET POLICY TOWARD INTERNATIONAL
CONTROL OF ATOMIC ENERGY. COM USA+45 WOR+45 INTELL
NAT/G ACT/RES DIPLOM EDU/PROP NUC/PWR TOTALISM
PERCEPT KNOWL PWR...TIME/SEQ COLD/WAR 20. PAGE 42
G0824
 B61 INT/ORG ATTIT ARMS/CONT USSR

DEUTSCH K.W.,"A NOTE ON THE APPEARANCE OF WISDOM IN
LARGE BUREAUCRATIC ORGANIZATIONS." ROUTINE PERSON
KNOWL SKILL...DECISION STAT. PAGE 15 G0299
 S61 ADMIN PROBABIL PROB/SOLV SIMUL

BROOKINGS INSTITUTION,DEVELOPMENT OF THE EMERGING
COUNTRIES: AN AGENDA FOR RESEARCH. WOR+45 AGRI
TEC/DEV FOR/AID EDU/PROP ADJUST HABITAT KNOWL...PSY
SOC ANTHOL 20 THIRD/WRLD. PAGE 9 G0175
 B62 ECO/UNDEV R+D SOCIETY PROB/SOLV

DUCKWORTH W.E.,A GUIDE TO OPERATIONAL RESEARCH.
INDUS PLAN PROB/SOLV EXEC EFFICIENCY PRODUC KNOWL
...MGT MATH STAT SIMUL METH 20 MONTECARLO. PAGE 16
G0319
 B62 OP/RES GAME DECISION ADMIN

GILPIN R.,AMERICAN SCIENTISTS AND NUCLEAR WEAPONS
POLICY. COM FUT USA+45 WOR+45 INT/ORG NAT/G
PROF/ORG CONSULT FORCES CREATE TEC/DEV BAL/PWR
EDU/PROP ARMS/CONT WAR PERCEPT KNOWL MORAL PWR
...PHIL/SCI SOC CONCPT GEN/LAWS 20. PAGE 21 G0417
 B62 INTELL ATTIT DETER NUC/PWR

OSGOOD C.E.,AN ALTERNATIVE TO WAR OR SURRENDER. FUT
UNIV CULTURE INTELL SOCIETY R+D INT/ORG CONSULT
DELIB/GP ACT/RES PLAN CHOOSE ATTIT PERCEPT KNOWL
...PHIL/SCI PSY SOC TREND GEN/LAWS 20. PAGE 43
G0849
 B62 ORD/FREE EDU/PROP PEACE WAR

ROSS R.,SYMBOLS AND CIVILIZATION. UNIV CULTURE SECT
 B62 PHIL/SCI

CREATE ALL/VALS MORAL ART/METH. PAGE 48 G0939
 KNOWL EPIST SOCIETY

SCHILLING W.R.,"SCIENTISTS, FOREIGN POLICY AND
POLITICS." WOR+45 WOR-45 INTELL INT/ORG CONSULT
TOP/EX ACT/RES PLAN ADMIN KNOWL...CONCPT OBS TREND
LEAGUE/NAT 20. PAGE 49 G0967
 S62 NAT/G TEC/DEV DIPLOM NUC/PWR

WALTER E.,"VERS UNE CLASSIFICATION SCIENTIFIQUE DE
LA SOCIOLOGIA." UNIV CULTURE INTELL SOCIETY R+D
ACT/RES LEGIT ROUTINE ATTIT KNOWL...JURID MGT TREND
GEN/LAWS 20. PAGE 62 G1208
 S62 PLAN CONCPT

PERLO V.,MILITARISM AND INDUSTRY. USA+45 INT/TRADE
EDU/PROP DETER KNOWL...CHARTS MAPS 20. PAGE 44
G0869
 B63 CIVMIL/REL INDUS LOBBY ARMS/CONT

REED E.,CHALLENGES TO DEMOCRACY: THE NEXT TEN
YEARS. FUT USA+45 ECO/DEV DELIB/GP TEC/DEV CONFER
GOV/REL KNOWL ORD/FREE...MAJORIT IDEA/COMP ANTHOL
20. PAGE 46 G0909
 B63 POLICY EDU/PROP ECO/TAC NAT/G

US ATOMIC ENERGY COMMISSION,ATOMIC ENERGY IN THE
SOVIET UNION: TRIP REPORT OF THE US ATOMIC ENERGY
DELEGATION, MAY 1933. USSR R+D NAT/G CONSULT CREATE
DIPLOM ADMIN ROUTINE EFFICIENCY PRODUC KNOWL SKILL
...NAT/COMP 20 AEC TRAVEL TREATY. PAGE 56 G1107
 B63 METH/COMP OP/RES TEC/DEV NUC/PWR

MCDOUGAL M.S.,"THE ENJOYMENT AND ACQUISITION OF
RESOURCES IN OUTER SPACE." CHRIST-17C FUT WOR+45
WOR-45 LAW EXTR/IND INT/ORG ACT/RES CREATE TEC/DEV
ECO/TAC LEGIT COERCE HEALTH KNOWL ORD/FREE PWR
WEALTH...JURID HIST/WRIT VAL/FREE. PAGE 37 G0738
 L63 PLAN TREND

BOULDING K.E.,"UNIVERSITY, SOCIETY, AND ARMS
CONTROL." WOR+45 WOR-45 ACADEM NAT/G CONSULT FORCES
ACT/RES PLAN TEC/DEV BAL/PWR ECO/TAC COERCE DETER
WAR ATTIT RIGID/FLEX KNOWL ORD/FREE PWR WEALTH
...CONCPT COLD/WAR TOT/POP 20. PAGE 8 G0159
 S63 SOCIETY ARMS/CONT

DUBRIDGE L.A.,"POLICY AND THE SCIENTISTS." ELITES
PROB/SOLV ROLE KNOWL PWR. PAGE 16 G0318
 S63 POLICY PHIL/SCI ACADEM DECISION

GARDNER R.N.,"COOPERATION IN OUTER SPACE." FUT USSR
WOR+45 AIR LAW COM/IND CONSULT DELIB/GP CREATE
KNOWL 20 TREATY. PAGE 21 G0410
 S63 INT/ORG ACT/RES PEACE SPACE

HOSKINS H.L.,"ARAB SOCIALISM IN THE UAR." ISLAM
USSR AGRI INDUS NAT/G TOP/EX CREATE DIPLOM EDU/PROP
DRIVE KNOWL PWR SOCISM...POLICY CONCPT TREND SUEZ
20. PAGE 27 G0530
 S63 ECO/DEV PLAN UAR

MASSART L.,"L'ORGANISATION DE LA RECHERCHE
SCIENTIFIQUE EN EUROPE." EUR+WWI WOR+45 ACT/RES
PLAN TEC/DEV EDU/PROP EXEC KNOWL...METH/CNCPT EEC
20. PAGE 36 G0718
 S63 R+D CREATE

PHELPS J.,"INFORMATION AND ARMS CONTROL." COM SPACE
USA+45 USSR WOR+45 R+D INT/ORG NAT/G DELIB/GP
DIPLOM ORD/FREE...CONCPT 20. PAGE 45 G0875
 S63 KNOWL ARMS/CONT NUC/PWR

WOHLSTETTER A.,"SCIENTISTS, SEERS AND STRATEGY."
USA+45 ELITES R+D NAT/G CONSULT FORCES TOP/EX
EDU/PROP ARMS/CONT KNOWL ORD/FREE...DECISION MYTH
20. PAGE 64 G1253
 S63 INTELL ACT/RES

ETZIONI A.,THE MOON-DOGGLE: DOMESTIC AND
INTERNATIONAL IMPLICATIONS OF THE SPACE RACE. FUT
USA+45 WOR+45 INTELL ECO/DEV INDUS VOL/ASSN
EX/STRUC FORCES LEGIS TOP/EX PLAN TEC/DEV ECO/TAC
EDU/PROP KNOWL ORD/FREE PWR RESPECT WEALTH
TIME/SEQ. PAGE 18 G0352
 B64 R+D NAT/G DIPLOM SPACE

RANSOM H.H.,CAN AMERICAN DEMOCRACY SURVIVE COLD
WAR. USA-45 CONSTN NAT/G CONSULT DELIB/GP LEGIS
ACT/RES LEGIT EXEC ATTIT KNOWL ORD/FREE PWR SKILL
 B64 USA+45 ROUTINE

...POLICY TIME/SEQ TREND GEN/LAWS 20 COLD/WAR.
PAGE 46 G0901

PAGE 16 G0306   CONCPT
ADMIN

ABT C.,"WAR GAMING." USA+45 NAT/G TOP/EX ACT/RES   FORCES   S64
TEC/DEV COERCE KNOWL ORD/FREE PWR...DECISION MATH   SIMUL
TIME/SEQ COMPUT/IR CHARTS LAB/EXP VAL/FREE. PAGE 2   WAR
G0026

GULICK M.C.,NONCONVENTIONAL INFORMATION SYSTEMS   BIBLIOG/A   B67
SERVING THE SOCIAL SCIENCES AND THE HUMANITIES; A   R+D
BIBLIOGRAPHIC ESSAY (PAPER). USA+45 COMPUTER CREATE   COMPUT/IR
EDU/PROP KNOWL...SOC METH 20. PAGE 23 G0462   HUM

MUMFORD L.,"AUTHORITARIAN AND DEMOCRATIC   ECO/DEV   S64
TECHNIQUES." INDUS PROC/MFG LG/CO SML/CO CREATE   TEC/DEV
PLAN KNOWL...POLICY TREND WORK 20. PAGE 40 G0794

HOROWITZ I.L.,THE RISE AND FALL OF PROJECT CAMELOT: NAT/G   B67
STUDIES IN THE RELATIONSHIP BETWEEN SOCIAL SCIENCE   ACADEM
AND PRACTICAL POLITICS. USA+45 WOR+45 CULTURE   ACT/RES
FORCES LEGIS EXEC CIVMIL/REL KNOWL...POLICY SOC   GP/REL
METH/CNCPT 20. PAGE 27 G0529

SPONSLER G.C.,"THE MILITARY ROLE IN SPACE." FUT   TEC/DEV   S64
USA+45 SEA AIR NAT/G ACT/RES PLAN COERCE NUC/PWR   FORCES
WEAPON KNOWL ORD/FREE PWR RESPECT...TREND 20.   SPACE
PAGE 52 G1026

NELSON R.R.,TECHNOLOGY, ECONOMIC GROWTH, AND PUBLIC   R+D   B67
POLICY. USA+45 PLAN GP/REL UTIL KNOWL...POLICY   CONSULT
PHIL/SCI CHARTS BIBLIOG 20. PAGE 41 G0817   CREATE
ACT/RES

KENT A.,SPECIALIZED INFORMATION CENTERS. INTELL R+D   COMPUT/IR   B65
VOL/ASSN CONSULT COMPUTER KNOWL...DECISION HUM   CREATE
PHIL/SCI METH/CNCPT TREND CHARTS 20. PAGE 30 G0593   TEC/DEV
METH/COMP

RIDKER R.G.,ECONOMIC COSTS OF AIR POLLUTION*   OP/RES   B67
STUDIES IN MEASUREMENT. R+D MUNIC GP/REL KNOWL   HABITAT
...OBS 20. PAGE 47 G0919   PHIL/SCI

NATIONAL SCIENCE FOUNDATION,CURRENT RESEARCH AND   BIBLIOG   B65
DEVELOPMENT IN SCIENTIFIC DOCUMENTATION - NO. 12.   COMPUT/IR
WOR+45 INTELL COM/IND NAT/G COMPUTER TEC/DEV   R+D
AUTOMAT KNOWL...PSY LING 20. PAGE 41 G0812   PHIL/SCI

WEINBERG A.M.,REFLECTIONS ON BIG SCIENCE. FUT   ACADEM   B67
USA+45 NAT/G EDU/PROP CHOOSE PERS/REL COST OPTIMAL   KNOWL
...PHIL/SCI TREND. PAGE 62 G1225   R+D
PLAN

SINGER J.D.,HUMAN BEHAVIOR AND INTERNATIONAL   DIPLOM   B65
POLITICS* CONTRIBUTIONS FROM THE SOCIAL-   PHIL/SCI
PSYCHOLOGICAL SCIENCES. ACT/RES PLAN EDU/PROP ADMIN   QUANT
KNOWL...DECISION PSY SOC NET/THEORY HYPO/EXP   SIMUL
LAB/EXP SOC/EXP GEN/METH ANTHOL BIBLIOG. PAGE 51
G1006

ZUCKERMAN S.,SCIENTISTS AND WAR. ELITES INDUS   R+D   B67
DIPLOM CENTRAL EFFICIENCY KNOWL 20. PAGE 65 G1271   CONSULT
ACT/RES
GP/REL

LASSWELL H.D.,"THE POLICY SCIENCES OF DEVELOPMENT."   PWR   L65
CULTURE SOCIETY EX/STRUC CREATE ADMIN ATTIT KNOWL   METH/CNCPT
...SOC CONCPT SIMUL GEN/METH. PAGE 33 G0644   DIPLOM

ALBAUM G.,"INFORMATION FLOW AND DECENTRALIZED   LG/CO   S67
DECISION MAKING IN MARKETING." EX/STRUC COMPUTER   ROUTINE
OP/RES PROB/SOLV EFFICIENCY OPTIMAL...METH/COMP   KNOWL
ORG/CHARTS 20. PAGE 2 G0033   MARKET

GRENIEWSKI H.,"INTENTION AND PERFORMANCE: A PRIMER   SIMUL   S65
OF CYBERNETICS OF PLANNING." EFFICIENCY OPTIMAL   GAME
KNOWL SKILL...DECISION MGT EQULIB. PAGE 23 G0448   GEN/METH
PLAN

BULMER-THOMAS I.,"SO, ON TO THE GREAT SOCIETY." FUT   PHIL/SCI   S67
UNIV TEC/DEV BAL/PWR WAR BIO/SOC KNOWL...ART/METH   SOCIETY
SOC PREDICT TREND WORSHIP 20 GREAT/SOC. PAGE 9   CREATE
G0185

MUMFORD L.,THE MYTH OF THE MACHINE: TECHNICS AND   WORKER   B66
HUMAN DEVELOPMENT. UNIV WOR-45 CREATE AUTOMAT   TEC/DEV
PERCEPT KNOWL...EPIST PHIL/SCI SOC LING TREND   SOCIETY
SOC/INTEG 20 MARX/KARL. PAGE 40 G0795

CRANBERG L.,"SCIENCE, ETHICS, AND LAW." UNIV CREATE   LAW   S67
PLAN EDU/PROP INGP/REL PERS/REL ADJUST RATIONAL   PHIL/SCI
KNOWL MORAL...CONCPT IDEA/COMP 20. PAGE 13 G0260   INTELL

NATIONAL SCIENCE FOUNDATION,SIXTEENTH ANNUAL REPORT   NAT/G   B66
FOR THE FISCAL YEAR ENDED JUNE 30, 1966. USA+45   EDU/PROP
CREATE BUDGET SKILL 20 NSF. PAGE 41 G0813   ACADEM
KNOWL

FOREIGN POLICY ASSOCIATION,"HOW WORLD LAW DEVELOPS*   INT/LAW   S67
A CASE STUDY OF THE OUTER SPACE TREATY." SPACE   DIPLOM
WOR+45 BAL/PWR NEUTRAL NUC/PWR PEACE KNOWL 20 UN   ARMS/CONT
TREATY. PAGE 19 G0380   INT/ORG

BUNGE M.,THE SEARCH FOR SYSTEM. VOL. 3, PART 1 OF   PHIL/SCI   B67
STUDIES IN THE FOUNDATIONS METHODOLOGY, AND   METH
PHILOSOPHY OF SCIENCE. UNIV LAW INTELL KNOWL.   GEN/LAWS
PAGE 10 G0187   CONCPT

HOFFER J.R.,"RELATIONSHIP OF NATURAL AND SOCIAL   PROB/SOLV   S67
SCIENCES TO SOCIAL PROBLEMS AND CONTRIBUTION OF...   SOCIETY
SCIENTISTS TO SOLUTIONS." USA+45 COMPUTER TEC/DEV   INTELL
GP/REL KNOWL...SOC TREND. PAGE 26 G0521   ACT/RES

BUNGE M.,THE SEARCH FOR TRUTH, VOL. 3, PART 2 OF   PHIL/SCI   B67
STUDIES IN THE FOUNDATIONS, METHODOLOGY, AND   TESTS
PHILOSOPHY OF SCIENCE. UNIV INTELL KNOWL...CONCPT   GEN/LAWS
OBS PREDICT METH. PAGE 10 G0188   RATIONAL

SLOAN P.,"FIFTY YEARS OF SOVIET RULE." USSR INDUS   CREATE   S67
EDU/PROP EFFICIENCY PRODUC HEALTH KNOWL MORAL   NAT/G
WEALTH MARXISM...POLICY 20. PAGE 51 G1011   PLAN
INSPECT

COMMONER B.,SCIENCE AND SURVIVAL. SOCIETY INDUS   PHIL/SCI   B67
PLAN NUC/PWR KNOWL PWR...SOC 20 AEC. PAGE 13 G0247   CONTROL
PROB/SOLV
EQUILIB

RENAN E.,THE FUTURE OF SCIENCE. WAR ORD/FREE WEALTH   PHIL/SCI   B91
...GOV/COMP IDEA/COMP GEN/LAWS 19. PAGE 46 G0913   KNOWL
SECT
PREDICT

CONNOLLY W.E.,POLITICAL SCIENCE AND IDEOLOGY.   PWR   B67
UTOPIA ATTIT KNOWL...MAJORIT EPIST PHIL/SCI SOC   PLURISM
IDEA/COMP HYPO/EXP GEN/LAWS METH HUME/D MARX/KARL.   ELITES
PAGE 13 G0250   CONCPT

DE JOUVENEL B.,THE ART OF CONJECTURE. WOR+45   FUT   B67
EFFICIENCY PERCEPT KNOWL...DECISION PHIL/SCI CONCPT   PREDICT
METH/COMP BIBLIOG 20. PAGE 15 G0285   SIMUL
METH

DONALD A.G.,MANAGEMENT, INFORMATION, AND SYSTEMS.   ROUTINE   B67
WOR+45 LG/CO PROB/SOLV CONTROL FEEDBACK KNOWL MGT.   TEC/DEV

SNYDER R.C.,FOREIGN POLICY DECISION-MAKING. FUT
KOREA WOR+45 R+D CREATE ADMIN ROUTINE PWR
...DECISION PSY SOC CONCPT METH/CNCPT CON/ANAL
CHARTS GEN/METH METH 20. PAGE 52 G1018
B62
TEC/DEV
HYPO/EXP
DIPLOM

BRODIE B.,ESCALATION AND THE NUCLEAR OPTION. ASIA
CUBA EUR+WWI KOREA USA+45 USSR VIETNAM RISK ATTIT
DRIVE PERCEPT PROBABIL. PAGE 9 G0172
B66
NUC/PWR
GUERRILLA
WAR
DETER

HILL R.,"SOCIAL ASPECTS OF FAMILY PLANNING." INDIA
KOREA TAIWAN ECO/UNDEV PLAN PROB/SOLV TEC/DEV
EDU/PROP CONTROL ATTIT DRIVE...HEAL PSY SOC 20
BIRTH/CON UN. PAGE 26 G0512
S67
FAM
BIO/SOC
GEOG
MARRIAGE

KOREA/N....NORTH KOREA

KOREA/S....SOUTH KOREA

KORNHAUSER W. G0614

KORNILOV/L....LAVR GEORGIEVICH KORNILOV

KOROL A.G. G0615

KRAFT J. G0616

KRANZBERG M. G0617

KRAUS J. G0618

KREITH K. G0619

KREPS J. G0620

KRICKUS R.J. G0621

KROECK P.C. G0850

KRUPP S. G0622

KRUSCHE H. G0623

KRUTILIA J.V. G0624

KU KLUX KLAN....SEE KKK

KUENNE R.E. G0625

KUOMINTANG....KUOMINTANG

KURAKOV I.G. G0626

KUWAIT....SEE ALSO ISLAM

INT. BANK RECONSTR. DEVELOP.,ECONOMIC DEVELOPMENT
OF KUWAIT. ISLAM KUWAIT AGRI FINAN MARKET EX/STRUC
TEC/DEV ECO/TAC ADMIN WEALTH...OBS CON/ANAL CHARTS
20. PAGE 28 G0548
B65
INDUS
NAT/G

KUZMACK A.M. G0627

KUZNETS....KUZNETS SCALE

KY/NGUYEN....NGUYEN KY

L

L/A+17C....LATIN AMERICA SINCE 1700; SEE ALSO APPROPRIATE
NATIONS

MARCHANT A.,INVESTIGATIONS IN PROGRESS IN THE
UNITED STATES IN THE FIELD OF LATIN AMERICAN
HUMANISTIC AND SOCIAL SCIENCE STUDIES. USA+45
ACADEM...QU ANTHOL. PAGE 36 G0702
B42
ACT/RES
SOC
R+D
L/A+17C

KISER M.,"ORGANIZATION OF AMERICAN STATES." L/A+17C
USA+45 ECO/UNDEV INT/ORG NAT/G PLAN TEC/DEV DIPLOM
ECO/TAC INT/TRADE EDU/PROP ADMIN ALL/VALS...POLICY
MGT RECORD ORG/CHARTS OAS 20. PAGE 30 G0601
L55
VOL/ASSN
ECO/DEV
REGION

MAYDA J.,ATOMIC ENERGY AND LAW. ECO/UNDEV FINAN
TEC/DEV FOR/AID EFFICIENCY PRODUC WEALTH...POLICY
TECHNIC 20. PAGE 37 G0723
B59
NUC/PWR
L/A+17C
LAW
ADMIN

JAFFEE A.J.,"POPULATION TRENDS AND CONTROLS IN
UNDERDEVELOPED COUNTRIES." AFR FUT ISLAM L/A+17C
S/ASIA CULTURE R+D FAM ACT/RES PLAN EDU/PROP
BIO/SOC RIGID/FLEX HEALTH...SOC STAT OBS CHARTS 20.
S60
ECO/UNDEV
GEOG

PAGE 28 G0555

MARTINS A.F.,REVOLUCAO BRANCA NO CAMPO. L/A+17C
SERV/IND DEMAND EFFICIENCY PRODUC...POLICY
METH/COMP. PAGE 36 G0717
B62
AGRI
ECO/UNDEV
TEC/DEV
NAT/COMP

FLORES E.,LAND REFORM AND THE ALLIANCE FOR PROGRESS
(PAMPHLET). L/A+17C USA+45 STRUCT ECO/UNDEV NAT/G
WORKER CREATE PLAN ECO/TAC COERCE REV 20. PAGE 19
G0373
B63
AGRI
INT/ORG
DIPLOM
POLICY

PANAMERICAN UNION,DOCUMENTOS OFICIALES DE LA
ORGANIZACION DE LOS ESTADOS AMERICANOS, INDICE Y
LISTA (VOL. III, 1962). L/A+17C DELIB/GP INT/TRADE
EDU/PROP REGION NUC/PWR...HEAL INT/LAW SOC/WK 20
OAS. PAGE 44 G0857
B63
BIBLIOG
INT/ORG
DIPLOM

ORGANIZATION AMERICAN STATES,ECONOMIC SURVEY OF
LATIN AMERICA, 1962. L/A+17C AGRI DIST/IND INDUS
MARKET PROC/MFG R+D PLAN TEC/DEV ECO/TAC REGION
BAL/PAY ALL/VALS...CON/ANAL ORG/CHARTS GEN/METH OAS
20. PAGE 43 G0844
B64
ECO/UNDEV
CHARTS

POWELSON J.P.,LATIN AMERICA: TODAY'S ECONOMIC AND
SOCIAL REVOLUTION. L/A+17C INTELL SOCIETY STRUCT
AGRI INDUS NAT/G DIPLOM ECO/TAC REV...POLICY 20.
PAGE 45 G0887
B64
ECO/UNDEV
WEALTH
ADJUST
PLAN

SCHOECK H.,CENTRAL PLANNING AND NEOMERCANTILISM.
L/A+17C UK WOR+45 BUDGET ECO/TAC PRICE CONTROL
GOV/REL UTOPIA 20. PAGE 49 G0974
B64
PLAN
CENTRAL
NAT/G
POLICY

HAAS E.B.,"ECONOMICS AND DIFFERENTIAL PATTERNS OF
POLITICAL INTEGRATION: PROJECTIONS ABOUT UNITY IN
LATIN AMERICA." SOCIETY NAT/G DELIB/GP ACT/RES
CREATE PLAN ECO/TAC REGION ROUTINE ATTIT DRIVE PWR
WEALTH...CONCPT TREND CHARTS LAFTA 20. PAGE 24
G0464
L64
L/A+17C
INT/ORG
MARKET

IANNI O.,ESTADO E CAPITALISMO. L/A+17C FINAN
TEC/DEV ECO/TAC ORD/FREE WEALTH POLICY. PAGE 28
G0542
B65
ECO/UNDEV
STRUCT
INDUS
NAT/G

WISH J.R.,ECONOMIC DEVELOPMENT IN LATIN AMERICA: AN
ANNOTATED BIBLIOGRAPHY. L/A+17C COM/IND MARKET R+D
CREATE CAP/ISM ATTIT...STAT METH 20. PAGE 64 G1250
B65
BIBLIOG/A
ECO/UNDEV
TEC/DEV
AGRI

SILVERT K.H.,"AMERICAN ACADEMIC ETHICS AND SOCIAL
RESEARCH ABROAD* THE LESSON OF PROJECT CAMELOT."
CHILE L/A+17C USA+45 FINAN ADMIN...PHIL/SCI SOC
GEN/LAWS CAMELOT. PAGE 51 G0998
S65
ACADEM
NAT/G
ACT/RES
POLICY

COHEN A.,"THE TECHNOLOGY/ELITE APPROACH TO THE
DEVELOPMENTAL PROCESS* PERUVIAN CASE STUDY."
L/A+17C STRUCT CREATE ECO/TAC FOR/AID CIVMIL/REL
MARXISM TECHRACY HYPO/EXP. PAGE 12 G0239
S66
ECO/UNDEV
ELITES
PERU

GARCIA ROBLES A.,THE DENUCLEARIZATION OF LATIN
AMERICA (TRANS. BY MARJORIE URQUIDI). LAW PLAN
DIPLOM...ANTHOL 20 TREATY UN. PAGE 21 G0409
B67
NUC/PWR
ARMS/CONT
L/A+17C
INT/ORG

LAMBERT J.,LATIN AMERICA: SOCIAL STRUCTURES AND
POLITICAL INSTITUTIONS. STRUCT TEC/DEV DIPLOM ADMIN
COLONIAL LEAD ATTIT...SOC CLASSIF NAT/COMP 17/20.
PAGE 32 G0631
B67
L/A+17C
NAT/G
ECO/UNDEV
SOCIETY

NASH M.,MACHINE AGE MAYA. GUATEMALA L/A+17C STRUCT
AGRI WORKER CREATE INCOME ATTIT RIGID/FLEX ROLE
...IDEA/COMP SOC/EXP WORSHIP 20 INDIAN/AM. PAGE 41
G0806
B67
INDUS
CULTURE
SOC
MUNIC

EINAUDI L.,"ANNOTATED BIBLIOGRAPHY OF LATIN
AMERICAN MILITARY JOURNALS" LAW TEC/DEV DOMIN
EDU/PROP COERCE WAR CIVMIL/REL 20. PAGE 17 G0336
L67
BIBLIOG/A
NAT/G
FORCES
L/A+17C

RUTH J.M.,"THE ADMINISTRATION OF WATER RESOURCES IN GUATEMALA." GUATEMALA L/A+17C DIST/IND LOC/G NAT/G EX/STRUC ADMIN GOV/REL DEMAND EQUILIB WEALTH...GEOG MGT 20. PAGE 48 G0952
EFFICIENCY ECO/UNDEV PLAN ACT/RES
L67

MCNAMARA R.L.,"THE NEED FOR INNOVATIVENESS IN DEVELOPING SOCIETIES." L/A+17C EDU/PROP ADMIN LEAD WEALTH...POLICY PSY SOC METH 20 COLOMB. PAGE 38 G0747
PROB/SOLV PLAN ECO/UNDEV NEW/IDEA
S67

STYCOS J.M.,"POLITICS AND POPULATION CONTROL IN LATIN AMERICA." USA+45 FAM NAT/G GP/REL AGE/C ATTIT CATHISM MARXISM...POLICY UN WHO. PAGE 53 G1045
PLAN CENSUS CONTROL L/A+17C
S67

US SENATE COMM ON FOREIGN REL,SURVEY OF THE ALLIANCE FOR PROGRESS; THE POLITICAL ASPECTS (PAMPHLET). CONSTN SOCIETY ECO/UNDEV INT/ORG TEC/DEV DIPLOM...CENSUS 20. PAGE 60 G1186
L/A+17C POLICY PROB/SOLV
N67

LA PORTE T. G0628

LAB/EXP....LABORATORY EXPERIMENTS

US ATOMIC ENERGY COMMISSION,ATOMIC ENERGY IN USE (PAMPHLET). R+D RISK EFFICIENCY HEALTH KNOWL ORD/FREE...PHIL/SCI CONCPT METH/CNCPT CHARTS LAB/EXP 20 AEC. PAGE 56 G1106
OP/RES TEC/DEV NUC/PWR CREATE
N19

SMYTH H.D.,ATOMIC ENERGY FOR MILITARY PURPOSES. USA-45 NAT/G PLAN TEC/DEV KNOWL...MATH CON/ANAL CHARTS LAB/EXP SIMUL 20. PAGE 52 G1017
R+D TIME/SEQ NUC/PWR
B45

BRADLEY D.,NO PLACE TO HIDE. USA+45 SOCIETY NAT/G FORCES TEC/DEV EDU/PROP DETER PEACE BIO/SOC ALL/VALS...POLICY PHIL/SCI OBS RECORD SAMP BIOG GEN/METH COLD/WAR 20. PAGE 8 G0162
R+D LAB/EXP ARMS/CONT NUC/PWR
B48

MILLER G.A.,"THE MAGICAL NUMBER SEVEN, PLUS OR MINUS TWO: SOME LIMITS ON OUR CAPACITY FOR PROCESSING INFORMATION." PERS/REL...PSY METH/CNCPT LING CHARTS BIBLIOG 20. PAGE 39 G0772
LAB/EXP KNOWL PERCEPT COMPUT/IR
S56

NEWELL A.C.,"ELEMENTS OF A THEORY OF HUMAN PROBLEM SOLVING" (BMR)" TASK PERCEPT...CONCPT LOG METH/COMP LAB/EXP BIBLIOG 20. PAGE 42 G0819
PROB/SOLV COMPUTER COMPUT/IR OP/RES
S58

US HOUSE COMM. SCI. ASTRONAUT.,OCEAN SCIENCES AND NATIONAL SECURITY. FUT SEA ECO/DEV EXTR/IND INT/ORG NAT/G FORCES ACT/RES TEC/DEV ECO/TAC COERCE WAR BIO/SOC KNOWL PWR...CONCPT RECORD LAB/EXP 20. PAGE 59 G1153
R+D ORD/FREE
B60

HOLZMAN B.G.,"BASIC RESEARCH FOR NATIONAL SURVIVAL." FUT USA+45 INTELL R+D ACT/RES OP/RES PLAN TEC/DEV EDU/PROP PERCEPT PERSON...PHIL/SCI METH/CNCPT NEW/IDEA MATH OBS RECORD TREND LAB/EXP 20. PAGE 27 G0525
FORCES STAT
L60

NAKICENOVIC S.,NUCLEAR ENERGY IN YUGOSLAVIA. YUGOSLAVIA AGRI INDUS CREATE OP/RES ROUTINE EFFICIENCY KNOWL...HEAL STAT CHARTS LAB/EXP BIBLIOG 20. PAGE 41 G0802
R+D ECO/DEV TEC/DEV NUC/PWR
B61

THOMSON G.P.,NUCLEAR ENERGY IN BRITAIN DURING THE LAST WAR: THE CHERWELL SIMON LECTURE (MONOGRAPH). UK R+D CONSULT FORCES PLAN DIPLOM TASK CIVMIL/REL ROLE...PHIL/SCI NEW/IDEA LAB/EXP 20 MAUD. PAGE 54 G1071
CREATE TEC/DEV WAR NUC/PWR
B62

FLOOD M.M.,"STOCHASTIC LEARNING THEORY APPLIED TO CHOICE EXPERIMENTS WITH RATS, DOGS, AND MEN."...PSY LAB/EXP METH. PAGE 19 G0372
DECISION COMPUTER HYPO/EXP TEC/DEV
S62

PEDERSEN E.S.,NUCLEAR ENERGY IN SPACE. FUT INTELL R+D CONSULT...NEW/IDEA CHARTS METH T 20. PAGE 44 G0864
SPACE TEC/DEV NUC/PWR LAB/EXP
B64

ABT C.,"WAR GAMING." USA+45 NAT/G TOP/EX ACT/RES TEC/DEV COERCE KNOWL ORD/FREE PWR...DECISION MATH TIME/SEQ COMPUT/IR CHARTS LAB/EXP VAL/FREE. PAGE 2 G0026
FORCES SIMUL WAR
S64

COOPER A.C.,"R&D IS MORE EFFICIENT IN SMALL COMPANIES." USA+45 LG/CO SML/CO WEALTH...RECORD INT LAB/EXP 20. PAGE 13 G0255
R+D INDUS CREATE GP/COMP
S64

SINGER J.D.,HUMAN BEHAVIOR AND INTERNATINAL POLITICS* CONTRIBUTIONS FROM THE SOCIAL-PSYCHOLOGICAL SCIENCES. ACT/RES PLAN EDU/PROP ADMIN KNOWL...DECISION PSY SOC NET/THEORY HYPO/EXP LAB/EXP SOC/EXP GEN/METH ANTHOL BIBLIOG. PAGE 51 G1006
DIPLOM PHIL/SCI QUANT SIMUL
B65

LABOR FORCE....SEE WORKER

LABOR RELATIONS....SEE LABOR, ALSO RELATIONS INDEX

LABOR UNIONS....SEE LABOR

LABOR....LABOR UNIONS (BUT NOT GUILDS)

FULLER G.A.,DEMOBILIZATION: A SELECTED LIST OF REFERENCES. USA+45 LAW AGRI LABOR WORKER ECO/TAC RATION RECEIVE EDU/PROP ROUTINE ARMS/CONT ALL/VALS 20. PAGE 20 G0398
BIBLIOG/A INDUS FORCES NAT/G
N

ADVANCED MANAGEMENT. INDUS EX/STRUC WORKER OP/RES ...DECISION BIBLIOG/A 20. PAGE 1 G0003
MGT ADMIN LABOR GP/REL
N

INDIA: A REFERENCE ANNUAL. INDIA CULTURE COM/IND R+D FORCES PLAN RECEIVE EDU/PROP HEALTH...STAT CHARTS BIBLIOG 20. PAGE 1 G0005
CONSTN LABOR INT/ORG
N

THE MANAGEMENT REVIEW. FINAN EX/STRUC PROFIT BIBLIOG/A. PAGE 1 G0007
LABOR MGT ADMIN MARKET
N

PERSONNEL. USA+45 LAW LABOR LG/CO WORKER CREATE GOV/REL PERS/REL ATTIT WEALTH. PAGE 1 G0010
BIBLIOG/A ADMIN MGT GP/REL
N

PRINCETON UNIVERSITY,SELECTED REFERENCES: INDUSTRIAL RELATIONS SECTION. USA+45 EX/STRUC WORKER TEC/DEV...MGT 20. PAGE 45 G0892
BIBLIOG/A LABOR INDUS GP/REL
N

RAND SCHOOL OF SOCIAL SCIENCE,INDEX TO LABOR ARTICLES. ECO/DEV INT/ORG LEGIS DIPLOM GP/REL ...NAT/COMP 20. PAGE 46 G0900
BIBLIOG LABOR MGT ADJUD
N

HECKSCHER G.,"GROUP ORGANIZATION IN SWEDEN." SWEDEN STRATA ECO/DEV AGRI INDUS LABOR NAT/G PROF/ORG ECO/TAC CENTRAL SOCISM...MGT 19/20. PAGE 25 G0499
LAISSEZ SOC
S39

HELLMAN F.S.,THE NEW DEAL: SELECTED LIST OF REFERENCES. USA-45 FINAN LABOR EX/STRUC CREATE INT/TRADE ADMIN CT/SYS 20 SUPREME/CT. PAGE 26 G0505
BIBLIOG/A ECO/TAC PLAN POLICY
B40

BAKER H.,PROBLEMS OF REEMPLOYMENT AND RETRAINING OF MANPOWER DURING THE TRANSITION FROM WAR TO PEACE. USA+45 INDUS LABOR LG/CO NAT/G PLAN ADMIN PEACE ...POLICY MGT 20. PAGE 5 G0086
BIBLIOG/A ADJUST WAR PROB/SOLV
B45

MAYO E.,THE SOCIAL PROBLEMS OF AN INDUSTRIAL CIVILIZATION. USA+45 SOCIETY LABOR CROWD PERS/REL LAISSEZ. PAGE 37 G0725
INDUS GP/REL MGT WORKER
B45

WILCOX J.K.,OFFICIAL DEFENSE PUBLICATIONS, 1941-1945 (NINE VOLS.). USA-45 AGRI INDUS R+D LABOR FORCES TEC/DEV EFFICIENCY PRODUC SKILL WEALTH 20.
BIBLIOG/A WAR CIVMIL/REL
B46

PAGE 63 G1238   ADMIN

B47

WHITEHEAD T.N.,LEADERSHIP IN A FREE SOCIETY; A   INDUS
STUDY IN HUMAN RELATIONS BASED ON AN ANALYSIS OF   LEAD
PRESENT-DAY INDUSTRIAL CIVILIZATION. WOR-45 STRUCT   ORD/FREE
R+D LABOR LG/CO SML/CO WORKER PLAN. PROB/SOLV   SOCIETY
TEC/DEV DRIVE...MGT 20. PAGE 63 G1234

B48

STEWART I.,ORGANIZING SCIENTIFIC RESEARCH FOR WAR: DELIB/GP
ADMINISTRATIVE HISTORY OF OFFICE OF SCIENTIFIC   ADMIN
RESEARCH AND DEVELOPMENT. USA-45 INTELL R+D LABOR   WAR
WORKER CREATE BUDGET WEAPON CIVMIL/REL GP/REL   TEC/DEV
EFFICIENCY...POLICY 20. PAGE 53 G1036

B50

BERNSTEIN I.,THE NEW DEAL COLLECTIVE BARGAINING   LABOR
PROCESS. USA-45 GOV/REL ATTIT...BIBLIOG 20   LEGIS
ROOSEVLT/F. PAGE 7 G0132   POLICY
                                                        NEW/LIB

B53

SAYLES L.R.,THE LOCAL UNION. CONSTN CULTURE   LABOR
DELIB/GP PARTIC CHOOSE GP/REL INGP/REL ATTIT ROLE   LEAD
...MAJORIT DECISION MGT. PAGE 49 G0958   ADJUD
                                                        ROUTINE

B53

TOMPKINS D.C.,CIVIL DEFENSE IN THE STATES: A   BIBLIOG
BIBLIOGRAPHY (DEFENSE BIBLIOGRAPHIES NO. 3;   WAR
PAMPHLET). USA+45 LABOR LOC/G NAT/G PROVS LEGIS.   ORD/FREE
PAGE 55 G1076   ADMIN

B54

MOSK S.A.,INDUSTRIAL REVOLUTION IN MEXICO. MARKET   INDUS
LABOR CREATE CAP/ISM ADMIN ATTIT SOCISM...POLICY 20   TEC/DEV
MEXIC/AMER. PAGE 40 G0789   ECO/UNDEV
                                                        NAT/G

B54

WILENSKY H.L.,SYLLABUS OF INDUSTRIAL RELATIONS: A   BIBLIOG
GUIDE TO READING AND RESEARCH. USA+45 MUNIC ADMIN   INDUS
INGP/REL...POLICY MGT PHIL/SCI 20. PAGE 63 G1239   LABOR
                                                        WORKER

C55

BONER H.A.,"HUNGRY GENERATIONS." UK WOR+45 WOR-45   ECO/DEV
STRATA INDUS FAM LABOR CAP/ISM...MGT BIBLIOG 19/20.   PHIL/SCI
PAGE 8 G0151   CONCPT
                                                        WEALTH

B58

DUBIN R.,THE WORLD OF WORK: INDUSTRIAL SOCIETY AND   WORKER
HUMAN RELATIONS. MARKET PROC/MFG LABOR TEC/DEV   ECO/TAC
CAP/ISM AUTOMAT TASK GP/REL EFFICIENCY...CONCPT   PRODUC
CHARTS BIBLIOG 20. PAGE 16 G0317   DRIVE

B59

DAHRENDORF R.,CLASS AND CLASS CONFLICT IN   VOL/ASSN
INDUSTRIAL SOCIETY. LABOR NAT/G COERCE ROLE PLURISM   STRUCT
...POLICY MGT CONCPT CLASSIF. PAGE 14 G0271   SOC
                                                        GP/REL

B60

APTHEKER H.,DISARMAMENT AND THE AMERICAN ECONOMY: A   MARXIST
SYMPOSIUM. FUT USA+45 ECO/DEV DIST/IND FINAN INDUS   ARMS/CONT
PROC/MFG LABOR NAT/G POL/PAR CONSULT PLAN CAP/ISM
INT/TRADE PEACE ATTIT MORAL WEALTH...TREND GEN/LAWS
TOT/POP 20. PAGE 3 G0063

B60

CRAUMER L.V.,BUSINESS PERIODICALS INDEX (8VOLS.).   BIBLIOG/A
USA+45 LABOR TAX 20. PAGE 13 G0262   FINAN
                                                        ECO/DEV
                                                        MGT

B60

PENTONY D.E.,THE UNDERDEVELOPED LANDS. FUT WOR+45   ECO/UNDEV
CULTURE AGRI FINAN INDUS MARKET INT/ORG LABOR NAT/G   POLICY
VOL/ASSN CONSULT TEC/DEV ECO/TAC EDU/PROP COLONIAL   FOR/AID
ATTIT WEALTH...OBS RECORD SAMP TREND GEN/METH WORK   INT/TRADE
UN 20. PAGE 44 G0867

B61

CARNELL F.,THE POLITICS OF THE NEW STATES: A SELECT   BIBLIOG/A
ANNOTATED BIBLIOGRAPHY WITH SPECIAL REFERENCE TO   AFR
THE COMMONWEALTH. CONSTN ELITES LABOR NAT/G POL/PAR   ASIA
EX/STRUC DIPLOM ADJUD ADMIN...GOV/COMP 20   COLONIAL
COMMONWLTH. PAGE 11 G0210

L61

TAUBENFELD H.J.,"A TREATY FOR ANTARCTICA." FUT   R+D
USA+45 INTELL INT/ORG LABOR 20 TREATY ANTARCTICA.   ACT/RES
PAGE 54 G1055   DIPLOM

B62

GRANICK D.,THE EUROPEAN EXECUTIVE. BELGIUM FRANCE   MGT
GERMANY/W UK INDUS LABOR LG/CO SML/CO EX/STRUC PLAN   ECO/DEV
TEC/DEV CAP/ISM COST DEMAND...POLICY CHARTS 20.   ECO/TAC
PAGE 22 G0441   EXEC

S62

VIETORISZ T.,"PRELIMINARY BIBLIOGRAPHY FOR   BIBLIOG/A
INDUSTRIAL DEVELOPMENT PROGRAMMING." ECO/DEV   TEC/DEV
ECO/UNDEV R+D LABOR PROB/SOLV AUTOMAT PRODUC.   ACT/RES
PAGE 61 G1198   PLAN

C62

JOINT ECONOMIC COMMITTEE,"DIMENSIONS OF SOVIET   ECO/DEV
ECONOMIC POWER." USSR R+D FORCES ACT/RES OP/RES   PLAN
TEC/DEV...GEOG STAT BIBLIOG 20. PAGE 29 G0565   PRODUC
                                                        LABOR

B63

KATZ S.M.,A SELECTED LIST OF US READINGS ON   BIBLIOG/A
DEVELOPMENT. AGRI COM/IND DIST/IND INDUS LABOR PLAN   ECO/UNDEV
FOR/AID EDU/PROP HEALTH...POLICY SOC/WK 20. PAGE 30   TEC/DEV
G0582   ACT/RES

B63

SCHOECK H.,THE NEW ARGUMENT IN ECONOMICS. UK USA+45   WELF/ST
INDUS MARKET LABOR NAT/G ECO/TAC ADMIN ROUTINE   FOR/AID
BAL/PAY PWR...POLICY BOLIV. PAGE 49 G0973   ECO/DEV
                                                        ALL/IDEOS

S63

VIETORISZ T.,"PRELIMINARY BIBLIOGRAPHY FOR   BIBLIOG/A
INDUSTRIAL DEVELOPMENT PROGRAMMING." ECO/DEV   TEC/DEV
ECO/UNDEV R+D LABOR PROB/SOLV AUTOMAT PRODUC.   ACT/RES
PAGE 61 G1199   PLAN

B64

HAZLEWOOD A.,THE ECONOMICS OF DEVELOPMENT: AN   BIBLIOG/A
ANNOTATED LIST OF BOOKS AND ARTICLES PUBLISHED   ECO/UNDEV
1958-1962. AGRI FINAN INDUS LABOR NAT/G DIPLOM   TEC/DEV
INT/TRADE INCOME...MGT 20. PAGE 25 G0497

B64

LI C.M.,INDUSTRIAL DEVELOPMENT IN COMMUNIST CHINA.   ASIA
CHINA/COM ECO/DEV AGRI FINAN INDUS MARKET   TEC/DEV
LABOR NAT/G ECO/TAC INT/TRADE EXEC ALL/VALS
...POLICY RELATIV TREND WORK TOT/POP VAL/FREE 20.
PAGE 34 G0665

B64

MILIBAND R.,THE SOCIALIST REGISTER: 1964. GERMANY/W   MARXISM
ITALY UK LABOR POL/PAR ECO/TAC FOR/AID NUC/PWR   SOCISM
...POLICY SOCIALIST IDEA/COMP 20 MAO NASSER/G.   CAP/ISM
PAGE 39 G0769   PROB/SOLV

S64

FLORINSKY M.T.,"TRENDS IN THE SOVIET ECONOMY." COM   ECO/DEV
USA+45 USSR INDUS LABOR NAT/G PLAN TEC/DEV ECO/TAC   AGRI
ALL/VALS SOCISM...MGT METH/CNCPT STYLE CON/ANAL
GEN/METH WORK 20. PAGE 19 G0374

B65

WHITE HOUSE CONFERENCE ON INTERNATIONAL   R+D
COOPERATION(VOL.II). SPACE WOR+45 EXTR/IND INT/ORG   CONFER
LABOR WORKER NUC/PWR PEACE AGE/Y...CENSUS ANTHOL 20   TEC/DEV
RESOURCE/N URBAN/RNWL PUB/TRANS. PAGE 1 G0019   DIPLOM

B65

BAILEY S.K.,AMERICAN POLITICS AND GOVERNMENT.   ANTHOL
USA+45 CONSTN FINAN LABOR POL/PAR DIPLOM ADMIN WAR   LEGIS
INGP/REL RACE/REL NEW/LIB 20 SUPREME/CT PRESIDENT   PWR
CONGRESS. PAGE 4 G0084

B65

CHENG C.-.Y.,SCIENTIFIC AND ENGINEERING MANPOWER IN   WORKER
COMMUNIST CHINA, 1949-1963. CHINA/COM USSR ELITES   CONSULT
ECO/DEV R+D ACADEM LABOR NAT/G EDU/PROP CONTROL   MARXISM
UTIL...POLICY BIBLIOG 20. PAGE 12 G0226   BIOG

B65

MORRIS M.D.,THE EMERGENCE OF AN INDUSTRIAL LABOR   INDUS
FORCE IN INDIA: A STUDY OF THE BOMBAY COTTON MILLS,   LABOR
1854-1947. INDIA WORKER OP/RES ADMIN 19/20. PAGE 40   ECO/UNDEV
G0784   CAP/ISM

B65

TURNER A.N.,INDUSTRIAL JOBS AND THE WORKER. USA+45   WORKER
CULTURE ECO/DEV LABOR MUNIC ACT/RES AUTOMAT TASK   INDUS
...CHARTS BIBLIOG 20. PAGE 55 G1082   ATTIT
                                                        TEC/DEV

B65

UN,SPACE ACTIVITIES AND RESOURCES: REVIEW OF UNITED   SPACE
NATION'S NATIONAL AND INTERNATIONAL PROGRAMS.   NUC/PWR
INT/ORG LABOR PLAN TEC/DEV DIPLOM EFFICIENCY HEALTH   FOR/AID
...GOV/COMP 20 UN. PAGE 55 G1086   PEACE

US LIBRARY OF CONGRESS,A DIRECTORY OF INFORMATION
RESOURCES IN THE UNITED STATES: SOCIAL SCIENCES.
USA+45 ACADEM INT/ORG LABOR PROF/ORG PUB/INST
SCHOOL SECT 20. PAGE 59 G1156
B65
BIBLIOG
R+D
COMPUT/IR

GOULD J.M.,THE TECHNICAL ELITE. INDUS LABOR
TECHRACY...POLICY DECISION STAT CHARTS 20. PAGE 22
G0437
B66
ECO/DEV
TEC/DEV
ELITES
TECHNIC

LINDFORS G.V.,INTERCOLLEGIATE BIBLIOGRAPHY; CASES
IN BUSINESS ADMINISTRATION (VOL. X). FINAN MARKET
LABOR CONSULT PLAN GP/REL PRODUC 20. PAGE 34 G0668
B66
BIBLIOG/A
ADMIN
MGT
OP/RES

ONYEMELUKWE C.C.,PROBLEMS OF INDUSTRIAL PLANNING
AND MANAGEMENT IN NIGERIA. AFR FINAN LABOR DELIB/GP
TEC/DEV ADJUST...MGT TREND BIBLIOG. PAGE 43 G0839
B66
ECO/UNDEV
ECO/TAC
INDUS
PLAN

PEIRCE W.S.,SELECTIVE MANPOWER POLICIES AND THE
TRADE-OFF BETWEEN RISING PRICES AND UNEMPLOYMENT
(DISSERTATION). ECO/DEV WORKER ACT/RES...PHIL/SCI
20. PAGE 44 G0865
B66
PRICE
LABOR
POLICY
ECO/TAC

US DEPARTMENT OF LABOR,PRODUCTIVITY: A
BIBLIOGRAPHY. ECO/DEV INDUS MARKET OP/RES AUTOMAT
COST...STAT 20. PAGE 57 G1119
B66
BIBLIOG/A
PRODUC
LABOR
PLAN

US DEPARTMENT OF LABOR,TECHNOLOGICAL TRENDS IN
MAJOR AMERICAN INDUSTRIES. USA+45 R+D LABOR GP/REL
PRODUC...MGT BIBLIOG 20. PAGE 57 G1120
B66
TEC/DEV
INDUS
TREND
AUTOMAT

PRINCETON U INDUSTRIAL REL SEC,RECENT MATERIAL ON
COLLECTIVE BARGAINING IN GOVERNMENT (PAMPHLET NO.
130). USA+45 ECO/DEV LABOR WORKER ECO/TAC GOV/REL
...MGT 20. PAGE 45 G0890
N66
BIBLIOG/A
BARGAIN
NAT/G
GP/REL

BUDER S.,PULLMAN: AN EXPERIMENT IN INDUSTRIAL ORDER
AND COMMUNITY PLANNING, 1880-1930. USA-45 SOCIETY
LABOR LG/CO CREATE PROB/SOLV CONTROL GP/REL
EFFICIENCY ATTIT...MGT BIBLIOG 19/20 PULLMAN.
PAGE 9 G0184
B67
DIST/IND
INDUS
MUNIC
PLAN

BUTLER J.,BOSTON UNIVERSITY PAPERS ON AFRICA*
TRANSITION IN AFRICAN POLITICS. AFR LAW CONSTN
LABOR POL/PAR TEC/DEV 20. PAGE 10 G0197
B67
IDEA/COMP
NAT/G
PWR

COLEMAN J.R.,THE CHANGING AMERICAN ECONOMY. USA+45
AGRI FINAN LABOR FOR/AID INT/TRADE AUTOMAT GP/REL
INGP/REL ANTHOL. PAGE 13 G0243
B67
BUDGET
ECO/TAC
ECO/DEV
WEALTH

NORTHRUP H.R.,RESTRICTIVE LABOR PRACTICES IN THE
SUPERMARKET INDUSTRY. USA+45 INDUS WORKER TEC/DEV
BARGAIN PAY CONTROL GP/REL COST...STAT CHARTS NLRB.
PAGE 42 G0827
B67
DIST/IND
MARKET
LABOR
MGT

UNIVERSAL REFERENCE SYSTEM,ECONOMIC REGULATION,
BUSINESS, AND GOVERNMENT (VOLUME VIII). WOR+45
WOR-45 ECO/DEV ECO/UNDEV FINAN LABOR TEC/DEV
ECO/TAC INT/TRADE GOV/REL...POLICY COMPUT/IR.
PAGE 56 G1099
B67
BIBLIOG/A
CONTROL
NAT/G

WARNER W.L.,THE EMERGENT AMERICAN SOCIETY VOL I,
LARGE-SCALE ORGANIZATIONS. USA+45 ACADEM USA-45
PROF/ORG SCHOOL SECT EX/STRUC TEC/DEV GP/REL
...TREND CHARTS. PAGE 62 G1215
B67
ANTHOL
NAT/G
LABOR
LG/CO

PRINCETON U INDUSTRIAL REL SEC,COLLECTIVE
BARGAINING IN THE PUBLIC SCHOOLS (PAMPHLET NO. 33).
USA+45 LABOR PROB/SOLV PWR MGT. PAGE 45 G0891
N67
BIBLIOG/A
SCHOOL
BARGAIN
GP/REL

LABOR/PAR....LABOR PARTY (ALL NATIONS)

LABORATORY EXPERIMENTS....SEE LAB/EXP

LAFTA....LATIN AMERICAN FREE TRADE ASSOCIATION; SEE ALSO
INT/ORG, VOL/ASSN, INT/TRADE

HAAS E.B.,"ECONOMICS AND DIFFERENTIAL PATTERNS OF
POLITICAL INTEGRATION: PROJECTIONS ABOUT UNITY IN
LATIN AMERICA." SOCIETY NAT/G DELIB/GP ACT/RES
CREATE PLAN ECO/TAC REGION ROUTINE ATTIT DRIVE PWR
WEALTH...CONCPT TREND CHARTS LAFTA 20. PAGE 24
G0464
L64
L/A+17C
INT/ORG
MARKET

LAGUARD/F....FIORELLO LAGUARDIA

LAHAYE R. G0629

LAISSEZ....LAISSEZ-FAIRE-ISM; SEE ALSO OLD/LIB

HECKSCHER G.,"GROUP ORGANIZATION IN SWEDEN." SWEDEN
STRATA ECO/DEV AGRI INDUS LABOR NAT/G PROF/ORG
ECO/TAC CENTRAL SOCISM...MGT 19/20. PAGE 25 G0499
S39
LAISSEZ
SOC

BEARD C.A.,PUBLIC POLICY AND THE GENERAL WELFARE.
USA-45 CONSTN LAISSEZ POPULISM...POLICY MAJORIT 20.
PAGE 6 G0108
B41
CONCPT
ORD/FREE
PWR
NAT/G

MAYO E.,THE SOCIAL PROBLEMS OF AN INDUSTRIAL
CIVILIZATION. USA+45 SOCIETY LABOR CROWD PERS/REL
LAISSEZ. PAGE 37 G0725
B45
INDUS
GP/REL
MGT
WORKER

SURANYI-UNGER T.,PRIVATE ENTERPRISE AND
GOVERNMENTAL PLANNING. STRUCT FINAN BAL/PWR
HAPPINESS DRIVE NEW/LIB PLURISM...MATH QUANT STAT
TREND BIBLIOG. PAGE 53 G1047
B50
PLAN
NAT/G
LAISSEZ
POLICY

ALLEN S.,LETTER TO A CONSERVATIVE. SOCIETY NAT/G
DIPLOM EDU/PROP NUC/PWR GP/REL ATTIT MORAL
...MAJORIT CONCPT 20. PAGE 2 G0044
B65
ORD/FREE
MARXISM
POLICY
LAISSEZ

SCOVILLE W.J.,"GOVERNMENT REGULATION AND GROWTH IN
THE FRENCH PAPER INDUSTRY DURING THE EIGHTEENTH
CENTURY." FRANCE MOD/EUR FINAN CAP/ISM TAX ADMIN
CONTROL PRIVIL LAISSEZ...POLICY 18. PAGE 50 G0985
S67
NAT/G
PROC/MFG
ECO/DEV
INGP/REL

LAKEWOOD....LAKEWOOD, CALIFORNIA

LAKOF S.A. G0323

LAKOFF/SA....SANFORD A. LAKOFF

LALL B.G. G0630

LAMBERT J. G0631

LAND REFORM....SEE AGRI + CREATE

LAND/LEAG....LAND LEAGUE (IRELAND)

LAND/VALUE....LAND VALUE TAX

LANDRAT....COUNTY CHIEF EXECUTIVE (GERMANY)

LANDRM/GRF....LANDRUM-GRIFFIN ACT

LANDRUM-GRIFFIN ACT....SEE LANDRM/GRF

LANG A.S. G0632

LANG D. G0633

LANGER W.L. G0634

LANGLEY....LANGLEY-PORTER NEUROPSYCHIATRIC INSTITUTE

LANGUAGE....SEE LING, ALSO LOGIC, MATHEMATICS, AND
LANGUAGE INDEX, P. XIV

LANGUEDOC....LANGUEDOC, SOUTHERN FRANCE

LAO/TZU....LAO TZU

LAOS....SEE ALSO S/ASIA

LAPP R.E. G0635

LARCENY....LARCENY

LARSEN K. G0636

LARTEH....LARTEH, GHANA

LASKI H.J. G0637

LASKI/H....HAROLD LASKI

LASSALLE/F....FERDINAND LASSALLE

LASSWELL H.D. G0638,G0639,G0641,G0642,G0643,G0644,G0658,G0737 , G0738,G0739,G0740

LASSWELL/H....HAROLD D. LASSWELL

LATIN AMERICA....SEE L/A+17C

LATIN AMERICAN FREE TRADE ASSOCIATION....SEE LAFTA

LATVIA....SEE ALSO USSR

LAURIER/W....SIR WILFRED LAURIER

LAW....LAW, ETHICAL DIRECTIVES IN A COMMUNITY; SEE ALSO JURID

FULLER G.A.,DEMOBILIZATION: A SELECTED LIST OF REFERENCES. USA+45 LAW AGRI LABOR WORKER ECO/TAC RATION RECEIVE EDU/PROP ROUTINE ARMS/CONT ALL/VALS 20. PAGE 20 G0398
N
BIBLIOG/A
INDUS
FORCES
NAT/G

PERSONNEL. USA+45 LAW LABOR LG/CO WORKER CREATE GOV/REL PERS/REL ATTIT WEALTH. PAGE 1 G0010
N
BIBLIOG/A
ADMIN
MGT
GP/REL

AMER COUNCIL OF LEARNED SOCIET,THE ACLS CONSTITUENT SOCIETY JOURNAL PROJECT. FUT USA+45 LAW NAT/G PLAN DIPLOM PHIL/SCI. PAGE 3 G0048
N
BIBLIOG/A
HUM
COMPUT/IR
COMPUTER

GT BRIT MIN OVERSEAS DEV, LIB, TECHNICAL CO-OPERATION -- A BIBLIOGRAPHY. UK LAW SOCIETY DIPLOM ECO/TAC FOR/AID...STAT 20 CMN/WLTH. PAGE 39 G0775
N
BIBLIOG
TEC/DEV
ECO/DEV
NAT/G

US SUPERINTENDENT OF DOCUMENTS,TRANSPORTATION: HIGHWAYS, ROADS, AND POSTAL SERVICE (PRICE LIST 25). PANAMA USA+45 LAW FORCES DIPLOM ADMIN GOV/REL HEALTH MGT. PAGE 61 G1188
N
BIBLIOG/A
DIST/IND
SERV/IND
NAT/G

ATOMIC INDUSTRIAL FORUM,COMMENTARY ON LEGISLATION TO PERMIT PRIVATE OWNERSHIP OF SPECIAL NUCLEAR MATERIAL (PAMPHLET). USA+45 DELIB/GP LEGIS PLAN OWN ...POLICY 20 AEC CONGRESS. PAGE 4 G0076
N19
NUC/PWR
MARKET
INDUS
LAW

LAWRENCE S.A.,THE BATTERY ADDITIVE CONTROVERSY (PAMPHLET). USA+45 LAW MARKET PROC/MFG R+D CAP/ISM CT/SYS GOV/REL OWN FTC CONGRESS BUR/STNDRD RITCHIE/JM. PAGE 33 G0645
N19
PHIL/SCI
LOBBY
INSPECT

HARPER S.N.,THE GOVERNMENT OF THE SOVIET UNION. COM USSR LAW CONSTN ECO/DEV PLAN TEC/DEV DIPLOM INT/TRADE ADMIN REV NAT/LISM...POLICY 20. PAGE 24 G0483
B38
MARXISM
NAT/G
LEAD
POL/PAR

US LIBRARY OF CONGRESS,CONDUCT OF THE WAR (APRIL 1941-MARCH 1942). USA-45 WOR-45 LAW INDUS PUB/INST TEC/DEV EDU/PROP CIVMIL/REL 20. PAGE 59 G1155
B42
BIBLIOG/A
WAR
FORCES
PLAN

FULLER G.H.,MILITARY GOVERNMENT: A LIST OF REFERENCES (A PAMPHLET). ITALY UK USA-45 WOR-45 LAW FORCES DOMIN ADMIN ARMS/CONT ORD/FREE PWR ...DECISION 20 CHINJAP. PAGE 21 G0404
B44
BIBLIOG
DIPLOM
CIVMIL/REL
SOVEREIGN

GRIFFITH E.S.,"THE CHANGING PATTERN OF PUBLIC POLICY FORMATION." MOD/EUR WOR+45 FINAN CHIEF CONFER ADMIN LEAD CONSERVE SOCISM TECHRACY...SOC CHARTS CONGRESS. PAGE 23 G0450
S44
LAW
POLICY
TEC/DEV

REVES E.,THE ANATOMY OF PEACE. WOR-45 LAW CULTURE NAT/G PLAN TEC/DEV EDU/PROP WAR NAT/LISM ATTIT ALL/VALS SOVEREIGN...POLICY HUM TIME/SEQ 20. PAGE 46 G0914
B45
ACT/RES
CONCPT
NUC/PWR
PEACE

AMERICAN DOCUMENTATION INST,CATALOGUE OF AUXILIARY PUBLICATIONS IN MICROFILMS AND PHOTOPRINTS. USA-45 LAW AGRI CREATE TEC/DEV ADMIN...GEOG LING MATH 20. PAGE 3 G0052
B46
BIBLIOG
EDU/PROP
PSY

TURNER R.H.,"THE NAVY DISBURSING OFFICER AS A BUREAUCRAT" (BMR)" USA-45 LAW STRATA DIST/IND WAR PWR...SOC 20 BUREAUCRCY. PAGE 55 G1083
S47
FORCES
ADMIN
PERSON
ROLE

PUBLIC ADMINISTRATION SERVICE,SOURCE MATERIALS IN PUBLIC ADMINISTRATION: A SELECTED BIBLIOGRAPHY (PAS PUBLICATION NO. 102). USA+45 LAW FINAN LOC/G MUNIC NAT/G PLAN RECEIVE EDU/PROP CT/SYS CHOOSE HEALTH 20. PAGE 45 G0895
B48
BIBLIOG/A
GOV/REL
MGT
ADMIN

HUXLEY J.,FREEDOM AND CULTURE. UNIV LAW SOCIETY R+D ACADEM SCHOOL CREATE SANCTION ATTIT KNOWL...HUM ANTHOL 20. PAGE 27 G0540
B51
CULTURE
ORD/FREE
PHIL/SCI
IDEA/COMP

CALDWELL L.K.,RESEARCH METHODS IN PUBLIC ADMINISTRATION; AN OUTLINE OF TOPICS AND READINGS (PAMPHLET). LAW ACT/RES COMPUTER KNOWL...SOC STAT GEN/METH 20. PAGE 10 G0201
B53
BIBLIOG/A
METH/COMP
ADMIN
OP/RES

LOCKLIN D.P.,ECONOMICS OF TRANSPORTATION (4TH ED.). USA+45 USA-45 SEA AIR LAW FINAN LG/CO EX/STRUC ADMIN CONTROL...STAT CHARTS 19/20 RAILROAD PUB/TRANS. PAGE 34 G0675
B54
ECO/DEV
DIST/IND
ECO/TAC
TEC/DEV

SCARROW H.A.,THE HIGHER PUBLIC SERVICE OF THE COMMONWEALTH OF AUSTRALIA. LAW SENIOR LOBBY ROLE 20 AUSTRAL CIVIL/SERV COMMONWLTH. PAGE 49 G0959
B57
ADMIN
NAT/G
EX/STRUC
GOV/COMP

ATOMIC INDUSTRIAL FORUM,MANAGEMENT AND ATOMIC ENERGY. WOR+45 SEA LAW MARKET NAT/G TEC/DEV INSPECT INT/TRADE CONFER PEACE HEALTH...ANTHOL 20. PAGE 4 G0078
B58
NUC/PWR
INDUS
MGT
ECO/TAC

HALEY A.G.,FIRST COLLOQUIUM ON THE LAW OF OUTER SPACE. WOR+45 INT/ORG ACT/RES PLAN BAL/PWR CONFER ATTIT PWR...POLICY JURID CHARTS ANTHOL 20. PAGE 24 G0468
B59
SPACE
LAW
SOVEREIGN
CONTROL

MAYDA J.,ATOMIC ENERGY AND LAW. ECO/UNDEV FINAN TEC/DEV FOR/AID EFFICIENCY PRODUC WEALTH...POLICY TECHNIC 20. PAGE 37 G0723
B59
NUC/PWR
L/A+17C
LAW
ADMIN

U OF MICHIGAN LAW SCHOOL,ATOMS AND THE LAW. USA+45 PROVS WORKER PROB/SOLV DIPLOM ADMIN GOV/REL ANTHOL. PAGE 55 G1085
B59
NUC/PWR
NAT/G
CONTROL
LAW

US CONGRESS JT ATOM ENRGY COMM,SELECTED MATERIALS ON FEDERAL-STATE COOPERATION IN THE ATOMIC ENERGY FIELD. USA+45 LAW LOC/G PROVS CONSULT LEGIS ADJUD ...POLICY BIBLIOG 20 AEC. PAGE 57 G1111
B59
NAT/G
NUC/PWR
GOV/REL
DELIB/GP

ALBI F.,TRATADO DE LOS MODOS DE GESTION DE LAS CORPORACIONES LOCALES. SPAIN FINAN NAT/G BUDGET CONTROL EXEC ROUTINE GOV/REL ORD/FREE SOVEREIGN ...MGT 20. PAGE 2 G0034
B60
LOC/G
LAW
ADMIN
MUNIC

CARPER E.T.,THE DEFENSE APPROPRIATIONS RIDER (PAMPHLET). USA+45 CONSTN CHIEF DELIB/GP LEGIS BUDGET LOBBY CIVMIL/REL...POLICY 20 CONGRESS EISNHWR/DD DEPT/DEFEN PRESIDENT BOSTON. PAGE 11 G0212
B60
GOV/REL
ADJUD
LAW
CONTROL

GOLDSEN J.M.,INTERNATIONAL POLITICAL IMPLICATIONS OF ACTIVITIES IN OUTER SPACE. FUT USA+45 WOR+45 AIR LAW ACT/RES LEGIT ATTIT KNOWL ORD/FREE PWR...CONCPT 20. PAGE 22 G0427
B60
R+D
SPACE

US SENATE COMM ON COMMERCE,URBAN MASS TRANSPORTATION. FUT USA+45 AIR ECO/DEV FINAN LOC/G MUNIC LEGIS CREATE PROB/SOLV TEC/DEV 20 PUB/TRANS.
B60
DIST/IND
PLAN
NAT/G

LAHAYE R.,LES ENTREPRISES PUBLIQUES AU MAROC.   NAT/G
FRANCE MOROCCO LAW DIST/IND EXTR/IND FINAN CONSULT   INDUS
PLAN TEC/DEV ADMIN AGREE CONTROL OWN...POLICY 20.   ECO/UNDEV
PAGE 32 G0629   ECO/TAC
                                                       B61

MURPHY E.F.,WATER PURITY: A STUDY IN LEGAL CONTROL   SEA
OF NATURAL RESOURCES. LOC/G ACT/RES PLAN TEC/DEV   LAW
LOBBY GP/REL COST ATTIT HEALTH ORD/FREE...HEAL   PROVS
JURID 20 WISCONSIN WATER. PAGE 40 G0797   CONTROL
                                                       B61

SMITH H.H.,THE CITIZEN'S GUIDE TO PLANNING. USA+45   MUNIC
LAW SCHOOL CREATE PROB/SOLV EDU/PROP GP/REL ROLE 20   PLAN
URBAN/RNWL OPEN/SPACE. PAGE 52 G1015   DELIB/GP
                                                       CONSULT
                                                       B61

MACHOWSKI K.,"SELECTED PROBLEMS OF NATIONAL   UNIV
SOVEREIGNTY WITH REFERENCE TO THE LAW OF OUTER   ACT/RES
SPACE." FUT WOR+45 AIR LAW INTELL SOCIETY ECO/DEV   NUC/PWR
PLAN EDU/PROP DETER DRIVE PERCEPT SOVEREIGN   SPACE
...POLICY INT/LAW OBS TREND TOT/POP 20. PAGE 35
G0689   S61

RICHSTEIN A.R.,"LEGAL RULES IN NUCLEAR WEAPONS   NUC/PWR
EMPLOYMENTS." FUT WOR+45 LAW SOCIETY FORCES PLAN   TEC/DEV
WEAPON RIGID/FLEX...HEAL CONCPT TREND VAL/FREE 20.   MORAL
PAGE 47 G0918   ARMS/CONT
                                                       S61

DUPRE J.S.,SCIENCE AND THE NATION: POLICY AND   R+D
POLITICS. USA+45 LAW ACADEM FORCES ADMIN CIVMIL/REL   INDUS
GOV/REL EFFICIENCY PEACE...TREND 20 SCI/ADVSRY.   TEC/DEV
PAGE 16 G0322   NUC/PWR
                                                       B62

KAHN H.,THINKING ABOUT THE UNTHINKABLE. FUT USA+45   INT/ORG
LAW NAT/G CONSULT FORCES ACT/RES CREATE PLAN   ORD/FREE
TEC/DEV BAL/PWR DIPLOM EDU/PROP ARMS/CONT DETER   NUC/PWR
ATTIT...CONCPT OBS TREND COLD/WAR 20. PAGE 29 G0570   PEACE
                                                       B62

STERN A.C.,AIR POLLUTION (2 VOLS.). LAW INDUS   AIR
PROB/SOLV TEC/DEV INSPECT RISK BIO/SOC HABITAT   OP/RES
...OBS/ENVIR TESTS SAMP 20 POLLUTION. PAGE 53 G1035   CONTROL
                                                       HEALTH
                                                       B62

STOVER C.F.,THE GOVERNMENT OF SCIENCE (PAMPHLET).   PHIL/SCI
USA+45 SOCIETY PROF/ORG EX/STRUC CREATE CONTROL   TEC/DEV
NUC/PWR WAR GOV/REL PEACE ORD/FREE 20. PAGE 53   LAW
G1041   NAT/G
                                                       B62

US CONGRESS,COMMUNICATIONS SATELLITE LEGISLATION: SPACE
HEARINGS BEFORE COMM ON AERON AND SPACE SCIENCES ON   COM/IND
BILLS S2550 AND 2814. WOR+45 LAW VOL/ASSN PLAN   ADJUD
DIPLOM CONTROL OWN PEACE...NEW/IDEA CONGRESS NASA.   GOV/REL
PAGE 56 G1110   B62

CRANE R.D.,"LAW AND STRATEGY IN SPACE." FUT USA+45   CONCPT
WOR+45 AIR LAW INT/ORG NAT/G FORCES ACT/RES PLAN   SPACE
BAL/PWR LEGIT ARMS/CONT COERCE ORD/FREE...POLICY
INT/LAW JURID SOC/EXP 20 TREATY. PAGE 13 G0261   S62

DALAND R.T.,PERSPECTIVES OF BRAZILIAN PUBLIC   ADMIN
ADMINISTRATION (VOL. I). BRAZIL LAW ECO/UNDEV   NAT/G
SCHOOL CHIEF TEC/DEV CONFER CONTROL GP/REL ATTIT   PLAN
ROLE PWR...ANTHOL 20. PAGE 14 G0272   GOV/REL
                                                       B63

GEERTZ C.,OLD SOCIETIES AND NEW STATES: THE QUEST   ECO/UNDEV
FOR MODERNITY IN ASIA AND AFRICA. AFR ASIA LAW   TEC/DEV
CULTURE SECT EDU/PROP REV...GOV/COMP NAT/COMP 20.   NAT/LISM
PAGE 21 G0415   SOVEREIGN
                                                       B63

HALEY A.G.,SPACE LAW AND GOVERNMENT. FUT USA+45   INT/ORG
WOR+45 LEGIS ACT/RES CREATE ATTIT RIGID/FLEX   LAW
ORD/FREE PWR SOVEREIGN...POLICY JURID CONCPT CHARTS   SPACE
VAL/FREE 20. PAGE 24 G0469   B63

HAUSMAN W.H.,MANAGING ECONOMIC DEVELOPMENT IN   ECO/UNDEV
AFRICA. AFR USA+45 LAW FINAN WORKER TEC/DEV WEALTH   PLAN
...ANTHOL 20. PAGE 25 G0492   FOR/AID
                                                       MGT

JACOB H.,GERMAN ADMINISTRATION SINCE BISMARCK: ADMIN
CENTRAL AUTHORITY VERSUS LOCAL AUTONOMY. GERMANY   NAT/G
GERMANY/W LAW POL/PAR CONTROL CENTRAL TOTALISM   LOC/G
FASCISM...MAJORIT DECISION STAT CHARTS GOV/COMP   POLICY
19/20 BISMARCK/O HITLER/A WEIMAR/REP. PAGE 28 G0551   B63

OTTOSON H.W.,LAND USE POLICY AND PROBLEMS IN THE   PROB/SOLV
UNITED STATES. USA+45 USA-45 LAW AGRI INDUS NAT/G   UTIL
GP/REL...CHARTS ANTHOL 19/20 HOMEST/ACT. PAGE 43   HABITAT
G0851   POLICY
                                                       B63

MCDOUGAL M.S.,"THE ENJOYMENT AND ACQUISITION OF   PLAN
RESOURCES IN OUTER SPACE." CHRIST-17C FUT WOR+45   TREND
WOR-45 LAW EXTR/IND INT/ORG ACT/RES CREATE TEC/DEV
ECO/TAC LEGIT COERCE HEALTH KNOWL ORD/FREE PWR
WEALTH...JURID HIST/WRIT VAL/FREE. PAGE 37 G0738   L63

CLEVELAND H.,"CRISIS DIPLOMACY." USA+45 WOR+45 LAW   DECISION
FORCES TASK NUC/PWR PWR 20. PAGE 12 G0235   DIPLOM
                                                       PROB/SOLV
                                                       POLICY
                                                       S63

GARDNER R.N.,"COOPERATION IN OUTER SPACE." FUT USSR   INT/ORG
WOR+45 AIR LAW COM/IND CONSULT DELIB/GP CREATE   ACT/RES
KNOWL 20 TREATY. PAGE 21 G0410   PEACE
                                                       SPACE
                                                       S63

BLOUSTEIN E.J.,NUCLEAR ENERGY, PUBLIC POLICY, AND   TEC/DEV
THE LAW. USA+45 NAT/G ADJUD ADMIN GP/REL OWN PEACE   LAW
ATTIT HEALTH...ANTHOL 20. PAGE 7 G0144   POLICY
                                                       NUC/PWR
                                                       B64

COHEN M.,LAW AND POLITICS IN SPACE: SPECIFIC AND   DELIB/GP
URGENT PROBLEMS IN THE LAW OF OUTER SPACE.   LAW
CHINA/COM COM USA+45 USSR WOR+45 COM/IND INT/ORG   INT/LAW
NAT/G LEGIT NUC/PWR ATTIT BIO/SOC...JURID CONCPT   SPACE
CONGRESS 20 STALIN/J. PAGE 12 G0241   B64

HEKHUIS D.J.,INTERNATIONAL STABILITY: MILITARY,   TEC/DEV
ECONOMIC AND POLITICAL DIMENSIONS. FUT WOR+45 LAW   DETER
ECO/UNDEV INT/ORG NAT/G VOL/ASSN FORCES ACT/RES   REGION
BAL/PWR PWR WEALTH...STAT UN 20. PAGE 25 G0503   B64

INST D'ETUDE POL L'U GRENOBLE,ADMINISTRATION   ADMIN
TRADITIONELLE ET PLANIFICATION REGIONALE. FRANCE   MUNIC
LAW POL/PAR PROB/SOLV ADJUST RIGID/FLEX...CHARTS   PLAN
ANTHOL BIBLIOG T 20 REFORMERS. PAGE 28 G0546   CREATE
                                                       B64

NASA,PROCEEDINGS OF CONFERENCE ON THE LAW OF SPACE   SPACE
AND OF SATELLITE COMMUNICATIONS: CHICAGO 1963. FUT   COM/IND
WOR+45 DELIB/GP PROB/SOLV TEC/DEV CONFER ADJUD   LAW
NUC/PWR...POLICY IDEA/COMP 20 NASA. PAGE 41 G0805   DIPLOM
                                                       B64

OSSENBECK F.J.,OPEN SPACE AND PEACE. CHINA/COM FUT   SPACE
USA+45 USSR LAW PROB/SOLV TEC/DEV EDU/PROP NEUTRAL   ORD/FREE
PEACE...AUD/VIS ANTHOL 20. PAGE 43 G0850   DIPLOM
                                                       CREATE
                                                       B64

PETERSON W.,THE POLITICS OF POPULATION. COM EUR+WWI   PLAN
FUT MOD/EUR S/ASIA USA+45 USA-45 WOR+45 LAW CULTURE   CENSUS
FAM SECT DOMIN EDU/PROP BIO/SOC HEALTH ORD/FREE   POLICY
...GEOG STAT TIME/SEQ TREND VAL/FREE. PAGE 44 G0871   B64

SCHWARTZ M.D.,CONFERENCE ON SPACE SCIENCE AND SPACE   SPACE
LAW. FUT COM/IND NAT/G FORCES ACT/RES PLAN BUDGET   LAW
DIPLOM NUC/PWR WEAPON...POLICY ANTHOL 20. PAGE 50   PEACE
G0983   TEC/DEV
                                                       B64

TAUBENFELD H.J.,SPACE AND SOCIETY. USA+45 LAW   SPACE
FORCES CREATE TEC/DEV ADJUD CONTROL COST PEACE   SOCIETY
...PREDICT ANTHOL 20. PAGE 54 G1057   ADJUST
                                                       DIPLOM
                                                       B64

US AIR FORCE ACADEMY ASSEMBLY,OUTER SPACE: FINAL   SPACE
REPORT APRIL 1-4, 1964. FUT USA+45 WOR+45 LAW   CIVMIL/REL
DELIB/GP CONFER ARMS/CONT WAR PEACE ATTIT MORAL   NUC/PWR
...ANTHOL 20 NASA. PAGE 56 G1104   DIPLOM
                                                       B64

BERKS R.N.,"THE US AND WEAPONS CONTROL." WOR+45 LAW   USA+45
INT/ORG NAT/G LEGIS EXEC COERCE PEACE ATTIT   PLAN
                                                       L64

RIGID/FLEX ALL/VALS PWR...POLICY TOT/POP 20. PAGE 7 ARMS/CONT
G0129

S64
MAGGS P.B.,"SOVIET VIEWPOINT ON NUCLEAR WEAPONS IN   COM
INTERNATIONAL LAW." USSR WOR+45 INT/ORG FORCES   LAW
DIPLOM ARMS/CONT ATTIT ORD/FREE PWR...POLICY JURID   INT/LAW
CONCPT OBS TREND CON/ANAL GEN/LAWS VAL/FREE 20.   NUC/PWR
PAGE 35 G0694

B65
US CONGRESS JT ATOM ENRGY COMM,ATOMIC ENERGY   NUC/PWR
LEGISLATION THROUGH 89TH CONGRESS, 1ST SESSION.   FORCES
USA+45 LAW INT/ORG DELIB/GP BUDGET DIPLOM 20 AEC   PEACE
CONGRESS CASEBOOK EURATOM IAEA. PAGE 57 G1114   LEGIS

B65
US CONGRESS JT ATOM ENRGY COMM,PROPOSED AMENDMENT   LAW
TO SECTION 271 OF THE ATOMIC ENERGY ACT OF 1954.   LEGIS
USA+45 CONSTRUC PLAN INSPECT CONTROL CT/SYS 20   DELIB/GP
CONGRESS AEC. PAGE 57 G1115   NUC/PWR

C65
SEARA M.V.,"COSMIC INTERNATIONAL LAW." LAW ACADEM   SPACE
ACT/RES DIPLOM COLONIAL CONTROL NUC/PWR SOVEREIGN   INT/LAW
...GEN/LAWS BIBLIOG UN. PAGE 50 G0987   IDEA/COMP
   INT/ORG

B66
DUNBAR L.W.,A REPUBLIC OF EQUALS. USA+45 CREATE   LAW
ADJUD PEACE NEW/LIB...POLICY 20 SOUTH/US   CONSTN
CIV/RIGHTS. PAGE 16 G0320   FEDERAL
   RACE/REL

B66
GRUNEWALD D.,PUBLIC POLICY AND THE MODERN   LG/CO
COOPERATION: SELECTED READINGS. USA+45 LAW MARKET   POLICY
VOL/ASSN CAP/ISM INT/TRADE CENTRAL OWN...SOC ANTHOL   NAT/G
20. PAGE 23 G0458   CONTROL

B66
HOPKINS J.F.K.,ARABIC PERIODICAL LITERATURE, 1961.   BIBLIOG/A
ISLAM LAW CULTURE SECT...GEOG HEAL PHIL/SCI PSY SOC   NAT/LISM
20. PAGE 27 G0528   TEC/DEV
   INDUS

B66
MARKHAM J.W.,AN ECONOMIC-MEDIA STUDY OF BOOK   PRESS
PUBLISHING. USA+45 LAW COM/IND ACADEM SCHOOL   ECO/TAC
EDU/PROP AUTOMAT CONTROL...DECISION STAT CHARTS 20   TEC/DEV
CONGRESS. PAGE 36 G0707   NAT/G

B67
BUNGE M.,THE SEARCH FOR SYSTEM. VOL. 3, PART 1 OF   PHIL/SCI
STUDIES IN THE FOUNDATIONS METHODOLOGY, AND   METH
PHILOSOPHY OF SCIENCE. UNIV LAW INTELL KNOWL.   GEN/LAWS
PAGE 10 G0187   CONCPT

B67
BURNS E.L.M.,MEGAMURDER. WOR+45 LAW INT/ORG NAT/G   FORCES
BAL/PWR DIPLOM DETER MURDER WEAPON CIVMIL/REL PEACE   PLAN
...INT/LAW TREND 20. PAGE 10 G0193   WAR
   NUC/PWR

B67
BUTLER J.,BOSTON UNIVERSITY PAPERS ON AFRICA*   IDEA/COMP
TRANSITION IN AFRICAN POLITICS. AFR LAW CONSTN   NAT/G
LABOR POL/PAR TEC/DEV 20. PAGE 10 G0197   PWR

B67
GARCIA ROBLES A.,THE DENUCLEARIZATION OF LATIN   NUC/PWR
AMERICA (TRANS. BY MARJORIE URQUIDI). LAW PLAN   ARMS/CONT
DIPLOM...ANTHOL 20 TREATY UN. PAGE 21 G0409   L/A+17C
   INT/ORG

B67
HODGKINSON R.G.,THE ORIGINS OF THE NATIONAL HEALTH   HEAL
SERVICE: THE MEDICAL SERVICES OF THE NEW POOR LAW,   NAT/G
1834-1871. UK INDUS MUNIC WORKER PROB/SOLV   POLICY
EFFICIENCY ATTIT HEALTH WEALTH SOCISM...JURID   LAW
SOC/WK 19/20. PAGE 26 G0519

B67
KAPLAN B.,AN UNHURRIED VIEW OF COPYRIGHT. FUT   TEC/DEV
...JURID 20. PAGE 29 G0575   LAW
   LICENSE

B67
ORLANS H.,CONTRACTING FOR ATOMS. USA+45 LAW INTELL   NUC/PWR
ACADEM LG/CO NAT/G PLAN TEC/DEV CONTROL DETER   R+D
...TREND 20 AEC. PAGE 43 G0845   PRODUC
   PEACE

B67
PADELFORD N.J.,THE DYNAMICS OF INTERNATIONAL   DIPLOM
POLITICS (2ND ED.). WOR+45 LAW INT/ORG FORCES   NAT/G

TEC/DEV REGION NAT/LISM PEACE ATTIT PWR ALL/IDEOS   POLICY
UN COLD/WAR NATO TREATY. PAGE 43 G0856   DECISION

B67
POMEROY W.J.,HALF A CENTURY OF SOCIALISM. USSR LAW   SOCISM
AGRI INDUS NAT/G CREATE DIPLOM EDU/PROP PERSON   MARXISM
ORD/FREE WEALTH...POLICY TREND 20. PAGE 45 G0884   COM
   SOCIETY

B67
UNIVERSAL REFERENCE SYSTEM,BIBLIOGRAPHY OF   BIBLIOG/A
BIBLIOGRAPHIES IN POLITICAL SCIENCE, GOVERNMENT,   NAT/G
AND PUBLIC POLICY (VOLUME III). WOR+45 WOR-45 LAW   DIPLOM
ADMIN...SOC CON/ANAL COMPUT/IR GEN/METH. PAGE 56   POLICY
G1095

B67
UNIVERSAL REFERENCE SYSTEM,PUBLIC POLICY AND THE   BIBLIOG/A
MANAGEMENT OF SCIENCE (VOLUME IX). FUT SPACE WOR+45   POLICY
LAW NAT/G TEC/DEV CONTROL NUC/PWR GOV/REL   MGT
...COMPUT/IR GEN/METH. PAGE 56 G1100   PHIL/SCI

B67
UNIVERSAL REFERENCE SYSTEM,LAW, JURISPRUDENCE, AND   BIBLIOG/A
JUDICIAL PROCESS (VOLUME VII). WOR+45 WOR-45 CONSTN   LAW
NAT/G LEGIS JUDGE CT/SYS...INT/LAW COMPUT/IR   JURID
GEN/METH METH. PAGE 56 G1101   ADJUD

B67
US PRES COMN LAW ENFORCE-JUS,THE CHALLENGE OF CRIME   CT/SYS
IN A FREE SOCIETY. LAW STRUCT CONSULT ACT/RES   PUB/INST
TEC/DEV INGP/REL...SOC/WK 20. PAGE 59 G1160   CRIMLGY
   CRIME

B67
US SENATE COMM ON FOREIGN REL,TREATY ON OUTER   SPACE
SPACE. WOR+45 AIR FORCES PROB/SOLV NUC/PWR SENATE   DIPLOM
TREATY UN. PAGE 60 G1182   ARMS/CONT
   LAW

B67
US SENATE COMM ON FOREIGN REL,FOREIGN ASSISTANCE   FOR/AID
ACT OF 1967. VIETNAM WOR+45 DELIB/GP CONFER CONTROL   LAW
WAR WEAPON BAL/PAY...CENSUS CHARTS SENATE. PAGE 60   DIPLOM
G1185   POLICY

B67
US SUPERINTENDENT OF DOCUMENTS,LIBRARY OF CONGRESS   BIBLIOG/A
(PRICE LIST 83). AFR ASIA EUR+WWI USA-45 USSR NAT/G   USA+45
DIPLOM CONFER CT/SYS WAR...DECISION PHIL/SCI   AUTOMAT
CLASSIF 19/20 CONGRESS PRESIDENT. PAGE 61 G1189   LAW

L67
BARRON J.A.,"ACCESS TO THE PRESS." USA+45 TEC/DEV   ORD/FREE
PRESS TV ADJUD AUD/VIS. PAGE 5 G0099   COM/IND
   EDU/PROP
   LAW

L67
CARMICHAEL D.M.,"FORTY YEARS OF WATER POLLUTION   HEALTH
CONTROL IN WISCONSIN: A CASE STUDY." LAW EXTR/IND   CONTROL
INDUS MUNIC DELIB/GP PLAN PROB/SOLV SANCTION   ADMIN
...CENSUS CHARTS 20 WISCONSIN. PAGE 11 G0207   ADJUD

L67
EINAUDI L.,"ANNOTATED BIBLIOGRAPHY OF LATIN   BIBLIOG/A
AMERICAN MILITARY JOURNALS" LAW TEC/DEV DOMIN   NAT/G
EDU/PROP COERCE WAR CIVMIL/REL 20. PAGE 17 G0336   FORCES
   L/A+17C

L67
NADER R.,"AUTOMOBILE DESIGN AND THE JUDICIAL   LAW
PROCESS." USA+45 CT/SYS SUPEGO JURID. PAGE 40 G0799   ADJUD
   TEC/DEV
   PROC/MFG

L67
SEABERG G.P.,"THE DRUG ABUSE PROBLEMS AND SOME   BIO/SOC
PROPOSALS." UK USA+45 MARKET SANCTION CRIME   LAW
...POLICY NEW/IDEA. PAGE 50 G0986   ADJUD
   PROB/SOLV

L67
TRAVERS H. JR.,"AN EXAMINATION OF THE CAB'S MERGER   ADJUD
POLICY." USA+45 USA-45 LAW NAT/G LEGIS PLAN ADMIN   LG/CO
...DECISION 20 CONGRESS. PAGE 55 G1078   POLICY
   DIST/IND

S67
ARONOWITZ D.S.,"CIVIL COMMITMENT OF NARCOTIC   PUB/INST
ADDICTS." USA+45 LAW INGP/REL DISCRIM MORAL...TREND   ACT/RES
20. PAGE 4 G0069   POLICY

S67
CARY G.D.,"THE QUIET REVOLUTION IN COPYRIGHT* THE   COM/IND
END OF THE 'PUBLICATION' CONCEPT." USA+45 LAW   POLICY

OP/RES TEC/DEV CONFER DEBATE EFFICIENCY...JURID
CONGRESS. PAGE 11 G0217
LICENSE
PRESS

CONWAY J.E.,"MAKING RESEARCH EFFECTIVE IN
LEGISLATION." LAW R+D CONSULT EX/STRUC PLAN CONFER
ADMIN LEAD ROUTINE TASK INGP/REL DECISION. PAGE 13
G0252
S67
ACT/RES
POLICY
LEGIS
PROB/SOLV

CRANBERG L.,"SCIENCE, ETHICS, AND LAW." UNIV CREATE
PLAN EDU/PROP INGP/REL PERS/REL ADJUST RATIONAL
KNOWL MORAL...CONCPT IDEA/COMP 20. PAGE 13 G0260
S67
LAW
PHIL/SCI
INTELL

GANZ G.,"THE CONTROL OF INDUSTRY BY ADMINISTRATIVE
PROCESS." UK DELIB/GP WORKER 20. PAGE 21 G0408
S67
INDUS
LAW
ADMIN
CONTROL

LAY S.H.,"EXCLUSIVE GOVERNMENTAL LIABILITY FOR
SPACE ACCIDENTS." USA+45 LAW FINAN SERV/IND TEC/DEV
ADJUD. PAGE 33 G0646
S67
NAT/G
SUPEGO
SPACE
PROB/SOLV

PENNEY N.,"BANK STATEMENTS, CANCELLED CHECKS, AND
ARTICLE FOUR IN THE ELECTRONIC AGE." USA+45 TEC/DEV
COST EFFICIENCY WEALTH. PAGE 44 G0866
S67
CREATE
LAW
ADJUD
FINAN

RICH G.S.,"THE PROPOSED PATENT LEGISLATION* SOME
COMMENTS." USA+45 LAW R+D ACT/RES TEC/DEV CONFER
EFFICIENCY OWN JURID. PAGE 46 G0916
S67
LICENSE
POLICY
CREATE
CAP/ISM

ROBINSON J.A.T.,"ABORTION* THE CASE FOR A FREE
DECISION." LAW PROB/SOLV SANCTION ATTIT MORAL...PSY
IDEA/COMP 20 ABORTION. PAGE 47 G0930
S67
PLAN
ILLEGIT
SEX
HEALTH

WHITTIER J.M.,"COMPULSORY POOLING AND UNITIZATION*
DIE-HARD KANSAS." LAW PLAN EDU/PROP ATTIT...POLICY
JURID PREDICT TREND METH/COMP 20. PAGE 63 G1236
S67
LEGIS
MUNIC
INDUS
ECO/TAC

BENTHAM J.,DEFENCE OF USURY (1787). UK LAW NAT/G
TEC/DEV ECO/TAC CONTROL ATTIT...CONCPT IDEA/COMP 18
SMITH/ADAM. PAGE 6 G0124
B88
TAX
FINAN
ECO/DEV
POLICY

LAW/ETHIC....ETHICS OF LAW AND COURT PROCESSES

LAWRENC/TE....THOMAS EDWARD LAWRENCE

LAWRENCE P.R. G1082

LAWRENCE S.A. G0645

LAWS R. G0620

LAY S.H. G0646

LAZARSFELD P.F. G0758

LAZRSFLD/P....PAUL LAZARSFELD (AND LAZARSFELD SCALE)

LE GHAIT E. G0647

LEAD....LEADING, CONTRIBUTING MORE THAN AVERAGE

CONOVER H.L.,CIVILIAN DEFENSE: A SELECTED LIST OF
RECENT REFERENCES (PAMPHLET). USA+45 LOC/G MUNIC
PROB/SOLV ADMIN LEAD TASK WEAPON GOV/REL...POLICY
CON/ANAL 20 CIV/DEFENS. PAGE 13 G0251
N
BIBLIOG
PLAN
WAR
CIVMIL/REL

WEIGLEY R.F.,HISTORY OF THE UNITED STATES ARMY.
USA+45 USA-45 SOCIETY NAT/G LEAD WAR GP/REL PWR
...SOC METH/COMP COLD/WAR. PAGE 62 G1222
N
FORCES
ADMIN
ROLE
CIVMIL/REL

BRITISH COMMONWEALTH BUR AGRI,WORLD AGRICULTURAL
ECONOMICS AND RURAL SOCIOLOGY ABSTRACTS. NAT/G
OP/RES PLAN TEC/DEV LEAD PRODUC...GEOG MGT NAT/COMP
20. PAGE 9 G0170
B
BIBLIOG/A
AGRI
SOC
WORKER

HARPER S.N.,THE GOVERNMENT OF THE SOVIET UNION. COM
USSR LAW CONSTN ECO/DEV PLAN TEC/DEV DIPLOM
INT/TRADE ADMIN REV NAT/LISM...POLICY 20. PAGE 24
G0483
B38
MARXISM
NAT/G
LEAD
POL/PAR

GRIFFITH E.S.,"THE CHANGING PATTERN OF PUBLIC
POLICY FORMATION." MOD/EUR WOR+45 FINAN CHIEF
CONFER ADMIN LEAD CONSERVE SOCISM TECHRACY...SOC
CHARTS CONGRESS. PAGE 23 G0450
S44
LAW
POLICY
TEC/DEV

BECK H.P.,MEN WHO CONTROL OUR UNIVERSITIES.
EX/STRUC CHOOSE INGP/REL DISCRIM PERSON WEALTH
...POLICY TREND CON/ANAL CHARTS BIBLIOG. PAGE 6
G0112
B47
EDU/PROP
ACADEM
CONTROL
LEAD

WHITEHEAD T.N.,LEADERSHIP IN A FREE SOCIETY; A
STUDY IN HUMAN RELATIONS BASED ON AN ANALYSIS OF
PRESENT-DAY INDUSTRIAL CIVILIZATION. WOR-45 STRUCT
R+D LABOR LG/CO SML/CO WORKER PLAN PROB/SOLV
TEC/DEV DRIVE...MGT 20. PAGE 63 G1234
B47
INDUS
LEAD
ORD/FREE
SOCIETY

KILE O.M.,THE FARM BUREAU MOVEMENT: THE FARM BUREAU
THROUGH THREE DECADES. NAT/G LEGIS LEAD LOBBY
GP/REL INCOME POLICY. PAGE 30 G0596
B48
AGRI
STRUCT
VOL/ASSN
DOMIN

HARDIN L.M.,"REFLECTIONS ON AGRICULTURAL POLICY
FORMATION IN THE UNITED STATES." LEGIS PLAN BUDGET
ECO/TAC LEAD CENTRAL...MGT SOC NEW/IDEA STAT FAO.
PAGE 24 G0480
S48
AGRI
POLICY
ADMIN
NEW/LIB

BAVELAS A.,"COMMUNICATION PATTERNS IN TASK-ORIENTED
GROUPS" (BMR)" R+D OP/RES INSPECT LEAD CENTRAL
EFFICIENCY HAPPINESS RIGID/FLEX...PROBABIL 20.
PAGE 6 G0106
S50
ACT/RES
PERS/REL
TASK
INGP/REL

WAGER P.W.,"COUNTY GOVERNMENT ACROSS THE NATION."
USA+45 CONSTN COM/IND FINAN SCHOOL DOMIN CT/SYS
LEAD GOV/REL...STAT BIBLIOG 20. PAGE 61 G1204
C50
LOC/G
PROVS
ADMIN
ROUTINE

MACRAE D.G.,"THE BOLSHEVIK IDEOLOGY; THE
INTELLECTUAL AND EMOTIONAL FACTORS IN COMMUNIST
AFFILIATION" (BMR)" COM LEAD REV ATTIT ORD/FREE
...SOC CON/ANAL 20 BOLSHEVISM. PAGE 35 G0693
S51
MARXISM
INTELL
PHIL/SCI
SECT

SAYLES L.R.,THE LOCAL UNION. CONSTN CULTURE
DELIB/GP PARTIC CHOOSE GP/REL INGP/REL ATTIT ROLE
...MAJORIT DECISION MGT. PAGE 49 G0958
B53
LABOR
LEAD
ADJUD
ROUTINE

HART B.H.L.,STRATEGY (REV. ED.). CHRIST-17C EUR+WWI
MEDIT-7 MOD/EUR TEC/DEV LEAD REV WEAPON...POLICY
CHARTS. PAGE 25 G0486
B54
WAR
PLAN
FORCES
PHIL/SCI

HOOPES T.,"CIVILIAN-MILITARY BALANCE." USA+45 CHIEF
FORCES PLAN CONTROL WAR GOV/REL GP/REL INGP/REL
...POLICY 19/20. PAGE 27 G0527
S54
CIVMIL/REL
LEAD
PWR
NAT/G

LONG N.E.,"PUBLIC POLICY AND ADMINISTRATION: THE
GOALS OF RATIONALITY AND RESPONSIBILITY." EX/STRUC
ADMIN LEAD 20. PAGE 34 G0676
S54
PROB/SOLV
EXEC
REPRESENT

VUCINICH A.,THE SOVIET ACADEMY OF SCIENCES. USSR
STRUCT ACADEM NAT/G EDU/PROP ADMIN LEAD ROLE
...BIBLIOG 20 ACADEM/SCI. PAGE 61 G1203
B56
PHIL/SCI
CREATE
INTELL
PROF/ORG

BAUMGARTEL H.,"LEADERSHIP STYLE AS A VARIABLE IN
RESEARCH ADMINISTRATION." USA+45 ADMIN REPRESENT
PERS/REL 20. PAGE 5 G0104
S57
LEAD
EXEC
MGT
INGP/REL

GODDARD V.,THE ENIGMA OF MENACE. WOR+45 SECT LEAD
NUC/PWR WAR WEAPON CHOOSE PERSON PWR...POLICY
PHIL/SCI PACIFIST 20 COLD/WAR. PAGE 22 G0423
B59
PEACE
ARMS/CONT
DIPLOM
ATTIT

SPANIER J.W.,THE TRUMAN-MACARTHUR CONTROVERSY AND THE KOREAN WAR. USA+45 TOP/EX PROB/SOLV LEAD ATTIT PWR...POLICY BIBLIOG/A UN. PAGE 52 G1023
B59
CIVMIL/REL
FORCES
CHIEF
WAR

VAN WAGENEN R.W.,SOME VIEWS OF AMERICAN DEFENSE OFFICIALS ABOUT THE UNITED NATIONS (PAPER). FUT USA+45 NAT/G DIPLOM WAR EFFICIENCY PEACE...POLICY INT 20 UN DEPT/DEFEN. PAGE 61 G1192
B59
INT/ORG
LEAD
ATTIT
FORCES

JANOWITZ M.,THE PROFESSIONAL SOLDIER. CULTURE STRATA STRUCT FAM PROB/SOLV TEC/DEV COERCE WAR CIVMIL/REL NAT/LISM AGE HEREDITY ALL/VALS CONSERVE ...MGT WORSHIP. PAGE 28 G0560
B60
FORCES
MYTH
LEAD
ELITES

KINGSTON-MCCLOUG E.,DEFENSE; POLICY AND STRATEGY. UK SEA AIR TEC/DEV DIPLOM ADMIN LEAD WAR ORD/FREE ...CHARTS 20. PAGE 30 G0597
B60
FORCES
PLAN
POLICY
DECISION

MCGREGOR D.,THE HUMAN SIDE OF ENTERPRISE. USA+45 LEAD ROUTINE GP/REL INGP/REL...CONCPT GEN/LAWS 20. PAGE 38 G0741
B60
MGT
ATTIT
SKILL
EDU/PROP

WILLIAUS T.H.,AMERICANS AT WAR: THE DEVELOPMENT OF THE AMERICAN MILITARY SYSTEM. USA+45 USA-45 EDU/PROP LEAD REV...GP/COMP BIBLIOG/A 18/20 PRESIDENT. PAGE 63 G1244
B60
FORCES
WAR
NAT/G
POLICY

JANOWITZ M.,COMMUNITY POLITICAL SYSTEMS. USA+45 SOCIETY INDUS VOL/ASSN TEC/DEV ADMIN LEAD CHOOSE ...SOC SOC/WK 20. PAGE 29 G0561
B61
MUNIC
STRUCT
POL/PAR

FAIR M.L.,"PORT AUTHORITIES IN THE UNITED STATES." PROB/SOLV ADMIN LEAD REPRESENT PWR...DECISION GEOG. PAGE 18 G0357
S61
MUNIC
REGION
LOC/G
GOV/REL

DODDS H.W.,THE ACADEMIC PRESIDENT "EDUCATOR OR CARETAKER? FINAN DELIB/GP EDU/PROP PARTIC ATTIT ROLE PWR...POLICY RECORD INT. PAGE 16 G0304
B62
ACADEM
ADMIN
LEAD
CONTROL

NEIBURG H.L.,"THE EISENHOWER AEC AND CONGRESS: A STUDY IN EXECUTIVE-LEGISLATIVE RELATIONS." USA+45 NAT/G POL/PAR DELIB/GP EX/STRUC TOP/EX ADMIN EXEC LEAD ROUTINE PWR...POLICY COLD/WAR CONGRESS PRESIDENT AEC. PAGE 41 G0816
L62
CHIEF
LEGIS
GOV/REL
NUC/PWR

HEYEL C.,THE ENCYCLOPEDIA OF MANAGEMENT. WOR+45 MARKET TOP/EX TEC/DEV AUTOMAT LEAD ADJUST...STAT CHARTS GAME ANTHOL BIBLIOG. PAGE 26 G0509
B63
MGT
INDUS
ADMIN
FINAN

LITTERER J.A.,ORGANIZATIONS: STRUCTURE AND BEHAVIOR. PLAN DOMIN CONTROL LEAD ROUTINE SANCTION INGP/REL EFFICIENCY PRODUC DRIVE RIGID/FLEX PWR. PAGE 34 G0674
B63
ADMIN
CREATE
MGT
ADJUST

MENEZES A.J.,SUBDESENVOLVIMENTO E POLITICA INTERNACIONAL. BRAZIL WOR+45 PLAN CONTROL LEAD NAT/LISM ORD/FREE 20 THIRD/WRLD. PAGE 38 G0754
B63
ECO/UNDEV
DIPLOM
POLICY
BAL/PWR

MILBRATH L.W.,THE WASHINGTON LOBBYISTS. CONSTN BAL/PWR CONTROL LEAD TASK CHOOSE SUPEGO...DECISION STAT CHARTS BIBLIOG. PAGE 39 G0767
B63
LOBBY
POLICY
PERS/REL

PEABODY R.L.,NEW PERSPECTIVES ON THE HOUSE OF REPRESENTATIVES. AGRI FINAN SCHOOL FORCES CONFER LEAD CHOOSE REPRESENT FEDERAL...POLICY DECISION HOUSE/REP. PAGE 44 G0862
B63
NEW/IDEA
LEGIS
PWR
ADMIN

US SENATE,DOCUMENTS ON INTERNATIONAL AS"ECTS OF EXPLORATION AND USE OF OUTER SPACE, 1954-62: STAFF REPORT FOR COMM AERON SPACE SCI. USA+45 USSR LEGIS LEAD CIVMIL/REL PEACE...POLICY INT/LAW ANTHOL 20 CONGRESS NASA KHRUSH/N. PAGE 59 G1162
B63
SPACE
UTIL
GOV/REL
DIPLOM

US SENATE COMM APPROPRIATIONS,PERSONNEL ADMINISTRATION AND OPERATIONS OF AGENCY FOR INTERNATIONAL DEVELOPMENT: SPECIAL HEARING. FINAN LEAD COST UTIL SKILL...CHARTS 20 CONGRESS AID CIVIL/SERV. PAGE 60 G1175
B63
ADMIN
FOR/AID
EFFICIENCY
DIPLOM

COMMITTEE ECONOMIC DEVELOPMENT,TAXES AND TRADE: 20 YEARS OF CED POLICY (PAMPHLET). USA+45 ECO/DEV PLAN BUDGET LEAD...POLICY KENNEDY/JF PRESIDENT. PAGE 13 G0246
N63
FINAN
ECO/TAC
NAT/G
DELIB/GP

SCHEINMAN L.,ATOMIC ENERGY POLICY IN FRANCE UNDER THE FOURTH REPUBLIC. FRANCE UK USA+45 ELITES POL/PAR PLAN PROB/SOLV DIPLOM LEAD GOV/REL ...BIBLIOG 20 DEGAULLE/C. PAGE 49 G0962
B65
NUC/PWR
NAT/G
DELIB/GP
POLICY

LEISERSON A.,"SCIENTISTS AND THE POLICY PROCESS." USA+45 NAT/G LEAD PARTIC REPRESENT. PAGE 33 G0654
S65
PHIL/SCI
ADMIN
EX/STRUC
EXEC

HALPIN A.W.,THEORY AND RESEARCH IN ADMINISTRATION. ACT/RES LEAD...MGT IDEA/COMP METH/COMP. PAGE 24 G0475
B66
GEN/LAWS
EDU/PROP
ADMIN
PHIL/SCI

ROSHOLT R.L.,AN ADMINISTRATIVE HISTORY OF NASA, 1958-1963. SPACE USA+45 FINAN LEAD...MGT CHARTS BIBLIOG 20 NASA. PAGE 48 G0938
B66
ADMIN
EX/STRUC
ADJUST
DELIB/GP

DOUGHERTY J.E.,"THE CATHOLIC CHURCH, WAR AND NUCLEAR WEAPONS." COM EUR+WWI SECT TOP/EX LEAD DETER ALL/VALS. PAGE 16 G0312
L66
CATHISM
MORAL
WAR
NUC/PWR

HEILBRONER R.L.,THE LIMITS OF AMERICAN CAPITALISM. FUT ECO/DEV INDUS LG/CO EX/STRUC LEAD PWR TECHRACY 20. PAGE 25 G0502
B67
ELITES
CREATE
TEC/DEV
CAP/ISM

LAMBERT J.,LATIN AMERICA: SOCIAL STRUCTURES AND POLITICAL INSTITUTIONS. STRUCT TEC/DEV DIPLOM ADMIN COLONIAL LEAD ATTIT...SOC CLASSIF NAT/COMP 17/20. PAGE 32 G0631
B67
L/A+17C
NAT/G
ECO/UNDEV
SOCIETY

MACKINTOSH J.M.,JUGGERNAUT. USSR NAT/G POL/PAR ADMIN LEAD CIVMIL/REL COST TOTALISM PWR MARXISM ...GOV/COMP 20. PAGE 35 G0691
B67
WAR
FORCES
COM
PROF/ORG

SCHEINMAN L.,EURATOM* NUCLEAR INTEGRATION IN EUROPE. EX/STRUC LEAD 20 EURATOM. PAGE 49 G0963
B67
INT/ORG
NAT/LISM
NUC/PWR
DIPLOM

YAMAMURA K.,ECONOMIC POLICY IN POSTWAR JAPAN. ASIA FINAN POL/PAR DIPLOM LEAD NAT/LISM ATTIT NEW/LIB POPULISM 20 CHINJAP. PAGE 64 G1262
B67
ECO/DEV
POLICY
NAT/G
TEC/DEV

DAVIS P.C.,"THE COMING CHINESE COMMUNIST NUCLEAR THREAT AND U.S. SEA BASED ABM OPTIONS." ASIA CHINA/COM FUT USA+45 SEA NAT/G FORCES PLAN TEC/DEV LEAD ARMS/CONT...GEOG METH/COMP 20 ABM/DEFSYS. PAGE 14 G0279
L67
NUC/PWR
DETER
WEAPON
DIPLOM

BENN W.,"TECHNOLOGY HAS AN INEXORABLE EFFECT." FUT UK ECO/DEV INT/ORG CONSULT PLAN EDU/PROP ADMIN LEAD GP/REL PRODUC...INT 20 EEC. PAGE 6 G0119
S67
R+D
LG/CO
TEC/DEV
INDUS

CARR E.H.,"REVOLUTION FROM ABOVE." USSR STRATA FINAN INDUS NAT/G DOMIN LEAD GP/REL INGP/REL OWN PRODUC PWR 20 STALIN/J. PAGE 11 G0214
S67
AGRI
POLICY
COM
EFFICIENCY

CHIU S.M.,"CHINA'S MILITARY POSTURE." CHINA/COM ELITES NAT/G POL/PAR TEC/DEV ECO/TAC DOMIN CONTROL LEAD REV MARXISM 20 MAO. PAGE 12 G0228
S67
FORCES
CIVMIL/REL
NUC/PWR

DIPLOM

CONWAY J.E.,"MAKING RESEARCH EFFECTIVE IN
LEGISLATION." LAW R+D CONSULT EX/STRUC PLAN CONFER
ADMIN LEAD ROUTINE TASK INGP/REL DECISION. PAGE 13
G0252
    S67
ACT/RES
POLICY
LEGIS
PROB/SOLV

DADDARIO E.Q.,"CONGRESS FACES SPACE POLICIES." R+D
NAT/G FORCES CREATE LEAD...DECISION CONGRESS NASA.
PAGE 14 G0269
    S67
SPACE
PLAN
BUDGET
POLICY

GOBER J.L.,"FEDERALISM AT WORK." USA+45 NAT/G
CONSULT ACT/RES PLAN CONFER ADMIN LEAD PARTIC
FEDERAL ATTIT. PAGE 21 G0422
    S67
MUNIC
TEC/DEV
R+D
GOV/REL

HABERER J.,"POLITICS AND THE COMMUNITY OF SCIENCE."
USA+45 SOCIETY ACT/RES PARTIC ATTIT PHIL/SCI.
PAGE 24 G0465
    S67
LEAD
SUPEGO
INTELL
LOBBY

MCNAMARA R.L.,"THE NEED FOR INNOVATIVENESS IN
DEVELOPING SOCIETIES." L/A+17C EDU/PROP ADMIN LEAD
WEALTH...POLICY PSY SOC METH 20 COLOMB. PAGE 38
G0747
    S67
PROB/SOLV
PLAN
ECO/UNDEV
NEW/IDEA

RICHMAN B.M.,"SOVIET MANAGEMENT IN TRANSITION."
USSR FINAN MARKET EX/STRUC PLAN PROB/SOLV TEC/DEV
CONTROL LEAD CENTRAL EFFICIENCY...METH/COMP 20
REFORMERS. PAGE 47 G0917
    S67
MGT
MARXISM
POLICY
AUTHORIT

LEADING....SEE LEAD

LEAGUE OF FREE NATIONS ASSOCIATION....SEE LFNA

LEAGUE OF WOMEN VOTERS....SEE LEAGUE/WV

LEAGUE/NAT....LEAGUE OF NATIONS; SEE ALSO INT/ORG

ARON R.,CENTURY OF TOTAL WAR. FUT WOR+45 WOR-45
SOCIETY INT/ORG NAT/G FORCES TOP/EX CREATE BAL/PWR
DOMIN EDU/PROP COERCE DETER PEACE TOTALISM PWR
...TIME/SEQ TREND COLD/WAR TOT/POP VAL/FREE
LEAGUE/NAT 20. PAGE 4 G0066
    B54
ATTIT
WAR

NOEL-BAKER D.,THE ARMS RACE. WOR+45 NAT/G DELIB/GP
ACT/RES TEC/DEV EDU/PROP NUC/PWR ATTIT KNOWL PWR
...CONCPT OBS LEAGUE/NAT 20 COLD/WAR. PAGE 42 G0823
    B58
FUT
INT/ORG
ARMS/CONT
PEACE

EINSTEIN A.,EINSTEIN ON PEACE. FUT WOR+45 WOR-45
SOCIETY NAT/G PLAN BAL/PWR CAP/ISM DIPLOM ARMS/CONT
DETER NAT/LISM...POLICY RELATIV HUM PHIL/SCI CONCPT
BIOG COLD/WAR LEAGUE/NAT NAZI. PAGE 17 G0338
    B60
INT/ORG
ATTIT
NUC/PWR
PEACE

US DEPARTMENT OF THE ARMY,DISARMAMENT: A
BIBLIOGRAPHIC RECORD: 1916-1960. DETER WAR WEAPON
PEACE 20 UN LEAGUE/NAT COLD/WAR NATO. PAGE 57 G1128
    B60
BIBLIOG/A
ARMS/CONT
NUC/PWR
DIPLOM

AIR FORCE ACADEMY LIBRARY,INTERNATIONAL
ORGANIZATIONS AND MILITARY SECURITY SYSTEMS
(PAMPHLET) (SPECIAL BIBLIOGRAPHY SERIES, NUMBER
25). DIPLOM FOR/AID INT/TRADE NUC/PWR PEACE 20 UN
NATO OAS SEATO LEAGUE/NAT. PAGE 2 G0031
    B62
BIBLIOG
INT/ORG
FORCES
DETER

SCHILLING W.R.,"SCIENTISTS, FOREIGN POLICY AND
POLITICS." WOR+45 WOR-45 INTELL INT/ORG CONSULT
TOP/EX ACT/RES PLAN ADMIN KNOWL...CONCPT OBS TREND
LEAGUE/NAT 20. PAGE 49 G0967
    S62
NAT/G
TEC/DEV
DIPLOM
NUC/PWR

WILTZ J.E.,IN SEARCH OF PEACE: THE SENATE MUNITIONS
INQUIRY, 1934-36. EUR+WWI USA-45 ELITES INDUS LG/CO
LEGIS INT/TRADE LOBBY NEUTRAL ARMS/CONT...POLICY
CONGRESS 20 LEAGUE/NAT PRESIDENT SENATE CONSCRIPTN.
PAGE 64 G1246
    B63
DELIB/GP
PROFIT
WAR
WEAPON

FALK S.L.,"DISARMAMENT IN HISTORICAL PERSPECTIVE."
WOR-45 NAT/G PLAN NUC/PWR PEACE ORD/FREE PWR
...TIME/SEQ AUD/VIS VAL/FREE LEAGUE/NAT 20. PAGE 18
G0360
    S64
INT/ORG
COERCE
ARMS/CONT

LEAGUE/WV....LEAGUE OF WOMEN VOTERS

LEAR J. G0648

LEARNING....SEE PERCEPT

LEASE....SEE RENT

LEBANON....SEE ALSO ISLAM

LECHT L. G0649

LECLERCQ H. G0650

LEDYARD/J....JOHN LEDYARD

LEE R.R. G0651

LEE/IVY....IVY LEE

LEEVILLE....LEEVILLE, TEXAS

LEFEVER E.W. G0652

LEFTON M. G0653

LEGAL SYSTEM....SEE LAW

LEGAL PERMIT....SEE LICENSE

LEGION OF DECENCY....SEE LEGION/DCY

LEGION/DCY....LEGION OF DECENCY

LEGIS....LEGISLATURES; SEE ALSO PARLIAMENT, CONGRESS

RAND SCHOOL OF SOCIAL SCIENCE,INDEX TO LABOR
ARTICLES. ECO/DEV INT/ORG LEGIS DIPLOM GP/REL
...NAT/COMP 20. PAGE 46 G0900
    N
BIBLIOG
LABOR
MGT
ADJUD

ATOMIC INDUSTRIAL FORUM,COMMENTARY ON LEGISLATION
TO PERMIT PRIVATE OWNERSHIP OF SPECIAL NUCLEAR
MATERIAL (PAMPHLET). USA+45 DELIB/GP LEGIS PLAN OWN
...POLICY 20 AEC CONGRESS. PAGE 4 G0076
    N19
NUC/PWR
MARKET
INDUS
LAW

MATHEWS J.M.,AMERICAN STATE GOVERNMENT. USA-45
LOC/G CHIEF EX/STRUC LEGIS ADJUD CONTROL CT/SYS
ROUTINE GOV/REL PWR 20 GOVERNOR. PAGE 37 G0721
    B25
PROVS
ADMIN
FEDERAL
CONSTN

BINGHAM A.M.,THE TECHNIQUES OF DEMOCRACY. USA-45
CONSTN STRUCT POL/PAR LEGIS PLAN PARTIC CHOOSE
REPRESENT NAT/LISM TOTALISM...MGT 20. PAGE 7 G0136
    B42
POPULISM
ORD/FREE
ADMIN
NAT/G

WHITE L.D.,"CONGRESSIONAL CONTROL OF THE PUBLIC
SERVICE." USA-45 NAT/G CONSULT DELIB/GP PLAN SENIOR
CONGRESS. PAGE 63 G1232
    S45
LEGIS
EXEC
POLICY
CONTROL

KILE O.M.,THE FARM BUREAU MOVEMENT: THE FARM BUREAU
THROUGH THREE DECADES. NAT/G LEGIS LEAD LOBBY
GP/REL INCOME POLICY. PAGE 30 G0596
    B48
AGRI
STRUCT
VOL/ASSN
DOMIN

HARDIN L.M.,"REFLECTIONS ON AGRICULTURAL POLICY
FORMATION IN THE UNITED STATES." LEGIS PLAN BUDGET
ECO/TAC LEAD CENTRAL...MGT SOC NEW/IDEA STAT FAO.
PAGE 24 G0480
    S48
AGRI
POLICY
ADMIN
NEW/LIB

ROSENHAUPT H.W.,HOW TO WAGE PEACE. USA+45 SOCIETY
STRATA STRUCT R+D INT/ORG POL/PAR LEGIS ACT/RES
CREATE PLAN EDU/PROP ADMIN EXEC ATTIT ALL/VALS
...TIME/SEQ TREND COLD/WAR 20. PAGE 48 G0937
    B49
INTELL
CONCPT
DIPLOM

BERNSTEIN I.,THE NEW DEAL COLLECTIVE BARGAINING
PROCESS. USA-45 GOV/REL ATTIT...BIBLIOG 20
ROOSEVLT/F. PAGE 7 G0132
    B50
LABOR
LEGIS
POLICY
NEW/LIB

HUZAR E.,THE PURSE AND THE SWORD: CONTROL OF THE
ARMY BY CONGRESS THROUGH MILITARY APPROPRIATIONS
1933-1950. NAT/G DELIB/GP EX/STRUC FORCES PROB/SOLV
BARGAIN CONFER ADMIN ROUTINE GOV/REL EFFICIENCY
...POLICY COLD/WAR. PAGE 27 G0541
    B50
CIVMIL/REL
BUDGET
CONTROL
LEGIS

B51

MAASS A.,MUDDY WATERS: THE ARMY ENGINEERS AND THE FORCES
NATIONS RIVERS. USA-45 PROF/ORG CONSULT LEGIS ADMIN GP/REL
EXEC ROLE PWR...SOC PRESIDENT 20. PAGE 35 G0682 LOBBY
CONSTRUC

B52

APPADORAI A.,THE SUBSTANCE OF POLITICS (6TH ED.). PHIL/SCI
EX/STRUC LEGIS DIPLOM CT/SYS CHOOSE FASCISM MARXISM NAT/G
SOCISM...BIBLIOG T. PAGE 3 G0062

B53

TOMPKINS D.C.,CIVIL DEFENSE IN THE STATES: A BIBLIOG
BIBLIOGRAPHY (DEFENSE BIBLIOGRAPHIES NO. 3; WAR
PAMPHLET). USA-45 LABOR LOC/G NAT/G PROVS LEGIS. ORD/FREE
PAGE 55 G1076 ADMIN

B54

TOMPKINS D.C.,STATE GOVERNMENT AND ADMINISTRATION: BIBLIOG/A
A BIBLIOGRAPHY. USA+45 USA-45 CONSTN LEGIS JUDGE LOC/G
BUDGET CT/SYS LOBBY...CHARTS 20. PAGE 55 G1077 PROVS
ADMIN

B54

WRIGHT Q.,PROBLEMS OF STABILITY AND PROGRESS IN INT/ORG
INTERNATIONAL RELATIONSHIPS. FUT WOR+45 WOR-45 CONCPT
SOCIETY LEGIS CREATE TEC/DEV ECO/TAC EDU/PROP ADJUD DIPLOM
WAR PEACE ORD/FREE PWR...KNO/TEST TREND GEN/LAWS
20. PAGE 64 G1257

C54

CALDWELL L.K.,"THE GOVERNMENT AND ADMINISTRATION OF PROVS
NEW YORK." LOC/G MUNIC POL/PAR SCHOOL CHIEF LEGIS ADMIN
PLAN TAX CT/SYS...MGT SOC/WK BIBLIOG 20 NEWYORK/C. CONSTN
PAGE 10 G0202 EX/STRUC

C54

ZELLER B.,"AMERICAN STATE LEGISLATURES: REPORT ON REPRESENT
THE COMMITTEE ON AMERICAN LEGISLATURES." CONSTN LEGIS
POL/PAR EX/STRUC CONFER ADMIN CONTROL EXEC LOBBY PROVS
ROUTINE GOV/REL...POLICY BIBLIOG 20. PAGE 65 G1267 APPORT

B55

SMITHIES A.,THE BUDGETARY PROCESS IN THE UNITED NAT/G
STATES. ECO/DEV AGRI EX/STRUC FORCES LEGIS ADMIN
PROB/SOLV TAX ROUTINE EFFICIENCY...MGT CONGRESS BUDGET
PRESIDENT. PAGE 52 G1016 GOV/REL

B56

KOENIG L.W.,THE TRUMAN ADMINISTRATION: ITS ADMIN
PRINCIPLES AND PRACTICE. USA-45 POL/PAR CHIEF LEGIS POLICY
DIPLOM DEATH NUC/PWR WAR CIVMIL/REL PEACE EX/STRUC
...DECISION 20 TRUMAN/HS PRESIDENT TREATY. PAGE 31 GOV/REL
G0610

B56

THOMAS M.,ATOMIC ENERGY AND CONGRESS. USA+45 NAT/G LEGIS
ACT/RES PLAN TEC/DEV EDU/PROP ROUTINE KNOWL PWR ADMIN
SKILL...PHIL/SCI NEW/IDEA TIME/SEQ CHARTS METH NUC/PWR
CONGRESS VAL/FREE 20 AEC. PAGE 54 G1067

S56

KNAPP D.C.,"CONGRESSIONAL CONTROL OF AGRICULTURAL LEGIS
CONSERVATION POLICY: A CASE STUDY OF THE AGRI
APPROPRIATIONS PROCESS." DELIB/GP PLAN PROB/SOLV BUDGET
CONFER PARL/PROC...POLICY INT CONGRESS. PAGE 31 CONTROL
G0607

S57

TAYLOR P.S.,"THE RELATION OF RESEARCH TO DECISION
LEGISLATIVE AND ADMINISTRATIVE DECISIONS." ELITES LEGIS
ACT/RES PLAN PROB/SOLV CONFER CHOOSE POLICY. MGT
PAGE 54 G1059 PWR

S58

MARCY C.,"THE RESEARCH PROGRAM OF THE SENATE DELIB/GP
COMMITTEE ON FOREIGN RELATIONS." EUR+WWI ECO/UNDEV LEGIS
ACT/RES PLAN PARL/PROC GOV/REL...GEOG CONFE FOR/AID
CONGRESS. PAGE 36 G0704 POLICY

B59

ATOMIC INDUSTRIAL FORUM,THE IMPACT OF THE PEACEFUL PROVS
USES OF ATOMIC ENERGY ON STATE AND LOCAL LOC/G
GOVERNMENT. USA+45 INDUS NAT/G LEGIS PLAN CONTROL NUC/PWR
GOV/REL. PAGE 4 G0079 PEACE

B59

US CONGRESS JT ATOM ENRGY COMM,SELECTED MATERIALS NAT/G
ON FEDERAL-STATE COOPERATION IN THE ATOMIC ENERGY NUC/PWR
FIELD. USA+45 LAW LOC/G PROVS CONSULT LEGIS ADJUD GOV/REL
...POLICY BIBLIOG 20 AEC. PAGE 57 G1111 DELIB/GP

B59

VERNEY D.V.,PUBLIC ENTERPRISE IN SWEDEN. FUT SWEDEN ECO/DEV
UK INDUS POL/PAR LEGIS PROB/SOLV CAP/ISM INT/TRADE POLICY

CONTROL SOCISM...MGT CONCPT NAT/COMP 20 SOCDEM/PAR LG/CO
CIVIL/SERV. PAGE 61 G1196 NAT/G

S59

SEIDMAN H.,"THE GOVERNMENT CORPORATION IN THE CONTROL
UNITED STATES." USA+45 LEGIS ADMIN PLURISM 20. GOV/REL
PAGE 50 G0988 EX/STRUC
EXEC

B60

BROOKINGS INSTITUTION,UNITED STATES FOREIGN POLICY: DIPLOM
STUDY NO 9: THE FORMULATION AND ADMINISTRATION OF INT/ORG
UNITED STATES FOREIGN POLICY. USA+45 WOR+45 CREATE
EX/STRUC LEGIS BAL/PWR FOR/AID EDU/PROP CIVMIL/REL
GOV/REL...INT COLD/WAR. PAGE 9 G0174

B60

CARPER E.T.,THE DEFENSE APPROPRIATIONS RIDER GOV/REL
(PAMPHLET). USA+45 CONSTN CHIEF DELIB/GP LEGIS ADJUD
BUDGET LOBBY CIVMIL/REL...POLICY 20 CONGRESS LAW
EISNHWR/DD DEPT/DEFEN PRESIDENT BOSTON. PAGE 11 CONTROL
G0212

B60

US SENATE COMM ON COMMERCE,URBAN MASS DIST/IND
TRANSPORTATION. FUT USA+45 AIR ECO/DEV FINAN LOC/G PLAN
MUNIC LEGIS CREATE PROB/SOLV TEC/DEV 20 PUB/TRANS. NAT/G
PAGE 60 G1180 LAW

S60

HUNTINGTON S.P.,"STRATEGIC PLANNING AND THE EXEC
POLITICAL PROCESS." USA+45 NAT/G DELIB/GP LEGIS FORCES
ACT/RES ECO/TAC LEGIT ROUTINE CHOOSE RIGID/FLEX PWR NUC/PWR
...POLICY MAJORIT MGT 20. PAGE 27 G0538 WAR

B62

BOCK E.A.,CASE STUDIES IN AMERICAN GOVERNMENT. POLICY
USA+45 ECO/DEV CHIEF EDU/PROP CT/SYS RACE/REL LEGIS
ORD/FREE...JURID MGT PHIL/SCI PRESIDENT CASEBOOK. IDEA/COMP
PAGE 8 G0146 NAT/G

B62

KARNJAHAPRAKORN C.,MUNICIPAL GOVERNMENT IN THAILAND LOC/G
AS AN INSTITUTION AND PROCESS OF SELF-GOVERNMENT. MUNIC
THAILAND CULTURE FINAN EX/STRUC LEGIS PLAN CONTROL ORD/FREE
GOV/REL EFFICIENCY ATTIT...POLICY 20. PAGE 29 G0578 ADMIN

B62

SCHILLING W.R.,STRATEGY, POLITICS, AND DEFENSE ROUTINE
BUDGETS. USA+45 R+D NAT/G CONSULT DELIB/GP FORCES POLICY
LEGIS ACT/RES PLAN BAL/PWR LEGIT EXEC NUC/PWR
RIGID/FLEX PWR...TREND COLD/WAR CONGRESS 20
EISNHWR/DD. PAGE 49 G0968

L62

NEIBURG H.L.,"THE EISENHOWER AEC AND CONGRESS: A CHIEF
STUDY IN EXECUTIVE-LEGISLATIVE RELATIONS." USA+45 LEGIS
NAT/G POL/PAR DELIB/GP EX/STRUC TOP/EX ADMIN EXEC GOV/REL
LEAD ROUTINE PWR...POLICY COLD/WAR CONGRESS NUC/PWR
PRESIDENT AEC. PAGE 41 G0816

S62

DAWSON R.H.,"CONGRESSIONAL INNOVATION AND LEGIS
INTERVENTION IN DEFENSE POLICY: LEGISLATIVE PWR
AUTHORIZATION OF WEAPONS SYSTEMS." CONSTN PLAN CONTROL
ARMS/CONT GOV/REL EFFICIENCY PEACE NEW/LIB OLD/LIB. WEAPON
PAGE 14 G0281

B63

GREEN H.P.,GOVERNMENT OF THE ATOM. USA+45 LEGIS GOV/REL
PROB/SOLV ADMIN CONTROL PWR...POLICY DECISION 20 EX/STRUC
PRESIDENT CONGRESS. PAGE 22 G0443 NUC/PWR
DELIB/GP

B63

HALEY A.G.,SPACE LAW AND GOVERNMENT. FUT USA+45 INT/ORG
WOR+45 LEGIS ACT/RES CREATE ATTIT RIGID/FLEX LAW
ORD/FREE PWR SOVEREIGN...POLICY JURID CONCPT CHARTS SPACE
VAL/FREE 20. PAGE 24 G0469

B63

HATHAWAY D.A.,GOVERNMENT AND AGRICULTURE: PUBLIC AGRI
POLICY IN A DEMOCRATIC SOCIETY. USA+45 LEGIS ADMIN GOV/REL
EXEC LOBBY REPRESENT PWR 20. PAGE 25 G0491 PROB/SOLV
EX/STRUC

B63

HERNDON J.,A SELECTED BIBLIOGRAPHY OF MATERIALS IN BIBLIOG
STATE GOVERNMENT AND POLITICS (PAMPHLET). USA+45 GOV/COMP
POL/PAR LEGIS ADMIN CHOOSE MGT. PAGE 26 G0507 PROVS
DECISION

B63

PEABODY R.L.,NEW PERSPECTIVES ON THE HOUSE OF NEW/IDEA
REPRESENTATIVES. AGRI FINAN SCHOOL FORCES CONFER LEGIS
LEAD CHOOSE REPRESENT FEDERAL...POLICY DECISION PWR

ADMIN

US SENATE,DOCUMENTS ON INTERNATIONAL AS"ECTS OF EXPLORATION AND USE OF OUTER SPACE, 1954-62: STAFF REPORT FOR COMM AERON SPACE SCI. USA+45 USSR LEGIS LEAD CIVMIL/REL PEACE...POLICY INT/LAW ANTHOL 20 CONGRESS NASA KHRUSH/N. PAGE 59 G1162
B63
SPACE
UTIL
GOV/REL
DIPLOM

WILTZ J.E.,IN SEARCH OF PEACE: THE SENATE MUNITIONS INQUIRY, 1934-36. EUR+WWI USA-45 ELITES INDUS LG/CO LEGIS INT/TRADE LOBBY NEUTRAL ARMS/CONT...POLICY CONGRESS 20 LEAGUE/NAT PRESIDENT SENATE CONSCRIPTN. PAGE 64 G1246
B63
DELIB/GP
PROFIT
WAR
WEAPON

NIEBURG H.,"EURATOM: A STUDY IN COALITION POLITICS." EUR+WWI UK USA+45 ELITES NAT/G DELIB/GP LEGIS TOP/EX ECO/TAC NUC/PWR ATTIT ORD/FREE PWR TOT/POP EEC OEEC 20 NATO EURATOM. PAGE 42 G0820
L63
VOL/ASSN
ACT/RES

KOLDZIEF E.A.,"CONGRESSIONAL RESPONSIBILITY FOR THE COMMON DEFENSE: THE MONEY PROBLEM." PLAN DEBATE EFFICIENCY ATTIT PWR DECISION. PAGE 31 G0612
S63
LEGIS
NAT/G
FORCES
POLICY

RECENT PUBLICATIONS ON GOVERNMENTAL PROBLEMS. FINAN INDUS ACADEM PLAN PROB/SOLV EDU/PROP ADJUD ADMIN BIO/SOC...MGT SOC. PAGE 1 G0017
B64
BIBLIOG
AUTOMAT
LEGIS
JURID

ETZIONI A.,THE MOON-DOGGLE: DOMESTIC AND INTERNATIONAL IMPLICATIONS OF THE SPACE RACE. FUT USA+45 WOR+45 INTELL ECO/DEV INDUS VOL/ASSN EX/STRUC FORCES LEGIS TOP/EX PLAN TEC/DEV ECO/TAC EDU/PROP KNOWL ORD/FREE PWR RESPECT WEALTH TIME/SEQ. PAGE 18 G0352
B64
R+D
NAT/G
DIPLOM
SPACE

RANSOM H.H.,CAN AMERICAN DEMOCRACY SURVIVE COLD WAR. USA-45 CONSTN NAT/G CONSULT DELIB/GP LEGIS ACT/RES LEGIT EXEC ATTIT KNOWL ORD/FREE PWR SKILL ...POLICY TIME/SEQ TREND GEN/LAWS 20 COLD/WAR. PAGE 46 G0901
B64
USA+45
ROUTINE

RIES J.C.,THE MANAGEMENT OF DEFENSE: ORGANIZATION AND CONTROL OF THE US ARMED SERVICES. PROF/ORG DELIB/GP EX/STRUC LEGIS GOV/REL PERS/REL CENTRAL RATIONAL PWR...POLICY TREND GOV/COMP BIBLIOG. PAGE 47 G0920
B64
FORCES
ACT/RES
DECISION
CONTROL

VAN DYKE V.,PRIDE AND POWER: THE RATIONALE OF THE SPACE PROGRAM. FUT USA+45 INTELL R+D NAT/G POL/PAR DELIB/GP EX/STRUC ACT/RES PLAN ECO/TAC POLICY EDU/PROP ORD/FREE PWR RESPECT SKILL...TIME/SEQ VAL/FREE. PAGE 61 G1191
B64
TEC/DEV
ATTIT
POLICY

BERKS R.N.,"THE US AND WEAPONS CONTROL." WOR+45 LAW INT/ORG NAT/G LEGIS EXEC COERCE PEACE ATTIT RIGID/FLEX ALL/VALS PWR...POLICY TOT/POP 20. PAGE 7 G0129
L64
USA+45
PLAN
ARMS/CONT

CARNEGIE ENDOWMENT INT. PEACE,"POLITICAL QUESTIONS (ISSUES BEFORE THE NINETEENTH GENERAL ASSEMBLY)." SPACE WOR+45 CONSTN FINAN NAT/G CONSULT DELIB/GP FORCES LEGIS TEC/DEV EDU/PROP LEGIT ARMS/CONT COERCE NUC/PWR ATTIT ALL/VALS...CONCPT OBS UN COLD/WAR 20. PAGE 11 G0208
L64
INT/ORG
PEACE

UNRUH J.M.,"SCIENTIFIC INPUTS TO LEGISLATIVE DECISION-MAKING (SUPPLEMENT)" USA+45 ACADEM NAT/G PROVS GOV/REL GOV/COMP. PAGE 56 G1102
S64
CREATE
DECISION
LEGIS
PARTIC

BAILEY S.K.,AMERICAN POLITICS AND GOVERNMENT. USA+45 CONSTN FINAN LABOR POL/PAR DIPLOM ADMIN WAR INGP/REL RACE/REL NEW/LIB 20 SUPREME/CT PRESIDENT CONGRESS. PAGE 4 G0084
B65
ANTHOL
LEGIS
PWR

BOBROW D.B.,COMPONENTS OF DEFENSE POLICY. ASIA EUR+WWI USA+45 WOR+45 INTELL INT/ORG NAT/G PROF/ORG CONSULT LEGIS ACT/RES CREATE ARMS/CONT COERCE ORD/FREE...DECISION SIMUL. PAGE 7 G0145
B65
DETER
NUC/PWR
PLAN
FORCES

LAPP R.E.,THE NEW PRIESTHOOD: THE SCIENTIFIC ELITE AND THE USES OF POWER. USA+45 ELITES INTELL SOCIETY R+D NAT/G CHIEF LEGIS CIVMIL/REL GP/REL PWR 20 PRESIDENT CONGRESS. PAGE 32 G0635
B65
TEC/DEV
TECHRACY
CONTROL
POPULISM

NATIONAL ACADEMY OF SCIENCES,BASIC RESEARCH AND NATIONAL GOALS. R+D ACADEM DELIB/GP PLAN EDU/PROP ...POLICY HEAL PHIL/SCI PSY SOC ANTHOL 20 CONGRESS HOUSE/REP HS/SCIASTR. PAGE 41 G0809
B65
LEGIS
BUDGET
NAT/G
CREATE

US CONGRESS JT ATOM ENRGY COMM,PEACEFUL APPLICATIONS OF NUCLEAR EXPLOSIVES: PLOWSHARE, HEARING. USA+45 LEGIS CREATE PLAN PEACE...CHARTS EXHIBIT BIBLIOG CONGRESS PANAMA/CNL. PAGE 57 G1113
B65
NUC/PWR
DELIB/GP
TEC/DEV
NAT/G

US CONGRESS JT ATOM ENRGY COMM,ATOMIC ENERGY LEGISLATION THROUGH 89TH CONGRESS, 1ST SESSION. USA+45 LAW INT/ORG DELIB/GP BUDGET DIPLOM 20 AEC CONGRESS CASEBOOK EURATOM IAEA. PAGE 57 G1114
B65
NUC/PWR
FORCES
PEACE
LEGIS

US CONGRESS JT ATOM ENRGY COMM,PROPOSED AMENDMENT TO SECTION 271 OF THE ATOMIC ENERGY ACT OF 1954. USA+45 CONSTRUC PLAN INSPECT CONTROL CT/SYS 20 CONGRESS AEC. PAGE 57 G1115
B65
LAW
LEGIS
DELIB/GP
NUC/PWR

US DEPARTMENT OF THE ARMY,MILITARY MANPOWER POLICY. USA+45 LEGIS EXEC WAR 20 CONGRESS. PAGE 58 G1132
B65
BIBLIOG/A
POLICY
FORCES
TREND

US SENATE COMM AERO SPACE SCI,NATIONAL SPACE GOALS FOR THE POST-APOLLO PERIOD. USA+45 CONSULT DELIB/GP TEC/DEV BUDGET GP/REL ATTIT...CHARTS IDEA/COMP TIME 20 DEPT/DEFEN NASA CONGRESS. PAGE 59 G1166
B65
SPACE
FUT
R+D
LEGIS

US SENATE COMM GOVT OPERATIONS,ORGANIZATION OF FEDERAL EXECUTIVE DEPARTMENTS AND AGENCIES: REPORT OF MARCH 23, 1965. USA+45 FORCES LEGIS DIPLOM ROUTINE CIVMIL/REL EFFICIENCY FEDERAL...MGT STAT. PAGE 60 G1179
B65
ADMIN
EX/STRUC
GOV/REL
ORG/CHARTS

ETZIONI A.,"ON THE NATIONAL GUIDANCE OF SCIENCE." USA+45 FINAN NAT/G LEGIS GIVE 20. PAGE 18 G0353
S65
PHIL/SCI
CREATE
POLICY
EFFICIENCY

GORDON G.,THE LEGISLATIVE PROCESS AND DIVIDED GOVERNMENT: A CASE STUDY OF THE 86TH CONGRESS. USA+45 POL/PAR PROVS PROB/SOLV BAL/PWR CHOOSE REPRESENT EFFICIENCY ATTIT...POLICY DECISION STAT 20 CONGRESS EISNHWR/DD. PAGE 22 G0434
B66
LEGIS
HABITAT
CHIEF
NAT/G

NIEBURG H.L.,IN THE NAME OF SCIENCE. USA+45 EX/STRUC LEGIS TEC/DEV BUDGET PAY AUTOMAT LOBBY PWR ...OBS 20. PAGE 42 G0822
B66
NAT/G
INDUS
TECHRACY

US HOUSE COMM ON JUDICIARY,CIVIL COMMITMENT AND TREATMENT OF NARCOTIC ADDICTS. USA+45 SOCIETY FINAN LEGIS PROB/SOLV GIVE CT/SYS SANCTION HEALTH ...POLICY HEAL 20. PAGE 58 G1141
B66
BIO/SOC
CRIME
IDEA/COMP
CONTROL

GREENBERG D.S.,"THE SCIENTIFIC PORK BARREL." USA+45 ECO/DEV PUB/INST CHIEF LEGIS BUDGET GIVE GP/REL PWR WEALTH 20. PAGE 23 G0445
S66
R+D
NAT/G
ACADEM
ATTIT

US HOUSE COMM SCI ASTRONAUT,INQUIRIES, LEGISLATION, POLICY STUDIES RE: SCIENCE AND TECHNOLOGY: REVIEW AND FORECAST (PAMPHLET). FUT WOR+45 DELIB/GP PROB/SOLV...POLICY JURID TREND 20 CONGRESS. PAGE 58 G1144
N66
TEC/DEV
R+D
PLAN
LEGIS

US HOUSE COMM SCI ASTRONAUT,THE ADEQUACY OF TECHNOLOGY FOR POLLUTION ABATEMENT (PAMPHLET). WOR+45 PLAN PROB/SOLV CONFER ADMIN...JURID 20 POLLUTION. PAGE 58 G1145
N66
HEALTH
POLICY
TEC/DEV
LEGIS

HOROWITZ I.L.,THE RISE AND FALL OF PROJECT CAMELOT: STUDIES IN THE RELATIONSHIP BETWEEN SOCIAL SCIENCE AND PRACTICAL POLITICS. USA+45 WOR+45 CULTURE
B67
NAT/G
ACADEM
ACT/RES

FORCES LEGIS EXEC CIVMIL/REL KNOWL...POLICY SOC   GP/REL
METH/CNCPT 20. PAGE 27 G0529

                                                        B67
MCBRIDE J.H.,THE TEST BAN TREATY: MILITARY,   ARMS/CONT
TECHNOLOGICAL, AND POLITICAL IMPLICATIONS. USA+45   DIPLOM
USSR DELIB/GP FORCES LEGIS TEC/DEV BAL/PWR TREATY.   NUC/PWR
PAGE 37 G0727

                                                        B67
UNIVERSAL REFERENCE SYSTEM,LEGISLATIVE PROCESS,   BIBLIOG/A
REPRESENTATION, AND DECISION-MAKING (VOLUME II).   LEGIS
WOR+45 WOR-45 CONSTN LOC/G NAT/G...POLICY CON/ANAL   REPRESENT
COMPUT/IR GEN/METH. PAGE 56 G1094   DECISION

                                                        B67
UNIVERSAL REFERENCE SYSTEM,LAW, JURISPRUDENCE, AND   BIBLIOG/A
JUDICIAL PROCESS (VOLUME VII). WOR+45 WOR-45 CONSTN   LAW
NAT/G LEGIS JUDGE CT/SYS...INT/LAW COMPUT/IR   JURID
GEN/METH METH. PAGE 56 G1101   ADJUD

                                                        B67
US DEPARTMENT OF THE ARMY,CIVILIAN IN PEACE,   BIBLIOG/A
SOLDIER IN WAR: A BIBLIOGRAPHIC SURVEY OF THE ARMY   FORCES
AND AIR NATIONAL GUARD (PAMPHLET, NOS. 130-2).   ROLE
USA+45 USA-45 LOC/G NAT/G PROVS LEGIS PLAN ADMIN   DIPLOM
ATTIT ORD/FREE...POLICY 19/20. PAGE 58 G1134

                                                        B67
US SENATE COMM AERO SPACE SCI,TREATY ON PRINCIPLES   SPACE
GOVERNING ACTIVITIES OF STATES IN EXPLORATION AND   INT/LAW
USE OF OUTER SPACE, INCLUDING...BODIES. DELIB/GP   ORD/FREE
FORCES LEGIS DIPLOM...JURID 20 DEPT/STATE NASA   PEACE
DEPT/DEFEN UN. PAGE 60 G1170

                                                        B67
US SENATE COMM AERO SPACE SCI,APOLLO ACCIDENT   PROB/SOLV
(PARTS 1-7). USA+45 DELIB/GP LEGIS...INT CHARTS   SPACE
NASA. PAGE 60 G1173   BUDGET
                                                        GOV/REL

                                                        L67
TRAVERS H. JR.,"AN EXAMINATION OF THE CAB'S MERGER   ADJUD
POLICY." USA+45 USA-45 LAW NAT/G LEGIS PLAN ADMIN   LG/CO
...DECISION 20 CONGRESS. PAGE 55 G1078   POLICY
                                                        DIST/IND

                                                        S67
CONWAY J.E.,"MAKING RESEARCH EFFECTIVE IN   ACT/RES
LEGISLATION." LAW R+D CONSULT EX/STRUC PLAN CONFER   POLICY
ADMIN LEAD ROUTINE TASK INGP/REL DECISION. PAGE 13   LEGIS
G0252   PROB/SOLV

                                                        S67
WHITTIER J.M.,"COMPULSORY POOLING AND UNITIZATION*   LEGIS
DIE-HARD KANSAS." LAW PLAN EDU/PROP ATTIT...POLICY   MUNIC
JURID PREDICT TREND METH/COMP 20. PAGE 63 G1236   INDUS
                                                        ECO/TAC

                                                        N67
US SENATE COMM ON PUBLIC WORKS,AIR QUALITY ACT OF   HEALTH
1967 (PAMPHLET). USA+45 INDUS R+D LEGIS SENATE.   AIR
PAGE 61 G1187   HABITAT
                                                        CONTROL

LEGISLATION....SEE CONGRESS, LEGIS, SENATE, HOUSE/REP

LEGISLATIVE APPORTIONMENT....SEE APPORT

LEGISLATURES....SEE LEGIS

LEGIT....LEGITIMACY

                                                        B34
EINSTEIN A.,THE WORLD AS I SEE IT. WOR-45 INTELL   SOCIETY
R+D INT/ORG NAT/G SECT VOL/ASSN FORCES CREATE   PHIL/SCI
EDU/PROP LEGIT ARMS/CONT WAR WEAPON NAT/LISM   DIPLOM
ALL/VALS...POLICY CONCPT 20. PAGE 17 G0337   PACIFISM

                                                        B46
NORTHROP F.S.C.,THE MEETING OF EAST AND WEST.   DRIVE
EUR+WWI FUT MOD/EUR UNIV WOR+45 WOR-45 INTELL   TREND
SOCIETY EX/STRUC TOP/EX ACT/RES LEGIT CHOOSE ATTIT   PEACE
PERCEPT RIGID/FLEX ALL/VALS...POLICY JURID OBS
TOT/POP. PAGE 42 G0826

                                                        B54
COMBS C.H.,DECISION PROCESSES. INTELL SOCIETY   MATH
DELIB/GP CREATE TEC/DEV DOMIN LEGIT EXEC CHOOSE   DECISION
DRIVE RIGID/FLEX KNOWL PWR...PHIL/SCI SOC
METH/CNCPT CONT/OBS REC/INT PERS/TEST SAMP/SIZ BIOG
SOC/EXP WORK. PAGE 13 G0245

                                                        S56
GORDON L.,"THE ORGANIZATION FOR EUROPEAN ECONOMIC   VOL/ASSN
COOPERATION." EUR+WWI INDUS INT/ORG NAT/G CONSULT   ECO/DEV

DELIB/GP ACT/RES CREATE PLAN TEC/DEV EDU/PROP LEGIT
WEALTH OEEC 20. PAGE 22 G0435

                                                        S58
DAVENPORT J.,"ARMS AND THE WELFARE STATE." INTELL   USA+45
STRUCT FORCES CREATE ECO/TAC FOR/AID DOMIN LEGIT   NAT/G
ADMIN WAR ORD/FREE PWR...POLICY SOC CONCPT MYTH OBS   USSR
TREND COLD/WAR TOT/POP 20. PAGE 14 G0276

                                                        S58
SINGER J.D.,"THREAT PERCEPTION AND THE ARMAMENT   PERCEPT
TENSION DILEMMA." WOR+45 WOR-45 ELITES INT/ORG   ARMS/CONT
NAT/G DELIB/GP PLAN LEGIT COERCE DETER ATTIT   BAL/PWR
RIGID/FLEX PWR...DECISION PSY 20. PAGE 51 G1002

                                                        S58
THOMPSON K.W.,"NATIONAL SECURITY IN A NUCLEAR AGE."   FORCES
USA+45 NAT/G INT/ORG NAT/G TOP/EX DIPLOM   PWR
DOMIN EDU/PROP LEGIT ARMS/CONT COERCE ORD/FREE   BAL/PWR
...TREND STERTYP TOT/POP VAL/FREE COLD/WAR 20.
PAGE 54 G1068

                                                        B59
AMRINE M.,THE GREAT DECISION: THE SECRET HISTORY OF   DECISION
THE ATOMIC BOMB. USA+45 TOP/EX EDU/PROP LEGIT   NAT/G
PERCEPT ORD/FREE PWR VAL/FREE HIROSHIMA. PAGE 3   NUC/PWR
G0055   FORCES

                                                        S59
STOESSINGER J.G.,"THE INTERNATIONAL ATOMIC ENERGY   INT/ORG
AGENCY: THE FIRST PHASE." FUT WOR+45 NAT/G VOL/ASSN   ECO/DEV
DELIB/GP BAL/PWR LEGIT ADMIN ROUTINE PWR...OBS   FOR/AID
CON/ANAL GEN/LAWS VAL/FREE 20 IAEA. PAGE 53 G1037   NUC/PWR

                                                        S59
WILLIAMS B.H.,"SCIENTIFIC METHOD IN FOREIGN   PLAN
POLICY." WOR+45 NAT/G FORCES TOP/EX DOMIN LEGIT   PHIL/SCI
COERCE PEACE ATTIT KNOWL ORD/FREE PWR...GEN/LAWS   DIPLOM
GEN/METH TOT/POP COLD/WAR NAZI. PAGE 63 G1241

                                                        B60
GOLDSEN J.M.,INTERNATIONAL POLITICAL IMPLICATIONS   R+D
OF ACTIVITIES IN OUTER SPACE. FUT USA+45 WOR+45 AIR   SPACE
LAW ACT/RES LEGIT ATTIT KNOWL ORD/FREE PWR...CONCPT
20. PAGE 22 G0427

                                                        S60
DOTY P.M.,"THE ROLE OF THE SMALLER POWERS." FUT   PWR
WOR+45 NAT/G TEC/DEV BAL/PWR DOMIN LEGIT CHOOSE   POLICY
DISPL DRIVE RESPECT...DECISION 20. PAGE 16 G0310   ARMS/CONT
                                                        NUC/PWR

                                                        S60
HAYTON R.D.,"THE ANTARCTIC SETTLEMENT OF 1959." FUT   DELIB/GP
USA+45 WOR+45 STRUCT R+D INT/ORG EX/STRUC   JURID
CREATE TEC/DEV LEGIT PEACE ATTIT SOVEREIGN   DIPLOM
...TIME/SEQ 20 TREATY IGY. PAGE 25 G0495   REGION

                                                        S60
HUNTINGTON S.P.,"STRATEGIC PLANNING AND THE   EXEC
POLITICAL PROCESS." USA+45 NAT/G DELIB/GP LEGIS   FORCES
ACT/RES ECO/TAC LEGIT ROUTINE CHOOSE RIGID/FLEX PWR   NUC/PWR
...POLICY MAJORIT MGT 20. PAGE 27 G0538   WAR

                                                        S60
IKLE F.C.,"NTH COUNTRIES AND DISARMAMENT." WOR+45   FUT
DELIB/GP ECO/TAC DOMIN EDU/PROP LEGIT ROUTINE   INT/ORG
COERCE RIGID/FLEX ORD/FREE...MARXIST TREND 20.   ARMS/CONT
PAGE 28 G0543   NUC/PWR

                                                        L61
TAUBENFELD H.J.,"A REGIME FOR OUTER SPACE." FUT   INT/ORG
UNIV R+D ACT/RES PLAN BAL/PWR LEGIT ARMS/CONT   ADJUD
ORD/FREE...POLICY JURID TREND UN TOT/POP 20   SPACE
COLD/WAR. PAGE 54 G1056

                                                        S61
SCHILLING W.R.,"THE H-BOMB: HOW TO DECIDE WITHOUT   PERSON
ACTUALLY CHOOSING." FUT USA+45 INTELL CONSULT ADMIN   LEGIT
CT/SYS MORAL...JURID OBS 20 TRUMAN/HS. PAGE 49   NUC/PWR
G0966

                                                        B62
MELMAN S.,DISARMAMENT: ITS POLITICS AND ECONOMICS.   NAT/G
WOR+45 DELIB/GP FORCES ECO/TAC DOMIN EDU/PROP LEGIT   ORD/FREE
COERCE PWR...POLICY CONCPT 20. PAGE 38 G0752   ARMS/CONT
                                                        NUC/PWR

                                                        B62
SCHILLING W.R.,STRATEGY, POLITICS, AND DEFENSE   ROUTINE
BUDGETS. USA+45 R+D NAT/G CONSULT DELIB/GP FORCES   POLICY
LEGIS ACT/RES PLAN BAL/PWR LEGIT EXEC NUC/PWR
RIGID/FLEX PWR...TREND COLD/WAR CONGRESS 20
EISNHWR/DD. PAGE 49 G0968

CRANE R.D.,"LAW AND STRATEGY IN SPACE." FUT USA+45 WOR+45 AIR LAW INT/ORG NAT/G FORCES ACT/RES PLAN BAL/PWR LEGIT ARMS/CONT COERCE ORD/FREE...POLICY INT/LAW JURID SOC/EXP 20 TREATY. PAGE 13 G0261
S62
CONCPT
SPACE

FINKELSTEIN L.S.,"THE UNITED NATIONS AND ORGANIZATIONS FOR CONTROL OF ARMAMENT." FUT WOR+45 VOL/ASSN DELIB/GP TOP/EX CREATE EDU/PROP LEGIT ADJUD NUC/PWR ATTIT RIGID/FLEX ORD/FREE...POLICY DECISION CONCPT OBS TREND GEN/LAWS TOT/POP COLD/WAR. PAGE 19 G0368
S62
INT/ORG
PWR
ARMS/CONT

FOSTER W.C.,"ARMS CONTROL AND DISARMAMENT IN A DIVIDED WORLD." COM FUT USA+45 WOR+45 INTELL INT/ORG NAT/G VOL/ASSN CONSULT CREATE PLAN TEC/DEV EDU/PROP LEGIT NUC/PWR ATTIT RIGID/FLEX...CONCPT TREND TOT/POP 20 UN. PAGE 20 G0387
S62
DELIB/GP
POLICY
ARMS/CONT
DIPLOM

NANES A.,"DISARMAMENT: THE LAST SEVEN YEARS." COM EUR+WWI USA+45 USSR INT/ORG FORCES TOP/EX CREATE LEGIT NUC/PWR DISPL ORD/FREE...CONCPT TIME/SEQ CON/ANAL 20. PAGE 41 G0803
S62
DELIB/GP
RIGID/FLEX
ARMS/CONT

WALTER E.,"VERS UNE CLASSIFICATION SCIENTIFIQUE DE LA SOCIOLOGIA." UNIV CULTURE INTELL SOCIETY R+D ACT/RES LEGIT ROUTINE ATTIT KNOWL...JURID MGT TREND GEN/LAWS 20. PAGE 62 G1208
S62
PLAN
CONCPT

MAYNE R.,THE COMMUNITY OF EUROPE. UK CONSTN NAT/G CONSULT DELIB/GP CREATE PLAN ECO/TAC LEGIT ADMIN ROUTINE ORD/FREE PWR WEALTH...CONCPT TIME/SEQ EEC EURATOM 20. PAGE 37 G0724
B63
EUR+WWI
INT/ORG
REGION

MCDOUGAL M.S.,"THE ENJOYMENT AND ACQUISITION OF RESOURCES IN OUTER SPACE." CHRIST-17C FUT WOR+45 WOR-45 LAW EXTR/IND INT/ORG ACT/RES CREATE TEC/DEV ECO/TAC LEGIT COERCE HEALTH KNOWL ORD/FREE PWR WEALTH...JURID HIST/WRIT VAL/FREE. PAGE 37 G0738
L63
PLAN
TREND

SCHMITT H.A.,"THE EUROPEAN COMMUNITIES." EUR+WWI FRANCE DELIB/GP EX/STRUC TOP/EX CREATE TEC/DEV ECO/TAC LEGIT REGION COERCE DRIVE ALL/VALS ...METH/CNCPT EEC 20. PAGE 49 G0972
S63
VOL/ASSN
ECO/DEV

COHEN M.,LAW AND POLITICS IN SPACE: SPECIFIC AND URGENT PROBLEMS IN THE LAW OF OUTER SPACE. CHINA/COM COM USA+45 USSR WOR+45 COM/IND INT/ORG NAT/G LEGIT NUC/PWR ATTIT BIO/SOC...JURID CONCPT CONGRESS 20 STALIN/J. PAGE 12 G0241
B64
DELIB/GP
LAW
INT/LAW
SPACE

RANSOM H.H.,CAN AMERICAN DEMOCRACY SURVIVE COLD WAR. USA+45 CONSTN NAT/G CONSULT DELIB/GP LEGIS ACT/RES LEGIT EXEC ATTIT KNOWL ORD/FREE PWR SKILL ...POLICY TIME/SEQ TREND GEN/LAWS 20 COLD/WAR. PAGE 46 G0901
B64
USA+45
ROUTINE

CARNEGIE ENDOWMENT INT. PEACE,"POLITICAL QUESTIONS (ISSUES BEFORE THE NINETEENTH GENERAL ASSEMBLY)." SPACE WOR+45 CONSTN FINAN NAT/G CONSULT DELIB/GP FORCES LEGIS TEC/DEV EDU/PROP LEGIT ARMS/CONT COERCE NUC/PWR ATTIT ALL/VALS...CONCPT OBS UN COLD/WAR 20. PAGE 11 G0208
L64
INT/ORG
PEACE

WARD C.,"THE 'NEW MYTHS' AND 'OLD REALITIES' OF NUCLEAR WAR." COM FUT USA+45 USSR WOR+45 INT/ORG NAT/G DOMIN LEGIT EXEC ATTIT PERCEPT ALL/VALS ...POLICY RELATIV PSY MYTH TREND 20. PAGE 62 G1212
L64
FORCES
COERCE
ARMS/CONT
NUC/PWR

LEIBNITZ/G....GOTTFRIED WILHELM VON LEIBNITZ

MCRAE R.,THE PROBLEM OF THE UNITY OF THE SCIENCES: BACON TO KANT. CREATE TASK KNOWL...PERS/COMP 16/18 BACON/F DESCARTE/R LEIBNITZ/G KANT/I DIDEROT/D. PAGE 38 G0748
B61
PHIL/SCI
IDEA/COMP
PERSON

LEIS A.C. G0142

LEISERSON A. G0654

LEISURE....UNOBLIGATED TIME EXPENDITURES

CROWE S.,THE LANDSCAPE OF POWER. UK CULTURE
B58
HABITAT

SERV/IND NAT/G CONSULT PARTIC NUC/PWR LEISURE...SOC EXHIBIT 20. PAGE 14 G0264
TEC/DEV
PLAN
CONTROL

BOWEN H.R.,AUTOMATION AND ECONOMIC PROGRESS. EUR+WWI USA+45 ECO/DEV INCOME ORD/FREE WEALTH ...POLICY ANTHOL 20. PAGE 8 G0160
B66
AUTOMAT
TEC/DEV
WORKER
LEISURE

LEVENSTEIN A.,"TECHNOLOGICAL CHANGE, WORK, AND HUMAN VALUES." WOR+45 SOCIETY AUTOMAT ROUTINE LEISURE INGP/REL ADJUST TECHRACY...MGT CONCPT. PAGE 33 G0660
S67
TEC/DEV
CULTURE
ALL/VALS
TIME/SEQ

LEND/LEASE....LEND-LEASE PROGRAM(S)

LENIN/VI....VLADIMIR ILYICH LENIN

LENTZ T.F. G0655

LEPAWSKY A. G0656

LERNER A.P. G0657

LERNER D. G0658,G0659

LESAGE/J.....J. LESAGE

LEVELLERS....LEVELLERS PARTY

LEVENSTEIN A. G0660

LEWIN K. G0661

LEWIS J.N. G0498

LEWIS R.L. G0662

LEWIS W.A. G0663

LEWIS/A.....ARTHUR LEWIS

LEWIS/JL....JOHN L. LEWIS

LEYDER J. G0664

LFNA....LEAGUE OF FREE NATIONS ASSOCIATION

LG/CO....LARGE COMPANY

PERSONNEL. USA+45 LAW LABOR LG/CO WORKER CREATE GOV/REL PERS/REL ATTIT WEALTH. PAGE 1 G0010
N
BIBLIOG/A
ADMIN
MGT
GP/REL

US CHAMBER OF COMMERCE,THE SIGNIFICANCE OF CONCENTRATION RATIOS (PAMPHLET). USA+45 FINAN INDUS ADMIN...METH/CNCPT SAMP CHARTS 20. PAGE 56 G1109
N19
MARKET
PREDICT
LG/CO
CONTROL

BAKER H.,PROBLEMS OF REEMPLOYMENT AND RETRAINING OF MANPOWER DURING THE TRANSITION FROM WAR TO PEACE. USA+45 INDUS LABOR LG/CO NAT/G PLAN ADMIN PEACE ...POLICY MGT 20. PAGE 5 G0086
B45
BIBLIOG/A
ADJUST
WAR
PROB/SOLV

WHITEHEAD T.N.,LEADERSHIP IN A FREE SOCIETY; A STUDY IN HUMAN RELATIONS BASED ON AN ANALYSIS OF PRESENT-DAY INDUSTRIAL CIVILIZATION. WOR-45 STRUCT R+D LABOR LG/CO SML/CO WORKER PLAN PROB/SOLV TEC/DEV DRIVE...MGT 20. PAGE 63 G1234
B47
INDUS
LEAD
ORD/FREE
SOCIETY

LEPAWSKY A.,ADMINISTRATION. FINAN INDUS LG/CO SML/CO INGP/REL PERS/REL COST EFFICIENCY OPTIMAL SKILL 20. PAGE 33 G0656
B49
ADMIN
MGT
WORKER
EX/STRUC

LOCKLIN D.P.,ECONOMICS OF TRANSPORTATION (4TH ED.). USA+45 USA-45 SEA AIR LAW FINAN LG/CO EX/STRUC ADMIN CONTROL...STAT CHARTS 19/20 RAILROAD PUB/TRANS. PAGE 34 G0675
B54
ECO/DEV
DIST/IND
ECO/TAC
TEC/DEV

CHEEK G.,ECONOMIC AND SOCIAL IMPLICATIONS OF AUTOMATION: A BIBLIOGRAPHIC REVIEW (PAMPHLET). USA+45 LG/CO WORKER CREATE PLAN CONTROL ROUTINE PERS/REL EFFICIENCY PRODUC...METH/COMP 20. PAGE 12 G0225
B58
BIBLIOG/A
SOCIETY
INDUS
AUTOMAT

ARGYRIS C.,"SOME PROBLEMS IN CONCEPTUALIZING   FINAN
ORGANIZATIONAL CLIMATE: A CASE STUDY OF A BANK"   CONCPT
(BMR)" USA+45 EX/STRUC ADMIN PERS/REL ADJUST PERSON   LG/CO
...POLICY HYPO/EXP SIMUL 20. PAGE 3 G0064   INGP/REL

_S58_

VERNEY D.V.,PUBLIC ENTERPRISE IN SWEDEN. FUT SWEDEN   ECO/DEV
UK INDUS POL/PAR LEGIS PROB/SOLV CAP/ISM INT/TRADE   POLICY
CONTROL SOCISM...MGT CONCPT NAT/COMP 20 SOCDEM/PAR   LG/CO
CIVIL/SERV. PAGE 61 G1196   NAT/G

_B59_

BOULDING K.E.,LINEAR PROGRAMMING AND THE THEORY OF   LG/CO
THE FIRM. ACT/RES PLAN...MGT MATH. PAGE 8 G0156   NEW/IDEA
                                                      COMPUTER

_B60_

SCHRAMM W.,"MASS COMMUNICATIONS: A BOOK OF READINGS   COM/IND
(2ND ED.)" LG/CO PRESS ADMIN CONTROL ROUTINE ATTIT   EDU/PROP
ROLE SUPEGO...CHARTS ANTHOL BIBLIOG 20. PAGE 50   CROWD
G0977   MAJORIT

_C60_

CHANDLER A.D.,STRATEGY AND STRUCTURE: CHAPTERS IN   LG/CO
THE HISTORY OF THE INDUSTRIAL ENTERPRISE. USA+45   PLAN
USA-45 ECO/DEV EX/STRUC ECO/TAC EXEC...DECISION 20.   ADMIN
PAGE 11 G0220   FINAN

_B62_

FERBER R.,RESEARCH METHODS IN ECONOMICS AND   ACT/RES
BUSINESS. ECO/DEV FINAN MARKET LG/CO SML/CO CONSULT   PROB/SOLV
CONTROL COST...STAT METH/COMP 20. PAGE 19 G0364   ECO/TAC
                                                      MGT

_B62_

GRANICK D.,THE EUROPEAN EXECUTIVE. BELGIUM FRANCE   MGT
GERMANY/W UK INDUS LABOR LG/CO SML/CO EX/STRUC PLAN   ECO/DEV
TEC/DEV CAP/ISM COST DEMAND...POLICY CHARTS 20.   ECO/TAC
PAGE 22 G0441   EXEC

_B62_

BROUDE H.W.,STEEL DECISIONS AND THE NATIONAL   PROC/MFG
ECONOMY. USA+45 LG/CO PLAN ADMIN COST DECISION.   NAT/G
PAGE 9 G0176   CONTROL
                                                      ECO/TAC

_B63_

KORNHAUSER W.,SCIENTISTS IN INDUSTRY: CONFLICT AND   CREATE
ACCOMMODATION. USA+45 R+D LG/CO NAT/G TEC/DEV   INDUS
CONTROL ADJUST ATTIT...MGT STAT INT BIBLIOG 20.   PROF/ORG
PAGE 31 G0614   GP/REL

_B63_

RAUDSEPP E.,MANAGING CREATIVE SCIENTISTS AND   MGT
ENGINEERS. USA+45 ECO/DEV LG/CO GP/REL PERS/REL   CREATE
PRODUC. PAGE 46 G0906   R+D
                                                      ECO/TAC

_B63_

THORELLI H.B.,INTOP: INTERNATIONAL OPERATIONS   GAME
SIMULATION: PLAYER'S MANUAL. BRAZIL FINAN OP/RES   INT/TRADE
ADMIN GP/REL INGP/REL PRODUC PERCEPT...DECISION MGT   EDU/PROP
EEC. PAGE 54 G1073   LG/CO

_B63_

WILTZ J.E.,IN SEARCH OF PEACE: THE SENATE MUNITIONS   DELIB/GP
INQUIRY, 1934-36. EUR+WWI USA-45 ELITES INDUS LG/CO   PROFIT
LEGIS INT/TRADE LOBBY NEUTRAL ARMS/CONT...POLICY   WAR
CONGRESS 20 LEAGUE/NAT PRESIDENT SENATE CONSCRIPTN.   WEAPON
PAGE 64 G1246

_B63_

BAUCHET P.,ECONOMIC PLANNING. FRANCE STRATA LG/CO   ECO/DEV
CAP/ISM ADMIN PARL/PROC DEMAND OPTIMAL ATTIT PWR   NAT/G
SOCISM...POLICY CHARTS 20. PAGE 5 G0102   PLAN
                                                      ECO/TAC

_B64_

MANSFIELD E.,MONOPOLY POWER AND ECONOMIC   LG/CO
PERFORMANCE: AN INTRODUCTION TO A CURRENT ISSUE OF   PWR
PUBLIC POLICY. ECO/DEV INDUS NAT/G CAP/ISM   ECO/TAC
PRICE CONTROL LOBBY EFFICIENCY PRODUC...POLICY 20   MARKET
CONGRESS KENNEDY/JF MONOPOLY. PAGE 36 G0701

_B64_

MARRIS R.,THE ECONOMIC THEORY OF "MANAGERIAL"   CAP/ISM
CAPITALISM. USA+45 ECO/DEV LG/CO ECO/TAC DEMAND   MGT
...CHARTS BIBLIOG 20. PAGE 36 G0709   CONTROL
                                                      OP/RES

_B64_

ORTH C.D.,ADMINISTERING RESEARCH AND DEVELOPMENT.   MGT
FINAN PLAN PROB/SOLV ADMIN ROUTINE...METH/CNCPT   R+D
STAT CHARTS METH 20. PAGE 43 G0847   LG/CO
                                                      INDUS

_B64_

COOPER A.C.,"R&D IS MORE EFFICIENT IN SMALL   R+D
COMPANIES." USA+45 LG/CO SML/CO WEALTH...RECORD INT   INDUS
LAB/EXP 20. PAGE 13 G0255   CREATE
                                                      GP/COMP

_S64_

MUMFORD L.,"AUTHORITARIAN AND DEMOCRATIC   ECO/DEV
TECHNIQUES." INDUS PROC/MFG LG/CO SML/CO CREATE   TEC/DEV
PLAN KNOWL...POLICY TREND WORK 20. PAGE 40 G0794

_S64_

STEINER G.A.,THE CREATIVE ORGANIZATION. ELITES   CREATE
LG/CO PLAN PROB/SOLV TEC/DEV INSPECT CAP/ISM   MGT
CONTROL EXEC PERSON...METH/COMP HYPO/EXP 20.   ADMIN
PAGE 52 G1034   SOC

_B65_

GRUNEWALD D.,PUBLIC POLICY AND THE MODERN   LG/CO
COOPERATION: SELECTED READINGS. USA+45 LAW MARKET   POLICY
VOL/ASSN CAP/ISM INT/TRADE CENTRAL OWN...SOC ANTHOL   NAT/G
20. PAGE 23 G0458   CONTROL

_B66_

BAUMOL W.J.,BUSINESS BEHAVIOR, VALUE AND GROWTH   ALL/IDEOS
(REV. ED.). WOR+45 FINAN LG/CO TEC/DEV CAP/ISM   PHIL/SCI
DEMAND EQUILIB...METH/COMP SIMUL 20. PAGE 5 G0105   PLAN
                                                      ECO/DEV

_B67_

BUDER S.,PULLMAN: AN EXPERIMENT IN INDUSTRIAL ORDER   DIST/IND
AND COMMUNITY PLANNING, 1880-1930. USA-45 SOCIETY   INDUS
LABOR LG/CO CREATE PROB/SOLV CONTROL GP/REL   MUNIC
EFFICIENCY ATTIT...MGT BIBLIOG 19/20 PULLMAN.   PLAN
PAGE 9 G0184

_B67_

DONALD A.G.,MANAGEMENT, INFORMATION, AND SYSTEMS.   ROUTINE
WOR+45 LG/CO PROB/SOLV CONTROL FEEDBACK KNOWL MGT.   TEC/DEV
PAGE 16 G0306   CONCPT
                                                      ADMIN

_B67_

HEILBRONER R.L.,THE LIMITS OF AMERICAN CAPITALISM.   ELITES
FUT ECO/DEV INDUS LG/CO EX/STRUC LEAD PWR TECHRACY   CREATE
20. PAGE 25 G0502   TEC/DEV
                                                      CAP/ISM

_B67_

ORLANS H.,CONTRACTING FOR ATOMS. USA+45 LAW INTELL   NUC/PWR
ACADEM LG/CO NAT/G PLAN TEC/DEV CONTROL DETER   R+D
...TREND 20 AEC. PAGE 43 G0845   PRODUC
                                                      PEACE

_B67_

UNIVERSAL REFERENCE SYSTEM,ADMINISTRATIVE   BIBLIOG/A
MANAGEMENT: PUBLIC AND PRIVATE BUREAUCRACY (VOLUME   MGT
IV). WOR+45 WOR-45 ECO/DEV LG/CO LOC/G PUB/INST   ADMIN
VOL/ASSN GOV/REL...COMPUT/IR GEN/METH. PAGE 56   NAT/G
G1096

_B67_

WARNER W.L.,THE EMERGENT AMERICAN SOCIETY VOL I,   ANTHOL
LARGE-SCALE ORGANIZATIONS. USA+45 USA-45 ACADEM   NAT/G
PROF/ORG SCHOOL SECT EX/STRUC TEC/DEV GP/REL   LABOR
...TREND CHARTS. PAGE 62 G1215   LG/CO

_L67_

TRAVERS H. JR.,"AN EXAMINATION OF THE CAB'S MERGER   ADJUD
POLICY." USA+45 USA-45 LAW NAT/G LEGIS PLAN ADMIN   LG/CO
...DECISION 20 CONGRESS. PAGE 55 G1078   POLICY
                                                      DIST/IND

_S67_

ALBAUM G.,"INFORMATION FLOW AND DECENTRALIZED   LG/CO
DECISION MAKING IN MARKETING." EX/STRUC COMPUTER   ROUTINE
OP/RES PROB/SOLV EFFICIENCY OPTIMAL...METH/COMP   KNOWL
ORG/CHARTS 20. PAGE 2 G0033   MARKET

_S67_

ALLISON D.,"THE GROWTH OF IDEAS." USA+45 LG/CO   R+D
ADMIN. PAGE 3 G0045   OP/RES
                                                      INDUS
                                                      TEC/DEV

_S67_

BARRO S.,"ECONOMIC IMPACT OF SPACE EXPENDITURES: SPACE
SOME BROAD ISSUES DEALING WITH COSTS AND BENEFITS."   FINAN
USA+45 PROC/MFG R+D LG/CO CONSULT COST PRODUC 20.   ECO/TAC
PAGE 5 G0098   NAT/G

_S67_

BENN W.,"TECHNOLOGY HAS AN INEXORABLE EFFECT." FUT   R+D
UK ECO/DEV INT/ORG CONSULT PLAN EDU/PROP ADMIN LEAD   LG/CO
GP/REL PRODUC...INT 20 EEC. PAGE 6 G0119   TEC/DEV

INDUS

ENKE S.,"GOVERNMENT-INDUSTRY DEVELOPMENT OF A
COMMERCIAL SUPERSONIC TRANSPORT." USA+45 ECO/DEV
R+D LG/CO NAT/G TEC/DEV PRICE RISK COST PROFIT.
PAGE 18 G0347
   S67 INDUS FINAN SERV/IND CAP/ISM

HAMBERG D.,"SIZE OF ENTERPRISE AND TECHNICAL
CHANGE." USA+45 LG/CO SML/CO CREATE OP/RES PROFIT
...TREND 20. PAGE 24 G0477
   S67 TEC/DEV INDUS R+D WEALTH

MORTON J.A.,"A SYSTEMS APPROACH TO THE INNOVATION
PROCESS: ITS USE IN THE BELL SYSTEM." USA+45 INTELL
INDUS LG/CO CONSULT WORKER COMPUTER AUTOMAT DEMAND
...MGT CHARTS 20. PAGE 40 G0787
   S67 TEC/DEV GEN/METH R+D COM/IND

WILLIAMS C.,"REGIONAL MANAGEMENT OVERSEAS." USA+45
WOR+45 DIST/IND LG/CO EX/STRUC INT/TRADE TARIFFS
ADMIN TASK CENTRAL. PAGE 63 G1242
   S67 MGT EUR+WWI ECO/DEV PLAN

BARAGWANATH L.E.,"SCIENTIFIC CO-OPERATION BETWEEN
THE UNIVERSITIES AND INDUSTRY - A RESEARCH NOTE."
UK LG/CO CREATE TEC/DEV EDU/PROP ATTIT...PHIL/SCI
STAT QU G0090. PAGE 5 G0090
   S68 R+D ACADEM INDUS GP/REL

LI C.M. G0665

LIB/INTRNT....LIBERAL INTERNATIONAL

LIB/PARTY....LIBERAL PARTY (ALL NATIONS)

LIBERALISM....SEE NEW/LIB, WELF/ST, OLD/LIB, LAISSEZ

LIBERIA....SEE ALSO AFR

LIBERTY....SEE ORD/FREE

LIBRARY....SEE OLD/STOR

LIBYA....SEE ALSO ISLAM

LICENSE....LEGAL PERMIT

KAPLAN B.,AN UNHURRIED VIEW OF COPYRIGHT. FUT
...JURID 20. PAGE 29 G0575
   B67 TEC/DEV LAW LICENSE

PIPER D.C.,THE INTERNATIONAL LAW OF THE GREAT
LAKES. CANADA EXTR/IND MUNIC LICENSE ARMS/CONT
CRIME...GEOG 19/20. PAGE 45 G0879
   B67 CONCPT DIPLOM INT/LAW

CARY G.D.,"THE QUIET REVOLUTION IN COPYRIGHT* THE
END OF THE 'PUBLICATION' CONCEPT." USA+45 LAW
OP/RES TEC/DEV CONFER DEBATE EFFICIENCY...JURID
CONGRESS. PAGE 11 G0217
   S67 COM/IND POLICY LICENSE PRESS

RICH G.S.,"THE PROPOSED PATENT LEGISLATION* SOME
COMMENTS." USA+45 LAW R+D ACT/RES TEC/DEV CONFER
EFFICIENCY OWN JURID. PAGE 46 G0916
   S67 LICENSE POLICY CREATE CAP/ISM

LIECHTENST....LIECHTENSTEIN; SEE ALSO APPROPRIATE
TIME/SPACE/CULTURE INDEX

LIGHTFT/PM....PHIL M. LIGHTFOOT

LIKERT/R....RENSIS LIKERT

LILIENTHAL D.E. G0666

LILLEY S. G0667

LIN/PIAO....LIN PIAO

LINCOLN G.A. G0856

LINCOLN/A....PRESIDENT ABRAHAM LINCOLN

LINDAHL/E....ERIK LINDAHL

LINDFORS G.V. G0668

LINDSAY F.A. G0669

LINDVEIT E.N. G0670

LING....LINGUISTICS, LANGUAGE

AMERICAN DOCUMENTATION INST,DOCUMENTATION
ABSTRACTS. WOR+45 NAT/G COMPUTER CREATE TEC/DEV
DIPLOM EDU/PROP REGION KNOWL...PHIL/SCI CLASSIF
LING. PAGE 3 G0051
   N BIBLIOG/A AUTOMAT COMPUT/IR R+D

COHEN M.R.,AN INTRODUCTION TO LOGIC AND SCIENTIFIC
METHOD....LING MATH CHARTS T 20. PAGE 12 G0242
   B34 LOG PHIL/SCI GEN/METH METH/CNCPT

KAPLAN A.,"CONTENT ANALYSIS AND THE THEORY OF
SIGNS" (BMR)" PERS/REL...PSY CONCPT LING IDEA/COMP
SIMUL BIBLIOG 20 MORRIS/CW. PAGE 29 G0573
   S43 LOG CON/ANAL STAT PHIL/SCI

KAUFMANN F.,METHODOLOGY OF THE SOCIAL SCIENCES.
PERSON...RELATIV PSY CONCPT LING METH 20. PAGE 30
G0585
   B44 SOC PHIL/SCI GEN/LAWS METH/CNCPT

AMERICAN DOCUMENTATION INST,CATALOGUE OF AUXILIARY
PUBLICATIONS IN MICROFILMS AND PHOTOPRINTS. USA-45
LAW AGRI CREATE TEC/DEV ADMIN...GEOG LING MATH 20.
PAGE 3 G0052
   B46 BIBLIOG EDU/PROP PSY

MACCORQUODALE K.,"ON A DISTINCTION BETWEEN
HYPOTHETICAL CONSTRUCTS AND INTERVENING VARIABLES."
...METH/CNCPT LING IDEA/COMP HYPO/EXP SOC/EXP
BIBLIOG 20. PAGE 35 G0686
   S48 PSY PHIL/SCI CONCPT GEN/METH

SPENCER R.F.,METHOD AND PERSPECTIVE IN ANTHROPOLOGY
....GEOG LING QUANT STAT TESTS SAMP/SIZ CON/ANAL
IDEA/COMP METH/COMP ANTHOL BIBLIOG 20. PAGE 52
G1025
   B54 PHIL/SCI SOC PSY METH

MILLER G.A.,"THE MAGICAL NUMBER SEVEN, PLUS OR
MINUS TWO: SOME LIMITS ON OUR CAPACITY FOR
PROCESSING INFORMATION." PERS/REL...PSY METH/CNCPT
LING CHARTS BIBLIOG 20. PAGE 39 G0772
   S56 LAB/EXP KNOWL PERCEPT COMPUT/IR

MCKINNEY E.R.,A BIBLIOGRAPHY OF CYBERNETICS AND
INFORMATION THEORY. COMPUTER OP/RES...DECISION
PHIL/SCI PSY LING LOG MATH PROBABIL GAME 20.
PAGE 38 G0743
   B57 BIBLIOG/A FEEDBACK SIMUL CONTROL

BORKOF H.,COMPUTER APPLICATIONS IN THE BEHAVIORAL
SCIENCES. AUTOMAT UTIL...DECISION PHIL/SCI PSY
METH/CNCPT LING LOG MATH STYLE NET/THEORY COMPUT/IR
PROG/TEAC SIMUL. PAGE 8 G0154
   B62 R+D COMPUTER PROB/SOLV FEEDBACK

ANTHONY R.N.,PLANNING AND CONTROL SYSTEMS. UNIV
OP/RES...DECISION MGT LING. PAGE 3 G0061
   B65 CONTROL PLAN METH HYPO/EXP

BENJAMIN A.C.,SCIENCE, TECHNOLOGY, AND HUMAN
VALUES. WOR+45 SECT EDU/PROP GP/REL ATTIT...TECHNIC
LING IDEA/COMP WORSHIP 20. PAGE 6 G0118
   B65 PHIL/SCI CREATE ROLE SOCIETY

NATIONAL SCIENCE FOUNDATION,CURRENT RESEARCH AND
DEVELOPMENT IN SCIENTIFIC DOCUMENTATION - NO. 12.
WOR+45 INTELL COM/IND NAT/G COMPUTER TEC/DEV
AUTOMAT KNOWL...PSY LING 20. PAGE 41 G0812
   B65 BIBLIOG COMPUT/IR R+D PHIL/SCI

MUMFORD L.,THE MYTH OF THE MACHINE: TECHNICS AND
HUMAN DEVELOPMENT. UNIV WOR-45 CREATE AUTOMAT
PERCEPT KNOWL...EPIST PHIL/SCI SOC LING TREND
SOC/INTEG 20 MARX/KARL. PAGE 40 G0795
   B66 WORKER TEC/DEV SOCIETY

SCHUMACHER B.G.,COMPUTER DYNAMICS IN PUBLIC
ADMINISTRATION. USA+45 CREATE PLAN TEC/DEV...MGT
LING CON/ANAL BIBLIOG/A 20. PAGE 50 G0980
   B67 COMPUTER COMPUT/IR ADMIN AUTOMAT

LINGUISTICS....SEE LING

LINK/AS....ARTHUR S. LINK

LINS L.J. G0671

LIPPITT R. G0672

LIPPMAN W. G0673

LIPPMANN/W....WALTER LIPPMANN

LIPSON L. G0736

LITERACY....ABILITY TO READ AND WRITE

FOSTER P..EDUCATION AND SOCIAL CHANGE IN GHANA. GHANA CULTURE STRUCT ECO/UNDEV TEC/DEV REGION EFFICIENCY LITERACY ALL/VALS SOVEREIGN...STAT METH/COMP 19/20 GOLD/COAST. PAGE 20 G0385
B65 SCHOOL CREATE SOCIETY

LITERARY ANALYSIS....SEE HUM

LITHUANIA....SEE ALSO USSR

LITTERER J.A. G0674

LIU/SHAO....LIU SHAO-CHI

LIVNGSTN/D....DAVID LIVINGSTON

LIVY....LIVY

LLOYD/HD....HENRY D. LLOYD

LLOYD-GEO/D....DAVID LLOYD GEORGE

LOANS....SEE RENT+GIVE+FOR/AID+FINAN

LOBBY....PRESSURE GROUP

LAWRENCE S.A..THE BATTERY ADDITIVE CONTROVERSY (PAMPHLET). USA+45 LAW MARKET PROC/MFG R+D CAP/ISM CT/SYS GOV/REL OWN FTC CONGRESS BUR/STNDRD RITCHIE/JM. PAGE 33 G0645
N19 PHIL/SCI LOBBY INSPECT

KILE O.M..THE FARM BUREAU MOVEMENT: THE FARM BUREAU THROUGH THREE DECADES. NAT/G LEGIS LEAD LOBBY GP/REL INCOME POLICY. PAGE 30 G0596
B48 AGRI STRUCT VOL/ASSN DOMIN

MAASS A..MUDDY WATERS: THE ARMY ENGINEERS AND THE NATIONS RIVERS. USA-45 PROF/ORG CONSULT LEGIS ADMIN EXEC ROLE PWR...SOC PRESIDENT 20. PAGE 35 G0682
B51 FORCES GP/REL LOBBY CONSTRUC

TOMPKINS D.C..STATE GOVERNMENT AND ADMINISTRATION: A BIBLIOGRAPHY. USA+45 USA-45 CONSTN LEGIS JUDGE BUDGET CT/SYS LOBBY...CHARTS 20. PAGE 55 G1077
B54 BIBLIOG/A LOC/G PROVS ADMIN

ZELLER B.."AMERICAN STATE LEGISLATURES: REPORT ON THE COMMITTEE ON AMERICAN LEGISLATURES." CONSTN POL/PAR EX/STRUC CONFER ADMIN CONTROL EXEC LOBBY ROUTINE GOV/REL...POLICY BIBLIOG 20. PAGE 65 G1267
C54 REPRESENT LEGIS PROVS APPORT

LIPPMAN W..THE PUBLIC PHILOSOPHY. EX/STRUC TOP/EX LOBBY RATIONAL POPULISM...POLICY SOC CONCPT PREDICT GP/COMP IDEA/COMP. PAGE 34 G0673
B55 MAJORIT STRUCT PWR TOTALISM

REDFORD E.S..PUBLIC ADMINISTRATION AND POLICY FORMATION: STUDIES IN OIL, GAS, BANKING, RIVER DEVELOPMENT AND CORPORATE INVESTIGATIONS. USA+45 CLIENT NAT/G ADMIN LOBBY REPRESENT GOV/REL INGP/REL 20. PAGE 46 G0908
B56 EX/STRUC PROB/SOLV CONTROL EXEC

SCARROW H.A..THE HIGHER PUBLIC SERVICE OF THE COMMONWEALTH OF AUSTRALIA. LAW SENIOR LOBBY ROLE 20 AUSTRAL CIVIL/SERV COMMONWLTH. PAGE 49 G0959
B57 ADMIN NAT/G EX/STRUC GOV/COMP

KEISER N.F.."PUBLIC RESPONSIBILITY AND FEDERAL ADVISORY GROUPS: A CASE STUDY." NAT/G ADMIN CONTROL ELITES LOBBY...POLICY 20. PAGE 30 G0590
S58 REPRESENT ELITES GP/REL EX/STRUC

CARPER E.T..THE DEFENSE APPROPRIATIONS RIDER (PAMPHLET). USA+45 CONSTN CHIEF DELIB/GP LEGIS
B60 GOV/REL ADJUD

BUDGET LOBBY CIVMIL/REL...POLICY 20 CONGRESS EISNHWR/DD DEPT/DEFEN PRESIDENT BOSTON. PAGE 11 G0212
LAW CONTROL

TAYLOR M.G.."THE ROLE OF THE MEDICAL PROFESSION IN THE FORMULATION AND EXECUTION OF PUBLIC POLICY" (BMR)" CANADA NAT/G CONSULT ADMIN REPRESENT GP/REL ROLE SOVEREIGN...DECISION 20 CMA. PAGE 54 G1058
S60 PROF/ORG HEALTH LOBBY POLICY

MURPHY E.F..WATER PURITY: A STUDY IN LEGAL CONTROL OF NATURAL RESOURCES. LOC/G ACT/RES PLAN TEC/DEV LOBBY GP/REL COST ATTIT HEALTH ORD/FREE...HEAL JURID 20 WISCONSIN WATER. PAGE 40 G0797
B61 SEA LAW PROVS CONTROL

COOKE E.F.."RESEARCH: AN INSTRUMENT OF POWER." VOL/ASSN PLAN TEC/DEV TAX LOBBY INGP/REL ROLE POLICY. PAGE 13 G0253
S61 R+D PROVS LOC/G DECISION

MAINZER L.C.."SCIENTIFIC FREEDOM IN GOVERNMENT-SPONSORED RESEARCH." USA+45 INTELL PUB/INST BUDGET LOBBY AUTHORIT PWR...POLICY PHIL/SCI 20 NIH NSF. PAGE 35 G0696
S61 CREATE ORD/FREE NAT/G R+D

REICH C.A..BUREAUCRACY AND THE FORESTS (PAMPHLET). USA+45 LOBBY...POLICY MGT 20. PAGE 46 G0910
B62 ADMIN CONTROL EX/STRUC REPRESENT

CAVERS D.F.."ADMINISTRATIVE DECISION-MAKING IN NUCLEAR FACILITIES LICENSING." USA+45 CLIENT ADMIN EXEC 20 AEC. PAGE 11 G0218
L62 REPRESENT LOBBY PWR CONTROL

NIEBURG H.L.."THE EISENHOWER ATOMIC ENERGY COMMISSION AND CONGRESS" R+D INT/ORG OP/RES DIPLOM ADMIN CONTROL 20 PRESIDENT CONGRESS AEC. PAGE 42 G0821
L62 NUC/PWR TOP/EX LOBBY DELIB/GP

HATHAWAY D.A..GOVERNMENT AND AGRICULTURE: PUBLIC POLICY IN A DEMOCRATIC SOCIETY. USA+45 LEGIS ADMIN EXEC LOBBY REPRESENT PWR 20. PAGE 25 G0491
B63 AGRI GOV/REL PROB/SOLV EX/STRUC

MILBRATH L.W..THE WASHINGTON LOBBYISTS. CONSTN BAL/PWR CONTROL LEAD TASK CHOOSE SUPEGO...DECISION STAT CHARTS BIBLIOG. PAGE 39 G0767
B63 LOBBY POLICY PERS/REL

PERLO V..MILITARISM AND INDUSTRY. USA+45 INT/TRADE EDU/PROP DETER KNOWL...CHARTS MAPS 20. PAGE 44 G0869
B63 CIVMIL/REL INDUS LOBBY ARMS/CONT

WILTZ J.E..IN SEARCH OF PEACE: THE SENATE MUNITIONS INQUIRY, 1934-36. EUR+WWI USA-45 ELITES INDUS LG/CO LEGIS INT/TRADE LOBBY NEUTRAL ARMS/CONT...POLICY CONGRESS 20 LEAGUE/NAT PRESIDENT SENATE CONSCRIPTN. PAGE 64 G1246
B63 DELIB/GP PROFIT WAR WEAPON

MANSFIELD E..MONOPOLY POWER AND ECONOMIC PERFORMANCE: AN INTRODUCTION TO A CURRENT ISSUE OF PUBLIC POLICY. ECO/DEV INDUS NAT/G PLAN CAP/ISM PRICE CONTROL LOBBY EFFICIENCY PRODUC...POLICY 20 CONGRESS KENNEDY/JF MONOPOLY. PAGE 36 G0701
B64 LG/CO PWR ECO/TAC MARKET

MASTERS N.A..STATE POLITICS AND THE PUBLIC SCHOOLS. STRUCT FINAN ADMIN LOBBY GP/REL PWR BIBLIOG. PAGE 36 G0720
B64 EDU/PROP PROVS DOMIN

CARPER E.T..REORGANIZATION OF THE U.S. PUBLIC HEALTH SERVICE. FUT USA+45 INTELL R+D LOBBY GP/REL INGP/REL PERS/REL RIGID/FLEX ROLE HEALTH...PHIL/SCI 20 CONGRESS PHS. PAGE 11 G0213
B65 HEAL PLAN NAT/G OP/RES

BOLTON R.E..DEFENSE AND DISARMAMENT: THE ECONOMICS OF TRANSITION. USA+45 R+D FORCES PLAN LOBBY DETER WAR COST PEACE...ANTHOL BIBLIOG 20. PAGE 8 G0150
B66 ARMS/CONT POLICY INDUS

NIEBURG H.L..IN THE NAME OF SCIENCE. USA+45 EX/STRUC LEGIS TEC/DEV BUDGET PAY AUTOMAT LOBBY PWR
B66 NAT/G INDUS

...OBS 20. PAGE 42 G0822   TECHRACY

                                                      S67
HABERER J.,"POLITICS AND THE COMMUNITY OF SCIENCE." LEAD
USA+45 SOCIETY ACT/RES PARTIC ATTIT PHIL/SCI.   SUPEGO
PAGE 24 G0465   INTELL
                                                     LOBBY

                                                      S67
TIVEY L.,"THE POLITICAL CONSEQUENCES OF ECONOMIC   PLAN
PLANNING." UK CONSTN INDUS ACT/RES ADMIN CONTROL   POLICY
LOBBY REPRESENT EFFICIENCY SUPEGO SOVEREIGN   NAT/G
...DECISION 20. PAGE 55 G1074

LOBBYING....SEE LOBBY

LOC/G....LOCAL GOVERNMENT

                                                      N
CONOVER H.L.,CIVILIAN DEFENSE: A SELECTED LIST OF   BIBLIOG
RECENT REFERENCES (PAMPHLET). USA+45 LOC/G MUNIC   PLAN
PROB/SOLV ADMIN LEAD TASK WEAPON GOV/REL...POLICY   WAR
CON/ANAL 20 CIV/DEFENS. PAGE 13 G0251   CIVMIL/REL

                                                      N19
GINZBERG E.,MANPOWER FOR GOVERNMENT (PAMPHLET).   WORKER
USA+45 FORCES PLAN PROB/SOLV PAY EDU/PROP ADMIN   CONSULT
GP/REL COST...MGT PREDICT TREND 20 CIVIL/SERV.   NAT/G
PAGE 21 G0418   LOC/G

                                                      N19
KAUFMAN J.L.,COMMUNITY RENEWAL PROGRAMS (PAMPHLET). LOC/G
USA+45 CONSTRUC PROVS CREATE PLAN CONTROL WEALTH 20 MUNIC
URBAN/RNWL. PAGE 30 G0584   ACT/RES
                                                     BIBLIOG

                                                      N19
VERNON R.,THE MYTH AND REALITY OF OUR URBAN   PLAN
PROBLEMS (PAMPHLET). USA+45 SOCIETY LOC/G ADMIN   MUNIC
COST 20 PRINCETN/U INTERVENT URBAN/RNWL. PAGE 61   HABITAT
G1197   PROB/SOLV

                                                      B25
MATHEWS J.M.,AMERICAN STATE GOVERNMENT. USA-45   PROVS
LOC/G CHIEF EX/STRUC LEGIS ADJUD CONTROL CT/SYS   ADMIN
ROUTINE GOV/REL PWR 20 GOVERNOR. PAGE 37 G0721   FEDERAL
                                                     CONSTN

                                                      B37
HODGSON J.G.,THE OFFICIAL PUBLICATIONS OF AMERICAN   BIBLIOG
COUNTIES: A UNION LIST. SCHOOL BUDGET...HEAL MGT   LOC/G
SOC/WK 19/20. PAGE 26 G0520   PUB/INST

                                                      B44
PUBLIC ADMINISTRATION SERVICE,YOUR BUSINESS OF   BIBLIOG
GOVERNMENT: A CATALOG OF PUBLICATIONS IN THE FIELD   ADMIN
OF PUBLIC ADMINISTRATION (PAMPHLET). FINAN R+D   NAT/G
LOC/G ACT/RES OP/RES PLAN 20. PAGE 45 G0894   MUNIC

                                                      B48
METZLER L.A.,INCOME, EMPLOYMENT, AND PUBLIC POLICY. INCOME
FINAN INDUS LOC/G NAT/G TAX GIVE PAY COST PRODUC   WEALTH
...MGT TIME/SEQ 20. PAGE 38 G0760   POLICY
                                                     ECO/TAC

                                                      B48
PUBLIC ADMINISTRATION SERVICE,SOURCE MATERIALS IN   BIBLIOG/A
PUBLIC ADMINISTRATION: A SELECTED BIBLIOGRAPHY (PAS GOV/REL
PUBLICATION NO. 102). USA+45 LAW FINAN LOC/G MUNIC   MGT
NAT/G PLAN RECEIVE EDU/PROP CT/SYS CHOOSE HEALTH   ADMIN
20. PAGE 45 G0895

                                                      L50
MAASS A.A.,"CONGRESS AND WATER RESOURCES." LOC/G   REGION
TEC/DEV CONTROL SANCTION...WELF/ST GEOG CONGRESS.   AGRI
PAGE 35 G0683   PLAN

                                                      C50
WAGER P.W.,"COUNTY GOVERNMENT ACROSS THE NATION."   LOC/G
USA+45 CONSTN COM/IND FINAN SCHOOL DOMIN CT/SYS   PROVS
LEAD GOV/REL...STAT BIBLIOG 20. PAGE 61 G1204   ADMIN
                                                     ROUTINE

                                                      L52
LASSWELL H.D.,"RESEARCH IN POLITICAL BEHAVIOR."   PHIL/SCI
LOC/G MUNIC POL/PAR CONSULT ADMIN PARTIC...CHARTS   METH
ANTHOL BIBLIOG/A 20. PAGE 32 G0641   R+D

                                                      B53
TOMPKINS D.C.,CIVIL DEFENSE IN THE STATES: A   BIBLIOG
BIBLIOGRAPHY (DEFENSE BIBLIOGRAPHIES NO. 3;   WAR
PAMPHLET). USA+45 LABOR LOC/G NAT/G PROVS LEGIS.   ORD/FREE
PAGE 55 G1076   ADMIN

                                                      B54
TOMPKINS D.C.,STATE GOVERNMENT AND ADMINISTRATION: BIBLIOG/A

A BIBLIOGRAPHY. USA+45 USA-45 CONSTN LEGIS JUDGE   LOC/G
BUDGET CT/SYS LOBBY...CHARTS 20. PAGE 55 G1077   PROVS
                                                     ADMIN

                                                      C54
CALDWELL L.K.,"THE GOVERNMENT AND ADMINISTRATION OF PROVS
NEW YORK." LOC/G MUNIC POL/PAR SCHOOL CHIEF LEGIS   ADMIN
PLAN TAX CT/SYS...MGT SOC/WK BIBLIOG 20 NEWYORK/C.   CONSTN
PAGE 10 G0202   EX/STRUC

                                                      B56
WASSERMAN P.,INFORMATION FOR ADMINISTRATORS: A   BIBLIOG
GUIDE TO PUBLICATIONS AND SERVICES FOR MANAGEMENT   MGT
IN BUSINESS AND GOVERNMENT. R+D LOC/G NAT/G   KNOWL
PROF/ORG VOL/ASSN PRESS...PSY SOC STAT 20. PAGE 62   EDU/PROP
G1219

                                                      B59
ATOMIC INDUSTRIAL FORUM,THE IMPACT OF THE PEACEFUL   PROVS
USES OF ATOMIC ENERGY ON STATE AND LOCAL   LOC/G
GOVERNMENT. USA+45 INDUS NAT/G LEGIS PLAN CONTROL   NUC/PWR
GOV/REL. PAGE 4 G0079   PEACE

                                                      B59
US CONGRESS JT ATOM ENRGY COMM,SELECTED MATERIALS   NAT/G
ON FEDERAL-STATE COOPERATION IN THE ATOMIC ENERGY   NUC/PWR
FIELD. USA+45 LAW LOC/G PROVS CONSULT LEGIS ADJUD   GOV/REL
...POLICY BIBLIOG 20 AEC. PAGE 57 G1111   DELIB/GP

                                                      B60
ALBI F.,TRATADO DE LOS MODOS DE GESTION DE LAS   LOC/G
CORPORACIONES LOCALES. SPAIN FINAN NAT/G BUDGET   LAW
CONTROL EXEC ROUTINE GOV/REL ORD/FREE SOVEREIGN   ADMIN
...MGT 20. PAGE 2 G0034   MUNIC

                                                      B60
US SENATE COMM ON COMMERCE,URBAN MASS   DIST/IND
TRANSPORTATION. FUT USA+45 AIR ECO/DEV FINAN LOC/G   PLAN
MUNIC LEGIS CREATE PROB/SOLV TEC/DEV 20 PUB/TRANS.   NAT/G
PAGE 60 G1180   LAW

                                                      B61
LEE R.R.,ENGINEERING-ECONOMIC PLANNING   BIBLIOG/A
MISCELLANEOUS SUBJECTS: A SELECTED BIBLIOGRAPHY   PLAN
(MIMEOGRAPHED). FINAN LOC/G NEIGH ADMIN   REGION
CONTROL INGP/REL HABITAT...GEOG MGT SOC/WK 20
RESOURCE/N. PAGE 33 G0651

                                                      B61
MURPHY E.F.,WATER PURITY: A STUDY IN LEGAL CONTROL   SEA
OF NATURAL RESOURCES. LOC/G ACT/RES PLAN TEC/DEV   LAW
LOBBY GP/REL COST ATTIT HEALTH ORD/FREE...HEAL   PROVS
JURID 20 WISCONSIN WATER. PAGE 40 G0797   CONTROL

                                                      S61
ANDREWS R.B.,"URBAN ECONOMICS: AN APPRAISAL OF   MUNIC
PROGRESS." LOC/G PROB/SOLV TEC/DEV...CONCPT   PHIL/SCI
OBS/ENVIR METH/COMP HYPO/EXP SOC/EXP SIMUL GEN/METH ECOMETRIC
METH 20. PAGE 3 G0058

                                                      S61
COOKE E.F.,"RESEARCH: AN INSTRUMENT OF POWER."   R+D
VOL/ASSN PLAN TEC/DEV TAX LOBBY INGP/REL ROLE   PROVS
POLICY. PAGE 13 G0253   LOC/G
                                                     DECISION

                                                      S61
DYKMAN J.W.,"REVIEW ARTICLE* PLANNING AND DECISION   DECISION
THEORY." ELITES LOC/G MUNIC CONSULT ADMIN...POLICY   PLAN
MGT. PAGE 17 G0327   RATIONAL

                                                      S61
FAIR M.L.,"PORT AUTHORITIES IN THE UNITED STATES."   MUNIC
PROB/SOLV ADMIN LEAD REPRESENT PWR...DECISION GEOG. REGION
PAGE 18 G0357   LOC/G
                                                     GOV/REL

                                                      B62
KARNJAHAPRAKORN C.,MUNICIPAL GOVERNMENT IN THAILAND LOC/G
AS AN INSTITUTION AND PROCESS OF SELF-GOVERNMENT.   MUNIC
THAILAND CULTURE FINAN EX/STRUC LEGIS PLAN CONTROL   ORD/FREE
GOV/REL EFFICIENCY ATTIT...POLICY 20. PAGE 29 G0578 ADMIN

                                                      B62
STAHL O.G.,PUBLIC PERSONNEL ADMINISTRATION. LOC/G   ADMIN
TOP/EX CREATE PLAN ROUTINE...TECHNIC MGT T. PAGE 52 WORKER
G1030   EX/STRUC
                                                     NAT/G

                                                      B63
BASS M.E.,SELECTIVE BIBLIOGRAPHY ON MUNICIPAL   BIBLIOG
GOVERNMENT FROM THE FILES OF THE MUNICIPAL   LOC/G
TECHNICAL ADVISORY SERVICE. USA+45 FINAN SERV/IND   ADMIN
PLAN 20. PAGE 5 G0100   MUNIC

METH/CNCPT

B63
JACOB H.,GERMAN ADMINISTRATION SINCE BISMARCK: ADMIN
CENTRAL AUTHORITY VERSUS LOCAL AUTONOMY. GERMANY   NAT/G
GERMANY/W LAW POL/PAR CONTROL CENTRAL TOTALISM   LOC/G
FASCISM...MAJORIT DECISION STAT CHARTS GOV/COMP   POLICY
19/20 BISMARCK/O HITLER/A WEIMAR/REP. PAGE 28 G0551

S64
NEEDHAM T.,"SCIENCE AND SOCIETY IN EAST AND WEST."   ASIA
INTELL STRATA R+D LOC/G NAT/G PROVS CONSULT ACT/RES   STRUCT
CREATE PLAN TEC/DEV EDU/PROP ADMIN ATTIT ALL/VALS
...POLICY RELATIV MGT CONCPT NEW/IDEA TIME/SEQ WORK
WORK. PAGE 41 G0815

B66
KLOTSCHE J.M.,THE URBAN UNIVERSITY AND THE FUTURE   ACADEM
OF OUR CITIES. FUT USA+45 USA-45 LOC/G NEIGH GIVE   MUNIC
19/20. PAGE 31 G0606   PROB/SOLV
                                                           TEC/DEV

B66
MURDOCK J.C.,RESEARCH AND REGIONS. AGRI FINAN INDUS   BIBLIOG
LOC/G MUNIC NAT/G PROB/SOLV TEC/DEV ADMIN REGION   ECO/DEV
20. PAGE 40 G0796   COMPUT/IR
                                                           R+D

B66
SCHURMANN F.,IDEOLOGY AND ORGANIZATION IN COMMUNIST   MARXISM
CHINA. CHINA/COM LOC/G MUNIC POL/PAR ECO/TAC   STRUCT
CONTROL ATTIT...MGT STERTYP 20 COM/PARTY. PAGE 50   ADMIN
G0981   NAT/G

S66
"FURTHER READING." INDIA LOC/G NAT/G PLAN ADMIN   BIBLIOG
WEALTH...GEOG SOC CONCPT CENSUS 20. PAGE 1 G0021   ECO/UNDEV
                                                           TEC/DEV
                                                           PROVS

B67
UNIVERSAL REFERENCE SYSTEM,LEGISLATIVE PROCESS,   BIBLIOG/A
REPRESENTATION, AND DECISION-MAKING (VOLUME II).   LEGIS
WOR+45 WOR-45 CONSTN LOC/G NAT/G...POLICY CON/ANAL   REPRESENT
COMPUT/IR GEN/METH. PAGE 56 G1094   DECISION

B67
UNIVERSAL REFERENCE SYSTEM,ADMINISTRATIVE   BIBLIOG/A
MANAGEMENT: PUBLIC AND PRIVATE BUREAUCRACY (VOLUME   MGT
IV). WOR+45 WOR-45 ECO/DEV LG/CO LOC/G PUB/INST   ADMIN
VOL/ASSN GOV/REL...COMPUT/IR GEN/METH. PAGE 56   NAT/G
G1096

B67
UNIVERSAL REFERENCE SYSTEM,CURRENT EVENTS AND   BIBLIOG/A
PROBLEMS OF MODERN SOCIETY (VOLUME V). WOR+45 LOC/G   SOCIETY
MUNIC NAT/G PLAN EDU/PROP CRIME RACE/REL WEALTH   PROB/SOLV
...COMPUT/IR GEN/METH. PAGE 56 G1097   ATTIT

B67
US DEPARTMENT OF THE ARMY,CIVILIAN IN PEACE,   BIBLIOG/A
SOLDIER IN WAR: A BIBLIOGRAPHIC SURVEY OF THE ARMY   FORCES
AND AIR NATIONAL GUARD (PAMPHLET. NOS. 130-2).   ROLE
USA+45 USA-45 LOC/G NAT/G PROVS LEGIS PLAN ADMIN   DIPLOM
ATTIT ORD/FREE...POLICY 19/20. PAGE 58 G1134

L67
RUTH J.M.,"THE ADMINISTRATION OF WATER RESOURCES IN   EFFICIENCY
GUATEMALA." GUATEMALA L/A+17C DIST/IND LOC/G NAT/G   ECO/UNDEV
EX/STRUC ADMIN GOV/REL DEMAND EQUILIB WEALTH...GEOG   PLAN
MGT 20. PAGE 48 G0952   ACT/RES

S67
DONAHO J.A.,"PLANNING-PROGRAMMING-BUDGETING   PLAN
SYSTEMS." USA+45 LOC/G NAT/G ROUTINE. PAGE 16 G0305   BUDGET
                                                           ADMIN
                                                           ECOMETRIC

S67
MYERS S.,"TECHNOLOGY AND URBAN TRANSIT: THE   R+D
ENORMOUS POTENTIAL OF BUS AND RAIL SYSTEMS." USA+45   TEC/DEV
FINAN LOC/G MUNIC WORKER PLAN PROB/SOLV PRICE   DIST/IND
AUTOMAT 20. PAGE 40 G0798   ACT/RES

LOCAL GOVERNMENT....SEE LOC/G

LOCKE/JOHN....JOHN LOCKE

LOCKLIN D.P. G0675

LODGE/HC....HENRY CABOT LODGE

LOG....LOGIC

B34
COHEN M.R.,AN INTRODUCTION TO LOGIC AND SCIENTIFIC   LOG
METHOD....LING MATH CHARTS T 20. PAGE 12 G0242   PHIL/SCI
                                                           GEN/METH

S43
KAPLAN A.,"CONTENT ANALYSIS AND THE THEORY OF   LOG
SIGNS" (BMR)" PERS/REL...PSY CONCPT LING IDEA/COMP   CON/ANAL
SIMUL BIBLIOG 20 MORRIS/CW. PAGE 29 G0573   STAT
                                                           PHIL/SCI

S51
BERGMANN G.,"IDEOLOGY" (BMR)" UNIV PERCEPT KNOWL   PHIL/SCI
...IDEA/COMP METH. PAGE 7 G0126   CONCPT
                                                           LOG
                                                           ALL/IDEOS

S55
DRUCKER P.F.,"'MANAGEMENT SCIENCE' AND THE   MGT
MANAGER." PLAN ROUTINE RIGID/FLEX...METH/CNCPT LOG   STRUCT
HYPO/EXP. PAGE 16 G0315   DECISION
                                                           RATIONAL

B57
MCKINNEY E.R.,A BIBLIOGRAPHY OF CYBERNETICS AND   BIBLIOG/A
INFORMATION THEORY. COMPUTER OP/RES...DECISION   FEEDBACK
PHIL/SCI PSY LING LOG MATH PROBABIL GAME 20.   SIMUL
PAGE 38 G0743   CONTROL

S58
NEWELL A.C.,"ELEMENTS OF A THEORY OF HUMAN PROBLEM   PROB/SOLV
SOLVING" (BMR)" TASK PERCEPT...CONCPT LOG METH/COMP   COMPUTER
LAB/EXP BIBLIOG 20. PAGE 42 G0819   COMPUT/IR
                                                           OP/RES

B62
BORKOF H.,COMPUTER APPLICATIONS IN THE BEHAVIORAL   R+D
SCIENCES. AUTOMAT UTIL...DECISION PHIL/SCI PSY   COMPUTER
METH/CNCPT LING LOG MATH STYLE NET/THEORY COMPUT/IR   PROB/SOLV
PROG/TEAC SIMUL. PAGE 8 G0154   FEEDBACK

LOGIC....SEE LOG

LOGIST/MGT....LOGISTICS MANAGEMENT INSTITUTE

LOGISTICS MANAGEMENT INSTITUTE....SEE LOGIST/MGT

LONDON....LONDON, ENGLAND

LONG N.E. G0676

LONG/FAMLY....THE LONG FAMILY OF LOUISIANA

LONGE/FD....F.D. LONGE

LOS/ANG....LOS ANGELES

LOUISIANA....LOUISIANA

LOUISVILLE....LOUISVILLE, KENTUCKY

LOUVERT/T....LOOUVERTURE TOUSSANT

LOVE....AFFECTION, FRIENDSHIP, SEX RELATIONS

LOVESTN/J....JAY LOVESTONE

LOWENSTEIN L. G0677

LOYALTY....SEE SUPEGO

LUA....LUA, OR LAWA: VILLAGE PEOPLES OF NORTHERN THAILAND

LUANDA....LUANDA, ANGOLA

LUBBOCK/TX....LUBBOCK, TEXAS

LUDWIG/BAV....LUDWIG THE BAVARIAN

LUMBERING....SEE EXTR/IND

LUNDBERG G.A. G0678,G0679

LUTHER/M....MARTIN LUTHER

LUTZ V. G0680

LUVALE....LUVALE TRIBE, CENTRAL AFRICA

LUXEMBOURG....SEE ALSO APPROPRIATE TIME/SPACE/CULTURE INDEX

LUZON....LUZON, PHILIPPINES

LYONS G.M. G0681

M

MAASS A.A. G0682,G0683

MACAO....MACAO

MACAPAGL/D....DIOSDADO MACAPAGAL

MACARTHR/D....DOUGLAS MACARTHUR

MACAVOY P.W. G0684

MACBRIDE R. G0685

MACCORQUODALE K. G0686

MACDONALD G.J.F. G0687

MACHIAVELL....NICCOLO MACHIAVELLI

MACHIAVELLISM....SEE REALPOL, MACHIAVELL

MACHLUP F. G0688

MACHOWSKI K. G0689

MACK R.T. G0690

MACKINTOSH J.M. G0691

MACLEISH/A....ARCHIBALD MACLEISH

MACMILLN/H....HAROLD MACMILLAN, PRIME MINISTER

MACPHERSON C. G0692

MACRAE D.G. G0693

MADAGASCAR....SEE ALSO AFR

MADERO/F....FRANCISCO MADERO

MADISON/J....PRESIDENT JAMES MADISON

MADOW W.G. G0299

MAFIA....MAFIA

MAGGS P.B. G0694

MAGHREB....SEE ALSO ISLAM

MAGNA/CART....MAGNA CARTA

MAGON/F....FLORES MAGON

MAHALANOBIS P.C. G0695

MAIMONIDES....MAIMONIDES

MAINE....MAINE

MAINZER L.C. G0696

MAITLAND/F....FREDERIC WILLIAM MAITLAND

B28
BARKER E.,POLITICAL THOUGHT IN ENGLAND: FROM   INTELL
HERBERT SPENCER TO THE PRESENT DAY. UK ALL/IDEOS GEN/LAWS
...PHIL/SCI 19/20 SPENCER/H GREEN/TH BENTHAM/J   IDEA/COMP
MAITLAND/F. PAGE 5 G0094

MAJORIT....MAJORITARIAN

B41
BEARD C.A.,PUBLIC POLICY AND THE GENERAL WELFARE. CONCPT
USA-45 CONSTN LAISSEZ POPULISM...POLICY MAJORIT 20. ORD/FREE
PAGE 6 G0108   PWR
                                                    NAT/G

B44
MERRIAM C.E.,PUBLIC AND PRIVATE GOVERNMENT.   NAT/G
VOL/ASSN EDU/PROP ADMIN REPRESENT EFFICIENCY PWR   NEIGH
PLURISM...MAJORIT CONCPT. PAGE 38 G0755   MGT
                                                    POLICY

B45
BUSH V.,SCIENCE, THE ENDLESS FRONTIER. FUT USA-45   R+D
INTELL STRATA ACT/RES CREATE PLAN EDU/PROP ADMIN   NAT/G
NUC/PWR PEACE ATTIT HEALTH KNOWL...MAJORIT HEAL MGT
PHIL/SCI CONCPT OBS TREND 20. PAGE 10 G0195

B46
BUSH V.,ENDLESS HORIZONS. FUT USA-45 INTELL NAT/G   R+D
CONSULT ACT/RES CREATE PLAN EDU/PROP DRIVE   KNOWL
...MAJORIT HEAL MGT PHIL/SCI CONCPT OBS TREND   PEACE
GEN/METH TOT/POP 20. PAGE 10 G0196

B53
SAYLES L.R.,THE LOCAL UNION. CONSTN CULTURE   LABOR
DELIB/GP PARTIC CHOOSE GP/REL INGP/REL ATTIT ROLE   LEAD
...MAJORIT DECISION MGT. PAGE 49 G0958   ADJUD
                                                    ROUTINE

B55
LIPPMAN W.,THE PUBLIC PHILOSOPHY. EX/STRUC TOP/EX   MAJORIT
LOBBY RATIONAL POPULISM...POLICY SOC CONCPT PREDICT STRUCT
GP/COMP IDEA/COMP. PAGE 34 G0673   PWR
                                                    TOTALISM

B55
MOCH J.,HUMAN FOLLY: DISARM OR PERISH. USA+45   FUT
WOR+45 SOCIETY INT/ORG NAT/G ACT/RES EDU/PROP ATTIT DELIB/GP
PERSON KNOWL ORD/FREE PWR...MAJORIT TOT/POP   ARMS/CONT
COLD/WAR 20. PAGE 39 G0776   NUC/PWR

S60
HUNTINGTON S.P.,"STRATEGIC PLANNING AND THE   EXEC
POLITICAL PROCESS." USA+45 NAT/G DELIB/GP LEGIS   FORCES
ACT/RES ECO/TAC LEGIT ROUTINE CHOOSE RIGID/FLEX PWR NUC/PWR
...POLICY MAJORIT MGT 20. PAGE 27 G0538   WAR

C60
SCHRAMM W.,"MASS COMMUNICATIONS: A BOOK OF READINGS COM/IND
(2ND ED.)" LG/CO PRESS ADMIN CONTROL ROUTINE ATTIT EDU/PROP
ROLE SUPEGO...CHARTS ANTHOL BIBLIOG 20. PAGE 50   CROWD
G0977   MAJORIT

B63
JACOB H.,GERMAN ADMINISTRATION SINCE BISMARCK: ADMIN
CENTRAL AUTHORITY VERSUS LOCAL AUTONOMY. GERMANY   NAT/G
GERMANY/W LAW POL/PAR CONTROL CENTRAL TOTALISM   LOC/G
FASCISM...MAJORIT DECISION STAT CHARTS GOV/COMP   POLICY
19/20 BISMARCK/O HITLER/A WEIMAR/REP. PAGE 28 G0551

B63
MULLER H.J.,FREEDOM IN THE WESTERN WORLD. PREHIST   ORD/FREE
CULTURE SECT CREATE TEC/DEV DOMIN PWR WEALTH   TIME/SEQ
...MAJORIT SOC CONCPT. PAGE 40 G0793   SOCIETY

B63
REED E.,CHALLENGES TO DEMOCRACY: THE NEXT TEN   POLICY
YEARS. FUT USA+45 ECO/DEV DELIB/GP TEC/DEV CONFER   EDU/PROP
GOV/REL KNOWL ORD/FREE...MAJORIT IDEA/COMP ANTHOL   ECO/TAC
20. PAGE 46 G0909   NAT/G

C64
SCHRAMM W.,"MASS MEDIA AND NATIONAL DEVELOPMENT: ECO/UNDEV
THE ROLE OF INFORMATION IN DEVELOPING COUNTRIES."   COM/IND
FINAN R+D ACT/RES PLAN TEC/DEV DIPLOM CHOOSE SUPEGO EDU/PROP
ORD/FREE...BIBLIOG 20. PAGE 50 G0978   MAJORIT

B65
ALLEN S.,LETTER TO A CONSERVATIVE. SOCIETY NAT/G   ORD/FREE
DIPLOM EDU/PROP NUC/PWR GP/REL ATTIT MORAL   MARXISM
...MAJORIT CONCPT 20. PAGE 2 G0044   POLICY
                                                    LAISSEZ

B67
CONNOLLY W.E.,POLITICAL SCIENCE AND IDEOLOGY.   PWR
UTOPIA ATTIT KNOWL...MAJORIT EPIST PHIL/SCI SOC   PLURISM
IDEA/COMP HYPO/EXP GEN/LAWS METH HUME/D MARX/KARL. ELITES
PAGE 13 G0250   CONCPT

B67
HALLE L.J.,THE COLD WAR AS HISTORY. USSR WOR+45   DIPLOM
ECO/TAC FOR/AID NUC/PWR WAR PEACE ORD/FREE   BAL/PWR
...MAJORIT TREND 20 COLD/WAR KENNEDY/JF KHRUSH/N
BERLIN/BLO. PAGE 24 G0470

MAJORITY....BEHAVIOR OF MAJOR PARTS OF A GROUP; SEE ALSO
    CONSEN, MAJORIT

S66
SIMON R.,"THE STATE OF PUBLIC RELATIONS SCHOLARLY   ACADEM
RESEARCH." TEC/DEV TASK MAJORITY PRODUC...TREND   CREATE
CHARTS BIBLIOG 20. PAGE 51 G1000   STAT
                                                    GP/REL

MALAWI....SEE ALSO AFR

MALAYA....MALAYA

MALAYSIA....SEE ALSO S/ASIA

MALCOLM/X....MALCOLM X

MALDIVE....MALDIVE ISLAND; SEE ALSO S/ASIA, COMMONWLTH

MALE/SEX....MALE SEX

MALENBAUM W. G0697

MALI....SEE ALSO AFR

MALONE D.K. G0698

MALTA....SEE ALSO APPROPRIATE TIME/SPACE/CULTURE INDEX

MALTHUS....THOMAS ROBERT MALTHUS

MANAGEMENT....SEE MGT, EX/STRUC, ADMIN

MANAGEMENT BY OBJECTIVES....SEE MGT/OBJECT

MANCHESTER....MANCHESTER, ENGLAND

MANCHU/DYN....MANCHU DYNASTY

MANGELSDORF J.E. G0699

MANGUM G.L. G0160

MANITOBA....MANITOBA, CANADA

MANNERS....SEE ETIQUET

MANNHEIM K. G0700

MANNHEIM/K....KARL MANNHEIM

MANPOWER....SEE LABOR

MANSFIELD E. G0701

MANTON/M....MART MANTON

MANUFACTURING INDUSTRY....SEE PROC/MFG

MAO....MAO TSE-TUNG

MILIBAND R.,THE SOCIALIST REGISTER: 1964. GERMANY/W MARXISM B64
ITALY UK LABOR POL/PAR ECO/TAC FOR/AID NUC/PWR SOCISM
...POLICY SOCIALIST IDEA/COMP 20 MAO NASSER/G. CAP/ISM
PAGE 39 G0769 PROB/SOLV

WYLIE J.C.,MILITARY STRATEGY: GENERAL THEORY OF FORCES B67
POWER CONTROL. CUBA USA+45 VIETNAM/N WOR+45 ELITES PLAN
CONTROL WAR PWR...POLICY METH/COMP 20 MAO. PAGE 64 DECISION
G1260 IDEA/COMP

CHIU S.M.,"CHINA'S MILITARY POSTURE." CHINA/COM FORCES S67
ELITES NAT/G POL/PAR TEC/DEV ECO/TAC DOMIN CONTROL CIVMIL/REL
LEAD REV MARXISM 20 MAO. PAGE 12 G0228 NUC/PWR
DIPLOM

CLEMENS W.C.,"CHINESE NUCLEAR TESTS: TRENDS AND NUC/PWR S67
PORTENTS." CHINA/COM USA+45 USSR FORCES PLAN WEAPON
TEC/DEV ARMS/CONT WAR PWR...DECISION 20 MAO POLICY
KHRUSH/N. PAGE 12 G0234 DIPLOM

MAPS....MAPS AND ATLASES; SEE ALSO CHARTS

PERLO V.,MILITARISM AND INDUSTRY. USA+45 INT/TRADE CIVMIL/REL B63
EDU/PROP DETER KNOWL...CHARTS MAPS 20. PAGE 44 INDUS
G0869 LOBBY
ARMS/CONT

MARAJO....MARAJO, A BRAZILIAN ISLAND

MARANHAO....MARANHAO, BRAZIL

MARCANT/V....VITO MARCANTONIO

MARCH J.G. G0267

MARCHANT A. G0702

MARCUSE H. G0703

MARCUSE/H....HERBERT MARCUSE

MARCY C. G0704

MARES V.E. G0705

MARITAIN/J....JACQUES MARITAIN

MARITIME....MARITIME PROVINCES

MARK M. G0706

MARKET RESEARCH....SEE MARKET

MARKET....MARKETING SYSTEM

THE MANAGEMENT REVIEW. FINAN EX/STRUC PROFIT LABOR N
BIBLIOG/A. PAGE 1 G0007 MGT
ADMIN
MARKET

MARKETING INFORMATION GUIDE. USA+45 ECO/DEV FINAN BIBLIOG/A N
ADMIN GP/REL. PAGE 1 G0008 DIST/IND
MARKET
ECO/TAC

ATOMIC INDUSTRIAL FORUM,COMMENTARY ON LEGISLATION NUC/PWR N19
TO PERMIT PRIVATE OWNERSHIP OF SPECIAL NUCLEAR MARKET
MATERIAL (PAMPHLET). USA+45 DELIB/GP LEGIS PLAN OWN INDUS
...POLICY 20 AEC CONGRESS. PAGE 4 G0076 LAW

LAWRENCE S.A.,THE BATTERY ADDITIVE CONTROVERSY PHIL/SCI N19
(PAMPHLET). USA+45 LAW MARKET PROC/MFG R+D CAP/ISM LOBBY
CT/SYS GOV/REL OWN FTC CONGRESS BUR/STNDRD INSPECT
RITCHIE/JM. PAGE 33 G0645

US CHAMBER OF COMMERCE,THE SIGNIFICANCE OF MARKET N19
CONCENTRATION RATIOS (PAMPHLET). USA+45 FINAN INDUS PREDICT
ADMIN...METH/CNCPT SAMP CHARTS 20. PAGE 56 G1109 LG/CO
CONTROL

ROBINSON E.A.G.,THE STRUCTURE OF COMPETITIVE INDUS B53
INDUSTRY. UK ECO/DEV DIST/IND MARKET TEC/DEV DIPLOM PRODUC
EDU/PROP ADMIN EFFICIENCY WEALTH...MGT 19/20. WORKER
PAGE 47 G0929 OPTIMAL

MOSK S.A.,INDUSTRIAL REVOLUTION IN MEXICO. MARKET INDUS B54
LABOR CREATE CAP/ISM ADMIN ATTIT SOCISM...POLICY 20 TEC/DEV
MEXIC/AMER. PAGE 40 G0789 ECO/UNDEV
NAT/G

FORM W.H.,"THE PLACE OF SOCIAL STRUCTURE IN THE HABITAT S54
DETERMINATION OF LAND USE: SOME IMPLICATIONS FOR A MARKET
THEORY OF URBAN ECOLOGY" (BMR)" STRUCT...GEOG ORD/FREE
PHIL/SCI SOC 20. PAGE 19 G0381 MUNIC

ATOMIC INDUSTRIAL FORUM,MANAGEMENT AND ATOMIC NUC/PWR B58
ENERGY. WOR+45 SEA LAW MARKET NAT/G TEC/DEV INSPECT INDUS
INT/TRADE CONFER PEACE HEALTH...ANTHOL 20. PAGE 4 MGT
G0078 ECO/TAC

DUBIN R.,THE WORLD OF WORK: INDUSTRIAL SOCIETY AND WORKER B58
HUMAN RELATIONS. MARKET PROC/MFG LABOR TEC/DEV ECO/TAC
CAP/ISM AUTOMAT TASK GP/REL EFFICIENCY...CONCPT PRODUC
CHARTS BIBLIOG 20. PAGE 16 G0317 DRIVE

EHRHARD J.,LE DESTIN DU COLONIALISME. AFR FRANCE COLONIAL B58
ECO/UNDEV AGRI FINAN MARKET CREATE PLAN TEC/DEV FOR/AID
BUDGET DIPLOM PRICE 20. PAGE 17 G0335 INT/TRADE
INDUS

FOLDES L.,"UNCERTAINTY, PROBABILITY AND POTENTIAL PROBABIL S58
SURPRISE." MARKET PROB/SOLV RISK PERSON...DECISION ADMIN
MGT HYPO/EXP GAME. PAGE 19 G0376 ROUTINE

WASSERMAN P.,MEASUREMENT AND ANALYSIS OF BIBLIOG/A B59
ORGANIZATIONAL PERFORMANCE. FINAN MARKET EX/STRUC ECO/TAC
TEC/DEV EDU/PROP CONTROL ROUTINE TASK...MGT 20. OP/RES
PAGE 62 G1220 EFFICIENCY

WELTON H.,THE THIRD WORLD WAR: TRADE AND INDUSTRY, INT/TRADE B59
THE NEW BATTLEGROUND. WOR+45 ECO/DEV INDUS MARKET PLAN
TASK...MGT IDEA/COMP COLD/WAR. PAGE 63 G1229 DIPLOM

PENTONY D.E.,THE UNDERDEVELOPED LANDS. FUT WOR+45 ECO/UNDEV B60
CULTURE AGRI FINAN INDUS MARKET INT/ORG LABOR NAT/G POLICY
VOL/ASSN CONSULT TEC/DEV ECO/TAC EDU/PROP COLONIAL FOR/AID
ATTIT WEALTH...OBS RECORD SAMP TREND GEN/METH WORK INT/TRADE
UN 20. PAGE 44 G0867

BRADY R.A.,ORGANIZATION, AUTOMATION, AND SOCIETY. TEC/DEV B61
USA+45 AGRI COM/IND DIST/IND MARKET CREATE INDUS
...DECISION MGT 20. PAGE 8 G0163 AUTOMAT
ADMIN

B61
HODGKINS J.A.,SOVIET POWER: ENERGY RESOURCES, GEOG
PRODUCTION AND POTENTIALS. USSR ECO/DEV INDUS EXTR/IND
MARKET...POLICY STAT CHARTS 20 RESOURCE/N. PAGE 26 TEC/DEV
G0518

B61
MCCRACKEN H.L.,KEYNESIAN ECONOMICS IN THE STREAM OF ECO/TAC
ECONOMIC THOUGHT. FINAN MARKET BARGAIN EFFICIENCY DEMAND
OPTIMAL...PHIL/SCI CONCPT IDEA/COMP BIBLIOG 18/20 ECOMETRIC
KEYNES/JM. PAGE 37 G0732

B62
FERBER R.,RESEARCH METHODS IN ECONOMICS AND ACT/RES
BUSINESS. ECO/DEV FINAN MARKET LG/CO SML/CO CONSULT PROB/SOLV
CONTROL COST...STAT METH/COMP 20. PAGE 19 G0364 ECO/TAC
MGT

B62
KRAFT J.,THE GRAND DESIGN. EUR+WWI USA+45 AGRI VOL/ASSN
FINAN INDUS MARKET INT/ORG NAT/G PLAN ECO/TAC ECO/DEV
TARIFFS REGION DRIVE ORD/FREE WEALTH...POLICY OBS INT/TRADE
TREND EEC 20. PAGE 31 G0616

B63
BONINI C.P.,SIMULATION OF INFORMATION AND DECISION INDUS
SYSTEMS IN THE FIRM. MARKET BUDGET DOMIN EDU/PROP SIMUL
ADMIN COST ATTIT HABITAT PERCEPT PWR...CONCPT DECISION
PROBABIL QUANT PREDICT HYPO/EXP BIBLIOG. PAGE 8 MGT
G0152

B63
HEYEL C.,THE ENCYCLOPEDIA OF MANAGEMENT. WOR+45 MGT
MARKET TOP/EX TEC/DEV AUTOMAT LEAD ADJUST...STAT INDUS
CHARTS GAME ANTHOL BIBLIOG. PAGE 26 G0509 ADMIN
FINAN

B63
SCHOECK H.,THE NEW ARGUMENT IN ECONOMICS. UK USA+45 WELF/ST
INDUS MARKET LABOR NAT/G ECO/TAC ADMIN ROUTINE FOR/AID
BAL/PAY PWR...POLICY BOLIV. PAGE 49 G0973 ECO/DEV
ALL/IDEOS

B63
WALES H.G.,A BASIC BIBLIOGRAPHY ON MARKETING BIBLIOG/A
RESEARCH (REV. ED.). ATTIT...MGT STAT INT QU SAMP MARKET
TREND 20. PAGE 62 G1206 OP/RES
METH/COMP

S63
WILES P.J.D.,"WILL CAPITALISM AND COMMUNISM PLAN
SPONTANEOUSLY CONVERGE." COM FUT USA+45 ECO/DEV TEC/DEV
DIST/IND MARKET CAP/ISM ECO/TAC RIGID/FLEX WEALTH USSR
MARXISM SOCISM...MATH STAT TREND COMPUT/IR 20.
PAGE 63 G1240

B64
FEI J.C.H.,DEVELOPMENT OF THE LABOR SURPLUS ECO/TAC
ECONOMY: THEORY AND POLICY. WOR+45 AGRI INDUS POLICY
MARKET PROB/SOLV TEC/DEV...STAT CHARTS GEN/LAWS WORKER
METH 20 THIRD/WRLD. PAGE 18 G0361 ECO/UNDEV

B64
LI C.M.,INDUSTRIAL DEVELOPMENT IN COMMUNIST CHINA. ASIA
CHINA/COM ECO/DEV ECO/UNDEV AGRI FINAN INDUS MARKET TEC/DEV
LABOR NAT/G ECO/TAC INT/TRADE EXEC ALL/VALS
...POLICY RELATIV TREND WORK TOT/POP VAL/FREE 20.
PAGE 34 G0665

B64
MANSFIELD E.,MONOPOLY POWER AND ECONOMIC LG/CO
PERFORMANCE: AN INTRODUCTION TO A CURRENT ISSUE OF PWR
PUBLIC POLICY. ECO/DEV INDUS NAT/G PLAN CAP/ISM ECO/TAC
PRICE CONTROL LOBBY EFFICIENCY PRODUC...POLICY 20 MARKET
CONGRESS KENNEDY/JF MONOPOLY. PAGE 36 G0701

B64
ORGANIZATION AMERICAN STATES,ECONOMIC SURVEY OF ECO/UNDEV
LATIN AMERICA, 1962. L/A+17C AGRI DIST/IND INDUS CHARTS
MARKET PROC/MFG R+D PLAN TEC/DEV ECO/TAC REGION
BAL/PAY ALL/VALS...CON/ANAL ORG/CHARTS GEN/METH OAS
20. PAGE 43 G0844

L64
HAAS E.B.,"ECONOMICS AND DIFFERENTIAL PATTERNS OF L/A+17C
POLITICAL INTEGRATION: PROJECTIONS ABOUT UNITY IN INT/ORG
LATIN AMERICA." SOCIETY NAT/G DELIB/GP ACT/RES MARKET
CREATE PLAN ECO/TAC REGION ROUTINE ATTIT DRIVE PWR
WEALTH...CONCPT TREND CHARTS LAFTA 20. PAGE 24
G0464

S64
GARDNER R.N.,"GATT AND THE UNITED NATIONS INT/ORG
CONFERENCE ON TRADE AND DEVELOPMENT." USA+45 WOR+45 INT/TRADE
SOCIETY ECO/UNDEV MARKET NAT/G DELIB/GP ACT/RES
PLAN ECO/TAC TARIFFS EDU/PROP ROUTINE DRIVE

RIGID/FLEX WEALTH...DECISION MGT TREND UN TOT/POP
20 GATT. PAGE 21 G0411

B65
INT. BANK RECONSTR. DEVELOP.,ECONOMIC DEVELOPMENT INDUS
OF KUWAIT. ISLAM KUWAIT AGRI FINAN MARKET EX/STRUC NAT/G
TEC/DEV ECO/TAC ADMIN WEALTH...OBS CON/ANAL CHARTS
20. PAGE 28 G0548

B65
WISH J.R.,ECONOMIC DEVELOPMENT IN LATIN AMERICA: AN BIBLIOG/A
ANNOTATED BIBLIOGRAPHY. L/A+17C COM/IND MARKET ECO/UNDEV
CREATE CAP/ISM ATTIT...STAT METH 20. PAGE 64 G1250 TEC/DEV
AGRI

B66
ECKSTEIN A.,COMMUNIST CHINA'S ECONOMIC GROWTH AND ASIA
FOREIGN TRADE* IMPLICATIONS FOR US POLICY. COM ECO/UNDEV
USA+45 USSR STRUCT INDUS MARKET DIPLOM ECO/TAC CREATE
FOR/AID INT/TRADE...STAT CHARTS. PAGE 17 G0332 PWR

B66
GRUNEWALD D.,PUBLIC POLICY AND THE MODERN LG/CO
COOPERATION: SELECTED READINGS. USA+45 LAW MARKET POLICY
VOL/ASSN CAP/ISM INT/TRADE CENTRAL OWN...SOC ANTHOL NAT/G
20. PAGE 23 G0458 CONTROL

B66
LINDFORS G.V.,INTERCOLLEGIATE BIBLIOGRAPHY; CASES BIBLIOG/A
IN BUSINESS ADMINISTRATION (VOL. X). FINAN MARKET ADMIN
LABOR CONSULT PLAN GP/REL PRODUC 20. PAGE 34 G0668 MGT
OP/RES

B66
US DEPARTMENT OF LABOR,PRODUCTIVITY: A BIBLIOG/A
BIBLIOGRAPHY. ECO/DEV INDUS MARKET OP/RES AUTOMAT PRODUC
COST...STAT 20. PAGE 57 G1119 LABOR
PLAN

S66
HANSON A.H.,"PLANNING AND THE POLITICIANS* SOME PLAN
REFLECTIONS ON ECONOMIC PLANNING IN WESTERN ECO/DEV
EUROPE." MARKET NAT/G TEC/DEV CONSEN ROLE EUR+WWI
...METH/COMP NAT/COMP. PAGE 24 G0479 ADMIN

B67
NORTHRUP H.R.,RESTRICTIVE LABOR PRACTICES IN THE DIST/IND
SUPERMARKET INDUSTRY. USA+45 INDUS WORKER TEC/DEV MARKET
BARGAIN PAY CONTROL GP/REL COST...STAT CHARTS NLRB. LABOR
PAGE 42 G0827 MGT

L67
SEABERG G.P.,"THE DRUG ABUSE PROBLEMS AND SOME BIO/SOC
PROPOSALS." UK USA+45 MARKET SANCTION CRIME LAW
...POLICY NEW/IDEA. PAGE 50 G0986 ADJUD
PROB/SOLV

S67
ALBAUM G.,"INFORMATION FLOW AND DECENTRALIZED LG/CO
DECISION MAKING IN MARKETING." EX/STRUC COMPUTER ROUTINE
OP/RES PROB/SOLV EFFICIENCY OPTIMAL...METH/COMP KNOWL
ORG/CHARTS 20. PAGE 2 G0033 MARKET

S67
RICHMAN B.M.,"SOVIET MANAGEMENT IN TRANSITION." MGT
USSR FINAN MARKET EX/STRUC PLAN PROB/SOLV TEC/DEV MARXISM
CONTROL LEAD CENTRAL EFFICIENCY...METH/COMP 20 POLICY
REFORMERS. PAGE 47 G0917 AUTHORIT

MARKETING SYSTEM....SEE MARKET

MARKHAM J.W. G0707

MARQUIS D.G. G0708

MARRIAGE....WEDLOCK; SEE ALSO LOVE

S67
HILL R.,"SOCIAL ASPECTS OF FAMILY PLANNING." INDIA FAM
KOREA TAIWAN ECO/UNDEV PLAN PROB/SOLV TEC/DEV BIO/SOC
EDU/PROP CONTROL ATTIT DRIVE...HEAL PSY SOC 20 GEOG
BIRTH/CON UN. PAGE 26 G0512 MARRIAGE

MARRIS R. G0709

MARS D. G0710

MARSCH P.E. G0711

MARSHALL/A....ALFRED MARSHALL

MARSHALL/J....JOHN MARSHALL

MARSHL/PLN....MARSHALL PLAN

JONES J.M.,THE FIFTEEN WEEKS (FEBRUARY 21-JUNE 5, 1947). EUR+WWI USA+45 PROB/SOLV BAL/PWR...POLICY TIME/SEQ 20 COLD/WAR MARSHL/PLN TRUMAN/HS WASHING/DC. PAGE 29 G0567 — DIPLOM ECO/TAC FOR/AID — B55

SCHMITT H.A.,THE PATH TO EUROPEAN UNITY. EUR+WWI USA+45 PLAN TEC/DEV DIPLOM FOR/AID CONFER...INT/LAW 20 EEC EURCOALSTL MARSHL/PLN UNIFICA. PAGE 49 G0971 — INT/ORG INT/TRADE REGION ECO/DEV — B62

MARSON C.C. G0613

MARTI/JOSE....JOSE MARTI

MARTIN A. G0712

MARTIN E.D. G0100

MARTIN L.W. G0713,G0714,G0715

MARTINO R.L. G0716

MARTINS A.F. G0717

MARX/KARL....KARL MARX

MUMFORD L.,THE MYTH OF THE MACHINE: TECHNICS AND HUMAN DEVELOPMENT. UNIV WOR-45 CREATE AUTOMAT PERCEPT KNOWL...EPIST PHIL/SCI SOC LING TREND SOC/INTEG 20 MARX/KARL. PAGE 40 G0795 — WORKER TEC/DEV SOCIETY — B66

CONNOLLY W.E.,POLITICAL SCIENCE AND IDEOLOGY. UTOPIA ATTIT MAJORIT EPIST PHIL/SCI SOC IDEA/COMP HYPO/EXP GEN/LAWS METH HUME/D MARX/KARL. PAGE 13 G0250 — PWR PLURISM ELITES CONCPT — B67

MARXISM....MARXISM, COMMUNISM; SEE ALSO MARXIST

HARPER S.N.,THE GOVERNMENT OF THE SOVIET UNION. COM USSR LAW CONSTN ECO/DEV PLAN TEC/DEV DIPLOM INT/TRADE ADMIN REV NAT/LISM...POLICY 20. PAGE 24 G0483 — MARXISM NAT/G LEAD POL/PAR — B38

LASKI H.J.,REFLECTIONS ON THE REVOLUTIONS OF OUR TIME. COM USSR NAT/G WORKER UTOPIA ORD/FREE WEALTH MARXISM SOCISM 19/20. PAGE 32 G0637 — CAP/ISM WELF/ST ECO/TAC POLICY — B43

MACRAE D.G.,"THE BOLSHEVIK IDEOLOGY; THE INTELLECTUAL AND EMOTIONAL FACTORS IN COMMUNIST AFFILIATION" (BMR)" COM LEAD REV ATTIT ORD/FREE ...SOC CON/ANAL 20 BOLSHEVISM. PAGE 35 G0693 — MARXISM INTELL PHIL/SCI SECT — S51

APPADORAI A.,THE SUBSTANCE OF POLITICS (6TH ED.). EX/STRUC LEGIS DIPLOM CT/SYS CHOOSE FASCISM MARXISM SOCISM...BIBLIOG T. PAGE 3 G0062 — PHIL/SCI NAT/G — B52

ANGELL N.,DEFENCE AND THE ENGLISH-SPEAKING ROLE. CHINA/COM UK USSR INT/ORG FORCES EDU/PROP NEUTRAL NUC/PWR NAT/LISM PEACE TOTALISM 20 COLD/WAR COEXIST. PAGE 3 G0059 — DIPLOM WAR MARXISM ORD/FREE — B58

MARCUSE H.,SOVIET MARXISM, A CRITICAL ANALYSIS. USSR CONSTN PLAN PRODUC RATIONAL SOCISM...IDEA/COMP 20 COM/PARTY. PAGE 36 G0703 — MARXISM ATTIT POLICY — B58

FRANCIS R.G.,THE PREDICTIVE PROCESS. PLAN MARXISM ...DECISION SOC CONCPT NAT/COMP 19/20. PAGE 20 G0390 — PREDICT PHIL/SCI TREND — B60

MCCLELLAND C.A.,NUCLEAR WEAPONS, MISSILES, AND FUTURE WAR: PROBLEM FOR THE SIXTIES. WOR+45 FORCES ARMS/CONT DETER MARXISM...POLICY ANTHOL COLD/WAR. PAGE 37 G0729 — DIPLOM NUC/PWR WAR WEAPON — B60

NOVE A.,THE SOVIET ECONOMY. USSR ECO/DEV FINAN NAT/G ECO/TAC PRICE ADMIN EFFICIENCY MARXISM ...TREND BIBLIOG 20. PAGE 42 G0828 — PLAN PRODUC POLICY — B61

BURKE A.E.,ENOUGH GOOD MEN. USA+45 WOR+45 ECO/UNDEV DIPLOM — B62

FORCES TEC/DEV GUERRILLA NUC/PWR REV WAR ORD/FREE MARXISM...GEOG 20 COLD/WAR. PAGE 10 G0189 — POLICY NAT/G TASK

FRIEDRICH-EBERT-STIFTUNG,THE SOVIET BLOC AND DEVELOPING COUNTRIES. CHINA/COM COM GERMANY/E USSR WOR+45 ECO/UNDEV INT/ORG NAT/G TEC/DEV NEUTRAL PWR ...POLICY 20. PAGE 20 G0394 — MARXISM DIPLOM ECO/TAC FOR/AID — B62

WALSTON H.,AGRICULTURE UNDER COMMUNISM. CHINA/COM COM PROB/SOLV HAPPINESS RIGID/FLEX...POLICY METH/COMP 20. PAGE 62 G1207 — AGRI MARXISM PLAN CREATE — B62

PACHTER H.M.,COLLISION COURSE; THE CUBAN MISSILE CRISIS AND COEXISTENCE. CUBA USA+45 DIPLOM ARMS/CONT PEACE MARXISM...DECISION INT/LAW 20 COLD/WAR KHRUSH/N KENNEDY/JF CASTRO/F. PAGE 43 G0854 — WAR BAL/PWR NUC/PWR DETER — B63

US DEPARTMENT OF THE ARMY,SOVIET RUSSIA: STRATEGIC SURVEY (PAMPHLET). USSR POL/PAR PLAN DOMIN EDU/PROP ARMS/CONT GUERRILLA WAR WEAPON...TREND CHARTS ORG/CHARTS 20. PAGE 57 G1129 — BIBLIOG/A MARXISM DIPLOM COERCE — B63

WILES P.J.D.,"WILL CAPITALISM AND COMMUNISM SPONTANEOUSLY CONVERGE." COM FUT USA+45 ECO/DEV DIST/IND MARKET CAP/ISM ECO/TAC RIGID/FLEX WEALTH MARXISM SOCISM...MATH STAT TREND COMPUT/IR 20. PAGE 63 G1240 — PLAN TEC/DEV USSR — S63

MILIBAND R.,THE SOCIALIST REGISTER: 1964. GERMANY/W ITALY UK LABOR POL/PAR ECO/TAC FOR/AID NUC/PWR ...POLICY SOCIALIST IDEA/COMP 20 MAO NASSER/G. PAGE 39 G0769 — MARXISM SOCISM CAP/ISM PROB/SOLV — B64

ALLEN S.,LETTER TO A CONSERVATIVE. SOCIETY NAT/G DIPLOM EDU/PROP NUC/PWR GP/REL ATTIT MORAL ...MAJORIT CONCPT 20. PAGE 2 G0044 — ORD/FREE MARXISM POLICY LAISSEZ — B65

CHENG C.-.Y.,SCIENTIFIC AND ENGINEERING MANPOWER IN COMMUNIST CHINA, 1949-1963. CHINA/COM USSR ELITES ECO/DEV R+D ACADEM LABOR NAT/G EDU/PROP CONTROL UTIL...POLICY BIBLIOG 20. PAGE 12 G0226 — WORKER CONSULT MARXISM BIOG — B65

HALPERIN M.H.,COMMUNIST CHINA AND ARMS CONTROL. CHINA/COM FUT USA+45 CULTURE FORCES TEC/DEV ECO/TAC WAR PEACE ORD/FREE MARXISM 20 COLD/WAR. PAGE 24 G0473 — ATTIT POLICY ARMS/CONT NUC/PWR — B65

JASNY H.,KHRUSHCHEV'S CROP POLICY. USSR ECO/DEV PLAN MARXISM...STAT 20 KHRUSH/N RESOURCE/N. PAGE 29 G0562 — AGRI NAT/G POLICY ECO/TAC — B65

ORG FOR ECO COOP AND DEVEL,THE MEDITERRANEAN REGIONAL PROJECT: YUGOSLAVIA; EDUCATION AND DEVELOPMENT. YUGOSLAVIA SOCIETY FINAN PROF/ORG PLAN ADMIN COST DEMAND MARXISM...STAT TREND CHARTS METH 20 OECD. PAGE 43 G0843 — EDU/PROP ACADEM SCHOOL ECO/UNDEV — B65

MARK M.,"BEYOND SOVEREIGNTY." WOR+45 WOR-45 ECO/UNDEV BAL/PWR INT/TRADE NUC/PWR REV WAR MARXISM NEW/LIB BIBLIOG. PAGE 36 G0706 — NAT/LISM NAT/G DIPLOM INTELL — C65

KURAKOV I.G.,SCIENCE, TECHNOLOGY AND COMMUNISM; SOME QUESTIONS OF DEVELOPMENT (TRANS. BY CARIN DEDIJER). USSR INDUS PLAN PROB/SOLV COST PRODUC ...MGT MATH CHARTS METH 20. PAGE 32 G0626 — CREATE TEC/DEV MARXISM ECO/TAC — B66

SCHURMANN F.,IDEOLOGY AND ORGANIZATION IN COMMUNIST CHINA. CHINA/COM LOC/G MUNIC POL/PAR ECO/TAC CONTROL ATTIT...MGT STERTYP 20 COM/PARTY. PAGE 50 G0981 — MARXISM STRUCT ADMIN NAT/G — B66

US DEPARTMENT OF THE ARMY,COMMUNIST CHINA: A STRATEGIC SURVEY: A BIBLIOGRAPHY (PAMPHLET NO. 20-67). CHINA/COM COM INDIA USSR NAT/G POL/PAR EX/STRUC FORCES NUC/PWR REV ATTIT...POLICY GEOG — BIBLIOG/A MARXISM S/ASIA DIPLOM — B66

CHARTS. PAGE 58 G1133

US SENATE COMM AERO SPACE SCI,SOVIET SPACE PROGRAMS, 1962-65; GOALS AND PURPOSES, ACHIEVEMENTS, PLANS, AND INTERNATIONAL IMPLICATIONS. USA+45 USSR R+D FORCES PLAN EDU/PROP PRESS ADJUD ARMS/CONT ATTIT MARXISM. PAGE 60 G1168 — B66 CONSULT SPACE FUT DIPLOM

WARD B.,NATIONALISM AND IDEOLOGY. ECO/UNDEV KIN CREATE CAP/ISM FOR/AID ALL/VALS MARXISM...POLICY SOC. PAGE 62 G1211 — B66 IDEA/COMP NAT/LISM ATTIT

COHEN A.,"THE TECHNOLOGY/ELITE APPROACH TO THE DEVELOPMENTAL PROCESS* PERUVIAN CASE STUDY." L/A+17C STRUCT CREATE ECO/TAC FOR/AID CIVMIL/REL MARXISM TECHRACY HYPO/EXP. PAGE 12 G0239 — S66 ECO/UNDEV ELITES PERU

FIELD M.G.,SOVIET SOCIALIZED MEDICINE. USSR FINAN R+D PROB/SOLV ADMIN SOCISM...MGT SOC CONCPT 20. PAGE 19 G0366 — B67 PUB/INST HEALTH NAT/G MARXISM

GROSSMAN G.,ECONOMIC SYSTEMS. USA+45 USA-45 USSR YUGOSLAVIA WORKER CAP/ISM PRICE GP/REL EQUILIB WEALTH MARXISM SOCISM...MGT METH/COMP 19/20. PAGE 23 G0456 — B67 ECO/DEV PLAN TEC/DEV DEMAND

MACKINTOSH J.M.,JUGGERNAUT. USSR NAT/G POL/PAR ADMIN LEAD CIVMIL/REL COST TOTALISM PWR MARXISM ...GOV/COMP 20. PAGE 35 G0691 — B67 WAR FORCES COM PROF/ORG

MAZOUR A.G.,SOVIET ECONOMIC DEVELOPMENT: OPERATION OUTSTRIP: 1921-1965. USSR ECO/UNDEV FINAN CHIEF WORKER PROB/SOLV CONTROL PRODUC MARXISM...CHARTS ORG/CHARTS 20 STALIN/J. PAGE 37 G0726 — B67 ECO/TAC AGRI INDUS PLAN

POMEROY W.J.,HALF A CENTURY OF SOCIALISM. USSR LAW AGRI INDUS NAT/G CREATE DIPLOM EDU/PROP PERSON ORD/FREE WEALTH...POLICY TREND 20. PAGE 45 G0884 — B67 SOCISM MARXISM COM SOCIETY

ROBINSON T.W.,"A NATIONAL INTEREST ANALYSIS OF SINO-SOVIET RELATIONS." CHINA/COM USSR NAT/G NUC/PWR ATTIT PWR...CONCPT CHARTS 20. PAGE 47 G0931 — L67 MARXISM DIPLOM SOVEREIGN GEN/LAWS

AVTORKHANOV A.,"A NEW AGRARIAN REVOLUTION." COM USSR ECO/DEV PLAN TEC/DEV ADMIN CONTROL OPTIMAL WEALTH SOCISM 20 KHRUSH/N STALIN/J. PAGE 4 G0082 — S67 AGRI METH/COMP MARXISM OWN

CHIU S.M.,"CHINA'S MILITARY POSTURE." CHINA/COM ELITES NAT/G POL/PAR TEC/DEV ECO/TAC DOMIN CONTROL LEAD REV MARXISM 20 MAO. PAGE 12 G0228 — S67 FORCES CIVMIL/REL NUC/PWR DIPLOM

FADDEYEV N.,"CMEA CO-OPERATION OF EQUAL NATIONS." COM R+D PLAN CAP/ISM DIPLOM FOR/AID WEALTH...POLICY MARXIST. PAGE 18 G0356 — S67 MARXISM ECO/TAC INT/ORG ECO/UNDEV

HAZARD J.N.,"POST-DISARMAMENT INTERNATIONAL LAW." FUT USSR WOR+45 INT/ORG DELIB/GP FORCES DETER EQUILIB SOVEREIGN MARXISM 20 UN. PAGE 25 G0496 — S67 INT/LAW ARMS/CONT PWR PLAN

KRAUS J.,"A MARXIST IN GHANA." GHANA ELITES CHIEF PROB/SOLV TEC/DEV DIPLOM ECO/TAC COLONIAL PARTIC PWR 20 NKRUMAH/K. PAGE 31 G0618 — S67 MARXISM PLAN ATTIT CREATE

RICHMAN B.M.,"SOVIET MANAGEMENT IN TRANSITION." USSR FINAN MARKET EX/STRUC PLAN PROB/SOLV TEC/DEV CONTROL LEAD CENTRAL EFFICIENCY...METH/COMP 20 REFORMERS. PAGE 47 G0917 — S67 MGT MARXISM POLICY AUTHORIT

SLOAN P.,"FIFTY YEARS OF SOVIET RULE." USSR INDUS EDU/PROP EFFICIENCY PRODUC HEALTH KNOWL MORAL WEALTH MARXISM...POLICY 20. PAGE 51 G1011 — S67 CREATE NAT/G PLAN

STYCOS J.M.,"POLITICS AND POPULATION CONTROL IN LATIN AMERICA." USA+45 FAM NAT/G GP/REL AGE/C ATTIT CATHISM MARXISM...POLICY UN WHO. PAGE 53 G1045 — S67 PLAN CENSUS CONTROL L/A+17C

TEKINER S.,"SINKIAN AND THE SINO-SOVIET CONFLICT." ASIA COM USSR FORCES PLAN BAL/PWR CONTROL NUC/PWR WAR WEAPON...DECISION 20. PAGE 54 G1060 — S67 DIPLOM PWR MARXISM

MARXIST....MARXIST

POKROVSKY G.I.,SCIENCE AND TECHNOLOGY IN CONTEMPORARY WAR. SPACE USSR WOR+45 NAT/G CONSULT ACT/RES PLAN DETER WEAPON...MARXIST METH/CNCPT CHARTS STERTYP COLD/WAR 20. PAGE 45 G0881 — B59 TEC/DEV FORCES NUC/PWR WAR

APTHEKER H.,DISARMAMENT AND THE AMERICAN ECONOMY: A SYMPOSIUM. FUT USA+45 ECO/DEV DIST/IND FINAN INDUS PROC/MFG LABOR NAT/G POL/PAR CONSULT PLAN CAP/ISM INT/TRADE PEACE ATTIT MORAL WEALTH...TREND GEN/LAWS TOT/POP 20. PAGE 3 G0063 — B60 MARXIST ARMS/CONT

IKLE F.C.,"NTH COUNTRIES AND DISARMAMENT." WOR+45 DELIB/GP ECO/TAC DOMIN EDU/PROP LEGIT ROUTINE COERCE RIGID/FLEX ORD/FREE...MARXIST TREND 20. PAGE 28 G0543 — S60 FUT INT/ORG ARMS/CONT NUC/PWR

FADDEYEV N.,"CMEA CO-OPERATION OF EQUAL NATIONS." COM R+D PLAN CAP/ISM DIPLOM FOR/AID WEALTH...POLICY MARXIST. PAGE 18 G0356 — S67 MARXISM ECO/TAC INT/ORG ECO/UNDEV

KRUSCHE H.,"THE STRIVING OF THE KIESINGER-STRAUS GOVERNMENT FOR NUCLEAR WEAPONS IS A THREAT TO EUROPEAN SECURITY." EUR+WWI GERMANY BAL/PWR SANCTION WEAPON PEACE ORD/FREE...MARXIST 20 NATO COLD/WAR. PAGE 32 G0623 — S67 ARMS/CONT INT/ORG NUC/PWR DIPLOM

REINTANZ G.,"THE SPACE TREATY." WOR+45 DIPLOM CONTROL ARMS/CONT NUC/PWR WAR...MARXIST 20 COLD/WAR UN TREATY. PAGE 46 G0911 — S67 SPACE INT/LAW INT/ORG PEACE

MARYLAND....MARYLAND

MASS MEDIA....SEE EDU/PROP, COM/IND

MASSACHU....MASSACHUSETTS

MASSART L. G0718

MASTERS D. G0719

MASTERS N.A. G0720

MATH....MATHEMATICS

AMERICAN DOCUMENTATION INST,AMERICAN DOCUMENTATION. PROF/ORG CONSULT PLAN PERCEPT...MATH STAT AUD/VIS CHARTS METH/COMP INDEX METH 20. PAGE 3 G0050 — N BIBLIOG TEC/DEV COM/IND COMPUT/IR

BERGSON H.,CREATIVE EVOLUTION. FUT WOR+45 WOR-45 INTELL AGRI R+D INTELL PERCEPT PERSON RIGID/FLEX ...RELATIV PHIL/SCI PSY METH/CNCPT MATH HIST/WRIT TREND HYPO/EXP TOT/POP. PAGE 7 G0127 — B11 BIO/SOC KNOWL

US FOOD AND DRUG ADMIN,CIVIL DEFENSE INFORMATION FOR FOOD AND DRUG OFFICIALS (2ND ED.) (PAMPHLET). USA+45 PROB/SOLV RISK HABITAT...MATH CHARTS DICTIONARY 20 CIV/DEFENS. PAGE 58 G1136 — N19 NUC/PWR WAR EATING HEALTH

COHEN M.R.,AN INTRODUCTION TO LOGIC AND SCIENTIFIC METHOD....LING MATH CHARTS T 20. PAGE 12 G0242 — B34 LOG PHIL/SCI GEN/METH METH/CNCPT

SMYTH H.D.,ATOMIC ENERGY FOR MILITARY PURPOSES. USA-45 NAT/G PLAN TEC/DEV KNOWL...MATH CON/ANAL CHARTS LAB/EXP SIMUL 20. PAGE 52 G1017 — B45 R+D TIME/SEQ NUC/PWR

B46

AMERICAN DOCUMENTATION INST.CATALOGUE OF AUXILIARY PUBLICATIONS IN MICROFILMS AND PHOTOPRINTS. USA-45 LAW AGRI CREATE TEC/DEV ADMIN...GEOG LING MATH 20. PAGE 3 G0052

BIBLIOG EDU/PROP PSY

B48

WEINER N.,CYBERNETICS. SOCIETY COMPUTER ADJUST EFFICIENCY UTIL PERCEPT...PSY MATH REGRESS TIME. PAGE 63 G1226

FEEDBACK AUTOMAT CONTROL TEC/DEV

B50

SURANYI-UNGER T.,PRIVATE ENTERPRISE AND GOVERNMENTAL PLANNING. STRUCT FINAN BAL/PWR HAPPINESS DRIVE NEW/LIB PLURISM...MATH QUANT STAT TREND BIBLIOG. PAGE 53 G1047

PLAN NAT/G LAISSEZ POLICY

S53

MILLER G.A.,"WHAT IS INFORMATION MEASUREMENT?" CREATE...CONCPT METH/CNCPT QUANT STAT CHARTS BIBLIOG/A 20. PAGE 39 G0771

COMPUTER TEC/DEV PSY MATH

B54

COMBS C.H.,DECISION PROCESSES. INTELL SOCIETY DELIB/GP CREATE TEC/DEV DOMIN LEGIT EXEC CHOOSE DRIVE RIGID/FLEX KNOWL PWR...PHIL/SCI SOC METH/CNCPT CONT/OBS REC/INT PERS/TEST SAMP/SIZ BIOG SOC/EXP WORK. PAGE 13 G0245

MATH DECISION

S54

DEUTSCH K.W.,"GAME THEORY AND POLITICS: SOME PROBLEMS OF APPLICATION." FUT WOR+45 SOCIETY R+D KNOWL PWR...CONCPT METH/CNCPT MATH QUANT GAME SIMUL VAL/FREE 20. PAGE 15 G0295

DECISION GEN/METH

B55

SHUBIK M.,READINGS IN GAME THEORY AND POLITICAL BEHAVIOR. WOR+45 FORCES CREATE ROUTINE WAR PEACE PERCEPT KNOWL PWR...PSY SOC CONCPT METH/CNCPT STAT CHARTS HYPO/EXP GAME METH VAL/FREE 20. PAGE 50 G0991

MATH DECISION DIPLOM

B57

MCKINNEY E.R.,A BIBLIOGRAPHY OF CYBERNETICS AND INFORMATION THEORY. COMPUTER OP/RES...DECISION PHIL/SCI PSY LING LOG MATH PROBABIL GAME 20. PAGE 38 G0743

BIBLIOG/A FEEDBACK SIMUL CONTROL

B58

OPERATIONS RESEARCH SOCIETY,A COMPREHENSIVE BIBLIOGRAPHY ON OPERATIONS RESEARCH: THROUGH 1956 WITH SUPPLEMENT FOR 1957. COM/IND DIST/IND INDUS ADMIN...DECISION MATH STAT METH 20. PAGE 43 G0840

BIBLIOG/A COMPUT/IR OP/RES MGT

B59

GUILBAUD G.T.,WHAT IS CYBERNETICS? COMPUTER OP/RES TEC/DEV AUTOMAT ROUTINE PERS/REL PERCEPT...PSY MATH COMPUT/IR SIMUL GEN/METH. PAGE 23 G0460

CONTROL COM/IND FEEDBACK NET/THEORY

B59

HARVARD UNIVERSITY LAW SCHOOL,INTERNATIONAL PROBLEMS OF FINANCIAL PROTECTION AGAINST NUCLEAR RISK. WOR+45 NAT/G DELIB/GP PROB/SOLV DIPLOM CONTROL ATTIT...POLICY INT/LAW MATH 20. PAGE 25 G0488

NUC/PWR ADJUD INDUS FINAN

S59

CYERT R.M.,"MODELS IN A BEHAVIORAL THEORY OF THE FIRM." ROUTINE...DECISION MGT METH/CNCPT MATH. PAGE 14 G0267

SIMUL GAME PREDICT INDUS

B60

ARROW K.J.,MATHEMATICAL METHODS IN THE SOCIAL SCIENCES, 1959. TEC/DEV CHOOSE UTIL PERCEPT ...KNO/TEST GAME SIMUL ANTHOL. PAGE 4 G0070

MATH PSY MGT

B60

BOULDING K.E.,LINEAR PROGRAMMING AND THE THEORY OF THE FIRM. ACT/RES PLAN...MGT MATH. PAGE 8 G0156

LG/CO NEW/IDEA COMPUTER

B60

RAPOPORT A.,FIGHTS, GAMES AND DEBATES. INTELL SOCIETY R+D EX/STRUC PERCEPT PERSON SKILL...PSY SOC GAME. PAGE 46 G0902

METH/CNCPT MATH DECISION CON/ANAL

B60

SLUCKIN W.,MINDS AND MACHINES (REV. ED.). PROB/SOLV TEC/DEV AUTOMAT TASK PERCEPT HEALTH KNOWL ...DECISION MATH PROBABIL COMPUT/IR GAME 20. PAGE 51 G1012

PSY COMPUTER PERSON SIMUL

L60

HOLZMAN B.G.,"BASIC RESEARCH FOR NATIONAL SURVIVAL." FUT USA+45 INTELL R+D ACT/RES OP/RES PLAN TEC/DEV EDU/PROP PERCEPT PERSON...PHIL/SCI METH/CNCPT NEW/IDEA MATH OBS RECORD TREND LAB/EXP 20. PAGE 27 G0525

FORCES STAT

S61

BENNION E.G.,"ECONOMETRICS FOR MANAGEMENT." USA+45 INDUS EX/STRUC ACT/RES COMPUTER UTIL...MATH STAT PREDICT METH/COMP HYPO/EXP. PAGE 6 G0122

ECOMETRIC MGT SIMUL DECISION

B62

BELLMAN R.,APPLIED DYNAMIC PROGRAMMING. OPTIMAL ...DECISION STAT SIMUL. PAGE 6 G0116

COMPUTER ECOMETRIC GAME MATH

B62

BORKOF H.,COMPUTER APPLICATIONS IN THE BEHAVIORAL SCIENCES. AUTOMAT UTIL...DECISION PHIL/SCI PSY METH/CNCPT LING LOG MATH STYLE NET/THEORY COMPUT/IR PROG/TEAC SIMUL. PAGE 8 G0154

R+D COMPUTER PROB/SOLV FEEDBACK

B62

BOULDING K.E.,CONFLICT AND DEFENSE: A GENERAL THEORY. FUT SOCIETY INT/ORG NAT/G CREATE BAL/PWR COERCE NAT/LISM DRIVE ALL/VALS...PLURIST DECISION CONCPT METH/CNCPT TREND HYPO/EXP TOT/POP 20. PAGE 8 G0157

MATH SIMUL PEACE WAR

B62

DUCKWORTH W.E.,A GUIDE TO OPERATIONAL RESEARCH. INDUS PLAN PROB/SOLV EXEC EFFICIENCY PRODUC KNOWL ...MGT MATH STAT SIMUL METH 20 MONTECARLO. PAGE 16 G0319

OP/RES GAME DECISION ADMIN

B62

RIKER W.H.,THE THEORY OF POLITICAL COALITIONS. WOR+45 INTELL NAT/G CREATE PLAN ATTIT DRIVE PERCEPT ...DECISION PSY SOC METH/CNCPT NEW/IDEA MATH CHARTS GAME TOT/POP 20. PAGE 47 G0921

FUT SIMUL

B63

BURSK E.C.,NEW DECISION-MAKING TOOLS FOR MANAGERS. COMPUTER PLAN PROB/SOLV ROUTINE COST. PAGE 10 G0194

DECISION MGT MATH RIGID/FLEX

B63

MULLENBACH P.,CIVILIAN NUCLEAR POWER: ECONOMIC ISSUES AND POLICY FORMATION. FINAN INT/ORG DELIB/GP ACT/RES ECO/TAC ATTIT SUPEGO HEALTH ORD/FREE PWR ...POLICY CONCPT MATH STAT CHARTS VAL/FREE 20 COLD/WAR. PAGE 40 G0792

USA+45 ECO/DEV NUC/PWR

S63

WILES P.J.D.,"WILL CAPITALISM AND COMMUNISM SPONTANEOUSLY CONVERGE." COM FUT USA+45 ECO/DEV DIST/IND MARKET CAP/ISM ECO/TAC RIGID/FLEX WEALTH MARXISM SOCISM...MATH STAT TREND COMPUT/IR 20. PAGE 63 G1240

PLAN TEC/DEV USSR

B64

BRILLOUIN L.,SCIENTIFIC UNCERTAINTY AND INFORMATION. PROB/SOLV AUTOMAT PERCEPT ORD/FREE ...MATH REGRESS STAT STYLE OBS IDEA/COMP SIMUL TIME. PAGE 9 G0169

PHIL/SCI NEW/IDEA METH/CNCPT CREATE

B64

COOMBS C.H.,A THEORY OF DATA....MGT PHIL/SCI SOC CLASSIF MATH PROBABIL STAT QU. PAGE 13 G0254

CON/ANAL GEN/METH TESTS PSY

B64

LANG A.S.,URBAN RAIL TRANSIT. OP/RES PLAN PROB/SOLV TEC/DEV AUTOMAT COST...TECHNIC MATH CON/ANAL CHARTS METH/COMP SIMUL 20 RAILROAD PUB/TRANS. PAGE 32 G0632

MUNIC DIST/IND ECOMETRIC

B64

MARTINO R.L.,PROJECT MANAGEMENT AND CONTROL: VOL. 2 APPLIED OPERATIONAL PLANNING. COMPUTER...MATH CHARTS SIMUL METH TIME. PAGE 36 G0716

DECISION PLAN TEC/DEV OP/RES

B64

SCHERER F.M.,THE WEAPONS ACQUISITION PROCESS: ECONOMIC INCENTIVES. BOSTON: DIVISION OF RESEARCH, GRADUATE SCHOOL OF BUSINESS. USA+45 FINAN NAT/G DELIB/GP ECO/TAC RIGID/FLEX WEALTH...MGT MATH STAT CHARTS VAL/FREE 20. PAGE 49 G0965

INDUS ACT/RES WEAPON

SHUBIK M.,GAME THEORY AND RELATED APPROACHES TO
SOCIAL BEHAVIOR: SELECTIONS. INTELL SOCIETY ACT/RES
CREATE PLAN PROB/SOLV...DECISION MATH. PAGE 50
G0994

SOC
SIMUL
GAME
PWR

B64

ABT C.,"WAR GAMING." USA+45 NAT/G TOP/EX ACT/RES
TEC/DEV COERCE KNOWL ORD/FREE PWR...DECISION MATH
TIME/SEQ COMPUT/IR CHARTS LAB/EXP VAL/FREE. PAGE 2
G0026

FORCES
SIMUL
WAR

S64

ALKER H.R. JR.,MATHEMATICS AND POLITICS. PROB/SOLV
...DECISION PHIL/SCI CLASSIF QUANT STAT GAME
GEN/LAWS INDEX. PAGE 2 G0042

GEN/METH
CONCPT
MATH

B65

KANTOROVICH L.V.,THE BEST USE OF ECONOMIC
RESOURCES. USSR SOCIETY FINAN ACT/RES TEC/DEV
ECO/TAC PRICE CONTROL COST DEMAND EFFICIENCY
OPTIMAL...MGT STAT. PAGE 29 G0572

PLAN
MATH
DECISION

B65

MCGUIRE M.C.,SECRECY AND THE ARMS RACE* A THEORY OF
THE ACCUMULATION OF STRATEGIC WEAPONS AND HOW
SECRECY AFFECTS IT. DIPLOM NUC/PWR WEAPON ISOLAT
RATIONAL ORD/FREE WEALTH...ECOMETRIC MATH GEN/LAWS.
PAGE 38 G0742

DETER
ARMS/CONT
SIMUL
GAME

B65

VEINOTT A.F. JR.,MATHEMATICAL STUDIES IN MANAGEMENT
SCIENCE. UNIV INDUS COMPUTER ADMIN...DECISION
NET/THEORY SIMUL 20. PAGE 61 G1193

MATH
MGT
PLAN
PRODUC

B65

BERND J.L.,MATHEMATICAL APPLICATIONS IN POLITICAL
SCIENCE. II. COMPUTER...PROBABIL STAT CHARTS.
PAGE 7 G0131

METH
MATH
METH/CNCPT

B66

KUENNE R.E.,THE POLARIS MISSILE STRIKE* A GENERAL
ECONOMIC SYSTEMS ANALYSIS. USA+45 USSR NAT/G
BAL/PWR ARMS/CONT WAR...MATH PROBABIL COMPUT/IR
CHARTS HYPO/EXP SIMUL. PAGE 32 G0625

NUC/PWR
FORCES
DETER
DIPLOM

B66

KURAKOV I.G.,SCIENCE, TECHNOLOGY AND COMMUNISM;
SOME QUESTIONS OF DEVELOPMENT (TRANS. BY CARIN
DEDIJER). USSR INDUS PLAN PROB/SOLV COST PRODUC
...MGT MATH CHARTS METH 20. PAGE 32 G0626

CREATE
TEC/DEV
MARXISM
ECO/TAC

B66

CHARLESWORTH J.C.,CONTEMPORARY POLITICAL ANALYSIS.
INTELL...DECISION METH/CNCPT MATH STYLE CON/ANAL
GAME ANTHOL 20. PAGE 11 G0222

R+D
IDEA/COMP
CONCPT
METH/COMP

B67

HARDT J.P.,MATHEMATICS AND COMPUTERS IN SOVIET
ECONOMIC PLANNING. COM USSR OP/RES PROB/SOLV
OPTIMAL...MODAL SIMUL 20. PAGE 24 G0481

PLAN
TEC/DEV
MATH
COMPUT/IR

B67

HARMAN H.H.,MODERN FACTOR ANALYSIS (2ND REV. ED.).
COMPUTER...DECISION CHARTS BIBLIOG T. PAGE 24 G0482

CON/ANAL
METH/CNCPT
SIMUL
MATH

B67

PORWIT K.,CENTRAL PLANNING: EVALUATION OF VARIANTS.
PRICE OPTIMAL PRODUC...DECISION MATH CHARTS SIMUL
BIBLIOG 20. PAGE 45 G0886

PLAN
MGT
ECOMETRIC

B67

MATHEMATICS....SEE MATH, ALSO LOGIC, MATHEMATICS, AND
LANGUAGE INDEX, P. XIV

MATHEWS J.M. G0721

MATTEI/E....ENRICO MATTEI

MATTHEWS M.A. G0722

MAU/MAU....MAU MAU

MAUD....MILITARY APPLICATIONS OF URANIUM DETONATION (MAUD)
(U.K. - WWII)

THOMSON G.P.,NUCLEAR ENERGY IN BRITAIN DURING THE
LAST WAR: THE CHERWELL SIMON LECTURE (MONOGRAPH).
UK R+D CONSULT FORCES PLAN DIPLOM TASK CIVMIL/REL
ROLE...PHIL/SCI NEW/IDEA LAB/EXP 20 MAUD. PAGE 54
G1071

CREATE
TEC/DEV
WAR
NUC/PWR

B62

MAURITANIA....SEE ALSO AFR

MAURRAS/C....CHARLES MAURRAS

MAYDA J. G0723

MAYNE R. G0724

MAYO E. G0725

MAYO/ELTON....ELTON MAYO

MAYOR....MAYOR; SEE ALSO MUNIC, CHIEF

MAZOUR A.G. G0726

MBEMBE....MBEMBE TRIBE

MCBRIDE J.H. G0727

MCCARTHY/E....EUGENE MCCARTHY

MCCARTHY/J....JOSEPH MCCARTHY

HOFSTADTER R.,ANTI-INTELLECTUALISM IN AMERICAN
LIFE. USA+45 AGRI INDUS ACADEM TEC/DEV EDU/PROP
INGP/REL ATTIT...SOC WORSHIP 20 MCCARTHY/J
STEVENSN/A. PAGE 26 G0522

INTELL
EPIST
CULTURE
SOCIETY

B63

MCCLELLAND C.A. G0728,G0729

MCCLELLN/J....JOHN MCCLELLAN

MCCLINTOCK C.G. G0503

MCCLINTOCK R. G0730

MCCLOSKEY J.F. G0731

MCCRACKEN H.L. G0732

MCDIARMID J. G0733

MCDONALD L.C. G0734

MCDONOUGH A.M. G0735

MCDOUGAL M.S. G0736,G0737,G0738,G0739,G0740

MCGOWEN F. G0582

MCGREGOR D. G0741

MCGUIRE M.C. G0742

MCKEAN R. G0514

MCKINLEY/W....PRESIDENT WILLIAM MCKINLEY

MCKINNELL H.A. G0946

MCKINNEY E.R. G0743

MCKINNEY R. G0744

MCLAUGHLIN M.R. G0745

MCLEAN J.M. G0746

MCLUHAN M. G0211

MCLUHAN/M....MARSHALL MCLUHAN

MCMAHON....MCMAHON LINE

MCNAMARA R.L. G0747

MCNAMARA/R....ROBERT MCNAMARA

US SENATE COMM GOVT OPERATIONS,ADMINISTRATION OF
NATIONAL SECURITY. USA+45 CHIEF PLAN PROB/SOLV
TEC/DEV DIPLOM ATTIT...POLICY DECISION 20
KENNEDY/JF RUSK/D MCNAMARA/R BUNDY/M HERTER/C.
PAGE 60 G1177

ORD/FREE
ADMIN
NAT/G
CONTROL

B62

KAUFMANN W.W.,THE MC NAMARA STRATEGY. TOP/EX
INSPECT BAL/PWR DIPLOM CONTROL DETER GUERRILLA
NUC/PWR WEAPON COST PWR...METH/COMP 20 MCNAMARA/R
KENNEDY/JF JOHNSON/LB NATO DEPT/DEFEN. PAGE 30
G0586

FORCES
WAR
PLAN
PROB/SOLV

B64

BALDWIN H.,"SLOW-DOWN IN THE PENTAGON." USA+45

RECORD

S65

CREATE PLAN GOV/REL CENTRAL COST EFFICIENCY PWR   R+D
...MGT MCNAMARA/R. PAGE 5 G0088   WEAPON
                                                       ADMIN

MCRAE R. G0748

MDTA....MANPOWER DEVELOPMENT AND TRAINING ACT (1962)

MEAD/GH....GEORGE HERBERT MEAD

MEAD/MARG....MARGARET MEAD

                                                                   B63
RUITENBEER H.M.,THE DILEMMA OF ORGANIZATIONAL   PERSON
SOCIETY. CULTURE ECO/DEV MUNIC SECT TEC/DEV   ROLE
EDU/PROP NAT/LISM ORD/FREE...NAT/COMP 20 RIESMAN/D   ADMIN
WHYTE/WF MERTON/R MEAD/MARG JASPERS/K. PAGE 48   WORKER
G0945

MEADVIL/PA....MEADVILLE, PA.

MEADVILLE, PA.....SEE MEADVIL/PA

MEANS G.C. G0749

MECRENSKY E. G0750

MEDIATION....SEE CONFER, CONSULT

MEDICAL CARE....SEE HEALTH

MEDITERRANEAN AND NEAR EAST, TO ISLAMIC PERIOD....SEE
    MEDIT-7

MEDIT-7....MEDITERRANEAN AND NEAR EAST TO THE ISLAMIC
    PERIOD (7TH CENTURY); SEE ALSO APPROPRIATE NATIONS

                                                                   B54
HART B.H.L.,STRATEGY (REV. ED.). CHRIST-17C EUR+WWI   WAR
MEDIT-7 MOD/EUR TEC/DEV LEAD REV WEAPON...POLICY   PLAN
CHARTS. PAGE 25 G0486   FORCES
                                                       PHIL/SCI

MEEHL P.E. G0686

MEHTA A. G0751

MEIJI....MEIJI: THE REIGN OF EMPEROR MUTSUHITO OF JAPAN
    (1868-1912)

MELANESIA....MELANESIA

MELMAN S. G0752,G0753

MENEZES A.J. G0754

MENON/KRSH....KRISHNA MENON

MENSHEVIK....MENSHEVIKS

MENTAL DISORDERS....SEE HEALTH

MENTAL HEALTH....SEE HEALTH, PSY

MENTAL INSTITUTION....SEE PUB/INST

MENZIES/RG....ROBERT G. MENZIES

MERCANTILISM....SEE ECO

MERCANTLST....MERCANTILIST ECONOMIC THEORY

MERCIER/E....ERNEST MERCIER

MEREDITH/J....JAMES MEREDITH

MERGERS....SEE INDUS, EX/STRUC, FINAN

MERRIAM C.E. G0755

MERTHYR....MERTHYR, WALES

MERTON R. G0756

MERTON R.K. G0757,G0759

MERTON/R....ROBERT MERTON

                                                                   B63
RUITENBEER H.M.,THE DILEMMA OF ORGANIZATIONAL   PERSON
SOCIETY. CULTURE ECO/DEV MUNIC SECT TEC/DEV   ROLE
EDU/PROP NAT/LISM ORD/FREE...NAT/COMP 20 RIESMAN/D   ADMIN
WHYTE/WF MERTON/R MEAD/MARG JASPERS/K. PAGE 48   WORKER
G0945

MESOPOTAM....MESOPOTAMIA

MESSICK S. G1075

METH....HEAVILY EMPHASIZED METHODOLOGY OR TECHNIQUE OF STUDY

                                                                   N
AMERICAN DOCUMENTATION INST,AMERICAN DOCUMENTATION.   BIBLIOG
PROF/ORG CONSULT PLAN PERCEPT...MATH STAT AUD/VIS   TEC/DEV
CHARTS METH/COMP INDEX METH 20. PAGE 3 G0050   COM/IND
                                                       COMPUT/IR

                                                                   B
US DEPT COMMERCE OFF TECH SERV,TECHNICAL   BIBLIOG
TRANSLATIONS. WOR+45 INDUS COMPUTER CREATE NUC/PWR   R+D
...PHIL/SCI COMPUT/IR METH/COMP METH. PAGE 58 G1135   TEC/DEV
                                                       AUTOMAT

                                                                   B34
BOWMAN I.,GEOGRAPHY IN RELATION TO THE SOCIAL   GEOG
SCIENCES. UNIV...SOC CONCPT METH. PAGE 8 G0161   CULTURE
                                                       ROUTINE
                                                       PHIL/SCI

                                                                   B40
PFIFFNER J.M.,RESEARCH METHODS IN PUBLIC   ADMIN
ADMINISTRATION. USA-45 R+D...MGT STAT INT QU T 20.   OP/RES
PAGE 44 G0872   METH
                                                       TEC/DEV

                                                                   B44
KAUFMANN F.,METHODOLOGY OF THE SOCIAL SCIENCES.   SOC
PERSON...RELATIV PSY CONCPT LING METH 20. PAGE 30   PHIL/SCI
G0585   GEN/LAWS
                                                       METH/CNCPT

                                                                   S44
HAWLEY A.H.,"ECOLOGY AND HUMAN ECOLOGY" WOR+45   HABITAT
INTELL ACADEM PLAN GP/REL ADJUST PERSON...PHIL/SCI   GEOG
SOC METH/CNCPT METH 20. PAGE 25 G0493   GEN/LAWS
                                                       METH/COMP

                                                                   S49
MERTON R.,"THE ROLE OF APPLIED SOCIAL SCIENCE IN   PLAN
THE FORMATION OF POLICY: A RESEARCH MEMORANDUM."   SOC
WOR+45 INDUS NAT/G EXEC ROUTINE CHOOSE ORD/FREE PWR   DIPLOM
SKILL...POLICY MGT PSY METH/CNCPT TESTS CHARTS METH
VAL/FREE 20. PAGE 38 G0756

                                                                   B50
CONTINUITIES IN SOCIAL RESEARCH; STUDIES IN SCOPE   SOC
AND METHOD OF "THE AMERICAN SOLDIER" USA+45 FORCES   PHIL/SCI
INGP/REL ATTIT...PSY SAMP CON/ANAL CHARTS GEN/LAWS   METH
ANTHOL 20. PAGE 38 G0758

                                                                   B51
CONANT J.B.,SCIENCE AND COMMON SENSE. WOR+45 WOR-45   CREATE
R+D SCHOOL CONSULT TEC/DEV EDU/PROP SKILL...PLURIST   PHIL/SCI
METH/CNCPT RECORD TIME/SEQ SIMUL GEN/METH METH.
PAGE 13 G0248

                                                                   B51
LEWIN K.,FIELD THEORY IN SOCIAL SCIENCE: SELECTED   PHIL/SCI
THEORETICAL PAPERS. UNIV CREATE DRIVE PERCEPT KNOWL   HYPO/EXP
...METH/CNCPT CONT/OBS CHARTS GEN/METH METH
VAL/FREE 20. PAGE 33 G0661

                                                                   S51
BERGMANN G.,"IDEOLOGY" (BMR)" UNIV PERCEPT KNOWL   PHIL/SCI
...IDEA/COMP METH. PAGE 7 G0126   CONCPT
                                                       LOG
                                                       ALL/IDEOS

                                                                   S51
LERNER D.,"THE POLICY SCIENCES: RECENT DEVELOPMENTS   CONSULT
IN SCOPE AND METHODS." R+D SERV/IND CREATE DIPLOM   SOC
ROUTINE PWR...METH/CNCPT TREND GEN/LAWS METH 20.
PAGE 33 G0658

                                                                   L52
ELDERSVELD S.J.,"RESEARCH IN POLITICAL BEHAVIOR"   ACT/RES
(BMR)" USA+45 PLAN TEC/DEV ATTIT...BIBLIOG/A METH   GEN/LAWS
20. PAGE 17 G0341   CREATE

                                                                   L52
LASSWELL H.D.,"RESEARCH IN POLITICAL BEHAVIOR."   PHIL/SCI
LOC/G MUNIC POL/PAR CONSULT ADMIN PARTIC...CHARTS   METH
ANTHOL BIBLIOG/A 20. PAGE 32 G0641   R+D

                                                                   S52
"SELECTED CRITICAL BIBLIOGRAPHY ON THE METHODS AND   BIBLIOG/A
TECHNIQUES OF POLITICAL BEHAVIOR RESEARCH."   METH
...PHIL/SCI OBS QU SYS/QU TESTS CON/ANAL. PAGE 1   SOC
G0012   EDU/PROP

SPENCER R.F.,METHOD AND PERSPECTIVE IN ANTHROPOLOGY
....GEOG LING QUANT STAT TESTS SAMP/SIZ CON/ANAL
IDEA/COMP METH/COMP ANTHOL BIBLIOG 20. PAGE 52
G1025
B54
PHIL/SCI
SOC
PSY
METH

SHUBIK M.,READINGS IN GAME THEORY AND POLITICAL
BEHAVIOR. WOR+45 FORCES CREATE ROUTINE WAR PEACE
PERCEPT KNOWL PWR...PSY SOC CONCPT METH/CNCPT STAT
CHARTS HYPO/EXP GAME METH VAL/FREE 20. PAGE 50
G0991
B55
MATH
DECISION
DIPLOM

THOMAS M.,ATOMIC ENERGY AND CONGRESS. USA+45 NAT/G
ACT/RES PLAN TEC/DEV EDU/PROP ROUTINE KNOWL PWR
SKILL...PHIL/SCI NEW/IDEA TIME/SEQ CHARTS METH
CONGRESS VAL/FREE 20 AEC. PAGE 54 G1067
B56
LEGIS
ADMIN
NUC/PWR

ALMOND G.A.,"COMPARATIVE POLITICAL SYSTEMS" (BMR)"
WOR+45 WOR-45 PROB/SOLV DIPLOM EFFICIENCY
...PHIL/SCI SOC METH 17/20. PAGE 3 G0046
S56
GOV/COMP
CONCPT
ALL/IDEOS
NAT/COMP

OPERATIONS RESEARCH SOCIETY,A COMPREHENSIVE
BIBLIOGRAPHY ON OPERATIONS RESEARCH; THROUGH 1956
WITH SUPPLEMENT FOR 1957. COM/IND DIST/IND INDUS
ADMIN...DECISION MATH STAT METH 20. PAGE 43 G0840
B58
BIBLIOG/A
COMPUT/IR
OP/RES
MGT

KLAPPER J.T.,"WHAT WE KNOW ABOUT THE EFFECTS OF
MASS COMMUNICATION: THE BRINK OF HOPE" (BMR)"
COM/IND KNOWL...METH/CNCPT GEN/LAWS BIBLIOG METH
20. PAGE 31 G0605
S58
ACT/RES
PERCEPT
CROWD
PHIL/SCI

BLOOMFIELD L.P.,"THREE EXPERIMENTS IN POLITICAL
GAMING." ACT/RES CREATE PWR...GAME GEN/METH METH.
PAGE 7 G0140
S59
TEC/DEV
METH/CNCPT
DECISION

GOLDHAMMER H.,"SOME OBSERVATIONS ON POLITICAL
GAMING." FUT WOR+45 R+D NAT/G ACT/RES CREATE CHOOSE
ATTIT PWR...POLICY CONCPT METH/CNCPT STYLE KNO/TEST
TREND HYPO/EXP GAME GEN/METH METH 20. PAGE 22 G0426
S59
COMPUT/IR
DECISION
DIPLOM

INSTITUTE PSYCHOLOGICAL RES,HUMAN ENGINEERING
BIBLIOGRAPHY, 1959-1960. USA+45 WORKER EDU/PROP
PERSON METH/COMP. PAGE 28 G0547
B61
BIBLIOG/A
METH
PSY
R+D

ROSENAU J.N.,INTERNATIONAL POLITICS AND FOREIGN
POLICY: A READER IN RESEARCH AND THEORY. ELITES
ATTIT SOVEREIGN...DECISION CHARTS HYPO/EXP GAME
SIMUL ANTHOL BIBLIOG METH 20. PAGE 48 G0936
B61
ACT/RES
DIPLOM
CONCPT
POLICY

ANDREWS R.B.,"URBAN ECONOMICS: AN APPRAISAL OF
PROGRESS." LOC/G PROB/SOLV TEC/DEV...CONCPT
OBS/ENVIR METH/COMP HYPO/EXP SOC/EXP SIMUL GEN/METH
METH 20. PAGE 3 G0058
S61
MUNIC
PHIL/SCI
ECOMETRIC

DALTON G.,"ECONOMIC THEORY AND PRIMITIVE SOCIETY"
(BMR)" UNIV AGRI KIN TEC/DEV ECO/TAC REGION HABITAT
SKILL...METH/COMP BIBLIOG. PAGE 14 G0274
S61
ECO/UNDEV
METH
PHIL/SCI
SOC

ASTIA,HUMAN ENGINEERING: A REPORT BIBLIOGRAPHY.
USA+45 R+D FORCES ACT/RES COMPUTER CREATE OP/RES
EDU/PROP CONTROL WEAPON...SOC NEW/IDEA. PAGE 4
G0073
B62
BIBLIOG/A
COM/IND
COMPUT/IR
METH

ASTIA,INFORMATION THEORY: A REPORT BIBLIOGRAPHY.
USA+45 COMPUTER CREATE OP/RES PLAN TEC/DEV CONTROL
...CONCPT METH/COMP. PAGE 4 G0074
B62
BIBLIOG/A
COM/IND
FORCES
METH

CHASE S.,THE PROPER STUDY OF MANKIND (2ND REV.
ED.). WOR+45 WOR-45 INTELL WAR...METH/CNCPT
SAMP/SIZ GEN/LAWS BIBLIOG METH 16/20. PAGE 11 G0224
B62
PHIL/SCI
SOC
PROB/SOLV
PERSON

DUCKWORTH W.E.,A GUIDE TO OPERATIONAL RESEARCH.
INDUS PLAN PROB/SOLV EXEC EFFICIENCY PRODUC KNOWL
...MGT MATH STAT SIMUL METH 20 MONTECARLO. PAGE 16
G0319
B62
OP/RES
GAME
DECISION
ADMIN

MARS D.,SUGGESTED LIBRARY IN PUBLIC ADMINISTRATION.
FINAN DELIB/GP EX/STRUC WORKER COMPUTER ADJUD
...DECISION PSY SOC METH/COMP 20. PAGE 36 G0710
B62
BIBLIOG
ADMIN
METH
MGT

SNYDER R.C.,FOREIGN POLICY DECISION-MAKING. FUT
KOREA WOR+45 R+D CREATE ADMIN ROUTINE PWR
...DECISION PSY SOC CONCPT METH/CNCPT CON/ANAL
CHARTS GEN/METH METH 20. PAGE 52 G1018
B62
TEC/DEV
HYPO/EXP
DIPLOM

FLOOD M.M.,"STOCHASTIC LEARNING THEORY APPLIED TO
CHOICE EXPERIMENTS WITH RATS, DOGS, AND MEN."...PSY
LAB/EXP METH. PAGE 19 G0372
S62
DECISION
COMPUTER
HYPO/EXP
TEC/DEV

NAFZIGER R.O.,INTRODUCTION TO MASS COMMUNICATIONS
RESEARCH (REV. ED.). ACT/RES...STAT CON/ANAL METH
20. PAGE 41 G0801
B63
COM/IND
CONCPT
PHIL/SCI
CREATE

FEI J.C.H.,DEVELOPMENT OF THE LABOR SURPLUS
ECONOMY: THEORY AND POLICY. WOR+45 AGRI INDUS
MARKET PROB/SOLV TEC/DEV...STAT CHARTS GEN/LAWS
METH 20 THIRD/WRLD. PAGE 18 G0361
B64
ECO/TAC
POLICY
WORKER
ECO/UNDEV

MARTINO R.L.,PROJECT MANAGEMENT AND CONTROL: VOL. 2
APPLIED OPERATIONAL PLANNING. COMPUTER...MATH
CHARTS SIMUL METH TIME. PAGE 36 G0716
B64
DECISION
PLAN
TEC/DEV
OP/RES

ORTH C.D.,ADMINISTERING RESEARCH AND DEVELOPMENT.
FINAN PLAN PROB/SOLV ADMIN ROUTINE...METH/CNCPT
STAT CHARTS METH 20. PAGE 43 G0847
B64
MGT
R+D
LG/CO
INDUS

PEDERSEN E.S.,NUCLEAR ENERGY IN SPACE. FUT INTELL
R+D CONSULT...NEW/IDEA CHARTS METH T 20. PAGE 44
G0864
B64
SPACE
TEC/DEV
NUC/PWR
LAB/EXP

ANTHONY R.N.,PLANNING AND CONTROL SYSTEMS. UNIV
OP/RES...DECISION MGT LING. PAGE 3 G0061
B65
CONTROL
PLAN
METH
HYPO/EXP

HASSON J.A.,THE ECONOMICS OF NUCLEAR POWER. INDIA
UK USA+45 WOR+45 INT/ORG TEC/DEV COST...SOC STAT
CHARTS 20 EURATOM. PAGE 25 G0490
B65
NUC/PWR
INDUS
ECO/DEV
METH

JANDA K.,DATA PROCESSING: APPLICATIONS TO POLITICAL
RESEARCH....STAT CON/ANAL. PAGE 28 G0557
B65
DECISION
COMPUTER
TEC/DEV
METH

OECD,THE MEDITERRANEAN REGIONAL PROJECT: PORTUGAL;
EDUCATION AND DEVELOPMENT. PORTUGAL SOCIETY STRATA
FINAN PROF/ORG WORKER PLAN PROB/SOLV ADMIN...POLICY
STAT CHARTS METH 20 OECD. PAGE 42 G0832
B65
EDU/PROP
SCHOOL
ACADEM
ECO/UNDEV

OECD,THE MEDITERRANEAN REGIONAL PROJECT: ITALY;
EDUCATION AND DEVELOPMENT. ITALY SOCIETY STRATA
FINAN NAT/G PROF/ORG WORKER PLAN PROB/SOLV ADMIN
...STAT CHARTS METH 20 OECD. PAGE 42 G0833
B65
SCHOOL
EDU/PROP
ECO/UNDEV
ACADEM

ORG FOR ECO COOP AND DEVEL,THE MEDITERRANEAN
REGIONAL PROJECT: YUGOSLAVIA; EDUCATION AND
DEVELOPMENT. YUGOSLAVIA SOCIETY FINAN PROF/ORG PLAN
ADMIN COST DEMAND MARXISM...STAT TREND CHARTS METH
20 OECD. PAGE 43 G0843
B65
EDU/PROP
ACADEM
SCHOOL
ECO/UNDEV

WISH J.R.,ECONOMIC DEVELOPMENT IN LATIN AMERICA: AN
ANNOTATED BIBLIOGRAPHY. L/A+17C COM/IND MARKET R+D
CREATE CAP/ISM ATTIT...STAT METH 20. PAGE 64 G1250
B65
BIBLIOG/A
ECO/UNDEV
TEC/DEV
AGRI

DECHERT C.R.,"THE DEVELOPMENT OF CYBERNETICS."
ACT/RES CREATE SKILL...STERTYP METH. PAGE 15 G0290
S65
SIMUL
COMPUT/IR
PLAN
DECISION

BERND J.L.,MATHEMATICAL APPLICATIONS IN POLITICAL SCIENCE. II. COMPUTER...PROBABIL STAT CHARTS. PAGE 7 G0131
B66
METH
MATH
METH/CNCPT

KURAKOV I.G.,SCIENCE, TECHNOLOGY AND COMMUNISM; SOME QUESTIONS OF DEVELOPMENT (TRANS. BY CARIN DEDIJER). USSR INDUS PLAN PROB/SOLV COST PRODUC ...MGT MATH CHARTS METH 20. PAGE 32 G0626
B66
CREATE
TEC/DEV
MARXISM
ECO/TAC

BARANSON J.,TECHNOLOGY FOR UNDERDEVELOPED AREAS: AN ANNOTATED BIBLIOGRAPHY. FUT WOR+45 CULTURE INDUS INT/ORG CREATE PROB/SOLV INT/TRADE EDU/PROP AUTOMAT ...CONCPT METH. PAGE 5 G0092
B67
BIBLIOG/A
ECO/UNDEV
TEC/DEV
R+D

BUNGE M.,THE SEARCH FOR SYSTEM. VOL. 3, PART 1 OF STUDIES IN THE FOUNDATIONS METHODOLOGY, AND PHILOSOPHY OF SCIENCE. UNIV LAW INTELL KNOWL. PAGE 10 G0187
B67
PHIL/SCI
METH
GEN/LAWS
CONCPT

BUNGE M.,THE SEARCH FOR TRUTH, VOL. 3, PART 2 OF STUDIES IN THE FOUNDATIONS, METHODOLOGY, AND PHILOSOPHY OF SCIENCE. UNIV INTELL KNOWL...CONCPT OBS PREDICT METH. PAGE 10 G0188
B67
PHIL/SCI
TESTS
GEN/LAWS
RATIONAL

CONNOLLY W.E.,POLITICAL SCIENCE AND IDEOLOGY. UTOPIA ATTIT KNOWL...MAJORIT EPIST PHIL/SCI SOC IDEA/COMP HYPO/EXP GEN/LAWS METH HUME/D MARX/KARL. PAGE 13 G0250
B67
PWR
PLURISM
ELITES
CONCPT

DAVIS V.,THE POLITICS OF INNOVATION: PATTERNS IN NAVY CASES (PAMPHLET). WOR+45 NAT/G CREATE WEAPON INGP/REL ATTIT...POLICY SOC METH/COMP METH. PAGE 14 G0280
B67
BIBLIOG
FORCES
NUC/PWR
TEC/DEV

DE BLIJ H.J.,SYSTEMATIC POLITICAL GEOGRAPHY. WOR+45 STRUCT INT/ORG NAT/G EDU/PROP ADMIN COLONIAL ROUTINE ORD/FREE PWR...IDEA/COMP T 20. PAGE 15 G0283
B67
GEOG
CONCPT
METH

DE JOUVENEL B.,THE ART OF CONJECTURE. WOR+45 EFFICIENCY PERCEPT KNOWL...DECISION PHIL/SCI CONCPT METH/COMP BIBLIOG 20. PAGE 15 G0285
B67
FUT
PREDICT
SIMUL
METH

GULICK M.C.,NONCONVENTIONAL INFORMATION SYSTEMS SERVING THE SOCIAL SCIENCES AND THE HUMANITIES; A BIBLIOGRAPHIC ESSAY (PAPER). USA+45 COMPUTER CREATE EDU/PROP KNOWL...SOC METH 20. PAGE 23 G0462
B67
BIBLIOG/A
R+D
COMPUT/IR
HUM

UNIVERSAL REFERENCE SYSTEM,LAW, JURISPRUDENCE, AND JUDICIAL PROCESS (VOLUME VII). WOR+45 WOR-45 CONSTN NAT/G LEGIS JUDGE CT/SYS...INT/LAW COMPUT/IR GEN/METH METH. PAGE 56 G1101
B67
BIBLIOG/A
LAW
JURID
ADJUD

MCNAMARA R.L.,"THE NEED FOR INNOVATIVENESS IN DEVELOPING SOCIETIES." L/A+17C EDU/PROP ADMIN LEAD WEALTH...POLICY PSY SOC METH 20 COLOMB. PAGE 38 G0747
S67
PROB/SOLV
PLAN
ECO/UNDEV
NEW/IDEA

TAGIL S.,"WEGENER, RAEDER, AND THE GERMAN NAVAL STRATEGY: VIEWPOINTS ON THE CONDITIONS FOR THE INFLUENCE OF IDEAS." GERMANY WOR-45...IDEA/COMP METH 20. PAGE 53 G1049
S67
SEA
POLICY
HIST/WRIT
CIVMIL/REL

METH/CNCPT....METHODOLOGICAL CONCEPTS

METH/COMP....COMPARISON OF METHODS

AMERICAN DOCUMENTATION INST,AMERICAN DOCUMENTATION. PROF/ORG CONSULT PLAN PERCEPT...MATH STAT AUD/VIS CHARTS METH/COMP INDEX METH 20. PAGE 3 G0050
N
BIBLIOG
TEC/DEV
COM/IND
COMPUT/IR

WEIGLEY R.F.,HISTORY OF THE UNITED STATES ARMY. USA+45 USA-45 SOCIETY NAT/G LEAD WAR GP/REL PWR ...SOC METH/COMP COLD/WAR. PAGE 62 G1222
N
FORCES
ADMIN
ROLE
CIVMIL/REL

US DEPT COMMERCE OFF TECH SERV,TECHNICAL
B
BIBLIOG

TRANSLATIONS. WOR+45 INDUS COMPUTER CREATE NUC/PWR ...PHIL/SCI COMPUT/IR METH/COMP METH. PAGE 58 G1135
R+D
TEC/DEV
AUTOMAT

FOLSOM M.B.,BETTER MANAGEMENT OF THE PUBLIC'S BUSINESS (PAMPHLET). USA+45 DELIB/GP PAY CONFER CONTROL REGION GP/REL...METH/COMP ANTHOL 20. PAGE 19 G0377
N1
ADMIN
NAT/G
MGT
PROB/SOLV

BOSANQUET B.,"SCIENCE AND PHILOSOPHY" IN J. MUIRHEAD AND R.B. BOSANQUET, EDS., SCIENCE AND PHILOSOPHY AND OTHER ESSAYS."...CONCPT METH/COMP GEN/METH. PAGE 8 G0155
C2
PHIL/SCI
CREATE
METH/CNCP
NEW/IDEA

GULICK L.,PAPERS ON THE SCIENCE OF ADMINISTRATION. INDUS PROB/SOLV TEC/DEV COST EFFICIENCY PRODUC HABITAT...PHIL/SCI METH/COMP 20. PAGE 23 G0461
B3
OP/RES
CONTROL
ADMIN
MGT

HAWLEY A.H.,"ECOLOGY AND HUMAN ECOLOGY" WOR+45 INTELL ACADEM PLAN GP/REL ADJUST PERSON...PHIL/SCI SOC METH/CNCPT METH 20. PAGE 25 G0493
S4
HABITAT
GEOG
GEN/LAWS
METH/COMP

MERTON R.K.,"THE BEARING OF EMPIRICAL RESEARCH UPON THE DEVELOPMENT OF SOCIAL THEORY" (BMR)"...SOC CONCPT QUANT METH/COMP HYPO/EXP 20. PAGE 38 G0757
S4
ACT/RES
SOC/EXP
OBS
PHIL/SCI

MCLEAN J.M.,THE PUBLIC SERVICE AND UNIVERSITY EDUCATION. UK USA-45 DELIB/GP EX/STRUC TOP/EX ADMIN ...GOV/COMP METH/COMP NAT/COMP ANTHOL 20. PAGE 38 G0746
B4
ACADEM
NAT/G
EXEC
EDU/PROP

CALDWELL L.K.,RESEARCH METHODS IN PUBLIC ADMINISTRATION: AN OUTLINE OF TOPICS AND READINGS (PAMPHLET). LAW ACT/RES COMPUTER KNOWL...SOC STAT GEN/METH 20. PAGE 10 G0201
B53
BIBLIOG/A
METH/COMP
ADMIN
OP/RES

MCCLOSKEY J.F.,OPERATIONS RESEARCH FOR MANAGEMENT. STRUCT COMPUTER ADMIN ROUTINE...PHIL/SCI CONCPT METH/CNCPT TREND ANTHOL BIBLIOG 20. PAGE 37 G0731
B54
OP/RES
MGT
METH/COMP
TEC/DEV

SPENCER R.F.,METHOD AND PERSPECTIVE IN ANTHROPOLOGY ....GEOG LING QUANT STAT TESTS SAMP/SIZ CON/ANAL IDEA/COMP METH/COMP ANTHOL BIBLIOG 20. PAGE 52 G1025
B54
PHIL/SCI
SOC
PSY
METH

BAUER P.T.,ECONOMIC ANALYSIS AND POLICY IN UNDERDEVELOPED COUNTRIES. WOR+45 AGRI INT/TRADE TAX PRICE...GEN/METH BIBLIOG/A 20 COMMONWLTH. PAGE 5 G0103
B57
ECO/UNDEV
METH/COMP
POLICY

CHEEK G.,ECONOMIC AND SOCIAL IMPLICATIONS OF AUTOMATION: A BIBLIOGRAPHIC REVIEW (PAMPHLET). USA+45 LG/CO WORKER CREATE PLAN CONTROL ROUTINE PERS/REL EFFICIENCY PRODUC...METH/COMP 20. PAGE 12 G0225
B58
BIBLIOG/A
SOCIETY
INDUS
AUTOMAT

MECRENSKY E.,SCIENTIFIC MANPOWER IN EUROPE. WOR+45 EDU/PROP GOV/REL SKILL...TECHNIC PHIL/SCI INT CHARTS BIBLIOG 20. PAGE 38 G0750
B58
ECO/TAC
TEC/DEV
METH/COMP
NAT/COMP

OGDEN F.D.,THE POLL TAX IN THE SOUTH. USA+45 USA-45 CONSTN ADJUD ADMIN PARTIC CRIME...TIME/SEQ GOV/COMP METH/COMP 18/20 SOUTH/US. PAGE 43 G0838
B58
TAX
CHOOSE
RACE/REL
DISCRIM

NEWELL A.C.,"ELEMENTS OF A THEORY OF HUMAN PROBLEM SOLVING" (BMR)" TASK PERCEPT...CONCPT LOG METH/COMP LAB/EXP BIBLIOG 20. PAGE 42 G0819
S58
PROB/SOLV
COMPUTER
COMPUT/IR
OP/RES

CLEAVELAND F.N.,SCIENCE AND STATE GOVERNMENT. AGRI EXTR/IND FINAN INDUS PROVS...METH/CNCPT STAT CHARTS 20 NEW/YORK CONNECTICT WISCONSIN CALIFORNIA NEW/MEXICO. PAGE 12 G0233
B59
TEC/DEV
PHIL/SCI
GOV/REL
METH/COMP

B59
ELDRIDGE H.T.,THE MATERIALS OF DEMOGRAPHY: A BIBLIOG/A
SELECTED AND ANNOTATED BIBLIOGRAPHY. R+D DEATH GEOG
...SAMP METH/COMP NAT/COMP 20. PAGE 18 G0343 STAT
TREND

B61
INSTITUTE PSYCHOLOGICAL RES.HUMAN ENGINEERING BIBLIOG/A
BIBLIOGRAPHY, 1959-1960. USA+45 WORKER EDU/PROP METH
PERSON METH/COMP. PAGE 28 G0547 PSY
R+D

S61
ANDREWS R.B.,"URBAN ECONOMICS: AN APPRAISAL OF MUNIC
PROGRESS." LOC/G PROB/SOLV TEC/DEV...CONCPT PHIL/SCI
OBS/ENVIR METH/COMP HYPO/EXP SOC/EXP SIMUL GEN/METH ECOMETRIC
METH 20. PAGE 3 G0058

S61
BENNION E.G.,"ECONOMETRICS FOR MANAGEMENT." USA+45 ECOMETRIC
INDUS EX/STRUC ACT/RES COMPUTER UTIL...MATH STAT MGT
PREDICT METH/COMP HYPO/EXP. PAGE 6 G0122 SIMUL
DECISION

S61
DALTON G.,"ECONOMIC THEORY AND PRIMITIVE SOCIETY" ECO/UNDEV
(BMR)" UNIV AGRI KIN TEC/DEV ECO/TAC REGION HABITAT METH
SKILL...METH/COMP BIBLIOG. PAGE 14 G0274 PHIL/SCI
SOC

B62
ASTIA,INFORMATION THEORY: A REPORT BIBLIOGRAPHY. BIBLIOG/A
USA+45 COMPUTER CREATE OP/RES PLAN TEC/DEV CONTROL COM/IND
...CONCPT METH/COMP. PAGE 4 G0074 FORCES
METH

B62
FERBER R.,RESEARCH METHODS IN ECONOMICS AND ACT/RES
BUSINESS. ECO/DEV FINAN MARKET LG/CO SML/CO CONSULT PROB/SOLV
CONTROL COST...STAT METH/COMP 20. PAGE 19 G0364 ECO/TAC
MGT

B62
HALPERIN M.H.,LIMITED WAR; AN ESSAY ON THE BIBLIOG/A
DEVELOPMENT OF THE THEORY AND AN ANNOTATED WAR
BIBLIOGRAPHY (OCCASIONAL PAPER NO. 3). WOR+45 ARMS/CONT
WOR-45 NUC/PWR...CONCPT IDEA/COMP METH/COMP 19/20. FORCES
PAGE 24 G0471

B62
MARS D.,SUGGESTED LIBRARY IN PUBLIC ADMINISTRATION. BIBLIOG
FINAN DELIB/GP EX/STRUC WORKER COMPUTER ADJUD ADMIN
...DECISION PSY SOC METH/COMP 20. PAGE 36 G0710 METH
MGT

B62
MARTINS A.F.,REVOLUCAO BRANCA NO CAMPO. L/A+17C AGRI
SERV/IND DEMAND EFFICIENCY PRODUC...POLICY ECO/UNDEV
METH/COMP. PAGE 36 G0717 TEC/DEV
NAT/COMP

B62
WALSTON H.,AGRICULTURE UNDER COMMUNISM. CHINA/COM AGRI
COM PROB/SOLV HAPPINESS RIGID/FLEX...POLICY MARXISM
METH/COMP 20. PAGE 62 G1207 PLAN
CREATE

B62
WENDT P.F.,HOUSING POLICY - THE SEARCH FOR PLAN
SOLUTIONS. GERMANY/W SWEDEN UK USA+45 OP/RES ADMIN
HABITAT WEALTH...SOC/WK CHARTS 20. PAGE 63 G1230 METH/COMP
NAT/G

N62
US CONGRESS JT ATOM ENRGY COMM,PEACEFUL USES OF NUC/PWR
ATOMIC ENERGY, HEARING. USA+45 USSR TEC/DEV ATTIT ACADEM
RIGID/FLEX...TESTS CHARTS EXHIBIT METH/COMP 20 SCHOOL
CONGRESS. PAGE 57 G1112 NAT/COMP

B63
MARSCH P.E.,FEDERAL AID TO SCIENCE EDUCATION: TWO EDU/PROP
PROGRAMS. USA+45 SCHOOL RECEIVE EFFICIENCY 20. PHIL/SCI
PAGE 36 G0711 NAT/G
METH/COMP

B63
US ATOMIC ENERGY COMMISSION,ATOMIC ENERGY IN THE METH/COMP
SOVIET UNION: TRIP REPORT OF THE US ATOMIC ENERGY OP/RES
DELEGATION, MAY 1933. USSR R+D NAT/G CONSULT CREATE TEC/DEV
DIPLOM ADMIN ROUTINE EFFICIENCY PRODUC KNOWL SKILL NUC/PWR
...NAT/COMP 20 AEC TRAVEL TREATY. PAGE 56 G1107

B63
WALES H.G.,A BASIC BIBLIOGRAPHY ON MARKETING BIBLIOG/A
RESEARCH (REV. ED.). ATTIT...MGT STAT INT QU SAMP MARKET
TREND 20. PAGE 62 G1206 OP/RES

B64
COENEN E.,LA "KONJUNKTURFORSCHUNG" EN ALLEMAGNE ET METH/COMP
EN AUTRICHE, 1925-1935. AUSTRIA GERMANY OP/RES PLAN R+D
COST PERCEPT...METH/CNCPT BIBLIOG 20. PAGE 12 G0237 ECO/TAC

B64
HODGETTS J.E.,ADMINISTERING THE ATOM FOR PEACE. PROB/SOLV
OP/RES TEC/DEV ADMIN...IDEA/COMP METH/COMP 20. NUC/PWR
PAGE 26 G0517 PEACE
MGT

B64
KAUFMANN W.W.,THE MC NAMARA STRATEGY. TOP/EX FORCES
INSPECT BAL/PWR DIPLOM CONTROL DETER GUERRILLA WAR
NUC/PWR WEAPON COST PWR...METH/COMP 20 MCNAMARA/R PLAN
KENNEDY/JF JOHNSON/LB NATO DEPT/DEFEN. PAGE 30 PROB/SOLV
G0586

B64
LANG A.S.,URBAN RAIL TRANSIT. OP/RES PLAN PROB/SOLV MUNIC
TEC/DEV AUTOMAT COST...TECHNIC MATH CON/ANAL CHARTS DIST/IND
METH/COMP SIMUL 20 RAILROAD PUB/TRANS. PAGE 32 ECOMETRIC
G0632

S64
STONE P.A.,"DECISION TECHNIQUES FOR TOWN OP/RES
DEVELOPMENT." PLAN COST PROFIT...DECISION MGT MUNIC
CON/ANAL CHARTS METH/COMP BIBLIOG 20. PAGE 53 G1039 ADMIN
PROB/SOLV

B65
FOSTER P.,EDUCATION AND SOCIAL CHANGE IN GHANA. SCHOOL
GHANA CULTURE STRUCT ECO/UNDEV TEC/DEV REGION CREATE
EFFICIENCY LITERACY ALL/VALS SOVEREIGN...STAT SOCIETY
METH/COMP 19/20 GOLD/COAST. PAGE 20 G0385

B65
KENT A.,SPECIALIZED INFORMATION CENTERS. INTELL R+D COMPUT/IR
VOL/ASSN CONSULT COMPUTER KNOWL...DECISION HUM CREATE
PHIL/SCI METH/CNCPT TREND CHARTS 20. PAGE 30 G0593 TEC/DEV
METH/COMP

B65
STEINER G.A.,THE CREATIVE ORGANIZATION. ELITES CREATE
LG/CO PLAN PROB/SOLV TEC/DEV INSPECT CAP/ISM MGT
CONTROL EXEC PERSON...METH/COMP HYPO/EXP 20. ADMIN
PAGE 52 G1034 SOC

B66
AMERICAN ASSEMBLY COLUMBIA U,A WORLD OF NUCLEAR NUC/PWR
POWERS? FUT WOR+45 ECO/DEV BAL/PWR ECO/TAC CONTROL DIPLOM
RISK EFFICIENCY ATTIT PWR...METH/COMP ANTHOL 20. TEC/DEV
PAGE 3 G0049 ARMS/CONT

B66
HALPIN A.W.,THEORY AND RESEARCH IN ADMINISTRATION. GEN/LAWS
ACT/RES LEAD...MGT IDEA/COMP METH/COMP. PAGE 24 EDU/PROP
G0475 ADMIN
PHIL/SCI

B66
SPULBER N.,THE STATE AND ECONOMIC DEVELOPMENT IN ECO/DEV
EASTERN EUROPE. BULGARIA COM CZECHOSLVK HUNGARY ECO/UNDEV
POLAND YUGOSLAVIA CULTURE PLAN CAP/ISM INT/TRADE NAT/G
CONTROL...POLICY CHARTS METH/COMP BIBLIOG/A 19/20. TOTALISM
PAGE 52 G1028

S66
HANSON A.H.,"PLANNING AND THE POLITICIANS* SOME PLAN
REFLECTIONS ON ECONOMIC PLANNING IN WESTERN ECO/DEV
EUROPE." MARKET NAT/G TEC/DEV CONSEN ROLE EUR+WWI
...METH/COMP NAT/COMP. PAGE 24 G0479 ADMIN

B67
BAUMOL W.J.,BUSINESS BEHAVIOR, VALUE AND GROWTH ALL/IDEOS
(REV. ED.). WOR+45 FINAN LG/CO TEC/DEV CAP/ISM PHIL/SCI
DEMAND EQUILIB...METH/COMP SIMUL 20. PAGE 5 G0105 PLAN
ECO/DEV

B67
CHARLESWORTH J.C.,CONTEMPORARY POLITICAL ANALYSIS. R+D
INTELL...DECISION METH/CNCPT MATH STYLE CON/ANAL IDEA/COMP
GAME ANTHOL 20. PAGE 11 G0222 CONCPT
METH/COMP

B67
DAVIS V.,THE POLITICS OF INNOVATION: PATTERNS IN BIBLIOG
NAVY CASES (PAMPHLET). WOR+45 NAT/G CREATE WEAPON FORCES
INGP/REL ATTIT...POLICY SOC METH/COMP METH. PAGE 14 NUC/PWR
G0280 TEC/DEV

B67
DE JOUVENEL B.,THE ART OF CONJECTURE. WOR+45 FUT
EFFICIENCY PERCEPT KNOWL...DECISION PHIL/SCI CONCPT PREDICT

METH/COMP BIBLIOG 20. PAGE 15 G0285 — SIMUL METH

B67
GROSSMAN G.,ECONOMIC SYSTEMS. USA+45 USA-45 USSR YUGOSLAVIA WORKER CAP/ISM PRICE GP/REL EQUILIB WEALTH MARXISM SOCISM...MGT METH/COMP 19/20. PAGE 23 G0456 — ECO/DEV PLAN TEC/DEV DEMAND

B67
HIRSCHMAN A.O.,DEVELOPMENT PROJECTS OBSERVED. INDUS INT/ORG CONSULT EX/STRUC CREATE OP/RES ECO/TAC DEMAND...POLICY MGT METH/COMP 20 WORLD/BANK. PAGE 26 G0513 — ECO/UNDEV R+D FINAN PLAN

B67
RUSSETT B.M.,ARMS CONTROL IN EUROPE: PROPOSALS AND POLITICAL CONSTRAINTS. GERMANY WOR+45 POL/PAR BARGAIN DIPLOM...TREND CHARTS 20 COLD/WAR. PAGE 48 G0950 — ARMS/CONT REGION METH/COMP

B67
SAPARINA Y.,CYBERNETICS WITHIN US. WOR+45 EDU/PROP FEEDBACK PERCEPT HEALTH...DECISION METH/CNCPT NEW/IDEA 20. PAGE 49 G0957 — COMPUTER METH/COMP CONTROL SIMUL

B67
WYLIE J.C.,MILITARY STRATEGY: GENERAL THEORY OF POWER CONTROL. CUBA USA+45 VIETNAM/N WOR+45 ELITES CONTROL WAR PWR...POLICY METH/COMP 20 MAO. PAGE 64 G1260 — FORCES PLAN DECISION IDEA/COMP

L67
DAVIS P.C.,"THE COMING CHINESE COMMUNIST NUCLEAR THREAT AND U.S. SEA BASED ABM OPTIONS." ASIA CHINA/COM FUT USA+45 SEA NAT/G FORCES PLAN TEC/DEV LEAD ARMS/CONT...GEOG METH/COMP 20 ABM/DEFSYS. PAGE 14 G0279 — NUC/PWR DETER WEAPON DIPLOM

S67
ALBAUM G.,"INFORMATION FLOW AND DECENTRALIZED DECISION MAKING IN MARKETING." EX/STRUC COMPUTER OP/RES PROB/SOLV EFFICIENCY OPTIMAL...METH/COMP ORG/CHARTS 20. PAGE 2 G0033 — LG/CO ROUTINE KNOWL MARKET

S67
AVTORKHANOV A.,"A NEW AGRARIAN REVOLUTION." COM USSR ECO/DEV PLAN TEC/DEV ADMIN CONTROL OPTIMAL WEALTH SOCISM 20 KHRUSH/N STALIN/J. PAGE 4 G0082 — AGRI METH/COMP MARXISM OWN

S67
BROWN W.B.,"MODEL-BUILDING AND ORGANIZATIONS." CONTROL FEEDBACK...PROBABIL CHARTS METH/COMP. PAGE 9 G0179 — MGT ADMIN GAME COMPUTER

S67
CETRON M.J.,"FORECASTING TECHNOLOGY." INDUS FORCES TASK UTIL...PHIL/SCI CONCPT CHARTS METH/COMP TIME. PAGE 11 G0219 — TEC/DEV FUT R+D PLAN

S67
GRIFFITHS F.,"THE POLITICAL SIDE OF 'DISARMAMENT'." FUT WOR+45 NUC/PWR NAT/LISM PEACE...NEW/IDEA PREDICT METH/COMP GEN/LAWS 20. PAGE 23 G0453 — ARMS/CONT DIPLOM

S67
RICHMAN B.M.,"SOVIET MANAGEMENT IN TRANSITION." USSR FINAN MARKET EX/STRUC PLAN PROB/SOLV TEC/DEV CONTROL LEAD CENTRAL EFFICIENCY...METH/COMP 20 REFORMERS. PAGE 47 G0917 — MGT MARXISM POLICY AUTHORIT

S67
WHITTIER J.M.,"COMPULSORY POOLING AND UNITIZATION* DIE-HARD KANSAS." LAW PLAN EDU/PROP ATTIT...POLICY JURID PREDICT TREND METH/COMP 20. PAGE 63 G1236 — LEGIS MUNIC INDUS ECO/TAC

METHOD, COMPARATIVE....SEE IDEA/COMP, METH/COMP

METHODOLOGY....SEE METH, PHIL/SCI, METHODOLOGICAL INDEXES, PP. XIII-XIV

METRO/COUN....METROPOLITAN COUNCIL

METROPOLITAN....SEE MUNIC

METROPOLITAN COUNCIL....SEE METRO/COUN

METTRNCH/K....PRINCE K. VON METTERNICH

METZLER L.A. G0760

MEXIC/AMER....MEXICAN-AMERICANS; SEE ALSO SPAN/AMER

B54
MOSK S.A.,INDUSTRIAL REVOLUTION IN MEXICO. MARKET LABOR CREATE CAP/ISM ADMIN ATTIT SOCISM...POLICY 20 MEXIC/AMER. PAGE 40 G0789 — INDUS TEC/DEV ECO/UNDEV NAT/G

MEXICO....SEE ALSO L/A+17C

MEZERIK A.G. G0761,G0762,G0763

MGT....MANAGEMENT

B
BRITISH COMMONWEALTH BUR AGRI,WORLD AGRICULTURAL ECONOMICS AND RURAL SOCIOLOGY ABSTRACTS. NAT/G OP/RES PLAN TEC/DEV LEAD PRODUC...GEOG MGT NAT/COMP 20. PAGE 9 G0170 — BIBLIOG/A AGRI SOC WORKER

N
ADVANCED MANAGEMENT. INDUS EX/STRUC WORKER OP/RES ...DECISION BIBLIOG/A 20. PAGE 1 G0003 — MGT ADMIN LABOR GP/REL

N
JOURNAL OF PUBLIC ADMINISTRATION: JOURNAL OF THE ROYAL INSTITUTE OF PUBLIC ADMINISTRATION. UK PLAN GP/REL INGP/REL 20. PAGE 1 G0006 — BIBLIOG/A ADMIN NAT/G MGT

N
THE MANAGEMENT REVIEW. FINAN EX/STRUC PROFIT BIBLIOG/A. PAGE 1 G0007 — LABOR MGT ADMIN MARKET

N
PERSONNEL. USA+45 LAW LABOR LG/CO WORKER CREATE GOV/REL PERS/REL ATTIT WEALTH. PAGE 1 G0010 — BIBLIOG/A ADMIN MGT GP/REL

N
PRINCETON UNIVERSITY,SELECTED REFERENCES: INDUSTRIAL RELATIONS SECTION. USA+45 EX/STRUC WORKER TEC/DEV...MGT 20. PAGE 45 G0892 — BIBLIOG/A LABOR INDUS GP/REL

N
RAND SCHOOL OF SOCIAL SCIENCE,INDEX TO LABOR ARTICLES. ECO/DEV INT/ORG LEGIS DIPLOM GP/REL ...NAT/COMP 20. PAGE 46 G0900 — BIBLIOG LABOR MGT ADJUD

N
US SUPERINTENDENT OF DOCUMENTS,TRANSPORTATION: HIGHWAYS, ROADS, AND POSTAL SERVICE (PRICE LIST 25). PANAMA USA+45 LAW FORCES DIPLOM ADMIN GOV/REL HEALTH MGT. PAGE 61 G1188 — BIBLIOG/A DIST/IND SERV/IND NAT/G

N19
DOTSON A.,PRODUCTION PLANNING IN THE PATENT OFFICE (PAMPHLET). USA+45 DIST/IND PROB/SOLV PRODUC...MGT PHIL/SCI 20 BUR/BUDGET PATENT/OFF. PAGE 16 G0309 — EFFICIENCY PLAN NAT/G ADMIN

N19
FOLSOM M.B.,BETTER MANAGEMENT OF THE PUBLIC'S BUSINESS (PAMPHLET). USA+45 DELIB/GP PAY CONFER CONTROL REGION GP/REL...METH/COMP ANTHOL 20. PAGE 19 G0377 — ADMIN NAT/G MGT PROB/SOLV

N19
GINZBERG E.,MANPOWER FOR GOVERNMENT (PAMPHLET). USA+45 FORCES PLAN PROB/SOLV PAY EDU/PROP ADMIN GP/REL COST...MGT PREDICT TREND 20 CIVIL/SERV. PAGE 21 G0418 — WORKER CONSULT NAT/G LOC/G

B37
GULICK L.,PAPERS ON THE SCIENCE OF ADMINISTRATION. INDUS PROB/SOLV TEC/DEV COST EFFICIENCY PRODUC HABITAT...PHIL/SCI METH/COMP 20. PAGE 23 G0461 — OP/RES CONTROL ADMIN MGT

B37
HODGSON J.G.,THE OFFICIAL PUBLICATIONS OF AMERICAN COUNTIES: A UNION LIST. SCHOOL BUDGET...HEAL MGT SOC/WK 19/20. PAGE 26 G0520 — BIBLIOG LOC/G PUB/INST

S39
HECKSCHER G.,"GROUP ORGANIZATION IN SWEDEN." SWEDEN STRATA ECO/DEV AGRI INDUS LABOR NAT/G PROF/ORG — LAISSEZ SOC

ECO/TAC CENTRAL SOCISM...MGT 19/20. PAGE 25 G0499

B40
MORSTEIN-MARX F.,PUBLIC MANAGEMENT IN THE NEW
DEMOCRACY. REPRESENT...MGT 20. PAGE 40 G0786
EX/STRUC
ADMIN
EXEC
PWR

B40
PFIFFNER J.M.,RESEARCH METHODS IN PUBLIC
ADMINISTRATION. USA-45 R+D...MGT STAT INT QU T 20.
PAGE 44 G0872
ADMIN
OP/RES
METH
TEC/DEV

B42
BINGHAM A.M.,THE TECHNIQUES OF DEMOCRACY. USA-45
CONSTN STRUCT POL/PAR LEGIS PLAN PARTIC CHOOSE
REPRESENT NAT/LISM TOTALISM...MGT 20. PAGE 7 G0136
POPULISM
ORD/FREE
ADMIN
NAT/G

B44
MERRIAM C.E.,PUBLIC AND PRIVATE GOVERNMENT.
VOL/ASSN EDU/PROP ADMIN REPRESENT EFFICIENCY PWR
PLURISM...MAJORIT CONCPT. PAGE 38 G0755
NAT/G
NEIGH
MGT
POLICY

B45
BAKER H.,PROBLEMS OF REEMPLOYMENT AND RETRAINING OF
MANPOWER DURING THE TRANSITION FROM WAR TO PEACE.
USA+45 INDUS LABOR LG/CO NAT/G PLAN ADMIN PEACE
...POLICY MGT 20. PAGE 5 G0086
BIBLIOG/A
ADJUST
WAR
PROB/SOLV

B45
BUSH V.,SCIENCE, THE ENDLESS FRONTIER. FUT USA-45
INTELL STRATA ACT/RES CREATE PLAN EDU/PROP ADMIN
NUC/PWR PEACE ATTIT HEALTH KNOWL...MAJORIT HEAL MGT
PHIL/SCI CONCPT OBS TREND 20. PAGE 10 G0195
R+D
NAT/G

B45
MAYO E.,THE SOCIAL PROBLEMS OF AN INDUSTRIAL
CIVILIZATION. USA+45 SOCIETY LABOR CROWD PERS/REL
LAISSEZ. PAGE 37 G0725
INDUS
GP/REL
MGT
WORKER

B46
BUSH V.,ENDLESS HORIZONS. FUT USA-45 INTELL NAT/G
CONSULT ACT/RES CREATE PLAN EDU/PROP DRIVE
...MAJORIT HEAL MGT PHIL/SCI CONCPT OBS TREND
GEN/METH TOT/POP 20. PAGE 10 G0196
R+D
KNOWL
PEACE

B47
WHITEHEAD T.N.,LEADERSHIP IN A FREE SOCIETY; A
STUDY IN HUMAN RELATIONS BASED ON AN ANALYSIS OF
PRESENT-DAY INDUSTRIAL CIVILIZATION. WOR-45 STRUCT
R+D LABOR LG/CO SML/CO WORKER PLAN PROB/SOLV
TEC/DEV DRIVE...MGT 20. PAGE 63 G1234
INDUS
LEAD
ORD/FREE
SOCIETY

B48
METZLER L.A.,INCOME, EMPLOYMENT, AND PUBLIC POLICY.
FINAN INDUS LOC/G NAT/G TAX GIVE PAY COST PRODUC
...MGT TIME/SEQ 20. PAGE 38 G0760
INCOME
WEALTH
POLICY
ECO/TAC

B48
PUBLIC ADMINISTRATION SERVICE,SOURCE MATERIALS IN
PUBLIC ADMINISTRATION: A SELECTED BIBLIOGRAPHY (PAS
PUBLICATION NO. 102). USA+45 LAW FINAN LOC/G MUNIC
NAT/G PLAN RECEIVE EDU/PROP CT/SYS CHOOSE HEALTH
20. PAGE 45 G0895
BIBLIOG/A
GOV/REL
MGT
ADMIN

S48
HARDIN L.M.,"REFLECTIONS ON AGRICULTURAL POLICY
FORMATION IN THE UNITED STATES." LEGIS PLAN BUDGET
ECO/TAC LEAD CENTRAL...MGT SOC NEW/IDEA STAT FAO.
PAGE 24 G0480
AGRI
POLICY
ADMIN
NEW/LIB

B49
LEPAWSKY A.,ADMINISTRATION. FINAN INDUS LG/CO
SML/CO INGP/REL PERS/REL COST EFFICIENCY OPTIMAL
SKILL 20. PAGE 33 G0656
ADMIN
MGT
WORKER
EX/STRUC

S49
MERTON R.,"THE ROLE OF APPLIED SOCIAL SCIENCE IN
THE FORMATION OF POLICY: A RESEARCH MEMORANDUM."
WOR+45 INDUS NAT/G EXEC ROUTINE CHOOSE ORD/FREE PWR
SKILL...POLICY MGT PSY METH/CNCPT TESTS CHARTS METH
VAL/FREE 20. PAGE 38 G0756
PLAN
SOC
DIPLOM

C51
HOMANS G.C.,"THE WESTERN ELECTRIC RESEARCHES" IN S.
HOSLETT, ED., HUMAN FACTORS IN MANAGEMENT (BMR)"
ACT/RES GP/REL HAPPINESS PRODUC DRIVE...MGT OBS 20.
PAGE 27 G0526
OP/RES
EFFICIENCY
SOC/EXP
WORKER

B52
DAY E.E.,EDUCATION FOR FREEDOM AND RESPONSIBILITY.
FUT USA+45 CULTURE CONSULT EDU/PROP ATTIT SKILL
...MGT CONCPT OBS GEN/LAWS COLD/WAR 20. PAGE 14
G0282
SCHOOL
KNOWL

L52
ROYAL INST. INT. AFF.,"ANNUAL REPORT OF THE
COUNCIL: 1951-1952." WOR+45 CREATE KNOWL...MGT
COLD/WAR CMN/WLTH TOT/POP VAL/FREE 20. PAGE 48
G0943
R+D
EDU/PROP

B53
LARSEN K.,NATIONAL BIBLIOGRAPHIC SERVICES: THEIR
CREATION AND OPERATION. WOR+45 COM/IND CREATE PLAN
DIPLOM PRESS ADMIN ROUTINE...MGT UNESCO. PAGE 32
G0636
BIBLIOG/A
INT/ORG
WRITING

B53
MACK R.T.,RAISING THE WORLDS STANDARD OF LIVING.
IRAN INT/ORG VOL/ASSN EX/STRUC ECO/TAC WEALTH...MGT
METH/CNCPT STAT CONT/OBS INT TOT/POP VAL/FREE 20
UN. PAGE 35 G0690
WOR+45
FOR/AID
INT/TRADE

B53
ROBINSON E.A.G.,THE STRUCTURE OF COMPETITIVE
INDUSTRY. UK ECO/DEV DIST/IND MARKET TEC/DEV DIPLOM
EDU/PROP ADMIN EFFICIENCY WEALTH...MGT 19/20.
PAGE 47 G0929
INDUS
PRODUC
WORKER
OPTIMAL

B53
SAYLES L.R.,THE LOCAL UNION. CONSTN CULTURE
DELIB/GP PARTIC CHOOSE GP/REL INGP/REL ATTIT ROLE
...MAJORIT DECISION MGT. PAGE 49 G0958
LABOR
LEAD
ADJUD
ROUTINE

B54
MCCLOSKEY J.F.,OPERATIONS RESEARCH FOR MANAGEMENT.
STRUCT COMPUTER ADMIN ROUTINE...PHIL/SCI CONCPT
METH/CNCPT TREND ANTHOL BIBLIOG 20. PAGE 37 G0731
OP/RES
MGT
METH/COMP
TEC/DEV

B54
PUBLIC ADMIN CLEARING HOUSE,PUBLIC ADMINISTRATIONS
ORGANIZATIONS: A DIRECTORY, 1954. USA+45 R+D PROVS
ACT/RES...MGT 20. PAGE 45 G0893
INDEX
VOL/ASSN
NAT/G
ADMIN

B54
WILENSKY H.L.,SYLLABUS OF INDUSTRIAL RELATIONS: A
GUIDE TO READING AND RESEARCH. USA+45 MUNIC ADMIN
INGP/REL...POLICY MGT PHIL/SCI 20. PAGE 63 G1239
BIBLIOG
INDUS
LABOR
WORKER

C54
CALDWELL L.K.,"THE GOVERNMENT AND ADMINISTRATION OF
NEW YORK." LOC/G MUNIC POL/PAR SCHOOL CHIEF LEGIS
PLAN TAX CT/SYS...MGT SOC/WK BIBLIOG 20 NEWYORK/C.
PAGE 10 G0202
PROVS
ADMIN
CONSTN
EX/STRUC

B55
RILEY V.,INTERINDUSTRY ECONOMIC STUDIES. USA+45
COMPUTER ADMIN OPTIMAL PRODUC...MGT CLASSIF STAT.
PAGE 47 G0922
BIBLIOG
ECO/DEV
PLAN
STRUCT

B55
SMITHIES A.,THE BUDGETARY PROCESS IN THE UNITED
STATES. ECO/DEV AGRI EX/STRUC FORCES LEGIS
PROB/SOLV TAX ROUTINE EFFICIENCY...MGT CONGRESS
PRESIDENT. PAGE 52 G1016
NAT/G
ADMIN
BUDGET
GOV/REL

L55
KISER M.,"ORGANIZATION OF AMERICAN STATES." L/A+17C
USA+45 ECO/UNDEV INT/ORG NAT/G PLAN TEC/DEV DIPLOM
ECO/TAC INT/TRADE EDU/PROP ADMIN ALL/VALS...POLICY
MGT RECORD ORG/CHARTS OAS 20. PAGE 30 G0601
VOL/ASSN
ECO/DEV
REGION

S55
DRUCKER P.F.,"'MANAGEMENT SCIENCE' AND THE
MANAGER." PLAN ROUTINE RIGID/FLEX...METH/CNCPT LOG
HYPO/EXP. PAGE 16 G0315
MGT
STRUCT
DECISION
RATIONAL

C55
BONER H.A.,"HUNGRY GENERATIONS." UK WOR+45 WOR-45
STRATA INDUS FAM LABOR CAP/ISM...MGT BIBLIOG 19/20.
PAGE 8 G0151
ECO/DEV
PHIL/SCI
CONCPT
WEALTH

B56
WASSERMAN P.,INFORMATION FOR ADMINISTRATORS: A
GUIDE TO PUBLICATIONS AND SERVICES FOR MANAGEMENT
IN BUSINESS AND GOVERNMENT. R+D LOC/G NAT/G
PROF/ORG VOL/ASSN PRESS...PSY SOC STAT 20. PAGE 62
G1219
BIBLIOG
MGT
KNOWL
EDU/PROP

S57

BAUMGARTEL H.,"LEADERSHIP STYLE AS A VARIABLE IN   LEAD
RESEARCH ADMINISTRATION." USA+45 ADMIN REPRESENT   EXEC
PERS/REL 20. PAGE 5 G0104   MGT
                                                         INGP/REL

S57

JANOWITZ M.,"MILITARY ELITES AND THE STUDY OF WAR."   FORCES
USA+45 WOR-45 STRATA NAT/G PROF/ORG TEC/DEV DOMIN   ELITES
EDU/PROP COERCE WAR ATTIT RIGID/FLEX PWR RESPECT
...MGT TREND STERTYP GEN/METH 20. PAGE 28 G0558

S57

TAYLOR P.S.,"THE RELATION OF RESEARCH TO   DECISION
LEGISLATIVE AND ADMINISTRATIVE DECISIONS." ELITES   LEGIS
ACT/RES PLAN PROB/SOLV CONFER CHOOSE POLICY.   MGT
PAGE 54 G1059   PWR

N57

US ARMY LIBRARY,THESES AND DISSERTATIONS IN THE   BIBLIOG
HOLDINGS OF THE ARMY LIBRARY (PAMPHLET). USA+45   FORCES
...INT/LAW PSY SOC 20. PAGE 56 G1105   MGT
                                                         CONTROL

B58

LIST OF PUBLICATIONS (PERIODICAL OR AD HOC) ISSUED   BIBLIOG
BY VARIOUS MINISTRIES OF THE GOVERNMENT OF INDIA   NAT/G
(3RD ED.). INDIA ECO/UNDEV PLAN...POLICY MGT 20.   ADMIN
PAGE 1 G0014

B58

ATOMIC INDUSTRIAL FORUM,MANAGEMENT AND ATOMIC   NUC/PWR
ENERGY. WOR+45 SEA LAW MARKET NAT/G TEC/DEV INSPECT   INDUS
INT/TRADE CONFER PEACE HEALTH...ANTHOL 20. PAGE 4   MGT
G0078   ECO/TAC

B58

GANGE J.,UNIVERSITY RESEARCH ON INTERNATIONAL   R+D
AFFAIRS. USA+45 ACADEM INT/ORG CONSULT CREATE EXEC   MGT
ROUTINE...QUANT STAT INT STERTYP GEN/METH TOT/POP   DIPLOM
VAL/FREE 20. PAGE 21 G0407

B58

OPERATIONS RESEARCH SOCIETY,A COMPREHENSIVE   BIBLIOG/A
BIBLIOGRAPHY ON OPERATIONS RESEARCH; THROUGH 1956   COMPUT/IR
WITH SUPPLEMENT FOR 1957. COM/IND DIST/IND INDUS   OP/RES
ADMIN...DECISION MATH STAT METH 20. PAGE 43 G0840   MGT

L58

FORRESTER J.W.,"INDUSTRIAL DYNAMICS* A MAJOR   INDUS
BREAKTHROUGH FOR DECISION MAKERS." COMPUTER OP/RES   ACT/RES
...DECISION CONCPT NEW/IDEA. PAGE 20 G0382   MGT
                                                         PROB/SOLV

S58

DEAN B.V.,"APPLICATION OF OPERATIONS RESEARCH TO   DECISION
MANAGERIAL DECISION MAKING" STRATA ACT/RES   OP/RES
PROB/SOLV ROLE...SOC PREDICT SIMUL 20. PAGE 15   MGT
G0288   METH/CNCPT

S58

FOLDES L.,"UNCERTAINTY, PROBABILITY AND POTENTIAL   PROBABIL
SURPRISE." MARKET PROB/SOLV RISK PERSON...DECISION   ADMIN
MGT HYPO/EXP GAME. PAGE 19 G0376   ROUTINE

B59

DAHRENDORF R.,CLASS AND CLASS CONFLICT IN   VOL/ASSN
INDUSTRIAL SOCIETY. LABOR NAT/G COERCE ROLE PLURISM   STRUCT
...POLICY MGT CONCPT CLASSIF. PAGE 14 G0271   SOC
                                                         GP/REL

B59

VERNEY D.V.,PUBLIC ENTERPRISE IN SWEDEN. FUT SWEDEN   ECO/DEV
UK INDUS POL/PAR LEGIS PROB/SOLV CAP/ISM INT/TRADE   POLICY
CONTROL SOCISM...MGT CONCPT NAT/COMP 20 SOCDEM/PAR   LG/CO
CIVIL/SERV. PAGE 61 G1196   NAT/G

B59

WASSERMAN P.,MEASUREMENT AND ANALYSIS OF   BIBLIOG/A
ORGANIZATIONAL PERFORMANCE. FINAN MARKET EX/STRUC   ECO/TAC
TEC/DEV EDU/PROP CONTROL ROUTINE TASK...MGT 20.   OP/RES
PAGE 62 G1220   EFFICIENCY

B59

WELTON H.,THE THIRD WORLD WAR; TRADE AND INDUSTRY,   INT/TRADE
THE NEW BATTLEGROUND. WOR+45 ECO/DEV INDUS MARKET   PLAN
TASK...MGT IDEA/COMP COLD/WAR. PAGE 63 G1229   DIPLOM

S59

BENDIX R.,"INDUSTRIALIZATION, IDEOLOGIES, AND   INDUS
SOCIAL STRUCTURE" (BMR)" UK USA-45 USSR STRUCT   ATTIT
WORKER GP/REL EFFICIENCY...IDEA/COMP 20. PAGE 6   MGT
G0117   ADMIN

S59

CALKINS R.D.,"THE DECISION PROCESS IN   ADMIN
ADMINISTRATION." EX/STRUC PROB/SOLV ROUTINE MGT.   OP/RES
PAGE 10 G0204   DECISION
                                                         CON/ANAL

S59

CYERT R.M.,"MODELS IN A BEHAVIORAL THEORY OF THE   SIMUL
FIRM." ROUTINE...DECISION MGT METH/CNCPT MATH.   GAME
PAGE 14 G0267   PREDICT
                                                         INDUS

B60

ALBI F.,TRATADO DE LOS MODOS DE GESTION DE LAS   LOC/G
CORPORACIONES LOCALES. SPAIN FINAN NAT/G BUDGET   LAW
CONTROL EXEC ROUTINE GOV/REL ORD/FREE SOVEREIGN   ADMIN
...MGT 20. PAGE 2 G0034   MUNIC

B60

ARROW K.J.,MATHEMATICAL METHODS IN THE SOCIAL   MATH
SCIENCES, 1959. TEC/DEV CHOOSE UTIL PERCEPT   PSY
...KNO/TEST GAME SIMUL ANTHOL. PAGE 4 G0070   MGT

B60

BOULDING K.E.,LINEAR PROGRAMMING AND THE THEORY OF   LG/CO
THE FIRM. ACT/RES PLAN...MGT MATH. PAGE 8 G0156   NEW/IDEA
                                                         COMPUTER

B60

CRAUMER L.V.,BUSINESS PERIODICALS INDEX (8VOLS.).   BIBLIOG/A
USA+45 LABOR TAX 20. PAGE 13 G0262   FINAN
                                                         ECO/DEV
                                                         MGT

B60

JANOWITZ M.,THE PROFESSIONAL SOLDIER. CULTURE   FORCES
STRATA STRUCT FAM PROB/SOLV TEC/DEV COERCE WAR   MYTH
CIVMIL/REL NAT/LISM AGE HEREDITY ALL/VALS CONSERVE   LEAD
...MGT WORSHIP. PAGE 28 G0560   ELITES

B60

MCGREGOR D.,THE HUMAN SIDE OF ENTERPRISE. USA+45   MGT
LEAD ROUTINE GP/REL INGP/REL...CONCPT GEN/LAWS 20.   ATTIT
PAGE 38 G0741   SKILL
                                                         EDU/PROP

B60

MORRIS W.T.,ENGINEERING ECONOMY. AUTOMAT RISK   OP/RES
RATIONAL...PROBABIL STAT CHARTS GAME SIMUL BIBLIOG   DECISION
T 20. PAGE 40 G0785   MGT
                                                         PROB/SOLV

B60

WEBSTER J.A.,A GENERAL STUDY OF THE DEPARTMENT OF   ORD/FREE
DEFENSE INTERNAL SECURITY PROGRAM. USA+45 WORKER   PLAN
TEC/DEV ADJUD CONTROL CT/SYS EXEC GOV/REL COST   ADMIN
...POLICY DECISION MGT 20 DEPT/DEFEN SUPREME/CT.   NAT/G
PAGE 62 G1221

B60

WOETZEL R.K.,THE INTERNATIONAL CONTROL OF AIRSPACE   INT/ORG
AND OUTERSPACE. FUT WOR+45 AIR CONSTN STRUCT   JURID
CONSULT PLAN TEC/DEV ADJUD RIGID/FLEX KNOWL   SPACE
ORD/FREE PWR...TECHNIC GEOG MGT NEW/IDEA TREND   INT/LAW
COMPUT/IR VAL/FREE 20 TREATY. PAGE 64 G1251

S60

HUNTINGTON S.P.,"STRATEGIC PLANNING AND THE   EXEC
POLITICAL PROCESS." USA+45 NAT/G DELIB/GP LEGIS   FORCES
ACT/RES ECO/TAC LEGIT ROUTINE CHOOSE RIGID/FLEX PWR   NUC/PWR
...POLICY MAJORIT MGT 20. PAGE 27 G0538   WAR

S60

HUTCHINSON C.E.,"AN INSTITUTE FOR NATIONAL SECURITY   POLICY
AFFAIRS." USA+45 R+D NAT/G CONSULT TOP/EX ACT/RES   METH/CNCPT
CREATE PLAN TEC/DEV EDU/PROP ROUTINE NUC/PWR ATTIT   ELITES
ORD/FREE PWR...DECISION MGT PHIL/SCI CONCPT RECORD   DIPLOM
GEN/LAWS GEN/METH 20. PAGE 27 G0539

S60

RAPP W.F.,"MANAGEMENT ANALYSIS AT THE HEADQUARTERS   INGP/REL
OF FEDERAL AGENCIES." USA+45 NAT/G 20. PAGE 46   ADMIN
G0903   EX/STRUC
                                                         MGT

S60

RIVKIN A.,"AFRICAN ECONOMIC DEVELOPMENT: ADVANCED   AFR
TECHNOLOGY AND THE STAGES OF GROWTH." CULTURE   TEC/DEV
ECO/UNDEV AGRI COM/IND EXTR/IND PLAN ECO/TAC ATTIT   FOR/AID
DRIVE RIGID/FLEX SKILL WEALTH...MGT SOC GEN/LAWS
WORK TOT/POP 20. PAGE 47 G0923

S60

SHUBIK M.,"BIBLIOGRAPHY ON SIMULATION, GAMING,   BIBLIOG
ARTIFICIAL INTELLIGENCE AND ALLIED TOPICS."   SIMUL
COMPUTER ROUTINE...DECISION MGT STAT 20. PAGE 50   GAME

G0992   OP/RES

                                                      B61
BRADY R.A.,ORGANIZATION, AUTOMATION, AND SOCIETY.   TEC/DEV
USA+45 AGRI COM/IND DIST/IND MARKET CREATE   INDUS
...DECISION MGT 20. PAGE 8 G0163   AUTOMAT
                                                    ADMIN

                                                      B61
CHAPPLE E.D.,THE MEASURE OF MANAGEMENT. USA+45   MGT
WORKER ADMIN GP/REL EFFICIENCY...DECISION   OP/RES
ORG/CHARTS SIMUL 20. PAGE 11 G0221   PLAN
                                                    METH/CNCPT

                                                      B61
GORDON W.J.J.,SYNECTICS; THE DEVELOPMENT OF   CREATE
CREATIVE CAPACITY. USA+45 PLAN TEC/DEV KNOWL WEALTH PROB/SOLV
...DECISION MGT 20. PAGE 22 G0436   ACT/RES
                                                    TOP/EX

                                                      B61
HELLER D.,THE KENNEDY CABINET--AMERICA'S MEN OF   EX/STRUC
DESTINY. NAT/G CHIEF CONSULT ADMIN CONTROL GOV/REL CONFER
...MGT 20 DEPT/LABOR DEPT/STATE DEPT/JUST   DELIB/GP
DEPT/DEFEN KENNEDY/J. PAGE 26 G0504   TOP/EX

                                                      B61
KRUPP S.,PATTERN IN ORGANIZATIONAL ANALYSIS: A   MGT
CRITICAL EXAMINATION. INGP/REL PERS/REL RATIONAL   CONTROL
ATTIT AUTHORIT DRIVE PWR...DECISION PHIL/SCI SOC   CONCPT
IDEA/COMP. PAGE 32 G0622   METH/CNCPT

                                                      B61
LEE R.R.,ENGINEERING-ECONOMIC PLANNING   BIBLIOG/A
MISCELLANEOUS SUBJECTS: A SELECTED BIBLIOGRAPHY   PLAN
(MIMEOGRAPHED). FINAN LOC/G MUNIC NEIGH ADMIN   REGION
CONTROL INGP/REL HABITAT...GEOG MGT SOC/WK 20
RESOURCE/N. PAGE 33 G0651

                                                      L61
COHEN K.J.,"THE ROLE OF MANAGEMENT GAMES IN   SOCIETY
EDUCATION AND RESEARCH." INTELL ECO/DEV FINAN   GAME
ACT/RES ECO/TAC DECISION. PAGE 12 G0240   MGT
                                                    EDU/PROP

                                                      L61
HERRING P.,"RESEARCH FOR PUBLIC POLICY: BROOKINGS   R+D
DEDICATION LECTURES." USA+45 CONSULT DELIB/GP   ACT/RES
ROUTINE PERCEPT SKILL...MGT 20. PAGE 26 G0508   DIPLOM

                                                      S61
BENNION E.G.,"ECONOMETRICS FOR MANAGEMENT." USA+45 ECOMETRIC
INDUS EX/STRUC ACT/RES COMPUTER UTIL...MATH STAT   MGT
PREDICT METH/COMP HYPO/EXP. PAGE 6 G0122   SIMUL
                                                    DECISION

                                                      S61
DYKMAN J.W.,"REVIEW ARTICLE* PLANNING AND DECISION DECISION
THEORY." ELITES LOC/G MUNIC CONSULT ADMIN...POLICY PLAN
MGT. PAGE 17 G0327   RATIONAL

                                                      S61
LINDSAY F.A.,"PLANNING IN FOREIGN AFFAIRS: THE   ECO/DEV
MISSING ELEMENT." FUT USA+45 ROUTINE SKILL...MGT   PLAN
TOT/POP 20. PAGE 34 G0669   DIPLOM

                                                      B62
BAKER G.W.,BEHAVIORAL SCIENCE AND CIVIL DEFENSE.   NUC/PWR
USA+45 PROB/SOLV ADMIN GP/REL INGP/REL PERS/REL   WAR
ANOMIE DRIVE PERSON...DECISION MGT SOC 20   POLICY
CIV/DEFENS. PAGE 4 G0085   ACT/RES

                                                      B62
BOCK E.A.,CASE STUDIES IN AMERICAN GOVERNMENT.   POLICY
USA+45 ECO/DEV CHIEF EDU/PROP CT/SYS RACE/REL   LEGIS
ORD/FREE...JURID MGT PHIL/SCI PRESIDENT CASEBOOK.   IDEA/COMP
PAGE 8 G0146   NAT/G

                                                      B62
DUCKWORTH W.E.,A GUIDE TO OPERATIONAL RESEARCH.   OP/RES
INDUS PLAN PROB/SOLV EXEC EFFICIENCY PRODUC KNOWL   GAME
...MGT MATH STAT SIMUL METH 20 MONTECARLO. PAGE 16 DECISION
G0319   ADMIN

                                                      B62
FERBER R.,RESEARCH METHODS IN ECONOMICS AND   ACT/RES
BUSINESS. ECO/DEV FINAN MARKET LG/CO SML/CO CONSULT PROB/SOLV
CONTROL COST...STAT METH/COMP 20. PAGE 19 G0364   ECO/TAC
                                                    MGT

                                                      B62
FORTUNE EDITORS,THE SPACE INDUSTRY: AMERICA'S   SPACE
NEWEST GIANT. USA+45 FINAN NAT/G BUDGET 20. PAGE 20 INDUS
G0383   TEC/DEV
                                                    MGT

                                                      B62
GRANICK D.,THE EUROPEAN EXECUTIVE. BELGIUM FRANCE   MGT
GERMANY/W UK INDUS LABOR LG/CO SML/CO EX/STRUC PLAN ECO/DEV
TEC/DEV CAP/ISM COST DEMAND...POLICY CHARTS 20.   ECO/TAC
PAGE 22 G0441   EXEC

                                                      B62
GUETZKOW H.,SIMULATION IN SOCIAL SCIENCE: READINGS. SIMUL
STRUCT OP/RES ADMIN AUTOMAT FEEDBACK...MGT PSY SOC TEC/DEV
STYLE BIBLIOG. PAGE 23 G0459   COMPUTER
                                                    GAME

                                                      B62
MARS D.,SUGGESTED LIBRARY IN PUBLIC ADMINISTRATION. BIBLIOG
FINAN DELIB/GP EX/STRUC WORKER COMPUTER ADJUD   ADMIN
...DECISION PSY SOC METH/COMP 20. PAGE 36 G0710   METH
                                                    MGT

                                                      B62
REICH C.A.,BUREAUCRACY AND THE FORESTS (PAMPHLET). ADMIN
USA+45 LOBBY...POLICY MGT 20. PAGE 46 G0910   CONTROL
                                                    EX/STRUC
                                                    REPRESENT

                                                      B62
STAHL O.G.,PUBLIC PERSONNEL ADMINISTRATION. LOC/G   ADMIN
TOP/EX CREATE PLAN ROUTINE...TECHNIC MGT T. PAGE 52 WORKER
G1030   EX/STRUC
                                                    NAT/G

                                                      B62
THANT U.,THE UNITED NATIONS' DEVELOPMENT DECADE: INT/ORG
PROPOSALS FOR ACTION. WOR+45 SOCIETY ECO/UNDEV AGRI ALL/VALS
COM/IND FINAN R+D MUNIC SCHOOL VOL/ASSN CONSULT
PLAN TEC/DEV ECO/TAC EDU/PROP ADMIN ROUTINE
RIGID/FLEX...MGT SOC CONCPT UNESCO UN TOT/POP
VAL/FREE. PAGE 54 G1064

                                                      L62
LINS L.J.,"BASIS FOR DECISION: A COMPOSITE OF   DECISION
CURRENT INSTITUTIONAL RESEARCH METHODS OF COLLEGES ACADEM
AND UNIVERSITIES" ADMIN MGT. PAGE 34 G0671   R+D
                                                    ACT/RES

                                                      S62
ALBONETTI A.,"IL SECONDO PROGRAMMA QUINQUENNALE   R+D
1963-67 ED IL BILANCIO RICERCHE ED INVESTIMENTI PER PLAN
IL 1963 DELL'ERATOM." EUR+WWI FUT ITALY WOR+45   NUC/PWR
ECO/DEV SERV/IND INT/ORG TEC/DEV ECO/TAC ATTIT
SKILL WEALTH...MGT TIME/SEQ OEEC 20. PAGE 2 G0035

                                                      S62
GORDON B.K.,"NUCLEAR WEAPONS: RUSSIAN AND   ORD/FREE
AMERICAN." COM USA+45 USSR NAT/G FORCES ACT/RES   COERCE
TEC/DEV PERCEPT RIGID/FLEX PWR SKILL...MGT   NUC/PWR
METH/CNCPT QUANT OBS TIME/SEQ CON/ANAL GEN/METH
TOT/POP VAL/FREE 20. PAGE 22 G0433

                                                      S62
WALTER E.,"VERS UNE CLASSIFICATION SCIENTIFIQUE DE PLAN
LA SOCIOLOGIA." UNIV CULTURE INTELL SOCIETY R+D   CONCPT
ACT/RES LEGIT ROUTINE ATTIT KNOWL...JURID MGT TREND
GEN/LAWS 20. PAGE 62 G1208

                                                      B63
ACKOFF R.L.,A MANAGER'S GUIDE TO OPERATIONS   OP/RES
RESEARCH. STRUCT INDUS PROB/SOLV ROUTINE 20. PAGE 2 MGT
G0028   GP/REL
                                                    ADMIN

                                                      B63
BONINI C.P.,SIMULATION OF INFORMATION AND DECISION INDUS
SYSTEMS IN THE FIRM. MARKET BUDGET DOMIN EDU/PROP   SIMUL
ADMIN COST ATTIT HABITAT PERCEPT PWR...CONCPT   DECISION
PROBABIL QUANT PREDICT HYPO/EXP BIBLIOG. PAGE 8   MGT
G0152

                                                      B63
BURSK E.C.,NEW DECISION-MAKING TOOLS FOR MANAGERS. DECISION
COMPUTER PLAN PROB/SOLV ROUTINE COST. PAGE 10 G0194 MGT
                                                    MATH
                                                    RIGID/FLEX

                                                      B63
DEAN A.L.,FEDERAL AGENCY APPROACHES TO FIELD   ADMIN
MANAGEMENT (PAMPHLET). R+D DELIB/GP EX/STRUC   MGT
PROB/SOLV GOV/REL...CLASSIF BIBLIOG 20 FAA NASA   NAT/G
DEPT/HEW POSTAL/SYS IRS. PAGE 15 G0287   OP/RES

                                                      B63
HAUSMAN W.H.,MANAGING ECONOMIC DEVELOPMENT IN   ECO/UNDEV
AFRICA. AFR USA+45 LAW FINAN WORKER TEC/DEV WEALTH PLAN
...ANTHOL 20. PAGE 25 G0492   FOR/AID
                                                    MGT

HERNDON J.,A SELECTED BIBLIOGRAPHY OF MATERIALS IN
STATE GOVERNMENT AND POLITICS (PAMPHLET). USA+45
POL/PAR LEGIS ADMIN CHOOSE MGT. PAGE 26 G0507
B63
BIBLIOG
GOV/COMP
PROVS
DECISION

HEYEL C.,THE ENCYCLOPEDIA OF MANAGEMENT. WOR+45
MARKET TOP/EX TEC/DEV AUTOMAT LEAD ADJUST...STAT
CHARTS GAME ANTHOL BIBLIOG. PAGE 26 G0509
B63
MGT
INDUS
ADMIN
FINAN

HOWER R.M.,MANAGERS AND SCIENTISTS. EX/STRUC CREATE
ADMIN REPRESENT ATTIT DRIVE ROLE PWR SKILL...SOC
INT. PAGE 27 G0532
B63
R+D
MGT
PERS/REL
INGP/REL

KAST F.E.,SCIENCE, TECHNOLOGY, AND MANAGEMENT.
SPACE USA+45 FORCES CONFER DETER NUC/PWR...PHIL/SCI
CHARTS ANTHOL BIBLIOG 20 NASA. PAGE 30 G0581
B63
MGT
PLAN
TEC/DEV
PROB/SOLV

KORNHAUSER W.,SCIENTISTS IN INDUSTRY: CONFLICT AND
ACCOMMODATION. USA+45 R+D LG/CO NAT/G TEC/DEV
CONTROL ADJUST ATTIT...MGT STAT INT BIBLIOG 20.
PAGE 31 G0614
B63
CREATE
INDUS
PROF/ORG
GP/REL

LITTERER J.A.,ORGANIZATIONS: STRUCTURE AND
BEHAVIOR. PLAN DOMIN CONTROL LEAD ROUTINE SANCTION
INGP/REL EFFICIENCY PRODUC DRIVE RIGID/FLEX PWR.
PAGE 34 G0674
B63
ADMIN
CREATE
MGT
ADJUST

MCDONOUGH A.M.,INFORMATION ECONOMICS AND MANAGEMENT
SYSTEMS. ECO/DEV OP/RES AUTOMAT EFFICIENCY 20.
PAGE 37 G0735
B63
COMPUT/IR
MGT
CONCPT
COMPUTER

RAUDSEPP E.,MANAGING CREATIVE SCIENTISTS AND
ENGINEERS. USA+45 ECO/DEV LG/CO GP/REL PERS/REL
PRODUC. PAGE 46 G0906
B63
MGT
CREATE
R+D
ECO/TAC

THORELLI H.B.,INTOP: INTERNATIONAL OPERATIONS
SIMULATION: PLAYER'S MANUAL. BRAZIL FINAN OP/RES
ADMIN GP/REL INGP/REL PRODUC PERCEPT...DECISION MGT
EEC. PAGE 54 G1073
B63
GAME
INT/TRADE
EDU/PROP
LG/CO

UN SECRETARY GENERAL,PLANNING FOR ECONOMIC
DEVELOPMENT. ECO/UNDEV FINAN BUDGET INT/TRADE
TARIFFS TAX ADMIN 20 UN. PAGE 55 G1089
B63
PLAN
ECO/TAC
MGT
NAT/COMP

WALES H.G.,A BASIC BIBLIOGRAPHY ON MARKETING
RESEARCH (REV. ED.). ATTIT...MGT STAT INT QU SAMP
TREND 20. PAGE 62 G1206
B63
BIBLIOG/A
MARKET
OP/RES
METH/COMP

GANDILHON J.,"LA SCIENCE ET LA TECHNIQUE A L'AIDE
DES REGIONS PEU DEVELOPPEES." FRANCE FUT WOR+45
ECO/DEV R+D PROF/ORG ACT/RES PLAN...MGT TOT/POP
VAL/FREE 20 UN. PAGE 21 G0406
S63
ECO/UNDEV
TEC/DEV
FOR/AID

NADLER E.B.,"SOME ECONOMIC DISADVANTAGES OF THE
ARMS RACE." USA+45 INDUS R+D FORCES PLAN TEC/DEV
ECO/TAC FOR/AID EDU/PROP PWR WEALTH...TREND
COLD/WAR 20. PAGE 41 G0800
S63
ECO/DEV
MGT
BAL/PAY

RECENT PUBLICATIONS ON GOVERNMENTAL PROBLEMS. FINAN
INDUS ACADEM PLAN PROB/SOLV EDU/PROP ADJUD ADMIN
BIO/SOC...MGT SOC. PAGE 1 G0017
B64
BIBLIOG
AUTOMAT
LEGIS
JURID

BRIGHT J.R.,RESEARCH, DEVELOPMENT AND TECHNOLOGICAL
INNOVATION. CULTURE R+D CREATE PLAN PROB/SOLV
AUTOMAT RISK PERSON...DECISION CONCPT PREDICT
BIBLIOG. PAGE 9 G0168
B64
TEC/DEV
NEW/IDEA
INDUS
MGT

COOMBS C.H.,A THEORY OF DATA....MGT PHIL/SCI SOC
CLASSIF MATH PROBABIL STAT QU. PAGE 13 G0254
B64
CON/ANAL
GEN/METH
TESTS
PSY

DIEBOLD J.,BEYOND AUTOMATION: MANAGERIAL PROBLEMS
OF AN EXPLODING TECHNOLOGY. SOCIETY ECO/DEV CREATE
ECO/TAC AUTOMAT SKILL...TECHNIC MGT WORK. PAGE 16
G0303
B64
FUT
INDUS
PROVS
NAT/G

EDELMAN M.,THE SYMBOLIC USES OF POWER. USA+45
EX/STRUC CONTROL GP/REL INGP/REL...MGT T. PAGE 17
G0333
B64
CLIENT
PWR
EXEC
ELITES

FALK L.A.,ADMINISTRATIVE ASPECTS OF GROUP PRACTICE.
USA+45 FINAN PROF/ORG PLAN MGT. PAGE 18 G0358
B64
BIBLIOG/A
HEAL
ADMIN
SERV/IND

HAMMOND P.E.,SOCIOLOGISTS AT WORK. VOL/ASSN OP/RES
TEC/DEV CONFER ROUTINE TASK EFFICIENCY...MGT
NEW/IDEA STYLE SAMP. PAGE 24 G0478
B64
R+D
BIOG
SOC

HAZLEWOOD A.,THE ECONOMICS OF DEVELOPMENT: AN
ANNOTATED LIST OF BOOKS AND ARTICLES PUBLISHED
1958-1962. AGRI FINAN INDUS LABOR NAT/G DIPLOM
INT/TRADE INCOME...MGT 20. PAGE 25 G0497
B64
BIBLIOG/A
ECO/UNDEV
TEC/DEV

HODGETTS J.E.,ADMINISTERING THE ATOM FOR PEACE.
OP/RES TEC/DEV ADMIN...IDEA/COMP METH/COMP 20.
PAGE 26 G0517
B64
PROB/SOLV
NUC/PWR
PEACE
MGT

MARRIS R.,THE ECONOMIC THEORY OF "MANAGERIAL"
CAPITALISM. USA+45 ECO/DEV LG/CO ECO/TAC DEMAND
...CHARTS BIBLIOG 20. PAGE 36 G0709
B64
CAP/ISM
MGT
CONTROL
OP/RES

ORTH C.D.,ADMINISTERING RESEARCH AND DEVELOPMENT.
FINAN PLAN PROB/SOLV ADMIN ROUTINE...METH/CNCPT
STAT CHARTS METH 20. PAGE 43 G0847
B64
MGT
R+D
LG/CO
INDUS

PARANJAPE H.K.,THE FLIGHT OF TECHNICAL PERSONNEL IN
PUBLIC UNDERTAKINGS. INDIA PAY DEMAND HAPPINESS
ORD/FREE...MGT QU 20 MIGRATION. PAGE 44 G0858
B64
ADMIN
NAT/G
WORKER
PLAN

SCHERER F.M.,THE WEAPONS ACQUISITION PROCESS:
ECONOMIC INCENTIVES. BOSTON: DIVISION OF RESEARCH,
GRADUATE SCHOOL OF BUSINESS. USA+45 FINAN NAT/G
DELIB/GP ECO/TAC RIGID/FLEX WEALTH...MGT MATH STAT
CHARTS VAL/FREE 20. PAGE 49 G0965
B64
INDUS
ACT/RES
WEAPON

FLORINSKY M.T.,"TRENDS IN THE SOVIET ECONOMY." COM
USA+45 USSR INDUS LABOR NAT/G TEC/DEV ECO/TAC
ALL/VALS SOCISM...MGT METH/CNCPT STYLE CON/ANAL
GEN/METH WORK 20. PAGE 19 G0374
S64
ECO/DEV
AGRI

GARDNER R.N.,"GATT AND THE UNITED NATIONS
CONFERENCE ON TRADE AND DEVELOPMENT." USA+45 WOR+45
SOCIETY ECO/UNDEV MARKET NAT/G DELIB/GP ACT/RES
PLAN ECO/TAC TARIFFS EDU/PROP ROUTINE DRIVE
RIGID/FLEX WEALTH...DECISION MGT TREND UN TOT/POP
20 GATT. PAGE 21 G0411
S64
INT/ORG
INT/TRADE

NEEDHAM T.,"SCIENCE AND SOCIETY IN EAST AND WEST."
INTELL STRATA R+D LOC/G NAT/G PROVS CONSULT ACT/RES
CREATE PLAN TEC/DEV EDU/PROP ADMIN ATTIT ALL/VALS
...POLICY RELATIV MGT CONCPT NEW/IDEA TIME/SEQ WORK
WORK. PAGE 41 G0815
S64
ASIA
STRUCT

STONE P.A.,"DECISION TECHNIQUES FOR TOWN
DEVELOPMENT." PLAN COST PROFIT...DECISION MGT
CON/ANAL CHARTS METH/COMP BIBLIOG 20. PAGE 53 G1039
S64
OP/RES
MUNIC
ADMIN
PROB/SOLV

THOMPSON V.A.,"ADMINISTRATIVE OBJECTIVES FOR
DEVELOPMENT ADMINISTRATION." WOR+45 CREATE PLAN
DOMIN EDU/PROP EXEC ROUTINE ATTIT ORD/FREE PWR
...POLICY GEN/LAWS VAL/FREE. PAGE 54 G1070
S64
ECO/UNDEV
MGT

ANTHONY R.N.,PLANNING AND CONTROL SYSTEMS. UNIV
OP/RES...DECISION MGT LING. PAGE 3 G0061
B65
CONTROL
PLAN

METH
HYPO/EXP

B65

BARISH N.N.,MANAGEMENT SCIENCES IN THE EMERGING
COUNTRIES. AFR CHINA/COM WOR+45 FINAN INDUS PLAN
PRODUC HABITAT...ANTHOL 20. PAGE 5 G0093

ECO/UNDEV
OP/RES
MGT
TEC/DEV

B65

DORFMAN R.,MEASURING BENEFITS OF GOVERNMENT
INVESTMENTS. ECO/DEV R+D ECO/TAC PROFIT UTIL...MGT
GEN/METH. PAGE 16 G0308

PLAN
RATION
EFFICIENCY
OPTIMAL

B65

FRUTKIN A.W.,SPACE AND THE INTERNATIONAL
COOPERATION YEAR: A NATIONAL CHALLENGE (PAMPHLET).
EUR+WWI USA+45 FINAN TEC/DEV BUDGET...MGT 20 NASA.
PAGE 20 G0396

SPACE
INDUS
NAT/G
DIPLOM

B65

INTERNATIONAL CITY MGRS ASSN,COUNCIL-MANAGER
GOVERNMENT, 1940-64: AN ANNOTATED BIBLIOGRAPHY.
USA+45 ADMIN GOV/REL ROLE...MGT 20. PAGE 28 G0549

BIBLIOG/A
MUNIC
CONSULT
PLAN

B65

KANTOROVICH L.V.,THE BEST USE OF ECONOMIC
RESOURCES. USSR SOCIETY FINAN ACT/RES TEC/DEV
ECO/TAC PRICE CONTROL COST DEMAND EFFICIENCY
OPTIMAL...MGT STAT. PAGE 29 G0572

PLAN
MATH
DECISION

B65

STEINER G.A.,THE CREATIVE ORGANIZATION. ELITES
LG/CO PLAN PROB/SOLV TEC/DEV INSPECT CAP/ISM
CONTROL EXEC PERSON...METH/COMP HYPO/EXP 20.
PAGE 52 G1034

CREATE
MGT
ADMIN
SOC

B65

US SENATE COMM GOVT OPERATIONS,ORGANIZATION OF
FEDERAL EXECUTIVE DEPARTMENTS AND AGENCIES: REPORT
OF MARCH 23, 1965. USA+45 FORCES LEGIS DIPLOM
ROUTINE CIVMIL/REL EFFICIENCY FEDERAL...MGT STAT.
PAGE 60 G1179

ADMIN
EX/STRUC
GOV/REL
ORG/CHARTS

B65

VEINOTT A.F. JR.,MATHEMATICAL STUDIES IN MANAGEMENT
SCIENCE. UNIV INDUS COMPUTER ADMIN...DECISION
NET/THEORY SIMUL 20. PAGE 61 G1193

MATH
MGT
PLAN
PRODUC

S65

BALDWIN H.,"SLOW-DOWN IN THE PENTAGON." USA+45
CREATE PLAN GOV/REL CENTRAL COST EFFICIENCY PWR
...MGT MCNAMARA/R. PAGE 5 G0088

RECORD
R+D
WEAPON
ADMIN

S65

DEAN B.V.,"CONTRACT RESEARCH PROPOSAL PREPARATION
STRATEGIES." ECO/TAC WEALTH...MGT SIMUL. PAGE 15
G0289

USA+45
PROC/MFG
R+D
PLAN

S65

GRENIEWSKI H.,"INTENTION AND PERFORMANCE: A PRIMER
OF CYBERNETICS OF PLANNING." EFFICIENCY OPTIMAL
KNOWL SKILL...DECISION MGT EQUILIB. PAGE 23 G0448

SIMUL
GAME
GEN/METH
PLAN

S65

HUGHES T.L.,"SCHOLARS AND FOREIGN POLICY* VARIETIES
OF RESEARCH EXPERIENCE." COM/IND DIPLOM ADMIN EXEC
ROUTINE...MGT OBS CONGRESS PRESIDENT CAMELOT.
PAGE 27 G0535

ACT/RES
ACADEM
CONTROL
NAT/G

S65

TENDLER J.D.,"TECHNOLOGY AND ECONOMIC DEVELOPMENT*
THE CASE OF HYDRO VS THERMAL POWER." CONSTRUC
DIST/IND CREATE TEC/DEV INT/TRADE CENTRAL PWR SKILL
WEALTH...MGT NAT/COMP ARGEN. PAGE 54 G1063

BRAZIL
INDUS
ECO/UNDEV

B66

ALEXANDER Y.,INTERNATIONAL TECHNICAL ASSISTANCE
EXPERTS* A CASE STUDY OF THE U.N. EXPERIENCE.
ECO/UNDEV CONSULT EX/STRUC CREATE PLAN DIPLOM
FOR/AID TASK EFFICIENCY...ORG/CHARTS UN. PAGE 2
G0038

ECO/TAC
INT/ORG
ADMIN
MGT

B66

GREEN P.,DEADLY LOGIC* THE THEORY OF NUCLEAR
DETERRENCE. USA+45 ACT/RES OP/RES NUC/PWR RATIONAL
ALL/VALS PWR...DECISION MGT PHIL/SCI QUANT
IDEA/COMP GAME. PAGE 23 G0444

DETER
ACADEM
GEN/LAWS
RECORD

B66

HALPIN A.W.,THEORY AND RESEARCH IN ADMINISTRATION.
ACT/RES LEAD...MGT IDEA/COMP METH/COMP. PAGE 24
G0475

GEN/LAWS
EDU/PROP
ADMIN
PHIL/SCI

B66

KURAKOV I.G.,SCIENCE, TECHNOLOGY AND COMMUNISM;
SOME QUESTIONS OF DEVELOPMENT (TRANS. BY CARIN
DEDIJER). USSR INDUS PLAN PROB/SOLV COST PRODUC
...MGT MATH CHARTS METH 20. PAGE 32 G0626

CREATE
TEC/DEV
MARXISM
ECO/TAC

B66

LINDFORS G.V.,INTERCOLLEGIATE BIBLIOGRAPHY; CASES
IN BUSINESS ADMINISTRATION (VOL. X). FINAN MARKET
LABOR CONSULT PLAN GP/REL PRODUC 20. PAGE 34 G0668

BIBLIOG/A
ADMIN
MGT
OP/RES

B66

ONYEMELUKWE C.C.,PROBLEMS OF INDUSTRIAL PLANNING
AND MANAGEMENT IN NIGERIA. AFR FINAN LABOR DELIB/GP
TEC/DEV ADJUST...MGT TREND BIBLIOG. PAGE 43 G0839

ECO/UNDEV
ECO/TAC
INDUS
PLAN

B66

ROSHOLT R.L.,AN ADMINISTRATIVE HISTORY OF NASA,
1958-1963. SPACE USA+45 FINAN LEAD...MGT CHARTS
BIBLIOG 20 NASA. PAGE 48 G0938

ADMIN
EX/STRUC
ADJUST
DELIB/GP

B66

SCHURMANN F.,IDEOLOGY AND ORGANIZATION IN COMMUNIST
CHINA. CHINA/COM LOC/G MUNIC POL/PAR ECO/TAC
CONTROL ATTIT...MGT STERTYP 20 COM/PARTY. PAGE 50
G0981

MARXISM
STRUCT
ADMIN
NAT/G

B66

US BUREAU OF THE BUDGET,THE ADMINISTRATION OF
GOVERNMENT SUPPORTED RESEARCH AT UNIVERSITIES
(PAMPHLET). USA+45 CONSULT TOP/EX ADMIN INCOME
WEALTH...MGT PHIL/SCI INT. PAGE 56 G1108

ACT/RES
NAT/G
ACADEM
GP/REL

B66

US DEPARTMENT OF LABOR,TECHNOLOGICAL TRENDS IN
MAJOR AMERICAN INDUSTRIES. USA+45 R+D LABOR GP/REL
PRODUC...MGT BIBLIOG 20. PAGE 57 G1120

TEC/DEV
INDUS
TREND
AUTOMAT

B66

YOUNG W.,EXISTING MECHANISMS OF ARMS CONTROL.
PROC/MFG OP/RES DIPLOM TASK CENTRAL...MGT TREATY.
PAGE 65 G1266

ARMS/CONT
ADMIN
NUC/PWR
ROUTINE

S66

FLEMING W.G.,"AUTHORITY, EFFICIENCY, AND ROLE
STRESS: PROBLEMS IN THE DEVELOPMENT OF EAST AFRICAN
BUREAUCRACIES." AFR UGANDA STRUCT PROB/SOLV ROUTINE
INGP/REL ROLE...MGT SOC GP/COMP GOV/COMP 20
TANGANYIKA AFRICA/E. PAGE 19 G0371

DOMIN
EFFICIENCY
COLONIAL
ADMIN

N66

PRINCETON U INDUSTRIAL REL SEC,RECENT MATERIAL ON
COLLECTIVE BARGAINING IN GOVERNMENT (PAMPHLET NO.
130). USA+45 ECO/DEV LABOR WORKER ECO/TAC GOV/REL
...MGT 20. PAGE 45 G0890

BIBLIOG/A
BARGAIN
NAT/G
GP/REL

B67

BENNETT J.W.,HUTTERIAN BRETHREN; THE AGRICULTURAL
ECONOMY AND SOCIAL ORGANIZATION OF A COMMUNAL
PEOPLE. USA+45 SOCIETY FAM KIN TEC/DEV ADJUST...MGT
AUD/VIS GP/COMP 20. PAGE 6 G0121

SECT
AGRI
STRUCT
GP/REL

B67

BUDER S.,PULLMAN: AN EXPERIMENT IN INDUSTRIAL ORDER
AND COMMUNITY PLANNING, 1880-1930. USA-45 SOCIETY
LABOR LG/CO CREATE PROB/SOLV CONTROL GP/REL
EFFICIENCY ATTIT...MGT BIBLIOG 19/20 PULLMAN.
PAGE 9 G0184

DIST/IND
INDUS
MUNIC
PLAN

B67

DICKSON P.G.M.,THE FINANCIAL REVOLUTION IN ENGLAND.
UK NAT/G TEC/DEV ADMIN GOV/REL...SOC METH/CNCPT
CHARTS GP/COMP BIBLIOG 17/18. PAGE 15 G0302

ECO/DEV
FINAN
CAP/ISM
MGT

B67

DONALD A.G.,MANAGEMENT, INFORMATION, AND SYSTEMS.
WOR+45 LG/CO PROB/SOLV CONTROL FEEDBACK KNOWL MGT.
PAGE 16 G0306

ROUTINE
TEC/DEV
CONCPT
ADMIN

B67

ELDREDGE H.W.,TAMING MEGALOPOLIS; HOW TO MANAGE AN
URBANIZED WORLD. WOR+45 SOCIETY ECO/DEV ECO/UNDEV
NAT/G COMPUTER CREATE PARTIC EFFICIENCY WEALTH

MUNIC
TEC/DEV
PLAN

...MGT ANTHOL. PAGE 17 G0342   PROB/SOLV

B67
ENKE S.,DEFENSE MANAGEMENT. USA+45 R+D FORCES   DECISION
WORKER PLAN ECO/TAC ADMIN NUC/PWR BAL/PAY UTIL   DELIB/GP
WEALTH...MGT DEPT/DEFEN. PAGE 18 G0348   EFFICIENCY
                                                     BUDGET

B67
FIELD M.G.,SOVIET SOCIALIZED MEDICINE. USSR FINAN   PUB/INST
R+D PROB/SOLV ADMIN SOCISM...MGT SOC CONCPT 20.   HEALTH
PAGE 19 G0366   NAT/G
                                                     MARXISM

B67
GOLEMBIEWSKI R.T.,ORGANIZING MEN AND POWER: ADMIN
PATTERNS OF BEHAVIOR AND LINESTAFF MODELS. WOR+45   CONTROL
EX/STRUC ACT/RES DOMIN PERS/REL...NEW/IDEA 20.   SIMUL
PAGE 22 G0431   MGT

B67
GROSSMAN G.,ECONOMIC SYSTEMS. USA+45 USA-45 USSR   ECO/DEV
YUGOSLAVIA WORKER CAP/ISM PRICE GP/REL EQUILIB   PLAN
WEALTH MARXISM SOCISM...MGT METH/COMP 19/20.   TEC/DEV
PAGE 23 G0456   DEMAND

B67
HIRSCHMAN A.O.,DEVELOPMENT PROJECTS OBSERVED. INDUS ECO/UNDEV
INT/ORG CONSULT EX/STRUC CREATE OP/RES ECO/TAC   R+D
DEMAND...POLICY MGT METH/COMP 20 WORLD/BANK.   FINAN
PAGE 26 G0513   PLAN

B67
NORTHRUP H.R.,RESTRICTIVE LABOR PRACTICES IN THE   DIST/IND
SUPERMARKET INDUSTRY. USA+45 INDUS WORKER TEC/DEV   MARKET
BARGAIN PAY CONTROL GP/REL COST...STAT CHARTS NLRB. LABOR
PAGE 42 G0827   MGT

B67
PORWIT K.,CENTRAL PLANNING: EVALUATION OF VARIANTS. PLAN
PRICE OPTIMAL PRODUC...DECISION MATH CHARTS SIMUL   MGT
BIBLIOG 20. PAGE 45 G0886   ECOMETRIC

B67
SCHUMACHER B.G.,COMPUTER DYNAMICS IN PUBLIC   COMPUTER
ADMINISTRATION. USA+45 CREATE PLAN TEC/DEV...MGT   COMPUT/IR
LING CON/ANAL BIBLIOG/A 20. PAGE 50 G0980   ADMIN
                                                     AUTOMAT

B67
UNIVERSAL REFERENCE SYSTEM,ADMINISTRATIVE   BIBLIOG/A
MANAGEMENT: PUBLIC AND PRIVATE BUREAUCRACY (VOLUME   MGT
IV). WOR+45 WOR-45 ECO/DEV LG/CO LOC/G PUB/INST   ADMIN
VOL/ASSN GOV/REL...COMPUT/IR GEN/METH. PAGE 56   NAT/G
G1096

B67
UNIVERSAL REFERENCE SYSTEM,PUBLIC POLICY AND THE   BIBLIOG/A
MANAGEMENT OF SCIENCE (VOLUME IX). FUT SPACE WOR+45 POLICY
LAW NAT/G TEC/DEV CONTROL NUC/PWR GOV/REL   MGT
...COMPUT/IR GEN/METH. PAGE 56 G1100   PHIL/SCI

B67
YAVITZ B.,AUTOMATION IN COMMERCIAL BANKING. USA+45   TEC/DEV
STRUCT WORKER CREATE OP/RES PLAN ROLE...DECISION   FINAN
SAMP/SIZ. PAGE 64 G1263   COMPUT/IR
                                                     MGT

L67
RUTH J.M.,"THE ADMINISTRATION OF WATER RESOURCES IN EFFICIENCY
GUATEMALA." GUATEMALA L/A+17C DIST/IND LOC/G NAT/G   ECO/UNDEV
EX/STRUC ADMIN GOV/REL DEMAND EQUILIB WEALTH...GEOG PLAN
MGT 20. PAGE 48 G0952   ACT/RES

S67
BROWN W.B.,"MODEL-BUILDING AND ORGANIZATIONS."   MGT
CONTROL FEEDBACK...PROBABIL CHARTS METH/COMP.   ADMIN
PAGE 9 G0179   GAME
                                                     COMPUTER

S67
LEVENSTEIN A.,"TECHNOLOGICAL CHANGE, WORK, AND   TEC/DEV
HUMAN VALUES." WOR+45 SOCIETY AUTOMAT ROUTINE   CULTURE
LEISURE INGP/REL ADJUST TECHRACY...MGT CONCPT.   ALL/VALS
PAGE 33 G0660   TIME/SEQ

S67
MACDONALD G.J.F.,"SCIENCE AND SPACE POLICY* HOW   SPACE
DOES IT GET PLANNED?" R+D CREATE TEC/DEV BUDGET   PLAN
ADMIN ROUTINE...DECISION NASA. PAGE 35 G0687   MGT
                                                     EX/STRUC

S67
MORTON J.A.,"A SYSTEMS APPROACH TO THE INNOVATION   TEC/DEV
PROCESS: ITS USE IN THE BELL SYSTEM." USA+45 INTELL GEN/METH
INDUS LG/CO CONSULT WORKER COMPUTER AUTOMAT DEMAND   R+D

...MGT CHARTS 20. PAGE 40 G0787   COM/IND

S67
RICHMAN B.M.,"SOVIET MANAGEMENT IN TRANSITION."   MGT
USSR FINAN MARKET EX/STRUC PLAN PROB/SOLV TEC/DEV   MARXISM
CONTROL LEAD CENTRAL EFFICIENCY...METH/COMP 20   POLICY
REFORMERS. PAGE 47 G0917   AUTHORIT

S67
ROBERTS E.B.,"THE PROBLEM OF AGING ORGANIZATIONS."   INDUS
INTELL PROB/SOLV ADMIN EXEC FEEDBACK EFFICIENCY   R+D
PRODUC...GEN/LAWS 20. PAGE 47 G0926   MGT
                                                     PLAN

S67
SKOLNIKOFF E.B.,"MAKING FOREIGN POLICY" PROB/SOLV   TEC/DEV
EFFICIENCY PERCEPT PWR...MGT METH/CNCPT CLASSIF 20. CONTROL
PAGE 51 G1009   USA+45
                                                     NAT/G

S67
VERGIN R.C.,"COMPUTER INDUCED ORGANIZATION   COMPUTER
CHANGES." FUT USA+45 R+D CREATE OP/RES TEC/DEV   DECISION
ADJUST CENTRAL...MGT INT CON/ANAL COMPUT/IR.   AUTOMAT
PAGE 61 G1194   EX/STRUC

S67
WEIL G.L.,"THE MERGER OF THE INSTITUTIONS OF THE   ECO/TAC
EUROPEAN COMMUNITIES" EUR+WWI ECO/DEV INT/TRADE   INT/ORG
CONSEN PLURISM...DECISION MGT 20 EEC EURATOM ECSC   CENTRAL
TREATY. PAGE 62 G1223   INT/LAW

S67
WILLIAMS C.,"REGIONAL MANAGEMENT OVERSEAS." USA+45   MGT
WOR+45 DIST/IND LG/CO EX/STRUC INT/TRADE TARIFFS   EUR+WWI
ADMIN TASK CENTRAL. PAGE 63 G1242   ECO/DEV
                                                     PLAN

N67
PRINCETON U INDUSTRIAL REL SEC,COLLECTIVE   BIBLIOG/A
BARGAINING IN THE PUBLIC SCHOOLS (PAMPHLET NO. 33). SCHOOL
USA+45 LABOR PROB/SOLV PWR MGT. PAGE 45 G0891   BARGAIN
                                                     GP/REL

N67
US CONGRESS JT COMM ECO GOVT,BACKGROUND MATERIAL ON BUDGET
ECONOMY IN GOVERNMENT 1967 (PAMPHLET). WOR+45   COST
ECO/DEV BARGAIN PRICE DEMAND OPTIMAL...STAT   MGT
DEPT/DEFEN. PAGE 57 G1116   NAT/G

MGT/OBJECT....MANAGEMENT BY OBJECTIVES

MICH/STA/U....MICHIGAN STATE UNIVERSITY

MICH/U....UNIVERSITY OF MICHIGAN

MICHAEL D.N. G0764

MICHIGAN STATE UNIVERSITY....SEE MICH/STA/U

MICHIGAN....MICHIGAN

MICRONESIA....MICRONESIA

MID/EAST....MIDDLE EAST

B64
THANT U.,TOWARD WORLD PEACE. DELIB/GP TEC/DEV   DIPLOM
EDU/PROP WAR SOVEREIGN...INT/LAW 20 UN MID/EAST.   BIOG
PAGE 54 G1065   PEACE
                                                     COERCE

MIDDLETOWN....MIDDLETOWN: LOCATION OF LYND STUDY

MIDWEST/US....MIDWESTERN UNITED STATES

MIGRATION....MIGRATION; IMMIGRATION AND EMIGRATION; SEE
    ALSO HABITAT, GEOG

B64
PARANJAPE H.K.,THE FLIGHT OF TECHNICAL PERSONNEL IN ADMIN
PUBLIC UNDERTAKINGS. INDIA PAY DEMAND HAPPINESS   NAT/G
ORD/FREE...MGT QU 20 MIGRATION. PAGE 44 G0858   WORKER
                                                     PLAN

MIKSCHE F.O. G0765,G0766

MIL/ACAD....MILITARY ACADEMY

MILBRATH L.W. G0767

MILBURN T.W. G0768

MILIBAND R. G0769

MILITARY....SEE FORCES

MILITARY APPLICATIONS OF URANIUM DETONATION....SEE MAUD

MILL/JAMES....JAMES MILL

MILL/JS....JOHN STUART MILL

MILLAR R. G0770

MILLER G.A. G0771,G0772

MILLER J.C. G0740

MILLER J.G. G0773

MILLER W.E. G0774

MILLS/CW....C. WRIGHT MILLS

MILNER/A....ALFRED MILNER

MILTON/J....MILTON, JOHN

MINING....SEE EXTR/IND

MINISTRY OF OVERSEAS DEVELOPME G0775

MINNESOTA....MINNESOTA

MINORITY....SEE RACE/REL

MISCEGEN....MISCEGENATION

MISSION....MISSIONARIES

MISSISSIPP....MISSISSIPPI

MISSOURI RIVER BASIN PLAN....SEE MO/BASIN

MISSOURI....MISSOURI

MNR....MOVIMIENTO NACIONALISTA REVOLUCIONARIO (BOLIVIA)

MO/BASIN....MISSOURI RIVER BASIN PLAN

MOB....SEE CROWD

MOBUTU/J....JOSEPH MOBUTU

MOCH J. G0776

MOCHE....MOCHE, PERU

MOD/EUR....MODERN EUROPE (1700-1918); SEE ALSO APPROPRIATE
    NATIONS

                                              C25

MOON P.T.,"SYLLABUS ON INTERNATIONAL RELATIONS."   INT/ORG
EUR+WWI MOD/EUR USA+45 FORCES COLONIAL WAR WEAPON   DIPLOM
NAT/LISM...POLICY BIBLIOG T 19/20. PAGE 39 G0778   NAT/G

                                              B28

SOROKIN P.,CONTEMPORARY SOCIOLOGICAL THEORIES.   CULTURE
MOD/EUR UNIV SOCIETY R+D SCHOOL ECO/TAC EDU/PROP   SOC
ROUTINE ATTIT DRIVE...PSY CONCPT TIME/SEQ TREND   WAR
GEN/LAWS 20. PAGE 52 G1021

                                              B39

FULLER G.H.,A SELECTED LIST OF REFERENCES ON THE   BIBLIOG
EXPANSION OF THE US NAVY, 1933-1939 (PAMPHLET).   FORCES
MOD/EUR USA-45 NAT/G PLAN DIPLOM DOMIN RISK   WEAPON
ARMS/CONT EQUILIB PWR 20 NAVY. PAGE 20 G0399   WAR

                                              B41

FULLER G.H.,DEFENSE FINANCING: A SELECTED LIST OF   BIBLIOG/A
REFERENCES (PAMPHLET). MOD/EUR USA-45 ECO/DEV NAT/G FINAN
DELIB/GP RATION ARMS/CONT WEAPON COST PEACE PWR 20   FORCES
CONGRESS. PAGE 20 G0401   BUDGET

                                              S44

GRIFFITH E.S.,"THE CHANGING PATTERN OF PUBLIC   LAW
POLICY FORMATION." MOD/EUR WOR+45 FINAN CHIEF   POLICY
CONFER ADMIN LEAD CONSERVE SOCISM TECHRACY...SOC   TEC/DEV
CHARTS CONGRESS. PAGE 23 G0450

                                              B46

BAXTER J.P.,SCIENTISTS AGAINST TIME. EUR+WWI   FORCES
MOD/EUR USA+45 USA-45 WOR+45 WOR-45 R+D NAT/G PLAN   WAR
ATTIT PWR...PHIL/SCI RECORD CON/ANAL 17/20. PAGE 6   NUC/PWR
G0107

                                              B46

NORTHROP F.S.C.,THE MEETING OF EAST AND WEST.   DRIVE
EUR+WWI FUT MOD/EUR UNIV WOR+45 WOR-45 INTELL   TREND
SOCIETY EX/STRUC TOP/EX ACT/RES LEGIT CHOOSE ATTIT   PEACE
PERCEPT RIGID/FLEX ALL/VALS...POLICY JURID OBS
TOT/POP. PAGE 42 G0826

                                              B54

GERMANY FOREIGN MINISTRY,DOCUMENTS ON GERMAN   NAT/G
FOREIGN POLICY 1918-1945, SERIES C (1933-1937)   DIPLOM
VOLS. I-V. GERMANY MOD/EUR FORCES PLAN ECO/TAC   POLICY
...FASCIST CHARTS ANTHOL 20. PAGE 21 G0416

                                              B54

HART B.H.L.,STRATEGY (REV. ED.). CHRIST-17C EUR+WWI   WAR
MEDIT-7 MOD/EUR TEC/DEV LEAD REV WEAPON...POLICY   PLAN
CHARTS. PAGE 25 G0486   FORCES
                                              PHIL/SCI

                                              S58

HUNTINGTON S.P.,"ARMS RACES: PREREQUISITES AND   FORCES
RESULTS." EUR+WWI MOD/EUR USA+45 WOR+45 WOR-45   PWR
NAT/G TEC/DEV BAL/PWR COERCE DETER ATTIT...POLICY   ARMS/CONT
TREND 20. PAGE 27 G0537

                                              B63

NORTH R.C.,CONTENT ANALYSIS: A HANDBOOK WITH   METH/CNCPT
APPLICATIONS FOR THE STUDY OF INTERNATIONAL CRISIS.   COMPUT/IR
ASIA COM EUR+WWI MOD/EUR INT/ORG TEC/DEV DOMIN   USSR
EDU/PROP ROUTINE COERCE PERCEPT RIGID/FLEX ALL/VALS
...QUANT TESTS CON/ANAL SIMUL GEN/LAWS VAL/FREE.
PAGE 42 G0825

                                              B64

PETERSON W.,THE POLITICS OF POPULATION. COM EUR+WWI   PLAN
FUT MOD/EUR S/ASIA USA+45 USA-45 WOR+45 LAW CULTURE CENSUS
FAM SECT DOMIN EDU/PROP BIO/SOC HEALTH ORD/FREE   POLICY
...GEOG STAT TIME/SEQ TREND VAL/FREE. PAGE 44 G0871

                                              B67

WOODRUFF W.,IMPACT OF WESTERN MAN. ECO/DEV INDUS   EUR+WWI
CREATE PLAN PROB/SOLV COLONIAL GOV/REL...CHARTS   MOD/EUR
GOV/COMP BIBLIOG 18/20. PAGE 64 G1256   CAP/ISM

                                              S67

SCOVILLE W.J.,"GOVERNMENT REGULATION AND GROWTH IN   NAT/G
THE FRENCH PAPER INDUSTRY DURING THE EIGHTEENTH   PROC/MFG
CENTURY." FRANCE MOD/EUR FINAN CAP/ISM TAX ADMIN   ECO/DEV
CONTROL PRIVIL LAISSEZ...POLICY 18. PAGE 50 G0985   INGP/REL

MODAL....MODAL TYPES, FASHIONS

                                              S59

LEFTON M.,"DECISION MAKING IN A MENTAL HOSPITAL: ACT/RES
REAL, PERCEIVED, AND IDEAL." R+D PUB/INST CONSULT   PROB/SOLV
CONFER INGP/REL PERCEPT...MODAL 20. PAGE 33 G0653   DECISION
                                              PSY

                                              B67

HARDT J.P.,MATHEMATICS AND COMPUTERS IN SOVIET   PLAN
ECONOMIC PLANNING. COM USSR OP/RES PROB/SOLV   TEC/DEV
OPTIMAL...MODAL SIMUL 20. PAGE 24 G0481   MATH
                                              COMPUT/IR

MODELS....SEE SIMUL, MATH, ALSO MODELS INDEX, P. XIV

MODELSKI G. G0777

MODERNIZATION....SEE MODERNIZE

MODERNIZE....MODERNIZATION

                                              B68

GALLAHER A. JR.,PERSPECTIVES IN DEVELOPMENTAL   TECHNIC
CHANGE. MUNIC PLAN INSPECT EDU/PROP...POLICY   TEC/DEV
DECISION GEOG PSY SOC IDEA/COMP ANTHOL 20   PROB/SOLV
MODERNIZE. PAGE 21 G0405   CREATE

MONACO....SEE ALSO APPROPRIATE TIME/SPACE/CULTURE INDEX

MONARCH....SEE CHIEF, KING

MONARCHY....SEE CONSERVE, CHIEF, KING

MONETARY POLICY....SEE FINAN, PLAN

MONEY....SEE FINAN, ECO

                                              B64

DUSCHA J.,ARMS, MONEY, AND POLITICS. USA+45 INDUS   NAT/G
POL/PAR ECO/TAC TAX DETER NUC/PWR WAR WEAPON   FORCES
GOV/REL ATTIT...BIBLIOG/A 20 CONGRESS MONEY   POLICY
DEPT/DEFEN. PAGE 17 G0326   BUDGET

MONGOLIA....SEE ALSO USSR

MONOPOLY....MONOPOLIES, OLIGOPOLIES, AND ANTI-TRUST ACTIONS

                                              B59

MEANS G.C.,ADMINISTRATIVE INFLATION AND PUBLIC   ECO/TAC
POLICY (PAMPHLET). USA+45 ECO/DEV FINAN INDUS   POLICY
WORKER PLAN BUDGET GOV/REL COST DEMAND WEALTH 20   RATION

CONGRESS MONOPOLY GOLD/STAND. PAGE 38 G0749   CONTROL

B64
MANSFIELD E.,MONOPOLY POWER AND ECONOMIC
PERFORMANCE: AN INTRODUCTION TO A CURRENT ISSUE OF
PUBLIC POLICY. ECO/DEV INDUS NAT/G PLAN CAP/ISM
PRICE CONTROL LOBBY EFFICIENCY PRODUC...POLICY 20
CONGRESS KENNEDY/JF MONOPOLY. PAGE 36 G0701
     LG/CO
     PWR
     ECO/TAC
     MARKET

MONROE/DOC....MONROE DOCTRINE

MONROE/J....PRESIDENT JAMES MONROE

MONTANA....MONTANA

MONTECARLO....MONTE CARLO - OPERATIONAL RESEARCH
DECISION-MAKING MODEL

B62
DUCKWORTH W.E.,A GUIDE TO OPERATIONAL RESEARCH.
INDUS PLAN PROB/SOLV EXEC EFFICIENCY PRODUC KNOWL
...MGT MATH STAT SIMUL METH 20 MONTECARLO. PAGE 16
G0319
     OP/RES
     GAME
     DECISION
     ADMIN

MONTESQ....MONTESQUIEU, CHARLES LOUIS DE SECONDAT

MONTGOMERY....MONTGOMERY, ALABAMA

MOON P.T. G0778

MOOR E.J. G0779

MOORE J.R. G0780

MORAL....RECTITUDE, MORALITY, GOODNESS (ALSO IMMORALITY)

B14
CRAIG J.,ELEMENTS OF POLITICAL SCIENCE (3 VOLS.).
CONSTN AGRI INDUS SCHOOL FORCES TAX CT/SYS SUFF
MORAL WEALTH...CONCPT 19 CIVIL/LIB. PAGE 13 G0259
     PHIL/SCI
     NAT/G
     ORD/FREE

B29
DEWEY J.,THE QUEST FOR CERTAINTY. GP/REL RATIONAL
UTOPIA ATTIT MORAL ORD/FREE PWR...MYTH HIST/WRIT.
PAGE 15 G0301
     PHIL/SCI
     PERSON
     PERCEPT
     KNOWL

B46
MORGENTHAU H.J.,SCIENTIFIC MAN VS POWER POLITICS.
USA+45 WOR+45 INTELL SOCIETY ACT/RES CREATE PLAN
EDU/PROP...CONCPT TREND TOT/POP 20. PAGE 40 G0782
     UNIV
     MORAL
     PEACE

B55
OPPENHEIMER R.,THE OPEN MIND. USA+45 WOR+45 NAT/G
DELIB/GP DETER MORAL ORD/FREE...MYTH GEN/LAWS 20.
PAGE 43 G0842
     CREATE
     PWR
     ARMS/CONT
     NUC/PWR

S55
SKINNER B.F.,"FREEDOM AND THE CONTROL OF MEN"
(BMR)" FUT WOR+45 CONTROL CHOOSE GP/REL ATTIT MORAL
PWR POPULISM...POLICY 20. PAGE 51 G1008
     ORD/FREE
     TEC/DEV
     PHIL/SCI
     INTELL

B57
KIETH-LUCAS A.,DECISIONS ABOUT PEOPLE IN NEED, A
STUDY OF ADMINISTRATIVE RESPONSIVENESS IN PUBLIC
ASSISTANCE. USA+45 GIVE RECEIVE INGP/REL PERS/REL
MORAL RESPECT WEALTH...SOC OBS BIBLIOG 20. PAGE 30
G0595
     ADMIN
     RIGID/FLEX
     SOC/WK
     DECISION

B58
JUNGK R.,BRIGHTER THAN A THOUSAND SUNS: THE MORAL
AND POLITICAL HISTORY OF THE ATOMIC SCIENTISTS.
WOR+45 WOR-45 CONSULT CREATE RISK UTIL DRIVE
PERCEPT PWR...INT 20. PAGE 29 G0568
     NUC/PWR
     MORAL
     GOV/REL
     PERSON

B59
LANG D.,FROM HIROSHIMA TO THE MOON: CHRONICLES OF
LIFE IN THE ATOMIC AGE. USA+45 OP/RES CONTROL
ARMS/CONT WAR CIVMIL/REL PEACE HABITAT MORAL PWR
...OBS INT 20 AEC. PAGE 32 G0633
     NUC/PWR
     SPACE
     HEALTH
     TEC/DEV

B59
RUSSELL B.,COMMON SENSE AND NUCLEAR WARFARE. WOR+45
INTELL SOCIETY STRATA NAT/G TOP/EX EDU/PROP ATTIT
PERSON KNOWL MORAL PWR...POLICY CONCPT MYTH
CON/ANAL COLD/WAR 20. PAGE 48 G0948
     ORD/FREE
     ARMS/CONT
     NUC/PWR

B60
APTHEKER H.,DISARMAMENT AND THE AMERICAN ECONOMY: A
SYMPOSIUM. FUT USA+45 ECO/DEV DIST/IND FINAN INDUS
PROC/MFG LABOR NAT/G POL/PAR CONSULT PLAN CAP/ISM
INT/TRADE PEACE ATTIT MORAL WEALTH...TREND GEN/LAWS
TOT/POP 20. PAGE 3 G0063
     MARXIST
     ARMS/CONT

B61
NATHAN O.,EINSTEIN ON PEACE. WOR+45 WOR-45 INTELL
NUC/PWR WAR PERSON MORAL...BIOG VAL/FREE NAZI 20
EINSTEIN/A. PAGE 41 G0807
     CONCPT
     PEACE

B61
STEIN W.,NUCLEAR WEAPONS: A CATHOLIC RESPONSE.
WOR+45 FORCES ARMS/CONT DETER MURDER MORAL...POLICY
CATH IDEA/COMP ANTHOL 20. PAGE 52 G1033
     NUC/PWR
     WAR
     CATHISM
     ATTIT

S61
RICHSTEIN A.R.,"LEGAL RULES IN NUCLEAR WEAPONS
EMPLOYMENTS." FUT WOR+45 LAW SOCIETY FORCES PLAN
WEAPON RIGID/FLEX...HEAL CONCPT TREND VAL/FREE 20.
PAGE 47 G0918
     NUC/PWR
     TEC/DEV
     MORAL
     ARMS/CONT

S61
SCHILLING W.R.,"THE H-BOMB: HOW TO DECIDE WITHOUT
ACTUALLY CHOOSING." FUT USA+45 INTELL CONSULT ADMIN
CT/SYS MORAL...JURID OBS 20 TRUMAN/HS. PAGE 49
G0966
     PERSON
     LEGIT
     NUC/PWR

B62
BENNETT J.C.,NUCLEAR WEAPONS AND THE CONFLICT OF
CONSCIENCE. WOR+45 PROB/SOLV DIPLOM WEAPON SUPEGO
MORAL...ANTHOL WORSHIP 20. PAGE 6 G0120
     POLICY
     NUC/PWR
     WAR

B62
GILPIN R.,AMERICAN SCIENTISTS AND NUCLEAR WEAPONS
POLICY. COM FUT USA+45 WOR+45 INT/ORG NAT/G
PROF/ORG CONSULT FORCES CREATE TEC/DEV BAL/PWR
EDU/PROP ARMS/CONT WAR PERCEPT KNOWL MORAL PWR
...PHIL/SCI SOC CONCPT GEN/LAWS 20. PAGE 21 G0417
     INTELL
     ATTIT
     DETER
     NUC/PWR

B62
ROSS R.,SYMBOLS AND CIVILIZATION. UNIV CULTURE SECT
CREATE ALL/VALS MORAL ART/METH. PAGE 48 G0939
     PHIL/SCI
     KNOWL
     EPIST
     SOCIETY

B64
ELLUL J.,THE TECHNOLOGICAL SOCIETY. FUT STRUCT
CREATE AUTOMAT ROUTINE STRANGE ANOMIE MORAL
PHIL/SCI. PAGE 18 G0344
     SOC
     SOCIETY
     TECHNIC
     TEC/DEV

B64
ROTHSCHILD J.H.,TOMORROW'S WEAPONS: CHEMICAL AND
BIOLOGICAL. FUT PROB/SOLV ARMS/CONT PEACE MORAL
...CHARTS BIBLIOG 20. PAGE 48 G0941
     WAR
     WEAPON
     BIO/SOC
     DETER

B64
US AIR FORCE ACADEMY ASSEMBLY,OUTER SPACE: FINAL
REPORT APRIL 1-4, 1964. FUT USA+45 WOR+45 LAW
DELIB/GP CONFER ARMS/CONT WAR PEACE ATTIT MORAL
...ANTHOL 20 NASA. PAGE 56 G1104
     SPACE
     CIVMIL/REL
     NUC/PWR
     DIPLOM

B65
ALLEN S.,LETTER TO A CONSERVATIVE. SOCIETY NAT/G
DIPLOM EDU/PROP NUC/PWR GP/REL ATTIT MORAL
...MAJORIT CONCPT 20. PAGE 2 G0044
     ORD/FREE
     MARXISM
     POLICY
     LAISSEZ

S65
KRICKUS R.J.,"ON THE MORALITY OF
CHEMICAL/BIOLOGICAL WAR." ECO/UNDEV ARMS/CONT DETER
NUC/PWR RIGID/FLEX HEALTH INT/LAW. PAGE 31 G0621
     MORAL
     BIO/SOC
     WEAPON
     WAR

L66
DOUGHERTY J.E.,"THE CATHOLIC CHURCH, WAR AND
NUCLEAR WEAPONS." COM EUR+WWI SECT TOP/EX LEAD
DETER ALL/VALS. PAGE 16 G0312
     CATHISM
     MORAL
     WAR
     NUC/PWR

S67
ARONOWITZ D.S.,"CIVIL COMMITMENT OF NARCOTIC
ADDICTS." USA+45 LAW INGP/REL DISCRIM MORAL...TREND
20. PAGE 4 G0069
     PUB/INST
     ACT/RES
     POLICY

S67
CRANBERG L.,"SCIENCE, ETHICS, AND LAW." UNIV CREATE
PLAN EDU/PROP INGP/REL PERS/REL ADJUST RATIONAL
KNOWL MORAL...CONCPT IDEA/COMP 20. PAGE 13 G0260
     LAW
     PHIL/SCI
     INTELL

S67
HARTIGAN R.S.,"NONCOMBAT IMMUNITY* REFLECTIONS ON
ITS ORIGINS AND PRESENT STATUS." WOR+45 PROB/SOLV
WAR PRIVIL MORAL...POLICY 20. PAGE 25 G0487
     INT/LAW
     NUC/PWR
     ARMS/CONT
     DIPLOM

S67
ROBINSON J.A.T.,"ABORTION* THE CASE FOR A FREE
DECISION." LAW PROB/SOLV SANCTION ATTIT MORAL...PSY
     PLAN
     ILLEGIT

IDEA/COMP 20 ABORTION. PAGE 47 G0930   SEX
                                         HEALTH

                                                    S67
SLOAN P.,"FIFTY YEARS OF SOVIET RULE." USSR INDUS   CREATE
EDU/PROP EFFICIENCY PRODUC HEALTH KNOWL MORAL   NAT/G
WEALTH MARXISM...POLICY 20. PAGE 51 G1011   PLAN
                                                    INSPECT

MORALITY....SEE MORAL, CULTURE, ALL/VALS, LAW/ETHIC

MORDAN H. G0338

MORE/THOM....SIR THOMAS MORE

MORGENSTERN O. G0608,G0781

MORGENTH/H.... HANS MORGENTHAU

MORGENTHAU H.J. G0782,G0783

MORL/MINTO....MORLEY-MINTO - ERA OF BRITISH RULE IN INDIA
    (1905-1910)

MORLEY/J....JOHN MORLEY

MORMON....MORMON PEOPLE AND MORMON FAITH

MOROCCO....SEE ALSO ISLAM

                                                    B61
LAHAYE R.,LES ENTREPRISES PUBLIQUES AU MAROC.   NAT/G
FRANCE MOROCCO LAW DIST/IND EXTR/IND FINAN CONSULT   INDUS
PLAN TEC/DEV ADMIN AGREE CONTROL OWN...POLICY 20.   ECO/UNDEV
PAGE 32 G0629   ECO/TAC

MORRIS M.D. G0784

MORRIS W.T. G0785

MORRIS/CW....C.W. MORRIS

                                                    S43
KAPLAN A.,"CONTENT ANALYSIS AND THE THEORY OF   LOG
SIGNS" (BMR)" PERS/REL...PSY CONCPT LING IDEA/COMP   CON/ANAL
SIMUL BIBLIOG 20 MORRIS/CW. PAGE 29 G0573   STAT
                                                    PHIL/SCI

MORRIS/G....G. MORRIS

MORROW/DW....DWIGHT W. MORROW

MORSE D. G1214

MORSTEIN-MARX F. G0786

MORTON J.A. G0787

MORTON L. G0788

MOSCA/G....GAETANO MOSCA

MOSCOW....MOSCOW, U.S.S.R.

MOSK S.A. G0789

MOSKOWITZ H. G0790

MOSLEY P.E. G0508

MOSS F.M. G0791

MOSSI....MOSSI TRIBE

MOTIVATION....SEE DRIVE

MOVIES....SEE FILM

MOVIMIENTO NACIONALISTA REVOLUCIONARIA (BOLIVIA)....SEE
    MNR

MOYNI/RPRT....MOYNIHAN REPORT

MOYNIHAN REPORT....SEE MOYNI/RPRT

MOZAMBIQUE LIBERATION FRONT....SEE FRELIMO

MOZAMBIQUE....MOZAMBIQUE

MUCKRAKER....MUCKRAKERS

MUGWUMP....MUGWUMP

MULATTO....MULATTO

MULLENBACH P. G0792

MULLER H.J. G0793

MULTIVAR....MULTIVARIATE ANALYSIS

MULTIVARIATE ANALYSIS....SEE MULTIVAR

MUMFORD L. G0794,G0795

MUNIC....CITIES, TOWNS, VILLAGES

                                                    N
CONOVER H.L.,CIVILIAN DEFENSE: A SELECTED LIST OF   BIBLIOG
RECENT REFERENCES (PAMPHLET). USA+45 LOC/G MUNIC   PLAN
PROB/SOLV ADMIN LEAD TASK WEAPON GOV/REL...POLICY   WAR
CON/ANAL 20 CIV/DEFENS. PAGE 13 G0251   CIVMIL/REL

                                                    N19
KAUFMAN J.L.,COMMUNITY RENEWAL PROGRAMS (PAMPHLET). LOC/G
USA+45 CONSTRUC PROVS CREATE PLAN CONTROL WEALTH 20   MUNIC
URBAN/RNWL. PAGE 30 G0584   ACT/RES
                                                    BIBLIOG

                                                    N19
VERNON R.,THE MYTH AND REALITY OF OUR URBAN   PLAN
PROBLEMS (PAMPHLET). USA+45 SOCIETY LOC/G ADMIN   MUNIC
COST 20 PRINCETN/U INTERVENT URBAN/RNWL. PAGE 61   HABITAT
G1197   PROB/SOLV

                                                    B36
US LIBRARY OF CONGRESS,CLASSIFIED GUIDE TO MATERIAL BIBLIOG
IN THE LIBRARY OF CONGRESS COVERING URBAN COMMUNITY   CLASSIF
DEVELOPMENT. USA+45 CREATE PROB/SOLV ADMIN 20.   MUNIC
PAGE 59 G1154   PLAN

                                                    B44
PUBLIC ADMINISTRATION SERVICE,YOUR BUSINESS OF   BIBLIOG
GOVERNMENT: A CATALOG OF PUBLICATIONS IN THE FIELD   ADMIN
OF PUBLIC ADMINISTRATION (PAMPHLET). FINAN R+D   NAT/G
LOC/G ACT/RES OP/RES PLAN 20. PAGE 45 G0894   MUNIC

                                                    B48
PUBLIC ADMINISTRATION SERVICE,SOURCE MATERIALS IN   BIBLIOG/A
PUBLIC ADMINISTRATION: A SELECTED BIBLIOGRAPHY (PAS GOV/REL
PUBLICATION NO. 102). USA+45 LAW FINAN LOC/G MUNIC   MGT
NAT/G PLAN RECEIVE EDU/PROP CT/SYS CHOOSE HEALTH   ADMIN
20. PAGE 45 G0895

                                                    B50
DEES J.W. JR.,URBAN SOCIOLOGY AND THE EMERGING   PLAN
ATOMIC MEGALOPOLIS, PART I. USA+45 TEC/DEV ADMIN   NEIGH
NUC/PWR HABITAT...SOC AUD/VIS CHARTS GEN/LAWS 20   MUNIC
WATER. PAGE 15 G0291   PROB/SOLV

                                                    L52
LASSWELL H.D.,"RESEARCH IN POLITICAL BEHAVIOR."   PHIL/SCI
LOC/G MUNIC POL/PAR CONSULT ADMIN PARTIC...CHARTS   METH
ANTHOL BIBLIOG/A 20. PAGE 32 G0641   R+D

                                                    B54
WILENSKY H.L.,SYLLABUS OF INDUSTRIAL RELATIONS: A   BIBLIOG
GUIDE TO READING AND RESEARCH. USA+45 MUNIC ADMIN   INDUS
INGP/REL...POLICY MGT PHIL/SCI 20. PAGE 63 G1239   LABOR
                                                    WORKER

                                                    S54
FORM W.H.,"THE PLACE OF SOCIAL STRUCTURE IN THE   HABITAT
DETERMINATION OF LAND USE: SOME IMPLICATIONS FOR A   MARKET
THEORY OF URBAN ECOLOGY" (BMR)" STRUCT...GEOG   ORD/FREE
PHIL/SCI SOC 20. PAGE 19 G0381   MUNIC

                                                    C54
CALDWELL L.K.,"THE GOVERNMENT AND ADMINISTRATION OF PROVS
NEW YORK." LOC/G MUNIC POL/PAR SCHOOL CHIEF LEGIS   ADMIN
PLAN TAX CT/SYS...MGT SOC/WK BIBLIOG 20 NEWYORK/C.   CONSTN
PAGE 10 G0202   EX/STRUC

                                                    B57
DRUCKER P.F.,AMERICA'S NEXT TWENTY YEARS. USA+45   WORKER
DIST/IND ACADEM MUNIC SCHOOL DIPLOM ECO/TAC AUTOMAT   FOR/AID
HABITAT HEALTH...SOC/WK TREND 20 URBAN/RNWL   CENSUS
PUB/TRANS. PAGE 16 G0316   GEOG

                                                    B60
ALBI F.,TRATADO DE LOS MODOS DE GESTION DE LAS   LOC/G
CORPORACIONES LOCALES. SPAIN FINAN NAT/G BUDGET   LAW
CONTROL EXEC ROUTINE GOV/REL ORD/FREE SOVEREIGN   ADMIN
...MGT 20. PAGE 2 G0034   MUNIC

                                                    B60
US SENATE COMM ON COMMERCE,URBAN MASS   DIST/IND
TRANSPORTATION. FUT USA+45 AIR ECO/DEV FINAN LOC/G   PLAN
MUNIC LEGIS CREATE PROB/SOLV TEC/DEV 20 PUB/TRANS.   NAT/G
PAGE 60 G1180   LAW

                                                    B60
WALDO D.,THE RESEARCH FUNCTION OF UNIVERSITY   ADMIN

BUREAUS AND INSTITUTES FOR GOVERNMENTAL-RELATED R+D
RESEARCH. FINAN ACADEM NAT/G INGP/REL ROLE...POLICY MUNIC
CLASSIF GOV/COMP. PAGE 61 G1205

B61
JANOWITZ M.,COMMUNITY POLITICAL SYSTEMS. USA+45 MUNIC
SOCIETY INDUS VOL/ASSN TEC/DEV ADMIN LEAD CHOOSE STRUCT
...SOC SOC/WK 20. PAGE 29 G0561 POL/PAR

B61
LEE R.R.,ENGINEERING-ECONOMIC PLANNING BIBLIOG/A
MISCELLANEOUS SUBJECTS: A SELECTED BIBLIOGRAPHY PLAN
(MIMEOGRAPHED). FINAN LOC/G MUNIC NEIGH ADMIN REGION
CONTROL INGP/REL HABITAT...GEOG MGT SOC/WK 20
RESOURCE/N. PAGE 33 G0651

B61
SMITH H.H.,THE CITIZEN'S GUIDE TO PLANNING. USA+45 MUNIC
LAW SCHOOL CREATE PROB/SOLV EDU/PROP GP/REL ROLE 20 PLAN
URBAN/RNWL OPEN/SPACE. PAGE 52 G1015 DELIB/GP
CONSULT

S61
ANDREWS R.B.,"URBAN ECONOMICS: AN APPRAISAL OF MUNIC
PROGRESS." LOC/G PROB/SOLV TEC/DEV...CONCPT PHIL/SCI
OBS/ENVIR METH/COMP HYPO/EXP SOC/EXP SIMUL GEN/METH ECOMETRIC
METH 20. PAGE 3 G0058

S61
DYKMAN J.W.,"REVIEW ARTICLE* PLANNING AND DECISION DECISION
THEORY." ELITES LOC/G MUNIC CONSULT ADMIN...POLICY PLAN
MGT. PAGE 17 G0327 RATIONAL

S61
FAIR M.L.,"PORT AUTHORITIES IN THE UNITED STATES." MUNIC
PROB/SOLV ADMIN LEAD REPRESENT PWR...DECISION GEOG. REGION
PAGE 18 G0357 LOC/G
GOV/REL

B62
KARNJAHAPRAKORN C.,MUNICIPAL GOVERNMENT IN THAILAND LOC/G
AS AN INSTITUTION AND PROCESS OF SELF-GOVERNMENT. MUNIC
THAILAND CULTURE FINAN EX/STRUC LEGIS PLAN CONTROL ORD/FREE
GOV/REL EFFICIENCY ATTIT...POLICY 20. PAGE 29 G0578 ADMIN

B62
THANT U.,THE UNITED NATIONS' DEVELOPMENT DECADE: INT/ORG
PROPOSALS FOR ACTION. WOR+45 SOCIETY ECO/UNDEV AGRI ALL/VALS
COM/IND FINAN R+D MUNIC SCHOOL VOL/ASSN CONSULT
PLAN TEC/DEV ECO/TAC EDU/PROP ADMIN ROUTINE
RIGID/FLEX...MGT SOC CONCPT UNESCO UN TOT/POP
VAL/FREE. PAGE 54 G1064

B63
BASS M.E.,SELECTIVE BIBLIOGRAPHY ON MUNICIPAL BIBLIOG
GOVERNMENT FROM THE FILES OF THE MUNICIPAL LOC/G
TECHNICAL ADVISORY SERVICE. USA+45 FINAN SERV/IND ADMIN
PLAN 20. PAGE 5 G0100 MUNIC

B63
NASA,CONFERENCE ON SPACE, SCIENCE, AND URBAN LIFE. MUNIC
USA+45 SOCIETY INDUS ACADEM ACT/RES ECO/TAC ADMIN SPACE
20. PAGE 41 G0804 TEC/DEV
PROB/SOLV

B63
RUITENBEER H.M.,THE DILEMMA OF ORGANIZATIONAL PERSON
SOCIETY. CULTURE ECO/DEV MUNIC SECT TEC/DEV ROLE
EDU/PROP NAT/LISM ORD/FREE...NAT/COMP 20 RIESMAN/D ADMIN
WHYTE/WF MERTON/R MEAD/MARG JASPERS/K. PAGE 48 WORKER
G0945

B64
GRAVIER J.F.,AMENAGEMENT DU TERRITOIRE ET L'AVENIR PLAN
DES REGIONS FRANCAISES. FRANCE ECO/DEV AGRI INDUS MUNIC
CREATE...GEOG CHARTS 20. PAGE 22 G0442 NEIGH
ADMIN

B64
INST D'ETUDE POL L'U GRENOBLE,ADMINISTRATION ADMIN
TRADITIONELLE ET PLANIFICATION REGIONALE. FRANCE MUNIC
LAW POL/PAR PROB/SOLV ADJUST RIGID/FLEX...CHARTS PLAN
ANTHOL BIBLIOG T 20 REFORMERS. PAGE 28 G0546 CREATE

B64
LANG A.S.,URBAN RAIL TRANSIT. OP/RES PLAN PROB/SOLV MUNIC
TEC/DEV AUTOMAT COST...TECHNIC MATH CON/ANAL CHARTS DIST/IND
METH/COMP SIMUL 20 RAILROAD PUB/TRANS. PAGE 32 ECOMETRIC
G0632

S64
STONE P.A.,"DECISION TECHNIQUES FOR TOWN OP/RES
DEVELOPMENT." PLAN COST PROFIT...DECISION MGT MUNIC
CON/ANAL CHARTS METH/COMP BIBLIOG 20. PAGE 53 G1039 ADMIN
PROB/SOLV

N64
NATIONAL ACADEMY OF SCIENCES,CIVIL DEFENSE: PROJECT NUC/PWR
HARBOR SUMMARY REPORT (PAMPHLET). USA+45 MUNIC FORCES
NAT/G ACT/RES BUDGET EDU/PROP DETER WEAPON EATING WAR
...GEOG 20. PAGE 41 G0808 PLAN

B65
ALTSHULER A.,A LAND-USE PLAN FOR ST. PAUL MUNIC
(PAMPHLET). USA+45 CREATE CAP/ISM RIGID/FLEX ROLE PLAN
...NEW/IDEA 20 ST/PAUL. PAGE 3 G0047 ECO/DEV
GEOG

B65
ARTHUR D LITTLE INC,SAN FRANCISCO COMMUNITY RENEWAL HABITAT
PROGRAM. USA+45 FINAN PROVS ADMIN INCOME...CHARTS MUNIC
20 CALIFORNIA SAN/FRAN URBAN/RNWL. PAGE 4 G0071 PLAN
PROB/SOLV

B65
INTERNATIONAL CITY MGRS ASSN,COUNCIL-MANAGER BIBLIOG/A
GOVERNMENT, 1940-64: AN ANNOTATED BIBLIOGRAPHY. MUNIC
USA+45 ADMIN GOV/REL ROLE...MGT 20. PAGE 28 G0549 CONSULT
PLAN

B65
TURNER A.N.,INDUSTRIAL JOBS AND THE WORKER. USA+45 WORKER
CULTURE ECO/DEV LABOR MUNIC ACT/RES AUTOMAT TASK INDUS
...CHARTS BIBLIOG 20. PAGE 55 G1082 ATTIT
TEC/DEV

B66
KLOTSCHE J.M.,THE URBAN UNIVERSITY AND THE FUTURE ACADEM
OF OUR CITIES. FUT USA+45 USA-45 LOC/G NEIGH GIVE MUNIC
19/20. PAGE 31 G0606 PROB/SOLV
TEC/DEV

B66
MURDOCK J.C.,RESEARCH AND REGIONS. AGRI FINAN INDUS BIBLIOG
LOC/G MUNIC NAT/G PROB/SOLV TEC/DEV ADMIN REGION ECO/DEV
20. PAGE 40 G0796 COMPUT/IR
R+D

B66
SCHURMANN F.,IDEOLOGY AND ORGANIZATION IN COMMUNIST MARXISM
CHINA. CHINA/COM LOC/G MUNIC POL/PAR ECO/TAC STRUCT
CONTROL ATTIT...MGT STERTYP 20 COM/PARTY. PAGE 50 ADMIN
G0981 NAT/G

B67
BUDER S.,PULLMAN: AN EXPERIMENT IN INDUSTRIAL ORDER DIST/IND
AND COMMUNITY PLANNING, 1880-1930. USA-45 SOCIETY INDUS
LABOR LG/CO CREATE PROB/SOLV CONTROL GP/REL MUNIC
EFFICIENCY ATTIT...MGT BIBLIOG 19/20 PULLMAN. PLAN
PAGE 9 G0184

B67
DEGLER C.N.,THE AGE OF THE ECONOMIC REVOLUTION INDUS
1876-1900. USA-45 AGRI MUNIC POL/PAR SECT ECO/TAC SOCIETY
CHOOSE...PHIL/SCI CHARTS NAT/COMP 19 NEGRO. PAGE 15 ECO/DEV
G0292 TEC/DEV

B67
ELDREDGE H.W.,TAMING MEGALOPOLIS: HOW TO MANAGE AN MUNIC
URBANIZED WORLD. WOR+45 SOCIETY ECO/DEV ECO/UNDEV TEC/DEV
NAT/G COMPUTER CREATE PARTIC EFFICIENCY WEALTH PLAN
...MGT ANTHOL. PAGE 17 G0342 PROB/SOLV

B67
HODGKINSON R.G.,THE ORIGINS OF THE NATIONAL HEALTH HEAL
SERVICE: THE MEDICAL SERVICES OF THE NEW POOR LAW, NAT/G
1834-1871. UK INDUS MUNIC WORKER PROB/SOLV POLICY
EFFICIENCY ATTIT HEALTH SOCISM...JURID LAW
SOC/WK 19/20. PAGE 26 G0519

B67
MACBRIDE R.,THE AUTOMATED STATE: COMPUTER SYSTEMS COMPUTER
AS A NEW FORCE IN SOCIETY. FUT WOR+45 FINAN MUNIC AUTOMAT
NAT/G WORKER PLAN TEC/DEV CONTROL PERS/REL RACE/REL PROB/SOLV
ADJUST. PAGE 35 G0685 SOCIETY

B67
NASH M.,MACHINE AGE MAYA. GUATEMALA L/A+17C STRUCT INDUS
AGRI WORKER CREATE INCOME ATTIT RIGID/FLEX ROLE CULTURE
...IDEA/COMP SOC/EXP WORSHIP 20 INDIAN/AM. PAGE 41 SOC
G0806 MUNIC

B67
PIPER D.C.,THE INTERNATIONAL LAW OF THE GREAT CONCPT
LAKES. CANADA EXTR/IND MUNIC LICENSE ARMS/CONT DIPLOM
CRIME...GEOG 19/20. PAGE 45 G0879 INT/LAW

B67
RIDKER R.G.,ECONOMIC COSTS OF AIR POLLUTION* OP/RES
STUDIES IN MEASUREMENT. R+D MUNIC GP/REL KNOWL HABITAT
...OBS 20. PAGE 47 G0919 PHIL/SCI

B67

ROTHENBERG J.,,ECONOMIC EVALUATION OF URBAN RENEWAL: PLAN
CONCEPTUAL FOUNDATION OF BENEFIT-COST ANALYSIS. MUNIC
USA+45 ECO/DEV NEIGH TEC/DEV ADMIN GEN/LAWS. PROB/SOLV
PAGE 48 G0940 COST

B67

UNIVERSAL REFERENCE SYSTEM,CURRENT EVENTS AND BIBLIOG/A
PROBLEMS OF MODERN SOCIETY (VOLUME V). WOR+45 LOC/G SOCIETY
MUNIC NAT/G PLAN EDU/PROP CRIME RACE/REL WEALTH PROB/SOLV
...COMPUT/IR GEN/METH. PAGE 56 G1097 ATTIT

L67

CARMICHAEL D.M.,"FORTY YEARS OF WATER POLLUTION HEALTH
CONTROL IN WISCONSIN: A CASE STUDY." LAW EXTR/IND CONTROL
INDUS MUNIC DELIB/GP PLAN PROB/SOLV SANCTION ADMIN
...CENSUS CHARTS 20 WISCONSIN. PAGE 11 G0207 ADJUD

S67

FRIED M.,"FUNCTIONS OF THE WORKING CLASS COMMUNITY CLASSIF
IN MODERN URBAN SOCIETY* IMPLICATIONS FOR FORCED WORKER
RELOCATION." USA+45 INDUS R+D NEIGH PLAN TEC/DEV MUNIC
PARTIC GP/REL ATTIT...SOC STAT CHARTS. PAGE 20 ADJUST
G0393

S67

GOBER J.L.,"FEDERALISM AT WORK." USA+45 NAT/G MUNIC
CONSULT ACT/RES PLAN CONFER ADMIN LEAD PARTIC TEC/DEV
FEDERAL ATTIT. PAGE 21 G0422 R+D
  GOV/REL

S67

MYERS S.,"TECHNOLOGY AND URBAN TRANSIT: THE R+D
ENORMOUS POTENTIAL OF BUS AND RAIL SYSTEMS." USA+45 TEC/DEV
FINAN LOC/G MUNIC WORKER PLAN PROB/SOLV PRICE DIST/IND
AUTOMAT 20. PAGE 40 G0798 ACT/RES

S67

WHITTIER J.M.,"COMPULSORY POOLING AND UNITIZATION* LEGIS
DIE-HARD KANSAS." LAW PLAN EDU/PROP ATTIT...POLICY MUNIC
JURID PREDICT TREND METH/COMP 20. PAGE 63 G1236 INDUS
  ECO/TAC

S67

WINSTON O.,"AN URBANIZATION PATTERN FOR THE US* USA+45
SOME CONSIDERATIONS FOR THE DECENTRALIZATION OF MUNIC
EXCELLENCE." FUT SOCIETY ECO/DEV R+D NEIGH ACT/RES PLAN
PROB/SOLV TEC/DEV. PAGE 64 G1247 HABITAT

N67

ASIAN STUDIES CENTER,FOUR ARTICLES ON POPULATION ASIA
AND FAMILY LIFE IN TAIWAN (ASIAN STUDIES PAPERS, FAM
REPRINT SERIES NO. 2). CULTURE STRATA ECO/UNDEV CENSUS
AGRI INDUS R+D KIN MUNIC...GEOG SOC CHARTS 20. ANTHOL
PAGE 4 G0072

B68

GALLAHER A. JR.,PERSPECTIVES IN DEVELOPMENTAL TECHNIC
CHANGE. MUNIC PLAN INSPECT EDU/PROP...POLICY TEC/DEV
DECISION GEOG PSY SOC IDEA/COMP ANTHOL 20 PROB/SOLV
MODERNIZE. PAGE 21 G0405 CREATE

MUNICH....MUNICH, GERMANY

MUNICIPALITIES....SEE MUNIC

MURDER....MURDER, ASSASSINATION; SEE ALSO CRIME

B61

STEIN W.,NUCLEAR WEAPONS: A CATHOLIC RESPONSE. NUC/PWR
WOR+45 FORCES ARMS/CONT DETER MURDER MORAL...POLICY WAR
CATH IDEA/COMP ANTHOL 20. PAGE 52 G1033 CATHISM
  ATTIT

B67

BURNS E.L.M.,MEGAMURDER. WOR+45 LAW INT/ORG NAT/G FORCES
BAL/PWR DIPLOM DETER MURDER WEAPON CIVMIL/REL PEACE PLAN
...INT/LAW TREND 20. PAGE 10 G0193 WAR
  NUC/PWR

S67

SALISBURY H.E.,"THE WAR IN VIETNAM." USA+45 POLICY
VIETNAM/N DIPLOM MURDER 20. PAGE 48 G0953 WAR
  FORCES
  OBS

MURDOCK J.C. G0796

MURNGIN....MURNGIN, AN AUSTRALIAN TRIBE

MURPHY E.F. G0797

MURRAY/JC....JOHN COURTNEY MURRAY

MUSCAT....MUSCAT AND OMAN; SEE ALSO ISLAM

MUSHRUSH G.J. G0358

MUSIC....MUSIC AND SONGS

MUSLIM....MUSLIM PEOPLE AND RELIGION

MUSLIM/LG....MUSLIM LEAGUE

MUSSOLIN/B....BENITO MUSSOLINI

MYERS S. G0798

MYRDAL/G....GUNNAR MYRDAL

MYSTIC....MYSTICAL

MYSTICISM....SEE MYSTISM

MYSTISM....MYSTICISM

MYTH....FICTION

B29

DEWEY J.,THE QUEST FOR CERTAINTY. GP/REL RATIONAL PHIL/SCI
UTOPIA ATTIT MORAL ORD/FREE PWR...MYTH HIST/WRIT. PERSON
PAGE 15 G0301 PERCEPT
  KNOWL

B55

OPPENHEIMER R.,THE OPEN MIND. USA+45 WOR+45 NAT/G CREATE
DELIB/GP DETER MORAL ORD/FREE...MYTH GEN/LAWS 20. PWR
PAGE 43 G0842 ARMS/CONT
  NUC/PWR

S56

MILLER W.E.,"PRESIDENTIAL COATTAILS: A STUDY IN CHIEF
POLITICAL MYTH AND METHODOLOGY" (BMR)" USA+45 CHOOSE
CREATE PARTIC ATTIT DRIVE PWR...DECISION CONCPT POL/PAR
CHARTS SIMUL 20 PRESIDENT CONGRESS. PAGE 39 G0774 MYTH

S58

DAVENPORT J.,"ARMS AND THE WELFARE STATE." INTELL USA+45
STRUCT FORCES CREATE ECO/TAC FOR/AID DOMIN LEGIT NAT/G
ADMIN WAR ORD/FREE PWR...POLICY SOC CONCPT MYTH OBS USSR
TREND COLD/WAR TOT/POP 20. PAGE 14 G0276

B59

RUSSELL B.,COMMON SENSE AND NUCLEAR WARFARE. WOR+45 ORD/FREE
INTELL SOCIETY STRATA NAT/G TOP/EX EDU/PROP ATTIT ARMS/CONT
PERSON KNOWL MORAL PWR...POLICY CONCPT MYTH NUC/PWR
CON/ANAL COLD/WAR 20. PAGE 48 G0948

S59

DEUTSCH K.W.,"THE IMPACT OF SCIENCE AND TECHNOLOGY PHIL/SCI
ON INTERNATIONAL POLITICS." UNIV INTELL NAT/G MYTH
ACT/RES CREATE TEC/DEV EDU/PROP EXEC KNOWL...CONCPT DIPLOM
TREND TOT/POP 20. PAGE 15 G0297 NAT/LISM

B60

JANOWITZ M.,THE PROFESSIONAL SOLDIER. CULTURE FORCES
STRATA STRUCT FAM PROB/SOLV TEC/DEV COERCE WAR MYTH
CIVMIL/REL NAT/LISM AGE HEREDITY ALL/VALS CONSERVE LEAD
...MGT WORSHIP. PAGE 28 G0560 ELITES

S60

DOUGHERTY J.E.,"KEY TO SECURITY: DISARMAMENT OR FORCES
ARMS STABILITY." COM USA+45 USSR INT/ORG NAT/G ORD/FREE
CREATE EDU/PROP COERCE DETER ATTIT PWR...DECISION ARMS/CONT
CONCPT MYTH NEW/IDEA TREND 20 COLD/WAR. PAGE 16 NUC/PWR
G0311

S62

FOSTER R.B.,"UNILATERAL ARMS CONTROL MEASURES AND PLAN
DISARMAMENT NEGOTIATION." WOR+45 VOL/ASSN DELIB/GP ORD/FREE
ACT/RES ECO/TAC EDU/PROP ATTIT RIGID/FLEX...CONCPT ARMS/CONT
MYTH TIME/SEQ COLD/WAR 20. PAGE 20 G0386 DETER

S62

PHIPPS T.E.,"THE CASE FOR DETERRENCE." FUT WOR+45 ATTIT
SOCIETY EX/STRUC FORCES ACT/RES CREATE PLAN TEC/DEV COERCE
ROUTINE RIGID/FLEX ORD/FREE...POLICY MYTH NEW/IDEA DETER
STERTYP COLD/WAR 20. PAGE 45 G0876 ARMS/CONT

S62

SINGER J.D.,"STABLE DETERRENCE AND ITS LIMITS." FUT NAT/G
WOR+45 R+D INT/ORG CONSULT ACT/RES TEC/DEV FORCES
ARMS/CONT COERCE DRIVE PERCEPT RIGID/FLEX ORD/FREE DETER
PWR...MYTH SIMUL TOT/POP 20. PAGE 51 G1004 NUC/PWR

B63

LILIENTHAL D.E.,CHANGE, HOPE, AND THE BOMB. USA+45 ATTIT
WOR+45 R+D INT/ORG NAT/G DELIB/GP FORCES ACT/RES MYTH
DETER RIGID/FLEX ORD/FREE...POLICY CONCPT OBS AEC ARMS/CONT
20. PAGE 34 G0666 NUC/PWR

S63
WOHLSTETTER A.,"SCIENTISTS, SEERS AND STRATEGY."   INTELL
USA+45 ELITES R+D NAT/G CONSULT FORCES TOP/EX   ACT/RES
EDU/PROP ARMS/CONT KNOWL ORD/FREE...DECISION MYTH
20. PAGE 64 G1253

B64
CONANT J.B.,TWO MODES OF THOUGHT: MY ENCOUNTERS   PHIL/SCI
WITH SCIENCE AND EDUCATION....ART/METH JURID SOC   SKILL
TREND. PAGE 13 G0249   MYTH
                                                      STYLE

B64
GROSSER G.H.,THE THREAT OF IMPENDING DISASTER: HEALTH
CONTRIBUTIONS TO THE PSYCHOLOGY OF STRESS. SPACE   PSY
UNIV SOCIETY R+D TEC/DEV EDU/PROP COERCE WAR ATTIT   NUC/PWR
BIO/SOC DISPL PERCEPT PERSON...SOC MYTH SELF/OBS
CONT/OBS BIOG CON/ANAL TOT/POP 20. PAGE 23 G0455

L64
WARD C.,"THE 'NEW MYTHS' AND 'OLD REALITIES' OF   FORCES
NUCLEAR WAR." COM FUT USA+45 USSR WOR+45 INT/ORG   COERCE
NAT/G DOMIN LEGIT EXEC ATTIT PERCEPT ALL/VALS   ARMS/CONT
...POLICY RELATIV PSY MYTH TREND 20. PAGE 62 G1212   NUC/PWR

S65
GRIFFITH S.B.,"COMMUNIST CHINA'S CAPACITY TO MAKE   FORCES
WAR." CHINA/COM COM NAT/G TOP/EX PLAN DOMIN COERCE   PWR
NUC/PWR ATTIT RESPECT SKILL...CONCPT MYTH TIME/SEQ   WEAPON
TREND COLD/WAR 20. PAGE 23 G0452   ASIA

B67
SCHON D.A.,TECHNOLOGY AND CHANGE* THE NEW   INDUS
HERACLITUS. TEC/DEV CONTROL COST DEMAND EFFICIENCY   PROB/SOLV
RIGID/FLEX...MYTH 20. PAGE 49 G0975   R+D
                                                      CREATE

B67
SILBERMAN C.E.,THE MYTHS OF AUTOMATION. INDUS   MYTH
WORKER COST PRODUC AGE WEALTH 20. PAGE 51 G0996   AUTOMAT
                                                      CHARTS

───────────────────────────── N ─────────────────────────────

NAACP....NATIONAL ASSOCIATION FOR THE ADVANCEMENT OF
COLORED PEOPLE

NABALOI....NABALOI TRIBE, PHILIPPINES

NADER R. G0799

NADLER E.B. G0800

NAFTA....NORTH ATLANTIC FREE TRADE AREA

NAFZIGER R.O. G0801

NAGEL E. G0242

NAKICENOVIC S. G0802

NAM....NATIONAL ASSOCIATION OF MANUFACTURERS

NAM/TIEN....NAM TIEN

NANES A. G0803

NAPOLEON/B....NAPOLEON BONAPARTE

NARAYAN/J....JAYPRAKASH NARAYAN

NARCO/ACT....UNIFORM NARCOTIC DRUG ACT

NASA G0804,G0805

NASA....NATIONAL AERONAUTIC AND SPACE ADMINISTRATION

B62
US CONGRESS,COMMUNICATIONS SATELLITE LEGISLATION: SPACE
HEARINGS BEFORE COMM ON AERON AND SPACE SCIENCES ON   COM/IND
BILLS S2550 AND 2814. WOR+45 LAW VOL/ASSN PLAN   ADJUD
DIPLOM CONTROL OWN PEACE...NEW/IDEA CONGRESS NASA.   GOV/REL
PAGE 56 G1110

B63
DEAN A.L.,FEDERAL AGENCY APPROACHES TO FIELD   ADMIN
MANAGEMENT (PAMPHLET). R+D DELIB/GP EX/STRUC   MGT
PROB/SOLV GOV/REL...CLASSIF BIBLIOG 20 FAA NASA   NAT/G
DEPT/HEW POSTAL/SYS IRS. PAGE 15 G0287   OP/RES

B63
KAST F.E.,SCIENCE, TECHNOLOGY, AND MANAGEMENT.   MGT
SPACE USA+45 FORCES CONFER DETER NUC/PWR...PHIL/SCI   PLAN
CHARTS ANTHOL BIBLIOG 20 NASA. PAGE 30 G0581   TEC/DEV
                                                      PROB/SOLV

B63
US SENATE,DOCUMENTS ON INTERNATIONAL AS"ECTS OF   SPACE
EXPLORATION AND USE OF OUTER SPACE, 1954-62: STAFF   UTIL
REPORT FOR COMM AERON SPACE SCI. USA+45 USSR LEGIS   GOV/REL
LEAD CIVMIL/REL PEACE...POLICY INT/LAW ANTHOL 20   DIPLOM
CONGRESS NASA KHRUSH/N. PAGE 59 G1162

B64
NASA,PROCEEDINGS OF CONFERENCE ON THE LAW OF SPACE   SPACE
AND OF SATELLITE COMMUNICATIONS: CHICAGO 1963. FUT   COM/IND
WOR+45 DELIB/GP PROB/SOLV TEC/DEV CONFER ADJUD   LAW
NUC/PWR...POLICY IDEA/COMP 20 NASA. PAGE 41 G0805   DIPLOM

B64
US AIR FORCE ACADEMY ASSEMBLY,OUTER SPACE: FINAL   SPACE
REPORT APRIL 1-4, 1964. FUT USA+45 WOR+45 LAW   CIVMIL/REL
DELIB/GP CONFER ARMS/CONT WAR PEACE ATTIT MORAL   NUC/PWR
...ANTHOL 20 NASA. PAGE 56 G1104   DIPLOM

B65
FRUTKIN A.W.,SPACE AND THE INTERNATIONAL   SPACE
COOPERATION YEAR: A NATIONAL CHALLENGE (PAMPHLET).   INDUS
EUR+WWI USA+45 FINAN TEC/DEV BUDGET...MGT 20 NASA.   NAT/G
PAGE 20 G0396   DIPLOM

B65
US SENATE,US INTERNATIONAL SPACE PROGRAMS, 1959-65:   SPACE
STAFF REPORT FOR COMM ON AERONAUTICAL AND SPACE   DIPLOM
SCIENCES. WOR+45 VOL/ASSN CIVMIL/REL 20 CONGRESS   PLAN
NASA TREATY. PAGE 59 G1163   GOV/REL

B65
US SENATE COMM AERO SPACE SCI,NATIONAL SPACE GOALS   SPACE
FOR THE POST-APOLLO PERIOD. USA+45 CONSULT DELIB/GP   FUT
TEC/DEV BUDGET GP/REL ATTIT...CHARTS IDEA/COMP TIME   R+D
20 DEPT/DEFEN NASA CONGRESS. PAGE 59 G1166   LEGIS

B65
US SENATE COMM AERO SPACE SCI,INTERNATIONAL   DIPLOM
COOPERATION AND ORGANIZATION FOR OUTER SPACE. FUT   SPACE
USA+45 WOR+45 PROF/ORG VOL/ASSN CONSULT DELIB/GP   R+D
PLAN TEC/DEV ARMS/CONT GP/REL PEACE 20 UN NASA.   NAT/G
PAGE 59 G1167

B66
ROSHOLT R.L.,AN ADMINISTRATIVE HISTORY OF NASA,   ADMIN
1958-1963. SPACE USA+45 FINAN LEAD...MGT CHARTS   EX/STRUC
BIBLIOG 20 NASA. PAGE 48 G0938   ADJUST
                                                      DELIB/GP

B66
US SENATE,POLICY PLANNING FOR AERONAUTICAL RESEARCH   SPACE
AND DEVELOPMENT: STAFF REPORT FOR COMM ON   CIVMIL/REL
AERONAUTICAL AND SPACE SCIENCES. USA+45 AIR   GOV/REL
DIST/IND PLAN...POLICY CHARTS 20 CONGRESS NASA.   R+D
PAGE 59 G1164

B67
US SENATE COMM AERO SPACE SCI,TREATY ON PRINCIPLES   SPACE
GOVERNING ACTIVITIES OF STATES IN EXPLORATION AND   INT/LAW
USE OF OUTER SPACE, INCLUDING...BODIES. DELIB/GP   ORD/FREE
FORCES LEGIS DIPLOM...JURID 20 DEPT/STATE NASA   PEACE
DEPT/DEFEN UN. PAGE 60 G1170

B67
US SENATE COMM AERO SPACE SCI,APOLLO ACCIDENT   PROB/SOLV
(PARTS 1-7). USA+45 DELIB/GP LEGIS...INT CHARTS   SPACE
NASA. PAGE 60 G1173   BUDGET
                                                      GOV/REL

S67
DADDARIO E.Q.,"CONGRESS FACES SPACE POLICIES." R+D   SPACE
NAT/G FORCES CREATE LEAD...DECISION CONGRESS NASA.   PLAN
PAGE 14 G0269   BUDGET
                                                      POLICY

S67
MACDONALD G.J.F.,"SCIENCE AND SPACE POLICY* HOW   SPACE
DOES IT GET PLANNED?" R+D CREATE TEC/DEV BUDGET   PLAN
ADMIN ROUTINE...DECISION NASA. PAGE 35 G0687   MGT
                                                      EX/STRUC

N67
US SUPERINTENDENT OF DOCUMENTS,SPACE: MISSILES, THE   BIBLIOG/A
MOON, NASA, AND SATELLITES (PRICE LIST 79A). USA+45   SPACE
COM/IND R+D NAT/G DIPLOM EDU/PROP ADMIN CONTROL   TEC/DEV
HEALTH...POLICY SIMUL NASA CONGRESS. PAGE 61 G1190   PEACE

N67
US HOUSE COMM SCI ASTRONAUT,AUTHORIZING   SPACE
APPROPRIATIONS TO THE NATIONAL AERONAUTICS AND   R+D
SPACE ADMINISTRATION (PAMPHLET). USA+45 NAT/G   PHIL/SCI
OP/RES TEC/DEV BUDGET NASA HOUSE/REP. PAGE 58 G1149   NUC/PWR

N67
US SENATE COMM AERO SPACE SCI,AERONAUTICAL RESEARCH AIR

AND DEVELOPMENT POLICY (PAMPHLET). SPACE USA+45 R+D
INDUS CIVMIL/REL CONGRESS PRESIDENT NASA SENATE. POLICY
PAGE 60 G1169 PLAN

N67
US SENATE COMM AERO SPACE SCI,AERONAUTICAL RESEARCH DIST/IND
AND DEVELOPMENT POLICY; HEARINGS, COMM ON SPACE
AERONAUTICAL AND SPACE SCIENCES...1967 (PAMPHLET). NAT/G
R+D PROB/SOLV EXEC GOV/REL 20 DEPT/DEFEN FAA NASA PLAN
CONGRESS. PAGE 60 G1174

NASH M. G0806

NASHVILLE....NASHVILLE, TENNESSEE

NASSER/G....GAMAL ABDEL NASSER

B64
MILIBAND R.,THE SOCIALIST REGISTER: 1964. GERMANY/W MARXISM
ITALY UK LABOR POL/PAR ECO/TAC FOR/AID NUC/PWR SOCISM
...POLICY SOCIALIST IDEA/COMP 20 MAO NASSER/G. CAP/ISM
PAGE 39 G0769 PROB/SOLV

NAT/COMP....COMPARISON OF NATIONS

B
BRITISH COMMONWEALTH BUR AGRI,WORLD AGRICULTURAL BIBLIOG/A
ECONOMICS AND RURAL SOCIOLOGY ABSTRACTS. NAT/G AGRI
OP/RES PLAN TEC/DEV LEAD PRODUC...GEOG MGT NAT/COMP SOC
20. PAGE 9 G0170 WORKER

N
RAND SCHOOL OF SOCIAL SCIENCE,INDEX TO LABOR BIBLIOG
ARTICLES. ECO/DEV INT/ORG LEGIS DIPLOM GP/REL LABOR
...NAT/COMP 20. PAGE 46 G0900 MGT
ADJUD

B49
MCLEAN J.M.,THE PUBLIC SERVICE AND UNIVERSITY ACADEM
EDUCATION. UK USA-45 DELIB/GP EX/STRUC TOP/EX ADMIN NAT/G
...GOV/COMP METH/COMP NAT/COMP ANTHOL 20. PAGE 38 EXEC
G0746 EDU/PROP

S56
ALMOND G.A.,"COMPARATIVE POLITICAL SYSTEMS" (BMR)" GOV/COMP
WOR+45 WOR-45 PROB/SOLV DIPLOM EFFICIENCY CONCPT
...PHIL/SCI SOC METH 17/20. PAGE 3 G0046 ALL/IDEOS
NAT/COMP

B58
MECRENSKY E.,SCIENTIFIC MANPOWER IN EUROPE. WOR+45 ECO/TAC
EDU/PROP GOV/REL SKILL...TECHNIC PHIL/SCI INT TEC/DEV
CHARTS BIBLIOG 20. PAGE 38 G0750 METH/COMP
NAT/COMP

B59
ELDRIDGE H.T.,THE MATERIALS OF DEMOGRAPHY: A BIBLIOG/A
SELECTED AND ANNOTATED BIBLIOGRAPHY. R+D DEATH GEOG
...SAMP METH/COMP NAT/COMP 20. PAGE 18 G0343 STAT
TREND

B59
EMME E.M.,THE IMPACT OF AIR POWER - NATIONAL DETER
SECURITY AND WORLD POLITICS. USA+45 USSR FORCES AIR
DIPLOM WEAPON PEACE TOTALISM...POLICY NAT/COMP 20 WAR
EUROPE. PAGE 18 G0346 ORD/FREE

B59
VERNEY D.V.,PUBLIC ENTERPRISE IN SWEDEN. FUT SWEDEN ECO/DEV
UK INDUS POL/PAR LEGIS PROB/SOLV CAP/ISM INT/TRADE POLICY
CONTROL SOCISM...MGT CONCPT NAT/COMP 20 SOCDEM/PAR LG/CO
CIVIL/SERV. PAGE 61 G1196 NAT/G

B60
FRANCIS R.G.,THE PREDICTIVE PROCESS. PLAN MARXISM PREDICT
...DECISION SOC CONCPT NAT/COMP 19/20. PAGE 20 PHIL/SCI
G0390 TREND

B62
FRYKLUND R.,100 MILLION LIVES: MAXIMUM SURVIVAL IN NUC/PWR
A NUCLEAR WAR. USA+45 USSR CONTROL WEAPON WAR
...IDEA/COMP NAT/COMP 20. PAGE 20 G0397 PLAN
DETER

B62
MARTINS A.F.,REVOLUCAO BRANCA NO CAMPO. L/A+17C AGRI
SERV/IND DEMAND EFFICIENCY PRODUC...POLICY ECO/UNDEV
METH/COMP. PAGE 36 G0717 TEC/DEV
NAT/COMP

N62
US CONGRESS JT ATOM ENRGY COMM,PEACEFUL USES OF NUC/PWR
ATOMIC ENERGY, HEARING. USA+45 USSR TEC/DEV ATTIT ACADEM
RIGID/FLEX...TESTS CHARTS EXHIBIT METH/COMP 20 SCHOOL
CONGRESS. PAGE 57 G1112 NAT/COMP

B63
GEERTZ C.,OLD SOCIETIES AND NEW STATES: THE QUEST ECO/UNDEV
FOR MODERNITY IN ASIA AND AFRICA. AFR ASIA LAW TEC/DEV
CULTURE SECT EDU/PROP REV...GOV/COMP NAT/COMP 20. NAT/LISM
PAGE 21 G0415 SOVEREIGN

B63
RUITENBEER H.M.,THE DILEMMA OF ORGANIZATIONAL PERSON
SOCIETY. CULTURE ECO/DEV MUNIC SECT TEC/DEV ROLE
EDU/PROP NAT/LISM ORD/FREE...NAT/COMP 20 RIESMAN/D ADMIN
WHYTE/WF MERTON/R MEAD/MARG JASPERS/K. PAGE 48 WORKER
G0945

B63
UN SECRETARY GENERAL,PLANNING FOR ECONOMIC PLAN
DEVELOPMENT. ECO/UNDEV FINAN BUDGET INT/TRADE ECO/TAC
TARIFFS TAX ADMIN 20 UN. PAGE 55 G1089 MGT
NAT/COMP

B63
US ATOMIC ENERGY COMMISSION,ATOMIC ENERGY IN THE METH/COMP
SOVIET UNION: TRIP REPORT OF THE US ATOMIC ENERGY OP/RES
DELEGATION, MAY 1933. USSR R+D NAT/G CONSULT CREATE TEC/DEV
DIPLOM ADMIN ROUTINE EFFICIENCY PRODUC KNOWL SKILL NUC/PWR
...NAT/COMP 20 AEC TRAVEL TREATY. PAGE 56 G1107

B64
BROWN N.,NUCLEAR WAR* THE IMPENDING STRATEGIC FORCES
DEADLOCK. USA+45 USSR TEC/DEV BUDGET RISK ARMS/CONT OP/RES
NUC/PWR WEAPON COST BIO/SOC...GEOG IDEA/COMP WAR
NAT/COMP GAME NATO WARSAW/P. PAGE 9 G0177 GEN/LAWS

B64
GUTMANN P.M.,ECONOMIC GROWTH: AN AMERICAN PROBLEM. WEALTH
USA+45 FINAN R+D...POLICY NAT/COMP ANTHOL BIBLIOG ECO/DEV
20. PAGE 24 G0463 CAP/ISM
ORD/FREE

B65
GRETTON P.,MARITIME STRATEGY - A STUDY OF DEFENSE FORCES
PROBLEMS. ASIA UK USSR DIPLOM COERCE DETER NUC/PWR PLAN
WEAPON...CONCPT NAT/COMP 20. PAGE 23 G0449 WAR
SEA

S65
BIRNBAUM K.,"SWEDEN'S NUCLEAR POLICY." WOR+45 SWEDEN
POL/PAR CREATE TEC/DEV NEUTRAL RISK WAR ORD/FREE NUC/PWR
...DECISION IDEA/COMP NAT/COMP TIME. PAGE 7 G0137 DIPLOM
ARMS/CONT

S65
MARTIN A.,"PROLIFERATION." FUT WOR+45 PROB/SOLV RECORD
REGION ADJUST...PREDICT NAT/COMP UN TREATY. PAGE 36 NUC/PWR
G0712 ARMS/CONT
VOL/ASSN

S65
TENDLER J.D.,"TECHNOLOGY AND ECONOMIC DEVELOPMENT* BRAZIL
THE CASE OF HYDRO VS THERMAL POWER." CONSTRUC INDUS
DIST/IND CREATE TEC/DEV INT/TRADE CENTRAL PWR SKILL ECO/UNDEV
WEALTH...MGT NAT/COMP ARGEN. PAGE 54 G1063

B66
OECD DEVELOPMENT CENTRE,CATALOGUE OF SOCIAL AND ECO/UNDEV
ECONOMIC DEVELOPMENT INSTITUTES AND PROGRAMMES* ECO/DEV
RESEARCH. ACT/RES PLAN TEC/DEV EDU/PROP...SOC R+D
GP/COMP NAT/COMP. PAGE 43 G0836 ACADEM

L66
ZOPPO C.E.,"NUCLEAR TECHNOLOGY, MULTIPOLARITY, AND NET/THEORY
INTERNATIONAL STABILITY." ASIA RUSSIA USA+45 STRUCT ORD/FREE
TOP/EX BAL/PWR DIPLOM DETER CIVMIL/REL NAT/COMP. DECISION
PAGE 65 G1270 NUC/PWR

S66
HANSON A.H.,"PLANNING AND THE POLITICIANS* SOME PLAN
REFLECTIONS ON ECONOMIC PLANNING IN WESTERN ECO/DEV
EUROPE." MARKET NAT/G TEC/DEV CONSEN ROLE EUR+WWI
...METH/COMP NAT/COMP. PAGE 24 G0479 ADMIN

S66
TURKEVICH J.,"SOVIET SCIENCE APPRAISED." USA+45 R+D USSR
ACADEM FORCES DIPLOM EDU/PROP WAR EFFICIENCY PEACE TEC/DEV
SKILL OBS. PAGE 55 G1081 NAT/COMP
ATTIT

B67
DEGLER C.N.,THE AGE OF THE ECONOMIC REVOLUTION INDUS
1876-1900. USA-45 AGRI MUNIC POL/PAR SECT ECO/TAC SOCIETY
CHOOSE...PHIL/SCI CHARTS NAT/COMP 19 NEGRO. PAGE 15 ECO/DEV
G0292 TEC/DEV

B67
LAMBERT J.,LATIN AMERICA: SOCIAL STRUCTURES AND L/A+17C
POLITICAL INSTITUTIONS. STRUCT TEC/DEV DIPLOM ADMIN NAT/G
COLONIAL LEAD ATTIT...SOC CLASSIF NAT/COMP 17/20. ECO/UNDEV

B67
MCCLINTOCK R.,THE MEANING OF LIMITED WAR. FUT   WAR
WOR+45 NAT/G FORCES GUERRILLA REV...POLICY SAMP/SIZ NUC/PWR
TREND NAT/COMP 45 COLD/WAR. PAGE 37 G0730   BAL/PWR
                                                   DIPLOM

B67
MCLAUGHLIN M.R.,RELIGIOUS EDUCATION AND THE STATE: SECT
DEMOCRACY FINDS A WAY. CANADA EUR+WWI GP/REL   NAT/G
POPULISM...CATH NAT/COMP 20 AUSTRAL. PAGE 38 G0745 EDU/PROP
                                                   POLICY

B67
OVERSEAS DEVELOPMENT INSTIT,EFFECTIVE AID. WOR+45   FOR/AID
INT/ORG TEC/DEV DIPLOM INT/TRADE ADMIN. PAGE 43   ECO/UNDEV
G0852   ECO/TAC
                                                   NAT/COMP

B67
UNESCO,PRINCIPLES AND PROBLEMS OF NATIONAL SCIENCE NAT/COMP
POLICIES. WOR+45 ECO/DEV ECO/UNDEV R+D INT/ORG   POLICY
PROB/SOLV CONFER...PHIL/SCI CHARTS 20 UNESCO UN.   TEC/DEV
PAGE 55 G1091   CREATE

NAT/FARMER....NATIONAL FARMERS' ASSOCIATION

NAT/G....NATIONAL GOVERNMENT

NAT/LISM....NATIONALISM

C25
MOON P.T.,"SYLLABUS ON INTERNATIONAL RELATIONS."   INT/ORG
EUR+WWI MOD/EUR USA-45 FORCES COLONIAL WAR WEAPON   DIPLOM
NAT/LISM...POLICY BIBLIOG T 19/20. PAGE 39 G0778   NAT/G

B34
EINSTEIN A.,THE WORLD AS I SEE IT. WOR-45 INTELL   SOCIETY
R+D INT/ORG NAT/G SECT VOL/ASSN FORCES CREATE   PHIL/SCI
EDU/PROP LEGIT ARMS/CONT WAR WEAPON NAT/LISM   DIPLOM
ALL/VALS...POLICY CONCPT 20. PAGE 17 G0337   PACIFISM

B35
FOREIGN AFFAIRS BIBLIOGRAPHY: A SELECTED AND   BIBLIOG/A
ANNOTATED LIST OF BOOKS ON INTERNATIONAL RELATIONS DIPLOM
1919-1962 (4 VOLS.). CONSTN FORCES COLONIAL   INT/ORG
ARMS/CONT WAR NAT/LISM PEACE ATTIT DRIVE...POLICY
INT/LAW 20. PAGE 1 G0011

B38
HARPER S.N.,THE GOVERNMENT OF THE SOVIET UNION. COM MARXISM
USSR LAW CONSTN ECO/DEV PLAN TEC/DEV DIPLOM   NAT/G
INT/TRADE ADMIN REV NAT/LISM...POLICY 20. PAGE 24   LEAD
G0483   POL/PAR

B42
BINGHAM A.M.,THE TECHNIQUES OF DEMOCRACY. USA-45   POPULISM
CONSTN STRUCT POL/PAR LEGIS PLAN PARTIC CHOOSE   ORD/FREE
REPRESENT NAT/LISM TOTALISM...MGT 20. PAGE 7 G0136 ADMIN
                                                   NAT/G

B45
REVES E.,THE ANATOMY OF PEACE. WOR-45 LAW CULTURE   ACT/RES
NAT/G PLAN TEC/DEV EDU/PROP WAR NAT/LISM ATTIT   CONCPT
ALL/VALS SOVEREIGN...POLICY HUM TIME/SEQ 20.   NUC/PWR
PAGE 46 G0914   PEACE

S54
PYE L.W.,"EASTERN NATIONALISM AND WESTERN POLICY." CREATE
ASIA S/ASIA USA+45 USA-45 SOCIETY PLAN DIPLOM KNOWL ACT/RES
TOT/POP 20. PAGE 46 G0896   NAT/LISM

B58
ANGELL N.,DEFENCE AND THE ENGLISH-SPEAKING ROLE.   DIPLOM
CHINA/COM UK USSR INT/ORG FORCES EDU/PROP NEUTRAL   WAR
NUC/PWR NAT/LISM PEACE TOTALISM 20 COLD/WAR   MARXISM
COEXIST. PAGE 3 G0059   ORD/FREE

B59
WARD B.,5 IDEAS THAT CHANGE THE WORLD. WOR+45   ECO/UNDEV
WOR-45 SOCIETY STRUCT AGRI INDUS INT/ORG NAT/G   ALL/VALS
FORCES ACT/RES ARMS/CONT TOTALISM ATTIT DRIVE   NAT/LISM
GEN/LAWS. PAGE 62 G1210   COLONIAL

S59
DEUTSCH K.W.,"THE IMPACT OF SCIENCE AND TECHNOLOGY PHIL/SCI
ON INTERNATIONAL POLITICS." UNIV INTELL NAT/G   MYTH
ACT/RES CREATE TEC/DEV EDU/PROP EXEC KNOWL...CONCPT DIPLOM
TREND TOT/POP 20. PAGE 15 G0297   NAT/LISM

B60
CHASE S.,LIVE AND LET LIVE. USA+45 ECO/DEV   NAT/G
PROB/SOLV TEC/DEV ECO/TAC ARMS/CONT NUC/PWR WAR   DIPLOM
NAT/LISM PEACE...GEOG TREND 20 COLD/WAR. PAGE 11   SOCIETY
G0223   TASK

B60
EINSTEIN A.,EINSTEIN ON PEACE. FUT WOR+45 WOR-45   INT/ORG
SOCIETY NAT/G PLAN BAL/PWR CAP/ISM DIPLOM ARMS/CONT ATTIT
DETER NAT/LISM...POLICY RELATIV HUM PHIL/SCI CONCPT NUC/PWR
BIOG COLD/WAR LEAGUE/NAT NAZI. PAGE 17 G0338   PEACE

B60
HEILBRONER R.L.,THE FUTURE AS HISTORY. USA+45   TEC/DEV
WOR+45 WOR-45 SOCIETY ECO/DEV ECO/UNDEV VOL/ASSN   TREND
PLAN CAP/ISM NUC/PWR CHOOSE NAT/LISM ATTIT ORD/FREE
RESPECT WEALTH SOCISM 20. PAGE 25 G0501

B60
JANOWITZ M.,THE PROFESSIONAL SOLDIER. CULTURE   FORCES
STRATA STRUCT FAM PROB/SOLV TEC/DEV COERCE WAR   MYTH
CIVMIL/REL NAT/LISM AGE HEREDITY ALL/VALS CONSERVE LEAD
...MGT WORSHIP. PAGE 28 G0560   ELITES

S60
KELLEY G.A.,"THE POLITICAL BACKGROUND OF THE FRENCH NAT/G
A-BOMB." EUR+WWI USSR FORCES TOP/EX TEC/DEV NUC/PWR RESPECT
ATTIT PWR...CONCPT OBS/ENVIR TREND 20. PAGE 30   NAT/LISM
G0591   FRANCE

B62
BOULDING K.E.,CONFLICT AND DEFENSE: A GENERAL   MATH
THEORY. FUT SOCIETY INT/ORG NAT/G CREATE BAL/PWR   SIMUL
COERCE NAT/LISM DRIVE ALL/VALS...PLURIST DECISION   PEACE
CONCPT METH/CNCPT TREND HYPO/EXP TOT/POP 20. PAGE 8 WAR
G0157

B63
GEERTZ C.,OLD SOCIETIES AND NEW STATES: THE QUEST   ECO/UNDEV
FOR MODERNITY IN ASIA AND AFRICA. AFR ASIA LAW   TEC/DEV
CULTURE SECT EDU/PROP REV...GOV/COMP NAT/COMP 20.   NAT/LISM
PAGE 21 G0415   SOVEREIGN

B63
MENEZES A.J.,SUBDESENVOLVIMENTO E POLITICA   ECO/UNDEV
INTERNACIONAL. BRAZIL WOR+45 PLAN CONTROL LEAD   DIPLOM
NAT/LISM ORD/FREE 20 THIRD/WRLD. PAGE 38 G0754   POLICY
                                                   BAL/PWR

B63
RUITENBEER H.M.,THE DILEMMA OF ORGANIZATIONAL   PERSON
SOCIETY. CULTURE ECO/DEV MUNIC SECT TEC/DEV   ROLE
EDU/PROP NAT/LISM ORD/FREE...NAT/COMP 20 RIESMAN/D ADMIN
WHYTE/WF MERTON/R MEAD/MARG JASPERS/K. PAGE 48   WORKER
G0945

B64
ROBERTS HL,FOREIGN AFFAIRS BIBLIOGRAPHY, 1952-1962. BIBLIOG/A
ECO/DEV SECT PLAN FOR/AID INT/TRADE ARMS/CONT   DIPLOM
NAT/LISM ATTIT...INT/LAW GOV/COMP IDEA/COMP 20.   INT/ORG
PAGE 47 G0928   WAR

S64
MARES V.E.,"EAST EUROPE'S SECOND CHANCE." COM   VOL/ASSN
EUR+WWI HUNGARY ROMANIA USSR YUGOSLAVIA ECO/UNDEV   ECO/TAC
NAT/G TOP/EX CREATE PLAN TEC/DEV REGION NAT/LISM
RIGID/FLEX PWR...CONCPT STAT COMECON 20. PAGE 36
G0705

S65
RUBINSTEIN A.Z.,"POLITICAL BARRIERS TO   COM
DISARMAMENT." FUT DIPLOM COERCE NUC/PWR WAR   USA+45
NAT/LISM ORD/FREE PREDICT. PAGE 48 G0944   ARMS/CONT
                                                   ATTIT

C65
MARK M.,"BEYOND SOVEREIGNTY." WOR+45 WOR-45   NAT/LISM
ECO/UNDEV BAL/PWR INT/TRADE NUC/PWR REV WAR MARXISM NAT/G
NEW/LIB BIBLIOG. PAGE 36 G0706   DIPLOM
                                                   INTELL

C65
SCHWEBEL M.,"BEHAVIORAL SCIENCE AND HUMAN   PEACE
SURVIVAL." FORCES ARMS/CONT COERCE NUC/PWR WAR   ACT/RES
GP/REL NAT/LISM PERCEPT...POLICY PSY ANTHOL   DIPLOM
BIBLIOG/A 20 COLD/WAR. PAGE 50 G0984   HEAL

B66
HOPKINS J.F.K.,ARABIC PERIODICAL LITERATURE, 1961. BIBLIOG/A
ISLAM LAW CULTURE SECT...GEOG HEAL PHIL/SCI PSY SOC NAT/LISM
20. PAGE 27 G0528   TEC/DEV
                                                   INDUS

B66
WARD B.,NATIONALISM AND IDEOLOGY. ECO/UNDEV KIN   IDEA/COMP
CREATE CAP/ISM FOR/AID ALL/VALS MARXISM...POLICY   NAT/LISM
SOC. PAGE 62 G1211   ATTIT

B67
PADELFORD N.J.,THE DYNAMICS OF INTERNATIONAL   DIPLOM
POLITICS (2ND ED.). WOR+45 LAW INT/ORG FORCES   NAT/G

TEC/DEV REGION NAT/LISM PEACE ATTIT PWR ALL/IDEOS   POLICY
UN COLD/WAR NATO TREATY. PAGE 43 G0856   DECISION

                                                                      B67
SCHEINMAN L.,EURATOM* NUCLEAR INTEGRATION IN   INT/ORG
EUROPE. EX/STRUC LEAD 20 EURATOM. PAGE 49 G0963   NAT/LISM
                                                         NUC/PWR
                                                         DIPLOM

                                                                      B67
YAMAMURA K.,ECONOMIC POLICY IN POSTWAR JAPAN. ASIA   ECO/DEV
FINAN POL/PAR DIPLOM LEAD NAT/LISM ATTIT NEW/LIB   POLICY
POPULISM 20 CHINJAP. PAGE 64 G1262   NAT/G
                                                        TEC/DEV

                                                                      S67
DOYLE S.E.,"COMMUNICATION SATELLITES* INTERNAL   TEC/DEV
ORGANIZATION FOR DEVELOPMENT AND CONTROL." USA+45   SPACE
R+D ACT/RES DIPLOM NAT/LISM...POLICY INT/LAW   COM/IND
PREDICT UN. PAGE 16 G0313   INT/ORG

                                                                      S67
GRIFFITHS F.,"THE POLITICAL SIDE OF 'DISARMAMENT'."   ARMS/CONT
FUT WOR+45 NUC/PWR NAT/LISM PEACE...NEW/IDEA   DIPLOM
PREDICT METH/COMP GEN/LAWS 20. PAGE 23 G0453

                                                                      S67
INGLIS D.R.,"MISSILE DEFENSE, NUCLEAR SPREAD, AND   NUC/PWR
VIETNAM." CHINA/COM USA+45 USSR VIETNAM INDUS   ARMS/CONT
BAL/PWR DETER WAR COST NAT/LISM PEACE. PAGE 28   DIPLOM
G0544   FORCES

                                                                      S67
JACKSON W.G.F.,"NUCLEAR PROLIFERATION AND THE GREAT   NUC/PWR
POWERS." FUT UK WOR+45 INT/ORG DOMIN ARMS/CONT   ATTIT
DETER ORD/FREE PACIFIST. PAGE 28 G0550   BAL/PWR
                                                        NAT/LISM

                                                                      N67
US HOUSE COMM FOREIGN AFFAIRS,REPORT OF SPECIAL   ISLAM
STUDY MISSION TO THE NEAR EAST (PAMPHLET). ISRAEL   DIPLOM
USA+45 YEMEN ECO/UNDEV INT/ORG FOR/AID ARMS/CONT   FORCES
WAR WEAPON NAT/LISM PEACE...GEOG 20 UN HOUSE/REP.
PAGE 58 G1138

NAT/SAFETY....NATIONAL SAFETY COUNCIL

NAT/SERV....COMPULSORY NATIONAL SERVICE

NAT/UNITY....NATIONAL UNITY COMMITTEE (TURKEY)

NATAL

NATHAN O. G0338,G0807

NATIONAL AERONAUTIC AND SPACE ADMINISTRATION....SEE NASA

NATIONAL ASSOCIATION FOR THE ADVANCEMENT OF COLORED
     PEOPLE....SEE NAACP

NATIONAL ASSOCIATION OF MANUFACTURERS....SEE NAM

NATIONAL BELLAS HESS....SEE BELLAS/HES

NATIONAL COUNCIL OF CHURCHES....SEE NCC

NATIONAL DEBT....SEE DEBT

NATIONAL DIRECTORY (IRELAND)....SEE DIRECT/NAT

NATIONAL EDUCATION ASSOCIATION....SEE NEA

NATIONAL FARMERS' ASSOCIATION....SEE NAT/FARMER

NATIONAL GUARD....SEE NATL/GUARD

NATIONAL INSTITUTE OF HEALTH....SEE NIH

NATIONAL INSTITUTE OF PUBLIC ADMINISTRATION....SEE NIPA

NATIONAL LABOR RELATIONS BOARD....SEE NLRB

NATIONAL LIBERATION COUNCIL IN GHANA....SEE NLC

NATIONAL LIBERATION FRONT (OF SOUTH VIETNAM)....SEE NLF

NATIONAL RECOVERY ADMINISTRATION....SEE NRA

NATIONAL SAFETY COUNCIL....SEE NAT/SAFETY

NATIONAL SCIENCE FOUNDATION....SEE NSF

NATIONAL SECURITY COUNCIL....SEE NSC

NATIONAL SECURITY....SEE ORD/FREE

NATIONAL SOCIAL SCIENCE FOUNDATION....SEE NSSF

NATIONAL UNITY COMMITTEE....SEE NUC

NATIONAL WEALTH....SEE NAT/G+WEALTH

NATIONAL ACADEMY OF SCIENCES G0808,G0809

NATIONAL PLANNING ASSOCIATION G0810

NATIONAL REFERRAL CENTER SCI G0811

NATIONAL SCIENCE FOUNDATION G0812,G0813,G0814

NATIONALISM....SEE NAT/LISM

NATIONALIST CHINA....SEE TAIWAN

NATIONALIZATION....SEE SOCISM

NATL/GUARD....NATIONAL GUARD

NATO....NORTH ATLANTIC TREATY ORGANIZATION; SEE ALSO
     VOL/ASSN, INT/ORG, FORCES, DETER

                                                                      B
CURRENT THOUGHT ON PEACE AND WAR. WOR+45 INT/ORG   BIBLIOG/A
FORCES PROB/SOLV DIPLOM NUC/PWR PERCEPT...POLICY   PEACE
SOC 20 UN NATO. PAGE 1 G0001   ATTIT
                                                        WAR

                                                                      B54
US DEPARTMENT OF STATE,PUBLICATIONS OF THE   BIBLIOG
DEPARTMENT OF STATE, OCTOBER 1,1929 TO JANUARY 1,   DIPLOM
1953. AGRI INT/ORG FORCES FOR/AID EDU/PROP
ARMS/CONT NUC/PWR ATTIT 20 DEPT/STATE OAS UN NATO.
PAGE 57 G1122

                                                                      B58
GAVIN J.M.,WAR AND PEACE IN THE SPACE AGE. SPACE   WAR
USA+45 USSR FORCES PLAN TEC/DEV BAL/PWR DIPLOM   DETER
ARMS/CONT WEAPON CIVMIL/REL...CHARTS GP/COMP 20   NUC/PWR
NATO COLD/WAR. PAGE 21 G0414   PEACE

                                                                      B58
ROCKEFELLER BROTH FUND INC,INTERNATIONAL SECURITY -   NUC/PWR
THE MILITARY ASPECT. USA+45 INT/ORG NAT/G BUDGET   DETER
ARMS/CONT WAR WEAPON PEACE ORD/FREE 20 NATO.   FORCES
PAGE 47 G0932   DIPLOM

                                                                      B58
US DEPARTMENT OF STATE,PUBLICATIONS OF THE   BIBLIOG
DEPARTMENT OF STATE, JANUARY 1,1953 TO DECEMBER 31,   DIPLOM
1957. AGRI INT/ORG FORCES FOR/AID EDU/PROP
ARMS/CONT NUC/PWR ATTIT 20 DEPT/STATE OAS UN NATO.
PAGE 57 G1123

                                                                      B60
HITCH C.J.,THE ECONOMICS OF DEFENSE IN THE NUCLEAR   R+D
AGE. USA+45 WOR+45 CREATE PLAN NUC/PWR ATTIT   FORCES
...CON/ANAL CHARTS HYPO/EXP NATO 20. PAGE 26 G0514

                                                                       B60
LE GHAIT E.,NO CARTE BLANCHE TO CAPRICORN; THE   DETER
FOLLY OF NUCLEAR WAR. WOR+45 INT/ORG BAL/PWR DIPLOM   NUC/PWR
RISK COERCE...CENSUS 20 NATO. PAGE 33 G0647   PLAN
                                                       DECISION

                                                                      B60
US DEPARTMENT OF THE ARMY,DISARMAMENT: A   BIBLIOG/A
BIBLIOGRAPHIC RECORD: 1916-1960. DETER WAR WEAPON   ARMS/CONT
PEACE 20 UN LEAGUE/NAT COLD/WAR NATO. PAGE 57 G1128   NUC/PWR
                                                       DIPLOM

                                                                      B61
SCHMIDT H.,VERTEIDIGUNG ODER VERGELTUNG. COM CUBA   PLAN
GERMANY/W USSR FORCES DIPLOM ARMS/CONT DETER   WAR
NUC/PWR...POLICY CHARTS HYPO/EXP SIMUL BIBLIOG 20   BAL/PWR
NATO COLD/WAR. PAGE 49 G0970   ORD/FREE

                                                                      S61
WOHLSTETTER A.,"NUCLEAR SHARING: NATO AND THE NTH   TREND
COUNTRY." EUR+WWI FUT SOCIETY DIPLOM EXEC DETER PWR   TEC/DEV
SKILL...POLICY TECHNIC CONCPT 20 NATO. PAGE 64   NUC/PWR
G1252   ARMS/CONT

                                                                      B62
AIR FORCE ACADEMY LIBRARY,INTERNATIONAL   BIBLIOG
ORGANIZATIONS AND MILITARY SECURITY SYSTEMS   INT/ORG
(PAMPHLET) (SPECIAL BIBLIOGRAPHY SERIES, NUMBER   FORCES
25). DIPLOM FOR/AID INT/TRADE NUC/PWR PEACE 20 UN   DETER
NATO OAS SEATO LEAGUE/NAT. PAGE 2 G0031

                                                                      L63
NIEBURG H.,"EURATOM: A STUDY IN COALITION   VOL/ASSN
POLITICS." EUR+WWI UK USA+45 ELITES NAT/G DELIB/GP   ACT/RES

LEGIS TOP/EX ECO/TAC NUC/PWR ATTIT ORD/FREE PWR
TOT/POP EEC OEEC 20 NATO EURATOM. PAGE 42 G0820

B64
BROWN N.,NUCLEAR WAR* THE IMPENDING STRATEGIC   FORCES
DEADLOCK. USA+45 USSR TEC/DEV BUDGET RISK ARMS/CONT   OP/RES
NUC/PWR WEAPON COST BIO/SOC...GEOG IDEA/COMP   WAR
NAT/COMP GAME NATO WARSAW/P. PAGE 9 G0177   GEN/LAWS

B64
FREYMOND J.,WESTERN EUROPE SINCE THE WAR. COM   INT/ORG
EUR+WWI USA+45 DIPLOM...BIBLIOG 20 NATO UN EEC.   POLICY
PAGE 20 G0392   ECO/DEV
                                                           ECO/TAC

B64
KAUFMANN W.W.,THE MC NAMARA STRATEGY. TOP/EX   FORCES
INSPECT BAL/PWR DIPLOM CONTROL DETER GUERRILLA   WAR
NUC/PWR WEAPON COST PWR...METH/COMP 20 MCNAMARA/R   PLAN
KENNEDY/JF JOHNSON/LB NATO DEPT/DEFEN. PAGE 30   PROB/SOLV
G0586

S64
BYRNES F.C.,"ASSIGNMENT TO AMBIGUITY: WORK   INTELL
PERFORMANCE IN CROSSCULTURAL TECHNICAL ASSISTANCE."   QU
USA+45 WOR+45 PROF/ORG CONSULT PLAN EDU/PROP ATTIT
DISPL PERCEPT PERSON ALL/VALS...POLICY INT CHARTS
NATO 20. PAGE 10 G0199

B65
MOSKOWITZ H.,US SECURITY, ARMS CONTROL, AND   BIBLIOG/A
DISARMAMENT 1961-1965. FORCES DIPLOM DETER WAR   ARMS/CONT
WEAPON...CHARTS 20 UN COLD/WAR NATO. PAGE 40 G0790   NUC/PWR
                                                          PEACE

B65
US DEPARTMENT OF DEFENSE,US SECURITY ARMS CONTROL,   BIBLIOG/A
AND DISARMAMENT 1961-1965 (PAMPHLET). COM COM   ARMS/CONT
GERMANY/W ISRAEL SPACE USA+45 USSR WOR+45 FORCES   NUC/PWR
EDU/PROP DETER EQUILIB PEACE ALL/VALS...GOV/COMP 20   DIPLOM
NATO. PAGE 57 G1118

B65
US DEPARTMENT OF THE ARMY,NUCLEAR WEAPONS AND THE   BIBLIOG/A
ATLANTIC ALLIANCE: A BIBLIOGRAPHIC SURVEY. ASIA COM   ARMS/CONT
EUR+WWI USA+45 FORCES DIPLOM WEAPON...STAT 20 NATO.   NUC/PWR
PAGE 58 G1131   BAL/PWR

S65
BEAUFRE A.,"THE SHARING OF NUCLEAR   DETER
RESPONSIBILITIES* A PROBLEM IN NEED OF SOLUTION."   RISK
FRANCE USA+45 INT/ORG NAT/G DELIB/GP FORCES CONTROL   ACT/RES
NUC/PWR RIGID/FLEX...CONCPT IDEA/COMP NATO. PAGE 6   WAR
G0110

S65
FOX A.B.,"NATO AND CONGRESS." CONSTN DELIB/GP   CONTROL
EX/STRUC FORCES TOP/EX BUDGET NUC/PWR GOV/REL   DIPLOM
...GP/COMP CONGRESS NATO TREATY. PAGE 20 G0388

S65
KINTNER W.P.,"THE PROSPECTS FOR WESTERN SCIENCE AND   TEC/DEV
TECHNOLOGY." EUR+WWI FRANCE USA+45 USSR R+D NUC/PWR   VOL/ASSN
NATO. PAGE 30 G0598   STAT
                                                        RECORD

S65
KOHL W.L.,"NUCLEAR SHARING IN NATO AND THE   ARMS/CONT
MULTILATERAL FORCE." FUT USSR VOL/ASSN TEC/DEV   OBS
DIPLOM NUC/PWR WAR WEAPON NATO. PAGE 31 G0611   IDEA/COMP

C65
US AIR FORCE ACADEMY,"AMERICAN DEFENSE POLICY." COM   PLAN
INT/ORG TEC/DEV FOR/AID ARMS/CONT DETER NUC/PWR   FORCES
...POLICY DECISION CONCPT ANTHOL BIBLIOG/A 20   WAR
COLD/WAR NATO. PAGE 56 G1103   COERCE

B67
PADELFORD N.J.,THE DYNAMICS OF INTERNATIONAL   DIPLOM
POLITICS (2ND ED.). WOR+45 LAW INT/ORG FORCES   NAT/G
TEC/DEV REGION NAT/LISM PEACE ATTIT PWR ALL/IDEOS   POLICY
UN COLD/WAR NATO TREATY. PAGE 43 G0856   DECISION

B67
ROACH J.R.,THE UNITED STATES AND THE ATLANTIC   INT/ORG
COMMUNITY; ISSUES AND PROSPECTS. WOR+45 TEC/DEV   POLICY
ECO/TAC COLONIAL REGION PEACE ROLE...ANTHOL NATO   ADJUST
COLD/WAR EEC. PAGE 47 G0925   DIPLOM

S67
DEUTSCH K.W.,"ARMS CONTROL AND EUROPEAN UNITY* THE   ARMS/CONT
NEXT TEN YEARS." USA+45 ELITES NAT/G BAL/PWR DIPLOM   PEACE
NUC/PWR...INT KNO/TEST NATO EEC. PAGE 15 G0300   REGION
                                                       PLAN

S67
KRUSCHE H.,"THE STRIVING OF THE KIESINGER-STRAUS   ARMS/CONT
GOVERNMENT FOR NUCLEAR WEAPONS IS A THREAT TO   INT/ORG
EUROPEAN SECURITY." EUR+WWI GERMANY BAL/PWR   NUC/PWR
SANCTION WEAPON PEACE ORD/FREE...MARXIST 20 NATO   DIPLOM
COLD/WAR. PAGE 32 G0623

S67
MARTIN L.W.,"BALLISTIC MISSILE DEFENSE AND EUROPE."   ATTIT
EUR+WWI USA+45 FORCES PLAN BAL/PWR DEBATE PEACE   ARMS/CONT
...POLICY COLD/WAR NATO. PAGE 36 G0715   NUC/PWR
                                                       DETER

S67
TELLER E.,"PLANNING FOR PEACE." CHINA/COM WOR+45   ARMS/CONT
DELIB/GP TEC/DEV RISK COERCE DETER WAR ATTIT   NUC/PWR
ORD/FREE 20 NATO. PAGE 54 G1061   PEACE
                                                       DOMIN

NATURL/LAW....NATURAL LAW

NAVAHO....NAVAHO INDIANS

NAVAL/RES....OFFICE OF NAVAL RESEARCH

NAVY....NAVY (ALL NATIONS)

B39
FULLER G.H.,A SELECTED LIST OF REFERENCES ON THE   BIBLIOG
EXPANSION OF THE US NAVY, 1933-1939 (PAMPHLET).   FORCES
MOD/EUR USA-45 NAT/G PLAN DIPLOM DOMIN RISK   WEAPON
ARMS/CONT EQUILIB PWR 20 NAVY. PAGE 20 G0399   WAR

NAYLOR T.H. G0230

NAZI....NAZI MOVEMENT (ALL NATIONS); SEE ALSO GERMANY,
     NAT/LISM, FASCIST

B47
LASSWELL H.D.,THE ANALYSIS OF POLITICAL BEHAVIOUR: R+D
AN EMPIRICAL APPROACH. WOR+45 CULTURE NAT/G FORCES   ACT/RES
EDU/PROP ADMIN ATTIT PERCEPT KNOWL...PHIL/SCI PSY   ELITES
SOC NEW/IDEA OBS INT GEN/METH NAZI 20. PAGE 32
G0639

S59
WILLIAMS B.H.,"SCIENTIFIC METHOD IN FOREIGN   PLAN
POLICY." WOR+45 NAT/G FORCES TOP/EX DOMIN LEGIT   PHIL/SCI
COERCE PEACE ATTIT KNOWL ORD/FREE PWR...GEN/LAWS   DIPLOM
GEN/METH TOT/POP COLD/WAR NAZI. PAGE 63 G1241

B60
EINSTEIN A.,EINSTEIN ON PEACE. FUT WOR+45 WOR-45   INT/ORG
SOCIETY NAT/G PLAN BAL/PWR CAP/ISM DIPLOM ARMS/CONT   ATTIT
DETER NAT/LISM...POLICY RELATIV HUM PHIL/SCI CONCPT   NUC/PWR
BIOG COLD/WAR LEAGUE/NAT NAZI. PAGE 17 G0338   PEACE

B61
NATHAN O.,EINSTEIN ON PEACE. WOR+45 WOR-45 INTELL   CONCPT
NUC/PWR WAR PERSON MORAL...BIOG VAL/FREE NAZI 20   PEACE
EINSTEIN/A. PAGE 41 G0807

NCC....NATIONAL COUNCIL OF CHURCHES

NE/WIN....NE WIN

NEA....NATIONAL EDUCATION ASSOCIATION

NEAR EAST....SEE MEDIT-7, ISLAM

NEBRASKA....NEBRASKA

NEEDHAM T. G0815

NEG/INCOME....NEGATIVE INCOME TAX

NEGATIVE INCOME TAX....SEE NEG/INCOME

NEGRITO....NEGRITO TRIBE, PHILIPPINES

NEGRO....NEGRO

B60
LEYDER J.,BIBLIOGRAPHIE DE L'ENSEIGNEMENT SUPERIEUR BIBLIOG/A
ET DE LA RECHERCHE SCIENTIFIQUE EN AFRIQUE   ACT/RES
INTERTROPICALE (2 VOLS.). AFR CULTURE ECO/UNDEV   ACADEM
AGRI PLAN EDU/PROP ADMIN COLONIAL...GEOG SOC/INTEG   R+D
20 NEGRO. PAGE 34 G0664

B65
HEER D.M.,AFTER NUCLEAR ATTACK: A DEMOGRAPHIC   GEOG
INQUIRY. USA+45 ECO/DEV SECT WORKER SEX...HEAL SOC   NUC/PWR
STAT PREDICT CHARTS 20 NEGRO. PAGE 25 G0500   CENSUS
                                                      WAR

B67
DEGLER C.N.,THE AGE OF THE ECONOMIC REVOLUTION   INDUS
1876-1900. USA-45 AGRI MUNIC POL/PAR SECT ECO/TAC   SOCIETY
CHOOSE...PHIL/SCI CHARTS NAT/COMP 19 NEGRO. PAGE 15 ECO/DEV
G0292   TEC/DEV

NEHRU/J....JAWAHARLAL NEHRU

NEHRU/PM....PANDIT MOTILAL NEHRU

NEIGH....NEIGHBORHOOD

B44
MERRIAM C.E.,PUBLIC AND PRIVATE GOVERNMENT.   NAT/G
VOL/ASSN EDU/PROP ADMIN REPRESENT EFFICIENCY PWR   NEIGH
PLURALISM...MAJORIT CONCPT. PAGE 38 G0755   MGT
                                                     POLICY

B50
DEES J.W. JR.,URBAN SOCIOLOGY AND THE EMERGING   PLAN
ATOMIC MEGALOPOLIS, PART I. USA-45 TEC/DEV ADMIN   NEIGH
NUC/PWR HABITAT...SOC AUD/VIS CHARTS GEN/LAWS 20   MUNIC
WATER. PAGE 15 G0291   PROB/SOLV

B54
ROSE A.M.,THEORY AND METHOD IN THE SOCIAL SCIENCES. CONCPT
STRATA R+D NEIGH PARTIC...METH/CNCPT GP/COMP.   SOC
PAGE 47 G0934   VOL/ASSN
                                                     ROLE

B61
LEE R.R.,ENGINEERING-ECONOMIC PLANNING   BIBLIOG/A
MISCELLANEOUS SUBJECTS: A SELECTED BIBLIOGRAPHY   PLAN
(MIMEOGRAPHED). FINAN LOC/G MUNIC NEIGH ADMIN   REGION
CONTROL INGP/REL HABITAT...GEOG MGT SOC/WK 20
RESOURCE/N. PAGE 33 G0651

B64
GRAVIER J.F.,AMENAGEMENT DU TERRITOIRE ET L'AVENIR   PLAN
DES REGIONS FRANCAISES. FRANCE ECO/DEV AGRI INDUS   MUNIC
CREATE...GEOG CHARTS 20. PAGE 22 G0442   NEIGH
                                                     ADMIN

B64
WIRTH L.,ON CITIES AND SOCIAL LIFE: SELECTED   GEN/LAWS
PAPERS. PLAN PROB/SOLV RACE/REL CONSEN ATTIT   SOCIETY
HABITAT PERSON...POLICY SOC CONCPT ANTHOL BIBLIOG   NEIGH
20. PAGE 64 G1249   STRUCT

B66
KLOTSCHE J.M.,THE URBAN UNIVERSITY AND THE FUTURE   ACADEM
OF OUR CITIES. FUT USA+45 USA-45 LOC/G NEIGH GIVE   MUNIC
19/20. PAGE 31 G0606   PROB/SOLV
                                                     TEC/DEV

B67
ROTHENBERG J.,ECONOMIC EVALUATION OF URBAN RENEWAL: PLAN
CONCEPTUAL FOUNDATION OF BENEFIT-COST ANALYSIS.   MUNIC
USA+45 ECO/DEV NEIGH TEC/DEV ADMIN GEN/LAWS.   PROB/SOLV
PAGE 48 G0940   COST

S67
FRIED M.,"FUNCTIONS OF THE WORKING CLASS COMMUNITY   CLASSIF
IN MODERN URBAN SOCIETY* IMPLICATIONS FOR FORCED   WORKER
RELOCATION." USA+45 INDUS R+D NEIGH PLAN TEC/DEV   MUNIC
PARTIC GP/REL ATTIT...SOC STAT CHARTS. PAGE 20   ADJUST
G0393

S67
WINSTON O.,"AN URBANIZATION PATTERN FOR THE US*   USA+45
SOME CONSIDERATIONS FOR THE DECENTRALIZATION OF   MUNIC
EXCELLENCE." FUT SOCIETY ECO/DEV R+D NEIGH ACT/RES   PLAN
PROB/SOLV TEC/DEV. PAGE 64 G1247   HABITAT

NELSON R.R. G0817

NEOLITHIC....NEOLITHIC PERIOD

NEPAL....SEE ALSO S/ASIA

NET/THEORY....NETWORK THEORY

B59
GUILBAUD G.T.,WHAT IS CYBERNETICS? COMPUTER OP/RES   CONTROL
TEC/DEV AUTOMAT ROUTINE PERS/REL PERCEPT...PSY MATH COM/IND
COMPUT/IR SIMUL GEN/METH. PAGE 23 G0460   FEEDBACK
                                                     NET/THEORY

B62
BORKOF H.,COMPUTER APPLICATIONS IN THE BEHAVIORAL   R+D
SCIENCES. AUTOMAT UTIL...DECISION PHIL/SCI PSY   COMPUTER
METH/CNCPT LING LOG MATH STYLE NET/THEORY COMPUT/IR PROB/SOLV
PROG/TEAC SIMUL. PAGE 8 G0154   FEEDBACK

B65
BLOOMFIELD L.,SOVIET INTERESTS IN ARMS CONTROL AND   USSR
DISARMAMENT* THE DECADE UNDER KHRUSHCHEV 1954-1964. ARMS/CONT
ASIA FORCES ACT/RES EDU/PROP DETER NUC/PWR WEAPON   DIPLOM
COST ATTIT...PHIL/SCI CLASSIF STAT NET/THEORY GAME   TREND
BIBLIOG. PAGE 7 G0139

B65
SINGER J.D.,HUMAN BEHAVIOR AND INTERNATINAL   DIPLOM
POLITICS* CONTRIBUTIONS FROM THE SOCIAL-   PHIL/SCI
PSYCHOLOGICAL SCIENCES. ACT/RES PLAN EDU/PROP ADMIN QUANT
KNOWL...DECISION PSY SOC NET/THEORY HYPO/EXP   SIMUL
LAB/EXP SOC/EXP GEN/METH ANTHOL BIBLIOG. PAGE 51
G1006

B65
VEINOTT A.F. JR.,MATHEMATICAL STUDIES IN MANAGEMENT MATH
SCIENCE. UNIV INDUS COMPUTER ADMIN...DECISION   MGT
NET/THEORY SIMUL 20. PAGE 61 G1193   PLAN
                                                     PRODUC

B66
FALK R.A.,ON MINIMIZING THE USE OF NUCLEAR WEAPONS; DIPLOM
THREE ESSAYS; RESEARCH MONOGRAPH NO. 23. WOR+45   EQUILIB
STRUCT CREATE NUC/PWR REV CONSERVE...POLICY   PHIL/SCI
NET/THEORY IDEA/COMP GEN/LAWS GEN/METH. PAGE 18   PROB/SOLV
G0359

L66
RASER J.R.,"DETERRENCE RESEARCH* PAST PROGRESS AND   DETER
FUTURE NEEDS." INTELL PLAN TEC/DEV NUC/PWR PERCEPT   BIBLIOG/A
...DECISION PSY SOC NET/THEORY. PAGE 46 G0905   FUT

L66
ZOPPO C.E.,"NUCLEAR TECHNOLOGY, MULTIPOLARITY, AND   NET/THEORY
INTERNATIONAL STABILITY." ASIA RUSSIA USA+45 STRUCT ORD/FREE
TOP/EX BAL/PWR DIPLOM DETER CIVMIL/REL NAT/COMP.   DECISION
PAGE 65 G1270   NUC/PWR

S66
KAPLAN M.A.,"THE NEW GREAT DEBATE* TRADITIONALISM   PHIL/SCI
VS SCIENCE IN INTERNATIONAL RELATIONS."...DECISION   CONSERVE
HUM QUANT STYLE NET/THEORY CON/ANAL STERTYP   DIPLOM
GEN/LAWS. PAGE 29 G0577   SIMUL

NETH/IND....NETHERLAND EAST INDIES (PRE-INDONESIA)

NETHERLAND....NETHERLANDS; SEE ALSO APPROPRIATE TIME/SPACE/
    CULTURE INDEX

B65
HICKMAN B.G.,QUANTITATIVE PLANNING OF ECONOMIC   PROB/SOLV
POLICY. FRANCE NETHERLAND OP/RES PRICE ROUTINE UTIL PLAN
...POLICY DECISION ECOMETRIC METH/CNCPT STAT STYLE   QUANT
CHINJAP. PAGE 26 G0511

N67
US HOUSE COMM SCI ASTRONAUT,GOVERNMENT, SCIENCE,   NAT/G
AND INTERNATIONAL POLICY (PAMPHLET). INDIA   POLICY
NETHERLAND ECO/DEV ECO/UNDEV R+D ACADEM PLAN DIPLOM CREATE
FOR/AID CONFER...PREDICT 20 CHINJAP. PAGE 59 G1152   TEC/DEV

NETWORK THEORY....SEE NET/THEORY

NEUTRAL....POLITICAL NONALIGNMENT, LEGAL NEUTRALITY

N47
FOX W.T.R.,UNITED STATES POLICY IN A TWO POWER   DIPLOM
WORLD. COM USA+45 USSR FORCES DOMIN AGREE NEUTRAL   FOR/AID
NUC/PWR ORD/FREE SOVEREIGN 20 COLD/WAR TREATY   POLICY
EUROPE/W INTERVENT. PAGE 20 G0389

B55
DAVIS E.,TWO MINUTES TO MIDNIGHT. WOR+45 PLAN   NUC/PWR
CONTROL NEUTRAL ARMS/CONT ATTIT ORD/FREE...PSY 20   WAR
COLD/WAR. PAGE 14 G0277   DETER
                                                     DIPLOM

B58
ANGELL N.,DEFENCE AND THE ENGLISH-SPEAKING ROLE.   DIPLOM
CHINA/COM UK USSR INT/ORG FORCES EDU/PROP NEUTRAL   WAR
NUC/PWR NAT/LISM PEACE TOTALISM 20 COLD/WAR   MARXISM
COEXIST. PAGE 3 G0059   ORD/FREE

B62
FRIEDRICH-EBERT-STIFTUNG,THE SOVIET BLOC AND   MARXISM
DEVELOPING COUNTRIES. CHINA/COM COM GERMANY/E USSR   DIPLOM
WOR+45 ECO/UNDEV INT/ORG NAT/G TEC/DEV NEUTRAL PWR   ECO/TAC
...POLICY 20. PAGE 20 G0394   FOR/AID

B63
WILTZ J.E.,IN SEARCH OF PEACE: THE SENATE MUNITIONS DELIB/GP
INQUIRY, 1934-36. EUR+WWI USA-45 ELITES INDUS LG/CO PROFIT
LEGIS INT/TRADE LOBBY NEUTRAL ARMS/CONT...POLICY   WAR
CONGRESS 20 LEAGUE/NAT PRESIDENT SENATE CONSCRIPTN. WEAPON
PAGE 64 G1246

PAGE 24 G0480   NEW/LIB

B64
OSSENBECK F.J.,OPEN SPACE AND PEACE. CHINA/COM FUT   SPACE
USA+45 USSR LAW PROB/SOLV TEC/DEV EDU/PROP NEUTRAL   ORD/FREE
PEACE...AUD/VIS ANTHOL 20. PAGE 43 G0850   DIPLOM
                                                     CREATE

S65
BIRNBAUM K.,"SWEDEN'S NUCLEAR POLICY." WOR+45   SWEDEN
POL/PAR CREATE TEC/DEV NEUTRAL RISK WAR ORD/FREE   NUC/PWR
...DECISION IDEA/COMP NAT/COMP TIME. PAGE 7 G0137   DIPLOM
                                                     ARMS/CONT

B66
DAENIKER G.,STRATEGIE DES KLEIN STAATS. SWITZERLND   NUC/PWR
ACT/RES CREATE DIPLOM NEUTRAL DETER WAR WEAPON PWR   PLAN
SOVEREIGN...IDEA/COMP 20 COLD/WAR. PAGE 14 G0270   FORCES
                                                     NAT/G

S67
FOREIGN POLICY ASSOCIATION."HOW WORLD LAW DEVELOPS*   INT/LAW
A CASE STUDY OF THE OUTER SPACE TREATY." SPACE   DIPLOM
WOR+45 BAL/PWR NEUTRAL NUC/PWR PEACE KNOWL 20 UN   ARMS/CONT
TREATY. PAGE 19 G0380   INT/ORG

S67
JOHNSTON D.M.,"LAW, TECHNOLOGY AND THE SEA." WOR+45   INT/LAW
PLAN PROB/SOLV TEC/DEV CONFER ADJUD ORD/FREE   INT/ORG
...POLICY JURID. PAGE 29 G0564   DIPLOM
                                                     NEUTRAL

S67
MEHTA A.,"INDIA* POVERTY AND CHANGE." STRATA INDUS   INDIA
CREATE ECO/TAC FOR/AID NEUTRAL GP/REL ADJUST INCOME   SOCIETY
...NEW/IDEA 20. PAGE 38 G0751   ECO/UNDEV
                                                     TEC/DEV

S67
VLASCIC I.A.,"THE SPACE TREATY* A PRELIMINARY   SPACE
EVALUATION." FUT USSR WOR+45 R+D ACT/RES TEC/DEV   INT/LAW
DIPLOM CONFER ARMS/CONT PEACE...PREDICT UN TREATY.   INT/ORG
PAGE 61 G1201   NEUTRAL

NEVADA....NEVADA

NEW ECONOMICS....SEE NEW/ECONOM

NEW LIBERALISM....SEE NEW/LIB

NEW STATES....SEE ECO/UNDEV+GEOGRAPHIC AREA+COLONIAL+
     NAT/LISM
NEW YORK CITY....SEE NEWYORK/C
NEW YORK TIMES....SEE NEWY/TIMES

NEW ZEALAND COMM OF ST SERVICE G0818

NEW/BRUNS....NEW BRUNSWICK, CANADA

NEW/DEAL....NEW DEAL OF F.D.R.'S ADMINISTRATION

B57
DUPREE A.H.,SCIENCE IN THE FEDERAL GOVERNMENT; A   NAT/G
HISTORY OF POLICIES AND ACTIVITIES TO 1940. USA-45   R+D
AGRI SCHOOL DELIB/GP WAR GOV/REL...PHIL/SCI BIBLIOG   CREATE
18/20 DEPRESSION NEW/DEAL WWI JEFFERSN/T. PAGE 17   TEC/DEV
G0324

NEW/DELHI....NEW DELHI (UNCTAD MEETING OF DEVELOPED AND
     UNDERDEVELOPED NATIONS IN 1968)

NEW/ECO/MN....NEW ECONOMIC MECHANISM OF HUNGARY

NEW/ECONOM....NEW ECONOMICS

NEW/ENGLND....NEW ENGLAND

NEW/FRONTR....NEW FRONTIER OF J.F.KENNEDY

NEW/GUINEA....NEW GUINEA

NEW/HAMPSH....NEW HAMPSHIRE

NEW/HEBRID....NEW HEBRIDES

NEW/IDEA....NEW CONCEPT

NEW/JERSEY....NEW JERSEY

NEW/LEFT....THE NEW LEFT

NEW/LIB....NEW LIBERALISM

S48
HARDIN L.M.,"REFLECTIONS ON AGRICULTURAL POLICY   AGRI
FORMATION IN THE UNITED STATES." LEGIS PLAN BUDGET   POLICY
ECO/TAC LEAD CENTRAL...MGT SOC NEW/IDEA STAT FAO.   ADMIN

B5
BERNSTEIN I.,THE NEW DEAL COLLECTIVE BARGAINING   LABOR
PROCESS. USA-45 GOV/REL ATTIT...BIBLIOG 20   LEGIS
ROOSEVLT/F. PAGE 7 G0132   POLICY
                                                     NEW/LIB

B5
SURANYI-UNGER T.,PRIVATE ENTERPRISE AND   PLAN
GOVERNMENTAL PLANNING. STRUCT FINAN BAL/PWR   NAT/G
HAPPINESS DRIVE NEW/LIB PLURISM...MATH QUANT STAT   LAISSEZ
TREND BIBLIOG. PAGE 53 G1047   POLICY

S6
DAWSON R.H.,"CONGRESSIONAL INNOVATION AND   LEGIS
INTERVENTION IN DEFENSE POLICY: LEGISLATIVE   PWR
AUTHORIZATION OF WEAPONS SYSTEMS." CONSTN PLAN   CONTROL
ARMS/CONT GOV/REL EFFICIENCY PEACE NEW/LIB OLD/LIB.   WEAPON
PAGE 14 G0281

B6
BAILEY S.K.,AMERICAN POLITICS AND GOVERNMENT.   ANTHOL
USA+45 CONSTN FINAN LABOR POL/PAR DIPLOM ADMIN WAR   LEGIS
INGP/REL RACE/REL NEW/LIB 20 SUPREME/CT PRESIDENT   PWR
CONGRESS. PAGE 4 G0084

C6
MARK M.,"BEYOND SOVEREIGNTY." WOR+45 WOR-45   NAT/LISM
ECO/UNDEV BAL/PWR INT/TRADE NUC/PWR REV WAR MARXISM   NAT/G
NEW/LIB BIBLIOG. PAGE 36 G0706   DIPLOM
                                                     INTELL

B6
DUNBAR L.W.,A REPUBLIC OF EQUALS. USA+45 CREATE   LAW
ADJUD PEACE NEW/LIB...POLICY 20 SOUTH/US   CONSTN
CIV/RIGHTS. PAGE 16 G0320   FEDERAL
                                                     RACE/REL

B6
YAMAMURA K.,ECONOMIC POLICY IN POSTWAR JAPAN. ASIA   ECO/DEV
FINAN POL/PAR DIPLOM LEAD NAT/LISM ATTIT NEW/LIB   POLICY
POPULISM 20 CHINJAP. PAGE 64 G1262   NAT/G
                                                     TEC/DEV

NEW/MEXICO....NEW MEXICO

B5
CLEAVELAND F.N.,SCIENCE AND STATE GOVERNMENT. AGRI   TEC/DEV
EXTR/IND FINAN INDUS PROVS...METH/CNCPT STAT CHARTS   PHIL/SCI
20 NEW/YORK CONNECTICT WISCONSIN CALIFORNIA   GOV/REL
NEW/MEXICO. PAGE 12 G0233   METH/COMP

B5
CLEAVELAND F.N.,SCIENCE AND STATE GOVERNMENT. AGRI   TEC/DEV
EXTR/IND FINAN INDUS PROVS...METH/CNCPT STAT CHARTS   PHIL/SCI
20 NEW/YORK CONNECTICT WISCONSIN CALIFORNIA   GOV/REL
NEW/MEXICO. PAGE 12 G0233   METH/COMP

NEW/YORK/C....NEW YORK CITY

NEW/ZEALND....NEW ZEALAND; SEE ALSO S/ASIA, COMMONWLTH

B6
NEW ZEALAND COMM OF ST SERVICE,THE STATE SERVICES   ADMIN
IN NEW ZEALAND. NEW/ZEALND CONSULT EX/STRUC ACT/RES   WORKER
...BIBLIOG 20. PAGE 42 G0818   TEC/DEV
                                                     NAT/G

NEWARK/NJ....NEWARK, N.J.

NEWELL A.C. G0819

NEWFNDLND....NEWFOUNDLAND, CANADA

NEWY/TIMES....NEW YORK TIMES

NEWYORK/C

C5
CALDWELL L.K.,"THE GOVERNMENT AND ADMINISTRATION OF   PROVS
NEW YORK." LOC/G MUNIC POL/PAR SCHOOL CHIEF LEGIS   ADMIN
PLAN TAX CT/SYS...MGT SOC/WK BIBLIOG 20 NEWYORK/C.   CONSTN
PAGE 10 G0202   EX/STRUC

B6
REISS A.J. JR.,SCHOOLS IN A CHANGING SOCIETY.   SCHOOL
CULTURE PROB/SOLV INSPECT DOMIN CONFER INGP/REL   EX/STRUC
RACE/REL AGE/C AGE/Y ALL/VALS...ANTHOL SOC/INTEG 20   ADJUST
NEWYORK/C. PAGE 46 G0912   ADMIN

NICARAGUA....NICARAGUA; SEE ALSO L/A+17C

NICHOLAS/I....CZAR NICHOLAS I

NICOLSON/A....SIR ARTHUR NICOLSON

NIEBUHR/R....REINHOLD NIEBUHR

NIEBURG H. G0820

NIEBURG H.L. G0816,G0821,G0822

NIEBURG/HL....H.L. NIEBURG

NIETZSCH/F....FRIEDRICH NIETZSCHE

NIGERIA....SEE ALSO AFR

NIH....NATIONAL INSTITUTE OF HEALTH

		S61
MAINZER L.C.,"SCIENTIFIC FREEDOM IN GOVERNMENT-	CREATE	
SPONSORED RESEARCH." USA+45 INTELL PUB/INST BUDGET	ORD/FREE	
LOBBY AUTHORIT PWR...POLICY PHIL/SCI 20 NIH NSF.	NAT/G	
PAGE 35 G0696	R+D	

		S62
STORER N.W.,"SOME SOCIOLOGICAL ASPECTS OF FEDERAL	POLICY	
SCIENCE POLICY." USA+45 INTELL PUB/INST PLAN GP/REL	CREATE	
PERS/REL DRIVE PERSON ROLE...PSY SOC SIMUL 20 NIH	NAT/G	
NSF. PAGE 53 G1040	ALL/VALS	

NIJKERK K.F. G0057

NIPA....NATIONAL INSTITUTE OF PUBLIC ADMINISTRATION

NISEI....NISEI: JAPANESE AMERICANS

NIXON/RM....PRESIDENT RICHARD M. NIXON

NKRUMAH/K....KWAME NKRUMAH

		S67
KRAUS J.,"A MARXIST IN GHANA." GHANA ELITES CHIEF	MARXISM	
PROB/SOLV TEC/DEV DIPLOM ECO/TAC COLONIAL PARTIC	PLAN	
PWR 20 NKRUMAH/K. PAGE 31 G0618	ATTIT	
	CREATE	

NLC....NATIONAL LIBERATION COUNCIL IN GHANA

NLF....NATIONAL LIBERATION FRONT OF SOUTH VIETNAM

NLRB....NATIONAL LABOR RELATIONS BOARD

		B67
NORTHRUP H.R.,RESTRICTIVE LABOR PRACTICES IN THE	DIST/IND	
SUPERMARKET INDUSTRY. USA+45 INDUS WORKER TEC/DEV	MARKET	
BARGAIN PAY CONTROL GP/REL COST...STAT CHARTS NLRB.	LABOR	
PAGE 42 G0827	MGT	

NOBILITY....SEE ELITES

NOEL-BAKER D. G0823

NOGEE J.L. G0824

NOMAD/MAX....MAX NOMAD

NOMADISM....SEE GEOG

NONALIGNED NATIONS....SEE THIRD/WRLD

NON-WHITE....SEE RACE/REL

NONVIOLENT....NONVIOLENCE (CONCEPT)

NORMS....SEE AVERAGE, ALSO APPROPRIATE VALUES AND DIMENSIONS
    OF GROUPS, STAT, LOG, ETC.

NORTH R.C. G0825

NORTH AFRICA....SEE AFRICA/N, ISLAM

NORTH ATLANTIC FREE TRADE AREA....SEE NAFTA

NORTH ATLANTIC TREATY ORGANIZATION....SEE NATO

NORTH KOREA....SEE KOREA/N

NORTH VIETNAM....SEE VIETNAM/N

NORTH/AMER....NORTH AMERICA, EXCLUSIVE OF CENTRAL AMERICA

NORTH/CAR....NORTH CAROLINA

		B66
SANFORD T.,BUT WHAT ABOUT THE PEOPLE? ACADEM SCHOOL	EDU/PROP	
BUDGET TAX CONTROL SKILL WEALTH 20 NORTH/CAR.	PROB/SOLV	
PAGE 49 G0956	POLICY	
	PROVS	

NORTH/DAK....NORTH DAKOTA

NORTH/US....NORTHERN UNITED STATES

NORTHERN RHODESIA....SEE ZAMBIA

NORTHROP F.S.C. G0826

NORTHRUP H.R. G0827

NORTHW/TER....NORTHWEST TERRITORIES, CANADA

NORTHWEST TERRITORIES, CANADA....SEE NORTHW/TER

NORTHWST/U....NORTHWESTERN UNIVERSITY

NORWAY....SEE ALSO APPROPRIATE TIME/SPACE/CULTURE INDEX

NOVA/SCOT....NOVA SCOTIA, CANADA

NOVE A. G0828

NOVOTNY/A....A. NOVOTNY

NRA....NATIONAL RECOVERY ADMINISTRATION

NSC....NATIONAL SECURITY COUNCIL

NSF....NATIONAL SCIENCE FOUNDATION

		S61
MAINZER L.C.,"SCIENTIFIC FREEDOM IN GOVERNMENT-	CREATE	
SPONSORED RESEARCH." USA+45 INTELL PUB/INST BUDGET	ORD/FREE	
LOBBY AUTHORIT PWR...POLICY PHIL/SCI 20 NIH NSF.	NAT/G	
PAGE 35 G0696	R+D	

		S62
STORER N.W.,"SOME SOCIOLOGICAL ASPECTS OF FEDERAL	POLICY	
SCIENCE POLICY." USA+45 INTELL PUB/INST PLAN GP/REL	CREATE	
PERS/REL DRIVE PERSON ROLE...PSY SOC SIMUL 20 NIH	NAT/G	
NSF. PAGE 53 G1040	ALL/VALS	

		B66
NATIONAL SCIENCE FOUNDATION,SIXTEENTH ANNUAL REPORT	NAT/G	
FOR THE FISCAL YEAR ENDED JUNE 30, 1966. USA+45	EDU/PROP	
CREATE BUDGET SKILL 20 NSF. PAGE 41 G0813	ACADEM	
	KNOWL	

		S67
HARRIS F.R.,"POLITICAL SCIENCE AND THE PROPOSAL FOR	PROF/ORG	
A NATIONAL SOCIAL SCIENCE FOUNDATION." FUT CONSULT	R+D	
DELIB/GP PLAN PROB/SOLV BUDGET CONFER SANCTION	CREATE	
CRIME...POLICY SOC/WK 20 NSF NSSF. PAGE 25 G0484	NAT/G	

		N67
US HOUSE COMM SCI ASTRONAUT,AMENDING NATIONAL	PHIL/SCI	
SCIENCE FOUNDATION ACT OF 1950 TO MAKE IMPROVEMENTS	DELIB/GP	
IN ORGANIZATION AND OPERATION OF FOUNDAT'N(PAMPH).	TEC/DEV	
USA+45 GIVE ADMIN...POLICY HOUSE/REP NSF. PAGE 58	R+D	
G1147		

NSSF....NATIONAL SOCIAL SCIENCE FOUNDATION

		S67
HARRIS F.R.,"POLITICAL SCIENCE AND THE PROPOSAL FOR	PROF/ORG	
A NATIONAL SOCIAL SCIENCE FOUNDATION." FUT CONSULT	R+D	
DELIB/GP PLAN PROB/SOLV BUDGET CONFER SANCTION	CREATE	
CRIME...POLICY SOC/WK 20 NSF NSSF. PAGE 25 G0484	NAT/G	

NUC....NATIONAL UNITY COMMITTEE (TURKEY)

NUC/PWR....NUCLEAR POWER, INCLUDING NUCLEAR WEAPONS

		B
CURRENT THOUGHT ON PEACE AND WAR. WOR+45 INT/ORG	BIBLIOG/A	
FORCES PROB/SOLV DIPLOM NUC/PWR PERCEPT...POLICY	PEACE	
SOC 20 UN NATO. PAGE 1 G0001	ATTIT	
	WAR	

		B
US DEPT COMMERCE OFF TECH SERV,TECHNICAL	BIBLIOG	
TRANSLATIONS. WOR+45 INDUS COMPUTER CREATE NUC/PWR	R+D	
...PHIL/SCI COMPUT/IR METH/COMP METH. PAGE 58 G1135	TEC/DEV	
	AUTOMAT	

		N
JOURNAL OF CONFLICT RESOLUTION. FUT WOR+45 INT/ORG	BIBLIOG/A	
NAT/G FORCES CREATE PROB/SOLV ARMS/CONT NUC/PWR	DIPLOM	
WEAPON SOC. PAGE 1 G0002	WAR	

		N
FOREIGN AFFAIRS. SPACE WOR+45 WOR-45 CULTURE	BIBLIOG	
ECO/UNDEV FINAN NAT/G TEC/DEV INT/TRADE ARMS/CONT	DIPLOM	
NUC/PWR...POLICY 20 UN EURATOM ECSC EEC. PAGE 1	INT/ORG	
G0004	INT/LAW	

AIR UNIVERSITY LIBRARY,INDEX TO MILITARY
PERIODICALS. FUT SPACE WOR+45 REGION ARMS/CONT
NUC/PWR WAR PEACE INT/LAW. PAGE 2 G0032

N
BIBLIOG/A
FORCES
NAT/G
DIPLOM

UNITED NATIONS,OFFICIAL RECORDS OF THE UNITED
NATIONS' ATOMIC ENERGY COMMISSION - DISARMAMENT
COMMISSION. WOR+45 TEC/DEV DIPLOM WRITING NUC/PWR
20 UN. PAGE 55 G1092

N
ARMS/CONT
INT/ORG
DELIB/GP
CONFER

ATOMIC INDUSTRIAL FORUM,COMMENTARY ON LEGISLATION
TO PERMIT PRIVATE OWNERSHIP OF SPECIAL NUCLEAR
MATERIAL (PAMPHLET). USA+45 DELIB/GP LEGIS PLAN OWN
...POLICY 20 AEC CONGRESS. PAGE 4 G0076

N19
NUC/PWR
MARKET
INDUS
LAW

BROWN W.M.,THE DESIGN AND PERFORMANCE OF "OPTIMUM"
BLAST SHELTER PROGRAMS (PAMPHLET). USA+45 ACT/RES
PLAN DEATH COST EFFICIENCY OPTIMAL...POLICY CHARTS
20. PAGE 9 G0180

N19
HABITAT
NUC/PWR
WAR
HEALTH

MEZERIK A.G.,ATOM TESTS AND RADIATION HAZARDS
(PAMPHLET). WOR+45 INT/ORG DIPLOM DETER 20 UN
TREATY. PAGE 39 G0761

N19
NUC/PWR
ARMS/CONT
CONFER
HEALTH

MEZERIK AG,OUTER SPACE: UN, US, USSR (PAMPHLET).
USSR DELIB/GP FORCES DETER NUC/PWR SOVEREIGN
...POLICY 20 UN TREATY. PAGE 39 G0763

N19
SPACE
CONTROL
DIPLOM
INT/ORG

US ATOMIC ENERGY COMMISSION,ATOMIC ENERGY IN USE
(PAMPHLET). R+D RISK EFFICIENCY HEALTH KNOWL
ORD/FREE...PHIL/SCI CONCPT METH/CNCPT CHARTS
LAB/EXP 20 AEC. PAGE 56 G1106

N19
OP/RES
TEC/DEV
NUC/PWR
CREATE

US FOOD AND DRUG ADMIN,CIVIL DEFENSE INFORMATION
FOR FOOD AND DRUG OFFICIALS (2ND ED.) (PAMPHLET).
USA+45 PROB/SOLV RISK HABITAT...MATH CHARTS
DICTIONARY 20 CIV/DEFENS. PAGE 58 G1136

N19
NUC/PWR
WAR
EATING
HEALTH

ZLOTNICK M.,WEAPONS IN SPACE (PAMPHLET). FUT WOR+45
TEC/DEV DIPLOM ARMS/CONT CIVMIL/REL PEACE HABITAT
...CONCPT NEW/IDEA CHARTS. PAGE 65 G1268

N19
SPACE
WEAPON
NUC/PWR
WAR

BUSH V.,SCIENCE, THE ENDLESS FRONTIER. FUT USA-45
INTELL STRATA ACT/RES CREATE PLAN EDU/PROP ADMIN
NUC/PWR PEACE ATTIT HEALTH KNOWL...MAJORIT HEAL MGT
PHIL/SCI CONCPT OBS TREND 20. PAGE 10 G0195

B45
R+D
NAT/G

REVES E.,THE ANATOMY OF PEACE. WOR-45 LAW CULTURE
NAT/G PLAN TEC/DEV EDU/PROP WAR NAT/LISM ATTIT
ALL/VALS SOVEREIGN...POLICY HUM TIME/SEQ 20.
PAGE 46 G0914

B45
ACT/RES
CONCPT
NUC/PWR
PEACE

SMYTH H.D.,ATOMIC ENERGY FOR MILITARY PURPOSES.
USA-45 NAT/G PLAN TEC/DEV KNOWL...MATH CON/ANAL
CHARTS LAB/EXP SIMUL 20. PAGE 52 G1017

B45
R+D
TIME/SEQ
NUC/PWR

BAXTER J.P.,SCIENTISTS AGAINST TIME. EUR+WWI
MOD/EUR USA+45 USA-45 WOR+45 WOR-45 R+D NAT/G PLAN
ATTIT PWR...PHIL/SCI RECORD CON/ANAL 17/20. PAGE 6
G0107

B46
FORCES
WAR
NUC/PWR

BRODIE B.,THE OBSOLETE WEAPON: ATOMIC POWER AND
WORLD ORDER. COM USA+45 USSR WOR+45 DELIB/GP PLAN
ORD/FREE PWR...CONCPT TIME/SEQ TREND UN 20. PAGE 9
G0171

B46
INT/ORG
TEC/DEV
ARMS/CONT
NUC/PWR

VINER J.,SYMPOSIUM ON ATOMIC ENERGY AND ITS
IMPLICATIONS. USA+45 WOR+45 SOCIETY DELIB/GP...SOC
CONCPT TIME/SEQ TOT/POP 20. PAGE 61 G1200

B46
R+D
RIGID/FLEX
NUC/PWR

MASTERS D.,"ONE WORLD OR NONE." FUT WOR+45 INTELL
INT/ORG ACT/RES EDU/PROP DETER ATTIT RIGID/FLEX
SUPEGO KNOWL...STAT TREND ORG/CHARTS 20. PAGE 36
G0719

L46
POLICY
PHIL/SCI
ARMS/CONT
NUC/PWR

BALDWIN H.W.,THE PRICE OF POWER. USA+45 FORCES PLAN

B47
PROB/SOLV

NUC/PWR ADJUST COST ORD/FREE...POLICY PSY BIBLIOG
20. PAGE 5 G0089

PWR
POPULISM
PRICE

SOCIAL SCIENCE RESEARCH COUN,PUBLIC REACTION TO THE
ATOMIC BOMB AND WORLD AFFAIRS. SOCIETY CONFER
ARMS/CONT...STAT QU SAMP CHARTS 20. PAGE 52 G1019

B47
ATTIT
NUC/PWR
DIPLOM
WAR

FOX W.T.R.,UNITED STATES POLICY IN A TWO POWER
WORLD. COM USA+45 USSR FORCES DOMIN AGREE NEUTRAL
NUC/PWR ORD/FREE SOVEREIGN 20 COLD/WAR TREATY
EUROPE/W INTERVENT. PAGE 20 G0389

N47
DIPLOM
FOR/AID
POLICY

BRADLEY D.,NO PLACE TO HIDE. USA+45 SOCIETY NAT/G
FORCES TEC/DEV EDU/PROP DETER PEACE BIO/SOC
ALL/VALS...POLICY PHIL/SCI OBS RECORD SAMP BIOG
GEN/METH COLD/WAR 20. PAGE 8 G0162

B48
R+D
LAB/EXP
ARMS/CONT
NUC/PWR

SOUERS S.W.,"POLICY FORMULATION FOR NATIONAL
SECURITY." EX/STRUC FORCES PROB/SOLV DIPLOM CONFER
EXEC ARMS/CONT DETER NUC/PWR GOV/REL PEACE
COLD/WAR. PAGE 52 G1022

S49
DELIB/GP
CHIEF
DECISION
POLICY

CROWTHER J.G.,SCIENCE AT WAR. EUR+WWI PLAN TEC/DEV
DOMIN COERCE NUC/PWR WEAPON KNOWL PWR...CONCPT OBS
TREND VAL/FREE 20. PAGE 14 G0265

B50
R+D
FORCES
WAR
UK

DEES J.W. JR.,URBAN SOCIOLOGY AND THE EMERGING
ATOMIC MEGALOPOLIS, PART I. USA+45 TEC/DEV ADMIN
NUC/PWR HABITAT...SOC AUD/VIS CHARTS GEN/LAWS 20
WATER. PAGE 15 G0291

B50
PLAN
NEIGH
MUNIC
PROB/SOLV

SCHAAF R.W.,DOCUMENTS OF INTERNATIONAL MEETINGS.
AGRI INDUS ACADEM DIPLOM NUC/PWR RACE/REL AGE/Y
HEALTH...SOC 20. PAGE 49 G0960

B53
BIBLIOG/A
DELIB/GP
INT/ORG
POLICY

BUTOW R.J.C.,JAPAN'S DECISION TO SURRENDER. USA-45
USSR CHIEF FORCES DOMIN NUC/PWR...BIBLIOG 20 TREATY
CHINJAP. PAGE 10 G0198

B54
ELITES
DIPLOM
WAR
PEACE

KENWORTHY L.S.,FREE AND INEXPENSIVE MATERIALS ON
WORLD AFFAIRS (PAMPHLET). WOR+45 CULTURE ECO/UNDEV
INT/TRADE ARMS/CONT NUC/PWR UN. PAGE 30 G0594

B54
BIBLIOG/A
NAT/G
INT/ORG
DIPLOM

US DEPARTMENT OF STATE,PUBLICATIONS OF THE
DEPARTMENT OF STATE, OCTOBER 1,1929 TO JANUARY 1,
1953. AGRI INT/ORG FORCES FOR/AID EDU/PROP
ARMS/CONT NUC/PWR ATTIT 20 DEPT/STATE OAS UN NATO.
PAGE 57 G1122

B54
BIBLIOG
DIPLOM

DAVIS E.,TWO MINUTES TO MIDNIGHT. WOR+45 PLAN
CONTROL NEUTRAL ARMS/CONT ATTIT ORD/FREE...PSY 20
COLD/WAR. PAGE 14 G0277

B55
NUC/PWR
WAR
DETER
DIPLOM

MIKSCHE F.O.,ATOMIC WEAPONS AND ARMIES. FUT WOR+45
WOR-45 SOCIETY COERCE DETER WEAPON PWR...POLICY
WELF/ST PSY CONCPT INT SYS/QU KNO/TEST TOT/POP 20.
PAGE 39 G0765

B55
TEC/DEV
FORCES
NUC/PWR

MOCH J.,HUMAN FOLLY: DISARM OR PERISH. USA+45
WOR+45 SOCIETY INT/ORG NAT/G ACT/RES EDU/PROP ATTIT
PERSON KNOWL ORD/FREE PWR...MAJORIT TOT/POP
COLD/WAR 20. PAGE 39 G0776

B55
FUT
DELIB/GP
ARMS/CONT
NUC/PWR

OPPENHEIMER R.,THE OPEN MIND. USA+45 WOR+45 NAT/G
DELIB/GP DETER MORAL ORD/FREE...MYTH GEN/LAWS 20.
PAGE 43 G0842

B55
CREATE
PWR
ARMS/CONT
NUC/PWR

VON NEUMANN J.,"CAN WE SURVIVE TECHNOLOGY?" WOR+45
AIR INDUS ADMIN ADJUST RIGID/FLEX...GEOG PHIL/SCI
NEW/IDEA 20. PAGE 61 G1202

S55
TEC/DEV
NUC/PWR
FUT
HABITAT

ATOMIC INDUSTRIAL FORUM.PUBLIC RELATIONS FOR THE
ATOMIC INDUSTRY. WOR+45 PLAN PROB/SOLV EDU/PROP
PRESS CONFER...AUD/VIS ANTHOL 20. PAGE 4 G0077
B56
NUC/PWR
INDUS
GP/REL
ATTIT

BLACKETT P.M.S..ATOMIC WEAPONS AND EAST-WEST
RELATIONS. FUT WOR+45 INT/ORG DELIB/GP COERCE ATTIT
RIGID/FLEX KNOWL...RELATIV HIST/WRIT TREND GEN/METH
COLD/WAR 20. PAGE 7 G0138
B56
FORCES
PWR
ARMS/CONT
NUC/PWR

KOENIG L.W..THE TRUMAN ADMINISTRATION: ITS
PRINCIPLES AND PRACTICE. USA+45 POL/PAR CHIEF LEGIS
DIPLOM DEATH NUC/PWR WAR CIVMIL/REL PEACE
...DECISION 20 TRUMAN/HS PRESIDENT TREATY. PAGE 31
G0610
B56
ADMIN
POLICY
EX/STRUC
GOV/REL

THOMAS M..ATOMIC ENERGY AND CONGRESS. USA+45 NAT/G
ACT/RES PLAN TEC/DEV EDU/PROP ROUTINE KNOWL PWR
SKILL...PHIL/SCI NEW/IDEA TIME/SEQ CHARTS METH
CONGRESS VAL/FREE 20 AEC. PAGE 54 G1067
B56
LEGIS
ADMIN
NUC/PWR

US DEPARTMENT OF THE ARMY.AMERICAN MILITARY
HISTORY. USA+45 USA-45 EX/STRUC PROB/SOLV TEC/DEV
DIPLOM NUC/PWR REV WAR WEAPON...PSY 18/20. PAGE 57
G1125
B56
BIBLIOG
FORCES
NAT/G

US DEPARTMENT OF THE ARMY.RESEARCH AND DEVELOPMENT
(AND RELATED ASPECTS) IN FOREIGN COUNTRIES. WOR+45
DIST/IND INDUS CONSULT FORCES CREATE EDU/PROP
AUTOMAT DETER WEAPON. PAGE 57 G1126
B56
BIBLIOG/A
R+D
TEC/DEV
NUC/PWR

GOLD N.L..REGIONAL ECONOMIC DEVELOPMENT AND NUCLEAR
POWER IN INDIA. FUT INDIA FINAN FOR/AID INT/TRADE
BAL/PAY EFFICIENCY OPTIMAL PRODUC WEALTH...PREDICT
20. PAGE 22 G0424
B57
ECO/UNDEV
TEC/DEV
NUC/PWR
INDUS

KISSINGER H.A..NUCLEAR WEAPONS AND FOREIGN POLICY.
FUT USA+45 WOR+45 INT/ORG FORCES ACT/RES TEC/DEV
DIPLOM ARMS/CONT COERCE ATTIT KNOWL PWR...DECISION
GEOG CHARTS 20. PAGE 31 G0602
B57
PLAN
DETER
NUC/PWR

SPEIER H..GERMAN REARMAMENT AND ATOMIC WAR: THE
VIEWS OF GERMAN MILITARY AND POLITICAL LEADERS. FUT
WOR+45 INT/ORG NAT/G WEAPON ATTIT PWR...INT QU
TOT/POP VAL/FREE COLD/WAR 20. PAGE 52 G1024
B57
TOP/EX
FORCES
NUC/PWR
GERMANY

MORTON L.."THE DECISION TO USE THE BOMB." FORCES
TOP/EX DOMIN COERCE PEACE. PAGE 40 G0788
S57
NUC/PWR
DIPLOM
WAR

ANGELL N..DEFENCE AND THE ENGLISH-SPEAKING ROLE.
CHINA/COM UK USSR INT/ORG FORCES EDU/PROP NEUTRAL
NUC/PWR NAT/LISM PEACE TOTALISM 20 COLD/WAR
COEXIST. PAGE 3 G0059
B58
DIPLOM
WAR
MARXISM
ORD/FREE

ARON R..ON WAR: ATOMIC WEAPONS AND GLOBAL DIPLOMACY
(TRANS. BY TERENCE KILMARTIN). WOR+45 SOCIETY
FORCES BAL/PWR WAR WEAPON PERSON...SOC 20. PAGE 4
G0067
B58
ARMS/CONT
NUC/PWR
COERCE
DIPLOM

ATOMIC INDUSTRIAL FORUM.MANAGEMENT AND ATOMIC
ENERGY. WOR+45 SEA LAW MARKET NAT/G TEC/DEV INSPECT
INT/TRADE CONFER PEACE HEALTH...ANTHOL 20. PAGE 4
G0078
B58
NUC/PWR
INDUS
MGT
ECO/TAC

CROWE S..THE LANDSCAPE OF POWER. UK CULTURE
SERV/IND NAT/G CONSULT PARTIC NUC/PWR LEISURE...SOC
EXHIBIT 20. PAGE 14 G0264
B58
HABITAT
TEC/DEV
PLAN
CONTROL

GAVIN J.M..WAR AND PEACE IN THE SPACE AGE. SPACE
USA+45 USSR FORCES PLAN TEC/DEV BAL/PWR DIPLOM
ARMS/CONT WEAPON CIVMIL/REL...CHARTS GP/COMP 20
NATO COLD/WAR. PAGE 21 G0414
B58
WAR
DETER
NUC/PWR
PEACE

JUNGK R..BRIGHTER THAN A THOUSAND SUNS: THE MORAL
AND POLITICAL HISTORY OF THE ATOMIC SCIENTISTS.
WOR+45 WOR-45 CONSULT CREATE RISK UTIL DRIVE
PERCEPT PWR...INT 20. PAGE 29 G0568
B58
NUC/PWR
MORAL
GOV/REL
PERSON

NATIONAL PLANNING ASSOCIATION.1970 WITHOUT ARMS
CONTROL (PAMPHLET). WOR+45 PROB/SOLV TEC/DEV DIPLOM
CONFER DETER NUC/PWR WAR...CHARTS 20 COLD/WAR.
PAGE 41 G0810
B58
ARMS/CONT
ORD/FREE
WEAPON
PREDICT

NOEL-BAKER D..THE ARMS RACE. WOR+45 NAT/G DELIB/GP
ACT/RES TEC/DEV EDU/PROP NUC/PWR ATTIT KNOWL PWR
...CONCPT OBS LEAGUE/NAT 20 COLD/WAR. PAGE 42 G0823
B58
FUT
INT/ORG
ARMS/CONT
PEACE

ROCKEFELLER BROTH FUND INC.INTERNATIONAL SECURITY -
THE MILITARY ASPECT. USA+45 INT/ORG NAT/G BUDGET
ARMS/CONT WAR WEAPON PEACE ORD/FREE 20 NATO.
PAGE 47 G0932
B58
NUC/PWR
DETER
FORCES
DIPLOM

TELLER E.A..OUR NUCLEAR FUTURE. SOCIETY FORCES
TEC/DEV EDU/PROP KNOWL ORD/FREE...STAND/INT SYS/QU
KNO/TEST AUD/VIS CHARTS SIMUL 20. PAGE 54 G1062
B58
FUT
PHIL/SCI
NUC/PWR
WAR

UN INTL CONF ON PEACEFUL USE.PROGRESS IN ATOMIC
ENERGY (VOL. I). WOR+45 R+D PLAN TEC/DEV CONFER
CONTROL PEACE SKILL...CHARTS ANTHOL 20 UN BAGHDAD.
PAGE 55 G1088
B58
NUC/PWR
DIPLOM
WORKER
EDU/PROP

US DEPARTMENT OF STATE.PUBLICATIONS OF THE
DEPARTMENT OF STATE, JANUARY 1.1953 TO DECEMBER 31,
1957. AGRI INT/ORG FORCES FOR/AID EDU/PROP
ARMS/CONT NUC/PWR ATTIT 20 DEPT/STATE OAS UN NATO.
PAGE 57 G1123
B58
BIBLIOG
DIPLOM

US DEPARTMENT OF THE ARMY.BIBLIOGRAPHY ON LIMITED
WAR (PAMPHLET). USA+45 TEC/DEV CONTROL RISK COERCE
DETER NUC/PWR WEAPON ADJUST PEACE ALL/VALS ORD/FREE
20. PAGE 57 G1127
B58
BIBLIOG/A
WAR
FORCES
CIVMIL/REL

US HOUSE COMM GOVT OPERATIONS.CIVIL DEFENSE. USA+45
FORCES...CHARTS 20 CONGRESS CIV/DEFENS HOLIFLD/C.
PAGE 58 G1139
B58
NUC/PWR
WAR
PLAN
ADJUST

BURNS A.L.."THE NEW WEAPONS AND INTERNATIONAL
RELATIONS." SPACE WOR+45 NAT/G VOL/ASSN FORCES
NUC/PWR 20. PAGE 10 G0190
S58
TEC/DEV
ARMS/CONT
DIPLOM

AMRINE M..THE GREAT DECISION: THE SECRET HISTORY OF
THE ATOMIC BOMB. USA+45 TOP/EX EDU/PROP LEGIT
PERCEPT ORD/FREE PWR VAL/FREE HIROSHIMA. PAGE 3
G0055
B59
DECISION
NAT/G
NUC/PWR
FORCES

ATOMIC INDUSTRIAL FORUM.THE IMPACT OF THE PEACEFUL
USES OF ATOMIC ENERGY ON STATE AND LOCAL
GOVERNMENT. USA+45 INDUS NAT/G LEGIS PLAN CONTROL
GOV/REL. PAGE 4 G0079
B59
PROVS
LOC/G
NUC/PWR
PEACE

GODDARD V..THE ENIGMA OF MENACE. WOR+45 SECT LEAD
NUC/PWR WAR WEAPON CHOOSE PERSON PWR...POLICY
PHIL/SCI PACIFIST 20 COLD/WAR. PAGE 22 G0423
B59
PEACE
ARMS/CONT
DIPLOM
ATTIT

GREENFIELD K.R..COMMAND DECISIONS. ASIA EUR+WWI
S/ASIA USA-45 WOR-45 NAT/G CONSULT DELIB/GP COERCE
NUC/PWR PWR...OBS 20 CHINJAP. PAGE 23 G0446
B59
PLAN
FORCES
WAR
WEAPON

HARVARD UNIVERSITY LAW SCHOOL.INTERNATIONAL
PROBLEMS OF FINANCIAL PROTECTION AGAINST NUCLEAR
RISK. WOR+45 NAT/G DELIB/GP PROB/SOLV DIPLOM
CONTROL ATTIT...POLICY INT/LAW MATH 20. PAGE 25
G0488
B59
NUC/PWR
ADJUD
INDUS
FINAN

HUGHES E.M..AMERICA THE VINCIBLE. USA+45 FOR/AID
ARMS/CONT NUC/PWR PERS/REL RATIONAL ATTIT ALL/VALS
20 COLD/WAR. PAGE 27 G0534
B59
ORD/FREE
DIPLOM
WAR

LANG D..FROM HIROSHIMA TO THE MOON: CHRONICLES OF
LIFE IN THE ATOMIC AGE. USA+45 OP/RES CONTROL
ARMS/CONT WAR CIVMIL/REL PEACE HABITAT MORAL PWR
...OBS INT 20 AEC. PAGE 32 G0633
B59
NUC/PWR
SPACE
HEALTH
TEC/DEV

B59
MAYDA J.,ATOMIC ENERGY AND LAW. ECO/UNDEV FINAN NUC/PWR
TEC/DEV FOR/AID EFFICIENCY PRODUC WEALTH...POLICY L/A+17C
TECHNIC 20. PAGE 37 G0723 LAW
ADMIN

B59
MIKSCHE F.O.,THE FAILURE OF ATOMIC STRATEGY. COM ACT/RES
EUR+WWI INTELL POL/PAR FORCES PLAN ECO/TAC NUC/PWR ORD/FREE
ATTIT DRIVE RIGID/FLEX PWR...DECISION GEOG PSY DIPLOM
CONCPT RECORD TREND CHARTS VAL/FREE 20. PAGE 39 ARMS/CONT
G0766

B59
MODELSKI G.,ATOMIC ENERGY IN THE COMMUNIST BLOC. TEC/DEV
FUT INT/ORG CONSULT FORCES ACT/RES PLAN KNOWL SKILL NUC/PWR
...PHIL/SCI STAT CHARTS 20. PAGE 39 G0777 USSR
COM

B59
POKROVSKY G.I.,SCIENCE AND TECHNOLOGY IN TEC/DEV
CONTEMPORARY WAR. SPACE USSR WOR+45 NAT/G CONSULT FORCES
ACT/RES PLAN DETER WEAPON...MARXIST METH/CNCPT NUC/PWR
CHARTS STERTYP COLD/WAR 20. PAGE 45 G0881 WAR

B59
RUSSELL B.,COMMON SENSE AND NUCLEAR WARFARE. WOR+45 ORD/FREE
INTELL SOCIETY STRATA NAT/G TOP/EX EDU/PROP ATTIT ARMS/CONT
PERSON KNOWL MORAL PWR...POLICY CONCPT MYTH NUC/PWR
CON/ANAL COLD/WAR 20. PAGE 48 G0948

B59
U OF MICHIGAN LAW SCHOOL.ATOMS AND THE LAW. USA+45 NUC/PWR
PROVS WORKER PROB/SOLV DIPLOM ADMIN GOV/REL ANTHOL. NAT/G
PAGE 55 G1085 CONTROL
LAW

B59
US CONGRESS JT ATOM ENRGY COMM,SELECTED MATERIALS NAT/G
ON FEDERAL-STATE COOPERATION IN THE ATOMIC ENERGY NUC/PWR
FIELD. USA+45 LAW LOC/G PROVS CONSULT LEGIS ADJUD GOV/REL
...POLICY BIBLIOG 20 AEC. PAGE 57 G1111 DELIB/GP

L59
BURNS A.L.,"THE RATIONALE OF CATALYTIC WAR." COM COERCE
USA+45 WOR+45 R+D NAT/G FORCES ACT/RES TEC/DEV PWR NUC/PWR
...DECISION HYPO/EXP TOT/POP 20. PAGE 10 G0191 WAR

L59
BURNS A.L.,"POWER POLITICS AND THE GROWING NUCLEAR FORCES
CLUB." FUT WOR+45 TEC/DEV EXEC ARMS/CONT COERCE BAL/PWR
DETER...DECISION HYPO/EXP 20. PAGE 10 G0192 NUC/PWR

S59
CORY R.H. JR.,"INTERNATIONAL INSPECTION FROM STRUCT
PROPOSALS TO REALIZATION." WOR+45 TEC/DEV ECO/TAC PSY
ADJUD ORD/FREE PWR WEALTH...RECORD VAL/FREE 20. ARMS/CONT
PAGE 13 G0258 NUC/PWR

S59
JANOWITZ M.,"CHANGING PATTERNS OF ORGANIZATIONAL FORCES
AUTHORITY: THE MILITARY ESTABLISHMENT" (BMR)" AUTHORIT
USA+45 ELITES STRUCT EX/STRUC PLAN DOMIN AUTOMAT ADMIN
NUC/PWR WEAPON 20. PAGE 28 G0559 TEC/DEV

S59
MILBURN T.W.,"WHAT CONSTITUTES EFFECTIVE INTELL
DETERRENCE." USA+45 USSR WOR+45 STRUCT FORCES ATTIT
ACT/RES PLAN SUPEGO KNOWL ORD/FREE PWR...RELATIV DETER
PSY CONCPT VAL/FREE 20 COLD/WAR. PAGE 39 G0768 NUC/PWR

S59
SIMONS H.,"WORLD-WIDE CAPABILITIES FOR PRODUCTION TEC/DEV
AND CONTROL OF NUCLEAR WEAPONS." FUT WOR+45 INDUS ARMS/CONT
INT/ORG NAT/G ECO/TAC ATTIT PWR SKILL...TREND NUC/PWR
CHARTS VAL/FREE 20. PAGE 51 G1001

S59
STOESSINGER J.G.,"THE INTERNATIONAL ATOMIC ENERGY INT/ORG
AGENCY: THE FIRST PHASE." FUT WOR+45 NAT/G VOL/ASSN ECO/DEV
DELIB/GP BAL/PWR LEGIT ADMIN ROUTINE PWR...OBS FOR/AID
CON/ANAL GEN/LAWS VAL/FREE 20 IAEA. PAGE 53 G1037 NUC/PWR

B60
ARMS CONTROL. FUT UNIV WOR+45 INTELL R+D INT/ORG DELIB/GP
NAT/G VOL/ASSN CONSULT CREATE EDU/PROP PEACE...HUM ORD/FREE
GEN/LAWS TOT/POP 20. PAGE 1 G0015 ARMS/CONT
NUC/PWR

B60
ATOMIC INDUSTRIAL FORUM,ATOMS FOR INDUSTRY: WORLD NUC/PWR
FORUM. WOR+45 FINAN COST UTIL...JURID ANTHOL 20. INDUS
PAGE 4 G0080 PLAN
PROB/SOLV

B60
BARNET R.,WHO WANTS DISARMAMENT. COM EUR+WWI USA+45 PLAN
USSR INT/ORG NAT/G BAL/PWR DIPLOM EDU/PROP COERCE FORCES
DETER NUC/PWR WAR WEAPON ATTIT PWR...TIME/SEQ ARMS/CONT
COLD/WAR CONGRESS 20. PAGE 5 G0096

B60
CHASE S.,LIVE AND LET LIVE. USA+45 ECO/DEV NAT/G
PROB/SOLV TEC/DEV ECO/TAC ARMS/CONT NUC/PWR WAR DIPLOM
NAT/LISM PEACE...GEOG TREND 20 COLD/WAR. PAGE 11 SOCIETY
G0223 TASK

B60
EINSTEIN A.,EINSTEIN ON PEACE. FUT WOR+45 WOR-45 INT/ORG
SOCIETY NAT/G PLAN BAL/PWR CAP/ISM DIPLOM ARMS/CONT ATTIT
DETER NAT/LISM...POLICY RELATIV HUM PHIL/SCI CONCPT NUC/PWR
BIOG COLD/WAR LEAGUE/NAT NAZI. PAGE 17 G0338 PEACE

B60
HEILBRONER R.L.,THE FUTURE AS HISTORY. USA+45 TEC/DEV
WOR+45 WOR-45 SOCIETY ECO/DEV ECO/UNDEV VOL/ASSN TREND
PLAN CAP/ISM NUC/PWR CHOOSE NAT/LISM ATTIT ORD/FREE
RESPECT WEALTH SOCISM 20. PAGE 25 G0501

B60
HITCH C.J.,THE ECONOMICS OF DEFENSE IN THE NUCLEAR R+D
AGE. USA+45 WOR+45 CREATE PLAN NUC/PWR ATTIT FORCES
...CON/ANAL CHARTS HYPO/EXP NATO 20. PAGE 26 G0514

B60
LE GHAIT E.,NO CARTE BLANCHE TO CAPRICORN; THE DETER
FOLLY OF NUCLEAR WAR. WOR+45 INT/ORG BAL/PWR DIPLOM NUC/PWR
RISK COERCE...CENSUS 20 NATO. PAGE 33 G0647 PLAN
DECISION

B60
MCCLELLAND C.A.,NUCLEAR WEAPONS, MISSILES, AND DIPLOM
FUTURE WAR: PROBLEM FOR THE SIXTIES. WOR+45 FORCES NUC/PWR
ARMS/CONT DETER MARXISM...POLICY ANTHOL COLD/WAR. WAR
PAGE 37 G0729 WEAPON

B60
MCKINNEY R.,REVIEW OF THE INTERNATIONAL ATOMIC NUC/PWR
POLICIES AND PROGRAMS OF THE UNITED STATES (5 PEACE
VOLS.). COM FUT USA+45 ECO/DEV ECO/UNDEV INT/ORG DIPLOM
DELIB/GP PLAN ADMIN 20 THIRD/WRLD. PAGE 38 G0744 POLICY

B60
PARRY A.,RUSSIA'S ROCKETS AND MISSILES. COM FUT PLAN
GERMANY USA+45 WOR+45 INTELL ECO/DEV ACT/RES TEC/DEV
NUC/PWR WEAPON ATTIT ALL/VALS...OBS TIME/SEQ SPACE
COLD/WAR 20. PAGE 44 G0859 USSR

B60
US DEPARTMENT OF THE ARMY,DISARMAMENT: A BIBLIOG/A
BIBLIOGRAPHIC RECORD: 1916-1960. DETER WAR WEAPON ARMS/CONT
PEACE 20 UN LEAGUE/NAT COLD/WAR NATO. PAGE 57 G1128 NUC/PWR
DIPLOM

L60
HOLTON G.,"ARMS CONTROL." FUT WOR+45 CULTURE ACT/RES
INT/ORG NAT/G FORCES TOP/EX PLAN EDU/PROP COERCE CONSULT
ATTIT RIGID/FLEX ORD/FREE...POLICY PHIL/SCI SOC ARMS/CONT
TREND COLD/WAR. PAGE 27 G0524 NUC/PWR

L60
JACOB P.E.,"THE DISARMAMENT CONSENSUS." USA+45 USSR DELIB/GP
WOR+45 INT/ORG NAT/G ACT/RES TEC/DEV BAL/PWR ATTIT
EDU/PROP ADMIN COERCE DETER NUC/PWR CONSEN ARMS/CONT
RIGID/FLEX PWR...CONCPT RECORD CHARTS COLD/WAR 20.
PAGE 28 G0552

S60
BRODY R.A.,"DETERRENCE STRATEGIES: AN ANNOTATED BIBLIOG/A
BIBLIOGRAPHY." WOR+45 PLAN ARMS/CONT NUC/PWR WAR FORCES
WEAPON DECISION. PAGE 9 G0173 DETER
DIPLOM

S60
DOTY P.M.,"THE ROLE OF THE SMALLER POWERS." FUT PWR
WOR+45 NAT/G TEC/DEV BAL/PWR DOMIN LEGIT CHOOSE POLICY
DISPL DRIVE RESPECT...DECISION 20. PAGE 16 G0310 ARMS/CONT
NUC/PWR

S60
DOUGHERTY J.E.,"KEY TO SECURITY: DISARMAMENT OR FORCES
ARMS STABILITY." COM USA+45 USSR INT/ORG NAT/G ORD/FREE
CREATE EDU/PROP COERCE DETER ATTIT PWR...DECISION ARMS/CONT
CONCPT MYTH NEW/IDEA TREND 20 COLD/WAR. PAGE 16 NUC/PWR
G0311

S60
DYSON F.J.,"THE FUTURE DEVELOPMENT OF NUCLEAR INT/ORG
WEAPONS." FUT WOR+45 DELIB/GP ACT/RES PLAN DETER ARMS/CONT
WEAPON ATTIT PWR...POLICY 20. PAGE 17 G0328 NUC/PWR

HUNTINGTON S.P.,"STRATEGIC PLANNING AND THE   EXEC
POLITICAL PROCESS." USA+45 NAT/G DELIB/GP LEGIS   FORCES
ACT/RES ECO/TAC LEGIT ROUTINE CHOOSE RIGID/FLEX PWR   NUC/PWR
...POLICY MAJORIT MGT 20. PAGE 27 G0538   WAR
                                                          S60

HUTCHINSON C.E.,"AN INSTITUTE FOR NATIONAL SECURITY   POLICY
AFFAIRS." USA+45 R+D NAT/G CONSULT TOP/EX ACT/RES   METH/CNCPT
CREATE PLAN TEC/DEV EDU/PROP ROUTINE NUC/PWR ATTIT   ELITES
ORD/FREE PWR...DECISION MGT PHIL/SCI CONCPT RECORD   DIPLOM
GEN/LAWS GEN/METH 20. PAGE 27 G0539
                                                          S60

IKLE F.C.,"NTH COUNTRIES AND DISARMAMENT." WOR+45   FUT
DELIB/GP ECO/TAC DOMIN EDU/PROP LEGIT ROUTINE   INT/ORG
COERCE RIGID/FLEX ORD/FREE...MARXIST TREND 20.   ARMS/CONT
PAGE 28 G0543   NUC/PWR
                                                          S60

KAPLAN M.A.,"THEORETICAL ANALYSIS OF THE BALANCE OF   CREATE
POWER." FUT USA+45 WOR+45 INTELL ECO/DEV INT/ORG   NEW/IDEA
NAT/G CONSULT TOP/EX ACT/RES PLAN TEC/DEV ATTIT   DIPLOM
ALL/VALS...METH/CNCPT TOT/POP 20. PAGE 29 G0576   NUC/PWR
                                                          S60

KELLEY G.A.,"THE POLITICAL BACKGROUND OF THE FRENCH   NAT/G
A-BOMB." EUR+WWI USSR FORCES TOP/EX TEC/DEV NUC/PWR   RESPECT
ATTIT PWR...CONCPT OBS/ENVIR TREND 20. PAGE 30   NAT/LISM
G0591   FRANCE
                                                          S60

KISSINGER H.A.,"ARMS CONTROL, INSPECTION AND   FORCES
SURPRISE ATTACK." COM USA+45 NAT/G ACT/RES PLAN   ORD/FREE
TEC/DEV DIPLOM EDU/PROP DETER WAR RIGID/FLEX   ARMS/CONT
...CONCPT GEN/METH TOT/POP 20. PAGE 31 G0603   NUC/PWR
                                                          S60

LEAR J.,"PEACE: SCIENCE'S NEXT GREAT EXPLORATION."   EX/STRUC
USA+45 INT/ORG TOP/EX TEC/DEV EDU/PROP ROUTINE   ARMS/CONT
PEACE KNOWL SKILL 20. PAGE 33 G0648   NUC/PWR
                                                          S60

OSGOOD C.E.,"A CASE FOR GRADUATED UNILATERAL   ATTIT
DISENGAGEMENT." FUT WOR+45 CULTURE SOCIETY NAT/G   EDU/PROP
NUC/PWR WAR PERSON SUPEGO ALL/VALS...POLICY PSY   ARMS/CONT
CONCPT COLD/WAR TOT/POP VAL/FREE 20. PAGE 43 G0848
                                                          S60

SANDERS R.,"NUCLEAR DYNAMITE: A NEW DIMENSION IN   INDUS
FOREIGN POLICY." FUT WOR+45 ECO/DEV CONSULT TEC/DEV   PWR
PERCEPT...CONT/OBS TIME/SEQ TREND GEN/LAWS TOT/POP   DIPLOM
20 TREATY. PAGE 49 G0955   NUC/PWR
                                                          S60

YEMELYANOV V.S.,"ATOMIC ENERGY FOR PEACE: THE USSR   VOL/ASSN
AND INTERNATIONAL CO-OPERATION." FUT USSR WOR+45   TEC/DEV
R+D CREATE EDU/PROP...CONCPT GEN/LAWS 20. PAGE 64   ARMS/CONT
G1264   NUC/PWR
                                                          B61

FRISCH D.,ARMS REDUCTION: PROGRAM AND ISSUES.   PLAN
USA+45 INT/ORG NAT/G ACT/RES REGION NUC/PWR ATTIT   FORCES
PWR...POLICY 20. PAGE 20 G0395   ARMS/CONT
                                                          DIPLOM
                                                          B61

HADLEY A.T.,THE NATIONS SAFETY AND ARMS CONTROL.   ACT/RES
FUT USA+45 WOR+45 TOP/EX PLAN TEC/DEV ATTIT DRIVE   ROUTINE
...CONCPT OBS TIME/SEQ TREND 20. PAGE 24 G0466   DETER
                                                          NUC/PWR
                                                          B61

HENKIN L.,ARMS CONTROL: ISSUES FOR THE PUBLIC.   WOR+45
EUR+WWI FUT USA+45 USSR INT/ORG NAT/G DIPLOM   DELIB/GP
EDU/PROP DETER NUC/PWR ATTIT PWR...CONCPT RECORD   ARMS/CONT
HIST/WRIT TIME/SEQ TOT/POP COLD/WAR 20. PAGE 26
G0506
                                                          B61

KAHN H.,ON THERMONUCLEAR WAR. FUT UNIV WOR+45   DETER
ECO/DEV CONSULT EX/STRUC TOP/EX ACT/RES CREATE PLAN   NUC/PWR
COERCE WAR PERSON ALL/VALS...POLICY GEOG CONCPT   SOCIETY
METH/CNCPT OBS TREND 20. PAGE 29 G0569
                                                          B61

KISSINGER H.A.,THE NECESSITY FOR CHOICE. FUT USA+45   TOP/EX
ECO/UNDEV NAT/G PLAN BAL/PWR ECO/TAC ARMS/CONT   TREND
DETER NUC/PWR ATTIT...POLICY CONCPT RECORD GEN/LAWS   DIPLOM
COLD/WAR 20. PAGE 31 G0604
                                                          B61

NAKICENOVIC S.,NUCLEAR ENERGY IN YUGOSLAVIA.   R+D
YUGOSLAVIA AGRI INDUS CREATE OP/RES ROUTINE   ECO/DEV
EFFICIENCY KNOWL...HEAL STAT CHARTS LAB/EXP BIBLIOG   TEC/DEV
20. PAGE 41 G0802   NUC/PWR

NATHAN O.,EINSTEIN ON PEACE. WOR+45 WOR-45 INTELL   CONCPT
NUC/PWR WAR PERSON MORAL...BIOG VAL/FREE NAZI 20   PEACE
EINSTEIN/A. PAGE 41 G0807
                                                          B61

NOGEE J.L.,SOVIET POLICY TOWARD INTERNATIONAL   INT/ORG
CONTROL OF ATOMIC ENERGY. COM USA+45 WOR+45 INTELL   ATTIT
NAT/G ACT/RES DIPLOM EDU/PROP NUC/PWR TOTALISM   ARMS/CONT
PERCEPT KNOWL PWR...TIME/SEQ COLD/WAR 20. PAGE 42   USSR
G0824
                                                          B61

RAMO S.,PEACETIME USES OF OUTER SPACE. FUT DIST/IND   PEACE
INT/ORG CONSULT NUC/PWR...AUD/VIS ANTHOL 20.   TEC/DEV
PAGE 46 G0898   SPACE
                                                          CREATE
                                                          B61

SCHMIDT H.,VERTEIDIGUNG ODER VERGELTUNG. COM CUBA   PLAN
GERMANY/W USSR FORCES DIPLOM ARMS/CONT DETER   WAR
NUC/PWR...POLICY CHARTS HYPO/EXP SIMUL BIBLIOG 20   BAL/PWR
NATO COLD/WAR. PAGE 49 G0970   ORD/FREE
                                                          B61

STEIN W.,NUCLEAR WEAPONS: A CATHOLIC RESPONSE.   NUC/PWR
WOR+45 FORCES ARMS/CONT DETER MURDER MORAL...POLICY   WAR
CATH IDEA/COMP ANTHOL 20. PAGE 52 G1033   CATHISM
                                                          ATTIT
                                                          B61

US SENATE COMM GOVT OPERATIONS,ORGANIZING FOR   POLICY
NATIONAL SECURITY. COM USA+45 BUDGET DIPLOM DETER   PLAN
NUC/PWR WAR WEAPON ORD/FREE...BIBLIOG 20 COLD/WAR.   FORCES
PAGE 60 G1176   COERCE
                                                          S61

MACHOWSKI K.,"SELECTED PROBLEMS OF NATIONAL   UNIV
SOVEREIGNTY WITH REFERENCE TO THE LAW OF OUTER   ACT/RES
SPACE." FUT WOR+45 AIR LAW INTELL SOCIETY ECO/DEV   NUC/PWR
PLAN EDU/PROP DETER DRIVE PERCEPT SOVEREIGN   SPACE
...POLICY INT/LAW OBS TREND TOT/POP 20. PAGE 35
G0689
                                                          S61

MORGENSTERN O.,"THE N-COUNTRY PROBLEM." EUR+WWI   FUT
UNIV USA+45 WOR+45 SOCIETY CONSULT TOP/EX ACT/RES   BAL/PWR
PLAN EDU/PROP ATTIT DRIVE...POLICY OBS TREND   NUC/PWR
TOT/POP 20. PAGE 40 G0781   TEC/DEV
                                                          S61

RICHSTEIN A.R.,"LEGAL RULES IN NUCLEAR WEAPONS   NUC/PWR
EMPLOYMENTS." FUT WOR+45 LAW SOCIETY FORCES PLAN   TEC/DEV
WEAPON RIGID/FLEX...HEAL CONCPT TREND VAL/FREE 20.   MORAL
PAGE 47 G0918   ARMS/CONT
                                                          S61

SCHILLING W.R.,"THE H-BOMB: HOW TO DECIDE WITHOUT   PERSON
ACTUALLY CHOOSING." FUT USA+45 INTELL CONSULT ADMIN   LEGIT
CT/SYS MORAL...JURID OBS 20 TRUMAN/HS. PAGE 49   NUC/PWR
G0966
                                                          S61

TAUBENFELD H.J.,"OUTER SPACE--PAST POLITICS AND   PLAN
FUTURE POLICY." FUT USA+45 USA-45 WOR+45 AIR INTELL   SPACE
STRUC ECO/DEV NAT/G TOP/EX ACT/RES ADMIN ROUTINE   INT/ORG
NUC/PWR ATTIT DRIVE...CONCPT TIME/SEQ TREND TOT/POP
20. PAGE 54 G1054
                                                          S61

WOHLSTETTER A.,"NUCLEAR SHARING: NATO AND THE NTH   TREND
COUNTRY." EUR+WWI FUT SOCIETY DIPLOM EXEC DETER PWR   TEC/DEV
SKILL...POLICY TECHNIC CONCPT 20 NATO. PAGE 64   NUC/PWR
G1252   ARMS/CONT
                                                          B62

SOVIET STAND ON DISARMAMENT. COM EUR+WWI FUT USA+45   ACT/RES
NAT/G TOP/EX NUC/PWR PEACE ATTIT...POLICY CONCPT   ORD/FREE
TOT/POP 20. PAGE 1 G0016   ARMS/CONT
                                                          USSR
                                                          B62

AIR FORCE ACADEMY LIBRARY,INTERNATIONAL   BIBLIOG
ORGANIZATIONS AND MILITARY SECURITY SYSTEMS   INT/ORG
(PAMPHLET) (SPECIAL BIBLIOGRAPHY SERIES, NUMBER   FORCES
25). DIPLOM FOR/AID INT/TRADE NUC/PWR PEACE 20 UN   DETER
NATO OAS SEATO LEAGUE/NAT. PAGE 2 G0031
                                                          B62

BAKER G.W.,BEHAVIORAL SCIENCE AND CIVIL DEFENSE.   NUC/PWR
USA+45 PROB/SOLV ADMIN GP/REL INGP/REL PERS/REL   WAR
ANOMIE DRIVE PERSON...DECISION MGT SOC 20   POLICY
CIV/DEFENS. PAGE 4 G0085   ACT/RES

B62
BENNETT J.C.,NUCLEAR WEAPONS AND THE CONFLICT OF   POLICY
CONSCIENCE. WOR+45 PROB/SOLV DIPLOM WEAPON SUPEGO   NUC/PWR
MORAL...ANTHOL WORSHIP 20. PAGE 6 G0120   WAR

B62
BURKE A.E.,ENOUGH GOOD MEN. USA+45 WOR+45 ECO/UNDEV   DIPLOM
FORCES TEC/DEV GUERRILLA NUC/PWR REV WAR ORD/FREE   POLICY
MARXISM...GEOG 20 COLD/WAR. PAGE 10 G0189   NAT/G
  TASK

B62
CALDER R.,LIVING WITH THE ATOM. FUT USA+45 WOR+45   TEC/DEV
R+D INT/ORG VOL/ASSN DELIB/GP ARMS/CONT...STYLE 20.   HEALTH
PAGE 10 G0200   NUC/PWR

B62
DUPRE J.S.,SCIENCE AND THE NATION: POLICY AND   R+D
POLITICS. USA+45 LAW ACADEM FORCES ADMIN CIVMIL/REL   INDUS
GOV/REL EFFICIENCY PEACE...TREND 20 SCI/ADVSRY.   TEC/DEV
PAGE 16 G0322   NUC/PWR

B62
FORBES H.W.,THE STRATEGY OF DISARMAMENT. FUT WOR+45   PLAN
INT/ORG VOL/ASSN CONSULT ARMS/CONT COERCE NUC/PWR   FORCES
WAR DRIVE RIGID/FLEX ORD/FREE PWR...POLICY CONCPT   DIPLOM
OBS TREND STERTYP 20. PAGE 19 G0378

B62
FRYKLUND R.,100 MILLION LIVES: MAXIMUM SURVIVAL IN   NUC/PWR
A NUCLEAR WAR. USA+45 USSR CONTROL WEAPON   WAR
...IDEA/COMP NAT/COMP 20. PAGE 20 G0397   PLAN
  DETER

B62
GILPIN R.,AMERICAN SCIENTISTS AND NUCLEAR WEAPONS   INTELL
POLICY. COM FUT USA+45 WOR+45 INT/ORG NAT/G   ATTIT
PROF/ORG CONSULT FORCES CREATE TEC/DEV BAL/PWR   DETER
EDU/PROP ARMS/CONT WAR PERCEPT KNOWL MORAL PWR   NUC/PWR
...PHIL/SCI SOC CONCPT GEN/LAWS 20. PAGE 21 G0417

B62
GOLOVINE M.N.,CONFLICT IN SPACE: A PATTERN OF WAR   CREATE
IN A NEW DIMENSION. FUT USA+45 WOR+45 AIR FORCES   TEC/DEV
PLAN DIPLOM DOMIN ATTIT...STAT AUD/VIS CHARTS   NUC/PWR
COLD/WAR 20. PAGE 22 G0432   SPACE

B62
HALPERIN M.H.,LIMITED WAR; AN ESSAY ON THE   BIBLIOG/A
DEVELOPMENT OF THE THEORY AND AN ANNOTATED   WAR
BIBLIOGRAPHY (OCCASIONAL PAPER NO. 3). WOR+45   ARMS/CONT
WOR-45 NUC/PWR...CONCPT IDEA/COMP METH/COMP 19/20.   FORCES
PAGE 24 G0471

B62
KAHN H.,THINKING ABOUT THE UNTHINKABLE. FUT USA+45   INT/ORG
LAW NAT/G CONSULT FORCES ACT/RES CREATE PLAN   ORD/FREE
TEC/DEV BAL/PWR DIPLOM EDU/PROP ARMS/CONT DETER   NUC/PWR
ATTIT...CONCPT OBS TREND COLD/WAR 20. PAGE 29 G0570 PEACE

B62
KENNEDY J.F.,TO TURN THE TIDE. SPACE AGRI INT/ORG   DIPLOM
FORCES TEC/DEV ADMIN NUC/PWR PEACE WEALTH...ANTHOL   CHIEF
20 KENNEDY/JF CIV/RIGHTS. PAGE 30 G0592   POLICY
  NAT/G

B62
MELMAN S.,DISARMAMENT: ITS POLITICS AND ECONOMICS.   NAT/G
WOR+45 DELIB/GP FORCES ECO/TAC DOMIN EDU/PROP LEGIT   ORD/FREE
COERCE PWR...POLICY CONCPT 20. PAGE 38 G0752   ARMS/CONT
  NUC/PWR

B62
PERRE J.,LES MUTATIONS DE LA GUERRE MODERNE: DE LA   WAR
REVOLUTION FRANCAISE A LA REVOLUTION NUCLEAIRE.   FORCES
DIPLOM ARMS/CONT DEATH REV WEAPON GP/REL PEACE   NUC/PWR
ATTIT...STAT PREDICT BIBLIOG 18/20 WWI. PAGE 44
G0870

B62
SCHILLING W.R.,STRATEGY, POLITICS, AND DEFENSE   ROUTINE
BUDGETS. USA+45 R+D NAT/G CONSULT DELIB/GP FORCES   POLICY
LEGIS ACT/RES PLAN BAL/PWR LEGIT EXEC NUC/PWR
RIGID/FLEX PWR...TREND COLD/WAR CONGRESS 20
EISNHWR/DD. PAGE 49 G0968

B62
SOHN L.B.,ZONAL DISARMAMENT: VARIATIONS ON A THEME.   ORD/FREE
FUT WOR+45 SOCIETY ACT/RES PLAN NUC/PWR PEACE ATTIT   NEW/IDEA
...POLICY GEOG CONT/OBS HYPO/EXP 20. PAGE 52 G1020   ARMS/CONT

B62
STOVER C.F.,THE GOVERNMENT OF SCIENCE (PAMPHLET).   PHIL/SCI
USA+45 SOCIETY PROF/ORG EX/STRUC CREATE CONTROL   TEC/DEV
NUC/PWR WAR GOV/REL PEACE ORD/FREE 20. PAGE 53   LAW
G1041   NAT/G

B62
STRAUSS L.L.,MEN AND DECISIONS. USA+45 USA-45 USSR   DECISION
CONSULT FORCES TOP/EX WAR PEACE 20. PAGE 53 G1042   PWR
  NUC/PWR
  DIPLOM

B62
THOMSON G.P.,NUCLEAR ENERGY IN BRITAIN DURING THE   CREATE
LAST WAR: THE CHERWELL SIMON LECTURE (MONOGRAPH).   TEC/DEV
UK R+D CONSULT FORCES PLAN DIPLOM TASK CIVMIL/REL   WAR
ROLE...PHIL/SCI NEW/IDEA LAB/EXP 20 MAUD. PAGE 54   NUC/PWR
G1071

L62
NEIBURG H.L.,"THE EISENHOWER AEC AND CONGRESS: A   CHIEF
STUDY IN EXECUTIVE-LEGISLATIVE RELATIONS." USA+45   LEGIS
NAT/G POL/PAR DELIB/GP EX/STRUC TOP/EX ADMIN EXEC   GOV/REL
LEAD ROUTINE PWR...POLICY COLD/WAR CONGRESS   NUC/PWR
PRESIDENT AEC. PAGE 41 G0816

L62
NIEBURG H.L.,"THE EISENHOWER ATOMIC ENERGY   NUC/PWR
COMMISSION AND CONGRESS" R+D INT/ORG OP/RES DIPLOM   TOP/EX
ADMIN CONTROL 20 PRESIDENT CONGRESS AEC. PAGE 42   LOBBY
G0821   DELIB/GP

S62
ALBONETTI A.,"IL SECONDO PROGRAMMA QUINQUENNALE   R+D
1963-67 ED IL BILANCIO RICERCHE ED INVESTIMENTI PER PLAN
IL 1963 DELL'ERATOM." EUR+WWI FUT ITALY WOR+45   NUC/PWR
ECO/DEV SERV/IND INT/ORG TEC/DEV ECO/TAC ATTIT
SKILL WEALTH...MGT TIME/SEQ OEEC 20. PAGE 2 G0035

S62
BETHE H.,"DISARMAMENT AND STRATEGY." COM USA+45   PLAN
USSR WOR+45 VOL/ASSN TEC/DEV EDU/PROP NUC/PWR   ORD/FREE
CHOOSE PEACE...POLICY DECISION NEW/IDEA OBS   ARMS/CONT
GEN/LAWS COLD/WAR 420. PAGE 7 G0133   DIPLOM

S62
FINKELSTEIN L.S.,"THE UNITED NATIONS AND   INT/ORG
ORGANIZATIONS FOR CONTROL OF ARMAMENT." FUT WOR+45   PWR
VOL/ASSN DELIB/GP TOP/EX CREATE EDU/PROP LEGIT   ARMS/CONT
ADJUD NUC/PWR ATTIT RIGID/FLEX ORD/FREE...POLICY
DECISION CONCPT OBS TREND GEN/LAWS TOT/POP
COLD/WAR. PAGE 19 G0368

S62
FOSTER W.C.,"ARMS CONTROL AND DISARMAMENT IN A   DELIB/GP
DIVIDED WORLD." COM FUT USA+45 USSR WOR+45 INTELL   POLICY
INT/ORG NAT/G VOL/ASSN CONSULT CREATE PLAN TEC/DEV   ARMS/CONT
EDU/PROP LEGIT NUC/PWR ATTIT RIGID/FLEX...CONCPT   DIPLOM
TREND TOT/POP 20 UN. PAGE 20 G0387

S62
GORDON B.K.,"NUCLEAR WEAPONS: RUSSIAN AND   ORD/FREE
AMERICAN." COM USA+45 USSR NAT/G FORCES ACT/RES   COERCE
TEC/DEV PERCEPT RIGID/FLEX PWR SKILL...MGT   NUC/PWR
METH/CNCPT QUANT OBS TIME/SEQ CON/ANAL GEN/METH
TOT/POP VAL/FREE 20. PAGE 22 G0433

S62
NANES A.,"DISARMAMENT: THE LAST SEVEN YEARS." COM   DELIB/GP
EUR+WWI USA+45 USSR INT/ORG FORCES TOP/EX CREATE   RIGID/FLEX
LEGIT NUC/PWR DISPL ORD/FREE...CONCPT TIME/SEQ   ARMS/CONT
CON/ANAL 20. PAGE 41 G0803

S62
PAULING L.,"GENETIC EFFECTS OF WEAPONS TESTS."   HEAL
WOR+45 SOCIETY FAM ACT/RES EDU/PROP AGE/C HEALTH   ARMS/CONT
ORD/FREE...GEOG STAT CONT/OBS PROJ/TEST CHARTS   NUC/PWR
TOT/POP 20. PAGE 44 G0861

S62
SCHILLING W.R.,"SCIENTISTS, FOREIGN POLICY AND   NAT/G
POLITICS." WOR+45 WOR-45 INTELL INT/ORG CONSULT   TEC/DEV
TOP/EX ACT/RES PLAN ADMIN KNOWL...CONCPT OBS TREND   DIPLOM
LEAGUE/NAT 20. PAGE 49 G0967   NUC/PWR

S62
SINGER J.D.,"STABLE DETERRENCE AND ITS LIMITS." FUT NAT/G
WOR+45 R+D INT/ORG CONSULT ACT/RES TEC/DEV   FORCES
ARMS/CONT COERCE DRIVE PERCEPT RIGID/FLEX ORD/FREE   DETER
PWR...MYTH SIMUL TOT/POP 20. PAGE 51 G1004   NUC/PWR

N62
US CONGRESS JT ATOM ENRGY COMM,PEACEFUL USES OF   NUC/PWR
ATOMIC ENERGY, HEARING. USA+45 USSR TEC/DEV ATTIT   ACADEM
RIGID/FLEX...TESTS CHARTS EXHIBIT METH/COMP 20   SCHOOL
CONGRESS. PAGE 57 G1112   NAT/COMP

B63
GREEN H.P.,GOVERNMENT OF THE ATOM. USA+45 LEGIS   GOV/REL
PROB/SOLV ADMIN CONTROL PWR...POLICY DECISION 20   EX/STRUC
PRESIDENT CONGRESS. PAGE 22 G0443   NUC/PWR

DELIB/GP

B63
KAST F.E.,SCIENCE, TECHNOLOGY, AND MANAGEMENT.   MGT
SPACE USA+45 FORCES CONFER DETER NUC/PWR...PHIL/SCI   PLAN
CHARTS ANTHOL BIBLIOG 20 NASA. PAGE 30 G0581   TEC/DEV
                                                       PROB/SOLV

B63
LILIENTHAL D.E.,CHANGE, HOPE, AND THE BOMB. USA+45   ATTIT
WOR+45 R+D INT/ORG NAT/G DELIB/GP FORCES ACT/RES   MYTH
DETER RIGID/FLEX ORD/FREE...POLICY CONCPT OBS AEC   ARMS/CONT
20. PAGE 34 G0666   NUC/PWR

B63
MULLENBACH P.,CIVILIAN NUCLEAR POWER: ECONOMIC   USA+45
ISSUES AND POLICY FORMATION. FINAN INT/ORG DELIB/GP   ECO/DEV
ACT/RES ECO/TAC ATTIT SUPEGO HEALTH ORD/FREE PWR   NUC/PWR
...POLICY CONCPT MATH STAT CHARTS VAL/FREE 20
COLD/WAR. PAGE 40 G0792

B63
PACHTER H.M.,COLLISION COURSE: THE CUBAN MISSILE   WAR
CRISIS AND COEXISTENCE. CUBA USA+45 DIPLOM   BAL/PWR
ARMS/CONT PEACE MARXISM...DECISION INT/LAW 20   NUC/PWR
COLD/WAR KHRUSH/N KENNEDY/JF CASTRO/F. PAGE 43   DETER
G0854

B63
PANAMERICAN UNION,DOCUMENTOS OFICIALES DE LA   BIBLIOG
ORGANIZACION DE LOS ESTADOS AMERICANOS, INDICE Y   INT/ORG
LISTA (VOL. III, 1962). L/A+17C DELIB/GP INT/TRADE   DIPLOM
EDU/PROP REGION NUC/PWR...HEAL INT/LAW SOC/WK 20
OAS. PAGE 44 G0857

B63
US ATOMIC ENERGY COMMISSION,ATOMIC ENERGY IN THE   METH/COMP
SOVIET UNION: TRIP REPORT OF THE US ATOMIC ENERGY   OP/RES
DELEGATION, MAY 1933. USSR R+D NAT/G CONSULT CREATE   TEC/DEV
DIPLOM ADMIN ROUTINE EFFICIENCY PRODUC KNOWL SKILL   NUC/PWR
...NAT/COMP 20 AEC TRAVEL TREATY. PAGE 56 G1107

B63
US DEPARTMENT OF THE ARMY,US OVERSEAS BASES: BIBLIOG/A
PRESENT STATUS AND FUTURE PROSPECTS (PAMPHLET).   WAR
USA+45 DIPLOM NUC/PWR ATTIT ORD/FREE...POLICY   BAL/PWR
CHARTS 20. PAGE 58 G1130   DETER

L63
NIEBURG H.,"EURATOM: A STUDY IN COALITION   VOL/ASSN
POLITICS." EUR+WWI UK USA+45 ELITES NAT/G DELIB/GP   ACT/RES
LEGIS TOP/EX ECO/TAC NUC/PWR ATTIT ORD/FREE PWR
TOT/POP EEC OEEC 20 NATO EURATOM. PAGE 42 G0820

L63
PHELPS J.,"STUDIES IN DETERRENCE VIII: MILITARY   FORCES
STABILITARY AND ARMS CONTROL: A CRITICAL SURVEY."   ORD/FREE
FUT WOR+45 INT/ORG ACT/RES EDU/PROP COERCE NUC/PWR   ARMS/CONT
WAR HEALTH PWR...POLICY TECHNIC TREND SIMUL TOT/POP   DETER
20. PAGE 44 G0874

S63
BOHN L.,"WHOSE NUCLEAR TEST: NON-PHYSICAL   ADJUD
INSPECTION AND TEST BAN." WOR+45 R+D INT/ORG   ARMS/CONT
VOL/ASSN ORD/FREE...GEN/LAWS GEN/METH COLD/WAR 20.   TEC/DEV
PAGE 8 G0148   NUC/PWR

S63
CLEVELAND H.,"CRISIS DIPLOMACY." USA+45 WOR+45 LAW   DECISION
FORCES TASK NUC/PWR PWR 20. PAGE 12 G0235   DIPLOM
                                                       PROB/SOLV
                                                       POLICY

S63
ENTHOVEN A.C.,"ECONOMIC ANALYSIS IN THE DEPARTMENT   PLAN
OF DEFENSE." USA+45 NAT/G DELIB/GP PROB/SOLV RATION   BUDGET
NUC/PWR WEAPON COST...DECISION 20 DEPT/DEFEN   ECO/TAC
RESOURCE/N. PAGE 18 G0349   FORCES

S63
ERSKINE H.G.,"THE POLLS: ATOMIC WEAPONS AND NUCLEAR   ATTIT
ENERGY." USA+45 COERCE ORD/FREE...POLICY SOC STAT   INT
CENSUS SAMP VAL/FREE 20. PAGE 18 G0350   NUC/PWR

S63
FERRETTI B.,"IMPORTANZA E PROSPETTIVE DELL ENERGIA   TEC/DEV
DI ORIGINE NUCLEARE." FUT ITALY WOR+45 INTELL R+D   EXEC
ACT/RES CREATE HEALTH WEALTH...METH/CNCPT TIME/SEQ   NUC/PWR
20. PAGE 19 G0365

S63
KAWALKOWSKI A.,"POUR UNE EUROPE INDEPENDENTE ET   R+D
REUNIFIEE." EUR+WWI FUT USA+45 USSR WOR+45 ECO/DEV   PLAN
PROC/MFG INT/ORG NAT/G ACT/RES TEC/DEV FEDERAL   NUC/PWR
RIGID/FLEX...CONCPT METH/CNCPT OEEC TOT/POP 20
DEGAULLE/C. PAGE 30 G0587

S63
PHELPS J.,"INFORMATION AND ARMS CONTROL." COM SPACE   KNOWL
USA+45 USSR WOR+45 R+D INT/ORG NAT/G DELIB/GP   ARMS/CONT
DIPLOM ORD/FREE...CONCPT 20. PAGE 45 G0875   NUC/PWR

B64
BLOUSTEIN E.J.,NUCLEAR ENERGY, PUBLIC POLICY, AND   TEC/DEV
THE LAW. USA+45 NAT/G ADJUD ADMIN GP/REL OWN PEACE   LAW
ATTIT HEALTH...ANTHOL 20. PAGE 7 G0144   POLICY
                                                       NUC/PWR

B64
BROWN N.,NUCLEAR WAR: THE IMPENDING STRATEGIC   FORCES
DEADLOCK. USA+45 USSR TEC/DEV BUDGET RISK ARMS/CONT   OP/RES
NUC/PWR WEAPON COST BIO/SOC...GEOG IDEA/COMP   WAR
NAT/COMP GAME NATO WARSAW/P. PAGE 9 G0177   GEN/LAWS

B64
COHEN M.,LAW AND POLITICS IN SPACE: SPECIFIC AND   DELIB/GP
URGENT PROBLEMS IN THE LAW OF OUTER SPACE.   LAW
CHINA/COM COM USA+45 USSR NAT/G DELIB/GP INT/ORG   INT/LAW
NAT/G LEGIT NUC/PWR ATTIT BIO/SOC...JURID CONCPT   SPACE
CONGRESS 20 STALIN/J. PAGE 12 G0241

B64
DUSCHA J.,ARMS, MONEY, AND POLITICS. USA+45 INDUS   NAT/G
POL/PAR ECO/TAC TAX DETER NUC/PWR WAR WEAPON   FORCES
GOV/REL ATTIT...BIBLIOG/A 20 CONGRESS MONEY   POLICY
DEPT/DEFEN. PAGE 17 G0326   BUDGET

B64
FOGELMAN E.,HIROSHIMA: THE DECISION TO USE THE A-   INTELL
BOMB. USA-45 DIPLOM EFFICIENCY PEACE...ANTHOL   DECISION
BIBLIOG T 20 CHINJAP. PAGE 19 G0375   NUC/PWR
                                                       WAR

B64
GOWING M.,BRITAIN AND ATOMIC ENERGY 1939-1945.   NUC/PWR
FRANCE UK USA+45 USA-45 NAT/G CREATE...PHIL/SCI 20   DIPLOM
AEA. PAGE 22 G0439   TEC/DEV

B64
GRODZINS M.,THE ATOMIC AGE: FORTY-FIVE SCIENTISTS   INTELL
AND SCHOLARS SPEAK ON NATIONAL AND WORLD AFFAIRS.   ARMS/CONT
FUT USA+45 R+D INT/ORG NAT/G CONSULT TEC/DEV NUC/PWR   NUC/PWR
EDU/PROP ATTIT PERSON ORD/FREE...HUM CONCPT
TIME/SEQ CON/ANAL. PAGE 23 G0454

B64
GROSSER G.H.,THE THREAT OF IMPENDING DISASTER: HEALTH
CONTRIBUTIONS TO THE PSYCHOLOGY OF STRESS. SPACE   PSY
UNIV SOCIETY R+D TEC/DEV EDU/PROP COERCE WAR ATTIT   NUC/PWR
BIO/SOC DISPL PERCEPT PERSON...SOC MYTH SELF/OBS
CONT/OBS BIOG CON/ANAL TOT/POP 20. PAGE 23 G0455

B64
HODGETTS J.E.,ADMINISTERING THE ATOM FOR PEACE.   PROB/SOLV
OP/RES TEC/DEV ADMIN...IDEA/COMP METH/COMP 20.   NUC/PWR
PAGE 26 G0517   PEACE
                                                       MGT

B64
KAUFMANN W.W.,THE MC NAMARA STRATEGY. TOP/EX   FORCES
INSPECT BAL/PWR DIPLOM CONTROL DETER GUERRILLA   WAR
NUC/PWR WEAPON COST PWR...METH/COMP 20 MCNAMARA/R   PLAN
KENNEDY/JF JOHNSON/LB NATO DEPT/DEFEN. PAGE 30   PROB/SOLV
G0586

B64
MILIBAND R.,THE SOCIALIST REGISTER: 1964. GERMANY/W   MARXISM
ITALY UK LABOR POL/PAR ECO/TAC FOR/AID NUC/PWR   SOCISM
...POLICY SOCIALIST IDEA/COMP 20 MAO NASSER/G.   CAP/ISM
PAGE 39 G0769   PROB/SOLV

B64
NASA,PROCEEDINGS OF CONFERENCE ON THE LAW OF SPACE   SPACE
AND OF SATELLITE COMMUNICATIONS: CHICAGO 1963. FUT   COM/IND
WOR+45 DELIB/GP PROB/SOLV TEC/DEV CONFER ADJUD   LAW
NUC/PWR...POLICY IDEA/COMP 20 NASA. PAGE 41 G0805   DIPLOM

B64
PEDERSEN E.S.,NUCLEAR ENERGY IN SPACE. FUT INTELL   SPACE
R+D CONSULT...NEW/IDEA CHARTS METH T 20. PAGE 44   TEC/DEV
G0864   NUC/PWR
                                                       LAB/EXP

B64
SCHWARTZ M.D.,CONFERENCE ON SPACE SCIENCE AND SPACE   SPACE
LAW. FUT COM/IND NAT/G FORCES ACT/RES PLAN BUDGET   LAW
DIPLOM NUC/PWR WEAPON...POLICY ANTHOL 20. PAGE 50   PEACE
G0983   TEC/DEV

B64
US AIR FORCE ACADEMY ASSEMBLY,OUTER SPACE: FINAL   SPACE
REPORT APRIL 1-4, 1964. FUT USA+45 WOR+45 LAW   CIVMIL/REL

DELIB/GP CONFER ARMS/CONT WAR PEACE ATTIT MORAL ...ANTHOL 20 NASA. PAGE 56 G1104
NUC/PWR
DIPLOM

WILLIAMS S.P.,TOWARD A GENUINE WORLD SECURITY SYSTEM (PAMPHLET). WOR+45 INT/ORG FORCES PLAN NUC/PWR ORD/FREE...INT/LAW CONCPT UN PRESIDENT. PAGE 63 G1243
B64
BIBLIOG/A
ARMS/CONT
DIPLOM
PEACE

CARNEGIE ENDOWMENT INT. PEACE,"POLITICAL QUESTIONS (ISSUES BEFORE THE NINETEENTH GENERAL ASSEMBLY)." SPACE WOR+45 CONSTN FINAN NAT/G CONSULT DELIB/GP FORCES LEGIS TEC/DEV EDU/PROP LEGIT ARMS/CONT COERCE NUC/PWR ATTIT ALL/VALS...CONCPT OBS UN COLD/WAR 20. PAGE 11 G0208
L64
INT/ORG
PEACE

GOLDBERG A.,"ATOMIC ORIGINS OF THE BRITISH NUCLEAR DETERRENT." EUR+WWI UK NAT/G TOP/EX PLAN BAL/PWR DOMIN DETER CHOOSE ATTIT DRIVE HEALTH ORD/FREE PWR RESPECT...CONCPT VAL/FREE COLD/WAR 20 CMN/WLTH. PAGE 22 G0425
L64
CREATE
FORCES
NUC/PWR

WARD C.,"THE 'NEW MYTHS' AND 'OLD REALITIES' OF NUCLEAR WAR." COM FUT USA+45 USSR WOR+45 INT/ORG NAT/G DOMIN LEGIT EXEC ATTIT PERCEPT ALL/VALS ...POLICY RELATIV PSY MYTH TREND 20. PAGE 62 G1212
L64
FORCES
COERCE
ARMS/CONT
NUC/PWR

FALK S.L.,"DISARMAMENT IN HISTORICAL PERSPECTIVE." WOR-45 NAT/G PLAN NUC/PWR ORD/FREE PWR ...TIME/SEQ AUD/VIS VAL/FREE LEAGUE/NAT 20. PAGE 18 G0360
S64
INT/ORG
COERCE
ARMS/CONT

LERNER A.P.,"NUCLEAR SYMMETRY AS A FRAMEWORK FOR COEXISTENCE." COM FUT USA+45 NAT/G ACT/RES CREATE PLAN DIPLOM EDU/PROP COERCE WAR RIGID/FLEX PWR SKILL...CONCPT METH/CNCPT GEN/LAWS TOT/POP VAL/FREE COLD/WAR 20. PAGE 33 G0657
S64
FORCES
ORD/FREE
DETER
NUC/PWR

MAGGS P.B.,"SOVIET VIEWPOINT ON NUCLEAR WEAPONS IN INTERNATIONAL LAW." USSR WOR+45 INT/ORG FORCES DIPLOM ARMS/CONT ATTIT ORD/FREE PWR...POLICY JURID CONCPT OBS TREND CON/ANAL GEN/LAWS VAL/FREE 20. PAGE 35 G0694
S64
COM
LAW
INT/LAW
NUC/PWR

SPONSLER G.C.,"THE MILITARY ROLE IN SPACE." FUT USA+45 SEA AIR NAT/G ACT/RES PLAN COERCE NUC/PWR WEAPON KNOWL ORD/FREE PWR RESPECT...TREND 20. PAGE 52 G1026
S64
TEC/DEV
FORCES
SPACE

NATIONAL ACADEMY OF SCIENCES,CIVIL DEFENSE: PROJECT HARBOR SUMMARY REPORT (PAMPHLET). USA+45 MUNIC NAT/G ACT/RES BUDGET EDU/PROP DETER WEAPON EATING ...GEOG 20. PAGE 41 G0808
N64
NUC/PWR
FORCES
WAR
PLAN

WHITE HOUSE CONFERENCE ON INTERNATIONAL COOPERATION(VOL.II). SPACE WOR+45 EXTR/IND INT/ORG LABOR WORKER NUC/PWR PEACE AGE/Y...CENSUS ANTHOL 20 RESOURCE/N URBAN/RNWL PUB/TRANS. PAGE 1 G0019
B65
R+D
CONFER
TEC/DEV
DIPLOM

PEACE RESEARCH ABSTRACTS. FUT WOR+45 R+D INT/ORG NAT/G PLAN TEC/DEV BAL/PWR DIPLOM FOR/AID NUC/PWR HEALTH. PAGE 1 G0020
B65
BIBLIOG/A
PEACE
ARMS/CONT
WAR

ALLEN S.,LETTER TO A CONSERVATIVE. SOCIETY NAT/G DIPLOM EDU/PROP NUC/PWR GP/REL ATTIT MORAL ...MAJORIT CONCPT 20. PAGE 2 G0044
B65
ORD/FREE
MARXISM
POLICY
LAISSEZ

ATOMIC INDUSTRIAL FORUM,SAFEGUARDS AGAINST DIVERSION OF NUCLEAR MATERIALS FROM PEACEFUL TO MILITARY PURPOSES. WOR+45 DELIB/GP FORCES PLAN DIPLOM CONFER PEACE...ANTHOL 20 IAEA. PAGE 4 G0081
B65
NUC/PWR
CIVMIL/REL
INSPECT
CONTROL

BEAUFRE A.,AN INTRODUCTION TO STRATEGY, WITH PARTICULAR REFERENCE TO PROBLEMS OF DEFENSE. POLITICS, ECONOMICS IN THE NUCLEAR AGE. WOR+45 FORCES DIPLOM DETER CIVMIL/REL GP/REL...NEW/IDEA IDEA/COMP 20. PAGE 6 G0111
B65
PLAN
NUC/PWR
WEAPON
DECISION

BLOOMFIELD L.,SOVIET INTERESTS IN ARMS CONTROL AND DISARMAMENT* THE DECADE UNDER KHRUSHCHEV 1954-1964.
B65
USSR
ARMS/CONT

ASIA FORCES ACT/RES EDU/PROP DETER NUC/PWR WEAPON COST ATTIT...PHIL/SCI CLASSIF STAT NET/THEORY GAME BIBLIOG. PAGE 7 G0139
DIPLOM
TREND

BOBROW D.B.,COMPONENTS OF DEFENSE POLICY. ASIA EUR+WWI USA+45 WOR+45 INTELL INT/ORG NAT/G PROF/ORG CONSULT LEGIS ACT/RES CREATE ARMS/CONT COERCE ORD/FREE...DECISION SIMUL. PAGE 7 G0145
B65
DETER
NUC/PWR
PLAN
FORCES

CORDIER A.W.,THE QUEST FOR PEACE. WOR+45 NAT/G PLAN BAL/PWR ECO/TAC ARMS/CONT NUC/PWR PWR...ANTHOL UN COLD/WAR. PAGE 13 G0256
B65
PEACE
DIPLOM
POLICY
INT/ORG

GRETTON P.,MARITIME STRATEGY - A STUDY OF DEFENSE PROBLEMS. EUR+WWI UK USSR DIPLOM COERCE DETER NUC/PWR WEAPON...CONCPT NAT/COMP 20. PAGE 23 G0449
B65
FORCES
PLAN
WAR
SEA

HALPERIN M.H.,CHINA AND THE BOMB. USA+45 USSR INT/ORG FORCES ARMS/CONT DETER PRODUC ORD/FREE PWR TREND. PAGE 24 G0472
B65
ASIA
NUC/PWR
WAR
DIPLOM

HALPERIN M.H.,COMMUNIST CHINA AND ARMS CONTROL. CHINA/COM FUT USA+45 CULTURE FORCES TEC/DEV ECO/TAC WAR PEACE ORD/FREE MARXISM 20 COLD/WAR. PAGE 24 G0473
B65
ATTIT
POLICY
ARMS/CONT
NUC/PWR

HASSON J.A.,THE ECONOMICS OF NUCLEAR POWER. INDIA UK USA+45 WOR+45 INT/ORG TEC/DEV COST...SOC STAT CHARTS 20 EURATOM. PAGE 25 G0490
B65
NUC/PWR
INDUS
ECO/DEV
METH

HEER D.M.,AFTER NUCLEAR ATTACK: A DEMOGRAPHIC INQUIRY. USA+45 ECO/DEV SECT WORKER SEX...HEAL SOC STAT PREDICT CHARTS 20 NEGRO. PAGE 25 G0500
B65
GEOG
NUC/PWR
CENSUS
WAR

MCGUIRE M.C.,SECRECY AND THE ARMS RACE* A THEORY OF THE ACCUMULATION OF STRATEGIC WEAPONS AND HOW SECRECY AFFECTS IT. DIPLOM NUC/PWR WEAPON ISOLAT RATIONAL ORD/FREE WEALTH...ECOMETRIC MATH GEN/LAWS. PAGE 38 G0742
B65
DETER
ARMS/CONT
SIMUL
GAME

MOSKOWITZ H.,US SECURITY, ARMS CONTROL, AND DISARMAMENT 1961-1965. FORCES DIPLOM DETER WAR WEAPON...CHARTS 20 UN COLD/WAR NATO. PAGE 40 G0790
B65
BIBLIOG/A
ARMS/CONT
NUC/PWR
PEACE

SCHEINMAN L.,ATOMIC ENERGY POLICY IN FRANCE UNDER THE FOURTH REPUBLIC. FRANCE UK USA+45 WOR+45 ELITES POL/PAR PLAN PROB/SOLV DIPLOM LEAD GOV/REL ...BIBLIOG 20 DEGAULLE/C. PAGE 49 G0962
B65
NUC/PWR
NAT/G
DELIB/GP
POLICY

UN,SPACE ACTIVITIES AND RESOURCES: REVIEW OF UNITED NATION'S NATIONAL AND INTERNATIONAL PROGRAMS. INT/ORG LABOR PLAN TEC/DEV DIPLOM EFFICIENCY HEALTH ...GOV/COMP 20 UN. PAGE 55 G1086
B65
SPACE
NUC/PWR
FOR/AID
PEACE

US CONGRESS JT ATOM ENRGY COMM,PEACEFUL APPLICATIONS OF NUCLEAR EXPLOSIVES: PLOWSHARE, HEARING. USA+45 LEGIS CREATE PLAN PEACE...CHARTS EXHIBIT BIBLIOG CONGRESS PANAMA/CNL. PAGE 57 G1113
B65
NUC/PWR
DELIB/GP
TEC/DEV
NAT/G

US CONGRESS JT ATOM ENRGY COMM,ATOMIC ENERGY LEGISLATION THROUGH 89TH CONGRESS, 1ST SESSION. USA+45 LAW INT/ORG DELIB/GP BUDGET DIPLOM 20 AEC CONGRESS CASEBOOK EURATOM IAEA. PAGE 57 G1114
B65
NUC/PWR
FORCES
PEACE
LEGIS

US CONGRESS JT ATOM ENRGY COMM,PROPOSED AMENDMENT TO SECTION 271 OF THE ATOMIC ENERGY ACT OF 1954. USA+45 CONSTRUC PLAN INSPECT CONTROL CT/SYS 20 CONGRESS AEC. PAGE 57 G1115
B65
LAW
LEGIS
DELIB/GP
NUC/PWR

US DEPARTMENT OF ARMY,MILITARY PROTECTIVE CONSTRUCTION: NUCLEAR WARFARE AND CHEMICAL AND BIOLOGICAL OPERATIONS (MANUAL). OP/RES TEC/DEV RISK COERCE NUC/PWR WAR WEAPON EFFICIENCY UTIL BIO/SOC HABITAT ORD/FREE 20. PAGE 57 G1117
B65
FORCES
CONSTRUC
TASK
HEALTH

B65

US DEPARTMENT OF DEFENSE.US SECURITY ARMS CONTROL, AND DISARMAMENT 1961-1965 (PAMPHLET). CHINA/COM COM GERMANY/W ISRAEL SPACE USA+45 USSR WOR+45 FORCES EDU/PROP DETER EQUILIB PEACE ALL/VALS...GOV/COMP 20 NATO. PAGE 57 G1118
BIBLIOG/A ARMS/CONT NUC/PWR DIPLOM

B65

US DEPARTMENT OF THE ARMY.NUCLEAR WEAPONS AND THE ATLANTIC ALLIANCE: A BIBLIOGRAPHIC SURVEY. ASIA COM EUR+WWI USA+45 FORCES DIPLOM WEAPON...STAT 20 NATO. PAGE 58 G1131
BIBLIOG/A ARMS/CONT NUC/PWR BAL/PWR

S65

ABT C.C.."CONTROLLING FUTURE ARMS." USSR PLAN BAL/PWR DIPLOM NUC/PWR COST...CLASSIF STAT CHARTS. PAGE 2 G0027
PREDICT FUT ARMS/CONT TEC/DEV

S65

BEAUFRE A.."THE SHARING OF NUCLEAR RESPONSIBILITIES* A PROBLEM IN NEED OF SOLUTION." FRANCE USA+45 INT/ORG NAT/G DELIB/GP FORCES CONTROL NUC/PWR RIGID/FLEX...CONCPT IDEA/COMP NATO. PAGE 6 G0110
DETER RISK ACT/RES WAR

S65

BIRNBAUM K.."SWEDEN'S NUCLEAR POLICY." WOR+45 POL/PAR CREATE TEC/DEV NEUTRAL RISK WAR ORD/FREE ...DECISION IDEA/COMP NAT/COMP TIME. PAGE 7 G0137
SWEDEN NUC/PWR DIPLOM ARMS/CONT

S65

BLOOMFIELD L.P.."ARMS CONTROL AND THE DEVELOPING COUNTRIES." AFR ISLAM S/ASIA USA+45 VOL/ASSN TEC/DEV DIPLOM REGION NUC/PWR...PREDICT TREND. PAGE 7 G0142
ARMS/CONT ECO/UNDEV HYPO/EXP OBS

S65

BOHN L.C.."ATOMS FOR PEACE AND ATOMS FOR WAR." WOR+45 INT/ORG TEC/DEV DIPLOM IDEA/COMP. PAGE 8 G0149
NUC/PWR ARMS/CONT RECORD

S65

DALKEY N.C.."SOLVABLE NUCLEAR WAR MODELS." FORCES BAL/PWR DIPLOM COERCE PEACE DECISION. PAGE 14 G0273
GAME SIMUL WAR NUC/PWR

S65

DESAI M.J.."INDIA AND NUCLEAR WEAPONS." ASIA BAL/PWR DIPLOM NUC/PWR WEAPON PEACE RECORD. PAGE 15 G0294
INDIA ARMS/CONT

S65

FOX A.B.."NATO AND CONGRESS." CONSTN DELIB/GP EX/STRUC FORCES TOP/EX BUDGET NUC/PWR GOV/REL ...GP/COMP CONGRESS NATO TREATY. PAGE 20 G0388
CONTROL DIPLOM

S65

GOLDSTEIN W.."KEEPING THE GENIE IN THE BOTTLE* THE FEASIBILITY OF A NUCLEAR NON-PROLIFERATION AGREEMENT." ASIA FRANCE UK USA+45 USSR WOR+45 ECO/UNDEV VOL/ASSN ACT/RES PLAN RISK ARMS/CONT WAR PEACE ATTIT PERCEPT...RECORD TREND TIME. PAGE 22 G0429
NUC/PWR CREATE COST

S65

GRIFFITH S.B.."COMMUNIST CHINA'S CAPACITY TO MAKE WAR." CHINA/COM COM NAT/G TOP/EX PLAN DOMIN COERCE NUC/PWR ATTIT RESPECT SKILL...CONCPT MYTH TIME/SEQ TREND COLD/WAR 20. PAGE 23 G0452
FORCES PWR WEAPON ASIA

S65

HARRISON S.L.."NTH NATION CHALLENGES* THE PRESENT PERSPECTIVE." EUR+WWI FUT USA+45 BAL/PWR CONTROL RISK COERCE WAR...PREDICT COLD/WAR. PAGE 25 G0485
ARMS/CONT NUC/PWR NAT/G DIPLOM

S65

HIBBS A.R.."SPACE TECHNOLOGY* THE THREAT AND THE PROMISE." FUT VOL/ASSN TEC/DEV NUC/PWR COST EFFICIENCY UTIL UN TREATY. PAGE 26 G0510
SPACE ARMS/CONT PREDICT

S65

HSIEH A.L.."THE SINO-SOVIET NUCLEAR DIALOGUE* 1963." S/ASIA USA+45 RISK DETER REV WAR SOVEREIGN IDEA/COMP. PAGE 27 G0533
ASIA USSR NUC/PWR

S65

KINTNER W.P.."THE PROSPECTS FOR WESTERN SCIENCE AND TECHNOLOGY." EUR+WWI FRANCE USA+45 USSR R+D NUC/PWR NATO. PAGE 30 G0598
TEC/DEV VOL/ASSN STAT RECORD

S65

KOHL W.L.."NUCLEAR SHARING IN NATO AND THE MULTILATERAL FORCE." FUT USSR VOL/ASSN TEC/DEV DIPLOM NUC/PWR WAR WEAPON NATO. PAGE 31 G0611
ARMS/CONT OBS IDEA/COMP

S65

KRICKUS R.J.."ON THE MORALITY OF CHEMICAL/BIOLOGICAL WAR." ECO/UNDEV ARMS/CONT DETER NUC/PWR RIGID/FLEX HEALTH INT/LAW. PAGE 31 G0621
MORAL BIO/SOC WEAPON WAR

S65

MARTIN A.."PROLIFERATION." FUT WOR+45 PROB/SOLV REGION ADJUST...PREDICT NAT/COMP UN TREATY. PAGE 36 G0712
RECORD ARMS/CONT VOL/ASSN

S65

RASER J.R.."WEAPONS DESIGN AND ARMS CONTROL* THE POLARIS EXAMPLE." DETER NUC/PWR WEAPON CHOOSE PERCEPT...STERTYP TIME. PAGE 46 G0904
ARMS/CONT R+D GEOG ACT/RES

S65

RUBINSTEIN A.Z.."POLITICAL BARRIERS TO DISARMAMENT." FUT DIPLOM COERCE NUC/PWR WAR NAT/LISM ORD/FREE PREDICT. PAGE 48 G0944
COM USA+45 ARMS/CONT ATTIT

C65

MARK M.."BEYOND SOVEREIGNTY." WOR+45 WOR-45 ECO/UNDEV BAL/PWR INT/TRADE NUC/PWR REV WAR MARXISM NEW/LIB BIBLIOG. PAGE 36 G0706
NAT/LISM NAT/G DIPLOM INTELL

C65

SCHWEBEL M.."BEHAVIORAL SCIENCE AND HUMAN SURVIVAL." FORCES ARMS/CONT COERCE NUC/PWR WAR GP/REL NAT/LISM PERCEPT...POLICY PSY ANTHOL BIBLIOG/A 20 COLD/WAR. PAGE 50 G0984
PEACE ACT/RES DIPLOM HEAL

C65

SEARA M.V.."COSMIC INTERNATIONAL LAW." LAW ACADEM ACT/RES DIPLOM COLONIAL CONTROL NUC/PWR SOVEREIGN ...GEN/LAWS BIBLIOG UN. PAGE 50 G0987
SPACE INT/LAW IDEA/COMP INT/ORG

C65

US AIR FORCE ACADEMY."AMERICAN DEFENSE POLICY." COM INT/ORG TEC/DEV FOR/AID ARMS/CONT DETER NUC/PWR ...POLICY DECISION CONCPT ANTHOL BIBLIOG/A 20 COLD/WAR NATO. PAGE 56 G1103
PLAN FORCES WAR COERCE

B66

AMERICAN ASSEMBLY COLUMBIA U.A WORLD OF NUCLEAR POWERS? FUT WOR+45 ECO/DEV BAL/PWR ECO/TAC CONTROL RISK EFFICIENCY ATTIT PWR...METH/COMP ANTHOL 20. PAGE 3 G0049
NUC/PWR DIPLOM TEC/DEV ARMS/CONT

B66

BEATON L..MUST THE BOMB SPREAD? WOR+45 TEC/DEV DIPLOM DRIVE ORD/FREE PWR...CHARTS 20. PAGE 6 G0109
NUC/PWR ARMS/CONT PLAN PROB/SOLV

B66

BLOOMFIELD L.P..KHRUSHCHEV AND THE ARMS RACE. USA+45 USSR ECO/DEV BAL/PWR EDU/PROP CONFER NUC/PWR ATTIT...CHARTS 20 KHRUSH/N. PAGE 7 G0143
ARMS/CONT COM POLICY DIPLOM

B66

BRODIE B..ESCALATION AND THE NUCLEAR OPTION. ASIA CUBA EUR+WWI KOREA USA+45 USSR VIETNAM RISK ATTIT DRIVE PERCEPT PROBABIL. PAGE 9 G0172
NUC/PWR GUERRILLA WAR DETER

B66

DAENIKER G..STRATEGIE DES KLEIN STAATS. SWITZERLND ACT/RES CREATE DIPLOM NEUTRAL DETER WAR WEAPON PWR SOVEREIGN...IDEA/COMP 20 COLD/WAR. PAGE 14 G0270
NUC/PWR PLAN FORCES NAT/G

B66

FALK R.A..ON MINIMIZING THE USE OF NUCLEAR WEAPONS; THREE ESSAYS; RESEARCH MONOGRAPH NO. 23. WOR+45 STRUCT CREATE NUC/PWR REV CONSERVE...POLICY NET/THEORY IDEA/COMP GEN/LAWS GEN/METH. PAGE 18 G0359
DIPLOM EQUILIB PHIL/SCI PROB/SOLV

B66

FEIS H..THE ATOMIC BOMB AND THE END OF WORLD WAR II. FORCES PLAN PROB/SOLV DIPLOM CONFER WAR ...TIME/SEQ TREND CHINJAP PRESIDENT TIME. PAGE 19 G0362
USA+45 PEACE NUC/PWR

FREIDEL F.,AMERICAN ISSUES IN THE TWENTIETH
CENTURY. SOCIETY FINAN ECO/TAC FOR/AID CONTROL
NUC/PWR WAR RACE/REL PEACE ATTIT...ANTHOL T 20
WILSON/W ROOSEVLT/F KENNEDY/JF TRUMAN/HS. PAGE 20
G0391

B66
DIPLOM
POLICY
NAT/G
ORD/FREE

GREEN P.,DEADLY LOGIC* THE THEORY OF NUCLEAR
DETERRENCE. USA+45 ACT/RES OP/RES NUC/PWR RATIONAL
ALL/VALS PWR...DECISION MGT PHIL/SCI QUANT
IDEA/COMP GAME. PAGE 23 G0444

B66
DETER
ACADEM
GEN/LAWS
RECORD

HALPERIN M.H.,CHINA AND NUCLEAR PROLIFERATION
(PAMPHLET). CHINA/COM FUT INDIA USA+45 USSR
ARMS/CONT WAR 20 CHINJAP. PAGE 24 G0474

B66
NUC/PWR
FORCES
POLICY
DIPLOM

JACOBSON H.K.,DIPLOMATS, SCIENTISTS, AND
POLITICIANS* THE UNITED STATES AND THE NUCLEAR TEST
BAN NEGOTIATIONS. USA+45 ACT/RES PLAN CONFER
DETER NUC/PWR CONSEN ORD/FREE...INT TREATY. PAGE 28
G0554

B66
DIPLOM
ARMS/CONT
TECHRACY
INT/ORG

KUENNE R.E.,THE POLARIS MISSILE STRIKE* A GENERAL
ECONOMIC SYSTEMS ANALYSIS. USA+45 USSR NAT/G
BAL/PWR ARMS/CONT WAR...MATH PROBABIL COMPUT/IR
CHARTS HYPO/EXP SIMUL. PAGE 32 G0625

B66
NUC/PWR
FORCES
DETER
DIPLOM

LILLEY S.,MEN, MACHINES AND HISTORY: THE STORY OF
TOOLS AND MACHINES IN RELATION TO SOCIAL PROGRESS.
PREHIST SPACE STRUCT COMPUTER AUTOMAT NUC/PWR
...POLICY SOC. PAGE 34 G0667

B66
AGRI
TEC/DEV
SOCIETY

VON BORCH H,FRIEDE TROTZ KRIEG. GERMANY USSR
WOR+45 PEACE ANOMIE ATTIT 20. PAGE 43 G0853

B66
DIPLOM
NUC/PWR
WAR
COERCE

POLLARD W.G.,ATOMIC ENERGY AND SOUTHERN SCIENCE.
USA+45 HEALTH. PAGE 45 G0883

B66
NUC/PWR
GP/REL
PHIL/SCI
CREATE

STONE J.J.,CONTAINING THE ARMS RACE* SOME SPECIFIC
PROPOSALS. ASIA USA+45 USSR PROB/SOLV BARGAIN
DIPLOM DETER NUC/PWR RATIONAL...GAME 20 DEPT/DEFEN
TREATY. PAGE 53 G1038

B66
ARMS/CONT
FEEDBACK
COST
ATTIT

UNITED NATIONS,INTERNATIONAL SPACE BIBLIOGRAPHY.
FUT INT/ORG TEC/DEV DIPLOM ARMS/CONT NUC/PWR
...JURID SOC UN. PAGE 56 G1093

B66
BIBLIOG
SPACE
PEACE
R+D

US DEPARTMENT OF THE ARMY,COMMUNIST CHINA: A
STRATEGIC SURVEY: A BIBLIOGRAPHY (PAMPHLET NO.
20-67). CHINA/COM COM INDIA USSR NAT/G POL/PAR
EX/STRUC FORCES NUC/PWR REV ATTIT...POLICY GEOG
CHARTS. PAGE 58 G1133

B66
BIBLIOG/A
MARXISM
S/ASIA
DIPLOM

US PRES COMM ECO IMPACT DEFENS,REPORT* JULY 1965.
USA+45 ECO/DEV INDUS DELIB/GP FORCES OP/RES
ARMS/CONT NUC/PWR WEAPON BAL/PAY...PREDICT SIMUL.
PAGE 59 G1159

B66
ACT/RES
STAT
WAR
BUDGET

WOLFERS A.,THE UNITED STATES IN A DISARMED WORLD: A
STUDY OF THE US OUTLINE FOR GENERAL AND COMPLETE
DISARMAMENT. USA+45 NAT/G CONTROL DETER NUC/PWR
EFFICIENCY...ANTHOL 20. PAGE 64 G1255

B66
ARMS/CONT
POLICY
FORCES
PEACE

YOUNG W.,EXISTING MECHANISMS OF ARMS CONTROL.
PROC/MFG OP/RES DIPLOM TASK CENTRAL...MGT TREATY.
PAGE 65 G1266

B66
ARMS/CONT
ADMIN
NUC/PWR
ROUTINE

DOUGHERTY J.E.,"THE CATHOLIC CHURCH, WAR AND
NUCLEAR WEAPONS." COM EUR+WWI SECT TOP/EX LEAD
DETER ALL/VALS. PAGE 16 G0312

L66
CATHISM
MORAL
WAR
NUC/PWR

RASER J.R.,"DETERRENCE RESEARCH* PAST PROGRESS AND
FUTURE NEEDS." INTELL PLAN TEC/DEV NUC/PWR PERCEPT

L66
DETER
BIBLIOG/A

...DECISION PSY SOC NET/THEORY. PAGE 46 G0905

FUT

ZOPPO C.E.,"NUCLEAR TECHNOLOGY, MULTIPOLARITY, AND
INTERNATIONAL STABILITY." ASIA RUSSIA USA+45 STRUCT
TOP/EX BAL/PWR DIPLOM DETER CIVMIL/REL NAT/COMP.
PAGE 65 G1270

L66
NET/THEORY
ORD/FREE
DECISION
NUC/PWR

BROWNLIE I.,"NUCLEAR PROLIFERATION* SOME PROBLEMS
OF CONTROL." USA+45 USSR ECO/UNDEV INT/ORG FORCES
TEC/DEV REGION CONSEN...RECORD TREATY. PAGE 9 G0181

S66
NUC/PWR
ARMS/CONT
VOL/ASSN
ORD/FREE

AMERICAN FRIENDS SERVICE COMM,IN PLACE OF WAR.
NAT/G ACT/RES DIPLOM ADMIN NUC/PWR EFFICIENCY
...POLICY 20. PAGE 3 G0053

B67
PEACE
PACIFISM
WAR
DETER

ARON R.,THE GREAT DEBATE: THEORIES OF NUCLEAR
STRATEGY. FRANCE USA+45 INT/ORG PLAN TREND. PAGE 4
G0068

B67
NUC/PWR
DETER
BAL/PWR
DIPLOM

BURNS E.L.M.,MEGAMURDER. WOR+45 LAW INT/ORG NAT/G
BAL/PWR DIPLOM DETER MURDER WEAPON CIVMIL/REL PEACE
...INT/LAW TREND 20. PAGE 10 G0193

B67
FORCES
PLAN
WAR
NUC/PWR

COMMONER B.,SCIENCE AND SURVIVAL. SOCIETY INDUS
PLAN NUC/PWR KNOWL PWR...SOC 20 AEC. PAGE 13 G0247

B67
PHIL/SCI
CONTROL
PROB/SOLV
EQUILIB

DAVIS V.,THE POLITICS OF INNOVATION: PATTERNS IN
NAVY CASES (PAMPHLET). WOR+45 NAT/G CREATE WEAPON
INGP/REL ATTIT...POLICY SOC METH/COMP METH. PAGE 14
G0280

B67
BIBLIOG
FORCES
NUC/PWR
TEC/DEV

ENKE S.,DEFENSE MANAGEMENT. USA+45 R+D FORCES
WORKER PLAN ECO/TAC ADMIN NUC/PWR BAL/PAY UTIL
WEALTH...MGT DEPT/DEFEN. PAGE 18 G0348

B67
DECISION
DELIB/GP
EFFICIENCY
BUDGET

GARCIA ROBLES A.,THE DENUCLEARIZATION OF LATIN
AMERICA (TRANS. BY MARJORIE URQUIDI). LAW PLAN
DIPLOM...ANTHOL 20 TREATY UN. PAGE 21 G0409

B67
NUC/PWR
ARMS/CONT
L/A+17C
INT/ORG

HALLE L.J.,THE COLD WAR AS HISTORY. USSR WOR+45
ECO/TAC FOR/AID NUC/PWR WAR PEACE ORD/FREE
...MAJORIT TREND 20 COLD/WAR KENNEDY/JF KHRUSH/N
BERLIN/BLO. PAGE 24 G0470

B67
DIPLOM
BAL/PWR

KINTNER W.R.,PEACE AND THE STRATEGY CONFLICT. PLAN
BAL/PWR DIPLOM CONTROL ARMS/CONT DETER WEAPON 20.
PAGE 30 G0599

B67
ROLE
PEACE
NUC/PWR
ORD/FREE

MCBRIDE J.H.,THE TEST BAN TREATY: MILITARY,
TECHNOLOGICAL, AND POLITICAL IMPLICATIONS. USA+45
USSR DELIB/GP FORCES LEGIS TEC/DEV BAL/PWR TREATY.
PAGE 37 G0727

B67
ARMS/CONT
DIPLOM
NUC/PWR

MCCLINTOCK R.,THE MEANING OF LIMITED WAR. FUT
WOR+45 NAT/G FORCES GUERRILLA REV...POLICY SAMP/SIZ
TREND NAT/COMP 45 COLD/WAR. PAGE 37 G0730

B67
WAR
NUC/PWR
BAL/PWR
DIPLOM

ORLANS H.,CONTRACTING FOR ATOMS. USA+45 LAW INTELL
ACADEM LG/CO NAT/G PLAN TEC/DEV CONTROL DETER
...TREND 20 AEC. PAGE 43 G0845

B67
NUC/PWR
R+D
PRODUC
PEACE

SCHEINMAN L.,EURATOM* NUCLEAR INTEGRATION IN
EUROPE. EX/STRUC LEAD 20 EURATOM. PAGE 49 G0963

B67
INT/ORG
NAT/LISM
NUC/PWR
DIPLOM

SKOLNIKOFF E.B.,SCIENCE, TECHNOLOGY, AND AMERICAN
FOREIGN POLICY. SPACE USA+45 INT/ORG TEC/DEV
ARMS/CONT NUC/PWR 29 DEPT/STATE. PAGE 51 G1010

B67
PHIL/SCI
DIPLOM
NAT/G

EFFICIENCY

UNIVERSAL REFERENCE SYSTEM.PUBLIC POLICY AND THE MANAGEMENT OF SCIENCE (VOLUME IX). FUT SPACE WOR+45 LAW NAT/G TEC/DEV CONTROL NUC/PWR GOV/REL ...COMPUT/IR GEN/METH. PAGE 56 G1100
B67
BIBLIOG/A
POLICY
MGT
PHIL/SCI

US SENATE COMM ON FOREIGN REL.TREATY ON OUTER SPACE. WOR+45 AIR FORCES PROB/SOLV NUC/PWR SENATE TREATY UN. PAGE 60 G1182
B67
SPACE
DIPLOM
ARMS/CONT
LAW

US SENATE COMM ON FOREIGN REL.UNITED STATES ARMAMENT AND DISARMAMENT PROBLEMS. USA+45 AIR BAL/PWR DIPLOM FOR/AID NUC/PWR ORD/FREE SENATE TREATY. PAGE 60 G1184
B67
ARMS/CONT
WEAPON
FORCES
PROB/SOLV

DAVIS P.C.,"THE COMING CHINESE COMMUNIST NUCLEAR THREAT AND U.S. SEA BASED ABM OPTIONS." ASIA CHINA/COM FUT USA+45 SEA NAT/G FORCES PLAN TEC/DEV LEAD ARMS/CONT...GEOG METH/COMP 20 ABM/DEFSYS. PAGE 14 G0279
L67
NUC/PWR
DETER
WEAPON
DIPLOM

PASLEY R.S.,"ORGANIZATIONAL CONFLICTS OF INTEREST IN GOVERNMENT CONTRACTS." ELITES R+D ROUTINE NUC/PWR DEMAND EFFICIENCY 20. PAGE 44 G0860
L67
NAT/G
ECO/TAC
RATION
CONTROL

ROBINSON T.W.,"A NATIONAL INTEREST ANALYSIS OF SINO-SOVIET RELATIONS." CHINA/COM USSR NAT/G NUC/PWR ATTIT PWR...CONCPT CHARTS 20. PAGE 47 G0931
L67
MARXISM
DIPLOM
SOVEREIGN
GEN/LAWS

"CHINESE STATEMENT ON NUCLEAR PROLIFERATION." CHINA/COM USA+45 USSR DOMIN COLONIAL PWR. PAGE 1 G0022
S67
NUC/PWR
BAL/PWR
ARMS/CONT
DIPLOM

BRETNOR R.,"DESTRUCTIVE FORCE AND THE MILITARY EQUATIONS." UNIV COMPUTER PLAN PROB/SOLV AUTOMAT CONTROL COERCE DETER NUC/PWR WEAPON DRIVE PWR. PAGE 9 G0166
S67
FORCES
TEC/DEV
DOMIN
WAR

CARROLL K.J.,"SECOND STEP TOWARD ARMS CONTROL." WOR+45 INT/ORG VOL/ASSN FORCES PROB/SOLV RISK WEAPON 20 COLD/WAR. PAGE 11 G0215
S67
ARMS/CONT
DIPLOM
PLAN
NUC/PWR

CHIU S.M.,"CHINA'S MILITARY POSTURE." CHINA/COM ELITES NAT/G POL/PAR TEC/DEV ECO/TAC DOMIN CONTROL LEAD REV MARXISM 20 MAO. PAGE 12 G0228
S67
FORCES
CIVMIL/REL
NUC/PWR
DIPLOM

CHRIST R.F.,"REORGANIZATION OF FRENCH ARMED FORCES." FRANCE CREATE PLAN TEC/DEV BAL/PWR DOMIN COERCE CENTRAL EFFICIENCY 20. PAGE 12 G0229
S67
CHIEF
DETER
NUC/PWR
FORCES

CLEMENS W.C.,"CHINESE NUCLEAR TESTS: TRENDS AND PORTENTS." CHINA/COM USA+45 USSR FORCES PLAN TEC/DEV ARMS/CONT WAR PWR...DECISION 20 MAO KHRUSH/N. PAGE 12 G0234
S67
NUC/PWR
WEAPON
POLICY
DIPLOM

COFFEY J.I.,"THE ANTI-BALLISTIC MISSILE DEBATE." USA+45 USSR TEC/DEV BAL/PWR 20. PAGE 12 G0238
S67
ARMS/CONT
NUC/PWR
DETER
DIPLOM

D'AMATO D.,"LEGAL ASPECTS OF THE FRENCH NUCLEAR TESTS." FRANCE WOR+45 ACT/RES COLONIAL RISK GOV/REL EQUILIB ORD/FREE PWR DECISION. PAGE 14 G0268
S67
INT/LAW
DIPLOM
NUC/PWR
ADJUD

DEUTSCH K.W.,"ARMS CONTROL AND EUROPEAN UNITY* THE NEXT TEN YEARS." USA+45 ELITES NAT/G BAL/PWR DIPLOM NUC/PWR...INT KNO/TEST NATO EEC. PAGE 15 G0300
S67
ARMS/CONT
PEACE
REGION
PLAN

EISENDRATH C.,"THE OUTER SPACE TREATY." CHINA/COM COM USA+45 DIPLOM CONTROL NUC/PWR...INT/LAW 20 UN
S67
SPACE
INT/ORG

COLD/WAR TREATY. PAGE 17 G0339
PEACO
ARMS/CONT

EYRAUD M.,"LA FRANCE FACE A UN EVENTUEL TRAITE DE NON DISSEMINATION DES ARMES NUCLEAIRES." FRANCE USA+45 EXTR/IND INDUS R+D INT/ORG ACT/RES TEC/DEV AGREE PRODUC ATTIT 20 TREATY AEC EURATOM. PAGE 18 G0355
S67
NUC/PWR
ARMS/CONT
POLICY

FELD B.T.,"A PLEDGE* NO FIRST USE." DELIB/GP BAL/PWR DOMIN DETER. PAGE 19 G0363
S67
ARMS/CONT
NUC/PWR
DIPLOM
PEACE

FOREIGN POLICY ASSOCIATION."HOW WORLD LAW DEVELOPS* A CASE STUDY OF THE OUTER SPACE TREATY." SPACE WOR+45 BAL/PWR NEUTRAL NUC/PWR PEACE KNOWL 20 UN TREATY. PAGE 19 G0380
S67
INT/LAW
DIPLOM
ARMS/CONT
INT/ORG

GAUSSENS J.,"THE APPLICATIONS OF NUCLEAR ENERGY - TECHNICAL, ECONOMIC AND SOCIAL ASPECTS." WOR+45 INDUS R+D ACT/RES EFFICIENCY PRODUC SKILL PREDICT. PAGE 21 G0413
S67
NUC/PWR
TEC/DEV
ECO/DEV
ADJUST

GRIFFITHS F.,"THE POLITICAL SIDE OF 'DISARMAMENT'." FUT WOR+45 NUC/PWR NAT/LISM PEACE...NEW/IDEA PREDICT METH/COMP GEN/LAWS 20. PAGE 23 G0453
S67
ARMS/CONT
DIPLOM

HARTIGAN R.S.,"NONCOMBAT IMMUNITY* REFLECTIONS ON ITS ORIGINS AND PRESENT STATUS." WOR+45 PROB/SOLV WAR PRIVIL MORAL...POLICY 20. PAGE 25 G0487
S67
INT/LAW
NUC/PWR
ARMS/CONT
DIPLOM

INGLIS D.R.,"MISSILE DEFENSE, NUCLEAR SPREAD, AND VIETNAM." CHINA/COM USA+45 USSR VIETNAM INDUS BAL/PWR DETER WAR COST NAT/LISM PEACE. PAGE 28 G0544
S67
NUC/PWR
ARMS/CONT
DIPLOM
FORCES

INGLIS D.R.,"PROSPECTS AND PROBLEMS: THE NONMILITARY USES OF NUCLEAR EXPLOSIVES." CREATE PROB/SOLV TEC/DEV AGREE PEACE...INT/LAW PHIL/SCI NEW/IDEA 20 TREATY. PAGE 28 G0545
S67
NUC/PWR
INDUS
ARMS/CONT
EXTR/IND

JACKSON W.G.F.,"NUCLEAR PROLIFERATION AND THE GREAT POWERS." FUT UK WOR+45 INT/ORG DOMIN ARMS/CONT DETER ORD/FREE PACIFIST. PAGE 28 G0550
S67
NUC/PWR
ATTIT
BAL/PWR
NAT/LISM

JAIN G.,"INDIA REJECTS THE POWER RACE* REALISM ABOUT NUCLEAR WEAPONS." FORCES PROB/SOLV FOR/AID ARMS/CONT COST PWR...GOV/COMP 20. PAGE 28 G0556
S67
INDIA
CHINA/COM
NUC/PWR
DIPLOM

KAHN H.,"CRITERIA FOR LONG-RANGE NUCLEAR CONTROL POLICIES." WOR+45 INT/ORG TEC/DEV DOMIN DETER WAR WEAPON ISOLAT ORD/FREE POLICY. PAGE 29 G0571
S67
NUC/PWR
ARMS/CONT
BAL/PWR
DIPLOM

KRUSCHE H.,"THE STRIVING OF THE KIESINGER-STRAUS GOVERNMENT FOR NUCLEAR WEAPONS IS A THREAT TO EUROPEAN SECURITY." EUR+WWI GERMANY BAL/PWR SANCTION WEAPON PEACE ORD/FREE...MARXIST 20 NATO COLD/WAR. PAGE 32 G0623
S67
ARMS/CONT
INT/ORG
NUC/PWR
DIPLOM

LALL B.G.,"GAPS IN THE ABM DEBATE." NAT/G DIPLOM DETER CIVMIL/REL 20. PAGE 32 G0630
S67
NUC/PWR
ARMS/CONT
EX/STRUC
FORCES

MARTIN L.,"THE AMERICAN ABM DECISION." ASIA COM EUR+WWI UK USA+45 USSR FORCES DIPLOM PEACE...POLICY 20 ABM/DEFSYS. PAGE 36 G0713
S67
WEAPON
DETER
NUC/PWR
WAR

MARTIN L.W.,"BALLISTIC MISSILE DEFENSE AND EUROPE." EUR+WWI USA+45 FORCES PLAN BAL/PWR DEBATE PEACE ...POLICY COLD/WAR NATO. PAGE 36 G0715
S67
ATTIT
ARMS/CONT
NUC/PWR
DETER

REINTANZ G.,"THE SPACE TREATY." WOR+45 DIPLOM
S67
SPACE

CONTROL ARMS/CONT NUC/PWR WAR...MARXIST 20 COLD/WAR INT/LAW UN TREATY. PAGE 46 G0911
INT/LAW
INT/ORG
PEACE

S67
ROMANIECKI L.,"THE ATOM AND INTERNATIONAL COOPERATION." PROB/SOLV DIPLOM PEACE ORD/FREE 20. PAGE 47 G0933
INT/ORG
NUC/PWR
ARMS/CONT
CONTROL

S67
ROTHSTEIN R.L.,"NUCLEAR PROLIFERATION AND AMERICAN POLICY." PROB/SOLV BAL/PWR DIPLOM ARMS/CONT EFFICIENCY 20. PAGE 48 G0942
NUC/PWR
CONTROL
DETER
WOR+45

S67
SHARP G.,"THE NEED OF A FUNCTIONAL SUBSTITUTE FOR WAR." FUT UNIV WOR+45 CULTURE SOCIETY INT/ORG CONSULT DELIB/GP ACT/RES CREATE BAL/PWR CONFER ARMS/CONT NUC/PWR 20. PAGE 50 G0989
PEACE
WAR
DIPLOM
PROB/SOLV

S67
SHULMAN M.D.,"'EUROPE' VERSUS 'DETENTE'." USA+45 USSR INT/ORG CONTROL ARMS/CONT DETER 20. PAGE 50 G0995
DIPLOM
BAL/PWR
NUC/PWR

S67
SUINN R.M.,"THE DISARMAMENT FANTASY* PSYCHOLOGICAL FACTORS THAT MAY PRODUCE WARFARE." DIPLOM RISK ARMS/CONT DETER ANOMIE PERSON GAME. PAGE 53 G1046
DECISION
NUC/PWR
WAR
PSY

S67
TEKINER S.,"SINKIAN AND THE SINO-SOVIET CONFLICT." ASIA COM USSR FORCES PLAN BAL/PWR CONTROL NUC/PWR WAR WEAPON...DECISION 20. PAGE 54 G1060
DIPLOM
PWR
MARXISM

S67
TELLER E.,"PLANNING FOR PEACE." CHINA/COM WOR+45 DELIB/GP TEC/DEV RISK COERCE DETER WAR ATTIT ORD/FREE 20 NATO. PAGE 54 G1061
ARMS/CONT
NUC/PWR
PEACE
DOMIN

S67
WALTERS R.E.,"THE ROLE OF NUCLEAR WEAPONS FOR THE WEST." ASIA UK USA+45 USSR DIPLOM COERCE WAR PEACE ...POLICY DECISION 20. PAGE 62 G1209
PLAN
NUC/PWR
WEAPON
FORCES

S67
WARE R.S.,"FORECAST A.D. 2000." SOCIETY STRATA ECO/UNDEV INDUS FORCES EDU/PROP AUTOMAT COERCE REV WEAPON ATTIT PREDICT. PAGE 62 G1213
NUC/PWR
GEOG
TEC/DEV
WAR

S67
WASHBURN A.M.,"NUCLEAR PROLIFERATION IN A REVOLUTIONARY INTERNATIONAL SYSTEM." WOR+45 NAT/G DELIB/GP PLAN TEC/DEV...POLICY 20. PAGE 62 G1216
ARMS/CONT
NUC/PWR
DIPLOM
CONFER

N67
US HOUSE COMM APPROPRIATIONS,PUBLIC WORKS AND ATOMIC ENERGY COMMISSION APPROPRIATION BILL, 1968 (PAMPHLET). USA+45 ECO/DEV NAT/G...GEOG DEEP/INT CHARTS HOUSE/REP AEC DEPT/DEFEN TVA. PAGE 58 G1137
BUDGET
NUC/PWR
PROVS
PLAN

N67
US HOUSE COMM SCI ASTRONAUT,AUTHORIZING APPROPRIATIONS TO THE NATIONAL AERONAUTICS AND SPACE ADMINISTRATION (PAMPHLET). USA+45 NAT/G OP/RES TEC/DEV BUDGET NASA HOUSE/REP. PAGE 58 G1149
SPACE
R+D
PHIL/SCI
NUC/PWR

N67
US SENATE,STATUS OF THE DEVELOPMENT OF THE ANTI-BALLISTIC MISSILE SYSTEMS IN THE UNITED STATES (PAMPHLET). FUT USA+45 R+D PLAN TEC/DEV DEPT/DEFEN. PAGE 59 G1165
FORCES
NUC/PWR
WAR
UTIL

NUCLEAR POWER....SEE NUC/PWR

NUCLEAR WAR....SEE NUC/PWR+COERCE, WAR

NUMERICAL INDICES....SEE INDEX

NUREMBERG....NUREMBERG WAR TRIALS; SEE ALSO WAR/TRIAL

NYASALAND....SEE MALAWI

NYATURU....NYATURU, A TRIBE OF TANGANYIKA

NYC....NEW YORK CITY

OAS....ORGANIZATION OF AMERICAN STATES; SEE ALSO INT/ORG, VOL/ASSN

B54
US DEPARTMENT OF STATE,PUBLICATIONS OF THE DEPARTMENT OF STATE, OCTOBER 1,1929 TO JANUARY 1, 1953. AGRI INT/ORG FORCES FOR/AID EDU/PROP ARMS/CONT NUC/PWR ATTIT 20 DEPT/STATE OAS UN NATO. PAGE 57 G1122
BIBLIOG
DIPLOM

L55
KISER M.,"ORGANIZATION OF AMERICAN STATES." L/A+17C USA+45 ECO/UNDEV INT/ORG NAT/G PLAN TEC/DEV DIPLOM ECO/TAC INT/TRADE EDU/PROP ADMIN ALL/VALS...POLICY MGT RECORD ORG/CHARTS OAS 20. PAGE 30 G0601
VOL/ASSN
ECO/DEV
REGION

B58
US DEPARTMENT OF STATE,PUBLICATIONS OF THE DEPARTMENT OF STATE, JANUARY 1,1953 TO DECEMBER 31, 1957. AGRI INT/ORG FORCES FOR/AID EDU/PROP ARMS/CONT NUC/PWR ATTIT 20 DEPT/STATE OAS UN NATO. PAGE 57 G1123
BIBLIOG
DIPLOM

B62
AIR FORCE ACADEMY LIBRARY,INTERNATIONAL ORGANIZATIONS AND MILITARY SECURITY SYSTEMS (PAMPHLET) (SPECIAL BIBLIOGRAPHY SERIES, NUMBER 25). DIPLOM FOR/AID INT/TRADE NUC/PWR PEACE 20 UN NATO OAS SEATO LEAGUE/NAT. PAGE 2 G0031
BIBLIOG
INT/ORG
FORCES
DETER

B63
PANAMERICAN UNION,DOCUMENTOS OFICIALES DE LA ORGANIZACION DE LOS ESTADOS AMERICANOS, INDICE Y LISTA (VOL. III, 1962). L/A+17C DELIB/GP INT/TRADE EDU/PROP REGION NUC/PWR...HEAL INT/LAW SOC/WK 20 OAS. PAGE 44 G0857
BIBLIOG
INT/ORG
DIPLOM

B64
ORGANIZATION AMERICAN STATES,ECONOMIC SURVEY OF LATIN AMERICA, 1962. L/A+17C AGRI DIST/IND INDUS MARKET PROC/MFG R+D PLAN TEC/DEV ECO/TAC REGION BAL/PAY ALL/VALS...CON/ANAL ORG/CHARTS GEN/METH OAS 20. PAGE 43 G0844
ECO/UNDEV
CHARTS

OAU....ORGANIZATION FOR AFRICAN UNITY

OBERLIN....OBERLIN, OHIO

OBESITY....SEE HEALTH, EATING

OBJECTIVE....OBJECTIVE, OBJECTIVITY

OBLIGATION....SEE SUPEGO

OBS....OBSERVATION; SEE ALSO DIRECT OBSERVATION METHOD INDEX, P. XIV

B23
DRAPER J.W.,HISTORY OF THE CONFLICT BETWEEN RELIGION AND SCIENCE. WOR+45 INTELL SOCIETY R+D CREATE PLAN TEC/DEV EDU/PROP ATTIT PWR...PHIL/SCI CONCPT OBS TIME/SEQ TREND GEN/LAWS TOT/POP. PAGE 16 G0314
SECT
KNOWL

B45
BUSH V.,SCIENCE, THE ENDLESS FRONTIER. FUT USA-45 INTELL STRATA ACT/RES CREATE PLAN EDU/PROP ADMIN NUC/PWR PEACE ATTIT HEALTH KNOWL...MAJORIT HEAL MGT PHIL/SCI CONCPT OBS TREND 20. PAGE 10 G0195
R+D
NAT/G

B46
BUSH V.,ENDLESS HORIZONS. FUT USA-45 INTELL NAT/G CONSULT ACT/RES CREATE PLAN EDU/PROP DRIVE ...MAJORIT HEAL MGT PHIL/SCI CONCPT OBS TREND GEN/METH TOT/POP 20. PAGE 10 G0196
R+D
KNOWL
PEACE

B46
NORTHROP F.S.C.,THE MEETING OF EAST AND WEST. EUR+WWI MOD/EUR UNIV WOR+45 INTELL SOCIETY EX/STRUC TOP/EX ACT/RES LEGIT CHOOSE ATTIT PERCEPT RIGID/FLEX ALL/VALS...POLICY JURID OBS TOT/POP. PAGE 42 G0826
DRIVE
TREND
PEACE

B47
LASSWELL H.D.,THE ANALYSIS OF POLITICAL BEHAVIOUR: AN EMPIRICAL APPROACH. WOR+45 CULTURE NAT/G FORCES EDU/PROP ADMIN ATTIT PERCEPT KNOWL...PHIL/SCI PSY SOC NEW/IDEA OBS INT GEN/METH NAZI 20. PAGE 32 G0639
R+D
ACT/RES
ELITES

B48
BRADLEY D.,NO PLACE TO HIDE. USA+45 SOCIETY NAT/G FORCES TEC/DEV EDU/PROP DETER PEACE BIO/SOC ALL/VALS...POLICY PHIL/SCI OBS RECORD SAMP BIOG GEN/METH COLD/WAR 20. PAGE 8 G0162
R+D
LAB/EXP
ARMS/CONT
NUC/PWR

S48
MERTON R.K.,"THE BEARING OF EMPIRICAL RESEARCH UPON THE DEVELOPMENT OF SOCIAL THEORY" (BMR)"...SOC
ACT/RES
SOC/EXP

CONCPT QUANT METH/COMP HYPO/EXP 20. PAGE 38 G0757 | OBS
PHIL/SCI

B50
CANTRIL H.,TENSIONS THAT CAUSE WAR. UNIV CULTURE | SOCIETY
R+D CREATE EDU/PROP DRIVE PERSON KNOWL ORD/FREE | PHIL/SCI
...HUM PSY SOC OBS CENSUS TREND CON/ANAL SOC/EXP | PEACE
SIMUL GEN/METH ANTHOL COLD/WAR TOT/POP. PAGE 11
G0206

B50
CROWTHER J.G.,SCIENCE AT WAR. EUR+WWI PLAN TEC/DEV | R+D
DOMIN COERCE NUC/PWR WEAPON KNOWL PWR...CONCPT OBS | FORCES
TREND VAL/FREE 20. PAGE 14 G0265 | WAR
UK

C51
HOMANS G.C.,"THE WESTERN ELECTRIC RESEARCHES" IN S. | OP/RES
HOSLETT, ED., HUMAN FACTORS IN MANAGEMENT (BMR)" | EFFICIENCY
ACT/RES GP/REL HAPPINESS PRODUC DRIVE...MGT OBS 20. | SOC/EXP
PAGE 27 G0526 | WORKER

B52
CURRENT TRENDS IN PSYCHOLOGY,PSYCHOLOGY IN THE | NAT/G
WORLD EMERGENCY. USA+45 CONSULT FORCES ACT/RES PLAN | PSY
SKILL...DECISION OBS APT/TEST KNO/TEST PERS/TEST
TREND CHARTS 20. PAGE 14 G0266

B52
DAY E.E.,EDUCATION FOR FREEDOM AND RESPONSIBILITY. | SCHOOL
FUT USA+45 CULTURE CONSULT EDU/PROP ATTIT SKILL | KNOWL
...MGT CONCPT OBS GEN/LAWS COLD/WAR 20. PAGE 14
G0282

B52
HAYEK F.A.,THE COUNTER-REVOLUTION OF SCIENCE. UNIV | PERCEPT
INTELL R+D VOL/ASSN CREATE EDU/PROP...PHIL/SCI SOC | KNOWL
OBS TIME/SEQ TREND GEN/METH. PAGE 25 G0494

S52
"SELECTED CRITICAL BIBLIOGRAPHY ON THE METHODS AND | BIBLIOG/A
TECHNIQUES OF POLITICAL BEHAVIOR RESEARCH." | METH
...PHIL/SCI OBS QU SYS/QU TESTS CON/ANAL. PAGE 1 | SOC
G0012 | EDU/PROP

S52
KECSKEMETI P.,"THE 'POLICY SCIENCES': ASPIRATION | CREATE
AND OUTLOOK." UNIV CULTURE INTELL SOCIETY STRUCT | NEW/IDEA
EDU/PROP ATTIT PERCEPT RIGID/FLEX KNOWL...PHIL/SCI
METH/CNCPT OBS 20. PAGE 30 G0589

S52
TRUMAN D.B.,"SELECTED CRITICAL BIBLIOGRAPHY ON THE | BIBLIOG/A
METHODS AND TECHNIQUES OF POLITICAL BEHAVIOR | ACT/RES
RESEARCH." R+D PARTIC...SOC OBS RECORD INT. PAGE 55 | METH/CNCPT
G1079

L54
OPLER M.E.,"SOCIAL ASPECTS OF TECHNICAL ASSISTANCE | INT/ORG
IN OPERATION." WOR+45 VOL/ASSN CREATE PLAN TEC/DEV | CONSULT
EDU/PROP ALL/VALS...METH/CNCPT OBS RECORD TREND UN | FOR/AID
20. PAGE 43 G0841

S55
ANGELL R.,"GOVERNMENTS AND PEOPLES AS A FOCI FOR | FUT
PEACE-ORIENTED RESEARCH." WOR+45 CULTURE SOCIETY | SOC
FACE/GP ACT/RES CREATE PLAN DIPLOM EDU/PROP ROUTINE | PEACE
ATTIT PERCEPT SKILL...POLICY CONCPT OBS TREND
GEN/METH 20. PAGE 3 G0060

B57
KIETH-LUCAS A.,DECISIONS ABOUT PEOPLE IN NEED, A | ADMIN
STUDY OF ADMINISTRATIVE RESPONSIVENESS IN PUBLIC | RIGID/FLEX
ASSISTANCE. USA+45 GIVE RECEIVE INGP/REL PERS/REL | SOC/WK
MORAL RESPECT WEALTH...SOC OBS BIBLIOG 20. PAGE 30 | DECISION
G0595

S57
MCDONALD L.C.,"VOEGELIN AND THE POSITIVISTS: A NEW | PHIL/SCI
SCIENCE OF POLITICS." WOR+45 WOR-45 INTELL CREATE | CONCPT
PLAN ATTIT...METH/CNCPT NEW/IDEA OBS VAL/FREE 20. | GEN/METH
PAGE 37 G0734

B58
NOEL-BAKER D.,THE ARMS RACE. WOR+45 NAT/G DELIB/GP | FUT
ACT/RES TEC/DEV EDU/PROP NUC/PWR ATTIT KNOWL PWR | INT/ORG
...CONCPT OBS LEAGUE/NAT 20 COLD/WAR. PAGE 42 G0823 | ARMS/CONT
PEACE

S58
DAVENPORT J.,"ARMS AND THE WELFARE STATE." INTELL | USA+45
STRUCT FORCES CREATE ECO/TAC FOR/AID DOMIN LEGIT | NAT/G
ADMIN WAR ORD/FREE PWR...POLICY SOC CONCPT MYTH OBS | USSR
TREND COLD/WAR TOT/POP 20. PAGE 14 G0276

B59
GREENFIELD K.R.,COMMAND DECISIONS. ASIA EUR+WWI | PLAN
S/ASIA USA-45 WOR-45 NAT/G CONSULT DELIB/GP COERCE | FORCES
NUC/PWR PWR...OBS 20 CHINJAP. PAGE 23 G0446 | WAR
WEAPON

B59
JACOBS N.,CULTURE FOR THE MILLIONS? INTELL SOCIETY | CULTURE
NAT/G...POLICY SOC OBS ANTHOL 20. PAGE 28 G0553 | COM/IND
PERF/ART
CONCPT

B59
LANG D.,FROM HIROSHIMA TO THE MOON: CHRONICLES OF | NUC/PWR
LIFE IN THE ATOMIC AGE. USA+45 OP/RES CONTROL | SPACE
ARMS/CONT WAR CIVMIL/REL PEACE HABITAT MORAL PWR | HEALTH
...OBS INT 20 AEC. PAGE 32 G0633 | TEC/DEV

S59
STOESSINGER J.G.,"THE INTERNATIONAL ATOMIC ENERGY | INT/ORG
AGENCY: THE FIRST PHASE." FUT WOR+45 NAT/G VOL/ASSN | ECO/DEV
DELIB/GP BAL/PWR LEGIT ADMIN ROUTINE PWR...OBS | FOR/AID
CON/ANAL GEN/LAWS VAL/FREE 20 IAEA. PAGE 53 G1037 | NUC/PWR

B60
PARRY A.,RUSSIA'S ROCKETS AND MISSILES. COM FUT | PLAN
GERMANY USA+45 WOR+45 INTELL ECO/DEV ACT/RES | TEC/DEV
NUC/PWR WEAPON ATTIT ALL/VALS...OBS TIME/SEQ | SPACE
COLD/WAR 20. PAGE 44 G0859 | USSR

B60
PENTONY D.E.,THE UNDERDEVELOPED LANDS. FUT WOR+45 | ECO/UNDEV
CULTURE AGRI FINAN INDUS MARKET INT/ORG LABOR NAT/G | POLICY
VOL/ASSN CONSULT TEC/DEV ECO/TAC EDU/PROP COLONIAL | FOR/AID
ATTIT WEALTH...OBS RECORD SAMP TREND GEN/METH WORK | INT/TRADE
UN 20. PAGE 44 G0867

L60
HOLZMAN B.G.,"BASIC RESEARCH FOR NATIONAL | FORCES
SURVIVAL." FUT USA+45 INTELL R+D ACT/RES OP/RES | STAT
PLAN TEC/DEV EDU/PROP PERCEPT PERSON...PHIL/SCI
METH/CNCPT NEW/IDEA MATH OBS RECORD TREND LAB/EXP
20. PAGE 27 G0525

L60
MACPHERSON C.,"TECHNICAL CHANGE AND POLITICAL | TEC/DEV
DECISION." WOR+45 NAT/G CREATE CAP/ISM DIPLOM | ADMIN
ROUTINE RIGID/FLEX...CONCPT OBS GEN/METH 20.
PAGE 35 G0692

L60
MCCLELLAND C.A.,"THE FUNCTION OF THEORY IN | INT/ORG
INTERNATIONAL RELATIONS." WOR+45 PLAN EDU/PROP | CONCPT
ROUTINE ORD/FREE...PHIL/SCI PSY SOC METH/CNCPT | DIPLOM
NEW/IDEA OBS TREND GEN/METH 20. PAGE 37 G0728

S60
JAFFEE A.J.,"POPULATION TRENDS AND CONTROLS IN | ECO/UNDEV
UNDERDEVELOPED COUNTRIES." AFR FUT ISLAM L/A+17C | GEOG
S/ASIA CULTURE R+D FAM ACT/RES PLAN EDU/PROP
BIO/SOC RIGID/FLEX HEALTH...SOC STAT OBS CHARTS 20.
PAGE 28 G0555

N60
US HOUSE COMM SCI ASTRONAUT,THE ORGANIZATION OF THE | ACT/RES
US NATIONAL SPACE EFFORT. USA+45 WOR+45 AIR ECO/DEV | SKILL
NAT/G PLAN TEC/DEV DIPLOM EDU/PROP ATTIT DRIVE PWR | SPACE
...OBS TIME/SEQ TREND TOT/POP 20. PAGE 58 G1142

B61
HADLEY A.T.,THE NATIONS SAFETY AND ARMS CONTROL. | ACT/RES
FUT USA+45 WOR+45 TOP/EX PLAN TEC/DEV ATTIT DRIVE | ROUTINE
...CONCPT OBS TIME/SEQ TREND 20. PAGE 24 G0466 | DETER
NUC/PWR

B61
KAHN H.,ON THERMONUCLEAR WAR. FUT UNIV WOR+45 | DETER
ECO/DEV CONSULT EX/STRUC TOP/EX ACT/RES CREATE PLAN | NUC/PWR
COERCE WAR PERSON ALL/VALS...POLICY GEOG CONCPT | SOCIETY
METH/CNCPT OBS TREND 20. PAGE 29 G0569

S61
MACHOWSKI K.,"SELECTED PROBLEMS OF NATIONAL | UNIV
SOVEREIGNTY WITH REFERENCE TO THE LAW OF OUTER | ACT/RES
SPACE." FUT WOR+45 AIR LAW INTELL SOCIETY ECO/DEV | NUC/PWR
PLAN EDU/PROP DETER DRIVE PERCEPT SOVEREIGN | SPACE
...POLICY INT/LAW OBS TREND TOT/POP 20. PAGE 35
G0689

S61
MORGENSTERN O.,"THE N-COUNTRY PROBLEM." EUR+WWI | FUT
UNIV USA+45 WOR+45 SOCIETY CONSULT TOP/EX ACT/RES | BAL/PWR
PLAN EDU/PROP ATTIT DRIVE...POLICY OBS TREND | NUC/PWR
TOT/POP 20. PAGE 40 G0781 | TEC/DEV

SCHILLING W.R.,,"THE H-BOMB: HOW TO DECIDE WITHOUT ACTUALLY CHOOSING." FUT USA+45 INTELL CONSULT ADMIN CT/SYS MORAL...JURID OBS 20 TRUMAN/HS. PAGE 49 G0966
S61
PERSON
LEGIT
NUC/PWR

FORBES H.W.,THE STRATEGY OF DISARMAMENT. FUT WOR+45 INT/ORG VOL/ASSN CONSULT ARMS/CONT COERCE NUC/PWR WAR DRIVE RIGID/FLEX ORD/FREE PWR...POLICY CONCPT OBS TREND STERTYP 20. PAGE 19 G0378
B62
PLAN
FORCES
DIPLOM

KAHN H.,THINKING ABOUT THE UNTHINKABLE. FUT USA+45 LAW NAT/G CONSULT FORCES ACT/RES CREATE PLAN TEC/DEV BAL/PWR DIPLOM EDU/PROP ARMS/CONT DETER ATTIT...CONCPT OBS TREND COLD/WAR 20. PAGE 29 G0570
B62
INT/ORG
ORD/FREE
NUC/PWR
PEACE

KRAFT J.,THE GRAND DESIGN. EUR+WWI USA+45 AGRI FINAN INDUS MARKET INT/ORG NAT/G PLAN ECO/TAC TARIFFS REGION DRIVE ORD/FREE WEALTH...POLICY OBS TREND EEC 20. PAGE 31 G0616
B62
VOL/ASSN
ECO/DEV
INT/TRADE

BETHE H.,,"DISARMAMENT AND STRATEGY." COM USA+45 USSR WOR+45 VOL/ASSN TEC/DEV EDU/PROP NUC/PWR CHOOSE PEACE...POLICY DECISION NEW/IDEA OBS GEN/LAWS COLD/WAR 420. PAGE 7 G0133
S62
PLAN
ORD/FREE
ARMS/CONT
DIPLOM

FINKELSTEIN L.S.,,"THE UNITED NATIONS AND ORGANIZATIONS FOR CONTROL OF ARMAMENT." FUT WOR+45 VOL/ASSN DELIB/GP TOP/EX CREATE EDU/PROP LEGIT ADJUD NUC/PWR ATTIT RIGID/FLEX ORD/FREE...POLICY DECISION CONCPT OBS TREND GEN/LAWS TOT/POP COLD/WAR. PAGE 19 G0368
S62
INT/ORG
PWR
ARMS/CONT

GORDON B.K.,,"NUCLEAR WEAPONS: RUSSIAN AND AMERICAN." COM USA+45 USSR NAT/G FORCES ACT/RES TEC/DEV PERCEPT RIGID/FLEX PWR SKILL...MGT METH/CNCPT QUANT OBS TIME/SEQ CON/ANAL GEN/METH TOT/POP VAL/FREE 20. PAGE 22 G0433
S62
ORD/FREE
COERCE
NUC/PWR

SCHILLING W.R.,,"SCIENTISTS, FOREIGN POLICY AND POLITICS." WOR+45 WOR-45 INTELL INT/ORG CONSULT TOP/EX ACT/RES PLAN ADMIN KNOWL...CONCPT OBS TREND LEAGUE/NAT 20. PAGE 49 G0967
S62
NAT/G
TEC/DEV
DIPLOM
NUC/PWR

LASSWELL H.D.,THE FUTURE OF POLITICAL SCIENCE. SOCIETY ECO/DEV ACADEM NAT/G PROB/SOLV...OBS SOC/INTEG. PAGE 33 G0643
B63
CREATE
ACT/RES
FUT

LILIENTHAL D.E.,CHANGE, HOPE, AND THE BOMB. USA+45 WOR+45 R+D INT/ORG NAT/G DELIB/GP FORCES ACT/RES DETER RIGID/FLEX ORD/FREE...POLICY CONCPT OBS AEC 20. PAGE 34 G0666
B63
ATTIT
MYTH
ARMS/CONT
NUC/PWR

WIGHTMAN D.,TOWARD ECONOMIC CO-OPERATION IN ASIA. ASIA S/ASIA VOL/ASSN ACT/RES PLAN TEC/DEV ECO/TAC EDU/PROP RIGID/FLEX SKILL...POLICY METH/CNCPT OBS INT GEN/LAWS UN 20 ECAFE. PAGE 63 G1237
B63
ECO/UNDEV
CREATE

BRILLOUIN L.,SCIENTIFIC UNCERTAINTY AND INFORMATION. PROB/SOLV AUTOMAT PERCEPT ORD/FREE ...MATH REGRESS STAT STYLE OBS IDEA/COMP SIMUL TIME. PAGE 9 G0169
B64
PHIL/SCI
NEW/IDEA
METH/CNCPT
CREATE

CARNEGIE ENDOWMENT INT. PEACE,"POLITICAL QUESTIONS (ISSUES BEFORE THE NINETEENTH GENERAL ASSEMBLY)." SPACE WOR+45 CONSTN FINAN NAT/G CONSULT DELIB/GP FORCES LEGIS TEC/DEV EDU/PROP LEGIT ARMS/CONT COERCE NUC/PWR ATTIT ALL/VALS...CONCPT OBS UN COLD/WAR 20. PAGE 11 G0208
L64
INT/ORG
PEACE

MAGGS P.B.,,"SOVIET VIEWPOINT ON NUCLEAR WEAPONS IN INTERNATIONAL LAW." USSR WOR+45 INT/ORG FORCES DIPLOM ARMS/CONT ATTIT ORD/FREE PWR...POLICY JURID CONCPT OBS TREND CON/ANAL GEN/LAWS VAL/FREE 20. PAGE 35 G0694
S64
COM
LAW
INT/LAW
NUC/PWR

INT. BANK RECONSTR. DEVELOP.,ECONOMIC DEVELOPMENT OF KUWAIT. ISLAM KUWAIT AGRI FINAN MARKET EX/STRUC TEC/DEV ECO/TAC ADMIN WEALTH...OBS CON/ANAL CHARTS 20. PAGE 28 G0548
B65
INDUS
NAT/G

BLOOMFIELD L.P.,,"ARMS CONTROL AND THE DEVELOPING COUNTRIES." AFR ISLAM S/ASIA USA+45 VOL/ASSN TEC/DEV DIPLOM REGION NUC/PWR...PREDICT TREND. PAGE 7 G0142
S65
ARMS/CONT
ECO/UNDEV
HYPO/EXP
OBS

HUGHES T.L.,,"SCHOLARS AND FOREIGN POLICY* VARIETIES OF RESEARCH EXPERIENCE." COM/IND DIPLOM ADMIN EXEC ROUTINE...MGT OBS CONGRESS PRESIDENT CAMELOT. PAGE 27 G0535
S65
ACT/RES
ACADEM
CONTROL
NAT/G

KOHL W.L.,,"NUCLEAR SHARING IN NATO AND THE MULTILATERAL FORCE." FUT USSR VOL/ASSN TEC/DEV DIPLOM NUC/PWR WAR WEAPON NATO. PAGE 31 G0611
S65
ARMS/CONT
OBS
IDEA/COMP

KREITH K.,,"PEACE RESEARCH AND GOVERNMENT POLICY." INTELL NAT/G DIPLOM ECO/TAC CONTROL ARMS/CONT WAR PERCEPT...DECISION IDEA/COMP. PAGE 31 G0619
S65
PEACE
STYLE
OBS

NIEBURG H.L.,IN THE NAME OF SCIENCE. USA+45 EX/STRUC LEGIS TEC/DEV BUDGET PAY AUTOMAT LOBBY PWR ...OBS 20. PAGE 42 G0822
B66
NAT/G
INDUS
TECHRACY

TURKEVICH J.,,"SOVIET SCIENCE APPRAISED." USA+45 R+D ACADEM FORCES DIPLOM EDU/PROP WAR EFFICIENCY PEACE SKILL OBS. PAGE 55 G1081
S66
USSR
TEC/DEV
NAT/COMP
ATTIT

BUNGE M.,THE SEARCH FOR TRUTH, VOL. 3, PART 2 OF STUDIES IN THE FOUNDATIONS, METHODOLOGY, AND PHILOSOPHY OF SCIENCE. UNIV INTELL KNOWL...CONCPT OBS PREDICT METH. PAGE 10 G0188
B67
PHIL/SCI
TESTS
GEN/LAWS
RATIONAL

RIDKER R.G.,ECONOMIC COSTS OF AIR POLLUTION* STUDIES IN MEASUREMENT. R+D MUNIC GP/REL KNOWL ...OBS 20. PAGE 47 G0919
B67
OP/RES
HABITAT
PHIL/SCI

SALISBURY H.E.,,"THE WAR IN VIETNAM." USA+45 VIETNAM/N DIPLOM MURDER 20. PAGE 48 G0953
S67
POLICY
WAR
FORCES
OBS

OBS/ENVIR....SOCIAL MILIEU OF AND RESISTANCES TO OBSERVATIONS

DEUTSCH K.W.,,"TOWARD AN INVENTORY OF BASIC TRENDS AND PATTERNS IN COMPARATIVE AND INTERNATIONAL POLITICS." UNIV WOR+45 SOCIETY STRUCT INT/ORG NAT/G CREATE PLAN EDU/PROP KNOWL...PHIL/SCI METH/CNCPT STAT SELF/OBS OBS/ENVIR SAMP TREND CON/ANAL CHARTS SOC/EXP GEN/METH 20. PAGE 15 G0298
L60
R+D
PERCEPT

KELLEY G.A.,,"THE POLITICAL BACKGROUND OF THE FRENCH A-BOMB." EUR+WWI USSR FORCES TOP/EX TEC/DEV NUC/PWR ATTIT PWR...CONCPT OBS/ENVIR TREND 20. PAGE 30 G0591
S60
NAT/G
RESPECT
NAT/LISM
FRANCE

ANDREWS R.B.,,"URBAN ECONOMICS: AN APPRAISAL OF PROGRESS." LOC/G PROB/SOLV TEC/DEV...CONCPT OBS/ENVIR METH/COMP HYPO/EXP SOC/EXP SIMUL GEN/METH METH 20. PAGE 3 G0058
S61
MUNIC
PHIL/SCI
ECOMETRIC

STERN A.C.,AIR POLLUTION (2 VOLS.). LAW INDUS PROB/SOLV TEC/DEV INSPECT RISK BIO/SOC HABITAT ...OBS/ENVIR TESTS SAMP 20 POLLUTION. PAGE 53 G1035
B62
AIR
OP/RES
CONTROL
HEALTH

ALEXANDER L.,,"PROTECTION OF PRIVACY IN BEHAVIORAL RESEARCH." WOR+45 ADJUD SANCTION ORD/FREE...JURID INT. PAGE 2 G0036
S67
ACT/RES
POLICY
OBS/ENVIR

OBSCENITY....OBSCENITY

OBSERVATION....SEE DIRECT-OBSERVATION METHOD INDEX, P. XIV

OBSOLESCENCE, PLANNED....SEE OBSOLESCNC

OBSOLESCNC....OBSOLESCENCE, PLANNED

OCCUPATION....SEE WORKER

OCEANIA....OCEANIA: AUSTRALIA, NEW ZEALAND, MALAYSIA,

MELANESIA, MICRONESIA, AND POLYNESIA

ODEGARD P.H. G0829

ODEGARD/P....PETER ODEGARD

ODINGA/O....OGINGA ODINGA

OECD G0830,G0831,G0832,G0833,G0834,G0835

OECD....ORGANIZATION FOR ECONOMIC COOPERATION AND DEVELOPMENT

OECD,MEDITERRANEAN REGIONAL PROJECT: TURKEY; EDUCATION AND DEVELOPMENT. FUT TURKEY SOCIETY STRATA FINAN NAT/G PROF/ORG PLAN PROB/SOLV ADMIN COST...STAT CHARTS 20 OECD. PAGE 42 G0831
B65
EDU/PROP
ACADEM
SCHOOL
ECO/UNDEV

OECD,THE MEDITERRANEAN REGIONAL PROJECT: PORTUGAL; EDUCATION AND DEVELOPMENT. PORTUGAL SOCIETY STRATA FINAN PROF/ORG WORKER PLAN PROB/SOLV ADMIN...POLICY STAT CHARTS METH 20 OECD. PAGE 42 G0832
B65
EDU/PROP
SCHOOL
ACADEM
ECO/UNDEV

OECD,THE MEDITERRANEAN REGIONAL PROJECT: ITALY; EDUCATION AND DEVELOPMENT. ITALY SOCIETY STRATA FINAN NAT/G PROF/ORG WORKER PLAN PROB/SOLV ADMIN ...STAT CHARTS METH 20 OECD. PAGE 42 G0833
B65
SCHOOL
EDU/PROP
ECO/UNDEV
ACADEM

OECD,THE MEDITERRANEAN REGIONAL PROJECT: GREECE; EDUCATION AND DEVELOPMENT. FUT GREECE SOCIETY AGRI FINAN NAT/G PROF/ORG WORKER PLAN PROB/SOLV ADMIN DEMAND ATTIT 20 OECD. PAGE 42 G0834
B65
EDU/PROP
SCHOOL
ACADEM
ECO/UNDEV

OECD,THE MEDITERRANEAN REGIONAL PROJECT: SPAIN; EDUCATION AND DEVELOPMENT. FUT SPAIN STRATA FINAN NAT/G WORKER PLAN PROB/SOLV ADMIN COST...POLICY STAT CHARTS 20 OECD. PAGE 42 G0835
B65
ECO/UNDEV
EDU/PROP
ACADEM
SCHOOL

ORG FOR ECO COOP AND DEVEL,THE MEDITERRANEAN REGIONAL PROJECT: YUGOSLAVIA; EDUCATION AND DEVELOPMENT. YUGOSLAVIA SOCIETY FINAN PROF/ORG PLAN ADMIN COST DEMAND MARXISM...STAT TREND CHARTS METH 20 OECD. PAGE 43 G0843
B65
EDU/PROP
ACADEM
SCHOOL
ECO/UNDEV

OECD DEVELOPMENT CENTRE G0836

OEEC....ORGANIZATION FOR EUROPEAN ECONOMIC COOPERATION; SEE ALSO VOL/ASSN, INT/ORG

GORDON L.,"THE ORGANIZATION FOR EUROPEAN ECONOMIC COOPERATION." EUR+WWI INDUS INT/ORG NAT/G CONSULT DELIB/GP ACT/RES CREATE PLAN TEC/DEV EDU/PROP LEGIT WEALTH OEEC 20. PAGE 22 G0435
S56
VOL/ASSN
ECO/DEV

ALBONETTI A.,"IL SECONDO PROGRAMMA QUINQUENNALE 1963-67 ED IL BILANCIO RICERCHE ED INVESTIMENTI PER IL 1963 DELL'ERATOM." EUR+WWI FUT ITALY WOR+45 ECO/DEV SERV/IND INT/ORG TEC/DEV ECO/TAC ATTIT SKILL WEALTH...MGT TIME/SEQ OEEC 20. PAGE 2 G0035
S62
R+D
PLAN
NUC/PWR

NIEBURG H.,"EURATOM: A STUDY IN COALITION POLITICS." EUR+WWI UK USA+45 ELITES NAT/G DELIB/GP LEGIS TOP/EX ECO/TAC NUC/PWR ATTIT ORD/FREE PWR TOT/POP EEC OEEC 20 NATO EURATOM. PAGE 42 G0820
L63
VOL/ASSN
ACT/RES

KAWALKOWSKI A.,"POUR UNE EUROPE INDEPENDENTE ET REUNIFIEE." EUR+WWI FUT USA+45 USSR WOR+45 ECO/DEV PROC/MFG INT/ORG NAT/G ACT/RES TEC/DEV FEDERAL RIGID/FLEX...CONCPT METH/CNCPT OEEC TOT/POP 20 DEGAULLE/C. PAGE 30 G0587
S63
R+D
PLAN
NUC/PWR

OEO....OFFICE OF ECONOMIC OPPORTUNITY

OEP....OFFICE OF EMERGENCY PLANNING

OFFICE OF ECONOMIC OPPORTUNITY....SEE OEO

OFFICE OF EMERGENCY PLANNING....SEE OEP

OFFICE OF PRICE ADMINISTRATION....SEE OPA

OFFICE OF WAR INFORMATION....SEE OWI

OGBURN W. G0837

OGDEN F.D. G0838

OHIO....OHIO

OHLIN/HECK....OHLIN-HECKSCHER THEORY OF COMMODITY TRADE

OKELLO/J....JOHN OKELLO

OKINAWA....OKINAWA

OKLAHOMA....OKLAHOMA

OLAS....ORGANIZATION FOR LATIN AMERICAN SOLIDARITY

OLD LIBERAL....SEE OLD/LIB

OLD/LIB....OLD LIBERAL

DAWSON R.H.,"CONGRESSIONAL INNOVATION AND INTERVENTION IN DEFENSE POLICY: LEGISLATIVE AUTHORIZATION OF WEAPONS SYSTEMS." CONSTN PLAN ARMS/CONT GOV/REL EFFICIENCY PEACE NEW/LIB OLD/LIB. PAGE 14 G0281
S62
LEGIS
PWR
CONTROL
WEAPON

OLD/STOR....CONVENTIONAL INFORMATION-STORAGE SYSTEMS

OLIGARCHY....SEE ELITES

OLIGOPOLY....SEE MONOPOLY

OLIN/MTHSN....OLIN MATHIESON

OLIVARES....OLIVARES, HEAD OF SPAIN DURING CATALAN REV., 1640

OMBUDSMAN....OMBUDSMAN; DOMESTIC GRIEVANCE ORGAN

ONTARIO....ONTARIO, CANADA

ONYEMELUKWE C.C. G0839

OP/RES....OPERATIONS RESEARCH; SEE ALSO CREATE

BRITISH COMMONWEALTH BUR AGRI,WORLD AGRICULTURAL ECONOMICS AND RURAL SOCIOLOGY ABSTRACTS. NAT/G OP/RES PLAN TEC/DEV LEAD PRODUC...GEOG MGT NAT/COMP 20. PAGE 9 G0170
B
BIBLIOG/A
AGRI
SOC
WORKER

ADVANCED MANAGEMENT. INDUS EX/STRUC WORKER OP/RES ...DECISION BIBLIOG/A 20. PAGE 1 G0003
N
MGT
ADMIN
LABOR
GP/REL

US ATOMIC ENERGY COMMISSION,ATOMIC ENERGY IN USE (PAMPHLET). R+D RISK EFFICIENCY HEALTH KNOWL ORD/FREE...PHIL/SCI CONCPT METH/CNCPT CHARTS LAB/EXP 20 AEC. PAGE 56 G1106
N19
OP/RES
TEC/DEV
NUC/PWR
CREATE

GULICK L.,PAPERS ON THE SCIENCE OF ADMINISTRATION. INDUS PROB/SOLV TEC/DEV COST EFFICIENCY PRODUC HABITAT...PHIL/SCI METH/COMP 20. PAGE 23 G0461
B37
OP/RES
CONTROL
ADMIN
MGT

PFIFFNER J.M.,RESEARCH METHODS IN PUBLIC ADMINISTRATION. USA-45 R+D...MGT STAT INT QU T 20. PAGE 44 G0872
B40
ADMIN
OP/RES
METH
TEC/DEV

PUBLIC ADMINISTRATION SERVICE,YOUR BUSINESS OF GOVERNMENT: A CATALOG OF PUBLICATIONS IN THE FIELD OF PUBLIC ADMINISTRATION (PAMPHLET). FINAN R+D LOC/G ACT/RES OP/RES PLAN 20. PAGE 45 G0894
B44
BIBLIOG
ADMIN
NAT/G
MUNIC

COCH L.,"OVERCOMING RESISTANCE TO CHANGE" (BMR)" USA+45 CONSULT ADMIN ROUTINE GP/REL EFFICIENCY PRODUC PERCEPT SKILL...CHARTS SOC/EXP 20. PAGE 12 G0236
S48
WORKER
OP/RES
PROC/MFG
RIGID/FLEX

BAVELAS A.,"COMMUNICATION PATTERNS IN TASK-ORIENTED GROUPS" (BMR)" R+D OP/RES INSPECT LEAD CENTRAL EFFICIENCY HAPPINESS RIGID/FLEX...PROBABIL 20. PAGE 6 G0106
S50
ACT/RES
PERS/REL
TASK
INGP/REL

KAPLAN A.,"THE PREDICTION OF SOCIAL AND TECHNOLOGICAL EVENTS." VOL/ASSN CONSULT ACT/RES CREATE OP/RES PLAN ROUTINE PERSON...POLICY METH/CNCPT STAT QU/SEMANT SYS/QU TESTS CENSUS TREND 20. PAGE 29 G0574
S50
PWR
KNO/TEST

HOMANS G.C.,"THE WESTERN ELECTRIC RESEARCHES" IN S. HOSLETT, ED., HUMAN FACTORS IN MANAGEMENT (BMR)" ACT/RES GP/REL HAPPINESS PRODUC DRIVE...MGT OBS 20. PAGE 27 G0526
C51
OP/RES
EFFICIENCY
SOC/EXP
WORKER

CALDWELL L.K.,RESEARCH METHODS IN PUBLIC ADMINISTRATION; AN OUTLINE OF TOPICS AND READINGS (PAMPHLET). LAW ACT/RES COMPUTER KNOWL...SOC STAT GEN/METH 20. PAGE 10 G0201
B53
BIBLIOG/A
METH/COMP
ADMIN
OP/RES

MCCLOSKEY J.F.,OPERATIONS RESEARCH FOR MANAGEMENT. STRUCT COMPUTER ADMIN ROUTINE...PHIL/SCI CONCPT METH/CNCPT TREND ANTHOL BIBLIOG 20. PAGE 37 G0731
B54
OP/RES
MGT
METH/COMP
TEC/DEV

WASHBURNE N.F.,INTERPRETING SOCIAL CHANGE IN AMERICA. USA+45 STRATA FAM NAT/G SECT OP/RES ECO/TAC EDU/PROP HABITAT...SOC TIME/SEQ TREND 20 BUREAUCRCY. PAGE 62 G1217
B54
CULTURE
STRUCT
CREATE
TEC/DEV

GOULDNER A.W.,"PATTERNS OF INDUSTRIAL BUREAUCRACY." GP/REL CONSEN ATTIT DRIVE...BIBLIOG 20. PAGE 22 G0438
C54
ADMIN
INDUS
OP/RES
WORKER

MILLER J.G.,"TOWARD A GENERAL THEORY FOR THE BEHAVIORAL SCIENCES" (BMR)" CREATE ALL/VALS KNOWL ...CON/ANAL CHARTS HYPO/EXP SIMUL BIBLIOG 20. PAGE 39 G0773
S55
CONCPT
OP/RES
METH/CNCPT
COMPUTER

MCKINNEY E.R.,A BIBLIOGRAPHY OF CYBERNETICS AND INFORMATION THEORY. COMPUTER OP/RES...DECISION PHIL/SCI PSY LING LOG MATH PROBABIL GAME 20. PAGE 38 G0743
B57
BIBLIOG/A
FEEDBACK
SIMUL
CONTROL

MERTON R.K.,SOCIAL THEORY AND SOCIAL STRUCTURE (REV. ED.). INTELL SECT WORKER OP/RES EDU/PROP ADMIN INGP/REL ANOMIE PERSON...AUD/VIS T 20 BUREAUCRCY. PAGE 38 G0759
B57
SOC
GEN/LAWS
SOCIETY
STRUCT

OPERATIONS RESEARCH SOCIETY,A COMPREHENSIVE BIBLIOGRAPHY ON OPERATIONS RESEARCH; THROUGH 1956 WITH SUPPLEMENT FOR 1957. COM/IND DIST/IND INDUS ADMIN...DECISION MATH STAT METH 20. PAGE 43 G0840
B58
BIBLIOG/A
COMPUT/IR
OP/RES
MGT

FORRESTER J.W.,"INDUSTRIAL DYNAMICS* A MAJOR BREAKTHROUGH FOR DECISION MAKERS." COMPUTER OP/RES ...DECISION CONCPT NEW/IDEA. PAGE 20 G0382
L58
INDUS
ACT/RES
MGT
PROB/SOLV

DEAN B.V.,"APPLICATION OF OPERATIONS RESEARCH TO MANAGERIAL DECISION MAKING" STRATA ACT/RES PROB/SOLV ROLE...SOC PREDICT SIMUL 20. PAGE 15 G0288
S58
DECISION
OP/RES
MGT
METH/CNCPT

NEWELL A.C.,"ELEMENTS OF A THEORY OF HUMAN PROBLEM SOLVING" (BMR)" TASK PERCEPT...CONCPT LOG METH/COMP LAB/EXP BIBLIOG 20. PAGE 42 G0819
S58
PROB/SOLV
COMPUTER
COMPUT/IR
OP/RES

GUILBAUD G.T.,WHAT IS CYBERNETICS? COMPUTER OP/RES TEC/DEV AUTOMAT ROUTINE PERS/REL PERCEPT...PSY MATH COMPUT/IR SIMUL GEN/METH. PAGE 23 G0460
B59
CONTROL
COM/IND
FEEDBACK
NET/THEORY

LANG D.,FROM HIROSHIMA TO THE MOON: CHRONICLES OF LIFE IN THE ATOMIC AGE. USA+45 OP/RES CONTROL ARMS/CONT WAR CIVMIL/REL PEACE HABITAT MORAL PWR ...OBS INT 20 AEC. PAGE 32 G0633
B59
NUC/PWR
SPACE
HEALTH
TEC/DEV

WASSERMAN P.,MEASUREMENT AND ANALYSIS OF ORGANIZATIONAL PERFORMANCE. FINAN MARKET EX/STRUC TEC/DEV EDU/PROP CONTROL ROUTINE TASK...MGT 20. PAGE 62 G1220
B59
BIBLIOG/A
ECO/TAC
OP/RES
EFFICIENCY

CALKINS R.D.,"THE DECISION PROCESS IN ADMINISTRATION." EX/STRUC PROB/SOLV ROUTINE MGT. PAGE 10 G0204
S59
ADMIN
OP/RES
DECISION
CON/ANAL

MORRIS W.T.,ENGINEERING ECONOMY. AUTOMAT RISK RATIONAL...PROBABIL STAT CHARTS GAME SIMUL BIBLIOG T 20. PAGE 40 G0785
B60
OP/RES
DECISION
MGT
PROB/SOLV

HOLZMAN B.G.,"BASIC RESEARCH FOR NATIONAL SURVIVAL." FUT USA+45 INTELL R+D ACT/RES OP/RES PLAN TEC/DEV EDU/PROP PERCEPT PERSON...PHIL/SCI METH/CNCPT NEW/IDEA MATH OBS RECORD TREND LAB/EXP 20. PAGE 27 G0525
L60
FORCES
STAT

SHUBIK M.,"BIBLIOGRAPHY ON SIMULATION, GAMING, ARTIFICIAL INTELLIGENCE AND ALLIED TOPICS." COMPUTER ROUTINE...DECISION MGT STAT 20. PAGE 50 G0992
S60
BIBLIOG
SIMUL
GAME
OP/RES

CHAPPLE E.D.,THE MEASURE OF MANAGEMENT. USA+45 WORKER ADMIN GP/REL EFFICIENCY...DECISION ORG/CHARTS SIMUL 20. PAGE 11 G0221
B61
MGT
OP/RES
PLAN
METH/CNCPT

NAKICENOVIC S.,NUCLEAR ENERGY IN YUGOSLAVIA. YUGOSLAVIA AGRI INDUS CREATE OP/RES ROUTINE EFFICIENCY KNOWL...HEAL STAT CHARTS LAB/EXP BIBLIOG 20. PAGE 41 G0802
B61
R+D
ECO/DEV
TEC/DEV
NUC/PWR

MANGELSDORF J.E.,"HUMAN DECISIONS IN MISSILE YSTEMS." OP/RES CHARTS. PAGE 35 G0699
S61
DECISION
PROB/SOLV
AUTOMAT
CONTROL

ASTIA,HUMAN ENGINEERING: A REPORT BIBLIOGRAPHY. USA+45 R+D FORCES ACT/RES COMPUTER CREATE OP/RES EDU/PROP CONTROL WEAPON...SOC NEW/IDEA. PAGE 4 G0073
B62
BIBLIOG/A
COM/IND
COMPUT/IR
METH

ASTIA,INFORMATION THEORY: A REPORT BIBLIOGRAPHY. USA+45 COMPUTER CREATE OP/RES PLAN TEC/DEV CONTROL ...CONCPT METH/COMP. PAGE 4 G0074
B62
BIBLIOG/A
COM/IND
FORCES
METH

BENNIS W.G.,THE PLANNING OF CHANGE: READINGS IN THE APPLIED BEHAVIORAL SCIENCES. CULTURE STRATA STRUCT PLAN GP/REL...SOC T. PAGE 6 G0123
B62
PROB/SOLV
CREATE
ACT/RES
OP/RES

DUCKWORTH W.E.,A GUIDE TO OPERATIONAL RESEARCH. INDUS PLAN PROB/SOLV EXEC EFFICIENCY PRODUC KNOWL ...MGT MATH STAT SIMUL METH 20 MONTECARLO. PAGE 16 G0319
B62
OP/RES
GAME
DECISION
ADMIN

GUETZKOW H.,SIMULATION IN SOCIAL SCIENCE: READINGS. STRUCT OP/RES ADMIN AUTOMAT FEEDBACK...MGT PSY SOC STYLE BIBLIOG. PAGE 23 G0459
B62
SIMUL
TEC/DEV
COMPUTER
GAME

STERN A.C.,AIR POLLUTION (2 VOLS.). LAW INDUS PROB/SOLV TEC/DEV INSPECT RISK BIO/SOC HABITAT ...OBS/ENVIR TESTS SAMP 20 POLLUTION. PAGE 53 G1035
B62
AIR
OP
OP/RES
CONTROL
HEALTH

WENDT P.F.,HOUSING POLICY - THE SEARCH FOR SOLUTIONS. GERMANY/W SWEDEN UK USA+45 OP/RES HABITAT WEALTH...SOC/WK CHARTS 20. PAGE 63 G1230
B62
PLAN
ADMIN
METH/COMP
NAT/G

NIEBURG H.L.,"THE EISENHOWER ATOMIC ENERGY COMMISSION AND CONGRESS" R+D INT/ORG OP/RES DIPLOM ADMIN CONTROL 20 PRESIDENT CONGRESS AEC. PAGE 42 G0821
L62
NUC/PWR
TOP/EX
LOBBY
DELIB/GP

JOINT ECONOMIC COMMITTEE,"DIMENSIONS OF SOVIET ECONOMIC POWER." USSR R+D FORCES ACT/RES OP/RES TEC/DEV...GEOG STAT BIBLIOG 20. PAGE 29 G0565
C62
ECO/DEV
PLAN
PRODUC
LABOR

ACKOFF R.L.,A MANAGER'S GUIDE TO OPERATIONS RESEARCH. STRUCT INDUS PROB/SOLV ROUTINE 20. PAGE 2 G0028
B6
OP/RES
MGT
GP/REL

ADMIN

DEAN A.L.,FEDERAL AGENCY APPROACHES TO FIELD
MANAGEMENT (PAMPHLET). R+D DELIB/GP EX/STRUC
PROB/SOLV GOV/REL...CLASSIF BIBLIOG 20 FAA NASA
DEPT/HEW POSTAL/SYS IRS. PAGE 15 G0287
B63
ADMIN
MGT
NAT/G
OP/RES

FOSKETT D.J.,CLASSIFICATION AND INDEXING IN THE
SOCIAL SCIENCES. WOR+45 R+D ACT/RES CREATE OP/RES
TEC/DEV AUTOMAT ROLE...SOC COMPUT/IR BIBLIOG.
PAGE 20 G0384
B63
PROB/SOLV
CON/ANAL
CLASSIF

MCDONOUGH A.M.,INFORMATION ECONOMICS AND MANAGEMENT
SYSTEMS. ECO/DEV OP/RES AUTOMAT EFFICIENCY 20.
PAGE 37 G0735
B63
COMPUT/IR
MGT
CONCPT
COMPUTER

THORELLI H.B.,INTOP: INTERNATIONAL OPERATIONS
SIMULATION: PLAYER'S MANUAL. BRAZIL FINAN OP/RES
ADMIN GP/REL INGP/REL PRODUC PERCEPT...DECISION MGT
EEC. PAGE 54 G1073
B63
GAME
INT/TRADE
EDU/PROP
LG/CO

US ATOMIC ENERGY COMMISSION,ATOMIC ENERGY IN THE
SOVIET UNION: TRIP REPORT OF THE US ATOMIC ENERGY
DELEGATION, MAY 1933. USSR R+D NAT/G CONSULT CREATE
DIPLOM ADMIN ROUTINE EFFICIENCY PRODUC KNOWL SKILL
...NAT/COMP 20 AEC TRAVEL TREATY. PAGE 56 G1107
B63
METH/COMP
OP/RES
TEC/DEV
NUC/PWR

US SENATE COMM GOVT OPERATIONS,ADMINISTRATION OF
NATIONAL SECURITY (9 PARTS). ADMIN...INT REC/INT
CHARTS 20 SENATE CONGRESS. PAGE 60 G1178
B63
DELIB/GP
NAT/G
OP/RES
ORD/FREE

WALES H.G.,A BASIC BIBLIOGRAPHY ON MARKETING
RESEARCH (REV. ED.). ATTIT...MGT STAT INT QU SAMP
TREND 20. PAGE 62 G1206
B63
BIBLIOG/A
MARKET
OP/RES
METH/COMP

TANNENBAUM P.H.,"COMMUNICATION OF SCIENCE
INFORMATION." USA+45 TEC/DEV ROUTINE...PHIL/SCI
STYLE 20. PAGE 53 G1051
S63
COM/IND
PRESS
OP/RES
METH/CNCPT

BROWN N.,NUCLEAR WAR* THE IMPENDING STRATEGIC
DEADLOCK. USA+45 USSR TEC/DEV BUDGET RISK ARMS/CONT
NUC/PWR WEAPON COST BIO/SOC...GEOG IDEA/COMP
NAT/COMP GAME NATO WARSAW/P. PAGE 9 G0177
B64
FORCES
OP/RES
WAR
GEN/LAWS

COENEN E.,LA "KONJUNKTURFORSCHUNG" EN ALLEMAGNE ET
EN AUTRICHE, 1925-1935. AUSTRIA GERMANY OP/RES PLAN
COST PERCEPT...METH/CNCPT BIBLIOG 20. PAGE 12 G0237
B64
METH/COMP
R+D
ECO/TAC

HAMMOND P.E.,SOCIOLOGISTS AT WORK. VOL/ASSN OP/RES
TEC/DEV CONFER ROUTINE TASK EFFICIENCY...MGT
NEW/IDEA STYLE SAMP. PAGE 24 G0478
B64
R+D
BIOG
SOC

HODGETTS J.E.,ADMINISTERING THE ATOM FOR PEACE.
OP/RES TEC/DEV ADMIN...IDEA/COMP METH/COMP 20.
PAGE 26 G0517
B64
PROB/SOLV
NUC/PWR
PEACE
MGT

LANG A.S.,URBAN RAIL TRANSIT. OP/RES PLAN PROB/SOLV
TEC/DEV AUTOMAT COST...TECHNIC MATH CON/ANAL CHARTS
METH/COMP SIMUL 20 RAILROAD PUB/TRANS. PAGE 32
G0632
B64
MUNIC
DIST/IND
ECOMETRIC

MARRIS R.,THE ECONOMIC THEORY OF "MANAGERIAL"
CAPITALISM. USA+45 ECO/DEV LG/CO ECO/TAC DEMAND
...CHARTS BIBLIOG 20. PAGE 36 G0709
B64
CAP/ISM
MGT
CONTROL
OP/RES

MARTINO R.L.,PROJECT MANAGEMENT AND CONTROL: VOL. 2
APPLIED OPERATIONAL PLANNING. COMPUTER...MATH
CHARTS SIMUL METH TIME. PAGE 36 G0716
B64
DECISION
PLAN
TEC/DEV
OP/RES

STONE P.A.,"DECISION TECHNIQUES FOR TOWN
DEVELOPMENT." PLAN COST PROFIT...DECISION MGT
CON/ANAL CHARTS METH/COMP BIBLIOG 20. PAGE 53 G1039
S64
OP/RES
MUNIC
ADMIN
PROB/SOLV

ANTHONY R.N.,PLANNING AND CONTROL SYSTEMS. UNIV
OP/RES...DECISION MGT LING. PAGE 3 G0061
B65
CONTROL
PLAN
METH
HYPO/EXP

BARISH N.N.,MANAGEMENT SCIENCES IN THE EMERGING
COUNTRIES. AFR CHINA/COM WOR+45 FINAN INDUS PLAN
PRODUC HABITAT...ANTHOL 20. PAGE 5 G0093
B65
ECO/UNDEV
OP/RES
MGT
TEC/DEV

CARPER E.T.,REORGANIZATION OF THE U.S. PUBLIC
HEALTH SERVICE. FUT USA+45 INTELL R+D LOBBY GP/REL
INGP/REL PERS/REL RIGID/FLEX ROLE HEALTH...PHIL/SCI
20 CONGRESS PHS. PAGE 11 G0213
B65
HEAL
PLAN
NAT/G
OP/RES

HICKMAN B.G.,QUANTITATIVE PLANNING OF ECONOMIC
POLICY. FRANCE NETHERLAND OP/RES PRICE ROUTINE UTIL
...POLICY DECISION ECOMETRIC METH/CNCPT STAT STYLE
CHINJAP. PAGE 26 G0511
B65
PROB/SOLV
PLAN
QUANT

HITCH C.J.,DECISION-MAKING FOR DEFENSE. USA+45
CREATE BUDGET COERCE WAR WEAPON EFFICIENCY...SIMUL
20. PAGE 26 G0515
B65
DECISION
OP/RES
PLAN
FORCES

MORRIS M.D.,THE EMERGENCE OF AN INDUSTRIAL LABOR
FORCE IN INDIA: A STUDY OF THE BOMBAY COTTON MILLS,
1854-1947. INDIA WORKER OP/RES ADMIN 19/20. PAGE 40
G0784
B65
INDUS
LABOR
ECO/UNDEV
CAP/ISM

THAYER F.C. JR.,AIR TRANSPORT POLICY AND NATIONAL
SECURITY: A POLITICAL, ECONOMIC, AND MILITARY
ANALYSIS. DIST/IND OP/RES PLAN TEC/DEV DIPLOM DETER
WAR COST EFFICIENCY...POLICY BIBLIOG 20 DEPT/DEFEN
FAA CAB. PAGE 54 G1066
B65
AIR
FORCES
CIVMIL/REL
ORD/FREE

US DEPARTMENT OF ARMY,MILITARY PROTECTIVE
CONSTRUCTION: NUCLEAR WARFARE AND CHEMICAL AND
BIOLOGICAL OPERATIONS (MANUAL). OP/RES TEC/DEV RISK
COERCE NUC/PWR WAR WEAPON EFFICIENCY UTIL BIO/SOC
HABITAT ORD/FREE 20. PAGE 57 G1117
B65
FORCES
CONSTRUC
TASK
HEALTH

CHU K.,"A DYNAMIC MODEL OF THE FIRM." OP/RES
PROB/SOLV...DECISION ECOMETRIC NEW/IDEA STAT GAME
ORG/CHARTS SIMUL. PAGE 12 G0230
S65
INDUS
COMPUTER
TEC/DEV

GREEN P.,DEADLY LOGIC* THE THEORY OF NUCLEAR
DETERRENCE. USA+45 ACT/RES OP/RES NUC/PWR RATIONAL
ALL/VALS PWR...DECISION MGT PHIL/SCI QUANT
IDEA/COMP GAME. PAGE 23 G0444
B66
DETER
ACADEM
GEN/LAWS
RECORD

LINDFORS G.V.,INTERCOLLEGIATE BIBLIOGRAPHY; CASES
IN BUSINESS ADMINISTRATION (VOL. X). FINAN MARKET
LABOR CONSULT PLAN GP/REL PRODUC 20. PAGE 34 G0668
B66
BIBLIOG/A
ADMIN
MGT
OP/RES

US DEPARTMENT OF LABOR,PRODUCTIVITY: A
BIBLIOGRAPHY. ECO/DEV INDUS MARKET OP/RES AUTOMAT
COST...STAT 20. PAGE 57 G1119
B66
BIBLIOG/A
PRODUC
LABOR
PLAN

US PRES COMM ECO IMPACT DEFENS,REPORT* JULY 1965.
USA+45 ECO/DEV INDUS DELIB/GP FORCES OP/RES
ARMS/CONT NUC/PWR WEAPON BAL/PAY...PREDICT SIMUL.
PAGE 59 G1159
B66
ACT/RES
STAT
WAR
BUDGET

YOUNG W.,EXISTING MECHANISMS OF ARMS CONTROL.
PROC/MFG OP/RES DIPLOM TASK CENTRAL...MGT TREATY.
PAGE 65 G1266
B66
ARMS/CONT
ADMIN
NUC/PWR
ROUTINE

HARDT J.P.,MATHEMATICS AND COMPUTERS IN SOVIET
ECONOMIC PLANNING. COM USSR OP/RES PROB/SOLV
OPTIMAL...MODAL SIMUL 20. PAGE 24 G0481
B67
PLAN
TEC/DEV
MATH
COMPUT/IR

HIRSCHMAN A.O.,DEVELOPMENT PROJECTS OBSERVED. INDUS
INT/ORG CONSULT EX/STRUC CREATE OP/RES ECO/TAC
DEMAND...POLICY MGT METH/COMP 20 WORLD/BANK.
B67
ECO/UNDEV
R+D
FINAN

PAGE 26 G0513   PLAN

                                                        B67
RIDKER R.G.,ECONOMIC COSTS OF AIR POLLUTION*   OP/RES
STUDIES IN MEASUREMENT. R+D MUNIC GP/REL KNOWL   HABITAT
...OBS 20. PAGE 47 G0919   PHIL/SCI

                                                        B67
US HOUSE COMM SCI ASTRONAUT,GOVERNMENT, SCIENCE,   ADMIN
AND INTERNATIONAL POLICY. R+D OP/RES PLAN 20.   PHIL/SCI
PAGE 58 G1146   ACT/RES
                                                        DIPLOM

                                                        B67
YAVITZ B.,AUTOMATION IN COMMERCIAL BANKING. USA+45   TEC/DEV
STRUCT WORKER CREATE OP/RES PLAN ROLE...DECISION   FINAN
SAMP/SIZ. PAGE 64 G1263   COMPUT/IR
                                                        MGT

                                                        S67
ALBAUM G.,"INFORMATION FLOW AND DECENTRALIZED   LG/CO
DECISION MAKING IN MARKETING." EX/STRUC COMPUTER   ROUTINE
OP/RES PROB/SOLV EFFICIENCY OPTIMAL...METH/COMP   KNOWL
ORG/CHARTS 20. PAGE 2 G0033   MARKET

                                                        S67
ALLISON D.,"THE GROWTH OF IDEAS." USA+45 LG/CO   R+D
ADMIN. PAGE 3 G0045   OP/RES
                                                        INDUS
                                                        TEC/DEV

                                                        S67
CARY G.D.,"THE QUIET REVOLUTION IN COPYRIGHT* THE   COM/IND
END OF THE 'PUBLICATION' CONCEPT." USA+45 LAW   POLICY
OP/RES TEC/DEV CONFER DEBATE EFFICIENCY...JURID   LICENSE
CONGRESS. PAGE 11 G0217   PRESS

                                                        S67
EDMONDS M.,"INTERNATIONAL COLLABORATION IN WEAPONS   DIPLOM
PROCUREMENT* THE IMPLICATIONS OF THE ANGLO-FRENCH   VOL/ASSN
CASE." FRANCE UK CONSULT OP/RES PROB/SOLV TEC/DEV   BAL/PWR
CONFER CONTROL EFFICIENCY 20. PAGE 17 G0334   ARMS/CONT

                                                        S67
HAMBERG D.,"SIZE OF ENTERPRISE AND TECHNICAL   TEC/DEV
CHANGE." USA+45 LG/CO SML/CO CREATE OP/RES PROFIT   INDUS
...TREND 20. PAGE 24 G0477   R+D
                                                        WEALTH

                                                        S67
KOMESAR N.K.,"SECURITY INTERESTS IN GOVERNMENT   POLICY
CONTRACTS* WHEREIN THE TORTOISE WINS THE RES."   CT/SYS
USA+45 INDUS NAT/G OP/RES SANCTION. PAGE 31 G0613   PRIVIL
                                                        JURID

                                                        S67
MALONE D.K.,"THE COMMANDER AND THE COMPUTER."   COMPUTER
USA+45 OP/RES PROB/SOLV TEC/DEV AUTOMAT CENTRAL 20.   FORCES
PAGE 35 G0698   ELITES
                                                        PLAN

                                                        S67
MOOR E.J.,"THE INTERNATIONAL IMPACT OF AUTOMATION."   TEC/DEV
WOR+45 ACT/RES COMPUTER CREATE PLAN CAP/ISM ROUTINE   OP/RES
EFFICIENCY PREDICT. PAGE 39 G0779   AUTOMAT
                                                        INDUS

                                                        S67
VERGIN R.C.,"COMPUTER INDUCED ORGANIZATION   COMPUTER
CHANGES." FUT USA+45 R+D CREATE OP/RES TEC/DEV   DECISION
ADJUST CENTRAL...MGT INT CON/ANAL COMPUT/IR.   AUTOMAT
PAGE 61 G1194   EX/STRUC

                                                        N67
US HOUSE COMM SCI ASTRONAUT,AUTHORIZING   SPACE
APPROPRIATIONS TO THE NATIONAL AERONAUTICS AND   R+D
SPACE ADMINISTRATION (PAMPHLET). USA+45 NAT/G   PHIL/SCI
OP/RES TEC/DEV BUDGET NASA HOUSE/REP. PAGE 58 G1149   NUC/PWR

                                                        N67
US SENATE COMM ON FOREIGN REL,ARMS SALES AND   ARMS/CONT
FOREIGN POLICY (PAMPHLET). FINAN FOR/AID CONTROL   ADMIN
20. PAGE 60 G1181   OP/RES
                                                        DIPLOM

OPA....OFFICE OF PRICE ADMINISTRATION

OPEN/SPACE....OPEN SPACE - TOWN AND COUNTRY PLANNING

                                                        B61
SMITH H.H.,THE CITIZEN'S GUIDE TO PLANNING. USA+45   MUNIC
LAW SCHOOL CREATE PROB/SOLV EDU/PROP GP/REL ROLE 20   PLAN
URBAN/RNWL OPEN/SPACE. PAGE 52 G1015   DELIB/GP
                                                        CONSULT

OPERATIONAL RESEARCH AND RELATED MANAGEMENT SCIENCE....

SEE OR/MS

OPERATIONS RESEARCH SOCIETY G0840

OPERATIONS RESEARCH....SEE OP/RES

OPINION TESTS AND POLLS....SEE KNO/TEST

OPINIONS....SEE ATTIT

OPLER M.E. G0841

OPPENHEIMER R. G0842

OPTIMAL....OPTIMALITY

                                                        N19
BROWN W.M.,THE DESIGN AND PERFORMANCE OF "OPTIMUM"   HABITAT
BLAST SHELTER PROGRAMS (PAMPHLET). USA+45 ACT/RES   NUC/PWR
PLAN DEATH COST EFFICIENCY OPTIMAL...POLICY CHARTS   WAR
20. PAGE 9 G0180   HEALTH

                                                        B49
LEPAWSKY A.,ADMINISTRATION. FINAN INDUS LG/CO   ADMIN
SML/CO INGP/REL PERS/REL COST EFFICIENCY OPTIMAL   MGT
SKILL 20. PAGE 33 G0656   WORKER
                                                        EX/STRUC

                                                        B53
ROBINSON E.A.G.,THE STRUCTURE OF COMPETITIVE   INDUS
INDUSTRY. UK ECO/DEV DIST/IND MARKET TEC/DEV DIPLOM   PRODUC
EDU/PROP ADMIN EFFICIENCY WEALTH...MGT 19/20.   WORKER
PAGE 47 G0929   OPTIMAL

                                                        B55
RILEY V.,INTERINDUSTRY ECONOMIC STUDIES. USA+45   BIBLIOG
COMPUTER ADMIN OPTIMAL PRODUC...MGT CLASSIF STAT.   ECO/DEV
PAGE 47 G0922   PLAN
                                                        STRUCT

                                                        B57
GOLD N.L.,REGIONAL ECONOMIC DEVELOPMENT AND NUCLEAR   ECO/UNDEV
POWER IN INDIA. FUT INDIA FINAN FOR/AID INT/TRADE   TEC/DEV
BAL/PAY EFFICIENCY OPTIMAL PRODUC WEALTH...PREDICT   NUC/PWR
20. PAGE 22 G0424   INDUS

                                                        B61
MCCRACKEN H.L.,KEYNESIAN ECONOMICS IN THE STREAM OF   ECO/TAC
ECONOMIC THOUGHT. FINAN MARKET BARGAIN EFFICIENCY   DEMAND
OPTIMAL...PHIL/SCI CONCPT IDEA/COMP BIBLIOG 18/20   ECOMETRIC
KEYNES/JM. PAGE 37 G0732

                                                        B62
BELLMAN R.,APPLIED DYNAMIC PROGRAMMING. OPTIMAL   COMPUTER
...DECISION STAT SIMUL. PAGE 6 G0116   ECOMETRIC
                                                        GAME
                                                        MATH

                                                        S62
MARTIN L.W.,"THE MARKET FOR STRATEGIC IDEAS IN   DIPLOM
BRITAIN: THE 'SANDYS ERA'" UK ARMS/CONT WAR GOV/REL   COERCE
OPTIMAL...POLICY DECISION GOV/COMP COLD/WAR   FORCES
CMN/WLTH. PAGE 36 G0714   PWR

                                                        B64
BAUCHET P.,ECONOMIC PLANNING. FRANCE STRATA LG/CO   ECO/DEV
CAP/ISM ADMIN PARL/PROC DEMAND OPTIMAL ATTIT PWR   NAT/G
SOCISM...POLICY CHARTS 20. PAGE 5 G0102   PLAN
                                                        ECO/TAC

                                                        B65
DORFMAN R.,MEASURING BENEFITS OF GOVERNMENT   PLAN
INVESTMENTS. ECO/DEV R+D ECO/TAC PROFIT UTIL...MGT   RATION
GEN/METH. PAGE 16 G0308   EFFICIENC
                                                        OPTIMAL

                                                        B65
KANTOROVICH L.V.,THE BEST USE OF ECONOMIC   PLAN
RESOURCES. USSR SOCIETY FINAN ACT/RES TEC/DEV   MATH
ECO/TAC PRICE CONTROL COST DEMAND EFFICIENCY   DECISION
OPTIMAL...MGT STAT. PAGE 29 G0572

                                                        B65
WARNER A.W.,THE IMPACT OF SCIENCE ON TECHNOLOGY.   DECISION
UNIV INTELL SOCIETY NAT/G ACT/RES PLAN PROB/SOLV   TEC/DEV
BUDGET OPTIMAL GEN/METH. PAGE 62 G1214   CREATE
                                                        POLICY

                                                        S6
GRENIEWSKI H.,"INTENTION AND PERFORMANCE: A PRIMER   SIMUL
OF CYBERNETICS OF PLANNING." EFFICIENCY OPTIMAL   GAME
KNOWL SKILL...DECISION MGT EQULIB. PAGE 23 G0448   GEN/METH
                                                        PLAN

                                                        B6
HARDT J.P.,MATHEMATICS AND COMPUTERS IN SOVIET   PLAN

ECONOMIC PLANNING. COM USSR OP/RES PROB/SOLV
OPTIMAL...MODAL SIMUL 20. PAGE 24 G0481

TEC/DEV
MATH
COMPUT/IR

B67
PORWIT K.,CENTRAL PLANNING: EVALUATION OF VARIANTS.
PRICE OPTIMAL PRODUC...DECISION MATH CHARTS SIMUL
BIBLIOG 20. PAGE 45 G0886

PLAN
MGT
ECOMETRIC

B67
WEINBERG A.M.,REFLECTIONS ON BIG SCIENCE. FUT
USA+45 NAT/G EDU/PROP CHOOSE PERS/REL COST OPTIMAL
...PHIL/SCI TREND. PAGE 62 G1225

ACADEM
KNOWL
R+D
PLAN

S67
ALBAUM G.,"INFORMATION FLOW AND DECENTRALIZED
DECISION MAKING IN MARKETING." EX/STRUC COMPUTER
OP/RES PROB/SOLV EFFICIENCY OPTIMAL...METH/COMP
ORG/CHARTS 20. PAGE 2 G0033

LG/CO
ROUTINE
KNOWL
MARKET

S67
AVTORKHANOV A.,"A NEW AGRARIAN REVOLUTION." COM
USSR ECO/DEV PLAN TEC/DEV ADMIN CONTROL OPTIMAL
WEALTH SOCISM 20 KHRUSH/N STALIN/J. PAGE 4 G0082

AGRI
METH/COMP
MARXISM
OWN

N67
US CONGRESS JT COMM ECO GOVT.BACKGROUND MATERIAL ON
ECONOMY IN GOVERNMENT 1967 (PAMPHLET). WOR+45
ECO/DEV BARGAIN PRICE DEMAND OPTIMAL...STAT
DEPT/DEFEN. PAGE 57 G1116

BUDGET
COST
MGT
NAT/G

OR/MS....OPERATIONAL RESEARCH AND RELATED MANAGEMENT
SCIENCE

ORANGE FREE STATE....SEE ORANGE/STA

ORANGE/STA....ORANGE FREE STATE

ORD/FREE....SECURITY, ORDER, RESTRAINT, LIBERTY, FREEDOM

B14
CRAIG J.,ELEMENTS OF POLITICAL SCIENCE (3 VOLS.).
CONSTN AGRI INDUS SCHOOL FORCES TAX CT/SYS SUFF
MORAL WEALTH...CONCPT 19 CIVIL/LIB. PAGE 13 G0259

PHIL/SCI
NAT/G
ORD/FREE

N19
US ATOMIC ENERGY COMMISSION.ATOMIC ENERGY IN USE
(PAMPHLET). R+D RISK EFFICIENCY HEALTH KNOWL
ORD/FREE...PHIL/SCI CONCPT METH/CNCPT CHARTS
LAB/EXP 20 AEC. PAGE 56 G1106

OP/RES
TEC/DEV
NUC/PWR
CREATE

B29
DEWEY J.,THE QUEST FOR CERTAINTY. GP/REL RATIONAL
UTOPIA ATTIT MORAL ORD/FREE PWR...MYTH HIST/WRIT.
PAGE 15 G0301

PHIL/SCI
PERSON
PERCEPT
KNOWL

B37
STAMP S.,THE SCIENCE OF SOCIAL ADJUSTMENT. WOR-45
ACT/RES CREATE PLAN PROB/SOLV TEC/DEV ECO/TAC
EFFICIENCY SOC/INTEG 20. PAGE 52 G1031

ADJUST
ORD/FREE
PHIL/SCI

B41
BEARD C.A.,PUBLIC POLICY AND THE GENERAL WELFARE.
USA-45 CONSTN LAISSEZ POPULISM...POLICY MAJORIT 20.
PAGE 6 G0108

CONCPT
ORD/FREE
PWR
NAT/G

B42
BINGHAM A.M.,THE TECHNIQUES OF DEMOCRACY. USA-45
CONSTN STRUCT POL/PAR LEGIS PLAN PARTIC CHOOSE
REPRESENT NAT/LISM TOTALISM...MGT 20. PAGE 7 G0136

POPULISM
ORD/FREE
ADMIN
NAT/G

B43
LASKI H.J.,REFLECTIONS ON THE REVOLUTIONS OF OUR
TIME. COM USSR NAT/G WORKER UTOPIA ORD/FREE WEALTH
MARXISM SOCISM 19/20. PAGE 32 G0637

CAP/ISM
WELF/ST
ECO/TAC
POLICY

B44
FULLER G.H.,MILITARY GOVERNMENT: A LIST OF
REFERENCES (A PAMPHLET). ITALY UK USA-45 WOR-45 LAW
FORCES DOMIN ADMIN ARMS/CONT ORD/FREE PWR
...DECISION 20 CHINJAP. PAGE 21 G0404

BIBLIOG
DIPLOM
CIVMIL/REL
SOVEREIGN

B46
BRODIE B.,THE OBSOLETE WEAPON: ATOMIC POWER AND
WORLD ORDER. COM USA+45 USSR WOR+45 DELIB/GP PLAN
ORD/FREE PWR...CONCPT TIME/SEQ TREND UN 20. PAGE 9
G0171

INT/ORG
TEC/DEV
ARMS/CONT
NUC/PWR

B47
BALDWIN H.W.,THE PRICE OF POWER. USA+45 FORCES PLAN PROB/SOLV

NUC/PWR ADJUST COST ORD/FREE...POLICY PSY BIBLIOG
20. PAGE 5 G0089

PWR
POPULISM
PRICE

B47
BRYSON L.,SCIENCE AND FREEDOM. WOR+45 ACT/RES
CREATE TECHRACY...TECHNIC SOC/INTEG. PAGE 9 G0183

CONCPT
ORD/FREE
CULTURE
SOC

B47
WHITEHEAD T.N.,LEADERSHIP IN A FREE SOCIETY; A
STUDY IN HUMAN RELATIONS BASED ON AN ANALYSIS OF
PRESENT-DAY INDUSTRIAL CIVILIZATION. WOR-45 STRUCT
R+D LABOR LG/CO SML/CO WORKER PLAN PROB/SOLV
TEC/DEV DRIVE...MGT 20. PAGE 63 G1234

INDUS
LEAD
ORD/FREE
SOCIETY

N47
FOX W.T.R.,UNITED STATES POLICY IN A TWO POWER
WORLD. COM USA+45 USSR FORCES DOMIN AGREE NEUTRAL
NUC/PWR ORD/FREE SOVEREIGN 20 COLD/WAR TREATY
EUROPE/W INTERVENT. PAGE 20 G0389

DIPLOM
FOR/AID
POLICY

S49
MERTON R.,"THE ROLE OF APPLIED SOCIAL SCIENCE IN
THE FORMATION OF POLICY: A RESEARCH MEMORANDUM."
WOR+45 INDUS NAT/G EXEC ROUTINE CHOOSE ORD/FREE PWR
SKILL...POLICY MGT PSY METH/CNCPT TESTS CHARTS METH
VAL/FREE 20. PAGE 38 G0756

PLAN
SOC
DIPLOM

B50
CANTRIL H.,TENSIONS THAT CAUSE WAR. UNIV CULTURE
R+D CREATE EDU/PROP DRIVE PERSON KNOWL ORD/FREE
...HUM PSY SOC OBS CENSUS TREND CON/ANAL SOC/EXP
SIMUL GEN/METH ANTHOL COLD/WAR TOT/POP. PAGE 11
G0206

SOCIETY
PHIL/SCI
PEACE

B51
HUXLEY J.,FREEDOM AND CULTURE. UNIV LAW SOCIETY R+D
ACADEM SCHOOL CREATE SANCTION ATTIT KNOWL...HUM
ANTHOL 20. PAGE 27 G0540

CULTURE
ORD/FREE
PHIL/SCI
IDEA/COMP

S51
MACRAE D.G.,"THE BOLSHEVIK IDEOLOGY; THE
INTELLECTUAL AND EMOTIONAL FACTORS IN COMMUNIST
AFFILIATION" (BMR)" COM LEAD REV ATTIT ORD/FREE
...SOC CON/ANAL 20 BOLSHEVISM. PAGE 35 G0693

MARXISM
INTELL
PHIL/SCI
SECT

B53
LANGER W.L.,THE UNDECLARED WAR, 1940-1941. EUR+WWI
GERMANY USA-45 USSR AIR FORCES TEC/DEV CONFER
CONTROL COERCE PERCEPT ORD/FREE PWR 20 CHINJAP
EUROPE. PAGE 32 G0634

WAR
POLICY
DIPLOM

B53
TOMPKINS D.C.,CIVIL DEFENSE IN THE STATES: A
BIBLIOGRAPHY (DEFENSE BIBLIOGRAPHIES NO. 3;
PAMPHLET). USA+45 LABOR LOC/G NAT/G PROVS LEGIS.
PAGE 55 G1076

BIBLIOG
WAR
ORD/FREE
ADMIN

S53
PERKINS J.A.,"ADMINISTRATION OF THE NATIONAL
SECURITY PROGRAM." USA+45 EX/STRUC FORCES ADMIN
CIVMIL/REL ORD/FREE 20. PAGE 44 G0868

CONTROL
GP/REL
REPRESENT
PROB/SOLV

B54
WRIGHT Q.,PROBLEMS OF STABILITY AND PROGRESS IN
INTERNATIONAL RELATIONSHIPS. FUT WOR+45 WOR-45
SOCIETY LEGIS CREATE TEC/DEV ECO/TAC EDU/PROP ADJUD
WAR PEACE ORD/FREE PWR...KNO/TEST TREND GEN/LAWS
20. PAGE 64 G1257

INT/ORG
CONCPT
DIPLOM

S54
FORM W.H.,"THE PLACE OF SOCIAL STRUCTURE IN THE
DETERMINATION OF LAND USE: SOME IMPLICATIONS FOR A
THEORY OF URBAN ECOLOGY" (BMR)" STRUCT...GEOG
PHIL/SCI SOC 20. PAGE 19 G0381

HABITAT
MARKET
ORD/FREE
MUNIC

B55
DAVIS E.,TWO MINUTES TO MIDNIGHT. WOR+45 PLAN
CONTROL NEUTRAL ARMS/CONT ATTIT ORD/FREE...PSY 20
COLD/WAR. PAGE 14 G0277

NUC/PWR
WAR
DETER
DIPLOM

B55
MOCH J.,HUMAN FOLLY: DISARM OR PERISH. USA+45
WOR+45 SOCIETY INT/ORG NAT/G ACT/RES EDU/PROP ATTIT
PERSON KNOWL ORD/FREE PWR...MAJORIT TOT/POP
COLD/WAR 20. PAGE 39 G0776

FUT
DELIB/GP
ARMS/CONT
NUC/PWR

B55
OPPENHEIMER R.,THE OPEN MIND. USA+45 WOR+45 NAT/G
DELIB/GP DETER MORAL ORD/FREE...MYTH GEN/LAWS 20.
PAGE 43 G0842

CREATE
PWR
ARMS/CONT

NUC/PWR

B55
US OFFICE OF THE PRESIDENT,REPORT TO CONGRESS ON THE MUTUAL SECURITY PROGRAM FOR THE SIX MONTHS ENDED JUNE 30, 1955. ECO/DEV INT/ORG NAT/G CREATE TEC/DEV BAL/PWR ECO/TAC AGREE DETER COST ORD/FREE 20 DEPT/STATE DEPT/DEFEN. PAGE 59 G1157
DIPLOM FORCES PLAN FOR/AID

S55
SKINNER B.F.,"FREEDOM AND THE CONTROL OF MEN" (BMR)" FUT WOR+45 CONTROL CHOOSE GP/REL ATTIT MORAL PWR POPULISM...POLICY 20. PAGE 51 G1008
ORD/FREE TEC/DEV PHIL/SCI INTELL

B56
US OFFICE OF THE PRESIDENT,REPORT TO CONGRESS ON THE MUTUAL SECURITY PROGRAM FOR THE SIX MONTHS ENDED DECEMBER 31, 1955. ASIA USSR ECO/DEV ECO/UNDEV INT/ORG CREATE TEC/DEV BAL/PWR ECO/TAC AGREE DETER COST ORD/FREE 20 DEPT/STATE DEPT/DEFEN EISNHWR/DD. PAGE 59 G1158
DIPLOM FORCES PLAN FOR/AID

S57
FISHMAN B.G.,"PUBLIC POLICY AND POLITICAL CONSIDERATIONS." USA+45 SOCIETY NAT/G ACT/RES CREATE PLAN DIPLOM KNOWL ORD/FREE...CONCPT GEN/METH 20. PAGE 19 G0370
ECO/DEV CONSULT

B58
ANGELL N.,DEFENCE AND THE ENGLISH-SPEAKING ROLE. CHINA/COM UK USSR INT/ORG FORCES EDU/PROP NEUTRAL NUC/PWR NAT/LISM PEACE TOTALISM 20 COLD/WAR COEXIST. PAGE 3 G0059
DIPLOM WAR MARXISM ORD/FREE

B58
LIPPITT R.,DYNAMICS OF PLANNED CHANGE. STRUCT ACT/RES ROUTINE INGP/REL PWR...POLICY METH/CNCPT BIBLIOG. PAGE 34 G0672
VOL/ASSN ORD/FREE PLAN CREATE

B58
NATIONAL PLANNING ASSOCIATION,1970 WITHOUT ARMS CONTROL (PAMPHLET). WOR+45 PROB/SOLV TEC/DEV DIPLOM CONFER DETER NUC/PWR WAR...CHARTS 20 COLD/WAR. PAGE 41 G0810
ARMS/CONT ORD/FREE WEAPON PREDICT

B58
ROCKEFELLER BROTH FUND INC,INTERNATIONAL SECURITY - THE MILITARY ASPECT. USA+45 INT/ORG NAT/G BUDGET ARMS/CONT WAR WEAPON PEACE ORD/FREE 20 NATO. PAGE 47 G0932
NUC/PWR DETER FORCES DIPLOM

B58
TELLER E.A.,OUR NUCLEAR FUTURE. SOCIETY FORCES TEC/DEV EDU/PROP KNOWL ORD/FREE...STAND/INT SYS/QU KNO/TEST AUD/VIS CHARTS SIMUL 20. PAGE 54 G1062
FUT PHIL/SCI NUC/PWR WAR

B58
US DEPARTMENT OF THE ARMY,BIBLIOGRAPHY ON LIMITED WAR (PAMPHLET). USA+45 TEC/DEV CONTROL RISK COERCE DETER NUC/PWR WEAPON ADJUST PEACE ALL/VALS ORD/FREE 20. PAGE 57 G1127
BIBLIOG/A WAR FORCES CIVMIL/REL

S58
DAVENPORT J.,"ARMS AND THE WELFARE STATE." INTELL STRUCT FORCES CREATE ECO/TAC FOR/AID DOMIN LEGIT ADMIN WAR ORD/FREE PWR...POLICY SOC CONCPT MYTH OBS TREND COLD/WAR TOT/POP 20. PAGE 14 G0276
USA+45 NAT/G USSR

S58
MCDOUGAL M.S.,"PERSPECTIVES FOR A LAW OF OUTER SPACE." FUT WOR+45 AIR CONSULT DELIB/GP TEC/DEV CT/SYS ORD/FREE...POLICY JURID 20 UN. PAGE 37 G0736
INT/ORG SPACE INT/LAW

S58
THOMPSON K.W.,"NATIONAL SECURITY IN A NUCLEAR AGE." USA+45 WOR+45 SOCIETY INT/ORG NAT/G TOP/EX DIPLOM DOMIN EDU/PROP LEGIT ARMS/CONT COERCE ORD/FREE ...TREND STERTYP TOT/POP VAL/FREE COLD/WAR 20. PAGE 54 G1068
FORCES PWR BAL/PWR

B59
AMRINE M.,THE GREAT DECISION: THE SECRET HISTORY OF THE ATOMIC BOMB. USA+45 TOP/EX EDU/PROP LEGIT PERCEPT ORD/FREE PWR VAL/FREE HIROSHIMA. PAGE 3 G0055
DECISION NAT/G NUC/PWR FORCES

B59
EMME E.M.,THE IMPACT OF AIR POWER - NATIONAL SECURITY AND WORLD POLITICS. USA+45 USSR FORCES DIPLOM WEAPON PEACE TOTALISM...POLICY NAT/COMP 20 EUROPE. PAGE 18 G0346
DETER AIR WAR ORD/FREE

B59
HUGHES E.M.,AMERICA THE VINCIBLE. USA+45 FOR/AID ARMS/CONT NUC/PWR PERS/REL RATIONAL ATTIT ALL/VALS 20 COLD/WAR. PAGE 27 G0534
ORD/FREE DIPLOM WAR

B59
MIKSCHE F.O.,THE FAILURE OF ATOMIC STRATEGY. COM EUR+WWI INTELL POL/PAR FORCES PLAN ECO/TAC NUC/PWR ATTIT DRIVE RIGID/FLEX PWR...DECISION GEOG PSY CONCPT RECORD TREND CHARTS VAL/FREE 20. PAGE 39 G0766
ACT/RES ORD/FREE DIPLOM ARMS/CONT

B59
RUSSELL B.,COMMON SENSE AND NUCLEAR WARFARE. WOR+45 INTELL SOCIETY STRATA NAT/G TOP/EX EDU/PROP ATTIT PERSON KNOWL MORAL PWR...POLICY CONCPT MYTH CON/ANAL COLD/WAR 20. PAGE 48 G0948
ORD/FREE ARMS/CONT NUC/PWR

S59
CORY R.H. JR.,"INTERNATIONAL INSPECTION FROM PROPOSALS TO REALIZATION." WOR+45 TEC/DEV ECO/TAC ADJUD ORD/FREE PWR WEALTH...RECORD VAL/FREE 20. PAGE 13 G0258
STRUCT PSY ARMS/CONT NUC/PWR

S59
MILBURN T.W.,"WHAT CONSTITUTES EFFECTIVE DETERRENCE." USA+45 WOR+45 STRUCT FORCES ACT/RES PLAN SUPEGO KNOWL ORD/FREE PWR...RELATIV PSY CONCPT VAL/FREE 20 COLD/WAR. PAGE 39 G0768
INTELL ATTIT DETER NUC/PWR

S59
WILLIAMS B.H.,"SCIENTIFIC METHOD IN FOREIGN POLICY." WOR+45 NAT/G FORCES TOP/EX DOMIN LEGIT COERCE PEACE ATTIT KNOWL ORD/FREE PWR...GEN/LAWS GEN/METH TOT/POP COLD/WAR NAZI. PAGE 63 G1241
PLAN PHIL/SCI DIPLOM

B60
ARMS CONTROL. FUT UNIV WOR+45 INTELL R+D INT/ORG NAT/G VOL/ASSN CONSULT CREATE EDU/PROP PEACE...HUM GEN/LAWS TOT/POP 20. PAGE 1 G0015
DELIB/GP ORD/FREE ARMS/CONT NUC/PWR

B60
ALBI F.,TRATADO DE LOS MODOS DE GESTION DE LAS CORPORACIONES LOCALES. SPAIN FINAN NAT/G BUDGET CONTROL EXEC ROUTINE GOV/REL ORD/FREE SOVEREIGN ...MGT 20. PAGE 2 G0034
LOC/G LAW ADMIN MUNIC

B60
GOLDSEN J.M.,INTERNATIONAL POLITICAL IMPLICATIONS OF ACTIVITIES IN OUTER SPACE. FUT USA+45 WOR+45 AIR LAW ACT/RES LEGIT ATTIT KNOWL ORD/FREE PWR...CONCPT 20. PAGE 22 G0427
R+D SPACE

B60
HEILBRONER R.L.,THE FUTURE AS HISTORY. USA+45 WOR+45 WOR-45 SOCIETY ECO/DEV ECO/UNDEV VOL/ASSN PLAN CAP/ISM NUC/PWR CHOOSE NAT/LISM ATTIT ORD/FREE RESPECT WEALTH SOCISM 20. PAGE 25 G0501
TEC/DEV TREND

B60
KINGSTON-MCCLOUG E.,DEFENSE; POLICY AND STRATEGY. UK SEA AIR TEC/DEV DIPLOM ADMIN LEAD WAR ORD/FREE ...CHARTS 20. PAGE 30 G0597
FORCES PLAN POLICY DECISION

B60
US HOUSE COMM. SCI. ASTRONAUT.,OCEAN SCIENCES AND NATIONAL SECURITY. FUT SEA ECO/DEV EXTR/IND INT/ORG NAT/G FORCES ACT/RES TEC/DEV ECO/TAC COERCE WAR BIO/SOC KNOWL PWR...CONCPT RECORD LAB/EXP 20. PAGE 59 G1153
R+D ORD/FREE

B60
WEBSTER J.A.,A GENERAL STUDY OF THE DEPARTMENT OF DEFENSE INTERNAL SECURITY PROGRAM. USA+45 WORKER TEC/DEV ADJUD CONTROL CT/SYS EXEC GOV/REL COST ...POLICY DECISION MGT 20 DEPT/DEFEN SUPREME/CT. PAGE 62 G1221
ORD/FREE PLAN ADMIN NAT/G

B60
WOETZEL R.K.,THE INTERNATIONAL CONTROL OF AIRSPACE AND OUTERSPACE. FUT WOR+45 AIR CONSTN STRUCT CONSULT PLAN TEC/DEV ADJUD RIGID/FLEX KNOWL ORD/FREE PWR...TECHNIC GEOG MGT NEW/IDEA TREND COMPUT/IR VAL/FREE 20 TREATY. PAGE 64 G1251
INT/ORG JURID SPACE INT/LAW

L60
HOLTON G.,"ARMS CONTROL." FUT WOR+45 CULTURE INT/ORG NAT/G FORCES TOP/EX PLAN EDU/PROP COERCE ATTIT RIGID/FLEX ORD/FREE...POLICY PHIL/SCI SOC TREND COLD/WAR. PAGE 27 G0524
ACT/RES CONSULT ARMS/CONT NUC/PWR

L60
MCCLELLAND C.A.,"THE FUNCTION OF THEORY IN INTERNATIONAL RELATIONS." WOR+45 PLAN EDU/PROP
INT/ORG CONCPT

ROUTINE ORD/FREE...PHIL/SCI PSY SOC METH/CNCPT   DIPLOM
NEW/IDEA OBS TREND GEN/METH 20. PAGE 37 G0728

S60
DOUGHERTY J.E.,"KEY TO SECURITY: DISARMAMENT OR   FORCES
ARMS STABILITY." COM USA+45 USSR INT/ORG NAT/G   ORD/FREE
CREATE EDU/PROP COERCE DETER ATTIT PWR...DECISION   ARMS/CONT
CONCPT MYTH NEW/IDEA TREND 20 COLD/WAR. PAGE 16   NUC/PWR
G0311

S60
HALSEY A.H.,"THE CHANGING FUNCTIONS OF UNIVERSITIES   ACADEM
IN ADVANCED INDUSTRIAL SOCIETIES." R+D EDU/PROP   CREATE
REPRESENT ROLE ORD/FREE PWR TREND. PAGE 24 G0476   CULTURE
   ADJUST

S60
HUTCHINSON C.E.,"AN INSTITUTE FOR NATIONAL SECURITY   POLICY
AFFAIRS." USA+45 R+D NAT/G CONSULT TOP/EX ACT/RES   METH/CNCPT
CREATE PLAN TEC/DEV EDU/PROP ROUTINE NUC/PWR ATTIT   ELITES
ORD/FREE PWR...DECISION MGT PHIL/SCI CONCPT RECORD   DIPLOM
GEN/LAWS GEN/METH 20. PAGE 27 G0539

S60
IKLE F.C.,"NTH COUNTRIES AND DISARMAMENT." WOR+45   FUT
DELIB/GP ECO/TAC DOMIN EDU/PROP LEGIT ROUTINE   INT/ORG
COERCE RIGID/FLEX ORD/FREE...MARXIST TREND 20.   ARMS/CONT
PAGE 28 G0543   NUC/PWR

S60
KISSINGER H.A.,"ARMS CONTROL, INSPECTION AND   FORCES
SURPRISE ATTACK." COM USA+45 NAT/G ACT/RES PLAN   ORD/FREE
TEC/DEV DIPLOM EDU/PROP DETER WAR RIGID/FLEX   ARMS/CONT
...CONCPT GEN/METH TOT/POP 20. PAGE 31 G0603   NUC/PWR

B61
BONNEFOUS M.,EUROPE ET TIERS MONDE. EUR+WWI SOCIETY   AFR
INT/ORG NAT/G VOL/ASSN ACT/RES TEC/DEV CAP/ISM   ECO/UNDEV
ECO/TAC ATTIT ORD/FREE SOVEREIGN...POLICY CONCPT   FOR/AID
TREND 20. PAGE 8 G0153   INT/TRADE

B61
MURPHY E.F.,WATER PURITY: A STUDY IN LEGAL CONTROL   SEA
OF NATURAL RESOURCES. LOC/G ACT/RES PLAN TEC/DEV   LAW
LOBBY GP/REL COST ATTIT HEALTH ORD/FREE...HEAL   PROVS
JURID 20 WISCONSIN WATER. PAGE 40 G0797   CONTROL

B61
SCHMIDT H.,VERTEIDIGUNG ODER VERGELTUNG. COM CUBA   PLAN
GERMANY/W USSR FORCES DIPLOM ARMS/CONT DETER   WAR
NUC/PWR...POLICY CHARTS HYPO/EXP SIMUL BIBLIOG 20   BAL/PWR
NATO COLD/WAR. PAGE 49 G0970   ORD/FREE

B61
US SENATE COMM GOVT OPERATIONS,ORGANIZING FOR   POLICY
NATIONAL SECURITY. COM USA+45 BUDGET DIPLOM DETER   PLAN
NUC/PWR WAR WEAPON ORD/FREE...BIBLIOG 20 COLD/WAR.   FORCES
PAGE 60 G1176   COERCE

L61
TAUBENFELD H.J.,"A REGIME FOR OUTER SPACE." FUT   INT/ORG
UNIV R+D ACT/RES PLAN BAL/PWR LEGIT ARMS/CONT   ADJUD
ORD/FREE...POLICY JURID TREND UN TOT/POP 20   SPACE
COLD/WAR. PAGE 54 G1056

S61
MAINZER L.C.,"SCIENTIFIC FREEDOM IN GOVERNMENT-   CREATE
SPONSORED RESEARCH." USA+45 INTELL PUB/INST BUDGET   ORD/FREE
LOBBY AUTHORIT PWR...POLICY PHIL/SCI 20 NIH NSF.   NAT/G
PAGE 35 G0696   R+D

B62
SOVIET STAND ON DISARMAMENT. COM EUR+WWI FUT USA+45   ACT/RES
NAT/G TOP/EX NUC/PWR PEACE ATTIT...POLICY CONCPT   ORD/FREE
TOT/POP 20. PAGE 1 G0016   ARMS/CONT
   USSR

B62
BOCK E.A.,CASE STUDIES IN AMERICAN GOVERNMENT.   POLICY
USA+45 ECO/DEV CHIEF EDU/PROP CT/SYS RACE/REL   LEGIS
ORD/FREE...JURID MGT PHIL/SCI PRESIDENT CASEBOOK.   IDEA/COMP
PAGE 8 G0146   NAT/G

B62
BURKE A.E.,ENOUGH GOOD MEN. USA+45 WOR+45 ECO/UNDEV   DIPLOM
FORCES TEC/DEV GUERRILLA NUC/PWR REV WAR ORD/FREE   POLICY
MARXISM...GEOG 20 COLD/WAR. PAGE 10 G0189   NAT/G
   TASK

B62
CARSON R.,SILENT SPRING. USA+45 AIR CULTURE AGRI   HABITAT
INDUS ADMIN ATTIT RIGID/FLEX ORD/FREE PWR...POLICY   TREND
20. PAGE 11 G0216   SOCIETY
   CONTROL

B62
DUPRE S.,SCIENCE AND THE NATION. USA+45 ECO/DEV   ARMS/CONT
ACADEM ORD/FREE TECHNIC. PAGE 17 G0323   DECISION
   TEC/DEV
   INDUS

B62
FORBES H.W.,THE STRATEGY OF DISARMAMENT. FUT WOR+45   PLAN
INT/ORG VOL/ASSN CONSULT ARMS/CONT COERCE NUC/PWR   FORCES
WAR DRIVE RIGID/FLEX ORD/FREE PWR...POLICY CONCPT   DIPLOM
OBS TREND STERTYP 20. PAGE 19 G0378

B62
KAHN H.,THINKING ABOUT THE UNTHINKABLE. FUT USA+45   INT/ORG
LAW NAT/G CONSULT FORCES ACT/RES CREATE PLAN   ORD/FREE
TEC/DEV BAL/PWR DIPLOM EDU/PROP ARMS/CONT DETER   NUC/PWR
ATTIT...CONCPT OBS TREND COLD/WAR 20. PAGE 29 G0570   PEACE

B62
KARNJAHAPRAKORN C.,MUNICIPAL GOVERNMENT IN THAILAND   LOC/G
AS AN INSTITUTION AND PROCESS OF SELF-GOVERNMENT.   MUNIC
THAILAND CULTURE FINAN EX/STRUC LEGIS PLAN CONTROL   ORD/FREE
GOV/REL EFFICIENCY ATTIT...POLICY 20. PAGE 29 G0578   ADMIN

B62
KRAFT J.,THE GRAND DESIGN. EUR+WWI USA+45 AGRI   VOL/ASSN
FINAN INDUS MARKET INT/ORG NAT/G PLAN ECO/DEV   ECO/DEV
TARIFFS REGION DRIVE ORD/FREE WEALTH...POLICY OBS   INT/TRADE
TREND EEC 20. PAGE 31 G0616

B62
LEFEVER E.W.,ARMS AND ARMS CONTROL. COM USA+45   ATTIT
INT/ORG TEC/DEV DIPLOM ORD/FREE 20. PAGE 33 G0652   PWR
   ARMS/CONT
   BAL/PWR

B62
MELMAN S.,DISARMAMENT: ITS POLITICS AND ECONOMICS.   NAT/G
WOR+45 DELIB/GP FORCES ECO/TAC DOMIN EDU/PROP LEGIT   ORD/FREE
COERCE PWR...POLICY CONCPT 20. PAGE 38 G0752   ARMS/CONT
   NUC/PWR

B62
OSGOOD C.E.,AN ALTERNATIVE TO WAR OR SURRENDER. FUT   ORD/FREE
UNIV CULTURE INTELL SOCIETY R+D INT/ORG CONSULT   EDU/PROP
DELIB/GP ACT/RES PLAN CHOOSE ATTIT PERCEPT KNOWL   PEACE
...PHIL/SCI PSY SOC TREND GEN/LAWS 20. PAGE 43   WAR
G0849

B62
SINGER J.D.,DETERRENCE, ARMS CONTROL AND   FUT
DISARMAMENT: TOWARD A SYNTHESIS IN NATIONAL   ACT/RES
SECURITY POLICY. COM USA+45 INT/ORG BAL/PWR DETER   ARMS/CONT
ORD/FREE...POLICY COLD/WAR 20. PAGE 51 G1003

B62
SOHN L.B.,ZONAL DISARMAMENT: VARIATIONS ON A THEME.   ORD/FREE
FUT WOR+45 SOCIETY ACT/RES PLAN NUC/PWR PEACE ATTIT   NEW/IDEA
...POLICY GEOG CONT/OBS HYPO/EXP 20. PAGE 52 G1020   ARMS/CONT

B62
STOVER C.F.,THE GOVERNMENT OF SCIENCE (PAMPHLET).   PHIL/SCI
USA+45 SOCIETY PROF/ORG EX/STRUC CREATE CONTROL   TEC/DEV
NUC/PWR WAR GOV/REL PEACE ORD/FREE 20. PAGE 53   LAW
G1041   NAT/G

B62
US SENATE COMM GOVT OPERATIONS,ADMINISTRATION OF   ORD/FREE
NATIONAL SECURITY. USA+45 CHIEF PLAN PROB/SOLV   ADMIN
TEC/DEV DIPLOM ATTIT...POLICY DECISION 20   NAT/G
KENNEDY/JF RUSK/D MCNAMARA/R BUNDY/M HERTER/C.   CONTROL
PAGE 60 G1177

B62
WRIGHT Q.,PREVENTING WORLD WAR THREE. FUT WOR+45   CREATE
CULTURE INT/ORG NAT/G CONSULT FORCES ADMIN   ATTIT
ARMS/CONT DRIVE RIGID/FLEX ORD/FREE SOVEREIGN
...POLICY CONCPT TREND STERTYP COLD/WAR 20. PAGE 64
G1259

B62
YALEN R.,REGIONALISM AND WORLD ORDER. EUR+WWI   ORD/FREE
WOR+45 WOR-45 INT/ORG VOL/ASSN DELIB/GP FORCES   POLICY
TOP/EX BAL/PWR DIPLOM DOMIN REGION ARMS/CONT PWR
...JURID HYPO/EXP COLD/WAR 20. PAGE 64 G1261

L62
FINKELSTEIN L.S.,"ARMS INSPECTION." FUT WOR+45   FORCES
NAT/G DIPLOM ATTIT PERCEPT RIGID/FLEX ORD/FREE   PWR
COLD/WAR 20. PAGE 19 G0369   ARMS/CONT

S62
BETHE H.,"DISARMAMENT AND STRATEGY." COM USA+45   PLAN
USSR WOR+45 VOL/ASSN TEC/DEV EDU/PROP NUC/PWR   ORD/FREE
CHOOSE PEACE...POLICY DECISION NEW/IDEA OBS   ARMS/CONT
GEN/LAWS COLD/WAR 420. PAGE 7 G0133   DIPLOM

BOULDING K.E.,"THE PREVENTION OF WORLD WAR THREE." FUT WOR+45 INT/ORG PLAN BAL/PWR PEACE ORD/FREE PWR ...NEW/IDEA TREND TOT/POP COLD/WAR 20. PAGE 8 G0158
`S62 VOL/ASSN NAT/G ARMS/CONT DIPLOM`

CRANE R.D.,"LAW AND STRATEGY IN SPACE." FUT USA+45 WOR+45 AIR LAW INT/ORG NAT/G FORCES ACT/RES PLAN BAL/PWR LEGIT ARMS/CONT COERCE ORD/FREE...POLICY INT/LAW JURID SOC/EXP 20 TREATY. PAGE 13 G0261
`S62 CONCPT SPACE`

FINKELSTEIN L.S.,"THE UNITED NATIONS AND ORGANIZATIONS FOR CONTROL OF ARMAMENT." FUT WOR+45 VOL/ASSN DELIB/GP TOP/EX CREATE EDU/PROP LEGIT ADJUD NUC/PWR ATTIT RIGID/FLEX ORD/FREE...POLICY DECISION CONCPT OBS TREND GEN/LAWS TOT/POP COLD/WAR. PAGE 19 G0368
`S62 INT/ORG PWR ARMS/CONT`

FOSTER R.B.,"UNILATERAL ARMS CONTROL MEASURES AND DISARMAMENT NEGOTIATION." WOR+45 VOL/ASSN DELIB/GP ACT/RES ECO/TAC EDU/PROP ATTIT RIGID/FLEX...CONCPT MYTH TIME/SEQ COLD/WAR 20. PAGE 20 G0386
`S62 PLAN ORD/FREE ARMS/CONT DETER`

GORDON B.K.,"NUCLEAR WEAPONS: RUSSIAN AND AMERICAN." COM USA+45 USSR NAT/G FORCES ACT/RES TEC/DEV PERCEPT RIGID/FLEX PWR SKILL...MGT METH/CNCPT QUANT OBS TIME/SEQ CON/ANAL GEN/METH TOT/POP VAL/FREE 20. PAGE 22 G0433
`S62 ORD/FREE COERCE NUC/PWR`

MORGENTHAU H.J.,"A POLITICAL THEORY OF FOREIGN AID." ECO/UNDEV NAT/G DELIB/GP PLAN ECO/TAC EDU/PROP EXEC ORD/FREE RESPECT WEALTH...METH/CNCPT TREND 20. PAGE 40 G0783
`S62 USA+45 PHIL/SCI FOR/AID`

NANES A.,"DISARMAMENT: THE LAST SEVEN YEARS." COM EUR+WWI USA+45 USSR INT/ORG FORCES TOP/EX CREATE LEGIT NUC/PWR DISPL ORD/FREE...CONCPT TIME/SEQ CON/ANAL 20. PAGE 41 G0803
`S62 DELIB/GP RIGID/FLEX ARMS/CONT`

PAULING L.,"GENETIC EFFECTS OF WEAPONS TESTS." WOR+45 SOCIETY FAM ACT/RES EDU/PROP AGE/C HEALTH ORD/FREE...GEOG STAT CONT/OBS PROJ/TEST CHARTS TOT/POP 20. PAGE 44 G0861
`S62 HEAL ARMS/CONT NUC/PWR`

PHIPPS T.E.,"THE CASE FOR DETERRENCE." FUT WOR+45 SOCIETY EX/STRUC FORCES ACT/RES CREATE PLAN TEC/DEV ROUTINE RIGID/FLEX ORD/FREE...POLICY MYTH NEW/IDEA STERTYP COLD/WAR 20. PAGE 45 G0876
`S62 ATTIT COERCE DETER ARMS/CONT`

SINGER J.D.,"STABLE DETERRENCE AND ITS LIMITS." FUT WOR+45 R+D INT/ORG CONSULT ACT/RES TEC/DEV ARMS/CONT COERCE DRIVE PERCEPT RIGID/FLEX ORD/FREE PWR...MYTH SIMUL TOT/POP 20. PAGE 51 G1004
`S62 NAT/G FORCES DETER NUC/PWR`

ABSHIRE D.M.,NATIONAL SECURITY: POLITICAL, MILITARY, AND ECONOMIC STRATEGIES IN THE DECADE AHEAD. ASIA COM USA+45 WOR+45 ECO/DEV ECO/UNDEV INT/ORG DELIB/GP FORCES ECO/TAC COERCE ATTIT RIGID/FLEX HEALTH ORD/FREE PWR WEALTH...POLICY STAT CHARTS ANTHOL COLD/WAR VAL/FREE. PAGE 1 G0024
`B63 FUT ACT/RES BAL/PWR`

GOLDSEN J.M.,OUTER SPACE IN WORLD POLITICS. COM USA+45 NAT/G FORCES ACT/RES PLAN DOMIN EDU/PROP COERCE ORD/FREE PWR...TECHNIC STAT INT SAMP TREND ANTHOL VAL/FREE 20. PAGE 22 G0428
`B63 TEC/DEV DIPLOM SPACE`

HALEY A.G.,SPACE LAW AND GOVERNMENT. FUT USA+45 WOR+45 LEGIS ACT/RES CREATE ATTIT RIGID/FLEX ORD/FREE PWR SOVEREIGN...POLICY JURID CONCPT CHARTS VAL/FREE 20. PAGE 24 G0469
`B63 INT/ORG LAW SPACE`

LILIENTHAL D.E.,CHANGE, HOPE, AND THE BOMB. USA+45 WOR+45 R+D INT/ORG NAT/G DELIB/GP FORCES ACT/RES DETER RIGID/FLEX ORD/FREE...POLICY CONCPT OBS AEC 20. PAGE 34 G0666
`B63 ATTIT MYTH ARMS/CONT NUC/PWR`

MAYNE R.,THE COMMUNITY OF EUROPE. UK CONSTN NAT/G CONSULT DELIB/GP CREATE PLAN ECO/TAC LEGIT ADMIN ROUTINE ORD/FREE PWR WEALTH...CONCPT TIME/SEQ EEC EURATOM 20. PAGE 37 G0724
`B63 EUR+WWI INT/ORG REGION`

MCDOUGAL M.S.,LAW AND PUBLIC ORDER IN SPACE. FUT USA+45 ACT/RES TEC/DEV ADJUD...POLICY INT/LAW JURID 20. PAGE 37 G0739
`B63 SPACE ORD/FREE DIPLOM DECISION`

MENEZES A.J.,SUBDESENVOLVIMENTO E POLITICA INTERNACIONAL. BRAZIL WOR+45 PLAN CONTROL LEAD NAT/LISM ORD/FREE 20 THIRD/WRLD. PAGE 38 G0754
`B63 ECO/UNDEV DIPLOM POLICY BAL/PWR`

MULLENBACH P.,CIVILIAN NUCLEAR POWER: ECONOMIC ISSUES AND POLICY FORMATION. FINAN INT/ORG DELIB/GP ACT/RES ECO/TAC ATTIT SUPEGO HEALTH ORD/FREE PWR ...POLICY CONCPT MATH STAT CHARTS VAL/FREE 20 COLD/WAR. PAGE 40 G0792
`B63 USA+45 ECO/DEV NUC/PWR`

MULLER H.J.,FREEDOM IN THE WESTERN WORLD. PREHIST CULTURE SECT CREATE TEC/DEV DOMIN PWR WEALTH ...MAJORIT SOC CONCPT. PAGE 40 G0793
`B63 ORD/FREE TIME/SEQ SOCIETY`

REED E.,CHALLENGES TO DEMOCRACY: THE NEXT TEN YEARS. FUT USA+45 ECO/DEV DELIB/GP TEC/DEV CONFER GOV/REL KNOWL ORD/FREE...MAJORIT IDEA/COMP ANTHOL 20. PAGE 46 G0909
`B63 POLICY EDU/PROP ECO/TAC NAT/G`

RUITENBEER H.M.,THE DILEMMA OF ORGANIZATIONAL SOCIETY. CULTURE ECO/DEV MUNIC SECT TEC/DEV EDU/PROP NAT/LISM ORD/FREE...NAT/COMP 20 RIESMAN/D WHYTE/WF MERTON/R MEAD/MARG JASPERS/K. PAGE 48 G0945
`B63 PERSON ROLE ADMIN WORKER`

US DEPARTMENT OF THE ARMY,US OVERSEAS BASES: PRESENT STATUS AND FUTURE PROSPECTS (PAMPHLET). USA+45 DIPLOM NUC/PWR ATTIT ORD/FREE...POLICY CHARTS 20. PAGE 58 G1130
`B63 BIBLIOG/A WAR BAL/PWR DETER`

US SENATE COMM GOVT OPERATIONS,ADMINISTRATION OF NATIONAL SECURITY (9 PARTS). ADMIN...INT REC/INT CHARTS 20 SENATE CONGRESS. PAGE 60 G1178
`B63 DELIB/GP NAT/G OP/RES ORD/FREE`

BRENNAN D.G.,"ARMS CONTROL AND CIVIL DEFENSE." USA+45 WOR+45 NAT/G BAL/PWR ROUTINE ATTIT RIGID/FLEX ORD/FREE...SOC TOT/POP 20. PAGE 8 G0165
`L63 PLAN HEALTH ARMS/CONT DETER`

MCDOUGAL M.S.,"THE ENJOYMENT AND ACQUISITION OF RESOURCES IN OUTER SPACE." CHRIST-17C FUT WOR+45 WOR-45 LAW EXTR/INT INT/ORG ACT/RES CREATE TEC/DEV ECO/TAC LEGIT COERCE HEALTH KNOWL ORD/FREE PWR WEALTH...JURID HIST/WRIT VAL/FREE. PAGE 37 G0738
`L63 PLAN TREND`

NIEBURG H.,"EURATOM: A STUDY IN COALITION POLITICS." EUR+WWI UK USA+45 ELITES NAT/G DELIB/GP LEGIS TOP/EX ECO/TAC NUC/PWR ATTIT ORD/FREE PWR TOT/POP EEC OEEC 20 NATO EURATOM. PAGE 42 G0820
`L63 VOL/ASSN ACT/RES`

PHELPS J.,"STUDIES IN DETERRENCE VIII: MILITARY STABILITARY AND ARMS CONTROL: A CRITICAL SURVEY." FUT WOR+45 INT/ORG ACT/RES EDU/PROP COERCE NUC/PWR WAR HEALTH PWR...POLICY TECHNIC TREND SIMUL TOT/POP 20. PAGE 44 G0874
`L63 FORCES ORD/FREE ARMS/CONT DETER`

ABT C.,"THE PROBLEMS AND POSSIBILITIES OF SPACE ARMS CONTROL." FUT USA+45 WOR+45 AIR SOCIETY NAT/G BAL/PWR EDU/PROP ATTIT PWR WEALTH...HYPO/EXP TOT/POP 20. PAGE 2 G0025
`S63 ACT/RES ORD/FREE ARMS/CONT SPACE`

BOHN L.,"WHOSE NUCLEAR TEST: NON-PHYSICAL INSPECTION AND TEST BAN." WOR+45 R+D INT/ORG VOL/ASSN ORD/FREE...GEN/LAWS GEN/METH COLD/WAR 20. PAGE 8 G0148
`S63 ADJUD ARMS/CONT TEC/DEV NUC/PWR`

BOULDING K.E.,"UNIVERSITY, SOCIETY, AND ARMS CONTROL." WOR+45 WOR-45 ACADEM NAT/G CONSULT FORCES ACT/RES PLAN TEC/DEV BAL/PWR ECO/TAC COERCE DETER WAR ATTIT RIGID/FLEX KNOWL ORD/FREE PWR WEALTH ...CONCPT COLD/WAR TOT/POP 20. PAGE 8 G0159
`S63 SOCIETY ARMS/CONT`

ERSKINE H.G.,"THE POLLS: ATOMIC WEAPONS AND NUCLEAR
`S6 ATTIT`

ENERGY." USA+45 COERCE ORD/FREE...POLICY SOC STAT
CENSUS SAMP VAL/FREE 20. PAGE 18 G0350
   INT
   NUC/PWR

S63
PHELPS J.,"INFORMATION AND ARMS CONTROL." COM SPACE
USA+45 USSR WOR+45 R+D INT/ORG NAT/G DELIB/GP
DIPLOM ORD/FREE...CONCPT 20. PAGE 45 G0875
   KNOWL
   ARMS/CONT
   NUC/PWR

S63
TASHJEAN J.E.,"RESEARCH ON ARMS CONTROL." COM
USA+45 USSR FORCES ACT/RES PLAN DOMIN COERCE
ORD/FREE PWR...TIME/SEQ GEN/LAWS 20 COLD/WAR.
PAGE 53 G1053
   NAT/G
   POLICY
   ARMS/CONT

S63
WOHLSTETTER A.,"SCIENTISTS, SEERS AND STRATEGY."
USA+45 ELITES R+D NAT/G CONSULT FORCES TOP/EX
EDU/PROP ARMS/CONT KNOWL ORD/FREE...DECISION MYTH
20. PAGE 64 G1253
   INTELL
   ACT/RES

B64
BRILLOUIN L.,SCIENTIFIC UNCERTAINTY AND
INFORMATION. PROB/SOLV AUTOMAT PERCEPT ORD/FREE
...MATH REGRESS STAT STYLE OBS IDEA/COMP SIMUL
TIME. PAGE 9 G0169
   PHIL/SCI
   NEW/IDEA
   METH/CNCPT
   CREATE

B64
ETZIONI A.,THE MOON-DOGGLE: DOMESTIC AND
INTERNATIONAL IMPLICATIONS OF THE SPACE RACE. FUT
USA+45 WOR+45 INTELL ECO/DEV INDUS VOL/ASSN
EX/STRUC FORCES LEGIS TOP/EX PLAN TEC/DEV ECO/TAC
EDU/PROP KNOWL ORD/FREE PWR RESPECT WEALTH
TIME/SEQ. PAGE 18 G0352
   R+D
   NAT/G
   DIPLOM
   SPACE

B64
GRODZINS M.,THE ATOMIC AGE: FORTY-FIVE SCIENTISTS
AND SCHOLARS SPEAK ON NATIONAL AND WORLD AFFAIRS.
FUT USA+45 WOR+45 R+D INT/ORG NAT/G CONSULT TEC/DEV
EDU/PROP ATTIT PERSON ORD/FREE...HUM CONCPT
TIME/SEQ CON/ANAL. PAGE 23 G0454
   INTELL
   ARMS/CONT
   NUC/PWR

B64
GUTMANN P.M.,ECONOMIC GROWTH: AN AMERICAN PROBLEM.
USA+45 FINAN R+D...POLICY NAT/COMP ANTHOL BIBLIOG
20. PAGE 24 G0463
   WEALTH
   ECO/DEV
   CAP/ISM
   ORD/FREE

B64
OSSENBECK F.J.,OPEN SPACE AND PEACE. CHINA/COM FUT
USA+45 USSR LAW PROB/SOLV TEC/DEV EDU/PROP NEUTRAL
PEACE...AUD/VIS ANTHOL 20. PAGE 43 G0850
   SPACE
   ORD/FREE
   DIPLOM
   CREATE

B64
PARANJAPE H.K.,THE FLIGHT OF TECHNICAL PERSONNEL IN
PUBLIC UNDERTAKINGS. INDIA PAY DEMAND HAPPINESS
ORD/FREE...MGT QU 20 MIGRATION. PAGE 44 G0858
   ADMIN
   NAT/G
   WORKER
   PLAN

B64
PETERSON W.,THE POLITICS OF POPULATION. COM EUR+WWI
FUT MOD/EUR S/ASIA USA+45 USA-45 WOR+45 LAW CULTURE
FAM SECT DOMIN EDU/PROP BIO/SOC HEALTH ORD/FREE
...GEOG STAT TIME/SEQ TREND VAL/FREE. PAGE 44 G0871
   PLAN
   CENSUS
   POLICY

B64
RANSOM H.H.,CAN AMERICAN DEMOCRACY SURVIVE COLD
WAR. USA-45 CONSTN NAT/G CONSULT DELIB/GP LEGIS
ACT/RES LEGIT EXEC ATTIT KNOWL ORD/FREE PWR SKILL
...POLICY TIME/SEQ TREND GEN/LAWS 20 COLD/WAR.
PAGE 46 G0901
   USA+45
   ROUTINE

B64
ROSECRANCE R.N.,THE DISPERSION OF NUCLEAR WEAPONS:
STRATEGY AND POLITICS. ASIA COM FUT S/ASIA USA+45
INT/ORG NAT/G DELIB/GP FORCES ACT/RES TEC/DEV
BAL/PWR COERCE DETER ATTIT RIGID/FLEX ORD/FREE
...POLICY CHARTS VAL/FREE. PAGE 48 G0935
   EUR+WWI
   PWR
   PEACE

B64
VAN DYKE V.,PRIDE AND POWER: THE RATIONALE OF THE
SPACE PROGRAM. FUT USA+45 INTELL R+D NAT/G POL/PAR
DELIB/GP EX/STRUC LEGIS TOP/EX ACT/RES PLAN ECO/TAC
EDU/PROP ORD/FREE PWR RESPECT SKILL...TIME/SEQ
VAL/FREE. PAGE 61 G1191
   TEC/DEV
   ATTIT
   POLICY

B64
WHEELER-BENNETT J.W.,THE NEMESIS OF POWER (2ND
ED.). EUR+WWI GERMANY TOP/EX TEC/DEV ADMIN WAR
PERS/REL RIGID/FLEX ROLE ORD/FREE PWR FASCISM 20
HITLER/A. PAGE 63 G1231
   FORCES
   NAT/G
   GP/REL
   STRUCT

B64
WILLIAMS S.P.,TOWARD A GENUINE WORLD SECURITY
SYSTEM (PAMPHLET). WOR+45 INT/ORG FORCES PLAN
NUC/PWR ORD/FREE...INT/LAW CONCPT UN PRESIDENT.
   BIBLIOG/A
   ARMS/CONT
   DIPLOM

PAGE 63 G1243

ORD/FREE
PEACE

L64
GOLDBERG A.,"ATOMIC ORIGINS OF THE BRITISH NUCLEAR
DETERRENT." EUR+WWI UK NAT/G TOP/EX PLAN BAL/PWR
DOMIN DETER CHOOSE ATTIT DRIVE HEALTH ORD/FREE PWR
RESPECT...CONCPT VAL/FREE COLD/WAR 20 CMN/WLTH.
PAGE 22 G0425
   CREATE
   FORCES
   NUC/PWR

S64
ABT C.,"WAR GAMING." USA+45 NAT/G TOP/EX ACT/RES
TEC/DEV COERCE KNOWL ORD/FREE PWR...DECISION MATH
TIME/SEQ COMPUT/IR CHARTS LAB/EXP VAL/FREE. PAGE 2
G0026
   FORCES
   SIMUL
   WAR

S64
FALK S.L.,"DISARMAMENT IN HISTORICAL PERSPECTIVE."
WOR-45 NAT/G PLAN NUC/PWR PEACE ORD/FREE PWR
...TIME/SEQ AUD/VIS VAL/FREE LEAGUE/NAT 20. PAGE 18
G0360
   INT/ORG
   COERCE
   ARMS/CONT

S64
KASSOF A.,"THE ADMINISTERED SOCIETY:
TOTALITARIANISM WITHOUT TERROR." COM USSR STRATA
AGRI INDUS NAT/G PERF/ART SCHOOL TOP/EX EDU/PROP
ADMIN ORD/FREE PWR...POLICY SOC TIME/SEQ GEN/LAWS
VAL/FREE 20. PAGE 29 G0580
   SOCIETY
   DOMIN
   TOTALISM

S64
LERNER A.P.,"NUCLEAR SYMMETRY AS A FRAMEWORK FOR
COEXISTENCE." COM FUT USA+45 NAT/G ACT/RES CREATE
PLAN DIPLOM EDU/PROP COERCE WAR RIGID/FLEX PWR
SKILL...CONCPT METH/CNCPT GEN/LAWS TOT/POP VAL/FREE
COLD/WAR 20. PAGE 33 G0657
   FORCES
   ORD/FREE
   DETER
   NUC/PWR

S64
MAGGS P.B.,"SOVIET VIEWPOINT ON NUCLEAR WEAPONS IN
INTERNATIONAL LAW." USSR WOR+45 INT/ORG FORCES
DIPLOM ARMS/CONT ATTIT ORD/FREE PWR...POLICY JURID
CONCPT OBS TREND CON/ANAL GEN/LAWS VAL/FREE 20.
PAGE 35 G0694
   COM
   LAW
   INT/LAW
   NUC/PWR

S64
MAHALANOBIS P.C.,"PERSPECTIVE PLANNING IN INDIA:
STATISTICAL TOOLS." INDIA S/ASIA STRATA AGRI
DIST/IND FINAN INDUS SERV/IND NAT/G ECO/TAC
ORD/FREE WEALTH...POLICY TREND SIMUL VAL/FREE 20.
PAGE 35 G0695
   PLAN
   STAT

S64
PILISUK M.,"STEPWISE DISARMAMENT & SUDDEN
DESTRUCTION IN A TWOPERSON GAME: A RESEARCH TOOL."
NAT/G FORCES ACT/RES ECO/TAC EDU/PROP EXEC ROUTINE
COERCE ORD/FREE...SIMUL GEN/LAWS VAL/FREE. PAGE 45
G0877
   PWR
   DECISION
   ARMS/CONT

S64
SPONSLER G.C.,"THE MILITARY ROLE IN SPACE." FUT
USA+45 SEA AIR NAT/G ACT/RES PLAN COERCE NUC/PWR
WEAPON KNOWL ORD/FREE PWR RESPECT...TREND 20.
PAGE 52 G1026
   TEC/DEV
   FORCES
   SPACE

S64
THOMPSON V.A.,"ADMINISTRATIVE OBJECTIVES FOR
DEVELOPMENT ADMINISTRATION." WOR+45 CREATE PLAN
DOMIN EDU/PROP EXEC ROUTINE ATTIT ORD/FREE PWR
...POLICY GEN/LAWS VAL/FREE. PAGE 54 G1070
   ECO/UNDEV
   MGT

C64
SCHRAMM W.,"MASS MEDIA AND NATIONAL DEVELOPMENT:
THE ROLE OF INFORMATION IN DEVELOPING COUNTRIES."
FINAN R+D ACT/RES PLAN TEC/DEV DIPLOM CHOOSE SUPEGO
ORD/FREE...BIBLIOG 20. PAGE 50 G0978
   ECO/UNDEV
   COM/IND
   EDU/PROP
   MAJORIT

B65
ALLEN S.,LETTER TO A CONSERVATIVE. SOCIETY NAT/G
DIPLOM EDU/PROP NUC/PWR GP/REL ATTIT MORAL
...MAJORIT CONCPT 20. PAGE 2 G0044
   ORD/FREE
   MARXISM
   POLICY
   LAISSEZ

B65
BOBROW D.B.,COMPONENTS OF DEFENSE POLICY. ASIA
EUR+WWI USA+45 WOR+45 INTELL INT/ORG NAT/G PROF/ORG
CONSULT LEGIS ACT/RES CREATE ARMS/CONT COERCE
ORD/FREE...DECISION SIMUL. PAGE 7 G0145
   DETER
   NUC/PWR
   PLAN
   FORCES

B65
HALPERIN M.H.,CHINA AND THE BOMB. USA+45 USSR
INT/ORG FORCES ARMS/CONT DETER PRODUC ORD/FREE PWR
TREND. PAGE 24 G0472
   ASIA
   NUC/PWR
   WAR
   DIPLOM

B65
HALPERIN M.H.,COMMUNIST CHINA AND ARMS CONTROL.
CHINA/COM FUT USA+45 CULTURE FORCES TEC/DEV ECO/TAC
WAR PEACE ORD/FREE MARXISM 20 COLD/WAR. PAGE 24
   ATTIT
   POLICY
   ARMS/CONT

G0473 NUC/PWR

B65
IANNI O.,ESTADO E CAPITALISMO. L/A+17C FINAN ECO/UNDEV
TEC/DEV ECO/TAC ORD/FREE WEALTH POLICY. PAGE 28 STRUCT
G0542 INDUS
NAT/G

B65
JENKS C.W.,SPACE LAW. DIPLOM DEBATE CONTROL SPACE
ORD/FREE TREATY 20 UN. PAGE 29 G0563 INT/LAW
JURID
INT/ORG

B65
LUTZ V.,FRENCH PLANNING. FRANCE TEC/DEV RIGID/FLEX PLAN
ORD/FREE 20. PAGE 34 G0680 ADMIN
FUT

B65
MCGUIRE M.C.,SECRECY AND THE ARMS RACE* A THEORY OF DETER
THE ACCUMULATION OF STRATEGIC WEAPONS AND HOW ARMS/CONT
SECRECY AFFECTS IT. DIPLOM NUC/PWR WEAPON ISOLAT SIMUL
RATIONAL ORD/FREE WEALTH...ECOMETRIC MATH GEN/LAWS. GAME
PAGE 38 G0742

B65
PYE L.W.,POLITICAL CULTURE AND DEVELOPMENT. WOR+45 PHIL/SCI
WOR-45 CULTURE ECO/UNDEV NAT/G ALL/VALS ORD/FREE TEC/DEV
PWR WEALTH ALL/IDEOS...TRADIT TREND 20. PAGE 46 SOCIETY
G0897

B65
SMITH E.A.,SOCIAL WELFARE: PRINCIPLES AND CONCEPTS. CONCPT
STRATA STRUCT CONSULT WORKER ACT/RES CREATE PLAN SOC/WK
TEC/DEV ROUTINE GP/REL UTOPIA...SOC 20. PAGE 51 RECEIVE
G1014 ORD/FREE

B65
THAYER F.C. JR.,AIR TRANSPORT POLICY AND NATIONAL AIR
SECURITY: A POLITICAL, ECONOMIC, AND MILITARY FORCES
ANALYSIS. DIST/IND OP/RES PLAN TEC/DEV DIPLOM DETER CIVMIL/REL
WAR COST EFFICIENCY...POLICY BIBLIOG 20 DEPT/DEFEN ORD/FREE
FAA CAB. PAGE 54 G1066

B65
US DEPARTMENT OF ARMY,MILITARY PROTECTIVE FORCES
CONSTRUCTION: NUCLEAR WARFARE AND CHEMICAL AND CONSTRUC
BIOLOGICAL OPERATIONS (MANUAL). OP/RES TEC/DEV RISK TASK
COERCE NUC/PWR WAR WEAPON EFFICIENCY UTIL BIO/SOC HEALTH
HABITAT ORD/FREE 20. PAGE 57 G1117

S65
BIRNBAUM K.,"SWEDEN'S NUCLEAR POLICY." WOR+45 SWEDEN
POL/PAR CREATE TEC/DEV NEUTRAL RISK WAR ORD/FREE NUC/PWR
...DECISION IDEA/COMP NAT/COMP TIME. PAGE 7 G0137 DIPLOM
ARMS/CONT

S65
RUBINSTEIN A.Z.,"POLITICAL BARRIERS TO COM
DISARMAMENT." FUT DIPLOM COERCE NUC/PWR WAR USA+45
NAT/LISM ORD/FREE PREDICT. PAGE 48 G0944 ARMS/CONT
ATTIT

S65
STAAR R.F.,"RETROGRESSION IN POLAND." COM USSR AGRI TOP/EX
INDUS NAT/G CREATE EDU/PROP TOTALISM RIGID/FLEX ECO/TAC
ORD/FREE PWR SOCISM...RECORD CHARTS 20. PAGE 52 POLAND
G1029

B66
ALI S.,PLANNING, DEVELOPMENT AND CHANGE: AN BIBLIOG/A
ANNOTATED BIBLIOGRAPHY ON DEVELOPMENTAL ADMIN
ADMINISTRATION. PAKISTAN SOCIETY ORD/FREE 20. ECO/UNDEV
PAGE 2 G0041 PLAN

B66
BEATON L.,MUST THE BOMB SPREAD? WOR+45 TEC/DEV NUC/PWR
DIPLOM DRIVE ORD/FREE PWR...CHARTS 20. PAGE 6 G0109 ARMS/CONT
PLAN
PROB/SOLV

B66
BOWEN H.R.,AUTOMATION AND ECONOMIC PROGRESS. AUTOMAT
EUR+WWI USA+45 ECO/DEV INCOME ORD/FREE WEALTH TEC/DEV
...POLICY ANTHOL 20. PAGE 8 G0160 WORKER
LEISURE

B66
FREIDEL F.,AMERICAN ISSUES IN THE TWENTIETH DIPLOM
CENTURY. SOCIETY FINAN ECO/TAC FOR/AID CONTROL POLICY
NUC/PWR WAR RACE/REL PEACE ATTIT...ANTHOL T 20 NAT/G
WILSON/W ROOSEVLT/F KENNEDY/JF TRUMAN/HS. PAGE 20 ORD/FREE
G0391

B66
JACOBSON H.K.,DIPLOMATS, SCIENTISTS, AND DIPLOM
POLITICIANS* THE UNITED STATES AND THE NUCLEAR TEST ARMS/CONT
BAN NEGOTIATIONS. USA+45 USSR ACT/RES PLAN CONFER TECHRACY
DETER NUC/PWR CONSEN ORD/FREE...INT TREATY. PAGE 28 INT/ORG
G0554

B66
US HOUSE COMM GOVT OPERATIONS,THE COMPUTER AND ORD/FREE
INVASION OF PRIVACY. USA+45 SOCIETY ALL/VALS...PSY COMPUTER
SOC CHARTS HOUSE/REP PRIVACY. PAGE 58 G1140 TEC/DEV
NAT/G

L66
ZOPPO C.E.,"NUCLEAR TECHNOLOGY, MULTIPOLARITY, AND NET/THEORY
INTERNATIONAL STABILITY." ASIA RUSSIA USA+45 STRUCT ORD/FREE
TOP/EX BAL/PWR DIPLOM DETER CIVMIL/REL NAT/COMP. DECISION
PAGE 65 G1270 NUC/PWR

S66
BROWNLIE I.,"NUCLEAR PROLIFERATION* SOME PROBLEMS NUC/PWR
OF CONTROL." USA+45 USSR ECO/UNDEV INT/ORG FORCES ARMS/CONT
TEC/DEV REGION CONSEN...RECORD TREATY. PAGE 9 G0181 VOL/ASSN
ORD/FREE

B67
DE BLIJ H.J.,SYSTEMATIC POLITICAL GEOGRAPHY. WOR+45 GEOG
STRUCT INT/ORG NAT/G EDU/PROP ADMIN COLONIAL CONCPT
ROUTINE ORD/FREE PWR...IDEA/COMP T 20. PAGE 15 METH
G0283

B67
HALLE L.J.,THE COLD WAR AS HISTORY. USSR WOR+45 DIPLOM
ECO/TAC FOR/AID NUC/PWR WAR PEACE ORD/FREE BAL/PWR
...MAJORIT TREND 20 COLD/WAR KENNEDY/JF KHRUSH/N
BERLIN/BLO. PAGE 24 G0470

B67
KINTNER W.R.,PEACE AND THE STRATEGY CONFLICT. PLAN ROLE
BAL/PWR DIPLOM CONTROL ARMS/CONT DETER WEAPON 20. PEACE
PAGE 30 G0599 NUC/PWR
ORD/FREE

B67
LERNER D.,COMMUNICATION AND CHANGE IN DEVELOPING EDU/PROP
COUNTRIES. CHINA/COM INDIA PHILIPPINE COM/IND ORD/FREE
CREATE TEC/DEV...ANTHOL 20. PAGE 33 G0659 PERCEPT
ECO/UNDEV

B67
POMEROY W.J.,HALF A CENTURY OF SOCIALISM. USSR LAW SOCISM
AGRI INDUS NAT/G CREATE DIPLOM EDU/PROP PERSON MARXISM
ORD/FREE WEALTH...POLICY TREND 20. PAGE 45 G0884 COM
SOCIETY

B67
US DEPARTMENT OF THE ARMY,CIVILIAN IN PEACE, BIBLIOG/A
SOLDIER IN WAR: A BIBLIOGRAPHIC SURVEY OF THE ARMY FORCES
AND AIR NATIONAL GUARD (PAMPHLET, NOS. 130-2). ROLE
USA+45 USA-45 LOC/G NAT/G PROVS LEGIS PLAN ADMIN DIPLOM
ATTIT ORD/FREE...POLICY 19/20. PAGE 58 G1134

B67
US SENATE COMM AERO SPACE SCI,TREATY ON PRINCIPLES SPACE
GOVERNING ACTIVITIES OF STATES IN EXPLORATION AND INT/LAW
USE OF OUTER SPACE, INCLUDING...BODIES. DELIB/GP ORD/FREE
FORCES LEGIS DIPLOM...JURID 20 DEPT/STATE NASA PEACE
DEPT/DEFEN UN. PAGE 60 G1170

B67
US SENATE COMM ON FOREIGN REL,UNITED STATES ARMS/CONT
ARMAMENT AND DISARMAMENT PROBLEMS. USA+45 AIR WEAPON
BAL/PWR DIPLOM FOR/AID NUC/PWR ORD/FREE SENATE FORCES
TREATY. PAGE 60 G1184 PROB/SOLV

L67
BARRON J.A.,"ACCESS TO THE PRESS." USA+45 TEC/DEV ORD/FREE
PRESS TV ADJUD AUD/VIS. PAGE 5 G0099 COM/IND
EDU/PROP
LAW

S67
ALEXANDER L.,"PROTECTION OF PRIVACY IN BEHAVIORAL ACT/RES
RESEARCH." WOR+45 ADJUD SANCTION ORD/FREE...JURID POLICY
INT. PAGE 2 G0036 OBS/ENVIR

S67
D'AMATO D.,"LEGAL ASPECTS OF THE FRENCH NUCLEAR INT/LAW
TESTS." FRANCE WOR+45 ACT/RES COLONIAL RISK GOV/REL DIPLOM
EQUILIB ORD/FREE PWR DECISION. PAGE 14 G0268 NUC/PWR
ADJUD

S67
DE NEUFVILLE R.,"EDUCATION AT THE ACADEMIES." FORCES
USA+45 ELITES CONSULT EX/STRUC COMPUTER PLAN ACADEM
PROB/SOLV TASK CIVMIL/REL ORD/FREE 20. PAGE 15 TEC/DEV

G0286   SKILL

S67

FOREIGN POLICY ASSOCIATION.."US CONCERN FOR WORLD   INT/LAW
LAW." USA+45 WOR+45 DELIB/GP JUDGE BAL/PWR CONFER   INT/ORG
PEACE ORD/FREE 20 UN. PAGE 19 G0379   DIPLOM
                                                      ARMS/CONT

S67

GOLDSTEIN W.."THE SCIENCE ESTABLISHMENT AND ITS   CREATE
POLITICAL CONTROL." WOR+45 SOCIETY GP/REL RATIONAL   ADJUST
ORD/FREE. PAGE 22 G0430   CONTROL

S67

JACKSON W.G.F.."NUCLEAR PROLIFERATION AND THE GREAT   NUC/PWR
POWERS." FUT UK WOR+45 INT/ORG DOMIN ARMS/CONT   ATTIT
DETER ORD/FREE PACIFIST. PAGE 28 G0550   BAL/PWR
                                                      NAT/LISM

S67

JOHNSTON D.M.."LAW, TECHNOLOGY AND THE SEA." WOR+45   INT/LAW
PLAN PROB/SOLV TEC/DEV CONFER ADJUD ORD/FREE   INT/ORG
...POLICY JURID. PAGE 29 G0564   DIPLOM
                                                      NEUTRAL

S67

KAHN H.."CRITERIA FOR LONG-RANGE NUCLEAR CONTROL   NUC/PWR
POLICIES." WOR+45 INT/ORG TEC/DEV DOMIN DETER WAR   ARMS/CONT
WEAPON ISOLAT ORD/FREE POLICY. PAGE 29 G0571   BAL/PWR
                                                      DIPLOM

S67

KRUSCHE H.."THE STRIVING OF THE KIESINGER-STRAUS   ARMS/CONT
GOVERNMENT FOR NUCLEAR WEAPONS IS A THREAT TO   INT/ORG
EUROPEAN SECURITY." EUR+WWI GERMANY BAL/PWR   NUC/PWR
SANCTION WEAPON PEACE ORD/FREE...MARXIST 20 NATO   DIPLOM
COLD/WAR. PAGE 32 G0623

S67

ROMANIECKI L.."THE ATOM AND INTERNATIONAL   INT/ORG
COOPERATION." PROB/SOLV DIPLOM PEACE ORD/FREE 20.   NUC/PWR
PAGE 47 G0933   ARMS/CONT
                                                      CONTROL

S67

TELLER E.."PLANNING FOR PEACE." CHINA/COM WOR+45   ARMS/CONT
DELIB/GP TEC/DEV RISK COERCE DETER WAR ATTIT   NUC/PWR
ORD/FREE 20 NATO. PAGE 54 G1061   PEACE
                                                      DOMIN

B91

RENAN E..THE FUTURE OF SCIENCE. WAR ORD/FREE WEALTH   PHIL/SCI
...GOV/COMP IDEA/COMP GEN/LAWS 19. PAGE 46 G0913   KNOWL
                                                      SECT
                                                      PREDICT

ORDER....SEE ORD/FREE

OREGON....OREGON

ORG FOR ECO COOP AND DEVEL G0843

ORG/CHARTS....ORGANIZATIONAL CHARTS, BLUEPRINTS

ORGANIZATION AMERICAN STATES G0844

ORGANIZATION FOR AFRICAN UNITY....SEE OAU

ORGANIZATION FOR ECONOMIC COOPERATION AND DEVELOPMENT....
    SEE OECD

ORGANIZATION FOR EUROPEAN ECONOMIC COOPERATION....SEE OEEC

ORGANIZATION FOR LATIN AMERICAN SOLIDARITY....SEE OLAS

ORGANIZATION OF AFRICAN STATES.... SEE AFR/STATES

ORGANIZATION OF AMERICAN STATES....SEE OAS

ORGANIZATION, INTERNATIONAL....SEE INT/ORG

ORGANIZATION, LABOR....SEE LABOR

ORGANIZATION, POLITICAL....SEE POL/PAR

ORGANIZATION, PROFESSIONAL....SEE PROF/ORG

ORGANIZATION, VOLUNTARY....SEE VOL/ASSN

ORGANIZATIONAL BEHAVIOR, NONEXECUTIVE....SEE ADMIN

ORGANIZATIONAL CHARTS....SEE ORG/CHARTS

ORLANS H. G0845

ORTEGA Y GASSET J. G0846

ORTH C.D. G0532,G0847

ORTHO/GK....GREEK ORTHODOX CHURCH

ORTHO/RUSS....RUSSIAN ORTHODOX CATHOLIC

ORTHODOX EASTERN CHURCH....SEE ORTHO/GK

ORWELL/G....GEORGE ORWELL

OSGOOD C.E. G0848,G0849

OSGOOD R.E. G1255

OSHOGBO....OSHOGBO, WEST AFRICA

OSSENBECK F.J. G0850

OTTOMAN....OTTOMAN EMPIRE

OTTOSON H.W. G0851

OUTER SPACE....SEE SPACE

OUTER/MONG....OUTER MONGOLIA

OVERSEAS DEVELOPMENT INSTITUTE....SEE OVRSEA/DEV

OVERSEAS DEVELOPMENT INSTIT G0852

OVIMBUNDU....OVIMBUNDU PEOPLES OF ANGOLA

OVRSEA/DEV....OVERSEAS DEVELOPMENT INSTITUTE

OWEN/RBT....ROBERT OWEN

OWI....OFFICE OF WAR INFORMATION

OWN....OWNERSHIP, OWNER

N19

ATOMIC INDUSTRIAL FORUM,COMMENTARY ON LEGISLATION   NUC/PWR
TO PERMIT PRIVATE OWNERSHIP OF SPECIAL NUCLEAR   MARKET
MATERIAL (PAMPHLET). USA+45 DELIB/GP LEGIS PLAN OWN   INDUS
...POLICY 20 AEC CONGRESS. PAGE 4 G0076   LAW

N19

LAWRENCE S.A..THE BATTERY ADDITIVE CONTROVERSY   PHIL/SCI
(PAMPHLET). USA+45 LAW MARKET PROC/MFG R+D CAP/ISM   LOBBY
CT/SYS GOV/REL OWN FTC CONGRESS BUR/STNDRD   INSPECT
RITCHIE/JM. PAGE 33 G0645

B61

LAHAYE R..LES ENTREPRISES PUBLIQUES AU MAROC.   NAT/G
FRANCE MOROCCO LAW DIST/IND EXTR/IND FINAN CONSULT   INDUS
PLAN TEC/DEV ADMIN AGREE CONTROL OWN...POLICY 20.   ECO/UNDEV
PAGE 32 G0629   ECO/TAC

B62

US CONGRESS,COMMUNICATIONS SATELLITE LEGISLATION: SPACE
HEARINGS BEFORE COMM ON AERON AND SPACE SCIENCES ON   COM/IND
BILLS S2550 AND 2814. WOR+45 LAW VOL/ASSN PLAN   ADJUD
DIPLOM CONTROL OWN PEACE...NEW/IDEA CONGRESS NASA.   GOV/REL
PAGE 56 G1110

B64

BLOUSTEIN E.J..NUCLEAR ENERGY, PUBLIC POLICY, AND   TEC/DEV
THE LAW. USA+45 NAT/G ADJUD ADMIN GP/REL OWN PEACE   LAW
ATTIT HEALTH...ANTHOL 20. PAGE 7 G0144   POLICY
                                                      NUC/PWR

B66

GRUNEWALD D..PUBLIC POLICY AND THE MODERN   LG/CO
COOPERATION: SELECTED READINGS. USA+45 LAW MARKET   POLICY
VOL/ASSN CAP/ISM INT/TRADE CENTRAL OWN...SOC ANTHOL   NAT/G
20. PAGE 23 G0458   CONTROL

S67

AVTORKHANOV A.."A NEW AGRARIAN REVOLUTION." COM   AGRI
USSR ECO/DEV PLAN TEC/DEV ADMIN CONTROL OPTIMAL   METH/COMP
WEALTH SOCISM 20 KHRUSH/N STALIN/J. PAGE 4 G0082   MARXISM
                                                      OWN

S67

CARR E.H.."REVOLUTION FROM ABOVE." USSR STRATA   AGRI
FINAN INDUS NAT/G DOMIN LEAD GP/REL INGP/REL OWN   POLICY
PRODUC PWR 20 STALIN/J. PAGE 11 G0214   COM
                                                      EFFICIENCY

S67

RAMSEY J.A.."THE STATUS OF INTERNATIONAL   INT/LAW
COPYRIGHTS." WOR+45 CREATE TEC/DEV DIPLOM CONFER   INT/ORG
CONTROL SANCTION OWN...POLICY JURID. PAGE 46 G0899   COM/IND
                                                      PRESS

RICH G.S.,"THE PROPOSED PATENT LEGISLATION* SOME COMMENTS." USA+45 LAW R+D ACT/RES TEC/DEV CONFER EFFICIENCY OWN JURID. PAGE 46 G0916
S67
LICENSE
POLICY
CREATE
CAP/ISM

OXFORD/GRP....OXFORD GROUP

P

PACHTER H.M. G0854

PACIFIC/IS....PACIFIC ISLANDS: US TRUST TERRITORY OF THE PACIFIC ISLANDS - CAROLINE ISLANDS, MARSHALL ISLANDS, AND MARIANA ISLANDS

PACIFISM....SEE ALSO ARMS/CONT, PEACE

EINSTEIN A.,THE WORLD AS I SEE IT. WOR-45 INTELL R+D INT/ORG NAT/G SECT VOL/ASSN FORCES CREATE EDU/PROP LEGIT ARMS/CONT WAR WEAPON NAT/LISM ALL/VALS...POLICY CONCPT 20. PAGE 17 G0337
B34
SOCIETY
PHIL/SCI
DIPLOM
PACIFISM

AMERICAN FRIENDS SERVICE COMM,IN PLACE OF WAR. NAT/G ACT/RES DIPLOM ADMIN NUC/PWR EFFICIENCY ...POLICY 20. PAGE 3 G0053
B67
PEACE
PACIFISM
WAR
DETER

PACIFIST....PACIFIST; SEE ALSO PEACE

GODDARD V.,THE ENIGMA OF MENACE. WOR+45 SECT LEAD NUC/PWR WAR WEAPON CHOOSE PERSON PWR...POLICY PHIL/SCI PACIFIST 20 COLD/WAR. PAGE 22 G0423
B59
PEACE
ARMS/CONT
DIPLOM
ATTIT

JACKSON W.G.F.,"NUCLEAR PROLIFERATION AND THE GREAT POWERS." FUT UK WOR+45 INT/ORG DOMIN ARMS/CONT DETER ORD/FREE PACIFIST. PAGE 28 G0550
S67
NUC/PWR
ATTIT
BAL/PWR
NAT/LISM

PACKENHAM R.A. G0855

PADELFORD N.J. G0140,G0856

PAGE J.A. G0799

PAIN....SEE HEALTH

PAKISTAN....SEE ALSO S/ASIA

"FURTHER READING." INDIA PAKISTAN SECT WAR PEACE ATTIT...POLICY 20. PAGE 1 G0018
S64
BIBLIOG
GP/REL
DIPLOM
NAT/G

ALI S.,PLANNING, DEVELOPMENT AND CHANGE: AN ANNOTATED BIBLIOGRAPHY ON DEVELOPMENTAL ADMINISTRATION. PAKISTAN SOCIETY ORD/FREE 20. PAGE 2 G0041
B66
BIBLIOG/A
ADMIN
ECO/UNDEV
PLAN

US SENATE COMM ON FOREIGN REL,ARMS SALES TO NEAR EAST AND SOUTH ASIAN COUNTRIES. INDIA IRAN PAKISTAN WOR+45 PROC/MFG BAL/PWR DIPLOM...DECISION SENATE. PAGE 60 G1183
B67
WEAPON
FOR/AID
FORCES
POLICY

PAKISTAN/E....EAST PAKISTAN

PALESTINE....PALESTINE (PRE-1948 ISRAEL); SEE ALSO ISRAEL

PAN AFRICAN FREEDOM MOVEMENT....SEE PANAF/FREE

PANAF/FREE....PAN AFRICAN FREEDOM MOVEMENT

PANAFR/ISM....PAN-AFRICANISM

PANAMA CANAL ZONE....SEE PANAMA/CNL

PANAMA....PANAMA

US SUPERINTENDENT OF DOCUMENTS,TRANSPORTATION: HIGHWAYS, ROADS, AND POSTAL SERVICE (PRICE LIST 25). PANAMA USA+45 LAW FORCES DIPLOM ADMIN GOV/REL HEALTH MGT. PAGE 61 G1188
N
BIBLIOG/A
DIST/IND
SERV/IND
NAT/G

PANAMA/CNL....PANAMA CANAL

US CONGRESS JT ATOM ENRGY COMM,PEACEFUL
B65
NUC/PWR

APPLICATIONS OF NUCLEAR EXPLOSIVES: PLOWSHARE, HEARING. USA+45 LEGIS CREATE PLAN PEACE...CHARTS EXHIBIT BIBLIOG CONGRESS PANAMA/CNL. PAGE 57 G1113
DELIB/GP
TEC/DEV
NAT/G

PANAMERICAN UNION G0857

PAN-AFRICANISM....SEE PANAFR/ISM

PANJAB, PANJABI PEOPLE....SEE PUNJAB

PAPUA....PAPUA

PARAGUAY....SEE ALSO L/A+17C

PARANJAPE H.K. G0858

PARETO/V....VILFREDO PARETO

PARIS....PARIS, FRANCE

PARITY....SEE ECO

PARK/R....ROBERT PARK

PARKER/H....HENRY PARKER

PARKFOREST....PARK FOREST, ILLINOIS

PARL/PROC....PARLIAMENTARY PROCESSES; SEE ALSO LEGIS

KNAPP D.C.,"CONGRESSIONAL CONTROL OF AGRICULTURAL CONSERVATION POLICY: A CASE STUDY OF THE APPROPRIATIONS PROCESS." DELIB/GP PLAN PROB/SOLV CONFER PARL/PROC...POLICY INT CONGRESS. PAGE 31 G0607
S56
LEGIS
AGRI
BUDGET
CONTROL

MARCY C.,"THE RESEARCH PROGRAM OF THE SENATE COMMITTEE ON FOREIGN RELATIONS." EUR+WWI ECO/UNDEV ACT/RES PLAN PARL/PROC GOV/REL...GEOG CONFE CONGRESS. PAGE 36 G0704
S58
DELIB/GP
LEGIS
FOR/AID
POLICY

BAUCHET P.,ECONOMIC PLANNING. FRANCE STRATA LG/CO CAP/ISM ADMIN PARL/PROC DEMAND OPTIMAL ATTIT PWR SOCISM...POLICY CHARTS 20. PAGE 5 G0102
B64
ECO/DEV
NAT/G
PLAN
ECO/TAC

PARLIAMENTARY PROCESSES....SEE PARL/PROC

PARLIAMENT....PARLIAMENT (ALL NATIONS); SEE ALSO LEGIS

PARNELL/CS....CHARLES STEWART PARNELL

PAROLE....SEE PUB/INST, ROUTINE, CRIME

PARRY A. G0859

PARSONS/T....TALCOTT PARSONS

PARTH/SASS....PARTHO-SASSANIAN EMPIRE

PARTIC....PARTICIPATION; CIVIC ACTIVITY AND NONACTIVITY

BINGHAM A.M.,THE TECHNIQUES OF DEMOCRACY. USA-45 CONSTN STRUCT POL/PAR LEGIS PLAN PARTIC CHOOSE REPRESENT NAT/LISM TOTALISM...MGT 20. PAGE 7 G0136
B42
POPULISM
ORD/FREE
ADMIN
NAT/G

WHITE L.D.,CIVIL SERVICE IN WARTIME. CONSULT DELIB/GP PARTIC WAR CHOOSE. PAGE 63 G1233
B45
REPRESENT
ADMIN
INTELL
NAT/G

LASSWELL H.D.,"RESEARCH IN POLITICAL BEHAVIOR." LOC/G MUNIC POL/PAR CONSULT ADMIN PARTIC...CHARTS ANTHOL BIBLIOG/A 20. PAGE 32 G0641
L52
PHIL/SCI
METH
R+D

TRUMAN D.B.,"SELECTED CRITICAL BIBLIOGRAPHY ON THE METHODS AND TECHNIQUES OF POLITICAL BEHAVIOR RESEARCH." R+D PARTIC...SOC OBS RECORD INT. PAGE 55 G1079
S52
BIBLIOG/A
ACT/RES
METH/CNCPT

SAYLES L.R.,THE LOCAL UNION. CONSTN CULTURE DELIB/GP PARTIC CHOOSE GP/REL INGP/REL ATTIT ROLE ...MAJORIT DECISION MGT. PAGE 49 G0958
B53
LABOR
LEAD
ADJUD
ROUTINE

ROSE A.M.,THEORY AND METHOD IN THE SOCIAL SCIENCES.
B54
CONCPT

STRATA R+D NEIGH PARTIC...METH/CNCPT GP/COMP.   SOC
PAGE 47 G0934   VOL/ASSN
                                                                ROLE

                                                        S56
MILLER W.E.,"PRESIDENTIAL COATTAILS: A STUDY IN   CHIEF
POLITICAL MYTH AND METHODOLOGY" (BMR)" USA+45   CHOOSE
CREATE PARTIC ATTIT DRIVE PWR...DECISION CONCPT   POL/PAR
CHARTS SIMUL 20 PRESIDENT CONGRESS. PAGE 39 G0774   MYTH

                                                        B58
CROWE S.,THE LANDSCAPE OF POWER. UK CULTURE   HABITAT
SERV/IND NAT/G CONSULT PARTIC NUC/PWR LEISURE...SOC   TEC/DEV
EXHIBIT 20. PAGE 14 G0264   PLAN
                                                                CONTROL

                                                        B58
OGDEN F.D.,THE POLL TAX IN THE SOUTH. USA+45 USA-45   TAX
CONSTN ADJUD ADMIN PARTIC CRIME...TIME/SEQ GOV/COMP   CHOOSE
METH/COMP 18/20 SOUTH/US. PAGE 43 G0838   RACE/REL
                                                                DISCRIM

                                                        S61
LYONS G.M.,"THE NEW CIVIL-MILITARY RELATIONS."   CIVMIL/REL
USA+45 NAT/G EX/STRUC TOP/EX PROB/SOLV ADMIN EXEC   PWR
PARTIC 20. PAGE 35 G0681   REPRESENT

                                                        B62
DODDS H.W.,THE ACADEMIC PRESIDENT "EDUCATOR OR   ACADEM
CARETAKER? FINAN DELIB/GP EDU/PROP PARTIC ATTIT   ADMIN
ROLE PWR...POLICY RECORD INT. PAGE 16 G0304   LEAD
                                                                CONTROL

                                                        S63
BUNDY M.,"THE SCIENTIST AND NATIONAL POLICY."   NAT/G
PROF/ORG PLAN PARTIC POLICY. PAGE 10 G0186   PHIL/SCI
                                                                DECISION

                                                        S64
UNRUH J.M.,"SCIENTIFIC INPUTS TO LEGISLATIVE   CREATE
DECISION-MAKING (SUPPLEMENT)" USA+45 ACADEM NAT/G   DECISION
PROVS GOV/REL GOV/COMP. PAGE 56 G1102   LEGIS
                                                                PARTIC

                                                        S65
LEISERSON A.,"SCIENTISTS AND THE POLICY PROCESS."   PHIL/SCI
USA+45 NAT/G LEAD PARTIC REPRESENT. PAGE 33 G0654   ADMIN
                                                                EX/STRUC
                                                                EXEC

                                                        B66
STREET D.,ORGANIZATION FOR TREATMENT. CLIENT PROVS   GP/COMP
PUB/INST PLAN CONTROL PARTIC REPRESENT ATTIT PWR   AGE/Y
...POLICY BIBLIOG. PAGE 53 G1044   ADMIN
                                                                VOL/ASSN

                                                        B67
ELDREDGE H.W.,TAMING MEGALOPOLIS; HOW TO MANAGE AN   MUNIC
URBANIZED WORLD. USA+45 SOCIETY ECO/DEV ECO/UNDEV   TEC/DEV
NAT/G COMPUTER CREATE PARTIC EFFICIENCY WEALTH   PLAN
...MGT ANTHOL. PAGE 17 G0342   PROB/SOLV

                                                        B67
UNIVERSAL REFERENCE SYSTEM,PUBLIC OPINION, MASS   BIBLIOG/A
BEHAVIOR, AND POLITICAL PSYCHOLOGY (VOLUME VI).   ATTIT
WOR+45 WOR-45 SOCIETY EDU/PROP PRESS PARTIC CHOOSE   CROWD
PERSON...TREND COMPUT/IR GEN/METH. PAGE 56 G1098   PSY

                                                        S67
FRIED M.,"FUNCTIONS OF THE WORKING CLASS COMMUNITY   CLASSIF
IN MODERN URBAN SOCIETY* IMPLICATIONS FOR FORCED   WORKER
RELOCATION." USA+45 INDUS R+D NEIGH PLAN TEC/DEV   MUNIC
PARTIC GP/REL ATTIT...SOC STAT CHARTS. PAGE 20   ADJUST
G0393

                                                        S67
GOBER J.L.,"FEDERALISM AT WORK." USA+45 NAT/G   MUNIC
CONSULT ACT/RES PLAN CONFER ADMIN LEAD PARTIC   TEC/DEV
FEDERAL ATTIT. PAGE 21 G0422   R+D
                                                                GOV/REL

                                                        S67
HABERER J.,"POLITICS AND THE COMMUNITY OF SCIENCE." LEAD
USA+45 SOCIETY ACT/RES PARTIC ATTIT PHIL/SCI.   SUPEGO
PAGE 24 G0465   INTELL
                                                                LOBBY

                                                        S67
KRAUS J.,"A MARXIST IN GHANA." GHANA ELITES CHIEF   MARXISM
PROB/SOLV TEC/DEV DIPLOM ECO/TAC COLONIAL PARTIC   PLAN
PWR 20 NKRUMAH/K. PAGE 31 G0618   ATTIT
                                                                CREATE

PARTIES, POLITICAL....SEE POL/PAR

PARTITION....PARTITIONS AND PARTITIONING - DIVISION OF AN

EXISTING POLITICAL-GEOGRAPHICAL ENTITY INTO TWO OR
MORE AUTONOMOUS ZONES

PASLEY R.S. G0860

PASSPORT....SEE LICENSE, TRAVEL

PATENT....PATENT

PATENT/OFF....U.S. PATENT OFFICE

                                                                N19
DOTSON A.,PRODUCTION PLANNING IN THE PATENT OFFICE   EFFICIENCY
(PAMPHLET). USA+45 DIST/IND PROB/SOLV PRODUC...MGT   PLAN
PHIL/SCI 20 BUR/BUDGET PATENT/OFF. PAGE 16 G0309   NAT/G
                                                                ADMIN

PATHAN....PATHAN PEOPLE (PAKISTAN, AFGHANISTAN)

PATHET/LAO....PATHET LAO

PATRIOTISM....SEE NAT/LISM

PAULING L. G0861

PAULING/L....LINUS PAULING

PAY....EARNINGS; SEE ALSO INCOME

                                                                N19
FOLSOM M.B.,BETTER MANAGEMENT OF THE PUBLIC'S   ADMIN
BUSINESS (PAMPHLET). USA+45 DELIB/GP PAY CONFER   NAT/G
CONTROL REGION GP/REL...METH/COMP ANTHOL 20.   MGT
PAGE 19 G0377   PROB/SOLV

                                                                N19
GINZBERG E.,MANPOWER FOR GOVERNMENT (PAMPHLET).   WORKER
USA+45 PROB/SOLV PAY EDU/PROP ADMIN   CONSULT
GP/REL COST...MGT PREDICT TREND 20 CIVIL/SERV.   NAT/G
PAGE 21 G0418   LOC/G

                                                                B48
METZLER L.A.,INCOME, EMPLOYMENT, AND PUBLIC POLICY.   INCOME
FINAN INDUS LOC/G NAT/G TAX GIVE PAY COST PRODUC   WEALTH
...MGT TIME/SEQ 20. PAGE 38 G0760   POLICY
                                                                ECO/TAC

                                                                B60
LINDVEIT E.N.,SCIENTISTS IN GOVERNMENT. USA+45 PAY   TEC/DEV
EDU/PROP ADMIN DRIVE HABITAT ROLE...TECHNIC BIBLIOG   ECO/TAC
20. PAGE 34 G0670   PHIL/SCI
                                                                GOV/REL

                                                                B64
PARANJAPE H.K.,THE FLIGHT OF TECHNICAL PERSONNEL IN   ADMIN
PUBLIC UNDERTAKINGS. INDIA PAY DEMAND HAPPINESS   NAT/G
ORD/FREE...MGT QU 20 MIGRATION. PAGE 44 G0858   WORKER
                                                                PLAN

                                                                B66
NIEBURG H.L.,IN THE NAME OF SCIENCE. USA+45   NAT/G
EX/STRUC LEGIS TEC/DEV BUDGET PAY AUTOMAT LOBBY PWR   INDUS
...OBS 20. PAGE 42 G0822   TECHRACY

                                                                B67
EISENMENGER R.W.,THE DYNAMICS OF GROWTH IN NEW   ECO/DEV
ENGLAND'S ECONOMY, 1870-1964. USA+45 USA-45 ECO/TAC   AGRI
TAX PAY AUTOMAT GOV/REL ADJUST HABITAT...STAT   INDUS
19/20. PAGE 17 G0340   CAP/ISM

                                                                B67
NORTHRUP H.R.,RESTRICTIVE LABOR PRACTICES IN THE   DIST/IND
SUPERMARKET INDUSTRY. USA+45 INDUS WORKER TEC/DEV   MARKET
BARGAIN PAY CONTROL GP/REL COST...STAT CHARTS NLRB.   LABOR
PAGE 42 G0827   MGT

PEABODY R.L. G0862

PEACE CORPS....SEE PEACE/CORP

PEACE....SEE ALSO ORD/FREE

                                                                B
CURRENT THOUGHT ON PEACE AND WAR. WOR+45 INT/ORG   BIBLIOG/A
FORCES PROB/SOLV DIPLOM NUC/PWR PERCEPT...POLICY   PEACE
SOC 20 UN NATO. PAGE 1 G0001   ATTIT
                                                                WAR

                                                                N
AIR UNIVERSITY LIBRARY,INDEX TO MILITARY   BIBLIOG/A
PERIODICALS. FUT SPACE WOR+45 REGION ARMS/CONT   FORCES
NUC/PWR WAR PEACE INT/LAW. PAGE 2 G0032   NAT/G
                                                                DIPLOM

N19
MEZERIK A.G..INTERNATIONAL POLICY 1965 (PAMPHLET).   DIPLOM
KASHMIR S/ASIA SPACE USA+45 VIETNAM WOR+45   INT/ORG
ARMS/CONT RACE/REL DISCRIM PEACE PWR 20 UN. PAGE 39   POLICY
G0762   WAR

N19
ZLOTNICK M..WEAPONS IN SPACE (PAMPHLET). FUT WOR+45   SPACE
TEC/DEV DIPLOM ARMS/CONT CIVMIL/REL PEACE HABITAT   WEAPON
...CONCPT NEW/IDEA CHARTS. PAGE 65 G1268   NUC/PWR
                                                       WAR

B35
FOREIGN AFFAIRS BIBLIOGRAPHY: A SELECTED AND   BIBLIOG/A
ANNOTATED LIST OF BOOKS ON INTERNATIONAL RELATIONS   DIPLOM
1919-1962 (4 VOLS.). CONSTN FORCES COLONIAL   INT/ORG
ARMS/CONT WAR NAT/LISM PEACE ATTIT DRIVE...POLICY
INT/LAW 20. PAGE 1 G0011

B40
FULLER G.H..SELECTED LIST OF RECENT REFERENCES ON   BIBLIOG
AMERICAN NATIONAL DEFENSE (PAMPHLET). USA-45 FINAN   CIVMIL/REL
NAT/G ARMS/CONT WAR GOV/REL CENTRAL COST PEACE PWR   FORCES
20. PAGE 20 G0400   WEAPON

B41
FULLER G.H..DEFENSE FINANCING: A SELECTED LIST OF   BIBLIOG/A
REFERENCES (PAMPHLET). MOD/EUR USA-45 ECO/DEV NAT/G   FINAN
DELIB/GP RATION ARMS/CONT WEAPON COST PEACE PWR 20   FORCES
CONGRESS. PAGE 20 G0401   BUDGET

B41
FULLER G.H..A LIST OF BIBLIOGRAPHIES ON QUESTIONS   BIBLIOG/A
RELATING TO NATIONAL DEFENSE (PAMPHLET). USA-45   FORCES
NAT/G ARMS/CONT WAR GOV/REL COST PEACE 20. PAGE 20   CIVMIL/REL
G0402   WEAPON

B42
FULLER G.H..DEFENSE FINANCING: A SUPPLEMENTARY LIST   BIBLIOG/A
OF REFERENCES (PAMPHLET). CANADA UK USA-45 ECO/DEV   FINAN
NAT/G DELIB/GP BUDGET ADJUD ARMS/CONT WEAPON COST   FORCES
PEACE PWR 20 AUSTRAL CHINJAP CONGRESS. PAGE 21   DIPLOM
G0403

B44
MATTHEWS M.A..INTERNATIONAL POLICE (PAMPHLET).   BIBLIOG
WOR-45 DIPLOM ARMS/CONT WAR 20. PAGE 37 G0722   INT/ORG
                                                       FORCES
                                                       PEACE

B45
BAKER H..PROBLEMS OF REEMPLOYMENT AND RETRAINING OF   BIBLIOG/A
MANPOWER DURING THE TRANSITION FROM WAR TO PEACE.   ADJUST
USA+45 INDUS LABOR LG/CO NAT/G PLAN ADMIN PEACE   WAR
...POLICY MGT 20. PAGE 5 G0086   PROB/SOLV

B45
BUSH V..SCIENCE, THE ENDLESS FRONTIER. FUT USA-45   R+D
INTELL STRATA ACT/RES CREATE PLAN EDU/PROP ADMIN   NAT/G
NUC/PWR PEACE ATTIT HEALTH KNOWL...MAJORIT HEAL MGT
PHIL/SCI CONCPT OBS TREND 20. PAGE 10 G0195

B45
REVES E..THE ANATOMY OF PEACE. WOR-45 LAW CULTURE   ACT/RES
NAT/G PLAN TEC/DEV EDU/PROP WAR NAT/LISM ATTIT   CONCPT
ALL/VALS SOVEREIGN...POLICY HUM TIME/SEQ 20.   NUC/PWR
PAGE 46 G0914   PEACE

B46
BUSH V..ENDLESS HORIZONS. FUT USA-45 INTELL NAT/G   R+D
CONSULT ACT/RES CREATE PLAN EDU/PROP DRIVE   KNOWL
...MAJORIT HEAL MGT PHIL/SCI CONCPT OBS TREND   PEACE
GEN/METH TOT/POP 20. PAGE 10 G0196

B46
MORGENTHAU H.J..SCIENTIFIC MAN VS POWER POLITICS.   UNIV
USA+45 WOR+45 INTELL SOCIETY ACT/RES CREATE PLAN   MORAL
EDU/PROP...CONCPT TREND TOT/POP 20. PAGE 40 G0782   PEACE

B46
NORTHROP F.S.C..THE MEETING OF EAST AND WEST.   DRIVE
EUR+WWI FUT MOD/EUR UNIV WOR+45 WOR-45 INTELL   TREND
SOCIETY EX/STRUC TOP/EX ACT/RES LEGIT CHOOSE ATTIT   PEACE
PERCEPT RIGID/FLEX ALL/VALS...POLICY JURID OBS
TOT/POP. PAGE 42 G0826

B48
BRADLEY D..NO PLACE TO HIDE. USA+45 SOCIETY NAT/G   R+D
FORCES TEC/DEV EDU/PROP DETER PEACE BIO/SOC   LAB/EXP
ALL/VALS...POLICY PHIL/SCI OBS RECORD SAMP BIOG   ARMS/CONT
GEN/METH COLD/WAR 20. PAGE 8 G0162   NUC/PWR

S49
SOUERS S.W.."POLICY FORMULATION FOR NATIONAL   DELIB/GP
SECURITY." EX/STRUC FORCES PROB/SOLV DIPLOM CONFER   CHIEF
EXEC ARMS/CONT DETER NUC/PWR GOV/REL PEACE   DECISION

COLD/WAR. PAGE 52 G1022   POLICY

B50
CANTRIL H..TENSIONS THAT CAUSE WAR. UNIV CULTURE   SOCIETY
R+D CREATE EDU/PROP DRIVE PERSON KNOWL ORD/FREE   PHIL/SCI
...HUM PSY SOC OBS CENSUS TREND CON/ANAL SOC/EXP   PEACE
SIMUL GEN/METH ANTHOL COLD/WAR TOT/POP. PAGE 11
G0206

B50
US DEPARTMENT OF STATE,POINT FOUR: COOPERATIVE   ECO/UNDEV
PROGRAM FOR AID IN THE DEVELOPMENT OF ECONOMICALLY   FOR/AID
UNDERDEVELOPED AREAS. WOR+45 AGRI INDUS INT/ORG   FINAN
PLAN TEC/DEV DIPLOM EDU/PROP ADMIN PEACE PRODUC   INT/TRADE
WEALTH 20 CONGRESS UN. PAGE 57 G1121

S53
CORY R.H. JR.."FORGING A PUBLIC INFORMATION POLICY   INT/ORG
FOR THE UNITED NATIONS." FUT WOR+45 SOCIETY ADMIN   EDU/PROP
PEACE ATTIT PERSON SKILL...CONCPT 20 UN. PAGE 13   BAL/PWR
G0257

B54
ARON R..CENTURY OF TOTAL WAR. FUT WOR+45 WOR-45   ATTIT
SOCIETY INT/ORG NAT/G FORCES TOP/EX CREATE BAL/PWR   WAR
DOMIN EDU/PROP COERCE DETER PEACE TOTALISM PWR
...TIME/SEQ TREND COLD/WAR TOT/POP VAL/FREE
LEAGUE/NAT 20. PAGE 4 G0066

B54
BUTOW R.J.C..JAPAN'S DECISION TO SURRENDER. USA-45   ELITES
USSR CHIEF FORCES DOMIN NUC/PWR...BIBLIOG 20 TREATY   DIPLOM
CHINJAP. PAGE 10 G0198   WAR
                                                       PEACE

B54
WRIGHT Q..PROBLEMS OF STABILITY AND PROGRESS IN   INT/ORG
INTERNATIONAL RELATIONSHIPS. FUT WOR+45 WOR-45   CONCPT
SOCIETY LEGIS CREATE TEC/DEV ECO/TAC EDU/PROP ADJUD   DIPLOM
WAR PEACE ORD/FREE PWR...KNO/TEST TREND GEN/LAWS
20. PAGE 64 G1257

B55
SHUBIK M..READINGS IN GAME THEORY AND POLITICAL   MATH
BEHAVIOR. WOR+45 FORCES CREATE ROUTINE WAR PEACE   DECISION
PERCEPT KNOWL PWR...PSY SOC CONCPT METH/CNCPT STAT   DIPLOM
CHARTS HYPO/EXP GAME METH VAL/FREE 20. PAGE 50
G0991

S55
ANGELL R.."GOVERNMENTS AND PEOPLES AS A FOCI FOR   FUT
PEACE-ORIENTED RESEARCH." WOR+45 CULTURE SOCIETY   SOC
FACE/GP ACT/RES CREATE PLAN DIPLOM EDU/PROP ROUTINE   PEACE
ATTIT PERCEPT SKILL...POLICY CONCPT OBS TREND
GEN/METH 20. PAGE 3 G0060

S55
WRIGHT Q.."THE PEACEFUL ADJUSTMENT OF INTERNATIONAL   R+D
RELATIONS: PROBLEMS AND RESEARCH APPROACHES." UNIV   METH/CNCPT
INTELL EDU/PROP ADJUD ROUTINE KNOWL SKILL...INT/LAW   PEACE
JURID PHIL/SCI CLASSIF 20. PAGE 64 G1258

B56
KOENIG L.W..THE TRUMAN ADMINISTRATION: ITS   ADMIN
PRINCIPLES AND PRACTICE. USA+45 POL/PAR CHIEF LEGIS   POLICY
DIPLOM DEATH NUC/PWR WAR CIVMIL/REL PEACE   EX/STRUC
...DECISION 20 TRUMAN/HS PRESIDENT TREATY. PAGE 31   GOV/REL
G0610

S57
MORTON L.."THE DECISION TO USE THE BOMB." FORCES   NUC/PWR
TOP/EX DOMIN COERCE PEACE. PAGE 40 G0788   DIPLOM
                                                       WAR

B58
ANGELL N..DEFENCE AND THE ENGLISH-SPEAKING ROLE.   DIPLOM
CHINA/COM UK USSR INT/ORG FORCES EDU/PROP NEUTRAL   WAR
NUC/PWR NAT/LISM PEACE TOTALISM 20 COLD/WAR   MARXISM
COEXIST. PAGE 3 G0059   ORD/FREE

B58
ATOMIC INDUSTRIAL FORUM,MANAGEMENT AND ATOMIC   NUC/PWR
ENERGY. WOR+45 SEA LAW MARKET NAT/G TEC/DEV INSPECT   INDUS
INT/TRADE CONFER PEACE HEALTH...ANTHOL 20. PAGE 4   MGT
G0078   ECO/TAC

B58
BIDWELL P.W..RAW MATERIALS: A STUDY OF AMERICAN   EXTR/IND
POLICY. USA+45 USA-45 ECO/UNDEV AGRI INDUS KIN   ECO/DEV
CREATE PLAN ECO/TAC WAR PEACE ATTIT DRIVE WEALTH
...STAT CHARTS CONGRESS VAL/FREE. PAGE 7 G0135

B58
GAVIN J.M..WAR AND PEACE IN THE SPACE AGE. SPACE   WAR
USA+45 USSR FORCES PLAN TEC/DEV BAL/PWR DIPLOM   DETER
ARMS/CONT WEAPON CIVMIL/REL...CHARTS GP/COMP 20   NUC/PWR

NATO COLD/WAR. PAGE 21 G0414

PEACE

B58
NOEL-BAKER D.,THE ARMS RACE. WOR+45 NAT/G DELIB/GP FUT
ACT/RES TEC/DEV EDU/PROP NUC/PWR ATTIT KNOWL PWR INT/ORG
...CONCPT OBS LEAGUE/NAT 20 COLD/WAR. PAGE 42 G0823 ARMS/CONT
PEACE

B58
ROCKEFELLER BROTH FUND INC,INTERNATIONAL SECURITY - NUC/PWR
THE MILITARY ASPECT. USA+45 INT/ORG NAT/G BUDGET DETER
ARMS/CONT WAR WEAPON PEACE ORD/FREE 20 NATO. FORCES
PAGE 47 G0932 DIPLOM

B58
UN INTL CONF ON PEACEFUL USE,PROGRESS IN ATOMIC NUC/PWR
ENERGY (VOL. I). WOR+45 R+D PLAN TEC/DEV CONFER DIPLOM
CONTROL PEACE SKILL...CHARTS ANTHOL 20 UN BAGHDAD. WORKER
PAGE 55 G1088 EDU/PROP

B58
US DEPARTMENT OF THE ARMY,BIBLIOGRAPHY ON LIMITED BIBLIOG/A
WAR (PAMPHLET). USA+45 TEC/DEV CONTROL RISK COERCE WAR
DETER NUC/PWR WEAPON ADJUST PEACE ALL/VALS ORD/FREE FORCES
20. PAGE 57 G1127 CIVMIL/REL

B59
ATOMIC INDUSTRIAL FORUM,THE IMPACT OF THE PEACEFUL PROVS
USES OF ATOMIC ENERGY ON STATE AND LOCAL LOC/G
GOVERNMENT. USA+45 INDUS NAT/G LEGIS PLAN CONTROL NUC/PWR
GOV/REL. PAGE 4 G0079 PEACE

B59
EMME E.M.,THE IMPACT OF AIR POWER - NATIONAL DETER
SECURITY AND WORLD POLITICS. USA+45 USSR FORCES AIR
DIPLOM WEAPON PEACE TOTALISM...POLICY NAT/COMP 20 WAR
EUROPE. PAGE 18 G0346 ORD/FREE

B59
GODDARD V.,THE ENIGMA OF MENACE. WOR+45 SECT LEAD PEACE
NUC/PWR WAR WEAPON CHOOSE PERSON PWR...POLICY ARMS/CONT
PHIL/SCI PACIFIST 20 COLD/WAR. PAGE 22 G0423 DIPLOM
ATTIT

B59
LANG D.,FROM HIROSHIMA TO THE MOON: CHRONICLES OF NUC/PWR
LIFE IN THE ATOMIC AGE. USA+45 OP/RES CONTROL SPACE
ARMS/CONT WAR CIVMIL/REL PEACE HABITAT MORAL PWR HEALTH
...OBS INT 20 AEC. PAGE 32 G0633 TEC/DEV

B59
STANFORD RESEARCH INSTITUTE,POSSIBLE NONMILITARY R+D
SCIENTIFIC DEVELOPMENTS AND THEIR POTENTIAL IMPACT TEC/DEV
ON FOREIGN POLICY PROBLEMS OF THE UNITED. FUT
USA+45 INT/ORG PROF/ORG CONSULT ACT/RES CREATE PLAN
PEACE KNOWL SKILL...TECHNIC PHIL/SCI NEW/IDEA
UNESCO 20. PAGE 52 G1032

B59
VAN WAGENEN R.W.,SOME VIEWS OF AMERICAN DEFENSE INT/ORG
OFFICIALS ABOUT THE UNITED NATIONS (PAPER). FUT LEAD
USA+45 NAT/G DIPLOM WAR EFFICIENCY PEACE...POLICY ATTIT
INT 20 UN DEPT/DEFEN. PAGE 61 G1192 FORCES

S59
WILLIAMS B.H.,"SCIENTIFIC METHOD IN FOREIGN PLAN
POLICY." WOR+45 NAT/G FORCES TOP/EX DOMIN LEGIT PHIL/SCI
COERCE PEACE ATTIT KNOWL ORD/FREE PWR...GEN/LAWS DIPLOM
GEN/METH TOT/POP COLD/WAR NAZI. PAGE 63 G1241

B60
ARMS CONTROL. FUT UNIV WOR+45 INTELL R+D INT/ORG DELIB/GP
NAT/G VOL/ASSN CONSULT CREATE EDU/PROP PEACE...HUM ORD/FREE
GEN/LAWS TOT/POP 20. PAGE 1 G0015 ARMS/CONT
NUC/PWR

B60
APTHEKER H.,DISARMAMENT AND THE AMERICAN ECONOMY: A MARXIST
SYMPOSIUM. FUT USA+45 ECO/DEV DIST/IND FINAN INDUS ARMS/CONT
PROC/MFG LABOR NAT/G POL/PAR CONSULT PLAN CAP/ISM
INT/TRADE PEACE ATTIT MORAL WEALTH...TREND GEN/LAWS
TOT/POP 20. PAGE 3 G0063

B60
CHASE S.,LIVE AND LET LIVE. USA+45 ECO/DEV NAT/G
PROB/SOLV TEC/DEV ECO/TAC ARMS/CONT NUC/PWR WAR DIPLOM
NAT/LISM PEACE...GEOG TREND 20 COLD/WAR. PAGE 11 SOCIETY
G0223 TASK

B60
EINSTEIN A.,EINSTEIN ON PEACE. FUT WOR+45 WOR-45 INT/ORG
SOCIETY NAT/G PLAN BAL/PWR CAP/ISM DIPLOM ARMS/CONT ATTIT
DETER NAT/LISM...POLICY RELATIV HUM PHIL/SCI CONCPT NUC/PWR
BIOG COLD/WAR LEAGUE/NAT NAZI. PAGE 17 G0338 PEACE

B60
MCKINNEY R.,REVIEW OF THE INTERNATIONAL ATOMIC NUC/PWR
POLICIES AND PROGRAMS OF THE UNITED STATES (5 PEACE
VOLS.). COM FUT USA+45 ECO/DEV ECO/UNDEV INT/ORG DIPLOM
DELIB/GP PLAN ADMIN 20 THIRD/WRLD. PAGE 38 G0744 POLICY

B60
US DEPARTMENT OF THE ARMY,DISARMAMENT: A BIBLIOG/A
BIBLIOGRAPHIC RECORD: 1916-1960. DETER WAR WEAPON ARMS/CONT
PEACE 20 UN LEAGUE/NAT COLD/WAR NATO. PAGE 57 G1128 NUC/PWR
DIPLOM

S60
HAYTON R.D.,"THE ANTARCTIC SETTLEMENT OF 1959." FUT DELIB/GP
USA+45 WOR+45 WOR-45 STRUCT R+D INT/ORG EX/STRUC JURID
CREATE TEC/DEV LEGIT PEACE ATTIT SOVEREIGN DIPLOM
...TIME/SEQ 20 TREATY IGY. PAGE 25 G0495 REGION

S60
LEAR J.,"PEACE: SCIENCE'S NEXT GREAT EXPLORATION." EX/STRUC
USA+45 INT/ORG TOP/EX TEC/DEV EDU/PROP ROUTINE ARMS/CONT
PEACE KNOWL SKILL 20. PAGE 33 G0648 NUC/PWR

B61
MICHAEL D.N.,PROPOSED STUDIES ON THE IMPLICATIONS FUT
OF PEACEFUL SPACE ACTIVITIES FOR HUMAN AFFAIRS. SPACE
COM/IND INDUS FORCES DIPLOM PEACE PERSON...PSY SOC ACT/RES
20. PAGE 39 G0764 PROB/SOLV

B61
NATHAN O.,EINSTEIN ON PEACE. WOR+45 WOR-45 INTELL CONCPT
NUC/PWR WAR PERSON MORAL...BIOG VAL/FREE NAZI 20 PEACE
EINSTEIN/A. PAGE 41 G0807

B61
RAMO S.,PEACETIME USES OF OUTER SPACE. FUT DIST/IND PEACE
INT/ORG CONSULT NUC/PWR...AUD/VIS ANTHOL 20. TEC/DEV
PAGE 46 G0898 SPACE
CREATE

B62
SOVIET STAND ON DISARMAMENT. COM EUR+WWI FUT USA+45 ACT/RES
NAT/G TOP/EX NUC/PWR PEACE ATTIT...POLICY CONCPT ORD/FREE
TOT/POP 20. PAGE 1 G0016 ARMS/CONT
USSR

B62
AIR FORCE ACADEMY LIBRARY,INTERNATIONAL BIBLIOG
ORGANIZATIONS AND MILITARY SECURITY SYSTEMS INT/ORG
(PAMPHLET) (SPECIAL BIBLIOGRAPHY SERIES, NUMBER FORCES
25). DIPLOM FOR/AID INT/TRADE NUC/PWR PEACE 20 UN DETER
NATO OAS SEATO LEAGUE/NAT. PAGE 2 G0031

B62
BOULDING K.E.,CONFLICT AND DEFENSE: A GENERAL MATH
THEORY. FUT SOCIETY INT/ORG NAT/G CREATE BAL/PWR SIMUL
COERCE NAT/LISM DRIVE ALL/VALS...PLURIST DECISION PEACE
CONCPT METH/CNCPT TREND HYPO/EXP TOT/POP 20. PAGE 8 WAR
G0157

B62
DUPRE J.S.,SCIENCE AND THE NATION: POLICY AND R+D
POLITICS. USA+45 LAW ACADEM FORCES ADMIN CIVMIL/REL INDUS
GOV/REL EFFICIENCY PEACE...TREND 20 SCI/ADVSRY. TEC/DEV
PAGE 16 G0322 NUC/PWR

B62
KAHN H.,THINKING ABOUT THE UNTHINKABLE. FUT USA+45 INT/ORG
LAW NAT/G CONSULT FORCES ACT/RES CREATE PLAN ORD/FREE
TEC/DEV BAL/PWR DIPLOM EDU/PROP ARMS/CONT DETER NUC/PWR
ATTIT...CONCPT OBS TREND COLD/WAR 20. PAGE 29 G0570 PEACE

B62
KENNEDY J.F.,TO TURN THE TIDE. SPACE AGRI INT/ORG DIPLOM
FORCES TEC/DEV ADMIN NUC/PWR PEACE WEALTH...ANTHOL CHIEF
20 KENNEDY/JF CIV/RIGHTS. PAGE 30 G0592 POLICY
NAT/G

B62
OSGOOD C.E.,AN ALTERNATIVE TO WAR OR SURRENDER. FUT ORD/FREE
UNIV CULTURE INTELL SOCIETY R+D INT/ORG CONSULT EDU/PROP
DELIB/GP ACT/RES PLAN CHOOSE ATTIT PERCEPT KNOWL PEACE
...PHIL/SCI PSY SOC TREND GEN/LAWS 20. PAGE 43 WAR
G0849

B62
PERRE J.,LES MUTATIONS DE LA GUERRE MODERNE: DE LA WAR
REVOLUTION FRANCAISE A LA REVOLUTION NUCLEAIRE. FORCES
DIPLOM ARMS/CONT DEATH REV WEAPON GP/REL PEACE NUC/PWR
ATTIT...STAT PREDICT BIBLIOG 18/20 WWI. PAGE 44
G0870

B62
SOHN L.B.,ZONAL DISARMAMENT: VARIATIONS ON A THEME. ORD/FREE
FUT WOR+45 SOCIETY ACT/RES PLAN NUC/PWR PEACE ATTIT NEW/IDEA
...POLICY GEOG CONT/OBS HYPO/EXP 20. PAGE 52 G1020 ARMS/CONT

STOVER C.F.,THE GOVERNMENT OF SCIENCE (PAMPHLET). | B62
USA+45 SOCIETY PROF/ORG EX/STRUC CREATE CONTROL | PHIL/SCI
NUC/PWR WAR GOV/REL PEACE ORD/FREE 20. PAGE 53 | TEC/DEV
G1041 | LAW
| NAT/G

STRAUSS L.L.,MEN AND DECISIONS. USA+45 USA-45 USSR | B62
CONSULT FORCES TOP/EX WAR PEACE 20. PAGE 53 G1042 | DECISION
| PWR
| NUC/PWR
| DIPLOM

US CONGRESS,COMMUNICATIONS SATELLITE LEGISLATION: | B62
HEARINGS BEFORE COMM ON AERON AND SPACE SCIENCES ON | SPACE
BILLS S2550 AND 2814. WOR+45 LAW VOL/ASSN PLAN | COM/IND
DIPLOM CONTROL OWN PEACE...NEW/IDEA CONGRESS NASA. | ADJUD
PAGE 56 G1110 | GOV/REL

BETHE H.,"DISARMAMENT AND STRATEGY." COM USA+45 | S62
USSR WOR+45 VOL/ASSN TEC/DEV EDU/PROP NUC/PWR | PLAN
CHOOSE PEACE...POLICY DECISION NEW/IDEA OBS | ORD/FREE
GEN/LAWS COLD/WAR 420. PAGE 7 G0133 | ARMS/CONT
| DIPLOM

BOULDING K.E.,"THE PREVENTION OF WORLD WAR THREE." | S62
FUT WOR+45 INT/ORG PLAN BAL/PWR PEACE ORD/FREE PWR | VOL/ASSN
...NEW/IDEA TREND TOT/POP COLD/WAR 20. PAGE 8 G0158 | NAT/G
| ARMS/CONT
| DIPLOM

DAWSON R.H.,"CONGRESSIONAL INNOVATION AND | S62
INTERVENTION IN DEFENSE POLICY: LEGISLATIVE | LEGIS
AUTHORIZATION OF WEAPONS SYSTEMS." CONSTN PLAN | PWR
ARMS/CONT GOV/REL EFFICIENCY PEACE NEW/LIB OLD/LIB. | CONTROL
PAGE 14 G0281 | WEAPON

PACHTER H.M.,COLLISION COURSE; THE CUBAN MISSILE | B63
CRISIS AND COEXISTENCE. CUBA USA+45 DIPLOM | WAR
ARMS/CONT PEACE MARXISM...DECISION INT/LAW 20 | BAL/PWR
COLD/WAR KHRUSH/N KENNEDY/JF CASTRO/F. PAGE 43 | NUC/PWR
G0854 | DETER

US SENATE,DOCUMENTS ON INTERNATIONAL AS"ECTS OF | B63
EXPLORATION AND USE OF OUTER SPACE, 1954-62: STAFF | SPACE
REPORT FOR COMM AERON SPACE SCI. USA+45 USSR LEGIS | UTIL
LEAD CIVMIL/REL PEACE...POLICY INT/LAW ANTHOL 20 | GOV/REL
CONGRESS NASA KHRUSH/N. PAGE 59 G1162 | DIPLOM

GARDNER R.N.,"COOPERATION IN OUTER SPACE." FUT USSR | S63
WOR+45 AIR LAW COM/IND CONSULT DELIB/GP CREATE | INT/ORG
KNOWL 20 TREATY. PAGE 21 G0410 | ACT/RES
| PEACE
| SPACE

BLOUSTEIN E.J.,NUCLEAR ENERGY, PUBLIC POLICY, AND | B64
THE LAW. USA+45 NAT/G ADJUD ADMIN GP/REL OWN PEACE | TEC/DEV
ATTIT HEALTH...ANTHOL 20. PAGE 7 G0144 | LAW
| POLICY
| NUC/PWR

FOGELMAN E.,HIROSHIMA: THE DECISION TO USE THE A- | B64
BOMB. USA-45 DIPLOM EFFICIENCY PEACE...ANTHOL | INTELL
BIBLIOG T 20 CHINJAP. PAGE 19 G0375 | DECISION
| NUC/PWR
| WAR

HODGETTS J.E.,ADMINISTERING THE ATOM FOR PEACE. | B64
OP/RES TEC/DEV ADMIN...IDEA/COMP METH/COMP 20. | PROB/SOLV
PAGE 26 G0517 | NUC/PWR
| PEACE
| MGT

OSSENBECK F.J.,OPEN SPACE AND PEACE. CHINA/COM FUT | B64
USA+45 USSR LAW PROB/SOLV TEC/DEV EDU/PROP NEUTRAL | SPACE
PEACE...AUD/VIS ANTHOL 20. PAGE 43 G0850 | ORD/FREE
| DIPLOM
| CREATE

ROSECRANCE R.N.,THE DISPERSION OF NUCLEAR WEAPONS: | B64
STRATEGY AND POLITICS. ASIA COM FUT S/ASIA USA+45 | EUR+WWI
INT/ORG NAT/G DELIB/GP FORCES ACT/RES TEC/DEV | PWR
BAL/PWR COERCE DETER ATTIT RIGID/FLEX ORD/FREE | PEACE
...POLICY CHARTS VAL/FREE. PAGE 48 G0935 |

ROTHSCHILD J.H.,TOMORROW'S WEAPONS: CHEMICAL AND | B64
BIOLOGICAL. FUT PROB/SOLV ARMS/CONT PEACE MORAL | WAR
...CHARTS BIBLIOG 20. PAGE 48 G0941 | WEAPON
| BIO/SOC
| DETER

SCHWARTZ M.D.,CONFERENCE ON SPACE SCIENCE AND SPACE | B64
LAW. FUT COM/IND NAT/G FORCES ACT/RES PLAN BUDGET | SPACE
DIPLOM NUC/PWR WEAPON...POLICY ANTHOL 20. PAGE 50 | LAW
G0983 | PEACE
| TEC/DEV

TAUBENFELD H.J.,SPACE AND SOCIETY. USA+45 LAW | B64
FORCES CREATE TEC/DEV ADJUD CONTROL COST PEACE | SPACE
...PREDICT ANTHOL 20. PAGE 54 G1057 | SOCIETY
| ADJUST
| DIPLOM

THANT U.,TOWARD WORLD PEACE. DELIB/GP TEC/DEV | B64
EDU/PROP WAR SOVEREIGN...INT/LAW 20 UN MID/EAST. | DIPLOM
PAGE 54 G1065 | BIOG
| PEACE
| COERCE

US AIR FORCE ACADEMY ASSEMBLY,OUTER SPACE: FINAL | B64
REPORT APRIL 1-4, 1964. FUT USA+45 WOR+45 LAW | SPACE
DELIB/GP CONFER ARMS/CONT WAR PEACE ATTIT MORAL | CIVMIL/REL
...ANTHOL 20 NASA. PAGE 56 G1104 | NUC/PWR
| DIPLOM

WILLIAMS S.P.,TOWARD A GENUINE WORLD SECURITY | B64
SYSTEM (PAMPHLET). WOR+45 INT/ORG FORCES PLAN | BIBLIOG/A
NUC/PWR ORD/FREE...INT/LAW CONCPT UN PRESIDENT. | ARMS/CONT
PAGE 63 G1243 | DIPLOM
| PEACE

BERKS R.N.,"THE US AND WEAPONS CONTROL." WOR+45 LAW | L64
INT/ORG NAT/G LEGIS EXEC COERCE PEACE ATTIT | USA+45
RIGID/FLEX ALL/VALS PWR...POLICY TOT/POP 20. PAGE 7 | PLAN
G0129 | ARMS/CONT

CARNEGIE ENDOWMENT INT. PEACE,"POLITICAL QUESTIONS | L64
(ISSUES BEFORE THE NINETEENTH GENERAL ASSEMBLY)." | INT/ORG
SPACE WOR+45 CONSTN FINAN NAT/G CONSULT DELIB/GP | PEACE
FORCES LEGIS TEC/DEV EDU/PROP LEGIT ARMS/CONT
COERCE NUC/PWR ATTIT ALL/VALS...CONCPT OBS UN
COLD/WAR 20. PAGE 11 G0208

"FURTHER READING." INDIA PAKISTAN SECT WAR PEACE | S64
ATTIT...POLICY 20. PAGE 1 G0018 | BIBLIOG
| GP/REL
| DIPLOM
| NAT/G

FALK S.L.,"DISARMAMENT IN HISTORICAL PERSPECTIVE." | S64
WOR-45 NAT/G PLAN NUC/PWR PEACE ORD/FREE PWR | INT/ORG
...TIME/SEQ AUD/VIS VAL/FREE LEAGUE/NAT 20. PAGE 18 | COERCE
G0360 | ARMS/CONT

WHITE HOUSE CONFERENCE ON INTERNATIONAL | B65
COOPERATION(VOL.II). SPACE WOR+45 EXTR/IND INT/ORG | R+D
LABOR WORKER NUC/PWR PEACE AGE/Y...CENSUS ANTHOL 20 | CONFER
RESOURCE/N URBAN/RNWL PUB/TRANS. PAGE 1 G0019 | TEC/DEV
| DIPLOM

PEACE RESEARCH ABSTRACTS. FUT WOR+45 R+D INT/ORG | B65
NAT/G PLAN TEC/DEV BAL/PWR DIPLOM FOR/AID NUC/PWR | BIBLIOG/A
HEALTH. PAGE 1 G0020 | PEACE
| ARMS/CONT
| WAR

ATOMIC INDUSTRIAL FORUM,SAFEGUARDS AGAINST | B65
DIVERSION OF NUCLEAR MATERIALS FROM PEACEFUL TO | NUC/PWR
MILITARY PURPOSES. WOR+45 DELIB/GP FORCES PLAN | CIVMIL/REL
DIPLOM CONFER PEACE...ANTHOL 20 IAEA. PAGE 4 G0081 | INSPECT
| CONTROL

CORDIER A.W.,THE QUEST FOR PEACE. WOR+45 NAT/G PLAN | B65
BAL/PWR ECO/TAC ARMS/CONT NUC/PWR PWR...ANTHOL UN | PEACE
COLD/WAR. PAGE 13 G0256 | DIPLOM
| POLICY
| INT/ORG

HALPERIN M.H.,COMMUNIST CHINA AND ARMS CONTROL. | B65
CHINA/COM FUT USA+45 CULTURE FORCES TEC/DEV ECO/TAC | ATTIT
WAR PEACE ORD/FREE MARXISM 20 COLD/WAR. PAGE 24 | POLICY
G0473 | ARMS/CONT
| NUC/PWR

MOSKOWITZ H.,US SECURITY, ARMS CONTROL, AND | B65
DISARMAMENT 1961-1965. FORCES DIPLOM DETER WAR | BIBLIOG/A
WEAPON...CHARTS 20 UN COLD/WAR NATO. PAGE 40 G0790 | ARMS/CONT
| NUC/PWR
| PEACE

UN,SPACE ACTIVITIES AND RESOURCES: REVIEW OF UNITED | B65
NATION'S NATIONAL AND INTERNATIONAL PROGRAMS. | SPACE
INT/ORG LABOR PLAN TEC/DEV DIPLOM EFFICIENCY HEALTH | NUC/PWR
| FOR/AID

...GOV/COMP 20 UN. PAGE 55 G1086   PEACE

B65
US CONGRESS JT ATOM ENRGY COMM,PEACEFUL   NUC/PWR
APPLICATIONS OF NUCLEAR EXPLOSIVES: PLOWSHARE.   DELIB/GP
HEARING. USA+45 LEGIS CREATE PLAN PEACE...CHARTS   TEC/DEV
EXHIBIT BIBLIOG CONGRESS PANAMA/CNL. PAGE 57 G1113   NAT/G

B65
US CONGRESS JT ATOM ENRGY COMM,ATOMIC ENERGY   NUC/PWR
LEGISLATION THROUGH 89TH CONGRESS, 1ST SESSION.   FORCES
USA+45 LAW INT/ORG DELIB/GP BUDGET DIPLOM 20 AEC   PEACE
CONGRESS CASEBOOK EURATOM IAEA. PAGE 57 G1114   LEGIS

B65
US DEPARTMENT OF DEFENSE,US SECURITY ARMS CONTROL,   BIBLIOG/A
AND DISARMAMENT 1961-1965 (PAMPHLET). CHINA/COM COM   ARMS/CONT
GERMANY/W ISRAEL SPACE USA+45 USSR WOR+45 FORCES   NUC/PWR
EDU/PROP DETER EQUILIB PEACE ALL/VALS...GOV/COMP 20   DIPLOM
NATO. PAGE 57 G1118

B65
US SENATE COMM AERO SPACE SCI,INTERNATIONAL   DIPLOM
COOPERATION AND ORGANIZATION FOR OUTER SPACE. FUT   SPACE
USA+45 WOR+45 PROF/ORG VOL/ASSN CONSULT DELIB/GP   R+D
PLAN TEC/DEV ARMS/CONT GP/REL PEACE 20 UN NASA.   NAT/G
PAGE 59 G1167

B65
WASKOW A.I.,KEEPING THE WORLD DISARMED. AFR   ARMS/CONT
GERMANY/E DIPLOM CONTROL WAR 20 UN. PAGE 62 G1218   PEACE
    FORCES
    PROB/SOLV

L65
PILISUK M.,"IS THERE A MILITARY INDUSTRIAL COMPLEX   ELITES
WHICH PREVENTS PEACE CONSENSUS; COUNTERVAILING   WEAPON
POWER IN PLURALIST SYSTEMS." INDUS R+D ACADEM   PEACE
FEEDBACK CIVMIL/REL ADJUST CONSEN ATTIT RIGID/FLEX   ARMS/CONT
...CENSUS IDEA/COMP BIBLIOG. PAGE 45 G0878

S65
DALKEY N.C.,"SOLVABLE NUCLEAR WAR MODELS." FORCES   GAME
BAL/PWR DIPLOM COERCE PEACE DECISION. PAGE 14 G0273   SIMUL
    WAR
    NUC/PWR

S65
DESAI M.J.,"INDIA AND NUCLEAR WEAPONS." ASIA   INDIA
BAL/PWR DIPLOM NUC/PWR WEAPON PEACE RECORD. PAGE 15   ARMS/CONT
G0294

S65
GOLDSTEIN W.,"KEEPING THE GENIE IN THE BOTTLE* THE   NUC/PWR
FEASIBILITY OF A NUCLEAR NON-PROLIFERATION   CREATE
AGREEMENT." ASIA FRANCE UK USA+45 USSR WOR+45   COST
ECO/UNDEV VOL/ASSN ACT/RES PLAN RISK ARMS/CONT WAR
PEACE ATTIT PERCEPT...RECORD TREND TIME. PAGE 22
G0429

S65
KREITH K.,"PEACE RESEARCH AND GOVERNMENT POLICY."   PEACE
INTELL NAT/G DIPLOM ECO/TAC CONTROL ARMS/CONT WAR   STYLE
PERCEPT...DECISION IDEA/COMP. PAGE 31 G0619   OBS

C65
SCHWEBEL M.,"BEHAVIORAL SCIENCE AND HUMAN   PEACE
SURVIVAL." FORCES ARMS/CONT COERCE NUC/PWR WAR   ACT/RES
GP/REL NAT/LISM PERCEPT...POLICY PSY ANTHOL   DIPLOM
BIBLIOG/A 20 COLD/WAR. PAGE 50 G0984   HEAL

B66
BOLTON R.E.,DEFENSE AND DISARMAMENT: THE ECONOMICS   ARMS/CONT
OF TRANSITION. USA+45 R+D FORCES PLAN LOBBY DETER   POLICY
WAR COST PEACE...ANTHOL BIBLIOG 20. PAGE 8 G0150   INDUS

B66
CLARK G.,WORLD PEACE THROUGH WORLD LAW; TWO   INT/LAW
ALTERNATIVE PLANS. WOR+45 DELIB/GP FORCES TAX   PEACE
CONFER ADJUD SANCTION ARMS/CONT WAR CHOOSE PRIVIL   PLAN
20 UN COLD/WAR. PAGE 12 G0231   INT/ORG

B66
DUNBAR L.W.,A REPUBLIC OF EQUALS. USA+45 CREATE   LAW
ADJUD PEACE NEW/LIB...POLICY 20 SOUTH/US   CONSTN
CIV/RIGHTS. PAGE 16 G0320   FEDERAL
    RACE/REL

B66
FEIS H.,THE ATOMIC BOMB AND THE END OF WORLD WAR   USA+45
II. FORCES PLAN PROB/SOLV DIPLOM CONFER WAR   PEACE
...TIME/SEQ TREND CHINJAP PRESIDENT TIME. PAGE 19   NUC/PWR
G0362

B66
FREIDEL F.,AMERICAN ISSUES IN THE TWENTIETH   DIPLOM

CENTURY. SOCIETY FINAN ECO/TAC FOR/AID CONTROL   POLICY
NUC/PWR WAR RACE/REL PEACE ATTIT...ANTHOL T 20   NAT/G
WILSON/W ROOSEVLT/F KENNEDY/JF TRUMAN/HS. PAGE 20   ORD/FREE
G0391

B66
VON BORCH H,FRIEDE TROTZ KRIEG. GERMANY USSR   DIPLOM
WOR+45 PEACE ANOMIE ATTIT 20. PAGE 43 G0853   NUC/PWR
    WAR
    COERCE

B66
UNITED NATIONS,INTERNATIONAL SPACE BIBLIOGRAPHY.   BIBLIOG
FUT INT/ORG TEC/DEV DIPLOM ARMS/CONT NUC/PWR   SPACE
...JURID SOC UN. PAGE 56 G1093   PEACE
    R+D

B66
WOLFERS A.,THE UNITED STATES IN A DISARMED WORLD: A   ARMS/CONT
STUDY OF THE US OUTLINE FOR GENERAL AND COMPLETE   POLICY
DISARMAMENT. USA+45 NAT/G CONTROL DETER NUC/PWR   FORCES
EFFICIENCY...ANTHOL 20. PAGE 64 G1255   PEACE

S66
TURKEVICH J.,"SOVIET SCIENCE APPRAISED." USA+45 R+D   USSR
ACADEM FORCES DIPLOM EDU/PROP WAR EFFICIENCY PEACE   TEC/DEV
SKILL OBS. PAGE 55 G1081   NAT/COMP
    ATTIT

B67
AMERICAN FRIENDS SERVICE COMM,IN PLACE OF WAR.   PEACE
NAT/G ACT/RES DIPLOM ADMIN NUC/PWR EFFICIENCY   PACIFISM
...POLICY 20. PAGE 3 G0053   WAR
    DETER

B67
BURNS E.L.M.,MEGAMURDER. WOR+45 LAW INT/ORG NAT/G   FORCES
BAL/PWR DIPLOM DETER MURDER WEAPON CIVMIL/REL PEACE   PLAN
...INT/LAW TREND 20. PAGE 10 G0193   WAR
    NUC/PWR

B67
HALLE L.J.,THE COLD WAR AS HISTORY. USSR WOR+45   DIPLOM
ECO/TAC FOR/AID NUC/PWR WAR PEACE ORD/FREE   BAL/PWR
...MAJORIT TREND 20 COLD/WAR KENNEDY/JF KHRUSH/N
BERLIN/BLO. PAGE 24 G0470

B67
KINTNER W.R.,PEACE AND THE STRATEGY CONFLICT. PLAN   ROLE
BAL/PWR DIPLOM CONTROL ARMS/CONT DETER WEAPON 20.   PEACE
PAGE 30 G0599   NUC/PWR
    ORD/FREE

B67
ORLANS H.,CONTRACTING FOR ATOMS. USA+45 LAW INTELL   NUC/PWR
ACADEM LG/CO NAT/G PLAN TEC/DEV CONTROL DETER   R+D
...TREND 20 AEC. PAGE 43 G0845   PRODUC
    PEACE

B67
PADELFORD N.J.,THE DYNAMICS OF INTERNATIONAL   DIPLOM
POLITICS (2ND ED.). WOR+45 LAW INT/ORG FORCES   NAT/G
TEC/DEV REGION NAT/LISM PEACE ATTIT PWR ALL/IDEOS   POLICY
UN COLD/WAR NATO TREATY. PAGE 43 G0856   DECISION

B67
ROACH J.R.,THE UNITED STATES AND THE ATLANTIC   INT/ORG
COMMUNITY; ISSUES AND PROSPECTS. WOR+45 TEC/DEV   POLICY
ECO/TAC COLONIAL REGION PEACE ROLE...ANTHOL NATO   ADJUST
COLD/WAR EEC. PAGE 47 G0925   DIPLOM

B67
US SENATE COMM AERO SPACE SCI,TREATY ON PRINCIPLES   SPACE
GOVERNING ACTIVITIES OF STATES IN EXPLORATION AND   INT/LAW
USE OF OUTER SPACE. INCLUDING...BODIES. DELIB/GP   ORD/FREE
FORCES LEGIS DIPLOM...JURID 20 DEPT/STATE NASA   PEACE
DEPT/DEFEN UN. PAGE 60 G1170

B67
DEUTSCH K.W.,"ARMS CONTROL AND EUROPEAN UNITY* THE   ARMS/CONT
NEXT TEN YEARS." USA+45 ELITES NAT/G BAL/PWR DIPLOM   PEACE
NUC/PWR...INT KNO/TEST NATO EEC. PAGE 15 G0300   REGION
    PLAN

S67
EISENDRATH C.,"THE OUTER SPACE TREATY." CHINA/COM   SPACE
COM USA+45 DIPLOM CONTROL NUC/PWR...INT/LAW 20 UN   INT/ORG
COLD/WAR TREATY. PAGE 17 G0339   PEACE
    ARMS/CONT

S67
FELD B.T.,"A PLEDGE* NO FIRST USE." DELIB/GP   ARMS/CONT
BAL/PWR DOMIN DETER. PAGE 19 G0363   NUC/PWR
    DIPLOM
    PEACE

S67

FOREIGN POLICY ASSOCIATION,"US CONCERN FOR WORLD   INT/LAW
LAW." USA+45 WOR+45 DELIB/GP JUDGE BAL/PWR CONFER   INT/ORG
PEACE ORD/FREE 20 UN. PAGE 19 G0379   DIPLOM
                                                       ARMS/CONT

S67

FOREIGN POLICY ASSOCIATION,"HOW WORLD LAW DEVELOPS*   INT/LAW
A CASE STUDY OF THE OUTER SPACE TREATY." SPACE   DIPLOM
WOR+45 BAL/PWR NEUTRAL NUC/PWR PEACE KNOWL 20 UN   ARMS/CONT
TREATY. PAGE 19 G0380   INT/ORG

S67

GRIFFITHS F.,"THE POLITICAL SIDE OF 'DISARMAMENT'."   ARMS/CONT
FUT WOR+45 NUC/PWR NAT/LISM PEACE...NEW/IDEA   DIPLOM
PREDICT METH/COMP GEN/LAWS 20. PAGE 23 G0453

S67

HULL E.W.S.,"THE POLITICAL OCEAN." FUT UNIV WOR+45   DIPLOM
EXTR/IND R+D VOL/ASSN PLAN BAL/PWR ECO/TAC PEACE   ECO/UNDEV
WEALTH 20 UN. PAGE 27 G0536   INT/ORG
                                                       INT/LAW

S67

INGLIS D.R.,"MISSILE DEFENSE, NUCLEAR SPREAD, AND   NUC/PWR
VIETNAM." CHINA/COM USA+45 USSR VIETNAM INDUS   ARMS/CONT
BAL/PWR DETER WAR COST NAT/LISM PEACE. PAGE 28   DIPLOM
G0544   FORCES

S67

INGLIS D.R.,"PROSPECTS AND PROBLEMS: THE   NUC/PWR
NONMILITARY USES OF NUCLEAR EXPLOSIVES." CREATE   INDUS
PROB/SOLV TEC/DEV AGREE PEACE...INT/LAW PHIL/SCI   ARMS/CONT
NEW/IDEA 20 TREATY. PAGE 28 G0545   EXTR/IND

S67

KRUSCHE H.,"THE STRIVING OF THE KIESINGER-STRAUS   ARMS/CONT
GOVERNMENT FOR NUCLEAR WEAPONS IS A THREAT TO   INT/ORG
EUROPEAN SECURITY." EUR+WWI GERMANY BAL/PWR   NUC/PWR
SANCTION WEAPON PEACE ORD/FREE...MARXIST 20 NATO   DIPLOM
COLD/WAR. PAGE 32 G0623

S67

MARTIN L.,"THE AMERICAN ABM DECISION." ASIA COM   WEAPON
EUR+WWI UK USA+45 USSR FORCES DIPLOM PEACE...POLICY   DETER
20 ABM/DEFSYS. PAGE 36 G0713   NUC/PWR
                                                       WAR

S67

MARTIN L.W.,"BALLISTIC MISSILE DEFENSE AND EUROPE."   ATTIT
EUR+WWI USA+45 FORCES PLAN BAL/PWR DEBATE PEACE   ARMS/CONT
...POLICY COLD/WAR NATO. PAGE 36 G0715   NUC/PWR
                                                       DETER

S67

REINTANZ G.,"THE SPACE TREATY." WOR+45 DIPLOM   SPACE
CONTROL ARMS/CONT NUC/PWR WAR...MARXIST 20 COLD/WAR   INT/LAW
UN TREATY. PAGE 46 G0911   INT/ORG
                                                       PEACE

S67

ROMANIECKI L.,"THE ATOM AND INTERNATIONAL   INT/ORG
COOPERATION." PROB/SOLV DIPLOM PEACE ORD/FREE 20.   NUC/PWR
PAGE 47 G0933   ARMS/CONT
                                                       CONTROL

S67

SHARP G.,"THE NEED OF A FUNCTIONAL SUBSTITUTE FOR   PEACE
WAR." FUT UNIV WOR+45 CULTURE SOCIETY INT/ORG   WAR
CONSULT DELIB/GP ACT/RES CREATE BAL/PWR CONFER   DIPLOM
ARMS/CONT NUC/PWR 20. PAGE 50 G0989   PROB/SOLV

S67

TELLER E.,"PLANNING FOR PEACE." CHINA/COM WOR+45   ARMS/CONT
DELIB/GP TEC/DEV RISK COERCE DETER WAR ATTIT   NUC/PWR
ORD/FREE 20 NATO. PAGE 54 G1061   PEACE
                                                       DOMIN

S67

VLASCIC I.A.,"THE SPACE TREATY* A PRELIMINARY   SPACE
EVALUATION." FUT USSR WOR+45 R+D ACT/RES TEC/DEV   INT/LAW
DIPLOM CONFER ARMS/CONT PEACE...PREDICT UN TREATY.   INT/ORG
PAGE 61 G1201   NEUTRAL

S67

WALTERS R.E.,"THE ROLE OF NUCLEAR WEAPONS FOR THE   PLAN
WEST." ASIA UK USA+45 USSR DIPLOM COERCE WAR PEACE   NUC/PWR
...POLICY DECISION 20. PAGE 62 G1209   WEAPON
                                                       FORCES

S67

YOUNG O.R.,"ACTIVE DEFENSE AND INTERNATIONAL   ARMS/CONT
ORDER." FORCES BAL/PWR DEBATE GAMBLE COST PEACE.   DETER
PAGE 64 G1265   PLAN
                                                       DECISION

N67

US SUPERINTENDENT OF DOCUMENTS,SPACE: MISSILES, THE   BIBLIOG/A
MOON, NASA, AND SATELLITES (PRICE LIST 79A). USA+45   SPACE
COM/IND R+D NAT/G DIPLOM EDU/PROP ADMIN CONTROL   TEC/DEV
HEALTH...POLICY SIMUL NASA CONGRESS. PAGE 61 G1190   PEACE

N67

US HOUSE COMM FOREIGN AFFAIRS,REPORT OF SPECIAL   ISLAM
STUDY MISSION TO THE NEAR EAST (PAMPHLET). ISRAEL   DIPLOM
USA+45 YEMEN ECO/UNDEV INT/ORG FOR/AID ARMS/CONT   FORCES
WAR WEAPON NAT/LISM PEACE...GEOG 20 UN HOUSE/REP.
PAGE 58 G1138

PEACE/CORP....PEACE CORPS

PEACEFUL COEXISTENCE....SEE PEACE+COLD/WAR

PEARSELL M. G0863

PEARSON/L....LESTER PEARSON

PEASNT/WAR....PEASANT WAR (1525)

PECK M.J. G0817

PEDERSEN E.S. G0864

PEIRCE W.S. G0865

PENN/WM....WILLIAM PENN

PENNEY N. G0866

PENNSYLVAN....PENNSYLVANIA

PENOLOGY....SEE CRIME

PENTAGON....PENTAGON

PENTONY D.E. G0867

PERCEPT....PERCEPTION AND COGNITION

N

AMERICAN DOCUMENTATION INST,AMERICAN DOCUMENTATION.   BIBLIOG
PROF/ORG CONSULT PLAN PERCEPT...MATH STAT AUD/VIS   TEC/DEV
CHARTS METH/COMP INDEX METH 20. PAGE 3 G0050   COM/IND
                                                       COMPUT/IR

B

CURRENT THOUGHT ON PEACE AND WAR. WOR+45 INT/ORG   BIBLIOG/A
FORCES PROB/SOLV DIPLOM NUC/PWR PERCEPT...POLICY   PEACE
SOC 20 UN NATO. PAGE 1 G0001   ATTIT
                                                       WAR

B11

BERGSON H.,CREATIVE EVOLUTION. FUT WOR+45 WOR-45   BIO/SOC
INTELL AGRI R+D ATTIT PERCEPT PERSON RIGID/FLEX   KNOWL
...RELATIV PHIL/SCI PSY METH/CNCPT MATH HIST/WRIT
TREND HYPO/EXP TOT/POP. PAGE 7 G0127

B29

DEWEY J.,THE QUEST FOR CERTAINTY. GP/REL RATIONAL   PHIL/SCI
UTOPIA ATTIT MORAL ORD/FREE PWR...MYTH HIST/WRIT.   PERSON
PAGE 15 G0301   PERCEPT
                                                       KNOWL

B46

NORTHROP F.S.C.,THE MEETING OF EAST AND WEST.   DRIVE
EUR+WWI FUT MOD/EUR UNIV WOR+45 WOR-45 INTELL   TREND
SOCIETY EX/STRUC TOP/EX ACT/RES LEGIT CHOOSE ATTIT   PEACE
PERCEPT RIGID/FLEX ALL/VALS...POLICY JURID OBS
TOT/POP. PAGE 42 G0826

B47

LASSWELL H.D.,THE ANALYSIS OF POLITICAL BEHAVIOUR: R+D
AN EMPIRICAL APPROACH. WOR+45 CULTURE NAT/G FORCES   ACT/RES
EDU/PROP ADMIN ATTIT PERCEPT KNOWL...PHIL/SCI PSY   ELITES
SOC NEW/IDEA OBS INT GEN/METH NAZI 20. PAGE 32
G0639

B48

WEINER N.,CYBERNETICS. SOCIETY COMPUTER ADJUST   FEEDBACK
EFFICIENCY UTIL PERCEPT...PSY MATH REGRESS TIME.   AUTOMAT
PAGE 63 G1226   CONTROL
                                                       TEC/DEV

S48

COCH L.,"OVERCOMING RESISTANCE TO CHANGE" (BMR)"   WORKER
USA+45 CONSULT ADMIN ROUTINE GP/REL EFFICIENCY   OP/RES
PRODUC PERCEPT SKILL...CHARTS SOC/EXP 20. PAGE 12   PROC/MFG
G0236   RIGID/FLEX

LEWIN K.,FIELD THEORY IN SOCIAL SCIENCE: SELECTED   B51
THEORETICAL PAPERS. UNIV CREATE DRIVE PERCEPT KNOWL   PHIL/SCI
...METH/CNCPT CONT/OBS CHARTS GEN/METH METH   HYPO/EXP
VAL/FREE 20. PAGE 33 G0661

BERGMANN G.,"IDEOLOGY" (BMR)" UNIV PERCEPT KNOWL   S51
...IDEA/COMP METH. PAGE 7 G0126   PHIL/SCI
                                                        CONCPT
                                                        LOG
                                                        ALL/IDEOS

CALLOT E.,LA SOCIETE ET SON ENVIRONNEMENT: ESSAI   B52
SUR LES PRINCIPES DES SCIENCES SOCIALES. GP/REL   SOCIETY
ADJUST CONSEN ISOLAT HABITAT PERCEPT PERSON   PHIL/SCI
...BIBLIOG SOC/INTEG 20. PAGE 10 G0205   CULTURE

HAYEK F.A.,THE COUNTER-REVOLUTION OF SCIENCE. UNIV   B52
INTELL R+D VOL/ASSN CREATE EDU/PROP...PHIL/SCI SOC   PERCEPT
OBS TIME/SEQ TREND GEN/METH. PAGE 25 G0494   KNOWL

KECSKEMETI P.,"THE 'POLICY SCIENCES': ASPIRATION   S52
AND OUTLOOK." UNIV CULTURE INTELL SOCIETY STRUCT   CREATE
EDU/PROP ATTIT PERCEPT RIGID/FLEX KNOWL...PHIL/SCI   NEW/IDEA
METH/CNCPT OBS 20. PAGE 30 G0589

EASTON D.,THE POLITICAL SYSTEM, AN INQUIRY INTO THE   B53
STATE POLITICAL SCIENCE. USA+45 INTELL CREATE   R+D
EDU/PROP RIGID/FLEX KNOWL SKILL...PHIL/SCI NEW/IDEA   PERCEPT
STERTYP TOT/POP 20. PAGE 17 G0329

LANGER W.L.,THE UNDECLARED WAR, 1940-1941. EUR+WWI   B53
GERMANY USA-45 USSR AIR FORCES TEC/DEV CONFER   WAR
CONTROL COERCE PERCEPT ORD/FREE PWR 20 CHINJAP   POLICY
EUROPE. PAGE 32 G0634   DIPLOM

SHUBIK M.,READINGS IN GAME THEORY AND POLITICAL   B55
BEHAVIOR. WOR+45 FORCES CREATE ROUTINE WAR PEACE   MATH
PERCEPT KNOWL PWR...PSY SOC CONCPT METH/CNCPT STAT   DECISION
CHARTS HYPO/EXP GAME METH VAL/FREE 20. PAGE 50   DIPLOM
G0991

ANGELL R.,"GOVERNMENTS AND PEOPLES AS A FOCI FOR   S55
PEACE-ORIENTED RESEARCH." WOR+45 CULTURE SOCIETY   FUT
FACE/GP ACT/RES CREATE PLAN DIPLOM EDU/PROP ROUTINE   SOC
ATTIT PERCEPT SKILL...POLICY CONCPT OBS TREND   PEACE
GEN/METH 20. PAGE 3 G0060

MILLER G.A.,"THE MAGICAL NUMBER SEVEN, PLUS OR   S56
MINUS TWO: SOME LIMITS ON OUR CAPACITY FOR   LAB/EXP
PROCESSING INFORMATION." PERS/REL...PSY METH/CNCPT   KNOWL
LING CHARTS BIBLIOG 20. PAGE 39 G0772   PERCEPT
                                                        COMPUT/IR

JUNGK R.,BRIGHTER THAN A THOUSAND SUNS: THE MORAL   B58
AND POLITICAL HISTORY OF THE ATOMIC SCIENTISTS.   NUC/PWR
WOR+45 WOR-45 CONSULT CREATE RISK UTIL DRIVE   MORAL
PERCEPT PWR...INT 20. PAGE 29 G0568   GOV/REL
                                                        PERSON

KLAPPER J.T.,"WHAT WE KNOW ABOUT THE EFFECTS OF   S58
MASS COMMUNICATION: THE BRINK OF HOPE" (BMR)"   ACT/RES
COM/IND KNOWL...METH/CNCPT GEN/LAWS BIBLIOG METH   PERCEPT
20. PAGE 31 G0605   CROWD
                                                        PHIL/SCI

LASSWELL H.D.,"THE SCIENTIFIC STUDY OF   S58
INTERNATIONAL RELATIONS." USA+45 INT/ORG CREATE   PHIL/SCI
EDU/PROP DETER ATTIT PERCEPT PWR...DECISION CONCPT   GEN/METH
METH/CNCPT STYLE CON/ANAL 20. PAGE 33 G0642   DIPLOM

NEWELL A.C.,"ELEMENTS OF A THEORY OF HUMAN PROBLEM   S58
SOLVING" (BMR)" TASK PERCEPT...CONCPT LOG METH/COMP   PROB/SOLV
LAB/EXP BIBLIOG 20. PAGE 42 G0819   COMPUTER
                                                        COMPUT/IR
                                                        OP/RES

SINGER J.D.,"THREAT PERCEPTION AND THE ARMAMENT   S58
TENSION DILEMMA." WOR+45 WOR-45 ELITES INT/ORG   PERCEPT
NAT/G DELIB/GP PLAN LEGIT COERCE DETER ATTIT   ARMS/CONT
RIGID/FLEX PWR...DECISION PSY 20. PAGE 51 G1002   BAL/PWR

AMRINE M.,THE GREAT DECISION: THE SECRET HISTORY OF   B59
THE ATOMIC BOMB. USA+45 TOP/EX EDU/PROP LEGIT   DECISION
PERCEPT ORD/FREE PWR VAL/FREE HIROSHIMA. PAGE 3   NAT/G
G0055   NUC/PWR
                                                        FORCES

GUILBAUD G.T.,WHAT IS CYBERNETICS? COMPUTER OP/RES   B59
TEC/DEV AUTOMAT ROUTINE PERS/REL PERCEPT...PSY MATH   CONTROL
COMPUT/IR SIMUL GEN/METH. PAGE 23 G0460   COM/IND
                                                        FEEDBACK
                                                        NET/THEORY

LEFTON M.,"DECISION MAKING IN A MENTAL HOSPITAL: S59
REAL, PERCEIVED, AND IDEAL." R+D PUB/INST CONSULT   ACT/RES
CONFER INGP/REL PERCEPT...MODAL 20. PAGE 33 G0653   PROB/SOLV
                                                        DECISION
                                                        PSY

ARROW K.J.,MATHEMATICAL METHODS IN THE SOCIAL   B60
SCIENCES, 1959. TEC/DEV CHOOSE UTIL PERCEPT   MATH
...KNO/TEST GAME SIMUL ANTHOL. PAGE 4 G0070   PSY
                                                        MGT

RAPOPORT A.,FIGHTS, GAMES AND DEBATES. INTELL   B60
SOCIETY R+D EX/STRUC PERCEPT PERSON SKILL...PSY SOC   METH/CNCPT
GAME. PAGE 46 G0902   MATH
                                                        DECISION
                                                        CON/ANAL

SLUCKIN W.,MINDS AND MACHINES (REV. ED.). PROB/SOLV   B60
TEC/DEV AUTOMAT TASK PERCEPT HEALTH KNOWL   PSY
...DECISION MATH PROBABIL COMPUT/IR GAME 20.   COMPUTER
PAGE 51 G1012   PERSON
                                                        SIMUL

DEUTSCH K.W.,"TOWARD AN INVENTORY OF BASIC TRENDS   L60
AND PATTERNS IN COMPARATIVE AND INTERNATIONAL   R+D
POLITICS." UNIV WOR+45 SOCIETY STRUCT INT/ORG NAT/G   PERCEPT
CREATE PLAN EDU/PROP KNOWL...PHIL/SCI METH/CNCPT
STAT SELF/OBS OBS/ENVIR SAMP TREND CON/ANAL CHARTS
SOC/EXP GEN/METH 20. PAGE 15 G0298

HOLZMAN B.G.,"BASIC RESEARCH FOR NATIONAL   L60
SURVIVAL." FUT USA+45 INTELL R+D ACT/RES OP/RES   FORCES
PLAN TEC/DEV EDU/PROP PERCEPT PERSON...PHIL/SCI   STAT
METH/CNCPT NEW/IDEA MATH OBS RECORD TREND LAB/EXP
20. PAGE 27 G0525

SANDERS R.,"NUCLEAR DYNAMITE: A NEW DIMENSION IN   S60
FOREIGN POLICY." FUT WOR+45 ECO/DEV CONSULT TEC/DEV   INDUS
PERCEPT...CONT/OBS TIME/SEQ TREND GEN/LAWS TOT/POP   PWR
20 TREATY. PAGE 49 G0955   DIPLOM
                                                        NUC/PWR

LUNDBERG G.A.,CAN SCIENCE SAVE US. UNIV CULTURE   B61
INTELL SOCIETY ECO/DEV R+D PLAN EDU/PROP ROUTINE   ACT/RES
CHOOSE ATTIT PERCEPT ALL/VALS...TREND 20. PAGE 34   CONCPT
G0679   TOTALISM

NOGEE J.L.,SOVIET POLICY TOWARD INTERNATIONAL   B61
CONTROL OF ATOMIC ENERGY. COM USA+45 WOR+45 INTELL   INT/ORG
NAT/G ACT/RES DIPLOM EDU/PROP NUC/PWR TOTALISM   ATTIT
PERCEPT KNOWL PWR...TIME/SEQ COLD/WAR 20. PAGE 42   ARMS/CONT
G0824   USSR

HERRING P.,"RESEARCH FOR PUBLIC POLICY: BROOKINGS   L61
DEDICATION LECTURES." USA+45 CONSULT DELIB/GP   R+D
ROUTINE PERCEPT SKILL...MGT 20. PAGE 26 G0508   ACT/RES
                                                        DIPLOM

MACHOWSKI K.,"SELECTED PROBLEMS OF NATIONAL   S61
SOVEREIGNTY WITH REFERENCE TO THE LAW OF OUTER   UNIV
SPACE." FUT WOR+45 AIR LAW INTELL SOCIETY ECO/DEV   ACT/RES
PLAN EDU/PROP DETER DRIVE PERCEPT SOVEREIGN   NUC/PWR
...POLICY INT/LAW OBS TREND TOT/POP 20. PAGE 35   SPACE
G0689

CLARKE A.C.,PROFILES OF THE FUTURE; AN INQUIRY INTO   FUT
THE LIMITS OF THE POSSIBLE. COM/IND DIST/IND PRODUC   TEC/DEV
AGE PERCEPT...TECHNIC NEW/IDEA TIME. PAGE 12 G0232   PREDICT   B62
                                                        SPACE

GILPIN R.,AMERICAN SCIENTISTS AND NUCLEAR WEAPONS   B62
POLICY. COM FUT USA+45 WOR+45 INT/ORG NAT/G   INTELL
PROF/ORG CONSULT FORCES CREATE TEC/DEV BAL/PWR   ATTIT
EDU/PROP ARMS/CONT WAR PERCEPT KNOWL MORAL PWR   DETER
...PHIL/SCI SOC CONCPT GEN/LAWS 20. PAGE 21 G0417   NUC/PWR

OSGOOD C.E.,AN ALTERNATIVE TO WAR OR SURRENDER. FUT   B62
UNIV CULTURE INTELL SOCIETY R+D INT/ORG CONSULT   ORD/FREE
DELIB/GP ACT/RES PLAN CHOOSE ATTIT PERCEPT KNOWL   EDU/PROP
...PHIL/SCI PSY SOC TREND GEN/LAWS 20. PAGE 43   PEACE
G0849   WAR

B62
RIKER W.H.,THE THEORY OF POLITICAL COALITIONS.   FUT
WOR+45 INTELL NAT/G CREATE PLAN ATTIT DRIVE PERCEPT   SIMUL
...DECISION PSY SOC METH/CNCPT NEW/IDEA MATH CHARTS
GAME TOT/POP 20. PAGE 47 G0921

L62
FINKELSTEIN L.S.,"ARMS INSPECTION." FUT WOR+45   FORCES
NAT/G DIPLOM ATTIT PERCEPT RIGID/FLEX ORD/FREE   PWR
COLD/WAR 20. PAGE 19 G0369   ARMS/CONT

S62
GORDON B.K.,"NUCLEAR WEAPONS: RUSSIAN AND   ORD/FREE
AMERICAN." COM USA+45 USSR NAT/G FORCES ACT/RES   COERCE
TEC/DEV PERCEPT RIGID/FLEX PWR SKILL...MGT   NUC/PWR
METH/CNCPT QUANT OBS TIME/SEQ CON/ANAL GEN/METH
TOT/POP VAL/FREE 20. PAGE 22 G0433

S62
SINGER J.D.,"STABLE DETERRENCE AND ITS LIMITS." FUT   NAT/G
WOR+45 R+D INT/ORG CONSULT ACT/RES TEC/DEV   FORCES
ARMS/CONT COERCE DRIVE PERCEPT RIGID/FLEX ORD/FREE   DETER
PWR...MYTH SIMUL TOT/POP 20. PAGE 51 G1004   NUC/PWR

B63
BONINI C.P.,SIMULATION OF INFORMATION AND DECISION   INDUS
SYSTEMS IN THE FIRM. MARKET BUDGET DOMIN EDU/PROP   SIMUL
ADMIN COST ATTIT HABITAT PERCEPT PWR...CONCPT   DECISION
PROBABIL QUANT PREDICT HYPO/EXP BIBLIOG. PAGE 8   MGT
G0152

B63
NORTH R.C.,CONTENT ANALYSIS: A HANDBOOK WITH   METH/CNCPT
APPLICATIONS FOR THE STUDY OF INTERNATIONAL CRISIS.   COMPUT/IR
ASIA COM EUR+WWI MOD/EUR INT/ORG TEC/DEV DOMIN   USSR
EDU/PROP ROUTINE COERCE PERCEPT RIGID/FLEX ALL/VALS
...QUANT TESTS CON/ANAL SIMUL GEN/LAWS VAL/FREE.
PAGE 42 G0825

B63
THORELLI H.B.,INTOP: INTERNATIONAL OPERATIONS   GAME
SIMULATION: PLAYER'S MANUAL. BRAZIL FINAN OP/RES   INT/TRADE
ADMIN GP/REL INGP/REL PRODUC PERCEPT...DECISION MGT   EDU/PROP
EEC. PAGE 54 G1073   LG/CO

B63
TOMKINS S.S.,COMPUTER SIMULATION OF PERSONALITY.   COMPUTER
R+D TEC/DEV AUTOMAT FEEDBACK ANOMIE PERCEPT...STYLE   PERSON
PERS/TEST PREDICT COMPUT/IR GP/COMP. PAGE 55 G1075   SIMUL
                                                               PROG/TEAC

S63
DE FOREST J.D.,"LOW LEVELS OF TECHNOLOGY AND   ECO/UNDEV
ECONOMIC DEVELOPMENT PROSPECTS." WOR+45 WOR-45   TEC/DEV
CULTURE ACT/RES CREATE PLAN ECO/TAC ROUTINE PERCEPT
WEALTH...METH/CNCPT GEN/LAWS 20. PAGE 15 G0284

B64
BRILLOUIN L.,SCIENTIFIC UNCERTAINTY AND   PHIL/SCI
INFORMATION. PROB/SOLV AUTOMAT PERCEPT ORD/FREE   NEW/IDEA
...MATH REGRESS STAT STYLE OBS IDEA/COMP SIMUL   METH/CNCPT
TIME. PAGE 9 G0169   CREATE

B64
COENEN E.,LA "KONJUNKTURFORSCHUNG" EN ALLEMAGNE ET   METH/COMP
EN AUTRICHE, 1925-1935. AUSTRIA GERMANY OP/RES PLAN   R+D
COST PERCEPT...METH/CNCPT BIBLIOG 20. PAGE 12 G0237   ECO/TAC

B64
GROSSER G.H.,THE THREAT OF IMPENDING DISASTER: HEALTH
CONTRIBUTIONS TO THE PSYCHOLOGY OF STRESS. SPACE   PSY
UNIV SOCIETY R+D TEC/DEV EDU/PROP COERCE WAR ATTIT   NUC/PWR
BIO/SOC DISPL PERCEPT PERSON...SOC MYTH SELF/OBS
CONT/OBS BIOG CON/ANAL TOT/POP. PAGE 23 G0455

L64
WARD C.,"THE 'NEW MYTHS' AND 'OLD REALITIES' OF   FORCES
NUCLEAR WAR." COM FUT USA+45 USSR WOR+45 INT/ORG   COERCE
NAT/G DOMIN LEGIT EXEC ATTIT PERCEPT ALL/VALS   ARMS/CONT
...POLICY RELATIV PSY MYTH TREND 20. PAGE 62 G1212   NUC/PWR

S64
BYRNES F.C.,"ASSIGNMENT TO AMBIGUITY: WORK   INTELL
PERFORMANCE IN CROSSCULTURAL TECHNICAL ASSISTANCE."   QU
USA+45 WOR+45 PROF/ORG CONSULT PLAN EDU/PROP ATTIT
DISPL PERCEPT PERSON ALL/VALS...POLICY INT CHARTS
NATO 20. PAGE 10 G0199

B65
ANDERSON C.A.,EDUCATION AND ECONOMIC DEVELOPMENT.   ANTHOL
INDUS R+D SCHOOL TEC/DEV ECO/TAC EDU/PROP AGE   ECO/DEV
HEREDITY PERCEPT SKILL 20. PAGE 3 G0056   ECO/UNDEV
                                                               WORKER

S65
GOLDSTEIN W.,"KEEPING THE GENIE IN THE BOTTLE* THE   NUC/PWR
FEASIBILITY OF A NUCLEAR NON-PROLIFERATION   CREATE
AGREEMENT." ASIA FRANCE UK USA+45 USSR WOR+45   COST
ECO/UNDEV VOL/ASSN ACT/RES PLAN RISK ARMS/CONT WAR
PEACE ATTIT PERCEPT...RECORD TREND TIME. PAGE 22
G0429

S65
KREITH K.,"PEACE RESEARCH AND GOVERNMENT POLICY."   PEACE
INTELL NAT/G DIPLOM ECO/TAC CONTROL ARMS/CONT WAR   STYLE
PERCEPT...DECISION IDEA/COMP. PAGE 31 G0619   OBS

S65
KUZMACK A.M.,"TECHNOLOGICAL CHANGE AND STABLE   R+D
DETERRENCE." CREATE EDU/PROP ARMS/CONT WEAPON   DETER
CHOOSE COST DRIVE PERCEPT...RECORD STERTYP TIME.   EQUILIB
PAGE 32 G0627

S65
RASER J.R.,"WEAPONS DESIGN AND ARMS CONTROL* THE   ARMS/CONT
POLARIS EXAMPLE." DETER NUC/PWR WEAPON CHOOSE   R+D
PERCEPT...STERTYP TIME. PAGE 46 G0904   GEOG
                                                               ACT/RES

C65
SCHWEBEL M.,"BEHAVIORAL SCIENCE AND HUMAN   PEACE
SURVIVAL." FORCES ARMS/CONT COERCE NUC/PWR WAR   ACT/RES
GP/REL NAT/LISM PERCEPT...POLICY PSY ANTHOL   DIPLOM
BIBLIOG/A 20 COLD/WAR. PAGE 50 G0984   HEAL

B66
BRODIE B.,ESCALATION AND THE NUCLEAR OPTION. ASIA   NUC/PWR
CUBA EUR+WWI KOREA USA+45 USSR VIETNAM RISK ATTIT   GUERRILLA
DRIVE PERCEPT PROBABIL. PAGE 9 G0172   WAR
                                                               DETER

B66
MUMFORD L.,THE MYTH OF THE MACHINE: TECHNICS AND   WORKER
HUMAN DEVELOPMENT. UNIV WOR-45 CREATE AUTOMAT   TEC/DEV
PERCEPT KNOWL...EPIST PHIL/SCI SOC LING TREND   SOCIETY
SOC/INTEG 20 MARX/KARL. PAGE 40 G0795

L66
RASER J.R.,"DETERRENCE RESEARCH* PAST PROGRESS AND   DETER
FUTURE NEEDS." INTELL PLAN TEC/DEV NUC/PWR PERCEPT   BIBLIOG/A
...DECISION PSY SOC NET/THEORY. PAGE 46 G0905   FUT

B67
DE JOUVENEL B.,THE ART OF CONJECTURE. WOR+45   FUT
EFFICIENCY PERCEPT KNOWL...DECISION PHIL/SCI CONCPT   PREDICT
METH/COMP BIBLIOG 20. PAGE 15 G0285   SIMUL
                                                               METH

B67
LERNER D.,COMMUNICATION AND CHANGE IN DEVELOPING   EDU/PROP
COUNTRIES. CHINA/COM INDIA PHILIPPINE COM/IND   ORD/FREE
CREATE TEC/DEV...ANTHOL 20. PAGE 33 G0659   PERCEPT
                                                               ECO/UNDEV

B67
SAPARINA Y.,CYBERNETICS WITHIN US. WOR+45 EDU/PROP   COMPUTER
FEEDBACK PERCEPT HEALTH...DECISION METH/CNCPT   METH/COMP
NEW/IDEA 20. PAGE 49 G0957   CONTROL
                                                               SIMUL

S67
SKOLNIKOFF E.B.,"MAKING FOREIGN POLICY" PROB/SOLV   TEC/DEV
EFFICIENCY PERCEPT PWR...MGT METH/CNCPT CLASSIF 20.   CONTROL
PAGE 51 G1009   USA+45
                                                               NAT/G

PERCEPTION....SEE PERCEPT

PERCY/CHAS....CHARLES PERCY

PERF/ART....PERFORMING ARTS

B59
JACOBS N.,CULTURE FOR THE MILLIONS? INTELL SOCIETY   CULTURE
NAT/G...POLICY SOC OBS ANTHOL 20. PAGE 28 G0553   COM/IND
                                                               PERF/ART
                                                               CONCPT

S64
KASSOF A.,"THE ADMINISTERED SOCIETY: SOCIETY
TOTALITARIANISM WITHOUT TERROR." COM USSR STRATA   DOMIN
AGRI INDUS NAT/G PERF/ART SCHOOL TOP/EX EDU/PROP   TOTALISM
ADMIN ORD/FREE PWR...POLICY SOC TIME/SEQ GEN/LAWS
VAL/FREE 20. PAGE 29 G0580

PERFORMING ARTS....SEE PERF/ART; ALSO ART/METH

PERKINS D.H. G0473

PERKINS J.A. G0868

PERLO V. G0869

PERON/JUAN....JUAN PERON

PERRE J. G0870

PERROW C. G1044

PERS/COMP....COMPARISON OF PERSONS

	B61
MCRAE R.,THE PROBLEM OF THE UNITY OF THE SCIENCES:	PHIL/SCI
BACON TO KANT. CREATE TASK KNOWL...PERS/COMP 16/18	IDEA/COMP
BACON/F DESCARTE/R LEIBNITZ/G KANT/I DIDEROT/D.	PERSON
PAGE 38 G0748	

PERS/REL....RELATIONS BETWEEN PERSONS AND INTERPERSONAL
   COMMUNICATION

	N
PERSONNEL. USA+45 LAW LABOR LG/CO WORKER CREATE	BIBLIOG/A
GOV/REL PERS/REL ATTIT WEALTH. PAGE 1 G0010	ADMIN
	MGT
	GP/REL

	S43
KAPLAN A.,"CONTENT ANALYSIS AND THE THEORY OF	LOG
SIGNS" (BMR)" PERS/REL...PSY CONCPT LING IDEA/COMP	CON/ANAL
SIMUL BIBLIOG 20 MORRIS/CW. PAGE 29 G0573	STAT
	PHIL/SCI

	B45
MAYO E.,THE SOCIAL PROBLEMS OF AN INDUSTRIAL	INDUS
CIVILIZATION. USA+45 SOCIETY LABOR CROWD PERS/REL	GP/REL
LAISSEZ. PAGE 37 G0725	MGT
	WORKER

	B49
LEPAWSKY A.,ADMINISTRATION. FINAN INDUS LG/CO	ADMIN
SML/CO INGP/REL PERS/REL COST EFFICIENCY OPTIMAL	MGT
SKILL 20. PAGE 33 G0656	WORKER
	EX/STRUC

	S50
BAVELAS A.,"COMMUNICATION PATTERNS IN TASK-ORIENTED	ACT/RES
GROUPS" (BMR)" R+D OP/RES INSPECT LEAD CENTRAL	PERS/REL
EFFICIENCY HAPPINESS RIGID/FLEX...PROBABIL 20.	TASK
PAGE 6 G0106	INGP/REL

	B54
SIMMONS L.W.,SOCIAL SCIENCE IN MEDICINE. USA+45	PUB/INST
USA-45 SOCIETY CONSULT PLAN PROB/SOLV CONTROL	HABITAT
PERS/REL...POLICY HEAL TREND BIBLIOG 20. PAGE 51	HEALTH
G0999	BIO/SOC

	S56
MILLER G.A.,"THE MAGICAL NUMBER SEVEN, PLUS OR	LAB/EXP
MINUS TWO: SOME LIMITS ON OUR CAPACITY FOR	KNOWL
PROCESSING INFORMATION." PERS/REL...PSY METH/CNCPT	PERCEPT
LING CHARTS BIBLIOG 20. PAGE 39 G0772	COMPUT/IR

	B57
KIETH-LUCAS A.,DECISIONS ABOUT PEOPLE IN NEED, A	ADMIN
STUDY OF ADMINISTRATIVE RESPONSIVENESS IN PUBLIC	RIGID/FLEX
ASSISTANCE. USA+45 GIVE RECEIVE INGP/REL PERS/REL	SOC/WK
MORAL RESPECT WEALTH...SOC OBS BIBLIOG 20. PAGE 30	DECISION
G0595	

	S57
BAUMGARTEL H.,"LEADERSHIP STYLE AS A VARIABLE IN	LEAD
RESEARCH ADMINISTRATION." USA+45 ADMIN REPRESENT	EXEC
PERS/REL 20. PAGE 5 G0104	MGT
	INGP/REL

	B58
CHEEK G.,ECONOMIC AND SOCIAL IMPLICATIONS OF	BIBLIOG/A
AUTOMATION: A BIBLIOGRAPHIC REVIEW (PAMPHLET).	SOCIETY
USA+45 LG/CO WORKER CREATE PLAN CONTROL ROUTINE	INDUS
PERS/REL EFFICIENCY PRODUC...METH/COMP 20. PAGE 12	AUTOMAT
G0225	

	S58
ARGYRIS C.,"SOME PROBLEMS IN CONCEPTUALIZING	FINAN
ORGANIZATIONAL CLIMATE: A CASE STUDY OF A BANK"	CONCPT
(BMR)" USA+45 EX/STRUC ADMIN PERS/REL ADJUST PERSON	LG/CO
...POLICY HYPO/EXP SIMUL 20. PAGE 3 G0064	INGP/REL

	B59
GUILBAUD G.T.,WHAT IS CYBERNETICS? COMPUTER OP/RES	CONTROL
TEC/DEV AUTOMAT ROUTINE PERS/REL PERCEPT...PSY MATH	COM/IND
COMPUT/IR SIMUL GEN/METH. PAGE 23 G0460	FEEDBACK
	NET/THEORY

	B59
HUGHES E.M.,AMERICA THE VINCIBLE. USA+45 FOR/AID	ORD/FREE
ARMS/CONT NUC/PWR PERS/REL RATIONAL ATTIT ALL/VALS	DIPLOM

20 COLD/WAR. PAGE 27 G0534	WAR

	B61
KRUPP S.,PATTERN IN ORGANIZATIONAL ANALYSIS: A	MGT
CRITICAL EXAMINATION. INGP/REL PERS/REL RATIONAL	CONTROL
ATTIT AUTHORIT DRIVE PWR...DECISION PHIL/SCI SOC	CONCPT
IDEA/COMP. PAGE 32 G0622	METH/CNCPT

	L61
THOMPSON V.A.,"HIERARACHY, SPECIALIZATION, AND	PERS/REL
ORGANIZATIONAL CONFLICT" (BMR)" WOR+45 STRATA	PROB/SOLV
STRUCT WORKER TEC/DEV GP/REL INGP/REL ATTIT	ADMIN
AUTHORIT 20 BUREAUCRCY. PAGE 54 G1069	EX/STRUC

	B62
BAKER G.W.,BEHAVIORAL SCIENCE AND CIVIL DEFENSE.	NUC/PWR
USA+45 PROB/SOLV ADMIN GP/REL INGP/REL PERS/REL	WAR
ANOMIE DRIVE PERSON...DECISION MGT SOC 20	POLICY
CIV/DEFENS. PAGE 4 G0085	ACT/RES

	S62
STORER N.W.,"SOME SOCIOLOGICAL ASPECTS OF FEDERAL	POLICY
SCIENCE POLICY." USA+45 INTELL PUB/INST PLAN GP/REL	CREATE
PERS/REL DRIVE PERSON ROLE...PSY SOC SIMUL 20 NIH	NAT/G
NSF. PAGE 53 G1040	ALL/VALS

	B63
HOWER R.M.,MANAGERS AND SCIENTISTS. EX/STRUC CREATE	R+D
ADMIN REPRESENT ATTIT DRIVE ROLE PWR SKILL...SOC	MGT
INT. PAGE 27 G0532	PERS/REL
	INGP/REL

	B63
MILBRATH L.W.,THE WASHINGTON LOBBYISTS. CONSTN	LOBBY
BAL/PWR CONTROL LEAD TASK CHOOSE SUPEGO...DECISION	POLICY
STAT CHARTS BIBLIOG. PAGE 39 G0767	PERS/REL

	B63
RAUDSEPP E.,MANAGING CREATIVE SCIENTISTS AND	MGT
ENGINEERS. USA+45 ECO/DEV LG/CO GP/REL PERS/REL	CREATE
PRODUC. PAGE 46 G0906	R+D
	ECO/TAC

	B64
RIES J.C.,THE MANAGEMENT OF DEFENSE: ORGANIZATION	FORCES
AND CONTROL OF THE US ARMED SERVICES. PROF/ORG	ACT/RES
DELIB/GP EX/STRUC LEGIS GOV/REL PERS/REL CENTRAL	DECISION
RATIONAL PWR...POLICY TREND GOV/COMP BIBLIOG.	CONTROL
PAGE 47 G0920	

	B64
WHEELER-BENNETT J.W.,THE NEMESIS OF POWER (2ND	FORCES
ED.). EUR+WWI GERMANY TOP/EX TEC/DEV ADMIN WAR	NAT/G
PERS/REL RIGID/FLEX ROLE ORD/FREE PWR FASCISM 20	GP/REL
HITLER/A. PAGE 63 G1231	STRUCT

	B65
CARPER E.T.,REORGANIZATION OF THE U.S. PUBLIC	HEAL
HEALTH SERVICE. FUT USA+45 INTELL R+D LOBBY GP/REL	PLAN
INGP/REL PERS/REL RIGID/FLEX ROLE HEALTH...PHIL/SCI	NAT/G
20 CONGRESS PHS. PAGE 11 G0213	OP/RES

	B67
GOLEMBIEWSKI R.T.,ORGANIZING MEN AND POWER:	ADMIN
PATTERNS OF BEHAVIOR AND LINESTAFF MODELS. WOR+45	CONTROL
EX/STRUC ACT/RES DOMIN PERS/REL...NEW/IDEA 20.	SIMUL
PAGE 22 G0431	MGT

	B67
MACBRIDE R.,THE AUTOMATED STATE: COMPUTER SYSTEMS	COMPUTER
AS A NEW FORCE IN SOCIETY. FUT WOR+45 FINAN MUNIC	AUTOMAT
NAT/G WORKER PLAN TEC/DEV CONTROL PERS/REL RACE/REL	PROB/SOLV
ADJUST. PAGE 35 G0685	SOCIETY

	B67
WEINBERG A.M.,REFLECTIONS ON BIG SCIENCE. FUT	ACADEM
USA+45 NAT/G EDU/PROP CHOOSE PERS/REL COST OPTIMAL	KNOWL
...PHIL/SCI TREND. PAGE 62 G1225	R+D
	PLAN

	S67
CRANBERG L.,"SCIENCE, ETHICS, AND LAW." UNIV CREATE	LAW
PLAN EDU/PROP INGP/REL PERS/REL ADJUST RATIONAL	PHIL/SCI
KNOWL MORAL...CONCPT IDEA/COMP 20. PAGE 13 G0260	INTELL

	S67
LA PORTE T.,"DIFFUSION AND DISCONTINUITY IN	INTELL
SCIENCE, TECHNOLOGY AND PUBLIC AFFAIRS: RESULTS OF	ADMIN
A SEARCH IN THE FIELD." USA+45 ACT/RES TEC/DEV	ACADEM
PERS/REL ATTIT PHIL/SCI. PAGE 32 G0628	GP/REL

PERS/TEST....PERSONALITY TESTS

	B52
CURRENT TRENDS IN PSYCHOLOGY.PSYCHOLOGY IN THE	NAT/G
WORLD EMERGENCY. USA+45 CONSULT FORCES ACT/RES PLAN	PSY

SKILL...DECISION OBS APT/TEST KNO/TEST PERS/TEST
TREND CHARTS 20. PAGE 14 G0266

B54
COMBS C.H..DECISION PROCESSES. INTELL SOCIETY   MATH
DELIB/GP CREATE TEC/DEV DOMIN LEGIT EXEC CHOOSE   DECISION
DRIVE RIGID/FLEX KNOWL PWR...PHIL/SCI SOC
METH/CNCPT CONT/OBS REC/INT PERS/TEST SAMP/SIZ BIOG
SOC/EXP WORK. PAGE 13 G0245

S58
ANDERSON N.."INTERNATIONAL SEMINARS: AN ANALYSIS   INT/ORG
AND AN EVALUATION." WOR+45 R+D ACT/RES CREATE PLAN   DELIB/GP
REGION ATTIT KNOWL SKILL...SOC REC/INT PERS/TEST
CHARTS 20. PAGE 3 G0057

B63
TOMKINS S.S..COMPUTER SIMULATION OF PERSONALITY.   COMPUTER
R+D TEC/DEV AUTOMAT FEEDBACK ANOMIE PERCEPT...STYLE   PERSON
PERS/TEST PREDICT COMPUT/IR GP/COMP. PAGE 55 G1075   SIMUL
                                                       PROG/TEAC

PERSIA....PERSIA: ANCIENT IRAN

PERSON....PERSONALITY AND HUMAN NATURE

B11
BERGSON H..CREATIVE EVOLUTION. FUT WOR+45 WOR-45   BIO/SOC
INTELL AGRI R+D ATTIT PERCEPT PERSON RIGID/FLEX   KNOWL
...RELATIV PHIL/SCI PSY METH/CNCPT MATH HIST/WRIT
TREND HYPO/EXP TOT/POP. PAGE 7 G0127

B29
DEWEY J..THE QUEST FOR CERTAINTY. GP/REL RATIONAL   PHIL/SCI
UTOPIA ATTIT MORAL ORD/FREE PWR...MYTH HIST/WRIT.   PERSON
PAGE 15 G0301   PERCEPT
                                                       KNOWL

B44
KAUFMANN F..METHODOLOGY OF THE SOCIAL SCIENCES.   SOC
PERSON...RELATIV PSY CONCPT LING METH 20. PAGE 30   PHIL/SCI
G0585   GEN/LAWS
                                                       METH/CNCPT

S44
HAWLEY A.H.."ECOLOGY AND HUMAN ECOLOGY" WOR+45   HABITAT
INTELL ACADEM PLAN GP/REL ADJUST PERSON...PHIL/SCI   GEOG
SOC METH/CNCPT METH 20. PAGE 25 G0493   GEN/LAWS
                                                       METH/COMP

C45
TRYTTEN M.H.."THE MOBILIZATION OF SCIENTISTS." IN   INTELL
L. WHITE. CIVIL SERVICE IN WARTIME." USA-45 R+D   WAR
FORCES ACT/RES PERSON ROLE 20. PAGE 55 G1080   TEC/DEV
                                                       NAT/G

B47
BECK H.P..MEN WHO CONTROL OUR UNIVERSITIES.   EDU/PROP
EX/STRUC CHOOSE INGP/REL DISCRIM PERSON WEALTH   ACADEM
...POLICY TREND CON/ANAL CHARTS BIBLIOG. PAGE 6   CONTROL
G0112   LEAD

S47
TURNER R.H.."THE NAVY DISBURSING OFFICER AS A   FORCES
BUREAUCRAT" (BMR)" USA-45 LAW STRATA DIST/IND WAR   ADMIN
PWR...SOC 20 BUREAUCRCY. PAGE 55 G1083   PERSON
                                                       ROLE

B50
CANTRIL H..TENSIONS THAT CAUSE WAR. UNIV CULTURE   SOCIETY
R+D CREATE EDU/PROP DRIVE PERSON KNOWL ORD/FREE   PHIL/SCI
...HUM PSY SOC OBS CENSUS TREND CON/ANAL SOC/EXP   PEACE
SIMUL GEN/METH ANTHOL COLD/WAR TOT/POP. PAGE 11
G0206

S50
KAPLAN A.."THE PREDICTION OF SOCIAL AND   PWR
TECHNOLOGICAL EVENTS." VOL/ASSN CONSULT ACT/RES   KNO/TEST
CREATE OP/RES PLAN ROUTINE PERSON...POLICY
METH/CNCPT STAT QU/SEMANT SYS/QU TESTS CENSUS TREND
20. PAGE 29 G0574

B52
CALLOT E.."LA SOCIETE ET SON ENVIRONNEMENT: ESSAI   SOCIETY
SUR LES PRINCIPES DES SCIENCES SOCIALES. GP/REL   PHIL/SCI
ADJUST CONSEN ISOLAT HABITAT PERCEPT PERSON   CULTURE
...BIBLIOG SOC/INTEG 20. PAGE 10 G0205

S53
CORY R.H. JR.."FORGING A PUBLIC INFORMATION POLICY   INT/ORG
FOR THE UNITED NATIONS." FUT WOR+45 SOCIETY ADMIN   EDU/PROP
PEACE ATTIT PERSON SKILL...CONCPT 20 UN. PAGE 13   BAL/PWR
G0257

B55
MOCH J..HUMAN FOLLY: DISARM OR PERISH. USA+45   FUT

WOR+45 SOCIETY INT/ORG NAT/G ACT/RES EDU/PROP ATTIT   DELIB/GP
PERSON KNOWL ORD/FREE PWR...MAJORIT TOT/POP   ARMS/CONT
COLD/WAR 20. PAGE 39 G0776   NUC/PWR

S55
GLADSTONE A.E.."THE POSSIBILITY OF PREDICTING   PHIL/SCI
REACTIONS TO INTERNATIONAL EVENTS." UNIV SOCIETY   CONCPT
NAT/G FORCES CREATE EDU/PROP COERCE WAR ATTIT
PERSON KNOWL PWR SKILL...METH/CNCPT NEW/IDEA
ORG/CHARTS. PAGE 21 G0420

B57
MERTON R.K..SOCIAL THEORY AND SOCIAL STRUCTURE   SOC
(REV. ED.). INTELL SECT WORKER OP/RES EDU/PROP   GEN/LAWS
ADMIN INGP/REL ANOMIE PERSON...AUD/VIS T 20   SOCIETY
BUREAUCRCY. PAGE 38 G0759   STRUCT

B58
ARON R..ON WAR: ATOMIC WEAPONS AND GLOBAL DIPLOMACY   ARMS/CONT
(TRANS. BY TERENCE KILMARTIN). WOR+45 SOCIETY   NUC/PWR
FORCES BAL/PWR WAR WEAPON PERSON...SOC 20. PAGE 4   COERCE
G0067   DIPLOM

B58
JUNGK R..BRIGHTER THAN A THOUSAND SUNS: THE MORAL   NUC/PWR
AND POLITICAL HISTORY OF THE ATOMIC SCIENTISTS.   MORAL
WOR+45 WOR-45 CONSULT CREATE RISK UTIL DRIVE   GOV/REL
PERCEPT PWR...INT 20. PAGE 29 G0568   PERSON

B58
ORTEGA Y GASSET J..MAN AND CRISIS. SECT CREATE   PHIL/SCI
PERSON CONSERVE...GEN/LAWS RENAISSAN. PAGE 43 G0846   CULTURE
                                                     CONCPT

S58
ARGYRIS C.."SOME PROBLEMS IN CONCEPTUALIZING   FINAN
ORGANIZATIONAL CLIMATE: A CASE STUDY OF A BANK"   CONCPT
(BMR)" USA+45 EX/STRUC ADMIN PERS/REL ADJUST PERSON   LG/CO
...POLICY HYPO/EXP SIMUL 20. PAGE 3 G0064   INGP/REL

S58
FOLDES L.."UNCERTAINTY, PROBABILITY AND POTENTIAL   PROBABIL
SURPRISE." MARKET PROB/SOLV RISK PERSON...DECISION   ADMIN
MGT HYPO/EXP GAME. PAGE 19 G0376   ROUTINE

B59
GODDARD V..THE ENIGMA OF MENACE. WOR+45 SECT LEAD   PEACE
NUC/PWR WAR WEAPON CHOOSE PERSON PWR...POLICY   ARMS/CONT
PHIL/SCI PACIFIST 20 COLD/WAR. PAGE 22 G0423   DIPLOM
                                                     ATTIT

B59
RUSSELL B..COMMON SENSE AND NUCLEAR WARFARE. WOR+45   ORD/FREE
INTELL SOCIETY STRATA NAT/G TOP/EX EDU/PROP ATTIT   ARMS/CONT
PERSON KNOWL MORAL PWR...POLICY CONCPT MYTH   NUC/PWR
CON/ANAL COLD/WAR 20. PAGE 48 G0948

B60
CARPENTER E..EXPLORATIONS IN COMMUNICATION. USSR   ANTHOL
CULTURE SCHOOL SECT EDU/PROP PRESS TV AUTOMAT   COM/IND
FEEDBACK ATTIT PERSON...ART/METH PSY 20. PAGE 11   TEC/DEV
G0211   WRITING

B60
RAPOPORT A..FIGHTS, GAMES AND DEBATES. INTELL   METH/CNCPT
SOCIETY R+D EX/STRUC PERCEPT PERSON SKILL...PSY SOC   MATH
GAME. PAGE 46 G0902   DECISION
                                                     CON/ANAL

B60
SLUCKIN W..MINDS AND MACHINES (REV. ED.). PROB/SOLV   PSY
TEC/DEV AUTOMAT TASK PERCEPT HEALTH KNOWL   COMPUTER
...DECISION MATH PROBABIL COMPUT/IR GAME 20.   PERSON
PAGE 51 G1012   SIMUL

L60
HOLZMAN B.G.."BASIC RESEARCH FOR NATIONAL   FORCES
SURVIVAL." FUT USA+45 INTELL R+D ACT/RES OP/RES   STAT
PLAN TEC/DEV EDU/PROP PERCEPT PERSON...PHIL/SCI
METH/CNCPT NEW/IDEA MATH OBS RECORD TREND LAB/EXP
20. PAGE 27 G0525

S60
OSGOOD C.E.."A CASE FOR GRADUATED UNILATERAL   ATTIT
DISENGAGEMENT." FUT WOR+45 CULTURE SOCIETY NAT/G   EDU/PROP
NUC/PWR WAR PERSON SUPEGO ALL/VALS...POLICY PSY   ARMS/CONT
CONCPT COLD/WAR TOT/POP VAL/FREE 20. PAGE 43 G0848

B61
INSTITUTE PSYCHOLOGICAL RES.HUMAN ENGINEERING   BIBLIOG/A
BIBLIOGRAPHY, 1959-1960. USA+45 WORKER EDU/PROP   METH
PERSON METH/COMP. PAGE 28 G0547   PSY
                                                     R+D

B61
KAHN H..ON THERMONUCLEAR WAR. FUT UNIV WOR+45   DETER

ECO/DEV CONSULT EX/STRUC TOP/EX ACT/RES CREATE PLAN NUC/PWR
COERCE WAR PERSON ALL/VALS...POLICY GEOG CONCPT SOCIETY
METH/CNCPT OBS TREND 20. PAGE 29 G0569

B61
MCRAE R.,THE PROBLEM OF THE UNITY OF THE SCIENCES: PHIL/SCI
BACON TO KANT. CREATE TASK KNOWL...PERS/COMP 16/18 IDEA/COMP
BACON/F DESCARTE/R LEIBNITZ/G KANT/I DIDEROT/D. PERSON
PAGE 38 G0748

B61
MICHAEL D.N.,PROPOSED STUDIES ON THE IMPLICATIONS FUT
OF PEACEFUL SPACE ACTIVITIES FOR HUMAN AFFAIRS. SPACE
COM/IND INDUS FORCES DIPLOM PEACE PERSON...PSY SOC ACT/RES
20. PAGE 39 G0764 PROB/SOLV

B61
NATHAN O.,EINSTEIN ON PEACE. WOR+45 WOR-45 INTELL CONCPT
NUC/PWR WAR PERSON MORAL...BIOG VAL/FREE NAZI 20 PEACE
EINSTEIN/A. PAGE 41 G0807

S61
DEUTSCH K.W.,"A NOTE ON THE APPEARANCE OF WISDOM IN ADMIN
LARGE BUREAUCRATIC ORGANIZATIONS." ROUTINE PERSON PROBABIL
KNOWL SKILL...DECISION STAT. PAGE 15 G0299 PROB/SOLV
SIMUL

S61
SCHILLING W.R.,"THE H-BOMB: HOW TO DECIDE WITHOUT PERSON
ACTUALLY CHOOSING." FUT USA+45 INTELL CONSULT ADMIN LEGIT
CT/SYS MORAL...JURID OBS 20 TRUMAN/HS. PAGE 49 NUC/PWR
G0966

B62
BAKER G.W.,BEHAVIORAL SCIENCE AND CIVIL DEFENSE. NUC/PWR
USA+45 PROB/SOLV ADMIN GP/REL INGP/REL PERS/REL WAR
ANOMIE DRIVE PERSON...DECISION MGT SOC 20 POLICY
CIV/DEFENS. PAGE 4 G0085 ACT/RES

B62
CHASE S.,THE PROPER STUDY OF MANKIND (2ND REV. PHIL/SCI
ED.). WOR+45 WOR-45 INTELL WAR...METH/CNCPT SOC
SAMP/SIZ GEN/LAWS BIBLIOG METH 16/20. PAGE 11 G0224 PROB/SOLV
PERSON

S62
STORER N.W.,"SOME SOCIOLOGICAL ASPECTS OF FEDERAL POLICY
SCIENCE POLICY." USA+45 INTELL PUB/INST PLAN GP/REL CREATE
PERS/REL DRIVE PERSON ROLE...PSY SOC SIMUL 20 NIH NAT/G
NSF. PAGE 53 G1040 ALL/VALS

B63
RUITENBEER H.M.,THE DILEMMA OF ORGANIZATIONAL PERSON
SOCIETY. CULTURE ECO/DEV MUNIC SECT TEC/DEV ROLE
EDU/PROP NAT/LISM ORD/FREE...NAT/COMP 20 RIESMAN/D ADMIN
WHYTE/WF MERTON/R MEAD/MARG JASPERS/K. PAGE 48 WORKER
G0945

B63
TOMKINS S.S.,COMPUTER SIMULATION OF PERSONALITY. COMPUTER
R+D TEC/DEV AUTOMAT FEEDBACK ANOMIE PERCEPT...STYLE PERSON
PERS/TEST PREDICT COMPUT/IR GP/COMP. PAGE 55 G1075 SIMUL
PROG/TEAC

B64
BRIGHT J.R.,RESEARCH, DEVELOPMENT AND TECHNOLOGICAL TEC/DEV
INNOVATION. CULTURE R+D CREATE PLAN PROB/SOLV NEW/IDEA
AUTOMAT RISK PERSON...DECISION CONCPT PREDICT INDUS
BIBLIOG. PAGE 9 G0168 MGT

B64
GRODZINS M.,THE ATOMIC AGE: FORTY-FIVE SCIENTISTS INTELL
AND SCHOLARS SPEAK ON NATIONAL AND WORLD AFFAIRS. ARMS/CONT
FUT USA+45 WOR+45 R+D INT/ORG NAT/G CONSULT TEC/DEV NUC/PWR
EDU/PROP ATTIT PERSON ORD/FREE...HUM CONCPT
TIME/SEQ CON/ANAL. PAGE 23 G0454

B64
GROSSER G.H.,THE THREAT OF IMPENDING DISASTER: HEALTH
CONTRIBUTIONS TO THE PSYCHOLOGY OF STRESS. SPACE PSY
UNIV SOCIETY R+D TEC/DEV EDU/PROP COERCE WAR ATTIT NUC/PWR
BIO/SOC DISPL PERCEPT PERSON...SOC MYTH SELF/OBS
CONT/OBS BIOG CON/ANAL TOT/POP 20. PAGE 23 G0455

B64
WIRTH L.,ON CITIES AND SOCIAL LIFE: SELECTED GEN/LAWS
PAPERS. PLAN PROB/SOLV RACE/REL CONSEN ATTIT SOCIETY
HABITAT PERSON...POLICY SOC CONCPT ANTHOL BIBLIOG NEIGH
20. PAGE 64 G1249 STRUCT

S64
BYRNES F.C.,"ASSIGNMENT TO AMBIGUITY: WORK INTELL
PERFORMANCE IN CROSSCULTURAL TECHNICAL ASSISTANCE." QU
USA+45 WOR+45 PROF/ORG CONSULT PLAN EDU/PROP ATTIT
DISPL PERCEPT PERSON ALL/VALS...POLICY INT CHARTS
NATO 20. PAGE 10 G0199

B65
STEINER G.A.,THE CREATIVE ORGANIZATION. ELITES CREATE
LG/CO PLAN PROB/SOLV TEC/DEV INSPECT CAP/ISM MGT
CONTROL EXEC PERSON...METH/COMP HYPO/EXP 20. ADMIN
PAGE 52 G1034 SOC

B67
POMEROY W.J.,HALF A CENTURY OF SOCIALISM. USSR LAW SOCISM
AGRI INDUS NAT/G CREATE DIPLOM EDU/PROP PERSON MARXISM
ORD/FREE WEALTH...POLICY TREND 20. PAGE 45 G0884 COM
SOCIETY

B67
UNIVERSAL REFERENCE SYSTEM,PUBLIC OPINION, MASS BIBLIOG/A
BEHAVIOR, AND POLITICAL PSYCHOLOGY (VOLUME VI). ATTIT
WOR+45 WOR-45 SOCIETY EDU/PROP PRESS PARTIC CHOOSE CROWD
PERSON...TREND COMPUT/IR GEN/METH. PAGE 56 G1098 PSY

S67
SUINN R.M.,"THE DISARMAMENT FANTASY* PSYCHOLOGICAL DECISION
FACTORS THAT MAY PRODUCE WARFARE." DIPLOM RISK NUC/PWR
ARMS/CONT DETER ANOMIE PERSON GAME. PAGE 53 G1046 WAR
PSY

PERSONAL RELATIONS....SEE PERS/REL

PERSONALITY....SEE PERSON, ALSO PERSONALITY INDEX, P. XIII

PERSONALITY TESTS....SEE PERS/TEST

PERSUASION....SEE LOBBY, EDU/PROP

PERU....SEE ALSO L/A+17C

S66
COHEN A.,"THE TECHNOLOGY/ELITE APPROACH TO THE ECO/UNDEV
DEVELOPMENTAL PROCESS* PERUVIAN CASE STUDY." ELITES
L/A+17C STRUCT CREATE ECO/TAC FOR/AID CIVMIL/REL PERU
MARXISM TECHRACY HYPO/EXP. PAGE 12 G0239

PETAIN/HP....H.P. PETAIN

PETERS....PETERS V. NEW YORK

PETERSON W. G0871

PFALTZGRAFF RL J.R. G0598

PFIFFNER J.M. G0872

PHELPS E.S. G0873

PHELPS J. G0874,G0875

PHIL/SCI....SCIENTIFIC METHOD AND PHILOSOPHY OF SCIENCE

N
AMERICAN DOCUMENTATION INST,DOCUMENTATION BIBLIOG/A
ABSTRACTS. WOR+45 NAT/G COMPUTER CREATE TEC/DEV AUTOMAT
DIPLOM EDU/PROP REGION KNOWL...PHIL/SCI CLASSIF COMPUT/IR
LING. PAGE 3 G0051 R+D

B
US DEPT COMMERCE OFF TECH SERV,TECHNICAL BIBLIOG
TRANSLATIONS. WOR+45 INDUS COMPUTER CREATE NUC/PWR R+D
...PHIL/SCI COMPUT/IR METH/COMP METH. PAGE 58 G1135 TEC/DEV
AUTOMAT

N
AMER COUNCIL OF LEARNED SOCIET,THE ACLS CONSTITUENT BIBLIOG/A
SOCIETY JOURNAL PROJECT. FUT USA+45 LAW NAT/G PLAN HUM
DIPLOM PHIL/SCI. PAGE 3 G0048 COMPUT/IR
COMPUTER

B11
BERGSON H.,CREATIVE EVOLUTION. FUT WOR+45 WOR-45 BIO/SOC
INTELL AGRI R+D ATTIT PERCEPT PERSON RIGID/FLEX KNOWL
...RELATIV PHIL/SCI PSY METH/CNCPT MATH HIST/WRIT
TREND HYPO/EXP TOT/POP. PAGE 7 G0127

B14
CRAIG J.,ELEMENTS OF POLITICAL SCIENCE (3 VOLS.). PHIL/SCI
CONSTN AGRI INDUS SCHOOL FORCES TAX CT/SYS SUFF NAT/G
MORAL WEALTH...CONCPT 19 CIVIL/LIB. PAGE 13 G0259 ORD/FREE

N19
DOTSON A.,PRODUCTION PLANNING IN THE PATENT OFFICE EFFICIENCY
(PAMPHLET). USA+45 DIST/IND PROB/SOLV PRODUC...MGT PLAN
PHIL/SCI 20 BUR/BUDGET PATENT/OFF. PAGE 16 G0309 NAT/G
ADMIN

N19
LAWRENCE S.A.,THE BATTERY ADDITIVE CONTROVERSY PHIL/SCI
(PAMPHLET). USA+45 LAW MARKET PROC/MFG R+D CAP/ISM LOBBY
CT/SYS GOV/REL OWN FTC CONGRESS BUR/STNDRD INSPECT

N19
US ATOMIC ENERGY COMMISSION,ATOMIC ENERGY IN USE
(PAMPHLET). R+D RISK EFFICIENCY HEALTH KNOWL
ORD/FREE...PHIL/SCI CONCPT METH/CNCPT CHARTS
LAB/EXP 20 AEC. PAGE 56 G1106
OP/RES
TEC/DEV
NUC/PWR
CREATE

B46
BAXTER J.P.,SCIENTISTS AGAINST TIME. EUR+WWI
MOD/EUR USA+45 USA-45 WOR+45 WOR-45 R+D NAT/G PLAN
ATTIT PWR...PHIL/SCI RECORD CON/ANAL 17/20. PAGE 6
G0107
FORCES
WAR
NUC/PWR

B23
DRAPER J.W.,HISTORY OF THE CONFLICT BETWEEN
RELIGION AND SCIENCE. WOR-45 INTELL SOCIETY R+D
CREATE PLAN TEC/DEV EDU/PROP ATTIT PWR...PHIL/SCI
CONCPT OBS TIME/SEQ TREND GEN/LAWS TOT/POP. PAGE 16
G0314
SECT
KNOWL

B46
BUSH V.,ENDLESS HORIZONS. FUT USA-45 INTELL NAT/G
CONSULT ACT/RES CREATE PLAN EDU/PROP DRIVE
...MAJORIT HEAL MGT PHIL/SCI CONCPT OBS TREND
GEN/METH TOT/POP 20. PAGE 10 G0196
R+D
KNOWL
PEACE

C27
BOSANQUET B.,"SCIENCE AND PHILOSOPHY" IN J.
MUIRHEAD AND R.B. BOSANQUET, EDS., SCIENCE AND
PHILOSOPHY AND OTHER ESSAYS."...CONCPT METH/COMP
GEN/METH. PAGE 8 G0155
PHIL/SCI
CREATE
METH/CNCPT
NEW/IDEA

L46
MASTERS D.,"ONE WORLD OR NONE." FUT WOR+45 INTELL
INT/ORG ACT/RES EDU/PROP DETER ATTIT RIGID/FLEX
SUPEGO KNOWL...STAT TREND ORG/CHARTS 20. PAGE 36
G0719
POLICY
PHIL/SCI
ARMS/CONT
NUC/PWR

B28
BARKER E.,POLITICAL THOUGHT IN ENGLAND: FROM
HERBERT SPENCER TO THE PRESENT DAY. UK ALL/IDEOS
...PHIL/SCI 19/20 SPENCER/H GREEN/TH BENTHAM/J
MAITLAND/F. PAGE 5 G0094
INTELL
GEN/LAWS
IDEA/COMP

B47
LASSWELL H.D.,THE ANALYSIS OF POLITICAL BEHAVIOUR:
AN EMPIRICAL APPROACH. WOR+45 CULTURE NAT/G FORCES
EDU/PROP ADMIN ATTIT PERCEPT KNOWL...PHIL/SCI PSY
SOC NEW/IDEA OBS INT GEN/METH NAZI 20. PAGE 32
G0639
R+D
ACT/RES
ELITES

B29
DEWEY J.,THE QUEST FOR CERTAINTY. GP/REL RATIONAL
UTOPIA ATTIT MORAL ORD/FREE PWR...MYTH HIST/WRIT.
PAGE 15 G0301
PHIL/SCI
PERSON
PERCEPT
KNOWL

B48
BRADLEY D.,NO PLACE TO HIDE. USA+45 SOCIETY NAT/G
FORCES TEC/DEV EDU/PROP DETER PEACE BIO/SOC
ALL/VALS...POLICY PHIL/SCI OBS RECORD SAMP BIOG
GEN/METH COLD/WAR 20. PAGE 8 G0162
R+D
LAB/EXP
ARMS/CONT
NUC/PWR

B34
BOWMAN I.,GEOGRAPHY IN RELATION TO THE SOCIAL
SCIENCES. UNIV...SOC CONCPT METH. PAGE 8 G0161
GEOG
CULTURE
ROUTINE
PHIL/SCI

B48
GRIFFITH E.S.,RESEARCH IN POLITICAL SCIENCE: THE
WORK OF PANELS OF RESEARCH COMMITTEE. APSA. WOR+45
WOR-45 COM/IND R+D FORCES ACT/RES WAR...GOV/COMP
ANTHOL 20. PAGE 23 G0451
BIBLIOG
PHIL/SCI
DIPLOM
JURID

B34
COHEN M.R.,AN INTRODUCTION TO LOGIC AND SCIENTIFIC
METHOD....LING MATH CHARTS T 20. PAGE 12 G0242
LOG
PHIL/SCI
GEN/METH
METH/CNCPT

S48
MACCORQUODALE K.,"ON A DISTINCTION BETWEEN
HYPOTHETICAL CONSTRUCTS AND INTERVENING VARIABLES."
...METH/CNCPT LING IDEA/COMP HYPO/EXP SOC/EXP
BIBLIOG 20. PAGE 35 G0686
PSY
PHIL/SCI
CONCPT
GEN/METH

B34
EINSTEIN A.,THE WORLD AS I SEE IT. WOR-45 INTELL
R+D INT/ORG NAT/G SECT VOL/ASSN FORCES CREATE
EDU/PROP LEGIT ARMS/CONT WAR WEAPON NAT/LISM
ALL/VALS...POLICY CONCPT 20. PAGE 17 G0337
SOCIETY
PHIL/SCI
DIPLOM
PACIFISM

S48
MERTON R.K.,"THE BEARING OF EMPIRICAL RESEARCH UPON
THE DEVELOPMENT OF SOCIAL THEORY" (BMR)"...SOC
CONCPT QUANT METH/COMP HYPO/EXP 20. PAGE 38 G0757
ACT/RES
SOC/EXP
OBS
PHIL/SCI

B37
GULICK L.,PAPERS ON THE SCIENCE OF ADMINISTRATION.
INDUS PROB/SOLV TEC/DEV COST EFFICIENCY PRODUC
HABITAT...PHIL/SCI METH/COMP 20. PAGE 23 G0461
OP/RES
CONTROL
ADMIN
MGT

B50
CANTRIL H.,TENSIONS THAT CAUSE WAR. UNIV CULTURE
R+D CREATE EDU/PROP DRIVE PERSON KNOWL ORD/FREE
...HUM PSY SOC OBS CENSUS TREND CON/ANAL SOC/EXP
SIMUL GEN/METH ANTHOL COLD/WAR TOT/POP. PAGE 11
G0206
SOCIETY
PHIL/SCI
PEACE

B37
STAMP S.,THE SCIENCE OF SOCIAL ADJUSTMENT. WOR-45
ACT/RES CREATE PLAN PROB/SOLV TEC/DEV ECO/TAC
EFFICIENCY SOC/INTEG 20. PAGE 52 G1031
ADJUST
ORD/FREE
PHIL/SCI

B50
CONTINUITIES IN SOCIAL RESEARCH; STUDIES IN SCOPE
AND METHOD OF "THE AMERICAN SOLDIER" USA+45 FORCES
INGP/REL ATTIT...PSY SAMP CON/ANAL CHARTS GEN/LAWS
ANTHOL 20. PAGE 38 G0758
SOC
PHIL/SCI
METH

S38
LUNDBERG G.A.,"THE CONCEPT OF LAW IN THE SOCIAL
SCIENCES"(BMR)" CULTURE INTELL SOCIETY STRUCT
CREATE...NEW/IDEA 20. PAGE 34 G0678
EPIST
GEN/LAWS
CONCPT
PHIL/SCI

B51
CONANT J.B.,SCIENCE AND COMMON SENSE. WOR+45 WOR-45 CREATE
R+D SCHOOL CONSULT TEC/DEV EDU/PROP SKILL...PLURIST PHIL/SCI
METH/CNCPT RECORD TIME/SEQ SIMUL GEN/METH METH.
PAGE 13 G0248

B40
ZNANIECKI F.,THE SOCIAL ROLE OF THE MAN OF
KNOWLEDGE. UNIV SOCIETY STRUCT TEC/DEV...EPIST
PHIL/SCI SOC NEW/IDEA 20. PAGE 65 G1269
ROLE
INTELL
KNOWL
INGP/REL

B51
HUXLEY J.,FREEDOM AND CULTURE. UNIV LAW SOCIETY R+D CULTURE
ACADEM SCHOOL CREATE SANCTION ATTIT KNOWL...HUM ORD/FREE
ANTHOL 20. PAGE 27 G0540
PHIL/SCI
IDEA/COMP

S43
KAPLAN A.,"CONTENT ANALYSIS AND THE THEORY OF
SIGNS" (BMR)" PERS/REL...PSY CONCPT LING IDEA/COMP
SIMUL BIBLIOG 20 MORRIS/CW. PAGE 29 G0573
LOG
CON/ANAL
STAT
PHIL/SCI

B51
LEWIN K.,FIELD THEORY IN SOCIAL SCIENCE: SELECTED PHIL/SCI
THEORETICAL PAPERS. UNIV CREATE DRIVE PERCEPT KNOWL HYPO/EXP
...METH/CNCPT CONT/OBS CHARTS GEN/METH METH
VAL/FREE 20. PAGE 33 G0661

B44
KAUFMANN F.,METHODOLOGY OF THE SOCIAL SCIENCES.
PERSON...RELATIV PSY CONCPT LING METH 20. PAGE 30
G0585
SOC
PHIL/SCI
GEN/LAWS
METH/CNCPT

S51
BERGMANN G.,"IDEOLOGY" (BMR)" UNIV PERCEPT KNOWL PHIL/SCI
...IDEA/COMP METH. PAGE 7 G0126
CONCPT
LOG
ALL/IDEOS

S44
HAWLEY A.H.,"ECOLOGY AND HUMAN ECOLOGY" WOR+45
INTELL ACADEM PLAN GP/REL ADJUST PERSON...PHIL/SCI
SOC METH/CNCPT METH 20. PAGE 25 G0493
HABITAT
GEOG
GEN/LAWS
METH/COMP

S51
MACRAE D.G.,"THE BOLSHEVIK IDEOLOGY; THE
INTELLECTUAL AND EMOTIONAL FACTORS IN COMMUNIST
AFFILIATION" (BMR)" COM LEAD REV ATTIT ORD/FREE
...SOC CON/ANAL 20 BOLSHEVISM. PAGE 35 G0693
MARXISM
INTELL
PHIL/SCI
SECT

B45
BUSH V.,SCIENCE, THE ENDLESS FRONTIER. FUT USA-45
INTELL STRATA ACT/RES CREATE PLAN EDU/PROP ADMIN
NUC/PWR PEACE ATTIT HEALTH KNOWL...MAJORIT HEAL MGT
R+D
NAT/G

B52
APPADORAI A.,THE SUBSTANCE OF POLITICS (6TH ED.).   PHIL/SCI

EX/STRUC LEGIS DIPLOM CT/SYS CHOOSE FASCISM MARXISM NAT/G
SOCISM...BIBLIOG T. PAGE 3 G0062

B52
CALLOT E..LA SOCIETE ET SON ENVIRONNEMENT: ESSAI
SUR LES PRINCIPES DES SCIENCES SOCIALES. GP/REL
ADJUST CONSEN ISOLAT HABITAT PERCEPT PERSON
...BIBLIOG SOC/INTEG 20. PAGE 10 G0205
SOCIETY
PHIL/SCI
CULTURE

B52
HAYEK F.A..THE COUNTER-REVOLUTION OF SCIENCE. UNIV
INTELL R+D VOL/ASSN CREATE EDU/PROP...PHIL/SCI SOC
OBS TIME/SEQ TREND GEN/METH. PAGE 25 G0494
PERCEPT
KNOWL

L52
LASSWELL H.D.."RESEARCH IN POLITICAL BEHAVIOR."
LOC/G MUNIC POL/PAR CONSULT ADMIN PARTIC...CHARTS
ANTHOL BIBLIOG/A 20. PAGE 32 G0641
PHIL/SCI
METH
R+D

S52
"SELECTED CRITICAL BIBLIOGRAPHY ON THE METHODS AND
TECHNIQUES OF POLITICAL BEHAVIOR RESEARCH."
...PHIL/SCI OBS QU SYS/QU TESTS CON/ANAL. PAGE 1
G0012
BIBLIOG/A
METH
SOC
EDU/PROP

S52
KECSKEMETI P..THE 'POLICY SCIENCES': ASPIRATION
AND OUTLOOK." UNIV CULTURE INTELL SOCIETY STRUCT
EDU/PROP ATTIT PERCEPT RIGID/FLEX KNOWL...PHIL/SCI
METH/CNCPT OBS 20. PAGE 30 G0589
CREATE
NEW/IDEA

B53
EASTON D..THE POLITICAL SYSTEM, AN INQUIRY INTO THE
STATE POLITICAL SCIENCE. USA+45 INTELL CREATE
EDU/PROP RIGID/FLEX KNOWL SKILL...PHIL/SCI NEW/IDEA
STERTYP TOT/POP 20. PAGE 17 G0329
R+D
PERCEPT

B54
COMBS C.H..DECISION PROCESSES. INTELL SOCIETY
DELIB/GP CREATE TEC/DEV DOMIN LEGIT EXEC CHOOSE
DRIVE RIGID/FLEX KNOWL PWR...PHIL/SCI SOC
METH/CNCPT CONT/OBS REC/INT PERS/TEST SAMP/SIZ BIOG
SOC/EXP WORK. PAGE 13 G0245
MATH
DECISION

B54
HART B.H.L..STRATEGY (REV. ED.). CHRIST-17C EUR+WWI
MEDIT-7 MOD/EUR TEC/DEV LEAD REV WEAPON...POLICY
CHARTS. PAGE 25 G0486
WAR
PLAN
FORCES
PHIL/SCI

B54
MCCLOSKEY J.F..OPERATIONS RESEARCH FOR MANAGEMENT.
STRUCT COMPUTER ADMIN ROUTINE...PHIL/SCI CONCPT
METH/CNCPT TREND ANTHOL BIBLIOG 20. PAGE 37 G0731
OP/RES
MGT
METH/COMP
TEC/DEV

B54
SPENCER R.F..METHOD AND PERSPECTIVE IN ANTHROPOLOGY
....GEOG LING QUANT STAT TESTS SAMP/SIZ CON/ANAL
IDEA/COMP METH/COMP ANTHOL BIBLIOG 20. PAGE 52
G1025
PHIL/SCI
SOC
PSY
METH

B54
SPROTT W.J.H..SCIENCE AND SOCIAL ACTION. STRUCT
ACT/RES CRIME GP/REL INGP/REL ANOMIE...PSY
SOC/INTEG 19/20. PAGE 52 G1027
SOC
CULTURE
PHIL/SCI

B54
WILENSKY H.L..SYLLABUS OF INDUSTRIAL RELATIONS: A
GUIDE TO READING AND RESEARCH. USA+45 MUNIC ADMIN
INGP/REL...POLICY MGT PHIL/SCI 20. PAGE 63 G1239
BIBLIOG
INDUS
LABOR
WORKER

S54
BATES J..A MODEL FOR THE SCIENCE OF DECISION."
UNIV ROUTINE...CONT/OBS CON/ANAL HYPO/EXP GAME.
PAGE 5 G0101
QUANT
DECISION
PHIL/SCI
METH/CNCPT

S54
FORM W.H..THE PLACE OF SOCIAL STRUCTURE IN THE
DETERMINATION OF LAND USE: SOME IMPLICATIONS FOR A
THEORY OF URBAN ECOLOGY" (BMR)" STRUCT...GEOG
PHIL/SCI SOC 20. PAGE 19 G0381
HABITAT
MARKET
ORD/FREE
MUNIC

S54
POLANYI M..ON THE INTRODUCTION OF SCIENCE INTO
MORAL SUBJECTS." FUT WOR+45 ACT/RES ATTIT KNOWL
...CONCPT NEW/IDEA 20. PAGE 45 G0882
INTELL
PHIL/SCI

S55
GLADSTONE A.E..THE POSSIBILITY OF PREDICTING
REACTIONS TO INTERNATIONAL EVENTS." UNIV SOCIETY
NAT/G FORCES CREATE EDU/PROP COERCE WAR ATTIT
PERSON KNOWL PWR SKILL...METH/CNCPT NEW/IDEA
ORG/CHARTS. PAGE 21 G0420
PHIL/SCI
CONCPT

S55
SKINNER B.F..FREEDOM AND THE CONTROL OF MEN"
(BMR)" FUT WOR+45 CONTROL CHOOSE GP/REL ATTIT MORAL
PWR POPULISM...POLICY 20. PAGE 51 G1008
ORD/FREE
TEC/DEV
PHIL/SCI
INTELL

S55
VON NEUMANN J..CAN WE SURVIVE TECHNOLOGY?" WOR+45
AIR INDUS ADMIN ADJUST RIGID/FLEX...GEOG PHIL/SCI
NEW/IDEA 20. PAGE 61 G1202
TEC/DEV
NUC/PWR
FUT
HABITAT

S55
WRIGHT Q..THE PEACEFUL ADJUSTMENT OF INTERNATIONAL
RELATIONS: PROBLEMS AND RESEARCH APPROACHES." UNIV
INTELL EDU/PROP ADJUD ROUTINE KNOWL SKILL...INT/LAW
JURID PHIL/SCI CLASSIF 20. PAGE 64 G1258
R+D
METH/CNCPT
PEACE

C55
BONER H.A..HUNGRY GENERATIONS." UK WOR+45 WOR-45
STRATA INDUS FAM LABOR CAP/ISM...MGT BIBLIOG 19/20.
PAGE 8 G0151
ECO/DEV
PHIL/SCI
CONCPT
WEALTH

B56
THOMAS M..ATOMIC ENERGY AND CONGRESS. USA+45 NAT/G
ACT/RES PLAN TEC/DEV PROB/SOLV ROUTINE KNOWL PWR
SKILL...PHIL/SCI NEW/IDEA TIME/SEQ CHARTS METH
CONGRESS VAL/FREE 20 AEC. PAGE 54 G1067
LEGIS
ADMIN
NUC/PWR

B56
VUCINICH A..THE SOVIET ACADEMY OF SCIENCES. USSR
STRUCT ACADEM NAT/G EDU/PROP ADMIN LEAD ROLE
...BIBLIOG 20 ACADEM/SCI. PAGE 61 G1203
PHIL/SCI
CREATE
INTELL
PROF/ORG

S56
ALMOND G.A..COMPARATIVE POLITICAL SYSTEMS" (BMR)"
WOR+45 WOR-45 PROB/SOLV DIPLOM EFFICIENCY
...PHIL/SCI SOC METH 17/20. PAGE 3 G0046
GOV/COMP
CONCPT
ALL/IDEOS
NAT/COMP

S56
EASTON D..LIMITS OF THE EQUILIBRIUM MODEL IN
SOCIAL RESEARCH." STRUCT GP/REL PWR...PHIL/SCI
CLASSIF. PAGE 17 G0330
METH/CNCPT
GEN/METH
R+D
QUANT

B57
DUPREE A.H..SCIENCE IN THE FEDERAL GOVERNMENT; A
HISTORY OF POLICIES AND ACTIVITIES TO 1940. USA-45
AGRI SCHOOL DELIB/GP WAR GOV/REL...PHIL/SCI BIBLIOG
18/20 DEPRESSION NEW/DEAL WWI JEFFERSN/T. PAGE 17
G0324
NAT/G
R+D
CREATE
TEC/DEV

B57
MCKINNEY E.R..A BIBLIOGRAPHY OF CYBERNETICS AND
INFORMATION THEORY. COMPUTER OP/RES...DECISION
PHIL/SCI PSY LING LOG MATH PROBABIL GAME 20.
PAGE 38 G0743
BIBLIOG/A
FEEDBACK
SIMUL
CONTROL

S57
DUNCAN O.D..THE MEASUREMENT OF POPULATION
DISTRIBUTION" (BMR)" WOR+45...QUANT STAT CENSUS
CHARTS 20. PAGE 16 G0321
GEOG
PHIL/SCI
PROB/SOLV
CLASSIF

S57
EASTON D..AN APPROACH TO THE ANALYSIS OF POLITICAL
SYSTEMS." R+D EDU/PROP KNOWL SKILL...POLICY SOC
METH/CNCPT NEW/IDEA SELF/OBS CHARTS GEN/METH
TOT/POP. PAGE 17 G0331
STRUCT
PHIL/SCI

S57
MCDONALD L.C..VOEGELIN AND THE POSITIVISTS: A NEW
SCIENCE OF POLITICS." WOR+45 WOR-45 INTELL CREATE
PLAN ATTIT...METH/CNCPT NEW/IDEA OBS VAL/FREE 20.
PAGE 37 G0734
PHIL/SCI
CONCPT
GEN/METH

B58
MECRENSKY E..SCIENTIFIC MANPOWER IN EUROPE. WOR+45
EDU/PROP GOV/REL SKILL...TECHNIC PHIL/SCI INT
CHARTS BIBLIOG 20. PAGE 38 G0750
ECO/TAC
TEC/DEV
METH/COMP
NAT/COMP

B58
ORTEGA Y GASSET J..MAN AND CRISIS. SECT CREATE
PERSON CONSERVE...GEN/LAWS RENAISSAN. PAGE 43 G0846
PHIL/SCI
CULTURE
CONCPT

B58
TELLER E.A..OUR NUCLEAR FUTURE. SOCIETY FORCES
TEC/DEV EDU/PROP KNOWL ORD/FREE...STAND/INT SYS/QU
KNO/TEST AUD/VIS CHARTS SIMUL 20. PAGE 54 G1062
FUT
PHIL/SCI
NUC/PWR
WAR

KLAPPER J.T.,"WHAT WE KNOW ABOUT THE EFFECTS OF MASS COMMUNICATION: THE BRINK OF HOPE" (BMR)" COM/IND KNOWL...METH/CNCPT GEN/LAWS BIBLIOG METH 20. PAGE 31 G0605
S58
ACT/RES
PERCEPT
CROWD
PHIL/SCI

LASSWELL H.D.,"THE SCIENTIFIC STUDY OF INTERNATIONAL RELATIONS." USA+45 INT/ORG CREATE EDU/PROP DETER ATTIT PERCEPT PWR...DECISION CONCPT METH/CNCPT STYLE CON/ANAL 20. PAGE 33 G0642
S58
PHIL/SCI
GEN/METH
DIPLOM

CLEAVELAND F.N.,SCIENCE AND STATE GOVERNMENT. AGRI EXTR/IND FINAN INDUS PROVS...METH/CNCPT STAT CHARTS 20 NEW/YORK CONNECTICT WISCONSIN CALIFORNIA NEW/MEXICO. PAGE 12 G0233
B59
TEC/DEV
PHIL/SCI
GOV/REL
METH/COMP

GODDARD V.,THE ENIGMA OF MENACE. WOR+45 SECT LEAD NUC/PWR WAR WEAPON CHOOSE PERSON PWR...POLICY PHIL/SCI PACIFIST 20 COLD/WAR. PAGE 22 G0423
B59
PEACE
ARMS/CONT
DIPLOM
ATTIT

MODELSKI G.,ATOMIC ENERGY IN THE COMMUNIST BLOC. FUT INT/ORG CONSULT FORCES ACT/RES PLAN KNOWL SKILL ...PHIL/SCI STAT CHARTS 20. PAGE 39 G0777
B59
TEC/DEV
NUC/PWR
USSR
COM

STANFORD RESEARCH INSTITUTE,POSSIBLE NONMILITARY SCIENTIFIC DEVELOPMENTS AND THEIR POTENTIAL IMPACT ON FOREIGN POLICY PROBLEMS OF THE UNITED. FUT USA+45 INT/ORG PROF/ORG CONSULT ACT/RES CREATE PLAN PEACE KNOWL SKILL...TECHNIC PHIL/SCI NEW/IDEA UNESCO 20. PAGE 52 G1032
B59
R+D
TEC/DEV

DEUTSCH K.W.,"THE IMPACT OF SCIENCE AND TECHNOLOGY ON INTERNATIONAL POLITICS." UNIV INTELL NAT/G ACT/RES CREATE TEC/DEV EDU/PROP EXEC KNOWL...CONCPT TREND TOT/POP 20. PAGE 15 G0297
S59
PHIL/SCI
MYTH
DIPLOM
NAT/LISM

WILLIAMS B.H.,"SCIENTIFIC METHOD IN FOREIGN POLICY." WOR+45 NAT/G FORCES TOP/EX DOMIN LEGIT COERCE PEACE ATTIT KNOWL ORD/FREE PWR...GEN/LAWS GEN/METH TOT/POP COLD/WAR NAZI. PAGE 63 G1241
S59
PLAN
PHIL/SCI
DIPLOM

EINSTEIN A.,EINSTEIN ON PEACE. FUT WOR+45 WOR-45 SOCIETY NAT/G PLAN BAL/PWR CAP/ISM DIPLOM ARMS/CONT DETER NAT/LISM...POLICY RELATIV HUM PHIL/SCI CONCPT BIOG COLD/WAR LEAGUE/NAT NAZI. PAGE 17 G0338
B60
INT/ORG
ATTIT
NUC/PWR
PEACE

FRANCIS R.G.,THE PREDICTIVE PROCESS. PLAN MARXISM ...DECISION SOC CONCPT NAT/COMP 19/20. PAGE 20 G0390
B60
PREDICT
PHIL/SCI
TREND

LINDVEIT E.N.,SCIENTISTS IN GOVERNMENT. USA+45 PAY EDU/PROP ADMIN DRIVE HABITAT ROLE...TECHNIC BIBLIOG 20. PAGE 34 G0670
B60
TEC/DEV
ECO/TAC
PHIL/SCI
GOV/REL

DEUTSCH K.W.,"TOWARD AN INVENTORY OF BASIC TRENDS AND PATTERNS IN COMPARATIVE AND INTERNATIONAL POLITICS." UNIV WOR+45 SOCIETY STRUCT INT/ORG NAT/G CREATE PLAN EDU/PROP KNOWL...PHIL/SCI METH/CNCPT STAT SELF/OBS OBS/ENVIR SAMP TREND CON/ANAL CHARTS SOC/EXP GEN/METH 20. PAGE 15 G0298
L60
R+D
PERCEPT

HOLTON G.,"ARMS CONTROL." FUT WOR+45 CULTURE INT/ORG NAT/G FORCES TOP/EX PLAN EDU/PROP COERCE ATTIT RIGID/FLEX ORD/FREE...POLICY PHIL/SCI SOC TREND COLD/WAR. PAGE 27 G0524
L60
ACT/RES
CONSULT
ARMS/CONT
NUC/PWR

HOLZMAN B.G.,"BASIC RESEARCH FOR NATIONAL SURVIVAL." FUT USA+45 INTELL R+D ACT/RES OP/RES PLAN TEC/DEV EDU/PROP PERCEPT PERSON...PHIL/SCI METH/CNCPT NEW/IDEA MATH OBS RECORD TREND LAB/EXP 20. PAGE 27 G0525
L60
FORCES
STAT

MCCLELLAND C.A.,"THE FUNCTION OF THEORY IN INTERNATIONAL RELATIONS." WOR+45 PLAN EDU/PROP ROUTINE ORD/FREE...PHIL/SCI PSY SOC METH/CNCPT NEW/IDEA OBS TREND GEN/METH 20. PAGE 37 G0728
L60
INT/ORG
CONCPT
DIPLOM

GARFINKEL H.,"THE RATIONAL PROPERTIES OF SCIENTIFIC AND COMMON SENSE ACTIVITIES." SOCIETY STRATA ACT/RES CHOOSE...SOC METH/CNCPT NEW/IDEA CONT/OBS SIMUL TOT/POP VAL/FREE. PAGE 21 G0412
S60
CREATE
PHIL/SCI

HUTCHINSON C.E.,"AN INSTITUTE FOR NATIONAL SECURITY AFFAIRS." USA+45 R+D CONSULT TOP/EX ACT/RES CREATE PLAN TEC/DEV EDU/PROP ROUTINE NUC/PWR ATTIT ORD/FREE PWR...DECISION MGT PHIL/SCI CONCPT RECORD GEN/LAWS GEN/METH 20. PAGE 27 G0539
S60
POLICY
METH/CNCPT
ELITES
DIPLOM

KRUPP S.,PATTERN IN ORGANIZATIONAL ANALYSIS: A CRITICAL EXAMINATION. INGP/REL PERS/REL RATIONAL ATTIT AUTHORIT DRIVE PWR...DECISION PHIL/SCI SOC IDEA/COMP. PAGE 32 G0622
B61
MGT
CONTROL
CONCPT
METH/CNCPT

MCCRACKEN H.L.,KEYNESIAN ECONOMICS IN THE STREAM OF ECONOMIC THOUGHT. FINAN MARKET BARGAIN EFFICIENCY OPTIMAL...PHIL/SCI CONCPT IDEA/COMP BIBLIOG 18/20 KEYNES/JM. PAGE 37 G0732
B61
ECO/TAC
DEMAND
ECOMETRIC

MCRAE R.,THE PROBLEM OF THE UNITY OF THE SCIENCES: BACON TO KANT. CREATE TASK KNOWL...PERS/COMP 16/18 BACON/F DESCARTE/R LEIBNITZ/G KANT/I DIDEROT/D. PAGE 38 G0748
B61
PHIL/SCI
IDEA/COMP
PERSON

ANDREWS R.B.,"URBAN ECONOMICS: AN APPRAISAL OF PROGRESS." LOC/G PROB/SOLV TEC/DEV...CONCPT OBS/ENVIR METH/COMP HYPO/EXP SOC/EXP SIMUL GEN/METH METH 20. PAGE 3 G0058
S61
MUNIC
PHIL/SCI
ECOMETRIC

DALTON G.,"ECONOMIC THEORY AND PRIMITIVE SOCIETY" (BMR)" UNIV AGRI KIN TEC/DEV ECO/TAC REGION HABITAT SKILL...METH/COMP BIBLIOG. PAGE 14 G0274
S61
ECO/UNDEV
METH
PHIL/SCI
SOC

MAINZER L.C.,"SCIENTIFIC FREEDOM IN GOVERNMENT-SPONSORED RESEARCH." USA+45 INTELL PUB/INST BUDGET LOBBY AUTHORIT PWR...POLICY PHIL/SCI 20 NIH NSF. PAGE 35 G0696
S61
CREATE
ORD/FREE
NAT/G
R+D

BOCK E.A.,CASE STUDIES IN AMERICAN GOVERNMENT. USA+45 ECO/DEV CHIEF EDU/PROP CT/SYS RACE/REL ORD/FREE...JURID MGT PHIL/SCI PRESIDENT CASEBOOK. PAGE 8 G0146
B62
POLICY
LEGIS
IDEA/COMP
NAT/G

BORKOF H.,COMPUTER APPLICATIONS IN THE BEHAVIORAL SCIENCES. AUTOMAT UTIL...DECISION PHIL/SCI PSY METH/CNCPT LING LOG MATH STYLE NET/THEORY COMPUT/IR PROG/TEAC SIMUL. PAGE 8 G0154
B62
R+D
COMPUTER
PROB/SOLV
FEEDBACK

CHASE S.,THE PROPER STUDY OF MANKIND (2ND REV. ED.). WOR+45 WOR-45 INTELL WAR...METH/CNCPT SAMP/SIZ GEN/LAWS BIBLIOG METH 16/20. PAGE 11 G0224
B62
PHIL/SCI
SOC
PROB/SOLV
PERSON

GILPIN R.,AMERICAN SCIENTISTS AND NUCLEAR WEAPONS POLICY. COM FUT USA+45 WOR+45 INT/ORG NAT/G PROF/ORG CONSULT FORCES CREATE TEC/DEV BAL/PWR EDU/PROP ARMS/CONT WAR PERCEPT KNOWL MORAL PWR ...PHIL/SCI SOC CONCPT GEN/LAWS 20. PAGE 21 G0417
B62
INTELL
ATTIT
DETER
NUC/PWR

OSGOOD C.E.,AN ALTERNATIVE TO WAR OR SURRENDER. FUT UNIV CULTURE INTELL SOCIETY R+D INT/ORG CONSULT DELIB/GP ACT/RES PLAN CHOOSE ATTIT PERCEPT KNOWL ...PHIL/SCI PSY SOC TREND GEN/LAWS 20. PAGE 43 G0849
B62
ORD/FREE
EDU/PROP
PEACE
WAR

ROSS R.,SYMBOLS AND CIVILIZATION. UNIV CULTURE SECT CREATE ALL/VALS MORAL ART/METH. PAGE 48 G0939
B62
PHIL/SCI
KNOWL
EPIST
SOCIETY

SCHWARTZ L.E.,INTERNATIONAL ORGANIZATIONS AND SPACE COOPERATION. VOL/ASSN CONSULT CREATE TEC/DEV SANCTION...POLICY INT/LAW PHIL/SCI 20 UN. PAGE 50 G0982
B62
INT/ORG
DIPLOM
R+D
SPACE

STOVER C.F.,THE GOVERNMENT OF SCIENCE (PAMPHLET). USA+45 SOCIETY PROF/ORG EX/STRUC CREATE CONTROL
B62
PHIL/SCI
TEC/DEV

NUC/PWR WAR GOV/REL PEACE ORD/FREE 20. PAGE 53
G1041
LAW
NAT/G

B62
THOMSON G.P.,NUCLEAR ENERGY IN BRITAIN DURING THE
LAST WAR: THE CHERWELL SIMON LECTURE (MONOGRAPH).
UK R+D CONSULT FORCES PLAN DIPLOM TASK CIVMIL/REL
ROLE...PHIL/SCI NEW/IDEA LAB/EXP 20 MAUD. PAGE 54
G1071
CREATE
TEC/DEV
WAR
NUC/PWR

B65
ALKER H.R. JR.,MATHEMATICS AND POLITICS. PROB/SOLV
...DECISION PHIL/SCI CLASSIF QUANT STAT GAME
GEN/LAWS INDEX. PAGE 2 G0042
GEN/METH
CONCPT
MATH

S62
MORGENTHAU H.J.,"A POLITICAL THEORY OF FOREIGN
AID." ECO/UNDEV NAT/G DELIB/GP PLAN ECO/TAC
EDU/PROP EXEC ORD/FREE RESPECT WEALTH...METH/CNCPT
TREND 20. PAGE 40 G0783
USA+45
PHIL/SCI
FOR/AID

B65
BENJAMIN A.C.,SCIENCE, TECHNOLOGY, AND HUMAN
VALUES. WOR+45 SECT EDU/PROP GP/REL ATTIT...TECHNIC
LING IDEA/COMP WORSHIP 20. PAGE 6 G0118
PHIL/SCI
CREATE
ROLE
SOCIETY

B63
KAST F.E.,SCIENCE, TECHNOLOGY, AND MANAGEMENT.
SPACE USA+45 FORCES CONFER DETER NUC/PWR...PHIL/SCI
CHARTS ANTHOL BIBLIOG 20 NASA. PAGE 30 G0581
MGT
PLAN
TEC/DEV
PROB/SOLV

B65
BLOOMFIELD L.,SOVIET INTERESTS IN ARMS CONTROL AND
DISARMAMENT* THE DECADE UNDER KHRUSHCHEV 1954-1964.
ASIA FORCES ACT/RES EDU/PROP DETER NUC/PWR WEAPON
COST ATTIT...PHIL/SCI CLASSIF STAT NET/THEORY GAME
BIBLIOG. PAGE 7 G0139
USSR
ARMS/CONT
DIPLOM
TREND

B63
MARSCH P.E.,FEDERAL AID TO SCIENCE EDUCATION: TWO
PROGRAMS. USA+45 SCHOOL RECEIVE EFFICIENCY 20.
PAGE 36 G0711
EDU/PROP
PHIL/SCI
NAT/G
METH/COMP

B65
CARPER E.T.,REORGANIZATION OF THE U.S. PUBLIC
HEALTH SERVICE. FUT USA+45 INTELL R+D LOBBY GP/REL
INGP/REL PERS/REL RIGID/FLEX ROLE HEALTH...PHIL/SCI
20 CONGRESS PHS. PAGE 11 G0213
HEAL
PLAN
NAT/G
OP/RES

B63
NAFZIGER R.O.,INTRODUCTION TO MASS COMMUNICATIONS
RESEARCH (REV. ED.). ACT/RES...STAT CON/ANAL METH
20. PAGE 41 G0801
COM/IND
CONCPT
PHIL/SCI
CREATE

B65
KENT A.,SPECIALIZED INFORMATION CENTERS. INTELL R+D
VOL/ASSN CONSULT COMPUTER KNOWL...DECISION HUM
PHIL/SCI METH/CNCPT TREND CHARTS 20. PAGE 30 G0593
COMPUT/IR
CREATE
TEC/DEV
METH/COMP

B63
OECD,SCIENCE AND THE POLICIES OF GOVERNMENTS: THE
IMPLICATIONS OF SCIENCE AND TECHNOLOGY FOR NATL AND
INTL AFFAIRS. WOR+45 INT/ORG EDU/PROP AUTOMAT
...POLICY PHIL/SCI 20. PAGE 42 G0830
CREATE
TEC/DEV
DIPLOM
NAT/G

B65
NATIONAL ACADEMY OF SCIENCES,BASIC RESEARCH AND
NATIONAL GOALS. R+D ACADEM DELIB/GP PLAN EDU/PROP
...POLICY HEAL PHIL/SCI PSY SOC ANTHOL 20 CONGRESS
HOUSE/REP HS/SCIASTR. PAGE 41 G0809
LEGIS
BUDGET
NAT/G
CREATE

S63
BUNDY M.,"THE SCIENTIST AND NATIONAL POLICY."
PROF/ORG PLAN PARTIC POLICY. PAGE 10 G0186
NAT/G
PHIL/SCI
DECISION

B65
NATIONAL SCIENCE FOUNDATION,CURRENT RESEARCH AND
DEVELOPMENT IN SCIENTIFIC DOCUMENTATION - NO. 12.
WOR+45 INTELL COM/IND NAT/G COMPUTER TEC/DEV
AUTOMAT KNOWL...PSY LING 20. PAGE 41 G0812
BIBLIOG
COMPUT/IR
R+D
PHIL/SCI

S63
DUBRIDGE L.A.,"POLICY AND THE SCIENTISTS." ELITES
PROB/SOLV ROLE KNOWL PWR. PAGE 16 G0318
POLICY
PHIL/SCI
ACADEM
DECISION

B65
PYE L.W.,POLITICAL CULTURE AND DEVELOPMENT. WOR+45
WOR-45 CULTURE ECO/UNDEV NAT/G ALL/VALS ORD/FREE
PWR WEALTH ALL/IDEOS...TRADIT TREND 20. PAGE 46
G0897
PHIL/SCI
TEC/DEV
SOCIETY

S63
TANNENBAUM P.H.,"COMMUNICATION OF SCIENCE
INFORMATION." USA+45 TEC/DEV ROUTINE...PHIL/SCI
STYLE 20. PAGE 53 G1051
COM/IND
PRESS
OP/RES
METH/CNCPT

B65
SINGER J.D.,HUMAN BEHAVIOR AND INTERNATIONAL
POLITICS* CONTRIBUTIONS FROM THE SOCIAL-
PSYCHOLOGICAL SCIENCES. ACT/RES PLAN EDU/PROP ADMIN
KNOWL...DECISION PSY SOC NET/THEORY HYPO/EXP
LAB/EXP SOC/EXP GEN/METH ANTHOL BIBLIOG. PAGE 51
G1006
DIPLOM
PHIL/SCI
QUANT
SIMUL

B64
BRILLOUIN L.,SCIENTIFIC UNCERTAINTY AND
INFORMATION. PROB/SOLV AUTOMAT PERCEPT ORD/FREE
...MATH REGRESS STAT STYLE OBS IDEA/COMP SIMUL
TIME. PAGE 9 G0169
PHIL/SCI
NEW/IDEA
METH/CNCPT
CREATE

B65
WEISNER J.B.,WHERE SCIENCE AND POLITICS MEET.
USA+45 ECO/DEV R+D FORCES PROB/SOLV DIPLOM FOR/AID
CONTROL...PHIL/SCI PRESIDENT KENNEDY/JF JOHNSON/LB.
PAGE 63 G1228
CHIEF
NAT/G
POLICY
TEC/DEV

B64
CONANT J.B.,TWO MODES OF THOUGHT: MY ENCOUNTERS
WITH SCIENCE AND EDUCATION....ART/METH JURID SOC
TREND. PAGE 13 G0249
PHIL/SCI
SKILL
MYTH
STYLE

S65
ETZIONI A.,"ON THE NATIONAL GUIDANCE OF SCIENCE."
USA+45 FINAN NAT/G LEGIS GIVE 20. PAGE 18 G0353
PHIL/SCI
CREATE
POLICY
EFFICIENCY

B64
COOMBS C.H.,A THEORY OF DATA....MGT PHIL/SCI SOC
CLASSIF MATH PROBABIL STAT QU. PAGE 13 G0254
CON/ANAL
GEN/METH
TESTS
PSY

S65
FINK C.F.,"MORE CALCULATIONS ABOUT DETERRENCE."
DRIVE...PHIL/SCI PSY STAT TIME/SEQ GAME GEN/LAWS.
PAGE 19 G0367
DETER
RECORD
PROBABIL
IDEA/COMP

B64
ELLUL J.,THE TECHNOLOGICAL SOCIETY. FUT STRUCT
CREATE AUTOMAT ROUTINE STRANGE ANOMIE MORAL
PHIL/SCI. PAGE 18 G0344
SOC
SOCIETY
TECHNIC
TEC/DEV

S65
GREGG P.M.,"DIMENSIONS OF POLITICAL SYSTEMS: FACTOR
ANALYSIS OF A CROSS POLITY SURVEY." TEC/DEV
...DECISION PHIL/SCI CONCPT STAT IDEA/COMP
GEN/LAWS. PAGE 23 G0447
SIMUL
GEN/METH
CLASSIF

B64
GOWING M.,BRITAIN AND ATOMIC ENERGY 1939-1945.
FRANCE UK USA+45 USA-45 NAT/G CREATE...PHIL/SCI 20
AEA. PAGE 22 G0439
NUC/PWR
DIPLOM
TEC/DEV

S65
LEISERSON A.,"SCIENTISTS AND THE POLICY PROCESS."
USA+45 NAT/G LEAD PARTIC REPRESENT. PAGE 33 G0654
PHIL/SCI
ADMIN
EX/STRUC
EXEC

B64
HASKINS C.P.,THE SCIENTIFIC REVOLUTION AND WORLD
POLITICS. COM FUT USA+45 ECO/DEV ECO/UNDEV ATTIT
...PHIL/SCI BIBLIOG 20 THIRD/WRLD. PAGE 25 G0489
TEC/DEV
POLICY
DIPLOM
TREND

S65
SILVERT K.H.,"AMERICAN ACADEMIC ETHICS AND SOCIAL
RESEARCH ABROAD* THE LESSON OF PROJECT CAMELOT."
CHILE L/A+17C USA+45 FINAN ADMIN...PHIL/SCI SOC
GEN/LAWS CAMELOT. PAGE 51 G0998
ACADEM
NAT/G
ACT/RES
POLICY

S64
CALDWELL L.K.,"BIOPOLITICS: SCIENCE, ETHICS, AND
PUBLIC POLICY." FUT USA+45 WOR+45 INTELL STRATA R+D
NAT/G CONSULT PLAN EDU/PROP ALL/VALS...RELATIV
TEC/DEV
POLICY

B66
AMERICAN LIBRARY ASSN,GUIDE TO JAPANESE REFERENCE
BIBLIOG/A

BOOKS....HUM 20 CHINJAP. PAGE 3 G0054
    SOC
    TEC/DEV
    PHIL/SCI

B66
FALK R.A.,ON MINIMIZING THE USE OF NUCLEAR WEAPONS; DIPLOM
THREE ESSAYS; RESEARCH MONOGRAPH NO. 23. WOR+45 EQUILIB
STRUCT CREATE NUC/PWR REV CONSERVE...POLICY PHIL/SCI
NET/THEORY IDEA/COMP GEN/LAWS GEN/METH. PAGE 18 PROB/SOLV
G0359

B66
GREEN P.,DEADLY LOGIC* THE THEORY OF NUCLEAR DETER
DETERRENCE. USA+45 ACT/RES OP/RES NUC/PWR RATIONAL ACADEM
ALL/VALS PWR...DECISION MGT PHIL/SCI QUANT GEN/LAWS
IDEA/COMP GAME. PAGE 23 G0444 RECORD

B66
HALPIN A.W.,THEORY AND RESEARCH IN ADMINISTRATION. GEN/LAWS
ACT/RES LEAD...MGT IDEA/COMP METH/COMP. PAGE 24 EDU/PROP
G0475 ADMIN
    PHIL/SCI

B66
HOPKINS J.F.K.,ARABIC PERIODICAL LITERATURE, 1961. BIBLIOG/A
ISLAM LAW CULTURE SECT...GEOG HEAL PHIL/SCI PSY SOC NAT/LISM
20. PAGE 27 G0528 TEC/DEV
    INDUS

B66
MUMFORD L.,THE MYTH OF THE MACHINE: TECHNICS AND WORKER
HUMAN DEVELOPMENT. UNIV WOR-45 CREATE AUTOMAT TEC/DEV
PERCEPT KNOWL...EPIST PHIL/SCI SOC LING TREND SOCIETY
SOC/INTEG 20 MARX/KARL. PAGE 40 G0795

B66
PEIRCE W.S.,SELECTIVE MANPOWER POLICIES AND THE PRICE
TRADE-OFF BETWEEN RISING PRICES AND UNEMPLOYMENT LABOR
(DISSERTATION). ECO/DEV WORKER ACT/RES...PHIL/SCI POLICY
20. PAGE 44 G0865 ECO/TAC

B66
POLLARD W.G.,ATOMIC ENERGY AND SOUTHERN SCIENCE. NUC/PWR
USA+45 HEALTH. PAGE 45 G0883 GP/REL
    PHIL/SCI
    CREATE

B66
US BUREAU OF THE BUDGET,THE ADMINISTRATION OF ACT/RES
GOVERNMENT SUPPORTED RESEARCH AT UNIVERSITIES NAT/G
(PAMPHLET). USA+45 CONSULT TOP/EX ADMIN INCOME ACADEM
WEALTH...MGT PHIL/SCI INT. PAGE 56 G1108 GP/REL

S66
KAPLAN M.A.,"THE NEW GREAT DEBATE* TRADITIONALISM PHIL/SCI
VS SCIENCE IN INTERNATIONAL RELATIONS."...DECISION CONSERVE
HUM QUANT STYLE NET/THEORY CON/ANAL STERTYP DIPLOM
GEN/LAWS. PAGE 29 G0577 SIMUL

S66
RIZOS E.J.,"SCIENCE AND TECHNOLOGY IN COUNTRY ADMIN
DEVELOPMENT* TOWARDS AN UNDERSTANDING OF THE ROLE TEC/DEV
OF PUBLIC ADMINISTRATION." WOR+45 STRUCT INT/ORG ECO/UNDEV
EX/STRUC CREATE PLAN PROB/SOLV EFFICIENCY ROLE PHIL/SCI
DECISION. PAGE 47 G0924

N66
US HOUSE COMM SCI ASTRONAUT,GOVERNMENT, SCIENCE, NAT/G
AND PUBLIC POLICY (PAMPHLET). R+D ACADEM DELIB/GP POLICY
COMPUTER BUDGET CONFER ADMIN...PHIL/SCI PREDICT TEC/DEV
TREND 20 CONGRESS HS/SCIASTR. PAGE 58 G1143 CREATE

B67
BAUMOL W.J.,BUSINESS BEHAVIOR, VALUE AND GROWTH ALL/IDEOS
(REV. ED.). WOR+45 FINAN LG/CO TEC/DEV CAP/ISM PHIL/SCI
DEMAND EQUILIB...METH/COMP SIMUL 20. PAGE 5 G0105 PLAN
    ECO/DEV

B67
BERNAL J.D.,THE SOCIAL FUNCTION OF SCIENCE. WOR+45 ROLE
WOR-45 R+D NAT/G PROB/SOLV DOMIN WAR...PHIL/SCI 20. TEC/DEV
PAGE 7 G0130 SOCIETY
    ADJUST

B67
BUNGE M.,THE SEARCH FOR SYSTEM. VOL. 3, PART 1 OF PHIL/SCI
STUDIES IN THE FOUNDATIONS METHODOLOGY, AND METH
PHILOSOPHY OF SCIENCE. UNIV LAW INTELL KNOWL. GEN/LAWS
PAGE 10 G0187 CONCPT

B67
BUNGE M.,THE SEARCH FOR TRUTH, VOL. 3, PART 2 OF PHIL/SCI
STUDIES IN THE FOUNDATIONS, METHODOLOGY, AND TESTS
PHILOSOPHY OF SCIENCE. UNIV INTELL KNOWL...CONCPT GEN/LAWS
OBS PREDICT METH. PAGE 10 G0188 RATIONAL

B67
COMMONER B.,SCIENCE AND SURVIVAL. SOCIETY INDUS PHIL/SCI
PLAN NUC/PWR KNOWL PWR...SOC 20 AEC. PAGE 13 G0247 CONTROL
    PROB/SOLV
    EQUILIB

B67
CONNOLLY W.E.,POLITICAL SCIENCE AND IDEOLOGY. PWR
UTOPIA ATTIT KNOWL...MAJORIT EPIST PHIL/SCI SOC PLURISM
IDEA/COMP HYPO/EXP GEN/LAWS METH HUME/D MARX/KARL. ELITES
PAGE 13 G0250 CONCPT

B67
CROSSON F.J.,SCIENCE AND CONTEMPORARY SOCIETY. FUT PHIL/SCI
WOR+45 SECT CREATE PROB/SOLV...HUM PREDICT TREND SOCIETY
IDEA/COMP ANTHOL. PAGE 14 G0263 TEC/DEV
    CONCPT

B67
DE JOUVENEL B.,THE ART OF CONJECTURE. WOR+45 FUT
EFFICIENCY PERCEPT KNOWL...DECISION PHIL/SCI CONCPT PREDICT
METH/COMP BIBLIOG 20. PAGE 15 G0285 SIMUL
    METH

B67
DEGLER C.N.,THE AGE OF THE ECONOMIC REVOLUTION INDUS
1876-1900. USA-45 AGRI MUNIC POL/PAR SECT ECO/TAC SOCIETY
CHOOSE...PHIL/SCI CHARTS NAT/COMP 19 NEGRO. PAGE 15 ECO/DEV
G0292 TEC/DEV

B67
NATIONAL SCIENCE FOUNDATION,DIRECTORY OF SELECTED INDEX
RESEARCH INSTITUTES IN EASTERN EUROPE. BULGARIA R+D
CZECHOSLVK HUNGARY POLAND ROMANIA INTELL ACADEM COM
NAT/G ACT/RES 20. PAGE 41 G0814 PHIL/SCI

B67
NELSON R.R.,TECHNOLOGY, ECONOMIC GROWTH, AND PUBLIC R+D
POLICY. USA+45 PLAN GP/REL UTIL KNOWL...POLICY CONSULT
PHIL/SCI CHARTS BIBLIOG 20. PAGE 41 G0817 CREATE
    ACT/RES

B67
RIDKER R.G.,ECONOMIC COSTS OF AIR POLLUTION* OP/RES
STUDIES IN MEASUREMENT. R+D MUNIC GP/REL KNOWL HABITAT
...OBS 20. PAGE 47 G0919 PHIL/SCI

B67
RUTGERS U GRADUATE SCH LIB SCI,BIBLIOGRAPHY OF BIBLIOG/A
RESEARCH RELATING TO THE COMMUNICATION OF COM/IND
SCIENTIFIC AND TECHNICAL INFORMATION. FUT CREATE R+D
FEEDBACK...PHIL/SCI NEW/IDEA COMPUT/IR HYPO/EXP. TEC/DEV
PAGE 48 G0951

B67
SKOLNIKOFF E.B.,SCIENCE, TECHNOLOGY, AND AMERICAN PHIL/SCI
FOREIGN POLICY. SPACE USA+45 INT/ORG TEC/DEV DIPLOM
ARMS/CONT NUC/PWR 29 DEPT/STATE. PAGE 51 G1010 NAT/G
    EFFICIENCY

B67
UNESCO,PRINCIPLES AND PROBLEMS OF NATIONAL SCIENCE NAT/COMP
POLICIES. WOR+45 ECO/DEV ECO/UNDEV R+D INT/ORG POLICY
PROB/SOLV CONFER...PHIL/SCI CHARTS 20 UNESCO UN. TEC/DEV
PAGE 55 G1091 CREATE

B67
UNIVERSAL REFERENCE SYSTEM,PUBLIC POLICY AND THE BIBLIOG/A
MANAGEMENT OF SCIENCE (VOLUME IX). FUT SPACE WOR+45 POLICY
LAW NAT/G TEC/DEV CONTROL NUC/PWR GOV/REL MGT
...COMPUT/IR GEN/METH. PAGE 56 G1100 PHIL/SCI

B67
US HOUSE COMM SCI ASTRONAUT,GOVERNMENT, SCIENCE, ADMIN
AND INTERNATIONAL POLICY. R+D OP/RES PLAN 20. PHIL/SCI
PAGE 58 G1146 ACT/RES
    DIPLOM

B67
US HOUSE COMM SCI ASTRONAUT,THE JUNIOR COLLEGE AND ACADEM
EDUCATION IN THE SCIENCES (PAMPHLET). USA+45 AGE/Y EDU/PROP
...CHARTS SIMUL HOUSE/REP. PAGE 58 G1148 PHIL/SCI
    R+D

B67
US HOUSE COMM SCI ASTRONAUT,AUTHORIZING SECY OF PHIL/SCI
COMMERCE TO PROVIDE FOR COLLECTION, COMPILATION, CON/ANAL
CRIT EVALUATION, PUBLICATION, SALE OF STD REF DATA. STAT
USA+45 TEC/DEV...COMPUT/IR HOUSE/REP. PAGE 59 G1150 R+D

B67
US SUPERINTENDENT OF DOCUMENTS,LIBRARY OF CONGRESS BIBLIOG/A
(PRICE LIST 83). AFR ASIA EUR+WWI USA-45 USSR NAT/G USA+45
DIPLOM CONFER CT/SYS WAR...DECISION PHIL/SCI AUTOMAT
CLASSIF 19/20 CONGRESS PRESIDENT. PAGE 61 G1189 LAW

WEINBERG A.M.,REFLECTIONS ON BIG SCIENCE. FUT
USA+45 NAT/G EDU/PROP CHOOSE PERS/REL COST OPTIMAL
...PHIL/SCI TREND. PAGE 62 G1225
| B67 |
| ACADEM |
| KNOWL |
| R+D |
| PLAN |

BRUNHILD G.,"THEORY OF 'TECHNICAL UNEMPLOYMENT'."
ECO/DEV ACT/RES PROB/SOLV DEMAND PRODUC...PHIL/SCI
20. PAGE 9 G0182
| S67 |
| WORKER |
| TEC/DEV |
| SKILL |
| INDUS |

BULMER-THOMAS I.,"SO, ON TO THE GREAT SOCIETY." FUT
UNIV TEC/DEV BAL/PWR WAR BIO/SOC KNOWL...ART/METH
SOC PREDICT TREND WORSHIP 20 GREAT/SOC. PAGE 9
G0185
| S67 |
| PHIL/SCI |
| SOCIETY |
| CREATE |

CETRON M.J.,"FORECASTING TECHNOLOGY." INDUS FORCES
TASK UTIL...PHIL/SCI CONCPT CHARTS METH/COMP TIME.
PAGE 11 G0219
| S67 |
| TEC/DEV |
| FUT |
| R+D |
| PLAN |

CRANBERG L.,"SCIENCE, ETHICS, AND LAW." UNIV CREATE
PLAN EDU/PROP INGP/REL PERS/REL ADJUST RATIONAL
KNOWL MORAL...CONCPT IDEA/COMP 20. PAGE 13 G0260
| S67 |
| LAW |
| PHIL/SCI |
| INTELL |

HABERER J.,"POLITICS AND THE COMMUNITY OF SCIENCE."
USA+45 SOCIETY ACT/RES PARTIC ATTIT PHIL/SCI.
PAGE 24 G0465
| S67 |
| LEAD |
| SUPEGO |
| INTELL |
| LOBBY |

INGLIS D.R.,"PROSPECTS AND PROBLEMS: THE
NONMILITARY USES OF NUCLEAR EXPLOSIVES." CREATE
PROB/SOLV TEC/DEV AGREE PEACE...INT/LAW PHIL/SCI
NEW/IDEA 20 TREATY. PAGE 28 G0545
| S67 |
| NUC/PWR |
| INDUS |
| ARMS/CONT |
| EXTR/IND |

LA PORTE T.,"DIFFUSION AND DISCONTINUITY IN
SCIENCE, TECHNOLOGY AND PUBLIC AFFAIRS: RESULTS OF
A SEARCH IN THE FIELD." USA+45 ACT/RES TEC/DEV
PERS/REL ATTIT PHIL/SCI. PAGE 32 G0628
| S67 |
| INTELL |
| ADMIN |
| ACADEM |
| GP/REL |

LEWIS R.L.,"GOAL AND NO GOAL* A NEW POLICY IN
SPACE." R+D BUDGET COST...POLICY DECISION PHIL/SCI.
PAGE 34 G0662
| S67 |
| SPACE |
| PLAN |
| EFFICIENCY |
| CREATE |

ROBERTS W.,"DIVERSITY, CONSENSUS, AND ECLECTICISM
IN POLITICAL SCIENCE"...PHIL/SCI 20. PAGE 47 G0927
| S67 |
| CONSEN |
| DEBATE |
| GEN/METH |

US HOUSE COMM SCI ASTRONAUT,AMENDING NATIONAL
SCIENCE FOUNDATION ACT OF 1950 TO MAKE IMPROVEMENTS
IN ORGANIZATION AND OPERATION OF FOUNDAT'N(PAMPH).
USA+45 GIVE ADMIN...POLICY HOUSE/REP NSF. PAGE 58
G1147
| N67 |
| PHIL/SCI |
| DELIB/GP |
| TEC/DEV |
| R+D |

US HOUSE COMM SCI ASTRONAUT,AUTHORIZING
APPROPRIATIONS TO THE NATIONAL AERONAUTICS AND
SPACE ADMINISTRATION (PAMPHLET). USA+45 NAT/G
OP/RES TEC/DEV BUDGET NASA HOUSE/REP. PAGE 58 G1149
| N67 |
| SPACE |
| R+D |
| PHIL/SCI |
| NUC/PWR |

BARAGWANATH L.E.,"SCIENTIFIC CO-OPERATION BETWEEN
THE UNIVERSITIES AND INDUSTRY - A RESEARCH NOTE."
UK LG/CO CREATE TEC/DEV EDU/PROP ATTIT...PHIL/SCI
STAT QU 20. PAGE 5 G0090
| S68 |
| R+D |
| ACADEM |
| INDUS |
| GP/REL |

RENAN E.,THE FUTURE OF SCIENCE. WAR ORD/FREE WEALTH
...GOV/COMP IDEA/COMP GEN/LAWS 19. PAGE 46 G0913
| B91 |
| PHIL/SCI |
| KNOWL |
| SECT |
| PREDICT |

PHILADELPH....PHILADELPHIA, PENNSYLVANIA

PHILANTHROPY....SEE GIVE+WEALTH

PHILIP/J....JOHN PHILIP

PHILIPPINE....PHILIPPINES; SEE ALSO S/ASIA

LERNER D.,COMMUNICATION AND CHANGE IN DEVELOPING
COUNTRIES. CHINA/COM INDIA PHILIPPINE COM/IND
| B67 |
| EDU/PROP |
| ORD/FREE |

CREATE TEC/DEV...ANTHOL 20. PAGE 33 G0659
| PERCEPT |
| ECO/UNDEV |

PHILIPPINES....SEE PHILIPPINE; S/ASIA

PHILLIP/IV....PHILLIP IV OF SPAIN

PHILLIPS/F....F. PHILLIPS - POLICE CHIEF, N.Y.C.

PHILOSOPHR....PHILOSOPHER

PHILOSOPHY....SEE GEN/LAWS. PHILOSOPHY OF SCIENCE....SEE
PHIL/SCI

PHILOSOPHY OF SCIENCE....SEE PHIL/SCI

PHIPPS T.E. G0876

PHOTOGRAPHS....SEE AUD/VIS

PHS....PUBLIC HEALTH SERVICE

CARPER E.T.,REORGANIZATION OF THE U.S. PUBLIC
HEALTH SERVICE. FUT USA+45 INTELL R+D LOBBY GP/REL
INGP/REL PERS/REL RIGID/FLEX ROLE HEALTH...PHIL/SCI
20 CONGRESS PHS. PAGE 11 G0213
| B65 |
| HEAL |
| PLAN |
| NAT/G |
| OP/RES |

PIERCE/F....PRESIDENT FRANKLIN PIERCE

PIGOU/AC....ARTHUR CECIL PIGOU

PILISUK M. G0877,G0878

PINCUS/J....JOHN PINCUS

PIPER D.C. G0879

PITTSBURGH....PITTSBURGH, PENNSYLVANIA

PLAN....PLANNING

AMERICAN DOCUMENTATION INST,AMERICAN DOCUMENTATION.
PROF/ORG CONSULT PLAN PERCEPT...MATH STAT AUD/VIS
CHARTS METH/COMP INDEX METH 20. PAGE 3 G0050
| N |
| BIBLIOG |
| TEC/DEV |
| COM/IND |
| COMPUT/IR |

CONOVER H.L.,CIVILIAN DEFENSE: A SELECTED LIST OF
RECENT REFERENCES (PAMPHLET). USA+45 LOC/G MUNIC
PROB/SOLV ADMIN LEAD TASK WEAPON GOV/REL...POLICY
CON/ANAL 20 CIV/DEFENS. PAGE 13 G0251
| N |
| BIBLIOG |
| PLAN |
| WAR |
| CIVMIL/REL |

BRITISH COMMONWEALTH BUR AGRI,WORLD AGRICULTURAL
ECONOMICS AND RURAL SOCIOLOGY ABSTRACTS. NAT/G
OP/RES PLAN TEC/DEV LEAD PRODUC...GEOG MGT NAT/COMP
20. PAGE 9 G0170
| B |
| BIBLIOG/A |
| AGRI |
| SOC |
| WORKER |

INDIA: A REFERENCE ANNUAL. INDIA CULTURE COM/IND
R+D FORCES PLAN RECEIVE EDU/PROP HEALTH...STAT
CHARTS BIBLIOG 20. PAGE 1 G0005
| N |
| CONSTN |
| LABOR |
| INT/ORG |

JOURNAL OF PUBLIC ADMINISTRATION: JOURNAL OF THE
ROYAL INSTITUTE OF PUBLIC ADMINISTRATION. UK PLAN
GP/REL INGP/REL 20. PAGE 1 G0006
| N |
| BIBLIOG/A |
| ADMIN |
| NAT/G |
| MGT |

PUBLIC ADMINISTRATION ABSTRACTS AND INDEX OF
ARTICLES. WOR+45 PLAN PROB/SOLV...POLICY 20. PAGE 1
G0009
| N |
| BIBLIOG/A |
| ADMIN |
| ECO/UNDEV |
| NAT/G |

AMER COUNCIL OF LEARNED SOCIET,THE ACLS CONSTITUENT
SOCIETY JOURNAL PROJECT. FUT USA+45 LAW NAT/G PLAN
DIPLOM PHIL/SCI. PAGE 3 G0048
| N |
| BIBLIOG/A |
| HUM |
| COMPUT/IR |
| COMPUTER |

ATOMIC INDUSTRIAL FORUM,COMMENTARY ON LEGISLATION
TO PERMIT PRIVATE OWNERSHIP OF SPECIAL NUCLEAR
MATERIAL (PAMPHLET). USA+45 DELIB/GP LEGIS PLAN OWN
...POLICY 20 AEC CONGRESS. PAGE 4 G0076
| N19 |
| NUC/PWR |
| MARKET |
| INDUS |
| LAW |

BELL J.R.,PERSONNEL PROBLEMS IN CONVERTING TO
AUTOMATION (PAMPHLET). USA+45 COMPUTER PLAN
...METH/CNCPT 20 CALIFORNIA. PAGE 6 G0115
| N19 |
| WORKER |
| AUTOMAT |
| PROB/SOLV |
| PROVS |

BROWN W.M.,THE DESIGN AND PERFORMANCE OF "OPTIMUM"
BLAST SHELTER PROGRAMS (PAMPHLET). USA+45 ACT/RES
| N19 |
| HABITAT |
| NUC/PWR |

PLAN DEATH COST EFFICIENCY OPTIMAL...POLICY CHARTS   WAR
20. PAGE 9 G0180   HEALTH

MANPOWER DURING THE TRANSITION FROM WAR TO PEACE.   ADJUST
USA+45 INDUS LABOR LG/CO NAT/G PLAN ADMIN PEACE   WAR
...POLICY MGT 20. PAGE 5 G0086   PROB/SOLV

N19
DOTSON A.,PRODUCTION PLANNING IN THE PATENT OFFICE   EFFICIENCY
(PAMPHLET). USA+45 DIST/IND PROB/SOLV PRODUC...MGT   PLAN
PHIL/SCI 20 BUR/BUDGET PATENT/OFF. PAGE 16 G0309   NAT/G
                                                         ADMIN

B45
BUSH V.,SCIENCE, THE ENDLESS FRONTIER. FUT USA-45   R+D
INTELL STRATA ACT/RES CREATE PLAN EDU/PROP ADMIN   NAT/G
NUC/PWR PEACE ATTIT HEALTH KNOWL...MAJORIT HEAL MGT
PHIL/SCI CONCPT OBS TREND 20. PAGE 10 G0195

N19
GINZBERG E.,MANPOWER FOR GOVERNMENT (PAMPHLET).   WORKER
USA+45 FORCES PLAN PROB/SOLV PAY EDU/PROP ADMIN   CONSULT
GP/REL COST...MGT PREDICT TREND 20 CIVIL/SERV.   NAT/G
PAGE 21 G0418   LOC/G

B45
REVES E.,THE ANATOMY OF PEACE. WOR-45 LAW CULTURE   ACT/RES
NAT/G PLAN TEC/DEV EDU/PROP WAR NAT/LISM ATTIT   CONCPT
ALL/VALS SOVEREIGN...POLICY HUM TIME/SEQ 20.   NUC/PWR
PAGE 46 G0914   PEACE

N19
KAUFMAN J.L.,COMMUNITY RENEWAL PROGRAMS (PAMPHLET).   LOC/G
USA+45 CONSTRUC PROVS CREATE PLAN CONTROL WEALTH 20   MUNIC
URBAN/RNWL. PAGE 30 G0584   ACT/RES
                                                         BIBLIOG

B45
SMYTH H.D.,ATOMIC ENERGY FOR MILITARY PURPOSES.   R+D
USA-45 NAT/G PLAN TEC/DEV KNOWL...MATH CON/ANAL   TIME/SEQ
CHARTS LAB/EXP SIMUL 20. PAGE 52 G1017   NUC/PWR

N19
VERNON R.,THE MYTH AND REALITY OF OUR URBAN   PLAN
PROBLEMS (PAMPHLET). USA+45 SOCIETY LOC/G ADMIN   MUNIC
COST 20 PRINCETN/U INTERVENT URBAN/RNWL. PAGE 61   HABITAT
G1197   PROB/SOLV

S45
WHITE L.D.,"CONGRESSIONAL CONTROL OF THE PUBLIC   LEGIS
SERVICE." USA-45 NAT/G CONSULT DELIB/GP PLAN SENIOR   EXEC
CONGRESS. PAGE 63 G1232   POLICY
                                                         CONTROL

B23
DRAPER J.W.,HISTORY OF THE CONFLICT BETWEEN   SECT
RELIGION AND SCIENCE. WOR-45 INTELL SOCIETY R+D   KNOWL
CREATE PLAN TEC/DEV EDU/PROP ATTIT PWR...PHIL/SCI
CONCPT OBS TIME/SEQ TREND GEN/LAWS TOT/POP. PAGE 16
G0314

B46
BAXTER J.P.,SCIENTISTS AGAINST TIME. EUR+WWI   FORCES
MOD/EUR USA+45 USA-45 WOR+45 WOR-45 R+D NAT/G PLAN   WAR
ATTIT PWR...PHIL/SCI RECORD CON/ANAL 17/20. PAGE 6   NUC/PWR
G0107

B36
US LIBRARY OF CONGRESS,CLASSIFIED GUIDE TO MATERIAL   BIBLIOG
IN THE LIBRARY OF CONGRESS COVERING URBAN COMMUNITY   CLASSIF
DEVELOPMENT. USA+45 CREATE PROB/SOLV ADMIN 20.   MUNIC
PAGE 59 G1154   PLAN

B46
BRODIE B.,THE OBSOLETE WEAPON: ATOMIC POWER AND   INT/ORG
WORLD ORDER. COM USA+45 USSR WOR+45 DELIB/GP PLAN   TEC/DEV
ORD/FREE PWR...CONCPT TIME/SEQ TREND UN 20. PAGE 9   ARMS/CONT
G0171   NUC/PWR

B37
STAMP S.,THE SCIENCE OF SOCIAL ADJUSTMENT. WOR-45   ADJUST
ACT/RES CREATE PLAN PROB/SOLV TEC/DEV ECO/TAC   ORD/FREE
EFFICIENCY SOC/INTEG 20. PAGE 52 G1031   PHIL/SCI

B46
BUSH V.,ENDLESS HORIZONS. FUT USA-45 INTELL NAT/G   R+D
CONSULT ACT/RES CREATE PLAN EDU/PROP DRIVE   KNOWL
...MAJORIT HEAL MGT PHIL/SCI CONCPT OBS TREND   PEACE
GEN/METH TOT/POP 20. PAGE 10 G0196

B38
HARPER S.N.,THE GOVERNMENT OF THE SOVIET UNION. COM   MARXISM
USSR LAW CONSTN ECO/DEV PLAN TEC/DEV DIPLOM   NAT/G
INT/TRADE ADMIN REV NAT/LISM...POLICY 20. PAGE 24   LEAD
G0483   POL/PAR

B46
MORGENTHAU H.J.,SCIENTIFIC MAN VS POWER POLITICS.   UNIV
USA+45 WOR+45 INTELL SOCIETY ACT/RES CREATE PLAN   MORAL
EDU/PROP...CONCPT TREND TOT/POP 20. PAGE 40 G0782   PEACE

B39
FULLER G.H.,A SELECTED LIST OF REFERENCES ON THE   BIBLIOG
EXPANSION OF THE US NAVY, 1933-1939 (PAMPHLET).   FORCES
MOD/EUR USA-45 NAT/G PLAN DIPLOM DOMIN RISK   WEAPON
ARMS/CONT EQUILIB PWR 20 NAVY. PAGE 20 G0399   WAR

B47
BALDWIN H.W.,THE PRICE OF POWER. USA+45 FORCES PLAN   PROB/SOLV
NUC/PWR ADJUST COST ORD/FREE...POLICY PSY BIBLIOG   PWR
20. PAGE 5 G0089   POPULISM
                                                         PRICE

B40
HELLMAN F.S.,THE NEW DEAL: SELECTED LIST OF   BIBLIOG/A
REFERENCES. USA-45 FINAN LABOR EX/STRUC CREATE   ECO/TAC
INT/TRADE ADMIN CT/SYS 20 SUPREME/CT. PAGE 26 G0505   PLAN
                                                         POLICY

B47
WHITEHEAD T.N.,LEADERSHIP IN A FREE SOCIETY; A   INDUS
STUDY IN HUMAN RELATIONS BASED ON AN ANALYSIS OF   LEAD
PRESENT-DAY INDUSTRIAL CIVILIZATION. WOR-45 STRUCT   ORD/FREE
R+D LABOR LG/CO SML/CO WORKER PLAN PROB/SOLV   SOCIETY
TEC/DEV DRIVE...MGT 20. PAGE 63 G1234

B42
BINGHAM A.M.,THE TECHNIQUES OF DEMOCRACY. USA-45   POPULISM
CONSTN STRUCT POL/PAR LEGIS PLAN PARTIC CHOOSE   ORD/FREE
REPRESENT NAT/LISM TOTALISM...MGT 20. PAGE 7 G0136   ADMIN
                                                         NAT/G

B48
PUBLIC ADMINISTRATION SERVICE,SOURCE MATERIALS IN   BIBLIOG/A
PUBLIC ADMINISTRATION: A SELECTED BIBLIOGRAPHY (PAS   GOV/REL
PUBLICATION NO. 102). USA+45 LAW FINAN LOC/G MUNIC   MGT
NAT/G PLAN RECEIVE EDU/PROP CT/SYS CHOOSE HEALTH   ADMIN
20. PAGE 45 G0895

B42
US LIBRARY OF CONGRESS,CONDUCT OF THE WAR (APRIL   BIBLIOG/A
1941-MARCH 1942). USA-45 WOR-45 LAW INDUS PUB/INST   WAR
TEC/DEV EDU/PROP CIVMIL/REL 20. PAGE 59 G1155   FORCES
                                                         PLAN

S48
HARDIN L.M.,"REFLECTIONS ON AGRICULTURAL POLICY   AGRI
FORMATION IN THE UNITED STATES." LEGIS PLAN BUDGET   POLICY
ECO/TAC LEAD CENTRAL...MGT SOC NEW/IDEA STAT FAO.   ADMIN
PAGE 24 G0480   NEW/LIB

S42
LASSWELL H.D.,"THE RELATION OF IDEOLOGICAL   ATTIT
INTELLIGENCE TO PUBLIC POLICY." WOR+45 WOR-45   DECISION
SOCIETY DELIB/GP ACT/RES CREATE PLAN DIPLOM
EDU/PROP CHOOSE KNOWL PWR...POLICY SOC TREND
GEN/LAWS 20. PAGE 32 G0638

S48
MARQUIS D.G.,"RESEARCH PLANNING AT THE FRONTIERS OF   PLAN
SCIENCE" (BMR)" INTELL ACADEM CREATE UTIL...PSY 20.   ACT/RES
PAGE 36 G0708   EFFICIENCY
                                                         GEN/METH

B44
PUBLIC ADMINISTRATION SERVICE,YOUR BUSINESS OF   BIBLIOG
GOVERNMENT: A CATALOG OF PUBLICATIONS IN THE FIELD   ADMIN
OF PUBLIC ADMINISTRATION (PAMPHLET). FINAN R+D   NAT/G
LOC/G ACT/RES OP/RES PLAN 20. PAGE 45 G0894   MUNIC

B49
OGBURN W.,TECHNOLOGY AND INTERNATIONAL RELATIONS.   TEC/DEV
WOR+45 WOR-45 ECO/DEV CREATE PLAN ECO/TAC EDU/PROP   DIPLOM
COERCE PWR SKILL WEALTH...TECHNIC PSY SOC NEW/IDEA   INT/ORG
CHARTS TOT/POP 20. PAGE 43 G0837

S44
HAWLEY A.H.,"ECOLOGY AND HUMAN ECOLOGY" WOR+45   HABITAT
INTELL ACADEM PLAN GP/REL ADJUST PERSON...PHIL/SCI   GEOG
SOC METH/CNCPT METH 20. PAGE 25 G0493   GEN/LAWS
                                                         METH/COMP

B49
ROSENHAUPT H.W.,HOW TO WAGE PEACE. USA+45 SOCIETY   INTELL
STRATA STRUCT R+D INT/ORG POL/PAR LEGIS ACT/RES   CONCPT
CREATE PLAN EDU/PROP ADMIN EXEC ATTIT ALL/VALS   DIPLOM
...TIME/SEQ TREND COLD/WAR 20. PAGE 48 G0937

B45
BAKER H.,PROBLEMS OF REEMPLOYMENT AND RETRAINING OF   BIBLIOG/A

S49
MERTON R.,"THE ROLE OF APPLIED SOCIAL SCIENCE IN   PLAN

THE FORMATION OF POLICY: A RESEARCH MEMORANDUM." SOC
WOR+45 INDUS NAT/G EXEC ROUTINE CHOOSE ORD/FREE PWR DIPLOM
SKILL...POLICY MGT PSY METH/CNCPT TESTS CHARTS METH
VAL/FREE 20. PAGE 38 G0756

B50
CROWTHER J.G.,SCIENCE AT WAR. EUR+WWI PLAN TEC/DEV R+D
DOMIN COERCE NUC/PWR WEAPON KNOWL PWR...CONCPT OBS FORCES
TREND VAL/FREE 20. PAGE 14 G0265 WAR
UK

B50
DEES J.W. JR.,URBAN SOCIOLOGY AND THE EMERGING PLAN
ATOMIC MEGALOPOLIS, PART I. USA+45 TEC/DEV ADMIN NEIGH
NUC/PWR HABITAT...SOC AUD/VIS CHARTS GEN/LAWS 20 MUNIC
WATER. PAGE 15 G0291 PROB/SOLV

B50
KOENIG L.W.,THE SALE OF THE TANKERS. USA+45 SEA NAT/G
DIST/IND POL/PAR DIPLOM ADMIN CIVMIL/REL ATTIT POLICY
...DECISION 20 PRESIDENT DEPT/STATE. PAGE 31 G0609 PLAN
GOV/REL

B50
MANNHEIM K.,FREEDOM, POWER, AND DEMOCRATIC TEC/DEV
PLANNING. FUT USSR WOR+45 ELITES INTELL SOCIETY PLAN
NAT/G EDU/PROP ROUTINE ATTIT DRIVE SUPEGO SKILL CAP/ISM
...POLICY PSY CONCPT TREND GEN/LAWS 20. PAGE 35 UK
G0700

B50
SURANYI-UNGER T.,PRIVATE ENTERPRISE AND PLAN
GOVERNMENTAL PLANNING. STRUCT FINAN BAL/PWR NAT/G
HAPPINESS DRIVE NEW/LIB PLURISM...MATH QUANT STAT LAISSEZ
TREND BIBLIOG. PAGE 53 G1047 POLICY

B50
US DEPARTMENT OF STATE,POINT FOUR: COOPERATIVE ECO/UNDEV
PROGRAM FOR AID IN THE DEVELOPMENT OF ECONOMICALLY FOR/AID
UNDERDEVELOPED AREAS. WOR+45 AGRI INDUS INT/ORG FINAN
PLAN TEC/DEV DIPLOM EDU/PROP ADMIN PEACE PRODUC INT/TRADE
WEALTH 20 CONGRESS UN. PAGE 57 G1121

L50
MAASS A.A.,"CONGRESS AND WATER RESOURCES." LOC/G REGION
TEC/DEV CONTROL SANCTION...WELF/ST GEOG CONGRESS. AGRI
PAGE 35 G0683 PLAN

S50
KAPLAN A.,"THE PREDICTION OF SOCIAL AND PWR
TECHNOLOGICAL EVENTS." VOL/ASSN CONSULT ACT/RES KNO/TEST
CREATE OP/RES PLAN ROUTINE PERSON...POLICY
METH/CNCPT STAT QU/SEMANT SYS/QU TESTS CENSUS TREND
20. PAGE 29 G0574

B52
CURRENT TRENDS IN PSYCHOLOGY,PSYCHOLOGY IN THE NAT/G
WORLD EMERGENCY. USA+45 CONSULT FORCES ACT/RES PLAN PSY
SKILL...DECISION OBS APT/TEST KNO/TEST PERS/TEST
TREND CHARTS 20. PAGE 14 G0266

L52
ELDERSVELD S.J.,"RESEARCH IN POLITICAL BEHAVIOR" ACT/RES
(BMR)" USA+45 PLAN TEC/DEV ATTIT...BIBLIOG/A METH GEN/LAWS
20. PAGE 17 G0341 CREATE

B53
LARSEN K.,NATIONAL BIBLIOGRAPHIC SERVICES: THEIR BIBLIOG/A
CREATION AND OPERATION. WOR+45 COM/IND CREATE PLAN INT/ORG
DIPLOM PRESS ADMIN ROUTINE...MGT UNESCO. PAGE 32 WRITING
G0636

B54
GERMANY FOREIGN MINISTRY,DOCUMENTS ON GERMAN NAT/G
FOREIGN POLICY 1918-1945, SERIES C (1933-1937) DIPLOM
VOLS. I-V. GERMANY MOD/EUR FORCES PLAN ECO/TAC POLICY
...FASCIST CHARTS ANTHOL 20. PAGE 21 G0416

B54
HART B.H.L.,STRATEGY (REV. ED.). CHRIST-17C EUR+WWI WAR
MEDIT-7 MOD/EUR TEC/DEV LEAD REV WEAPON...POLICY PLAN
CHARTS. PAGE 25 G0486 FORCES
PHIL/SCI

B54
SIMMONS L.W.,SOCIAL SCIENCE IN MEDICINE. USA+45 PUB/INST
USA-45 SOCIETY CONSULT PLAN PROB/SOLV CONTROL HABITAT
PERS/REL...POLICY HEAL TREND BIBLIOG 20. PAGE 51 HEALTH
G0999 BIO/SOC

L54
OPLER M.E.,"SOCIAL ASPECTS OF TECHNICAL ASSISTANCE INT/ORG
IN OPERATION." WOR+45 VOL/ASSN CREATE PLAN TEC/DEV CONSULT
EDU/PROP ALL/VALS...METH/CNCPT OBS RECORD TREND UN FOR/AID
20. PAGE 43 G0841

S54
HOOPES T.,"CIVILIAN-MILITARY BALANCE." USA+45 CHIEF CIVMIL/REL
FORCES PLAN CONTROL WAR GOV/REL GP/REL INGP/REL LEAD
...POLICY 19/20. PAGE 27 G0527 PWR
NAT/G

S54
PYE L.W.,"EASTERN NATIONALISM AND WESTERN POLICY." CREATE
ASIA S/ASIA USA+45 USA-45 SOCIETY PLAN DIPLOM KNOWL ACT/RES
TOT/POP 20. PAGE 46 G0896 NAT/LISM

C54
CALDWELL L.K.,"THE GOVERNMENT AND ADMINISTRATION OF PROVS
NEW YORK." LOC/G MUNIC POL/PAR SCHOOL CHIEF LEGIS ADMIN
PLAN TAX CT/SYS...MGT SOC/WK BIBLIOG 20 NEWYORK/C. CONSTN
PAGE 10 G0202 EX/STRUC

B55
DAVIS E.,TWO MINUTES TO MIDNIGHT. WOR+45 PLAN NUC/PWR
CONTROL NEUTRAL ARMS/CONT ATTIT ORD/FREE...PSY 20 WAR
COLD/WAR. PAGE 14 G0277 DETER
DIPLOM

B55
RILEY V.,INTERINDUSTRY ECONOMIC STUDIES. USA+45 BIBLIOG
COMPUTER ADMIN OPTIMAL PRODUC...MGT CLASSIF STAT. ECO/DEV
PAGE 47 G0922 PLAN
STRUCT

B55
US OFFICE OF THE PRESIDENT,REPORT TO CONGRESS ON DIPLOM
THE MUTUAL SECURITY PROGRAM FOR THE SIX MONTHS FORCES
ENDED JUNE 30, 1955. ECO/DEV INT/ORG NAT/G CREATE PLAN
TEC/DEV BAL/PWR ECO/TAC AGREE DETER COST ORD/FREE FOR/AID
20 DEPT/STATE DEPT/DEFEN. PAGE 59 G1157

L55
KISER M.,"ORGANIZATION OF AMERICAN STATES." L/A+17C VOL/ASSN
USA+45 ECO/UNDEV INT/ORG NAT/G PLAN TEC/DEV DIPLOM ECO/DEV
ECO/TAC INT/TRADE EDU/PROP ADMIN ALL/VALS...POLICY REGION
MGT RECORD ORG/CHARTS OAS 20. PAGE 30 G0601

S55
ANGELL R.,"GOVERNMENTS AND PEOPLES AS A FOCI FOR FUT
PEACE-ORIENTED RESEARCH." WOR+45 CULTURE SOCIETY SOC
FACE/GP ACT/RES CREATE PLAN DIPLOM EDU/PROP ROUTINE PEACE
ATTIT PERCEPT SKILL...POLICY CONCPT OBS TREND
GEN/METH 20. PAGE 3 G0060

S55
DRUCKER P.F.,"'MANAGEMENT SCIENCE' AND THE MGT
MANAGER." PLAN ROUTINE RIGID/FLEX...METH/CNCPT LOG STRUCT
HYPO/EXP. PAGE 16 G0315 DECISION
RATIONAL

B56
ATOMIC INDUSTRIAL FORUM,PUBLIC RELATIONS FOR THE NUC/PWR
ATOMIC INDUSTRY. WOR+45 PLAN PROB/SOLV EDU/PROP INDUS
PRESS CONFER...AUD/VIS ANTHOL 20. PAGE 4 G0077 GP/REL
ATTIT

B56
ESTEP R.,AN AIR POWER BIBLIOGRAPHY. USA+45 TEC/DEV BIBLIOG/A
BUDGET DIPLOM EDU/PROP DETER CIVMIL/REL...DECISION FORCES
INT/LAW 20. PAGE 18 G0351 WEAPON
PLAN

B56
THOMAS M.,ATOMIC ENERGY AND CONGRESS. USA+45 NAT/G LEGIS
ACT/RES PLAN TEC/DEV EDU/PROP ROUTINE KNOWL PWR ADMIN
SKILL...PHIL/SCI NEW/IDEA TIME/SEQ CHARTS METH NUC/PWR
CONGRESS VAL/FREE 20 AEC. PAGE 54 G1067

B56
US OFFICE OF THE PRESIDENT,REPORT TO CONGRESS ON DIPLOM
THE MUTUAL SECURITY PROGRAM FOR THE SIX MONTHS FORCES
ENDED DECEMBER 31, 1955. ASIA USSR ECO/DEV PLAN
ECO/UNDEV INT/ORG CREATE TEC/DEV BAL/PWR ECO/TAC FOR/AID
AGREE DETER COST ORD/FREE 20 DEPT/STATE DEPT/DEFEN
EISNHWR/DD. PAGE 59 G1158

S56
GORDON L.,"THE ORGANIZATION FOR EUROPEAN ECONOMIC VOL/ASSN
COOPERATION." EUR+WWI INDUS INT/ORG NAT/G CONSULT ECO/DEV
DELIB/GP ACT/RES CREATE PLAN TEC/DEV EDU/PROP LEGIT
WEALTH OEEC 20. PAGE 22 G0435

S56
KNAPP D.C.,"CONGRESSIONAL CONTROL OF AGRICULTURAL LEGIS
CONSERVATION POLICY: A CASE STUDY OF THE AGRI
APPROPRIATIONS PROCESS." DELIB/GP PLAN PROB/SOLV BUDGET
CONFER PARL/PROC...POLICY INT CONGRESS. PAGE 31 CONTROL
G0607

B57
KISSINGER H.A.,NUCLEAR WEAPONS AND FOREIGN POLICY. PLAN

FUT USA+45 WOR+45 INT/ORG FORCES ACT/RES TEC/DEV DIPLOM ARMS/CONT COERCE ATTIT KNOWL PWR...DECISION GEOG CHARTS 20. PAGE 31 G0602
DETER
NUC/PWR

FISHMAN B.G.,"PUBLIC POLICY AND POLITICAL CONSIDERATIONS." USA+45 SOCIETY NAT/G ACT/RES CREATE PLAN DIPLOM KNOWL ORD/FREE...CONCPT GEN/METH 20. PAGE 19 G0370
S57
ECO/DEV
CONSULT

MCDONALD L.C.,"VOEGELIN AND THE POSITIVISTS: A NEW SCIENCE OF POLITICS." WOR+45 WOR-45 INTELL CREATE PLAN ATTIT...METH/CNCPT NEW/IDEA OBS VAL/FREE 20. PAGE 37 G0734
S57
PHIL/SCI
CONCPT
GEN/METH

TAYLOR P.S.,"THE RELATION OF RESEARCH TO LEGISLATIVE AND ADMINISTRATIVE DECISIONS." ELITES ACT/RES PLAN PROB/SOLV CONFER CHOOSE POLICY. PAGE 54 G1059
S57
DECISION
LEGIS
MGT
PWR

LIST OF PUBLICATIONS (PERIODICAL OR AD HOC) ISSUED BY VARIOUS MINISTRIES OF THE GOVERNMENT OF INDIA (3RD ED.). INDIA ECO/UNDEV PLAN...POLICY MGT 20. PAGE 1 G0014
B58
BIBLIOG
NAT/G
ADMIN

BIDWELL P.W.,RAW MATERIALS: A STUDY OF AMERICAN POLICY. USA+45 USA-45 ECO/UNDEV AGRI INDUS KIN CREATE PLAN ECO/TAC WAR PEACE ATTIT DRIVE WEALTH ...STAT CHARTS CONGRESS VAL/FREE. PAGE 7 G0135
B58
EXTR/IND
ECO/DEV

CHEEK G.,ECONOMIC AND SOCIAL IMPLICATIONS OF AUTOMATION: A BIBLIOGRAPHIC REVIEW (PAMPHLET). USA+45 LG/CO WORKER CREATE PLAN CONTROL ROUTINE PERS/REL EFFICIENCY PRODUC...METH/COMP 20. PAGE 12 G0225
B58
BIBLIOG/A
SOCIETY
INDUS
AUTOMAT

CROWE S.,THE LANDSCAPE OF POWER. UK CULTURE SERV/IND NAT/G CONSULT PARTIC NUC/PWR LEISURE...SOC EXHIBIT 20. PAGE 14 G0264
B58
HABITAT
TEC/DEV
PLAN
CONTROL

EHRHARD J.,LE DESTIN DU COLONIALISME. AFR FRANCE ECO/UNDEV AGRI FINAN MARKET CREATE PLAN TEC/DEV BUDGET DIPLOM PRICE 20. PAGE 17 G0335
B58
COLONIAL
FOR/AID
INT/TRADE
INDUS

GAVIN J.M.,WAR AND PEACE IN THE SPACE AGE. SPACE USA+45 USSR FORCES PLAN TEC/DEV BAL/PWR DIPLOM ARMS/CONT WEAPON CIVMIL/REL...CHARTS GP/COMP 20 NATO COLD/WAR. PAGE 21 G0414
B58
WAR
DETER
NUC/PWR
PEACE

LIPPITT R.,DYNAMICS OF PLANNED CHANGE. STRUCT ACT/RES ROUTINE INGP/REL PWR...POLICY METH/CNCPT BIBLIOG. PAGE 34 G0672
B58
VOL/ASSN
ORD/FREE
PLAN
CREATE

MARCUSE H.,SOVIET MARXISM, A CRITICAL ANALYSIS. USSR CONSTN PLAN PRODUC RATIONAL SOCISM...IDEA/COMP 20 COM/PARTY. PAGE 36 G0703
B58
MARXISM
ATTIT
POLICY

UN INTL CONF ON PEACEFUL USE,PROGRESS IN ATOMIC ENERGY (VOL. I). WOR+45 R+D PLAN TEC/DEV CONFER CONTROL PEACE SKILL...CHARTS ANTHOL 20 UN BAGHDAD. PAGE 55 G1088
B58
NUC/PWR
DIPLOM
WORKER
EDU/PROP

US HOUSE COMM GOVT OPERATIONS,CIVIL DEFENSE. USA+45 FORCES...CHARTS 20 CONGRESS CIV/DEFENS HOLIFLD/C. PAGE 58 G1139
B58
NUC/PWR
WAR
PLAN
ADJUST

ANDERSON N.,"INTERNATIONAL SEMINARS: AN ANALYSIS AND AN EVALUATION." WOR+45 R+D ACT/RES CREATE PLAN REGION ATTIT KNOWL SKILL...SOC REC/INT PERS/TEST CHARTS 20. PAGE 3 G0057
S58
INT/ORG
DELIB/GP

MARCY C.,"THE RESEARCH PROGRAM OF THE SENATE COMMITTEE ON FOREIGN RELATIONS." EUR+WWI ECO/UNDEV ACT/RES PLAN PARL/PROC GOV/REL...GEOG CONFE CONGRESS. PAGE 36 G0704
S58
DELIB/GP
LEGIS
FOR/AID
POLICY

SINGER J.D.,"THREAT PERCEPTION AND THE ARMAMENT
S58
PERCEPT

TENSION DILEMMA." WOR+45 WOR-45 ELITES INT/ORG NAT/G DELIB/GP PLAN LEGIT COERCE DETER ATTIT RIGID/FLEX PWR...DECISION PSY 20. PAGE 51 G1002
ARMS/CONT
BAL/PWR

AIR FORCE ACADEMY ASSEMBLY '59,INTERNATIONAL STABILITY AND PROGRESS (PAMPHLET). USA+45 USSR ECO/UNDEV PROB/SOLV BUDGET DIPLOM ADMIN DETER COST ATTIT...TREND 20. PAGE 2 G0030
B59
FOR/AID
FORCES
WAR
PLAN

ATOMIC INDUSTRIAL FORUM,THE IMPACT OF THE PEACEFUL USES OF ATOMIC ENERGY ON STATE AND LOCAL GOVERNMENT. USA+45 INDUS NAT/G LEGIS PLAN CONTROL GOV/REL. PAGE 4 G0079
B59
PROVS
LOC/G
NUC/PWR
PEACE

GREENFIELD K.R.,COMMAND DECISIONS. ASIA EUR+WWI S/ASIA USA-45 WOR-45 NAT/G CONSULT DELIB/GP COERCE NUC/PWR PWR...OBS 20 CHINJAP. PAGE 23 G0446
B59
PLAN
FORCES
WAR
WEAPON

HALEY A.G.,FIRST COLLOQUIUM ON THE LAW OF OUTER SPACE. WOR+45 INT/ORG ACT/RES PLAN BAL/PWR CONFER ATTIT PWR...POLICY JURID CHARTS ANTHOL 20. PAGE 24 G0468
B59
SPACE
LAW
SOVEREIGN
CONTROL

MEANS G.C.,ADMINISTRATIVE INFLATION AND PUBLIC POLICY (PAMPHLET). USA+45 ECO/DEV FINAN INDUS WORKER PLAN BUDGET GOV/REL COST DEMAND WEALTH 20 CONGRESS MONOPOLY GOLD/STAND. PAGE 38 G0749
B59
ECO/TAC
POLICY
RATION
CONTROL

MIKSCHE F.O.,THE FAILURE OF ATOMIC STRATEGY. COM EUR+WWI INTELL POL/PAR FORCES PLAN ECO/TAC NUC/PWR ATTIT DRIVE RIGID/FLEX PWR...DECISION GEOG PSY CONCPT RECORD TREND CHARTS VAL/FREE 20. PAGE 39 G0766
B59
ACT/RES
ORD/FREE
DIPLOM
ARMS/CONT

MODELSKI G.,ATOMIC ENERGY IN THE COMMUNIST BLOC. FUT INT/ORG CONSULT FORCES ACT/RES PLAN KNOWL SKILL ...PHIL/SCI STAT CHARTS 20. PAGE 39 G0777
B59
TEC/DEV
NUC/PWR
USSR
COM

POKROVSKY G.I.,SCIENCE AND TECHNOLOGY IN CONTEMPORARY WAR. SPACE USSR WOR+45 NAT/G CONSULT ACT/RES PLAN DETER WEAPON...MARXIST METH/CNCPT CHARTS STERTYP COLD/WAR 20. PAGE 45 G0881
B59
TEC/DEV
FORCES
NUC/PWR
WAR

COLUMBIA U BUREAU APPL SOC R, ATTITUDES OF PROMINENT AMERICANS TOWARD "WORLD PEACE THROUGH WORLD LAW" (SUPRA-NATL ORGANIZATION FOR WAR PREVENTION). USA+45 USSR ELITES FORCES PLAN PROB/SOLV CONTROL WAR PWR...POLICY SOC QU IDEA/COMP 20 UN. PAGE 45 G0888
B59
ATTIT
ACT/RES
INT/LAW
STAT

STANFORD RESEARCH INSTITUTE,POSSIBLE NONMILITARY SCIENTIFIC DEVELOPMENTS AND THEIR POTENTIAL IMPACT ON FOREIGN POLICY PROBLEMS OF THE UNITED. FUT USA+45 INT/ORG PROF/ORG CONSULT ACT/RES CREATE PLAN PEACE KNOWL SKILL...TECHNIC PHIL/SCI NEW/IDEA UNESCO 20. PAGE 52 G1032
B59
R+D
TEC/DEV

WELTON H.,THE THIRD WORLD WAR; TRADE AND INDUSTRY, THE NEW BATTLEGROUND. WOR+45 ECO/DEV INDUS MARKET TASK...MGT IDEA/COMP COLD/WAR. PAGE 63 G1229
B59
INT/TRADE
PLAN
DIPLOM

JANOWITZ M.,"CHANGING PATTERNS OF ORGANIZATIONAL AUTHORITY: THE MILITARY ESTABLISHMENT" (BMR)" USA+45 ELITES STRUCT EX/STRUC PLAN DOMIN AUTOMAT NUC/PWR WEAPON 20. PAGE 28 G0559
S59
FORCES
AUTHORIT
ADMIN
TEC/DEV

MILBURN T.W.,"WHAT CONSTITUTES EFFECTIVE DETERRENCE." USA+45 USSR WOR+45 STRUCT FORCES ACT/RES PLAN SUPEGO KNOWL ORD/FREE PWR...RELATIV PSY CONCPT VAL/FREE 20 COLD/WAR. PAGE 39 G0768
S59
INTELL
ATTIT
DETER
NUC/PWR

WILLIAMS B.H.,"SCIENTIFIC METHOD IN FOREIGN POLICY." WOR+45 NAT/G FORCES TOP/EX DOMIN LEGIT COERCE PEACE ATTIT KNOWL ORD/FREE PWR...GEN/LAWS GEN/METH TOT/POP COLD/WAR NAZI. PAGE 63 G1241
S59
PLAN
PHIL/SCI
DIPLOM

APTHEKER H.,DISARMAMENT AND THE AMERICAN ECONOMY: A SYMPOSIUM. FUT USA+45 ECO/DEV DIST/IND FINAN INDUS PROC/MFG LABOR NAT/G POL/PAR CONSULT PLAN CAP/ISM
B60
MARXIST
ARMS/CONT

INT/TRADE PEACE ATTIT MORAL WEALTH...TREND GEN/LAWS
TOT/POP 20. PAGE 3 G0063

B60
ATOMIC INDUSTRIAL FORUM,ATOMS FOR INDUSTRY: WORLD NUC/PWR
FORUM. WOR+45 FINAN COST UTIL...JURID ANTHOL 20. INDUS
PAGE 4 G0080 PLAN
PROB/SOLV

B60
BARNET R.,WHO WANTS DISARMAMENT. COM EUR+WWI USA+45 PLAN
USSR INT/ORG NAT/G BAL/PWR DIPLOM EDU/PROP COERCE FORCES
DETER NUC/PWR WAR WEAPON ATTIT PWR...TIME/SEQ ARMS/CONT
COLD/WAR CONGRESS 20. PAGE 5 G0096

B60
BOULDING K.E.,LINEAR PROGRAMMING AND THE THEORY OF LG/CO
THE FIRM. ACT/RES PLAN...MGT MATH. PAGE 8 G0156 NEW/IDEA
COMPUTER

B60
EINSTEIN A.,EINSTEIN ON PEACE. FUT WOR+45 WOR-45 INT/ORG
SOCIETY NAT/G PLAN BAL/PWR CAP/ISM DIPLOM ARMS/CONT ATTIT
DETER NAT/LISM...POLICY RELATIV HUM PHIL/SCI CONCPT NUC/PWR
BIOG COLD/WAR LEAGUE/NAT NAZI. PAGE 17 G0338 PEACE

B60
FRANCIS R.G.,THE PREDICTIVE PROCESS. PLAN MARXISM PREDICT
...DECISION SOC CONCPT NAT/COMP 19/20. PAGE 20 PHIL/SCI
G0390 TREND

B60
GRANICK D.,THE RED EXECUTIVE. COM USA+45 SOCIETY PWR
ECO/DEV INDUS NAT/G POL/PAR EX/STRUC PLAN ECO/TAC STRATA
EDU/PROP ADMIN EXEC ATTIT DRIVE...GP/COMP 20. USSR
PAGE 22 G0440 ELITES

B60
HEILBRONER R.L.,THE FUTURE AS HISTORY. USA+45 TEC/DEV
WOR+45 WOR-45 SOCIETY ECO/DEV ECO/UNDEV VOL/ASSN TREND
PLAN CAP/ISM NUC/PWR CHOOSE NAT/LISM ATTIT ORD/FREE
RESPECT WEALTH SOCISM 20. PAGE 25 G0501

B60
HITCH C.J.,THE ECONOMICS OF DEFENSE IN THE NUCLEAR R+D
AGE. USA+45 WOR+45 CREATE PLAN NUC/PWR ATTIT FORCES
...CON/ANAL CHARTS HYPO/EXP NATO 20. PAGE 26 G0514

B60
KINGSTON-MCCLOUG E.,DEFENSE: POLICY AND STRATEGY. FORCES
UK SEA AIR TEC/DEV DIPLOM ADMIN LEAD WAR ORD/FREE PLAN
...CHARTS 20. PAGE 30 G0597 POLICY
DECISION

B60
LE GHAIT E.,NO CARTE BLANCHE TO CAPRICORN; THE DETER
FOLLY OF NUCLEAR WAR. WOR+45 INT/ORG BAL/PWR DIPLOM NUC/PWR
RISK COERCE...CENSUS 20 NATO. PAGE 33 G0647 PLAN
DECISION

B60
LEYDER J.,BIBLIOGRAPHIE DE L'ENSEIGNEMENT SUPERIEUR BIBLIOG/A
ET DE LA RECHERCHE SCIENTIFIQUE EN AFRIQUE ACT/RES
INTERTROPICALE (2 VOLS.). AFR CULTURE ECO/UNDEV ACADEM
AGRI PLAN EDU/PROP ADMIN COLONIAL...GEOG SOC/INTEG R+D
20 NEGRO. PAGE 34 G0664

B60
MCKINNEY R.,REVIEW OF THE INTERNATIONAL ATOMIC NUC/PWR
POLICIES AND PROGRAMS OF THE UNITED STATES (5 PEACE
VOLS.). COM FUT USA+45 ECO/DEV ECO/UNDEV INT/ORG DIPLOM
DELIB/GP PLAN ADMIN 20 THIRD/WRLD. PAGE 38 G0744 POLICY

B60
PARRY A.,RUSSIA'S ROCKETS AND MISSILES. COM FUT PLAN
GERMANY USA+45 WOR+45 INTELL ECO/DEV ACT/RES TEC/DEV
NUC/PWR WEAPON ATTIT ALL/VALS...OBS TIME/SEQ SPACE
COLD/WAR 20. PAGE 44 G0859 USSR

B60
US SENATE COMM ON COMMERCE,URBAN MASS DIST/IND
TRANSPORTATION. FUT USA+45 AIR ECO/DEV FINAN LOC/G PLAN
MUNIC LEGIS CREATE PROB/SOLV TEC/DEV 20 PUB/TRANS. NAT/G
PAGE 60 G1180 LAW

B60
WEBSTER J.A.,A GENERAL STUDY OF THE DEPARTMENT OF ORD/FREE
DEFENSE INTERNAL SECURITY PROGRAM. USA+45 WORKER PLAN
TEC/DEV ADJUD CONTROL CT/SYS EXEC GOV/REL COST ADMIN
...POLICY DECISION MGT 20 DEPT/DEFEN SUPREME/CT. NAT/G
PAGE 62 G1221

B60
WOETZEL R.K.,THE INTERNATIONAL CONTROL OF AIRSPACE INT/ORG
AND OUTERSPACE. FUT WOR+45 AIR CONSTN STRUCT JURID
CONSULT PLAN TEC/DEV ADJUD RIGID/FLEX KNOWL SPACE

ORD/FREE PWR...TECHNIC GEOG MGT NEW/IDEA TREND INT/LAW
COMPUT/IR VAL/FREE 20 TREATY. PAGE 64 G1251

L60
BRENNAN D.G.,"SETTING AND GOALS OF ARMS CONTROL." FORCES
FUT USA+45 USSR WOR+45 INTELL INT/ORG NAT/G COERCE
VOL/ASSN CONSULT PLAN DIPLOM ECO/TAC ADMIN KNOWL ARMS/CONT
PWR...POLICY CONCPT TREND COLD/WAR 20. PAGE 8 G0164 DETER

L60
DEUTSCH K.W.,"TOWARD AN INVENTORY OF BASIC TRENDS R+D
AND PATTERNS IN COMPARATIVE AND INTERNATIONAL PERCEPT
POLITICS." UNIV WOR+45 SOCIETY STRUCT INT/ORG NAT/G
CREATE PLAN EDU/PROP KNOWL...PHIL/SCI METH/CNCPT
STAT SELF/OBS OBS/ENVIR SAMP TREND CON/ANAL CHARTS
SOC/EXP GEN/METH 20. PAGE 15 G0298

L60
HOLTON G.,"ARMS CONTROL." FUT WOR+45 CULTURE ACT/RES
INT/ORG NAT/G FORCES TOP/EX PLAN EDU/PROP COERCE CONSULT
ATTIT RIGID/FLEX ORD/FREE...POLICY PHIL/SCI SOC ARMS/CONT
TREND COLD/WAR. PAGE 27 G0524 NUC/PWR

L60
HOLZMAN B.G.,"BASIC RESEARCH FOR NATIONAL FORCES
SURVIVAL." FUT USA+45 INTELL R+D ACT/RES OP/RES STAT
PLAN TEC/DEV EDU/PROP PERCEPT PERSON...PHIL/SCI
METH/CNCPT NEW/IDEA MATH OBS RECORD TREND LAB/EXP
20. PAGE 27 G0525

L60
MCCLELLAND C.A.,"THE FUNCTION OF THEORY IN INT/ORG
INTERNATIONAL RELATIONS." WOR+45 PLAN EDU/PROP CONCPT
ROUTINE ORD/FREE...PHIL/SCI PSY SOC METH/CNCPT DIPLOM
NEW/IDEA OBS TREND GEN/METH 20. PAGE 37 G0728

S60
BARNETT H.J.,"RESEARCH AND DEVELOPMENT, ECONOMIC ACT/RES
GROWTH, AND NATIONAL SECURITY." USA+45 R+D CREATE PLAN
ECO/TAC ATTIT DRIVE PWR...POLICY SOC METH/CNCPT
QUANT STAT TIME/SEQ ORG/CHARTS COLD/WAR 20. PAGE 5
G0097

S60
BECKER A.S.,"COMPARISIONS OF UNITED STATES AND USSR STAT
NATIONAL OUTPUT: SOME RULES OF THE GAME." COM USSR
USA+45 ECO/DEV AGRI DIST/IND INDUS R+D CONSULT PLAN
ECO/TAC RIGID/FLEX KNOWL...METH/CNCPT CHARTS 20.
PAGE 6 G0113

S60
BRODY R.A.,"DETERRENCE STRATEGIES: AN ANNOTATED BIBLIOG/A
BIBLIOGRAPHY." WOR+45 PLAN ARMS/CONT NUC/PWR WAR FORCES
WEAPON DECISION. PAGE 9 G0173 DETER
DIPLOM

S60
DYSON F.J.,"THE FUTURE DEVELOPMENT OF NUCLEAR INT/ORG
WEAPONS." FUT WOR+45 DELIB/GP ACT/RES PLAN DETER ARMS/CONT
WEAPON ATTIT PWR...POLICY 20. PAGE 17 G0328 NUC/PWR

S60
HUTCHINSON C.E.,"AN INSTITUTE FOR NATIONAL SECURITY POLICY
AFFAIRS." USA+45 R+D NAT/G CONSULT TOP/EX ACT/RES METH/CNCPT
CREATE PLAN TEC/DEV EDU/PROP ROUTINE NUC/PWR ATTIT ELITES
ORD/FREE PWR...DECISION MGT PHIL/SCI CONCPT RECORD DIPLOM
GEN/LAWS GEN/METH 20. PAGE 27 G0539

S60
JAFFEE A.J.,"POPULATION TRENDS AND CONTROLS IN ECO/UNDEV
UNDERDEVELOPED COUNTRIES." AFR FUT ISLAM L/A+17C GEOG
S/ASIA CULTURE R+D FAM ACT/RES PLAN EDU/PROP
BIO/SOC RIGID/FLEX HEALTH...SOC STAT OBS CHARTS 20.
PAGE 28 G0555

S60
KAPLAN M.A.,"THEORETICAL ANALYSIS OF THE BALANCE OF CREATE
POWER." FUT USA+45 WOR+45 INTELL ECO/DEV INT/ORG NEW/IDEA
NAT/G CONSULT TOP/EX ACT/RES PLAN TEC/DEV ATTIT DIPLOM
ALL/VALS...METH/CNCPT TOT/POP 20. PAGE 29 G0576 NUC/PWR

S60
KISSINGER H.A.,"ARMS CONTROL, INSPECTION AND FORCES
SURPRISE ATTACK." COM USA+45 NAT/G ACT/RES PLAN ORD/FREE
TEC/DEV DIPLOM EDU/PROP DETER WAR RIGID/FLEX ARMS/CONT
...CONCPT GEN/METH TOT/POP 20. PAGE 31 G0603 NUC/PWR

S60
RIVKIN A.,"AFRICAN ECONOMIC DEVELOPMENT: ADVANCED AFR
TECHNOLOGY AND THE STAGES OF GROWTH." CULTURE TEC/DEV
ECO/UNDEV AGRI COM/IND EXTR/IND PLAN ECO/TAC ATTIT FOR/AID
DRIVE RIGID/FLEX SKILL WEALTH...MGT SOC GEN/LAWS
WORK TOT/POP 20. PAGE 47 G0923

N60
US HOUSE COMM SCI ASTRONAUT,THE ORGANIZATION OF THE ACT/RES

US NATIONAL SPACE EFFORT. USA+45 WOR+45 AIR ECO/DEV SKILL
NAT/G PLAN TEC/DEV DIPLOM EDU/PROP ATTIT DRIVE PWR SPACE
...OBS TIME/SEQ TREND TOT/POP 20. PAGE 58 G1142

    SKILL
    SPACE

B61
CHAPPLE E.D.,THE MEASURE OF MANAGEMENT. USA+45 MGT
WORKER ADMIN GP/REL EFFICIENCY...DECISION OP/RES
ORG/CHARTS SIMUL 20. PAGE 11 G0221 PLAN
    METH/CNCPT

B61
FRISCH D.,ARMS REDUCTION: PROGRAM AND ISSUES. PLAN
USA+45 INT/ORG NAT/G ACT/RES REGION NUC/PWR ATTIT FORCES
PWR...POLICY 20. PAGE 20 G0395 ARMS/CONT
    DIPLOM

B61
GORDON W.J.J.,SYNECTICS; THE DEVELOPMENT OF CREATE
CREATIVE CAPACITY. USA+45 PLAN TEC/DEV KNOWL WEALTH PROB/SOLV
...DECISION MGT 20. PAGE 22 G0436 ACT/RES
    TOP/EX

B61
HADLEY A.T.,THE NATIONS SAFETY AND ARMS CONTROL. ACT/RES
FUT USA+45 WOR+45 TOP/EX PLAN TEC/DEV ATTIT DRIVE ROUTINE
...CONCPT OBS TIME/SEQ TREND 20. PAGE 24 G0466 DETER
    NUC/PWR

B61
KAHN H.,ON THERMONUCLEAR WAR. FUT UNIV WOR+45 DETER
ECO/DEV CONSULT EX/STRUC TOP/EX ACT/RES CREATE PLAN NUC/PWR
COERCE WAR PERSON ALL/VALS...POLICY GEOG CONCPT SOCIETY
METH/CNCPT OBS TREND 20. PAGE 29 G0569

B61
KISSINGER H.A.,THE NECESSITY FOR CHOICE. FUT USA+45 TOP/EX
ECO/UNDEV NAT/G PLAN BAL/PWR ECO/TAC ARMS/CONT TREND
DETER NUC/PWR ATTIT...POLICY CONCPT RECORD GEN/LAWS DIPLOM
COLD/WAR 20. PAGE 31 G0604

B61
LAHAYE R.,LES ENTREPRISES PUBLIQUES AU MAROC. NAT/G
FRANCE MOROCCO LAW DIST/IND EXTR/IND FINAN CONSULT INDUS
PLAN TEC/DEV ADMIN AGREE CONTROL OWN...POLICY 20. ECO/UNDEV
PAGE 32 G0629 ECO/TAC

B61
LEE R.R.,ENGINEERING-ECONOMIC PLANNING BIBLIOG/A
MISCELLANEOUS SUBJECTS: A SELECTED BIBLIOGRAPHY PLAN
(MIMEOGRAPHED). FINAN LOC/G MUNIC NEIGH ADMIN REGION
CONTROL INGP/REL HABITAT...GEOG MGT SOC/WK 20
RESOURCE/N. PAGE 33 G0651

B61
LUNDBERG G.A.,CAN SCIENCE SAVE US. UNIV CULTURE ACT/RES
INTELL SOCIETY ECO/DEV R+D PLAN EDU/PROP ROUTINE CONCPT
CHOOSE ATTIT PERCEPT ALL/VALS...TREND 20. PAGE 34 TOTALISM
G0679

B61
MURPHY E.F.,WATER PURITY: A STUDY IN LEGAL CONTROL SEA
OF NATURAL RESOURCES. LOC/G ACT/RES PLAN TEC/DEV LAW
LOBBY GP/REL COST ATTIT HEALTH ORD/FREE...HEAL PROVS
JURID 20 WISCONSIN WATER. PAGE 40 G0797 CONTROL

B61
NOVE A.,THE SOVIET ECONOMY. USSR ECO/DEV FINAN PLAN
NAT/G ECO/TAC PRICE ADMIN EFFICIENCY MARXISM PRODUC
...TREND BIBLIOG 20. PAGE 42 G0828 POLICY

B61
SCHMIDT H.,VERTEIDIGUNG ODER VERGELTUNG. COM CUBA PLAN
GERMANY/W USSR FORCES DIPLOM ARMS/CONT DETER WAR
NUC/PWR...POLICY CHARTS HYPO/EXP SIMUL BIBLIOG 20 BAL/PWR
NATO COLD/WAR. PAGE 49 G0970 ORD/FREE

B61
SMITH H.H.,THE CITIZEN'S GUIDE TO PLANNING. USA+45 MUNIC
LAW SCHOOL CREATE PROB/SOLV EDU/PROP GP/REL ROLE 20 PLAN
URBAN/RNWL OPEN/SPACE. PAGE 52 G1015 DELIB/GP
    CONSULT

B61
US SENATE COMM GOVT OPERATIONS,ORGANIZING FOR POLICY
NATIONAL SECURITY. COM USA+45 BUDGET DIPLOM DETER PLAN
NUC/PWR WAR WEAPON ORD/FREE...BIBLIOG 20 COLD/WAR. FORCES
PAGE 60 G1176 COERCE

L61
TAUBENFELD H.J.,"A REGIME FOR OUTER SPACE." FUT INT/ORG
UNIV R+D ACT/RES PLAN BAL/PWR LEGIT ARMS/CONT ADJUD
ORD/FREE...POLICY JURID TREND UN TOT/POP 20 SPACE
COLD/WAR. PAGE 54 G1056

S61
COOKE E.F.,"RESEARCH: AN INSTRUMENT OF POWER." R+D

VOL/ASSN PLAN TEC/DEV TAX LOBBY INGP/REL ROLE PROVS
POLICY. PAGE 13 G0253 LOC/G
    DECISION

S61
DYKMAN J.W.,"REVIEW ARTICLE* PLANNING AND DECISION DECISION
THEORY." ELITES LOC/G MUNIC CONSULT ADMIN...POLICY PLAN
MGT. PAGE 17 G0327 RATIONAL

S61
LINDSAY F.A.,"PLANNING IN FOREIGN AFFAIRS: THE ECO/DEV
MISSING ELEMENT." FUT USA+45 ROUTINE SKILL...MGT PLAN
TOT/POP 20. PAGE 34 G0669 DIPLOM

S61
MACHOWSKI K.,"SELECTED PROBLEMS OF NATIONAL UNIV
SOVEREIGNTY WITH REFERENCE TO THE LAW OF OUTER ACT/RES
SPACE." FUT WOR+45 AIR LAW INTELL SOCIETY ECO/DEV NUC/PWR
PLAN EDU/PROP DETER DRIVE PERCEPT SOVEREIGN SPACE
...POLICY INT/LAW OBS TREND TOT/POP 20. PAGE 35
G0689

S61
MORGENSTERN O.,"THE N-COUNTRY PROBLEM." EUR+WWI FUT
UNIV USA+45 WOR+45 SOCIETY CONSULT TOP/EX ACT/RES BAL/PWR
PLAN EDU/PROP ATTIT DRIVE...POLICY OBS TREND NUC/PWR
TOT/POP 20. PAGE 40 G0781 TEC/DEV

S61
RICHSTEIN A.R.,"LEGAL RULES IN NUCLEAR WEAPONS NUC/PWR
EMPLOYMENTS." FUT WOR+45 LAW SOCIETY FORCES PLAN TEC/DEV
WEAPON RIGID/FLEX...HEAL CONCPT TREND VAL/FREE 20. MORAL
PAGE 47 G0918 ARMS/CONT

S61
TAUBENFELD H.J.,"OUTER SPACE--PAST POLITICS AND PLAN
FUTURE POLICY." FUT USA+45 USA-45 WOR+45 AIR INTELL SPACE
STRUCT ECO/DEV NAT/G TOP/EX ACT/RES ADMIN ROUTINE INT/ORG
NUC/PWR ATTIT DRIVE...CONCPT TIME/SEQ TREND TOT/POP
20. PAGE 54 G1054

B62
ASTIA,INFORMATION THEORY: A REPORT BIBLIOGRAPHY. BIBLIOG/A
USA+45 COMPUTER CREATE OP/RES PLAN TEC/DEV CONTROL COM/IND
...CONCPT METH/COMP. PAGE 4 G0074 FORCES
    METH

B62
BENNIS W.G.,THE PLANNING OF CHANGE: READINGS IN THE PROB/SOLV
APPLIED BEHAVIORAL SCIENCES. CULTURE STRATA STRUCT CREATE
PLAN GP/REL...SOC T. PAGE 6 G0123 ACT/RES
    OP/RES

B62
CHANDLER A.D.,STRATEGY AND STRUCTURE: CHAPTERS IN LG/CO
THE HISTORY OF THE INDUSTRIAL ENTERPRISE. USA+45 PLAN
USA-45 ECO/DEV EX/STRUC ECO/TAC EXEC...DECISION 20. ADMIN
PAGE 11 G0220 FINAN

B62
DUCKWORTH W.E.,A GUIDE TO OPERATIONAL RESEARCH. OP/RES
INDUS PLAN PROB/SOLV EXEC EFFICIENCY PRODUC KNOWL GAME
...MGT MATH STAT SIMUL METH 20 MONTECARLO. PAGE 16 DECISION
G0319 ADMIN

B62
FORBES H.W.,THE STRATEGY OF DISARMAMENT. FUT WOR+45 PLAN
INT/ORG VOL/ASSN CONSULT ARMS/CONT COERCE NUC/PWR FORCES
WAR DRIVE RIGID/FLEX ORD/FREE PWR...POLICY CONCPT DIPLOM
OBS TREND STERTYP 20. PAGE 19 G0378

B62
FRYKLUND R.,100 MILLION LIVES: MAXIMUM SURVIVAL IN NUC/PWR
A NUCLEAR WAR. USA+45 USSR CONTROL WEAPON WAR
...IDEA/COMP NAT/COMP 20. PAGE 20 G0397 PLAN
    DETER

B62
GOLOVINE M.N.,CONFLICT IN SPACE: A PATTERN OF WAR CREATE
IN A NEW DIMENSION. FUT USA+45 WOR+45 AIR FORCES TEC/DEV
PLAN DIPLOM DOMIN ATTIT...STAT AUD/VIS CHARTS NUC/PWR
COLD/WAR 20. PAGE 22 G0432 SPACE

B62
GRANICK D.,THE EUROPEAN EXECUTIVE. BELGIUM FRANCE MGT
GERMANY/W UK INDUS LABOR LG/CO SML/CO EX/STRUC PLAN ECO/DEV
TEC/DEV CAP/ISM COST DEMAND...POLICY CHARTS 20. ECO/TAC
PAGE 22 G0441 EXEC

B62
KAHN H.,THINKING ABOUT THE UNTHINKABLE. FUT USA+45 INT/ORG
LAW NAT/G CONSULT FORCES ACT/RES CREATE PLAN ORD/FREE
TEC/DEV BAL/PWR DIPLOM EDU/PROP ARMS/CONT DETER NUC/PWR
ATTIT...CONCPT OBS TREND COLD/WAR 20. PAGE 29 G0570 PEACE

B62

KARNJAHAPRAKORN C.,MUNICIPAL GOVERNMENT IN THAILAND LOC/G
AS AN INSTITUTION AND PROCESS OF SELF-GOVERNMENT.   MUNIC
THAILAND CULTURE FINAN EX/STRUC LEGIS PLAN CONTROL   ORD/FREE
GOV/REL EFFICIENCY ATTIT...POLICY 20. PAGE 29 G0578   ADMIN

B62

KRAFT J.,THE GRAND DESIGN. EUR+WWI USA+45 AGRI   VOL/ASSN
FINAN INDUS MARKET INT/ORG NAT/G PLAN ECO/TAC   ECO/DEV
TARIFFS REGION DRIVE ORD/FREE WEALTH...POLICY OBS   INT/TRADE
TREND EEC 20. PAGE 31 G0616

B62

OSGOOD C.E.,AN ALTERNATIVE TO WAR OR SURRENDER. FUT   ORD/FREE
UNIV CULTURE INTELL SOCIETY R+D INT/ORG CONSULT   EDU/PROP
DELIB/GP ACT/RES PLAN CHOOSE ATTIT PERCEPT KNOWL   PEACE
...PHIL/SCI PSY SOC TREND GEN/LAWS 20. PAGE 43   WAR
G0849

B62

RIKER W.H.,THE THEORY OF POLITICAL COALITIONS.   FUT
WOR+45 INTELL NAT/G CREATE PLAN ATTIT DRIVE PERCEPT   SIMUL
...DECISION PSY SOC METH/CNCPT NEW/IDEA MATH CHARTS
GAME TOT/POP 20. PAGE 47 G0921

B62

SCHILLING W.R.,STRATEGY, POLITICS, AND DEFENSE   ROUTINE
BUDGETS. USA+45 R+D NAT/G FORCES DELIB/GP FORCES   POLICY
LEGIS ACT/RES PLAN BAL/PWR LEGIT EXEC NUC/PWR
RIGID/FLEX PWR...TREND COLD/WAR CONGRESS 20
EISNHWR/DD. PAGE 49 G0968

B62

SCHMITT H.A.,THE PATH TO EUROPEAN UNITY. EUR+WWI   INT/ORG
USA+45 PLAN TEC/DEV DIPLOM FOR/AID CONFER...INT/LAW   INT/TRADE
20 EEC EURCOALSTL MARSHL/PLN UNIFICA. PAGE 49 G0971   REGION
                                                          ECO/DEV

B62

SOHN L.B.,ZONAL DISARMAMENT: VARIATIONS ON A THEME.   ORD/FREE
FUT WOR+45 SOCIETY ACT/RES PLAN NUC/PWR PEACE ATTIT   NEW/IDEA
...POLICY GEOG CONT/OBS HYPO/EXP 20. PAGE 52 G1020   ARMS/CONT

B62

STAHL O.G.,PUBLIC PERSONNEL ADMINISTRATION. LOC/G   ADMIN
TOP/EX CREATE PLAN ROUTINE...TECHNIC MGT T. PAGE 52   WORKER
G1030   EX/STRUC
                                                          NAT/G

B62

THANT U.,THE UNITED NATIONS' DEVELOPMENT DECADE: INT/ORG
PROPOSALS FOR ACTION. WOR+45 ECO/UNDEV AGRI   ALL/VALS
COM/IND FINAN R+D MUNIC SCHOOL VOL/ASSN CONSULT
PLAN TEC/DEV ECO/TAC EDU/PROP ADMIN ROUTINE
RIGID/FLEX...MGT SOC CONCPT UNESCO UN TOT/POP
VAL/FREE. PAGE 54 G1064

B62

THOMSON G.P.,NUCLEAR ENERGY IN BRITAIN DURING THE   CREATE
LAST WAR: THE CHERWELL SIMON LECTURE (MONOGRAPH).   TEC/DEV
UK R+D CONSULT FORCES PLAN DIPLOM TASK CIVMIL/REL   WAR
ROLE...PHIL/SCI NEW/IDEA LAB/EXP 20 MAUD. PAGE 54   NUC/PWR
G1071

B62

US CONGRESS,COMMUNICATIONS SATELLITE LEGISLATION: SPACE
HEARINGS BEFORE COMM ON AERON AND SPACE SCIENCES ON   COM/IND
BILLS S2550 AND 2814. WOR+45 LAW VOL/ASSN PLAN   ADJUD
DIPLOM CONTROL OWN PEACE...NEW/IDEA CONGRESS NASA.   GOV/REL
PAGE 56 G1110

B62

US SENATE COMM GOVT OPERATIONS,ADMINISTRATION OF   ORD/FREE
NATIONAL SECURITY. USA+45 CHIEF PLAN PROB/SOLV   ADMIN
TEC/DEV DIPLOM ATTIT...POLICY DECISION 20   NAT/G
KENNEDY/JF RUSK/D MCNAMARA/R BUNDY/M HERTER/C.   CONTROL
PAGE 60 G1177

B62

WALSTON H.,AGRICULTURE UNDER COMMUNISM. CHINA/COM   AGRI
COM PROB/SOLV HAPPINESS RIGID/FLEX...POLICY   MARXISM
METH/COMP 20. PAGE 62 G1207   PLAN
                                                          CREATE

B62

WENDT P.F.,HOUSING POLICY - THE SEARCH FOR   PLAN
SOLUTIONS. GERMANY/W SWEDEN UK USA+45 OP/RES   ADMIN
HABITAT WEALTH...SOC/WK CHARTS 20. PAGE 63 G1230   METH/COMP
                                                          NAT/G

L62

BETTEN J.K.,"ARMS CONTROL AND THE PROBLEM OF   NAT/G
EVASION." WOR+45 FORCES CREATE DIPLOM DETER PWR   PLAN
...PSY TREND GEN/LAWS COLD/WAR 20. PAGE 7 G0134   ARMS/CONT

S62

ALBONETTI A.,"IL SECONDO PROGRAMMA QUINQUENNALE   R+D
1963-67 ED IL BILANCIO RICERCHE ED INVESTIMENTI PER   PLAN
IL 1963 DELL'ERATOM." EUR+WWI FUT ITALY WOR+45   NUC/PWR
ECO/DEV SERV/IND INT/ORG TEC/DEV ECO/TAC ATTIT
SKILL WEALTH...MGT TIME/SEQ OEEC 20. PAGE 2 G0035

S62

BETHE H.,"DISARMAMENT AND STRATEGY." COM USA+45   PLAN
USSR WOR+45 VOL/ASSN TEC/DEV EDU/PROP NUC/PWR   ORD/FREE
CHOOSE PEACE...POLICY DECISION NEW/IDEA OBS   ARMS/CONT
GEN/LAWS COLD/WAR 420. PAGE 7 G0133   DIPLOM

S62

BOULDING K.E.,"THE PREVENTION OF WORLD WAR THREE."   VOL/ASSN
FUT WOR+45 INT/ORG PLAN BAL/PWR PEACE ORD/FREE PWR   NAT/G
...NEW/IDEA TREND TOT/POP COLD/WAR 20. PAGE 8 G0158   ARMS/CONT
                                                          DIPLOM

S62

CRANE R.D.,"LAW AND STRATEGY IN SPACE." FUT USA+45   CONCPT
WOR+45 AIR LAW INT/ORG NAT/G FORCES ACT/RES PLAN   SPACE
BAL/PWR LEGIT ARMS/CONT COERCE ORD/FREE...POLICY
INT/LAW JURID SOC/EXP 20 TREATY. PAGE 13 G0261

S62

DAWSON R.H.,"CONGRESSIONAL INNOVATION AND   LEGIS
INTERVENTION IN DEFENSE POLICY: LEGISLATIVE   PWR
AUTHORIZATION OF WEAPONS SYSTEMS." CONSTN PLAN   CONTROL
ARMS/CONT GOV/REL EFFICIENCY PEACE NEW/LIB OLD/LIB.   WEAPON
PAGE 14 G0281

S62

FOSTER R.B.,"UNILATERAL ARMS CONTROL MEASURES AND   PLAN
DISARMAMENT NEGOTIATION." WOR+45 VOL/ASSN DELIB/GP   ORD/FREE
ACT/RES ECO/TAC EDU/PROP ATTIT RIGID/FLEX...CONCPT   ARMS/CONT
MYTH TIME/SEQ COLD/WAR 20. PAGE 20 G0386   DETER

S62

FOSTER W.C.,"ARMS CONTROL AND DISARMAMENT IN A   DELIB/GP
DIVIDED WORLD." COM FUT USA+45 USSR WOR+45 INTELL   POLICY
INT/ORG NAT/G VOL/ASSN CONSULT CREATE PLAN TEC/DEV   ARMS/CONT
EDU/PROP LEGIT NUC/PWR ATTIT RIGID/FLEX...CONCPT   DIPLOM
TREND TOT/POP 20 UN. PAGE 20 G0387

S62

MORGENTHAU H.J.,"A POLITICAL THEORY OF FOREIGN   USA+45
AID." ECO/UNDEV NAT/G DELIB/GP PLAN ECO/TAC   PHIL/SCI
EDU/PROP EXEC ORD/FREE RESPECT WEALTH...METH/CNCPT   FOR/AID
TREND 20. PAGE 40 G0783

S62

PHIPPS T.E.,"THE CASE FOR DETERRENCE." FUT WOR+45   ATTIT
SOCIETY EX/STRUC FORCES ACT/RES CREATE PLAN TEC/DEV   COERCE
ROUTINE RIGID/FLEX ORD/FREE...POLICY MYTH NEW/IDEA   DETER
STERTYP COLD/WAR 20. PAGE 45 G0876   ARMS/CONT

S62

SCHILLING W.R.,"SCIENTISTS, FOREIGN POLICY AND   NAT/G
POLITICS." WOR+45 INTELL INT/ORG CONSULT   TEC/DEV
TOP/EX ACT/RES PLAN ADMIN KNOWL...CONCPT OBS TREND   DIPLOM
LEAGUE/NAT 20. PAGE 49 G0967   NUC/PWR

S62

STORER N.W.,"SOME SOCIOLOGICAL ASPECTS OF FEDERAL   POLICY
SCIENCE POLICY." USA+45 INTELL PUB/INST PLAN GP/REL   CREATE
PERS/REL DRIVE PERSON ROLE...PSY SOC SIMUL 20 NIH   NAT/G
NSF. PAGE 53 G1040   ALL/VALS

S62

VIETORISZ T.,"PRELIMINARY BIBLIOGRAPHY FOR   BIBLIOG/A
INDUSTRIAL DEVELOPMENT PROGRAMMING." ECO/DEV   TEC/DEV
ECO/UNDEV R+D LABOR PROB/SOLV AUTOMAT PRODUC.   ACT/RES
PAGE 61 G1198   PLAN

S62

WALTER E.,"VERS UNE CLASSIFICATION SCIENTIFIQUE DE   PLAN
LA SOCIOLOGIA." UNIV CULTURE INTELL SOCIETY R+D   CONCPT
ACT/RES LEGIT ROUTINE ATTIT KNOWL...JURID MGT TREND
GEN/LAWS 20. PAGE 62 G1208

C62

JOINT ECONOMIC COMMITTEE,"DIMENSIONS OF SOVIET   ECO/DEV
ECONOMIC POWER." USSR R+D FORCES ACT/RES OP/RES   PLAN
TEC/DEV...GEOG STAT BIBLIOG 20. PAGE 29 G0565   PRODUC
                                                          LABOR

B63

BASS M.E.,SELECTIVE BIBLIOGRAPHY ON MUNICIPAL   BIBLIOG
GOVERNMENT FROM THE FILES OF THE MUNICIPAL   LOC/G
TECHNICAL ADVISORY SERVICE. USA+45 FINAN SERV/IND   ADMIN
PLAN 20. PAGE 5 G0100   MUNIC

B63

BROUDE H.W.,STEEL DECISIONS AND THE NATIONAL   PROC/MFG
ECONOMY. USA+45 LG/CO PLAN ADMIN COST DECISION.   NAT/G

PAGE 9 G0176   CONTROL
                                                      ECO/TAC

                                                         B63
BURSK E.C.,NEW DECISION-MAKING TOOLS FOR MANAGERS.   DECISION
COMPUTER PLAN PROB/SOLV ROUTINE COST. PAGE 10 G0194   MGT
                                                      MATH
                                                      RIGID/FLEX
                                                         B63
DALAND R.T.,PERSPECTIVES OF BRAZILIAN PUBLIC   ADMIN
ADMINISTRATION (VOL. I). BRAZIL LAW ECO/UNDEV   NAT/G
SCHOOL CHIEF TEC/DEV CONFER CONTROL GP/REL ATTIT   PLAN
ROLE PWR...ANTHOL 20. PAGE 14 G0272   GOV/REL
                                                         B63
FLORES E.,LAND REFORM AND THE ALLIANCE FOR PROGRESS   AGRI
(PAMPHLET). L/A+17C USA+45 STRUCT ECO/UNDEV NAT/G   INT/ORG
WORKER CREATE PLAN ECO/TAC COERCE REV 20. PAGE 19   DIPLOM
G0373   POLICY
                                                         B63
GOLDSEN J.M.,OUTER SPACE IN WORLD POLITICS. COM   TEC/DEV
USA+45 NAT/G FORCES ACT/RES PLAN DOMIN EDU/PROP   DIPLOM
COERCE ORD/FREE PWR...TECHNIC STAT INT SAMP TREND   SPACE
ANTHOL VAL/FREE 20. PAGE 22 G0428
                                                         B63
HAUSMAN W.H.,MANAGING ECONOMIC DEVELOPMENT IN   ECO/UNDEV
AFRICA. AFR USA+45 LAW FINAN WORKER TEC/DEV WEALTH   PLAN
...ANTHOL 20. PAGE 25 G0492   FOR/AID
                                                      MGT
                                                         B63
KAST F.E.,SCIENCE, TECHNOLOGY, AND MANAGEMENT.   MGT
SPACE USA+45 FORCES CONFER DETER NUC/PWR...PHIL/SCI   PLAN
CHARTS ANTHOL BIBLIOG 20 NASA. PAGE 30 G0581   TEC/DEV
                                                      PROB/SOLV
                                                         B63
KATZ S.M.,A SELECTED LIST OF US READINGS ON   BIBLIOG/A
DEVELOPMENT. AGRI COM/IND DIST/IND INDUS LABOR PLAN   ECO/UNDEV
FOR/AID EDU/PROP HEALTH...POLICY SOC/WK 20. PAGE 30   TEC/DEV
G0582   ACT/RES
                                                         B63
LITTERER J.A.,ORGANIZATIONS: STRUCTURE AND   ADMIN
BEHAVIOR. PLAN DOMIN CONTROL LEAD ROUTINE SANCTION   CREATE
INGP/REL EFFICIENCY PRODUC DRIVE RIGID/FLEX PWR.   MGT
PAGE 34 G0674   ADJUST
                                                         B63
MAYNE R.,THE COMMUNITY OF EUROPE. UK CONSTN NAT/G   EUR+WWI
CONSULT DELIB/GP CREATE PLAN ECO/TAC LEGIT ADMIN   INT/ORG
ROUTINE ORD/FREE PWR WEALTH...CONCPT TIME/SEQ EEC   REGION
EURATOM 20. PAGE 37 G0724
                                                         B63
MENEZES A.J.,SUBDESENVOLVIMENTO E POLITICA   ECO/UNDEV
INTERNACIONAL. BRAZIL WOR+45 PLAN CONTROL LEAD   DIPLOM
NAT/LISM ORD/FREE 20 THIRD/WRLD. PAGE 38 G0754   POLICY
                                                      BAL/PWR
                                                         B63
SCHRADER R.,SCIENCE AND POLICY. WOR+45 ECO/DEV   TEC/DEV
ECO/UNDEV R+D FORCES PLAN DIPLOM GOV/REL TECHRACY   NAT/G
BIBLIOG. PAGE 50 G0976   POLICY
                                                      ADMIN
                                                         B63
UN SECRETARY GENERAL,PLANNING FOR ECONOMIC   PLAN
DEVELOPMENT. ECO/UNDEV FINAN BUDGET INT/TRADE   ECO/TAC
TARIFFS TAX ADMIN 20 UN. PAGE 55 G1089   MGT
                                                      NAT/COMP
                                                         B63
US DEPARTMENT OF THE ARMY,SOVIET RUSSIA: STRATEGIC   BIBLIOG/A
SURVEY (PAMPHLET). USSR POL/PAR PLAN DOMIN EDU/PROP MARXISM
ARMS/CONT GUERRILLA WAR WEAPON...TREND CHARTS   DIPLOM
ORG/CHARTS 20. PAGE 57 G1129   COERCE
                                                         B63
WIGHTMAN D.,TOWARD ECONOMIC CO-OPERATION IN ASIA.   ECO/UNDEV
ASIA S/ASIA VOL/ASSN ACT/RES PLAN TEC/DEV ECO/TAC   CREATE
EDU/PROP RIGID/FLEX SKILL...POLICY METH/CNCPT OBS
INT GEN/LAWS UN 20 ECAFE. PAGE 63 G1237
                                                         L63
BRENNAN D.G.,"ARMS CONTROL AND CIVIL DEFENSE."   PLAN
USA+45 WOR+45 NAT/G BAL/PWR ROUTINE ATTIT   HEALTH
RIGID/FLEX ORD/FREE...SOC TOT/POP 20. PAGE 8 G0165   ARMS/CONT
                                                      DETER
                                                         L63
MCDOUGAL M.S.,"THE ENJOYMENT AND ACQUISITION OF   PLAN
RESOURCES IN OUTER SPACE." CHRIST-17C FUT WOR+45   TREND

WOR-45 LAW EXTR/IND INT/ORG ACT/RES CREATE TEC/DEV
ECO/TAC LEGIT COERCE HEALTH KNOWL ORD/FREE PWR
WEALTH...JURID HIST/WRIT VAL/FREE. PAGE 37 G0738
                                                         S63
BOULDING K.E.,"UNIVERSITY, SOCIETY, AND ARMS   SOCIETY
CONTROL." WOR+45 WOR+45 ACADEM NAT/G CONSULT FORCES ARMS/CONT
ACT/RES PLAN TEC/DEV BAL/PWR ECO/TAC COERCE DETER
WAR ATTIT RIGID/FLEX KNOWL ORD/FREE PWR WEALTH
...CONCPT COLD/WAR TOT/POP 20. PAGE 8 G0159
                                                         S63
BUNDY M.,"THE SCIENTIST AND NATIONAL POLICY."   NAT/G
PROF/ORG PLAN PARTIC POLICY. PAGE 10 G0186   PHIL/SCI
                                                      DECISION
                                                         S63
DE FOREST J.D.,"LOW LEVELS OF TECHNOLOGY AND   ECO/UNDEV
ECONOMIC DEVELOPMENT PROSPECTS." WOR+45 WOR-45   TEC/DEV
CULTURE ACT/RES CREATE PLAN ECO/TAC ROUTINE PERCEPT
WEALTH...METH/CNCPT GEN/LAWS 20. PAGE 15 G0284
                                                         S63
ENTHOVEN A.C.,"ECONOMIC ANALYSIS IN THE DEPARTMENT PLAN
OF DEFENSE." USA+45 NAT/G DELIB/GP PROB/SOLV RATION BUDGET
NUC/PWR WEAPON COST...DECISION 20 DEPT/DEFEN   ECO/TAC
RESOURCE/N. PAGE 18 G0349   FORCES
                                                         S63
GANDILHON J.,"LA SCIENCE ET LA TECHNIQUE A L'AIDE   ECO/UNDEV
DES REGIONS PEU DEVELOPPEES." FRANCE FUT WOR+45   TEC/DEV
ECO/DEV R+D PROF/ORG ACT/RES PLAN...MGT TOT/POP   FOR/AID
VAL/FREE 20 UN. PAGE 21 G0406
                                                         S63
HOSKINS H.L.,"ARAB SOCIALISM IN THE UAR." ISLAM   ECO/DEV
USSR AGRI INDUS NAT/G TOP/EX CREATE DIPLOM EDU/PROP PLAN
DRIVE KNOWL PWR SOCISM...POLICY CONCPT TREND SUEZ   UAR
20. PAGE 27 G0530
                                                         S63
KAWALKOWSKI A.,"POUR UNE EUROPE INDEPENDENTE ET   R+D
REUNIFIEE." EUR+WWI FUT USA+45 USSR WOR+45 ECO/DEV   PLAN
PROC/MFG INT/ORG NAT/G ACT/RES TEC/DEV FEDERAL   NUC/PWR
RIGID/FLEX...CONCPT METH/CNCPT OEEC TOT/POP 20
DEGAULLE/C. PAGE 30 G0587
                                                         S63
KOLDZIEF E.A.,"CONGRESSIONAL RESPONSIBILITY FOR THE LEGIS
COMMON DEFENSE: THE MONEY PROBLEM." PLAN DEBATE   NAT/G
EFFICIENCY ATTIT PWR DECISION. PAGE 31 G0612   FORCES
                                                      POLICY
                                                         S63
MASSART L.,"L'ORGANISATION DE LA RECHERCHE   R+D
SCIENTIFIQUE EN EUROPE." EUR+WWI WOR+45 ACT/RES   CREATE
PLAN TEC/DEV EDU/PROP EXEC KNOWL...METH/CNCPT EEC
20. PAGE 36 G0718
                                                         S63
NADLER E.B.,"SOME ECONOMIC DISADVANTAGES OF THE   ECO/DEV
ARMS RACE." USA+45 INDUS R+D FORCES PLAN TEC/DEV   MGT
ECO/TAC FOR/AID EDU/PROP PWR WEALTH...TREND   BAL/PAY
COLD/WAR 20. PAGE 41 G0800
                                                         S63
TASHJEAN J.E.,"RESEARCH ON ARMS CONTROL." COM   NAT/G
USA+45 USSR FORCES ACT/RES PLAN DOMIN COERCE   POLICY
ORD/FREE PWR...TIME/SEQ GEN/LAWS 20 COLD/WAR.   ARMS/CONT
PAGE 53 G1053
                                                         S63
VIETORISZ T.,"PRELIMINARY BIBLIOGRAPHY FOR   BIBLIOG/A
INDUSTRIAL DEVELOPMENT PROGRAMMING." ECO/DEV   TEC/DEV
ECO/UNDEV R+D LABOR PROB/SOLV AUTOMAT PRODUC.   ACT/RES
PAGE 61 G1199   PLAN
                                                         S63
WILES P.J.D.,"WILL CAPITALISM AND COMMUNISM   PLAN
SPONTANEOUSLY CONVERGE." COM FUT USA+45 ECO/DEV   TEC/DEV
DIST/IND MARKET CAP/ISM ECO/TAC RIGID/FLEX WEALTH   USSR
MARXISM SOCISM...MATH STAT TREND COMPUT/IR 20.
PAGE 63 G1240
                                                         N63
COMMITTEE ECONOMIC DEVELOPMENT,TAXES AND TRADE: 20   FINAN
YEARS OF CED POLICY (PAMPHLET). USA+45 ECO/DEV PLAN ECO/TAC
BUDGET LEAD...POLICY KENNEDY/JF PRESIDENT. PAGE 13   NAT/G
G0246   DELIB/GP
                                                         B64
RECENT PUBLICATIONS ON GOVERNMENTAL PROBLEMS. FINAN BIBLIOG
INDUS ACADEM PLAN PROB/SOLV EDU/PROP ADJUD ADMIN   AUTOMAT
BIO/SOC...MGT SOC. PAGE 1 G0017   LEGIS
                                                      JURID

BALASSA B.,TRADE PROSPECTS FOR DEVELOPING
COUNTRIES. WOR+45 ECO/DEV AGRI EXTR/IND INDUS
CREATE PLAN PRICE...ECOMETRIC CLASSIF TIME/SEQ
GEN/METH. PAGE 5 G0087
INT/TRADE
ECO/UNDEV
TREND
STAT
B64

BAUCHET P.,ECONOMIC PLANNING. FRANCE STRATA LG/CO
CAP/ISM ADMIN PARL/PROC DEMAND OPTIMAL ATTIT PWR
SOCISM...POLICY CHARTS 20. PAGE 5 G0102
ECO/DEV
NAT/G
PLAN
ECO/TAC
B64

BRIGHT J.R.,RESEARCH, DEVELOPMENT AND TECHNOLOGICAL
INNOVATION. CULTURE R+D CREATE PLAN PROB/SOLV
AUTOMAT RISK PERSON...DECISION CONCPT PREDICT
BIBLIOG. PAGE 9 G0168
TEC/DEV
NEW/IDEA
INDUS
MGT
B64

COENEN E.,LA "KONJUNKTURFORSCHUNG" EN ALLEMAGNE ET
EN AUTRICHE, 1925-1935. AUSTRIA GERMANY OP/RES PLAN
COST PERCEPT...METH/CNCPT BIBLIOG 20. PAGE 12 G0237
METH/COMP
R+D
ECO/TAC
B64

ETZIONI A.,THE MOON-DOGGLE: DOMESTIC AND
INTERNATIONAL IMPLICATIONS OF THE SPACE RACE. FUT
USA+45 WOR+45 INTELL ECO/DEV INDUS VOL/ASSN
EX/STRUC FORCES LEGIS TOP/EX PLAN TEC/DEV ECO/TAC
EDU/PROP KNOWL ORD/FREE PWR RESPECT WEALTH
TIME/SEQ. PAGE 18 G0352
R+D
NAT/G
DIPLOM
SPACE
B64

FALK L.A.,ADMINISTRATIVE ASPECTS OF GROUP PRACTICE.
USA+45 FINAN PROF/ORG PLAN MGT. PAGE 18 G0358
BIBLIOG/A
HEAL
ADMIN
SERV/IND
B64

GRAVIER J.F.,AMENAGEMENT DU TERRITOIRE ET L'AVENIR
DES REGIONS FRANCAISES. FRANCE ECO/DEV AGRI INDUS
CREATE...GEOG CHARTS 20. PAGE 22 G0442
PLAN
MUNIC
NEIGH
ADMIN
B64

INST D'ETUDE POL L'U GRENOBLE,ADMINISTRATION
TRADITIONELLE ET PLANIFICATION REGIONALE. FRANCE
LAW POL/PAR PROB/SOLV ADJUST RIGID/FLEX...CHARTS
ANTHOL BIBLIOG T 20 REFORMERS. PAGE 28 G0546
ADMIN
MUNIC
PLAN
CREATE
B64

KAUFMANN W.W.,THE MC NAMARA STRATEGY. TOP/EX
INSPECT BAL/PWR DIPLOM CONTROL DETER GUERRILLA
NUC/PWR WEAPON COST PWR...METH/COMP 20 MCNAMARA/R
KENNEDY/JF JOHNSON/LB NATO DEPT/DEFEN. PAGE 30
G0586
FORCES
WAR
PLAN
PROB/SOLV
B64

LANG A.S.,URBAN RAIL TRANSIT. OP/RES PLAN PROB/SOLV
TEC/DEV AUTOMAT COST...TECHNIC MATH CON/ANAL CHARTS
METH/COMP SIMUL 20 RAILROAD PUB/TRANS. PAGE 32
G0632
MUNIC
DIST/IND
ECOMETRIC
B64

MANSFIELD E.,MONOPOLY POWER AND ECONOMIC
PERFORMANCE: AN INTRODUCTION TO A CURRENT ISSUE OF
PUBLIC POLICY. ECO/DEV INDUS NAT/G PLAN CAP/ISM
PRICE CONTROL LOBBY EFFICIENCY PRODUC...POLICY 20
CONGRESS KENNEDY/JF MONOPOLY. PAGE 36 G0701
LG/CO
PWR
ECO/TAC
MARKET
B64

MARTINO R.L.,PROJECT MANAGEMENT AND CONTROL: VOL. 2
APPLIED OPERATIONAL PLANNING. COMPUTER...MATH
CHARTS SIMUL METH TIME. PAGE 36 G0716
DECISION
PLAN
TEC/DEV
OP/RES
B64

ORGANIZATION AMERICAN STATES,ECONOMIC SURVEY OF
LATIN AMERICA, 1962. L/A+17C AGRI DIST/IND INDUS
MARKET PROC/MFG R+D PLAN TEC/DEV ECO/TAC REGION
BAL/PAY ALL/VALS...CON/ANAL ORG/CHARTS GEN/METH OAS
20. PAGE 43 G0844
ECO/UNDEV
CHARTS
B64

ORTH C.D.,ADMINISTERING RESEARCH AND DEVELOPMENT.
FINAN PLAN PROB/SOLV ADMIN ROUTINE...METH/CNCPT
STAT CHARTS METH 20. PAGE 43 G0847
MGT
R+D
LG/CO
INDUS
B64

PARANJAPE H.K.,THE FLIGHT OF TECHNICAL PERSONNEL IN
PUBLIC UNDERTAKINGS. INDIA PAY DEMAND HAPPINESS
ORD/FREE...MGT QU 20 MIGRATION. PAGE 44 G0858
ADMIN
NAT/G
WORKER
PLAN
B64

PETERSON W.,THE POLITICS OF POPULATION. COM EUR+WWI
PLAN

FUT MOD/EUR S/ASIA USA+45 USA-45 WOR+45 LAW CULTURE
FAM SECT DOMIN EDU/PROP BIO/SOC HEALTH ORD/FREE
...GEOG STAT TIME/SEQ TREND VAL/FREE. PAGE 44 G0871
CENSUS
POLICY
B64

POWELSON J.P.,LATIN AMERICA: TODAY'S ECONOMIC AND
SOCIAL REVOLUTION. L/A+17C INTELL SOCIETY STRUCT
AGRI INDUS NAT/G DIPLOM ECO/TAC REV...POLICY 20.
PAGE 45 G0887
ECO/UNDEV
WEALTH
ADJUST
PLAN
B64

ROBERTS HL,FOREIGN AFFAIRS BIBLIOGRAPHY, 1952-1962.
ECO/DEV SECT PLAN FOR/AID INT/TRADE ARMS/CONT
NAT/LISM ATTIT...INT/LAW GOV/COMP IDEA/COMP 20.
PAGE 47 G0928
BIBLIOG/A
DIPLOM
INT/ORG
WAR
B64

SCHOECK H.,CENTRAL PLANNING AND NEOMERCANTILISM.
L/A+17C UK WOR+45 BUDGET ECO/TAC PRICE CONTROL
GOV/REL UTOPIA 20. PAGE 49 G0974
PLAN
CENTRAL
NAT/G
POLICY
B64

SCHWARTZ M.D.,CONFERENCE ON SPACE SCIENCE AND SPACE
LAW. FUT COM/IND NAT/G FORCES ACT/RES PLAN BUDGET
DIPLOM NUC/PWR WEAPON...POLICY ANTHOL 20. PAGE 50
G0983
SPACE
LAW
PEACE
TEC/DEV
B64

SHUBIK M.,GAME THEORY AND RELATED APPROACHES TO
SOCIAL BEHAVIOR: SELECTIONS. INTELL SOCIETY ACT/RES
CREATE PLAN PROB/SOLV...DECISION MATH. PAGE 50
G0994
SOC
SIMUL
GAME
PWR
B64

VAN DYKE V.,PRIDE AND POWER: THE RATIONALE OF THE
SPACE PROGRAM. FUT USA+45 INTELL R+D NAT/G POL/PAR
DELIB/GP EX/STRUC LEGIS TOP/EX ACT/RES PLAN ECO/TAC
EDU/PROP ORD/FREE PWR RESPECT SKILL...TIME/SEQ
VAL/FREE. PAGE 61 G1191
TEC/DEV
ATTIT
POLICY
B64

WILLIAMS S.P.,TOWARD A GENUINE WORLD SECURITY
SYSTEM (PAMPHLET). WOR+45 INT/ORG FORCES PLAN
NUC/PWR ORD/FREE...INT/LAW CONCPT UN PRESIDENT.
PAGE 63 G1243
BIBLIOG/A
ARMS/CONT
DIPLOM
PEACE
B64

WIRTH L.,ON CITIES AND SOCIAL LIFE: SELECTED
PAPERS. PLAN PROB/SOLV RACE/REL CONSEN ATTIT
HABITAT PERSON...POLICY SOC CONCPT ANTHOL BIBLIOG
20. PAGE 64 G1249
GEN/LAWS
SOCIETY
NEIGH
STRUCT
B64

BERKS R.N.,"THE US AND WEAPONS CONTROL." WOR+45 LAW
INT/ORG NAT/G LEGIS EXEC COERCE PEACE ATTIT
RIGID/FLEX ALL/VALS PWR...POLICY TOT/POP 20. PAGE 7
G0129
USA+45
PLAN
ARMS/CONT
L64

CARNEGIE ENDOWMENT INT. PEACE,"ECONOMIC AND SOCIAL
QUESTION (ISSUES BEFORE THE NINETEENTH GENERAL
ASSEMBLY)." WOR+45 ECO/DEV ECO/UNDEV INDUS R+D
DELIB/GP CREATE PLAN TEC/DEV ECO/TAC FOR/AID
BAL/PAY...RECORD UN 20. PAGE 11 G0209
INT/ORG
INT/TRADE
L64

GOLDBERG A.,"ATOMIC ORIGINS OF THE BRITISH NUCLEAR
DETERRENT." EUR+WWI UK NAT/G TOP/EX PLAN BAL/PWR
DOMIN DETER CHOOSE ATTIT DRIVE HEALTH ORD/FREE PWR
RESPECT...CONCPT VAL/FREE COLD/WAR 20 CMN/WLTH.
PAGE 22 G0425
CREATE
FORCES
NUC/PWR
L64

HAAS E.B.,"ECONOMICS AND DIFFERENTIAL PATTERNS OF
POLITICAL INTEGRATION: PROJECTIONS ABOUT UNITY IN
LATIN AMERICA." SOCIETY NAT/G DELIB/GP ACT/RES
CREATE PLAN ECO/TAC REGION ROUTINE ATTIT DRIVE PWR
WEALTH...CONCPT TREND CHARTS LAFTA 20. PAGE 24
G0464
L/A+17C
INT/ORG
MARKET
L64

BYRNES F.C.,"ASSIGNMENT TO AMBIGUITY: WORK
PERFORMANCE IN CROSSCULTURAL TECHNICAL ASSISTANCE."
USA+45 WOR+45 PROF/ORG CONSULT PLAN EDU/PROP ATTIT
DISPL PERCEPT PERSON ALL/VALS...POLICY INT CHARTS
NATO 20. PAGE 10 G0199
INTELL
QU
S64

CALDWELL L.K.,"BIOPOLITICS: SCIENCE, ETHICS, AND
PUBLIC POLICY." FUT USA+45 WOR+45 INTELL STRATA R+D
NAT/G CONSULT PLAN EDU/PROP ALL/VALS...RELATIV
PHIL/SCI 20. PAGE 10 G0203
TEC/DEV
POLICY
S64

FALK S.L.,"DISARMAMENT IN HISTORICAL PERSPECTIVE."
INT/ORG
S64

WOR-45 NAT/G PLAN NUC/PWR PEACE ORD/FREE PWR   COERCE
...TIME/SEQ AUD/VIS VAL/FREE LEAGUE/NAT 20. PAGE 18 ARMS/CONT
G0360

                                                      S64
FLORINSKY M.T.,"TRENDS IN THE SOVIET ECONOMY." COM   ECO/DEV
USA+45 USSR INDUS LABOR NAT/G PLAN TEC/DEV ECO/TAC   AGRI
ALL/VALS SOCISM...MGT METH/CNCPT STYLE CON/ANAL
GEN/METH WORK 20. PAGE 19 G0374

                                                      S64
GARDNER R.N.,"GATT AND THE UNITED NATIONS   INT/ORG
CONFERENCE ON TRADE AND DEVELOPMENT." USA+45 WOR+45   INT/TRADE
SOCIETY ECO/UNDEV MARKET NAT/G DELIB/GP ACT/RES
PLAN ECO/TAC TARIFFS EDU/PROP ROUTINE DRIVE
RIGID/FLEX WEALTH...DECISION MGT TREND UN TOT/POP
20 GATT. PAGE 21 G0411

                                                      S64
LERNER A.P.,"NUCLEAR SYMMETRY AS A FRAMEWORK FOR   FORCES
COEXISTENCE." COM FUT USA+45 NAT/G ACT/RES CREATE   ORD/FREE
PLAN DIPLOM EDU/PROP COERCE WAR RIGID/FLEX PWR   DETER
SKILL...CONCPT METH/CNCPT GEN/LAWS TOT/POP VAL/FREE   NUC/PWR
COLD/WAR 20. PAGE 33 G0657

                                                      S64
MAHALANOBIS P.C.,"PERSPECTIVE PLANNING IN INDIA: PLAN
STATISTICAL TOOLS." INDIA S/ASIA STRATA AGRI   STAT
DIST/IND FINAN INDUS SERV/IND NAT/G ECO/TAC
ORD/FREE WEALTH...POLICY TREND SIMUL VAL/FREE 20.
PAGE 35 G0695

                                                      S64
MARES V.E.,"EAST EUROPE'S SECOND CHANCE." COM   VOL/ASSN
EUR+WWI HUNGARY ROMANIA USSR YUGOSLAVIA ECO/UNDEV   ECO/TAC
NAT/G TOP/EX CREATE PLAN TEC/DEV REGION NAT/LISM
RIGID/FLEX PWR...CONCPT STAT COMECON 20. PAGE 36
G0705

                                                      S64
MUMFORD L.,"AUTHORITARIAN AND DEMOCRATIC   ECO/DEV
TECHNIQUES." INDUS PROC/MFG LG/CO SML/CO CREATE   TEC/DEV
PLAN KNOWL...POLICY TREND WORK 20. PAGE 40 G0794

                                                      S64
NEEDHAM T.,"SCIENCE AND SOCIETY IN EAST AND WEST."   ASIA
INTELL STRATA R+D LOC/G NAT/G PROVS CONSULT ACT/RES   STRUCT
CREATE PLAN TEC/DEV EDU/PROP ADMIN ATTIT ALL/VALS
...POLICY RELATIV MGT CONCPT NEW/IDEA TIME/SEQ WORK
WORK. PAGE 41 G0815

                                                      S64
PLATT J.R.,"RESEARCH AND DEVELOPMENT FOR SOCIAL   R+D
PROBLEMS." INTELL SOCIETY PROB/SOLV GP/REL ATTIT   ACT/RES
ALL/VALS CONT/OBS. PAGE 45 G0880   PLAN
                                                        SOC

                                                      S64
SPONSLER G.C.,"THE MILITARY ROLE IN SPACE." FUT   TEC/DEV
USA+45 SEA AIR NAT/G ACT/RES PLAN COERCE NUC/PWR   FORCES
WEAPON KNOWL ORD/FREE PWR RESPECT...TREND 20.   SPACE
PAGE 52 G1026

                                                      S64
STONE P.A.,"DECISION TECHNIQUES FOR TOWN   OP/RES
DEVELOPMENT." PLAN COST PROFIT...DECISION MGT   MUNIC
CON/ANAL CHARTS METH/COMP BIBLIOG 20. PAGE 53 G1039   ADMIN
                                                        PROB/SOLV

                                                      S64
THOMPSON V.A.,"ADMINISTRATIVE OBJECTIVES FOR   ECO/UNDEV
DEVELOPMENT ADMINISTRATION." WOR+45 CREATE PLAN   MGT
DOMIN EDU/PROP EXEC ROUTINE ATTIT ORD/FREE PWR
...POLICY GEN/LAWS VAL/FREE. PAGE 54 G1070

                                                      C64
SCHRAMM W.,"MASS MEDIA AND NATIONAL DEVELOPMENT: ECO/UNDEV
THE ROLE OF INFORMATION IN DEVELOPING COUNTRIES."   COM/IND
FINAN R+D ACT/RES PLAN TEC/DEV DIPLOM CHOOSE SUPEGO   EDU/PROP
ORD/FREE...BIBLIOG 20. PAGE 50 G0978   MAJORIT

                                                      N64
NATIONAL ACADEMY OF SCIENCES,CIVIL DEFENSE: PROJECT   NUC/PWR
HARBOR SUMMARY REPORT (PAMPHLET). USA+45 MUNIC   FORCES
NAT/G ACT/RES BUDGET EDU/PROP DETER WEAPON EATING   WAR
...GEOG 20. PAGE 41 G0808   PLAN

                                                      B65
PEACE RESEARCH ABSTRACTS. FUT WOR+45 R+D INT/ORG   BIBLIOG/A
NAT/G PLAN TEC/DEV BAL/PWR DIPLOM FOR/AID NUC/PWR   PEACE
HEALTH. PAGE 1 G0020   ARMS/CONT
                                                        WAR

                                                      B65
ALTSHULER A.,A LAND-USE PLAN FOR ST. PAUL   MUNIC
(PAMPHLET). USA+45 CREATE CAP/ISM RIGID/FLEX ROLE   PLAN

...NEW/IDEA 20 ST/PAUL. PAGE 3 G0047   ECO/DEV
                                                        GEOG

                                                      B65
ANTHONY R.N.,PLANNING AND CONTROL SYSTEMS. UNIV   CONTROL
OP/RES...DECISION MGT LING. PAGE 3 G0061   PLAN
                                                        METH
                                                        HYPO/EXP

                                                      B65
ARTHUR D LITTLE INC,SAN FRANCISCO COMMUNITY RENEWAL   HABITAT
PROGRAM. USA+45 FINAN PROVS ADMIN INCOME...CHARTS   MUNIC
20 CALIFORNIA SAN/FRAN URBAN/RNWL. PAGE 4 G0071   PLAN
                                                        PROB/SOLV

                                                      B65
ATOMIC INDUSTRIAL FORUM,SAFEGUARDS AGAINST   NUC/PWR
DIVERSION OF NUCLEAR MATERIALS FROM PEACEFUL TO   CIVMIL/REL
MILITARY PURPOSES. WOR+45 DELIB/GP FORCES PLAN   INSPECT
DIPLOM CONFER PEACE...ANTHOL 20 IAEA. PAGE 4 G0081   CONTROL

                                                      B65
BARISH N.N.,MANAGEMENT SCIENCES IN THE EMERGING   ECO/UNDEV
COUNTRIES. AFR CHINA/COM WOR+45 FINAN INDUS PLAN   OP/RES
PRODUC HABITAT...ANTHOL 20. PAGE 5 G0093   MGT
                                                        TEC/DEV

                                                      B65
BEAUFRE A.,AN INTRODUCTION TO STRATEGY, WITH   PLAN
PARTICULAR REFERENCE TO PROBLEMS OF DEFENSE,   NUC/PWR
POLITICS, ECONOMICS IN THE NUCLEAR AGE. WOR+45   WEAPON
FORCES DIPLOM DETER CIVMIL/REL GP/REL...NEW/IDEA   DECISION
IDEA/COMP 20. PAGE 6 G0111

                                                      B65
BOBROW D.B.,COMPONENTS OF DEFENSE POLICY. ASIA   DETER
EUR+WWI USA+45 WOR+45 INTELL INT/ORG NAT/G PROF/ORG   NUC/PWR
CONSULT LEGIS ACT/RES CREATE ARMS/CONT COERCE   PLAN
ORD/FREE...DECISION SIMUL. PAGE 7 G0145   FORCES

                                                      B65
CARPER E.T.,REORGANIZATION OF THE U.S. PUBLIC   HEAL
HEALTH SERVICE. FUT USA+45 INTELL R+D LOBBY GP/REL   PLAN
INGP/REL PERS/REL RIGID/FLEX ROLE HEALTH...PHIL/SCI   NAT/G
20 CONGRESS PHS. PAGE 11 G0213   OP/RES

                                                      B65
CORDIER A.W.,THE QUEST FOR PEACE. WOR+45 NAT/G PLAN   PEACE
BAL/PWR ECO/TAC ARMS/CONT NUC/PWR PWR...ANTHOL UN   DIPLOM
COLD/WAR. PAGE 13 G0256   POLICY
                                                        INT/ORG

                                                      B65
DORFMAN R.,MEASURING BENEFITS OF GOVERNMENT   PLAN
INVESTMENTS. ECO/DEV R+D ECO/TAC PROFIT UTIL...MGT   RATION
GEN/METH. PAGE 16 G0308   EFFICIENCY
                                                        OPTIMAL

                                                      B65
GRETTON P.,MARITIME STRATEGY - A STUDY OF DEFENSE   FORCES
PROBLEMS. ASIA UK USSR DIPLOM COERCE DETER NUC/PWR   PLAN
WEAPON...CONCPT NAT/COMP 20. PAGE 23 G0449   WAR
                                                        SEA

                                                      B65
HICKMAN B.G.,QUANTITATIVE PLANNING OF ECONOMIC   PROB/SOLV
POLICY. FRANCE NETHERLAND OP/RES PRICE ROUTINE UTIL   PLAN
...POLICY DECISION ECOMETRIC METH/CNCPT STAT STYLE   QUANT
CHINJAP. PAGE 26 G0511

                                                      B65
HITCH C.J.,DECISION-MAKING FOR DEFENSE. USA+45   DECISION
CREATE BUDGET COERCE WAR WEAPON EFFICIENCY...SIMUL   OP/RES
20. PAGE 26 G0515   PLAN
                                                        FORCES

                                                      B65
INTERNATIONAL CITY MGRS ASSN,COUNCIL-MANAGER   BIBLIOG/A
GOVERNMENT, 1940-64: AN ANNOTATED BIBLIOGRAPHY.   MUNIC
USA+45 ADMIN GOV/REL ROLE...MGT 20. PAGE 28 G0549   CONSULT
                                                        PLAN

                                                      B65
JASNY H.,KHRUSHCHEV'S CROP POLICY. USSR ECO/DEV   AGRI
PLAN MARXISM...STAT 20 KHRUSH/N RESOURCE/N. PAGE 29   NAT/G
G0562   POLICY
                                                        ECO/TAC

                                                      B65
KANTOROVICH L.V.,THE BEST USE OF ECONOMIC   PLAN
RESOURCES. USSR SOCIETY FINAN ACT/RES TEC/DEV   MATH
ECO/TAC PRICE CONTROL COST DEMAND EFFICIENCY   DECISION
OPTIMAL...MGT STAT. PAGE 29 G0572

                                                      B65
KASER M.,COMECON* INTEGRATION PROBLEMS OF THE   PLAN

PLANNED ECONOMIES. INT/ORG TEC/DEV INT/TRADE PRICE ECO/DEV
ADMIN ADJUST CENTRAL...STAT TIME/SEQ ORG/CHARTS COM
COMECON. PAGE 29 G0579 REGION

B65
KNORR K.,SCIENCE AND DEFENSE: SOME CRITICAL CIVMIL/REL
THOUGHTS ON MILITARY RESEARCH AND DEVELOPMENT. R+D
USA+45 ACT/RES CREATE BUDGET ECO/TAC DEMAND FORCES
DECISION. PAGE 31 G0608 PLAN

B65
LUTZ V.,FRENCH PLANNING. FRANCE TEC/DEV RIGID/FLEX PLAN
ORD/FREE 20. PAGE 34 G0680 ADMIN
FUT

B65
NATIONAL ACADEMY OF SCIENCES,BASIC RESEARCH AND LEGIS
NATIONAL GOALS. R+D ACADEM DELIB/GP PLAN EDU/PROP BUDGET
...POLICY HEAL PHIL/SCI PSY SOC ANTHOL 20 CONGRESS NAT/G
HOUSE/REP HS/SCIASTR. PAGE 41 G0809 CREATE

B65
OECD,MEDITERRANEAN REGIONAL PROJECT: TURKEY; EDU/PROP
EDUCATION AND DEVELOPMENT. FUT TURKEY SOCIETY ACADEM
STRATA FINAN NAT/G PROF/ORG PLAN PROB/SOLV ADMIN SCHOOL
COST...STAT CHARTS 20 OECD. PAGE 42 G0831 ECO/UNDEV

B65
OECD,THE MEDITERRANEAN REGIONAL PROJECT: PORTUGAL; EDU/PROP
EDUCATION AND DEVELOPMENT. PORTUGAL SOCIETY STRATA SCHOOL
FINAN PROF/ORG WORKER PLAN PROB/SOLV ADMIN...POLICY ACADEM
STAT CHARTS METH 20 OECD. PAGE 42 G0832 ECO/UNDEV

B65
OECD,THE MEDITERRANEAN REGIONAL PROJECT: ITALY; SCHOOL
EDUCATION AND DEVELOPMENT. ITALY SOCIETY STRATA EDU/PROP
FINAN NAT/G PROF/ORG WORKER PLAN PROB/SOLV ADMIN ECO/UNDEV
...STAT CHARTS METH 20 OECD. PAGE 42 G0833 ACADEM

B65
OECD,THE MEDITERRANEAN REGIONAL PROJECT: GREECE; EDU/PROP
EDUCATION AND DEVELOPMENT. FUT GREECE SOCIETY AGRI SCHOOL
FINAN NAT/G PROF/ORG WORKER PLAN PROB/SOLV ADMIN ACADEM
DEMAND ATTIT 20 OECD. PAGE 42 G0834 ECO/UNDEV

B65
OECD,THE MEDITERRANEAN REGIONAL PROJECT: SPAIN; ECO/UNDEV
EDUCATION AND DEVELOPMENT. FUT SPAIN STRATA FINAN EDU/PROP
NAT/G WORKER PLAN PROB/SOLV ADMIN COST...POLICY ACADEM
STAT CHARTS 20 OECD. PAGE 42 G0835 SCHOOL

B65
ORG FOR ECO COOP AND DEVEL,THE MEDITERRANEAN EDU/PROP
REGIONAL PROJECT: YUGOSLAVIA; EDUCATION AND ACADEM
DEVELOPMENT. YUGOSLAVIA SOCIETY FINAN PROF/ORG PLAN SCHOOL
ADMIN COST DEMAND MARXISM...STAT TREND CHARTS METH ECO/UNDEV
20 OECD. PAGE 43 G0843

B65
PHELPS E.S.,PRIVATE WANTS AND PUBLIC NEEDS - AN NAT/G
INTRODUCTION TO A CURRENT ISSUE OF PUBLIC POLICY POLICY
(REV. ED.). USA+45 PLAN CAP/ISM INGP/REL ROLE DEMAND
...DECISION TIME/SEQ 20. PAGE 44 G0873

B65
SCHEINMAN L.,ATOMIC ENERGY POLICY IN FRANCE UNDER NUC/PWR
THE FOURTH REPUBLIC. FRANCE UK USA+45 ELITES NAT/G
POL/PAR PLAN PROB/SOLV DIPLOM LEAD GOV/REL DELIB/GP
...BIBLIOG 20 DEGAULLE/C. PAGE 49 G0962 POLICY

B65
SINGER J.D.,HUMAN BEHAVIOR AND INTERNATIONAL DIPLOM
POLITICS* CONTRIBUTIONS FROM THE SOCIAL- PHIL/SCI
PSYCHOLOGICAL SCIENCES. ACT/RES PLAN EDU/PROP ADMIN QUANT
KNOWL...DECISION PSY SOC NET/THEORY HYPO/EXP SIMUL
LAB/EXP SOC/EXP GEN/METH ANTHOL BIBLIOG. PAGE 51
G1006

B65
SMITH E.A.,SOCIAL WELFARE: PRINCIPLES AND CONCEPTS. CONCPT
STRATA STRUCT CONSULT WORKER ACT/RES CREATE PLAN SOC/WK
TEC/DEV ROUTINE GP/REL UTOPIA...SOC 20. PAGE 51 RECEIVE
G1014 ORD/FREE

B65
STEINER G.A.,THE CREATIVE ORGANIZATION. ELITES CREATE
LG/CO PLAN PROB/SOLV TEC/DEV INSPECT CAP/ISM MGT
CONTROL EXEC PERSON...METH/COMP HYPO/EXP 20. ADMIN
PAGE 52 G1034 SOC

B65
THAYER F.C. JR.,AIR TRANSPORT POLICY AND NATIONAL AIR
SECURITY: A POLITICAL, ECONOMIC, AND MILITARY FORCES
ANALYSIS. DIST/IND OP/RES PLAN TEC/DEV DIPLOM DETER CIVMIL/REL
WAR COST EFFICIENCY...POLICY BIBLIOG 20 DEPT/DEFEN ORD/FREE
FAA CAB. PAGE 54 G1066

B65
UN,SPACE ACTIVITIES AND RESOURCES: REVIEW OF UNITED SPACE
NATION'S NATIONAL AND INTERNATIONAL PROGRAMS. NUC/PWR
INT/ORG LABOR PLAN TEC/DEV DIPLOM EFFICIENCY HEALTH FOR/AID
...GOV/COMP 20 UN. PAGE 55 G1086 PEACE

B65
US CONGRESS JT ATOM ENRGY COMM,PEACEFUL NUC/PWR
APPLICATIONS OF NUCLEAR EXPLOSIVES: PLOWSHARE, DELIB/GP
HEARING. USA+45 LEGIS CREATE PLAN PEACE...CHARTS TEC/DEV
EXHIBIT BIBLIOG CONGRESS PANAMA/CNL. PAGE 57 G1113 NAT/G

B65
US CONGRESS JT ATOM ENRGY COMM,PROPOSED AMENDMENT LAW
TO SECTION 271 OF THE ATOMIC ENERGY ACT OF 1954. LEGIS
USA+45 CONSTRUC PLAN INSPECT CONTROL CT/SYS 20 DELIB/GP
CONGRESS AEC. PAGE 57 G1115 NUC/PWR

B65
US SENATE,US INTERNATIONAL SPACE PROGRAMS, 1959-65: SPACE
STAFF REPORT FOR COMM ON AERONAUTICAL AND SPACE DIPLOM
SCIENCES. WOR+45 VOL/ASSN CIVMIL/REL 20 CONGRESS PLAN
NASA TREATY. PAGE 59 G1163 GOV/REL

B65
US SENATE COMM AERO SPACE SCI,INTERNATIONAL DIPLOM
COOPERATION AND ORGANIZATION FOR OUTER SPACE. FUT SPACE
USA+45 WOR+45 PROF/ORG VOL/ASSN CONSULT DELIB/GP R+D
PLAN TEC/DEV ARMS/CONT GP/REL PEACE 20 UN NASA. NAT/G
PAGE 59 G1167

B65
VEINOTT A.F. JR.,MATHEMATICAL STUDIES IN MANAGEMENT MATH
SCIENCE. UNIV INDUS COMPUTER ADMIN...DECISION MGT
NET/THEORY SIMUL 20. PAGE 61 G1193 PLAN
PRODUC

B65
VERMOT-GAUCHY M.,L'EDUCATION NATIONALE DANS LA ACADEM
FRANCE DE 1975. FRANCE FUT CULTURE ELITES R+D CREATE
SCHOOL PLAN EDU/PROP EFFICIENCY...POLICY PREDICT TREND
CHARTS INDEX 20. PAGE 61 G1195 INTELL

B65
WARNER A.W.,THE IMPACT OF SCIENCE ON TECHNOLOGY. DECISION
UNIV INTELL SOCIETY NAT/G ACT/RES PLAN PROB/SOLV TEC/DEV
BUDGET OPTIMAL GEN/METH. PAGE 62 G1214 CREATE
POLICY

S65
ABT C.C.,"CONTROLLING FUTURE ARMS." USSR PLAN PREDICT
BAL/PWR DIPLOM NUC/PWR COST...CLASSIF STAT CHARTS. FUT
PAGE 2 G0027 ARMS/CONT
TEC/DEV

S65
BALDWIN H.,"SLOW-DOWN IN THE PENTAGON." USA+45 RECORD
CREATE PLAN GOV/REL CENTRAL COST EFFICIENCY PWR R+D
...MGT MCNAMARA/R. PAGE 5 G0088 WEAPON
ADMIN

S65
DEAN B.V.,"CONTRACT RESEARCH PROPOSAL PREPARATION USA+45
STRATEGIES." ECO/TAC WEALTH...MGT SIMUL. PAGE 15 PROC/MFG
G0289 R+D
PLAN

S65
DECHERT C.R.,"THE DEVELOPMENT OF CYBERNETICS." SIMUL
ACT/RES CREATE SKILL...STERTYP METH. PAGE 15 G0290 COMPUT/IR
PLAN
DECISION

S65
GOLDSTEIN W.,"KEEPING THE GENIE IN THE BOTTLE* THE NUC/PWR
FEASIBILITY OF A NUCLEAR NON-PROLIFERATION CREATE
AGREEMENT." ASIA FRANCE UK USA+45 USSR WOR+45 COST
ECO/UNDEV VOL/ASSN ACT/RES PLAN RISK ARMS/CONT WAR
PEACE ATTIT PERCEPT...RECORD TREND TIME. PAGE 22
G0429

S65
GRENIEWSKI H.,"INTENTION AND PERFORMANCE: A PRIMER SIMUL
OF CYBERNETICS OF PLANNING." EFFICIENCY OPTIMAL GAME
KNOWL SKILL...DECISION MGT EQUILIB. PAGE 23 G0448 GEN/METH
PLAN

S65
GRIFFITH S.B.,"COMMUNIST CHINA'S CAPACITY TO MAKE FORCES
WAR." CHINA/COM COM NAT/G TOP/EX PLAN DOMIN COERCE PWR
NUC/PWR ATTIT RESPECT SKILL...CONCPT MYTH TIME/SEQ WEAPON
TREND COLD/WAR 20. PAGE 23 G0452 ASIA

S65
LECLERCQ H.,"ECONOMIC RESEARCH AND DEVELOPMENT IN AFR

TROPICAL AFRICA." ECO/UNDEV INT/ORG CREATE PLAN UN. R+D
PAGE 33 G0650   ACADEM
                                                      ECO/TAC

                                                          C65
US AIR FORCE ACADEMY,"AMERICAN DEFENSE POLICY." COM PLAN
INT/ORG TEC/DEV FOR/AID ARMS/CONT DETER NUC/PWR   FORCES
...POLICY DECISION CONCPT ANTHOL BIBLIOG/A 20   WAR
COLD/WAR NATO. PAGE 56 G1103   COERCE

                                                          B66
ALEXANDER Y.,INTERNATIONAL TECHNICAL ASSISTANCE   ECO/TAC
EXPERTS* A CASE STUDY OF THE U.N. EXPERIENCE.   INT/ORG
ECO/UNDEV CONSULT EX/STRUC CREATE PLAN DIPLOM   ADMIN
FOR/AID TASK EFFICIENCY...ORG/CHARTS UN. PAGE 2   MGT
G0038

                                                          B66
ALEXANDER Y.,INTERNATIONAL TECHNICAL ASSISTANCE   SKILL
EXPERTS: A CASE STUDY OF THE U.N. EXPERIENCE.   INT/ORG
USA+45 WOR+45 WORKER CREATE PLAN PROB/SOLV ECO/TAC TEC/DEV
FOR/AID GIVE EDU/PROP...CHARTS BIBLIOG 20 UN.   CONSULT
PAGE 2 G0039

                                                          B66
ALI S.,PLANNING, DEVELOPMENT AND CHANGE: AN   BIBLIOG/A
ANNOTATED BIBLIOGRAPHY ON DEVELOPMENTAL   ADMIN
ADMINISTRATION. PAKISTAN SOCIETY ORD/FREE 20.   ECO/UNDEV
PAGE 2 G0041   PLAN

                                                          B66
BEATON L.,MUST THE BOMB SPREAD? WOR+45 TEC/DEV   NUC/PWR
DIPLOM DRIVE ORD/FREE PWR...CHARTS 20. PAGE 6 G0109 ARMS/CONT
                                                    PLAN
                                                    PROB/SOLV

                                                          B66
BOLTON R.E.,DEFENSE AND DISARMAMENT: THE ECONOMICS ARMS/CONT
OF TRANSITION. USA+45 R+D FORCES PLAN LOBBY DETER   POLICY
WAR COST PEACE...ANTHOL BIBLIOG 20. PAGE 8 G0150   INDUS

                                                          B66
CLARK G.,WORLD PEACE THROUGH WORLD LAW; TWO   INT/LAW
ALTERNATIVE PLANS. WOR+45 DELIB/GP FORCES TAX   PEACE
CONFER ADJUD SANCTION ARMS/CONT WAR CHOOSE PRIVIL   PLAN
20 UN COLD/WAR. PAGE 12 G0231   INT/ORG

                                                          B66
DAENIKER G.,STRATEGIE DES KLEIN STAATS. SWITZERLND NUC/PWR
ACT/RES CREATE DIPLOM NEUTRAL DETER WAR WEAPON PWR PLAN
SOVEREIGN...IDEA/COMP 20 COLD/WAR. PAGE 14 G0270   FORCES
                                                    NAT/G

                                                          B66
FEIS H.,THE ATOMIC BOMB AND THE END OF WORLD WAR   USA+45
II. FORCES PLAN PROB/SOLV DIPLOM CONFER WAR   PEACE
...TIME/SEQ TREND CHINJAP PRESIDENT TIME. PAGE 19   NUC/PWR
G0362

                                                          B66
GLAZER M.,THE FEDERAL GOVERNMENT AND THE   BIBLIOG/A
UNIVERSITY. CHILE PROB/SOLV DIPLOM GIVE ADMIN WAR   NAT/G
...POLICY SOC 20. PAGE 21 G0421   PLAN
                                                    ACADEM

                                                          B66
JACOBSON H.K.,DIPLOMATS, SCIENTISTS, AND   DIPLOM
POLITICIANS* THE UNITED STATES AND THE NUCLEAR TEST ARMS/CONT
BAN NEGOTIATIONS. USA+45 USSR ACT/RES PLAN CONFER   TECHRACY
DETER NUC/PWR CONSEN ORD/FREE...INT TREATY. PAGE 28 INT/ORG
G0554

                                                          B66
KURAKOV I.G.,SCIENCE, TECHNOLOGY AND COMMUNISM;   CREATE
SOME QUESTIONS OF DEVELOPMENT (TRANS. BY CARIN   TEC/DEV
DEDIJER). USSR INDUS PLAN PROB/SOLV COST PRODUC   MARXISM
...MGT MATH CHARTS METH 20. PAGE 32 G0626   ECO/TAC

                                                          B66
LECHT L.,GOAL, PRIORITIES, AND DOLLARS: THE NEXT   IDEA/COMP
DECADE. SPACE USA+45 SOCIETY AGRI BUDGET FOR/AID   POLICY
...HEAL SOC/WK STAT CHARTS 20 URBAN/RNWL PUB/TRANS. CONSEN
PAGE 33 G0649   PLAN

                                                          B66
LEWIS W.A.,DEVELOPMENT PLANNING; THE ESSENTIALS OF PLAN
ECONOMIC POLICY. USA+45 FINAN INDUS NAT/G WORKER   ECO/DEV
FOR/AID INT/TRADE ADMIN ROUTINE WEALTH...CONCPT   POLICY
STAT. PAGE 34 G0663   CREATE

                                                          B66
LINDFORS G.V.,INTERCOLLEGIATE BIBLIOGRAPHY; CASES   BIBLIOG/A
IN BUSINESS ADMINISTRATION (VOL. X). FINAN MARKET   ADMIN
LABOR CONSULT PLAN GP/REL PRODUC 20. PAGE 34 G0668 MGT
                                                    OP/RES

                                                          B66
OECD DEVELOPMENT CENTRE,CATALOGUE OF SOCIAL AND   ECO/UNDEV
ECONOMIC DEVELOPMENT INSTITUTES AND PROGRAMMES*   ECO/DEV
RESEARCH. ACT/RES PLAN TEC/DEV EDU/PROP...SOC   R+D
GP/COMP NAT/COMP. PAGE 43 G0836   ACADEM

                                                          B66
ONYEMELUKWE C.C.,PROBLEMS OF INDUSTRIAL PLANNING   ECO/UNDEV
AND MANAGEMENT IN NIGERIA. AFR FINAN LABOR DELIB/GP ECO/TAC
TEC/DEV ADJUST...MGT TREND BIBLIOG. PAGE 43 G0839   INDUS
                                                    PLAN

                                                          B66
PRINCETON U INDUSTRIAL REL SEC,THE FEDERAL   BIBLIOG/A
GOVERNMENT AND THE UNIVERSITY: SUPPORT FOR SOCIAL   NAT/G
SCIENCE RESEARCH AND THE IMPACT OF PROJECT CAMELOT. ACADEM
USA+45 ACT/RES CONTROL GP/REL PWR...POLICY 20.   PLAN
PAGE 45 G0889

                                                          B66
RUPPENTHAL K.M.,TRANSPORTATION AND TOMORROW. FUT   DIST/IND
SPACE USA+45 SEA AIR FORCES TEC/DEV INT/TRADE   PLAN
...ANTHOL 20 RAILROAD. PAGE 48 G0946   CIVMIL/REL
                                                    PREDICT

                                                          B66
SPULBER N.,THE STATE AND ECONOMIC DEVELOPMENT IN   ECO/DEV
EASTERN EUROPE. BULGARIA COM CZECHOSLVK HUNGARY   ECO/UNDEV
POLAND YUGOSLAVIA CULTURE PLAN CAP/ISM INT/TRADE   NAT/G
CONTROL...POLICY CHARTS METH/COMP BIBLIOG/A 19/20. TOTALISM
PAGE 52 G1028

                                                          B66
STREET D.,ORGANIZATION FOR TREATMENT. CLIENT PROVS GP/COMP
PUB/INST PLAN CONTROL PARTIC REPRESENT ATTIT PWR   AGE/Y
...POLICY BIBLIOG. PAGE 53 G1044   ADMIN
                                                    VOL/ASSN

                                                          B66
US DEPARTMENT OF LABOR,PRODUCTIVITY: A   BIBLIOG/A
BIBLIOGRAPHY. ECO/DEV INDUS MARKET OP/RES AUTOMAT   PRODUC
COST...STAT 20. PAGE 57 G1119   LABOR
                                                    PLAN

                                                          B66
US SENATE,POLICY PLANNING FOR AERONAUTICAL RESEARCH SPACE
AND DEVELOPMENT: STAFF REPORT FOR COMM ON   CIVMIL/REL
AERONAUTICAL AND SPACE SCIENCES. USA+45 AIR   GOV/REL
DIST/IND PLAN...POLICY CHARTS 20 CONGRESS NASA.   R+D
PAGE 59 G1164

                                                          B66
US SENATE COMM AERO SPACE SCI,SOVIET SPACE   CONSULT
PROGRAMS, 1962-65; GOALS AND PURPOSES,   SPACE
ACHIEVEMENTS, PLANS, AND INTERNATIONAL   FUT
IMPLICATIONS. USA+45 USSR R+D FORCES PLAN EDU/PROP DIPLOM
PRESS ADJUD ARMS/CONT ATTIT MARXISM. PAGE 60 G1168

                                                          L66
RASER J.R.,"DETERRENCE RESEARCH* PAST PROGRESS AND DETER
FUTURE NEEDS." INTELL PLAN TEC/DEV NUC/PWR PERCEPT BIBLIOG/A
...DECISION PSY SOC NET/THEORY. PAGE 46 G0905   FUT

                                                          S66
"FURTHER READING." INDIA LOC/G NAT/G PLAN ADMIN   BIBLIOG
WEALTH...GEOG SOC CONCPT CENSUS 20. PAGE 1 G0021   ECO/UNDEV
                                                    TEC/DEV
                                                    PROVS

                                                          S66
HANSON A.H.,"PLANNING AND THE POLITICIANS* SOME   PLAN
REFLECTIONS ON ECONOMIC PLANNING IN WESTERN   ECO/DEV
EUROPE." MARKET NAT/G TEC/DEV CONSEN ROLE   EUR+WWI
...METH/COMP NAT/COMP. PAGE 24 G0479   ADMIN

                                                          S66
MALENBAUM W.,"GOVERNMENT, ENTREPRENEURSHIP, AND   ECO/TAC
ECONOMIC GROWTH IN POOR LANDS." ELITES ECO/UNDEV   PLAN
INDUS CREATE DRIVE. PAGE 35 G0697   CONSERVE
                                                    NAT/G

                                                          S66
RIZOS E.J.,"SCIENCE AND TECHNOLOGY IN COUNTRY   ADMIN
DEVELOPMENT* TOWARDS AN UNDERSTANDING OF THE ROLE   TEC/DEV
OF PUBLIC ADMINISTRATION." WOR+45 STRUCT INT/ORG   ECO/UNDEV
EX/STRUC CREATE PLAN PROB/SOLV EFFICIENCY ROLE   PHIL/SCI
DECISION. PAGE 47 G0924

                                                          N66
US HOUSE COMM SCI ASTRONAUT,INQUIRIES, LEGISLATION, TEC/DEV
POLICY STUDIES RE: SCIENCE AND TECHNOLOGY: REVIEW   R+D
AND FORECAST (PAMPHLET). FUT WOR+45 DELIB/GP   PLAN
PROB/SOLV...POLICY JURID TREND 20 CONGRESS. PAGE 58 LEGIS
G1144

US HOUSE COMM SCI ASTRONAUT,THE ADEQUACY OF
TECHNOLOGY FOR POLLUTION ABATEMENT (PAMPHLET).
WOR+45 PLAN PROB/SOLV CONFER ADMIN...JURID 20
POLLUTION. PAGE 58 G1145

HEALTH
POLICY
TEC/DEV
LEGIS

N66

ARON R.,THE GREAT DEBATE: THEORIES OF NUCLEAR
STRATEGY. FRANCE USA+45 INT/ORG PLAN TREND. PAGE 4
G0068

NUC/PWR
DETER
BAL/PWR
DIPLOM

B67

BAUMOL W.J.,BUSINESS BEHAVIOR, VALUE AND GROWTH
(REV. ED.). WOR+45 FINAN LG/CO TEC/DEV CAP/ISM
DEMAND EQUILIB...METH/COMP SIMUL 20. PAGE 5 G0105

ALL/IDEOS
PHIL/SCI
PLAN
ECO/DEV

B67

BUDER S.,PULLMAN: AN EXPERIMENT IN INDUSTRIAL ORDER
AND COMMUNITY PLANNING, 1880-1930. USA-45 SOCIETY
LABOR LG/CO CREATE PROB/SOLV CONTROL GP/REL
EFFICIENCY ATTIT...MGT BIBLIOG 19/20 PULLMAN.
PAGE 9 G0184

DIST/IND
INDUS
MUNIC
PLAN

B67

BURNS E.L.M.,MEGAMURDER. WOR+45 LAW INT/ORG NAT/G
BAL/PWR DIPLOM DETER MURDER WEAPON CIVMIL/REL PEACE
...INT/LAW TREND 20. PAGE 10 G0193

FORCES
PLAN
WAR
NUC/PWR

B67

COMMONER B.,SCIENCE AND SURVIVAL. SOCIETY INDUS
PLAN NUC/PWR KNOWL PWR...SOC 20 AEC. PAGE 13 G0247

PHIL/SCI
CONTROL
PROB/SOLV
EQUILIB

B67

ELDREDGE H.W.,TAMING MEGALOPOLIS: HOW TO MANAGE AN
URBANIZED WORLD. WOR+45 SOCIETY ECO/DEV ECO/UNDEV
NAT/G COMPUTER CREATE PARTIC EFFICIENCY WEALTH
...MGT ANTHOL. PAGE 17 G0342

MUNIC
TEC/DEV
PLAN
PROB/SOLV

B67

ENKE S.,DEFENSE MANAGEMENT. USA+45 R+D FORCES
WORKER PLAN ECO/TAC ADMIN NUC/PWR BAL/PAY UTIL
WEALTH...MGT DEPT/DEFEN. PAGE 18 G0348

DECISION
DELIB/GP
EFFICIENCY
BUDGET

B67

GARCIA ROBLES A.,THE DENUCLEARIZATION OF LATIN
AMERICA (TRANS. BY MARJORIE URQUIDI). LAW PLAN
DIPLOM...ANTHOL 20 TREATY UN. PAGE 21 G0409

NUC/PWR
ARMS/CONT
L/A+17C
INT/ORG

B67

GROSSMAN G.,ECONOMIC SYSTEMS. USA+45 USA-45 USSR
YUGOSLAVIA WORKER CAP/ISM PRICE GP/REL EQUILIB
WEALTH MARXISM SOCISM...MGT METH/COMP 19/20.
PAGE 23 G0456

ECO/DEV
PLAN
TEC/DEV
DEMAND

B67

HARDT J.P.,MATHEMATICS AND COMPUTERS IN SOVIET
ECONOMIC PLANNING. COM USSR OP/RES PROB/SOLV
OPTIMAL...MODAL SIMUL 20. PAGE 24 G0481

PLAN
TEC/DEV
MATH
COMPUT/IR

B67

HIRSCHMAN A.O.,DEVELOPMENT PROJECTS OBSERVED. INDUS
INT/ORG CONSULT EX/STRUC CREATE OP/RES ECO/TAC
DEMAND...POLICY MGT METH/COMP 20 WORLD/BANK.
PAGE 26 G0513

ECO/UNDEV
R+D
FINAN
PLAN

B67

KINTNER W.R.,PEACE AND THE STRATEGY CONFLICT. PLAN
BAL/PWR DIPLOM CONTROL ARMS/CONT DETER WEAPON 20.
PAGE 30 G0599

ROLE
PEACE
NUC/PWR
ORD/FREE

B67

MACBRIDE R.,THE AUTOMATED STATE: COMPUTER SYSTEMS
AS A NEW FORCE IN SOCIETY. FUT WOR+45 FINAN MUNIC
NAT/G WORKER PLAN TEC/DEV CONTROL PERS/REL RACE/REL
ADJUST. PAGE 35 G0685

COMPUTER
AUTOMAT
PROB/SOLV
SOCIETY

B67

MAZOUR A.G.,SOVIET ECONOMIC DEVELOPMENT: OPERATION
OUTSTRIP: 1921-1965. USSR ECO/UNDEV FINAN CHIEF
WORKER PROB/SOLV CONTROL PRODUC MARXISM...CHARTS
ORG/CHARTS 20 STALIN/J. PAGE 37 G0726

ECO/TAC
AGRI
INDUS
PLAN

B67

MOORE J.R.,THE ECONOMIC IMPACT OF THE TVA. AGRI
INDUS PLAN BARGAIN CONTROL REGION GOV/REL DEMAND
EFFICIENCY SOCISM 20 TVA. PAGE 40 G0780

ECO/UNDEV
ECO/DEV
NAT/G
CREATE

B67

NELSON R.R.,TECHNOLOGY, ECONOMIC GROWTH, AND PUBLIC
POLICY. USA+45 PLAN GP/REL UTIL KNOWL...POLICY
PHIL/SCI CHARTS BIBLIOG 20. PAGE 41 G0817

R+D
CONSULT
CREATE
ACT/RES

B67

ORLANS H.,CONTRACTING FOR ATOMS. USA+45 LAW INTELL
ACADEM LG/CO NAT/G PLAN TEC/DEV CONTROL DETER
...TREND 20 AEC. PAGE 43 G0845

NUC/PWR
R+D
PRODUC
PEACE

B67

PORWIT K.,CENTRAL PLANNING: EVALUATION OF VARIANTS.
PRICE OPTIMAL PRODUC...DECISION MATH CHARTS SIMUL
BIBLIOG 20. PAGE 45 G0886

PLAN
MGT
ECOMETRIC

B67

ROTHENBERG J.,ECONOMIC EVALUATION OF URBAN RENEWAL:
CONCEPTUAL FOUNDATION OF BENEFIT-COST ANALYSIS.
USA+45 ECO/DEV NEIGH TEC/DEV ADMIN GEN/LAWS.
PAGE 48 G0940

PLAN
MUNIC
PROB/SOLV
COST

B67

SCHUMACHER B.G.,COMPUTER DYNAMICS IN PUBLIC
ADMINISTRATION. USA+45 CREATE PLAN TEC/DEV...MGT
LING CON/ANAL BIBLIOG/A 20. PAGE 50 G0980

COMPUTER
COMPUT/IR
ADMIN
AUTOMAT

B67

UNIVERSAL REFERENCE SYSTEM,CURRENT EVENTS AND
PROBLEMS OF MODERN SOCIETY (VOLUME V). WOR+45 LOC/G
MUNIC NAT/G PLAN EDU/PROP CRIME RACE/REL WEALTH
...COMPUT/IR GEN/METH. PAGE 56 G1097

BIBLIOG/A
SOCIETY
PROB/SOLV
ATTIT

B67

US DEPARTMENT OF THE ARMY,CIVILIAN IN PEACE,
SOLDIER IN WAR: A BIBLIOGRAPHIC SURVEY OF THE ARMY
AND AIR NATIONAL GUARD (PAMPHLET, NOS. 130-2).
USA+45 USA-45 LOC/G NAT/G PROVS LEGIS PLAN ADMIN
ATTIT ORD/FREE...POLICY 19/20. PAGE 58 G1134

BIBLIOG/A
FORCES
ROLE
DIPLOM

B67

US HOUSE COMM SCI ASTRONAUT,GOVERNMENT, SCIENCE,
AND INTERNATIONAL POLICY. R+D OP/RES PLAN 20.
PAGE 58 G1146

ADMIN
PHIL/SCI
ACT/RES
DIPLOM

B67

WEINBERG A.M.,REFLECTIONS ON BIG SCIENCE. FUT
USA+45 NAT/G EDU/PROP CHOOSE PERS/REL COST OPTIMAL
...PHIL/SCI TREND. PAGE 62 G1225

ACADEM
KNOWL
R+D
PLAN

B67

WOODRUFF W.,IMPACT OF WESTERN MAN. ECO/DEV INDUS
CREATE PLAN PROB/SOLV COLONIAL GOV/REL...CHARTS
GOV/COMP BIBLIOG 18/20. PAGE 64 G1256

EUR+WWI
MOD/EUR
CAP/ISM

B67

WYLIE J.C.,MILITARY STRATEGY: GENERAL THEORY OF
POWER CONTROL. CUBA USA+45 VIETNAM/N WOR+45 ELITES
CONTROL WAR PWR...POLICY METH/COMP 20 MAO. PAGE 64
G1260

FORCES
PLAN
DECISION
IDEA/COMP

B67

YAVITZ B.,AUTOMATION IN COMMERCIAL BANKING. USA+45
STRUCT WORKER CREATE OP/RES PLAN ROLE...DECISION
SAMP/SIZ. PAGE 64 G1263

TEC/DEV
FINAN
COMPUT/IR
MGT

B67

"POLITICAL PARTIES ON FOREIGN POLICY IN THE INTER-
ELECTION YEARS 1962-66." ASIA COM INDIA USA+45 PLAN
ATTIT...DECISION 20. PAGE 1 G0023

POL/PAR
DIPLOM
POLICY

L67

CARMICHAEL D.M.,"FORTY YEARS OF WATER POLLUTION
CONTROL IN WISCONSIN: A CASE STUDY." LAW EXTR/IND
INDUS MUNIC DELIB/GP PLAN PROB/SOLV SANCTION
...CENSUS CHARTS 20 WISCONSIN. PAGE 11 G0207

HEALTH
CONTROL
ADMIN
ADJUD

L67

DAVIS P.C.,"THE COMING CHINESE COMMUNIST NUCLEAR
THREAT AND U.S. SEA BASED ABM OPTIONS." ASIA
CHINA/COM FUT USA+45 SEA NAT/G FORCES PLAN TEC/DEV
LEAD ARMS/CONT...GEOG METH/COMP 20 ABM/DEFSYS.
PAGE 14 G0279

NUC/PWR
DETER
WEAPON
DIPLOM

L67

RUTH J.M.,"THE ADMINISTRATION OF WATER RESOURCES IN
GUATEMALA." GUATEMALA L/A+17C DIST/IND LOC/G NAT/G
EX/STRUC ADMIN GOV/REL DEMAND EQUILIB WEALTH...GEOG
MGT 20. PAGE 48 G0952

EFFICIENCY
ECO/UNDEV
PLAN
ACT/RES

L67

L67

TRAVERS H. JR.,"AN EXAMINATION OF THE CAB'S MERGER   ADJUD
POLICY." USA+45 USA-45 LAW NAT/G LEGIS PLAN ADMIN   LG/CO
...DECISION 20 CONGRESS. PAGE 55 G1078   POLICY
                                                      DIST/IND

S67

ALLEE D.,"AMERICAN AGRICULTURE - ITS RESOURCE   AGRI
ISSUES FOR THE COMING YEARS." FUT USA+45 PLAN   SOCIETY
PROB/SOLV 20. PAGE 2 G0043   EFFICIENCY
                                                      AUTOMAT

S67

ATKIN J.M.,"THE FEDERAL GOVERNMENT, BIG BUSINESS,   SCHOOL
AND COLLEGES OF EDUCATION." PROF/ORG CONSULT CREATE   ACADEM
PLAN PROB/SOLV ADMIN EFFICIENCY. PAGE 4 G0075   NAT/G
                                                      INDUS

S67

AVTORKHANOV A.,"A NEW AGRARIAN REVOLUTION." COM   AGRI
USSR ECO/DEV PLAN TEC/DEV ADMIN CONTROL OPTIMAL   METH/COMP
WEALTH SOCISM 20 KHRUSH/N STALIN/J. PAGE 4 G0082   MARXISM
                                                      OWN

S67

BARAN P.,"THE FUTURE COMPUTER UTILITY." USA+45   COMPUTER
NAT/G PLAN CONTROL COST...POLICY 20. PAGE 5 G0091   UTIL
                                                      FUT
                                                      TEC/DEV

S67

BENN W.,"TECHNOLOGY HAS AN INEXORABLE EFFECT." FUT   R+D
UK ECO/DEV INT/ORG CONSULT PLAN EDU/PROP ADMIN LEAD   LG/CO
GP/REL PRODUC...INT 20 EEC. PAGE 6 G0119   TEC/DEV
                                                      INDUS

S67

BRETNOR R.,"DESTRUCTIVE FORCE AND THE MILITARY   FORCES
EQUATIONS." UNIV COMPUTER PLAN PROB/SOLV AUTOMAT   TEC/DEV
CONTROL COERCE DETER NUC/PWR WEAPON DRIVE PWR.   DOMIN
PAGE 9 G0166   WAR

S67

BROWN N.,"BRITISH ARMS AND THE SWITCH TOWARD   FORCES
EUROPE." EUR+WWI UK ARMS/CONT. PAGE 9 G0178   PLAN
                                                      DIPLOM
                                                      INT/ORG

S67

CARROLL K.J.,"SECOND STEP TOWARD ARMS CONTROL."   ARMS/CONT
WOR+45 INT/ORG VOL/ASSN FORCES PROB/SOLV RISK   DIPLOM
WEAPON 20 COLD/WAR. PAGE 11 G0215   PLAN
                                                      NUC/PWR

S67

CETRON M.J.,"FORECASTING TECHNOLOGY." INDUS FORCES   TEC/DEV
TASK UTIL...PHIL/SCI CONCPT CHARTS METH/COMP TIME.   FUT
PAGE 11 G0219   R+D
                                                      PLAN

S67

CHRIST R.F.,"REORGANIZATION OF FRENCH ARMED   CHIEF
FORCES." FRANCE CREATE PLAN TEC/DEV BAL/PWR DOMIN   DETER
COERCE CENTRAL EFFICIENCY 20. PAGE 12 G0229   NUC/PWR
                                                      FORCES

S67

CLEMENS W.C.,"CHINESE NUCLEAR TESTS: TRENDS AND   NUC/PWR
PORTENTS." CHINA/COM USA+45 USSR FORCES PLAN   WEAPON
TEC/DEV ARMS/CONT WAR PWR...DECISION 20 MAO   POLICY
KHRUSH/N. PAGE 12 G0234   DIPLOM

S67

CONWAY J.E.,"MAKING RESEARCH EFFECTIVE IN   ACT/RES
LEGISLATION." LAW R+D CONSULT EX/STRUC PLAN CONFER   POLICY
ADMIN LEAD ROUTINE TASK INGP/REL DECISION. PAGE 13   LEGIS
G0252   PROB/SOLV

S67

CRANBERG L.,"SCIENCE, ETHICS, AND LAW." UNIV CREATE   LAW
PLAN EDU/PROP INGP/REL PERS/REL ADJUST RATIONAL   PHIL/SCI
KNOWL MORAL...CONCPT IDEA/COMP 20. PAGE 13 G0260   INTELL

S67

DADDARIO E.Q.,"CONGRESS FACES SPACE POLICIES." R+D   SPACE
NAT/G FORCES CREATE LEAD...DECISION CONGRESS NASA.   PLAN
PAGE 14 G0269   BUDGET
                                                      POLICY

S67

DE NEUFVILLE R.,"EDUCATION AT THE ACADEMIES."   FORCES
USA+45 ELITES CONSULT EX/STRUC COMPUTER PLAN   ACADEM
PROB/SOLV TASK CIVMIL/REL ORD/FREE 20. PAGE 15   TEC/DEV
G0286   SKILL

S67

DEUTSCH K.W.,"ARMS CONTROL AND EUROPEAN UNITY* THE   ARMS/CONT
NEXT TEN YEARS." USA+45 ELITES NAT/G BAL/PWR DIPLOM   PEACE
NUC/PWR...INT KNO/TEST NATO EEC. PAGE 15 G0300   REGION
                                                      PLAN

S67

DONAHO J.A.,"PLANNING-PROGRAMMING-BUDGETING   PLAN
SYSTEMS." USA+45 LOC/G NAT/G ROUTINE. PAGE 16 G0305   BUDGET
                                                      ADMIN
                                                      ECOMETRIC

S67

FADDEYEV N.,"CMEA CO-OPERATION OF EQUAL NATIONS."   MARXISM
COM R+D PLAN CAP/ISM DIPLOM FOR/AID WEALTH...POLICY   ECO/TAC
MARXIST. PAGE 18 G0356   INT/ORG
                                                      ECO/UNDEV

S67

FRIED M.,"FUNCTIONS OF THE WORKING CLASS COMMUNITY   CLASSIF
IN MODERN URBAN SOCIETY* IMPLICATIONS FOR FORCED   WORKER
RELOCATION." USA+45 INDUS R+D NEIGH PLAN TEC/DEV   MUNIC
PARTIC GP/REL ATTIT...SOC STAT CHARTS. PAGE 20   ADJUST
G0393

S67

GOBER J.L.,"FEDERALISM AT WORK." USA+45 NAT/G   MUNIC
CONSULT ACT/RES PLAN CONFER ADMIN LEAD PARTIC   TEC/DEV
FEDERAL ATTIT. PAGE 21 G0422   R+D
                                                      GOV/REL

S67

HARRIS F.R.,"POLITICAL SCIENCE AND THE PROPOSAL FOR   PROF/ORG
A NATIONAL SOCIAL SCIENCE FOUNDATION." FUT CONSULT   R+D
DELIB/GP PLAN PROB/SOLV BUDGET CONFER SANCTION   CREATE
CRIME...POLICY SOC/WK 20 NSF NSSF. PAGE 25 G0484   NAT/G

S67

HAZARD J.N.,"POST-DISARMAMENT INTERNATIONAL LAW."   INT/LAW
FUT USSR WOR+45 INT/ORG DELIB/GP FORCES DETER   ARMS/CONT
EQUILIB SOVEREIGN MARXISM 20 UN. PAGE 25 G0496   PWR
                                                      PLAN

S67

HILL R.,"SOCIAL ASPECTS OF FAMILY PLANNING." INDIA   FAM
KOREA TAIWAN ECO/UNDEV PLAN PROB/SOLV TEC/DEV   BIO/SOC
EDU/PROP CONTROL ATTIT DRIVE...HEAL PSY SOC 20   GEOG
BIRTH/CON UN. PAGE 26 G0512   MARRIAGE

S67

HULL E.W.S.,"THE POLITICAL OCEAN." FUT UNIV WOR+45   DIPLOM
EXTR/IND R+D VOL/ASSN PLAN BAL/PWR ECO/TAC PEACE   ECO/UNDEV
WEALTH 20 UN. PAGE 27 G0536   INT/ORG
                                                      INT/LAW

S67

JOHNSTON D.M.,"LAW, TECHNOLOGY AND THE SEA." WOR+45   INT/LAW
PLAN PROB/SOLV TEC/DEV CONFER ADJUD ORD/FREE   INT/ORG
...POLICY JURID. PAGE 29 G0564   DIPLOM
                                                      NEUTRAL

S67

JONES G.S.,"STRATEGIC PLANNING." USA+45 EX/STRUC   PLAN
FORCES DETER WAR 20 PRESIDENT. PAGE 29 G0566   DECISION
                                                      DELIB/GP
                                                      POLICY

S67

KAYSEN C.,"DATA BANKS AND DOSSIERS." FUT USA+45   CENTRAL
COM/IND NAT/G PLAN PROB/SOLV TEC/DEV BUDGET ADMIN   EFFICIENCY
ROUTINE. PAGE 30 G0588   CENSUS
                                                      ACT/RES

S67

KRAUS J.,"A MARXIST IN GHANA." GHANA ELITES CHIEF   MARXISM
PROB/SOLV TEC/DEV DIPLOM ECO/TAC COLONIAL PARTIC   PLAN
PWR 20 NKRUMAH/K. PAGE 31 G0618   ATTIT
                                                      CREATE

S67

LEWIS R.L.,"GOAL AND NO GOAL* A NEW POLICY IN   SPACE
SPACE." R+D BUDGET COST...POLICY DECISION PHIL/SCI.   PLAN
PAGE 34 G0662   EFFICIENCY
                                                      CREATE

S67

MACDONALD G.J.F.,"SCIENCE AND SPACE POLICY* HOW   SPACE
DOES IT GET PLANNED?" R+D CREATE TEC/DEV BUDGET   PLAN
ADMIN ROUTINE...DECISION NASA. PAGE 35 G0687   MGT
                                                      EX/STRUC

S67

MALONE D.K.,"THE COMMANDER AND THE COMPUTER."   COMPUTER
USA+45 OP/RES PROB/SOLV TEC/DEV AUTOMAT CENTRAL 20.   FORCES
PAGE 35 G0698   ELITES
                                                      PLAN

S67

MARTIN L.W.,"BALLISTIC MISSILE DEFENSE AND EUROPE." ATTIT
EUR+WWI USA+45 FORCES PLAN BAL/PWR DEBATE PEACE   ARMS/CONT
...POLICY COLD/WAR NATO. PAGE 36 G0715   NUC/PWR
                                                          DETER

S67

MCNAMARA R.L.,"THE NEED FOR INNOVATIVENESS IN   PROB/SOLV
DEVELOPING SOCIETIES." L/A+17C EDU/PROP ADMIN LEAD   PLAN
WEALTH...POLICY PSY SOC METH 20 COLOMB. PAGE 38   ECO/UNDEV
G0747   NEW/IDEA

S67

MOOR E.J.,"THE INTERNATIONAL IMPACT OF AUTOMATION."   TEC/DEV
WOR+45 ACT/RES COMPUTER CREATE PLAN CAP/ISM ROUTINE   OP/RES
EFFICIENCY PREDICT. PAGE 39 G0779   AUTOMAT
                                                        INDUS

S67

MYERS S.,"TECHNOLOGY AND URBAN TRANSIT: THE   R+D
ENORMOUS POTENTIAL OF BUS AND RAIL SYSTEMS." USA+45   TEC/DEV
FINAN LOC/G MUNIC WORKER PLAN PROB/SOLV PRICE   DIST/IND
AUTOMAT 20. PAGE 40 G0798   ACT/RES

S67

RICHMAN B.M.,"SOVIET MANAGEMENT IN TRANSITION."   MGT
USSR FINAN MARKET EX/STRUC PLAN PROB/SOLV TEC/DEV   MARXISM
CONTROL LEAD CENTRAL EFFICIENCY...METH/COMP 20   POLICY
REFORMERS. PAGE 47 G0917   AUTHORIT

S67

ROBERTS E.B.,"THE PROBLEM OF AGING ORGANIZATIONS."   INDUS
INTELL PROB/SOLV ADMIN EXEC FEEDBACK EFFICIENCY   R+D
PRODUC...GEN/LAWS 20. PAGE 47 G0926   MGT
                                                      PLAN

S67

ROBINSON J.A.T.,"ABORTION* THE CASE FOR A FREE   PLAN
DECISION." LAW PROB/SOLV SANCTION ATTIT MORAL...PSY   ILLEGIT
IDEA/COMP 20 ABORTION. PAGE 47 G0930   SEX
                                                      HEALTH

S67

SCHACTER O.,"SCIENTIFIC ADVANCES AND INTERNATIONAL   TEC/DEV
LAWMAKING." FUT R+D PLAN PROB/SOLV CONFER CONTROL   INT/LAW
...POLICY PREDICT 20 UN. PAGE 49 G0961   INT/ORG
                                                      ACT/RES

S67

SINGH B.,"ITALIAN EXPERIENCE IN REGIONAL ECONOMIC   ECO/UNDEV
DEVELOPMENT AND LESSONS FOR OTHER COUNTRIES."   PLAN
EUR+WWI ITALY INDUS NAT/G ACT/RES REGION GP/REL   ECO/TAC
EFFICIENCY EQUILIB PRODUC WEALTH. PAGE 51 G1007   CONTROL

S67

SLOAN P.,"FIFTY YEARS OF SOVIET RULE." USSR INDUS   CREATE
EDU/PROP EFFICIENCY PRODUC HEALTH KNOWL MORAL   NAT/G
WEALTH MARXISM...POLICY 20. PAGE 51 G1011   PLAN
                                                      INSPECT

S67

STYCOS J.M.,"POLITICS AND POPULATION CONTROL IN   PLAN
LATIN AMERICA." USA+45 FAM NAT/G GP/REL AGE/C ATTIT   CENSUS
CATHISM MARXISM...POLICY UN WHO. PAGE 53 G1045   CONTROL
                                                      L/A+17C

S67

TEKINER S.,"SINKIAN AND THE SINO-SOVIET CONFLICT."   DIPLOM
ASIA COM USSR FORCES PLAN BAL/PWR CONTROL NUC/PWR   PWR
WAR WEAPON...DECISION 20. PAGE 54 G1060   MARXISM

S67

TIVEY L.,"THE POLITICAL CONSEQUENCES OF ECONOMIC   PLAN
PLANNING." UK CONSTN INDUS ACT/RES ADMIN CONTROL   POLICY
LOBBY REPRESENT EFFICIENCY SUPEGO SOVEREIGN   NAT/G
...DECISION 20. PAGE 55 G1074

S67

WALTERS R.E.,"THE ROLE OF NUCLEAR WEAPONS FOR THE   PLAN
WEST." ASIA UK USA+45 USSR DIPLOM COERCE WAR PEACE   NUC/PWR
...POLICY DECISION 20. PAGE 62 G1209   WEAPON
                                                      FORCES

S67

WASHBURN A.M.,"NUCLEAR PROLIFERATION IN A   ARMS/CONT
REVOLUTIONARY INTERNATIONAL SYSTEM." WOR+45 NAT/G   NUC/PWR
DELIB/GP PLAN TEC/DEV...POLICY 20. PAGE 62 G1216   DIPLOM
                                                      CONFER

S67

WHITTIER J.M.,"COMPULSORY POOLING AND UNITIZATION*   LEGIS
DIE-HARD KANSAS." LAW PLAN EDU/PROP ATTIT...POLICY   MUNIC
JURID PREDICT TREND METH/COMP 20. PAGE 63 G1236   INDUS
                                                      ECO/TAC

S67

WILLIAMS C.,"REGIONAL MANAGEMENT OVERSEAS." USA+45   MGT
WOR+45 DIST/IND LG/CO EX/STRUC INT/TRADE TARIFFS   EUR+WWI
ADMIN TASK CENTRAL. PAGE 63 G1242   ECO/DEV
                                                      PLAN

S67

WINSTON O.,"AN URBANIZATION PATTERN FOR THE US*   USA+45
SOME CONSIDERATIONS FOR THE DECENTRALIZATION OF   MUNIC
EXCELLENCE." FUT SOCIETY ECO/DEV R+D NEIGH ACT/RES   PLAN
PROB/SOLV TEC/DEV. PAGE 64 G1247   HABITAT

S67

WOLFE T.W.,"SOVIET MILITARY POLICY AT THE FIFTY   FORCES
YEAR MARK." USSR VIETNAM WOR+45 RATION AGREE WAR   POLICY
WEAPON CIVMIL/REL TREATY. PAGE 64 G1254   TIME/SEQ
                                                      PLAN

S67

YOUNG O.R.,"ACTIVE DEFENSE AND INTERNATIONAL   ARMS/CONT
ORDER." FORCES BAL/PWR DEBATE GAMBLE COST PEACE.   DETER
PAGE 64 G1265   PLAN
                                                      DECISION

N67

US HOUSE COMM APPROPRIATIONS,PUBLIC WORKS AND   BUDGET
ATOMIC ENERGY COMMISSION APPROPRIATION BILL, 1968   NUC/PWR
(PAMPHLET). USA+45 ECO/DEV NAT/G...GEOG DEEP/INT   PROVS
CHARTS HOUSE/REP AEC DEPT/DEFEN TVA. PAGE 58 G1137   PLAN

N67

US HOUSE COMM SCI ASTRONAUT,GOVERNMENT, SCIENCE,   NAT/G
AND INTERNATIONAL POLICY (PAMPHLET). INDIA   POLICY
NETHERLAND ECO/DEV ECO/UNDEV R+D ACADEM PLAN DIPLOM   CREATE
FOR/AID CONFER...PREDICT 20 CHINJAP. PAGE 59 G1152   TEC/DEV

N67

US SENATE,STATUS OF THE DEVELOPMENT OF THE ANTI-   FORCES
BALLISTIC MISSILE SYSTEMS IN THE UNITED STATES   NUC/PWR
(PAMPHLET). FUT USA+45 R+D PLAN TEC/DEV DEPT/DEFEN.   WAR
PAGE 59 G1165   UTIL

N67

US SENATE COMM AERO SPACE SCI,AERONAUTICAL RESEARCH   AIR
AND DEVELOPMENT POLICY (PAMPHLET). SPACE USA+45   R+D
INDUS CIVMIL/REL CONGRESS PRESIDENT NASA SENATE.   POLICY
PAGE 60 G1169   PLAN

N67

US SENATE COMM AERO SPACE SCI,POLICY PLANNING FOR   TEC/DEV
TECHNOLOGY TRANSFER (PAMPHLET). WOR+45 INDUS CREATE   POLICY
PLAN EFFICIENCY ATTIT. PAGE 60 G1171   NAT/G
                                                      ECO/DEV

N67

US SENATE COMM AERO SPACE SCI,HEARINGS BEFORE THE   NAT/G
COMMITTEE ON AERONAUTICAL AND SPACE SCIENCES UNITED   DELIB/GP
STATES SENATE NINETIETH CONGRESS (PAMPHLET). USA+45   SPACE
CONSULT PLAN CONFER EFFICIENCY SENATE. PAGE 60   CREATE
G1172

N67

US SENATE COMM AERO SPACE SCI,AERONAUTICAL RESEARCH   DIST/IND
AND DEVELOPMENT POLICY: HEARINGS, COMM ON   SPACE
AERONAUTICAL AND SPACE SCIENCES...1967 (PAMPHLET).   NAT/G
R+D PROB/SOLV EXEC GOV/REL 20 DEPT/DEFEN FAA NASA   PLAN
CONGRESS. PAGE 60 G1174

B68

GALLAHER A. JR.,PERSPECTIVES IN DEVELOPMENTAL   TECHNIC
CHANGE. MUNIC PLAN INSPECT EDU/PROP...POLICY   TEC/DEV
DECISION GEOG PSY SOC IDEA/COMP ANTHOL 20   PROB/SOLV
MODERNIZE. PAGE 21 G0405   CREATE

PLAN/UNIT....PLANNED UNIT DEVELOPMENT

PLATO....PLATO

PLATT J.R. G0880

PLEKHNV/GV....G.V. PLEKHANOV

PLUNKITT/G....G.W. PLUNKITT, TAMMANY BOSS

PLURALISM....SEE PLURISM, PLURIST

PLURISM....PLURALISM, SOCIO-POLITICAL ORDER OF AUTONOMOUS
    GROUPS

B44

MERRIAM C.E.,PUBLIC AND PRIVATE GOVERNMENT.   NAT/G
VOL/ASSN EDU/PROP ADMIN REPRESENT EFFICIENCY PWR   NEIGH
PLURISM...MAJORIT CONCPT. PAGE 38 G0755   MGT
                                                      POLICY

SURANYI-UNGER T.,PRIVATE ENTERPRISE AND B50
GOVERNMENTAL PLANNING. STRUCT FINAN BAL/PWR PLAN
HAPPINESS DRIVE NEW/LIB PLURISM...MATH QUANT STAT NAT/G
TREND BIBLIOG. PAGE 53 G1047 LAISSEZ
POLICY

DAHRENDORF R.,CLASS AND CLASS CONFLICT IN B59
INDUSTRIAL SOCIETY. LABOR NAT/G COERCE ROLE PLURISM VOL/ASSN
...POLICY MGT CONCPT CLASSIF. PAGE 14 G0271 STRUCT
SOC
GP/REL

SEIDMAN H.,"THE GOVERNMENT CORPORATION IN THE S59
UNITED STATES." USA+45 LEGIS ADMIN PLURISM 20. CONTROL
PAGE 50 G0988 GOV/REL
EX/STRUC
EXEC

CONNOLLY W.E.,POLITICAL SCIENCE AND IDEOLOGY. B67
UTOPIA ATTIT KNOWL...MAJORIT EPIST PHIL/SCI SOC PWR
IDEA/COMP HYPO/EXP GEN/LAWS METH HUME/D MARX/KARL. PLURISM
PAGE 13 G0250 ELITES
CONCPT

WEIL G.L.,"THE MERGER OF THE INSTITUTIONS OF THE S67
EUROPEAN COMMUNITIES" EUR+WWI ECO/DEV INT/TRADE ECO/TAC
CONSEN PLURISM...DECISION MGT 20 EEC EURATOM ECSC INT/ORG
TREATY. PAGE 62 G1223 CENTRAL
INT/LAW

PLURIST....PLURALIST

CONANT J.B.,SCIENCE AND COMMON SENSE. WOR+45 WOR-45 B51
R+D SCHOOL CONSULT TEC/DEV EDU/PROP SKILL...PLURIST CREATE
METH/CNCPT RECORD TIME/SEQ SIMUL GEN/METH METH. PHIL/SCI
PAGE 13 G0248

BOULDING K.E.,CONFLICT AND DEFENSE: A GENERAL B62
THEORY. FUT SOCIETY INT/ORG NAT/G CREATE BAL/PWR MATH
COERCE NAT/LISM DRIVE ALL/VALS...PLURIST DECISION SIMUL
CONCPT METH/CNCPT TREND HYPO/EXP TOT/POP 20. PAGE 8 PEACE
G0157 WAR

POKROVSKY G.I. G0881

POL....POLITICAL AND POWER PROCESS

POL/PAR....POLITICAL PARTIES

HARPER S.N.,THE GOVERNMENT OF THE SOVIET UNION. COM B38
USSR LAW CONSTN ECO/DEV PLAN TEC/DEV DIPLOM MARXISM
INT/TRADE ADMIN REV NAT/LISM...POLICY 20. PAGE 24 NAT/G
G0483 LEAD
POL/PAR

BINGHAM A.M.,THE TECHNIQUES OF DEMOCRACY. USA-45 B42
CONSTN STRUCT POL/PAR LEGIS PLAN PARTIC CHOOSE POPULISM
REPRESENT NAT/LISM TOTALISM...MGT 20. PAGE 7 G0136 ORD/FREE
ADMIN
NAT/G

ROSENHAUPT H.W.,HOW TO WAGE PEACE. USA+45 SOCIETY B49
STRATA STRUCT R+D INT/ORG POL/PAR LEGIS ACT/RES INTELL
CREATE PLAN EDU/PROP ADMIN EXEC ATTIT ALL/VALS CONCPT
...TIME/SEQ TREND COLD/WAR 20. PAGE 48 G0937 DIPLOM

KOENIG L.W.,THE SALE OF THE TANKERS. USA+45 SEA B50
DIST/IND POL/PAR DIPLOM ADMIN CIVMIL/REL ATTIT NAT/G
...DECISION 20 PRESIDENT DEPT/STATE. PAGE 31 G0609 POLICY
PLAN
GOV/REL

LASSWELL H.D.,"RESEARCH IN POLITICAL BEHAVIOR." L52
LOC/G MUNIC POL/PAR CONSULT ADMIN PARTIC...CHARTS PHIL/SCI
ANTHOL BIBLIOG/A 20. PAGE 32 G0641 METH
R+D

REYNOLDS P.A.,BRITISH FOREIGN POLICY IN THE INTER- B54
WAR YEARS. CZECHOSLVK GERMANY POLAND UK USA-45 DIPLOM
POL/PAR FORCES ECO/TAC ARMS/CONT WAR ATTIT 20. POLICY
PAGE 46 G0915 NAT/G

CALDWELL L.K.,"THE GOVERNMENT AND ADMINISTRATION OF C54
NEW YORK." LOC/G MUNIC POL/PAR SCHOOL CHIEF LEGIS PROVS
PLAN TAX CT/SYS...MGT SOC/WK BIBLIOG 20 NEWYORK/C. ADMIN
PAGE 10 G0202 CONSTN
EX/STRUC

ZELLER B.,"AMERICAN STATE LEGISLATURES: REPORT ON C54
THE COMMITTEE ON AMERICAN LEGISLATURES." CONSTN REPRESENT
POL/PAR EX/STRUC CONFER ADMIN CONTROL EXEC LOBBY LEGIS
PROVS

ROUTINE GOV/REL...POLICY BIBLIOG 20. PAGE 65 G1267 APPORT

KOENIG L.W.,THE TRUMAN ADMINISTRATION: ITS B56
PRINCIPLES AND PRACTICE. USA+45 POL/PAR CHIEF LEGIS ADMIN
DIPLOM DEATH NUC/PWR WAR CIVMIL/REL PEACE POLICY
...DECISION 20 TRUMAN/HS PRESIDENT TREATY. PAGE 31 EX/STRUC
G0610 GOV/REL

MILLER W.E.,"PRESIDENTIAL COATTAILS: A STUDY IN S56
POLITICAL MYTH AND METHODOLOGY" (BMR)" USA+45 CHIEF
CREATE PARTIC ATTIT DRIVE PWR...DECISION CONCPT CHOOSE
CHARTS SIMUL 20 PRESIDENT CONGRESS. PAGE 39 G0774 POL/PAR
MYTH

MIKSCHE F.O.,THE FAILURE OF ATOMIC STRATEGY. COM B59
EUR+WWI INTELL POL/PAR FORCES PLAN ECO/TAC NUC/PWR ACT/RES
ATTIT DRIVE RIGID/FLEX PWR...DECISION GEOG PSY ORD/FREE
CONCPT RECORD TREND CHARTS VAL/FREE 20. PAGE 39 DIPLOM
G0766 ARMS/CONT

VERNEY D.V.,PUBLIC ENTERPRISE IN SWEDEN. FUT SWEDEN B59
UK INDUS POL/PAR LEGIS PROB/SOLV CAP/ISM INT/TRADE ECO/DEV
CONTROL SOCISM...MGT CONCPT NAT/COMP 20 SOCDEM/PAR POLICY
CIVIL/SERV. PAGE 61 G1196 LG/CO
NAT/G

APTHEKER H.,DISARMAMENT AND THE AMERICAN ECONOMY: A B60
SYMPOSIUM. FUT USA+45 ECO/DEV DIST/IND FINAN INDUS MARXIST
PROC/MFG LABOR NAT/G POL/PAR CONSULT PLAN CAP/ISM ARMS/CONT
INT/TRADE PEACE ATTIT MORAL WEALTH...TREND GEN/LAWS
TOT/POP 20. PAGE 3 G0063

GRANICK D.,THE RED EXECUTIVE. COM USA+45 SOCIETY B60
ECO/DEV INDUS NAT/G POL/PAR EX/STRUC PLAN ECO/TAC PWR
EDU/PROP ADMIN EXEC ATTIT DRIVE...GP/COMP 20. STRATA
PAGE 22 G0440 USSR
ELITES

CARNELL F.,THE POLITICS OF THE NEW STATES: A SELECT B61
ANNOTATED BIBLIOGRAPHY WITH SPECIAL REFERENCE TO BIBLIOG/A
THE COMMONWEALTH. CONSTN ELITES LABOR NAT/G POL/PAR AFR
EX/STRUC DIPLOM ADJUD ADMIN...GOV/COMP 20 ASIA
COMMONWLTH. PAGE 11 G0210 COLONIAL

JANOWITZ M.,COMMUNITY POLITICAL SYSTEMS. USA+45 B61
SOCIETY INDUS VOL/ASSN TEC/DEV ADMIN LEAD CHOOSE MUNIC
...SOC SOC/WK 20. PAGE 29 G0561 STRUCT
POL/PAR

NEIBURG H.L.,"THE EISENHOWER AEC AND CONGRESS: A L62
STUDY IN EXECUTIVE-LEGISLATIVE RELATIONS." USA+45 CHIEF
NAT/G POL/PAR DELIB/GP EX/STRUC TOP/EX ADMIN EXEC LEGIS
LEAD ROUTINE PWR...POLICY COLD/WAR CONGRESS GOV/REL
PRESIDENT AEC. PAGE 41 G0816 NUC/PWR

HERNDON J.,A SELECTED BIBLIOGRAPHY OF MATERIALS IN B63
STATE GOVERNMENT AND POLITICS (PAMPHLET). USA+45 BIBLIOG
POL/PAR LEGIS ADMIN CHOOSE MGT. PAGE 26 G0507 GOV/COMP
PROVS
DECISION

JACOB H.,GERMAN ADMINISTRATION SINCE BISMARCK: B63
CENTRAL AUTHORITY VERSUS LOCAL AUTONOMY. GERMANY ADMIN
GERMANY/W LAW POL/PAR CONTROL CENTRAL TOTALISM NAT/G
FASCISM...MAJORIT DECISION STAT CHARTS GOV/COMP LOC/G
19/20 BISMARCK/O HITLER/A WEIMAR/REP. PAGE 28 G0551 POLICY

US DEPARTMENT OF THE ARMY,SOVIET RUSSIA: STRATEGIC B63
SURVEY (PAMPHLET). USSR POL/PAR PLAN DOMIN EDU/PROP BIBLIOG/A
ARMS/CONT GUERRILLA WAR WEAPON...TREND CHARTS MARXISM
ORG/CHARTS 20. PAGE 57 G1129 DIPLOM
COERCE

DELLIN L.A.D.,"BULGARIA UNDER SOVIET LEADERSHIP." S63
BULGARIA COM USA+45 USSR ECO/DEV INDUS POL/PAR AGRI
EX/STRUC TOP/EX COERCE ATTIT RIGID/FLEX...POLICY NAT/G
TIME/SEQ 20. PAGE 15 G0293 TOTALISM

DUSCHA J.,ARMS, MONEY, AND POLITICS. USA+45 INDUS B64
POL/PAR ECO/TAC TAX DETER NUC/PWR WAR WEAPON NAT/G
GOV/REL ATTIT...BIBLIOG/A 20 CONGRESS MONEY FORCES
DEPT/DEFEN. PAGE 17 G0326 POLICY
BUDGET

INST D'ETUDE POL L'U GRENOBLE,ADMINISTRATION B64
TRADITIONELLE ET PLANIFICATION REGIONALE. FRANCE ADMIN
LAW POL/PAR PROB/SOLV ADJUST RIGID/FLEX...CHARTS MUNIC
ANTHOL BIBLIOG T 20 REFORMERS. PAGE 28 G0546 PLAN
CREATE

B64
MILIBAND R.,THE SOCIALIST REGISTER: 1964. GERMANY/W MARXISM
ITALY UK LABOR POL/PAR ECO/TAC FOR/AID NUC/PWR SOCISM
...POLICY SOCIALIST IDEA/COMP 20 MAO NASSER/G. CAP/ISM
PAGE 39 G0769 PROB/SOLV

B64
VAN DYKE V.,PRIDE AND POWER: THE RATIONALE OF THE TEC/DEV
SPACE PROGRAM. FUT USA+45 INTELL R+D NAT/G POL/PAR ATTIT
DELIB/GP EX/STRUC LEGIS TOP/EX ACT/RES PLAN ECO/TAC POLICY
EDU/PROP ORD/FREE PWR RESPECT SKILL...TIME/SEQ
VAL/FREE. PAGE 61 G1191

B65
BAILEY S.K.,AMERICAN POLITICS AND GOVERNMENT. ANTHOL
USA+45 CONSTN FINAN LABOR POL/PAR DIPLOM ADMIN WAR LEGIS
INGP/REL RACE/REL NEW/LIB 20 SUPREME/CT PRESIDENT PWR
CONGRESS. PAGE 4 G0084

B65
SCHEINMAN L.,ATOMIC ENERGY POLICY IN FRANCE UNDER NUC/PWR
THE FOURTH REPUBLIC. FRANCE UK USA+45 ELITES NAT/G
POL/PAR PLAN PROB/SOLV DIPLOM LEAD GOV/REL DELIB/GP
...BIBLIOG 20 DEGAULLE/C. PAGE 49 G0962 POLICY

S65
BIRNBAUM K.,"SWEDEN'S NUCLEAR POLICY." WOR+45 SWEDEN
POL/PAR CREATE TEC/DEV NEUTRAL RISK WAR ORD/FREE NUC/PWR
...DECISION IDEA/COMP NAT/COMP TIME. PAGE 7 G0137 DIPLOM
ARMS/CONT

B66
GORDON G.,THE LEGISLATIVE PROCESS AND DIVIDED LEGIS
GOVERNMENT; A CASE STUDY OF THE 86TH CONGRESS. HABITAT
USA+45 POL/PAR PROVS PROB/SOLV BAL/PWR CHOOSE CHIEF
REPRESENT EFFICIENCY ATTIT...POLICY DECISION STAT NAT/G
20 CONGRESS EISNHWR/DD. PAGE 22 G0434

B66
SCHURMANN F.,IDEOLOGY AND ORGANIZATION IN COMMUNIST MARXISM
CHINA. CHINA/COM LOC/G MUNIC POL/PAR ECO/TAC STRUCT
CONTROL ATTIT...MGT STERTYP 20 COM/PARTY. PAGE 50 ADMIN
G0981 NAT/G

B66
US DEPARTMENT OF THE ARMY,COMMUNIST CHINA: A BIBLIOG/A
STRATEGIC SURVEY: A BIBLIOGRAPHY (PAMPHLET NO. MARXISM
20-67). CHINA/COM COM INDIA USSR NAT/G POL/PAR S/ASIA
EX/STRUC FORCES NUC/PWR REV ATTIT...POLICY GEOG DIPLOM
CHARTS. PAGE 58 G1133

B67
BUTLER J.,BOSTON UNIVERSITY PAPERS ON AFRICA* IDEA/COMP
TRANSITION IN AFRICAN POLITICS. AFR LAW CONSTN NAT/G
LABOR POL/PAR TEC/DEV 20. PAGE 10 G0197 PWR

B67
DEGLER C.N.,THE AGE OF THE ECONOMIC REVOLUTION INDUS
1876-1900. USA-45 AGRI MUNIC POL/PAR SECT ECO/TAC SOCIETY
CHOOSE...PHIL/SCI CHARTS NAT/COMP 19 NEGRO. PAGE 15 ECO/DEV
G0292 TEC/DEV

B67
MACKINTOSH J.M.,JUGGERNAUT. USSR NAT/G POL/PAR WAR
ADMIN LEAD CIVMIL/REL COST TOTALISM PWR MARXISM FORCES
...GOV/COMP 20. PAGE 35 G0691 COM
PROF/ORG

B67
RUSSETT B.M.,ARMS CONTROL IN EUROPE: PROPOSALS AND ARMS/CONT
POLITICAL CONSTRAINTS. GERMANY WOR+45 POL/PAR REGION
BARGAIN DIPLOM...TREND CHARTS 20 COLD/WAR. PAGE 48 METH/COMP
G0950

B67
YAMAMURA K.,ECONOMIC POLICY IN POSTWAR JAPAN. ASIA ECO/DEV
FINAN POL/PAR DIPLOM LEAD NAT/LISM ATTIT NEW/LIB POLICY
POPULISM 20 CHINJAP. PAGE 64 G1262 NAT/G
TEC/DEV

L67
"POLITICAL PARTIES ON FOREIGN POLICY IN THE INTER- POL/PAR
ELECTION YEARS 1962-66." ASIA COM INDIA USA+45 PLAN DIPLOM
ATTIT...DECISION 20. PAGE 1 G0023 POLICY

S67
CHIU S.M.,"CHINA'S MILITARY POSTURE." CHINA/COM FORCES
ELITES NAT/G POL/PAR TEC/DEV ECO/TAC DOMIN CONTROL CIVMIL/REL
LEAD REV MARXISM 20 MAO. PAGE 12 G0228 NUC/PWR
DIPLOM

POLAND....SEE ALSO COM

B54
REYNOLDS P.A.,BRITISH FOREIGN POLICY IN THE INTER- DIPLOM

POLICY
WAR YEARS. CZECHOSLVK GERMANY POLAND UK USA-45 NAT/G
POL/PAR FORCES ECO/TAC ARMS/CONT WAR ATTIT 20.
PAGE 46 G0915

S65
STAAR R.F.,"RETROGRESSION IN POLAND." COM USSR AGRI TOP/EX
INDUS NAT/G CREATE EDU/PROP TOTALSM RIGID/FLEX ECO/TAC
ORD/FREE PWR SOCISM...RECORD CHARTS 20. PAGE 52 POLAND
G1029

B66
SPULBER N.,THE STATE AND ECONOMIC DEVELOPMENT IN ECO/DEV
EASTERN EUROPE. BULGARIA COM CZECHOSLVK HUNGARY ECO/UNDEV
POLAND YUGOSLAVIA CULTURE PLAN CAP/ISM INT/TRADE NAT/G
CONTROL...POLICY CHARTS METH/COMP BIBLIOG/A 19/20. TOTALISM
PAGE 52 G1028

B67
NATIONAL SCIENCE FOUNDATION,DIRECTORY OF SELECTED INDEX
RESEARCH INSTITUTES IN EASTERN EUROPE. BULGARIA R+D
CZECHOSLVK HUNGARY POLAND ROMANIA INTELL ACADEM COM
NAT/G ACT/RES 20. PAGE 41 G0814 PHIL/SCI

POLANYI M. G0882

POLICE....SEE FORCES

POLICY....ETHICS OF PUBLIC POLICIES

POLIT/ACTN....POLITICAL ACTION COMMITTEE

POLITBURO....POLITBURO (U.S.S.R.)

POLITICAL BEHAVIOR....SEE POL

POLITICAL FINANCING....SEE POL+FINAN

POLITICAL MACHINE....SEE POL+ADMIN

POLITICAL MOVEMENT....SEE IDEOLOGICAL TOPIC INDEX

POLITICAL ORGANIZATION....SEE POL/PAR

POLITICAL PROCESS....SEE LEGIS, POL

POLITICAL SCIENCE....SEE POL

POLITICAL SYSTEMS....SEE IDEOLOGICAL TOPIC INDEX

POLITICAL SYSTEMS THEORY....SEE GEN/LAWS+NET/THEORY+POL

POLITICAL THEORY....SEE IDEOLOGICAL TOPIC INDEX

POLITICS....SEE POL

POLK/JAMES....PRESIDENT JAMES POLK

POLLACK N. G0391

POLLACK/N....NORMAN POLLACK

POLLARD W.G. G0883

POLLUTION....AIR OR WATER POLLUTION

B62
STERN A.C.,AIR POLLUTION (2 VOLS.). LAW INDUS AIR
PROB/SOLV TEC/DEV INSPECT RISK BIO/SOC HABITAT OP/RES
...OBS/ENVIR TESTS SAMP 20 POLLUTION. PAGE 53 G1035 CONTROL
HEALTH

N66
US HOUSE COMM SCI ASTRONAUT,THE ADEQUACY OF HEALTH
TECHNOLOGY FOR POLLUTION ABATEMENT (PAMPHLET). POLICY
WOR+45 PLAN PROB/SOLV CONFER ADMIN...JURID 20 TEC/DEV
POLLUTION. PAGE 58 G1145 LEGIS

POLSBY N.W. G0862

POLYNESIA....POLYNESIA

POMEROY W.J. G0884

PONTECORVO G. G0885

POOLE R.E. G0646

POONA....POONA, INDIA

POPE....POPE

POPPER/K....KARL POPPER

POPULATION....SEE GEOG, CENSUS

POPULISM....MAJORITARIANISM

BEARD C.A.,PUBLIC POLICY AND THE GENERAL WELFARE. **CONCPT** **B41**
USA-45 CONSTN LAISSEZ POPULISM...POLICY MAJORIT 20. **ORD/FREE**
PAGE 6 G0108 **PWR**
NAT/G

BINGHAM A.M.,THE TECHNIQUES OF DEMOCRACY. USA-45 **POPULISM** **B42**
CONSTN STRUCT POL/PAR LEGIS PLAN PARTIC CHOOSE **ORD/FREE**
REPRESENT NAT/LISM TOTALISM...MGT 20. PAGE 7 G0136 **ADMIN**
NAT/G

BALDWIN H.W.,THE PRICE OF POWER. USA+45 FORCES PLAN **PROB/SOLV** **B47**
NUC/PWR ADJUST COST ORD/FREE...POLICY PSY BIBLIOG **PWR**
20. PAGE 5 G0089 **POPULISM**
PRICE

LIPPMAN W.,THE PUBLIC PHILOSOPHY. EX/STRUC TOP/EX **MAJORIT** **B55**
LOBBY RATIONAL POPULISM...POLICY SOC CONCPT PREDICT **STRUCT**
GP/COMP IDEA/COMP. PAGE 34 G0673 **PWR**
TOTALISM

SKINNER B.F.,"FREEDOM AND THE CONTROL OF MEN" **ORD/FREE** **S55**
(BMR)" FUT WOR+45 CONTROL CHOOSE GP/REL ATTIT MORAL **TEC/DEV**
PWR POPULISM...POLICY 20. PAGE 51 G1008 **PHIL/SCI**
INTELL

LAPP R.E.,THE NEW PRIESTHOOD; THE SCIENTIFIC ELITE **TEC/DEV** **B65**
AND THE USES OF POWER. USA+45 ELITES INTELL SOCIETY **TECHRACY**
R+D NAT/G CHIEF LEGIS CIVMIL/REL GP/REL PWR 20 **CONTROL**
PRESIDENT CONGRESS. PAGE 32 G0635 **POPULISM**

MCLAUGHLIN M.R.,RELIGIOUS EDUCATION AND THE STATE: **SECT** **B67**
DEMOCRACY FINDS A WAY. CANADA EUR+WWI GP/REL **NAT/G**
POPULISM...CATH NAT/COMP 20 AUSTRAL. PAGE 38 G0745 **EDU/PROP**
POLICY

YAMAMURA K.,ECONOMIC POLICY IN POSTWAR JAPAN. ASIA **ECO/DEV** **B67**
FINAN POL/PAR DIPLOM LEAD NAT/LISM ATTIT NEW/LIB **POLICY**
POPULISM 20 CHINJAP. PAGE 64 G1262 **NAT/G**
TEC/DEV

PORTUGAL....SEE ALSO APPROPRIATE TIME/SPACE/CULTURE INDEX

OECD,THE MEDITERRANEAN REGIONAL PROJECT: PORTUGAL; **EDU/PROP** **B65**
EDUCATION AND DEVELOPMENT. PORTUGAL SOCIETY STRATA **SCHOOL**
FINAN PROF/ORG WORKER PLAN PROB/SOLV ADMIN...POLICY **ACADEM**
STAT CHARTS METH 20 OECD. PAGE 42 G0832 **ECO/UNDEV**

PORWIT K. G0886

POSITIVISM....SEE GEN/METH

POSTAL/SYS....POSTAL SYSTEMS

DEAN A.L.,FEDERAL AGENCY APPROACHES TO FIELD **ADMIN** **B63**
MANAGEMENT (PAMPHLET). R+D DELIB/GP EX/STRUC **MGT**
PROB/SOLV GOV/REL...CLASSIF BIBLIOG 20 FAA NASA **NAT/G**
DEPT/HEW POSTAL/SYS IRS. PAGE 15 G0287 **OP/RES**

POSTOFFICE....POST OFFICE DEPARTMENT

POTSDAM....POTSDAM

POUND/ROS....ROSCOE POUND

POVERTY....SEE WEALTH, INCOME

POVRTY/WAR....WAR ON POVERTY; SEE ALSO JOHNSON/LB

POWELL/AC....ADAM CLAYTON POWELL

POWELSON J.P. G0887

POWER....SEE PWR

PPBS....PLANNING-PROGRAMMING-BUDGETING SYSTEM

PRAGMATICS....SEE LOG

PRE/AMER....PRE-EUROPEAN AMERICAS

PRE/US/AM....PRE-1776 UNITED STATES (THE COLONIES)

PREDICT....PREDICTION OF FUTURE EVENTS, SEE ALSO FUT

GINZBERG E.,MANPOWER FOR GOVERNMENT (PAMPHLET). **WORKER** **N19**
USA+45 FORCES PLAN PROB/SOLV PAY EDU/PROP ADMIN **CONSULT**
GP/REL COST...MGT PREDICT TREND 20 CIVIL/SERV. **NAT/G**
PAGE 21 G0418 **LOC/G**

US CHAMBER OF COMMERCE,THE SIGNIFICANCE OF **MARKET** **N19**
CONCENTRATION RATIOS (PAMPHLET). USA+45 FINAN INDUS **PREDICT**
ADMIN...METH/CNCPT SAMP CHARTS 20. PAGE 56 G1109 **LG/CO**
CONTROL

LIPPMAN W.,THE PUBLIC PHILOSOPHY. EX/STRUC TOP/EX **MAJORIT** **B55**
LOBBY RATIONAL POPULISM...POLICY SOC CONCPT PREDICT **STRUCT**
GP/COMP IDEA/COMP. PAGE 34 G0673 **PWR**
TOTALISM

GOLD N.L.,REGIONAL ECONOMIC DEVELOPMENT AND NUCLEAR **ECO/UNDEV** **B57**
POWER IN INDIA. FUT INDIA FINAN FOR/AID INT/TRADE **TEC/DEV**
BAL/PAY EFFICIENCY OPTIMAL PRODUC WEALTH...PREDICT **NUC/PWR**
20. PAGE 22 G0424 **INDUS**

NATIONAL PLANNING ASSOCIATION,1970 WITHOUT ARMS **ARMS/CONT** **B58**
CONTROL (PAMPHLET). WOR+45 PROB/SOLV TEC/DEV DIPLOM **ORD/FREE**
CONFER DETER NUC/PWR WAR...CHARTS 20 COLD/WAR. **WEAPON**
PAGE 41 G0810 **PREDICT**

DEAN B.V.,"APPLICATION OF OPERATIONS RESEARCH TO **DECISION** **S58**
MANAGERIAL DECISION MAKING" STRATA ACT/RES **OP/RES**
PROB/SOLV ROLE...SOC PREDICT SIMUL 20. PAGE 15 **MGT**
G0288 **METH/CNCPT**

ADAMS E.W.,"A MODEL OF RISKLESS CHOICE." CREATE **GAME** **S59**
PROB/SOLV UTIL...PROBABIL PREDICT HYPO/EXP. PAGE 2 **SIMUL**
G0029 **RISK**
DECISION

CYERT R.M.,"MODELS IN A BEHAVIORAL THEORY OF THE **SIMUL** **S59**
FIRM." ROUTINE...DECISION MGT METH/CNCPT MATH. **GAME**
PAGE 14 G0267 **PREDICT**
INDUS

FRANCIS R.G.,THE PREDICTIVE PROCESS. PLAN MARXISM **PREDICT** **B60**
...DECISION SOC CONCPT NAT/COMP 19/20. PAGE 20 **PHIL/SCI**
G0390 **TREND**

BENNION E.G.,"ECONOMETRICS FOR MANAGEMENT." USA+45 **ECOMETRIC** **S61**
INDUS EX/STRUC ACT/RES COMPUTER UTIL...MATH STAT **MGT**
PREDICT METH/COMP HYPO/EXP. PAGE 6 G0122 **SIMUL**
DECISION

CLARKE A.C.,PROFILES OF THE FUTURE; AN INQUIRY INTO **FUT** **B62**
THE LIMITS OF THE POSSIBLE. COM/IND DIST/IND PRODUC **TEC/DEV**
AGE PERCEPT...TECHNIC NEW/IDEA TIME. PAGE 12 G0232 **PREDICT**
SPACE

PERRE J.,LES MUTATIONS DE LA GUERRE MODERNE: DE LA **WAR** **B62**
REVOLUTION FRANCAISE A LA REVOLUTION NUCLEAIRE. **FORCES**
DIPLOM ARMS/CONT DEATH REV WEAPON GP/REL PEACE **NUC/PWR**
ATTIT...STAT PREDICT BIBLIOG 18/20 WWI. PAGE 44
G0870

BONINI C.P.,SIMULATION OF INFORMATION AND DECISION **INDUS** **B63**
SYSTEMS IN THE FIRM. MARKET BUDGET DOMIN EDU/PROP **SIMUL**
ADMIN COST ATTIT HABITAT PERCEPT PWR...CONCPT **DECISION**
PROBABIL QUANT PREDICT HYPO/EXP BIBLIOG. PAGE 8 **MGT**
G0152

TOMKINS S.S.,COMPUTER SIMULATION OF PERSONALITY. **COMPUTER** **B63**
R+D TEC/DEV AUTOMAT FEEDBACK ANOMIE PERCEPT...STYLE **PERSON**
PERS/TEST PREDICT COMPUT/IR GP/COMP. PAGE 55 G1075 **SIMUL**
PROG/TEAC

BRIGHT J.R.,RESEARCH, DEVELOPMENT AND TECHNOLOGICAL **TEC/DEV** **B64**
INNOVATION. CULTURE R+D CREATE PLAN PROB/SOLV **NEW/IDEA**
AUTOMAT RISK PERSON...DECISION CONCPT PREDICT **INDUS**
BIBLIOG. PAGE 9 G0168 **MGT**

TAUBENFELD H.J.,SPACE AND SOCIETY. USA+45 LAW **SPACE** **B64**
FORCES CREATE TEC/DEV ADJUD CONTROL COST PEACE **SOCIETY**
...PREDICT ANTHOL 20. PAGE 54 G1057 **ADJUST**
DIPLOM

HEER D.M.,AFTER NUCLEAR ATTACK: A DEMOGRAPHIC INQUIRY. USA+45 ECO/DEV SECT WORKER SEX...HEAL SOC STAT PREDICT CHARTS 20 NEGRO. PAGE 25 G0500
B65 GEOG NUC/PWR CENSUS WAR

VERMOT-GAUCHY M.,L'EDUCATION NATIONALE DANS LA FRANCE DE 1975. FRANCE FUT CULTURE ELITES R+D SCHOOL PLAN EDU/PROP EFFICIENCY...POLICY PREDICT CHARTS INDEX 20. PAGE 61 G1195
B65 ACADEM CREATE TREND INTELL

ABT C.C.,"CONTROLLING FUTURE ARMS." USSR PLAN BAL/PWR DIPLOM NUC/PWR COST...CLASSIF STAT CHARTS. PAGE 2 G0027
S65 PREDICT FUT ARMS/CONT TEC/DEV

BLOOMFIELD L.P.,"ARMS CONTROL AND THE DEVELOPING COUNTRIES." AFR ISLAM S/ASIA USA+45 VOL/ASSN TEC/DEV DIPLOM REGION NUC/PWR...PREDICT TREND. PAGE 7 G0142
S65 ARMS/CONT ECO/UNDEV HYPO/EXP OBS

HARRISON S.L.,"NTH NATION CHALLENGES* THE PRESENT PERSPECTIVE." EUR+WWI FUT USA+45 BAL/PWR CONTROL RISK COERCE WAR...PREDICT COLD/WAR. PAGE 25 G0485
S65 ARMS/CONT NUC/PWR NAT/G DIPLOM

HIBBS A.R.,"SPACE TECHNOLOGY* THE THREAT AND THE PROMISE." FUT VOL/ASSN TEC/DEV NUC/PWR COST EFFICIENCY UTIL UN TREATY. PAGE 26 G0510
S65 SPACE ARMS/CONT PREDICT

MARTIN A.,"PROLIFERATION." FUT WOR+45 PROB/SOLV REGION ADJUST...PREDICT NAT/COMP UN TREATY. PAGE 36 G0712
S65 RECORD NUC/PWR ARMS/CONT VOL/ASSN

RUBINSTEIN A.Z.,"POLITICAL BARRIERS TO DISARMAMENT." FUT DIPLOM COERCE NUC/PWR WAR NAT/LISM ORD/FREE PREDICT. PAGE 48 G0944
S65 COM USA+45 ARMS/CONT ATTIT

RUPPENTHAL K.M.,TRANSPORTATION AND TOMORROW. FUT SPACE USA+45 SEA AIR FORCES TEC/DEV INT/TRADE ...ANTHOL 20 RAILROAD. PAGE 48 G0946
B66 DIST/IND PLAN CIVMIL/REL PREDICT

US PRES COMM ECO IMPACT DEFENS,REPORT* JULY 1965. USA+45 ECO/DEV INDUS DELIB/GP FORCES OP/RES ARMS/CONT NUC/PWR WEAPON BAL/PAY...PREDICT SIMUL. PAGE 59 G1159
B66 ACT/RES STAT WAR BUDGET

US HOUSE COMM SCI ASTRONAUT,GOVERNMENT, SCIENCE, AND PUBLIC POLICY (PAMPHLET). R+D ACADEM DELIB/GP COMPUTER BUDGET CONFER ADMIN...PHIL/SCI PREDICT TREND 20 CONGRESS HS/SCIASTR. PAGE 58 G1143
N66 NAT/G POLICY TEC/DEV CREATE

BUNGE M.,THE SEARCH FOR TRUTH, VOL. 3, PART 2 OF STUDIES IN THE FOUNDATIONS, METHODOLOGY, AND PHILOSOPHY OF SCIENCE. UNIV INTELL KNOWL...CONCPT OBS PREDICT METH. PAGE 10 G0188
B67 PHIL/SCI TESTS GEN/LAWS RATIONAL

CROSSON F.J.,SCIENCE AND CONTEMPORARY SOCIETY. FUT WOR+45 SECT CREATE PROB/SOLV...HUM PREDICT TREND IDEA/COMP ANTHOL. PAGE 14 G0263
B67 PHIL/SCI SOCIETY TEC/DEV CONCPT

DE JOUVENEL B.,THE ART OF CONJECTURE. WOR+45 EFFICIENCY PERCEPT KNOWL...DECISION PHIL/SCI CONCPT METH/COMP BIBLIOG 20. PAGE 15 G0285
B67 FUT PREDICT SIMUL METH

BULMER-THOMAS I.,"SO, ON TO THE GREAT SOCIETY." FUT UNIV TEC/DEV BAL/PWR WAR BIO/SOC KNOWL...ART/METH SOC PREDICT TREND WORSHIP 20 GREAT/SOC. PAGE 9 G0185
S67 PHIL/SCI SOCIETY CREATE

DOYLE S.E.,"COMMUNICATION SATELLITES* INTERNAL ORGANIZATION FOR DEVELOPMENT AND CONTROL." USA+45 R+D ACT/RES DIPLOM NAT/LISM...POLICY INT/LAW PREDICT UN. PAGE 16 G0313
S67 TEC/DEV SPACE COM/IND INT/ORG

GAUSSENS J.,"THE APPLICATIONS OF NUCLEAR ENERGY - TECHNICAL, ECONOMIC AND SOCIAL ASPECTS." WOR+45 INDUS R+D ACT/RES EFFICIENCY PRODUC SKILL PREDICT. PAGE 21 G0413
S67 NUC/PWR TEC/DEV ECO/DEV ADJUST

GRIFFITHS F.,"THE POLITICAL SIDE OF 'DISARMAMENT'." FUT WOR+45 NUC/PWR NAT/LISM PEACE...NEW/IDEA PREDICT METH/COMP GEN/LAWS 20. PAGE 23 G0453
S67 ARMS/CONT DIPLOM

MOOR E.J.,"THE INTERNATIONAL IMPACT OF AUTOMATION." WOR+45 ACT/RES COMPUTER CREATE PLAN CAP/ISM ROUTINE EFFICIENCY PREDICT. PAGE 39 G0779
S67 TEC/DEV OP/RES AUTOMAT INDUS

SCHACTER O.,"SCIENTIFIC ADVANCES AND INTERNATIONAL LAWMAKING." FUT R+D PLAN PROB/SOLV CONFER CONTROL ...POLICY PREDICT 20 UN. PAGE 49 G0961
S67 TEC/DEV INT/LAW INT/ORG ACT/RES

VLASCIC I.A.,"THE SPACE TREATY* A PRELIMINARY EVALUATION." FUT USSR WOR+45 R+D ACT/RES TEC/DEV DIPLOM CONFER ARMS/CONT PEACE...PREDICT UN TREATY. PAGE 61 G1201
S67 SPACE INT/LAW INT/ORG NEUTRAL

WARE R.S.,"FORECAST A.D. 2000." SOCIETY STRATA ECO/UNDEV INDUS FORCES EDU/PROP AUTOMAT COERCE REV WEAPON ATTIT PREDICT. PAGE 62 G1213
S67 NUC/PWR GEOG TEC/DEV WAR

WHITTIER J.M.,"COMPULSORY POOLING AND UNITIZATION* DIE-HARD KANSAS." LAW PLAN EDU/PROP ATTIT...POLICY JURID PREDICT TREND METH/COMP 20. PAGE 63 G1236
S67 LEGIS MUNIC INDUS ECO/TAC

US HOUSE COMM SCI ASTRONAUT,GOVERNMENT, SCIENCE, AND INTERNATIONAL POLICY (PAMPHLET). INDIA NETHERLAND ECO/DEV ECO/UNDEV R+D ACADEM PLAN DIPLOM FOR/AID CONFER...PREDICT 20 CHINJAP. PAGE 59 G1152
N67 NAT/G POLICY CREATE TEC/DEV

RENAN E.,THE FUTURE OF SCIENCE. WAR ORD/FREE WEALTH ...GOV/COMP IDEA/COMP GEN/LAWS 19. PAGE 46 G0913
B91 PHIL/SCI KNOWL SECT PREDICT

PREDICTION....SEE PREDICT, FUT

PREFECT....PREFECTS AND PREFECTORALISM

PREHIST....PREHISTORIC SOCIETY, PRIOR TO 3000 B.C.

MULLER H.J.,FREEDOM IN THE WESTERN WORLD. PREHIST CULTURE SECT CREATE TEC/DEV DOMIN PWR WEALTH ...MAJORIT SOC CONCPT. PAGE 40 G0793
B63 ORD/FREE TIME/SEQ SOCIETY

LILLEY S.,MEN, MACHINES AND HISTORY: THE STORY OF TOOLS AND MACHINES IN RELATION TO SOCIAL PROGRESS. PREHIST SPACE STRUCT COMPUTER AUTOMAT NUC/PWR ...POLICY SOC. PAGE 34 G0667
B66 AGRI TEC/DEV SOCIETY

PREHISTORIC SOCIETY....SEE PREHIST

PREJUDICE....SEE DISCRIM

PRESIDENT....PRESIDENCY (ALL NATIONS); SEE ALSO CHIEF

KOENIG L.W.,THE SALE OF THE TANKERS. USA+45 SEA DIST/IND POL/PAR DIPLOM ADMIN CIVMIL/REL ATTIT ...DECISION 20 PRESIDENT DEPT/STATE. PAGE 31 G0609
B50 NAT/G POLICY PLAN GOV/REL

MAASS A.,MUDDY WATERS: THE ARMY ENGINEERS AND THE NATIONS RIVERS. USA-45 PROF/ORG CONSULT LEGIS ADMIN EXEC ROLE PWR...SOC PRESIDENT 20. PAGE 35 G0682
B51 FORCES GP/REL LOBBY CONSTRUC

SMITHIES A.,THE BUDGETARY PROCESS IN THE UNITED STATES. ECO/DEV AGRI EX/STRUC FORCES LEGIS PROB/SOLV TAX ROUTINE EFFICIENCY...MGT CONGRESS PRESIDENT. PAGE 52 G1016
B55 NAT/G ADMIN BUDGET GOV/REL

KOENIG L.W.,THE TRUMAN ADMINISTRATION: ITS
B56 ADMIN

PRINCIPLES AND PRACTICE. USA+45 POL/PAR CHIEF LEGIS POLICY
DIPLOM DEATH NUC/PWR WAR CIVMIL/REL PEACE
...DECISION 20 TRUMAN/HS PRESIDENT TREATY. PAGE 31 GOV/REL
G0610 | POLICY EX/STRUC GOV/REL

S56
MILLER W.E.,"PRESIDENTIAL COATTAILS: A STUDY IN CHIEF
POLITICAL MYTH AND METHODOLOGY" (BMR)" USA+45 CHOOSE
CREATE PARTIC ATTIT DRIVE PWR...DECISION CONCPT POL/PAR
CHARTS SIMUL 20 PRESIDENT CONGRESS. PAGE 39 G0774 MYTH

B60
CARPER E.T.,THE DEFENSE APPROPRIATIONS RIDER GOV/REL
(PAMPHLET). USA+45 CONSTN CHIEF DELIB/GP LEGIS ADJUD
BUDGET LOBBY CIVMIL/REL...POLICY 20 CONGRESS LAW
EISNHWR/DD DEPT/DEFEN PRESIDENT BOSTON. PAGE 11 CONTROL
G0212

B60
WILLIAUS T.H.,AMERICANS AT WAR: THE DEVELOPMENT OF FORCES
THE AMERICAN MILITARY SYSTEM. USA+45 USA-45 WAR
EDU/PROP LEAD REV...GP/COMP BIBLIOG/A 18/20 NAT/G
PRESIDENT. PAGE 63 G1244 POLICY

B62
BOCK E.A.,CASE STUDIES IN AMERICAN GOVERNMENT. POLICY
USA+45 ECO/DEV CHIEF EDU/PROP CT/SYS RACE/REL LEGIS
ORD/FREE...JURID MGT PHIL/SCI PRESIDENT CASEBOOK. IDEA/COMP
PAGE 8 G0146 NAT/G

L62
NEIBURG H.L.,"THE EISENHOWER AEC AND CONGRESS: A CHIEF
STUDY IN EXECUTIVE-LEGISLATIVE RELATIONS." USA+45 LEGIS
NAT/G POL/PAR DELIB/GP EX/STRUC TOP/EX ADMIN EXEC GOV/REL
LEAD ROUTINE PWR...POLICY COLD/WAR CONGRESS NUC/PWR
PRESIDENT AEC. PAGE 41 G0816

L62
NIEBURG H.L.,"THE EISENHOWER ATOMIC ENERGY NUC/PWR
COMMISSION AND CONGRESS" R+D INT/ORG OP/RES DIPLOM TOP/EX
ADMIN CONTROL 20 PRESIDENT CONGRESS AEC. PAGE 42 LOBBY
G0821 DELIB/GP

B63
GREEN H.P.,GOVERNMENT OF THE ATOM. USA+45 LEGIS GOV/REL
PROB/SOLV ADMIN CONTROL PWR...POLICY DECISION 20 EX/STRUC
PRESIDENT CONGRESS. PAGE 22 G0443 NUC/PWR
DELIB/GP

B63
WILTZ J.E.,IN SEARCH OF PEACE: THE SENATE MUNITIONS DELIB/GP
INQUIRY, 1934-36. EUR+WWI USA-45 ELITES INDUS LG/CO PROFIT
LEGIS INT/TRADE LOBBY NEUTRAL ARMS/CONT...POLICY WAR
CONGRESS 20 LEAGUE/NAT PRESIDENT SENATE CONSCRIPTN. WEAPON
PAGE 64 G1246

N63
COMMITTEE ECONOMIC DEVELOPMENT,TAXES AND TRADE: 20 FINAN
YEARS OF CED POLICY (PAMPHLET). USA+45 ECO/DEV PLAN ECO/TAC
BUDGET LEAD...POLICY KENNEDY/JF PRESIDENT. PAGE 13 NAT/G
G0246 DELIB/GP

B64
WILLIAMS S.P.,TOWARD A GENUINE WORLD SECURITY BIBLIOG/A
SYSTEM (PAMPHLET). WOR+45 INT/ORG FORCES PLAN ARMS/CONT
NUC/PWR ORD/FREE...INT/LAW CONCPT UN PRESIDENT. DIPLOM
PAGE 63 G1243 PEACE

B65
BAILEY S.K.,AMERICAN POLITICS AND GOVERNMENT. ANTHOL
USA+45 CONSTN FINAN LABOR POL/PAR DIPLOM ADMIN WAR LEGIS
INGP/REL RACE/REL NEW/LIB 20 SUPREME/CT PRESIDENT PWR
CONGRESS. PAGE 4 G0084

B65
LAPP R.E.,THE NEW PRIESTHOOD; THE SCIENTIFIC ELITE TEC/DEV
AND THE USES OF POWER. USA+45 ELITES INTELL SOCIETY TECHRACY
R+D NAT/G CHIEF LEGIS CIVMIL/REL GP/REL PWR 20 CONTROL
PRESIDENT CONGRESS. PAGE 32 G0635 POPULISM

B65
WEISNER J.B.,WHERE SCIENCE AND POLITICS MEET. CHIEF
USA+45 ECO/DEV R+D FORCES PROB/SOLV DIPLOM FOR/AID NAT/G
CONTROL...PHIL/SCI PRESIDENT KENNEDY/JF JOHNSON/LB. POLICY
PAGE 63 G1228 TEC/DEV

S65
HUGHES T.L.,"SCHOLARS AND FOREIGN POLICY* VARIETIES ACT/RES
OF RESEARCH EXPERIENCE." COM/IND DIPLOM ADMIN EXEC ACADEM
ROUTINE...MGT OBS CONGRESS PRESIDENT CAMELOT. CONTROL
PAGE 27 G0535 NAT/G

B66
FEIS H.,THE ATOMIC BOMB AND THE END OF WORLD WAR USA+45
II. FORCES PLAN PROB/SOLV DIPLOM CONFER WAR PEACE
...TIME/SEQ TREND CHINJAP PRESIDENT TIME. PAGE 19 NUC/PWR

G0362

B67
US SUPERINTENDENT OF DOCUMENTS,LIBRARY OF CONGRESS BIBLIOG/A
(PRICE LIST 83). AFR ASIA EUR+WWI USA-45 USSR NAT/G USA+45
DIPLOM CONFER CT/SYS WAR...DECISION PHIL/SCI AUTOMAT
CLASSIF 19/20 CONGRESS PRESIDENT. PAGE 61 G1189 LAW

S67
JONES G.S.,"STRATEGIC PLANNING." USA+45 EX/STRUC PLAN
FORCES DETER WAR 20 PRESIDENT. PAGE 29 G0566 DECISION
DELIB/GP
POLICY

N67
US SENATE COMM AERO SPACE SCI,AERONAUTICAL RESEARCH AIR
AND DEVELOPMENT POLICY (PAMPHLET). SPACE USA+45 R+D
INDUS CIVMIL/REL CONGRESS PRESIDENT NASA SENATE. POLICY
PAGE 60 G1169 PLAN

PRESS C. G0507

PRESS....PRESS, OPERATIONS OF ALL PRINTED MEDIA, EXCEPT
FILM AND TV (Q.V.), JOURNALISM; SEE ALSO COM/IND

B53
LARSEN K.,NATIONAL BIBLIOGRAPHIC SERVICES: THEIR BIBLIOG/A
CREATION AND OPERATION. WOR+45 COM/IND CREATE PLAN INT/ORG
DIPLOM PRESS ADMIN ROUTINE...MGT UNESCO. PAGE 32 WRITING
G0636

B56
ATOMIC INDUSTRIAL FORUM,PUBLIC RELATIONS FOR THE NUC/PWR
ATOMIC INDUSTRY. WOR+45 PLAN PROB/SOLV EDU/PROP INDUS
PRESS CONFER...AUD/VIS ANTHOL 20. PAGE 4 G0077 GP/REL
ATTIT

B56
WASSERMAN P.,INFORMATION FOR ADMINISTRATORS: A BIBLIOG
GUIDE TO PUBLICATIONS AND SERVICES FOR MANAGEMENT MGT
IN BUSINESS AND GOVERNMENT. R+D LOC/G NAT/G KNOWL
PROF/ORG VOL/ASSN PRESS...PSY SOC STAT 20. PAGE 62 EDU/PROP
G1219

B60
CARPENTER E.,EXPLORATIONS IN COMMUNICATION. USSR ANTHOL
CULTURE SCHOOL SECT EDU/PROP PRESS TV AUTOMAT COM/IND
FEEDBACK ATTIT PERSON...ART/METH PSY 20. PAGE 11 TEC/DEV
G0211 WRITING

C60
SCHRAMM W.,"MASS COMMUNICATIONS: A BOOK OF READINGS COM/IND
(2ND ED.)" LG/CO PRESS ADMIN CONTROL ROUTINE ATTIT EDU/PROP
ROLE SUPEGO...CHARTS ANTHOL BIBLIOG 20. PAGE 50 CROWD
G0977 MAJORIT

S63
TANNENBAUM P.H.,"COMMUNICATION OF SCIENCE COM/IND
INFORMATION." USA+45 TEC/DEV ROUTINE...PHIL/SCI PRESS
STYLE 20. PAGE 53 G1051 OP/RES
METH/CNCPT

B65
UNESCO,HANDBOOK OF INTERNATIONAL EXCHANGES. COM/IND INDEX
R+D ACADEM PROF/ORG VOL/ASSN CREATE TEC/DEV INT/ORG
EDU/PROP AGREE 20 TREATY. PAGE 55 G1090 DIPLOM
PRESS

B66
MARKHAM J.W.,AN ECONOMIC-MEDIA STUDY OF BOOK PRESS
PUBLISHING. USA+45 LAW COM/IND ACADEM SCHOOL ECO/TAC
EDU/PROP AUTOMAT CONTROL...DECISION STAT CHARTS 20 TEC/DEV
CONGRESS. PAGE 36 G0707 NAT/G

B66
US SENATE COMM AERO SPACE SCI,SOVIET SPACE CONSULT
PROGRAMS, 1962-65: GOALS AND PURPOSES, SPACE
ACHIEVEMENTS, PLANS, AND INTERNATIONAL FUT
IMPLICATIONS. USA+45 USSR R+D FORCES PLAN EDU/PROP DIPLOM
PRESS ADJUD ARMS/CONT ATTIT MARXISM. PAGE 60 G1168

B67
UNIVERSAL REFERENCE SYSTEM,PUBLIC OPINION, MASS BIBLIOG/A
BEHAVIOR, AND POLITICAL PSYCHOLOGY (VOLUME VI). ATTIT
WOR+45 WOR-45 SOCIETY EDU/PROP PRESS PARTIC CHOOSE CROWD
PERSON...TREND COMPUT/IR GEN/METH. PAGE 56 G1098 PSY

L67
BARRON J.A.,"ACCESS TO THE PRESS." USA+45 TEC/DEV ORD/FREE
PRESS TV ADJUD AUD/VIS. PAGE 5 G0099 COM/IND
EDU/PROP
LAW

S67
CARY G.D.,"THE QUIET REVOLUTION IN COPYRIGHT* THE COM/IND
END OF THE 'PUBLICATION' CONCEPT." USA+45 LAW POLICY

OP/RES TEC/DEV CONFER DEBATE EFFICIENCY...JURID
CONGRESS. PAGE 11 G0217

LICENSE
PRESS

RAMSEY J.A.,"THE STATUS OF INTERNATIONAL
COPYRIGHTS." WOR+45 CREATE TEC/DEV DIPLOM CONFER
CONTROL SANCTION OWN...POLICY JURID. PAGE 46 G0899

S67
INT/LAW
INT/ORG
COM/IND
PRESS

PRESSURE GROUPS....SEE LOBBY

PRICE D.K. G0377

PRICE CONTROL....SEE PRICE, COST, PLAN, RATION

PRICE....SEE ALSO COST

BALDWIN H.W.,THE PRICE OF POWER. USA+45 FORCES PLAN
NUC/PWR ADJUST COST ORD/FREE...POLICY PSY BIBLIOG
20. PAGE 5 G0089

B47
PROB/SOLV
PWR
POPULISM
PRICE

BAUER P.T.,ECONOMIC ANALYSIS AND POLICY IN
UNDERDEVELOPED COUNTRIES. WOR+45 AGRI INT/TRADE TAX
PRICE...GEN/METH BIBLIOG/A 20 COMMONWLTH. PAGE 5
G0103

B57
ECO/UNDEV
METH/COMP
POLICY

EHRHARD J.,LE DESTIN DU COLONIALISME. AFR FRANCE
ECO/UNDEV AGRI FINAN MARKET CREATE PLAN TEC/DEV
BUDGET DIPLOM PRICE 20. PAGE 17 G0335

B58
COLONIAL
FOR/AID
INT/TRADE
INDUS

SILK L.S.,THE RESEARCH REVOLUTION. USA+45 FINAN
CAP/ISM ECO/TAC PRICE EQUILIB PRODUC...STAT TREND
CHARTS. PAGE 51 G0997

B60
ECO/DEV
R+D
TEC/DEV
PROB/SOLV

NOVE A.,THE SOVIET ECONOMY. USSR ECO/DEV FINAN
NAT/G ECO/TAC PRICE ADMIN EFFICIENCY MARXISM
...TREND BIBLIOG 20. PAGE 42 G0828

B61
PLAN
PRODUC
POLICY

BALASSA B.,TRADE PROSPECTS FOR DEVELOPING
COUNTRIES. WOR+45 ECO/DEV AGRI EXTR/IND INDUS
CREATE PLAN PRICE...ECOMETRIC CLASSIF TIME/SEQ
GEN/METH. PAGE 5 G0087

B64
INT/TRADE
ECO/UNDEV
TREND
STAT

MANSFIELD E.,MONOPOLY POWER AND ECONOMIC
PERFORMANCE: AN INTRODUCTION TO A CURRENT ISSUE OF
PUBLIC POLICY. ECO/DEV INDUS NAT/G PLAN CAP/ISM
PRICE CONTROL LOBBY EFFICIENCY PRODUC...POLICY 20
CONGRESS KENNEDY/JF MONOPOLY. PAGE 36 G0701

B64
LG/CO
PWR
ECO/TAC
MARKET

SCHOECK H.,CENTRAL PLANNING AND NEOMERCANTILISM.
L/A+17C UK WOR+45 BUDGET ECO/TAC PRICE CONTROL
GOV/REL UTOPIA 20. PAGE 49 G0974

B64
PLAN
CENTRAL
NAT/G
POLICY

HICKMAN B.G.,QUANTITATIVE PLANNING OF ECONOMIC
POLICY. FRANCE NETHERLAND OP/RES PRICE ROUTINE UTIL
...POLICY DECISION ECOMETRIC METH/CNCPT STAT STYLE
CHINJAP. PAGE 26 G0511

B65
PROB/SOLV
PLAN
QUANT

KANTOROVICH L.V.,THE BEST USE OF ECONOMIC
RESOURCES. USSR SOCIETY FINAN ACT/RES TEC/DEV
ECO/TAC PRICE CONTROL COST DEMAND EFFICIENCY
OPTIMAL...MGT STAT. PAGE 29 G0572

B65
PLAN
MATH
DECISION

KASER M.,COMECON* INTEGRATION PROBLEMS OF THE
PLANNED ECONOMIES. INT/ORG TEC/DEV INT/TRADE PRICE
ADMIN ADJUST CENTRAL...STAT TIME/SEQ ORG/CHARTS
COMECON. PAGE 29 G0579

B65
PLAN
ECO/DEV
COM
REGION

PEIRCE W.S.,SELECTIVE MANPOWER POLICIES AND THE
TRADE-OFF BETWEEN RISING PRICES AND UNEMPLOYMENT
(DISSERTATION). ECO/DEV WORKER ACT/RES...PHIL/SCI
20. PAGE 44 G0865

B66
PRICE
LABOR
POLICY
ECO/TAC

GROSSMAN G.,ECONOMIC SYSTEMS. USA+45 USA-45 USSR
YUGOSLAVIA WORKER CAP/ISM PRICE GP/REL EQUILIB
WEALTH MARXISM SOCISM...MGT METH/COMP 19/20.
PAGE 23 G0456

B67
ECO/DEV
PLAN
TEC/DEV
DEMAND

MACAVOY P.W.,REGULATION OF TRANSPORT INNOVATION.
ACT/RES ADJUD COST DEMAND...POLICY CHARTS 20.
PAGE 35 G0684

B67
DIST/IND
CONTROL
PRICE
PROFIT

PORWIT K.,CENTRAL PLANNING: EVALUATION OF VARIANTS.
PRICE OPTIMAL PRODUC...DECISION MATH CHARTS SIMUL
BIBLIOG 20. PAGE 45 G0886

B67
PLAN
MGT
ECOMETRIC

ENKE S.,"GOVERNMENT-INDUSTRY DEVELOPMENT OF A
COMMERCIAL SUPERSONIC TRANSPORT." USA+45 ECO/DEV
R+D LG/CO NAT/G TEC/DEV PRICE RISK COST PROFIT.
PAGE 18 G0347

S67
INDUS
FINAN
SERV/IND
CAP/ISM

MYERS S.,"TECHNOLOGY AND URBAN TRANSIT: THE
ENORMOUS POTENTIAL OF BUS AND RAIL SYSTEMS." USA+45
FINAN LOC/G MUNIC WORKER PLAN PROB/SOLV PRICE
AUTOMAT 20. PAGE 40 G0798

S67
R+D
TEC/DEV
DIST/IND
ACT/RES

US CONGRESS JT COMM ECO GOVT,BACKGROUND MATERIAL ON
ECONOMY IN GOVERNMENT 1967 (PAMPHLET). WOR+45
ECO/DEV BARGAIN PRICE DEMAND OPTIMAL...STAT
DEPT/DEFEN. PAGE 57 G1116

N67
BUDGET
COST
MGT
NAT/G

PRICING....SEE PRICE, ECO, ACT/RES

PRIMARIES....ELECTORAL PRIMARIES

PRIME/MIN....PRIME MINISTER

PRINCETN/U....PRINCETON UNIVERSITY

VERNON R.,THE MYTH AND REALITY OF OUR URBAN
PROBLEMS (PAMPHLET). USA+45 SOCIETY LOC/G ADMIN
COST 20 PRINCETN/U INTERVENT URBAN/RNWL. PAGE 61
G1197

N19
PLAN
MUNIC
HABITAT
PROB/SOLV

PRINCETON U INDUSTRIAL REL SEC G0889,G0890,G0891

PRINCETON UNIVERSITY G0892

PRISON....PRISONS; SEE ALSO PUB/INST

PRIVACY....PRIVACY AND ITS INVASION

US HOUSE COMM GOVT OPERATIONS,THE COMPUTER AND
INVASION OF PRIVACY. USA+45 SOCIETY ALL/VALS...PSY
SOC CHARTS HOUSE/REP PRIVACY. PAGE 58 G1140

B66
ORD/FREE
COMPUTER
TEC/DEV
NAT/G

PRIVIL....PRIVILEGED, AS CONDITION

CLARK G.,WORLD PEACE THROUGH WORLD LAW; TWO
ALTERNATIVE PLANS. WOR+45 DELIB/GP FORCES TAX
CONFER ADJUD SANCTION ARMS/CONT WAR CHOOSE PRIVIL
20 UN COLD/WAR. PAGE 12 G0231

B66
INT/LAW
PEACE
PLAN
INT/ORG

ALEXANDER L.M.,THE LAW OF THE SEA: OFFSHORE
BOUNDARIES AND ZONES. WOR+45 INT/ORG TEC/DEV
CONTROL PRIVIL HABITAT SOVEREIGN...CON/ANAL CHARTS
ANTHOL. PAGE 2 G0037

B67
SEA
INT/LAW
EXTR/IND

HARTIGAN R.S.,"NONCOMBAT IMMUNITY* REFLECTIONS ON
ITS ORIGINS AND PRESENT STATUS." WOR+45 PROB/SOLV
WAR PRIVIL MORAL...POLICY 20. PAGE 25 G0487

S67
INT/LAW
NUC/PWR
ARMS/CONT
DIPLOM

KOMESAR N.K.,"SECURITY INTERESTS IN GOVERNMENT
CONTRACTS* WHEREIN THE TORTOISE WINS THE RES."
USA+45 INDUS NAT/G OP/RES SANCTION. PAGE 31 G0613

S67
POLICY
CT/SYS
PRIVIL
JURID

SCOVILLE W.J.,"GOVERNMENT REGULATION AND GROWTH IN
THE FRENCH PAPER INDUSTRY DURING THE EIGHTEENTH
CENTURY." FRANCE MOD/EUR FINAN CAP/ISM TAX ADMIN
CONTROL PRIVIL LAISSEZ...POLICY 18. PAGE 50 G0985

S67
NAT/G
PROC/MFG
ECO/DEV
INGP/REL

PRIVILEGE....SEE PRIVIL

PROB/SOLV....PROBLEM SOLVING

CONOVER H.L.,CIVILIAN DEFENSE: A SELECTED LIST OF
RECENT REFERENCES (PAMPHLET). USA+45 LOC/G MUNIC

N
BIBLIOG
PLAN

PROB/SOLV ADMIN LEAD TASK WEAPON GOV/REL...POLICY CON/ANAL 20 CIV/DEFENS. PAGE 13 G0251 — WAR CIVMIL/REL

KRUTILIA J.V.,CONSERVATION RECONSIDERED. USA+45 CREATE EDU/PROP. PAGE 32 G0624 — N PROB/SOLV POLICY HABITAT GEOG

CURRENT THOUGHT ON PEACE AND WAR. WOR+45 INT/ORG FORCES PROB/SOLV DIPLOM NUC/PWR PERCEPT...POLICY SOC 20 UN NATO. PAGE 1 G0001 — B BIBLIOG/A PEACE ATTIT WAR

JOURNAL OF CONFLICT RESOLUTION. FUT WOR+45 INT/ORG NAT/G FORCES CREATE PROB/SOLV ARMS/CONT NUC/PWR WEAPON SOC. PAGE 1 G0002 — N BIBLIOG/A DIPLOM WAR

PUBLIC ADMINISTRATION ABSTRACTS AND INDEX OF ARTICLES. WOR+45 PLAN PROB/SOLV...POLICY 20. PAGE 1 G0009 — N BIBLIOG/A ADMIN ECO/UNDEV NAT/G

BELL J.R.,PERSONNEL PROBLEMS IN CONVERTING TO AUTOMATION (PAMPHLET). USA+45 COMPUTER PLAN ...METH/CNCPT 20 CALIFORNIA. PAGE 6 G0115 — N19 WORKER AUTOMAT PROB/SOLV PROVS

DOTSON A.,PRODUCTION PLANNING IN THE PATENT OFFICE (PAMPHLET). USA+45 DIST/IND PROB/SOLV PRODUC...MGT PHIL/SCI 20 BUR/BUDGET PATENT/OFF. PAGE 16 G0309 — N19 EFFICIENCY PLAN NAT/G ADMIN

FOLSOM M.B.,BETTER MANAGEMENT OF THE PUBLIC'S BUSINESS (PAMPHLET). USA+45 DELIB/GP PAY CONFER CONTROL REGION GP/REL...METH/COMP ANTHOL 20. PAGE 19 G0377 — N19 ADMIN NAT/G MGT PROB/SOLV

GINZBERG E.,MANPOWER FOR GOVERNMENT (PAMPHLET). USA+45 FORCES PLAN PROB/SOLV PAY EDU/PROP ADMIN GP/REL COST...MGT PREDICT TREND 20 CIVIL/SERV. PAGE 21 G0418 — N19 WORKER CONSULT NAT/G LOC/G

US FOOD AND DRUG ADMIN.CIVIL DEFENSE INFORMATION FOR FOOD AND DRUG OFFICIALS (2ND ED.) (PAMPHLET). USA+45 PROB/SOLV RISK HABITAT...MATH CHARTS DICTIONARY 20 CIV/DEFENS. PAGE 58 G1136 — N19 NUC/PWR WAR EATING HEALTH

VERNON R.,THE MYTH AND REALITY OF OUR URBAN PROBLEMS (PAMPHLET). USA+45 SOCIETY LOC/G ADMIN COST 20 PRINCETN/U INTERVENT URBAN/RNWL. PAGE 61 G1197 — N19 PLAN MUNIC HABITAT PROB/SOLV

US LIBRARY OF CONGRESS.CLASSIFIED GUIDE TO MATERIAL IN THE LIBRARY OF CONGRESS COVERING URBAN COMMUNITY DEVELOPMENT. USA+45 CREATE PROB/SOLV ADMIN 20. PAGE 59 G1154 — B36 BIBLIOG CLASSIF MUNIC PLAN

GULICK L.,PAPERS ON THE SCIENCE OF ADMINISTRATION. INDUS PROB/SOLV TEC/DEV COST EFFICIENCY PRODUC HABITAT...PHIL/SCI METH/COMP 20. PAGE 23 G0461 — B37 OP/RES CONTROL ADMIN MGT

STAMP S.,THE SCIENCE OF SOCIAL ADJUSTMENT. WOR-45 ACT/RES CREATE PLAN PROB/SOLV TEC/DEV ECO/TAC EFFICIENCY SOC/INTEG 20. PAGE 52 G1031 — B37 ADJUST ORD/FREE PHIL/SCI

BAKER H.,PROBLEMS OF REEMPLOYMENT AND RETRAINING OF MANPOWER DURING THE TRANSITION FROM WAR TO PEACE. USA+45 INDUS LABOR LG/CO NAT/G PLAN ADMIN PEACE ...POLICY MGT 20. PAGE 5 G0086 — B45 BIBLIOG/A ADJUST WAR PROB/SOLV

BALDWIN H.W.,THE PRICE OF POWER. USA+45 FORCES PLAN NUC/PWR ADJUST COST ORD/FREE...POLICY PSY BIBLIOG 20. PAGE 5 G0089 — B47 PROB/SOLV PWR POPULISM PRICE

WHITEHEAD T.N.,LEADERSHIP IN A FREE SOCIETY; A STUDY IN HUMAN RELATIONS BASED ON AN ANALYSIS OF PRESENT-DAY INDUSTRIAL CIVILIZATION. WOR-45 STRUCT R+D LABOR LG/CO SML/CO WORKER PLAN PROB/SOLV — B47 INDUS LEAD ORD/FREE SOCIETY

TEC/DEV DRIVE...MGT 20. PAGE 63 G1234

SOUERS S.W.,"POLICY FORMULATION FOR NATIONAL SECURITY." EX/STRUC FORCES PROB/SOLV DIPLOM CONFER EXEC ARMS/CONT DETER NUC/PWR GOV/REL PEACE COLD/WAR. PAGE 52 G1022 — S49 DELIB/GP CHIEF DECISION POLICY

DEES J.W. JR.,URBAN SOCIOLOGY AND THE EMERGING ATOMIC MEGALOPOLIS. PART I. USA+45 TEC/DEV ADMIN NUC/PWR HABITAT...SOC AUD/VIS CHARTS GEN/LAWS 20 WATER. PAGE 15 G0291 — B50 PLAN NEIGH MUNIC PROB/SOLV

HUZAR E.,THE PURSE AND THE SWORD: CONTROL OF THE ARMY BY CONGRESS THROUGH MILITARY APPROPRIATIONS 1933-1950. NAT/G DELIB/GP EX/STRUC FORCES PROB/SOLV BARGAIN CONFER ADMIN ROUTINE GOV/REL EFFICIENCY ...POLICY COLD/WAR. PAGE 27 G0541 — B50 CIVMIL/REL BUDGET CONTROL LEGIS

PERKINS J.A.,"ADMINISTRATION OF THE NATIONAL SECURITY PROGRAM." USA+45 EX/STRUC FORCES ADMIN CIVMIL/REL ORD/FREE 20. PAGE 44 G0868 — S53 CONTROL GP/REL REPRESENT PROB/SOLV

SIMMONS L.W.,SOCIAL SCIENCE IN MEDICINE. USA+45 USA-45 SOCIETY CONSULT PLAN PROB/SOLV CONTROL PERS/REL...POLICY HEAL TREND BIBLIOG 20. PAGE 51 G0999 — B54 PUB/INST HABITAT HEALTH BIO/SOC

LONG N.E.,"PUBLIC POLICY AND ADMINISTRATION: THE GOALS OF RATIONALITY AND RESPONSIBILITY." EX/STRUC ADMIN LEAD 20. PAGE 34 G0676 — S54 PROB/SOLV EXEC REPRESENT

JONES J.M.,THE FIFTEEN WEEKS (FEBRUARY 21-JUNE 5, 1947). EUR+WWI USA+45 PROB/SOLV BAL/PWR...POLICY TIME/SEQ 20 COLD/WAR MARSHL/PLN TRUMAN/HS WASHING/DC. PAGE 29 G0567 — B55 DIPLOM ECO/TAC FOR/AID

SMITHIES A.,THE BUDGETARY PROCESS IN THE UNITED STATES. ECO/DEV AGRI EX/STRUC FORCES LEGIS PROB/SOLV TAX ROUTINE EFFICIENCY...MGT CONGRESS PRESIDENT. PAGE 52 G1016 — B55 NAT/G ADMIN BUDGET GOV/REL

ATOMIC INDUSTRIAL FORUM.PUBLIC RELATIONS FOR THE ATOMIC INDUSTRY. WOR+45 PLAN PROB/SOLV EDU/PROP PRESS CONFER...AUD/VIS ANTHOL 20. PAGE 4 G0077 — B56 NUC/PWR INDUS GP/REL ATTIT

REDFORD E.S.,PUBLIC ADMINISTRATION AND POLICY FORMATION: STUDIES IN OIL, GAS, BANKING, RIVER DEVELOPMENT AND CORPORATE INVESTIGATIONS. USA+45 CLIENT NAT/G ADMIN LOBBY REPRESENT GOV/REL INGP/REL EXEC 20. PAGE 46 G0908 — B56 EX/STRUC PROB/SOLV CONTROL EXEC

US DEPARTMENT OF THE ARMY.AMERICAN MILITARY HISTORY. USA+45 USA-45 EX/STRUC PROB/SOLV TEC/DEV DIPLOM NUC/PWR REV WAR WEAPON...PSY 18/20. PAGE 57 G1125 — B56 BIBLIOG FORCES NAT/G

ALMOND G.A.,"COMPARATIVE POLITICAL SYSTEMS" (BMR)" WOR+45 WOR-45 PROB/SOLV DIPLOM EFFICIENCY ...PHIL/SCI SOC METH 17/20. PAGE 3 G0046 — S56 GOV/COMP CONCPT ALL/IDEOS NAT/COMP

KNAPP D.C.,"CONGRESSIONAL CONTROL OF AGRICULTURAL CONSERVATION POLICY: A CASE STUDY OF THE APPROPRIATIONS PROCESS." DELIB/GP PLAN PROB/SOLV CONFER PARL/PROC...POLICY INT CONGRESS. PAGE 31 G0607 — S56 LEGIS AGRI BUDGET CONTROL

DUNCAN O.D.,"THE MEASUREMENT OF POPULATION DISTRIBUTION" (BMR)" WOR+45...QUANT STAT CENSUS CHARTS 20. PAGE 16 G0321 — S57 GEOG PHIL/SCI PROB/SOLV CLASSIF

TAYLOR P.S.,"THE RELATION OF RESEARCH TO LEGISLATIVE AND ADMINISTRATIVE DECISIONS." ELITES ACT/RES PLAN PROB/SOLV CONFER CHOOSE POLICY. PAGE 54 G1059 — S57 DECISION LEGIS MGT PWR

DAVIS K.C.,ADMINISTRATIVE LAW TREATISE (VOLS. I AND — B58 ADMIN

IV). NAT/G JUDGE PROB/SOLV ADJUD GP/REL 20 SUPREME/CT. PAGE 14 G0278
JURID
CT/SYS
EX/STRUC

B58
NATIONAL PLANNING ASSOCIATION,1970 WITHOUT ARMS CONTROL (PAMPHLET). WOR+45 PROB/SOLV TEC/DEV DIPLOM CONFER DETER NUC/PWR WAR...CHARTS 20 COLD/WAR. PAGE 41 G0810
ARMS/CONT
ORD/FREE
WEAPON
PREDICT

L58
FORRESTER J.W.,"INDUSTRIAL DYNAMICS* A MAJOR BREAKTHROUGH FOR DECISION MAKERS." COMPUTER OP/RES ...DECISION CONCPT NEW/IDEA. PAGE 20 G0382
INDUS
ACT/RES
MGT
PROB/SOLV

S58
DEAN B.V.,"APPLICATION OF OPERATIONS RESEARCH TO MANAGERIAL DECISION MAKING" STRATA ACT/RES PROB/SOLV ROLE...SOC PREDICT SIMUL 20. PAGE 15 G0288
DECISION
OP/RES
MGT
METH/CNCPT

S58
FOLDES L.,"UNCERTAINTY, PROBABILITY AND POTENTIAL SURPRISE." MARKET PROB/SOLV RISK PERSON...DECISION MGT HYPO/EXP GAME. PAGE 19 G0376
PROBABIL
ADMIN
ROUTINE

S58
NEWELL A.C.,"ELEMENTS OF A THEORY OF HUMAN PROBLEM SOLVING" (BMR)" TASK PERCEPT...CONCPT LOG METH/COMP LAB/EXP BIBLIOG 20. PAGE 42 G0819
PROB/SOLV
COMPUTER
COMPUT/IR
OP/RES

B59
AIR FORCE ACADEMY ASSEMBLY '59,INTERNATIONAL STABILITY AND PROGRESS (PAMPHLET). USA+45 USSR ECO/UNDEV PROB/SOLV BUDGET DIPLOM ADMIN DETER COST ATTIT...TREND 20. PAGE 2 G0030
FOR/AID
FORCES
WAR
PLAN

B59
HARVARD UNIVERSITY LAW SCHOOL,INTERNATIONAL PROBLEMS OF FINANCIAL PROTECTION AGAINST NUCLEAR RISK. WOR+45 NAT/G DELIB/GP PROB/SOLV DIPLOM CONTROL ATTIT...POLICY INT/LAW MATH 20. PAGE 25 G0488
NUC/PWR
ADJUD
INDUS
FINAN

B59
COLUMBIA U BUREAU APPL SOC R, ATTITUDES OF PROMINENT AMERICANS TOWARD "WORLD PEACE THROUGH WORLD LAW" (SUPRA-NATL ORGANIZATION FOR WAR PREVENTION). USA+45 USSR ELITES FORCES PLAN PROB/SOLV CONTROL WAR PWR...POLICY SOC QU IDEA/COMP 20 UN. PAGE 45 G0888
ATTIT
ACT/RES
INT/LAW
STAT

B59
SPANIER J.W.,THE TRUMAN-MACARTHUR CONTROVERSY AND THE KOREAN WAR. USA+45 TOP/EX PROB/SOLV LEAD ATTIT PWR...POLICY BIBLIOG/A UN. PAGE 52 G1023
CIVMIL/REL
FORCES
CHIEF
WAR

B59
U OF MICHIGAN LAW SCHOOL,ATOMS AND THE LAW. USA+45 PROVS WORKER PROB/SOLV DIPLOM ADMIN GOV/REL ANTHOL. PAGE 55 G1085
NUC/PWR
NAT/G
CONTROL
LAW

B59
VERNEY D.V.,PUBLIC ENTERPRISE IN SWEDEN. FUT SWEDEN UK INDUS POL/PAR LEGIS PROB/SOLV CAP/ISM INT/TRADE CONTROL SOCISM...MGT CONCPT NAT/COMP 20 SOCDEM/PAR CIVIL/SERV. PAGE 61 G1196
ECO/DEV
POLICY
LG/CO
NAT/G

S59
ADAMS E.W.,"A MODEL OF RISKLESS CHOICE." CREATE PROB/SOLV UTIL...PROBABIL PREDICT HYPO/EXP. PAGE 2 G0029
GAME
SIMUL
RISK
DECISION

S59
CALKINS R.D.,"THE DECISION PROCESS IN ADMINISTRATION." EX/STRUC PROB/SOLV ROUTINE MGT. PAGE 10 G0204
ADMIN
OP/RES
DECISION
CON/ANAL

S59
LEFTON M.,"DECISION MAKING IN A MENTAL HOSPITAL: REAL, PERCEIVED, AND IDEAL." R+D PUB/INST CONSULT CONFER INGP/REL PERCEPT...MODAL 20. PAGE 33 G0653
ACT/RES
PROB/SOLV
DECISION
PSY

B60
ATOMIC INDUSTRIAL FORUM,ATOMS FOR INDUSTRY: WORLD FORUM. WOR+45 FINAN COST UTIL...JURID ANTHOL 20. PAGE 4 G0080
NUC/PWR
INDUS
PLAN
PROB/SOLV

B60
CHASE S.,LIVE AND LET LIVE. USA+45 ECO/DEV PROB/SOLV TEC/DEV ECO/TAC ARMS/CONT NUC/PWR WAR NAT/LISM PEACE...GEOG TREND 20 COLD/WAR. PAGE 11 G0223
NAT/G
DIPLOM
SOCIETY
TASK

B60
JANOWITZ M.,THE PROFESSIONAL SOLDIER. CULTURE STRATA STRUCT FAM PROB/SOLV TEC/DEV COERCE WAR CIVMIL/REL NAT/LISM AGE HEREDITY ALL/VALS CONSERVE ...MGT WORSHIP. PAGE 28 G0560
FORCES
MYTH
LEAD
ELITES

B60
MORRIS W.T.,ENGINEERING ECONOMY. AUTOMAT RISK RATIONAL...PROBABIL STAT CHARTS GAME SIMUL BIBLIOG T 20. PAGE 40 G0785
OP/RES
DECISION
MGT
PROB/SOLV

B60
SILK L.S.,THE RESEARCH REVOLUTION. USA+45 FINAN CAP/ISM ECO/TAC PRICE EQUILIB PRODUC...STAT TREND CHARTS. PAGE 51 G0997
ECO/DEV
R+D
TEC/DEV
PROB/SOLV

B60
SLUCKIN W.,MINDS AND MACHINES (REV. ED.). PROB/SOLV TEC/DEV AUTOMAT TASK PERCEPT HEALTH KNOWL ...DECISION MATH PROBABIL COMPUT/IR GAME 20. PAGE 51 G1012
PSY
COMPUTER
PERSON
SIMUL

B60
US SENATE COMM ON COMMERCE,URBAN MASS TRANSPORTATION. FUT USA+45 AIR ECO/DEV FINAN LOC/G MUNIC LEGIS CREATE PROB/SOLV TEC/DEV 20 PUB/TRANS. PAGE 60 G1180
DIST/IND
PLAN
NAT/G
LAW

B61
GORDON W.J.J.,SYNECTICS; THE DEVELOPMENT OF CREATIVE CAPACITY. USA+45 PLAN TEC/DEV KNOWL WEALTH ...DECISION MGT 20. PAGE 22 G0436
CREATE
PROB/SOLV
ACT/RES
TOP/EX

B61
MICHAEL D.N.,PROPOSED STUDIES ON THE IMPLICATIONS OF PEACEFUL SPACE ACTIVITIES FOR HUMAN AFFAIRS. COM/IND INDUS FORCES DIPLOM PEACE PERSON...PSY SOC 20. PAGE 39 G0764
FUT
SPACE
ACT/RES
PROB/SOLV

B61
SMITH H.H.,THE CITIZEN'S GUIDE TO PLANNING. USA+45 LAW SCHOOL CREATE PROB/SOLV EDU/PROP GP/REL ROLE 20 URBAN/RNWL OPEN/SPACE. PAGE 52 G1015
MUNIC
PLAN
DELIB/GP
CONSULT

L61
THOMPSON V.A.,"HIERARACHY, SPECIALIZATION, AND ORGANIZATIONAL CONFLICT" (BMR)" WOR+45 STRATA STRUCT WORKER TEC/DEV GP/REL INGP/REL ATTIT AUTHORIT 20 BUREAUCRCY. PAGE 54 G1069
PERS/REL
PROB/SOLV
ADMIN
EX/STRUC

S61
ANDREWS R.B.,"URBAN ECONOMICS: AN APPRAISAL OF PROGRESS." LOC/G PROB/SOLV TEC/DEV...CONCPT OBS/ENVIR METH/COMP HYPO/EXP SOC/EXP SIMUL GEN/METH METH 20. PAGE 3 G0058
MUNIC
PHIL/SCI
ECOMETRIC

S61
DEUTSCH K.W.,"A NOTE ON THE APPEARANCE OF WISDOM IN LARGE BUREAUCRATIC ORGANIZATIONS." ROUTINE PERSON KNOWL SKILL...DECISION STAT. PAGE 15 G0299
ADMIN
PROBABIL
PROB/SOLV
SIMUL

S61
FAIR M.L.,"PORT AUTHORITIES IN THE UNITED STATES." PROB/SOLV ADMIN LEAD REPRESENT PWR...DECISION GEOG. PAGE 18 G0357
MUNIC
REGION
LOC/G
GOV/REL

S61
HAINES G.,"THE COMPUTER AS A SMALL-GROUP MEMBER." DELIB/GP BAL/PWR TASK 20. PAGE 24 G0467
INGP/REL
COMPUTER
PROB/SOLV
EFFICIENCY

S61
LYONS G.M.,"THE NEW CIVIL-MILITARY RELATIONS." USA+45 NAT/G EX/STRUC TOP/EX PROB/SOLV ADMIN EXEC PARTIC 20. PAGE 35 G0681
CIVMIL/REL
PWR
REPRESENT

S61
MANGELSDORF J.E.,"HUMAN DECISIONS IN MISSILE YSTEMS." OP/RES CHARTS. PAGE 35 G0699
DECISION
PROB/SOLV
AUTOMAT
CONTROL

B62
BAKER G.W.,BEHAVIORAL SCIENCE AND CIVIL DEFENSE.   NUC/PWR
USA+45 PROB/SOLV ADMIN GP/REL INGP/REL PERS/REL   WAR
ANOMIE DRIVE PERSON...DECISION MGT SOC 20   POLICY
CIV/DEFENS. PAGE 4 G0085   ACT/RES

B62
BENNETT J.C.,NUCLEAR WEAPONS AND THE CONFLICT OF   POLICY
CONSCIENCE. WOR+45 PROB/SOLV DIPLOM WEAPON SUPEGO   NUC/PWR
MORAL...ANTHOL WORSHIP 20. PAGE 6 G0120   WAR

B62
BENNIS W.G.,THE PLANNING OF CHANGE: READINGS IN THE   PROB/SOLV
APPLIED BEHAVIORAL SCIENCES. CULTURE STRATA STRUCT   CREATE
PLAN GP/REL...SOC T. PAGE 6 G0123   ACT/RES
                                                         OP/RES

B62
BORKOF H.,COMPUTER APPLICATIONS IN THE BEHAVIORAL   R+D
SCIENCES. AUTOMAT UTIL...DECISION PHIL/SCI PSY   COMPUTER
METH/CNCPT LING LOG MATH STYLE NET/THEORY COMPUT/IR   PROB/SOLV
PROG/TEAC SIMUL. PAGE 8 G0154   FEEDBACK

B62
BROOKINGS INSTITUTION,DEVELOPMENT OF THE EMERGING   ECO/UNDEV
COUNTRIES; AN AGENDA FOR RESEARCH. WOR+45 AGRI   R+D
TEC/DEV FOR/AID EDU/PROP ADJUST HABITAT KNOWL...PSY   SOCIETY
SOC ANTHOL 20 THIRD/WRLD. PAGE 9 G0175   PROB/SOLV

B62
CHASE S.,THE PROPER STUDY OF MANKIND (2ND REV.   PHIL/SCI
ED.). WOR+45 WOR-45 INTELL WAR...METH/CNCPT   SOC
SAMP/SIZ GEN/LAWS BIBLIOG METH 16/20. PAGE 11 G0224   PROB/SOLV
                                                         PERSON

B62
DUCKWORTH W.E.,A GUIDE TO OPERATIONAL RESEARCH.   OP/RES
INDUS PLAN PROB/SOLV EXEC EFFICIENCY PRODUC KNOWL   GAME
...MGT MATH STAT SIMUL METH 20 MONTECARLO. PAGE 16   DECISION
G0319   ADMIN

B62
FERBER R.,RESEARCH METHODS IN ECONOMICS AND   ACT/RES
BUSINESS. ECO/DEV FINAN MARKET LG/CO SML/CO CONSULT   PROB/SOLV
CONTROL COST...STAT METH/COMP 20. PAGE 19 G0364   ECO/TAC
                                                         MGT

B62
STERN A.C.,AIR POLLUTION (2 VOLS.). LAW INDUS   AIR
PROB/SOLV TEC/DEV INSPECT RISK BIO/SOC HABITAT   OP/RES
...OBS/ENVIR TESTS SAMP 20 POLLUTION. PAGE 53 G1035   CONTROL
                                                         HEALTH

B62
US SENATE COMM GOVT OPERATIONS,ADMINISTRATION OF   ORD/FREE
NATIONAL SECURITY. USA+45 CHIEF PLAN PROB/SOLV   ADMIN
TEC/DEV DIPLOM ATTIT...POLICY DECISION 20   NAT/G
KENNEDY/JF RUSK/D MCNAMARA/R BUNDY/M HERTER/C.   CONTROL
PAGE 60 G1177

B62
WALSTON H.,AGRICULTURE UNDER COMMUNISM. CHINA/COM   AGRI
COM PROB/SOLV HAPPINESS RIGID/FLEX...POLICY   MARXISM
METH/COMP 20. PAGE 62 G1207   PLAN
                                                         CREATE

S62
VIETORISZ T.,"PRELIMINARY BIBLIOGRAPHY FOR   BIBLIOG/A
INDUSTRIAL DEVELOPMENT PROGRAMMING." ECO/DEV   TEC/DEV
ECO/UNDEV R+D LABOR PROB/SOLV AUTOMAT PRODUC.   ACT/RES
PAGE 61 G1198   PLAN

B63
ACKOFF R.L.,A MANAGER'S GUIDE TO OPERATIONS   OP/RES
RESEARCH. STRUCT INDUS PROB/SOLV ROUTINE 20. PAGE 2   MGT
G0028   GP/REL
                                                         ADMIN

B63
BURSK E.C.,NEW DECISION-MAKING TOOLS FOR MANAGERS.   DECISION
COMPUTER PLAN PROB/SOLV ROUTINE COST. PAGE 10 G0194   MGT
                                                         MATH
                                                         RIGID/FLEX

B63
DEAN A.L.,FEDERAL AGENCY APPROACHES TO FIELD   ADMIN
MANAGEMENT (PAMPHLET). R+D DELIB/GP EX/STRUC   MGT
PROB/SOLV GOV/REL...CLASSIF BIBLIOG 20 FAA NASA   NAT/G
DEPT/HEW POSTAL/SYS IRS. PAGE 15 G0287   OP/RES

B63
FOSKETT D.J.,CLASSIFICATION AND INDEXING IN THE   PROB/SOLV
SOCIAL SCIENCES. WOR+45 R+D ACT/RES CREATE OP/RES   CON/ANAL
TEC/DEV AUTOMAT ROLE...SOC COMPUT/IR BIBLIOG.   CLASSIF
PAGE 20 G0384

B63
GREEN H.P.,GOVERNMENT OF THE ATOM. USA+45 LEGIS   GOV/REL
PROB/SOLV ADMIN CONTROL PWR...POLICY DECISION 20   EX/STRUC
PRESIDENT CONGRESS. PAGE 22 G0443   NUC/PWR
                                                         DELIB/GP

B63
HATHAWAY D.A.,GOVERNMENT AND AGRICULTURE: PUBLIC   AGRI
POLICY IN A DEMOCRATIC SOCIETY. USA+45 LEGIS ADMIN   GOV/REL
EXEC LOBBY REPRESENT PWR 20. PAGE 25 G0491   PROB/SOLV
                                                         EX/STRUC

B63
KAST F.E.,SCIENCE, TECHNOLOGY, AND MANAGEMENT.   MGT
SPACE USA+45 FORCES CONFER DETER NUC/PWR...PHIL/SCI   PLAN
CHARTS ANTHOL BIBLIOG 20 NASA. PAGE 30 G0581   TEC/DEV
                                                         PROB/SOLV

B63
LASSWELL H.D.,THE FUTURE OF POLITICAL SCIENCE.   CREATE
SOCIETY ECO/DEV ACADEM NAT/G PROB/SOLV...OBS   ACT/RES
SOC/INTEG. PAGE 33 G0643   FUT

B63
NASA,CONFERENCE ON SPACE, SCIENCE, AND URBAN LIFE.   MUNIC
USA+45 SOCIETY INDUS ACADEM ACT/RES ECO/TAC ADMIN   SPACE
20. PAGE 41 G0804   TEC/DEV
                                                         PROB/SOLV

B63
OTTOSON H.W.,LAND USE POLICY AND PROBLEMS IN THE   PROB/SOLV
UNITED STATES. USA+45 USA-45 LAW AGRI INDUS NAT/G   UTIL
GP/REL...CHARTS ANTHOL 19/20 HOMEST/ACT. PAGE 43   HABITAT
G0851   POLICY

S63
CLEVELAND H.,"CRISIS DIPLOMACY." USA+45 WOR+45 LAW   DECISION
FORCES TASK NUC/PWR PWR 20. PAGE 12 G0235   DIPLOM
                                                         PROB/SOLV
                                                         POLICY

S63
DUBRIDGE L.A.,"POLICY AND THE SCIENTISTS." ELITES   POLICY
PROB/SOLV ROLE KNOWL PWR. PAGE 16 G0318   PHIL/SCI
                                                         ACADEM
                                                         DECISION

S63
ENTHOVEN A.C.,"ECONOMIC ANALYSIS IN THE DEPARTMENT   PLAN
OF DEFENSE." USA+45 NAT/G DELIB/GP PROB/SOLV RATION   BUDGET
NUC/PWR WEAPON COST...DECISION 20 DEPT/DEFEN   ECO/TAC
RESOURCE/N. PAGE 18 G0349   FORCES

S63
VIETORISZ T.,"PRELIMINARY BIBLIOGRAPHY FOR   BIBLIOG/A
INDUSTRIAL DEVELOPMENT PROGRAMMING." ECO/DEV   TEC/DEV
ECO/UNDEV R+D LABOR PROB/SOLV AUTOMAT PRODUC.   ACT/RES
PAGE 61 G1199   PLAN

B64
RECENT PUBLICATIONS ON GOVERNMENTAL PROBLEMS. FINAN   BIBLIOG
INDUS ACADEM PLAN PROB/SOLV EDU/PROP ADJUD ADMIN   AUTOMAT
BIO/SOC...MGT SOC. PAGE 1 G0017   LEGIS
                                                         JURID

B64
BRIGHT J.R.,RESEARCH, DEVELOPMENT AND TECHNOLOGICAL   TEC/DEV
INNOVATION. CULTURE R+D CREATE PLAN PROB/SOLV   NEW/IDEA
AUTOMAT RISK PERSON...DECISION CONCPT PREDICT   INDUS
BIBLIOG. PAGE 9 G0168   MGT

B64
BRILLOUIN L.,SCIENTIFIC UNCERTAINTY AND   PHIL/SCI
INFORMATION. PROB/SOLV AUTOMAT PERCEPT ORD/FREE   NEW/IDEA
...MATH REGRESS STAT STYLE OBS IDEA/COMP SIMUL   METH/CNCPT
TIME. PAGE 9 G0169   CREATE

B64
FEI J.C.H.,DEVELOPMENT OF THE LABOR SURPLUS   ECO/TAC
ECONOMY: THEORY AND POLICY. WOR+45 AGRI INDUS   POLICY
MARKET PROB/SOLV TEC/DEV...STAT CHARTS GEN/LAWS   WORKER
METH 20 THIRD/WRLD. PAGE 18 G0361   ECO/UNDEV

B64
HODGETTS J.E.,ADMINISTERING THE ATOM FOR PEACE.   PROB/SOLV
OP/RES TEC/DEV ADMIN...IDEA/COMP METH/COMP 20.   NUC/PWR
PAGE 26 G0517   PEACE
                                                         MGT

B64
INST D'ETUDE POL L'U GRENOBLE,ADMINISTRATION   ADMIN
TRADITIONELLE ET PLANIFICATION REGIONALE. FRANCE   MUNIC
LAW POL/PAR PROB/SOLV ADJUST RIGID/FLEX...CHARTS   PLAN
ANTHOL BIBLIOG T 20 REFORMERS. PAGE 28 G0546   CREATE

KAUFMANN W.W.,,THE MC NAMARA STRATEGY. TOP/EX
INSPECT BAL/PWR DIPLOM CONTROL DETER GUERRILLA
NUC/PWR WEAPON COST PWR...METH/COMP 20 MCNAMARA/R
KENNEDY/JF JOHNSON/LB NATO DEPT/DEFEN. PAGE 30
G0586
B64
FORCES
WAR
PLAN
PROB/SOLV

LANG A.S.,,URBAN RAIL TRANSIT. OP/RES PLAN PROB/SOLV
TEC/DEV AUTOMAT COST...TECHNIC MATH CON/ANAL CHARTS
METH/COMP SIMUL 20 RAILROAD PUB/TRANS. PAGE 32
G0632
B64
MUNIC
DIST/IND
ECOMETRIC

MILIBAND R.,,THE SOCIALIST REGISTER: 1964. GERMANY/W
ITALY UK LABOR POL/PAR ECO/TAC FOR/AID NUC/PWR
...POLICY SOCIALIST IDEA/COMP 20 MAO NASSER/G.
PAGE 39 G0769
B64
MARXISM
SOCISM
CAP/ISM
PROB/SOLV

NASA,PROCEEDINGS OF CONFERENCE ON THE LAW OF SPACE
AND OF SATELLITE COMMUNICATIONS: CHICAGO 1963. FUT
WOR+45 DELIB/GP PROB/SOLV TEC/DEV CONFER ADJUD
NUC/PWR...POLICY IDEA/COMP 20 NASA. PAGE 41 G0805
B64
SPACE
COM/IND
LAW
DIPLOM

ORTH C.D.,,ADMINISTERING RESEARCH AND DEVELOPMENT.
FINAN PLAN PROB/SOLV ADMIN ROUTINE...METH/CNCPT
STAT CHARTS METH 20. PAGE 43 G0847
B64
MGT
R+D
LG/CO
INDUS

OSSENBECK F.J.,,OPEN SPACE AND PEACE. CHINA/COM FUT
USA+45 USSR LAW PROB/SOLV TEC/DEV EDU/PROP NEUTRAL
PEACE...AUD/VIS ANTHOL 20. PAGE 43 G0850
B64
SPACE
ORD/FREE
DIPLOM
CREATE

ROTHSCHILD J.H.,,TOMORROW'S WEAPONS: CHEMICAL AND
BIOLOGICAL. FUT PROB/SOLV ARMS/CONT PEACE MORAL
...CHARTS BIBLIOG 20. PAGE 48 G0941
B64
WAR
WEAPON
BIO/SOC
DETER

SHUBIK M.,,GAME THEORY AND RELATED APPROACHES TO
SOCIAL BEHAVIOR: SELECTIONS. INTELL SOCIETY ACT/RES
CREATE PLAN PROB/SOLV...DECISION MATH. PAGE 50
G0994
B64
SOC
SIMUL
GAME
PWR

WIRTH L.,,ON CITIES AND SOCIAL LIFE: SELECTED
PAPERS. PLAN PROB/SOLV RACE/REL CONSEN ATTIT
HABITAT PERSON...POLICY SOC CONCPT ANTHOL BIBLIOG
20. PAGE 64 G1249
B64
GEN/LAWS
SOCIETY
NEIGH
STRUCT

PLATT J.R.,,"RESEARCH AND DEVELOPMENT FOR SOCIAL
PROBLEMS." INTELL SOCIETY PROB/SOLV GP/REL ATTIT
ALL/VALS CONT/OBS. PAGE 45 G0880
S64
R+D
ACT/RES
PLAN
SOC

STONE P.A.,,"DECISION TECHNIQUES FOR TOWN
DEVELOPMENT." PLAN COST PROFIT...DECISION MGT
CON/ANAL CHARTS METH/COMP BIBLIOG 20. PAGE 53 G1039
S64
OP/RES
MUNIC
ADMIN
PROB/SOLV

ALKER H.R. JR.,,MATHEMATICS AND POLITICS. PROB/SOLV
...DECISION PHIL/SCI CLASSIF QUANT STAT GAME
GEN/LAWS INDEX. PAGE 2 G0042
B65
GEN/METH
CONCPT
MATH

ARTHUR D LITTLE INC,SAN FRANCISCO COMMUNITY RENEWAL
PROGRAM. USA+45 FINAN PROVS ADMIN INCOME...CHARTS
20 CALIFORNIA SAN/FRAN URBAN/RNWL. PAGE 4 G0071
B65
HABITAT
MUNIC
PLAN
PROB/SOLV

BENTWICH J.S.,,EDUCATION IN ISRAEL. ISRAEL CULTURE
STRATA PROB/SOLV TEC/DEV ADJUST ALL/VALS 20 JEWS.
PAGE 7 G0125
B65
SECT
EDU/PROP
ACADEM
SCHOOL

HICKMAN B.G.,,QUANTITATIVE PLANNING OF ECONOMIC
POLICY. FRANCE NETHERLAND OP/RES PRICE ROUTINE UTIL
...POLICY DECISION ECOMETRIC METH/CNCPT STAT STYLE
CHINJAP. PAGE 26 G0511
B65
PROB/SOLV
PLAN
QUANT

OECD,MEDITERRANEAN REGIONAL PROJECT: TURKEY;
EDUCATION AND DEVELOPMENT. FUT TURKEY SOCIETY
STRATA FINAN NAT/G PROF/ORG PLAN PROB/SOLV ADMIN
COST...STAT CHARTS 20 OECD. PAGE 42 G0831
B65
EDU/PROP
ACADEM
SCHOOL
ECO/UNDEV

OECD,THE MEDITERRANEAN REGIONAL PROJECT: PORTUGAL;
EDUCATION AND DEVELOPMENT. PORTUGAL SOCIETY STRATA
FINAN PROF/ORG WORKER PLAN PROB/SOLV ADMIN...POLICY
STAT CHARTS METH 20 OECD. PAGE 42 G0832
B65
EDU/PROP
SCHOOL
ACADEM
ECO/UNDEV

OECD,THE MEDITERRANEAN REGIONAL PROJECT: ITALY;
EDUCATION AND DEVELOPMENT. ITALY SOCIETY STRATA
FINAN NAT/G PROF/ORG WORKER PLAN PROB/SOLV ADMIN
...STAT CHARTS METH 20 OECD. PAGE 42 G0833
B65
SCHOOL
EDU/PROP
ECO/UNDEV
ACADEM

OECD,THE MEDITERRANEAN REGIONAL PROJECT: GREECE;
EDUCATION AND DEVELOPMENT. FUT GREECE SOCIETY AGRI
FINAN NAT/G PROF/ORG WORKER PLAN PROB/SOLV ADMIN
DEMAND ATTIT 20 OECD. PAGE 42 G0834
B65
EDU/PROP
SCHOOL
ACADEM
ECO/UNDEV

OECD,THE MEDITERRANEAN REGIONAL PROJECT: SPAIN;
EDUCATION AND DEVELOPMENT. FUT SPAIN STRATA FINAN
NAT/G WORKER PLAN PROB/SOLV ADMIN COST...POLICY
STAT CHARTS 20 OECD. PAGE 42 G0835
B65
ECO/UNDEV
EDU/PROP
ACADEM
SCHOOL

REISS A.J. JR.,,SCHOOLS IN A CHANGING SOCIETY.
CULTURE PROB/SOLV INSPECT DOMIN CONFER INGP/REL
RACE/REL AGE/C AGE/Y ALL/VALS...ANTHOL SOC/INTEG 20
NEWYORK/C. PAGE 46 G0912
B65
SCHOOL
EX/STRUC
ADJUST
ADMIN

SCHEINMAN L.,,ATOMIC ENERGY POLICY IN FRANCE UNDER
THE FOURTH REPUBLIC. FRANCE UK USA+45 ELITES
POL/PAR PLAN PROB/SOLV DIPLOM LEAD GOV/REL
...BIBLIOG 20 DEGAULLE/C. PAGE 49 G0962
B65
NUC/PWR
NAT/G
DELIB/GP
POLICY

STEINER G.A.,,THE CREATIVE ORGANIZATION. ELITES
LG/CO PLAN PROB/SOLV TEC/DEV INSPECT CAP/ISM
CONTROL EXEC PERSON...METH/COMP HYPO/EXP 20.
PAGE 52 G1034
B65
CREATE
MGT
ADMIN
SOC

WARNER A.W.,,THE IMPACT OF SCIENCE ON TECHNOLOGY.
UNIV INTELL SOCIETY NAT/G ACT/RES PLAN PROB/SOLV
BUDGET OPTIMAL GEN/METH. PAGE 62 G1214
B65
DECISION
TEC/DEV
CREATE
POLICY

WASKOW A.I.,,KEEPING THE WORLD DISARMED. AFR
GERMANY/E DIPLOM CONTROL WAR 20 UN. PAGE 62 G1218
B65
ARMS/CONT
PEACE
FORCES
PROB/SOLV

WEISNER J.B.,,WHERE SCIENCE AND POLITICS MEET.
USA+45 ECO/DEV R+D FORCES PROB/SOLV DIPLOM FOR/AID
CONTROL...PHIL/SCI PRESIDENT KENNEDY/JF JOHNSON/LB.
PAGE 63 G1228
B65
CHIEF
NAT/G
POLICY
TEC/DEV

CHU K.,,"A DYNAMIC MODEL OF THE FIRM." OP/RES
PROB/SOLV...DECISION ECOMETRIC NEW/IDEA STAT GAME
ORG/CHARTS SIMUL. PAGE 12 G0230
S65
INDUS
COMPUTER
TEC/DEV

MARTIN A.,,"PROLIFERATION." FUT WOR+45 PROB/SOLV
REGION ADJUST...PREDICT NAT/COMP UN TREATY. PAGE 36
G0712
S65
RECORD
NUC/PWR
ARMS/CONT
VOL/ASSN

ALEXANDER Y.,,INTERNATIONAL TECHNICAL ASSISTANCE
EXPERTS: A CASE STUDY OF THE U.N. EXPERIENCE.
USA+45 WOR+45 WORKER CREATE PLAN PROB/SOLV ECO/TAC
FOR/AID GIVE EDU/PROP...CHARTS BIBLIOG 20 UN.
PAGE 2 G0039
B66
SKILL
INT/ORG
TEC/DEV
CONSULT

BEATON L.,,MUST THE BOMB SPREAD? WOR+45 TEC/DEV
DIPLOM DRIVE ORD/FREE PWR...CHARTS 20. PAGE 6 G0109
B66
NUC/PWR
ARMS/CONT
PLAN
PROB/SOLV

FALK R.A.,,ON MINIMIZING THE USE OF NUCLEAR WEAPONS;
THREE ESSAYS; RESEARCH MONOGRAPH NO. 23. WOR+45
STRUCT CREATE NUC/PWR REV CONSERVE...POLICY
NET/THEORY IDEA/COMP GEN/LAWS GEN/METH. PAGE 18
G0359
B66
DIPLOM
EQUILIB
PHIL/SCI
PROB/SOLV

FEIS H.,,THE ATOMIC BOMB AND THE END OF WORLD WAR
II. FORCES PLAN PROB/SOLV DIPLOM CONFER WAR
...TIME/SEQ TREND CHINJAP PRESIDENT TIME. PAGE 19
G0362
B66
USA+45
PEACE
NUC/PWR

GLAZER M.,THE FEDERAL GOVERNMENT AND THE
UNIVERSITY. CHILE PROB/SOLV DIPLOM GIVE ADMIN WAR
...POLICY SOC 20. PAGE 21 G0421

B66
BIBLIOG/A
NAT/G
PLAN
ACADEM

GORDON G.,THE LEGISLATIVE PROCESS AND DIVIDED
GOVERNMENT; A CASE STUDY OF THE 86TH CONGRESS.
USA+45 POL/PAR PROVS PROB/SOLV BAL/PWR CHOOSE
REPRESENT EFFICIENCY ATTIT...POLICY DECISION STAT
20 CONGRESS EISNHWR/DD. PAGE 22 G0434

B66
LEGIS
HABITAT
CHIEF
NAT/G

KLOTSCHE J.M.,THE URBAN UNIVERSITY AND THE FUTURE
OF OUR CITIES. FUT USA+45 USA-45 LOC/G NEIGH GIVE
19/20. PAGE 31 G0606

B66
ACADEM
MUNIC
PROB/SOLV
TEC/DEV

KURAKOV I.G.,SCIENCE, TECHNOLOGY AND COMMUNISM;
SOME QUESTIONS OF DEVELOPMENT (TRANS. BY CARIN
DEDIJER). USSR INDUS PLAN PROB/SOLV COST PRODUC
...MGT MATH CHARTS METH 20. PAGE 32 G0626

B66
CREATE
TEC/DEV
MARXISM
ECO/TAC

MURDOCK J.C.,RESEARCH AND REGIONS. AGRI FINAN INDUS
LOC/G MUNIC NAT/G PROB/SOLV TEC/DEV ADMIN REGION
20. PAGE 40 G0796

B66
BIBLIOG
ECO/DEV
COMPUT/IR
R+D

SANFORD T.,BUT WHAT ABOUT THE PEOPLE? ACADEM SCHOOL
BUDGET TAX CONTROL SKILL WEALTH 20 NORTH/CAR.
PAGE 49 G0956

B66
EDU/PROP
PROB/SOLV
POLICY
PROVS

STONE J.J.,CONTAINING THE ARMS RACE* SOME SPECIFIC
PROPOSALS. ASIA USA+45 USSR PROB/SOLV BARGAIN
DIPLOM DETER NUC/PWR RATIONAL...GAME 20 DEPT/DEFEN
TREATY. PAGE 53 G1038

B66
ARMS/CONT
FEEDBACK
COST
ATTIT

US HOUSE COMM ON JUDICIARY,CIVIL COMMITMENT AND
TREATMENT OF NARCOTIC ADDICTS. USA+45 SOCIETY FINAN
LEGIS PROB/SOLV GIVE CT/SYS SANCTION HEALTH
...POLICY HEAL 20. PAGE 58 G1141

B66
BIO/SOC
CRIME
IDEA/COMP
CONTROL

FLEMING W.G.,"AUTHORITY, EFFICIENCY, AND ROLE
STRESS: PROBLEMS IN THE DEVELOPMENT OF EAST AFRICAN
BUREAUCRACIES." AFR UGANDA STRUCT PROB/SOLV ROUTINE
INGP/REL ROLE...MGT SOC GP/COMP GOV/COMP 20
TANGANYIKA AFRICA/E. PAGE 19 G0371

S66
DOMIN
EFFICIENCY
COLONIAL
ADMIN

RIZOS E.J.,"SCIENCE AND TECHNOLOGY IN COUNTRY
DEVELOPMENT* TOWARDS AN UNDERSTANDING OF THE ROLE
OF PUBLIC ADMINISTRATION." WOR+45 STRUCT INT/ORG
EX/STRUC CREATE PLAN PROB/SOLV EFFICIENCY ROLE
DECISION. PAGE 47 G0924

S66
ADMIN
TEC/DEV
ECO/UNDEV
PHIL/SCI

US HOUSE COMM SCI ASTRONAUT,INQUIRIES, LEGISLATION,
POLICY STUDIES RE: SCIENCE AND TECHNOLOGY: REVIEW
AND FORECAST (PAMPHLET). FUT WOR+45 DELIB/GP
PROB/SOLV...POLICY JURID TREND 20 CONGRESS. PAGE 58
G1144

N66
TEC/DEV
R+D
PLAN
LEGIS

US HOUSE COMM SCI ASTRONAUT,THE ADEQUACY OF
TECHNOLOGY FOR POLLUTION ABATEMENT (PAMPHLET).
WOR+45 PLAN PROB/SOLV CONFER ADMIN...JURID 20
POLLUTION. PAGE 58 G1145

N66
HEALTH
POLICY
TEC/DEV
LEGIS

BARANSON J.,TECHNOLOGY FOR UNDERDEVELOPED AREAS: AN
ANNOTATED BIBLIOGRAPHY. FUT WOR+45 CULTURE INDUS
INT/ORG CREATE PROB/SOLV INT/TRADE EDU/PROP AUTOMAT
...CONCPT METH. PAGE 5 G0092

B67
BIBLIOG/A
ECO/UNDEV
TEC/DEV
R+D

BERNAL J.D.,THE SOCIAL FUNCTION OF SCIENCE. WOR+45
WOR-45 R+D NAT/G PROB/SOLV DOMIN WAR...PHIL/SCI 20.
PAGE 7 G0130

B67
ROLE
TEC/DEV
SOCIETY
ADJUST

BUDER S.,PULLMAN: AN EXPERIMENT IN INDUSTRIAL ORDER
AND COMMUNITY PLANNING, 1880-1930. USA-45 SOCIETY
LABOR LG/CO CREATE PROB/SOLV CONTROL GP/REL
EFFICIENCY ATTIT...MGT BIBLIOG 19/20 PULLMAN.
PAGE 9 G0184

B67
DIST/IND
INDUS
MUNIC
PLAN

COMMONER B.,SCIENCE AND SURVIVAL. SOCIETY INDUS
PLAN NUC/PWR KNOWL PWR...SOC 20 AEC. PAGE 13 G0247

B67
PHIL/SCI
CONTROL
PROB/SOLV
EQUILIB

CROSSON F.J.,SCIENCE AND CONTEMPORARY SOCIETY. FUT
WOR+45 SECT CREATE PROB/SOLV...HUM PREDICT TREND
IDEA/COMP ANTHOL. PAGE 14 G0263

B67
PHIL/SCI
SOCIETY
TEC/DEV
CONCPT

DONALD A.G.,MANAGEMENT, INFORMATION, AND SYSTEMS.
WOR+45 LG/CO PROB/SOLV CONTROL FEEDBACK KNOWL MGT.
PAGE 16 G0306

B67
ROUTINE
TEC/DEV
CONCPT
ADMIN

ELDREDGE H.W.,TAMING MEGALOPOLIS: HOW TO MANAGE AN
URBANIZED WORLD. WOR+45 SOCIETY ECO/DEV ECO/UNDEV
NAT/G COMPUTER CREATE PARTIC EFFICIENCY WEALTH
...MGT ANTHOL. PAGE 17 G0342

B67
MUNIC
TEC/DEV
PLAN
PROB/SOLV

FIELD M.G.,SOVIET SOCIALIZED MEDICINE. USSR FINAN
R+D PROB/SOLV ADMIN SOCISM...MGT SOC CONCPT 20.
PAGE 19 G0366

B67
PUB/INST
HEALTH
NAT/G
MARXISM

HARDT J.P.,MATHEMATICS AND COMPUTERS IN SOVIET
ECONOMIC PLANNING. COM USSR OP/RES PROB/SOLV
OPTIMAL...MODAL SIMUL 20. PAGE 24 G0481

B67
PLAN
TEC/DEV
MATH
COMPUT/IR

HODGKINSON R.G.,THE ORIGINS OF THE NATIONAL HEALTH
SERVICE: THE MEDICAL SERVICES OF THE NEW POOR LAW,
1834-1871. UK INDUS MUNIC WORKER PROB/SOLV
EFFICIENCY ATTIT HEALTH WEALTH SOCISM...JURID
SOC/WK 19/20. PAGE 26 G0519

B67
HEAL
NAT/G
POLICY
LAW

MACBRIDE R.,THE AUTOMATED STATE; COMPUTER SYSTEMS
AS A NEW FORCE IN SOCIETY. FUT WOR+45 FINAN MUNIC
NAT/G WORKER PLAN TEC/DEV CONTROL PERS/REL RACE/REL
ADJUST. PAGE 35 G0685

B67
COMPUTER
AUTOMAT
PROB/SOLV
SOCIETY

MAZOUR A.G.,SOVIET ECONOMIC DEVELOPMENT: OPERATION
OUTSTRIP: 1921-1965. USSR ECO/UNDEV FINAN CHIEF
WORKER PROB/SOLV CONTROL PRODUC MARXISM...CHARTS
ORG/CHARTS 20 STALIN/J. PAGE 37 G0726

B67
ECO/TAC
AGRI
INDUS
PLAN

MCDOUGAL M.S.,THE INTERPRETATION OF AGREEMENTS AND
WORLD PUBLIC ORDER: PRINCIPLES OF CONTENT AND
PROCEDURE. WOR+45 CONSTN PROB/SOLV TEC/DEV
...CON/ANAL TREATY. PAGE 37 G0740

B67
INT/LAW
STRUCT
ECO/UNDEV
DIPLOM

MOSS F.M.,THE WATER CRISIS. PROB/SOLV CONTROL
...POLICY NEW/IDEA. PAGE 40 G0791

B67
GEOG
ACT/RES
PRODUC
WEALTH

ROTHENBERG J.,ECONOMIC EVALUATION OF URBAN RENEWAL:
CONCEPTUAL FOUNDATION OF BENEFIT-COST ANALYSIS.
USA+45 ECO/DEV NEIGH TEC/DEV ADMIN GEN/LAWS.
PAGE 48 G0940

B67
PLAN
MUNIC
PROB/SOLV
COST

SCHON D.A.,TECHNOLOGY AND CHANGE* THE NEW
HERACLITUS. TEC/DEV CONTROL COST DEMAND EFFICIENCY
RIGID/FLEX...MYTH 20. PAGE 49 G0975

B67
INDUS
PROB/SOLV
R+D
CREATE

UNESCO,PRINCIPLES AND PROBLEMS OF NATIONAL SCIENCE
POLICIES. WOR+45 ECO/DEV ECO/UNDEV R+D INT/ORG
PROB/SOLV CONFER...PHIL/SCI CHARTS 20 UNESCO UN.
PAGE 55 G1091

B67
NAT/COMP
POLICY
TEC/DEV
CREATE

UNIVERSAL REFERENCE SYSTEM,CURRENT EVENTS AND
PROBLEMS OF MODERN SOCIETY (VOLUME V). WOR+45 LOC/G
MUNIC NAT/G PLAN EDU/PROP CRIME RACE/REL WEALTH
...COMPUT/IR GEN/METH. PAGE 56 G1097

B67
BIBLIOG/A
SOCIETY
PROB/SOLV
ATTIT

US SENATE COMM AERO SPACE SCI,APOLLO ACCIDENT
(PARTS 1-7). USA+45 DELIB/GP LEGIS...INT CHARTS
NASA. PAGE 60 G1173

B67
PROB/SOLV
SPACE
BUDGET
GOV/REL

US SENATE COMM ON FOREIGN REL,TREATY ON OUTER
SPACE. WOR+45 AIR FORCES PROB/SOLV NUC/PWR SENATE
TREATY UN. PAGE 60 G1182

B67
SPACE
DIPLOM
ARMS/CONT
LAW

US SENATE COMM ON FOREIGN REL,UNITED STATES
ARMAMENT AND DISARMAMENT PROBLEMS. USA+45 AIR
BAL/PWR DIPLOM FOR/AID NUC/PWR ORD/FREE SENATE
TREATY. PAGE 60 G1184

B67
ARMS/CONT
WEAPON
FORCES
PROB/SOLV

WOODRUFF W.,IMPACT OF WESTERN MAN. ECO/DEV INDUS
CREATE PLAN PROB/SOLV COLONIAL GOV/REL...CHARTS
GOV/COMP BIBLIOG 18/20. PAGE 64 G1256

B67
EUR+WWI
MOD/EUR
CAP/ISM

CARMICHAEL D.M.,"FORTY YEARS OF WATER POLLUTION
CONTROL IN WISCONSIN: A CASE STUDY." LAW EXTR/IND
INDUS MUNIC DELIB/GP PLAN PROB/SOLV SANCTION
...CENSUS CHARTS 20 WISCONSIN. PAGE 11 G0207

L67
HEALTH
CONTROL
ADMIN
ADJUD

SEABERG G.P.,"THE DRUG ABUSE PROBLEMS AND SOME
PROPOSALS." UK USA+45 MARKET SANCTION CRIME
...POLICY NEW/IDEA. PAGE 50 G0986

L67
BIO/SOC
LAW
ADJUD
PROB/SOLV

ALBAUM G.,"INFORMATION FLOW AND DECENTRALIZED
DECISION MAKING IN MARKETING." EX/STRUC COMPUTER
OP/RES PROB/SOLV EFFICIENCY OPTIMAL...METH/COMP
ORG/CHARTS 20. PAGE 2 G0033

S67
LG/CO
ROUTINE
KNOWL
MARKET

ALLEE D.,"AMERICAN AGRICULTURE - ITS RESOURCE
ISSUES FOR THE COMING YEARS." FUT USA+45 PLAN
PROB/SOLV 20. PAGE 2 G0043

S67
AGRI
SOCIETY
EFFICIENCY
AUTOMAT

ATKIN J.M.,"THE FEDERAL GOVERNMENT, BIG BUSINESS,
AND COLLEGES OF EDUCATION." PROF/ORG CONSULT CREATE
PLAN PROB/SOLV ADMIN EFFICIENCY. PAGE 4 G0075

S67
SCHOOL
ACADEM
NAT/G
INDUS

BRETNOR R.,"DESTRUCTIVE FORCE AND THE MILITARY
EQUATIONS." UNIV COMPUTER PLAN PROB/SOLV AUTOMAT
CONTROL COERCE DETER NUC/PWR WEAPON DRIVE PWR.
PAGE 9 G0166

S67
FORCES
TEC/DEV
DOMIN
WAR

BRUNHILD G.,"THEORY OF 'TECHNICAL UNEMPLOYMENT'."
ECO/DEV ACT/RES PROB/SOLV DEMAND PRODUC...PHIL/SCI
20. PAGE 9 G0182

S67
WORKER
TEC/DEV
SKILL
INDUS

CARROLL K.J.,"SECOND STEP TOWARD ARMS CONTROL."
WOR+45 INT/ORG VOL/ASSN FORCES PROB/SOLV RISK
WEAPON 20 COLD/WAR. PAGE 11 G0215

S67
ARMS/CONT
DIPLOM
PLAN
NUC/PWR

CONWAY J.E.,"MAKING RESEARCH EFFECTIVE IN
LEGISLATION." LAW R+D CONSULT EX/STRUC PLAN CONFER
ADMIN LEAD ROUTINE TASK INGP/REL DECISION. PAGE 13
G0252

S67
ACT/RES
POLICY
LEGIS
PROB/SOLV

DE NEUFVILLE R.,"EDUCATION AT THE ACADEMIES."
USA+45 ELITES CONSULT EX/STRUC COMPUTER PLAN
PROB/SOLV TASK CIVMIL/REL ORD/FREE 20. PAGE 15
G0286

S67
FORCES
ACADEM
TEC/DEV
SKILL

EDMONDS M.,"INTERNATIONAL COLLABORATION IN WEAPONS
PROCUREMENT* THE IMPLICATIONS OF THE ANGLO-FRENCH
CASE." FRANCE UK CONSULT OP/RES PROB/SOLV TEC/DEV
CONFER CONTROL EFFICIENCY 20. PAGE 17 G0334

S67
DIPLOM
VOL/ASSN
BAL/PWR
ARMS/CONT

HARRIS F.R.,"POLITICAL SCIENCE AND THE PROPOSAL FOR
A NATIONAL SOCIAL SCIENCE FOUNDATION." FUT CONSULT
DELIB/GP PLAN PROB/SOLV BUDGET CONFER SANCTION
CRIME...POLICY SOC/WK 20 NSF NSSF. PAGE 25 G0484

S67
PROF/ORG
R+D
CREATE
NAT/G

HARTIGAN R.S.,"NONCOMBAT IMMUNITY* REFLECTIONS ON
ITS ORIGINS AND PRESENT STATUS." WOR+45 PROB/SOLV
WAR PRIVIL MORAL...POLICY 20. PAGE 25 G0487

S67
INT/LAW
NUC/PWR
ARMS/CONT
DIPLOM

HILL R.,"SOCIAL ASPECTS OF FAMILY PLANNING." INDIA
KOREA TAIWAN ECO/UNDEV PLAN PROB/SOLV TEC/DEV
EDU/PROP CONTROL ATTIT DRIVE...HEAL PSY SOC 20
BIRTH/CON UN. PAGE 26 G0512

S67
FAM
BIO/SOC
GEOG
MARRIAGE

HOFFER J.R.,"RELATIONSHIP OF NATURAL AND SOCIAL
SCIENCES TO SOCIAL PROBLEMS AND CONTRIBUTION OF...
SCIENTISTS TO SOLUTIONS." USA+45 COMPUTER TEC/DEV
GP/REL KNOWL...SOC TREND. PAGE 26 G0521

S67
PROB/SOLV
SOCIETY
INTELL
ACT/RES

INGLIS D.R.,"PROSPECTS AND PROBLEMS: THE
NONMILITARY USES OF NUCLEAR EXPLOSIVES." CREATE
PROB/SOLV TEC/DEV AGREE PEACE...INT/LAW PHIL/SCI
NEW/IDEA 20 TREATY. PAGE 28 G0545

S67
NUC/PWR
INDUS
ARMS/CONT
EXTR/IND

JAIN G.,"INDIA REJECTS THE POWER RACE* REALISM
ABOUT NUCLEAR WEAPONS." FORCES PROB/SOLV FOR/AID
ARMS/CONT COST PWR...GOV/COMP 20. PAGE 28 G0556

S67
INDIA
CHINA/COM
NUC/PWR
DIPLOM

JOHNSTON D.M.,"LAW, TECHNOLOGY AND THE SEA." WOR+45
PLAN PROB/SOLV TEC/DEV CONFER ADJUD ORD/FREE
...POLICY JURID. PAGE 29 G0564

S67
INT/LAW
INT/ORG
DIPLOM
NEUTRAL

KAYSEN C.,"DATA BANKS AND DOSSIERS." FUT USA+45
COM/IND NAT/G PLAN PROB/SOLV TEC/DEV BUDGET ADMIN
ROUTINE. PAGE 30 G0588

S67
CENTRAL
EFFICIENCY
CENSUS
ACT/RES

KRAUS J.,"A MARXIST IN GHANA." GHANA ELITES CHIEF
PROB/SOLV TEC/DEV DIPLOM ECO/TAC COLONIAL PARTIC
PWR 20 NKRUMAH/K. PAGE 31 G0618

S67
MARXISM
PLAN
ATTIT
CREATE

LAY S.H.,"EXCLUSIVE GOVERNMENTAL LIABILITY FOR
SPACE ACCIDENTS." USA+45 LAW FINAN SERV/IND TEC/DEV
ADJUD. PAGE 33 G0646

S67
NAT/G
SUPEGO
SPACE
PROB/SOLV

MALONE D.K.,"THE COMMANDER AND THE COMPUTER."
USA+45 OP/RES PROB/SOLV TEC/DEV AUTOMAT CENTRAL 20.
PAGE 35 G0698

S67
COMPUTER
FORCES
ELITES
PLAN

MCNAMARA R.L.,"THE NEED FOR INNOVATIVENESS IN
DEVELOPING SOCIETIES." L/A+17C EDU/PROP ADMIN LEAD
WEALTH...POLICY PSY SOC METH 20 COLOMB. PAGE 38
G0747

S67
PROB/SOLV
PLAN
ECO/UNDEV
NEW/IDEA

MYERS S.,"TECHNOLOGY AND URBAN TRANSIT: THE
ENORMOUS POTENTIAL OF BUS AND RAIL SYSTEMS." USA+45
FINAN LOC/G MUNIC WORKER PLAN PROB/SOLV PRICE
AUTOMAT 20. PAGE 40 G0798

S67
R+D
TEC/DEV
DIST/IND
ACT/RES

RICHMAN B.M.,"SOVIET MANAGEMENT IN TRANSITION."
USSR FINAN MARKET EX/STRUC PLAN PROB/SOLV TEC/DEV
CONTROL LEAD CENTRAL EFFICIENCY...METH/COMP 20
REFORMERS. PAGE 47 G0917

S67
MGT
MARXISM
POLICY
AUTHORIT

ROBERTS E.B.,"THE PROBLEM OF AGING ORGANIZATIONS."
INTELL PROB/SOLV ADMIN EXEC FEEDBACK EFFICIENCY
PRODUC...GEN/LAWS 20. PAGE 47 G0926

S67
INDUS
R+D
MGT
PLAN

ROBINSON J.A.T.,"ABORTION* THE CASE FOR A FREE
DECISION." LAW PROB/SOLV SANCTION ATTIT MORAL...PSY
IDEA/COMP 20 ABORTION. PAGE 47 G0930

S67
PLAN
ILLEGIT
SEX
HEALTH

ROMANIECKI L.,"THE ATOM AND INTERNATIONAL
COOPERATION." PROB/SOLV DIPLOM PEACE ORD/FREE 20.
PAGE 47 G0933

S67
INT/ORG
NUC/PWR
ARMS/CONT
CONTROL

ROTHSTEIN R.L.,"NUCLEAR PROLIFERATION AND AMERICAN
POLICY." PROB/SOLV BAL/PWR DIPLOM ARMS/CONT
EFFICIENCY 20. PAGE 48 G0942

S67
NUC/PWR
CONTROL
DETER
WOR+45

SCHACTER O.,"SCIENTIFIC ADVANCES AND INTERNATIONAL LAWMAKING." FUT R+D PLAN PROB/SOLV CONFER CONTROL ...POLICY PREDICT 20 UN. PAGE 49 G0961
S67 TEC/DEV INT/LAW INT/ORG ACT/RES

SHARP G.,"THE NEED OF A FUNCTIONAL SUBSTITUTE FOR WAR." FUT UNIV WOR+45 CULTURE SOCIETY INT/ORG CONSULT DELIB/GP ACT/RES CREATE BAL/PWR CONFER ARMS/CONT NUC/PWR 20. PAGE 50 G0989
S67 PEACE WAR DIPLOM PROB/SOLV

SKOLNIKOFF E.B.,"MAKING FOREIGN POLICY" PROB/SOLV EFFICIENCY PERCEPT PWR...MGT METH/CNCPT CLASSIF 20. PAGE 51 G1009
S67 TEC/DEV CONTROL USA+45 NAT/G

WEINBERG A.M.,"CAN TECHNOLOGY REPLACE SOCIAL ENGINEERING?" SPACE USA+45 SOCIETY ACADEM GP/REL. PAGE 62 G1224
S67 TEC/DEV ACT/RES PROB/SOLV INTELL

WINSTON O.,"AN URBANIZATION PATTERN FOR THE US* SOME CONSIDERATIONS FOR THE DECENTRALIZATION OF EXCELLENCE." FUT SOCIETY ECO/DEV R+D NEIGH ACT/RES PROB/SOLV TEC/DEV. PAGE 64 G1247
S67 USA+45 MUNIC PLAN HABITAT

WINTHROP H.,"THE MEANING OF DECENTRALIZATION FOR TWENTIETH-CENTURY MAN." FUT WOR+45 SOCIETY TEC/DEV. PAGE 64 G1248
S67 ADMIN STRUCT CENTRAL PROB/SOLV

PRINCETON U INDUSTRIAL REL SEC,COLLECTIVE BARGAINING IN THE PUBLIC SCHOOLS (PAMPHLET NO. 33). USA+45 LABOR PROB/SOLV PWR MGT. PAGE 45 G0891
N67 BIBLIOG/A SCHOOL BARGAIN GP/REL

US SENATE COMM AERO SPACE SCI,AERONAUTICAL RESEARCH AND DEVELOPMENT POLICY; HEARINGS, COMM ON AERONAUTICAL AND SPACE SCIENCES...1967 (PAMPHLET). R+D PROB/SOLV EXEC GOV/REL 20 DEPT/DEFEN FAA NASA CONGRESS. PAGE 60 G1174
N67 DIST/IND SPACE NAT/G PLAN

US SENATE COMM ON FOREIGN REL,SURVEY OF THE ALLIANCE FOR PROGRESS; THE POLITICAL ASPECTS (PAMPHLET). CONSTN SOCIETY ECO/UNDEV INT/ORG TEC/DEV DIPLOM...CENSUS 20. PAGE 60 G1186
N67 L/A+17C POLICY PROB/SOLV

GALLAHER A. JR.,PERSPECTIVES IN DEVELOPMENTAL CHANGE. MUNIC PLAN INSPECT EDU/PROP...POLICY DECISION GEOG PSY SOC IDEA/COMP ANTHOL 20 MODERNIZE. PAGE 21 G0405
B68 TECHNIC TEC/DEV PROB/SOLV CREATE

PROBABIL....PROBABILITY; SEE ALSO GAMBLE

BAVELAS A.,"COMMUNICATION PATTERNS IN TASK-ORIENTED GROUPS" (BMR)" R+D OP/RES INSPECT LEAD CENTRAL EFFICIENCY HAPPINESS RIGID/FLEX...PROBABIL 20. PAGE 6 G0106
S50 ACT/RES PERS/REL TASK INGP/REL

MCKINNEY E.R.,A BIBLIOGRAPHY OF CYBERNETICS AND INFORMATION THEORY. COMPUTER OP/RES...DECISION PHIL/SCI PSY LING LOG MATH PROBABIL GAME 20. PAGE 38 G0743
B57 BIBLIOG/A FEEDBACK SIMUL CONTROL

FOLDES L.,"UNCERTAINTY, PROBABILITY AND POTENTIAL SURPRISE." MARKET PROB/SOLV RISK PERSON...DECISION MGT HYPO/EXP GAME. PAGE 19 G0376
S58 PROBABIL ADMIN ROUTINE

ADAMS E.W.,"A MODEL OF RISKLESS CHOICE." CREATE PROB/SOLV UTIL...PROBABIL PREDICT HYPO/EXP. PAGE 2 G0029
S59 GAME SIMUL RISK DECISION

MORRIS W.T.,ENGINEERING ECONOMY. AUTOMAT RISK RATIONAL...PROBABIL STAT CHARTS GAME SIMUL BIBLIOG T 20. PAGE 40 G0785
B60 OP/RES DECISION MGT PROB/SOLV

SLUCKIN W.,MINDS AND MACHINES (REV. ED.). PROB/SOLV TEC/DEV AUTOMAT TASK PERCEPT HEALTH KNOWL ...DECISION MATH PROBABIL COMPUT/IR GAME 20.
B60 PSY COMPUTER PERSON

PAGE 51 G1012
SIMUL

DEUTSCH K.W.,"A NOTE ON THE APPEARANCE OF WISDOM IN LARGE BUREAUCRATIC ORGANIZATIONS." ROUTINE PERSON KNOWL SKILL...DECISION STAT. PAGE 15 G0299
S61 ADMIN PROBABIL PROB/SOLV SIMUL

BONINI C.P.,SIMULATION OF INFORMATION AND DECISION SYSTEMS IN THE FIRM. MARKET BUDGET DOMIN EDU/PROP ADMIN COST ATTIT HABITAT PERCEPT PWR...CONCPT PROBABIL QUANT PREDICT HYPO/EXP BIBLIOG. PAGE 8 G0152
B63 INDUS SIMUL DECISION MGT

COOMBS C.H.,A THEORY OF DATA....MGT PHIL/SCI SOC CLASSIF MATH PROBABIL STAT QU. PAGE 13 G0254
B64 CON/ANAL GEN/METH TESTS PSY

FINK C.F.,"MORE CALCULATIONS ABOUT DETERRENCE." DRIVE...PHIL/SCI PSY STAT TIME/SEQ GAME GEN/LAWS. PAGE 19 G0367
B65 DETER RECORD PROBABIL IDEA/COMP

BERND J.L.,MATHEMATICAL APPLICATIONS IN POLITICAL SCIENCE, II. COMPUTER...PROBABIL STAT CHARTS. PAGE 7 G0131
B66 METH MATH METH/CNCPT

BRODIE B.,ESCALATION AND THE NUCLEAR OPTION. ASIA CUBA EUR+WWI KOREA USA+45 USSR VIETNAM RISK ATTIT DRIVE PERCEPT PROBABIL. PAGE 9 G0172
B66 NUC/PWR GUERRILLA WAR DETER

KUENNE R.E.,THE POLARIS MISSILE STRIKE* A GENERAL ECONOMIC SYSTEMS ANALYSIS. USA+45 USSR NAT/G BAL/PWR ARMS/CONT WAR...MATH PROBABIL COMPUT/IR CHARTS HYPO/EXP SIMUL. PAGE 32 G0625
B66 NUC/PWR FORCES DETER DIPLOM

BROWN W.B.,"MODEL-BUILDING AND ORGANIZATIONS." CONTROL FEEDBACK...PROBABIL CHARTS METH/COMP. PAGE 9 G0179
S67 MGT ADMIN GAME COMPUTER

PROBLEM SOLVING....SEE PROB/SOLV

PROC/MFG....PROCESSING OR MANUFACTURING INDUSTRIES

LAWRENCE S.A.,THE BATTERY ADDITIVE CONTROVERSY (PAMPHLET). USA+45 LAW MARKET PROC/MFG R+D CAP/ISM CT/SYS GOV/REL OWN FTC CONGRESS BUR/STNDRD RITCHIE/JM. PAGE 33 G0645
N19 PHIL/SCI LOBBY INSPECT

COCH L.,"OVERCOMING RESISTANCE TO CHANGE" (BMR)" USA+45 CONSULT ADMIN ROUTINE GP/REL EFFICIENCY PRODUC PERCEPT SKILL...CHARTS SOC/EXP 20. PAGE 12 G0236
S48 WORKER OP/RES PROC/MFG RIGID/FLEX

DUBIN R.,THE WORLD OF WORK: INDUSTRIAL SOCIETY AND HUMAN RELATIONS. MARKET PROC/MFG LABOR TEC/DEV CAP/ISM AUTOMAT TASK GP/REL EFFICIENCY...CONCPT CHARTS BIBLIOG 20. PAGE 16 G0317
B58 WORKER ECO/TAC PRODUC DRIVE

APTHEKER H.,DISARMAMENT AND THE AMERICAN ECONOMY: A SYMPOSIUM. FUT USA+45 ECO/DEV DIST/IND FINAN INDUS PROC/MFG LABOR NAT/G POL/PAR CONSULT PLAN CAP/ISM INT/TRADE PEACE ATTIT MORAL WEALTH...TREND GEN/LAWS TOT/POP 20. PAGE 3 G0063
B60 MARXIST ARMS/CONT

BROUDE H.W.,STEEL DECISIONS AND THE NATIONAL ECONOMY. USA+45 LG/CO PLAN ADMIN COST DECISION. PAGE 9 G0176
B63 PROC/MFG NAT/G CONTROL ECO/TAC

KAWALKOWSKI A.,"POUR UNE EUROPE INDEPENDENTE ET REUNIFIEE." EUR+WWI FUT USA+45 USSR WOR+45 ECO/DEV PROC/MFG INT/ORG NAT/G ACT/RES TEC/DEV FEDERAL RIGID/FLEX...CONCPT METH/CNCPT OEEC TOT/POP 20 DEGAULLE/C. PAGE 30 G0587
S63 R+D PLAN NUC/PWR

ORGANIZATION AMERICAN STATES,ECONOMIC SURVEY OF
B64 ECO/UNDEV

LATIN AMERICA, 1962. L/A+17C AGRI DIST/IND INDUS MARKET PROC/MFG R+D PLAN TEC/DEV ECO/TAC REGION BAL/PAY ALL/VALS...CON/ANAL ORG/CHARTS GEN/METH OAS 20. PAGE 43 G0844 — CHARTS

S64
MUMFORD L.,"AUTHORITARIAN AND DEMOCRATIC TECHNIQUES." INDUS PROC/MFG LG/CO SML/CO CREATE PLAN KNOWL...POLICY TREND WORK 20. PAGE 40 G0794 — ECO/DEV TEC/DEV

S65
DEAN B.V.,"CONTRACT RESEARCH PROPOSAL PREPARATION STRATEGIES." ECO/TAC WEALTH...MGT SIMUL. PAGE 15 G0289 — USA+45 PROC/MFG R+D PLAN

B66
YOUNG W.,EXISTING MECHANISMS OF ARMS CONTROL. PROC/MFG OP/RES DIPLOM TASK CENTRAL...MGT TREATY. PAGE 65 G1266 — ARMS/CONT ADMIN NUC/PWR ROUTINE

B67
US SENATE COMM ON FOREIGN REL,ARMS SALES TO NEAR EAST AND SOUTH ASIAN COUNTRIES. INDIA IRAN PAKISTAN WOR+45 PROC/MFG BAL/PWR DIPLOM...DECISION SENATE. PAGE 60 G1183 — WEAPON FOR/AID FORCES POLICY

L67
NADER R.,"AUTOMOBILE DESIGN AND THE JUDICIAL PROCESS." USA+45 CT/SYS SUPEGO JURID. PAGE 40 G0799 — LAW ADJUD TEC/DEV PROC/MFG

S67
BARRO S.,"ECONOMIC IMPACT OF SPACE EXPENDITURES: SOME BROAD ISSUES DEALING WITH COSTS AND BENEFITS." USA+45 PROC/MFG R+D LG/CO CONSULT COST PRODUC 20. PAGE 5 G0098 — SPACE FINAN ECO/TAC NAT/G

S67
SCOVILLE W.J.,"GOVERNMENT REGULATION AND GROWTH IN THE FRENCH PAPER INDUSTRY DURING THE EIGHTEENTH CENTURY." FRANCE MOD/EUR FINAN CAP/ISM TAX ADMIN CONTROL PRIVIL LAISSEZ...POLICY 18. PAGE 50 G0985 — NAT/G PROC/MFG ECO/DEV INGP/REL

PROCEDURAL SYSTEMS....SEE ROUTINE, ALSO PROCESSES AND PRACTICES INDEX

PROCESSING OR MANUFACTURING INDUSTRY....SEE PROC/MFG

PRODUC....PRODUCTIVITY; SEE ALSO PLAN

B
BRITISH COMMONWEALTH BUR AGRI,WORLD AGRICULTURAL ECONOMICS AND RURAL SOCIOLOGY ABSTRACTS. NAT/G OP/RES PLAN TEC/DEV LEAD PRODUC...GEOG MGT NAT/COMP 20. PAGE 9 G0170 — BIBLIOG/A AGRI SOC WORKER

N19
DOTSON A.,PRODUCTION PLANNING IN THE PATENT OFFICE (PAMPHLET). USA+45 DIST/IND PROB/SOLV PRODUC...MGT PHIL/SCI 20 BUR/BUDGET PATENT/OFF. PAGE 16 G0309 — EFFICIENCY PLAN NAT/G ADMIN

B37
GULICK L.,PAPERS ON THE SCIENCE OF ADMINISTRATION. INDUS PROB/SOLV TEC/DEV COST EFFICIENCY PRODUC HABITAT...PHIL/SCI METH/COMP 20. PAGE 23 G0461 — OP/RES CONTROL ADMIN MGT

B46
WILCOX J.K.,OFFICIAL DEFENSE PUBLICATIONS, 1941-1945 (NINE VOLS.). USA-45 AGRI INDUS R+D LABOR FORCES TEC/DEV EFFICIENCY PRODUC SKILL WEALTH 20. PAGE 63 G1238 — BIBLIOG/A WAR CIVMIL/REL ADMIN

B48
METZLER L.A.,INCOME, EMPLOYMENT, AND PUBLIC POLICY. FINAN INDUS LOC/G NAT/G TAX GIVE PAY COST PRODUC ...MGT TIME/SEQ 20. PAGE 38 G0760 — INCOME WEALTH POLICY ECO/TAC

S48
COCH L.,"OVERCOMING RESISTANCE TO CHANGE" (BMR)." USA+45 CONSULT ADMIN ROUTINE GP/REL EFFICIENCY PRODUC PERCEPT SKILL...CHARTS SOC/EXP 20. PAGE 12 G0236 — WORKER OP/RES PROC/MFG RIGID/FLEX

B50
US DEPARTMENT OF STATE,POINT FOUR: COOPERATIVE PROGRAM FOR AID IN THE DEVELOPMENT OF ECONOMICALLY UNDERDEVELOPED AREAS. WOR+45 AGRI INDUS INT/ORG PLAN TEC/DEV DIPLOM EDU/PROP ADMIN PEACE PRODUC WEALTH 20 CONGRESS UN. PAGE 57 G1121 — ECO/UNDEV FOR/AID FINAN INT/TRADE

C51
HOMANS G.C.,"THE WESTERN ELECTRIC RESEARCHES" IN S. HOSLETT, ED.," HUMAN FACTORS IN MANAGEMENT (BMR)" ACT/RES GP/REL HAPPINESS PRODUC DRIVE...MGT OBS 20. PAGE 27 G0526 — OP/RES EFFICIENCY SOC/EXP WORKER

B53
ROBINSON E.A.G.,THE STRUCTURE OF COMPETITIVE INDUSTRY. UK ECO/DEV DIST/IND MARKET TEC/DEV DIPLOM EDU/PROP ADMIN EFFICIENCY WEALTH...MGT 19/20. PAGE 47 G0929 — INDUS PRODUC WORKER OPTIMAL

B55
RILEY V.,INTERINDUSTRY ECONOMIC STUDIES. USA+45 COMPUTER ADMIN OPTIMAL PRODUC...MGT CLASSIF STAT. PAGE 47 G0922 — BIBLIOG ECO/DEV PLAN STRUCT

B57
GOLD N.L.,REGIONAL ECONOMIC DEVELOPMENT AND NUCLEAR POWER IN INDIA. FUT INDIA FINAN FOR/AID INT/TRADE BAL/PAY EFFICIENCY OPTIMAL PRODUC WEALTH...PREDICT 20. PAGE 22 G0424 — ECO/UNDEV TEC/DEV NUC/PWR INDUS

B58
CHEEK G.,ECONOMIC AND SOCIAL IMPLICATIONS OF AUTOMATION: A BIBLIOGRAPHIC REVIEW (PAMPHLET). USA+45 LG/CO WORKER CREATE PLAN CONTROL ROUTINE PERS/REL EFFICIENCY PRODUC...METH/COMP 20. PAGE 12 G0225 — BIBLIOG/A SOCIETY INDUS AUTOMAT

B58
DUBIN R.,THE WORLD OF WORK: INDUSTRIAL SOCIETY AND HUMAN RELATIONS. MARKET PROC/MFG LABOR TEC/DEV CAP/ISM AUTOMAT TASK GP/REL EFFICIENCY...CONCPT CHARTS BIBLIOG 20. PAGE 16 G0317 — WORKER ECO/TAC PRODUC DRIVE

B58
MARCUSE H.,SOVIET MARXISM, A CRITICAL ANALYSIS. USSR CONSTN PLAN PRODUC RATIONAL SOCISM...IDEA/COMP 20 COM/PARTY. PAGE 36 G0703 — MARXISM ATTIT POLICY

B59
MAYDA J.,ATOMIC ENERGY AND LAW. ECO/UNDEV FINAN TEC/DEV FOR/AID EFFICIENCY PRODUC WEALTH...POLICY TECHNIC 20. PAGE 37 G0723 — NUC/PWR L/A+17C LAW ADMIN

B60
SILK L.S.,THE RESEARCH REVOLUTION. USA+45 FINAN CAP/ISM ECO/TAC PRICE EQUILIB PRODUC...STAT TREND CHARTS. PAGE 51 G0997 — ECO/DEV R+D TEC/DEV PROB/SOLV

B61
NOVE A.,THE SOVIET ECONOMY. USSR ECO/DEV FINAN NAT/G ECO/TAC PRICE ADMIN EFFICIENCY MARXISM ...TREND BIBLIOG 20. PAGE 42 G0828 — PLAN PRODUC POLICY

B62
CLARKE A.C.,PROFILES OF THE FUTURE; AN INQUIRY INTO THE LIMITS OF THE POSSIBLE. COM/IND DIST/IND PRODUC AGE PERCEPT...TECHNIC NEW/IDEA TIME. PAGE 12 G0232 — FUT TEC/DEV PREDICT SPACE

B62
DUCKWORTH W.E.,A GUIDE TO OPERATIONAL RESEARCH. INDUS PLAN PROB/SOLV EXEC EFFICIENCY PRODUC KNOWL ...MGT MATH STAT SIMUL METH 20 MONTECARLO. PAGE 16 G0319 — OP/RES GAME DECISION ADMIN

B62
MARTINS A.F.,REVOLUCAO BRANCA NO CAMPO. L/A+17C SERV/IND DEMAND EFFICIENCY PRODUC...POLICY METH/COMP. PAGE 36 G0717 — AGRI ECO/UNDEV TEC/DEV NAT/COMP

S62
VIETORISZ T.,"PRELIMINARY BIBLIOGRAPHY FOR INDUSTRIAL DEVELOPMENT PROGRAMMING." ECO/DEV ECO/UNDEV R+D LABOR PROB/SOLV AUTOMAT PRODUC. PAGE 61 G1198 — BIBLIOG/A TEC/DEV ACT/RES PLAN

C62
JOINT ECONOMIC COMMITTEE,"DIMENSIONS OF SOVIET ECONOMIC POWER." USSR R+D FORCES ACT/RES OP/RES TEC/DEV...GEOG STAT BIBLIOG 20. PAGE 29 G0565 — ECO/DEV PLAN PRODUC LABOR

B63
LITTERER J.A.,ORGANIZATIONS: STRUCTURE AND BEHAVIOR. PLAN DOMIN CONTROL LEAD ROUTINE SANCTION INGP/REL EFFICIENCY PRODUC DRIVE RIGID/FLEX PWR. PAGE 34 G0674 — ADMIN CREATE MGT ADJUST

RAUDSEPP E.,MANAGING CREATIVE SCIENTISTS AND
ENGINEERS. USA+45 ECO/DEV LG/CO GP/REL PERS/REL
PRODUC. PAGE 46 G0906

B63
MGT
CREATE
R+D
ECO/TAC

THORELLI H.B.,INTOP: INTERNATIONAL OPERATIONS
SIMULATION: PLAYER'S MANUAL. BRAZIL FINAN OP/RES
ADMIN GP/REL INGP/REL PRODUC PERCEPT...DECISION MGT
EEC. PAGE 54 G1073

B63
GAME
INT/TRADE
EDU/PROP
LG/CO

US ATOMIC ENERGY COMMISSION,ATOMIC ENERGY IN THE
SOVIET UNION: TRIP REPORT OF THE US ATOMIC ENERGY
DELEGATION, MAY 1933. USSR R+D NAT/G CONSULT CREATE
DIPLOM ADMIN ROUTINE EFFICIENCY PRODUC KNOWL SKILL
...NAT/COMP 20 AEC TRAVEL TREATY. PAGE 56 G1107

B63
METH/COMP
OP/RES
TEC/DEV
NUC/PWR

VIETORISZ T.,"PRELIMINARY BIBLIOGRAPHY FOR
INDUSTRIAL DEVELOPMENT PROGRAMMING." ECO/DEV
ECO/UNDEV R+D LABOR PROB/SOLV AUTOMAT PRODUC.
PAGE 61 G1199

S63
BIBLIOG/A
TEC/DEV
ACT/RES
PLAN

MANSFIELD E.,MONOPOLY POWER AND ECONOMIC
PERFORMANCE: AN INTRODUCTION TO A CURRENT ISSUE OF
PUBLIC POLICY. ECO/DEV INDUS NAT/G PLAN CAP/ISM
PRICE CONTROL LOBBY EFFICIENCY PRODUC...POLICY 20
CONGRESS KENNEDY/JF MONOPOLY. PAGE 36 G0701

B64
LG/CO
PWR
ECO/TAC
MARKET

BARISH N.N.,MANAGEMENT SCIENCES IN THE EMERGING
COUNTRIES. AFR CHINA/COM WOR+45 FINAN INDUS PLAN
PRODUC HABITAT...ANTHOL 20. PAGE 5 G0093

B65
ECO/UNDEV
OP/RES
MGT
TEC/DEV

HALPERIN M.H.,CHINA AND THE BOMB. USA+45 USSR
INT/ORG FORCES ARMS/CONT DETER PRODUC ORD/FREE PWR
TREND. PAGE 24 G0472

B65
ASIA
NUC/PWR
WAR
DIPLOM

VEINOTT A.F. JR.,MATHEMATICAL STUDIES IN MANAGEMENT
SCIENCE. UNIV INDUS COMPUTER ADMIN...DECISION
NET/THEORY SIMUL 20. PAGE 61 G1193

B65
MATH
MGT
PLAN
PRODUC

KURAKOV I.G.,SCIENCE, TECHNOLOGY AND COMMUNISM;
SOME QUESTIONS OF DEVELOPMENT (TRANS. BY CARIN
DEDIJER). USSR INDUS PLAN PROB/SOLV COST PRODUC
...MGT MATH CHARTS METH 20. PAGE 32 G0626

B66
CREATE
TEC/DEV
MARXISM
ECO/TAC

LINDFORS G.V.,INTERCOLLEGIATE BIBLIOGRAPHY; CASES
IN BUSINESS ADMINISTRATION (VOL. X). FINAN MARKET
LABOR CONSULT PLAN GP/REL PRODUC 20. PAGE 34 G0668

B66
BIBLIOG/A
ADMIN
MGT
OP/RES

US DEPARTMENT OF LABOR,PRODUCTIVITY: A
BIBLIOGRAPHY. ECO/DEV INDUS MARKET OP/RES AUTOMAT
COST...STAT 20. PAGE 57 G1119

B66
BIBLIOG/A
PRODUC
LABOR
PLAN

US DEPARTMENT OF LABOR,TECHNOLOGICAL TRENDS IN
MAJOR AMERICAN INDUSTRIES. USA+45 R+D LABOR GP/REL
PRODUC...MGT BIBLIOG 20. PAGE 57 G1120

B66
TEC/DEV
INDUS
TREND
AUTOMAT

SIMON R.,"THE STATE OF PUBLIC RELATIONS SCHOLARLY
RESEARCH." TEC/DEV TASK MAJORITY PRODUC...TREND
CHARTS BIBLIOG 20. PAGE 51 G1000

S66
ACADEM
CREATE
STAT
GP/REL

COLM G.,THE ECONOMY OF THE AMERICAN PEOPLE. USA+45
ECO/DEV FINAN WORKER INT/TRADE AUTOMAT GP/REL.
PAGE 13 G0244

B67
ECO/TAC
PRODUC
TREND
TEC/DEV

ELSNER H.,THE TECHNOCRATS, PROPHETS OF AUTOMATION.
SOCIETY INDUS VOL/ASSN COST INCOME ATTIT 20.
PAGE 18 G0345

B67
AUTOMAT
TECHRACY
PRODUC
HIST/WRIT

MAZOUR A.G.,SOVIET ECONOMIC DEVELOPMENT: OPERATION
OUTSTRIP: 1921-1965. USSR ECO/UNDEV FINAN CHIEF
WORKER PROB/SOLV CONTROL PRODUC MARXISM...CHARTS

B67
ECO/TAC
AGRI
INDUS

ORG/CHARTS 20 STALIN/J. PAGE 37 G0726

PLAN

MOSS F.M.,THE WATER CRISIS. PROB/SOLV CONTROL
...POLICY NEW/IDEA. PAGE 40 G0791

B67
GEOG
ACT/RES
PRODUC
WEALTH

ORLANS H.,CONTRACTING FOR ATOMS. USA+45 LAW INTELL
ACADEM LG/CO NAT/G PLAN TEC/DEV CONTROL DETER
...TREND 20 AEC. PAGE 43 G0845

B67
NUC/PWR
R+D
PRODUC
PEACE

PORWIT K.,CENTRAL PLANNING: EVALUATION OF VARIANTS.
PRICE OPTIMAL PRODUC...DECISION MATH CHARTS SIMUL
BIBLIOG 20. PAGE 45 G0886

B67
PLAN
MGT
ECOMETRIC

SILBERMAN C.E.,THE MYTHS OF AUTOMATION. INDUS
WORKER COST PRODUC AGE WEALTH 20. PAGE 51 G0996

B67
MYTH
AUTOMAT
CHARTS
TEC/DEV

BARRO S.,"ECONOMIC IMPACT OF SPACE EXPENDITURES:
SOME BROAD ISSUES DEALING WITH COSTS AND BENEFITS."
USA+45 PROC/MFG R+D LG/CO CONSULT COST PRODUC 20.
PAGE 5 G0098

S67
SPACE
FINAN
ECO/TAC
NAT/G

BENN W.,"TECHNOLOGY HAS AN INEXORABLE EFFECT." FUT
UK ECO/DEV INT/ORG CONSULT PLAN EDU/PROP ADMIN LEAD
GP/REL PRODUC...INT 20 EEC. PAGE 6 G0119

S67
R+D
LG/CO
TEC/DEV
INDUS

BRUNHILD G.,"THEORY OF 'TECHNICAL UNEMPLOYMENT'."
ECO/DEV ACT/RES PROB/SOLV DEMAND PRODUC...PHIL/SCI
20. PAGE 9 G0182

S67
WORKER
TEC/DEV
SKILL
INDUS

CARR E.H.,"REVOLUTION FROM ABOVE." USSR STRATA
FINAN INDUS NAT/G DOMIN LEAD GP/REL INGP/REL OWN
PRODUC PWR 20 STALIN/J. PAGE 11 G0214

S67
AGRI
POLICY
COM
EFFICIENCY

EYRAUD M.,"LA FRANCE FACE A UN EVENTUEL TRAITE DE
NON DISSEMINATION DES ARMES NUCLEAIRES." FRANCE
USA+45 EXTR/IND INDUS R+D INT/ORG ACT/RES TEC/DEV
AGREE PRODUC ATTIT 20 TREATY AEC EURATOM. PAGE 18
G0355

S67
NUC/PWR
ARMS/CONT
POLICY

GAUSSENS J.,"THE APPLICATIONS OF NUCLEAR ENERGY -
TECHNICAL, ECONOMIC AND SOCIAL ASPECTS." WOR+45
INDUS R+D ACT/RES EFFICIENCY PRODUC SKILL PREDICT.
PAGE 21 G0413

S67
NUC/PWR
TEC/DEV
ECO/DEV
ADJUST

ROBERTS E.B.,"THE PROBLEM OF AGING ORGANIZATIONS."
INTELL PROB/SOLV ADMIN EXEC FEEDBACK EFFICIENCY
PRODUC...GEN/LAWS 20. PAGE 47 G0926

S67
INDUS
R+D
MGT
PLAN

SINGH B.,"ITALIAN EXPERIENCE IN REGIONAL ECONOMIC
DEVELOPMENT AND LESSONS FOR OTHER COUNTRIES."
EUR+WWI ITALY INDUS NAT/G ACT/RES REGION GP/REL
EFFICIENCY EQUILIB PRODUC WEALTH. PAGE 51 G1007

S67
ECO/UNDEV
PLAN
ECO/TAC
CONTROL

SLOAN P.,"FIFTY YEARS OF SOVIET RULE." USSR INDUS
EDU/PROP EFFICIENCY PRODUC HEALTH KNOWL MORAL
WEALTH MARXISM...POLICY 20. PAGE 51 G1011

S67
CREATE
NAT/G
PLAN
INSPECT

PRODUCTIVITY....SEE PRODUC

PROF/ORG....PROFESSIONAL ORGANIZATIONS

AMERICAN DOCUMENTATION INST,AMERICAN DOCUMENTATION.
PROF/ORG CONSULT PLAN PERCEPT...MATH STAT AUD/VIS
CHARTS METH/COMP INDEX METH 20. PAGE 3 G0050

N
BIBLIOG
TEC/DEV
COM/IND
COMPUT/IR

HECKSCHER G.,"GROUP ORGANIZATION IN SWEDEN." SWEDEN
STRATA ECO/DEV AGRI INDUS LABOR NAT/G PROF/ORG
ECO/TAC CENTRAL SOCISM...MGT 19/20. PAGE 25 G0499

S39
LAISSEZ
SOC

B51
MAASS A.,MUDDY WATERS: THE ARMY ENGINEERS AND THE
NATIONS RIVERS. USA-45 PROF/ORG CONSULT LEGIS ADMIN
EXEC ROLE PWR...SOC PRESIDENT 20. PAGE 35 G0682
FORCES
GP/REL
LOBBY
CONSTRUC

B56
VUCINICH A.,THE SOVIET ACADEMY OF SCIENCES. USSR
STRUCT ACADEM NAT/G EDU/PROP ADMIN LEAD ROLE
...BIBLIOG 20 ACADEM/SCI. PAGE 61 G1203
PHIL/SCI
CREATE
INTELL
PROF/ORG

B56
WASSERMAN P.,INFORMATION FOR ADMINISTRATORS: A
GUIDE TO PUBLICATIONS AND SERVICES FOR MANAGEMENT
IN BUSINESS AND GOVERNMENT. R+D LOC/G NAT/G
PROF/ORG VOL/ASSN PRESS...PSY SOC STAT 20. PAGE 62
G1219
BIBLIOG
MGT
KNOWL
EDU/PROP

S57
JANOWITZ M.,"MILITARY ELITES AND THE STUDY OF WAR."
USA+45 WOR-45 STRATA NAT/G PROF/ORG TEC/DEV DOMIN
EDU/PROP COERCE WAR ATTIT RIGID/FLEX PWR RESPECT
...MGT TREND STERTYP GEN/METH 20. PAGE 28 G0558
FORCES
ELITES

B59
STANFORD RESEARCH INSTITUTE,POSSIBLE NONMILITARY
SCIENTIFIC DEVELOPMENTS AND THEIR POTENTIAL IMPACT
ON FOREIGN POLICY PROBLEMS OF THE UNITED. FUT
USA+45 INT/ORG PROF/ORG CONSULT ACT/RES CREATE PLAN
PEACE KNOWL SKILL...TECHNIC PHIL/SCI NEW/IDEA
UNESCO 20. PAGE 52 G1032
R+D
TEC/DEV

S60
TAYLOR M.G.,"THE ROLE OF THE MEDICAL PROFESSION IN
THE FORMULATION AND EXECUTION OF PUBLIC POLICY"
(BMR)" CANADA NAT/G CONSULT ADMIN REPRESENT GP/REL
ROLE SOVEREIGN...DECISION 20 CMA. PAGE 54 G1058
PROF/ORG
HEALTH
LOBBY
POLICY

B62
GILPIN R.,AMERICAN SCIENTISTS AND NUCLEAR WEAPONS
POLICY. COM FUT USA+45 WOR+45 INT/ORG NAT/G
PROF/ORG CONSULT FORCES CREATE TEC/DEV BAL/PWR
EDU/PROP ARMS/CONT WAR PERCEPT KNOWL MORAL PWR
...PHIL/SCI SOC CONCPT GEN/LAWS 20. PAGE 21 G0417
INTELL
ATTIT
DETER
NUC/PWR

B62
STOVER C.F.,THE GOVERNMENT OF SCIENCE (PAMPHLET).
USA+45 SOCIETY PROF/ORG EX/STRUC CREATE CONTROL
NUC/PWR WAR GOV/REL PEACE ORD/FREE 20. PAGE 53
G1041
PHIL/SCI
TEC/DEV
LAW
NAT/G

B63
KORNHAUSER W.,SCIENTISTS IN INDUSTRY: CONFLICT AND
ACCOMMODATION. USA+45 R+D LG/CO NAT/G TEC/DEV
CONTROL ADJUST ATTIT...MGT STAT INT BIBLIOG 20.
PAGE 31 G0614
CREATE
INDUS
PROF/ORG
GP/REL

S63
BUNDY M.,"THE SCIENTIST AND NATIONAL POLICY."
PROF/ORG PLAN PARTIC POLICY. PAGE 10 G0186
NAT/G
PHIL/SCI
DECISION

S63
GANDILHON J.,"LA SCIENCE ET LA TECHNIQUE A L'AIDE
DES REGIONS PEU DEVELOPPEES." FRANCE FUT WOR+45
ECO/DEV R+D PROF/ORG ACT/RES PLAN...MGT TOT/POP
VAL/FREE 20 UN. PAGE 21 G0406
ECO/UNDEV
TEC/DEV
FOR/AID

B64
FALK L.A.,ADMINISTRATIVE ASPECTS OF GROUP PRACTICE.
USA+45 FINAN PROF/ORG PLAN MGT. PAGE 18 G0358
BIBLIOG/A
HEAL
ADMIN
SERV/IND

B64
RIES J.C.,THE MANAGEMENT OF DEFENSE: ORGANIZATION
AND CONTROL OF THE US ARMED SERVICES. PROF/ORG
DELIB/GP EX/STRUC LEGIS GOV/REL PERS/REL CENTRAL
RATIONAL PWR...POLICY TREND GOV/COMP BIBLIOG.
PAGE 47 G0920
FORCES
ACT/RES
DECISION
CONTROL

B64
RUSHING W.A.,THE PSYCHIATRIC PROFESSIONS. DOMIN
INGP/REL DRIVE RIGID/FLEX ROLE HEALTH PWR...POLICY
GP/COMP. PAGE 48 G0947
ATTIT
PUB/INST
PROF/ORG
BAL/PWR

S64
BYRNES F.C.,"ASSIGNMENT TO AMBIGUITY: WORK
PERFORMANCE IN CROSSCULTURAL TECHNICAL ASSISTANCE."
USA+45 WOR+45 PROF/ORG CONSULT PLAN EDU/PROP ATTIT
DISPL PERCEPT PERSON ALL/VALS...POLICY INT CHARTS
NATO 20. PAGE 10 G0199
INTELL
QU

B65
BOBROW D.B.,COMPONENTS OF DEFENSE POLICY. ASIA
EUR+WWI USA+45 WOR+45 INTELL INT/ORG NAT/G PROF/ORG
CONSULT LEGIS ACT/RES CREATE ARMS/CONT COERCE
ORD/FREE...DECISION SIMUL. PAGE 7 G0145
DETER
NUC/PWR
PLAN
FORCES

B65
NATIONAL REFERRAL CENTER SCI,A DIRECTORY OF
INFORMATION RESOURCES IN THE UNITED STATES; SOCIAL
SCIENCES. USA+45 PROF/ORG...PSY SOC 20. PAGE 41
G0811
INDEX
R+D
ACADEM
ACT/RES

B65
OECD,MEDITERRANEAN REGIONAL PROJECT: TURKEY;
EDUCATION AND DEVELOPMENT. FUT TURKEY SOCIETY
STRATA FINAN NAT/G PROF/ORG PLAN PROB/SOLV ADMIN
COST...STAT CHARTS 20 OECD. PAGE 42 G0831
EDU/PROP
ACADEM
SCHOOL
ECO/UNDEV

B65
OECD,THE MEDITERRANEAN REGIONAL PROJECT: PORTUGAL;
EDUCATION AND DEVELOPMENT. PORTUGAL SOCIETY STRATA
FINAN PROF/ORG WORKER PLAN PROB/SOLV ADMIN...POLICY
STAT CHARTS METH 20 OECD. PAGE 42 G0832
EDU/PROP
SCHOOL
ACADEM
ECO/UNDEV

B65
OECD,THE MEDITERRANEAN REGIONAL PROJECT: ITALY;
EDUCATION AND DEVELOPMENT. ITALY SOCIETY STRATA
FINAN NAT/G PROF/ORG WORKER PLAN PROB/SOLV ADMIN
...STAT CHARTS METH 20 OECD. PAGE 42 G0833
SCHOOL
EDU/PROP
ECO/UNDEV
ACADEM

B65
OECD,THE MEDITERRANEAN REGIONAL PROJECT: GREECE;
EDUCATION AND DEVELOPMENT. FUT GREECE SOCIETY AGRI
FINAN NAT/G PROF/ORG WORKER PLAN PROB/SOLV ADMIN
DEMAND ATTIT 20 OECD. PAGE 42 G0834
EDU/PROP
SCHOOL
ACADEM
ECO/UNDEV

B65
ORG FOR ECO COOP AND DEVEL,THE MEDITERRANEAN
REGIONAL PROJECT: YUGOSLAVIA; EDUCATION AND
DEVELOPMENT. YUGOSLAVIA SOCIETY FINAN PROF/ORG PLAN
ADMIN COST DEMAND MARXISM...STAT TREND CHARTS METH
20 OECD. PAGE 43 G0843
EDU/PROP
ACADEM
SCHOOL
ECO/UNDEV

B65
UNESCO,HANDBOOK OF INTERNATIONAL EXCHANGES. COM/IND
R+D ACADEM PROF/ORG VOL/ASSN CREATE TEC/DEV
EDU/PROP AGREE 20 TREATY. PAGE 55 G1090
INDEX
INT/ORG
DIPLOM
PRESS

B65
US LIBRARY OF CONGRESS,A DIRECTORY OF INFORMATION
RESOURCES IN THE UNITED STATES: SOCIAL SCIENCES.
USA+45 ACADEM INT/ORG LABOR PROF/ORG PUB/INST
SCHOOL SECT 20. PAGE 59 G1156
BIBLIOG
R+D
COMPUT/IR

B65
US SENATE COMM AERO SPACE SCI,INTERNATIONAL
COOPERATION AND ORGANIZATION FOR OUTER SPACE. FUT
USA+45 WOR+45 PROF/ORG VOL/ASSN CONSULT DELIB/GP
PLAN TEC/DEV ARMS/CONT GP/REL PEACE 20 UN NASA.
PAGE 59 G1167
DIPLOM
SPACE
R+D
NAT/G

B67
MACKINTOSH J.M.,JUGGERNAUT. USSR NAT/G POL/PAR
ADMIN LEAD CIVMIL/REL COST TOTALISM PWR MARXISM
...GOV/COMP 20. PAGE 35 G0691
WAR
FORCES
COM
PROF/ORG

B67
WARNER W.L.,THE EMERGENT AMERICAN SOCIETY VOL I,
LARGE-SCALE ORGANIZATIONS. USA+45 USA-45 ACADEM
PROF/ORG SCHOOL SECT EX/STRUC TEC/DEV GP/REL
...TREND CHARTS. PAGE 62 G1215
ANTHOL
NAT/G
LABOR
LG/CO

S67
ATKIN J.M.,"THE FEDERAL GOVERNMENT, BIG BUSINESS,
AND COLLEGES OF EDUCATION." PROF/ORG CONSULT CREATE
PLAN PROB/SOLV ADMIN EFFICIENCY. PAGE 4 G0075
SCHOOL
ACADEM
NAT/G
INDUS

S67
HARRIS F.R.,"POLITICAL SCIENCE AND THE PROPOSAL FOR
A NATIONAL SOCIAL SCIENCE FOUNDATION." FUT CONSULT
DELIB/GP PLAN PROB/SOLV BUDGET CONFER SANCTION
CRIME...POLICY SOC/WK 20 NSF NSSF. PAGE 25 G0484
PROF/ORG
R+D
CREATE
NAT/G

PROFESSIONAL ORGANIZATION....SEE PROF/ORG

PROFIT

N
THE MANAGEMENT REVIEW. FINAN EX/STRUC PROFIT
BIBLIOG/A. PAGE 1 G0007
LABOR
MGT
ADMIN
MARKET

B63
WILTZ J.E.,IN SEARCH OF PEACE: THE SENATE MUNITIONS DELIB/GP
INQUIRY, 1934-36. EUR+WWI USA-45 ELITES INDUS LG/CO PROFIT
LEGIS INT/TRADE LOBBY NEUTRAL ARMS/CONT...POLICY WAR
CONGRESS 20 LEAGUE/NAT PRESIDENT SENATE CONSCRIPTN. WEAPON
PAGE 64 G1246

S64
STONE P.A.,"DECISION TECHNIQUES FOR TOWN OP/RES
DEVELOPMENT." PLAN COST PROFIT...DECISION MGT MUNIC
CON/ANAL CHARTS METH/COMP BIBLIOG 20. PAGE 53 G1039 ADMIN
PROB/SOLV

B65
DORFMAN R.,MEASURING BENEFITS OF GOVERNMENT PLAN
INVESTMENTS. ECO/DEV R+D ECO/TAC PROFIT UTIL...MGT RATION
GEN/METH. PAGE 16 G0308 EFFICIENCY
OPTIMAL

B65
TYBOUT R.A.,ECONOMICS OF RESEARCH AND DEVELOPMENT. R+D
ECO/DEV ECO/UNDEV INDUS PROFIT DECISION. PAGE 55 FORCES
G1084 ADMIN
DIPLOM

B67
MACAVOY P.W.,REGULATION OF TRANSPORT INNOVATION. DIST/IND
ACT/RES ADJUD COST DEMAND...POLICY CHARTS 20. CONTROL
PAGE 35 G0684 PRICE
PROFIT

S67
ENKE S.,"GOVERNMENT-INDUSTRY DEVELOPMENT OF A INDUS
COMMERCIAL SUPERSONIC TRANSPORT." USA+45 ECO/DEV FINAN
R+D LG/CO NAT/G TEC/DEV PRICE RISK COST PROFIT. SERV/IND
PAGE 18 G0347 CAP/ISM

S67
HAMBERG D.,"SIZE OF ENTERPRISE AND TECHNICAL TEC/DEV
CHANGE." USA+45 LG/CO SML/CO CREATE OP/RES PROFIT INDUS
...TREND 20. PAGE 24 G0477 R+D
WEALTH

PROFUMO/J....JOHN PROFUMO, THE PROFUMO AFFAIR

PROG/TEAC....PROGRAMMED INSTRUCTION

B62
BORKOF H.,COMPUTER APPLICATIONS IN THE BEHAVIORAL R+D
SCIENCES. AUTOMAT UTIL...DECISION PHIL/SCI PSY COMPUTER
METH/CNCPT LING LOG MATH STYLE NET/THEORY COMPUT/IR PROB/SOLV
PROG/TEAC SIMUL. PAGE 8 G0154 FEEDBACK

B63
TOMKINS S.S.,COMPUTER SIMULATION OF PERSONALITY. COMPUTER
R+D TEC/DEV AUTOMAT FEEDBACK ANOMIE PERCEPT...STYLE PERSON
PERS/TEST PREDICT COMPUT/IR GP/COMP. PAGE 55 G1075 SIMUL
PROG/TEAC

S66
EWALD R.F.,"ONE OF MANY POSSIBLE GAMES." ACADEM SIMUL
INT/ORG ARMS/CONT...INT/LAW GAME. PAGE 18 G0354 HYPO/EXP
PROG/TEAC
RECORD

PROGRAMMED INSTRUCTION....SEE PROG/TEAC

PROGRAMMING....SEE COMPUTER

PROGRSV/M....PROGRESSIVE MOVEMENT (ALL NATIONS)

PROJ/TEST....PROJECTIVE TESTS

S62
PAULING L.,"GENETIC EFFECTS OF WEAPONS TESTS." HEAL
WOR+45 SOCIETY FAM ACT/RES EDU/PROP AGE/C HEALTH ARMS/CONT
ORD/FREE...GEOG STAT CONT/OBS PROJ/TEST CHARTS NUC/PWR
TOT/POP 20. PAGE 44 G0861

PROJECTION....SEE DISPL

PROPAGANDA....SEE EDU/PROP

PROPERTY TAX....SEE PROPERTY/TX

PROPERTY/TX....PROPERTY TAX

PROSTITUTN....SEE ALSO SEX + CRIME

PROTECTIONISM....SEE PROTECTNSM

PROTECTNSM....PROTECTIONISM

PROTEST....SEE COERCE

PROTESTANT....PROTESTANTS, PROTESTANTISM

PROUDHON/P....PIERRE JOSEPH PROUDHON

PROVS....STATE AND PROVINCES

N19
BELL J.R.,PERSONNEL PROBLEMS IN CONVERTING TO WORKER
AUTOMATION (PAMPHLET). USA+45 COMPUTER PLAN AUTOMAT
...METH/CNCPT 20 CALIFORNIA. PAGE 6 G0115 PROB/SOLV
PROVS

N19
KAUFMAN J.L.,COMMUNITY RENEWAL PROGRAMS (PAMPHLET). LOC/G
USA+45 CONSTRUC PROVS CREATE PLAN CONTROL WEALTH 20 MUNIC
URBAN/RNWL. PAGE 30 G0584 ACT/RES
BIBLIOG

B25
MATHEWS J.M.,AMERICAN STATE GOVERNMENT. USA-45 PROVS
LOC/G CHIEF EX/STRUC LEGIS ADJUD CONTROL CT/SYS ADMIN
ROUTINE GOV/REL PWR 20 GOVERNOR. PAGE 37 G0721 FEDERAL
CONSTN

C50
WAGER P.W.,"COUNTY GOVERNMENT ACROSS THE NATION." LOC/G
USA+45 CONSTN COM/IND FINAN SCHOOL DOMIN CT/SYS PROVS
LEAD GOV/REL...STAT BIBLIOG 20. PAGE 61 G1204 ADMIN
ROUTINE

B53
TOMPKINS D.C.,CIVIL DEFENSE IN THE STATES: A BIBLIOG
BIBLIOGRAPHY (DEFENSE BIBLIOGRAPHIES NO. 3; WAR
PAMPHLET). USA+45 LABOR LOC/G NAT/G PROVS LEGIS. ORD/FREE
PAGE 55 G1076 ADMIN

B54
PUBLIC ADMIN CLEARING HOUSE,PUBLIC ADMINISTRATIONS INDEX
ORGANIZATIONS: A DIRECTORY, 1954. USA+45 R+D PROVS VOL/ASSN
ACT/RES...MGT 20. PAGE 45 G0893 NAT/G
ADMIN

B54
TOMPKINS D.C.,STATE GOVERNMENT AND ADMINISTRATION: BIBLIOG/A
A BIBLIOGRAPHY. USA+45 USA-45 CONSTN LEGIS JUDGE LOC/G
BUDGET CT/SYS LOBBY...CHARTS 20. PAGE 55 G1077 PROVS
ADMIN

C54
CALDWELL L.K.,"THE GOVERNMENT AND ADMINISTRATION OF PROVS
NEW YORK." LOC/G MUNIC POL/PAR SCHOOL CHIEF LEGIS ADMIN
PLAN TAX CT/SYS...MGT SOC/WK BIBLIOG 20 NEWYORK/C. CONSTN
PAGE 10 G0202 EX/STRUC

C54
ZELLER B.,"AMERICAN STATE LEGISLATURES: REPORT ON REPRESENT
THE COMMITTEE ON AMERICAN LEGISLATURES." CONSTN LEGIS
POL/PAR EX/STRUC CONFER ADMIN CONTROL EXEC LOBBY PROVS
ROUTINE GOV/REL...POLICY BIBLIOG 20. PAGE 65 G1267 APPORT

B59
ATOMIC INDUSTRIAL FORUM,THE IMPACT OF THE PEACEFUL PROVS
USES OF ATOMIC ENERGY ON STATE AND LOCAL LOC/G
GOVERNMENT. USA+45 INDUS NAT/G LEGIS PLAN CONTROL NUC/PWR
GOV/REL. PAGE 4 G0079 PEACE

B59
CLEAVELAND F.N.,SCIENCE AND STATE GOVERNMENT. AGRI TEC/DEV
EXTR/IND FINAN INDUS PROVS...METH/CNCPT STAT CHARTS PHIL/SCI
20 NEW/YORK CONNECTICT WISCONSIN CALIFORNIA GOV/REL
NEW/MEXICO. PAGE 12 G0233 METH/COMP

B59
U OF MICHIGAN LAW SCHOOL,ATOMS AND THE LAW. USA+45 NUC/PWR
PROVS WORKER PROB/SOLV DIPLOM ADMIN GOV/REL ANTHOL. NAT/G
PAGE 55 G1085 CONTROL
LAW

B59
US CONGRESS JT ATOM ENRGY COMM,SELECTED MATERIALS NAT/G
ON FEDERAL-STATE COOPERATION IN THE ATOMIC ENERGY NUC/PWR
FIELD. USA+45 LAW LOC/G PROVS CONSULT LEGIS ADJUD GOV/REL
...POLICY BIBLIOG 20 AEC. PAGE 57 G1111 DELIB/GP

B61
MURPHY E.F.,WATER PURITY: A STUDY IN LEGAL CONTROL SEA
OF NATURAL RESOURCES. LOC/G ACT/RES PLAN TEC/DEV LAW
LOBBY GP/REL COST ATTIT HEALTH ORD/FREE...HEAL PROVS
JURID 20 WISCONSIN WATER. PAGE 40 G0797 CONTROL

S61
COOKE E.F.,"RESEARCH: AN INSTRUMENT OF POWER." R+D
VOL/ASSN PLAN TEC/DEV TAX LOBBY INGP/REL ROLE PROVS
POLICY. PAGE 13 G0253 LOC/G
DECISION

B63
HERNDON J.,A SELECTED BIBLIOGRAPHY OF MATERIALS IN BIBLIOG

STATE GOVERNMENT AND POLITICS (PAMPHLET). USA+45 POL/PAR LEGIS ADMIN CHOOSE MGT. PAGE 26 G0507
GOV/COMP
PROVS
DECISION

B64
DIEBOLD J.,BEYOND AUTOMATION: MANAGERIAL PROBLEMS OF AN EXPLODING TECHNOLOGY. SOCIETY ECO/DEV CREATE ECO/TAC AUTOMAT SKILL...TECHNIC MGT WORK. PAGE 16 G0303
FUT
INDUS
PROVS
NAT/G

B64
MASTERS N.A.,STATE POLITICS AND THE PUBLIC SCHOOLS. STRUCT FINAN ADMIN LOBBY GP/REL PWR BIBLIOG. PAGE 36 G0720
EDU/PROP
PROVS
DOMIN

S64
NEEDHAM T.,"SCIENCE AND SOCIETY IN EAST AND WEST." INTELL STRATA R+D LOC/G NAT/G PROVS CONSULT ACT/RES CREATE PLAN TEC/DEV EDU/PROP ADMIN ATTIT ALL/VALS ...POLICY RELATIV MGT CONCPT NEW/IDEA TIME/SEQ WORK WORK. PAGE 41 G0815
ASIA
STRUCT

S64
UNRUH J.M.,"SCIENTIFIC INPUTS TO LEGISLATIVE DECISION-MAKING (SUPPLEMENT)" USA+45 ACADEM NAT/G PROVS GOV/REL GOV/COMP. PAGE 56 G1102
CREATE
DECISION
LEGIS
PARTIC

B65
ARTHUR D LITTLE INC,SAN FRANCISCO COMMUNITY RENEWAL PROGRAM. USA+45 FINAN PROVS ADMIN INCOME...CHARTS 20 CALIFORNIA SAN/FRAN URBAN/RNWL. PAGE 4 G0071
HABITAT
MUNIC
PLAN
PROB/SOLV

B66
GORDON G.,THE LEGISLATIVE PROCESS AND DIVIDED GOVERNMENT; A CASE STUDY OF THE 86TH CONGRESS. USA+45 POL/PAR PROVS PROB/SOLV BAL/PWR CHOOSE REPRESENT EFFICIENCY ATTIT...POLICY DECISION STAT 20 CONGRESS EISNHWR/DD. PAGE 22 G0434
LEGIS
HABITAT
CHIEF
NAT/G

B66
SANFORD T.,BUT WHAT ABOUT THE PEOPLE? ACADEM SCHOOL BUDGET TAX CONTROL SKILL WEALTH 20 NORTH/CAR. PAGE 49 G0956
EDU/PROP
PROB/SOLV
POLICY
PROVS

B66
STREET D.,ORGANIZATION FOR TREATMENT. CLIENT PROVS PUB/INST PLAN CONTROL PARTIC REPRESENT ATTIT PWR ...POLICY BIBLIOG. PAGE 53 G1044
GP/COMP
AGE/Y
ADMIN
VOL/ASSN

S66
"FURTHER READING." INDIA LOC/G NAT/G PLAN ADMIN WEALTH...GEOG SOC CONCPT CENSUS 20. PAGE 1 G0021
BIBLIOG
ECO/UNDEV
TEC/DEV
PROVS

B67
US DEPARTMENT OF THE ARMY,CIVILIAN IN PEACE, SOLDIER IN WAR: A BIBLIOGRAPHIC SURVEY OF THE ARMY AND AIR NATIONAL GUARD (PAMPHLET, NOS. 130-2). USA+45 USA-45 LOC/G NAT/G PROVS LEGIS PLAN ADMIN ATTIT ORD/FREE...POLICY 19/20. PAGE 58 G1134
BIBLIOG/A
FORCES
ROLE
DIPLOM

N67
US HOUSE COMM APPROPRIATIONS,PUBLIC WORKS AND ATOMIC ENERGY COMMISSION APPROPRIATION BILL, 1968 (PAMPHLET). USA+45 ECO/DEV NAT/G...GEOG DEEP/INT CHARTS HOUSE/REP AEC DEPT/DEFEN TVA. PAGE 58 G1137
BUDGET
NUC/PWR
PROVS
PLAN

PRUITT/DG....DEAN G. PRUITT

PRUSSIA....PRUSSIA

PSY....PSYCHOLOGY

B11
BERGSON H.,CREATIVE EVOLUTION. FUT WOR+45 WOR-45 INTELL AGRI R+D ATTIT PERCEPT PERSON RIGID/FLEX ...RELATIV PHIL/SCI PSY METH/CNCPT MATH HIST/WRIT TREND HYPO/EXP TOT/POP. PAGE 7 G0127
BIO/SOC
KNOWL

B28
SOROKIN P.,CONTEMPORARY SOCIOLOGICAL THEORIES. MOD/EUR UNIV SOCIETY R+D SCHOOL ECO/TAC EDU/PROP ROUTINE ATTIT DRIVE...PSY CONCPT TIME/SEQ TREND GEN/LAWS 20. PAGE 52 G1021
CULTURE
SOC
WAR

S43
KAPLAN A.,"CONTENT ANALYSIS AND THE THEORY OF SIGNS" (BMR)" PERS/REL...PSY CONCPT LING IDEA/COMP SIMUL BIBLIOG 20 MORRIS/CW. PAGE 29 G0573
LOG
CON/ANAL
STAT
PHIL/SCI

B44
KAUFMANN F.,METHODOLOGY OF THE SOCIAL SCIENCES. PERSON...RELATIV PSY CONCPT LING METH 20. PAGE 30 G0585
SOC
PHIL/SCI
GEN/LAWS
METH/CNCPT

B46
AMERICAN DOCUMENTATION INST,CATALOGUE OF AUXILIARY PUBLICATIONS IN MICROFILMS AND PHOTOPRINTS. USA-45 LAW AGRI CREATE TEC/DEV ADMIN...GEOG LING MATH 20. PAGE 3 G0052
BIBLIOG
EDU/PROP
PSY

B47
BALDWIN H.W.,THE PRICE OF POWER. USA+45 FORCES PLAN NUC/PWR ADJUST COST ORD/FREE...POLICY PSY BIBLIOG 20. PAGE 5 G0089
PROB/SOLV
PWR
POPULISM
PRICE

B47
LASSWELL H.D.,THE ANALYSIS OF POLITICAL BEHAVIOUR: AN EMPIRICAL APPROACH. WOR+45 CULTURE NAT/G FORCES EDU/PROP ADMIN ATTIT PERCEPT KNOWL...PHIL/SCI PSY SOC NEW/IDEA OBS INT GEN/METH NAZI 20. PAGE 32 G0639
R+D
ACT/RES
ELITES

B48
WEINER N.,CYBERNETICS. SOCIETY COMPUTER ADJUST EFFICIENCY UTIL PERCEPT...PSY MATH REGRESS TIME. PAGE 63 G1226
FEEDBACK
AUTOMAT
CONTROL
TEC/DEV

S48
MACCORQUODALE K.,"ON A DISTINCTION BETWEEN HYPOTHETICAL CONSTRUCTS AND INTERVENING VARIABLES." ...METH/CNCPT LING IDEA/COMP HYPO/EXP SOC/EXP BIBLIOG 20. PAGE 35 G0686
PSY
PHIL/SCI
CONCPT
GEN/METH

S48
MARQUIS D.G.,"RESEARCH PLANNING AT THE FRONTIERS OF SCIENCE" (BMR)" INTELL ACADEM CREATE UTIL...PSY 20. PAGE 36 G0708
PLAN
ACT/RES
EFFICIENCY
GEN/METH

B49
OGBURN W.,TECHNOLOGY AND INTERNATIONAL RELATIONS. WOR+45 WOR-45 ECO/DEV CREATE PLAN ECO/TAC EDU/PROP COERCE PWR SKILL WEALTH...TECHNIC PSY SOC NEW/IDEA CHARTS TOT/POP 20. PAGE 43 G0837
TEC/DEV
DIPLOM
INT/ORG

S49
MERTON R.,"THE ROLE OF APPLIED SOCIAL SCIENCE IN THE FORMATION OF POLICY: A RESEARCH MEMORANDUM." WOR+45 INDUS NAT/G EXEC ROUTINE CHOOSE ORD/FREE PWR SKILL...POLICY MGT PSY METH/CNCPT TESTS CHARTS METH VAL/FREE 20. PAGE 38 G0756
PLAN
SOC
DIPLOM

B50
CANTRIL H.,TENSIONS THAT CAUSE WAR. UNIV CULTURE R+D CREATE EDU/PROP DRIVE PERSON KNOWL ORD/FREE ...HUM PSY SOC OBS CENSUS TREND CON/ANAL SOC/EXP SIMUL GEN/METH ANTHOL COLD/WAR TOT/POP. PAGE 11 G0206
SOCIETY
PHIL/SCI
PEACE

B50
MANNHEIM K.,FREEDOM, POWER, AND DEMOCRATIC PLANNING. FUT USSR WOR+45 ELITES INTELL SOCIETY NAT/G EDU/PROP ROUTINE ATTIT DRIVE SUPEGO SKILL ...POLICY PSY CONCPT TREND GEN/LAWS 20. PAGE 35 G0700
TEC/DEV
PLAN
CAP/ISM
UK

B50
CONTINUITIES IN SOCIAL RESEARCH; STUDIES IN SCOPE AND METHOD OF "THE AMERICAN SOLDIER" USA+45 FORCES INGP/REL ATTIT...PSY SAMP CON/ANAL CHARTS GEN/LAWS ANTHOL 20. PAGE 38 G0758
SOC
PHIL/SCI
METH

S50
LENTZ T.F.,"REPORT ON A SURVEY OF SOCIAL SCIENTISTS CONDUCTED BY THE ATTITUDE RESEARCH LABORATORY." FUT WOR+45 CREATE EDU/PROP...PSY STAT RECORD SYS/QU SAMP/SIZ CON/ANAL VAL/FREE 20. PAGE 33 G0655
ACT/RES
ATTIT
DIPLOM

B52
CURRENT TRENDS IN PSYCHOLOGY,PSYCHOLOGY IN THE WORLD EMERGENCY. USA+45 CONSULT FORCES ACT/RES PLAN SKILL...DECISION OBS APT/TEST KNO/TEST PERS/TEST TREND CHARTS 20. PAGE 14 G0266
NAT/G
PSY

B53
HOVLAND C.I.,COMMUNICATION AND PERSUASION: PSYCHOLOGICAL STUDIES OF OPINION CHANGE. INTELL SOCIETY ECO/DEV COM/IND R+D SERV/IND CREATE TEC/DEV ATTIT RIGID/FLEX KNOWL NEW/IDEA. PAGE 27 G0531
PSY
EDU/PROP

S53
MILLER G.A.,"WHAT IS INFORMATION MEASUREMENT?"
COMPUTER

CREATE...CONCPT METH/CNCPT QUANT STAT CHARTS
BIBLIOG/A 20. PAGE 39 G0771
TEC/DEV
PSY
MATH

B54
SPENCER R.F.,METHOD AND PERSPECTIVE IN ANTHROPOLOGY
...GEOG LING QUANT STAT TESTS SAMP/SIZ CON/ANAL
IDEA/COMP METH/COMP ANTHOL BIBLIOG 20. PAGE 52
G1025
PHIL/SCI
SOC
PSY
METH

B54
SPROTT W.J.H.,SCIENCE AND SOCIAL ACTION. STRUCT
ACT/RES CRIME GP/REL INGP/REL ANOMIE...PSY
SOC/INTEG 19/20. PAGE 52 G1027
SOC
CULTURE
PHIL/SCI

B55
DAVIS E.,TWO MINUTES TO MIDNIGHT. WOR+45 PLAN
CONTROL NEUTRAL ARMS/CONT ATTIT ORD/FREE...PSY 20
COLD/WAR. PAGE 14 G0277
NUC/PWR
WAR
DETER
DIPLOM

B55
MIKSCHE F.O.,ATOMIC WEAPONS AND ARMIES. FUT WOR+45
WOR-45 SOCIETY COERCE DETER WEAPON PWR...POLICY
WELF/ST PSY CONCPT INT SYS/QU KNO/TEST TOT/POP 20.
PAGE 39 G0765
TEC/DEV
FORCES
NUC/PWR

B55
SHUBIK M.,READINGS IN GAME THEORY AND POLITICAL
BEHAVIOR. WOR+45 FORCES CREATE ROUTINE WAR PEACE
PERCEPT KNOWL PWR...PSY SOC CONCPT METH/CNCPT STAT
CHARTS HYPO/EXP GAME METH VAL/FREE 20. PAGE 50
G0991
MATH
DECISION
DIPLOM

B56
US DEPARTMENT OF THE ARMY,AMERICAN MILITARY
HISTORY. USA+45 USA-45 EX/STRUC PROB/SOLV TEC/DEV
DIPLOM NUC/PWR REV WAR WEAPON...PSY 18/20. PAGE 57
G1125
BIBLIOG
FORCES
NAT/G

B56
WASSERMAN P.,INFORMATION FOR ADMINISTRATORS: A
GUIDE TO PUBLICATIONS AND SERVICES FOR MANAGEMENT
IN BUSINESS AND GOVERNMENT. R+D LOC/G NAT/G
PROF/ORG VOL/ASSN PRESS...PSY SOC STAT 20. PAGE 62
G1219
BIBLIOG
MGT
KNOWL
EDU/PROP

S56
MILLER G.A.,"THE MAGICAL NUMBER SEVEN, PLUS OR
MINUS TWO: SOME LIMITS ON OUR CAPACITY FOR
PROCESSING INFORMATION." PERS/REL...PSY METH/CNCPT
LING CHARTS BIBLIOG 20. PAGE 39 G0772
LAB/EXP
KNOWL
PERCEPT
COMPUT/IR

B57
MCKINNEY E.R.,A BIBLIOGRAPHY OF CYBERNETICS AND
INFORMATION THEORY. COMPUTER OP/RES...DECISION
PHIL/SCI PSY LING LOG MATH PROBABIL GAME 20.
PAGE 38 G0743
BIBLIOG/A
FEEDBACK
SIMUL
CONTROL

N57
US ARMY LIBRARY,THESES AND DISSERTATIONS IN THE
HOLDINGS OF THE ARMY LIBRARY (PAMPHLET). USA+45
...INT/LAW PSY SOC 20. PAGE 56 G1105
BIBLIOG
FORCES
MGT
CONTROL

S58
SINGER J.D.,"THREAT PERCEPTION AND THE ARMAMENT
TENSION DILEMMA." WOR+45 WOR-45 ELITES INT/ORG
NAT/G DELIB/GP PLAN LEGIT COERCE DETER ATTIT
RIGID/FLEX PWR...DECISION PSY 20. PAGE 51 G1002
PERCEPT
ARMS/CONT
BAL/PWR

B59
GUILBAUD G.T.,WHAT IS CYBERNETICS? COMPUTER OP/RES
TEC/DEV AUTOMAT ROUTINE PERS/REL PERCEPT...PSY MATH
COMPUT/IR SIMUL GEN/METH. PAGE 23 G0460
CONTROL
COM/IND
FEEDBACK
NET/THEORY

B59
MIKSCHE F.O.,THE FAILURE OF ATOMIC STRATEGY. COM
EUR+WWI INTELL POL/PAR FORCES PLAN ECO/TAC NUC/PWR
ATTIT DRIVE RIGID/FLEX PWR...DECISION GEOG PSY
CONCPT RECORD TREND CHARTS VAL/FREE 20. PAGE 39
G0766
ACT/RES
ORD/FREE
DIPLOM
ARMS/CONT

S59
CORY R.H. JR.,"INTERNATIONAL INSPECTION FROM
PROPOSALS TO REALIZATION." WOR+45 TEC/DEV ECO/TAC
ADJUD ORD/FREE PWR WEALTH...RECORD VAL/FREE 20.
PAGE 13 G0258
STRUCT
PSY
ARMS/CONT
NUC/PWR

S59
LEFTON M.,"DECISION MAKING IN A MENTAL HOSPITAL:
REAL, PERCEIVED, AND IDEAL." R+D PUB/INST CONSULT
CONFER INGP/REL PERCEPT...MODAL 20. PAGE 33 G0653
ACT/RES
PROB/SOLV
DECISION
PSY

S59
MILBURN T.W.,"WHAT CONSTITUTES EFFECTIVE
DETERRENCE." USA+45 USSR WOR+45 STRUCT FORCES
ACT/RES PLAN SUPEGO KNOWL ORD/FREE PWR...RELATIV
PSY CONCPT VAL/FREE 20 COLD/WAR. PAGE 39 G0768
INTELL
ATTIT
DETER
NUC/PWR

B60
ARROW K.J.,MATHEMATICAL METHODS IN THE SOCIAL
SCIENCES, 1959. TEC/DEV CHOOSE UTIL PERCEPT
...KNO/TEST GAME SIMUL ANTHOL. PAGE 4 G0070
MATH
PSY
MGT

B60
CARPENTER E.,EXPLORATIONS IN COMMUNICATION. USSR
CULTURE SCHOOL SECT EDU/PROP PRESS TV AUTOMAT
FEEDBACK ATTIT PERSON...ART/METH PSY 20. PAGE 11
G0211
ANTHOL
COM/IND
TEC/DEV
WRITING

B60
RAPOPORT A.,FIGHTS, GAMES AND DEBATES. INTELL
SOCIETY R+D EX/STRUC PERCEPT PERSON SKILL...PSY SOC
GAME. PAGE 46 G0902
METH/CNCPT
MATH
DECISION
CON/ANAL

B60
SLUCKIN W.,MINDS AND MACHINES (REV. ED.). PROB/SOLV
TEC/DEV AUTOMAT TASK PERCEPT HEALTH KNOWL
...DECISION MATH PROBABIL COMPUT/IR GAME 20.
PAGE 51 G1012
PSY
COMPUTER
PERSON
SIMUL

L60
MCCLELLAND C.A.,"THE FUNCTION OF THEORY IN
INTERNATIONAL RELATIONS." WOR+45 PLAN EDU/PROP
ROUTINE ORD/FREE...PHIL/SCI PSY SOC METH/CNCPT
NEW/IDEA OBS TREND GEN/METH 20. PAGE 37 G0728
INT/ORG
CONCPT
DIPLOM

S60
OSGOOD C.E.,"A CASE FOR GRADUATED UNILATERAL
DISENGAGEMENT." FUT WOR+45 CULTURE SOCIETY NAT/G
NUC/PWR WAR PERSON SUPEGO ALL/VALS...POLICY PSY
CONCPT COLD/WAR TOT/POP VAL/FREE 20. PAGE 43 G0848
ATTIT
EDU/PROP
ARMS/CONT

B61
INSTITUTE PSYCHOLOGICAL RES,HUMAN ENGINEERING
BIBLIOGRAPHY, 1959-1960. USA+45 WORKER EDU/PROP
PERSON METH/COMP. PAGE 28 G0547
BIBLIOG/A
METH
PSY
R+D

B61
MICHAEL D.N.,PROPOSED STUDIES ON THE IMPLICATIONS
OF PEACEFUL SPACE ACTIVITIES FOR HUMAN AFFAIRS.
COM/IND INDUS FORCES DIPLOM PEACE PERSON...PSY SOC
20. PAGE 39 G0764
FUT
SPACE
ACT/RES
PROB/SOLV

B62
BORKOF H.,COMPUTER APPLICATIONS IN THE BEHAVIORAL
SCIENCES. AUTOMAT UTIL...DECISION PHIL/SCI PSY
METH/CNCPT LING LOG MATH STYLE NET/THEORY COMPUT/IR
PROG/TEAC SIMUL. PAGE 8 G0154
R+D
COMPUTER
PROB/SOLV
FEEDBACK

B62
BROOKINGS INSTITUTION,DEVELOPMENT OF THE EMERGING
COUNTRIES: AN AGENDA FOR RESEARCH. WOR+45 AGRI
TEC/DEV FOR/AID EDU/PROP ADJUST HABITAT KNOWL...PSY
SOC ANTHOL 20 THIRD/WRLD. PAGE 9 G0175
ECO/UNDEV
R+D
SOCIETY
PROB/SOLV

B62
GUETZKOW H.,SIMULATION IN SOCIAL SCIENCE: READINGS.
STRUCT OP/RES ADMIN AUTOMAT FEEDBACK...MGT PSY SOC
STYLE BIBLIOG. PAGE 23 G0459
SIMUL
TEC/DEV
COMPUTER
GAME

B62
MARS D.,SUGGESTED LIBRARY IN PUBLIC ADMINISTRATION.
FINAN DELIB/GP EX/STRUC WORKER COMPUTER ADJUD
...DECISION PSY SOC METH/COMP 20. PAGE 36 G0710
BIBLIOG
ADMIN
METH
MGT

B62
OSGOOD C.E.,AN ALTERNATIVE TO WAR OR SURRENDER. FUT
UNIV CULTURE INTELL SOCIETY R+D INT/ORG CONSULT
DELIB/GP ACT/RES PLAN CHOOSE ATTIT PERCEPT KNOWL
...PHIL/SCI PSY SOC TREND GEN/LAWS 20. PAGE 43
G0849
ORD/FREE
EDU/PROP
PEACE
WAR

B62
RIKER W.H.,THE THEORY OF POLITICAL COALITIONS.
WOR+45 INTELL NAT/G CREATE PLAN ATTIT DRIVE PERCEPT
...DECISION PSY SOC METH/CNCPT NEW/IDEA MATH CHARTS
GAME TOT/POP 20. PAGE 47 G0921
FUT
SIMUL

B62
SNYDER R.C.,FOREIGN POLICY DECISION-MAKING. FUT
KOREA WOR+45 R+D CREATE ADMIN ROUTINE PWR
...DECISION PSY SOC CONCPT METH/CNCPT CON/ANAL
CHARTS GEN/METH METH 20. PAGE 52 G1018
TEC/DEV
HYPO/EXP
DIPLOM

BETTEN J.K.,"ARMS CONTROL AND THE PROBLEM OF
EVASION." WOR+45 FORCES CREATE DIPLOM DETER PWR
...PSY TREND GEN/LAWS COLD/WAR 20. PAGE 7 G0134
L62 NAT/G PLAN ARMS/CONT

FLOOD M.M.,"STOCHASTIC LEARNING THEORY APPLIED TO
CHOICE EXPERIMENTS WITH RATS, DOGS, AND MEN."...PSY
LAB/EXP METH. PAGE 19 G0372
S62 DECISION COMPUTER HYPO/EXP TEC/DEV

STORER N.W.,"SOME SOCIOLOGICAL ASPECTS OF FEDERAL
SCIENCE POLICY." USA+45 INTELL PUB/INST PLAN GP/REL
PERS/REL DRIVE PERSON ROLE...PSY SOC SIMUL 20 NIH
NSF. PAGE 53 G1040
S62 POLICY CREATE NAT/G ALL/VALS

PEARSELL M.,MEDICAL BEHAVIORAL SCIENCE: A SELECTED
BIBLIOGRAPHY OF CULTURAL ANTHROPOLOGY, SOCIAL
PSYCHOLOGY, AND SOCIOLOGY... USA+45 USA-45 R+D
ATTIT ROLE 20. PAGE 44 G0863
B63 BIBLIOG SOC PSY HEALTH

COOMBS C.H.,A THEORY OF DATA....MGT PHIL/SCI SOC
CLASSIF MATH PROBABIL STAT QU. PAGE 13 G0254
B64 CON/ANAL GEN/METH TESTS PSY

GROSSER G.H.,THE THREAT OF IMPENDING DISASTER:
CONTRIBUTIONS TO THE PSYCHOLOGY OF STRESS. SPACE
UNIV SOCIETY R+D TEC/DEV EDU/PROP COERCE WAR ATTIT
BIO/SOC DISPL PERCEPT PERSON...SOC MYTH SELF/OBS
CONT/OBS BIOG CON/ANAL TOT/POP 20. PAGE 23 G0455
B64 HEALTH PSY NUC/PWR

WARD C.,"THE 'NEW MYTHS' AND 'OLD REALITIES' OF
NUCLEAR WAR." COM FUT USA+45 USSR WOR+45 INT/ORG
NAT/G DOMIN LEGIT EXEC ATTIT PERCEPT ALL/VALS
...POLICY RELATIV PSY MYTH TREND 20. PAGE 62 G1212
L64 FORCES COERCE ARMS/CONT NUC/PWR

NATIONAL ACADEMY OF SCIENCES,BASIC RESEARCH AND
NATIONAL GOALS. R+D ACADEM DELIB/GP PLAN EDU/PROP
...POLICY HEAL PHIL/SCI PSY SOC ANTHOL 20 CONGRESS
HOUSE/REP HS/SCIASTR. PAGE 41 G0809
B65 LEGIS BUDGET NAT/G CREATE

NATIONAL REFERRAL CENTER SCI,A DIRECTORY OF
INFORMATION RESOURCES IN THE UNITED STATES; SOCIAL
SCIENCES. USA+45 PROF/ORG...PSY SOC 20. PAGE 41
G0811
B65 INDEX R+D ACADEM ACT/RES

NATIONAL SCIENCE FOUNDATION,CURRENT RESEARCH AND
DEVELOPMENT IN SCIENTIFIC DOCUMENTATION - NO. 12.
WOR+45 INTELL COM/IND NAT/G COMPUTER TEC/DEV
AUTOMAT KNOWL...PSY LING 20. PAGE 41 G0812
B65 BIBLIOG COMPUT/IR R+D PHIL/SCI

SINGER J.D.,HUMAN BEHAVIOR AND INTERNATIONAL
POLITICS* CONTRIBUTIONS FROM THE SOCIAL-
PSYCHOLOGICAL SCIENCES. ACT/RES PLAN EDU/PROP ADMIN
KNOWL...DECISION PSY SOC NET/THEORY HYPO/EXP
LAB/EXP SOC/EXP GEN/METH ANTHOL BIBLIOG. PAGE 51
G1006
B65 DIPLOM PHIL/SCI QUANT SIMUL

FINK C.F.,"MORE CALCULATIONS ABOUT DETERRENCE."
DRIVE...PHIL/SCI PSY STAT TIME/SEQ GAME GEN/LAWS.
PAGE 19 G0367
S65 DETER RECORD PROBABIL IDEA/COMP

SCHWEBEL M.,"BEHAVIORAL SCIENCE AND HUMAN
SURVIVAL." FORCES ARMS/CONT COERCE NUC/PWR WAR
GP/REL NAT/LISM PERCEPT...POLICY PSY ANTHOL
BIBLIOG/A 20 COLD/WAR. PAGE 50 G0984
C65 PEACE ACT/RES DIPLOM HEAL

HOPKINS J.F.K.,ARABIC PERIODICAL LITERATURE, 1961.
ISLAM LAW CULTURE SECT...GEOG HEAL PHIL/SCI PSY SOC
20. PAGE 27 G0528
B66 BIBLIOG/A NAT/LISM TEC/DEV INDUS

US HOUSE COMM GOVT OPERATIONS,THE COMPUTER AND
INVASION OF PRIVACY. USA+45 SOCIETY ALL/VALS...PSY
SOC CHARTS HOUSE/REP PRIVACY. PAGE 58 G1140
B66 ORD/FREE COMPUTER TEC/DEV NAT/G

RASER J.R.,"DETERRENCE RESEARCH* PAST PROGRESS AND
FUTURE NEEDS." INTELL PLAN TEC/DEV NUC/PWR PERCEPT
...DECISION PSY SOC NET/THEORY. PAGE 46 G0905
L66 DETER BIBLIOG/A FUT

UNIVERSAL REFERENCE SYSTEM,PUBLIC OPINION, MASS
BEHAVIOR, AND POLITICAL PSYCHOLOGY (VOLUME VI).
WOR+45 WOR-45 SOCIETY EDU/PROP PRESS PARTIC CHOOSE
PERSON...TREND COMPUT/IR GEN/METH. PAGE 56 G1098
B67 BIBLIOG/A ATTIT CROWD PSY

US DEPARTMENT OF STATE,FOREIGN AFFAIRS RESEARCH
(PAMPHLET). USA+45 WOR+45 ACADEM NAT/G...PSY SOC
CHARTS 20. PAGE 57 G1124
B67 BIBLIOG INDEX R+D DIPLOM

HILL R.,"SOCIAL ASPECTS OF FAMILY PLANNING." INDIA
KOREA TAIWAN ECO/UNDEV PLAN PROB/SOLV TEC/DEV
EDU/PROP CONTROL ATTIT DRIVE...HEAL PSY SOC 20
BIRTH/CON UN. PAGE 26 G0512
S67 FAM BIO/SOC GEOG MARRIAGE

MCNAMARA R.L.,"THE NEED FOR INNOVATIVENESS IN
DEVELOPING SOCIETIES." L/A+17C EDU/PROP ADMIN LEAD
WEALTH...POLICY PSY SOC METH 20 COLOMB. PAGE 38
G0747
S67 PROB/SOLV PLAN ECO/UNDEV NEW/IDEA

ROBINSON J.A.T.,"ABORTION* THE CASE FOR A FREE
DECISION." LAW PROB/SOLV SANCTION ATTIT MORAL...PSY
IDEA/COMP 20 ABORTION. PAGE 47 G0930
S67 PLAN ILLEGIT SEX HEALTH

SUINN R.M.,"THE DISARMAMENT FANTASY* PSYCHOLOGICAL
FACTORS THAT MAY PRODUCE WARFARE." DIPLOM RISK
ARMS/CONT DETER ANOMIE PERSON GAME. PAGE 53 G1046
S67 DECISION NUC/PWR WAR PSY

GALLAHER A. JR.,PERSPECTIVES IN DEVELOPMENTAL
CHANGE. MUNIC PLAN INSPECT EDU/PROP...POLICY
DECISION GEOG PSY SOC IDEA/COMP ANTHOL 20
MODERNIZE. PAGE 21 G0405
B68 TECHNIC TEC/DEV PROB/SOLV CREATE

PSY/WAR....PSYCHOLOGICAL WARFARE; SEE ALSO PSY + EDU/PROP +
WAR

PSYCHIATRY....SEE PSY

PSYCHOANALYSIS....SEE BIOG, PSY

PSYCHO-DRAMA....SEE SELF/OBS

PSYCHOLOGICAL WARFARE....SEE PSY+EDU/PROP+WAR

PSYCHOLOGY....SEE PSY

PUB/INST....MENTAL, CORRECTIONAL, AND OTHER HABITATIONAL
    INSTITUTIONS

HODGSON J.G.,THE OFFICIAL PUBLICATIONS OF AMERICAN
COUNTIES: A UNION LIST. SCHOOL BUDGET...HEAL MGT
SOC/WK 19/20. PAGE 26 G0520
B37 BIBLIOG LOC/G PUB/INST

US LIBRARY OF CONGRESS,CONDUCT OF THE WAR (APRIL
1941-MARCH 1942). USA-45 WOR-45 LAW INDUS PUB/INST
TEC/DEV EDU/PROP CIVMIL/REL 20. PAGE 59 G1155
B42 BIBLIOG/A WAR FORCES PLAN

SIMMONS L.W.,SOCIAL SCIENCE IN MEDICINE. USA+45
USA-45 SOCIETY CONSULT PLAN PROB/SOLV CONTROL
PERS/REL...POLICY HEAL TREND BIBLIOG 20. PAGE 51
G0999
B54 PUB/INST HABITAT HEALTH BIO/SOC

LEFTON M.,"DECISION MAKING IN A MENTAL HOSPITAL:
REAL, PERCEIVED, AND IDEAL." R+D PUB/INST CONSULT
CONFER INGP/REL PERCEPT...MODAL 20. PAGE 33 G0653
S59 ACT/RES PROB/SOLV DECISION PSY

MAINZER L.C.,"SCIENTIFIC FREEDOM IN GOVERNMENT-
SPONSORED RESEARCH." USA+45 INTELL PUB/INST BUDGET
LOBBY AUTHORIT PWR...POLICY PHIL/SCI 20 NIH NSF.
PAGE 35 G0696
S61 CREATE ORD/FREE NAT/G R+D

STORER N.W.,"SOME SOCIOLOGICAL ASPECTS OF FEDERAL
SCIENCE POLICY." USA+45 INTELL PUB/INST PLAN GP/REL
PERS/REL DRIVE PERSON ROLE...PSY SOC SIMUL 20 NIH
NSF. PAGE 53 G1040
S62 POLICY CREATE NAT/G ALL/VALS

RUSHING W.A.,THE PSYCHIATRIC PROFESSIONS. DOMIN
B64 ATTIT

INGP/REL DRIVE RIGID/FLEX ROLE HEALTH PWR...POLICY GP/COMP. PAGE 48 G0947
PUB/INST
PROF/ORG
BAL/PWR

B65
US LIBRARY OF CONGRESS,A DIRECTORY OF INFORMATION RESOURCES IN THE UNITED STATES: SOCIAL SCIENCES. USA+45 ACADEM INT/ORG LABOR PROF/ORG PUB/INST SCHOOL SECT 20. PAGE 59 G1156
BIBLIOG
R+D
COMPUT/IR

B66
STREET D.,ORGANIZATION FOR TREATMENT. CLIENT PROVS PUB/INST PLAN CONTROL PARTIC REPRESENT ATTIT PWR ...POLICY BIBLIOG. PAGE 53 G1044
GP/COMP
AGE/Y
ADMIN
VOL/ASSN

S66
GREENBERG D.S.,"THE SCIENTIFIC PORK BARREL." USA+45 ECO/DEV PUB/INST CHIEF LEGIS BUDGET GIVE GP/REL PWR WEALTH 20. PAGE 23 G0445
R+D
NAT/G
ACADEM
ATTIT

B67
FIELD M.G.,SOVIET SOCIALIZED MEDICINE. USSR FINAN R+D PROB/SOLV ADMIN SOCISM...MGT SOC CONCPT 20. PAGE 19 G0366
PUB/INST
HEALTH
NAT/G
MARXISM

B67
UNIVERSAL REFERENCE SYSTEM,ADMINISTRATIVE MANAGEMENT: PUBLIC AND PRIVATE BUREAUCRACY (VOLUME IV). WOR+45 WOR-45 ECO/DEV LG/CO LOC/G PUB/INST VOL/ASSN GOV/REL...COMPUT/IR GEN/METH. PAGE 56 G1096
BIBLIOG/A
MGT
ADMIN
NAT/G

B67
US PRES COMN LAW ENFORCE-JUS,THE CHALLENGE OF CRIME IN A FREE SOCIETY. LAW STRUCT CONSULT ACT/RES TEC/DEV INGP/REL...SOC/WK 20. PAGE 59 G1160
CT/SYS
PUB/INST
CRIMLGY
CRIME

S67
ARONOWITZ D.S.,"CIVIL COMMITMENT OF NARCOTIC ADDICTS." USA+45 LAW INGP/REL DISCRIM MORAL...TREND 20. PAGE 4 G0069
PUB/INST
ACT/RES
POLICY

PUB/TRANS....PUBLIC TRANSPORTATION

B54
LOCKLIN D.P.,ECONOMICS OF TRANSPORTATION (4TH ED.). USA+45 USA-45 SEA AIR LAW FINAN LG/CO EX/STRUC ADMIN CONTROL...STAT CHARTS 19/20 RAILROAD PUB/TRANS. PAGE 34 G0675
ECO/DEV
DIST/IND
ECO/TAC
TEC/DEV

B57
DRUCKER P.F.,AMERICA'S NEXT TWENTY YEARS. USA+45 DIST/IND ACADEM MUNIC SCHOOL DIPLOM ECO/TAC AUTOMAT HABITAT HEALTH...SOC/WK TREND 20 URBAN/RNWL PUB/TRANS. PAGE 16 G0316
WORKER
FOR/AID
CENSUS
GEOG

B60
US SENATE COMM ON COMMERCE,URBAN MASS TRANSPORTATION. FUT USA+45 AIR ECO/DEV FINAN LOC/G MUNIC LEGIS CREATE PROB/SOLV TEC/DEV 20 PUB/TRANS. PAGE 60 G1180
DIST/IND
PLAN
NAT/G
LAW

B64
LANG A.S.,URBAN RAIL TRANSIT. OP/RES PLAN PROB/SOLV TEC/DEV AUTOMAT COST...TECHNIC MATH CON/ANAL CHARTS METH/COMP SIMUL 20 RAILROAD PUB/TRANS. PAGE 32 G0632
MUNIC
DIST/IND
ECOMETRIC

B65
WHITE HOUSE CONFERENCE ON INTERNATIONAL COOPERATION(VOL.II). SPACE WOR+45 EXTR/IND INT/ORG LABOR WORKER NUC/PWR PEACE AGE/Y...CENSUS ANTHOL 20 RESOURCE/N URBAN/RNWL PUB/TRANS. PAGE 1 G0019
R+D
CONFER
TEC/DEV
DIPLOM

B66
LECHT L.,GOAL, PRIORITIES, AND DOLLARS: THE NEXT DECADE. SPACE USA+45 SOCIETY AGRI BUDGET FOR/AID ...HEAL SOC/WK STAT CHARTS 20 URBAN/RNWL PUB/TRANS. PAGE 33 G0649
IDEA/COMP
POLICY
CONSEN
PLAN

PUBL/WORKS....PUBLIC WORKS

PUBLIC ADMINISTRATION....SEE ADMIN

PUBLIC HEALTH SERVICE....SEE PHS

PUBLIC OPINION....SEE ATTIT

PUBLIC POLICY....SEE NAT/G+PLAN

PUBLIC RELATIONS....SEE NAT/G+RELATIONS INDEX

PUBLIC WORKS....SEE PUBL/WORKS

PUBLIC ADMIN CLEARING HOUSE G0893

PUBLIC ADMINISTRATION SERVICE G0894,G0895

PUBLIC/EDU....PUBLIC EDUCATION ASSOCIATION

PUBLIC/REL....PUBLIC RELATIONS; SEE ALSO NAT/G + RELATIONS INDEX

PUBLIC/USE....PUBLIC USE

PUEBLO....PUEBLO INCIDENT; SEE ALSO KOREA/N

PUERT/RICN....PUERTO RICAN

PUERT/RICO....PUERTO RICO; SEE ALSO L/A+17C

PUERTO RICANS....SEE PUERT/RICN

PULLMAN....PULLMAN, ILLINOIS

B67
BUDER S.,PULLMAN: AN EXPERIMENT IN INDUSTRIAL ORDER AND COMMUNITY PLANNING, 1880-1930. USA-45 SOCIETY LABOR LG/CO CREATE PROB/SOLV CONTROL GP/REL EFFICIENCY ATTIT...MGT BIBLIOG 19/20 PULLMAN. PAGE 9 G0184
DIST/IND
INDUS
MUNIC
PLAN

PUNISHMENT....SEE ADJUD, LAW, LEGIT, SANCTION

PUNJAB....THE PUNJAB AND ITS PEOPLES

PUNTA DEL ESTE....SEE PUNTA/ESTE

PUNTA/ESTE....PUNTA DEL ESTE

PURGE....PURGES

PURHAM/M....MARGERY PURHAM

PURITAN....PURITANS

PURSELL G.W.E. G0617

PWR....POWER, PARTICIPATION IN DECISION-MAKING

N
WEIGLEY R.F.,HISTORY OF THE UNITED STATES ARMY. USA+45 USA-45 SOCIETY NAT/G LEAD WAR GP/REL PWR ...SOC METH/COMP COLD/WAR. PAGE 62 G1222
FORCES
ADMIN
ROLE
CIVMIL/REL

N19
MEZERIK A.G.,INTERNATIONAL POLICY 1965 (PAMPHLET). KASHMIR S/ASIA SPACE USA+45 VIETNAM WOR+45 ARMS/CONT RACE/REL DISCRIM PEACE PWR 20 UN. PAGE 39 G0762
DIPLOM
INT/ORG
POLICY
WAR

B23
DRAPER J.W.,HISTORY OF THE CONFLICT BETWEEN RELIGION AND SCIENCE. WOR-45 INTELL SOCIETY R+D CREATE PLAN TEC/DEV EDU/PROP ATTIT PWR...PHIL/SCI CONCPT OBS TIME/SEQ TREND GEN/LAWS TOT/POP. PAGE 16 G0314
SECT
KNOWL

B25
MATHEWS J.M.,AMERICAN STATE GOVERNMENT. USA-45 LOC/G CHIEF EX/STRUC LEGIS ADJUD CONTROL CT/SYS ROUTINE GOV/REL PWR 20 GOVERNOR. PAGE 37 G0721
PROVS
ADMIN
FEDERAL
CONSTN

B29
DEWEY J.,THE QUEST FOR CERTAINTY. GP/REL RATIONAL UTOPIA ATTIT MORAL ORD/FREE PWR...MYTH HIST/WRIT. PAGE 15 G0301
PHIL/SCI
PERSON
PERCEPT
KNOWL

B39
FULLER G.H.,A SELECTED LIST OF REFERENCES ON THE EXPANSION OF THE US NAVY, 1933-1939 (PAMPHLET). MOD/EUR USA-45 NAT/G PLAN DIPLOM DOMIN RISK ARMS/CONT EQUILIB PWR 20 NAVY. PAGE 20 G0399
BIBLIOG
FORCES
WEAPON
WAR

B40
FULLER G.H.,SELECTED LIST OF RECENT REFERENCES ON AMERICAN NATIONAL DEFENSE (PAMPHLET). USA-45 FINAN NAT/G ARMS/CONT WAR GOV/REL CENTRAL COST PEACE PWR 20. PAGE 20 G0400
BIBLIOG
CIVMIL/REL
FORCES
WEAPON

B40
MORSTEIN-MARX F.,PUBLIC MANAGEMENT IN THE NEW DEMOCRACY. REPRESENT...MGT 20. PAGE 40 G0786
EX/STRUC
ADMIN
EXEC
PWR

BEARD C.A.,PUBLIC POLICY AND THE GENERAL WELFARE. B41
USA-45 CONSTN LAISSEZ POPULISM...POLICY MAJORIT 20.
PAGE 6 G0108

CONCPT
ORD/FREE
PWR
NAT/G

FULLER G.H.,DEFENSE FINANCING: A SELECTED LIST OF B41
REFERENCES (PAMPHLET). MOD/EUR USA-45 ECO/DEV NAT/G
DELIB/GP RATION ARMS/CONT WEAPON COST PEACE PWR 20
CONGRESS. PAGE 20 G0401

BIBLIOG/A
FINAN
FORCES
BUDGET

FULLER G.H.,DEFENSE FINANCING: A SUPPLEMENTARY LIST B42
OF REFERENCES (PAMPHLET). CANADA UK USA-45 ECO/DEV
NAT/G DELIB/GP BUDGET ADJUD ARMS/CONT WEAPON COST
PEACE PWR 20 AUSTRAL CHINJAP CONGRESS. PAGE 21
G0403

BIBLIOG/A
FINAN
FORCES
DIPLOM

LASSWELL H.D.,"THE RELATION OF IDEOLOGICAL S42
INTELLIGENCE TO PUBLIC POLICY." WOR+45 WOR-45
SOCIETY DELIB/GP ACT/RES CREATE PLAN DIPLOM
EDU/PROP CHOOSE KNOWL PWR...POLICY SOC TREND
GEN/LAWS 20. PAGE 32 G0638

ATTIT
DECISION

FULLER G.H.,MILITARY GOVERNMENT: A LIST OF B44
REFERENCES (A PAMPHLET). ITALY UK USA-45 WOR-45 LAW
FORCES DOMIN ADMIN ARMS/CONT ORD/FREE PWR
...DECISION 20 CHINJAP. PAGE 21 G0404

BIBLIOG
DIPLOM
CIVMIL/REL
SOVEREIGN

MERRIAM C.E.,PUBLIC AND PRIVATE GOVERNMENT. B44
VOL/ASSN EDU/PROP ADMIN REPRESENT EFFICIENCY PWR
PLURISM...MAJORIT CONCPT. PAGE 38 G0755

NAT/G
NEIGH
MGT
POLICY

BAXTER J.P.,SCIENTISTS AGAINST TIME. EUR+WWI B46
MOD/EUR USA+45 USA-45 WOR+45 WOR-45 R+D NAT/G PLAN
ATTIT PWR...PHIL/SCI RECORD CON/ANAL 17/20. PAGE 6
G0107

FORCES
WAR
NUC/PWR

BRODIE B.,THE OBSOLETE WEAPON: ATOMIC POWER AND B46
WORLD ORDER. COM USA+45 USSR WOR+45 DELIB/GP PLAN
ORD/FREE PWR...CONCPT TIME/SEQ TREND UN 20. PAGE 9
G0171

INT/ORG
TEC/DEV
ARMS/CONT
NUC/PWR

BALDWIN H.W.,THE PRICE OF POWER. USA+45 FORCES PLAN B47
NUC/PWR ADJUST COST ORD/FREE...POLICY PSY BIBLIOG
20. PAGE 5 G0089

PROB/SOLV
PWR
POPULISM
PRICE

TURNER R.H.,"THE NAVY DISBURSING OFFICER AS A S47
BUREAUCRAT" (BMR)" USA-45 LAW STRATA DIST/IND WAR
PWR...SOC 20 BUREAUCRCY. PAGE 55 G1083

FORCES
ADMIN
PERSON
ROLE

OGBURN W.,TECHNOLOGY AND INTERNATIONAL RELATIONS. B49
WOR+45 WOR-45 ECO/DEV CREATE PLAN ECO/TAC EDU/PROP
COERCE PWR SKILL WEALTH...TECHNIC PSY SOC NEW/IDEA
CHARTS TOT/POP 20. PAGE 43 G0837

TEC/DEV
DIPLOM
INT/ORG

MERTON R.,"THE ROLE OF APPLIED SOCIAL SCIENCE IN S49
THE FORMATION OF POLICY: A RESEARCH MEMORANDUM."
WOR+45 INDUS NAT/G EXEC ROUTINE CHOOSE ORD/FREE PWR
SKILL...POLICY MGT PSY METH/CNCPT TESTS CHARTS METH
VAL/FREE 20. PAGE 38 G0756

PLAN
SOC
DIPLOM

CROWTHER J.G.,SCIENCE AT WAR. EUR+WWI PLAN TEC/DEV B50
DOMIN COERCE NUC/PWR WEAPON KNOWL PWR...CONCPT OBS
TREND VAL/FREE 20. PAGE 14 G0265

R+D
FORCES
WAR
UK

KAPLAN A.,"THE PREDICTION OF SOCIAL AND S50
TECHNOLOGICAL EVENTS." VOL/ASSN CONSULT ACT/RES
CREATE OP/RES PLAN ROUTINE PERSON...POLICY
METH/CNCPT STAT QU/SEMANT SYS/QU TESTS CENSUS TREND
20. PAGE 29 G0574

PWR
KNO/TEST

MAASS A.,MUDDY WATERS: THE ARMY ENGINEERS AND THE B51
NATIONS RIVERS. USA-45 PROF/ORG CONSULT LEGIS ADMIN
EXEC ROLE PWR...SOC PRESIDENT 20. PAGE 35 G0682

FORCES
GP/REL
LOBBY
CONSTRUC

LERNER D.,"THE POLICY SCIENCES: RECENT DEVELOPMENTS S51
IN SCOPE AND METHODS." R+D SERV/IND CREATE DIPLOM
ROUTINE PWR...METH/CNCPT TREND GEN/LAWS METH 20.
PAGE 33 G0658

CONSULT
SOC

LANGER W.L.,THE UNDECLARED WAR, 1940-1941. EUR+WWI B53
GERMANY USA-45 USSR AIR FORCES TEC/DEV CONFER
CONTROL COERCE PERCEPT ORD/FREE PWR 20 CHINJAP
EUROPE. PAGE 32 G0634

WAR
POLICY
DIPLOM

ARON R.,CENTURY OF TOTAL WAR. FUT WOR+45 WOR-45 B54
SOCIETY INT/ORG NAT/G FORCES TOP/EX CREATE BAL/PWR
DOMIN EDU/PROP COERCE DETER PEACE TOTALISM PWR
...TIME/SEQ TREND COLD/WAR TOT/POP VAL/FREE
LEAGUE/NAT 20. PAGE 4 G0066

ATTIT
WAR

COMBS C.H.,DECISION PROCESSES. INTELL SOCIETY B54
DELIB/GP CREATE TEC/DEV DOMIN LEGIT EXEC CHOOSE
DRIVE RIGID/FLEX KNOWL PWR...PHIL/SCI SOC
METH/CNCPT CONT/OBS REC/INT PERS/TEST SAMP/SIZ BIOG
SOC/EXP WORK. PAGE 13 G0245

MATH
DECISION

WRIGHT Q.,PROBLEMS OF STABILITY AND PROGRESS IN B54
INTERNATIONAL RELATIONSHIPS. FUT WOR+45 WOR-45
SOCIETY LEGIS CREATE TEC/DEV ECO/TAC EDU/PROP ADJUD
WAR PEACE ORD/FREE PWR...KNO/TEST TREND GEN/LAWS
20. PAGE 64 G1257

INT/ORG
CONCPT
DIPLOM

DEUTSCH K.W.,"GAME THEORY AND POLITICS: SOME S54
PROBLEMS OF APPLICATION." FUT WOR+45 SOCIETY R+D
KNOWL PWR...CONCPT METH/CNCPT MATH QUANT GAME SIMUL
VAL/FREE 20. PAGE 15 G0295

DECISION
GEN/METH

HOOPES T.,"CIVILIAN-MILITARY BALANCE." USA+45 CHIEF S54
FORCES PLAN CONTROL WAR GOV/REL GP/REL INGP/REL
...POLICY 19/20. PAGE 27 G0527

CIVMIL/REL
LEAD
PWR
NAT/G

LIPPMAN W.,THE PUBLIC PHILOSOPHY. EX/STRUC TOP/EX B55
LOBBY RATIONAL POPULISM...POLICY SOC CONCPT PREDICT
GP/COMP IDEA/COMP. PAGE 34 G0673

MAJORIT
STRUCT
PWR
TOTALISM

MIKSCHE F.O.,ATOMIC WEAPONS AND ARMIES. FUT WOR+45 B55
WOR-45 SOCIETY COERCE DETER WEAPON PWR...POLICY
WELF/ST PSY CONCPT INT SYS/QU KNO/TEST TOT/POP 20.
PAGE 39 G0765

TEC/DEV
FORCES
NUC/PWR

MOCH J.,HUMAN FOLLY: DISARM OR PERISH. USA+45 B55
WOR+45 SOCIETY INT/ORG NAT/G ACT/RES EDU/PROP ATTIT
PERSON KNOWL ORD/FREE PWR...MAJORIT TOT/POP
COLD/WAR 20. PAGE 39 G0776

FUT
DELIB/GP
ARMS/CONT
NUC/PWR

OPPENHEIMER R.,THE OPEN MIND. USA+45 WOR+45 NAT/G B55
DELIB/GP DETER MORAL ORD/FREE...MYTH GEN/LAWS 20.
PAGE 43 G0842

CREATE
PWR
ARMS/CONT
NUC/PWR

SHUBIK M.,READINGS IN GAME THEORY AND POLITICAL B55
BEHAVIOR. WOR+45 FORCES CREATE ROUTINE WAR PEACE
PERCEPT KNOWL PWR...PSY SOC CONCPT METH/CNCPT STAT
CHARTS HYPO/EXP GAME METH VAL/FREE 20. PAGE 50
G0991

MATH
DECISION
DIPLOM

GLADSTONE A.E.,"THE POSSIBILITY OF PREDICTING S55
REACTIONS TO INTERNATIONAL EVENTS." UNIV SOCIETY
NAT/G FORCES CREATE EDU/PROP COERCE WAR ATTIT
PERSON KNOWL PWR SKILL...METH/CNCPT NEW/IDEA
ORG/CHARTS. PAGE 21 G0420

PHIL/SCI
CONCPT

SKINNER B.F.,"FREEDOM AND THE CONTROL OF MEN" S55
(BMR)" FUT WOR+45 CONTROL CHOOSE GP/REL ATTIT MORAL
PWR POPULISM...POLICY 20. PAGE 51 G1008

ORD/FREE
TEC/DEV
PHIL/SCI
INTELL

BLACKETT P.M.S.,ATOMIC WEAPONS AND EAST-WEST B56
RELATIONS. FUT WOR+45 INT/ORG DELIB/GP COERCE ATTIT
RIGID/FLEX KNOWL...RELATIV HIST/WRIT TREND GEN/METH
COLD/WAR 20. PAGE 7 G0138

FORCES
PWR
ARMS/CONT
NUC/PWR

THOMAS M.,ATOMIC ENERGY AND CONGRESS. USA+45 NAT/G | B56 | LEGIS
ACT/RES PLAN TEC/DEV EDU/PROP ROUTINE KNOWL PWR | ADMIN
SKILL...PHIL/SCI NEW/IDEA TIME/SEQ CHARTS METH | NUC/PWR
CONGRESS VAL/FREE 20 AEC. PAGE 54 G1067

EASTON D.,"LIMITS OF THE EQUILIBRIUM MODEL IN | S56 | METH/CNCPT
SOCIAL RESEARCH." STRUCT GP/REL PWR...PHIL/SCI | GEN/METH
CLASSIF. PAGE 17 G0330 | R+D
QUANT

MILLER W.E.,"PRESIDENTIAL COATTAILS: A STUDY IN | S56 | CHIEF
POLITICAL MYTH AND METHODOLOGY" (BMR)" USA+45 | CHOOSE
CREATE PARTIC ATTIT DRIVE PWR...DECISION CONCPT | POL/PAR
CHARTS SIMUL 20 PRESIDENT CONGRESS. PAGE 39 G0774 | MYTH

KISSINGER H.A.,NUCLEAR WEAPONS AND FOREIGN POLICY. | B57 | PLAN
FUT WOR+45 INT/ORG FORCES ACT/RES TEC/DEV | DETER
DIPLOM ARMS/CONT COERCE ATTIT KNOWL PWR...DECISION | NUC/PWR
GEOG CHARTS 20. PAGE 31 G0602

SPEIER H.,GERMAN REARMAMENT AND ATOMIC WAR: THE | B57 | TOP/EX
VIEWS OF GERMAN MILITARY AND POLITICAL LEADERS. FUT | FORCES
WOR+45 INT/ORG NAT/G WEAPON ATTIT PWR...INT QU | NUC/PWR
TOT/POP VAL/FREE COLD/WAR 20. PAGE 52 G1024 | GERMANY

JANOWITZ M.,"MILITARY ELITES AND THE STUDY OF WAR." | S57 | FORCES
USA+45 WOR-45 STRATA NAT/G PROF/ORG TEC/DEV DOMIN | ELITES
EDU/PROP COERCE WAR ATTIT RIGID/FLEX PWR RESPECT
...MGT TREND STERTYP GEN/METH 20. PAGE 28 G0558

TAYLOR P.S.,"THE RELATION OF RESEARCH TO | S57 | DECISION
LEGISLATIVE AND ADMINISTRATIVE DECISIONS." ELITES | LEGIS
ACT/RES PLAN PROB/SOLV CONFER CHOOSE POLICY. | MGT
PAGE 54 G1059 | PWR

JUNGK R.,BRIGHTER THAN A THOUSAND SUNS: THE MORAL | B58 | NUC/PWR
AND POLITICAL HISTORY OF THE ATOMIC SCIENTISTS. | MORAL
WOR+45 WOR-45 CONSULT CREATE RISK UTIL DRIVE | GOV/REL
PERCEPT PWR...INT 20. PAGE 29 G0568 | PERSON

LIPPITT R.,DYNAMICS OF PLANNED CHANGE. STRUCT | B58 | VOL/ASSN
ACT/RES ROUTINE INGP/REL PWR...POLICY METH/CNCPT | ORD/FREE
BIBLIOG. PAGE 34 G0672 | PLAN
CREATE

NOEL-BAKER D.,THE ARMS RACE. WOR+45 NAT/G DELIB/GP | B58 | FUT
ACT/RES TEC/DEV EDU/PROP NUC/PWR ATTIT KNOWL PWR | INT/ORG
...CONCPT OBS LEAGUE/NAT 20 COLD/WAR. PAGE 42 G0823 | ARMS/CONT
PEACE

DAVENPORT J.,"ARMS AND THE WELFARE STATE." INTELL | S58 | USA+45
STRUCT FORCES CREATE ECO/TAC FOR/AID DOMIN LEGIT | NAT/G
ADMIN WAR ORD/FREE PWR...POLICY SOC CONCPT MYTH OBS | USSR
TREND COLD/WAR TOT/POP 20. PAGE 14 G0276

HUNTINGTON S.P.,"ARMS RACES: PREREQUISITES AND | S58 | FORCES
RESULTS." EUR+WWI MOD/EUR USA+45 WOR+45 WOR-45 | PWR
NAT/G TEC/DEV BAL/PWR COERCE DETER ATTIT...POLICY | ARMS/CONT
TREND 20. PAGE 27 G0537

LASSWELL H.D.,"THE SCIENTIFIC STUDY OF | S58 | PHIL/SCI
INTERNATIONAL RELATIONS." USA+45 INT/ORG CREATE | GEN/METH
EDU/PROP DETER ATTIT PERCEPT PWR...DECISION CONCPT | DIPLOM
METH/CNCPT STYLE CON/ANAL 20. PAGE 33 G0642

SINGER J.D.,"THREAT PERCEPTION AND THE ARMAMENT | S58 | PERCEPT
TENSION DILEMMA." WOR+45 WOR-45 ELITES INT/ORG | ARMS/CONT
NAT/G DELIB/GP PLAN LEGIT COERCE DETER ATTIT | BAL/PWR
RIGID/FLEX PWR...DECISION PSY 20. PAGE 51 G1002

THOMPSON K.W.,"NATIONAL SECURITY IN A NUCLEAR AGE." | S58 | FORCES
USA+45 WOR+45 SOCIETY INT/ORG NAT/G TOP/EX DIPLOM | PWR
DOMIN EDU/PROP LEGIT ARMS/CONT COERCE ORD/FREE | BAL/PWR
...TREND STERTYP TOT/POP VAL/FREE COLD/WAR 20.
PAGE 54 G1068

AMRINE M.,THE GREAT DECISION: THE SECRET HISTORY OF | B59 | DECISION
THE ATOMIC BOMB. USA+45 TOP/EX EDU/PROP LEGIT | NAT/G
PERCEPT ORD/FREE PWR VAL/FREE HIROSHIMA. PAGE 3 | NUC/PWR
G0055 | FORCES

GODDARD V.,THE ENIGMA OF MENACE. WOR+45 SECT LEAD | B59 | PEACE
NUC/PWR WAR WEAPON CHOOSE PERSON PWR...POLICY | ARMS/CONT
PHIL/SCI PACIFIST 20 COLD/WAR. PAGE 22 G0423 | DIPLOM
ATTIT

GREENFIELD K.R.,COMMAND DECISIONS. ASIA EUR+WWI | B59 | PLAN
S/ASIA USA-45 WOR-45 NAT/G CONSULT DELIB/GP COERCE | FORCES
NUC/PWR PWR...OBS 20 CHINJAP. PAGE 23 G0446 | WAR
WEAPON

HALEY A.G.,FIRST COLLOQUIUM ON THE LAW OF OUTER | B59 | SPACE
SPACE. WOR+45 INT/ORG ACT/RES PLAN BAL/PWR CONFER | LAW
ATTIT PWR...POLICY JURID CHARTS ANTHOL 20. PAGE 24 | SOVEREIGN
G0468 | CONTROL

LANG D.,FROM HIROSHIMA TO THE MOON: CHRONICLES OF | B59 | NUC/PWR
LIFE IN THE ATOMIC AGE. USA+45 OP/RES CONTROL | SPACE
ARMS/CONT WAR CIVMIL/REL PEACE HABITAT MORAL PWR | HEALTH
...OBS INT 20 AEC. PAGE 32 G0633 | TEC/DEV

MIKSCHE F.O.,THE FAILURE OF ATOMIC STRATEGY. COM | B59 | ACT/RES
EUR+WWI INTELL POL/PAR FORCES PLAN ECO/TAC NUC/PWR | ORD/FREE
ATTIT DRIVE RIGID/FLEX PWR...DECISION GEOG PSY | DIPLOM
CONCPT RECORD TREND CHARTS VAL/FREE 20. PAGE 39 | ARMS/CONT
G0766

COLUMBIA U BUREAU APPL SOC R, ATTITUDES OF | B59 | ATTIT
PROMINENT AMERICANS TOWARD "WORLD PEACE THROUGH | ACT/RES
WORLD LAW" (SUPRA-NATL ORGANIZATION FOR WAR | INT/LAW
PREVENTION). USA+45 USSR ELITES FORCES PLAN | STAT
PROB/SOLV CONTROL WAR PWR...POLICY SOC QU IDEA/COMP
20 UN. PAGE 45 G0888

RUSSELL B.,COMMON SENSE AND NUCLEAR WARFARE. WOR+45 | B59 | ORD/FREE
INTELL SOCIETY STRATA NAT/G TOP/EX EDU/PROP ATTIT | ARMS/CONT
PERSON KNOWL MORAL PWR...POLICY CONCPT MYTH | NUC/PWR
CON/ANAL COLD/WAR 20. PAGE 48 G0948

SPANIER J.W.,THE TRUMAN-MACARTHUR CONTROVERSY AND | B59 | CIVMIL/REL
THE KOREAN WAR. USA+45 TOP/EX PROB/SOLV LEAD ATTIT | FORCES
PWR...POLICY BIBLIOG/A UN. PAGE 52 G1023 | CHIEF
WAR

BURNS A.L.,"THE RATIONALE OF CATALYTIC WAR." COM | L59 | COERCE
USA+45 WOR+45 R+D NAT/G FORCES ACT/RES TEC/DEV PWR | NUC/PWR
...DECISION HYPO/EXP TOT/POP 20. PAGE 10 G0191 | WAR

BLOOMFIELD L.P.,"THREE EXPERIMENTS IN POLITICAL | S59 | TEC/DEV
GAMING." ACT/RES CREATE PWR...GAME GEN/METH METH. | METH/CNCPT
PAGE 7 G0140 | DECISION

CORY R.H. JR.,"INTERNATIONAL INSPECTION FROM | S59 | STRUCT
PROPOSALS TO REALIZATION." WOR+45 TEC/DEV ECO/TAC | PSY
ADJUD ORD/FREE PWR WEALTH...RECORD VAL/FREE 20. | ARMS/CONT
PAGE 13 G0258 | NUC/PWR

GOLDHAMMER H.,"SOME OBSERVATIONS ON POLITICAL | S59 | COMPUT/IR
GAMING." FUT WOR+45 R+D NAT/G ACT/RES CREATE CHOOSE | DECISION
ATTIT PWR...POLICY CONCPT METH/CNCPT STYLE KNO/TEST | DIPLOM
TREND HYPO/EXP GAME GEN/METH METH 20. PAGE 22 G0426

MILBURN T.W.,"WHAT CONSTITUTES EFFECTIVE | S59 | INTELL
DETERRENCE." USA+45 USSR WOR+45 STRUCT FORCES | ATTIT
ACT/RES PLAN SUPEGO KNOWL ORD/FREE PWR...RELATIV | DETER
PSY CONCPT VAL/FREE 20 COLD/WAR. PAGE 39 G0768 | NUC/PWR

SIMONS H.,"WORLD-WIDE CAPABILITIES FOR PRODUCTION | S59 | TEC/DEV
AND CONTROL OF NUCLEAR WEAPONS." FUT WOR+45 INDUS | ARMS/CONT
INT/ORG NAT/G ECO/TAC ATTIT PWR SKILL...TREND | NUC/PWR
CHARTS VAL/FREE 20. PAGE 51 G1001

STOESSINGER J.G.,"THE INTERNATIONAL ATOMIC ENERGY | S59 | INT/ORG
AGENCY: THE FIRST PHASE." FUT WOR+45 NAT/G VOL/ASSN | ECO/DEV
DELIB/GP BAL/PWR LEGIT ADMIN ROUTINE PWR...OBS | FOR/AID
CON/ANAL GEN/LAWS VAL/FREE 20 IAEA. PAGE 53 G1037 | NUC/PWR

WILLIAMS B.H.,"SCIENTIFIC METHOD IN FOREIGN | S59 | PLAN
POLICY." WOR+45 NAT/G FORCES TOP/EX DOMIN LEGIT | PHIL/SCI
COERCE PEACE ATTIT KNOWL ORD/FREE PWR...GEN/LAWS | DIPLOM

BARNET R.,WHO WANTS DISARMAMENT. COM EUR+WWI USA+45 PLAN
USSR INT/ORG NAT/G BAL/PWR DIPLOM EDU/PROP COERCE FORCES
DETER NUC/PWR WAR WEAPON ATTIT PWR...TIME/SEQ ARMS/CONT
COLD/WAR CONGRESS 20. PAGE 5 G0096
B60

GOLDSEN J.M.,INTERNATIONAL POLITICAL IMPLICATIONS R+D
OF ACTIVITIES IN OUTER SPACE. FUT USA+45 WOR+45 AIR SPACE
LAW ACT/RES LEGIT KNOWL ORD/FREE PWR...CONCPT
20. PAGE 22 G0427
B60

GRANICK D.,THE RED EXECUTIVE. COM USA+45 SOCIETY PWR
ECO/DEV INDUS NAT/G POL/PAR EX/STRUC PLAN ECO/TAC STRATA
EDU/PROP ADMIN EXEC ATTIT DRIVE...GP/COMP 20. USSR
PAGE 22 G0440 ELITES
B60

US HOUSE COMM. SCI. ASTRONAUT.,OCEAN SCIENCES AND R+D
NATIONAL SECURITY. FUT SEA ECO/DEV EXTR/IND INT/ORG ORD/FREE
NAT/G FORCES ACT/RES TEC/DEV ECO/TAC COERCE WAR
BIO/SOC KNOWL PWR...CONCPT RECORD LAB/EXP 20.
PAGE 59 G1153
B60

WOETZEL R.K.,THE INTERNATIONAL CONTROL OF AIRSPACE INT/ORG
AND OUTERSPACE. FUT WOR+45 AIR CONSTN STRUCT JURID
CONSULT PLAN TEC/DEV ADJUD RIGID/FLEX KNOWL SPACE
ORD/FREE PWR...TECHNIC GEOG MGT NEW/IDEA TREND INT/LAW
COMPUT/IR VAL/FREE 20 TREATY. PAGE 64 G1251
B60

BRENNAN D.G.,"SETTING AND GOALS OF ARMS CONTROL." FORCES
FUT USA+45 USSR WOR+45 INTELL INT/ORG NAT/G COERCE
VOL/ASSN CONSULT PLAN DIPLOM ECO/TAC ADMIN KNOWL ARMS/CONT
PWR...POLICY CONCPT TREND COLD/WAR 20. PAGE 8 G0164 DETER
L60

JACOB P.E.,"THE DISARMAMENT CONSENSUS." USA+45 USSR DELIB/GP
WOR+45 INT/ORG NAT/G ACT/RES TEC/DEV BAL/PWR ATTIT
EDU/PROP ADMIN COERCE DETER NUC/PWR CONSEN ARMS/CONT
RIGID/FLEX PWR...CONCPT RECORD CHARTS COLD/WAR 20.
PAGE 28 G0552
L60

BARNETT H.J.,"RESEARCH AND DEVELOPMENT, ECONOMIC ACT/RES
GROWTH, AND NATIONAL SECURITY." USA+45 R+D CREATE PLAN
ECO/TAC ATTIT DRIVE PWR...POLICY SOC METH/CNCPT
QUANT STAT TIME/SEQ ORG/CHARTS COLD/WAR 20. PAGE 5
G0097
S60

DOTY P.M.,"THE ROLE OF THE SMALLER POWERS." FUT PWR
WOR+45 NAT/G TEC/DEV BAL/PWR DOMIN LEGIT CHOOSE POLICY
DISPL DRIVE RESPECT...DECISION 20. PAGE 16 G0310 ARMS/CONT
NUC/PWR
S60

DOUGHERTY J.E.,"KEY TO SECURITY: DISARMAMENT OR FORCES
ARMS STABILITY." COM USA+45 USSR INT/ORG NAT/G ORD/FREE
CREATE EDU/PROP COERCE DETER ATTIT PWR...DECISION ARMS/CONT
CONCPT MYTH NEW/IDEA TREND 20 COLD/WAR. PAGE 16 NUC/PWR
G0311
S60

DYSON F.J.,"THE FUTURE DEVELOPMENT OF NUCLEAR INT/ORG
WEAPONS." FUT WOR+45 DELIB/GP ACT/RES PLAN DETER ARMS/CONT
WEAPON ATTIT PWR...POLICY 20. PAGE 17 G0328 NUC/PWR
S60

HALSEY A.H.,"THE CHANGING FUNCTIONS OF UNIVERSITIES ACADEM
IN ADVANCED INDUSTRIAL SOCIETIES." R+D EDU/PROP CREATE
REPRESENT ROLE ORD/FREE PWR TREND. PAGE 24 G0476 CULTURE
ADJUST
S60

HUNTINGTON S.P.,"STRATEGIC PLANNING AND THE EXEC
POLITICAL PROCESS." USA+45 NAT/G DELIB/GP LEGIS FORCES
ACT/RES ECO/TAC LEGIT ROUTINE CHOOSE RIGID/FLEX PWR NUC/PWR
...POLICY MAJORIT MGT 20. PAGE 27 G0538 WAR
S60

HUTCHINSON C.E.,"AN INSTITUTE FOR NATIONAL SECURITY POLICY
AFFAIRS." USA+45 R+D NAT/G CONSULT TOP/EX ACT/RES METH/CNCPT
CREATE PLAN TEC/DEV EDU/PROP ROUTINE NUC/PWR ATTIT ELITES
ORD/FREE PWR...DECISION MGT PHIL/SCI CONCPT RECORD DIPLOM
GEN/LAWS GEN/METH 20. PAGE 27 G0539
S60

KELLEY G.A.,"THE POLITICAL BACKGROUND OF THE FRENCH NAT/G
A-BOMB." EUR+WWI USSR FORCES TOP/EX TEC/DEV NUC/PWR RESPECT
ATTIT PWR...CONCPT OBS/ENVIR TREND 20. PAGE 30 NAT/LISM
G0591 FRANCE
S60

SANDERS R.,"NUCLEAR DYNAMITE: A NEW DIMENSION IN INDUS
FOREIGN POLICY." FUT WOR+45 ECO/DEV CONSULT TEC/DEV PWR
PERCEPT...CONT/OBS TIME/SEQ TREND GEN/LAWS TOT/POP DIPLOM
20 TREATY. PAGE 49 G0955 NUC/PWR
S60

US HOUSE COMM SCI ASTRONAUT.THE ORGANIZATION OF THE ACT/RES
US NATIONAL SPACE EFFORT. USA+45 WOR+45 AIR ECO/DEV SKILL
NAT/G PLAN TEC/DEV DIPLOM EDU/PROP ATTIT DRIVE PWR SPACE
...OBS TIME/SEQ TREND TOT/POP 20. PAGE 58 G1142
N60

FRISCH D.,ARMS REDUCTION: PROGRAM AND ISSUES. PLAN
USA+45 INT/ORG NAT/G ACT/RES REGION NUC/PWR ATTIT FORCES
PWR...POLICY 20. PAGE 20 G0395 ARMS/CONT
DIPLOM
B61

HENKIN L.,ARMS CONTROL: ISSUES FOR THE PUBLIC. WOR+45
EUR+WWI FUT USA+45 USSR INT/ORG NAT/G DIPLOM DELIB/GP
EDU/PROP DETER NUC/PWR ATTIT PWR...CONCPT RECORD ARMS/CONT
HIST/WRIT TIME/SEQ TOT/POP COLD/WAR 20. PAGE 26
G0506
B61

KRUPP S.,PATTERN IN ORGANIZATIONAL ANALYSIS: A MGT
CRITICAL EXAMINATION. INGP/REL PERS/REL RATIONAL CONTROL
ATTIT AUTHORIT DRIVE PWR...DECISION PHIL/SCI SOC CONCPT
IDEA/COMP. PAGE 32 G0622 METH/CNCPT
B61

NOGEE J.L.,SOVIET POLICY TOWARD INTERNATIONAL INT/ORG
CONTROL OF ATOMIC ENERGY. COM USA+45 WOR+45 INTELL ATTIT
NAT/G ACT/RES DIPLOM EDU/PROP NUC/PWR TOTALISM ARMS/CONT
PERCEPT KNOWL PWR...TIME/SEQ COLD/WAR 20. PAGE 42 USSR
G0824
B61

FAIR M.L.,"PORT AUTHORITIES IN THE UNITED STATES." MUNIC
PROB/SOLV ADMIN LEAD REPRESENT PWR...DECISION GEOG. REGION
PAGE 18 G0357 LOC/G
GOV/REL
S61

LYONS G.M.,"THE NEW CIVIL-MILITARY RELATIONS." CIVMIL/REL
USA+45 NAT/G EX/STRUC TOP/EX PROB/SOLV ADMIN EXEC PWR
PARTIC 20. PAGE 35 G0681 REPRESENT
S61

MAINZER L.C.,"SCIENTIFIC FREEDOM IN GOVERNMENT- CREATE
SPONSORED RESEARCH." USA+45 INTELL PUB/INST BUDGET ORD/FREE
LOBBY AUTHORIT PWR...POLICY PHIL/SCI 20 NIH NSF. NAT/G
PAGE 35 G0696 R+D
S61

WOHLSTETTER A.,"NUCLEAR SHARING: NATO AND THE NTH TREND
COUNTRY." EUR+WWI FUT SOCIETY DIPLOM EXEC DETER PWR TEC/DEV
SKILL...POLICY TECHNIC CONCPT 20 NATO. PAGE 64 NUC/PWR
G1252 ARMS/CONT
S61

BLOOMFIELD L.P.,OUTER SPACE: A PATTERN OF WAR IN A CREATE
NEW DIMENSION. FUT USA+45 AIR TEC/DEV PWR ACT/RES
...DECISION CONCPT GEN/LAWS 20. PAGE 7 G0141 ARMS/CONT
SPACE
B62

CARSON R.,SILENT SPRING. USA+45 AIR CULTURE AGRI HABITAT
INDUS ADMIN ATTIT RIGID/FLEX ORD/FREE PWR...POLICY TREND
20. PAGE 11 G0216 SOCIETY
CONTROL
B62

DODDS H.W.,THE ACADEMIC PRESIDENT "EDUCATOR OR ACADEM
CARETAKER? FINAN DELIB/GP EDU/PROP PARTIC ATTIT ADMIN
ROLE PWR...POLICY RECORD INT. PAGE 16 G0304 LEAD
CONTROL
B62

FORBES H.W.,THE STRATEGY OF DISARMAMENT. FUT WOR+45 PLAN
INT/ORG VOL/ASSN CONSULT ARMS/CONT COERCE NUC/PWR FORCES
WAR DRIVE RIGID/FLEX ORD/FREE PWR...POLICY CONCPT DIPLOM
OBS TREND STERTYP 20. PAGE 19 G0378
B62

FRIEDRICH-EBERT-STIFTUNG,THE SOVIET BLOC AND MARXISM
DEVELOPING COUNTRIES. CHINA/COM COM GERMANY/E USSR DIPLOM
WOR+45 ECO/UNDEV INT/ORG NAT/G TEC/DEV NEUTRAL PWR ECO/TAC
...POLICY 20. PAGE 20 G0394 FOR/AID
B62

GILPIN R.,AMERICAN SCIENTISTS AND NUCLEAR WEAPONS INTELL
POLICY. COM FUT USA+45 WOR+45 INT/ORG NAT/G ATTIT
PROF/ORG CONSULT FORCES CREATE TEC/DEV BAL/PWR DETER
B62

EDU/PROP ARMS/CONT WAR PERCEPT KNOWL MORAL PWR   NUC/PWR
...PHIL/SCI SOC CONCPT GEN/LAWS 20. PAGE 21 G0417

B62

LEFEVER E.W.,ARMS AND ARMS CONTROL. COM USA+45   ATTIT
INT/ORG TEC/DEV DIPLOM ORD/FREE 20. PAGE 33 G0652   PWR
    ARMS/CONT
    BAL/PWR

B62

MELMAN S.,DISARMAMENT: ITS POLITICS AND ECONOMICS.   NAT/G
WOR+45 DELIB/GP FORCES ECO/TAC DOMIN EDU/PROP LEGIT   ORD/FREE
COERCE PWR...POLICY CONCPT 20. PAGE 38 G0752   ARMS/CONT
    NUC/PWR

B62

SCHILLING W.R.,STRATEGY, POLITICS, AND DEFENSE   ROUTINE
BUDGETS. USA+45 R+D NAT/G CONSULT DELIB/GP FORCES   POLICY
LEGIS ACT/RES PLAN BAL/PWR LEGIT EXEC NUC/PWR
RIGID/FLEX PWR...TREND COLD/WAR CONGRESS 20
EISNHWR/DD. PAGE 49 G0968

B62

SNYDER R.C.,FOREIGN POLICY DECISION-MAKING. FUT   TEC/DEV
KOREA WOR+45 R+D CREATE ADMIN ROUTINE PWR   HYPO/EXP
...DECISION PSY SOC CONCPT METH/CNCPT CON/ANAL   DIPLOM
CHARTS GEN/METH METH 20. PAGE 52 G1018

B62

STRAUSS L.L.,MEN AND DECISIONS. USA+45 USA-45 USSR   DECISION
CONSULT FORCES TOP/EX WAR PEACE 20. PAGE 53 G1042   PWR
    NUC/PWR
    DIPLOM

B62

YALEN R.,REGIONALISM AND WORLD ORDER. EUR+WWI   ORD/FREE
WOR+45 INT/ORG VOL/ASSN DELIB/GP FORCES   POLICY
TOP/EX BAL/PWR DIPLOM DOMIN REGION ARMS/CONT PWR
...JURID HYPO/EXP COLD/WAR 20. PAGE 64 G1261

L62

BETTEN J.K.,"ARMS CONTROL AND THE PROBLEM OF   NAT/G
EVASION." WOR+45 FORCES CREATE DIPLOM DETER PWR   PLAN
...PSY TREND GEN/LAWS COLD/WAR 20. PAGE 7 G0134   ARMS/CONT

L62

CAVERS D.F.,"ADMINISTRATIVE DECISION-MAKING IN   REPRESENT
NUCLEAR FACILITIES LICENSING." USA+45 CLIENT ADMIN   LOBBY
EXEC 20 AEC. PAGE 11 G0218   PWR
    CONTROL

L62

FINKELSTEIN L.S.,"ARMS INSPECTION." FUT WOR+45   FORCES
NAT/G DIPLOM ATTIT PERCEPT RIGID/FLEX ORD/FREE   PWR
COLD/WAR 20. PAGE 19 G0369   ARMS/CONT

L62

NEIBURG H.L.,"THE EISENHOWER AEC AND CONGRESS: A   CHIEF
STUDY IN EXECUTIVE-LEGISLATIVE RELATIONS." USA+45   LEGIS
NAT/G POL/PAR DELIB/GP EX/STRUC TOP/EX ADMIN EXEC   GOV/REL
LEAD ROUTINE PWR...POLICY COLD/WAR CONGRESS   NUC/PWR
PRESIDENT AEC. PAGE 41 G0816

S62

BOULDING K.E.,"THE PREVENTION OF WORLD WAR THREE."   VOL/ASSN
FUT WOR+45 INT/ORG PLAN BAL/PWR PEACE ORD/FREE PWR   NAT/G
...NEW/IDEA TREND TOT/POP COLD/WAR 20. PAGE 8 G0158   ARMS/CONT
    DIPLOM

S62

DAWSON R.H.,"CONGRESSIONAL INNOVATION AND   LEGIS
INTERVENTION IN DEFENSE POLICY: LEGISLATIVE   PWR
AUTHORIZATION OF WEAPONS SYSTEMS." CONSTN PLAN   CONTROL
ARMS/CONT GOV/REL EFFICIENCY PEACE NEW/LIB OLD/LIB.   WEAPON
PAGE 14 G0281

S62

FINKELSTEIN L.S.,"THE UNITED NATIONS AND   INT/ORG
ORGANIZATIONS FOR CONTROL OF ARMAMENT." FUT WOR+45   PWR
VOL/ASSN DELIB/GP TOP/EX CREATE EDU/PROP LEGIT   ARMS/CONT
ADJUD NUC/PWR ATTIT RIGID/FLEX ORD/FREE...POLICY
DECISION CONCPT OBS TREND GEN/LAWS TOT/POP
COLD/WAR. PAGE 19 G0368

S62

GORDON B.K.,"NUCLEAR WEAPONS: RUSSIAN AND   ORD/FREE
AMERICAN." COM USA+45 USSR NAT/G FORCES ACT/RES   COERCE
TEC/DEV PERCEPT RIGID/FLEX PWR SKILL...MGT   NUC/PWR
METH/CNCPT QUANT OBS TIME/SEQ CON/ANAL GEN/METH
TOT/POP VAL/FREE 20. PAGE 22 G0433

S62

MARTIN L.W.,"THE MARKET FOR STRATEGIC IDEAS IN   DIPLOM
BRITAIN: THE 'SANDYS ERA'." UK ARMS/CONT WAR GOV/REL   COERCE
OPTIMAL...POLICY DECISION GOV/COMP COLD/WAR   FORCES
CMN/WLTH. PAGE 36 G0714   PWR

S62

SINGER J.D.,"STABLE DETERRENCE AND ITS LIMITS." FUT   NAT/G
WOR+45 R+D INT/ORG CONSULT ACT/RES TEC/DEV   FORCES
ARMS/CONT COERCE DRIVE PERCEPT RIGID/FLEX ORD/FREE   DETER
PWR...MYTH SIMUL TOT/POP 20. PAGE 51 G1004   NUC/PWR

B63

ABSHIRE D.M.,NATIONAL SECURITY: POLITICAL,   FUT
MILITARY, AND ECONOMIC STRATEGIES IN THE DECADE   ACT/RES
AHEAD. ASIA COM USA+45 WOR+45 ECO/DEV ECO/UNDEV   BAL/PWR
INT/ORG DELIB/GP FORCES ECO/TAC COERCE ATTIT
RIGID/FLEX HEALTH ORD/FREE PWR WEALTH...POLICY STAT
CHARTS ANTHOL COLD/WAR VAL/FREE. PAGE 1 G0024

B63

BONINI C.P.,SIMULATION OF INFORMATION AND DECISION   INDUS
SYSTEMS IN THE FIRM. MARKET BUDGET DOMIN EDU/PROP   SIMUL
ADMIN COST ATTIT HABITAT PERCEPT PWR...CONCPT   DECISION
PROBABIL QUANT PREDICT HYPO/EXP BIBLIOG. PAGE 8   MGT
G0152

B63

DALAND R.T.,PERSPECTIVES OF BRAZILIAN PUBLIC   ADMIN
ADMINISTRATION (VOL. I). BRAZIL LAW ECO/UNDEV   NAT/G
SCHOOL CHIEF TEC/DEV CONFER CONTROL GP/REL ATTIT   PLAN
ROLE PWR...ANTHOL 20. PAGE 14 G0272   GOV/REL

B63

GOLDSEN J.M.,OUTER SPACE IN WORLD POLITICS. COM   TEC/DEV
USA+45 NAT/G FORCES ACT/RES PLAN DOMIN EDU/PROP   DIPLOM
COERCE ORD/FREE PWR...TECHNIC STAT INT SAMP TREND   SPACE
ANTHOL VAL/FREE 20. PAGE 22 G0428

B63

GREEN H.P.,GOVERNMENT OF THE ATOM. USA+45 LEGIS   GOV/REL
PROB/SOLV ADMIN CONTROL PWR...POLICY DECISION 20   EX/STRUC
PRESIDENT CONGRESS. PAGE 22 G0443   NUC/PWR
    DELIB/GP

B63

HALEY A.G.,SPACE LAW AND GOVERNMENT. FUT USA+45   INT/ORG
WOR+45 LEGIS ACT/RES CREATE ATTIT RIGID/FLEX   LAW
ORD/FREE PWR SOVEREIGN...POLICY JURID CONCPT CHARTS   SPACE
VAL/FREE 20. PAGE 24 G0469

B63

HATHAWAY D.A.,GOVERNMENT AND AGRICULTURE: PUBLIC   AGRI
POLICY IN A DEMOCRATIC SOCIETY. USA+45 LEGIS ADMIN   GOV/REL
EXEC LOBBY REPRESENT PWR 20. PAGE 25 G0491   PROB/SOLV
    EX/STRUC

B63

HOWER R.M.,MANAGERS AND SCIENTISTS. EX/STRUC CREATE   R+D
ADMIN REPRESENT ATTIT DRIVE ROLE PWR SKILL...SOC   MGT
INT. PAGE 27 G0532   PERS/REL
    INGP/REL

B63

LITTERER J.A.,ORGANIZATIONS: STRUCTURE AND   ADMIN
BEHAVIOR. PLAN DOMIN CONTROL LEAD ROUTINE SANCTION   CREATE
INGP/REL EFFICIENCY PRODUC DRIVE RIGID/FLEX PWR.   MGT
PAGE 34 G0674   ADJUST

B63

MAYNE R.,THE COMMUNITY OF EUROPE. UK CONSTN NAT/G   EUR+WWI
CONSULT DELIB/GP CREATE PLAN ECO/TAC LEGIT ADMIN   INT/ORG
ROUTINE ORD/FREE PWR WEALTH...CONCPT TIME/SEQ EEC   REGION
EURATOM 20. PAGE 37 G0724

B63

MULLENBACH P.,CIVILIAN NUCLEAR POWER: ECONOMIC   USA+45
ISSUES AND POLICY FORMATION. FINAN INT/ORG DELIB/GP   ECO/DEV
ACT/RES ECO/TAC ATTIT SUPEGO HEALTH ORD/FREE PWR   NUC/PWR
...POLICY CONCPT MATH STAT CHARTS VAL/FREE 20
COLD/WAR. PAGE 40 G0792

B6

MULLER H.J.,FREEDOM IN THE WESTERN WORLD. PREHIST   ORD/FREE
CULTURE SECT CREATE TEC/DEV DOMIN PWR WEALTH   TIME/SEQ
...MAJORIT SOC CONCPT. PAGE 40 G0793   SOCIETY

B6

PEABODY R.L.,NEW PERSPECTIVES ON THE HOUSE OF   NEW/IDEA
REPRESENTATIVES. AGRI FINAN SCHOOL FORCES CONFER   LEGIS
LEAD CHOOSE REPRESENT FEDERAL...POLICY DECISION   PWR
HOUSE/REP. PAGE 44 G0862   ADMIN

B6

SCHOECK H.,THE NEW ARGUMENT IN ECONOMICS. UK USA+45   WELF/ST
INDUS MARKET LABOR NAT/G ECO/TAC ADMIN ROUTINE   FOR/AID
BAL/PAY PWR...POLICY BOLIV. PAGE 49 G0973   ECO/DEV
    ALL/IDEOS

L6

MCDOUGAL M.S.,"THE ENJOYMENT AND ACQUISITION OF   PLAN

RESOURCES IN OUTER SPACE." CHRIST-17C FUT WOR+45   TREND
WOR-45 LAW EXTR/IND INT/ORG ACT/RES CREATE TEC/DEV
ECO/TAC LEGIT COERCE HEALTH KNOWL ORD/FREE PWR
WEALTH...JURID HIST/WRIT VAL/FREE. PAGE 37 G0738

NIEBURG H.,"EURATOM: A STUDY IN COALITION   L63
POLITICS." EUR+WWI UK USA+45 ELITES NAT/G DELIB/GP   VOL/ASSN
LEGIS TOP/EX ECO/TAC NUC/PWR ATTIT ORD/FREE PWR   ACT/RES
TOT/POP EEC OEEC 20 NATO EURATOM. PAGE 42 G0820

PHELPS J.,"STUDIES IN DETERRENCE VIII: MILITARY   L63
STABILITARY AND ARMS CONTROL: A CRITICAL SURVEY."   FORCES
FUT WOR+45 INT/ORG ACT/RES EDU/PROP COERCE NUC/PWR   ORD/FREE
WAR HEALTH PWR...POLICY TECHNIC TREND SIMUL TOT/POP   ARMS/CONT
20. PAGE 44 G0874   DETER

ABT C.,"THE PROBLEMS AND POSSIBILITIES OF SPACE   S63
ARMS CONTROL." FUT USA+45 WOR+45 AIR SOCIETY NAT/G   ACT/RES
BAL/PWR EDU/PROP ATTIT PWR WEALTH...HYPO/EXP   ORD/FREE
TOT/POP 20. PAGE 2 G0025   ARMS/CONT
  SPACE

BOULDING K.E.,"UNIVERSITY, SOCIETY, AND ARMS   S63
CONTROL." WOR+45 WOR-45 ACADEM NAT/G CONSULT FORCES   SOCIETY
ACT/RES PLAN TEC/DEV BAL/PWR ECO/TAC COERCE DETER   ARMS/CONT
WAR ATTIT RIGID/FLEX KNOWL ORD/FREE PWR WEALTH
...CONCPT COLD/WAR TOT/POP 20. PAGE 8 G0159

CLEVELAND H.,"CRISIS DIPLOMACY." USA+45 WOR+45 LAW   S63
FORCES TASK NUC/PWR PWR 20. PAGE 12 G0235   DECISION
  DIPLOM
  PROB/SOLV
  POLICY

DUBRIDGE L.A.,"POLICY AND THE SCIENTISTS." ELITES   S63
PROB/SOLV ROLE KNOWL PWR. PAGE 16 G0318   POLICY
  PHIL/SCI
  ACADEM
  DECISION

HOSKINS H.L.,"ARAB SOCIALISM IN THE UAR." ISLAM   S63
USSR AGRI INDUS NAT/G TOP/EX CREATE DIPLOM EDU/PROP   ECO/DEV
DRIVE KNOWL PWR SOCISM...POLICY CONCPT TREND SUEZ   PLAN
20. PAGE 27 G0530   UAR

KOLDZIEF E.A.,"CONGRESSIONAL RESPONSIBILITY FOR THE   S63
COMMON DEFENSE: THE MONEY PROBLEM." PLAN DEBATE   LEGIS
EFFICIENCY ATTIT PWR DECISION. PAGE 31 G0612   NAT/G
  FORCES
  POLICY

NADLER E.B.,"SOME ECONOMIC DISADVANTAGES OF THE   S63
ARMS RACE." USA+45 INDUS R+D FORCES PLAN TEC/DEV   ECO/DEV
ECO/TAC FOR/AID EDU/PROP PWR WEALTH...TREND   MGT
COLD/WAR 20. PAGE 41 G0800   BAL/PAY

SMITH D.O.,"WHAT IS A WAR DETERRENT." FUT GERMANY   S63
HUNGARY UK USA+45 WOR-45 NAT/G TEC/DEV   ACT/RES
BAL/PWR PWR...CONCPT GEN/LAWS COLD/WAR 20. PAGE 51   FORCES
G1013   ARMS/CONT
  DETER

TASHJEAN J.E.,"RESEARCH ON ARMS CONTROL." COM   S63
USA+45 USSR FORCES ACT/RES PLAN DOMIN COERCE   NAT/G
ORD/FREE PWR...TIME/SEQ GEN/LAWS 20 COLD/WAR.   POLICY
PAGE 53 G1053   ARMS/CONT

BAUCHET P.,ECONOMIC PLANNING. FRANCE STRATA LG/CO   B64
CAP/ISM ADMIN PARL/PROC DEMAND OPTIMAL ATTIT PWR   ECO/DEV
SOCISM...POLICY CHARTS 20. PAGE 5 G0102   NAT/G
  PLAN
  ECO/TAC

EDELMAN M.,THE SYMBOLIC USES OF POWER. USA+45   B64
EX/STRUC CONTROL GP/REL INGP/REL...MGT T. PAGE 17   CLIENT
G0333   PWR
  EXEC
  ELITES

ETZIONI A.,THE MOON-DOGGLE: DOMESTIC AND   B64
INTERNATIONAL IMPLICATIONS OF THE SPACE RACE. FUT   R+D
USA+45 WOR+45 INTELL ECO/DEV INDUS VOL/ASSN   NAT/G
EX/STRUC FORCES LEGIS TOP/EX PLAN TEC/DEV ECO/TAC   DIPLOM
EDU/PROP KNOWL ORD/FREE PWR RESPECT WEALTH   SPACE
TIME/SEQ. PAGE 18 G0352

HEKHUIS D.J.,INTERNATIONAL STABILITY: MILITARY,   B64
ECONOMIC AND POLITICAL DIMENSIONS. FUT WOR+45 LAW   TEC/DEV
  DETER

ECO/UNDEV INT/ORG NAT/G VOL/ASSN FORCES ACT/RES   REGION
BAL/PWR PWR WEALTH...STAT UN 20. PAGE 25 G0503

KAUFMANN W.W.,THE MC NAMARA STRATEGY. TOP/EX   B64
INSPECT BAL/PWR DIPLOM CONTROL DETER GUERRILLA   FORCES
NUC/PWR WEAPON COST PWR...METH/COMP 20 MCNAMARA/R   WAR
KENNEDY/JF JOHNSON/LB NATO DEPT/DEFEN. PAGE 30   PLAN
G0586   PROB/SOLV

MANSFIELD E.,MONOPOLY POWER AND ECONOMIC   B64
PERFORMANCE: AN INTRODUCTION TO A CURRENT ISSUE OF   LG/CO
PUBLIC POLICY. ECO/DEV INDUS NAT/G PLAN CAP/ISM   PWR
PRICE CONTROL LOBBY EFFICIENCY PRODUC...POLICY 20   ECO/TAC
CONGRESS KENNEDY/JF MONOPOLY. PAGE 36 G0701   MARKET

MASTERS N.A.,STATE POLITICS AND THE PUBLIC SCHOOLS.   EDU/PROP
STRUCT FINAN ADMIN LOBBY GP/REL PWR BIBLIOG.   PROVS
PAGE 36 G0720   DOMIN

RANSOM H.H.,CAN AMERICAN DEMOCRACY SURVIVE COLD   B64
WAR. USA+45 CONSTN NAT/G CONSULT DELIB/GP LEGIS   USA+45
ACT/RES LEGIT EXEC ATTIT KNOWL ORD/FREE PWR SKILL   ROUTINE
...POLICY TIME/SEQ TREND GEN/LAWS 20 COLD/WAR.
PAGE 46 G0901

RIES J.C.,THE MANAGEMENT OF DEFENSE: ORGANIZATION   B64
AND CONTROL OF THE US ARMED SERVICES. PROF/ORG   FORCES
DELIB/GP EX/STRUC LEGIS GOV/REL PERS/REL CENTRAL   ACT/RES
RATIONAL PWR...POLICY TREND GOV/COMP BIBLIOG.   DECISION
PAGE 47 G0920   CONTROL

ROSECRANCE R.N.,THE DISPERSION OF NUCLEAR WEAPONS: B64
STRATEGY AND POLITICS. ASIA COM FUT S/ASIA USA+45   EUR+WWI
INT/ORG NAT/G DELIB/GP FORCES ACT/RES TEC/DEV   PWR
BAL/PWR COERCE DETER ATTIT RIGID/FLEX ORD/FREE   PEACE
...POLICY CHARTS VAL/FREE. PAGE 48 G0935

RUSHING W.A.,THE PSYCHIATRIC PROFESSIONS. DOMIN   B64
INGP/REL DRIVE RIGID/FLEX ROLE HEALTH PWR...POLICY   ATTIT
GP/COMP. PAGE 48 G0947   PUB/INST
  PROF/ORG
  BAL/PWR

SHUBIK M.,GAME THEORY AND RELATED APPROACHES TO   B64
SOCIAL BEHAVIOR: SELECTIONS. INTELL SOCIETY ACT/RES   SOC
CREATE PLAN PROB/SOLV...DECISION MATH. PAGE 50   SIMUL
G0994   GAME
  PWR

VAN DYKE V.,PRIDE AND POWER: THE RATIONALE OF THE   B64
SPACE PROGRAM. FUT USA+45 INTELL R+D NAT/G POL/PAR   TEC/DEV
DELIB/GP EX/STRUC LEGIS TOP/EX ACT/RES PLAN ECO/TAC   ATTIT
EDU/PROP ORD/FREE PWR RESPECT SKILL...TIME/SEQ   POLICY
VAL/FREE. PAGE 61 G1191

WHEELER-BENNETT J.W.,THE NEMESIS OF POWER (2ND   B64
ED.). EUR+WWI GERMANY TOP/EX TEC/DEV ADMIN WAR   FORCES
PERS/REL RIGID/FLEX ROLE ORD/FREE PWR FASCISM 20   NAT/G
HITLER/A. PAGE 63 G1231   GP/REL
  STRUCT

BERKS R.N.,"THE US AND WEAPONS CONTROL." WOR+45 LAW   USA+45
INT/ORG NAT/G LEGIS EXEC COERCE PEACE ATTIT   PLAN
RIGID/FLEX ALL/VALS PWR...POLICY TOT/POP 20. PAGE 7   ARMS/CONT
G0129

GOLDBERG A.,"ATOMIC ORIGINS OF THE BRITISH NUCLEAR   CREATE
DETERRENT." EUR+WWI UK NAT/G TOP/EX PLAN BAL/PWR   FORCES
DOMIN DETER CHOOSE ATTIT DRIVE HEALTH ORD/FREE PWR   NUC/PWR
RESPECT...CONCPT VAL/FREE COLD/WAR 20 CMN/WLTH.
PAGE 22 G0425

HAAS E.B.,"ECONOMICS AND DIFFERENTIAL PATTERNS OF   L/A+17C
POLITICAL INTEGRATION: PROJECTIONS ABOUT UNITY IN   INT/ORG
LATIN AMERICA." SOCIETY NAT/G DELIB/GP ACT/RES   MARKET
CREATE PLAN ECO/TAC REGION ROUTINE ATTIT DRIVE PWR
WEALTH...CONCPT TREND CHARTS LAFTA 20. PAGE 24
G0464

ABT C.,"WAR GAMING." USA+45 NAT/G TOP/EX ACT/RES   S64
TEC/DEV COERCE KNOWL ORD/FREE PWR...DECISION MATH   FORCES
TIME/SEQ COMPUT/IR CHARTS LAB/EXP VAL/FREE. PAGE 2   SIMUL
G0026   WAR

FALK S.L.,"DISARMAMENT IN HISTORICAL PERSPECTIVE." **S64** INT/ORG
WOR-45 NAT/G PLAN NUC/PWR PEACE ORD/FREE PWR COERCE
...TIME/SEQ AUD/VIS VAL/FREE LEAGUE/NAT 20. PAGE 18 ARMS/CONT
G0360

KASSOF A.,"THE ADMINISTERED SOCIETY: **S64** SOCIETY
TOTALITARIANISM WITHOUT TERROR." COM USSR STRATA DOMIN
AGRI INDUS NAT/G PERF/ART SCHOOL TOP/EX EDU/PROP TOTALISM
ADMIN ORD/FREE PWR...POLICY SOC TIME/SEQ GEN/LAWS
VAL/FREE 20. PAGE 29 G0580

LERNER A.P.,"NUCLEAR SYMMETRY AS A FRAMEWORK FOR **S64** FORCES
COEXISTENCE." COM FUT USA+45 NAT/G ACT/RES CREATE ORD/FREE
PLAN DIPLOM EDU/PROP COERCE WAR RIGID/FLEX PWR DETER
SKILL...CONCPT METH/CNCPT GEN/LAWS TOT/POP VAL/FREE NUC/PWR
COLD/WAR 20. PAGE 33 G0657

MAGGS P.B.,"SOVIET VIEWPOINT ON NUCLEAR WEAPONS IN **S64** COM
INTERNATIONAL LAW." USSR WOR+45 INT/ORG FORCES LAW
DIPLOM ARMS/CONT ATTIT ORD/FREE PWR...POLICY JURID INT/LAW
CONCPT OBS TREND CON/ANAL GEN/LAWS VAL/FREE 20. NUC/PWR
PAGE 35 G0694

MARES V.E.,"EAST EUROPE'S SECOND CHANCE." COM **S64** VOL/ASSN
EUR+WWI HUNGARY ROMANIA USSR YUGOSLAVIA ECO/UNDEV ECO/TAC
NAT/G TOP/EX CREATE PLAN TEC/DEV REGION NAT/LISM
RIGID/FLEX PWR...CONCPT STAT COMECON 20. PAGE 36
G0705

PILISUK M.,"STEPWISE DISARMAMENT & SUDDEN **S64** PWR
DESTRUCTION IN A TWOPERSON GAME: A RESEARCH TOOL." DECISION
NAT/G FORCES ACT/RES ECO/TAC EDU/PROP EXEC ROUTINE ARMS/CONT
COERCE ORD/FREE...SIMUL GEN/LAWS VAL/FREE. PAGE 45
G0877

SPONSLER G.C.,"THE MILITARY ROLE IN SPACE." FUT **S64** TEC/DEV
USA+45 SEA AIR NAT/G ACT/RES PLAN COERCE NUC/PWR FORCES
WEAPON KNOWL ORD/FREE PWR RESPECT...TREND 20. SPACE
PAGE 52 G1026

THOMPSON V.A.,"ADMINISTRATIVE OBJECTIVES FOR **S64** ECO/UNDEV
DEVELOPMENT ADMINISTRATION." WOR+45 CREATE PLAN MGT
DOMIN EDU/PROP EXEC ROUTINE ATTIT ORD/FREE PWR
...POLICY GEN/LAWS VAL/FREE. PAGE 54 G1070

BAILEY S.K.,AMERICAN POLITICS AND GOVERNMENT. **B65** ANTHOL
USA+45 CONSTN FINAN LABOR POL/PAR DIPLOM ADMIN WAR LEGIS
INGP/REL RACE/REL NEW/LIB 20 SUPREME/CT PRESIDENT PWR
CONGRESS. PAGE 4 G0084

CORDIER A.W.,THE QUEST FOR PEACE. WOR+45 NAT/G PLAN **B65** PEACE
BAL/PWR ECO/TAC ARMS/CONT NUC/PWR PWR...ANTHOL UN DIPLOM
COLD/WAR. PAGE 13 G0256 POLICY
INT/ORG

HALPERIN M.H.,CHINA AND THE BOMB. USA+45 USSR **B65** ASIA
INT/ORG FORCES ARMS/CONT DETER PRODUC ORD/FREE PWR NUC/PWR
TREND. PAGE 24 G0472 WAR
DIPLOM

LAPP R.E.,THE NEW PRIESTHOOD: THE SCIENTIFIC ELITE **B65** TEC/DEV
AND THE USES OF POWER. USA+45 ELITES INTELL SOCIETY TECHRACY
R+D NAT/G CHIEF LEGIS CIVMIL/REL GP/REL PWR 20 CONTROL
PRESIDENT CONGRESS. PAGE 32 G0635 POPULISM

PYE L.W.,POLITICAL CULTURE AND DEVELOPMENT. WOR+45 **B65** PHIL/SCI
WOR-45 CULTURE ECO/UNDEV NAT/G ALL/VALS ORD/FREE TEC/DEV
PWR WEALTH ALL/IDEOS...TRADIT TREND 20. PAGE 46 SOCIETY
G0897

LASSWELL H.D.,"THE POLICY SCIENCES OF DEVELOPMENT." **L65** PWR
CULTURE SOCIETY EX/STRUC CREATE ADMIN ATTIT KNOWL METH/CNCPT
...SOC CONCPT SIMUL GEN/METH. PAGE 33 G0644 DIPLOM

BALDWIN H.,"SLOW-DOWN IN THE PENTAGON." USA+45 **S65** RECORD
CREATE PLAN GOV/REL CENTRAL COST EFFICIENCY PWR R+D
...MGT MCNAMARA/R. PAGE 5 G0088 WEAPON
ADMIN

GRIFFITH S.B.,"COMMUNIST CHINA'S CAPACITY TO MAKE **S65** FORCES

WAR." CHINA/COM COM NAT/G TOP/EX PLAN DOMIN COERCE PWR
NUC/PWR ATTIT RESPECT SKILL...CONCPT MYTH TIME/SEQ WEAPON
TREND COLD/WAR 20. PAGE 23 G0452 ASIA

STAAR R.F.,"RETROGRESSION IN POLAND." COM USSR AGRI **S65** TOP/EX
INDUS NAT/G CREATE EDU/PROP TOTALSM RIGID/FLEX ECO/TAC
ORD/FREE PWR SOCISM...RECORD CHARTS 20. PAGE 52 POLAND
G1029

TENDLER J.D.,"TECHNOLOGY AND ECONOMIC DEVELOPMENT* **S65** BRAZIL
THE CASE OF HYDRO VS THERMAL POWER." CONSTRUC INDUS
DIST/IND CREATE TEC/DEV INT/TRADE CENTRAL PWR SKILL ECO/UNDEV
WEALTH...MGT NAT/COMP ARGEN. PAGE 54 G1063

AMERICAN ASSEMBLY COLUMBIA U,A WORLD OF NUCLEAR **B66** NUC/PWR
POWERS? FUT WOR+45 ECO/DEV BAL/PWR ECO/TAC CONTROL DIPLOM
RISK EFFICIENCY ATTIT PWR...METH/COMP ANTHOL 20. TEC/DEV
PAGE 3 G0049 ARMS/CONT

BEATON L.,MUST THE BOMB SPREAD? WOR+45 TEC/DEV **B66** NUC/PWR
DIPLOM DRIVE ORD/FREE PWR...CHARTS 20. PAGE 6 G0109 ARMS/CONT
PLAN
PROB/SOLV

DAENIKER G.,STRATEGIE DES KLEIN STAATS. SWITZERLND **B66** NUC/PWR
ACT/RES CREATE DIPLOM NEUTRAL DETER WAR WEAPON PWR PLAN
SOVEREIGN...IDEA/COMP 20 COLD/WAR. PAGE 14 G0270 FORCES
NAT/G

ECKSTEIN A.,COMMUNIST CHINA'S ECONOMIC GROWTH AND **B66** ASIA
FOREIGN TRADE* IMPLICATIONS FOR US POLICY. COM ECO/UNDEV
USA+45 USSR STRUCT INDUS MARKET DIPLOM ECO/TAC CREATE
FOR/AID INT/TRADE...STAT CHARTS. PAGE 17 G0332 PWR

GREEN P.,DEADLY LOGIC* THE THEORY OF NUCLEAR **B66** DETER
DETERRENCE. USA+45 ACT/RES OP/RES NUC/PWR RATIONAL ACADEM
ALL/VALS PWR...DECISION MGT PHIL/SCI QUANT GEN/LAWS
IDEA/COMP GAME. PAGE 23 G0444 RECORD

NIEBURG H.L.,IN THE NAME OF SCIENCE. USA+45 **B66** NAT/G
EX/STRUC LEGIS TEC/DEV BUDGET PAY AUTOMAT LOBBY PWR INDUS
...OBS 20. PAGE 42 G0822 TECHRACY

ODEGARD P.H.,POLITICAL POWER AND SOCIAL CHANGE. **B66** PWR
UNIV NAT/G CREATE ALL/IDEOS...POLICY GEOG SOC TEC/DEV
CENSUS TREND. PAGE 42 G0829 IDEA/COMP

PRINCETON U INDUSTRIAL REL SEC,THE FEDERAL **B66** BIBLIOG/A
GOVERNMENT AND THE UNIVERSITY: SUPPORT FOR SOCIAL NAT/G
SCIENCE RESEARCH AND THE IMPACT OF PROJECT CAMELOT. ACADEM
USA+45 ACT/RES CONTROL GP/REL PWR...POLICY 20. PLAN
PAGE 45 G0889

STREET D.,ORGANIZATION FOR TREATMENT. CLIENT PROVS **B66** GP/COMP
PUB/INST PLAN CONTROL PARTIC REPRESENT ATTIT PWR AGE/Y
...POLICY BIBLIOG. PAGE 53 G1044 ADMIN
VOL/ASSN

GREENBERG D.S.,"THE SCIENTIFIC PORK BARREL." USA+45 **S66** R+D
ECO/DEV PUB/INST CHIEF LEGIS BUDGET GIVE GP/REL PWR NAT/G
WEALTH 20. PAGE 23 G0445 ACADEM
ATTIT

BUTLER J.,BOSTON UNIVERSITY PAPERS ON AFRICA* **B67** IDEA/COMP
TRANSITION IN AFRICAN POLITICS. AFR LAW CONSTN NAT/G
LABOR POL/PAR TEC/DEV 20. PAGE 10 G0197 PWR

COMMONER B.,SCIENCE AND SURVIVAL. SOCIETY INDUS **B67** PHIL/SCI
PLAN NUC/PWR KNOWL PWR...SOC 20 AEC. PAGE 13 G0247 CONTROL
PROB/SOLV
EQUILIB

CONNOLLY W.E.,POLITICAL SCIENCE AND IDEOLOGY. **B67** PWR
UTOPIA ATTIT KNOWL...MAJORIT EPIST PHIL/SCI SOC PLURISM
IDEA/COMP HYPO/EXP GEN/LAWS METH HUME/D MARX/KARL. ELITES
PAGE 13 G0250 CONCPT

DE BLIJ H.J.,SYSTEMATIC POLITICAL GEOGRAPHY. WOR+45 **B67** GEOG
STRUCT INT/ORG NAT/G EDU/PROP ADMIN COLONIAL CONCPT
ROUTINE ORD/FREE PWR...IDEA/COMP T 20. PAGE 15 METH

G0283

B67

HEILBRONER R.L.,THE LIMITS OF AMERICAN CAPITALISM. ELITES
FUT ECO/DEV INDUS LG/CO EX/STRUC LEAD PWR TECHRACY CREATE
20. PAGE 25 G0502 TEC/DEV
CAP/ISM

B67

MACKINTOSH J.M.,JUGGERNAUT. USSR NAT/G POL/PAR WAR
ADMIN LEAD CIVMIL/REL COST TOTALISM PWR MARXISM FORCES
...GOV/COMP 20. PAGE 35 G0691 COM
PROF/ORG

B67

PADELFORD N.J.,THE DYNAMICS OF INTERNATIONAL DIPLOM
POLITICS (2ND ED.). WOR+45 LAW INT/ORG FORCES NAT/G
TEC/DEV REGION NAT/LISM PEACE ATTIT PWR ALL/IDEOS POLICY
UN COLD/WAR NATO TREATY. PAGE 43 G0856 DECISION

B67

RAWLINSON J.L.,CHINA'S STRUGGLE FOR NAVAL SEA
DEVELOPMENT 1839-1895. ASIA DIPLOM ADMIN WAR FORCES
...BIBLIOG DICTIONARY 19 CHINJAP. PAGE 46 G0907 PWR

B67

WYLIE J.C.,MILITARY STRATEGY: GENERAL THEORY OF FORCES
POWER CONTROL. CUBA USA+45 VIETNAM/N WOR+45 ELITES PLAN
CONTROL WAR PWR...POLICY METH/COMP 20 MAO. PAGE 64 DECISION
G1260 IDEA/COMP

L67

ROBINSON T.W.,"A NATIONAL INTEREST ANALYSIS OF MARXISM
SINO-SOVIET RELATIONS." CHINA/COM USSR NAT/G DIPLOM
NUC/PWR ATTIT PWR...CONCPT CHARTS 20. PAGE 47 G0931 SOVEREIGN
GEN/LAWS

S67

"CHINESE STATEMENT ON NUCLEAR PROLIFERATION." NUC/PWR
CHINA/COM USA+45 USSR DOMIN COLONIAL PWR. PAGE 1 BAL/PWR
G0022 ARMS/CONT
DIPLOM

S67

BRETNOR R.,"DESTRUCTIVE FORCE AND THE MILITARY FORCES
EQUATIONS." UNIV COMPUTER PLAN PROB/SOLV AUTOMAT TEC/DEV
CONTROL COERCE DETER NUC/PWR WEAPON DRIVE PWR. DOMIN
PAGE 9 G0166 WAR

S67

CARR E.H.,"REVOLUTION FROM ABOVE." USSR STRATA AGRI
FINAN INDUS NAT/G DOMIN LEAD GP/REL INGP/REL OWN POLICY
PRODUC PWR 20 STALIN/J. PAGE 11 G0214 COM
EFFICIENCY

S67

CLEMENS W.C.,"CHINESE NUCLEAR TESTS: TRENDS AND NUC/PWR
PORTENTS." CHINA/COM USA+45 USSR FORCES PLAN WEAPON
TEC/DEV ARMS/CONT WAR PWR...DECISION 20 MAO POLICY
KHRUSH/N. PAGE 12 G0234 DIPLOM

S67

D'AMATO D.,"LEGAL ASPECTS OF THE FRENCH NUCLEAR INT/LAW
TESTS." FRANCE WOR+45 ACT/RES COLONIAL RISK GOV/REL DIPLOM
EQUILIB ORD/FREE PWR DECISION. PAGE 14 G0268 NUC/PWR
ADJUD

S67

HAZARD J.N.,"POST-DISARMAMENT INTERNATIONAL LAW." INT/LAW
FUT USSR WOR+45 INT/ORG DELIB/GP FORCES DETER ARMS/CONT
EQUILIB SOVEREIGN MARXISM 20 UN. PAGE 25 G0496 PWR
PLAN

S67

JAIN G.,"INDIA REJECTS THE POWER RACE* REALISM INDIA
ABOUT NUCLEAR WEAPONS." FORCES PROB/SOLV FOR/AID CHINA/COM
ARMS/CONT COST PWR...GOV/COMP 20. PAGE 28 G0556 NUC/PWR
DIPLOM

S67

KRAUS J.,"A MARXIST IN GHANA." GHANA ELITES CHIEF MARXISM
PROB/SOLV TEC/DEV DIPLOM ECO/TAC COLONIAL PARTIC PLAN
PWR 20 NKRUMAH/K. PAGE 31 G0618 ATTIT
CREATE

S67

SKOLNIKOFF E.B.,"MAKING FOREIGN POLICY" PROB/SOLV TEC/DEV
EFFICIENCY PERCEPT PWR...MGT METH/CNCPT CLASSIF 20. CONTROL
PAGE 51 G1009 USA+45
NAT/G

S67

TEKINER S.,"SINKIAN AND THE SINO-SOVIET CONFLICT." DIPLOM
ASIA COM USSR FORCES PLAN BAL/PWR CONTROL NUC/PWR PWR
WAR WEAPON...DECISION 20. PAGE 54 G1060 MARXISM

N67

PRINCETON U INDUSTRIAL REL SEC,COLLECTIVE BIBLIOG/A
BARGAINING IN THE PUBLIC SCHOOLS (PAMPHLET NO. 33). SCHOOL
USA+45 LABOR PROB/SOLV PWR MGT. PAGE 45 G0891 BARGAIN
GP/REL

PYE L.W. G0896,G0897 —————— Q ——————

QU....QUESTIONNAIRES; SEE ALSO QUESTIONNAIRES INDEX, P. XIV

B40

PFIFFNER J.M.,RESEARCH METHODS IN PUBLIC ADMIN
ADMINISTRATION. USA-45 R+D...MGT STAT INT QU T 20. OP/RES
PAGE 44 G0872 METH
TEC/DEV

B42

MARCHANT A.,INVESTIGATIONS IN PROGRESS IN THE ACT/RES
UNITED STATES IN THE FIELD OF LATIN AMERICAN SOC
HUMANISTIC AND SOCIAL SCIENCE STUDIES. USA+45 R+D
ACADEM...QU ANTHOL. PAGE 36 G0702 L/A+17C

B47

SOCIAL SCIENCE RESEARCH COUN,PUBLIC REACTION TO THE ATTIT
ATOMIC BOMB AND WORLD AFFAIRS. SOCIETY CONFER NUC/PWR
ARMS/CONT...STAT QU SAMP CHARTS 20. PAGE 52 G1019 DIPLOM
WAR

S52

"SELECTED CRITICAL BIBLIOGRAPHY ON THE METHODS AND BIBLIOG/A
TECHNIQUES OF POLITICAL BEHAVIOR RESEARCH." METH
...PHIL/SCI OBS QU SYS/QU TESTS CON/ANAL. PAGE 1 SOC
G0012 EDU/PROP

B57

SPEIER H.,GERMAN REARMAMENT AND ATOMIC WAR: THE TOP/EX
VIEWS OF GERMAN MILITARY AND POLITICAL LEADERS. FUT FORCES
WOR+45 INT/ORG NAT/G WEAPON ATTIT PWR...INT QU NUC/PWR
TOT/POP VAL/FREE COLD/WAR 20. PAGE 52 G1024 GERMANY

B59

COLUMBIA U BUREAU APPL SOC R, ATTITUDES OF ATTIT
PROMINENT AMERICANS TOWARD "WORLD PEACE THROUGH ACT/RES
WORLD LAW" (SUPRA-NATL ORGANIZATION FOR WAR INT/LAW
PREVENTION). USA+45 USSR ELITES FORCES PLAN STAT
PROB/SOLV CONTROL WAR PWR...POLICY SOC QU IDEA/COMP
20 UN. PAGE 45 G0888

B63

WALES H.G.,A BASIC BIBLIOGRAPHY ON MARKETING BIBLIOG/A
RESEARCH (REV. ED.). ATTIT...MGT STAT INT QU SAMP MARKET
TREND 20. PAGE 62 G1206 OP/RES
METH/COMP

B64

COOMBS C.H.,A THEORY OF DATA....MGT PHIL/SCI SOC CON/ANAL
CLASSIF MATH PROBABIL STAT QU. PAGE 13 G0254 GEN/METH
TESTS
PSY

B64

PARANJAPE H.K.,THE FLIGHT OF TECHNICAL PERSONNEL IN ADMIN
PUBLIC UNDERTAKINGS. INDIA PAY DEMAND HAPPINESS NAT/G
ORD/FREE...MGT QU 20 MIGRATION. PAGE 44 G0858 WORKER
PLAN

S64

BYRNES F.C.,"ASSIGNMENT TO AMBIGUITY: WORK INTELL
PERFORMANCE IN CROSSCULTURAL TECHNICAL ASSISTANCE." QU
USA+45 PROF/ORG CONSULT PLAN EDU/PROP ATTIT
DISPL PERCEPT PERSON ALL/VALS...POLICY INT CHARTS
NATO 20. PAGE 10 G0199

S68

BARAGWANATH L.E.,"SCIENTIFIC CO-OPERATION BETWEEN R+D
THE UNIVERSITIES AND INDUSTRY - A RESEARCH NOTE." ACADEM
UK LG/CO CREATE TEC/DEV EDU/PROP ATTIT...PHIL/SCI INDUS
STAT QU 20. PAGE 5 G0090 GP/REL

QU/SEMANT.....SEMANTIC AND SOCIAL PROBLEMS OF QUESTIONNAIRES

S50

KAPLAN A.,"THE PREDICTION OF SOCIAL AND PWR
TECHNOLOGICAL EVENTS." VOL/ASSN CONSULT ACT/RES KNO/TEST
CREATE OP/RES PLAN ROUTINE PERSON...POLICY
METH/CNCPT STAT QU/SEMANT SYS/QU TESTS CENSUS TREND
20. PAGE 29 G0574

QUAKER....QUAKER

QUANDT R.E. G0576

QUANT....QUANTIFICATION

S48

MERTON R.K.,"THE BEARING OF EMPIRICAL RESEARCH UPON ACT/RES

THE DEVELOPMENT OF SOCIAL THEORY" (BMR)"...SOC
CONCPT QUANT METH/COMP HYPO/EXP 20. PAGE 38 G0757

SOC/EXP
OBS
PHIL/SCI

B50

SURANYI-UNGER T.,PRIVATE ENTERPRISE AND
GOVERNMENTAL PLANNING. STRUCT FINAN BAL/PWR
HAPPINESS DRIVE NEW/LIB PLURISM...MATH QUANT STAT
TREND BIBLIOG. PAGE 53 G1047

PLAN
NAT/G
LAISSEZ
POLICY

S53

MILLER G.A.,"WHAT IS INFORMATION MEASUREMENT?"
CREATE...CONCPT METH/CNCPT QUANT STAT CHARTS
BIBLIOG/A 20. PAGE 39 G0771

COMPUTER
TEC/DEV
PSY
MATH

B54

SPENCER R.F.,METHOD AND PERSPECTIVE IN ANTHROPOLOGY
....GEOG LING QUANT STAT TESTS SAMP/SIZ CON/ANAL
IDEA/COMP METH/COMP ANTHOL BIBLIOG 20. PAGE 52
G1025

PHIL/SCI
SOC
PSY
METH

S54

BATES J.,"A MODEL FOR THE SCIENCE OF DECISION."
UNIV ROUTINE...CONT/OBS CON/ANAL HYPO/EXP GAME.
PAGE 5 G0101

QUANT
DECISION
PHIL/SCI
METH/CNCPT

S54

DEUTSCH K.W.,"GAME THEORY AND POLITICS: SOME
PROBLEMS OF APPLICATION." FUT WOR+45 SOCIETY R+D
KNOWL PWR...CONCPT METH/CNCPT MATH QUANT GAME SIMUL
VAL/FREE 20. PAGE 15 G0295

DECISION
GEN/METH

S56

EASTON D.,"LIMITS OF THE EQUILIBRIUM MODEL IN
SOCIAL RESEARCH." STRUCT GP/REL PWR...PHIL/SCI
CLASSIF. PAGE 17 G0330

METH/CNCPT
GEN/METH
R+D
QUANT

S57

DUNCAN O.D.,"THE MEASUREMENT OF POPULATION
DISTRIBUTION" (BMR)" WOR+45...QUANT STAT CENSUS
CHARTS 20. PAGE 16 G0321

GEOG
PHIL/SCI
PROB/SOLV
CLASSIF

B58

GANGE J.,UNIVERSITY RESEARCH ON INTERNATIONAL
AFFAIRS. USA+45 ACADEM INT/ORG CONSULT CREATE EXEC
ROUTINE...QUANT STAT INT STERTYP GEN/METH TOT/POP
VAL/FREE 20. PAGE 21 G0407

R+D
MGT
DIPLOM

S60

BARNETT H.J.,"RESEARCH AND DEVELOPMENT, ECONOMIC
GROWTH, AND NATIONAL SECURITY." USA+45 R+D CREATE
ECO/TAC ATTIT DRIVE PWR...POLICY SOC METH/CNCPT
QUANT STAT TIME/SEQ ORG/CHARTS COLD/WAR 20. PAGE 5
G0097

ACT/RES
PLAN

S62

GORDON B.K.,"NUCLEAR WEAPONS: RUSSIAN AND
AMERICAN." COM USA+45 USSR NAT/G FORCES ACT/RES
TEC/DEV PERCEPT RIGID/FLEX PWR SKILL...MGT
METH/CNCPT QUANT OBS TIME/SEQ CON/ANAL GEN/METH
TOT/POP VAL/FREE 20. PAGE 22 G0433

ORD/FREE
COERCE
NUC/PWR

B63

BONINI C.P.,SIMULATION OF INFORMATION AND DECISION
SYSTEMS IN THE FIRM. MARKET BUDGET DOMIN EDU/PROP
ADMIN COST ATTIT HABITAT PERCEPT PWR...CONCPT
PROBABIL QUANT PREDICT HYPO/EXP BIBLIOG. PAGE 8
G0152

INDUS
SIMUL
DECISION
MGT

B63

NORTH R.C.,CONTENT ANALYSIS: A HANDBOOK WITH
APPLICATIONS FOR THE STUDY OF INTERNATIONAL CRISIS.
ASIA COM EUR+WWI MOD/EUR INT/ORG TEC/DEV DOMIN
EDU/PROP ROUTINE COERCE PERCEPT RIGID/FLEX ALL/VALS
...QUANT TESTS CON/ANAL SIMUL GEN/LAWS VAL/FREE.
PAGE 42 G0825

METH/CNCPT
COMPUT/IR
USSR

B65

ALKER H.R. JR.,MATHEMATICS AND POLITICS. PROB/SOLV
...DECISION PHIL/SCI CLASSIF QUANT STAT GAME
GEN/LAWS INDEX. PAGE 2 G0042

GEN/METH
CONCPT
MATH

B65

HICKMAN B.G.,QUANTITATIVE PLANNING OF ECONOMIC
POLICY. FRANCE NETHERLAND OP/RES PRICE ROUTINE UTIL
...POLICY DECISION ECOMETRIC METH/CNCPT STAT STYLE
CHINJAP. PAGE 26 G0511

PROB/SOLV
PLAN
QUANT

B65

SINGER J.D.,HUMAN BEHAVIOR AND INTERNATIONAL
POLITICS* CONTRIBUTIONS FROM THE SOCIAL-
PSYCHOLOGICAL SCIENCES. ACT/RES PLAN EDU/PROP ADMIN

DIPLOM
PHIL/SCI
QUANT

KNOWL...DECISION PSY SOC NET/THEORY HYPO/EXP
LAB/EXP SOC/EXP GEN/METH ANTHOL BIBLIOG. PAGE 51
G1006

SIMUL

B60

GREEN P.,DEADLY LOGIC* THE THEORY OF NUCLEAR
DETERRENCE. USA+45 ACT/RES OP/RES NUC/PWR RATIONAL
ALL/VALS PWR...DECISION MGT PHIL/SCI QUANT
IDEA/COMP GAME. PAGE 23 G0444

DETER
ACADEM
GEN/LAWS
RECORD

S66

KAPLAN M.A.,"THE NEW GREAT DEBATE* TRADITIONALISM
VS SCIENCE IN INTERNATIONAL RELATIONS."...DECISION
HUM QUANT STYLE NET/THEORY CON/ANAL STERTYP
GEN/LAWS. PAGE 29 G0577

PHIL/SCI
CONSERVE
DIPLOM
SIMUL

QUANTIFICATION....SEE QUANT

QUANTITATIVE CONTENT ANALYSIS....SEE CON/ANAL

QUEBEC....QUEBEC, CANADA

QUESTIONNAIRES....SEE QU

R

R+D....RESEARCH AND DEVELOPMENT GROUP

AMERICAN DOCUMENTATION INST,DOCUMENTATION
ABSTRACTS. WOR+45 NAT/G COMPUTER CREATE TEC/DEV
DIPLOM EDU/PROP REGION KNOWL...PHIL/SCI CLASSIF
LING. PAGE 3 G0051

N
BIBLIOG/A
AUTOMAT
COMPUT/IR
R+D

B

US DEPT COMMERCE OFF TECH SERV,TECHNICAL
TRANSLATIONS. WOR+45 INDUS COMPUTER CREATE NUC/PWR
...PHIL/SCI COMPUT/IR METH/COMP METH. PAGE 58 G1135

BIBLIOG
R+D
TEC/DEV
AUTOMAT

N

INDIA: A REFERENCE ANNUAL. INDIA CULTURE COM/IND
R+D FORCES PLAN RECEIVE EDU/PROP HEALTH...STAT
CHARTS BIBLIOG 20. PAGE 1 G0005

CONSTN
LABOR
INT/ORG

B1

BERGSON H.,CREATIVE EVOLUTION. FUT WOR+45 WOR-45
INTELL AGRI R+D ATTIT PERCEPT PERSON RIGID/FLEX
...RELATIV PHIL/SCI PSY METH/CNCPT MATH HIST/WRIT
TREND HYPO/EXP TOT/POP. PAGE 7 G0127

BIO/SOC
KNOWL

N1

LAWRENCE S.A.,THE BATTERY ADDITIVE CONTROVERSY
(PAMPHLET). USA+45 LAW MARKET PROC/MFG R+D CAP/ISM
CT/SYS GOV/REL OWN FTC CONGRESS BUR/STNDRD
RITCHIE/JM. PAGE 33 G0645

PHIL/SCI
LOBBY
INSPECT

N1

US ATOMIC ENERGY COMMISSION,ATOMIC ENERGY IN USE
(PAMPHLET). R+D RISK EFFICIENCY HEALTH KNOWL
ORD/FREE...PHIL/SCI CONCPT METH/CNCPT CHARTS
LAB/EXP 20 AEC. PAGE 56 G1106

OP/RES
TEC/DEV
NUC/PWR
CREATE

B2

DRAPER J.W.,HISTORY OF THE CONFLICT BETWEEN
RELIGION AND SCIENCE. WOR-45 INTELL SOCIETY R+D
CREATE PLAN TEC/DEV EDU/PROP ATTIT PWR...PHIL/SCI
CONCPT OBS TIME/SEQ TREND GEN/LAWS TOT/POP. PAGE 16
G0314

SECT
KNOWL

B2

SOROKIN P.,CONTEMPORARY SOCIOLOGICAL THEORIES.
MOD/EUR UNIV SOCIETY R+D SCHOOL ECO/TAC EDU/PROP
ROUTINE ATTIT DRIVE...PSY CONCPT TIME/SEQ TREND
GEN/LAWS 20. PAGE 52 G1021

CULTURE
SOC
WAR

B3

EINSTEIN A.,THE WORLD AS I SEE IT. WOR-45 INTELL
R+D INT/ORG NAT/G SECT VOL/ASSN FORCES CREATE
EDU/PROP LEGIT ARMS/CONT WAR WEAPON NAT/LISM
ALL/VALS...POLICY CONCPT 20. PAGE 17 G0337

SOCIETY
PHIL/SCI
DIPLOM
PACIFISM

B4

PFIFFNER J.M.,RESEARCH METHODS IN PUBLIC
ADMINISTRATION. USA-45 R+D...MGT STAT INT QU T 20.
PAGE 44 G0872

ADMIN
OP/RES
METH
TEC/DEV

B4

MARCHANT A.,INVESTIGATIONS IN PROGRESS IN THE
UNITED STATES IN THE FIELD OF LATIN AMERICAN
HUMANISTIC AND SOCIAL SCIENCE STUDIES. USA+45
ACADEM...QU ANTHOL. PAGE 36 G0702

ACT/RES
SOC
R+D
L/A+17C

B4

PUBLIC ADMINISTRATION SERVICE,YOUR BUSINESS OF
GOVERNMENT: A CATALOG OF PUBLICATIONS IN THE FIELD
OF PUBLIC ADMINISTRATION (PAMPHLET). FINAN R+D

BIBLIOG
ADMIN
NAT/G

LOC/G ACT/RES OP/RES PLAN 20. PAGE 45 G0894   MUNIC

UK

B45
BUSH V.,SCIENCE, THE ENDLESS FRONTIER. FUT USA-45 R+D
INTELL STRATA ACT/RES CREATE PLAN EDU/PROP ADMIN NAT/G
NUC/PWR PEACE ATTIT HEALTH KNOWL...MAJORIT HEAL MGT
PHIL/SCI CONCPT OBS TREND 20. PAGE 10 G0195

S50
BAVELAS A.,"COMMUNICATION PATTERNS IN TASK-ORIENTED ACT/RES
GROUPS" (BMR)" R+D OP/RES INSPECT LEAD CENTRAL PERS/REL
EFFICIENCY HAPPINESS RIGID/FLEX...PROBABIL 20. TASK
PAGE 6 G0106 INGP/REL

B45
SCHULTZ T.H.,FOOD FOR THE WORLD. UNIV SOCIETY INDUS AGRI
R+D ECO/TAC...GEOG TREND GEN/LAWS 20. PAGE 50 G0979 TEC/DEV

B51
CONANT J.B.,SCIENCE AND COMMON SENSE. WOR+45 WOR-45 CREATE
R+D SCHOOL CONSULT TEC/DEV EDU/PROP SKILL...PLURIST PHIL/SCI
METH/CNCPT RECORD TIME/SEQ SIMUL GEN/METH METH.
PAGE 13 G0248

B45
SMYTH H.D.,ATOMIC ENERGY FOR MILITARY PURPOSES. R+D
USA-45 NAT/G PLAN TEC/DEV KNOWL...MATH CON/ANAL TIME/SEQ
CHARTS LAB/EXP SIMUL 20. PAGE 52 G1017 NUC/PWR

B51
HUXLEY J.,FREEDOM AND CULTURE. UNIV LAW SOCIETY R+D CULTURE
ACADEM SCHOOL CREATE SANCTION ATTIT KNOWL...HUM ORD/FREE
ANTHOL 20. PAGE 27 G0540 PHIL/SCI
  IDEA/COMP

C45
TRYTTEN M.H.,"THE MOBILIZATION OF SCIENTISTS," IN INTELL
L. WHITE, CIVIL SERVICE IN WARTIME." USA-45 R+D WAR
FORCES ACT/RES PERSON ROLE 20. PAGE 55 G1080 TEC/DEV
  NAT/G

S51
LERNER D.,"THE POLICY SCIENCES: RECENT DEVELOPMENTS CONSULT
IN SCOPE AND METHODS." R+D SERV/IND CREATE DIPLOM SOC
ROUTINE PWR...METH/CNCPT TREND GEN/LAWS METH 20.
PAGE 33 G0658

B46
BAXTER J.P.,SCIENTISTS AGAINST TIME. EUR+WWI FORCES
MOD/EUR USA+45 USA-45 WOR+45 WOR-45 R+D NAT/G PLAN WAR
ATTIT PWR...PHIL/SCI RECORD CON/ANAL 17/20. PAGE 6 NUC/PWR
G0107

B52
HAYEK F.A.,THE COUNTER-REVOLUTION OF SCIENCE. UNIV PERCEPT
INTELL R+D VOL/ASSN CREATE EDU/PROP...PHIL/SCI SOC KNOWL
OBS TIME/SEQ TREND GEN/METH. PAGE 25 G0494

B46
BUSH V.,ENDLESS HORIZONS. FUT USA-45 INTELL NAT/G R+D
CONSULT ACT/RES CREATE PLAN EDU/PROP DRIVE KNOWL
...MAJORIT HEAL MGT PHIL/SCI CONCPT OBS TREND PEACE
GEN/METH TOT/POP 20. PAGE 10 G0196

L52
LASSWELL H.D.,"RESEARCH IN POLITICAL BEHAVIOR." PHIL/SCI
LOC/G MUNIC POL/PAR CONSULT ADMIN PARTIC...CHARTS METH
ANTHOL BIBLIOG/A 20. PAGE 32 G0641 R+D

B46
VINER J.,SYMPOSIUM ON ATOMIC ENERGY AND ITS R+D
IMPLICATIONS. USA+45 WOR+45 SOCIETY DELIB/GP...SOC RIGID/FLEX
CONCPT TIME/SEQ TOT/POP 20. PAGE 61 G1200 NUC/PWR

L52
ROYAL INST. INT. AFF.,"ANNUAL REPORT OF THE R+D
COUNCIL: 1951-1952." WOR+45 CREATE KNOWL...MGT EDU/PROP
COLD/WAR CMN/WLTH TOT/POP VAL/FREE 20. PAGE 48
G0943

B46
WILCOX J.K.,OFFICIAL DEFENSE PUBLICATIONS, BIBLIOG/A
1941-1945 (NINE VOLS.). USA-45 AGRI INDUS R+D LABOR WAR
FORCES TEC/DEV EFFICIENCY PRODUC SKILL WEALTH 20. CIVMIL/REL
PAGE 63 G1238 ADMIN

S52
TRUMAN D.B.,"SELECTED CRITICAL BIBLIOGRAPHY ON THE BIBLIOG/A
METHODS AND TECHNIQUES OF POLITICAL BEHAVIOR ACT/RES
RESEARCH." R+D PARTIC...SOC OBS RECORD INT. PAGE 55 METH/CNCPT
G1079

B47
LASSWELL H.D.,THE ANALYSIS OF POLITICAL BEHAVIOUR: R+D
AN EMPIRICAL APPROACH. WOR+45 CULTURE NAT/G FORCES ACT/RES
EDU/PROP ADMIN ATTIT PERCEPT KNOWL...PHIL/SCI PSY ELITES
SOC NEW/IDEA OBS INT GEN/METH NAZI 20. PAGE 32
G0639

B53
EASTON D.,THE POLITICAL SYSTEM, AN INQUIRY INTO THE R+D
STATE POLITICAL SCIENCE. USA+45 INTELL CREATE PERCEPT
EDU/PROP RIGID/FLEX KNOWL SKILL...PHIL/SCI NEW/IDEA
STERTYP TOT/POP 20. PAGE 17 G0329

B47
WHITEHEAD T.N.,LEADERSHIP IN A FREE SOCIETY; A INDUS
STUDY IN HUMAN RELATIONS BASED ON AN ANALYSIS OF LEAD
PRESENT-DAY INDUSTRIAL CIVILIZATION. WOR-45 STRUCT ORD/FREE
R+D LABOR LG/CO SML/CO WORKER PLAN PROB/SOLV SOCIETY
TEC/DEV DRIVE...MGT 20. PAGE 63 G1234

B53
HOVLAND C.I.,COMMUNICATION AND PERSUASION: PSY
PSYCHOLOGICAL STUDIES OF OPINION CHANGE. INTELL EDU/PROP
SOCIETY ECO/DEV COM/IND R+D SERV/IND CREATE TEC/DEV
ATTIT RIGID/FLEX KNOWL NEW/IDEA. PAGE 27 G0531

B48
BRADLEY D.,NO PLACE TO HIDE. USA+45 SOCIETY NAT/G R+D
FORCES TEC/DEV EDU/PROP DETER PEACE BIO/SOC LAB/EXP
ALL/VALS...POLICY PHIL/SCI OBS RECORD SAMP BIOG ARMS/CONT
GEN/METH COLD/WAR 20. PAGE 8 G0162 NUC/PWR

B54
PUBLIC ADMIN CLEARING HOUSE,PUBLIC ADMINISTRATIONS INDEX
ORGANIZATIONS: A DIRECTORY, 1954. USA+45 R+D PROVS VOL/ASSN
ACT/RES...MGT 20. PAGE 45 G0893 NAT/G
  ADMIN

B48
GRIFFITH E.S.,RESEARCH IN POLITICAL SCIENCE: THE BIBLIOG
WORK OF PANELS OF RESEARCH COMMITTEE, APSA. WOR+45 PHIL/SCI
WOR-45 COM/IND R+D FORCES ACT/RES WAR...GOV/COMP DIPLOM
ANTHOL 20. PAGE 23 G0451 JURID

B54
ROSE A.M.,THEORY AND METHOD IN THE SOCIAL SCIENCES. CONCPT
STRATA R+D NEIGH PARTIC...METH/CNCPT GP/COMP. SOC
PAGE 47 G0934 VOL/ASSN
  ROLE

B48
STEWART I.,ORGANIZING SCIENTIFIC RESEARCH FOR WAR: DELIB/GP
ADMINISTRATIVE HISTORY OF OFFICE OF SCIENTIFIC ADMIN
RESEARCH AND DEVELOPMENT. USA-45 INTELL R+D LABOR WAR
WORKER CREATE BUDGET WEAPON CIVMIL/REL GP/REL TEC/DEV
EFFICIENCY...POLICY 20. PAGE 53 G1036

S54
DEUTSCH K.W.,"GAME THEORY AND POLITICS: SOME DECISION
PROBLEMS OF APPLICATION." FUT WOR+45 SOCIETY R+D GEN/METH
KNOWL PWR...CONCPT METH/CNCPT MATH QUANT GAME SIMUL
VAL/FREE 20. PAGE 15 G0295

B49
ROSENHAUPT H.W.,HOW TO WAGE PEACE. USA+45 SOCIETY INTELL
STRATA STRUCT R+D INT/ORG POL/PAR LEGIS ACT/RES CONCPT
CREATE PLAN EDU/PROP ADMIN EXEC ATTIT ALL/VALS DIPLOM
...TIME/SEQ TREND COLD/WAR 20. PAGE 48 G0937

S55
WRIGHT Q.,"THE PEACEFUL ADJUSTMENT OF INTERNATIONAL R+D
RELATIONS: PROBLEMS AND RESEARCH APPROACHES." UNIV METH/CNCPT
INTELL EDU/PROP ADJUD ROUTINE KNOWL SKILL...INT/LAW PEACE
JURID PHIL/SCI CLASSIF 20. PAGE 64 G1258

B50
CANTRIL H.,TENSIONS THAT CAUSE WAR. UNIV CULTURE SOCIETY
R+D CREATE EDU/PROP DRIVE PERSON KNOWL ORD/FREE PHIL/SCI
...HUM PSY SOC OBS CENSUS TREND CON/ANAL SOC/EXP PEACE
SIMUL GEN/METH ANTHOL COLD/WAR TOT/POP. PAGE 11
G0206

B56
UN HEADQUARTERS LIBRARY,BIBLIOGRAPHY OF BIBLIOG
INDUSTRIALIZATION IN UNDERDEVELOPED COUNTRIES ECO/UNDEV
(BIBLIOGRAPHICAL SERIES NO. 6). WOR+45 R+D ACADEM TEC/DEV
INT/ORG NAT/G. PAGE 55 G1087

B50
CROWTHER J.G.,SCIENCE AT WAR. EUR+WWI PLAN TEC/DEV R+D
DOMIN COERCE NUC/PWR WEAPON KNOWL PWR...CONCPT OBS FORCES
TREND VAL/FREE 20. PAGE 14 G0265 WAR

B56
US DEPARTMENT OF THE ARMY,RESEARCH AND DEVELOPMENT BIBLIOG/A
(AND RELATED ASPECTS) IN FOREIGN COUNTRIES. WOR+45 R+D
DIST/IND INDUS CONSULT FORCES CREATE EDU/PROP TEC/DEV
AUTOMAT DETER WEAPON. PAGE 57 G1126 NUC/PWR

WASSERMAN P.,INFORMATION FOR ADMINISTRATORS: A GUIDE TO PUBLICATIONS AND SERVICES FOR MANAGEMENT IN BUSINESS AND GOVERNMENT. R+D LOC/G NAT/G PROF/ORG VOL/ASSN PRESS...PSY SOC STAT 20. PAGE 62 G1219
B56 BIBLIOG MGT KNOWL EDU/PROP

EASTON D.,"LIMITS OF THE EQUILIBRIUM MODEL IN SOCIAL RESEARCH." STRUCT GP/REL PWR...PHIL/SCI CLASSIF. PAGE 17 G0330
S56 METH/CNCPT GEN/METH R+D QUANT

DUPREE A.H.,SCIENCE IN THE FEDERAL GOVERNMENT; A HISTORY OF POLICIES AND ACTIVITIES TO 1940. USA-45 AGRI SCHOOL DELIB/GP WAR GOV/REL...PHIL/SCI BIBLIOG 18/20 DEPRESSION NEW/DEAL WWI JEFFERSN/T. PAGE 17 G0324
B57 NAT/G R+D CREATE TEC/DEV

EASTON D.,"AN APPROACH TO THE ANALYSIS OF POLITICAL SYSTEMS." R+D EDU/PROP KNOWL SKILL...POLICY SOC METH/CNCPT NEW/IDEA SELF/OBS CHARTS GEN/METH TOT/POP. PAGE 17 G0331
S57 STRUCT PHIL/SCI

GANGE J.,UNIVERSITY RESEARCH ON INTERNATIONAL AFFAIRS. USA+45 ACADEM INT/ORG CONSULT CREATE EXEC ROUTINE...QUANT STAT INT STERTYP GEN/METH TOT/POP VAL/FREE 20. PAGE 21 G0407
B58 R+D MGT DIPLOM

UN INTL CONF ON PEACEFUL USE,PROGRESS IN ATOMIC ENERGY (VOL. I). WOR+45 R+D PLAN TEC/DEV CONFER CONTROL PEACE SKILL...CHARTS ANTHOL 20 UN BAGHDAD. PAGE 55 G1088
B58 NUC/PWR DIPLOM WORKER EDU/PROP

ANDERSON N.,"INTERNATIONAL SEMINARS: AN ANALYSIS AND AN EVALUATION." WOR+45 R+D ACT/RES CREATE PLAN REGION ATTIT KNOWL SKILL...SOC REC/INT PERS/TEST CHARTS 20. PAGE 3 G0057
S58 INT/ORG DELIB/GP

ELDRIDGE H.T.,THE MATERIALS OF DEMOGRAPHY: A SELECTED AND ANNOTATED BIBLIOGRAPHY. R+D DEATH ...SAMP METH/COMP NAT/COMP 20. PAGE 18 G0343
B59 BIBLIOG/A GEOG STAT TREND

STANFORD RESEARCH INSTITUTE,POSSIBLE NONMILITARY SCIENTIFIC DEVELOPMENTS AND THEIR POTENTIAL IMPACT ON FOREIGN POLICY PROBLEMS OF THE UNITED. FUT USA+45 INT/ORG PROF/ORG CONSULT ACT/RES CREATE PLAN PEACE KNOWL SKILL...TECHNIC PHIL/SCI NEW/IDEA UNESCO 20. PAGE 52 G1032
B59 R+D TEC/DEV

BURNS A.L.,"THE RATIONALE OF CATALYTIC WAR." COM USA+45 WOR+45 R+D NAT/G FORCES ACT/RES TEC/DEV PWR ...DECISION HYPO/EXP TOT/POP 20. PAGE 10 G0191
L59 COERCE NUC/PWR WAR

GOLDHAMMER H.,"SOME OBSERVATIONS ON POLITICAL GAMING." FUT WOR+45 R+D NAT/G ACT/RES CREATE CHOOSE ATTIT PWR...POLICY CONCPT METH/CNCPT STYLE KNO/TEST TREND HYPO/EXP GAME GEN/METH METH 20. PAGE 22 G0426
S59 COMPUT/IR DECISION DIPLOM

LEFTON M.,"DECISION MAKING IN A MENTAL HOSPITAL: REAL, PERCEIVED, AND IDEAL." R+D PUB/INST CONSULT CONFER INGP/REL PERCEPT...MODAL 20. PAGE 33 G0653
S59 ACT/RES PROB/SOLV DECISION PSY

ARMS CONTROL. FUT UNIV WOR+45 INTELL R+D INT/ORG NAT/G VOL/ASSN CONSULT CREATE EDU/PROP PEACE...HUM GEN/LAWS TOT/POP 20. PAGE 1 G0015
B60 DELIB/GP ORD/FREE ARMS/CONT NUC/PWR

GOLDSEN J.M.,INTERNATIONAL POLITICAL IMPLICATIONS OF ACTIVITIES IN OUTER SPACE. FUT USA+45 WOR+45 AIR LAW ACT/RES LEGIT ATTIT KNOWL ORD/FREE PWR...CONCPT 20. PAGE 22 G0427
B60 R+D SPACE

HITCH C.J.,THE ECONOMICS OF DEFENSE IN THE NUCLEAR AGE. USA+45 WOR+45 CREATE PLAN NUC/PWR ATTIT ...CON/ANAL CHARTS HYPO/EXP NATO 20. PAGE 26 G0514
B60 R+D FORCES

LEYDER J.,BIBLIOGRAPHIE DE L'ENSEIGNEMENT SUPERIEUR ET DE LA RECHERCHE SCIENTIFIQUE EN AFRIQUE INTERTROPICALE (2 VOLS.). AFR CULTURE ECO/UNDEV
B60 BIBLIOG/A ACT/RES ACADEM

AGRI PLAN EDU/PROP ADMIN COLONIAL...GEOG SOC/INTEG 20 NEGRO. PAGE 34 G0664
R+D

RAPOPORT A.,FIGHTS, GAMES AND DEBATES. INTELL SOCIETY R+D EX/STRUC PERCEPT PERSON SKILL...PSY SOC GAME. PAGE 46 G0902
B60 METH/CNCPT MATH DECISION CON/ANAL

SILK L.S.,THE RESEARCH REVOLUTION. USA+45 FINAN CAP/ISM ECO/TAC PRICE EQUILIB PRODUC...STAT TREND CHARTS. PAGE 51 G0997
B60 ECO/DEV R+D TEC/DEV PROB/SOLV

US HOUSE COMM. SCI. ASTRONAUT.,OCEAN SCIENCES AND NATIONAL SECURITY. FUT SEA ECO/DEV EXTR/IND INT/ORG NAT/G FORCES ACT/RES TEC/DEV ECO/TAC COERCE WAR BIO/SOC KNOWL PWR...CONCPT RECORD LAB/EXP 20. PAGE 59 G1153
B60 R+D ORD/FREE

WALDO D.,THE RESEARCH FUNCTION OF UNIVERSITY BUREAUS AND INSTITUTES FOR GOVERNMENTAL-RELATED RESEARCH. FINAN ACADEM NAT/G INGP/REL ROLE...POLICY CLASSIF GOV/COMP. PAGE 61 G1205
B60 ADMIN R+D MUNIC

DEUTSCH K.W.,"TOWARD AN INVENTORY OF BASIC TRENDS AND PATTERNS IN COMPARATIVE AND INTERNATIONAL POLITICS." UNIV WOR+45 SOCIETY STRUCT INT/ORG NAT/G CREATE PLAN EDU/PROP KNOWL...PHIL/SCI METH/CNCPT STAT SELF/OBS OBS/ENVIR SAMP TREND CON/ANAL CHARTS SOC/EXP GEN/METH 20. PAGE 15 G0298
L60 R+D PERCEPT

HOLZMAN B.G.,"BASIC RESEARCH FOR NATIONAL SURVIVAL." FUT USA+45 INTELL R+D ACT/RES OP/RES PLAN TEC/DEV EDU/PROP PERCEPT PERSON...PHIL/SCI METH/CNCPT NEW/IDEA MATH OBS RECORD TREND LAB/EXP 20. PAGE 27 G0525
L60 FORCES STAT

BARNETT H.J.,"RESEARCH AND DEVELOPMENT, ECONOMIC GROWTH, AND NATIONAL SECURITY." USA+45 R+D CREATE ECO/TAC ATTIT DRIVE PWR...POLICY SOC METH/CNCPT QUANT STAT TIME/SEQ ORG/CHARTS COLD/WAR 20. PAGE 5 G0097
S60 ACT/RES PLAN

BECKER A.S.,"COMPARISIONS OF UNITED STATES AND USSR NATIONAL OUTPUT: SOME RULES OF THE GAME." COM USA+45 ECO/DEV AGRI DIST/IND INDUS R+D CONSULT PLAN ECO/TAC RIGID/FLEX KNOWL...METH/CNCPT CHARTS 20. PAGE 6 G0113
S60 STAT USSR

HALSEY A.H.,"THE CHANGING FUNCTIONS OF UNIVERSITIES IN ADVANCED INDUSTRIAL SOCIETIES." R+D EDU/PROP REPRESENT ROLE ORD/FREE PWR TREND. PAGE 24 G0476
S60 ACADEM CREATE CULTURE ADJUST

HAYTON R.D.,"THE ANTARCTIC SETTLEMENT OF 1959." FUT USA+45 WOR+45 STRUCT R+D INT/ORG EX/STRUC CREATE TEC/DEV LEGIT PEACE ATTIT SOVEREIGN ...TIME/SEQ 20 TREATY IGY. PAGE 25 G0495
S60 DELIB/GP JURID DIPLOM REGION

HUTCHINSON C.E.,"AN INSTITUTE FOR NATIONAL SECURITY AFFAIRS." USA+45 R+D NAT/G CONSULT TOP/EX ACT/RES CREATE PLAN TEC/DEV EDU/PROP ROUTINE NUC/PWR ATTIT ORD/FREE PWR...DECISION MGT PHIL/SCI CONCPT RECORD GEN/LAWS GEN/METH 20. PAGE 27 G0539
S60 POLICY METH/CNCPT ELITES DIPLOM

JAFFEE A.J.,"POPULATION TRENDS AND CONTROLS IN UNDERDEVELOPED COUNTRIES." AFR FUT ISLAM L/A+17C S/ASIA CULTURE R+D FAM ACT/RES PLAN EDU/PROP BIO/SOC RIGID/FLEX HEALTH...SOC STAT OBS CHARTS 20. PAGE 28 G0555
S60 ECO/UNDEV GEOG

YEMELYANOV V.S.,"ATOMIC ENERGY FOR PEACE: THE USSR AND INTERNATIONAL CO-OPERATION." FUT USSR WOR+45 R+D CREATE EDU/PROP...CONCPT GEN/LAWS 20. PAGE 64 G1264
S60 VOL/ASSN TEC/DEV ARMS/CONT NUC/PWR

INSTITUTE PSYCHOLOGICAL RES.,HUMAN ENGINEERING BIBLIOGRAPHY, 1959-1960. USA+45 WORKER EDU/PROP PERSON METH/COMP. PAGE 28 G0547
B61 BIBLIOG/A METH PSY R+D

LUNDBERG G.A.,,CAN SCIENCE SAVE US. UNIV CULTURE
INTELL SOCIETY ECO/DEV R+D PLAN EDU/PROP ROUTINE
CHOOSE ATTIT PERCEPT ALL/VALS...TREND 20. PAGE 34
G0679

B61
ACT/RES
CONCPT
TOTALISM

NAKICENOVIC S.,NUCLEAR ENERGY IN YUGOSLAVIA.
YUGOSLAVIA AGRI INDUS CREATE OP/RES ROUTINE
EFFICIENCY KNOWL...HEAL STAT CHARTS LAB/EXP BIBLIOG
20. PAGE 41 G0802

B61
R+D
ECO/DEV
TEC/DEV
NUC/PWR

HERRING P.,"RESEARCH FOR PUBLIC POLICY: BROOKINGS
DEDICATION LECTURES." USA+45 CONSULT DELIB/GP
ROUTINE PERCEPT SKILL...MGT 20. PAGE 26 G0508

L61
R+D
ACT/RES
DIPLOM

TAUBENFELD H.J.,"A TREATY FOR ANTARCTICA." FUT
USA+45 INTELL INT/ORG LABOR 20 TREATY ANTARCTICA.
PAGE 54 G1055

L61
R+D
ACT/RES
DIPLOM

TAUBENFELD H.J.,"A REGIME FOR OUTER SPACE." FUT
UNIV R+D ACT/RES PLAN BAL/PWR LEGIT ARMS/CONT
ORD/FREE...POLICY JURID TREND UN TOT/POP 20
COLD/WAR. PAGE 54 G1056

L61
INT/ORG
ADJUD
SPACE

COOKE E.F.,"RESEARCH: AN INSTRUMENT OF POWER."
VOL/ASSN PLAN TEC/DEV TAX LOBBY INGP/REL ROLE
POLICY. PAGE 13 G0253

S61
R+D
PROVS
LOC/G
DECISION

MAINZER L.C.,"SCIENTIFIC FREEDOM IN GOVERNMENT-
SPONSORED RESEARCH." USA+45 INTELL PUB/INST BUDGET
LOBBY AUTHORIT PWR...POLICY PHIL/SCI 20 NIH NSF.
PAGE 35 G0696

S61
CREATE
ORD/FREE
NAT/G
R+D

ASTIA,HUMAN ENGINEERING: A REPORT BIBLIOGRAPHY.
USA+45 R+D FORCES ACT/RES COMPUTER CREATE OP/RES
EDU/PROP CONTROL WEAPON...SOC NEW/IDEA. PAGE 4
G0073

B62
BIBLIOG/A
COM/IND
COMPUT/IR
METH

BORKOF H.,COMPUTER APPLICATIONS IN THE BEHAVIORAL
SCIENCES. AUTOMAT UTIL...DECISION PHIL/SCI PSY
METH/CNCPT LING LOG MATH STYLE NET/THEORY COMPUT/IR
PROG/TEAC SIMUL. PAGE 8 G0154

B62
R+D
COMPUTER
PROB/SOLV
FEEDBACK

BROOKINGS INSTITUTION,DEVELOPMENT OF THE EMERGING
COUNTRIES; AN AGENDA FOR RESEARCH. WOR+45 AGRI
TEC/DEV FOR/AID EDU/PROP ADJUST HABITAT KNOWL...PSY
SOC ANTHOL 20 THIRD/WRLD. PAGE 9 G0175

B62
ECO/UNDEV
R+D
SOCIETY
PROB/SOLV

CALDER R.,LIVING WITH THE ATOM. FUT USA+45 WOR+45
R+D INT/ORG VOL/ASSN DELIB/GP ARMS/CONT...STYLE 20.
PAGE 10 G0200

B62
TEC/DEV
HEALTH
NUC/PWR

DUPRE J.S.,SCIENCE AND THE NATION: POLICY AND
POLITICS. USA+45 LAW ACADEM FORCES ADMIN CIVMIL/REL
GOV/REL EFFICIENCY PEACE...TREND 20 SCI/ADVSRY.
PAGE 16 G0322

B62
R+D
INDUS
TEC/DEV
NUC/PWR

MACHLUP F.,THE PRODUCTION AND DISTRIBUTION OF
KNOWLEDGE IN THE UNITED STATES. USA+45 COM/IND
INDUS SCHOOL SECT WORKER COMPUTER CREATE CIVMIL/REL
COST EFFICIENCY WEALTH 20. PAGE 35 G0688

B62
ACADEM
TEC/DEV
EDU/PROP
R+D

OSGOOD C.E.,AN ALTERNATIVE TO WAR OR SURRENDER. FUT
UNIV CULTURE INTELL SOCIETY R+D INT/ORG CONSULT
DELIB/GP ACT/RES PLAN CHOOSE ATTIT PERCEPT KNOWL
...PHIL/SCI PSY SOC TREND GEN/LAWS 20. PAGE 43
G0849

B62
ORD/FREE
EDU/PROP
PEACE
WAR

SCHILLING W.R.,STRATEGY, POLITICS, AND DEFENSE
BUDGETS. USA+45 R+D NAT/G CONSULT DELIB/GP FORCES
LEGIS ACT/RES PLAN BAL/PWR LEGIT EXEC NUC/PWR
RIGID/FLEX PWR...TREND COLD/WAR CONGRESS 20
EISNHWR/DD. PAGE 49 G0968

B62
ROUTINE
POLICY

SCHWARTZ L.E.,INTERNATIONAL ORGANIZATIONS AND SPACE
COOPERATION. VOL/ASSN CONSULT CREATE TEC/DEV
SANCTION...POLICY INT/LAW PHIL/SCI 20 UN. PAGE 50
G0982

B62
INT/ORG
DIPLOM
R+D
SPACE

SNYDER R.C.,FOREIGN POLICY DECISION-MAKING. FUT
KOREA WOR+45 R+D CREATE ADMIN ROUTINE PWR
...DECISION PSY SOC CONCPT METH/CNCPT CON/ANAL
CHARTS GEN/METH METH 20. PAGE 52 G1018

B62
TEC/DEV
HYPO/EXP
DIPLOM

THANT U.,THE UNITED NATIONS' DEVELOPMENT DECADE:
PROPOSALS FOR ACTION. WOR+45 SOCIETY ECO/UNDEV AGRI
COM/IND FINAN R+D MUNIC SCHOOL VOL/ASSN CONSULT
PLAN TEC/DEV ECO/TAC EDU/PROP ADMIN ROUTINE
RIGID/FLEX...MGT SOC CONCPT UNESCO UN TOT/POP
VAL/FREE. PAGE 54 G1064

B62
INT/ORG
ALL/VALS

THOMSON G.P.,NUCLEAR ENERGY IN BRITAIN DURING THE
LAST WAR: THE CHERWELL SIMON LECTURE (MONOGRAPH).
UK R+D CONSULT FORCES PLAN DIPLOM TASK CIVMIL/REL
ROLE...PHIL/SCI NEW/IDEA LAB/EXP 20 MAUD. PAGE 54
G1071

B62
CREATE
TEC/DEV
WAR
NUC/PWR

LINS L.J.,"BASIS FOR DECISION: A COMPOSITE OF
CURRENT INSTITUTIONAL RESEARCH METHODS OF COLLEGES
AND UNIVERSITIES" ADMIN MGT. PAGE 34 G0671

L62
DECISION
ACADEM
R+D
ACT/RES

NIEBURG H.L.,"THE EISENHOWER ATOMIC ENERGY
COMMISSION AND CONGRESS" R+D INT/ORG OP/RES DIPLOM
ADMIN CONTROL 20 PRESIDENT CONGRESS AEC. PAGE 42
G0821

L62
NUC/PWR
TOP/EX
LOBBY
DELIB/GP

ALBONETTI A.,"IL SECONDO PROGRAMMA QUINQUENNALE
1963-67 ED IL BILANCIO RICERCHE ED INVESTIMENTI PER
IL 1963 DELL'ERATOM." EUR+WWI FUT ITALY WOR+45
ECO/DEV SERV/IND INT/ORG TEC/DEV ECO/TAC ATTIT
SKILL WEALTH...MGT TIME/SEQ OEEC 20. PAGE 2 G0035

S62
R+D
PLAN
NUC/PWR

SINGER J.D.,"STABLE DETERRENCE AND ITS LIMITS." FUT
WOR+45 R+D INT/ORG CONSULT ACT/RES TEC/DEV
ARMS/CONT COERCE DRIVE PERCEPT RIGID/FLEX ORD/FREE
PWR...MYTH SIMUL TOT/POP 20. PAGE 51 G1004

S62
NAT/G
FORCES
DETER
NUC/PWR

VIETORISZ T.,"PRELIMINARY BIBLIOGRAPHY FOR
INDUSTRIAL DEVELOPMENT PROGRAMMING." ECO/DEV
ECO/UNDEV R+D LABOR PROB/SOLV AUTOMAT PRODUC.
PAGE 61 G1198

S62
BIBLIOG/A
TEC/DEV
ACT/RES
PLAN

WALTER E.,"VERS UNE CLASSIFICATION SCIENTIFIQUE DE
LA SOCIOLOGIA." UNIV CULTURE INTELL SOCIETY R+D
ACT/RES LEGIT ROUTINE ATTIT KNOWL...JURID MGT TREND
GEN/LAWS 20. PAGE 62 G1208

S62
PLAN
CONCPT

JOINT ECONOMIC COMMITTEE,"DIMENSIONS OF SOVIET
ECONOMIC POWER." USSR R+D FORCES ACT/RES OP/RES
TEC/DEV...GEOG STAT BIBLIOG 20. PAGE 29 G0565

C62
ECO/DEV
PLAN
PRODUC
LABOR

DEAN A.L.,FEDERAL AGENCY APPROACHES TO FIELD
MANAGEMENT (PAMPHLET). R+D DELIB/GP EX/STRUC
PROB/SOLV GOV/REL...CLASSIF BIBLIOG 20 FAA NASA
DEPT/HEW POSTAL/SYS IRS. PAGE 15 G0287

B63
ADMIN
MGT
NAT/G
OP/RES

FOSKETT D.J.,CLASSIFICATION AND INDEXING IN THE
SOCIAL SCIENCES. WOR+45 R+D ACT/RES CREATE OP/RES
TEC/DEV AUTOMAT ROLE...SOC COMPUT/IR BIBLIOG.
PAGE 20 G0384

B63
PROB/SOLV
CON/ANAL
CLASSIF

HOWER R.M.,MANAGERS AND SCIENTISTS. EX/STRUC CREATE
ADMIN REPRESENT ATTIT DRIVE ROLE PWR SKILL...SOC
INT. PAGE 27 G0532

B63
R+D
MGT
PERS/REL
INGP/REL

KORNHAUSER W.,SCIENTISTS IN INDUSTRY: CONFLICT AND
ACCOMMODATION. USA+45 R+D LG/CO NAT/G TEC/DEV
CONTROL ADJUST ATTIT...MGT STAT INT BIBLIOG 20.
PAGE 31 G0614

B63
CREATE
INDUS
PROF/ORG
GP/REL

LILIENTHAL D.E.,CHANGE, HOPE, AND THE BOMB. USA+45
WOR+45 R+D INT/ORG NAT/G DELIB/GP FORCES ACT/RES
DETER RIGID/FLEX ORD/FREE...POLICY CONCPT OBS AEC
20. PAGE 34 G0666

B63
ATTIT
MYTH
ARMS/CONT
NUC/PWR

PEARSELL M.,MEDICAL BEHAVIORAL SCIENCE: A SELECTED

B63
BIBLIOG

BIBLIOGRAPHY OF CULTURAL ANTHROPOLOGY, SOCIAL
PSYCHOLOGY, AND SOCIOLOGY... USA+45 USA-45 R+D
ATTIT ROLE 20. PAGE 44 G0863
SOC
PSY
HEALTH

B63
RAUDSEPP E.,MANAGING CREATIVE SCIENTISTS AND
ENGINEERS. USA+45 ECO/DEV LG/CO GP/REL PERS/REL
PRODUC. PAGE 46 G0906
MGT
CREATE
R+D
ECO/TAC

B63
SCHRADER R.,SCIENCE AND POLICY. WOR+45 ECO/DEV
ECO/UNDEV R+D FORCES PLAN DIPLOM GOV/REL TECHRACY
BIBLIOG. PAGE 50 G0976
TEC/DEV
NAT/G
POLICY
ADMIN

B63
TOMKINS S.S.,COMPUTER SIMULATION OF PERSONALITY.
R+D TEC/DEV AUTOMAT FEEDBACK ANOMIE PERCEPT...STYLE
PERS/TEST PREDICT COMPUT/IR GP/COMP. PAGE 55 G1075
COMPUTER
PERSON
SIMUL
PROG/TEAC

B63
US ATOMIC ENERGY COMMISSION,ATOMIC ENERGY IN THE
SOVIET UNION: TRIP REPORT OF THE US ATOMIC ENERGY
DELEGATION, MAY 1933. USSR R+D NAT/G CONSULT CREATE
DIPLOM ADMIN ROUTINE EFFICIENCY PRODUC KNOWL SKILL
...NAT/COMP 20 AEC TRAVEL TREATY. PAGE 56 G1107
METH/COMP
OP/RES
TEC/DEV
NUC/PWR

L63
BEGUIN H.,"ASPECTS GEOGRAPHIQUE DE LA
POLARISATION." FUT WOR+45 SOCIETY STRUCT ECO/DEV
R+D BAL/PWR ADMIN ATTIT RIGID/FLEX HEALTH WEALTH
...CHARTS 20. PAGE 6 G0114
ECO/UNDEV
GEOG
DIPLOM

S63
BOHN L.,"WHOSE NUCLEAR TEST: NON-PHYSICAL
INSPECTION AND TEST BAN." WOR+45 R+D INT/ORG
VOL/ASSN ORD/FREE...GEN/LAWS GEN/METH COLD/WAR 20.
PAGE 8 G0148
ADJUD
ARMS/CONT
TEC/DEV
NUC/PWR

S63
FERRETTI B.,"IMPORTANZA E PROSPETTIVE DELL ENERGIA
DI ORIGINE NUCLEARE." FUT ITALY WOR+45 INTELL R+D
ACT/RES CREATE HEALTH WEALTH...METH/CNCPT TIME/SEQ
20. PAGE 19 G0365
TEC/DEV
EXEC
NUC/PWR

S63
GANDILHON J.,"LA SCIENCE ET LA TECHNIQUE A L'AIDE
DES REGIONS PEU DEVELOPPEES." FRANCE FUT WOR+45
ECO/DEV R+D PROF/ORG ACT/RES PLAN...MGT TOT/POP
VAL/FREE 20 UN. PAGE 21 G0406
ECO/UNDEV
TEC/DEV
FOR/AID

S63
KAWALKOWSKI A.,"POUR UNE EUROPE INDEPENDENTE ET
REUNIFIEE." EUR+WWI FUT USA+45 USSR WOR+45 ECO/DEV
PROC/MFG INT/ORG NAT/G ACT/RES TEC/DEV FEDERAL
RIGID/FLEX...CONCPT METH/CNCPT OEEC TOT/POP 20
DEGAULLE/C. PAGE 30 G0587
R+D
PLAN
NUC/PWR

S63
MASSART L.,"L'ORGANISATION DE LA RECHERCHE
SCIENTIFIQUE EN EUROPE." EUR+WWI WOR+45 ACT/RES
PLAN TEC/DEV EDU/PROP EXEC KNOWL...METH/CNCPT EEC
20. PAGE 36 G0718
R+D
CREATE

S63
NADLER E.B.,"SOME ECONOMIC DISADVANTAGES OF THE
ARMS RACE." USA+45 INDUS R+D FORCES PLAN TEC/DEV
ECO/TAC FOR/AID EDU/PROP PWR WEALTH...TREND
COLD/WAR 20. PAGE 41 G0800
ECO/DEV
MGT
BAL/PAY

S63
PHELPS J.,"INFORMATION AND ARMS CONTROL." COM SPACE
USA+45 USSR WOR+45 R+D INT/ORG NAT/G DELIB/GP
DIPLOM ORD/FREE...CONCPT 20. PAGE 45 G0875
KNOWL
ARMS/CONT
NUC/PWR

S63
VIETORISZ T.,"PRELIMINARY BIBLIOGRAPHY FOR
INDUSTRIAL DEVELOPMENT PROGRAMMING." ECO/DEV
ECO/UNDEV R+D LABOR PROB/SOLV AUTOMAT PRODUC.
PAGE 61 G1199
BIBLIOG/A
TEC/DEV
ACT/RES
PLAN

S63
WOHLSTETTER A.,"SCIENTISTS, SEERS AND STRATEGY."
USA+45 ELITES R+D NAT/G CONSULT FORCES TOP/EX
EDU/PROP ARMS/CONT KNOWL ORD/FREE...DECISION MYTH
20. PAGE 64 G1253
INTELL
ACT/RES

B64
BRIGHT J.R.,RESEARCH, DEVELOPMENT AND TECHNOLOGICAL
INNOVATION. CULTURE R+D CREATE PLAN PROB/SOLV
AUTOMAT RISK PERSON...DECISION CONCPT PREDICT
BIBLIOG. PAGE 9 G0168
TEC/DEV
NEW/IDEA
INDUS
MGT

B64
COENEN E.,LA "KONJUNKTURFORSCHUNG" EN ALLEMAGNE ET
EN AUTRICHE, 1925-1935. AUSTRIA GERMANY OP/RES PLAN
COST PERCEPT...METH/CNCPT BIBLIOG 20. PAGE 12 G0237
METH/COMP
R+D
ECO/TAC

B64
ETZIONI A.,THE MOON-DOGGLE: DOMESTIC AND
INTERNATIONAL IMPLICATIONS OF THE SPACE RACE. FUT
USA+45 WOR+45 INTELL ECO/DEV INDUS VOL/ASSN
EX/STRUC FORCES LEGIS TOP/EX PLAN TEC/DEV ECO/TAC
EDU/PROP KNOWL ORD/FREE PWR RESPECT WEALTH
TIME/SEQ. PAGE 18 G0352
R+D
NAT/G
DIPLOM
SPACE

B64
GRODZINS M.,THE ATOMIC AGE: FORTY-FIVE SCIENTISTS
AND SCHOLARS SPEAK ON NATIONAL AND WORLD AFFAIRS.
FUT USA+45 WOR+45 R+D INT/ORG NAT/G CONSULT TEC/DEV
EDU/PROP ATTIT PERSON ORD/FREE...HUM CONCPT
TIME/SEQ CON/ANAL. PAGE 23 G0454
INTELL
ARMS/CONT
NUC/PWR

B64
GROSSER G.H.,THE THREAT OF IMPENDING DISASTER:
CONTRIBUTIONS TO THE PSYCHOLOGY OF STRESS. SPACE
UNIV SOCIETY R+D TEC/DEV EDU/PROP COERCE WAR ATTIT
BIO/SOC DISPL PERCEPT PERSON...SOC MYTH SELF/OBS
CONT/OBS BIOG CON/ANAL TOT/POP 20. PAGE 23 G0455
HEALTH
PSY
NUC/PWR

B64
GUTMANN P.M.,ECONOMIC GROWTH: AN AMERICAN PROBLEM.
USA+45 FINAN R+D...POLICY NAT/COMP ANTHOL BIBLIOG
20. PAGE 24 G0463
WEALTH
ECO/DEV
CAP/ISM
ORD/FREE

B64
HAMMOND P.E.,SOCIOLOGISTS AT WORK. VOL/ASSN OP/RES
TEC/DEV CONFER ROUTINE TASK EFFICIENCY...MGT
NEW/IDEA STYLE SAMP. PAGE 24 G0478
R+D
BIOG
SOC

B64
ORGANIZATION AMERICAN STATES,ECONOMIC SURVEY OF
LATIN AMERICA, 1962. L/A+17C AGRI DIST/IND INDUS
MARKET PROC/MFG R+D PLAN TEC/DEV ECO/TAC REGION
BAL/PAY ALL/VALS...CON/ANAL ORG/CHARTS GEN/METH OAS
20. PAGE 43 G0844
ECO/UNDEV
CHARTS

B64
ORTH C.D.,ADMINISTERING RESEARCH AND DEVELOPMENT.
FINAN PLAN PROB/SOLV ADMIN ROUTINE...METH/CNCPT
STAT CHARTS METH 20. PAGE 43 G0847
MGT
R+D
LG/CO
INDUS

B64
PEDERSEN E.S.,NUCLEAR ENERGY IN SPACE. FUT INTELL
R+D CONSULT...NEW/IDEA CHARTS METH T 20. PAGE 44
G0864
SPACE
TEC/DEV
NUC/PWR
LAB/EXP

B64
VAN DYKE V.,PRIDE AND POWER: THE RATIONALE OF THE
SPACE PROGRAM. FUT USA+45 INTELL R+D NAT/G POL/PAR
DELIB/GP EX/STRUC LEGIS TOP/EX ACT/RES PLAN ECO/TAC
EDU/PROP ORD/FREE PWR RESPECT SKILL...TIME/SEQ
VAL/FREE. PAGE 61 G1191
TEC/DEV
ATTIT
POLICY

L64
CARNEGIE ENDOWMENT INT. PEACE,"ECONOMIC AND SOCIAL
QUESTION (ISSUES BEFORE THE NINETEENTH GENERAL
ASSEMBLY)." WOR+45 ECO/DEV ECO/UNDEV INDUS R+D
DELIB/GP CREATE PLAN TEC/DEV ECO/TAC FOR/AID
BAL/PAY...RECORD UN 20. PAGE 11 G0209
INT/ORG
INT/TRADE

S64
CALDWELL L.K.,"BIOPOLITICS: SCIENCE, ETHICS, AND
PUBLIC POLICY." FUT USA+45 WOR+45 INTELL STRATA R+D
NAT/G CONSULT PLAN EDU/PROP ALL/VALS...RELATIV
PHIL/SCI 20. PAGE 10 G0203
TEC/DEV
POLICY

S64
COOPER A.C.,"R&D IS MORE EFFICIENT IN SMALL
COMPANIES." USA+45 LG/CO SML/CO WEALTH...RECORD INT
LAB/EXP 20. PAGE 13 G0255
R+D
INDUS
CREATE
GP/COMP

S64
NEEDHAM T.,"SCIENCE AND SOCIETY IN EAST AND WEST."
INTELL STRATA R+D LOC/G NAT/G PROVS CONSULT ACT/RES
CREATE PLAN TEC/DEV EDU/PROP ADMIN ATTIT ALL/VALS
...POLICY RELATIV MGT CONCPT NEW/IDEA TIME/SEQ WORK
WORK. PAGE 41 G0815
ASIA
STRUCT

S64
PLATT J.R.,"RESEARCH AND DEVELOPMENT FOR SOCIAL
PROBLEMS." INTELL SOCIETY PROB/SOLV GP/REL ATTIT
ALL/VALS CONT/OBS. PAGE 45 G0880
R+D
ACT/RES
PLAN
SOC

SCHRAMM W.,"MASS MEDIA AND NATIONAL DEVELOPMENT:
THE ROLE OF INFORMATION IN DEVELOPING COUNTRIES."
FINAN R+D ACT/RES PLAN TEC/DEV DIPLOM CHOOSE SUPEGO
ORD/FREE...BIBLIOG 20. PAGE 50 G0978
C64
ECO/UNDEV
COM/IND
EDU/PROP
MAJORIT

WHITE HOUSE CONFERENCE ON INTERNATIONAL
COOPERATION(VOL.II). SPACE WOR+45 EXTR/IND INT/ORG
LABOR WORKER NUC/PWR PEACE AGE/Y...CENSUS ANTHOL 20
RESOURCE/N URBAN/RNWL PUB/TRANS. PAGE 1 G0019
B65
R+D
CONFER
TEC/DEV
DIPLOM

PEACE RESEARCH ABSTRACTS. FUT WOR+45 R+D INT/ORG
NAT/G PLAN TEC/DEV BAL/PWR DIPLOM FOR/AID NUC/PWR
HEALTH. PAGE 1 G0020
B65
BIBLIOG/A
PEACE
ARMS/CONT
WAR

ANDERSON C.A.,EDUCATION AND ECONOMIC DEVELOPMENT.
INDUS R+D SCHOOL TEC/DEV ECO/TAC EDU/PROP AGE
HEREDITY PERCEPT SKILL 20. PAGE 3 G0056
B65
ANTHOL
ECO/DEV
ECO/UNDEV
WORKER

CARPER E.T.,REORGANIZATION OF THE U.S. PUBLIC
HEALTH SERVICE. FUT USA+45 INTELL R+D LOBBY GP/REL
INGP/REL PERS/REL RIGID/FLEX ROLE HEALTH...PHIL/SCI
20 CONGRESS PHS. PAGE 11 G0213
B65
HEAL
PLAN
NAT/G
OP/RES

CHENG C.-.Y.,SCIENTIFIC AND ENGINEERING MANPOWER IN
COMMUNIST CHINA: 1949-1963. CHINA/COM USSR ELITES
ECO/DEV R+D ACADEM LABOR NAT/G EDU/PROP CONTROL
UTIL...POLICY BIBLIOG 20. PAGE 12 G0226
B65
WORKER
CONSULT
MARXISM
BIOG

DORFMAN R.,MEASURING BENEFITS OF GOVERNMENT
INVESTMENTS. ECO/DEV R+D ECO/TAC PROFIT UTIL...MGT
GEN/METH. PAGE 16 G0308
B65
PLAN
RATION
EFFICIENCY
OPTIMAL

KENT A.,SPECIALIZED INFORMATION CENTERS. INTELL R+D
VOL/ASSN CONSULT COMPUTER KNOWL...DECISION HUM
PHIL/SCI METH/CNCPT TREND CHARTS 20. PAGE 30 G0593
B65
COMPUT/IR
CREATE
TEC/DEV
METH/COMP

KNORR K.,SCIENCE AND DEFENSE: SOME CRITICAL
THOUGHTS ON MILITARY RESEARCH AND DEVELOPMENT.
USA+45 ACT/RES CREATE BUDGET ECO/TAC DEMAND
DECISION. PAGE 31 G0608
B65
CIVMIL/REL
R+D
FORCES
PLAN

KOROL A.G.,SOVIET RESEARCH AND DEVELOPMENT. USSR
ACADEM SCHOOL WORKER ROUTINE COST...STAT T 20.
PAGE 31 G0615
B65
COM
R+D
FINAN
DIST/IND

LAPP R.E.,THE NEW PRIESTHOOD; THE SCIENTIFIC ELITE
AND THE USES OF POWER. USA+45 ELITES INTELL SOCIETY
R+D NAT/G CHIEF LEGIS CIVMIL/REL GP/REL PWR 20
PRESIDENT CONGRESS. PAGE 32 G0635
B65
TEC/DEV
TECHRACY
CONTROL
POPULISM

LOWENSTEIN L.,GOVERNMENT RESOURCES AVAILABLE FOR
FOREIGN AFFAIRS RESEARCH. NAT/G DIPLOM GOV/REL.
PAGE 34 G0677
B65
R+D
ACADEM
ACT/RES
BIBLIOG/A

NATIONAL ACADEMY OF SCIENCES,BASIC RESEARCH AND
NATIONAL GOALS. R+D ACADEM DELIB/GP PLAN EDU/PROP
...POLICY HEAL PHIL/SCI PSY SOC ANTHOL 20 CONGRESS
HOUSE/REP HS/SCIASTR. PAGE 41 G0809
B65
LEGIS
BUDGET
NAT/G
CREATE

NATIONAL REFERRAL CENTER SCI,A DIRECTORY OF
INFORMATION RESOURCES IN THE UNITED STATES; SOCIAL
SCIENCES. USA+45 PROF/ORG...PSY SOC 20. PAGE 41
G0811
B65
INDEX
R+D
ACADEM
ACT/RES

NATIONAL SCIENCE FOUNDATION,CURRENT RESEARCH AND
DEVELOPMENT IN SCIENTIFIC DOCUMENTATION - NO. 12.
WOR+45 INTELL COM/IND NAT/G COMPUTER TEC/DEV
AUTOMAT KNOWL...PSY LING 20. PAGE 41 G0812
B65
BIBLIOG
COMPUT/IR
R+D
PHIL/SCI

TYBOUT R.A.,ECONOMICS OF RESEARCH AND DEVELOPMENT.
ECO/DEV ECO/UNDEV INDUS PROFIT DECISION. PAGE 55
G1084
B65
R+D
FORCES
ADMIN
DIPLOM

UNESCO,HANDBOOK OF INTERNATIONAL EXCHANGES. COM/IND
R+D ACADEM PROF/ORG VOL/ASSN CREATE TEC/DEV
EDU/PROP AGREE 20 TREATY. PAGE 55 G1090
B65
INDEX
INT/ORG
DIPLOM
PRESS

US LIBRARY OF CONGRESS,A DIRECTORY OF INFORMATION
RESOURCES IN THE UNITED STATES: SOCIAL SCIENCES.
USA+45 ACADEM INT/ORG LABOR PROF/ORG PUB/INST
SCHOOL SECT 20. PAGE 59 G1156
B65
BIBLIOG
R+D
COMPUT/IR

US SENATE COMM AERO SPACE SCI,NATIONAL SPACE GOALS
FOR THE POST-APOLLO PERIOD. USA+45 CONSULT DELIB/GP
TEC/DEV BUDGET GP/REL ATTIT...CHARTS IDEA/COMP TIME
20 DEPT/DEFEN NASA CONGRESS. PAGE 59 G1166
B65
SPACE
FUT
R+D
LEGIS

US SENATE COMM AERO SPACE SCI,INTERNATIONAL
COOPERATION AND ORGANIZATION FOR OUTER SPACE. FUT
USA+45 WOR+45 PROF/ORG VOL/ASSN CONSULT DELIB/GP
PLAN TEC/DEV ARMS/CONT GP/REL PEACE 20 UN NASA.
PAGE 59 G1167
B65
DIPLOM
SPACE
R+D
NAT/G

VERMOT-GAUCHY M.,L'EDUCATION NATIONALE DANS LA
FRANCE DE 1975. FRANCE FUT CULTURE ELITES R+D
SCHOOL PLAN EDU/PROP EFFICIENCY...POLICY PREDICT
CHARTS INDEX 20. PAGE 61 G1195
B65
ACADEM
CREATE
TREND
INTELL

WEISNER J.B.,WHERE SCIENCE AND POLITICS MEET.
USA+45 ECO/DEV R+D FORCES PROB/SOLV DIPLOM FOR/AID
CONTROL...PHIL/SCI PRESIDENT KENNEDY/JF JOHNSON/LB.
PAGE 63 G1228
B65
CHIEF
NAT/G
POLICY
TEC/DEV

WISH J.R.,ECONOMIC DEVELOPMENT IN LATIN AMERICA: AN
ANNOTATED BIBLIOGRAPHY. L/A+17C COM/IND MARKET R+D
CREATE CAP/ISM ATTIT...STAT METH 20. PAGE 64 G1250
B65
BIBLIOG/A
ECO/UNDEV
TEC/DEV
AGRI

PILISUK M.,"IS THERE A MILITARY INDUSTRIAL COMPLEX
WHICH PREVENTS PEACE CONSENSUS; COUNTERVAILING
POWER IN PLURALIST SYSTEMS." INDUS R+D ACADEM
FEEDBACK CIVMIL/REL ADJUST CONSEN ATTIT RIGID/FLEX
...CENSUS IDEA/COMP BIBLIOG. PAGE 45 G0878
L65
ELITES
WEAPON
PEACE
ARMS/CONT

BALDWIN H.,"SLOW-DOWN IN THE PENTAGON." USA+45
CREATE PLAN GOV/REL CENTRAL COST EFFICIENCY PWR
...MGT MCNAMARA/R. PAGE 5 G0088
S65
RECORD
R+D
WEAPON
ADMIN

DEAN B.V.,"CONTRACT RESEARCH PROPOSAL PREPARATION
STRATEGIES." ECO/TAC WEALTH...MGT SIMUL. PAGE 15
G0289
S65
USA+45
PROC/MFG
R+D
PLAN

KINTNER W.P.,"THE PROSPECTS FOR WESTERN SCIENCE AND
TECHNOLOGY." EUR+WWI FRANCE USA+45 USSR R+D NUC/PWR
NATO. PAGE 30 G0598
S65
TEC/DEV
VOL/ASSN
STAT
RECORD

KUZMACK A.M.,"TECHNOLOGICAL CHANGE AND STABLE
DETERRENCE." CREATE EDU/PROP ARMS/CONT WEAPON
CHOOSE COST DRIVE PERCEPT...RECORD STERTYP TIME.
PAGE 32 G0627
S65
R+D
DETER
EQUILIB

LECLERCQ H.,"ECONOMIC RESEARCH AND DEVELOPMENT IN
TROPICAL AFRICA." ECO/UNDEV INT/ORG CREATE PLAN UN.
PAGE 33 G0650
S65
AFR
R+D
ACADEM
ECO/TAC

RASER J.R.,"WEAPONS DESIGN AND ARMS CONTROL* THE
POLARIS EXAMPLE." DETER NUC/PWR WEAPON CHOOSE
PERCEPT...STERTYP TIME. PAGE 46 G0904
S65
ARMS/CONT
R+D
GEOG
ACT/RES

SCHELLING T.C.,"SIGNALS AND FEEDBACK IN THE ARMS
DIALOGUE." USA+45 USSR R+D ACADEM FORCES ACT/RES
ADJUST COST GEN/LAWS. PAGE 49 G0964
S65
FEEDBACK
DETER
EDU/PROP
ARMS/CONT

BOLTON R.E.,DEFENSE AND DISARMAMENT: THE ECONOMICS
OF TRANSITION. USA+45 R+D FORCES PLAN LOBBY DETER
WAR COST PEACE...ANTHOL BIBLIOG 20. PAGE 8 G0150
B66
ARMS/CONT
POLICY
INDUS

B66
MURDOCK J.C.,RESEARCH AND REGIONS. AGRI FINAN INDUS BIBLIOG
LOC/G MUNIC NAT/G PROB/SOLV TEC/DEV ADMIN REGION ECO/DEV
20. PAGE 40 G0796 COMPUT/IR
R+D

B66
OECD DEVELOPMENT CENTRE,CATALOGUE OF SOCIAL AND ECO/UNDEV
ECONOMIC DEVELOPMENT INSTITUTES AND PROGRAMMES* ECO/DEV
RESEARCH. ACT/RES PLAN TEC/DEV EDU/PROP...SOC R+D
GP/COMP NAT/COMP. PAGE 43 G0836 ACADEM

B66
UNITED NATIONS,INTERNATIONAL SPACE BIBLIOGRAPHY. BIBLIOG
FUT INT/ORG TEC/DEV DIPLOM ARMS/CONT NUC/PWR SPACE
...JURID SOC UN. PAGE 56 G1093 PEACE
R+D

B66
US DEPARTMENT OF LABOR,TECHNOLOGICAL TRENDS IN TEC/DEV
MAJOR AMERICAN INDUSTRIES. USA+45 R+D LABOR GP/REL INDUS
PRODUC...MGT BIBLIOG 20. PAGE 57 G1120 TREND
AUTOMAT

B66
US SENATE,POLICY PLANNING FOR AERONAUTICAL RESEARCH SPACE
AND DEVELOPMENT: STAFF REPORT FOR COMM ON CIVMIL/REL
AERONAUTICAL AND SPACE SCIENCES. USA+45 AIR GOV/REL
DIST/IND PLAN...POLICY CHARTS 20 CONGRESS NASA. R+D
PAGE 59 G1164

B66
US SENATE COMM AERO SPACE SCI,SOVIET SPACE CONSULT
PROGRAMS, 1962-65; GOALS AND PURPOSES, SPACE
ACHIEVEMENTS, PLANS, AND INTERNATIONAL FUT
IMPLICATIONS. USA+45 USSR R+D FORCES PLAN EDU/PROP DIPLOM
PRESS ADJUD ARMS/CONT ATTIT MARXISM. PAGE 60 G1168

L66
PACKENHAM R.A.,"POLITICAL-DEVELOPMENT DOCTRINES IN FOR/AID
THE AMERICAN FOREIGN AID PROGRAM." STRUCT R+D ECO/UNDEV
CREATE DIPLOM AID. PAGE 43 G0855 GEN/LAWS

S66
GREENBERG D.S.,"THE SCIENTIFIC PORK BARREL." USA+45 R+D
ECO/DEV PUB/INST CHIEF LEGIS BUDGET GIVE GP/REL PWR NAT/G
WEALTH 20. PAGE 23 G0445 ACADEM
ATTIT

S66
TURKEVICH J.,"SOVIET SCIENCE APPRAISED." USA+45 R+D USSR
ACADEM FORCES DIPLOM EDU/PROP WAR EFFICIENCY PEACE TEC/DEV
SKILL OBS. PAGE 55 G1081 NAT/COMP
ATTIT

N66
US HOUSE COMM SCI ASTRONAUT,GOVERNMENT, SCIENCE, NAT/G
AND PUBLIC POLICY (PAMPHLET). R+D ACADEM DELIB/GP POLICY
COMPUTER BUDGET CONFER ADMIN...PHIL/SCI PREDICT TEC/DEV
TREND 20 CONGRESS HS/SCIASTR. PAGE 58 G1143 CREATE

N66
US HOUSE COMM SCI ASTRONAUT,INQUIRIES, LEGISLATION, TEC/DEV
POLICY STUDIES RE: SCIENCE AND TECHNOLOGY: REVIEW R+D
AND FORECAST (PAMPHLET). FUT WOR+45 DELIB/GP PLAN
PROB/SOLV...POLICY JURID TREND 20 CONGRESS. PAGE 58 LEGIS
G1144

B67
BARANSON J.,TECHNOLOGY FOR UNDERDEVELOPED AREAS: AN BIBLIOG/A
ANNOTATED BIBLIOGRAPHY. FUT WOR+45 CULTURE INDUS ECO/UNDEV
INT/ORG CREATE PROB/SOLV INT/TRADE EDU/PROP AUTOMAT TEC/DEV
...CONCPT METH. PAGE 5 G0092 R+D

B67
BERNAL J.D.,THE SOCIAL FUNCTION OF SCIENCE. WOR+45 ROLE
WOR-45 R+D NAT/G PROB/SOLV DOMIN WAR...PHIL/SCI 20. TEC/DEV
PAGE 7 G0130 SOCIETY
ADJUST

B67
CHARLESWORTH J.C.,CONTEMPORARY POLITICAL ANALYSIS. R+D
INTELL...DECISION METH/CNCPT MATH STYLE CON/ANAL IDEA/COMP
GAME ANTHOL 20. PAGE 11 G0222 CONCPT
METH/COMP

B67
ENKE S.,DEFENSE MANAGEMENT. USA+45 R+D FORCES DECISION
WORKER PLAN ECO/TAC ADMIN NUC/PWR BAL/PAY UTIL DELIB/GP
WEALTH...MGT DEPT/DEFEN. PAGE 18 G0348 EFFICIENCY
BUDGET

B67
FIELD M.G.,SOVIET SOCIALIZED MEDICINE. USSR FINAN PUB/INST
R+D PROB/SOLV ADMIN SOCISM...MGT SOC CONCPT 20. HEALTH

PAGE 19 G0366 NAT/G
MARXISM

B67
GULICK M.C.,NONCONVENTIONAL INFORMATION SYSTEMS BIBLIOG/A
SERVING THE SOCIAL SCIENCES AND THE HUMANITIES; A R+D
BIBLIOGRAPHIC ESSAY (PAPER). USA+45 COMPUTER CREATE COMPUT/IR
EDU/PROP KNOWL...SOC METH 20. PAGE 23 G0462 HUM

B67
HIRSCHMAN A.O.,DEVELOPMENT PROJECTS OBSERVED. INDUS ECO/UNDEV
INT/ORG CONSULT EX/STRUC CREATE OP/RES ECO/TAC R+D
DEMAND...POLICY MGT METH/COMP 20 WORLD/BANK. FINAN
PAGE 26 G0513 PLAN

B67
NATIONAL SCIENCE FOUNDATION,DIRECTORY OF SELECTED INDEX
RESEARCH INSTITUTES IN EASTERN EUROPE. BULGARIA R+D
CZECHOSLVK HUNGARY POLAND ROMANIA INTELL ACADEM COM
NAT/G ACT/RES 20. PAGE 41 G0814 PHIL/SCI

B67
NELSON R.R.,TECHNOLOGY, ECONOMIC GROWTH, AND PUBLIC R+D
POLICY. USA+45 PLAN GP/REL UTIL KNOWL...POLICY CONSULT
PHIL/SCI CHARTS BIBLIOG 20. PAGE 41 G0817 CREATE
ACT/RES

B67
ORLANS H.,CONTRACTING FOR ATOMS. USA+45 LAW INTELL NUC/PWR
ACADEM LG/CO NAT/G PLAN TEC/DEV CONTROL DETER R+D
...TREND 20 AEC. PAGE 43 G0845 PRODUC
PEACE

B67
RIDKER R.G.,ECONOMIC COSTS OF AIR POLLUTION* OP/RES
STUDIES IN MEASUREMENT. R+D MUNIC GP/REL KNOWL HABITAT
...OBS 20. PAGE 47 G0919 PHIL/SCI

B67
RUTGERS U GRADUATE SCH LIB SCI,BIBLIOGRAPHY OF BIBLIOG/A
RESEARCH RELATING TO THE COMMUNICATION OF COM/IND
SCIENTIFIC AND TECHNICAL INFORMATION. FUT CREATE R+D
FEEDBACK...PHIL/SCI NEW/IDEA COMPUT/IR HYPO/EXP. TEC/DEV
PAGE 48 G0951

B67
SCHON D.A.,TECHNOLOGY AND CHANGE* THE NEW INDUS
HERACLITUS. TEC/DEV CONTROL COST DEMAND EFFICIENCY PROB/SOLV
RIGID/FLEX...MYTH 20. PAGE 49 G0975 R+D
CREATE

B67
UNESCO,PRINCIPLES AND PROBLEMS OF NATIONAL SCIENCE NAT/COMP
POLICIES. WOR+45 ECO/DEV ECO/UNDEV R+D INT/ORG POLICY
PROB/SOLV CONFER...PHIL/SCI CHARTS 20 UNESCO UN. TEC/DEV
PAGE 55 G1091 CREATE

B67
US DEPARTMENT OF STATE,FOREIGN AFFAIRS RESEARCH BIBLIOG
(PAMPHLET). USA+45 WOR+45 ACADEM NAT/G...PSY SOC INDEX
CHARTS 20. PAGE 57 G1124 R+D
DIPLOM

B67
US HOUSE COMM SCI ASTRONAUT,GOVERNMENT, SCIENCE, ADMIN
AND INTERNATIONAL POLICY. R+D OP/RES PLAN 20. PHIL/SCI
PAGE 58 G1146 ACT/RES
DIPLOM

B67
US HOUSE COMM SCI ASTRONAUT,THE JUNIOR COLLEGE AND ACADEM
EDUCATION IN THE SCIENCES (PAMPHLET). USA+45 AGE/Y EDU/PROP
...CHARTS SIMUL HOUSE/REP. PAGE 58 G1148 PHIL/SCI
R+D

B67
US HOUSE COMM SCI ASTRONAUT,AUTHORIZING SECY OF PHIL/SCI
COMMERCE TO PROVIDE FOR COLLECTION, COMPILATION, CON/ANAL
CRIT EVALUATION, PUBLICATION, SALE OF STD REF DATA. STAT
USA+45 TEC/DEV...COMPUT/IR HOUSE/REP. PAGE 59 G1150 R+D

B67
WEINBERG A.M.,REFLECTIONS ON BIG SCIENCE. FUT ACADEM
USA+45 NAT/G EDU/PROP CHOOSE PERS/REL COST OPTIMAL KNOWL
...PHIL/SCI TREND. PAGE 62 G1225 R+D
PLAN

B67
ZUCKERMAN S.,SCIENTISTS AND WAR. ELITES INDUS R+D
DIPLOM CENTRAL EFFICIENCY KNOWL 20. PAGE 65 G1271 CONSULT
ACT/RES
GP/REL

L67
PASLEY R.S.,"ORGANIZATIONAL CONFLICTS OF INTEREST NAT/G
IN GOVERNMENT CONTRACTS." ELITES R+D ROUTINE ECO/TAC

NUC/PWR DEMAND EFFICIENCY 20. PAGE 44 G0860   RATION
CONTROL

S67
ALLISON D.,"THE GROWTH OF IDEAS." USA+45 LG/CO   R+D
ADMIN. PAGE 3 G0045   OP/RES
INDUS
TEC/DEV

S67
BARRO S.,"ECONOMIC IMPACT OF SPACE EXPENDITURES: SPACE
SOME BROAD ISSUES DEALING WITH COSTS AND BENEFITS."   FINAN
USA+45 PROC/MFG R+D LG/CO CONSULT COST PRODUC 20.   ECO/TAC
PAGE 5 G0098   NAT/G

S67
BENN W.,"TECHNOLOGY HAS AN INEXORABLE EFFECT." FUT   R+D
UK ECO/DEV INT/ORG CONSULT PLAN EDU/PROP ADMIN LEAD   LG/CO
GP/REL PRODUC...INT 20 EEC. PAGE 6 G0119   TEC/DEV
INDUS

S67
CETRON M.J.,"FORECASTING TECHNOLOGY." INDUS FORCES   TEC/DEV
TASK UTIL...PHIL/SCI CONCPT CHARTS METH/COMP TIME.   FUT
PAGE 11 G0219   R+D
PLAN

S67
CONWAY J.E.,"MAKING RESEARCH EFFECTIVE IN   ACT/RES
LEGISLATION." LAW R+D CONSULT EX/STRUC PLAN CONFER   POLICY
ADMIN LEAD ROUTINE TASK INGP/REL DECISION. PAGE 13   LEGIS
G0252   PROB/SOLV

S67
DADDARIO E.Q.,"CONGRESS FACES SPACE POLICIES." R+D   SPACE
NAT/G FORCES CREATE LEAD...DECISION CONGRESS NASA.   PLAN
PAGE 14 G0269   BUDGET
POLICY

S67
DOYLE S.E.,"COMMUNICATION SATELLITES* INTERNAL   TEC/DEV
ORGANIZATION FOR DEVELOPMENT AND CONTROL." USA+45   SPACE
R+D ACT/RES DIPLOM NAT/LISM...POLICY INT/LAW   COM/IND
PREDICT UN. PAGE 16 G0313   INT/ORG

S67
ENKE S.,"GOVERNMENT-INDUSTRY DEVELOPMENT OF A   INDUS
COMMERCIAL SUPERSONIC TRANSPORT." USA+45 ECO/DEV   FINAN
R+D LG/CO NAT/G TEC/DEV PRICE RISK COST PROFIT.   SERV/IND
PAGE 18 G0347   CAP/ISM

S67
EYRAUD M.,"LA FRANCE FACE A UN EVENTUEL TRAITE DE   NUC/PWR
NON DISSEMINATION DES ARMES NUCLEAIRES." FRANCE   ARMS/CONT
USA+45 EXTR/IND INDUS R+D INT/ORG ACT/RES TEC/DEV   POLICY
AGREE PRODUC ATTIT 20 TREATY AEC EURATOM. PAGE 18
G0355

S67
FADDEYEV N.,"CMEA CO-OPERATION OF EQUAL NATIONS."   MARXISM
COM R+D PLAN CAP/ISM DIPLOM FOR/AID WEALTH...POLICY   ECO/TAC
MARXIST. PAGE 18 G0356   INT/ORG
ECO/UNDEV

S67
FRIED M.,"FUNCTIONS OF THE WORKING CLASS COMMUNITY   CLASSIF
IN MODERN URBAN SOCIETY* IMPLICATIONS FOR FORCED   WORKER
RELOCATION." USA+45 INDUS R+D NEIGH PLAN TEC/DEV   MUNIC
PARTIC GP/REL ATTIT...SOC STAT CHARTS. PAGE 20   ADJUST
G0393

S67
GAUSSENS J.,"THE APPLICATIONS OF NUCLEAR ENERGY -   NUC/PWR
TECHNICAL, ECONOMIC AND SOCIAL ASPECTS." WOR+45   TEC/DEV
INDUS R+D ACT/RES EFFICIENCY PRODUC SKILL PREDICT.   ECO/DEV
PAGE 21 G0413   ADJUST

S67
GOBER J.L.,"FEDERALISM AT WORK." USA+45 NAT/G   MUNIC
CONSULT ACT/RES PLAN CONFER ADMIN LEAD PARTIC   TEC/DEV
FEDERAL ATTIT. PAGE 21 G0422   R+D
GOV/REL

S67
HAMBERG D.,"SIZE OF ENTERPRISE AND TECHNICAL   TEC/DEV
CHANGE." USA+45 LG/CO SML/CO CREATE OP/RES PROFIT   INDUS
...TREND 20. PAGE 24 G0477   R+D
WEALTH

S67
HARRIS F.R.,"POLITICAL SCIENCE AND THE PROPOSAL FOR   PROF/ORG
A NATIONAL SOCIAL SCIENCE FOUNDATION." FUT CONSULT   R+D
DELIB/GP PLAN PROB/SOLV BUDGET CONFER SANCTION   CREATE
CRIME...POLICY SOC/WK 20 NSF NSSF. PAGE 25 G0484   NAT/G

S67
HULL E.W.S.,"THE POLITICAL OCEAN." FUT UNIV WOR+45   DIPLOM
EXTR/IND R+D VOL/ASSN PLAN BAL/PWR ECO/TAC PEACE   ECO/UNDEV
WEALTH 20 UN. PAGE 27 G0536   INT/ORG
INT/LAW

S67
LEWIS R.L.,"GOAL AND NO GOAL* A NEW POLICY IN   SPACE
SPACE." R+D BUDGET COST...POLICY DECISION PHIL/SCI.   PLAN
PAGE 34 G0662   EFFICIENCY
CREATE

S67
MACDONALD G.J.F.,"SCIENCE AND SPACE POLICY* HOW   SPACE
DOES IT GET PLANNED?" R+D CREATE TEC/DEV BUDGET   PLAN
ADMIN ROUTINE...DECISION NASA. PAGE 35 G0687   MGT
EX/STRUC

S67
MORTON J.A.,"A SYSTEMS APPROACH TO THE INNOVATION   TEC/DEV
PROCESS: ITS USE IN THE BELL SYSTEM." USA+45 INTELL   GEN/METH
INDUS LG/CO CONSULT WORKER COMPUTER AUTOMAT DEMAND   R+D
...MGT CHARTS 20. PAGE 40 G0787   COM/IND

S67
MYERS S.,"TECHNOLOGY AND URBAN TRANSIT: THE   R+D
ENORMOUS POTENTIAL OF BUS AND RAIL SYSTEMS." USA+45   TEC/DEV
FINAN LOC/G MUNIC WORKER PLAN PROB/SOLV PRICE   DIST/IND
AUTOMAT 20. PAGE 40 G0798   ACT/RES

S67
RICH G.S.,"THE PROPOSED PATENT LEGISLATION* SOME   LICENSE
COMMENTS." USA+45 LAW R+D ACT/RES TEC/DEV CONFER   POLICY
EFFICIENCY OWN JURID. PAGE 46 G0916   CREATE
CAP/ISM

S67
ROBERTS E.B.,"THE PROBLEM OF AGING ORGANIZATIONS."   INDUS
INTELL PROB/SOLV ADMIN EXEC FEEDBACK EFFICIENCY   R+D
PRODUC...GEN/LAWS 20. PAGE 47 G0926   MGT
PLAN

S67
SCHACTER O.,"SCIENTIFIC ADVANCES AND INTERNATIONAL   TEC/DEV
LAWMAKING." FUT R+D PLAN PROB/SOLV CONFER CONTROL   INT/LAW
...POLICY PREDICT 20 UN. PAGE 49 G0961   INT/ORG
ACT/RES

S67
VERGIN R.C.,"COMPUTER INDUCED ORGANIZATION   COMPUTER
CHANGES." FUT USA+45 R+D CREATE OP/RES TEC/DEV   DECISION
ADJUST CENTRAL...MGT INT CON/ANAL COMPUT/IR.   AUTOMAT
PAGE 61 G1194   EX/STRUC

S67
VLASCIC I.A.,"THE SPACE TREATY* A PRELIMINARY   SPACE
EVALUATION." FUT USSR WOR+45 R+D ACT/RES TEC/DEV   INT/LAW
DIPLOM CONFER ARMS/CONT PEACE...PREDICT UN TREATY.   INT/ORG
PAGE 61 G1201   NEUTRAL

S67
WINSTON O.,"AN URBANIZATION PATTERN FOR THE US*   USA+45
SOME CONSIDERATIONS FOR THE DECENTRALIZATION OF   MUNIC
EXCELLENCE." FUT SOCIETY ECO/DEV R+D NEIGH ACT/RES   PLAN
PROB/SOLV TEC/DEV. PAGE 64 G1247   HABITAT

N67
ASIAN STUDIES CENTER,FOUR ARTICLES ON POPULATION   ASIA
AND FAMILY LIFE IN TAIWAN (ASIAN STUDIES PAPERS,   FAM
REPRINT SERIES NO. 2). CULTURE STRATA ECO/UNDEV   CENSUS
AGRI INDUS R+D KIN MUNIC...GEOG SOC CHARTS 20.   ANTHOL
PAGE 4 G0072

N67
US SUPERINTENDENT OF DOCUMENTS,SPACE: MISSILES, THE   BIBLIOG/A
MOON, NASA, AND SATELLITES (PRICE LIST 79A). USA+45   SPACE
COM/IND R+D NAT/G DIPLOM EDU/PROP ADMIN CONTROL   TEC/DEV
HEALTH...POLICY SIMUL NASA CONGRESS. PAGE 61 G1190   PEACE

N67
US HOUSE COMM SCI ASTRONAUT,AMENDING NATIONAL   PHIL/SCI
SCIENCE FOUNDATION ACT OF 1950 TO MAKE IMPROVEMENTS   DELIB/GP
IN ORGANIZATION AND OPERATION OF FOUNDAT'N(PAMPH).   TEC/DEV
USA+45 GIVE ADMIN...POLICY HOUSE/REP NSF. PAGE 58   R+D
G1147

N67
US HOUSE COMM SCI ASTRONAUT,AUTHORIZING   SPACE
APPROPRIATIONS TO THE NATIONAL AERONAUTICS AND   R+D
SPACE ADMINISTRATION (PAMPHLET). USA+45 NAT/G   PHIL/SCI
OP/RES TEC/DEV BUDGET NASA HOUSE/REP. PAGE 58 G1149   NUC/PWR

N67
US HOUSE COMM SCI ASTRONAUT,GOVERNMENT, SCIENCE,   NAT/G
AND INTERNATIONAL POLICY (PAMPHLET). INDIA   POLICY
NETHERLAND ECO/DEV ECO/UNDEV R+D ACADEM PLAN DIPLOM   CREATE

FOR/AID CONFER...PREDICT 20 CHINJAP. PAGE 59 G1152   TEC/DEV

N67

US SENATE,STATUS OF THE DEVELOPMENT OF THE ANTI-   FORCES
BALLISTIC MISSILE SYSTEMS IN THE UNITED STATES   NUC/PWR
(PAMPHLET). FUT USA+45 R+D PLAN TEC/DEV DEPT/DEFEN.   WAR
PAGE 59 G1165   UTIL

N67

US SENATE COMM AERO SPACE SCI,AERONAUTICAL RESEARCH   AIR
AND DEVELOPMENT POLICY (PAMPHLET). SPACE USA+45   R+D
INDUS CIVMIL/REL CONGRESS PRESIDENT NASA SENATE.   POLICY
PAGE 60 G1169   PLAN

N67

US SENATE COMM AERO SPACE SCI,AERONAUTICAL RESEARCH   DIST/IND
AND DEVELOPMENT POLICY; HEARINGS, COMM ON   SPACE
AERONAUTICAL AND SPACE SCIENCES...1967 (PAMPHLET).   NAT/G
R+D PROB/SOLV EXEC GOV/REL 20 DEPT/DEFEN FAA NASA   PLAN
CONGRESS. PAGE 60 G1174

N67

US SENATE COMM ON PUBLIC WORKS,AIR QUALITY ACT OF   HEALTH
1967 (PAMPHLET). USA+45 INDUS R+D LEGIS SENATE.   AIR
PAGE 61 G1187   HABITAT
    CONTROL

S68

BARAGWANATH L.E.,"SCIENTIFIC CO-OPERATION BETWEEN   R+D
THE UNIVERSITIES AND INDUSTRY - A RESEARCH NOTE."   ACADEM
UK LG/CO CREATE TEC/DEV EDU/PROP ATTIT...PHIL/SCI   INDUS
STAT QU 20. PAGE 5 G0090   GP/REL

RABINOWITCH E. G0454

RACE....SEE RACE/REL, KIN

RACE/REL....RACE RELATIONS; SEE ALSO DISCRIM, ISOLAT, KIN

N19

MEZERIK A.G.,INTERNATIONAL POLICY 1965 (PAMPHLET).   DIPLOM
KASHMIR S/ASIA SPACE USA+45 VIETNAM WOR+45   INT/ORG
ARMS/CONT RACE/REL DISCRIM PEACE PWR 20 UN. PAGE 39   POLICY
G0762   WAR

B53

SCHAAF R.W.,DOCUMENTS OF INTERNATIONAL MEETINGS.   BIBLIOG/A
AGRI INDUS ACADEM DIPLOM NUC/PWR RACE/REL AGE/Y   DELIB/GP
HEALTH...SOC 20. PAGE 49 G0960   INT/ORG
    POLICY

B58

OGDEN F.D.,THE POLL TAX IN THE SOUTH. USA+45 USA-45   TAX
CONSTN ADJUD ADMIN PARTIC CRIME...TIME/SEQ GOV/COMP   CHOOSE
METH/COMP 18/20 SOUTH/US. PAGE 43 G0838   RACE/REL
    DISCRIM

B62

BOCK E.A.,CASE STUDIES IN AMERICAN GOVERNMENT.   POLICY
USA+45 ECO/DEV CHIEF EDU/PROP CT/SYS RACE/REL   LEGIS
ORD/FREE...JURID MGT PHIL/SCI PRESIDENT CASEBOOK.   IDEA/COMP
PAGE 8 G0146   NAT/G

B64

WIRTH L.,ON CITIES AND SOCIAL LIFE: SELECTED   GEN/LAWS
PAPERS. PLAN PROB/SOLV RACE/REL CONSEN ATTIT   SOCIETY
HABITAT PERSON...POLICY SOC CONCPT ANTHOL BIBLIOG   NEIGH
20. PAGE 64 G1249   STRUCT

B65

BAILEY S.K.,AMERICAN POLITICS AND GOVERNMENT.   ANTHOL
USA+45 CONSTN FINAN LABOR POL/PAR DIPLOM ADMIN WAR   LEGIS
INGP/REL RACE/REL NEW/LIB 20 SUPREME/CT PRESIDENT   PWR
CONGRESS. PAGE 4 G0084

B65

REISS A.J. JR.,SCHOOLS IN A CHANGING SOCIETY.   SCHOOL
CULTURE PROB/SOLV INSPECT DOMIN CONFER INGP/REL   EX/STRUC
RACE/REL AGE/C AGE/Y ALL/VALS...ANTHOL SOC/INTEG 20   ADJUST
NEWYORK/C. PAGE 46 G0912   ADMIN

B66

DUNBAR L.W.,A REPUBLIC OF EQUALS. USA+45 CREATE   LAW
ADJUD PEACE NEW/LIB...POLICY 20 SOUTH/US   CONSTN
CIV/RIGHTS. PAGE 16 G0320   FEDERAL
    RACE/REL

B66

FREIDEL F.,AMERICAN ISSUES IN THE TWENTIETH   DIPLOM
CENTURY. SOCIETY FINAN ECO/TAC FOR/AID CONTROL   POLICY
NUC/PWR WAR RACE/REL PEACE ATTIT...ANTHOL T 20   NAT/G
WILSON/W ROOSEVLT/F KENNEDY/JF TRUMAN/HS. PAGE 20   ORD/FREE
G0391

B67

MACBRIDE R.,THE AUTOMATED STATE: COMPUTER SYSTEMS   COMPUTER

AS A NEW FORCE IN SOCIETY. FUT WOR+45 FINAN MUNIC   AUTOMAT
NAT/G WORKER PLAN TEC/DEV CONTROL PERS/REL RACE/REL   PROB/SOLV
ADJUST. PAGE 35 G0685   SOCIETY

B67

RUSSELL B.,WAR CRIMES IN VIETNAM. USA+45 VIETNAM   WAR
FORCES DIPLOM WEAPON RACE/REL DISCRIM ISOLAT   CRIME
BIO/SOC 20 COLD/WAR RUSSELL/B. PAGE 48 G0949   ATTIT
    POLICY

B67

UNIVERSAL REFERENCE SYSTEM,CURRENT EVENTS AND   BIBLIOG/A
PROBLEMS OF MODERN SOCIETY (VOLUME V). WOR+45 LOC/G   SOCIETY
MUNIC NAT/G PLAN EDU/PROP CRIME RACE/REL WEALTH   PROB/SOLV
...COMPUT/IR GEN/METH. PAGE 56 G1097   ATTIT

RAF....ROYAL AIR FORCE

RAHMAN/TA....TUNKU ABDUL RAHMAN

RAILROAD....RAILROADS AND RAILWAY SYSTEMS

B54

LOCKLIN D.P.,ECONOMICS OF TRANSPORTATION (4TH ED.).   ECO/DEV
USA+45 USA-45 SEA AIR LAW FINAN LG/CO EX/STRUC   DIST/IND
ADMIN CONTROL...STAT CHARTS 19/20 RAILROAD   ECO/TAC
PUB/TRANS. PAGE 34 G0675   TEC/DEV

B64

LANG A.S.,URBAN RAIL TRANSIT. OP/RES PLAN PROB/SOLV   MUNIC
TEC/DEV AUTOMAT COST...TECHNIC MATH CON/ANAL CHARTS   DIST/IND
METH/COMP SIMUL 20 RAILROAD PUB/TRANS. PAGE 32   ECOMETRIC
G0632

B66

RUPPENTHAL K.M.,TRANSPORTATION AND TOMORROW. FUT   DIST/IND
SPACE USA+45 SEA AIR FORCES TEC/DEV INT/TRADE   PLAN
...ANTHOL 20 RAILROAD. PAGE 48 G0946   CIVMIL/REL
    PREDICT

RAJARATAM/S....S. RAJARATAM

RAJASTHAN....RAJASTHAN

RAMO S. G0898

RAMSEY J.A. G0899

RAND SCHOOL OF SOCIAL SCIENCE G0900

RANDOMNESS....SEE PROB/SOLV

RANIS G. G0361

RANKE/L....LEOPOLD VON RANKE

RANKING SYSTEMS....SEE SENIOR

RANKOVIC/A....ALEXANDER RANKOVIC, YUGOSLAVIA'S FORMER VICE
    PRESIDENT

RANSOM H.H. G0901

RAPOPORT A. G0877,G0902

RAPP W.F. G0903

RASER J.R. G0904,G0905

RATION....RATIONING

N

FULLER G.A.,DEMOBILIZATION: A SELECTED LIST OF   BIBLIOG/A
REFERENCES. USA+45 LAW AGRI LABOR WORKER ECO/TAC   INDUS
RATION RECEIVE EDU/PROP ROUTINE ARMS/CONT ALL/VALS   FORCES
20. PAGE 20 G0398   NAT/G

B41

FULLER G.H.,DEFENSE FINANCING: A SELECTED LIST OF   BIBLIOG/A
REFERENCES (PAMPHLET). MOD/EUR USA-45 ECO/DEV NAT/G   FINAN
DELIB/GP RATION ARMS/CONT WEAPON COST PEACE PWR 20   FORCES
CONGRESS. PAGE 20 G0401   BUDGET

B59

MEANS G.C.,ADMINISTRATIVE INFLATION AND PUBLIC   ECO/TAC
POLICY (PAMPHLET). USA+45 ECO/DEV FINAN INDUS   POLICY
WORKER PLAN BUDGET GOV/REL COST DEMAND WEALTH 20   RATION
CONGRESS MONOPOLY GOLD/STAND. PAGE 38 G0749   CONTROL

S63

ENTHOVEN A.C.,"ECONOMIC ANALYSIS IN THE DEPARTMENT   PLAN
OF DEFENSE." USA+45 NAT/G DELIB/GP PROB/SOLV RATION   BUDGET
NUC/PWR WEAPON COST...DECISION 20 DEPT/DEFEN   ECO/TAC
RESOURCE/N. PAGE 18 G0349   FORCES

DORFMAN R.,MEASURING BENEFITS OF GOVERNMENT INVESTMENTS. ECO/DEV R+D ECO/TAC PROFIT UTIL...MGT GEN/METH. PAGE 16 G0308
B65
PLAN
RATION
EFFICIENCY
OPTIMAL

PASLEY R.S.,"ORGANIZATIONAL CONFLICTS OF INTEREST IN GOVERNMENT CONTRACTS," ELITES R+D ROUTINE NUC/PWR DEMAND EFFICIENCY 20. PAGE 44 G0860
L67
NAT/G
ECO/TAC
RATION
CONTROL

WOLFE T.W.,"SOVIET MILITARY POLICY AT THE FIFTY YEAR MARK." USSR VIETNAM WOR+45 RATION AGREE WAR WEAPON CIVMIL/REL TREATY. PAGE 64 G1254
S67
FORCES
POLICY
TIME/SEQ
PLAN

RATIONAL....RATIONALITY

DEWEY J.,THE QUEST FOR CERTAINTY. GP/REL RATIONAL UTOPIA ATTIT MORAL ORD/FREE PWR...MYTH HIST/WRIT. PAGE 15 G0301
B29
PHIL/SCI
PERSON
PERCEPT
KNOWL

LIPPMAN W.,THE PUBLIC PHILOSOPHY. EX/STRUC TOP/EX LOBBY RATIONAL POPULISM...POLICY SOC CONCPT PREDICT GP/COMP IDEA/COMP. PAGE 34 G0673
B55
MAJORIT
STRUCT
PWR
TOTALISM

DRUCKER P.F.,"'MANAGEMENT SCIENCE' AND THE MANAGER." PLAN ROUTINE RIGID/FLEX...METH/CNCPT LOG HYPO/EXP. PAGE 16 G0315
S55
MGT
STRUCT
DECISION
RATIONAL

MARCUSE H.,SOVIET MARXISM, A CRITICAL ANALYSIS. USSR CONSTN PLAN PRODUC RATIONAL SOCISM...IDEA/COMP 20 COM/PARTY. PAGE 36 G0703
B58
MARXISM
ATTIT
POLICY

HUGHES E.M.,AMERICA THE VINCIBLE. USA+45 FOR/AID ARMS/CONT NUC/PWR PERS/REL RATIONAL ATTIT ALL/VALS 20 COLD/WAR. PAGE 27 G0534
B59
ORD/FREE
DIPLOM
WAR

MORRIS W.T.,ENGINEERING ECONOMY. AUTOMAT RISK RATIONAL...PROBABIL STAT CHARTS GAME SIMUL BIBLIOG T 20. PAGE 40 G0785
B60
OP/RES
DECISION
MGT
PROB/SOLV

KRUPP S.,PATTERN IN ORGANIZATIONAL ANALYSIS: A CRITICAL EXAMINATION. INGP/REL PERS/REL RATIONAL ATTIT AUTHORIT DRIVE PWR...DECISION PHIL/SCI SOC IDEA/COMP. PAGE 32 G0622
B61
MGT
CONTROL
CONCPT
METH/CNCPT

DYKMAN J.W.,"REVIEW ARTICLE* PLANNING AND DECISION THEORY." ELITES LOC/G MUNIC CONSULT ADMIN...POLICY MGT. PAGE 17 G0327
S61
DECISION
PLAN
RATIONAL

RIES J.C.,THE MANAGEMENT OF DEFENSE: ORGANIZATION AND CONTROL OF THE US ARMED SERVICES. PROF/ORG DELIB/GP EX/STRUC LEGIS GOV/REL PERS/REL CENTRAL RATIONAL PWR...POLICY TREND GOV/COMP BIBLIOG. PAGE 47 G0920
B64
FORCES
ACT/RES
DECISION
CONTROL

MCGUIRE M.C.,SECRECY AND THE ARMS RACE* A THEORY OF THE ACCUMULATION OF STRATEGIC WEAPONS AND HOW SECRECY AFFECTS IT. DIPLOM NUC/PWR WEAPON ISOLAT RATIONAL ORD/FREE WEALTH...ECOMETRIC MATH GEN/LAWS. PAGE 38 G0742
B65
DETER
ARMS/CONT
SIMUL
GAME

GREEN P.,DEADLY LOGIC* THE THEORY OF NUCLEAR DETERRENCE. USA+45 ACT/RES OP/RES NUC/PWR RATIONAL ALL/VALS PWR...DECISION MGT PHIL/SCI QUANT IDEA/COMP GAME. PAGE 23 G0444
B66
DETER
ACADEM
GEN/LAWS
RECORD

STONE J.J.,CONTAINING THE ARMS RACE* SOME SPECIFIC PROPOSALS. ASIA USA+45 USSR PROB/SOLV BARGAIN DIPLOM DETER NUC/PWR RATIONAL...GAME 20 DEPT/DEFEN TREATY. PAGE 53 G1038
B66
ARMS/CONT
FEEDBACK
COST
ATTIT

BUNGE M.,THE SEARCH FOR TRUTH, VOL. 3, PART 2 OF STUDIES IN THE FOUNDATIONS, METHODOLOGY, AND PHILOSOPHY OF SCIENCE. UNIV INTELL KNOWL...CONCPT OBS PREDICT METH. PAGE 10 G0188
B67
PHIL/SCI
TESTS
GEN/LAWS
RATIONAL

CRANBERG L.,"SCIENCE, ETHICS, AND LAW." UNIV CREATE PLAN EDU/PROP INGP/REL PERS/REL ADJUST RATIONAL KNOWL MORAL...CONCPT IDEA/COMP 20. PAGE 13 G0260
S67
LAW
PHIL/SCI
INTELL

GOLDSTEIN W.,"THE SCIENCE ESTABLISHMENT AND ITS POLITICAL CONTROL." WOR+45 SOCIETY GP/REL RATIONAL ORD/FREE. PAGE 22 G0430
S67
CREATE
ADJUST
CONTROL

RAUDSEPP E. G0906

RAWLINSON J.L. G0907

REAGAN/RON....RONALD REAGAN

REALPOL....REALPOLITIK, PRACTICAL POLITICS

REALPOLITIK....SEE REALPOL

REC/INT....RECORDING OF INTERVIEWS

COMBS C.H.,DECISION PROCESSES. INTELL SOCIETY DELIB/GP CREATE TEC/DEV DOMIN LEGIT EXEC CHOOSE DRIVE RIGID/FLEX KNOWL PWR...PHIL/SCI SOC METH/CNCPT CONT/OBS REC/INT PERS/TEST SAMP/SIZ BIOG SOC/EXP WORK. PAGE 13 G0245
B54
MATH
DECISION

ANDERSON N.,"INTERNATIONAL SEMINARS: AN ANALYSIS AND AN EVALUATION." WOR+45 R+D ACT/RES CREATE PLAN REGION ATTIT KNOWL SKILL...SOC REC/INT PERS/TEST CHARTS 20. PAGE 3 G0057
S58
INT/ORG
DELIB/GP

US SENATE COMM GOVT OPERATIONS,ADMINISTRATION OF NATIONAL SECURITY (9 PARTS). ADMIN...INT REC/INT CHARTS 20 SENATE CONGRESS. PAGE 60 G1178
B63
DELIB/GP
NAT/G
OP/RES
ORD/FREE

RECALL....RECALL PROCEDURE

RECEIVE....RECEIVING (IN WELFARE SENSE)

FULLER G.A.,DEMOBILIZATION: A SELECTED LIST OF REFERENCES. USA+45 LAW AGRI LABOR WORKER ECO/TAC RATION RECEIVE EDU/PROP ROUTINE ARMS/CONT ALL/VALS 20. PAGE 20 G0398
N
BIBLIOG/A
INDUS
FORCES
NAT/G

INDIA: A REFERENCE ANNUAL. INDIA CULTURE COM/IND R+D FORCES PLAN RECEIVE EDU/PROP HEALTH...STAT CHARTS BIBLIOG 20. PAGE 1 G0005
N
CONSTN
LABOR
INT/ORG

PUBLIC ADMINISTRATION SERVICE,SOURCE MATERIALS IN PUBLIC ADMINISTRATION: A SELECTED BIBLIOGRAPHY (PAS PUBLICATION NO. 102). USA+45 LAW FINAN LOC/G MUNIC NAT/G PLAN RECEIVE EDU/PROP CT/SYS CHOOSE HEALTH 20. PAGE 45 G0895
B48
BIBLIOG/A
GOV/REL
MGT
ADMIN

KIETH-LUCAS A.,DECISIONS ABOUT PEOPLE IN NEED, A STUDY OF ADMINISTRATIVE RESPONSIVENESS IN PUBLIC ASSISTANCE. USA+45 GIVE RECEIVE INGP/REL PERS/REL MORAL RESPECT WEALTH...SOC OBS BIBLIOG 20. PAGE 30 G0595
B57
ADMIN
RIGID/FLEX
SOC/WK
DECISION

MARSCH P.E.,FEDERAL AID TO SCIENCE EDUCATION: TWO PROGRAMS. USA+45 SCHOOL RECEIVE EFFICIENCY 20. PAGE 36 G0711
B63
EDU/PROP
PHIL/SCI
NAT/G
METH/COMP

SMITH E.A.,SOCIAL WELFARE: PRINCIPLES AND CONCEPTS. STRATA STRUCT CONSULT WORKER ACT/RES CREATE PLAN TEC/DEV ROUTINE GP/REL UTOPIA...SOC 20. PAGE 51 G1014
B65
CONCPT
SOC/WK
RECEIVE
ORD/FREE

RECIFE....RECIFE, BRAZIL

RECIPROCITY....SEE SANCTION

RECORD....RECORDING OF DIRECT OBSERVATIONS

BAXTER J.P.,SCIENTISTS AGAINST TIME. EUR+WWI MOD/EUR USA+45 USA-45 WOR+45 WOR-45 R+D NAT/G PLAN ATTIT PWR...PHIL/SCI RECORD CON/ANAL 17/20. PAGE 6 G0107
B46
FORCES
WAR
NUC/PWR

B48
BRADLEY D..NO PLACE TO HIDE. USA+45 SOCIETY NAT/G   R+D
FORCES TEC/DEV EDU/PROP DETER PEACE BIO/SOC   LAB/EXP
ALL/VALS...POLICY PHIL/SCI OBS RECORD SAMP BIOG   ARMS/CONT
GEN/METH COLD/WAR 20. PAGE 8 G0162   NUC/PWR

S50
LENTZ T.F.."REPORT ON A SURVEY OF SOCIAL SCIENTISTS ACT/RES
CONDUCTED BY THE ATTITUDE RESEARCH LABORATORY." FUT   ATTIT
WOR+45 CREATE EDU/PROP...PSY STAT RECORD SYS/QU   DIPLOM
SAMP/SIZ CON/ANAL VAL/FREE 20. PAGE 33 G0655

B51
CONANT J.B..SCIENCE AND COMMON SENSE. WOR+45 WOR-45 CREATE
R+D SCHOOL CONSULT TEC/DEV EDU/PROP SKILL...PLURIST PHIL/SCI
METH/CNCPT RECORD TIME/SEQ SIMUL GEN/METH METH.
PAGE 13 G0248

S52
TRUMAN D.B.."SELECTED CRITICAL BIBLIOGRAPHY ON THE BIBLIOG/A
METHODS AND TECHNIQUES OF POLITICAL BEHAVIOR   ACT/RES
RESEARCH." R+D PARTIC...SOC OBS RECORD INT. PAGE 55 METH/CNCPT
G1079

L54
OPLER M.E.."SOCIAL ASPECTS OF TECHNICAL ASSISTANCE INT/ORG
IN OPERATION." WOR+45 VOL/ASSN CREATE PLAN TEC/DEV CONSULT
EDU/PROP ALL/VALS...METH/CNCPT OBS RECORD TREND UN FOR/AID
20. PAGE 43 G0841

L55
KISER M.."ORGANIZATION OF AMERICAN STATES." L/A+17C VOL/ASSN
USA+45 ECO/UNDEV INT/ORG NAT/G PLAN TEC/DEV DIPLOM ECO/DEV
ECO/TAC INT/TRADE EDU/PROP ADMIN ALL/VALS...POLICY REGION
MGT RECORD ORG/CHARTS OAS 20. PAGE 30 G0601

B59
MIKSCHE F.O..THE FAILURE OF ATOMIC STRATEGY. COM   ACT/RES
EUR+WWI INTELL POL/PAR FORCES PLAN ECO/TAC NUC/PWR ORD/FREE
ATTIT DRIVE RIGID/FLEX PWR...DECISION GEOG PSY   DIPLOM
CONCPT RECORD TREND CHARTS VAL/FREE 20. PAGE 39   ARMS/CONT
G0766

S59
CORY R.H. JR.."INTERNATIONAL INSPECTION FROM   STRUCT
PROPOSALS TO REALIZATION." WOR+45 TEC/DEV ECO/TAC PSY
ADJUD ORD/FREE PWR WEALTH...RECORD VAL/FREE 20.   ARMS/CONT
PAGE 13 G0258   NUC/PWR

B60
PENTONY D.E..THE UNDERDEVELOPED LANDS. FUT WOR+45 ECO/UNDEV
CULTURE AGRI FINAN INDUS MARKET INT/ORG LABOR NAT/G POLICY
VOL/ASSN CONSULT TEC/DEV ECO/TAC EDU/PROP COLONIAL FOR/AID
ATTIT WEALTH...OBS RECORD SAMP TREND GEN/METH WORK INT/TRADE
UN 20. PAGE 44 G0867

B60
US HOUSE COMM. SCI. ASTRONAUT..OCEAN SCIENCES AND R+D
NATIONAL SECURITY. FUT SEA ECO/DEV EXTR/IND INT/ORG ORD/FREE
NAT/G FORCES ACT/RES TEC/DEV ECO/TAC COERCE WAR
BIO/SOC KNOWL PWR...CONCPT RECORD LAB/EXP 20.
PAGE 59 G1153

L60
HOLZMAN B.G.."BASIC RESEARCH FOR NATIONAL   FORCES
SURVIVAL." FUT USA+45 INTELL R+D ACT/RES OP/RES STAT
PLAN TEC/DEV EDU/PROP PERCEPT PERSON...PHIL/SCI
METH/CNCPT NEW/IDEA MATH OBS RECORD TREND LAB/EXP
20. PAGE 27 G0525

L60
JACOB P.E.."THE DISARMAMENT CONSENSUS." USA+45 USSR DELIB/GP
WOR+45 INT/ORG NAT/G ACT/RES TEC/DEV BAL/PWR   ATTIT
EDU/PROP ADMIN COERCE DETER NUC/PWR CONSEN   ARMS/CONT
RIGID/FLEX PWR...CONCPT RECORD CHARTS COLD/WAR 20.
PAGE 28 G0552

S60
HUTCHINSON C.E.."AN INSTITUTE FOR NATIONAL SECURITY POLICY
AFFAIRS." USA+45 R+D NAT/G CONSULT TOP/EX ACT/RES METH/CNCPT
CREATE PLAN TEC/DEV EDU/PROP ROUTINE NUC/PWR ATTIT ELITES
ORD/FREE PWR...DECISION MGT PHIL/SCI CONCPT RECORD DIPLOM
GEN/LAWS GEN/METH 20. PAGE 27 G0539

B61
HENKIN L.,ARMS CONTROL: ISSUES FOR THE PUBLIC.   WOR+45
EUR+WWI FUT USA+45 USSR INT/ORG NAT/G DIPLOM   DELIB/GP
EDU/PROP DETER NUC/PWR ATTIT PWR...CONCPT RECORD ARMS/CONT
HIST/WRIT TIME/SEQ TOT/POP COLD/WAR 20. PAGE 26
G0506

B61
KISSINGER H.A..THE NECESSITY FOR CHOICE. FUT USA+45 TOP/EX
ECO/UNDEV NAT/G PLAN BAL/PWR ECO/TAC ARMS/CONT   TREND
DETER NUC/PWR ATTIT...POLICY CONCPT RECORD GEN/LAWS DIPLOM

COLD/WAR 20. PAGE 31 G0604

B62
DODDS H.W..THE ACADEMIC PRESIDENT "EDUCATOR OR   ACADEM
CARETAKER? FINAN DELIB/GP EDU/PROP PARTIC ATTIT   ADMIN
ROLE PWR...POLICY RECORD INT. PAGE 16 G0304   LEAD
   CONTROL

L64
CARNEGIE ENDOWMENT INT. PEACE.."ECONOMIC AND SOCIAL INT/ORG
QUESTION (ISSUES BEFORE THE NINETEENTH GENERAL   INT/TRADE
ASSEMBLY)." WOR+45 ECO/DEV ECO/UNDEV INDUS R+D
DELIB/GP CREATE PLAN TEC/DEV ECO/TAC FOR/AID
BAL/PAY...RECORD UN 20. PAGE 11 G0209

S64
COOPER A.C.."R&D IS MORE EFFICIENT IN SMALL   R+D
COMPANIES." USA+45 LG/CO SML/CO WEALTH...RECORD INT INDUS
LAB/EXP 20. PAGE 13 G0255   CREATE
   GP/COMP

S65
BALDWIN H.."SLOW-DOWN IN THE PENTAGON." USA+45   RECORD
CREATE PLAN GOV/REL CENTRAL COST EFFICIENCY PWR   R+D
...MGT MCNAMARA/R. PAGE 5 G0088   WEAPON
   ADMIN

S65
BOHN L.C.."ATOMS FOR PEACE AND ATOMS FOR WAR."   NUC/PWR
WOR+45 INT/ORG TEC/DEV DIPLOM IDEA/COMP. PAGE 8   ARMS/CONT
G0149   RECORD

S65
DESAI M.J.."INDIA AND NUCLEAR WEAPONS." ASIA   INDIA
BAL/PWR DIPLOM NUC/PWR WEAPON PEACE RECORD. PAGE 15 ARMS/CONT
G0294

S65
FINK C.F.."MORE CALCULATIONS ABOUT DETERRENCE."   DETER
DRIVE...PHIL/SCI PSY STAT TIME/SEQ GAME GEN/LAWS.   RECORD
PAGE 19 G0367   PROBABIL
   IDEA/COMP

S65
GOLDSTEIN W.."KEEPING THE GENIE IN THE BOTTLE* THE NUC/PWR
FEASIBILITY OF A NUCLEAR NON-PROLIFERATION   CREATE
AGREEMENT." ASIA FRANCE UK USA+45 USSR WOR+45   COST
ECO/UNDEV VOL/ASSN ACT/RES PLAN RISK ARMS/CONT WAR
PEACE ATTIT PERCEPT...RECORD TREND TIME. PAGE 22
G0429

S65
KINTNER W.P.."THE PROSPECTS FOR WESTERN SCIENCE AND TEC/DEV
TECHNOLOGY." EUR+WWI FRANCE USA+45 USSR R+D NUC/PWR VOL/ASSN
NATO. PAGE 30 G0598   STAT
   RECORD

S65
KUZMACK A.M.."TECHNOLOGICAL CHANGE AND STABLE   R+D
DETERRENCE." CREATE EDU/PROP ARMS/CONT WEAPON   DETER
CHOOSE COST DRIVE PERCEPT...RECORD STERTYP TIME.   EQUILIB
PAGE 32 G0627

S65
MARTIN A.."PROLIFERATION." FUT WOR+45 PROB/SOLV   RECORD
REGION ADJUST...PREDICT NAT/COMP UN TREATY. PAGE 36 NUC/PWR
G0712   ARMS/CONT
   VOL/ASSN

S65
STAAR R.F.."RETROGRESSION IN POLAND." COM USSR AGRI TOP/EX
INDUS NAT/G CREATE EDU/PROP TOTALISM RIGID/FLEX   ECO/TAC
ORD/FREE PWR SOCISM...RECORD CHARTS 20. PAGE 52   POLAND
G1029

B66
GREEN P..DEADLY LOGIC* THE THEORY OF NUCLEAR   DETER
DETERRENCE. USA+45 ACT/RES OP/RES NUC/PWR RATIONAL ACADEM
ALL/VALS PWR...DECISION MGT PHIL/SCI QUANT   GEN/LAWS
IDEA/COMP GAME. PAGE 23 G0444   RECORD

S66
BROWNLIE I.."NUCLEAR PROLIFERATION* SOME PROBLEMS   NUC/PWR
OF CONTROL." USA+45 USSR ECO/UNDEV INT/ORG FORCES ARMS/CONT
TEC/DEV REGION CONSEN...RECORD TREATY. PAGE 9 G0181 VOL/ASSN
   ORD/FREE

S66
EWALD R.F.."ONE OF MANY POSSIBLE GAMES." ACADEM   SIMUL
INT/ORG ARMS/CONT...INT/LAW GAME. PAGE 18 G0354   HYPO/EXP
   PROG/TEAC
   RECORD

RECORDING OF INTERVIEWS....SEE REC/INT

RECTITUDE....SEE MORAL

RED/GUARD....RED GUARD

REDFIELD/R....ROBERT REDFIELD

REDFORD E.S. G0908

REED E. G0909

REED/STAN....JUSTICE STANLEY REED

REFERENDUM....REFERENDUM; SEE ALSO PARTIC

REFORMERS....REFORMERS

B64
INST D'ETUDE POL L'U GRENOBLE,ADMINISTRATION ADMIN
TRADITIONELLE ET PLANIFICATION REGIONALE. FRANCE MUNIC
LAW POL/PAR PROB/SOLV ADJUST RIGID/FLEX...CHARTS PLAN
ANTHOL BIBLIOG T 20 REFORMERS. PAGE 28 G0546 CREATE

S67
RICHMAN B.M.,"SOVIET MANAGEMENT IN TRANSITION." MGT
USSR FINAN MARKET EX/STRUC PLAN PROB/SOLV TEC/DEV MARXISM
CONTROL LEAD CENTRAL EFFICIENCY...METH/COMP 20 POLICY
REFORMERS. PAGE 47 G0917 AUTHORIT

REGION....REGIONALISM

N
AMERICAN DOCUMENTATION INST,DOCUMENTATION BIBLIOG/A
ABSTRACTS. WOR+45 NAT/G COMPUTER CREATE TEC/DEV AUTOMAT
DIPLOM EDU/PROP REGION KNOWL...PHIL/SCI CLASSIF COMPUT/IR
LING. PAGE 3 G0051 R+D

N
AIR UNIVERSITY LIBRARY,INDEX TO MILITARY BIBLIOG/A
PERIODICALS. FUT SPACE WOR+45 REGION ARMS/CONT FORCES
NUC/PWR WAR PEACE INT/LAW. PAGE 2 G0032 NAT/G
DIPLOM

N19
FOLSOM M.B.,BETTER MANAGEMENT OF THE PUBLIC'S ADMIN
BUSINESS (PAMPHLET). USA+45 DELIB/GP PAY CONFER NAT/G
CONTROL REGION GP/REL...METH/COMP ANTHOL 20. MGT
PAGE 19 G0377 PROB/SOLV

L50
MAASS A.A.,"CONGRESS AND WATER RESOURCES." LOC/G REGION
TEC/DEV CONTROL SANCTION...WELF/ST GEOG CONGRESS. AGRI
PAGE 35 G0683 PLAN

L55
KISER M.,"ORGANIZATION OF AMERICAN STATES." L/A+17C VOL/ASSN
USA+45 ECO/UNDEV INT/ORG NAT/G PLAN TEC/DEV DIPLOM ECO/DEV
ECO/TAC INT/TRADE EDU/PROP ADMIN ALL/VALS...POLICY REGION
MGT RECORD ORG/CHARTS OAS 20. PAGE 30 G0601

S58
ANDERSON N.,"INTERNATIONAL SEMINARS: AN ANALYSIS INT/ORG
AND AN EVALUATION." WOR+45 R+D ACT/RES CREATE PLAN DELIB/GP
REGION ATTIT KNOWL SKILL...SOC REC/INT PERS/TEST
CHARTS 20. PAGE 3 G0057

S60
HAYTON R.D.,"THE ANTARCTIC SETTLEMENT OF 1959." FUT DELIB/GP
USA+45 WOR-45 STRUCT R+D INT/ORG EX/STRUC JURID
CREATE TEC/DEV LEGIT PEACE ATTIT SOVEREIGN DIPLOM
...TIME/SEQ 20 TREATY IGY. PAGE 25 G0495 REGION

B61
FRISCH D.,ARMS REDUCTION: PROGRAM AND ISSUES. PLAN
USA+45 INT/ORG NAT/G ACT/RES REGION NUC/PWR ATTIT FORCES
PWR...POLICY 20. PAGE 20 G0395 ARMS/CONT
DIPLOM

B61
LEE R.R.,ENGINEERING-ECONOMIC PLANNING BIBLIOG/A
MISCELLANEOUS SUBJECTS: A SELECTED BIBLIOGRAPHY PLAN
(MIMEOGRAPHED). FINAN LOC/G MUNIC NEIGH ADMIN REGION
CONTROL INGP/REL HABITAT...GEOG MGT SOC/WK 20
RESOURCE/N. PAGE 33 G0651

S61
DALTON G.,"ECONOMIC THEORY AND PRIMITIVE SOCIETY" ECO/UNDEV
(BMR)" UNIV AGRI KIN TEC/DEV ECO/TAC REGION HABITAT METH
SKILL...METH/COMP BIBLIOG. PAGE 14 G0274 PHIL/SCI
SOC

S61
FAIR M.L.,"PORT AUTHORITIES IN THE UNITED STATES." MUNIC
PROB/SOLV ADMIN LEAD REPRESENT PWR...DECISION GEOG. REGION
PAGE 18 G0357 LOC/G
GOV/REL

B62
KRAFT J.,THE GRAND DESIGN. EUR+WWI USA+45 AGRI VOL/ASSN
FINAN INDUS MARKET INT/ORG NAT/G PLAN ECO/TAC ECO/DEV
TARIFFS REGION DRIVE ORD/FREE WEALTH...POLICY OBS INT/TRADE
TREND EEC 20. PAGE 31 G0616

B62
SCHMITT H.A.,THE PATH TO EUROPEAN UNITY. EUR+WWI INT/ORG
USA+45 PLAN TEC/DEV DIPLOM FOR/AID CONFER...INT/LAW INT/TRADE
20 EEC EURCOALSTL MARSHL/PLN UNIFICA. PAGE 49 G0971 REGION
ECO/DEV

B62
YALEN R.,REGIONALISM AND WORLD ORDER. EUR+WWI ORD/FREE
WOR+45 WOR-45 INT/ORG VOL/ASSN DELIB/GP FORCES POLICY
TOP/EX BAL/PWR DIPLOM DOMIN REGION ARMS/CONT PWR
...JURID HYPO/EXP COLD/WAR 20. PAGE 64 G1261

B63
MAYNE R.,THE COMMUNITY OF EUROPE. UK CONSTN NAT/G EUR+WWI
CONSULT DELIB/GP CREATE PLAN ECO/TAC LEGIT ADMIN INT/ORG
ROUTINE ORD/FREE PWR WEALTH...CONCPT TIME/SEQ EEC REGION
EURATOM 20. PAGE 37 G0724

B63
PANAMERICAN UNION,DOCUMENTOS OFICIALES DE LA BIBLIOG
ORGANIZACION DE LOS ESTADOS AMERICANOS, INDICE Y INT/ORG
LISTA (VOL. III, 1962). L/A+17C DELIB/GP INT/TRADE DIPLOM
EDU/PROP REGION NUC/PWR...HEAL INT/LAW SOC/WK 20
OAS. PAGE 44 G0857

S63
SCHMITT H.A.,"THE EUROPEAN COMMUNITIES." EUR+WWI VOL/ASSN
FRANCE DELIB/GP EX/STRUC TOP/EX CREATE TEC/DEV ECO/DEV
ECO/TAC LEGIT REGION COERCE DRIVE ALL/VALS
...METH/CNCPT EEC 20. PAGE 49 G0972

B64
HEKHUIS D.J.,INTERNATIONAL STABILITY: MILITARY, TEC/DEV
ECONOMIC AND POLITICAL DIMENSIONS. FUT WOR+45 LAW DETER
ECO/UNDEV INT/ORG NAT/G VOL/ASSN FORCES ACT/RES REGION
BAL/PWR PWR WEALTH...STAT UN 20. PAGE 25 G0503

B64
ORGANIZATION AMERICAN STATES,ECONOMIC SURVEY OF ECO/UNDEV
LATIN AMERICA, 1962. L/A+17C AGRI DIST/IND INDUS CHARTS
MARKET PROC/MFG R+D PLAN TEC/DEV ECO/TAC REGION
BAL/PAY ALL/VALS...CON/ANAL ORG/CHARTS GEN/METH OAS
20. PAGE 43 G0844

L64
HAAS E.B.,"ECONOMICS AND DIFFERENTIAL PATTERNS OF L/A+17C
POLITICAL INTEGRATION: PROJECTIONS ABOUT UNITY IN INT/ORG
LATIN AMERICA." SOCIETY NAT/G DELIB/GP ACT/RES MARKET
CREATE PLAN ECO/TAC REGION ROUTINE ATTIT DRIVE PWR
WEALTH...CONCPT TREND CHARTS LAFTA 20. PAGE 24
G0464

S64
MARES V.E.,"EAST EUROPE'S SECOND CHANCE." COM VOL/ASSN
EUR+WWI HUNGARY ROMANIA USSR YUGOSLAVIA ECO/UNDEV ECO/TAC
NAT/G TOP/EX CREATE PLAN TEC/DEV REGION NAT/LISM
RIGID/FLEX PWR...CONCPT STAT COMECON 20. PAGE 36
G0705

B65
FOSTER P.,EDUCATION AND SOCIAL CHANGE IN GHANA. SCHOOL
GHANA CULTURE STRUC ECO/UNDEV TEC/DEV REGION CREATE
EFFICIENCY LITERACY ALL/VALS SOVEREIGN...STAT SOCIETY
METH/COMP 19/20 GOLD/COAST. PAGE 20 G0385

B65
KASER M.,COMECON* INTEGRATION PROBLEMS OF THE PLAN
PLANNED ECONOMIES. INT/ORG TEC/DEV INT/TRADE PRICE ECO/DEV
ADMIN ADJUST CENTRAL...STAT TIME/SEQ ORG/CHARTS COM
COMECON. PAGE 29 G0579 REGION

S65
BLOOMFIELD L.P.,"ARMS CONTROL AND THE DEVELOPING ARMS/CONT
COUNTRIES." AFR ISLAM S/ASIA USA+45 VOL/ASSN ECO/UNDEV
TEC/DEV DIPLOM REGION NUC/PWR...PREDICT TREND. HYPO/EXP
PAGE 7 G0142 OBS

S65
HOLSTI O.R.,"EAST-WEST CONFLICT AND SINO-SOVIET VOL/ASSN
RELATIONS" CHINA/COM USSR COMPUTER REGION DECISION. DIPLOM
PAGE 27 G0523 CON/ANAL
COM

S65
MARTIN A.,"PROLIFERATION." FUT WOR+45 PROB/SOLV RECORD
REGION ADJUST...PREDICT NAT/COMP UN TREATY. PAGE 36 NUC/PWR
G0712 ARMS/CONT
VOL/ASSN

B66

MURDOCK J.C.,RESEARCH AND REGIONS. AGRI FINAN INDUS LOC/G MUNIC NAT/G PROB/SOLV TEC/DEV ADMIN REGION 20. PAGE 40 G0796

BIBLIOG
ECO/DEV
COMPUT/IR
R+D

S66

BROWNLIE I.,"NUCLEAR PROLIFERATION* SOME PROBLEMS OF CONTROL." USA+45 USSR ECO/UNDEV INT/ORG FORCES TEC/DEV REGION CONSEN...RECORD TREATY. PAGE 9 G0181

NUC/PWR
ARMS/CONT
VOL/ASSN
ORD/FREE

B67

MOORE J.R.,THE ECONOMIC IMPACT OF THE TVA. AGRI INDUS PLAN BARGAIN CONTROL REGION GOV/REL DEMAND EFFICIENCY SOCISM 20 TVA. PAGE 40 G0780

ECO/UNDEV
ECO/DEV
NAT/G
CREATE

B67

PADELFORD N.J.,THE DYNAMICS OF INTERNATIONAL POLITICS (2ND ED.). WOR+45 LAW INT/ORG FORCES TEC/DEV REGION NAT/LISM PEACE ATTIT PWR ALL/IDEOS UN COLD/WAR NATO TREATY. PAGE 43 G0856

DIPLOM
NAT/G
POLICY
DECISION

B67

ROACH J.R.,THE UNITED STATES AND THE ATLANTIC COMMUNITY; ISSUES AND PROSPECTS. WOR+45 TEC/DEV ECO/TAC COLONIAL REGION PEACE ROLE...ANTHOL NATO COLD/WAR EEC. PAGE 47 G0925

INT/ORG
POLICY
ADJUST
DIPLOM

B67

RUSSETT B.M.,ARMS CONTROL IN EUROPE: PROPOSALS AND POLITICAL CONSTRAINTS. GERMANY WOR+45 POL/PAR BARGAIN DIPLOM...TREND CHARTS 20 COLD/WAR. PAGE 48 G0950

ARMS/CONT
REGION
METH/COMP

S67

DEUTSCH K.W.,"ARMS CONTROL AND EUROPEAN UNITY* THE NEXT TEN YEARS." USA+45 ELITES NAT/G BAL/PWR DIPLOM NUC/PWR...INT KNO/TEST NATO EEC. PAGE 15 G0300

ARMS/CONT
PEACE
REGION
PLAN

S67

SINGH B.,"ITALIAN EXPERIENCE IN REGIONAL ECONOMIC DEVELOPMENT AND LESSONS FOR OTHER COUNTRIES." EUR+WWI ITALY INDUS NAT/G ACT/RES REGION GP/REL EFFICIENCY EQUILIB PRODUC WEALTH. PAGE 51 G1007

ECO/UNDEV
PLAN
ECO/TAC
CONTROL

REGRESS....REGRESSION ANALYSIS; SEE ALSO CON/ANAL

B48

WEINER N.,CYBERNETICS. SOCIETY COMPUTER ADJUST EFFICIENCY UTIL PERCEPT...PSY MATH REGRESS TIME. PAGE 63 G1226

FEEDBACK
AUTOMAT
CONTROL
TEC/DEV

B64

BRILLOUIN L.,SCIENTIFIC UNCERTAINTY AND INFORMATION. PROB/SOLV AUTOMAT PERCEPT ORD/FREE ...MATH REGRESS STAT STYLE OBS IDEA/COMP SIMUL TIME. PAGE 9 G0169

PHIL/SCI
NEW/IDEA
METH/CNCPT
CREATE

REGRESSION ANALYSIS....SEE REGRESS

REHABILITATION....SEE REHABILITN

REHABILITN....REHABILITATION

REICH C.A. G0910

REINTANZ G. G0911

REISS A.J. G0912

RELATIONS AMONG GROUPS....SEE GP/REL

RELATISM....RELATIVISM

RELATIV....RELATIVITY

B11

BERGSON H.,CREATIVE EVOLUTION. FUT WOR+45 WOR-45 INTELL AGRI R+D ATTIT PERCEPT PERSON RIGID/FLEX ...RELATIV PHIL/SCI PSY METH/CNCPT MATH HIST/WRIT TREND HYPO/EXP TOT/POP. PAGE 7 G0127

BIO/SOC
KNOWL

B44

KAUFMANN F.,METHODOLOGY OF THE SOCIAL SCIENCES. PERSON...RELATIV PSY CONCPT LING METH 20. PAGE 30 G0585

SOC
PHIL/SCI
GEN/LAWS
METH/CNCPT

B56

BLACKETT P.M.S.,ATOMIC WEAPONS AND EAST-WEST RELATIONS. FUT WOR+45 INT/ORG DELIB/GP COERCE ATTIT RIGID/FLEX KNOWL...RELATIV HIST/WRIT TREND GEN/METH

FORCES
PWR
ARMS/CONT

COLD/WAR 20. PAGE 7 G0138

NUC/PWR

S59

MILBURN T.W.,"WHAT CONSTITUTES EFFECTIVE DETERRENCE." USA+45 USSR WOR+45 STRUCT FORCES ACT/RES PLAN SUPEGO KNOWL ORD/FREE PWR...RELATIV PSY CONCPT VAL/FREE 20 COLD/WAR. PAGE 39 G0768

INTELL
ATTIT
DETER
NUC/PWR

B60

EINSTEIN A.,EINSTEIN ON PEACE. FUT WOR+45 WOR-45 SOCIETY NAT/G PLAN BAL/PWR CAP/ISM DIPLOM ARMS/CONT DETER NAT/LISM...POLICY RELATIV HUM PHIL/SCI CONCPT BIOG COLD/WAR LEAGUE/NAT NAZI. PAGE 17 G0338

INT/ORG
ATTIT
NUC/PWR
PEACE

B64

LI C.M.,INDUSTRIAL DEVELOPMENT IN COMMUNIST CHINA. CHINA/COM ECO/DEV ECO/UNDEV AGRI FINAN INDUS MARKET LABOR NAT/G ECO/TAC INT/TRADE EXEC ALL/VALS ...POLICY RELATIV TREND WORK TOT/POP VAL/FREE 20. PAGE 34 G0665

ASIA
TEC/DEV

L64

WARD C.,"THE 'NEW MYTHS' AND 'OLD REALITIES' OF NUCLEAR WAR." COM FUT USA+45 USSR WOR+45 INT/ORG NAT/G DOMIN LEGIT EXEC ATTIT PERCEPT ALL/VALS ...POLICY RELATIV PSY MYTH TREND 20. PAGE 62 G1212

FORCES
COERCE
ARMS/CONT
NUC/PWR

S64

CALDWELL L.K.,"BIOPOLITICS: SCIENCE, ETHICS, AND PUBLIC POLICY." FUT USA+45 WOR+45 INTELL STRATA R+D NAT/G CONSULT PLAN EDU/PROP ALL/VALS...RELATIV PHIL/SCI 20. PAGE 10 G0203

TEC/DEV
POLICY

S64

NEEDHAM T.,"SCIENCE AND SOCIETY IN EAST AND WEST." INTELL STRATA R+D LOC/G NAT/G PROVS CONSULT ACT/RES CREATE PLAN TEC/DEV EDU/PROP ADMIN ATTIT ALL/VALS ...POLICY RELATIV MGT CONCPT NEW/IDEA TIME/SEQ WORK WORK. PAGE 41 G0815

ASIA
STRUCT

RELATIVISM....SEE RELATISM, RELATIV

RELATIVITY....SEE RELATIV

RELIABILITY....SEE METH/CNCPT

RELIGION....SEE SECT, WORSHIP

RELIGIOUS GROUP....SEE SECT

REMINGTON D. G0467

RENAISSAN....RENAISSANCE

B58

ORTEGA Y GASSET J.,MAN AND CRISIS. SECT CREATE PERSON CONSERVE...GEN/LAWS RENAISSAN. PAGE 43 G0846

PHIL/SCI
CULTURE
CONCPT

RENAN E. G0913

RENT....RENTING

REP/CONVEN....REPUBLICAN (PARTY - U.S.) NATIONAL CONVENTION

REPAR....REPARATIONS; SEE ALSO INT/REL, SANCTION

REPARATIONS....SEE REPAR

REPRESENT....REPRESENTATION; SEE ALSO LEGIS

B40

MORSTEIN-MARX F.,PUBLIC MANAGEMENT IN THE NEW DEMOCRACY. REPRESENT...MGT 20. PAGE 40 G0786

EX/STRUC
ADMIN
EXEC
PWR

B42

BINGHAM A.M.,THE TECHNIQUES OF DEMOCRACY. USA-45 CONSTN STRUCT POL/PAR LEGIS PLAN PARTIC CHOOSE REPRESENT NAT/LISM TOTALISM...MGT 20. PAGE 7 G0136

POPULISM
ORD/FREE
ADMIN
NAT/G

B44

BARKER E.,THE DEVELOPMENT OF PUBLIC SERVICES IN WESTERN WUROPE: 1660-1930. FRANCE GERMANY UK SCHOOL CONTROL REPRESENT ROLE...WELF/ST 17/20. PAGE 5 G0095

GOV/COMP
ADMIN
EX/STRUC

B44

MERRIAM C.E.,PUBLIC AND PRIVATE GOVERNMENT. VOL/ASSN EDU/PROP ADMIN REPRESENT EFFICIENCY PWR PLURALISM...MAJORIT CONCPT. PAGE 38 G0755

NAT/G
NEIGH
MGT
POLICY

B45
WHITE L.D.,CIVIL SERVICE IN WARTIME. CONSULT REPRESENT
DELIB/GP PARTIC WAR CHOOSE. PAGE 63 G1233 ADMIN
INTELL
NAT/G

S53
PERKINS J.A.,"ADMINISTRATION OF THE NATIONAL CONTROL
SECURITY PROGRAM." USA+45 EX/STRUC FORCES ADMIN GP/REL
CIVMIL/REL ORD/FREE 20. PAGE 44 G0868 REPRESENT
PROB/SOLV

S54
LONG N.E.,"PUBLIC POLICY AND ADMINISTRATION: THE PROB/SOLV
GOALS OF RATIONALITY AND RESPONSIBILITY." EX/STRUC EXEC
ADMIN LEAD 20. PAGE 34 G0676 REPRESENT

C54
ZELLER B.,"AMERICAN STATE LEGISLATURES: REPORT ON REPRESENT
THE COMMITTEE ON AMERICAN LEGISLATURES." CONSTN LEGIS
POL/PAR EX/STRUC CONFER ADMIN CONTROL EXEC LOBBY PROVS
ROUTINE GOV/REL...POLICY BIBLIOG 20. PAGE 65 G1267 APPORT

B56
REDFORD E.S.,PUBLIC ADMINISTRATION AND POLICY EX/STRUC
FORMATION: STUDIES IN OIL, GAS, BANKING, RIVER PROB/SOLV
DEVELOPMENT AND CORPORATE INVESTIGATIONS. USA+45 CONTROL
CLIENT NAT/G ADMIN LOBBY REPRESENT GOV/REL INGP/REL EXEC
20. PAGE 46 G0908

S57
BAUMGARTEL H.,"LEADERSHIP STYLE AS A VARIABLE IN LEAD
RESEARCH ADMINISTRATION." USA+45 ADMIN REPRESENT EXEC
PERS/REL 20. PAGE 5 G0104 MGT
INGP/REL

S58
KEISER N.F.,"PUBLIC RESPONSIBILITY AND FEDERAL REPRESENT
ADVISORY GROUPS: A CASE STUDY." NAT/G ADMIN CONTROL ELITES
LOBBY...POLICY 20. PAGE 30 G0590 GP/REL
EX/STRUC

S59
SHEENAN D.,"PUBLIC CORPORATIONS AND PUBLIC ACTION." ECO/DEV
UK ADMIN CONTROL REPRESENT SOCISM 20. PAGE 50 G0990 EFFICIENCY
EX/STRUC
EXEC

S59
STREAT R.,"GOVERNMENT CONSULTATION WITH INDUSTRY." REPRESENT
UK 20. PAGE 53 G1043 ADMIN
EX/STRUC
INDUS

S60
HALSEY A.H.,"THE CHANGING FUNCTIONS OF UNIVERSITIES ACADEM
IN ADVANCED INDUSTRIAL SOCIETIES." R+D EDU/PROP CREATE
REPRESENT ROLE ORD/FREE PWR TREND. PAGE 24 G0476 CULTURE
ADJUST

S60
TAYLOR M.G.,"THE ROLE OF THE MEDICAL PROFESSION IN PROF/ORG
THE FORMULATION AND EXECUTION OF PUBLIC POLICY" HEALTH
(BMR)" CANADA NAT/G CONSULT ADMIN REPRESENT GP/REL LOBBY
ROLE SOVEREIGN...DECISION 20 CMA. PAGE 54 G1058 POLICY

S61
FAIR M.L.,"PORT AUTHORITIES IN THE UNITED STATES." MUNIC
PROB/SOLV ADMIN LEAD REPRESENT PWR...DECISION GEOG. REGION
PAGE 18 G0357 LOC/G
GOV/REL

S61
LYONS G.M.,"THE NEW CIVIL-MILITARY RELATIONS." CIVMIL/REL
USA+45 NAT/G EX/STRUC TOP/EX PROB/SOLV ADMIN EXEC PWR
PARTIC 20. PAGE 35 G0681 REPRESENT

B62
REICH C.A.,BUREAUCRACY AND THE FORESTS (PAMPHLET). ADMIN
USA+45 LOBBY...POLICY MGT 20. PAGE 46 G0910 CONTROL
EX/STRUC
REPRESENT

L62
CAVERS D.F.,"ADMINISTRATIVE DECISION-MAKING IN REPRESENT
NUCLEAR FACILITIES LICENSING." USA+45 CLIENT ADMIN LOBBY
EXEC 20 AEC. PAGE 11 G0218 PWR
CONTROL

B63
HATHAWAY D.A.,GOVERNMENT AND AGRICULTURE: PUBLIC AGRI
POLICY IN A DEMOCRATIC SOCIETY. USA+45 LEGIS ADMIN GOV/REL
EXEC LOBBY REPRESENT PWR 20. PAGE 25 G0491 PROB/SOLV
EX/STRUC

B63
HOWER R.M.,MANAGERS AND SCIENTISTS. EX/STRUC CREATE R+D
ADMIN REPRESENT ATTIT DRIVE ROLE PWR SKILL...SOC MGT
INT. PAGE 27 G0532 PERS/REL
INGP/REL

B63
PEABODY R.L.,NEW PERSPECTIVES ON THE HOUSE OF NEW/IDEA
REPRESENTATIVES. AGRI FINAN SCHOOL FORCES CONFER LEGIS
LEAD CHOOSE REPRESENT FEDERAL...POLICY DECISION PWR
HOUSE/REP. PAGE 44 G0862 ADMIN

S65
LEISERSON A.,"SCIENTISTS AND THE POLICY PROCESS." PHIL/SCI
USA+45 NAT/G LEAD PARTIC REPRESENT. PAGE 33 G0654 ADMIN
EX/STRUC
EXEC

B66
GORDON G.,THE LEGISLATIVE PROCESS AND DIVIDED LEGIS
GOVERNMENT: A CASE STUDY OF THE 86TH CONGRESS. HABITAT
USA+45 POL/PAR PROVS PROB/SOLV BAL/PWR CHOOSE CHIEF
REPRESENT EFFICIENCY ATTIT...POLICY DECISION STAT NAT/G
20 CONGRESS EISNHWR/DD. PAGE 22 G0434

B66
STREET D.,ORGANIZATION FOR TREATMENT. CLIENT PROVS GP/COMP
PUB/INST PLAN CONTROL PARTIC REPRESENT ATTIT PWR AGE/Y
...POLICY BIBLIOG. PAGE 53 G1044 ADMIN
VOL/ASSN

B67
UNIVERSAL REFERENCE SYSTEM.LEGISLATIVE PROCESS, BIBLIOG/A
REPRESENTATION, AND DECISION-MAKING (VOLUME II). LEGIS
WOR+45 WOR-45 CONSTN LOC/G NAT/G...POLICY CON/ANAL REPRESENT
COMPUT/IR GEN/METH. PAGE 56 G1094 DECISION

S67
TIVEY L.,"THE POLITICAL CONSEQUENCES OF ECONOMIC PLAN
PLANNING." UK CONSTN INDUS ACT/RES ADMIN CONTROL POLICY
LOBBY REPRESENT EFFICIENCY SUPEGO SOVEREIGN NAT/G
...DECISION 20. PAGE 55 G1074

REPUBLIC OF CHINA....SEE TAIWAN

REPUBLICAN....REPUBLICAN PARTY (ALL NATIONS)

RESEARCH....SEE ACT/RES, OP/RES, R+D, CREATE

RESEARCH AND DEVELOPMENT GROUP....SEE R+D

RESIST/INT....SOCIAL RESISTANCE TO INTERVIEWS

RESOURCE/N....NATURAL RESOURCES

B61
HODGKINS J.A.,SOVIET POWER: ENERGY RESOURCES, GEOG
PRODUCTION AND POTENTIALS. USSR ECO/DEV INDUS EXTR/IND
MARKET...POLICY STAT CHARTS 20 RESOURCE/N. PAGE 26 TEC/DEV
G0518

B61
LEE R.R.,ENGINEERING-ECONOMIC PLANNING BIBLIOG/A
MISCELLANEOUS SUBJECTS: A SELECTED BIBLIOGRAPHY PLAN
(MIMEOGRAPHED). FINAN LOC/G MUNIC NEIGH ADMIN REGION
CONTROL INGP/REL HABITAT...GEOG MGT SOC/WK 20
RESOURCE/N. PAGE 33 G0651

S63
ENTHOVEN A.C.,"ECONOMIC ANALYSIS IN THE DEPARTMENT PLAN
OF DEFENSE." USA+45 NAT/G DELIB/GP PROB/SOLV RATION BUDGET
NUC/PWR WEAPON COST...DECISION 20 DEPT/DEFEN ECO/TAC
RESOURCE/N. PAGE 18 G0349 FORCES

B65
WHITE HOUSE CONFERENCE ON INTERNATIONAL R+D
COOPERATION(VOL.II). SPACE WOR+45 EXTR/IND INT/ORG CONFER
LABOR WORKER NUC/PWR PEACE AGE/Y...CENSUS ANTHOL 20 TEC/DEV
RESOURCE/N URBAN/RNWL PUB/TRANS. PAGE 1 G0019 DIPLOM

B65
JASNY H.,KHRUSHCHEV'S CROP POLICY. USSR ECO/DEV AGRI
PLAN MARXISM...STAT 20 KHRUSH/N RESOURCE/N. PAGE 29 NAT/G
G0562 POLICY
ECO/TAC

RESPECT....RESPECT, SOCIAL CLASS, STRATIFICATION (CONTEMPT)

B57
KIETH-LUCAS A.,DECISIONS ABOUT PEOPLE IN NEED, A ADMIN
STUDY OF ADMINISTRATIVE RESPONSIVENESS IN PUBLIC RIGID/FLEX
ASSISTANCE. USA+45 GIVE RECEIVE INGP/REL PERS/REL SOC/WK
MORAL RESPECT WEALTH...SOC OBS BIBLIOG 20. PAGE 30 DECISION
G0595

S57
JANOWITZ M.,"MILITARY ELITES AND THE STUDY OF WAR."   FORCES
USA+45 WOR+45 STRATA NAT/G PROF/ORG TEC/DEV DOMIN   ELITES
EDU/PROP COERCE WAR ATTIT RIGID/FLEX PWR RESPECT
...MGT TREND STERTYP GEN/METH 20. PAGE 28 G0558

B60
HEILBRONER R.L.,THE FUTURE AS HISTORY. USA+45   TEC/DEV
WOR+45 WOR-45 SOCIETY ECO/DEV ECO/UNDEV VOL/ASSN   TREND
PLAN CAP/ISM NUC/PWR CHOOSE NAT/LISM ATTIT ORD/FREE
RESPECT WEALTH SOCISM 20. PAGE 25 G0501

S60
DOTY P.M.,"THE ROLE OF THE SMALLER POWERS." FUT   PWR
WOR+45 NAT/G TEC/DEV BAL/PWR DOMIN LEGIT CHOOSE   POLICY
DISPL DRIVE RESPECT...DECISION 20. PAGE 16 G0310   ARMS/CONT
                                                      NUC/PWR

S60
KELLEY G.A.,"THE POLITICAL BACKGROUND OF THE FRENCH   NAT/G
A-BOMB." EUR+WWI USSR FORCES TOP/EX TEC/DEV NUC/PWR   RESPECT
ATTIT PWR...CONCPT OBS/ENVIR TREND 20. PAGE 30   NAT/LISM
G0591   FRANCE

S62
MORGENTHAU H.J.,"A POLITICAL THEORY OF FOREIGN   USA+45
AID." ECO/UNDEV NAT/G DELIB/GP PLAN ECO/TAC   PHIL/SCI
EDU/PROP EXEC ORD/FREE RESPECT WEALTH...METH/CNCPT   FOR/AID
TREND 20. PAGE 40 G0783

B64
ETZIONI A.,THE MOON-DOGGLE: DOMESTIC AND   R+D
INTERNATIONAL IMPLICATIONS OF THE SPACE RACE. FUT   NAT/G
USA+45 WOR+45 INTELL ECO/DEV INDUS VOL/ASSN   DIPLOM
EX/STRUC FORCES LEGIS TOP/EX PLAN TEC/DEV ECO/TAC   SPACE
EDU/PROP KNOWL ORD/FREE PWR RESPECT WEALTH
TIME/SEQ. PAGE 18 G0352

B64
VAN DYKE V.,PRIDE AND POWER: THE RATIONALE OF THE   TEC/DEV
SPACE PROGRAM. FUT USA+45 INTELL R+D NAT/G POL/PAR   ATTIT
DELIB/GP EX/STRUC LEGIS TOP/EX ACT/RES PLAN ECO/TAC   POLICY
EDU/PROP ORD/FREE PWR RESPECT SKILL...TIME/SEQ
VAL/FREE. PAGE 61 G1191

L64
GOLDBERG A.,"ATOMIC ORIGINS OF THE BRITISH NUCLEAR   CREATE
DETERRENT." EUR+WWI UK NAT/G TOP/EX PLAN BAL/PWR   FORCES
DOMIN DETER CHOOSE ATTIT DRIVE HEALTH ORD/FREE PWR   NUC/PWR
RESPECT...CONCPT VAL/FREE COLD/WAR 20 CMN/WLTH.
PAGE 22 G0425

S64
SPONSLER G.C.,"THE MILITARY ROLE IN SPACE." FUT   TEC/DEV
USA+45 SEA AIR NAT/G ACT/RES PLAN COERCE NUC/PWR   FORCES
WEAPON KNOWL ORD/FREE PWR RESPECT...TREND 20.   SPACE
PAGE 52 G1026

S65
GRIFFITH S.B.,"COMMUNIST CHINA'S CAPACITY TO MAKE   FORCES
WAR." CHINA/COM COM NAT/G TOP/EX PLAN DOMIN COERCE   PWR
NUC/PWR ATTIT RESPECT SKILL...CONCPT MYTH TIME/SEQ   WEAPON
TREND COLD/WAR 20. PAGE 23 G0452   ASIA

RESPONSIBILITY....SEE SUPEGO, RESPECT

RESPONSIVENESS....SEE RIGID/FLEX

RESTRAINT....SEE ORD/FREE

RETAILING....SEE MARKET

RETIREMENT....SEE SENIOR, ADMIN

REUTHER/W....WALTER REUTHER

REV....REVOLUTION; SEE ALSO WAR

B38
HARPER S.N.,THE GOVERNMENT OF THE SOVIET UNION. COM   MARXISM
USSR LAW CONSTN ECO/DEV PLAN TEC/DEV DIPLOM   NAT/G
INT/TRADE ADMIN REV NAT/LISM...POLICY 20. PAGE 24   LEAD
G0483   POL/PAR

S51
MACRAE D.G.,"THE BOLSHEVIK IDEOLOGY; THE   MARXISM
INTELLECTUAL AND EMOTIONAL FACTORS IN COMMUNIST   INTELL
AFFILIATION" (BMR)" COM LEAD REV ATTIT ORD/FREE   PHIL/SCI
...SOC CON/ANAL 20 BOLSHEVISM. PAGE 35 G0693   SECT

B54
HART B.H.L.,STRATEGY (REV. ED.). CHRIST-17C EUR+WWI   WAR
MEDIT-7 MOD/EUR TEC/DEV LEAD REV WEAPON...POLICY   PLAN
CHARTS. PAGE 25 G0486   FORCES
                                                      PHIL/SCI

B56
US DEPARTMENT OF THE ARMY,AMERICAN MILITARY   BIBLIOG
HISTORY. USA+45 USA-45 EX/STRUC PROB/SOLV TEC/DEV   FORCES
DIPLOM NUC/PWR REV WAR WEAPON...PSY 18/20. PAGE 57   NAT/G
G1125

B60
WILLIAUS T.H.,AMERICANS AT WAR: THE DEVELOPMENT OF   FORCES
THE AMERICAN MILITARY SYSTEM. USA+45 USA-45   WAR
EDU/PROP LEAD REV...GP/COMP BIBLIOG/A 18/20   NAT/G
PRESIDENT. PAGE 63 G1244   POLICY

B62
BURKE A.E.,ENOUGH GOOD MEN. USA+45 WOR+45 ECO/UNDEV   DIPLOM
FORCES TEC/DEV GUERRILLA NUC/PWR REV WAR ORD/FREE   POLICY
MARXISM...GEOG 20 COLD/WAR. PAGE 10 G0189   NAT/G
                                                      TASK

B62
PERRE J.,LES MUTATIONS DE LA GUERRE MODERNE: DE LA   WAR
REVOLUTION FRANCAISE A LA REVOLUTION NUCLEAIRE.   FORCES
DIPLOM ARMS/CONT DEATH REV WEAPON GP/REL PEACE   NUC/PWR
ATTIT...STAT PREDICT BIBLIOG 18/20 WWI. PAGE 44
G0870

B63
FLORES E.,LAND REFORM AND THE ALLIANCE FOR PROGRESS   AGRI
(PAMPHLET). L/A+17C USA+45 STRUCT ECO/UNDEV NAT/G   INT/ORG
WORKER CREATE PLAN ECO/TAC COERCE REV 20. PAGE 19   DIPLOM
G0373   POLICY

B63
GEERTZ C.,OLD SOCIETIES AND NEW STATES: THE QUEST   ECO/UNDEV
FOR MODERNITY IN ASIA AND AFRICA. AFR ASIA LAW   TEC/DEV
CULTURE SECT EDU/PROP REV...GOV/COMP NAT/COMP 20.   NAT/LISM
PAGE 21 G0415   SOVEREIGN

B64
POWELSON J.P.,LATIN AMERICA: TODAY'S ECONOMIC AND   ECO/UNDEV
SOCIAL REVOLUTION. L/A+17C INTELL SOCIETY STRUCT   WEALTH
AGRI INDUS NAT/G DIPLOM ECO/TAC REV...POLICY 20.   ADJUST
PAGE 45 G0887   PLAN

S65
HSIEH A.L.,"THE SINO-SOVIET NUCLEAR DIALOGUE*   ASIA
1963." S/ASIA USA+45 RISK DETER REV WAR SOVEREIGN   USSR
IDEA/COMP. PAGE 27 G0533   NUC/PWR

C65
MARK M.,"BEYOND SOVEREIGNTY." WOR+45 WOR-45   NAT/LISM
ECO/UNDEV BAL/PWR INT/TRADE NUC/PWR REV WAR MARXISM   NAT/G
NEW/LIB BIBLIOG. PAGE 36 G0706   DIPLOM
                                                      INTELL

B66
FALK R.A.,ON MINIMIZING THE USE OF NUCLEAR WEAPONS;   DIPLOM
THREE ESSAYS; RESEARCH MONOGRAPH NO. 23. WOR+45   EQUILIB
STRUCT CREATE NUC/PWR REV CONSERVE...POLICY   PHIL/SCI
NET/THEORY IDEA/COMP GEN/LAWS GEN/METH. PAGE 18   PROB/SOLV
G0359

B66
US DEPARTMENT OF THE ARMY,COMMUNIST CHINA: A   BIBLIOG/A
STRATEGIC SURVEY: A BIBLIOGRAPHY (PAMPHLET NO.   MARXISM
20-67). CHINA/COM COM INDIA USSR NAT/G POL/PAR   S/ASIA
EX/STRUC FORCES NUC/PWR REV ATTIT...POLICY GEOG   DIPLOM
CHARTS. PAGE 58 G1133

B67
MCCLINTOCK R.,THE MEANING OF LIMITED WAR. FUT   WAR
WOR+45 NAT/G FORCES GUERRILLA REV...POLICY SAMP/SIZ   NUC/PWR
TREND NAT/COMP 45 COLD/WAR. PAGE 37 G0730   BAL/PWR
                                                      DIPLOM

S67
CHIU S.M.,"CHINA'S MILITARY POSTURE." CHINA/COM   FORCES
ELITES NAT/G POL/PAR TEC/DEV ECO/TAC DOMIN CONTROL   CIVMIL/REL
LEAD REV MARXISM 20 MAO. PAGE 12 G0228   NUC/PWR
                                                      DIPLOM

S67
WARE R.S.,"FORECAST A.D. 2000." SOCIETY STRATA   NUC/PWR
ECO/UNDEV INDUS FORCES EDU/PROP AUTOMAT COERCE REV   GEOG
WEAPON ATTIT PREDICT. PAGE 62 G1213   TEC/DEV
                                                      WAR

REVES E. G0914

REVOLUTION....SEE REV

REWARD....SEE SANCTION

REYNOLDS P.A. G0915

RHENMAN E. G0240

RHODE/ISL....RHODE ISLAND

RHODES/C....CECIL RHODES

RHODESIA....SEE ALSO AFR

RICARDO/D....DAVID RICARDO

RICH G.S. G0916

RICHARD/H....HENRY RICHARD (WELSH POLITICIAN - 19TH CENTURY)

RICHMAN B.M. G0917

RICHSTEIN A.R. G0918

RIDKER R.G. G0919

RIES J.C. G0920

RIESMAN/D....DAVID RIESMAN

B63
RUITENBEER H.M.,THE DILEMMA OF ORGANIZATIONAL SOCIETY. CULTURE ECO/DEV MUNIC SECT TEC/DEV EDU/PROP NAT/LISM ORD/FREE...NAT/COMP 20 RIESMAN/D WHYTE/WF MERTON/R MEAD/MARG JASPERS/K. PAGE 48 G0945 — PERSON ROLE ADMIN WORKER

RIGGS/FRED....FRED W. RIGGS

RIGHTS/MAN....RIGHTS OF MAN

RIGID/FLEX....DEGREE OF RESPONSIVENESS TO NEW IDEAS, METHODS, AND PEOPLE

B11
BERGSON H.,CREATIVE EVOLUTION. FUT WOR+45 WOR-45 INTELL AGRI R+D ATTIT PERCEPT PERSON RIGID/FLEX ...RELATIV PHIL/SCI PSY METH/CNCPT MATH HIST/WRIT TREND HYPO/EXP TOT/POP. PAGE 7 G0127 — BIO/SOC KNOWL

B46
NORTHROP F.S.C.,THE MEETING OF EAST AND WEST. EUR+WWI FUT MOD/EUR UNIV WOR+45 WOR-45 INTELL SOCIETY EX/STRUC TOP/EX ACT/RES LEGIT CHOOSE ATTIT PERCEPT RIGID/FLEX ALL/VALS...POLICY JURID OBS TOT/POP. PAGE 42 G0826 — DRIVE TREND PEACE

B46
VINER J.,SYMPOSIUM ON ATOMIC ENERGY AND ITS IMPLICATIONS. USA+45 WOR+45 SOCIETY DELIB/GP...SOC CONCPT TIME/SEQ TOT/POP 20. PAGE 61 G1200 — R+D RIGID/FLEX NUC/PWR

L46
MASTERS D.,"ONE WORLD OR NONE." FUT WOR+45 INTELL INT/ORG ACT/RES EDU/PROP DETER ATTIT RIGID/FLEX SUPEGO KNOWL...STAT TREND ORG/CHARTS 20. PAGE 36 G0719 — POLICY PHIL/SCI ARMS/CONT NUC/PWR

S48
COCH L.,"OVERCOMING RESISTANCE TO CHANGE" (BMR)" USA+45 CONSULT ADMIN ROUTINE GP/REL EFFICIENCY PRODUC PERCEPT SKILL...CHARTS SOC/EXP 20. PAGE 12 G0236 — WORKER OP/RES PROC/MFG RIGID/FLEX

S50
BAVELAS A.,"COMMUNICATION PATTERNS IN TASK-ORIENTED GROUPS" (BMR)" R+D OP/RES INSPECT LEAD CENTRAL EFFICIENCY HAPPINESS RIGID/FLEX...PROBABIL 20. PAGE 6 G0106 — ACT/RES PERS/REL TASK INGP/REL

S52
KECSKEMETI P.,"THE 'POLICY SCIENCES': ASPIRATION AND OUTLOOK." UNIV CULTURE INTELL SOCIETY STRUCT EDU/PROP ATTIT PERCEPT RIGID/FLEX KNOWL...PHIL/SCI METH/CNCPT OBS 20. PAGE 30 G0589 — CREATE NEW/IDEA

B53
EASTON D.,THE POLITICAL SYSTEM, AN INQUIRY INTO THE STATE POLITICAL SCIENCE. USA+45 INTELL CREATE EDU/PROP RIGID/FLEX KNOWL SKILL...PHIL/SCI NEW/IDEA STERTYP TOT/POP 20. PAGE 17 G0329 — R+D PERCEPT

B53
HOVLAND C.I.,COMMUNICATION AND PERSUASION: PSYCHOLOGICAL STUDIES OF OPINION CHANGE. INTELL SOCIETY ECO/DEV COM/IND R+D SERV/IND CREATE TEC/DEV ATTIT RIGID/FLEX KNOWL NEW/IDEA. PAGE 27 G0531 — PSY EDU/PROP

B54
COMBS C.H.,DECISION PROCESSES. INTELL SOCIETY DELIB/GP CREATE TEC/DEV DOMIN LEGIT EXEC CHOOSE DRIVE RIGID/FLEX KNOWL PWR...PHIL/SCI SOC METH/CNCPT CONT/OBS REC/INT PERS/TEST SAMP/SIZ BIOG SOC/EXP WORK. PAGE 13 G0245 — MATH DECISION

S55
DRUCKER P.F.,"'MANAGEMENT SCIENCE' AND THE MANAGER." PLAN ROUTINE RIGID/FLEX...METH/CNCPT LOG HYPO/EXP. PAGE 16 G0315 — MGT STRUCT DECISION RATIONAL

S55
VON NEUMANN J.,"CAN WE SURVIVE TECHNOLOGY?" WOR+45 AIR INDUS ADMIN ADJUST RIGID/FLEX...GEOG PHIL/SCI NEW/IDEA 20. PAGE 61 G1202 — TEC/DEV NUC/PWR FUT HABITAT

B56
BLACKETT P.M.S.,ATOMIC WEAPONS AND EAST-WEST RELATIONS. FUT WOR+45 INT/ORG DELIB/GP COERCE ATTIT RIGID/FLEX KNOWL...RELATIV HIST/WRIT TREND GEN/METH COLD/WAR 20. PAGE 7 G0138 — FORCES PWR ARMS/CONT NUC/PWR

B57
KIETH-LUCAS A.,DECISIONS ABOUT PEOPLE IN NEED, A STUDY OF ADMINISTRATIVE RESPONSIVENESS IN PUBLIC ASSISTANCE. USA+45 GIVE RECEIVE INGP/REL PERS/REL MORAL RESPECT WEALTH...SOC OBS BIBLIOG 20. PAGE 30 G0595 — ADMIN RIGID/FLEX SOC/WK DECISION

S57
JANOWITZ M.,"MILITARY ELITES AND THE STUDY OF WAR." USA+45 WOR-45 STRATA NAT/G PROF/ORG TEC/DEV DOMIN EDU/PROP COERCE WAR ATTIT RIGID/FLEX PWR RESPECT ...MGT TREND STERTYP GEN/METH 20. PAGE 28 G0558 — FORCES ELITES

S58
SINGER J.D.,"THREAT PERCEPTION AND THE ARMAMENT TENSION DILEMMA." WOR+45 WOR-45 ELITES INT/ORG NAT/G DELIB/GP PLAN LEGIT COERCE DETER ATTIT RIGID/FLEX PWR...DECISION PSY 20. PAGE 51 G1002 — PERCEPT ARMS/CONT BAL/PWR

B59
MIKSCHE F.O.,THE FAILURE OF ATOMIC STRATEGY. COM EUR+WWI INTELL POL/PAR FORCES PLAN ECO/TAC NUC/PWR ATTIT DRIVE RIGID/FLEX PWR...DECISION GEOG PSY CONCPT RECORD TREND CHARTS VAL/FREE 20. PAGE 39 G0766 — ACT/RES ORD/FREE DIPLOM ARMS/CONT

B60
WOETZEL R.K.,THE INTERNATIONAL CONTROL OF AIRSPACE AND OUTERSPACE. FUT WOR+45 AIR CONSTN STRUCT CONSULT PLAN TEC/DEV ADJUD RIGID/FLEX KNOWL ORD/FREE PWR...TECHNIC GEOG MGT NEW/IDEA TREND COMPUT/IR VAL/FREE 20 TREATY. PAGE 64 G1251 — INT/ORG JURID SPACE INT/LAW

L60
HOLTON G.,"ARMS CONTROL." FUT WOR+45 CULTURE INT/ORG NAT/G FORCES TOP/EX PLAN EDU/PROP COERCE ATTIT RIGID/FLEX ORD/FREE...POLICY PHIL/SCI SOC TREND COLD/WAR. PAGE 27 G0524 — ACT/RES CONSULT ARMS/CONT NUC/PWR

L60
JACOB P.E.,"THE DISARMAMENT CONSENSUS." USA+45 USSR WOR+45 INT/ORG NAT/G ACT/RES TEC/DEV BAL/PWR EDU/PROP ADMIN COERCE DETER NUC/PWR CONSEN RIGID/FLEX PWR...CONCPT RECORD CHARTS COLD/WAR 20. PAGE 28 G0552 — DELIB/GP ATTIT ARMS/CONT

L60
MACPHERSON C.,"TECHNICAL CHANGE AND POLITICAL DECISION." WOR+45 NAT/G CREATE CAP/ISM DIPLOM ROUTINE RIGID/FLEX...CONCPT OBS GEN/METH 20. PAGE 35 G0692 — TEC/DEV ADMIN

S60
BECKER A.S.,"COMPARISIONS OF UNITED STATES AND USSR NATIONAL OUTPUT: SOME RULES OF THE GAME." COM USA+45 ECO/DEV AGRI DIST/IND INDUS R+D CONSULT PLAN ECO/TAC RIGID/FLEX KNOWL...METH/CNCPT CHARTS 20. PAGE 6 G0113 — STAT USSR

S60
HUNTINGTON S.P.,"STRATEGIC PLANNING AND THE POLITICAL PROCESS." USA+45 NAT/G DELIB/GP LEGIS ACT/RES ECO/TAC LEGIT ROUTINE CHOOSE RIGID/FLEX PWR ...POLICY MAJORIT MGT 20. PAGE 27 G0538 — EXEC FORCES NUC/PWR WAR

S60
IKLE F.C.,"NTH COUNTRIES AND DISARMAMENT." WOR+45 DELIB/GP ECO/TAC DOMIN EDU/PROP LEGIT ROUTINE COERCE RIGID/FLEX ORD/FREE...MARXIST TREND 20. PAGE 28 G0543 — FUT INT/ORG ARMS/CONT NUC/PWR

S60
JAFFEE A.J.,"POPULATION TRENDS AND CONTROLS IN UNDERDEVELOPED COUNTRIES." AFR FUT ISLAM L/A+17C S/ASIA CULTURE R+D FAM ACT/RES PLAN EDU/PROP BIO/SOC RIGID/FLEX HEALTH...SOC STAT OBS CHARTS 20. PAGE 28 G0555 — ECO/UNDEV GEOG

TOT/POP VAL/FREE 20. PAGE 22 G0433

KISSINGER H.A.,"ARMS CONTROL, INSPECTION AND
SURPRISE ATTACK." COM USA+45 NAT/G ACT/RES PLAN
TEC/DEV DIPLOM EDU/PROP DETER WAR RIGID/FLEX
...CONCPT GEN/METH TOT/POP 20. PAGE 31 G0603
S60
FORCES
ORD/FREE
ARMS/CONT
NUC/PWR

RIVKIN A.,"AFRICAN ECONOMIC DEVELOPMENT: ADVANCED
TECHNOLOGY AND THE STAGES OF GROWTH." CULTURE
ECO/UNDEV AGRI COM/IND EXTR/IND PLAN ECO/TAC ATTIT
DRIVE RIGID/FLEX SKILL WEALTH...MGT SOC GEN/LAWS
WORK TOT/POP 20. PAGE 47 G0923
S60
AFR
TEC/DEV
FOR/AID

SWIFT R.,"THE UNITED NATIONS AND ITS PUBLIC."
WOR+45 CONSTN FINAN CONSULT DELIB/GP ACT/RES ADMIN
ROUTINE RIGID/FLEX SKILL UN 20. PAGE 53 G1048
S60
INT/ORG
EDU/PROP

RICHSTEIN A.R.,"LEGAL RULES IN NUCLEAR WEAPONS
EMPLOYMENTS." FUT WOR+45 LAW SOCIETY FORCES PLAN
WEAPON RIGID/FLEX...HEAL CONCPT TREND VAL/FREE 20.
PAGE 47 G0918
S61
NUC/PWR
TEC/DEV
MORAL
ARMS/CONT

CARSON R.,SILENT SPRING. USA+45 AIR CULTURE AGRI
INDUS ADMIN ATTIT RIGID/FLEX ORD/FREE PWR...POLICY
20. PAGE 11 G0216
B62
HABITAT
TREND
SOCIETY
CONTROL

FORBES H.W.,THE STRATEGY OF DISARMAMENT. FUT WOR+45
INT/ORG VOL/ASSN CONSULT ARMS/CONT COERCE NUC/PWR
WAR DRIVE RIGID/FLEX ORD/FREE PWR...POLICY CONCPT
OBS TREND STERTYP 20. PAGE 19 G0378
B62
PLAN
FORCES
DIPLOM

SCHILLING W.R.,STRATEGY, POLITICS, AND DEFENSE
BUDGETS. USA+45 R+D NAT/G CONSULT DELIB/GP FORCES
LEGIS ACT/RES PLAN BAL/PWR LEGIT EXEC NUC/PWR
RIGID/FLEX PWR...TREND COLD/WAR CONGRESS 20
EISNHWR/DD. PAGE 49 G0968
B62
ROUTINE
POLICY

THANT U.,THE UNITED NATIONS' DEVELOPMENT DECADE:
PROPOSALS FOR ACTION. WOR+45 SOCIETY ECO/UNDEV AGRI
COM/IND FINAN R+D MUNIC SCHOOL VOL/ASSN CONSULT
PLAN TEC/DEV ECO/TAC EDU/PROP ADMIN ROUTINE
RIGID/FLEX...MGT SOC CONCPT UNESCO UN TOT/POP
VAL/FREE. PAGE 54 G1064
B62
INT/ORG
ALL/VALS

WALSTON H.,AGRICULTURE UNDER COMMUNISM. CHINA/COM
COM PROB/SOLV HAPPINESS RIGID/FLEX...POLICY
METH/COMP 20. PAGE 62 G1207
B62
AGRI
MARXISM
PLAN
CREATE

WRIGHT Q.,PREVENTING WORLD WAR THREE. FUT WOR+45
CULTURE INT/ORG NAT/G CONSULT FORCES ADMIN
ARMS/CONT DRIVE RIGID/FLEX ORD/FREE SOVEREIGN
...POLICY CONCPT TREND STERTYP COLD/WAR 20. PAGE 64
G1259
B62
CREATE
ATTIT

FINKELSTEIN L.S.,"ARMS INSPECTION." FUT WOR+45
NAT/G DIPLOM ATTIT PERCEPT RIGID/FLEX ORD/FREE
COLD/WAR 20. PAGE 19 G0369
L62
FORCES
PWR
ARMS/CONT

FINKELSTEIN L.S.,"THE UNITED NATIONS AND
ORGANIZATIONS FOR CONTROL OF ARMAMENT." FUT WOR+45
VOL/ASSN DELIB/GP TOP/EX CREATE EDU/PROP LEGIT
ADJUD NUC/PWR ATTIT RIGID/FLEX ORD/FREE...POLICY
DECISION CONCPT OBS TREND GEN/LAWS TOT/POP
COLD/WAR. PAGE 19 G0368
S62
INT/ORG
PWR
ARMS/CONT

FOSTER R.B.,"UNILATERAL ARMS CONTROL MEASURES AND
DISARMAMENT NEGOTIATION." WOR+45 VOL/ASSN DELIB/GP
ACT/RES ECO/TAC EDU/PROP ATTIT RIGID/FLEX...CONCPT
MYTH TIME/SEQ COLD/WAR 20. PAGE 20 G0386
S62
PLAN
ORD/FREE
ARMS/CONT
DETER

FOSTER W.C.,"ARMS CONTROL AND DISARMAMENT IN A
DIVIDED WORLD." COM FUT USA+45 USSR WOR+45 INTELL
INT/ORG NAT/G VOL/ASSN CONSULT CREATE PLAN TEC/DEV
EDU/PROP LEGIT NUC/PWR ATTIT RIGID/FLEX...CONCPT
TREND TOT/POP 20 UN. PAGE 20 G0387
S62
DELIB/GP
POLICY
ARMS/CONT
DIPLOM

GORDON B.K.,"NUCLEAR WEAPONS: RUSSIAN AND
AMERICAN." COM USA+45 USSR NAT/G FORCES ACT/RES
TEC/DEV PERCEPT RIGID/FLEX PWR SKILL...MGT
METH/CNCPT QUANT OBS TIME/SEQ CON/ANAL GEN/METH
S62
ORD/FREE
COERCE
NUC/PWR

NANES A.,"DISARMAMENT: THE LAST SEVEN YEARS." COM
EUR+WWI USA+45 USSR INT/ORG FORCES TOP/EX CREATE
LEGIT NUC/PWR DISPL ORD/FREE...CONCPT TIME/SEQ
CON/ANAL 20. PAGE 41 G0803
S62
DELIB/GP
RIGID/FLEX
ARMS/CONT

PHIPPS T.E.,"THE CASE FOR DETERRENCE." FUT WOR+45
SOCIETY EX/STRUC FORCES ACT/RES CREATE PLAN TEC/DEV
ROUTINE RIGID/FLEX ORD/FREE...POLICY MYTH NEW/IDEA
STERTYP COLD/WAR 20. PAGE 45 G0876
S62
ATTIT
COERCE
DETER
ARMS/CONT

SINGER J.D.,"STABLE DETERRENCE AND ITS LIMITS." FUT
WOR+45 INT/ORG CONSULT ACT/RES TEC/DEV
ARMS/CONT COERCE DRIVE PERCEPT RIGID/FLEX ORD/FREE
PWR...MYTH SIMUL TOT/POP 20. PAGE 51 G1004
S62
NAT/G
FORCES
DETER
NUC/PWR

US CONGRESS JT ATOM ENRGY COMM,PEACEFUL USES OF
ATOMIC ENERGY. HEARING. USA+45 USSR TEC/DEV ATTIT
RIGID/FLEX...TESTS CHARTS EXHIBIT METH/COMP 20
CONGRESS. PAGE 57 G1112
N62
NUC/PWR
ACADEM
SCHOOL
NAT/COMP

ABSHIRE D.M.,NATIONAL SECURITY: POLITICAL,
MILITARY, AND ECONOMIC STRATEGIES IN THE DECADE
AHEAD. ASIA COM USA+45 WOR+45 ECO/DEV ECO/UNDEV
INT/ORG DELIB/GP FORCES ECO/TAC COERCE ATTIT
RIGID/FLEX HEALTH ORD/FREE PWR WEALTH...POLICY STAT
CHARTS ANTHOL COLD/WAR VAL/FREE. PAGE 1 G0024
B63
FUT
ACT/RES
BAL/PWR

BURSK E.C.,NEW DECISION-MAKING TOOLS FOR MANAGERS.
COMPUTER PLAN PROB/SOLV ROUTINE COST. PAGE 10 G0194
B63
DECISION
MGT
MATH
RIGID/FLEX

HALEY A.G.,SPACE LAW AND GOVERNMENT. FUT USA+45
WOR+45 LEGIS ACT/RES CREATE ATTIT RIGID/FLEX
ORD/FREE PWR SOVEREIGN...POLICY JURID CONCPT CHARTS
VAL/FREE 20. PAGE 24 G0469
B63
INT/ORG
LAW
SPACE

LILIENTHAL D.E.,CHANGE, HOPE, AND THE BOMB. USA+45
WOR+45 R+D INT/ORG NAT/G DELIB/GP FORCES ACT/RES
DETER RIGID/FLEX ORD/FREE...POLICY CONCPT OBS AEC
20. PAGE 34 G0666
B63
ATTIT
MYTH
ARMS/CONT
NUC/PWR

LITTERER J.A.,ORGANIZATIONS: STRUCTURE AND
BEHAVIOR. PLAN DOMIN CONTROL LEAD ROUTINE SANCTION
INGP/REL EFFICIENCY PRODUC DRIVE RIGID/FLEX PWR.
PAGE 34 G0674
B63
ADMIN
CREATE
MGT
ADJUST

NORTH R.C.,CONTENT ANALYSIS: A HANDBOOK WITH
APPLICATIONS FOR THE STUDY OF INTERNATIONAL CRISIS.
ASIA COM EUR+WWI MOD/EUR INT/ORG DOMIN
EDU/PROP ROUTINE COERCE PERCEPT RIGID/FLEX ALL/VALS
...QUANT TESTS CON/ANAL SIMUL GEN/LAWS VAL/FREE.
PAGE 42 G0825
B63
METH/CNCPT
COMPUT/IR
USSR

WIGHTMAN D.,TOWARD ECONOMIC CO-OPERATION IN ASIA.
ASIA S/ASIA VOL/ASSN ACT/RES PLAN TEC/DEV ECO/TAC
EDU/PROP RIGID/FLEX SKILL...POLICY METH/CNCPT OBS
INT GEN/LAWS UN 20 ECAFE. PAGE 63 G1237
B63
ECO/UNDEV
CREATE

BEGUIN H.,"ASPECTS GEOGRAPHIQUE DE LA
POLARISATION." FUT WOR+45 SOCIETY STRUCT ECO/DEV
R+D BAL/PWR ADMIN ATTIT RIGID/FLEX HEALTH WEALTH
...CHARTS 20. PAGE 6 G0114
L63
ECO/UNDEV
GEOG
DIPLOM

BRENNAN D.G.,"ARMS CONTROL AND CIVIL DEFENSE."
USA+45 WOR+45 NAT/G BAL/PWR ROUTINE ATTIT
RIGID/FLEX ORD/FREE...SOC TOT/POP 20. PAGE 8 G0165
L63
PLAN
HEALTH
ARMS/CONT
DETER

BOULDING K.E.,"UNIVERSITY, SOCIETY, AND ARMS
CONTROL." WOR+45 WOR-45 ACADEM NAT/G CONSULT FORCES
ACT/RES PLAN TEC/DEV BAL/PWR ECO/TAC COERCE DETER
WAR ATTIT RIGID/FLEX KNOWL ORD/FREE PWR WEALTH
...CONCPT COLD/WAR TOT/POP 20. PAGE 8 G0159
S63
SOCIETY
ARMS/CONT

DELLIN L.A.D.,"BULGARIA UNDER SOVIET LEADERSHIP."
BULGARIA COM USA+45 USSR ECO/DEV INDUS POL/PAR
EX/STRUC TOP/EX COERCE ATTIT RIGID/FLEX...POLICY
TIME/SEQ 20. PAGE 15 G0293
S63
AGRI
NAT/G
TOTALISM

KAWALKOWSKI A.,"POUR UNE EUROPE INDEPENDENTE ET
REUNIFIEE." EUR+WWI FUT USA+45 USSR WOR+45 ECO/DEV
PROC/MFG INT/ORG NAT/G ACT/RES TEC/DEV FEDERAL
RIGID/FLEX...CONCPT METH/CNCPT OEEC TOT/POP 20
DEGAULLE/C. PAGE 30 G0587
S63 R+D PLAN NUC/PWR

WILES P.J.D.,"WILL CAPITALISM AND COMMUNISM
SPONTANEOUSLY CONVERGE." COM FUT USA+45 ECO/DEV
DIST/IND MARKET CAP/ISM ECO/TAC RIGID/FLEX WEALTH
MARXISM SOCISM...MATH STAT TREND COMPUT/IR 20.
PAGE 63 G1240
S63 PLAN TEC/DEV USSR

INST D'ETUDE POL L'U GRENOBLE,ADMINISTRATION
TRADITIONELLE ET PLANIFICATION REGIONALE. FRANCE
LAW POL/PAR PROB/SOLV ADJUST RIGID/FLEX...CHARTS
ANTHOL BIBLIOG T 20 REFORMERS. PAGE 28 G0546
B64 ADMIN MUNIC PLAN CREATE

ROSECRANCE R.N.,THE DISPERSION OF NUCLEAR WEAPONS:
STRATEGY AND POLITICS. ASIA COM FUT S/ASIA USA+45
INT/ORG NAT/G DELIB/GP FORCES ACT/RES TEC/DEV
BAL/PWR COERCE DETER ATTIT RIGID/FLEX ORD/FREE
...POLICY CHARTS VAL/FREE. PAGE 48 G0935
B64 EUR+WWI PWR PEACE

RUSHING W.A.,THE PSYCHIATRIC PROFESSIONS. DOMIN
INGP/REL DRIVE RIGID/FLEX ROLE HEALTH PWR...POLICY
GP/COMP. PAGE 48 G0947
B64 ATTIT PUB/INST PROF/ORG BAL/PWR

SCHERER F.M.,THE WEAPONS ACQUISITION PROCESS:
ECONOMIC INCENTIVES. BOSTON: DIVISION OF RESEARCH,
GRADUATE SCHOOL OF BUSINESS. USA+45 FINAN NAT/G
DELIB/GP ECO/TAC RIGID/FLEX WEALTH...MGT MATH STAT
CHARTS VAL/FREE 20. PAGE 49 G0965
B64 INDUS ACT/RES WEAPON

WHEELER-BENNETT J.W.,THE NEMESIS OF POWER (2ND
ED.). EUR+WWI GERMANY TOP/EX TEC/DEV ADMIN WAR
PERS/REL RIGID/FLEX ROLE ORD/FREE PWR FASCISM 20
HITLER/A. PAGE 63 G1231
B64 FORCES NAT/G GP/REL STRUCT

BERKS R.N.,"THE US AND WEAPONS CONTROL." WOR+45 LAW
INT/ORG NAT/G LEGIS EXEC COERCE PEACE ATTIT
RIGID/FLEX ALL/VALS PWR...POLICY TOT/POP 20. PAGE 7
G0129
L64 USA+45 PLAN ARMS/CONT

GARDNER R.N.,"GATT AND THE UNITED NATIONS
CONFERENCE ON TRADE AND DEVELOPMENT." USA+45 WOR+45
SOCIETY ECO/UNDEV MARKET NAT/G DELIB/GP ACT/RES
PLAN ECO/TAC TARIFFS EDU/PROP ROUTINE DRIVE
RIGID/FLEX WEALTH...DECISION MGT TREND UN TOT/POP
20 GATT. PAGE 21 G0411
S64 INT/ORG INT/TRADE

LERNER A.P.,"NUCLEAR SYMMETRY AS A FRAMEWORK FOR
COEXISTENCE." COM FUT USA+45 NAT/G ACT/RES CREATE
PLAN DIPLOM EDU/PROP COERCE WAR RIGID/FLEX PWR
SKILL...CONCPT METH/CNCPT GEN/LAWS TOT/POP VAL/FREE
COLD/WAR 20. PAGE 33 G0657
S64 FORCES ORD/FREE DETER NUC/PWR

MARES V.E.,"EAST EUROPE'S SECOND CHANCE." COM
EUR+WWI HUNGARY ROMANIA USSR YUGOSLAVIA ECO/UNDEV
NAT/G TOP/EX CREATE PLAN TEC/DEV REGION NAT/LISM
RIGID/FLEX PWR...CONCPT STAT COMECON 20. PAGE 36
G0705
S64 VOL/ASSN ECO/TAC

ALTSHULER A.,A LAND-USE PLAN FOR ST. PAUL
(PAMPHLET). USA+45 CREATE CAP/ISM RIGID/FLEX ROLE
...NEW/IDEA 20 ST/PAUL. PAGE 3 G0047
B65 MUNIC PLAN ECO/DEV GEOG

CARPER E.T.,REORGANIZATION OF THE U.S. PUBLIC
HEALTH SERVICE. FUT USA+45 INTELL R+D LOBBY GP/REL
INGP/REL PERS/REL RIGID/FLEX ROLE HEALTH...PHIL/SCI
20 CONGRESS PHS. PAGE 11 G0213
B65 HEAL INGP/REL NAT/G OP/RES

LUTZ V.,FRENCH PLANNING. FRANCE TEC/DEV RIGID/FLEX
ORD/FREE 20. PAGE 34 G0680
B65 PLAN ADMIN FUT

PILISUK M.,"IS THERE A MILITARY INDUSTRIAL COMPLEX
WHICH PREVENTS PEACE CONSENSUS; COUNTERVAILING
POWER IN PLURALIST SYSTEMS." INDUS R+D ACADEM
L65 ELITES WEAPON PEACE

FEEDBACK CIVMIL/REL ADJUST CONSEN ATTIT RIGID/FLEX
...CENSUS IDEA/COMP BIBLIOG. PAGE 45 G0878
ARMS/CONT

BEAUFRE A.,"THE SHARING OF NUCLEAR
RESPONSIBILITIES* A PROBLEM IN NEED OF SOLUTION."
FRANCE USA+45 INT/ORG NAT/G DELIB/GP FORCES CONTROL
NUC/PWR RIGID/FLEX...CONCPT IDEA/COMP NATO. PAGE 6
G0110
S65 DETER RISK ACT/RES WAR

KRICKUS R.J.,"ON THE MORALITY OF
CHEMICAL/BIOLOGICAL WAR." ECO/UNDEV ARMS/CONT DETER
NUC/PWR RIGID/FLEX HEALTH INT/LAW. PAGE 31 G0621
S65 MORAL BIO/SOC WEAPON WAR

STAAR R.F.,"RETROGRESSION IN POLAND." COM USSR AGRI
INDUS NAT/G CREATE EDU/PROP TOTALISM RIGID/FLEX
ORD/FREE PWR SOCISM...RECORD CHARTS 20. PAGE 52
G1029
S65 TOP/EX ECO/TAC POLAND

NASH M.,MACHINE AGE MAYA. GUATEMALA L/A+17C STRUCT
AGRI WORKER CREATE INCOME ATTIT RIGID/FLEX ROLE
...IDEA/COMP SOC/EXP WORSHIP 20 INDIAN/AM. PAGE 41
G0806
B67 INDUS CULTURE SOC MUNIC

SCHON D.A.,TECHNOLOGY AND CHANGE* THE NEW
HERACLITUS. TEC/DEV CONTROL COST DEMAND EFFICIENCY
RIGID/FLEX...MYTH 20. PAGE 49 G0975
B67 INDUS PROB/SOLV R+D CREATE

RIKER W.H. G0921

RILEY V. G0922

RIO/PACT....RIO PACT

RIOT....RIOTS; SEE ALSO CROWD

RISK....SEE ALSO GAMBLE

US ATOMIC ENERGY COMMISSION,ATOMIC ENERGY IN USE
(PAMPHLET). R+D RISK EFFICIENCY HEALTH KNOWL
ORD/FREE...PHIL/SCI CONCPT METH/CNCPT CHARTS
LAB/EXP 20 AEC. PAGE 56 G1106
N19 OP/RES TEC/DEV NUC/PWR CREATE

US FOOD AND DRUG ADMIN,CIVIL DEFENSE INFORMATION
FOR FOOD AND DRUG OFFICIALS (2ND ED.) (PAMPHLET).
USA+45 PROB/SOLV RISK HABITAT...MATH CHARTS
DICTIONARY 20 CIV/DEFENS. PAGE 58 G1136
N19 NUC/PWR WAR EATING HEALTH

FULLER G.H.,A SELECTED LIST OF REFERENCES ON THE
EXPANSION OF THE US NAVY, 1933-1939 (PAMPHLET).
MOD/EUR USA-45 NAT/G PLAN DIPLOM DOMIN RISK
ARMS/CONT EQUILIB PWR 20 NAVY. PAGE 20 G0399
B39 BIBLIOG FORCES WEAPON WAR

JUNGK R.,BRIGHTER THAN A THOUSAND SUNS: THE MORAL
AND POLITICAL HISTORY OF THE ATOMIC SCIENTISTS.
WOR+45 WOR-45 CONSULT CREATE RISK UTIL DRIVE
PERCEPT PWR...INT 20. PAGE 29 G0568
B58 NUC/PWR MORAL GOV/REL PERSON

US DEPARTMENT OF THE ARMY,BIBLIOGRAPHY ON LIMITED
WAR (PAMPHLET). USA+45 TEC/DEV CONTROL RISK COERCE
DETER NUC/PWR WEAPON ADJUST PEACE ALL/VALS ORD/FREE
20. PAGE 57 G1127
B58 BIBLIOG/A WAR FORCES CIVMIL/REL

FOLDES L.,"UNCERTAINTY, PROBABILITY AND POTENTIAL
SURPRISE." MARKET PROB/SOLV RISK PERSON...DECISION
MGT HYPO/EXP GAME. PAGE 19 G0376
S58 PROBABIL ADMIN ROUTINE

ADAMS E.W.,"A MODEL OF RISKLESS CHOICE." CREATE
PROB/SOLV UTIL...PROBABIL PREDICT HYPO/EXP. PAGE 2
G0029
S59 GAME SIMUL RISK DECISION

LE GHAIT E.,NO CARTE BLANCHE TO CAPRICORN; THE
FOLLY OF NUCLEAR WAR. WOR+45 INT/ORG BAL/PWR DIPLOM
RISK COERCE...CENSUS 20 NATO. PAGE 33 G0647
B60 DETER NUC/PWR PLAN DECISION

MORRIS W.T.,ENGINEERING ECONOMY. AUTOMAT RISK
RATIONAL...PROBABIL STAT CHARTS GAME SIMUL BIBLIOG
T 20. PAGE 40 G0785
B60 OP/RES DECISION MGT PROB/SOLV

STERN A.C.,AIR POLLUTION (2 VOLS.). LAW INDUS
PROB/SOLV TEC/DEV INSPECT RISK BIO/SOC HABITAT
...OBS/ENVIR TESTS SAMP 20 POLLUTION. PAGE 53 G1035
B62 AIR OP/RES CONTROL HEALTH

BRIGHT J.R.,RESEARCH, DEVELOPMENT AND TECHNOLOGICAL
INNOVATION. CULTURE R+D CREATE PLAN PROB/SOLV
AUTOMAT RISK PERSON...DECISION CONCPT PREDICT
BIBLIOG. PAGE 9 G0168
B64 TEC/DEV NEW/IDEA INDUS MGT

BROWN N.,NUCLEAR WAR* THE IMPENDING STRATEGIC
DEADLOCK. USA+45 USSR TEC/DEV BUDGET RISK ARMS/CONT
NUC/PWR WEAPON COST BIO/SOC...GEOG IDEA/COMP
NAT/COMP GAME NATO WARSAW/P. PAGE 9 G0177
B64 FORCES OP/RES WAR GEN/LAWS

US DEPARTMENT OF ARMY,MILITARY PROTECTIVE
CONSTRUCTION: NUCLEAR WARFARE AND CHEMICAL AND
BIOLOGICAL OPERATIONS (MANUAL). OP/RES TEC/DEV RISK
COERCE NUC/PWR WAR WEAPON EFFICIENCY UTIL BIO/SOC
HABITAT ORD/FREE 20. PAGE 57 G1117
B65 FORCES CONSTRUC TASK HEALTH

BEAUFRE A.,"THE SHARING OF NUCLEAR
RESPONSIBILITIES* A PROBLEM IN NEED OF SOLUTION."
FRANCE USA+45 INT/ORG NAT/G DELIB/GP FORCES CONTROL
NUC/PWR RIGID/FLEX...CONCPT IDEA/COMP NATO. PAGE 6
G0110
S65 DETER RISK ACT/RES WAR

BIRNBAUM K.,"SWEDEN'S NUCLEAR POLICY." WOR+45
POL/PAR CREATE TEC/DEV NEUTRAL RISK WAR ORD/FREE
...DECISION IDEA/COMP NAT/COMP TIME. PAGE 7 G0137
S65 SWEDEN NUC/PWR DIPLOM ARMS/CONT

GOLDSTEIN W.,"KEEPING THE GENIE IN THE BOTTLE* THE
FEASIBILITY OF A NUCLEAR NON-PROLIFERATION
AGREEMENT." ASIA FRANCE UK USA+45 USSR WOR+45
ECO/UNDEV VOL/ASSN ACT/RES PLAN RISK ARMS/CONT WAR
PEACE ATTIT PERCEPT...RECORD TREND TIME. PAGE 22
G0429
S65 NUC/PWR CREATE COST

HARRISON S.L.,"NTH NATION CHALLENGES* THE PRESENT
PERSPECTIVE." EUR+WWI FUT USA+45 BAL/PWR CONTROL
RISK COERCE WAR...PREDICT COLD/WAR. PAGE 25 G0485
S65 ARMS/CONT NUC/PWR NAT/G DIPLOM

HSIEH A.L.,"THE SINO-SOVIET NUCLEAR DIALOGUE*
1963." S/ASIA USA+45 RISK DETER REV WAR SOVEREIGN
IDEA/COMP. PAGE 27 G0533
S65 ASIA USSR NUC/PWR

AMERICAN ASSEMBLY COLUMBIA U,A WORLD OF NUCLEAR
POWERS? FUT WOR+45 ECO/DEV BAL/PWR ECO/TAC CONTROL
RISK EFFICIENCY ATTIT PWR...METH/COMP ANTHOL 20.
PAGE 3 G0049
B66 NUC/PWR DIPLOM TEC/DEV ARMS/CONT

BRODIE B.,ESCALATION AND THE NUCLEAR OPTION. ASIA
CUBA EUR+WWI KOREA USA+45 USSR VIETNAM RISK ATTIT
DRIVE PERCEPT PROBABIL. PAGE 9 G0172
B66 NUC/PWR GUERRILLA WAR DETER

CARROLL K.J.,"SECOND STEP TOWARD ARMS CONTROL."
WOR+45 INT/ORG VOL/ASSN FORCES PROB/SOLV RISK
WEAPON 20 COLD/WAR. PAGE 11 G0215
S67 ARMS/CONT DIPLOM PLAN NUC/PWR

D'AMATO D.,"LEGAL ASPECTS OF THE FRENCH NUCLEAR
TESTS." FRANCE WOR+45 ACT/RES COLONIAL RISK GOV/REL
EQUILIB ORD/FREE PWR DECISION. PAGE 14 G0268
S67 INT/LAW DIPLOM NUC/PWR ADJUD

ENKE S.,"GOVERNMENT-INDUSTRY DEVELOPMENT OF A
COMMERCIAL SUPERSONIC TRANSPORT." USA+45 ECO/DEV
R+D LG/CO NAT/G TEC/DEV PRICE RISK COST PROFIT.
PAGE 18 G0347
S67 INDUS FINAN SERV/IND CAP/ISM

HODGE G.,"THE RISE AND DEMISE OF THE UN TECHNICAL
ASSISTANCE ADMINISTRATION." RISK TASK INGP/REL
CONSEN EFFICIENCY 20 UN. PAGE 26 G0516
S67 ADMIN TEC/DEV EX/STRUC INT/ORG

SUINN R.M.,"THE DISARMAMENT FANTASY* PSYCHOLOGICAL
S67 DECISION

FACTORS THAT MAY PRODUCE WARFARE." DIPLOM RISK
ARMS/CONT DETER ANOMIE PERSON GAME. PAGE 53 G1046
NUC/PWR WAR PSY

TELLER E.,"PLANNING FOR PEACE." CHINA/COM WOR+45
DELIB/GP TEC/DEV RISK COERCE DETER WAR ATTIT
ORD/FREE 20 NATO. PAGE 54 G1061
S67 ARMS/CONT NUC/PWR PEACE DOMIN

RITCHIE/JM....JESS M. RITCHIE

LAWRENCE S.A.,THE BATTERY ADDITIVE CONTROVERSY
(PAMPHLET). USA+45 LAW MARKET PROC/MFG R+D CAP/ISM
CT/SYS GOV/REL OWN FTC CONGRESS BUR/STNDRD
RITCHIE/JM. PAGE 33 G0645
N19 PHIL/SCI LOBBY INSPECT

RITSCHL/H....HANS RITSCHL

RITUAL....RITUALS AND SYMBOLIC CEREMONIES; SEE ALSO WORSHIP,
SECT

RIVETT P. G0028

RIVKIN A. G0923

RIZOS E.J. G0924

RKFDV....REICHSKOMMISSARIAT FUR DIE FESTIGUNG DEUTSCHEN
VOLKSTUMS

RKO....R.K.O.

ROACH J.R. G0925

ROBERTS E.B. G0926

ROBERTS J. G0790

ROBERTS W. G0927

ROBERTS HL G0928

ROBESPR/M....MAXIMILIAN FRANCOIS ROBESPIERRE

ROBINSN/JH....JAMES HARVEY ROBINSON

ROBINSON E.A.G. G0929

ROBINSON J.A.T. G0930

ROBINSON T.W. G0931

ROBINSON/H....HENRY ROBINSON

ROCKEFELLER BROTHERS FUND INC G0932

RODBRTUS/C....CARL RODBERTUS

ROGGEVEEN V.J. G0651

ROLE....ROLE, REFERENCE GROUP, CROSS-PRESSURES

WEIGLEY R.F.,HISTORY OF THE UNITED STATES ARMY.
USA+45 USA-45 SOCIETY NAT/G LEAD WAR GP/REL PWR
...SOC METH/COMP COLD/WAR. PAGE 62 G1222
N FORCES ADMIN ROLE CIVMIL/REL

ZNANIECKI F.,THE SOCIAL ROLE OF THE MAN OF
KNOWLEDGE. UNIV SOCIETY STRUCT TEC/DEV...EPIST
PHIL/SCI SOC NEW/IDEA 20. PAGE 65 G1269
B40 ROLE INTELL KNOWL INGP/REL

BARKER E.,THE DEVELOPMENT OF PUBLIC SERVICES IN
WESTERN WUROPE: 1660-1930. FRANCE GERMANY UK SCHOOL
CONTROL REPRESENT ROLE...WELF/ST 17/20. PAGE 5
G0095
B44 GOV/COMP ADMIN EX/STRUC

TRYTTEN M.H.,"THE MOBILIZATION OF SCIENTISTS," IN
L. WHITE, CIVIL SERVICE IN WARTIME." USA-45 R+D
FORCES ACT/RES PERSON ROLE 20. PAGE 55 G1080
C45 INTELL WAR TEC/DEV NAT/G

TURNER R.H.,"THE NAVY DISBURSING OFFICER AS A
BUREAUCRAT" (BMR)" USA-45 LAW STRATA DIST/IND WAR
PWR...SOC 20 BUREAUCRCY. PAGE 55 G1083
S47 FORCES ADMIN PERSON ROLE

MAASS A.,MUDDY WATERS: THE ARMY ENGINEERS AND THE
B51 FORCES

NATIONS RIVERS. USA-45 PROF/ORG CONSULT LEGIS ADMIN GP/REL
EXEC ROLE PWR...SOC PRESIDENT 20. PAGE 35 G0682 LOBBY
CONSTRUC

B53
SAYLES L.R.,THE LOCAL UNION. CONSTN CULTURE LABOR
DELIB/GP PARTIC CHOOSE GP/REL INGP/REL ATTIT ROLE LEAD
...MAJORIT DECISION MGT. PAGE 49 G0958 ADJUD
ROUTINE

B54
ROSE A.M.,THEORY AND METHOD IN THE SOCIAL SCIENCES. CONCPT
STRATA R+D NEIGH PARTIC...METH/CNCPT GP/COMP. SOC
PAGE 47 G0934 VOL/ASSN
ROLE

B56
VUCINICH A.,THE SOVIET ACADEMY OF SCIENCES. USSR PHIL/SCI
STRUCT ACADEM NAT/G EDU/PROP ADMIN LEAD ROLE CREATE
...BIBLIOG 20 ACADEM/SCI. PAGE 61 G1203 INTELL
PROF/ORG

B57
SCARROW H.A.,THE HIGHER PUBLIC SERVICE OF THE ADMIN
COMMONWEALTH OF AUSTRALIA. LAW SENIOR LOBBY ROLE 20 NAT/G
AUSTRAL CIVIL/SERV COMMONWLTH. PAGE 49 G0959 EX/STRUC
GOV/COMP

S58
DEAN B.V.,"APPLICATION OF OPERATIONS RESEARCH TO DECISION
MANAGERIAL DECISION MAKING" STRATA ACT/RES OP/RES
PROB/SOLV ROLE...SOC PREDICT SIMUL 20. PAGE 15 MGT
G0288 METH/CNCPT

B59
DAHRENDORF R.,CLASS AND CLASS CONFLICT IN VOL/ASSN
INDUSTRIAL SOCIETY. LABOR NAT/G COERCE ROLE PLURISM STRUCT
...POLICY MGT CONCPT CLASSIF. PAGE 14 G0271 SOC
GP/REL

B60
LINDVEIT E.N.,SCIENTISTS IN GOVERNMENT. USA+45 PAY TEC/DEV
EDU/PROP ADMIN DRIVE HABITAT ROLE...TECHNIC BIBLIOG ECO/TAC
20. PAGE 34 G0670 PHIL/SCI
GOV/REL

B60
WALDO D.,THE RESEARCH FUNCTION OF UNIVERSITY ADMIN
BUREAUS AND INSTITUTES FOR GOVERNMENTAL-RELATED R+D
RESEARCH. FINAN ACADEM NAT/G INGP/REL ROLE...POLICY MUNIC
CLASSIF GOV/COMP. PAGE 61 G1205

S60
HALSEY A.H.,"THE CHANGING FUNCTIONS OF UNIVERSITIES ACADEM
IN ADVANCED INDUSTRIAL SOCIETIES." R+D EDU/PROP CREATE
REPRESENT ROLE ORD/FREE PWR TREND. PAGE 24 G0476 CULTURE
ADJUST

S60
TAYLOR M.G.,"THE ROLE OF THE MEDICAL PROFESSION IN PROF/ORG
THE FORMULATION AND EXECUTION OF PUBLIC POLICY" HEALTH
(BMR)" CANADA NAT/G CONSULT ADMIN REPRESENT GP/REL LOBBY
ROLE SOVEREIGN...DECISION 20 CMA. PAGE 54 G1058 POLICY

C60
SCHRAMM W.,"MASS COMMUNICATIONS: A BOOK OF READINGS COM/IND
(2ND ED.)" LG/CO PRESS ADMIN CONTROL ROUTINE ATTIT EDU/PROP
ROLE SUPEGO...CHARTS ANTHOL BIBLIOG 20. PAGE 50 CROWD
G0977 MAJORIT

B61
SMITH H.H.,THE CITIZEN'S GUIDE TO PLANNING. USA+45 MUNIC
LAW SCHOOL CREATE PROB/SOLV EDU/PROP GP/REL ROLE 20 PLAN
URBAN/RNWL OPEN/SPACE. PAGE 52 G1015 DELIB/GP
CONSULT

S61
COOKE E.F.,"RESEARCH: AN INSTRUMENT OF POWER." R+D
VOL/ASSN PLAN TEC/DEV TAX LOBBY INGP/REL ROLE PROVS
POLICY. PAGE 13 G0253 LOC/G
DECISION

B62
DODDS H.W.,THE ACADEMIC PRESIDENT "EDUCATOR OR ACADEM
CARETAKER? FINAN DELIB/GP EDU/PROP PARTIC ATTIT ADMIN
ROLE PWR...POLICY RECORD INT. PAGE 16 G0304 LEAD
CONTROL

B62
THOMSON G.P.,NUCLEAR ENERGY IN BRITAIN DURING THE CREATE
LAST WAR: THE CHERWELL SIMON LECTURE (MONOGRAPH). TEC/DEV
UK R+D CONSULT FORCES PLAN DIPLOM TASK CIVMIL/REL WAR
ROLE...PHIL/SCI NEW/IDEA LAB/EXP 20 MAUD. PAGE 54 NUC/PWR
G1071

S62
STORER N.W.,"SOME SOCIOLOGICAL ASPECTS OF FEDERAL POLICY
SCIENCE POLICY." USA+45 INTELL PUB/INST PLAN GP/REL CREATE
PERS/REL DRIVE PERSON ROLE...PSY SOC SIMUL 20 NIH NAT/G
NSF. PAGE 53 G1040 ALL/VALS

B63
DALAND R.T.,PERSPECTIVES OF BRAZILIAN PUBLIC ADMIN
ADMINISTRATION (VOL. I). BRAZIL LAW ECO/UNDEV NAT/G
SCHOOL CHIEF TEC/DEV CONFER CONTROL GP/REL ATTIT PLAN
ROLE PWR...ANTHOL 20. PAGE 14 G0272 GOV/REL

B63
FOSKETT D.J.,CLASSIFICATION AND INDEXING IN THE PROB/SOLV
SOCIAL SCIENCES. WOR+45 R+D ACT/RES CREATE OP/RES CON/ANAL
TEC/DEV AUTOMAT ROLE...SOC COMPUT/IR BIBLIOG. CLASSIF
PAGE 20 G0384

B63
HOWER R.M.,MANAGERS AND SCIENTISTS. EX/STRUC CREATE R+D
ADMIN REPRESENT ATTIT DRIVE ROLE PWR SKILL...SOC MGT
INT. PAGE 27 G0532 PERS/REL
INGP/REL

B63
PEARSELL M.,MEDICAL BEHAVIORAL SCIENCE: A SELECTED BIBLIOG
BIBLIOGRAPHY OF CULTURAL ANTHROPOLOGY, SOCIAL SOC
PSYCHOLOGY, AND SOCIOLOGY... USA+45 USA-45 R+D PSY
ATTIT ROLE 20. PAGE 44 G0863 HEALTH

B63
RUITENBEER H.M.,THE DILEMMA OF ORGANIZATIONAL PERSON
SOCIETY. CULTURE ECO/DEV MUNIC SECT TEC/DEV ROLE
EDU/PROP NAT/LISM ORD/FREE...NAT/COMP 20 RIESMAN/D ADMIN
WHYTE/WF MERTON/R MEAD/MARG JASPERS/K. PAGE 48 WORKER
G0945

S63
DUBRIDGE L.A.,"POLICY AND THE SCIENTISTS." ELITES POLICY
PROB/SOLV ROLE KNOWL PWR. PAGE 16 G0318 PHIL/SCI
ACADEM
DECISION

B64
RUSHING W.A.,THE PSYCHIATRIC PROFESSIONS. DOMIN ATTIT
INGP/REL DRIVE RIGID/FLEX ROLE HEALTH PWR...POLICY PUB/INST
GP/COMP. PAGE 48 G0947 PROF/ORG
BAL/PWR

B64
WHEELER-BENNETT J.W.,THE NEMESIS OF POWER (2ND FORCES
ED.). EUR+WWI GERMANY TOP/EX TEC/DEV ADMIN WAR NAT/G
PERS/REL RIGID/FLEX ROLE ORD/FREE PWR FASCISM 20 GP/REL
HITLER/A. PAGE 63 G1231 STRUCT

B65
ALTSHULER A.,A LAND-USE PLAN FOR ST. PAUL MUNIC
(PAMPHLET). USA+45 CREATE CAP/ISM RIGID/FLEX ROLE PLAN
...NEW/IDEA 20 ST/PAUL. PAGE 3 G0047 ECO/DEV
GEOG

B65
BENJAMIN A.C.,SCIENCE, TECHNOLOGY, AND HUMAN PHIL/SCI
VALUES. WOR+45 SECT EDU/PROP GP/REL ATTIT...TECHNIC CREATE
LING IDEA/COMP WORSHIP 20. PAGE 6 G0118 ROLE
SOCIETY

B65
CARPER E.T.,REORGANIZATION OF THE U.S. PUBLIC HEAL
HEALTH SERVICE. FUT USA+45 INTELL R+D LOBBY GP/REL PLAN
INGP/REL PERS/REL RIGID/FLEX ROLE HEALTH...PHIL/SCI NAT/G
20 CONGRESS PHS. PAGE 11 G0213 OP/RES

B65
INTERNATIONAL CITY MGRS ASSN,COUNCIL-MANAGER BIBLIOG/A
GOVERNMENT, 1940-64: AN ANNOTATED BIBLIOGRAPHY. MUNIC
USA+45 ADMIN GOV/REL ROLE...MGT 20. PAGE 28 G0549 CONSULT
PLAN

B65
PHELPS E.S.,PRIVATE WANTS AND PUBLIC NEEDS - AN NAT/G
INTRODUCTION TO A CURRENT ISSUE OF PUBLIC POLICY POLICY
(REV. ED.). USA+45 PLAN CAP/ISM INGP/REL ROLE DEMAND
...DECISION TIME/SEQ 20. PAGE 44 G0873

S66
FLEMING W.G.,"AUTHORITY, EFFICIENCY, AND ROLE DOMIN
STRESS: PROBLEMS IN THE DEVELOPMENT OF EAST AFRICAN EFFICIENCY
BUREAUCRACIES." AFR UGANDA STRUCT PROB/SOLV ROUTINE COLONIAL
INGP/REL ROLE...MGT SOC GP/COMP GOV/COMP 20 ADMIN
TANGANYIKA AFRICA/E. PAGE 19 G0371

S66
HANSON A.H.,"PLANNING AND THE POLITICIANS* SOME PLAN
REFLECTIONS ON ECONOMIC PLANNING IN WESTERN ECO/DEV
EUROPE." MARKET NAT/G TEC/DEV CONSEN ROLE EUR+WWI

...METH/COMP NAT/COMP. PAGE 24 G0479   ADMIN

S66

RIZOS E.J.,"SCIENCE AND TECHNOLOGY IN COUNTRY   ADMIN
DEVELOPMENT* TOWARDS AN UNDERSTANDING OF THE ROLE   TEC/DEV
OF PUBLIC ADMINISTRATION." WOR+45 STRUCT INT/ORG   ECO/UNDEV
EX/STRUC CREATE PLAN PROB/SOLV EFFICIENCY ROLE   PHIL/SCI
DECISION. PAGE 47 G0924

B67

BERNAL J.D.,THE SOCIAL FUNCTION OF SCIENCE. WOR+45   ROLE
WOR-45 R+D NAT/G PROB/SOLV DOMIN WAR...PHIL/SCI 20.   TEC/DEV
PAGE 7 G0130   SOCIETY
                                                        ADJUST

B67

KINTNER W.R.,PEACE AND THE STRATEGY CONFLICT. PLAN   ROLE
BAL/PWR DIPLOM CONTROL ARMS/CONT DETER WEAPON 20.   PEACE
PAGE 30 G0599   NUC/PWR
                                                        ORD/FREE

B67

NASH M.,MACHINE AGE MAYA. GUATEMALA L/A+17C STRUCT   INDUS
AGRI WORKER CREATE INCOME ATTIT RIGID/FLEX ROLE   CULTURE
...IDEA/COMP SOC/EXP WORSHIP 20 INDIAN/AM. PAGE 41   SOC
G0806   MUNIC

B67

ROACH J.R.,THE UNITED STATES AND THE ATLANTIC   INT/ORG
COMMUNITY: ISSUES AND PROSPECTS. WOR+45 TEC/DEV   POLICY
ECO/TAC COLONIAL REGION PEACE ROLE...ANTHOL NATO   ADJUST
COLD/WAR EEC. PAGE 47 G0925   DIPLOM

B67

US DEPARTMENT OF THE ARMY,CIVILIAN IN PEACE,   BIBLIOG/A
SOLDIER IN WAR: A BIBLIOGRAPHIC SURVEY OF THE ARMY   FORCES
AND AIR NATIONAL GUARD (PAMPHLET. NOS. 130-2).   ROLE
USA+45 USA-45 LOC/G NAT/G PROVS LEGIS PLAN ADMIN   DIPLOM
ATTIT ORD/FREE...POLICY 19/20. PAGE 58 G1134

B67

YAVITZ B.,AUTOMATION IN COMMERCIAL BANKING. USA+45   TEC/DEV
STRUCT WORKER CREATE OP/RES PLAN ROLE...DECISION   FINAN
SAMP/SIZ. PAGE 64 G1263   COMPUT/IR
                                                        MGT

ROLL E. G0377

ROMAN CATHOLIC....SEE CATH, CATHISM

ROMAN/EMP....ROMAN EMPIRE

ROMAN/LAW....ROMAN LAW

ROMAN/REP....ROMAN REPUBLIC

ROMANIA....SEE ALSO COM

S64

MARES V.E.,"EAST EUROPE'S SECOND CHANCE." COM   VOL/ASSN
EUR+WWI HUNGARY ROMANIA USSR YUGOSLAVIA ECO/UNDEV   ECO/TAC
NAT/G TOP/EX CREATE PLAN TEC/DEV REGION NAT/LISM
RIGID/FLEX PWR...CONCPT STAT COMECON 20. PAGE 36
G0705

B67

NATIONAL SCIENCE FOUNDATION.DIRECTORY OF SELECTED   INDEX
RESEARCH INSTITUTES IN EASTERN EUROPE. BULGARIA   R+D
CZECHOSLVK HUNGARY POLAND ROMANIA INTELL ACADEM   COM
NAT/G ACT/RES 20. PAGE 41 G0814   PHIL/SCI

ROMANIECKI L. G0933

ROME....ROME

ROME/ANC....ANCIENT ROME; SEE ALSO ROM/REP, ROM/EMP

ROMNEY/GEO....GEORGE ROMNEY

ROOSEVLT/F....PRESIDENT FRANKLIN D. ROOSEVELT

B50

BERNSTEIN I.,THE NEW DEAL COLLECTIVE BARGAINING   LABOR
PROCESS. USA-45 GOV/REL ATTIT...BIBLIOG 20   LEGIS
ROOSEVLT/F. PAGE 7 G0132   POLICY
                                                       NEW/LIB

B66

FREIDEL F.,AMERICAN ISSUES IN THE TWENTIETH   DIPLOM
CENTURY. SOCIETY FINAN ECO/TAC FOR/AID CONTROL   POLICY
NUC/PWR WAR RACE/REL PEACE ATTIT...ANTHOL T 20   NAT/G
WILSON/W ROOSEVLT/F KENNEDY/JF TRUMAN/HS. PAGE 20   ORD/FREE
G0391

B67

SALMOND J.A.,THE CIVILIAN CONSERVATION CORPS,   ADMIN

1933-1942. USA-45 NAT/G CREATE EXEC EFFICIENCY   ECO/TAC
WEALTH...BIBLIOG 20 ROOSEVLT/F. PAGE 48 G0954   TASK
                                                       AGRI

ROOSEVLT/T....PRESIDENT THEODORE ROOSEVELT

ROSE A.M. G0934

ROSECRANCE R.N. G0935

ROSENAU J.N. G0936

ROSENHAUPT H.W. G0937

ROSENTHAL A. G0443

ROSENWEIG J.E. G0581

ROSHOLT R.L. G0938

ROSS R. G0939

ROSS/EH....EDWARD H. ROSS

ROSSMOOR....ROSSMOOR LEISURE WORLD, SEAL BEACH, CAL.

ROTHENBERG J. G0940

ROTHSCHILD J.H. G0941

ROTHSTEIN R.L. G0942

ROUSSEAU/J....JEAN JACQUES ROUSSEAU

ROUTINE....PROCEDURAL AND WORK SYSTEMS

N

FULLER G.A.,DEMOBILIZATION: A SELECTED LIST OF   BIBLIOG/A
REFERENCES. USA+45 LAW AGRI LABOR WORKER ECO/TAC   INDUS
RATION RECEIVE EDU/PROP ROUTINE ARMS/CONT ALL/VALS   FORCES
20. PAGE 20 G0398   NAT/G

B25

MATHEWS J.M.,AMERICAN STATE GOVERNMENT. USA-45   PROVS
LOC/G CHIEF EX/STRUC LEGIS ADJUD CONTROL CT/SYS   ADMIN
ROUTINE GOV/REL PWR 20 GOVERNOR. PAGE 37 G0721   FEDERAL
                                                       CONSTN

B28

SOROKIN P.,CONTEMPORARY SOCIOLOGICAL THEORIES.   CULTURE
MOD/EUR UNIV SOCIETY R+D SCHOOL ECO/TAC EDU/PROP   SOC
ROUTINE ATTIT DRIVE...PSY CONCPT TIME/SEQ TREND   WAR
GEN/LAWS 20. PAGE 52 G1021

B34

BOWMAN I.,GEOGRAPHY IN RELATION TO THE SOCIAL   GEOG
SCIENCES. UNIV...SOC CONCPT METH. PAGE 8 G0161   CULTURE
                                                       ROUTINE
                                                       PHIL/SCI

B48

CHILDS J.R.,AMERICAN FOREIGN SERVICE. USA+45   DIPLOM
SOCIETY NAT/G ROUTINE GOV/REL 20 DEPT/STATE   ADMIN
CIVIL/SERV. PAGE 12 G0227   GP/REL

S48

COCH L.,"OVERCOMING RESISTANCE TO CHANGE" (BMR)"   WORKER
USA+45 CONSULT ADMIN ROUTINE GP/REL EFFICIENCY   OP/RES
PRODUC PERCEPT SKILL...CHARTS SOC/EXP 20. PAGE 12   PROC/MFG
G0236   RIGID/FLEX

S49

MERTON R.,"THE ROLE OF APPLIED SOCIAL SCIENCE IN   PLAN
THE FORMATION OF POLICY: A RESEARCH MEMORANDUM."   SOC
WOR+45 INDUS NAT/G EXEC ROUTINE CHOOSE ORD/FREE PWR   DIPLOM
SKILL...POLICY MGT PSY METH/CNCPT TESTS CHARTS METH
VAL/FREE 20. PAGE 38 G0756

B50

HUZAR E.,THE PURSE AND THE SWORD: CONTROL OF THE   CIVMIL/REL
ARMY BY CONGRESS THROUGH MILITARY APPROPRIATIONS   BUDGET
1933-1950. NAT/G DELIB/GP EX/STRUC FORCES PROB/SOLV   CONTROL
BARGAIN CONFER ADMIN ROUTINE GOV/REL EFFICIENCY   LEGIS
...POLICY COLD/WAR. PAGE 27 G0541

B50

MANNHEIM K.,FREEDOM, POWER, AND DEMOCRATIC   TEC/DEV
PLANNING. FUT USSR WOR+45 ELITES INTELL SOCIETY   PLAN
NAT/G EDU/PROP ROUTINE ATTIT DRIVE SUPEGO SKILL   CAP/ISM
...POLICY PSY CONCPT TREND GEN/LAWS 20. PAGE 35   UK
G0700

S50

KAPLAN A.,"THE PREDICTION OF SOCIAL AND   PWR
TECHNOLOGICAL EVENTS." VOL/ASSN CONSULT ACT/RES   KNO/TEST
CREATE OP/RES PLAN ROUTINE PERSON...POLICY

METH/CNCPT STAT QU/SEMANT SYS/QU TESTS CENSUS TREND
20. PAGE 29 G0574

C50
WAGER P.W.,"COUNTY GOVERNMENT ACROSS THE NATION." LOC/G
USA+45 CONSTN COM/IND FINAN SCHOOL DOMIN CT/SYS PROVS
LEAD GOV/REL...STAT BIBLIOG 20. PAGE 61 G1204 ADMIN
ROUTINE

S51
LERNER D.,"THE POLICY SCIENCES: RECENT DEVELOPMENTS CONSULT
IN SCOPE AND METHODS." R+D SERV/IND CREATE DIPLOM SOC
ROUTINE PWR...METH/CNCPT TREND GEN/LAWS METH 20.
PAGE 33 G0658

B53
LARSEN K.,NATIONAL BIBLIOGRAPHIC SERVICES: THEIR BIBLIOG/A
CREATION AND OPERATION. WOR+45 COM/IND CREATE PLAN INT/ORG
DIPLOM PRESS ADMIN ROUTINE...MGT UNESCO. PAGE 32 WRITING
G0636

B53
SAYLES L.R.,THE LOCAL UNION. CONSTN CULTURE LABOR
DELIB/GP PARTIC CHOOSE GP/REL INGP/REL ATTIT ROLE LEAD
...MAJORIT DECISION MGT. PAGE 49 G0958 ADJUD
ROUTINE

B54
MCCLOSKEY J.F.,OPERATIONS RESEARCH FOR MANAGEMENT. OP/RES
STRUCT COMPUTER ADMIN ROUTINE...PHIL/SCI CONCPT MGT
METH/CNCPT TREND ANTHOL BIBLIOG 20. PAGE 37 G0731 METH/COMP
TEC/DEV

S54
BATES J.,"A MODEL FOR THE SCIENCE OF DECISION." QUANT
UNIV ROUTINE...CONT/OBS CON/ANAL HYPO/EXP GAME. DECISION
PAGE 5 G0101 PHIL/SCI
METH/CNCPT

C54
ZELLER B.,"AMERICAN STATE LEGISLATURES: REPORT ON REPRESENT
THE COMMITTEE ON AMERICAN LEGISLATURES." CONSTN LEGIS
POL/PAR EX/STRUC CONFER ADMIN CONTROL EXEC LOBBY PROVS
ROUTINE GOV/REL...POLICY BIBLIOG 20. PAGE 65 G1267 APPORT

B55
SHUBIK M.,READINGS IN GAME THEORY AND POLITICAL MATH
BEHAVIOR. WOR+45 FORCES CREATE ROUTINE WAR PEACE DECISION
PERCEPT KNOWL PWR...PSY SOC CONCPT METH/CNCPT STAT DIPLOM
CHARTS HYPO/EXP GAME METH VAL/FREE 20. PAGE 50
G0991

B55
SMITHIES A.,THE BUDGETARY PROCESS IN THE UNITED NAT/G
STATES. ECO/DEV AGRI EX/STRUC FORCES LEGIS ADMIN
PROB/SOLV TAX ROUTINE EFFICIENCY...MGT CONGRESS BUDGET
PRESIDENT. PAGE 52 G1016 GOV/REL

S55
ANGELL R.,"GOVERNMENTS AND PEOPLES AS A FOCI FOR FUT
PEACE-ORIENTED RESEARCH." WOR+45 CULTURE SOCIETY SOC
FACE/GP ACT/RES CREATE PLAN DIPLOM EDU/PROP ROUTINE PEACE
ATTIT PERCEPT SKILL...POLICY CONCPT OBS TREND
GEN/METH 20. PAGE 3 G0060

S55
DRUCKER P.F.,"'MANAGEMENT SCIENCE' AND THE MGT
MANAGER." PLAN ROUTINE RIGID/FLEX...METH/CNCPT LOG STRUCT
HYPO/EXP. PAGE 16 G0315 DECISION
RATIONAL

S55
WRIGHT Q.,"THE PEACEFUL ADJUSTMENT OF INTERNATIONAL R+D
RELATIONS: PROBLEMS AND RESEARCH APPROACHES." UNIV METH/CNCPT
INTELL EDU/PROP ADJUD ROUTINE KNOWL SKILL...INT/LAW PEACE
JURID PHIL/SCI CLASSIF 20. PAGE 64 G1258

B56
THOMAS M.,ATOMIC ENERGY AND CONGRESS. USA+45 NAT/G LEGIS
ACT/RES PLAN TEC/DEV EDU/PROP ROUTINE KNOWL PWR ADMIN
SKILL...PHIL/SCI NEW/IDEA TIME/SEQ CHARTS METH NUC/PWR
CONGRESS VAL/FREE 20 AEC. PAGE 54 G1067

C56
DUPUY R.E.,"MILITARY HERITAGE OF AMERICA." USA+45 FORCES
USA-45 TEC/DEV DIPLOM ROUTINE...POLICY TREND CHARTS WAR
IDEA/COMP BIBLIOG COLD/WAR. PAGE 17 G0325 CONCPT

B58
CHEEK G.,ECONOMIC AND SOCIAL IMPLICATIONS OF BIBLIOG/A
AUTOMATION: A BIBLIOGRAPHIC REVIEW (PAMPHLET). SOCIETY
USA+45 LG/CO WORKER CREATE PLAN CONTROL ROUTINE INDUS
PERS/REL EFFICIENCY PRODUC...METH/COMP 20. PAGE 12 AUTOMAT
G0225

B58
GANGE J.,UNIVERSITY RESEARCH ON INTERNATIONAL R+D
AFFAIRS. USA+45 ACADEM INT/ORG CONSULT CREATE EXEC MGT
ROUTINE...QUANT STAT INT STERTYP GEN/METH TOT/POP DIPLOM
VAL/FREE 20. PAGE 21 G0407

B58
LIPPITT R.,DYNAMICS OF PLANNED CHANGE. STRUCT VOL/ASSN
ACT/RES ROUTINE INGP/REL PWR...POLICY METH/CNCPT ORD/FREE
BIBLIOG. PAGE 34 G0672 PLAN
CREATE

S58
FOLDES L.,"UNCERTAINTY, PROBABILITY AND POTENTIAL PROBABIL
SURPRISE." MARKET PROB/SOLV RISK PERSON...DECISION ADMIN
MGT HYPO/EXP GAME. PAGE 19 G0376 ROUTINE

B59
GUILBAUD G.T.,WHAT IS CYBERNETICS? COMPUTER OP/RES CONTROL
TEC/DEV AUTOMAT ROUTINE PERS/REL PERCEPT...PSY MATH COM/IND
COMPUT/IR SIMUL GEN/METH. PAGE 23 G0460 FEEDBACK
NET/THEORY

B59
WASSERMAN P.,MEASUREMENT AND ANALYSIS OF BIBLIOG/A
ORGANIZATIONAL PERFORMANCE. FINAN MARKET EX/STRUC ECO/TAC
TEC/DEV EDU/PROP CONTROL ROUTINE TASK...MGT 20. OP/RES
PAGE 62 G1220 EFFICIENCY

S59
CALKINS R.D.,"THE DECISION PROCESS IN ADMIN
ADMINISTRATION." EX/STRUC PROB/SOLV ROUTINE MGT. OP/RES
PAGE 10 G0204 DECISION
CON/ANAL

S59
CYERT R.M.,"MODELS IN A BEHAVIORAL THEORY OF THE SIMUL
FIRM." ROUTINE...DECISION MGT METH/CNCPT MATH. GAME
PAGE 14 G0267 PREDICT
INDUS

S59
STOESSINGER J.G.,"THE INTERNATIONAL ATOMIC ENERGY INT/ORG
AGENCY: THE FIRST PHASE." FUT WOR+45 NAT/G VOL/ASSN ECO/DEV
DELIB/GP BAL/PWR LEGIT ADMIN ROUTINE PWR...OBS FOR/AID
CON/ANAL GEN/LAWS VAL/FREE 20 IAEA. PAGE 53 G1037 NUC/PWR

B60
ALBI F.,TRATADO DE LOS MODOS DE GESTION DE LAS LOC/G
CORPORACIONES LOCALES. SPAIN FINAN NAT/G BUDGET LAW
CONTROL EXEC ROUTINE ORD/FREE GOV/REL SOVEREIGN ADMIN
...MGT 20. PAGE 2 G0034 MUNIC

B60
MCGREGOR D.,THE HUMAN SIDE OF ENTERPRISE. USA+45 MGT
LEAD ROUTINE GP/REL INGP/REL...CONCPT GEN/LAWS 20. ATTIT
PAGE 38 G0741 SKILL
EDU/PROP

L60
MACPHERSON C.,"TECHNICAL CHANGE AND POLITICAL TEC/DEV
DECISION." WOR+45 NAT/G CREATE CAP/ISM DIPLOM ADMIN
ROUTINE RIGID/FLEX...CONCPT OBS GEN/METH 20.
PAGE 35 G0692

L60
MCCLELLAND C.A.,"THE FUNCTION OF THEORY IN INT/ORG
INTERNATIONAL RELATIONS." WOR+45 PLAN EDU/PROP CONCPT
ROUTINE ORD/FREE...PHIL/SCI PSY SOC METH/CNCPT DIPLOM
NEW/IDEA OBS TREND GEN/METH 20. PAGE 37 G0728

S60
HUNTINGTON S.P.,"STRATEGIC PLANNING AND THE EXEC
POLITICAL PROCESS." USA+45 NAT/G DELIB/GP LEGIS FORCES
ACT/RES ECO/TAC LEGIT ROUTINE CHOOSE RIGID/FLEX PWR NUC/PWR
...POLICY MAJORIT MGT 20. PAGE 27 G0538 WAR

S60
HUTCHINSON C.E.,"AN INSTITUTE FOR NATIONAL SECURITY POLICY
AFFAIRS." USA+45 R+D NAT/G CONSULT TOP/EX ACT/RES METH/CNCPT
CREATE PLAN TEC/DEV EDU/PROP ROUTINE NUC/PWR ATTIT ELITES
ORD/FREE PWR...DECISION MGT PHIL/SCI CONCPT RECORD DIPLOM
GEN/LAWS GEN/METH 20. PAGE 27 G0539

S60
IKLE F.C.,"NTH COUNTRIES AND DISARMAMENT." WOR+45 FUT
DELIB/GP ECO/TAC DOMIN EDU/PROP LEGIT ROUTINE INT/ORG
COERCE RIGID/FLEX ORD/FREE...MARXIST TREND 20. ARMS/CONT
PAGE 28 G0543 NUC/PWR

S60
LEAR J.,"PEACE: SCIENCE'S NEXT GREAT EXPLORATION." EX/STRUC
USA+45 INT/ORG TOP/EX TEC/DEV EDU/PROP ROUTINE ARMS/CONT
PEACE KNOWL SKILL 20. PAGE 33 G0648 NUC/PWR

SHUBIK M.,"BIBLIOGRAPHY ON SIMULATION, GAMING, | BIBLIOG
ARTIFICIAL INTELLIGENCE AND ALLIED TOPICS." | SIMUL
COMPUTER ROUTINE...DECISION MGT STAT 20. PAGE 50 | GAME
G0992 | OP/RES
S60

SWIFT R.,"THE UNITED NATIONS AND ITS PUBLIC." | INT/ORG
WOR+45 CONSTN FINAN CONSULT DELIB/GP ACT/RES ADMIN | EDU/PROP
ROUTINE RIGID/FLEX SKILL UN 20. PAGE 53 G1048
S60

SCHRAMM W.,"MASS COMMUNICATIONS: A BOOK OF READINGS | COM/IND
(2ND ED.)" LG/CO PRESS ADMIN CONTROL ROUTINE ATTIT | EDU/PROP
ROLE SUPEGO...CHARTS ANTHOL BIBLIOG 20. PAGE 50 | CROWD
G0977 | MAJORIT
C60

HADLEY A.T.,THE NATIONS SAFETY AND ARMS CONTROL. | ACT/RES
FUT USA+45 WOR+45 TOP/EX PLAN TEC/DEV ATTIT DRIVE | ROUTINE
...CONCPT OBS TIME/SEQ TREND 20. PAGE 24 G0466 | DETER
B61 | NUC/PWR

LUNDBERG G.A.,CAN SCIENCE SAVE US. UNIV CULTURE | ACT/RES
INTELL SOCIETY ECO/DEV R+D PLAN EDU/PROP ROUTINE | CONCPT
CHOOSE ATTIT PERCEPT ALL/VALS...TREND 20. PAGE 34 | TOTALISM
G0679
B61

NAKICENOVIC S.,NUCLEAR ENERGY IN YUGOSLAVIA. | R+D
YUGOSLAVIA AGRI INDUS CREATE OP/RES ROUTINE | ECO/DEV
EFFICIENCY KNOWL...HEAL STAT CHARTS LAB/EXP BIBLIOG | TEC/DEV
20. PAGE 41 G0802 | NUC/PWR
B61

HERRING P.,"RESEARCH FOR PUBLIC POLICY: BROOKINGS | R+D
DEDICATION LECTURES." USA+45 CONSULT DELIB/GP | ACT/RES
ROUTINE PERCEPT SKILL...MGT 20. PAGE 26 G0508 | DIPLOM
L61

DEUTSCH K.W.,"A NOTE ON THE APPEARANCE OF WISDOM IN | ADMIN
LARGE BUREAUCRATIC ORGANIZATIONS." ROUTINE PERSON | PROBABIL
KNOWL SKILL...DECISION STAT. PAGE 15 G0299 | PROB/SOLV
S61 | SIMUL

LINDSAY F.A.,"PLANNING IN FOREIGN AFFAIRS: THE | ECO/DEV
MISSING ELEMENT." FUT USA+45 ROUTINE SKILL...MGT | PLAN
TOT/POP 20. PAGE 34 G0669 | DIPLOM
S61

TAUBENFELD H.J.,"OUTER SPACE--PAST POLITICS AND | PLAN
FUTURE POLICY." FUT USA+45 USA-45 WOR+45 AIR INTELL | SPACE
STRUCT ECO/DEV NAT/G TOP/EX ACT/RES ADMIN ROUTINE | INT/ORG
NUC/PWR ATTIT DRIVE...CONCPT TIME/SEQ TREND TOT/POP
20. PAGE 54 G1054
S61

SCHILLING W.R.,STRATEGY, POLITICS, AND DEFENSE | ROUTINE
BUDGETS. USA+45 R+D NAT/G CONSULT DELIB/GP FORCES | POLICY
LEGIS ACT/RES PLAN BAL/PWR LEGIT EXEC NUC/PWR
RIGID/FLEX PWR...TREND COLD/WAR CONGRESS 20
EISNHWR/DD. PAGE 49 G0968
B62

SNYDER R.C.,FOREIGN POLICY DECISION-MAKING. FUT | TEC/DEV
KOREA WOR+45 R+D CREATE ADMIN ROUTINE PWR | HYPO/EXP
...DECISION PSY SOC CONCPT METH/CNCPT CON/ANAL | DIPLOM
CHARTS GEN/METH METH 20. PAGE 52 G1018
B62

STAHL O.G.,PUBLIC PERSONNEL ADMINISTRATION. LOC/G | ADMIN
TOP/EX CREATE PLAN ROUTINE...TECHNIC MGT T. PAGE 52 | WORKER
G1030 | EX/STRUC
| NAT/G
B62

THANT U.,THE UNITED NATIONS' DEVELOPMENT DECADE: | INT/ORG
PROPOSALS FOR ACTION. WOR+45 SOCIETY ECO/UNDEV AGRI | ALL/VALS
COM/IND FINAN R+D MUNIC SCHOOL VOL/ASSN CONSULT
PLAN TEC/DEV ECO/TAC EDU/PROP ADMIN ROUTINE
RIGID/FLEX...MGT SOC CONCPT UNESCO UN TOT/POP
VAL/FREE. PAGE 54 G1064
B62

NEIBURG H.L.,"THE EISENHOWER AEC AND CONGRESS: A | CHIEF
STUDY IN EXECUTIVE-LEGISLATIVE RELATIONS." USA+45 | LEGIS
NAT/G POL/PAR DELIB/GP EX/STRUC TOP/EX ADMIN EXEC | GOV/REL
LEAD ROUTINE PWR...POLICY COLD/WAR CONGRESS | NUC/PWR
PRESIDENT AEC. PAGE 41 G0816
L62

DONNELLY D.,"THE POLITICS AND ADMINISTRATION OF | GOV/REL
PLANNING." UK ROUTINE FEDERAL 20. PAGE 16 G0307 | EFFICIENCY
| ADMIN
S62

S62

PHIPPS T.E.,"THE CASE FOR DETERRENCE." FUT WOR+45 | ATTIT
SOCIETY EX/STRUC FORCES ACT/RES CREATE PLAN TEC/DEV | COERCE
ROUTINE RIGID/FLEX ORD/FREE...POLICY MYTH NEW/IDEA | DETER
STERTYP COLD/WAR 20. PAGE 45 G0876 | ARMS/CONT
S62

WALTER E.,"VERS UNE CLASSIFICATION SCIENTIFIQUE DE | PLAN
LA SOCIOLOGIA." UNIV CULTURE INTELL SOCIETY R+D | CONCPT
ACT/RES LEGIT ROUTINE ATTIT KNOWL...JURID MGT TREND
GEN/LAWS 20. PAGE 62 G1208
B63

ACKOFF R.L.,A MANAGER'S GUIDE TO OPERATIONS | OP/RES
RESEARCH. STRUCT INDUS PROB/SOLV ROUTINE 20. PAGE 2 | MGT
G0028 | GP/REL
| ADMIN
B63

BURSK E.C.,NEW DECISION-MAKING TOOLS FOR MANAGERS. | DECISION
COMPUTER PLAN PROB/SOLV ROUTINE COST. PAGE 10 G0194 | MGT
| MATH
| RIGID/FLEX
B63

LITTERER J.A.,ORGANIZATIONS: STRUCTURE AND | ADMIN
BEHAVIOR. PLAN DOMIN CONTROL LEAD ROUTINE SANCTION | CREATE
INGP/REL EFFICIENCY PRODUC DRIVE RIGID/FLEX PWR. | MGT
PAGE 34 G0674 | ADJUST
B63

MAYNE R.,THE COMMUNITY OF EUROPE. UK CONSTN NAT/G | EUR+WWI
CONSULT DELIB/GP CREATE PLAN ECO/TAC LEGIT ADMIN | INT/ORG
ROUTINE ORD/FREE PWR WEALTH...CONCPT TIME/SEQ EEC | REGION
EURATOM 20. PAGE 37 G0724
B63

NORTH R.C.,CONTENT ANALYSIS: A HANDBOOK WITH | METH/CNCPT
APPLICATIONS FOR THE STUDY OF INTERNATIONAL CRISIS. | COMPUT/IR
ASIA COM EUR+WWI MOD/EUR INT/ORG EDU/PROP DOMIN | USSR
EDU/PROP ROUTINE COERCE PERCEPT RIGID/FLEX ALL/VALS
...QUANT TESTS CON/ANAL SIMUL GEN/LAWS VAL/FREE.
PAGE 42 G0825
B63

SCHOECK H.,THE NEW ARGUMENT IN ECONOMICS. UK USA+45 | WELF/ST
INDUS MARKET LABOR NAT/G ECO/TAC ADMIN ROUTINE | FOR/AID
BAL/PAY PWR...POLICY BOLIV. PAGE 49 G0973 | ECO/DEV
| ALL/IDEOS
B63

US ATOMIC ENERGY COMMISSION.ATOMIC ENERGY IN THE | METH/COMP
SOVIET UNION: TRIP REPORT OF THE US ATOMIC ENERGY | OP/RES
DELEGATION, MAY 1933. USSR R+D NAT/G CONSULT CREATE | TEC/DEV
DIPLOM ADMIN ROUTINE EFFICIENCY PRODUC KNOWL SKILL | NUC/PWR
...NAT/COMP 20 AEC TRAVEL TREATY. PAGE 56 G1107
L63

BRENNAN D.G.,"ARMS CONTROL AND CIVIL DEFENSE." | PLAN
USA+45 WOR+45 NAT/G BAL/PWR ROUTINE ATTIT | HEALTH
RIGID/FLEX ORD/FREE...SOC TOT/POP 20. PAGE 8 G0165 | ARMS/CONT
| DETER
S63

DE FOREST J.D.,"LOW LEVELS OF TECHNOLOGY AND | ECO/UNDEV
ECONOMIC DEVELOPMENT PROSPECTS." WOR+45 WOR-45 | TEC/DEV
CULTURE ACT/RES CREATE PLAN ECO/TAC ROUTINE PERCEPT
WEALTH...METH/CNCPT GEN/LAWS 20. PAGE 15 G0284
S63

TANNENBAUM P.H.,"COMMUNICATION OF SCIENCE | COM/IND
INFORMATION." USA+45 TEC/DEV ROUTINE...PHIL/SCI | PRESS
STYLE 20. PAGE 53 G1051 | OP/RES
| METH/CNCPT
B64

ELLUL J.,THE TECHNOLOGICAL SOCIETY. FUT STRUCT | SOC
CREATE AUTOMAT ROUTINE STRANGE ANOMIE MORAL | SOCIETY
PHIL/SCI. PAGE 18 G0344 | TECHNIC
| TEC/DEV
B64

HAMMOND P.E.,SOCIOLOGISTS AT WORK. VOL/ASSN OP/RES | R+D
TEC/DEV CONFER ROUTINE TASK EFFICIENCY...MGT | BIOG
NEW/IDEA STYLE SAMP. PAGE 24 G0478 | SOC
B64

ORTH C.D.,ADMINISTERING RESEARCH AND DEVELOPMENT. | MGT
FINAN PLAN PROB/SOLV ADMIN ROUTINE...METH/CNCPT | R+D
STAT CHARTS METH 20. PAGE 43 G0847 | LG/CO
| INDUS
B64

RANSOM H.H.,CAN AMERICAN DEMOCRACY SURVIVE COLD | USA+45
B64

WAR. USA-45 CONSTN NAT/G CONSULT DELIB/GP LEGIS   ROUTINE
ACT/RES LEGIT EXEC ATTIT KNOWL ORD/FREE PWR SKILL
...POLICY TIME/SEQ TREND GEN/LAWS 20 COLD/WAR.
PAGE 46 G0901

L64
HAAS E.B.,"ECONOMICS AND DIFFERENTIAL PATTERNS OF   L/A+17C
POLITICAL INTEGRATION: PROJECTIONS ABOUT UNITY IN   INT/ORG
LATIN AMERICA." SOCIETY NAT/G DELIB/GP ACT/RES   MARKET
CREATE PLAN ECO/TAC REGION ROUTINE ATTIT DRIVE PWR
WEALTH...CONCPT TREND CHARTS LAFTA 20. PAGE 24
G0464

S64
GARDNER R.N.,"GATT AND THE UNITED NATIONS   INT/ORG
CONFERENCE ON TRADE AND DEVELOPMENT." USA+45 WOR+45 INT/TRADE
SOCIETY ECO/UNDEV MARKET NAT/G DELIB/GP ACT/RES
PLAN ECO/TAC TARIFFS EDU/PROP ROUTINE DRIVE
RIGID/FLEX WEALTH...DECISION MGT TREND UN TOT/POP
20 GATT. PAGE 21 G0411

S64
PILISUK M.,"STEPWISE DISARMAMENT & SUDDEN   PWR
DESTRUCTION IN A TWOPERSON GAME: A RESEARCH TOOL."   DECISION
NAT/G FORCES ACT/RES ECO/TAC EDU/PROP EXEC ROUTINE   ARMS/CONT
COERCE ORD/FREE...SIMUL GEN/LAWS VAL/FREE. PAGE 45
G0877

S64
THOMPSON V.A.,"ADMINISTRATIVE OBJECTIVES FOR   ECO/UNDEV
DEVELOPMENT ADMINISTRATION." WOR+45 CREATE PLAN   MGT
DOMIN EDU/PROP EXEC ROUTINE ATTIT ORD/FREE PWR
...POLICY GEN/LAWS VAL/FREE. PAGE 54 G1070

B65
HICKMAN B.G.,QUANTITATIVE PLANNING OF ECONOMIC   PROB/SOLV
POLICY. FRANCE NETHERLAND OP/RES PRICE ROUTINE UTIL PLAN
...POLICY DECISION ECOMETRIC METH/CNCPT STAT STYLE   QUANT
CHINJAP. PAGE 26 G0511

B65
KOROL A.G.,SOVIET RESEARCH AND DEVELOPMENT. USSR   COM
ACADEM SCHOOL WORKER ROUTINE COST...STAT T 20.   R+D
PAGE 31 G0615   FINAN
                                                     DIST/IND

B65
SMITH E.A.,SOCIAL WELFARE: PRINCIPLES AND CONCEPTS. CONCPT
STRATA STRUCT CONSULT WORKER ACT/RES CREATE PLAN   SOC/WK
TEC/DEV ROUTINE GP/REL UTOPIA...SOC 20. PAGE 51   RECEIVE
G1014   ORD/FREE

B65
US SENATE COMM GOVT OPERATIONS,ORGANIZATION OF   ADMIN
FEDERAL EXECUTIVE DEPARTMENTS AND AGENCIES: REPORT   EX/STRUC
OF MARCH 23, 1965. USA+45 FORCES LEGIS DIPLOM   GOV/REL
ROUTINE CIVMIL/REL EFFICIENCY FEDERAL...MGT STAT.   ORG/CHARTS
PAGE 60 G1179

S65
HUGHES T.L.,"SCHOLARS AND FOREIGN POLICY* VARIETIES ACT/RES
OF RESEARCH EXPERIENCE." COM/IND DIPLOM ADMIN EXEC   ACADEM
ROUTINE...MGT OBS CONGRESS PRESIDENT CAMELOT.   CONTROL
PAGE 27 G0535   NAT/G

B66
LEWIS W.A.,DEVELOPMENT PLANNING: THE ESSENTIALS OF   PLAN
ECONOMIC POLICY. USA+45 FINAN INDUS NAT/G WORKER   ECO/DEV
FOR/AID INT/TRADE ADMIN ROUTINE WEALTH...CONCPT   POLICY
STAT. PAGE 34 G0663   CREATE

B66
WHITNAH D.R.,SAFER SKYWAYS. DIST/IND DELIB/GP   ADMIN
FORCES TOP/EX WORKER TEC/DEV ROUTINE WAR CIVMIL/REL NAT/G
COST...TIME/SEQ 20 FAA CAB. PAGE 63 G1235   AIR
                                                     GOV/REL

B66
YOUNG W.,EXISTING MECHANISMS OF ARMS CONTROL.   ARMS/CONT
PROC/MFG OP/RES DIPLOM TASK CENTRAL...MGT TREATY.   ADMIN
PAGE 65 G1266   NUC/PWR
                                                     ROUTINE

S66
FLEMING W.G.,"AUTHORITY, EFFICIENCY, AND ROLE   DOMIN
STRESS: PROBLEMS IN THE DEVELOPMENT OF EAST AFRICAN EFFICIENCY
BUREAUCRACIES." AFR UGANDA STRUCT PROB/SOLV ROUTINE COLONIAL
INGP/REL ROLE...MGT SOC GP/COMP GOV/COMP 20   ADMIN
TANGANYIKA AFRICA/E. PAGE 19 G0371

B67
DE BLIJ H.J.,SYSTEMATIC POLITICAL GEOGRAPHY. WOR+45 GEOG
STRUCT INT/ORG NAT/G EDU/PROP ADMIN COLONIAL   CONCPT
ROUTINE ORD/FREE PWR...IDEA/COMP T 20. PAGE 15   METH
G0283

B67
DONALD A.G.,MANAGEMENT, INFORMATION, AND SYSTEMS.   ROUTINE
WOR+45 LG/CO PROB/SOLV CONTROL FEEDBACK KNOWL MGT.   TEC/DEV
PAGE 16 G0306   CONCPT
                                                     ADMIN

L67
PASLEY R.S.,"ORGANIZATIONAL CONFLICTS OF INTEREST   NAT/G
IN GOVERNMENT CONTRACTS." ELITES R+D ROUTINE   ECO/TAC
NUC/PWR DEMAND EFFICIENCY 20. PAGE 44 G0860   RATION
                                                     CONTROL

S67
ALBAUM G.,"INFORMATION FLOW AND DECENTRALIZED   LG/CO
DECISION MAKING IN MARKETING." EX/STRUC COMPUTER   ROUTINE
OP/RES PROB/SOLV EFFICIENCY OPTIMAL...METH/COMP   KNOWL
ORG/CHARTS 20. PAGE 2 G0033   MARKET

S67
CONWAY J.E.,"MAKING RESEARCH EFFECTIVE IN   ACT/RES
LEGISLATION." LAW R+D CONSULT EX/STRUC PLAN CONFER   POLICY
ADMIN LEAD ROUTINE TASK INGP/REL DECISION. PAGE 13   LEGIS
G0252   PROB/SOLV

S67
DONAHO J.A.,"PLANNING-PROGRAMMING-BUDGETING   PLAN
SYSTEMS." USA+45 LOC/G NAT/G ROUTINE. PAGE 16 G0305 BUDGET
                                                     ADMIN
                                                     ECOMETRIC

S67
KAYSEN C.,"DATA BANKS AND DOSSIERS." FUT USA+45   CENTRAL
COM/IND NAT/G PLAN PROB/SOLV TEC/DEV BUDGET ADMIN   EFFICIENCY
ROUTINE. PAGE 30 G0588   CENSUS
                                                     ACT/RES

S67
LEVENSTEIN A.,"TECHNOLOGICAL CHANGE, WORK, AND   TEC/DEV
HUMAN VALUES." WOR+45 SOCIETY AUTOMAT ROUTINE   CULTURE
LEISURE INGP/REL ADJUST TECHRACY...MGT CONCPT.   ALL/VALS
PAGE 33 G0660   TIME/SEQ

S67
MACDONALD G.J.F.,"SCIENCE AND SPACE POLICY* HOW   SPACE
DOES IT GET PLANNED?" R+D CREATE TEC/DEV BUDGET   PLAN
ADMIN ROUTINE...DECISION NASA. PAGE 35 G0687   MGT
                                                     EX/STRUC

S67
MOOR E.J.,"THE INTERNATIONAL IMPACT OF AUTOMATION." TEC/DEV
WOR+45 ACT/RES COMPUTER CREATE PLAN CAP/ISM ROUTINE OP/RES
EFFICIENCY PREDICT. PAGE 39 G0779   AUTOMAT
                                                     INDUS

ROY/MN....M.N. ROY

ROYAL AIR FORCE....SEE RAF

ROYAL INST. INT. AFF. G0943

RUBINSTEIN A.Z. G0944

RUEF/ABE....ABRAHAM RUEF

RUITENBEER H.M. G0945

RULES/COMM....RULES COMMITTEES OF CONGRESS

RUMOR....SEE ALSO PERS/REL

RUPPENTHAL K.M. G0946

RURAL....RURAL AREAS, PEOPLE, ETC.

RUSHING W.A. G0947

RUSK/D

B62
US SENATE COMM GOVT OPERATIONS,ADMINISTRATION OF   ORD/FREE
NATIONAL SECURITY. USA+45 CHIEF PLAN PROB/SOLV   ADMIN
TEC/DEV DIPLOM ATTIT...POLICY DECISION 20   NAT/G
KENNEDY/JF RUSK/D MCNAMARA/R BUNDY/M HERTER/C.   CONTROL
PAGE 60 G1177

RUSK/DEAN....DEAN RUSK

RUSKIN/J....JOHN RUSKIN

RUSSELL B. G0948,G0949

RUSSELL/B....BERTRAND RUSSELL

B67
RUSSELL B.,WAR CRIMES IN VIETNAM. USA+45 VIETNAM   WAR
FORCES DIPLOM WEAPON RACE/REL DISCRIM ISOLAT   CRIME

BIO/SOC 20 COLD/WAR RUSSELL/B. PAGE 48 G0949   ATTIT
POLICY

RUSSETT B.M. G0950

RUSSIA....PRE-REVOLUTIONARY RUSSIA; SEE ALSO APPROPRIATE
    TIME/SPACE/CULTURE INDEX

                                                       L66
ZOPPO C.E.,"NUCLEAR TECHNOLOGY, MULTIPOLARITY, AND   NET/THEORY
INTERNATIONAL STABILITY." ASIA RUSSIA USA+45 STRUCT ORD/FREE
TOP/EX BAL/PWR DIPLOM DETER CIVMIL/REL NAT/COMP.   DECISION
PAGE 65 G1270   NUC/PWR

RUTGERS U GRADUATE SCH LIB SCI G0951

RUTH J.M. G0952

RWANDA....SEE ALSO AFR

RYUKYUS....RYUKYU ISLANDS

S

S/AFR....SOUTH AFRICA, SEE ALSO AFR

S/ASIA....SOUTHEAST ASIA; SEE ALSO APPROPRIATE NATIONS

                                                        N19
MEZERIK A.G.,INTERNATIONAL POLICY 1965 (PAMPHLET).   DIPLOM
KASHMIR S/ASIA SPACE USA+45 VIETNAM WOR+45   INT/ORG
ARMS/CONT RACE/REL DISCRIM PEACE PWR 20 UN. PAGE 39 POLICY
G0762   WAR

                                                        S54
PYE L.W.,"EASTERN NATIONALISM AND WESTERN POLICY."   CREATE
ASIA S/ASIA USA+45 USA-45 SOCIETY PLAN DIPLOM KNOWL ACT/RES
TOT/POP 20. PAGE 46 G0896   NAT/LISM

                                                        B59
GREENFIELD K.R.,COMMAND DECISIONS. ASIA EUR+WWI   PLAN
S/ASIA USA-45 WOR-45 NAT/G CONSULT DELIB/GP COERCE FORCES
NUC/PWR PWR...OBS 20 CHINJAP. PAGE 23 G0446   WAR
                                                        WEAPON

                                                        S60
JAFFEE A.J.,"POPULATION TRENDS AND CONTROLS IN   ECO/UNDEV
UNDERDEVELOPED COUNTRIES." AFR FUT ISLAM L/A+17C   GEOG
S/ASIA CULTURE R+D FAM ACT/RES PLAN EDU/PROP
BIO/SOC RIGID/FLEX HEALTH...SOC STAT OBS CHARTS 20.
PAGE 28 G0555

                                                        B63
WIGHTMAN D.,TOWARD ECONOMIC CO-OPERATION IN ASIA.   ECO/UNDEV
ASIA S/ASIA VOL/ASSN ACT/RES PLAN TEC/DEV ECO/TAC CREATE
EDU/PROP RIGID/FLEX SKILL...POLICY METH/CNCPT OBS
INT GEN/LAWS UN 20 ECAFE. PAGE 63 G1237

                                                        B64
PETERSON W.,THE POLITICS OF POPULATION. COM EUR+WWI PLAN
FUT MOD/EUR S/ASIA USA+45 USA-45 WOR+45 LAW CULTURE CENSUS
FAM SECT DOMIN EDU/PROP BIO/SOC HEALTH ORD/FREE   POLICY
...GEOG STAT TIME/SEQ TREND VAL/FREE. PAGE 44 G0871

                                                        B64
ROSECRANCE R.N.,THE DISPERSION OF NUCLEAR WEAPONS: EUR+WWI
STRATEGY AND POLITICS. ASIA COM FUT S/ASIA USA+45 PWR
INT/ORG NAT/G DELIB/GP FORCES ACT/RES TEC/DEV   PEACE
BAL/PWR COERCE DETER ATTIT RIGID/FLEX ORD/FREE
...POLICY CHARTS VAL/FREE. PAGE 48 G0935

                                                        S64
MAHALANOBIS P.C.,"PERSPECTIVE PLANNING IN INDIA: PLAN
STATISTICAL TOOLS." INDIA S/ASIA STRATA AGRI   STAT
DIST/IND FINAN INDUS SERV/IND NAT/G ECO/TAC
ORD/FREE WEALTH...POLICY TREND SIMUL VAL/FREE 20.
PAGE 35 G0695

                                                        S65
BLOOMFIELD L.P.,"ARMS CONTROL AND THE DEVELOPING   ARMS/CONT
COUNTRIES." AFR ISLAM S/ASIA USA+45 VOL/ASSN   ECO/UNDEV
TEC/DEV DIPLOM REGION NUC/PWR...PREDICT TREND.   HYPO/EXP
PAGE 7 G0142   OBS

                                                        S65
HSIEH A.L.,"THE SINO-SOVIET NUCLEAR DIALOGUE*   ASIA
1963." S/ASIA USA+45 RISK DETER REV WAR SOVEREIGN USSR
IDEA/COMP. PAGE 27 G0533   NUC/PWR

                                                        B66
US DEPARTMENT OF THE ARMY,COMMUNIST CHINA: A   BIBLIOG/A
STRATEGIC SURVEY: A BIBLIOGRAPHY (PAMPHLET NO.   MARXISM
20-67). CHINA/COM COM INDIA USSR NAT/G POL/PAR   S/ASIA
EX/STRUC FORCES NUC/PWR REV ATTIT...POLICY GEOG   DIPLOM
CHARTS. PAGE 58 G1133

S/EASTASIA....SOUTHEAST ASIA: CAMBODIA, LAOS, NORTH AND
    SOUTH VIETNAM, AND THAILAND

SABAH....SABAH, MALAYSIA

SABBATINO....SABBATINO CASE

SAINT AUGUSTINE....SEE AUGUSTINE

SAINT/PIER....JACQUES SAINT-PIERRE

SAINTSIMON....COMTE DE SAINT-SIMON

SALARY....SEE WORKER, WEALTH, ROUTINE

SALAZAR/A....ANTONIO DE OLIVERA SALAZAR

SALIENCE....SALIENCE

SALINGER/P....PIERRE SALINGER

SALISBURY H.E. G0953

SALISBURY R.H. G0720

SALMOND J.A. G0954

SALO....SALO REPUBLIC

SAMBURU....SAMBURU TRIBE OF EAST AFRICA

SAMOA....SEE ALSO WEST/SAMOA

SAMP....SAMPLE SURVEY

                                                        N19
US CHAMBER OF COMMERCE,THE SIGNIFICANCE OF   MARKET
CONCENTRATION RATIOS (PAMPHLET). USA+45 FINAN INDUS PREDICT
ADMIN...METH/CNCPT SAMP CHARTS 20. PAGE 56 G1109   LG/CO
                                                        CONTROL

                                                        B47
SOCIAL SCIENCE RESEARCH COUN,PUBLIC REACTION TO THE ATTIT
ATOMIC BOMB AND WORLD AFFAIRS. SOCIETY CONFER   NUC/PWR
ARMS/CONT...STAT QU SAMP CHARTS 20. PAGE 52 G1019   DIPLOM
                                                        WAR

                                                        B48
BRADLEY D.,NO PLACE TO HIDE. USA+45 SOCIETY NAT/G   R+D
FORCES TEC/DEV EDU/PROP DETER PEACE BIO/SOC   LAB/EXP
ALL/VALS...POLICY PHIL/SCI OBS RECORD SAMP BIOG   ARMS/CONT
GEN/METH COLD/WAR 20. PAGE 8 G0162   NUC/PWR

                                                        B50
CONTINUITIES IN SOCIAL RESEARCH; STUDIES IN SCOPE   SOC
AND METHOD OF "THE AMERICAN SOLDIER" USA+45 FORCES PHIL/SCI
INGP/REL ATTIT...PSY SAMP CON/ANAL CHARTS GEN/LAWS METH
ANTHOL 20. PAGE 38 G0758

                                                        B59
ELDRIDGE H.T.,THE MATERIALS OF DEMOGRAPHY: A   BIBLIOG/A
SELECTED AND ANNOTATED BIBLIOGRAPHY. R+D DEATH   GEOG
...SAMP METH/COMP NAT/COMP 20. PAGE 18 G0343   STAT
                                                        TREND

                                                        B60
PENTONY D.E.,THE UNDERDEVELOPED LANDS. FUT WOR+45   ECO/UNDEV
CULTURE AGRI FINAN INDUS MARKET INT/ORG LABOR NAT/G POLICY
VOL/ASSN CONSULT TEC/DEV ECO/TAC EDU/PROP COLONIAL FOR/AID
ATTIT WEALTH...OBS RECORD SAMP TREND GEN/METH WORK INT/TRADE
UN 20. PAGE 44 G0867

                                                        L60
DEUTSCH K.W.,"TOWARD AN INVENTORY OF BASIC TRENDS   R+D
AND PATTERNS IN COMPARATIVE AND INTERNATIONAL   PERCEPT
POLITICS." UNIV WOR+45 SOCIETY STRUCT INT/ORG NAT/G
CREATE PLAN EDU/PROP KNOWL...PHIL/SCI METH/CNCPT
STAT SELF/OBS OBS/ENVIR SAMP TREND CON/ANAL CHARTS
SOC/EXP GEN/METH 20. PAGE 15 G0298

                                                        B62
STERN A.C.,AIR POLLUTION (2 VOLS.). LAW INDUS   AIR
PROB/SOLV TEC/DEV INSPECT RISK BIO/SOC HABITAT   OP/RES
...OBS/ENVIR TESTS SAMP 20 POLLUTION. PAGE 53 G1035 CONTROL
                                                        HEALTH

                                                        B63
GOLDSEN J.M.,OUTER SPACE IN WORLD POLITICS. COM   TEC/DEV
USA+45 NAT/G FORCES ACT/RES PLAN DOMIN EDU/PROP   DIPLOM
COERCE ORD/FREE PWR...TECHNIC STAT INT SAMP TREND SPACE
ANTHOL VAL/FREE 20. PAGE 22 G0428

                                                        B63
WALES H.G.,A BASIC BIBLIOGRAPHY ON MARKETING   BIBLIOG/A
RESEARCH (REV. ED.). ATTIT...MGT STAT INT QU SAMP MARKET
TREND 20. PAGE 62 G1206   OP/RES
                                                        METH/COMP

S63
ERSKINE H.G.,"THE POLLS: ATOMIC WEAPONS AND NUCLEAR ATTIT
ENERGY." USA+45 COERCE ORD/FREE...POLICY SOC STAT INT
CENSUS SAMP VAL/FREE 20. PAGE 18 G0350   NUC/PWR

B64
HAMMOND P.E.,SOCIOLOGISTS AT WORK. VOL/ASSN OP/RES R+D
TEC/DEV CONFER ROUTINE TASK EFFICIENCY...MGT   BIOG
NEW/IDEA STYLE SAMP. PAGE 24 G0478   SOC

SAMP/SIZ....SIZES AND TECHNIQUES OF SAMPLING

S50
LENTZ T.F.,"REPORT ON A SURVEY OF SOCIAL SCIENTISTS ACT/RES
CONDUCTED BY THE ATTITUDE RESEARCH LABORATORY." FUT ATTIT
WOR+45 CREATE EDU/PROP...PSY STAT RECORD SYS/QU DIPLOM
SAMP/SIZ CON/ANAL VAL/FREE 20. PAGE 33 G0655

B54
COMBS C.H.,DECISION PROCESSES. INTELL SOCIETY MATH
DELIB/GP CREATE TEC/DEV DOMIN LEGIT EXEC CHOOSE DECISION
DRIVE RIGID/FLEX KNOWL PWR...PHIL/SCI SOC
METH/CNCPT CONT/OBS REC/INT PERS/TEST SAMP/SIZ BIOG
SOC/EXP WORK. PAGE 13 G0245

B54
SPENCER R.F.,METHOD AND PERSPECTIVE IN ANTHROPOLOGY PHIL/SCI
....GEOG LING QUANT STAT TESTS SAMP/SIZ CON/ANAL SOC
IDEA/COMP METH/COMP ANTHOL BIBLIOG 20. PAGE 52 PSY
G1025   METH

B62
CHASE S.,THE PROPER STUDY OF MANKIND (2ND REV. PHIL/SCI
ED.). WOR+45 WOR-45 INTELL WAR...METH/CNCPT SOC
SAMP/SIZ GEN/LAWS BIBLIOG METH 16/20. PAGE 11 G0224 PROB/SOLV
PERSON

B67
MCCLINTOCK R.,THE MEANING OF LIMITED WAR. FUT WAR
WOR+45 NAT/G FORCES GUERRILLA REV...POLICY SAMP/SIZ NUC/PWR
TREND NAT/COMP 45 COLD/WAR. PAGE 37 G0730 BAL/PWR
DIPLOM

B67
YAVITZ B.,AUTOMATION IN COMMERCIAL BANKING. USA+45 TEC/DEV
STRUCT WORKER CREATE OP/RES PLAN ROLE...DECISION FINAN
SAMP/SIZ. PAGE 64 G1263   COMPUT/IR
MGT

SAMPLE....SEE SAMP

SAMPLE AND SAMPLING....SEE UNIVERSES AND SAMPLING INDEX,
    P. XIV

SAMUEL CLEMENS....SEE TWAIN/MARK

SAMUELSN/P....PAUL SAMUELSON

SAN/FRAN....SAN FRANCISCO

B65
ARTHUR D LITTLE INC.SAN FRANCISCO COMMUNITY RENEWAL HABITAT
PROGRAM. USA+45 FINAN PROVS ADMIN INCOME...CHARTS MUNIC
20 CALIFORNIA SAN/FRAN URBAN/RNWL. PAGE 4 G0071 PLAN
PROB/SOLV

SAN/MARINO....SAN MARINO

SAN/MARTIN....JOSE DE SAN MARTIN

SAN/QUENTN....SAN QUENTIN PRISON

SANCTION....SANCTION OF LAW AND SEMI-LEGAL PRIVATE
    ASSOCIATIONS AND SOCIAL GROUPS

L50
MAASS A.A.,"CONGRESS AND WATER RESOURCES." LOC/G REGION
TEC/DEV CONTROL SANCTION...WELF/ST GEOG CONGRESS. AGRI
PAGE 35 G0683   PLAN

B51
HUXLEY J.,FREEDOM AND CULTURE. UNIV LAW SOCIETY R+D CULTURE
ACADEM SCHOOL CREATE SANCTION ATTIT KNOWL...HUM ORD/FREE
ANTHOL 20. PAGE 27 G0540   PHIL/SCI
IDEA/COMP

B62
SCHWARTZ L.E.,INTERNATIONAL ORGANIZATIONS AND SPACE INT/ORG
COOPERATION. VOL/ASSN CONSULT CREATE TEC/DEV DIPLOM
SANCTION...POLICY INT/LAW PHIL/SCI 20 UN. PAGE 50 R+D
G0982   SPACE

B63
LITTERER J.A.,ORGANIZATIONS: STRUCTURE AND ADMIN
BEHAVIOR. PLAN DOMIN CONTROL LEAD ROUTINE SANCTION CREATE

INGP/REL EFFICIENCY PRODUC DRIVE RIGID/FLEX PWR. MGT
PAGE 34 G0674   ADJUST

B66
CLARK G.,WORLD PEACE THROUGH WORLD LAW; TWO INT/LAW
ALTERNATIVE PLANS. WOR+45 DELIB/GP FORCES TAX PEACE
CONFER ADJUD SANCTION ARMS/CONT WAR CHOOSE PRIVIL PLAN
20 UN COLD/WAR. PAGE 12 G0231   INT/ORG

B66
US HOUSE COMM ON JUDICIARY.CIVIL COMMITMENT AND BIO/SOC
TREATMENT OF NARCOTIC ADDICTS. USA+45 SOCIETY FINAN CRIME
LEGIS PROB/SOLV GIVE CT/SYS SANCTION HEALTH IDEA/COMP
...POLICY HEAL 20. PAGE 58 G1141   CONTROL

L67
CARMICHAEL D.M.,"FORTY YEARS OF WATER POLLUTION HEALTH
CONTROL IN WISCONSIN: A CASE STUDY." LAW EXTR/IND CONTROL
INDUS MUNIC DELIB/GP PLAN PROB/SOLV SANCTION ADMIN
...CENSUS CHARTS 20 WISCONSIN. PAGE 11 G0207 ADJUD

L67
SEABERG G.P.,"THE DRUG ABUSE PROBLEMS AND SOME BIO/SOC
PROPOSALS." UK USA+45 MARKET SANCTION CRIME LAW
...POLICY NEW/IDEA. PAGE 50 G0986   ADJUD
PROB/SOLV

S67
ALEXANDER L.,"PROTECTION OF PRIVACY IN BEHAVIORAL ACT/RES
RESEARCH." WOR+45 ADJUD SANCTION ORD/FREE...JURID POLICY
INT. PAGE 2 G0036   OBS/ENVIR

S67
HARRIS F.R.,"POLITICAL SCIENCE AND THE PROPOSAL FOR PROF/ORG
A NATIONAL SOCIAL SCIENCE FOUNDATION." FUT CONSULT R+D
DELIB/GP PLAN PROB/SOLV BUDGET CONFER SANCTION CREATE
CRIME...POLICY SOC/WK 20 NSF NSSF. PAGE 25 G0484 NAT/G

S67
KOMESAR N.K.,"SECURITY INTERESTS IN GOVERNMENT POLICY
CONTRACTS* WHEREIN THE TORTOISE WINS THE RES." CT/SYS
USA+45 INDUS NAT/G OP/RES SANCTION. PAGE 31 G0613 PRIVIL
JURID

S67
KRUSCHE H.,"THE STRIVING OF THE KIESINGER-STRAUS ARMS/CONT
GOVERNMENT FOR NUCLEAR WEAPONS IS A THREAT TO INT/ORG
EUROPEAN SECURITY." EUR+WWI GERMANY BAL/PWR NUC/PWR
SANCTION WEAPON PEACE ORD/FREE...MARXIST 20 NATO DIPLOM
COLD/WAR. PAGE 32 G0623

S67
RAMSEY J.A.,"THE STATUS OF INTERNATIONAL INT/LAW
COPYRIGHTS." WOR+45 CREATE TEC/DEV DIPLOM CONFER INT/ORG
CONTROL SANCTION OWN...POLICY JURID. PAGE 46 G0899 COM/IND
PRESS

S67
ROBINSON J.A.T.,"ABORTION* THE CASE FOR A FREE PLAN
DECISION." LAW PROB/SOLV SANCTION ATTIT MORAL...PSY ILLEGIT
IDEA/COMP 20 ABORTION. PAGE 47 G0930   SEX
HEALTH

SANDERS R. G0955

SANDLER C.R. G0545

SANFORD S.A. G0322

SANFORD T. G0956

SANTAYAN/G....GEORGE SANTAYANA

SAO/PAULO....SAO PAULO, BRAZIL

SAPARINA Y. G0957

SAPIN B. G1018

SAPIR/EDW....EDWARD SAPIR

SARAWAK....SARAWAK, MALAYSIA

SARTRE/J....JEAN-PAUL SARTRE

SARVODAYA....SARVODAYA - GANDHIAN SOCIALIST POLITICAL IDEAL
    OF UNIVERSAL MATERIAL AND SPIRITUAL WELFARE; SEE ALSO
    GANDHI/M

SASKATCH....SASKATCHEWAN, CANADA

SASKATCHEWAN, CANADA...SEE SASKATCH

SATELLITE....SPACE SATELLITES

SATISFACTION....SEE HAPPINESS

SAUDI/ARAB....SAUDI ARABIA; SEE ALSO ISLAM

SAVILLE J. G0769

SAX/JOSEPH....JOSEPH SAX

SAY/EMIL....EMIL SAY

SAYLES L.R. G0221,G0958

SBA....SMALL BUSINESS ADMINISTRATION

SCALES....SEE TESTS AND SCALES INDEX, P. XIV

SCANDINAV....SCANDINAVIAN COUNTRIES

SCANLON/H....HUGH SCANLON

SCARROW H.A. G0959

SCHAAF R.W. G0960

SCHACHTER O.G0961

SCHEINMAN L. G0962,G0963

SCHELLING T.C. G0964

SCHERER F.M. G0965

SCHEURER/K....AUGUSTE SCHEURER-KESTNER

SCHEURER-KESTNER, AUGUSTE....SEE SCHEURER/K

SCHILLING W.R. G0966,G0967,G0968

SCHINDLR/P....PAULINE SCHINDLER

SCHIZO....SCHIZOPHRENIA

SCHMIDT H. G0970

SCHMITT H.A. G0971,G0972

SCHMITTER P.C. G0464

SCHOECK H. G0973,G0974

SCHOLASTIC....SCHOLASTICISM (MEDIEVAL)

SCHON D.A. G0975

SCHOOL....SCHOOLS, EXCEPT UNIVERSITIES

B14
CRAIG J.,ELEMENTS OF POLITICAL SCIENCE (3 VOLS.). PHIL/SCI
CONSTN AGRI INDUS SCHOOL FORCES TAX CT/SYS SUFF NAT/G
MORAL WEALTH...CONCPT 19 CIVIL/LIB. PAGE 13 G0259 ORD/FREE

B28
SOROKIN P.,CONTEMPORARY SOCIOLOGICAL THEORIES. CULTURE
MOD/EUR UNIV SOCIETY R+D SCHOOL ECO/TAC EDU/PROP SOC
ROUTINE ATTIT DRIVE...PSY CONCPT TIME/SEQ TREND WAR
GEN/LAWS 20. PAGE 52 G1021

B37
HODGSON J.G.,THE OFFICIAL PUBLICATIONS OF AMERICAN BIBLIOG
COUNTIES: A UNION LIST. SCHOOL BUDGET...HEAL MGT LOC/G
SOC/WK 19/20. PAGE 26 G0520 PUB/INST

B44
BARKER E.,THE DEVELOPMENT OF PUBLIC SERVICES IN GOV/COMP
WESTERN WUROPE: 1660-1930. FRANCE GERMANY UK SCHOOL ADMIN
CONTROL REPRESENT ROLE...WELF/ST 17/20. PAGE 5 EX/STRUC
G0095

C50
WAGER P.W.,"COUNTY GOVERNMENT ACROSS THE NATION." LOC/G
USA+45 CONSTN COM/IND FINAN SCHOOL DOMIN CT/SYS PROVS
LEAD GOV/REL...STAT BIBLIOG 20. PAGE 61 G1204 ADMIN
ROUTINE

B51
CONANT J.B.,SCIENCE AND COMMON SENSE. WOR+45 WOR-45 CREATE
R+D SCHOOL CONSULT TEC/DEV EDU/PROP SKILL...PLURIST PHIL/SCI
METH/CNCPT RECORD TIME/SEQ SIMUL GEN/METH METH.
PAGE 13 G0248

B51
HUXLEY J.,FREEDOM AND CULTURE. UNIV LAW SOCIETY R+D CULTURE
ACADEM SCHOOL CREATE SANCTION ATTIT KNOWL...HUM ORD/FREE
ANTHOL 20. PAGE 27 G0540 PHIL/SCI
IDEA/COMP

B52
DAY E.E.,EDUCATION FOR FREEDOM AND RESPONSIBILITY. SCHOOL

FUT USA+45 CULTURE CONSULT EDU/PROP ATTIT SKILL KNOWL
...MGT CONCPT OBS GEN/LAWS COLD/WAR 20. PAGE 14
G0282

C54
CALDWELL L.K.,"THE GOVERNMENT AND ADMINISTRATION OF PROVS
NEW YORK." LOC/G MUNIC POL/PAR SCHOOL CHIEF LEGIS ADMIN
PLAN TAX CT/SYS...MGT SOC/WK BIBLIOG 20 NEWYORK/C. CONSTN
PAGE 10 G0202 EX/STRUC

B57
DRUCKER P.F.,AMERICA'S NEXT TWENTY YEARS. USA+45 WORKER
DIST/IND ACADEM MUNIC SCHOOL DIPLOM ECO/TAC AUTOMAT FOR/AID
HABITAT HEALTH...SOC/WK TREND 20 URBAN/RNWL CENSUS
PUB/TRANS. PAGE 16 G0316 GEOG

B57
DUPREE A.H.,SCIENCE IN THE FEDERAL GOVERNMENT; A NAT/G
HISTORY OF POLICIES AND ACTIVITIES TO 1940. USA-45 R+D
AGRI SCHOOL DELIB/GP WAR GOV/REL...PHIL/SCI BIBLIOG CREATE
18/20 DEPRESSION NEW/DEAL WWI JEFFERSN/T. PAGE 17 TEC/DEV
G0324

B60
CARPENTER E.,EXPLORATIONS IN COMMUNICATION. USSR ANTHOL
CULTURE SCHOOL SECT EDU/PROP PRESS TV AUTOMAT COM/IND
FEEDBACK ATTIT PERSON...ART/METH PSY 20. PAGE 11 TEC/DEV
G0211 WRITING

B61
SMITH H.H.,THE CITIZEN'S GUIDE TO PLANNING. USA+45 MUNIC
LAW SCHOOL CREATE PROB/SOLV EDU/PROP GP/REL ROLE 20 PLAN
URBAN/RNWL OPEN/SPACE. PAGE 52 G1015 DELIB/GP
CONSULT

B62
MACHLUP F.,THE PRODUCTION AND DISTRIBUTION OF ACADEM
KNOWLEDGE IN THE UNITED STATES. USA+45 COM/IND TEC/DEV
INDUS SCHOOL SECT WORKER COMPUTER CREATE CIVMIL/REL EDU/PROP
COST EFFICIENCY WEALTH 20. PAGE 35 G0688 R+D

B62
THANT U.,THE UNITED NATIONS' DEVELOPMENT DECADE: INT/ORG
PROPOSALS FOR ACTION. WOR+45 SOCIETY ECO/UNDEV AGRI ALL/VALS
COM/IND FINAN R+D MUNIC SCHOOL VOL/ASSN CONSULT
PLAN TEC/DEV ECO/TAC EDU/PROP ADMIN ROUTINE
RIGID/FLEX...MGT SOC CONCPT UNESCO UN TOT/POP
VAL/FREE. PAGE 54 G1064

N62
US CONGRESS JT ATOM ENRGY COMM,PEACEFUL USES OF NUC/PWR
ATOMIC ENERGY, HEARING. USA+45 USSR TEC/DEV ATTIT ACADEM
RIGID/FLEX...TESTS CHARTS EXHIBIT METH/COMP 20 SCHOOL
CONGRESS. PAGE 57 G1112 NAT/COMP

B63
DALAND R.T.,PERSPECTIVES OF BRAZILIAN PUBLIC ADMIN
ADMINISTRATION (VOL. I). BRAZIL LAW ECO/UNDEV NAT/G
SCHOOL CHIEF TEC/DEV CONFER CONTROL GP/REL ATTIT PLAN
ROLE PWR...ANTHOL 20. PAGE 14 G0272 GOV/REL

B63
MARSCH P.E.,FEDERAL AID TO SCIENCE EDUCATION: TWO EDU/PROP
PROGRAMS. USA+45 SCHOOL RECEIVE EFFICIENCY 20. PHIL/SCI
PAGE 36 G0711 NAT/G
METH/COMP

B63
PEABODY R.L.,NEW PERSPECTIVES ON THE HOUSE OF NEW/IDEA
REPRESENTATIVES. AGRI FINAN SCHOOL FORCES CONFER LEGIS
LEAD CHOOSE REPRESENT FEDERAL...POLICY DECISION PWR
HOUSE/REP. PAGE 44 G0862 ADMIN

S64
KASSOF A.,"THE ADMINISTERED SOCIETY: SOCIETY
TOTALITARIANISM WITHOUT TERROR." COM USSR STRATA DOMIN
AGRI INDUS NAT/G PERF/ART SCHOOL TOP/EX EDU/PROP TOTALISM
ADMIN ORD/FREE PWR...POLICY SOC TIME/SEQ GEN/LAWS
VAL/FREE 20. PAGE 29 G0580

B65
ANDERSON C.A.,EDUCATION AND ECONOMIC DEVELOPMENT. ANTHOL
INDUS R+D SCHOOL TEC/DEV ECO/TAC EDU/PROP AGE ECO/DEV
HEREDITY PERCEPT SKILL 20. PAGE 3 G0056 ECO/UNDEV
WORKER

B65
BENTWICH J.S.,EDUCATION IN ISRAEL. ISRAEL CULTURE SECT
STRATA PROB/SOLV TEC/DEV ADJUST ALL/VALS 20 JEWS. EDU/PROP
PAGE 7 G0125 ACADEM
SCHOOL

B65
FOSTER P.,EDUCATION AND SOCIAL CHANGE IN GHANA. SCHOOL
GHANA CULTURE STRUCT ECO/UNDEV TEC/DEV REGION CREATE
EFFICIENCY LITERACY ALL/VALS SOVEREIGN...STAT SOCIETY

METH/COMP 19/20 GOLD/COAST. PAGE 20 G0385

B65
KOROL A.G.,SOVIET RESEARCH AND DEVELOPMENT. USSR   COM
ACADEM SCHOOL WORKER ROUTINE COST...STAT T 20.   R+D
PAGE 31 G0615   FINAN
  DIST/IND

B65
OECD,MEDITERRANEAN REGIONAL PROJECT: TURKEY;   EDU/PROP
EDUCATION AND DEVELOPMENT. FUT TURKEY SOCIETY   ACADEM
STRATA FINAN NAT/G PROF/ORG PLAN PROB/SOLV ADMIN   SCHOOL
COST...STAT CHARTS 20 OECD. PAGE 42 G0831   ECO/UNDEV

B65
OECD,THE MEDITERRANEAN REGIONAL PROJECT: PORTUGAL;   EDU/PROP
EDUCATION AND DEVELOPMENT. PORTUGAL SOCIETY STRATA   SCHOOL
FINAN PROF/ORG WORKER PLAN PROB/SOLV ADMIN...POLICY   ACADEM
STAT CHARTS METH 20 OECD. PAGE 42 G0832   ECO/UNDEV

B65
OECD,THE MEDITERRANEAN REGIONAL PROJECT: ITALY;   SCHOOL
EDUCATION AND DEVELOPMENT. ITALY SOCIETY STRATA   EDU/PROP
FINAN NAT/G PROF/ORG WORKER PLAN PROB/SOLV ADMIN   ECO/UNDEV
...STAT CHARTS METH 20 OECD. PAGE 42 G0833   ACADEM

B65
OECD,THE MEDITERRANEAN REGIONAL PROJECT: GREECE;   EDU/PROP
EDUCATION AND DEVELOPMENT. FUT GREECE SOCIETY AGRI   SCHOOL
FINAN NAT/G PROF/ORG WORKER PLAN PROB/SOLV ADMIN   ACADEM
DEMAND ATTIT 20 OECD. PAGE 42 G0834   ECO/UNDEV

B65
OECD,THE MEDITERRANEAN REGIONAL PROJECT: SPAIN;   ECO/UNDEV
EDUCATION AND DEVELOPMENT. FUT SPAIN STRATA FINAN   EDU/PROP
NAT/G WORKER PLAN PROB/SOLV ADMIN COST...POLICY   ACADEM
STAT CHARTS 20 OECD. PAGE 42 G0835   SCHOOL

B65
ORG FOR ECO COOP AND DEVEL,THE MEDITERRANEAN   EDU/PROP
REGIONAL PROJECT: YUGOSLAVIA; EDUCATION AND   ACADEM
DEVELOPMENT. YUGOSLAVIA SOCIETY FINAN PROF/ORG PLAN   SCHOOL
ADMIN COST DEMAND MARXISM...STAT TREND CHARTS METH   ECO/UNDEV
20 OECD. PAGE 43 G0843

B65
REISS A.J. JR.,SCHOOLS IN A CHANGING SOCIETY.   SCHOOL
CULTURE PROB/SOLV INSPECT DOMIN CONFER INGP/REL   EX/STRUC
RACE/REL AGE/C AGE/Y ALL/VALS...ANTHOL SOC/INTEG 20   ADJUST
NEWYORK/C. PAGE 46 G0912   ADMIN

B65
US LIBRARY OF CONGRESS,A DIRECTORY OF INFORMATION   BIBLIOG
RESOURCES IN THE UNITED STATES: SOCIAL SCIENCES.   R+D
USA+45 ACADEM INT/ORG LABOR PROF/ORG PUB/INST   COMPUT/IR
SCHOOL SECT 20. PAGE 59 G1156

B65
VERMOT-GAUCHY M.,L'EDUCATION NATIONALE DANS LA   ACADEM
FRANCE DE 1975. FRANCE FUT CULTURE ELITES R+D   CREATE
SCHOOL PLAN EDU/PROP EFFICIENCY...POLICY PREDICT   TREND
CHARTS INDEX 20. PAGE 61 G1195   INTELL

B66
MARKHAM J.W.,AN ECONOMIC-MEDIA STUDY OF BOOK   PRESS
PUBLISHING. USA+45 LAW COM/IND ACADEM SCHOOL   ECO/TAC
EDU/PROP AUTOMAT CONTROL...DECISION STAT CHARTS 20   TEC/DEV
CONGRESS. PAGE 36 G0707   NAT/G

B66
SANFORD T.,BUT WHAT ABOUT THE PEOPLE? ACADEM SCHOOL   EDU/PROP
BUDGET TAX CONTROL SKILL WEALTH 20 NORTH/CAR.   PROB/SOLV
PAGE 49 G0956   POLICY
  PROVS

B67
WARNER W.L.,THE EMERGENT AMERICAN SOCIETY VOL I,   ANTHOL
LARGE-SCALE ORGANIZATIONS. USA+45 USA-45 ACADEM   NAT/G
PROF/ORG SCHOOL SECT EX/STRUC TEC/DEV GP/REL   LABOR
...TREND CHARTS. PAGE 62 G1215   LG/CO

S67
ATKIN J.M.,"THE FEDERAL GOVERNMENT, BIG BUSINESS,   SCHOOL
AND COLLEGES OF EDUCATION." PROF/ORG CONSULT CREATE   ACADEM
PLAN PROB/SOLV ADMIN EFFICIENCY. PAGE 4 G0075   NAT/G
  INDUS

N67
PRINCETON U INDUSTRIAL REL SEC,COLLECTIVE   BIBLIOG/A
BARGAINING IN THE PUBLIC SCHOOLS (PAMPHLET NO. 33).   SCHOOL
USA+45 LABOR PROB/SOLV PWR MGT. PAGE 45 G0891   BARGAIN
  GP/REL

SCHRADER R. G0976

SCHRAMM W. G0659,G0977,G0978

SCHULTZ T.H. G0979

SCHUMACHER B.G. G0980

SCHUMCHR/K....KURT SCHUMACHER

SCHUMPTR/J....JOSEPH SCHUMPETER

SCHURMANN F. G0981

SCHWARTZ L.E. G0982

SCHWARTZ M.D. G0983

SCHWEBEL M. G0984

SCHWINN....ARNOLD, SCHWINN + COMPANY

SCI/ADVSRY....SCIENCE ADVISORY COMMISSION

B62
DUPRE J.S.,SCIENCE AND THE NATION: POLICY AND   R+D
POLITICS. USA+45 LAW ACADEM FORCES ADMIN CIVMIL/REL   INDUS
GOV/REL EFFICIENCY PEACE...TREND 20 SCI/ADVSRY.   TEC/DEV
PAGE 16 G0322   NUC/PWR

SCIENCE....SEE PHIL/SCI, CREATE

SCIENCE ADVISORY COMMISSION....SEE SCI/ADVSRY

SCIENTIFIC METHOD....SEE PHIL/SCI

SCOT/YARD....SCOTLAND YARD - LONDON POLICE HEADQUARTERS AND
    DETECTIVE BUREAU

SCOTLAND....SCOTLAND

SCOVILLE W.J. G0985

SCREENING AND SELECTION....SEE CHOOSE, SAMP

SDR....SPECIAL DRAWING RIGHTS

SDS....STUDENTS FOR A DEMOCRATIC SOCIETY

SEA....LOCALE OF SUBJECT ACTIVITY IS AQUATIC

B50
KOENIG L.W.,THE SALE OF THE TANKERS. USA+45 SEA   NAT/G
DIST/IND POL/PAR DIPLOM ADMIN CIVMIL/REL ATTIT   POLICY
...DECISION 20 PRESIDENT DEPT/STATE. PAGE 31 G0609   PLAN
  GOV/REL

B54
LOCKLIN D.P.,ECONOMICS OF TRANSPORTATION (4TH ED.).   ECO/DEV
USA+45 USA-45 SEA AIR LAW FINAN LG/CO EX/STRUC   DIST/IND
ADMIN CONTROL...STAT CHARTS 19/20 RAILROAD   ECO/TAC
PUB/TRANS. PAGE 34 G0675   TEC/DEV

B58
ATOMIC INDUSTRIAL FORUM,MANAGEMENT AND ATOMIC   NUC/PWR
ENERGY. WOR+45 SEA LAW MARKET NAT/G TEC/DEV INSPECT   INDUS
INT/TRADE CONFER PEACE HEALTH...ANTHOL 20. PAGE 4   MGT
G0078   ECO/TAC

B60
KINGSTON-MCCLOUG E.,DEFENSE; POLICY AND STRATEGY.   FORCES
UK SEA AIR TEC/DEV DIPLOM ADMIN LEAD WAR ORD/FREE   PLAN
...CHARTS 20. PAGE 30 G0597   POLICY
  DECISION

B60
US HOUSE COMM. SCI. ASTRONAUT.,OCEAN SCIENCES AND   R+D
NATIONAL SECURITY. FUT SEA ECO/DEV EXTR/IND INT/ORG   ORD/FREE
NAT/G FORCES ACT/RES TEC/DEV ECO/TAC COERCE WAR
BIO/SOC KNOWL PWR...CONCPT RECORD LAB/EXP 20.
PAGE 59 G1153

B61
MURPHY E.F.,WATER PURITY: A STUDY IN LEGAL CONTROL   SEA
OF NATURAL RESOURCES. LOC/G ACT/RES PLAN TEC/DEV   LAW
LOBBY GP/REL COST ATTIT HEALTH ORD/FREE...HEAL   PROVS
JURID 20 WISCONSIN WATER. PAGE 40 G0797   CONTROL

S64
SPONSLER G.C.,"THE MILITARY ROLE IN SPACE." FUT   TEC/DEV
USA+45 SEA AIR NAT/G ACT/RES PLAN COERCE NUC/PWR   FORCES
WEAPON KNOWL ORD/FREE PWR RESPECT...TREND 20.   SPACE
PAGE 52 G1026

B65
GRETTON P.,MARITIME STRATEGY - A STUDY OF DEFENSE   FORCES
PROBLEMS. ASIA UK USSR DIPLOM COERCE DETER NUC/PWR   PLAN
WEAPON...CONCPT NAT/COMP 20. PAGE 23 G0449   WAR
  SEA

RUPPENTHAL K.M.,TRANSPORTATION AND TOMORROW. FUT SPACE USA+45 SEA AIR FORCES TEC/DEV INT/TRADE ...ANTHOL 20 RAILROAD. PAGE 48 G0946
B66
DIST/IND
PLAN
CIVMIL/REL
PREDICT

ALEXANDER L.M.,THE LAW OF THE SEA: OFFSHORE BOUNDARIES AND ZONES. WOR+45 INT/ORG TEC/DEV CONTROL PRIVIL HABITAT SOVEREIGN...CON/ANAL CHARTS ANTHOL. PAGE 2 G0037
B67
SEA
INT/LAW
EXTR/IND

RAWLINSON J.L.,CHINA'S STRUGGLE FOR NAVAL DEVELOPMENT 1839-1895. ASIA DIPLOM ADMIN WAR ...BIBLIOG DICTIONARY 19 CHINJAP. PAGE 46 G0907
B67
SEA
FORCES
PWR

DAVIS P.C.,"THE COMING CHINESE COMMUNIST NUCLEAR THREAT AND U.S. SEA BASED ABM OPTIONS." ASIA CHINA/COM FUT USA+45 SEA NAT/G FORCES PLAN TEC/DEV LEAD ARMS/CONT...GEOG METH/COMP 20 ABM/DEFSYS. PAGE 14 G0279
L67
NUC/PWR
DETER
WEAPON
DIPLOM

PONTECORVO G.,"THE LAW OF THE SEA." ECO/DEV ECO/UNDEV TEC/DEV GEOG. PAGE 45 G0885
S67
CONFER
INT/LAW
EXTR/IND
SEA

TAGIL S.,"WEGENER, RAEDER, AND THE GERMAN NAVAL STRATEGY: VIEWPOINTS ON THE CONDITIONS FOR THE INFLUENCE OF IDEAS." GERMANY WOR-45...IDEA/COMP METH 20. PAGE 53 G1049
S67
SEA
POLICY
HIST/WRIT
CIVMIL/REL

SEABERG G.P. G0986

SEARA M.V. G0987

SEATO....SOUTH EAST ASIA TREATY ORGANIZATION; SEE ALSO INT/ORG, VOL/ASSN, FORCES, DETER

AIR FORCE ACADEMY LIBRARY,INTERNATIONAL ORGANIZATIONS AND MILITARY SECURITY SYSTEMS (PAMPHLET) (SPECIAL BIBLIOGRAPHY SERIES, NUMBER 25). DIPLOM FOR/AID INT/TRADE NUC/PWR PEACE 20 UN NATO OAS SEATO LEAGUE/NAT. PAGE 2 G0031
B62
BIBLIOG
INT/ORG
FORCES
DETER

SEATTLE....SEATTLE, WASHINGTON

SEC/EXCHNG....SECURITY EXCHANGE COMMISSION

SEC/REFORM....SECOND REFORM ACT OF 1867 (U.K.)

SEC/STATE....U.S. SECRETARY OF STATE

SECOND REFORM ACT OF 1867 (U.K.)....SEE SEC/REFORM

SECRETARY OF STATE (U.S.)....SEE SEC/STATE

SECT....CHURCH, SECT, RELIGIOUS GROUP

DRAPER J.W.,HISTORY OF THE CONFLICT BETWEEN RELIGION AND SCIENCE. WOR-45 INTELL SOCIETY R+D CREATE PLAN TEC/DEV EDU/PROP ATTIT PWR...PHIL/SCI CONCPT OBS TIME/SEQ TREND GEN/LAWS TOT/POP. PAGE 16 G0314
B23
SECT
KNOWL

EINSTEIN A.,THE WORLD AS I SEE IT. WOR-45 INTELL R+D INT/ORG NAT/G SECT VOL/ASSN FORCES CREATE EDU/PROP LEGIT ARMS/CONT WAR WEAPON NAT/LISM ALL/VALS...POLICY CONCPT 20. PAGE 17 G0337
B34
SOCIETY
PHIL/SCI
DIPLOM
PACIFISM

MACRAE D.G.,"THE BOLSHEVIK IDEOLOGY; THE INTELLECTUAL AND EMOTIONAL FACTORS IN COMMUNIST AFFILIATION" (BMR)" COM LEAD REV ATTIT ORD/FREE ...SOC CON/ANAL 20 BOLSHEVISM. PAGE 35 G0693
S51
MARXISM
INTELL
PHIL/SCI
SECT

WASHBURNE N.F.,INTERPRETING SOCIAL CHANGE IN AMERICA. USA+45 STRATA FAM NAT/G SECT OP/RES ECO/TAC EDU/PROP HABITAT...SOC TIME/SEQ TREND 20 BUREAUCRCY. PAGE 62 G1217
B54
CULTURE
STRUCT
CREATE
TEC/DEV

MERTON R.K.,SOCIAL THEORY AND SOCIAL STRUCTURE (REV. ED.). INTELL SECT WORKER OP/RES EDU/PROP ADMIN INGP/REL ANOMIE PERSON...AUD/VIS T 20 BUREAUCRCY. PAGE 38 G0759
B57
SOC
GEN/LAWS
SOCIETY
STRUCT

ORTEGA Y GASSET J.,MAN AND CRISIS. SECT CREATE PERSON CONSERVE...GEN/LAWS RENAISSAN. PAGE 43 G0846
B58
PHIL/SCI
CULTURE
CONCPT

GODDARD V.,THE ENIGMA OF MENACE. WOR+45 SECT LEAD NUC/PWR WAR WEAPON CHOOSE PERSON PWR...POLICY PHIL/SCI PACIFIST 20 COLD/WAR. PAGE 22 G0423
B59
PEACE
ARMS/CONT
DIPLOM
ATTIT

CARPENTER E.,EXPLORATIONS IN COMMUNICATION. USSR CULTURE SCHOOL SECT EDU/PROP PRESS TV AUTOMAT FEEDBACK ATTIT PERSON...ART/METH PSY 20. PAGE 11 G0211
B60
ANTHOL
COM/IND
TEC/DEV
WRITING

MACHLUP F.,THE PRODUCTION AND DISTRIBUTION OF KNOWLEDGE IN THE UNITED STATES. USA+45 COM/IND INDUS SCHOOL SECT WORKER COMPUTER CREATE CIVMIL/REL COST EFFICIENCY WEALTH 20. PAGE 35 G0688
B62
ACADEM
TEC/DEV
EDU/PROP
R+D

ROSS R.,SYMBOLS AND CIVILIZATION. UNIV CULTURE SECT CREATE ALL/VALS MORAL ART/METH. PAGE 48 G0939
B62
PHIL/SCI
KNOWL
EPIST
SOCIETY

GEERTZ C.,OLD SOCIETIES AND NEW STATES: THE QUEST FOR MODERNITY IN ASIA AND AFRICA. AFR ASIA LAW CULTURE SECT EDU/PROP REV...GOV/COMP NAT/COMP 20. PAGE 21 G0415
B63
ECO/UNDEV
TEC/DEV
NAT/LISM
SOVEREIGN

MULLER H.J.,FREEDOM IN THE WESTERN WORLD. PREHIST CULTURE SECT CREATE TEC/DEV DOMIN PWR WEALTH ...MAJORIT SOC CONCPT. PAGE 40 G0793
B63
ORD/FREE
TIME/SEQ
SOCIETY

RUITENBEER H.M.,THE DILEMMA OF ORGANIZATIONAL SOCIETY. CULTURE ECO/DEV MUNIC SECT TEC/DEV EDU/PROP NAT/LISM ORD/FREE...NAT/COMP 20 RIESMAN/D WHYTE/WF MERTON/R MEAD/MARG JASPERS/K. PAGE 48 G0945
B63
PERSON
ROLE
ADMIN
WORKER

PETERSON W.,THE POLITICS OF POPULATION. COM EUR+WWI FUT MOD/EUR S/ASIA USA+45 USA-45 WOR+45 LAW CULTURE FAM SECT DOMIN EDU/PROP BIO/SOC HEALTH ORD/FREE ...GEOG STAT TIME/SEQ TREND VAL/FREE. PAGE 44 G0871
B64
PLAN
CENSUS
POLICY

ROBERTS HL,FOREIGN AFFAIRS BIBLIOGRAPHY, 1952-1962. ECO/DEV SECT PLAN FOR/AID INT/TRADE ARMS/CONT NAT/LISM ATTIT...INT/LAW GOV/COMP IDEA/COMP 20. PAGE 47 G0928
B64
BIBLIOG/A
DIPLOM
INT/ORG
WAR

"FURTHER READING." INDIA PAKISTAN SECT WAR PEACE ATTIT...POLICY 20. PAGE 1 G0018
S64
BIBLIOG
GP/REL
DIPLOM
NAT/G

BENJAMIN A.C.,SCIENCE, TECHNOLOGY, AND HUMAN VALUES. WOR+45 SECT EDU/PROP GP/REL ATTIT...TECHNIC LING IDEA/COMP WORSHIP 20. PAGE 6 G0118
B65
PHIL/SCI
CREATE
ROLE
SOCIETY

BENTWICH J.S.,EDUCATION IN ISRAEL. ISRAEL CULTURE STRATA PROB/SOLV TEC/DEV ADJUST ALL/VALS 20 JEWS. PAGE 7 G0125
B65
SECT
EDU/PROP
ACADEM
SCHOOL

HEER D.M.,AFTER NUCLEAR ATTACK: A DEMOGRAPHIC INQUIRY. USA+45 ECO/DEV SECT WORKER SEX...HEAL SOC STAT PREDICT CHARTS 20 NEGRO. PAGE 25 G0500
B65
GEOG
NUC/PWR
CENSUS
WAR

US LIBRARY OF CONGRESS,A DIRECTORY OF INFORMATION RESOURCES IN THE UNITED STATES: SOCIAL SCIENCES. USA+45 ACADEM INT/ORG LABOR PROF/ORG PUB/INST SCHOOL SECT 20. PAGE 59 G1156
B65
BIBLIOG
R+D
COMPUT/IR

HOPKINS J.F.K.,ARABIC PERIODICAL LITERATURE, 1961. ISLAM LAW CULTURE SECT...GEOG HEAL PHIL/SCI PSY SOC 20. PAGE 27 G0528
B66
BIBLIOG/A
NAT/LISM
TEC/DEV
INDUS

L66
DOUGHERTY J.E.,"THE CATHOLIC CHURCH, WAR AND   CATHISM
NUCLEAR WEAPONS." COM EUR+WWI SECT TOP/EX LEAD   MORAL
DETER ALL/VALS. PAGE 16 G0312   WAR
                                                      NUC/PWR

B67
BENNETT J.W.,HUTTERIAN BRETHREN; THE AGRICULTURAL   SECT
ECONOMY AND SOCIAL ORGANIZATION OF A COMMUNAL   AGRI
PEOPLE. USA+45 SOCIETY FAM KIN TEC/DEV ADJUST...MGT   STRUCT
AUD/VIS GP/COMP 20. PAGE 6 G0121   GP/REL

B67
CROSSON F.J.,SCIENCE AND CONTEMPORARY SOCIETY. FUT   PHIL/SCI
WOR+45 SECT CREATE PROB/SOLV...HUM PREDICT TREND   SOCIETY
IDEA/COMP ANTHOL. PAGE 14 G0263   TEC/DEV
                                                      CONCPT

B67
DEGLER C.N.,THE AGE OF THE ECONOMIC REVOLUTION   INDUS
1876-1900. USA-45 AGRI MUNIC POL/PAR SECT ECO/TAC   SOCIETY
CHOOSE...PHIL/SCI CHARTS NAT/COMP 19 NEGRO. PAGE 15   ECO/DEV
G0292   TEC/DEV

B67
MCLAUGHLIN M.R.,RELIGIOUS EDUCATION AND THE STATE: SECT
DEMOCRACY FINDS A WAY. CANADA EUR+WWI GP/REL   NAT/G
POPULISM...CATH NAT/COMP 20 AUSTRAL. PAGE 38 G0745   EDU/PROP
                                                      POLICY

B67
WARNER W.L.,THE EMERGENT AMERICAN SOCIETY VOL I,   ANTHOL
LARGE-SCALE ORGANIZATIONS. USA+45 USA-45 ACADEM   NAT/G
PROF/ORG SCHOOL SECT EX/STRUC TEC/DEV GP/REL   LABOR
...TREND CHARTS. PAGE 62 G1215   LG/CO

B91
RENAN E.,THE FUTURE OF SCIENCE. WAR ORD/FREE WEALTH   PHIL/SCI
...GOV/COMP IDEA/COMP GEN/LAWS 19. PAGE 46 G0913   KNOWL
                                                      SECT
                                                      PREDICT

SECUR/COUN....UNITED NATIONS SECURITY COUNCIL

SECUR/PROG....SECURITY PROGRAM

SECURITIES....SEE FINAN

SECURITY....SEE ORD/FREE

SECURITY COUNCIL....SEE UN+DELIB/GP+PWR

SECURITY PROGRAM....SEE SECUR/PROG

SEDITION....SEDITION

SEEK....SEARCH FOR EDUCATION, ELEVATION, AND KNOWLEDGE

SEGREGATION....SEE NEGRO, SOUTH/US, RACE/REL, SOC/INTEG,
    CIV/RIGHTS, DISCRIM, MISCEGEN, ISOLAT, SCHOOL,
    STRANGE, ANOMIE

SEIDMAN H. G0988

SELASSIE/H....HAILE SELASSIE

SELBORNE/W....WILLIAM SELBORNE

SELEC/SERV....SELECTIVE SERVICE

SELF/OBS....SELF/OBSERVATION

S57
EASTON D.,"AN APPROACH TO THE ANALYSIS OF POLITICAL   STRUCT
SYSTEMS." R+D EDU/PROP KNOWL SKILL...POLICY SOC   PHIL/SCI
METH/CNCPT NEW/IDEA SELF/OBS CHARTS GEN/METH
TOT/POP. PAGE 17 G0331

L60
DEUTSCH K.W.,"TOWARD AN INVENTORY OF BASIC TRENDS   R+D
AND PATTERNS IN COMPARATIVE AND INTERNATIONAL   PERCEPT
POLITICS." UNIV WOR+45 SOCIETY STRUCT INT/ORG NAT/G
CREATE PLAN EDU/PROP KNOWL...PHIL/SCI METH/CNCPT
STAT SELF/OBS OBS/ENVIR SAMP TREND CON/ANAL CHARTS
SOC/EXP GEN/METH 20. PAGE 15 G0298

B64
GROSSER G.H.,THE THREAT OF IMPENDING DISASTER: HEALTH
CONTRIBUTIONS TO THE PSYCHOLOGY OF STRESS. SPACE   PSY
UNIV SOCIETY R+D TEC/DEV EDU/PROP COERCE WAR ATTIT   NUC/PWR
BIO/SOC DISPL PERCEPT PERSON...SOC MYTH SELF/OBS
CONT/OBS BIOG CON/ANAL TOT/POP 20. PAGE 23 G0455

SEMANTICS...SEE LOG

SEN/SPACE....UNITED STATES SENATE SPECIAL COMMITTEE ON
    SPACE ASTRONAUTICS

N19
US SEN SPEC COMM SPACE ASTRO,SPACE LAW; A SYMPOSIUM   SPACE
(PAMPHLET). USA+45 TEC/DEV CONFER CONTROL SOVEREIGN   ADJUD
...INT/LAW 20 SEN/SPACE. PAGE 59 G1161   DIPLOM
                                                      INT/ORG

SENATE SPECIAL COMMITTEE ON SPACE ASTRONAUTICS....SEE
    SEN/SPACE

SENATE....SENATE (ALL NATIONS); SEE ALSO CONGRESS, LEGIS

B63
US SENATE COMM GOVT OPERATIONS,ADMINISTRATION OF   DELIB/GP
NATIONAL SECURITY (9 PARTS). ADMIN...INT REC/INT   NAT/G
CHARTS 20 SENATE CONGRESS. PAGE 60 G1178   OP/RES
                                                      ORD/FREE

B63
WILTZ J.E.,IN SEARCH OF PEACE: THE SENATE MUNITIONS   DELIB/GP
INQUIRY, 1934-36. EUR+WWI USA-45 ELITES INDUS LG/CO   PROFIT
LEGIS INT/TRADE LOBBY NEUTRAL ARMS/CONT...POLICY   WAR
CONGRESS 20 LEAGUE/NAT PRESIDENT SENATE CONSCRIPTN.   WEAPON
PAGE 64 G1246

B67
US SENATE COMM ON FOREIGN REL,TREATY ON OUTER   SPACE
SPACE. WOR+45 AIR FORCES PROB/SOLV NUC/PWR SENATE   DIPLOM
TREATY UN. PAGE 60 G1182   ARMS/CONT
                                                      LAW

B67
US SENATE COMM ON FOREIGN REL,ARMS SALES TO NEAR   WEAPON
EAST AND SOUTH ASIAN COUNTRIES. INDIA IRAN PAKISTAN   FOR/AID
WOR+45 PROC/MFG BAL/PWR DIPLOM...DECISION SENATE.   FORCES
PAGE 60 G1183   POLICY

B67
US SENATE COMM ON FOREIGN REL,UNITED STATES   ARMS/CONT
ARMAMENT AND DISARMAMENT PROBLEMS. USA+45 AIR   WEAPON
BAL/PWR DIPLOM FOR/AID NUC/PWR ORD/FREE SENATE   FORCES
TREATY. PAGE 60 G1184   PROB/SOLV

B67
US SENATE COMM ON FOREIGN REL,FOREIGN ASSISTANCE   FOR/AID
ACT OF 1967. VIETNAM WOR+45 DELIB/GP CONFER CONTROL   LAW
WAR WEAPON BAL/PAY...CENSUS CHARTS SENATE. PAGE 60   DIPLOM
G1185   POLICY

N67
US SENATE COMM AERO SPACE SCI,AERONAUTICAL RESEARCH   AIR
AND DEVELOPMENT POLICY (PAMPHLET). SPACE USA+45   R+D
INDUS CIVMIL/REL CONGRESS PRESIDENT NASA SENATE.   POLICY
PAGE 60 G1169   PLAN

N67
US SENATE COMM AERO SPACE SCI,HEARINGS BEFORE THE   NAT/G
COMMITTEE ON AERONAUTICAL AND SPACE SCIENCES UNITED   DELIB/GP
STATES SENATE NINETIETH CONGRESS (PAMPHLET). USA+45   SPACE
CONSULT PLAN CONFER EFFICIENCY SENATE. PAGE 60   CREATE
G1172

N67
US SENATE COMM ON PUBLIC WORKS,AIR QUALITY ACT OF   HEALTH
1967 (PAMPHLET). USA+45 INDUS R+D LEGIS SENATE.   AIR
PAGE 61 G1187   HABITAT
                                                      CONTROL

SENEGAL....SEE ALSO AFR

SENIOR....SENIORITY; SEE ALSO ADMIN, ROUTINE

S45
WHITE L.D.,"CONGRESSIONAL CONTROL OF THE PUBLIC   LEGIS
SERVICE." USA-45 NAT/G CONSULT DELIB/GP PLAN SENIOR   EXEC
CONGRESS. PAGE 63 G1232   POLICY
                                                      CONTROL

B57
SCARROW H.A.,THE HIGHER PUBLIC SERVICE OF THE   ADMIN
COMMONWEALTH OF AUSTRALIA. LAW SENIOR LOBBY ROLE 20   NAT/G
AUSTRAL CIVIL/SERV COMMONWLTH. PAGE 49 G0959   EX/STRUC
                                                      GOV/COMP

SEPARATION....SEE ISOLAT, DISCRIM, RACE/REL

SERBIA....SERBIA

SERV/IND....SERVICE INDUSTRY

N
US SUPERINTENDENT OF DOCUMENTS,TRANSPORTATION: BIBLIOG/A
HIGHWAYS, ROADS, AND POSTAL SERVICE (PRICE LIST   DIST/IND
25). PANAMA USA+45 LAW FORCES DIPLOM ADMIN GOV/REL   SERV/IND

HEALTH MGT. PAGE 61 G1188   NAT/G

S51
LERNER D.,"THE POLICY SCIENCES: RECENT DEVELOPMENTS CONSULT
IN SCOPE AND METHODS." R+D SERV/IND CREATE DIPLOM SOC
ROUTINE PWR...METH/CNCPT TREND GEN/LAWS METH 20.
PAGE 33 G0658

B53
HOVLAND C.I.,COMMUNICATION AND PERSUASION: PSY
PSYCHOLOGICAL STUDIES OF OPINION CHANGE. INTELL EDU/PROP
SOCIETY ECO/DEV COM/IND R+D SERV/IND CREATE TEC/DEV
ATTIT RIGID/FLEX KNOWL NEW/IDEA. PAGE 27 G0531

B58
CROWE S.,THE LANDSCAPE OF POWER. UK CULTURE HABITAT
SERV/IND NAT/G CONSULT PARTIC NUC/PWR LEISURE...SOC TEC/DEV
EXHIBIT 20. PAGE 14 G0264 PLAN
CONTROL

B62
MARTINS A.F.,REVOLUCAO BRANCA NO CAMPO. L/A+17C AGRI
SERV/IND DEMAND EFFICIENCY PRODUC...POLICY ECO/UNDEV
METH/COMP. PAGE 36 G0717 TEC/DEV
NAT/COMP

S62
ALBONETTI A.,"IL SECONDO PROGRAMMA QUINQUENNALE R+D
1963-67 ED IL BILANCIO RICERCHE ED INVESTIMENTI PER PLAN
IL 1963 DELL'ERATOM." EUR+WWI FUT ITALY WOR+45 NUC/PWR
ECO/DEV SERV/IND INT/ORG TEC/DEV ECO/TAC ATTIT
SKILL WEALTH...MGT TIME/SEQ OEEC 20. PAGE 2 G0035

B63
BASS M.E.,SELECTIVE BIBLIOGRAPHY ON MUNICIPAL BIBLIOG
GOVERNMENT FROM THE FILES OF THE MUNICIPAL LOC/G
TECHNICAL ADVISORY SERVICE. USA+45 FINAN SERV/IND ADMIN
PLAN 20. PAGE 5 G0100 MUNIC

B64
FALK L.A.,ADMINISTRATIVE ASPECTS OF GROUP PRACTICE. BIBLIOG/A
USA+45 FINAN PROF/ORG PLAN MGT. PAGE 18 G0358 HEAL
ADMIN
SERV/IND

S64
MAHALANOBIS P.C.,"PERSPECTIVE PLANNING IN INDIA: PLAN
STATISTICAL TOOLS." INDIA S/ASIA STRATA AGRI STAT
DIST/IND FINAN INDUS SERV/IND NAT/G ECO/TAC
ORD/FREE WEALTH...POLICY TREND SIMUL VAL/FREE 20.
PAGE 35 G0695

S67
ENKE S.,"GOVERNMENT-INDUSTRY DEVELOPMENT OF A INDUS
COMMERCIAL SUPERSONIC TRANSPORT." USA+45 ECO/DEV FINAN
R+D LG/CO NAT/G TEC/DEV PRICE RISK COST PROFIT. SERV/IND
PAGE 18 G0347 CAP/ISM

S67
LAY S.H.,"EXCLUSIVE GOVERNMENTAL LIABILITY FOR NAT/G
SPACE ACCIDENTS." USA+45 LAW FINAN SERV/IND TEC/DEV SUPEGO
ADJUD. PAGE 33 G0646 SPACE
PROB/SOLV

SERVAN/JJ....JEAN JACQUES SERVAN-SCHREIBER

SERVAN-SCHREIBER, JEAN-JACQUES....SEE SERVAN/JJ

SERVICE INDUSTRY....SEE SERV/IND

SET THEORY....SEE CLASSIF

SEVENTHDAY....SEVENTH DAY ADVENTISTS

SEX DIFFERENCES....SEE SEX

SEX....SEE ALSO BIO/SOC

B65
HEER D.M.,AFTER NUCLEAR ATTACK: A DEMOGRAPHIC GEOG
INQUIRY. USA+45 ECO/DEV SECT WORKER SEX...HEAL SOC NUC/PWR
STAT PREDICT CHARTS 20 NEGRO. PAGE 25 G0500 CENSUS
WAR

S67
ROBINSON J.A.T.,"ABORTION* THE CASE FOR A FREE PLAN
DECISION." LAW PROB/SOLV SANCTION ATTIT MORAL...PSY ILLEGIT
IDEA/COMP 20 ABORTION. PAGE 47 G0930 SEX
HEALTH

SEXUAL BEHAVIOR....SEE SEX, PERSON

SHANGHAI....SHANGHAI

SHARP G. G0989

SHASTRI/LB....LAL BAHADUR SHASTRI

SHAW J.C. G0819

SHEEHAN D. G0990

SHELBY C. G0702

SHEPPARD/S....SAMUEL SHEPPARD

SHERMN/ACT....SHERMAN ANTI-TRUST ACT; SEE ALSO MONOPOLY

SHORT TAKE-OFF AND LANDING AIRCRAFT....SEE STOL

SHOUP/C....C. SHOUP

SHRIVER/S....SARGENT SHRIVER

SHUBIK M. G0991,G0992,G0994

SHULMAN M.D. G0995

SIBERIA....SIBERIA

SIBRON....SIBRON V. NEW YORK

SICILY....SICILY

SICKNESS....SEE HEALTH

SIDGWICK/H....HENRY SIDGWICK

SIER/LEONE....SIERRA LEONE; SEE ALSO AFR

SIHANOUK....NORODOM SIHANOUK

SIKKIM....SEE ALSO S/ASIA

SILBERMAN C.E. G0996

SILK L.S. G0997

SILVER....SILVER STANDARD AND POLICIES RELATING TO SILVER

SILVERT K.H. G0998

SIMMEL/G....GEORG SIMMEL

SIMMONS L.W. G0999

SIMON H.A. G0819

SIMON R. G1000

SIMONS H. G1001

SIMPSON....SIMPSON V. UNION OIL COMPANY

SIMUL....SCIENTIFIC MODELS

S43
KAPLAN A.,"CONTENT ANALYSIS AND THE THEORY OF LOG
SIGNS" (BMR)" PERS/REL...PSY CONCPT LING IDEA/COMP CON/ANAL
SIMUL BIBLIOG 20 MORRIS/CW. PAGE 29 G0573 STAT
PHIL/SCI

B45
SMYTH H.D.,ATOMIC ENERGY FOR MILITARY PURPOSES. R+D
USA-45 NAT/G PLAN TEC/DEV KNOWL...MATH CON/ANAL TIME/SEQ
CHARTS LAB/EXP SIMUL 20. PAGE 52 G1017 NUC/PWR

B50
CANTRIL H.,TENSIONS THAT CAUSE WAR. UNIV CULTURE SOCIETY
R+D CREATE EDU/PROP DRIVE PERSON KNOWL ORD/FREE PHIL/SCI
...HUM PSY SOC OBS CENSUS TREND CON/ANAL SOC/EXP PEACE
SIMUL GEN/METH ANTHOL COLD/WAR TOT/POP. PAGE 11
G0206

B51
CONANT J.B.,SCIENCE AND COMMON SENSE. WOR+45 WOR-45 CREATE
R+D SCHOOL CONSULT TEC/DEV EDU/PROP SKILL...PLURIST PHIL/SCI
METH/CNCPT RECORD TIME/SEQ SIMUL GEN/METH METH.
PAGE 13 G0248

S54
DEUTSCH K.W.,"GAME THEORY AND POLITICS: SOME DECISION
PROBLEMS OF APPLICATION." FUT WOR+45 SOCIETY R+D GEN/METH
KNOWL PWR...CONCPT METH/CNCPT MATH QUANT GAME SIMUL
VAL/FREE 20. PAGE 15 G0295

S55
MILLER J.G.,"TOWARD A GENERAL THEORY FOR THE CONCPT
BEHAVIORAL SCIENCES" (BMR)" CREATE ALL/VALS KNOWL OP/RES
...CON/ANAL CHARTS HYPO/EXP SIMUL BIBLIOG 20. METH/CNCPT
PAGE 39 G0773 COMPUTER

S56

MILLER W.E.,"PRESIDENTIAL COATTAILS: A STUDY IN
POLITICAL MYTH AND METHODOLOGY" (BMR)" USA+45
CREATE PARTIC ATTIT DRIVE PWR...DECISION CONCPT
CHARTS SIMUL 20 PRESIDENT CONGRESS. PAGE 39 G0774

CHIEF
CHOOSE
POL/PAR
MYTH

B57

MCKINNEY E.R.,A BIBLIOGRAPHY OF CYBERNETICS AND
INFORMATION THEORY. COMPUTER OP/RES...DECISION
PHIL/SCI PSY LING LOG MATH PROBABIL GAME 20.
PAGE 38 G0743

BIBLIOG/A
FEEDBACK
SIMUL
CONTROL

B58

TELLER E.A.,OUR NUCLEAR FUTURE. SOCIETY FORCES
TEC/DEV EDU/PROP KNOWL ORD/FREE...STAND/INT SYS/QU
KNO/TEST AUD/VIS CHARTS SIMUL 20. PAGE 54 G1062

FUT
PHIL/SCI
NUC/PWR
WAR

S58

ARGYRIS C.,"SOME PROBLEMS IN CONCEPTUALIZING
ORGANIZATIONAL CLIMATE: A CASE STUDY OF A BANK"
(BMR)" USA+45 EX/STRUC ADMIN PERS/REL ADJUST PERSON
...POLICY HYPO/EXP SIMUL 20. PAGE 3 G0064

FINAN
CONCPT
LG/CO
INGP/REL

S58

DEAN B.V.,"APPLICATION OF OPERATIONS RESEARCH TO
MANAGERIAL DECISION MAKING" STRATA ACT/RES
PROB/SOLV ROLE...SOC PREDICT SIMUL 20. PAGE 15
G0288

DECISION
OP/RES
MGT
METH/CNCPT

B59

GUILBAUD G.T.,WHAT IS CYBERNETICS? COMPUTER OP/RES
TEC/DEV AUTOMAT ROUTINE PERS/REL PERCEPT...PSY MATH
COMPUT/IR SIMUL GEN/METH. PAGE 23 G0460

CONTROL
COM/IND
FEEDBACK
NET/THEORY

S59

ADAMS E.W.,"A MODEL OF RISKLESS CHOICE." CREATE
PROB/SOLV UTIL...PROBABIL PREDICT HYPO/EXP. PAGE 2
G0029

GAME
SIMUL
RISK
DECISION

S59

CYERT R.M.,"MODELS IN A BEHAVIORAL THEORY OF THE
FIRM." ROUTINE...DECISION MGT METH/CNCPT MATH.
PAGE 14 G0267

SIMUL
GAME
PREDICT
INDUS

B60

ARROW K.J.,MATHEMATICAL METHODS IN THE SOCIAL
SCIENCES, 1959. TEC/DEV CHOOSE UTIL PERCEPT
...KNO/TEST GAME SIMUL ANTHOL. PAGE 4 G0070

MATH
PSY
MGT

B60

MORRIS W.T.,ENGINEERING ECONOMY. AUTOMAT RISK
RATIONAL...PROBABIL STAT CHARTS GAME SIMUL BIBLIOG
T 20. PAGE 40 G0785

OP/RES
DECISION
MGT
PROB/SOLV

B60

SLUCKIN W.,MINDS AND MACHINES (REV. ED.). PROB/SOLV
TEC/DEV AUTOMAT TASK PERCEPT HEALTH KNOWL
...DECISION MATH PROBABIL COMPUT/IR GAME 20.
PAGE 51 G1012

PSY
COMPUTER
PERSON
SIMUL

S60

GARFINKEL H.,"THE RATIONAL PROPERTIES OF SCIENTIFIC
AND COMMON SENSE ACTIVITIES." SOCIETY STRATA
ACT/RES CHOOSE...SOC METH/CNCPT NEW/IDEA CONT/OBS
SIMUL TOT/POP VAL/FREE. PAGE 21 G0412

CREATE
PHIL/SCI

S60

SHUBIK M.,"BIBLIOGRAPHY ON SIMULATION, GAMING,
ARTIFICIAL INTELLIGENCE AND ALLIED TOPICS."
COMPUTER ROUTINE...DECISION MGT STAT 20. PAGE 50
G0992

BIBLIOG
SIMUL
GAME
OP/RES

B61

CHAPPLE E.D.,THE MEASURE OF MANAGEMENT. USA+45
WORKER ADMIN GP/REL EFFICIENCY...DECISION
ORG/CHARTS SIMUL 20. PAGE 11 G0221

MGT
OP/RES
PLAN
METH/CNCPT

B61

ROSENAU J.N.,INTERNATIONAL POLITICS AND FOREIGN
POLICY: A READER IN RESEARCH AND THEORY. ELITES
ATTIT SOVEREIGN...DECISION CHARTS HYPO/EXP GAME
SIMUL ANTHOL BIBLIOG METH 20. PAGE 48 G0936

ACT/RES
DIPLOM
CONCPT
POLICY

B61

SCHMIDT H.,VERTEIDIGUNG ODER VERGELTUNG. COM CUBA
GERMANY/W USSR FORCES DIPLOM ARMS/CONT DETER
NUC/PWR...POLICY CHARTS HYPO/EXP SIMUL BIBLIOG 20
NATO COLD/WAR. PAGE 49 G0970

PLAN
WAR
BAL/PWR
ORD/FREE

S61

ANDREWS R.B.,"URBAN ECONOMICS: AN APPRAISAL OF
PROGRESS." LOC/G PROB/SOLV TEC/DEV...CONCPT
OBS/ENVIR METH/COMP HYPO/EXP SOC/EXP SIMUL GEN/METH
METH 20. PAGE 3 G0058

MUNIC
PHIL/SCI
ECOMETRIC

S61

BENNION E.G.,"ECONOMETRICS FOR MANAGEMENT." USA+45
INDUS EX/STRUC ACT/RES COMPUTER UTIL...MATH STAT
PREDICT METH/COMP HYPO/EXP. PAGE 6 G0122

ECOMETRIC
MGT
SIMUL
DECISION

S61

DEUTSCH K.W.,"A NOTE ON THE APPEARANCE OF WISDOM IN
LARGE BUREAUCRATIC ORGANIZATIONS." ROUTINE PERSON
KNOWL SKILL...DECISION STAT. PAGE 15 G0299

ADMIN
PROBABIL
PROB/SOLV
SIMUL

B62

BELLMAN R.,APPLIED DYNAMIC PROGRAMMING. OPTIMAL
...DECISION STAT SIMUL. PAGE 6 G0116

COMPUTER
ECOMETRIC
GAME
MATH

B62

BORKOF H.,COMPUTER APPLICATIONS IN THE BEHAVIORAL
SCIENCES. AUTOMAT UTIL...DECISION PHIL/SCI PSY
METH/CNCPT LING LOG MATH STYLE NET/THEORY COMPUT/IR
PROG/TEAC SIMUL. PAGE 8 G0154

R+D
COMPUTER
PROB/SOLV
FEEDBACK

B62

BOULDING K.E.,CONFLICT AND DEFENSE: A GENERAL
THEORY. FUT SOCIETY INT/ORG NAT/G CREATE BAL/PWR
COERCE NAT/LISM DRIVE ALL/VALS...PLURIST DECISION
CONCPT METH/CNCPT TREND HYPO/EXP TOT/POP 20. PAGE 8
G0157

MATH
SIMUL
PEACE
WAR

B62

DUCKWORTH W.E.,A GUIDE TO OPERATIONAL RESEARCH.
INDUS PLAN PROB/SOLV EXEC EFFICIENCY PRODUC KNOWL
...MGT MATH STAT SIMUL METH 20 MONTECARLO. PAGE 16
G0319

OP/RES
GAME
DECISION
ADMIN

B62

GUETZKOW H.,SIMULATION IN SOCIAL SCIENCE: READINGS.
STRUCT OP/RES ADMIN AUTOMAT FEEDBACK...MGT PSY SOC
STYLE BIBLIOG. PAGE 23 G0459

SIMUL
TEC/DEV
COMPUTER
GAME

B62

RIKER W.H.,THE THEORY OF POLITICAL COALITIONS.
WOR+45 INTELL NAT/G CREATE PLAN ATTIT DRIVE PERCEPT
...DECISION PSY SOC METH/CNCPT NEW/IDEA MATH CHARTS
GAME TOT/POP 20. PAGE 47 G0921

FUT
SIMUL

S62

SINGER J.D.,"STABLE DETERRENCE AND ITS LIMITS." FUT
WOR+45 R+D INT/ORG CONSULT ACT/RES TEC/DEV
ARMS/CONT COERCE DRIVE PERCEPT RIGID/FLEX ORD/FREE
PWR...MYTH SIMUL TOT/POP 20. PAGE 51 G1004

NAT/G
FORCES
DETER
NUC/PWR

S62

STORER N.W.,"SOME SOCIOLOGICAL ASPECTS OF FEDERAL
SCIENCE POLICY." USA+45 INTELL PUB/INST PLAN GP/REL
PERS/REL DRIVE PERSON ROLE...PSY SOC SIMUL 20 NIH
NSF. PAGE 53 G1040

POLICY
CREATE
NAT/G
ALL/VALS

S62

THORELLI H.B.,"THE INTERNATIONAL OPERATIONS
SIMULATION AT THE UNIVERSITY OF CHICAGO." FUT
USA+45 WOR+45 ECO/DEV DIST/IND FINAN INDUS INT/ORG
DELIB/GP ACT/RES CREATE TEC/DEV WEALTH...STAT
VAL/FREE 20. PAGE 54 G1072

ECO/TAC
SIMUL
INT/TRADE

B63

BONINI C.P.,SIMULATION OF INFORMATION AND DECISION
SYSTEMS IN THE FIRM. MARKET BUDGET DOMIN EDU/PROP
ADMIN COST ATTIT HABITAT PERCEPT PWR...CONCPT
PROBABIL QUANT PREDICT HYPO/EXP BIBLIOG. PAGE 8
G0152

INDUS
SIMUL
DECISION
MGT

B63

NORTH R.C.,CONTENT ANALYSIS: A HANDBOOK WITH
APPLICATIONS FOR THE STUDY OF INTERNATIONAL CRISIS.
ASIA COM EUR+WWI MOD/EUR INT/ORG TEC/DEV DOMIN
EDU/PROP ROUTINE COERCE PERCEPT RIGID/FLEX ALL/VALS
...QUANT TESTS CON/ANAL SIMUL GEN/LAWS VAL/FREE.
PAGE 42 G0825

METH/CNCPT
COMPUT/IR
USSR

B63

TOMKINS S.S.,COMPUTER SIMULATION OF PERSONALITY.
R+D TEC/DEV AUTOMAT FEEDBACK ANOMIE PERCEPT...STYLE
PERS/TEST PREDICT COMPUT/IR GP/COMP. PAGE 55 G1075

COMPUTER
PERSON
SIMUL
PROG/TEAC

PHELPS J.,"STUDIES IN DETERRENCE VIII: MILITARY STABILITY AND ARMS CONTROL: A CRITICAL SURVEY." FUT WOR+45 INT/ORG ACT/RES EDU/PROP COERCE NUC/PWR WAR HEALTH PWR...POLICY TECHNIC TREND SIMUL TOT/POP 20. PAGE 44 G0874
L'63
FORCES
ORD/FREE
ARMS/CONT
DETER

BRILLOUIN L.,SCIENTIFIC UNCERTAINTY AND INFORMATION. PROB/SOLV AUTOMAT PERCEPT ORD/FREE ...MATH REGRESS STAT STYLE OBS IDEA/COMP SIMUL TIME. PAGE 9 G0169
B64
PHIL/SCI
NEW/IDEA
METH/CNCPT
CREATE

LANG A.S.,URBAN RAIL TRANSIT. OP/RES PLAN PROB/SOLV TEC/DEV AUTOMAT COST...TECHNIC MATH CON/ANAL CHARTS METH/COMP SIMUL 20 RAILROAD PUB/TRANS. PAGE 32 G0632
B64
MUNIC
DIST/IND
ECOMETRIC

MARTINO R.L.,PROJECT MANAGEMENT AND CONTROL: VOL. 2 APPLIED OPERATIONAL PLANNING. COMPUTER...MATH CHARTS SIMUL METH TIME. PAGE 36 G0716
B64
DECISION
PLAN
TEC/DEV
OP/RES

SHUBIK M.,GAME THEORY AND RELATED APPROACHES TO SOCIAL BEHAVIOR: SELECTIONS. INTELL SOCIETY ACT/RES CREATE PLAN PROB/SOLV...DECISION MATH. PAGE 50 G0994
B64
SOC
SIMUL
GAME
PWR

ABT C.,"WAR GAMING." USA+45 NAT/G TOP/EX ACT/RES TEC/DEV COERCE KNOWL ORD/FREE PWR...DECISION MATH TIME/SEQ COMPUT/IR CHARTS LAB/EXP VAL/FREE. PAGE 2 G0026
S64
FORCES
SIMUL
WAR

MAHALANOBIS P.C.,"PERSPECTIVE PLANNING IN INDIA: STATISTICAL TOOLS." INDIA S/ASIA STRATA AGRI DIST/IND FINAN INDUS SERV/IND NAT/G ECO/TAC ORD/FREE WEALTH...POLICY TREND SIMUL VAL/FREE 20. PAGE 35 G0695
S64
PLAN
STAT

PILISUK M.,"STEPWISE DISARMAMENT & SUDDEN DESTRUCTION IN A TWOPERSON GAME: A RESEARCH TOOL." NAT/G FORCES ACT/RES ECO/TAC EDU/PROP EXEC ROUTINE COERCE ORD/FREE...SIMUL GEN/LAWS VAL/FREE. PAGE 45 G0877
S64
PWR
DECISION
ARMS/CONT

BOBROW D.B.,COMPONENTS OF DEFENSE POLICY. ASIA EUR+WWI USA+45 WOR+45 INTELL INT/ORG NAT/G PROF/ORG CONSULT LEGIS ACT/RES CREATE ARMS/CONT COERCE ORD/FREE...DECISION SIMUL. PAGE 7 G0145
B65
DETER
NUC/PWR
PLAN
FORCES

HITCH C.J.,DECISION-MAKING FOR DEFENSE. USA+45 CREATE BUDGET COERCE WAR WEAPON EFFICIENCY...SIMUL 20. PAGE 26 G0515
B65
DECISION
OP/RES
PLAN
FORCES

MCGUIRE M.C.,SECRECY AND THE ARMS RACE* A THEORY OF THE ACCUMULATION OF STRATEGIC WEAPONS AND HOW SECRECY AFFECTS IT. DIPLOM NUC/PWR WEAPON ISOLAT RATIONAL ORD/FREE WEALTH...ECOMETRIC MATH GEN/LAWS. PAGE 38 G0742
B65
DETER
ARMS/CONT
SIMUL
GAME

SINGER J.D.,HUMAN BEHAVIOR AND INTERNATIONAL POLITICS* CONTRIBUTIONS FROM THE SOCIAL-PSYCHOLOGICAL SCIENCES. ACT/RES PLAN EDU/PROP ADMIN KNOWL...DECISION PSY SOC NET/THEORY HYPO/EXP LAB/EXP SOC/EXP GEN/METH ANTHOL BIBLIOG. PAGE 51 G1006
B65
DIPLOM
PHIL/SCI
QUANT
SIMUL

VEINOTT A.F. JR.,MATHEMATICAL STUDIES IN MANAGEMENT SCIENCE. UNIV INDUS COMPUTER ADMIN...DECISION NET/THEORY SIMUL 20. PAGE 61 G1193
B65
MATH
MGT
PLAN
PRODUC

LASSWELL H.D.,"THE POLICY SCIENCES OF DEVELOPMENT." CULTURE SOCIETY EX/STRUC CREATE ADMIN ATTIT KNOWL ...SOC CONCPT SIMUL GEN/METH. PAGE 33 G0644
L65
PWR
METH/CNCPT
DIPLOM

CHU K.,"A DYNAMIC MODEL OF THE FIRM." OP/RES PROB/SOLV...DECISION ECOMETRIC NEW/IDEA STAT GAME ORG/CHARTS SIMUL. PAGE 12 G0230
S65
INDUS
COMPUTER
TEC/DEV

DALKEY N.C.,"SOLVABLE NUCLEAR WAR MODELS." FORCES
S65
GAME

BAL/PWR DIPLOM COERCE PEACE DECISION. PAGE 14 G0273
SIMUL
WAR
NUC/PWR

DEAN B.V.,"CONTRACT RESEARCH PROPOSAL PREPARATION STRATEGIES." ECO/TAC WEALTH...MGT SIMUL. PAGE 15 G0289
S65
USA+45
PROC/MFG
R+D
PLAN

DECHERT C.R.,"THE DEVELOPMENT OF CYBERNETICS." ACT/RES CREATE SKILL...STERTYP METH. PAGE 15 G0290
S65
SIMUL
COMPUT/IR
PLAN
DECISION

GREGG P.M.,"DIMENSIONS OF POLITICAL SYSTEMS: FACTOR ANALYSIS OF A CROSS POLITY SURVEY." TEC/DEV ...DECISION PHIL/SCI CONCPT STAT IDEA/COMP GEN/LAWS. PAGE 23 G0447
S65
SIMUL
GEN/METH
CLASSIF

GRENIEWSKI H.,"INTENTION AND PERFORMANCE: A PRIMER OF CYBERNETICS OF PLANNING." EFFICIENCY OPTIMAL KNOWL SKILL...DECISION MGT EQULIB. PAGE 23 G0448
S65
SIMUL
GAME
GEN/METH
PLAN

KUENNE R.E.,THE POLARIS MISSILE STRIKE* A GENERAL ECONOMIC SYSTEMS ANALYSIS. USA+45 USSR NAT/G BAL/PWR ARMS/CONT WAR...MATH PROBABIL COMPUT/IR CHARTS HYPO/EXP SIMUL. PAGE 32 G0625
B66
NUC/PWR
FORCES
DETER
DIPLOM

US PRES COMM ECO IMPACT DEFENS,REPORT* JULY 1965. USA+45 ECO/DEV INDUS DELIB/GP FORCES OP/RES ARMS/CONT NUC/PWR WEAPON BAL/PAY...PREDICT SIMUL. PAGE 59 G1159
B66
ACT/RES
STAT
WAR
BUDGET

EWALD R.F.,"ONE OF MANY POSSIBLE GAMES." ACADEM INT/ORG ARMS/CONT...INT/LAW GAME. PAGE 18 G0354
S66
SIMUL
HYPO/EXP
PROG/TEAC
RECORD

KAPLAN M.A.,"THE NEW GREAT DEBATE* TRADITIONALISM VS SCIENCE IN INTERNATIONAL RELATIONS."...DECISION HUM QUANT STYLE NET/THEORY CON/ANAL STERTYP GEN/LAWS. PAGE 29 G0577
S66
PHIL/SCI
CONSERVE
DIPLOM
SIMUL

BAUMOL W.J.,BUSINESS BEHAVIOR, VALUE AND GROWTH (REV. ED.). WOR+45 FINAN LG/CO TEC/DEV CAP/ISM DEMAND EQULIB...METH/COMP SIMUL 20. PAGE 5 G0105
B67
ALL/IDEOS
PHIL/SCI
PLAN
ECO/DEV

DE JOUVENEL B.,THE ART OF CONJECTURE. WOR+45 EFFICIENCY PERCEPT KNOWL...DECISION PHIL/SCI CONCPT METH/COMP BIBLIOG 20. PAGE 15 G0285
B67
FUT
PREDICT
SIMUL
METH

GOLEMBIEWSKI R.T.,ORGANIZING MEN AND POWER: PATTERNS OF BEHAVIOR AND LINESTAFF MODELS. WOR+45 EX/STRUC ACT/RES DOMIN PERS/REL...NEW/IDEA 20. PAGE 22 G0431
B67
ADMIN
CONTROL
SIMUL
MGT

HARDT J.P.,MATHEMATICS AND COMPUTERS IN SOVIET ECONOMIC PLANNING. COM USSR OP/RES PROB/SOLV OPTIMAL...MODAL SIMUL 20. PAGE 24 G0481
B67
PLAN
TEC/DEV
MATH
COMPUT/IR

HARMAN H.H.,MODERN FACTOR ANALYSIS (2ND REV. ED.). COMPUTER...DECISION CHARTS BIBLIOG T. PAGE 24 G0482
B67
CON/ANAL
METH/CNCPT
SIMUL
MATH

PORWIT K.,CENTRAL PLANNING: EVALUATION OF VARIANTS. PRICE OPTIMAL PRODUC...DECISION MATH CHARTS SIMUL BIBLIOG 20. PAGE 45 G0886
B67
PLAN
MGT
ECOMETRIC

SAPARINA Y.,CYBERNETICS WITHIN US. WOR+45 EDU/PROP FEEDBACK PERCEPT HEALTH...DECISION METH/CNCPT NEW/IDEA 20. PAGE 49 G0957
B67
COMPUTER
METH/COMP
CONTROL
SIMUL

US HOUSE COMM SCI ASTRONAUT,THE JUNIOR COLLEGE AND EDUCATION IN THE SCIENCES (PAMPHLET). USA+45 AGE/Y
B67
ACADEM
EDU/PROP

...CHARTS SIMUL HOUSE/REP. PAGE 58 G1148 — PHIL/SCI R+D

N67
US SUPERINTENDENT OF DOCUMENTS,SPACE: MISSILES, THE MOON, NASA, AND SATELLITES (PRICE LIST 79A). USA+45 COM/IND R+D NAT/G DIPLOM EDU/PROP ADMIN CONTROL HEALTH...POLICY SIMUL NASA CONGRESS. PAGE 61 G1190 — BIBLIOG/A SPACE TEC/DEV PEACE

SIMULATION....SEE SIMUL, MODELS INDEX

SINAI....SINAI

SIND....SIND - REGION OF PAKISTAN

SINGAPORE....SINGAPORE; SEE ALSO MALAYSIA

SINGER J.D. G1002,G1003,G1004,G1005,G1006

SINGH B. G1007

SINO/SOV....SINO-SOVIET RELATIONSHIPS

SINO-SOVIET RELATIONS....SEE SINO/SOV

SINYAVSK/A....ANDREY SINYAVSKY

SIRS....SALARY INFORMATION RETRIEVAL SYSTEM

SKILL....DEXTERITY

B46
WILCOX J.K.,OFFICIAL DEFENSE PUBLICATIONS, 1941-1945 (NINE VOLS.). USA-45 AGRI INDUS R+D LABOR FORCES TEC/DEV EFFICIENCY PRODUC SKILL WEALTH 20. PAGE 63 G1238 — BIBLIOG/A WAR CIVMIL/REL ADMIN

S48
COCH L.,"OVERCOMING RESISTANCE TO CHANGE" (BMR)" USA+45 CONSULT ADMIN ROUTINE GP/REL EFFICIENCY PRODUC PERCEPT SKILL...CHARTS SOC/EXP 20. PAGE 12 G0236 — WORKER OP/RES PROC/MFG RIGID/FLEX

B49
LEPAWSKY A.,ADMINISTRATION. FINAN INDUS LG/CO SML/CO INGP/REL PERS/REL COST EFFICIENCY OPTIMAL SKILL 20. PAGE 33 G0656 — ADMIN MGT WORKER EX/STRUC

B49
OGBURN W.,TECHNOLOGY AND INTERNATIONAL RELATIONS. WOR+45 WOR-45 ECO/DEV CREATE PLAN ECO/TAC EDU/PROP COERCE PWR SKILL WEALTH...TECHNIC PSY SOC NEW/IDEA CHARTS TOT/POP 20. PAGE 43 G0837 — TEC/DEV DIPLOM INT/ORG

S49
MERTON R.,"THE ROLE OF APPLIED SOCIAL SCIENCE IN THE FORMATION OF POLICY: A RESEARCH MEMORANDUM." WOR+45 INDUS NAT/G EXEC ROUTINE CHOOSE ORD/FREE PWR SKILL...POLICY MGT PSY METH/CNCPT TESTS CHARTS METH VAL/FREE 20. PAGE 38 G0756 — PLAN SOC DIPLOM

B50
MANNHEIM K.,FREEDOM, POWER, AND DEMOCRATIC PLANNING. FUT USSR WOR+45 ELITES INTELL SOCIETY NAT/G EDU/PROP ROUTINE ATTIT DRIVE SUPEGO SKILL ...POLICY PSY CONCPT TREND GEN/LAWS 20. PAGE 35 G0700 — TEC/DEV PLAN CAP/ISM UK

B51
CONANT J.B.,SCIENCE AND COMMON SENSE. WOR+45 WOR-45 R+D SCHOOL CONSULT TEC/DEV EDU/PROP SKILL...PLURIST METH/CNCPT RECORD TIME/SEQ SIMUL GEN/METH METH. PAGE 13 G0248 — CREATE PHIL/SCI

B52
CURRENT TRENDS IN PSYCHOLOGY,PSYCHOLOGY IN THE WORLD EMERGENCY. USA+45 CONSULT FORCES ACT/RES PLAN SKILL...DECISION OBS APT/TEST KNO/TEST PERS/TEST TREND CHARTS 20. PAGE 14 G0266 — NAT/G PSY

B52
DAY E.E.,EDUCATION FOR FREEDOM AND RESPONSIBILITY. FUT USA+45 CULTURE CONSULT EDU/PROP ATTIT SKILL ...MGT CONCPT OBS GEN/LAWS COLD/WAR 20. PAGE 14 G0282 — SCHOOL KNOWL

B53
EASTON D.,THE POLITICAL SYSTEM, AN INQUIRY INTO THE STATE POLITICAL SCIENCE. USA+45 INTELL CREATE EDU/PROP RIGID/FLEX KNOWL SKILL...PHIL/SCI NEW/IDEA STERTYP TOT/POP 20. PAGE 17 G0329 — R+D PERCEPT

S53
CORY R.H. JR.,"FORGING A PUBLIC INFORMATION POLICY FOR THE UNITED NATIONS." FUT WOR+45 SOCIETY ADMIN — INT/ORG EDU/PROP

PEACE ATTIT PERSON SKILL...CONCPT 20 UN. PAGE 13 G0257 — BAL/PWR

S55
ANGELL R.,"GOVERNMENTS AND PEOPLES AS A FOCI FOR PEACE-ORIENTED RESEARCH." WOR+45 CULTURE SOCIETY FACE/GP ACT/RES CREATE PLAN DIPLOM EDU/PROP ROUTINE ATTIT PERCEPT SKILL...POLICY CONCPT OBS TREND GEN/METH 20. PAGE 3 G0060 — FUT SOC PEACE

S55
GLADSTONE A.E.,"THE POSSIBILITY OF PREDICTING REACTIONS TO INTERNATIONAL EVENTS." UNIV SOCIETY NAT/G FORCES CREATE EDU/PROP COERCE WAR ATTIT PERSON KNOWL PWR SKILL...METH/CNCPT NEW/IDEA ORG/CHARTS. PAGE 21 G0420 — PHIL/SCI CONCPT

S55
WRIGHT Q.,"THE PEACEFUL ADJUSTMENT OF INTERNATIONAL RELATIONS: PROBLEMS AND RESEARCH APPROACHES." UNIV INTELL EDU/PROP ADJUD ROUTINE KNOWL SKILL...INT/LAW JURID PHIL/SCI CLASSIF 20. PAGE 64 G1258 — R+D METH/CNCPT PEACE

B56
THOMAS M.,ATOMIC ENERGY AND CONGRESS. USA+45 NAT/G ACT/RES PLAN TEC/DEV EDU/PROP ROUTINE KNOWL PWR SKILL...PHIL/SCI NEW/IDEA TIME/SEQ CHARTS METH CONGRESS VAL/FREE 20 AEC. PAGE 54 G1067 — LEGIS ADMIN NUC/PWR

S57
EASTON D.,"AN APPROACH TO THE ANALYSIS OF POLITICAL SYSTEMS." R+D EDU/PROP KNOWL SKILL...POLICY SOC METH/CNCPT NEW/IDEA SELF/OBS CHARTS GEN/METH TOT/POP. PAGE 17 G0331 — STRUCT PHIL/SCI

B58
MECRENSKY E.,SCIENTIFIC MANPOWER IN EUROPE. WOR+45 EDU/PROP GOV/REL SKILL...TECHNIC PHIL/SCI INT CHARTS BIBLIOG 20. PAGE 38 G0750 — ECO/TAC TEC/DEV METH/COMP NAT/COMP

B58
UN INTL CONF ON PEACEFUL USE,PROGRESS IN ATOMIC ENERGY (VOL. I). WOR+45 R+D PLAN TEC/DEV CONFER CONTROL PEACE SKILL...CHARTS ANTHOL 20 UN BAGHDAD. PAGE 55 G1088 — NUC/PWR DIPLOM WORKER EDU/PROP

S58
ANDERSON N.,"INTERNATIONAL SEMINARS: AN ANALYSIS AND AN EVALUATION." WOR+45 R+D ACT/RES CREATE PLAN REGION ATTIT KNOWL SKILL...SOC REC/INT PERS/TEST CHARTS 20. PAGE 3 G0057 — INT/ORG DELIB/GP

B59
MODELSKI G.,ATOMIC ENERGY IN THE COMMUNIST BLOC. FUT INT/ORG CONSULT FORCES ACT/RES PLAN KNOWL SKILL ...PHIL/SCI STAT CHARTS 20. PAGE 39 G0777 — TEC/DEV NUC/PWR USSR COM

B59
STANFORD RESEARCH INSTITUTE,POSSIBLE NONMILITARY SCIENTIFIC DEVELOPMENTS AND THEIR POTENTIAL IMPACT ON FOREIGN POLICY PROBLEMS OF THE UNITED. FUT USA+45 INT/ORG PROF/ORG CONSULT ACT/RES CREATE PLAN PEACE KNOWL SKILL...TECHNIC PHIL/SCI NEW/IDEA UNESCO 20. PAGE 52 G1032 — R+D TEC/DEV

S59
SIMONS H.,"WORLD-WIDE CAPABILITIES FOR PRODUCTION AND CONTROL OF NUCLEAR WEAPONS." FUT WOR+45 INDUS INT/ORG NAT/G ECO/TAC ATTIT PWR SKILL...TREND CHARTS VAL/FREE 20. PAGE 51 G1001 — TEC/DEV ARMS/CONT NUC/PWR

B60
MCGREGOR D.,THE HUMAN SIDE OF ENTERPRISE. USA+45 LEAD ROUTINE GP/REL INGP/REL...CONCPT GEN/LAWS 20. PAGE 38 G0741 — MGT ATTIT SKILL EDU/PROP

B60
RAPOPORT A.,FIGHTS, GAMES AND DEBATES. INTELL SOCIETY R+D EX/STRUC PERCEPT PERSON SKILL...PSY SOC GAME. PAGE 46 G0902 — METH/CNCPT MATH DECISION CON/ANAL

S60
LEAR J.,"PEACE: SCIENCE'S NEXT GREAT EXPLORATION." USA+45 INT/ORG TOP/EX TEC/DEV EDU/PROP ROUTINE PEACE KNOWL SKILL 20. PAGE 33 G0648 — EX/STRUC ARMS/CONT NUC/PWR

S60
RIVKIN A.,"AFRICAN ECONOMIC DEVELOPMENT: ADVANCED TECHNOLOGY AND THE STAGES OF GROWTH." CULTURE ECO/UNDEV AGRI COM/IND EXTR/IND PLAN ECO/TAC ATTIT DRIVE RIGID/FLEX SKILL WEALTH...MGT SOC GEN/LAWS WORK TOT/POP 20. PAGE 47 G0923 — AFR TEC/DEV FOR/AID

S60
SWIFT R.,"THE UNITED NATIONS AND ITS PUBLIC." INT/ORG
WOR+45 CONSTN FINAN CONSULT DELIB/GP ACT/RES ADMIN EDU/PROP
ROUTINE RIGID/FLEX SKILL UN 20. PAGE 53 G1048

N60
US HOUSE COMM SCI ASTRONAUT,THE ORGANIZATION OF THE ACT/RES
US NATIONAL SPACE EFFORT. USA+45 WOR+45 AIR ECO/DEV SKILL
NAT/G PLAN TEC/DEV DIPLOM EDU/PROP ATTIT DRIVE PWR SPACE
...OBS TIME/SEQ TREND TOT/POP 20. PAGE 58 G1142

B61
GRUBER R.,SCIENCE AND THE NEW NATIONS. WOR+45 NAT/G ECO/UNDEV
CREATE SKILL...CONCPT GEN/LAWS 20. PAGE 23 G0457 KNOWL

L61
HERRING P.,"RESEARCH FOR PUBLIC POLICY: BROOKINGS R+D
DEDICATION LECTURES." USA+45 CONSULT DELIB/GP ACT/RES
ROUTINE PERCEPT SKILL...MGT 20. PAGE 26 G0508 DIPLOM

S61
DALTON G.,"ECONOMIC THEORY AND PRIMITIVE SOCIETY" ECO/UNDEV
(BMR)" UNIV AGRI KIN TEC/DEV ECO/TAC REGION HABITAT METH
SKILL...METH/COMP BIBLIOG. PAGE 14 G0274 PHIL/SCI
SOC

S61
DEUTSCH K.W.,"A NOTE ON THE APPEARANCE OF WISDOM IN ADMIN
LARGE BUREAUCRATIC ORGANIZATIONS." ROUTINE PERSON PROBABIL
KNOWL SKILL...DECISION STAT. PAGE 15 G0299 PROB/SOLV
SIMUL

S61
LINDSAY F.A.,"PLANNING IN FOREIGN AFFAIRS: THE ECO/DEV
MISSING ELEMENT." FUT USA+45 ROUTINE SKILL...MGT PLAN
TOT/POP 20. PAGE 34 G0669 DIPLOM

S61
WOHLSTETTER A.,"NUCLEAR SHARING: NATO AND THE NTH TREND
COUNTRY." EUR+WWI FUT SOCIETY DIPLOM EXEC DETER PWR TEC/DEV
SKILL...POLICY TECHNIC CONCPT 20 NATO. PAGE 64 NUC/PWR
G1252 ARMS/CONT

S62
ALBONETTI A.,"IL SECONDO PROGRAMMA QUINQUENNALE R+D
1963-67 ED IL BILANCIO RICERCHE ED INVESTIMENTI PER PLAN
IL 1963 DELL'ERATOM." EUR+WWI FUT ITALY WOR+45 NUC/PWR
ECO/DEV SERV/IND INT/ORG TEC/DEV ECO/TAC ATTIT
SKILL WEALTH...MGT TIME/SEQ OEEC 20. PAGE 2 G0035

S62
GORDON B.K.,"NUCLEAR WEAPONS: RUSSIAN AND ORD/FREE
AMERICAN." COM USA+45 USSR NAT/G FORCES ACT/RES COERCE
TEC/DEV PERCEPT RIGID/FLEX PWR SKILL...MGT NUC/PWR
METH/CNCPT QUANT OBS TIME/SEQ CON/ANAL GEN/METH
TOT/POP VAL/FREE 20. PAGE 22 G0433

B63
HOWER R.M.,MANAGERS AND SCIENTISTS. EX/STRUC CREATE R+D
ADMIN REPRESENT ATTIT DRIVE ROLE PWR SKILL...SOC MGT
INT. PAGE 27 G0532 PERS/REL
INGP/REL

B63
US ATOMIC ENERGY COMMISSION,ATOMIC ENERGY IN THE METH/COMP
SOVIET UNION: TRIP REPORT OF THE US ATOMIC ENERGY OP/RES
DELEGATION, MAY 1933. USSR R+D NAT/G CONSULT CREATE TEC/DEV
DIPLOM ADMIN ROUTINE EFFICIENCY PRODUC KNOWL SKILL NUC/PWR
...NAT/COMP 20 AEC TRAVEL TREATY. PAGE 56 G1107

B63
US SENATE COMM APPROPRIATIONS,PERSONNEL ADMIN
ADMINISTRATION AND OPERATIONS OF AGENCY FOR FOR/AID
INTERNATIONAL DEVELOPMENT: SPECIAL HEARING. FINAN EFFICIENCY
LEAD COST UTIL SKILL...CHARTS 20 CONGRESS AID DIPLOM
CIVIL/SERV. PAGE 60 G1175

B63
WIGHTMAN D.,TOWARD ECONOMIC CO-OPERATION IN ASIA. ECO/UNDEV
ASIA S/ASIA VOL/ASSN ACT/RES PLAN TEC/DEV ECO/TAC CREATE
EDU/PROP RIGID/FLEX SKILL...POLICY METH/CNCPT OBS
INT GEN/LAWS UN 20 ECAFE. PAGE 63 G1237

B64
CONANT J.B.,TWO MODES OF THOUGHT: MY ENCOUNTERS PHIL/SCI
WITH SCIENCE AND EDUCATION....ART/METH JURID SOC SKILL
TREND. PAGE 13 G0249 MYTH
STYLE

B64
DIEBOLD J.,BEYOND AUTOMATION: MANAGERIAL PROBLEMS FUT
OF AN EXPLODING TECHNOLOGY. SOCIETY ECO/DEV CREATE INDUS
ECO/TAC AUTOMAT SKILL...TECHNIC MGT WORK. PAGE 16 PROVS
G0303 NAT/G

B64
RANSOM H.H.,CAN AMERICAN DEMOCRACY SURVIVE COLD USA+45
WAR. USA-45 CONSTN NAT/G CONSULT DELIB/GP LEGIS ROUTINE
ACT/RES LEGIT EXEC ATTIT KNOWL ORD/FREE PWR SKILL
...POLICY TIME/SEQ TREND GEN/LAWS 20 COLD/WAR.
PAGE 46 G0901

B64
VAN DYKE V.,PRIDE AND POWER: THE RATIONALE OF THE TEC/DEV
SPACE PROGRAM. FUT USA+45 INTELL R+D NAT/G POL/PAR ATTIT
DELIB/GP EX/STRUC LEGIS TOP/EX ACT/RES PLAN ECO/TAC POLICY
EDU/PROP ORD/FREE PWR RESPECT SKILL...TIME/SEQ
VAL/FREE. PAGE 61 G1191

S64
LERNER A.P.,"NUCLEAR SYMMETRY AS A FRAMEWORK FOR FORCES
COEXISTENCE." COM FUT USA+45 NAT/G ACT/RES CREATE ORD/FREE
PLAN DIPLOM EDU/PROP COERCE WAR RIGID/FLEX PWR DETER
SKILL...CONCPT METH/CNCPT GEN/LAWS TOT/POP VAL/FREE NUC/PWR
COLD/WAR 20. PAGE 33 G0657

B65
ANDERSON C.A.,EDUCATION AND ECONOMIC DEVELOPMENT. ANTHOL
INDUS R+D SCHOOL TEC/DEV ECO/TAC EDU/PROP AGE ECO/DEV
HEREDITY PERCEPT SKILL 20. PAGE 3 G0056 ECO/UNDEV
WORKER

S65
DECHERT C.R.,"THE DEVELOPMENT OF CYBERNETICS." SIMUL
ACT/RES CREATE SKILL...STERTYP METH. PAGE 15 G0290 COMPUT/IR
PLAN
DECISION

S65
GRENIEWSKI H.,"INTENTION AND PERFORMANCE: A PRIMER SIMUL
OF CYBERNETICS OF PLANNING." EFFICIENCY OPTIMAL GAME
KNOWL SKILL...DECISION MGT EQULIB. PAGE 23 G0448 GEN/METH
PLAN

S65
GRIFFITH S.B.,"COMMUNIST CHINA'S CAPACITY TO MAKE FORCES
WAR." CHINA/COM COM NAT/G TOP/EX PLAN DOMIN COERCE PWR
NUC/PWR ATTIT RESPECT SKILL...CONCPT MYTH TIME/SEQ WEAPON
TREND COLD/WAR 20. PAGE 23 G0452 ASIA

S65
TENDLER J.D.,"TECHNOLOGY AND ECONOMIC DEVELOPMENT* BRAZIL
THE CASE OF HYDRO VS THERMAL POWER." CONSTRUC INDUS
DIST/IND CREATE TEC/DEV INT/TRADE CENTRAL PWR SKILL ECO/UNDEV
WEALTH...MGT NAT/COMP ARGEN. PAGE 54 G1063

B66
ALEXANDER Y.,INTERNATIONAL TECHNICAL ASSISTANCE SKILL
EXPERTS: A CASE STUDY OF THE U.N. EXPERIENCE. INT/ORG
USA+45 WOR+45 WORKER CREATE PLAN PROB/SOLV ECO/TAC TEC/DEV
FOR/AID GIVE EDU/PROP...CHARTS BIBLIOG 20 UN. CONSULT
PAGE 2 G0039

B66
NATIONAL SCIENCE FOUNDATION,SIXTEENTH ANNUAL REPORT NAT/G
FOR THE FISCAL YEAR ENDED JUNE 30, 1966. USA+45 EDU/PROP
CREATE BUDGET SKILL 20 NSF. PAGE 41 G0813 ACADEM
KNOWL

B66
SANFORD T.,BUT WHAT ABOUT THE PEOPLE? ACADEM SCHOOL EDU/PROP
BUDGET TAX CONTROL SKILL WEALTH 20 NORTH/CAR. PROB/SOLV
PAGE 49 G0956 POLICY
PROVS

S66
TURKEVICH J.,"SOVIET SCIENCE APPRAISED." USA+45 R+D USSR
ACADEM FORCES DIPLOM EDU/PROP WAR EFFICIENCY PEACE TEC/DEV
SKILL OBS. PAGE 55 G1081 NAT/COMP
ATTIT

B67
KRANZBERG M.,TECHNOLOGY IN WESTERN CIVILIZATION TEC/DEV
VOLUME ONE. UNIV INDUS SKILL. PAGE 31 G0617 ACT/RES
AUTOMAT
POLICY

S67
BRUNHILD G.,"THEORY OF 'TECHNICAL UNEMPLOYMENT'." WORKER
ECO/DEV ACT/RES PROB/SOLV DEMAND PRODUC...PHIL/SCI TEC/DEV
20. PAGE 9 G0182 SKILL
INDUS

S67
DE NEUFVILLE R.,"EDUCATION AT THE ACADEMIES." FORCES
USA+45 ELITES CONSULT EX/STRUC COMPUTER PLAN ACADEM
PROB/SOLV TASK CIVMIL/REL ORD/FREE 20. PAGE 15 TEC/DEV
G0286 SKILL

S67
GAUSSENS J.,"THE APPLICATIONS OF NUCLEAR ENERGY - NUC/PWR

TECHNICAL, ECONOMIC AND SOCIAL ASPECTS." WOR+45   TEC/DEV
INDUS R+D ACT/RES EFFICIENCY PRODUC SKILL PREDICT.   ECO/DEV
PAGE 21 G0413   ADJUST

SKINNER B.F. G1008

SKOGSTAD A.L. G0574

SKOLNIKOFF E.B. G1009,G1010

SKRIVANEK M.S. G0358

SLAV/MACED....SLAVO-MACEDONIANS

SLAVERY....SEE ORD/FREE, DOMIN

SLAVS....SLAVS - PERTAINING TO THE SLAVIC PEOPLE AND
    SLAVOPHILISM

SLEEP....SLEEPING AND FATIGUE

SLOAN P. G1011

SLOSS J. G0684

SLUCKIN W. G1012

SLUMS....SLUMS

SMITH D.O. G1013

SMITH E.A. G1014

SMITH E.B. G0090

SMITH H.H. G1015

SMITH/ACT....SMITH ACT

SMITH/ADAM....ADAM SMITH

B88
BENTHAM J.,DEFENCE OF USURY (1787). UK LAW NAT/G   TAX
TEC/DEV ECO/TAC CONTROL ATTIT...CONCPT IDEA/COMP 18   FINAN
SMITH/ADAM. PAGE 6 G0124   ECO/DEV
   POLICY

SMITH/ALF....ALFRED E. SMITH

SMITH/IAN....IAN SMITH

SMITH/JOS....JOSEPH SMITH

SMITH/LEVR....SMITH-LEVER ACT

SMITHIES A. G1016

SML/CO....SMALL COMPANY

B47
WHITEHEAD T.N.,LEADERSHIP IN A FREE SOCIETY; A   INDUS
STUDY IN HUMAN RELATIONS BASED ON AN ANALYSIS OF   LEAD
PRESENT-DAY INDUSTRIAL CIVILIZATION. WOR-45 STRUCT   ORD/FREE
R+D LABOR LG/CO SML/CO WORKER PLAN PROB/SOLV   SOCIETY
TEC/DEV DRIVE...MGT 20. PAGE 63 G1234

B49
LEPAWSKY A.,ADMINISTRATION. FINAN INDUS LG/CO   ADMIN
SML/CO INGP/REL PERS/REL COST EFFICIENCY OPTIMAL   MGT
SKILL 20. PAGE 33 G0656   WORKER
   EX/STRUC

B62
FERBER R.,RESEARCH METHODS IN ECONOMICS AND   ACT/RES
BUSINESS. ECO/DEV FINAN MARKET LG/CO SML/CO CONSULT   PROB/SOLV
CONTROL COST...STAT METH/COMP 20. PAGE 19 G0364   ECO/TAC
   MGT

B62
GRANICK D.,THE EUROPEAN EXECUTIVE. BELGIUM FRANCE   MGT
GERMANY/W UK INDUS LABOR LG/CO SML/CO EX/STRUC PLAN   ECO/DEV
TEC/DEV CAP/ISM COST DEMAND...POLICY CHARTS 20.   ECO/TAC
PAGE 22 G0441   EXEC

S64
COOPER A.C.,"R&D IS MORE EFFICIENT IN SMALL   R+D
COMPANIES." USA+45 LG/CO SML/CO WEALTH...RECORD INT   INDUS
LAB/EXP 20. PAGE 13 G0255   CREATE
   GP/COMP

S64
MUMFORD L.,"AUTHORITARIAN AND DEMOCRATIC   ECO/DEV
TECHNIQUES." INDUS PROC/MFG LG/CO SML/CO CREATE   TEC/DEV
PLAN KNOWL...POLICY TREND WORK 20. PAGE 40 G0794

S67
HAMBERG D.,"SIZE OF ENTERPRISE AND TECHNICAL   TEC/DEV
CHANGE." USA+45 LG/CO SML/CO CREATE OP/RES PROFIT   INDUS
...TREND 20. PAGE 24 G0477   R+D
   WEALTH

SMUTS/JAN....JAN CHRISTIAN SMUTS

SMYTH H.D. G1017

SNCC....STUDENT NONVIOLENT COORDINATING COMMITTEE

SNYDER O.H. G0968

SNYDER R.C. G1018

SOBERMAN R.M. G0632

SOC....SOCIOLOGY

N
WEIGLEY R.F.,HISTORY OF THE UNITED STATES ARMY.   FORCES
USA+45 USA-45 SOCIETY NAT/G LEAD WAR GP/REL PWR   ADMIN
...SOC METH/COMP COLD/WAR. PAGE 62 G1222   ROLE
   CIVMIL/REL

B
CURRENT THOUGHT ON PEACE AND WAR. WOR+45 INT/ORG   BIBLIOG/A
FORCES PROB/SOLV DIPLOM NUC/PWR PERCEPT...POLICY   PEACE
SOC 20 UN NATO. PAGE 1 G0001   ATTIT
   WAR

B
BRITISH COMMONWEALTH BUR AGRI,WORLD AGRICULTURAL   BIBLIOG/A
ECONOMICS AND RURAL SOCIOLOGY ABSTRACTS. NAT/G   AGRI
OP/RES PLAN TEC/DEV LEAD PRODUC...GEOG MGT NAT/COMP   SOC
20. PAGE 9 G0170   WORKER

N
JOURNAL OF CONFLICT RESOLUTION. FUT WOR+45 INT/ORG   BIBLIOG/A
NAT/G FORCES CREATE PROB/SOLV ARMS/CONT NUC/PWR   DIPLOM
WEAPON SOC. PAGE 1 G0002   WAR

B28
SOROKIN P.,CONTEMPORARY SOCIOLOGICAL THEORIES.   CULTURE
MOD/EUR UNIV SOCIETY R+D SCHOOL ECO/TAC EDU/PROP   SOC
ROUTINE ATTIT DRIVE...PSY CONCPT TIME/SEQ TREND   WAR
GEN/LAWS 20. PAGE 52 G1021

B34
BOWMAN I.,GEOGRAPHY IN RELATION TO THE SOCIAL   GEOG
SCIENCES. UNIV...SOC CONCPT METH. PAGE 8 G0161   CULTURE
   ROUTINE
   PHIL/SCI

S39
HECKSCHER G.,"GROUP ORGANIZATION IN SWEDEN." SWEDEN   LAISSEZ
STRATA ECO/DEV AGRI INDUS LABOR NAT/G PROF/ORG   SOC
ECO/TAC CENTRAL SOCISM...MGT 19/20. PAGE 25 G0499

B40
ZNANIECKI F.,THE SOCIAL ROLE OF THE MAN OF   ROLE
KNOWLEDGE. UNIV SOCIETY STRUCT TEC/DEV...EPIST   INTELL
PHIL/SCI SOC NEW/IDEA 20. PAGE 65 G1269   KNOWL
   INGP/REL

B42
MARCHANT A.,INVESTIGATIONS IN PROGRESS IN THE   ACT/RES
UNITED STATES IN THE FIELD OF LATIN AMERICAN   SOC
HUMANISTIC AND SOCIAL SCIENCE STUDIES. USA+45   R+D
ACADEM...QU ANTHOL. PAGE 36 G0702   L/A+17C

S42
LASSWELL H.D.,"THE RELATION OF IDEOLOGICAL   ATTIT
INTELLIGENCE TO PUBLIC POLICY." WOR+45 WOR-45   DECISION
SOCIETY DELIB/GP ACT/RES CREATE PLAN DIPLOM
EDU/PROP CHOOSE KNOWL PWR...POLICY SOC TREND
GEN/LAWS 20. PAGE 32 G0638

B44
KAUFMANN F.,METHODOLOGY OF THE SOCIAL SCIENCES.   SOC
PERSON...RELATIV PSY CONCPT LING METH 20. PAGE 30   PHIL/SCI
G0585   GEN/LAWS
   METH/CNCPT

S44
GRIFFITH E.S.,"THE CHANGING PATTERN OF PUBLIC   LAW
POLICY FORMATION." MOD/EUR WOR+45 FINAN CHIEF   POLICY
CONFER ADMIN LEAD CONSERVE SOCISM TECHRACY...SOC   TEC/DEV
CHARTS CONGRESS. PAGE 23 G0450

S44
HAWLEY A.H.,"ECOLOGY AND HUMAN ECOLOGY" WOR+45   HABITAT
INTELL ACADEM PLAN GP/REL ADJUST PERSON...PHIL/SCI   GEOG

SOC METH/CNCPT METH 20. PAGE 25 G0493 — GEN/LAWS METH/COMP

C45
MCDIARMID J.,"THE MOBILIZATION OF SOCIAL SCIENTISTS," IN L. WHITE'S CIVIL CIVIL SERVICE IN WARTIME." USA+45 TEC/DEV CENTRAL...SOC 20 CIVIL/SERV. PAGE 37 G0733 — INTELL WAR DELIB/GP ADMIN

B46
VINER J.,SYMPOSIUM ON ATOMIC ENERGY AND ITS IMPLICATIONS. USA+45 WOR+45 SOCIETY DELIB/GP...SOC CONCPT TIME/SEQ TOT/POP 20. PAGE 61 G1200 — R+D RIGID/FLEX NUC/PWR

B47
BRYSON L.,SCIENCE AND FREEDOM. WOR+45 ACT/RES CREATE TECHRACY...TECHNIC SOC/INTEG. PAGE 9 G0183 — CONCPT ORD/FREE CULTURE SOC

B47
LASSWELL H.D.,THE ANALYSIS OF POLITICAL BEHAVIOUR: AN EMPIRICAL APPROACH. WOR+45 CULTURE NAT/G FORCES EDU/PROP ADMIN ATTIT PERCEPT KNOWL...PHIL/SCI PSY SOC NEW/IDEA OBS INT GEN/METH NAZI 20. PAGE 32 G0639 — R+D ACT/RES ELITES

S47
TURNER R.H.,"THE NAVY DISBURSING OFFICER AS A BUREAUCRAT" (BMR)" USA-45 LAW STRATA DIST/IND WAR PWR...SOC 20 BUREAUCRCY. PAGE 55 G1083 — FORCES ADMIN PERSON ROLE

S48
HARDIN L.M.,"REFLECTIONS ON AGRICULTURAL POLICY FORMATION IN THE UNITED STATES." LEGIS PLAN BUDGET ECO/TAC LEAD CENTRAL...MGT SOC NEW/IDEA STAT FAO. PAGE 24 G0480 — AGRI POLICY ADMIN NEW/LIB

S48
MERTON R.K.,"THE BEARING OF EMPIRICAL RESEARCH UPON THE DEVELOPMENT OF SOCIAL THEORY" (BMR)"...SOC CONCPT QUANT METH/COMP HYPO/EXP 20. PAGE 38 G0757 — ACT/RES SOC/EXP OBS PHIL/SCI

B49
OGBURN W.,TECHNOLOGY AND INTERNATIONAL RELATIONS. WOR+45 WOR-45 ECO/DEV CREATE PLAN ECO/TAC EDU/PROP COERCE PWR SKILL WEALTH...TECHNIC PSY SOC NEW/IDEA CHARTS TOT/POP 20. PAGE 43 G0837 — TEC/DEV DIPLOM INT/ORG

S49
MERTON R.,"THE ROLE OF APPLIED SOCIAL SCIENCE IN THE FORMATION OF POLICY: A RESEARCH MEMORANDUM." WOR+45 INDUS NAT/G EXEC ROUTINE CHOOSE ORD/FREE PWR SKILL...POLICY MGT PSY METH/CNCPT TESTS CHARTS METH VAL/FREE 20. PAGE 38 G0756 — PLAN SOC DIPLOM

B50
CANTRIL H.,TENSIONS THAT CAUSE WAR. UNIV CULTURE R+D CREATE EDU/PROP DRIVE PERSON KNOWL ORD/FREE ...HUM PSY SOC OBS CENSUS TREND CON/ANAL SOC/EXP SIMUL GEN/METH ANTHOL COLD/WAR TOT/POP. PAGE 11 G0206 — SOCIETY PHIL/SCI PEACE

B50
DEES J.W. JR.,URBAN SOCIOLOGY AND THE EMERGING ATOMIC MEGALOPOLIS, PART I. USA+45 TEC/DEV ADMIN NUC/PWR HABITAT...SOC AUD/VIS CHARTS GEN/LAWS 20 WATER. PAGE 15 G0291 — PLAN NEIGH MUNIC PROB/SOLV

B50
CONTINUITIES IN SOCIAL RESEARCH; STUDIES IN SCOPE AND METHOD OF "THE AMERICAN SOLDIER" USA+45 FORCES INGP/REL ATTIT...PSY SAMP CON/ANAL CHARTS GEN/LAWS ANTHOL 20. PAGE 38 G0758 — SOC PHIL/SCI METH

B51
MAASS A.,MUDDY WATERS: THE ARMY ENGINEERS AND THE NATIONS RIVERS. USA-45 PROF/ORG CONSULT LEGIS ADMIN EXEC ROLE PWR...SOC PRESIDENT 20. PAGE 35 G0682 — FORCES GP/REL LOBBY CONSTRUC

S51
LERNER D.,"THE POLICY SCIENCES: RECENT DEVELOPMENTS IN SCOPE AND METHODS." R+D SERV/IND CREATE DIPLOM ROUTINE PWR...METH/CNCPT TREND GEN/LAWS METH 20. PAGE 33 G0658 — CONSULT SOC

S51
MACRAE D.G.,"THE BOLSHEVIK IDEOLOGY; THE INTELLECTUAL AND EMOTIONAL FACTORS IN COMMUNIST AFFILIATION" (BMR)" COM LEAD REV ATTIT ORD/FREE ...SOC CON/ANAL 20 BOLSHEVISM. PAGE 35 G0693 — MARXISM INTELL PHIL/SCI SECT

B52
HAYEK F.A.,THE COUNTER-REVOLUTION OF SCIENCE. UNIV INTELL R+D VOL/ASSN CREATE EDU/PROP...PHIL/SCI SOC OBS TIME/SEQ TREND GEN/METH. PAGE 25 G0494 — PERCEPT KNOWL

S52
"SELECTED CRITICAL BIBLIOGRAPHY ON THE METHODS AND TECHNIQUES OF POLITICAL BEHAVIOR RESEARCH." ...PHIL/SCI OBS QU SYS/QU TESTS CON/ANAL. PAGE 1 G0012 — BIBLIOG/A METH SOC EDU/PROP

S52
TRUMAN D.B.,"SELECTED CRITICAL BIBLIOGRAPHY ON THE METHODS AND TECHNIQUES OF POLITICAL BEHAVIOR RESEARCH." R+D PARTIC...SOC OBS RECORD INT. PAGE 55 G1079 — BIBLIOG/A ACT/RES METH/CNCPT

B53
CALDWELL L.K.,RESEARCH METHODS IN PUBLIC ADMINISTRATION; AN OUTLINE OF TOPICS AND READINGS (PAMPHLET). LAW ACT/RES COMPUTER KNOWL...SOC STAT GEN/METH 20. PAGE 10 G0201 — BIBLIOG/A METH/COMP ADMIN OP/RES

B53
SCHAAF R.W.,DOCUMENTS OF INTERNATIONAL MEETINGS. AGRI INDUS ACADEM DIPLOM NUC/PWR RACE/REL AGE/Y HEALTH...SOC 20. PAGE 49 G0960 — BIBLIOG/A DELIB/GP INT/ORG POLICY

B54
COMBS C.H.,DECISION PROCESSES. INTELL SOCIETY DELIB/GP CREATE TEC/DEV DOMIN LEGIT EXEC CHOOSE DRIVE RIGID/FLEX KNOWL PWR...PHIL/SCI SOC METH/CNCPT CONT/OBS REC/INT PERS/TEST SAMP/SIZ BIOG SOC/EXP WORK. PAGE 13 G0245 — MATH DECISION

B54
ROSE A.M.,THEORY AND METHOD IN THE SOCIAL SCIENCES. STRATA R+D NEIGH PARTIC...METH/CNCPT GP/COMP. PAGE 47 G0934 — CONCPT SOC VOL/ASSN ROLE

B54
SPENCER R.F.,METHOD AND PERSPECTIVE IN ANTHROPOLOGY ....GEOG LING QUANT STAT TESTS SAMP/SIZ CON/ANAL IDEA/COMP METH/COMP ANTHOL BIBLIOG 20. PAGE 52 G1025 — PHIL/SCI SOC PSY METH

B54
SPROTT W.J.H.,SCIENCE AND SOCIAL ACTION. STRUCT ACT/RES CRIME GP/REL INGP/REL ANOMIE...PSY SOC/INTEG 19/20. PAGE 52 G1027 — SOC CULTURE PHIL/SCI

B54
WASHBURNE N.F.,INTERPRETING SOCIAL CHANGE IN AMERICA. USA+45 STRATA FAM NAT/G SECT OP/RES ECO/TAC EDU/PROP HABITAT...SOC TIME/SEQ TREND 20 BUREAUCRCY. PAGE 62 G1217 — CULTURE STRUCT CREATE TEC/DEV

S54
FORM W.H.,"THE PLACE OF SOCIAL STRUCTURE IN THE DETERMINATION OF LAND USE: SOME IMPLICATIONS FOR A THEORY OF URBAN ECOLOGY" (BMR)" STRUCT...GEOG PHIL/SCI SOC 20. PAGE 19 G0381 — HABITAT MARKET ORD/FREE MUNIC

B55
LIPPMAN W.,THE PUBLIC PHILOSOPHY. EX/STRUC TOP/EX LOBBY RATIONAL POPULISM...POLICY SOC CONCPT PREDICT GP/COMP IDEA/COMP. PAGE 34 G0673 — MAJORIT STRUCT PWR TOTALISM

B55
SHUBIK M.,READINGS IN GAME THEORY AND POLITICAL BEHAVIOR. WOR+45 FORCES CREATE ROUTINE WAR PEACE PERCEPT KNOWL PWR...PSY SOC CONCPT METH/CNCPT STAT CHARTS HYPO/EXP GAME METH VAL/FREE 20. PAGE 50 G0991 — MATH DECISION DIPLOM

S55
ANGELL R.,"GOVERNMENTS AND PEOPLES AS A FOCI FOR PEACE-ORIENTED RESEARCH." WOR+45 CULTURE SOCIETY FACE/GP ACT/RES CREATE PLAN DIPLOM EDU/PROP ROUTINE ATTIT PERCEPT SKILL...POLICY CONCPT OBS TREND GEN/METH 20. PAGE 3 G0060 — FUT SOC PEACE

B56
HISTORICAL ABSTRACTS. NAT/G CREATE DIPLOM ATTIT ...SOC DICTIONARY INDEX 18/20. PAGE 1 G0013 — WOR-45 COMPUT/IR BIBLIOG/A

B56
WASSERMAN P.,INFORMATION FOR ADMINISTRATORS: A GUIDE TO PUBLICATIONS AND SERVICES FOR MANAGEMENT IN BUSINESS AND GOVERNMENT. R+D LOC/G NAT/G PROF/ORG VOL/ASSN PRESS...PSY SOC STAT 20. PAGE 62 G1219 — BIBLIOG MGT KNOWL EDU/PROP

ALMOND G.A.,"COMPARATIVE POLITICAL SYSTEMS" (BMR)"
WOR+45 WOR-45 PROB/SOLV DIPLOM EFFICIENCY
...PHIL/SCI SOC METH 17/20. PAGE 3 G0046
GOV/COMP CONCPT ALL/IDEOS NAT/COMP S56

KIETH-LUCAS A.,DECISIONS ABOUT PEOPLE IN NEED, A
STUDY OF ADMINISTRATIVE RESPONSIVENESS IN PUBLIC
ASSISTANCE. USA+45 GIVE RECEIVE INGP/REL PERS/REL
MORAL RESPECT WEALTH...SOC OBS BIBLIOG 20. PAGE 30
G0595
B57 ADMIN RIGID/FLEX SOC/WK DECISION

MERTON R.K.,SOCIAL THEORY AND SOCIAL STRUCTURE
(REV. ED.). INTELL SECT WORKER OP/RES EDU/PROP
ADMIN INGP/REL ANOMIE PERSON...AUD/VIS T 20
BUREAUCRCY. PAGE 38 G0759
B57 SOC GEN/LAWS SOCIETY STRUCT

EASTON D.,"AN APPROACH TO THE ANALYSIS OF POLITICAL
SYSTEMS." R+D EDU/PROP KNOWL SKILL...POLICY SOC
METH/CNCPT NEW/IDEA SELF/OBS CHARTS GEN/METH
TOT/POP. PAGE 17 G0331
S57 STRUCT PHIL/SCI

US ARMY LIBRARY,THESES AND DISSERTATIONS IN THE
HOLDINGS OF THE ARMY LIBRARY (PAMPHLET). USA+45
...INT/LAW PSY SOC 20. PAGE 56 G1105
N57 BIBLIOG FORCES MGT CONTROL

ARON R.,ON WAR: ATOMIC WEAPONS AND GLOBAL DIPLOMACY
(TRANS. BY TERENCE KILMARTIN). WOR+45 SOCIETY
FORCES BAL/PWR WAR WEAPON PERSON...SOC 20. PAGE 4
G0067
B58 ARMS/CONT NUC/PWR COERCE DIPLOM

CROWE S.,THE LANDSCAPE OF POWER. UK CULTURE
SERV/IND NAT/G CONSULT PARTIC NUC/PWR LEISURE...SOC
EXHIBIT 20. PAGE 14 G0264
B58 HABITAT TEC/DEV PLAN CONTROL

ANDERSON N.,"INTERNATIONAL SEMINARS: AN ANALYSIS
AND AN EVALUATION." WOR+45 R+D ACT/RES CREATE PLAN
REGION ATTIT KNOWL SKILL...SOC REC/INT PERS/TEST
CHARTS 20. PAGE 3 G0057
S58 INT/ORG DELIB/GP

DAVENPORT J.,"ARMS AND THE WELFARE STATE." INTELL
STRUCT FORCES CREATE ECO/TAC FOR/AID DOMIN LEGIT
ADMIN WAR ORD/FREE PWR...POLICY SOC CONCPT MYTH OBS
TREND COLD/WAR TOT/POP 20. PAGE 14 G0276
S58 USA+45 NAT/G USSR

DEAN B.V.,"APPLICATION OF OPERATIONS RESEARCH TO
MANAGERIAL DECISION MAKING" STRATA ACT/RES
PROB/SOLV ROLE...SOC PREDICT SIMUL 20. PAGE 15
G0288
S58 DECISION OP/RES MGT METH/CNCPT

DAHRENDORF R.,CLASS AND CLASS CONFLICT IN
INDUSTRIAL SOCIETY. LABOR NAT/G COERCE ROLE PLURISM
...POLICY MGT CONCPT CLASSIF. PAGE 14 G0271
B59 VOL/ASSN STRUCT SOC GP/REL

JACOBS N.,CULTURE FOR THE MILLIONS? INTELL SOCIETY
NAT/G...POLICY SOC OBS ANTHOL 20. PAGE 28 G0553
B59 CULTURE COM/IND PERF/ART CONCPT

COLUMBIA U BUREAU APPL SOC R, ATTITUDES OF
PROMINENT AMERICANS TOWARD "WORLD PEACE THROUGH
WORLD LAW" (SUPRA-NATL ORGANIZATION FOR WAR
PREVENTION). USA+45 USSR ELITES FORCES PLAN
PROB/SOLV CONTROL WAR PWR...POLICY SOC QU IDEA/COMP
20 UN. PAGE 45 G0888
B59 ATTIT ACT/RES INT/LAW STAT

FRANCIS R.G.,THE PREDICTIVE PROCESS. PLAN MARXISM
...DECISION SOC CONCPT NAT/COMP 19/20. PAGE 20
G0390
B60 PREDICT PHIL/SCI TREND

RAPOPORT A.,FIGHTS, GAMES AND DEBATES. INTELL
SOCIETY R+D EX/STRUC PERCEPT PERSON SKILL...PSY SOC
GAME. PAGE 46 G0902
B60 METH/CNCPT MATH DECISION CON/ANAL

HOLTON G.,"ARMS CONTROL." FUT WOR+45 CULTURE
INT/ORG NAT/G FORCES TOP/EX PLAN EDU/PROP COERCE
L60 ACT/RES CONSULT

ATTIT RIGID/FLEX ORD/FREE...POLICY PHIL/SCI SOC
TREND COLD/WAR. PAGE 27 G0524
ARMS/CONT NUC/PWR

MCCLELLAND C.A.,"THE FUNCTION OF THEORY IN
INTERNATIONAL RELATIONS." WOR+45 PLAN EDU/PROP
ROUTINE ORD/FREE...PHIL/SCI PSY SOC METH/CNCPT
NEW/IDEA OBS TREND GEN/METH 20. PAGE 37 G0728
L60 INT/ORG CONCPT DIPLOM

BARNETT H.J.,"RESEARCH AND DEVELOPMENT, ECONOMIC
GROWTH, AND NATIONAL SECURITY." USA+45 R+D CREATE
ECO/TAC ATTIT DRIVE PWR...POLICY SOC METH/CNCPT
QUANT STAT TIME/SEQ ORG/CHARTS COLD/WAR 20. PAGE 5
G0097
S60 ACT/RES PLAN

GARFINKEL H.,"THE RATIONAL PROPERTIES OF SCIENTIFIC
AND COMMON SENSE ACTIVITIES." SOCIETY STRATA
ACT/RES CHOOSE...SOC METH/CNCPT NEW/IDEA CONT/OBS
SIMUL TOT/POP VAL/FREE. PAGE 21 G0412
S60 CREATE PHIL/SCI

JAFFEE A.J.,"POPULATION TRENDS AND CONTROLS IN
UNDERDEVELOPED COUNTRIES." AFR FUT ISLAM L/A+17C
S/ASIA CULTURE R+D FAM ACT/RES PLAN EDU/PROP
BIO/SOC RIGID/FLEX HEALTH...SOC STAT OBS CHARTS 20.
PAGE 28 G0555
S60 ECO/UNDEV GEOG

RIVKIN A.,"AFRICAN ECONOMIC DEVELOPMENT: ADVANCED
TECHNOLOGY AND THE STAGES OF GROWTH." CULTURE
ECO/UNDEV AGRI COM/IND EXTR/IND PLAN ECO/TAC ATTIT
DRIVE RIGID/FLEX SKILL WEALTH...MGT SOC GEN/LAWS
WORK TOT/POP 20. PAGE 47 G0923
S60 AFR TEC/DEV FOR/AID

JANOWITZ M.,COMMUNITY POLITICAL SYSTEMS. USA+45
SOCIETY INDUS VOL/ASSN TEC/DEV ADMIN LEAD CHOOSE
...SOC SOC/WK 20. PAGE 29 G0561
B61 MUNIC STRUCT POL/PAR

KRUPP S.,PATTERN IN ORGANIZATIONAL ANALYSIS: A
CRITICAL EXAMINATION. INGP/REL PERS/REL RATIONAL
ATTIT AUTHORIT DRIVE PWR...DECISION PHIL/SCI SOC
IDEA/COMP. PAGE 32 G0622
B61 MGT CONTROL CONCPT METH/CNCPT

MICHAEL D.N.,PROPOSED STUDIES ON THE IMPLICATIONS
OF PEACEFUL SPACE ACTIVITIES FOR HUMAN AFFAIRS.
COM/IND INDUS FORCES DIPLOM PEACE PERSON...PSY SOC
20. PAGE 39 G0764
B61 FUT SPACE ACT/RES PROB/SOLV

DALTON G.,"ECONOMIC THEORY AND PRIMITIVE SOCIETY"
(BMR)" UNIV AGRI KIN TEC/DEV ECO/TAC REGION HABITAT
SKILL...METH/COMP BIBLIOG. PAGE 14 G0274
S61 ECO/UNDEV METH PHIL/SCI SOC

ASTIA,HUMAN ENGINEERING: A REPORT BIBLIOGRAPHY.
USA+45 R+D FORCES ACT/RES COMPUTER CREATE OP/RES
EDU/PROP CONTROL WEAPON...SOC NEW/IDEA. PAGE 4
G0073
B62 BIBLIOG/A COM/IND COMPUT/IR METH

BAKER G.W.,BEHAVIORAL SCIENCE AND CIVIL DEFENSE.
USA+45 PROB/SOLV ADMIN GP/REL INGP/REL PERS/REL
ANOMIE DRIVE PERSON...DECISION MGT SOC 20
CIV/DEFENS. PAGE 4 G0085
B62 NUC/PWR WAR POLICY ACT/RES

BENNIS W.G.,THE PLANNING OF CHANGE: READINGS IN THE
APPLIED BEHAVIORAL SCIENCES. CULTURE STRATA STRUCT
PLAN GP/REL...SOC T. PAGE 6 G0123
B62 PROB/SOLV CREATE ACT/RES OP/RES

BERKELEY E.C.,THE COMPUTER REVOLUTION. WOR+45
CREATE TEC/DEV EFFICIENCY TECHRACY...SOC TREND 20.
PAGE 7 G0128
B62 COMPUTER CONTROL AUTOMAT SOCIETY

BROOKINGS INSTITUTION,DEVELOPMENT OF THE EMERGING
COUNTRIES: AN AGENDA FOR RESEARCH. WOR+45 AGRI
TEC/DEV FOR/AID EDU/PROP ADJUST HABITAT KNOWL...PSY
SOC ANTHOL 20 THIRD/WRLD. PAGE 9 G0175
B62 ECO/UNDEV R+D SOCIETY PROB/SOLV

CHASE S.,THE PROPER STUDY OF MANKIND (2ND REV.
ED.). WOR+45 WOR-45 INTELL WAR...METH/CNCPT
SAMP/SIZ GEN/LAWS BIBLIOG METH 16/20. PAGE 11 G0224
B62 PHIL/SCI SOC PROB/SOLV PERSON

GILPIN R.,AMERICAN SCIENTISTS AND NUCLEAR WEAPONS POLICY. COM FUT USA+45 WOR+45 INT/ORG NAT/G PROF/ORG CONSULT FORCES CREATE TEC/DEV BAL/PWR EDU/PROP ARMS/CONT WAR PERCEPT KNOWL MORAL PWR ...PHIL/SCI SOC CONCPT GEN/LAWS 20. PAGE 21 G0417
B62 INTELL ATTIT DETER NUC/PWR

GUETZKOW H.,SIMULATION IN SOCIAL SCIENCE: READINGS. STRUCT OP/RES ADMIN AUTOMAT FEEDBACK...MGT PSY SOC STYLE BIBLIOG. PAGE 23 G0459
B62 SIMUL TEC/DEV COMPUTER GAME

MARS D.,SUGGESTED LIBRARY IN PUBLIC ADMINISTRATION. FINAN DELIB/GP EX/STRUC WORKER COMPUTER ADJUD ...DECISION PSY SOC METH/COMP 20. PAGE 36 G0710
B62 BIBLIOG ADMIN METH MGT

OSGOOD C.E.,AN ALTERNATIVE TO WAR OR SURRENDER. FUT UNIV CULTURE INTELL SOCIETY R+D INT/ORG CONSULT DELIB/GP ACT/RES PLAN CHOOSE ATTIT PERCEPT KNOWL ...PHIL/SCI PSY SOC TREND GEN/LAWS 20. PAGE 43 G0849
B62 ORD/FREE EDU/PROP PEACE WAR

RIKER W.H.,THE THEORY OF POLITICAL COALITIONS. WOR+45 INTELL NAT/G CREATE PLAN ATTIT DRIVE PERCEPT ...DECISION PSY SOC METH/CNCPT NEW/IDEA MATH CHARTS GAME TOT/POP 20. PAGE 47 G0921
B62 FUT SIMUL

SNYDER R.C.,FOREIGN POLICY DECISION-MAKING. FUT KOREA WOR+45 R+D CREATE ADMIN ROUTINE PWR ...DECISION PSY SOC CONCPT METH/CNCPT CON/ANAL CHARTS GEN/METH METH 20. PAGE 52 G1018
B62 TEC/DEV HYPO/EXP DIPLOM

THANT U.,THE UNITED NATIONS' DEVELOPMENT DECADE: PROPOSALS FOR ACTION. WOR+45 SOCIETY ECO/UNDEV AGRI COM/IND FINAN R+D MUNIC SCHOOL VOL/ASSN CONSULT PLAN TEC/DEV ECO/TAC EDU/PROP ADMIN ROUTINE RIGID/FLEX...MGT SOC CONCPT UNESCO UN TOT/POP VAL/FREE. PAGE 54 G1064
B62 INT/ORG ALL/VALS

STORER N.W.,"SOME SOCIOLOGICAL ASPECTS OF FEDERAL SCIENCE POLICY." USA+45 INTELL PUB/INST PLAN GP/REL PERS/REL DRIVE PERSON ROLE...PSY SOC SIMUL 20 NIH NSF. PAGE 53 G1040
S62 POLICY CREATE NAT/G ALL/VALS

FOSKETT D.J.,CLASSIFICATION AND INDEXING IN THE SOCIAL SCIENCES. WOR+45 R+D ACT/RES CREATE OP/RES TEC/DEV AUTOMAT ROLE...SOC COMPUT/IR BIBLIOG. PAGE 20 G0384
B63 PROB/SOLV CON/ANAL CLASSIF

HOFSTADTER R.,ANTI-INTELLECTUALISM IN AMERICAN LIFE. USA+45 AGRI INDUS ACADEM TEC/DEV EDU/PROP INGP/REL ATTIT...SOC WORSHIP 20 MCCARTHY/J STEVENSN/A. PAGE 26 G0522
B63 INTELL EPIST CULTURE SOCIETY

HOWER R.M.,MANAGERS AND SCIENTISTS. EX/STRUC CREATE ADMIN REPRESENT ATTIT DRIVE ROLE PWR SKILL...SOC INT. PAGE 27 G0532
B63 R+D MGT PERS/REL INGP/REL

MULLER H.J.,FREEDOM IN THE WESTERN WORLD. PREHIST CULTURE SECT CREATE TEC/DEV DOMIN PWR WEALTH ...MAJORIT SOC CONCPT. PAGE 40 G0793
B63 ORD/FREE TIME/SEQ SOCIETY

PEARSELL M.,MEDICAL BEHAVIORAL SCIENCE: A SELECTED BIBLIOGRAPHY OF CULTURAL ANTHROPOLOGY, SOCIAL PSYCHOLOGY, AND SOCIOLOGY... USA+45 USA-45 R+D ATTIT ROLE 20. PAGE 44 G0863
B63 BIBLIOG SOC PSY HEALTH

BRENNAN D.G.,"ARMS CONTROL AND CIVIL DEFENSE." USA+45 WOR+45 NAT/G BAL/PWR ROUTINE ATTIT RIGID/FLEX ORD/FREE...SOC TOT/POP 20. PAGE 8 G0165
L63 PLAN HEALTH ARMS/CONT DETER

ERSKINE H.G.,"THE POLLS: ATOMIC WEAPONS AND NUCLEAR ENERGY." USA+45 COERCE ORD/FREE...POLICY SOC STAT CENSUS SAMP VAL/FREE 20. PAGE 18 G0350
S63 ATTIT INT NUC/PWR

RECENT PUBLICATIONS ON GOVERNMENTAL PROBLEMS. FINAN INDUS ACADEM PLAN PROB/SOLV EDU/PROP ADJUD ADMIN BIO/SOC...MGT SOC. PAGE 1 G0017
B64 BIBLIOG AUTOMAT LEGIS

CONANT J.B.,TWO MODES OF THOUGHT: MY ENCOUNTERS WITH SCIENCE AND EDUCATION....ART/METH JURID SOC TREND. PAGE 13 G0249
B64 PHIL/SCI SKILL MYTH STYLE

COOMBS C.H.,A THEORY OF DATA....MGT PHIL/SCI SOC CLASSIF MATH PROBABIL STAT QU. PAGE 13 G0254
B64 CON/ANAL GEN/METH TESTS PSY

ELLUL J.,THE TECHNOLOGICAL SOCIETY. FUT STRUCT CREATE AUTOMAT ROUTINE STRANGE ANOMIE MORAL PHIL/SCI. PAGE 18 G0344
B64 SOC SOCIETY TECHNIC TEC/DEV

GROSSER G.H.,THE THREAT OF IMPENDING DISASTER: CONTRIBUTIONS TO THE PSYCHOLOGY OF STRESS. SPACE UNIV SOCIETY R+D TEC/DEV EDU/PROP COERCE WAR ATTIT BIO/SOC DISPL PERCEPT PERSON...SOC MYTH SELF/OBS CONT/OBS BIOG CON/ANAL TOT/POP 20. PAGE 23 G0455
B64 HEALTH PSY NUC/PWR

HAMMOND P.E.,SOCIOLOGISTS AT WORK. VOL/ASSN OP/RES TEC/DEV CONFER ROUTINE TASK EFFICIENCY...MGT NEW/IDEA STYLE SAMP. PAGE 24 G0478
B64 R+D BIOG SOC

SHUBIK M.,GAME THEORY AND RELATED APPROACHES TO SOCIAL BEHAVIOR: SELECTIONS. INTELL SOCIETY ACT/RES CREATE PLAN PROB/SOLV...DECISION MATH. PAGE 50 G0994
B64 SOC SIMUL GAME PWR

WIRTH L.,ON CITIES AND SOCIAL LIFE: SELECTED PAPERS. PLAN PROB/SOLV RACE/REL CONSEN ATTIT HABITAT PERSON...POLICY SOC CONCPT ANTHOL BIBLIOG 20. PAGE 64 G1249
B64 GEN/LAWS SOCIETY NEIGH STRUCT

KASSOF A.,"THE ADMINISTERED SOCIETY: TOTALITARIANISM WITHOUT TERROR." COM USSR STRATA AGRI INDUS NAT/G PERF/ART SCHOOL TOP/EX EDU/PROP ADMIN ORD/FREE PWR...POLICY SOC TIME/SEQ GEN/LAWS VAL/FREE 20. PAGE 29 G0580
S64 SOCIETY DOMIN TOTALISM

PLATT J.R.,"RESEARCH AND DEVELOPMENT FOR SOCIAL PROBLEMS." INTELL SOCIETY PROB/SOLV GP/REL ATTIT ALL/VALS CONT/OBS. PAGE 45 G0880
S64 R+D ACT/RES PLAN SOC

HASSON J.A.,THE ECONOMICS OF NUCLEAR POWER. INDIA UK USA+45 WOR+45 INT/ORG TEC/DEV COST...SOC STAT CHARTS 20 EURATOM. PAGE 25 G0490
B65 NUC/PWR INDUS ECO/DEV METH

HEER D.M.,AFTER NUCLEAR ATTACK: A DEMOGRAPHIC INQUIRY. USA+45 ECO/DEV SECT WORKER SEX...HEAL SOC STAT PREDICT CHARTS 20 NEGRO. PAGE 25 G0500
B65 GEOG NUC/PWR CENSUS WAR

NATIONAL ACADEMY OF SCIENCES,BASIC RESEARCH AND NATIONAL GOALS. R+D ACADEM DELIB/GP PLAN EDU/PROP ...POLICY HEAL PHIL/SCI PSY SOC ANTHOL 20 CONGRESS HOUSE/REP HS/SCIASTR. PAGE 41 G0809
B65 LEGIS BUDGET NAT/G CREATE

NATIONAL REFERRAL CENTER SCI,A DIRECTORY OF INFORMATION RESOURCES IN THE UNITED STATES; SOCIAL SCIENCES. USA+45 PROF/ORG...PSY SOC 20. PAGE 41 G0811
B65 INDEX R+D ACADEM ACT/RES

SINGER J.D.,HUMAN BEHAVIOR AND INTERNATIONAL POLITICS* CONTRIBUTIONS FROM THE SOCIAL-PSYCHOLOGICAL SCIENCES. ACT/RES PLAN EDU/PROP ADMIN KNOWL...DECISION PSY SOC NET/THEORY HYPO/EXP LAB/EXP SOC/EXP GEN/METH ANTHOL BIBLIOG. PAGE 51 G1006
B65 DIPLOM PHIL/SCI QUANT SIMUL

SMITH E.A.,SOCIAL WELFARE: PRINCIPLES AND CONCEPTS. STRATA STRUCT CONSULT WORKER ACT/RES CREATE PLAN TEC/DEV ROUTINE GP/REL UTOPIA...SOC 20. PAGE 51 G1014
B65 CONCPT SOC/WK RECEIVE ORD/FREE

B65
STEINER G.A.,THE CREATIVE ORGANIZATION. ELITES
LG/CO PLAN PROB/SOLV TEC/DEV INSPECT CAP/ISM
CONTROL EXEC PERSON...METH/COMP HYPO/EXP 20.
PAGE 52 G1034
CREATE
MGT
ADMIN
SOC

L65
LASSWELL H.D.,"THE POLICY SCIENCES OF DEVELOPMENT."
CULTURE SOCIETY EX/STRUC CREATE ADMIN ATTIT KNOWL
...SOC CONCPT SIMUL GEN/METH. PAGE 33 G0644
PWR
METH/CNCPT
DIPLOM

S65
SILVERT K.H.,"AMERICAN ACADEMIC ETHICS AND SOCIAL
RESEARCH ABROAD* THE LESSON OF PROJECT CAMELOT."
CHILE L/A+17C USA+45 FINAN ADMIN...PHIL/SCI SOC
GEN/LAWS CAMELOT. PAGE 51 G0998
ACADEM
NAT/G
ACT/RES
POLICY

B66
AMERICAN LIBRARY ASSN,GUIDE TO JAPANESE REFERENCE
BOOKS....HUM 20 CHINJAP. PAGE 3 G0054
BIBLIOG/A
SOC
TEC/DEV
PHIL/SCI

B66
GLAZER M.,THE FEDERAL GOVERNMENT AND THE
UNIVERSITY. CHILE PROB/SOLV DIPLOM GIVE ADMIN WAR
...POLICY SOC 20. PAGE 21 G0421
BIBLIOG/A
NAT/G
PLAN
ACADEM

B66
GRUNEWALD D.,PUBLIC POLICY AND THE MODERN
COOPERATION: SELECTED READINGS. USA+45 LAW MARKET
VOL/ASSN CAP/ISM INT/TRADE CENTRAL OWN...SOC ANTHOL
20. PAGE 23 G0458
LG/CO
POLICY
NAT/G
CONTROL

B66
HOPKINS J.F.K.,ARABIC PERIODICAL LITERATURE, 1961.
ISLAM LAW CULTURE SECT...GEOG HEAL PHIL/SCI PSY SOC
20. PAGE 27 G0528
BIBLIOG/A
NAT/LISM
TEC/DEV
INDUS

B66
LILLEY S.,MEN, MACHINES AND HISTORY: THE STORY OF
TOOLS AND MACHINES IN RELATION TO SOCIAL PROGRESS.
PREHIST SPACE STRUCT COMPUTER AUTOMAT NUC/PWR
...POLICY SOC. PAGE 34 G0667
AGRI
TEC/DEV
SOCIETY

B66
MUMFORD L.,THE MYTH OF THE MACHINE: TECHNICS AND
HUMAN DEVELOPMENT. UNIV WOR-45 CREATE AUTOMAT
PERCEPT KNOWL...EPIST PHIL/SCI SOC LING TREND
SOC/INTEG 20 MARX/KARL. PAGE 40 G0795
WORKER
TEC/DEV
SOCIETY

B66
ODEGARD P.H.,POLITICAL POWER AND SOCIAL CHANGE.
UNIV NAT/G CREATE ALL/IDEOS...POLICY GEOG SOC
CENSUS TREND. PAGE 42 G0829
PWR
TEC/DEV
IDEA/COMP

B66
OECD DEVELOPMENT CENTRE,CATALOGUE OF SOCIAL AND
ECONOMIC DEVELOPMENT INSTITUTES AND PROGRAMMES*
RESEARCH. ACT/RES PLAN TEC/DEV EDU/PROP...SOC
GP/COMP NAT/COMP. PAGE 43 G0836
ECO/UNDEV
ECO/DEV
R+D
ACADEM

B66
UNITED NATIONS,INTERNATIONAL SPACE BIBLIOGRAPHY.
FUT INT/ORG TEC/DEV DIPLOM ARMS/CONT NUC/PWR
...JURID SOC UN. PAGE 56 G1093
BIBLIOG
SPACE
PEACE
R+D

B66
US HOUSE COMM GOVT OPERATIONS,THE COMPUTER AND
INVASION OF PRIVACY. USA+45 SOCIETY ALL/VALS...PSY
SOC CHARTS HOUSE/REP PRIVACY. PAGE 58 G1140
ORD/FREE
COMPUTER
TEC/DEV
NAT/G

B66
WARD B.,NATIONALISM AND IDEOLOGY. ECO/UNDEV KIN
CREATE CAP/ISM FOR/AID ALL/VALS MARXISM...POLICY
SOC. PAGE 62 G1211
IDEA/COMP
NAT/LISM
ATTIT

L66
RASER J.R.,"DETERRENCE RESEARCH* PAST PROGRESS AND
FUTURE NEEDS." INTELL PLAN TEC/DEV NUC/PWR PERCEPT
...DECISION PSY SOC NET/THEORY. PAGE 46 G0905
DETER
BIBLIOG/A
FUT

S66
"FURTHER READING." INDIA LOC/G NAT/G PLAN ADMIN
WEALTH...GEOG SOC CONCPT CENSUS 20. PAGE 1 G0021
BIBLIOG
ECO/UNDEV
TEC/DEV
PROVS

S66
FLEMING W.G.,"AUTHORITY, EFFICIENCY, AND ROLE
STRESS: PROBLEMS IN THE DEVELOPMENT OF EAST AFRICAN
BUREAUCRACIES." AFR UGANDA STRUCT PROB/SOLV ROUTINE
DOMIN
EFFICIENCY
COLONIAL

INGP/REL ROLE...MGT SOC GP/COMP GOV/COMP 20
TANGANYIKA AFRICA/E. PAGE 19 G0371
ADMIN

B67
COMMONER B.,SCIENCE AND SURVIVAL. SOCIETY INDUS
PLAN NUC/PWR KNOWL PWR...SOC 20 AEC. PAGE 13 G0247
PHIL/SCI
CONTROL
PROB/SOLV
EQUILIB

B67
CONNOLLY W.E.,POLITICAL SCIENCE AND IDEOLOGY.
UTOPIA ATTIT KNOWL...MAJORIT EPIST PHIL/SCI SOC
IDEA/COMP HYPO/EXP GEN/LAWS METH HUME/D MARX/KARL.
PAGE 13 G0250
PWR
PLURISM
ELITES
CONCPT

B67
DAVIS V.,THE POLITICS OF INNOVATION: PATTERNS IN
NAVY CASES (PAMPHLET). WOR+45 NAT/G CREATE WEAPON
INGP/REL ATTIT...POLICY SOC METH/COMP METH. PAGE 14
G0280
BIBLIOG
FORCES
NUC/PWR
TEC/DEV

B67
DICKSON P.G.M.,THE FINANCIAL REVOLUTION IN ENGLAND.
UK NAT/G TEC/DEV ADMIN GOV/REL...SOC METH/CNCPT
CHARTS GP/COMP BIBLIOG 17/18. PAGE 15 G0302
ECO/DEV
FINAN
CAP/ISM
MGT

B67
FIELD M.G.,SOVIET SOCIALIZED MEDICINE. USSR FINAN
R+D PROB/SOLV ADMIN SOCISM...MGT SOC CONCPT 20.
PAGE 19 G0366
PUB/INST
HEALTH
NAT/G
MARXISM

B67
GULICK M.C.,NONCONVENTIONAL INFORMATION SYSTEMS
SERVING THE SOCIAL SCIENCES AND THE HUMANITIES; A
BIBLIOGRAPHIC ESSAY (PAPER). USA+45 COMPUTER CREATE
EDU/PROP KNOWL...SOC METH 20. PAGE 23 G0462
BIBLIOG/A
R+D
COMPUT/IR
HUM

B67
HOROWITZ I.L.,THE RISE AND FALL OF PROJECT CAMELOT:
STUDIES IN THE RELATIONSHIP BETWEEN SOCIAL SCIENCE
AND PRACTICAL POLITICS. USA+45 WOR+45 CULTURE
FORCES LEGIS EXEC CIVMIL/REL KNOWL...POLICY SOC
METH/CNCPT 20. PAGE 27 G0529
NAT/G
ACADEM
ACT/RES
GP/REL

B67
LAMBERT J.,LATIN AMERICA: SOCIAL STRUCTURES AND
POLITICAL INSTITUTIONS. STRUCT TEC/DEV DIPLOM ADMIN
COLONIAL LEAD ATTIT...SOC CLASSIF NAT/COMP 17/20.
PAGE 32 G0631
L/A+17C
NAT/G
ECO/UNDEV
SOCIETY

B67
NASH M.,MACHINE AGE MAYA. GUATEMALA L/A+17C STRUCT
AGRI WORKER CREATE INCOME ATTIT RIGID/FLEX ROLE
...IDEA/COMP SOC/EXP WORSHIP 20 INDIAN/AM. PAGE 41
G0806
INDUS
CULTURE
SOC
MUNIC

B67
UNIVERSAL REFERENCE SYSTEM,BIBLIOGRAPHY OF
BIBLIOGRAPHIES IN POLITICAL SCIENCE, GOVERNMENT,
AND PUBLIC POLICY (VOLUME III). WOR+45 WOR-45 LAW
ADMIN...SOC CON/ANAL COMPUT/IR GEN/METH. PAGE 56
G1095
BIBLIOG/A
NAT/G
DIPLOM
POLICY

B67
US DEPARTMENT OF STATE,FOREIGN AFFAIRS RESEARCH
(PAMPHLET). USA+45 WOR+45 ACADEM NAT/G...PSY SOC
CHARTS 20. PAGE 57 G1124
BIBLIOG
INDEX
R+D
DIPLOM

S67
BULMER-THOMAS I.,"SO, ON TO THE GREAT SOCIETY." FUT
UNIV TEC/DEV BAL/PWR WAR BIO/SOC KNOWL...ART/METH
SOC PREDICT TREND WORSHIP 20 GREAT/SOC. PAGE 9
G0185
PHIL/SCI
SOCIETY
CREATE

S67
FRIED M.,"FUNCTIONS OF THE WORKING CLASS COMMUNITY
IN MODERN URBAN SOCIETY* IMPLICATIONS FOR FORCED
RELOCATION." USA+45 INDUS R+D NEIGH PLAN TEC/DEV
PARTIC GP/REL ATTIT...SOC STAT CHARTS. PAGE 20
G0393
CLASSIF
WORKER
MUNIC
ADJUST

S67
HILL R.,"SOCIAL ASPECTS OF FAMILY PLANNING." INDIA
KOREA TAIWAN ECO/UNDEV PLAN PROB/SOLV TEC/DEV
EDU/PROP CONTROL ATTIT DRIVE...HEAL PSY SOC 20
BIRTH/CON UN. PAGE 26 G0512
FAM
BIO/SOC
GEOG
MARRIAGE

S67
HOFFER J.R.,"RELATIONSHIP OF NATURAL AND SOCIAL
SCIENCES TO SOCIAL PROBLEMS AND CONTRIBUTION OF...
SCIENTISTS TO SOLUTIONS." USA+45 COMPUTER TEC/DEV
GP/REL KNOWL...SOC TREND. PAGE 26 G0521
PROB/SOLV
SOCIETY
INTELL
ACT/RES

MCNAMARA R.L.,"THE NEED FOR INNOVATIVENESS IN
DEVELOPING SOCIETIES." L/A+17C EDU/PROP ADMIN LEAD
WEALTH...POLICY PSY SOC METH 20 COLOMB. PAGE 38
G0747
S67 PROB/SOLV PLAN ECO/UNDEV NEW/IDEA

ASIAN STUDIES CENTER,FOUR ARTICLES ON POPULATION
AND FAMILY LIFE IN TAIWAN (ASIAN STUDIES PAPERS,
REPRINT SERIES NO. 2). CULTURE STRATA ECO/UNDEV
AGRI INDUS R+D KIN MUNIC...GEOG SOC CHARTS 20.
PAGE 4 G0072
N67 ASIA FAM CENSUS ANTHOL

GALLAHER A. JR.,PERSPECTIVES IN DEVELOPMENTAL
CHANGE. MUNIC PLAN INSPECT EDU/PROP...POLICY
DECISION GEOG PSY SOC IDEA/COMP ANTHOL 20
MODERNIZE. PAGE 21 G0405
B68 TECHNIC TEC/DEV PROB/SOLV CREATE

SOC/DEMPAR....SOCIAL DEMOCRATIC PARTY (USE WITH SPECIFIC
NATION)

SOC/EXP...."SOCIAL" EXPERIMENTATION UNDER UNCONTROLLED
CONDITIONS

COCH L.,"OVERCOMING RESISTANCE TO CHANGE" (BMR)"
USA+45 CONSULT ADMIN ROUTINE GP/REL EFFICIENCY
PRODUC PERCEPT SKILL...CHARTS SOC/EXP 20. PAGE 12
G0236
S48 WORKER OP/RES PROC/MFG RIGID/FLEX

MACCORQUODALE K.,"ON A DISTINCTION BETWEEN
HYPOTHETICAL CONSTRUCTS AND INTERVENING VARIABLES."
...METH/CNCPT LING IDEA/COMP HYPO/EXP SOC/EXP
BIBLIOG 20. PAGE 35 G0686
S48 PSY PHIL/SCI CONCPT GEN/METH

MERTON R.K.,"THE BEARING OF EMPIRICAL RESEARCH UPON
THE DEVELOPMENT OF SOCIAL THEORY" (BMR)"...SOC
CONCPT QUANT METH/COMP HYPO/EXP 20. PAGE 38 G0757
S48 ACT/RES SOC/EXP OBS PHIL/SCI

CANTRIL H.,TENSIONS THAT CAUSE WAR. UNIV CULTURE
R+D CREATE EDU/PROP DRIVE PERSON KNOWL ORD/FREE
...HUM PSY SOC OBS CENSUS TREND CON/ANAL SOC/EXP
SIMUL GEN/METH ANTHOL COLD/WAR TOT/POP. PAGE 11
G0206
B50 SOCIETY PHIL/SCI PEACE

HOMANS G.C.,"THE WESTERN ELECTRIC RESEARCHES" IN S.
HOSLETT, ED., HUMAN FACTORS IN MANAGEMENT (BMR)"
ACT/RES GP/REL HAPPINESS PRODUC DRIVE...MGT OBS 20.
PAGE 27 G0526
C51 OP/RES EFFICIENCY SOC/EXP WORKER

COMBS C.H.,DECISION PROCESSES. INTELL SOCIETY
DELIB/GP CREATE TEC/DEV DOMIN LEGIT EXEC CHOOSE
DRIVE RIGID/FLEX KNOWL PWR...PHIL/SCI SOC
METH/CNCPT CONT/OBS REC/INT PERS/TEST SAMP/SIZ BIOG
SOC/EXP WORK. PAGE 13 G0245
B54 MATH DECISION

DEUTSCH K.W.,"TOWARD AN INVENTORY OF BASIC TRENDS
AND PATTERNS IN COMPARATIVE AND INTERNATIONAL
POLITICS." UNIV WOR+45 SOCIETY STRUCT INT/ORG NAT/G
CREATE PLAN EDU/PROP KNOWL...PHIL/SCI METH/CNCPT
STAT SELF/OBS OBS/ENVIR SAMP TREND CON/ANAL CHARTS
SOC/EXP GEN/METH 20. PAGE 15 G0298
L60 R+D PERCEPT

ANDREWS R.B.,"URBAN ECONOMICS: AN APPRAISAL OF
PROGRESS." LOC/G PROB/SOLV TEC/DEV...CONCPT
OBS/ENVIR METH/COMP HYPO/EXP SOC/EXP SIMUL GEN/METH
METH 20. PAGE 3 G0058
S61 MUNIC PHIL/SCI ECOMETRIC

CRANE R.D.,"LAW AND STRATEGY IN SPACE." FUT USA+45
WOR+45 AIR LAW INT/ORG NAT/G FORCES ACT/RES PLAN
BAL/PWR LEGIT ARMS/CONT COERCE ORD/FREE...POLICY
INT/LAW JURID SOC/EXP 20 TREATY. PAGE 13 G0261
S62 CONCPT SPACE

SINGER J.D.,HUMAN BEHAVIOR AND INTERNATIONAL
POLITICS* CONTRIBUTIONS FROM THE SOCIAL-
PSYCHOLOGICAL SCIENCES. ACT/RES PLAN EDU/PROP ADMIN
KNOWL...DECISION PSY SOC NET/THEORY HYPO/EXP
LAB/EXP SOC/EXP GEN/METH ANTHOL BIBLIOG. PAGE 51
G1006
B65 DIPLOM PHIL/SCI QUANT SIMUL

NASH M.,MACHINE AGE MAYA. GUATEMALA L/A+17C STRUCT
AGRI WORKER CREATE INCOME ATTIT RIGID/FLEX ROLE
...IDEA/COMP SOC/EXP WORSHIP 20 INDIAN/AM. PAGE 41
G0806
B67 INDUS CULTURE SOC MUNIC

SOC/INTEG....SOCIAL INTEGRATION; SEE ALSO CONSEN, RACE/REL

STAMP S.,THE SCIENCE OF SOCIAL ADJUSTMENT. WOR-45
ACT/RES CREATE PLAN PROB/SOLV TEC/DEV ECO/TAC
EFFICIENCY SOC/INTEG 20. PAGE 52 G1031
B3? ADJUST ORD/FREE PHIL/SCI

BRYSON L.,SCIENCE AND FREEDOM. WOR+45 ACT/RES
CREATE TECHRACY...TECHNIC SOC/INTEG. PAGE 9 G0183
B4? CONCPT ORD/FREE CULTURE SOC

CALLOT E.,LA SOCIETE ET SON ENVIRONNEMENT: ESSAI
SUR LES PRINCIPES DES SCIENCES SOCIALES. GP/REL
ADJUST CONSEN ISOLAT HABITAT PERCEPT PERSON
...BIBLIOG SOC/INTEG 20. PAGE 10 G0205
B52 SOCIETY PHIL/SCI CULTURE

SPROTT W.J.H.,SCIENCE AND SOCIAL ACTION. STRUCT
ACT/RES CRIME GP/REL INGP/REL ANOMIE...PSY
SOC/INTEG 19/20. PAGE 52 G1027
B54 SOC CULTURE PHIL/SCI

LEYDER J.,BIBLIOGRAPHIE DE L'ENSEIGNEMENT SUPERIEUR
ET DE LA RECHERCHE SCIENTIFIQUE EN AFRIQUE
INTERTROPICALE (2 VOLS.). AFR CULTURE ECO/UNDEV
AGRI PLAN EDU/PROP ADMIN COLONIAL...GEOG SOC/INTEG
20 NEGRO. PAGE 34 G0664
B60 BIBLIOG ACT/RES ACADEM R+D

LASSWELL H.D.,THE FUTURE OF POLITICAL SCIENCE.
SOCIETY ECO/DEV ACADEM NAT/G PROB/SOLV...OBS
SOC/INTEG. PAGE 33 G0643
B63 CREATE ACT/RES FUT

REISS A.J. JR.,SCHOOLS IN A CHANGING SOCIETY.
CULTURE PROB/SOLV INSPECT DOMIN CONFER INGP/REL
RACE/REL AGE/C AGE/Y ALL/VALS...ANTHOL SOC/INTEG 20
NEWYORK/C. PAGE 46 G0912
B65 SCHOOL EX/STRUC ADJUST ADMIN

MILLAR R.,THE NEW CLASSES. UK ELITES SOCIETY INDUS
AUTOMAT GP/REL SOC/INTEG 20 INDUS/REV. PAGE 39
G0770
B66 STRUCT STRATA TEC/DEV CREATE

MUMFORD L.,THE MYTH OF THE MACHINE: TECHNICS AND
HUMAN DEVELOPMENT. UNIV WOR-45 CREATE AUTOMAT
PERCEPT KNOWL...EPIST PHIL/SCI SOC LING TREND
SOC/INTEG 20 MARX/KARL. PAGE 40 G0795
B66 WORKER TEC/DEV SOCIETY

SOC/PAR....SOCIALIST PARTY (USE WITH SPECIFIC NATION)

SOC/REVPAR....SOCIALIST REVOLUTIONARY PARTY (USE WITH
SPECIFIC NATION)

SOC/SECUR....SOCIAL SECURITY

SOC/WK....SOCIAL WORK, SOCIAL SERVICE ORGANIZATION

HODGSON J.G.,THE OFFICIAL PUBLICATIONS OF AMERICAN
COUNTIES: A UNION LIST. SCHOOL BUDGET...HEAL MGT
SOC/WK 19/20. PAGE 26 G0520
B37 BIBLIOG LOC/G PUB/INST

CALDWELL L.K.,"THE GOVERNMENT AND ADMINISTRATION OF
NEW YORK." LOC/G MUNIC POL/PAR SCHOOL CHIEF LEGIS
PLAN TAX CT/SYS...MGT SOC/WK BIBLIOG 20 NEWYORK/C.
PAGE 10 G0202
C54 PROVS ADMIN CONSTN EX/STRUC

DRUCKER P.F.,AMERICA'S NEXT TWENTY YEARS. USA+45
DIST/IND ACADEM MUNIC SCHOOL DIPLOM ECO/TAC AUTOMAT
HABITAT HEALTH...SOC/WK TREND 20 URBAN/RNWL
PUB/TRANS. PAGE 16 G0316
B57 WORKER FOR/AID CENSUS GEOG

KIETH-LUCAS A.,DECISIONS ABOUT PEOPLE IN NEED, A
STUDY OF ADMINISTRATIVE RESPONSIVENESS IN PUBLIC
ASSISTANCE. USA+45 GIVE RECEIVE INGP/REL PERS/REL
MORAL RESPECT WEALTH...SOC OBS BIBLIOG 20. PAGE 30
G0595
B57 ADMIN RIGID/FLEX SOC/WK DECISION

JANOWITZ M.,COMMUNITY POLITICAL SYSTEMS. USA+45
SOCIETY INDUS VOL/ASSN TEC/DEV ADMIN LEAD CHOOSE
...SOC SOC/WK 20. PAGE 29 G0561
B61 MUNIC STRUCT POL/PAR

LEE R.R.,ENGINEERING-ECONOMIC PLANNING
MISCELLANEOUS SUBJECTS: A SELECTED BIBLIOGRAPHY
(MIMEOGRAPHED). FINAN LOC/G MUNIC NEIGH ADMIN
B61 BIBLIOG/A PLAN REGION

CONTROL INGP/REL HABITAT...GEOG MGT SOC/WK 20
RESOURCE/N. PAGE 33 G0651

B62
WENDT P.F.,HOUSING POLICY - THE SEARCH FOR   PLAN
SOLUTIONS. GERMANY/W SWEDEN UK USA+45 OP/RES   ADMIN
HABITAT WEALTH...SOC/WK CHARTS 20. PAGE 63 G1230 METH/COMP
                                                  NAT/G

B63
KATZ S.M.,A SELECTED LIST OF US READINGS ON   BIBLIOG/A
DEVELOPMENT. AGRI COM/IND DIST/IND INDUS LABOR PLAN ECO/UNDEV
FOR/AID EDU/PROP HEALTH...POLICY SOC/WK 20. PAGE 30 TEC/DEV
G0582   ACT/RES

B63
PANAMERICAN UNION,DOCUMENTOS OFICIALES DE LA   BIBLIOG
ORGANIZACION DE LOS ESTADOS AMERICANOS, INDICE Y   INT/ORG
LISTA (VOL. III, 1962). L/A+17C DELIB/GP INT/TRADE DIPLOM
EDU/PROP REGION NUC/PWR...HEAL INT/LAW SOC/WK 20
OAS. PAGE 44 G0857

B65
SMITH E.A.,SOCIAL WELFARE: PRINCIPLES AND CONCEPTS. CONCPT
STRATA STRUCT CONSULT WORKER ACT/RES CREATE PLAN   SOC/WK
TEC/DEV ROUTINE GP/REL UTOPIA...SOC 20. PAGE 51   RECEIVE
G1014   ORD/FREE

B66
LECHT L.,GOAL, PRIORITIES, AND DOLLARS: THE NEXT   IDEA/COMP
DECADE. SPACE USA+45 SOCIETY AGRI BUDGET FOR/AID   POLICY
...HEAL SOC/WK STAT CHARTS 20 URBAN/RNWL PUB/TRANS. CONSEN
PAGE 33 G0649   PLAN

B67
HODGKINSON R.G.,THE ORIGINS OF THE NATIONAL HEALTH HEAL
SERVICE: THE MEDICAL SERVICES OF THE NEW POOR LAW, NAT/G
1834-1871. UK INDUS MUNIC WORKER PROB/SOLV   POLICY
EFFICIENCY ATTIT HEALTH WEALTH SOCISM...JURID   LAW
SOC/WK 19/20. PAGE 26 G0519

B67
US PRES COMN LAW ENFORCE-JUS,THE CHALLENGE OF CRIME CT/SYS
IN A FREE SOCIETY. LAW STRUCT CONSULT ACT/RES   PUB/INST
TEC/DEV INGP/REL...SOC/WK 20. PAGE 59 G1160   CRIMLGY
                                                  CRIME

S67
HARRIS F.R.,"POLITICAL SCIENCE AND THE PROPOSAL FOR PROF/ORG
A NATIONAL SOCIAL SCIENCE FOUNDATION." FUT CONSULT R+D
DELIB/GP PLAN PROB/SOLV BUDGET CONFER SANCTION   CREATE
CRIME...POLICY SOC/WK 20 NSF NSSF. PAGE 25 G0484   NAT/G

SOCDEM/PAR

B59
VERNEY D.V.,PUBLIC ENTERPRISE IN SWEDEN. FUT SWEDEN ECO/DEV
UK INDUS POL/PAR LEGIS PROB/SOLV CAP/ISM INT/TRADE POLICY
CONTROL SOCISM...MGT CONCPT NAT/COMP 20 SOCDEM/PAR LG/CO
CIVIL/SERV. PAGE 61 G1196   NAT/G

SOCIAL ANALYSIS....SEE SOC

SOCIAL DEMOCRATIC PARTY (ALL NATIONS)....SEE SOC/DEMPAR

SOCIAL CLASS....SEE STRATA

SOCIAL INSTITUTIONS....SEE INSTITUTIONAL INDEX

SOCIAL MOBILITY....SEE STRATA

SOCIAL PSYCHOLOGY (GROUPS)....SEE SOC

SOCIAL PSYCHOLOGY (INDIVIDUALS)....SEE PSY

SOCIAL STRUCTURE....SEE STRUCT

SOCIAL WORK....SEE SOC/WK

SOCIAL STRUCTURE....SEE STRUCT, STRATA

SOCIAL SCIENCE RESEARCH COUN G1019

SOCIALISM....SEE SOCISM, SOCIALIST

SOCIALIST....NON-COMMUNIST SOCIALIST; SEE ALSO SOCISM

B64
MILIBAND R.,THE SOCIALIST REGISTER: 1964. GERMANY/W MARXISM
ITALY UK LABOR POL/PAR ECO/TAC FOR/AID NUC/PWR   SOCISM
...POLICY SOCIALIST IDEA/COMP 20 MAO NASSER/G.   CAP/ISM
PAGE 39 G0769   PROB/SOLV

SOCIALIZATION....SEE ADJUST

SOCIETY....SOCIETY AS A WHOLE

SOCIOLOGY....SEE SOC

SOCIOLOGY OF KNOWLEDGE....SEE EPIST

SOCISM....SOCIALISM; SEE ALSO SOCIALIST

S39
HECKSCHER G.,"GROUP ORGANIZATION IN SWEDEN." SWEDEN LAISSEZ
STRATA ECO/DEV AGRI INDUS LABOR NAT/G PROF/ORG   SOC
ECO/TAC CENTRAL SOCISM...MGT 19/20. PAGE 25 G0499

B43
LASKI H.J.,REFLECTIONS ON THE REVOLUTIONS OF OUR   CAP/ISM
TIME. COM USSR NAT/G WORKER UTOPIA ORD/FREE WEALTH WELF/ST
MARXISM SOCISM 19/20. PAGE 32 G0637   ECO/TAC
                                                  POLICY

S44
GRIFFITH E.S.,"THE CHANGING PATTERN OF PUBLIC   LAW
POLICY FORMATION." MOD/EUR WOR+45 FINAN CHIEF   POLICY
CONFER ADMIN LEAD CONSERVE SOCISM TECHRACY...SOC   TEC/DEV
CHARTS CONGRESS. PAGE 23 G0450

B52
APPADORAI A.,THE SUBSTANCE OF POLITICS (6TH ED.). PHIL/SCI
EX/STRUC LEGIS DIPLOM CT/SYS CHOOSE FASCISM MARXISM NAT/G
SOCISM...BIBLIOG T. PAGE 3 G0062

B54
MOSK S.A.,INDUSTRIAL REVOLUTION IN MEXICO. MARKET INDUS
LABOR CREATE CAP/ISM ADMIN ATTIT SOCISM...POLICY 20 TEC/DEV
MEXIC/AMER. PAGE 40 G0789   ECO/UNDEV
                                                  NAT/G

B58
MARCUSE H.,SOVIET MARXISM, A CRITICAL ANALYSIS.   MARXISM
USSR CONSTN PLAN PRODUC RATIONAL SOCISM...IDEA/COMP ATTIT
20 COM/PARTY. PAGE 36 G0703   POLICY

B59
VERNEY D.V.,PUBLIC ENTERPRISE IN SWEDEN. FUT SWEDEN ECO/DEV
UK INDUS POL/PAR LEGIS PROB/SOLV CAP/ISM INT/TRADE POLICY
CONTROL SOCISM...MGT CONCPT NAT/COMP 20 SOCDEM/PAR LG/CO
CIVIL/SERV. PAGE 61 G1196   NAT/G

S59
SHEENAN D.,"PUBLIC CORPORATIONS AND PUBLIC ACTION." ECO/DEV
UK ADMIN CONTROL REPRESENT SOCISM 20. PAGE 50 G0990 EFFICIENCY
                                                  EX/STRUC
                                                  EXEC

B60
HEILBRONER R.L.,THE FUTURE AS HISTORY. USA+45   TEC/DEV
WOR+45 WOR-45 SOCIETY ECO/DEV ECO/UNDEV VOL/ASSN   TREND
PLAN CAP/ISM NUC/PWR CHOOSE NAT/LISM ATTIT ORD/FREE
RESPECT WEALTH SOCISM 20. PAGE 25 G0501

S63
HOSKINS H.L.,"ARAB SOCIALISM IN THE UAR." ISLAM   ECO/DEV
USSR AGRI INDUS NAT/G TOP/EX CREATE DIPLOM EDU/PROP PLAN
DRIVE KNOWL PWR SOCISM...POLICY CONCPT TREND SUEZ UAR
20. PAGE 27 G0530

S63
WILES P.J.D.,"WILL CAPITALISM AND COMMUNISM   PLAN
SPONTANEOUSLY CONVERGE." COM FUT USA+45 ECO/DEV   TEC/DEV
DIST/IND MARKET CAP/ISM ECO/TAC RIGID/FLEX WEALTH USSR
MARXISM SOCISM...MATH STAT TREND COMPUT/IR 20.
PAGE 63 G1240

B64
BAUCHET P.,ECONOMIC PLANNING. FRANCE STRATA LG/CO ECO/DEV
CAP/ISM ADMIN PARL/PROC DEMAND OPTIMAL ATTIT PWR   NAT/G
SOCISM...POLICY CHARTS 20. PAGE 5 G0102   PLAN
                                                  ECO/TAC

B64
MILIBAND R.,THE SOCIALIST REGISTER: 1964. GERMANY/W MARXISM
ITALY UK LABOR POL/PAR ECO/TAC FOR/AID NUC/PWR   SOCISM
...POLICY SOCIALIST IDEA/COMP 20 MAO NASSER/G.   CAP/ISM
PAGE 39 G0769   PROB/SOLV

S64
FLORINSKY M.T.,"TRENDS IN THE SOVIET ECONOMY." COM ECO/DEV
USA+45 USSR INDUS LABOR NAT/G PLAN TEC/DEV ECO/TAC AGRI
ALL/VALS SOCISM...MGT METH/CNCPT STYLE CON/ANAL
GEN/METH WORK 20. PAGE 19 G0374

S65
STAAR R.F.,"RETROGRESSION IN POLAND." COM USSR AGRI TOP/EX
INDUS NAT/G CREATE EDU/PROP TOTALISM RIGID/FLEX   ECO/TAC
ORD/FREE PWR SOCISM...RECORD CHARTS 20. PAGE 52   POLAND

G1029

                                                                                                                N19
                                                        MEZERIK AG,OUTER SPACE: UN, US, USSR (PAMPHLET).   SPACE
                                                        USSR DELIB/GP FORCES DETER NUC/PWR SOVEREIGN   CONTROL
                                                        ...POLICY 20 UN TREATY. PAGE 39 G0763   DIPLOM
                                                                                                             INT/ORG

                                                                                                                B67
FIELD M.G.,SOVIET SOCIALIZED MEDICINE. USSR FINAN   PUB/INST
R+D PROB/SOLV ADMIN SOCISM...MGT SOC CONCPT 20.   HEALTH
PAGE 19 G0366   NAT/G
                                                       MARXISM
                                                                                                                N19
                                                        US SEN SPEC COMM SPACE ASTRO,SPACE LAW; A SYMPOSIUM SPACE
                                                        (PAMPHLET). USA+45 TEC/DEV CONFER CONTROL SOVEREIGN ADJUD
                                                        ...INT/LAW 20 SEN/SPACE. PAGE 59 G1161   DIPLOM
                                                                                                             INT/ORG
                                                       B67
GROSSMAN G.,ECONOMIC SYSTEMS. USA+45 USA-45 USSR   ECO/DEV
YUGOSLAVIA WORKER CAP/ISM PRICE GP/REL EQUILIB   PLAN
WEALTH MARXISM SOCISM...MGT METH/COMP 19/20.   TEC/DEV
PAGE 23 G0456   DEMAND
                                                                                                                B44
                                                        FULLER G.H.,MILITARY GOVERNMENT: A LIST OF   BIBLIOG
                                                        REFERENCES (A PAMPHLET). ITALY UK USA+45 WOR-45 LAW BIOG
                                                        FORCES DOMIN ADMIN ARMS/CONT ORD/FREE PWR   CIVMIL/REL
                                                        ...DECISION 20 CHINJAP. PAGE 21 G0404   SOVEREIGN
                                                       B67
HODGKINSON R.G.,THE ORIGINS OF THE NATIONAL HEALTH   HEAL
SERVICE: THE MEDICAL SERVICES OF THE NEW POOR LAW,   NAT/G
1834-1871. UK INDUS MUNIC WORKER PROB/SOLV   POLICY
EFFICIENCY ATTIT HEALTH WEALTH SOCISM...JURID   LAW
SOC/WK 19/20. PAGE 26 G0519   B45
                                                        REVES E.,THE ANATOMY OF PEACE. WOR-45 LAW CULTURE   ACT/RES
                                                        NAT/G TEC/DEV EDU/PROP WAR NAT/LISM ATTIT   CONCPT
                                                        ALL/VALS SOVEREIGN...POLICY HUM TIME/SEQ 20.   NUC/PWR
                                                       B67 PAGE 46 G0914   PEACE
MOORE J.R.,THE ECONOMIC IMPACT OF THE TVA. AGRI   ECO/UNDEV
INDUS PLAN BARGAIN CONTROL REGION GOV/REL DEMAND   ECO/DEV
EFFICIENCY SOCISM 20 TVA. PAGE 40 G0780   NAT/G
                                                      CREATE   N47
                                                        FOX W.T.R.,UNITED STATES POLICY IN A TWO POWER   DIPLOM
                                                        WORLD. COM USA+45 USSR FORCES DOMIN AGREE NEUTRAL   FOR/AID
                                                       B67 NUC/PWR ORD/FREE SOVEREIGN 20 COLD/WAR TREATY   POLICY
POMEROY W.J.,HALF A CENTURY OF SOCIALISM. USSR LAW   SOCISM EUROPE/W INTERVENT. PAGE 20 G0389
AGRI INDUS NAT/G CREATE DIPLOM EDU/PROP PERSON   MARXISM
ORD/FREE WEALTH...POLICY TREND 20. PAGE 45 G0884   COM
                                                      SOCIETY   B59
                                                        HALEY A.G.,FIRST COLLOQUIUM ON THE LAW OF OUTER   SPACE
                                                        SPACE. WOR+45 INT/ORG ACT/RES PLAN BAL/PWR CONFER   LAW
                                                       S67 ATTIT PWR...POLICY JURID CHARTS ANTHOL 20. PAGE 24 SOVEREIGN
AVTORKHANOV A.,"A NEW AGRARIAN REVOLUTION." COM   AGRI G0468   CONTROL
USSR ECO/DEV PLAN TEC/DEV ADMIN CONTROL OPTIMAL   METH/COMP
WEALTH SOCISM 20 KHRUSH/N STALIN/J. PAGE 4 G0082   MARXISM
                                                      OWN   B60
                                                        ALBI F.,TRATADO DE LOS MODOS DE GESTION DE LAS   LOC/G
                                                        CORPORACIONES LOCALES. SPAIN FINAN NAT/G BUDGET   LAW
SOCRATES....SOCRATES   CONTROL EXEC ROUTINE GOV/REL ORD/FREE SOVEREIGN   ADMIN
                                                        ...MGT 20. PAGE 2 G0034   MUNIC
SOHN L.B. G0231,G1020

SOLOMONS....THE SOLOMON ISLANDS   S60
                                                        HAYTON R.D.,"THE ANTARCTIC SETTLEMENT OF 1959." FUT DELIB/GP
SOMALIA....SOMALIA; SEE ALSO AFR   USA+45 WOR+45 WOR-45 STRUCT R+D INT/ORG EX/STRUC   JURID
                                                        CREATE TEC/DEV LEGIT PEACE ATTIT SOVEREIGN   DIPLOM
SONGAI....SONGAI EMPIRES (AFRICA)   ...TIME/SEQ 20 TREATY IGY. PAGE 25 G0495   REGION

SOREL/G....GEORGES SOREL   S60
                                                        TAYLOR M.G.,"THE ROLE OF THE MEDICAL PROFESSION IN PROF/ORG
SOROKIN P. G1021   THE FORMULATION AND EXECUTION OF PUBLIC POLICY"   HEALTH
                                                        (BMR)" CANADA NAT/G CONSULT ADMIN REPRESENT GP/REL   LOBBY
SOUERS S.W. G1022   ROLE SOVEREIGN...DECISION 20 CMA. PAGE 54 G1058   POLICY

SOUPHANGOU....PRINCE SOUPHANGOU-VONG (LEADER OF PATHET LAO)   B61
                                                        BONNEFOUS M.,EUROPE ET TIERS MONDE. EUR+WWI SOCIETY AFR
SOUTH AFRICA....SEE S/AFR   INT/ORG NAT/G VOL/ASSN ACT/RES TEC/DEV CAP/ISM   ECO/UNDEV
                                                        ECO/TAC ATTIT ORD/FREE SOVEREIGN...POLICY CONCPT   FOR/AID
SOUTH ARABIA....SEE ARABIA/SOU   TREND 20. PAGE 8 G0153   INT/TRADE

SOUTH KOREA....SEE KOREA/S   B61
                                                        ROSENAU J.N.,INTERNATIONAL POLITICS AND FOREIGN   ACT/RES
                                                        POLICY: A READER IN RESEARCH AND THEORY. ELITES   DIPLOM
SOUTH WEST AFRICA....SEE AFRICA/SW   ATTIT SOVEREIGN...DECISION CHARTS HYPO/EXP GAME   CONCPT
                                                        SIMUL ANTHOL BIBLIOG METH 20. PAGE 48 G0936   POLICY
SOUTH/AFR....UNION OF SOUTH AFRICA

SOUTH/AMER....SOUTH AMERICA   S61
                                                        MACHOWSKI K.,"SELECTED PROBLEMS OF NATIONAL   UNIV
SOUTH/CAR....SOUTH CAROLINA   SOVEREIGNTY WITH REFERENCE TO THE LAW OF OUTER   ACT/RES
                                                        SPACE." FUT WOR+45 AIR LAW INTELL SOCIETY ECO/DEV   NUC/PWR
SOUTH/DAK....SOUTH DAKOTA   PLAN EDU/PROP DETER DRIVE PERCEPT SOVEREIGN   SPACE
                                                        ...POLICY INT/LAW OBS TREND TOT/POP 20. PAGE 35
SOUTH/US....SOUTH (UNITED STATES)   G0689

                                                       B58
OGDEN F.D.,THE POLL TAX IN THE SOUTH. USA+45 USA-45 TAX   B62
CONSTN ADJUD ADMIN PARTIC CRIME...TIME/SEQ GOV/COMP CHOOSE WRIGHT Q.,PREVENTING WORLD WAR THREE. FUT WOR+45 CREATE
METH/COMP 18/20 SOUTH/US. PAGE 43 G0838   RACE/REL CULTURE INT/ORG NAT/G CONSULT FORCES ADMIN   ATTIT
                                                    DISCRIM ARMS/CONT DRIVE RIGID/FLEX ORD/FREE SOVEREIGN
                                                             ...POLICY CONCPT TREND STERTYP COLD/WAR 20. PAGE 64
                                                       B66 G1259
DUNBAR L.W.,A REPUBLIC OF EQUALS. USA+45 CREATE   LAW
ADJUD PEACE NEW/LIB...POLICY 20 SOUTH/US   CONSTN   B63
CIV/RIGHTS. PAGE 16 G0320   FEDERAL GEERTZ C.,OLD SOCIETIES AND NEW STATES: THE QUEST ECO/UNDEV
                                                    RACE/REL FOR MODERNITY IN ASIA AND AFRICA. AFR ASIA LAW   TEC/DEV
                                                             CULTURE SECT EDU/PROP REV...GOV/COMP NAT/COMP 20. NAT/LISM
SOUTHEAST ASIA....SEE S/EASTASIA, S/ASIA   PAGE 21 G0415   SOVEREIGN

SOUTHEAST ASIA TREATY ORGANIZATION....SEE SEATO   B63
                                                        HALEY A.G.,SPACE LAW AND GOVERNMENT. FUT USA+45   INT/ORG
SOUTHERN RHODESIA....SEE RHODESIA, COMMONWLTH   WOR+45 LEGIS ACT/RES CREATE ATTIT RIGID/FLEX   LAW
                                                        ORD/FREE PWR SOVEREIGN...POLICY JURID CONCPT CHARTS SPACE
SOVEREIGN....SOVEREIGNTY   VAL/FREE 20. PAGE 24 G0469

                                                                                                                B64
                                                        THANT U.,TOWARD WORLD PEACE. DELIB/GP TEC/DEV   DIPLOM
                                                        EDU/PROP WAR SOVEREIGN...INT/LAW 20 UN MID/EAST.   BIOG

PAGE 54 G1065   PEACE COERCE

B65
FOSTER P.,EDUCATION AND SOCIAL CHANGE IN GHANA. GHANA CULTURE STRUCT ECO/UNDEV TEC/DEV REGION EFFICIENCY LITERACY ALL/VALS SOVEREIGN...STAT METH/COMP 19/20 GOLD/COAST. PAGE 20 G0385   SCHOOL CREATE SOCIETY

S65
HSIEH A.L.,"THE SINO-SOVIET NUCLEAR DIALOGUE* 1963." S/ASIA USA+45 RISK DETER REV WAR SOVEREIGN IDEA/COMP. PAGE 27 G0533   ASIA USSR NUC/PWR

C65
SEARA M.V.,"COSMIC INTERNATIONAL LAW." LAW ACADEM ACT/RES DIPLOM COLONIAL CONTROL NUC/PWR SOVEREIGN ...GEN/LAWS BIBLIOG UN. PAGE 50 G0987   SPACE INT/LAW IDEA/COMP INT/ORG

B66
DAENIKER G.,STRATEGIE DES KLEIN STAATS. SWITZERLND ACT/RES CREATE DIPLOM NEUTRAL DETER WAR WEAPON PWR SOVEREIGN...IDEA/COMP 20 COLD/WAR. PAGE 14 G0270   NUC/PWR PLAN FORCES NAT/G

B67
ALEXANDER L.M.,THE LAW OF THE SEA: OFFSHORE BOUNDARIES AND ZONES. WOR+45 INT/ORG TEC/DEV CONTROL PRIVIL HABITAT SOVEREIGN...CON/ANAL CHARTS ANTHOL. PAGE 2 G0037   SEA INT/LAW EXTR/IND

L67
ROBINSON T.W.,"A NATIONAL INTEREST ANALYSIS OF SINO-SOVIET RELATIONS." CHINA/COM USSR NAT/G NUC/PWR ATTIT PWR...CONCPT CHARTS 20. PAGE 47 G0931   MARXISM DIPLOM SOVEREIGN GEN/LAWS

S67
HAZARD J.N.,"POST-DISARMAMENT INTERNATIONAL LAW." FUT USSR WOR+45 INT/ORG DELIB/GP FORCES DETER EQUILIB SOVEREIGN MARXISM 20 UN. PAGE 25 G0496   INT/LAW ARMS/CONT PWR PLAN

S67
TIVEY L.,"THE POLITICAL CONSEQUENCES OF ECONOMIC PLANNING." UK CONSTN INDUS ACT/RES ADMIN CONTROL LOBBY REPRESENT EFFICIENCY SUPEGO SOVEREIGN ...DECISION 20. PAGE 55 G1074   PLAN POLICY NAT/G

SOVEREIGNTY....SEE SOVEREIGN

SOVIET UNION....SEE USSR

SPACE....OUTER SPACE, SPACE LAW

N
FOREIGN AFFAIRS. SPACE WOR+45 WOR-45 CULTURE ECO/UNDEV FINAN NAT/G TEC/DEV INT/TRADE ARMS/CONT NUC/PWR...POLICY 20 UN EURATOM ECSC EEC. PAGE 1 G0004   BIBLIOG DIPLOM INT/ORG INT/LAW

N
AIR UNIVERSITY LIBRARY,INDEX TO MILITARY PERIODICALS. FUT SPACE WOR+45 REGION ARMS/CONT NUC/PWR WAR PEACE INT/LAW. PAGE 2 G0032   BIBLIOG/A FORCES NAT/G DIPLOM

N19
MEZERIK A.G.,INTERNATIONAL POLICY 1965 (PAMPHLET). KASHMIR S/ASIA SPACE USA+45 VIETNAM WOR+45 ARMS/CONT RACE/REL DISCRIM PEACE PWR 20 UN. PAGE 39 G0762   DIPLOM INT/ORG POLICY WAR

N19
MEZERIK AG,OUTER SPACE: UN, US, USSR (PAMPHLET). USSR DELIB/GP FORCES DETER NUC/PWR SOVEREIGN ...POLICY 20 UN TREATY. PAGE 39 G0763   SPACE CONTROL DIPLOM INT/ORG

N19
US SEN SPEC COMM SPACE ASTRO,SPACE LAW: A SYMPOSIUM (PAMPHLET). USA+45 TEC/DEV CONFER CONTROL SOVEREIGN ...INT/LAW 20 SEN/SPACE. PAGE 59 G1161   SPACE ADJUD DIPLOM INT/ORG

N19
ZLOTNICK M.,WEAPONS IN SPACE (PAMPHLET). FUT WOR+45 TEC/DEV DIPLOM ARMS/CONT CIVMIL/REL PEACE HABITAT ...CONCPT NEW/IDEA CHARTS. PAGE 65 G1268   SPACE WEAPON NUC/PWR WAR

B58
GAVIN J.M.,WAR AND PEACE IN THE SPACE AGE. SPACE USA+45 USSR FORCES PLAN TEC/DEV BAL/PWR DIPLOM ARMS/CONT WEAPON CIVMIL/REL...CHARTS GP/COMP 20   WAR DETER NUC/PWR

NATO COLD/WAR. PAGE 21 G0414   PEACE

S58
BURNS A.L.,"THE NEW WEAPONS AND INTERNATIONAL RELATIONS." SPACE WOR+45 NAT/G VOL/ASSN FORCES NUC/PWR 20. PAGE 10 G0190   TEC/DEV ARMS/CONT DIPLOM

S58
MCDOUGAL M.S.,"PERSPECTIVES FOR A LAW OF OUTER SPACE." FUT WOR+45 AIR CONSULT DELIB/GP TEC/DEV CT/SYS ORD/FREE...POLICY JURID 20 UN. PAGE 37 G0736   INT/ORG SPACE INT/LAW

B59
HALEY A.G.,FIRST COLLOQUIUM ON THE LAW OF OUTER SPACE. WOR+45 INT/ORG ACT/RES PLAN BAL/PWR CONFER ATTIT PWR...POLICY JURID CHARTS ANTHOL 20. PAGE 24 G0468   SPACE LAW SOVEREIGN CONTROL

B59
LANG D.,FROM HIROSHIMA TO THE MOON: CHRONICLES OF LIFE IN THE ATOMIC AGE. USA+45 OP/RES CONTROL ARMS/CONT WAR CIVMIL/REL PEACE HABITAT MORAL PWR ...OBS INT 20 AEC. PAGE 32 G0633   NUC/PWR SPACE HEALTH TEC/DEV

B59
POKROVSKY G.I.,SCIENCE AND TECHNOLOGY IN CONTEMPORARY WAR. SPACE USSR WOR+45 NAT/G CONSULT ACT/RES PLAN DETER WEAPON...MARXIST METH/CNCPT CHARTS STERTYP COLD/WAR 20. PAGE 45 G0881   TEC/DEV FORCES NUC/PWR WAR

B60
GOLDSEN J.M.,INTERNATIONAL POLITICAL IMPLICATIONS OF ACTIVITIES IN OUTER SPACE. FUT USA+45 WOR+45 AIR LAW ACT/RES LEGIT ATTIT KNOWL ORD/FREE PWR...CONCPT 20. PAGE 22 G0427   R+D SPACE

B60
PARRY A.,RUSSIA'S ROCKETS AND MISSILES. COM FUT GERMANY USA+45 WOR+45 ACT/RES NUC/PWR WEAPON ATTIT ALL/VALS...OBS TIME/SEQ COLD/WAR 20. PAGE 44 G0859   PLAN TEC/DEV SPACE USSR

B60
WOETZEL R.K.,THE INTERNATIONAL CONTROL OF AIRSPACE AND OUTERSPACE. FUT WOR+45 AIR CONSTN STRUCT CONSULT PLAN TEC/DEV ADJUD RIGID/FLEX KNOWL ORD/FREE PWR...TECHNIC GEOG MGT NEW/IDEA TREND COMPUT/IR VAL/FREE 20 TREATY. PAGE 64 G1251   INT/ORG JURID SPACE INT/LAW

N60
US HOUSE COMM SCI ASTRONAUT,THE ORGANIZATION OF THE US NATIONAL SPACE EFFORT. USA+45 WOR+45 AIR ECO/DEV NAT/G PLAN TEC/DEV DIPLOM EDU/PROP ATTIT DRIVE PWR ...OBS TIME/SEQ TREND TOT/POP 20. PAGE 58 G1142   ACT/RES SKILL SPACE

B61
MICHAEL D.N.,PROPOSED STUDIES ON THE IMPLICATIONS OF PEACEFUL SPACE ACTIVITIES FOR HUMAN AFFAIRS. COM/IND INDUS FORCES DIPLOM PEACE PERSON...PSY SOC 20. PAGE 39 G0764   FUT SPACE ACT/RES PROB/SOLV

B61
RAMO S.,PEACETIME USES OF OUTER SPACE. FUT DIST/IND INT/ORG CONSULT NUC/PWR...AUD/VIS ANTHOL 20. PAGE 46 G0898   PEACE TEC/DEV SPACE CREATE

L61
TAUBENFELD H.J.,"A REGIME FOR OUTER SPACE." FUT UNIV R+D ACT/RES PLAN BAL/PWR LEGIT ARMS/CONT ORD/FREE...POLICY JURID TREND UN TOT/POP 20 COLD/WAR. PAGE 54 G1056   INT/ORG ADJUD SPACE

S61
MACHOWSKI K.,"SELECTED PROBLEMS OF NATIONAL SOVEREIGNTY WITH REFERENCE TO THE LAW OF OUTER SPACE." FUT WOR+45 AIR LAW INTELL SOCIETY ECO/DEV PLAN EDU/PROP DETER DRIVE PERCEPT SOVEREIGN ...POLICY INT/LAW OBS TREND TOT/POP 20. PAGE 35 G0689   UNIV ACT/RES NUC/PWR SPACE

S61
TAUBENFELD H.J.,"OUTER SPACE--PAST POLITICS AND FUTURE POLICY." FUT USA+45 USA-45 WOR+45 AIR INTELL STRUCT ECO/DEV NAT/G TOP/EX ACT/RES ADMIN ROUTINE NUC/PWR ATTIT DRIVE...CONCPT TIME/SEQ TREND TOT/POP 20. PAGE 54 G1054   PLAN SPACE INT/ORG

B62
BLOOMFIELD L.P.,OUTER SPACE: A PATTERN OF WAR IN A NEW DIMENSION. FUT USA+45 AIR TEC/DEV PWR ...DECISION CONCPT GEN/LAWS 20. PAGE 7 G0141   CREATE ACT/RES ARMS/CONT SPACE

B62
CLARKE A.C.,PROFILES OF THE FUTURE; AN INQUIRY INTO FUT

THE LIMITS OF THE POSSIBLE. COM/IND DIST/IND PRODUC TEC/DEV
AGE PERCEPT...TECHNIC NEW/IDEA TIME. PAGE 12 G0232   PREDICT
                                                       SPACE

                                                          B62
FORTUNE EDITORS,THE SPACE INDUSTRY: AMERICA'S   SPACE
NEWEST GIANT. USA+45 FINAN NAT/G BUDGET 20. PAGE 20   INDUS
G0383   TEC/DEV
                                                       MGT

                                                          B62
GOLOVINE M.N.,CONFLICT IN SPACE: A PATTERN OF WAR   CREATE
IN A NEW DIMENSION. FUT USA+45 WOR+45 AIR FORCES   TEC/DEV
PLAN DIPLOM DOMIN ATTIT...STAT AUD/VIS CHARTS   NUC/PWR
COLD/WAR 20. PAGE 22 G0432   SPACE

                                                          B62
KENNEDY J.F.,TO TURN THE TIDE. SPACE AGRI INT/ORG   DIPLOM
FORCES TEC/DEV ADMIN NUC/PWR PEACE WEALTH...ANTHOL   CHIEF
20 KENNEDY/JF CIV/RIGHTS. PAGE 30 G0592   POLICY
                                                       NAT/G

                                                          B62
SCHWARTZ L.E.,INTERNATIONAL ORGANIZATIONS AND SPACE   INT/ORG
COOPERATION. VOL/ASSN CONSULT CREATE TEC/DEV   DIPLOM
SANCTION...POLICY INT/LAW PHIL/SCI 20 UN. PAGE 50   R+D
G0982   SPACE

                                                          B62
US CONGRESS,COMMUNICATIONS SATELLITE LEGISLATION: SPACE
HEARINGS BEFORE COMM ON AERON AND SPACE SCIENCES ON   COM/IND
BILLS S2550 AND 2814. WOR+45 LAW VOL/ASSN PLAN   ADJUD
DIPLOM CONTROL OWN PEACE...NEW/IDEA CONGRESS NASA.   GOV/REL
PAGE 56 G1110

                                                          S62
CRANE R.D.,"LAW AND STRATEGY IN SPACE." FUT USA+45   CONCPT
WOR+45 AIR LAW INT/ORG NAT/G FORCES ACT/RES PLAN   SPACE
BAL/PWR LEGIT ARMS/CONT COERCE ORD/FREE...POLICY
INT/LAW JURID SOC/EXP 20 TREATY. PAGE 13 G0261

                                                          B63
GOLDSEN J.M.,OUTER SPACE IN WORLD POLITICS. COM   TEC/DEV
USA+45 NAT/G FORCES ACT/RES PLAN DOMIN EDU/PROP   DIPLOM
COERCE ORD/FREE PWR...TECHNIC STAT INT SAMP TREND   SPACE
ANTHOL VAL/FREE 20. PAGE 22 G0428

                                                          B63
HALEY A.G.,SPACE LAW AND GOVERNMENT. FUT USA+45   INT/ORG
WOR+45 LEGIS ACT/RES CREATE ATTIT RIGID/FLEX   LAW
ORD/FREE PWR SOVEREIGN...POLICY JURID CONCPT CHARTS   SPACE
VAL/FREE 20. PAGE 24 G0469

                                                          B63
KAST F.E.,SCIENCE, TECHNOLOGY, AND MANAGEMENT.   MGT
SPACE USA+45 FORCES CONFER DETER NUC/PWR...PHIL/SCI   PLAN
CHARTS ANTHOL BIBLIOG 20 NASA. PAGE 30 G0581   TEC/DEV
                                                       PROB/SOLV

                                                          B63
MCDOUGAL M.S.,LAW AND PUBLIC ORDER IN SPACE. FUT   SPACE
USA+45 ACT/RES TEC/DEV ADJUD...POLICY INT/LAW JURID   ORD/FREE
20. PAGE 37 G0739   DIPLOM
                                                       DECISION

                                                          B63
NASA,CONFERENCE ON SPACE, SCIENCE, AND URBAN LIFE.   MUNIC
USA+45 SOCIETY INDUS ACADEM ACT/RES ECO/TAC ADMIN   SPACE
20. PAGE 41 G0804   TEC/DEV
                                                       PROB/SOLV

                                                          B63
US SENATE,DOCUMENTS ON INTERNATIONAL AS"ECTS OF   SPACE
EXPLORATION AND USE OF OUTER SPACE, 1954-62: STAFF   UTIL
REPORT FOR COMM AERON SPACE SCI. USA+45 USSR LEGIS   GOV/REL
LEAD CIVMIL/REL PEACE...POLICY INT/LAW ANTHOL 20   DIPLOM
CONGRESS NASA KHRUSH/N. PAGE 59 G1162

                                                          S63
ABT C.,"THE PROBLEMS AND POSSIBILITIES OF SPACE   ACT/RES
ARMS CONTROL." FUT USA+45 WOR+45 AIR SOCIETY NAT/G   ORD/FREE
BAL/PWR EDU/PROP ATTIT PWR WEALTH...HYPO/EXP   ARMS/CONT
TOT/POP 20. PAGE 2 G0025   SPACE

                                                          S63
GARDNER R.N.,"COOPERATION IN OUTER SPACE." FUT USSR   INT/ORG
WOR+45 AIR LAW COM/IND CONSULT DELIB/GP CREATE   ACT/RES
KNOWL 20 TREATY. PAGE 21 G0410   PEACE
                                                       SPACE

                                                          S63
PHELPS J.,"INFORMATION AND ARMS CONTROL." COM SPACE   KNOWL
USA+45 USSR WOR+45 R+D INT/ORG NAT/G DELIB/GP   ARMS/CONT
DIPLOM ORD/FREE...CONCPT 20. PAGE 45 G0875   NUC/PWR

                                                          B64
COHEN M.,LAW AND POLITICS IN SPACE: SPECIFIC AND   DELIB/GP
URGENT PROBLEMS IN THE LAW OF OUTER SPACE.   LAW
CHINA/COM COM USA+45 USSR WOR+45 COM/IND INT/ORG   INT/LAW
NAT/G LEGIT NUC/PWR ATTIT BIO/SOC...JURID CONCPT   SPACE
CONGRESS 20 STALIN/J. PAGE 12 G0241

                                                          B64
ETZIONI A.,THE MOON-DOGGLE: DOMESTIC AND   R+D
INTERNATIONAL IMPLICATIONS OF THE SPACE RACE. FUT   NAT/G
USA+45 WOR+45 INTELL ECO/DEV INDUS VOL/ASSN   DIPLOM
EX/STRUC FORCES LEGIS TOP/EX PLAN TEC/DEV ECO/TAC   SPACE
EDU/PROP KNOWL ORD/FREE PWR RESPECT WEALTH
TIME/SEQ. PAGE 18 G0352

                                                          B64
GROSSER G.H.,THE THREAT OF IMPENDING DISASTER: HEALTH
CONTRIBUTIONS TO THE PSYCHOLOGY OF STRESS. SPACE   PSY
UNIV SOCIETY R+D TEC/DEV EDU/PROP COERCE WAR ATTIT   NUC/PWR
BIO/SOC DISPL PERCEPT PERSON...SOC MYTH SELF/OBS
CONT/OBS BIOG CON/ANAL TOT/POP 20. PAGE 23 G0455

                                                          B64
NASA,PROCEEDINGS OF CONFERENCE ON THE LAW OF SPACE   SPACE
AND OF SATELLITE COMMUNICATIONS: CHICAGO 1963. FUT   COM/IND
WOR+45 DELIB/GP PROB/SOLV TEC/DEV CONFER ADJUD   LAW
NUC/PWR...POLICY IDEA/COMP 20 NASA. PAGE 41 G0805   DIPLOM

                                                          B64
OSSENBECK F.J.,OPEN SPACE AND PEACE. CHINA/COM FUT   SPACE
USA+45 USSR LAW PROB/SOLV TEC/DEV EDU/PROP NEUTRAL   ORD/FREE
PEACE...AUD/VIS ANTHOL 20. PAGE 43 G0850   DIPLOM
                                                       CREATE

                                                          B64
PEDERSEN E.S.,NUCLEAR ENERGY IN SPACE. FUT INTELL   SPACE
R+D CONSULT...NEW/IDEA CHARTS METH T 20. PAGE 44   TEC/DEV
G0864   NUC/PWR
                                                       LAB/EXP

                                                          B64
SCHWARTZ M.D.,CONFERENCE ON SPACE SCIENCE AND SPACE   SPACE
LAW. FUT COM/IND NAT/G FORCES ACT/RES PLAN BUDGET   LAW
DIPLOM NUC/PWR WEAPON...POLICY ANTHOL 20. PAGE 50   PEACE
G0983   TEC/DEV

                                                          B64
TAUBENFELD H.J.,SPACE AND SOCIETY. USA+45 LAW   SPACE
FORCES CREATE TEC/DEV ADJUD CONTROL COST PEACE   SOCIETY
...PREDICT ANTHOL 20. PAGE 54 G1057   ADJUST
                                                       DIPLOM

                                                          B64
US AIR FORCE ACADEMY ASSEMBLY,OUTER SPACE: FINAL   SPACE
REPORT APRIL 1-4, 1964. FUT USA+45 WOR+45 LAW   CIVMIL/REL
DELIB/GP CONFER ARMS/CONT WAR PEACE ATTIT MORAL   NUC/PWR
...ANTHOL 20 NASA. PAGE 56 G1104   DIPLOM

                                                          L64
CARNEGIE ENDOWMENT INT. PEACE,"POLITICAL QUESTIONS   INT/ORG
(ISSUES BEFORE THE NINETEENTH GENERAL ASSEMBLY)."   PEACE
SPACE WOR+45 CONSTN FINAN NAT/G CONSULT DELIB/GP
FORCES LEGIS TEC/DEV EDU/PROP LEGIT ARMS/CONT
COERCE NUC/PWR ATTIT ALL/VALS...CONCPT OBS UN
COLD/WAR 20. PAGE 11 G0208

                                                          S64
SPONSLER G.C.,"THE MILITARY ROLE IN SPACE." FUT   TEC/DEV
USA+45 SEA AIR NAT/G ACT/RES PLAN COERCE NUC/PWR   FORCES
WEAPON KNOWL ORD/FREE PWR RESPECT...TREND 20.   SPACE
PAGE 52 G1026

                                                          B65
WHITE HOUSE CONFERENCE ON INTERNATIONAL   R+D
COOPERATION(VOL.II). SPACE WOR+45 EXTR/IND INT/ORG   CONFER
LABOR WORKER NUC/PWR PEACE AGE/Y...CENSUS ANTHOL 20   TEC/DEV
RESOURCE/N URBAN/RNWL PUB/TRANS. PAGE 1 G0019   DIPLOM

                                                          B65
FRUTKIN A.W.,SPACE AND THE INTERNATIONAL   SPACE
COOPERATION YEAR: A NATIONAL CHALLENGE (PAMPHLET).   INDUS
EUR+WWI USA+45 FINAN TEC/DEV BUDGET...MGT 20 NASA.   NAT/G
PAGE 20 G0396   DIPLOM

                                                          B65
JENKS C.W.,SPACE LAW. DIPLOM DEBATE CONTROL   SPACE
ORD/FREE TREATY 20 UN. PAGE 29 G0563   INT/LAW
                                                       JURID
                                                       INT/ORG

                                                          B65
MELMANS S.,OUR DEPLETED SOCIETY. SPACE USA+45   CIVMIL/REL
ECO/DEV FORCES BUDGET ECO/TAC ADMIN WEAPON   INDUS
EFFICIENCY 20 COLD/WAR. PAGE 38 G0753   EDU/PROP
                                                       CONTROL

B65
UN,SPACE ACTIVIIIES AND RESOURCES: REVIEW OF UNITED SPACE
NATION'S NATIONAL AND INTERNATIONAL PROGRAMS. NUC/PWR
INT/ORG LABOR PLAN TEC/DEV DIPLOM EFFICIENCY HEALTH FOR/AID
...GOV/COMP 20 UN. PAGE 55 G1086 PEACE

B65
US DEPARTMENT OF DEFENSE,US SECURITY ARMS CONTROL, BIBLIOG/A
AND DISARMAMENT 1961-1965 (PAMPHLET). CHINA/COM COM ARMS/CONT
GERMANY/W ISRAEL SPACE USA+45 USSR WOR+45 FORCES NUC/PWR
EDU/PROP DETER EQUILIB PEACE ALL/VALS...GOV/COMP 20 DIPLOM
NATO. PAGE 57 G1118

B65
US SENATE,US INTERNATIONAL SPACE PROGRAMS, 1959-65: SPACE
STAFF REPORT FOR COMM ON AERONAUTICAL AND SPACE DIPLOM
SCIENCES. WOR+45 VOL/ASSN CIVMIL/REL 20 CONGRESS PLAN
NASA TREATY. PAGE 59 G1163 GOV/REL

B65
US SENATE COMM AERO SPACE SCI,NATIONAL SPACE GOALS SPACE
FOR THE POST-APOLLO PERIOD. USA+45 CONSULT DELIB/GP FUT
TEC/DEV BUDGET GP/REL ATTIT...CHARTS IDEA/COMP TIME R+D
20 DEPT/DEFEN NASA CONGRESS. PAGE 59 G1166 LEGIS

B65
US SENATE COMM AERO SPACE SCI,INTERNATIONAL DIPLOM
COOPERATION AND ORGANIZATION FOR OUTER SPACE. FUT SPACE
USA+45 WOR+45 PROF/ORG VOL/ASSN CONSULT DELIB/GP R+D
PLAN TEC/DEV ARMS/CONT GP/REL PEACE 20 UN NASA. NAT/G
PAGE 59 G1167

S65
HIBBS A.R.,"SPACE TECHNOLOGY* THE THREAT AND THE SPACE
PROMISE." FUT VOL/ASSN TEC/DEV NUC/PWR COST ARMS/CONT
EFFICIENCY UTIL UN TREATY. PAGE 26 G0510 PREDICT

C65
SEARA M.V.,"COSMIC INTERNATIONAL LAW." LAW ACADEM SPACE
ACT/RES DIPLOM COLONIAL CONTROL NUC/PWR SOVEREIGN INT/LAW
...GEN/LAWS BIBLIOG UN. PAGE 50 G0987 IDEA/COMP
INT/ORG

B66
LECHT L.,GOAL, PRIORITIES, AND DOLLARS: THE NEXT IDEA/COMP
DECADE. SPACE USA+45 SOCIETY AGRI BUDGET FOR/AID POLICY
...HEAL SOC/WK STAT CHARTS 20 URBAN/RNWL PUB/TRANS. CONSEN
PAGE 33 G0649 PLAN

B66
LILLEY S.,MEN, MACHINES AND HISTORY: THE STORY OF AGRI
TOOLS AND MACHINES IN RELATION TO SOCIAL PROGRESS. TEC/DEV
PREHIST SPACE STRUCT COMPUTER AUTOMAT NUC/PWR SOCIETY
...POLICY SOC. PAGE 34 G0667

B66
ROSHOLT R.L.,AN ADMINISTRATIVE HISTORY OF NASA, ADMIN
1958-1963. SPACE USA+45 FINAN LEAD...MGT CHARTS EX/STRUC
BIBLIOG 20 NASA. PAGE 48 G0938 ADJUST
DELIB/GP

B66
RUPPENTHAL K.M.,TRANSPORTATION AND TOMORROW. FUT DIST/IND
SPACE USA+45 SEA AIR FORCES TEC/DEV INT/TRADE PLAN
...ANTHOL 20 RAILROAD. PAGE 48 G0946 CIVMIL/REL
PREDICT

B66
UNITED NATIONS,INTERNATIONAL SPACE BIBLIOGRAPHY. BIBLIOG
FUT INT/ORG TEC/DEV DIPLOM ARMS/CONT NUC/PWR SPACE
...JURID SOC UN. PAGE 56 G1093 PEACE
R+D

B66
US SENATE,POLICY PLANNING FOR AERONAUTICAL RESEARCH SPACE
AND DEVELOPMENT: STAFF REPORT FOR COMM ON CIVMIL/REL
AERONAUTICAL AND SPACE SCIENCES. USA+45 AIR GOV/REL
DIST/IND PLAN...POLICY CHARTS 20 CONGRESS NASA. R+D
PAGE 59 G1164

B66
US SENATE COMM AERO SPACE SCI,SOVIET SPACE CONSULT
PROGRAMS, 1962-65; GOALS AND PURPOSES, SPACE
ACHIEVEMENTS, PLANS, AND INTERNATIONAL FUT
IMPLICATIONS. USA+45 USSR R+D FORCES PLAN EDU/PROP DIPLOM
PRESS ADJUD ARMS/CONT ATTIT MARXISM. PAGE 60 G1168

B67
SKOLNIKOFF E.B.,SCIENCE, TECHNOLOGY, AND AMERICAN PHIL/SCI
FOREIGN POLICY. SPACE USA+45 INT/ORG TEC/DEV DIPLOM
ARMS/CONT NUC/PWR 29 DEPT/STATE. PAGE 51 G1010 NAT/G
EFFICIENCY

B67
UNIVERSAL REFERENCE SYSTEM,PUBLIC POLICY AND THE BIBLIOG/A
MANAGEMENT OF SCIENCE (VOLUME IX). FUT SPACE WOR+45 POLICY

LAW NAT/G TEC/DEV CONTROL NUC/PWR GOV/REL MGT
...COMPUT/IR GEN/METH. PAGE 56 G1100 PHIL/SCI

B67
US SENATE COMM AERO SPACE SCI,TREATY ON PRINCIPLES SPACE
GOVERNING ACTIVITIES OF STATES IN EXPLORATION AND INT/LAW
USE OF OUTER SPACE, INCLUDING...BODIES. DELIB/GP ORD/FREE
FORCES LEGIS DIPLOM...JURID 20 DEPT/STATE NASA PEACE
DEPT/DEFEN UN. PAGE 60 G1170

B67
US SENATE COMM AERO SPACE SCI,APOLLO ACCIDENT PROB/SOLV
(PARTS 1-7). USA+45 DELIB/GP LEGIS...INT CHARTS SPACE
NASA. PAGE 60 G1173 BUDGET
GOV/REL

B67
US SENATE COMM ON FOREIGN REL,TREATY ON OUTER SPACE
SPACE. WOR+45 AIR FORCES PROB/SOLV NUC/PWR SENATE DIPLOM
TREATY UN. PAGE 60 G1182 ARMS/CONT
LAW

S67
BARRO S.,"ECONOMIC IMPACT OF SPACE EXPENDITURES: SPACE
SOME BROAD ISSUES DEALING WITH COSTS AND BENEFITS." FINAN
USA+45 PROC/MFG R+D LG/CO CONSULT COST PRODUC 20. ECO/TAC
PAGE 5 G0098 NAT/G

S67
DADDARIO E.Q.,"CONGRESS FACES SPACE POLICIES." R+D SPACE
NAT/G FORCES CREATE LEAD...DECISION CONGRESS NASA. PLAN
PAGE 14 G0269 BUDGET
POLICY

S67
DOYLE S.E.,"COMMUNICATION SATELLITES* INTERNAL TEC/DEV
ORGANIZATION FOR DEVELOPMENT AND CONTROL." USA+45 SPACE
R+D ACT/RES DIPLOM NAT/LISM...POLICY INT/LAW COM/IND
PREDICT UN. PAGE 16 G0313 INT/ORG

S67
EISENDRATH C.,"THE OUTER SPACE TREATY." CHINA/COM SPACE
COM USA+45 DIPLOM CONTROL NUC/PWR...INT/LAW 20 UN INT/ORG
COLD/WAR TREATY. PAGE 17 G0339 PEACE
ARMS/CONT

S67
FOREIGN POLICY ASSOCIATION,"HOW WORLD LAW DEVELOPS* INT/LAW
A CASE STUDY OF THE OUTER SPACE TREATY." SPACE DIPLOM
WOR+45 BAL/PWR NEUTRAL NUC/PWR PEACE KNOWL 20 UN ARMS/CONT
TREATY. PAGE 19 G0380 INT/ORG

S67
LAY S.H.,"EXCLUSIVE GOVERNMENTAL LIABILITY FOR NAT/G
SPACE ACCIDENTS." USA+45 LAW FINAN SERV/IND TEC/DEV SUPEGO
ADJUD. PAGE 33 G0646 SPACE
PROB/SOLV

S67
LEWIS R.L.,"GOAL AND NO GOAL* A NEW POLICY IN SPACE
SPACE." R+D BUDGET COST...POLICY DECISION PHIL/SCI. PLAN
PAGE 34 G0662 EFFICIENCY
CREATE

S67
MACDONALD G.J.F.,"SCIENCE AND SPACE POLICY* HOW SPACE
DOES IT GET PLANNED?" R+D CREATE TEC/DEV BUDGET PLAN
ADMIN ROUTINE...DECISION NASA. PAGE 35 G0687 MGT
EX/STRUC

S67
REINTANZ G.,"THE SPACE TREATY." WOR+45 DIPLOM SPACE
CONTROL ARMS/CONT NUC/PWR WAR...MARXIST 20 COLD/WAR INT/LAW
UN TREATY. PAGE 46 G0911 INT/ORG
PEACE

S67
VLASCIC I.A.,"THE SPACE TREATY* A PRELIMINARY SPACE
EVALUATION." FUT USSR WOR+45 R+D ACT/RES TEC/DEV INT/LAW
DIPLOM CONFER ARMS/CONT PEACE...PREDICT UN TREATY. INT/ORG
PAGE 61 G1201 NEUTRAL

S67
WEINBERG A.M.,"CAN TECHNOLOGY REPLACE SOCIAL TEC/DEV
ENGINEERING?" SPACE USA+45 SOCIETY ACADEM GP/REL. ACT/RES
PAGE 62 G1224 PROB/SOLV
INTELL

N67
US SUPERINTENDENT OF DOCUMENTS,SPACE: MISSILES, THE BIBLIOG/A
MOON, NASA, AND SATELLITES (PRICE LIST 79A). USA+45 SPACE
COM/IND R+D NAT/G DIPLOM EDU/PROP ADMIN CONTROL TEC/DEV
HEALTH...POLICY SIMUL NASA CONGRESS. PAGE 61 G1190 PEACE

N67
US HOUSE COMM SCI ASTRONAUT,AUTHORIZING SPACE

APPROPRIATIONS TO THE NATIONAL AERONAUTICS AND SPACE ADMINISTRATION (PAMPHLET). USA+45 NAT/G OP/RES TEC/DEV BUDGET NASA HOUSE/REP. PAGE 58 G1149 — R+D PHIL/SCI NUC/PWR

N67
US SENATE COMM AERO SPACE SCI,AERONAUTICAL RESEARCH AND DEVELOPMENT POLICY (PAMPHLET). SPACE USA+45 INDUS CIVMIL/REL CONGRESS PRESIDENT NASA SENATE. PAGE 60 G1169 — AIR R+D POLICY PLAN

N67
US SENATE COMM AERO SPACE SCI,HEARINGS BEFORE THE COMMITTEE ON AERONAUTICAL AND SPACE SCIENCES UNITED STATES SENATE NINETIETH CONGRESS (PAMPHLET). USA+45 CONSULT PLAN CONFER EFFICIENCY SENATE. PAGE 60 G1172 — NAT/G DELIB/GP SPACE CREATE

N67
US SENATE COMM AERO SPACE SCI,AERONAUTICAL RESEARCH AND DEVELOPMENT POLICY; HEARINGS, COMM ON AERONAUTICAL AND SPACE SCIENCES...1967 (PAMPHLET). R+D PROB/SOLV EXEC GOV/REL 20 DEPT/DEFEN FAA NASA CONGRESS. PAGE 60 G1174 — DIST/IND SPACE NAT/G PLAN

SPAIN....SPAIN

B60
ALBI F.,TRATADO DE LOS MODOS DE GESTION DE LAS CORPORACIONES LOCALES. SPAIN FINAN NAT/G BUDGET CONTROL EXEC ROUTINE GOV/REL ORD/FREE SOVEREIGN ...MGT 20. PAGE 2 G0034 — LOC/G LAW ADMIN MUNIC

B65
OECD,THE MEDITERRANEAN REGIONAL PROJECT: SPAIN; EDUCATION AND DEVELOPMENT. FUT SPAIN STRATA FINAN NAT/G WORKER PLAN PROB/SOLV ADMIN COST...POLICY STAT CHARTS 20 OECD. PAGE 42 G0835 — ECO/UNDEV EDU/PROP ACADEM SCHOOL

SPAN/AMER....SPANISH-AMERICAN CULTURE

SPANIER J.W. G1023

SPEAKER OF THE HOUSE....SEE CONGRESS, HOUSE/REP, LEGIS, PARLIAMENT

SPEAR/BRWN....SPEARMAN BROWN PREDICTION FORMULA

SPECIALIZATION....SEE TASK, SKILL

SPECULATION....SEE GAMBLE, RISK

SPEIER H. G0426,G1024

SPENCER R.F. G1025

SPENCER/H....HERBERT SPENCER

B28
BARKER E.,POLITICAL THOUGHT IN ENGLAND: FROM HERBERT SPENCER TO THE PRESENT DAY. UK ALL/IDEOS ...PHIL/SCI 19/20 SPENCER/H GREEN/TH BENTHAM/J MAITLAND/F. PAGE 5 G0094 — INTELL GEN/LAWS IDEA/COMP

SPENGLER/O....OSWALD SPENGLER

SPINOZA/B....BARUCH (OR BENEDICT) SPINOZA

SPIVEY W.A. G0156

SPOCK/B....BENJAMIN SPOCK

SPONSLER G.C. G1026

SPORTS....SPORTS AND ATHLETIC COMPETITIONS

SPROTT W.J.H. G1027

SPULBER N. G1028

SRAFFA/P....PIERO SRAFFA

SST....SUPERSONIC TRANSPORT

ST/LOUIS....ST. LOUIS, MO.

ST/PAUL....SAINT PAUL, MINNESOTA

B65
ALTSHULER A.,A LAND-USE PLAN FOR ST. PAUL (PAMPHLET). USA+45 CREATE CAP/ISM RIGID/FLEX ROLE ...NEW/IDEA 20 ST/PAUL. PAGE 3 G0047 — MUNIC PLAN ECO/DEV GEOG

STAAR R.F. G1029

STAGES....SEE TIME/SEQ

STAHL O.G. G1030

STALIN/J....JOSEPH STALIN

B64
COHEN M.,LAW AND POLITICS IN SPACE: SPECIFIC AND URGENT PROBLEMS IN THE LAW OF OUTER SPACE. CHINA/COM COM USA+45 USSR WOR+45 COM/IND INT/ORG NAT/G LEGIT NUC/PWR ATTIT BIO/SOC...JURID CONCPT CONGRESS 20 STALIN/J. PAGE 12 G0241 — DELIB/GP LAW INT/LAW SPACE

B67
MAZOUR A.G.,SOVIET ECONOMIC DEVELOPMENT: OPERATION OUTSTRIP: 1921-1965. USSR ECO/UNDEV FINAN CHIEF WORKER PROB/SOLV CONTROL PRODUC MARXISM...CHARTS ORG/CHARTS 20 STALIN/J. PAGE 37 G0726 — ECO/TAC AGRI INDUS PLAN

S67
AVTORKHANOV A.,"A NEW AGRARIAN REVOLUTION." COM USSR ECO/DEV PLAN TEC/DEV ADMIN CONTROL OPTIMAL WEALTH SOCISM 20 KHRUSH/N STALIN/J. PAGE 4 G0082 — AGRI METH/COMP MARXISM OWN

S67
CARR E.H.,"REVOLUTION FROM ABOVE." USSR STRATA FINAN INDUS NAT/G DOMIN LEAD GP/REL INGP/REL OWN PRODUC PWR 20 STALIN/J. PAGE 11 G0214 — AGRI POLICY COM EFFICIENCY

STAMMLER/R....RUDOLF STAMMLER

STAMP S. G1031

STAND/INT....STANDARDIZED INTERVIEWS

B58
TELLER E.A.,OUR NUCLEAR FUTURE. SOCIETY FORCES TEC/DEV EDU/PROP KNOWL ORD/FREE...STAND/INT SYS/QU KNO/TEST AUD/VIS CHARTS SIMUL 20. PAGE 54 G1062 — FUT PHIL/SCI NUC/PWR WAR

STANDARDIZED INTERVIEWS....SEE STAND/INT

STANFORD RESEARCH INSTITUTE G1032

STANFORD/U....STANFORD UNIVERSITY

STANKIEW/W....W.J. STANKIEWICZ

STANKIEWICZ, W.J.....SEE STANKIEW/W

STAR/CARR....STAR-CARR, A PREHISTORIC SOCIETY

STAT....STATISTICS

N
AMERICAN DOCUMENTATION INST,AMERICAN DOCUMENTATION. PROF/ORG CONSULT PLAN PERCEPT...MATH STAT AUD/VIS CHARTS METH/COMP INDEX METH 20. PAGE 3 G0050 — BIBLIOG TEC/DEV COM/IND COMPUT/IR

N
INDIA: A REFERENCE ANNUAL. INDIA CULTURE COM/IND R+D FORCES PLAN RECEIVE EDU/PROP HEALTH...STAT CHARTS BIBLIOG 20. PAGE 1 G0005 — CONSTN LABOR INT/ORG

N
GT BRIT MIN OVERSEAS DEV, LIB, TECHNICAL CO-OPERATION -- A BIBLIOGRAPHY. UK LAW SOCIETY DIPLOM ECO/TAC FOR/AID...STAT 20 CMN/WLTH. PAGE 39 G0775 — BIBLIOG TEC/DEV ECO/DEV NAT/G

B40
PFIFFNER J.M.,RESEARCH METHODS IN PUBLIC ADMINISTRATION. USA-45 R+D...MGT STAT INT QU T 20. PAGE 44 G0872 — ADMIN OP/RES METH TEC/DEV

S43
KAPLAN A.,"CONTENT ANALYSIS AND THE THEORY OF SIGNS" (BMR)" PERS/REL...PSY CONCPT LING IDEA/COMP SIMUL BIBLIOG 20 MORRIS/CW. PAGE 29 G0573 — LOG CON/ANAL STAT PHIL/SCI

L46
MASTERS D.,"ONE WORLD OR NONE." FUT WOR+45 INTELL INT/ORG ACT/RES EDU/PROP DETER ATTIT RIGID/FLEX SUPEGO KNOWL...STAT TREND ORG/CHARTS 20. PAGE 36 G0719 — POLICY PHIL/SCI ARMS/CONT NUC/PWR

B47
SOCIAL SCIENCE RESEARCH COUN,PUBLIC REACTION TO THE ATOMIC BOMB AND WORLD AFFAIRS. SOCIETY CONFER ARMS/CONT...STAT QU SAMP CHARTS 20. PAGE 52 G1019 — ATTIT NUC/PWR DIPLOM

WAR

S48

HARDIN L.M.,"REFLECTIONS ON AGRICULTURAL POLICY
FORMATION IN THE UNITED STATES." LEGIS PLAN BUDGET
ECO/TAC LEAD CENTRAL...MGT SOC NEW/IDEA STAT FAO.
PAGE 24 G0480

AGRI
POLICY
ADMIN
NEW/LIB

B50

SURANYI-UNGER T.,PRIVATE ENTERPRISE AND
GOVERNMENTAL PLANNING. STRUCT FINAN BAL/PWR
HAPPINESS DRIVE NEW/LIB PLURISM...MATH QUANT STAT
TREND BIBLIOG. PAGE 53 G1047

PLAN
NAT/G
LAISSEZ
POLICY

S50

KAPLAN A.,"THE PREDICTION OF SOCIAL AND
TECHNOLOGICAL EVENTS." VOL/ASSN CONSULT ACT/RES
CREATE OP/RES PLAN ROUTINE PERSON...POLICY
METH/CNCPT STAT QU/SEMANT SYS/QU TESTS CENSUS TREND
20. PAGE 29 G0574

PWR
KNO/TEST

S50

LENTZ T.F.,"REPORT ON A SURVEY OF SOCIAL SCIENTISTS
CONDUCTED BY THE ATTITUDE RESEARCH LABORATORY."FUT
WOR+45 CREATE EDU/PROP...PSY STAT RECORD SYS/QU
SAMP/SIZ CON/ANAL VAL/FREE 20. PAGE 33 G0655

ACT/RES
ATTIT
DIPLOM

C50

WAGER P.W.,"COUNTY GOVERNMENT ACROSS THE NATION."
USA+45 CONSTN COM/IND FINAN SCHOOL DOMIN CT/SYS
LEAD GOV/REL...STAT BIBLIOG 20. PAGE 61 G1204

LOC/G
PROVS
ADMIN
ROUTINE

B53

CALDWELL L.K.,RESEARCH METHODS IN PUBLIC
ADMINISTRATION; AN OUTLINE OF TOPICS AND READINGS
(PAMPHLET). LAW ACT/RES COMPUTER KNOWL...SOC STAT
GEN/METH 20. PAGE 10 G0201

BIBLIOG/A
METH/COMP
ADMIN
OP/RES

B53

MACK R.T.,RAISING THE WORLDS STANDARD OF LIVING.
IRAN INT/ORG VOL/ASSN EX/STRUC ECO/TAC WEALTH...MGT
METH/CNCPT STAT CONT/OBS INT TOT/POP VAL/FREE 20
UN. PAGE 35 G0690

WOR+45
FOR/AID
INT/TRADE

S53

MILLER G.A.,"WHAT IS INFORMATION MEASUREMENT?"
CREATE...CONCPT METH/CNCPT QUANT STAT CHARTS
BIBLIOG/A 20. PAGE 39 G0771

COMPUTER
TEC/DEV
PSY
MATH

B54

LOCKLIN D.P.,ECONOMICS OF TRANSPORTATION (4TH ED.).
USA+45 USA-45 SEA AIR LAW FINAN LG/CO EX/STRUC
ADMIN CONTROL...STAT CHARTS 19/20 RAILROAD
PUB/TRANS. PAGE 34 G0675

ECO/DEV
DIST/IND
ECO/TAC
TEC/DEV

B54

SPENCER R.F.,METHOD AND PERSPECTIVE IN ANTHROPOLOGY
....GEOG LING QUANT STAT TESTS SAMP/SIZ CON/ANAL
IDEA/COMP METH/COMP ANTHOL BIBLIOG 20. PAGE 52
G1025

PHIL/SCI
SOC
PSY
METH

B55

RILEY V.,INTERINDUSTRY ECONOMIC STUDIES. USA+45
COMPUTER ADMIN OPTIMAL PRODUC...MGT CLASSIF STAT.
PAGE 47 G0922

BIBLIOG
ECO/DEV
PLAN
STRUCT

B55

SHUBIK M.,READINGS IN GAME THEORY AND POLITICAL
BEHAVIOR. WOR+45 FORCES CREATE ROUTINE WAR PEACE
PERCEPT KNOWL PWR...PSY SOC CONCPT METH/CNCPT STAT
CHARTS HYPO/EXP GAME METH VAL/FREE 20. PAGE 50
G0991

MATH
DECISION
DIPLOM

B56

WASSERMAN P.,INFORMATION FOR ADMINISTRATORS: A
GUIDE TO PUBLICATIONS AND SERVICES FOR MANAGEMENT
IN BUSINESS AND GOVERNMENT. R+D LOC/G NAT/G
PROF/ORG VOL/ASSN PRESS...PSY SOC STAT 20. PAGE 62
G1219

BIBLIOG
MGT
KNOWL
EDU/PROP

S57

DUNCAN O.D.,"THE MEASUREMENT OF POPULATION
DISTRIBUTION" (BMR)" WOR+45...QUANT STAT CENSUS
CHARTS 20. PAGE 16 G0321

GEOG
PHIL/SCI
PROB/SOLV
CLASSIF

B58

BIDWELL P.W.,RAW MATERIALS: A STUDY OF AMERICAN
POLICY. USA+45 USA-45 ECO/UNDEV AGRI INDUS KIN
CREATE PLAN ECO/TAC WAR PEACE ATTIT DRIVE WEALTH
...STAT CHARTS CONGRESS VAL/FREE. PAGE 7 G0135

EXTR/IND
ECO/DEV

B58

GANGE J.,UNIVERSITY RESEARCH ON INTERNATIONAL
AFFAIRS. USA+45 ACADEM INT/ORG CONSULT CREATE EXEC
ROUTINE...QUANT STAT INT STERTYP GEN/METH TOT/POP
VAL/FREE 20. PAGE 21 G0407

R+D
MGT
DIPLOM

B58

OPERATIONS RESEARCH SOCIETY,A COMPREHENSIVE
BIBLIOGRAPHY ON OPERATIONS RESEARCH; THROUGH 1956
WITH SUPPLEMENT FOR 1957. COM/IND DIST/IND INDUS
ADMIN...DECISION MATH STAT METH 20. PAGE 43 G0840

BIBLIOG/A
COMPUT/IR
OP/RES
MGT

B59

CLEAVELAND F.N.,SCIENCE AND STATE GOVERNMENT. AGRI
EXTR/IND FINAN INDUS PROVS...METH/CNCPT STAT CHARTS
20 NEW/YORK CONNECTICT WISCONSIN CALIFORNIA
NEW/MEXICO. PAGE 12 G0233

TEC/DEV
R+D
PHIL/SCI
GOV/REL
METH/COMP

B59

ELDRIDGE H.T.,THE MATERIALS OF DEMOGRAPHY: A
SELECTED AND ANNOTATED BIBLIOGRAPHY. R+D DEATH
...SAMP METH/COMP NAT/COMP 20. PAGE 18 G0343

BIBLIOG/A
GEOG
STAT
TREND

B59

MODELSKI G.,ATOMIC ENERGY IN THE COMMUNIST BLOC.
FUT INT/ORG CONSULT FORCES ACT/RES PLAN KNOWL SKILL
...PHIL/SCI STAT CHARTS 20. PAGE 39 G0777

TEC/DEV
NUC/PWR
USSR
COM

B59

COLUMBIA U BUREAU APPL SOC R, ATTITUDES OF
PROMINENT AMERICANS TOWARD "WORLD PEACE THROUGH
WORLD LAW" (SUPRA-NATL ORGANIZATION FOR WAR
PREVENTION). USA+45 USSR ELITES FORCES PLAN
PROB/SOLV CONTROL WAR PWR...POLICY SOC QU IDEA/COMP
20 UN. PAGE 45 G0888

ATTIT
ACT/RES
INT/LAW
STAT

B60

MORRIS W.T.,ENGINEERING ECONOMY. AUTOMAT RISK
RATIONAL...PROBABIL STAT CHARTS GAME SIMUL BIBLIOG
T 20. PAGE 40 G0785

OP/RES
DECISION
MGT
PROB/SOLV

B60

SILK L.S.,THE RESEARCH REVOLUTION. USA+45 FINAN
CAP/ISM ECO/TAC PRICE EQUILIB PRODUC...STAT TREND
CHARTS. PAGE 51 G0997

ECO/DEV
R+D
TEC/DEV
PROB/SOLV

L60

DEUTSCH K.W.,"TOWARD AN INVENTORY OF BASIC TRENDS
AND PATTERNS IN COMPARATIVE AND INTERNATIONAL
POLITICS." UNIV WOR+45 SOCIETY STRUCT INT/ORG NAT/G
CREATE PLAN EDU/PROP KNOWL...PHIL/SCI METH/CNCPT
STAT SELF/OBS OBS/ENVIR SAMP TREND CON/ANAL CHARTS
SOC/EXP GEN/METH 20. PAGE 15 G0298

R+D
PERCEPT

L60

HOLZMAN B.G.,"BASIC RESEARCH FOR NATIONAL
SURVIVAL." FUT USA+45 INTELL R+D ACT/RES OP/RES
PLAN TEC/DEV EDU/PROP PERCEPT PERSON...PHIL/SCI
METH/CNCPT NEW/IDEA MATH OBS RECORD TREND LAB/EXP
20. PAGE 27 G0525

FORCES
STAT

S60

BARNETT H.J.,"RESEARCH AND DEVELOPMENT, ECONOMIC
GROWTH, AND NATIONAL SECURITY." USA+45 R+D CREATE
ECO/TAC ATTIT DRIVE PWR...POLICY SOC METH/CNCPT
QUANT STAT TIME/SEQ ORG/CHARTS COLD/WAR 20. PAGE 5
G0097

ACT/RES
PLAN

S60

BECKER A.S.,"COMPARISIONS OF UNITED STATES AND USSR
NATIONAL OUTPUT: SOME RULES OF THE GAME." COM
USA+45 ECO/DEV AGRI DIST/IND INDUS R+D CONSULT PLAN
ECO/TAC RIGID/FLEX KNOWL...METH/CNCPT CHARTS 20.
PAGE 6 G0113

STAT
USSR

S60

JAFFEE A.J.,"POPULATION TRENDS AND CONTROLS IN
UNDERDEVELOPED COUNTRIES." AFR FUT ISLAM L/A+17C
S/ASIA CULTURE R+D FAM ACT/RES PLAN EDU/PROP
BIO/SOC RIGID/FLEX HEALTH...SOC STAT OBS CHARTS 20.
PAGE 28 G0555

ECO/UNDEV
GEOG

S60

SHUBIK M.,"BIBLIOGRAPHY ON SIMULATION, GAMING,
ARTIFICIAL INTELLIGENCE AND ALLIED TOPICS."
COMPUTER ROUTINE...DECISION MGT STAT 20. PAGE 50
G0992

BIBLIOG
SIMUL
GAME
OP/RES

B61

HODGKINS J.A.,SOVIET POWER: ENERGY RESOURCES,
PRODUCTION AND POTENTIALS. USSR ECO/DEV INDUS
MARKET...POLICY STAT CHARTS 20 RESOURCE/N. PAGE 26

GEOG
EXTR/IND
TEC/DEV

G0518

B61
NAKICENOVIC S.,NUCLEAR ENERGY IN YUGOSLAVIA.   R+D
YUGOSLAVIA AGRI INDUS CREATE OP/RES ROUTINE   ECO/DEV
EFFICIENCY KNOWL...HEAL STAT CHARTS LAB/EXP BIBLIOG   TEC/DEV
20. PAGE 41 G0802   NUC/PWR

B61
WEISBROD B.A.,ECONOMICS OF PUBLIC HEALTH. USA+45   SOCIETY
INGP/REL HABITAT...POLICY STAT 20. PAGE 63 G1227   HEALTH
                                                      NEW/IDEA
                                                      ECO/DEV

S61
BENNION E.G.,"ECONOMETRICS FOR MANAGEMENT." USA+45   ECOMETRIC
INDUS EX/STRUC ACT/RES COMPUTER UTIL...MATH STAT   MGT
PREDICT METH/COMP HYPO/EXP. PAGE 6 G0122   SIMUL
                                                      DECISION

S61
DEUTSCH K.W.,"A NOTE ON THE APPEARANCE OF WISDOM IN   ADMIN
LARGE BUREAUCRATIC ORGANIZATIONS." ROUTINE PERSON   PROBABIL
KNOWL SKILL...DECISION STAT. PAGE 15 G0299   PROB/SOLV
                                                      SIMUL

B62
BELLMAN R.,APPLIED DYNAMIC PROGRAMMING. OPTIMAL   COMPUTER
...DECISION STAT SIMUL. PAGE 6 G0116   ECOMETRIC
                                                      GAME
                                                      MATH

B62
DUCKWORTH W.E.,A GUIDE TO OPERATIONAL RESEARCH.   OP/RES
INDUS PLAN PROB/SOLV EXEC EFFICIENCY PRODUC KNOWL   GAME
...MGT MATH STAT SIMUL METH 20 MONTECARLO. PAGE 16   DECISION
G0319   ADMIN

B62
FERBER R.,RESEARCH METHODS IN ECONOMICS AND   ACT/RES
BUSINESS. ECO/DEV FINAN MARKET LG/CO SML/CO CONSULT   PROB/SOLV
CONTROL COST...STAT METH/COMP 20. PAGE 19 G0364   ECO/TAC
                                                      MGT

B62
GOLOVINE M.N.,CONFLICT IN SPACE: A PATTERN OF WAR   CREATE
IN A NEW DIMENSION. FUT USA+45 WOR+45 AIR FORCES   TEC/DEV
PLAN DIPLOM DOMIN ATTIT...STAT AUD/VIS CHARTS   NUC/PWR
COLD/WAR 20. PAGE 22 G0432   SPACE

B62
PERRE J.,LES MUTATIONS DE LA GUERRE MODERNE: DE LA   WAR
REVOLUTION FRANCAISE A LA REVOLUTION NUCLEAIRE.   FORCES
DIPLOM ARMS/CONT DEATH REV WEAPON GP/REL PEACE   NUC/PWR
ATTIT...STAT PREDICT BIBLIOG 18/20 WWI. PAGE 44
G0870

S62
PAULING L.,"GENETIC EFFECTS OF WEAPONS TESTS."   HEAL
WOR+45 SOCIETY FAM ACT/RES EDU/PROP AGE/C HEALTH   ARMS/CONT
ORD/FREE...GEOG STAT CONT/OBS PROJ/TEST CHARTS   NUC/PWR
TOT/POP 20. PAGE 44 G0861

S62
THORELLI H.B.,"THE INTERNATIONAL OPERATIONS   ECO/TAC
SIMULATION AT THE UNIVERSITY OF CHICAGO." FUT   SIMUL
USA+45 WOR+45 ECO/DEV DIST/IND FINAN INDUS INT/ORG   INT/TRADE
DELIB/GP ACT/RES CREATE TEC/DEV WEALTH...STAT
VAL/FREE 20. PAGE 54 G1072

C62
JOINT ECONOMIC COMMITTEE,"DIMENSIONS OF SOVIET   ECO/DEV
ECONOMIC POWER." USSR R+D FORCES ACT/RES OP/RES   PLAN
TEC/DEV...GEOG STAT BIBLIOG 20. PAGE 29 G0565   PRODUC
                                                      LABOR

B63
ABSHIRE D.M.,NATIONAL SECURITY: POLITICAL,   FUT
MILITARY, AND ECONOMIC STRATEGIES IN THE DECADE   ACT/RES
AHEAD. ASIA COM USA+45 WOR+45 ECO/DEV ECO/UNDEV   BAL/PWR
INT/ORG DELIB/GP FORCES ECO/TAC COERCE ATTIT
RIGID/FLEX HEALTH ORD/FREE PWR WEALTH...POLICY STAT
CHARTS ANTHOL COLD/WAR VAL/FREE. PAGE 1 G0024

B63
GOLDSEN J.M.,OUTER SPACE IN WORLD POLITICS. COM   TEC/DEV
USA+45 NAT/G FORCES ACT/RES PLAN EDU/PROP   DIPLOM
COERCE ORD/FREE PWR...TECHNIC STAT INT SAMP TREND   SPACE
ANTHOL VAL/FREE 20. PAGE 22 G0428

B63
HEYEL C.,THE ENCYCLOPEDIA OF MANAGEMENT. WOR+45   MGT
MARKET TOP/EX TEC/DEV AUTOMAT LEAD ADJUST...STAT   INDUS
CHARTS GAME ANTHOL BIBLIOG. PAGE 26 G0509   ADMIN
                                                      FINAN

B63
JACOB H.,GERMAN ADMINISTRATION SINCE BISMARCK: ADMIN
CENTRAL AUTHORITY VERSUS LOCAL AUTONOMY. GERMANY   NAT/G
GERMANY/W LAW POL/PAR CONTROL CENTRAL TOTALISM   LOC/G
FASCISM...MAJORIT DECISION STAT CHARTS GOV/COMP   POLICY
19/20 BISMARCK/O HITLER/A WEIMAR/REP. PAGE 28 G0551

B63
KORNHAUSER W.,SCIENTISTS IN INDUSTRY: CONFLICT AND   CREATE
ACCOMMODATION. USA+45 R+D LG/CO NAT/G TEC/DEV   INDUS
CONTROL ADJUST ATTIT...MGT STAT INT BIBLIOG 20.   PROF/ORG
PAGE 31 G0614   GP/REL

B63
MILBRATH L.W.,THE WASHINGTON LOBBYISTS. CONSTN   LOBBY
BAL/PWR CONTROL LEAD TASK CHOOSE SUPEGO...DECISION   POLICY
STAT CHARTS BIBLIOG. PAGE 39 G0767   PERS/REL

B63
MULLENBACH P.,CIVILIAN NUCLEAR POWER: ECONOMIC   USA+45
ISSUES AND POLICY FORMATION. FINAN INT/ORG DELIB/GP   ECO/DEV
ACT/RES ECO/TAC ATTIT SUPEGO HEALTH ORD/FREE PWR   NUC/PWR
...POLICY CONCPT MATH STAT CHARTS VAL/FREE 20
COLD/WAR. PAGE 40 G0792

B63
NAFZIGER R.O.,INTRODUCTION TO MASS COMMUNICATIONS   COM/IND
RESEARCH (REV. ED.). ACT/RES...STAT CON/ANAL METH   CONCPT
20. PAGE 41 G0801   PHIL/SCI
                                                      CREATE

B63
WALES H.G.,A BASIC BIBLIOGRAPHY ON MARKETING   BIBLIOG/A
RESEARCH (REV. ED.). ATTIT...MGT STAT INT QU SAMP   MARKET
TREND 20. PAGE 62 G1206   OP/RES
                                                      METH/COMP

S63
ERSKINE H.G.,"THE POLLS: ATOMIC WEAPONS AND NUCLEAR   ATTIT
ENERGY." USA+45 COERCE ORD/FREE...POLICY SOC STAT   INT
CENSUS SAMP VAL/FREE 20. PAGE 18 G0350   NUC/PWR

S63
WILES P.J.D.,"WILL CAPITALISM AND COMMUNISM   PLAN
SPONTANEOUSLY CONVERGE." COM FUT USA+45 ECO/DEV   TEC/DEV
DIST/IND MARKET CAP/ISM ECO/TAC RIGID/FLEX WEALTH   USSR
MARXISM SOCISM...MATH STAT TREND COMPUT/IR 20.
PAGE 63 G1240

B64
BALASSA B.,TRADE PROSPECTS FOR DEVELOPING   INT/TRADE
COUNTRIES. WOR+45 ECO/DEV AGRI EXTR/IND INDUS   ECO/UNDEV
CREATE PLAN PRICE...ECOMETRIC CLASSIF TIME/SEQ   TREND
GEN/METH. PAGE 5 G0087   STAT

B64
BRILLOUIN L.,SCIENTIFIC UNCERTAINTY AND   PHIL/SCI
INFORMATION. PROB/SOLV AUTOMAT PERCEPT ORD/FREE   NEW/IDEA
...MATH REGRESS STAT STYLE OBS IDEA/COMP SIMUL   METH/CNCPT
TIME. PAGE 9 G0169   CREATE

B64
COOMBS C.H.,A THEORY OF DATA....MGT PHIL/SCI SOC   CON/ANAL
CLASSIF MATH PROBABIL STAT QU. PAGE 13 G0254   GEN/METH
                                                      TESTS
                                                      PSY

B64
FEI J.C.H.,DEVELOPMENT OF THE LABOR SURPLUS   ECO/TAC
ECONOMY: THEORY AND POLICY. WOR+45 AGRI INDUS   POLICY
MARKET PROB/SOLV TEC/DEV...STAT CHARTS GEN/LAWS   WORKER
METH 20 THIRD/WRLD. PAGE 18 G0361   ECO/UNDEV

B64
HEKHUIS D.J.,INTERNATIONAL STABILITY: MILITARY,   TEC/DEV
ECONOMIC AND POLITICAL DIMENSIONS. FUT WOR+45 LAW   DETER
ECO/UNDEV INT/ORG NAT/G VOL/ASSN FORCES ACT/RES   REGION
BAL/PWR PWR WEALTH...STAT UN 20. PAGE 25 G0503

B64
ORTH C.D.,ADMINISTERING RESEARCH AND DEVELOPMENT.   MGT
FINAN PLAN PROB/SOLV ADMIN ROUTINE...METH/CNCPT   R+D
STAT CHARTS METH 20. PAGE 43 G0847   LG/CO
                                                      INDUS

B64
PETERSON W.,THE POLITICS OF POPULATION. COM EUR+WWI   PLAN
FUT MOD/EUR S/ASIA USA+45 USA-45 WOR+45 LAW CULTURE   CENSUS
FAM SECT DOMIN EDU/PROP BIO/SOC HEALTH ORD/FREE   POLICY
...GEOG STAT TIME/SEQ TREND VAL/FREE. PAGE 44 G0871

B64
SCHERER F.M.,THE WEAPONS ACQUISITION PROCESS: INDUS
ECONOMIC INCENTIVES. BOSTON: DIVISION OF RESEARCH,   ACT/RES
GRADUATE SCHOOL OF BUSINESS. USA+45 FINAN NAT/G   WEAPON
DELIB/GP ECO/TAC RIGID/FLEX WEALTH...MGT MATH STAT

CHARTS VAL/FREE 20. PAGE 49 G0965

S64

MAHALANOBIS P.C.,"PERSPECTIVE PLANNING IN INDIA: STATISTICAL TOOLS." INDIA S/ASIA STRATA AGRI DIST/IND FINAN INDUS SERV/IND NAT/G ECO/TAC ORD/FREE WEALTH...POLICY TREND SIMUL VAL/FREE 20. PAGE 35 G0695

PLAN
STAT

S64

MARES V.E.,"EAST EUROPE'S SECOND CHANCE." COM EUR+WWI HUNGARY ROMANIA USSR YUGOSLAVIA ECO/UNDEV NAT/G TOP/EX CREATE PLAN TEC/DEV REGION NAT/LISM RIGID/FLEX PWR...CONCPT STAT COMECON 20. PAGE 36 G0705

VOL/ASSN
ECO/TAC

B65

ALKER H.R. JR.,MATHEMATICS AND POLITICS. PROB/SOLV ...DECISION PHIL/SCI CLASSIF QUANT STAT GAME GEN/LAWS INDEX. PAGE 2 G0042

GEN/METH
CONCPT
MATH

B65

BLOOMFIELD L.,SOVIET INTERESTS IN ARMS CONTROL AND DISARMAMENT* THE DECADE UNDER KHRUSHCHEV 1954-1964. ASIA FORCES ACT/RES EDU/PROP DETER NUC/PWR WEAPON COST ATTIT...PHIL/SCI CLASSIF STAT NET/THEORY GAME BIBLIOG. PAGE 7 G0139

USSR
ARMS/CONT
DIPLOM
TREND

B65

FOSTER P.,EDUCATION AND SOCIAL CHANGE IN GHANA. GHANA CULTURE STRUCT ECO/UNDEV TEC/DEV REGION EFFICIENCY LITERACY ALL/VALS SOVEREIGN...STAT METH/COMP 19/20 GOLD/COAST. PAGE 20 G0385

SCHOOL
CREATE
SOCIETY

B65

HASSON J.A.,THE ECONOMICS OF NUCLEAR POWER. INDIA UK USA+45 WOR+45 INT/ORG TEC/DEV COST...SOC STAT CHARTS 20 EURATOM. PAGE 25 G0490

NUC/PWR
INDUS
ECO/DEV
METH

B65

HEER D.M.,AFTER NUCLEAR ATTACK: A DEMOGRAPHIC INQUIRY. USA+45 ECO/DEV SECT WORKER SEX...HEAL SOC STAT PREDICT CHARTS 20 NEGRO. PAGE 25 G0500

GEOG
NUC/PWR
CENSUS
WAR

B65

HICKMAN B.G.,QUANTITATIVE PLANNING OF ECONOMIC POLICY. FRANCE NETHERLAND OP/RES PRICE ROUTINE UTIL ...POLICY DECISION ECOMETRIC METH/CNCPT STAT STYLE CHINJAP. PAGE 26 G0511

PROB/SOLV
PLAN
QUANT

B65

JANDA K.,DATA PROCESSING: APPLICATIONS TO POLITICAL RESEARCH....STAT CON/ANAL. PAGE 28 G0557

DECISION
COMPUTER
TEC/DEV
METH

B65

JASNY H.,KHRUSHCHEV'S CROP POLICY. USSR ECO/DEV PLAN MARXISM...STAT 20 KHRUSH/N RESOURCE/N. PAGE 29 G0562

AGRI
NAT/G
POLICY
ECO/TAC

B65

KANTOROVICH L.V.,THE BEST USE OF ECONOMIC RESOURCES. USSR SOCIETY FINAN ACT/RES TEC/DEV ECO/TAC PRICE CONTROL COST DEMAND EFFICIENCY OPTIMAL...MGT STAT. PAGE 29 G0572

PLAN
MATH
DECISION

B65

KASER M.,COMECON* INTEGRATION PROBLEMS OF THE PLANNED ECONOMIES. INT/ORG TEC/DEV INT/TRADE PRICE ADMIN ADJUST CENTRAL...STAT TIME/SEQ ORG/CHARTS COMECON. PAGE 29 G0579

PLAN
ECO/DEV
COM
REGION

B65

KOROL A.G.,SOVIET RESEARCH AND DEVELOPMENT. USSR ACADEM SCHOOL WORKER ROUTINE COST...STAT T 20. PAGE 31 G0615

COM
R+D
FINAN
DIST/IND

B65

OECD,MEDITERRANEAN REGIONAL PROJECT: TURKEY; EDUCATION AND DEVELOPMENT. FUT TURKEY SOCIETY STRATA FINAN NAT/G PROF/ORG PLAN PROB/SOLV ADMIN COST...STAT CHARTS 20 OECD. PAGE 42 G0831

EDU/PROP
ACADEM
SCHOOL
ECO/UNDEV

B65

OECD,THE MEDITERRANEAN REGIONAL PROJECT: PORTUGAL; EDUCATION AND DEVELOPMENT. PORTUGAL SOCIETY STRATA FINAN PROF/ORG WORKER PLAN PROB/SOLV ADMIN...POLICY STAT CHARTS METH 20 OECD. PAGE 42 G0832

EDU/PROP
SCHOOL
ACADEM
ECO/UNDEV

B65

OECD,THE MEDITERRANEAN REGIONAL PROJECT: ITALY;

SCHOOL

EDUCATION AND DEVELOPMENT. ITALY SOCIETY STRATA FINAN NAT/G PROF/ORG WORKER PLAN PROB/SOLV ADMIN ...STAT CHARTS METH 20 OECD. PAGE 42 G0833

EDU/PROP
ECO/UNDEV
ACADEM

B65

OECD,THE MEDITERRANEAN REGIONAL PROJECT: SPAIN; EDUCATION AND DEVELOPMENT. FUT SPAIN STRATA FINAN NAT/G WORKER PLAN PROB/SOLV ADMIN COST...POLICY STAT CHARTS 20 OECD. PAGE 42 G0835

ECO/UNDEV
EDU/PROP
ACADEM
SCHOOL

B65

ORG FOR ECO COOP AND DEVEL,THE MEDITERRANEAN REGIONAL PROJECT: YUGOSLAVIA; EDUCATION AND DEVELOPMENT. YUGOSLAVIA SOCIETY FINAN PROF/ORG PLAN ADMIN COST DEMAND MARXISM...STAT TREND CHARTS METH 20 OECD. PAGE 43 G0843

EDU/PROP
ACADEM
SCHOOL
ECO/UNDEV

B65

US DEPARTMENT OF THE ARMY,NUCLEAR WEAPONS AND THE ATLANTIC ALLIANCE: A BIBLIOGRAPHIC SURVEY. ASIA COM EUR+WWI USA+45 FORCES DIPLOM WEAPON...STAT 20 NATO. PAGE 58 G1131

BIBLIOG/A
NUC/PWR
BAL/PWR

B65

US SENATE COMM GOVT OPERATIONS,ORGANIZATION OF FEDERAL EXECUTIVE DEPARTMENTS AND AGENCIES: REPORT OF MARCH 23, 1965. USA+45 FORCES LEGIS DIPLOM ROUTINE CIVMIL/REL EFFICIENCY FEDERAL...MGT STAT. PAGE 60 G1179

ADMIN
EX/STRUC
GOV/REL
ORG/CHARTS

B65

WISH J.R.,ECONOMIC DEVELOPMENT IN LATIN AMERICA: AN ANNOTATED BIBLIOGRAPHY. L/A+17C COM/IND MARKET R+D CREATE CAP/ISM ATTIT...STAT METH 20. PAGE 64 G1250

BIBLIOG/A
ECO/UNDEV
TEC/DEV
AGRI

S65

ABT C.C.,"CONTROLLING FUTURE ARMS." USSR PLAN BAL/PWR DIPLOM NUC/PWR COST...CLASSIF STAT CHARTS. PAGE 2 G0027

PREDICT
FUT
ARMS/CONT
TEC/DEV

S65

CHU K.,"A DYNAMIC MODEL OF THE FIRM." OP/RES PROB/SOLV...DECISION ECOMETRIC NEW/IDEA STAT GAME ORG/CHARTS SIMUL. PAGE 12 G0230

INDUS
COMPUTER
TEC/DEV

S65

FINK C.F.,"MORE CALCULATIONS ABOUT DETERRENCE." DRIVE...PHIL/SCI PSY STAT TIME/SEQ GAME GEN/LAWS. PAGE 19 G0367

DETER
RECORD
PROBABIL
IDEA/COMP

S65

GREGG P.M.,"DIMENSIONS OF POLITICAL SYSTEMS: FACTOR ANALYSIS OF A CROSS POLITY SURVEY." TEC/DEV ...DECISION PHIL/SCI CONCPT STAT IDEA/COMP GEN/LAWS. PAGE 23 G0447

SIMUL
GEN/METH
CLASSIF

S65

KINTNER W.P.,"THE PROSPECTS FOR WESTERN SCIENCE AND TECHNOLOGY." EUR+WWI FRANCE USA+45 USSR R+D NUC/PWR NATO. PAGE 30 G0598

TEC/DEV
VOL/ASSN
STAT
RECORD

B66

BERND J.L.,MATHEMATICAL APPLICATIONS IN POLITICAL SCIENCE, II. COMPUTER...PROBABIL STAT CHARTS. PAGE 7 G0131

METH
MATH
METH/CNCPT

B66

ECKSTEIN A.,COMMUNIST CHINA'S ECONOMIC GROWTH AND FOREIGN TRADE* IMPLICATIONS FOR US POLICY. COM USA+45 USSR STRUCT INDUS MARKET DIPLOM ECO/TAC FOR/AID INT/TRADE...STAT CHARTS. PAGE 17 G0332

ASIA
ECO/UNDEV
CREATE
PWR

B66

GORDON G.,THE LEGISLATIVE PROCESS AND DIVIDED GOVERNMENT; A CASE STUDY OF THE 86TH CONGRESS. USA+45 POL/PAR PROVS PROB/SOLV BAL/PWR CHOOSE REPRESENT EFFICIENCY ATTIT...POLICY DECISION STAT 20 CONGRESS EISNHWR/DD. PAGE 22 G0434

LEGIS
HABITAT
CHIEF
NAT/G

B66

GOULD J.M.,THE TECHNICAL ELITE. INDUS LABOR TECHRACY...POLICY DECISION STAT CHARTS 20. PAGE 22 G0437

ECO/DEV
TEC/DEV
ELITES
TECHNIC

B66

LECHT L.,GOAL, PRIORITIES, AND DOLLARS: THE NEXT DECADE. SPACE USA+45 SOCIETY AGRI BUDGET FOR/AID ...HEAL SOC/WK STAT CHARTS 20 URBAN/RNWL PUB/TRANS. PAGE 33 G0649

IDEA/COMP
POLICY
CONSEN
PLAN

LEWIS W.A.,DEVELOPMENT PLANNING: THE ESSENTIALS OF   PLAN
ECONOMIC POLICY. USA+45 FINAN INDUS NAT/G WORKER   ECO/DEV
FOR/AID INT/TRADE ADMIN ROUTINE WEALTH...CONCPT   POLICY
STAT. PAGE 34 G0663   CREATE
                                                      B66

MARKHAM J.W.,AN ECONOMIC-MEDIA STUDY OF BOOK   PRESS
PUBLISHING. USA+45 LAW COM/IND ACADEM SCHOOL   ECO/TAC
EDU/PROP AUTOMAT CONTROL...DECISION STAT CHARTS 20   TEC/DEV
CONGRESS. PAGE 36 G0707   NAT/G
                                                      B66

US DEPARTMENT OF LABOR,PRODUCTIVITY: A   BIBLIOG/A
BIBLIOGRAPHY. ECO/DEV INDUS MARKET OP/RES AUTOMAT   PRODUC
COST...STAT 20. PAGE 57 G1119   LABOR
                                                      PLAN
                                                      B66

US PRES COMM ECO IMPACT DEFENS,REPORT* JULY 1965.   ACT/RES
USA+45 ECO/DEV INDUS DELIB/GP FORCES OP/RES   STAT
ARMS/CONT NUC/PWR WEAPON BAL/PAY...PREDICT SIMUL.   WAR
PAGE 59 G1159   BUDGET
                                                      S66

SIMON R.,"THE STATE OF PUBLIC RELATIONS SCHOLARLY   ACADEM
RESEARCH." TEC/DEV TASK MAJORITY PRODUC...TREND   CREATE
CHARTS BIBLIOG 20. PAGE 51 G1000   STAT
                                                      GP/REL
                                                      B67

EISENMENGER R.W.,THE DYNAMICS OF GROWTH IN NEW   ECO/DEV
ENGLAND'S ECONOMY, 1870-1964. USA+45 USA-45 ECO/TAC   AGRI
TAX PAY AUTOMAT GOV/REL ADJUST HABITAT...STAT   INDUS
19/20. PAGE 17 G0340   CAP/ISM
                                                      B67

NORTHRUP H.R.,RESTRICTIVE LABOR PRACTICES IN THE   DIST/IND
SUPERMARKET INDUSTRY. USA+45 INDUS WORKER TEC/DEV   MARKET
BARGAIN PAY CONTROL GP/REL COST...STAT CHARTS NLRB.   LABOR
PAGE 42 G0827   MGT
                                                      B67

US HOUSE COMM SCI ASTRONAUT,AUTHORIZING SECY OF   PHIL/SCI
COMMERCE TO PROVIDE FOR COLLECTION, COMPILATION,   CON/ANAL
CRIT EVALUATION, PUBLICATION, SALE OF STD REF DATA.   STAT
USA+45 TEC/DEV...COMPUT/IR HOUSE/REP. PAGE 59 G1150   R+D
                                                      S67

FRIED M.,"FUNCTIONS OF THE WORKING CLASS COMMUNITY   CLASSIF
IN MODERN URBAN SOCIETY* IMPLICATIONS FOR FORCED   WORKER
RELOCATION." USA+45 INDUS R+D NEIGH PLAN TEC/DEV   MUNIC
PARTIC GP/REL ATTIT...SOC STAT CHARTS. PAGE 20   ADJUST
G0393
                                                      N67

US CONGRESS JT COMM ECO GOVT,BACKGROUND MATERIAL ON   BUDGET
ECONOMY IN GOVERNMENT 1967 (PAMPHLET). WOR+45   COST
ECO/DEV BARGAIN PRICE DEMAND OPTIMAL...STAT   MGT
DEPT/DEFEN. PAGE 57 G1116   NAT/G
                                                      S68

BARAGWANATH L.E.,"SCIENTIFIC CO-OPERATION BETWEEN   R+D
THE UNIVERSITIES AND INDUSTRY - A RESEARCH NOTE."   ACADEM
UK LG/CO CREATE TEC/DEV EDU/PROP ATTIT...PHIL/SCI   INDUS
STAT QU 20. PAGE 5 G0090   GP/REL

STATE GOVERNMENT....SEE PROVS

STATE DEPARTMENT....SEE DEPT/STATE

STATISTICS....SEE STAT, ALSO LOGIC, MATHEMATICS, AND
    LANGUAGE INDEX, P. XIV

STEEDMAN L.B. G0115

STEIN E. G0554

STEIN W. G1033

STEINER G.A. G1034

STEREOTYPE....SEE STERTYP

STERN A.C. G1035

STERN/GANG....STERN GANG (PALESTINE)

STEROTYPE....SEE STERTYP

STERTYP....STEREOTYPE

                                                      B53
EASTON D.,THE POLITICAL SYSTEM, AN INQUIRY INTO THE   R+D
STATE POLITICAL SCIENCE. USA+45 INTELL CREATE   PERCEPT
EDU/PROP RIGID/FLEX KNOWL SKILL...PHIL/SCI NEW/IDEA

STERTYP TOT/POP 20. PAGE 17 G0329
                                                      S57

JANOWITZ M.,"MILITARY ELITES AND THE STUDY OF WAR."   FORCES
USA+45 WOR-45 STRATA NAT/G PROF/ORG TEC/DEV DOMIN   ELITES
EDU/PROP COERCE WAR ATTIT RIGID/FLEX PWR RESPECT
...MGT TREND STERTYP GEN/METH 20. PAGE 28 G0558
                                                      B58

GANGE J.,UNIVERSITY RESEARCH ON INTERNATIONAL   R+D
AFFAIRS. USA+45 ACADEM INT/ORG CONSULT CREATE EXEC   MGT
ROUTINE...QUANT STAT INT STERTYP GEN/METH TOT/POP   DIPLOM
VAL/FREE 20. PAGE 21 G0407
                                                      S58

THOMPSON K.W.,"NATIONAL SECURITY IN A NUCLEAR AGE."   FORCES
USA+45 WOR+45 SOCIETY INT/ORG NAT/G TOP/EX DIPLOM   PWR
DOMIN EDU/PROP LEGIT ARMS/CONT COERCE ORD/FREE   BAL/PWR
...TREND STERTYP TOT/POP VAL/FREE COLD/WAR 20.
PAGE 54 G1068
                                                      B59

POKROVSKY G.I.,SCIENCE AND TECHNOLOGY IN   TEC/DEV
CONTEMPORARY WAR. SPACE USSR WOR+45 NAT/G CONSULT   FORCES
ACT/RES PLAN DETER WEAPON...MARXIST METH/CNCPT   NUC/PWR
CHARTS STERTYP COLD/WAR 20. PAGE 45 G0881   WAR
                                                      B62

FORBES H.W.,THE STRATEGY OF DISARMAMENT. FUT WOR+45   PLAN
INT/ORG VOL/ASSN CONSULT ARMS/CONT COERCE NUC/PWR   FORCES
WAR DRIVE RIGID/FLEX ORD/FREE PWR...POLICY CONCPT   DIPLOM
OBS TREND STERTYP 20. PAGE 19 G0378
                                                      B62

WRIGHT Q.,PREVENTING WORLD WAR THREE. FUT WOR+45   CREATE
CULTURE INT/ORG NAT/G CONSULT FORCES ADMIN   ATTIT
ARMS/CONT DRIVE RIGID/FLEX ORD/FREE SOVEREIGN
...POLICY CONCPT TREND STERTYP COLD/WAR 20. PAGE 64
G1259
                                                      S62

PHIPPS T.E.,"THE CASE FOR DETERRENCE." FUT WOR+45   ATTIT
SOCIETY EX/STRUC FORCES ACT/RES CREATE PLAN TEC/DEV   COERCE
ROUTINE RIGID/FLEX ORD/FREE...POLICY MYTH NEW/IDEA   DETER
STERTYP COLD/WAR 20. PAGE 45 G0876   ARMS/CONT
                                                      S65

DECHERT C.R.,"THE DEVELOPMENT OF CYBERNETICS."   SIMUL
ACT/RES CREATE SKILL...STERTYP METH. PAGE 15 G0290   COMPUT/IR
                                                      PLAN
                                                      DECISION
                                                      S65

KUZMACK A.M.,"TECHNOLOGICAL CHANGE AND STABLE   R+D
DETERRENCE." CREATE EDU/PROP ARMS/CONT WEAPON   DETER
CHOOSE COST DRIVE PERCEPT...RECORD STERTYP TIME.   EQUILIB
PAGE 32 G0627
                                                      S65

RASER J.R.,"WEAPONS DESIGN AND ARMS CONTROL* THE   ARMS/CONT
POLARIS EXAMPLE." DETER NUC/PWR WEAPON CHOOSE   R+D
PERCEPT...STERTYP TIME. PAGE 46 G0904   GEOG
                                                      ACT/RES
                                                      B66

SCHURMANN F.,IDEOLOGY AND ORGANIZATION IN COMMUNIST   MARXISM
CHINA. CHINA/COM LOC/G MUNIC POL/PAR ECO/TAC   STRUCT
CONTROL ATTIT...MGT STERTYP 20 COM/PARTY. PAGE 50   ADMIN
G0981   NAT/G
                                                      S66

KAPLAN M.A.,"THE NEW GREAT DEBATE* TRADITIONALISM   PHIL/SCI
VS SCIENCE IN INTERNATIONAL RELATIONS."...DECISION   CONSERVE
HUM QUANT STYLE NET/THEORY CON/ANAL STERTYP   DIPLOM
GEN/LAWS. PAGE 29 G0577   SIMUL

STEVENSN/A....ADLAI STEVENSON
                                                      B63

HOFSTADTER R.,ANTI-INTELLECTUALISM IN AMERICAN   INTELL
LIFE. USA+45 AGRI INDUS ACADEM TEC/DEV EDU/PROP   EPIST
INGP/REL ATTIT...SOC WORSHIP 20 MCCARTHY/J   CULTURE
STEVENSN/A. PAGE 26 G0522   SOCIETY

STEWARD/JH....JULIAN H. STEWARD

STEWART I. G1036

STIMSON/HL....HENRY L. STIMSON

STOCHASTIC PROCESSES....SEE PROB/SOLV, MODELS INDEX

STOCKHOLM....STOCKHOLM

STOESSINGER J.G. G1037

STOKES/CB....CARL B. STOKES

STOL....SHORT TAKE-OFF AND LANDING AIRCRAFT

STONE J.J. G1038

STONE P.A. G1039

STONE/HF....HARLAN FISKE STONE

STONE/IF....I.F. STONE

STORER N.W. G1040

STORING/HJ....H.J. STORING

STOVER C.F. G1041

STRANGE....ESTRANGEMENT, ALIENATION, IMPERSONALITY

B64
ELLUL J.,THE TECHNOLOGICAL SOCIETY. FUT STRUCT SOC
CREATE AUTOMAT ROUTINE STRANGE ANOMIE MORAL SOCIETY
PHIL/SCI. PAGE 18 G0344 TECHNIC
TEC/DEV

STRASBOURG....STRASBOURG PLAN

STRATA....SOCIAL STRATA, CLASS DIVISION

S39
HECKSCHER G.,"GROUP ORGANIZATION IN SWEDEN." SWEDEN LAISSEZ
STRATA ECO/DEV AGRI INDUS LABOR NAT/G PROF/ORG SOC
ECO/TAC CENTRAL SOCISM...MGT 19/20. PAGE 25 G0499

B45
BUSH V.,SCIENCE, THE ENDLESS FRONTIER. FUT USA-45 R+D
INTELL STRATA ACT/RES CREATE PLAN EDU/PROP ADMIN NAT/G
NUC/PWR PEACE ATTIT HEALTH KNOWL...MAJORIT HEAL MGT
PHIL/SCI CONCPT OBS TREND 20. PAGE 10 G0195

S47
TURNER R.H.,"THE NAVY DISBURSING OFFICER AS A FORCES
BUREAUCRAT" (BMR)" USA-45 LAW STRATA DIST/IND WAR ADMIN
PWR...SOC 20 BUREAUCRCY. PAGE 55 G1083 PERSON
ROLE

B49
ROSENHAUPT H.W.,HOW TO WAGE PEACE. USA+45 SOCIETY INTELL
STRATA STRUCT R+D INT/ORG POL/PAR LEGIS ACT/RES CONCPT
CREATE PLAN EDU/PROP ADMIN EXEC ATTIT ALL/VALS DIPLOM
...TIME/SEQ TREND COLD/WAR 20. PAGE 48 G0937

B54
ROSE A.M.,THEORY AND METHOD IN THE SOCIAL SCIENCES. CONCPT
STRATA R+D NEIGH PARTIC...METH/CNCPT GP/COMP. SOC
PAGE 47 G0934 VOL/ASSN
ROLE

B54
WASHBURNE N.F.,INTERPRETING SOCIAL CHANGE IN CULTURE
AMERICA. USA+45 STRATA FAM NAT/G SECT OP/RES STRUCT
ECO/TAC EDU/PROP HABITAT...SOC TIME/SEQ TREND 20 CREATE
BUREAUCRCY. PAGE 62 G1217 TEC/DEV

C55
BONER H.A.,"HUNGRY GENERATIONS." UK WOR+45 WOR-45 ECO/DEV
STRATA INDUS FAM LABOR CAP/ISM...MGT BIBLIOG 19/20. PHIL/SCI
PAGE 8 G0151 CONCPT
WEALTH

S57
JANOWITZ M.,"MILITARY ELITES AND THE STUDY OF WAR." FORCES
USA+45 WOR-45 STRATA NAT/G PROF/ORG TEC/DEV DOMIN ELITES
EDU/PROP COERCE WAR ATTIT RIGID/FLEX PWR RESPECT
...MGT TREND STERTYP GEN/METH 20. PAGE 28 G0558

S58
DEAN B.V.,"APPLICATION OF OPERATIONS RESEARCH TO DECISION
MANAGERIAL DECISION MAKING" STRATA ACT/RES OP/RES
PROB/SOLV ROLE...SOC PREDICT SIMUL 20. PAGE 15 MGT
G0288 METH/CNCPT

B59
RUSSELL B.,COMMON SENSE AND NUCLEAR WARFARE. WOR+45 ORD/FREE
INTELL SOCIETY STRATA NAT/G TOP/EX EDU/PROP ATTIT ARMS/CONT
PERSON KNOWL MORAL PWR...POLICY CONCPT MYTH NUC/PWR
CON/ANAL COLD/WAR 20. PAGE 48 G0948

B60
GRANICK D.,THE RED EXECUTIVE. COM USA+45 SOCIETY PWR
ECO/DEV INDUS NAT/G POL/PAR EX/STRUC PLAN ECO/TAC STRATA
EDU/PROP ADMIN EXEC ATTIT DRIVE...GP/COMP 20. USSR
PAGE 22 G0440 ELITES

B60
JANOWITZ M.,THE PROFESSIONAL SOLDIER. CULTURE FORCES
STRATA STRUCT FAM PROB/SOLV TEC/DEV COERCE WAR MYTH
CIVMIL/REL NAT/LISM AGE HEREDITY ALL/VALS CONSERVE LEAD
...MGT WORSHIP. PAGE 28 G0560 ELITES

S60
GARFINKEL H.,"THE RATIONAL PROPERTIES OF SCIENTIFIC CREATE
AND COMMON SENSE ACTIVITIES." SOCIETY STRATA PHIL/SCI
ACT/RES CHOOSE...SOC METH/CNCPT NEW/IDEA CONT/OBS
SIMUL TOT/POP VAL/FREE. PAGE 21 G0412

L61
THOMPSON V.A.,"HIERARACHY, SPECIALIZATION, AND PERS/REL
ORGANIZATIONAL CONFLICT" (BMR)" WOR+45 STRATA PROB/SOLV
STRUCT WORKER TEC/DEV GP/REL INGP/REL ATTIT ADMIN
AUTHORIT 20 BUREAUCRCY. PAGE 54 G1069 EX/STRUC

B62
BENNIS W.G.,THE PLANNING OF CHANGE: READINGS IN THE PROB/SOLV
APPLIED BEHAVIORAL SCIENCES. CULTURE STRATA STRUCT CREATE
PLAN GP/REL...SOC T. PAGE 6 G0123 ACT/RES
OP/RES

B64
BAUCHET P.,ECONOMIC PLANNING. FRANCE STRATA LG/CO ECO/DEV
CAP/ISM ADMIN PARL/PROC DEMAND OPTIMAL ATTIT PWR NAT/G
SOCISM...POLICY CHARTS 20. PAGE 5 G0102 PLAN
ECO/TAC

S64
CALDWELL L.K.,"BIOPOLITICS: SCIENCE, ETHICS, AND TEC/DEV
PUBLIC POLICY." FUT USA+45 WOR+45 INTELL STRATA R+D POLICY
NAT/G CONSULT PLAN EDU/PROP ALL/VALS...RELATIV
PHIL/SCI 20. PAGE 10 G0203

S64
KASSOF A.,"THE ADMINISTERED SOCIETY: SOCIETY
TOTALITARIANISM WITHOUT TERROR." COM USSR STRATA DOMIN
AGRI INDUS NAT/G PERF/ART SCHOOL TOP/EX EDU/PROP TOTALSM
ADMIN ORD/FREE PWR...POLICY SOC TIME/SEQ GEN/LAWS
VAL/FREE 20. PAGE 29 G0580

S64
MAHALANOBIS P.C.,"PERSPECTIVE PLANNING IN INDIA: PLAN
STATISTICAL TOOLS." INDIA S/ASIA STRATA AGRI STAT
DIST/IND INDUS SERV/IND NAT/G ECO/TAC
ORD/FREE WEALTH...POLICY TREND SIMUL VAL/FREE 20.
PAGE 35 G0695

S64
NEEDHAM T.,"SCIENCE AND SOCIETY IN EAST AND WEST." ASIA
INTELL STRATA R+D LOC/G NAT/G PROVS CONSULT ACT/RES STRUCT
CREATE PLAN TEC/DEV EDU/PROP ADMIN ATTIT ALL/VALS
...POLICY RELATIV MGT CONCPT NEW/IDEA TIME/SEQ WORK
WORK. PAGE 41 G0815

B65
BENTWICH J.S.,EDUCATION IN ISRAEL. ISRAEL CULTURE SECT
STRATA PROB/SOLV TEC/DEV ADJUST ALL/VALS 20 JEWS. EDU/PROP
PAGE 7 G0125 ACADEM
SCHOOL

B65
OECD,MEDITERRANEAN REGIONAL PROJECT: TURKEY; EDU/PROP
EDUCATION AND DEVELOPMENT. FUT TURKEY SOCIETY ACADEM
STRATA FINAN NAT/G PROF/ORG PLAN PROB/SOLV ADMIN SCHOOL
COST...STAT CHARTS 20 OECD. PAGE 42 G0831 ECO/UNDEV

B65
OECD,THE MEDITERRANEAN REGIONAL PROJECT: PORTUGAL; EDU/PROP
EDUCATION AND DEVELOPMENT. PORTUGAL SOCIETY STRATA SCHOOL
FINAN PROF/ORG WORKER PLAN PROB/SOLV ADMIN...POLICY ACADEM
STAT CHARTS METH 20 OECD. PAGE 42 G0832 ECO/UNDEV

B65
OECD,THE MEDITERRANEAN REGIONAL PROJECT: ITALY; SCHOOL
EDUCATION AND DEVELOPMENT. ITALY SOCIETY STRATA EDU/PROP
FINAN NAT/G PROF/ORG WORKER PLAN PROB/SOLV ADMIN ECO/UNDEV
...STAT CHARTS METH 20 OECD. PAGE 42 G0833 ACADEM

B65
OECD,THE MEDITERRANEAN REGIONAL PROJECT: SPAIN; ECO/UNDEV
EDUCATION AND DEVELOPMENT. FUT SPAIN STRATA FINAN EDU/PROP
NAT/G WORKER PLAN PROB/SOLV ADMIN COST...POLICY ACADEM
STAT CHARTS 20 OECD. PAGE 42 G0835 SCHOOL

B65
SMITH E.A.,SOCIAL WELFARE: PRINCIPLES AND CONCEPTS. CONCPT
STRATA STRUCT CONSULT WORKER ACT/RES CREATE PLAN SOC/WK
TEC/DEV ROUTINE GP/REL UTOPIA...SOC 20. PAGE 51 RECEIVE
G1014 ORD/FREE

B66
MILLAR R.,THE NEW CLASSES. UK ELITES SOCIETY INDUS STRUCT
AUTOMAT GP/REL SOC/INTEG 20 INDUS/REV. PAGE 39 STRATA

G0770   TEC/DEV
                                                         CREATE

                                                              S67
CARR E.H.,"REVOLUTION FROM ABOVE." USSR STRATA   AGRI
FINAN INDUS NAT/G DOMIN LEAD GP/REL INGP/REL OWN   POLICY
PRODUC PWR 20 STALIN/J. PAGE 11 G0214   COM
                                                         EFFICIENCY

                                                              S67
MEHTA A.,"INDIA* POVERTY AND CHANGE." STRATA INDUS   INDIA
CREATE ECO/TAC FOR/AID NEUTRAL GP/REL ADJUST INCOME   SOCIETY
...NEW/IDEA 20. PAGE 38 G0751   ECO/UNDEV
                                                         TEC/DEV

                                                              S67
WARE R.S.,"FORECAST A.D. 2000." SOCIETY STRATA   NUC/PWR
ECO/UNDEV INDUS FORCES EDU/PROP AUTOMAT COERCE REV   GEOG
WEAPON ATTIT PREDICT. PAGE 62 G1213   TEC/DEV
                                                         WAR

                                                              N67
ASIAN STUDIES CENTER,FOUR ARTICLES ON POPULATION   ASIA
AND FAMILY LIFE IN TAIWAN (ASIAN STUDIES PAPERS,   FAM
REPRINT SERIES NO. 2). CULTURE STRATA ECO/UNDEV   CENSUS
AGRI INDUS R+D KIN MUNIC...GEOG SOC CHARTS 20.   ANTHOL
PAGE 4 G0072

STRATEGY....SEE PLAN, DECISION

STRATIFICATION....SEE STRATA

STRAUSS G. G0958

STRAUSS L.L. G1042

STREAT R. G1043

STREET D. G1044

STRESEMANN, GUSTAV....SEE STRESEMN/G

STRESEMN/G....GUSTAV STRESEMANN

                                                              B53
BRETTON H.L.,STRESEMANN AND THE REVISION OF   POLICY
VERSAILLES: A FIGHT FOR REASON. EUR+WWI GERMANY   DIPLOM
FORCES BUDGET ARMS/CONT WAR SUPEGO...BIBLIOG 20   BIOG
TREATY VERSAILLES STRESEMN/G. PAGE 9 G0167

STRESS....SEE PERSON, DRIVE

STRIKE....STRIKE OF WORKERS

STRIKES....SEE LABOR, GP/REL, FINAN

STRUC/FUNC....STRUCTURAL-FUNCTIONAL THEORY

STRUCT...SOCIAL STRUCTURE

                                                              S38
LUNDBERG G.A.,"THE CONCEPT OF LAW IN THE SOCIAL   EPIST
SCIENCES"(BMR)" CULTURE INTELL SOCIETY STRUCT   GEN/LAWS
CREATE...NEW/IDEA 20. PAGE 34 G0678   CONCPT
                                                         PHIL/SCI

                                                              B40
ZNANIECKI F.,THE SOCIAL ROLE OF THE MAN OF   ROLE
KNOWLEDGE. UNIV SOCIETY STRUCT TEC/DEV...EPIST   INTELL
PHIL/SCI SOC NEW/IDEA 20. PAGE 65 G1269   KNOWL
                                                         INGP/REL

                                                              B42
BINGHAM A.M.,THE TECHNIQUES OF DEMOCRACY. USA-45   POPULISM
CONSTN STRUCT POL/PAR LEGIS PLAN PARTIC CHOOSE   ORD/FREE
REPRESENT NAT/LISM TOTALISM...MGT 20. PAGE 7 G0136   ADMIN
                                                         NAT/G

                                                              B47
WHITEHEAD T.N.,LEADERSHIP IN A FREE SOCIETY; A   INDUS
STUDY IN HUMAN RELATIONS BASED ON AN ANALYSIS OF   LEAD
PRESENT-DAY INDUSTRIAL CIVILIZATION. WOR-45 STRUCT   ORD/FREE
R+D LABOR LG/CO SML/CO WORKER PLAN PROB/SOLV   SOCIETY
TEC/DEV DRIVE...MGT 20. PAGE 63 G1234

                                                              B48
KILE O.M.,THE FARM BUREAU MOVEMENT: THE FARM BUREAU   AGRI
THROUGH THREE DECADES. NAT/G LEGIS LEAD LOBBY   STRUCT
GP/REL INCOME POLICY. PAGE 30 G0596   VOL/ASSN
                                                         DOMIN

                                                              B49
ROSENHAUPT H.W.,HOW TO WAGE PEACE. USA+45 SOCIETY   INTELL
STRATA STRUCT R+D INT/ORG POL/PAR LEGIS ACT/RES   CONCPT
CREATE PLAN EDU/PROP ADMIN EXEC ATTIT ALL/VALS   DIPLOM
...TIME/SEQ TREND COLD/WAR 20. PAGE 48 G0937

                                                              B50
SURANYI-UNGER T.,PRIVATE ENTERPRISE AND   PLAN
GOVERNMENTAL PLANNING. STRUCT FINAN BAL/PWR   NAT/G
HAPPINESS DRIVE NEW/LIB PLURISM...MATH QUANT STAT   LAISSEZ
TREND BIBLIOG. PAGE 53 G1047   POLICY

                                                              S52
KECSKEMETI P.,"THE 'POLICY SCIENCES': ASPIRATION   CREATE
AND OUTLOOK." UNIV CULTURE INTELL SOCIETY STRUCT   NEW/IDEA
EDU/PROP ATTIT PERCEPT RIGID/FLEX KNOWL...PHIL/SCI
METH/CNCPT OBS 20. PAGE 30 G0589

                                                              B54
MCCLOSKEY J.F.,OPERATIONS RESEARCH FOR MANAGEMENT.   OP/RES
STRUCT COMPUTER ADMIN ROUTINE...PHIL/SCI CONCPT   MGT
METH/CNCPT TREND ANTHOL BIBLIOG 20. PAGE 37 G0731   METH/COMP
                                                         TEC/DEV

                                                              B54
SPROTT W.J.H.,SCIENCE AND SOCIAL ACTION. STRUCT   SOC
ACT/RES CRIME GP/REL INGP/REL ANOMIE...PSY   CULTURE
SOC/INTEG 19/20. PAGE 52 G1027   PHIL/SCI

                                                              B54
WASHBURNE N.F.,INTERPRETING SOCIAL CHANGE IN   CULTURE
AMERICA. USA+45 STRATA FAM NAT/G SECT OP/RES   STRUCT
ECO/TAC EDU/PROP HABITAT...SOC TIME/SEQ TREND 20   CREATE
BUREAUCRCY. PAGE 62 G1217   TEC/DEV

                                                              S54
FORM W.H.,"THE PLACE OF SOCIAL STRUCTURE IN THE   HABITAT
DETERMINATION OF LAND USE: SOME IMPLICATIONS FOR A   MARKET
THEORY OF URBAN ECOLOGY" (BMR)" STRUCT...GEOG   ORD/FREE
PHIL/SCI SOC 20. PAGE 19 G0381   MUNIC

                                                              B55
LIPPMAN W.,THE PUBLIC PHILOSOPHY. EX/STRUC TOP/EX   MAJORIT
LOBBY RATIONAL POPULISM...POLICY SOC CONCPT PREDICT   STRUCT
GP/COMP IDEA/COMP. PAGE 34 G0673   PWR
                                                         TOTALISM

                                                              B55
RILEY V.,INTERINDUSTRY ECONOMIC STUDIES. USA+45   BIBLIOG
COMPUTER ADMIN OPTIMAL PRODUC...MGT CLASSIF STAT.   ECO/DEV
PAGE 47 G0922   PLAN
                                                         STRUCT

                                                              S55
DRUCKER P.F.,"'MANAGEMENT SCIENCE' AND THE   MGT
MANAGER." PLAN ROUTINE RIGID/FLEX...METH/CNCPT LOG   STRUCT
HYPO/EXP. PAGE 16 G0315   DECISION
                                                         RATIONAL

                                                              B56
VUCINICH A.,THE SOVIET ACADEMY OF SCIENCES. USSR   PHIL/SCI
STRUCT ACADEM NAT/G EDU/PROP ADMIN LEAD ROLE   CREATE
...BIBLIOG 20 ACADEM/SCI. PAGE 61 G1203   INTELL
                                                         PROF/ORG

                                                              S56
EASTON D.,"LIMITS OF THE EQUILIBRIUM MODEL IN   METH/CNCPT
SOCIAL RESEARCH." STRUCT GP/REL PWR...PHIL/SCI   GEN/METH
CLASSIF. PAGE 17 G0330   R+D
                                                         QUANT

                                                              B57
MERTON R.K.,SOCIAL THEORY AND SOCIAL STRUCTURE   SOC
(REV. ED.). INTELL SECT WORKER OP/RES EDU/PROP   GEN/LAWS
ADMIN INGP/REL ANOMIE PERSON...AUD/VIS T 20   SOCIETY
BUREAUCRCY. PAGE 38 G0759   STRUCT

                                                              S57
EASTON D.,"AN APPROACH TO THE ANALYSIS OF POLITICAL   STRUCT
SYSTEMS." R+D EDU/PROP KNOWL SKILL...POLICY SOC   PHIL/SCI
METH/CNCPT NEW/IDEA SELF/OBS CHARTS GEN/METH
TOT/POP. PAGE 17 G0331

                                                              B58
LIPPITT R.,DYNAMICS OF PLANNED CHANGE. STRUCT   VOL/ASSN
ACT/RES ROUTINE INGP/REL PWR...POLICY METH/CNCPT   ORD/FREE
BIBLIOG. PAGE 34 G0672   PLAN
                                                         CREATE

                                                              S58
DAVENPORT J.,"ARMS AND THE WELFARE STATE." INTELL   USA+45
STRUCT FORCES CREATE ECO/TAC FOR/AID DOMIN LEGIT   NAT/G
ADMIN WAR ORD/FREE PWR...POLICY SOC CONCPT MYTH OBS   USSR
TREND COLD/WAR TOT/POP 20. PAGE 14 G0276

                                                              B59
DAHRENDORF R.,CLASS AND CLASS CONFLICT IN   VOL/ASSN
INDUSTRIAL SOCIETY. LABOR NAT/G COERCE ROLE PLURISM   STRUCT
...POLICY MGT CONCPT CLASSIF. PAGE 14 G0271   SOC
                                                         GP/REL

WARD B.,5 IDEAS THAT CHANGE THE WORLD. WOR+45
WOR-45 SOCIETY STRUCT AGRI INDUS INT/ORG NAT/G
FORCES ACT/RES ARMS/CONT TOTALISM ATTIT DRIVE
GEN/LAWS. PAGE 62 G1210

B59
ECO/UNDEV
ALL/VALS
NAT/LISM
COLONIAL

BENDIX R.,"INDUSTRIALIZATION, IDEOLOGIES, AND
SOCIAL STRUCTURE" (BMR)" UK USA-45 USSR STRUCT
WORKER GP/REL EFFICIENCY...IDEA/COMP 20. PAGE 6
G0117

S59
INDUS
ATTIT
MGT
ADMIN

CORY R.H. JR.,"INTERNATIONAL INSPECTION FROM
PROPOSALS TO REALIZATION." WOR+45 TEC/DEV ECO/TAC
ADJUD ORD/FREE PWR WEALTH...RECORD VAL/FREE 20.
PAGE 13 G0258

S59
STRUCT
PSY
ARMS/CONT
NUC/PWR

JANOWITZ M.,"CHANGING PATTERNS OF ORGANIZATIONAL
AUTHORITY: THE MILITARY ESTABLISHMENT" (BMR)"
USA+45 ELITES STRUCT EX/STRUC PLAN DOMIN AUTOMAT
NUC/PWR WEAPON 20. PAGE 28 G0559

S59
FORCES
AUTHORIT
ADMIN
TEC/DEV

MILBURN T.W.,"WHAT CONSTITUTES EFFECTIVE
DETERRENCE." USA+45 USSR WOR+45 STRUCT FORCES
ACT/RES PLAN SUPEGO KNOWL ORD/FREE PWR...RELATIV
PSY CONCPT VAL/FREE 20 COLD/WAR. PAGE 39 G0768

S59
INTELL
ATTIT
DETER
NUC/PWR

JANOWITZ M.,THE PROFESSIONAL SOLDIER. CULTURE
STRATA STRUCT FAM PROB/SOLV TEC/DEV COERCE WAR
CIVMIL/REL NAT/LISM AGE HEREDITY ALL/VALS CONSERVE
...MGT WORSHIP. PAGE 28 G0560

B60
FORCES
MYTH
LEAD
ELITES

WOETZEL R.K.,THE INTERNATIONAL CONTROL OF AIRSPACE
AND OUTERSPACE. FUT WOR+45 AIR CONSTN STRUCT
CONSULT PLAN TEC/DEV ADJUD RIGID/FLEX KNOWL
ORD/FREE PWR...TECHNIC GEOG MGT NEW/IDEA TREND
COMPUT/IR VAL/FREE 20 TREATY. PAGE 64 G1251

B60
INT/ORG
JURID
SPACE
INT/LAW

DEUTSCH K.W.,"TOWARD AN INVENTORY OF BASIC TRENDS
AND PATTERNS IN COMPARATIVE AND INTERNATIONAL
POLITICS." UNIV WOR+45 SOCIETY STRUCT INT/ORG NAT/G
CREATE PLAN EDU/PROP KNOWL...PHIL/SCI METH/CNCPT
STAT SELF/OBS OBS/ENVIR SAMP TREND CON/ANAL CHARTS
SOC/EXP GEN/METH 20. PAGE 15 G0298

L60
R+D
PERCEPT

HAYTON R.D.,"THE ANTARCTIC SETTLEMENT OF 1959." FUT
USA+45 WOR+45 STRUCT R+D INT/ORG EX/STRUC
CREATE TEC/DEV LEGIT PEACE ATTIT SOVEREIGN
...TIME/SEQ 20 TREATY IGY. PAGE 25 G0495

S60
DELIB/GP
JURID
DIPLOM
REGION

JANOWITZ M.,COMMUNITY POLITICAL SYSTEMS. USA+45
SOCIETY INDUS VOL/ASSN TEC/DEV ADMIN LEAD CHOOSE
...SOC SOC/WK 20. PAGE 29 G0561

B61
MUNIC
STRUCT
POL/PAR

THOMPSON V.A.,"HIERARACHY, SPECIALIZATION, AND
ORGANIZATIONAL CONFLICT" (BMR)" WOR+45 STRATA
STRUCT WORKER TEC/DEV GP/REL INGP/REL ATTIT
AUTHORIT 20 BUREAUCRCY. PAGE 54 G1069

L61
PERS/REL
PROB/SOLV
ADMIN
EX/STRUC

TAUBENFELD H.J.,"OUTER SPACE--PAST POLITICS AND
FUTURE POLICY." FUT USA+45 USA-45 WOR+45 AIR INTELL
STRUCT ECO/DEV NAT/G TOP/EX ACT/RES ADMIN ROUTINE
NUC/PWR ATTIT DRIVE...CONCPT TIME/SEQ TREND TOT/POP
20. PAGE 54 G1054

S61
PLAN
SPACE
INT/ORG

BENNIS W.G.,THE PLANNING OF CHANGE: READINGS IN THE
APPLIED BEHAVIORAL SCIENCES. CULTURE STRATA STRUCT
PLAN GP/REL...SOC T. PAGE 6 G0123

B62
PROB/SOLV
CREATE
ACT/RES
OP/RES

GUETZKOW H.,SIMULATION IN SOCIAL SCIENCE: READINGS.
STRUCT OP/RES ADMIN AUTOMAT FEEDBACK...MGT PSY SOC
STYLE BIBLIOG. PAGE 23 G0459

B62
SIMUL
TEC/DEV
COMPUTER
GAME

ACKOFF R.L.,A MANAGER'S GUIDE TO OPERATIONS
RESEARCH. STRUCT INDUS PROB/SOLV ROUTINE 20. PAGE 2
G0028

B63
OP/RES
MGT
GP/REL
ADMIN

FLORES E.,LAND REFORM AND THE ALLIANCE FOR PROGRESS
(PAMPHLET). L/A+17C USA+45 STRUCT ECO/UNDEV NAT/G

B63
AGRI
INT/ORG

WORKER CREATE PLAN ECO/TAC COERCE REV 20. PAGE 19
G0373

DIPLOM
POLICY

KREPS J.,AUTOMATION AND THE OLDER WORKER: AN
ANNOTATED BIBLIOGRAPHY (PAMPHLET). USA+45 STRUCT
ECO/DEV INDUS TEC/DEV. PAGE 31 G0620

B63
BIBLIOG/A
WORKER
AGE/O
AUTOMAT

BEGUIN H.,"ASPECTS GEOGRAPHIQUE DE LA
POLARISATION." FUT WOR+45 SOCIETY STRUCT ECO/DEV
R+D BAL/PWR ADMIN ATTIT RIGID/FLEX HEALTH WEALTH
...CHARTS 20. PAGE 6 G0114

L63
ECO/UNDEV
GEOG
DIPLOM

ELLUL J.,THE TECHNOLOGICAL SOCIETY. FUT STRUCT
CREATE AUTOMAT ROUTINE STRANGE ANOMIE MORAL
PHIL/SCI. PAGE 18 G0344

B64
SOC
SOCIETY
TECHNIC
TEC/DEV

MASTERS N.A.,STATE POLITICS AND THE PUBLIC SCHOOLS.
STRUCT FINAN ADMIN LOBBY GP/REL PWR BIBLIOG.
PAGE 36 G0720

B64
EDU/PROP
PROVS
DOMIN

POWELSON J.P.,LATIN AMERICA: TODAY'S ECONOMIC AND
SOCIAL REVOLUTION. L/A+17C INTELL SOCIETY STRUCT
AGRI INDUS NAT/G DIPLOM ECO/TAC REV...POLICY 20.
PAGE 45 G0887

B64
ECO/UNDEV
WEALTH
ADJUST
PLAN

WHEELER-BENNETT J.W.,THE NEMESIS OF POWER (2ND
ED.). EUR+WWI GERMANY TOP/EX TEC/DEV ADMIN WAR
PERS RIGID/FLEX ROLE ORD/FREE PWR FASCISM 20
HITLER/A. PAGE 63 G1231

B64
FORCES
NAT/G
GP/REL
STRUCT

WIRTH L.,ON CITIES AND SOCIAL LIFE: SELECTED
PAPERS. PLAN PROB/SOLV RACE/REL CONSEN ATTIT
HABITAT PERSON...POLICY SOC CONCPT ANTHOL BIBLIOG
20. PAGE 64 G1249

B64
GEN/LAWS
SOCIETY
NEIGH
STRUCT

NEEDHAM T.,"SCIENCE AND SOCIETY IN EAST AND WEST."
INTELL STRATA R+D LOC/G NAT/G PROVS CONSULT ACT/RES
CREATE PLAN TEC/DEV EDU/PROP ADMIN ATTIT ALL/VALS
...POLICY RELATIV MGT CONCPT NEW/IDEA TIME/SEQ WORK
WORK. PAGE 41 G0815

S64
ASIA
STRUCT

FOSTER P.,EDUCATION AND SOCIAL CHANGE IN GHANA.
GHANA CULTURE STRUCT ECO/UNDEV TEC/DEV REGION
EFFICIENCY LITERACY ALL/VALS SOVEREIGN...STAT
METH/COMP 19/20 GOLD/COAST. PAGE 20 G0385

B65
SCHOOL
CREATE
SOCIETY

IANNI O.,ESTADO E CAPITALISMO. L/A+17C FINAN
TEC/DEV ECO/TAC ORD/FREE WEALTH POLICY. PAGE 28
G0542

B65
ECO/UNDEV
STRUCT
INDUS
NAT/G

SMITH E.A.,SOCIAL WELFARE: PRINCIPLES AND CONCEPTS.
STRATA STRUCT CONSULT WORKER ACT/RES CREATE PLAN
TEC/DEV ROUTINE GP/REL UTOPIA...SOC 20. PAGE 51
G1014

B65
CONCPT
SOC/WK
RECEIVE
ORD/FREE

ECKSTEIN A.,COMMUNIST CHINA'S ECONOMIC GROWTH AND
FOREIGN TRADE* IMPLICATIONS FOR US POLICY. COM
USA+45 USSR STRUCT INDUS MARKET DIPLOM ECO/TAC
FOR/AID INT/TRADE...STAT CHARTS. PAGE 17 G0332

B66
ASIA
ECO/UNDEV
CREATE
PWR

FALK R.A.,ON MINIMIZING THE USE OF NUCLEAR WEAPONS;
THREE ESSAYS; RESEARCH MONOGRAPH NO. 23. WOR+45
STRUCT CREATE NUC/PWR REV CONSERVE...POLICY
NET/THEORY IDEA/COMP GEN/LAWS GEN/METH. PAGE 18
G0359

B66
DIPLOM
EQUILIB
PHIL/SCI
PROB/SOLV

LILLEY S.,MEN, MACHINES AND HISTORY: THE STORY OF
TOOLS AND MACHINES IN RELATION TO SOCIAL PROGRESS.
PREHIST SPACE STRUCT COMPUTER AUTOMAT NUC/PWR
...POLICY SOC. PAGE 34 G0667

B66
AGRI
TEC/DEV
SOCIETY

MILLAR R.,THE NEW CLASSES. UK ELITES SOCIETY INDUS
AUTOMAT GP/REL SOC/INTEG 20 INDUS/REV. PAGE 39
G0770

B66
STRUCT
STRATA
TEC/DEV
CREATE

SCHURMANN F.,IDEOLOGY AND ORGANIZATION IN COMMUNIST

B66
MARXISM

CHINA. CHINA/COM LOC/G MUNIC POL/PAR ECO/TAC
CONTROL ATTIT...MGT STERTYP 20 COM/PARTY. PAGE 50
G0981
STRUCT
ADMIN
NAT/G

L66
PACKENHAM R.A.,"POLITICAL-DEVELOPMENT DOCTRINES IN
THE AMERICAN FOREIGN AID PROGRAM." STRUCT R+D
CREATE DIPLOM AID. PAGE 43 G0855
FOR/AID
ECO/UNDEV
GEN/LAWS

L66
ZOPPO C.E.,"NUCLEAR TECHNOLOGY, MULTIPOLARITY, AND
INTERNATIONAL STABILITY." ASIA RUSSIA USA+45 STRUCT
TOP/EX BAL/PWR DIPLOM DETER CIVMIL/REL NAT/COMP.
PAGE 65 G1270
NET/THEORY
ORD/FREE
DECISION
NUC/PWR

S66
COHEN A.,"THE TECHNOLOGY/ELITE APPROACH TO THE
DEVELOPMENTAL PROCESS* PERUVIAN CASE STUDY."
L/A+17C STRUCT CREATE ECO/TAC FOR/AID CIVMIL/REL
MARXISM TECHRACY HYPO/EXP. PAGE 12 G0239
ECO/UNDEV
ELITES
PERU

S66
FLEMING W.G.,"AUTHORITY, EFFICIENCY, AND ROLE
STRESS: PROBLEMS IN THE DEVELOPMENT OF EAST AFRICAN
BUREAUCRACIES." AFR UGANDA STRUCT PROB/SOLV ROUTINE
INGP/REL ROLE...MGT SOC GP/COMP GOV/COMP 20
TANGANYIKA AFRICA/E. PAGE 19 G0371
DOMIN
EFFICIENCY
COLONIAL
ADMIN

S66
RIZOS E.J.,"SCIENCE AND TECHNOLOGY IN COUNTRY
DEVELOPMENT* TOWARDS AN UNDERSTANDING OF THE ROLE
OF PUBLIC ADMINISTRATION." WOR+45 STRUCT INT/ORG
EX/STRUC CREATE PLAN PROB/SOLV EFFICIENCY ROLE
DECISION. PAGE 47 G0924
ADMIN
TEC/DEV
ECO/UNDEV
PHIL/SCI

B67
BENNETT J.W.,HUTTERIAN BRETHREN; THE AGRICULTURAL
ECONOMY AND SOCIAL ORGANIZATION OF A COMMUNAL
PEOPLE. USA+45 SOCIETY FAM KIN TEC/DEV ADJUST...MGT
AUD/VIS GP/COMP 20. PAGE 6 G0121
SECT
AGRI
STRUCT
GP/REL

B67
DE BLIJ H.J.,SYSTEMATIC POLITICAL GEOGRAPHY. WOR+45
STRUCT INT/ORG NAT/G EDU/PROP ADMIN COLONIAL
ROUTINE ORD/FREE PWR...IDEA/COMP T 20. PAGE 15
G0283
GEOG
CONCPT
METH

B67
LAMBERT J.,LATIN AMERICA: SOCIAL STRUCTURES AND
POLITICAL INSTITUTIONS. STRUCT TEC/DEV DIPLOM ADMIN
COLONIAL LEAD ATTIT...SOC CLASSIF NAT/COMP 17/20.
PAGE 32 G0631
L/A+17C
NAT/G
ECO/UNDEV
SOCIETY

B67
MCDOUGAL M.S.,THE INTERPRETATION OF AGREEMENTS AND
WORLD PUBLIC ORDER: PRINCIPLES OF CONTENT AND
PROCEDURE. WOR+45 CONSTN PROB/SOLV TEC/DEV
...CON/ANAL TREATY. PAGE 37 G0740
INT/LAW
STRUCT
ECO/UNDEV
DIPLOM

B67
NASH M.,MACHINE AGE MAYA. GUATEMALA L/A+17C STRUCT
AGRI WORKER CREATE INCOME ATTIT RIGID/FLEX ROLE
...IDEA/COMP SOC/EXP WORSHIP 20 INDIAN/AM. PAGE 41
G0806
INDUS
CULTURE
SOC
MUNIC

B67
US PRES COMN LAW ENFORCE-JUS,THE CHALLENGE OF CRIME
IN A FREE SOCIETY. LAW STRUCT CONSULT ACT/RES
TEC/DEV INGP/REL...SOC/WK 20. PAGE 59 G1160
CT/SYS
PUB/INST
CRIMLGY
CRIME

B67
YAVITZ B.,AUTOMATION IN COMMERCIAL BANKING. USA+45
STRUCT WORKER CREATE OP/RES PLAN ROLE...DECISION
SAMP/SIZ. PAGE 64 G1263
TEC/DEV
FINAN
COMPUT/IR
MGT

S67
WINTHROP H.,"THE MEANING OF DECENTRALIZATION FOR
TWENTIETH-CENTURY MAN." FUT WOR+45 SOCIETY TEC/DEV.
PAGE 64 G1248
ADMIN
STRUCT
CENTRAL
PROB/SOLV

STRUVE/P....PETER STRUVE

STUART DYNASTY....SEE STUART/DYN

STUART/DYN....THE STUART DYNASTY

STUDENTS FOR A DEMOCRATIC SOCIETY....SEE SDS

STUDNT/PWR....STUDENT POWER: STUDENT PROTESTS AND PROTEST
MOVEMENTS

STYCOS J.M. G1045

STYLE....STYLES OF SCIENTIFIC COMMUNICATION

S58
LASSWELL H.D.,"THE SCIENTIFIC STUDY OF
INTERNATIONAL RELATIONS." USA+45 INT/ORG CREATE
EDU/PROP DETER ATTIT PERCEPT PWR...DECISION CONCPT
METH/CNCPT STYLE CON/ANAL 20. PAGE 33 G0642
PHIL/SCI
GEN/METH
DIPLOM

S59
GOLDHAMMER H.,"SOME OBSERVATIONS ON POLITICAL
GAMING." FUT WOR+45 R+D NAT/G ACT/RES CREATE CHOOSE
ATTIT PWR...POLICY CONCPT METH/CNCPT STYLE KNO/TEST
TREND HYPO/EXP GAME GEN/METH METH 20. PAGE 22 G0426
COMPUT/IR
DECISION
DIPLOM

B62
BORKOF H.,COMPUTER APPLICATIONS IN THE BEHAVIORAL
SCIENCES. AUTOMAT UTIL...DECISION PHIL/SCI PSY
METH/CNCPT LING LOG MATH STYLE NET/THEORY COMPUT/IR
PROG/TEAC SIMUL. PAGE 8 G0154
R+D
COMPUTER
PROB/SOLV
FEEDBACK

B62
CALDER R.,LIVING WITH THE ATOM. FUT USA+45 WOR+45
R+D INT/ORG VOL/ASSN DELIB/GP ARMS/CONT...STYLE 20.
PAGE 10 G0200
TEC/DEV
HEALTH
NUC/PWR

B62
GUETZKOW H.,SIMULATION IN SOCIAL SCIENCE: READINGS.
STRUCT OP/RES ADMIN AUTOMAT FEEDBACK...MGT PSY SOC
STYLE BIBLIOG. PAGE 23 G0459
SIMUL
TEC/DEV
COMPUTER
GAME

B63
TOMKINS S.S.,COMPUTER SIMULATION OF PERSONALITY.
R+D TEC/DEV AUTOMAT FEEDBACK ANOMIE PERCEPT...STYLE
PERS/TEST PREDICT COMPUT/IR GP/COMP. PAGE 55 G1075
COMPUTER
PERSON
SIMUL
PROG/TEAC

S63
TANNENBAUM P.H.,"COMMUNICATION OF SCIENCE
INFORMATION." USA+45 TEC/DEV ROUTINE...PHIL/SCI
STYLE 20. PAGE 53 G1051
COM/IND
PRESS
OP/RES
METH/CNCPT

B64
BRILLOUIN L.,SCIENTIFIC UNCERTAINTY AND
INFORMATION. PROB/SOLV AUTOMAT PERCEPT ORD/FREE
...MATH REGRESS STAT STYLE OBS IDEA/COMP SIMUL
TIME. PAGE 9 G0169
PHIL/SCI
NEW/IDEA
METH/CNCPT
CREATE

B64
CONANT J.B.,TWO MODES OF THOUGHT: MY ENCOUNTERS
WITH SCIENCE AND EDUCATION....ART/METH JURID SOC
TREND. PAGE 13 G0249
PHIL/SCI
SKILL
MYTH
STYLE

B64
HAMMOND P.E.,SOCIOLOGISTS AT WORK. VOL/ASSN OP/RES
TEC/DEV CONFER ROUTINE TASK EFFICIENCY...MGT
NEW/IDEA STYLE SAMP. PAGE 24 G0478
R+D
BIOG
SOC

S64
FLORINSKY M.T.,"TRENDS IN THE SOVIET ECONOMY." COM
USA+45 USSR INDUS LABOR NAT/G PLAN TEC/DEV ECO/TAC
ALL/VALS SOCISM...MGT METH/CNCPT STYLE CON/ANAL
GEN/METH WORK 20. PAGE 19 G0374
ECO/DEV
AGRI

B65
HICKMAN B.G.,QUANTITATIVE PLANNING OF ECONOMIC
POLICY. FRANCE NETHERLAND OP/RES PRICE ROUTINE UTIL
...POLICY DECISION ECOMETRIC METH/CNCPT STAT STYLE
CHINJAP. PAGE 26 G0511
PROB/SOLV
PLAN
QUANT

S65
KREITH K.,"PEACE RESEARCH AND GOVERNMENT POLICY."
INTELL NAT/G DIPLOM ECO/TAC CONTROL ARMS/CONT WAR
PERCEPT...DECISION IDEA/COMP. PAGE 31 G0619
PEACE
STYLE
OBS

S66
KAPLAN M.A.,"THE NEW GREAT DEBATE* TRADITIONALISM
VS SCIENCE IN INTERNATIONAL RELATIONS."...DECISION
HUM QUANT STYLE NET/THEORY CON/ANAL STERTYP
GEN/LAWS. PAGE 29 G0577
PHIL/SCI
CONSERVE
DIPLOM
SIMUL

B67
CHARLESWORTH J.C.,CONTEMPORARY POLITICAL ANALYSIS.
INTELL...DECISION METH/CNCPT MATH STYLE CON/ANAL
GAME ANTHOL 20. PAGE 11 G0222
R+D
IDEA/COMP
CONCPT
METH/COMP

SUAREZ/F....FRANCISCO SUAREZ

SUBMARINE....SUBMARINES AND SUBMARINE WARFARE

SUBSIDIES....SEE FINAN

SUBURBS....SUBURBS

SUBVERT....SUBVERSION

SUCCESSION....SUCCESSION (POLITICAL)

SUDAN....SEE ALSO AFR

SUDETENLND....SUDETENLAND

SUEZ CRISIS....SEE NAT/LISM+COERCE, ALSO INDIVIDUAL
   NATIONS, SUEZ

SUEZ....SUEZ CANAL

HOSKINS H.L.,"ARAB SOCIALISM IN THE UAR." ISLAM   ECO/DEV   S63
USSR AGRI INDUS NAT/G TOP/EX CREATE DIPLOM EDU/PROP PLAN
DRIVE KNOWL PWR SOCISM...POLICY CONCPT TREND SUEZ   UAR
20. PAGE 27 G0530

SUFF....SUFFRAGE; SEE ALSO CHOOSE

CRAIG J.,ELEMENTS OF POLITICAL SCIENCE (3 VOLS.). PHIL/SCI   B14
CONSTN AGRI INDUS SCHOOL FORCES TAX CT/SYS SUFF   NAT/G
MORAL WEALTH...CONCPT 19 CIVIL/LIB. PAGE 13 G0259 ORD/FREE

SUFFRAGE....SEE SUFF

SUICIDE....SUICIDE AND RELATED SELF-DESTRUCTIVENESS

SUINN R.M. G1046

SUKARNO/A....ACHMED SUKARNO

SUMATRA....SUMATRA

SUMER....SUMER, A PRE- OR EARLY HISTORIC SOCIETY

SUN/YAT....SUN YAT SEN

SUPEGO....CONSCIENCE, SUPEREGO, RESPONSIBILITY

MASTERS D.,"ONE WORLD OR NONE." FUT WOR+45 INTELL POLICY   L46
INT/ORG ACT/RES EDU/PROP DETER ATTIT RIGID/FLEX   PHIL/SCI
SUPEGO KNOWL...STAT TREND ORG/CHARTS 20. PAGE 36 ARMS/CONT
G0719   NUC/PWR

MANNHEIM K.,FREEDOM, POWER, AND DEMOCRATIC   TEC/DEV   B50
PLANNING. FUT USSR WOR+45 ELITES INTELL SOCIETY   PLAN
NAT/G EDU/PROP ROUTINE ATTIT DRIVE SUPEGO SKILL   CAP/ISM
...POLICY PSY CONCPT TREND GEN/LAWS 20. PAGE 35 UK
G0700

BRETTON H.L.,STRESEMANN AND THE REVISION OF   POLICY   B53
VERSAILLES: A FIGHT FOR REASON. EUR+WWI GERMANY   DIPLOM
FORCES BUDGET ARMS/CONT WAR SUPEGO...BIBLIOG 20   BIOG
TREATY VERSAILLES STRESEMN/G. PAGE 9 G0167

MILBURN T.W.,"WHAT CONSTITUTES EFFECTIVE   INTELL   S59
DETERRENCE." USA+45 USSR WOR+45 STRUCT FORCES   ATTIT
ACT/RES PLAN SUPEGO KNOWL ORD/FREE PWR...RELATIV DETER
PSY CONCPT VAL/FREE 20 COLD/WAR. PAGE 39 G0768   NUC/PWR

OSGOOD C.E.,"A CASE FOR GRADUATED UNILATERAL   ATTIT   S60
DISENGAGEMENT." FUT WOR+45 CULTURE SOCIETY NAT/G EDU/PROP
NUC/PWR WAR PERSON SUPEGO ALL/VALS...POLICY PSY ARMS/CONT
CONCPT COLD/WAR TOT/POP VAL/FREE 20. PAGE 43 G0848

SCHRAMM W.,"MASS COMMUNICATIONS: A BOOK OF READINGS COM/IND   C60
(2ND ED.)" LG/CO PRESS ADMIN CONTROL ROUTINE ATTIT EDU/PROP
ROLE SUPEGO...CHARTS ANTHOL BIBLIOG 20. PAGE 50 CROWD
G0977   MAJORIT

BENNETT J.C.,NUCLEAR WEAPONS AND THE CONFLICT OF POLICY   B62
CONSCIENCE. WOR+45 PROB/SOLV DIPLOM WEAPON SUPEGO NUC/PWR
MORAL...ANTHOL WORSHIP 20. PAGE 6 G0120   WAR

MILBRATH L.W.,THE WASHINGTON LOBBYISTS. CONSTN   LOBBY   B63
BAL/PWR CONTROL LEAD TASK CHOOSE SUPEGO...DECISION POLICY
STAT CHARTS BIBLIOG. PAGE 39 G0767   PERS/REL

MULLENBACH P.,CIVILIAN NUCLEAR POWER: ECONOMIC   USA+45   B63
ISSUES AND POLICY FORMATION. FINAN INT/ORG DELIB/GP ECO/DEV
ACT/RES ECO/TAC ATTIT SUPEGO HEALTH ORD/FREE PWR NUC/PWR
...POLICY CONCPT MATH STAT CHARTS VAL/FREE 20
COLD/WAR. PAGE 40 G0792

SCHRAMM W.,"MASS MEDIA AND NATIONAL DEVELOPMENT: ECO/UNDEV C64
THE ROLE OF INFORMATION IN DEVELOPING COUNTRIES." COM/IND
FINAN R+D ACT/RES PLAN TEC/DEV DIPLOM CHOOSE SUPEGO EDU/PROP
ORD/FREE...BIBLIOG 20. PAGE 50 G0978   MAJORIT

NADER R.,"AUTOMOBILE DESIGN AND THE JUDICIAL   LAW   L67
PROCESS." USA+45 CT/SYS SUPEGO JURID. PAGE 40 G0799 ADJUD
  TEC/DEV
  PROC/MFG

HABERER J.,"POLITICS AND THE COMMUNITY OF SCIENCE." LEAD   S67
USA+45 SOCIETY ACT/RES PARTIC ATTIT PHIL/SCI.   SUPEGO
PAGE 24 G0465   INTELL
  LOBBY

LAY S.H.,"EXCLUSIVE GOVERNMENTAL LIABILITY FOR   NAT/G   S67
SPACE ACCIDENTS." USA+45 LAW FINAN SERV/IND TEC/DEV SUPEGO
ADJUD. PAGE 33 G0646   SPACE
  PROB/SOLV

TIVEY L.,"THE POLITICAL CONSEQUENCES OF ECONOMIC PLAN   S67
PLANNING." UK CONSTN INDUS ACT/RES ADMIN CONTROL POLICY
LOBBY REPRESENT EFFICIENCY SUPEGO SOVEREIGN   NAT/G
...DECISION 20. PAGE 55 G1074

SUPERVISION....SEE EXEC, CONTROL, LEAD, TASK

SUPPES P. G0070

SUPREME/CT....SUPREME COURT (ALL NATIONS)

HELLMAN F.S.,THE NEW DEAL: SELECTED LIST OF   BIBLIOG/A   B40
REFERENCES. USA-45 FINAN LABOR EX/STRUC CREATE   ECO/TAC
INT/TRADE ADMIN CT/SYS 20 SUPREME/CT. PAGE 26 G0505 PLAN
  POLICY

DAVIS K.C.,ADMINISTRATIVE LAW TREATISE (VOLS. I AND ADMIN   B58
IV). NAT/G JUDGE PROB/SOLV ADJUD GP/REL 20   JURID
SUPREME/CT. PAGE 14 G0278   CT/SYS
  EX/STRUC

WEBSTER J.A.,A GENERAL STUDY OF THE DEPARTMENT OF ORD/FREE   B60
DEFENSE INTERNAL SECURITY PROGRAM. USA+45 WORKER PLAN
TEC/DEV ADJUD CONTROL CT/SYS EXEC GOV/REL COST   ADMIN
...POLICY DECISION MGT 20 DEPT/DEFEN SUPREME/CT. NAT/G
PAGE 62 G1221

BAILEY S.K.,AMERICAN POLITICS AND GOVERNMENT.   ANTHOL   B65
USA+45 CONSTN FINAN LABOR POL/PAR DIPLOM ADMIN WAR LEGIS
INGP/REL RACE/REL NEW/LIB 20 SUPREME/CT PRESIDENT PWR
CONGRESS. PAGE 4 G0084

SURANYI-UNGER T. G1047

SURPLUS....SEE DEMAND,PLAN

SURVEY ANALYSIS....SEE SAMP/SIZ

SWATANTRA....SWATANTRA - COALITION RIGHT-WING PARTY IN INDIA

SWEDEN....SEE ALSO APPROPRIATE TIME/SPACE/CULTURE INDEX

HECKSCHER G.,"GROUP ORGANIZATION IN SWEDEN." SWEDEN LAISSEZ   S39
STRATA ECO/DEV AGRI INDUS LABOR NAT/G PROF/ORG   SOC
ECO/TAC CENTRAL SOCISM...MGT 19/20. PAGE 25 G0499

VERNEY D.V.,PUBLIC ENTERPRISE IN SWEDEN. FUT SWEDEN ECO/DEV   B59
UK INDUS POL/PAR LEGIS PROB/SOLV CAP/ISM INT/TRADE POLICY
CONTROL SOCISM...MGT CONCPT NAT/COMP 20 SOCDEM/PAR LG/CO
CIVIL/SERV. PAGE 61 G1196   NAT/G

WENDT P.F.,HOUSING POLICY - THE SEARCH FOR   PLAN   B62
SOLUTIONS. GERMANY/W SWEDEN UK USA+45 OP/RES   ADMIN
HABITAT WEALTH...SOC/WK CHARTS 20. PAGE 63 G1230 METH/COMP
  NAT/G

S65
BIRNBAUM K.,"SWEDEN'S NUCLEAR POLICY." WOR+45   SWEDEN
POL/PAR CREATE TEC/DEV NEUTRAL RISK WAR ORD/FREE   NUC/PWR
...DECISION IDEA/COMP NAT/COMP TIME. PAGE 7 G0137   DIPLOM
                                                      ARMS/CONT

SWIFT R. G1048

SWITZERLND....SWITZERLAND; SEE ALSO APPROPRIATE TIME/SPACE/
     CULTURE INDEX

                                                      B66
DAENIKER G.,STRATEGIE DES KLEIN STAATS. SWITZERLND   NUC/PWR
ACT/RES CREATE DIPLOM NEUTRAL DETER WAR WEAPON PWR   PLAN
SOVEREIGN...IDEA/COMP 20 COLD/WAR. PAGE 14 G0270   FORCES
                                                      NAT/G

SYNANON....SYNANON: COMMUNITY OF FORMER DRUG ADDICTS AND
     CRIMINALS

SYNTAX....SEE LOG

SYRIA....SEE ALSO UAR

SYS/QU....SYSTEMATIZING AND ANALYZING QUESTIONNAIRES

                                                      S50
KAPLAN A.,"THE PREDICTION OF SOCIAL AND   PWR
TECHNOLOGICAL EVENTS." VOL/ASSN CONSULT ACT/RES   KNO/TEST
CREATE OP/RES PLAN ROUTINE PERSON...POLICY
METH/CNCPT STAT QU/SEMANT SYS/QU TESTS CENSUS TREND
20. PAGE 29 G0574

                                                      S50
LENTZ T.F.,"REPORT ON A SURVEY OF SOCIAL SCIENTISTS   ACT/RES
CONDUCTED BY THE ATTITUDE RESEARCH LABORATORY." FUT   ATTIT
WOR+45 CREATE EDU/PROP...PSY STAT RECORD SYS/QU   DIPLOM
SAMP/SIZ CON/ANAL VAL/FREE 20. PAGE 33 G0655

                                                      S52
"SELECTED CRITICAL BIBLIOGRAPHY ON THE METHODS AND   BIBLIOG/A
TECHNIQUES OF POLITICAL BEHAVIOR RESEARCH."   METH
...PHIL/SCI OBS QU SYS/QU TESTS CON/ANAL. PAGE 1   SOC
G0012   EDU/PROP

                                                      B55
MIKSCHE F.O.,ATOMIC WEAPONS AND ARMIES. FUT WOR+45   TEC/DEV
WOR-45 SOCIETY COERCE DETER WEAPON PWR...POLICY   FORCES
WELF/ST PSY CONCPT INT SYS/QU KNO/TEST TOT/POP 20.   NUC/PWR
PAGE 39 G0765

                                                      B58
TELLER E.A.,OUR NUCLEAR FUTURE. SOCIETY FORCES   FUT
TEC/DEV EDU/PROP KNOWL ORD/FREE...STAND/INT SYS/QU   PHIL/SCI
KNO/TEST AUD/VIS CHARTS SIMUL 20. PAGE 54 G1062   NUC/PWR
                                                      WAR

SYSTEMS....SEE ROUTINE, COMPUTER

SZASZ/T....THOMAS SZASZ
——————————————————— T ———————————————————
T....TEXTBOOK

                                                      C25
MOON P.T.,"SYLLABUS ON INTERNATIONAL RELATIONS."   INT/ORG
EUR+WWI MOD/EUR USA-45 FORCES COLONIAL WAR WEAPON   DIPLOM
NAT/LISM...POLICY BIBLIOG T 19/20. PAGE 39 G0778   NAT/G

                                                      B34
COHEN M.R.,AN INTRODUCTION TO LOGIC AND SCIENTIFIC   LOG
METHOD....LING MATH CHARTS T 20. PAGE 12 G0242   PHIL/SCI
                                                      GEN/METH
                                                      METH/CNCPT

                                                      B40
PFIFFNER J.M.,RESEARCH METHODS IN PUBLIC   ADMIN
ADMINISTRATION. USA-45 R+D...MGT STAT INT QU T 20.   OP/RES
PAGE 44 G0872   METH
                                                      TEC/DEV

                                                      B52
APPADORAI A.,THE SUBSTANCE OF POLITICS (6TH ED.).   PHIL/SCI
EX/STRUC LEGIS DIPLOM CT/SYS CHOOSE FASCISM MARXISM   NAT/G
SOCISM...BIBLIOG T. PAGE 3 G0062

                                                      B57
MERTON R.K.,SOCIAL THEORY AND SOCIAL STRUCTURE   SOC
(REV. ED.). INTELL SECT WORKER OP/RES EDU/PROP   GEN/LAWS
ADMIN INGP/REL ANOMIE PERSON...AUD/VIS T 20   SOCIETY
BUREAUCRCY. PAGE 38 G0759   STRUCT

                                                      B60
MORRIS W.T.,ENGINEERING ECONOMY. AUTOMAT RISK   OP/RES
RATIONAL...PROBABIL STAT CHARTS GAME SIMUL BIBLIOG   DECISION
T 20. PAGE 40 G0785   MGT

                                                      B62
BENNIS W.G.,THE PLANNING OF CHANGE: READINGS IN THE   PROB/SOLV
APPLIED BEHAVIORAL SCIENCES. CULTURE STRATA STRUCT   CREATE
PLAN GP/REL...SOC T. PAGE 6 G0123   ACT/RES
                                                      OP/RES

                                                      B62
STAHL O.G.,PUBLIC PERSONNEL ADMINISTRATION. LOC/G   ADMIN
TOP/EX CREATE PLAN ROUTINE...TECHNIC MGT T. PAGE 52   WORKER
G1030   EX/STRUC
                                                      NAT/G

                                                      B64
EDELMAN M.,THE SYMBOLIC USES OF POWER. USA+45   CLIENT
EX/STRUC CONTROL GP/REL INGP/REL...MGT T. PAGE 17   PWR
G0333   EXEC
                                                      ELITES

                                                      B64
FOGELMAN E.,HIROSHIMA: THE DECISION TO USE THE A-   INTELL
BOMB. USA-45 DIPLOM EFFICIENCY PEACE...ANTHOL   DECISION
BIBLIOG T 20 CHINJAP. PAGE 19 G0375   NUC/PWR
                                                      WAR

                                                      B64
INST D'ETUDE POL L'U GRENOBLE,ADMINISTRATION   ADMIN
TRADITIONELLE ET PLANIFICATION REGIONALE. FRANCE   MUNIC
LAW POL/PAR PROB/SOLV ADJUST RIGID/FLEX...CHARTS   PLAN
ANTHOL BIBLIOG T 20 REFORMERS. PAGE 28 G0546   CREATE

                                                      B64
PEDERSEN E.S.,NUCLEAR ENERGY IN SPACE. FUT INTELL   SPACE
R+D CONSULT...NEW/IDEA CHARTS METH T 20. PAGE 44   TEC/DEV
G0864   NUC/PWR
                                                      LAB/EXP

                                                      B65
KOROL A.G.,SOVIET RESEARCH AND DEVELOPMENT. USSR   COM
ACADEM SCHOOL WORKER ROUTINE COST...STAT T 20.   R+D
PAGE 31 G0615   FINAN
                                                      DIST/IND

                                                      B66
FREIDEL F.,AMERICAN ISSUES IN THE TWENTIETH   DIPLOM
CENTURY. SOCIETY FINAN ECO/TAC FOR/AID CONTROL   POLICY
NUC/PWR WAR RACE/REL PEACE ATTIT...ANTHOL T 20   NAT/G
WILSON/W ROOSEVLT/F KENNEDY/JF TRUMAN/HS. PAGE 20   ORD/FREE
G0391

                                                      B67
DE BLIJ H.J.,SYSTEMATIC POLITICAL GEOGRAPHY. WOR+45   GEOG
STRUCT INT/ORG NAT/G EDU/PROP ADMIN COLONIAL   CONCPT
ROUTINE ORD/FREE PWR...IDEA/COMP T 20. PAGE 15   METH
G0283

                                                      B67
HARMAN H.H.,MODERN FACTOR ANALYSIS (2ND REV. ED.).   CON/ANAL
COMPUTER...DECISION CHARTS BIBLIOG T. PAGE 24 G0482   METH/CNCPT
                                                      SIMUL
                                                      MATH

TABOOS....SEE CULTURE

TAFT/HART....TAFT-HARTLEY ACT

TAFT/RA....ROBERT A. TAFT

TAFT/WH....PRESIDENT WILLIAM HOWARD TAFT

TAGIL S. G1049

TAHITI....TAHITI

TAIWAN....TAIWAN AND REPUBLIC OF CHINA

                                                      S67
HILL R.,"SOCIAL ASPECTS OF FAMILY PLANNING." INDIA   FAM
KOREA TAIWAN ECO/UNDEV PLAN PROB/SOLV TEC/DEV   BIO/SOC
EDU/PROP CONTROL ATTIT DRIVE...HEAL PSY SOC 20   GEOG
BIRTH/CON UN. PAGE 26 G0512   MARRIAGE

TAMMANY....TAMMANY HALL

TANGANYIKA....SEE TANZANIA

                                                      S66
FLEMING W.G.,"AUTHORITY, EFFICIENCY, AND ROLE   DOMIN
STRESS: PROBLEMS IN THE DEVELOPMENT OF EAST AFRICAN   EFFICIENCY
BUREAUCRACIES." AFR UGANDA STRUCT PROB/SOLV ROUTINE   COLONIAL
INGP/REL ROLE...MGT SOC GP/COMP GOV/COMP 20   ADMIN
TANGANYIKA AFRICA/E. PAGE 19 G0371

TANNENBAUM P.H. G1051

TANZANIA....TANZANIA; SEE ALSO AFR

PROB/SOLV
EFFICIENCY

TARIFFS....SEE ALSO ECO, INT/TRADE, GATT

B62

KRAFT J.,THE GRAND DESIGN. EUR+WWI USA+45 AGRI
FINAN INDUS MARKET INT/ORG NAT/G PLAN ECO/TAC
TARIFFS REGION DRIVE ORD/FREE WEALTH...POLICY OBS
TREND EEC 20. PAGE 31 G0616
VOL/ASSN
ECO/DEV
INT/TRADE

B63

UN SECRETARY GENERAL.PLANNING FOR ECONOMIC
DEVELOPMENT. ECO/UNDEV FINAN BUDGET INT/TRADE
TARIFFS TAX ADMIN 20 UN. PAGE 55 G1089
PLAN
ECO/TAC
MGT
NAT/COMP

S64

GARDNER R.N.,"GATT AND THE UNITED NATIONS
CONFERENCE ON TRADE AND DEVELOPMENT." USA+45 WOR+45
SOCIETY ECO/UNDEV MARKET NAT/G DELIB/GP ACT/RES
PLAN ECO/TAC TARIFFS RIGID/FLEX WEALTH...DECISION MGT TREND UN TOT/POP
20 GATT. PAGE 21 G0411
INT/ORG
INT/TRADE

S67

WILLIAMS C.,"REGIONAL MANAGEMENT OVERSEAS." USA+45
WOR+45 DIST/IND LG/CO EX/STRUC INT/TRADE TARIFFS
ADMIN TASK CENTRAL. PAGE 63 G1242
MGT
EUR+WWI
ECO/DEV
PLAN

TARKOWSKI Z.M. G1052

TARTARS....TARTARS

TASHJEAN J.E. G1053

TASK....SPECIFIC SELF-ASSIGNED OR OTHER ASSIGNED OPERATIONS

N

CONOVER H.L.,CIVILIAN DEFENSE: A SELECTED LIST OF
RECENT REFERENCES (PAMPHLET). USA+45 LOC/G MUNIC
PROB/SOLV ADMIN LEAD TASK WEAPON GOV/REL...POLICY
CON/ANAL 20 CIV/DEFENS. PAGE 13 G0251
BIBLIOG
PLAN
WAR
CIVMIL/REL

S50

BAVELAS A.,"COMMUNICATION PATTERNS IN TASK-ORIENTED
GROUPS" (BMR)" R+D OP/RES INSPECT LEAD CENTRAL
EFFICIENCY HAPPINESS RIGID/FLEX...PROBABIL 20.
PAGE 6 G0106
ACT/RES
PERS/REL
TASK
INGP/REL

B58

DUBIN R.,THE WORLD OF WORK: INDUSTRIAL SOCIETY AND
HUMAN RELATIONS. MARKET PROC/MFG LABOR TEC/DEV
CAP/ISM AUTOMAT TASK GP/REL EFFICIENCY...CONCPT
CHARTS BIBLIOG 20. PAGE 16 G0317
WORKER
ECO/TAC
PRODUC
DRIVE

S58

NEWELL A.C.,"ELEMENTS OF A THEORY OF HUMAN PROBLEM
SOLVING" (BMR)" TASK PERCEPT...CONCPT LOG METH/COMP
LAB/EXP BIBLIOG 20. PAGE 42 G0819
PROB/SOLV
COMPUTER
COMPUT/IR
OP/RES

B59

WASSERMAN P.,MEASUREMENT AND ANALYSIS OF
ORGANIZATIONAL PERFORMANCE. FINAN MARKET EX/STRUC
TEC/DEV EDU/PROP CONTROL ROUTINE TASK...MGT 20.
PAGE 62 G1220
BIBLIOG/A
ECO/TAC
OP/RES
EFFICIENCY

B59

WELTON H.,THE THIRD WORLD WAR: TRADE AND INDUSTRY,
THE NEW BATTLEGROUND. WOR+45 ECO/DEV INDUS MARKET
TASK...MGT IDEA/COMP COLD/WAR. PAGE 63 G1229
INT/TRADE
PLAN
DIPLOM

B60

CHASE S.,LIVE AND LET LIVE. USA+45 ECO/DEV
PROB/SOLV TEC/DEV ECO/TAC ARMS/CONT NUC/PWR WAR
NAT/LISM PEACE...GEOG TREND 20 COLD/WAR. PAGE 11
G0223
NAT/G
DIPLOM
SOCIETY
TASK

B60

SLUCKIN W.,MINDS AND MACHINES (REV. ED.). PROB/SOLV
TEC/DEV AUTOMAT TASK PERCEPT HEALTH KNOWL
...DECISION MATH PROBABIL COMPUT/IR GAME 20.
PAGE 51 G1012
PSY
COMPUTER
PERSON
SIMUL

B61

MCRAE R.,THE PROBLEM OF THE UNITY OF THE SCIENCES:
BACON TO KANT. CREATE TASK KNOWL...PERS/COMP 16/18
BACON/F DESCARTE/R LEIBNITZ/G KANT/I DIDEROT/D.
PAGE 38 G0748
PHIL/SCI
IDEA/COMP
PERSON

S61

HAINES G.,"THE COMPUTER AS A SMALL-GROUP MEMBER."
DELIB/GP BAL/PWR TASK 20. PAGE 24 G0467
INGP/REL
COMPUTER

B62

BURKE A.E.,ENOUGH GOOD MEN. USA+45 WOR+45 ECO/UNDEV
FORCES TEC/DEV GUERRILLA NUC/PWR REV WAR ORD/FREE
MARXISM...GEOG 20 COLD/WAR. PAGE 10 G0189
DIPLOM
POLICY
NAT/G
TASK

B62

THOMSON G.P.,NUCLEAR ENERGY IN BRITAIN DURING THE
LAST WAR: THE CHERWELL SIMON LECTURE (MONOGRAPH).
UK R+D CONSULT FORCES PLAN DIPLOM TASK CIVMIL/REL
ROLE...PHIL/SCI NEW/IDEA LAB/EXP 20 MAUD. PAGE 54
G1071
CREATE
TEC/DEV
WAR
NUC/PWR

B63

MILBRATH L.W.,THE WASHINGTON LOBBYISTS. CONSTN
BAL/PWR CONTROL LEAD TASK CHOOSE SUPEGO...DECISION
STAT CHARTS BIBLIOG. PAGE 39 G0767
LOBBY
POLICY
PERS/REL

S63

CLEVELAND H.,"CRISIS DIPLOMACY." USA+45 WOR+45 LAW
FORCES TASK NUC/PWR PWR 20. PAGE 12 G0235
DECISION
DIPLOM
PROB/SOLV
POLICY

B64

HAMMOND P.E.,SOCIOLOGISTS AT WORK. VOL/ASSN OP/RES
TEC/DEV CONFER ROUTINE TASK EFFICIENCY...MGT
NEW/IDEA STYLE SAMP. PAGE 24 G0478
R+D
BIOG
SOC

B65

TURNER A.N.,INDUSTRIAL JOBS AND THE WORKER. USA+45
CULTURE ECO/DEV LABOR MUNIC ACT/RES AUTOMAT TASK
...CHARTS BIBLIOG 20. PAGE 55 G1082
WORKER
INDUS
ATTIT
TEC/DEV

B65

US DEPARTMENT OF ARMY.MILITARY PROTECTIVE
CONSTRUCTION: NUCLEAR WARFARE AND CHEMICAL AND
BIOLOGICAL OPERATIONS (MANUAL). OP/RES TEC/DEV RISK
COERCE NUC/PWR WAR WEAPON EFFICIENCY UTIL BIO/SOC
HABITAT ORD/FREE 20. PAGE 57 G1117
FORCES
CONSTRUC
TASK
HEALTH

B66

ALEXANDER Y.,INTERNATIONAL TECHNICAL ASSISTANCE
EXPERTS* A CASE STUDY OF THE U.N. EXPERIENCE.
ECO/UNDEV CONSULT EX/STRUC CREATE PLAN DIPLOM
FOR/AID TASK EFFICIENCY...ORG/CHARTS UN. PAGE 2
G0038
ECO/TAC
INT/ORG
ADMIN
MGT

B66

YOUNG W.,EXISTING MECHANISMS OF ARMS CONTROL.
PROC/MFG OP/RES DIPLOM TASK CENTRAL...MGT TREATY.
PAGE 65 G1266
ARMS/CONT
ADMIN
NUC/PWR
ROUTINE

S66

SIMON R.,"THE STATE OF PUBLIC RELATIONS SCHOLARLY
RESEARCH." TEC/DEV TASK MAJORITY PRODUC...TREND
CHARTS BIBLIOG 20. PAGE 51 G1000
ACADEM
CREATE
STAT
GP/REL

B67

SALMOND J.A.,THE CIVILIAN CONSERVATION CORPS,
1933-1942. USA-45 NAT/G CREATE EXEC EFFICIENCY
WEALTH...BIBLIOG 20 ROOSEVLT/F. PAGE 48 G0954
ADMIN
ECO/TAC
TASK
AGRI

S67

CETRON M.J.,"FORECASTING TECHNOLOGY." INDUS FORCES
TASK UTIL...PHIL/SCI CONCPT CHARTS METH/COMP TIME.
PAGE 11 G0219
TEC/DEV
FUT
R+D
PLAN

S67

CONWAY J.E.,"MAKING RESEARCH EFFECTIVE IN
LEGISLATION." LAW R+D CONSULT EX/STRUC PLAN CONFER
ADMIN LEAD ROUTINE TASK INGP/REL DECISION. PAGE 13
G0252
ACT/RES
POLICY
LEGIS
PROB/SOLV

S67

DE NEUFVILLE R.,"EDUCATION AT THE ACADEMIES."
USA+45 ELITES CONSULT EX/STRUC COMPUTER PLAN
PROB/SOLV TASK CIVMIL/REL ORD/FREE 20. PAGE 15
G0286
FORCES
ACADEM
TEC/DEV
SKILL

S67

HODGE G.,"THE RISE AND DEMISE OF THE UN TECHNICAL
ASSISTANCE ADMINISTRATION." RISK TASK INGP/REL
CONSEN EFFICIENCY 20 UN. PAGE 26 G0516
ADMIN
TEC/DEV
EX/STRUC
INT/ORG

S67

WILLIAMS C.,"REGIONAL MANAGEMENT OVERSEAS." USA+45
MGT

WOR+45 DIST/IND LG/CO EX/STRUC INT/TRADE TARIFFS
ADMIN TASK CENTRAL. PAGE 63 G1242
EUR+WWI
ECO/DEV
PLAN

TAUBENFELD H.J. G1054,G1055,G1056,G1057

TAX....TAXING, TAXATION

B14
CRAIG J.,ELEMENTS OF POLITICAL SCIENCE (3 VOLS.).
CONSTN AGRI INDUS SCHOOL FORCES TAX CT/SYS SUFF
MORAL WEALTH...CONCPT 19 CIVIL/LIB. PAGE 13 G0259
PHIL/SCI
NAT/G
ORD/FREE

B48
METZLER L.A.,INCOME, EMPLOYMENT, AND PUBLIC POLICY.
FINAN INDUS LOC/G NAT/G TAX GIVE PAY COST PRODUC
...MGT TIME/SEQ 20. PAGE 38 G0760
INCOME
WEALTH
POLICY
ECO/TAC

C54
CALDWELL L.K.,"THE GOVERNMENT AND ADMINISTRATION OF
NEW YORK." LOC/G MUNIC POL/PAR SCHOOL CHIEF LEGIS
PLAN TAX CT/SYS...MGT SOC/WK BIBLIOG 20 NEWYORK/C.
PAGE 10 G0202
PROVS
ADMIN
CONSTN
EX/STRUC

B55
SMITHIES A.,THE BUDGETARY PROCESS IN THE UNITED
STATES. ECO/DEV AGRI EX/STRUC FORCES LEGIS
PROB/SOLV TAX ROUTINE EFFICIENCY...MGT CONGRESS
PRESIDENT. PAGE 52 G1016
NAT/G
ADMIN
BUDGET
GOV/REL

B57
BAUER P.T.,ECONOMIC ANALYSIS AND POLICY IN
UNDERDEVELOPED COUNTRIES. WOR+45 AGRI INT/TRADE TAX
PRICE...GEN/METH BIBLIOG/A 20 COMMONWLTH. PAGE 5
G0103
ECO/UNDEV
METH/COMP
POLICY

B58
OGDEN F.D.,THE POLL TAX IN THE SOUTH. USA+45 USA-45
CONSTN ADJUD ADMIN PARTIC CRIME...TIME/SEQ GOV/COMP
METH/COMP 18/20 SOUTH/US. PAGE 43 G0838
TAX
CHOOSE
RACE/REL
DISCRIM

B60
CRAUMER L.V.,BUSINESS PERIODICALS INDEX (8VOLS.).
USA+45 LABOR TAX 20. PAGE 13 G0262
BIBLIOG/A
FINAN
ECO/DEV
MGT

S61
COOKE E.F.,"RESEARCH: AN INSTRUMENT OF POWER."
VOL/ASSN PLAN TEC/DEV TAX LOBBY INGP/REL ROLE
POLICY. PAGE 13 G0253
R+D
PROVS
LOC/G
DECISION

B63
UN SECRETARY GENERAL,PLANNING FOR ECONOMIC
DEVELOPMENT. ECO/UNDEV FINAN BUDGET INT/TRADE
TARIFFS TAX ADMIN 20 UN. PAGE 55 G1089
PLAN
ECO/TAC
MGT
NAT/COMP

B64
DUSCHA J.,ARMS, MONEY, AND POLITICS. USA+45 INDUS
POL/PAR ECO/TAC TAX DETER NUC/PWR WAR WEAPON
GOV/REL ATTIT...BIBLIOG/A 20 CONGRESS MONEY
DEPT/DEFEN. PAGE 17 G0326
NAT/G
FORCES
POLICY
BUDGET

B66
CLARK G.,WORLD PEACE THROUGH WORLD LAW; TWO
ALTERNATIVE PLANS. WOR+45 DELIB/GP FORCES TAX
CONFER ADJUD SANCTION ARMS/CONT WAR CHOOSE PRIVIL
20 UN COLD/WAR. PAGE 12 G0231
INT/LAW
PEACE
PLAN
INT/ORG

B66
SANFORD T.,BUT WHAT ABOUT THE PEOPLE? ACADEM SCHOOL
BUDGET TAX CONTROL SKILL WEALTH 20 NORTH/CAR.
PAGE 49 G0956
EDU/PROP
PROB/SOLV
POLICY
PROVS

B67
EISENMENGER R.W.,THE DYNAMICS OF GROWTH IN NEW
ENGLAND'S ECONOMY, 1870-1964. USA+45 USA-45 ECO/TAC
TAX PAY AUTOMAT GOV/REL ADJUST HABITAT...STAT
19/20. PAGE 17 G0340
ECO/DEV
AGRI
INDUS
CAP/ISM

S67
SCOVILLE W.J.,"GOVERNMENT REGULATION AND GROWTH IN
THE FRENCH PAPER INDUSTRY DURING THE EIGHTEENTH
CENTURY." FRANCE MOD/EUR FINAN CAP/ISM TAX ADMIN
CONTROL PRIVIL LAISSEZ...POLICY 18. PAGE 50 G0985
NAT/G
PROC/MFG
ECO/DEV
INGP/REL

B88
BENTHAM J.,DEFENCE OF USURY (1787). UK LAW NAT/G
TEC/DEV ECO/TAC CONTROL ATTIT...CONCPT IDEA/COMP 18
SMITH/ADAM. PAGE 6 G0124
TAX
FINAN
ECO/DEV
POLICY

TAYLOR M.G. G1058

TAYLOR P.S. G1059

TAYLOR/AJP....A.J.P. TAYLOR

TAYLOR/Z....PRESIDENT ZACHARY TAYLOR

TEC/DEV....DEVELOPMENT OF TECHNIQUES

N
AMERICAN DOCUMENTATION INST,AMERICAN DOCUMENTATION.
PROF/ORG CONSULT PLAN PERCEPT...MATH STAT AUD/VIS
CHARTS METH/COMP INDEX METH 20. PAGE 3 G0050
BIBLIOG
TEC/DEV
COM/IND
COMPUT/IR

C54
AMERICAN DOCUMENTATION INST,DOCUMENTATION
ABSTRACTS. WOR+45 NAT/G COMPUTER CREATE TEC/DEV
DIPLOM EDU/PROP REGION KNOWL...PHIL/SCI CLASSIF
LING. PAGE 3 G0051
BIBLIOG/A
AUTOMAT
COMPUT/IR
R+D

B
BRITISH COMMONWEALTH BUR AGRI,WORLD AGRICULTURAL
ECONOMICS AND RURAL SOCIOLOGY ABSTRACTS. NAT/G
OP/RES PLAN TEC/DEV LEAD PRODUC...GEOG MGT NAT/COMP
20. PAGE 9 G0170
BIBLIOG/A
AGRI
SOC
WORKER

B
US DEPT COMMERCE OFF TECH SERV,TECHNICAL
TRANSLATIONS. WOR+45 INDUS COMPUTER CREATE NUC/PWR
...PHIL/SCI COMPUT/IR METH/COMP METH. PAGE 58 G1135
BIBLIOG
R+D
TEC/DEV
AUTOMAT

N
FOREIGN AFFAIRS. SPACE WOR+45 WOR-45 CULTURE
ECO/UNDEV FINAN NAT/G TEC/DEV INT/TRADE ARMS/CONT
NUC/PWR...POLICY 20 UN EURATOM ECSC EEC. PAGE 1
G0004
BIBLIOG
DIPLOM
INT/ORG
INT/LAW

N
GT BRIT MIN OVERSEAS DEV, LIB, TECHNICAL CO-
OPERATION -- A BIBLIOGRAPHY. UK LAW SOCIETY DIPLOM
ECO/TAC FOR/AID...STAT 20 CMN/WLTH. PAGE 39 G0775
BIBLIOG
TEC/DEV
ECO/DEV
NAT/G

N
PRINCETON UNIVERSITY,SELECTED REFERENCES:
INDUSTRIAL RELATIONS SECTION. USA+45 EX/STRUC
WORKER TEC/DEV...MGT 20. PAGE 45 G0892
BIBLIOG/A
LABOR
INDUS
GP/REL

N
UNITED NATIONS,OFFICIAL RECORDS OF THE UNITED
NATIONS' ATOMIC ENERGY COMMISSION - DISARMAMENT
COMMISSION. WOR+45 TEC/DEV DIPLOM WRITING NUC/PWR
20 UN. PAGE 55 G1092
ARMS/CONT
INT/ORG
DELIB/GP
CONFER

N19
US ATOMIC ENERGY COMMISSION,ATOMIC ENERGY IN USE
(PAMPHLET). R+D RISK EFFICIENCY HEALTH KNOWL
ORD/FREE...PHIL/SCI CONCPT METH/CNCPT CHARTS
LAB/EXP 20 AEC. PAGE 56 G1106
OP/RES
TEC/DEV
NUC/PWR
CREATE

N19
US SEN SPEC COMM SPACE ASTRO,SPACE LAW; A SYMPOSIUM
(PAMPHLET). USA+45 TEC/DEV CONFER CONTROL SOVEREIGN
...INT/LAW 20 SEN/SPACE. PAGE 59 G1161
SPACE
ADJUD
DIPLOM
INT/ORG

N19
ZLOTNICK M.,WEAPONS IN SPACE (PAMPHLET). FUT WOR+45
TEC/DEV DIPLOM ARMS/CONT CIVMIL/REL PEACE HABITAT
...CONCPT NEW/IDEA CHARTS. PAGE 65 G1268
SPACE
WEAPON
NUC/PWR
WAR

B23
DRAPER J.W.,HISTORY OF THE CONFLICT BETWEEN
RELIGION AND SCIENCE. WOR-45 INTELL SOCIETY R+D
CREATE PLAN TEC/DEV EDU/PROP ATTIT PWR...PHIL/SCI
CONCPT OBS TIME/SEQ TREND GEN/LAWS TOT/POP. PAGE 16
G0314
SECT
KNOWL

B37
GULICK L.,PAPERS ON THE SCIENCE OF ADMINISTRATION.
INDUS PROB/SOLV TEC/DEV COST EFFICIENCY PRODUC
HABITAT...PHIL/SCI METH/COMP 20. PAGE 23 G0461
OP/RES
CONTROL
ADMIN
MGT

B37
STAMP S.,THE SCIENCE OF SOCIAL ADJUSTMENT. WOR-45
ACT/RES CREATE PLAN PROB/SOLV TEC/DEV ECO/TAC
EFFICIENCY SOC/INTEG 20. PAGE 52 G1031
ADJUST
ORD/FREE
PHIL/SCI

B38
HARPER S.N.,THE GOVERNMENT OF THE SOVIET UNION. COM MARXISM
USSR LAW CONSTN ECO/DEV PLAN TEC/DEV DIPLOM NAT/G
INT/TRADE ADMIN REV NAT/LISM...POLICY 20. PAGE 24 LEAD
G0483 POL/PAR

B40
PFIFFNER J.M.,RESEARCH METHODS IN PUBLIC ADMIN
ADMINISTRATION. USA-45 R+D...MGT STAT INT QU T 20. OP/RES
PAGE 44 G0872 METH
TEC/DEV

B40
ZNANIECKI F.,THE SOCIAL ROLE OF THE MAN OF ROLE
KNOWLEDGE. UNIV SOCIETY STRUCT TEC/DEV...EPIST INTELL
PHIL/SCI SOC NEW/IDEA 20. PAGE 65 G1269 KNOWL
INGP/REL

B42
US LIBRARY OF CONGRESS,CONDUCT OF THE WAR (APRIL BIBLIOG/A
1941-MARCH 1942). USA-45 WOR-45 LAW INDUS PUB/INST WAR
TEC/DEV EDU/PROP CIVMIL/REL 20. PAGE 59 G1155 FORCES
PLAN

S44
GRIFFITH E.S.,"THE CHANGING PATTERN OF PUBLIC LAW
POLICY FORMATION." MOD/EUR WOR+45 FINAN CHIEF POLICY
CONFER ADMIN LEAD CONSERVE SOCISM TECHRACY...SOC TEC/DEV
CHARTS CONGRESS. PAGE 23 G0450

B45
REVES E.,THE ANATOMY OF PEACE. WOR-45 LAW CULTURE ACT/RES
NAT/G PLAN TEC/DEV EDU/PROP WAR NAT/LISM ATTIT CONCPT
ALL/VALS SOVEREIGN...POLICY HUM TIME/SEQ 20. NUC/PWR
PAGE 46 G0914 PEACE

B45
SCHULTZ T.H.,FOOD FOR THE WORLD. UNIV SOCIETY INDUS AGRI
R+D ECO/TAC...GEOG TREND GEN/LAWS 20. PAGE 50 G0979 TEC/DEV

B45
SMYTH H.D.,ATOMIC ENERGY FOR MILITARY PURPOSES. R+D
USA-45 NAT/G PLAN TEC/DEV KNOWL...MATH CON/ANAL TIME/SEQ
CHARTS LAB/EXP SIMUL 20. PAGE 52 G1017 NUC/PWR

C45
MCDIARMID J.,"THE MOBILIZATION OF SOCIAL INTELL
SCIENTISTS," IN L. WHITE'S CIVIL CIVIL SERVICE IN WAR
WARTIME." USA-45 TEC/DEV CENTRAL...SOC 20 DELIB/GP
CIVIL/SERV. PAGE 37 G0733 ADMIN

C45
TRYTTEN M.H.,"THE MOBILIZATION OF SCIENTISTS," IN INTELL
L. WHITE, CIVIL SERVICE IN WARTIME." USA-45 R+D WAR
FORCES ACT/RES PERSON ROLE 20. PAGE 55 G1080 TEC/DEV
NAT/G

B46
AMERICAN DOCUMENTATION INST,CATALOGUE OF AUXILIARY BIBLIOG
PUBLICATIONS IN MICROFILMS AND PHOTOPRINTS. USA-45 EDU/PROP
LAW AGRI CREATE TEC/DEV ADMIN...GEOG LING MATH 20. PSY
PAGE 3 G0052

B46
BRODIE B.,THE OBSOLETE WEAPON: ATOMIC POWER AND INT/ORG
WORLD ORDER. COM USA+45 USSR WOR+45 DELIB/GP PLAN TEC/DEV
ORD/FREE PWR...CONCPT TIME/SEQ TREND UN 20. PAGE 9 ARMS/CONT
G0171 NUC/PWR

B46
WILCOX J.K.,OFFICIAL DEFENSE PUBLICATIONS, BIBLIOG/A
1941-1945 (NINE VOLS.). USA-45 AGRI INDUS R+D LABOR WAR
FORCES TEC/DEV EFFICIENCY PRODUC SKILL WEALTH 20. CIVMIL/REL
PAGE 63 G1238 ADMIN

B47
WHITEHEAD T.N.,LEADERSHIP IN A FREE SOCIETY; A INDUS
STUDY IN HUMAN RELATIONS BASED ON AN ANALYSIS OF LEAD
PRESENT-DAY INDUSTRIAL CIVILIZATION. WOR-45 STRUCT ORD/FREE
R+D LABOR LG/CO SML/CO WORKER PLAN PROB/SOLV SOCIETY
TEC/DEV DRIVE...MGT 20. PAGE 63 G1234

B48
BRADLEY D.,NO PLACE TO HIDE. USA+45 SOCIETY NAT/G R+D
FORCES TEC/DEV EDU/PROP DETER PEACE BIO/SOC LAB/EXP
ALL/VALS...POLICY PHIL/SCI OBS RECORD SAMP BIOG ARMS/CONT
GEN/METH COLD/WAR 20. PAGE 8 G0162 NUC/PWR

B48
STEWART I.,ORGANIZING SCIENTIFIC RESEARCH FOR WAR: DELIB/GP
ADMINISTRATIVE HISTORY OF OFFICE OF SCIENTIFIC ADMIN
RESEARCH AND DEVELOPMENT. USA-45 INTELL R+D LABOR WAR
WORKER CREATE BUDGET WEAPON CIVMIL/REL GP/REL TEC/DEV
EFFICIENCY...POLICY 20. PAGE 53 G1036

B48
WEINER N.,CYBERNETICS. SOCIETY COMPUTER ADJUST FEEDBACK
EFFICIENCY UTIL PERCEPT...PSY MATH REGRESS TIME. AUTOMAT
PAGE 63 G1226 CONTROL
TEC/DEV

B49
OGBURN W.,TECHNOLOGY AND INTERNATIONAL RELATIONS. TEC/DEV
WOR+45 ECO/DEV CREATE PLAN ECO/TAC EDU/PROP DIPLOM
COERCE PWR SKILL WEALTH...TECHNIC PSY SOC NEW/IDEA INT/ORG
CHARTS TOT/POP 20. PAGE 43 G0837

B50
CROWTHER J.G.,SCIENCE AT WAR. EUR+WWI PLAN TEC/DEV R+D
DOMIN COERCE NUC/PWR WEAPON KNOWL PWR...CONCPT OBS FORCES
TREND VAL/FREE 20. PAGE 14 G0265 WAR
UK

B50
DEES J.W. JR.,URBAN SOCIOLOGY AND THE EMERGING PLAN
ATOMIC MEGALOPOLIS. PART I. USA+45 TEC/DEV ADMIN NEIGH
NUC/PWR HABITAT...SOC AUD/VIS CHARTS GEN/LAWS 20 MUNIC
WATER. PAGE 15 G0291 PROB/SOLV

B50
MANNHEIM K.,FREEDOM, POWER, AND DEMOCRATIC TEC/DEV
PLANNING. FUT USSR WOR+45 ELITES INTELL SOCIETY PLAN
NAT/G EDU/PROP ROUTINE ATTIT DRIVE SUPEGO SKILL CAP/ISM
...POLICY PSY CONCPT TREND GEN/LAWS 20. PAGE 35 UK
G0700

B50
US DEPARTMENT OF STATE,POINT FOUR: COOPERATIVE ECO/UNDEV
PROGRAM FOR AID IN THE DEVELOPMENT OF ECONOMICALLY FOR/AID
UNDERDEVELOPED AREAS. WOR+45 AGRI INDUS INT/ORG FINAN
PLAN TEC/DEV DIPLOM EDU/PROP ADMIN PEACE PRODUC INT/TRADE
WEALTH 20 CONGRESS UN. PAGE 57 G1121

L50
MAASS A.A.,"CONGRESS AND WATER RESOURCES." LOC/G REGION
TEC/DEV CONTROL SANCTION...WELF/ST GEOG CONGRESS. AGRI
PAGE 35 G0683 PLAN

B51
CONANT J.B.,SCIENCE AND COMMON SENSE. WOR+45 WOR-45 CREATE
R+D SCHOOL CONSULT TEC/DEV EDU/PROP SKILL...PLURIST PHIL/SCI
METH/CNCPT RECORD TIME/SEQ SIMUL GEN/METH METH.
PAGE 13 G0248

L52
ELDERSVELD S.J.,"RESEARCH IN POLITICAL BEHAVIOR" ACT/RES
(BMR)" USA+45 PLAN TEC/DEV ATTIT...BIBLIOG/A METH GEN/LAWS
20. PAGE 17 G0341 CREATE

B53
HOVLAND C.I.,COMMUNICATION AND PERSUASION: PSY
PSYCHOLOGICAL STUDIES OF OPINION CHANGE. INTELL EDU/PROP
SOCIETY ECO/DEV COM/IND R+D SERV/IND CREATE TEC/DEV
ATTIT RIGID/FLEX KNOWL NEW/IDEA. PAGE 27 G0531

B53
LANGER W.L.,THE UNDECLARED WAR, 1940-1941. EUR+WWI WAR
GERMANY USA-45 USSR AIR FORCES TEC/DEV CONFER POLICY
CONTROL COERCE PERCEPT ORD/FREE PWR 20 CHINJAP DIPLOM
EUROPE. PAGE 32 G0634

B53
ROBINSON E.A.G.,THE STRUCTURE OF COMPETITIVE INDUS
INDUSTRY. UK ECO/DEV DIST/IND MARKET TEC/DEV DIPLOM PRODUC
EDU/PROP ADMIN EFFICIENCY WEALTH...MGT 19/20. WORKER
PAGE 47 G0929 OPTIMAL

S53
MILLER G.A.,"WHAT IS INFORMATION MEASUREMENT?" COMPUTER
CREATE...CONCPT METH/CNCPT QUANT STAT CHARTS TEC/DEV
BIBLIOG/A 20. PAGE 39 G0771 PSY
MATH

B54
COMBS C.H.,DECISION PROCESSES. INTELL SOCIETY MATH
DELIB/GP CREATE TEC/DEV DOMIN LEGIT EXEC CHOOSE DECISION
DRIVE RIGID/FLEX KNOWL PWR...PHIL/SCI SOC
METH/CNCPT CONT/OBS REC/INT PERS/TEST SAMP/SIZ BIOG
SOC/EXP WORK. PAGE 13 G0245

B54
HART B.H.L.,STRATEGY (REV. ED.). CHRIST-17C EUR+WWI WAR
MEDIT-7 MOD/EUR TEC/DEV LEAD REV WEAPON...POLICY PLAN
CHARTS. PAGE 25 G0486 FORCES
PHIL/SCI

B54
LOCKLIN D.P.,ECONOMICS OF TRANSPORTATION (4TH ED.). ECO/DEV
USA+45 USA-45 SEA AIR LAW FINAN LG/CO EX/STRUC DIST/IND
ADMIN CONTROL...STAT CHARTS 19/20 RAILROAD ECO/TAC
PUB/TRANS. PAGE 34 G0675 TEC/DEV

MCCLOSKEY J.F.,OPERATIONS RESEARCH FOR MANAGEMENT. STRUCT COMPUTER ADMIN ROUTINE...PHIL/SCI CONCPT METH/CNCPT TREND ANTHOL BIBLIOG 20. PAGE 37 G0731
B54
OP/RES MGT METH/COMP TEC/DEV

MOSK S.A.,INDUSTRIAL REVOLUTION IN MEXICO. MARKET LABOR CREATE CAP/ISM ADMIN ATTIT SOCISM...POLICY 20 MEXIC/AMER. PAGE 40 G0789
B54
INDUS TEC/DEV ECO/UNDEV NAT/G

WASHBURNE N.F.,INTERPRETING SOCIAL CHANGE IN AMERICA. USA+45 STRATA FAM NAT/G SECT OP/RES ECO/TAC EDU/PROP HABITAT...SOC TIME/SEQ TREND 20 BUREAUCRCY. PAGE 62 G1217
B54
CULTURE STRUCT CREATE TEC/DEV

WRIGHT Q.,PROBLEMS OF STABILITY AND PROGRESS IN INTERNATIONAL RELATIONSHIPS. FUT WOR+45 WOR-45 SOCIETY LEGIS CREATE TEC/DEV ECO/TAC EDU/PROP ADJUD WAR PEACE ORD/FREE PWR...KNO/TEST TREND GEN/LAWS 20. PAGE 64 G1257
B54
INT/ORG CONCPT DIPLOM

OPLER M.E.,"SOCIAL ASPECTS OF TECHNICAL ASSISTANCE IN OPERATION." WOR+45 VOL/ASSN CREATE PLAN TEC/DEV EDU/PROP ALL/VALS...METH/CNCPT OBS RECORD TREND UN 20. PAGE 43 G0841
L54
INT/ORG CONSULT FOR/AID

MIKSCHE F.O.,ATOMIC WEAPONS AND ARMIES. FUT WOR+45 WOR-45 SOCIETY COERCE DETER WEAPON PWR...POLICY WELF/ST PSY CONCPT INT SYS/QU KNO/TEST TOT/POP 20. PAGE 39 G0765
B55
TEC/DEV FORCES NUC/PWR

US OFFICE OF THE PRESIDENT,REPORT TO CONGRESS ON THE MUTUAL SECURITY PROGRAM FOR THE SIX MONTHS ENDED JUNE 30, 1955. ECO/DEV INT/ORG NAT/G CREATE TEC/DEV BAL/PWR ECO/TAC AGREE DETER COST ORD/FREE 20 DEPT/STATE DEPT/DEFEN. PAGE 59 G1157
B55
DIPLOM FORCES PLAN FOR/AID

KISER M.,"ORGANIZATION OF AMERICAN STATES." L/A+17C USA+45 ECO/UNDEV INT/ORG NAT/G PLAN TEC/DEV DIPLOM ECO/TAC INT/TRADE EDU/PROP ADMIN ALL/VALS...POLICY MGT RECORD ORG/CHARTS OAS 20. PAGE 30 G0601
L55
VOL/ASSN ECO/DEV REGION

SKINNER B.F.,"FREEDOM AND THE CONTROL OF MEN" (BMR)" FUT WOR+45 CONTROL CHOOSE GP/REL ATTIT MORAL PWR POPULISM...POLICY 20. PAGE 51 G1008
S55
ORD/FREE TEC/DEV PHIL/SCI INTELL

VON NEUMANN J.,"CAN WE SURVIVE TECHNOLOGY?" WOR+45 AIR INDUS ADMIN ADJUST RIGID/FLEX...GEOG PHIL/SCI NEW/IDEA 20. PAGE 61 G1202
S55
TEC/DEV NUC/PWR FUT HABITAT

ESTEP R.,AN AIR POWER BIBLIOGRAPHY. USA+45 TEC/DEV BUDGET DIPLOM EDU/PROP DETER CIVMIL/REL...DECISION INT/LAW 20. PAGE 18 G0351
B56
BIBLIOG/A FORCES WEAPON PLAN

THOMAS M.,ATOMIC ENERGY AND CONGRESS. USA+45 NAT/G ACT/RES PLAN TEC/DEV EDU/PROP ROUTINE KNOWL PWR SKILL...PHIL/SCI NEW/IDEA TIME/SEQ CHARTS METH CONGRESS VAL/FREE 20 AEC. PAGE 54 G1067
B56
LEGIS ADMIN NUC/PWR

UN HEADQUARTERS LIBRARY,BIBLIOGRAPHY OF INDUSTRIALIZATION IN UNDERDEVELOPED COUNTRIES (BIBLIOGRAPHICAL SERIES NO. 6). WOR+45 R+D ACADEM INT/ORG NAT/G. PAGE 55 G1087
B56
BIBLIOG ECO/UNDEV TEC/DEV

US DEPARTMENT OF THE ARMY,AMERICAN MILITARY HISTORY. USA+45 USA-45 EX/STRUC PROB/SOLV TEC/DEV DIPLOM NUC/PWR REV WAR WEAPON...PSY 18/20. PAGE 57 G1125
B56
BIBLIOG FORCES NAT/G

US DEPARTMENT OF THE ARMY,RESEARCH AND DEVELOPMENT (AND RELATED ASPECTS) IN FOREIGN COUNTRIES. WOR+45 DIST/IND INDUS CONSULT FORCES CREATE EDU/PROP AUTOMAT DETER WEAPON. PAGE 57 G1126
B56
BIBLIOG/A R+D TEC/DEV NUC/PWR

US OFFICE OF THE PRESIDENT,REPORT TO CONGRESS ON THE MUTUAL SECURITY PROGRAM FOR THE SIX MONTHS
B56
DIPLOM FORCES

ENDED DECEMBER 31, 1955. ASIA USSR ECO/DEV ECO/UNDEV INT/ORG CREATE TEC/DEV BAL/PWR ECO/TAC AGREE DETER COST ORD/FREE 20 DEPT/STATE DEPT/DEFEN EISNHWR/DD. PAGE 59 G1158
PLAN FOR/AID

GORDON L.,"THE ORGANIZATION FOR EUROPEAN ECONOMIC COOPERATION." EUR+WWI INDUS INT/ORG NAT/G CONSULT DELIB/GP ACT/RES CREATE PLAN TEC/DEV EDU/PROP LEGIT WEALTH OEEC 20. PAGE 22 G0435
S56
VOL/ASSN ECO/DEV

DUPUY R.E.,"MILITARY HERITAGE OF AMERICA." USA+45 USA-45 TEC/DEV DIPLOM ROUTINE...POLICY TREND CHARTS IDEA/COMP BIBLIOG COLD/WAR. PAGE 17 G0325
C56
FORCES WAR CONCPT

DUPREE A.H.,SCIENCE IN THE FEDERAL GOVERNMENT; A HISTORY OF POLICIES AND ACTIVITIES TO 1940. USA+45 AGRI SCHOOL DELIB/GP WAR GOV/REL...PHIL/SCI BIBLIOG 18/20 DEPRESSION NEW/DEAL WWI JEFFERSN/T. PAGE 17 G0324
B57
NAT/G R+D CREATE TEC/DEV

GOLD N.L.,REGIONAL ECONOMIC DEVELOPMENT AND NUCLEAR POWER IN INDIA. FUT INDIA FINAN FOR/AID INT/TRADE BAL/PAY EFFICIENCY OPTIMAL PRODUC WEALTH...PREDICT 20. PAGE 22 G0424
B57
ECO/UNDEV TEC/DEV NUC/PWR INDUS

KISSINGER H.A.,NUCLEAR WEAPONS AND FOREIGN POLICY. FUT USA+45 WOR+45 INT/ORG FORCES ACT/RES TEC/DEV DIPLOM ARMS/CONT COERCE ATTIT KNOWL PWR...DECISION GEOG CHARTS 20. PAGE 31 G0602
B57
PLAN DETER NUC/PWR

JANOWITZ M.,"MILITARY ELITES AND THE STUDY OF WAR." USA+45 WOR-45 STRATA NAT/G PROF/ORG TEC/DEV DOMIN EDU/PROP COERCE WAR ATTIT RIGID/FLEX PWR RESPECT ...MGT TREND STERTYP GEN/METH 20. PAGE 28 G0558
S57
FORCES ELITES

ATOMIC INDUSTRIAL FORUM,MANAGEMENT AND ATOMIC ENERGY. WOR+45 SEA LAW MARKET NAT/G TEC/DEV INSPECT INT/TRADE CONFER PEACE HEALTH...ANTHOL 20. PAGE 4 G0078
B58
NUC/PWR INDUS MGT ECO/TAC

CROWE S.,THE LANDSCAPE OF POWER. UK CULTURE SERV/IND NAT/G CONSULT PARTIC NUC/PWR LEISURE...SOC EXHIBIT 20. PAGE 14 G0264
B58
HABITAT TEC/DEV PLAN CONTROL

DUBIN R.,THE WORLD OF WORK: INDUSTRIAL SOCIETY AND HUMAN RELATIONS. MARKET PROC/MFG LABOR TEC/DEV CAP/ISM AUTOMAT TASK GP/REL EFFICIENCY...CONCPT CHARTS BIBLIOG 20. PAGE 16 G0317
B58
WORKER ECO/TAC PRODUC DRIVE

EHRHARD J.,LE DESTIN DU COLONIALISME. AFR FRANCE ECO/UNDEV AGRI FINAN MARKET CREATE PLAN TEC/DEV BUDGET DIPLOM PRICE 20. PAGE 17 G0335
B58
COLONIAL FOR/AID INT/TRADE INDUS

GAVIN J.M.,WAR AND PEACE IN THE SPACE AGE. SPACE USA+45 USSR FORCES PLAN TEC/DEV BAL/PWR DIPLOM ARMS/CONT WEAPON CIVMIL/REL...CHARTS GP/COMP 20 NATO COLD/WAR. PAGE 21 G0414
B58
WAR DETER NUC/PWR PEACE

MECRENSKY E.,SCIENTIFIC MANPOWER IN EUROPE. WOR+45 EDU/PROP GOV/REL SKILL...TECHNIC PHIL/SCI INT CHARTS BIBLIOG 20. PAGE 38 G0750
B58
ECO/TAC TEC/DEV METH/COMP NAT/COMP

NATIONAL PLANNING ASSOCIATION,1970 WITHOUT ARMS CONTROL (PAMPHLET). WOR+45 PROB/SOLV TEC/DEV DIPLOM CONFER DETER NUC/PWR WAR...CHARTS 20 COLD/WAR. PAGE 41 G0810
B58
ARMS/CONT ORD/FREE WEAPON PREDICT

NOEL-BAKER D.,THE ARMS RACE. WOR+45 NAT/G DELIB/GP ACT/RES TEC/DEV EDU/PROP NUC/PWR ATTIT KNOWL PWR ...CONCPT OBS LEAGUE/NAT 20 COLD/WAR. PAGE 42 G0823
B58
FUT INT/ORG ARMS/CONT PEACE

TELLER E.A.,OUR NUCLEAR FUTURE. SOCIETY FORCES TEC/DEV EDU/PROP KNOWL ORD/FREE...STAND/INT SYS/QU KNO/TEST AUD/VIS CHARTS SIMUL 20. PAGE 54 G1062
B58
FUT PHIL/SCI NUC/PWR WAR

UN INTL CONF ON PEACEFUL USE.PROGRESS IN ATOMIC
ENERGY (VOL. I). WOR+45 R+D PLAN TEC/DEV CONFER
CONTROL PEACE SKILL...CHARTS ANTHOL 20 UN BAGHDAD.
PAGE 55 G1088

B58
NUC/PWR
DIPLOM
WORKER
EDU/PROP

US DEPARTMENT OF THE ARMY,BIBLIOGRAPHY ON LIMITED
WAR (PAMPHLET). USA+45 TEC/DEV CONTROL RISK COERCE
DETER NUC/PWR WEAPON ADJUST PEACE ALL/VALS ORD/FREE
20. PAGE 57 G1127

B58
BIBLIOG/A
WAR
FORCES
CIVMIL/REL

BURNS A.L.,"THE NEW WEAPONS AND INTERNATIONAL
RELATIONS." SPACE WOR+45 NAT/G VOL/ASSN FORCES
NUC/PWR 20. PAGE 10 G0190

S58
TEC/DEV
ARMS/CONT
DIPLOM

HUNTINGTON S.P.,"ARMS RACES: PREREQUISITES AND
RESULTS." EUR+WWI MOD/EUR USA+45 WOR+45 WOR-45
NAT/G TEC/DEV BAL/PWR COERCE DETER ATTIT...POLICY
TREND 20. PAGE 27 G0537

S58
FORCES
PWR
ARMS/CONT

MCDOUGAL M.S.,"PERSPECTIVES FOR A LAW OF OUTER
SPACE." FUT WOR+45 AIR CONSULT DELIB/GP TEC/DEV
CT/SYS ORD/FREE...POLICY JURID 20 UN. PAGE 37 G0736

S58
INT/ORG
SPACE
INT/LAW

CLEAVELAND F.N.,SCIENCE AND STATE GOVERNMENT. AGRI
EXTR/IND FINAN INDUS PROVS...METH/CNCPT STAT CHARTS
20 NEW/YORK CONNECTICT WISCONSIN CALIFORNIA
NEW/MEXICO. PAGE 12 G0233

B59
TEC/DEV
PHIL/SCI
GOV/REL
METH/COMP

GUILBAUD G.T.,WHAT IS CYBERNETICS? COMPUTER OP/RES
TEC/DEV AUTOMAT ROUTINE PERS/REL PERCEPT...PSY MATH
COMPUT/IR SIMUL GEN/METH. PAGE 23 G0460

B59
CONTROL
COM/IND
FEEDBACK
NET/THEORY

LANG D.,FROM HIROSHIMA TO THE MOON: CHRONICLES OF
LIFE IN THE ATOMIC AGE. USA+45 OP/RES CONTROL
ARMS/CONT WAR CIVMIL/REL PEACE HABITAT MORAL PWR
...OBS INT 20 AEC. PAGE 32 G0633

B59
NUC/PWR
SPACE
HEALTH
TEC/DEV

MAYDA J.,ATOMIC ENERGY AND LAW. ECO/UNDEV FINAN
TEC/DEV FOR/AID EFFICIENCY PRODUC WEALTH...POLICY
TECHNIC 20. PAGE 37 G0723

B59
NUC/PWR
L/A+17C
LAW
ADMIN

MODELSKI G.,ATOMIC ENERGY IN THE COMMUNIST BLOC.
FUT INT/ORG CONSULT FORCES ACT/RES PLAN KNOWL SKILL
...PHIL/SCI STAT CHARTS 20. PAGE 39 G0777

B59
TEC/DEV
NUC/PWR
USSR
COM

POKROVSKY G.I.,SCIENCE AND TECHNOLOGY IN
CONTEMPORARY WAR. SPACE USSR WOR+45 NAT/G CONSULT
ACT/RES PLAN DETER WEAPON...MARXIST METH/CNCPT
CHARTS STERTYP COLD/WAR 20. PAGE 45 G0881

B59
TEC/DEV
FORCES
NUC/PWR
WAR

STANFORD RESEARCH INSTITUTE,POSSIBLE NONMILITARY
SCIENTIFIC DEVELOPMENTS AND THEIR POTENTIAL IMPACT
ON FOREIGN POLICY PROBLEMS OF THE UNITED. FUT
USA+45 INT/ORG PROF/ORG CONSULT ACT/RES CREATE PLAN
PEACE KNOWL SKILL...TECHNIC PHIL/SCI NEW/IDEA
UNESCO 20. PAGE 52 G1032

B59
R+D
TEC/DEV

WASSERMAN P.,MEASUREMENT AND ANALYSIS OF
ORGANIZATIONAL PERFORMANCE. FINAN MARKET EX/STRUC
TEC/DEV EDU/PROP CONTROL ROUTINE TASK...MGT 20.
PAGE 62 G1220

B59
BIBLIOG/A
ECO/TAC
OP/RES
EFFICIENCY

BURNS A.L.,"THE RATIONALE OF CATALYTIC WAR." COM
USA+45 WOR+45 R+D NAT/G FORCES ACT/RES TEC/DEV PWR
...DECISION HYPO/EXP TOT/POP 20. PAGE 10 G0191

L59
COERCE
NUC/PWR
WAR

BURNS A.L.,"POWER POLITICS AND THE GROWING NUCLEAR
CLUB." FUT WOR+45 TEC/DEV EXEC ARMS/CONT COERCE
DETER...DECISION HYPO/EXP 20. PAGE 10 G0192

L59
FORCES
BAL/PWR
NUC/PWR

BLOOMFIELD L.P.,"THREE EXPERIMENTS IN POLITICAL
GAMING." ACT/RES CREATE PWR...GAME GEN/METH METH.
PAGE 7 G0140

S59
TEC/DEV
METH/CNCPT
DECISION

CORY R.H. JR.,"INTERNATIONAL INSPECTION FROM
PROPOSALS TO REALIZATION." WOR+45 TEC/DEV ECO/TAC

S59
STRUCT
PSY

ADJUD ORD/FREE PWR WEALTH...RECORD VAL/FREE 20.
PAGE 13 G0258

ARMS/CONT
NUC/PWR

DEUTSCH K.W.,"THE IMPACT OF SCIENCE AND TECHNOLOGY
ON INTERNATIONAL POLITICS." UNIV INTELL NAT/G
ACT/RES CREATE TEC/DEV EDU/PROP EXEC KNOWL...CONCPT
TREND TOT/POP 20. PAGE 15 G0297

S59
PHIL/SCI
MYTH
DIPLOM
NAT/LISM

JANOWITZ M.,"CHANGING PATTERNS OF ORGANIZATIONAL
AUTHORITY: THE MILITARY ESTABLISHMENT" (BMR)"
USA+45 ELITES STRUCT EX/STRUC PLAN DOMIN AUTOMAT
NUC/PWR WEAPON 20. PAGE 28 G0559

S59
FORCES
AUTHORIT
ADMIN
TEC/DEV

SIMONS H.,"WORLD-WIDE CAPABILITIES FOR PRODUCTION
AND CONTROL OF NUCLEAR WEAPONS." FUT WOR+45 INDUS
INT/ORG NAT/G ECO/TAC ATTIT PWR SKILL...TREND
CHARTS VAL/FREE 20. PAGE 51 G1001

S59
TEC/DEV
ARMS/CONT
NUC/PWR

ARROW K.J.,MATHEMATICAL METHODS IN THE SOCIAL
SCIENCES. 1959. TEC/DEV CHOOSE UTIL PERCEPT
...KNO/TEST GAME SIMUL ANTHOL. PAGE 4 G0070

B60
MATH
PSY
MGT

CARPENTER E.,EXPLORATIONS IN COMMUNICATION. USSR
CULTURE SCHOOL SECT EDU/PROP PRESS TV AUTOMAT
FEEDBACK ATTIT PERSON...ART/METH PSY 20. PAGE 11
G0211

B60
ANTHOL
COM/IND
TEC/DEV
WRITING

CHASE S.,LIVE AND LET LIVE. USA+45 ECO/DEV
PROB/SOLV TEC/DEV ECO/TAC ARMS/CONT NUC/PWR WAR
NAT/LISM PEACE...GEOG TREND 20 COLD/WAR. PAGE 11
G0223

B60
NAT/G
DIPLOM
SOCIETY
TASK

HEILBRONER R.L.,THE FUTURE AS HISTORY. USA+45
WOR+45 WOR-45 SOCIETY ECO/DEV ECO/UNDEV VOL/ASSN
PLAN CAP/ISM NUC/PWR CHOOSE NAT/LISM ATTIT ORD/FREE
RESPECT WEALTH SOCISM 20. PAGE 25 G0501

B60
TEC/DEV
TREND

JANOWITZ M.,THE PROFESSIONAL SOLDIER. CULTURE
STRATA STRUCT FAM PROB/SOLV TEC/DEV COERCE WAR
CIVMIL/REL NAT/LISM AGE HEREDITY ALL/VALS CONSERVE
...MGT WORSHIP. PAGE 28 G0560

B60
FORCES
MYTH
LEAD
ELITES

KINGSTON-MCCLOUG E.,DEFENSE; POLICY AND STRATEGY.
UK SEA AIR TEC/DEV DIPLOM ADMIN LEAD WAR ORD/FREE
...CHARTS 20. PAGE 30 G0597

B60
FORCES
PLAN
POLICY
DECISION

LINDVEIT E.N.,SCIENTISTS IN GOVERNMENT. USA+45 PAY
EDU/PROP ADMIN DRIVE HABITAT ROLE...TECHNIC BIBLIOG
20. PAGE 34 G0670

B60
TEC/DEV
ECO/TAC
PHIL/SCI
GOV/REL

PARRY A.,RUSSIA'S ROCKETS AND MISSILES. COM FUT
GERMANY USA+45 WOR+45 INTELL ECO/DEV ACT/RES
NUC/PWR WEAPON ATTIT ALL/VALS...OBS TIME/SEQ
COLD/WAR 20. PAGE 44 G0859

B60
PLAN
TEC/DEV
SPACE
USSR

PENTONY D.E.,THE UNDERDEVELOPED LANDS. FUT WOR+45
CULTURE AGRI FINAN INDUS MARKET INT/ORG LABOR NAT/G
VOL/ASSN CONSULT TEC/DEV ECO/TAC EDU/PROP COLONIAL
ATTIT WEALTH...OBS RECORD SAMP TREND GEN/METH WORK
UN 20. PAGE 44 G0867

B60
ECO/UNDEV
POLICY
FOR/AID
INT/TRADE

SILK L.S.,THE RESEARCH REVOLUTION. USA+45 FINAN
CAP/ISM ECO/TAC PRICE EQUILIB PRODUC...STAT TREND
CHARTS. PAGE 51 G0997

B60
ECO/DEV
R+D
TEC/DEV
PROB/SOLV

SLUCKIN W.,MINDS AND MACHINES (REV. ED.). PROB/SOLV
TEC/DEV AUTOMAT TASK PERCEPT HEALTH KNOWL
...DECISION MATH PROBABIL COMPUT/IR GAME 20.
PAGE 51 G1012

B60
PSY
COMPUTER
PERSON
SIMUL

US HOUSE COMM. SCI. ASTRONAUT.,OCEAN SCIENCES AND
NATIONAL SECURITY. FUT SEA ECO/DEV EXTR/IND INT/ORG
NAT/G FORCES ACT/RES TEC/DEV ECO/TAC COERCE WAR
BIO/SOC KNOWL PWR...CONCPT RECORD LAB/EXP 20.
PAGE 59 G1153

B60
R+D
ORD/FREE

US SENATE COMM ON COMMERCE,URBAN MASS

B60
DIST/IND

TRANSPORTATION. FUT USA+45 AIR ECO/DEV FINAN LOC/G PLAN
MUNIC LEGIS CREATE PROB/SOLV TEC/DEV 20 PUB/TRANS. NAT/G
PAGE 60 G1180 LAW

B60
WEBSTER J.A.,A GENERAL STUDY OF THE DEPARTMENT OF ORD/FREE
DEFENSE INTERNAL SECURITY PROGRAM. USA+45 WORKER PLAN
TEC/DEV ADJUD CONTROL CT/SYS EXEC GOV/REL COST ADMIN
...POLICY DECISION MGT 20 DEPT/DEFEN SUPREME/CT. NAT/G
PAGE 62 G1221

B60
WOETZEL R.K.,THE INTERNATIONAL CONTROL OF AIRSPACE INT/ORG
AND OUTERSPACE. FUT WOR+45 AIR CONSTN STRUCT JURID
CONSULT PLAN TEC/DEV ADJUD RIGID/FLEX KNOWL SPACE
ORD/FREE PWR...TECHNIC GEOG MGT NEW/IDEA TREND INT/LAW
COMPUT/IR VAL/FREE 20 TREATY. PAGE 64 G1251

L60
HOLZMAN B.G.,"BASIC RESEARCH FOR NATIONAL FORCES
SURVIVAL." FUT USA+45 INTELL R+D ACT/RES OP/RES STAT
PLAN TEC/DEV EDU/PROP PERCEPT PERSON...PHIL/SCI
METH/CNCPT NEW/IDEA MATH OBS RECORD TREND LAB/EXP
20. PAGE 27 G0525

L60
JACOB P.E.,"THE DISARMAMENT CONSENSUS." USA+45 USSR DELIB/GP
WOR+45 INT/ORG NAT/G ACT/RES TEC/DEV BAL/PWR ATTIT
EDU/PROP ADMIN COERCE DETER NUC/PWR CONSEN ARMS/CONT
RIGID/FLEX PWR...CONCPT RECORD CHARTS COLD/WAR 20.
PAGE 28 G0552

L60
MACPHERSON C.,"TECHNICAL CHANGE AND POLITICAL TEC/DEV
DECISION." WOR+45 NAT/G CREATE CAP/ISM DIPLOM ADMIN
ROUTINE RIGID/FLEX...CONCPT OBS GEN/METH 20.
PAGE 35 G0692

S60
DOTY P.M.,"THE ROLE OF THE SMALLER POWERS." FUT PWR
WOR+45 NAT/G TEC/DEV BAL/PWR DOMIN LEGIT CHOOSE POLICY
DISPL DRIVE RESPECT...DECISION 20. PAGE 16 G0310 ARMS/CONT
NUC/PWR

S60
HAYTON R.D.,"THE ANTARCTIC SETTLEMENT OF 1959." FUT DELIB/GP
USA+45 WOR+45 WOR-45 STRUCT R+D INT/ORG EX/STRUC JURID
CREATE TEC/DEV LEGIT PEACE ATTIT SOVEREIGN DIPLOM
...TIME/SEQ 20 TREATY IGY. PAGE 25 G0495 REGION

S60
HUTCHINSON C.E.,"AN INSTITUTE FOR NATIONAL SECURITY POLICY
AFFAIRS." USA+45 R+D NAT/G CONSULT TOP/EX ACT/RES METH/CNCPT
CREATE PLAN TEC/DEV EDU/PROP ROUTINE NUC/PWR ATTIT ELITES
ORD/FREE PWR...DECISION MGT PHIL/SCI CONCPT RECORD DIPLOM
GEN/LAWS GEN/METH 20. PAGE 27 G0539

S60
KAPLAN M.A.,"THEORETICAL ANALYSIS OF THE BALANCE OF CREATE
POWER." FUT USA+45 WOR+45 INTELL ECO/DEV INT/ORG NEW/IDEA
NAT/G CONSULT TOP/EX ACT/RES PLAN TEC/DEV ATTIT DIPLOM
ALL/VALS...METH/CNCPT TOT/POP 20. PAGE 29 G0576 NUC/PWR

S60
KELLEY G.A.,"THE POLITICAL BACKGROUND OF THE FRENCH NAT/G
A-BOMB." EUR+WWI USSR FORCES TOP/EX TEC/DEV NUC/PWR RESPECT
ATTIT PWR...CONCPT OBS/ENVIR TREND 20. PAGE 30 NAT/LISM
G0591 FRANCE

S60
KISSINGER H.A.,"ARMS CONTROL, INSPECTION AND FORCES
SURPRISE ATTACK." COM USA+45 NAT/G ACT/RES PLAN ORD/FREE
TEC/DEV DIPLOM EDU/PROP DETER WAR RIGID/FLEX ARMS/CONT
...CONCPT GEN/METH TOT/POP 20. PAGE 31 G0603 NUC/PWR

S60
LEAR J.,"PEACE: SCIENCE'S NEXT GREAT EXPLORATION." EX/STRUC
USA+45 INT/ORG TOP/EX TEC/DEV EDU/PROP ROUTINE ARMS/CONT
PEACE KNOWL SKILL 20. PAGE 33 G0648 NUC/PWR

S60
RIVKIN A.,"AFRICAN ECONOMIC DEVELOPMENT: ADVANCED AFR
TECHNOLOGY AND THE STAGES OF GROWTH." CULTURE TEC/DEV
ECO/UNDEV AGRI COM/IND EXTR/IND PLAN ECO/TAC ATTIT FOR/AID
DRIVE RIGID/FLEX SKILL WEALTH...MGT SOC GEN/LAWS
WORK TOT/POP 20. PAGE 47 G0923

S60
SANDERS R.,"NUCLEAR DYNAMITE: A NEW DIMENSION IN INDUS
FOREIGN POLICY." FUT WOR+45 ECO/DEV CONSULT TEC/DEV PWR
PERCEPT...CONT/OBS TIME/SEQ TREND GEN/LAWS TOT/POP DIPLOM
20 TREATY. PAGE 49 G0955 NUC/PWR

S60
YEMELYANOV V.S.,"ATOMIC ENERGY FOR PEACE: THE USSR VOL/ASSN
AND INTERNATIONAL CO-OPERATION." FUT USSR WOR+45 TEC/DEV

R+D CREATE EDU/PROP...CONCPT GEN/LAWS 20. PAGE 64 ARMS/CONT
G1264 NUC/PWR

N60
US HOUSE COMM SCI ASTRONAUT,THE ORGANIZATION OF THE ACT/RES
US NATIONAL SPACE EFFORT. USA+45 WOR+45 AIR ECO/DEV SKILL
NAT/G PLAN TEC/DEV DIPLOM EDU/PROP ATTIT DRIVE PWR SPACE
...OBS TIME/SEQ TREND TOT/POP 20. PAGE 58 G1142

B61
BONNEFOUS M.,EUROPE ET TIERS MONDE. EUR+WWI SOCIETY AFR
INT/ORG NAT/G VOL/ASSN ACT/RES TEC/DEV CAP/ISM ECO/UNDEV
ECO/TAC ATTIT ORD/FREE SOVEREIGN...POLICY CONCPT FOR/AID
TREND 20. PAGE 8 G0153 INT/TRADE

B61
BRADY R.A.,ORGANIZATION, AUTOMATION, AND SOCIETY. TEC/DEV
USA+45 AGRI COM/IND DIST/IND MARKET CREATE INDUS
...DECISION MGT 20. PAGE 8 G0163 AUTOMAT
ADMIN

B61
GORDON W.J.J.,SYNECTICS: THE DEVELOPMENT OF CREATE
CREATIVE CAPACITY. USA+45 PLAN TEC/DEV KNOWL WEALTH PROB/SOLV
...DECISION MGT 20. PAGE 22 G0436 ACT/RES
TOP/EX

B61
HADLEY A.T.,THE NATIONS SAFETY AND ARMS CONTROL. ACT/RES
FUT USA+45 WOR+45 TOP/EX PLAN TEC/DEV ATTIT DRIVE ROUTINE
...CONCPT OBS TIME/SEQ TREND 20. PAGE 24 G0466 DETER
NUC/PWR

B61
HODGKINS J.A.,SOVIET POWER: ENERGY RESOURCES, GEOG
PRODUCTION AND POTENTIALS. USSR ECO/DEV INDUS EXTR/IND
MARKET...POLICY STAT CHARTS 20 RESOURCE/N. PAGE 26 TEC/DEV
G0518

B61
JANOWITZ M.,COMMUNITY POLITICAL SYSTEMS. USA+45 MUNIC
SOCIETY INDUS VOL/ASSN TEC/DEV ADMIN LEAD CHOOSE STRUCT
...SOC SOC/WK 20. PAGE 29 G0561 POL/PAR

B61
LAHAYE R.,LES ENTREPRISES PUBLIQUES AU MAROC. NAT/G
FRANCE MOROCCO LAW DIST/IND EXTR/IND FINAN CONSULT INDUS
PLAN TEC/DEV ADMIN AGREE CONTROL OWN...POLICY 20. ECO/UNDEV
PAGE 32 G0629 ECO/TAC

B61
MURPHY E.F.,WATER PURITY: A STUDY IN LEGAL CONTROL SEA
OF NATURAL RESOURCES. LOC/G ACT/RES PLAN TEC/DEV LAW
LOBBY GP/REL COST ATTIT HEALTH ORD/FREE...HEAL PROVS
JURID 20 WISCONSIN WATER. PAGE 40 G0797 CONTROL

B61
NAKICENOVIC S.,NUCLEAR ENERGY IN YUGOSLAVIA. R+D
YUGOSLAVIA AGRI INDUS CREATE OP/RES ROUTINE ECO/DEV
EFFICIENCY KNOWL...HEAL STAT CHARTS LAB/EXP BIBLIOG TEC/DEV
20. PAGE 41 G0802 NUC/PWR

B61
RAMO S.,PEACETIME USES OF OUTER SPACE. FUT DIST/IND PEACE
INT/ORG CONSULT NUC/PWR...AUD/VIS ANTHOL 20. TEC/DEV
PAGE 46 G0898 SPACE
CREATE

L61
THOMPSON V.A.,"HIERARCHY, SPECIALIZATION, AND PERS/REL
ORGANIZATIONAL CONFLICT" (BMR)" WOR+45 STRATA PROB/SOLV
STRUCT WORKER TEC/DEV GP/REL INGP/REL ATTIT ADMIN
AUTHORIT 20 BUREAUCRCY. PAGE 54 G1069 EX/STRUC

S61
ANDREWS R.B.,"URBAN ECONOMICS: AN APPRAISAL OF MUNIC
PROGRESS." LOC/G PROB/SOLV TEC/DEV...CONCPT PHIL/SCI
OBS/ENVIR METH/COMP HYPO/EXP SOC/EXP SIMUL GEN/METH ECOMETRIC
METH 20. PAGE 3 G0058

S61
COOKE E.F.,"RESEARCH: AN INSTRUMENT OF POWER." R+D
VOL/ASSN PLAN TEC/DEV TAX LOBBY INGP/REL ROLE PROVS
POLICY. PAGE 13 G0253 LOC/G
DECISION

S61
DALTON G.,"ECONOMIC THEORY AND PRIMITIVE SOCIETY" ECO/UNDEV
(BMR)" UNIV AGRI KIN TEC/DEV ECO/TAC REGION HABITAT METH
SKILL...METH/COMP BIBLIOG. PAGE 14 G0274 PHIL/SCI
SOC

S61
MORGENSTERN O.,"THE N-COUNTRY PROBLEM." EUR+WWI FUT
UNIV USA+45 WOR+45 SOCIETY CONSULT TOP/EX ACT/RES BAL/PWR
PLAN EDU/PROP ATTIT DRIVE...POLICY OBS TREND NUC/PWR

TOT/POP 20. PAGE 40 G0781   TEC/DEV

RICHSTEIN A.R.,"LEGAL RULES IN NUCLEAR WEAPONS   NUC/PWR
EMPLOYMENTS." FUT WOR+45 LAW SOCIETY FORCES PLAN   S61
WEAPON RIGID/FLEX...HEAL CONCPT TREND VAL/FREE 20.   TEC/DEV
PAGE 47 G0918   MORAL
       ARMS/CONT

WOHLSTETTER A.,"NUCLEAR SHARING: NATO AND THE NTH   S61
COUNTRY." EUR+WWI FUT SOCIETY DIPLOM EXEC DETER PWR   TREND
SKILL...POLICY TECHNIC CONCPT 20 NATO. PAGE 64   TEC/DEV
G1252   NUC/PWR
       ARMS/CONT

ASTIA,INFORMATION THEORY: A REPORT BIBLIOGRAPHY.   B62
USA+45 COMPUTER CREATE OP/RES PLAN TEC/DEV CONTROL   BIBLIOG/A
...CONCPT METH/COMP. PAGE 4 G0074   COM/IND
       FORCES
       METH

BERKELEY E.C.,THE COMPUTER REVOLUTION. WOR+45   B62
CREATE TEC/DEV EFFICIENCY TECHRACY...SOC TREND 20.   COMPUTER
PAGE 7 G0128   CONTROL
       AUTOMAT
       SOCIETY

BLOOMFIELD L.P.,OUTER SPACE: A PATTERN OF WAR IN A   B62
NEW DIMENSION. FUT USA+45 AIR TEC/DEV PWR   CREATE
...DECISION CONCPT GEN/LAWS 20. PAGE 7 G0141   ACT/RES
       ARMS/CONT
       SPACE

BROOKINGS INSTITUTION,DEVELOPMENT OF THE EMERGING   B62
COUNTRIES; AN AGENDA FOR RESEARCH. WOR+45 AGRI   ECO/UNDEV
TEC/DEV FOR/AID EDU/PROP ADJUST HABITAT KNOWL...PSY   R+D
SOC ANTHOL 20 THIRD/WRLD. PAGE 9 G0175   SOCIETY
       PROB/SOLV

BURKE A.E.,ENOUGH GOOD MEN. USA+45 WOR+45 ECO/UNDEV   B62
FORCES TEC/DEV GUERRILLA NUC/PWR REV WAR ORD/FREE   DIPLOM
MARXISM...GEOG 20 COLD/WAR. PAGE 10 G0189   POLICY
       NAT/G
       TASK

CALDER R.,LIVING WITH THE ATOM. FUT USA+45 WOR+45   B62
R+D INT/ORG VOL/ASSN DELIB/GP ARMS/CONT...STYLE 20.   TEC/DEV
PAGE 10 G0200   HEALTH
       NUC/PWR

CLARKE A.C.,PROFILES OF THE FUTURE; AN INQUIRY INTO   B62
THE LIMITS OF THE POSSIBLE. COM/IND DIST/IND PRODUC   FUT
AGE PERCEPT...TECHNIC NEW/IDEA TIME. PAGE 12 G0232   TEC/DEV
       PREDICT
       SPACE

DUPRE J.S.,SCIENCE AND THE NATION: POLICY AND   B62
POLITICS. USA+45 LAW ACADEM FORCES ADMIN CIVMIL/REL   R+D
GOV/REL EFFICIENCY PEACE...TREND 20 SCI/ADVSRY.   INDUS
PAGE 16 G0322   TEC/DEV
       NUC/PWR

DUPRE S.,SCIENCE AND THE NATION. USA+45 ECO/DEV   B62
ACADEM ORD/FREE TECHNIC. PAGE 17 G0323   ARMS/CONT
       DECISION
       TEC/DEV
       INDUS

FORTUNE EDITORS,THE SPACE INDUSTRY: AMERICA'S   B62
NEWEST GIANT. USA+45 FINAN NAT/G BUDGET 20. PAGE 20   SPACE
G0383   INDUS
       TEC/DEV
       MGT

FRIEDRICH-EBERT-STIFTUNG,THE SOVIET BLOC AND   B62
DEVELOPING COUNTRIES. CHINA/COM COM GERMANY/E USSR   MARXISM
WOR+45 ECO/UNDEV INT/ORG NAT/G TEC/DEV NEUTRAL PWR   DIPLOM
...POLICY 20. PAGE 20 G0394   ECO/TAC
       FOR/AID

GILPIN R.,AMERICAN SCIENTISTS AND NUCLEAR WEAPONS   B62
POLICY. COM FUT USA+45 WOR+45 INT/ORG NAT/G   INTELL
PROF/ORG CONSULT FORCES CREATE TEC/DEV BAL/PWR   ATTIT
EDU/PROP ARMS/CONT WAR PERCEPT KNOWL MORAL PWR   DETER
...PHIL/SCI SOC CONCPT GEN/LAWS 20. PAGE 21 G0417   NUC/PWR

GOLOVINE M.N.,CONFLICT IN SPACE: A PATTERN OF WAR   B62
IN A NEW DIMENSION. FUT USA+45 WOR+45 AIR FORCES   CREATE
PLAN DIPLOM DOMIN ATTIT...STAT AUD/VIS CHARTS   TEC/DEV
COLD/WAR 20. PAGE 22 G0432   NUC/PWR
       SPACE

GRANICK D.,THE EUROPEAN EXECUTIVE. BELGIUM FRANCE   B62
GERMANY/W UK INDUS LABOR LG/CO SML/CO EX/STRUC PLAN   MGT
TEC/DEV CAP/ISM COST DEMAND...POLICY CHARTS 20.   ECO/DEV
       ECO/TAC

PAGE 22 G0441   TEC/DEV
       EXEC

GUETZKOW H.,SIMULATION IN SOCIAL SCIENCE: READINGS.   B62
STRUCT OP/RES ADMIN AUTOMAT FEEDBACK...MGT PSY SOC   SIMUL
STYLE BIBLIOG. PAGE 23 G0459   TEC/DEV
       COMPUTER
       GAME

KAHN H.,THINKING ABOUT THE UNTHINKABLE. FUT USA+45   B62
LAW NAT/G CONSULT FORCES ACT/RES CREATE PLAN   INT/ORG
TEC/DEV BAL/PWR DIPLOM EDU/PROP ARMS/CONT DETER   ORD/FREE
ATTIT...CONCPT OBS TREND COLD/WAR 20. PAGE 29 G0570   NUC/PWR
       PEACE

KENNEDY J.F.,TO TURN THE TIDE. SPACE AGRI INT/ORG   B62
FORCES TEC/DEV ADMIN NUC/PWR PEACE WEALTH...ANTHOL   DIPLOM
20 KENNEDY/JF CIV/RIGHTS. PAGE 30 G0592   CHIEF
       POLICY
       NAT/G

LEFEVER E.W.,ARMS AND ARMS CONTROL. COM USA+45   B62
INT/ORG TEC/DEV DIPLOM ORD/FREE 20. PAGE 33 G0652   ATTIT
       PWR
       ARMS/CONT
       BAL/PWR

MACHLUP F.,THE PRODUCTION AND DISTRIBUTION OF   B62
KNOWLEDGE IN THE UNITED STATES. USA+45 COM/IND   ACADEM
INDUS SCHOOL SECT WORKER COMPUTER CREATE CIVMIL/REL   TEC/DEV
COST EFFICIENCY WEALTH 20. PAGE 35 G0688   EDU/PROP
       R+D

MARTINS A.F.,REVOLUCAO BRANCA NO CAMPO. L/A+17C   B62
SERV/IND DEMAND EFFICIENCY PRODUC...POLICY   AGRI
METH/COMP. PAGE 36 G0717   ECO/UNDEV
       TEC/DEV
       NAT/COMP

NEW ZEALAND COMM OF ST SERVICE,THE STATE SERVICES   B62
IN NEW ZEALAND. NEW/ZEALND CONSULT EX/STRUC ACT/RES   ADMIN
...BIBLIOG 20. PAGE 42 G0818   WORKER
       TEC/DEV
       NAT/G

SCHMITT H.A.,THE PATH TO EUROPEAN UNITY. EUR+WWI   B62
USA+45 PLAN TEC/DEV DIPLOM FOR/AID CONFER...INT/LAW   INT/ORG
20 EEC EURCOALSTL MARSHL/PLN UNIFICA. PAGE 49 G0971   INT/TRADE
       REGION
       ECO/DEV

SCHWARTZ L.E.,INTERNATIONAL ORGANIZATIONS AND SPACE   B62
COOPERATION. VOL/ASSN CONSULT CREATE TEC/DEV   INT/ORG
SANCTION...POLICY INT/LAW PHIL/SCI 20 UN. PAGE 50   DIPLOM
G0982   R+D
       SPACE

SNYDER R.C.,FOREIGN POLICY DECISION-MAKING. FUT   B62
KOREA WOR+45 R+D CREATE ADMIN ROUTINE PWR   TEC/DEV
...DECISION PSY SOC CONCPT METH/CNCPT CON/ANAL   HYPO/EXP
CHARTS GEN/METH METH 20. PAGE 52 G1018   DIPLOM

STERN A.C.,AIR POLLUTION (2 VOLS.). LAW INDUS   B62
PROB/SOLV TEC/DEV INSPECT RISK BIO/SOC HABITAT   AIR
...OBS/ENVIR TESTS SAMP 20 POLLUTION. PAGE 53 G1035   OP/RES
       CONTROL
       HEALTH

STOVER C.F.,THE GOVERNMENT OF SCIENCE (PAMPHLET).   B62
USA+45 SOCIETY PROF/ORG EX/STRUC CREATE CONTROL   PHIL/SCI
NUC/PWR WAR GOV/REL PEACE ORD/FREE 20. PAGE 53   TEC/DEV
G1041   LAW
       NAT/G

THANT U.,THE UNITED NATIONS' DEVELOPMENT DECADE: B62
PROPOSALS FOR ACTION. WOR+45 SOCIETY ECO/UNDEV AGRI   INT/ORG
COM/IND FINAN R+D MUNIC SCHOOL VOL/ASSN CONSULT   ALL/VALS
PLAN TEC/DEV ECO/TAC EDU/PROP ADMIN ROUTINE
RIGID/FLEX...MGT SOC CONCPT UNESCO UN TOT/POP
VAL/FREE. PAGE 54 G1064

THOMSON G.P.,NUCLEAR ENERGY IN BRITAIN DURING THE   B62
LAST WAR: THE CHERWELL SIMON LECTURE (MONOGRAPH).   CREATE
UK R+D CONSULT FORCES PLAN DIPLOM TASK CIVMIL/REL   TEC/DEV
ROLE...PHIL/SCI NEW/IDEA LAB/EXP 20 MAUD. PAGE 54   WAR
G1071   NUC/PWR

US SENATE COMM GOVT OPERATIONS,ADMINISTRATION OF   B62
NATIONAL SECURITY. USA+45 CHIEF PLAN PROB/SOLV   ORD/FREE
TEC/DEV DIPLOM ATTIT...POLICY DECISION 20   ADMIN
KENNEDY/JF RUSK/D MCNAMARA/R BUNDY/M HERTER/C.   NAT/G
PAGE 60 G1177   CONTROL

S62

ALBONETTI A.,"IL SECONDO PROGRAMMA QUINQUENNALE   R+D
1963-67 ED IL BILANCIO RICERCHE ED INVESTIMENTI PER PLAN
IL 1963 DELL'ERATOM." EUR+WWI FUT ITALY WOR+45   NUC/PWR
ECO/DEV SERV/IND INT/ORG TEC/DEV ECO/TAC ATTIT
SKILL WEALTH...MGT TIME/SEQ OEEC 20. PAGE 2 G0035

S62

BETHE H.,"DISARMAMENT AND STRATEGY." COM USA+45   PLAN
USSR WOR+45 VOL/ASSN TEC/DEV EDU/PROP NUC/PWR   ORD/FREE
CHOOSE PEACE...POLICY DECISION NEW/IDEA OBS   ARMS/CONT
GEN/LAWS COLD/WAR 420. PAGE 7 G0133   DIPLOM

S62

FLOOD M.M.,"STOCHASTIC LEARNING THEORY APPLIED TO DECISION
CHOICE EXPERIMENTS WITH RATS, DOGS, AND MEN."...PSY COMPUTER
LAB/EXP METH. PAGE 19 G0372   HYPO/EXP
                                     TEC/DEV

S62

FOSTER W.C.,"ARMS CONTROL AND DISARMAMENT IN A   DELIB/GP
DIVIDED WORLD." COM FUT USA+45 USSR WOR+45 INTELL POLICY
INT/ORG NAT/G VOL/ASSN CONSULT CREATE PLAN TEC/DEV ARMS/CONT
EDU/PROP LEGIT NUC/PWR ATTIT RIGID/FLEX...CONCPT   DIPLOM
TREND TOT/POP 20 UN. PAGE 20 G0387

S62

GORDON B.K.,"NUCLEAR WEAPONS: RUSSIAN AND   ORD/FREE
AMERICAN." COM USA+45 USSR NAT/G FORCES ACT/RES   COERCE
TEC/DEV PERCEPT RIGID/FLEX PWR SKILL...MGT   NUC/PWR
METH/CNCPT QUANT OBS TIME/SEQ CON/ANAL GEN/METH
TOT/POP VAL/FREE 20. PAGE 22 G0433

S62

PHIPPS T.E.,"THE CASE FOR DETERRENCE." FUT WOR+45 ATTIT
SOCIETY EX/STRUC FORCES ACT/RES CREATE PLAN TEC/DEV COERCE
ROUTINE RIGID/FLEX ORD/FREE...POLICY MYTH NEW/IDEA DETER
STERTYP COLD/WAR 20. PAGE 45 G0876   ARMS/CONT

S62

SCHILLING W.R.,"SCIENTISTS, FOREIGN POLICY AND   NAT/G
POLITICS." WOR+45 WOR-45 INTELL INT/ORG CONSULT   TEC/DEV
TOP/EX ACT/RES PLAN ADMIN KNOWL...CONCPT OBS TREND DIPLOM
LEAGUE/NAT 20. PAGE 49 G0967   NUC/PWR

S62

SINGER J.D.,"STABLE DETERRENCE AND ITS LIMITS." FUT NAT/G
WOR+45 R+D INT/ORG CONSULT ACT/RES TEC/DEV   FORCES
ARMS/CONT COERCE DRIVE PERCEPT RIGID/FLEX ORD/FREE DETER
PWR...MYTH SIMUL TOT/POP 20. PAGE 51 G1004   NUC/PWR

S62

THORELLI H.B.,"THE INTERNATIONAL OPERATIONS   ECO/TAC
SIMULATION AT THE UNIVERSITY OF CHICAGO." FUT   SIMUL
USA+45 WOR+45 ECO/DEV DIST/IND FINAN INDUS INT/ORG INT/TRADE
DELIB/GP ACT/RES CREATE TEC/DEV WEALTH...STAT
VAL/FREE 20. PAGE 54 G1072

S62

VIETORISZ T.,"PRELIMINARY BIBLIOGRAPHY FOR   BIBLIOG/A
INDUSTRIAL DEVELOPMENT PROGRAMMING." ECO/DEV   TEC/DEV
ECO/UNDEV R+D LABOR PROB/SOLV AUTOMAT PRODUC.   ACT/RES
PAGE 61 G1198   PLAN

C62

JOINT ECONOMIC COMMITTEE,"DIMENSIONS OF SOVIET   ECO/DEV
ECONOMIC POWER." USSR R+D FORCES ACT/RES OP/RES   PLAN
TEC/DEV...GEOG STAT BIBLIOG 20. PAGE 29 G0565   PRODUC
                                     LABOR

N62

US CONGRESS JT ATOM ENRGY COMM,PEACEFUL USES OF   NUC/PWR
ATOMIC ENERGY, HEARING. USA+45 USSR TEC/DEV ATTIT ACADEM
RIGID/FLEX...TESTS CHARTS EXHIBIT METH/COMP 20   SCHOOL
CONGRESS. PAGE 57 G1112   NAT/COMP

B63

DALAND R.T.,PERSPECTIVES OF BRAZILIAN PUBLIC   ADMIN
ADMINISTRATION (VOL. I). BRAZIL LAW ECO/UNDEV   NAT/G
SCHOOL CHIEF TEC/DEV CONFER CONTROL GP/REL ATTIT   PLAN
ROLE PWR...ANTHOL 20. PAGE 14 G0272   GOV/REL

B63

FOSKETT D.J.,CLASSIFICATION AND INDEXING IN THE   PROB/SOLV
SOCIAL SCIENCES. WOR+45 R+D ACT/RES CREATE OP/RES CON/ANAL
TEC/DEV AUTOMAT ROLE...SOC COMPUT/IR BIBLIOG.   CLASSIF
PAGE 20 G0384

B63

GEERTZ C.,OLD SOCIETIES AND NEW STATES: THE QUEST ECO/UNDEV
FOR MODERNITY IN ASIA AND AFRICA. AFR ASIA LAW   TEC/DEV
CULTURE SECT EDU/PROP REV...GOV/COMP NAT/COMP 20. NAT/LISM
PAGE 21 G0415   SOVEREIGN

B63

GOLDSEN J.M.,OUTER SPACE IN WORLD POLITICS. COM   TEC/DEV

USA+45 NAT/G FORCES ACT/RES PLAN DOMIN EDU/PROP   DIPLOM
COERCE ORD/FREE PWR...TECHNIC STAT INT SAMP TREND SPACE
ANTHOL VAL/FREE 20. PAGE 22 G0428

B63

HAUSMAN W.H.,MANAGING ECONOMIC DEVELOPMENT IN   ECO/UNDEV
AFRICA. AFR USA+45 LAW FINAN WORKER TEC/DEV WEALTH PLAN
...ANTHOL 20. PAGE 25 G0492   FOR/AID
                                     MGT

B63

HEYEL C.,THE ENCYCLOPEDIA OF MANAGEMENT. WOR+45   MGT
MARKET TOP/EX TEC/DEV AUTOMAT LEAD ADJUST...STAT   INDUS
CHARTS GAME ANTHOL BIBLIOG. PAGE 26 G0509   ADMIN
                                     FINAN

B63

HOFSTADTER R.,ANTI-INTELLECTUALISM IN AMERICAN   INTELL
LIFE. USA+45 AGRI INDUS ACADEM TEC/DEV EDU/PROP   EPIST
INGP/REL ATTIT...SOC WORSHIP 20 MCCARTHY/J   CULTURE
STEVENSN/A. PAGE 26 G0522   SOCIETY

B63

KAST F.E.,SCIENCE, TECHNOLOGY, AND MANAGEMENT.   MGT
SPACE USA+45 FORCES CONFER DETER NUC/PWR...PHIL/SCI PLAN
CHARTS ANTHOL BIBLIOG 20 NASA. PAGE 30 G0581   TEC/DEV
                                     PROB/SOLV

B63

KATZ S.M.,A SELECTED LIST OF US READINGS ON   BIBLIOG/A
DEVELOPMENT. AGRI COM/IND DIST/IND INDUS LABOR PLAN ECO/UNDEV
FOR/AID EDU/PROP HEALTH...POLICY SOC/WK 20. PAGE 30 TEC/DEV
G0582   ACT/RES

B63

KORNHAUSER W.,SCIENTISTS IN INDUSTRY: CONFLICT AND CREATE
ACCOMMODATION. USA+45 R+D LG/CO NAT/G TEC/DEV   INDUS
CONTROL ADJUST ATTIT...MGT STAT INT BIBLIOG 20.   PROF/ORG
PAGE 31 G0614   GP/REL

B63

KREPS J.,AUTOMATION AND THE OLDER WORKER: AN   BIBLIOG/A
ANNOTATED BIBLIOGRAPHY (PAMPHLET). USA+45 STRUCT   WORKER
ECO/DEV INDUS TEC/DEV. PAGE 31 G0620   AGE/O
                                     AUTOMAT

B63

MCDOUGAL M.S.,LAW AND PUBLIC ORDER IN SPACE. FUT   SPACE
USA+45 ACT/RES TEC/DEV ADJUD...POLICY INT/LAW JURID ORD/FREE
20. PAGE 37 G0739   DIPLOM
                                     DECISION

B63

MULLER H.J.,FREEDOM IN THE WESTERN WORLD. PREHIST ORD/FREE
CULTURE SECT CREATE TEC/DEV DOMIN PWR WEALTH   TIME/SEQ
...MAJORIT SOC CONCPT. PAGE 40 G0793   SOCIETY

B63

NASA,CONFERENCE ON SPACE, SCIENCE, AND URBAN LIFE. MUNIC
USA+45 SOCIETY INDUS ACADEM ACT/RES ECO/TAC ADMIN   SPACE
20. PAGE 41 G0804   TEC/DEV
                                     PROB/SOLV

B63

NORTH R.C.,CONTENT ANALYSIS: A HANDBOOK WITH   METH/CNCPT
APPLICATIONS FOR THE STUDY OF INTERNATIONAL CRISIS. COMPUT/IR
ASIA COM EUR+WWI MOD/EUR INT/ORG TEC/DEV DOMIN   USSR
EDU/PROP ROUTINE COERCE PERCEPT RIGID/FLEX ALL/VALS
...QUANT TESTS CON/ANAL SIMUL GEN/LAWS VAL/FREE.
PAGE 42 G0825

B63

OECD,SCIENCE AND THE POLICIES OF GOVERNMENTS: THE CREATE
IMPLICATIONS OF SCIENCE AND TECHNOLOGY FOR NATL AND TEC/DEV
INTL AFFAIRS. WOR+45 INT/ORG EDU/PROP AUTOMAT   DIPLOM
...POLICY PHIL/SCI 20. PAGE 42 G0830   NAT/G

B63

REED E.,CHALLENGES TO DEMOCRACY: THE NEXT TEN   POLICY
YEARS. FUT USA+45 ECO/DEV DELIB/GP TEC/DEV CONFER EDU/PROP
GOV/REL KNOWL ORD/FREE...MAJORIT IDEA/COMP ANTHOL ECO/TAC
20. PAGE 46 G0909   NAT/G

B63

RUITENBEER H.M.,THE DILEMMA OF ORGANIZATIONAL   PERSON
SOCIETY. CULTURE ECO/DEV MUNIC SECT TEC/DEV   ROLE
EDU/PROP NAT/LISM ORD/FREE...NAT/COMP 20 RIESMAN/D ADMIN
WHYTE/WF MERTON/R MEAD/MARG JASPERS/K. PAGE 48   WORKER
G0945

B63

SCHRADER R.,SCIENCE AND POLICY. WOR+45 ECO/DEV   TEC/DEV
ECO/UNDEV R+D FORCES PLAN DIPLOM GOV/REL TECHRACY NAT/G
BIBLIOG. PAGE 50 G0976   POLICY
                                     ADMIN

TOMKINS S.S.,COMPUTER SIMULATION OF PERSONALITY. B63
R+D TEC/DEV AUTOMAT FEEDBACK ANOMIE PERCEPT...STYLE
PERS/TEST PREDICT COMPUT/IR GP/COMP. PAGE 55 G1075
COMPUTER
PERSON
SIMUL
PROG/TEAC

US ATOMIC ENERGY COMMISSION,ATOMIC ENERGY IN THE B63
SOVIET UNION: TRIP REPORT OF THE US ATOMIC ENERGY
DELEGATION, MAY 1933. USSR R+D NAT/G CONSULT CREATE
DIPLOM ADMIN ROUTINE EFFICIENCY PRODUC KNOWL SKILL
...NAT/COMP 20 AEC TRAVEL TREATY. PAGE 56 G1107
METH/COMP
OP/RES
TEC/DEV
NUC/PWR

WIGHTMAN D.,TOWARD ECONOMIC CO-OPERATION IN ASIA. B63
ASIA S/ASIA VOL/ASSN ACT/RES PLAN TEC/DEV ECO/TAC
EDU/PROP RIGID/FLEX SKILL...POLICY METH/CNCPT OBS
INT GEN/LAWS UN 20 ECAFE. PAGE 63 G1237
ECO/UNDEV
CREATE

MCDOUGAL M.S.,"THE ENJOYMENT AND ACQUISITION OF L63
RESOURCES IN OUTER SPACE." CHRIST-17C FUT WOR+45
WOR-45 LAW EXTR/IND INT/ORG ACT/RES CREATE TEC/DEV
ECO/TAC LEGIT COERCE HEALTH KNOWL ORD/FREE PWR
WEALTH...JURID HIST/WRIT VAL/FREE. PAGE 37 G0738
PLAN
TREND

BOHN L.,"WHOSE NUCLEAR TEST: NON-PHYSICAL S63
INSPECTION AND TEST BAN." WOR+45 R+D INT/ORG
VOL/ASSN ORD/FREE...GEN/LAWS GEN/METH COLD/WAR 20.
PAGE 8 G0148
ADJUD
ARMS/CONT
TEC/DEV
NUC/PWR

BOULDING K.E.,"UNIVERSITY, SOCIETY, AND ARMS S63
CONTROL." WOR+45 WOR-45 ACADEM NAT/G CONSULT FORCES
ACT/RES PLAN TEC/DEV BAL/PWR ECO/TAC COERCE DETER
WAR ATTIT RIGID/FLEX KNOWL ORD/FREE PWR WEALTH
...CONCPT COLD/WAR TOT/POP 20. PAGE 8 G0159
SOCIETY
ARMS/CONT

DE FOREST J.D.,"LOW LEVELS OF TECHNOLOGY AND S63
ECONOMIC DEVELOPMENT PROSPECTS." WOR+45 WOR-45
CULTURE ACT/RES CREATE PLAN ECO/TAC ROUTINE PERCEPT
WEALTH...METH/CNCPT GEN/LAWS 20. PAGE 15 G0284
ECO/UNDEV
TEC/DEV

FERRETTI B.,"IMPORTANZA E PROSPETTIVE DELL ENERGIA S63
DI ORIGINE NUCLEARE." FUT ITALY WOR+45 INTELL R+D
ACT/RES CREATE HEALTH WEALTH...METH/CNCPT TIME/SEQ
20. PAGE 19 G0365
TEC/DEV
EXEC
NUC/PWR

GANDILHON J.,"LA SCIENCE ET LA TECHNIQUE A L'AIDE S63
DES REGIONS PEU DEVELOPPEES." FRANCE FUT WOR+45
ECO/DEV R+D PROF/ORG ACT/RES PLAN...MGT TOT/POP
VAL/FREE 20 UN. PAGE 21 G0406
ECO/UNDEV
TEC/DEV
FOR/AID

KAWALKOWSKI A.,"POUR UNE EUROPE INDEPENDENTE ET S63
REUNIFIEE." EUR+WWI FUT USA+45 USSR WOR+45 ECO/DEV
PROC/MFG INT/ORG NAT/G ACT/RES TEC/DEV FEDERAL
RIGID/FLEX...CONCPT METH/CNCPT OEEC TOT/POP 20
DEGAULLE/C. PAGE 30 G0587
R+D
PLAN
NUC/PWR

MASSART L.,"L'ORGANISATION DE LA RECHERCHE S63
SCIENTIFIQUE EN EUROPE." EUR+WWI WOR+45 ACT/RES
PLAN TEC/DEV EDU/PROP EXEC KNOWL...METH/CNCPT EEC
20. PAGE 36 G0718
R+D
CREATE

NADLER E.B.,"SOME ECONOMIC DISADVANTAGES OF THE S63
ARMS RACE." USA+45 INDUS R+D FORCES PLAN TEC/DEV
ECO/TAC FOR/AID EDU/PROP PWR WEALTH...TREND
COLD/WAR 20. PAGE 41 G0800
ECO/DEV
MGT
BAL/PAY

SCHMITT H.A.,"THE EUROPEAN COMMUNITIES." EUR+WWI S63
FRANCE GERMANY DELIB/GP EX/STRUC TOP/EX CREATE TEC/DEV
ECO/TAC LEGIT REGION COERCE DRIVE ALL/VALS
...METH/CNCPT EEC 20. PAGE 49 G0972
VOL/ASSN
ECO/DEV

SMITH D.O.,"WHAT IS A WAR DETERRENT." FUT GERMANY S63
HUNGARY UK USA+45 WOR+45 WOR-45 NAT/G TEC/DEV
BAL/PWR PWR...CONCPT GEN/LAWS COLD/WAR 20. PAGE 51
G1013
ACT/RES
FORCES
ARMS/CONT
DETER

TANNENBAUM P.H.,"COMMUNICATION OF SCIENCE S63
INFORMATION." USA+45 TEC/DEV ROUTINE...PHIL/SCI
STYLE 20. PAGE 53 G1051
COM/IND
PRESS
OP/RES
METH/CNCPT

VIETORISZ T.,"PRELIMINARY BIBLIOGRAPHY FOR S63
BIBLIOG/A

INDUSTRIAL DEVELOPMENT PROGRAMMING." ECO/DEV
ECO/UNDEV R+D LABOR PROB/SOLV AUTOMAT PRODUC.
PAGE 61 G1199
TEC/DEV
ACT/RES
PLAN

WILES P.J.D.,"WILL CAPITALISM AND COMMUNISM S63
SPONTANEOUSLY CONVERGE." COM FUT USA+45 ECO/DEV
DIST/IND MARKET CAP/ISM ECO/TAC RIGID/FLEX WEALTH
MARXISM SOCISM...MATH STAT TREND COMPUT/IR 20.
PAGE 63 G1240
PLAN
TEC/DEV
USSR

BLOUSTEIN E.J.,NUCLEAR ENERGY, PUBLIC POLICY, AND B64
THE LAW. USA+45 NAT/G ADJUD ADMIN GP/REL OWN PEACE
ATTIT HEALTH...ANTHOL 20. PAGE 7 G0144
TEC/DEV
LAW
POLICY
NUC/PWR

BRIGHT J.R.,RESEARCH, DEVELOPMENT AND TECHNOLOGICAL B64
INNOVATION. CULTURE R+D CREATE PLAN PROB/SOLV
AUTOMAT RISK PERSON...DECISION CONCPT PREDICT
BIBLIOG. PAGE 9 G0168
TEC/DEV
NEW/IDEA
INDUS
MGT

BROWN N.,NUCLEAR WAR: THE IMPENDING STRATEGIC B64
DEADLOCK. USA+45 USSR TEC/DEV BUDGET RISK ARMS/CONT
NUC/PWR WEAPON COST BIO/SOC...GEOG IDEA/COMP
NAT/COMP GAME NATO WARSAW/P. PAGE 9 G0177
FORCES
OP/RES
WAR
GEN/LAWS

ELLUL J.,THE TECHNOLOGICAL SOCIETY. FUT STRUCT B64
CREATE AUTOMAT ROUTINE STRANGE ANOMIE MORAL
PHIL/SCI. PAGE 18 G0344
SOC
SOCIETY
TECHNIC
TEC/DEV

ETZIONI A.,THE MOON-DOGGLE: DOMESTIC AND B64
INTERNATIONAL IMPLICATIONS OF THE SPACE RACE. FUT
USA+45 WOR+45 INTELL ECO/DEV INDUS VOL/ASSN
EX/STRUC FORCES LEGIS TOP/EX PLAN TEC/DEV ECO/TAC
EDU/PROP KNOWL ORD/FREE PWR RESPECT WEALTH
TIME/SEQ. PAGE 18 G0352
R+D
NAT/G
DIPLOM
SPACE

FEI J.C.H.,DEVELOPMENT OF THE LABOR SURPLUS B64
ECONOMY: THEORY AND POLICY. WOR+45 AGRI INDUS
MARKET PROB/SOLV TEC/DEV...STAT CHARTS GEN/LAWS
METH 20 THIRD/WRLD. PAGE 18 G0361
ECO/TAC
POLICY
WORKER
ECO/UNDEV

GOWING M.,BRITAIN AND ATOMIC ENERGY 1939-1945. B64
FRANCE UK USA+45 USA-45 NAT/G CREATE...PHIL/SCI 20
AEA. PAGE 22 G0439
NUC/PWR
DIPLOM
TEC/DEV

GRODZINS M.,THE ATOMIC AGE: FORTY-FIVE SCIENTISTS B64
AND SCHOLARS SPEAK ON NATIONAL AND WORLD AFFAIRS.
FUT USA+45 WOR+45 R+D INT/ORG NAT/G CONSULT TEC/DEV
EDU/PROP ATTIT PERSON ORD/FREE...HUM CONCPT
TIME/SEQ CON/ANAL. PAGE 23 G0454
INTELL
ARMS/CONT
NUC/PWR

GROSSER G.H.,THE THREAT OF IMPENDING DISASTER: B64
CONTRIBUTIONS TO THE PSYCHOLOGY OF STRESS. SPACE
UNIV SOCIETY R+D TEC/DEV EDU/PROP COERCE WAR ATTIT
BIO/SOC DISPL PERCEPT PERSON...SOC MYTH SELF/OBS
CONT/OBS BIOG CON/ANAL TOT/POP 20. PAGE 23 G0455
HEALTH
PSY
NUC/PWR

HAMMOND P.E.,SOCIOLOGISTS AT WORK. VOL/ASSN OP/RES B64
TEC/DEV CONFER ROUTINE TASK EFFICIENCY...MGT
NEW/IDEA STYLE SAMP. PAGE 24 G0478
R+D
BIOG
SOC

HASKINS C.P.,THE SCIENTIFIC REVOLUTION AND WORLD B64
POLITICS. COM FUT USA+45 ECO/DEV ECO/UNDEV ATTIT
...PHIL/SCI BIBLIOG 20 THIRD/WRLD. PAGE 25 G0489
TEC/DEV
POLICY
DIPLOM
TREND

HAZLEWOOD A.,THE ECONOMICS OF DEVELOPMENT: AN B64
ANNOTATED LIST OF BOOKS AND ARTICLES PUBLISHED
1958-1962. AGRI FINAN INDUS LABOR NAT/G DIPLOM
INT/TRADE INCOME...MGT 20. PAGE 25 G0497
BIBLIOG/A
ECO/UNDEV
TEC/DEV

HEKHUIS D.J.,INTERNATIONAL STABILITY: MILITARY, B64
ECONOMIC AND POLITICAL DIMENSIONS. FUT WOR+45 LAW
ECO/UNDEV INT/ORG NAT/G VOL/ASSN FORCES ACT/RES
BAL/PWR PWR WEALTH...STAT UN 20. PAGE 25 G0503
TEC/DEV
DETER
REGION

HODGETTS J.E.,ADMINISTERING THE ATOM FOR PEACE. B64
OP/RES TEC/DEV ADMIN...IDEA/COMP METH/COMP 20.
PAGE 26 G0517
PROB/SOLV
NUC/PWR
PEACE
MGT

LANG A.S.,URBAN RAIL TRANSIT. OP/RES PLAN PROB/SOLV MUNIC
TEC/DEV AUTOMAT COST...TECHNIC MATH CON/ANAL CHARTS DIST/IND
METH/COMP SIMUL 20 RAILROAD PUB/TRANS. PAGE 32 ECOMETRIC
G0632
B64

LI C.M.,INDUSTRIAL DEVELOPMENT IN COMMUNIST CHINA. ASIA
CHINA/COM ECO/DEV ECO/UNDEV AGRI FINAN INDUS MARKET TEC/DEV
LABOR NAT/G ECO/TAC INT/TRADE EXEC ALL/VALS
...POLICY RELATIV TREND WORK TOT/POP VAL/FREE 20.
PAGE 34 G0665
B64

MARTINO R.L.,PROJECT MANAGEMENT AND CONTROL: VOL. 2 DECISION
APPLIED OPERATIONAL PLANNING. COMPUTER...MATH PLAN
CHARTS SIMUL METH TIME. PAGE 36 G0716 TEC/DEV
OP/RES
B64

NASA,PROCEEDINGS OF CONFERENCE ON THE LAW OF SPACE SPACE
AND OF SATELLITE COMMUNICATIONS: CHICAGO 1963. FUT COM/IND
WOR+45 DELIB/GP PROB/SOLV TEC/DEV CONFER ADJUD LAW
NUC/PWR...POLICY IDEA/COMP 20 NASA. PAGE 41 G0805 DIPLOM
B64

ORGANIZATION AMERICAN STATES,ECONOMIC SURVEY OF ECO/UNDEV
LATIN AMERICA, 1962. L/A+17C AGRI DIST/IND INDUS CHARTS
MARKET PROC/MFG R+D PLAN TEC/DEV ECO/TAC REGION
BAL/PAY ALL/VALS...CON/ANAL ORG/CHARTS GEN/METH OAS
20. PAGE 43 G0844

OSSENBECK F.J.,OPEN SPACE AND PEACE. CHINA/COM FUT SPACE
USA+45 USSR LAW PROB/SOLV TEC/DEV EDU/PROP NEUTRAL ORD/FREE
PEACE...AUD/VIS ANTHOL 20. PAGE 43 G0850 DIPLOM
CREATE
B64

PEDERSEN E.S.,NUCLEAR ENERGY IN SPACE. FUT INTELL SPACE
R+D CONSULT...NEW/IDEA CHARTS METH T 20. PAGE 44 TEC/DEV
G0864 NUC/PWR
LAB/EXP
B64

ROSECRANCE R.N.,THE DISPERSION OF NUCLEAR WEAPONS: EUR+WWI
STRATEGY AND POLITICS. ASIA COM FUT S/ASIA USA+45 PWR
INT/ORG NAT/G DELIB/GP FORCES ACT/RES TEC/DEV PEACE
BAL/PWR COERCE DETER ATTIT RIGID/FLEX ORD/FREE
...POLICY CHARTS VAL/FREE. PAGE 48 G0935
B64

SCHWARTZ M.D.,CONFERENCE ON SPACE SCIENCE AND SPACE SPACE
LAW. FUT COM/IND NAT/G FORCES ACT/RES PLAN BUDGET LAW
DIPLOM NUC/PWR WEAPON...POLICY ANTHOL 20. PAGE 50 PEACE
G0983 TEC/DEV
B64

TAUBENFELD H.J.,SPACE AND SOCIETY. USA+45 LAW SPACE
FORCES CREATE TEC/DEV ADJUD CONTROL COST PEACE SOCIETY
...PREDICT ANTHOL 20. PAGE 54 G1057 ADJUST
DIPLOM
B64

THANT U.,TOWARD WORLD PEACE. DELIB/GP TEC/DEV DIPLOM
EDU/PROP WAR SOVEREIGN...INT/LAW 20 UN MID/EAST. BIOG
PAGE 54 G1065 PEACE
COERCE
B64

VAN DYKE V.,PRIDE AND POWER: THE RATIONALE OF THE TEC/DEV
SPACE PROGRAM. FUT USA+45 INTELL R+D NAT/G POL/PAR ATTIT
DELIB/GP EX/STRUC LEGIS TOP/EX ACT/RES PLAN ECO/TAC POLICY
EDU/PROP ORD/FREE PWR RESPECT SKILL...TIME/SEQ
VAL/FREE. PAGE 61 G1191
B64

WHEELER-BENNETT J.W.,THE NEMESIS OF POWER (2ND FORCES
ED.). EUR+WWI GERMANY TOP/EX TEC/DEV ADMIN WAR NAT/G
PERS/REL RIGID/FLEX ROLE ORD/FREE PWR FASCISM 20 GP/REL
HITLER/A. PAGE 63 G1231 STRUCT
B64

CARNEGIE ENDOWMENT INT. PEACE,"POLITICAL QUESTIONS INT/ORG
(ISSUES BEFORE THE NINETEENTH GENERAL ASSEMBLY)." PEACE
SPACE WOR+45 CONSTN FINAN NAT/G CONSULT DELIB/GP
FORCES LEGIS TEC/DEV EDU/PROP LEGIT ARMS/CONT
COERCE NUC/PWR ATTIT ALL/VALS...CONCPT OBS UN
COLD/WAR 20. PAGE 11 G0208
L64

CARNEGIE ENDOWMENT INT. PEACE,"ECONOMIC AND SOCIAL INT/ORG
QUESTION (ISSUES BEFORE THE NINETEENTH GENERAL INT/TRADE
ASSEMBLY)." WOR+45 ECO/DEV ECO/UNDEV INDUS R+D
DELIB/GP CREATE PLAN TEC/DEV ECO/TAC FOR/AID
L64

BAL/PAY...RECORD UN 20. PAGE 11 G0209

ABT C.,"WAR GAMING." USA+45 NAT/G TOP/EX ACT/RES FORCES
TEC/DEV COERCE KNOWL ORD/FREE PWR...DECISION MATH SIMUL
TIME/SEQ COMPUT/IR CHARTS LAB/EXP VAL/FREE. PAGE 2 WAR
G0026
S64

CALDWELL L.K.,"BIOPOLITICS: SCIENCE, ETHICS, AND TEC/DEV
PUBLIC POLICY." FUT USA+45 WOR+45 INTELL STRATA R+D POLICY
NAT/G CONSULT PLAN EDU/PROP ALL/VALS...RELATIV
PHIL/SCI 20. PAGE 10 G0203
S64

FLORINSKY M.T.,"TRENDS IN THE SOVIET ECONOMY." COM ECO/DEV
USA+45 USSR INDUS LABOR NAT/G PLAN TEC/DEV ECO/TAC AGRI
ALL/VALS SOCISM...MGT METH/CNCPT STYLE CON/ANAL
GEN/METH WORK 20. PAGE 19 G0374
S64

MARES V.E.,"EAST EUROPE'S SECOND CHANCE." COM VOL/ASSN
EUR+WWI HUNGARY ROMANIA USSR YUGOSLAVIA ECO/UNDEV ECO/TAC
NAT/G TOP/EX CREATE PLAN TEC/DEV REGION NAT/LISM
RIGID/FLEX PWR...CONCPT STAT COMECON 20. PAGE 36
G0705
S64

MUMFORD L.,"AUTHORITARIAN AND DEMOCRATIC ECO/DEV
TECHNIQUES." INDUS PROC/MFG LG/CO SML/CO CREATE TEC/DEV
PLAN KNOWL...POLICY TREND WORK 20. PAGE 40 G0794
S64

NEEDHAM T.,"SCIENCE AND SOCIETY IN EAST AND WEST." ASIA
INTELL STRATA R+D LOC/G NAT/G PROVS CONSULT ACT/RES STRUCT
CREATE PLAN TEC/DEV EDU/PROP ADMIN ATTIT ALL/VALS
...POLICY RELATIV MGT CONCPT NEW/IDEA TIME/SEQ WORK
WORK. PAGE 41 G0815
S64

SPONSLER G.C.,"THE MILITARY ROLE IN SPACE." FUT TEC/DEV
USA+45 SEA AIR NAT/G ACT/RES PLAN COERCE NUC/PWR FORCES
WEAPON KNOWL ORD/FREE PWR RESPECT...TREND 20. SPACE
PAGE 52 G1026
S64

SCHRAMM W.,"MASS MEDIA AND NATIONAL DEVELOPMENT: ECO/UNDEV
THE ROLE OF INFORMATION IN DEVELOPING COUNTRIES." COM/IND
FINAN R+D ACT/RES PLAN TEC/DEV DIPLOM CHOOSE SUPEGO EDU/PROP
ORD/FREE...BIBLIOG 20. PAGE 50 G0978 MAJORIT
C64

WHITE HOUSE CONFERENCE ON INTERNATIONAL R+D
COOPERATION(VOL.II). SPACE WOR+45 EXTR/IND INT/ORG CONFER
LABOR WORKER NUC/PWR PEACE AGE/Y...CENSUS ANTHOL 20 TEC/DEV
RESOURCE/N URBAN/RNWL PUB/TRANS. PAGE 1 G0019 DIPLOM
B65

PEACE RESEARCH ABSTRACTS. FUT WOR+45 R+D INT/ORG BIBLIOG/A
NAT/G PLAN TEC/DEV BAL/PWR DIPLOM FOR/AID NUC/PWR PEACE
HEALTH. PAGE 1 G0020 ARMS/CONT
WAR
B65

ANDERSON C.A.,EDUCATION AND ECONOMIC DEVELOPMENT. ANTHOL
INDUS R+D SCHOOL TEC/DEV ECO/TAC EDU/PROP AGE ECO/DEV
HEREDITY PERCEPT SKILL 20. PAGE 3 G0056 ECO/UNDEV
WORKER
B65

BARISH N.N.,MANAGEMENT SCIENCES IN THE EMERGING ECO/UNDEV
COUNTRIES. AFR CHINA/COM WOR+45 FINAN INDUS PLAN OP/RES
PRODUC HABITAT...ANTHOL 20. PAGE 5 G0093 MGT
TEC/DEV
B65

BENTWICH J.S.,EDUCATION IN ISRAEL. ISRAEL CULTURE SECT
STRATA PROB/SOLV TEC/DEV ADJUST ALL/VALS 20 JEWS. EDU/PROP
PAGE 7 G0125 ACADEM
SCHOOL
B65

FOSTER P.,EDUCATION AND SOCIAL CHANGE IN GHANA. SCHOOL
GHANA CULTURE STRUCT ECO/UNDEV TEC/DEV REGION CREATE
EFFICIENCY LITERACY ALL/VALS SOVEREIGN...STAT SOCIETY
METH/COMP 19/20 GOLD/COAST. PAGE 20 G0385
B65

FRUTKIN A.W.,SPACE AND THE INTERNATIONAL SPACE
COOPERATION YEAR: A NATIONAL CHALLENGE (PAMPHLET). INDUS
EUR+WWI USA+45 FINAN TEC/DEV BUDGET...MGT 20 NASA. NAT/G
PAGE 20 G0396 DIPLOM
B65

HALPERIN M.H.,COMMUNIST CHINA AND ARMS CONTROL. ATTIT
CHINA/COM FUT USA+45 CULTURE FORCES TEC/DEV ECO/TAC POLICY

WAR PEACE ORD/FREE MARXISM 20 COLD/WAR. PAGE 24   ARMS/CONT
G0473   NUC/PWR

         B65
HASSON J.A.,THE ECONOMICS OF NUCLEAR POWER. INDIA   NUC/PWR
UK USA+45 WOR+45 INT/ORG TEC/DEV COST...SOC STAT   INDUS
CHARTS 20 EURATOM. PAGE 25 G0490   ECO/DEV
    METH

         B65
IANNI O.,ESTADO E CAPITALISMO. L/A+17C FINAN   ECO/UNDEV
TEC/DEV ECO/TAC ORD/FREE WEALTH POLICY. PAGE 28   STRUCT
G0542   INDUS
    NAT/G

         B65
INT. BANK RECONSTR. DEVELOP.,ECONOMIC DEVELOPMENT   INDUS
OF KUWAIT. ISLAM KUWAIT AGRI FINAN MARKET EX/STRUC   NAT/G
TEC/DEV ECO/TAC ADMIN WEALTH...OBS CON/ANAL CHARTS
20. PAGE 28 G0548

         B65
JANDA K.,DATA PROCESSING: APPLICATIONS TO POLITICAL   DECISION
RESEARCH....STAT CON/ANAL. PAGE 28 G0557   COMPUTER
    TEC/DEV
    METH

         B65
KANTOROVICH L.V.,THE BEST USE OF ECONOMIC   PLAN
RESOURCES. USSR SOCIETY FINAN ACT/RES TEC/DEV   MATH
ECO/TAC PRICE CONTROL COST DEMAND EFFICIENCY   DECISION
OPTIMAL...MGT STAT. PAGE 29 G0572

         B65
KASER M.,COMECON* INTEGRATION PROBLEMS OF THE   PLAN
PLANNED ECONOMIES. INT/ORG TEC/DEV INT/TRADE PRICE   ECO/DEV
ADMIN ADJUST CENTRAL...STAT TIME/SEQ ORG/CHARTS   COM
COMECON. PAGE 29 G0579   REGION

         B65
KENT A.,SPECIALIZED INFORMATION CENTERS. INTELL R+D   COMPUT/IR
VOL/ASSN CONSULT COMPUTER KNOWL...DECISION HUM   CREATE
PHIL/SCI METH/CNCPT TREND CHARTS 20. PAGE 30 G0593   TEC/DEV
    METH/COMP

         B65
LAPP R.E.,THE NEW PRIESTHOOD; THE SCIENTIFIC ELITE   TEC/DEV
AND THE USES OF POWER. USA+45 ELITES INTELL SOCIETY   TECHRACY
R+D NAT/G CHIEF LEGIS CIVMIL/REL GP/REL PWR 20   CONTROL
PRESIDENT CONGRESS. PAGE 32 G0635   POPULISM

         B65
LUTZ V.,FRENCH PLANNING. FRANCE TEC/DEV RIGID/FLEX   PLAN
ORD/FREE 20. PAGE 34 G0680   ADMIN
    FUT

         B65
NATIONAL SCIENCE FOUNDATION,CURRENT RESEARCH AND   BIBLIOG
DEVELOPMENT IN SCIENTIFIC DOCUMENTATION - NO. 12.   COMPUT/IR
WOR+45 INTELL COM/IND NAT/G COMPUTER TEC/DEV   R+D
AUTOMAT KNOWL...PSY LING 20. PAGE 41 G0812   PHIL/SCI

         B65
PYE L.W.,POLITICAL CULTURE AND DEVELOPMENT. WOR+45   PHIL/SCI
WOR-45 CULTURE ECO/UNDEV NAT/G ALL/VALS ORD/FREE   TEC/DEV
PWR WEALTH ALL/IDEOS...TRADIT TREND 20. PAGE 46   SOCIETY
G0897

         B65
SMITH E.A.,SOCIAL WELFARE: PRINCIPLES AND CONCEPTS.   CONCPT
STRATA STRUCT CONSULT WORKER ACT/RES CREATE PLAN   SOC/WK
TEC/DEV ROUTINE GP/REL UTOPIA...SOC 20. PAGE 51   RECEIVE
G1014   ORD/FREE

         B65
STEINER G.A.,THE CREATIVE ORGANIZATION. ELITES   CREATE
LG/CO PLAN PROB/SOLV TEC/DEV INSPECT CAP/ISM   MGT
CONTROL EXEC PERSON...METH/COMP HYPO/EXP 20.   ADMIN
PAGE 52 G1034   SOC

         B65
THAYER F.C. JR.,AIR TRANSPORT POLICY AND NATIONAL   AIR
SECURITY: A POLITICAL, ECONOMIC, AND MILITARY   FORCES
ANALYSIS. DIST/IND OP/RES PLAN TEC/DEV DIPLOM DETER   CIVMIL/REL
WAR COST EFFICIENCY...POLICY BIBLIOG 20 DEPT/DEFEN   ORD/FREE
FAA CAB. PAGE 54 G1066

         B65
TURNER A.N.,INDUSTRIAL JOBS AND THE WORKER. USA+45   WORKER
CULTURE ECO/DEV LABOR MUNIC ACT/RES AUTOMAT TASK   INDUS
...CHARTS BIBLIOG 20. PAGE 55 G1082   ATTIT
    TEC/DEV

         B65
UN,SPACE ACTIVITIES AND RESOURCES: REVIEW OF UNITED   SPACE
NATION'S NATIONAL AND INTERNATIONAL PROGRAMS.   NUC/PWR

INT/ORG LABOR PLAN TEC/DEV DIPLOM EFFICIENCY HEALTH   FOR/AID
...GOV/COMP 20 UN. PAGE 55 G1086   PEACE

         B65
UNESCO,HANDBOOK OF INTERNATIONAL EXCHANGES. COM/IND   INDEX
R+D ACADEM PROF/ORG VOL/ASSN CREATE TEC/DEV   INT/ORG
EDU/PROP AGREE 20 TREATY. PAGE 55 G1090   DIPLOM
    PRESS

         B65
US CONGRESS JT ATOM ENRGY COMM,PEACEFUL   NUC/PWR
APPLICATIONS OF NUCLEAR EXPLOSIVES: PLOWSHARE.   DELIB/GP
HEARING. USA+45 LEGIS CREATE PLAN PEACE...CHARTS   TEC/DEV
EXHIBIT BIBLIOG CONGRESS PANAMA/CNL. PAGE 57 G1113   NAT/G

         B65
US DEPARTMENT OF ARMY,MILITARY PROTECTIVE   FORCES
CONSTRUCTION: NUCLEAR WARFARE AND CHEMICAL AND   CONSTRUC
BIOLOGICAL OPERATIONS (MANUAL). OP/RES TEC/DEV RISK   TASK
COERCE NUC/PWR WAR WEAPON EFFICIENCY UTIL BIO/SOC   HEALTH
HABITAT ORD/FREE 20. PAGE 57 G1117

         B65
US SENATE COMM AERO SPACE SCI,NATIONAL SPACE GOALS   SPACE
FOR THE POST-APOLLO PERIOD. USA+45 CONSULT DELIB/GP   FUT
TEC/DEV BUDGET GP/REL ATTIT...CHARTS IDEA/COMP TIME   R+D
20 DEPT/DEFEN NASA CONGRESS. PAGE 59 G1166   LEGIS

         B65
US SENATE COMM AERO SPACE SCI,INTERNATIONAL   DIPLOM
COOPERATION AND ORGANIZATION FOR OUTER SPACE. FUT   SPACE
USA+45 WOR+45 PROF/ORG VOL/ASSN CONSULT DELIB/GP   R+D
PLAN TEC/DEV ARMS/CONT GP/REL PEACE 20 UN NASA.   NAT/G
PAGE 59 G1167

         B65
WARNER A.W.,THE IMPACT OF SCIENCE ON TECHNOLOGY.   DECISION
UNIV INTELL SOCIETY NAT/G ACT/RES PLAN PROB/SOLV   TEC/DEV
BUDGET OPTIMAL GEN/METH. PAGE 62 G1214   CREATE
    POLICY

         B65
WEISNER J.B.,WHERE SCIENCE AND POLITICS MEET.   CHIEF
USA+45 ECO/DEV R+D FORCES PROB/SOLV DIPLOM FOR/AID   NAT/G
CONTROL...PHIL/SCI PRESIDENT KENNEDY/JF JOHNSON/LB.   POLICY
PAGE 63 G1228   TEC/DEV

         B65
WISH J.R.,ECONOMIC DEVELOPMENT IN LATIN AMERICA: AN   BIBLIOG/A
ANNOTATED BIBLIOGRAPHY. L/A+17C COM/IND MARKET R+D   ECO/UNDEV
CREATE CAP/ISM ATTIT...STAT METH 20. PAGE 64 G1250   TEC/DEV
    AGRI

         S65
ABT C.C.,"CONTROLLING FUTURE ARMS." USSR PLAN   PREDICT
BAL/PWR DIPLOM NUC/PWR COST...CLASSIF STAT CHARTS.   FUT
PAGE 2 G0027   ARMS/CONT
    TEC/DEV

         S65
BIRNBAUM K.,"SWEDEN'S NUCLEAR POLICY." WOR+45   SWEDEN
POL/PAR CREATE TEC/DEV NEUTRAL RISK WAR ORD/FREE   NUC/PWR
...DECISION IDEA/COMP NAT/COMP TIME. PAGE 7 G0137   DIPLOM
    ARMS/CONT

         S65
BLOOMFIELD L.P.,"ARMS CONTROL AND THE DEVELOPING   ARMS/CONT
COUNTRIES." AFR ISLAM S/ASIA USA+45 VOL/ASSN   ECO/UNDEV
TEC/DEV DIPLOM REGION NUC/PWR...PREDICT TREND.   HYPO/EXP
PAGE 7 G0142   OBS

         S65
BOHN L.C.,"ATOMS FOR PEACE AND ATOMS FOR WAR."   NUC/PWR
WOR+45 INT/ORG TEC/DEV DIPLOM IDEA/COMP. PAGE 8   ARMS/CONT
G0149   RECORD

         S65
CHU K.,"A DYNAMIC MODEL OF THE FIRM." OP/RES   INDUS
PROB/SOLV...DECISION ECOMETRIC NEW/IDEA STAT GAME   COMPUTER
ORG/CHARTS SIMUL. PAGE 12 G0230   TEC/DEV

         S65
GREGG P.M.,"DIMENSIONS OF POLITICAL SYSTEMS: FACTOR   SIMUL
ANALYSIS OF A CROSS POLITY SURVEY." TEC/DEV   GEN/METH
...DECISION PHIL/SCI CONCPT STAT IDEA/COMP   CLASSIF
GEN/LAWS. PAGE 23 G0447

         S65
HIBBS A.R.,"SPACE TECHNOLOGY* THE THREAT AND THE   SPACE
PROMISE." FUT VOL/ASSN TEC/DEV NUC/PWR COST   ARMS/CONT
EFFICIENCY UTIL UN TREATY. PAGE 26 G0510   PREDICT

         S65
KINTNER W.P.,"THE PROSPECTS FOR WESTERN SCIENCE AND   TEC/DEV
TECHNOLOGY." EUR+WWI FRANCE USA+45 USSR R+D NUC/PWR   VOL/ASSN
NATO. PAGE 30 G0598   STAT

RECORD

S65
KOHL W.L.,"NUCLEAR SHARING IN NATO AND THE
MULTILATERAL FORCE." FUT USSR VOL/ASSN TEC/DEV
DIPLOM NUC/PWR WAR WEAPON NATO. PAGE 31 G0611
ARMS/CONT
OBS
IDEA/COMP

S65
TENDLER J.D.,"TECHNOLOGY AND ECONOMIC DEVELOPMENT*
THE CASE OF HYDRO VS THERMAL POWER." CONSTRUC
DIST/IND CREATE TEC/DEV INT/TRADE CENTRAL PWR SKILL
WEALTH...MGT NAT/COMP ARGEN. PAGE 54 G1063
BRAZIL
INDUS
ECO/UNDEV

C65
US AIR FORCE ACADEMY.,"AMERICAN DEFENSE POLICY." COM
INT/ORG TEC/DEV FOR/AID ARMS/CONT DETER NUC/PWR
...POLICY DECISION CONCPT ANTHOL BIBLIOG/A 20
COLD/WAR NATO. PAGE 56 G1103
PLAN
FORCES
WAR
COERCE

B66
ALEXANDER Y.,INTERNATIONAL TECHNICAL ASSISTANCE
EXPERTS: A CASE STUDY OF THE U.N. EXPERIENCE.
USA+45 WOR+45 WORKER CREATE PLAN PROB/SOLV ECO/TAC
FOR/AID GIVE EDU/PROP...CHARTS BIBLIOG 20 UN.
PAGE 2 G0039
SKILL
INT/ORG
TEC/DEV
CONSULT

B66
AMERICAN ASSEMBLY COLUMBIA U.A WORLD OF NUCLEAR
POWERS? FUT WOR+45 ECO/DEV BAL/PWR ECO/TAC CONTROL
RISK EFFICIENCY ATTIT PWR...METH/COMP ANTHOL 20.
PAGE 3 G0049
NUC/PWR
DIPLOM
TEC/DEV
ARMS/CONT

B66
AMERICAN LIBRARY ASSN.GUIDE TO JAPANESE REFERENCE
BOOKS....HUM 20 CHINJAP. PAGE 3 G0054
BIBLIOG/A
SOC
TEC/DEV
PHIL/SCI

B66
BEATON L.,MUST THE BOMB SPREAD? WOR+45 TEC/DEV
DIPLOM DRIVE ORD/FREE PWR...CHARTS 20. PAGE 6 G0109
NUC/PWR
ARMS/CONT
PLAN
PROB/SOLV

B66
BOWEN H.R.,AUTOMATION AND ECONOMIC PROGRESS.
EUR+WWI USA+45 ECO/DEV INCOME ORD/FREE WEALTH
...POLICY ANTHOL 20. PAGE 8 G0160
AUTOMAT
TEC/DEV
WORKER
LEISURE

B66
GOULD J.M.,THE TECHNICAL ELITE. INDUS LABOR
TECHRACY...POLICY DECISION STAT CHARTS 20. PAGE 22
G0437
ECO/DEV
TEC/DEV
ELITES
TECHNIC

B66
HOPKINS J.F.K.,ARABIC PERIODICAL LITERATURE, 1961.
ISLAM LAW CULTURE SECT...GEOG HEAL PHIL/SCI PSY SOC
20. PAGE 27 G0528
BIBLIOG/A
NAT/LISM
TEC/DEV
INDUS

B66
KLOTSCHE J.M.,THE URBAN UNIVERSITY AND THE FUTURE
OF OUR CITIES. FUT USA+45 USA-45 LOC/G NEIGH GIVE
19/20. PAGE 31 G0606
ACADEM
MUNIC
PROB/SOLV
TEC/DEV

B66
KURAKOV I.G.,SCIENCE, TECHNOLOGY AND COMMUNISM;
SOME QUESTIONS OF DEVELOPMENT (TRANS. BY CARIN
DEDIJER). USSR INDUS PLAN PROB/SOLV COST PRODUC
...MGT MATH CHARTS METH 20. PAGE 32 G0626
CREATE
TEC/DEV
MARXISM
ECO/TAC

B66
LILLEY S.,MEN, MACHINES AND HISTORY: THE STORY OF
TOOLS AND MACHINES IN RELATION TO SOCIAL PROGRESS.
PREHIST SPACE STRUCT COMPUTER AUTOMAT NUC/PWR
...POLICY SOC. PAGE 34 G0667
AGRI
TEC/DEV
SOCIETY

B66
MARKHAM J.W.,AN ECONOMIC-MEDIA STUDY OF BOOK
PUBLISHING. USA+45 LAW COM/IND ACADEM SCHOOL
EDU/PROP AUTOMAT CONTROL...DECISION STAT CHARTS 20
CONGRESS. PAGE 36 G0707
PRESS
ECO/TAC
TEC/DEV
NAT/G

B66
MILLAR R.,THE NEW CLASSES. UK ELITES SOCIETY INDUS
AUTOMAT GP/REL SOC/INTEG 20 INDUS/REV. PAGE 39
G0770
STRUCT
STRATA
TEC/DEV
CREATE

B66
MUMFORD L.,THE MYTH OF THE MACHINE: TECHNICS AND
HUMAN DEVELOPMENT. UNIV WOR-45 CREATE AUTOMAT
PERCEPT KNOWL...EPIST PHIL/SCI SOC LING TREND
WORKER
TEC/DEV
SOCIETY

B66
MURDOCK J.C.,RESEARCH AND REGIONS. AGRI FINAN INDUS
LOC/G MUNIC NAT/G PROB/SOLV TEC/DEV ADMIN REGION
20. PAGE 40 G0796
BIBLIOG
ECO/DEV
COMPUT/IR
R+D

B66
NIEBURG H.L.,IN THE NAME OF SCIENCE. USA+45
EX/STRUC LEGIS TEC/DEV BUDGET PAY AUTOMAT LOBBY PWR
...OBS 20. PAGE 42 G0822
NAT/G
INDUS
TECHRACY

B66
ODEGARD P.H.,POLITICAL POWER AND SOCIAL CHANGE.
UNIV NAT/G CREATE ALL/IDEOS...POLICY GEOG SOC
CENSUS TREND. PAGE 42 G0829
PWR
TEC/DEV
IDEA/COMP

B66
OECD DEVELOPMENT CENTRE.CATALOGUE OF SOCIAL AND
ECONOMIC DEVELOPMENT INSTITUTES AND PROGRAMMES*
RESEARCH. ACT/RES PLAN TEC/DEV EDU/PROP...SOC
GP/COMP NAT/COMP. PAGE 43 G0836
ECO/UNDEV
ECO/DEV
R+D
ACADEM

B66
ONYEMELUKWE C.C.,PROBLEMS OF INDUSTRIAL PLANNING
AND MANAGEMENT IN NIGERIA. AFR FINAN LABOR DELIB/GP
TEC/DEV ADJUST...MGT TREND BIBLIOG. PAGE 43 G0839
ECO/UNDEV
ECO/TAC
INDUS
PLAN

B66
RUPPENTHAL K.M.,TRANSPORTATION AND TOMORROW. FUT
SPACE USA+45 SEA AIR FORCES TEC/DEV INT/TRADE
...ANTHOL 20 RAILROAD. PAGE 48 G0946
DIST/IND
PLAN
CIVMIL/REL
PREDICT

B66
UNITED NATIONS.INTERNATIONAL SPACE BIBLIOGRAPHY.
FUT INT/ORG TEC/DEV DIPLOM ARMS/CONT NUC/PWR
...JURID SOC UN. PAGE 56 G1093
BIBLIOG
SPACE
PEACE
R+D

B66
US DEPARTMENT OF LABOR.TECHNOLOGICAL TRENDS IN
MAJOR AMERICAN INDUSTRIES. USA+45 R+D LABOR GP/REL
PRODUC...MGT BIBLIOG 20. PAGE 57 G1120
TEC/DEV
INDUS
TREND
AUTOMAT

B66
US HOUSE COMM GOVT OPERATIONS.THE COMPUTER AND
INVASION OF PRIVACY. USA+45 SOCIETY ALL/VALS...PSY
SOC CHARTS HOUSE/REP PRIVACY. PAGE 58 G1140
ORD/FREE
COMPUTER
TEC/DEV
NAT/G

B66
WHITNAH D.R.,SAFER SKYWAYS. DIST/IND DELIB/GP
FORCES TOP/EX WORKER TEC/DEV ROUTINE WAR CIVMIL/REL
COST...TIME/SEQ 20 FAA CAB. PAGE 63 G1235
ADMIN
NAT/G
AIR
GOV/REL

L66
RASER J.R.,"DETERRENCE RESEARCH* PAST PROGRESS AND
FUTURE NEEDS." INTELL PLAN TEC/DEV NUC/PWR PERCEPT
...DECISION PSY SOC NET/THEORY. PAGE 46 G0905
DETER
BIBLIOG/A
FUT

S66
"FURTHER READING." INDIA LOC/G NAT/G PLAN ADMIN
WEALTH...GEOG SOC CONCPT CENSUS 20. PAGE 1 G0021
BIBLIOG
ECO/UNDEV
TEC/DEV
PROVS

S66
BROWNLIE I.,"NUCLEAR PROLIFERATION* SOME PROBLEMS
OF CONTROL." USA+45 USSR ECO/UNDEV INT/ORG FORCES
TEC/DEV REGION CONSEN...RECORD TREATY. PAGE 9 G0181
NUC/PWR
ARMS/CONT
VOL/ASSN
ORD/FREE

S66
HANSON A.H.,"PLANNING AND THE POLITICIANS* SOME
REFLECTIONS ON ECONOMIC PLANNING IN WESTERN
EUROPE." MARKET NAT/G TEC/DEV CONSEN ROLE
...METH/COMP NAT/COMP. PAGE 24 G0479
PLAN
ECO/DEV
EUR+WWI
ADMIN

S66
RIZOS E.J.,"SCIENCE AND TECHNOLOGY IN COUNTRY
DEVELOPMENT* TOWARDS AN UNDERSTANDING OF THE ROLE
OF PUBLIC ADMINISTRATION." WOR+45 STRUCT INT/ORG
EX/STRUC CREATE PLAN PROB/SOLV EFFICIENCY ROLE
DECISION. PAGE 47 G0924
ADMIN
TEC/DEV
ECO/UNDEV
PHIL/SCI

S66
SIMON R.,"THE STATE OF PUBLIC RELATIONS SCHOLARLY
RESEARCH." TEC/DEV TASK MAJORITY PRODUC...TREND
CHARTS BIBLIOG 20. PAGE 51 G1000
ACADEM
CREATE
STAT
GP/REL

TURKEVICH J.,"SOVIET SCIENCE APPRAISED." USA+45 R+D USSR ACADEM FORCES DIPLOM EDU/PROP WAR EFFICIENCY PEACE SKILL OBS. PAGE 55 G1081
S66
USSR
TEC/DEV
NAT/COMP
ATTIT

US HOUSE COMM SCI ASTRONAUT,GOVERNMENT, SCIENCE, AND PUBLIC POLICY (PAMPHLET). R+D ACADEM DELIB/GP COMPUTER BUDGET CONFER ADMIN...PHIL/SCI PREDICT TREND 20 CONGRESS HS/SCIASTR. PAGE 58 G1143
N66
NAT/G
POLICY
TEC/DEV
CREATE

US HOUSE COMM SCI ASTRONAUT,INQUIRIES, LEGISLATION, POLICY STUDIES RE: SCIENCE AND TECHNOLOGY: REVIEW AND FORECAST (PAMPHLET). FUT WOR+45 DELIB/GP PROB/SOLV...POLICY JURID TREND 20 CONGRESS. PAGE 58 G1144
N66
TEC/DEV
R+D
PLAN
LEGIS

US HOUSE COMM SCI ASTRONAUT,THE ADEQUACY OF TECHNOLOGY FOR POLLUTION ABATEMENT (PAMPHLET). WOR+45 PLAN PROB/SOLV CONFER ADMIN...JURID 20 POLLUTION. PAGE 58 G1145
N66
HEALTH
POLICY
TEC/DEV
LEGIS

ALEXANDER L.M.,THE LAW OF THE SEA: OFFSHORE BOUNDARIES AND ZONES. WOR+45 INT/ORG TEC/DEV CONTROL PRIVIL HABITAT SOVEREIGN...CON/ANAL CHARTS ANTHOL. PAGE 2 G0037
B67
SEA
INT/LAW
EXTR/IND

BARANSON J.,TECHNOLOGY FOR UNDERDEVELOPED AREAS: AN ANNOTATED BIBLIOGRAPHY. FUT WOR+45 CULTURE INDUS INT/ORG CREATE PROB/SOLV INT/TRADE EDU/PROP AUTOMAT ...CONCPT METH. PAGE 5 G0092
B67
BIBLIOG/A
ECO/UNDEV
TEC/DEV
R+D

BAUMOL W.J.,BUSINESS BEHAVIOR, VALUE AND GROWTH (REV. ED.). WOR+45 FINAN LG/CO TEC/DEV CAP/ISM DEMAND EQUILIB...METH/COMP SIMUL 20. PAGE 5 G0105
B67
ALL/IDEOS
PHIL/SCI
PLAN
ECO/DEV

BENNETT J.W.,HUTTERIAN BRETHREN; THE AGRICULTURAL ECONOMY AND SOCIAL ORGANIZATION OF A COMMUNAL PEOPLE. USA+45 SOCIETY FAM KIN TEC/DEV ADJUST...MGT AUD/VIS GP/COMP 20. PAGE 6 G0121
B67
SECT
AGRI
STRUCT
GP/REL

BERNAL J.D.,THE SOCIAL FUNCTION OF SCIENCE. WOR+45 WOR-45 R+D NAT/G PROB/SOLV DOMIN WAR...PHIL/SCI 20. PAGE 7 G0130
B67
ROLE
TEC/DEV
SOCIETY
ADJUST

BUTLER J.,BOSTON UNIVERSITY PAPERS ON AFRICA* TRANSITION IN AFRICAN POLITICS. AFR LAW CONSTN LABOR POL/PAR TEC/DEV 20. PAGE 10 G0197
B67
IDEA/COMP
NAT/G
PWR

COLM G.,THE ECONOMY OF THE AMERICAN PEOPLE. USA+45 ECO/DEV FINAN WORKER INT/TRADE AUTOMAT GP/REL. PAGE 13 G0244
B67
ECO/TAC
PRODUC
TREND
TEC/DEV

CROSSON F.J.,SCIENCE AND CONTEMPORARY SOCIETY. FUT WOR+45 SECT CREATE PROB/SOLV...HUM PREDICT TREND IDEA/COMP ANTHOL. PAGE 14 G0263
B67
PHIL/SCI
SOCIETY
TEC/DEV
CONCPT

DAVIS V.,THE POLITICS OF INNOVATION: PATTERNS IN NAVY CASES (PAMPHLET). WOR+45 NAT/G CREATE WEAPON INGP/REL ATTIT...POLICY SOC METH/COMP METH. PAGE 14 G0280
B67
BIBLIOG
FORCES
NUC/PWR
TEC/DEV

DEGLER C.N.,THE AGE OF THE ECONOMIC REVOLUTION 1876-1900. USA-45 AGRI MUNIC POL/PAR SECT ECO/TAC CHOOSE...PHIL/SCI CHARTS NAT/COMP 19 NEGRO. PAGE 15 G0292
B67
INDUS
SOCIETY
ECO/DEV
TEC/DEV

DICKSON P.G.M.,THE FINANCIAL REVOLUTION IN ENGLAND. UK NAT/G TEC/DEV ADMIN GOV/REL...SOC METH/CNCPT CHARTS GP/COMP BIBLIOG 17/18. PAGE 15 G0302
B67
ECO/DEV
FINAN
CAP/ISM
MGT

DONALD A.G.,MANAGEMENT, INFORMATION, AND SYSTEMS. WOR+45 LG/CO PROB/SOLV CONTROL FEEDBACK KNOWL MGT. PAGE 16 G0306
B67
ROUTINE
TEC/DEV
CONCPT
ADMIN

ELDREDGE H.W.,TAMING MEGALOPOLIS; HOW TO MANAGE AN URBANIZED WORLD. WOR+45 SOCIETY ECO/DEV ECO/UNDEV NAT/G COMPUTER CREATE PARTIC EFFICIENCY WEALTH ...MGT ANTHOL. PAGE 17 G0342
B67
MUNIC
TEC/DEV
PLAN
PROB/SOLV

GROSSMAN G.,ECONOMIC SYSTEMS. USA+45 USA-45 USSR YUGOSLAVIA WORKER CAP/ISM PRICE GP/REL EQUILIB WEALTH MARXISM SOCISM...MGT METH/COMP 19/20. PAGE 23 G0456
B67
ECO/DEV
PLAN
TEC/DEV
DEMAND

HARDT J.P.,MATHEMATICS AND COMPUTERS IN SOVIET ECONOMIC PLANNING. COM USSR OP/RES PROB/SOLV OPTIMAL...MODAL SIMUL 20. PAGE 24 G0481
B67
PLAN
TEC/DEV
MATH
COMPUT/IR

HEADLEY J.C.,PESTICIDE PROBLEM: AN ECONOMIC APPROACH TO PUBLIC POLICY. AGRI TEC/DEV GOV/REL COST ATTIT CHARTS. PAGE 25 G0498
B67
HABITAT
POLICY
BIO/SOC
CONTROL

HEILBRONER R.L.,THE LIMITS OF AMERICAN CAPITALISM. FUT ECO/DEV INDUS LG/CO EX/STRUC LEAD PWR TECHRACY 20. PAGE 25 G0502
B67
ELITES
CREATE
TEC/DEV
CAP/ISM

KAPLAN B.,AN UNHURRIED VIEW OF COPYRIGHT. FUT ...JURID 20. PAGE 29 G0575
B67
TEC/DEV
LAW
LICENSE

KRANZBERG M.,TECHNOLOGY IN WESTERN CIVILIZATION VOLUME ONE. UNIV INDUS SKILL. PAGE 31 G0617
B67
TEC/DEV
ACT/RES
AUTOMAT
POLICY

LAMBERT J.,LATIN AMERICA: SOCIAL STRUCTURES AND POLITICAL INSTITUTIONS. STRUCT TEC/DEV DIPLOM ADMIN COLONIAL LEAD ATTIT...SOC CLASSIF NAT/COMP 17/20. PAGE 32 G0631
B67
L/A+17C
NAT/G
ECO/UNDEV
SOCIETY

LERNER D.,COMMUNICATION AND CHANGE IN DEVELOPING COUNTRIES. CHINA/COM INDIA PHILIPPINE COM/IND CREATE TEC/DEV...ANTHOL 20. PAGE 33 G0659
B67
EDU/PROP
ORD/FREE
PERCEPT
ECO/UNDEV

MACBRIDE R.,THE AUTOMATED STATE; COMPUTER SYSTEMS AS A NEW FORCE IN SOCIETY. FUT WOR+45 FINAN MUNIC NAT/G WORKER PLAN TEC/DEV CONTROL PERS/REL RACE/REL ADJUST. PAGE 35 G0685
B67
COMPUTER
AUTOMAT
PROB/SOLV
SOCIETY

MCBRIDE J.H.,THE TEST BAN TREATY: MILITARY, TECHNOLOGICAL, AND POLITICAL IMPLICATIONS. USA+45 USSR DELIB/GP FORCES LEGIS TEC/DEV BAL/PWR TREATY. PAGE 37 G0727
B67
ARMS/CONT
DIPLOM
NUC/PWR

MCDOUGAL M.S.,THE INTERPRETATION OF AGREEMENTS AND WORLD PUBLIC ORDER: PRINCIPLES OF CONTENT AND PROCEDURE. WOR+45 CONSTN PROB/SOLV TEC/DEV ...CON/ANAL TREATY. PAGE 37 G0740
B67
INT/LAW
STRUCT
ECO/UNDEV
DIPLOM

NORTHRUP H.R.,RESTRICTIVE LABOR PRACTICES IN THE SUPERMARKET INDUSTRY. USA+45 INDUS WORKER TEC/DEV BARGAIN PAY CONTROL GP/REL COST...STAT CHARTS NLRB. PAGE 42 G0827
B67
DIST/IND
MARKET
LABOR
MGT

ORLANS H.,CONTRACTING FOR ATOMS. USA+45 LAW INTELL ACADEM LG/CO NAT/G PLAN TEC/DEV CONTROL DETER ...TREND 20 AEC. PAGE 43 G0845
B67
NUC/PWR
R+D
PRODUC
PEACE

OVERSEAS DEVELOPMENT INSTIT,EFFECTIVE AID. WOR+45 INT/ORG TEC/DEV DIPLOM INT/TRADE ADMIN. PAGE 43 G0852
B67
FOR/AID
ECO/UNDEV
ECO/TAC
NAT/COMP

PADELFORD N.J.,THE DYNAMICS OF INTERNATIONAL POLITICS (2ND ED.). WOR+45 LAW INT/ORG FORCES TEC/DEV REGION NAT/LISM PEACE ATTIT PWR ALL/IDEOS UN COLD/WAR NATO TREATY. PAGE 43 G0856
B67
DIPLOM
NAT/G
POLICY
DECISION

ROACH J.R.,THE UNITED STATES AND THE ATLANTIC
COMMUNITY; ISSUES AND PROSPECTS. WOR+45 TEC/DEV
ECO/TAC COLONIAL REGION PEACE ROLE...ANTHOL NATO
COLD/WAR EEC. PAGE 47 G0925
INT/ORG
POLICY
ADJUST
DIPLOM
B67

ROTHENBERG J.,ECONOMIC EVALUATION OF URBAN RENEWAL:
CONCEPTUAL FOUNDATION OF BENEFIT-COST ANALYSIS.
USA+45 ECO/DEV NEIGH TEC/DEV ADMIN GEN/LAWS.
PAGE 48 G0940
PLAN
MUNIC
PROB/SOLV
COST
B67

RUTGERS U GRADUATE SCH LIB SCI,BIBLIOGRAPHY OF
RESEARCH RELATING TO THE COMMUNICATION OF
SCIENTIFIC AND TECHNICAL INFORMATION. FUT CREATE
FEEDBACK...PHIL/SCI NEW/IDEA COMPUT/IR HYPO/EXP.
PAGE 48 G0951
BIBLIOG/A
COM/IND
R+D
TEC/DEV
B67

SCHON D.A.,TECHNOLOGY AND CHANGE* THE NEW
HERACLITUS. TEC/DEV CONTROL COST DEMAND EFFICIENCY
RIGID/FLEX...MYTH 20. PAGE 49 G0975
INDUS
PROB/SOLV
R+D
CREATE
B67

SCHUMACHER B.G.,COMPUTER DYNAMICS IN PUBLIC
ADMINISTRATION. USA+45 CREATE PLAN TEC/DEV...MGT
LING CON/ANAL BIBLIOG/A 20. PAGE 50 G0980
COMPUTER
COMPUT/IR
ADMIN
AUTOMAT
B67

SILBERMAN C.E.,THE MYTHS OF AUTOMATION. INDUS
WORKER COST PRODUC AGE WEALTH 20. PAGE 51 G0996
MYTH
AUTOMAT
CHARTS
TEC/DEV
B67

SKOLNIKOFF E.B.,SCIENCE, TECHNOLOGY, AND AMERICAN
FOREIGN POLICY. SPACE USA+45 INT/ORG TEC/DEV
ARMS/CONT NUC/PWR 29 DEPT/STATE. PAGE 51 G1010
PHIL/SCI
DIPLOM
NAT/G
EFFICIENCY
B67

UNESCO,PRINCIPLES AND PROBLEMS OF NATIONAL SCIENCE
POLICIES. WOR+45 ECO/DEV ECO/UNDEV R+D INT/ORG
PROB/SOLV CONFER...PHIL/SCI CHARTS 20 UNESCO UN.
PAGE 55 G1091
NAT/COMP
POLICY
TEC/DEV
CREATE
B67

UNIVERSAL REFERENCE SYSTEM,ECONOMIC REGULATION,
BUSINESS, AND GOVERNMENT (VOLUME VIII). WOR+45
WOR-45 ECO/DEV ECO/UNDEV FINAN LABOR TEC/DEV
ECO/TAC INT/TRADE GOV/REL...POLICY COMPUT/IR.
PAGE 56 G1099
BIBLIOG/A
CONTROL
NAT/G
B67

UNIVERSAL REFERENCE SYSTEM,PUBLIC POLICY AND THE
MANAGEMENT OF SCIENCE (VOLUME IX). FUT SPACE WOR+45
LAW NAT/G TEC/DEV CONTROL NUC/PWR GOV/REL
...COMPUT/IR GEN/METH. PAGE 56 G1100
BIBLIOG/A
POLICY
MGT
PHIL/SCI
B67

US HOUSE COMM SCI ASTRONAUT,AUTHORIZING SECY OF
COMMERCE TO PROVIDE FOR COLLECTION, COMPILATION,
CRIT EVALUATION, PUBLICATION, SALE OF STD REF DATA.
USA+45 TEC/DEV...COMPUT/IR HOUSE/REP. PAGE 59 G1150
PHIL/SCI
CON/ANAL
STAT
R+D
B67

US HOUSE COMM SCI ASTRONAUT,SCIENCE, TECHNOLOGY,
AND PUBLIC POLICY DURING THE 89TH CONGRESS,
JANUARY, 1965 THROUGH DECEMBER, 1966. USA+45
...CHARTS BIBLIOG. PAGE 59 G1151
POLICY
TEC/DEV
CREATE
NAT/G
B67

US PRES COMN LAW ENFORCE-JUS,THE CHALLENGE OF CRIME
IN A FREE SOCIETY. LAW STRUCT CONSULT ACT/RES
TEC/DEV INGP/REL...SOC/WK 20. PAGE 59 G1160
CT/SYS
PUB/INST
CRIMLGY
CRIME
B67

WARNER W.L.,THE EMERGENT AMERICAN SOCIETY VOL I,
LARGE-SCALE ORGANIZATIONS. USA+45 USA-45 ACADEM
PROF/ORG SCHOOL SECT EX/STRUC TEC/DEV GP/REL
...TREND CHARTS. PAGE 62 G1215
ANTHOL
NAT/G
LABOR
LG/CO
B67

YAMAMURA K.,ECONOMIC POLICY IN POSTWAR JAPAN. ASIA
FINAN POL/PAR DIPLOM LEAD NAT/LISM ATTIT NEW/LIB
POPULISM 20 CHINJAP. PAGE 64 G1262
ECO/DEV
POLICY
NAT/G
TEC/DEV
B67

YAVITZ B.,AUTOMATION IN COMMERCIAL BANKING. USA+45
STRUCT WORKER CREATE OP/RES PLAN ROLE...DECISION
SAMP/SIZ. PAGE 64 G1263
TEC/DEV
FINAN
COMPUT/IR

MGT

BARRON J.A.,"ACCESS TO THE PRESS." USA+45 TEC/DEV
PRESS TV ADJUD AUD/VIS. PAGE 5 G0099
ORD/FREE
COM/IND
EDU/PROP
LAW
L67

DAVIS P.C.,"THE COMING CHINESE COMMUNIST NUCLEAR
THREAT AND U.S. SEA BASED ABM OPTIONS." ASIA
CHINA/COM FUT USA+45 SEA NAT/G FORCES PLAN TEC/DEV
LEAD ARMS/CONT...GEOG METH/COMP 20 ABM/DEFSYS.
PAGE 14 G0279
NUC/PWR
DETER
WEAPON
DIPLOM
L67

EINAUDI L.,"ANNOTATED BIBLIOGRAPHY OF LATIN
AMERICAN MILITARY JOURNALS" LAW TEC/DEV DOMIN
EDU/PROP COERCE WAR CIVMIL/REL 20. PAGE 17 G0336
BIBLIOG/A
NAT/G
FORCES
L/A+17C
L67

NADER R.,"AUTOMOBILE DESIGN AND THE JUDICIAL
PROCESS." USA+45 CT/SYS SUPEGO JURID. PAGE 40 G0799
LAW
ADJUD
TEC/DEV
PROC/MFG
L67

ALLISON D.,"THE GROWTH OF IDEAS." USA+45 LG/CO
ADMIN. PAGE 3 G0045
R+D
OP/RES
INDUS
TEC/DEV
S67

AVTORKHANOV A.,"A NEW AGRARIAN REVOLUTION." COM
USSR ECO/DEV PLAN TEC/DEV ADMIN CONTROL OPTIMAL
WEALTH SOCISM 20 KHRUSH/N STALIN/J. PAGE 4 G0082
AGRI
METH/COMP
MARXISM
OWN
S67

BARAN P.,"THE FUTURE COMPUTER UTILITY." USA+45
NAT/G PLAN CONTROL COST...POLICY 20. PAGE 5 G0091
COMPUTER
UTIL
FUT
TEC/DEV
S67

BENN W.,"TECHNOLOGY HAS AN INEXORABLE EFFECT." FUT
UK ECO/DEV INT/ORG CONSULT PLAN EDU/PROP ADMIN LEAD
GP/REL PRODUC...INT 20 EEC. PAGE 6 G0119
R+D
LG/CO
TEC/DEV
INDUS
S67

BRETNOR R.,"DESTRUCTIVE FORCE AND THE MILITARY
EQUATIONS." UNIV COMPUTER PLAN PROB/SOLV AUTOMAT
CONTROL COERCE DETER NUC/PWR WEAPON DRIVE PWR.
PAGE 9 G0166
FORCES
TEC/DEV
DOMIN
WAR
S67

BRUNHILD G.,"THEORY OF 'TECHNICAL UNEMPLOYMENT'."
ECO/DEV ACT/RES PROB/SOLV DEMAND PRODUC...PHIL/SCI
20. PAGE 9 G0182
WORKER
TEC/DEV
SKILL
INDUS
S67

BULMER-THOMAS I.,"SO, ON TO THE GREAT SOCIETY." FUT
UNIV TEC/DEV BAL/PWR WAR BIO/SOC KNOWL...ART/METH
SOC PREDICT TREND WORSHIP 20 GREAT/SOC. PAGE 9
G0185
PHIL/SCI
SOCIETY
CREATE
S67

CARY G.D.,"THE QUIET REVOLUTION IN COPYRIGHT* THE
END OF THE 'PUBLICATION' CONCEPT." USA+45 LAW
OP/RES TEC/DEV CONFER DEBATE EFFICIENCY...JURID
CONGRESS. PAGE 11 G0217
COM/IND
POLICY
LICENSE
PRESS
S67

CETRON M.J.,"FORECASTING TECHNOLOGY." INDUS FORCES
TASK UTIL...PHIL/SCI CONCPT CHARTS METH/COMP TIME.
PAGE 11 G0219
TEC/DEV
FUT
R+D
PLAN
S67

CHIU S.M.,"CHINA'S MILITARY POSTURE." CHINA/COM
ELITES NAT/G POL/PAR TEC/DEV ECO/TAC DOMIN CONTROL
LEAD REV MARXISM 20 MAO. PAGE 12 G0228
FORCES
CIVMIL/REL
NUC/PWR
DIPLOM
S67

CHRIST R.F.,"REORGANIZATION OF FRENCH ARMED
FORCES." FRANCE CREATE PLAN TEC/DEV BAL/PWR DOMIN
COERCE CENTRAL EFFICIENCY 20. PAGE 12 G0229
CHIEF
DETER
NUC/PWR
FORCES
S67

CLEMENS W.C.,"CHINESE NUCLEAR TESTS: TRENDS AND
PORTENTS." CHINA/COM USA+45 USSR FORCES PLAN
NUC/PWR
WEAPON

TEC/DEV ARMS/CONT WAR PWR...DECISION 20 MAO KHRUSH/N. PAGE 12 G0234
POLICY
DIPLOM

S67
COFFEY J.I.,"THE ANTI-BALLISTIC MISSILE DEBATE." USA+45 USSR TEC/DEV BAL/PWR 20. PAGE 12 G0238
ARMS/CONT
NUC/PWR
DETER
DIPLOM

S67
DE NEUFVILLE R.,"EDUCATION AT THE ACADEMIES." USA+45 ELITES CONSULT EX/STRUC COMPUTER PLAN PROB/SOLV TASK CIVMIL/REL ORD/FREE 20. PAGE 15 G0286
FORCES
ACADEM
TEC/DEV
SKILL

S67
DOYLE S.E.,"COMMUNICATION SATELLITES* INTERNAL ORGANIZATION FOR DEVELOPMENT AND CONTROL." USA+45 R+D ACT/RES DIPLOM NAT/LISM...POLICY INT/LAW PREDICT UN. PAGE 16 G0313
TEC/DEV
SPACE
COM/IND
INT/ORG

S67
EDMONDS M.,"INTERNATIONAL COLLABORATION IN WEAPONS PROCUREMENT* THE IMPLICATIONS OF THE ANGLO-FRENCH CASE." FRANCE UK CONSULT OP/RES PROB/SOLV TEC/DEV CONFER CONTROL EFFICIENCY 20. PAGE 17 G0334
DIPLOM
VOL/ASSN
BAL/PWR
ARMS/CONT

S67
ENKE S.,"GOVERNMENT-INDUSTRY DEVELOPMENT OF A COMMERCIAL SUPERSONIC TRANSPORT." USA+45 ECO/DEV R+D LG/CO NAT/G TEC/DEV PRICE RISK COST PROFIT. PAGE 18 G0347
INDUS
FINAN
SERV/IND
CAP/ISM

S67
EYRAUD M.,"LA FRANCE FACE A UN EVENTUEL TRAITE DE NON DISSEMINATION DES ARMES NUCLEAIRES." FRANCE USA+45 EXTR/IND INDUS R+D INT/ORG ACT/RES TEC/DEV AGREE PRODUC ATTIT 20 TREATY AEC EURATOM. PAGE 18 G0355
NUC/PWR
ARMS/CONT
POLICY

S67
FRIED M.,"FUNCTIONS OF THE WORKING CLASS COMMUNITY IN MODERN URBAN SOCIETY* IMPLICATIONS FOR FORCED RELOCATION." USA+45 INDUS R+D NEIGH PLAN TEC/DEV PARTIC GP/REL ATTIT...SOC STAT CHARTS. PAGE 20 G0393
CLASSIF
WORKER
MUNIC
ADJUST

S67
GAUSSENS J.,"THE APPLICATIONS OF NUCLEAR ENERGY - TECHNICAL, ECONOMIC AND SOCIAL ASPECTS." WOR+45 INDUS R+D ACT/RES EFFICIENCY PRODUC SKILL PREDICT. PAGE 21 G0413
NUC/PWR
TEC/DEV
ECO/DEV
ADJUST

S67
GOBER J.L.,"FEDERALISM AT WORK." USA+45 NAT/G CONSULT ACT/RES PLAN CONFER ADMIN LEAD PARTIC FEDERAL ATTIT. PAGE 21 G0422
MUNIC
TEC/DEV
R+D
GOV/REL

S67
HAMBERG D.,"SIZE OF ENTERPRISE AND TECHNICAL CHANGE." USA+45 LG/CO SML/CO CREATE OP/RES PROFIT ...TREND 20. PAGE 24 G0477
TEC/DEV
INDUS
R+D
WEALTH

S67
HILL R.,"SOCIAL ASPECTS OF FAMILY PLANNING." INDIA KOREA TAIWAN ECO/UNDEV PLAN PROB/SOLV TEC/DEV EDU/PROP CONTROL ATTIT DRIVE...HEAL PSY SOC 20 BIRTH/CON UN. PAGE 26 G0512
FAM
BIO/SOC
GEOG
MARRIAGE

S67
HODGE G.,"THE RISE AND DEMISE OF THE UN TECHNICAL ASSISTANCE ADMINISTRATION." RISK TASK INGP/REL CONSEN EFFICIENCY 20 UN. PAGE 26 G0516
ADMIN
TEC/DEV
EX/STRUC
INT/ORG

S67
HOFFER J.R.,"RELATIONSHIP OF NATURAL AND SOCIAL SCIENCES TO SOCIAL PROBLEMS AND CONTRIBUTION OF... SCIENTISTS TO SOLUTIONS." USA+45 COMPUTER TEC/DEV GP/REL KNOWL...SOC TREND. PAGE 26 G0521
PROB/SOLV
SOCIETY
INTELL
ACT/RES

S67
INGLIS D.R.,"PROSPECTS AND PROBLEMS: THE NONMILITARY USES OF NUCLEAR EXPLOSIVES." CREATE PROB/SOLV TEC/DEV AGREE PEACE...INT/LAW PHIL/SCI NEW/IDEA 20 TREATY. PAGE 28 G0545
NUC/PWR
INDUS
ARMS/CONT
EXTR/IND

S67
JOHNSTON D.M.,"LAW, TECHNOLOGY AND THE SEA." WOR+45 PLAN PROB/SOLV TEC/DEV CONFER ADJUD ORD/FREE ...POLICY JURID. PAGE 29 G0564
INT/LAW
INT/ORG
DIPLOM
NEUTRAL

S67
KAHN H.,"CRITERIA FOR LONG-RANGE NUCLEAR CONTROL POLICIES." WOR+45 INT/ORG TEC/DEV DOMIN DETER WAR WEAPON ISOLAT ORD/FREE POLICY. PAGE 29 G0571
NUC/PWR
ARMS/CONT
BAL/PWR
DIPLOM

S67
KAYSEN C.,"DATA BANKS AND DOSSIERS." FUT USA+45 COM/IND NAT/G PLAN PROB/SOLV TEC/DEV BUDGET ADMIN ROUTINE. PAGE 30 G0588
CENTRAL
EFFICIENCY
CENSUS
ACT/RES

S67
KRAUS J.,"A MARXIST IN GHANA." GHANA ELITES CHIEF PROB/SOLV TEC/DEV DIPLOM ECO/TAC COLONIAL PARTIC PWR 20 NKRUMAH/K. PAGE 31 G0618
MARXISM
PLAN
ATTIT
CREATE

S67
LA PORTE T.,"DIFFUSION AND DISCONTINUITY IN SCIENCE, TECHNOLOGY AND PUBLIC AFFAIRS: RESULTS OF A SEARCH IN THE FIELD." USA+45 ACT/RES TEC/DEV PERS/REL ATTIT PHIL/SCI. PAGE 32 G0628
INTELL
ADMIN
ACADEM
GP/REL

S67
LAY S.H.,"EXCLUSIVE GOVERNMENTAL LIABILITY FOR SPACE ACCIDENTS." USA+45 LAW FINAN SERV/IND TEC/DEV ADJUD. PAGE 33 G0646
NAT/G
SUPEGO
SPACE
PROB/SOLV

S67
LEVENSTEIN A.,"TECHNOLOGICAL CHANGE, WORK, AND HUMAN VALUES." WOR+45 SOCIETY AUTOMAT ROUTINE LEISURE INGP/REL ADJUST TECHRACY...MGT CONCPT. PAGE 33 G0660
TEC/DEV
CULTURE
ALL/VALS
TIME/SEQ

S67
MACDONALD G.J.F.,"SCIENCE AND SPACE POLICY* HOW DOES IT GET PLANNED?" R+D CREATE TEC/DEV BUDGET ADMIN ROUTINE...DECISION NASA. PAGE 35 G0687
SPACE
PLAN
MGT
EX/STRUC

S67
MALONE D.K.,"THE COMMANDER AND THE COMPUTER." USA+45 OP/RES PROB/SOLV TEC/DEV AUTOMAT CENTRAL 20. PAGE 35 G0698
COMPUTER
FORCES
ELITES
PLAN

S67
MEHTA A.,"INDIA* POVERTY AND CHANGE." STRATA INDUS CREATE ECO/TAC FOR/AID NEUTRAL GP/REL ADJUST INCOME ...NEW/IDEA 20. PAGE 38 G0751
INDIA
SOCIETY
ECO/UNDEV
TEC/DEV

S67
MOOR E.J.,"THE INTERNATIONAL IMPACT OF AUTOMATION." WOR+45 ACT/RES COMPUTER CREATE PLAN CAP/ISM ROUTINE EFFICIENCY PREDICT. PAGE 39 G0779
TEC/DEV
OP/RES
AUTOMAT
INDUS

S67
MORTON J.A.,"A SYSTEMS APPROACH TO THE INNOVATION PROCESS: ITS USE IN THE BELL SYSTEM." USA+45 INTELL INDUS LG/CO CONSULT WORKER COMPUTER AUTOMAT DEMAND ...MGT CHARTS 20. PAGE 40 G0787
TEC/DEV
GEN/METH
R+D
COM/IND

S67
MYERS S.,"TECHNOLOGY AND URBAN TRANSIT: THE ENORMOUS POTENTIAL OF BUS AND RAIL SYSTEMS." USA+45 FINAN LOC/G MUNIC WORKER PLAN PROB/SOLV PRICE AUTOMAT 20. PAGE 40 G0798
R+D
TEC/DEV
DIST/IND
ACT/RES

S67
PENNEY N.,"BANK STATEMENTS, CANCELLED CHECKS, AND ARTICLE FOUR IN THE ELECTRONIC AGE." USA+45 TEC/DEV COST EFFICIENCY WEALTH. PAGE 44 G0866
CREATE
LAW
ADJUD
FINAN

S67
PONTECORVO G.,"THE LAW OF THE SEA." ECO/DEV ECO/UNDEV TEC/DEV GEOG. PAGE 45 G0885
CONFER
INT/LAW
EXTR/IND
SEA

S67
RAMSEY J.A.,"THE STATUS OF INTERNATIONAL COPYRIGHTS." WOR+45 CREATE TEC/DEV DIPLOM CONFER CONTROL SANCTION OWN...POLICY JURID. PAGE 46 G0899
INT/LAW
INT/ORG
COM/IND
PRESS

S67
RICH G.S.,"THE PROPOSED PATENT LEGISLATION* SOME COMMENTS." USA+45 LAW R+D ACT/RES TEC/DEV CONFER EFFICIENCY OWN JURID. PAGE 46 G0916
LICENSE
POLICY
CREATE
CAP/ISM

RICHMAN B.M.,"SOVIET MANAGEMENT IN TRANSITION." USSR FINAN MARKET EX/STRUC PLAN PROB/SOLV TEC/DEV CONTROL LEAD CENTRAL EFFICIENCY...METH/COMP 20 REFORMERS. PAGE 47 G0917
S67
MGT
MARXISM
POLICY
AUTHORIT

SCHACTER O.,"SCIENTIFIC ADVANCES AND INTERNATIONAL LAWMAKING." FUT R+D PLAN PROB/SOLV CONFER CONTROL ...POLICY PREDICT 20 UN. PAGE 49 G0961
S67
TEC/DEV
INT/LAW
INT/ORG
ACT/RES

SKOLNIKOFF E.B.,"MAKING FOREIGN POLICY" PROB/SOLV EFFICIENCY PERCEPT PWR...MGT METH/CNCPT CLASSIF 20. PAGE 51 G1009
S67
TEC/DEV
CONTROL
USA+45
NAT/G

TELLER E.,"PLANNING FOR PEACE." CHINA/COM WOR+45 DELIB/GP TEC/DEV RISK COERCE DETER WAR ATTIT ORD/FREE 20 NATO. PAGE 54 G1061
S67
ARMS/CONT
NUC/PWR
PEACE
DOMIN

VERGIN R.C.,"COMPUTER INDUCED ORGANIZATION CHANGES." FUT USA+45 R+D CREATE OP/RES TEC/DEV ADJUST CENTRAL...MGT INT CON/ANAL COMPUT/IR. PAGE 61 G1194
S67
COMPUTER
DECISION
AUTOMAT
EX/STRUC

VLASCIC I.A.,"THE SPACE TREATY* A PRELIMINARY EVALUATION." FUT USSR WOR+45 R+D ACT/RES TEC/DEV DIPLOM CONFER ARMS/CONT PEACE...PREDICT UN TREATY. PAGE 61 G1201
S67
SPACE
INT/LAW
INT/ORG
NEUTRAL

WARE R.S.,"FORECAST A.D. 2000." SOCIETY STRATA ECO/UNDEV INDUS FORCES EDU/PROP AUTOMAT COERCE REV WEAPON ATTIT PREDICT. PAGE 62 G1213
S67
NUC/PWR
GEOG
TEC/DEV
WAR

WASHBURN A.M.,"NUCLEAR PROLIFERATION IN A REVOLUTIONARY INTERNATIONAL SYSTEM." WOR+45 NAT/G DELIB/GP PLAN TEC/DEV...POLICY 20. PAGE 62 G1216
S67
ARMS/CONT
NUC/PWR
DIPLOM
CONFER

WEINBERG A.M.,"CAN TECHNOLOGY REPLACE SOCIAL ENGINEERING?" SPACE USA+45 SOCIETY ACADEM GP/REL. PAGE 62 G1224
S67
TEC/DEV
ACT/RES
PROB/SOLV
INTELL

WINSTON O.,"AN URBANIZATION PATTERN FOR THE US* SOME CONSIDERATIONS FOR THE DECENTRALIZATION OF EXCELLENCE." FUT SOCIETY ECO/DEV R+D NEIGH ACT/RES PROB/SOLV TEC/DEV. PAGE 64 G1247
S67
USA+45
MUNIC
PLAN
HABITAT

WINTHROP H.,"THE MEANING OF DECENTRALIZATION FOR TWENTIETH-CENTURY MAN." FUT WOR+45 SOCIETY TEC/DEV. PAGE 64 G1248
S67
ADMIN
STRUCT
CENTRAL
PROB/SOLV

US SUPERINTENDENT OF DOCUMENTS,SPACE: MISSILES, THE MOON, NASA, AND SATELLITES (PRICE LIST 79A). USA+45 COM/IND R+D NAT/G DIPLOM EDU/PROP ADMIN CONTROL HEALTH...POLICY SIMUL NASA CONGRESS. PAGE 61 G1190
N67
BIBLIOG/A
SPACE
TEC/DEV
PEACE

US HOUSE COMM SCI ASTRONAUT,AMENDING NATIONAL SCIENCE FOUNDATION ACT OF 1950 TO MAKE IMPROVEMENTS IN ORGANIZATION AND OPERATION OF FOUNDAT'N(PAMPH). USA+45 GIVE ADMIN...POLICY HOUSE/REP NSF. PAGE 58 G1147
N67
PHIL/SCI
DELIB/GP
TEC/DEV
R+D

US HOUSE COMM SCI ASTRONAUT,AUTHORIZING APPROPRIATIONS TO THE NATIONAL AERONAUTICS AND SPACE ADMINISTRATION (PAMPHLET). USA+45 NAT/G OP/RES TEC/DEV BUDGET NASA HOUSE/REP. PAGE 58 G1149
N67
SPACE
R+D
PHIL/SCI
NUC/PWR

US HOUSE COMM SCI ASTRONAUT,GOVERNMENT, SCIENCE, AND INTERNATIONAL POLICY (PAMPHLET). INDIA NETHERLAND ECO/DEV ECO/UNDEV R+D ACADEM PLAN DIPLOM FOR/AID CONFER...PREDICT 20 CHINJAP. PAGE 59 G1152
N67
NAT/G
POLICY
CREATE
TEC/DEV

US SENATE,STATUS OF THE DEVELOPMENT OF THE ANTI-BALLISTIC MISSILE SYSTEMS IN THE UNITED STATES (PAMPHLET). FUT USA+45 R+D PLAN TEC/DEV DEPT/DEFEN. PAGE 59 G1165
N67
FORCES
NUC/PWR
WAR
UTIL

US SENATE COMM AERO SPACE SCI,POLICY PLANNING FOR TECHNOLOGY TRANSFER (PAMPHLET). WOR+45 INDUS CREATE PLAN EFFICIENCY ATTIT. PAGE 60 G1171
N67
TEC/DEV
POLICY
NAT/G
ECO/DEV

US SENATE COMM ON FOREIGN REL,SURVEY OF THE ALLIANCE FOR PROGRESS; THE POLITICAL ASPECTS (PAMPHLET). CONSTN SOCIETY ECO/UNDEV INT/ORG TEC/DEV DIPLOM...CENSUS 20. PAGE 60 G1186
N67
L/A+17C
POLICY
PROB/SOLV

GALLAHER A. JR.,PERSPECTIVES IN DEVELOPMENTAL CHANGE. MUNIC PLAN INSPECT EDU/PROP...POLICY DECISION GEOG PSY SOC IDEA/COMP ANTHOL 20 MODERNIZE. PAGE 21 G0405
B68
TECHNIC
TEC/DEV
PROB/SOLV
CREATE

BARAGWANATH L.E.,"SCIENTIFIC CO-OPERATION BETWEEN THE UNIVERSITIES AND INDUSTRY - A RESEARCH NOTE." UK LG/CO CREATE TEC/DEV EDU/PROP ATTIT...PHIL/SCI STAT QU 20. PAGE 5 G0090
S68
R+D
ACADEM
INDUS
GP/REL

BENTHAM J.,DEFENCE OF USURY (1787). UK LAW NAT/G TEC/DEV ECO/TAC CONTROL ATTIT...CONCPT IDEA/COMP 18 SMITH/ADAM. PAGE 6 G0124
B88
TAX
FINAN
ECO/DEV
POLICY

TECHNIC....TECHNOCRATIC

BRYSON L.,SCIENCE AND FREEDOM. WOR+45 ACT/RES CREATE TECHRACY...TECHNIC SOC/INTEG. PAGE 9 G0183
B47
CONCPT
ORD/FREE
CULTURE
SOC

OGBURN W.,TECHNOLOGY AND INTERNATIONAL RELATIONS. WOR+45 WOR-45 ECO/DEV CREATE PLAN ECO/TAC EDU/PROP COERCE PWR SKILL WEALTH...TECHNIC PSY SOC NEW/IDEA CHARTS TOT/POP 20. PAGE 43 G0837
B49
TEC/DEV
DIPLOM
INT/ORG

MECRENSKY E.,SCIENTIFIC MANPOWER IN EUROPE. WOR+45 EDU/PROP GOV/REL SKILL...TECHNIC PHIL/SCI INT CHARTS BIBLIOG 20. PAGE 38 G0750
B58
ECO/TAC
TEC/DEV
METH/COMP
NAT/COMP

MAYDA J.,ATOMIC ENERGY AND LAW. ECO/UNDEV FINAN TEC/DEV FOR/AID EFFICIENCY PRODUC WEALTH...POLICY TECHNIC 20. PAGE 37 G0723
B59
NUC/PWR
L/A+17C
LAW
ADMIN

STANFORD RESEARCH INSTITUTE,POSSIBLE NONMILITARY SCIENTIFIC DEVELOPMENTS AND THEIR POTENTIAL IMPACT ON FOREIGN POLICY PROBLEMS OF THE UNITED. FUT USA+45 INT/ORG PROF/ORG CONSULT ACT/RES CREATE PLAN PEACE KNOWL SKILL...TECHNIC PHIL/SCI NEW/IDEA UNESCO 20. PAGE 52 G1032
B59
R+D
TEC/DEV

LINDVEIT E.N.,SCIENTISTS IN GOVERNMENT. USA+45 PAY EDU/PROP ADMIN DRIVE HABITAT ROLE...TECHNIC BIBLIOG 20. PAGE 34 G0670
B60
TEC/DEV
ECO/TAC
PHIL/SCI
GOV/REL

WOETZEL R.K.,THE INTERNATIONAL CONTROL OF AIRSPACE AND OUTERSPACE. FUT WOR+45 AIR CONSTN STRUCT CONSULT PLAN TEC/DEV ADJUD RIGID/FLEX KNOWL ORD/FREE PWR...TECHNIC GEOG MGT NEW/IDEA TREND COMPUT/IR VAL/FREE 20 TREATY. PAGE 64 G1251
B60
INT/ORG
JURID
SPACE
INT/LAW

WOHLSTETTER A.,"NUCLEAR SHARING: NATO AND THE NTH COUNTRY." EUR+WWI FUT SOCIETY DIPLOM EXEC DETER PWR SKILL...POLICY TECHNIC CONCPT 20 NATO. PAGE 64 G1252
S61
TREND
TEC/DEV
NUC/PWR
ARMS/CONT

CLARKE A.C.,PROFILES OF THE FUTURE; AN INQUIRY INTO THE LIMITS OF THE POSSIBLE. COM/IND DIST/IND PRODUC AGE PERCEPT...TECHNIC NEW/IDEA TIME. PAGE 12 G0232
B62
FUT
TEC/DEV
PREDICT
SPACE

DUPRE S.,SCIENCE AND THE NATION. USA+45 ECO/DEV ACADEM ORD/FREE TECHNIC. PAGE 17 G0323
B62
ARMS/CONT
DECISION
TEC/DEV
INDUS

B62
STAHL O.G.,PUBLIC PERSONNEL ADMINISTRATION. LOC/G   ADMIN
TOP/EX CREATE PLAN ROUTINE...TECHNIC MGT T. PAGE 52   WORKER
G1030   EX/STRUC
                                                      NAT/G

B63
GOLDSEN J.M.,OUTER SPACE IN WORLD POLITICS. COM   TEC/DEV
USA+45 NAT/G FORCES ACT/RES PLAN DIPLOM EDU/PROP   DIPLOM
COERCE ORD/FREE PWR...TECHNIC STAT INT SAMP TREND   SPACE
ANTHOL VAL/FREE 20. PAGE 22 G0428

L63
PHELPS J.,"STUDIES IN DETERRENCE VIII: MILITARY   FORCES
STABILITY AND ARMS CONTROL: A CRITICAL SURVEY."   ORD/FREE
FUT WOR+45 INT/ORG ACT/RES EDU/PROP COERCE NUC/PWR   ARMS/CONT
WAR HEALTH PWR...POLICY TECHNIC TREND SIMUL TOT/POP   DETER
20. PAGE 44 G0874

B64
DIEBOLD J.,BEYOND AUTOMATION: MANAGERIAL PROBLEMS   FUT
OF AN EXPLODING TECHNOLOGY. SOCIETY ECO/DEV CREATE   INDUS
ECO/TAC AUTOMAT SKILL...TECHNIC MGT WORK. PAGE 16   PROVS
G0303   NAT/G

B64
ELLUL J.,THE TECHNOLOGICAL SOCIETY. FUT STRUCT   SOC
CREATE AUTOMAT ROUTINE STRANGE ANOMIE MORAL   SOCIETY
PHIL/SCI. PAGE 18 G0344   TECHNIC
                                                      TEC/DEV

B64
LANG A.S.,URBAN RAIL TRANSIT. OP/RES PLAN PROB/SOLV   MUNIC
TEC/DEV AUTOMAT COST...TECHNIC MATH CON/ANAL CHARTS   DIST/IND
METH/COMP SIMUL 20 RAILROAD PUB/TRANS. PAGE 32   ECOMETRIC
G0632

B65
BENJAMIN A.C.,SCIENCE, TECHNOLOGY, AND HUMAN   PHIL/SCI
VALUES. WOR+45 SECT EDU/PROP GP/REL ATTIT...TECHNIC   CREATE
LING IDEA/COMP WORSHIP 20. PAGE 6 G0118   ROLE
                                                      SOCIETY

B66
GOULD J.M.,THE TECHNICAL ELITE. INDUS LABOR   ECO/DEV
TECHRACY...POLICY DECISION STAT CHARTS 20. PAGE 22   TEC/DEV
G0437   ELITES
                                                      TECHNIC

B68
GALLAHER A. JR.,PERSPECTIVES IN DEVELOPMENTAL   TECHNIC
CHANGE. MUNIC PLAN INSPECT EDU/PROP...POLICY   TEC/DEV
DECISION GEOG PSY SOC IDEA/COMP ANTHOL 20   PROB/SOLV
MODERNIZE. PAGE 21 G0405   CREATE

TECHNIQUES....SEE TEC/DEV, METHODOLOGICAL INDEXES,
     PP. XIII-XIV

TECHNOCRACY....SEE TECHRACY, TECHNIC

TECHNOLOGY....SEE COMPUTER, TECHNIC, TEC/DEV

TECHRACY....SOCIO-POLITICAL ORDER DOMINATED BY TECHNICIANS

S44
GRIFFITH E.S.,"THE CHANGING PATTERN OF PUBLIC   LAW
POLICY FORMATION." MOD/EUR WOR+45 FINAN CHIEF   POLICY
CONFER ADMIN LEAD CONSERVE SOCISM TECHRACY...SOC   TEC/DEV
CHARTS CONGRESS. PAGE 23 G0450

B47
BRYSON L.,SCIENCE AND FREEDOM. WOR+45 ACT/RES   CONCPT
CREATE TECHRACY...TECHNIC SOC/INTEG. PAGE 9 G0183   ORD/FREE
                                                      CULTURE
                                                      SOC

B62
BERKELEY E.C.,THE COMPUTER REVOLUTION. WOR+45   COMPUTER
CREATE TEC/DEV EFFICIENCY TECHRACY...SOC TREND 20.   CONTROL
PAGE 7 G0128   AUTOMAT
                                                      SOCIETY

B63
SCHRADER R.,SCIENCE AND POLICY. WOR+45 ECO/DEV   TEC/DEV
ECO/UNDEV R+D FORCES PLAN DIPLOM GOV/REL TECHRACY   NAT/G
BIBLIOG. PAGE 50 G0976   POLICY
                                                      ADMIN

B65
LAPP R.E.,THE NEW PRIESTHOOD; THE SCIENTIFIC ELITE   TEC/DEV
AND THE USES OF POWER. USA+45 ELITES INTELL SOCIETY   TECHRACY
R+D NAT/G CHIEF LEGIS CIVMIL/REL GP/REL PWR 20   CONTROL
PRESIDENT CONGRESS. PAGE 32 G0635   POPULISM

B66
GOULD J.M.,THE TECHNICAL ELITE. INDUS LABOR   ECO/DEV

TECHRACY...POLICY DECISION STAT CHARTS 20. PAGE 22   TEC/DEV
G0437   ELITES
                                                      TECHNIC

B66
JACOBSON H.K.,DIPLOMATS, SCIENTISTS, AND   DIPLOM
POLITICIANS* THE UNITED STATES AND THE NUCLEAR TEST ARMS/CONT
BAN NEGOTIATIONS. USA+45 USSR ACT/RES PLAN CONFER   TECHRACY
DETER NUC/PWR CONSEN ORD/FREE...INT TREATY. PAGE 28 INT/ORG
G0554

B66
NIEBURG H.L.,IN THE NAME OF SCIENCE. USA+45   NAT/G
EX/STRUC LEGIS TEC/DEV BUDGET PAY AUTOMAT LOBBY PWR INDUS
...OBS 20. PAGE 42 G0822   TECHRACY

S66
COHEN A.,"THE TECHNOLOGY/ELITE APPROACH TO THE   ECO/UNDEV
DEVELOPMENTAL PROCESS* PERUVIAN CASE STUDY."   ELITES
L/A+17C STRUCT CREATE ECO/TAC FOR/AID CIVMIL/REL   PERU
MARXISM TECHRACY HYPO/EXP. PAGE 12 G0239

B67
ELSNER H.,THE TECHNOCRATS, PROPHETS OF AUTOMATION.   AUTOMAT
SOCIETY INDUS VOL/ASSN COST INCOME ATTIT 20.   TECHRACY
PAGE 18 G0345   PRODUC
                                                     HIST/WRIT

B67
HEILBRONER R.L.,THE LIMITS OF AMERICAN CAPITALISM.   ELITES
FUT ECO/DEV INDUS LG/CO EX/STRUC LEAD PWR TECHRACY   CREATE
20. PAGE 25 G0502   TEC/DEV
                                                     CAP/ISM

S67
LEVENSTEIN A.,"TECHNOLOGICAL CHANGE, WORK, AND   TEC/DEV
HUMAN VALUES." WOR+45 SOCIETY AUTOMAT ROUTINE   CULTURE
LEISURE INGP/REL ADJUST TECHRACY...MGT CONCPT.   ALL/VALS
PAGE 33 G0660   TIME/SEQ

TEHERAN....TEHERAN CONFERENCE

TEKINER S. G1060

TELLER E. G1061,G1062

TEMPERANCE....TEMPERANCE MOVEMENTS

TENDLER J.D. G1063

TENNESSEE VALLEY AUTHORITY....SEE TVA

TENNESSEE....TENNESSEE

TERRELL/G....GLENN TERRELL

TERRY V. OHIO....SEE TERRY

TERRY....TERRY V. OHIO

TESTS....THEORY AND USES OF TESTS AND SCALES; SEE ALSO
     TESTS AND SCALES INDEX, P. XIV

S4.
MERTON R.,"THE ROLE OF APPLIED SOCIAL SCIENCE IN   PLAN
THE FORMATION OF POLICY: A RESEARCH MEMORANDUM."   SOC
WOR+45 INDUS NAT/G EXEC ROUTINE CHOOSE ORD/FREE PWR DIPLOM
SKILL...POLICY MGT PSY METH/CNCPT TESTS CHARTS METH
VAL/FREE 20. PAGE 38 G0756

S50
KAPLAN A.,"THE PREDICTION OF SOCIAL AND   PWR
TECHNOLOGICAL EVENTS." VOL/ASSN CONSULT ACT/RES   KNO/TEST
CREATE OP/RES PLAN ROUTINE PERSON...POLICY
METH/CNCPT STAT QU/SEMANT SYS/QU TESTS CENSUS TREND
20. PAGE 29 G0574

S52
"SELECTED CRITICAL BIBLIOGRAPHY ON THE METHODS AND   BIBLIOG/A
TECHNIQUES OF POLITICAL BEHAVIOR RESEARCH."   METH
...PHIL/SCI OBS QU SYS/QU TESTS CON/ANAL. PAGE 1   SOC
G0012   EDU/PROP

B54
SPENCER R.F.,METHOD AND PERSPECTIVE IN ANTHROPOLOGY PHIL/SCI
....GEOG LING QUANT STAT TESTS SAMP/SIZ CON/ANAL   SOC
IDEA/COMP METH/COMP ANTHOL BIBLIOG 20. PAGE 52   PSY
G1025   METH

B62
STERN A.C.,AIR POLLUTION (2 VOLS.). LAW INDUS   AIR
PROB/SOLV TEC/DEV INSPECT RISK BIO/SOC HABITAT   OP/RES
...OBS/ENVIR TESTS SAMP 20 POLLUTION. PAGE 53 G1035 CONTROL
                                                     HEALTH

N62
US CONGRESS JT ATOM ENRGY COMM.PEACEFUL USES OF   NUC/PWR
ATOMIC ENERGY, HEARING. USA+45 USSR TEC/DEV ATTIT   ACADEM
RIGID/FLEX...TESTS CHARTS EXHIBIT METH/COMP 20   SCHOOL
CONGRESS. PAGE 57 G1112   NAT/COMP

B63
NORTH R.C..CONTENT ANALYSIS: A HANDBOOK WITH   METH/CNCPT
APPLICATIONS FOR THE STUDY OF INTERNATIONAL CRISIS.   COMPUT/IR
ASIA COM EUR+WWI MOD/EUR INT/ORG TEC/DEV DOMIN   USSR
EDU/PROP ROUTINE COERCE PERCEPT RIGID/FLEX ALL/VALS
...QUANT TESTS CON/ANAL SIMUL GEN/LAWS VAL/FREE.
PAGE 42 G0825

B64
COOMBS C.H..A THEORY OF DATA....MGT PHIL/SCI SOC   CON/ANAL
CLASSIF MATH PROBABIL STAT QU. PAGE 13 G0254   GEN/METH
                                                         TESTS
                                                         PSY

B67
BUNGE M..THE SEARCH FOR TRUTH. VOL. 3, PART 2 OF   PHIL/SCI
STUDIES IN THE FOUNDATIONS, METHODOLOGY, AND   TESTS
PHILOSOPHY OF SCIENCE. UNIV INTELL KNOWL...CONCPT   GEN/LAWS
OBS PREDICT METH. PAGE 10 G0188   RATIONAL

TEXAS....TEXAS

THAILAND....THAILAND; SEE ALSO S/ASIA

B62
KARNJAHAPRAKORN C..MUNICIPAL GOVERNMENT IN THAILAND   LOC/G
AS AN INSTITUTION AND PROCESS OF SELF-GOVERNMENT.   MUNIC
THAILAND CULTURE FINAN EX/STRUC LEGIS PLAN CONTROL   ORD/FREE
GOV/REL EFFICIENCY ATTIT...POLICY 20. PAGE 29 G0578   ADMIN

THANT U. G1064,G1065

THAYER F.C. G1066

THERAPY....SEE SPECIFICS, SUCH AS PROJ/TEST, DEEP/INT,
    SOC/EXP; ALSO SEE DIFFERENT VALUES (E.G., LOVE) AND
    TOPICAL TERMS (E.G., PRESS)

THING/STOR....ARTIFACTS AND MATERIAL EVIDENCE

THIRD/WRLD....THIRD WORLD - NONALIGNED NATIONS

B60
MCKINNEY R..REVIEW OF THE INTERNATIONAL ATOMIC   NUC/PWR
POLICIES AND PROGRAMS OF THE UNITED STATES (5   PEACE
VOLS.). COM FUT USA+45 ECO/DEV ECO/UNDEV INT/ORG   DIPLOM
DELIB/GP PLAN ADMIN 20 THIRD/WRLD. PAGE 38 G0744   POLICY

B62
BROOKINGS INSTITUTION.DEVELOPMENT OF THE EMERGING   ECO/UNDEV
COUNTRIES; AN AGENDA FOR RESEARCH. WOR+45 AGRI   R+D
TEC/DEV FOR/AID EDU/PROP ADJUST HABITAT KNOWL...PSY   SOCIETY
SOC ANTHOL 20 THIRD/WRLD. PAGE 9 G0175   PROB/SOLV

B63
MENEZES A.J..SUBDESENVOLVIMENTO E POLITICA   ECO/UNDEV
INTERNACIONAL. BRAZIL WOR+45 PLAN CONTROL LEAD   DIPLOM
NAT/LISM ORD/FREE 20 THIRD/WRLD. PAGE 38 G0754   POLICY
                                                        BAL/PWR

B64
FEI J.C.H..DEVELOPMENT OF THE LABOR SURPLUS   ECO/TAC
ECONOMY: THEORY AND POLICY. WOR+45 AGRI INDUS   POLICY
MARKET PROB/SOLV TEC/DEV...STAT CHARTS GEN/LAWS   WORKER
METH 20 THIRD/WRLD. PAGE 18 G0361   ECO/UNDEV

B64
HASKINS C.P..THE SCIENTIFIC REVOLUTION AND WORLD   TEC/DEV
POLITICS. COM FUT USA+45 ECO/DEV ECO/UNDEV ATTIT   POLICY
...PHIL/SCI BIBLIOG 20 THIRD/WRLD. PAGE 25 G0489   DIPLOM
                                                        TREND

THOMAS M. G1067

THOMAS/FA....F.A. THOMAS

THOMAS/N....NORMAN THOMAS

THOMAS/TK....TREVOR K. THOMAS

THOMPSON K.W. G1068

THOMPSON V.A. G1069,G1070

THOMSON G.P. G1071

THOREAU/H....HENRY THOREAU

THORELLI H.B. G1072,G1073

THORNTN/WT....WILLIAM T. THORNTON

THRALL R.M. G0245

THUCYDIDES....THUCYDIDES

THURSTON/L....LOUIS LEON THURSTONE

TIBET....TIBET; SEE ALSO ASIA, CHINA

TILLICH/P....PAUL TILLICH

TIME....TIMING, TIME FACTOR; SEE ALSO ANALYSIS OF TEMPORAL
    SEQUENCES INDEX, P. XIV

B48
WEINER N..CYBERNETICS. SOCIETY COMPUTER ADJUST   FEEDBACK
EFFICIENCY UTIL PERCEPT...PSY MATH REGRESS TIME.   AUTOMAT
PAGE 63 G1226   CONTROL
                                                        TEC/DEV

B62
CLARKE A.C..PROFILES OF THE FUTURE; AN INQUIRY INTO   FUT
THE LIMITS OF THE POSSIBLE. COM/IND DIST/IND PRODUC   TEC/DEV
AGE PERCEPT...TECHNIC NEW/IDEA TIME. PAGE 12 G0232   PREDICT
                                                        SPACE

B64
BRILLOUIN L..SCIENTIFIC UNCERTAINTY AND   PHIL/SCI
INFORMATION. PROB/SOLV AUTOMAT PERCEPT ORD/FREE   NEW/IDEA
...MATH REGRESS STAT STYLE OBS IDEA/COMP SIMUL   METH/CNCPT
TIME. PAGE 9 G0169   CREATE

B64
MARTINO R.L..PROJECT MANAGEMENT AND CONTROL: VOL. 2   DECISION
APPLIED OPERATIONAL PLANNING. COMPUTER...MATH   PLAN
CHARTS SIMUL METH TIME. PAGE 36 G0716   TEC/DEV
                                                        OP/RES

B65
US SENATE COMM AERO SPACE SCI.NATIONAL SPACE GOALS   SPACE
FOR THE POST-APOLLO PERIOD. USA+45 CONSULT DELIB/GP   FUT
TEC/DEV BUDGET GP/REL ATTIT...CHARTS IDEA/COMP TIME   R+D
20 DEPT/DEFEN NASA CONGRESS. PAGE 59 G1166   LEGIS

S65
BIRNBAUM K.."SWEDEN'S NUCLEAR POLICY." WOR+45   SWEDEN
POL/PAR CREATE TEC/DEV NEUTRAL RISK WAR ORD/FREE   NUC/PWR
...DECISION IDEA/COMP NAT/COMP TIME. PAGE 7 G0137   DIPLOM
                                                        ARMS/CONT

S65
GOLDSTEIN W.."KEEPING THE GENIE IN THE BOTTLE* THE   NUC/PWR
FEASIBILITY OF A NUCLEAR NON-PROLIFERATION   CREATE
AGREEMENT." ASIA FRANCE UK USA+45 USSR WOR+45   COST
ECO/UNDEV VOL/ASSN ACT/RES PLAN RISK ARMS/CONT WAR
PEACE ATTIT PERCEPT...RECORD TREND TIME. PAGE 22
G0429

S65
KUZMACK A.M.."TECHNOLOGICAL CHANGE AND STABLE   R+D
DETERRENCE." CREATE EDU/PROP ARMS/CONT WEAPON   DETER
CHOOSE COST DRIVE PERCEPT...RECORD STERTYP TIME.   EQUILIB
PAGE 32 G0627

S65
RASER J.R.."WEAPONS DESIGN AND ARMS CONTROL* THE   ARMS/CONT
POLARIS EXAMPLE." DETER NUC/PWR WEAPON CHOOSE   R+D
PERCEPT...STERTYP TIME. PAGE 46 G0904   GEOG
                                                        ACT/RES

B66
FEIS H..THE ATOMIC BOMB AND THE END OF WORLD WAR   USA+45
II. FORCES PLAN PROB/SOLV DIPLOM CONFER WAR   PEACE
...TIME/SEQ TREND CHINJAP PRESIDENT TIME. PAGE 19   NUC/PWR
G0362

S67
CETRON M.J.."FORECASTING TECHNOLOGY." INDUS FORCES   TEC/DEV
TASK UTIL...PHIL/SCI CONCPT CHARTS METH/COMP TIME.   FUT
PAGE 11 G0219   R+D
                                                        PLAN

TIME/SEQ....CHRONOLOGY AND GENETIC SERIES

B23
DRAPER J.W..HISTORY OF THE CONFLICT BETWEEN   SECT
RELIGION AND SCIENCE. WOR-45 INTELL SOCIETY R+D   KNOWL
CREATE PLAN TEC/DEV EDU/PROP ATTIT PWR...PHIL/SCI
CONCPT OBS TIME/SEQ TREND GEN/LAWS TOT/POP. PAGE 16
G0314

B28
SOROKIN P..CONTEMPORARY SOCIOLOGICAL THEORIES.   CULTURE

MOD/EUR UNIV SOCIETY R+D SCHOOL ECO/TAC EDU/PROP
ROUTINE ATTIT DRIVE...PSY CONCPT TIME/SEQ TREND
GEN/LAWS 20. PAGE 52 G1021
SOC
WAR

B45
REVES E.,THE ANATOMY OF PEACE. WOR-45 LAW CULTURE
NAT/G PLAN TEC/DEV EDU/PROP WAR NAT/LISM ATTIT
ALL/VALS SOVEREIGN...POLICY HUM TIME/SEQ 20.
PAGE 46 G0914
ACT/RES
CONCPT
NUC/PWR
PEACE

B45
SMYTH H.D.,ATOMIC ENERGY FOR MILITARY PURPOSES.
USA-45 NAT/G PLAN TEC/DEV KNOWL...MATH CON/ANAL
CHARTS LAB/EXP SIMUL 20. PAGE 52 G1017
R+D
TIME/SEQ
NUC/PWR

B46
BRODIE B.,THE OBSOLETE WEAPON: ATOMIC POWER AND
WORLD ORDER. COM USA+45 USSR WOR+45 DELIB/GP PLAN
ORD/FREE PWR...CONCPT TIME/SEQ TREND UN 20. PAGE 9
G0171
INT/ORG
TEC/DEV
ARMS/CONT
NUC/PWR

B46
VINER J.,SYMPOSIUM ON ATOMIC ENERGY AND ITS
IMPLICATIONS. USA+45 WOR+45 SOCIETY DELIB/GP...SOC
CONCPT TIME/SEQ TOT/POP 20. PAGE 61 G1200
R+D
RIGID/FLEX
NUC/PWR

B48
METZLER L.A.,INCOME, EMPLOYMENT, AND PUBLIC POLICY.
FINAN INDUS LOC/G NAT/G TAX GIVE PAY COST PRODUC
...MGT TIME/SEQ 20. PAGE 38 G0760
INCOME
WEALTH
POLICY
ECO/TAC

B49
ROSENHAUPT H.W.,HOW TO WAGE PEACE. USA+45 SOCIETY
STRATA STRUCT R+D INT/ORG POL/PAR LEGIS ACT/RES
CREATE PLAN EDU/PROP ADMIN EXEC ATTIT ALL/VALS
...TIME/SEQ TREND COLD/WAR 20. PAGE 48 G0937
INTELL
CONCPT
DIPLOM

B51
CONANT J.B.,SCIENCE AND COMMON SENSE. WOR+45 WOR-45
R+D SCHOOL CONSULT TEC/DEV EDU/PROP SKILL...PLURIST
METH/CNCPT RECORD TIME/SEQ SIMUL GEN/METH METH.
PAGE 13 G0248
CREATE
PHIL/SCI

B52
HAYEK F.A.,THE COUNTER-REVOLUTION OF SCIENCE. UNIV
INTELL R+D VOL/ASSN CREATE EDU/PROP...PHIL/SCI SOC
OBS TIME/SEQ TREND GEN/METH. PAGE 25 G0494
PERCEPT
KNOWL

B54
ARON R.,CENTURY OF TOTAL WAR. FUT WOR+45 WOR-45
SOCIETY INT/ORG NAT/G FORCES TOP/EX CREATE BAL/PWR
DOMIN EDU/PROP COERCE DETER PEACE TOTALISM PWR
...TIME/SEQ TREND COLD/WAR TOT/POP VAL/FREE
LEAGUE/NAT 20. PAGE 4 G0066
ATTIT
WAR

B54
WASHBURNE N.F.,INTERPRETING SOCIAL CHANGE IN
AMERICA. USA+45 STRATA FAM NAT/G SECT OP/RES
ECO/TAC EDU/PROP HABITAT...SOC TIME/SEQ TREND 20
BUREAUCRCY. PAGE 62 G1217
CULTURE
STRUCT
CREATE
TEC/DEV

B55
JONES J.M.,THE FIFTEEN WEEKS (FEBRUARY 21-JUNE 5,
1947). EUR+WWI USA+45 PROB/SOLV BAL/PWR...POLICY
TIME/SEQ 20 COLD/WAR MARSHL/PLN TRUMAN/HS
WASHING/DC. PAGE 29 G0567
DIPLOM
ECO/TAC
FOR/AID

B56
THOMAS M.,ATOMIC ENERGY AND CONGRESS. USA+45 NAT/G
ACT/RES PLAN TEC/DEV EDU/PROP ROUTINE KNOWL PWR
SKILL...PHIL/SCI NEW/IDEA TIME/SEQ CHARTS METH
CONGRESS VAL/FREE 20 AEC. PAGE 54 G1067
LEGIS
ADMIN
NUC/PWR

B58
OGDEN F.D.,THE POLL TAX IN THE SOUTH. USA+45 USA-45
CONSTN ADJUD ADMIN PARTIC CRIME...TIME/SEQ GOV/COMP
METH/COMP 18/20 SOUTH/US. PAGE 43 G0838
TAX
CHOOSE
RACE/REL
DISCRIM

B60
BARNET R.,WHO WANTS DISARMAMENT. COM EUR+WWI USA+45
USSR INT/ORG NAT/G BAL/PWR DIPLOM EDU/PROP COERCE
DETER NUC/PWR WAR WEAPON ATTIT PWR...TIME/SEQ
COLD/WAR CONGRESS 20. PAGE 5 G0096
PLAN
FORCES
ARMS/CONT

B60
PARRY A.,RUSSIA'S ROCKETS AND MISSILES. COM FUT
GERMANY USA+45 WOR+45 INTELL ECO/DEV ACT/RES
NUC/PWR WEAPON ATTIT ALL/VALS...OBS TIME/SEQ
COLD/WAR 20. PAGE 44 G0859
PLAN
TEC/DEV
SPACE
USSR

S60
BARNETT H.J.,"RESEARCH AND DEVELOPMENT, ECONOMIC
GROWTH, AND NATIONAL SECURITY." USA+45 R+D CREATE
ECO/TAC ATTIT DRIVE PWR...POLICY SOC METH/CNCPT
ACT/RES
PLAN

QUANT STAT TIME/SEQ ORG/CHARTS COLD/WAR 20. PAGE 5
G0097

S60
HAYTON R.D.,"THE ANTARCTIC SETTLEMENT OF 1959." FUT
USA+45 WOR+45 WOR-45 STRUCT R+D INT/ORG EX/STRUC
CREATE TEC/DEV LEGIT PEACE ATTIT SOVEREIGN
...TIME/SEQ 20 TREATY IGY. PAGE 25 G0495
DELIB/GP
JURID
DIPLOM
REGION

S60
SANDERS R.,"NUCLEAR DYNAMITE: A NEW DIMENSION IN
FOREIGN POLICY." FUT WOR+45 ECO/DEV CONSULT TEC/DEV
PERCEPT...CONT/OBS TIME/SEQ TREND GEN/LAWS TOT/POP
20 TREATY. PAGE 49 G0955
INDUS
PWR
DIPLOM
NUC/PWR

N60
US HOUSE COMM SCI ASTRONAUT,THE ORGANIZATION OF THE
US NATIONAL SPACE EFFORT. USA+45 WOR+45 AIR ECO/DEV
NAT/G PLAN TEC/DEV DIPLOM EDU/PROP ATTIT DRIVE PWR
...OBS TIME/SEQ TREND TOT/POP 20. PAGE 58 G1142
ACT/RES
SKILL
SPACE

B61
HADLEY A.T.,THE NATIONS SAFETY AND ARMS CONTROL.
FUT USA+45 WOR+45 TOP/EX PLAN TEC/DEV ATTIT DRIVE
...CONCPT OBS TIME/SEQ TREND 20. PAGE 24 G0466
ACT/RES
ROUTINE
DETER
NUC/PWR

B61
HENKIN L.,ARMS CONTROL: ISSUES FOR THE PUBLIC.
EUR+WWI FUT USA+45 USSR INT/ORG NAT/G DIPLOM
EDU/PROP DETER NUC/PWR ATTIT PWR...CONCPT RECORD
HIST/WRIT TIME/SEQ TOT/POP COLD/WAR 20. PAGE 26
G0506
WOR+45
DELIB/GP
ARMS/CONT

B61
NOGEE J.L.,SOVIET POLICY TOWARD INTERNATIONAL
CONTROL OF ATOMIC ENERGY. COM USA+45 WOR+45 INTELL
NAT/G ACT/RES DIPLOM EDU/PROP NUC/PWR TOTALISM
PERCEPT KNOWL PWR...TIME/SEQ COLD/WAR 20. PAGE 42
G0824
INT/ORG
ATTIT
ARMS/CONT
USSR

S61
TAUBENFELD H.J.,"OUTER SPACE--PAST POLITICS AND
FUTURE POLICY." FUT USA+45 USA-45 WOR+45 AIR INTELL
STRUCT ECO/DEV NAT/G TOP/EX ACT/RES ADMIN ROUTINE
NUC/PWR ATTIT DRIVE...CONCPT TIME/SEQ TREND TOT/POP
20. PAGE 54 G1054
PLAN
SPACE
INT/ORG

S62
ALBONETTI A.,"IL SECONDO PROGRAMMA QUINQUENNALE
1963-67 ED IL BILANCIO RICERCHE ED INVESTIMENTI PER
IL 1963 DELL'ERATOM." EUR+WWI FUT ITALY WOR+45
ECO/DEV SERV/IND INT/ORG TEC/DEV ECO/TAC ATTIT
SKILL WEALTH...MGT TIME/SEQ OEEC 20. PAGE 2 G0035
R+D
PLAN
NUC/PWR

S62
FOSTER R.B.,"UNILATERAL ARMS CONTROL MEASURES AND
DISARMAMENT NEGOTIATION." WOR+45 VOL/ASSN DELIB/GP
ACT/RES ECO/TAC EDU/PROP ATTIT RIGID/FLEX...CONCPT
MYTH TIME/SEQ COLD/WAR 20. PAGE 20 G0386
PLAN
ORD/FREE
ARMS/CONT
DETER

S62
GORDON B.K.,"NUCLEAR WEAPONS: RUSSIAN AND
AMERICAN." COM USA+45 USSR NAT/G FORCES ACT/RES
TEC/DEV PERCEPT RIGID/FLEX PWR SKILL...MGT
METH/CNCPT QUANT OBS TIME/SEQ CON/ANAL GEN/METH
TOT/POP VAL/FREE 20. PAGE 22 G0433
ORD/FREE
COERCE
NUC/PWR

S62
NANES A.,"DISARMAMENT: THE LAST SEVEN YEARS." COM
EUR+WWI USA+45 USSR INT/ORG FORCES TOP/EX CREATE
LEGIT NUC/PWR DISPL ORD/FREE...CONCPT TIME/SEQ
CON/ANAL 20. PAGE 41 G0803
DELIB/GP
RIGID/FLEX
ARMS/CONT

B63
MAYNE R.,THE COMMUNITY OF EUROPE. UK CONSTN NAT/G
CONSULT DELIB/GP CREATE PLAN ECO/TAC LEGIT ADMIN
ROUTINE ORD/FREE PWR WEALTH...CONCPT TIME/SEQ EEC
EURATOM 20. PAGE 37 G0724
EUR+WWI
INT/ORG
REGION

B63
MULLER H.J.,FREEDOM IN THE WESTERN WORLD. PREHIST
CULTURE SECT CREATE TEC/DEV DOMIN PWR WEALTH
...MAJORIT SOC CONCPT. PAGE 40 G0793
ORD/FREE
TIME/SEQ
SOCIETY

S63
DELLIN L.A.D.,"BULGARIA UNDER SOVIET LEADERSHIP."
BULGARIA COM USA+45 USSR ECO/DEV INDUS POL/PAR
EX/STRUC TOP/EX COERCE ATTIT RIGID/FLEX...POLICY
TIME/SEQ 20. PAGE 15 G0293
AGRI
NAT/G
TOTALISM

S63
FERRETTI B.,"IMPORTANZA E PROSPETTIVE DELL ENERGIA
DI ORIGINE NUCLEARE." FUT ITALY WOR+45 INTELL R+D
ACT/RES CREATE HEALTH WEALTH...METH/CNCPT TIME/SEQ
20. PAGE 19 G0365
TEC/DEV
EXEC
NUC/PWR

TASHJEAN J.E.,"RESEARCH ON ARMS CONTROL." COM   NAT/G   S63
USA+45 USSR FORCES ACT/RES PLAN DOMIN COERCE   POLICY
ORD/FREE PWR...TIME/SEQ GEN/LAWS 20 COLD/WAR.   ARMS/CONT
PAGE 53 G1053

BALASSA B.,TRADE PROSPECTS FOR DEVELOPING   INT/TRADE   B64
COUNTRIES. WOR+45 ECO/DEV AGRI EXTR/IND INDUS   ECO/UNDEV
CREATE PLAN PRICE...ECOMETRIC CLASSIF TIME/SEQ TREND
GEN/METH. PAGE 5 G0087   STAT

ETZIONI A.,THE MOON-DOGGLE: DOMESTIC AND   R+D   B64
INTERNATIONAL IMPLICATIONS OF THE SPACE RACE. FUT NAT/G
USA+45 WOR+45 INTELL ECO/DEV INDUS VOL/ASSN   DIPLOM
EX/STRUC FORCES LEGIS PLAN TEC/DEV ECO/TAC   SPACE
EDU/PROP KNOWL ORD/FREE PWR RESPECT WEALTH
TIME/SEQ. PAGE 18 G0352

GRODZINS M.,THE ATOMIC AGE: FORTY-FIVE SCIENTISTS INTELL   B64
AND SCHOLARS SPEAK ON NATIONAL AND WORLD AFFAIRS. ARMS/CONT
FUT USA+45 WOR+45 R+D INT/ORG NAT/G CONSULT TEC/DEV NUC/PWR
EDU/PROP ATTIT PERSON ORD/FREE...HUM CONCPT
TIME/SEQ CON/ANAL. PAGE 23 G0454

PETERSON W.,THE POLITICS OF POPULATION. COM EUR+WWI PLAN   B64
FUT MOD/EUR S/ASIA USA+45 WOR+45 LAW CULTURE   CENSUS
FAM SECT DOMIN EDU/PROP BIO/SOC HEALTH ORD/FREE POLICY
...GEOG STAT TIME/SEQ TREND VAL/FREE. PAGE 44 G0871

RANSOM H.H.,CAN AMERICAN DEMOCRACY SURVIVE COLD   USA+45   B64
WAR. USA-45 CONSTN NAT/G CONSULT DELIB/GP LEGIS ROUTINE
ACT/RES LEGIT EXEC ATTIT KNOWL ORD/FREE PWR SKILL
...POLICY TIME/SEQ TREND GEN/LAWS 20 COLD/WAR.
PAGE 46 G0901

VAN DYKE V.,PRIDE AND POWER: THE RATIONALE OF THE TEC/DEV   B64
SPACE PROGRAM. FUT USA+45 INTELL R+D NAT/G POL/PAR ATTIT
DELIB/GP EX/STRUC LEGIS TOP/EX ACT/RES PLAN ECO/TAC POLICY
EDU/PROP ORD/FREE PWR RESPECT SKILL...TIME/SEQ
VAL/FREE. PAGE 61 G1191

ABT C.,"WAR GAMING." USA+45 NAT/G TOP/EX ACT/RES   FORCES   S64
TEC/DEV COERCE KNOWL ORD/FREE PWR...DECISION MATH SIMUL
TIME/SEQ COMPUT/IR CHARTS LAB/EXP VAL/FREE. PAGE 2 WAR
G0026

FALK S.L.,"DISARMAMENT IN HISTORICAL PERSPECTIVE." INT/ORG   S64
WOR-45 NAT/G PLAN NUC/PWR PEACE ORD/FREE PWR   COERCE
...TIME/SEQ AUD/VIS VAL/FREE LEAGUE/NAT 20. PAGE 18 ARMS/CONT
G0360

KASSOF A.,"THE ADMINISTERED SOCIETY: SOCIETY   S64
TOTALITARIANISM WITHOUT TERROR." COM USSR STRATA DOMIN
AGRI INDUS NAT/G PERF/ART SCHOOL TOP/EX EDU/PROP TOTALISM
ADMIN ORD/FREE PWR...POLICY SOC TIME/SEQ GEN/LAWS
VAL/FREE 20. PAGE 29 G0580

NEEDHAM T.,"SCIENCE AND SOCIETY IN EAST AND WEST." ASIA   S64
INTELL STRATA R+D LOC/G NAT/G PROVS CONSULT ACT/RES STRUCT
CREATE PLAN TEC/DEV EDU/PROP ADMIN ATTIT ALL/VALS
...POLICY RELATIV MGT CONCPT NEW/IDEA TIME/SEQ WORK
WORK. PAGE 41 G0815

KASER M.,COMECON* INTEGRATION PROBLEMS OF THE   PLAN   B65
PLANNED ECONOMIES. INT/ORG TEC/DEV INT/TRADE PRICE ECO/DEV
ADMIN ADJUST CENTRAL...STAT TIME/SEQ ORG/CHARTS COM
COMECON. PAGE 29 G0579   REGION

PHELPS E.S.,PRIVATE WANTS AND PUBLIC NEEDS - AN   NAT/G   B65
INTRODUCTION TO A CURRENT ISSUE OF PUBLIC POLICY POLICY
(REV. ED.). USA+45 PLAN CAP/ISM INGP/REL ROLE   DEMAND
...DECISION TIME/SEQ 20. PAGE 44 G0873

FINK C.F.,"MORE CALCULATIONS ABOUT DETERRENCE."   DETER   S65
DRIVE...PHIL/SCI PSY STAT TIME/SEQ GAME GEN/LAWS. RECORD
PAGE 19 G0367   PROBABIL
                              IDEA/COMP

GRIFFITH S.B.,"COMMUNIST CHINA'S CAPACITY TO MAKE FORCES   S65
WAR." CHINA/COM COM NAT/G TOP/EX PLAN DOMIN COERCE PWR
NUC/PWR ATTIT RESPECT SKILL...CONCPT MYTH TIME/SEQ WEAPON

TREND COLD/WAR 20. PAGE 23 G0452   ASIA

FEIS H.,THE ATOMIC BOMB AND THE END OF WORLD WAR   USA+45   B66
II. FORCES PLAN PROB/SOLV DIPLOM CONFER WAR   PEACE
...TIME/SEQ TREND CHINJAP PRESIDENT TIME. PAGE 19 NUC/PWR
G0362

WHITNAH D.R.,SAFER SKYWAYS. DIST/IND DELIB/GP   ADMIN   B66
FORCES TOP/EX WORKER TEC/DEV ROUTINE WAR CIVMIL/REL NAT/G
COST...TIME/SEQ 20 FAA CAB. PAGE 63 G1235   AIR
                              GOV/REL

LEVENSTEIN A.,"TECHNOLOGICAL CHANGE, WORK, AND   TEC/DEV   S67
HUMAN VALUES." WOR+45 SOCIETY AUTOMAT ROUTINE   CULTURE
LEISURE INGP/REL ADJUST TECHRACY...MGT CONCPT.   ALL/VALS
PAGE 33 G0660   TIME/SEQ

WOLFE T.W.,"SOVIET MILITARY POLICY AT THE FIFTY   FORCES   S67
YEAR MARK." USSR VIETNAM WOR+45 RATION AGREE WAR POLICY
WEAPON CIVMIL/REL TREATY. PAGE 64 G1254   TIME/SEQ
                              PLAN

TIMING....SEE TIME

TITO/MARSH....JOSIP BROZ TITO

TIVEY L. G1074

TIZARD/H....HENRY TIZARD

TOBAGO....SEE TRINIDAD

TOCQUEVILL....ALEXIS DE TOCQUEVILLE

TOGO....SEE ALSO AFR

TOLEDO/O....TOLEDO, OHIO

TOMKINS S.S. G1075

TOMPKINS D.C. G1076,G1077

TONGA....TONGA

TOP/EX....TOP EXECUTIVES

NORTHROP F.S.C.,THE MEETING OF EAST AND WEST.   DRIVE   B46
EUR+WWI FUT MOD/EUR UNIV WOR+45 WOR-45 INTELL   TREND
SOCIETY EX/STRUC TOP/EX ACT/RES LEGIT CHOOSE ATTIT PEACE
PERCEPT RIGID/FLEX ALL/VALS...POLICY JURID OBS
TOT/POP. PAGE 42 G0826

MCLEAN J.M.,THE PUBLIC SERVICE AND UNIVERSITY   ACADEM   B49
EDUCATION. UK USA-45 DELIB/GP EX/STRUC TOP/EX ADMIN NAT/G
...GOV/COMP METH/COMP NAT/COMP ANTHOL 20. PAGE 38 EXEC
G0746   EDU/PROP

ARON R.,CENTURY OF TOTAL WAR. FUT WOR+45 WOR-45   ATTIT   B54
SOCIETY INT/ORG NAT/G FORCES TOP/EX CREATE BAL/PWR WAR
DOMIN EDU/PROP COERCE DETER PEACE TOTALISM PWR
...TIME/SEQ TREND COLD/WAR TOT/POP VAL/FREE
LEAGUE/NAT 20. PAGE 4 G0066

LIPPMAN W.,THE PUBLIC PHILOSOPHY. EX/STRUC TOP/EX   MAJORIT   B55
LOBBY RATIONAL POPULISM...POLICY SOC CONCPT PREDICT STRUCT
GP/COMP IDEA/COMP. PAGE 34 G0673   PWR
                              TOTALISM

SPEIER H.,GERMAN REARMAMENT AND ATOMIC WAR: THE   TOP/EX   B57
VIEWS OF GERMAN MILITARY AND POLITICAL LEADERS. FUT FORCES
WOR+45 INT/ORG NAT/G WEAPON ATTIT PWR...INT QU   NUC/PWR
TOT/POP VAL/FREE COLD/WAR 20. PAGE 52 G1024   GERMANY

MORTON L.,"THE DECISION TO USE THE BOMB." FORCES   NUC/PWR   S57
TOP/EX DOMIN COERCE PEACE. PAGE 40 G0788   DIPLOM
                              WAR

THOMPSON K.W.,"NATIONAL SECURITY IN A NUCLEAR AGE." FORCES   S58
USA+45 WOR+45 SOCIETY INT/ORG NAT/G TOP/EX DIPLOM PWR
DOMIN EDU/PROP LEGIT ARMS/CONT COERCE ORD/FREE   BAL/PWR
...TREND STERTYP TOT/POP VAL/FREE COLD/WAR 20.
PAGE 54 G1068

AMRINE M.,THE GREAT DECISION: THE SECRET HISTORY OF DECISION   B59

THE ATOMIC BOMB. USA+45 TOP/EX EDU/PROP LEGIT
PERCEPT ORD/FREE PWR VAL/FREE HIROSHIMA. PAGE 3
G0055

NAT/G
NUC/PWR
FORCES

B59
RUSSELL B.,COMMON SENSE AND NUCLEAR WARFARE. WOR+45
INTELL SOCIETY STRATA NAT/G TOP/EX EDU/PROP ATTIT
PERSON KNOWL MORAL PWR...POLICY CONCPT MYTH
CON/ANAL COLD/WAR 20. PAGE 48 G0948

ORD/FREE
ARMS/CONT
NUC/PWR

B59
SPANIER J.W.,THE TRUMAN-MACARTHUR CONTROVERSY AND
THE KOREAN WAR. USA+45 TOP/EX PROB/SOLV LEAD ATTIT
PWR...POLICY BIBLIOG/A UN. PAGE 52 G1023

CIVMIL/REL
FORCES
CHIEF
WAR

S59
WILLIAMS B.H.,"SCIENTIFIC METHOD IN FOREIGN
POLICY." WOR+45 NAT/G FORCES TOP/EX DOMIN LEGIT
COERCE PEACE ATTIT KNOWL ORD/FREE PWR...GEN/LAWS
GEN/METH TOT/POP COLD/WAR NAZI. PAGE 63 G1241

PLAN
PHIL/SCI
DIPLOM

L60
HOLTON G.,"ARMS CONTROL." FUT WOR+45 CULTURE
INT/ORG FORCES TOP/EX PLAN EDU/PROP COERCE
ATTIT RIGID/FLEX ORD/FREE...POLICY PHIL/SCI SOC
TREND COLD/WAR. PAGE 27 G0524

ACT/RES
CONSULT
ARMS/CONT
NUC/PWR

S60
HUTCHINSON C.E.,"AN INSTITUTE FOR NATIONAL SECURITY
AFFAIRS." USA+45 R+D NAT/G CONSULT TOP/EX ACT/RES
CREATE PLAN TEC/DEV EDU/PROP ROUTINE NUC/PWR ATTIT
ORD/FREE PWR...DECISION MGT PHIL/SCI CONCPT RECORD
GEN/LAWS GEN/METH 20. PAGE 27 G0539

POLICY
METH/CNCPT
ELITES
DIPLOM

S60
KAPLAN M.A.,"THEORETICAL ANALYSIS OF THE BALANCE OF
POWER." FUT USA+45 WOR+45 INTELL ECO/DEV INT/ORG
NAT/G CONSULT TOP/EX ACT/RES PLAN TEC/DEV ATTIT
ALL/VALS...METH/CNCPT TOT/POP 20. PAGE 29 G0576

CREATE
NEW/IDEA
DIPLOM
NUC/PWR

S60
KELLEY G.A.,"THE POLITICAL BACKGROUND OF THE FRENCH
A-BOMB." EUR+WWI USSR FORCES TOP/EX TEC/DEV NUC/PWR
ATTIT PWR...CONCPT OBS/ENVIR TREND 20. PAGE 30
G0591

NAT/G
RESPECT
NAT/LISM
FRANCE

S60
LEAR J.,"PEACE: SCIENCE'S NEXT GREAT EXPLORATION."
USA+45 INT/ORG TOP/EX TEC/DEV EDU/PROP ROUTINE
PEACE KNOWL SKILL 20. PAGE 33 G0648

EX/STRUC
ARMS/CONT
NUC/PWR

B61
GORDON W.J.J.,SYNECTICS; THE DEVELOPMENT OF
CREATIVE CAPACITY. USA+45 PLAN TEC/DEV KNOWL WEALTH
...DECISION MGT 20. PAGE 22 G0436

CREATE
PROB/SOLV
ACT/RES
TOP/EX

B61
HADLEY A.T.,THE NATIONS SAFETY AND ARMS CONTROL.
FUT USA+45 WOR+45 TOP/EX PLAN TEC/DEV ATTIT DRIVE
...CONCPT OBS TIME/SEQ TREND 20. PAGE 24 G0466

ACT/RES
ROUTINE
DETER
NUC/PWR

B61
HELLER D.,THE KENNEDY CABINET--AMERICA'S MEN OF
DESTINY. NAT/G CHIEF CONSULT ADMIN CONTROL GOV/REL
...MGT 20 DEPT/LABOR DEPT/STATE DEPT/JUST
DEPT/DEFEN KENNEDY/J. PAGE 26 G0504

EX/STRUC
CONFER
DELIB/GP
TOP/EX

B61
KAHN H.,ON THERMONUCLEAR WAR. FUT UNIV WOR+45
ECO/DEV CONSULT EX/STRUC TOP/EX ACT/RES CREATE PLAN
COERCE WAR PERSON ALL/VALS...POLICY GEOG CONCPT
METH/CNCPT OBS TREND 20. PAGE 29 G0569

DETER
NUC/PWR
SOCIETY

B61
KISSINGER H.A.,THE NECESSITY FOR CHOICE. FUT USA+45
ECO/UNDEV NAT/G PLAN BAL/PWR ECO/TAC ARMS/CONT
DETER NUC/PWR ATTIT...POLICY CONCPT RECORD GEN/LAWS
COLD/WAR 20. PAGE 31 G0604

TOP/EX
TREND
DIPLOM

S61
LYONS G.M.,"THE NEW CIVIL-MILITARY RELATIONS."
USA+45 NAT/G EX/STRUC TOP/EX PROB/SOLV ADMIN EXEC
PARTIC 20. PAGE 35 G0681

CIVMIL/REL
PWR
REPRESENT

S61
MORGENSTERN O.,"THE N-COUNTRY PROBLEM." EUR+WWI
UNIV USA+45 WOR+45 SOCIETY CONSULT TOP/EX ACT/RES
PLAN EDU/PROP ATTIT DRIVE...POLICY OBS TREND
TOT/POP 20. PAGE 40 G0781

FUT
BAL/PWR
NUC/PWR
TEC/DEV

S61
TAUBENFELD H.J.,"OUTER SPACE--PAST POLITICS AND
FUTURE POLICY." FUT USA+45 USA-45 WOR+45 AIR INTELL

PLAN
SPACE

STRUCT ECO/DEV NAT/G TOP/EX ACT/RES ADMIN ROUTINE
NUC/PWR ATTIT DRIVE...CONCPT TIME/SEQ TREND TOT/POP
20. PAGE 54 G1054

INT/ORG

B62
SOVIET STAND ON DISARMAMENT. COM EUR+WWI FUT USA+45
NAT/G TOP/EX NUC/PWR PEACE ATTIT...POLICY CONCPT
TOT/POP 20. PAGE 1 G0016

ACT/RES
ORD/FREE
ARMS/CONT
USSR

B62
STAHL O.G.,PUBLIC PERSONNEL ADMINISTRATION. LOC/G
TOP/EX CREATE PLAN ROUTINE...TECHNIC MGT T. PAGE 52
G1030

ADMIN
WORKER
EX/STRUC
NAT/G

B62
STRAUSS L.L.,MEN AND DECISIONS. USA+45 USA-45 USSR
CONSULT FORCES TOP/EX WAR PEACE 20. PAGE 53 G1042

DECISION
PWR
NUC/PWR
DIPLOM

B62
YALEN R.,REGIONALISM AND WORLD ORDER. EUR+WWI
WOR+45 WOR-45 INT/ORG VOL/ASSN DELIB/GP FORCES
TOP/EX BAL/PWR DIPLOM DOMIN REGION ARMS/CONT PWR
...JURID HYPO/EXP COLD/WAR 20. PAGE 64 G1261

ORD/FREE
POLICY

L62
NEIBURG H.L.,"THE EISENHOWER AEC AND CONGRESS: A
STUDY IN EXECUTIVE-LEGISLATIVE RELATIONS." USA+45
NAT/G POL/PAR DELIB/GP EX/STRUC TOP/EX ADMIN EXEC
LEAD ROUTINE PWR...POLICY COLD/WAR CONGRESS
PRESIDENT AEC. PAGE 41 G0816

CHIEF
LEGIS
GOV/REL
NUC/PWR

L62
NIEBURG H.L.,"THE EISENHOWER ATOMIC ENERGY
COMMISSION AND CONGRESS" R+D INT/ORG OP/RES DIPLOM
ADMIN CONTROL 20 PRESIDENT CONGRESS AEC. PAGE 42
G0821

NUC/PWR
TOP/EX
LOBBY
DELIB/GP

S62
FINKELSTEIN L.S.,"THE UNITED NATIONS AND
ORGANIZATIONS FOR CONTROL OF ARMAMENT." FUT WOR+45
VOL/ASSN DELIB/GP TOP/EX CREATE EDU/PROP LEGIT
ADJUD NUC/PWR ATTIT RIGID/FLEX ORD/FREE...POLICY
DECISION CONCPT OBS TREND GEN/LAWS TOT/POP
COLD/WAR. PAGE 19 G0368

INT/ORG
PWR
ARMS/CONT

S62
NANES A.,"DISARMAMENT: THE LAST SEVEN YEARS." COM
EUR+WWI USA+45 USSR NAT/G FORCES TOP/EX CREATE
LEGIT NUC/PWR DISPL ORD/FREE...CONCPT TIME/SEQ
CON/ANAL 20. PAGE 41 G0803

DELIB/GP
RIGID/FLEX
ARMS/CONT

S62
SCHILLING W.R.,"SCIENTISTS, FOREIGN POLICY AND
POLITICS." WOR+45 WOR-45 INTELL INT/ORG CONSULT
TOP/EX ACT/RES PLAN ADMIN KNOWL...CONCPT OBS TREND
LEAGUE/NAT 20. PAGE 49 G0967

NAT/G
TEC/DEV
DIPLOM
NUC/PWR

B63
HEYEL C.,THE ENCYCLOPEDIA OF MANAGEMENT. WOR+45
MARKET TOP/EX TEC/DEV AUTOMAT LEAD ADJUST...STAT
CHARTS GAME ANTHOL BIBLIOG. PAGE 26 G0509

MGT
INDUS
ADMIN
FINAN

L63
NIEBURG H.,"EURATOM: A STUDY IN COALITION
POLITICS." EUR+WWI UK USA+45 ELITES NAT/G DELIB/GP
LEGIS TOP/EX ECO/TAC NUC/PWR ATTIT ORD/FREE PWR
TOT/POP EEC OEEC 20 NATO EURATOM. PAGE 42 G0820

VOL/ASSN
ACT/RES

S63
DELLIN L.A.D.,"BULGARIA UNDER SOVIET LEADERSHIP."
BULGARIA COM USA+45 USSR ECO/DEV INDUS POL/PAR
EX/STRUC TOP/EX COERCE ATTIT RIGID/FLEX...POLICY
TIME/SEQ 20. PAGE 15 G0293

AGRI
NAT/G
TOTALISM

S63
HOSKINS H.L.,"ARAB SOCIALISM IN THE UAR." ISLAM
USSR AGRI INDUS NAT/G TOP/EX CREATE DIPLOM EDU/PROP
DRIVE KNOWL PWR SOCISM...POLICY CONCPT TREND SUEZ
20. PAGE 27 G0530

ECO/DEV
PLAN
UAR

S63
SCHMITT H.A.,"THE EUROPEAN COMMUNITIES." EUR+WWI
FRANCE DELIB/GP EX/STRUC TOP/EX CREATE TEC/DEV
ECO/TAC LEGIT REGION COERCE DRIVE ALL/VALS
...METH/CNCPT EEC 20. PAGE 49 G0972

VOL/ASSN
ECO/DEV

S63
WOHLSTETTER A.,"SCIENTISTS, SEERS AND STRATEGY."
USA+45 ELITES R+D NAT/G CONSULT FORCES TOP/EX
EDU/PROP ARMS/CONT KNOWL ORD/FREE...DECISION MYTH
20. PAGE 64 G1253

INTELL
ACT/RES

ETZIONI A.,THE MOON-DOGGLE: DOMESTIC AND   R+D
INTERNATIONAL IMPLICATIONS OF THE SPACE RACE. FUT   NAT/G
USA+45 WOR+45 INTELL ECO/DEV INDUS VOL/ASSN   DIPLOM
EX/STRUC FORCES LEGIS TOP/EX PLAN TEC/DEV ECO/TAC   SPACE
EDU/PROP KNOWL ORD/FREE PWR RESPECT WEALTH
TIME/SEQ. PAGE 18 G0352

KAUFMANN W.W.,THE MC NAMARA STRATEGY. TOP/EX   FORCES
INSPECT BAL/PWR DIPLOM CONTROL DETER GUERRILLA   WAR
NUC/PWR WEAPON COST PWR...METH/COMP 20 MCNAMARA/R PLAN
KENNEDY/JF JOHNSON/LB NATO DEPT/DEFEN. PAGE 30   PROB/SOLV
G0586

VAN DYKE V.,PRIDE AND POWER: THE RATIONALE OF THE TEC/DEV
SPACE PROGRAM. FUT USA+45 INTELL R+D NAT/G POL/PAR ATTIT
DELIB/GP EX/STRUC LEGIS TOP/EX ACT/RES PLAN ECO/TAC POLICY
EDU/PROP ORD/FREE PWR RESPECT SKILL...TIME/SEQ
VAL/FREE. PAGE 61 G1191

WHEELER-BENNETT J.W.,THE NEMESIS OF POWER (2ND   FORCES
ED.). EUR+WWI GERMANY TOP/EX TEC/DEV ADMIN WAR   NAT/G
PERS/REL RIGID/FLEX ROLE ORD/FREE PWR FASCISM 20   GP/REL
HITLER/A. PAGE 63 G1231   STRUCT

GOLDBERG A.,"ATOMIC ORIGINS OF THE BRITISH NUCLEAR CREATE
DETERRENT." EUR+WWI UK NAT/G TOP/EX PLAN BAL/PWR   FORCES
DOMIN DETER CHOOSE ATTIT DRIVE HEALTH ORD/FREE PWR NUC/PWR
RESPECT...CONCPT VAL/FREE COLD/WAR 20 CMN/WLTH.
PAGE 22 G0425

ABT C.,"WAR GAMING." USA+45 NAT/G TOP/EX ACT/RES   FORCES
TEC/DEV COERCE KNOWL ORD/FREE PWR...DECISION MATH SIMUL
TIME/SEQ COMPUT/IR CHARTS LAB/EXP VAL/FREE. PAGE 2 WAR
G0026

KASSOF A.,"THE ADMINISTERED SOCIETY: SOCIETY
TOTALITARIANISM WITHOUT TERROR." COM USSR STRATA   DOMIN
AGRI INDUS NAT/G PERF/ART SCHOOL TOP/EX EDU/PROP   TOTALISM
ADMIN ORD/FREE PWR...POLICY SOC TIME/SEQ GEN/LAWS
VAL/FREE 20. PAGE 29 G0580

MARES V.E.,"EAST EUROPE'S SECOND CHANCE." COM   VOL/ASSN
EUR+WWI HUNGARY ROMANIA USSR YUGOSLAVIA ECO/UNDEV ECO/TAC
NAT/G TOP/EX CREATE PLAN TEC/DEV REGION NAT/LISM
RIGID/FLEX PWR...CONCPT STAT COMECON 20. PAGE 36
G0705

FOX A.B.,"NATO AND CONGRESS." CONSTN DELIB/GP   CONTROL
EX/STRUC FORCES TOP/EX BUDGET NUC/PWR GOV/REL   DIPLOM
...GP/COMP CONGRESS NATO TREATY. PAGE 20 G0388

GRIFFITH S.B.,"COMMUNIST CHINA'S CAPACITY TO MAKE FORCES
WAR." CHINA/COM COM NAT/G TOP/EX PLAN DOMIN COERCE PWR
NUC/PWR ATTIT RESPECT SKILL...CONCPT MYTH TIME/SEQ WEAPON
TREND COLD/WAR 20. PAGE 23 G0452   ASIA

STAAR R.F.,"RETROGRESSION IN POLAND." COM USSR AGRI TOP/EX
INDUS NAT/G CREATE EDU/PROP TOTALISM RIGID/FLEX   ECO/TAC
ORD/FREE PWR SOCISM...RECORD CHARTS 20. PAGE 52   POLAND
G1029

US BUREAU OF THE BUDGET,THE ADMINISTRATION OF   ACT/RES
GOVERNMENT SUPPORTED RESEARCH AT UNIVERSITIES   NAT/G
(PAMPHLET). USA+45 CONSULT TOP/EX ADMIN INCOME   ACADEM
WEALTH...MGT PHIL/SCI INT. PAGE 56 G1108   GP/REL

WHITNAH D.R.,SAFER SKYWAYS. DIST/IND DELIB/GP   ADMIN
FORCES TOP/EX WORKER TEC/DEV ROUTINE WAR CIVMIL/REL NAT/G
COST...TIME/SEQ 20 FAA CAB. PAGE 63 G1235   AIR
                                        GOV/REL

DOUGHERTY J.E.,"THE CATHOLIC CHURCH, WAR AND   CATHISM
NUCLEAR WEAPONS." COM EUR+WWI SECT TOP/EX LEAD   MORAL
DETER ALL/VALS. PAGE 16 G0312   WAR
                                        NUC/PWR

ZOPPO C.E.,"NUCLEAR TECHNOLOGY, MULTIPOLARITY, AND NET/THEORY
INTERNATIONAL STABILITY." ASIA RUSSIA USA+45 STRUCT ORD/FREE
TOP/EX BAL/PWR DIPLOM DETER CIVMIL/REL NAT/COMP.   DECISION
PAGE 65 G1270   NUC/PWR

TORONTO....TORONTO, ONTARIO

TORY/PARTY....TORY PARTY

TOTALISM....TOTALITARIANISM

BINGHAM A.M.,THE TECHNIQUES OF DEMOCRACY. USA-45   POPULISM
CONSTN STRUCT POL/PAR LEGIS PLAN PARTIC CHOOSE   ORD/FREE
REPRESENT NAT/LISM TOTALISM...MGT 20. PAGE 7 G0136 ADMIN
                                        NAT/G

ARON R.,CENTURY OF TOTAL WAR. FUT WOR+45 WOR-45   ATTIT
SOCIETY INT/ORG NAT/G FORCES TOP/EX CREATE BAL/PWR WAR
DOMIN EDU/PROP COERCE DETER PEACE TOTALISM PWR
...TIME/SEQ TREND COLD/WAR TOT/POP VAL/FREE
LEAGUE/NAT 20. PAGE 4 G0066

LIPPMAN W.,THE PUBLIC PHILOSOPHY. EX/STRUC TOP/EX MAJORIT
LOBBY RATIONAL POPULISM...POLICY SOC CONCPT PREDICT STRUCT
GP/COMP IDEA/COMP. PAGE 34 G0673   PWR
                                        TOTALISM

ANGELL N.,DEFENCE AND THE ENGLISH-SPEAKING ROLE.   DIPLOM
CHINA/COM UK USSR INT/ORG FORCES EDU/PROP NEUTRAL   WAR
NUC/PWR NAT/LISM PEACE TOTALISM 20 COLD/WAR   MARXISM
COEXIST. PAGE 3 G0059   ORD/FREE

EMME E.M.,THE IMPACT OF AIR POWER - NATIONAL   DETER
SECURITY AND WORLD POLITICS. USA+45 USSR FORCES   AIR
DIPLOM WEAPON PEACE TOTALISM...POLICY NAT/COMP 20   WAR
EUROPE. PAGE 18 G0346   ORD/FREE

WARD B.,5 IDEAS THAT CHANGE THE WORLD. WOR+45   ECO/UNDEV
WOR-45 SOCIETY STRUCT AGRI INDUS INT/ORG NAT/G   ALL/VALS
FORCES ACT/RES ARMS/CONT TOTALISM ATTIT DRIVE   NAT/LISM
GEN/LAWS. PAGE 62 G1210   COLONIAL

LUNDBERG G.A.,CAN SCIENCE SAVE US. UNIV CULTURE   ACT/RES
INTELL SOCIETY ECO/DEV R+D PLAN EDU/PROP ROUTINE   CONCPT
CHOOSE ATTIT PERCEPT ALL/VALS...TREND 20. PAGE 34   TOTALISM
G0679

NOGEE J.L.,SOVIET POLICY TOWARD INTERNATIONAL   INT/ORG
CONTROL OF ATOMIC ENERGY. COM USA+45 WOR+45 INTELL ATTIT
NAT/G ACT/RES DIPLOM EDU/PROP NUC/PWR TOTALISM   ARMS/CONT
PERCEPT KNOWL PWR...TIME/SEQ COLD/WAR 20. PAGE 42   USSR
G0824

JACOB H.,GERMAN ADMINISTRATION SINCE BISMARCK: ADMIN
CENTRAL AUTHORITY VERSUS LOCAL AUTONOMY. GERMANY   NAT/G
GERMANY/W LAW POL/PAR CONTROL CENTRAL TOTALISM   LOC/G
FASCISM...MAJORIT DECISION STAT CHARTS GOV/COMP   POLICY
19/20 BISMARCK/O HITLER/A WEIMAR/REP. PAGE 28 G0551

DELLIN L.A.D.,"BULGARIA UNDER SOVIET LEADERSHIP."   AGRI
BULGARIA COM USA+45 USSR ECO/DEV INDUS POL/PAR   NAT/G
EX/STRUC TOP/EX COERCE ATTIT RIGID/FLEX...POLICY   TOTALISM
TIME/SEQ 20. PAGE 15 G0293

KASSOF A.,"THE ADMINISTERED SOCIETY: SOCIETY
TOTALITARIANISM WITHOUT TERROR." COM USSR STRATA   DOMIN
AGRI INDUS NAT/G PERF/ART SCHOOL TOP/EX EDU/PROP   TOTALISM
ADMIN ORD/FREE PWR...POLICY SOC TIME/SEQ GEN/LAWS
VAL/FREE 20. PAGE 29 G0580

STAAR R.F.,"RETROGRESSION IN POLAND." COM USSR AGRI TOP/EX
INDUS NAT/G CREATE EDU/PROP TOTALISM RIGID/FLEX   ECO/TAC
ORD/FREE PWR SOCISM...RECORD CHARTS 20. PAGE 52   POLAND
G1029

SPULBER N.,THE STATE AND ECONOMIC DEVELOPMENT IN   ECO/DEV
EASTERN EUROPE. BULGARIA COM CZECHOSLVK HUNGARY   ECO/UNDEV
POLAND YUGOSLAVIA CULTURE PLAN CAP/ISM INT/TRADE   NAT/G
CONTROL...POLICY CHARTS METH/COMP BIBLIOG/A 19/20. TOTALISM
PAGE 52 G1028

MACKINTOSH J.M.,JUGGERNAUT. USSR NAT/G POL/PAR   WAR
ADMIN LEAD CIVMIL/REL COST TOTALISM PWR MARXISM   FORCES
...GOV/COMP 20. PAGE 35 G0691   COM
                                        PROF/ORG

TOTALITARIANISM....SEE TOTALISM

TOURISM....SEE TRAVEL

TOUSSAIN/P....PIERRE DOMINIQUE TOUSSAINT L'OUVERTURE

TOWNS....SEE MUNIC

TOWNSD/PLN....TOWNSEND PLAN

TOWNSEND PLAN....SEE TOWNSD/PLN

TOYNBEE/A....ARNOLD TOYNBEE

TRADE, INTERNATIONAL....SEE INT/TRADE

TRADIT....TRADITIONAL AND ARISTOCRATIC

                B65
 PYE L.W.,POLITICAL CULTURE AND DEVELOPMENT. WOR+45 PHIL/SCI
 WOR-45 CULTURE ECO/UNDEV NAT/G ALL/VALS ORD/FREE TEC/DEV
 PWR WEALTH ALL/IDEOS...TRADIT TREND 20. PAGE 46   SOCIETY
 G0897

TRADITIONAL....SEE CONSERVE, TRADIT

TRAINING....SEE SCHOOL, ACADEM, SKILL, EDU/PROP

TRANSFER....TRANSFER

TRANSITIVITY OF CHOICE....SEE DECISION

TRANSKEI....TRANSKEI

TRANSPORTATION....SEE DIST/IND

TRAVEL....TRAVEL AND TOURISM

                B63
 US ATOMIC ENERGY COMMISSION,ATOMIC ENERGY IN THE METH/COMP
 SOVIET UNION: TRIP REPORT OF THE US ATOMIC ENERGY OP/RES
 DELEGATION, MAY 1933. USSR R+D NAT/G CONSULT CREATE TEC/DEV
 DIPLOM ADMIN ROUTINE EFFICIENCY PRODUC KNOWL SKILL NUC/PWR
 ...NAT/COMP 20 AEC TRAVEL TREATY. PAGE 56 G1107

TRAVERS H. G1078

TREASURY DEPARTMENT....SEE DEPT/TREAS

TREATY....TREATIES; INTERNATIONAL AGREEMENTS

                N19
 MEZERIK A.G.,ATOM TESTS AND RADIATION HAZARDS   NUC/PWR
 (PAMPHLET). WOR+45 INT/ORG DIPLOM DETER 20 UN   ARMS/CONT
 TREATY. PAGE 39 G0761   CONFER
                HEALTH

                N19
 MEZERIK AG,OUTER SPACE: UN, US, USSR (PAMPHLET). SPACE
 USSR DELIB/GP FORCES DETER NUC/PWR SOVEREIGN   CONTROL
 ...POLICY 20 UN TREATY. PAGE 39 G0763   DIPLOM
                INT/ORG

                N47
 FOX W.T.R.,UNITED STATES POLICY IN A TWO POWER   DIPLOM
 WORLD. COM USA+45 USSR FORCES DOMIN AGREE NEUTRAL FOR/AID
 NUC/PWR ORD/FREE SOVEREIGN 20 COLD/WAR TREATY   POLICY
 EUROPE/W INTERVENT. PAGE 20 G0389

                B53
 BRETTON H.L.,STRESEMANN AND THE REVISION OF   POLICY
 VERSAILLES: A FIGHT FOR REASON. EUR+WWI GERMANY DIPLOM
 FORCES BUDGET ARMS/CONT WAR SUPEGO...BIBLIOG 20 BIOG
 TREATY VERSAILLES STRESEMN/G. PAGE 9 G0167

                B54
 BUTOW R.J.C.,JAPAN'S DECISION TO SURRENDER. USA-45 ELITES
 USSR CHIEF FORCES DOMIN NUC/PWR...BIBLIOG 20 TREATY DIPLOM
 CHINJAP. PAGE 10 G0198   WAR
                PEACE

                B56
 KOENIG L.W.,THE TRUMAN ADMINISTRATION: ITS   ADMIN
 PRINCIPLES AND PRACTICE. USA+45 POL/PAR CHIEF LEGIS POLICY
 DIPLOM DEATH NUC/PWR WAR CIVMIL/REL PEACE   EX/STRUC
 ...DECISION 20 TRUMAN/HS PRESIDENT TREATY. PAGE 31 GOV/REL
 G0610

                B60
 WOETZEL R.K.,THE INTERNATIONAL CONTROL OF AIRSPACE INT/ORG
 AND OUTERSPACE. FUT WOR+45 AIR CONSTN STRUCT   JURID
 CONSULT PLAN TEC/DEV ADJUD RIGID/FLEX KNOWL   SPACE
 ORD/FREE PWR...TECHNIC GEOG MGT NEW/IDEA TREND INT/LAW
 COMPUT/IR VAL/FREE 20 TREATY. PAGE 64 G1251

                S60
 HAYTON R.D.,"THE ANTARCTIC SETTLEMENT OF 1959." FUT DELIB/GP
 USA+45 WOR+45 WOR-45 STRUCT R+D INT/ORG EX/STRUC JURID

CREATE TEC/DEV LEGIT PEACE ATTIT SOVEREIGN   DIPLOM
...TIME/SEQ 20 TREATY IGY. PAGE 25 G0495   REGION

                S60
 SANDERS R.,"NUCLEAR DYNAMITE: A NEW DIMENSION IN INDUS
 FOREIGN POLICY." FUT WOR+45 ECO/DEV CONSULT TEC/DEV PWR
 PERCEPT...CONT/OBS TIME/SEQ TREND GEN/LAWS TOT/POP DIPLOM
 20 TREATY. PAGE 49 G0955   NUC/PWR

                L61
 TAUBENFELD H.J.,"A TREATY FOR ANTARCTICA." FUT   R+D
 USA+45 INTELL INT/ORG LABOR 20 TREATY ANTARCTICA. ACT/RES
 PAGE 54 G1055   DIPLOM

                S62
 CRANE R.D.,"LAW AND STRATEGY IN SPACE." FUT USA+45 CONCPT
 WOR+45 AIR LAW INT/ORG NAT/G FORCES ACT/RES PLAN SPACE
 BAL/PWR LEGIT ARMS/CONT COERCE ORD/FREE...POLICY
 INT/LAW JURID SOC/EXP 20 TREATY. PAGE 13 G0261

                B63
 US ATOMIC ENERGY COMMISSION,ATOMIC ENERGY IN THE METH/COMP
 SOVIET UNION: TRIP REPORT OF THE US ATOMIC ENERGY OP/RES
 DELEGATION, MAY 1933. USSR R+D NAT/G CONSULT CREATE TEC/DEV
 DIPLOM ADMIN ROUTINE EFFICIENCY PRODUC KNOWL SKILL NUC/PWR
 ...NAT/COMP 20 AEC TRAVEL TREATY. PAGE 56 G1107

                S63
 GARDNER R.N.,"COOPERATION IN OUTER SPACE." FUT USSR INT/ORG
 WOR+45 AIR LAW COM/IND CONSULT DELIB/GP CREATE   ACT/RES
 KNOWL 20 TREATY. PAGE 21 G0410   PEACE
                SPACE

                B65
 JENKS C.W.,SPACE LAW. DIPLOM DEBATE CONTROL   SPACE
 ORD/FREE TREATY 20 UN. PAGE 29 G0563   INT/LAW
                JURID
                INT/ORG

                B65
 UNESCO,HANDBOOK OF INTERNATIONAL EXCHANGES. COM/IND INDEX
 R+D ACADEM PROF/ORG VOL/ASSN CREATE TEC/DEV   INT/ORG
 EDU/PROP AGREE 20 TREATY. PAGE 55 G1090   DIPLOM
                PRESS

                B65
 US SENATE,US INTERNATIONAL SPACE PROGRAMS, 1959-65: SPACE
 STAFF REPORT FOR COMM ON AERONAUTICAL AND SPACE DIPLOM
 SCIENCES. WOR+45 VOL/ASSN CIVMIL/REL 20 CONGRESS PLAN
 NASA TREATY. PAGE 59 G1163   GOV/REL

                S65
 FOX A.B.,"NATO AND CONGRESS." CONSTN DELIB/GP   CONTROL
 EX/STRUC FORCES TOP/EX BUDGET NUC/PWR GOV/REL   DIPLOM
 ...GP/COMP CONGRESS NATO TREATY. PAGE 20 G0388

                S65
 HIBBS A.R.,"SPACE TECHNOLOGY* THE THREAT AND THE SPACE
 PROMISE." FUT VOL/ASSN TEC/DEV NUC/PWR COST   ARMS/CONT
 EFFICIENCY UTIL UN TREATY. PAGE 26 G0510   PREDICT

                S65
 MARTIN A.,"PROLIFERATION." FUT WOR+45 PROB/SOLV RECORD
 REGION ADJUST...PREDICT NAT/COMP UN TREATY. PAGE 36 NUC/PWR
 G0712   ARMS/CONT
                VOL/ASSN

                B66
 JACOBSON H.K.,DIPLOMATS, SCIENTISTS, AND   DIPLOM
 POLITICIANS* THE UNITED STATES AND THE NUCLEAR TEST ARMS/CONT
 BAN NEGOTIATIONS. USA+45 USSR ACT/RES PLAN CONFER TECHRACY
 DETER NUC/PWR CONSEN ORD/FREE...INT TREATY. PAGE 28 INT/ORG
 G0554

                B66
 STONE J.J.,CONTAINING THE ARMS RACE* SOME SPECIFIC ARMS/CONT
 PROPOSALS. ASIA USA+45 USSR PROB/SOLV BARGAIN   FEEDBACK
 DIPLOM DETER NUC/PWR RATIONAL...GAME 20 DEPT/DEFEN COST
 TREATY. PAGE 53 G1038   ATTIT

                B66
 YOUNG W.,EXISTING MECHANISMS OF ARMS CONTROL.   ARMS/CONT
 PROC/MFG OP/RES DIPLOM TASK CENTRAL...MGT TREATY. ADMIN
 PAGE 65 G1266   NUC/PWR
                ROUTINE

                S66
 BROWNLIE I.,"NUCLEAR PROLIFERATION* SOME PROBLEMS NUC/PWR
 OF CONTROL." USA+45 USSR ECO/UNDEV INT/ORG FORCES ARMS/CONT
 TEC/DEV REGION CONSEN...RECORD TREATY. PAGE 9 G0181 VOL/ASSN
                ORD/FREE

                B67
 GARCIA ROBLES A.,THE DENUCLEARIZATION OF LATIN   NUC/PWR
 AMERICA (TRANS. BY MARJORIE URQUIDI). LAW PLAN   ARMS/CONT
 DIPLOM...ANTHOL 20 TREATY UN. PAGE 21 G0409   L/A+17C

MCBRIDE J.H.,THE TEST BAN TREATY: MILITARY, TECHNOLOGICAL, AND POLITICAL IMPLICATIONS. USA+45 USSR DELIB/GP FORCES LEGIS TEC/DEV BAL/PWR TREATY. PAGE 37 G0727
INT/ORG
B67
ARMS/CONT
DIPLOM
NUC/PWR

MCDOUGAL M.S.,THE INTERPRETATION OF AGREEMENTS AND WORLD PUBLIC ORDER: PRINCIPLES OF CONTENT AND PROCEDURE. WOR+45 CONSTN PROB/SOLV TEC/DEV ...CON/ANAL TREATY. PAGE 37 G0740
B67
INT/LAW
STRUCT
ECO/UNDEV
DIPLOM

PADELFORD N.J.,THE DYNAMICS OF INTERNATIONAL POLITICS (2ND ED.). WOR+45 LAW INT/ORG FORCES TEC/DEV REGION NAT/LISM PEACE ATTIT PWR ALL/IDEOS UN COLD/WAR NATO TREATY. PAGE 43 G0856
B67
DIPLOM
NAT/G
POLICY
DECISION

US SENATE COMM ON FOREIGN REL,TREATY ON OUTER SPACE. WOR+45 AIR FORCES PROB/SOLV NUC/PWR SENATE TREATY UN. PAGE 60 G1182
B67
SPACE
DIPLOM
ARMS/CONT
LAW

US SENATE COMM ON FOREIGN REL,UNITED STATES ARMAMENT AND DISARMAMENT PROBLEMS. USA+45 AIR BAL/PWR DIPLOM FOR/AID NUC/PWR ORD/FREE SENATE TREATY. PAGE 60 G1184
B67
ARMS/CONT
WEAPON
FORCES
PROB/SOLV

EISENDRATH C.,"THE OUTER SPACE TREATY." CHINA/COM COM USA+45 DIPLOM CONTROL NUC/PWR...INT/LAW 20 UN COLD/WAR TREATY. PAGE 17 G0339
S67
SPACE
INT/ORG
PEACE
ARMS/CONT

EYRAUD M.,"LA FRANCE FACE A UN EVENTUEL TRAITE DE NON DISSEMINATION DES ARMES NUCLEAIRES." FRANCE USA+45 EXTR/IND INDUS R+D INT/ORG ACT/RES TEC/DEV AGREE PRODUC ATTIT 20 TREATY AEC EURATOM. PAGE 18 G0355
S67
NUC/PWR
ARMS/CONT
POLICY

FOREIGN POLICY ASSOCIATION,"HOW WORLD LAW DEVELOPS* A CASE STUDY OF THE OUTER SPACE TREATY." SPACE WOR+45 BAL/PWR NEUTRAL NUC/PWR PEACE KNOWL 20 UN TREATY. PAGE 19 G0380
S67
INT/LAW
DIPLOM
ARMS/CONT
INT/ORG

INGLIS D.R.,"PROSPECTS AND PROBLEMS: THE NONMILITARY USES OF NUCLEAR EXPLOSIVES." CREATE PROB/SOLV TEC/DEV AGREE PEACE...INT/LAW PHIL/SCI NEW/IDEA 20 TREATY. PAGE 28 G0545
S67
NUC/PWR
INDUS
ARMS/CONT
EXTR/IND

REINTANZ G.,"THE SPACE TREATY." WOR+45 DIPLOM CONTROL ARMS/CONT NUC/PWR WAR...MARXIST 20 COLD/WAR UN TREATY. PAGE 46 G0911
S67
SPACE
INT/LAW
INT/ORG
PEACE

VLASCIC I.A.,"THE SPACE TREATY* A PRELIMINARY EVALUATION." FUT USSR WOR+45 R+D ACT/RES TEC/DEV DIPLOM CONFER ARMS/CONT PEACE...PREDICT UN TREATY. PAGE 61 G1201
S67
SPACE
INT/LAW
INT/ORG
NEUTRAL

WEIL G.L.,"THE MERGER OF THE INSTITUTIONS OF THE EUROPEAN COMMUNITIES" EUR+WWI ECO/DEV INT/TRADE CONSEN PLURISM...DECISION MGT 20 EEC EURATOM ECSC TREATY. PAGE 62 G1223
S67
ECO/TAC
INT/ORG
CENTRAL
INT/LAW

WOLFE T.W.,"SOVIET MILITARY POLICY AT THE FIFTY YEAR MARK." USSR VIETNAM WOR+45 RATION AGREE WAR WEAPON CIVMIL/REL TREATY. PAGE 64 G1254
S67
FORCES
POLICY
TIME/SEQ
PLAN

TREFETHEN F.N. G0731

TREND....PROJECTION OF HISTORICAL TRENDS

BERGSON H.,CREATIVE EVOLUTION. FUT WOR+45 WOR-45 INTELL AGRI R+D ATTIT PERCEPT PERSON RIGID/FLEX ...RELATIV PHIL/SCI PSY METH/CNCPT MATH HIST/WRIT TREND HYPO/EXP TOT/POP. PAGE 7 G0127
B11
BIO/SOC
KNOWL

GINZBERG E.,MANPOWER FOR GOVERNMENT (PAMPHLET). USA+45 FORCES PLAN PROB/SOLV PAY EDU/PROP ADMIN GP/REL COST...MGT PREDICT TREND 20 CIVIL/SERV. PAGE 21 G0418
N19
WORKER
CONSULT
NAT/G
LOC/G

DRAPER J.W.,HISTORY OF THE CONFLICT BETWEEN RELIGION AND SCIENCE. WOR-45 INTELL SOCIETY R+D CREATE PLAN TEC/DEV EDU/PROP ATTIT PWR...PHIL/SCI CONCPT OBS TIME/SEQ TREND GEN/LAWS TOT/POP. PAGE 16 G0314
B23
SECT
KNOWL

SOROKIN P.,CONTEMPORARY SOCIOLOGICAL THEORIES. MOD/EUR UNIV SOCIETY R+D SCHOOL ECO/TAC EDU/PROP ROUTINE ATTIT DRIVE...PSY CONCPT TIME/SEQ TREND GEN/LAWS 20. PAGE 52 G1021
B28
CULTURE
SOC
WAR

LASSWELL H.D.,"THE RELATION OF IDEOLOGICAL INTELLIGENCE TO PUBLIC POLICY." WOR+45 WOR-45 SOCIETY DELIB/GP ACT/RES CREATE PLAN DIPLOM EDU/PROP CHOOSE KNOWL PWR...POLICY SOC TREND GEN/LAWS 20. PAGE 32 G0638
S42
ATTIT
DECISION

BUSH V.,SCIENCE, THE ENDLESS FRONTIER. FUT USA-45 INTELL STRATA ACT/RES CREATE PLAN EDU/PROP ADMIN NUC/PWR PEACE ATTIT HEALTH KNOWL...MAJORIT HEAL MGT PHIL/SCI CONCPT OBS TREND 20. PAGE 10 G0195
B45
R+D
NAT/G

SCHULTZ T.H.,FOOD FOR THE WORLD. UNIV SOCIETY INDUS R+D ECO/TAC...GEOG TREND GEN/LAWS 20. PAGE 50 G0979
B45
AGRI
TEC/DEV

BRODIE B.,THE OBSOLETE WEAPON: ATOMIC POWER AND WORLD ORDER. COM USA+45 USSR WOR+45 DELIB/GP PLAN ORD/FREE PWR...CONCPT TIME/SEQ TREND UN 20. PAGE 9 G0171
B46
INT/ORG
TEC/DEV
ARMS/CONT
NUC/PWR

BUSH V.,ENDLESS HORIZONS. FUT USA-45 INTELL NAT/G CONSULT ACT/RES CREATE PLAN EDU/PROP DRIVE ...MAJORIT HEAL MGT PHIL/SCI CONCPT OBS TREND GEN/METH TOT/POP 20. PAGE 10 G0196
B46
R+D
KNOWL
PEACE

MORGENTHAU H.J.,SCIENTIFIC MAN VS POWER POLITICS. USA+45 WOR+45 INTELL SOCIETY ACT/RES CREATE PLAN EDU/PROP...CONCPT TREND TOT/POP 20. PAGE 40 G0782
B46
UNIV
MORAL
PEACE

NORTHROP F.S.C.,THE MEETING OF EAST AND WEST. EUR+WWI FUT MOD/EUR UNIV WOR+45 WOR-45 INTELL SOCIETY EX/STRUC TOP/EX ACT/RES LEGIT CHOOSE ATTIT PERCEPT RIGID/FLEX ALL/VALS...POLICY JURID OBS TOT/POP. PAGE 42 G0826
B46
DRIVE
TREND
PEACE

MASTERS D.,"ONE WORLD OR NONE." FUT WOR+45 INTELL INT/ORG ACT/RES EDU/PROP DETER ATTIT RIGID/FLEX SUPEGO KNOWL...STAT TREND ORG/CHARTS 20. PAGE 36 G0719
L46
POLICY
PHIL/SCI
ARMS/CONT
NUC/PWR

BECK H.P.,MEN WHO CONTROL OUR UNIVERSITIES. EX/STRUC CHOOSE INGP/REL DISCRIM PERSON WEALTH ...POLICY TREND CON/ANAL CHARTS BIBLIOG. PAGE 6 G0112
B47
EDU/PROP
ACADEM
CONTROL
LEAD

ROSENHAUPT H.W.,HOW TO WAGE PEACE. USA+45 SOCIETY STRATA STRUCT R+D INT/ORG POL/PAR LEGIS ACT/RES CREATE PLAN EDU/PROP ADMIN EXEC ATTIT ALL/VALS ...TIME/SEQ TREND COLD/WAR 20. PAGE 48 G0937
B49
INTELL
CONCPT
DIPLOM

CANTRIL H.,TENSIONS THAT CAUSE WAR. UNIV CULTURE R+D CREATE EDU/PROP DRIVE PERSON KNOWL ORD/FREE ...HUM PSY SOC OBS CENSUS TREND CON/ANAL SOC/EXP SIMUL GEN/METH ANTHOL COLD/WAR TOT/POP. PAGE 11 G0206
B50
SOCIETY
PHIL/SCI
PEACE

CROWTHER J.G.,SCIENCE AT WAR. EUR+WWI PLAN TEC/DEV DOMIN COERCE NUC/PWR WEAPON KNOWL PWR...CONCPT OBS TREND VAL/FREE 20. PAGE 14 G0265
B50
R+D
FORCES
WAR
UK

MANNHEIM K.,FREEDOM, POWER, AND DEMOCRATIC PLANNING. FUT USSR WOR+45 ELITES INTELL SOCIETY NAT/G EDU/PROP ROUTINE ATTIT DRIVE SUPEGO SKILL ...POLICY PSY CONCPT TREND GEN/LAWS 20. PAGE 35 G0700
B50
TEC/DEV
PLAN
CAP/ISM
UK

SURANYI-UNGER T.,PRIVATE ENTERPRISE AND GOVERNMENTAL PLANNING. STRUCT FINAN BAL/PWR
B50
PLAN
NAT/G

HAPPINESS DRIVE NEW/LIB PLURISM...MATH QUANT STAT TREND BIBLIOG. PAGE 53 G1047 — LAISSEZ POLICY

S50
KAPLAN A.,"THE PREDICTION OF SOCIAL AND TECHNOLOGICAL EVENTS." VOL/ASSN CONSULT ACT/RES CREATE OP/RES PLAN ROUTINE PERSON...POLICY METH/CNCPT STAT QU/SEMANT SYS/QU TESTS CENSUS TREND 20. PAGE 29 G0574 — PWR KNO/TEST

S51
LERNER D.,"THE POLICY SCIENCES: RECENT DEVELOPMENTS IN SCOPE AND METHODS." R+D SERV/IND CREATE DIPLOM ROUTINE PWR...METH/CNCPT TREND GEN/LAWS METH 20. PAGE 33 G0658 — CONSULT SOC

B52
CURRENT TRENDS IN PSYCHOLOGY,PSYCHOLOGY IN THE WORLD EMERGENCY. USA+45 CONSULT FORCES ACT/RES PLAN SKILL...DECISION OBS APT/TEST KNO/TEST PERS/TEST TREND CHARTS 20. PAGE 14 G0266 — NAT/G PSY

B52
HAYEK F.A.,THE COUNTER-REVOLUTION OF SCIENCE. UNIV INTELL R+D VOL/ASSN CREATE EDU/PROP...PHIL/SCI SOC OBS TIME/SEQ TREND GEN/METH. PAGE 25 G0494 — PERCEPT KNOWL

B54
ARON R.,CENTURY OF TOTAL WAR. FUT WOR+45 WOR-45 SOCIETY INT/ORG NAT/G FORCES TOP/EX CREATE BAL/PWR DOMIN EDU/PROP COERCE DETER PEACE TOTALISM PWR...TIME/SEQ TREND COLD/WAR TOT/POP VAL/FREE LEAGUE/NAT 20. PAGE 4 G0066 — ATTIT WAR

B54
MCCLOSKEY J.F.,OPERATIONS RESEARCH FOR MANAGEMENT. STRUCT COMPUTER ADMIN ROUTINE...PHIL/SCI CONCPT METH/CNCPT TREND ANTHOL BIBLIOG 20. PAGE 37 G0731 — OP/RES MGT METH/COMP TEC/DEV

B54
SIMMONS L.W.,SOCIAL SCIENCE IN MEDICINE. USA+45 USA-45 SOCIETY CONSULT PLAN PROB/SOLV CONTROL PERS/REL...POLICY HEAL TREND BIBLIOG 20. PAGE 51 G0999 — PUB/INST HABITAT HEALTH BIO/SOC

B54
WASHBURNE N.F.,INTERPRETING SOCIAL CHANGE IN AMERICA. USA+45 STRATA FAM NAT/G SECT OP/RES ECO/TAC EDU/PROP HABITAT...SOC TIME/SEQ TREND 20 BUREAUCRCY. PAGE 62 G1217 — CULTURE STRUCT CREATE TEC/DEV

B54
WRIGHT Q.,PROBLEMS OF STABILITY AND PROGRESS IN INTERNATIONAL RELATIONSHIPS. FUT WOR+45 WOR-45 SOCIETY LEGIS CREATE TEC/DEV ECO/TAC EDU/PROP ADJUD WAR PEACE ORD/FREE PWR...KNO/TEST TREND GEN/LAWS 20. PAGE 64 G1257 — INT/ORG CONCPT DIPLOM

L54
OPLER M.E.,"SOCIAL ASPECTS OF TECHNICAL ASSISTANCE IN OPERATION." WOR+45 VOL/ASSN CREATE PLAN TEC/DEV EDU/PROP ALL/VALS...METH/CNCPT OBS RECORD TREND UN 20. PAGE 43 G0841 — INT/ORG CONSULT FOR/AID

S55
ANGELL R.,"GOVERNMENTS AND PEOPLES AS A FOCI FOR PEACE-ORIENTED RESEARCH." WOR+45 CULTURE SOCIETY FACE/GP ACT/RES CREATE PLAN DIPLOM EDU/PROP ROUTINE ATTIT PERCEPT SKILL...POLICY CONCPT OBS TREND GEN/METH 20. PAGE 3 G0060 — FUT SOC PEACE

B56
BLACKETT P.M.S.,ATOMIC WEAPONS AND EAST-WEST RELATIONS. FUT WOR+45 INT/ORG DELIB/GP COERCE ATTIT RIGID/FLEX KNOWL...RELATIV HIST/WRIT TREND GEN/METH COLD/WAR 20. PAGE 7 G0138 — FORCES PWR ARMS/CONT NUC/PWR

C56
DUPUY R.E.,"MILITARY HERITAGE OF AMERICA." USA+45 USA-45 TEC/DEV DIPLOM ROUTINE...POLICY TREND CHARTS IDEA/COMP BIBLIOG COLD/WAR. PAGE 17 G0325 — FORCES WAR CONCPT

B57
DRUCKER P.F.,AMERICA'S NEXT TWENTY YEARS. USA+45 DIST/IND ACADEM MUNIC SCHOOL DIPLOM ECO/TAC AUTOMAT HABITAT HEALTH...SOC/WK TREND 20 URBAN/RNWL PUB/TRANS. PAGE 16 G0316 — WORKER FOR/AID CENSUS GEOG

S57
JANOWITZ M.,"MILITARY ELITES AND THE STUDY OF WAR." USA+45 WOR-45 STRATA NAT/G PROF/ORG TEC/DEV DOMIN EDU/PROP COERCE WAR ATTIT RIGID/FLEX PWR RESPECT...MGT TREND STERTYP GEN/METH 20. PAGE 28 G0558 — FORCES ELITES

S58
DAVENPORT J.,"ARMS AND THE WELFARE STATE." INTELL STRUCT FORCES CREATE ECO/TAC FOR/AID DOMIN LEGIT ADMIN WAR ORD/FREE PWR...POLICY SOC CONCPT MYTH OBS TREND COLD/WAR TOT/POP 20. PAGE 14 G0276 — USA+45 NAT/G USSR

S58
HUNTINGTON S.P.,"ARMS RACES: PREREQUISITES AND RESULTS." EUR+WWI MOD/EUR WOR+45 WOR-45 NAT/G TEC/DEV BAL/PWR COERCE DETER ATTIT...POLICY TREND 20. PAGE 27 G0537 — FORCES PWR ARMS/CONT

S58
THOMPSON K.W.,"NATIONAL SECURITY IN A NUCLEAR AGE." USA+45 WOR+45 SOCIETY INT/ORG NAT/G TOP/EX DIPLOM DOMIN EDU/PROP LEGIT ARMS/CONT COERCE ORD/FREE...TREND STERTYP TOT/POP VAL/FREE COLD/WAR 20. PAGE 54 G1068 — FORCES PWR BAL/PWR

B59
AIR FORCE ACADEMY ASSEMBLY '59,INTERNATIONAL STABILITY AND PROGRESS (PAMPHLET). USA+45 USSR ECO/UNDEV PROB/SOLV BUDGET DIPLOM ADMIN DETER COST ATTIT...TREND 20. PAGE 2 G0030 — FOR/AID FORCES WAR PLAN

B59
ELDRIDGE H.T.,THE MATERIALS OF DEMOGRAPHY: A SELECTED AND ANNOTATED BIBLIOGRAPHY. R+D DEATH...SAMP METH/COMP NAT/COMP 20. PAGE 18 G0343 — BIBLIOG/A GEOG STAT TREND

B59
MIKSCHE F.O.,THE FAILURE OF ATOMIC STRATEGY. COM EUR+WWI INTELL POL/PAR FORCES PLAN ECO/TAC NUC/PWR ATTIT DRIVE RIGID/FLEX PWR...DECISION GEOG PSY CONCPT RECORD TREND CHARTS VAL/FREE 20. PAGE 39 G0766 — ACT/RES ORD/FREE DIPLOM ARMS/CONT

S59
DEUTSCH K.W.,"THE IMPACT OF SCIENCE AND TECHNOLOGY ON INTERNATIONAL POLITICS." UNIV INTELL NAT/G ACT/RES CREATE TEC/DEV EDU/PROP EXEC KNOWL...CONCPT TREND TOT/POP 20. PAGE 15 G0297 — PHIL/SCI MYTH DIPLOM NAT/LISM

S59
GOLDHAMMER H.,"SOME OBSERVATIONS ON POLITICAL GAMING." FUT WOR+45 R+D NAT/G ACT/RES CREATE CHOOSE ATTIT PWR...POLICY CONCPT METH/CNCPT STYLE KNO/TEST TREND HYPO/EXP GAME GEN/METH METH 20. PAGE 22 G0426 — COMPUT/IR DECISION DIPLOM

S59
SIMONS H.,"WORLD-WIDE CAPABILITIES FOR PRODUCTION AND CONTROL OF NUCLEAR WEAPONS." FUT WOR+45 INDUS INT/ORG NAT/G ECO/TAC ATTIT PWR SKILL...TREND CHARTS VAL/FREE 20. PAGE 51 G1001 — TEC/DEV ARMS/CONT NUC/PWR

B60
APTHEKER H.,DISARMAMENT AND THE AMERICAN ECONOMY: A SYMPOSIUM. FUT USA+45 ECO/DEV DIST/IND INDUS PROC/MFG LABOR NAT/G POL/PAR CONSULT PLAN CAP/ISM INT/TRADE PEACE ATTIT MORAL WEALTH...TREND GEN/LAWS TOT/POP 20. PAGE 3 G0063 — MARXIST ARMS/CONT

B60
CHASE S.,LIVE AND LET LIVE. USA+45 ECO/DEV PROB/SOLV TEC/DEV ECO/TAC ARMS/CONT NUC/PWR WAR NAT/LISM PEACE...GEOG TREND 20 COLD/WAR. PAGE 11 G0223 — NAT/G DIPLOM SOCIETY TASK

B60
FRANCIS R.G.,THE PREDICTIVE PROCESS. PLAN MARXISM...DECISION SOC CONCPT NAT/COMP 19/20. PAGE 20 G0390 — PREDICT PHIL/SCI TREND

B60
HEILBRONER R.L.,THE FUTURE AS HISTORY. USA+45 WOR+45 WOR-45 SOCIETY ECO/DEV ECO/UNDEV VOL/ASSN PLAN CAP/ISM NUC/PWR CHOOSE NAT/LISM ATTIT ORD/FREE RESPECT WEALTH SOCISM 20. PAGE 25 G0501 — TEC/DEV TREND

B60
PENTONY D.E.,THE UNDERDEVELOPED LANDS. FUT WOR+45 CULTURE AGRI FINAN INDUS MARKET INT/ORG LABOR NAT/G VOL/ASSN CONSULT TEC/DEV ECO/TAC EDU/PROP COLONIAL ATTIT WEALTH...OBS RECORD SAMP TREND GEN/METH WORK UN 20. PAGE 44 G0867 — ECO/UNDEV POLICY FOR/AID INT/TRADE

B60
SILK L.S.,THE RESEARCH REVOLUTION. USA+45 FINAN CAP/ISM ECO/TAC PRICE EQUILIB PRODUC...STAT TREND CHARTS. PAGE 51 G0997 — ECO/DEV R+D TEC/DEV PROB/SOLV

B60
WOETZEL R.K.,THE INTERNATIONAL CONTROL OF AIRSPACE AND OUTERSPACE. FUT WOR+45 AIR CONSTN STRUCT — INT/ORG JURID

CONSULT PLAN TEC/DEV ADJUD RIGID/FLEX KNOWL   SPACE
ORD/FREE PWR...TECHNIC GEOG MGT NEW/IDEA TREND   INT/LAW
COMPUT/IR VAL/FREE 20 TREATY. PAGE 64 G1251

                                                     L60
BRENNAN D.G.,"SETTING AND GOALS OF ARMS CONTROL."   FORCES
FUT USA+45 USSR WOR+45 INTELL INT/ORG NAT/G   COERCE
VOL/ASSN CONSULT PLAN DIPLOM ECO/TAC ADMIN KNOWL   ARMS/CONT
PWR...POLICY CONCPT TREND COLD/WAR 20. PAGE 8 G0164 DETER

                                                     L60
DEUTSCH K.W.,"TOWARD AN INVENTORY OF BASIC TRENDS   R+D
AND PATTERNS IN COMPARATIVE AND INTERNATIONAL   PERCEPT
POLITICS." UNIV WOR+45 SOCIETY STRUCT INT/ORG NAT/G
CREATE PLAN EDU/PROP KNOWL...PHIL/SCI METH/CNCPT
STAT SELF/OBS OBS/ENVIR SAMP TREND CON/ANAL CHARTS
SOC/EXP GEN/METH 20. PAGE 15 G0298

                                                     L60
HOLTON G.,"ARMS CONTROL." FUT WOR+45 CULTURE   ACT/RES
INT/ORG NAT/G FORCES TOP/EX PLAN EDU/PROP COERCE   CONSULT
ATTIT RIGID/FLEX ORD/FREE...POLICY PHIL/SCI SOC   ARMS/CONT
TREND COLD/WAR. PAGE 27 G0524   NUC/PWR

                                                     L60
HOLZMAN B.G.,"BASIC RESEARCH FOR NATIONAL   FORCES
SURVIVAL." FUT USA+45 INTELL R+D ACT/RES OP/RES   STAT
PLAN TEC/DEV EDU/PROP PERCEPT PERSON...PHIL/SCI
METH/CNCPT NEW/IDEA MATH OBS RECORD TREND LAB/EXP
20. PAGE 27 G0525

                                                     L60
MCCLELLAND C.A.,"THE FUNCTION OF THEORY IN   INT/ORG
INTERNATIONAL RELATIONS." WOR+45 PLAN EDU/PROP   CONCPT
ROUTINE ORD/FREE...PHIL/SCI PSY SOC METH/CNCPT   DIPLOM
NEW/IDEA OBS TREND GEN/METH 20. PAGE 37 G0728

                                                     S60
DOUGHERTY J.E.,"KEY TO SECURITY: DISARMAMENT OR   FORCES
ARMS STABILITY." COM USA+45 USSR INT/ORG NAT/G   ORD/FREE
CREATE EDU/PROP COERCE DETER ATTIT PWR...DECISION   ARMS/CONT
CONCPT MYTH NEW/IDEA TREND 20 COLD/WAR. PAGE 16   NUC/PWR
G0311

                                                     S60
HALSEY A.H.,"THE CHANGING FUNCTIONS OF UNIVERSITIES ACADEM
IN ADVANCED INDUSTRIAL SOCIETIES." R+D EDU/PROP   CREATE
REPRESENT ROLE ORD/FREE PWR TREND. PAGE 24 G0476   CULTURE
                                                     ADJUST

                                                     S60
IKLE F.C.,"NTH COUNTRIES AND DISARMAMENT." WOR+45   FUT
DELIB/GP ECO/TAC DOMIN EDU/PROP LEGIT ROUTINE   INT/ORG
COERCE RIGID/FLEX ORD/FREE...MARXIST TREND 20.   ARMS/CONT
PAGE 28 G0543   NUC/PWR

                                                     S60
KELLEY G.A.,"THE POLITICAL BACKGROUND OF THE FRENCH NAT/G
A-BOMB." EUR+WWI USSR FORCES TOP/EX TEC/DEV NUC/PWR RESPECT
ATTIT PWR...CONCPT OBS/ENVIR TREND 20. PAGE 30   NAT/LISM
G0591   FRANCE

                                                     S60
SANDERS R.,"NUCLEAR DYNAMITE: A NEW DIMENSION IN   INDUS
FOREIGN POLICY." FUT WOR+45 ECO/DEV CONSULT TEC/DEV PWR
PERCEPT...CONT/OBS TIME/SEQ TREND GEN/LAWS TOT/POP   DIPLOM
20 TREATY. PAGE 49 G0955   NUC/PWR

                                                     N60
US HOUSE COMM SCI ASTRONAUT,THE ORGANIZATION OF THE ACT/RES
US NATIONAL SPACE EFFORT. USA+45 WOR+45 AIR ECO/DEV SKILL
NAT/G PLAN TEC/DEV DIPLOM EDU/PROP ATTIT DRIVE PWR   SPACE
...OBS TIME/SEQ TREND TOT/POP 20. PAGE 58 G1142

                                                     B61
BONNEFOUS M.,EUROPE ET TIERS MONDE. EUR+WWI SOCIETY AFR
INT/ORG NAT/G VOL/ASSN ACT/RES TEC/DEV CAP/ISM   ECO/UNDEV
ECO/TAC ATTIT ORD/FREE SOVEREIGN...POLICY CONCPT   FOR/AID
TREND 20. PAGE 8 G0153   INT/TRADE

                                                     B61
HADLEY A.T.,THE NATIONS SAFETY AND ARMS CONTROL.   ACT/RES
FUT USA+45 WOR+45 TOP/EX PLAN TEC/DEV ATTIT DRIVE   ROUTINE
...CONCPT OBS TIME/SEQ TREND 20 G0466   DETER
                                                     NUC/PWR

                                                     B61
KAHN H.,ON THERMONUCLEAR WAR. FUT UNIV WOR+45   DETER
ECO/DEV CONSULT EX/STRUC TOP/EX ACT/RES CREATE PLAN NUC/PWR
COERCE WAR PERSON ALL/VALS...POLICY GEOG CONCPT   SOCIETY
METH/CNCPT OBS TREND 20. PAGE 29 G0569

                                                     B61
KISSINGER H.A.,THE NECESSITY FOR CHOICE. FUT USA+45 TOP/EX
ECO/UNDEV NAT/G PLAN BAL/PWR ECO/TAC ARMS/CONT   TREND
DETER NUC/PWR ATTIT...POLICY CONCPT RECORD GEN/LAWS DIPLOM

COLD/WAR 20. PAGE 31 G0604

                                                     B61
LUNDBERG G.A.,CAN SCIENCE SAVE US. UNIV CULTURE   ACT/RES
INTELL SOCIETY ECO/DEV R+D PLAN EDU/PROP ROUTINE   CONCPT
CHOOSE ATTIT PERCEPT ALL/VALS...TREND 20. PAGE 34   TOTALISM
G0679

                                                     B61
NOVE A.,THE SOVIET ECONOMY. USSR ECO/DEV FINAN   PLAN
NAT/G ECO/TAC PRICE ADMIN EFFICIENCY MARXISM   PRODUC
...TREND BIBLIOG 20. PAGE 42 G0828   POLICY

                                                     L61
TAUBENFELD H.J.,"A REGIME FOR OUTER SPACE." FUT   INT/ORG
UNIV R+D ACT/RES PLAN BAL/PWR LEGIT ARMS/CONT   ADJUD
ORD/FREE...POLICY JURID TREND UN TOT/POP 20   SPACE
COLD/WAR. PAGE 54 G1056

                                                     S61
MACHOWSKI K.,"SELECTED PROBLEMS OF NATIONAL   UNIV
SOVEREIGNTY WITH REFERENCE TO THE LAW OF OUTER   ACT/RES
SPACE." FUT WOR+45 AIR LAW INTELL SOCIETY ECO/DEV   NUC/PWR
PLAN EDU/PROP DETER DRIVE PERCEPT SOVEREIGN   SPACE
...POLICY INT/LAW OBS TREND TOT/POP 20. PAGE 35
G0689

                                                     S61
MORGENSTERN O.,"THE N-COUNTRY PROBLEM." EUR+WWI   FUT
UNIV USA+45 WOR+45 SOCIETY CONSULT TOP/EX ACT/RES   BAL/PWR
PLAN EDU/PROP ATTIT DRIVE...POLICY OBS TREND   NUC/PWR
TOT/POP 20. PAGE 40 G0781   TEC/DEV

                                                     S61
RICHSTEIN A.R.,"LEGAL RULES IN NUCLEAR WEAPONS   NUC/PWR
EMPLOYMENTS." FUT WOR+45 LAW SOCIETY FORCES PLAN   TEC/DEV
WEAPON RIGID/FLEX...HEAL CONCPT TREND VAL/FREE 20.   MORAL
PAGE 47 G0918   ARMS/CONT

                                                     S61
TAUBENFELD H.J.,"OUTER SPACE--PAST POLITICS AND   PLAN
FUTURE POLICY." FUT USA+45 USA-45 WOR+45 AIR INTELL SPACE
STRUCT ECO/DEV NAT/G TOP/EX ACT/RES ADMIN ROUTINE   INT/ORG
NUC/PWR ATTIT DRIVE...CONCPT TIME/SEQ TREND TOT/POP
20. PAGE 54 G1054

                                                     S61
WOHLSTETTER A.,"NUCLEAR SHARING: NATO AND THE NTH   TREND
COUNTRY." EUR+WWI FUT SOCIETY DIPLOM EXEC DETER PWR TEC/DEV
SKILL...POLICY TECHNIC CONCPT 20 NATO. PAGE 64   NUC/PWR
G1252   ARMS/CONT

                                                     B62
BERKELEY E.C.,THE COMPUTER REVOLUTION. WOR+45   COMPUTER
CREATE TEC/DEV EFFICIENCY TECHRACY...SOC TREND 20.   CONTROL
PAGE 7 G0128   AUTOMAT
                                                     SOCIETY

                                                     B62
BOULDING K.E.,CONFLICT AND DEFENSE: A GENERAL   MATH
THEORY. FUT SOCIETY INT/ORG NAT/G CREATE BAL/PWR   SIMUL
COERCE NAT/LISM DRIVE ALL/VALS...PLURIST DECISION   PEACE
CONCPT METH/CNCPT TREND HYPO/EXP TOT/POP 20. PAGE 8 WAR
G0157

                                                     B62
CARSON R.,SILENT SPRING. USA+45 AIR CULTURE AGRI   HABITAT
INDUS ADMIN ATTIT RIGID/FLEX ORD/FREE PWR...POLICY   TREND
20. PAGE 11 G0216   SOCIETY
                                                     CONTROL

                                                     B62
DUPRE J.S.,SCIENCE AND THE NATION: POLICY AND   R+D
POLITICS. USA+45 LAW ACADEM FORCES ADMIN CIVMIL/REL INDUS
GOV/REL EFFICIENCY PEACE...TREND 20 SCI/ADVSRY.   TEC/DEV
PAGE 16 G0322   NUC/PWR

                                                     B62
FORBES H.W.,THE STRATEGY OF DISARMAMENT. FUT WOR+45 PLAN
INT/ORG VOL/ASSN CONSULT ARMS/CONT COERCE NUC/PWR   FORCES
WAR DRIVE RIGID/FLEX ORD/FREE PWR...POLICY CONCPT   DIPLOM
OBS TREND STERTYP 20. PAGE 19 G0378

                                                     B62
KAHN H.,THINKING ABOUT THE UNTHINKABLE. FUT USA+45   INT/ORG
LAW NAT/G CONSULT FORCES ACT/RES CREATE PLAN   ORD/FREE
TEC/DEV BAL/PWR DIPLOM EDU/PROP ARMS/CONT DETER   NUC/PWR
ATTIT...CONCPT OBS TREND COLD/WAR 20. PAGE 29 G0570 PEACE

                                                     B62
KRAFT J.,THE GRAND DESIGN. EUR+WWI USA+45 AGRI   VOL/ASSN
FINAN INDUS MARKET INT/ORG NAT/G PLAN ECO/TAC   ECO/DEV
TARIFFS REGION DRIVE ORD/FREE WEALTH...POLICY OBS   INT/TRADE
TREND EEC 20. PAGE 31 G0616

OSGOOD C.E.,AN ALTERNATIVE TO WAR OR SURRENDER. FUT UNIV CULTURE INTELL SOCIETY R+D INT/ORG CONSULT DELIB/GP ACT/RES PLAN CHOOSE ATTIT PERCEPT KNOWL ...PHIL/SCI PSY SOC TREND GEN/LAWS 20. PAGE 43 G0849 — B62 ORD/FREE EDU/PROP PEACE WAR

SCHILLING W.R.,STRATEGY, POLITICS, AND DEFENSE BUDGETS. USA+45 R+D NAT/G CONSULT DELIB/GP FORCES LEGIS ACT/RES PLAN BAL/PWR LEGIT EXEC NUC/PWR RIGID/FLEX PWR...TREND COLD/WAR CONGRESS 20 EISNHWR/DD. PAGE 49 G0968 — B62 ROUTINE POLICY

WRIGHT Q.,PREVENTING WORLD WAR THREE. FUT CULTURE INT/ORG NAT/G CONSULT FORCES ADMIN ARMS/CONT DRIVE RIGID/FLEX ORD/FREE SOVEREIGN ...POLICY CONCPT TREND STERTYP COLD/WAR 20. PAGE 64 G1259 — B62 CREATE ATTIT

BETTEN J.K.,"ARMS CONTROL AND THE PROBLEM OF EVASION." WOR+45 FORCES CREATE DIPLOM DETER PWR ...PSY TREND GEN/LAWS COLD/WAR 20. PAGE 7 G0134 — L62 NAT/G PLAN ARMS/CONT

BOULDING K.E.,"THE PREVENTION OF WORLD WAR THREE." FUT WOR+45 INT/ORG PLAN BAL/PWR PEACE ORD/FREE PWR ...NEW/IDEA TREND TOT/POP COLD/WAR 20. PAGE 8 G0158 — S62 VOL/ASSN NAT/G ARMS/CONT DIPLOM

FINKELSTEIN L.S.,"THE UNITED NATIONS AND ORGANIZATIONS FOR CONTROL OF ARMAMENT." FUT WOR+45 VOL/ASSN DELIB/GP TOP/EX CREATE DIPLOM NUC/PWR ATTIT RIGID/FLEX ORD/FREE...POLICY DECISION CONCPT OBS TREND GEN/LAWS TOT/POP COLD/WAR. PAGE 19 G0368 — S62 INT/ORG PWR ARMS/CONT

FOSTER W.C.,"ARMS CONTROL AND DISARMAMENT IN A DIVIDED WORLD." COM FUT USA+45 USSR WOR+45 INTELL INT/ORG NAT/G VOL/ASSN CONSULT CREATE PLAN TEC/DEV EDU/PROP LEGIT NUC/PWR ATTIT RIGID/FLEX...CONCPT TREND TOT/POP 20 UN. PAGE 20 G0387 — S62 DELIB/GP POLICY ARMS/CONT DIPLOM

MORGENTHAU H.J.,"A POLITICAL THEORY OF FOREIGN AID." ECO/UNDEV NAT/G DELIB/GP PLAN ECO/TAC EDU/PROP EXEC ORD/FREE RESPECT WEALTH...METH/CNCPT TREND 20. PAGE 40 G0783 — S62 USA+45 PHIL/SCI FOR/AID

SCHILLING W.R.,"SCIENTISTS, FOREIGN POLICY AND POLITICS." WOR+45 WOR-45 INTELL INT/ORG CONSULT TOP/EX ACT/RES PLAN ADMIN KNOWL...CONCPT OBS TREND LEAGUE/NAT 20. PAGE 49 G0967 — S62 NAT/G TEC/DEV DIPLOM NUC/PWR

WALTER E.,"VERS UNE CLASSIFICATION SCIENTIFIQUE DE LA SOCIOLOGIA." UNIV CULTURE INTELL SOCIETY R+D ACT/RES LEGIT ROUTINE ATTIT KNOWL...JURID MGT TREND GEN/LAWS 20. PAGE 62 G1208 — S62 PLAN CONCPT

GOLDSEN J.M.,OUTER SPACE IN WORLD POLITICS. COM USA+45 NAT/G FORCES ACT/RES PLAN DOMIN EDU/PROP COERCE ORD/FREE PWR...TECHNIC STAT INT SAMP TREND ANTHOL VAL/FREE 20. PAGE 22 G0428 — B63 TEC/DEV DIPLOM SPACE

US DEPARTMENT OF THE ARMY,SOVIET RUSSIA: STRATEGIC SURVEY (PAMPHLET). USSR POL/PAR PLAN DOMIN EDU/PROP ARMS/CONT GUERRILLA WAR WEAPON...TREND CHARTS ORG/CHARTS 20. PAGE 57 G1129 — B63 BIBLIOG/A MARXISM DIPLOM COERCE

WALES H.G.,A BASIC BIBLIOGRAPHY ON MARKETING RESEARCH (REV. ED.). ATTIT...MGT STAT INT QU SAMP TREND 20. PAGE 62 G1206 — B63 BIBLIOG/A MARKET OP/RES METH/COMP

MCDOUGAL M.S.,"THE ENJOYMENT AND ACQUISITION OF RESOURCES IN OUTER SPACE." CHRIST-17C FUT WOR+45 WOR-45 LAW EXTR/IND INT/ORG ACT/RES CREATE TEC/DEV ECO/TAC LEGIT COERCE HEALTH KNOWL ORD/FREE PWR WEALTH...JURID HIST/WRIT VAL/FREE. PAGE 37 G0738 — L63 PLAN TREND

PHELPS J.,"STUDIES IN DETERRENCE VIII: MILITARY STABILITARY AND ARMS CONTROL: A CRITICAL SURVEY." FUT WOR+45 INT/ORG ACT/RES EDU/PROP COERCE NUC/PWR WAR HEALTH PWR...POLICY TECHNIC TREND SIMUL TOT/POP 20. PAGE 44 G0874 — L63 FORCES ORD/FREE ARMS/CONT DETER

HOSKINS H.L.,"ARAB SOCIALISM IN THE UAR." ISLAM USSR AGRI INDUS NAT/G TOP/EX CREATE DIPLOM EDU/PROP DRIVE KNOWL PWR SOCISM...POLICY CONCPT TREND SUEZ 20. PAGE 27 G0530 — S63 ECO/DEV PLAN UAR

NADLER E.B.,"SOME ECONOMIC DISADVANTAGES OF THE ARMS RACE." USA+45 INDUS R+D FORCES PLAN TEC/DEV ECO/TAC FOR/AID EDU/PROP PWR WEALTH...TREND COLD/WAR 20. PAGE 41 G0800 — S63 ECO/DEV MGT BAL/PAY

WILES P.J.D.,"WILL CAPITALISM AND COMMUNISM SPONTANEOUSLY CONVERGE." COM FUT USA+45 ECO/DEV DIST/IND MARKET CAP/ISM ECO/TAC RIGID/FLEX WEALTH MARXISM SOCISM...MATH STAT TREND COMPUT/IR 20. PAGE 63 G1240 — S63 PLAN TEC/DEV USSR

BALASSA B.,TRADE PROSPECTS FOR DEVELOPING COUNTRIES. WOR+45 ECO/DEV AGRI EXTR/IND INDUS CREATE PLAN PRICE...ECOMETRIC CLASSIF TIME/SEQ GEN/METH. PAGE 5 G0087 — B64 INT/TRADE ECO/UNDEV TREND STAT

CONANT J.B.,TWO MODES OF THOUGHT: MY ENCOUNTERS WITH SCIENCE AND EDUCATION....ART/METH JURID SOC TREND. PAGE 13 G0249 — B64 PHIL/SCI SKILL MYTH STYLE

HASKINS C.P.,THE SCIENTIFIC REVOLUTION AND WORLD POLITICS. COM FUT USA+45 ECO/DEV ECO/UNDEV ATTIT ...PHIL/SCI BIBLIOG 20 THIRD/WRLD. PAGE 25 G0489 — B64 TEC/DEV POLICY DIPLOM TREND

LI C.M.,INDUSTRIAL DEVELOPMENT IN COMMUNIST CHINA. CHINA/COM ECO/DEV ECO/UNDEV AGRI FINAN INDUS MARKET LABOR NAT/G ECO/TAC INT/TRADE EXEC ALL/VALS ...POLICY RELATIV TREND WORK TOT/POP VAL/FREE 20. PAGE 34 G0665 — B64 ASIA TEC/DEV

PETERSON W.,THE POLITICS OF POPULATION. COM EUR+WWI FUT MOD/EUR S/ASIA USA+45 USA-45 WOR+45 LAW CULTURE FAM SECT DOMIN EDU/PROP BIO/SOC HEALTH ORD/FREE ...GEOG STAT TIME/SEQ TREND VAL/FREE. PAGE 44 G0871 — B64 PLAN CENSUS POLICY

RANSOM H.H.,CAN AMERICAN DEMOCRACY SURVIVE COLD WAR. USA-45 CONSTN NAT/G CONSULT DELIB/GP LEGIS ACT/RES LEGIT EXEC ATTIT KNOWL ORD/FREE PWR SKILL ...POLICY TIME/SEQ TREND GEN/LAWS 20 COLD/WAR. PAGE 46 G0901 — B64 USA+45 ROUTINE

RIES J.C.,THE MANAGEMENT OF DEFENSE: ORGANIZATION AND CONTROL OF THE US ARMED SERVICES. PROF/ORG DELIB/GP EX/STRUC LEGIS GOV/REL PERS/REL CENTRAL RATIONAL PWR...POLICY TREND GOV/COMP BIBLIOG. PAGE 47 G0920 — B64 FORCES ACT/RES DECISION CONTROL

HAAS E.B.,"ECONOMICS AND DIFFERENTIAL PATTERNS OF POLITICAL INTEGRATION: PROJECTIONS ABOUT UNITY IN LATIN AMERICA." SOCIETY NAT/G DELIB/GP ACT/RES CREATE PLAN ECO/TAC REGION ROUTINE ATTIT DRIVE PWR WEALTH...CONCPT TREND CHARTS LAFTA 20. PAGE 24 G0464 — L/A+17C INT/ORG MARKET

WARD C.,"THE 'NEW MYTHS' AND 'OLD REALITIES' OF NUCLEAR WAR." COM FUT USA+45 USSR WOR+45 INT/ORG NAT/G DOMIN LEGIT EXEC ATTIT PERCEPT ALL/VALS ...POLICY RELATIV PSY MYTH TREND 20. PAGE 62 G1212 — L64 FORCES COERCE ARMS/CONT NUC/PWR

GARDNER R.N.,"GATT AND THE UNITED NATIONS CONFERENCE ON TRADE AND DEVELOPMENT." USA+45 WOR+45 SOCIETY ECO/UNDEV MARKET NAT/G DELIB/GP ACT/RES PLAN ECO/TAC TARIFFS EDU/PROP ROUTINE DRIVE RIGID/FLEX WEALTH...DECISION MGT TREND UN TOT/POP 20 GATT. PAGE 21 G0411 — S64 INT/ORG INT/TRADE

MAGGS P.B.,"SOVIET VIEWPOINT ON NUCLEAR WEAPONS IN INTERNATIONAL LAW." USSR WOR+45 INT/ORG FORCES DIPLOM ARMS/CONT ATTIT ORD/FREE PWR...POLICY JURID CONCPT OBS TREND CON/ANAL GEN/LAWS VAL/FREE 20. PAGE 35 G0694 — S64 COM LAW INT/LAW NUC/PWR

MAHALANOBIS P.C.,"PERSPECTIVE PLANNING IN INDIA: — S64 PLAN

STATISTICAL TOOLS." INDIA S/ASIA STRATA AGRI
DIST/IND FINAN INDUS SERV/IND NAT/G ECO/TAC
ORD/FREE WEALTH...POLICY TREND SIMUL VAL/FREE 20.
PAGE 35 G0695
STAT

S64
MUMFORD L.,"AUTHORITARIAN AND DEMOCRATIC
TECHNIQUES." INDUS PROC/MFG LG/CO SML/CO CREATE
PLAN KNOWL...POLICY TREND WORK 20. PAGE 40 G0794
ECO/DEV
TEC/DEV

S64
SPONSLER G.C.,"THE MILITARY ROLE IN SPACE." FUT
USA+45 SEA AIR NAT/G ACT/RES PLAN COERCE NUC/PWR
WEAPON KNOWL ORD/FREE PWR RESPECT...TREND 20.
PAGE 52 G1026
TEC/DEV
FORCES
SPACE

B65
BLOOMFIELD L.,SOVIET INTERESTS IN ARMS CONTROL AND
DISARMAMENT* THE DECADE UNDER KHRUSHCHEV 1954-1964.
ASIA FORCES ACT/RES EDU/PROP DETER NUC/PWR WEAPON
COST ATTIT...PHIL/SCI CLASSIF STAT NET/THEORY GAME
BIBLIOG. PAGE 7 G0139
USSR
ARMS/CONT
DIPLOM
TREND

B65
HALPERIN M.H.,CHINA AND THE BOMB. USA+45 USSR
INT/ORG FORCES ARMS/CONT DETER PRODUC ORD/FREE PWR
TREND. PAGE 24 G0472
ASIA
NUC/PWR
WAR
DIPLOM

B65
KENT A.,SPECIALIZED INFORMATION CENTERS. INTELL R+D
VOL/ASSN CONSULT COMPUTER KNOWL...DECISION HUM
PHIL/SCI METH/CNCPT TREND CHARTS 20. PAGE 30 G0593
COMPUT/IR
CREATE
TEC/DEV
METH/COMP

B65
ORG FOR ECO COOP AND DEVEL,THE MEDITERRANEAN
REGIONAL PROJECT: YUGOSLAVIA; EDUCATION AND
DEVELOPMENT. YUGOSLAVIA SOCIETY FINAN PROF/ORG PLAN
ADMIN COST DEMAND MARXISM...STAT TREND CHARTS METH
20 OECD. PAGE 43 G0843
EDU/PROP
ACADEM
SCHOOL
ECO/UNDEV

B65
PYE L.W.,POLITICAL CULTURE AND DEVELOPMENT. WOR+45
WOR-45 CULTURE ECO/UNDEV NAT/G ALL/VALS ORD/FREE
PWR WEALTH ALL/IDEOS...TRADIT TREND 20. PAGE 46
G0897
PHIL/SCI
TEC/DEV
SOCIETY

B65
US DEPARTMENT OF THE ARMY,MILITARY MANPOWER POLICY.
USA+45 LEGIS EXEC WAR 20 CONGRESS. PAGE 58 G1132
BIBLIOG/A
POLICY
FORCES
TREND

B65
VERMOT-GAUCHY M.,L'EDUCATION NATIONALE DANS LA
FRANCE DE 1975. FRANCE FUT CULTURE ELITES R+D
SCHOOL PLAN EDU/PROP EFFICIENCY...POLICY PREDICT
CHARTS INDEX 20. PAGE 61 G1195
ACADEM
CREATE
TREND
INTELL

S65
BLOOMFIELD L.P.,"ARMS CONTROL AND THE DEVELOPING
COUNTRIES." AFR ISLAM S/ASIA USA+45 VOL/ASSN
TEC/DEV DIPLOM REGION NUC/PWR...PREDICT TREND.
PAGE 7 G0142
ARMS/CONT
ECO/UNDEV
HYPO/EXP
OBS

S65
GOLDSTEIN W.,"KEEPING THE GENIE IN THE BOTTLE* THE
FEASIBILITY OF A NUCLEAR NON-PROLIFERATION
AGREEMENT." ASIA FRANCE UK USA+45 USSR WOR+45
ECO/UNDEV VOL/ASSN ACT/RES PLAN RISK ARMS/CONT WAR
PEACE ATTIT PERCEPT...RECORD TREND TIME. PAGE 22
G0429
NUC/PWR
CREATE
COST

S65
GRIFFITH S.B.,"COMMUNIST CHINA'S CAPACITY TO MAKE
WAR." CHINA/COM COM NAT/G TOP/EX PLAN DOMIN COERCE
NUC/PWR ATTIT RESPECT SKILL...CONCPT MYTH TIME/SEQ
TREND COLD/WAR 20. PAGE 23 G0452
FORCES
PWR
WEAPON
ASIA

B66
FEIS H.,THE ATOMIC BOMB AND THE END OF WORLD WAR
II. FORCES PLAN PROB/SOLV DIPLOM CONFER WAR
...TIME/SEQ TREND CHINJAP PRESIDENT TIME. PAGE 19
G0362
USA+45
PEACE
NUC/PWR

B66
MUMFORD L.,THE MYTH OF THE MACHINE: TECHNICS AND
HUMAN DEVELOPMENT. UNIV WOR-45 CREATE AUTOMAT
PERCEPT KNOWL...EPIST PHIL/SCI SOC LING TREND
SOC/INTEG 20 MARX/KARL. PAGE 40 G0795
WORKER
TEC/DEV
SOCIETY

B66
ODEGARD P.H.,POLITICAL POWER AND SOCIAL CHANGE.
UNIV NAT/G CREATE ALL/IDEOS...POLICY GEOG SOC
CENSUS TREND. PAGE 42 G0829
PWR
TEC/DEV
IDEA/COMP

B66
ONYEMELUKWE C.C.,PROBLEMS OF INDUSTRIAL PLANNING
AND MANAGEMENT IN NIGERIA. AFR FINAN LABOR DELIB/GP
TEC/DEV ADJUST...MGT TREND BIBLIOG. PAGE 43 G0839
ECO/UNDEV
ECO/TAC
INDUS
PLAN

B66
US DEPARTMENT OF LABOR,TECHNOLOGICAL TRENDS IN
MAJOR AMERICAN INDUSTRIES. USA+45 R+D LABOR GP/REL
PRODUC...MGT BIBLIOG 20. PAGE 57 G1120
TEC/DEV
INDUS
TREND
AUTOMAT

S66
SIMON R.,"THE STATE OF PUBLIC RELATIONS SCHOLARLY
RESEARCH." TEC/DEV TASK MAJORITY PRODUC...TREND
CHARTS BIBLIOG 20. PAGE 51 G1000
ACADEM
CREATE
STAT
GP/REL

N66
US HOUSE COMM SCI ASTRONAUT,GOVERNMENT, SCIENCE,
AND PUBLIC POLICY (PAMPHLET). R+D ACADEM DELIB/GP
COMPUTER BUDGET CONFER ADMIN...PHIL/SCI PREDICT
TREND 20 CONGRESS HS/SCIASTR. PAGE 58 G1143
NAT/G
POLICY
TEC/DEV
CREATE

N66
US HOUSE COMM SCI ASTRONAUT,INQUIRIES, LEGISLATION,
POLICY STUDIES RE: SCIENCE AND TECHNOLOGY: REVIEW
AND FORECAST (PAMPHLET). FUT WOR+45 DELIB/GP
PROB/SOLV...POLICY JURID TREND 20 CONGRESS. PAGE 58
G1144
TEC/DEV
R+D
PLAN
LEGIS

B67
ARON R.,THE GREAT DEBATE: THEORIES OF NUCLEAR
STRATEGY. FRANCE USA+45 INT/ORG PLAN TREND. PAGE 4
G0068
NUC/PWR
DETER
BAL/PWR
DIPLOM

B67
BURNS E.L.M.,MEGAMURDER. WOR+45 LAW INT/ORG NAT/G
BAL/PWR DIPLOM DETER MURDER WEAPON CIVMIL/REL PEACE
...INT/LAW TREND 20. PAGE 10 G0193
FORCES
PLAN
WAR
NUC/PWR

B67
COLM G.,THE ECONOMY OF THE AMERICAN PEOPLE. USA+45
ECO/DEV FINAN WORKER INT/TRADE AUTOMAT GP/REL.
PAGE 13 G0244
ECO/TAC
PRODUC
TREND
TEC/DEV

B67
CROSSON F.J.,SCIENCE AND CONTEMPORARY SOCIETY. FUT
WOR+45 SECT CREATE PROB/SOLV...HUM PREDICT TREND
IDEA/COMP ANTHOL. PAGE 14 G0263
PHIL/SCI
SOCIETY
TEC/DEV
CONCPT

B67
HALLE L.J.,THE COLD WAR AS HISTORY. USSR WOR+45
ECO/TAC FOR/AID NUC/PWR WAR PEACE ORD/FREE
...MAJORIT TREND 20 COLD/WAR KENNEDY/JF KHRUSH/N
BERLIN/BLO. PAGE 24 G0470
DIPLOM
BAL/PWR

B67
MCCLINTOCK R.,THE MEANING OF LIMITED WAR. FUT
WOR+45 NAT/G FORCES GUERRILLA REV...POLICY SAMP/SIZ
TREND NAT/COMP 45 COLD/WAR. PAGE 37 G0730
WAR
NUC/PWR
BAL/PWR
DIPLOM

B67
ORLANS H.,CONTRACTING FOR ATOMS. USA+45 LAW INTELL
ACADEM LG/CO NAT/G PLAN TEC/DEV CONTROL DETER
...TREND 20 AEC. PAGE 43 G0845
NUC/PWR
R+D
PRODUC
PEACE

B67
POMEROY W.J.,HALF A CENTURY OF SOCIALISM. USSR LAW
AGRI INDUS NAT/G CREATE DIPLOM EDU/PROP PERSON
ORD/FREE WEALTH...POLICY TREND 20. PAGE 45 G0884
SOCISM
MARXISM
COM
SOCIETY

B67
RUSSETT B.M.,ARMS CONTROL IN EUROPE: PROPOSALS AND
POLITICAL CONSTRAINTS. GERMANY WOR+45 POL/PAR
BARGAIN DIPLOM...TREND CHARTS 20 COLD/WAR. PAGE 48
G0950
ARMS/CONT
REGION
METH/COMP

B67
UNIVERSAL REFERENCE SYSTEM,PUBLIC OPINION, MASS
BEHAVIOR, AND POLITICAL PSYCHOLOGY (VOLUME VI).
WOR+45 WOR-45 SOCIETY EDU/PROP PRESS PARTIC CHOOSE
PERSON...TREND COMPUT/IR GEN/METH. PAGE 56 G1098
BIBLIOG/A
ATTIT
CROWD
PSY

B67
WARNER W.L.,THE EMERGENT AMERICAN SOCIETY VOL I,
LARGE-SCALE ORGANIZATIONS. USA+45 USA-45 ACADEM
PROF/ORG SCHOOL SECT EX/STRUC TEC/DEV GP/REL
ANTHOL
NAT/G
LABOR

...TREND CHARTS. PAGE 62 G1215   LG/CO

B67
WEINBERG A.M.,REFLECTIONS ON BIG SCIENCE. FUT   ACADEM
USA+45 NAT/G EDU/PROP CHOOSE PERS/REL COST OPTIMAL   KNOWL
...PHIL/SCI TREND. PAGE 62 G1225   R+D
                                                       PLAN

S67
ARONOWITZ D.S.,"CIVIL COMMITMENT OF NARCOTIC   PUB/INST
ADDICTS." USA+45 LAW INGP/REL DISCRIM MORAL...TREND   ACT/RES
20. PAGE 4 G0069   POLICY

S67
BULMER-THOMAS I.,"SO, ON TO THE GREAT SOCIETY." FUT   PHIL/SCI
UNIV TEC/DEV BAL/PWR WAR BIO/SOC KNOWL...ART/METH   SOCIETY
SOC PREDICT TREND WORSHIP 20 GREAT/SOC. PAGE 9   CREATE
G0185

S67
HAMBERG D.,"SIZE OF ENTERPRISE AND TECHNICAL   TEC/DEV
CHANGE." USA+45 LG/CO SML/CO CREATE OP/RES PROFIT   INDUS
...TREND 20. PAGE 24 G0477   R+D
                                                      WEALTH

S67
HOFFER J.R.,"RELATIONSHIP OF NATURAL AND SOCIAL   PROB/SOLV
SCIENCES TO SOCIAL PROBLEMS AND CONTRIBUTION OF...   SOCIETY
SCIENTISTS TO SOLUTIONS." USA+45 COMPUTER TEC/DEV   INTELL
GP/REL KNOWL...SOC TREND. PAGE 26 G0521   ACT/RES

S67
WHITTIER J.M.,"COMPULSORY POOLING AND UNITIZATION*   LEGIS
DIE-HARD KANSAS." LAW PLAN EDU/PROP ATTIT...POLICY   MUNIC
JURID PREDICT TREND METH/COMP 20. PAGE 63 G1236   INDUS
                                                      ECO/TAC

TRIBAL....SEE KIN

TRIESTE....TRIESTE

TRINIDAD AND TOBAGO....SEE TRINIDAD

TRINIDAD....TRINIDAD AND TOBAGO; SEE ALSO L/A+17C

TROBRIAND....TROBRIAND ISLANDS AND ISLANDERS

TROTSKY/L....LEON TROTSKY

TRUJILLO/R....RAFAEL TRUJILLO

TRUMAN D.B. G1079

TRUMAN DOCTRINE....SEE TRUMAN/DOC

TRUMAN/DOC....TRUMAN DOCTRINE

TRUMAN/HS....PRESIDENT HARRY S. TRUMAN

B55
JONES J.M.,THE FIFTEEN WEEKS (FEBRUARY 21-JUNE 5,   DIPLOM
1947). EUR+WWI USA+45 PROB/SOLV BAL/PWR...POLICY   ECO/TAC
TIME/SEQ 20 COLD/WAR MARSHL/PLN TRUMAN/HS   FOR/AID
WASHING/DC. PAGE 29 G0567

B56
KOENIG L.W.,THE TRUMAN ADMINISTRATION: ITS   ADMIN
PRINCIPLES AND PRACTICE. USA+45 POL/PAR CHIEF LEGIS   POLICY
DIPLOM DEATH NUC/PWR WAR CIVMIL/REL PEACE   EX/STRUC
...DECISION 20 TRUMAN/HS PRESIDENT TREATY. PAGE 31   GOV/REL
G0610

S61
SCHILLING W.R.,"THE H-BOMB: HOW TO DECIDE WITHOUT   PERSON
ACTUALLY CHOOSING." FUT USA+45 INTELL CONSULT ADMIN   LEGIT
CT/SYS MORAL...JURID OBS 20 TRUMAN/HS. PAGE 49   NUC/PWR
G0966

B66
FREIDEL F.,AMERICAN ISSUES IN THE TWENTIETH   DIPLOM
CENTURY. SOCIETY FINAN ECO/TAC FOR/AID CONTROL   POLICY
NUC/PWR WAR RACE/REL PEACE ATTIT...ANTHOL T 20   NAT/G
WILSON/W ROOSEVLT/F KENNEDY/JF TRUMAN/HS. PAGE 20   ORD/FREE
G0391

TRUST, PERSONAL....SEE RESPECT, SUPEGO

TRUST/TERR....TRUST TERRITORY

TRYTTEN M.H. G1080

TSHOMBE/M....MOISE TSHOMBE

TUCKER R.C. G0359

TULANE/U....TULANE UNIVERSITY

TUNISIA....SEE ALSO ISLAM, AFR

TURKESTAN....TURKESTAN

TURKEVICH J. G1081

TURKEY....TURKEY; SEE ALSO ISLAM

B65
OECD,MEDITERRANEAN REGIONAL PROJECT: TURKEY;   EDU/PROP
EDUCATION AND DEVELOPMENT. FUT TURKEY SOCIETY   ACADEM
STRATA FINAN NAT/G PROF/ORG PLAN PROB/SOLV ADMIN   SCHOOL
COST...STAT CHARTS 20 OECD. PAGE 42 G0831   ECO/UNDEV

TURKIC....TURKIC PEOPLES

TURNBULL A.V. G1052

TURNER A.N. G1082

TURNER R.H. G1083

TUSKEGEE....TUSKEGEE, ALABAMA

TV....TELEVISION; SEE ALSO PRESS, COM/IND

B60
CARPENTER E.,EXPLORATIONS IN COMMUNICATION. USSR   ANTHOL
CULTURE SCHOOL SECT EDU/PROP PRESS TV AUTOMAT   COM/IND
FEEDBACK ATTIT PERSON...ART/METH PSY 20. PAGE 11   TEC/DEV
G0211   WRITING

L67
BARRON J.A.,"ACCESS TO THE PRESS." USA+45 TEC/DEV   ORD/FREE
PRESS TV ADJUD AUD/VIS. PAGE 5 G0099   COM/IND
                                                      EDU/PROP
                                                      LAW

TVA....TENNESSEE VALLEY AUTHORITY

B67
MOORE J.R.,THE ECONOMIC IMPACT OF THE TVA. AGRI   ECO/UNDEV
INDUS PLAN BARGAIN CONTROL REGION GOV/REL DEMAND   ECO/DEV
EFFICIENCY SOCISM 20 TVA. PAGE 40 G0780   NAT/G
                                                      CREATE

N67
US HOUSE COMM APPROPRIATIONS,PUBLIC WORKS AND   BUDGET
ATOMIC ENERGY COMMISSION APPROPRIATION BILL, 1968   NUC/PWR
(PAMPHLET). USA+45 ECO/DEV NAT/G...GEOG DEEP/INT   PROVS
CHARTS HOUSE/REP AEC DEPT/DEFEN TVA. PAGE 58 G1137   PLAN

TWAIN/MARK....MARK TWAIN (SAMUEL CLEMENS)

TYBOUT R.A. G1084

TYLER/JOHN....PRESIDENT JOHN TYLER

TYPOLOGY....SEE CLASSIF

U

U.S. DEPARTMENT OF LABOR....SEE DEPT/LABOR

U OF MICHIGAN LAW SCHOOL G1085

U/THANT....U THANT

UA/PAR....UNITED AUSTRALIAN PARTY

UAM....UNION AFRICAINE ET MALGACHE; ALSO OCAM

UAR....UNITED ARAB REPUBLIC (EGYPT AND SYRIA 1958-1961,
    EGYPT AFTER 1958); SEE ALSO EGYPT, ISLAM

563
HOSKINS H.L.,"ARAB SOCIALISM IN THE UAR." ISLAM   ECO/DEV
USSR AGRI INDUS NAT/G TOP/EX CREATE DIPLOM EDU/PROP   PLAN
DRIVE KNOWL PWR SOCISM...POLICY CONCPT TREND SUEZ   UAR
20. PAGE 27 G0530

UAW....UNITED AUTO WORKERS

UDR....UNION POUR LA DEFENSE DE LA REPUBLIQUE (FRANCE)

UGANDA....SEE ALSO AFR

S66
FLEMING W.G.,"AUTHORITY, EFFICIENCY, AND ROLE   DOMIN
STRESS: PROBLEMS IN THE DEVELOPMENT OF EAST AFRICAN EFFICIENCY
BUREAUCRACIES." AFR UGANDA STRUCT PROB/SOLV ROUTINE   COLONIAL
INGP/REL ROLE...MGT SOC GP/COMP GOV/COMP 20   ADMIN
TANGANYIKA AFRICA/E. PAGE 19 G0371

UK....UNITED KINGDOM; SEE ALSO APPROPRIATE TIME/SPACE/
CULTURE INDEX, COMMONWLTH

JOURNAL OF PUBLIC ADMINISTRATION: JOURNAL OF THE
ROYAL INSTITUTE OF PUBLIC ADMINISTRATION. UK PLAN
GP/REL INGP/REL 20. PAGE 1 G0006
 N
 BIBLIOG/A
 ADMIN
 NAT/G
 MGT

GT BRIT MIN OVERSEAS DEV, LIB,TECHNICAL CO-
OPERATION -- A BIBLIOGRAPHY. UK LAW SOCIETY DIPLOM
ECO/TAC FOR/AID...STAT 20 CMN/WLTH. PAGE 39 G0775
 N
 BIBLIOG
 TEC/DEV
 ECO/DEV
 NAT/G

BARKER E.,POLITICAL THOUGHT IN ENGLAND: FROM
HERBERT SPENCER TO THE PRESENT DAY. UK ALL/IDEOS
...PHIL/SCI 19/20 SPENCER/H GREEN/TH BENTHAM/J
MAITLAND/F. PAGE 5 G0094
 B28
 INTELL
 GEN/LAWS
 IDEA/COMP

FULLER G.H.,DEFENSE FINANCING: A SUPPLEMENTARY LIST
OF REFERENCES (PAMPHLET). CANADA UK USA-45 ECO/DEV
NAT/G DELIB/GP BUDGET ADJUD ARMS/CONT WEAPON COST
PEACE PWR 20 AUSTRAL CHINJAP CONGRESS. PAGE 21
G0403
 B42
 BIBLIOG/A
 FINAN
 FORCES
 DIPLOM

BARKER E.,THE DEVELOPMENT OF PUBLIC SERVICES IN
WESTERN WUROPE: 1660-1930. FRANCE GERMANY UK SCHOOL
CONTROL REPRESENT ROLE...WELF/ST 17/20. PAGE 5
G0095
 B44
 GOV/COMP
 ADMIN
 EX/STRUC

FULLER G.H.,MILITARY GOVERNMENT: A LIST OF
REFERENCES (A PAMPHLET). ITALY UK USA-45 WOR-45 LAW
FORCES DOMIN ADMIN ARMS/CONT ORD/FREE PWR
...DECISION 20 CHINJAP. PAGE 21 G0404
 B44
 BIBLIOG
 DIPLOM
 CIVMIL/REL
 SOVEREIGN

MCLEAN J.M.,THE PUBLIC SERVICE AND UNIVERSITY
EDUCATION. UK USA-45 DELIB/GP EX/STRUC TOP/EX ADMIN
...GOV/COMP METH/COMP NAT/COMP ANTHOL 20. PAGE 38
G0746
 B49
 ACADEM
 NAT/G
 EXEC
 EDU/PROP

CROWTHER J.G.,SCIENCE AT WAR. EUR+WWI PLAN TEC/DEV
DOMIN COERCE NUC/PWR WEAPON KNOWL PWR...CONCPT OBS
TREND VAL/FREE 20. PAGE 14 G0265
 B50
 R+D
 FORCES
 WAR
 UK

MANNHEIM K.,FREEDOM, POWER, AND DEMOCRATIC
PLANNING. FUT USSR WOR+45 ELITES INTELL SOCIETY
NAT/G EDU/PROP ROUTINE ATTIT DRIVE SUPEGO SKILL
...POLICY PSY CONCPT TREND GEN/LAWS 20. PAGE 35
G0700
 B50
 TEC/DEV
 PLAN
 CAP/ISM
 UK

ROBINSON E.A.G.,THE STRUCTURE OF COMPETITIVE
INDUSTRY. UK ECO/DEV DIST/IND MARKET TEC/DEV DIPLOM
EDU/PROP ADMIN EFFICIENCY WEALTH...MGT 19/20.
PAGE 47 G0929
 B53
 INDUS
 PRODUC
 WORKER
 OPTIMAL

REYNOLDS P.A.,BRITISH FOREIGN POLICY IN THE INTER-
WAR YEARS. CZECHOSLVK GERMANY POLAND UK USA-45
POL/PAR FORCES ECO/TAC ARMS/CONT WAR ATTIT 20.
PAGE 46 G0915
 B54
 DIPLOM
 POLICY
 NAT/G

BONER H.A.,"HUNGRY GENERATIONS." UK WOR+45 WOR-45
STRATA INDUS FAM LABOR CAP/ISM...MGT BIBLIOG 19/20.
PAGE 8 G0151
 C55
 ECO/DEV
 PHIL/SCI
 CONCPT
 WEALTH

ANGELL N.,DEFENCE AND THE ENGLISH-SPEAKING ROLE.
CHINA/COM UK USSR INT/ORG FORCES EDU/PROP NEUTRAL
NUC/PWR NAT/LISM PEACE TOTALISM 20 COLD/WAR
COEXIST. PAGE 3 G0059
 B58
 DIPLOM
 WAR
 MARXISM
 ORD/FREE

CROWE S.,THE LANDSCAPE OF POWER. UK CULTURE
SERV/IND NAT/G CONSULT PARTIC NUC/PWR LEISURE...SOC
EXHIBIT 20. PAGE 14 G0264
 B58
 HABITAT
 TEC/DEV
 PLAN
 CONTROL

VERNEY D.V.,PUBLIC ENTERPRISE IN SWEDEN. FUT SWEDEN
UK INDUS POL/PAR LEGIS PROB/SOLV CAP/ISM INT/TRADE
CONTROL SOCISM...MGT CONCPT NAT/COMP 20 SOCDEM/PAR
CIVIL/SERV. PAGE 61 G1196
 B59
 ECO/DEV
 POLICY
 LG/CO
 NAT/G

TARKOWSKI Z.M.,"SCIENTISTS VERSUS ADMINISTRATORS:
AN APPROACH TOWARD ACHIEVING GREATER
UNDERSTANDING." UK EXEC EFFICIENCY 20. PAGE 53
G1052
 L5?
 INGP/REL
 GP/REL
 ADMIN
 EX/STRUC

BENDIX R.,"INDUSTRIALIZATION, IDEOLOGIES, AND
SOCIAL STRUCTURE" (BMR)" UK USA-45 USSR STRUCT
WORKER GP/REL EFFICIENCY...IDEA/COMP 20. PAGE 6
G0117
 S5?
 INDUS
 ATTIT
 MGT
 ADMIN

SHEENAN D.,"PUBLIC CORPORATIONS AND PUBLIC ACTION."
UK ADMIN CONTROL REPRESENT SOCISM 20. PAGE 50 G0990
 S5?
 ECO/DEV
 EFFICIENCY
 EX/STRUC
 EXEC

STREAT R.,"GOVERNMENT CONSULTATION WITH INDUSTRY."
UK 20. PAGE 53 G1043
 S5?
 REPRESENT
 ADMIN
 EX/STRUC
 INDUS

KINGSTON-MCCLOUG E.,DEFENSE; POLICY AND STRATEGY.
UK SEA AIR TEC/DEV DIPLOM ADMIN LEAD WAR ORD/FREE
...CHARTS 20. PAGE 30 G0597
 B60
 FORCES
 PLAN
 POLICY
 DECISION

GLADDEN E.N.,BRITISH PUBLIC SERVICE ADMINISTRATION.
UK...CHARTS 20. PAGE 21 G0419
 B61
 EFFICIENCY
 ADMIN
 EX/STRUC
 EXEC

GRANICK D.,THE EUROPEAN EXECUTIVE. BELGIUM FRANCE
GERMANY/W UK INDUS LABOR LG/CO SML/CO EX/STRUC PLAN
TEC/DEV CAP/ISM COST DEMAND...POLICY CHARTS 20.
PAGE 22 G0441
 B62
 MGT
 ECO/DEV
 ECO/TAC
 EXEC

THOMSON G.P.,NUCLEAR ENERGY IN BRITAIN DURING THE
LAST WAR: THE CHERWELL SIMON LECTURE (MONOGRAPH).
UK R+D CONSULT FORCES PLAN DIPLOM TASK CIVMIL/REL
ROLE...PHIL/SCI NEW/IDEA LAB/EXP 20 MAUD. PAGE 54
G1071
 B62
 CREATE
 TEC/DEV
 WAR
 NUC/PWR

WENDT P.F.,HOUSING POLICY - THE SEARCH FOR
SOLUTIONS. GERMANY/W SWEDEN UK USA+45 OP/RES
HABITAT WEALTH...SOC/WK CHARTS 20. PAGE 63 G1230
 B62
 PLAN
 ADMIN
 METH/COMP
 NAT/G

DONNELLY D.,"THE POLITICS AND ADMINISTRATION OF
PLANNING." UK ROUTINE FEDERAL 20. PAGE 16 G0307
 S62
 GOV/REL
 EFFICIENCY
 ADMIN
 EX/STRUC

MARTIN L.W.,"THE MARKET FOR STRATEGIC IDEAS IN
BRITAIN: THE 'SANDYS ERA'" UK ARMS/CONT WAR GOV/REL
OPTIMAL...POLICY DECISION GOV/COMP COLD/WAR
CMN/WLTH. PAGE 36 G0714
 S62
 DIPLOM
 COERCE
 FORCES
 PWR

MAYNE R.,THE COMMUNITY OF EUROPE. UK CONSTN NAT/G
CONSULT DELIB/GP CREATE PLAN ECO/TAC LEGIT ADMIN
ROUTINE ORD/FREE PWR WEALTH...CONCPT TIME/SEQ EEC
EURATOM 20. PAGE 37 G0724
 B63
 EUR+WWI
 INT/ORG
 REGION

SCHOECK H.,THE NEW ARGUMENT IN ECONOMICS. UK USA+45
INDUS MARKET LABOR NAT/G ECO/TAC ADMIN ROUTINE
BAL/PAY PWR...POLICY BOLIV. PAGE 49 G0973
 B63
 WELF/ST
 FOR/AID
 ECO/DEV
 ALL/IDEOS

NIEBURG H.,"EURATOM: A STUDY IN COALITION
POLITICS." EUR+WWI UK USA+45 ELITES NAT/G DELIB/GP
LEGIS TOP/EX ECO/TAC NUC/PWR ATTIT ORD/FREE PWR
TOT/POP EEC OEEC 20 NATO EURATOM. PAGE 42 G0820
 L63
 VOL/ASSN
 ACT/RES

SMITH D.O.,"WHAT IS A WAR DETERRENT." FUT GERMANY
HUNGARY UK USA+45 WOR+45 WOR-45 NAT/G TEC/DEV
BAL/PWR...CONCPT GEN/LAWS COLD/WAR 20. PAGE 51
G1013
 S63
 ACT/RES
 FORCES
 ARMS/CONT
 DETER

GOWING M.,BRITAIN AND ATOMIC ENERGY 1939-1945.
FRANCE UK USA+45 USA-45 NAT/G CREATE...PHIL/SCI 20
AEA. PAGE 22 G0439
 B64
 NUC/PWR
 DIPLOM
 TEC/DEV

MILIBAND R.,THE SOCIALIST REGISTER: 1964. GERMANY/W MARXISM
ITALY UK LABOR POL/PAR ECO/TAC FOR/AID NUC/PWR   SOCISM
...POLICY SOCIALIST IDEA/COMP 20 MAO NASSER/G.   CAP/ISM
PAGE 39 G0769   PROB/SOLV
                        B64

SCHOECK H.,CENTRAL PLANNING AND NEOMERCANTILISM.   PLAN
L/A+17C UK WOR+45 BUDGET ECO/TAC PRICE CONTROL   CENTRAL
GOV/REL UTOPIA 20. PAGE 49 G0974   NAT/G
                        B64 POLICY

GOLDBERG A.,"ATOMIC ORIGINS OF THE BRITISH NUCLEAR   CREATE
DETERRENT." EUR+WWI UK NAT/G TOP/EX PLAN BAL/PWR   FORCES
DOMIN DETER CHOOSE ATTIT DRIVE HEALTH ORD/FREE PWR   NUC/PWR
RESPECT...CONCPT VAL/FREE COLD/WAR 20 CMN/WLTH.
PAGE 22 G0425
                        L64

GRETTON P.,MARITIME STRATEGY - A STUDY OF DEFENSE   FORCES
PROBLEMS. ASIA UK USSR DIPLOM COERCE DETER NUC/PWR   PLAN
WEAPON...CONCPT NAT/COMP 20. PAGE 23 G0449   WAR
                        B65 SEA

HASSON J.A.,THE ECONOMICS OF NUCLEAR POWER. INDIA   NUC/PWR
UK USA+45 WOR+45 INT/ORG TEC/DEV COST...SOC STAT   INDUS
CHARTS 20 EURATOM. PAGE 25 G0490   ECO/DEV
                        B65 METH

SCHEINMAN L.,ATOMIC ENERGY POLICY IN FRANCE UNDER   NUC/PWR
THE FOURTH REPUBLIC. FRANCE UK USA+45 ELITES   NAT/G
POL/PAR PLAN PROB/SOLV DIPLOM LEAD GOV/REL   DELIB/GP
...BIBLIOG 20 DEGAULLE/C. PAGE 49 G0962   POLICY

GOLDSTEIN W.,"KEEPING THE GENIE IN THE BOTTLE* THE   NUC/PWR
FEASIBILITY OF A NUCLEAR NON-PROLIFERATION   CREATE
AGREEMENT." ASIA FRANCE UK USA+45 USSR WOR+45   COST
ECO/UNDEV VOL/ASSN ACT/RES PLAN RISK ARMS/CONT WAR
PEACE ATTIT PERCEPT...RECORD TREND TIME. PAGE 22
G0429
                        S65

MILLAR R.,THE NEW CLASSES. UK ELITES SOCIETY INDUS   STRUCT
AUTOMAT SOC/REL SOC/INTEG 20 INDUS/REV. PAGE 39   STRATA
G0770   TEC/DEV
                        B66 CREATE

DICKSON P.G.M.,THE FINANCIAL REVOLUTION IN ENGLAND. ECO/DEV
UK NAT/G TEC/DEV ADMIN GOV/REL...SOC METH/CNCPT   FINAN
CHARTS GP/COMP BIBLIOG 17/18. PAGE 15 G0302   CAP/ISM
                        B67 MGT

HODGKINSON R.G.,THE ORIGINS OF THE NATIONAL HEALTH   HEAL
SERVICE: THE MEDICAL SERVICES OF THE NEW POOR LAW,   NAT/G
1834-1871. UK INDUS MUNIC WORKER PROB/SOLV   POLICY
EFFICIENCY ATTIT HEALTH WEALTH SOCISM...JURID   LAW
SOC/WK 19/20. PAGE 26 G0519
                        L67

SEABERG G.P.,"THE DRUG ABUSE PROBLEMS AND SOME   BIO/SOC
PROPOSALS." UK USA+45 MARKET SANCTION CRIME   LAW
...POLICY NEW/IDEA. PAGE 50 G0986   ADJUD
                        S67 PROB/SOLV

BENN W.,"TECHNOLOGY HAS AN INEXORABLE EFFECT." FUT   R+D
UK ECO/DEV INT/ORG CONSULT PLAN EDU/PROP ADMIN LEAD LG/CO
GP/REL PRODUC...INT 20 EEC. PAGE 6 G0119   TEC/DEV
                        S67 INDUS

BROWN N.,"BRITISH ARMS AND THE SWITCH TOWARD   FORCES
EUROPE." EUR+WWI UK ARMS/CONT. PAGE 9 G0178   PLAN
                           DIPLOM
                           INT/ORG

EDMONDS M.,"INTERNATIONAL COLLABORATION IN WEAPONS   DIPLOM
PROCUREMENT* THE IMPLICATIONS OF THE ANGLO-FRENCH   VOL/ASSN
CASE." FRANCE UK CONSULT OP/RES PROB/SOLV TEC/DEV   BAL/PWR
CONFER CONTROL EFFICIENCY 20. PAGE 17 G0334   ARMS/CONT
                        S67

GANZ G.,"THE CONTROL OF INDUSTRY BY ADMINISTRATIVE   INDUS
PROCESS." UK DELIB/GP WORKER 20. PAGE 21 G0408   LAW
                           ADMIN
                           CONTROL

                        S67
JACKSON W.G.F.,"NUCLEAR PROLIFERATION AND THE GREAT NUC/PWR

POWERS." FUT UK WOR+45 INT/ORG DOMIN ARMS/CONT   ATTIT
DETER ORD/FREE PACIFIST. PAGE 28 G0550   BAL/PWR
                           NAT/LISM
                        S67

MARTIN L.,"THE AMERICAN ABM DECISION." ASIA COM   WEAPON
EUR+WWI UK USA+45 USSR FORCES DIPLOM PEACE...POLICY DETER
20 ABM/DEFSYS. PAGE 36 G0713   NUC/PWR
                           WAR
                        S67

TIVEY L.,"THE POLITICAL CONSEQUENCES OF ECONOMIC   PLAN
PLANNING." UK CONSTN INDUS ACT/RES ADMIN CONTROL   POLICY
LOBBY REPRESENT EFFICIENCY SUPEGO SOVEREIGN   NAT/G
...DECISION 20. PAGE 55 G1074
                        S67

WALTERS R.E.,"THE ROLE OF NUCLEAR WEAPONS FOR THE   PLAN
WEST." ASIA UK USA+45 USSR DIPLOM COERCE WAR PEACE   NUC/PWR
...POLICY DECISION 20. PAGE 62 G1209   WEAPON
                           FORCES
                        S68

BARAGWANATH L.E.,"SCIENTIFIC CO-OPERATION BETWEEN   R+D
THE UNIVERSITIES AND INDUSTRY - A RESEARCH NOTE."   ACADEM
UK LG/CO CREATE TEC/DEV EDU/PROP ATTIT...PHIL/SCI   INDUS
STAT QU 20. PAGE 5 G0090   GP/REL
                        B88

BENTHAM J.,DEFENCE OF USURY (1787). UK LAW NAT/G   TAX
TEC/DEV ECO/TAC CONTROL ATTIT...CONCPT IDEA/COMP 18 FINAN
SMITH/ADAM. PAGE 6 G0124   ECO/DEV
                           POLICY

UN G1086

UN....UNITED NATIONS; SEE ALSO INT/ORG, VOL/ASSN, INT/REL

CURRENT THOUGHT ON PEACE AND WAR. WOR+45 INT/ORG   BIBLIOG/A
FORCES PROB/SOLV DIPLOM NUC/PWR PERCEPT...POLICY   PEACE
SOC 20 UN NATO. PAGE 1 G0001   ATTIT
                         WAR

FOREIGN AFFAIRS. SPACE WOR+45 WOR-45 CULTURE   BIBLIOG
ECO/UNDEV FINAN NAT/G TEC/DEV INT/TRADE ARMS/CONT   DIPLOM
NUC/PWR...POLICY 20 UN EURATOM ECSC EEC. PAGE 1   INT/ORG
G0004   INT/LAW
                        N

UNITED NATIONS,OFFICIAL RECORDS OF THE UNITED   ARMS/CONT
NATIONS' ATOMIC ENERGY COMMISSION - DISARMAMENT   INT/ORG
COMMISSION. WOR+45 TEC/DEV DIPLOM WRITING NUC/PWR   DELIB/GP
20 UN. PAGE 55 G1092   CONFER
                        N19

MEZERIK A.G.,ATOM TESTS AND RADIATION HAZARDS   NUC/PWR
(PAMPHLET). WOR+45 INT/ORG DIPLOM DETER 20 UN   ARMS/CONT
TREATY. PAGE 39 G0761   CONFER
                           HEALTH
                        N19

MEZERIK A.G.,INTERNATIONAL POLICY 1965 (PAMPHLET).   DIPLOM
KASHMIR S/ASIA SPACE USA+45 VIETNAM WOR+45   INT/ORG
ARMS/CONT RACE/REL DISCRIM PEACE PWR 20 UN. PAGE 39 POLICY
G0762   WAR
                        N19

MEZERIK AG,OUTER SPACE: UN, US, USSR (PAMPHLET).   SPACE
USSR DELIB/GP FORCES DETER NUC/PWR SOVEREIGN   CONTROL
...POLICY 20 UN TREATY. PAGE 39 G0763   DIPLOM
                           INT/ORG
                        B46

BRODIE B.,THE OBSOLETE WEAPON: ATOMIC POWER AND   INT/ORG
WORLD ORDER. COM USA+45 USSR WOR+45 DELIB/GP PLAN   TEC/DEV
ORD/FREE PWR...CONCPT TIME/SEQ TREND UN 20. PAGE 9   ARMS/CONT
G0171   NUC/PWR
                        B50

US DEPARTMENT OF STATE,POINT FOUR: COOPERATIVE   ECO/UNDEV
PROGRAM FOR AID IN THE DEVELOPMENT OF ECONOMICALLY   FOR/AID
UNDERDEVELOPED AREAS. WOR+45 AGRI INDUS INT/ORG   FINAN
PLAN TEC/DEV DIPLOM EDU/PROP ADMIN PEACE PRODUC   INT/TRADE
WEALTH 20 CONGRESS UN. PAGE 57 G1121
                        B53

MACK R.T.,RAISING THE WORLDS STANDARD OF LIVING.   WOR+45
IRAN INT/ORG VOL/ASSN EX/STRUC ECO/TAC WEALTH...MGT FOR/AID
METH/CNCPT STAT CONT/OBS INT TOT/POP VAL/FREE 20   INT/TRADE
UN. PAGE 35 G0690
                        S53

CORY R.H. JR.,"FORGING A PUBLIC INFORMATION POLICY   INT/ORG
FOR THE UNITED NATIONS." FUT WOR+45 SOCIETY ADMIN   EDU/PROP

PEACE ATTIT PERSON SKILL...CONCPT 20 UN. PAGE 13   BAL/PWR
G0257

KENWORTHY L.S.,FREE AND INEXPENSIVE MATERIALS ON   BIBLIOG/A
WORLD AFFAIRS (PAMPHLET). WOR+45 CULTURE ECO/UNDEV   NAT/G
INT/TRADE ARMS/CONT NUC/PWR UN. PAGE 30 G0594   INT/ORG
                                                      DIPLOM
                                               B54

US DEPARTMENT OF STATE,PUBLICATIONS OF THE   BIBLIOG
DEPARTMENT OF STATE, OCTOBER 1,1929 TO JANUARY 1,   DIPLOM
1953. AGRI INT/ORG FORCES FOR/AID EDU/PROP
ARMS/CONT NUC/PWR ATTIT 20 DEPT/STATE OAS UN NATO.
PAGE 57 G1122

                                               L54
OPLER M.E.,"SOCIAL ASPECTS OF TECHNICAL ASSISTANCE   INT/ORG
IN OPERATION." WOR+45 VOL/ASSN CREATE PLAN TEC/DEV   CONSULT
EDU/PROP ALL/VALS...METH/CNCPT OBS RECORD TREND UN   FOR/AID
20. PAGE 43 G0841

                                               B58
UN INTL CONF ON PEACEFUL USE,PROGRESS IN ATOMIC   NUC/PWR
ENERGY (VOL. I). WOR+45 R+D PLAN TEC/DEV CONFER   DIPLOM
CONTROL PEACE SKILL...CHARTS ANTHOL 20 UN BAGHDAD.   WORKER
PAGE 55 G1088   EDU/PROP

                                               B58
US DEPARTMENT OF STATE,PUBLICATIONS OF THE   BIBLIOG
DEPARTMENT OF STATE, JANUARY 1,1953 TO DECEMBER 31,   DIPLOM
1957. AGRI INT/ORG FORCES FOR/AID EDU/PROP
ARMS/CONT NUC/PWR ATTIT 20 DEPT/STATE OAS UN NATO.
PAGE 57 G1123

                                               S58
MCDOUGAL M.S.,"PERSPECTIVES FOR A LAW OF OUTER   INT/ORG
SPACE." FUT WOR+45 AIR CONSULT DELIB/GP TEC/DEV   SPACE
CT/SYS ORD/FREE...POLICY JURID 20 UN. PAGE 37 G0736   INT/LAW

                                               B59
COLUMBIA U BUREAU APPL SOC R, ATTITUDES OF   ATTIT
PROMINENT AMERICANS TOWARD "WORLD PEACE THROUGH   ACT/RES
WORLD LAW" (SUPRA-NATL ORGANIZATION FOR WAR   INT/LAW
PREVENTION). USA+45 USSR ELITES FORCES PLAN   STAT
PROB/SOLV CONTROL WAR PWR...POLICY SOC QU IDEA/COMP
20 UN. PAGE 45 G0888

                                               B59
SPANIER J.W.,THE TRUMAN-MACARTHUR CONTROVERSY AND   CIVMIL/REL
THE KOREAN WAR. USA+45 TOP/EX PROB/SOLV LEAD ATTIT   FORCES
PWR...POLICY BIBLIOG/A UN. PAGE 52 G1023   CHIEF
                                                      WAR
                                               B59
VAN WAGENEN R.W.,SOME VIEWS OF AMERICAN DEFENSE   INT/ORG
OFFICIALS ABOUT THE UNITED NATIONS (PAPER). FUT   LEAD
USA+45 NAT/G DIPLOM WAR EFFICIENCY PEACE...POLICY   ATTIT
INT 20 UN DEPT/DEFEN. PAGE 61 G1192   FORCES

                                               B60
PENTONY D.E.,THE UNDERDEVELOPED LANDS. FUT WOR+45   ECO/UNDEV
CULTURE AGRI FINAN INDUS MARKET INT/ORG LABOR NAT/G   POLICY
VOL/ASSN CONSULT TEC/DEV ECO/TAC EDU/PROP COLONIAL   FOR/AID
ATTIT WEALTH...OBS RECORD SAMP TREND GEN/METH WORK   INT/TRADE
UN 20. PAGE 44 G0867

                                               B60
US DEPARTMENT OF THE ARMY,DISARMAMENT: A   BIBLIOG/A
BIBLIOGRAPHIC RECORD: 1916-1960. DETER WAR WEAPON   ARMS/CONT
PEACE 20 UN LEAGUE/NAT COLD/WAR NATO. PAGE 57 G1128   NUC/PWR
                                                      DIPLOM
                                               S60
SWIFT R.,"THE UNITED NATIONS AND ITS PUBLIC."   INT/ORG
WOR+45 CONSTN FINAN CONSULT DELIB/GP ACT/RES ADMIN   EDU/PROP
ROUTINE RIGID/FLEX SKILL UN 20. PAGE 53 G1048

                                               L61
TAUBENFELD H.J.,"A REGIME FOR OUTER SPACE." FUT   INT/ORG
UNIV R+D ACT/RES PLAN BAL/PWR LEGIT ARMS/CONT   ADJUD
ORD/FREE...POLICY JURID TREND UN TOT/POP 20   SPACE
COLD/WAR. PAGE 54 G1056

                                               B62
AIR FORCE ACADEMY LIBRARY,INTERNATIONAL   BIBLIOG
ORGANIZATIONS AND MILITARY SECURITY SYSTEMS   INT/ORG
(PAMPHLET) (SPECIAL BIBLIOGRAPHY SERIES, NUMBER   FORCES
25). DIPLOM FOR/AID INT/TRADE NUC/PWR PEACE 20 UN   DETER
NATO OAS SEATO LEAGUE/NAT. PAGE 2 G0031

                                               B62
SCHWARTZ L.E.,INTERNATIONAL ORGANIZATIONS AND SPACE INT/ORG
COOPERATION. VOL/ASSN CONSULT CREATE TEC/DEV   DIPLOM
SANCTION...POLICY INT/LAW PHIL/SCI 20 UN. PAGE 50   R+D
G0982   SPACE

                                               B62
THANT U.,THE UNITED NATIONS' DEVELOPMENT DECADE: INT/ORG
PROPOSALS FOR ACTION. WOR+45 SOCIETY ECO/UNDEV AGRI   ALL/VALS
COM/IND FINAN R+D MUNIC SCHOOL VOL/ASSN CONSULT
PLAN TEC/DEV ECO/TAC EDU/PROP ADMIN ROUTINE
RIGID/FLEX...MGT SOC CONCPT UNESCO UN TOT/POP
VAL/FREE. PAGE 54 G1064

                                               S62
FOSTER W.C.,"ARMS CONTROL AND DISARMAMENT IN A   DELIB/GP
DIVIDED WORLD." COM FUT USA+45 USSR WOR+45 INTELL   POLICY
INT/ORG NAT/G VOL/ASSN CONSULT CREATE PLAN TEC/DEV   ARMS/CONT
EDU/PROP LEGIT NUC/PWR ATTIT RIGID/FLEX...CONCPT   DIPLOM
TREND TOT/POP 20 UN. PAGE 20 G0387

                                               B63
UN SECRETARY GENERAL,PLANNING FOR ECONOMIC   PLAN
DEVELOPMENT. ECO/UNDEV FINAN BUDGET INT/TRADE   ECO/TAC
TARIFFS TAX ADMIN 20 UN. PAGE 55 G1089   MGT
                                                      NAT/COMP
                                               B63
WIGHTMAN D.,TOWARD ECONOMIC CO-OPERATION IN ASIA.   ECO/UNDEV
ASIA S/ASIA VOL/ASSN ACT/RES PLAN TEC/DEV ECO/TAC   CREATE
EDU/PROP RIGID/FLEX SKILL...POLICY METH/CNCPT OBS
INT GEN/LAWS UN 20 ECAFE. PAGE 63 G1237

                                               S63
GANDILHON J.,"LA SCIENCE ET LA TECHNIQUE A L'AIDE   ECO/UNDEV
DES REGIONS PEU DEVELOPPEES." FRANCE FUT WOR+45   TEC/DEV
ECO/DEV R+D PROF/ORG ACT/RES PLAN...MGT TOT/POP   FOR/AID
VAL/FREE 20 UN. PAGE 21 G0406

                                               B64
FREYMOND J.,WESTERN EUROPE SINCE THE WAR. COM   INT/ORG
EUR+WWI USA+45 DIPLOM...BIBLIOG 20 NATO UN EEC.   POLICY
PAGE 20 G0392   ECO/DEV
                                                      ECO/TAC
                                               B64
HEKHUIS D.J.,INTERNATIONAL STABILITY: MILITARY,   TEC/DEV
ECONOMIC AND POLITICAL DIMENSIONS. FUT WOR+45 LAW   DETER
ECO/UNDEV INT/ORG NAT/G VOL/ASSN FORCES ACT/RES   REGION
BAL/PWR PWR WEALTH...STAT UN 20. PAGE 25 G0503

                                               B64
THANT U.,TOWARD WORLD PEACE. DELIB/GP TEC/DEV   DIPLOM
EDU/PROP WAR SOVEREIGN...INT/LAW 20 UN MID/EAST.   BIOG
PAGE 54 G1065   PEACE
                                                      COERCE
                                               B64
WILLIAMS S.P.,TOWARD A GENUINE WORLD SECURITY   BIBLIOG/A
SYSTEM (PAMPHLET). WOR+45 INT/ORG FORCES PLAN   ARMS/CONT
NUC/PWR ORD/FREE...INT/LAW CONCPT UN PRESIDENT.   DIPLOM
PAGE 63 G1243   PEACE

                                               L64
CARNEGIE ENDOWMENT INT. PEACE,"POLITICAL QUESTIONS   INT/ORG
(ISSUES BEFORE THE NINETEENTH GENERAL ASSEMBLY)."   PEACE
SPACE WOR+45 CONSTN FINAN NAT/G CONSULT DELIB/GP
FORCES LEGIS TEC/DEV EDU/PROP LEGIT ARMS/CONT
COERCE NUC/PWR ATTIT ALL/VALS...CONCPT OBS UN
COLD/WAR 20. PAGE 11 G0208

                                               L64
CARNEGIE ENDOWMENT INT. PEACE,"ECONOMIC AND SOCIAL   INT/ORG
QUESTION (ISSUES BEFORE THE NINETEENTH GENERAL   INT/TRADE
ASSEMBLY)." WOR+45 ECO/DEV ECO/UNDEV INDUS R+D
DELIB/GP CREATE PLAN TEC/DEV ECO/TAC FOR/AID
BAL/PAY...RECORD UN 20. PAGE 11 G0209

                                               S64
GARDNER R.N.,"GATT AND THE UNITED NATIONS   INT/ORG
CONFERENCE ON TRADE AND DEVELOPMENT." USA+45 WOR+45   INT/TRADE
SOCIETY ECO/UNDEV MARKET NAT/G DELIB/GP ACT/RES
PLAN ECO/TAC TARIFFS EDU/PROP ROUTINE DRIVE
RIGID/FLEX WEALTH...DECISION MGT TREND UN TOT/POP
20 GATT. PAGE 21 G0411

                                               B65
CORDIER A.W.,THE QUEST FOR PEACE. WOR+45 NAT/G PLAN PEACE
BAL/PWR ECO/TAC ARMS/CONT NUC/PWR PWR...ANTHOL UN   DIPLOM
COLD/WAR. PAGE 13 G0256   POLICY
                                                      INT/ORG
                                               B65
JENKS C.W.,SPACE LAW. DIPLOM DEBATE CONTROL   SPACE
ORD/FREE TREATY 20 UN. PAGE 29 G0563   INT/LAW
                                                      JURID
                                                      INT/ORG
                                               B65
MOSKOWITZ H.,US SECURITY, ARMS CONTROL, AND   BIBLIOG/A
DISARMAMENT 1961-1965. FORCES DIPLOM DETER WAR   ARMS/CONT

WEAPON...CHARTS 20 UN COLD/WAR NATO. PAGE 40 G0790   NUC/PWR
                                                      PEACE

                                                      B65
UN.SPACE ACTIVITIES AND RESOURCES: REVIEW OF UNITED   SPACE
NATION'S NATIONAL AND INTERNATIONAL PROGRAMS.   NUC/PWR
INT/ORG LABOR PLAN TEC/DEV DIPLOM EFFICIENCY HEALTH   FOR/AID
...GOV/COMP 20 UN. PAGE 55 G1086   PEACE

                                                      B65
US SENATE COMM AERO SPACE SCI,INTERNATIONAL   DIPLOM
COOPERATION AND ORGANIZATION FOR OUTER SPACE. FUT   SPACE
USA+45 WOR+45 PROF/ORG VOL/ASSN CONSULT DELIB/GP   R+D
PLAN TEC/DEV ARMS/CONT GP/REL PEACE 20 UN NASA.   NAT/G
PAGE 59 G1167

                                                      B65
WASKOW A.I.,KEEPING THE WORLD DISARMED. AFR   ARMS/CONT
GERMANY/E DIPLOM CONTROL WAR 20 UN. PAGE 62 G1218   PEACE
                                                      FORCES
                                                      PROB/SOLV

                                                      S65
HIBBS A.R.,"SPACE TECHNOLOGY* THE THREAT AND THE   SPACE
PROMISE." FUT VOL/ASSN TEC/DEV NUC/PWR COST   ARMS/CONT
EFFICIENCY UTIL UN TREATY. PAGE 26 G0510   PREDICT

                                                      S65
LECLERCQ H.,"ECONOMIC RESEARCH AND DEVELOPMENT IN   AFR
TROPICAL AFRICA." ECO/UNDEV INT/ORG CREATE PLAN UN.   R+D
PAGE 33 G0650   ACADEM
                                                      ECO/TAC

                                                      S65
MARTIN A.,"PROLIFERATION." FUT WOR+45 PROB/SOLV   RECORD
REGION ADJUST...PREDICT NAT/COMP UN TREATY. PAGE 36   NUC/PWR
G0712   ARMS/CONT
                                                      VOL/ASSN

                                                      C65
SEARA M.V.,"COSMIC INTERNATIONAL LAW." LAW ACADEM   SPACE
ACT/RES DIPLOM COLONIAL CONTROL NUC/PWR SOVEREIGN   INT/LAW
...GEN/LAWS BIBLIOG UN. PAGE 50 G0987   IDEA/COMP
                                                      INT/ORG

                                                      B66
ALEXANDER Y.,INTERNATIONAL TECHNICAL ASSISTANCE   ECO/TAC
EXPERTS* A CASE STUDY OF THE U.N. EXPERIENCE.   INT/ORG
ECO/UNDEV CONSULT EX/STRUC CREATE PLAN DIPLOM   ADMIN
FOR/AID TASK EFFICIENCY...ORG/CHARTS UN. PAGE 2   MGT
G0038

                                                      B66
ALEXANDER Y.,INTERNATIONAL TECHNICAL ASSISTANCE   SKILL
EXPERTS: A CASE STUDY OF THE U.N. EXPERIENCE.   INT/ORG
USA+45 WOR+45 WORKER CREATE PLAN PROB/SOLV ECO/TAC   TEC/DEV
FOR/AID GIVE EDU/PROP...CHARTS BIBLIOG 20 UN.   CONSULT
PAGE 2 G0039

                                                      B66
CLARK G.,WORLD PEACE THROUGH WORLD LAW; TWO   INT/LAW
ALTERNATIVE PLANS. WOR+45 DELIB/GP FORCES TAX   PEACE
CONFER ADJUD SANCTION ARMS/CONT WAR CHOOSE PRIVIL   PLAN
20 UN COLD/WAR. PAGE 12 G0231   INT/ORG

                                                      B66
UNITED NATIONS,INTERNATIONAL SPACE BIBLIOGRAPHY.   BIBLIOG
FUT INT/ORG TEC/DEV DIPLOM ARMS/CONT NUC/PWR   SPACE
...JURID SOC UN. PAGE 56 G1093   PEACE
                                                      R+D

                                                      B67
GARCIA ROBLES A.,THE DENUCLEARIZATION OF LATIN   NUC/PWR
AMERICA (TRANS. BY MARJORIE URQUIDI). LAW PLAN   ARMS/CONT
DIPLOM...ANTHOL 20 TREATY UN. PAGE 21 G0409   L/A+17C
                                                      INT/ORG

                                                      B67
PADELFORD N.J.,THE DYNAMICS OF INTERNATIONAL   DIPLOM
POLITICS (2ND ED.). WOR+45 LAW INT/ORG FORCES   NAT/G
TEC/DEV REGION NAT/LISM PEACE ATTIT PWR ALL/IDEOS   POLICY
UN COLD/WAR NATO TREATY. PAGE 43 G0856   DECISION

                                                      B67
UNESCO,PRINCIPLES AND PROBLEMS OF NATIONAL SCIENCE   NAT/COMP
POLICIES. WOR+45 ECO/DEV ECO/UNDEV R+D INT/ORG   POLICY
PROB/SOLV CONFER...PHIL/SCI CHARTS 20 UNESCO UN.   TEC/DEV
PAGE 55 G1091   CREATE

                                                      B67
US SENATE COMM AERO SPACE SCI,TREATY ON PRINCIPLES   SPACE
GOVERNING ACTIVITIES OF STATES IN EXPLORATION AND   INT/LAW
USE OF OUTER SPACE. INCLUDING...BODIES. DELIB/GP   ORD/FREE
FORCES LEGIS DIPLOM...JURID 20 DEPT/STATE NASA   PEACE
DEPT/DEFEN UN. PAGE 60 G1170

                                                      B67
US SENATE COMM ON FOREIGN REL,TREATY ON OUTER   SPACE
SPACE. WOR+45 AIR FORCES PROB/SOLV NUC/PWR SENATE   DIPLOM
TREATY UN. PAGE 60 G1182   ARMS/CONT
                                                      LAW

                                                      S67
DOYLE S.E.,"COMMUNICATION SATELLITES* INTERNAL   TEC/DEV
ORGANIZATION FOR DEVELOPMENT AND CONTROL." USA+45   SPACE
R+D ACT/RES DIPLOM NAT/LISM...POLICY INT/LAW   COM/IND
PREDICT UN. PAGE 16 G0313   INT/ORG

                                                      S67
EISENDRATH C.,"THE OUTER SPACE TREATY." CHINA/COM   SPACE
COM USA+45 DIPLOM CONTROL NUC/PWR...INT/LAW 20 UN   INT/ORG
COLD/WAR TREATY. PAGE 17 G0339   PEACE
                                                      ARMS/CONT

                                                      S67
FOREIGN POLICY ASSOCIATION,"US CONCERN FOR WORLD   INT/LAW
LAW." USA+45 WOR+45 DELIB/GP JUDGE BAL/PWR CONFER   INT/ORG
PEACE ORD/FREE 20 UN. PAGE 19 G0379   DIPLOM
                                                      ARMS/CONT

                                                      S67
FOREIGN POLICY ASSOCIATION,"HOW WORLD LAW DEVELOPS*   INT/LAW
A CASE STUDY OF THE OUTER SPACE TREATY." SPACE   DIPLOM
WOR+45 BAL/PWR NEUTRAL NUC/PWR PEACE KNOWL 20 UN   ARMS/CONT
TREATY. PAGE 19 G0380   INT/ORG

                                                      S67
HAZARD J.N.,"POST-DISARMAMENT INTERNATIONAL LAW."   INT/LAW
FUT USSR WOR+45 INT/ORG DELIB/GP FORCES DETER   ARMS/CONT
EQUILIB SOVEREIGN MARXISM 20 UN. PAGE 25 G0496   PWR
                                                      PLAN

                                                      S67
HILL R.,"SOCIAL ASPECTS OF FAMILY PLANNING." INDIA   FAM
KOREA TAIWAN ECO/UNDEV PLAN PROB/SOLV TEC/DEV   BIO/SOC
EDU/PROP CONTROL ATTIT DRIVE...HEAL PSY SOC 20   GEOG
BIRTH/CON UN. PAGE 26 G0512   MARRIAGE

                                                      S67
HODGE G.,"THE RISE AND DEMISE OF THE UN TECHNICAL   ADMIN
ASSISTANCE ADMINISTRATION." RISK TASK INGP/REL   TEC/DEV
CONSEN EFFICIENCY 20 UN. PAGE 26 G0516   EX/STRUC
                                                      INT/ORG

                                                      S67
HULL E.W.S.,"THE POLITICAL OCEAN." FUT UNIV WOR+45   DIPLOM
EXTR/IND R+D VOL/ASSN PLAN BAL/PWR ECO/TAC PEACE   ECO/UNDEV
WEALTH 20 UN. PAGE 27 G0536   INT/ORG
                                                      INT/LAW

                                                      S67
REINTANZ G.,"THE SPACE TREATY." WOR+45 DIPLOM   SPACE
CONTROL ARMS/CONT NUC/PWR WAR...MARXIST 20 COLD/WAR   INT/LAW
UN TREATY. PAGE 46 G0911   INT/ORG
                                                      PEACE

                                                      S67
SCHACTER O.,"SCIENTIFIC ADVANCES AND INTERNATIONAL   TEC/DEV
LAWMAKING." FUT R+D PLAN PROB/SOLV CONFER CONTROL   INT/LAW
...POLICY PREDICT 20 UN. PAGE 49 G0961   INT/ORG
                                                      ACT/RES

                                                      S67
STYCOS J.M.,"POLITICS AND POPULATION CONTROL IN   PLAN
LATIN AMERICA." USA+45 FAM NAT/G GP/REL AGE/C ATTIT   CENSUS
CATHISM MARXISM...POLICY UN WHO. PAGE 53 G1045   CONTROL
                                                      L/A+17C

                                                      S67
VLASCIC I.A.,"THE SPACE TREATY* A PRELIMINARY   SPACE
EVALUATION." FUT USSR WOR+45 R+D ACT/RES TEC/DEV   INT/LAW
DIPLOM CONFER ARMS/CONT PEACE...PREDICT UN TREATY.   INT/ORG
PAGE 61 G1201   NEUTRAL

                                                      N67
US HOUSE COMM FOREIGN AFFAIRS,REPORT OF SPECIAL   ISLAM
STUDY MISSION TO THE NEAR EAST (PAMPHLET). ISRAEL   DIPLOM
USA+45 YEMEN ECO/UNDEV INT/ORG FOR/AID ARMS/CONT   FORCES
WAR WEAPON NAT/LISM PEACE...GEOG 20 UN HOUSE/REP.
PAGE 58 G1138

UN HEADQUARTERS LIBRARY G1087

UN INTL CONF ON PEACEFUL USE G1088

UN SECRETARY GENERAL G1089

UN/ILC....UNITED NATIONS INTERNATIONAL LAW COMMISSION

UN/SEC/GEN....UNITED NATIONS SECRETARY GENERAL

UNCSAT....UNITED NATIONS CONFERENCE ON THE APPLICATION OF

SCIENCE AND TECHNOLOGY FOR THE BENEFIT OF THE LESS
DEVELOPED AREAS

UNCTAD....UNITED NATIONS COMMISSION ON TRADE, AID, AND
DEVELOPMENT

UNDERDEVELOPED COUNTRIES....SEE ECO/UNDEV

UNDP....UNITED NATIONS DEVELOPMENT PROGRAM

UNEF....UNITED NATIONS EMERGENCY FORCE

UNESCO G1090,G1091

UNESCO....UNITED NATIONS EDUCATIONAL, SCIENTIFIC, AND
CULTURAL ORGANIZATION; SEE ALSO UN, INT/ORG

LARSEN K.,NATIONAL BIBLIOGRAPHIC SERVICES: THEIR   B53
CREATION AND OPERATION. WOR+45 COM/IND CREATE PLAN   BIBLIOG/A
DIPLOM PRESS ADMIN ROUTINE...MGT UNESCO. PAGE 32   INT/ORG
G0636   WRITING

STANFORD RESEARCH INSTITUTE,POSSIBLE NONMILITARY   B59
SCIENTIFIC DEVELOPMENTS AND THEIR POTENTIAL IMPACT   R+D
ON FOREIGN POLICY PROBLEMS OF THE UNITED. FUT   TEC/DEV
USA+45 INT/ORG PROF/ORG CONSULT ACT/RES CREATE PLAN
PEACE KNOWL SKILL...TECHNIC PHIL/SCI NEW/IDEA
UNESCO 20. PAGE 52 G1032

THANT U.,THE UNITED NATIONS' DEVELOPMENT DECADE: B62
PROPOSALS FOR ACTION. WOR+45 SOCIETY ECO/UNDEV AGRI   INT/ORG
COM/IND FINAN R+D MUNIC SCHOOL VOL/ASSN CONSULT   ALL/VALS
PLAN TEC/DEV ECO/TAC EDU/PROP ADMIN ROUTINE
RIGID/FLEX...MGT SOC CONCPT UNESCO UN TOT/POP
VAL/FREE. PAGE 54 G1064

UNESCO,PRINCIPLES AND PROBLEMS OF NATIONAL SCIENCE   B67
POLICIES. WOR+45 ECO/DEV ECO/UNDEV R+D INT/ORG   NAT/COMP
PROB/SOLV CONFER...PHIL/SCI CHARTS 20 UNESCO UN.   POLICY
PAGE 55 G1091   TEC/DEV
                                                       CREATE

UNIDO....UNITED NATIONS INDUSTRIAL DEVELOPMENT ORGANIZATION

UNIFICA....UNIFICATION AND REUNIFICATION OF GEOGRAPHIC-
POLITICAL ENTITIES

SCHMITT H.A.,THE PATH TO EUROPEAN UNITY. EUR+WWI   B62
USA+45 PLAN TEC/DEV DIPLOM FOR/AID CONFER...INT/LAW   INT/ORG
20 EEC EURCOALSTL MARSHL/PLN UNIFICA. PAGE 49 G0971   INT/TRADE
                                                       REGION
                                                       ECO/DEV

UNIFORM NARCOTIC DRUG ACT....SEE NARCO/ACT

UNION AFRICAINE ET MALGACHE, ALSO OCAM....SEE UAM

UNION FOR THE NEW REPUBLIC....SEE UNR

UNION OF SOUTH AFRICA....SEE SOUTH/AFR

UNION OF SOVIET SOCIALIST REPUBLICS....SEE USSR

UNIONS....SEE LABOR

UNITED ARAB REPUBLIC....SEE UAR

UNITED AUTO WORKERS....SEE UAW

UNITED KINGDOM....SEE UK, COMMONWLTH

UNITED NATIONS....SEE UN

UNITED NATIONS INTERNATIONAL LAW COMMISSION....SEE UN/ILC

UNITED NATIONS SECURITY COUNCIL....SEE SECUR/COUN

UNITED NATIONS SPECIAL FUND....SEE UNSF

UNITED STATES ARMS CONTROL AND DISARMAMENT AGENCY....SEE
ACD

UNITED STATES FEDERAL POWER COMMISSION....SEE FPC

UNITED STATES HOUSING CORPORATION....SEE US/HOUSING

UNITED STATES MILITARY ACADEMY....SEE WEST/POINT

UNITED STATES SENATE COMMITTEE ON FOREIGN RELATIONS....SEE
FOREIGNREL

UNITED NATIONS G1092,G1093

UNIV....UNIVERSAL TO MAN

UNIVERSAL REFERENCE SYSTEM G1094,G1095,G1096,G1097,G1098,G1099,
G1100,G1101

UNIVERSES....SEE UNIVERSES AND SAMPLING INDEX, P. XIV

UNIVERSITIES....SEE ACADEM

UNIVERSITIES RESEARCH ASSOCIATION, INC.....SEE UNIVS/RES

UNIVS/RES....UNIVERSITIES RESEARCH ASSOCIATION, INC.

UNLABR/PAR....UNION LABOR PARTY

UNPLAN/INT....IMPROMPTU INTERVIEW

UNR....UNION FOR THE NEW REPUBLIC

UNRRA....UNITED NATIONS RELIEF AND REHABILITATION AGENCY

UNRUH J.M. G1102

UNRWA....UNITED NATIONS RELIEF AND WORKS AGENCY

UNSF....UNITED NATIONS SPECIAL FUND

UPPER VOLTA....SEE UPPER/VOLT

UPPER/VOLT....UPPER VOLTA; SEE ALSO AFR

URBAN/LEAG....URBAN LEAGUE

URBAN/RNWL....URBAN RENEWAL

KAUFMAN J.L.,COMMUNITY RENEWAL PROGRAMS (PAMPHLET).   N19
USA+45 CONSTRUC PROVS CREATE PLAN CONTROL WEALTH 20   LOC/G
URBAN/RNWL. PAGE 30 G0584   MUNIC
                                                       ACT/RES
                                                       BIBLIOG

VERNON R.,THE MYTH AND REALITY OF OUR URBAN   N19
PROBLEMS (PAMPHLET). USA+45 SOCIETY LOC/G ADMIN   PLAN
COST 20 PRINCETN/U INTERVENT URBAN/RNWL. PAGE 61   MUNIC
G1197   HABITAT
                                                       PROB/SOLV

DRUCKER P.F.,AMERICA'S NEXT TWENTY YEARS. USA+45   B57
DIST/IND ACADEM MUNIC SCHOOL DIPLOM ECO/TAC AUTOMAT   WORKER
HABITAT HEALTH...SOC/WK TREND 20 URBAN/RNWL   FOR/AID
PUB/TRANS. PAGE 16 G0316   CENSUS
                                                       GEOG

SMITH H.H.,THE CITIZEN'S GUIDE TO PLANNING. USA+45   B61
LAW SCHOOL CREATE PROB/SOLV EDU/PROP GP/REL ROLE 20 MUNIC
URBAN/RNWL OPEN/SPACE. PAGE 52 G1015   PLAN
                                                       DELIB/GP
                                                       CONSULT

WHITE HOUSE CONFERENCE ON INTERNATIONAL   B65
COOPERATION(VOL.II). SPACE WOR+45 EXTR/IND INT/ORG   R+D
LABOR WORKER NUC/PWR PEACE AGE/Y...CENSUS ANTHOL 20   CONFER
RESOURCE/N URBAN/RNWL PUB/TRANS. PAGE 1 G0019   TEC/DEV
                                                       DIPLOM

ARTHUR D LITTLE INC,SAN FRANCISCO COMMUNITY RENEWAL   B65
PROGRAM. USA+45 FINAN PROVS ADMIN INCOME...CHARTS   HABITAT
20 CALIFORNIA SAN/FRAN URBAN/RNWL. PAGE 4 G0071   MUNIC
                                                       PLAN
                                                       PROB/SOLV

LECHT L.,GOAL, PRIORITIES, AND DOLLARS: THE NEXT   B66
DECADE. SPACE USA+45 SOCIETY AGRI BUDGET FOR/AID   IDEA/COMP
...HEAL SOC/WK STAT CHARTS 20 URBAN/RNWL PUB/TRANS.   POLICY
PAGE 33 G0649   CONSEN
                                                       PLAN

URUGUAY....URUGUAY

URWICK L. G0461

US AGENCY FOR INTERNATIONAL DEVELOPMENT....SEE US/AID

US ATOMIC ENERGY COMMISSION....SEE AEC

US ATTORNEY GENERAL....SEE ATTRNY/GEN

US BUREAU OF STANDARDS....SEE BUR/STNDRD

US BUREAU OF THE BUDGET....SEE BUR/BUDGET

US CIVIL AERONAUTICS BOARD....SEE CAB

US CONGRESS RULES COMMITTEES....SEE RULES/COMM

US DEPARTMENT OF AGRICULTURE....SEE DEPT/AGRI

US DEPARTMENT OF COMMERCE....SEE DEPT/COM

US DEPARTMENT OF DEFENSE....SEE DEPT/DEFEN

US DEPARTMENT OF HEALTH, EDUCATION, AND WELFARE....SEE DEPT/HEW

US DEPARTMENT OF HOUSING AND URBAN DEVELOPMENT....SEE DEPT/HUD

US DEPARTMENT OF JUSTICE....SEE DEPT/JUST

US DEPARTMENT OF LABOR AND INDUSTRY....SEE DEPT/LABOR

US DEPARTMENT OF STATE....SEE DEPT/STATE

US DEPARTMENT OF THE INTERIOR....SEE DEPT/INTER

US DEPARTMENT OF THE TREASURY....SEE DEPT/TREAS

US FEDERAL AVIATION AGENCY....SEE FAA

US FEDERAL BUREAU OF INVESTIGATION....SEE FBI

US FEDERAL COMMUNICATIONS COMMISSION....SEE FCC

US FEDERAL COUNCIL FOR SCIENCE AND TECHNOLOGY....SEE FEDSCI/TEC

US FEDERAL HOUSING ADMINISTRATION....SEE FHA

US FEDERAL OPEN MARKET COMMITTEE....SEE FED/OPNMKT

US FEDERAL RESERVE SYSTEM....SEE FED/RESERV

US FEDERAL TRADE COMMISSION....SEE FTC

US HOUSE COMMITTEE ON SCIENCE AND ASTRONAUTICS....SEE HS/SCIASTR

US HOUSE COMMITTEE ON UNAMERICAN ACTIVITIES....SEE HUAC

US HOUSE OF REPRESENTATIVES....SEE HOUSE/REP

US INFORMATION AGENCY....SEE USIA

US INTERNAL REVENUE SERVICE....SEE IRS

US INTERNATIONAL COOPERATION ADMINISTRATION....SEE ICA

US INTERSTATE COMMERCE COMMISSION....SEE ICC

US MILITARY ACADEMY....SEE WEST/POINT

US NATIONAL AERONAUTICS AND SPACE ADMINISTRATION....SEE NASA

US OFFICE OF ECONOMIC OPPORTUNITY....SEE OEO

US OFFICE OF NAVAL RESEARCH....SEE NAVAL/RES

US OFFICE OF PRICE ADMINISTRATION....SEE OPA

US OFFICE OF WAR INFORMATION....SEE OWI

US PATENT OFFICE....SEE PATENT/OFF

US PEACE CORPS....SEE PEACE/CORP

US SECRETARY OF STATE....SEE SEC/STATE

US SECURITIES AND EXCHANGE COMMISSION....SEE SEC/EXCHNG

US SENATE COMMITTEE ON AERONAUTICS AND SPACE....SEE SEN/SPACE

US SENATE SCIENCE ADVISORY COMMISSION....SEE SCI/ADVSRY

US SENATE....SEE SENATE

US SMALL BUSINESS ADMINISTRATION....SEE SBA

US SOUTH....SEE SOUTH/US

US STEEL CORPORATION....SEE US/STEEL

US AIR FORCE ACADEMY G1103

US AIR FORCE ACADEMY ASSEMBLY G1104

US ARMY LIBRARY G1105

US ATOMIC ENERGY COMMISSION G1106,G1107

US BUREAU OF THE BUDGET G1108

US CHAMBER OF COMMERCE G1109

US CONGRESS JT ATOM ENRGY COMM G1111,G1112,G1113,G1114,G1115

US CONGRESS JT COMM ECO GOVT G1116

US DEPARTMENT OF DEFENSE G1118

US DEPARTMENT OF LABOR G1119,G1120

US DEPARTMENT OF STATE G1121,G1122,G1123,G1124

US DEPARTMENT OF THE ARMY G1117, G1125,G1126,G1127,G1128,G1129, G1130,G1131,G1132,G1133,G1134

US DEPT COMMERCE OFF TECH SERV G1135

US FOOD AND DRUG ADMIN G1136

US HOUSE COMM APPROPRIATIONS G1137

US HOUSE COMM FOREIGN AFFAIRS G1138

US HOUSE COMM GOVT OPERATIONS G1139,G1140

US HOUSE COMM ON JUDICIARY G1141

US HOUSE COMM SCI ASTRONAUT G1142,G1143,G1144,G1145,G1146,G1147 G1148,G1149,G1150,G1151,G1152 ,G1153

US LIBRARY OF CONGRESS G1154,G1155,G1156

US OFFICE OF THE PRESIDENT G1157,G1158

US PRES COMM ECO IMPACT DEFENS G1159

US PRES COMN LAW ENFORCE-JUS G1160

US SEN SPEC COMM SPACE ASTRO G1161

US SENATE COMM AERO SPACE SCI G1110,G1162,G1163,G1164,G1165,G1166 G1167,G1168,G1169,G1170,G1171,G1172,G1173,G1174

US SENATE COMM APPROPRIATIONS G1175

US SENATE COMM GOVT OPERATIONS G1176,G1177,G1178,G1179

US SENATE COMM ON COMMERCE G1180

US SENATE COMM ON FOREIGN REL G1181,G1182,G1183,G1184,G1185 , G1186

US SENATE COMM ON PUBLIC WORKS G1187

US SUPERINTENDENT OF DOCUMENTS G1188,G1189,G1190

US/AID....UNITED STATES AGENCY FOR INTERNATIONAL DEVELOPMENT

US/HOUSING....UNITED STATES HOUSING CORPORATION

US/STEEL....UNITED STATES STEEL CORPORATION

US/WEST....WESTERN UNITED STATES

USA+45....UNITED STATES, 1945 TO PRESENT

USA-45....UNITED STATES, 1700 TO 1945

USIA....UNITED STATES INFORMATION AGENCY

USPNSKII/G....GLEB USPENSKII

USSR....UNION OF SOVIET SOCIALIST REPUBLICS; SEE ALSO RUSSIA, APPROPRIATE TIME/SPACE/CULTURE INDEX

N19
MEZERIK AG,OUTER SPACE: UN, US, USSR (PAMPHLET). SPACE
USSR DELIB/GP FORCES DETER NUC/PWR SOVEREIGN CONTROL
...POLICY 20 UN TREATY. PAGE 39 G0763 DIPLOM
INT/ORG

B38
HARPER S.N.,THE GOVERNMENT OF THE SOVIET UNION. COM MARXISM
USSR LAW CONSTN ECO/DEV PLAN TEC/DEV DIPLOM NAT/G
INT/TRADE ADMIN REV NAT/LISM...POLICY 20. PAGE 24 LEAD
G0483 POL/PAR

LASKI H.J.,REFLECTIONS ON THE REVOLUTIONS OF OUR TIME. COM USSR NAT/G WORKER UTOPIA ORD/FREE WEALTH MARXISM SOCISM 19/20. PAGE 32 G0637
CAP/ISM WELF/ST ECO/TAC POLICY
B43

BRODIE B.,THE OBSOLETE WEAPON: ATOMIC POWER AND WORLD ORDER. COM USA+45 USSR WOR+45 DELIB/GP PLAN ORD/FREE PWR...CONCPT TIME/SEQ TREND UN 20. PAGE 9 G0171
INT/ORG TEC/DEV ARMS/CONT NUC/PWR
B46

FOX W.T.R.,UNITED STATES POLICY IN A TWO POWER WORLD. COM USA+45 USSR FORCES DOMIN AGREE NEUTRAL NUC/PWR ORD/FREE SOVEREIGN 20 COLD/WAR TREATY EUROPE/W INTERVENT. PAGE 20 G0389
DIPLOM FOR/AID POLICY
N47

MANNHEIM K.,FREEDOM, POWER, AND DEMOCRATIC PLANNING. FUT USSR WOR+45 ELITES INTELL SOCIETY NAT/G EDU/PROP ROUTINE ATTIT DRIVE SUPEGO SKILL ...POLICY PSY CONCPT TREND GEN/LAWS 20. PAGE 35 G0700
TEC/DEV PLAN CAP/ISM UK
B50

LANGER W.L.,THE UNDECLARED WAR, 1940-1941. EUR+WWI GERMANY USA-45 USSR AIR FORCES TEC/DEV CONFER CONTROL COERCE PERCEPT ORD/FREE PWR 20 CHINJAP EUROPE. PAGE 32 G0634
WAR POLICY DIPLOM
B53

BUTOW R.J.C.,JAPAN'S DECISION TO SURRENDER. USA-45 USSR CHIEF FORCES DOMIN NUC/PWR...BIBLIOG 20 TREATY CHINJAP. PAGE 10 G0198
ELITES DIPLOM WAR PEACE
B54

US OFFICE OF THE PRESIDENT,REPORT TO CONGRESS ON THE MUTUAL SECURITY PROGRAM FOR THE SIX MONTHS ENDED DECEMBER 31, 1955. ASIA USSR ECO/DEV ECO/UNDEV INT/ORG CREATE TEC/DEV BAL/PWR ECO/TAC AGREE DETER COST ORD/FREE 20 DEPT/STATE DEPT/DEFEN EISNHWR/DD. PAGE 59 G1158
DIPLOM FORCES PLAN FOR/AID
B56

VUCINICH A.,THE SOVIET ACADEMY OF SCIENCES. USSR STRUCT ACADEM NAT/G EDU/PROP ADMIN LEAD ROLE ...BIBLIOG 20 ACADEM/SCI. PAGE 61 G1203
PHIL/SCI CREATE INTELL PROF/ORG
B56

ANGELL N.,DEFENCE AND THE ENGLISH-SPEAKING ROLE. CHINA/COM UK USSR INT/ORG FORCES EDU/PROP NEUTRAL NUC/PWR NAT/LISM PEACE TOTALISM 20 COLD/WAR COEXIST. PAGE 3 G0059
DIPLOM WAR MARXISM ORD/FREE
B58

GAVIN J.M.,WAR AND PEACE IN THE SPACE AGE. SPACE USA+45 USSR FORCES PLAN TEC/DEV BAL/PWR DIPLOM ARMS/CONT WEAPON CIVMIL/REL...CHARTS GP/COMP 20 NATO COLD/WAR. PAGE 21 G0414
WAR DETER NUC/PWR PEACE
B58

MARCUSE H.,SOVIET MARXISM, A CRITICAL ANALYSIS. USSR CONSTN PLAN PRODUC RATIONAL SOCISM...IDEA/COMP 20 COM/PARTY. PAGE 36 G0703
MARXISM ATTIT POLICY
B58

DAVENPORT J.,"ARMS AND THE WELFARE STATE." INTELL STRUCT FORCES CREATE ECO/TAC FOR/AID DOMIN LEGIT ADMIN WAR ORD/FREE PWR...POLICY SOC CONCPT MYTH OBS TREND COLD/WAR TOT/POP 20. PAGE 14 G0276
USA+45 NAT/G USSR
S58

AIR FORCE ACADEMY ASSEMBLY '59,INTERNATIONAL STABILITY AND PROGRESS (PAMPHLET). USA+45 USSR ECO/UNDEV PROB/SOLV BUDGET DIPLOM ADMIN DETER COST ATTIT...TREND 20. PAGE 2 G0030
FOR/AID FORCES WAR PLAN
B59

EMME E.M.,THE IMPACT OF AIR POWER - NATIONAL SECURITY AND WORLD POLITICS. USA+45 USSR FORCES DIPLOM WEAPON PEACE TOTALISM...POLICY NAT/COMP 20 EUROPE. PAGE 18 G0346
DETER AIR WAR ORD/FREE
B59

MODELSKI G.,ATOMIC ENERGY IN THE COMMUNIST BLOC. FUT INT/ORG CONSULT FORCES ACT/RES PLAN KNOWL SKILL ...PHIL/SCI STAT CHARTS 20. PAGE 39 G0777
TEC/DEV NUC/PWR USSR COM
B59

POKROVSKY G.I.,SCIENCE AND TECHNOLOGY IN CONTEMPORARY WAR. SPACE USSR WOR+45 NAT/G CONSULT FORCES
TEC/DEV FORCES
B59

ACT/RES PLAN DETER WEAPON...MARXIST METH/CNCPT CHARTS STERTYP COLD/WAR 20. PAGE 45 G0881
NUC/PWR WAR

COLUMBIA U BUREAU APPL SOC R, ATTITUDES OF PROMINENT AMERICANS TOWARD "WORLD PEACE THROUGH WORLD LAW" (SUPRA-NATL ORGANIZATION FOR WAR PREVENTION). USA+45 USSR ELITES FORCES PLAN PROB/SOLV CONTROL WAR PWR...POLICY SOC QU IDEA/COMP 20 UN. PAGE 45 G0888
ATTIT ACT/RES INT/LAW STAT
B59

BENDIX R.,"INDUSTRIALIZATION, IDEOLOGIES, AND SOCIAL STRUCTURE" (BMR)" UK USA-45 USSR STRUCT WORKER GP/REL EFFICIENCY...IDEA/COMP 20. PAGE 6 G0117
INDUS ATTIT MGT ADMIN
S59

MILBURN T.W.,"WHAT CONSTITUTES EFFECTIVE DETERRENCE." USA+45 USSR WOR+45 STRUCT FORCES ACT/RES PLAN SUPEGO KNOWL ORD/FREE PWR...RELATIV PSY CONCPT VAL/FREE 20 COLD/WAR. PAGE 39 G0768
INTELL ATTIT DETER NUC/PWR
S59

BARNET R.,WHO WANTS DISARMAMENT. COM EUR+WWI USA+45 USSR INT/ORG NAT/G BAL/PWR DIPLOM EDU/PROP COERCE DETER NUC/PWR WAR WEAPON ATTIT PWR...TIME/SEQ COLD/WAR CONGRESS 20. PAGE 5 G0096
PLAN FORCES ARMS/CONT
B60

CARPENTER E.,EXPLORATIONS IN COMMUNICATION. USSR CULTURE SCHOOL SECT EDU/PROP PRESS TV AUTOMAT FEEDBACK ATTIT PERSON...ART/METH PSY 20. PAGE 11 G0211
ANTHOL COM/IND TEC/DEV WRITING
B60

GRANICK D.,THE RED EXECUTIVE. COM USA+45 SOCIETY ECO/DEV INDUS NAT/G POL/PAR EX/STRUC PLAN ECO/TAC EDU/PROP ADMIN EXEC ATTIT DRIVE...GP/COMP 20. PAGE 22 G0440
PWR STRATA USSR ELITES
B60

PARRY A.,RUSSIA'S ROCKETS AND MISSILES. COM FUT GERMANY USA+45 WOR+45 INTELL ECO/DEV ACT/RES NUC/PWR WEAPON ATTIT ALL/VALS...OBS TIME/SEQ COLD/WAR 20. PAGE 44 G0859
PLAN TEC/DEV SPACE USSR
B60

BRENNAN D.G.,"SETTING AND GOALS OF ARMS CONTROL." FUT USA+45 USSR WOR+45 INTELL INT/ORG NAT/G VOL/ASSN CONSULT PLAN DIPLOM ECO/TAC ADMIN KNOWL PWR...POLICY CONCPT TREND COLD/WAR 20. PAGE 8 G0164
FORCES COERCE ARMS/CONT DETER
L60

JACOB P.E.,"THE DISARMAMENT CONSENSUS." USA+45 USSR WOR+45 INT/ORG NAT/G ACT/RES TEC/DEV BAL/PWR EDU/PROP ADMIN COERCE DETER NUC/PWR CONSEN RIGID/FLEX PWR...CONCPT RECORD CHARTS COLD/WAR 20. PAGE 28 G0552
DELIB/GP ATTIT ARMS/CONT
L60

BECKER A.S.,"COMPARISIONS OF UNITED STATES AND USSR NATIONAL OUTPUT: SOME RULES OF THE GAME." COM USA+45 ECO/DEV AGRI DIST/IND INDUS R+D CONSULT PLAN ECO/TAC RIGID/FLEX KNOWL...METH/CNCPT CHARTS 20. PAGE 6 G0113
STAT USSR
S60

DOUGHERTY J.E.,"KEY TO SECURITY: DISARMAMENT OR ARMS STABILITY." COM USA+45 USSR INT/ORG NAT/G CREATE EDU/PROP COERCE DETER ATTIT PWR...DECISION CONCPT MYTH NEW/IDEA TREND 20 COLD/WAR. PAGE 16 G0311
FORCES ORD/FREE ARMS/CONT NUC/PWR
S60

KELLEY G.A.,"THE POLITICAL BACKGROUND OF THE FRENCH A-BOMB." EUR+WWI USSR FORCES TOP/EX TEC/DEV NUC/PWR ATTIT PWR...CONCPT OBS/ENVIR TREND 20. PAGE 30 G0591
NAT/G RESPECT NAT/LISM FRANCE
S60

YEMELYANOV V.S.,"ATOMIC ENERGY FOR PEACE: THE USSR AND INTERNATIONAL CO-OPERATION." FUT USSR WOR+45 R+D CREATE EDU/PROP...CONCPT GEN/LAWS 20. PAGE 64 G1264
VOL/ASSN TEC/DEV ARMS/CONT NUC/PWR
S60

HENKIN L.,ARMS CONTROL: ISSUES FOR THE PUBLIC. EUR+WWI FUT USA+45 USSR INT/ORG NAT/G DIPLOM EDU/PROP DETER NUC/PWR ATTIT PWR...CONCPT RECORD HIST/WRIT TIME/SEQ TOT/POP COLD/WAR 20. PAGE 26 G0506
WOR+45 DELIB/GP ARMS/CONT
B61

HODGKINS J.A.,SOVIET POWER: ENERGY RESOURCES, PRODUCTION AND POTENTIALS. USSR ECO/DEV INDUS
GEOG EXTR/IND
B61

MARKET...POLICY STAT CHARTS 20 RESOURCE/N. PAGE 26 TEC/DEV
G0518

B61
NOGEE J.L.,SOVIET POLICY TOWARD INTERNATIONAL INT/ORG
CONTROL OF ATOMIC ENERGY. COM USA+45 WOR+45 INTELL ATTIT
NAT/G ACT/RES DIPLOM EDU/PROP NUC/PWR TOTALISM ARMS/CONT
PERCEPT KNOWL PWR...TIME/SEQ COLD/WAR 20. PAGE 42 USSR
G0824

B61
NOVE A.,THE SOVIET ECONOMY. USSR ECO/DEV FINAN PLAN
NAT/G ECO/TAC PRICE ADMIN EFFICIENCY MARXISM PRODUC
...TREND BIBLIOG 20. PAGE 42 G0828 POLICY

B61
SCHMIDT H.,VERTEIDIGUNG ODER VERGELTUNG. COM CUBA PLAN
GERMANY/W USSR FORCES DIPLOM ARMS/CONT DETER WAR
NUC/PWR...POLICY CHARTS HYPO/EXP SIMUL BIBLIOG 20 BAL/PWR
NATO COLD/WAR. PAGE 49 G0970 ORD/FREE

B62
SOVIET STAND ON DISARMAMENT. COM EUR+WWI FUT USA+45 ACT/RES
NAT/G TOP/EX NUC/PWR PEACE ATTIT...POLICY CONCPT ORD/FREE
TOT/POP 20. PAGE 1 G0016 ARMS/CONT
USSR

B62
FRIEDRICH-EBERT-STIFTUNG,THE SOVIET BLOC AND MARXISM
DEVELOPING COUNTRIES. CHINA/COM COM GERMANY/E USSR DIPLOM
WOR+45 ECO/UNDEV INT/ORG NAT/G TEC/DEV NEUTRAL PWR ECO/TAC
...POLICY 20. PAGE 20 G0394 FOR/AID

B62
FRYKLUND R.,100 MILLION LIVES: MAXIMUM SURVIVAL IN NUC/PWR
A NUCLEAR WAR. USA+45 USSR CONTROL WEAPON WAR
...IDEA/COMP NAT/COMP 20. PAGE 20 G0397 PLAN
DETER

B62
STRAUSS L.L.,MEN AND DECISIONS. USA+45 USA-45 USSR DECISION
CONSULT FORCES TOP/EX WAR PEACE 20. PAGE 53 G1042 PWR
NUC/PWR
DIPLOM

S62
BETHE H.,"DISARMAMENT AND STRATEGY." COM USA+45 PLAN
USSR WOR+45 VOL/ASSN TEC/DEV EDU/PROP NUC/PWR ORD/FREE
CHOOSE PEACE...POLICY DECISION NEW/IDEA OBS ARMS/CONT
GEN/LAWS COLD/WAR 420. PAGE 7 G0133 DIPLOM

S62
FOSTER W.C.,"ARMS CONTROL AND DISARMAMENT IN A DELIB/GP
DIVIDED WORLD." COM FUT USA+45 USSR WOR+45 INTELL POLICY
INT/ORG NAT/G VOL/ASSN CONSULT CREATE PLAN TEC/DEV ARMS/CONT
EDU/PROP LEGIT NUC/PWR ATTIT RIGID/FLEX...CONCPT DIPLOM
TREND TOT/POP 20 UN. PAGE 20 G0387

S62
GORDON B.K.,"NUCLEAR WEAPONS: RUSSIAN AND ORD/FREE
AMERICAN." COM USA+45 USSR NAT/G FORCES ACT/RES COERCE
TEC/DEV PERCEPT RIGID/FLEX PWR SKILL...MGT NUC/PWR
METH/CNCPT QUANT OBS TIME/SEQ CON/ANAL GEN/METH
TOT/POP VAL/FREE 20. PAGE 22 G0433

S62
NANES A.,"DISARMAMENT: THE LAST SEVEN YEARS." COM DELIB/GP
EUR+WWI USA+45 USSR INT/ORG FORCES TOP/EX CREATE RIGID/FLEX
LEGIT NUC/PWR DISPL ORD/FREE...CONCPT TIME/SEQ ARMS/CONT
CON/ANAL 20. PAGE 41 G0803

C62
JOINT ECONOMIC COMMITTEE,"DIMENSIONS OF SOVIET ECO/DEV
ECONOMIC POWER." USSR R+D FORCES ACT/RES OP/RES PLAN
TEC/DEV...GEOG STAT BIBLIOG 20. PAGE 29 G0565 PRODUC
LABOR

N62
US CONGRESS JT ATOM ENRGY COMM,PEACEFUL USES OF NUC/PWR
ATOMIC ENERGY. HEARING. USA+45 USSR TEC/DEV ATTIT ACADEM
RIGID/FLEX...TESTS CHARTS EXHIBIT METH/COMP 20 SCHOOL
CONGRESS. PAGE 57 G1112 NAT/COMP

B63
NORTH R.C.,CONTENT ANALYSIS: A HANDBOOK WITH METH/CNCPT
APPLICATIONS FOR THE STUDY OF INTERNATIONAL CRISIS. COMPUT/IR
ASIA COM EUR+WWI MOD/EUR INT/ORG TEC/DEV DOMIN USSR
EDU/PROP ROUTINE COERCE PERCEPT RIGID/FLEX ALL/VALS
...QUANT TESTS CON/ANAL SIMUL GEN/LAWS VAL/FREE.
PAGE 42 G0825

B63
US ATOMIC ENERGY COMMISSION,ATOMIC ENERGY IN THE METH/COMP
SOVIET UNION: TRIP REPORT OF THE US ATOMIC ENERGY OP/RES
DELEGATION, MAY 1933. USSR R+D NAT/G CONSULT CREATE TEC/DEV
DIPLOM ADMIN ROUTINE EFFICIENCY PRODUC KNOWL SKILL NUC/PWR

...NAT/COMP 20 AEC TRAVEL TREATY. PAGE 56 G1107

B63
US DEPARTMENT OF THE ARMY,SOVIET RUSSIA: STRATEGIC BIBLIOG/A
SURVEY (PAMPHLET). USSR POL/PAR PLAN DOMIN EDU/PROP MARXISM
ARMS/CONT GUERRILLA WAR WEAPON...TREND CHARTS DIPLOM
ORG/CHARTS 20. PAGE 57 G1129 COERCE

B63
US SENATE,DOCUMENTS ON INTERNATIONAL ASPECTS OF SPACE
EXPLORATION AND USE OF OUTER SPACE. 1954-62: STAFF UTIL
REPORT FOR COMM AERON SPACE SCI. USA+45 USSR LEGIS GOV/REL
LEAD CIVMIL/REL PEACE...POLICY INT/LAW ANTHOL 20 DIPLOM
CONGRESS NASA KHRUSH/N. PAGE 59 G1162

S63
DELLIN L.A.D.,"BULGARIA UNDER SOVIET LEADERSHIP." AGRI
BULGARIA COM USA+45 USSR ECO/DEV INDUS POL/PAR NAT/G
EX/STRUC TOP/EX COERCE ATTIT RIGID/FLEX...POLICY TOTALISM
TIME/SEQ 20. PAGE 15 G0293

S63
GARDNER R.N.,"COOPERATION IN OUTER SPACE." FUT USSR INT/ORG
WOR+45 AIR LAW COM/IND CONSULT DELIB/GP CREATE ACT/RES
KNOWL 20 TREATY. PAGE 21 G0410 PEACE
SPACE

S63
HOSKINS H.L.,"ARAB SOCIALISM IN THE UAR." ISLAM ECO/DEV
USSR AGRI INDUS NAT/G TOP/EX CREATE DIPLOM EDU/PROP PLAN
DRIVE KNOWL PWR SOCISM...POLICY CONCPT TREND SUEZ UAR
20. PAGE 27 G0530

S63
KAWALKOWSKI A.,"POUR UNE EUROPE INDEPENDENTE ET R+D
REUNIFIEE." EUR+WWI FUT USA+45 USSR WOR+45 ECO/DEV PLAN
PROC/MFG INT/ORG NAT/G ACT/RES TEC/DEV FEDERAL NUC/PWR
RIGID/FLEX...CONCPT METH/CNCPT OEEC TOT/POP 20
DEGAULLE/C. PAGE 30 G0587

S63
PHELPS J.,"INFORMATION AND ARMS CONTROL." COM SPACE KNOWL
USA+45 USSR WOR+45 R+D INT/ORG NAT/G DELIB/GP ARMS/CONT
DIPLOM ORD/FREE...CONCPT 20. PAGE 45 G0875 NUC/PWR

S63
TASHJEAN J.E.,"RESEARCH ON ARMS CONTROL." COM NAT/G
USA+45 USSR FORCES ACT/RES PLAN DOMIN COERCE POLICY
ORD/FREE PWR...TIME/SEQ GEN/LAWS 20 COLD/WAR. ARMS/CONT
PAGE 53 G1053

S63
WILES P.J.D.,"WILL CAPITALISM AND COMMUNISM PLAN
SPONTANEOUSLY CONVERGE." COM FUT USA+45 ECO/DEV TEC/DEV
DIST/IND MARKET CAP/ISM ECO/TAC RIGID/FLEX WEALTH USSR
MARXISM SOCISM...MATH STAT TREND COMPUT/IR 20.
PAGE 63 G1240

B64
BROWN N.,NUCLEAR WAR* THE IMPENDING STRATEGIC FORCES
DEADLOCK. USA+45 USSR TEC/DEV BUDGET RISK ARMS/CONT OP/RES
NUC/PWR WEAPON COST BIO/SOC...GEOG IDEA/COMP WAR
NAT/COMP GAME NATO WARSAW/P. PAGE 9 G0177 GEN/LAWS

B64
COHEN M.,LAW AND POLITICS IN SPACE: SPECIFIC AND DELIB/GP
URGENT PROBLEMS IN THE LAW OF OUTER SPACE. LAW
CHINA/COM COM USA+45 USSR WOR+45 COM/IND INT/ORG INT/LAW
NAT/G LEGIT NUC/PWR ATTIT BIO/SOC...JURID CONCPT SPACE
CONGRESS 20 STALIN/J. PAGE 12 G0241

B64
OSSENBECK F.J.,OPEN SPACE AND PEACE. CHINA/COM FUT SPACE
USA+45 USSR LAW PROB/SOLV TEC/DEV EDU/PROP NEUTRAL ORD/FREE
PEACE...AUD/VIS ANTHOL 20. PAGE 43 G0850 DIPLOM
CREATE

L64
WARD C.,"THE 'NEW MYTHS' AND 'OLD REALITIES' OF FORCES
NUCLEAR WAR." COM FUT USA+45 USSR WOR+45 INT/ORG COERCE
NAT/G DOMIN LEGIT EXEC ATTIT PERCEPT ALL/VALS ARMS/CONT
...POLICY RELATIV PSY MYTH TREND 20. PAGE 62 G1212 NUC/PWR

S64
FLORINSKY M.T.,"TRENDS IN THE SOVIET ECONOMY." COM ECO/DEV
USA+45 USSR INDUS LABOR NAT/G PLAN TEC/DEV ECO/TAC AGRI
ALL/VALS SOCISM...MGT METH/CNCPT STYLE CON/ANAL
GEN/METH WORK 20. PAGE 19 G0374

S64
KASSOF A.,"THE ADMINISTERED SOCIETY: SOCIETY
TOTALITARIANISM WITHOUT TERROR." COM USSR STRATA DOMIN
AGRI INDUS NAT/G PERF/ART SCHOOL TOP/EX EDU/PROP TOTALISM
ADMIN ORD/FREE PWR...POLICY SOC TIME/SEQ GEN/LAWS
VAL/FREE 20. PAGE 29 G0580

S64

MAGGS P.B.,"SOVIET VIEWPOINT ON NUCLEAR WEAPONS IN INTERNATIONAL LAW." USSR WOR+45 INT/ORG FORCES DIPLOM ARMS/CONT ATTIT ORD/FREE PWR...POLICY JURID CONCPT OBS TREND CON/ANAL GEN/LAWS VAL/FREE 20. PAGE 35 G0694
COM
LAW
INT/LAW
NUC/PWR

S64

MARES V.E.,"EAST EUROPE'S SECOND CHANCE." COM EUR+WWI HUNGARY ROMANIA USSR YUGOSLAVIA ECO/UNDEV NAT/G TOP/EX CREATE PLAN TEC/DEV REGION NAT/LISM RIGID/FLEX PWR...CONCPT STAT COMECON 20. PAGE 36 G0705
VOL/ASSN
ECO/TAC

B65

BLOOMFIELD L.,SOVIET INTERESTS IN ARMS CONTROL AND DISARMAMENT* THE DECADE UNDER KHRUSHCHEV 1954-1964. ASIA FORCES ACT/RES EDU/PROP DETER NUC/PWR WEAPON COST ATTIT...PHIL/SCI CLASSIF STAT NET/THEORY GAME BIBLIOG. PAGE 7 G0139
USSR
ARMS/CONT
DIPLOM
TREND

B65

CHENG C.-.Y.,SCIENTIFIC AND ENGINEERING MANPOWER IN COMMUNIST CHINA. 1949-1963. CHINA/COM USSR ELITES ECO/DEV R+D ACADEM LABOR NAT/G EDU/PROP CONTROL UTIL...POLICY BIBLIOG 20. PAGE 12 G0226
WORKER
CONSULT
MARXISM
BIOG

B65

GRETTON P.,MARITIME STRATEGY - A STUDY OF DEFENSE PROBLEMS. ASIA UK USSR DIPLOM COERCE DETER NUC/PWR WEAPON...CONCPT NAT/COMP 20. PAGE 23 G0449
FORCES
PLAN
WAR
SEA

B65

HALPERIN M.H.,CHINA AND THE BOMB. USA+45 USSR INT/ORG FORCES ARMS/CONT DETER PRODUC ORD/FREE PWR TREND. PAGE 24 G0472
ASIA
NUC/PWR
WAR
DIPLOM

B65

JASNY H.,KHRUSHCHEV'S CROP POLICY. USSR ECO/DEV PLAN MARXISM...STAT 20 KHRUSH/N RESOURCE/N. PAGE 29 G0562
AGRI
NAT/G
POLICY
ECO/TAC

B65

KANTOROVICH L.V.,THE BEST USE OF ECONOMIC RESOURCES. USSR SOCIETY FINAN ACT/RES TEC/DEV ECO/TAC PRICE CONTROL COST DEMAND EFFICIENCY OPTIMAL...MGT STAT. PAGE 29 G0572
PLAN
MATH
DECISION

B65

KOROL A.G.,SOVIET RESEARCH AND DEVELOPMENT. USSR ACADEM SCHOOL WORKER ROUTINE COST...STAT T 20. PAGE 31 G0615
COM
R+D
FINAN
DIST/IND

B65

US DEPARTMENT OF DEFENSE,US SECURITY ARMS CONTROL, AND DISARMAMENT 1961-1965 (PAMPHLET). CHINA/COM COM GERMANY/W ISRAEL SPACE USA+45 USSR WOR+45 FORCES EDU/PROP DETER EQUILIB PEACE ALL/VALS...GOV/COMP 20 NATO. PAGE 57 G1118
BIBLIOG/A
ARMS/CONT
NUC/PWR
DIPLOM

S65

ABT C.C.,"CONTROLLING FUTURE ARMS." USSR PLAN BAL/PWR DIPLOM NUC/PWR COST...CLASSIF STAT CHARTS. PAGE 2 G0027
PREDICT
FUT
ARMS/CONT
TEC/DEV

S65

GOLDSTEIN W.,"KEEPING THE GENIE IN THE BOTTLE* THE FEASIBILITY OF A NUCLEAR NON-PROLIFERATION AGREEMENT." ASIA FRANCE UK USA+45 USSR WOR+45 ECO/UNDEV VOL/ASSN ACT/RES PLAN RISK ARMS/CONT WAR PEACE ATTIT PERCEPT...RECORD TREND TIME. PAGE 22 G0429
NUC/PWR
CREATE
COST

S65

HOLSTI O.R.,"EAST-WEST CONFLICT AND SINO-SOVIET RELATIONS" CHINA/COM USSR COMPUTER REGION DECISION. PAGE 27 G0523
VOL/ASSN
DIPLOM
CON/ANAL
COM

S65

HSIEH A.L.,"THE SINO-SOVIET NUCLEAR DIALOGUE* 1963." S/ASIA USA+45 RISK DETER REV WAR SOVEREIGN IDEA/COMP. PAGE 27 G0533
ASIA
USSR
NUC/PWR

S65

KINTNER W.P.,"THE PROSPECTS FOR WESTERN SCIENCE AND TECHNOLOGY." EUR+WWI FRANCE USA+45 USSR R+D NUC/PWR NATO. PAGE 30 G0598
TEC/DEV
VOL/ASSN
STAT
RECORD

S65

KOHL W.L.,"NUCLEAR SHARING IN NATO AND THE MULTILATERAL FORCE." FUT USSR VOL/ASSN TEC/DEV DIPLOM NUC/PWR WAR WEAPON NATO. PAGE 31 G0611
ARMS/CONT
OBS
IDEA/COMP

S65

SCHELLING T.C.,"SIGNALS AND FEEDBACK IN THE ARMS DIALOGUE." USA+45 USSR R+D ACADEM FORCES ACT/RES ADJUST COST GEN/LAWS. PAGE 49 G0964
FEEDBACK
DETER
EDU/PROP
ARMS/CONT

S65

STAAR R.F.,"RETROGRESSION IN POLAND." COM USSR AGRI INDUS NAT/G CREATE EDU/PROP TOTALISM RIGID/FLEX ORD/FREE PWR SOCISM...RECORD CHARTS 20. PAGE 52 G1029
TOP/EX
ECO/TAC
POLAND

B66

BLOOMFIELD L.P.,KHRUSHCHEV AND THE ARMS RACE. USA+45 USSR ECO/DEV BAL/PWR EDU/PROP CONFER NUC/PWR ATTIT...CHARTS 20 KHRUSH/N. PAGE 7 G0143
ARMS/CONT
COM
POLICY
DIPLOM

B66

BRODIE B.,ESCALATION AND THE NUCLEAR OPTION. ASIA CUBA EUR+WWI KOREA USA+45 USSR VIETNAM RISK ATTIT DRIVE PERCEPT PROBABIL. PAGE 9 G0172
NUC/PWR
GUERRILLA
WAR
DETER

B66

ECKSTEIN A.,COMMUNIST CHINA'S ECONOMIC GROWTH AND FOREIGN TRADE* IMPLICATIONS FOR US POLICY. COM USA+45 USSR STRUCT INDUS MARKET DIPLOM ECO/TAC FOR/AID INT/TRADE...STAT CHARTS. PAGE 17 G0332
ASIA
ECO/UNDEV
CREATE
PWR

B66

HALPERIN M.H.,CHINA AND NUCLEAR PROLIFERATION (PAMPHLET). CHINA/COM FUT INDIA USA+45 USSR ARMS/CONT WAR 20 CHINJAP. PAGE 24 G0474
NUC/PWR
FORCES
POLICY
DIPLOM

B66

JACOBSON H.K.,DIPLOMATS, SCIENTISTS, AND POLITICIANS* THE UNITED STATES AND THE NUCLEAR TEST BAN NEGOTIATIONS. USA+45 USSR ACT/RES PLAN CONFER DETER NUC/PWR CONSEN ORD/FREE...INT TREATY. PAGE 28 G0554
DIPLOM
ARMS/CONT
TECHRACY
INT/ORG

B66

KUENNE R.E.,THE POLARIS MISSILE STRIKE* A GENERAL ECONOMIC SYSTEMS ANALYSIS. USA+45 USSR NAT/G BAL/PWR ARMS/CONT WAR...MATH PROBABIL COMPUT/IR CHARTS HYPO/EXP SIMUL. PAGE 32 G0625
NUC/PWR
FORCES
DETER
DIPLOM

B66

KURAKOV I.G.,SCIENCE, TECHNOLOGY AND COMMUNISM; SOME QUESTIONS OF DEVELOPMENT (TRANS. BY CARIN DEDIJER). USSR INDUS PLAN PROB/SOLV COST PRODUC ...MGT MATH CHARTS METH 20. PAGE 32 G0626
CREATE
TEC/DEV
MARXISM
ECO/TAC

B66

VON BORCH H,FRIEDE TROTZ KRIEG. GERMANY USSR WOR+45 PEACE ANOMIE ATTIT 20. PAGE 43 G0853
DIPLOM
NUC/PWR
WAR
COERCE

B66

STONE J.J.,CONTAINING THE ARMS RACE* SOME SPECIFIC PROPOSALS. ASIA USA+45 USSR PROB/SOLV BARGAIN DIPLOM DETER NUC/PWR RATIONAL...GAME 20 DEPT/DEFEN TREATY. PAGE 53 G1038
ARMS/CONT
FEEDBACK
COST
ATTIT

B66

US DEPARTMENT OF THE ARMY,COMMUNIST CHINA: A STRATEGIC SURVEY: A BIBLIOGRAPHY (PAMPHLET NO. 20-67). CHINA/COM COM INDIA USSR NAT/G POL/PAR EX/STRUC FORCES NUC/PWR REV ATTIT...POLICY GEOG CHARTS. PAGE 58 G1133
BIBLIOG/A
MARXISM
S/ASIA
DIPLOM

B66

US SENATE COMM AERO SPACE SCI,SOVIET SPACE PROGRAMS, 1962-65; GOALS AND PURPOSES, ACHIEVEMENTS, PLANS, AND INTERNATIONAL IMPLICATIONS. USA+45 USSR R+D FORCES PLAN EDU/PROP PRESS ADJUD ARMS/CONT ATTIT MARXISM. PAGE 60 G1168
CONSULT
SPACE
FUT
DIPLOM

S66

BROWNLIE I.,"NUCLEAR PROLIFERATION* SOME PROBLEMS OF CONTROL." USA+45 USSR ECO/UNDEV INT/ORG FORCES TEC/DEV REGION CONSEN...RECORD TREATY. PAGE 9 G0181
NUC/PWR
ARMS/CONT
VOL/ASSN
ORD/FREE

S66

TURKEVICH J.,"SOVIET SCIENCE APPRAISED." USA+45 R+D USSR ACADEM FORCES DIPLOM EDU/PROP WAR EFFICIENCY PEACE SKILL OBS. PAGE 55 G1081
TEC/DEV
NAT/COMP

ATTIT

PLAN

B67
FIELD M.G.,SOVIET SOCIALIZED MEDICINE. USSR FINAN
R+D PROB/SOLV ADMIN SOCISM...MGT SOC CONCPT 20.
PAGE 19 G0366
PUB/INST
HEALTH
NAT/G
MARXISM

B67
GROSSMAN G.,ECONOMIC SYSTEMS. USA+45 USA-45 USSR
YUGOSLAVIA WORKER CAP/ISM PRICE GP/REL EQUILIB
WEALTH MARXISM SOCISM...MGT METH/COMP 19/20.
PAGE 23 G0456
ECO/DEV
PLAN
TEC/DEV
DEMAND

B67
HALLE L.J.,THE COLD WAR AS HISTORY. USSR WOR+45
ECO/TAC FOR/AID NUC/PWR WAR PEACE ORD/FREE
...MAJORIT TREND 20 COLD/WAR KENNEDY/JF KHRUSH/N
BERLIN/BLO. PAGE 24 G0470
DIPLOM
BAL/PWR

B67
HARDT J.P.,MATHEMATICS AND COMPUTERS IN SOVIET
ECONOMIC PLANNING. COM USSR OP/RES PROB/SOLV
OPTIMAL...MODAL SIMUL 20. PAGE 24 G0481
PLAN
TEC/DEV
MATH
COMPUT/IR

B67
MACKINTOSH J.M.,JUGGERNAUT. USSR NAT/G POL/PAR
ADMIN LEAD CIVMIL/REL COST TOTALISM PWR MARXISM
...GOV/COMP 20. PAGE 35 G0691
WAR
FORCES
COM
PROF/ORG

B67
MAZOUR A.G.,SOVIET ECONOMIC DEVELOPMENT: OPERATION
OUTSTRIP: 1921-1965. USSR ECO/UNDEV FINAN CHIEF
WORKER PROB/SOLV CONTROL PRODUC MARXISM...CHARTS
ORG/CHARTS 20 STALIN/J. PAGE 37 G0726
ECO/TAC
AGRI
INDUS
PLAN

B67
MCBRIDE J.H.,THE TEST BAN TREATY: MILITARY,
TECHNOLOGICAL, AND POLITICAL IMPLICATIONS. USA+45
USSR DELIB/GP FORCES LEGIS TEC/DEV BAL/PWR TREATY.
PAGE 37 G0727
ARMS/CONT
DIPLOM
NUC/PWR

B67
POMEROY W.J.,HALF A CENTURY OF SOCIALISM. USSR LAW
AGRI INDUS NAT/G CREATE DIPLOM EDU/PROP PERSON
ORD/FREE WEALTH...POLICY TREND 20. PAGE 45 G0884
SOCISM
MARXISM
COM
SOCIETY

B67
US SUPERINTENDENT OF DOCUMENTS,LIBRARY OF CONGRESS
(PRICE LIST 83). AFR ASIA EUR+WWI USA-45 USSR NAT/G
DIPLOM CONFER CT/SYS WAR...DECISION PHIL/SCI
CLASSIF 19/20 CONGRESS PRESIDENT. PAGE 61 G1189
BIBLIOG/A
USA+45
AUTOMAT
LAW

L67
ROBINSON T.W.,"A NATIONAL INTEREST ANALYSIS OF
SINO-SOVIET RELATIONS." CHINA/COM USSR NAT/G
NUC/PWR ATTIT PWR...CONCPT CHARTS 20. PAGE 47 G0931
MARXISM
DIPLOM
SOVEREIGN
GEN/LAWS

S67
"CHINESE STATEMENT ON NUCLEAR PROLIFERATION."
CHINA/COM USA+45 USSR DOMIN COLONIAL PWR. PAGE 1
G0022
NUC/PWR
BAL/PWR
ARMS/CONT
DIPLOM

S67
AVTORKHANOV A.,"A NEW AGRARIAN REVOLUTION." COM
USSR ECO/DEV PLAN TEC/DEV ADMIN CONTROL OPTIMAL
WEALTH SOCISM 20 KHRUSH/N STALIN/J. PAGE 4 G0082
AGRI
METH/COMP
MARXISM
OWN

S67
CARR E.H.,"REVOLUTION FROM ABOVE." USSR STRATA
FINAN INDUS NAT/G DOMIN LEAD GP/REL INGP/REL OWN
PRODUC PWR 20 STALIN/J. PAGE 11 G0214
AGRI
POLICY
COM
EFFICIENCY

S67
CLEMENS W.C.,"CHINESE NUCLEAR TESTS: TRENDS AND
PORTENTS." CHINA/COM USA+45 USSR FORCES PLAN
TEC/DEV ARMS/CONT WAR PWR...DECISION 20 MAO
KHRUSH/N. PAGE 12 G0234
NUC/PWR
WEAPON
POLICY
DIPLOM

S67
COFFEY J.I.,"THE ANTI-BALLISTIC MISSILE DEBATE."
USA+45 USSR TEC/DEV BAL/PWR 20. PAGE 12 G0238
ARMS/CONT
NUC/PWR
DETER
DIPLOM

S67
HAZARD J.N.,"POST-DISARMAMENT INTERNATIONAL LAW."
FUT USSR WOR+45 INT/ORG DELIB/GP FORCES DETER
EQUILIB SOVEREIGN MARXISM 20 UN. PAGE 25 G0496
INT/LAW
ARMS/CONT
PWR

S67
INGLIS D.R.,"MISSILE DEFENSE, NUCLEAR SPREAD, AND
VIETNAM." CHINA/COM USA+45 USSR VIETNAM INDUS
BAL/PWR DETER WAR COST NAT/LISM PEACE. PAGE 28
G0544
NUC/PWR
ARMS/CONT
DIPLOM
FORCES

S67
MARTIN L.,"THE AMERICAN ABM DECISION." ASIA COM
EUR+WWI UK USA+45 USSR FORCES DIPLOM PEACE...POLICY
20 ABM/DEFSYS. PAGE 36 G0713
WEAPON
DETER
NUC/PWR
WAR

S67
RICHMAN B.M.,"SOVIET MANAGEMENT IN TRANSITION."
USSR FINAN MARKET EX/STRUC PLAN PROB/SOLV TEC/DEV
CONTROL LEAD CENTRAL EFFICIENCY...METH/COMP 20
REFORMERS. PAGE 47 G0917
MGT
MARXISM
POLICY
AUTHORIT

S67
SHULMAN M.D.,"'EUROPE' VERSUS 'DETENTE'." USA+45
USSR INT/ORG CONTROL ARMS/CONT DETER 20. PAGE 50
G0995
DIPLOM
BAL/PWR
NUC/PWR

S67
SLOAN P.,"FIFTY YEARS OF SOVIET RULE." USSR INDUS
EDU/PROP EFFICIENCY PRODUC HEALTH KNOWL MORAL
WEALTH MARXISM...POLICY 20. PAGE 51 G1011
CREATE
NAT/G
PLAN
INSPECT

S67
TEKINER S.,"SINKIAN AND THE SINO-SOVIET CONFLICT."
ASIA COM USSR FORCES PLAN BAL/PWR CONTROL NUC/PWR
WAR WEAPON...DECISION 20. PAGE 54 G1060
DIPLOM
PWR
MARXISM

S67
VLASCIC I.A.,"THE SPACE TREATY* A PRELIMINARY
EVALUATION." FUT USSR WOR+45 R+D ACT/RES TEC/DEV
DIPLOM CONFER ARMS/CONT PEACE...PREDICT UN TREATY.
PAGE 61 G1201
SPACE
INT/LAW
INT/ORG
NEUTRAL

S67
WALTERS R.E.,"THE ROLE OF NUCLEAR WEAPONS FOR THE
WEST." ASIA UK USA+45 USSR DIPLOM COERCE WAR PEACE
...POLICY DECISION 20. PAGE 62 G1209
PLAN
NUC/PWR
WEAPON
FORCES

S67
WOLFE T.W.,"SOVIET MILITARY POLICY AT THE FIFTY
YEAR MARK." USSR VIETNAM WOR+45 RATION AGREE WAR
WEAPON CIVMIL/REL TREATY. PAGE 64 G1254
FORCES
POLICY
TIME/SEQ
PLAN

UTAH....UTAH

UTIL....UTILITY, USEFULNESS

B48
WEINER N.,CYBERNETICS. SOCIETY COMPUTER ADJUST
EFFICIENCY UTIL PERCEPT...PSY MATH REGRESS TIME.
PAGE 63 G1226
FEEDBACK
AUTOMAT
CONTROL
TEC/DEV

S48
MARQUIS D.G.,"RESEARCH PLANNING AT THE FRONTIERS OF
SCIENCE" (BMR)" INTELL ACADEM CREATE UTIL...PSY 20.
PAGE 36 G0708
PLAN
ACT/RES
EFFICIENCY
GEN/METH

B58
JUNGK R.,BRIGHTER THAN A THOUSAND SUNS: THE MORAL
AND POLITICAL HISTORY OF THE ATOMIC SCIENTISTS.
WOR+45 WOR-45 CONSULT CREATE RISK UTIL DRIVE
PERCEPT PWR...INT 20. PAGE 29 G0568
NUC/PWR
MORAL
GOV/REL
PERSON

S59
ADAMS E.W.,"A MODEL OF RISKLESS CHOICE." CREATE
PROB/SOLV UTIL...PROBABIL PREDICT HYPO/EXP. PAGE 2
G0029
GAME
SIMUL
RISK
DECISION

B60
ARROW K.J.,MATHEMATICAL METHODS IN THE SOCIAL
SCIENCES, 1959. TEC/DEV CHOOSE UTIL PERCEPT
...KNO/TEST GAME SIMUL ANTHOL. PAGE 4 G0070
MATH
PSY
MGT

B60
ATOMIC INDUSTRIAL FORUM,ATOMS FOR INDUSTRY: WORLD
FORUM. WOR+45 FINAN COST UTIL...JURID ANTHOL 20.
PAGE 4 G0080
NUC/PWR
INDUS
PLAN
PROB/SOLV

S61
BENNION E.G.,"ECONOMETRICS FOR MANAGEMENT." USA+45
INDUS EX/STRUC ACT/RES COMPUTER UTIL...MATH STAT
ECOMETRIC
MGT

PREDICT METH/COMP HYPO/EXP. PAGE 6 G0122
SIMUL
DECISION

B62
BORKOF H.,COMPUTER APPLICATIONS IN THE BEHAVIORAL
SCIENCES. AUTOMAT UTIL...DECISION PHIL/SCI PSY
METH/CNCPT LING LOG MATH STYLE NET/THEORY COMPUT/IR
PROG/TEAC SIMUL. PAGE 8 G0154
R+D
COMPUTER
PROB/SOLV
FEEDBACK

B63
OTTOSON H.W.,LAND USE POLICY AND PROBLEMS IN THE
UNITED STATES. USA+45 USA-45 LAW AGRI INDUS NAT/G
GP/REL...CHARTS ANTHOL 19/20 HOMEST/ACT. PAGE 43
G0851
PROB/SOLV
UTIL
HABITAT
POLICY

B63
US SENATE,DOCUMENTS ON INTERNATIONAL AS"ECTS OF
EXPLORATION AND USE OF OUTER SPACE, 1954-62: STAFF
REPORT FOR COMM AERON SPACE SCI. USA+45 USSR LEGIS
LEAD CIVMIL/REL PEACE...POLICY INT/LAW ANTHOL 20
CONGRESS NASA KHRUSH/N. PAGE 59 G1162
SPACE
UTIL
GOV/REL
DIPLOM

B63
US SENATE COMM APPROPRIATIONS,PERSONNEL
ADMINISTRATION AND OPERATIONS OF AGENCY FOR
INTERNATIONAL DEVELOPMENT: SPECIAL HEARING. FINAN
LEAD COST UTIL SKILL...CHARTS 20 CONGRESS AID
CIVIL/SERV. PAGE 60 G1175
ADMIN
FOR/AID
EFFICIENCY
DIPLOM

B65
CHENG C.-Y.,SCIENTIFIC AND ENGINEERING MANPOWER IN
COMMUNIST CHINA. 1949-1963. CHINA/COM USSR ELITES
ECO/DEV R+D ACADEM LABOR NAT/G EDU/PROP CONTROL
UTIL...POLICY BIBLIOG 20. PAGE 12 G0226
WORKER
CONSULT
MARXISM
BIOG

B65
DORFMAN R.,MEASURING BENEFITS OF GOVERNMENT
INVESTMENTS. ECO/DEV R+D ECO/TAC PROFIT UTIL...MGT
GEN/METH. PAGE 16 G0308
PLAN
RATION
EFFICIENCY
OPTIMAL

B65
HICKMAN B.G.,QUANTITATIVE PLANNING OF ECONOMIC
POLICY. FRANCE NETHERLAND OP/RES PRICE ROUTINE UTIL
...POLICY DECISION ECOMETRIC METH/CNCPT STAT STYLE
CHINJAP. PAGE 26 G0511
PROB/SOLV
PLAN
QUANT

B65
US DEPARTMENT OF ARMY,MILITARY PROTECTIVE
CONSTRUCTION: NUCLEAR WARFARE AND CHEMICAL AND
BIOLOGICAL OPERATIONS (MANUAL). OP/RES TEC/DEV RISK
COERCE NUC/PWR WAR WEAPON EFFICIENCY UTIL BIO/SOC
HABITAT ORD/FREE 20. PAGE 57 G1117
FORCES
CONSTRUC
TASK
HEALTH

S65
HIBBS A.R.,"SPACE TECHNOLOGY* THE THREAT AND THE
PROMISE." FUT VOL/ASSN TEC/DEV NUC/PWR COST
EFFICIENCY UTIL UN TREATY. PAGE 26 G0510
SPACE
ARMS/CONT
PREDICT

B67
ENKE S.,DEFENSE MANAGEMENT. USA+45 R+D FORCES
WORKER PLAN ECO/TAC ADMIN NUC/PWR BAL/PAY UTIL
WEALTH...MGT DEPT/DEFEN. PAGE 18 G0348
DECISION
DELIB/GP
EFFICIENCY
BUDGET

B67
NELSON R.R.,TECHNOLOGY, ECONOMIC GROWTH, AND PUBLIC
POLICY. USA+45 PLAN GP/REL UTIL KNOWL...POLICY
PHIL/SCI CHARTS BIBLIOG 20. PAGE 41 G0817
R+D
CONSULT
CREATE
ACT/RES

S67
BARAN P.,"THE FUTURE COMPUTER UTILITY." USA+45
NAT/G PLAN CONTROL COST...POLICY 20. PAGE 5 G0091
COMPUTER
UTIL
FUT
TEC/DEV

S67
CETRON M.J.,"FORECASTING TECHNOLOGY." INDUS FORCES
TASK UTIL...PHIL/SCI CONCPT CHARTS METH/COMP TIME.
PAGE 11 G0219
TEC/DEV
FUT
R+D
PLAN

N67
US SENATE,STATUS OF THE DEVELOPMENT OF THE ANTI-
BALLISTIC MISSILE SYSTEMS IN THE UNITED STATES
(PAMPHLET). FUT USA+45 R+D PLAN TEC/DEV DEPT/DEFEN.
PAGE 59 G1165
FORCES
NUC/PWR
WAR
UTIL

UTILITAR....UTILITARIANISM

UTILITARIANISM....SEE UTILITAR

UTILITY....SEE UTIL

UTOPIA....ENVISIONED GENERAL SOCIAL CONDITIONS; SEE ALSO

STERTYP

B29
DEWEY J.,THE QUEST FOR CERTAINTY. GP/REL RATIONAL
UTOPIA ATTIT MORAL ORD/FREE PWR...MYTH HIST/WRIT.
PAGE 15 G0301
PHIL/SCI
PERSON
PERCEPT
KNOWL

B43
LASKI H.J.,REFLECTIONS ON THE REVOLUTIONS OF OUR
TIME. COM USSR NAT/G WORKER UTOPIA ORD/FREE WEALTH
MARXISM SOCISM 19/20. PAGE 32 G0637
CAP/ISM
WELF/ST
ECO/TAC
POLICY

B64
SCHOECK H.,CENTRAL PLANNING AND NEOMERCANTILISM.
L/A+17C UK WOR+45 BUDGET ECO/TAC PRICE CONTROL
GOV/REL UTOPIA 20. PAGE 49 G0974
PLAN
CENTRAL
NAT/G
POLICY

B65
SMITH E.A.,SOCIAL WELFARE: PRINCIPLES AND CONCEPTS.
STRATA STRUCT CONSULT WORKER ACT/RES CREATE PLAN
TEC/DEV ROUTINE GP/REL UTOPIA...SOC 20. PAGE 51
G1014
CONCPT
SOC/WK
RECEIVE
ORD/FREE

B67
CONNOLLY W.E.,POLITICAL SCIENCE AND IDEOLOGY.
UTOPIA ATTIT KNOWL...MAJORIT EPIST PHIL/SCI SOC
IDEA/COMP HYPO/EXP GEN/LAWS METH HUME/D MARX/KARL.
PAGE 13 G0250
PWR
PLURISM
ELITES
CONCPT

UTTAR/PRAD....UTTAR PRADESH, INDIA

V

VALIDITY (AS CONCEPT)....SEE METH/CNCPT

VALUE ADDED TAX....SEE VALUE/ADD

VALUE/ADD....VALUE ADDED TAX

VALUE-FREE THOUGHT....SEE OBJECTIVE

VALUES....SEE VALUES INDEX, P. XIII

VAN DYKE V. G1191

VAN WAGENEN R.W. G1192

VANBUREN/M....PRESIDENT MARTIN VAN BUREN

VATICAN....VATICAN

VEBLEN/T....THORSTEIN VEBLEN

VEINOTT A.F. G1193

VENETIAN REPUBLIC....SEE VENICE

VENEZUELA....VENEZUELA; SEE ALSO L/A+17C

VENICE....VENETIAN REPUBLIC

VERBA S. G0897

VERDOORN P.J. G0364

VERGIN R.C. G1194

VERHULST M. G0093

VERMONT....VERMONT

VERMOT-GAUCHY M. G1195

VERNEY D.V. G1196

VERNON R. G1197

VERSAILLES....VERSAILLES, FRANCE

B53
BRETTON H.L.,STRESEMANN AND THE REVISION OF
VERSAILLES: A FIGHT FOR REASON. EUR+WWI GERMANY
FORCES BUDGET ARMS/CONT WAR SUPEGO...BIBLIOG 20
TREATY VERSAILLES STRESEMN/G. PAGE 9 G0167
POLICY
DIPLOM
BIOG

VERTICAL TAKE-OFF AND LANDING AIRCRAFT....SEE VTOL

VERWOERD/H....HENDRIK VERWOERD

VETO....VETO AND VETOING

VICE/PRES....VICE-PRESIDENCY (ALL NATIONS)

VICEREGAL....VICEROYALTY; VICEROY SYSTEM

UBLIC POLICY AND THE MANAGEMENT OF SCIENCE

ICHY....VICHY, FRANCE

ICTORIA/Q....QUEEN VICTORIA

IENNA/CNV....VIENNA CONVENTION ON CONSULAR RELATIONS

IET MINH....SEE VIETNAM, GUERRILLA, COLONIAL

IET/CONG....VIET CONG

IETNAM....VIETNAM IN GENERAL; SEE ALSO S/ASIA, VIETNAM/N,
    VIETNAM/S

N19
MEZERIK A.G.,INTERNATIONAL POLICY 1965 (PAMPHLET). DIPLOM
KASHMIR S/ASIA SPACE USA+45 VIETNAM WOR+45   INT/ORG
ARMS/CONT RACE/REL DISCRIM PEACE PWR 20 UN. PAGE 39 POLICY
G0762   WAR

B66
BRODIE B.,ESCALATION AND THE NUCLEAR OPTION. ASIA   NUC/PWR
CUBA EUR+WWI KOREA USA+45 USSR VIETNAM RISK ATTIT   GUERRILLA
DRIVE PERCEPT PROBABIL. PAGE 9 G0172   WAR
                                                    DETER

B67
RUSSELL B.,WAR CRIMES IN VIETNAM. USA+45 VIETNAM   WAR
FORCES DIPLOM WEAPON RACE/REL DISCRIM ISOLAT   CRIME
BIO/SOC 20 COLD/WAR RUSSELL/B. PAGE 48 G0949   ATTIT
                                                    POLICY

B67
US SENATE COMM ON FOREIGN REL.FOREIGN ASSISTANCE   FOR/AID
ACT OF 1967. VIETNAM WOR+45 DELIB/GP CONFER CONTROL LAW
WAR WEAPON BAL/PAY...CENSUS CHARTS SENATE. PAGE 60 DIPLOM
G1185   POLICY

S67
INGLIS D.R.,"MISSILE DEFENSE, NUCLEAR SPREAD, AND   NUC/PWR
VIETNAM." CHINA/COM USA+45 USSR VIETNAM INDUS   ARMS/CONT
BAL/PWR DETER WAR COST NAT/LISM PEACE. PAGE 28   DIPLOM
G0544   FORCES

S67
WOLFE T.W.,"SOVIET MILITARY POLICY AT THE FIFTY   FORCES
YEAR MARK." USSR VIETNAM WOR+45 RATION AGREE WAR   POLICY
WEAPON CIVMIL/REL TREATY. PAGE 64 G1254   TIME/SEQ
                                                    PLAN

IETNAM/N....NORTH VIETNAM

B67
WYLIE J.C.,MILITARY STRATEGY: GENERAL THEORY OF   FORCES
POWER CONTROL. CUBA USA+45 VIETNAM/N WOR+45 ELITES PLAN
CONTROL WAR PWR...POLICY METH/COMP 20 MAO. PAGE 64 DECISION
G1260   IDEA/COMP

S67
SALISBURY H.E.,"THE WAR IN VIETNAM." USA+45   POLICY
VIETNAM/N DIPLOM MURDER 20. PAGE 48 G0953   WAR
                                                    FORCES
                                                    OBS

VIETNAM/S....SOUTH VIETNAM

VIETORISZ T. G1198,G1199

VILLA/P....PANCHO VILLA

VILLAGE....SEE MUNIC

VILLARD/OG....OSWALD GARRISON VILLARD

VINER J. G1200

VINER/J....JACOB VINER

VINTER R.D. G1044

VIOLENCE....SEE COERCE, ALSO PROCESSES AND PRACTICES INDEX,
    PART G, PAGE XIII

VIRGIN/ISL....VIRGIN ISLANDS

VIRGINIA....VIRGINIA

VISTA....VOLUNTEERS IN SERVICE TO AMERICA (VISTA)

VLASIC I.A. G0739,G1201

VOL/ASSN....VOLUNTARY ASSOCIATION

B34
EINSTEIN A.,THE WORLD AS I SEE IT. WOR-45 INTELL   SOCIETY

R+D INT/ORG NAT/G SECT VOL/ASSN FORCES CREATE   PHIL/SCI
EDU/PROP LEGIT ARMS/CONT WAR WEAPON NAT/LISM   DIPLOM
ALL/VALS...POLICY CONCPT 20. PAGE 17 G0337   PACIFISM

B44
MERRIAM C.E.,PUBLIC AND PRIVATE GOVERNMENT.   NAT/G
VOL/ASSN EDU/PROP ADMIN REPRESENT EFFICIENCY PWR   NEIGH
PLURISM...MAJORIT CONCPT. PAGE 38 G0755   MGT
                                                    POLICY

B48
KILE O.M.,THE FARM BUREAU MOVEMENT: THE FARM BUREAU AGRI
THROUGH THREE DECADES. NAT/G LEGIS LEAD LOBBY   STRUCT
GP/REL INCOME POLICY. PAGE 30 G0596   VOL/ASSN
                                                    DOMIN

S50
KAPLAN A.,"THE PREDICTION OF SOCIAL AND   PWR
TECHNOLOGICAL EVENTS." VOL/ASSN CONSULT ACT/RES   KNO/TEST
CREATE OP/RES PLAN ROUTINE PERSON...POLICY
METH/CNCPT STAT QU/SEMANT SYS/QU TESTS CENSUS TREND
20. PAGE 29 G0574

B52
HAYEK F.A.,THE COUNTER-REVOLUTION OF SCIENCE. UNIV PERCEPT
INTELL R+D VOL/ASSN CREATE EDU/PROP...PHIL/SCI SOC KNOWL
OBS TIME/SEQ TREND GEN/METH. PAGE 25 G0494

B53
MACK R.T.,RAISING THE WORLDS STANDARD OF LIVING.   WOR+45
IRAN INT/ORG VOL/ASSN EX/STRUC ECO/TAC WEALTH...MGT FOR/AID
METH/CNCPT STAT CONT/OBS INT TOT/POP VAL/FREE 20   INT/TRADE
UN. PAGE 35 G0690

B54
PUBLIC ADMIN CLEARING HOUSE,PUBLIC ADMINISTRATIONS INDEX
ORGANIZATIONS: A DIRECTORY, 1954. USA+45 R+D PROVS VOL/ASSN
ACT/RES...MGT 20. PAGE 45 G0893   NAT/G
                                                    ADMIN

B54
ROSE A.M.,THEORY AND METHOD IN THE SOCIAL SCIENCES. CONCPT
STRATA R+D NEIGH PARTIC...METH/CNCPT GP/COMP.   SOC
PAGE 47 G0934   VOL/ASSN
                                                    ROLE

L54
OPLER M.E.,"SOCIAL ASPECTS OF TECHNICAL ASSISTANCE INT/ORG
IN OPERATION." WOR+45 VOL/ASSN CREATE PLAN TEC/DEV CONSULT
EDU/PROP ALL/VALS...METH/CNCPT OBS RECORD TREND UN FOR/AID
20. PAGE 43 G0841

L55
KISER M.,"ORGANIZATION OF AMERICAN STATES." L/A+17C VOL/ASSN
USA+45 ECO/UNDEV INT/ORG NAT/G PLAN TEC/DEV DIPLOM ECO/DEV
ECO/TAC INT/TRADE EDU/PROP ADMIN ALL/VALS...POLICY REGION
MGT RECORD ORG/CHARTS OAS 20. PAGE 30 G0601

B56
WASSERMAN P.,INFORMATION FOR ADMINISTRATORS: A   BIBLIOG
GUIDE TO PUBLICATIONS AND SERVICES FOR MANAGEMENT   MGT
IN BUSINESS AND GOVERNMENT. R+D LOC/G NAT/G   KNOWL
PROF/ORG VOL/ASSN PRESS...PSY SOC STAT 20. PAGE 62 EDU/PROP
G1219

S56
GORDON L.,"THE ORGANIZATION FOR EUROPEAN ECONOMIC   VOL/ASSN
COOPERATION." EUR+WWI INDUS INT/ORG NAT/G CONSULT   ECO/DEV
DELIB/GP ACT/RES CREATE PLAN TEC/DEV EDU/PROP LEGIT
WEALTH OEEC 20. PAGE 22 G0435

B58
LIPPITT R.,DYNAMICS OF PLANNED CHANGE. STRUCT   VOL/ASSN
ACT/RES ROUTINE INGP/REL PWR...POLICY METH/CNCPT   ORD/FREE
BIBLIOG. PAGE 34 G0672   PLAN
                                                    CREATE

B58
BURNS A.L.,"THE NEW WEAPONS AND INTERNATIONAL   TEC/DEV
RELATIONS." SPACE WOR+45 NAT/G VOL/ASSN FORCES   ARMS/CONT
NUC/PWR 20. PAGE 10 G0190   DIPLOM

B59
DAHRENDORF R.,CLASS AND CLASS CONFLICT IN   VOL/ASSN
INDUSTRIAL SOCIETY. LABOR NAT/G COERCE ROLE PLURISM STRUCT
...POLICY MGT CONCPT CLASSIF. PAGE 14 G0271   SOC
                                                    GP/REL

S59
STOESSINGER J.G.,"THE INTERNATIONAL ATOMIC ENERGY   INT/ORG
AGENCY: THE FIRST PHASE." FUT WOR+45 NAT/G VOL/ASSN ECO/DEV
DELIB/GP BAL/PWR LEGIT ADMIN ROUTINE PWR...OBS   FOR/AID
CON/ANAL GEN/LAWS VAL/FREE 20 IAEA. PAGE 53 G1037   NUC/PWR

B60
ARMS CONTROL. FUT UNIV WOR+45 INTELL R+D INT/ORG   DELIB/GP

NAT/G VOL/ASSN CONSULT CREATE EDU/PROP PEACE...HUM   ORD/FREE
GEN/LAWS TOT/POP 20. PAGE 1 G0015   ARMS/CONT
                                                     NUC/PWR

                                                     B60
HEILBRONER R.L.,THE FUTURE AS HISTORY. USA+45   TEC/DEV
WOR+45 WOR-45 SOCIETY ECO/DEV ECO/UNDEV VOL/ASSN   TREND
PLAN CAP/ISM NUC/PWR CHOOSE NAT/LISM ATTIT ORD/FREE
RESPECT WEALTH SOCISM 20. PAGE 25 G0501

                                                     B60
PENTONY D.E.,THE UNDERDEVELOPED LANDS. FUT WOR+45   ECO/UNDEV
CULTURE AGRI FINAN INDUS MARKET INT/ORG LABOR NAT/G POLICY
VOL/ASSN CONSULT TEC/DEV ECO/TAC EDU/PROP COLONIAL   FOR/AID
ATTIT WEALTH...OBS RECORD SAMP TREND GEN/METH WORK   INT/TRADE
UN 20. PAGE 44 G0867

                                                     L60
BRENNAN D.G.,"SETTING AND GOALS OF ARMS CONTROL."   FORCES
FUT USA+45 USSR WOR+45 INT/ORG PLAN BAL/PWR   COERCE
VOL/ASSN CONSULT PLAN DIPLOM ECO/TAC ADMIN KNOWL   ARMS/CONT
PWR...POLICY CONCPT TREND COLD/WAR 20. PAGE 8 G0164 DETER

                                                     S60
YEMELYANOV V.S.,"ATOMIC ENERGY FOR PEACE: THE USSR   VOL/ASSN
AND INTERNATIONAL CO-OPERATION." FUT USSR WOR+45   TEC/DEV
R+D CREATE EDU/PROP...CONCPT GEN/LAWS 20. PAGE 64   ARMS/CONT
G1264   NUC/PWR

                                                     B61
BONNEFOUS M.,EUROPE ET TIERS MONDE. EUR+WWI SOCIETY AFR
INT/ORG NAT/G VOL/ASSN ACT/RES TEC/DEV CAP/ISM   ECO/UNDEV
ECO/TAC ATTIT ORD/FREE SOVEREIGN...POLICY CONCPT   FOR/AID
TREND 20. PAGE 8 G0153   INT/TRADE

                                                     B61
JANOWITZ M.,COMMUNITY POLITICAL SYSTEMS. USA+45   MUNIC
SOCIETY INDUS VOL/ASSN TEC/DEV ADMIN LEAD CHOOSE   STRUCT
...SOC SOC/WK 20. PAGE 29 G0561   POL/PAR

                                                     S61
COOKE E.F.,"RESEARCH: AN INSTRUMENT OF POWER."   R+D
VOL/ASSN PLAN TEC/DEV TAX LOBBY INGP/REL ROLE   PROVS
POLICY. PAGE 13 G0253   LOC/G
                                                     DECISION

                                                     B62
CALDER R.,LIVING WITH THE ATOM. FUT USA+45 WOR+45   TEC/DEV
R+D INT/ORG VOL/ASSN DELIB/GP ARMS/CONT...STYLE 20. HEALTH
PAGE 10 G0200   NUC/PWR

                                                     B62
FORBES H.W.,THE STRATEGY OF DISARMAMENT. FUT WOR+45 PLAN
INT/ORG VOL/ASSN CONSULT ARMS/CONT COERCE NUC/PWR   FORCES
WAR DRIVE RIGID/FLEX ORD/FREE PWR...POLICY CONCPT   DIPLOM
OBS TREND STERTYP 20. PAGE 19 G0378

                                                     B62
KRAFT J.,THE GRAND DESIGN. EUR+WWI USA+45 AGRI   VOL/ASSN
FINAN INDUS MARKET INT/ORG NAT/G PLAN ECO/TAC   ECO/DEV
TARIFFS REGION DRIVE ORD/FREE WEALTH...POLICY OBS   INT/TRADE
TREND EEC 20. PAGE 31 G0616

                                                     B62
SCHWARTZ L.E.,INTERNATIONAL ORGANIZATIONS AND SPACE INT/ORG
COOPERATION. VOL/ASSN CONSULT CREATE TEC/DEV   DIPLOM
SANCTION...POLICY INT/LAW PHIL/SCI 20 UN. PAGE 50   R+D
G0982   SPACE

                                                     B62
THANT U.,THE UNITED NATIONS' DEVELOPMENT DECADE: INT/ORG
PROPOSALS FOR ACTION. WOR+45 SOCIETY ECO/UNDEV AGRI ALL/VALS
COM/IND FINAN R+D MUNIC SCHOOL VOL/ASSN CONSULT
PLAN TEC/DEV ECO/TAC EDU/PROP ADMIN ROUTINE
RIGID/FLEX...MGT SOC CONCPT UNESCO UN TOT/POP
VAL/FREE. PAGE 54 G1064

                                                     B62
US CONGRESS,COMMUNICATIONS SATELLITE LEGISLATION: SPACE
HEARINGS BEFORE COMM ON AERON AND SPACE SCIENCES ON COM/IND
BILLS S2550 AND 2814. WOR+45 LAW VOL/ASSN PLAN   ADJUD
DIPLOM CONTROL OWN PEACE...NEW/IDEA CONGRESS NASA.   GOV/REL
PAGE 56 G1110

                                                     B62
YALEN R.,REGIONALISM AND WORLD ORDER. EUR+WWI   ORD/FREE
WOR+45 WOR-45 INT/ORG VOL/ASSN DELIB/GP FORCES   POLICY
TOP/EX BAL/PWR DIPLOM DOMIN REGION ARMS/CONT PWR
...JURID HYPO/EXP COLD/WAR 20. PAGE 64 G1261

                                                     S62
BETHE H.,"DISARMAMENT AND STRATEGY." COM USA+45   PLAN
USSR WOR+45 VOL/ASSN TEC/DEV EDU/PROP NUC/PWR   ORD/FREE
CHOOSE PEACE...POLICY DECISION NEW/IDEA OBS   ARMS/CONT
GEN/LAWS COLD/WAR 420. PAGE 7 G0133   DIPLOM

                                                     S62
BOULDING K.E.,"THE PREVENTION OF WORLD WAR THREE."   VOL/ASSN
FUT WOR+45 INT/ORG PLAN BAL/PWR PEACE ORD/FREE PWR   NAT/G
...NEW/IDEA TREND TOT/POP COLD/WAR 20. PAGE 8 G0158 ARMS/CONT
                                                     DIPLOM

                                                     S62
FINKELSTEIN L.S.,"THE UNITED NATIONS AND   INT/ORG
ORGANIZATIONS FOR CONTROL OF ARMAMENT." FUT WOR+45   PWR
VOL/ASSN DELIB/GP TOP/EX CREATE EDU/PROP LEGIT   ARMS/CONT
ADJUD NUC/PWR ATTIT RIGID/FLEX ORD/FREE...POLICY
DECISION CONCPT OBS TREND GEN/LAWS TOT/POP
COLD/WAR. PAGE 19 G0368

                                                     S62
FOSTER R.B.,"UNILATERAL ARMS CONTROL MEASURES AND   PLAN
DISARMAMENT NEGOTIATION." WOR+45 VOL/ASSN DELIB/GP   ORD/FREE
ACT/RES ECO/TAC EDU/PROP ATTIT RIGID/FLEX...CONCPT   ARMS/CONT
MYTH TIME/SEQ COLD/WAR 20. PAGE 20 G0386   DETER

                                                     S62
FOSTER W.C.,"ARMS CONTROL AND DISARMAMENT IN A   DELIB/GP
DIVIDED WORLD." COM FUT USA+45 USSR WOR+45 INTELL   POLICY
INT/ORG NAT/G VOL/ASSN CONSULT CREATE PLAN TEC/DEV   ARMS/CONT
EDU/PROP LEGIT NUC/PWR ATTIT RIGID/FLEX...CONCPT   DIPLOM
TREND TOT/POP 20 UN. PAGE 20 G0387

                                                     B63
WIGHTMAN D.,TOWARD ECONOMIC CO-OPERATION IN ASIA.   ECO/UNDEV
ASIA S/ASIA VOL/ASSN ACT/RES PLAN TEC/DEV ECO/TAC   CREATE
EDU/PROP RIGID/FLEX SKILL...POLICY METH/CNCPT OBS
INT GEN/LAWS UN 20 ECAFE. PAGE 63 G1237

                                                     L63
NIEBURG H.,"EURATOM: A STUDY IN COALITION   VOL/ASSN
POLITICS." EUR+WWI UK USA+45 ELITES NAT/G DELIB/GP   ACT/RES
LEGIS TOP/EX ECO/TAC NUC/PWR ATTIT ORD/FREE PWR
TOT/POP EEC OEEC 20 NATO EURATOM. PAGE 42 G0820

                                                     S63
BOHN L.,"WHOSE NUCLEAR TEST: NON-PHYSICAL   ADJUD
INSPECTION AND TEST BAN." WOR+45 R+D INT/ORG   ARMS/CONT
VOL/ASSN ORD/FREE...GEN/LAWS GEN/METH COLD/WAR 20.   TEC/DEV
PAGE 8 G0148   NUC/PWR

                                                     S63
SCHMITT H.A.,"THE EUROPEAN COMMUNITIES." EUR+WWI   VOL/ASSN
FRANCE DELIB/GP EX/STRUC TOP/EX CREATE TEC/DEV   ECO/DEV
ECO/TAC LEGIT REGION COERCE DRIVE ALL/VALS
...METH/CNCPT EEC 20. PAGE 49 G0972

                                                     B64
ETZIONI A.,THE MOON-DOGGLE: DOMESTIC AND   R+D
INTERNATIONAL IMPLICATIONS OF THE SPACE RACE. FUT   NAT/G
USA+45 WOR+45 INTELL ECO/DEV INDUS VOL/ASSN   DIPLOM
EX/STRUC FORCES LEGIS TOP/EX PLAN TEC/DEV ECO/TAC   SPACE
EDU/PROP KNOWL ORD/FREE PWR RESPECT WEALTH
TIME/SEQ. PAGE 18 G0352

                                                     B64
HAMMOND P.E.,SOCIOLOGISTS AT WORK. VOL/ASSN OP/RES   R+D
TEC/DEV CONFER ROUTINE TASK EFFICIENCY...MGT   BIOG
NEW/IDEA STYLE SAMP. PAGE 24 G0478   SOC

                                                     B64
HEKHUIS D.J.,INTERNATIONAL STABILITY: MILITARY,   TEC/DEV
ECONOMIC AND POLITICAL DIMENSIONS. FUT WOR+45 LAW   DETER
ECO/UNDEV INT/ORG NAT/G VOL/ASSN FORCES ACT/RES   REGION
BAL/PWR PWR WEALTH...STAT UN 20. PAGE 25 G0503

                                                     S64
MARES V.E.,"EAST EUROPE'S SECOND CHANCE." COM   VOL/ASSN
EUR+WWI HUNGARY ROMANIA USSR YUGOSLAVIA ECO/UNDEV   ECO/TAC
NAT/G TOP/EX CREATE PLAN TEC/DEV REGION NAT/LISM
RIGID/FLEX PWR...CONCPT STAT COMECON 20. PAGE 36
G0705

                                                     B65
KENT A.,SPECIALIZED INFORMATION CENTERS. INTELL R+D COMPUT/IR
VOL/ASSN CONSULT COMPUTER KNOWL...DECISION HUM   CREATE
PHIL/SCI METH/CNCPT TREND CHARTS 20. PAGE 30 G0593   TEC/DEV
                                                     METH/COMP

                                                     B65
UNESCO,HANDBOOK OF INTERNATIONAL EXCHANGES. COM/IND INDEX
R+D ACADEM PROF/ORG VOL/ASSN CREATE TEC/DEV   INT/ORG
EDU/PROP AGREE 20 TREATY. PAGE 55 G1090   DIPLOM
                                                     PRESS

                                                     B65
US SENATE,US INTERNATIONAL SPACE PROGRAMS, 1959-65: SPACE
STAFF REPORT FOR COMM ON AERONAUTICAL AND SPACE   DIPLOM
SCIENCES. WOR+45 VOL/ASSN CIVMIL/REL 20 CONGRESS   PLAN
NASA TREATY. PAGE 59 G1163   GOV/REL

US SENATE COMM AERO SPACE SCI.INTERNATIONAL COOPERATION AND ORGANIZATION FOR OUTER SPACE. FUT USA+45 WOR+45 PROF/ORG VOL/ASSN CONSULT DELIB/GP PLAN TEC/DEV ARMS/CONT GP/REL PEACE 20 UN NASA. PAGE 59 G1167
B65
DIPLOM
SPACE
R+D
NAT/G

BLOOMFIELD L.P.."ARMS CONTROL AND THE DEVELOPING COUNTRIES." AFR ISLAM S/ASIA USA+45 VOL/ASSN TEC/DEV DIPLOM REGION NUC/PWR...PREDICT TREND. PAGE 7 G0142
S65
ARMS/CONT
ECO/UNDEV
HYPO/EXP
OBS

GOLDSTEIN W.."KEEPING THE GENIE IN THE BOTTLE* THE FEASIBILITY OF A NUCLEAR NON-PROLIFERATION AGREEMENT." ASIA FRANCE UK USA+45 USSR WOR+45 ECO/UNDEV VOL/ASSN ACT/RES PLAN RISK ARMS/CONT WAR PEACE ATTIT PERCEPT...RECORD TREND TIME. PAGE 22 G0429
S65
NUC/PWR
CREATE
COST

HIBBS A.R.."SPACE TECHNOLOGY* THE THREAT AND THE PROMISE." FUT VOL/ASSN TEC/DEV NUC/PWR COST EFFICIENCY UTIL UN TREATY. PAGE 26 G0510
S65
SPACE
ARMS/CONT
PREDICT

HOLSTI O.R.."EAST-WEST CONFLICT AND SINO-SOVIET RELATIONS" CHINA/COM USSR COMPUTER REGION DECISION. PAGE 27 G0523
S65
VOL/ASSN
DIPLOM
CON/ANAL
COM

KINTNER W.P.."THE PROSPECTS FOR WESTERN SCIENCE AND TECHNOLOGY." EUR+WWI FRANCE USA+45 USSR R+D NUC/PWR NATO. PAGE 30 G0598
S65
TEC/DEV
VOL/ASSN
STAT
RECORD

KOHL W.L.."NUCLEAR SHARING IN NATO AND THE MULTILATERAL FORCE." FUT USSR VOL/ASSN TEC/DEV DIPLOM NUC/PWR WAR WEAPON NATO. PAGE 31 G0611
S65
ARMS/CONT
OBS
IDEA/COMP

MARTIN A.."PROLIFERATION." FUT WOR+45 PROB/SOLV REGION ADJUST...PREDICT NAT/COMP UN TREATY. PAGE 36 G0712
S65
RECORD
NUC/PWR
ARMS/CONT
VOL/ASSN

GRUNEWALD D..PUBLIC POLICY AND THE MODERN COOPERATION: SELECTED READINGS. USA+45 LAW MARKET VOL/ASSN CAP/ISM INT/TRADE CENTRAL OWN...SOC ANTHOL 20. PAGE 23 G0458
B66
LG/CO
POLICY
NAT/G
CONTROL

STREET D..ORGANIZATION FOR TREATMENT. CLIENT PROVS PUB/INST PLAN CONTROL PARTIC REPRESENT ATTIT PWR ...POLICY BIBLIOG. PAGE 53 G1044
B66
GP/COMP
AGE/Y
ADMIN
VOL/ASSN

BROWNLIE I.."NUCLEAR PROLIFERATION* SOME PROBLEMS OF CONTROL." USA+45 USSR ECO/UNDEV INT/ORG FORCES TEC/DEV REGION CONSEN...RECORD TREATY. PAGE 9 G0181
S66
NUC/PWR
ARMS/CONT
VOL/ASSN
ORD/FREE

ELSNER H..THE TECHNOCRATS, PROPHETS OF AUTOMATION. SOCIETY INDUS VOL/ASSN COST INCOME ATTIT 20. PAGE 18 G0345
B67
AUTOMAT
TECHRACY
PRODUC
HIST/WRIT

UNIVERSAL REFERENCE SYSTEM.ADMINISTRATIVE MANAGEMENT: PUBLIC AND PRIVATE BUREAUCRACY (VOLUME IV). WOR+45 WOR-45 ECO/DEV LG/CO LOC/G PUB/INST VOL/ASSN GOV/REL...COMPUT/IR GEN/METH. PAGE 56 G1096
B67
BIBLIOG/A
MGT
ADMIN
NAT/G

CARROLL K.J.."SECOND STEP TOWARD ARMS CONTROL." WOR+45 INT/ORG VOL/ASSN FORCES PROB/SOLV RISK WEAPON 20 COLD/WAR. PAGE 11 G0215
S67
ARMS/CONT
DIPLOM
PLAN
NUC/PWR

EDMONDS M.."INTERNATIONAL COLLABORATION IN WEAPONS PROCUREMENT* THE IMPLICATIONS OF THE ANGLO-FRENCH CASE." FRANCE UK CONSULT OP/RES PROB/SOLV TEC/DEV CONFER CONTROL EFFICIENCY 20. PAGE 17 G0334
S67
DIPLOM
VOL/ASSN
BAL/PWR
ARMS/CONT

HULL E.W.S.."THE POLITICAL OCEAN." FUT UNIV WOR+45 EXTR/IND R+D VOL/ASSN PLAN BAL/PWR ECO/TAC PEACE WEALTH 20 UN. PAGE 27 G0536
S67
DIPLOM
ECO/UNDEV
INT/ORG

VOLTAIRE....VOLTAIRE (FRANCOIS MARIE AROUET)

VOLUNTARY ASSOCIATIONS....SEE VOL/ASSN

VOLUNTEERS IN SERVICE TO AMERICA (VISTA)....SEE VISTA
VON BORCH H. G0853
VON NEUMANN J. G1202

VON/TRESCK....VON TRESCKOW

VOTING....SEE CHOOSE, SUFF

VTOL....VERTICAL TAKE-OFF AND LANDING AIRCRAFT

VUCINICH A. G1203

─────────────W─────────────

WAGER P.W. G1204

WAGES....SEE PRICE, WORKER, WEALTH

WAGNER/A....ADOLPH WAGNER

WALDO D. G1205

WALES H.G. G1206

WALES....WALES

WALKER/E....EDWIN WALKER

WALLACE/G....GEORGE WALLACE

WALLACE/HA....HENRY A. WALLACE

WALSTON H. G1207

WALTER E. G1208

WALTERS R.E. G1209

WALTZ/KN....KENNETH N. WALTZ

WAR....SEE ALSO COERCE

CONOVER H.L..CIVILIAN DEFENSE: A SELECTED LIST OF RECENT REFERENCES (PAMPHLET). USA+45 LOC/G MUNIC PROB/SOLV ADMIN LEAD TASK WEAPON GOV/REL...POLICY CON/ANAL 20 CIV/DEFENS. PAGE 13 G0251
N
BIBLIOG
PLAN
WAR
CIVMIL/REL

WEIGLEY R.F..HISTORY OF THE UNITED STATES ARMY. USA+45 USA-45 SOCIETY NAT/G LEAD WAR GP/REL PWR ...SOC METH/COMP COLD/WAR. PAGE 62 G1222
N
FORCES
ADMIN
ROLE
CIVMIL/REL

CURRENT THOUGHT ON PEACE AND WAR. WOR+45 INT/ORG FORCES PROB/SOLV DIPLOM NUC/PWR PERCEPT...POLICY SOC 20 UN NATO. PAGE 1 G0001
B
BIBLIOG/A
PEACE
ATTIT
WAR

JOURNAL OF CONFLICT RESOLUTION. FUT WOR+45 INT/ORG NAT/G FORCES CREATE PROB/SOLV ARMS/CONT NUC/PWR WEAPON SOC. PAGE 1 G0002
N
BIBLIOG/A
DIPLOM
WAR

AIR UNIVERSITY LIBRARY.INDEX TO MILITARY PERIODICALS. FUT SPACE WOR+45 REGION ARMS/CONT NUC/PWR WAR PEACE INT/LAW. PAGE 2 G0032
N
BIBLIOG/A
FORCES
NAT/G
DIPLOM

BROWN W.M..THE DESIGN AND PERFORMANCE OF "OPTIMUM" BLAST SHELTER PROGRAMS (PAMPHLET). USA+45 ACT/RES PLAN DEATH COST EFFICIENCY OPTIMAL...POLICY CHARTS 20. PAGE 9 G0180
N19
HABITAT
NUC/PWR
WAR
HEALTH

MEZERIK A.G..INTERNATIONAL POLICY 1965 (PAMPHLET). KASHMIR S/ASIA SPACE USA+45 VIETNAM WOR+45 ARMS/CONT RACE/REL DISCRIM PEACE PWR 20 UN. PAGE 39 G0762
N19
DIPLOM
INT/ORG
POLICY
WAR

US FOOD AND DRUG ADMIN.CIVIL DEFENSE INFORMATION FOR FOOD AND DRUG OFFICIALS (2ND ED.) (PAMPHLET). USA+45 PROB/SOLV RISK HABITAT...MATH CHARTS DICTIONARY 20 CIV/DEFENS. PAGE 58 G1136
N19
NUC/PWR
WAR
EATING
HEALTH

ZLOTNICK M..WEAPONS IN SPACE (PAMPHLET). FUT WOR+45 TEC/DEV DIPLOM ARMS/CONT CIVMIL/REL PEACE HABITAT
N19
SPACE
WEAPON

...CONCPT NEW/IDEA CHARTS. PAGE 65 G1268
NUC/PWR
WAR

C25

MOON P.T.,"SYLLABUS ON INTERNATIONAL RELATIONS."
INT/ORG
EUR+WWI MOD/EUR USA-45 FORCES COLONIAL WAR WEAPON
DIPLOM
NAT/LISM...POLICY BIBLIOG T 19/20. PAGE 39 G0778
NAT/G

B28

SOROKIN P.,CONTEMPORARY SOCIOLOGICAL THEORIES.
CULTURE
MOD/EUR UNIV SOCIETY R+D SCHOOL ECO/TAC EDU/PROP
SOC
ROUTINE ATTIT DRIVE...PSY CONCPT TIME/SEQ TREND
WAR
GEN/LAWS 20. PAGE 52 G1021

B34

EINSTEIN A.,THE WORLD AS I SEE IT. WOR-45 INTELL
SOCIETY
R+D INT/ORG NAT/G SECT VOL/ASSN FORCES CREATE
PHIL/SCI
EDU/PROP LEGIT ARMS/CONT WAR WEAPON NAT/LISM
DIPLOM
ALL/VALS...POLICY CONCPT 20. PAGE 17 G0337
PACIFISM

B35

FOREIGN AFFAIRS BIBLIOGRAPHY: A SELECTED AND
BIBLIOG/A
ANNOTATED LIST OF BOOKS ON INTERNATIONAL RELATIONS
DIPLOM
1919-1962 (4 VOLS.). CONSTN FORCES COLONIAL
INT/ORG
ARMS/CONT WAR NAT/LISM PEACE ATTIT DRIVE...POLICY
INT/LAW 20. PAGE 1 G0011

B39

FULLER G.H.,A SELECTED LIST OF REFERENCES ON THE
BIBLIOG
EXPANSION OF THE US NAVY, 1933-1939 (PAMPHLET).
FORCES
MOD/EUR USA-45 NAT/G PLAN DIPLOM DOMIN RISK
WEAPON
ARMS/CONT EQUILIB PWR 20 NAVY. PAGE 20 G0399
WAR

B40

FULLER G.H.,SELECTED LIST OF RECENT REFERENCES ON
BIBLIOG
AMERICAN NATIONAL DEFENSE (PAMPHLET). USA-45 FINAN
CIVMIL/REL
NAT/G ARMS/CONT WAR GOV/REL CENTRAL COST PEACE PWR
FORCES
20. PAGE 20 G0400
WEAPON

B41

FULLER G.H.,A LIST OF BIBLIOGRAPHIES ON QUESTIONS
BIBLIOG/A
RELATING TO NATIONAL DEFENSE (PAMPHLET). USA-45
FORCES
NAT/G ARMS/CONT WAR GOV/REL COST PEACE 20. PAGE 20
CIVMIL/REL
G0402
WEAPON

B42

US LIBRARY OF CONGRESS,CONDUCT OF THE WAR (APRIL
BIBLIOG/A
1941-MARCH 1942). USA-45 WOR-45 LAW INDUS PUB/INST
WAR
TEC/DEV EDU/PROP CIVMIL/REL 20. PAGE 59 G1155
FORCES
PLAN

B44

MATTHEWS M.A.,INTERNATIONAL POLICE (PAMPHLET).
BIBLIOG
WOR-45 DIPLOM ARMS/CONT WAR 20. PAGE 37 G0722
INT/ORG
FORCES
PEACE

B45

BAKER H.,PROBLEMS OF REEMPLOYMENT AND RETRAINING OF
BIBLIOG/A
MANPOWER DURING THE TRANSITION FROM WAR TO PEACE.
ADJUST
USA+45 INDUS LABOR LG/CO NAT/G PLAN ADMIN PEACE
WAR
...POLICY MGT 20. PAGE 5 G0086
PROB/SOLV

B45

REVES E.,THE ANATOMY OF PEACE. WOR-45 LAW CULTURE
ACT/RES
NAT/G PLAN TEC/DEV EDU/PROP WAR NAT/LISM ATTIT
CONCPT
ALL/VALS SOVEREIGN...POLICY HUM TIME/SEQ 20.
NUC/PWR
PAGE 46 G0914
PEACE

B45

WHITE L.D.,CIVIL SERVICE IN WARTIME. CONSULT
REPRESENT
DELIB/GP PARTIC WAR CHOOSE. PAGE 63 G1233
ADMIN
INTELL
NAT/G

C45

MCDIARMID J.,"THE MOBILIZATION OF SOCIAL
INTELL
SCIENTISTS," IN L. WHITE'S CIVIL CIVIL SERVICE IN
WAR
WARTIME." USA-45 TEC/DEV CENTRAL...SOC 20
DELIB/GP
CIVIL/SERV. PAGE 37 G0733
ADMIN

C45

TRYTTEN M.H.,"THE MOBILIZATION OF SCIENTISTS," IN
INTELL
L. WHITE. CIVIL SERVICE IN WARTIME." USA-45 R+D
WAR
FORCES ACT/RES PERSON ROLE 20. PAGE 55 G1080
TEC/DEV
NAT/G

B46

BAXTER J.P.,SCIENTISTS AGAINST TIME. EUR+WWI
FORCES
MOD/EUR USA+45 USA-45 WOR+45 WOR-45 R+D NAT/G PLAN
WAR
ATTIT PWR...PHIL/SCI RECORD CON/ANAL 17/20. PAGE 6
NUC/PWR
G0107

B46

WILCOX J.K.,OFFICIAL DEFENSE PUBLICATIONS,
1941-1945 (NINE VOLS.). USA-45 AGRI INDUS R+D LABOR WAR
BIBLIOG/A

FORCES TEC/DEV EFFICIENCY PRODUC SKILL WEALTH 20.
CIVMIL/REL
PAGE 63 G1238
ADMIN

B47

SOCIAL SCIENCE RESEARCH COUN,PUBLIC REACTION TO THE
ATTIT
ATOMIC BOMB AND WORLD AFFAIRS. SOCIETY CONFER
NUC/PWR
ARMS/CONT...STAT QU SAMP CHARTS 20. PAGE 52 G1019
DIPLOM
WAR

S47

TURNER R.H.,"THE NAVY DISBURSING OFFICER AS A
FORCES
BUREAUCRAT" (BMR)" USA-45 LAW STRATA DIST/IND WAR
ADMIN
PWR...SOC 20 BUREAUCRCY. PAGE 55 G1083
PERSON
ROLE

B48

GRIFFITH E.S.,RESEARCH IN POLITICAL SCIENCE: THE
BIBLIOG
WORK OF PANELS OF RESEARCH COMMITTEE, APSA. WOR+45
PHIL/SCI
WOR-45 COM/IND R+D FORCES ACT/RES WAR...GOV/COMP
DIPLOM
ANTHOL 20. PAGE 23 G0451
JURID

B48

STEWART I.,ORGANIZING SCIENTIFIC RESEARCH FOR WAR:
DELIB/GP
ADMINISTRATIVE HISTORY OF OFFICE OF SCIENTIFIC
ADMIN
RESEARCH AND DEVELOPMENT. USA-45 INTELL R+D LABOR
WAR
WORKER CREATE BUDGET WEAPON CIVMIL/REL GP/REL
TEC/DEV
EFFICIENCY...POLICY 20. PAGE 53 G1036

B50

CROWTHER J.G.,SCIENCE AT WAR. EUR+WWI PLAN TEC/DEV
R+D
DOMIN COERCE NUC/PWR WEAPON KNOWL PWR...CONCPT OBS
FORCES
TREND VAL/FREE 20. PAGE 14 G0265
WAR
UK

B53

BRETTON H.L.,STRESEMANN AND THE REVISION OF
POLICY
VERSAILLES: A FIGHT FOR REASON. EUR+WWI GERMANY
DIPLOM
FORCES BUDGET ARMS/CONT WAR SUPEGO...BIBLIOG 20
BIOG
TREATY VERSAILLES STRESEMN/G. PAGE 9 G0167

B53

LANGER W.L.,THE UNDECLARED WAR, 1940-1941. EUR+WWI
WAR
GERMANY USA-45 USSR AIR FORCES TEC/DEV CONFER
POLICY
CONTROL COERCE PERCEPT ORD/FREE PWR 20 CHINJAP
DIPLOM
EUROPE. PAGE 32 G0634

B53

TOMPKINS D.C.,CIVIL DEFENSE IN THE STATES: A
BIBLIOG
BIBLIOGRAPHY (DEFENSE BIBLIOGRAPHIES NO. 3;
WAR
PAMPHLET). USA+45 LABOR LOC/G NAT/G PROVS LEGIS.
ORD/FREE
PAGE 55 G1076
ADMIN

B54

ARON R.,CENTURY OF TOTAL WAR. FUT WOR+45 WOR-45
ATTIT
SOCIETY INT/ORG NAT/G FORCES TOP/EX CREATE BAL/PWR
WAR
DOMIN EDU/PROP COERCE DETER PEACE TOTALISM PWR
...TIME/SEQ TREND COLD/WAR TOT/POP VAL/FREE
LEAGUE/NAT 20. PAGE 4 G0066

B54

BUTOW R.J.C.,JAPAN'S DECISION TO SURRENDER. USA-45
ELITES
USSR CHIEF FORCES DOMIN NUC/PWR...BIBLIOG 20 TREATY
DIPLOM
CHINJAP. PAGE 10 G0198
WAR
PEACE

B54

HART B.H.L.,STRATEGY (REV. ED.). CHRIST-17C EUR+WWI
WAR
MEDIT-7 MOD/EUR TEC/DEV LEAD REV WEAPON...POLICY
PLAN
CHARTS. PAGE 25 G0486
FORCES
PHIL/SCI

B54

REYNOLDS P.A.,BRITISH FOREIGN POLICY IN THE INTER-
DIPLOM
WAR YEARS. CZECHOSLVK GERMANY POLAND UK USA-45
POLICY
POL/PAR FORCES ECO/TAC ARMS/CONT WAR ATTIT 20.
NAT/G
PAGE 46 G0915

B54

WRIGHT Q.,PROBLEMS OF STABILITY AND PROGRESS IN
INT/ORG
INTERNATIONAL RELATIONSHIPS. FUT WOR+45 WOR-45
CONCPT
SOCIETY LEGIS CREATE TEC/DEV ECO/TAC EDU/PROP ADJUD
DIPLOM
WAR PEACE ORD/FREE PWR...KNO/TEST TREND GEN/LAWS
20. PAGE 64 G1257

S54

HOOPES T.,"CIVILIAN-MILITARY BALANCE." USA+45 CHIEF
CIVMIL/REL
FORCES PLAN CONTROL WAR GOV/REL GP/REL INGP/REL
LEAD
...POLICY 19/20. PAGE 27 G0527
PWR
NAT/G

B55

DAVIS E.,TWO MINUTES TO MIDNIGHT. WOR+45 PLAN
NUC/PWR
CONTROL NEUTRAL ARMS/CONT ATTIT ORD/FREE...PSY 20
WAR
COLD/WAR. PAGE 14 G0277
DETER
DIPLOM

B55
SHUBIK M.,READINGS IN GAME THEORY AND POLITICAL   MATH
BEHAVIOR. WOR+45 FORCES CREATE ROUTINE WAR PEACE   DECISION
PERCEPT KNOWL PWR...PSY SOC CONCPT METH/CNCPT STAT   DIPLOM
CHARTS HYPO/EXP GAME METH VAL/FREE 20. PAGE 50
G0991

S55
GLADSTONE A.E.,"THE POSSIBILITY OF PREDICTING   PHIL/SCI
REACTIONS TO INTERNATIONAL EVENTS." UNIV SOCIETY   CONCPT
NAT/G FORCES CREATE EDU/PROP COERCE WAR ATTIT
PERSON KNOWL PWR SKILL...METH/CNCPT NEW/IDEA
ORG/CHARTS. PAGE 21 G0420

B56
KOENIG L.W.,THE TRUMAN ADMINISTRATION: ITS   ADMIN
PRINCIPLES AND PRACTICE. USA+45 POL/PAR CHIEF LEGIS   POLICY
DIPLOM DEATH NUC/PWR WAR CIVMIL/REL PEACE   EX/STRUC
...DECISION 20 TRUMAN/HS PRESIDENT TREATY. PAGE 31   GOV/REL
G0610

B56
US DEPARTMENT OF THE ARMY,AMERICAN MILITARY   BIBLIOG
HISTORY. USA+45 USA-45 EX/STRUC PROB/SOLV TEC/DEV   FORCES
DIPLOM NUC/PWR REV WAR WEAPON...PSY 18/20. PAGE 57   NAT/G
G1125

C56
DUPUY R.E.,"MILITARY HERITAGE OF AMERICA." USA+45   FORCES
USA-45 TEC/DEV DIPLOM ROUTINE...POLICY TREND CHARTS   WAR
IDEA/COMP BIBLIOG COLD/WAR. PAGE 17 G0325   CONCPT

B57
DUPREE A.H.,SCIENCE IN THE FEDERAL GOVERNMENT; A   NAT/G
HISTORY OF POLICIES AND ACTIVITIES TO 1940. USA-45   R+D
AGRI SCHOOL DELIB/GP WAR GOV/REL...PHIL/SCI BIBLIOG   CREATE
18/20 DEPRESSION NEW/DEAL WWI JEFFERSN/T. PAGE 17   TEC/DEV
G0324

S57
JANOWITZ M.,"MILITARY ELITES AND THE STUDY OF WAR."   FORCES
USA+45 WOR-45 STRATA NAT/G PROF/ORG TEC/DEV DOMIN   ELITES
EDU/PROP COERCE WAR ATTIT RIGID/FLEX PWR RESPECT
...MGT TREND STERTYP GEN/METH 20. PAGE 28 G0558

S57
MORTON L.,"THE DECISION TO USE THE BOMB." FORCES   NUC/PWR
TOP/EX DOMIN COERCE PEACE. PAGE 40 G0788   DIPLOM
                                                      WAR

B58
ANGELL N.,DEFENCE AND THE ENGLISH-SPEAKING ROLE.   DIPLOM
CHINA/COM UK USSR INT/ORG FORCES EDU/PROP NEUTRAL   WAR
NUC/PWR NAT/LISM PEACE TOTALISM 20 COLD/WAR   MARXISM
COEXIST. PAGE 3 G0059   ORD/FREE

B58
ARON R.,ON WAR: ATOMIC WEAPONS AND GLOBAL DIPLOMACY   ARMS/CONT
(TRANS. BY TERENCE KILMARTIN). WOR+45 SOCIETY   NUC/PWR
FORCES BAL/PWR WAR WEAPON PERSON...SOC 20. PAGE 4   COERCE
G0067   DIPLOM

B58
BIDWELL P.W.,RAW MATERIALS: A STUDY OF AMERICAN   EXTR/IND
POLICY. USA+45 USA-45 ECO/UNDEV AGRI INDUS KIN   ECO/DEV
CREATE PLAN ECO/TAC WAR PEACE ATTIT DRIVE WEALTH
...STAT CHARTS CONGRESS VAL/FREE. PAGE 7 G0135

B58
GAVIN J.M.,WAR AND PEACE IN THE SPACE AGE. SPACE   WAR
USA+45 USSR FORCES PLAN TEC/DEV BAL/PWR DIPLOM   DETER
ARMS/CONT WEAPON CIVMIL/REL...CHARTS GP/COMP 20   NUC/PWR
NATO COLD/WAR. PAGE 21 G0414   PEACE

B58
NATIONAL PLANNING ASSOCIATION,1970 WITHOUT ARMS   ARMS/CONT
CONTROL (PAMPHLET). WOR+45 PROB/SOLV TEC/DEV DIPLOM   ORD/FREE
CONFER DETER NUC/PWR WAR...CHARTS 20 COLD/WAR.   WEAPON
PAGE 41 G0810   PREDICT

B58
ROCKEFELLER BROTH FUND INC,INTERNATIONAL SECURITY -   NUC/PWR
THE MILITARY ASPECT. USA+45 INT/ORG NAT/G BUDGET   DETER
ARMS/CONT WAR WEAPON PEACE ORD/FREE 20 NATO.   FORCES
PAGE 47 G0932   DIPLOM

B58
TELLER E.A.,OUR NUCLEAR FUTURE. SOCIETY FORCES   FUT
TEC/DEV EDU/PROP KNOWL ORD/FREE...STAND/INT SYS/QU   PHIL/SCI
KNO/TEST AUD/VIS CHARTS SIMUL 20. PAGE 54 G1062   NUC/PWR
                                                      WAR

B58
US DEPARTMENT OF THE ARMY,BIBLIOGRAPHY ON LIMITED   BIBLIOG/A
WAR (PAMPHLET). USA+45 TEC/DEV CONTROL RISK COERCE   WAR
DETER NUC/PWR WEAPON ADJUST PEACE ALL/VALS ORD/FREE   FORCES

20. PAGE 57 G1127   CIVMIL/REL

B58
US HOUSE COMM GOVT OPERATIONS,CIVIL DEFENSE. USA+45   NUC/PWR
FORCES...CHARTS 20 CONGRESS CIV/DEFENS HOLIFLD/C.   WAR
PAGE 58 G1139   PLAN
                                                      ADJUST

S58
DAVENPORT J.,"ARMS AND THE WELFARE STATE." INTELL   USA+45
STRUCT FORCES CREATE ECO/TAC FOR/AID DOMIN LEGIT   NAT/G
ADMIN WAR ORD/FREE PWR...POLICY SOC CONCPT MYTH OBS   USSR
TREND COLD/WAR TOT/POP 20. PAGE 14 G0276

B59
AIR FORCE ACADEMY ASSEMBLY '59,INTERNATIONAL   FOR/AID
STABILITY AND PROGRESS (PAMPHLET). USA+45 USSR   FORCES
ECO/UNDEV PROB/SOLV BUDGET DIPLOM ADMIN DETER COST   WAR
ATTIT...TREND 20. PAGE 2 G0030   PLAN

B59
EMME E.M.,THE IMPACT OF AIR POWER - NATIONAL   DETER
SECURITY AND WORLD POLITICS. USA+45 USSR FORCES   AIR
DIPLOM WEAPON PEACE TOTALISM...POLICY NAT/COMP 20   WAR
EUROPE. PAGE 18 G0346   ORD/FREE

B59
GODDARD V.,THE ENIGMA OF MENACE. WOR+45 SECT LEAD   PEACE
NUC/PWR WAR WEAPON CHOOSE PERSON PWR...POLICY   ARMS/CONT
PHIL/SCI PACIFIST 20 COLD/WAR. PAGE 22 G0423   DIPLOM
                                                      ATTIT

B59
GREENFIELD K.R.,COMMAND DECISIONS. ASIA EUR+WWI   PLAN
S/ASIA USA-45 WOR-45 NAT/G CONSULT DELIB/GP COERCE   FORCES
NUC/PWR PWR...OBS 20 CHINJAP. PAGE 23 G0446   WAR
                                                      WEAPON

B59
HUGHES E.M.,AMERICA THE VINCIBLE. USA+45 FOR/AID   ORD/FREE
ARMS/CONT NUC/PWR PERS/REL RATIONAL ATTIT ALL/VALS   DIPLOM
20 COLD/WAR. PAGE 27 G0534   WAR

B59
LANG D.,FROM HIROSHIMA TO THE MOON: CHRONICLES OF   NUC/PWR
LIFE IN THE ATOMIC AGE. USA+45 OP/RES CONTROL   SPACE
ARMS/CONT WAR CIVMIL/REL PEACE HABITAT MORAL PWR   HEALTH
...OBS INT 20 AEC. PAGE 32 G0633   TEC/DEV

B59
POKROVSKY G.I.,SCIENCE AND TECHNOLOGY IN   TEC/DEV
CONTEMPORARY WAR. SPACE USSR WOR+45 NAT/G CONSULT   FORCES
ACT/RES PLAN DETER WEAPON...MARXIST METH/CNCPT   NUC/PWR
CHARTS STERTYP COLD/WAR 20. PAGE 45 G0881   WAR

B59
COLUMBIA U BUREAU APPL SOC R, ATTITUDES OF   ATTIT
PROMINENT AMERICANS TOWARD "WORLD PEACE THROUGH   ACT/RES
WORLD LAW" (SUPRA-NATL ORGANIZATION FOR WAR   INT/LAW
PREVENTION). USA+45 USSR ELITES FORCES PLAN   STAT
PROB/SOLV CONTROL WAR PWR...POLICY SOC QU IDEA/COMP
20 UN. PAGE 45 G0888

B59
SPANIER J.W.,THE TRUMAN-MACARTHUR CONTROVERSY AND   CIVMIL/REL
THE KOREAN WAR. USA+45 TOP/EX PROB/SOLV LEAD ATTIT   FORCES
PWR...POLICY BIBLIOG/A UN. PAGE 52 G1023   CHIEF
                                                      WAR

B59
VAN WAGENEN R.W.,SOME VIEWS OF AMERICAN DEFENSE   INT/ORG
OFFICIALS ABOUT THE UNITED NATIONS (PAPER). FUT   LEAD
USA+45 NAT/G DIPLOM WAR EFFICIENCY PEACE...POLICY   ATTIT
INT 20 UN DEPT/DEFEN. PAGE 61 G1192   FORCES

L59
BURNS A.L.,"THE RATIONALE OF CATALYTIC WAR." COM   COERCE
USA+45 WOR+45 R+D NAT/G FORCES ACT/RES TEC/DEV PWR   NUC/PWR
...DECISION HYPO/EXP TOT/POP 20. PAGE 10 G0191   WAR

B60
BARNET R.,WHO WANTS DISARMAMENT. COM EUR+WWI USA+45   PLAN
USSR INT/ORG NAT/G BAL/PWR DIPLOM EDU/PROP COERCE   FORCES
DETER NUC/PWR WAR WEAPON ATTIT PWR...TIME/SEQ   ARMS/CONT
COLD/WAR CONGRESS 20. PAGE 5 G0096

B60
CHASE S.,LIVE AND LET LIVE. USA+45 ECO/DEV   NAT/G
PROB/SOLV TEC/DEV ECO/TAC ARMS/CONT NUC/PWR WAR   DIPLOM
NAT/LISM PEACE...GEOG TREND 20 COLD/WAR. PAGE 11   SOCIETY
G0223   TASK

B60
JANOWITZ M.,THE PROFESSIONAL SOLDIER. CULTURE   FORCES
STRATA STRUCT FAM PROB/SOLV TEC/DEV COERCE WAR   MYTH
CIVMIL/REL NAT/LISM AGE HEREDITY ALL/VALS CONSERVE   LEAD

...MGT WORSHIP. PAGE 28 G0560   ELITES

B60
KINGSTON-MCCLOUG E.,DEFENSE; POLICY AND STRATEGY.   FORCES
UK SEA AIR TEC/DEV DIPLOM ADMIN LEAD WAR ORD/FREE   PLAN
...CHARTS 20. PAGE 30 G0597   POLICY
                                                     DECISION

B60
MCCLELLAND C.A.,NUCLEAR WEAPONS, MISSILES, AND   DIPLOM
FUTURE WAR: PROBLEM FOR THE SIXTIES. WOR+45 FORCES   NUC/PWR
ARMS/CONT DETER MARXISM...POLICY ANTHOL COLD/WAR.   WAR
PAGE 37 G0729   WEAPON

B60
US DEPARTMENT OF THE ARMY,DISARMAMENT: A   BIBLIOG/A
BIBLIOGRAPHIC RECORD: 1916-1960. DETER WAR WEAPON   ARMS/CONT
PEACE 20 UN LEAGUE/NAT COLD/WAR NATO. PAGE 57 G1128 NUC/PWR
                                                     DIPLOM

B60
US HOUSE COMM. SCI. ASTRONAUT.,OCEAN SCIENCES AND   R+D
NATIONAL SECURITY. FUT SEA ECO/DEV EXTR/IND INT/ORG ORD/FREE
NAT/G FORCES ACT/RES TEC/DEV ECO/TAC COERCE WAR
BIO/SOC KNOWL PWR...CONCPT RECORD LAB/EXP 20.
PAGE 59 G1153

B60
WILLIAUS T.H.,AMERICANS AT WAR: THE DEVELOPMENT OF   FORCES
THE AMERICAN MILITARY SYSTEM. USA+45 USA-45   WAR
EDU/PROP LEAD REV...GP/COMP BIBLIOG/A 18/20   NAT/G
PRESIDENT. PAGE 63 G1244   POLICY

S60
BRODY R.A.,"DETERRENCE STRATEGIES: AN ANNOTATED   BIBLIOG/A
BIBLIOGRAPHY." WOR+45 PLAN ARMS/CONT NUC/PWR WAR   FORCES
WEAPON DECISION. PAGE 9 G0173   DETER
                                                     DIPLOM

S60
HUNTINGTON S.P.,"STRATEGIC PLANNING AND THE   EXEC
POLITICAL PROCESS." USA+45 NAT/G DELIB/GP LEGIS   FORCES
ACT/RES ECO/TAC LEGIT ROUTINE CHOOSE RIGID/FLEX PWR NUC/PWR
...POLICY MAJORIT MGT 20. PAGE 27 G0538   WAR

S60
KISSINGER H.A.,"ARMS CONTROL, INSPECTION AND   FORCES
SURPRISE ATTACK." COM USA+45 NAT/G ACT/RES PLAN   ORD/FREE
TEC/DEV DIPLOM EDU/PROP DETER WAR RIGID/FLEX   ARMS/CONT
...CONCPT GEN/METH TOT/POP 20. PAGE 31 G0603   NUC/PWR

S60
OSGOOD C.E.,"A CASE FOR GRADUATED UNILATERAL   ATTIT
DISENGAGEMENT." FUT WOR+45 CULTURE SOCIETY NAT/G   EDU/PROP
NUC/PWR WAR PERSON SUPEGO ALL/VALS...POLICY PSY   ARMS/CONT
CONCPT COLD/WAR TOT/POP VAL/FREE 20. PAGE 43 G0848

B61
KAHN H.,ON THERMONUCLEAR WAR. FUT UNIV WOR+45   DETER
ECO/DEV CONSULT EX/STRUC TOP/EX ACT/RES CREATE PLAN NUC/PWR
COERCE WAR PERSON ALL/VALS...POLICY GEOG CONCPT   SOCIETY
METH/CNCPT OBS TREND 20. PAGE 29 G0569

B61
NATHAN O.,EINSTEIN ON PEACE. WOR+45 WOR-45 INTELL   CONCPT
NUC/PWR WAR PERSON MORAL...BIOG VAL/FREE NAZI 20   PEACE
EINSTEIN/A. PAGE 41 G0807

B61
SCHMIDT H.,VERTEIDIGUNG ODER VERGELTUNG. COM CUBA   PLAN
GERMANY/W USSR FORCES DIPLOM ARMS/CONT DETER   WAR
NUC/PWR...POLICY CHARTS HYPO/EXP SIMUL BIBLIOG 20   BAL/PWR
NATO COLD/WAR. PAGE 49 G0970   ORD/FREE

B61
STEIN W.,NUCLEAR WEAPONS: A CATHOLIC RESPONSE.   NUC/PWR
WOR+45 FORCES ARMS/CONT DETER MURDER MORAL...POLICY WAR
CATH IDEA/COMP ANTHOL 20. PAGE 52 G1033   CATHISM
                                                     ATTIT

B61
US SENATE COMM GOVT OPERATIONS,ORGANIZING FOR   POLICY
NATIONAL SECURITY. COM USA+45 BUDGET DIPLOM DETER   PLAN
NUC/PWR WAR WEAPON ORD/FREE...BIBLIOG 20 COLD/WAR.   FORCES
PAGE 60 G1176   COERCE

B62
BAKER G.W.,BEHAVIORAL SCIENCE AND CIVIL DEFENSE.   NUC/PWR
USA+45 PROB/SOLV ADMIN GP/REL INGP/REL PERS/REL   WAR
ANOMIE DRIVE PERSON...DECISION MGT SOC 20   POLICY
CIV/DEFENS. PAGE 4 G0085   ACT/RES

B62
BENNETT J.C.,NUCLEAR WEAPONS AND THE CONFLICT OF   POLICY
CONSCIENCE. WOR+45 PROB/SOLV DIPLOM WEAPON SUPEGO   NUC/PWR
MORAL...ANTHOL WORSHIP 20. PAGE 6 G0120   WAR

B62
BOULDING K.E.,CONFLICT AND DEFENSE: A GENERAL   MATH
THEORY. FUT SOCIETY INT/ORG NAT/G CREATE BAL/PWR   SIMUL
COERCE NAT/LISM DRIVE ALL/VALS...PLURIST DECISION   PEACE
CONCPT METH/CNCPT TREND HYPO/EXP TOT/POP 20. PAGE 8 WAR
G0157

B62
BURKE A.E.,ENOUGH GOOD MEN. USA+45 WOR+45 ECO/UNDEV DIPLOM
FORCES TEC/DEV GUERRILLA NUC/PWR REV WAR ORD/FREE   POLICY
MARXISM...GEOG 20 COLD/WAR. PAGE 10 G0189   NAT/G
                                                     TASK

B62
CHASE S.,THE PROPER STUDY OF MANKIND (2ND REV.   PHIL/SCI
ED.). WOR+45 WOR-45 INTELL WAR...METH/CNCPT   SOC
SAMP/SIZ GEN/LAWS BIBLIOG METH 16/20. PAGE 11 G0224 PROB/SOLV
                                                     PERSON

B62
FORBES H.W.,THE STRATEGY OF DISARMAMENT. FUT WOR+45 PLAN
INT/ORG VOL/ASSN CONSULT ARMS/CONT COERCE NUC/PWR   FORCES
WAR DRIVE RIGID/FLEX ORD/FREE PWR...POLICY CONCPT   DIPLOM
OBS TREND STERTYP 20. PAGE 19 G0378

B62
FRYKLUND R.,100 MILLION LIVES: MAXIMUM SURVIVAL IN   NUC/PWR
A NUCLEAR WAR. USA+45 USSR CONTROL WEAPON   WAR
...IDEA/COMP NAT/COMP 20. PAGE 20 G0397   PLAN
                                                     DETER

B62
GILPIN R.,AMERICAN SCIENTISTS AND NUCLEAR WEAPONS   INTELL
POLICY. COM FUT USA+45 WOR+45 INT/ORG NAT/G   ATTIT
PROF/ORG CONSULT FORCES CREATE TEC/DEV BAL/PWR   DETER
EDU/PROP ARMS/CONT WAR PERCEPT KNOWL MORAL PWR   NUC/PWR
...PHIL/SCI SOC CONCPT GEN/LAWS 20. PAGE 21 G0417

B62
HALPERIN M.H.,LIMITED WAR; AN ESSAY ON THE   BIBLIOG/A
DEVELOPMENT OF THE THEORY AND AN ANNOTATED   WAR
BIBLIOGRAPHY (OCCASIONAL PAPER NO. 3). WOR+45   ARMS/CONT
WOR-45 NUC/PWR...CONCPT IDEA/COMP METH/COMP 19/20.   FORCES
PAGE 24 G0471

B62
OSGOOD C.E.,AN ALTERNATIVE TO WAR OR SURRENDER. FUT ORD/FREE
UNIV CULTURE INTELL SOCIETY R+D INT/ORG CONSULT   EDU/PROP
DELIB/GP ACT/RES PLAN CHOOSE ATTIT PERCEPT KNOWL   PEACE
...PHIL/SCI PSY SOC TREND GEN/LAWS 20. PAGE 43   WAR
G0849

B62
PERRE J.,LES MUTATIONS DE LA GUERRE MODERNE: DE LA   WAR
REVOLUTION FRANCAISE A LA REVOLUTION NUCLEAIRE.   FORCES
DIPLOM ARMS/CONT DEATH REV WEAPON GP/REL PEACE   NUC/PWR
ATTIT...STAT PREDICT BIBLIOG 18/20 WWI. PAGE 44
G0870

B62
STOVER C.F.,THE GOVERNMENT OF SCIENCE (PAMPHLET).   PHIL/SCI
USA+45 SOCIETY PROF/ORG EX/STRUC CREATE CONTROL   TEC/DEV
NUC/PWR WAR GOV/REL PEACE ORD/FREE 20. PAGE 53   LAW
G1041   NAT/G

B62
STRAUSS L.L.,MEN AND DECISIONS. USA+45 USA-45 USSR   DECISION
CONSULT FORCES TOP/EX WAR PEACE 20. PAGE 53 G1042   PWR
                                                     NUC/PWR
                                                     DIPLOM

B62
THOMSON G.P.,NUCLEAR ENERGY IN BRITAIN DURING THE   CREATE
LAST WAR: THE CHERWELL SIMON LECTURE (MONOGRAPH).   TEC/DEV
UK R+D CONSULT FORCES PLAN DIPLOM TASK CIVMIL/REL   WAR
ROLE...PHIL/SCI NEW/IDEA LAB/EXP 20 MAUD. PAGE 54   NUC/PWR
G1071

S62
MARTIN L.W.,"THE MARKET FOR STRATEGIC IDEAS IN   DIPLOM
BRITAIN: THE 'SANDYS ERA'" UK ARMS/CONT WAR GOV/REL COERCE
OPTIMAL...POLICY DECISION GOV/COMP COLD/WAR   FORCES
CMN/WLTH. PAGE 36 G0714   PWR

B63
PACHTER H.M.,COLLISION COURSE; THE CUBAN MISSILE   WAR
CRISIS AND COEXISTENCE. CUBA USA+45 DIPLOM   BAL/PWR
ARMS/CONT PEACE MARXISM...DECISION INT/LAW 20   NUC/PWR
COLD/WAR KHRUSH/N KENNEDY/JF CASTRO/F. PAGE 43   DETER
G0854

B63
US DEPARTMENT OF THE ARMY,SOVIET RUSSIA: STRATEGIC   BIBLIOG/A
SURVEY (PAMPHLET). USSR POL/PAR PLAN DOMIN EDU/PROP MARXISM
ARMS/CONT GUERRILLA WAR WEAPON...TREND CHARTS   DIPLOM

ORG/CHARTS 20. PAGE 57 G1129   COERCE

B63
US DEPARTMENT OF THE ARMY,US OVERSEAS BASES: PRESENT STATUS AND FUTURE PROSPECTS (PAMPHLET). USA+45 DIPLOM NUC/PWR ATTIT ORD/FREE...POLICY CHARTS 20. PAGE 58 G1130
BIBLIOG/A WAR BAL/PWR DETER

B63
WILTZ J.E.,IN SEARCH OF PEACE: THE SENATE MUNITIONS INQUIRY, 1934-36. EUR+WWI USA-45 ELITES INDUS LG/CO LEGIS INT/TRADE LOBBY NEUTRAL ARMS/CONT...POLICY CONGRESS 20 LEAGUE/NAT PRESIDENT SENATE CONSCRIPTN. PAGE 64 G1246
DELIB/GP PROFIT WAR WEAPON

L63
PHELPS J.,"STUDIES IN DETERRENCE VIII: MILITARY STABILITY AND ARMS CONTROL: A CRITICAL SURVEY." FUT WOR+45 INT/ORG ACT/RES EDU/PROP COERCE NUC/PWR WAR HEALTH PWR...POLICY TECHNIC TREND SIMUL TOT/POP 20. PAGE 44 G0874
FORCES ORD/FREE ARMS/CONT DETER

S63
BOULDING K.E.,"UNIVERSITY, SOCIETY, AND ARMS CONTROL." WOR+45 WOR-45 ACADEM NAT/G CONSULT FORCES ACT/RES PLAN TEC/DEV BAL/PWR ECO/TAC COERCE DETER WAR ATTIT RIGID/FLEX KNOWL ORD/FREE PWR WEALTH ...CONCPT COLD/WAR TOT/POP 20. PAGE 8 G0159
SOCIETY ARMS/CONT

B64
BROWN N.,NUCLEAR WAR* THE IMPENDING STRATEGIC DEADLOCK. USA+45 USSR TEC/DEV BUDGET RISK ARMS/CONT NUC/PWR WEAPON COST BIO/SOC...GEOG IDEA/COMP NAT/COMP GAME NATO WARSAW/P. PAGE 9 G0177
FORCES OP/RES WAR GEN/LAWS

B64
DUSCHA J.,ARMS, MONEY, AND POLITICS. USA+45 INDUS POL/PAR ECO/TAC TAX DETER NUC/PWR WAR WEAPON GOV/REL ATTIT...BIBLIOG/A 20 CONGRESS MONEY DEPT/DEFEN. PAGE 17 G0326
NAT/G FORCES POLICY BUDGET

B64
FOGELMAN E.,HIROSHIMA: THE DECISION TO USE THE A-BOMB. USA-45 DIPLOM EFFICIENCY PEACE...ANTHOL BIBLIOG T 20 CHINJAP. PAGE 19 G0375
INTELL DECISION NUC/PWR WAR

B64
GROSSER G.H.,THE THREAT OF IMPENDING DISASTER: CONTRIBUTIONS TO THE PSYCHOLOGY OF STRESS. SPACE UNIV SOCIETY R+D TEC/DEV EDU/PROP COERCE WAR ATTIT BIO/SOC DISPL PERCEPT PERSON...SOC MYTH SELF/OBS CONT/OBS BIOG CON/ANAL TOT/POP 20. PAGE 23 G0455
HEALTH PSY NUC/PWR

B64
KAUFMANN W.W.,THE MC NAMARA STRATEGY. TOP/EX INSPECT BAL/PWR DIPLOM CONTROL DETER GUERRILLA NUC/PWR WEAPON COST PWR...METH/COMP 20 MCNAMARA/R KENNEDY/JF JOHNSON/LB NATO DEPT/DEFEN. PAGE 30 G0586
FORCES WAR PLAN PROB/SOLV

B64
ROBERTS HL,FOREIGN AFFAIRS BIBLIOGRAPHY, 1952-1962. ECO/DEV SECT PLAN FOR/AID INT/TRADE ARMS/CONT NAT/LISM ATTIT...INT/LAW GOV/COMP IDEA/COMP 20. PAGE 47 G0928
BIBLIOG/A DIPLOM INT/ORG WAR

B64
ROTHSCHILD J.H.,TOMORROW'S WEAPONS: CHEMICAL AND BIOLOGICAL. FUT PROB/SOLV ARMS/CONT PEACE MORAL ...CHARTS BIBLIOG 20. PAGE 48 G0941
WAR WEAPON BIO/SOC DETER

B64
THANT U.,TOWARD WORLD PEACE. DELIB/GP TEC/DEV EDU/PROP WAR SOVEREIGN...INT/LAW 20 UN MID/EAST. PAGE 54 G1065
DIPLOM BIOG PEACE COERCE

B64
US AIR FORCE ACADEMY ASSEMBLY,OUTER SPACE: FINAL REPORT APRIL 1-4, 1964. FUT USA+45 WOR+45 LAW DELIB/GP CONFER ARMS/CONT WAR PEACE ATTIT MORAL ...ANTHOL 20 NASA. PAGE 56 G1104
SPACE CIVMIL/REL NUC/PWR DIPLOM

B64
WHEELER-BENNETT J.W.,THE NEMESIS OF POWER (2ND ED.). EUR+WWI GERMANY TOP/EX TEC/DEV ADMIN WAR PERS/REL RIGID/FLEX ROLE ORD/FREE PWR FASCISM 20 HITLER/A. PAGE 63 G1231
FORCES NAT/G GP/REL STRUCT

S64
"FURTHER READING." INDIA PAKISTAN SECT WAR PEACE ATTIT...POLICY 20. PAGE 1 G0018
BIBLIOG GP/REL DIPLOM NAT/G

S64
ABT C.,"WAR GAMING." USA+45 NAT/G TOP/EX ACT/RES TEC/DEV COERCE KNOWL ORD/FREE PWR...DECISION MATH TIME/SEQ COMPUT/IR CHARTS LAB/EXP VAL/FREE. PAGE 2 G0026
FORCES SIMUL WAR

S64
LERNER A.P.,"NUCLEAR SYMMETRY AS A FRAMEWORK FOR COEXISTENCE." COM FUT USA+45 NAT/G ACT/RES CREATE PLAN DIPLOM EDU/PROP COERCE WAR RIGID/FLEX PWR SKILL...CONCPT METH/CNCPT GEN/LAWS TOT/POP VAL/FREE COLD/WAR 20. PAGE 33 G0657
FORCES ORD/FREE DETER NUC/PWR

N64
NATIONAL ACADEMY OF SCIENCES,CIVIL DEFENSE: PROJECT HARBOR SUMMARY REPORT (PAMPHLET). USA+45 MUNIC NAT/G ACT/RES BUDGET EDU/PROP DETER WEAPON EATING ...GEOG 20. PAGE 41 G0808
NUC/PWR FORCES WAR PLAN

B65
PEACE RESEARCH ABSTRACTS. FUT WOR+45 R+D INT/ORG NAT/G PLAN TEC/DEV BAL/PWR DIPLOM FOR/AID NUC/PWR HEALTH. PAGE 1 G0020
BIBLIOG/A PEACE ARMS/CONT WAR

B65
BAILEY S.K.,AMERICAN POLITICS AND GOVERNMENT. USA+45 CONSTN FINAN LABOR POL/PAR DIPLOM ADMIN WAR INGP/REL RACE/REL NEW/LIB 20 SUPREME/CT PRESIDENT CONGRESS. PAGE 4 G0084
ANTHOL LEGIS PWR

B65
GRETTON P.,MARITIME STRATEGY - A STUDY OF DEFENSE PROBLEMS. ASIA UK USSR DIPLOM COERCE DETER NUC/PWR WEAPON...CONCPT NAT/COMP 20. PAGE 23 G0449
FORCES PLAN WAR SEA

B65
HALPERIN M.H.,CHINA AND THE BOMB. USA+45 USSR INT/ORG FORCES ARMS/CONT DETER PRODUC ORD/FREE PWR TREND. PAGE 24 G0472
ASIA NUC/PWR WAR DIPLOM

B65
HALPERIN M.H.,COMMUNIST CHINA AND ARMS CONTROL. CHINA/COM FUT USA+45 CULTURE FORCES TEC/DEV ECO/TAC WAR PEACE ORD/FREE MARXISM 20 COLD/WAR. PAGE 24 G0473
ATTIT POLICY ARMS/CONT NUC/PWR

B65
HEER D.M.,AFTER NUCLEAR ATTACK: A DEMOGRAPHIC INQUIRY. USA+45 ECO/DEV SECT WORKER SEX...HEAL SOC STAT PREDICT CHARTS 20 NEGRO. PAGE 25 G0500
GEOG NUC/PWR CENSUS WAR

B65
HITCH C.J.,DECISION-MAKING FOR DEFENSE. USA+45 CREATE BUDGET COERCE WAR WEAPON EFFICIENCY...SIMUL 20. PAGE 26 G0515
DECISION OP/RES PLAN FORCES

B65
MOSKOWITZ H.,US SECURITY, ARMS CONTROL, AND DISARMAMENT 1961-1965. FORCES DIPLOM DETER WAR WEAPON...CHARTS 20 UN COLD/WAR NATO. PAGE 40 G0790
BIBLIOG/A ARMS/CONT NUC/PWR PEACE

B65
THAYER F.C. JR.,AIR TRANSPORT POLICY AND NATIONAL SECURITY: A POLITICAL, ECONOMIC, AND MILITARY ANALYSIS. DIST/IND OP/RES PLAN TEC/DEV DIPLOM DETER WAR COST EFFICIENCY...POLICY BIBLIOG 20 DEPT/DEFEN FAA CAB. PAGE 54 G1066
AIR FORCES CIVMIL/REL ORD/FREE

B65
US DEPARTMENT OF ARMY,MILITARY PROTECTIVE CONSTRUCTION: NUCLEAR WARFARE AND CHEMICAL AND BIOLOGICAL OPERATIONS (MANUAL). OP/RES TEC/DEV RISK COERCE NUC/PWR WAR WEAPON EFFICIENCY UTIL BIO/SOC HABITAT ORD/FREE 20. PAGE 57 G1117
FORCES CONSTRUC TASK HEALTH

B65
US DEPARTMENT OF THE ARMY,MILITARY MANPOWER POLICY. USA+45 LEGIS EXEC WAR 20 CONGRESS. PAGE 58 G1132
BIBLIOG/A POLICY FORCES TREND

B65
WASKOW A.I.,KEEPING THE WORLD DISARMED. AFR GERMANY/E DIPLOM CONTROL WAR 20 UN. PAGE 62 G1218
ARMS/CONT PEACE FORCES PROB/SOLV

S65
BEAUFRE A.,"THE SHARING OF NUCLEAR   DETER

RESPONSIBILITIES* A PROBLEM IN NEED OF SOLUTION.."   RISK
FRANCE USA+45 INT/ORG NAT/G DELIB/GP FORCES CONTROL   ACT/RES
NUC/PWR RIGID/FLEX...CONCPT IDEA/COMP NATO. PAGE 6   WAR
G0110

                                                          S65
BIRNBAUM K.,"SWEDEN'S NUCLEAR POLICY." WOR+45   SWEDEN
POL/PAR CREATE TEC/DEV NEUTRAL RISK WAR ORD/FREE   NUC/PWR
...DECISION IDEA/COMP NAT/COMP TIME. PAGE 7 G0137   DIPLOM
                                                          ARMS/CONT

                                                          S65
DALKEY N.C.,"SOLVABLE NUCLEAR WAR MODELS." FORCES   GAME
BAL/PWR DIPLOM COERCE PEACE DECISION. PAGE 14 G0273   SIMUL
                                                          WAR
                                                          NUC/PWR

                                                          S65
GOLDSTEIN W.,"KEEPING THE GENIE IN THE BOTTLE* THE   NUC/PWR
FEASIBILITY OF A NUCLEAR NON-PROLIFERATION   CREATE
AGREEMENT." ASIA FRANCE UK USA+45 USSR WOR+45   COST
ECO/UNDEV VOL/ASSN ACT/RES PLAN RISK ARMS/CONT WAR
PEACE ATTIT PERCEPT...RECORD TREND TIME. PAGE 22
G0429

                                                          S65
HARRISON S.L.,"NTH NATION CHALLENGES* THE PRESENT   ARMS/CONT
PERSPECTIVE." EUR+WWI FUT USA+45 BAL/PWR CONTROL   NUC/PWR
RISK COERCE WAR...PREDICT COLD/WAR. PAGE 25 G0485   NAT/G
                                                          DIPLOM

                                                          S65
HSIEH A.L.,"THE SINO-SOVIET NUCLEAR DIALOGUE*   ASIA
1963." S/ASIA USA+45 RISK DETER REV WAR SOVEREIGN   USSR
IDEA/COMP. PAGE 27 G0533   NUC/PWR

                                                          S65
KOHL W.L.,"NUCLEAR SHARING IN NATO AND THE   ARMS/CONT
MULTILATERAL FORCE." FUT USSR VOL/ASSN TEC/DEV   OBS
DIPLOM NUC/PWR WAR WEAPON NATO. PAGE 31 G0611   IDEA/COMP

                                                          S65
KREITH K.,"PEACE RESEARCH AND GOVERNMENT POLICY."   PEACE
INTELL NAT/G DIPLOM ECO/TAC CONTROL ARMS/CONT WAR   STYLE
PERCEPT...DECISION IDEA/COMP. PAGE 31 G0619   OBS

                                                          S65
KRICKUS R.J.,"ON THE MORALITY OF   MORAL
CHEMICAL/BIOLOGICAL WAR." ECO/UNDEV ARMS/CONT DETER   BIO/SOC
NUC/PWR RIGID/FLEX HEALTH INT/LAW. PAGE 31 G0621   WEAPON
                                                          WAR

                                                          S65
RUBINSTEIN A.Z.,"POLITICAL BARRIERS TO   COM
DISARMAMENT." FUT DIPLOM COERCE NUC/PWR WAR   USA+45
NAT/LISM ORD/FREE PREDICT. PAGE 48 G0944   ARMS/CONT
                                                          ATTIT

                                                          C65
MARK M.,"BEYOND SOVEREIGNTY." WOR+45 WOR-45   NAT/LISM
ECO/UNDEV BAL/PWR INT/TRADE NUC/PWR REV WAR MARXISM   NAT/G
NEW/LIB BIBLIOG. PAGE 36 G0706   DIPLOM
                                                          INTELL

                                                          C65
SCHWEBEL M.,"BEHAVIORAL SCIENCE AND HUMAN   PEACE
SURVIVAL." FORCES ARMS/CONT COERCE NUC/PWR WAR   ACT/RES
GP/REL NAT/LISM PERCEPT...POLICY PSY ANTHOL   DIPLOM
BIBLIOG/A 20 COLD/WAR. PAGE 50 G0984   HEAL

                                                          C65
US AIR FORCE ACADEMY,"AMERICAN DEFENSE POLICY." COM   PLAN
INT/ORG TEC/DEV FOR/AID ARMS/CONT DETER NUC/PWR   FORCES
...POLICY DECISION CONCPT ANTHOL BIBLIOG/A 20   WAR
COLD/WAR NATO. PAGE 56 G1103   COERCE

                                                          B66
BOLTON R.E.,DEFENSE AND DISARMAMENT: THE ECONOMICS   ARMS/CONT
OF TRANSITION. USA+45 R+D FORCES PLAN LOBBY DETER   POLICY
WAR COST PEACE...ANTHOL BIBLIOG 20. PAGE 8 G0150   INDUS

                                                          B66
BRODIE B.,ESCALATION AND THE NUCLEAR OPTION. ASIA   NUC/PWR
CUBA EUR+WWI KOREA USA+45 USSR VIETNAM RISK ATTIT   GUERRILLA
DRIVE PERCEPT PROBABIL. PAGE 9 G0172   WAR
                                                          DETER

                                                          B66
CLARK G.,WORLD PEACE THROUGH WORLD LAW; TWO   INT/LAW
ALTERNATIVE PLANS. WOR+45 DELIB/GP FORCES TAX   PEACE
CONFER ADJUD SANCTION ARMS/CONT WAR CHOOSE PRIVIL   PLAN
20 UN COLD/WAR. PAGE 12 G0231   INT/ORG

                                                          B66
DAENIKER G.,STRATEGIE DES KLEIN STAATS. SWITZERLND   NUC/PWR
ACT/RES CREATE DIPLOM NEUTRAL DETER WAR WEAPON PWR   PLAN

SOVEREIGN...IDEA/COMP 20 COLD/WAR. PAGE 14 G0270   FORCES
                                                          NAT/G

                                                          B66
FEIS H.,THE ATOMIC BOMB AND THE END OF WORLD WAR   USA+45
II. FORCES PLAN PROB/SOLV DIPLOM CONFER WAR   PEACE
...TIME/SEQ TREND CHINJAP PRESIDENT TIME. PAGE 19   NUC/PWR
G0362

                                                          B66
FREIDEL F.,AMERICAN ISSUES IN THE TWENTIETH   DIPLOM
CENTURY. SOCIETY FINAN ECO/TAC FOR/AID CONTROL   POLICY
NUC/PWR WAR RACE/REL PEACE ATTIT...ANTHOL T 20   NAT/G
WILSON/W ROOSEVLT/F KENNEDY/JF TRUMAN/HS. PAGE 20   ORD/FREE
G0391

                                                          B66
GLAZER M.,THE FEDERAL GOVERNMENT AND THE   BIBLIOG/A
UNIVERSITY. CHILE PROB/SOLV DIPLOM GIVE ADMIN WAR   NAT/G
...POLICY SOC 20. PAGE 21 G0421   PLAN
                                                          ACADEM

                                                          B66
HALPERIN M.H.,CHINA AND NUCLEAR PROLIFERATION   NUC/PWR
(PAMPHLET). CHINA/COM FUT INDIA USA+45 USSR   FORCES
ARMS/CONT WAR 20 CHINJAP. PAGE 24 G0474   POLICY
                                                          DIPLOM

                                                          B66
KUENNE R.E.,THE POLARIS MISSILE STRIKE* A GENERAL   NUC/PWR
ECONOMIC SYSTEMS ANALYSIS. USA+45 USSR NAT/G   FORCES
BAL/PWR ARMS/CONT WAR...MATH PROBABIL COMPUT/IR   DETER
CHARTS HYPO/EXP SIMUL. PAGE 32 G0625   DIPLOM

                                                          B66
VON BORCH H,FRIEDE TROTZ KRIEG. GERMANY USSR   DIPLOM
WOR+45 PEACE ANOMIE ATTIT 20. PAGE 43 G0853   NUC/PWR
                                                          WAR
                                                          COERCE

                                                          B66
US PRES COMM ECO IMPACT DEFENS,REPORT* JULY 1965.   ACT/RES
USA+45 ECO/DEV INDUS DELIB/GP FORCES OP/RES   STAT
ARMS/CONT NUC/PWR WEAPON BAL/PAY...PREDICT SIMUL.   WAR
PAGE 59 G1159   BUDGET

                                                          B66
WHITNAH D.R.,SAFER SKYWAYS. DIST/IND DELIB/GP   ADMIN
FORCES TOP/EX WORKER TEC/DEV ROUTINE WAR CIVMIL/REL   NAT/G
COST...TIME/SEQ 20 FAA CAB. PAGE 63 G1235   AIR
                                                          GOV/REL

                                                          L66
DOUGHERTY J.E.,"THE CATHOLIC CHURCH, WAR AND   CATHISM
NUCLEAR WEAPONS." COM EUR+WWI SECT TOP/EX LEAD   MORAL
DETER ALL/VALS. PAGE 16 G0312   WAR
                                                          NUC/PWR

                                                          S66
TURKEVICH J.,"SOVIET SCIENCE APPRAISED." USA+45 R+D USSR
ACADEM FORCES DIPLOM EDU/PROP WAR EFFICIENCY PEACE   TEC/DEV
SKILL OBS. PAGE 55 G1081   NAT/COMP
                                                          ATTIT

                                                          B67
AMERICAN FRIENDS SERVICE COMM,IN PLACE OF WAR.   PEACE
NAT/G ACT/RES DIPLOM ADMIN NUC/PWR EFFICIENCY   PACIFISM
...POLICY 20. PAGE 3 G0053   WAR
                                                          DETER

                                                          B67
BERNAL J.D.,THE SOCIAL FUNCTION OF SCIENCE. WOR+45   ROLE
WOR-45 R+D NAT/G PROB/SOLV DOMIN WAR...PHIL/SCI 20.   TEC/DEV
PAGE 7 G0130   SOCIETY
                                                          ADJUST

                                                          B67
BURNS E.L.M.,MEGAMURDER. WOR+45 LAW INT/ORG NAT/G   FORCES
BAL/PWR DIPLOM DETER MURDER WEAPON CIVMIL/REL PEACE   PLAN
...INT/LAW TREND 20. PAGE 10 G0193   WAR
                                                          NUC/PWR

                                                          B67
HALLE L.J.,THE COLD WAR AS HISTORY. USSR WOR+45   DIPLOM
ECO/TAC FOR/AID NUC/PWR WAR PEACE ORD/FREE   BAL/PWR
...MAJORIT TREND 20 COLD/WAR KENNEDY/JF KHRUSH/N
BERLIN/BLO. PAGE 24 G0470

                                                          B67
MACKINTOSH J.M.,JUGGERNAUT. USSR NAT/G POL/PAR   WAR
ADMIN LEAD CIVMIL/REL COST TOTALISM PWR MARXISM   FORCES
...GOV/COMP 20. PAGE 35 G0691   COM
                                                          PROF/ORG

                                                          B67
MCCLINTOCK R.,THE MEANING OF LIMITED WAR. FUT   WAR

WOR+45 NAT/G FORCES GUERRILLA REV...POLICY SAMP/SIZ NUC/PWR
TREND NAT/COMP 45 COLD/WAR. PAGE 37 G0730   BAL/PWR
DIPLOM

B67
RAWLINSON J.L.,CHINA'S STRUGGLE FOR NAVAL   SEA
DEVELOPMENT 1839-1895. ASIA DIPLOM ADMIN WAR   FORCES
...BIBLIOG DICTIONARY 19 CHINJAP. PAGE 46 G0907   PWR

B67
RUSSELL B.,WAR CRIMES IN VIETNAM. USA+45 VIETNAM   WAR
FORCES DIPLOM WEAPON RACE/REL DISCRIM ISOLAT   CRIME
BIO/SOC 20 COLD/WAR RUSSELL/B. PAGE 48 G0949   ATTIT
POLICY

B67
US SENATE COMM ON FOREIGN REL,FOREIGN ASSISTANCE   FOR/AID
ACT OF 1967. VIETNAM WOR+45 DELIB/GP CONFER CONTROL   LAW
WAR WEAPON BAL/PAY...CENSUS CHARTS SENATE. PAGE 60   DIPLOM
G1185   POLICY

B67
US SUPERINTENDENT OF DOCUMENTS,LIBRARY OF CONGRESS   BIBLIOG/A
(PRICE LIST 83). AFR ASIA EUR+WWI USA-45 USSR NAT/G   USA+45
DIPLOM CONFER CT/SYS WAR...DECISION PHIL/SCI   AUTOMAT
CLASSIF 19/20 CONGRESS PRESIDENT. PAGE 61 G1189   LAW

B67
WYLIE J.C.,MILITARY STRATEGY: GENERAL THEORY OF   FORCES
POWER CONTROL. CUBA USA+45 VIETNAM/N WOR+45 ELITES   PLAN
CONTROL WAR PWR...POLICY METH/COMP 20 MAO. PAGE 64   DECISION
G1260   IDEA/COMP

L67
EINAUDI L.,"ANNOTATED BIBLIOGRAPHY OF LATIN   BIBLIOG/A
AMERICAN MILITARY JOURNALS" LAW TEC/DEV DOMIN   NAT/G
EDU/PROP COERCE WAR CIVMIL/REL 20. PAGE 17 G0336   FORCES
L/A+17C

S67
BRETNOR R.,"DESTRUCTIVE FORCE AND THE MILITARY   FORCES
EQUATIONS." UNIV COMPUTER PLAN PROB/SOLV AUTOMAT   TEC/DEV
CONTROL COERCE DETER NUC/PWR WEAPON DRIVE PWR.   DOMIN
PAGE 9 G0166   WAR

S67
BULMER-THOMAS I.,"SO, ON TO THE GREAT SOCIETY." FUT   PHIL/SCI
UNIV TEC/DEV BAL/PWR WAR BIO/SOC KNOWL...ART/METH   SOCIETY
SOC PREDICT TREND WORSHIP 20 GREAT/SOC. PAGE 9   CREATE
G0185

S67
CLEMENS W.C.,"CHINESE NUCLEAR TESTS: TRENDS AND   NUC/PWR
PORTENTS." CHINA/COM USA+45 USSR FORCES PLAN   WEAPON
TEC/DEV ARMS/CONT WAR PWR...DECISION 20 MAO   POLICY
KHRUSH/N. PAGE 12 G0234   DIPLOM

S67
HARTIGAN R.S.,"NONCOMBAT IMMUNITY* REFLECTIONS ON   INT/LAW
ITS ORIGINS AND PRESENT STATUS." WOR+45 PROB/SOLV   NUC/PWR
WAR PRIVIL MORAL...POLICY 20. PAGE 25 G0487   ARMS/CONT
DIPLOM

S67
INGLIS D.R.,"MISSILE DEFENSE, NUCLEAR SPREAD, AND   NUC/PWR
VIETNAM." CHINA/COM USA+45 USSR VIETNAM INDUS   ARMS/CONT
BAL/PWR DETER WAR COST NAT/LISM PEACE. PAGE 28   DIPLOM
G0544   FORCES

S67
JONES G.S.,"STRATEGIC PLANNING." USA+45 EX/STRUC   PLAN
FORCES DETER WAR 20 PRESIDENT. PAGE 29 G0566   DECISION
DELIB/GP
POLICY

S67
KAHN H.,"CRITERIA FOR LONG-RANGE NUCLEAR CONTROL   NUC/PWR
POLICIES." WOR+45 INT/ORG TEC/DEV DOMIN DETER WAR   ARMS/CONT
WEAPON ISOLAT ORD/FREE POLICY. PAGE 29 G0571   BAL/PWR
DIPLOM

S67
MARTIN L.,"THE AMERICAN ABM DECISION." ASIA COM   WEAPON
EUR+WWI UK USA+45 USSR FORCES DIPLOM PEACE...POLICY   DETER
20 ABM/DEFSYS. PAGE 36 G0713   NUC/PWR
WAR

S67
REINTANZ G.,"THE SPACE TREATY." WOR+45 DIPLOM   SPACE
CONTROL ARMS/CONT NUC/PWR WAR...MARXIST 20 COLD/WAR   INT/LAW
UN TREATY. PAGE 46 G0911   INT/ORG
PEACE

S67
SALISBURY H.E.,"THE WAR IN VIETNAM." USA+45   POLICY
VIETNAM/N DIPLOM MURDER 20. PAGE 48 G0953   WAR

FORCES
OBS

S67
SHARP G.,"THE NEED OF A FUNCTIONAL SUBSTITUTE FOR   PEACE
WAR." FUT UNIV WOR+45 CULTURE SOCIETY INT/ORG   WAR
CONSULT DELIB/GP ACT/RES CREATE BAL/PWR CONFER   DIPLOM
ARMS/CONT NUC/PWR 20. PAGE 50 G0989   PROB/SOLV

S67
SUINN R.M.,"THE DISARMAMENT FANTASY* PSYCHOLOGICAL   DECISION
FACTORS THAT MAY PRODUCE WARFARE." DIPLOM RISK   NUC/PWR
ARMS/CONT DETER ANOMIE PERSON GAME. PAGE 53 G1046   WAR
PSY

S67
TEKINER S.,"SINKIAN AND THE SINO-SOVIET CONFLICT."   DIPLOM
ASIA COM USSR FORCES PLAN BAL/PWR CONTROL NUC/PWR   PWR
WAR WEAPON...DECISION 20. PAGE 54 G1060   MARXISM

S67
TELLER E.,"PLANNING FOR PEACE." CHINA/COM WOR+45   ARMS/CONT
DELIB/GP TEC/DEV RISK COERCE DETER WAR ATTIT   NUC/PWR
ORD/FREE 20 NATO. PAGE 54 G1061   PEACE
DOMIN

S67
WALTERS R.E.,"THE ROLE OF NUCLEAR WEAPONS FOR THE   PLAN
WEST." ASIA UK USA+45 USSR DIPLOM COERCE WAR PEACE   NUC/PWR
...POLICY DECISION 20. PAGE 62 G1209   WEAPON
FORCES

S67
WARE R.S.,"FORECAST A.D. 2000." SOCIETY STRATA   NUC/PWR
ECO/UNDEV INDUS FORCES EDU/PROP AUTOMAT COERCE REV   GEOG
WEAPON ATTIT PREDICT. PAGE 62 G1213   TEC/DEV
WAR

S67
WOLFE T.W.,"SOVIET MILITARY POLICY AT THE FIFTY   FORCES
YEAR MARK." USSR VIETNAM WOR+45 RATION AGREE WAR   POLICY
WEAPON CIVMIL/REL TREATY. PAGE 64 G1254   TIME/SEQ
PLAN

N67
US HOUSE COMM FOREIGN AFFAIRS,REPORT OF SPECIAL   ISLAM
STUDY MISSION TO THE NEAR EAST (PAMPHLET). ISRAEL   DIPLOM
USA+45 YEMEN ECO/UNDEV INT/ORG FOR/AID ARMS/CONT   FORCES
WAR WEAPON NAT/LISM PEACE...GEOG 20 UN HOUSE/REP.
PAGE 58 G1138

N67
US SENATE,STATUS OF THE DEVELOPMENT OF THE ANTI-   FORCES
BALLISTIC MISSILE SYSTEMS IN THE UNITED STATES   NUC/PWR
(PAMPHLET). FUT USA+45 R+D PLAN TEC/DEV DEPT/DEFEN.   WAR
PAGE 59 G1165   UTIL

B91
RENAN E.,THE FUTURE OF SCIENCE. WAR ORD/FREE WEALTH   PHIL/SCI
...GOV/COMP IDEA/COMP GEN/LAWS 19. PAGE 46 G0913   KNOWL
SECT
PREDICT

B64
BROWN N.,NUCLEAR WAR* THE IMPENDING STRATEGIC   FORCES
DEADLOCK. USA+45 USSR TEC/DEV BUDGET RISK ARMS/CONT   OP/RES
NUC/PWR WEAPON COST BIO/SOC...GEOG IDEA/COMP   WAR
NAT/COMP GAME NATO WARSAW/P. PAGE 9 G0177   GEN/LAWS

WASHBURN A.M. G1216

WASHBURNE N.F. G1217

WASHING/BT....BOOKER T. WASHINGTON

WASHING/DC....WASHINGTON, D.C.

B55
JONES J.M.,THE FIFTEEN WEEKS (FEBRUARY 21-JUNE 5, 1947). EUR+WWI USA+45 PROB/SOLV BAL/PWR...POLICY TIME/SEQ 20 COLD/WAR MARSHL/PLN TRUMAN/HS WASHING/DC. PAGE 29 G0567
DIPLOM ECO/TAC FOR/AID

WASHINGT/G....PRESIDENT GEORGE WASHINGTON

WASHINGTON....WASHINGTON, STATE OF

WASKOW A.I. G1218

WASP....WHITE-ANGLO-SAXON-PROTESTANT ESTABLISHMENT

WASSERMAN P. G1219,G1220

WATER POLLUTION....SEE POLLUTION

WATER....PERTAINING TO ALL NON-SALT WATER

B50
DEES J.W. JR.,URBAN SOCIOLOGY AND THE EMERGING ATOMIC MEGALOPOLIS, PART I. USA+45 TEC/DEV ADMIN NUC/PWR HABITAT...SOC AUD/VIS CHARTS GEN/LAWS 20 WATER. PAGE 15 G0291
PLAN NEIGH MUNIC PROB/SOLV

B61
MURPHY E.F.,WATER PURITY: A STUDY IN LEGAL CONTROL OF NATURAL RESOURCES. LOC/G ACT/RES PLAN TEC/DEV LOBBY GP/REL COST ATTIT HEALTH ORD/FREE...HEAL JURID 20 WISCONSIN WATER. PAGE 40 G0797
SEA LAW PROVS CONTROL

WATSON J. G0672

WATTS....WATTS,LOS ANGELES

WCC....WORLD COUNCIL CHURCHES

WCTU....WOMAN'S CHRISTIAN TEMPERANCE UNION

WEALTH....ACCESS TO GOODS AND SERVICES (ALSO POVERTY)

N
PERSONNEL. USA+45 LAW LABOR LG/CO WORKER CREATE GOV/REL PERS/REL ATTIT WEALTH. PAGE 1 G0010
BIBLIOG/A ADMIN MGT GP/REL

B14
CRAIG J.,ELEMENTS OF POLITICAL SCIENCE (3 VOLS.). CONSTN AGRI INDUS SCHOOL FORCES TAX CT/SYS SUFF MORAL WEALTH...CONCPT 19 CIVIL/LIB. PAGE 13 G0259
PHIL/SCI NAT/G ORD/FREE

N19
KAUFMAN J.L.,COMMUNITY RENEWAL PROGRAMS (PAMPHLET). USA+45 CONSTRUC PROVS CREATE PLAN CONTROL WEALTH 20 URBAN/RNWL. PAGE 30 G0584
LOC/G MUNIC ACT/RES BIBLIOG

B43
LASKI H.J.,REFLECTIONS ON THE REVOLUTIONS OF OUR TIME. COM USSR NAT/G WORKER UTOPIA ORD/FREE WEALTH MARXISM SOCISM 19/20. PAGE 32 G0637
CAP/ISM WELF/ST ECO/TAC POLICY

B46
WILCOX J.K.,OFFICIAL DEFENSE PUBLICATIONS, 1941-1945 (NINE VOLS.). USA-45 AGRI INDUS R+D LABOR FORCES TEC/DEV EFFICIENCY PRODUC SKILL WEALTH 20. PAGE 63 G1238
BIBLIOG/A WAR CIVMIL/REL ADMIN

B47
BECK H.P.,MEN WHO CONTROL OUR UNIVERSITIES. EX/STRUC CHOOSE INGP/REL DISCRIM PERSON WEALTH ...POLICY TREND CON/ANAL CHARTS BIBLIOG. PAGE 6 G0112
EDU/PROP ACADEM CONTROL LEAD

B48
METZLER L.A.,INCOME, EMPLOYMENT, AND PUBLIC POLICY. FINAN INDUS LOC/G NAT/G TAX GIVE PAY COST PRODUC ...MGT TIME/SEQ 20. PAGE 38 G0760
INCOME WEALTH POLICY ECO/TAC

B49
OGBURN W.,TECHNOLOGY AND INTERNATIONAL RELATIONS. WOR+45 WOR-45 ECO/DEV CREATE PLAN ECO/TAC EDU/PROP COERCE PWR SKILL WEALTH...TECHNIC PSY SOC NEW/IDEA CHARTS TOT/POP 20. PAGE 43 G0837
TEC/DEV DIPLOM INT/ORG

B50
US DEPARTMENT OF STATE,POINT FOUR: COOPERATIVE PROGRAM FOR AID IN THE DEVELOPMENT OF ECONOMICALLY UNDERDEVELOPED AREAS. WOR+45 AGRI INDUS INT/ORG PLAN TEC/DEV DIPLOM EDU/PROP ADMIN PEACE PRODUC WEALTH 20 CONGRESS UN. PAGE 57 G1121
ECO/UNDEV FOR/AID FINAN INT/TRADE

B53
MACK R.T.,RAISING THE WORLDS STANDARD OF LIVING. IRAN INT/ORG VOL/ASSN EX/STRUC ECO/TAC WEALTH...MGT METH/CNCPT STAT CONT/OBS INT TOT/POP VAL/FREE 20 UN. PAGE 35 G0690
WOR+45 FOR/AID INT/TRADE

B53
ROBINSON E.A.G.,THE STRUCTURE OF COMPETITIVE INDUSTRY. UK ECO/DEV DIST/IND MARKET TEC/DEV DIPLOM EDU/PROP ADMIN EFFICIENCY WEALTH...MGT 19/20. PAGE 47 G0929
INDUS PRODUC WORKER OPTIMAL

C55
BONER H.A.,"HUNGRY GENERATIONS." UK WOR+45 WOR-45 STRATA INDUS FAM LABOR CAP/ISM...MGT BIBLIOG 19/20. PAGE 8 G0151
ECO/DEV PHIL/SCI CONCPT WEALTH

S56
GORDON L.,"THE ORGANIZATION FOR EUROPEAN ECONOMIC COOPERATION." EUR+WWI INDUS INT/ORG NAT/G CONSULT DELIB/GP ACT/RES CREATE PLAN TEC/DEV EDU/PROP LEGIT WEALTH OEEC 20. PAGE 22 G0435
VOL/ASSN ECO/DEV

B57
GOLD N.L.,REGIONAL ECONOMIC DEVELOPMENT AND NUCLEAR POWER IN INDIA. FUT INDIA FINAN FOR/AID INT/TRADE BAL/PAY EFFICIENCY OPTIMAL PRODUC WEALTH...PREDICT 20. PAGE 22 G0424
ECO/UNDEV TEC/DEV NUC/PWR INDUS

B57
KIETH-LUCAS A.,DECISIONS ABOUT PEOPLE IN NEED, A STUDY OF ADMINISTRATIVE RESPONSIVENESS IN PUBLIC ASSISTANCE. USA+45 GIVE RECEIVE INGP/REL PERS/REL MORAL RESPECT WEALTH...SOC OBS BIBLIOG 20. PAGE 30 G0595
ADMIN RIGID/FLEX SOC/WK DECISION

B58
BIDWELL P.W.,RAW MATERIALS: A STUDY OF AMERICAN POLICY. USA+45 USA-45 ECO/UNDEV AGRI INDUS KIN CREATE PLAN ECO/TAC WAR PEACE ATTIT DRIVE WEALTH ...STAT CHARTS CONGRESS VAL/FREE. PAGE 7 G0135
EXTR/IND ECO/DEV

B59
MAYDA J.,ATOMIC ENERGY AND LAW. ECO/UNDEV FINAN TEC/DEV FOR/AID EFFICIENCY PRODUC WEALTH...POLICY TECHNIC 20. PAGE 37 G0723
NUC/PWR L/A+17C LAW ADMIN

B59
MEANS G.C.,ADMINISTRATIVE INFLATION AND PUBLIC POLICY (PAMPHLET). USA+45 ECO/DEV FINAN INDUS WORKER PLAN BUDGET GOV/REL COST DEMAND WEALTH 20 CONGRESS MONOPOLY GOLD/STAND. PAGE 38 G0749
ECO/TAC POLICY RATION CONTROL

S59
CORY R.H. JR.,"INTERNATIONAL INSPECTION FROM PROPOSALS TO REALIZATION." WOR+45 TEC/DEV ECO/TAC ADJUD ORD/FREE PWR WEALTH...RECORD VAL/FREE 20. PAGE 13 G0258
STRUCT PSY ARMS/CONT NUC/PWR

B60
APTHEKER H.,DISARMAMENT AND THE AMERICAN ECONOMY: A SYMPOSIUM. FUT USA+45 ECO/DEV DIST/IND FINAN INDUS PROC/MFG LABOR NAT/G POL/PAR CONSULT PLAN CAP/ISM INT/TRADE PEACE ATTIT MORAL WEALTH...TREND GEN/LAWS TOT/POP 20. PAGE 3 G0063
MARXIST ARMS/CONT

B60
HEILBRONER R.L.,THE FUTURE AS HISTORY. USA+45 WOR+45 WOR-45 SOCIETY ECO/DEV ECO/UNDEV VOL/ASSN PLAN CAP/ISM NUC/PWR CHOOSE NAT/LISM ATTIT ORD/FREE RESPECT WEALTH SOCISM 20. PAGE 25 G0501
TEC/DEV TREND

B60
PENTONY D.E.,THE UNDERDEVELOPED LANDS. FUT WOR+45 CULTURE AGRI FINAN INDUS MARKET INT/ORG LABOR NAT/G VOL/ASSN CONSULT TEC/DEV ECO/TAC EDU/PROP COLONIAL ATTIT WEALTH...OBS RECORD SAMP TREND GEN/METH WORK UN 20. PAGE 44 G0867
ECO/UNDEV POLICY FOR/AID INT/TRADE

S60
RIVKIN A.,"AFRICAN ECONOMIC DEVELOPMENT: ADVANCED TECHNOLOGY AND THE STAGES OF GROWTH." CULTURE ECO/UNDEV AGRI COM/IND EXTR/IND PLAN ECO/TAC ATTIT DRIVE RIGID/FLEX SKILL WEALTH...MGT SOC GEN/LAWS WORK TOT/POP 20. PAGE 47 G0923
AFR TEC/DEV FOR/AID

B61
GORDON W.J.J.,SYNECTICS; THE DEVELOPMENT OF   CREATE
CREATIVE CAPACITY. USA+45 PLAN TEC/DEV KNOWL WEALTH PROB/SOLV
...DECISION MGT 20. PAGE 22 G0436   ACT/RES
                                                    TOP/EX

B62
KENNEDY J.F.,TO TURN THE TIDE. SPACE AGRI INT/ORG   DIPLOM
FORCES TEC/DEV ADMIN NUC/PWR PEACE WEALTH...ANTHOL   CHIEF
20 KENNEDY/JF CIV/RIGHTS. PAGE 30 G0592   POLICY
                                                    NAT/G

B62
KRAFT J.,THE GRAND DESIGN. EUR+WWI USA+45 AGRI   VOL/ASSN
FINAN INDUS MARKET INT/ORG NAT/G PLAN ECO/TAC   ECO/DEV
TARIFFS REGION DRIVE ORD/FREE WEALTH...POLICY OBS   INT/TRADE
TREND EEC 20. PAGE 31 G0616

B62
MACHLUP F.,THE PRODUCTION AND DISTRIBUTION OF   ACADEM
KNOWLEDGE IN THE UNITED STATES. USA+45 COM/IND   TEC/DEV
INDUS SCHOOL SECT WORKER COMPUTER CREATE CIVMIL/REL EDU/PROP
COST EFFICIENCY WEALTH 20. PAGE 35 G0688   R+D

B62
WENDT P.F.,HOUSING POLICY - THE SEARCH FOR   PLAN
SOLUTIONS. GERMANY/W SWEDEN UK USA+45 OP/RES   ADMIN
HABITAT WEALTH...SOC/WK CHARTS 20. PAGE 63 G1230   METH/COMP
                                                    NAT/G

S62
ALBONETTI A.,"IL SECONDO PROGRAMMA QUINQUENNALE   R+D
1963-67 ED IL BILANCIO RICERCHE ED INVESTIMENTI PER PLAN
IL 1963 DELL'ERATOM." EUR+WWI FUT ITALY WOR+45   NUC/PWR
ECO/DEV SERV/IND INT/ORG TEC/DEV ECO/TAC ATTIT
SKILL WEALTH...MGT TIME/SEQ OEEC 20. PAGE 2 G0035

S62
MORGENTHAU H.J.,"A POLITICAL THEORY OF FOREIGN   USA+45
AID." ECO/UNDEV NAT/G DELIB/GP PLAN ECO/TAC   PHIL/SCI
EDU/PROP EXEC ORD/FREE RESPECT WEALTH...METH/CNCPT   FOR/AID
TREND 20. PAGE 40 G0783

S62
THORELLI H.B.,"THE INTERNATIONAL OPERATIONS   ECO/TAC
SIMULATION AT THE UNIVERSITY OF CHICAGO." FUT   SIMUL
USA+45 ECO/DEV DIST/IND FINAN INDUS INT/ORG   INT/TRADE
DELIB/GP ACT/RES CREATE TEC/DEV WEALTH...STAT
VAL/FREE 20. PAGE 54 G1072

B63
ABSHIRE D.M.,NATIONAL SECURITY: POLITICAL,   FUT
MILITARY, AND ECONOMIC STRATEGIES IN THE DECADE   ACT/RES
AHEAD. ASIA COM USA+45 WOR+45 ECO/DEV ECO/UNDEV   BAL/PWR
INT/ORG DELIB/GP FORCES ECO/TAC COERCE ATTIT
RIGID/FLEX HEALTH ORD/FREE PWR WEALTH...POLICY STAT
CHARTS ANTHOL COLD/WAR VAL/FREE. PAGE 1 G0024

B63
HAUSMAN W.H.,MANAGING ECONOMIC DEVELOPMENT IN   ECO/UNDEV
AFRICA. AFR USA+45 LAW FINAN WORKER TEC/DEV WEALTH   PLAN
...ANTHOL 20. PAGE 25 G0492   FOR/AID
                                                    MGT

B63
MAYNE R.,THE COMMUNITY OF EUROPE. UK CONSTN NAT/G   EUR+WWI
CONSULT DELIB/GP CREATE PLAN ECO/TAC LEGIT ADMIN   INT/ORG
ROUTINE ORD/FREE PWR WEALTH...CONCPT TIME/SEQ EEC   REGION
EURATOM 20. PAGE 37 G0724

B63
MULLER H.J.,FREEDOM IN THE WESTERN WORLD. PREHIST   ORD/FREE
CULTURE SECT CREATE TEC/DEV DOMIN PWR WEALTH   TIME/SEQ
...MAJORIT SOC CONCPT. PAGE 40 G0793   SOCIETY

L63
BEGUIN H.,"ASPECTS GEOGRAPHIQUE DE LA   ECO/UNDEV
POLARISATION." FUT WOR+45 SOCIETY STRUCT ECO/DEV   GEOG
R+D BAL/PWR ADMIN ATTIT RIGID/FLEX HEALTH WEALTH   DIPLOM
...CHARTS 20. PAGE 6 G0114

L63
MCDOUGAL M.S.,"THE ENJOYMENT AND ACQUISITION OF   PLAN
RESOURCES IN OUTER SPACE." CHRIST-17C FUT WOR+45   TREND
WOR-45 LAW EXTR/IND INT/ORG ACT/RES CREATE TEC/DEV
ECO/TAC LEGIT COERCE HEALTH KNOWL ORD/FREE PWR
WEALTH...JURID HIST/WRIT VAL/FREE. PAGE 37 G0738

S63
ABT C.,"THE PROBLEMS AND POSSIBILITIES OF SPACE   ACT/RES
ARMS CONTROL." FUT USA+45 WOR+45 AIR SOCIETY NAT/G   ORD/FREE
BAL/PWR EDU/PROP ATTIT PWR WEALTH...HYPO/EXP   ARMS/CONT
TOT/POP 20. PAGE 2 G0025   SPACE

S63
BOULDING K.E.,"UNIVERSITY, SOCIETY, AND ARMS   SOCIETY

CONTROL." WOR+45 WOR-45 ACADEM NAT/G CONSULT FORCES ARMS/CONT
ACT/RES PLAN TEC/DEV BAL/PWR ECO/TAC COERCE DETER
WAR ATTIT RIGID/FLEX KNOWL ORD/FREE PWR WEALTH
...CONCPT COLD/WAR TOT/POP 20. PAGE 8 G0159

S63
DE FOREST J.D.,"LOW LEVELS OF TECHNOLOGY AND   ECO/UNDEV
ECONOMIC DEVELOPMENT PROSPECTS." WOR+45 WOR-45   TEC/DEV
CULTURE ACT/RES CREATE PLAN ECO/TAC ROUTINE PERCEPT
WEALTH...METH/CNCPT GEN/LAWS 20. PAGE 15 G0284

S63
FERRETTI B.,"IMPORTANZA E PROSPETTIVE DELL ENERGIA   TEC/DEV
DI ORIGINE NUCLEARE." FUT ITALY WOR+45 INTELL R+D   EXEC
ACT/RES CREATE HEALTH WEALTH...METH/CNCPT TIME/SEQ   NUC/PWR
20. PAGE 19 G0365

S63
NADLER E.B.,"SOME ECONOMIC DISADVANTAGES OF THE   ECO/DEV
ARMS RACE." USA+45 INDUS R+D FORCES PLAN TEC/DEV   MGT
ECO/TAC FOR/AID EDU/PROP PWR WEALTH...TREND   BAL/PAY
COLD/WAR 20. PAGE 41 G0800

S63
WILES P.J.D.,"WILL CAPITALISM AND COMMUNISM   PLAN
SPONTANEOUSLY CONVERGE." COM FUT USA+45 ECO/DEV   TEC/DEV
DIST/IND MARKET CAP/ISM ECO/TAC RIGID/FLEX WEALTH   USSR
MARXISM SOCISM...MATH STAT TREND COMPUT/IR 20.
PAGE 63 G1240

B64
ETZIONI A.,THE MOON-DOGGLE: DOMESTIC AND   R+D
INTERNATIONAL IMPLICATIONS OF THE SPACE RACE. FUT   NAT/G
USA+45 WOR+45 INTELL ECO/DEV INDUS VOL/ASSN   DIPLOM
EX/STRUC FORCES LEGIS TOP/EX PLAN TEC/DEV ECO/TAC   SPACE
EDU/PROP KNOWL ORD/FREE PWR RESPECT WEALTH
TIME/SEQ. PAGE 18 G0352

B64
GUTMANN P.M.,ECONOMIC GROWTH: AN AMERICAN PROBLEM.   WEALTH
USA+45 FINAN R+D...POLICY NAT/COMP ANTHOL BIBLIOG   ECO/DEV
20. PAGE 24 G0463   CAP/ISM
                                                    ORD/FREE

B64
HEKHUIS D.J.,INTERNATIONAL STABILITY: MILITARY,   TEC/DEV
ECONOMIC AND POLITICAL DIMENSIONS. FUT WOR+45 LAW   DETER
ECO/UNDEV INT/ORG NAT/G VOL/ASSN FORCES ACT/RES   REGION
BAL/PWR PWR WEALTH...STAT UN 20. PAGE 25 G0503

B64
POWELSON J.P.,LATIN AMERICA: TODAY'S ECONOMIC AND   ECO/UNDEV
SOCIAL REVOLUTION. L/A+17C INTELL SOCIETY STRUCT   WEALTH
AGRI INDUS NAT/G DIPLOM ECO/TAC REV...POLICY 20.   ADJUST
PAGE 45 G0887   PLAN

B64
SCHERER F.M.,THE WEAPONS ACQUISITION PROCESS: INDUS
ECONOMIC INCENTIVES. BOSTON: DIVISION OF RESEARCH,   ACT/RES
GRADUATE SCHOOL OF BUSINESS. USA+45 FINAN NAT/G   WEAPON
DELIB/GP ECO/TAC RIGID/FLEX WEALTH...MGT MATH STAT
CHARTS VAL/FREE 20. PAGE 49 G0965

L64
HAAS E.B.,"ECONOMICS AND DIFFERENTIAL PATTERNS OF   L/A+17C
POLITICAL INTEGRATION: PROJECTIONS ABOUT UNITY IN   INT/ORG
LATIN AMERICA." SOCIETY NAT/G DELIB/GP ACT/RES   MARKET
CREATE PLAN ECO/TAC REGION ROUTINE ATTIT DRIVE PWR
WEALTH...CONCPT TREND CHARTS LAFTA 20. PAGE 24
G0464

S64
COOPER A.C.,"R&D IS MORE EFFICIENT IN SMALL   R+D
COMPANIES." USA+45 LG/CO SML/CO WEALTH...RECORD INT INDUS
LAB/EXP 20. PAGE 13 G0255   CREATE
                                                    GP/COMP

S64
GARDNER R.N.,"GATT AND THE UNITED NATIONS   INT/ORG
CONFERENCE ON TRADE AND DEVELOPMENT." USA+45 WOR+45 INT/TRADE
SOCIETY ECO/UNDEV MARKET NAT/G DELIB/GP ACT/RES
PLAN ECO/TAC TARIFFS EDU/PROP ROUTINE DRIVE
RIGID/FLEX WEALTH...DECISION MGT TREND UN TOT/POP
20 GATT. PAGE 21 G0411

S64
MAHALANOBIS P.C.,"PERSPECTIVE PLANNING IN INDIA: PLAN
STATISTICAL TOOLS." INDIA S/ASIA STRATA AGRI   STAT
DIST/IND FINAN INDUS SERV/IND NAT/G ECO/TAC
ORD/FREE WEALTH...POLICY TREND SIMUL VAL/FREE 20.
PAGE 35 G0695

B65
IANNI O.,ESTADO E CAPITALISMO. L/A+17C FINAN   ECO/UNDEV
TEC/DEV ECO/TAC ORD/FREE WEALTH POLICY. PAGE 28   STRUCT
G0542   INDUS

NAT/G
B65

INT. BANK RECONSTR. DEVELOP..ECONOMIC DEVELOPMENT   INDUS
OF KUWAIT. ISLAM KUWAIT AGRI FINAN MARKET EX/STRUC   NAT/G
TEC/DEV ECO/TAC ADMIN WEALTH...OBS CON/ANAL CHARTS
20. PAGE 28 G0548

B65

MCGUIRE M.C.,SECRECY AND THE ARMS RACE* A THEORY OF   DETER
THE ACCUMULATION OF STRATEGIC WEAPONS AND HOW   ARMS/CONT
SECRECY AFFECTS IT. DIPLOM NUC/PWR WEAPON ISOLAT   SIMUL
RATIONAL ORD/FREE WEALTH...ECOMETRIC MATH GEN/LAWS.   GAME
PAGE 38 G0742

B65

PYE L.W.,POLITICAL CULTURE AND DEVELOPMENT. WOR+45   PHIL/SCI
WOR-45 CULTURE ECO/UNDEV NAT/G ALL/VALS ORD/FREE   TEC/DEV
PWR WEALTH ALL/IDEOS...TRADIT TREND 20. PAGE 46   SOCIETY
G0897

S65

DEAN B.V.,"CONTRACT RESEARCH PROPOSAL PREPARATION   USA+45
STRATEGIES." ECO/TAC WEALTH...MGT SIMUL. PAGE 15   PROC/MFG
G0289   R+D
                                                         PLAN

S65

TENDLER J.D.,"TECHNOLOGY AND ECONOMIC DEVELOPMENT*   BRAZIL
THE CASE OF HYDRO VS THERMAL POWER." CONSTRUC   INDUS
DIST/IND CREATE TEC/DEV INT/TRADE CENTRAL PWR SKILL   ECO/UNDEV
WEALTH...MGT NAT/COMP ARGEN. PAGE 54 G1063

B66

BOWEN H.R.,AUTOMATION AND ECONOMIC PROGRESS.   AUTOMAT
EUR+WWI USA+45 ECO/DEV INCOME ORD/FREE WEALTH   TEC/DEV
...POLICY ANTHOL 20. PAGE 8 G0160   WORKER
                                                         LEISURE

B66

LEWIS W.A.,DEVELOPMENT PLANNING: THE ESSENTIALS OF   PLAN
ECONOMIC POLICY. USA+45 FINAN INDUS NAT/G WORKER   ECO/DEV
FOR/AID INT/TRADE ADMIN ROUTINE WEALTH...CONCPT   POLICY
STAT. PAGE 34 G0663   CREATE

B66

SANFORD T.,BUT WHAT ABOUT THE PEOPLE? ACADEM SCHOOL   EDU/PROP
BUDGET TAX CONTROL SKILL WEALTH 20 NORTH/CAR.   PROB/SOLV
PAGE 49 G0956   POLICY
                                                         PROVS

B66

US BUREAU OF THE BUDGET,THE ADMINISTRATION OF   ACT/RES
GOVERNMENT SUPPORTED RESEARCH AT UNIVERSITIES   NAT/G
(PAMPHLET). USA+45 CONSULT TOP/EX ADMIN INCOME   ACADEM
WEALTH...MGT PHIL/SCI INT. PAGE 56 G1108   GP/REL

S66

"FURTHER READING." INDIA LOC/G NAT/G PLAN ADMIN   BIBLIOG
WEALTH...GEOG SOC CONCPT CENSUS 20. PAGE 1 G0021   ECO/UNDEV
                                                         TEC/DEV
                                                         PROVS

S66

GREENBERG D.S.,"THE SCIENTIFIC PORK BARREL." USA+45   R+D
ECO/DEV PUB/INST CHIEF LEGIS BUDGET GIVE GP/REL PWR   NAT/G
WEALTH 20. PAGE 23 G0445   ACADEM
                                                         ATTIT

B67

COLEMAN J.R.,THE CHANGING AMERICAN ECONOMY. USA+45   BUDGET
AGRI FINAN LABOR FOR/AID INT/TRADE AUTOMAT GP/REL   ECO/TAC
INGP/REL ANTHOL. PAGE 13 G0243   ECO/DEV
                                                         WEALTH

B67

ELDREDGE H.W.,TAMING MEGALOPOLIS: HOW TO MANAGE AN   MUNIC
URBANIZED WORLD. WOR+45 SOCIETY ECO/DEV ECO/UNDEV   TEC/DEV
NAT/G COMPUTER CREATE PARTIC EFFICIENCY WEALTH   PLAN
...MGT ANTHOL. PAGE 17 G0342   PROB/SOLV

B67

ENKE S.,DEFENSE MANAGEMENT. USA+45 R+D FORCES   DECISION
WORKER PLAN ECO/TAC ADMIN NUC/PWR BAL/PAY UTIL   DELIB/GP
WEALTH...MGT DEPT/DEFEN. PAGE 18 G0348   EFFICIENCY
                                                         BUDGET

B67

GROSSMAN G.,ECONOMIC SYSTEMS. USA+45 USA-45 USSR   ECO/DEV
YUGOSLAVIA WORKER CAP/ISM PRICE GP/REL EQUILIB   PLAN
WEALTH MARXISM SOCISM...MGT METH/COMP 19/20.   TEC/DEV
PAGE 23 G0456   DEMAND

B67

HODGKINSON R.G.,THE ORIGINS OF THE NATIONAL HEALTH   HEAL
SERVICE: THE MEDICAL SERVICES OF THE NEW POOR LAW,   NAT/G

1834-1871. UK INDUS MUNIC WORKER PROB/SOLV   POLICY
EFFICIENCY ATTIT HEALTH WEALTH SOCISM...JURID   LAW
SOC/WK 19/20. PAGE 26 G0519

B67

MOSS F.M.,THE WATER CRISIS. PROB/SOLV CONTROL   GEOG
...POLICY NEW/IDEA. PAGE 40 G0791   ACT/RES
                                                        PRODUC
                                                        WEALTH

B67

POMEROY W.J.,HALF A CENTURY OF SOCIALISM. USSR LAW   SOCISM
AGRI INDUS NAT/G CREATE DIPLOM EDU/PROP PERSON   MARXISM
ORD/FREE WEALTH...POLICY TREND 20. PAGE 45 G0884   COM
                                                        SOCIETY

B67

SALMOND J.A.,THE CIVILIAN CONSERVATION CORPS,   ADMIN
1933-1942. USA-45 NAT/G CREATE EXEC EFFICIENCY   ECO/TAC
WEALTH...BIBLIOG 20 ROOSEVLT/F. PAGE 48 G0954   TASK
                                                        AGRI

B67

SILBERMAN C.E.,THE MYTHS OF AUTOMATION. INDUS   MYTH
WORKER COST PRODUC AGE WEALTH 20. PAGE 51 G0996   AUTOMAT
                                                        CHARTS
                                                        TEC/DEV

B67

UNIVERSAL REFERENCE SYSTEM,CURRENT EVENTS AND   BIBLIOG/A
PROBLEMS OF MODERN SOCIETY (VOLUME V). WOR+45 LOC/G   SOCIETY
MUNIC NAT/G PLAN EDU/PROP CRIME RACE/REL WEALTH   PROB/SOLV
...COMPUT/IR GEN/METH. PAGE 56 G1097   ATTIT

L67

RUTH J.M.,"THE ADMINISTRATION OF WATER RESOURCES IN   EFFICIENCY
GUATEMALA." GUATEMALA L/A+17C DIST/IND LOC/G NAT/G   ECO/UNDEV
EX/STRUC ADMIN GOV/REL DEMAND EQUILIB WEALTH...GEOG   PLAN
MGT 20. PAGE 48 G0952   ACT/RES

S67

AVTORKHANOV A.,"A NEW AGRARIAN REVOLUTION." COM   AGRI
USSR ECO/DEV PLAN TEC/DEV ADMIN CONTROL OPTIMAL   METH/COMP
WEALTH SOCISM 20 KHRUSH/N STALIN/J. PAGE 4 G0082   MARXISM
                                                        OWN

S67

FADDEYEV N.,"CMEA CO-OPERATION OF EQUAL NATIONS."   MARXISM
COM R+D PLAN CAP/ISM DIPLOM FOR/AID WEALTH...POLICY   ECO/TAC
MARXIST. PAGE 18 G0356   INT/ORG
                                                        ECO/UNDEV

S67

HAMBERG D.,"SIZE OF ENTERPRISE AND TECHNICAL   TEC/DEV
CHANGE." USA+45 LG/CO SML/CO CREATE OP/RES PROFIT   INDUS
...TREND 20. PAGE 24 G0477   R+D
                                                        WEALTH

S67

HULL E.W.S.,"THE POLITICAL OCEAN." FUT UNIV WOR+45   DIPLOM
EXTR/IND R+D VOL/ASSN PLAN BAL/PWR ECO/TAC PEACE   ECO/UNDEV
WEALTH 20 UN. PAGE 27 G0536   INT/ORG
                                                        INT/LAW

S67

MCNAMARA R.L.,"THE NEED FOR INNOVATIVENESS IN   PROB/SOLV
DEVELOPING SOCIETIES." L/A+17C EDU/PROP ADMIN LEAD   PLAN
WEALTH...POLICY PSY SOC METH 20 COLOMB. PAGE 38   ECO/UNDEV
G0747   NEW/IDEA

S67

PENNEY N.,"BANK STATEMENTS, CANCELLED CHECKS, AND   CREATE
ARTICLE FOUR IN THE ELECTRONIC AGE." USA+45 TEC/DEV   LAW
COST EFFICIENCY WEALTH. PAGE 44 G0866   ADJUD
                                                        FINAN

S67

SINGH B.,"ITALIAN EXPERIENCE IN REGIONAL ECONOMIC   ECO/UNDEV
DEVELOPMENT AND LESSONS FOR OTHER COUNTRIES."   PLAN
EUR+WWI ITALY INDUS NAT/G ACT/RES REGION GP/REL   ECO/TAC
EFFICIENCY EQUILIB PRODUC WEALTH. PAGE 51 G1007   CONTROL

S67

SLOAN P.,"FIFTY YEARS OF SOVIET RULE." USSR INDUS   CREATE
EDU/PROP EFFICIENCY PRODUC HEALTH KNOWL MORAL   NAT/G
WEALTH MARXISM...POLICY 20. PAGE 51 G1011   PLAN
                                                        INSPECT

B91

RENAN E.,THE FUTURE OF SCIENCE. WAR ORD/FREE WEALTH   PHIL/SCI
...GOV/COMP IDEA/COMP GEN/LAWS 19. PAGE 46 G0913   KNOWL
                                                        SECT
                                                        PREDICT

WEAPON....NON-NUCLEAR WEAPONS

CONOVER H.L.,CIVILIAN DEFENSE: A SELECTED LIST OF RECENT REFERENCES (PAMPHLET). USA+45 LOC/G MUNIC PROB/SOLV ADMIN LEAD TASK WEAPON GOV/REL...POLICY CON/ANAL 20 CIV/DEFENS. PAGE 13 G0251
BIBLIOG N PLAN WAR CIVMIL/REL

JOURNAL OF CONFLICT RESOLUTION. FUT WOR+45 INT/ORG NAT/G FORCES CREATE PROB/SOLV ARMS/CONT NUC/PWR WEAPON SOC. PAGE 1 G0002
BIBLIOG/A N DIPLOM WAR

ZLOTNICK M.,WEAPONS IN SPACE (PAMPHLET). FUT WOR+45 TEC/DEV DIPLOM ARMS/CONT CIVMIL/REL PEACE HABITAT ...CONCPT NEW/IDEA CHARTS. PAGE 65 G1268
SPACE N19 WEAPON NUC/PWR WAR

MOON P.T.,"SYLLABUS ON INTERNATIONAL RELATIONS." EUR+WWI MOD/EUR USA-45 FORCES COLONIAL WAR WEAPON NAT/LISM...POLICY BIBLIOG T 19/20. PAGE 39 G0778
INT/ORG C25 DIPLOM NAT/G

EINSTEIN A.,THE WORLD AS I SEE IT. WOR-45 INTELL R+D INT/ORG NAT/G SECT VOL/ASSN FORCES CREATE EDU/PROP LEGIT ARMS/CONT WAR WEAPON NAT/LISM ALL/VALS...POLICY CONCPT 20. PAGE 17 G0337
SOCIETY B34 PHIL/SCI DIPLOM PACIFISM

FULLER G.H.,A SELECTED LIST OF REFERENCES ON THE EXPANSION OF THE US NAVY, 1933-1939 (PAMPHLET). MOD/EUR USA-45 NAT/G PLAN DIPLOM DOMIN RISK ARMS/CONT EQUILIB PWR 20 NAVY. PAGE 20 G0399
BIBLIOG B39 FORCES WEAPON WAR

FULLER G.H.,SELECTED LIST OF RECENT REFERENCES ON AMERICAN NATIONAL DEFENSE (PAMPHLET). USA-45 FINAN NAT/G ARMS/CONT WAR GOV/REL CENTRAL COST PEACE PWR 20. PAGE 20 G0400
BIBLIOG B40 CIVMIL/REL FORCES WEAPON

FULLER G.H.,DEFENSE FINANCING: A SELECTED LIST OF REFERENCES (PAMPHLET). MOD/EUR USA-45 ECO/DEV NAT/G DELIB/GP RATION ARMS/CONT WEAPON COST PEACE PWR 20 CONGRESS. PAGE 20 G0401
BIBLIOG/A B41 FINAN FORCES BUDGET

FULLER G.H.,A LIST OF BIBLIOGRAPHIES ON QUESTIONS RELATING TO NATIONAL DEFENSE (PAMPHLET). USA-45 NAT/G ARMS/CONT WAR GOV/REL COST PEACE 20. PAGE 20 G0402
BIBLIOG/A B41 FORCES CIVMIL/REL WEAPON

FULLER G.H.,DEFENSE FINANCING: A SUPPLEMENTARY LIST OF REFERENCES (PAMPHLET). CANADA UK USA-45 ECO/DEV NAT/G DELIB/GP BUDGET ADJUD ARMS/CONT WEAPON COST PEACE PWR 20 AUSTRAL CHINJAP CONGRESS. PAGE 21 G0403
BIBLIOG/A B42 FINAN FORCES DIPLOM

STEWART I.,ORGANIZING SCIENTIFIC RESEARCH FOR WAR: ADMINISTRATIVE HISTORY OF OFFICE OF SCIENTIFIC RESEARCH AND DEVELOPMENT. USA-45 INTELL R+D LABOR WORKER CREATE BUDGET WEAPON CIVMIL/REL GP/REL EFFICIENCY...POLICY 20. PAGE 53 G1036
DELIB/GP B48 ADMIN WAR TEC/DEV

CROWTHER J.G.,SCIENCE AT WAR. EUR+WWI PLAN TEC/DEV DOMIN COERCE NUC/PWR WEAPON KNOWL PWR...CONCPT OBS TREND VAL/FREE 20. PAGE 14 G0265
R+D B50 FORCES WAR UK

HART B.H.L.,STRATEGY (REV. ED.). CHRIST-17C EUR+WWI MEDIT-7 MOD/EUR TEC/DEV LEAD REV WEAPON...POLICY CHARTS. PAGE 25 G0486
WAR B54 PLAN FORCES PHIL/SCI

MIKSCHE F.O.,ATOMIC WEAPONS AND ARMIES. FUT WOR+45 WOR-45 SOCIETY COERCE DETER WEAPON PWR...POLICY WELF/ST PSY CONCPT INT SYS/QU KNO/TEST TOT/POP 20. PAGE 39 G0765
TEC/DEV B55 FORCES NUC/PWR

ESTEP R.,AN AIR POWER BIBLIOGRAPHY. USA+45 TEC/DEV BUDGET DIPLOM EDU/PROP DETER CIVMIL/REL...DECISION INT/LAW 20. PAGE 18 G0351
BIBLIOG/A B56 FORCES WEAPON PLAN

US DEPARTMENT OF THE ARMY,AMERICAN MILITARY HISTORY. USA+45 USA-45 EX/STRUC PROB/SOLV TEC/DEV DIPLOM NUC/PWR REV WAR WEAPON...PSY 18/20. PAGE 57 G1125
BIBLIOG B56 FORCES NAT/G

US DEPARTMENT OF THE ARMY,RESEARCH AND DEVELOPMENT (AND RELATED ASPECTS) IN FOREIGN COUNTRIES. WOR+45 DIST/IND INDUS CONSULT FORCES CREATE EDU/PROP AUTOMAT DETER WEAPON. PAGE 57 G1126
BIBLIOG/A B56 R+D TEC/DEV NUC/PWR

SPEIER H.,GERMAN REARMAMENT AND ATOMIC WAR: THE VIEWS OF GERMAN MILITARY AND POLITICAL LEADERS. FUT WOR+45 INT/ORG NAT/G WEAPON ATTIT PWR...INT QU TOT/POP VAL/FREE COLD/WAR 20. PAGE 52 G1024
TOP/EX B57 FORCES NUC/PWR GERMANY

ARON R.,ON WAR: ATOMIC WEAPONS AND GLOBAL DIPLOMACY (TRANS. BY TERENCE KILMARTIN). WOR+45 SOCIETY FORCES BAL/PWR WAR WEAPON PERSON...SOC 20. PAGE 4 G0067
ARMS/CONT B58 NUC/PWR COERCE DIPLOM

GAVIN J.M.,WAR AND PEACE IN THE SPACE AGE. SPACE USA+45 USSR FORCES PLAN TEC/DEV BAL/PWR DIPLOM ARMS/CONT WEAPON CIVMIL/REL...CHARTS GP/COMP 20 NATO COLD/WAR. PAGE 21 G0414
WAR B58 DETER NUC/PWR PEACE

NATIONAL PLANNING ASSOCIATION,1970 WITHOUT ARMS CONTROL (PAMPHLET). WOR+45 PROB/SOLV TEC/DEV DIPLOM CONFER DETER NUC/PWR WAR...CHARTS 20 COLD/WAR. PAGE 41 G0810
ARMS/CONT B58 ORD/FREE WEAPON PREDICT

ROCKEFELLER BROTH FUND INC,INTERNATIONAL SECURITY - THE MILITARY ASPECT. USA+45 INT/ORG NAT/G BUDGET ARMS/CONT WAR WEAPON PEACE ORD/FREE 20 NATO. PAGE 47 G0932
NUC/PWR B58 DETER FORCES DIPLOM

US DEPARTMENT OF THE ARMY,BIBLIOGRAPHY ON LIMITED WAR (PAMPHLET). USA+45 TEC/DEV CONTROL RISK COERCE DETER NUC/PWR WEAPON ADJUST PEACE ALL/VALS ORD/FREE 20. PAGE 57 G1127
BIBLIOG/A B58 WAR FORCES CIVMIL/REL

EMME E.M.,THE IMPACT OF AIR POWER - NATIONAL SECURITY AND WORLD POLITICS. USA+45 USSR FORCES DIPLOM WEAPON PEACE TOTALISM...POLICY NAT/COMP 20 EUROPE. PAGE 18 G0346
DETER B59 AIR WAR ORD/FREE

GODDARD V.,THE ENIGMA OF MENACE. WOR+45 SECT LEAD NUC/PWR WAR WEAPON CHOOSE PERSON PWR...POLICY PHIL/SCI PACIFIST 20 COLD/WAR. PAGE 22 G0423
PEACE B59 ARMS/CONT DIPLOM ATTIT

GREENFIELD K.R.,COMMAND DECISIONS. ASIA EUR+WWI S/ASIA USA-45 WOR-45 NAT/G CONSULT DELIB/GP COERCE NUC/PWR PWR...OBS 20 CHINJAP. PAGE 23 G0446
PLAN B59 FORCES WAR WEAPON

POKROVSKY G.I.,SCIENCE AND TECHNOLOGY IN CONTEMPORARY WAR. SPACE USSR WOR+45 NAT/G CONSULT ACT/RES PLAN DETER WEAPON...MARXIST METH/CNCPT CHARTS STERTYP COLD/WAR 20. PAGE 45 G0881
TEC/DEV B59 FORCES NUC/PWR WAR

JANOWITZ M.,"CHANGING PATTERNS OF ORGANIZATIONAL AUTHORITY: THE MILITARY ESTABLISHMENT" (BMR)" USA+45 ELITES STRUCT EX/STRUC PLAN DOMIN AUTOMAT NUC/PWR WEAPON 20. PAGE 28 G0559
FORCES S59 AUTHORIT ADMIN TEC/DEV

BARNET R.,WHO WANTS DISARMAMENT. COM EUR+WWI USA+45 USSR INT/ORG NAT/G BAL/PWR DIPLOM EDU/PROP COERCE DETER NUC/PWR WAR WEAPON ATTIT PWR...TIME/SEQ COLD/WAR CONGRESS 20. PAGE 5 G0096
PLAN B60 FORCES ARMS/CONT

MCCLELLAND C.A.,NUCLEAR WEAPONS, MISSILES, AND FUTURE WAR: PROBLEM FOR THE SIXTIES. WOR+45 FORCES ARMS/CONT DETER MARXISM...POLICY ANTHOL COLD/WAR. PAGE 37 G0729
DIPLOM B60 NUC/PWR WAR WEAPON

PARRY A.,RUSSIA'S ROCKETS AND MISSILES. COM FUT GERMANY USA+45 WOR+45 INTELL ECO/DEV ACT/RES NUC/PWR WEAPON ATTIT ALL/VALS...OBS TIME/SEQ COLD/WAR 20. PAGE 44 G0859
PLAN B60 TEC/DEV SPACE USSR

US DEPARTMENT OF THE ARMY,DISARMAMENT: A BIBLIOGRAPHIC RECORD: 1916-1960. DETER WAR WEAPON PEACE 20 UN LEAGUE/NAT COLD/WAR NATO. PAGE 57 G1128
BIBLIOG/A B60 ARMS/CONT NUC/PWR DIPLOM

S60

BRODY R.A.,"DETERRENCE STRATEGIES: AN ANNOTATED | BIBLIOG/A
BIBLIOGRAPHY." WOR+45 PLAN ARMS/CONT NUC/PWR WAR | FORCES
WEAPON DECISION. PAGE 9 G0173 | DETER
| DIPLOM

B64

SCHERER F.M.,THE WEAPONS ACQUISITION PROCESS: | INDUS
ECONOMIC INCENTIVES. BOSTON: DIVISION OF RESEARCH, | ACT/RES
GRADUATE SCHOOL OF BUSINESS. USA+45 FINAN NAT/G | WEAPON
DELIB/GP ECO/TAC RIGID/FLEX WEALTH...MGT MATH STAT
CHARTS VAL/FREE 20. PAGE 49 G0965

S60

DYSON F.J.,"THE FUTURE DEVELOPMENT OF NUCLEAR | INT/ORG
WEAPONS." FUT WOR+45 DELIB/GP ACT/RES PLAN DETER | ARMS/CONT
WEAPON ATTIT PWR...POLICY 20. PAGE 17 G0328 | NUC/PWR

B64

SCHWARTZ M.D.,CONFERENCE ON SPACE SCIENCE AND SPACE | SPACE
LAW. FUT COM/IND NAT/G FORCES ACT/RES PLAN BUDGET | LAW
DIPLOM NUC/PWR WEAPON...POLICY ANTHOL 20. PAGE 50 | PEACE
G0983 | TEC/DEV

B61

US SENATE COMM GOVT OPERATIONS,ORGANIZING FOR | POLICY
NATIONAL SECURITY. COM USA+45 BUDGET DIPLOM DETER | PLAN
NUC/PWR WAR WEAPON ORD/FREE...BIBLIOG 20 COLD/WAR. | FORCES
PAGE 60 G1176 | COERCE

S64

SPONSLER G.C.,"THE MILITARY ROLE IN SPACE." FUT | TEC/DEV
USA+45 SEA AIR NAT/G ACT/RES PLAN COERCE NUC/PWR | FORCES
WEAPON KNOWL ORD/FREE PWR RESPECT...TREND 20. | SPACE
PAGE 52 G1026

S61

RICHSTEIN A.R.,"LEGAL RULES IN NUCLEAR WEAPONS | NUC/PWR
EMPLOYMENTS." FUT WOR+45 LAW SOCIETY FORCES PLAN | TEC/DEV
WEAPON RIGID/FLEX...HEAL CONCPT TREND VAL/FREE 20. | MORAL
PAGE 47 G0918 | ARMS/CONT

N64

NATIONAL ACADEMY OF SCIENCES,CIVIL DEFENSE: PROJECT | NUC/PWR
HARBOR SUMMARY REPORT (PAMPHLET). USA+45 MUNIC | FORCES
NAT/G ACT/RES BUDGET EDU/PROP DETER WEAPON EATING | WAR
...GEOG 20. PAGE 41 G0808 | PLAN

B62

ASTIA,HUMAN ENGINEERING: A REPORT BIBLIOGRAPHY. | BIBLIOG/A
USA+45 R+D FORCES ACT/RES COMPUTER CREATE OP/RES | COM/IND
EDU/PROP CONTROL WEAPON...SOC NEW/IDEA. PAGE 4 | COMPUT/IR
G0073 | METH

B65

BEAUFRE A.,AN INTRODUCTION TO STRATEGY, WITH | PLAN
PARTICULAR REFERENCE TO PROBLEMS OF DEFENSE, | NUC/PWR
POLITICS, ECONOMICS IN THE NUCLEAR AGE. WOR+45 | WEAPON
FORCES DIPLOM DETER CIVMIL/REL GP/REL...NEW/IDEA | DECISION
IDEA/COMP 20. PAGE 6 G0111

B62

BENNETT J.C.,NUCLEAR WEAPONS AND THE CONFLICT OF | POLICY
CONSCIENCE. WOR+45 PROB/SOLV DIPLOM WEAPON SUPEGO | NUC/PWR
MORAL...ANTHOL WORSHIP 20. PAGE 6 G0120 | WAR

B65

BLOOMFIELD L.,SOVIET INTERESTS IN ARMS CONTROL AND | USSR
DISARMAMENT* THE DECADE UNDER KHRUSHCHEV 1954-1964. | ARMS/CONT
ASIA FORCES ACT/RES EDU/PROP DETER NUC/PWR WEAPON | DIPLOM
COST ATTIT...PHIL/SCI CLASSIF STAT NET/THEORY GAME | TREND
BIBLIOG. PAGE 7 G0139

B62

FRYKLUND R.,100 MILLION LIVES: MAXIMUM SURVIVAL IN | NUC/PWR
A NUCLEAR WAR. USA+45 USSR CONTROL WEAPON | WAR
...IDEA/COMP NAT/COMP 20. PAGE 20 G0397 | PLAN
| DETER

B65

GRETTON P.,MARITIME STRATEGY - A STUDY OF DEFENSE | FORCES
PROBLEMS. ASIA UK USSR DIPLOM COERCE DETER NUC/PWR | PLAN
WEAPON...CONCPT NAT/COMP 20. PAGE 23 G0449 | WAR
| SEA

B62

PERRE J.,LES MUTATIONS DE LA GUERRE MODERNE: DE LA | WAR
REVOLUTION FRANCAISE A LA REVOLUTION NUCLEAIRE. | FORCES
DIPLOM ARMS/CONT DEATH REV WEAPON GP/REL PEACE | NUC/PWR
ATTIT...STAT PREDICT BIBLIOG 18/20 WWI. PAGE 44
G0870

B65

HITCH C.J.,DECISION-MAKING FOR DEFENSE. USA+45 | DECISION
CREATE BUDGET COERCE WAR WEAPON EFFICIENCY...SIMUL | OP/RES
20. PAGE 26 G0515 | PLAN
| FORCES

S62

DAWSON R.H.,"CONGRESSIONAL INNOVATION AND | LEGIS
INTERVENTION IN DEFENSE POLICY: LEGISLATIVE | PWR
AUTHORIZATION OF WEAPONS SYSTEMS." CONSTN PLAN | CONTROL
ARMS/CONT GOV/REL EFFICIENCY PEACE NEW/LIB OLD/LIB. | WEAPON
PAGE 14 G0281

B65

MCGUIRE M.C.,SECRECY AND THE ARMS RACE* A THEORY OF | DETER
THE ACCUMULATION OF STRATEGIC WEAPONS AND HOW | ARMS/CONT
SECRECY AFFECTS IT. DIPLOM NUC/PWR WEAPON ISOLAT | SIMUL
RATIONAL ORD/FREE WEALTH...ECOMETRIC MATH GEN/LAWS. | GAME
PAGE 38 G0742

B63

US DEPARTMENT OF THE ARMY,SOVIET RUSSIA: STRATEGIC | BIBLIOG/A
SURVEY (PAMPHLET). USSR POL/PAR PLAN DOMIN EDU/PROP | MARXISM
ARMS/CONT GUERRILLA WAR WEAPON...TREND CHARTS | DIPLOM
ORG/CHARTS 20. PAGE 57 G1129 | COERCE

B65

MELMANS S.,OUR DEPLETED SOCIETY. SPACE USA+45 | CIVMIL/REL
ECO/DEV FORCES BUDGET ECO/TAC ADMIN WEAPON | INDUS
EFFICIENCY 20 COLD/WAR. PAGE 38 G0753 | EDU/PROP
| CONTROL

B63

WILTZ J.E.,IN SEARCH OF PEACE: THE SENATE MUNITIONS | DELIB/GP
INQUIRY, 1934-36. EUR+WWI USA+45 ELITES INDUS LG/CO | PROFIT
LEGIS INT/TRADE LOBBY NEUTRAL ARMS/CONT...POLICY | WAR
CONGRESS 20 LEAGUE/NAT PRESIDENT SENATE CONSCRIPTN. | WEAPON
PAGE 64 G1246

B65

MOSKOWITZ H.,US SECURITY, ARMS CONTROL, AND | BIBLIOG/A
DISARMAMENT 1961-1965. FORCES DIPLOM DETER WAR | ARMS/CONT
WEAPON...CHARTS 20 UN COLD/WAR NATO. PAGE 40 G0790 | NUC/PWR
| PEACE

S63

ENTHOVEN A.C.,"ECONOMIC ANALYSIS IN THE DEPARTMENT | PLAN
OF DEFENSE." USA+45 NAT/G DELIB/GP PROB/SOLV RATION | BUDGET
NUC/PWR WEAPON COST...DECISION 20 DEPT/DEFEN | ECO/TAC
RESOURCE/N. PAGE 18 G0349 | FORCES

B65

US DEPARTMENT OF ARMY,MILITARY PROTECTIVE | FORCES
CONSTRUCTION: NUCLEAR WARFARE AND CHEMICAL AND | CONSTRUC
BIOLOGICAL OPERATIONS (MANUAL). OP/RES TEC/DEV RISK | TASK
COERCE NUC/PWR WAR WEAPON EFFICIENCY UTIL BIO/SOC | HEALTH
HABITAT ORD/FREE 20. PAGE 57 G1117

B64

BROWN N.,NUCLEAR WAR* THE IMPENDING STRATEGIC | FORCES
DEADLOCK. USA+45 USSR TEC/DEV BUDGET RISK ARMS/CONT | OP/RES
NUC/PWR WEAPON COST BIO/SOC...GEOG IDEA/COMP | WAR
NAT/COMP GAME NATO WARSAW/P. PAGE 9 G0177 | GEN/LAWS

B65

US DEPARTMENT OF THE ARMY,NUCLEAR WEAPONS AND THE | BIBLIOG/A
ATLANTIC ALLIANCE: A BIBLIOGRAPHIC SURVEY. ASIA COM | ARMS/CONT
EUR+WWI USA+45 FORCES DIPLOM WEAPON...STAT 20 NATO. | NUC/PWR
PAGE 58 G1131 | BAL/PWR

B64

DUSCHA J.,ARMS, MONEY, AND POLITICS. USA+45 INDUS | NAT/G
POL/PAR ECO/TAC TAX DETER NUC/PWR WAR WEAPON | FORCES
GOV/REL ATTIT...BIBLIOG/A 20 CONGRESS MONEY | POLICY
DEPT/DEFEN. PAGE 17 G0326 | BUDGET

L65

PILISUK M.,"IS THERE A MILITARY INDUSTRIAL COMPLEX | ELITES
WHICH PREVENTS PEACE CONSENSUS; COUNTERVAILING | WEAPON
POWER IN PLURALIST SYSTEMS." INDUS R+D ACADEM | PEACE
FEEDBACK CIVMIL/REL ADJUST CONSEN ATTIT RIGID/FLEX | ARMS/CONT
...CENSUS IDEA/COMP BIBLIOG. PAGE 45 G0878

B64

KAUFMANN W.W.,THE MC NAMARA STRATEGY. TOP/EX | FORCES
INSPECT BAL/PWR DIPLOM CONTROL DETER GUERRILLA | WAR
NUC/PWR WEAPON COST PWR...METH/COMP 20 MCNAMARA/R | PLAN
KENNEDY/JF JOHNSON/LB NATO DEPT/DEFEN. PAGE 30 | PROB/SOLV
G0586

S65

BALDWIN H.,"SLOW-DOWN IN THE PENTAGON." USA+45 | RECORD
CREATE PLAN GOV/REL CENTRAL COST EFFICIENCY PWR | R+D
...MGT MCNAMARA/R. PAGE 5 G0088 | WEAPON

B64

ROTHSCHILD J.H.,TOMORROW'S WEAPONS: CHEMICAL AND | WAR
BIOLOGICAL. FUT PROB/SOLV ARMS/CONT PEACE MORAL | WEAPON
...CHARTS BIBLIOG 20. PAGE 48 G0941 | BIO/SOC

ADMIN

S65
DESAI M.J.,"INDIA AND NUCLEAR WEAPONS." ASIA
BAL/PWR DIPLOM NUC/PWR WEAPON PEACE RECORD. PAGE 15
G0294
INDIA
ARMS/CONT

S65
GRIFFITH S.B.,"COMMUNIST CHINA'S CAPACITY TO MAKE
WAR." CHINA/COM COM NAT/G TOP/EX PLAN DOMIN COERCE
NUC/PWR ATTIT RESPECT SKILL...CONCPT MYTH TIME/SEQ
TREND COLD/WAR. PAGE 23 G0452
FORCES
PWR
WEAPON
ASIA

S65
KOHL W.L.,"NUCLEAR SHARING IN NATO AND THE
MULTILATERAL FORCE." FUT USSR VOL/ASSN TEC/DEV
DIPLOM NUC/PWR WAR WEAPON NATO. PAGE 31 G0611
ARMS/CONT
OBS
IDEA/COMP

S65
KRICKUS R.J.,"ON THE MORALITY OF
CHEMICAL/BIOLOGICAL WAR." ECO/UNDEV ARMS/CONT DETER
NUC/PWR RIGID/FLEX HEALTH INT/LAW. PAGE 31 G0621
MORAL
BIO/SOC
WEAPON
WAR

S65
KUZMACK A.M.,"TECHNOLOGICAL CHANGE AND STABLE
DETERRENCE." CREATE EDU/PROP ARMS/CONT WEAPON
CHOOSE COST DRIVE PERCEPT...RECORD STERTYP TIME.
PAGE 32 G0627
R+D
DETER
EQUILIB

S65
RASER J.R.,"WEAPONS DESIGN AND ARMS CONTROL* THE
POLARIS EXAMPLE." DETER NUC/PWR WEAPON CHOOSE
PERCEPT...STERTYP TIME. PAGE 46 G0904
ARMS/CONT
R+D
GEOG
ACT/RES

B66
DAENIKER G.,STRATEGIE DES KLEIN STAATS. SWITZERLND
ACT/RES CREATE DIPLOM NEUTRAL DETER WAR WEAPON PWR
SOVEREIGN...IDEA/COMP 20 COLD/WAR. PAGE 14 G0270
NUC/PWR
PLAN
FORCES
NAT/G

B66
US PRES COMM ECO IMPACT DEFENS,REPORT* JULY 1965.
USA+45 ECO/DEV INDUS DELIB/GP FORCES OP/RES
ARMS/CONT NUC/PWR WEAPON BAL/PAY...PREDICT SIMUL.
PAGE 59 G1159
ACT/RES
STAT
WAR
BUDGET

B67
BURNS E.L.M.,MEGAMURDER. WOR+45 LAW INT/ORG NAT/G
BAL/PWR DIPLOM DETER MURDER WEAPON CIVMIL/REL PEACE
...INT/LAW TREND 20. PAGE 10 G0193
FORCES
PLAN
WAR
NUC/PWR

B67
DAVIS V.,THE POLITICS OF INNOVATION: PATTERNS IN
NAVY CASES (PAMPHLET). WOR+45 NAT/G CREATE WEAPON
INGP/REL ATTIT...POLICY SOC METH/COMP METH. PAGE 14
G0280
BIBLIOG
FORCES
NUC/PWR
TEC/DEV

B67
KINTNER W.R.,PEACE AND THE STRATEGY CONFLICT. PLAN
BAL/PWR DIPLOM CONTROL ARMS/CONT DETER WEAPON 20.
PAGE 30 G0599
ROLE
PEACE
NUC/PWR
ORD/FREE

B67
RUSSELL B.,WAR CRIMES IN VIETNAM. USA+45 VIETNAM
FORCES DIPLOM WEAPON RACE/REL DISCRIM ISOLAT
BIO/SOC 20 COLD/WAR RUSSELL/B. PAGE 48 G0949
WAR
CRIME
ATTIT
POLICY

B67
US SENATE COMM ON FOREIGN REL,ARMS SALES TO NEAR
EAST AND SOUTH ASIAN COUNTRIES. INDIA IRAN PAKISTAN
WOR+45 PROC/MFG BAL/PWR DIPLOM...DECISION SENATE.
PAGE 60 G1183
WEAPON
FOR/AID
FORCES
POLICY

B67
US SENATE COMM ON FOREIGN REL,UNITED STATES
ARMAMENT AND DISARMAMENT PROBLEMS. USA+45 AIR
BAL/PWR DIPLOM FOR/AID NUC/PWR ORD/FREE SENATE
TREATY. PAGE 60 G1184
ARMS/CONT
WEAPON
FORCES
PROB/SOLV

B67
US SENATE COMM ON FOREIGN REL,FOREIGN ASSISTANCE
ACT OF 1967. VIETNAM WOR+45 DELIB/GP CONFER CONTROL
WAR WEAPON BAL/PAY...CENSUS CHARTS SENATE. PAGE 60
G1185
FOR/AID
LAW
DIPLOM
POLICY

L67
DAVIS P.C.,"THE COMING CHINESE COMMUNIST NUCLEAR
THREAT AND U.S. SEA BASED ABM OPTIONS." ASIA
CHINA/COM FUT USA+45 SEA NAT/G FORCES PLAN TEC/DEV
LEAD ARMS/CONT...GEOG METH/COMP 20 ABM/DEFSYS.
PAGE 14 G0279
NUC/PWR
DETER
WEAPON
DIPLOM

S67
BRETNOR R.,"DESTRUCTIVE FORCE AND THE MILITARY
EQUATIONS." UNIV COMPUTER PLAN PROB/SOLV AUTOMAT
CONTROL COERCE DETER NUC/PWR WEAPON DRIVE PWR.
PAGE 9 G0166
FORCES
TEC/DEV
DOMIN
WAR

S67
CARROLL K.J.,"SECOND STEP TOWARD ARMS CONTROL."
WOR+45 INT/ORG VOL/ASSN FORCES PROB/SOLV RISK
WEAPON 20 COLD/WAR. PAGE 11 G0215
ARMS/CONT
DIPLOM
PLAN
NUC/PWR

S67
CLEMENS W.C.,"CHINESE NUCLEAR TESTS: TRENDS AND
PORTENTS." CHINA/COM USA+45 USSR FORCES PLAN
TEC/DEV ARMS/CONT WAR PWR...DECISION 20 MAO
KHRUSH/N. PAGE 12 G0234
NUC/PWR
WEAPON
POLICY
DIPLOM

S67
KAHN H.,"CRITERIA FOR LONG-RANGE NUCLEAR CONTROL
POLICIES." WOR+45 INT/ORG TEC/DEV DOMIN DETER WAR
WEAPON ISOLAT ORD/FREE POLICY. PAGE 29 G0571
NUC/PWR
ARMS/CONT
BAL/PWR
DIPLOM

S67
KRUSCHE H.,"THE STRIVING OF THE KIESINGER-STRAUS
GOVERNMENT FOR NUCLEAR WEAPONS IS A THREAT TO
EUROPEAN SECURITY." EUR+WWI GERMANY BAL/PWR
SANCTION WEAPON PEACE ORD/FREE...MARXIST 20 NATO
COLD/WAR. PAGE 32 G0623
ARMS/CONT
INT/ORG
NUC/PWR
DIPLOM

S67
MARTIN L.,"THE AMERICAN ABM DECISION." ASIA COM
EUR+WWI UK USA+45 USSR FORCES DIPLOM PEACE...POLICY
20 ABM/DEFSYS. PAGE 36 G0713
WEAPON
DETER
NUC/PWR
WAR

S67
TEKINER S.,"SINKIAN AND THE SINO-SOVIET CONFLICT."
ASIA COM USSR FORCES PLAN BAL/PWR CONTROL NUC/PWR
WAR WEAPON...DECISION 20. PAGE 54 G1060
DIPLOM
PWR
MARXISM

S67
WALTERS R.E.,"THE ROLE OF NUCLEAR WEAPONS FOR THE
WEST." ASIA UK USA+45 USSR DIPLOM COERCE WAR PEACE
...POLICY DECISION 20. PAGE 62 G1209
PLAN
NUC/PWR
WEAPON
FORCES

S67
WARE R.S.,"FORECAST A.D. 2000." SOCIETY STRATA
ECO/UNDEV INDUS FORCES EDU/PROP AUTOMAT COERCE REV
WEAPON ATTIT PREDICT. PAGE 62 G1213
NUC/PWR
GEOG
TEC/DEV
WAR

S67
WOLFE T.W.,"SOVIET MILITARY POLICY AT THE FIFTY
YEAR MARK." USSR VIETNAM WOR+45 RATION AGREE WAR
WEAPON CIVMIL/REL TREATY. PAGE 64 G1254
FORCES
POLICY
TIME/SEQ
PLAN

N67
US HOUSE COMM FOREIGN AFFAIRS,REPORT OF SPECIAL
STUDY MISSION TO THE NEAR EAST (PAMPHLET). ISRAEL
USA+45 YEMEN ECO/UNDEV INT/ORG FOR/AID ARMS/CONT
WAR WEAPON NAT/LISM PEACE...GEOG 20 UN HOUSE/REP.
PAGE 58 G1138
ISLAM
DIPLOM
FORCES

WEATHER....WEATHER

WEBER/MAX....MAX WEBER

WEBSTER J.A. G1221

WEIGLEY R.F. G1222

WEIL G.L. G1223

WEIMAR/REP....WEIMAR REPUBLIC

B63
JACOB H.,GERMAN ADMINISTRATION SINCE BISMARCK:
CENTRAL AUTHORITY VERSUS LOCAL AUTONOMY. GERMANY
GERMANY/W LAW POL/PAR CONTROL CENTRAL TOTALISM
FASCISM...MAJORIT DECISION STAT CHARTS GOV/COMP
19/20 BISMARCK/O HITLER/A WEIMAR/REP. PAGE 28 G0551
ADMIN
NAT/G
LOC/G
POLICY

WEINBERG A.M. G1224,G1225

WEINER N. G1226

WEISBROD B.A. G1227

WEISNER J.B. G1228

WELF/ST....WELFARE STATE ADVOCATE

LASKI H.J.,REFLECTIONS ON THE REVOLUTIONS OF OUR   CAP/ISM   B43
TIME. COM USSR NAT/G WORKER UTOPIA ORD/FREE WEALTH   WELF/ST
MARXISM SOCISM 19/20. PAGE 32 G0637   ECO/TAC
                                                        POLICY

BARKER E.,THE DEVELOPMENT OF PUBLIC SERVICES IN   GOV/COMP   B44
WESTERN WUROPE: 1660-1930. FRANCE GERMANY UK SCHOOL   ADMIN
CONTROL REPRESENT ROLE...WELF/ST 17/20. PAGE 5   EX/STRUC
G0095

MAASS A.A.,"CONGRESS AND WATER RESOURCES." LOC/G   REGION   L50
TEC/DEV CONTROL SANCTION...WELF/ST GEOG CONGRESS.   AGRI
PAGE 35 G0683   PLAN

MIKSCHE F.O.,ATOMIC WEAPONS AND ARMIES. FUT WOR+45   TEC/DEV   B55
WOR-45 SOCIETY COERCE DETER WEAPON PWR...POLICY   FORCES
WELF/ST PSY CONCPT INT SYS/QU KNO/TEST TOT/POP 20.   NUC/PWR
PAGE 39 G0765

SCHOECK H.,THE NEW ARGUMENT IN ECONOMICS. UK USA+45   WELF/ST   B63
INDUS MARKET LABOR NAT/G ECO/TAC ADMIN ROUTINE   FOR/AID
BAL/PAY PWR...POLICY BOLIV. PAGE 49 G0973   ECO/DEV
                                                        ALL/IDEOS

WELFARE....SEE RECEIVE, NEW/LIB, WELF/ST

WELFARE STATE....SEE NEW/LIB, WELF/ST

WELTON H. G1229

WENDT P.F. G1230

WEST R.L. G0650

WEST AFRICA....SEE AFRICA/W

WEST GERMANY....SEE GERMANY/W

WEST/EDWRD....SIR EDWARD WEST

WEST/IND....WEST INDIES; SEE ALSO L/A+17C

WEST/POINT....UNITED STATES MILITARY ACADEMY

WEST/SAMOA....WESTERN SAMOA; SEE ALSO S/ASIA

WEST/VIRGN....WEST VIRGINIA

WESTERN ELECTRIC....SEE AT+T

WESTERN EUROPE....SEE EUROPE/W

WESTERN SAMOA....SEE WEST/SAMOA

WESTERN UNITED STATES....SEE US/WEST

WESTLEY B. G0672

WESTMINSTER HALL, COURTS OF....SEE CTS/WESTM

WESTPHALIA....PEACE OF WESTPHALIA

WHEELER-BENNETT J.W. G1231

WHIDDINGTON R. G0265

WHIG/PARTY....WHIG PARTY (USE WITH SPECIFIC NATION)

WHIP....SEE LEGIS, CONG, ROUTINE

WHITE D.M. G0801

WHITE L.D. G1232,G1233

WHITE/SUP....WHITE SUPREMACY - PERSONS, GROUPS, AND IDEAS

WHITE/T....THEODORE WHITE

WHITE/WA....WILLIAM ALLEN WHITE

WHITEHD/AN....ALFRED NORTH WHITEHEAD

WHITEHEAD T.N. G1234

WHITMAN/W....WALT WHITMAN

WHITNAH D.R. G1235

WHITTIER J.M. G1236

WHO....WORLD HEALTH ORGANIZATION

STYCOS J.M.,"POLITICS AND POPULATION CONTROL IN   PLAN   S67
LATIN AMERICA." USA+45 FAM NAT/G GP/REL AGE/C ATTIT   CENSUS
CATHISM MARXISM...POLICY UN WHO. PAGE 53 G1045   CONTROL
                                                        L/A+17C

WHYTE/WF....WILLIAM FOOTE WHYTE

RUITENBEER H.M.,THE DILEMMA OF ORGANIZATIONAL   PERSON   B63
SOCIETY. CULTURE ECO/DEV MUNIC SECT TEC/DEV   ROLE
EDU/PROP NAT/LISM ORD/FREE...NAT/COMP 20 RIESMAN/D   ADMIN
WHYTE/WF MERTON/R MEAD/MARG JASPERS/K. PAGE 48   WORKER
G0945

WIGGINS J.W. G0973,G0974

WIGHTMAN D. G1237

WILCOX J.K. G1238

WILENSKY H.L. G1239

WILES P.J.D. G1240

WILHELM/I....WILHELM I (KAISER)

WILHELM/II....WILHELM II (KAISER)

WILKINS/R....ROY WILKINS

WILLIAM/3....WILLIAM III (PRINCE OF ORANGE)

WILLIAMS B.H. G1241

WILLIAMS C. G1242

WILLIAMS D.P. G0507

WILLIAMS S.P. G1243

WILLIAMS/R....ROGER WILLIAMS

WILLIAUS T.H. G1244

WILLOW/RUN....WILLOW RUN, MICHIGAN

WILLS....WILLS AND TESTAMENTS

WILSON/H....HAROLD WILSON

WILSON/J....JAMES WILSON

WILSON/W....PRESIDENT WOODROW WILSON

FREIDEL F.,AMERICAN ISSUES IN THE TWENTIETH   DIPLOM   B66
CENTURY. SOCIETY FINAN ECO/TAC FOR/AID CONTROL   POLICY
NUC/PWR WAR RACE/REL PEACE ATTIT...ANTHOL T 20   NAT/G
WILSON/W ROOSEVLT/F KENNEDY/JF TRUMAN/HS. PAGE 20   ORD/FREE
G0391

WILTZ J.E. G1246

WINSTON O. G1247

WINTHROP H. G1248

WIRETAPPING....SEE PRIVACY

WIRTH L. G1249

WISCONSIN....WISCONSIN

CLEAVELAND F.N.,SCIENCE AND STATE GOVERNMENT. AGRI   TEC/DEV   B59
EXTR/IND FINAN INDUS PROVS...METH/CNCPT STAT CHARTS   PHIL/SCI
20 NEW/YORK CONNECTICT WISCONSIN CALIFORNIA   GOV/REL
NEW/MEXICO. PAGE 12 G0233   METH/COMP

MURPHY E.F.,WATER PURITY: A STUDY IN LEGAL CONTROL   SEA   B61
OF NATURAL RESOURCES. LOC/G ACT/RES PLAN TEC/DEV   LAW
LOBBY GP/REL COST ATTIT HEALTH ORD/FREE...HEAL   PROVS
JURID 20 WISCONSIN WATER. PAGE 40 G0797   CONTROL

CARMICHAEL D.M.,"FORTY YEARS OF WATER POLLUTION   HEALTH   L67
CONTROL IN WISCONSIN: A CASE STUDY." LAW EXTR/IND   CONTROL
INDUS MUNIC DELIB/GP PLAN PROB/SOLV SANCTION   ADMIN
...CENSUS CHARTS 20 WISCONSIN. PAGE 11 G0207   ADJUD

WISCONSN/U....WISCONSIN STATE UNIVERSITY

WISH J.R. G1250

WITTGEN/L....LUDWIG WITTGENSTEIN

WOETZEL R.K. G1251

WOHLSTETTER A. G1252,G1253

WOLEK F.W. G0847

WOLFE H.G. G0999

WOLFE T.W. G1254

WOLFERS A. G1255

WOLFF/C....CHRISTIAN WOLFF

WOLFF/RP....ROBERT PAUL WOLFF

WOMAN....SEE FEMALE/SEX

WOMEN'S CHRISTIAN TEMPERANCE UNION....SEE WCTU

WOOD/CHAS....SIR CHARLES WOOD

WOODRUFF W. G1256

WOR+45....WORLDWIDE, 1945 TO PRESENT

WOR-45....WORLDWIDE, TO 1945

WORK....SEE WORKER

WORK PROJECTS ADMINISTRATION....SEE WPA

B54
COMBS C.H.,DECISION PROCESSES. INTELL SOCIETY   MATH
DELIB/GP CREATE TEC/DEV DOMIN LEGIT EXEC CHOOSE   DECISION
DRIVE RIGID/FLEX KNOWL PWR...PHIL/SCI SOC
METH/CNCPT CONT/OBS REC/INT PERS/TEST SAMP/SIZ BIOG
SOC/EXP WORK. PAGE 13 G0245

B60
PENTONY D.E.,THE UNDERDEVELOPED LANDS. FUT WOR+45   ECO/UNDEV
CULTURE AGRI FINAN INDUS MARKET INT/ORG LABOR NAT/G POLICY
VOL/ASSN CONSULT TEC/DEV ECO/TAC EDU/PROP COLONIAL FOR/AID
ATTIT WEALTH...OBS RECORD SAMP TREND GEN/METH WORK INT/TRADE
UN 20. PAGE 44 G0867

S60
RIVKIN A.,"AFRICAN ECONOMIC DEVELOPMENT: ADVANCED AFR
TECHNOLOGY AND THE STAGES OF GROWTH." CULTURE   TEC/DEV
ECO/UNDEV AGRI COM/IND EXTR/IND PLAN ECO/TAC ATTIT FOR/AID
DRIVE RIGID/FLEX SKILL WEALTH...MGT SOC GEN/LAWS
WORK TOT/POP 20. PAGE 47 G0923

B64
DIEBOLD J.,BEYOND AUTOMATION: MANAGERIAL PROBLEMS   FUT
OF AN EXPLODING TECHNOLOGY. SOCIETY ECO/DEV CREATE INDUS
ECO/TAC AUTOMAT SKILL...TECHNIC MGT WORK. PAGE 16   PROVS
G0303   NAT/G

B64
LI C.M.,INDUSTRIAL DEVELOPMENT IN COMMUNIST CHINA. ASIA
CHINA/COM ECO/DEV ECO/UNDEV AGRI FINAN INDUS MARKET TEC/DEV
LABOR NAT/G ECO/TAC INT/TRADE EXEC ALL/VALS
...POLICY RELATIV TREND WORK TOT/POP VAL/FREE 20.
PAGE 34 G0665

S64
FLORINSKY M.T.,"TRENDS IN THE SOVIET ECONOMY." COM ECO/DEV
USA+45 USSR INDUS LABOR NAT/G PLAN TEC/DEV ECO/TAC AGRI
ALL/VALS SOCISM...MGT METH/CNCPT STYLE CON/ANAL
GEN/METH WORK 20. PAGE 19 G0374

S64
MUMFORD L.,"AUTHORITARIAN AND DEMOCRATIC   ECO/DEV
TECHNIQUES." INDUS PROC/MFG LG/CO SML/CO CREATE   TEC/DEV
PLAN KNOWL...POLICY TREND WORK 20. PAGE 40 G0794

S64
NEEDHAM T.,"SCIENCE AND SOCIETY IN EAST AND WEST." ASIA
INTELL STRATA R+D LOC/G NAT/G PROVS CONSULT ACT/RES STRUCT
CREATE PLAN TEC/DEV EDU/PROP ADMIN ATTIT ALL/VALS
...POLICY RELATIV MGT CONCPT NEW/IDEA TIME/SEQ WORK
WORK. PAGE 41 G0815

S64
NEEDHAM T.,"SCIENCE AND SOCIETY IN EAST AND WEST." ASIA
INTELL STRATA R+D LOC/G NAT/G PROVS CONSULT ACT/RES STRUCT
CREATE PLAN TEC/DEV EDU/PROP ADMIN ATTIT ALL/VALS
...POLICY RELATIV MGT CONCPT NEW/IDEA TIME/SEQ WORK
WORK. PAGE 41 G0815

WORKER....WORKER, LABORER

N
FULLER G.A.,DEMOBILIZATION: A SELECTED LIST OF   BIBLIOG/A
REFERENCES. USA+45 LAW AGRI LABOR WORKER ECO/TAC   INDUS
RATION RECEIVE EDU/PROP ROUTINE ARMS/CONT ALL/VALS FORCES
20. PAGE 20 G0398   NAT/G

B
BRITISH COMMONWEALTH BUR AGRI,WORLD AGRICULTURAL   BIBLIOG/A
ECONOMICS AND RURAL SOCIOLOGY ABSTRACTS. NAT/G   AGRI
OP/RES PLAN TEC/DEV LEAD PRODUC...GEOG MGT NAT/COMP SOC
20. PAGE 9 G0170   WORKER

N
ADVANCED MANAGEMENT. INDUS EX/STRUC WORKER OP/RES   MGT
...DECISION BIBLIOG/A 20. PAGE 1 G0003   ADMIN
                                                    LABOR
                                                    GP/REL

N
PERSONNEL. USA+45 LAW LABOR LG/CO WORKER CREATE   BIBLIOG/A
GOV/REL PERS/REL ATTIT WEALTH. PAGE 1 G0010   ADMIN
                                                    MGT
                                                    GP/REL

N
PRINCETON UNIVERSITY,SELECTED REFERENCES: BIBLIOG/A
INDUSTRIAL RELATIONS SECTION. USA+45 EX/STRUC   LABOR
WORKER TEC/DEV...MGT 20. PAGE 45 G0892   INDUS
                                                    GP/REL

N19
BELL J.R.,PERSONNEL PROBLEMS IN CONVERTING TO   WORKER
AUTOMATION (PAMPHLET). USA+45 COMPUTER PLAN   AUTOMAT
...METH/CNCPT 20 CALIFORNIA. PAGE 6 G0115   PROB/SOLV
                                                    PROVS

N19
GINZBERG E.,MANPOWER FOR GOVERNMENT (PAMPHLET).   WORKER
USA+45 FORCES PLAN PROB/SOLV PAY EDU/PROP ADMIN   CONSULT
GP/REL COST...MGT PREDICT TREND 20 CIVIL/SERV.   NAT/G
PAGE 21 G0418   LOC/G

B43
LASKI H.J.,REFLECTIONS ON THE REVOLUTIONS OF OUR   CAP/ISM
TIME. COM USSR NAT/G WORKER UTOPIA ORD/FREE WEALTH WELF/ST
MARXISM SOCISM 19/20. PAGE 32 G0637   ECO/TAC
                                                    POLICY

B45
MAYO E.,THE SOCIAL PROBLEMS OF AN INDUSTRIAL   INDUS
CIVILIZATION. USA+45 SOCIETY LABOR CROWD PERS/REL   GP/REL
LAISSEZ. PAGE 37 G0725   MGT
                                                    WORKER

B47
WHITEHEAD T.N.,LEADERSHIP IN A FREE SOCIETY; A   INDUS
STUDY IN HUMAN RELATIONS BASED ON AN ANALYSIS OF   LEAD
PRESENT-DAY INDUSTRIAL CIVILIZATION. WOR-45 STRUCT ORD/FREE
R+D LABOR LG/CO SML/CO WORKER PLAN PROB/SOLV   SOCIETY
TEC/DEV DRIVE...MGT 20. PAGE 63 G1234

B48
STEWART I.,ORGANIZING SCIENTIFIC RESEARCH FOR WAR: DELIB/GP
ADMINISTRATIVE HISTORY OF OFFICE OF SCIENTIFIC   ADMIN
RESEARCH AND DEVELOPMENT. USA-45 INTELL R+D LABOR   WAR
WORKER CREATE BUDGET WEAPON CIVMIL/REL GP/REL   TEC/DEV
EFFICIENCY...POLICY 20. PAGE 53 G1036

S48
COCH L.,"OVERCOMING RESISTANCE TO CHANGE" (BMR)"   WORKER
USA+45 CONSULT ADMIN ROUTINE GP/REL EFFICIENCY   OP/RES
PRODUC PERCEPT SKILL...CHARTS SOC/EXP 20. PAGE 12   PROC/MFG
G0236   RIGID/FLEX

B49
LEPAWSKY A.,ADMINISTRATION. FINAN INDUS LG/CO   ADMIN
SML/CO INGP/REL PERS/REL COST EFFICIENCY OPTIMAL   MGT
SKILL 20. PAGE 33 G0656   WORKER
                                                    EX/STRUC

C51
HOMANS G.C.,"THE WESTERN ELECTRIC RESEARCHES" IN S. OP/RES
HOSLETT, ED., HUMAN FACTORS IN MANAGEMENT (BMR)"   EFFICIENCY
ACT/RES GP/REL HAPPINESS PRODUC DRIVE...MGT OBS 20. SOC/EXP
PAGE 27 G0526   WORKER

B53
ROBINSON E.A.G.,THE STRUCTURE OF COMPETITIVE   INDUS
INDUSTRY. UK ECO/DEV DIST/IND MARKET TEC/DEV DIPLOM PRODUC
EDU/PROP ADMIN EFFICIENCY WEALTH...MGT 19/20.   WORKER
PAGE 47 G0929   OPTIMAL

B54
WILENSKY H.L.,SYLLABUS OF INDUSTRIAL RELATIONS: A   BIBLIOG

GUIDE TO READING AND RESEARCH. USA+45 MUNIC ADMIN
INGP/REL...POLICY MGT PHIL/SCI 20. PAGE 63 G1239
  INDUS
  LABOR
  WORKER

C54
GOULDNER A.W.,"PATTERNS OF INDUSTRIAL BUREAUCRACY."
GP/REL CONSEN ATTIT DRIVE...BIBLIOG 20. PAGE 22
G0438
  ADMIN
  INDUS
  OP/RES
  WORKER

B57
DRUCKER P.F.,AMERICA'S NEXT TWENTY YEARS. USA+45
DIST/IND ACADEM MUNIC SCHOOL DIPLOM ECO/TAC AUTOMAT
HABITAT HEALTH...SOC/WK TREND 20 URBAN/RNWL
PUB/TRANS. PAGE 16 G0316
  WORKER
  FOR/AID
  CENSUS
  GEOG

B57
MERTON R.K.,SOCIAL THEORY AND SOCIAL STRUCTURE
(REV. ED.). INTELL SECT WORKER OP/RES EDU/PROP
ADMIN INGP/REL ANOMIE PERSON...AUD/VIS T 20
BUREAUCRCY. PAGE 38 G0759
  SOC
  GEN/LAWS
  SOCIETY
  STRUCT

B58
CHEEK G.,ECONOMIC AND SOCIAL IMPLICATIONS OF
AUTOMATION: A BIBLIOGRAPHIC REVIEW (PAMPHLET).
USA+45 LG/CO WORKER CREATE PLAN CONTROL ROUTINE
PERS/REL EFFICIENCY PRODUC...METH/COMP 20. PAGE 12
G0225
  BIBLIOG/A
  SOCIETY
  INDUS
  AUTOMAT

B58
DUBIN R.,THE WORLD OF WORK: INDUSTRIAL SOCIETY AND
HUMAN RELATIONS. MARKET PROC/MFG LABOR TEC/DEV
CAP/ISM AUTOMAT TASK GP/REL EFFICIENCY...CONCPT
CHARTS BIBLIOG 20. PAGE 16 G0317
  WORKER
  ECO/TAC
  PRODUC
  DRIVE

B58
UN INTL CONF ON PEACEFUL USE,PROGRESS IN ATOMIC
ENERGY (VOL. I). WOR+45 R+D PLAN TEC/DEV CONFER
CONTROL PEACE SKILL...CHARTS ANTHOL 20 UN BAGHDAD.
PAGE 55 G1088
  NUC/PWR
  DIPLOM
  WORKER
  EDU/PROP

B59
MEANS G.C.,ADMINISTRATIVE INFLATION AND PUBLIC
POLICY (PAMPHLET). USA+45 ECO/DEV FINAN INDUS
WORKER PLAN BUDGET GOV/REL COST DEMAND WEALTH 20
CONGRESS MONOPOLY GOLD/STAND. PAGE 38 G0749
  ECO/TAC
  POLICY
  RATION
  CONTROL

B59
U OF MICHIGAN LAW SCHOOL,ATOMS AND THE LAW. USA+45
PROVS WORKER PROB/SOLV DIPLOM ADMIN GOV/REL ANTHOL.
PAGE 55 G1085
  NUC/PWR
  NAT/G
  CONTROL
  LAW

S59
BENDIX R.,"INDUSTRIALIZATION, IDEOLOGIES, AND
SOCIAL STRUCTURE" (BMR)" UK USA-45 USSR STRUCT
WORKER GP/REL EFFICIENCY...IDEA/COMP 20. PAGE 6
G0117
  INDUS
  ATTIT
  MGT
  ADMIN

B60
WEBSTER J.A.,A GENERAL STUDY OF THE DEPARTMENT OF
DEFENSE INTERNAL SECURITY PROGRAM. USA+45 WORKER
TEC/DEV ADJUD CONTROL CT/SYS EXEC GOV/REL COST
...POLICY DECISION MGT 20 DEPT/DEFEN SUPREME/CT.
PAGE 62 G1221
  ORD/FREE
  PLAN
  ADMIN
  NAT/G

B61
CHAPPLE E.D.,THE MEASURE OF MANAGEMENT. USA+45
WORKER ADMIN GP/REL EFFICIENCY...DECISION
ORG/CHARTS SIMUL 20. PAGE 11 G0221
  MGT
  OP/RES
  PLAN
  METH/CNCPT

B61
INSTITUTE PSYCHOLOGICAL RES,HUMAN ENGINEERING
BIBLIOGRAPHY, 1959-1960. USA+45 WORKER EDU/PROP
PERSON METH/COMP. PAGE 28 G0547
  BIBLIOG/A
  METH
  PSY
  R+D

L61
THOMPSON V.A.,"HIERARACHY, SPECIALIZATION, AND
ORGANIZATIONAL CONFLICT" (BMR)" WOR+45 STRATA
STRUCT WORKER TEC/DEV GP/REL INGP/REL ATTIT
AUTHORIT 20 BUREAUCRCY. PAGE 54 G1069
  PERS/REL
  PROB/SOLV
  ADMIN
  EX/STRUC

B62
MACHLUP F.,THE PRODUCTION AND DISTRIBUTION OF
KNOWLEDGE IN THE UNITED STATES. USA+45 COM/IND
INDUS SCHOOL SECT WORKER COMPUTER CREATE CIVMIL/REL
COST EFFICIENCY WEALTH 20. PAGE 35 G0688
  ACADEM
  TEC/DEV
  EDU/PROP
  R+D

B62
MARS D.,SUGGESTED LIBRARY IN PUBLIC ADMINISTRATION.
FINAN DELIB/GP EX/STRUC WORKER COMPUTER ADJUD
...DECISION PSY SOC METH/COMP 20. PAGE 36 G0710
  BIBLIOG
  ADMIN
  METH
  MGT

B62
NEW ZEALAND COMM OF ST SERVICE,THE STATE SERVICES
IN NEW ZEALAND. NEW/ZEALND CONSULT EX/STRUC ACT/RES
...BIBLIOG 20. PAGE 42 G0818
  ADMIN
  WORKER
  TEC/DEV
  NAT/G

B62
STAHL O.G.,PUBLIC PERSONNEL ADMINISTRATION. LOC/G
TOP/EX CREATE PLAN ROUTINE...TECHNIC MGT T. PAGE 52
G1030
  ADMIN
  WORKER
  EX/STRUC
  NAT/G

B63
FLORES E.,LAND REFORM AND THE ALLIANCE FOR PROGRESS
(PAMPHLET). L/A+17C USA+45 STRUCT ECO/UNDEV NAT/G
WORKER CREATE PLAN ECO/TAC COERCE REV 20. PAGE 19
G0373
  AGRI
  INT/ORG
  DIPLOM
  POLICY

B63
HAUSMAN W.H.,MANAGING ECONOMIC DEVELOPMENT IN
AFRICA. AFR USA+45 LAW FINAN WORKER TEC/DEV WEALTH
...ANTHOL 20. PAGE 25 G0492
  ECO/UNDEV
  PLAN
  FOR/AID
  MGT

B63
KREPS J.,AUTOMATION AND THE OLDER WORKER: AN
ANNOTATED BIBLIOGRAPHY (PAMPHLET). USA+45 STRUCT
ECO/DEV INDUS TEC/DEV. PAGE 31 G0620
  BIBLIOG/A
  WORKER
  AGE/O
  AUTOMAT

B63
RUITENBEER H.M.,THE DILEMMA OF ORGANIZATIONAL
SOCIETY. CULTURE ECO/DEV MUNIC SECT TEC/DEV
EDU/PROP NAT/LISM ORD/FREE...NAT/COMP 20 RIESMAN/D
WHYTE/WF MERTON/R MEAD/MARG JASPERS/K. PAGE 48
G0945
  PERSON
  ROLE
  ADMIN
  WORKER

B64
FEI J.C.H.,DEVELOPMENT OF THE LABOR SURPLUS
ECONOMY: THEORY AND POLICY. WOR+45 AGRI INDUS
MARKET PROB/SOLV TEC/DEV...STAT CHARTS GEN/LAWS
METH 20 THIRD/WRLD. PAGE 18 G0361
  ECO/TAC
  POLICY
  WORKER
  ECO/UNDEV

B64
PARANJAPE H.K.,THE FLIGHT OF TECHNICAL PERSONNEL IN
PUBLIC UNDERTAKINGS. INDIA PAY DEMAND HAPPINESS
ORD/FREE...MGT QU 20 MIGRATION. PAGE 44 G0858
  ADMIN
  NAT/G
  WORKER
  PLAN

B65
WHITE HOUSE CONFERENCE ON INTERNATIONAL
COOPERATION(VOL.II). SPACE WOR+45 EXTR/IND INT/ORG
LABOR WORKER NUC/PWR PEACE AGE/Y...CENSUS ANTHOL 20
RESOURCE/N URBAN/RNWL PUB/TRANS. PAGE 1 G0019
  R+D
  CONFER
  TEC/DEV
  DIPLOM

B65
ANDERSON C.A.,EDUCATION AND ECONOMIC DEVELOPMENT.
INDUS R+D SCHOOL TEC/DEV ECO/TAC EDU/PROP AGE
HEREDITY PERCEPT SKILL 20. PAGE 3 G0056
  ANTHOL
  ECO/DEV
  ECO/UNDEV
  WORKER

B65
CHENG C.-.Y.,SCIENTIFIC AND ENGINEERING MANPOWER IN
COMMUNIST CHINA, 1949-1963. CHINA/COM USSR ELITES
ECO/DEV R+D ACADEM LABOR NAT/G EDU/PROP CONTROL
UTIL...POLICY BIBLIOG 20. PAGE 12 G0226
  WORKER
  CONSULT
  MARXISM
  BIOG

B65
HEER D.M.,AFTER NUCLEAR ATTACK: A DEMOGRAPHIC
INQUIRY. USA+45 ECO/DEV SECT WORKER SEX...HEAL SOC
STAT PREDICT CHARTS 20 NEGRO. PAGE 25 G0500
  GEOG
  NUC/PWR
  CENSUS
  WAR

B65
KOROL A.G.,SOVIET RESEARCH AND DEVELOPMENT. USSR
ACADEM SCHOOL WORKER ROUTINE COST...STAT T 20.
PAGE 31 G0615
  COM
  R+D
  FINAN
  DIST/IND

B65
MORRIS M.D.,THE EMERGENCE OF AN INDUSTRIAL LABOR
FORCE IN INDIA: A STUDY OF THE BOMBAY COTTON MILLS,
1854-1947. INDIA WORKER OP/RES ADMIN 19/20. PAGE 40
G0784
  INDUS
  LABOR
  ECO/UNDEV
  CAP/ISM

B65
OECD,THE MEDITERRANEAN REGIONAL PROJECT: PORTUGAL;
EDUCATION AND DEVELOPMENT. PORTUGAL SOCIETY STRATA
FINAN PROF/ORG WORKER PLAN PROB/SOLV ADMIN...POLICY
STAT CHARTS METH 20 OECD. PAGE 42 G0832
  EDU/PROP
  SCHOOL
  ACADEM
  ECO/UNDEV

B65
OECD,THE MEDITERRANEAN REGIONAL PROJECT: ITALY;
EDUCATION AND DEVELOPMENT. ITALY SOCIETY STRATA
FINAN NAT/G PROF/ORG WORKER PLAN PROB/SOLV ADMIN
...STAT CHARTS METH 20 OECD. PAGE 42 G0833
  SCHOOL
  EDU/PROP
  ECO/UNDEV
  ACADEM

OECD,THE MEDITERRANEAN REGIONAL PROJECT: GREECE;
EDUCATION AND DEVELOPMENT. FUT GREECE SOCIETY AGRI
FINAN NAT/G PROF/ORG WORKER PLAN PROB/SOLV ADMIN
DEMAND ATTIT 20 OECD. PAGE 42 G0834
B65
EDU/PROP
SCHOOL
ACADEM
ECO/UNDEV

OECD,THE MEDITERRANEAN REGIONAL PROJECT: SPAIN;
EDUCATION AND DEVELOPMENT. FUT SPAIN STRATA FINAN
NAT/G WORKER PLAN PROB/SOLV ADMIN COST...POLICY
STAT CHARTS 20 OECD. PAGE 42 G0835
B65
ECO/UNDEV
EDU/PROP
ACADEM
SCHOOL

SMITH E.A.,SOCIAL WELFARE: PRINCIPLES AND CONCEPTS.
STRATA STRUCT CONSULT WORKER ACT/RES CREATE PLAN
TEC/DEV ROUTINE GP/REL UTOPIA...SOC 20. PAGE 51
G1014
B65
CONCPT
SOC/WK
RECEIVE
ORD/FREE

TURNER A.N.,INDUSTRIAL JOBS AND THE WORKER. USA+45
CULTURE ECO/DEV LABOR MUNIC ACT/RES AUTOMAT TASK
...CHARTS BIBLIOG 20. PAGE 55 G1082
B65
WORKER
INDUS
ATTIT
TEC/DEV

ALEXANDER Y.,INTERNATIONAL TECHNICAL ASSISTANCE
EXPERTS: A CASE STUDY OF THE U.N. EXPERIENCE.
USA+45 WOR+45 WORKER CREATE PLAN PROB/SOLV ECO/TAC
FOR/AID GIVE EDU/PROP...CHARTS BIBLIOG 20 UN.
PAGE 2 G0039
B66
SKILL
INT/ORG
TEC/DEV
CONSULT

BOWEN H.R.,AUTOMATION AND ECONOMIC PROGRESS.
EUR+WWI USA+45 ECO/DEV INCOME ORD/FREE WEALTH
...POLICY ANTHOL 20. PAGE 8 G0160
B66
AUTOMAT
TEC/DEV
WORKER
LEISURE

LEWIS W.A.,DEVELOPMENT PLANNING; THE ESSENTIALS OF
ECONOMIC POLICY. USA+45 FINAN INDUS NAT/G WORKER
FOR/AID INT/TRADE ADMIN ROUTINE WEALTH...CONCPT
STAT. PAGE 34 G0663
B66
PLAN
ECO/DEV
POLICY
CREATE

MUMFORD L.,THE MYTH OF THE MACHINE: TECHNICS AND
HUMAN DEVELOPMENT. UNIV WOR-45 CREATE AUTOMAT
PERCEPT KNOWL...EPIST PHIL/SCI SOC LING TREND
SOC/INTEG 20 MARX/KARL. PAGE 40 G0795
B66
WORKER
TEC/DEV
SOCIETY

PEIRCE W.S.,SELECTIVE MANPOWER POLICIES AND THE
TRADE-OFF BETWEEN RISING PRICES AND UNEMPLOYMENT
(DISSERTATION). ECO/DEV WORKER ACT/RES...PHIL/SCI
20. PAGE 44 G0865
B66
PRICE
LABOR
POLICY
ECO/TAC

WHITNAH D.R.,SAFER SKYWAYS. DIST/IND DELIB/GP
FORCES TOP/EX WORKER TEC/DEV ROUTINE WAR CIVMIL/REL
COST...TIME/SEQ 20 FAA CAB. PAGE 63 G1235
B66
ADMIN
NAT/G
AIR
GOV/REL

PRINCETON U INDUSTRIAL REL SEC,RECENT MATERIAL ON
COLLECTIVE BARGAINING IN GOVERNMENT (PAMPHLET NO.
130). USA+45 ECO/DEV LABOR WORKER ECO/TAC GOV/REL
...MGT 20. PAGE 45 G0890
N66
BIBLIOG/A
BARGAIN
NAT/G
GP/REL

COLM G.,THE ECONOMY OF THE AMERICAN PEOPLE. USA+45
ECO/DEV FINAN WORKER INT/TRADE AUTOMAT GP/REL.
PAGE 13 G0244
B67
ECO/TAC
PRODUC
TREND
TEC/DEV

ENKE S.,DEFENSE MANAGEMENT. USA+45 R+D FORCES
WORKER PLAN ECO/TAC ADMIN NUC/PWR BAL/PAY UTIL
WEALTH...MGT DEPT/DEFEN. PAGE 18 G0348
B67
DECISION
DELIB/GP
EFFICIENCY
BUDGET

GROSSMAN G.,ECONOMIC SYSTEMS. USA+45 USA-45 USSR
YUGOSLAVIA WORKER CAP/ISM PRICE GP/REL EQUILIB
WEALTH MARXISM SOCISM...MGT METH/COMP 19/20.
PAGE 23 G0456
B67
ECO/DEV
PLAN
TEC/DEV
DEMAND

HODGKINSON R.G.,THE ORIGINS OF THE NATIONAL HEALTH
SERVICE: THE MEDICAL SERVICES OF THE NEW POOR LAW,
1834-1871. UK INDUS MUNIC WORKER PROB/SOLV
EFFICIENCY ATTIT HEALTH WEALTH SOCISM...JURID
SOC/WK 19/20. PAGE 26 G0519
B67
HEAL
NAT/G
POLICY
LAW

MACBRIDE R.,THE AUTOMATED STATE; COMPUTER SYSTEMS
AS A NEW FORCE IN SOCIETY. FUT WOR+45 FINAN MUNIC
B67
COMPUTER
AUTOMAT

NAT/G WORKER PLAN TEC/DEV CONTROL PERS/REL RACE/REL
ADJUST. PAGE 35 G0685
PROB/SOLV
SOCIETY

MAZOUR A.G.,SOVIET ECONOMIC DEVELOPMENT: OPERATION
OUTSTRIP: 1921-1965. USSR ECO/UNDEV FINAN CHIEF
WORKER PROB/SOLV CONTROL PRODUC MARXISM...CHARTS
ORG/CHARTS 20 STALIN/J. PAGE 37 G0726
B67
ECO/TAC
AGRI
INDUS
PLAN

NASH M.,MACHINE AGE MAYA. GUATEMALA L/A+17C STRUCT
AGRI WORKER CREATE INCOME ATTIT RIGID/FLEX ROLE
...IDEA/COMP SOC/EXP WORSHIP 20 INDIAN/AM. PAGE 41
G0806
B67
INDUS
CULTURE
SOC
MUNIC

NORTHRUP H.R.,RESTRICTIVE LABOR PRACTICES IN THE
SUPERMARKET INDUSTRY. USA+45 INDUS WORKER TEC/DEV
BARGAIN PAY CONTROL GP/REL COST...STAT CHARTS NLRB.
PAGE 42 G0827
B67
DIST/IND
MARKET
LABOR
MGT

SILBERMAN C.E.,THE MYTHS OF AUTOMATION. INDUS
WORKER COST PRODUC AGE WEALTH 20. PAGE 51 G0996
B67
MYTH
AUTOMAT
CHARTS
TEC/DEV

YAVITZ B.,AUTOMATION IN COMMERCIAL BANKING. USA+45
STRUCT WORKER CREATE OP/RES PLAN ROLE...DECISION
SAMP/SIZ. PAGE 64 G1263
B67
TEC/DEV
FINAN
COMPUT/IR
MGT

BRUNHILD G.,"THEORY OF 'TECHNICAL UNEMPLOYMENT'."
ECO/DEV ACT/RES PROB/SOLV DEMAND PRODUC...PHIL/SCI
20. PAGE 9 G0182
S67
WORKER
TEC/DEV
SKILL
INDUS

FRIED M.,"FUNCTIONS OF THE WORKING CLASS COMMUNITY
IN MODERN URBAN SOCIETY* IMPLICATIONS FOR FORCED
RELOCATION." USA+45 INDUS R+D NEIGH PLAN TEC/DEV
PARTIC GP/REL ATTIT...SOC STAT CHARTS. PAGE 20
G0393
S67
CLASSIF
WORKER
MUNIC
ADJUST

GANZ G.,"THE CONTROL OF INDUSTRY BY ADMINISTRATIVE
PROCESS." UK DELIB/GP WORKER 20. PAGE 21 G0408
S67
INDUS
LAW
ADMIN
CONTROL

MORTON J.A.,"A SYSTEMS APPROACH TO THE INNOVATION
PROCESS: ITS USE IN THE BELL SYSTEM." USA+45 INTELL
INDUS LG/CO CONSULT WORKER COMPUTER AUTOMAT DEMAND
...MGT CHARTS 20. PAGE 40 G0787
S67
TEC/DEV
GEN/METH
R+D
COM/IND

MYERS S.,"TECHNOLOGY AND URBAN TRANSIT: THE
ENORMOUS POTENTIAL OF BUS AND RAIL SYSTEMS." USA+45
FINAN LOC/G MUNIC WORKER PLAN PROB/SOLV PRICE
AUTOMAT 20. PAGE 40 G0798
S67
R+D
TEC/DEV
DIST/IND
ACT/RES

WORKING....SEE ROUTINE

WORLD HEALTH ORGANIZATION....SEE WHO

WORLD WAR I....SEE WWI

WORLD WAR II....SEE WWII

WORLD/BANK....WORLD BANK

HIRSCHMAN A.O.,DEVELOPMENT PROJECTS OBSERVED. INDUS
INT/ORG CONSULT EX/STRUC CREATE OP/RES ECO/TAC
DEMAND...POLICY MGT METH/COMP 20 WORLD/BANK.
PAGE 26 G0513
B67
ECO/UNDEV
R+D
FINAN
PLAN

WORLD/CONG....WORLD CONGRESS

WORLD/CT....WORLD COURT; SEE ALSO ICJ

WORLDUNITY....WORLD UNITY, WORLD FEDERATION (EXCLUDING UN
AND LEAGUE OF NATIONS)

WORSHIP....SEE ALSO SECT

JANOWITZ M.,THE PROFESSIONAL SOLDIER. CULTURE
STRATA STRUCT FAM PROB/SOLV TEC/DEV COERCE WAR
CIVMIL/REL NAT/LISM AGE HEREDITY ALL/VALS CONSERVE
...MGT WORSHIP. PAGE 28 G0560
B60
FORCES
MYTH
LEAD
ELITES

BENNETT J.C.,NUCLEAR WEAPONS AND THE CONFLICT OF CONSCIENCE. WOR+45 PROB/SOLV DIPLOM WEAPON SUPEGO MORAL...ANTHOL WORSHIP 20. PAGE 6 G0120
POLICY NUC/PWR WAR
B62

HOFSTADTER R.,ANTI-INTELLECTUALISM IN AMERICAN LIFE. USA+45 AGRI INDUS ACADEM TEC/DEV EDU/PROP INGP/REL ATTIT...SOC WORSHIP 20 MCCARTHY/J STEVENSN/A. PAGE 26 G0522
INTELL EPIST CULTURE SOCIETY
B63

BENJAMIN A.C.,SCIENCE, TECHNOLOGY, AND HUMAN VALUES. WOR+45 SECT EDU/PROP GP/REL ATTIT...TECHNIC LING IDEA/COMP WORSHIP 20. PAGE 6 G0118
PHIL/SCI CREATE ROLE SOCIETY
B65

NASH M.,MACHINE AGE MAYA. GUATEMALA L/A+17C STRUCT AGRI WORKER CREATE INCOME ATTIT RIGID/FLEX ROLE ...IDEA/COMP SOC/EXP WORSHIP 20 INDIAN/AM. PAGE 41 G0806
INDUS CULTURE SOC MUNIC
B67

BULMER-THOMAS I.,"SO, ON TO THE GREAT SOCIETY." FUT UNIV TEC/DEV BAL/PWR WAR BIO/SOC KNOWL...ART/METH SOC PREDICT TREND WORSHIP 20 GREAT/SOC. PAGE 9 G0185
PHIL/SCI SOCIETY CREATE
S67

WPA....WORK PROJECTS ADMINISTRATION

WRIGHT Q. G1257,G1258,G1259

WRITING....SEE ALSO HIST/WRIT

UNITED NATIONS,OFFICIAL RECORDS OF THE UNITED NATIONS' ATOMIC ENERGY COMMISSION - DISARMAMENT COMMISSION. WOR+45 TEC/DEV DIPLOM WRITING NUC/PWR 20 UN. PAGE 55 G1092
ARMS/CONT INT/ORG DELIB/GP CONFER
N

LARSEN K.,NATIONAL BIBLIOGRAPHIC SERVICES: THEIR CREATION AND OPERATION. WOR+45 COM/IND CREATE PLAN DIPLOM PRESS ADMIN ROUTINE...MGT UNESCO. PAGE 32 G0636
BIBLIOG/A INT/ORG WRITING
B53

CARPENTER E.,EXPLORATIONS IN COMMUNICATION. USSR CULTURE SCHOOL SECT EDU/PROP PRESS TV AUTOMAT FEEDBACK ATTIT PERSON...ART/METH PSY 20. PAGE 11 G0211
ANTHOL COM/IND TEC/DEV WRITING
B60

WWI....WORLD WAR I

DUPREE A.H.,SCIENCE IN THE FEDERAL GOVERNMENT; A HISTORY OF POLICIES AND ACTIVITIES TO 1940. USA-45 AGRI SCHOOL DELIB/GP WAR GOV/REL...PHIL/SCI BIBLIOG 18/20 DEPRESSION NEW/DEAL WWI JEFFERSN/T. PAGE 17 G0324
NAT/G R+D CREATE TEC/DEV
B57

PERRE J.,LES MUTATIONS DE LA GUERRE MODERNE: DE LA REVOLUTION FRANCAISE A LA REVOLUTION NUCLEAIRE. DIPLOM ARMS/CONT DEATH REV WEAPON GP/REL PEACE ATTIT...STAT PREDICT BIBLIOG 18/20 WWI. PAGE 44 G0870
WAR FORCES NUC/PWR
B62

WWII....WORLD WAR II

WYLIE J.C. G1260

WYOMING....WYOMING

X

XENOPHOBIA....SEE NAT/LISM

XENOPHON....XENOPHON

XHOSA....XHOSA TRIBE (SOUTH AFRICA)

Y

YALE/U....YALE UNIVERSITY

YALEN R.J. G1261

YALTA....YALTA CONFERENCE

YAMAMURA K. G1262

YANKEE/C....YANKEE CITY - LOCATION OF W.L. WARNER'S STUDY OF SAME NAME

YARBROGH/R....RALPH YARBOROUGH

YAVITZ B. G1263

YAZOO....YAZOO LAND SCANDAL

YEMELYANOV V.S. G1264

YEMEN....SEE ALSO ISLAM

US HOUSE COMM FOREIGN AFFAIRS,REPORT OF SPECIAL STUDY MISSION TO THE NEAR EAST (PAMPHLET). ISRAEL USA+45 YEMEN ECO/UNDEV INT/ORG FOR/AID ARMS/CONT WAR WEAPON NAT/LISM PEACE...GEOG 20 UN HOUSE/REP. PAGE 58 G1138
ISLAM DIPLOM FORCES
N67

YORUBA....YORUBA TRIBE

YOUNG O.R. G0359,G1265

YOUNG W. G0712,G1266

YOUNG/TURK....YOUNG TURK POLITICAL PARTY

YOUTH....SEE AGE/Y

YUDELMAN/M....MONTEGU YUDELMAN

YUGOSLAVIA....YUGOSLAVIA; SEE ALSO COM

NAKICENOVIC S.,NUCLEAR ENERGY IN YUGOSLAVIA. YUGOSLAVIA AGRI INDUS CREATE OP/RES ROUTINE EFFICIENCY KNOWL...HEAL STAT CHARTS LAB/EXP BIBLIOG 20. PAGE 41 G0802
R+D ECO/DEV TEC/DEV NUC/PWR
B61

MARES V.E.,"EAST EUROPE'S SECOND CHANCE." COM EUR+WWI HUNGARY ROMANIA USSR YUGOSLAVIA ECO/UNDEV NAT/G TOP/EX CREATE PLAN TEC/DEV REGION NAT/LISM RIGID/FLEX PWR...CONCPT STAT COMECON 20. PAGE 36 G0705
VOL/ASSN ECO/TAC
S64

ORG FOR ECO COOP AND DEVEL,THE MEDITERRANEAN REGIONAL PROJECT: YUGOSLAVIA; EDUCATION AND DEVELOPMENT. YUGOSLAVIA SOCIETY FINAN PROF/ORG PLAN ADMIN COST DEMAND MARXISM...STAT TREND CHARTS METH 20 OECD. PAGE 43 G0843
EDU/PROP ACADEM SCHOOL ECO/UNDEV
B65

SPULBER N.,THE STATE AND ECONOMIC DEVELOPMENT IN EASTERN EUROPE. BULGARIA COM CZECHOSLVK HUNGARY POLAND YUGOSLAVIA CULTURE PLAN CAP/ISM INT/TRADE CONTROL...POLICY CHARTS METH/COMP BIBLIOG/A 19/20. PAGE 52 G1028
ECO/DEV ECO/UNDEV NAT/G TOTALISM
B66

GROSSMAN G.,ECONOMIC SYSTEMS. USA+45 USA-45 USSR YUGOSLAVIA WORKER CAP/ISM PRICE GP/REL EQUILIB WEALTH MARXISM SOCISM...MGT METH/COMP 19/20. PAGE 23 G0456
ECO/DEV PLAN TEC/DEV DEMAND
B67

YUKON....YUKON, CANADA

Z

ZAMBIA....SEE ALSO AFR

ZANDE....ZANDE, AFRICA

ZANZIBAR....SEE TANZANIA

ZELLER B. G1267

ZIONISM....SEE ISRAEL, NAT/LISM

ZLATOVRT/N....NIKOLAI ZLATOVRATSKII

ZLOTNICK M. G1268

ZNANIECKI F. G1269

ZONING....ZONING REGULATIONS

ZOPPO C.E. G1270

ZUCKERMAN S. G1271

ZULU....ZULU - MEMBER OF BANTU NATION (SOUTHEAST AFRICA)

ZUNI....ZUNI - NEW MEXICAN INDIAN TRIBE

ZWINGLI/U....ULRICH ZWINGLI

Directory of Publishers

Abelard-Schuman Ltd., New York
Abeledo-Perrot, Buenos Aires
Abingdon Press, Nashville, Tenn.; New York
Academic Press, London; New York
Academy of the Rumanian People's Republic Scientific Documentation Center, Bucharest
Academy Publishers, New York
Accra Government Printer, Accra, Ghana
Acharya Book Depot, Baroda, India
Acorn Press, Phoenix, Ariz.
Action Housing, Inc., Pittsburgh, Pa.
Adams & Charles Black, London
Addison-Wesley Publishing Co., Inc., Reading, Mass.
Adelphi, Greenberg, New York
Adelphi Terrace, London
Advertising Research Foundation, New York
Advisory Committee on Intergovernmental Relations, Washington
Africa Bureau, London
Africa 1960 Committee, London
African Bibliographical Center, Inc., Washington
African Research Ltd., Exeter, England
Agarwal Press, Allahabad, India
Agathon Press, New York
Agency for International Development, Washington
Agrupacion Bibliotecalogica, Montevideo
Aguilar, S. A. de Ediciones, Madrid
Air University, Montgomery, Ala.
Akademiai Kiado, Budapest
Akademische Druck-und Verlagsanstalt, Graz, Austria
Akhil Bharat Sarva Seva Sangh, Rajghat, Varanasi, India; Rajghat, Kashi, India
Al Jadidah Press, Cairo
Alba House, New York
Eberhard Albert Verlag, Freiburg, Germany
Alcan, Paris
Aldine Publishing Co., Chicago
Aligarh Muslim University, Department of History, Aligarh, India
All-India Congress Committee, New Delhi
Allen and Unwin, Ltd., London
Howard Allen, Inc., Cleveland, Ohio
W. H. Allen & Co., Ltd., London
Alliance Inc., New York
Allied Publishers, Private, Ltd., Bombay; New Delhi
Allyn and Bacon, Inc., Boston
Almquist-Wiksell, Stockholm; Upsala
Ambassador Books, Ltd., Toronto, Ontario
American Academy of Arts and Sciences, Harvard University, Cambridge, Mass.
American Academy of Political and Social Science, Philadelphia
American Anthropological Association, Washington, D. C.
American Arbitration Association, New York
American-Asian Educational Exchange, New York
American Assembly, New York
American Association for the Advancement of Science, Washington, D. C.
American Association for the United Nations, New York
American Association of University Women, Washington, D. C.
American Bankers Association, New York
American Bar Association, Chicago
American Bar Foundation, Chicago
American Bibliographical Center-Clio Press, Santa Barbara, Calif.
American Bibliographic Service, Darien, Conn.
American Book Company, New York
American Civil Liberties Union, New York
American Council of Learned Societies, New York
American Council on Education, Washington
American Council on Public Affairs, Washington
American Data Processing, Inc., Detroit, Mich.
American Documentation Institute, Washington
American Economic Association, Evanston, Ill.
American Elsevier Publishing Co., Inc., New York
American Enterprise Institute for Public Policy Research, Washington, D. C.
American Features, New York
American Federation of Labor & Congress of Industrial Organizations, Washington, D. C.

American Foreign Law Association, Chicago
American Forest Products Industries, Washington, D. C.
American Friends of Vietnam, New York
American Friends Service Committee, New York
American Historical Association, Washington, D. C.
American Historical Society, New York
American Institute for Economic Research, Great Barrington, Mass.
American Institute of Consulting Engineers, New York
American Institute of Pacific Relations, New York
American International College, Springfield, Mass.
American Jewish Archives, Hebrew Union College—Jewish Institute of Religion, Cincinnati, Ohio
American Jewish Committee Institute of Human Relations, New York
American Judicature Society, Chicago
American Law Institute, Philadelphia
American Library Association, Chicago
American Management Association, New York
American Marketing Association, Inc., Chicago
American Municipal Association, Washington
American Museum of Natural History Press, New York
American Nepal Education Foundation, Eugene, Oregon
American Newspaper Publishers' Association, New York
American Opinion, Belmont, Mass.
American Philosophical Society, Philadelphia
American Political Science Association, Washington
American Psychiatric Association, New York
American Public Welfare Association, Chicago
American Research Council, Larchmont, N. Y.
American Society of African Culture, New York
American Society of International Law, Chicago
American Society for Public Administration, Chicago; Washington
American Textbook Publishers Council, New York
American Universities Field Staff, New York
American University, Washington, D. C.
American University of Beirut, Beirut
American University of Cairo, Cairo
American University Press, Washington
American University Press Services, Inc., New York
Ampersand Press, Inc., London, New York
Amsterdam Stock Exchange, Amsterdam
Anchor Books, New York
Anderson Kramer Association, Washington, D. C.
Anglo-Israel Association, London
Angus and Robertson, Sydney, Australia
Ann Arbor Publications, Ann Arbor, Mich.
Anthropological Publications, Oosterhout, Netherlands
Anti-Defamation League of B'nai B'rith, New York
Antioch Press, Yellow Springs, Ohio
Antwerp Institut Universitaire des Territoires d'Outre-Mer, Antwerp, Belgium
APEC Editora, Rio de Janeiro
Apollo Editions, New York
Ludwig Appel Verlag, Hamburg
Appleton-Century-Crofts, New York
Aqueduct Books, Rochester, N. Y.
Arbeitsgemeinschaft fur Forschung des Landes Nordrhein-Westfalen, Dusseldorf, Germany
Arcadia, New York
Architectural Press, London
Archon Books, Hamden, Conn.
Arco Publishing Company, New York
Arizona Department of Library and Archives, Tucson
Arizona State University, Bureau of Government Research, Tucson
Arlington House, New Rochelle, N. Y.
Arnold Foundation, Southern Methodist University, Dallas
Edward Arnold Publishers, Ltd., London
J. W. Arrowsmith, Ltd., London
Artes Graficas, Buenos Aires
Artes Graficas Industrias Reunidas SA, Rio de Janeiro
Asia Foundation, San Francisco
Asia Publishing House, Bombay; Calcutta; London; New York
Asia Society, New York
Asian Studies Center, Michigan State University, East Lansing, Mich.
Asian Studies Press, Bombay
Associated College Presses, New York

Associated Lawyers Publishing Co., Newark, N. J.
Association for Asian Studies, Ann Arbor
Association of National Advertisers, New York
Association of the Bar of the City of New York, New York
Association Press, New York
Associated University Bureaus of Business and Economic Research, Eugene, Ore.
M. L. Atallah, Rotterdam
Atheneum Publishers, New York
Atherton Press, New York
Athlone Press, London
Atlanta University Press, Atlanta, Ga.
The Atlantic Institute, Boulogne-sur-Seine
Atlantic Provinces Research Board, Fredericton, Newfoundland
Atma Ram & Sons, New Delhi
Atomic Industrial Forum, New York
Augustan Reprint Society, Los Angeles, Calif.
Augustana College Library, Rock Island, Ill.
Augustana Press, Rock Island, Ill.
J. J. Augustin, New York
Augustinus Verlag, Wurzburg
Australian National Research Council, Melbourne
Australian National University, Canberra
Australian Public Affairs Information Service, Sydney
Australian War Memorial, Canberra
Avi Publishing Co., Westport, Conn.
Avtoreferaty Dissertatsii, Moscow
N. W. Ayer and Sons, Inc., Philadelphia, Pa.
Aymon, Paris

La Baconniere, Neuchatel; Paris
Richard G. Badger, Boston
Baker Book House, Grand Rapids, Mich.
Baker, Vorhis, and Co., Boston
John Baker, London
A. A. Balkema, Capetown
Ballantine Books, Inc., New York
James Ballantine and Co., London
Baltimore Sun, Baltimore, Md.
Banco Central de Venezuela, Caracas
Bank for International Settlements, Basel
Bank of Finland Institute for Economic Research, Helsinki
Bank of Italy, Rome
Bankers Publishing Co., Boston
George Banta Publishing Co., Menasha, Wis.
Bantam Books, Inc., New York
A. S. Barnes and Co., Inc., Cranbury, N. J.
Barnes and Noble, Inc., New York
Barre Publishers, Barre, Mass.
Basic Books, Inc., New York
Batchworth Press Ltd., London
Bayerische Akademie der Wissenschaften, Munich
Bayerischer Schulbuch Verlag, Munich
Ebenezer Baylis and Son, Ltd., Worcester, England
Baylor University Press, Waco, Texas
Beacon Press, Boston
Bechte Verlag, Esslingen, Germany
H. Beck, Dresden
Bedminster Press, Inc., Totowa, N. J.
Beechhurst Press, New York
Behavioral Research Council, Great Barrington, Mass.
Belknap Press, Cambridge, Mass.
G. Bell & Sons, London
Bellman Publishing Co., Inc., Cambridge, Mass.
Matthew Bender and Co., Albany, New York
Bengal Publishers, Ltd., Calcutta
Marshall Benick, New York
Ernest Benn, Ltd., London
J. Bensheimer, Berlin; Leipzig; Mannheim
Benziger Brothers, New York
Berkley Publishing Corporation, New York
Bernard und Graefe Verlag fur Wehrwesen, Frankfurt
C. Bertelsmann Verlag, Gutersloh
Bharati Bhawan, Bankipore, India
Bharatiyi Vidya Bhavan, Bombay
G. R. Bhatkal for Popular Prakashan, Bombay
Bibliographical Society, London
Bibliographical Society of America, New York
Bibliographie des Staats, Dresden
Biblioteca de la II feria del libro exposicion nacional del periodismo, Panuco, Mexico
Biblioteca Nacional, Bogota

Biblioteka Imeni V. I. Lenina, Moscow
Bibliotheque des Temps Nouveaux, Paris
Bibliotheque Nationale, Paris
Adams & Charles Black, London
Basil Blackwell, Oxford
William Blackwood, Edinburgh
Blaisdell Publishing Co., Inc., Waltham, Mass.
Blanford Press, London
Blass, S. A., Madrid
Geoffrey Bles, London
BNA, Inc. (Bureau of National Affairs), Washington, D. C.
Board of Trade and Industry Estates Management Corp., London
T. V. Boardman and Co., London
Bobbs-Merrill Company, Inc., Indianapolis, Ind.
The Bodley Head, London
Bogen-Verlag, Munich
Bohlau-Verlag, Cologne; Graz; Tubingen
H. G. Bohn, London
Boni and Gaer, New York
Bonn University, Bonn
The Book of the Month Club, Johannesburg
Bookcraft, Inc., Salt Lake City, Utah
Bookfield House, New York
Bookland Private, Ltd., Calcutta; London
Bookmailer, New York
Bookman Associates, Record Press, New York
Books for Libraries, Inc., Freeport, N. Y.
Books International, Jullundur City, India
Borsenverein der deutschen Buchhandler, Leipzig
Bossange, Paris
Boston Book Co., Boston
Boston College Library, Chestnut Hill, Boston
Boston University, African Research Program, Boston
Boston University Press, Boston
H. Bouvier Verlag, Bonn
Bowes and Bowes, Ltd., Cambridge, England
R. R. Bowker Co., New York
John Bradburn, New York
George Braziller, Inc., New York
Brentano's, New York
Brigham Young University, Provo, Utah
E. J. Brill, Leyden
British Borneo Research Project, London
British Broadcasting Corp., London
British Council, London
British Liberal Party Organization, London
British Museum, London
Broadman Press, Nashville, Tenn.
The Brookings Institution, Washington
Brown University Press, Providence, R. I.
A. Brown and Sons, Ltd., London
William C. Brown Co., Dubuque, Iowa
Brown-White-Lowell Press, Kansas City
Bruce Publishing Co., Milwaukee, Wis.
Buchdruckerei Meier, Bulach, Germany
Buchhandler-Vereinigung, Frankfurt
Buijten & Schipperheijn, Amsterdam
Building Contractors Council, Chicago
Bureau of Public Printing, Manila
Bureau of Social Science Research, Washington, D. C.
Business Economists Group, Oxford
Business Publications, Inc., Chicago
Business Service Corp., Detroit, Mich.
Buttenheim Publishing Corp., New York
Butterworth's, London; Washington, D. C.; Toronto

Anne Cabbott, Manchester, England
California, Assembly of the State of, Sacramento, Calif.
California State Library, Sacramento
Calman Levy, Paris
Camara Oficial del Libro, Madrid
Cambridge Book Co., Inc., Bronxville, N. Y.
Cambridge University Press, Cambridge; London; New York
Camelot Press Ltd., London
Campion Press, London
M. Campos, Rio de Janeiro
Canada, Civil Service Commission, Ottawa
Canada, Civil Service Commission, Organization Division, Ottawa
Canada, Ministry of National Health and Welfare, Ottawa
Canada, National Joint Council of the Public Service, Ottawa

578

Canadian Dept. of Mines and Technical Surveys, Ottawa
Canadian Institute of International Affairs, Toronto
Canadian Peace Research Institute, Clarkson, Ont.
Canadian Trade Committee, Montreal
Candour Publishing Co., London
Jonathan Cape, London
Cape and Smith, New York
Capricorn Books, New York
Caribbean Commission, Port-of-Spain, Trinidad
Carleton University Library, Ottawa
Erich Carlsohn, Leipzig
Carnegie Endowment for International Peace, New York
Carnegie Endowment for International Peace, Washington, D. C.
Carnegie Foundation for the Advancement of Teaching, New York
Carnegie Press, Pittsburgh, Pa.
Carswell Co., Ltd., Toronto, Canada
Casa de las Americas, Havana
Case Institute of Technology, Cleveland, Ohio
Frank Cass & Co., Ltd., London
Cassell & Co., Ltd., London
Castle Press, Pasadena, Calif.
Catholic Historical Society of Philadelphia, Philadelphia
Catholic Press, Beirut
Catholic Students Mission Crusade Press, Cincinnati, Ohio
Catholic University Press, Washington
The Caxton Printers, Ltd., Caldwell, Idaho
Cedesa, Brussels
Cellar Book Shop, Detroit, Mich.
Center for Applied Research in Education, New York
Center for Applied Research in Education, Washington, D. C.
Center for Research on Economic Development, Ann Arbor, Mich.
Center for the Study of Democratic Institutions, Santa Barbara, Calif.
Center of Foreign Policy Research, Washington, D. C.
Center of International Studies, Princeton
Center of Planning and Economic Research, Athens, Greece; Washington, D. C.
Central Asian Research Centre, London
Central Bank of Egypt, Cairo
Central Book Co., Inc., Brooklyn, N. Y.
Central Book Department, Allahabad, India
Central Law Book Supply, Inc., Manila
Central News Agency, Ltd., Capetown, S. Afr.
Central Publicity Commission, Indian National Congress, New Delhi
Centre de Documentation CNRS, Paris
Centre de Documentation Economique et Sociale Africaine, Brussels
Centre d'Etudes de Politique Etrangere, Paris
Centre de Recherches sur l'URSS et les pays de l'est, Strasbourg
Centro de Estudios Monetarios Latino-Americanos, Mexico City
Centro Editorial, Guatemala City
Centro Mexicano de Escritores, Mexico City
Centro Para el "Desarrollo Economico y Social de America Latina", Santiago, Chile
The Century Co., New York
Century House, Inc., Watkins Glen, N. Y.
Cercle de la Librairie, Paris
Leon Chaillez Editeur, Paris
Chaitanya Publishing House, Allahabad, India
Chamber of Commerce of the United States, Washington, D. C.
S. Chand and Co., New Delhi
Chandler Publishing Co., San Francisco
Chandler-Davis, Lexington, Mass.
Chandler-Davis Publishing Co., West Trenton, N. J.
Channel Press, Inc., Great Neck, N. Y.
Chapman and Hall, London
Geoffrey Chapman, London
Chatham College, Pittsburgh, Pa.
Chatto and Windus, Ltd., London
F. W. Cheshire, London
Chestnut Hill, Boston College Library, Boston
Chicago Joint Reference Library, Chicago
Chilean Development Corp., New York
Chilmark Press, New York
Chilton Books, New York
China Viewpoints, Hong Kong
Chinese-American Publishing Co., Shanghai

Chiswick Press, London
Christian Crusade, Tulsa, Okla.
Georg Christiansen, Itzehoe, Germany
Christopher Publishing House, Boston
Chulalongkorn University, Bangkok
Church League of America, Wheaton, Ill.
C. I. Associates, New York
Cincinnati Civil Service, Cincinnati, Ohio
Citadel Press, New York
City of Johannesburg Public Library, Johannesburg
Citizens Research Foundation, Paris
Citizens Research Foundation, Princeton, N. J.
Ciudad Universitaria, San Jose, Calif.
Ciudad y Espiritu, Buenos Aires
Claremont Colleges, Claremont, Calif.
Clarendon Press, London
Clark, Irwin and Co., Ltd., Toronto
Clark University Press, Worcester, Mass.
Classics Press, New York
Clay and Sons, London
Cleveland Civil Service Commission, Cleveland
Clio Press, Santa Barbara, Calif.
William Clowes and Sons, Ltd., London
Colin (Librairie Armand) Paris
College and University Press, New Haven
Collet's Holdings, Ltd., London
Colliers, New York
F. Collin, Brussels
Collins, London
Colloquium Verlag, Berlin
Colombo Plan Bureau, Colombo, Ceylon
Colonial Press Inc., Northport, Ala.; New York
Colorado Bibliographic Institute, Denver
Colorado Legislature Council, Denver
Colorado State Board of Library Commissioners, Denver
Columbia University, New York
Columbia University, Bureau of Applied Social Research, New York
Columbia University, Center for Urban Education, New York
Columbia University, East Asian Institute, New York
Columbia University, Graduate School of Business, New York
Columbia University, Institute of French Studies, New York
Columbia University, Institute of Public Administration, New York
Columbia University, Institute of Russian Studies, New York
Columbia University, Institute of War-Peace Studies, New York
Columbia University, Law Library, New York
Columbia University, Parker School, New York
Columbia University, School of International Affairs, New York
Columbia University, School of Library Service, New York
Columbia University Press, New York
Columbia University Teachers College, New York
Combat Forces Press, Washington, D. C.
Comet Press, New York
Comision Nacional Ejecutiva, Buenos Aires
Commerce Clearing House, Chicago; Washington; New York
Commercial Credit Co., Baltimore, Md.
Commissao do iv Centenario de Ciudade, Sao Paulo
Commission for Technical Cooperation, Lahore
Commission to Study the Organization of Peace, New York
Committee for Economic Development, New York
Committee on Africa, New York
Committee on Federal Tax Policy, New York
Committee on Near East Studies, Washington
Committee on Public Administration, Washington, D. C.
Committee to Frame World Constitution, New York
Common Council for American Unity, New York
Commonwealth Agricultural Bureau, London
Commonwealth Economic Commission, London
Community Publications, Manila
Community Renewal Program, San Francisco
Community Studies, Inc., Kansas City
Companhia Editora Forense, Rio de Janeiro
Companhia Editora Nacional, Sao Paulo
Compass Books, New York
Concordia Publishing House, St. Louis, Mo.
Confederate Publishing Co., Tuscaloosa, Ala.
Conference on Economic Progress, Washington, D. C.
Conference on State and Economic Enterprise in Modern Japan, Estes Park, Colo.
Congress for Cultural Freedom, Prabhakar

Congressional Quarterly Service, Washington
Connecticut Personnel Department, Hartford
Connecticut State Civil Service Commission, Hartford
Conseil d'Etat, Paris
Conservative Political Centre, London
Constable and Co., London
Archibald Constable and Co., Edinburgh
Cooper Square Publishers, New York
U. Cooper and Partners, Ltd., London
Corinth Books, New York
Cornell University, Dept. of Asian Studies, Ithaca
Cornell University, Graduate School of Business and Public
 Administration, Ithaca
Cornell University Press, Ithaca
Cornell University, School of Industry and Labor Planning,
 Ithaca
Council for Economic Education, Bombay
Council of Education, Johannesburg
Council of Europe, Strasbourg
Council of State Governments, Chicago, Ill.
Council of the British National Bibliography, Ltd., London
Council on Foreign Relations, New York
Council on Public Affairs, Washington, D. C.
Council on Religion and International Affairs, New York
Council on Social Work Education, Washington, D. C.
Covici, Friede, Inc., New York
Coward-McCann, Inc., New York
Cresset Press, London
Crestwood Books, Springfield, Va.
Criterion Books, Inc., New York
S. Crofts and Co., New York
Crosby, Lockwood, and Sons, Ltd., London
Crosscurrents Press, New York
Thomas Y. Crowell Co., New York
Crowell-Collier and MacMillan, New York
Crown Publishers, Inc., New York
C.S.I.C., Madrid
Cuadernos de la Facultad de Derecho Universidad
 Veracruzana, Mexico City
Cuerpo Facultativo de Archiveros, Bibliotecarios y
 Argueologos, Madrid
Cultural Center of the French Embassy, New York
Current Scene, Hong Kong
Current Thought, Inc., Durham, N. C.
Czechoslovak Foreign Institute in Exile, Chicago

Da Capo Press, New York
Daguin Freres, Editeurs, Paris
Daily Telegraph, London
Daily Worker Publishing Co., Chicago
Dalloz, Paris
Damascus Bar Association, Damascus
Dangary Publishing Co., Baltimore
David Davies Memorial Institute of Political Studies,
 London
David-Stewart, New York
John Day Co., Inc., New York
John de Graff, Inc., Tuckahoe, N. Y.
La Decima Conferencia Interamericana, Caracas
Delacorte Press, New York
Dell Publishing Co., New York
T. S. Denison & Co., Inc., Minneapolis, Minn.
J. M. Dent, London
Departamento de Imprensa Nacional, Rio de Janeiro
Deseret Book Co., Salt Lake City, Utah
Desert Research Institute Publications' Office, Reno, Nev.
Deus Books, Paulist Press, Glen Rock, N. J.
Andre Deutsch, Ltd., London
Deutsche Afrika Gesellschaft, Bonn
Deutsche Bibliographie, Frankfurt am Main
Deutsche Bucherei, Leipzig
Deutsche Gesellschaft fur Volkerrecht, Karlsruhe
Deutsche Gesellschaft fur Auswartige Politik, Bonn
Deutsche Verlagsanstalt, Stuttgart
Deutscher Taschenbuch Verlag, Munich
Deva Datta Shastri, Hoshiarpur
Development Loan Fund, Washington, D. C.
Devin-Adair, Co., New York
Diablo Press, Inc., Berkeley, Calif.
Dial Press, Inc., New York
Dibco Press, San Jose, Cal.
Dickenson Publishing Co., Inc., Belmont, Calif.
Didier Publishers, New York

Firmin Didot Freres, Paris
Dietz Verlag, Berlin
Difusao Europeia do Livro, Sao Paulo
Diplomatic Press, London
Direccion General de Accion Social, Lisbon
District of Columbia, Office of Urban Renewal,
 Washington, D. C.
Djambatan, Amsterdam
Dennis Dobson, London
Dobunken Co., Ltd., Tokyo
La Documentation Francaise, Paris
Documents Index, Arlington, Virginia
Dodd, Mead and Co., New York
Octave Doin et Fils, Paris
Dolphin Books, Inc., New York
Dominion Press, Chicago
Walter Doon Verlag, Bremen
George H. Doran Co., New York
Dorrance and Co., Inc., Philadelphia, Pa.
Dorsey Press, Homewood, Illinois
Doubleday and Co., Inc., Garden City, N. Y.
Dover Publications, New York
Dow Jones and Co., Inc., New York
Dragonfly Books, Hong Kong
Drei Masken Verlag, Munich
Droemersche Verlagsanstalt, Zurich
Droste Verlag, Dusseldorf
Druck und Verlag von Carl Gerolds Sohn, Vienna
Guy Drummond, Montreal
The Dryden Press, New York
Dryfus Conference on Public Affairs, Hanover, N. H.
Duckworth, London
Duell, Sloan & Pearce, New York
Dufour Editions, Inc., Chester Springs, Pa.
Carl Duisburg-Gesellschaft fur Nachwuchsforderung, Cologne
Duke University, School of Law, Durham, N. C.
Duke University Press, Durham, N. C.
Dulau and Co., London
Duncker und Humblot, Berlin
Duquesne University Press, Pittsburgh, Pa.
R. Dutt, London
E. P. Dutton and Co., Inc., Garden City, N. Y.

E. P. & Commercial Printing Co., Durban, S. Africa
East Africa Publishing House, Nairobi
East European Fund, Inc., New York
East-West Center Press, Honolulu
Eastern Kentucky Regional Development Commission,
 Frankfort, Ky.
Eastern World, Ltd., London
Emil Ebering, Berlin
Echter-Verlag, Wurzburg
Ecole Francaise d'Extreme Orient, Paris
Ecole Nationale d'Administration, Paris
Econ Verlag, Dusseldorf; Vienna
Economic Research Corp., Ltd., Montreal
Economic Society of South Africa, Johannesburg
The Economist, London
Edicao Saraiva, Sao Paulo
Ediciones Ariel, Barcelona
Ediciones Cultura Hispanica, Madrid
Ediciones del Movimiento, Borgos, Spain
Ediciones Nuestro Tiempo, Montevideo
Ediciones Rialp, Madrid
Ediciones Riaz, Lima
Ediciones Siglo Veinte, Buenos Aires
Ediciones Tercer Mundo, Bogota
Edicoes de Revista de Estudes Politos, Rio de Janeiro
Edicoes Do Val, Rio de Janeiro
Edicoes GRD, Rio de Janeiro
Edicoes o Cruzeiro, Rio de Janeiro
Edicoes Tempo Brasileiro, Ltda., Rio de Janeiro
Edinburgh House Press, Edinburgh
Editions Albin Michel, Paris
Editions Alsatia, Paris
Editions Berger-Levrault, Paris
Editions Cujas, Paris
Editions de l'Epargne, Paris
Editions de l'Institut de Sociologie de l'Universite Libre de
 Bruxelles, Brussels
Editions d'Organisation, Paris
Editions Denoel, Paris
Editions John Didier, Paris

Editions du Carrefour, Paris
Editions du Cerf, Paris
Editions du Livre, Monte Carlo
Editions du Monde, Paris
Editions du Rocher, Monaco
Editions du Seuil, Paris
Editions du Tiers-Monde, Algiers
Editions du Vieux Colombier, Paris
Editions Eyrolles, Paris
Editions Internationales, Paris
Editions Mont Chrestien, Paris
Editions Nauwelaerts, Louvain
Editions Ouvrieres, Paris
Editions A. Pedone, Paris
Editions Presence Africaine, Paris
Editions Rouff, Paris
Editions Sedif, Paris
Editions Sirey, Paris
Editions Sociales, Paris
Editions Techniques Nord Africaines, Rabat
Editions Universitaires, Paris
Editora Brasiliense, Sao Paulo
Editora Civilizacao Brasileira S. A., Rio de Janeiro
Editora Fulgor, Sao Paulo
Editora Saga, Rio de Janerio
Editores letras e artes, Rio de Janeiro
Editores Mexicanos, Mexico City
Editores Mexicanos Unidos, Mexico City
Editorial AIP, Miami
Editorial Amerinda, Buenos Aires
Editorial Columbia, Buenos Aires
Editorial Freeland, Buenos Aires
Editorial Gustavo Gili, Barcelona
Editorial Jus, Mexico City, Mexico
Editorial Lex, Havana
Editorial Losa da Buenos Aires, Buenos Aires
Editorial Marymar, Buenos Aires
Editorial Mentora, Barcelona
Editorial Nascimento, Santiago
Editorial Palestra, Buenos Aires
Editorial Patria, Mexico City
Editorial Pax, Bogota
Editorial Pax-Mexico, Mexico City
Editorial Platina, Buenos Aires
Editorial Porrua, Mexico City
Editorial Stylo Durangozgo, Mexico City
Editorial Universitaria de Buenos Aires, Buenos Aires
Editorial Universitaria de Puerto Rico, San Jose
Editorial Universitaria Santiago, Santiago
Le Edizioni de Favoro, Rome
Edizioni di Storia e Letteratura, Rome
Edizioni Scientifiche Italiane, Naples
Education and World Affairs, New York
Educational Heritage, Yonkers, N. Y.
Edwards Brothers, Ann Arbor
Effingham Wilson Publishers, London
Egyptian Library Press, Cairo
Egyptian Society of International Law, Cairo
Elex Books, London
Elsevier Publishing Co., Ltd., London
EMECE Editores, Buenos Aires
Emerson Books, New York
Empresa Editora Austral, Ltd., Santiago
Encyclopedia Britannica, Inc., Chicago
English Universities Press, London
Ferdinand Enke Verlag, Bonn; Erlangen; Stuttgart
Horst Erdmann Verlag, Schwarzwald
Paul Eriksson, Inc., New York
Escorpion, Buenos Aires
Escuela de Historia Moderna, Madrid
Escuela Nacional de Ciencias Politicas y Sociales,
    Mexico City
Escuela Superior de Administracion Publica America Central,
    San Jose, Costa Rica
Essener Verlagsanstalt, Essen
Essential Books, Ltd., London
Ethiopia, Ministry of Information, Addis Ababa
Etudes, Paris
Euroamerica, Madrid
Europa-Archiv, Frankfurt am Main
Europa Publications Ltd., London
Europa Verlag, Zurich; Vienna
Europaische Verlagsanstalt, Frankfurt

European Committee for Economic and Social Progress,
    Milan
European Free Trade Association, Geneva
Evangelischer Verlag, Zurich
Edward Evans and Sons, Shanghai
Everline Press, Princeton
Excerpta Criminologica Foundation, Leyden, Netherlands
Exchange Bibliographies, Eugene, Ore.
Export Press, Belgrade
Exposition Press, Inc., New York
Eyre and Spottiswoode, Ltd., London
Extending Horizon Books, Boston

F. and T. Publishers, Seattle, Washington
Faber and Faber, Ltd., London
Fabian Society, London
Facing Reality Publishing Corporation, Detroit, Mich.
Facts on File, Inc., New York
Fairchild Publishing, Inc., New York
Fairleigh Dickinson Press, Rutherford, N. J.
Falcon Press, London
Family Service Association of America, New York
Farrar and Rinehart, New York
Farrar, Strauss & Giroux, Inc., New York
Fawcett World Library, New York
F. W. Faxon Co., Inc., Boston
Fayard, Paris
Federal Legal Publications, Inc., New York
Federal Reserve Bank of New York, New York
Federal Trust for Education and Research, London
Fellowship Publications, New York
Feltrinelli Giangiacomo (Editore), Milan
Au Fil d'Ariadne, Paris
Filipiniana Book Guild, Manila
Financial Index Co., New York
Finnish Political Science Association, Helsinki
Fischer Bucherei, Frankfurt
Fischer Verlag, Stuttgart
Gustav Fischer Verlag, Jena
Flammarion, Paris
Fleet Publishing Co., New York
Fletcher School of Law and Diplomacy, Boston
R. Flint and Co., London
Florida State University, Tallahassee
Follett Publishing Co., Chicago
Fondation Nationale des Sciences Politiques, Paris
Fondo Historico y Bibliografico Jose Foribio, Medina,
    Santiago
Fondo de Cultura Economica, Mexico
B. C. Forbes and Sons, New York
Ford Foundation, New York
Fordham University Press, New York
Foreign Affairs Association of Japan, Tokyo
Foreign Affairs Bibliography, New York
Foreign Language Press, Peking
Foreign Language Publishing House, Moscow
Foreign Policy Association, New York
Foreign Policy Clearing House, Washington, D. C.
Foreign Policy Research Institute, University of
    Pennsylvania, Philadelphia, Pa.
Foreign Trade Library, Philadelphia
Arnold Forni Editore, Bologna
Forschungs-Berichte des Landes Nordrhein-Westfalen, Dussel-
    dorf, Germany
Fortress Press, Philadelphia, Pa.
Foundation for Economic Education, Irvington-on-Hudson,
    N. Y.
Foundation for Social Research, Los Angeles, Calif.
Foundation Press, Inc., Brooklyn, N. Y.; Mineola, N. Y.
Foundation Press, Inc., Chicago
Foundation for Research on Human Behavior, New York
France Editions Nouvelles, Paris
France, Ministere de l'Education Nationale, Paris
France, Ministere d'Etat aux Affaires Culturelles, Paris
France, Ministere des Finances et des Affaires Economiques,
    Paris
Francois Maspera, Paris
Francke Verlag, Munich
Ben Franklin Press, Pittsfield, Mass.
Burt Franklin, New York
Free Europe Committee, New York
Free Press, New York
Free Press of Glencoe, Glencoe, Ill.; New York

Free Speech League, New York
Freedom Books, New York
Freedom Press, London
Ira J. Friedman, Inc., Port Washington, N. Y.
Friends General Conference, Philadelphia, Pa.
Friendship Press, New York
M. L. Fuert, Los Angeles
Fund for the Republic, New York
Fundacao Getulio Vargas, Rio de Janeiro
Funk and Wagnalls Co., Inc., New York
Orell Fuessli Verlag, Zurich

Galaxy Books, Oxford
Gale Research Co., Detroit
Galton Publishing Co., New York
A. R. Geoghegan, Buenos Aires
George Washington University, Population Research Project, Washington, D. C.
Georgetown University Press, Washington, D. C.
Georgia State College, Atlanta, Ga.
Georgia State Library, Atlanta, Ga.
Germany (Territory under Allied Occupation, 1945—U. S. Zone) Office of Public Information, Information Control Division, Bonn
Germany, Bundesministerium fur Vertriebene, Fluechtlinge, und Kriegsbeschadigte (Federal Ministry for Expellees, Refugees, and War Victims), Bonn
Gerold & Co. Verlag, Vienna, Austria
Ghana University Press, Accra, Ghana
Gideon Press, Beirut
Gustavo Gili, Barcelona
Ginn and Co., Boston
Glanville Publishing Co., New York
Glasgow University Press, Glasgow
Gleditsch Brockhaus, Leipzig
Glencoe Free Press, London
Golden Bell Press, Denver, Colo.
Victor Gollancz, Ltd., London
Gordon and Breach Science Publications, New York
Gothic Printing Co., Capetown, S. Afr.
Gould Publications, Jamaica, N. Y.
Government Affairs Foundation, Albany, N. Y.
Government Data Publications, New York
Government of India National Library, Calcutta
Government Printing Office, Washington
Government Publications of Political Literature, Moscow
Government Research Institute, Cleveland
Grafica Americana, Caracas
Grafica Editorial Souza, Rio de Janeiro
Graficas Gonzales, Madrid
Graficas Uguina, Madrid
Graphic, New York
H. W. Gray, Inc., New York
Great Britain, Administrative Staff College, London
Great Britain, Committee on Ministers' Powers, London
Great Britain, Department of Technical Cooperation, London
Great Britain, Foreign Office, London
Great Britain, Ministry of Overseas Development, London
Great Britain, Treasury, London
Greater Bridgeport Region, Planning Agency, Trumbull
W. Green and Son, Edinburgh
Green Pagoda Press, Hong Kong
Greenwich Book Publications, New York
Greenwood Periodicals, New York
Griffin Press, Adelaide, Australia
Grolier, Inc., New York
J. Groning, Hamburg
Grosset and Dunlap, Inc., New York
Grossman Publishers, New York
G. Grote'sche Verlagsbuchhandlung, Rastatt, Germany
Group for the Advancement of Psychiatry, New York
Grove Press, Inc., New York
Grune and Stratton, New York
Gruyter and Co., Walter de, Berlin
E. Guilmato, Paris
Democratic Party of Guinea, Guinea
Gulf Publishing Co., Houston, Texas
J. Chr. Gunderson Boktrykkeri og Bokbinderi, Oslo
Hans E. Gunther Verlag, Stuttgart
Gutersloher Verlagshaus, Gutersloh

Hadar Publishing Co., Tel-Aviv
Hafner Publishing Co., Inc., New York

G. K. Hall, Boston
Robert Hall, London
Charles Hallberg and Co., Chicago
Hamburgisches Wirtschafts Archiv, Hamburg
Hamilton & Co., London
Hamilton County Research Foundation, Cincinnati
Hamish Hamilton, London
Hanover House, New York
Hansard Society, London
Harcourt, Brace and World, New York
Harlo Press, Detroit, Mich.
Harper and Row Publishers, New York; London
George Harrap and Co., London
Otto Harrassowitz, Wiesbaden
Harrison Co., Atlanta, Ga.
Rupert Hart-Davis, London
Hartford Printing Co., Hartford, Conn.
Harvard Center for International Affairs, Cambridge, Mass.
Harvard Law School, Cambridge, Mass.
Harvard Law Review Association, Cambridge, Mass.
Harvard University Center for East Asian Studies, Cambridge, Mass.
Harvard University, Center for Russian Research and Studies, Cambridge, Mass.
Harvard University, Graduate School of Business Administration, Cambridge, Mass.
Harvard University, Peabody Museum, Cambridge, Mass.
Harvard University, Widener Library, Cambridge
Harvard University Press, Cambridge
V. Hase und Kohler Verlag, Mainz
Hastings House, New York
Hauser Press, New Orleans, La.
Hawthorne Books, Inc., New York
Hayden Book Company, New York
The John Randolph Haynes and Dora Haynes Foundation, Los Angeles
The Edward D. Hazen Foundation, New Haven, Conn.
D. C. Heath and Co., Boston
Hebrew University Press, Jerusalem
Heffer and Sons Ltd., Cambridge, England
William S. Hein and Co., Buffalo
James H. Heineman, Inc., New York
Heinemann Ltd., London
Heirsemann, Leipzig
A. Hepple, Johannesburg
Helicon Press, Inc., Baltimore, Md.
Herald Press, Scottdale, Penna.
Herder and Herder, New York
Herder Book Co., New York, St. Louis
Johann Gottfried Herder, Marburg, Germany
Heritage Foundation, Chicago
The Heritage Press, New York
Hermitage Press, Inc., New York
Heron House Winslow, Washington, D. C.
Herzl Press, New York
Carl Heymanns Verlag, Berlin
Hill and Wang, Inc., New York
Hillary House Publishers, Ltd., New York
Hind Kitabs, Ltd., Bombay
Hinds, Noble, and Eldridge, New York
Ferdinand Hirt, Kiel, Germany
Historical Society of New Mexico, Albuquerque, N. M.
H. M. Stationery Office, London
Hobart and William Smith Colleges, Geneva, N. Y.
Hobbs, Dorman and Co., New York
Hodden and Staughton, London
William Hodge and Co., Ltd., London
Hodges Figgis and Co., Ltd., Dublin
J. G. Hodgson, Fort Collins, Colo.
Hogarth Press, London
The Hokuseido Press, Tokyo
Holborn Publishing House, London
Hollis and Carter, London
Hollywood A.S.P. Council, Hollywood, Calif.
Holt and Williams, New York
Holt, Rinehart and Winston, New York
Henry Holt and Co., New York
Holzner Verlag, Wurzburg
Home and Van Thal, London
Hong Kong Government Press, Hong Kong
Hong Kong University Press, Hong Kong
Hoover Institute on War, Revolution and Peace, Stanford, Calif.

Hope College, Holland, Mich.
Horizon Press, Inc., New York
Houghton, Mifflin Co., Boston
Houlgate House, Los Angeles
Howard University Press, Washington
Howell, Sosbin and Co., New York
Hudson Institute, Inc., Harmon-on-Hudson, New York
B. W. Huebsch, Inc., New York
H. Hugendubel Verlag, Munich
Human Relations Area Files Press (HRAF), New Haven
Human Rights Publications, Caulfield, Victoria, Australia
Human Sciences Research, Inc., Arlington, Va.
Humanities Press, New York
Humon and Rousseau, Capetown
Hungarian Academy of Science, Publishing House of, Budapest
Hunter College Library, New York
R. Hunter, London
Huntington Library, San Marino, Calif.
Hutchinson and Co., London
Hutchinson University Library, London

Ibadan University Press, Ibadan, Nigeria
Iberia Publishing Company, New York
Ibero-American Institute, Stockholm
Illini Union Bookstore, Champaign, Ill.
Illinois State Publications, Springfield
Ilmgau Verlag, Pfaffenhofen
Imago Publishing Co., Ltd., London
Imprenta Calderon, Honduras
Imprenta Mossen Alcover, Mallorca
Imprenta Nacional, Caracas
Imprimerie d'Extreme Orient, Hanoi
Imprimerie Nationale, Paris
Imprimerie Sefan, Tunis
Imprimerie Fr. Van Muysewinkel, Brussels
Incentivist Publications, Greenwich, Conn.
Index Society, New York
India and Pakistan: Combined Interservice Historical
    Section, New Delhi
India, Government of, Press, New Delhi
India, Ministry of Community Development, New Delhi
India, Ministry of Finance, New Delhi
India, Ministry of Health, New Delhi
India, Ministry of Home Affairs, New Delhi
India, Ministry of Information and Broadcasting, Faridabad;
    New Delhi
India, Ministry of Law, New Delhi
Indian Council on World Affairs, New Delhi
Indian Institute of Public Administration, New Delhi
Indian Ministry of Information and Broadcasting, New Delhi
Indian Press, Ltd., Allahabad
Indian School of International Studies, New Delhi
Indiana University, Bureau of Government Research,
    Bloomington
Indiana University, Institute of Training for Public
    Service, Department of Government, Bloomington
Indiana University Press, Bloomington
Indraprastha Estate, New Delhi
Industrial Areas Foundations, Chicago
Industrial Council for Social and Economic Studies, Upsala
Industrial Press, New York
Infantry Journal Press, Washington, D. C.
Information Bulletin Ltd., London
Insel Verlag, Frankfurt
Institut Afro-Asiatique d'Etudes Syndicales, Tel Aviv
Institut de Droit International, Paris
Institut des Hautes Etudes de l'Amerique Latine,
    Rio de Janeiro
Institut des Relations Internationales, Brussels
Institut fur Kulturwissenschaftliche Forschung, Freiburg
Institut fur Politische Wissenschaft, Frankfurt
Institut International de Collaboration Philosophique, Paris
Institute for Comparative Study of Political Systems,
    Washington, D. C.
Institute for Defense Analyses, Washington, D. C.
Institute for International Politics and Economics, Prague
Institute for International Social Research, Princeton, N. J.
Institute for Mediterranean Affairs, New York
Institute for Monetary Research, Washington, D. C.
Institute for Social Science Research, Washington, D. C.
Institute of Brazilian Studies, Rio de Janeiro
Institute of Early American History and Culture,
    Williamsburg, Va.

Institute of Economic Affairs, London
Institute of Ethiopian Studies, Addis Ababa
Institute of Human Relations Press, New York
Institute of Islamic Culture, Lahore
Institute of Labor and Industrial Relations, Urbana, Ill.
Institute of Judicial Administration, New York
Institute of National Planning, Cairo
Institute of Pacific Relations, New York
Institute of Professional Civil Servants, London
Institute of Public Administration, Dublin
Instituto de Antropologia e Etnologia de Para, Belem, Para,
    Brazil
Instituto Brasileiro de Estudos Afro-Asiaticos,
    Rio de Janeiro
Instituto Caro y Cuervo, Bogota
Instituto de Derecho Comparedo, Barcelona
Instituto de Estudios Africanos, Madrid
Instituto de Estudios Politicos, Madrid
Instituto de Investigaciones Historicas, Mexico City
Instituto Guatemalteco-Americano, Guatemala City
Instituto Internacional de Ciencias Administrativas,
    Rio de Janeiro
Instituto Nacional do Livro, Rio de Janeiro
Instituto Nazionale di Cultura Fascista, Firenze
Instituto Pan Americano de Geografia e Historia, Mexico City
Integrated Education Associates, Chicago
Inter-American Bibliographical and Library Association,
    Gainesville, Fla.
Inter-American Development Bank, Buenos Aires
Inter-American Statistical Institute, Washington
Intercollegiate Case Clearing House, Boston
International African Institute, London
International Association for Research in Income and Wealth,
    New Haven, Conn.
International Atomic Energy Commission, Vienna
International Bank for Reconstruction and Development,
    Washington, D. C.
International Center for African Economic and Social
    Documentation, Brussels
International Chamber of Commerce, New York
International City Managers' Association, Chicago
International Commission of Jurists, Geneva
International Committee for Peaceful Investment,
    Washington, D. C.
International Congress of History of Discoveries, Lisbon
International Congress of Jurists, Rio de Janeiro
International Cotton Advisory Committee, Washington, D. C.
International Court of Justice, The Hague
International Development Association, Washington, D. C.
International Economic Policy Association, Washington, D. C.
International Editions, New York
International Federation for Documentation, The Hague
International Federation for Housing and Planning, The Hague
International Finance, Princeton, N. J.
International Institute of Administrative Science, Brussels
International Institute of Differing Civilizations, Brussels
International Labour Office, Geneva
International Managers' Association, Chicago
International Monetary Fund, Washington
International Press Institute, Zurich
International Publications Service, New York
International Publishers Co., New York
International Publishing House, Meerat, India
International Review Service, New York
International Textbook Co., Scranton, Penna.
International Union for Scientific Study of Population,
    New York
International Universities Press, Inc., New York
Interstate Printers and Publishers, Danville, Ill.
Iowa State University, Center for Agricultural and Economic
    Development, Ames
Iowa State University Press, Ames
Irish Manuscripts Commission, Dublin
Richard D. Irwin, Inc., Homewood, Ill.
Isar Verlag, Munich
Isbister and Co., London
Italian Library of Information, New York; Rome
Italy, Council of Ministers, Rome

Jacaranda Press, Melbourne
Mouriel Jacobs, Inc., Philadelphia
Al Jadidah Press, Cairo
Jain General House, Jullundur, India
Japan, Ministry of Education, Tokyo

Japan, Ministry of Justice, Tokyo
Japanese National Commission for UNESCO, Tokyo
Jarrolds Publishers, Ltd., London
Jewish Publication Society of America, Philadelphia, Pa.
Johns Hopkins Press, Baltimore
Johns Hopkins School of Advanced International Studies, Baltimore
Johns Hopkins School of Hygiene, Baltimore
Johnson Publishing Co., Chicago
Christopher Johnson Publishers, Ltd., London
Johnstone and Hunter, London
Joint Center for Urban Studies, Cambridge, Mass.
Joint Committee on Slavic Studies, New York
Joint Council on Economic Education, New York
Joint Library of IMF and IBRD, Washington
Joint Reference Library, Chicago
Jonathan Cape, London
Jones and Evans Book Shop, Ltd., London
Marshall Jones, Boston
Jornal do Commercio, Rio de Janeiro
Michael Joseph, Ltd., London
Jowett, Leeds, England
Juilliard Publishers, Paris
Junker und Dunnhaupt Verlag, Berlin
Juta and Co., Ltd., Capetown, South Africa

Kallman Publishing Co., Gainesville, Fla.
Karl Karusa, Washington, D. C.
Katzman Verlag, Tubingen
Kay Publishing Co., Salt Lake City
Nicholas Kaye, London
Calvin K. Kazanjian Economics Foundation, Westport, Conn.
Kegan, Paul and Co., Ltd., London
P. G. Keller, Winterthur, Switz.
Augustus M. Kelley, Publishers, New York
Kelly and Walsh, Ltd., Baltimore, Md.
P. J. Kenedy, New York
Kennikat Press, Port Washington, N. Y.
Kent House, Port-of-Spain
Kent State University Bureau of Economic and Business Research, Kent, Ohio
Kentucky State Archives and Records Service, Frankfort
Kentucky State Planning Commission, Frankfort
Kenya Ministry of Economic Planning and Development, Nairobi
Charles H. Kerr and Co., Chicago
Khadiand Village Industries Commission, Bombay
Khayat's, Beirut
Khun Aroon, Bangkok
P. S. King and Son, Ltd., London
King's College, Cambridge
King's Crown Press, New York
Kino Kuniva Bookstore Co., Ltd., Tokyo
Kitab Mahal, Allahabad, India
Kitabistan, Allahabad
B. Klein and Co., New York
Ernst Klett Verlag, Stuttgart
V. Klostermann, Frankfurt
Fritz Knapp Verlag, Frankfurt
Alfred Knopf, New York
John Knox Press, Richmond, Va.
Kodansha International, Ltd., Tokyo
W. Kohlhammer Verlag, Stuttgart; Berlin; Cologne; Mainz
Korea Researcher and Publisher, Inc., Seoul
Korea, Ministry of Reconstruction, Seoul
Korea, Republic of, Seoul
Korea University, Asiatic Research Center, Seoul
Korean Conflict Research Foundation, Albany, N. Y.
Kosel Verlag, Munich
Kossuth Foundation, New York
Guillermo Kraft, Ltd., Buenos Aires
John F. Kraft, Inc., New York
Krasnzi Proletarii, Moscow
Kraus, Ltd., Dresden
Kraus Reprint Co., Vaduz, Liechtenstein
Kreuz-Verlag, Stuttgart
Kumasi College of Technology, The Library, Kumasi, Ghana
Kuwait, Arabia, Government Printing Press, Kuwait

Labor News Co., New York
Robert Laffont, Paris
Lambarde Press, Sidcup, Kent, England
Albert D. and Mary Lasker Foundation, Washington, D. C.

Harold Laski Institute of Political Science, Ahmedabad
Guiseppe Laterza e Figli, Bari, Italy
T. Werner Laurie, Ltd., London
Lawrence Brothers, Ltd., London
Lawrence and Wishart, London
Lawyers Co-operative Publishing Co., Rochester, N. Y.
League for Industrial Democracy, New York
League of Independent Voters, New Haven
League of Nations, Geneva
League of Women Voters, Cambridge
League of Women Voters of U. S., Washington, D. C.
Leeds University Press, Leeds, Engand
J. F. Lehmanns Verlag, Munich
Leicester University Press, London
F. Leitz, Frankfurt
Lemcke, Lemcke and Beuchner, New York
Michel Levy Freres, Paris
Lexington Publishing Co., New York
Liberal Arts Press, Inc., New York
Liberia Altiplano, La Paz
Liberia Anticuaria, Barcelona
Liberia Campos, San Juan
Liberia Panamericana, Buenos Aires
Liberty Bell Press, Jefferson City, Mo.
Librairie Academique Perrin, Paris
Librairie Artheme Fayard, Paris
Librairie Beauchemin, Montreal
Librairie Armand Colin, Paris
Librairie Firmin Didot et Cie., Paris
Librairie Droz, Geneva
Librairie de Medicis, Paris
Librairie de la Societe du Recueil Sirey, Paris
Librairie des Sciences Politiques et Sociales, Paris
Librairie Felix Alcan, Paris
Librairie Gallimard, Paris
Librairie Hachette et Cie., Paris
Librairie Julius Abel, Greiswald
Librairie La Rose, Paris
Librairie Letouzey, Paris
Librairie Payot, Paris
Librairie Philosophique J. Vrin, Paris
Librairie Plon, Paris
Librairie Marcel Riviere et Cie., Paris
Librairie Stock Delamain et Boutelleau, Paris
Library, Kumasi College of Technology, Kumasi
Library Association, London
Library of Congress, Washington
Library House, London
Library of International Relations, Chicago
Libyan Publishing, Tripoli
Light and Life Press, Winona Lake, Ind.
Lincoln University, Lincoln, Pa.
J. B. Lippincott Co., New York, Philadelphia
Little, Brown and Co., Boston
Liverpool University Press, Liverpool
Horace Liveright, New York
Living Books, New York
Livraria Agir Editora, Rio de Janeiro
Livraria Editora da Casa di Estudante do Brazil, Sao Paulo
Livraria Jose Olympio Editora, Rio de Janeiro
Livraria Martins Editora, Sao Paulo
Lok Sabha Secretariat, New Delhi
London Conservative Political Centre, London
London Historical Association, London
London Institute of World Affairs, London
London Library Association, London
London School of Economics, London
London Times, Inc., London
London University, School of Oriental and African Studies, London
Roy Long and Richard R. Smith, Inc., New York
Long House, New Canaan, Conn.
Longmans, Green and Co., New York, London
Los Angeles Board of Civil Service Commissioners, Los Angeles
Louisiana State Legislature, Baton Rouge
Louisiana State University Press, Baton Rouge
Loyola University Press, Chicago
Lucas Brothers, Columbia
Herman Luchterhand Verlag, Neuwied am Rhein
Lyle Stuart, Inc., New York

MIT Center of International Studies, Cambridge

MIT Press, Cambridge
MIT School of Industrial Management, Cambridge
Macfadden-Bartwell Corp., New York
MacGibbon and Kee, Ltd., London
Macmillan Co., New York; London
Macmillan Co., of Canada, Ltd., Toronto
Macrae Smith Co., Philadelphia, Pa.
Magistrats Druckerei, Berlin
Magnes Press, Jerusalem
S. P. Maisonneuve et La Rose, Paris
Malaysia Publications, Ltd., Singapore
Malhorta Brothers, New Delhi
Manager Government of India Press, Kosib
Manaktalas, Bombay
Manchester University Press, Manchester, England
Manhattan Publishing Co., New York
Manzsche Verlag, Vienna
Marathon Oil Co., Findlay, Ohio
Marisal, Madrid
Marquette University Press, Milwaukee
Marshall Benick, New York
Marzani and Munsell, New York
Marzun Kabushiki Kaisha, Tokyo
Mascat Publications, Ltd., Calcutta
Francois Maspera, Paris
Massachusetts Mass Transportation Commission, Boston
Masses and McInstream, New York
Maurice Falk Institute for Economic Research, Jerusalem
Maxwell Air Force Base, Montgomery, Ala.
Robert Maxwell and Co., Ltd., London
McBride, Nast and Co., New York
McClelland and Stewart, Ltd., London
McClure and Co., Chicago
McClure, Phillips and Co., New York
McCutchan Publishing Corp., Berkeley
McDonald and Evans, Ltd., London
McDowell, Obolensky, New York
McFadden Bartwell Corp., New York
McGill University Industrial Relations Section, Montreal
McGill University, Institute of Islamic Studies, Montreal
McGill University Press, Montreal
McGraw Hill Book Co., New York
David McKay Co., Inc., New York
McKinley Publishing Co., Philadelphia
George J. McLeod, Ltd., Toronto
McMullen Books, Inc., New York
Meador Publishing Co., Boston
Mediaeval Academy of Americana, Cambridge
Felix Meiner Verlag, Hamburg
Melbourne University Press, Melbourne, Victoria, Australia
Mendonca, Lisbon
Mental Health Materials Center, New York
Mentor Books, New York
Meredith Press, Des Moines
Meridian Books, New York
Merit Publishers, New York
The Merlin Press, Ltd., London
Charles E. Merrill Publishing Co., Inc., Columbus
Methuen and Co., Ltd., London
Metropolitan Book Co., Ltd., New Delhi
Metropolitan Housing and Planning Council, Chicago
Metropolitan Police District, Scotland Yard, London
Alfred Metzner Verlag, Frankfurt
Meyer London Memorial Library, London
Miami University Press, Oxford, Ohio
Michie Co., Charlottesville, Va.
Michigan Municipal League, Ann Arbor
Michigan State University, Agricultural Experiment Station,
  East Lansing
Michigan State University, Bureau of Business and Economic
  Research, East Lansing
Michigan State University, Bureau of Social and Political
  Research, East Lansing
Michigan State University, Governmental Research Bureau,
  East Lansing
Michigan State University, Institute for Community
  Development and Services, East Lansing
Michigan State University, Institute for Social Research,
  East Lansing
Michigan State University, Labor and Industrial Relations
  Center, East Lansing
Michigan State University Press, East Lansing

Michigan State University School of Business Administration,
  East Lansing
Michigan State University, Vietnam Advisory Group,
  East Lansing
Mid-European Studies Center, Free European Committee,
  New York
Middle East Institute, Washington
Middle East Research Associates, Arlington, Va.
Middlebury College, Middlebury, Vt.
Midwest Administration Center, Chicago
Midwest Beach Co., Sioux Falls
Milbank Memorial Fund, New York
M. S. Mill and Co., Inc., Division of William Morrow and
  Co., Inc., New York
Ministere de l'Education Nationale, Paris
Ministere d'Etat aux Affaires Culturelles, Paris
Ministerio de Educacao e Cultura, Rio de Janeiro
Ministerio de Relaciones Exteriores, Havana
Minnesota Efficiency in Government Commission, St. Paul
Minton, Balch and Co., New York
Missionary Research Library, New York
Ernst Siegfried Mittler und Sohn, Berlin
Modern Humanities Research Association, Chicago
T. C. B. Mohr, Tubingen
Moira Books, Detroit
Monarch Books, Inc., Derby, Conn.
Monthly Review, New York
Mont Pelerin Society, University of Chicago, Chicago
Hugh Moore Fund, New York
T. G. Moran's Sons, Inc., Baton Rouge
William Morrow and Co., Inc., New York
Morus Verlag, Berlin
Mosaik Verlag, Hamburg
Motilal Banarsidass, New Delhi
Mouton and Co., The Hague; Paris
C. F. Mueller Verlag, Karlsruhe, Germany
Muhammad Mosque of Islam #2, Chicago
Firma K. L. Mukhopadhyaz, Calcutta
F. A. W. Muldener, Gottingen, Germany
Frederick Muller, Ltd., London
Municipal Finance Officers Association of the United States
  and Canada, Chicago
Munksgaard International Booksellers and Publishers,
  Copenhagen
John Murray, London
Museum fur Volkerkunde, Vienna
Museum of Honolulu, Honolulu
Musterschmidt Verlag, Gottingen

NA Tipographia do Panorama, Lisbon
Nassau County Planning Committee, Long Island
Natal Witness, Ltd., Pietermaritzburg
The Nation Associates, New York
National Academy of Sciences-National Research Council,
  Washington, D. C.
National Archives of Rhodesia and Nyasaland, Salisbury
National Assembly on Teaching The Principles of the Bill of
  Rights, Washington
National Association of Counties Research Foundation,
  Washington, D. C.
National Association of County Officials, Chicago
National Association of Home Builders, Washington, D. C.
National Association of Local Government Officers, London
National Association of State Libraries, Boston
National Bank of Egypt, Cairo
National Bank of Libya, Tripoli
National Board of YMCA, New York
National Book League, London
National Bureau of Economic Research, New York
National Capitol Publishers, Manassas, Va.
National Central Library, London
National Citizens' Commission on International Cooperation,
  Washington, D. C.
National Council for the Social Sciences, New York
National Council for the Social Studies, New York
National Council of Applied Economic Research, New Delhi
National Council of Churches of Christ in USA, New York
National Council of National Front of Democratic Germany,
  Berlin
National Council on Aging, New York
National Council on Crime and Delinquency, New York
National Economic and Social Planning Agency,
  Washington

National Education Association, Washington
National Home Library Foundation, Washington, D. C.
National Industrial Conference Board, New York
National Institute for Personnel Research, Johannesburg
National Institute of Administration, Saigon
National Institute of Economic Research, Stockholm
National Labor Relations Board Library, Washington
National Labour Press, London
National Library of Canada, Ottawa
National Library Press, Ottawa
National Municipal League, New York
National Observer, Silver Springs, Md.
National Opinion Research Center, Chicago
National Peace Council, London
National Planning Association, Washington, D. C.
National Press, Palo Alto, Calif.
National Review, New York
National Science Foundation Scientific Information, Washington, D. C.
Natural History Press, Garden City, N. Y.
Nauka Publishing House, Moscow
Navahind, Hyderabad
Navajiran Publishing House, Ahmedabad
Thomas Nelson and Sons, London; New York
Neukirchener Verlag des Erziehungsvereins, Neukirchen
New American Library, New York
New Century Publishers, New York
New Jersey Department of Agriculture, Rural Advisory Council, Trenton
New Jersey Department of Civil Service, Trenton
New Jersey Department of Conservation and Economic Development, Trenton
New Jersey Division of State and Regional Planning, Trenton
New Jersey Housing and Renewal, Trenton
New Jersey State Department of Education, Trenton
New Jersey State Legislature, Trenton
New Republic, Washington, D. C.
New School of Social Research, New York
New World Press, New York
New York City College Institute for Pacific Relations, New York
New York City Department of Correction, New York
New York City Temporary Committee on City Finance, New York
New York Public Library, New York
New York State College of Agriculture, Ithaca
New York State Library, Albany
New York State School of Industrial and Labor Relations, Cornell University, Ithaca
New York, State University of, at Albany, Albany
New York, State University of, State Education Department, Albany
New York, State University of, State Education Department, Office of Foreign Area Studies, Albany
New York Times, New York
New York University School of Commerce, Accounts and Finance, New York
New York University, School of Law, New York
New York University Press, New York
Newark Public Library, Newark
Newman Press, Westminster, Md.
Martinus Nijhoff, The Hague; Geneva
James Nisbet and Co., Ltd., Welwyn, Herts, England
Noonday Press, New York
North American Review Publishing Co., New York
North Atlantic Treaty Organization, Brussels
North Holland Publishing Co., Amsterdam, Holland
Northern California Friends Committee on Legislation, San Francisco
Northern Michigan University Press, Marquette
Northwestern University, Evanston
Northwestern University, African Department, Evanston, Ill.
Northwestern University, International Relations Conference, Chicago
Northwestern University Press, Evanston, Ill.
W. W. Norton and Co., Inc., New York
Norwegian Institute of International Affairs, Oslo
Norwegian University Press, Oslo
Nouvelle Librairie Nationale, Paris
John Nuveen and Co., Chicago
Novelty and Co., Patna, India

Novostii Press Agency Publishing House, Moscow
Nymphenburger Verlagsbuchhandlung, Munich

Oak Publications, New York
Oak Ridge Associated Universities, Oak Ridge, Tenn.
Oceana Publishing Co., Dobbs Ferry, N. Y.
Octagon Publishing Co., New York
Odyssey Press, New York
Oesterreichische Ethnologische Gesellschaft, Vienna
Oficina Internacional de Investigaciones Sociales de Freres, Madrid
W.E.R. O'Gorman, Glendale, Calif.
O'Hare, Flanders, N. J.
Ohio State University, Columbus
Ohio State University, College of Commerce and Administration, Bureau of Business Research, Columbus
Ohio State University Press, Columbus
Ohio University Press, Athens
Old Lyme Press, Old Lyme, Conn.
R. Oldenbourg, Munich
Oliver and Boyd, London, Edinburgh
Guenter Olzog Verlag, Munich
Open Court Publishing Co., La Salle, Ill.
Operation America, Inc., Los Angeles
Operations and Policy Research, Inc., Washington, D. C.
Oregon Historical Society, Portland
Organization for European Economic Cooperation and Development (OEEC), Paris
Organization of African Unity, Addis Ababa
Organization of American States, Rio de Janeiro
Organization of Economic Aid, Washington, D. C.
Orient Longman's, Bombay
Oriole Press, Berkeley Heights, N. J.
P. O'Shey, New York
Osaka University of Commerce, Tokyo
James R. Osgood and Co., Boston
Oslo University Press, Oslo
Oswald-Wolff, London
John Ousley, Ltd., London
George Outram Co., Ltd., Glasgow
Overseas Development Institute, Ltd., London
R. E. Owen, Wellington, N. Z.
Oxford Book Co., New York
Oxford University Press, Capetown; London; Madras; Melbourne; New York

Pacific Books, Palo Alto, Calif.
Pacific Coast Publishing Co., Menlo Park, Calif.
Pacific Philosophy Institute, Stockton, Calif.
Pacific Press Publishing Association, Mountain View, Calif.
Pacifist Research Bureau, Philadelphia
Padma Publications, Ltd., Bombay
Hermann Paetel Verlag, Berlin
Pageant Press, New York
Paine-Whitman, New York
Pakistan Academy for Rural Development, Peshawar
Pakistan Association for Advancement of Science, Lahore
Pakistan Bibliographical Working Group, Karachi
Pakistan Educational Publishers, Ltd., Karachi
Pakistan Ministry of Finance, Rawalpindi
Pall Mall Press, London
Pan American Union, Washington
Pantheon Books, Inc., New York
John W. Parker, London
Patna University Press, Madras
B. G. Paul and Co., Madras
Paulist Press, Glen Rock, N. J.
Payne Fund, New York
Peabody Museum, Cambridge
Peace Publications, New York
Peace Society, London
P. Pearlman, Washington
Pegasus, New York
Peking Review, Peking
Pelican Books, Ltd., Hammonsworth, England
Pemberton Press, Austin
Penguin Books, Baltimore
Penn.-N.J.-Del. Metropolitan Project, Philadelphia, Pa.
Pennsylvania German Society, Lancaster, Pa.
Pennsylvania Historical and Museum Commission, Harrisburg
Pennsylvania State University, Department of Religious Studies, University Park, Pa.

Pennsylvania State University, Institute of Public Administration, University Park, Pa.
Pennsylvania State University Press, University Park, Pa.
People's Publishing House, Ltd., New Delhi
Pergamon Press, Inc., New York
Permanent Secretariat, AAPS Conference, Cairo
Perrine Book Co., Minneapolis
Personnel Administration, Washington
Personnel Research Association, New York
George A. Pflaum Publishers, Inc., Dayton, Ohio
Phelps-Stokes Fund, Capetown; New York
Philadelphia Bibliographical Center, Philadelphia
George Philip & Son, London
Philippine Historical Society, Manila
Philippine Islands Bureau of Science, Manila
Philosophical Library Inc., New York
Phoenix House, Ltd., London
Pichon et Durand-Auzias, Paris
B. M. Pickering, London
Oskar Piest, New York
Pilot Press, London
Pioneer Publishers, New York
R. Piper and Co. Verlag, Munich
Pitman Publishing Corp., New York
Plimpton Press, Norwood, Mass.
PLJ Publications, Manila
Pocket Books, Inc., New York
Polish Scientific Publishers, Warsaw
Polygraphischer Verlag, Zurich
The Polynesian Society, Inc., Wellington, N. Z.
Popular Book Depot, Bombay
Popular Prakashan, Bombay
Population Association of America, Washington
Population Council, New York
Post Printing Co., New York
Post Publishing Co., Bangkok
Potomac Books, Washington, D. C.
Clarkson N. Potter, Inc., New York
Prabhakar Sahityalok, Lucknow, India
Practicing Law Institute, New York
Frederick A. Praeger, Inc., New York
Prager, Berlin
Prensa Latino Americana, Santiago
Prentice Hall, Inc., Englewood Cliffs, N. J.
Prentice-Hall International, London
Presence Afrique, Paris
President's Press, New Delhi
Press & Information Division of the French Embassy, New York
The Press of Case Western Reserve University, Cleveland
Presses de l'Ecole des Hautes Etudes Commerciales, Montreal
Presses Universitaires de Bruxelles, Brussels
Presses Universitaires de France, Paris
Presseverband der Evangelischen Kirche im Rheinland, Dusseldorf
Princeton Research Publishing Co., Princeton
Princeton University, Princeton, N. J.
Princeton University, Center of International Studies, Woodrow Wilson School of Public and International Affairs, Princeton, N. J.
Princeton University, Department of Economics, Princeton, N. J.
Princeton University, Department of History, Princeton, N. J.
Princeton University, Department of Oriental Studies, Princeton, N. J.
Princeton University, Department of Philosophy, Princeton, N. J.
Princeton University, Department of Politics, Princeton, N. J.
Princeton University, Department of Psychology, Princeton
Princeton University, Department of Sociology, Princeton, N. J.
Princeton University, Econometric Research Program, Princeton, N. J.
Princeton University, Firestone Library, Princeton, N. J.
Princeton University, Industrial Relations Center, Princeton
Princeton University, International Finance Section, Princeton, N. J.
Princeton University, Princeton Public Opinion Research Project, Princeton, N. J.
Princeton University Press, Princeton
Edouard Privat, Toulouse

Arthur Probsthain, London
Professional Library Press, West Haven, Conn.
Programa Interamericano de Informacion Popular, San Jose
Progress Publishing Co., Indianapolis
Progressive Education Association, New York
Prolog Research and Publishing Association, New York
Prometheus Press, New York
Psycho-Sociological Press, New York
Public Administration Clearing House, Chicago
Public Administration Institute, Ankara
Public Administration Service, Chicago
Public Affairs Forum, Bombay
Public Affairs Press, Washington
Public Enterprises, Tequcigalpa
Public Personnel Association, Chicago
Publications Centre, University of British Columbia, Vancouver
Publications de l'Institut Pedagogique National, Paris
Publications de l'Institut Universitaire des Hautes Etudes Internationales, Paris
Publications du CNRS, Paris
Publisher's Circular, Ltd., London,, England
Publisher's Weekly, Inc., New York
Publishing House Jugoslavia, Belgrade
Punjab University, Pakistan
Punjab University Extension Library, Ludhiana, Punjab
Purdue University Press, Lafayette, Ind.
Purnell and Sons, Capetown
G. P. Putnam and Sons, New York

Quadrangle Books, Inc., Chicago
Bernard Quaritch, London
Queen's Printer, Ottawa
Queen's University, Belfast
Quell Verlag, Stuttgart, Germany
Quelle und Meyer, Heidelberg
Queromon Editores, Mexico City

Atma Ram and Sons, New Delhi
Ramsey-Wallace Corporation, Ramsey, New Jersey
Rand Corporation, Publications of the Social Science Department, New York
Rand McNally and Co., Skokie, Ill.
Random House, Inc., New York
Regents Publishing House, Inc., New York
Regional Planning Association, New York
Regional Science Research Institute, Philadelphia
Henry Regnery Co., Chicago
D. Reidel Publishing Co., Dordrecht, Holland
E. Reinhardt Verlag, Munich
Reinhold Publishing Corp., New York; London
Remsen Press, New York
La Renaissance de Loire, Paris
Eugen Rentsch Verlag, Stuttgart
Republican National Committee, Washington, D. C.
Research Institute on Sino-Soviet Bloc, Washington, D. C.
Research Microfilm Publications, Inc., Annapolis
Resources for the Future, Inc., Washington, D. C.
Revista de Occidente, Madrid
Revue Administrative, Paris
Renyal and Co., Inc., New York
Reynal & Hitchcock, New York
Rheinische Friedrich Wilhelms Universitat, Bonn
Rice University, Fondren Library, Houston
Richards Rosen Press, New York
The Ridge Press, Inc., New York
Rinehart, New York
Ring-Verlag, Stuttgart
Riverside Editions, Cambridge
Robinson and Co., Durban, South Africa
J. A. Rogers, New York
Roques Roman, Trujillo
Rudolf M. Rohrer, Leipzig
Ludwig Rohrscheid Verlag, Bonn
Walter Roming and Co., Detroit
Ronald Press Co., New York
Roper Public Opinion Poll Research Center, New York
Ross and Haine, Inc., Minneapolis, Minn.
Fred B. Rothman and Co., S. Hackensack, N. J.
Rotterdam University Press, Rotterdam
Routledge and Kegan Paul, London
George Routledge and Sons, Ltd., London
Row-Peterson Publishing Co., Evanston, Ill.

Rowohlt, Hamburg
Roy Publishers, Inc., New York
Royal African Society, London
Royal Anthropological Institute, London
Royal Colonial Institute, London
Royal Commission of Canada's Economic Prospects, Ottawa
Royal Commonwealth Society, London
Royal Geographical Society, London
Royal Greek Embassy Information Service, Washington, D. C.
Royal Institute of International Affairs, London; New York
Royal Institute of Public Administration, London
Royal Netherlands Printing Office, Schiedam
Royal Statistical Society, London
Rubin Mass, Jerusalem
Rule of Law Press, Durham
Rupert Hart-Davis, London
Russell and Russell, Inc., New York
Russell Sage College, Institute for Advanced Study in Crisis, NDEA Institute, Troy, N. Y.
Russell Sage Foundation, New York
Rutgers University, New Brunswick, N. J.
Rutgers University Bureau of Government Research, New Brunswick, N. J.
Rutgers University, Institute of Management and Labor Relations, New Brunswick, N. J.
Rutgers University, Urban Studies Conference, New Brunswick, N. J.
Rutgers University Press, New Brunswick, N. J.
Rutten und Loening Verlag, Munich
Ryerson Press, Toronto

Sage Publications, Beverly Hills, Calif.
Sahitya Akademi, Bombay
St. Andrews College, Drygrange, Scotland
St. Clement's Press, London
St. George Press, Los Angeles
St. John's University Bookstore, Annapolis
St. John's University Press, Jamaica, N. Y.
St. Louis Post-Dispatch, St. Louis
St. Martin's Press, New York
St. Michael's College, Toronto
San Diego State College Library, San Diego
San Francisco State College, San Francisco
The Sapir Memorial Publication Fund, Menasha, Wis.
Sarah Lawrence College, New York
Sarah Lawrence College, Institute for Community Studies, New York
Porter Sargent, Publishers, Boston, Mass.
Sauerlaender and Co., Aarau, Switz.
Saunders and Ottey, London
W. B. Saunders Co., Philadelphia, Pa.
Scandinavian University Books, Copenhagen
Scarecrow Press, Metuchen, N. J.
L. N. Schaffrath, Geldern, Germany
Robert Schalkenbach Foundation, New York
Schenkman Publishing Co., Cambridge
P. Schippers, N. V., Amsterdam
Schocken Books, Inc., New York
Henry Schuman, Inc., New York
Carl Schunemann Verlag, Bremen
Curt E. Schwab, Stuttgart
Otto Schwartz und Co., Gottingen
Science and Behavior Books, Palo Alto, Calif.
Science Council of Japan, Tokyo
Science of Society Foundation, Baltimore, Md.
Science Press, New York
Science Research Associates, Inc., Chicago
Scientia Verlag, Aalen, Germany
SCM Press, London
Scott, Foresman and Co., Chicago
Scottish League for European Freedom, Edinburgh
Chas. Scribner's Sons, New York
Seabury Press, New York
Sears Publishing Co., Inc., New York
Secker and Warburg, Ltd., London
Secretaria del Consejo Nacional Economia, Tegucigalpa
Securities Study Project, Vancouver, Wash.
Seewald Verlag, Munich; Stuttgart
Selbstverlag Jakob Rosner, Vienna
Seldon Society, London
Robert C. Sellers and Associates, Washington, D. C.
Thomas Seltzer Inc., New York
Seminar, New Delhi

C. Serbinis Press, Athens
Service Bibliographique des Messageries Hachette, Paris
Service Center for Teaching of History, Washington, D. C.
Servicos de Imprensa e Informacao da Exbaixada, Lisbon
Sheed and Ward, New York
Shoestring Press, Hamden, Conn.
Shuter and Shooter, Pietermaritzburg
Siam Society, Bangkok
Sidgewick and Jackson, London
K. G. Siegler & Co., Bonn
Signet Books, New York
A. W. Sijthoff, Leyden, Netherlands
Silver Burdett, Morristown, N. J.
Simmons Boardman Publishing Co., New York
Simon and Schuster, Inc., New York
Simpkin, Marshall, et al., London
Sino-American Cultural Society, Washington
William Sloane Associates, New York
Small, Maynard and Co., Boston
Smith-Brook Printing Co., Denver
Smith College, Northampton, Mass.
Smith, Elder and Co., London
Smith, Keynes and Marshall, Buffalo, N. Y.
Allen Smith Co., Indianapolis, Ind.
Peter Smith, Gloucester, Mass.
Richard R. Smith Co. Inc., Peterborough, N. H.
Smithsonian Institute, Washington, D. C.
Social Science Research Center, Rio Piedras, Puerto Rico
Social Science Research Council, New York
Social Science Research Council, Committee on the Economy of China, Berkeley, Calif.
Social Science Research Council of Australia, Sydney
The Social Sciences, Mexico City
Societa Editrice del "Foro Italiano", Rome
Societas Bibliographica, Lausanne, Switzerland
Societe d'Edition d'Enseignement Superieur, Paris
Societe Francaise d'Imprimerie et Librairie, Paris
Society for Advancement of Management, New York
Society for Promoting Christian Knowledge, London
Society for the Study of Social Problems, Kalamazoo, Mich.
Society of Comparative Legislative and International Law, London
Sociological Abstracts, New York
Solidaridad Publishing House, Manila
Somerset Press, Inc., Somerville, N. J.
Soney and Sage Co., Newark, N. J.
South Africa Commission on Future Government, Capetown
South Africa State Library, Pretoria
South African Congress of Democrats, Johannesburg
South African Council for Scientific and Industrial Research, Pretoria
South African Institute of International Affairs, Johannesburg
South African Institute of Race Relations, Johannesburg
South African Public Library, Johannesburg
South Carolina Archives, State Library, Columbia
South Pacific Commission, Noumea, New Caledonia
South Western Publishing Co., Cincinnati, Ohio
Southern Illinois University Press, Carbondale, Ill.
Southern Methodist University Press, Dallas, Tex.
Southern Political Science Association, New York
Southworth Anthoensen Press, Portland, Maine
Sovetskaia Rossiia, Moscow
Soviet and East European Research and Translation Service, New York
Spartan Books, Washington, D. C.
Special Libraries Association, New York
Specialty Press of South Africa, Johannesburg
Robert Speller and Sons, New York
Lorenz Spindler Verlag, Nuremberg
Julius Springer, Berlin
Springer-Verlag, New York; Stuttgart; Gottingen; Vienna
Stackpole Co., New York
Gerhard Stalling, Oldenburg, Germany
Stanford Bookstore, Stanford
Stanford University Comparative Education Center, Stanford, Calif.
Stanford University Institute for Communications Research, Stanford
Stanford University, Institute of Hispanic-American and Luso-Brazilian Studies, Stanford, Calif.
Stanford University, Project on Engineering-Economic Planning, Stanford, Calif.

Stanford University Research Institute, Menlo Park, Calif.
Stanford University, School of Business Administration,
   Stanford, Calif.
Stanford University, School of Education, Stanford, Calif.
Stanford University Press, Stanford, Cal.
Staples Press, New York
State University of New York at Albany, Albany
Stein & Day Publishers, New York
Franz Steiner Verlag, Wiesbaden
Ulrich Steiner Verlag, Wurttemburg
H. E. Stenfert Kroese, Leyden
Sterling Printing and Publishing Co., Ltd., Karachi
Sterling Publishers, Ltd., London
Stevens and Hayes, London
Stevens and Sons, Ltd., London
George W. Stewart, Inc., New York
George Stilke Berlin
Frederick A. Stokes Publishing Co., New York
C. Struik, Capetown
Stuttgarter Verlags Kantor, Stuttgart
Summy-Birchard Co., Evanston, Ill.
Swann Sonnenschein and Co., London
Philip Swartzwelder, Pittsburgh, Pa.
Sweet and Maxwell, Ltd., London
Swiss Eastern Institute, Berne
Sydney University Press, Sydney, Australia
Syracuse University, Maxwell School of Citizenship and
   Public Affairs, Syracuse, N. Y.
Syracuse University Press, Syracuse
Szczesnez Verlag, Munich

Talleres Graficos de Manuel Casas, Mexico City
Talleres de Impresion de Estampillas y Valores, Mexico City
Taplinger Publishing Co., New York
Tavistock, London
Tax Foundation, New York
Teachers' College, Bureau of Publications, Columbia
   University, New York
Technical Assistance Information Clearing House, New York
Technology Press, Cambridge
de Tempel, Bruges, Belgium
B. G. Teubner, Berlin; Leipzig
Texas College of Arts and Industries, Kingsville
Texas Western Press, Dallas
Texian Press, Waco, Texas
Thacker's Press and Directories, Ltd., Calcutta
Thailand, National Office of Statistics, Bangkok
Thailand National Economic Development Board, Bangkok
Thames and Hudson, Ltd., London
Thammasat University Institute of Public Administration,
   Bangkok, Thailand
E. J. Theisen, East Orange, N. J.
Charles C. Thomas, Publisher, Springfield, Ill.
Tilden Press, New York
Time, Inc., New York
Time-Life Books, New York
Times Mirror Printing and Binding, New York
Tipografia de Archivos, Madrid
Tipografia Mendonca, Lisbon
Tipografia Nacional, Guatemala, Guatemala City
Tipographia Nacional Guatemala, Guatemala City
H. D. Tjeenk Willink, Haarlem, Netherlands
J. C. Topping, Cambridge, Mass.
Transatlantic Arts, Inc., New York
Trejos Hermanos, San Jose
Trenton State College, Trenton
Tri-Ocean Books, San Francisco
Trident Press, New York
Trowitzsch and Son, Berlin
Truebner and Co., London
Tufts University Press, Medford, Mass.
Tulane University, School of Business Administration,
   New Orleans, La.
Tulane University Press, New Orleans
Turnstile Press, London
Tuskegee Institute, Tuskegee, Ala.
Charles E. Tuttle Co., Tokyo
Twayne Publishers Inc., New York
The Twentieth Century Fund, New York
Twin Circle Publishing Co.. New York
Typographische Anstalt, Vienna
Tyrolia Verlag, Innsbruck

UNESCO, Paris
N. V. Uitgeverij W. Van Hoeve, The Hague
Frederick Ungar Publishing Co., Inc., New York
Union Federaliste Inter-Universitaire, Paris
Union of American Hebrew Congregations, New York
Union of International Associations, Brussels
Union of Japanese Societies of Law and Politics, Tokyo
Union of South Africa, Capetown
Union of South Africa, Government Information Office,
   New York
Union Press, Hong Kong
Union Research Institute, Hong Kong
United Arab Republic, Information Department, Cairo
United Nations Economic Commission for Asia and the
   Far East, Secretariat of Bangkok, Bangkok
United Nations Educational, Scientific and Cultural Organi-
   zation, Paris
United Nations Food and Agriculture Organization, Rome
United Nations International Conference on Peaceful Uses
   of Atomic Energy, Geneva
United Nations Publishing Service, New York
United States Air Force Academy, Colorado Springs, Colo.
United States Bureau of the Census, Washington, D. C.
United States Business and Defense Services Administration,
   Washington D.C.
United States Civil Rights Commission, Washington, D. C.
United States Civil Service Commission, Washington, D. C.
United States Consulate General, Hong Kong
United States Department of Agriculture, Washington, D. C.
United States Department of the Army, Washington
United States Department of the Army, Office of Chief of
   Military History, Washington, D. C.
United States Department of Correction, New York
United States Department of State, Washington
United States Department of State, Government Printing
   Office, Washington, D. C.
United States Government Printing Office, Washington
United States Housing and Home Financing Agency,
   Washington, D. C.
United States Mutual Security Agency, Washington, D. C.
United States National Archives General Services,
   Washington, D. C.
United States National Referral Center for Science and
   Technology, Washington, D. C.
United States National Resources Committee,
   Washington, D. C.
United States Naval Academy, Annapolis, Md.
United States Naval Institute, Annapolis, Md.
United States Naval Officers Training School, China Lake, Cal.
United States Operations Mission to Vietnam,
   Washington, D. C.
United States President's Committee to Study Military
   Assistance, Washington, D. C.
United States Small Business Administration,
   Washington, D. C.
United World Federalists, Boston
Universal Reference System; see Princeton Research
   Publishing Co., Princeton, N.J.
Universidad Central de Venezuela, Caracas
Universidad de Buenos Aires, Instituto Sociologia,
   Buenos Aires
Universidad de Chile, Santiago
Universidad de el Salvador, El Salvador
Universidad Nacional Autonomo de Mexico, Direccion General
   de Publicaciones, Mexico
Universidad Nacional de la Plata, Argentina
Universidad Nacional Instituto de Historia Antonoma de
   Mexico, Mexico City
Universidad Nacional Mayor de San Marcos, Lima
Universidad de Antioquia, Medellin, Colombia
Universite de Rabat, Rabat, Morocco
Universite Fouad I, Cairo
Universite Libre de Bruxelles, Brussels
Universite Mohammed V, Rabat, Morocco
University Books, Inc., Hyde Park, New York
University Bookstore, Hong Kong
University Microfilms, Inc., Ann Arbor
University of Alabama, Bureau of Public Administration,
   University, Ala.
University of Alabama Press, University, Ala.
University of Ankara, Ankara
University of Arizona Press, Tucson
University of Bombay, Bombay

University of Bonn, Bonn
University of British Columbia Press, Vancouver
University of California, Berkeley, Calif.
University of California at Los Angeles, Bureau of Government Research, Los Angeles
University of California at Los Angeles, Near Eastern Center, Los Angeles
University of California, Bureau of Business and Economic Research, Berkeley, Calif.
University of California, Bureau of Government Research, Los Angeles
University of California, Bureau of Public Administration, Berkeley
University of California, Department of Psychology, Los Angeles
University of California, Institute for International Studies, Berkeley, Calif.
University of California, Institute of East Asiatic Studies, Berkeley, Calif.
University of California, Institute of Governmental Affairs, Davis
University of California, Institute of Governmental Studies, Berkeley
University of California, Institute of Urban and Regional Development, Berkeley, Calif.
University of California, Latin American Center, Los Angeles
University of California Library, Berkeley, Calif.
University of California Press, Berkeley
University of California Survey Research Center, Berkeley, Calif.
University of Canterbury, Christchurch, New Zealand
University of Capetown, Capetown
University of Chicago, Chicago
University of Chicago, Center for Policy Study, Chicago
University of Chicago, Center for Program in Government Administration, Chicago
University of Chicago, Center of Race Relations, Chicago
University of Chicago, Graduate School of Business, Chicago
University of Chicago Law School, Chicago
University of Chicago, Politics Department, Chicago
University of Chicago Press, Chicago
University of Cincinnati, Cincinnati
University of Cincinnati, Center for Study of United States Foreign Policy, Cincinnati
University of Colorado Press, Boulder
University of Connecticut, Institute of Public Service, Storrs, Conn.
University of Dar es Salaam, Institute of Public Administration, Dar es Salaam
University of Denver, Denver
University of Detroit Press, Detroit
University of Edinburgh, Edinburgh, Scotland
University of Florida, Public Administration Clearing Service, Gainesville, Fla.
University of Florida, School of Inter-American Studies, Gainesville, Fla.
University of Florida Libraries, Gainesville
University of Florida Press, Gainesville
University of Georgia, Institute of Community and Area Development, Athens, Georgia
University of Georgia Press, Athens
University of Glasgow Press, Glasgow, Scotland
University of Glasgow Press, Fredericton, New Brunswick, Canada
University of Hawaii Press, Honolulu
University of Hong Kong Press, Hong Kong
University of Houston, Houston
University of Illinois, Champaign
University of Illinois, Graduate School of Library Science, Urbana
University of Illinois, Institute for Labor and Industrial Relations, Urbana
University of Illinois, Institute of Government and Public Affairs, Urbana, Ill.
University of Illinois Press, Urbana
University of Iowa, Center for Labor and Management, Iowa City
University of Iowa, School of Journalism, Iowa City
University of Iowa Press, Iowa City
University of Kansas, Bureau of Government Research, Lawrence, Kans.
University of Kansas Press, Lawrence
University of Karachi, Institute of Business and Public

Administration, Karachi
University of Karachi Press, Karachi
University of Kentucky, Bureau of Governmental Research, Lexington
University of Kentucky Press, Lexington
University of London, Institute of Advanced Legal Studies, London
University of London, Institute of Commonwealth Studies, London
University of London, Institute of Education, London
University of London, School of Oriental and African Studies, London
University of London Press, London
University of Lund, Lund, Sweden
University of Maine Studies, Augusta, Me.
University of Malaya, Kualalumpur
University of Manchester Press, Manchester, England
University of Maryland, Bureau of Governmental Research, College of Business and Public Administration, College Park, Md.
University of Maryland, Department of Agriculture and Extension Education, College Park, Md.
University of Massachusetts, Bureau of Government Research, Amherst, Mass.
University of Massachusetts Press, Amherst
University of Melbourne Press, Melbourne, Australia
University of Miami Law Library, Coral Gables
University of Miami Press, Coral Gables
University of Michigan, Center for Research on Conflict Resolution, Ann Arbor
University of Michigan, Department of History and Political Science, Ann Arbor
University of Michigan, Graduate School of Business Administration, Ann Arbor
University of Michigan, Institute for Social Research, Ann Arbor
University of Michigan, Institute of Public Administration, Ann Arbor
University of Michigan Law School, Ann Arbor
University of Michigan, Survey Research Center, Ann Arbor
University of Michigan Press, Ann Arbor
University of Minnesota, St. Paul; Duluth
University of Minnesota, Industrial Relations Center, Minneapolis
University of Minnesota Press, Minneapolis
University of Mississippi, Bureau of Public Administration, University, Miss.
University of Missouri, Research Center, School of Business and Public Administration, Columbia
University of Missouri Press, Columbia
University of Natal Press, Pietermaritzburg
University of Nebraska Press, Lincoln
University of New England, Grafton, Australia
University of New Mexico, Department of Government, Albuquerque, N. Mex.
University of New Mexico, School of Law, Albuquerque
University of New Mexico Press, Albuquerque
University of North Carolina, Department of City and Regional Planning, Chapel Hill
University of North Carolina, Institute for International Studies, Chapel Hill
University of North Carolina, Institute for Research in the Social Sciences, Center for Urban and Regional Studies, Chapel Hill
University of North Carolina, Institute of Government, Chapel Hill
University of North Carolina Library, Chapel Hill
University of North Carolina Press, Chapel Hill
University of Notre Dame, Notre Dame, Ind.
University of Notre Dame Press, Notre Dame, Ind.
University of Oklahoma Press, Norman
University of Oregon Press, Eugene
University of Panama, Panama City
University of Paris (Conferences du Palais de la Decouverte), Paris
University of Pennsylvania, Philadelphia, Pa.
University of Pennsylvania, Department of Translations, Philadelphia
University of Pennsylvania Law School, Philadelphia, Pa.
University of Pennsylvania Press, Philadelphia
University of Pittsburgh, Institute of Local Government, Pittsburgh, Pa.
University of Pittsburgh Book Centers, Pittsburgh
University of Pittsburgh Press, Pittsburgh

University of Puerto Rico, San Juan
University of Rochester, Rochester, N. Y.
University of Santo Tomas, Manila
University of South Africa, Pretoria
University of South Carolina Press, Columbia
University of Southern California, Middle East and North Africa Program, Los Angeles
University of Southern California, School of International Relations, Los Angeles
University of Southern California Press, Los Angeles
University of Southern California, School of Public Administration, Los Angeles
University of State of New York, State Education Department, Albany
University of Sussex, Sussex, England
University of Sydney, Department of Government and Public Administration, Sydney
University of Tennessee, Knoxville
University of Tennessee, Bureau of Public Administration, Knoxville
University of Tennessee, Municipal Technical Advisory Service, Division of University Extension, Knoxville
University of Tennessee Press, Knoxville
University of Texas, Austin
University of Texas, Bureau of Business Research, Austin
University of Texas Press, Austin
University of the Philippines, Quezon City
University of the Punjab, Department of Public Administration, Lahore, Pakistan
University of the Witwatersrand, Johannesburg
University of Toronto, Toronto
University of Toronto Press, Toronto; Buffalo, N. Y.
University of Utah Press, Salt Lake City
University of Vermont, Burlington
University of Virginia, Bureau of Public Administration, Charlottesville
University of Wales Press, Cardiff
University of Washington, Bureau of Governmental Research and Services, Seattle
University of Washington Press, Seattle
University of Wisconsin, Madison
University of Wisconsin Press, Madison
University Press, University of the South, Sewanee, Tenn.
University Press of Virginia, Charlottesville
University Publishers, Inc., New York
University Publishing Co., Lincoln, Nebr.
University Society, Inc., Ridgewood, N. J.
Unwin University Books, London
T. Fisher Unwin, Ltd., London
Upjohn Institute for Employment Research, Kalamazoo, Mich; Los Angeles; Washington, D. C.
Urban America, New York
Urban Studies Center, New Brunswick, N. J.

VEB Verlag fur Buch-und Bibliothekwesen, Leipzig
Franz Vahlen, Berlin
Vallentine, Mitchell and Co., London
Van Nostrand Co., Inc., Princeton
Van Rees Press, New York
Vandenhoeck und Ruprecht, Gottingen
Vanderbilt University Press, Nashville, Tenn.
Vanguard Press, Inc., New York
E. C. Vann, Richmond, Va.
Vantage Press, New York
G. Velgaminov, New York
Verein fur Sozial Politik, Berlin
Vergara Editorial, Barcelona
Verlag Karl Alber, Freiburg
Verlag Georg D. W. Callwey, Munich
Verlag der Wiener Volksbuchhandlung, Vienna
Verlag der Wirtschaft, Berlin
Verlag Deutsche Polizei, Hamburg
Verlag Felix Dietrich, Osnabrueck
Verlag Kurt Dosch, Vienna
Verlag Gustav Fischer, Jena
Verlag Huber Frauenfeld, Stuttgart
Verlag fur Buch- und Bibliothekwesen, Leipzig
Verlag fur Literatur und Zeitgeschehen, Hannover, Germany
Verlag fur Recht und Gesellschaft, Basel
Verein fuer Sozialpolitik, Wirtschaft und Statistik, Berlin
Verlag Anton Hain, Meisenheim
Verlag Hans Krach, Mainz
Verlag Edward Krug, Wurttemburg

Verlag Helmut Kupper, Godesberg
Verlag August Lutzeyer, Baden-Baden
Verlag Mensch und Arbeit, Bruckmann, Munich
Verlag C. F. Muller, Karlsruhe
Verlag Anton Pustet, Munich
Verlag Rombach und Co., Freiburg
Verlag Heinrich Scheffler, Frankfurt
Verlag Hans Schellenberg, Winterthur, Switz.
Verlag P. Schippers, Amsterdam
Verlag Lambert Schneider, Heidelberg
Verlag K. W. Schutz, Gottingen
Verlag Styria, Graz, Austria
Lawrence Verry, Publishers, Mystic, Conn.
Viking Press, New York
Villanova Law School, Philadelphia
J. Villanueva, Buenos Aires
Vintage Books, New York
Virginia Commission on Constitutional Government, Richmond
Virginia State Library, Richmond
Vishveshvaranand Vedic Research Institute, Hoshiarpur
Vista Books, London
F. & J. Voglrieder, Munich
Voigt und Gleibner, Frankfurt
Voltaire Verlag, Berlin
Von Engelhorn, Stuttgart
Vora and Co. Publishers, Bombay
J. Vrin, Paris

Karl Wachholtz Verlag, Neumunster
Wadsworth Publishing Co., Belmont, Cal.
Walker and Co., New York
Ives Washburn, Inc., New York
Washington State University Press, Pullman
Washington University Libraries, Washington
Franklin Watts, Inc., New York
Waverly Press, Inc., Baltimore, Md.
Wayne State University Press, Detroit, Mich.
Christian Wegner Verlag, Hamburg
Weidenfield and Nicolson, London
R. Welch, Belmont, Mass.
Wellesley College, Wellesley, Mass.
Herbert Wendler & Co., Berlin
Wenner-Gren Foundation for Anthropological Research, New York
Wesleyan University Press, Middletown, Conn.
West Publishing Co., St. Paul, Minn.
Westdeutscher Verlag, Cologne
Western Islands Publishing Co., Belmont, Mass.
Western Publishing Co., Inc., Racine, Wis.
Western Reserve University Press, Cleveland
Westminster Press, Philadelphia, Pa.
J. Whitaker and Sons, Ltd., London
Whitcombe and Tombs, Ltd., Christchurch
Whiteside, Inc., New York
Thomas Wilcox, Los Angeles
John Wiley and Sons, Inc., New York
William-Frederick Press, New York
Williams and Vorgate, Ltd., London
Williams and Wilkins Co., Baltimore, Md.
Wilshire Book Co., Hollywood, Calif.
H. W. Wilson Co., New York
Winburn Press, Lexington, Ky.
Allan Wingate, Ltd., London
Carl Winters Universitats-Buchhandlung, Heidelberg
Wisconsin State University Press, River Falls
Wisconsin State Historical Society, Madison
Witwatersrand University Press, Capetown
Woking Muslim Mission and Literary Trust, Surrey
Wolters, Groningen, Netherlands
Woodrow Wilson Foundation, New York
Woodrow Wilson Memorial Library, New York
World Law Fund, New York
World Peace Foundation, Boston
World Press, Ltd., Calcutta
World Publishing Co., Cleveland
World Trade Academy Press, New York
World University Library, New York

Yale University, New Haven, Conn.
Yale University, Department of Industrial Administration, New Haven, Conn.

Yale University, Harvard Foundation, New Haven, Conn.
Yale University, Institute of Advanced Studies, New Haven, Conn.
Yale University Press, New Haven
Yale University, Southeast Asia Studies, New Haven
Yeshiva University Press, New York
Thomas Yoseloff, New York

T. L. Yuan, Tokyo

Zambia, Government Printer, Lusaka
Otto Zeller, Osnabruck, Germany
Zentral Verlag der NSDAP, Munich
Zwingli Verlag, Zurich

List of Periodicals Cited in this Volume

Academy of Management Journal
Administrative Science Quarterly
Air University Quarterly Review
American Anthropologist
American Bar Association Journal
American Behavioral Scientist
American Documentation
American Economic Review
American Journal of Economics and Sociology
American Journal of International Law
American Political Science Review
American Psychologist
American Scholar
American Society of International Law, Proceedings
American Sociological Review
Annals of the American Academy of Political and Social Science
Annals of the New York Academy of Sciences
Anti-Trust Law and Economic Review
Australian Outlook
Background (now International Studies Quarterly)
Behavioral Science
Bulletin of the Atomic Scientists
Business Horizons
Business Topics
California Law Review
California Management Review
Cambridge Journal
Canadian Journal of Economics and Political Science
Canadian Public Administration
China Quarterly
Co-Existence
Columbia Law Review
Cooperation and Conflict
Current History
Daedalus
Dialectica
Dissent
Economic Development and Cultural Change
Economica
Educational Forum
Encounter
Ethics
Foreign Affairs
Foreign Service Journal
Fortune
George Washington Law Review
German Foreign Policy
Harper's Magazine
Harvard Business Review
Human Organization
Human Relations
Impact of Science on Society
India Quarterly
Institut zur Erforschung der UdSSR, Bulletin
Inter-American Economic Affairs
Intercom
International Affairs (U.K.)

International Conciliation
International Journal
International Journal of Opinion and Attitude Research
International Organization
International Relations
International Review of Administrative Sciences
International Science and Technology
International Social Science Journal
International Studies Quarterly (formerly Background)
Journal of the Acoustical Society of America
Journal of the American Institute of Planners
Journal of the American Statistical Association
Journal of Applied Behavioral Science
Journal of Arms Control
Journal of Business
Journal of Conflict Resolution
Journal of Criminal Law, Criminology, and Police Science
Journal of Experimental Education
Journal of Human Relations
Journal of Management Studies
Journal of Peace Research
Journal of Politics
Journal of Social Issues
Land Economics
Law and Contemporary Problems
Lex et Scientia
Management Science
Midwestern Journal of Political Science
Military Review
Mulino
Municipal Finance
National Civic Review
New Left Review
Northwestern University Law Review
Operational Research Quarterly
Orbis
Parliamentary Affairs
Philosophy of Science
Polish Perspectives
Political Quarterly
Political Research: Organization and Design (PROD)
Political Science Quarterly
Politique Etrangere
Population Studies
Problems of Communism
Psychological Review
Public Administration
Public Administration Review
Public and International Affairs
Public Interest
Public Opinion Quarterly
Public Policy
Public Relations Journal
Quarterly Review
Round Table
Royal United Service Institution, Journal
Rural Sociology

Saturday Review
Science
Science and Society
Science and Technology
Seminar
Social Forces
Social Research
Social Science
Southern Humanities Review
Southwestern Social Science Quarterly
Survival
Table Ronde
Tiers-Monde

Twentieth Century
United Nations Industrialization and Productivity
  Bulletin
University of Chicago Law Review
University of Kansas Law Journal
University of Pennsylvania Law Review
Virginia Quarterly Review
Western Political Quarterly
Wisconsin Law Review
World Justice
World Politics
Yale Review
Yearbook of World Affairs

Now, a ten-volume series of bibliographies

SPEEDS ACCESS TO ALL SIGNIFICANT PUBLISHED LITERATURE IN THE POLITICAL AND BEHAVIORAL SCIENCES

Available for immediate delivery is the Universal Reference System *Political Science Series,* a 10-volume compilation of deeply-indexed books, papers, articles and documents published in the political, social and behavioral sciences.

Compiled by professional political scientists, and computer-processed into organized format, the URS provides the professional political scientist, administrative management, the political psychologist, the jurist, author, ecologist, humanist and student with ultrafast, multifaceted access to substantive published literature in their fields.

The Universal Reference System is easy to use, and reduces literature search time from hours or days to just minutes. The search is more fruitful, and brings to the researcher's attention many more significant works than would ordinarily be uncovered under any other type of organized literature search. Moreover, the researcher can quickly assess the relevance of any piece of literature because each reference includes a clear, concise summary of the document in question.

The ten-volume basic library is available for immediate delivery and covers the following political and behavioral science subfields:

I International Affairs

II Legislative Process, Representation and Decision Making

III Bibliography of Bibliographies in Political Science, Government and Public Policy

IV Administrative Management: Public and Private Bureaucracy

V Current Events and Problems of Modern Society

VI Public Opinion, Mass Behavior and Political Psychology

VII Law, Jurisprudence and Judicial Process

VIII Economic Regulation: Business and Government

IX Public Policy and the Management of Science

X Comparative Government and Cultures

Each volume (referred to as a CODEX) contains approximately 1,200 8½ x 11 inch pages and cites between 2,000-4,000 books, articles, papers and documents. Covered in the library are the books of about 2,400 publishers throughout the world. Each CODEX includes a list of periodicals cited in that volume. CODEXES are attractively bound in gold-stamped brown and green buckram.

Price of the complete library is $550.

Each year, three newsprint supplements—each covering all ten political science subfields with a single alphabetical Index—will alert scholar, researcher, student and professional political scientist to the most recent literature and current research activities in relevant categories. Each quarterly supplement cumulates the material in the preceding quarterly(s). The year-end quarterly cumulates the entire year's material which will cover—in addition to books, articles and papers—about 700 journals screened for material in all ten political science subfields. The fourth quarterly will be published in two bound volumes. In keeping with good encyclopedic practice, these will be easily differentiated from the basic library by the use of reverse color in their bindings.

Price for the cumulative quarterlies and the year-end pair of bound volumes is $250.

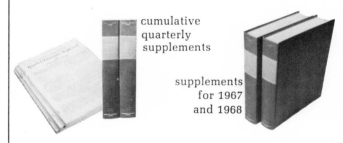

cumulative quarterly supplements

supplements for 1967 and 1968

Bound annual supplements for 1967 and 1968 cumulate the deeply-indexed annotations of all the significant journal articles and books published during these years. Two bound volumes—alphabetically indexed to embrace all ten subfields—contain the literary reference output for each year, and are distinguished from the basic library by reverse color in their bindings.

Price for the two 2-volume sets is $200.

To order your copies of the Universal Reference System *Political Science Series . . .*

The ten-volume basic library $550

Cumulative quarterly supplements for one year including bound volumes $250

Bound annual supplements for 1967 and 1968 .... $200 Complete

Prices effective May 1969

Make check payable to Universal Reference System and send to Universal Reference System, 32 Nassau Street, Princeton, New Jersey 08540.